PUBLISHED EVERY
YEAR SINCE 1864

136TH YEAR

WISDEN

CRICKETERS' ALMANACK

1999

EDITED BY MATTHEW ENGEL

PUBLISHED BY JOHN WISDEN & CO LTD
25 DOWN ROAD, MERROW
GUILDFORD, SURREY GU1 2PY

Cased edition ISBN 0 947766 50 2   £28.00

Soft cover edition ISBN 0 947766 51 0   £28.00

Leatherbound edition ISBN 0 947766 52 9   £200
(Limited edition of 150)

Published in 1999 by
JOHN WISDEN & CO LTD
25 Down Road, Merrow, Guildford, Surrey GU1 2PY
Tel: 01483 570358   Fax: 01483 533153
E-mail: wisden@ndirect.co.uk

WISDEN CRICKETERS' ALMANACK

Editor: Matthew Engel, The Oaks, Newton St Margarets, Herefordshire HR2 0QN.

Deputy editor: Harriet Monkhouse. Editorial assistant: Lawrence Booth.
Managing editor: Hugh Chevallier.
Production co-ordinator: Peter Bather. Chief typesetter: Mike Smith.
Advertisement sales by Colin Ackehurst and by London and Edinburgh Publishing plc.
Managing director: Christopher Lane.

Computer typeset by LazerType, Colchester

Printed and bound in Great Britain by Clays Ltd, St Ives plc
Distributed by The Penguin Group
Distributed in Australia by Hardie Grant Books, Melbourne

PREFACE

The first *Wisden* of more than 500 pages was in 1896; the 1,000 mark was first passed in 1924. In the years since then, editors have become cannier about making the most of the space available. But this year, it has finally happened: the first 1,500-page *Wisden*. I suppose the correct cricketing response is to acknowledge graciously anyone who might feel moved to applaud, then take fresh guard and aim for 2,000. We will not be rushing it.

This growth is partly deliberate. As regular readers know, *Wisden* is far more than a mass of statistics. This may not be obvious to every casual browser, however, and we are anxious to make the Almanack less intimidating and even, in a small way, more pictorial. Significant parts of the book should now be easier on the eye. The Records section accretes, as a matter of course. And there is an awful lot of cricket. In general, I believe that the more cricket there is, the better the world. Unfortunately, this growth is mainly in one-day internationals, a form of the game which is now debased and corrupted.

Wisden has expanded outside its covers as well as inside. In November 1998 came the first edition of *Wisden Cricketers' Almanack Australia*, sporting a natty green cover and already over 800 pages, all of them designed to be complementary to this volume rather than a replacement. This is intended to fill a gaping hole in Australian cricket culture, and initial response suggests it will fill it very well. Readers aware of the current value of our own 1864 edition might think it worthwhile to be in on the start of our Aussie counterpart.

We are also continuing to push ahead in the newest medium. John Wisden and Co has two web sites. One (www.wisden.com) provides a growing records service, a range of articles from the current edition of *Wisden Cricket Monthly* and a chance to order publications. The main site (www.cricketunlimited.co.uk) is operated jointly with *The Guardian* and provides full, lively and authoritative coverage of the game.

It has been a year of personnel changes too. Hugh Chevallier, *Wisden's* new managing editor, has oozed calm and efficiency ever since he took the job. I am hugely grateful to him and the deputy editor Harriet Monkhouse for their immense help and hard work through a difficult period. Special thanks also go to Sir Paul Getty and the board and management committee of John Wisden and Co, especially Christopher Lane; to Lawrence Booth, Simon Briggs, Gordon Burling, Gordon Vince, Philip Bailey, Peter Bather, Mike Smith and everyone at our new typesetters LazerType; to our colleagues at *Wisden Cricket Monthly* and my own on *The Guardian*. Above all, I salute the love and tolerance of my wife Hilary, my son Laurie and my new and gorgeous daughter Victoria.

MATTHEW ENGEL

Newton St Margarets, Herefordshire,
February 1998

4

LIST OF CONTRIBUTORS

Paul Allott
Andy Arlidge
Chris Aspin
Jack Bailey
Philip Bailey
Jack Bannister
Peter Bather
Marcus Berkmann
Mike Berry
Scyld Berry
Edward Bevan
J. Watson Blair
Henry Blofeld
Mihir Bose
Simon Briggs
Robert Brooke
Colin Bryden
Winston Bynorth
Don Cameron
Graham Chadwick
Mick Cheney
Marion Collin
Frank Coppi
Ted Corbett
Craig Cozier
Tony Cozier
Robert Craddock
Brian Croudy
Ben Curtis

John Curtis
Martin Davidson
Nigel Davies
Geoffrey Dean
Ralph Dellor
Tim de Lisle
Norman de Mesquita
Patrick Eagar
Philip Eden
Colin Evans
James Ferguson
David Foot
Stu Forster
Bill Frindall
Nigel Fuller
Andrew Gidley
Chris Goddard
Laurence Griffiths
Julian Guyer
David Hallett
David Hardy
Peter S. Hargreaves
Norman Harris
Les Hatton
Peter Hayter
Murray Hedgcock
Michael Henderson
Mike Hewitt
Myles Hodgson

Jim Holden
Grenville Holland
David Hopps
Gerald Howat
Peter Johnson
Abid Ali Kazi
Paul Kelso
Malcolm Knox
Mark Lawson
David Leggat
David Llewellyn
Nick Lucy
Steven Lynch
John MacKinnon
Bill McLeod
Neil Manthorp
Vic Marks
Clive Mason
Allan Massie
Fazeer Mohammed
R. Mohan
Graham Morris
Gerald Mortimer
Adrian Murrell
Graham Otway
Michael Owen-Smith
Gordon Phillips
Terry Power
Craig Prentis

Qamar Ahmed
Andrew Radd
Ben Radford
Peter Roebuck
Graham Russell
Dicky Rutnagur
Carol Salmon
Andrew Samson
Derek Scott
Mike Selvey
Shane Seneviratne
Utpal Shuvro
Jasmer Singh
Bill Smith
John Stern
Micky Stewart
Pat Symes
Sa'adi Thawfeeq
Andrew Tong
Jim Tucker
Sudhir Vaidya
Gerry Vaidyasekera
Gordon Vince
Ian Waldie
John Ward
David Warner
Paul Weaver
Tim Wellock
Simon Wilde

Round the World: Stephen Bates, Trevor Bayley, Trent Bouts, Anthony Bradbury, Mike Coward, John Cribbin, Olivier de Braekeleer, Geoff Edwards, Brian Fell, T. J. Finlayson, Simone Gambino, Bob Gibb, Richard Heller, Simon Hewitt, S. Azmat Hussain, Francis King, Pierre Naudi, Stanley Perlman, Laurie Pieters, Ken Sainsbury, Jai Kumar Shah, C. Sivanandan, Derek Thursby and Colin Wolfe.

Thanks are accorded to the following for checking the scorecards of first-class matches: Keith Booth, Len Chandler, Alex Davis, Byron Denning, Jack Foley, Keith Gerrish, Sam Hale, Neil Harris, Brian Hewes, Brian Hunt, Vic Isaacs, David Kendix, Tony Kingston, Reg May, David Norris, David Oldam, Gordon Stringfellow, Stan Tacey, Tony Weld, Alan West, Roy Wilkinson and Graham York.

The editor also acknowledges with gratitude assistance from the following: Bill Andersson, David Armstrong, Brian Austin, Kevin Boller, Jack Burrell, Ray Burrows, Gerry Byrne, Duncan Cameron, John Campbell, Donald Carr, Richard Colbey, Prakash Dahatonde, Robert Eastaway, Andrew Evans, Ric Finlay, Alexander Flint, Christine Forrest, Sujoy Ghosh, Ghulam Mustafa Khan, Ray Goble, Peter Griffiths, C. W. Haigh, Kate Hanson, Bob Harragan, Leo Harrison, John Hartridge, Col. Malcolm Havergal, Keith Hayhurst, Andrew Hignell, Paul Holden, Robin Isherwood, Mohammad Ali Jafri, Robert Kay, Frank Keating, Rajesh Kumar, David Lamming, Tony Lewis, Malcolm Lorimer, Mahendra Mapagunaratne, Mohandas Menon, Allan Miller, Edd Oliver, Francis Payne, Ken Piesse, S. Pervez Qaiser, Donald Rich, Earl W. Robinson, Major R. W. K. Ross-Hurst, Lokendra Pratap Sahi, Geoffrey Saulez, S. Simon, Neville Smith, Philip Snow, Mike Turner, Mike Vimpany, David Walsh, Charlie Wat, Wendy Wimbush, Michael Wolton, John Woodcock and Peter Wynne-Thomas.

The production of *Wisden* would not be possible without the support and co-operation of many other cricket officials, writers and lovers of the game. To them all, many thanks.

CONTENTS

Part One: Comment

Part Two: The World Cup

Part Three: The Players

Part Four: Records

Part Five: English Cricket in 1998

Part Six: Overseas Cricket in 1997-98

Part Seven: Administration and Laws

Part Eight: Miscellaneous

Addresses of first-class and minor counties can be found on pages 1383-1384.

Index of Fillers and Inserts

PART ONE: COMMENT

NOTES BY THE EDITOR

On a couple of occasions last November, *The Times*, a newspaper which made its reputation by not exaggerating, said cricket faced "its worst crisis in 20 years" – the Kerry Packer schism being the benchmark for modern cricketing crises. The paper was right, but not in the way it intended. The supposed "worst crisis" was the bizarre industrial dispute in which the West Indian players refused to start their tour of South Africa and instead holed up in a London hotel for a week. It was settled soon enough.

At the time, the real crisis was being ignored. Justice Qayyum, a Pakistani judge, was in Lahore conducting his investigation into the tangled skein of allegations about gambling and match-fixing. But elsewhere in the cricket world, no one was listening.

A month later, the Australian Cricket Board was finally forced to admit something it had known, and covered up, since February 1995. Mark Waugh and Shane Warne, who had made the original allegations of attempted match-fixing against the former Pakistan captain Salim Malik, had themselves accepted thousands of dollars from an Indian bookmaker for providing apparently innocuous information.

Of itself, what Waugh and Warne did was only borderline-reprehensible. My own hunch is that it was a sting that went wrong: the bookmaker, using old spymasters' techniques, tried to draw them into a web of deceit from which there could be no escape, but was far too unsubtle. The Waugh–Warne case is just a small but rocky outcrop of the mountain range of corruption that almost certainly still lies shrouded in the mists elsewhere.

But its emergence at last galvanised public opinion, and – on the face of it – the administrators. Suddenly, the Australian Board announced that it would hold an investigation. So did the International Cricket Council. "Unfortunately," said ICC chairman Jagmohan Dalmiya, "the very fabric of the great game is being damaged." Yet both bodies had known about Waugh and Warne for four years, since the ACB had informed ICC officials (but no one else) at the time. The fabric, apparently, was damaged only when the public found out.

Cricket-watchers have never had much faith in the game's administrators. But what they expect is incompetence, not cynicism. In fact, the ICC investigation never materialised as such. The national boards, obsessed by territorial imperative, refused to allow it. Instead, a supervisory body was to be set up, although, outside Australia and Pakistan, there were no investigations to supervise.

This did at least appear to constitute an acceptance that the rotten apples had to be removed from the barrel. But that misses the point. The poison is in the barrel itself, and it is likely to seep out again and again in the years ahead. The known facts about match-fixing are bad enough. What is suspected is terrible. If even a fraction of the rumours doing the rounds are true, it would be diabolical.

It is not easy to understand the new world of cricket if you sit in London or even Melbourne. Go to Dalmiya's own patch, though, to a hotel room or a middle-class home with satellite TV, pretty well anywhere in South Asia. There nearly always seems to be a game being broadcast from somewhere, usually a one-day international (India played 48 in 1997-98), otherwise another one-day game. Yes, these matches do have some spectator appeal. But they have as much lasting resonance as the afternoon greyhound meetings staged in Britain for the benefit of betting shops. And since cricket goes on longer than a dog race, it makes better, more cost-effective, visual wallpaper without losing its power as a gambling medium.

This crisis is not merely the worst in 20 years. It is doing more damage than anything since Bodyline because it is eating away at cricket's most vital asset: its reputation for fair play. And Bodyline was easily solved by amending the Laws. This one is far harder to control.

I like a punt myself: I would be sorry if cricket betting had to end. But it is an ironclad rule that unregulated gambling leads to gangsterism, and, when that gets a grip on a game, then radical action is the only solution. It happened in baseball after the First World War. To clean up, the game required strong moral leadership at the time, and constant vigilance thereafter. Cricket's response so far has been pathetic, almost frivolous. Dalmiya almost split world cricket trying to take charge of ICC. Having succeeded, he has given the game no leadership whatever. He should resign and be replaced by someone capable of providing that leadership.

The Taylor years

But the game goes on. In the very week *Wisden* went to press, Anil Kumble of India emphasised the global supremacy of wrist-spin by becoming the second player in Test history to take ten wickets in an innings. Just before that, the Australian captain Mark Taylor departed from international cricket, not so much retiring as ascending to post-cricket heaven in a fiery chariot: no captain since Mike Brearley has left the game with a higher reputation. And in Taylor's case, tactical skill was a smaller part of the mix. Even the media failed to disturb his equilibrium. He was straight-talking, straight-forward, dignified, a very fine batsman in his own right and – like all great leaders – damn lucky. He took over an Australian squad of remarkable (and perhaps unprecedented) ability and depth, at a time when England were groggily trying to stand upright but were still vulnerable to the merest sucker punch, and West Indies were plummeting towards the canvas.

Taylor is perhaps the only cricketer of the decade to acquire stature round the cricket world as a human being as well as a mere games player. Several of the world's most gifted batsmen and bowlers have lately been attracting more bad publicity than good: Wasim Akram, Brian Lara, Muttiah Muralitharan and Shane Warne. Meanwhile, Sachin Tendulkar kept himself squeaky-clean but had now become such a huge star in India that it was difficult to see the real person who might exist beneath the advertising icon.

Everyone agreed, even in England, that the game's most urgent need was for cricketers with enough personality to enthuse the public. The trouble is

that when such people do appear, everyone spends their time s
off, the career of Ian Botham providing a particularly graphi
Since Botham retired, England have had very few perso
slagging off.

Lord MacLaurin, the chairman of the England and Wales Cricket Board
(ECB), has his own views on this. His major public pronouncement of 1998
was an article in the *Sunday Telegraph*, sending Mike Atherton, who had
just resigned as England captain, on his way with a sharp kick: ". . . the
general behaviour of cricketers and their appearance has to be addressed.
No longer should we see international cricketers appearing on television
unshaven, chewing gum and looking slovenly." Mark Taylor chewed gum,
by the way, about as incessantly as cricket administrators miss the point.

Eight days in Dhaka

The most positive event in world cricket in 1998 was probably the first Mini
World Cup, held at the end of October and won by South Africa. In itself,
it was nothing special. The idea of raising funds for the game's international
development was praiseworthy but, in the context of the current, insane,
number of one-day internationals, this looked like another unnecessary
tournament. Many top players were absent, including the entire England
Ashes party. What mattered was the venue.

The tournament was held in Bangladesh almost by accident. The original
plan was to fulfil ICC's fantasy and play in Florida. Then it was going to
be Sharjah. But going to Dhaka validated the entire exercise. Only a few
weeks earlier, the country had been ravaged by floods that were bad even
by Bangladesh's own terrible standards, and some thought it was tasteless
to go on. Nothing of the kind. Nowhere has ever been more grateful to see
cricket. People told me, without a trace of irony, that it was the biggest event
– not merely the biggest *sporting* event – ever to take place there. It was
something to counteract the floods, cyclones, droughts, coups and earthquakes
which normally bring the country to world attention.

On all the evidence so far, Bangladesh's playing standards place it a long
way below Test status, and its players desperately need to learn the disciplines
of three and four-day cricket before it can get there. But all that was true
of Sri Lanka 30 years ago. The enthusiasm and potential here are even
greater. Bangladesh is the ninth most populous country in the world. And,
even in villages without electricity, people spent the week of the tournament
huddled round transistor radios listening to commentary. The players who
went, expecting to find who-knew-what, were cosseted in a first-rate hotel
and an excellent stadium. A week there should be an obligatory side-trip on
all future tours of the subcontinent.

A Batty summer

The hero of the English cricket season of 1998 may well have been someone
who is not even a cricketer: one David Batty. Batty was the England footballer

.o missed the crucial penalty in the shoot-out after the World Cup match against Argentina. England had only reached the last 16, but an atmosphere had built up that was already close to hysterical: every competing leisure activity, from eating out to theatre-going, was bleeding as the country went football-mad. English cricket seemed to be haemorrhaging.

It was a cold, damp spring. The Test team was doing badly. The County Championship was hardly registering. If the football team had got to the final, public reaction would probably have surpassed the Relief of Mafeking and VE Day put together: we live in a trivial age. More to the point, had they reached the quarter-final, the game would have been played on Saturday afternoon, in the midst of the Third Test against South Africa.

As it was, the England cricket team got booed off the field at Old Trafford that day. Had there been direct competition from a football match, there might not have been anyone there to boo. These were bleak hours for English cricket. If the papers noticed the game at all, it was usually to print feature articles announcing that it was finished, and that football was now the national summer sport. The ECB issued statements trying to show that cricket was actually doing jolly well, really, but failed to sound as if it had convinced even itself.

The weather got better. So did the Test team. Football went away for a week or two. But May–June 1999 is now looming as the most crucial period the English game has ever faced. The World Cup – the cricket one, that is – comes to Britain for the first time in 16 years. It will not return for a generation. No one inside the game needs reminding what a crucial opportunity this is. The weather has to stay fine; we need a lot of close finishes, preferably in those games that are on terrestrial TV rather than satellite; England have to excel themselves. But, gosh, what if the players start chewing gum?

Strength through joy

The most remarkable event of 1998-99 was not Australia's sixth successive Ashes, which had been pretty much universally predicted, but what happened when the West Indians were finally shoved on to their flight to Johannesburg: they lost to South Africa 5-0, a rainbow-wash. But the decline of West Indian cricket will become real to some people only when they finally lose a series to England. In the spring, they won the Wisden Trophy for the 13th successive time, which finally ended the reign of the unshaven, gum-chewing Atherton and brought in Alec Stewart, the only contemporary English cricketer who looks as though he might have done National Service.

In all other respects, the change was seamless: the team's strengths and weaknesses remained much the same. England's troubles were more chronic than the West Indians', but less acute. And after that grim Saturday at Old Trafford they went into remission. England saved the match, dramatically. They won the Fourth Test, ditto. And then the Fifth – and thus the series – when, on the final morning, 10,000 crowded into Headingley to see the last two South African wickets fall. Momentarily, the cricketers, not the footballers, were getting the headlines, and admiring ones at that.

It was indeed momentary. Three weeks later, England were routed by the Sri Lankan spinner Muralitharan. They then went to Australia to face a team that would be without Warne, their nemesis in the three previous Ashes series, until the last Test. It was a curious series, in that England were highly competitive most of the time, only to revert to their old ways for short but decisive periods. These happened mostly against Warne's deputies: Stuart MacGill, a leg-spinner who had been temperamentally unsound in English league cricket, and Colin Miller, a happy-go-lucky journeyman seamer who had started experimenting late in life with off-breaks. Both would probably have been regarded as too oddball to make an England team.

Technically, England might have had bowlers to match them. But Miller and MacGill bowled with exuberance and panache, as though they would take a wicket any minute. England's spinners conveyed the air of men about to be straight-driven for four. There were gifted cricketers in the England team. But the England players were numbed by inhibition, as though fear (of failure, of being dropped, of being insulted by the crowd or the press) had drained all their zest for the game. It was the same off the field, too: the team seemed to take little pleasure from the experience of touring – with some reason, since the slightest indiscretion can be picked on by one of the more sanctimonious papers. There are several aspects of Australian cricket that England ought to emulate, but the studied nonchalance of Taylor's team was perhaps the least attainable.

One problem dealt with ...

The replay screens at the Tests in England last year were sponsored by the car firm Citroën. And so, during intervals at the Lord's Test, the screen kept showing Citroën's current advert, which consisted of the model Claudia Schiffer descending a staircase and getting into a car while simultaneously removing every item of her clothing. She did this, in about twice life-size, in full view of the Lord's pavilion. It was a remarkable disjunction.

At the time, a blocking minority of MCC had just ensured the continuation of the club's ban on women members. In normal times, that might have been the end of the subject for another generation. But an unusually determined MCC President, Colin Ingleby-Mackenzie, accompanied by threatening noises from the sports minister, Tony Banks, had a remarkable effect. Essentially, members were told to keep thinking and voting until they came up with the right decision. In September, they did: 69.8 per cent of those who voted were in favour of change, above the two-thirds majority required, compared with 55.7 per cent in February. And in early 1999 five women were duly invited to become playing members.

The first vote had come at a time when two cases that were nothing to do with MCC (see Cricket and the Law, pages 1468–1469) had added to the perception that this was a game in serious need of sexual re-education. What was notable about the continuing debate was that the arguments advanced against the admission of women were generally stupid, mostly peevish and entirely selfish. The minority never explained how a game battling against heavy odds to retain its place in British hearts could do so if its most famous organisation so wantonly alienated half the population. What they talked about were their own privileges.

The change has come, and it is very welcome. But in practice, of course, MCC discriminates against almost all the population. The 57 million Britons who are not members have second-class access to the game's greatest occasions, as the World Cup final in June will show yet again, even though, on that occasion, members will actually have to pay their way. A random elite is still accorded privileges that would be unthinkable if the game were to start from scratch. What MCC needs to ask itself is what its function is to be in the 21st century. If it did not happen to own England's biggest and most historic cricket ground (an increasingly well-appointed one), MCC's entrance requirements would be of no more interest than those of Free Foresters or I Zingari. But it does matter, because Lord's matters. Does MCC exist primarily for the benefit of cricket as a whole? Or is it just a rich organisation whose first obligation is to its own members? Admitting women is a start. But only a start.

... another untouched

In the midst of South Africa's triumphant series against West Indies, the South African selectors were informed that the team was not good enough. Steve Tshwete, the sports minister, said that if an all-white side were sent to the World Cup "it will be difficult for me to support them". The United Cricket Board has been obliged to respond with a policy of positive discrimination, fumbling and unclear at national level, overt and clear-cut below that.

The initial objection to the old South Africa was that its teams were not chosen on merit. That is true once again. There is exquisite irony here, but it still makes me feel uneasy. What value is a South African cap to a player who knows he is not there on his own ability?

Other countries have racial difficulties, too. In an informal, unspoken, very English way, cricketing apartheid has become accepted practice in England. The anti-racist banner has been picked up, but mainly by people whose love of sloganising far exceeds their love of the game. This does not invalidate their essential point. I know of nothing that constitutes active racial discrimination in English recreational cricket. But there is a great deal of what might be called passive discrimination, a refusal to go the extra inch and welcome outsiders into a club's often clannish atmosphere.

It has become normal for ethnic-minority players to gravitate towards their own clubs, and there is now clear-cut evidence of segregation operating, informally, in both Yorkshire and Essex. There is some element of choice about this on both sides: a report from the University of East London into the Essex situation showed that many non-whites think the traditional local leagues are too sociable and soft. Whites, on the other hand, regard Pakistanis, in particular, as standoffish because so few of them drink.

But the effect is that black and Asian players are operating outside the official structure. They have become second-class in all kinds of little ways.

They play on poor pitches. And every week in summer, the *Yorkshire Post* reports the scores from about 50 leagues around the county, but the Bradford-based Quaid-e-Azam League is not one of them: "They can't get the results to us in time for Monday's paper," said a spokesman.

English cricket should now be reaping great benefit from the generation born here of parents who came to Britain in the great wave of post-war migration from the subcontinent and the Caribbean. England's first crop of West Indian players were nearly all born overseas. The new fast bowler Alex Tudor ought to be the harbinger of a galaxy of stars. But most of his black contemporaries have already been seduced by football, and many inner-city kids regard cricket as "an Asian game". Indeed, county scorecards are starting to be enriched by names like Habib and Mirza and Sheriyar, all English-born. But there would be a great deal more if the white majority made a greater effort to encourage them. This is a moral issue. But for English cricket, it is also a question of self-interest.

The house divided

The entire country was opposed to the introduction of two divisions in the County Championship. Unfortunately, the country concerned was Wales. Glamorgan were against the idea in the vote at the First-Class Forum last December, but were swamped by the English. Durham and Essex abstained; all the other counties voted for the plan. Many did so not from conviction but from a weary certainty that this was an idea which would not go away, and that (a little like the MCC members) they would keep getting beaten over the head until they acquiesced. Thus the top nine counties of 1999 will form a First Division in 2000.

It was the culmination of a debate notable for its intellectual incoherence. Lord MacLaurin, as ECB chairman, made no public case for the change, but forced the counties into accepting it by going around badmouthing the existing Championship more effectively than any media critic. One county chairman accused him of turning into Gerald Ratner, the jeweller who lost his empire after describing the products as "crap".

Those who argued for two divisions did so for contradictory reasons; indeed some often contradicted themselves in the same breath. On the one hand, the reform was supposed to pep up the County Championship. On the other, reformers wanted the best players formally taken away from their counties and placed under the England selectors' control. Indeed, the new programme of seven Tests and a ten-game triangular one-day international tournament means that the bigger names will effectively take no part at all in county cricket. What kind of championship is that?

We will see how enthusiastic the supporters of change are when their team gets relegated (as is certain to happen) because they have given over their best players to England, or because of one freakish declaration, or rotten luck with the weather. How will the players feel when they find themselves capriciously relegated? How will the selectors evaluate form in the different divisions? Already, counties are finding parents of promising teenagers demanding assurances: "I don't want my boy joining a Second Division club, you know."

The system, as introduced, makes no sense whatever. Six teams out of 18 will shift divisions each year. That will create confusion, not an elite. And the transfer system is to remain in its present rudimentary state, so players will have extreme difficulty bettering themselves.

The County Championship has to fulfil three functions. It is a competition, a public entertainment, and a preparatory ground for cricketers trying to climb to international level. Of late, quite obviously, it has been failing on each count (Championship attendances fell by almost ten per cent in 1998); and competitiveness and public interest may indeed perk up a fraction. But the third function is by far the most important, and in my judgment two divisions will work heavily against that, forcing counties into short-term decision-making as they duck and dive for immediate advantage. The young spinners England desperately need will get little chance to perfect their craft. This system, incidentally, is the absolute antithesis of what happens through-out Australian cricket, where the emphasis is on individual competition and mobility, while the clubs themselves remain static.

The whole scheme makes sense only for those who believe the counties should be heavily weeded, and reduced to a handful of big-city teams. It is a useful way-station on the road to that objective. I happen to think that would be a disaster, and that English cricket must be maintained and nurtured by 18 counties with full-time professional cricket. The counties have been bamboozled into a reform born of panic.

Getting the picture

When the dust from the World Cup settles, cricket followers in England will wake up to a very different world. The BBC has lost its immemorial right to cover home Test matches, and deservedly so. For many years, its presentation of cricket has been (as with other sports) complacent and dreary. Many new techniques for broadcasting the game have been developed in the past two decades – from the blindingly obvious (showing the score continuously) to the technically magical (super slo-mo). So far as I am aware, not a single one has emanated from the BBC, though they cheerfully pinched the ideas from others.

The viewing figures will probably fall when Tests move to Channel 4 (and they will plummet for the one Test a year to be shown live only on Sky TV, which is unavailable in most homes), though I am not sure cricket will lose anyone who has really been watching. The coverage may or may not be an improvement. But it was a reasonable gamble by the ECB, which will enliven future bidding rounds without shunting too much of the game into the ghetto of satellite TV. The BBC lost out not because of its poverty, but because of its poverty of ideas.

So what has Channel 4 got to show first time out, on the bounce from what everyone hopes will be a successful World Cup? A clutch of Tests against New Zealand, the world's least charismatic team. It was an absurdity to give them four Tests this year, having allowed Sri Lanka only one in

1998. But there should be two occasions that would be a little bit special: 1999 marks the centenary of Test cricket at both Headingley and Trent Bridge. However, you'll never guess which two grounds have not been awarded Test matches this year. Oh, you've guessed, haven't you?

Fast-medium is the message

Careful readers will notice that among the innovations in this year's *Wisden* is an extra column in the first-class bowling averages. For the first time, we are using the widely understood initials (RF, RFM, RM, OB, SLA etc.) that denote bowling styles, to give readers an extra and important piece of information about a player. We hope, in time, to extend this service into overseas averages as well, but it is particularly interesting for the 1998 season given the absolutely wretched record of even the best-known English spinners.

The exercise proved a great deal harder than might be imagined. Spin bowlers are relatively easy to categorise, though both Saqlain Mushtaq and Sachin Tendulkar are now mixing up off-breaks and leg-breaks, like Sonny Ramadhin before them. Seam bowlers, though, create a problem. The distinction between a fast bowler, a fast-medium one and a medium-pacer is essentially one of opinion. Some reference books have started using an extra category, medium-fast, which is apparently somewhere between medium and fast-medium. An eight-year-old cricket fan (they do exist) asked me what the difference was between fast-medium and medium-fast. About one mile an hour, I supposed.

No human can measure bowling that accurately, and thus the medium-fast category will not appear in *Wisden*. The Speedster machine, a popular diversion at last year's Tests, is a help, but even that can be misleading here, since a bowler's average speed may disguise all kinds of possibilities: one may be very fast in the morning and slower as he tires; another may use the slower ball as a deliberate tactic; another may have just the odd really fast delivery.

To compile our list, we talked to umpires, coaches and batsmen. They frequently disagreed with each other, and sometimes we had to make a difficult judgment, which may be rather galling for a fast bowler who finds himself relegated from RF to RFM. Bowlers change, of course. Our view was that Dean Headley bowled fast towards the end of the 1998-99 Ashes series, but that in 1998 he was essentially fast-medium. Maybe fast fast-medium. But not medium-fast, or medium fast-medium. We will try to keep it simple.

Austin joins the maestros

The old maxim "Never complain, never explain" is a reasonable one, especially for *Wisden* editors. But, speaking as a bit of an old whinger myself, I also accept that there are some decisions that come better with an explanation.

The Five Cricketers of the Year are traditionally chosen by democratic election, by an electorate of one – the editor. In my own mind, there were at least five other cricketers who were not chosen but who, on their form in the 1998 season, warranted very serious consideration: Mark Butcher, Andrew Caddick, John Crawley, Hansie Cronje and Nasser Hussain. But there is also a tradition that *Wisden* editors feel free to ignore the obvious dictates of form and look for other qualities.

The current generation of cricketers is the most anonymous in history. Players hide behind their helmets and their agents, cocooned in their dressing-rooms, understanding little either of cricket's unimportance, or its importance. English county professionals are becoming increasingly assertive in small ways, but as a group they have failed miserably at projecting themselves.

Old *Wisdens* are full of the names of men who were local heroes even if they never played international cricket. Nowadays, it is a rarity for someone to come along and establish a special rapport even with his home crowd. Ian Austin is an exception. He is Lancashire to the marrow. When he succeeds, there is a special cheer in the Old Trafford pavilion because they regard him as one of their own. There ought to be dozens like him, but there aren't. That's why he is a Cricketer of the Year.

Throwing mud

Two more of our new Cricketers of the Year began 1999 mired in controversy. The Australian umpire Ross Emerson called Muttiah Muralitharan for throwing in a one-day international against England at Adelaide; the vigorous and uncricketlike response of his captain, Arjuna Ranatunga, caused widespread criticism. The main blame must attach to Emerson who ignored both ICC and common sense by no-balling Muralitharan from apparent premeditation, rather than because one ball was delivered in a different way from any of the others.

This was the behaviour of a man with his own agenda. The quality of Australian cricketers may be unsurpassed at present, but their umpires could use a little humility concerning their own limitations. Australia cannot even reliably provide competent TV umpires – not an especially arduous duty – for Test matches.

The issue of throwing recurs in cricket history like outbreaks of flu. In 1898 and 1899 these Notes were simply headed "A Note By the Editor", and it was solely on this subject. Yet the real problem in modern cricket is not the persistent thrower, who has mostly been eradicated, but the occasional deceitful chucker who throws the odd faster ball or bouncer. Such people are never called.

Muralitharan is a special case. Assuming his assertion – that he cannot unbend his arm – is correct, and it has not been disproved, then under Law 24 his action is legal. In my view, the Law is badly drafted, and there is a case for changing the wording. A bowler whose arm is bent has an extra advantage because he can clearly get extra snap from his wrist. But a man's entire career is at stake here. It is not a matter that can sensibly be dealt with by an umpire/show-off at a one-day international.

A change for the better

The one thing nobody noticed when Emerson thrust out his arm was many runs England got for the no-ball. But Law 24 is badly drafted on this point too. Traditionally, a team gets no reward for a single off a no-ball except that the run moves out of the Extras line and is credited to the striker. This is unjust, and a minor – if long-standing – distortion of the game.

The experimental playing condition recently used in competitions like the County Championship and Sheffield Shield gives the batting side two extras for the no-ball plus anything that is scored from the delivery. This goes too far, and smacks of trying to teach the bowlers a lesson. The new ICC regulation, which applies in Tests and one-day internationals, awards one extra plus anything that is scored. This actually makes sense, and constitutes a small improvement. It should be incorporated in the forthcoming revision of the Laws.

Graceless, sort of

Within the past two years, two cricketers, the former West Indian Test player Winston Davis and the young Yorkshireman Jamie Hood, have both been left tetraplegics by tragic accidents. Yet the game had no mechanism to respond to their plight. Cricket's attitude to charity – distorted by the benefit system – is hopeless. Normal human kindness seems to have been tossed overboard by the way the benefit system forces the able-bodied to beg.

The match played at Lord's on July 18 last year, on the 150th anniversary of W. G. Grace's birth, was billed, ludicrously, as a Diana, Princess of Wales Memorial Match. This nonsense was attacked in these Notes last year and, by the time the game was staged (quite successfully), MCC had back-pedalled a little, and the two names had almost become a pair: Trueman and Statham; Laker and Lock; W. G. and Diana.

The worst of it was what happened to the money. The day raised £520,000 for the princess's memorial fund. This fund had already got more than £70 million; another half a million was neither here nor there, gobbled without a thought, barely touching the sides. When one thinks how much could have been done by sensible application of that money to causes close to cricket, one could weep.

It broadens the mind

Neville Cardus first went to Australia to report the 1936-37 tour. He was not far off 50. "When the ambition of a lifetime is fulfilled," he wrote later, "when a boy's dream comes true, something has gone from one's life." These days, as our Schools section makes clear, teams of teenagers regularly fly off to matches in the furthest corners of the globe. There are Under-19 Tests, an Under-15 World Cup even. This may help explain why professional cricketers who come up through the system get so blasé about the opportunities for travel that are part of their job, and turn into bored and boring tourists. "Where are we going on our tour?" one public schoolboy was overheard asking another last year. "Barbados," he was told. "Oh, no!" came the reply. "Not again!"

THE WISDEN FIVE HUNDRED

It all began very tentatively: "It has been thought appropriate, in consequence of the exceptional quality and effectiveness of last season's bowling, to publish some medallion portraits of prominent men." Thus *Wisden* 1889 began what has become the Almanack's most distinctive feature: the Wisden Five.

Actually, since cricket is a game of evolving complexities rather than neat rigidities, it started with six, all of them bowlers, and all of them names that are still resonant in the Records section today: Briggs, Ferris, Lohmann, Peel, Turner, Woods. They were photographed by E. Hawkins and Co. of Brighton "who have made cricket photography their speciality, and whose reputation will certainly not suffer by the present specimen of their ability".

The following year, the editor, Charles Pardon, felt emboldened to try again, this time with nine batsmen. In 1891 *Wisden* went for wicket-keepers, and settled for five. And there the number has stayed. No choices were made for part of the First War and the whole of the Second. And there were four early years when a "special portrait" appeared, and only one player was honoured – including 1913 when the Almanack's founder, John Wisden, was chosen, 50 years after he retired from first-class cricket and 29 years after his death.

And so, with the publication of *Wisden* 1999, the number of Cricketers of the Year has passed 500. A total of 504 portraits have appeared, but two of the special portraits were of Sir Pelham Warner and Sir Jack Hobbs, who had already been chosen in the normal way. Since 1927, the number has been fixed at five, and the rule that no one can be chosen twice has remained inviolate. So 502 different players have now been chosen; it is impossible to say officially who the 500th is, since the Five are all equal.

The story of the first 100 years of Cricketers of the Year by Anthony Bradbury appeared in *Wisden* 1989. He pointed out some of the most glaring omissions and selected 1977 as perhaps the most vintage of all *Wisden* vintages. The full list of Cricketers of the Year appears on pages 181-183. From 1996 to 1998, this was followed by Robert Brooke's analysis of those chosen since the Second World War. He has now analysed the full list, and his findings appear on page 183. Gideon Haigh's notional listing of past Australian Cricketers of the Year appears on page 1470.

FIVE CRICKETERS OF THE CENTURY

By MATTHEW ENGEL

The 1900 edition of *Wisden* makes no reference to the start of the 20th century. At the time, pedantry held sway, and the new century was generally held to start in 1901. But *Wisden* 1901 seems silent on the subject as well.

There were, at the time, other preoccupations. "At the moment of writing one hears nothing but War! War! War!" wrote A. G. Steel in *Wisden* 1900. "What numbers of gallant young soldier cricketers have gone to the front, eager for the chance; well, the true wishes of all cricketers and readers of *Wisden* will go with them." The year 2000 is scheduled to dawn with England preparing for a Test match at the Cape rather than a battle, so that at least represents human progress.

This date is apparently being ignored by no one, and *Wisden* feels obliged to join in. So *Wisden* 2000 – the 137th edition – will include, in addition to the customary Five Cricketers of the Year, our list of Five Cricketers of the Century.

The Cricketers of the Year have traditionally been chosen by the editor. For the Cricketers of the Century, it seemed right to multiply the electorate a hundredfold. The choice will be made by a panel of 100 players, writers, umpires, historians and other watchers of the game from all the major cricketing countries. They will vote during 1999; the results, and appreciations of the top five, will appear next year in our Millennium Edition.

The voters will be asked to set aside any bias towards their own countries, and their own eras, before coming up with five people "whose excellence at cricket during the 20th century has made the greatest contribution to the game". Excellence can be interpreted broadly; it is legitimate to take into account leadership qualities, personality, character and impact on the public. (We believe, by the way, that W. G. Grace is a Cricketer of the 19th Century, and is not eligible.)

Not everyone can be invited on to the panel. However, all *Wisden* readers have the opportunity to join in by entering our special competition and trying to guess the names of the winners.

A leaflet with full details of this contest should be included in every copy of *Wisden*. If you do not have a form, please send a stamped addressed envelope (or international reply coupon) to: Cricketers of the Century, John Wisden and Co, 25 Down Road, Merrow, Guildford, Surrey GU1 2PY, England. No proof of purchase is necessary but, please, only one entry per person.

In 1900, by the way, A. G. Steel was deeply worried, and not by the Boer War. Cricket, he wrote, "is in the very direst peril of degenerating from the finest of all summer games into an exhibition of dullness and weariness". I think, as soon as one begins to consider the candidates for this very special Five, one can take pride in the fact that the century turned out better than he feared.

THE WISDEN WORLD CHAMPIONSHIP

The Wisden World Championship – intended as a temporary measure while the International Cricket Council decided the form of an official Championship – is beginning to assume an ominous air of permanence.

Though ICC has agreed on the idea of a Championship, it yet again proved unable to agree on its form at the executive meeting in January 1999, and so the *Wisden* version goes on, if necessary indefinitely. At the top of the table, Australia are also beginning to assume an air of permanence, ominous for everyone else. When they won a series in Pakistan in October 1998, they reached 25 points out of 28, having won their last home series against all their opponents, and their last away series against everyone except India (where they lost in March 1998) and New Zealand (where they drew in March 1993). They were still to play a Test against Zimbabwe.

There was one major change in the organisation of the Championship in 1998. The basic system remains the same: the most recent series, both home and away, between each pair of countries count. Teams receive two points for winning a series, and one for drawing. And a one-off Test counts as a series. But not everyone has played everyone else.

Originally the *Wisden* table was determined by the difference between series played and points won. But this created an apparent anomaly at the foot of the table, because New Zealand have fulfilled all their fixtures while Zimbabwe (through absolutely no fault of their own) are not even close. Following many protests from New Zealand, *Wisden* agreed to decide the table on the average points per series instead. It did New Zealand little good. After triumphing in Pakistan, Zimbabwe leapfrogged back over the New Zealanders, and indeed began to threaten England in seventh place. Sri Lanka are the biggest climbers, having risen from seventh to fourth in six months.

It was also decided that, in future, series not renewed after seven years would be excluded from the table, recalculation to take place in September each year. The current table includes series played since September 1991. As *Wisden* went to press, we were finalising plans as to how to incorporate the neutral ground Test – the first in 87 years – that was scheduled for Dhaka in 1999 as the culmination of the Asian Test Championship.

THE WISDEN CHAMPIONSHIP TABLE

(as at February 4, 1999)

		Series played	Points	Average
1.	Australia	14	25	1.79
2.	South Africa	15	19	1.27
3.	West Indies	14	17	1.21
4.	Sri Lanka	16	15	0.94
5.	India	14	13	0.93
6.	Pakistan	13	11	0.85
7.	England	14	10	0.71
8.	Zimbabwe	10	7	0.70
9.	New Zealand	16	9	0.56

Previous leaders: October 13–December 12, 1996 South Africa; December 12–January 28, 1997 Australia, South Africa and West Indies (joint); Australia have led since January 28, 1997.

The standings are updated regularly in *Wisden Cricket Monthly* and on Wisden's web site, www.wisden.com.

THE CORRUPTION OF CRICKET

By MIHIR BOSE

It had been obvious for some time that cricket's great bribery saga was far from over. The wholly unexpected twist of December 1998 was that the goodies threatened to change places with the baddies.

The original accusation was that the Australians Shane Warne, Tim May and Mark Waugh had been approached by Salim Malik, who allegedly offered them $200,000 bribes to throw matches in October 1994. This first alerted a dozing cricket world to the heavy illegal betting going on in the subcontinent and Sharjah, and to the possibility that players were being bribed to rig matches.

More than four years later, it finally emerged that Warne and Waugh had their own involvement with subcontinental bookmakers and that the Australian Cricket Board knew about this and had covered it up all that time. Suddenly, the rights and wrongs seemed a great deal muddier.

Until the new Australian revelations, the affair had followed a predictable pattern. The Pakistanis had held three inquiries into the allegations, the Indians had held one, Malik had denied everything, nothing had been proven and in four years the only victim had been a journalist. This was Ramaswamy Mohan, for 18 years the cricket correspondent of *The Hindu*, one of India's leading newspapers. The paper has never officially commented on Mohan's departure, although one source there said: *"The Hindu* had to think of the credibility of the paper." *

But everyone's credibility was at stake. In 1997 the Delhi-based magazine *Outlook* published claims by the former Indian Test cricketer Manoj Prabhakar that he was offered 2.5 million rupees (about £40,000) by a teammate "to play below my usual standards". Prabhakar said the incident happened just before the India–Pakistan fixture (which was rained off anyway) in the Singer World Series in Sri Lanka in September 1994. "I told him to get out of my room," Prabhakar said.

Until then, the Indian Board had been looking on Pakistan's difficulties on this issue with a slightly smug and superior air. Now it asked Mr Justice Chandrachud, a former Chief Justice of India, to examine the Prabhakar story. But Prabhakar refused to name the player concerned, so Chandrachud concluded in December 1997 that there was nothing to report. This limp-wristed conclusion pleased no one. The general feeling by now was that betting and match-throwing were part of the subcontinent's cricket culture, and that nothing could be done about it. People began to accept the resigned comment of a Bombay police investigator: "Every side with the exception of Australia and England can be purchased."

This remained the accepted wisdom for another year. In the meantime, the Pakistanis did begin a far more serious inquiry into the issue. Justice

---

* *Editor's note:* Mohan admits having bet on cricket and having passed on routine information, but denies acting as a linkman between players and bookmakers, or any involvement in match-fixing. In the absence of any evidence that would justify his removal, he remains as *Wisden's* Indian correspondent.

Malik Mohammad Qayyum sat in Lahore while Pakistan's cricketing elite made depositions. Inexorably, a picture of casual corruption built up. The International Cricket Council privately promised that, once Qayyum had finished, it would take action. But it was, the rest of the cricketing world thought, primarily Pakistan's problem.

Then, on December 8, 1998, the former Australian cricketer David Hookes mentioned to a Melbourne radio station that two Australians had given information to an Indian bookmaker. This turned the whole story on its head. The new revelation was that, during the same tournament in Sri Lanka in 1994, Waugh and Warne had been approached by an Indian bookmaker identified only as "John", who had asked them to begin giving him apparently innocent information about the weather and the state of the pitch – less, said the players, than they might routinely give free to journalists. For this, Waugh was paid $A6,000 (about £2,500) and Warne $A5,000.

The players had admitted this after making their original allegations about Malik to the Australian Cricket Board, which then fined them slightly more than John paid them ($A10,000 for Waugh and $A8,000 for Warne). But the ACB had said nothing about this publicly for almost four years. However, it informed ICC at the time, telling Sir Clyde Walcott, the then chairman, and David Richards, the chief executive, to keep it secret, which they did. The news incensed the Australian public, and Waugh was booed during the Adelaide Test against England. Warne escaped this because he was injured. But letter-writers to Australian papers demanded that both be drummed out of the game. Warne and Waugh admitted being "naive and stupid" but insisted they had not been involved in match-fixing in any way.

The news also incensed the Pakistanis. Justice Qayyum's inquiry was just nearing its end. Two months earlier, Waugh and Mark Taylor (representing Warne) had given evidence to him during Australia's tour of Pakistan. The Pakistanis had made special arrangements to accommodate their wishes, assembling a special court in a private house. Waugh and Taylor promised to tell the truth, the whole truth and nothing but the truth. They were not asked about John and (though Taylor was in on the secret) neither said anything. They did speak loftily about their cricketing ideals, and Justice Qayyum was much impressed by Waugh's testimony – until the news broke. "If he did not have a legal obligation, he had a moral duty to bring it to our notice, and it casts doubt on his credibility," Qayyum said.

Pakistani officials were also angered by ICC's connivance in the Australian cover-up. "We felt the way ICC was constituted, we could not inform Pakistan," said Richards. "We were of the view that the onus was on the ACB to disseminate the information." Yet when the first Pakistan inquiry, under Justice Fakhruddin G. Ebrahim, suggested that the Australians had concocted their complaints against Malik, the Australians had demanded that ICC hold its own inquiry under Rule 2 of the Code of Conduct.

Now it was the Pakistanis who were making demands. They wanted Waugh and Warne to return to Pakistan to give further evidence. The compromise was that the Pakistani court travelled instead, at the Australian Board's expense. A hearing was arranged in Melbourne; it was in effect a Pakistani court, sitting under Pakistani law. Ali Sibtain Fazli, the Pakistan Board's

[*MCC Photo Library*   [*Ben Curtis, PA News*

Gambling with their careers: William Lambert, depicted by Paul Falconer Poole, years after being banned from cricket in the match-fixing scandal of 1817. Shane Warne, at a press conference in Adelaide in December 1998, after his dealings with an Indian bookmaker were revealed.

lawyer, closely questioned Warne and Waugh about the match that was now felt to be the key to the whole affair. This was the one-day international in Colombo on September 7, 1994, eight days before the washed-out India–Pakistan match, and immediately preceding the Australian Test tour when Malik allegedly made his approach. Australia had scored just 179 for seven; Pakistan, captained by Malik and going well until Saeed Anwar retired with a hamstring injury, had lost by 28 runs. The Singer World Series involved India, who went on to win it, and Sri Lanka as well. It was rapidly becoming the centre of the many allegations; and it was after this tournament that the Pakistani Board banned mobile telephones from the dressing-room. A Pakistani bookmaker had previously told the commission in secret that he had given money to two players to fix this game. Both denied it.

When Warne and Waugh were given a grilling by the Pakistani investigators, no new information emerged. And the sense of anticlimax was heightened two days later when ICC held its much-heralded executive meeting. This was billed as the occasion when the organisation would finally come of age and take some of the powers of policing invested in similar international sporting organisations. Instead, ICC announced a three-man commission to supervise the investigation of such allegations but left the initial responsibility with the domestic boards.

The belief that this is a Pakistani issue remains deeply ingrained. Yet in the month before the meeting, one Australian – Ricky Ponting – and two England players – Adam Hollioake and Dougie Brown – said they had received approaches from bookmakers. The approach to Ponting was made at a Sydney dog track, a long way from Pakistan. In 1817, it was easy for MCC to ban the miscreant William Lambert and expel the bookmakers from Lord's. The world is a more complex place in 1999. There seemed little sign of this sorry story ever ending, let alone soon.

Mihir Bose is sports news correspondent of the Daily Telegraph.

WHAT THEY SAID

Extracts from statements made by players and officials, on oath, to Justice Qayyum's inquiry in Lahore, and to its special sitting in Melbourne:

I was absolutely sure that match-fixing and betting was going on in Pakistani team.
Javed Burki, former Pakistan captain and chairman of ad hoc committee running Pakistani cricket 1994-95

In July 1997, I took over charge as coach of senior Pakistani team. Even before that there was talk about match-fixing and betting. I cannot say with certainty whether any match was fixed or not. During my tenure as coach, there were some matches which I, as a cricketer, felt should have been won by Pakistan but they lost. In my opinion, those matches were thrown away.
Haroon Rashid, former Pakistan player and coach

In my view, although I have no positive proof, there is match-fixing and betting prevalent in Pakistani team. In 1994, at Sharjah, the betting was going on in full swing.   *Aqib Javed, former Pakistan player*

I have been writing about cricket since 1987. . . I have come to the conclusion that more and more players, who are leading ones, are involved in corruption, with the result that the entire team is being polluted.
Fareshteh Gati, Pakistani journalist

I was never myself contacted for match-fixing nor did I indulge in betting. When I was captain, I have no proof that any player was involved in these nefarious activities.
Ramiz Raja, former Pakistan captain

The allegations against me regarding match-fixing are totally wrong and baseless. If the figures are compared it will be seen that the maximum number of matches was won under my captaincy, which itself shows the allegations are false.
Salim Malik, former Pakistan captain

I now believe that I spoke to John on approximately ten occasions. The information I gave him was no more than anyone could receive by listening to expert commentators on radio or television or to pre-match interviews with cricketers.
Mark Waugh, Australian player

I next heard from John in Melbourne just before the Boxing Day Test later that year. He telephoned me in the hotel at Melbourne. He said: "G'day, it's John. I met you in Sri Lanka. I'm just wishing you a Merry Christmas. . . what's the MCG pitch like?" I said: "Mate, it's a typical MCG pitch. It should be a good batting wicket. It should turn a bit and keep a bit low towards the end of the game." He said: "Is it going to rain?" I said: "I don't know, you can never tell in Melbourne, but I don't think so." He said: "Well OK, have a good Christmas."
Shane Warne, Australian player

THE LIGHT THAT FLICKERED

By PETER ROEBUCK

Upon the abandonment of the match in which he scored his 100th hundred, Graeme Hick walked across a damp and emptying ground in Worcester and into the arms of his daughters. It was an ordinary thing to do, but it was noticed because it said something about a cricketer who had once seemed a fearless gladiator, but whose confidence had slowly been eroded.

Always he had seemed distant. A fellow could watch him bat a hundred times and still not feel close. Suddenly, he seemed human, warm and vulnerable, a quiet man in a noisy place. Watching him, it was hard to believe he really wanted to throw himself back into the hurly-burly.

Hick was seen again, two months later, sitting alone upon the ridiculously exposed area that serves as the players' balcony in Leeds. A Test match hung in the balance and much depended on his contribution. He had been recalled after scoring heavily at Worcester, an amiable place which he has made his home. The teams threw themselves at each other, and the crowd was transfixed. Here was a chance for Hick to impose himself, to use his power, to turn the match, and to secure a place in the team for Australia. It was not to be. Twice Hick fell cheaply, caught in the covers off poorly executed strokes. Throughout, he seemed stiff. Of course, he was not alone in his failures. But his failures have always been noticed, because of the expectations, and his appearance, and his extraordinary successes.

He played again at The Oval, against Sri Lanka, and hit a century. A place on the Ashes tour beckoned – until he was upstaged by a bigger hundred from John Crawley. Hedging their bets, the selectors put Hick on standby. He was duly summoned and thrown into the hotpot in Perth. After an embarrassing failure in the first innings to a stroke played with bat and body far apart, he contributed a rousing effort in a lost cause, hooking and driving without inhibition and with immense force. But power and authority are not the same. In Sydney, in the final Test, the whole series seemed to rest on his shoulders. Perhaps it was an unfair burden. All England willed him to punch his weight. Instead, he held back: tightening, trying too hard, uncertain of his tempo. Perhaps he is too conscientious, and accordingly unable to take the brave decision or to execute it with his whole heart.

It may be his fate to be remembered as a remarkable cricketer and a monumental scorer of runs, as a player fit and reliable, yet incapable of taking the extra step; in short, a player whose finest moments came along at times of their own choosing. Considering his achievements, it might seem a harsh judgment. More leeway is given elsewhere. Sport forgives those who cannot contain themselves on the field, whose careers consist of flashes of brilliance, calling them charming and romantic and misunderstood. Sport also forgives those who must scrape around for their runs. But it will not smile upon those who do not deliver upon their promises, even if they did not make those promises themselves.

It was Hick's fate to be given an ability that did not suit his temperament. It took him on a long journey, across the world and into himself, took him further than he cared to go. His upbringing was simple and secure, and did not prepare him for the conflict. He grew up on a tobacco farm in Trelawney, not so far from Harare. His family had an English heritage and lots of Yorkshire blood, and his father played for the local cricket team, though not terribly well. Hick was confident in these surroundings, with the sunshine and the emotional warmth. He hung a cricket ball from a tree and began practising in his uncreased way, building a game that had no nooks or crannies, no subtleties, a game founded upon straight lines and trust. He has always been a performer rather than a downright competitor.

Hick attended prep school and Prince Edward High School, ordered places with a sense of right and wrong. Although an uninspired student, he was obedient and respectful, as he has been throughout his career in cricket. It is hard to recall any tantrums, and he has not been greedy or vainglorious or obsessed with figures. To the contrary: he has batted at first wicket down for his club, hardly missing a match, taking catches at second slip or fielding in the deep, and showing an athleticism astonishing in such a big man. And yet something was held back. Hick has not been a leader, clapping his hands upon the field or grabbing the ball at a telling moment. Significantly, he has been reluctant to work upon his gentle off-spinners, which is not the approach taken by Viv or Sachin or Steve Waugh. Perhaps he could not imagine anyone losing his wicket to such nonsense. Or perhaps he was unwilling to put himself in places where he might be vulnerable.

The feeling arises that Hick is being criticised when he ought to be celebrated. It is hard to stop this mood creeping in. We had thought he belonged in the highest class and judged him by its standards. Perhaps we were misguided. Our expectations may have been too high. It did not help Hick that he cut such an impressive figure, and it was easy to forget that he had been a sickly stick insect in his boyhood, and that meningitis had bedevilled his teenage years. Only in young adulthood did he blossom.

Expectation did not rest easily upon him. Any hopes he had of a quiet entry into county cricket were swiftly ended. English cricket was in the doldrums. Nor did it help that Hick found himself in Worcester and not London, where he might have been pushed and cursed. And he had a long time to wait before he could play Test cricket. It would hardly be surprising if something went missing in those seven years, waiting to qualify for England. Had he played at 21 or 22, he might have risen to the heights. Most great players burst into Test cricket at an early age, before adulthood has brought its doubts. Provoked by Hick's reputation, the top bowlers of the age probed for weaknesses, waited for their man.

Conceivably, those years in county cricket lulled him, and the rest of us, into a false sense of security. Faults were not confronted and corrected. Hick may also have felt comfortable within the confines and privacies of the county game. Only the most ruthless analysts detected important faults. Most particularly, they saw a heaviness of foot and shot that made late movement an enemy. They saw, too, that Hick had a weakness against balls rising sharply at his shoulders. Torn between hooking, ducking, parrying and evading, he could appear confused, even frozen. Between them, the long wait and the problems posed by bumpers bit into Hick's confidence. At times,

[*Patrick Eagar*

Largely impassive ... Hick is out for eight in the first innings of the 1998-99 Adelaide Test.

he has looked alarmingly baffled, bewildered by the game's betrayals and shaken by its scrutiny. He has not relished the critical world. Nor has he been able to resolve his own difficulties. Whatever his technical flaws, his limitations are mental.

Happily, there is much to be said on Hick's behalf. His cultured and forceful strokeplay has given enormous enjoyment to crowds across the world. He has hardly ever let his supporters down, or his team-mates, or the game itself. He has scored a mountain of runs, few of them given away. The regularity with which hundreds came along said much about his fitness, discipline and concentration. He has been an impressive and largely impassive professional, one of the heaviest scorers to appear in the last 20 years, and one of the best tall batsmen. His accomplishments are extraordinary. Only in Test cricket has Hick been found wanting, and even there his record is not so bad. None the less, something was missing, a spark, an ability to be himself in the most demanding situations.

It has not been Hick's fate to enjoy the fierceness of Test cricket. He was given almost all the characteristics demanded by greatness. Conviction alone was missing. It says much for him that he has remained unbowed by dismay. He has been a punishing and faithful cricketer, commanding where he is comfortable, and quiet elsewhere. Throughout, he has searched for the contentment and simplicity he knew in his early days, and he has found it in the same place, at home with his family. It might sound like a defeat but it isn't a defeat at all. Indeed, it's a sort of victory.

Peter Roebuck, the former Somerset captain, is cricket columnist for the Sydney Morning Herald. *His classic account of fielding while Hick scored 405 is in* Wisden 1989.

THE CENTURIONS

Age on scoring their hundredth hundred

	Season	Age	Innings
W. R. Hammond	1935	31 years 359 days	679
G. A. Hick	**1998**	**32 years 8 days**	**574**
D. C. S. Compton	1952	34 years 19 days	552
G. M. Turner	1982	35 years 3 days	779
L. Hutton	1951	35 years 23 days	619
Zaheer Abbas	1982-83	35 years 140 days	658
I. V. A. Richards	1988-89	36 years 251 days	658
G. Boycott	1977	36 years 294 days	645
T. W. Graveney	1964	37 years 50 days	940
H. Sutcliffe	1932	37 years 227 days	700
D. G. Bradman	1947-48	39 years 80 days	295
G. A. Gooch	1992-93	39 years 184 days	820
E. H. Hendren	1928-29	39 years 272 days	740
J. H. Edrich	1977	40 years 21 days	945
C. P. Mead	1927	40 years 132 days	892
J. B. Hobbs	1923	40 years 143 days	821
M. C. Cowdrey	1973	40 years 193 days	1,035
T. W. Hayward	1913	42 years 90 days	1,076
F. E. Woolley	1929	42 years 93 days	1,031
D. L. Amiss	1986	43 years 113 days	1,081
L. E. G. Ames	1950	44 years 251 days	915
A. Sandham	1935	44 years 355 days	871
E. Tyldesley	1934	45 years 152 days	919
W. G. Grace	1895	46 years 303 days	1,113

HICK'S HUNDREDS

Graeme Hick had scored 104 first-class hundreds by the start of 1999.

75 for Worcestershire (v Somerset 8, Glam, Glos and Sussex 7, Surrey 6, Northants 5, Hants and Lancs 4, Essex, Kent, Middx and Warwicks 3, Leics, Notts, Yorks and Oxford U. 2, Derbys, Durham, Australians, Indians, West Indians, Pakistan A and MCC 1)

10 for Northern Districts (v Wellington 3, Auckland and Canterbury 2, Central Districts, England XI and Otago 1)

7 for England XI on tour (v Australian XI, Central Districts, Minor Associations' XI, NZ Emerging Players, South Australia, Victoria and Western Australia 1)

5 for England (v South Africa 2, India, Sri Lanka and West Indies 1)

4 for Zimbabweans (v Young Australians 2, Glam and Oxford U. 1)

3 for Queensland (v New South Wales, Tasmania and Western Australia 1)

HICK'S DOUBLE-HUNDREDS

Graeme Hick had scored 11 double-hundreds by the start of 1999.

405*	Worcestershire v Somerset at Taunton	1988
303*	Worcestershire v Hampshire at Southampton	1997
252*	Worcestershire v Glamorgan at Abergavenny	1990
230	Zimbabweans v Oxford University at Oxford	1985
227*	Worcestershire v Nottinghamshire at Worcester	1986
219*	Worcestershire v Glamorgan at Neath	1986
215	Worcestershire v Lancashire at Manchester	1994
215	Worcestershire v Indians at Worcester	1996
213*	Worcestershire v Nottinghamshire at Nottingham	1992
212	Worcestershire v Lancashire at Manchester	1988
211*	Northern Districts v Auckland at Auckland	1988-89

THE HISTORY OF MYSTERY

By SIMON WILDE

The splendid Australian batsmen, those active, clear-eyed men who could smile at our fast bowling and make the best of our slow bowlers seem simple, were absolutely at sea. Here was something of which they had never heard, for which they had never prepared, and which was unlike anything in the history of cricket. Spedegue had got his fifty-foot trajectory to a nicety, bowling over the wicket with a marked curve from the leg. Every ball fell on or near the top of the stumps. He was as accurate as a human howitzer pitching shells.

Sadly, Spedegue, who claims 15 wickets on debut to rout Australia and clinch the Ashes, only exists in fiction, the eponymous hero of Arthur Conan Doyle's *The Story of Spedegue's Dropper*, published in 1929. How the real England team could have done with him last winter.

An unknown schoolteacher who the selectors risked playing after a secret 4 a.m. trial, Spedegue was the ultimate "mystery" bowler – the spinner who, armed with a novel method, deceives and destroys the opposition. Such players exist in real life, but they rarely spring from nowhere. The true mystery bowler is often attempting to resurrect a career that has foundered or never even got under way, and he will do well to make it last.

Other mystery men start younger. In the past two seasons, Saqlain Mushtaq, the Pakistani off-spinner, enjoyed great success with Surrey, and one reason was a delivery which few batsmen could pick: a ball that not merely drifted towards first slip – the off-spinner's traditional variation – but turned sharply, with no discernible change of action. This was a weapon that the Sri Lankan Muttiah Muralitharan also possessed, although "Murali" had many more tricks up his sleeve when he faced England, for the first time in a five-day game since 1993, in a one-off Test match at The Oval.

That this most unorthodox of orthodox spinners bamboozled the England batsmen was quickly evident from their leaden footwork and tentative strokes. He achieved a corkscrew effect from his wrist, and the ball turned and bounced as though dancing to wild, unfathomable music. Dav Whatmore, formerly Sri Lanka's coach, claimed Murali's wrist rotation was unmatched in history.

Like Shane Warne and a growing corps of leg-spin bowlers, Muralitharan and Saqlain have benefited from the general inability of modern batsmen to cope with slow bowling. Brought up with covered pitches, fast bowling, heavy bats and helmets, many have been so ignorant that not only skilled practitioners but modest part-time "rollers" took on the guise of little green men from the planet Zog.

Muralitharan and Saqlain have the pedigree to carry on doing well, but they may need new tricks if they are to stay ahead. Almost 50 years ago, another off-spinner, Sonny Ramadhin, swept all before him. With shirtsleeves and cap pulled down, spinning the ball either way with his fingers, and using an extraordinarily fast, windmilling action, he was the conjuror personified. Then Peter May and Colin Cowdrey countered him by getting outside the line and playing every delivery as an off-break. Ramadhin was never the same again.

Historically, off-spin has been short of innovation, though it can be claimed that its inventor, a farmer called Lamborn from Hambledon days, was the first mystery bowler in history. Then, all bowling was underarm and the natural break from leg, but Lamborn, a "plain-spoken little bumpkin", possessed a gift for spinning the ball past leg stump, much to his advantage.

Mystery bowling does not have to be new, just different. The underarm method was exhausted when players turned to roundarm bowling early in the 19th century, but it soon reappeared as a surprise tactic against batsmen attuned to facing tearaway roundarmers. And it survived as a shock weapon past the First World War – its final fling did not come until Trevor Chappell nearly ruptured relations between Australia and New Zealand by bowling a grubber as the last ball of a one-day international in 1980-81.

The research of R. J. Reynolds has revealed several interesting cases (see *The Cricket Statistician*, Spring 1997) in the last third of the 19th century. There was David Buchanan, who turned to lobs in his late thirties, and, on behalf of the Gentlemen, time and again gulled the Players, whose respectfulness suggested they were unaware that he was routinely punished by the schoolboys of Rugby. E. M. Grace frequently mixed lobs with roundarm, and nearly caused a riot when he bowled Harry Jupp, one of England's leading batsmen, with a high full toss at The Oval in 1865.

Nor was it uncommon during the 1870s to see bowlers resorting to "daisy-cutters". C. I. Thornton opened the bowling with them for Gentlemen of the South at The Oval in 1871 and, six years later, in the first-ever Test match at Melbourne, Thomas Armitage attempted to break Charles Bannerman's concentration with a spell of full tosses and grubbers – without success.

It may be no coincidence that lob bowling died out at around the time that the most brilliant and successful mystery ball in history, the googly, was developed. Tradition credits B. J. T. Bosanquet, another fast bowler grown weary of his work, as its creator; more likely, "Bosie" was the first who developed the ball – an off-break that looked like a leg-break – with the deliberate intention of misleading batsmen. "It is not unfair," he once said of his googly, "only immoral". In finest mystery tradition, Bosanquet's early efforts were greeted as an amusing diversion. His first googly to claim a county wicket in 1900 reportedly bounced four times before a bemused Samuel Coe, of Leicestershire, was stumped off it for 98, but within a few years Bosanquet had helped England win two Tests, and the power of the googly was established.

It proved a costly export. Bosanquet tutored Reggie Schwarz, who played with him at Middlesex, but took the secret to South Africa, where he in turn encouraged Albert Vogler and Aubrey Faulkner, who took 65 wickets between them when South Africa beat England 3-2 in 1909-10. (In that series, George Simpson-Hayward claimed 23 victims for England with lobs.) More damagingly, Bosanquet inspired the great tradition of Australian googly-bowling, which is still tormenting England in 1999.

Bosanquet's English imitators were numerous but erratic, though some who showed promise rose swiftly. Douglas Carr was an ordinary middle-aged club cricketer and schoolteacher who converted to googly bowling in his mid-thirties. Plucked from obscurity to play for Kent in 1909, within weeks he found himself representing England in a deciding Test match against Australia, and rapidly took the first three Australian wickets. But the parallels with Spedegue did not go that far. He was bowled into the ground by his captain, Archie MacLaren, and England failed to win.

[Hutton Getty Picture Collection   *[Hulton Getty Picture Collection*

Great deceivers: B. J. T. Bosanquet (*left*); Jack Iverson (*right*), pictured at net practice in 1950.

Not that the googly was always enough, even for the best exponents. Few were clever enough to disguise it completely, and positive, quick-footed batsmen such as Jack Hobbs showed how the threat could be negated. Subtle variations were much prized. Clarrie Grimmett, whose early googly was relatively easy to pick, spent years perfecting the "flipper", the ball that hurried through, and dreamed of developing a "wrong wrong 'un", a delivery that looked like his googly but broke from leg – truly a riddle wrapped in a mystery inside an enigma.

Generally, the googly came out of the back of the hand rather than the front, but not always. While on army service during the Second World War, Jack Iverson, a lumbering fast bowler from Victoria, hit on a strange technique of spinning the ball by discharging it from between thumb and bent middle finger, and used it to baffle Freddie Brown's touring side in 1950-51. He was soon found to be vulnerable under fire, but his method did not perish with his short career. In the 1960s, Johnny Gleeson, a useful batsman/wicket-keeper at club level in Tamworth, New South Wales, saw a photograph of Iverson's bizarre grip and had a go at imitating it. He played 29 Tests for Australia and lived up to the tag of "mystery man" better than most.

The left-arm wrist-spinner's stock ball, the "chinaman", developed on the back of the right-arm googly craze, but has remained a rare art. Historically, chinaman bowlers have struggled for control even more than their right-arm counterparts. It may be significant that two of the better practitioners, Johnny Wardle and Garry Sobers, bowled other styles as well, and before Paul Adams appeared for South Africa in 1995 they had been unrepresented in Test cricket for almost 20 years. With an action that was even more exotic than his technique, Adams was a doubly perplexing proposition.

Of course, problems flourish in batsmen's minds, and a clever bowler knows that he need not necessarily invent a mystery ball, just talk about one. Shane Warne terrified England in 1994-95 by threatening them with his "zooter" (rhyming with footer rather than hooter). This is an Australian term for a flipper bowled from the front of the hand, though there remain people who insist that it is a figment of the imagination. As Gleeson pointed out: "You can only do three things: spin from the leg, spin from the off, or go in straight. The ball can't disappear or explode."

The crowd had begun by cheering and laughing, but now they had got beyond it and sat in a sort of awed silence as people might who were contemplating a miracle ... The slogging bumpkin from the village green would have made a better job of Spedegue than did these great cricketers, to whom the orthodox method was the only way. Every rule learned, every experience endured, had in a moment become useless. How could you play with a straight bat at a ball that fell from the clouds?

Simon Wilde is cricket correspondent of the Sunday Times.

THE YEAR THE CITADEL FELL

By PETER HAYTER

What was a woman to think? Or a chap? The messages being thrown at women in cricket during 1998 were so confused and confusing that they made the head spin. In the early months of the year came three items of news that suggested that all the old attitudes were alive and well and living at Lord's.

In March, an industrial tribunal upheld a claim for sex discrimination by Theresa Harrild, a receptionist formerly employed by the England and Wales Cricket Board, who said she had been pressured and paid by the Board to have an abortion after becoming pregnant by a colleague.

Harrild's evidence – regarding the attitude of certain high-ranking Board officials towards women in their offices and in cricket at large – was damning. The ECB got into even more trouble when it denied her allegations after the hearing, having declined to contest them. This came only weeks after a case in which Geoffrey Boycott, one of the game's most public figures, was convicted by a French court of assaulting a girlfriend in a Riviera hotel room.

To the public, the conclusion that there was no smoke without fire was all but irresistible. Why would the man, or woman, in the street think otherwise? To them, all the available evidence, outside as well as inside the courtrooms, pointed to the same conclusion: the majority of men in cricket regarded women as simply fodder for jokes about maidens, tickles to fine legs and bouncers – or worse.

It was made all the more relevant because of events in the Marylebone Cricket Club barely a fortnight before the Harrild case. A blocking minority

James Ferguson's view in the *Financial Times*.

of the all-male MCC membership had voted against the proposal of their committee – pushed by the President, Colin Ingleby-Mackenzie – to admit persons of the opposite gender. They thus reaffirmed the club's 211-year-old position: not in here, madam.

By the end of the year, so much had changed that those of a cynical disposition might have been tempted to believe Rachael Heyhoe-Flint had been busy putting something in the gin-and-tonics at NW8. Ingleby-Mackenzie, having refused to take no for an answer, urged the members to think and vote again and, on September 28, they did, momentously. Just how influential in their final decision was the president's warning that no women meant no lottery money, who can tell? In the meantime, the Women's Cricket Association had voted to become an integral part of the ECB, thus establishing a single governing body for all cricket in the country. Women in MCC, and the ECB, as equals? Whatever next?

In the short term, some answers please, for those who play. Shirley Taylor, the manager of the England women's cricket team that was defeated 5-0 in their one-day international series with Australia but battled to draw the three-Test series 0-0, believes, that although some progress has been made, the road to real recognition will be long and arduous. "I do think we are being taken more seriously," she says, "but there is a lot of work to be done.

"You will still find the armchair critics with nothing better to do than have a go. Everyone who has taken the trouble to come and watch us play has been impressed, not only with our enthusiasm and commitment, but also with the level of skill we reach."

My own experience of the women's game was, until 1998, limited to one match at Lord's in 1987, a one-day game between England and Australia ruined by rain and by grim clichés about naked ladies in the pavilion. But when I went to watch the 1998 "Ashes" Test at Worcester, I was enormously impressed by the quality of play. Clearly, the bowling is not as fast as in the men's game, but the batting, in particular, was of a high standard. Indeed, the thought occurred and then grew that, given the opportunity, almost all of the Australian bats, and many of the English, had the technical skill not only to survive in men's county cricket, but to prosper. Predictably, when I put that proposition to a current England Test cricketer (male), his reaction was: "Oh, yes. And how would they deal with the quick stuff?" It would be interesting to find out.

ECB figures suggest that interest, at least, is on the increase. They state that 3,600 women are playing, as are 475,000 school girls, three-quarters of them at primary school. There are more than 150 women's clubs, and women's sections in nearly 100 other clubs – 27 clubs or sections have been formed in the past two years.

All well and good. But the disparity between England's cricketers and their Australian counterparts is best illustrated by some other statistics. There are 80 women's cricket clubs in Melbourne alone, and Australia, with a third of the population, has almost seven times as many women playing: 23,000. At the start of the 1998-99 season, the cover of the big-selling *Australian Women's Weekly* proclaimed that a full list of Australian domestic and international cricket fixtures (male) was included. Admittedly, the magazine is owned by Kerry Packer, who has a vested interest. But it is hard to believe cricket would be used as a selling point in any English equivalent.

[*Craig Prentis, Allsport*

Playing at their own game: Belinda Clark of Australia is caught by Sue Redfern of England in the women's Test at Guildford in 1998.

For the lot of the English woman cricketer to be significantly improved, it will not be enough for a few token members to be admitted to MCC. Nor is it enough for the Board – and their Test sponsors Vodafone who, for no obvious publicity benefit, pushed money the way of the women in 1998 – to repeat the dose and leave it at that. At the moment, it seems that women in cricket are themselves unsure how to pitch their campaign for recognition. To some, Vodafone's publicity gimmick to drum up media interest in the women's "Ashes" might have been considered retrograde in tone: journalists were sent a bunch of red roses with a card reading "Eleven English roses playing cricket – watch this space." And even Rachael Heyhoe-Flint's comments in celebrating women's admission to MCC sounded peculiar: "Perhaps now," she suggested, "you will be able to buy MCC nighties and fluffy slippers as well as pyjamas."

If there is an inferiority complex at work here, it will only be shattered by strong women with confidence and belief in their place in the sport – separate, but entitled to equal respect and opportunity. That's why, the extraordinary nature of its events notwithstanding, 1998 must be only the beginning.

Peter Hayter is cricket correspondent of the Mail on Sunday.

THE SPEEDOMETER SUMMER

By PAUL ALLOTT

Speed excites the spectator. Crowds love to see fast bowlers in full cry. The sound of the ball thudding into the wicket-keeper's gloves, the batsman hopping and off-balance – his equilibrium disturbed by sheer pace – will always encourage gasps and roars of approval from packed Test match grounds. Fast bowling is all about raw aggression, power and domination. But how fast is fast?

Until the 1998 season in England, no one really knew. There had been attempts to measure the speed of bowlers before, using the kind of radar guns police point at speeding cars. There were trials in the 1950s when Frank Tyson was in full cry, and again during World Series Cricket 20 years ago when Jeff Thomson was declared the fastest of all. But the technology was uncertain. And a similar exercise at the Lord's Test against Pakistan in 1996 produced implausible results and public derision. The machine was soon switched off.

However, in the last English summer, the technology took a giant leap forward. The Yellow Pages Speedster appeared at Test grounds, telling spectators – and the players – the speed of a delivery moments after it had been bowled. And this time the technology seemed unassailable. It was still pooh-poohed, mainly by former quick bowlers. Surely, the argument went, there are enough visual keys for the spectator without an electronic read-out. But people like to grasp something tangible: how fast their car gets from nought to 60 mph – or how often Allan Donald bowls at over 90. It was a popular innovation.

The Speedster is a spin-off from the arms trade. It was developed by a firm in Stellenbosch, South Africa, using technology originally intended to measure the speed of bullets. The breakthrough, it is claimed, is that the speed is measured in two dimensions rather than one. The system measures the vertical speed of the ball as well as the horizontal speed, which gives a much truer indication of its actual velocity. What that means in practice is that two people sit huddled round a bank of computer screens which receive information from a small box behind the bowler's arm. A computer 400 times faster than the average home PC verifies all the readings, and only then will it allow the speed to be displayed. All this takes about a second, by which time the batsman can check whether he has faced a very fast delivery or not – as if he did not already know.

But the bowler really might not know. During the series against South Africa, when Donald was confirmed as comfortably the fastest bowler on either side, David Lloyd, the England coach, mischievously suggested that the Speedster ought to be turned down when Darren Gough was bowling to encourage him to try even harder. For most of the summer, Donald regularly clocked 90 mph, and averaged 86. Gough only occasionally touched 90. For other, slower, bowlers, it could all be a trifle embarrassing. There was Donald exploding the ball into the turf, and there was Angus Fraser, steaming in with every ounce of effort he possessed, to get the needle up to about 78. Still, Gough and Fraser had the last laugh: England won the series.

Prior to the Speedster, cricketers talked of pace in terms of yards, not mph. And this concept is useful to put the new-fangled device into context. Bowlers have often yearned for "an extra yard" of pace: over the 20 yards the ball travels between bowler and batsman, the yard is significant. The extra yard makes batsmen hurry. Get two yards quicker, and that is some achievement.

The difference between Donald's average of 86 mph and Fraser's of 78 is about ten per cent – or two yards. It may not sound a stunning statistic but, in terms of professional cricket, it is significant. Many spectators were surprised to see that players they regarded as trundlers were also breaking the motorway speed limit: Hansie Cronje, for instance, averaged 74, but that is another half-yard slower than Fraser.

There is far more to bowling than sheer speed, as Fraser showed. But the Speedster is likely to increase the emphasis on raw pace. A 100 mph delivery would be two yards faster than Donald. That is fast, very fast. What price someone breaking the barrier? If it happens, the crowd's applause is likely to be wilder than anything that greets a more conventional century.

Paul Allott bowled in 13 Tests for England in the 1980s without ever quite reaching 100 mph. He is now a freelance writer and commentator on Sky TV.

SPEEDSTER STATS

England v South Africa 1998

England	Miles per hour Fastest ball	Average speed	South Africa	Miles per hour Fastest ball	Average speed
Darren Gough	90	84	Allan Donald	92	86
Dean Headley	88	82	Lance Klusener	89	84
Dominic Cork	85	79	Makhaya Ntini	88	84
Angus Fraser	83	78	Shaun Pollock	90	83
Mark Ealham	81	77	Steve Elworthy	87	83
Andrew Flintoff	79	76	Jacques Kallis	87	80
Mark Butcher	79	73	Brian McMillan	83	76
Ashley Giles	65	56	Hansie Cronje	78	74
Robert Croft	57	55	Paul Adams	61	50
Mark Ramprakash	53	49	Daryll Cullinan	50	48
Ian Salisbury	51	48			

Australia v England 1998-99

Fastest ball bowled (Melbourne and Sydney Tests only)

Australia: Damien Fleming 88 mph; Glenn McGrath 88; Matt Nicholson 88; Colin Miller 83; Steve Waugh 80; Shane Warne 60; Mark Waugh 56; Stuart MacGill 55.

England: Darren Gough 91 mph; Dean Headley 91; Alex Tudor 88; Alan Mullally 86; Angus Fraser 81; Mark Ramprakash 54; Peter Such 54.

FIVE CRICKETERS OF THE YEAR

IAN AUSTIN

In the final of the 1998 NatWest Trophy, an event in which the team batting first customarily falls to pieces at once, Lancashire found themselves in unexpected trouble. Rain had delayed play until late in the afternoon, and the Derbyshire opening pair, Michael Slater and Kim Barnett, astonished the great Wasim Akram by hitting him and Peter Martin all round Lord's. Then Ian Austin came on to bowl.

If he produced a bad ball, the batsmen never spotted it. He finished with the astonishing figures of 10–5–14–3, and that included four overthrows. Martin suddenly became inspired too, and took four wickets himself. Both moved the ball around ferociously. Derbyshire collapsed from 70 for nought to 108 all out. On the Sunday, Lancashire completed victory and Austin was named man of the match, joining a very select list (Asif Iqbal, Vic Marks, Clive Radley, Viv Richards, Robin Smith) to have won the awards in both one-day finals. And when his name was announced, a very special cheer rang round the remnants of Lancashire supporters. It was as though the honour had not gone to one of their players, but to one of them. It was a reward for a very special kind of cricketing virtue.

The next day, Lancashire won the Sunday League, and they went on to finish second in the Championship. Just three weeks earlier, Austin had been plucked from the middle of a Roses match at Headingley and brought into the England one-day team for the Triangular Tournament against South Africa and Sri Lanka. It was a memorable summer for him.

His success confounded a few people. Cricketers are not supposed to look like Ian Austin any more. He is a burly man and, though he is fit, still has the air of an old-fashioned pie-and-chips player. Mike Selvey once compared him to a stoker on a merchant steamer and his team-mates call him "Bully", which is meant affectionately. He proved that, in a game trying desperately hard to sell itself as something young and trendy in readiness for the World Cup, there is still room for the old-fashioned county stalwart who looks as if he has stepped off the village green. If cricketers can be divided into occupants of the lounge bar or the tap-room, there isn't much doubt which door Austin emerged from.

IAN DAVID AUSTIN was born in Haslingden on May 30, 1966. Haslingden is a small town at the entrance to the Rossendale Valley, where icy winds blow in August, and the cricketers have to be rugged and robust. The local team has built a reputation as the Manchester United of the Lancashire League. Their overseas players have included George Headley, Clive Lloyd and Dennis Lillee, and the locals have included both Ian and his father Jack. Some of Lancashire's best cricketers and characters have come from the Haslingden/Accrington area: Jack Simmons, David Lloyd, Graeme Fowler.

He joined the county in 1986, making his first-class debut a year later. He was viewed at first as a batsman, and then mainly as a one-day player, and became frustrated by his failure to gain a regular place. "I said 'give me a run in the side, and if I don't perform then let me go. I'll hold up my hand if I don't do it.'" The 1990 season, in which Lancashire became the first county to win both one-day knockout cups in the same year, was important for him. Six years later, when they repeated the feat, he was opening the bowling. In between, he played a big role in the 1995 Benson and Hedges victory, when he ended Aravinda de Silva's magnificent innings in the nick of time.

Austin was now acknowledged to be as reliable a one-day bowler as any in England. Indeed, Wasim has called him "the best death bowler I have ever seen". He has a remarkable ability to produce yorker after yorker and, even though batsmen may expect it, just as they may expect a great fast bowler's bouncer, it is still not easy to cope. But he is also a very skilful user of the new ball, especially the white one, because of his accuracy and swing. And he has developed into a batsman who scores runs when it matters most.

"He's so phlegmatic," says the Lancashire cricket secretary, Dave Edmundson. "He never seems wound up in any situation. We can be 90 for nine chasing 210, and he will just quietly assume he's got the ability to do it. He'll just nudge and nurdle, and then suddenly dob it for six." He is used to being underrated in a team of international performers. Not for him the publicity that attended Andrew Flintoff's rise to prominence last summer, in his first full season, when Lancashire used the young all-rounder as publicity material to sell their Sunday games. Not for him the coverage devoted to Mike Atherton and John Crawley. Instead, something of the old pro attaches itself to Austin, something of the game as it was before fads, diets and personal counselling.

The last Lancashire cricketer to catch the public imagination in the same way was Simmons, who did not enter the professional game until he was 27, and was still playing it 20 years later. Lancashire loved Flat Jack, and he remains in high regard as the chairman of the club. Austin still has some distance to travel to match his record. But he has established himself as someone rare, perhaps unique in modern cricket. "He's a cricketer's cricketer," says Edmundson, "and a people's cricketer." – MICHAEL HENDERSON.

DARREN GOUGH

There are two different England teams these days. This is nothing to do with the increasingly disparate Test and one-day sides, because the difference affects them both. One lot is the downbeat, fatalistic crew who have become all too familiar: heads bowed, expecting the worst. The other is seen when Darren Gough is fit and firing.

At Old Trafford against New Zealand in 1994, Gough made one of the most sensational Test debuts of modern times. He took a wicket in his first over and had figures of four for 47. Earlier, he had gone out and hit a rousing 65, with ten fours. He was 23 years old. Everyone yelled "New Botham", which was not a Yorkshire mining village but already a cliché, and later a rather sad joke.

That winter, with England having been humiliated in the Melbourne Test, they went to Sydney looking hopeless. One young man took the game by the scruff. England 309 (Gough 51, and a thrilling 51 at that). Australia 116 all out (Gough six for 49). The Test was not quite won, but its hero was suddenly the hottest property in English sport. He was young, good-looking, an authentic Yorkshireman with that air of sleeves-up defiance which the nation adores. Vast wealth as well as glory looked a certainty.

But Gough had felt pain in his left foot even while the cheers were echoing. He ignored it. In a one-day international a few days later, he broke down and went home with his foot in plaster. It took four years to recapture that exuberance, in which time his career veered between wretched injuries and fated comebacks. His batting form went to pieces. And at the start of England's next Ashes tour, he became the sort of bowler everyone drops catches off, which was never Botham's fate. He was a star who twinkled rather than blazed.

And yet the omens of 1994 have been proved right. And in 1998 he delivered. At Headingley, with his home crowd roaring him on, he ripped through South Africa's second innings to settle the series: six for 42 – three of them in a dramatic opening burst. Then he was at the heart of England's epic win in Melbourne before starting 1999 with a hat-trick in the Sydney Test. In any case, Gough's contribution to the team cannot merely be computed. He is an inspirational cricketer in an uninspiring era. And his successes make the Tests he has missed even more poignant.

DARREN GOUGH was born at Barnsley on September 18, 1970. No town in cricket has such a rich tradition of character and characters: Geoffrey Boycott, Dickie Bird, Michael Parkinson. Gough was not born straight into the tradition. His father, a pest control officer, was a sports fan rather than a performer. But young Darren quickly established himself as a breathtakingly good sportsman and, at school, was captain of football, rugby and athletics as well as cricket.

Football came first, and was the centre of Gough's early ambitions as he went through the Barnsley FC youth system and then became a Government-funded trainee at Rotherham United. He was a midfielder – "stylish" he insists – modelling himself on Glenn Hoddle, and dreaming of a transfer to Tottenham. It never happened. "It was a time when football was all about quick runners, and I wasn't good enough." But then came another traineeship: this time with Yorkshire. And the club thought enough of him to give him a go in the first team right at the start of the 1989 season. The side travelled from Leeds to Lord's by train. Darren's dad took him to the station; David Bairstow, the captain, gave the lad, just 18, a big bearhug and promised Dad he would look after him. Pressure can override promises. Gough had to bowl 13 consecutive overs in the second innings. He ended up injured, and played only once more all season.

As seems to be Gough's fate, fulfilment came slower than expected. He remained a member of the first-team squad, considered too valuable to be wasted much in the Second Eleven, but he was not getting enough chances to be kept happy. At the start of 1993, he thought he would give it one more season before thinking about another county. Then the opportunities came, and he grabbed them: 57 first-class wickets that season, followed by an A tour to South Africa, and his Test debut. But the glory was transient. He played again in 1995 when not quite ready. For a while, he ceased to be a certain choice, and was ignored (mysteriously) through the summer of 1996. In 1997, he began to feel pains in his left leg and was forced to pull out of the West Indies tour. When he reappeared, at Edgbaston, he broke a finger.

But the selectors knew now how much they wanted him: David Graveney, the chairman, called him "the pulse of the team". And when Gough came back into the South Africa series, so did England. His bowling was highly skilled by now. Though he could not match Allan Donald on the speedometer, he was consistently quicker than anyone else, and was able to offer just about every other weapon in the fast bowling armoury as well – with the possible exception of really telling bounce. Pace bowlers like Gough who are not six-footers tend to produce deliveries that skid rather than leap.

Above all, though, in a team of brooders and worriers, he stood out for his bullish enthusiasm. England need Darren Gough, and not just for his wickets. – MATTHEW ENGEL.

MUTTIAH MURALITHARAN

Maybe the whispers and rumours will never cease; maybe Muttiah Muralitharan will forever have to lure international batsmen to their doom with a murky cloud of suspicion over his twirling arm. It would be a shame, though – for cricket in general, and for the off-spin assassin who bewitched players and spectators alike at The Oval last summer when taking 16 for 220 to give Sri Lanka their first Test victory in England.

These remarkable figures were the fifth best of all time in Test cricket, yet Murali's cunning strategies, his marathon patience and his sporting instincts were overshadowed by controversy. David Lloyd, the England coach, made remarks on television that implicitly suggested a problem with his bowling action. It was another day, another victory, tainted. Murali's response to the doubters is emphatic. "I don't care what anyone says now," he protests, the insistence in his gentle voice as sharp as the spin he imparts on a cricket ball. "I know I am not a cheat. It has been medically proved that I am not chucking." The 16 wickets at The Oval took Murali past 200 in Test matches, second only to Lance Gibbs among off-spinners. His new target is 300. A sense of history and a sense of injustice have now become powerful twin motivating factors to his career.

The eternal problem for Murali is that his action does look distinctly odd. First impressions are that he must be a chucker. The arm is bent, the wrist action is generous, to say the least. But that is nature, not nurture. The deformity in his right arm was there at birth. His three brothers, Sridaran, Sasidaran and Prabgaran, have exactly the same "bend". His wrist is also especially flexible, which means extra leverage on the ball. Yes, it may give him an advantage over other slow bowlers, but it is not an unfair one, according to ICC, which commissioned many hours of analysis into Muralitharan's action and found that it conformed to Law 24 because his arm does not straighten.

MUTTIAH MURALITHARAN was born on April 17, 1972, in Kandy, Sri Lanka, the first of four sons for Sinnasami and Laxmi Muttiah, who still run the Lucky Land biscuit and confectionery firm in the city. It proved to be a lucky land for young Murali, whose first cricketing memories are of street and park games with other children. His formal sporting education came at St Anthony's College in Kandy. "I started going to cricket practice at the age of eight," he recalls. "I was a medium-pacer, until the age of 13. But then the coach, Sunil Fernando, suggested I try off-spin and it seemed to work much better. One year I took 127 wickets in a schools competition, and the national selectors showed an interest." Until that time, Murali says, he had never considered the fact that he had a bent arm. It was just the way he was; but he soon discovered life and sport could never be simple again.

His progress through the Sri Lankan A team to the full international side was rapid, and he made his Test debut against Australia in August 1992. After one wicket in the first innings, he dismissed Tom Moody and Mark Waugh with successive deliveries in the second. Seven months later, Murali had his first bittersweet taste of triumph and trauma. He took five wickets in the match as Sri Lanka decisively defeated England in Colombo. However, as *Wisden* noted, there were murmurings about his action.

England's players were privately scathing, but refused to go public. Various umpires and match referees subsequently kept their suspicions out of the public domain too, until the dam burst on Boxing Day 1995, in the Melbourne Test against Australia. After 22 Tests, Murali was suddenly "called" for throwing seven times by umpire Darrell Hair. Ten days later, he was again repeatedly no-balled by umpire Ross Emerson in a one-day international.

His world fell apart. "It affected everything, my friends and family, all those who believed in me," he says. "It was very cruel. Everyone was watching me for all the wrong reasons, thinking I was cheating. I wasn't." For a short time he considered quitting cricket and retreating to the family business, a life of selling candy to Kandy. Instead, with support from the Sri Lankan board, Murali decided to fight back.

Medical experts gave evidence about his bent arm, the bowling action was filmed from 27 different angles, and ICC eventually sided with the Sri Lankan view that the "problem" was an optical illusion. The murmurings never ceased, but no umpire called him again until Emerson reappeared at Adelaide in January 1999. The general opinion was that the umpire discredited himself more than the bowler. What the whole process has done is give Murali an enviable mental toughness to complement his fiendish array of deliveries: the prodigious off-breaks, the occasional leg-break, the startling top-spinner that goes on yet bounces high at the batsman. It has made him an even more formidable cricketer.

Consistent success has flowed since, including the 1996 World Cup triumph, culminating in the waterfall of wickets at The Oval last summer. England captain Alec Stewart gave a gracious tribute afterwards, saying: "It was a very special performance, and clearly here is a bowler of great quality." Whatever the arguments, no one can deny that. – JIM HOLDEN.

ARJUNA RANATUNGA

Almost two decades ago, the Indian player Ravi Shastri, now a commentator, took an Indian youth team to Sri Lanka and came up against a 17-year-old schoolboy, who scored an unbeaten hundred. "He was the same tubby chap, the same clever batsman, the same streetwise cricketer we have been watching in Test cricket all these years," Shastri recalled. "He has had a magnificent career, and I often think that in many ways he *is* Sri Lankan cricket."

ARJUNA RANATUNGA was born on December 1, 1963, in Colombo, Sri Lanka. He was still at Ananda College, just over a year after he made Shastri suffer, when he appeared in Sri Lanka's first Test, against England, and scored their first Test fifty. He assumed the captaincy in 1989 and has held it ever since, apart from a brief interruption while he was in dispute with the Sri Lankan board. By the time he led his country to victory over England at The Oval in August 1998, he had played in 82 of their 87 Tests, and had captained them in all but two of their 14 victories. They had also become the world's one-day champions, winning the World Cup and six other multilateral tournaments inside three years.

Ranatunga's guiding hand can be seen in every success the side has had in the past few years. That, as much as his batting, which by the end of the Oval Test had produced 4,595 Test runs (or walks, since so many were strolled), has brought about his selection as one of *Wisden's* Five Cricketers of the Year. Five Sri Lankans have now been chosen, four of them in the past four years. Among the others was Sanath Jayasuriya, and Ranatunga's faith played a major part in his success. He wanted to use more cricketers from outside Colombo, he believed in Jayasuriya's ability and was prepared to experiment with a middlingly successful middle-order all-rounder in the hope he would turn into a ferocious opening batsman. Even Ranatunga could not imagine how well that theory would work.

The obvious high point of Ranatunga's career came when he coaxed and cajoled his side to their World Cup success in 1996. But he ranks the performance in England in 1998 close to it. Sri Lanka pulled off a spectacular double, winning first the Triangular Tournament and then crushing England by ten wickets at The Oval. This was his crowning moment as a strategist: he was derided when he put England in on a good pitch, especially after they scored 445. "I knew we had to rely entirely on Murali's bowling for victory and that I could not enforce a follow-on because of the amount of work that was likely to fall on his shoulders," he said. Was this a sublime piece of captaincy or a lucky chance? Or a subtle piece of spin doctoring? Whichever, the result was another memorable moment in the rise and rise of Sri Lankan cricket.

Ranatunga attributes his success to building a family atmosphere in the Sri Lankan dressing-room. "I call the boys *malli* – which is young brother in Sinhalese – and they call me *aiya*, or elder brother." He understands about family atmosphere. Two of his brothers, Dhammika and Sanjeewa, have also played Test cricket for Sri Lanka; a third, Nishantha, has appeared in one-day internationals. Comparisons with the Grace brothers come to mind. Dhammika, a year older than Arjuna, is now chief executive of the Sri Lankan board. If, as is popularly rumoured, Arjuna wants to enter the political arena like his father and another brother, Prasanna, he may do so by way of cricket administration too.

In 1998, despite briefly using a bat bizarrely advertising Sam's Chicken and Ribs, Ranatunga lost 12 kilos. He argues that, if the new Sri Lanka is to succeed, the young players must also follow his lead in self-denial. "In the old days it was fine for a young player to make his name in the team with some spectacular shot. But now the new boys will have to be fit and to be good fielders too. The rest of the world was happy for us to be the attractive cricketers who never won anything. Now they have to respect us for our skill and dedication and professionalism."

He believes that the new, aggressive, Sri Lankan attitude dates to 1995-96 when they first faced trouble in Australia over Muttiah Muralitharan's bowling action. The Sri Lankans created a stir by answering each sledge with one of their own. When they returned to Australia for the one-day series early in 1999, Ranatunga became even more aggressive after Ross Emerson no-balled Muralitharan again. He wagged his finger at the umpire and led his team off. But he believes a captain must defend his players, come what may. Throughout this unnecessary crisis – despite the booing, the tasteless banners and the one-sided abuse in Australian newspapers – Ranatunga lost his impressive mien only briefly. The most touching sight of the resulting disciplinary hearing was the arrival of his team demonstrating their loyalty to a much-loved captain. – TED CORBETT.

JONTY RHODES

There were many sceptics when 22-year-old Jonty Rhodes was selected for South Africa's 1992 World Cup squad. He could field, but could he bat? At best, he was regarded as someone who might be useful in a one-day team. Rhodes, however, was already thinking ahead and said his ambition was "to be a good Test player".

Six years later, on South Africa's first full tour of England in nearly 40 years, cricket followers in both countries thrilled to the best of him. By now, he was accepted as the best outfielder in cricket – if anything, better than he was as a youngster – and indispensable in one-day cricket. It was Rhodes the batsman who was a revelation. He scored 367 runs in five Tests against England at an average of 52.42, despite being unlucky with three umpiring decisions.

Three of his innings were memorable. He made his team's top score, 95, at Edgbaston, and took South Africa to safety with positive strokeplay. He played even better at Lord's, where he hit 117, his second Test century, and with Hansie Cronje steered South Africa from the peril of 46 for four to a platform from which they gained a crushing win. In the deciding Test at Headingley, he made a glorious 85 which helped South Africa from 27 for five to the brink of an improbable – but ultimately unattainable – triumph.

Back in May, Rhodes had confirmed his status as a one-day player when he took the man of the series award in the Texaco Trophy. He rounded off his summer in the Triangular Tournament with a miraculous leaping catch at short cover to dismiss Robert Croft off a full-blooded drive. At least, it would have been miraculous for anyone else.

JONATHAN NEIL RHODES was born in Pietermaritzburg on July 27, 1969. Sport was always a part of his life. His mother Tish played tennis.

His father Digby, a former athlete and rugby scrum half, was deputy headmaster of Merchiston primary school, where young Rhodes played in the First Eleven. Rhodes senior was a firm believer in the value of fielding. "If you didn't come off with grass stains on your flannels he thought you hadn't done your job," says Jonty.

He made a century for Natal in the under-13 provincial cricket week, but soccer was his first love: he was the leading scorer at a junior provincial tournament. "Kevin Keegan and Pele were my heroes and I dreamed of playing in England." At Maritzburg College, he switched his goal-scoring skills to hockey, was selected for the national hockey squad before the end of cricketing isolation and, as recently as 1996, was invited to try out for the Atlanta Olympic Games but suffered an untimely hamstring injury.

Although his rise in cricket was not as rapid or spectacular, in 1987 he became vice-captain to Cronje in the South African Schools XI and made a century on his first-class debut, for Natal against Western Province in 1988-89. But it was his fielding and ability to score quickly, rather than weight of runs, that earned him selection for the World Cup, and there was some surprise when he was preferred to Cronje for South Africa's first post-isolation home Test, against India at Kingsmead in 1992-93. Rhodes, however, maintained an average above 40 for his first 15 Tests, making a match-saving century against Sri Lanka in Moratuwa in 1993-94.

Gradually, though, his batting performances dwindled. "I didn't have the best technique in the world," he admits. Test bowlers refused to allow him his favourite cut and pull shots. When Bob Woolmer took over as national team coach in 1994-95, he worked with Rhodes on playing straighter. Natal coach Graham Ford oversaw a slight change in grip, to reduce the amount of bottom hand, while Woolmer's simple advice to focus on the ball was invaluable. But it was only in England that he re-established himself as a first-choice Test player.

He has runs on his side, however, whether he scores any or not. Steve Waugh, for instance, says that there is a lessening of intensity whenever Rhodes is not playing for South Africa. He is often described as the best fielder in the world, but Rhodes shrugs this off: "There are so many different aspects of fielding. I don't believe you can say any one person is the best. I like to think I am one of the best stoppers. My strengths are stopping runs, holding catches and putting pressure on opponents."

As he nears his 30th birthday, he admits there is a physical toll. "I enjoy diving, but when I use both hands I land on my chest and it causes whiplash to my neck. I visit a chiropractor once a month. There will come a time when the body says 'no more'." Before regaining his Test place, he thought the 1999 World Cup might be his swansong, but now he will take each season as it comes. Enjoyment is paramount. "It is a game," he says. "I play cricket because I love it."

Religion, though, is crucial in his life. He says he will always walk if he knows he is out, and recall a batsman if he takes a catch on the bounce. "The Lord doesn't like cheating," he says. Such a policy makes bad decisions doubly cruel, but Rhodes says: "Averages are not everything, it's also about that old thing of how you played the game." In 1998, Jonty Rhodes played it exceedingly well. – COLIN BRYDEN.

AND THAT'S THAT – YET AGAIN

[*Stu Forster, Allsport*

Nasser Hussain gives a return catch to Stuart MacGill at Sydney in the final innings of the 1998-99 Ashes. And England know they have lost the series for the sixth time running.

DO NOT ADJUST YOUR SET.

Test cricket and the NatWest Trophy on Channel 4.

WAR OF WORDS

[*Clive Mason, Allsport*]

Allan Donald sweet-talks Mike Atherton during the 1998 Trent Bridge Test after Atherton had controversially survived an appeal for caught behind.

CROFT'S LAST STAND

[*Adrian Murrell, Allsport*

Robert Croft is congratulated by England captain Alec Stewart on his match-saving innings at the
1998 Old Trafford Test. Croft was promptly dropped, and did not play in England's two victories.

OLD HAT, NEW HAT

[Patrick Eagar

Above: Jack Russell in the scruffy sunhat banned by England when they introduced uniform headgear. Russell followed his hat into retirement from international cricket in October 1998.
Below: Russell keeping wicket in a helmet as Phil Tufnell tries to pitch into the rough outside Carl Hooper's leg stump during the Second Test at Port-of-Spain in February 1998.

[Graham Morris

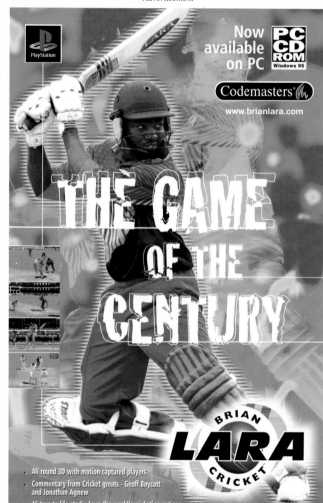

COME AS YOU AREN'T

[*Graham Morris*

Spectators at the 1998 Edgbaston Test indulging in the latest and most bizarre cricket craze: watching in drag.

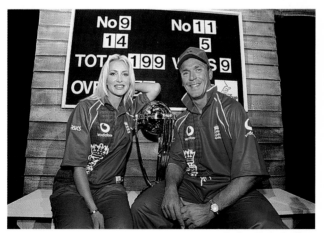

[*Graham Chadwick, Allsport*

Model Caprice poses in the gear the England (men's) team are due to wear in the 1999 World Cup. Alec Stewart keeps her company.

KEEPING THE FLAG FLYING

[*Ian Waldie, Popperfoto/Reuters*

An England supporter waves the Union Jack to celebrate the only thing worth cheering in the early part of the 1998-99 Ashes series: the thunderstorm at Brisbane which prevented a certain Australian victory.

[*Patrick Eagar*

Dean Headley on his way to six for 60 in the second innings of the Melbourne Test, which gave England a stunning 12-run win.

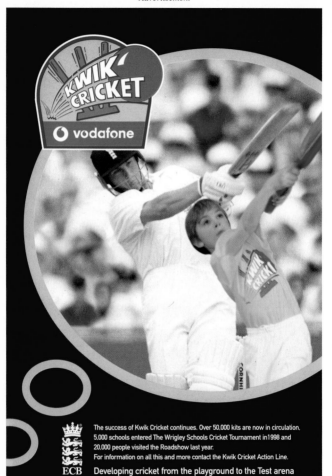

THE DAY OF THE BUTCHERS

[*Patrick Eagar*

Mark Butcher reaches his maiden Test century against South Africa at Headingley . . .

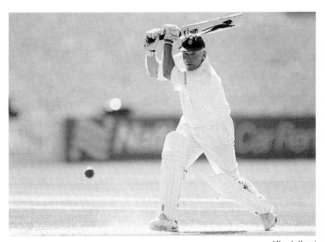

[*Frank Coppi*

. . . on the very day his 44-year-old father Alan is recalled by Surrey from his job as Second Eleven coach to play his first Championship match since 1992.

THE GOLDEN BOYS

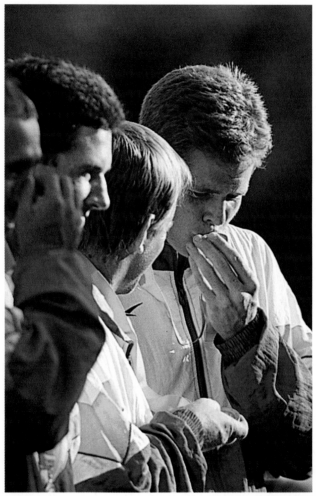

[Laurence Griffiths, Allsport

Shaun Pollock, captain of South Africa as they win the first-ever Commonwealth Games cricket
tournament, kisses the gold medal at the presentation ceremony.

FIVE CRICKETERS OF THE YEAR

[*Adrian Murrell, Allsport*

JONTY RHODES

FIVE CRICKETERS OF THE YEAR

[Graham Morris

IAN AUSTIN

FIVE CRICKETERS OF THE YEAR

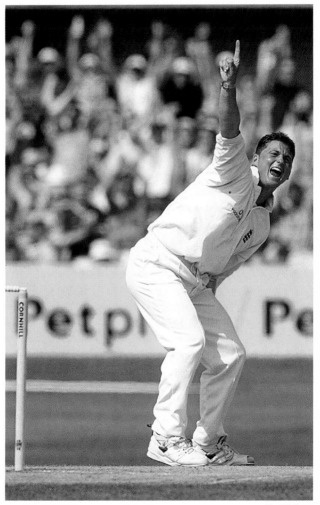

[*Patrick Eagar*

DARREN GOUGH

FIVE CRICKETERS OF THE YEAR

[*Graham Morris*

ARJUNA RANATUNGA

FIVE CRICKETERS OF THE YEAR

[*Shane Seneviratne*

MUTTIAH MURALITHARAN

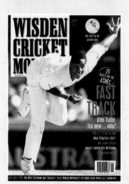

CASTING A LONG SHADOW

[Ian Waldie, Popperfoto/Reuters

Dickie Bird returns from a pitch inspection on his last day as a first-class umpire: a Sunday game between Yorkshire and Warwickshire at Headingley.

ALL THE WINNERS

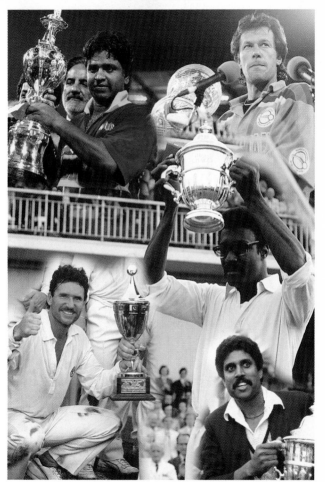

[*Pictures: Patrick Eagar; Montage: Nigel Davies*

The five captains who have led their teams to victory in World Cup finals show off the trophies.
Clockwise from top left: Arjuna Ranatunga (Sri Lanka, 1996); Imran Khan (Pakistan, 1992);
Clive Lloyd (West Indies, 1975 – he led them to victory again in 1979); Kapil Dev (India, 1983);
Allan Border (1987).

Advertisement

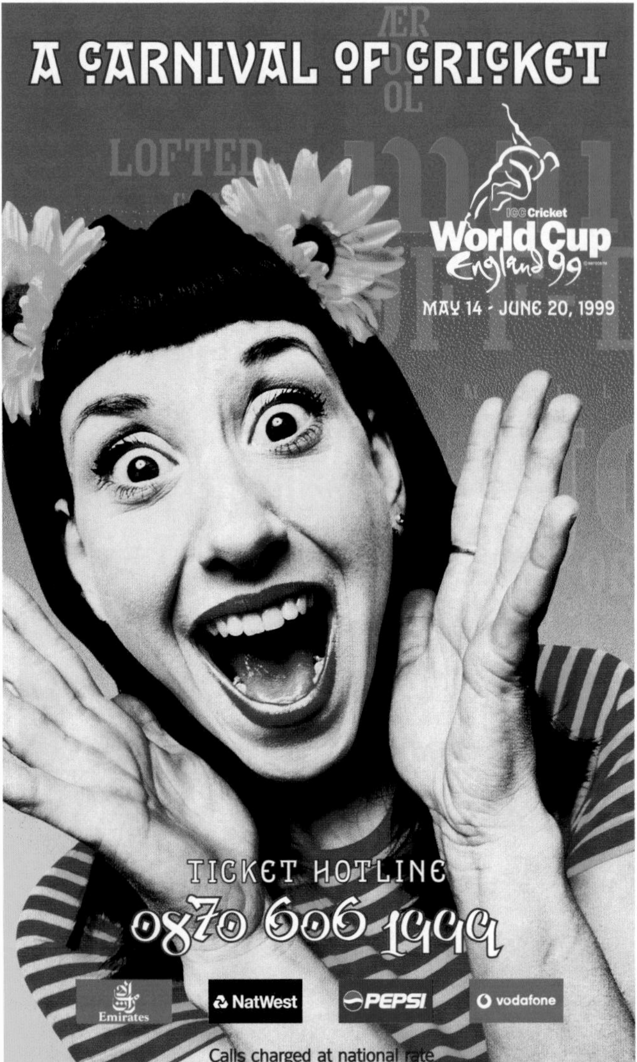

PART TWO: THE WORLD CUP

AND NOW FOR SOMETHING COMPLETELY DIFFERENT

By SCYLD BERRY

Twenty years ago – no more – England's opening batsmen walked out to bat in the World Cup final. They were the 38-year-old Geoffrey Boycott and the 37-year-old Michael Brearley, conventional batsmen both: not even at a pinch could you have called them hitters. They proceeded to prove as much: in pursuit of a target of 287 to beat West Indies, they consumed 235 balls to score 121 runs between them.

England's opening pair were not alone, however, in erring on the side of the pedestrian and conventional in that 1979 World Cup. New Zealand's batting was opened by John Wright and Bruce Edgar, India's by Sunil Gavaskar – the same Gavaskar who had batted through 60 overs in the previous World Cup for 36 runs, albeit largely out of bloody-mindedness – and the studious Anshuman Gaekwad (slow and bespectacled batsmen are always "studious").

One-day international cricket in those days was for Test players letting their often-greying hair down. England's wicket-keeper in the 1979 World Cup was Bob Taylor; the only player resembling a one-day specialist was Brian McKechnie – but then New Zealand were usually short of a full hand of Test players. Nobody did anything cunning like change the batting around (England could have opened in that final with Graham Gooch and Wayne Larkins, or Ian Botham and Derek Randall). It was still an age of innocence, cricketing and commercial, and perhaps more enjoyable for being so.

Now the World Cup is a strapping young man of 24 years, who has grown and grown until he is able to look the World Cups of other sports in the eye. Every feature of cricket's World Cup has expanded enormously since those first two modest tournaments in England in the 1970s. They both consisted of 15 games played by eight teams over 15 days. In 1983, again in England, there were 27 games over 17 days. In 1987, there were still 27 matches played by eight countries, but this time they were spread over the length and breadth of India and Pakistan, regardless of the travelling hardships for the players, and the tournament took five weeks to stage.

In Australia in 1992, 39 matches were played by nine countries in the best format conceived to date, as every country played the others once. In 1996, back in the subcontinent, the number of competitors expanded to 12 as three non-Test sides were included, and Kenya produced the biggest giant-killing act of all when they defeated a disunited West Indian team. This time there will be 42 matches, the most yet, with six teams going through, and being whittled down to four via a complex system called the "Super Six", to determine the semi-finalists.

Crowds have expanded too, from 158,000 to an expected 500,000 for this summer's event in England, and untold millions for the two Cups staged in the subcontinent. Profits too have grown a little, from £150,000 in the original competition to millions of rupees which were again untold in the last World Cup, as the accounts were not subjected to external auditing. The International Cricket Council has decided never to repeat that mistake, and will wisely oversee this and all future World Cups.

If the entrepreneurial horizons have expanded hugely, so too have those of the cricketers themselves, and particularly of batsmen. The first three tournaments were much of a muchness, all of them 60-over events on pitches where the ball did a bit. Even as late as 1983, England were opening with Chris Tavaré – in his dogged England mode, not his sometimes free county style. You built your innings as you would in any other match, kept wickets in hand for "the slog", and only clubbed and clattered in the last few overs. A rate of four runs an over after 60 overs was pretty good, except if you were whopping the likes of Canada, East Africa or Sri Lanka (yes, the 1996 winners were non-Test tiddlers in the first two Cups). Only three totals above 250 were recorded in the 1979 tournament; unsurprisingly, England in the final failed to offer one of those instances.

Each of the next three Cups saw a significant step forward in batting. The 1987 competition was held on the grassless pitches of India and Pakistan. The fact that the innings had to be reduced to 50 overs, to allow for shorter hours of daylight than in England in midsummer, was soon forgotten; the number of totals above 250 was now up to 16. Batsmen cut out pedantic introductions in the first ten overs. West Indies and Viv Richards went further by hitting Sri Lanka for 360 for four and 181 respectively in their Karachi qualifier.

Seam bowlers had been safe from assault in England, unless you were as aggressive as Dennis Lillee and tried to bounce out Alvin Kallicharran, even though it was a limited-overs game (Kalli hit Lillee for 35 from ten balls in a 1975 qualifier). Now, in 1987, such canny exponents as Courtney Walsh and Derek Pringle were carted, especially at the end of a long hot session: the three breaks in leisurely England had been reduced to one between innings. Line and length were no longer enough. Change of pace was in, as exemplified by Steve Waugh, who rolled his wrist and fingers and frequently got that ball up in the blockhole. But spin too had a major say for the first time in the 1987 Cup. Whereas not one over of it was bowled in the 1975 final, seven of the nine most economical bowlers in the qualifying round of 1987 were spinners.

As the 1992 tournament was staged largely in Australia, the ACB introduced floodlit cricket, coloured clothes, white balls and the fielding restriction which had been a feature of their one-day internationals at home since World Series: only two fielders allowed outside the semi-circles in the first 15 overs, so that television viewers would be glued to their seats from the start. In the previous World Cup, Geoff Marsh and David Boon of victorious Australia had been the exemplars of one-day opening, running those quick singles: their coach Bobby Simpson had calculated that 90 per cent of internationals were won by the side which scored off the greater number of balls, never mind the boundaries. Soon that was a load of old helmet. England opened with Ian Botham, India with Kris Srikkanth, West Indies with Brian Lara, to cash in while the field was up, but none of them did so with such effect as Mark Greatbatch of New Zealand.

Nobody could legally bowl him a bouncer (the definition of what was too high and wide had been tightened up for the 1983 competition onwards), so he put his foot down the wicket and bounced the ball off the terracing of New Zealand's cricket-cum-rugby grounds. One-day batting could not be confused with the Test-match style of Boycott and Brearley any more. The vogue was to use a pinch-hitter to get that scoring-rate up and keep it up. The counter, especially in New Zealand where pitches were slow, was to take all the pace off the ball – as the Indians had done in 1983 – even to the extent of opening the bowling with Dipak Patel.

In 1995-96, Sri Lanka were playing in the one-day series in Australia when one of their regular openers, Roshan Mahanama, was injured (their other opener was called Sanath Jayasuriya). So the Sri Lankans' manager Duleep Mendis asked the coach Dav Whatmore what he thought about promoting the wicket-keeper Romesh Kaluwitharana, who had been batting down the order and getting caught in the deep. "I love it," replied Whatmore. Thus was born the Sri Lankan ploy of two pinch-hitters, except that Jayasuriya and Kaluwitharana were not in any sense mere hitters; one already had a Test century against Australia, the other would get his within a few weeks. They were able to bat with greater freedom than specialist batsmen because they were all-rounders with more than one bow-string.

With five specialist batsmen to follow – Mahanama now served as insurance against any batting collapses at No. 7 – the Sri Lankans scored freely in the 1996 Cup, not only when they clattered Kenya for a record total of 398 but even when they made bad starts in the semi-final and final. Whatmore and his Australian vigour had already made Sri Lanka into the first accomplished all-round fielding side the subcontinent had produced (Asia had seen some wonderful specialists before, of course, but there was always someone less than zealous or reluctant to dive). Throw in four spinners who took the pace off the ball, and mature composure from the senior players, and the World Cup was deservedly Sri Lanka's. The Australian argument that they were handicapped by dew in the day/night final in Lahore does not bear much scrutiny, as they had underperformed with the bat in broad daylight.

This growth in run-scoring may cease in 1999 as the young man reaches his mid-twenties. The three previous World Cups in England were staged in June, but this one will begin on May 14. Specialist pace bowlers will be necessary to make full use of the conditions, and specialist top-order batsmen to withstand them. Everything else should keep on growing though, like the excellence of the fielding, and the sponsorship money, and the television revenues, and the media coverage, and the worldwide interest. It will be a mature man of the world who goes to South Africa in 2003.

Scyld Berry is cricket correspondent of the Sunday Telegraph.

SLOW, SLOW, QUICK, QUICK, SLOWIE: THE EVOLUTION OF ONE-DAY STRATEGY

By MICKY STEWART

Back in the 1950s and early 1960s, it was my privilege to play in the Surrey side with the late Bernard Constable, one of the most knowledgeable cricketers I have known. He was a real professional, with great respect for the game, but was never really happy unless he had something to moan about. If anyone ever declared against us and set a target of around 90 runs an hour, you knew how Bernie would react: "What kind of declaration is that supposed to be then?" he would demand loudly.

A fair asking-rate in those days was thought to be 80 runs an hour. All targets then were set against the clock: the number of overs was hardly ever mentioned, although the average was around 20 per hour. Bernie was a free scorer himself, but he still expected a good three hours to chase 250, about four runs an over. And yet today's cricketers will gladly chase five an over in any form of cricket. Over shorter periods, six an over is thought reasonable, and seven or eight or even more possible.

My first year as captain of Surrey was 1963, the start of what became the Gillette Cup, when teams had 65 overs to bat – yet 250 was passed only five times. In 1969, the first year of the 40-over Sunday League, Lancashire's highest score was 204, with a run-rate all season of barely four an over. And they were the champions. One-day cricket created a different set of demands from those of the longer game. These were understood only slowly, and players are still adapting to them today.

Many of the tactical innovations, however, are not new ones. To begin with batting, the role of the "anchor-man" existed long before the one-day game. And the idea that one player should bat through, allowing others to take risks, was one of the very first one-day strategies to emerge. It is fine as long as the anchor-man's scoring-rate gradually accelerates throughout the innings, and he does not get bogged down.

The term pinch-hitter has only recently been borrowed from baseball, where it means a substitute batter. In one-day cricket, it means the promotion of a hard-hitting batsman up the order, especially to take advantage of the rule allowing only two fielders outside the circle in the first 15 overs. Again, the idea is not new at all. Surrey would promote Arthur McIntyre during run-chases in the 1950s; Sussex later did the same with John Snow – long before the 15-over rule. Soon after it came in, England used Ian Botham as opener towards the end of the 1986-87 World Series in Australia, and again in the 1992 World Cup, with qualified success. Now players have become specialists in the role.

The skills acquired in one-day cricket can feed through into the longer game. During my playing years, Peter May and Jim Parks stood out as players who would regularly explore the aerial route over extra cover. Nowadays it is a stroke employed by many batsmen. But I cringe when I see it attempted against off-spinners on a turning pitch. Running between

[*Alpha*

One-day cricket ancient . . . (*above*) Jim Parks drives Doug Slade in the classic manner
during the first Gillette Cup final . . . and modern (*below*) Romesh Kaluwitharana tries to stump
Michael Bevan in the 1996 World Cup final.

[*Patrick Eagar*

the wickets and rotating the strike have both improved enormously. As England team manager, I sat down with the captain, Graham Gooch, to discuss how to improve this aspect of the game. I then discovered from my statistics that Graham himself was near the top of the league for dot balls. He hit so many boundaries that this had not been obvious to either of us.

Many batsmen now try to go for big shots all the time. My own preference is for controlled aggression from the first ball of an innings, using all the skills, from perhaps having to play a maiden over to positive running between the wickets, good placement of the ball between fielders and crisp striking to the boundary. This formula, put together in partnerships, usually produces winning totals. I am all for innovation to produce these totals, including the reverse sweep, as long as those putting it into practice have worked long and hard at it before playing it in the middle.

After that first Gillette Cup, *Wisden* noted that spin bowlers were normally "despised" in one-day cricket. And, as the game developed, those who did play usually concentrated on a leg-stump line with a quicker pace, little spin and a flat trajectory. Pat Pocock and John Emburey were very successful one-day bowlers through adopting these tactics. Outstanding bowlers though they were, it was detrimental to their effectiveness in the longer game, especially in their ability to bowl a more attacking line to take wickets. To counter the leg-stump line ploy, the Australians were the first to introduce the restriction on leg-side fielders: only five allowed. Before that, the six-three field was the norm, and at times seven-two was used.

Back in the 1960s, the line adopted by pace bowlers was no different than it is today i.e. off stump and *just* outside. Too much width has always been taboo, and very good bowlers have often held the ball across the seam if they could not control their direction. For some bowlers, such as Allan Donald, this problem has increased since the introduction of the white ball. After the initial onslaught, the length adopted was usually either very full, to strike the toe of the bat, or a fraction short of a length to hit the splice. Again, this has changed very little.

What has changed is the much greater emphasis on the use of variation of pace by the quicker bowlers, and regular use of the slower ball, the "slowie". Again, good control is paramount: an early exponent was Steve Waugh, when he was in his bowling prime. He could hit the pitch really hard when he wanted to, but he also had great control of the slower ball, which was particularly useful when the slog was on towards the end of an innings. In the early days, the usual tactic was a succession of straight yorkers, but as the batsmen became more effective at making room to hit full-length deliveries over the off side, pace variation was introduced to confuse the striker. Hence the more common use of the slowie. Spin bowlers also vary their pace more in one-day cricket these days, and the restriction of fielders on the leg side has encouraged them to revert to variations of spin and flight. There are also bowlers whose whole method rests on bowling as slowly as possible: this only works on a very bland surface, and on a pitch with any pace in it they can be murdered.

Of course, unless all the bowlers are supported by the highest-quality fielding, no side is going to be an effective one-day unit. Limited-overs cricket has improved all areas of outfielding over the years, and the longer game has benefited too. Much more practice time is spent working at fielding, and this, combined with a greater emphasis on general fitness, has produced higher standards. It was nearly ten years ago, before the England team went to the West Indies in 1989-90, that I introduced a general fitness programme for the touring party. Most of the media, and others in the game, referred to Gooch and myself as the "tracksuit regime". But even then we were playing catch-up with the Australians and West Indies, who had been running similar programmes for some time.

I know that the current England coach, David Lloyd, and his staff have now spent hours and hours on fitness and fielding. But since the South Africans have come back into the fold, I believe they have overtaken the Australians as fielders, and Jonty Rhodes has taken fielding on to a different plane, developing into a role model for budding young cricketers everywhere. He is not a freak: there is no reason why others cannot aspire to be as good.

In the old days, fielding, and especially throwing, was sadly neglected in England. Not so now. Many hours are spent practising both old and new skills, the sliding pick-up and the baseball throw amongst them. It is only four years since I first contacted a baseball coach and got him to work with the England Under-15s at Lilleshall. There was a huge improvement in half an hour.

The Australians Neil Harvey and Norman O'Neill were throwing the ball baseball-style years ago. The method is that the elbow has to be at least level with, or preferably above, the throwing shoulder. This ensures that all the joints involved are revolving in the same direction as the throw, so reducing the injury risk and producing a stronger, more accurate result. It is now included in our national coaching programme at all levels, and has also been introduced at a number of counties. I hope that I will never again hear that overseas cricketers throw better than the average English player because they grew up in a hotter climate.

In Surrey's very first Gillette game at Worcester, 36 years ago, Bernie Constable said to me: "We've got a lot to learn about this game." We are still learning. And by the time the 1999 World Cup is over, we will doubtless have learned even more.

Micky Stewart was captain of Surrey when the Gillette Cup started in 1963. He subsequently became the club's cricket manager (1979-86), England team manager (1986-92) and ECB director of coaching (1992-97).

THE SCOTTISH CONNECTION

By ALLAN MASSIE

Our local newspaper in Selkirk, just inside the Scottish border, runs one of those "100 Years Ago" columns. Last year, it told of how, in 1898, the Selkirk cricket XI, returning from a victory over Hawick which had enabled them to win the Border League for the third time in its four-year history, were greeted in the market square by the town band and an exuberant crowd. The story would surprise many who think of cricket as a game with shallow roots in Scotland.

It didn't surprise me. My first cricketing heroes were Bill Edrich, Jim Donald and Davie Ewen. Bill Edrich needs no introduction; it was his defiance of the Australian attack in 1946-47 which won him my regard. Jim Donald and Davie Ewen are rather different. They played for Kintore in the Aberdeenshire Grades. Davie Ewen was a postman who bowled fast off a very long run. Jim Donald, who was the school janitor and whose wife used to come to clean for my mother, was a tall left-hander who always promised to hit sixes over long-on into the neighbouring hayfield, and sometimes did so. Cricket was played and followed with great intensity in Aberdeenshire. Kintore, a small burgh with a population of 800, then fielded two XIs every week. The Aberdeenshire Grades – three or four divisions with promotion and relegation, and a Reserve Grade too – were very competitive. I suppose the term "Grade" was borrowed from Australia, though I have occasionally played with the fancy that the Aussies took it from Aberdeenshire.

I soon found myself also watching cricket in Aberdeen, at Mannofield, where Aberdeenshire played in, and then usually won, the Scottish County Championship (founded in 1902). There I got myself a new hero – Alma Hunt, the club's Bermudan professional, a fast bowler and fast-scoring left-handed bat. In those days, trams used to run up and down Aberdeen's Union Street with a placard proclaiming "To and From the Cricket Match". A crowd of 5,000 was not uncommon. Further south, the Perthshire–Forfarshire derby games would draw almost twice that many. Gradually, in the 1950s, television, the greater variety of occupations, the disappearance of petrol rationing, and the encroachment of football either end of summer, killed Scottish club cricket as a spectator sport.

Interest in cricket of course survived. More people, it is claimed, play club cricket in Scotland today than play rugby. Certainly cricket clubs are older than either rugby or football clubs. If 18th-century matches recorded in Scotland were mostly between teams drawn from regiments stationed here, there are nevertheless clubs which can trace a continuous existence since the first half of the 19th century: Perthshire and Grange (in Edinburgh) both date from the 1830s.

Most of Scotland was playing competitive league cricket by the end of the century. The Western Union was founded in 1893; so was the North of Scotland League. The Border League followed in 1895, the County Championship in 1902, and the Strathmore Union (covering the north-east)

[*The Highland Council, Nairn*

Beyond the border: cricket at Nairn, by the Moray Firth.

in 1929. Only Edinburgh, until 1953, held out against league cricket. The Edinburgh clubs prided themselves on a gentlemanly approach, Grange being known as the MCC of Scotland.

For this reason they disdained professionals. Other leagues permitted each club to field one professional. Some were very distinguished. The young Wilfred Rhodes played two seasons, 1896 and 1897, for Gala in the Border League before being required by Yorkshire. It was Galashiels folklore that they taught him all he knew. Rhodes finished his career in Scotland too, in 1931, with Perthshire, and was still taking wickets for less than ten apiece.

Scottish cricket owes much to English county pros, especially to Yorkshiremen like Tom Lodge, who contributed to Perthshire's great record in the 1950s, and now to Jim Love, the Scottish Cricket Union's director of cricket, who has played a very big part in Scotland's emergence in international one-day cricket. Apart from their playing ability, veteran county pros have helped by their talk to make Scottish cricketers feel they belong to the great family of cricket. No great performer myself, I still got a touch of this from our school pro, Frank Matthews, a Nottinghamshire fast bowler of the 1920s. His memories of George Gunn and Arthur Carr were as much part of my cricket education as reading Cardus.

Recently, fewer pros have been old county players, as clubs have looked overseas instead: to Australia, India, Pakistan, as well as the West Indies. These pros are usually young, regarding a season or two in the British Isles as part of their cricketing education. They have included Test players like Kim Hughes, Sadiq Mohammad, Abdul Qadir, and Bob Massie, who went on to take 16 England wickets in the 1972 Lord's Test. He wasn't always so successful when he played for Kilmarnock. Middle-aged men in Perthshire still like to recall how one of the Laing brothers gave him stick in a Rothman's Quaich match.

There have been plenty of good native cricketers. Foremost must be the great John Kerr of Greenock, whose 147 against Warwick Armstrong's 1921 Australians was reckoned by them to be as fine an innings as any played against them that summer. Kerr also hit four centuries in Scotland's annual three-day "Test" match against Ireland. Then there was, after the Second World War, the Rev. James Aitchison, a Church of Scotland minister who, on his best days, played as if the Calvinist doctrine of predestination ensured he would make a century; which indeed he often did, notably against the 1956 Australians. There can have been few more complete cricketers than Jimmy Allan, slow left-arm bowler and dogged bat. He took 171 wickets for Scotland over 20 years at an average of 22 and, in 1955, one of his few complete first-class seasons for Oxford University and Kent, finished only five wickets short of the Double. He was followed into the Kent team by Mike Denness, who went on, of course, to captain England.

No surprise there; though some Scottish nationalists may delight in supporting whoever is playing against England, the majority of Scottish cricketers and cricket followers have agonised over England's fortunes and misfortunes as intensely as anyone in Yorkshire, Lancashire or Surrey. Indeed, most cricketers in Scotland keenly support an English county, selected for some reason or other. Since Len Hutton superseded Bill Edrich as my boyhood hero, there has scarcely been a day in the cricket season when I haven't looked first to see how Yorkshire are faring. My elder son, however, supports Somerset, on account of Botham, and my younger identified from an early age with Kent, for reasons neither he nor I can recall.

The climate does often make cricket hard going in Scotland, calling for the exercise of Spartan virtues, and enough sweaters to make fieldsmen resemble the Michelin man. More damagingly to the standard, wickets are usually slow, at least till late July, and in recent seasons summer rain has shown a dismal habit of concentrating on Saturdays and Sundays. Nevertheless, cricket is widely played. I have even heard of games in Orkney and Shetland, though organised club cricket tails off north of Inverness, and in the West little is played north of the Firth of Clyde.

Crowds may have gone, as they have, of course, even from county cricket in England; and the development of the game has certainly been hampered by a lack of media interest, sometimes, it seems, founded on the prejudice against cricket as "not a Scottish game". Historically untrue, this has been rendered absurd by the recent improvement in the level attained by the national side, first in domestic one-day tournaments, and now demonstrated in Scotland's qualification for the World Cup. That was no mean achievement.

It is unlikely that a full-scale professional game will ever develop in Scotland, and participation at Test level is still well beyond the capabilities of Scottish cricket. Until even a couple of years ago it would indeed have seemed an absurd ambition. But who knows? The same would have been said of Sri Lanka and Zimbabwe not long ago. Now, in a world where Sri Lanka can beat England by ten wickets, and Zimbabwe win a series in Pakistan, anything seems, suddenly, possible and no ambition unrealistic.

Allan Massie is a novelist and journalist, occasionally permitted to write about sport for The Scotsman. *In his youth he bowled chinamen, more relished by batsmen than by his captain.*

WISDEN COMPETITION

CHOOSE YOUR FIVE CRICKETERS OF THE CENTURY

Even before the 20th century started, *Wisden* was choosing its Five Cricketers of the Year. As it ends, *Wisden* will also be naming its **Five Cricketers of the Century.**

The choice is to be made by a panel of 100 players and pundits from all the major cricketing countries, and will be announced in our millennium edition: *Wisden 2000.* The concept is explained in detail on page 21 of *Wisden 1999.*

We are inviting readers to guess who they believe the panel will choose. Alongside the Five Cricketers of the Century, we will name five competition winners who will each receive a personalised de-luxe leatherbound copy of the Millennium Edition, which would normally be priced at £200. Ten runners-up will receive a copy of the limited-edition *Wisden* Millennium calendar of cricket (details overleaf).

Wisden 2000 will focus on the past 100 years of cricket. While you're waiting to read it, you can think about the century's great players, and make your selection.

RULES

1. One entry per person, please. Entries may be made on a sheet of paper, provided you include your name, address and phone number.

2. Please post entries to *Wisden* Competition, 25 Down Road, Merrow, Guildford, Surrey GU1 2PY. Entries must be received on or before SEPTEMBER 30, 1999.

3. The main prize winners will be the first five entries drawn whose choice is identical to the five cricketers selected by *Wisden's* panel of 100. The next ten all-correct entries will win the runners-up prizes. If insufficient all-correct entries are received, then prizes will be awarded to entrants with four correct, then three etc., as appropriate.

4. In any dispute the decision of the editor of *Wisden* will be final.

The names of the winners, and the runners-up, will be announced along with the names of the Five Cricketers of the Century in *Wisden 2000,* to be published in April 2000.

MY PREDICTIONS FOR THE WISDEN CRICKETERS OF THE CENTURY ARE:-

1

2

3

4

5

NAME

ADDRESS

TELEPHONE

Send to: **Wisden Competition, 25 Down Road, Merrow, Guildford, Surrey GU1 2PY**

Closing date 30 September 1999

☐ Tick if you do not want to be on any mailing list to be passed to selected other companies.

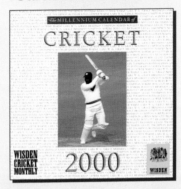

WORLD CUP RECORDS 1975-1996

WORLD CUP FINALS

1975	WEST INDIES (291-8) beat Australia (274) by 17 runs.	Lord's
1979	WEST INDIES (286-9) beat England (194) by 92 runs	Lord's
1983	INDIA (183) beat West Indies (140) by 43 runs.	Lord's
1987-88	AUSTRALIA (253-5) beat England (246-8) by seven runs.	Calcutta
1991-92	PAKISTAN (249-6) beat England (227) by 22 runs.	Melbourne
1995-96	SRI LANKA (245-3) beat Australia (241-7) by seven wickets.	Lahore

TEAM RESULTS 1975-1996

	Rounds reached				Matches		
	W	F	SF	P	W	L	NR
West Indies (6)	2	3	4	38	25	12	1
England (6).	0	3	5	40	25	14	1
Australia (6)	1	3	3	37	22	15	0
Pakistan (6).	1	1	4	37	21	15	1
New Zealand (6)	0	0	3	35	19	16	0
India (6).	1	1	3	36	18	17	1
South Africa (2).	0	0	1	15	10	5	0
Sri Lanka (6).	1	1	1	32	10	20	2
Zimbabwe (4)	0	0	0	25	3	22	0
Kenya (1)	0	0	0	5	1	4	0
United Arab Emirates (1).	0	0	0	5	1	4	0
Canada (1)	0	0	0	3	0	3	0
East Africa (1).	0	0	0	3	0	3	0
Holland (1)	0	0	0	5	0	5	0

The number of tournaments each team has played in is shown in brackets.

BATTING RECORDS

Most Runs

	M	I	NO	R	HS	100s	Avge
Javed Miandad (P). . . .	33	30	5	1,083	103	1	43.32
I. V. A. Richards (WI) .	23	21	5	1,013	181	3	63.31
G. A. Gooch (E)	21	21	1	897	115	1	44.85
M. D. Crowe (NZ). . . .	21	21	5	880	100*	1	55.00
D. L. Haynes (WI)	25	25	2	854	105	1	37.13
A. Ranatunga (SL). . . .	25	24	8	835	88*	0	52.18
D. C. Boon (A).	16	16	1	815	100	2	54.33
S. R. Tendulkar (I). . . .	15	14	2	806	137	2	67.16

Highest Scores

188*	G. Kirsten	South Africa v United Arab Emirates at Rawalpindi. . .	1995-96
181	I. V. A. Richards	West Indies v Sri Lanka at Karachi.	1987-88
175*	Kapil Dev	India v Zimbabwe at Tunbridge Wells.	1983
171*	G. M. Turner†	New Zealand v East Africa at Birmingham	1975
161	A. C. Hudson	South Africa v Holland at Rawalpindi.	1995-96
145	P. A. de Silva	Sri Lanka v Kenya at Kandy.	1995-96
142	D. L. Houghton	Zimbabwe v New Zealand at Hyderabad (India)	1987-88

Highest scores for other Test-playing countries:

137	D. L. Amiss†	England v India at Lord's	1975
130	M. E. Waugh	Australia v Kenya at Vishakhapatnam	1995-96
119*	Ramiz Raja	Pakistan v New Zealand at Christchurch	1991-92

† *Amiss scored 137 and Turner 171* on the opening day of the inaugural World Cup in 1975; both remain national records.*

Hundred Before Lunch

101	A. Turner	Australia v Sri Lanka at The Oval	1975

Most Hundreds

3   I. V. A. Richards (WI), Ramiz Raja (P), M. E. Waugh (A)

Highest Partnership for Each Wicket

186	for 1st	G. Kirsten and A. C. Hudson	SA v H	Rawalpindi	1995-96
176	for 2nd	D. L. Amiss and K. W. R. Fletcher	E v I	Lord's	1975
207	for 3rd	M. E. Waugh and S. R. Waugh	A v K	Vishakhapatnam	1995-96
168	for 4th	L. K. Germon and C. Z. Harris	NZ v A	Madras	1995-96
145*	for 5th	A. Flower and A. C. Waller	Z v SL	New Plymouth	1991-92
144	for 6th	Imran Khan and Shahid Mahboob	P v SL	Leeds	1983
75*	for 7th	D. A. G. Fletcher and I. P. Butchart	Z v A	Nottingham	1983
117	for 8th	D. L. Houghton and I. P. Butchart	Z v NZ	Hyderabad (India)	1987-88
126*	for 9th	Kapil Dev and S. M. H. Kirmani	I v Z	Tunbridge Wells	1983
71	for 10th	A. M. E. Roberts and J. Garner	WI v I	Manchester	1983

BOWLING RECORDS

Most Wickets

	O	R	W	BB	4W/i	Avge
Imran Khan (P)	169.3	655	34	4-37	2	19.26
I. T. Botham (E)	222	762	30	4-31	1	25.40
Kapil Dev (I)	237	892	28	5-43	1	31.85
Wasim Akram (P)	186.2	768	28	4-32	1	27.42
C. J. McDermott (A) . . .	149	599	27	5-44	2	22.18
Mushtaq Ahmed (P)	135	549	26	3-16	0	21.11
A. M. E. Roberts (WI) . .	170.1	552	26	3-32	0	21.23

Best Bowling

7-51	W. W. Davis	West Indies v Australia at Leeds	1983
6-14	G. J. Gilmour	Australia v England at Leeds	1975
6-39	K. H. MacLeay	Australia v India at Nottingham	1983
5-21	A. G. Hurst	Australia v Canada at Birmingham	1979
5-21	P. A. Strang	Zimbabwe v Kenya at Patna	1995-96
5-25	R. J. Hadlee	New Zealand v Sri Lanka at Bristol	1983
5-29	S. Dukanwala	United Arab Emirates v Holland at Lahore	1995-96
5-32	A. L. F. de Mel	Sri Lanka v New Zealand at Derby	1983

Best analyses for other Test-playing countries:

5-39	V. J. Marks	England v Sri Lanka at Taunton	1983
5-43	Kapil Dev	India v Australia at Nottingham	1983
5-44	Abdul Qadir	Pakistan v Sri Lanka at Leeds	1983
4-11	M. W. Pringle	South Africa v West Indies at Christchurch	1991-92

Other Bowling Records

Hat-trick: Chetan Sharma, India v New Zealand at Nagpur, 1987-88.
Most economical bowling: 12–8–6–1; B. S. Bedi, India v East Africa at Leeds, 1975.
Most expensive bowling: 12–1–105–2; M. C. Snedden, New Zealand v England at The Oval, 1983.

WICKET-KEEPING RECORDS
Most Dismissals

Wasim Bari (P)	22 (18 ct, 4 st)	R. W. Marsh (A)	18 (17 ct, 1 st)
P. J. L. Dujon (WI).	20 (19 ct, 1 st)	K. S. More (I)	18 (12 ct, 6 st)
I. A. Healy (A)	20 (17 ct, 3 st)		

Most Dismissals in an Innings

5 (5 ct)	S. M. H. Kirmani	India v Zimbabwe at Leicester	1983
5 (4 ct, 1st)	J. C. Adams	West Indies v Kenya at Pune	1995-96
5 (4 ct, 1st)	Rashid Latif	Pakistan v New Zealand at Lahore	1995-96

FIELDING RECORDS
Most Catches

12 C. H. Lloyd (WI), Kapil Dev (I), D. L. Haynes (WI); 11 C. L. Cairns (NZ); 10 I. T. Botham (E), A. R. Border (A).

MOST APPEARANCES

33 Javed Miandad (P); 28 Imran Khan (P); 26 Kapil Dev (I); 25 A. R. Border (A), D. L. Haynes (WI), A. Ranatunga (SL).

TEAM RECORDS

Highest Total	398-5	Sri Lanka v Kenya	Kandy	1995-96
Batting Second	313-7	Sri Lanka v Zimbabwe	New Plymouth	1991-92
Lowest Total	45	Canada v England	Manchester	1979
Highest Aggregate	652-12	Sri Lanka v Kenya	Kandy	1995-96
Largest Victories	10 wkts	India beat East Africa	Leeds	1975
	10 wkts	West Indies beat Zimbabwe	Birmingham	1983
	10 wkts	West Indies beat Pakistan	Melbourne	1991-92
	202 runs	England beat India	Lord's	1975
Narrowest Victories	1 wkt	West Indies beat Pakistan	Birmingham	1975
	1 wkt	Pakistan beat West Indies	Lahore	1987-88
	1 run	Australia beat India	Madras	1987-88
	1 run	Australia beat India	Brisbane	1991-92

WORLD CUP FIXTURES, 1999
WARM-UP MATCHES
MAY

7–Kent v England (Canterbury); Leics v Indians (Leicester); Northants v Sri Lankans (Northampton); Somerset v Kenya (Taunton); Sussex.v South Africans (Hove); Worcs v Zimbabweans (Worcester).

8–Derbys v Pakistanis (Derby); Durham v Scotland (Chester-le-Street); Essex v Bangladesh (Chelmsford); Glam v Australians (Cardiff); Glos v West Indians (Bristol); Hants v New Zealanders (Southampton).

9–Derbys v Zimbabweans (Derby); Essex v England (Chelmsford); Glos v Kenya (Bristol); Kent v South Africans (Canterbury); Notts v Sri Lankans (Nottingham); Yorks v Indians (Harrogate).

10–Durham v Pakistanis (Chester-le-Street); Lancs v Scotland (Manchester); Middx v Bangladesh (Southgate); Surrey v New Zealanders (The Oval); Warwicks v West Indians (Birmingham); Worcs v Australians (Worcester).

11–Glam v Kenya (Cardiff); Hants v England (Southampton); Leics v Sri Lankans (Leicester); Middx v South Africans (Southgate); Notts v Indians (Nottingham); Warwicks v Zimbabweans (Birmingham).

12 –Lancs v Pakistanis (Manchester); Northants v Bangladesh (Northampton); Somerset v Australians (Taunton); Surrey v West Indians (The Oval); Sussex v New Zealanders (Arundel); Yorks v Scotland (Scarborough).

WORLD CUP

Group A

MAY

14	Lord's†	England v Sri Lanka
15	Hove†	India v South Africa
15	Taunton†	Kenya v Zimbabwe
18	Canterbury*	England v Kenya
19	Leicester†	India v Zimbabwe
19	Northampton†	South Africa v Sri Lanka
22	The Oval*	England v South Africa
22	Worcester*	Sri Lanka v Zimbabwe
23	Bristol†	India v Kenya
25	Nottingham†	England v Zimbabwe
26	Taunton*	India v Sri Lanka
26	Amstelveen*	Kenya v South Africa
29	Birmingham†	England v India
29	Chelmsford†	South Africa v Zimbabwe
30	Southampton*	Kenya v Sri Lanka

Group B

MAY

16	Worcester*	Australia v Scotland
16	Bristol*	Pakistan v West Indies
17	Chelmsford†	Bangladesh v New Zealand
20	Cardiff*	Australia v New Zealand
20	Chester-le-Street*	Pakistan v Scotland
21	Dublin†	Bangladesh v West Indies
23	Leeds†	Australia v Pakistan
24	Southampton*	New Zealand v West Indies
24	Edinburgh*	Scotland v Bangladesh
27	Chester-le-Street†	Australia v Bangladesh
27	Leicester†	Scotland v West Indies
28	Derby†	New Zealand v Pakistan
30	Manchester*	Australia v West Indies
31	Northampton†	Bangladesh v Pakistan
31	Edinburgh†	Scotland v New Zealand

The top three teams from each group advance to the Super Six round, taking with them the points they gained against the other teams that progress. Each of them will then play the three teams from the other group.

SUPER SIX

JUNE

4	The Oval†	Group A 2nd v Group B 2nd
5	Nottingham*	Group A 1st v Group B 1st
6	Leeds†	Group A 3rd v Group B 3rd
8	Manchester†	Group A 2nd v Group B 1st
9	Lord's*	Group A 3rd v Group B 2nd
10	Birmingham†	Group A 1st v Group B 3rd
11	The Oval*	Group A 3rd v Group B 1st
12	Nottingham*	Group A 2nd v Group B 3rd
13	Leeds†	Group A 1st v Group B 2nd

SEMI-FINALS

Wednesday, June 16		**Thursday, June 17**	
Manchester	First v Fourth of Super Six	Birmingham	Second v Third of Super Six

The World Cup Final will be played on Sunday, June 20, 1999, at Lord's.

* To be televised by the BBC; † to be televised by Sky TV. The BBC and Sky will each show one semi-final; Sky has first choice. Both will broadcast the final.

PART THREE: THE PLAYERS

TEST CRICKETERS

FULL LIST FROM 1877 TO AUGUST 31, 1998

These lists have been compiled on a home and abroad basis, appearances abroad being printed in *italics*.

Abbreviations. E: England. A: Australia. SA: South Africa. WI: West Indies. NZ: New Zealand. In: India. P: Pakistan. SL: Sri Lanka. Z: Zimbabwe.

All appearances are placed in this order of seniority. Hence, any England cricketer playing against Australia in England has that achievement recorded first and the remainder of his appearances at home (if any) set down before passing to matches abroad. The figures immediately following each name represent the total number of appearances in *all* Tests.

Where the season embraces two different years, the first year is given; i.e. 1876 indicates 1876-77.

ENGLAND

Number of Test cricketers: 591

Abel, R. 13: v A 1888 (3) 1896 (3) 1902 (2); *v A 1891 (3); v SA 1888 (2)*
Absolom, C. A. 1: *v A 1878*
Agnew, J. P. 3: v A 1985 (1); v WI 1984 (1); v SL 1984 (1)
Allen, D. A. 39: v A 1961 (4) 1964 (1); v SA 1960 (2); v WI 1963 (2) 1966 (1); v P 1962 (4); *v A 1962 (1) 1965 (4); v SA 1964 (4); v WI 1959 (5); v NZ 1965 (3); v In 1961 (5); v P 1961 (3)*
Allen, G. O. B. 25: v A 1930 (1) 1934 (2); v WI 1933 (1); v NZ 1931 (3); v In 1936 (3); *v A 1932 (5) 1936 (5); v WI 1947 (3); v NZ 1932 (2)*
Allom, M. J. C. 5: *v SA 1930 (1); v NZ 1929 (4)*
Allott, P. J. W. 13: v A 1981 (1) 1985 (4); v WI 1984 (3); v In 1982 (2); v SL 1984 (1); *v In 1981 (1); v SL 1981 (1)*
Ames, L. E. G. 47: v A 1934 (5) 1938 (2); v SA 1929 (1) 1935 (4); v WI 1933 (3); v NZ 1931 (3) 1937 (3); v In 1932 (1); *v A 1932 (5) 1936 (5); v SA 1938 (5); v WI 1929 (4) 1934 (4); v NZ 1932 (2)*
Amiss, D. L. 50: v A 1968 (1) 1975 (2) 1977 (2); v WI 1966 (1) 1973 (3) 1976 (1); v NZ 1973 (3); v In 1967 (2) 1971 (1) 1974 (3); v P 1967 (1) 1971 (3) 1974 (3); *v A 1974 (5) 1976 (1); v WI 1973 (5); v NZ 1974 (2); v In 1972 (3) 1976 (5); v P 1972 (3)*
Andrew, K. V. 2: v WI 1963 (1); *v A 1954 (1)*
Appleyard, R. 9: v A 1956 (1); v SA 1955 (1); v P 1954 (1); *v A 1954 (4); v NZ 1954 (2)*
Archer, A. G. 1: *v SA 1898*
Armitage, T. 2: *v A 1876 (2)*
Arnold, E. G. 10: v A 1905 (4); v SA 1907 (2); *v A 1903 (4)*
Arnold, G. G. 34: v A 1972 (3) 1975 (1); v WI 1973 (3); v NZ 1969 (1) 1973 (3); v In 1974 (2); v P 1967 (2) 1974 (3); *v A 1974 (4); v WI 1973 (3); v NZ 1974 (2); v In 1972 (4); v P 1972 (3)*
Arnold, J. 1: v NZ 1931
Astill, W. E. 9: *v SA 1927 (5); v WI 1929 (4)*
Atherton, M. A. 84: v A 1989 (2) 1993 (6) 1997 (6); v SA 1994 (3) 1998 (5); v WI 1991 (5) 1995 (6); v NZ 1990 (3) 1994 (3); v In 1990 (3) 1996 (3); v P 1992 (3) 1996 (3); *v A 1990 (5) 1994 (5); v SA 1995 (5); v WI 1993 (5) 1997 (6); v NZ 1996 (3); v In 1992 (1); v SL 1992 (1); v Z 1996 (2)*
Athey, C. W. J. 23: v A 1980 (1); v WI 1988 (1); v NZ 1986 (3); v In 1986 (2); v P 1987 (4); *v A 1986 (5) 1987 (1); v WI 1980 (2); v NZ 1987 (1); v P 1987 (3)*
Attewell, W. 10: v A 1890 (1); *v A 1884 (5) 1887 (1) 1891 (3)*

Bailey, R. J. 4: v WI 1988 (1); *v WI 1989 (3)*

Bailey, T. E. 61: v A 1953 (5) 1956 (4); v SA 1951 (2) 1955 (5); v WI 1950 (2) 1957 (4); v NZ 1949 (4) 1958 (4); v P 1954 (3); *v A 1950 (4) 1954 (5) 1958 (5); v SA 1956 (5); v WI 1953 (5); v NZ 1950 (2) 1954 (2)*

Bairstow, D. L. 4: v A 1980 (1); v WI 1980 (1); v In 1979 (1); *v WI 1980 (1)*

Bakewell, A. H. 6: v SA 1935 (2); v WI 1933 (1); v NZ 1931 (2); *v In 1933 (1)*

Balderstone, J. C. 2: v WI 1976 (2)

Barber, R. W. 28: v A 1964 (1) 1968 (1); v SA 1960 (1) 1965 (3); v WI 1966 (2); v NZ 1965 (3); *v A 1965 (5); v SA 1964 (4); v In 1961 (5); v P 1961 (3)*

Barber, W. 2: v SA 1935 (2)

Barlow, G. D. 3: v A 1977 (1); *v In 1976 (2)*

Barlow, R. G. 17: v A 1882 (1) 1884 (3) 1886 (3); *v A 1881 (4) 1882 (4) 1886 (2)*

Barnes, S. F. 27: v A 1902 (1) 1909 (3) 1912 (3); v SA 1912 (3); *v A 1901 (3) 1907 (5) 1911 (5); v SA 1913 (4)*

Barnes, W. 21: v A 1880 (1) 1882 (1) 1884 (2) 1886 (2) 1888 (3) 1890 (2); *v A 1882 (4) 1884 (5) 1886 (1)*

Barnett, C. J. 20: v A 1938 (3) 1948 (1); v SA 1947 (3); v WI 1933 (1); v NZ 1937 (3); v In 1936 (1); *v A 1936 (5); v In 1933 (3)*

Barnett, K. J. 4: v A 1989 (3); v SL 1988 (1)

Barratt, F. 5: v SA 1929 (1); *v NZ 1929 (4)*

Barrington, K. F. 82: v A 1961 (5) 1964 (5) 1968 (3); v SA 1955 (2) 1960 (4) 1965 (3); v WI 1963 (5) 1966 (2); v NZ 1965 (2); v In 1959 (5) 1967 (3); v P 1962 (4) 1967 (3); *v A 1962 (5) 1965 (5); v SA 1964 (5); v WI 1959 (5) 1967 (5); v NZ 1962 (3); v In 1961 (5) 1963 (1); v P 1961 (2)*

Barton, V. A. 1: *v SA 1891*

Bates, W. 15: *v A 1881 (4) 1882 (4) 1884 (5) 1886 (2)*

Bean, G. 3: *v A 1891 (3)*

Bedser, A. V. 51: v A 1948 (5) 1953 (5); v SA 1947 (2) 1951 (5) 1955 (1); v WI 1950 (3); v NZ 1949 (2); v In 1946 (3) 1952 (4); v P 1954 (2); *v A 1946 (5) 1950 (5) 1954 (1); v SA 1948 (5); v NZ 1946 (1) 1950 (2)*

Benjamin, J. E. 1: v SA 1994

Benson, M. R. 1: v In 1986

Berry, R. 2: v WI 1950 (2)

Bicknell, M. P. 2: v A 1993 (2)

Binks, J. G. 2: *v In 1963 (2)*

Bird, M. C. 10: *v SA 1909 (5) 1913 (5)*

Birkenshaw, J. 5: *v WI 1973 (2); v In 1972 (2); v P 1972 (1)*

Blakey, R. J. 2: *v In 1992 (2)*

Bligh, Hon. I. F. W. 4: *v A 1882 (4)*

Blythe, C. 19: v A 1905 (1) 1909 (2); v SA 1907 (3); *v A 1901 (5) 1907 (1); v SA 1905 (5) 1909 (2)*

Board, J. H. 6: *v SA 1898 (2) 1905 (4)*

Bolus, J. B. 7: v WI 1963 (2); *v In 1963 (5)*

Booth, M. W. 2: *v SA 1913 (2)*

Bosanquet, B. J. T. 7: v A 1905 (3); *v A 1903 (4)*

Botham, I. T. 102: v A 1977 (2) 1980 (1) 1981 (6) 1985 (6) 1989 (3); v WI 1980 (5) 1984 (5) 1991 (1); v NZ 1978 (3) 1983 (4) 1986 (1); v In 1979 (4) 1982 (3); v P 1978 (3) 1982 (3) 1987 (5) 1992 (2); v SL 1984 (1) 1991 (1); *v A 1978 (6) 1979 (3) 1982 (5) 1986 (4); v WI 1980 (4) 1985 (5); v NZ 1977 (3) 1983 (3) 1991 (1); v In 1979 (1) 1981 (6); v P 1983 (1); v SL 1981 (1)*

Bowden, M. P. 2: *v SA 1888 (2)*

Bowes, W. E. 15: v A 1934 (3) 1938 (2); v SA 1935 (4); v WI 1939 (2); v In 1932 (1) 1946 (1); *v A 1932 (1); v NZ 1932 (1)*

Bowley, E. H. 5: v SA 1929 (2); *v NZ 1929 (3)*

Boycott, G. 108: v A 1964 (4) 1968 (3) 1972 (2) 1977 (3) 1980 (1) 1981 (6); v SA 1965 (2); v WI 1966 (4) 1969 (3) 1973 (3) 1980 (2); v NZ 1965 (2) 1969 (3) 1973 (3) 1978 (2); v In 1967 (2) 1971 (1) 1974 (1) 1979 (4); v P 1967 (1) 1971 (2); *v A 1965 (5) 1970 (5) 1978 (6) 1979 (3); v SA 1964 (5); v WI 1967 (5) 1973 (5) 1980 (4); v NZ 1965 (2) 1977 (3); v In 1979 (1) 1981 (4); v P 1977 (2)*

Bradley, W. M. 2: v A 1899 (2)

Braund, L. C. 23: v A 1902 (5); v SA 1907 (3); *v A 1901 (5) 1903 (5) 1907 (5)*

Brearley, J. M. 39: v A 1977 (5) 1981 (4); v WI 1976 (2); v NZ 1978 (3); v In 1979 (4); v P 1978 (3); *v A 1976 (1) 1978 (6) 1979 (3); v In 1976 (5) 1979 (1); v P 1977 (2)*

Brearley, W. 4: v A 1905 (2) 1909 (1); v SA 1912 (1)

Brennan, D. V. 2: v SA 1951 (2)

Briggs, John 33: v A 1886 (3) 1888 (3) 1893 (2) 1896 (1) 1899 (1); *v A 1884 (5) 1886 (2) 1887 (1) 1891 (3) 1894 (5) 1897 (5); v SA 1888 (2)*

Broad, B. C. 25: v A 1989 (2); v WI 1984 (4) 1988 (2); v P 1987 (4); v SL 1984 (1); *v A 1986 (5) 1987 (1); v NZ 1987 (3); v P 1987 (3)*

Brockwell, W. 7: v A 1893 (1) 1899 (1); *v A 1894 (5)*

Bromley-Davenport, H. R. 4: *v SA 1895 (3) 1898 (1)*

Brookes, D. 1: *v WI 1947*

Brown, A. 2: *v In 1961 (1); v P 1961 (1)*

Brown, D. J. 26: v A 1968 (4); v SA 1965 (2); v WI 1966 (1) 1969 (3); v NZ 1969 (1); v In 1967 (2); *v A 1965 (4); v WI 1967 (4); v NZ 1965 (2); v P 1968 (3)*

Brown, F. R. 22: v A 1953 (1); v SA 1951 (5); v WI 1950 (1); v NZ 1931 (2) 1937 (1) 1949 (2); v In 1932 (1); *v A 1950 (5); v NZ 1932 (2) 1950 (2)*

Brown, G. 7: v A 1921 (3); *v SA 1922 (4)*

Brown, J. T. 8: v A 1896 (2) 1899 (1); *v A 1894 (5)*

Brown, S. J. E. 1: v P 1996

Buckenham, C. P. 4: *v SA 1909 (4)*

Butcher, A. R. 1: v In 1979

Butcher, M. A. 14: v A 1997 (5); v SA 1998 (3); v SL 1998 (1); *v WI 1997 (5)*

Butcher, R. O. 3: *v WI 1980 (3)*

Butler, H. J. 2: v SA 1947 (1); *v WI 1947 (1)*

Butt, H. R. 3: *v SA 1895 (3)*

Caddick, A. R. 21: v A 1993 (4) 1997 (5); v P 1996 (1); *v WI 1993 (4) 1997 (5); v NZ 1996 (2)*

Calthorpe, Hon. F. S. G. 4: *v WI 1929 (4)*

Capel, D. J. 15: v A 1989 (1); v WI 1988 (2); v P 1987 (1); *v A 1987 (1); v WI 1989 (4); v NZ 1987 (3); v P 1987 (3)*

Carr, A. W. 11: v A 1926 (4); v SA 1929 (2); *v SA 1922 (5)*

Carr, D. B. 2: *v In 1951 (2)*

Carr, D. W. 1: v A 1909

Cartwright, T. W. 5: v A 1964 (2); v SA 1965 (1); v NZ 1965 (1); *v SA 1964 (1)*

Chapman, A. P. F. 26: v A 1926 (4) 1930 (4); v SA 1924 (2); v WI 1928 (3); *v A 1924 (4) 1928 (4); v SA 1930 (5)*

Charlwood, H. R. J. 2: *v A 1876 (2)*

Chatterton, W. 1: *v SA 1891*

Childs, J. H. 2: v WI 1988 (2)

Christopherson, S. 1: v A 1884

Clark, E. W. 8: v A 1934 (2); v SA 1929 (1); v WI 1933 (2); *v In 1933 (3)*

Clay, J. C. 1: v SA 1935

Close, D. B. 22: v A 1961 (1); v SA 1955 (1); v WI 1957 (2) 1963 (5) 1966 (1) 1976 (3); v NZ 1949 (1); v In 1959 (1) 1967 (3); v P 1967 (3); *v A 1950 (1)*

Coldwell, L. J. 7: v A 1964 (2); v P 1962 (2); *v A 1962 (2); v NZ 1962 (1)*

Compton, D. C. S. 78: v A 1938 (4) 1948 (5) 1953 (5) 1956 (1); v SA 1947 (5) 1951 (4) 1955 (5); v WI 1939 (3) 1950 (1); v NZ 1937 (1) 1949 (4); v In 1946 (3) 1952 (2); v P 1954 (4); *v A 1946 (5) 1950 (4) 1954 (4); v SA 1948 (5) 1956 (5); v WI 1953 (5); v NZ 1946 (1) 1950 (2)*

Cook, C. 1: v SA 1947

Cook, G. 7: v In 1982 (3); *v A 1982 (3); v SL 1981 (1)*

Cook, N. G. B. 15: v A 1989 (3); v WI 1984 (3); v NZ 1983 (2); *v NZ 1983 (1); v P 1983 (3) 1987 (3)*

Cope, G. A. 3: *v P 1977 (3)*

Copson, W. H. 3: v SA 1947 (1); v WI 1939 (2)

Cork, D. G. 25: v A 1998 (5); v WI 1995 (5); v In 1996 (3); v P 1996 (3); v SL 1998 (1); *v SA 1995 (5); v NZ 1996 (3)*

Cornford, W. L. 4: *v NZ 1929 (4)*

Cottam, R. M. H. 4: *v In 1972 (2); v P 1968 (2)*

Coventry, Hon. C. J. 2: *v SA 1888 (2)*

Cowans, N. G. 19: v A 1985 (1); v WI 1984 (1); v NZ 1983 (4); *v A 1982 (4); v NZ 1983 (2); v In 1984 (5); v P 1983 (2)*

Cowdrey, C. S. 6: v WI 1988 (1); *v In 1984 (5)*

Cowdrey, M. C. 114: v A 1956 (5) 1961 (4) 1964 (3) 1968 (4); v SA 1955 (1) 1960 (5) 1965 (3); v WI 1957 (5) 1963 (2) 1966 (4); v NZ 1958 (4) 1965 (3); v In 1959 (5); v P 1962 (4) 1967 (2) 1971 (1); *v A 1954 (5) 1958 (5) 1962 (5) 1965 (4) 1970 (3) 1974 (5); v SA 1956 (5); v WI 1959 (5) 1967 (5); v NZ 1954 (2) 1958 (2) 1962 (3) 1965 (3) 1970 (1); v In 1963 (3); v P 1968 (3)*

Coxon, A. 1: v A 1948

Cranston, J. 1: v A 1890

Cranston, K. 8: v A 1948 (1); v SA 1947 (3); *v WI 1947 (4)*

Crapp, J. F. 7: v A 1948 (3); *v SA 1948 (4)*

Crawford, J. N. 12: v SA 1907 (2); *v A 1907 (5); v SA 1905 (5)*

Crawley, J. P. 26: v A 1997 (5); v SA 1994 (3); v WI 1995 (3); v P 1996 (2); v SL 1998 (1); *v A 1994 (3); v SA 1995 (1); v WI 1997 (3); v NZ 1996 (3); v Z 1996 (2)*

Croft, R. D. B. 14: v A 1997 (5); v SA 1998 (3); v P 1996 (1); *v WI 1997 (1); v NZ 1996 (2); v Z 1996 (2)*

Curtis, T. S. 5: v A 1989 (3); v WI 1988 (2)

Cuttell, W. R. 2: *v SA 1898 (2)*

Dawson, E. W. 5: *v SA 1927 (1); v NZ 1929 (4)*

Dean, H. 3: v A 1912 (2); v SA 1912 (1)

DeFreitas, P. A. J. 44: v A 1989 (1) 1993 (1); v SA 1994 (3); v WI 1988 (3) 1991 (5) 1995 (1); v NZ 1990 (2) 1994 (3); v P 1987 (1) 1992 (2); v SL 1991 (1); *v A 1986 (4) 1990 (3) 1994 (4); v WI 1989 (2); v NZ 1987 (2) 1991 (3); v In 1992 (1); v P 1987 (2)*

Denness, M. H. 28: v A 1975 (1); v NZ 1969 (1); v In 1974 (3); v P 1974 (3); *v A 1974 (5); v WI 1973 (5); v NZ 1974 (2); v In 1972 (5); v P 1972 (3)*

Denton, D. 11: v A 1905 (1); *v SA 1905 (5) 1909 (5)*

Dewes, J. G. 5: v A 1948 (1); v WI 1950 (2); *v A 1950 (2)*

Dexter, E. R. 62: v A 1961 (5) 1964 (5) 1968 (2); v SA 1960 (5); v WI 1963 (5); v NZ 1958 (1) 1965 (2); v In 1959 (2); v P 1962 (5); *v A 1958 (2) 1962 (5); v WI 1959 (5); v NZ 1958 (2) 1962 (3); v In 1961 (5); v P 1961 (3)*

Dilley, G. R. 41: v A 1981 (3) 1989 (2); v WI 1980 (3) 1988 (4); v In 1983 (1) 1986 (2); v NZ 1983 (1) 1986 (3); v P 1987 (1); *v A 1979 (2) 1986 (4) 1987 (1); v WI 1980 (4); v NZ 1987 (3); v In 1981 (4); v P 1983 (1) 1987 (1)*

Dipper, A. E. 1: v A 1921

Doggart, G. H. G. 2: v WI 1950 (2)

D'Oliveira, B. L. 44: v A 1968 (2) 1972 (5); v WI 1966 (4) 1969 (2); v NZ 1969 (1); v In 1967 (2) 1971 (3); v P 1967 (3) 1971 (3); *v A 1970 (6); v WI 1967 (5); v NZ 1970 (2); v P 1968 (3)*

Dollery, H. E. 4: v A 1948 (2); v SA 1947 (1); v WI 1950 (1)

Dolphin, A. 1: *v A 1920*

Douglas, J. W. H. T. 23: v A 1912 (1) 1921 (5); v SA 1924 (1); *v A 1911 (5) 1920 (5) 1924 (1); v SA 1913 (5)*

Downton, P. R. 30: v A 1981 (1) 1985 (6); v WI 1984 (5) 1988 (3); v In 1986 (1); v SL 1984 (1); *v WI 1980 (3) 1985 (5); v In 1984 (5)*

Druce, N. F. 5: *v A 1897 (5)*

Ducat, A. 1: v A 1921

Duckworth, G. 24: v A 1930 (5); v SA 1924 (1) 1929 (4) 1935 (1); v WI 1928 (1); v In 1936 (3); *v A 1928 (5); v SA 1930 (3); v NZ 1932 (1)*

Duleepsinhji, K. S. 12: v A 1930 (4); v SA 1929 (3); v NZ 1931 (3); *v NZ 1929 (4)*

Durston, F. J. 1: v A 1921

Ealham, M. A. 8: v A 1997 (4); v SA 1998 (2); v In 1996 (1); v P 1996 (1)

Edmonds, P. H. 51: v A 1975 (2) 1985 (5); v NZ 1978 (3) 1983 (2) 1986 (3); v In 1979 (4) 1982 (3) 1986 (2); v P 1978 (3) 1987 (5); *v A 1978 (1) 1986 (5); v WI 1985 (3); v NZ 1977 (3); v In 1984 (5); v P 1977 (2)*

Edrich, J. H. 77: v A 1964 (3) 1968 (5) 1972 (5) 1975 (4); v SA 1965 (1); v WI 1963 (3) 1966 (1) 1969 (3) 1976 (2); v NZ 1965 (1) 1969 (3); v In 1967 (2) 1971 (3) 1974 (3); v P 1971 (3) 1974 (3); *v A 1965 (3) 1970 (6) 1974 (4); v WI 1967 (5); v NZ 1965 (3) 1970 (2) 1974 (2); v In 1963 (3); v P 1968 (3)*

Edrich, W. J. 39: v A 1938 (4) 1948 (5) 1953 (3); v SA 1947 (4); v WI 1950 (2); v NZ 1949 (4); v In 1946 (1); v P 1954 (1); *v A 1946 (5) 1954 (4); v SA 1938 (5); v NZ 1946 (1)*

Elliott, H. 4: v WI 1928 (1); *v SA 1927 (1); v In 1933 (2)*

Ellison, R. M. 11: v A 1985 (2); v WI 1984 (1); v In 1986 (1); v SL 1984 (1); *v WI 1985 (3); v In 1984 (3)*

Emburey, J. E. 64: v A 1980 (1) 1981 (4) 1985 (6) 1989 (3) 1993 (1); v WI 1980 (3) 1988 (3) 1995 (1); v NZ 1978 (1) 1986 (2); v In 1986 (3); v P 1987 (4); v SL 1988 (1); *v A 1978 (4) 1986 (5) 1987 (1); v WI 1980 (4) 1985 (4); v NZ 1987 (3); v In 1979 (1) 1981 (3) 1992 (1); v P 1987 (3); v SL 1981 (1) 1992 (1)*

Emmett, G. M. 1: v A 1948

Emmett, T. 7: *v A 1876 (2) 1878 (1) 1881 (4)*

Evans, A. J. 1: v A 1921

Evans, T. G. 91: v A 1948 (5) 1953 (5) 1956 (5); v SA 1947 (5) 1951 (3) 1955 (3); v WI 1950 (3) 1957 (5); v NZ 1949 (4) 1958 (5); v In 1946 (1) 1952 (4) 1959 (2); v P 1954 (4); *v A 1946 (4) 1950 (5) 1954 (4) 1958 (3); v SA 1948 (3) 1956 (5); v WI 1947 (4) 1953 (4); v NZ 1946 (1) 1950 (2) 1954 (2)*

Fagg, A. E. 5: v WI 1939 (1); v In 1936 (2); *v A 1936 (2)*

Fairbrother, N. H. 10: v NZ 1990 (3); v P 1987 (1); *v NZ 1987 (2); v In 1992 (2); v P 1987 (1); v SL 1992 (1)*

Fane, F. L. 14: *v A 1907 (4); v SA 1905 (5) 1909 (5)*

Farnes, K. 15: v A 1934 (2) 1938 (4); *v A 1936 (2); v SA 1938 (5); v WI 1934 (2)*

Farrimond, W. 4: v SA 1935 (1); *v SA 1930 (2); v WI 1934 (1)*

Fender, P. G. H. 13: v A 1921 (2); v SA 1924 (2) 1929 (1); *v A 1920 (3); v SA 1922 (5)*

Ferris, J. J. 1: *v SA 1891*

Fielder, A. 6: *v A 1903 (2) 1907 (4)*

Fishlock, L. B. 4: v In 1936 (2) 1946 (1); *v A 1946 (1)*

Flavell, J. A. 4: v A 1961 (2) 1964 (2)

Fletcher, K. W. R. 59: v A 1968 (1) 1972 (1) 1975 (2); v WI 1973 (3); v NZ 1969 (2) 1973 (3); v In 1971 (2) 1974 (3); v P 1974 (3); *v A 1970 (5) 1974 (5) 1976 (1); v WI 1973 (4); v NZ 1970 (1) 1974 (2); v In 1972 (5) 1976 (3) 1981 (6); v P 1968 (3) 1972 (3); v SL 1981 (1)*

Flintoff, A. 2: v SA 1998 (2)

Flowers, W. 8: v A 1893 (1); *v A 1884 (5) 1886 (2)*

Ford, F. G. J. 5: *v A 1894 (5)*

Foster, F. R. 11: v A 1912 (3); v SA 1912 (3); *v A 1911 (5)*

Foster, N. A. 29: v A 1985 (1) 1989 (3) 1993 (1); v WI 1984 (1) 1988 (2); v NZ 1983 (1) 1986 (1); v In 1986 (1); v P 1987 (5); v SL 1988 (1); *v A 1987 (1); v WI 1985 (3); v NZ 1983 (2); v In 1984 (2); v P 1983 (2) 1987 (2)*

Foster, R. E. 8: v SA 1907 (3); *v A 1903 (5)*

Fothergill, A. J. 2: *v SA 1888 (2)*

Fowler, G. 21: v WI 1984 (5); v NZ 1983 (1); v P 1982 (1); v SL 1984 (1); *v A 1982 (3); v NZ 1983 (2); v In 1984 (5); v P 1983 (2)*

Fraser, A. R. C. 44: v A 1989 (3) 1993 (1); v SA 1994 (2) 1998 (5); v WI 1995 (5); v NZ 1994 (3); v In 1990 (3); v SL 1998 (1); *v A 1990 (3) 1994 (3); v SA 1995 (3); v WI 1989 (2) 1993 (4) 1997 (6)*

Freeman, A. P. 12: v A 1929 (3); v WI 1928 (3); *v A 1924 (2); v SA 1927 (4)*

French, B. N. 16: v NZ 1986 (3); v In 1986 (2); v P 1987 (4); *v A 1987 (1); v NZ 1987 (3); v P 1987 (3)*

Fry, C. B. 26: v A 1899 (5) 1902 (3) 1905 (4) 1909 (3) 1912 (3); v SA 1907 (3) 1912 (3); *v SA 1895 (2)*

Gallian, J. E. R. 3: v WI 1995 (2); *v SA 1995 (1)*

Gatting, M. W. 79: v A 1980 (1) 1981 (6) 1985 (6) 1989 (1) 1993 (2); v WI 1980 (4) 1984 (1) 1988 (2); v NZ 1983 (2) 1986 (3); v In 1986 (3); v P 1982 (3) 1987 (5); *v A 1986 (5) 1987 (3) 1994 (5); v WI 1980 (1) 1985 (1); v NZ 1977 (1) 1983 (2) 1987 (3); v In 1981 (3) 1984 (5) 1992 (3); v P 1977 (1) 1983 (3) 1987 (3); v SL 1992 (1)*

Gay, L. H. 1: *v A 1894*

Geary, G. 14: v A 1926 (2) 1930 (1) 1934 (2); v SA 1924 (1) 1929 (2); *v A 1928 (4); v SA 1927(2)*

Gibb, P. A. 8: v In 1946 (2); *v A 1946 (1); v SA 1938 (5)*

Gifford, N. 15: v A 1964 (2) 1972 (3); v NZ 1973 (2); v In 1971 (3); v P 1971 (2); *v In 1972 (2); v P 1972 (2)*

Giles, A. F. 1: v SA 1998

Gilligan, A. E. R. 11: v SA 1924 (4); *v A 1924 (5); v SA 1922 (2)*

Gilligan, A. H. H. 4: *v NZ 1929 (4)*

Gimblett, H. 3: v WI 1939 (1); v In 1936 (2)

Gladwin, C. 8: v SA 1947 (2); v NZ 1949 (1); *v SA 1948 (5)*

Goddard, T. W. 8: v A 1930 (1); v WI 1939 (2); v NZ 1937 (2); v SA 1938 (3)

Gooch, G. A. 118: v A 1975 (2) 1980 (1) 1981 (5) 1985 (6) 1989 (5) 1993 (6); v WI 1980 (5) 1988 (5) 1991 (5); v NZ 1978 (3) 1986 (3) 1990 (3) 1994 (3); v In 1979 (4) 1986 (3) 1990 (3); v P 1978 (2) 1992 (5); v SL 1988 (1) 1991 (1); v A 1978 (6) 1979 (2) 1990 (4) 1994 (5); v WI 1980 (4) 1985 (5) 1989 (2); v NZ 1991 (3); v In 1979 (1) 1981 (6) 1992 (2); v P 1987 (3); v SL 1981 (1)

Gough, D. 26: v A 1997 (4); v SA 1994 (3) 1998 (4); v WI 1995 (3); v NZ 1994 (1); v SL 1998 (1); v A 1994 (3); v SA 1995 (2); v NZ 1996 (3); v Z 1996 (2)

Gover, A. R. 4: v NZ 1937 (2); v In 1936 (1) 1946 (1)

Gower, D. I. 117: v A 1980 (1) 1981 (5) 1985 (6) 1989 (6); v WI 1980 (1) 1984 (5) 1988 (4); v NZ 1978 (3) 1983 (4) 1986 (3); v In 1979 (4) 1982 (3) 1986 (2) 1990 (3); v P 1978 (3) 1982 (3) 1987 (5) 1992 (3); v SL 1984 (1); v A 1978 (6) 1979 (3) 1982 (5) 1986 (5) 1990 (5); v WI 1980 (4) 1985 (5); v NZ 1983 (3); v In 1979 (1) 1981 (6) 1984 (5); v P 1983 (3); v SL 1981 (1)

Grace, E. M. 1: v A 1880

Grace, G. F. 1: v A 1880

Grace, W. G. 22: v A 1880 (1) 1882 (1) 1884 (1) 1886 (3) 1888 (3) 1890 (2) 1893 (2) 1896 (3) 1899 (1); v A 1891 (3)

Graveney, T. W. 79: v A 1953 (5) 1956 (2) 1968 (5); v SA 1951 (1) 1955 (5); v WI 1957 (4) 1966 (4) 1969 (1); v NZ 1958 (4); v In 1952 (4) 1967 (3); v P 1954 (3) 1962 (4) 1967 (3); v A 1954 (2) 1958 (5) 1962 (3); v WI 1953 (5) 1967 (5); v NZ 1954 (2) 1958 (2); v In 1951 (4); v P 1968 (3)

Greenhough, T. 4: v SA 1960 (1); v In 1959 (3)

Greenwood, A. 2: v A 1876 (2)

Greig, A. W. 58: v A 1972 (5) 1975 (4) 1977 (5); v WI 1973 (3) 1976 (5); v NZ 1973 (3); v In 1974 (3); v P 1974 (3); v A 1974 (6) 1976 (1); v WI 1973 (3); v NZ 1974 (2); v In 1972 (5) 1976 (5); v P 1972 (3)

Greig, I. A. 2: v P 1982 (2)

Grieve, B. A. F. 2: v SA 1888 (2)

Griffith, S. C. 3: v SA 1948 (2); v WI 1947 (1)

Gunn, G. 15: v A 1909 (1); v A 1907 (5) 1911 (5); v WI 1929 (4)

Gunn, J. 6: v A 1905 (1); v A 1901 (5)

Gunn, W. 11: v A 1888 (2) 1890 (2) 1893 (3) 1896 (1) 1899 (1); v A 1886 (2)

Haig, N. E. 5: v A 1921 (1); v WI 1929 (4)

Haigh, S. 11: v A 1905 (2) 1909 (1) 1912 (1); v SA 1898 (2) 1905 (5)

Hallows, C. 2: v A 1921 (1); v WI 1928 (1)

Hammond, W. R. 85: v A 1930 (5) 1934 (5) 1938 (4); v SA 1929 (4) 1935 (5); v WI 1928 (3) 1933 (3) 1939 (3); v NZ 1931 (3) 1937 (3); v In 1932 (1) 1936 (2) 1946 (3); v A 1928 (5) 1932 (5) 1936 (5) 1946 (4); v SA 1927 (5) 1930 (5) 1938 (5); v WI 1934 (4); v NZ 1932 (2) 1946 (1)

Hampshire, J. H. 8: v A 1972 (1) 1975 (1); v WI 1969 (2); v A 1970 (2); v NZ 1970 (2)

Hardinge, H. T. W. 1: v A 1921

Hardstaff, J. 5: v A 1907 (5)

Hardstaff, J. jun. 23: v A 1938 (2) 1948 (1); v SA 1935 (1); v WI 1939 (3); v NZ 1937 (3); v In 1936 (2) 1946 (2); v A 1936 (5) 1946 (1); v WI 1947 (3)

Harris, Lord 4: v A 1880 (1) 1884 (2); v A 1878 (1)

Hartley, J. C. 2: v SA 1905 (2)

Hawke, Lord 5: v SA 1895 (3) 1898 (2)

Hayes, E. G. 5: v A 1909 (1); v SA 1912 (1); v SA 1905 (3)

Hayes, F. C. 9: v WI 1973 (3) 1976 (2); v WI 1973 (4)

Hayward, T. W. 35: v A 1896 (2) 1899 (5) 1902 (1) 1905 (5) 1909 (3); v SA 1907 (3); v A 1897 (5) 1901 (5) 1903 (5); v SA 1895 (3)

Headley, D. W. 10: v A 1997 (3); v SA 1998 (1); v WI 1997 (6)

Hearne, A. 1: v SA 1891

Hearne, F. 2: v SA 1888 (2)

Hearne, G. G. 1: v SA 1891

Hearne, J. T. 12: v A 1896 (3) 1899 (3); v A 1897 (5); v SA 1891 (1)

Hearne, J. W. 24: v A 1912 (3) 1921 (1) 1926 (1); v SA 1912 (1) 1924 (3); v A 1911 (5) 1920 (2) 1924 (4); v SA 1913 (3)

Hemmings, E. E. 16: v A 1989 (1); v NZ 1990 (3); v In 1990 (3); v P 1982 (2); v A 1982 (3) 1987 (1) 1990 (1); v NZ 1987 (1); v P 1987 (1)

Hendren, E. H. 51: v A 1921 (2) 1926 (5) 1930 (2) 1934 (4); v SA 1924 (5) 1929 (4); v WI 1928 (1); v A 1920 (5) 1924 (5) 1928 (5); v SA 1930 (5); v WI 1929 (4) 1934 (4)

Hendrick, M. 30: v A 1977 (3) 1980 (1) 1981 (2); v WI 1976 (2) 1980 (2); v NZ 1978 (2); v In 1974 (3) 1979 (4); v P 1974 (2); *v A 1974 (2) 1978 (5); v NZ 1974 (1) 1977 (1)*

Heseltine, C. 2: *v SA 1895 (2)*

Hick, G. A. 49: v A 1993 (3); v SA 1994 (3) 1998 (2); v WI 1991 (4) 1995 (5); v NZ 1994 (3); v In 1996 (3); v P 1992 (4) 1996 (1); v SL 1998 (1); *v A 1994 (3); v SA 1995 (5); v WI 1993 (5); v NZ 1991 (1); v In 1992 (3); v SL 1992 (1)*

Higgs, K. 15: v A 1968 (1); v WI 1966 (5); v SA 1965 (1); v In 1967 (1); v P 1967 (3); *v A 1965 (1); v NZ 1965 (3)*

Hill, A. 2: *v A 1876 (2)*

Hill, A. J. L. 3: *v SA 1895 (3)*

Hilton, M. J. 4: v SA 1951 (1); v WI 1950 (1); *v In 1951 (2)*

Hirst, G. H. 24: v A 1899 (1) 1902 (4) 1905 (3) 1909 (4); v SA 1907 (3); *v A 1897 (4) 1903 (5)*

Hitch, J. W. 7: v A 1912 (1) 1921 (1); v SA 1912 (1); *v A 1911 (3) 1920 (1)*

Hobbs, J. B. 61: v A 1909 (3) 1912 (3) 1921 (1) 1926 (5) 1930 (5); v SA 1912 (3) 1924 (1) 1929 (1); v WI 1928 (2); *v A 1907 (4) 1911 (5) 1920 (5) 1924 (5) 1928 (5); v SA 1909 (5) 1913 (5)*

Hobbs, R. N. S. 7: v In 1967 (3); v P 1967 (1) 1971 (1); *v WI 1967 (1); v P 1968 (1)*

Hollies, W. E. 13: v A 1948 (1); v SA 1947 (1); v WI 1950 (1); v NZ 1949 (4); *v WI 1934 (3)*

Hollioake, A. J. 4: v A 1997 (2); *v WI 1997 (2)*

Hollioake, B. C. 2: v A 1997 (1); *v SL 1998 (1)*

Holmes, E. R. T. 5: v SA 1935 (1); *v WI 1934 (4)*

Holmes, P. 7: v A 1921 (1); v In 1932 (1); *v SA 1927 (5)*

Hone, L. 1: *v A 1878*

Hopwood, J. L. 2: v A 1934 (2)

Hornby, A. N. 3: v A 1882 (1) 1884 (1); *v A 1878 (1)*

Horton, M. J. 2: v In 1959 (2)

Howard, N. D. 4: *v In 1951 (4)*

Howell, H. 5: v A 1921 (1); v SA 1924 (1); *v A 1920 (3)*

Howorth, R. 5: v SA 1947 (1); *v WI 1947 (4)*

Humphries, J. 3: *v A 1907 (3)*

Hunter, J. 5: *v A 1884 (5)*

Hussain, N. 34: v A 1993 (4) 1997 (6); v SA 1998 (5); v In 1996 (3); v P 1996 (2); *v WI 1989 (3) 1997 (6); v NZ 1996 (3); v Z 1996 (2)*

Hutchings, K. L. 7: v A 1909 (2); *v A 1907 (5)*

Hutton, L. 79: v A 1938 (3) 1948 (4) 1953 (5); v SA 1947 (5) 1951 (5); v WI 1939 (3) 1950 (5); v NZ 1937 (3) 1949 (4); v In 1946 (3) 1952 (4); v P 1954 (2); *v A 1946 (5) 1950 (5) 1954 (5); v SA 1938 (4) 1948 (5); v WI 1947 (2) 1953 (5); v NZ 1950 (2) 1954 (2)*

Hutton, R. A. 5: v In 1971 (3); v P 1971 (2)

Iddon, J. 5: v SA 1935 (1); *v WI 1934 (4)*

Igglesden, A. P. 3: v A 1989 (1); *v WI 1993 (2)*

Ikin, J. T. 18: v SA 1951 (3) 1955 (1); v In 1946 (2) 1952 (2); *v A 1946 (5); v NZ 1946 (1); v WI 1947 (4)*

Illingworth, R. 61: v A 1961 (2) 1968 (3) 1972 (5); v SA 1960 (4); v WI 1966 (2) 1969 (3) 1973 (3); v NZ 1958 (1) 1965 (1) 1969 (3) 1973 (3); v In 1959 (2) 1967 (3) 1971 (3); v P 1962 (1) 1967 (1) 1971 (3); *v A 1962 (2) 1970 (6); v WI 1959 (5); v NZ 1962 (3) 1970 (2)*

Illingworth, R. K. 9: v WI 1991 (2) 1995 (4); *v SA 1995 (3)*

Ilott, M. C. 5: v A 1993 (3); *v SA 1995 (2)*

Insole, D. J. 9: v A 1956 (1); v SA 1955 (1); v WI 1950 (1) 1957 (1); *v SA 1956 (5)*

Irani, R. C. 2: v In 1996 (2)

Jackman, R. D. 4: v P 1982 (2); *v WI 1980 (2)*

Jackson, F. S. 20: v A 1893 (2) 1896 (3) 1899 (5) 1902 (5) 1905 (5)

Jackson, H. L. 2: v A 1961 (1); v NZ 1949 (1)

James, S. P. 2: v SA 1998 (1); v SL 1998 (1)

Jameson, J. A. 4: v In 1971 (2); *v WI 1973 (2)*

Jardine, D. R. 22: v WI 1928 (2) 1933 (2); v NZ 1931 (3); v In 1932 (1); *v A 1928 (5) 1932 (5); v NZ 1932 (1); v In 1933 (3)*

Jarvis, P. W. 9: v A 1989 (2); v WI 1988 (2); *v NZ 1987 (2); v In 1992 (2), v SL 1992 (1)*

Jenkins, R. O. 9: v WI 1950 (2); v In 1952 (2); *v SA 1948 (5)*

Jessop, G. L. 18: v A 1899 (1) 1902 (4) 1905 (1) 1909 (2); v SA 1907 (3) 1912 (2); *v A 1901 (5)*

Jones, A. O. 12: v A 1899 (1) 1905 (2) 1909 (2); *v A 1901 (5) 1907 (2)*

Jones, I. J. 15: v WI 1966 (2); *v A 1965 (4)*; *v WI 1967 (5)*; *v NZ 1965 (3)*; *v In 1963 (1)*
Jupp, H. 2: *v A 1876 (2)*
Jupp, V. W. C. 8: v A 1921 (2); v WI 1928 (2); *v SA 1922 (4)*

Keeton, W. W. 2: v A 1934 (1); v WI 1939 (1)
Kennedy, A. S. 5: *v SA 1922 (5)*
Kenyon, D. 8: v A 1953 (2); v SA 1955 (3); *v In 1951 (3)*
Killick, E. T. 2: v SA 1929 (2)
Kilner, R. 9: v A 1926 (4); v SA 1924 (2); *v A 1924 (3)*
King, J. H. 1: v A 1909
Kinneir, S. P. 1: *v A 1911*
Knight, A. E. 3: *v A 1903 (3)*
Knight, B. R. 29: v A 1968 (2); v WI 1966 (1) 1969 (3); v NZ 1969 (2); v P 1962 (2); *v A 1962 (1) 1965 (2)*; *v NZ 1962 (3) 1965 (2)*; *v In 1961 (4) 1963 (5)*; *v P 1961 (2)*
Knight, D. J. 2: v A 1921 (2)
Knight, N. V. 12: v SA 1998 (1); v WI 1995 (2); v In 1996 (1); v P 1996 (3); *v NZ 1996 (3)*; *v Z 1996 (2)*
Knott, A. P. E. 95: v A 1968 (5) 1972 (5) 1975 (4) 1977 (5) 1981 (2); v WI 1969 (3) 1973 (3) 1976 (5) 1980 (4); v NZ 1969 (3) 1973 (3); v In 1971 (3) 1974 (3); v P 1967 (2) 1971 (3) 1974 (3); *v A 1970 (6) 1974 (6) 1976 (1)*; *v WI 1967 (2) 1973 (5)*; *v NZ 1970 (1) 1974 (2)*; *v In 1972 (5) 1976 (5)*; *v P 1968 (3) 1972 (3)*
Knox, N. A. 2: v SA 1907 (2)

Laker, J. C. 46: v A 1948 (3) 1953 (3) 1956 (5); v SA 1951 (2) 1955 (1); v WI 1950 (1) 1957 (4); v NZ 1949 (1) 1958 (4); v In 1952 (4); v P 1954 (1); *v A 1958 (4)*; *v SA 1956 (5)*; *v WI 1947 (4) 1953 (4)*
Lamb, A. J. 79: v A 1985 (6) 1989 (1); v WI 1984 (5) 1988 (4) 1991 (4); v NZ 1983 (4) 1986 (1) 1990 (3); v In 1982 (3) 1986 (2) 1990 (3); v P 1982 (3) 1992 (2); v SL 1984 (1) 1988 (1); *v A 1982 (5) 1986 (5) 1990 (3)*; *v WI 1985 (5) 1989 (4)*; *v NZ 1983 (3) 1991 (3)*; *v In 1984 (5)*; *v P 1983 (3)*
Langridge, James 8: v SA 1935 (1); v WI 1933 (2); v In 1936 (1) 1946 (1); *v In 1933 (3)*
Larkins, W. 13: v A 1981 (1); v WI 1980 (3); *v A 1979 (1) 1990 (3)*; *v WI 1989 (4)*; *v In 1979 (1)*
Larter, J. D. F. 10: v SA 1965 (2); v NZ 1965 (1); v P 1962 (1); *v NZ 1962 (3)*; *v In 1963 (3)*
Larwood, H. 21: v A 1926 (2) 1930 (3); v SA 1929 (3); v WI 1928 (2); v NZ 1931 (1); *v A 1928 (5) 1932 (5)*
Lathwell, M. N. 2: v A 1993 (2)
Lawrence, D. V. 5: v WI 1991 (2); v SL 1988 (1) 1991 (1); *v NZ 1991 (1)*
Leadbeater, E. 2: *v In 1951 (2)*
Lee, H. W. 1: *v SA 1930*
Lees, W. S. 5: *v SA 1905 (5)*
Legge, G. B. 5: *v SA 1927 (1)*; *v NZ 1929 (4)*
Leslie, C. F. H. 4: *v A 1882 (4)*
Lever, J. K. 21: v A 1977 (3); v WI 1980 (1); v In 1979 (1) 1986 (1); *v A 1976 (1) 1978 (1) 1979 (1)*; *v NZ 1977 (1)*; *v In 1976 (5) 1979 (1) 1981 (2)*; *v P 1977 (3)*
Lever, P. 17: v A 1972 (1) 1975 (1); v In 1971 (1); v P 1971 (3); *v A 1970 (5) 1974 (2)*; *v NZ 1970 (2) 1974 (2)*
Leveson Gower, H. D. G. 3: *v SA 1909 (3)*
Levett, W. H. V. 1: *v In 1933*
Lewis, A. R. 9: v NZ 1973 (1); *v In 1972 (5)*; *v P 1972 (3)*
Lewis, C. C. 32: v A 1993 (2); v WI 1991 (2); v NZ 1990 (1); v In 1990 (2) 1996 (3); v P 1992 (5) 1996 (2); v SL 1991 (1); *v A 1990 (1) 1994 (2)*; *v WI 1993 (5)*; *v NZ 1991 (2)*; *v In 1992 (3)*; *v SL 1992 (1)*
Leyland, M. 41: v A 1930 (3) 1934 (5) 1938 (1); v SA 1929 (5) 1935 (4); v WI 1928 (1) 1933 (1); v In 1936 (2); *v A 1928 (1) 1932 (5) 1936 (5)*; *v SA 1930 (5)*; *v WI 1934 (3)*
Lilley, A. A. 35: v A 1896 (3) 1899 (4) 1902 (5) 1905 (5) 1909 (5); v SA 1907 (3); *v A 1901 (5) 1903 (5)*
Lillywhite, James jun. 2: *v A 1876 (2)*
Lloyd, D. 9: v In 1974 (2); v P 1974 (3); *v A 1974 (4)*
Lloyd, T. A. 1: v WI 1984
Loader, P. J. 13: v SA 1955 (1); v WI 1957 (2); v NZ 1958 (3); v P 1954 (1); *v A 1958 (2)*; *v SA 1956 (4)*

Lock, G. A. R. 49: v A 1953 (2) 1956 (4) 1961 (3); v SA 1955 (3); v WI 1957 (3) 1963 (3); v NZ
    1958 (5); v In 1952 (2); v P 1962 (3); *v A 1958 (4); v SA 1956 (1); v WI 1953 (5) 1967 (2); v NZ*
    1958 (5); v In 1961 (5); v P 1961 (2)
Lockwood, W. H. 12: v A 1893 (2) 1899 (1) 1902 (4); *v A 1894 (5)*
Lohmann, G. A. 18: v A 1886 (3) 1888 (3) 1890 (2) 1896 (1); *v A 1886 (2) 1887 (1) 1891 (3); v SA*
    1895 (3)
Lowson, F. A. 7: v SA 1951 (2) 1955 (1); *v In 1951 (4)*
Lucas, A. P. 5: v A 1880 (1) 1882 (1) 1884 (2); *v A 1878 (1)*
Luckhurst, B. W. 21: v A 1972 (4); v WI 1973 (3); v In 1971 (3); v P 1971 (3); *v A 1970 (5)*
    1974 (2); v NZ 1970 (2)
Lyttelton, Hon. A. 4: v A 1880 (1) 1882 (1) 1884 (2)

Macaulay, G. G. 8: v A 1926 (1); v SA 1924 (1); v WI 1933 (2); *v SA 1922 (4)*
MacBryan, J. C. W. 1: v SA 1924
McCague, M. J. 3: v A 1993 (2); *v A 1994 (1)*
McConnon, J. E. 2: v P 1954 (2)
McGahey, C. P. 2: *v A 1901 (2)*
MacGregor, G. 8: v A 1890 (2) 1893 (3); *v A 1891 (3)*
McIntyre, A. J. W. 3: v SA 1955 (1); v WI 1950 (1); *v A 1950 (1)*
MacKinnon, F. A. 1: *v A 1878*
MacLaren, A. C. 35: v A 1896 (2) 1899 (4) 1902 (5) 1905 (4) 1909 (5); *v A 1894 (5) 1897 (5)*
    1901 (5)
McMaster, J. E. P. 1: *v SA 1888*
Makepeace, J. W. H. 4: *v A 1920 (4)*
Malcolm, D. E. 40: v A 1989 (1) 1993 (1) 1997 (4); v SA 1994 (1); v WI 1991 (2) 1995 (2); v NZ
    1990 (3) 1994 (1); v In 1990 (3); v P 1992 (3); *v A 1990 (5) 1994 (4); v SA 1995 (2); v WI*
    1989 (4) 1993 (1); v In 1992 (2); v SL 1992 (1)
Mallender, N. A. 2: v P 1992 (2)
Mann, F. G. 7: v NZ 1949 (2); *v SA 1948 (5)*
Mann, F. T. 5: *v SA 1922 (5)*
Marks, V. J. 6: v NZ 1983 (1); v P 1982 (1); *v NZ 1983 (1); v P 1983 (3)*
Marriott, C. S. 1: v WI 1933
Martin, F. 2: v A 1890 (1); *v SA 1891 (1)*
Martin, J. W. 1: v SA 1947
Martin, P. J. 8: v A 1997 (1); v WI 1995 (3); v In 1996 (1); *v SA 1995 (3)*
Mason, J. R. 5: *v A 1897 (5)*
Matthews, A. D. G. 1: v NZ 1937
May, P. B. H. 66: v A 1953 (2) 1956 (5) 1961 (4); v SA 1951 (2) 1955 (5); v WI 1957 (5); v NZ
    1958 (5); v In 1952 (4) 1959 (3); v P 1954 (4); *v A 1954 (5) 1958 (5); v SA 1956 (5); v WI*
    1953 (5) 1959 (3); v NZ 1954 (2) 1958 (2)
Maynard, M. P. 4: v A 1993 (2); v WI 1988 (1); *v WI 1993 (1)*
Mead, C. P. 17: v A 1921 (2); *v A 1911 (4) 1928 (1); v SA 1913 (5) 1922 (5)*
Mead, W. 1: v A 1899
Midwinter, W. E. 4: *v A 1881 (4)*
Milburn, C. 9: v A 1968 (2); v WI 1966 (4); v In 1967 (1); v P 1967 (1); *v P 1968 (1)*
Miller, A. M. 1: *v SA 1895*
Miller, G. 34: v A 1977 (2); v WI 1976 (1) 1984 (2); v NZ 1978 (2); v In 1979 (3) 1982 (1); v P
    1978 (3) 1982 (1); *v A 1978 (6) 1979 (1) 1982 (5); v WI 1980 (1); v NZ 1977 (3); v P 1977 (3)*
Milligan, F. W. 2: *v SA 1898 (2)*
Millman, G. 6: v P 1962 (2); *v In 1961 (2); v P 1961 (2)*
Milton, C. A. 6: v NZ 1958 (2); v In 1959 (2); *v A 1958 (2)*
Mitchell, A. 6: v SA 1935 (2); v In 1936 (1); *v In 1933 (3)*
Mitchell, F. 2: *v SA 1898 (2)*
Mitchell, T. B. 5: v A 1934 (2); v SA 1935 (1); *v A 1932 (1); v NZ 1932 (1)*
Mitchell-Innes, N. S. 1: v SA 1935
Mold, A. W. 3: v A 1893 (3)
Moon, L. J. 4: *v SA 1905 (4)*
Morley, F. 4: v A 1880 (1); *v A 1882 (3)*
Morris, H. 3: v WI 1991 (2); v SL 1991 (1)
Morris, J. E. 3: v In 1990 (3)
Mortimore, J. B. 9: v A 1964 (1); v In 1959 (2); *v A 1958 (1); v NZ 1958 (2); v In 1963 (3)*

Moss, A. E. 9: v A 1956 (1); v SA 1960 (2); v In 1959 (3); *v WI 1953 (1) 1959 (2)*

Moxon, M. D. 10: v A 1989 (1); v WI 1988 (2); v NZ 1986 (2); v P 1987 (1); *v A 1987 (1); v NZ 1987 (3)*

Mullally, A. D. 9: v In 1996 (3); v P 1996 (3); *v NZ 1996 (1); v Z 1996 (2)*

Munton, T. A. 2: v P 1992 (2)

Murdoch, W. L. 1: *v SA 1891*

Murray, J. T. 21: v A 1961 (5); v WI 1966 (1); v In 1967 (3); v P 1962 (3) 1967 (1); *v A 1962 (1); v SA 1964 (1); v NZ 1962 (1) 1965 (1); v In 1961 (3); v P 1961 (1)*

Newham, W. 1: *v A 1887*

Newport, P. J. 3: v A 1989 (1); v SL 1988 (1); *v A 1990 (1)*

Nichols, M. S. 14: v A 1930 (1); v SA 1935 (4); v WI 1933 (1) 1939 (1); *v NZ 1929 (4); v In 1933 (3)*

Oakman, A. S. M. 2: v A 1956 (2)

O'Brien, Sir T. C. 5: v A 1884 (1) 1888 (1); *v SA 1895 (3)*

O'Connor, J. 4: v SA 1929 (1); *v WI 1929 (3)*

Old, C. M. 46: v A 1975 (3) 1977 (2) 1980 (1) 1981 (2); v WI 1973 (1) 1976 (2) 1980 (1); v NZ 1973 (2) 1978 (1); v In 1974 (3); v P 1974 (3) 1978 (3); *v A 1974 (2) 1976 (1) 1978 (1); v WI 1973 (4) 1980 (1); v NZ 1974 (1) 1977 (2); v In 1972 (4) 1976 (4); v P 1972 (1) 1977 (1)*

Oldfield, N. 1: v WI 1939

Padgett, D. E. V. 2: v SA 1960 (2)

Paine, G. A. E. 4: *v WI 1934 (4)*

Palairet, L. C. H. 2: v A 1902 (2)

Palmer, C. H. 1: *v WI 1953*

Palmer, K. E. 1: *v SA 1964*

Parfitt, P. H. 37: v A 1964 (4) 1972 (3); v SA 1965 (2); v WI 1969 (1); v NZ 1965 (1); v P 1962 (5); *v A 1962 (2); v SA 1964 (5); v NZ 1962 (3) 1965 (3); v In 1961 (2) 1963 (3); v P 1961 (2)*

Parker, C. W. L. 1: v A 1921

Parker, P. W. G. 1: v A 1981

Parkhouse, W. G. A. 7: v WI 1950 (2); v In 1959 (2); *v A 1950 (2); v NZ 1950 (1)*

Parkin, C. H. 10: v A 1921 (4); v SA 1924 (1); *v A 1920 (5)*

Parks, J. H. 1: v NZ 1937

Parks, J. M. 46: v A 1964 (5); v SA 1960 (5) 1965 (3); v WI 1963 (4) 1966 (4); v NZ 1965 (3); v P 1954 (1); *v A 1965 (5); v SA 1964 (5); v WI 1959 (1) 1967 (3); v NZ 1965 (2); v In 1963 (5)*

Pataudi sen., Nawab of, 3: v A 1934 (1); *v A 1932 (2)*

Patel, M. M. 2: v In 1996 (2)

Paynter, E. 20: v A 1938 (4); v WI 1939 (2); v NZ 1931 (1) 1937 (2); v In 1932 (1); *v A 1932 (3); v SA 1938 (5); v NZ 1932 (2)*

Peate, E. 9: v A 1882 (1) 1884 (3) 1886 (1); *v A 1881 (4)*

Peebles, I. A. R. 13: v A 1930 (2); v NZ 1931 (3); *v SA 1927 (4) 1930 (4)*

Peel, R. 20: v A 1888 (3) 1890 (1) 1893 (1) 1896 (1); *v A 1884 (5) 1887 (1) 1891 (3) 1894 (5)*

Penn, F. 1: v A 1880

Perks, R. T. D. 2: v WI 1939 (1); *v SA 1938 (1)*

Philipson, H. 5: *v A 1891 (1) 1894 (4)*

Pigott, A. C. S. 1: *v NZ 1983*

Pilling, R. 8: v A 1884 (1) 1886 (1) 1888 (1); *v A 1881 (4) 1887 (1)*

Place, W. 3: *v WI 1947 (3)*

Pocock, P. I. 25: v A 1968 (1); v WI 1976 (2) 1984 (2); v SL 1984 (1); *v WI 1967 (2) 1973 (4); v In 1972 (4) 1984 (5); v P 1968 (1) 1972 (3)*

Pollard, R. 4: v A 1948 (2); v In 1946 (1); *v NZ 1946 (1)*

Poole, C. J. 3: *v In 1951 (3)*

Pope, G. H. 1: v SA 1947

Pougher, A. D. 1: *v SA 1891*

Price, J. S. E. 15: v A 1964 (2) 1972 (1); v In 1971 (3); v P 1971 (1); *v SA 1964 (4); v In 1963 (4)*

Price, W. F. F. 1: v A 1938

Prideaux, R. M. 3: v A 1968 (1); *v P 1968 (2)*

Pringle, D. R. 30: v A 1989 (2); v WI 1984 (3) 1988 (4) 1991 (4); v NZ 1986 (1); v In 1982 (3) 1986 (3); v P 1982 (1) 1992 (3); v SL 1988 (1); *v A 1982 (3); v NZ 1991 (2)*

Pullar, G. 28: v A 1961 (5); v SA 1960 (3); v In 1959 (3); v P 1962 (2); *v A 1962 (4); v WI 1959 (5); v In 1961 (3); v P 1961 (3)*

Quaife, W. G. 7: v A 1899 (2); *v A 1901 (5)*

Radford, N. V. 3: v NZ 1986 (1); v In 1986 (1); *v NZ 1987 (1)*
Radley, C. T. 8: v NZ 1978 (3); v P 1978 (3); *v NZ 1977 (2)*
Ramprakash, M. R. 29: v A 1993 (1) 1997 (1); v WI 1991 (5) 1995 (2); v P 1992 (3); v SL 1991 (1) 1998 (1); *v A 1994 (1); v WI 1993 (4) 1997 (3); v SA 1995 (2)*
Randall, D. W. 47: v A 1977 (5); v WI 1984 (1); v NZ 1983 (3); v In 1979 (3) 1982 (3); v P 1982 (3); *v A 1976 (1) 1978 (6) 1979 (2) 1982 (4); v NZ 1977 (3) 1983 (3); v In 1976 (4); v P 1977 (3) 1983 (3)*
Ranjitsinhji, K. S. 15: v A 1896 (2) 1899 (3) 1902 (3); *v A 1897 (5)*
Read, H. D. 1: v SA 1935
Read, J. M. 17: v A 1882 (1) 1890 (2) 1893 (1); *v A 1884 (5) 1886 (2) 1887 (1) 1891 (3); v SA 1888 (2)*
Read, W. W. 18: v A 1884 (2) 1886 (3) 1888 (3) 1890 (2) 1893 (2); *v A 1882 (4) 1887 (1); v SA 1891 (1)*
Reeve, D. A. 3: *v NZ 1991 (3)*
Relf, A. E. 13: v A 1909 (1); *v A 1903 (2); v SA 1905 (5) 1913 (5)*
Rhodes, H. J. 2: v In 1959 (2)
Rhodes, S. J. 11: v SA 1994 (3); v NZ 1994 (3); *v A 1994 (5)*
Rhodes, W. 58: v A 1899 (3) 1902 (5) 1905 (4) 1909 (4) 1912 (3) 1921 (1) 1926 (1); v SA 1912 (3); *v A 1903 (5) 1907 (5) 1911 (5) 1920 (5); v SA 1909 (5) 1913 (5); v WI 1929 (4)*
Richards, C. J. 8: v WI 1988 (2); v P 1987 (1); *v A 1986 (5)*
Richardson, D. W. 1: v WI 1957
Richardson, P. E. 34: v A 1956 (5); v WI 1957 (5) 1963 (1); v NZ 1958 (4); *v A 1958 (4); v SA 1956 (5); v NZ 1958 (2); v In 1961 (5); v P 1961 (3)*
Richardson, T. 14: v A 1893 (1) 1896 (3); *v A 1894 (5) 1897 (5)*
Richmond, T. L. 1: v A 1921
Ridgway, F. 5: *v In 1951 (5)*
Robertson, J. D. 11: v SA 1947 (1); v NZ 1949 (1); *v WI 1947 (4); v In 1951 (5)*
Robins, R. W. V. 19: v A 1930 (2); v SA 1929 (1) 1935 (3); v WI 1933 (2); v NZ 1931 (1) 1937 (3); v In 1932 (1) 1936 (2); *v A 1936 (4)*
Robinson, R. T. 29: v A 1985 (6) 1989 (1); v In 1986 (1); v P 1987 (5); v SL 1988 (1); *v A 1987 (1); v WI 1985 (4); v NZ 1987 (3); v In 1984 (5); v P 1987 (2)*
Roope, G. R. J. 21: v A 1975 (1) 1977 (2); v WI 1973 (1); v NZ 1973 (3) 1978 (1); v P 1978 (3); *v NZ 1977 (2); v In 1972 (2); v P 1972 (2) 1977 (3)*
Root, C. F. 3: v A 1926 (3)
Rose, B. C. 9: v WI 1980 (3); *v WI 1980 (3); v NZ 1977 (2); v P 1977 (3)*
Royle, V. P. F. A. 1: *v A 1878*
Rumsey, F. E. 5: v A 1964 (1); v SA 1965 (1); v NZ 1965 (3)
Russell, A. C. 10: v A 1921 (2); *v A 1920 (4); v SA 1922 (4)*
Russell, R. C. 54: v A 1989 (6); v WI 1991 (4) 1995 (3); v NZ 1990 (3); v In 1990 (3) 1996 (3); v P 1992 (3) 1996 (2); v SL 1988 (1) 1991 (1); *v A 1990 (3); v SA 1995 (5); v WI 1989 (4) 1993 (5) 1997 (5); v NZ 1991 (3)*
Russell, W. E. 10: v SA 1965 (1); v WI 1966 (2); v P 1967 (1); *v A 1965 (1); v NZ 1965 (3); v In 1961 (1); v P 1961 (1)*

Salisbury, I. D. K. 12: v SA 1994 (1) 1998 (2); v P 1992 (2) 1996 (2); v SL 1998 (1); *v WI 1993 (2); v In 1992 (2)*
Sandham, A. 14: v A 1921 (1); v SA 1924 (2); *v A 1924 (2); v SA 1922 (5); v WI 1929 (4)*
Schultz, S. S. 1: *v A 1878*
Scotton, W. H. 15: v A 1884 (1) 1886 (3); *v A 1881 (4) 1884 (5) 1886 (2)*
Selby, J. 6: *v A 1876 (2) 1881 (4)*
Selvey, M. W. W. 3: v WI 1976 (2); *v In 1976 (1)*
Shackleton, D. 7: v SA 1951 (1); v WI 1950 (1) 1963 (4); *v In 1951 (1)*
Sharp, J. 3: v A 1909 (3)
Sharpe, J. W. 3: v A 1890 (1); *v A 1891 (2)*
Sharpe, P. J. 12: v A 1964 (2); v WI 1963 (3) 1969 (3); v NZ 1969 (3); *v In 1963 (1)*
Shaw, A. 7: v A 1880 (1); *v A 1876 (2) 1881 (4)*

Sheppard, Rev. D. S. 22: v A 1956 (2); v WI 1950 (1) 1957 (2); v In 1952 (2); v P 1954 (2) 1962 (2); *v A 1950 (2) 1962 (5); v NZ 1950 (1) 1963 (3)*

Sherwin, M. 3: v A 1888 (1); *v A 1886 (2)*

Shrewsbury, A. 23: v A 1884 (3) 1886 (3) 1890 (2) 1893 (3); *v A 1881 (4) 1884 (5) 1886 (2) 1887 (1)*

Shuter, J. 1: v A 1888

Shuttleworth, K. 5: v P 1971 (1); *v A 1970 (2); v NZ 1970 (2)*

Sidebottom, A. 1: v A 1985

Silverwood, C. E. W. 1: *v Z 1996*

Simpson, R. T. 27: v A 1953 (3); v SA 1951 (3); v WI 1950 (3); v NZ 1949 (2); v In 1952 (2); v P 1954 (3); *v A 1950 (5) 1954 (1); v SA 1948 (1); v NZ 1950 (2) 1954 (2)*

Simpson-Hayward, G. H. 5: *v SA 1909 (5)*

Sims, J. M. 4: v SA 1935 (1); v In 1936 (1); *v A 1936 (2)*

Sinfield, R. A. 1: v A 1938

Slack, W. N. 3: v In 1986 (1); *v WI 1985 (2)*

Smailes, T. F. 1: v In 1946

Small, G. C. 17: v A 1989 (1); v WI 1988 (1); v NZ 1986 (2) 1990 (3); *v A 1986 (2) 1990 (4); v WI 1989 (4)*

Smith, A. C. 6: *v A 1962 (4); v NZ 1962 (2)*

Smith, A. M. 1: v A 1997

Smith, C. A. 1: *v SA 1888*

Smith, C. I. J. 5: v NZ 1937 (1); *v WI 1934 (4)*

Smith, C. L. 8: v NZ 1983 (2); v In 1986 (1); *v NZ 1983 (2); v P 1983 (3)*

Smith, D. 2: v SA 1935 (2)

Smith, D. M. 2: *v WI 1985 (2)*

Smith, D. R. 5: *v In 1961 (5)*

Smith, D. V. 3: v WI 1957 (3)

Smith, E. J. 11: v A 1912 (3); v SA 1912 (3); *v A 1911 (4); v SA 1913 (1)*

Smith, H. 1: v WI 1928

Smith, M. J. K. 50: v A 1961 (1) 1972 (3); v SA 1960 (4) 1965 (3); v WI 1966 (1); v NZ 1958 (3) 1965 (3); v In 1959 (2); *v A 1965 (5); v SA 1964 (5); v WI 1959 (5); v NZ 1965 (3); v In 1961 (4) 1963 (5); v P 1961 (3)*

Smith, R. A. 62: v A 1989 (5) 1993 (5); v WI 1988 (2) 1991 (4) 1995 (4); v NZ 1990 (3) 1994 (3); v In 1990 (3); v P 1992 (5); v SL 1988 (1) 1991 (1); *v A 1990 (5); v SA 1995 (5); v WI 1989 (4) 1993 (5); v NZ 1991 (3); v In 1992 (3); v SL 1992 (1)*

Smith, T. P. B. 4: v In 1946 (1); *v A 1946 (2); v NZ 1946 (1)*

Smithson, G. A. 2: *v WI 1947 (2)*

Snow, J. A. 49: v A 1968 (5) 1972 (5) 1975 (4); v SA 1965 (1); v WI 1966 (3) 1969 (3) 1973 (1) 1976 (3); v NZ 1965 (1) 1969 (2) 1973 (3); v In 1967 (3) 1971 (2); v P 1967 (1); *v A 1970 (6); v WI 1967 (4); v P 1968 (2)*

Southerton, J. 2: *v A 1876 (2)*

Spooner, R. H. 10: v A 1905 (2) 1909 (2) 1912 (3); v SA 1912 (3)

Spooner, R. T. 7: v SA 1955 (1); *v In 1951 (5); v WI 1953 (1)*

Stanyforth, R. T. 4: *v SA 1927 (4)*

Staples, S. J. 3: *v SA 1927 (3)*

Statham, J. B. 70: v A 1953 (1) 1956 (3) 1961 (4); v SA 1951 (2) 1955 (4) 1960 (5) 1965 (1); v WI 1957 (3) 1963 (2); v NZ 1958 (2); v In 1959 (3); v P 1954 (4) 1962 (3); *v A 1954 (5) 1958 (4) 1962 (5); v SA 1956 (4); v WI 1953 (4) 1959 (3); v NZ 1950 (1) 1954 (2); v In 1951 (5)*

Steel, A. G. 13: v A 1880 (1) 1882 (1) 1884 (3) 1886 (3) 1888 (1); *v A 1882 (4)*

Steele, D. S. 8: v A 1975 (3); v WI 1976 (5)

Stephenson, J. P. 1: v A 1989

Stevens, G. T. S. 10: v A 1926 (2); *v SA 1922 (1) 1927 (5); v WI 1929 (2)*

Stevenson, G. B. 2: *v WI 1980 (1); v In 1979 (1)*

Stewart, A. J. 81: v A 1993 (6) 1997 (6); v SA 1994 (3) 1998 (5); v WI 1991 (1) 1995 (3); v NZ 1990 (3) 1994 (3); v In 1996 (2); v P 1992 (5) 1996 (3); v SL 1991 (1) 1998 (1); *v A 1990 (5) 1994 (2); v SA 1995 (5); v WI 1989 (4) 1993 (5) 1997 (6); v NZ 1991 (3) 1996 (3); v In 1992 (3); v SL 1992 (1); v Z 1996 (2)*

Stewart, M. J. 8: v WI 1963 (4); v P 1962 (2); *v In 1963 (2)*

Stoddart, A. E. 16: v A 1893 (3) 1896 (2); *v A 1887 (1) 1891 (3) 1894 (5) 1897 (2)*

Storer, W. 6: v A 1899 (1); *v A 1897 (5)*

Street, G. B. 1: *v SA 1922*

Strudwick, H. 28: v A 1921 (2) 1926 (5); v SA 1924 (1); *v A 1911 (1) 1920 (4) 1924 (5); v SA 1909 (5) 1913 (5)*

Studd, C. T. 5: v A 1882 (1); *v A 1882 (4)*

Studd, G. B. 4: *v A 1882 (4)*

Subba Row, R. 13: v A 1961 (5); v SA 1960 (4); v NZ 1958 (1); v In 1959 (1); *v WI 1959 (2)*

Such, P. M. 8: v A 1993 (5); v NZ 1994 (3)

Sugg, F. H. 2: v A 1888 (2)

Sutcliffe, H. 54: v A 1926 (5) 1930 (4) 1934 (4); v SA 1924 (5) 1929 (5) 1935 (2); v WI 1928 (3) 1933 (2); v NZ 1931 (2); v In 1932 (1); *v A 1924 (5) 1928 (4) 1932 (5); v SA 1927 (5); v NZ 1932 (2)*

Swetman, R. 11: v In 1959 (3); *v A 1958 (2); v WI 1959 (4); v NZ 1958 (2)*

Tate, F. W. 1: v A 1902

Tate, M. W. 39: v A 1926 (5) 1930 (5); v SA 1924 (5) 1929 (3) 1935 (1); v WI 1928 (3); v NZ 1931 (1); *v A 1924 (5) 1928 (5); v SA 1930 (5); v NZ 1932 (1)*

Tattersall, R. 16: v A 1953 (1); v SA 1951 (5); v P 1954 (1); *v A 1950 (2); v NZ 1950 (2); v In 1951 (5)*

Tavaré, C. J. 31: v A 1981 (2) 1989 (1); v WI 1980 (2) 1984 (1); v NZ 1983 (4); v In 1982 (3); v P 1982 (3); v SL 1984 (1); *v A 1982 (5); v NZ 1983 (2); v In 1981 (6); v SL 1981 (1)*

Taylor, J. P. 2: v NZ 1994 (1); *v In 1992 (1)*

Taylor, K. 3: v A 1964 (1); v In 1959 (2)

Taylor, L. B. 2: v A 1985 (2)

Taylor, R. W. 57: v A 1981 (3); v NZ 1978 (3) 1983 (3); v In 1979 (3) 1982 (3); v P 1978 (3) 1982 (3); *v A 1978 (6) 1979 (3) 1982 (5); v NZ 1970 (1) 1977 (3) 1983 (3); v In 1979 (1) 1981 (6); v P 1977 (3) 1983 (3); v SL 1981 (1)*

Tennyson, Hon. L. H. 9: v A 1921 (4); *v SA 1913 (5)*

Terry, V. P. 2: v WI 1984 (2)

Thomas, J. G. 5: v NZ 1986 (1); *v WI 1985 (4)*

Thompson, G. J. 6: v A 1909 (1); *v SA 1909 (5)*

Thomson, N. I. 5: *v SA 1964 (5)*

Thorpe, G. P. 52: v A 1993 (3) 1997 (6); v SA 1994 (2) 1998 (3); v WI 1995 (6); v In 1996 (3); v P 1996 (3); *v A 1994 (5); v SA 1995 (5); v WI 1993 (5) 1997 (6); v NZ 1996 (3); v Z 1996 (2)*

Titmus, F. J. 53: v A 1964 (5); v SA 1955 (2) 1965 (3); v WI 1963 (4) 1966 (3); v NZ 1965 (3); v P 1962 (3) 1967 (2); *v A 1962 (5) 1965 (5) 1974 (4); v SA 1964 (5); v WI 1967 (2); v NZ 1962 (3); v In 1963 (5)*

Tolchard, R. W. 4: *v In 1976 (4)*

Townsend, C. L. 2: v A 1899 (2)

Townsend, D. C. H. 3: *v WI 1934 (3)*

Townsend, L. F. 4: *v WI 1929 (1); v In 1933 (3)*

Tremlett, M. F. 3: *v WI 1947 (3)*

Trott, A. E. 2: *v SA 1898 (2)*

Trueman, F. S. 67: v A 1953 (1) 1956 (2) 1961 (4) 1964 (4); v SA 1955 (1) 1960 (5); v WI 1957 (5) 1963 (5); v NZ 1958 (5) 1965 (2); v In 1952 (4) 1959 (5); v P 1962 (4); *v A 1958 (3) 1962 (5); v WI 1953 (3) 1959 (5); v NZ 1958 (2) 1962 (2)*

Tufnell, N. C. 1: *v SA 1909*

Tufnell, P. C/R. 34: v A 1993 (2) 1997 (1); v SA 1994 (1); v WI 1991 (1); v P 1992 (1); v SL 1991 (1); *v A 1990 (4) 1994 (4); v WI 1993 (2) 1997 (6); v NZ 1991 (3) 1996 (3); v In 1992 (2); v SL 1992 (1); v Z 1996 (2)*

Turnbull, M. J. 9: v WI 1933 (2); v In 1936 (1); *v SA 1930 (5); v NZ 1929 (1)*

Tyldesley, E. 14: v A 1921 (3) 1926 (1); v SA 1924 (1); v WI 1928 (3); *v A 1928 (1); v SA 1927 (5)*

Tyldesley, J. T. 31: v A 1899 (2) 1902 (5) 1905 (5) 1909 (4); v SA 1907 (3); *v A 1901 (5) 1903 (5); v SA 1898 (2)*

Tyldesley, R. K. 7: v A 1930 (2); v SA 1924 (4); *v A 1924 (1)*

Tylecote, E. F. S. 6: v A 1886 (2); *v A 1882 (4)*

Tyler, E. J. 1: *v SA 1895*

Tyson, F. H. 17: v A 1956 (1); v SA 1955 (2); v P 1954 (1); *v A 1954 (5) 1958 (2); v SA 1956 (2); v NZ 1954 (2) 1958 (2)*

Ulyett, G. 25: v A 1882 (1) 1884 (3) 1886 (3) 1888 (2) 1890 (1); *v A 1876 (2) 1878 (1) 1881 (4) 1884 (5) 1887 (1)*; *v SA 1888 (2)*

Underwood, D. L. 86: v A 1968 (4) 1972 (2) 1975 (4) 1977 (5); v WI 1966 (2) 1969 (2) 1973 (3) 1976 (5) 1980 (1); v NZ 1969 (3) 1973 (1); v In 1971 (1) 1974 (3); v P 1967 (2) 1971 (1) 1974 (3); *v A 1970 (5) 1974 (5) 1976 (1) 1979 (3); v WI 1973 (4); v NZ 1970 (2) 1974 (2); v In 1972 (4) 1976 (5) 1979 (1) 1981 (6); v P 1968 (3) 1972 (2); v SL 1981 (1)*

Valentine, B. H. 7: *v SA 1938 (5); v In 1933 (2)*

Verity, H. 40: v A 1934 (5) 1938 (4); v SA 1935 (4); v WI 1933 (2) 1939 (1); v NZ 1931 (1) 1937 (1); v In 1936 (3); *v A 1932 (4) 1936 (5); v SA 1938 (5); v NZ 1932 (1); v In 1933 (3)*

Vernon, G. F. 1: *v A 1882*

Vine, J. 2: *v A 1911 (2)*

Voce, W. 27: v NZ 1931 (1) 1937 (1); v In 1932 (1) 1936 (1) 1946 (1); *v A 1932 (4) 1936 (5) 1946 (2); v SA 1930 (5); v WI 1929 (4); v NZ 1932 (2)*

Waddington, A. 2: *v A 1920 (2)*

Wainwright, E. 5: v A 1893 (1); *v A 1897 (4)*

Walker, P. M. 3: v SA 1960 (3)

Walters, C. F. 11: v A 1934 (5); v WI 1933 (3); *v In 1933 (3)*

Ward, A. 5: v WI 1976 (1); v NZ 1969 (3); v P 1971 (1)

Ward, A. 7: v A 1893 (2); *v A 1894 (5)*

Wardle, J. H. 28: v A 1953 (3) 1956 (1); v SA 1951 (2) 1955 (3); v WI 1950 (1) 1957 (1); v P 1954 (4); *v A 1954 (4); v SA 1956 (4); v WI 1947 (1) 1953 (2); v NZ 1954 (2)*

Warner, P. F. 15: v A 1909 (1) 1912 (1); v SA 1912 (1); *v A 1903 (5); v SA 1898 (2) 1905 (5)*

Warr, J. J. 2: *v A 1950 (2)*

Warren, A. R. 1: v A 1905

Washbrook, C. 37: v A 1948 (4) 1956 (3); v SA 1947 (5); v WI 1950 (2); v NZ 1937 (1) 1949 (2); v In 1946 (3); *v A 1946 (5) 1950 (5); v SA 1948 (5); v NZ 1946 (1) 1950 (1)*

Watkin, S. L. 3: v A 1993 (1); v WI 1991 (2)

Watkins, A. J. 15: v A 1948 (1); v NZ 1949 (1); v In 1952 (3); *v SA 1948 (5); v In 1951 (5)*

Watkinson, M. 4: v WI 1995 (3); *v SA 1995 (1)*

Watson, W. 23: v A 1953 (3) 1956 (2); v SA 1951 (5) 1955 (1); v NZ 1958 (2); v In 1952 (1); *v A 1958 (2); v NZ 1958 (2)*

Webbe, A. J. 1: *v A 1878*

Wellard, A. W. 2: v A 1938 (1); v NZ 1937 (1)

Wells, A. P. 1: v WI 1995

Wharton, A. 1: v NZ 1949

Whitaker, J. J. 1: *v A 1986*

White, C. 8: v A 1994 (1); v WI 1995 (2); v NZ 1994 (3); *v NZ 1996 (1); v Z 1996 (1)*

White, D. W. 2: *v P 1961 (2)*

White, J. C. 15: v A 1921 (1) 1930 (1); v SA 1929 (3); v WI 1928 (1); *v A 1928 (5); v SA 1930 (4)*

Whysall, W. W. 4: v A 1930 (1); *v A 1924 (3)*

Wilkinson, L. L. 3: *v SA 1938 (3)*

Willey, P. 26: v A 1980 (1) 1981 (4) 1985 (1); v WI 1976 (1) 1980 (5); v NZ 1986 (1); v In 1979 (1); *v A 1979 (3); v WI 1980 (4) 1985 (4)*

Williams, N. F. 1: v In 1990

Willis, R. G. D. 90: v A 1977 (5) 1981 (6); v WI 1973 (1) 1976 (2) 1980 (4) 1984 (3); v NZ 1978 (3) 1983 (4); v In 1974 (1) 1979 (3) 1982 (3); v P 1974 (1) 1978 (3) 1982 (2); *v A 1970 (4) 1974 (5) 1976 (1) 1978 (6) 1979 (3) 1982 (5); v WI 1973 (3); v NZ 1970 (1) 1977 (3) 1983 (3); v In 1976 (5) 1981 (5); v P 1977 (3) 1983 (1); v SL 1981 (1)*

Wilson, C. E. M. 2: *v SA 1898 (2)*

Wilson, D. 6: *v NZ 1970 (1); v In 1963 (5)*

Wilson, E. R. 1: *v A 1920*

Wood, A. 4: v A 1938 (1); v WI 1939 (3)

Wood, B. 12: v A 1972 (1) 1975 (3); v WI 1976 (1); v P 1978 (1); *v NZ 1974 (2); v In 1972 (3); v P 1972 (1)*

Wood, G. E. C. 3: v SA 1924 (3)

Wood, H. 4: v A 1888 (1); *v SA 1888 (2) 1891 (1)*

Wood, R. 1: *v A 1886*

Woods S. M. J. 3: *v SA 1895 (3)*

Woolley, F. E. 64: v A 1909 (1) 1912 (3) 1921 (5) 1926 (5) 1930 (2) 1934 (1); v SA 1912 (3) 1924 (5) 1929 (3); v NZ 1931 (1); v In 1932 (1); *v A 1911 (5) 1920 (5) 1924 (5); v SA 1909 (5) 1913 (5) 1922 (5); v NZ 1929 (4)*

Woolmer, R. A. 19: v A 1975 (2) 1977 (5) 1981 (2); v WI 1976 (5) 1980 (2); *v A 1976 (1); v In 1976 (2)*

Worthington, T. S. 9: v In 1936 (2); *v A 1936 (3); v NZ 1929 (4)*

Wright, C. W. 3: *v SA 1895 (3)*

Wright, D. V. P. 34: v A 1938 (3) 1948 (1); v SA 1947 (4); v WI 1939 (3) 1950 (1); v NZ 1949 (1); v In 1946 (2); *v A 1946 (5) 1950 (5); v SA 1938 (3) 1948 (3); v NZ 1946 (1) 1950 (2)*

Wyatt, R. E. S. 40: v A 1930 (1) 1934 (4); v SA 1929 (2) 1935 (5); v WI 1933 (2); v In 1936 (1); *v A 1932 (5) 1936 (2); v SA 1927 (5) 1930 (5); v WI 1929 (2) 1934 (4); v NZ 1932 (2)*

Wynyard, E. G. 3: v A 1896 (1); *v SA 1905 (2)*

Yardley, N. W. D. 20: v A 1948 (5); v SA 1947 (5); v WI 1950 (3); *v A 1946 (5); v SA 1938 (1); v NZ 1946 (1)*

Young, H. I. 2: v A 1899 (2)

Young, J. A. 8: v A 1948 (3); v SA 1947 (1); v NZ 1949 (2); *v SA 1948 (2)*

Young, R. A. 2: *v A 1907 (2)*

AUSTRALIA

Number of Test cricketers: 378

a'Beckett, E. L. 4: v E 1928 (2); v SA 1931 (1); *v E 1930 (1)*

Alderman, T. M. 41: v E 1982 (1) 1990 (4); v WI 1981 (2) 1984 (3) 1988 (2); v NZ 1989 (1); v P 1981 (3) 1989 (2); v SL 1989 (2); *v E 1981 (6) 1989 (6); v WI 1983 (3) 1990 (1); v NZ 1981 (3) 1989 (1); v P 1982 (1)*

Alexander, G. 2: v E 1884 (1); *v E 1880 (1)*

Alexander, H. H. 1: v E 1932

Allan, F. E. 1: v E 1878

Allan, P. J. 1: v E 1965

Allen, R. C. 1: v E 1886

Andrews, T. J. E. 16: v E 1924 (3); *v E 1921 (5) 1926 (5); v SA 1921 (3)*

Angel, J. 4: v E 1994 (1); v WI 1992 (1); *v P 1994 (2)*

Archer, K. A. 5: v E 1950 (3); v WI 1951 (2)

Archer, R. G. 19: v E 1954 (4); v SA 1952 (1); *v E 1953 (3) 1956 (5); v WI 1954 (5); v P 1956 (1)*

Armstrong, W. W. 50: v E 1901 (4) 1903 (3) 1907 (5) 1911 (5) 1920 (5); v SA 1910 (5); *v E 1902 (5) 1905 (5) 1909 (5) 1921 (5); v SA 1902 (3)*

Badcock, C. L. 7: v E 1936 (3); *v E 1938 (4)*

Bannerman, A. C. 28: v E 1878 (1) 1881 (3) 1882 (4) 1884 (4) 1886 (1) 1887 (1) 1891 (3); *v E 1880 (1) 1882 (1) 1884 (3) 1888 (3) 1893 (3)*

Bannerman, C. 3: v E 1876 (2) 1878 (1)

Bardsley, W. 41: v E 1911 (4) 1920 (5) 1924 (3); v SA 1910 (5); *v E 1909 (5) 1912 (3) 1921 (5) 1926 (5); v SA 1912 (3) 1921 (3)*

Barnes, S. G. 13: v E 1946 (4); v In 1947 (3); *v E 1938 (1) 1948 (4); v NZ 1945 (1)*

Barnett, B. A. 4: *v E 1938 (4)*

Barrett, J. E. 2: *v E 1890 (2)*

Beard, G. R. 3: *v P 1979 (3)*

Benaud, J. 3: v P 1972 (2); *v WI 1972 (1)*

Benaud, R. 63: v E 1954 (5) 1958 (5) 1962 (5); v SA 1952 (5) 1963 (4); v WI 1951 (1) 1960 (5); *v E 1953 (3) 1956 (5) 1961 (4); v SA 1957 (5); v WI 1954 (5); v In 1956 (3) 1959 (5); v P 1956 (1) 1959 (3)*

Bennett, M. J. 3: v WI 1984 (2); *v E 1985 (1)*

Bevan, M. G. 18: v E 1994 (3); v SA 1997 (1); v WI 1996 (4); *v E 1997 (3); v SA 1996 (3); v In 1996 (1); v P 1994 (3)*

Bichel, A. J. 3: v SA 1997 (1); v WI 1996 (2)

78   *Test Cricketers – Australia*

Blackham, J. McC. 35: v E 1876 (2) 1878 (1) 1881 (4) 1882 (4) 1884 (2) 1886 (1) 1887 (1) 1891 (3) 1894 (1); *v E 1880 (1) 1882 (1) 1884 (3) 1886 (3) 1888 (3) 1890 (2) 1893 (3)*

Blackie, D. D. 3: v E 1928 (3)

Blewett, G. S. 31: v E 1994 (2); v SA 1997 (3); v WI 1996 (4); v NZ 1997 (3); v P 1995 (3); *v E 1997 (6); v SA 1996 (3); v WI 1994 (4); v In 1997 (3)*

Bonnor, G. J. 17: v E 1882 (4) 1884 (3); *v E 1880 (1) 1882 (1) 1884 (3) 1886 (3) 1888 (3)*

Boon, D. C. 107: v E 1986 (4) 1987 (1) 1990 (5) 1994 (5); v SA 1993 (3); v WI 1984 (3) 1988 (5) 1992 (5); v NZ 1985 (3) 1987 (3) 1989 (1) 1993 (3); v In 1985 (3) 1991 (5); v P 1989 (2) 1995 (3); v SL 1987 (1) 1989 (2) 1995 (3); *v E 1985 (4) 1989 (6) 1993 (6); v SA 1993 (3); v WI 1990 (5) 1994 (4); v NZ 1985 (3) 1989 (1) 1992 (3); v In 1986 (3); v P 1988 (3) 1994 (3); v SL 1992 (3)*

Booth, B. C. 29: v E 1962 (5) 1965 (3); v SA 1963 (4); v P 1964 (1); *v E 1961 (2) 1964 (5); v WI 1964 (5); v In 1964 (3); v P 1964 (1)*

Border, A. R. 156: v E 1978 (3) 1979 (3) 1982 (5) 1986 (5) 1987 (1) 1990 (5); v SA 1993 (3); v WI 1979 (3) 1981 (3) 1984 (5) 1988 (5) 1992 (5); v NZ 1980 (3) 1985 (3) 1987 (3) 1989 (1) 1993 (3); v In 1980 (3) 1985 (3) 1991 (5); v P 1978 (2) 1981 (3) 1983 (5) 1989 (3); v SL 1987 (1) 1989 (2); *v E 1980 (1) 1981 (6) 1985 (6) 1989 (6) 1993 (6); v SA 1993 (3); v WI 1983 (5) 1990 (5); v NZ 1981 (3) 1985 (3) 1989 (1) 1992 (3); v In 1979 (5) 1986 (3); v P 1979 (3) 1982 (3) 1988 (3); v SL 1982 (1) 1992 (3)*

Boyle, H. F. 12: v E 1878 (1) 1881 (4) 1882 (1) 1884 (1); *v E 1880 (1) 1882 (1) 1884 (3)*

Bradman, D. G. 52: v E 1928 (4) 1932 (4) 1936 (5) 1946 (5); v SA 1931 (5); v WI 1930 (5); v In 1947 (5); *v E 1930 (5) 1934 (5) 1938 (4) 1948 (5)*

Bright, R. J. 25: v E 1979 (1); v WI 1979 (1); v NZ 1985 (1); v In 1985 (3); *v E 1977 (3) 1980 (1) 1981 (5); v NZ 1985 (2); v In 1986 (3); v P 1979 (3) 1982 (2)*

Bromley, E. H. 2: v E 1932 (1); *v E 1934 (1)*

Brown, W. A. 22: v E 1936 (2); v In 1947 (1); *v E 1934 (5) 1938 (4) 1948 (2); v SA 1935 (5); v NZ 1945 (1)*

Bruce, W. 14: v E 1884 (2) 1891 (3) 1894 (4); *v E 1886 (2) 1893 (3)*

Burge, P. J. 42: v E 1954 (1) 1958 (1) 1962 (3) 1965 (4); v SA 1963 (5); v WI 1960 (2); *v E 1956 (3) 1961 (5) 1964 (5); v SA 1957 (1); v WI 1954 (1); v In 1956 (3) 1959 (2) 1964 (3); v P 1959 (2) 1964 (1)*

Burke, J. W. 24: v E 1950 (2) 1954 (2) 1958 (5); v WI 1951 (1); *v E 1956 (5); v SA 1957 (5); v In 1956 (3); v P 1956 (1)*

Burn, K. E. 2: *v E 1890 (2)*

Burton, F. J. 2: v E 1886 (1) 1887 (1)

Callaway, S. T. 3: v E 1891 (2) 1894 (1)

Callen, I. W. 1: v In 1977

Campbell, G. D. 4: v P 1989 (1); v SL 1989 (1); *v E 1989 (1); v NZ 1989 (1)*

Carkeek, W. 6: *v E 1912 (3); v SA 1912 (3)*

Carlson, P. H. 2: v E 1978 (2)

Carter, H. 28: v E 1907 (5) 1911 (5) 1920 (2); v SA 1910 (5); *v E 1909 (5) 1921 (4); v SA 1921 (2)*

Chappell, G. S. 87: v E 1970 (5) 1974 (6) 1976 (1) 1979 (3) 1982 (5); v WI 1975 (6) 1979 (3) 1981 (3); v NZ 1973 (3) 1980 (3); v In 1980 (3); v P 1972 (3) 1976 (3) 1981 (3) 1983 (5); *v E 1972 (5) 1975 (4) 1977 (5) 1980 (1); v WI 1972 (5); v NZ 1973 (3) 1976 (2) 1981 (3); v P 1979 (3); v SL 1982 (1)*

Chappell, I. M. 75: v E 1965 (2) 1970 (6) 1974 (6) 1979 (2); v WI 1968 (5) 1975 (6) 1979 (1); v NZ 1973 (3); v In 1967 (4); v P 1964 (1) 1972 (3); *v E 1968 (5) 1972 (5) 1975 (4); v SA 1966 (5) 1969 (4); v WI 1972 (5); v NZ 1973 (3); v In 1969 (5)*

Chappell, T. M. 3: *v E 1981 (3)*

Charlton, P. C. 2: *v E 1890 (2)*

Chipperfield, A. G. 14: v E 1936 (3); *v E 1934 (5) 1938 (1); v SA 1935 (5)*

Clark, W. M. 10: v In 1977 (5); v P 1978 (1); *v WI 1977 (4)*

Colley, D. J. 3: *v E 1972 (3)*

Collins, H. L. 19: v E 1920 (5) 1924 (5); *v E 1921 (3) 1926 (3); v SA 1921 (3)*

Coningham, A. 1: v E 1894

Connolly, A. N. 29: v E 1965 (1) 1970 (1); v SA 1963 (3); v WI 1968 (5); v In 1967 (3); *v E 1968 (5); v SA 1969 (4); v In 1964 (2) 1969 (5)*

Cook, S. H. 2: v NZ 1997 (2)

Cooper, B. B. 1: v E 1876

Cooper, W. H. 2: v E 1881 (1) 1884 (1)

Corling, G. E. 5: v E *1964 (5)*

Cosier, G. J. 18: v E 1976 (1) 1978 (2); v WI 1975 (3); v In 1977 (4); v P 1976 (3); *v WI 1977 (3); v NZ 1976 (2)*

Cottam, J. T. 1: v E 1886

Cotter, A. 21: v E 1903 (2) 1907 (2) 1911 (4); v SA 1910 (5); *v E 1905 (3) 1909 (5)*

Coulthard, G. 1: v E 1881

Cowper, R. M. 27: v E 1965 (4); v In 1967 (4); v P 1964 (1); *v E 1964 (1) 1968 (4); v SA 1966 (5); v WI 1964 (5); v In 1966 (2); v P 1964 (1)*

Craig, I. D. 11: v SA 1952 (1); *v E 1956 (2); v SA 1957 (5); v In 1956 (2); v P 1956 (1)*

Crawford, P. 4: *v E 1956 (1); v In 1956 (3)*

Dale, A. C. 1: *v In 1997*

Darling, J. 34: v E 1894 (5) 1897 (5) 1901 (3); *v E 1896 (3) 1899 (5) 1902 (5) 1905 (5); v SA 1902 (3)*

Darling, L. S. 12: v E 1932 (2) 1936 (1); *v E 1934 (4); v SA 1935 (5)*

Darling, W. M. 14: v E 1978 (4); v In 1977 (1); v P 1978 (1); *v WI 1977 (3); v In 1979 (5)*

Davidson, A. K. 44: v E 1954 (3) 1958 (5) 1962 (5); v WI 1960 (4); *v E 1953 (5) 1956 (2) 1961 (5); v SA 1957 (3); v In 1956 (1) 1959 (5); v P 1956 (1) 1959 (3)*

Davis, I. C. 15: v E 1976 (1); v NZ 1973 (3); v P 1976 (3); *v E 1977 (3); v NZ 1973 (3) 1976 (2)*

Davis, S. P. 1: *v NZ 1985*

De Courcy, J. H. 3: *v E 1953 (3)*

Dell, A. R. 2: v E 1970 (1); v NZ 1973 (1)

Dodemaide, A. I. C. 10: v E 1987 (1); v WI 1988 (2); v NZ 1987 (1); v SL 1987 (1); *v P 1988 (3); v SL 1992 (2)*

Donnan, H. 5: v E 1891 (2); *v E 1896 (3)*

Dooland, B. 3: v E 1946 (2); v In 1947 (1)

Duff, R. A. 22: v E 1901 (4) 1903 (5); *v E 1902 (5) 1905 (5); v SA 1902 (3)*

Duncan, J. R. F. 1: v E 1970

Dyer, G. C. 6: v E 1986 (1) 1987 (1); v NZ 1987 (3); v SL 1987 (1)

Dymock, G. 21: v E 1974 (1) 1978 (3) 1979 (3); v WI 1979 (2); v NZ 1973 (3); v P 1978 (1); *v NZ 1973 (2); v In 1979 (5); v P 1979 (3)*

Dyson, J. 30: v E 1982 (5); v WI 1981 (2) 1984 (3); v NZ 1980 (3); v In 1977 (3) 1980 (3); *v E 1981 (5); v NZ 1981 (3); v P 1982 (3)*

Eady, C. J. 2: v E 1901 (1); *v E 1896 (1)*

Eastwood, K. H. 1: v E 1970

Ebeling, H. I. 1: *v E 1934*

Edwards, J. D. 3: *v E 1888 (3)*

Edwards, R. 20: v E 1974 (5); v P 1972 (2); *v E 1972 (4) 1975 (4); v WI 1972 (5)*

Edwards, W. J. 3: v E 1974 (3)

Elliott, M. T. G. 17: v SA 1997 (3); v WI 1996 (2); v NZ 1997 (3); *v E 1997 (6); v SA 1996 (3)*

Emery, P. A. 1: *v P 1994*

Emery, S. H. 4: *v E 1912 (2); v SA 1912 (2)*

Evans, E. 6: v E 1881 (2) 1882 (1) 1884 (1); *v E 1886 (2)*

Fairfax, A. G. 10: v E 1928 (1); v WI 1930 (5); *v E 1930 (4)*

Favell, L. E. 19: v E 1954 (4) 1958 (2); v WI 1960 (4); *v WI 1954 (2); v In 1959 (4); v P 1959 (3)*

Ferris, J. J. 8: v E 1886 (2) 1887 (1); *v E 1888 (3) 1890 (2)*

Fingleton, J. H. 18: v E 1932 (3) 1936 (5); v SA 1931 (1); *v E 1938 (4); v SA 1935 (5)*

Fleetwood-Smith, L. O'B. 10: v E 1936 (3); *v E 1938 (4); v SA 1935 (3)*

Fleming, D. W. 4: v E 1994 (3); *v P 1994 (1)*

Francis, B. C. 3: *v E 1972 (3)*

Freeman, E. W. 11: v WI 1968 (4); v In 1967 (2); *v E 1968 (2); v SA 1969 (2); v In 1969 (1)*

Freer, F. W. 1: v E 1946

Gannon, J. B. 3: v In 1977 (3)

Garrett, T. W. 19: v E 1876 (2) 1878 (1) 1881 (3) 1882 (3) 1884 (3) 1886 (2) 1887 (1); *v E 1882 (1) 1886 (3)*

Gaunt, R. A. 3: v SA 1963 (1); *v E 1961 (1); v SA 1957 (1)*

Gehrs, D. R. A. 6: v E 1903 (1); v SA 1910 (4); *v E 1905 (1)*

Giffen, G. 31: v E 1881 (3) 1882 (4) 1884 (3) 1891 (3) 1894 (5); *v E 1882 (1) 1884 (3) 1886 (3) 1893 (3) 1896 (3)*

Giffen, W. F. 3: v E 1886 (1) 1891 (2)

Gilbert, D. R. 9: v NZ 1985 (3); v In 1985 (2); *v E 1985 (1); v NZ 1985 (1); v In 1986 (2)*

Gillespie, J. N. 9: v WI 1996 (2); *v E 1997 (4); v SA 1996 (3)*

Gilmour, G. J. 15: v E 1976 (1); v WI 1975 (5); v NZ 1973 (2); v P 1976 (3); *v E 1975 (1); v NZ 1973 (1) 1976 (2)*

Gleeson, J. W. 29: v E 1970 (5); v WI 1968 (5); v In 1967 (4); *v E 1968 (5) 1972 (3); v SA 1969 (4); v In 1969 (3)*

Graham, H. 6: v E 1894 (2); *v E 1893 (3) 1896 (1)*

Gregory, D. W. 3: v E 1876 (2) 1878 (1)

Gregory, E. J. 1: v E 1876

Gregory, J. M. 24: v E 1920 (5) 1924 (5) 1928 (1); *v E 1921 (5) 1926 (5); v SA 1921 (3)*

Gregory, R. G. 2: v E 1936 (2)

Gregory, S. E. 58: v E 1891 (1) 1894 (5) 1897 (5) 1901 (5) 1903 (4) 1907 (2) 1911 (1); *v E 1890 (2) 1893 (3) 1896 (3) 1899 (5) 1902 (5) 1905 (3) 1909 (5) 1912 (3); v SA 1902 (3) 1912 (3)*

Grimmett, C. V. 37: v E 1924 (1) 1928 (5) 1932 (3); v SA 1931 (5); v WI 1930 (5); *v E 1926 (3) 1930 (5) 1934 (5); v SA 1935 (5)*

Groube, T. U. 1: *v E 1880*

Grout, A. T. W. 51: v E 1958 (5) 1962 (2) 1965 (5); v SA 1963 (5); v WI 1960 (5); *v E 1961 (5) 1964 (5); v SA 1957 (5); v WI 1964 (5); v In 1959 (4) 1964 (1); v P 1959 (3) 1964 (1)*

Guest, C. E. J. 1: v E 1962

Hamence, R. A. 3: v E 1946 (1); v In 1947 (2)

Hammond, J. R. 5: *v WI 1972 (5)*

Harry, J. 1: v E 1894

Hartigan, R. J. 2: v E 1907 (2)

Hartkopf, A. E. V. 1: v E 1924

Harvey, M. R. 1: v E 1946

Harvey, R. N. 79: v E 1950 (5) 1954 (5) 1958 (5) 1962 (5); v SA 1952 (5); v WI 1951 (5) 1960 (4); v In 1947 (2); *v E 1948 (2) 1953 (5) 1956 (5) 1961 (5); v SA 1949 (5) 1957 (4); v WI 1954 (5); v In 1956 (3) 1959 (5); v P 1956 (1) 1959 (3)*

Hassett, A. L. 43: v E 1946 (5) 1950 (5); v SA 1952 (5); v WI 1951 (4); v In 1947 (4); *v E 1938 (4) 1948 (5) 1953 (5); v SA 1949 (5); v NZ 1945 (1)*

Hawke, N. J. N. 27: v E 1962 (1) 1965 (4); v SA 1963 (4); v In 1967 (1); v P 1964 (1); *v E 1964 (5) 1968 (2); v SA 1966 (2); v WI 1964 (5); v In 1964 (1); v P 1964 (1)*

Hayden, M. L. 7: v WI 1996 (3); *v SA 1993 (1) 1996 (3)*

Hazlitt, G. R. 9: v E 1907 (2) 1911 (1); *v E 1912 (3); v SA 1912 (3)*

Healy, I. A. 103: v E 1990 (5) 1994 (5); v SA 1993 (3) 1997 (3); v WI 1988 (5) 1992 (5) 1996 (5); v NZ 1989 (1) 1993 (3) 1997 (3); v In 1991 (5); v P 1989 (1) 1995 (3); v SL 1989 (2) 1995 (3); *v E 1989 (6) 1993 (6) 1997 (6); v SA 1993 (3) 1996 (3); v WI 1990 (5) 1994 (4); v NZ 1989 (1) 1992 (3); v In 1996 (1) 1997 (3); v P 1988 (3) 1994 (2); v SL 1992 (3)*

Hendry, H. L. 11: v E 1924 (1) 1928 (4); *v E 1921 (4); v SA 1921 (2)*

Hibbert, P. A. 1: v In 1977

Higgs, J. D. 22: v E 1978 (5) 1979 (1); v WI 1979 (1); v NZ 1980 (3); v In 1980 (2); *v WI 1977 (4); v In 1979 (6)*

Hilditch, A. M. J. 18: v E 1978 (1); v WI 1984 (2); v NZ 1985 (1); v P 1978 (2); *v E 1985 (6); v In 1979 (6)*

Hill, C. 49: v E 1897 (5) 1901 (5) 1903 (5) 1907 (5) 1911 (5); v SA 1910 (5); *v E 1896 (3) 1899 (3) 1902 (5) 1905 (5); v SA 1902 (3)*

Hill, J. C. 3: *v E 1953 (2); v WI 1954 (1)*

Hoare, D. E. 1: v WI 1960

Hodges, J. 2: v E 1876 (2)

Hogan, T. G. 7: v P 1983 (1); *v WI 1983 (5); v SL 1982 (1)*

Hogg, G. B. 1: *v In 1996*

Hogg, R. M. 38: v E 1978 (6) 1982 (3); v WI 1979 (2) 1984 (4); v NZ 1980 (2); v In 1980 (2); v P 1978 (2) 1983 (4); *v E 1981 (2); v WI 1983 (4); v In 1979 (6); v SL 1982 (1)*

Hohns, T. V. 7: v WI 1988 (2); *v E 1989 (5)*

Hole, G. B. 18: v E 1950 (1) 1954 (3); v SA 1952 (4); v WI 1951 (5); *v E 1953 (5)*

Holland, R. G. 11: v WI 1984 (3); v NZ 1985 (3); v In 1985 (1); *v E 1985 (4)*

Hookes, D. W. 23: v E 1976 (1) 1982 (5); v WI 1979 (1); v NZ 1985 (2); *v E 1977 (5); v WI 1983 (5); v P 1979 (1); v SL 1982 (1)*

Hopkins, A. J. 20: v E 1901 (2) 1903 (5); *v E 1902 (5) 1905 (3) 1909 (2); v SA 1902 (3)*

Horan, T. P. 15: v E 1876 (1) 1878 (1) 1881 (4) 1882 (4) 1884 (4); *v E 1882 (1)*

Hordern, H. V. 7: v E 1911 (5); v SA 1910 (2)

Hornibrook, P. M. 6: v E 1928 (1); *v E 1930 (5)*

Howell, W. P. 18: v E 1897 (3) 1901 (4) 1903 (3); *v E 1899 (5) 1902 (1); v SA 1902 (2)*

Hughes, K. J. 70: v E 1978 (6) 1979 (3) 1982 (5); v WI 1979 (3) 1981 (3) 1984 (2); v NZ 1980 (3); v In 1977 (2) 1980 (3); v P 1978 (2) 1981 (3) 1983 (5); *v E 1977 (1) 1980 (1) 1981 (6); v WI 1983 (5); v NZ 1981 (3); v In 1979 (6); v P 1979 (3) 1982 (3)*

Hughes, M. G. 53: v E 1986 (4) 1990 (4); v WI 1988 (4) 1992 (5); v NZ 1987 (1) 1989 (1); v In 1985 (1) 1991 (5); v P 1989 (3); v SL 1987 (1) 1989 (2); *v E 1989 (6) 1993 (6); v SA 1993 (2); v WI 1990 (5); v NZ 1992 (3)*

Hunt, W. A. 1: v SA 1931

Hurst, A. G. 12: v E 1978 (6); v NZ 1973 (1); v In 1977 (1); v P 1978 (2); *v In 1979 (2)*

Hurwood, A. 2: v WI 1930 (2)

Inverarity, R. J. 6: v WI 1968 (1); *v E 1968 (2) 1972 (2)*

Iredale, F. A. 14: v E 1894 (5) 1897 (4); *v E 1896 (2) 1899 (3)*

Ironmonger, H. 14: v E 1928 (2) 1932 (4); v SA 1931 (4); v WI 1930 (4)

Iverson, J. B. 5: v E 1950 (5)

Jackson, A. A. 8: v E 1928 (2); v WI 1930 (4); *v E 1930 (2)*

Jarman, B. N. 19: v E 1962 (3); v WI 1968 (4); v In 1967 (4); v P 1964 (1); *v E 1968 (4); v In 1959 (1) 1964 (2)*

Jarvis, A. H. 11: v E 1884 (3) 1894 (4); *v E 1886 (2) 1888 (2)*

Jenner, T. J. 9: v E 1970 (2) 1974 (2); v WI 1975 (1); *v WI 1972 (4)*

Jennings, C. B. 6: *v E 1912 (3); v SA 1912 (3)*

Johnson I. W. 45: v E 1946 (4) 1950 (5) 1954 (4); v SA 1952 (1); v WI 1951 (4); v In 1947 (4); *v E 1948 (4) 1956 (5); v SA 1949 (5); v WI 1954 (5); v NZ 1945 (1); v In 1956 (2); v P 1956 (1)*

Johnson, L. J. 1: v In 1947

Johnston W. A. 40: v E 1950 (5) 1954 (4); v SA 1952 (5); v WI 1951 (5); v In 1947 (4); *v E 1948 (5) 1953 (3); v SA 1949 (5); v WI 1954 (4)*

Jones, D. M. 52: v E 1986 (5) 1987 (1) 1990 (5); v WI 1988 (3); v NZ 1987 (3) 1989 (1); v In 1991 (5); v P 1989 (3); v SL 1987 (1) 1989 (2); *v E 1989 (6); v WI 1983 (2) 1990 (5); v NZ 1989 (1); v In 1986 (3); v P 1988 (3); v SL 1992 (3)*

Jones, E. 19: v E 1894 (1) 1897 (5) 1901 (2); *v E 1896 (3) 1899 (5) 1902 (2); v SA 1902 (1)*

Jones, S. P. 12: v E 1881 (2) 1884 (4) 1886 (1) 1887 (1); *v E 1882 (1) 1886 (3)*

Joslin, L. R. 1: v In 1967

Julian, B. P. 7: v SL 1995 (1); *v E 1993 (2); v WI 1994 (4)*

Kasprowicz, M. S. 13: v SA 1997 (2); v WI 1996 (2); v NZ 1997 (3); *v E 1997 (3); v In 1997 (3)*

Kelleway, C. 26: v E 1911 (4) 1920 (5) 1924 (5) 1928 (1); v SA 1910 (5); *v E 1912 (3); v SA 1912 (3)*

Kelly, J. J. 36: v E 1897 (5) 1901 (5) 1903 (5); *v E 1896 (3) 1899 (5) 1902 (5) 1905 (3); v SA 1902 (3)*

Kelly, T. J. D. 2: v E 1876 (1) 1878 (1)

Kendall, T. 2: v E 1876 (2)

Kent, M. F. 3: *v E 1981 (3)*

Kerr, R. B. 2: v NZ 1985 (2)

Kippax, A. F. 22: v E 1924 (1) 1928 (5) 1932 (1); v SA 1931 (4); v WI 1930 (4); *v E 1930 (5) 1934 (1)*

Kline L. F. 13: v E 1958 (2); v WI 1960 (1); *v SA 1957 (5); v In 1959 (3); v P 1959 (1)*

Laird, B. M. 21: v E 1979 (2); v WI 1979 (3) 1981 (3); v P 1981 (3); *v E 1980 (1); v NZ 1981 (3); v P 1979 (3) 1982 (3)*

Langer, J. L. 8: v WI 1992 (2) 1996 (2); *v NZ 1992 (3); v P 1994 (1)*

Langley, G. R. A. 26: v E 1954 (2); v SA 1952 (5); v WI 1951 (5); *v E 1953 (4) 1956 (3); v WI 1954 (4); v In 1956 (2); v P 1956 (1)*

Laughlin, T. J. 3: v E 1978 (1); *v WI 1977 (2)*

Laver, F. 15: v E 1901 (1) 1903 (1); *v E 1899 (4) 1905 (5) 1909 (4)*

Law, S. G. 1: v SL 1995

Lawry, W. M. 67: v E 1962 (5) 1965 (5) 1970 (5); v SA 1963 (5); v WI 1968 (5); v In 1967 (4); v P 1964 (1); *v E 1961 (5) 1964 (5) 1968 (4); v SA 1966 (5) 1969 (4); v WI 1964 (5); v In 1964 (3) 1969 (5); v P 1964 (1)*

Lawson, G. F. 46: v E 1982 (5) 1986 (1); v WI 1981 (1) 1984 (5) 1988 (1); v NZ 1980 (1) 1985 (2) 1989 (1); v P 1983 (5); v SL 1989 (1); *v E 1981 (3) 1985 (6) 1989 (6); v WI 1983 (5); v P 1982 (3)*

Lee, P. K. 2: v E 1932 (1); v SA 1931 (1)

Lehmann, D. S. 1: *v In 1997*

Lillee, D. K. 70: v E 1970 (2) 1974 (6) 1976 (1) 1979 (3) 1982 (1); v WI 1975 (5) 1979 (5) 1981 (3); v NZ 1980 (3); v In 1980 (3); v P 1972 (3) 1976 (3) 1981 (3) 1983 (5); *v E 1972 (5) 1975 (4) 1980 (1) 1981 (6); v WI 1972 (1); v NZ 1976 (2) 1981 (3); v P 1979 (3); v SL 1982 (1)*

Lindwall, R. R. 61: v E 1946 (4) 1950 (5) 1954 (4) 1958 (2); v SA 1952 (4); v WI 1951 (5); v In 1947 (5); *v E 1948 (5) 1953 (5) 1956 (4); v SA 1949 (4); v WI 1954 (5); v NZ 1945 (1); v In 1956 (3) 1959 (2); v P 1956 (1) 1959 (2)*

Love, H. S. B. 1: v E 1932

Loxton, S. J. E. 12: v E 1950 (3); v In 1947 (1); *v E 1948 (3); v SA 1949 (5)*

Lyons, J. J. 14: v E 1886 (1) 1891 (3) 1894 (3) 1897 (1); *v E 1888 (1) 1890 (2) 1893 (3)*

McAlister, P. A. 8: v E 1903 (2) 1907 (4); *v E 1909 (2)*

Macartney, C. G. 35: v E 1907 (5) 1911 (5) 1920 (2); v SA 1910 (4); *v E 1909 (5) 1912 (3) 1921 (5) 1926 (5); v SA 1912 (3) 1921 (2)*

McCabe, S. J. 39: v E 1932 (5) 1936 (5); v SA 1931 (5); v WI 1930 (5); *v E 1930 (5) 1934 (5) 1938 (4); v SA 1935 (5)*

McCool, C. L. 14: v E 1946 (5); v In 1947 (3); *v SA 1949 (5); v NZ 1945 (1)*

McCormick, E. L. 12: v E 1936 (4); *v E 1938 (3); v SA 1935 (5)*

McCosker, R. B. 25: v E 1974 (3) 1976 (1) 1979 (2); v WI 1975 (4) 1979 (1); v P 1976 (3); *v E 1975 (4) 1977 (5); v NZ 1976 (2)*

McDermott, C. J. 71: v E 1986 (1) 1987 (1) 1990 (2) 1994 (5); v SA 1993 (3); v WI 1984 (2) 1988 (2) 1992 (5); v NZ 1985 (2) 1987 (3) 1993 (3); v In 1985 (2) 1991 (5); v P 1995 (3); v SL 1987 (1) 1995 (3); *v E 1985 (6) 1993 (2); v SA 1993 (3); v WI 1990 (5); v NZ 1985 (2) 1992 (3); v In 1986 (2); v P 1994 (2); v SL 1992 (3)*

McDonald, C. C. 47: v E 1954 (2) 1958 (5); v SA 1952 (5); v WI 1951 (1) 1960 (5); *v E 1956 (5) 1961 (3); v SA 1957 (5); v WI 1954 (5); v In 1956 (2) 1959 (5); v P 1956 (1) 1959 (3)*

McDonald, E. A. 11: v E 1920 (3); *v E 1921 (5); v SA 1921 (3)*

McDonnell, P. S. 19: v E 1881 (4) 1882 (3) 1884 (2) 1886 (2) 1887 (1); *v E 1880 (1) 1884 (3) 1888 (3)*

MacGill, S. C. G. 1: v SA 1997

McGrath, G. D. 37: v E 1994 (2); v SA 1993 (1) 1997 (2); v WI 1996 (5); v NZ 1993 (2) 1997 (1); v P 1995 (3); v SL 1995 (3); *v E 1997 (6); v SA 1993 (2) 1996 (3); v WI 1994 (4); v In 1996 (1); v P 1994 (2)*

McIlwraith, J. 1: *v E 1886*

McIntyre, P. E. 2: v E 1994 (1); *v In 1996 (1)*

Mackay, K. D. 37: v E 1958 (5) 1962 (3); v WI 1960 (5); *v E 1956 (3) 1961 (5); v SA 1957 (5); v In 1956 (3) 1959 (5); v P 1959 (3)*

McKenzie, G. D. 60: v E 1962 (5) 1965 (4) 1970 (3); v SA 1963 (3); v WI 1968 (5); v In 1967 (2); v P 1964 (1); *v E 1961 (3) 1964 (5) 1968 (5); v SA 1966 (5) 1969 (5); v WI 1964 (5); v In 1964 (3) 1969 (5); v P 1964 (1)*

McKibbin, T. R. 5: v E 1894 (1) 1897 (2); *v E 1896 (2)*

McLaren, J. W. 1: v E 1911

Maclean, J. A. 4: v E 1978 (4)

McLeod, C. E. 17: v E 1894 (1) 1897 (5) 1901 (2) 1903 (3); *v E 1899 (1) 1905 (5)*

McLeod, R. W. 6: v E 1891 (3); *v E 1893 (3)*

McShane, P. G. 3: v E 1884 (1) 1886 (1) 1887 (1)

Maddocks, L. V. 7: v E 1954 (3); *v E 1956 (2); v WI 1954 (1); v In 1956 (1)*

Maguire, J. N. 3: v P 1983 (1); *v WI 1983 (2)*

Mailey, A. A. 21: v E 1920 (5) 1924 (5); *v E 1921 (3) 1926 (5); v SA 1921 (3)*

Mallett, A. A. 38: v E 1970 (2) 1974 (5) 1979 (1); v WI 1968 (1) 1975 (6) 1979 (1); v NZ 1973 (3); v P 1972 (2); *v E 1968 (1) 1972 (2) 1975 (4) 1980 (1); v SA 1969 (1); v NZ 1973 (3); v In 1969 (5)*

Malone, M. F. 1: *v E 1977*

Mann, A. L. 4: v In 1977 (4)

Marr, A. P. 1: v E 1884

Marsh, G. R. 50: v E 1986 (5) 1987 (1) 1990 (5); v WI 1988 (5); v NZ 1987 (3); v In 1985 (3) 1991 (4); v P 1989 (2); v SL 1987 (1); *v E 1989 (6); v WI 1990 (5); v NZ 1985 (3) 1989 (1); v In 1986 (3); v P 1988 (3)*

Marsh, R. W. 96: v E 1970 (6) 1974 (6) 1976 (1) 1979 (3) 1982 (5); v WI 1975 (6) 1979 (3) 1981 (3); v NZ 1973 (3) 1980 (3); v In 1980 (3); v P 1972 (3) 1976 (3) 1981 (3) 1983 (5); *v E 1972 (5) 1975 (4) 1977 (5) 1980 (1) 1981 (6); v WI 1972 (5); v NZ 1973 (3) 1976 (2) 1981 (3); v P 1979 (3) 1982 (3)*

Martin, J. W. 8: v SA 1963 (1); v WI 1960 (3); *v SA 1966 (1); v In 1964 (2); v P 1964 (1)*

Martyn, D. R. 7: v SA 1993 (2); v WI 1992 (4); *v NZ 1992 (1)*

Massie, H. H. 9: v E 1881 (4) 1882 (3) 1884 (1); *v E 1882 (1)*

Massie, R. A. L. 6: v P 1972 (2); *v E 1972 (4)*

Matthews, C. D. 3: v E 1986 (2); v WI 1988 (1)

Matthews, G. R. J. 33: v E 1986 (4) 1990 (5); v WI 1984 (1) 1992 (2); v NZ 1985 (3); v In 1985 (3); v P 1983 (2); *v WI 1985 (1); v WI 1983 (1) 1990 (2); v NZ 1985 (3); v In 1986 (3); v SL 1992 (3)*

Matthews, T. J. 8: v E 1911 (2); *v E 1912 (3); v SA 1912 (3)*

May, T. B. A. 24: v E 1994 (3); v SA 1993 (3); v WI 1988 (3) 1992 (1); v NZ 1987 (1) 1993 (2); *v E 1993 (5); v SA 1993 (1); v P 1988 (3) 1994 (2)*

Mayne, E. R. 4: *v E 1912 (1); v SA 1912 (1) 1921 (2)*

Mayne, L. C. 6: v SA 1969 (2); *v WI 1964 (3); v In 1969 (1)*

Meckiff, I. 18: v E 1958 (4); v WI 1960 (2); *v SA 1957 (4); v In 1959 (5); v P 1959 (2)*

Meuleman, K. D. 1: *v NZ 1945*

Midwinter, W. E. 8: v E 1876 (2) 1882 (1) 1886 (2); *v E 1884 (3)*

Miller, K. R. 55: v E 1946 (5) 1950 (5) 1954 (4); v SA 1952 (4); v WI 1951 (5); v In 1947 (5); *v E 1948 (5) 1953 (5) 1956 (5); v SA 1949 (5); v WI 1954 (5); v NZ 1945 (1); v P 1956 (1)*

Minnett, R. B. 9: v E 1911 (5); *v E 1912 (1); v SA 1912 (3)*

Misson, F. M. 5: v WI 1960 (3); *v E 1961 (2)*

Moody, T. M. 8: v NZ 1989 (1); v In 1991 (1); v P 1989 (1); v SL 1989 (2); *v SL 1992 (3)*

Moroney, J. 7: v E 1950 (1); v WI 1951 (1); *v SA 1949 (5)*

Morris, A. R. 46: v E 1946 (5) 1950 (5) 1954 (4); v SA 1952 (5); v WI 1951 (5); v In 1947 (4); *v E 1948 (5) 1953 (5); v SA 1949 (5); v WI 1954 (4)*

Morris, S. 1: v E 1884

Moses, H. 6: v E 1886 (2) 1887 (1) 1891 (2) 1894 (1)

Moss, J. K. 1: v P 1978

Moule, W. H. 1: *v E 1880*

Murdoch, W. L. 18: v E 1876 (1) 1878 (1) 1881 (4) 1882 (4) 1884 (1); *v E 1880 (1) 1882 (1) 1884 (3) 1890 (2)*

Musgrove, H. 1: v E 1884

Nagel, L. E. 1: v E 1932

Nash, L. J. 2: v E 1936 (1); v SA 1931 (1)

Nitschke, H. C. 2: v SA 1931 (2)

Noble, M. A. 42: v E 1897 (4) 1901 (5) 1903 (5) 1907 (5); *v E 1899 (5) 1902 (5) 1905 (5) 1909 (5); v SA 1902 (3)*

Noblet, G. 3: v SA 1952 (1); v WI 1951 (1); *v SA 1949 (1)*

Nothling, O. E. 1: v E 1928

O'Brien, L. P. J. 5: v E 1932 (2) 1936 (1); *v SA 1935 (2)*

O'Connor, J. D. A. 4: v E 1907 (3); *v E 1909 (1)*

O'Donnell, S. P. 6: v NZ 1985 (1); *v E 1985 (5)*

Ogilvie, A. D. 5: v In 1977 (3); *v WI 1977 (2)*

O'Keeffe, K. J. 24: v E 1970 (2) 1976 (1); v NZ 1973 (3); v P 1972 (2) 1976 (3); *v E 1977 (3); v WI 1972 (5); v NZ 1973 (3) 1976 (2)*

Oldfield, W. A. 54: v E 1920 (3) 1924 (5) 1928 (5) 1932 (4) 1936 (5); v SA 1931 (5); v WI 1930 (5); *v E 1921 (1) 1926 (5) 1930 (5) 1934 (5); v SA 1921 (1) 1935 (5)*

O'Neill, N. C. 42: v E 1958 (5) 1962 (5); v SA 1963 (4); v WI 1960 (5); *v E 1961 (5) 1964 (4); v WI 1964 (4); v In 1959 (5) 1964 (2); v P 1959 (3)*

O'Reilly, W. J. 27: v E 1932 (5) 1936 (5); v SA 1931 (2); *v E 1934 (5) 1938 (4); v SA 1935 (5); v NZ 1945 (1)*

Oxenham, R. K. 7: v E 1928 (3); v SA 1931 (1); v WI 1930 (3)

Palmer, G. E. 17: v E 1881 (4) 1882 (4) 1884 (2); *v E 1880 (1) 1884 (3) 1886 (3)*

Park, R. L. 1: v E 1920

Pascoe, L. S. 14: v E 1979 (2); v WI 1979 (1) 1981 (1); v NZ 1980 (3); v In 1980 (3); *v E 1977 (3) 1980 (1)*

Pellew, C. E. 10: v E 1920 (4); *v E 1921 (5); v SA 1921 (1)*

Phillips, W. B. 27: v WI 1984 (2); v NZ 1985 (3); v In 1985 (3); v P 1983 (5); *v E 1985 (6); v WI 1983 (5); v NZ 1985 (3)*

Phillips, W. N. 1: v In 1991

Philpott, P. I. 8: v E 1965 (3); *v WI 1964 (5)*

Ponsford, W. H. 29: v E 1924 (5) 1928 (2) 1932 (3); v SA 1931 (4); v WI 1930 (5); *v E 1926 (2) 1930 (4) 1934 (4)*

Ponting, R. T. 18: v SA 1997 (3); v WI 1996 (2); v NZ 1997 (3); v SL 1995 (3); *v E 1997 (3); v In 1996 (1) 1997 (3)*

Pope, R. J. 1: v E 1884

Rackemann, C. G. 12: v E 1982 (1) 1990 (1); v WI 1984 (1); v NZ 1989 (1); v P 1983 (2) 1989 (3); v SL 1989 (1); *v WI 1983 (1); v NZ 1989 (1)*

Ransford, V. S. 20: v E 1907 (5) 1911 (5); v SA 1910 (3); *v E 1909 (5)*

Redpath, I. R. 66: v E 1965 (1) 1970 (6) 1974 (6); v WI 1968 (5) 1975 (6); v In 1967 (3); v P 1972 (3); *v E 1964 (5) 1968 (5); v SA 1966 (5) 1969 (4); v WI 1972 (5); v NZ 1973 (3); v In 1964 (2) 1969 (5); v P 1964 (1)*

Reedman, J. C. 1: v E 1894

Reid, B. A. 27: v E 1986 (5) 1990 (4); v WI 1992 (1); v NZ 1987 (2); v In 1985 (3) 1991 (2); *v WI 1990 (2); v NZ 1985 (3); v In 1986 (2); v P 1988 (3)*

Reiffel, P. R. 35: v SA 1993 (2) 1997 (2); v WI 1996 (3); v NZ 1993 (2) 1997 (3); v In 1991 (1); v P 1995 (3); v SL 1995 (2); *v E 1993 (3) 1997 (4); v SA 1993 (1); v WI 1994 (4); v NZ 1992 (3); v In 1996 (1) 1997 (1)*

Renneberg, D. A. 8: v In 1967 (3); *v SA 1966 (5)*

Richardson, A. J. 9: v E 1924 (4); *v E 1926 (5)*

Richardson, V. Y. 19: v E 1924 (3) 1928 (2) 1932 (5); *v E 1930 (4); v SA 1935 (5)*

Rigg, K. E. 8: v E 1936 (3); v SA 1931 (4); v WI 1930 (1)

Ring, D. T. 13: v SA 1952 (5); v WI 1951 (5); v In 1947 (1); *v E 1948 (1) 1953 (1)*

Ritchie, G. M. 30: v E 1986 (4); v WI 1984 (1); v NZ 1985 (3); v In 1985 (2); *v E 1985 (6); v WI 1983 (5); v NZ 1985 (3); v In 1986 (3); v P 1982 (3)*

Rixon, S. J. 13: v WI 1984 (3); v In 1977 (5); *v WI 1977 (5)*

Robertson, G. R. 3: *v In 1997 (3)*

Robertson, W. R. 1: v E 1884

Robinson, R. D. 3: *v E 1977 (3)*

Robinson, R. H. 1: v E 1936

Rorke, G. F. 4: v E 1958 (2); *v In 1959 (2)*

Rutherford, J. W. 1: *v In 1956*

Ryder, J. 20: v E 1920 (5) 1924 (3) 1928 (5); *v E 1926 (4); v SA 1921 (3)*

Saggers, R. A. 6: *v E 1948 (1); v SA 1949 (5)*

Saunders, J. V. 14: v E 1901 (1) 1903 (2) 1907 (5); *v E 1902 (4); v SA 1902 (2)*

Scott, H. J. H. 8: v E 1884 (2); *v E 1884 (3) 1886 (3)*

Sellers, R. H. D. 1: *v In 1964*

Serjeant, C. S. 12: v In 1977 (4); *v E 1977 (3); v WI 1977 (5)*

Sheahan, A. P. 31: v E 1970 (2); v WI 1968 (5); v NZ 1973 (2); v In 1967 (4); v P 1972 (2); *v E 1968 (5) 1972 (2); v SA 1969 (4); v In 1969 (5)*

Shepherd, B. K. 9: v E 1962 (2); v SA 1963 (4); v P 1964 (1); *v WI 1964 (2)*

Sievers, M. W. 3: v E 1936 (3)

Simpson, R. B. 62: v E 1958 (1) 1962 (5) 1965 (3); v SA 1963 (5); v WI 1960 (5); v In 1967 (3) 1977 (5); v P 1964 (1); *v E 1961 (5) 1964 (5); v SA 1957 (5) 1966 (5); v WI 1964 (5) 1977 (5); v In 1964 (3); v P 1964 (1)*

Sincock, D. J. 3: v E 1965 (1); v P 1964 (1); *v WI 1964 (1)*

Slater, K. N. 1: v E 1958

Slater, M. J. 37: v E 1994 (5); v SA 1993 (3); v NZ 1993 (3); v P 1995 (3); v SL 1995 (3); *v E 1993 (6); v SA 1993 (3); v WI 1994 (4); v In 1996 (1) 1997 (3); v P 1994 (3)*

Sleep, P. R. 14: v E 1986 (3) 1987 (1); v NZ 1987 (3); v P 1978 (1) 1989 (1); v SL 1989 (1); *v In 1979 (2); v P 1982 (1) 1988 (1)*

Slight, J. 1: *v E 1880*

Smith, D. B. M. 2: *v E 1912 (2)*

Smith, S. B. 3: *v WI 1983 (3)*

Spofforth, F. R. 18: v E 1876 (1) 1878 (1) 1881 (1) 1882 (4) 1884 (3) 1886 (1); *v E 1882 (1) 1884 (3) 1886 (3)*

Stackpole, K. R. 43: v E 1965 (2) 1970 (6); v WI 1968 (5); v NZ 1973 (3); v P 1972 (1); *v E 1972 (5); v SA 1966 (5) 1969 (4); v WI 1972 (4); v NZ 1973 (3); v In 1969 (5)*

Stevens, G. B. 4: *v In 1959 (2); v P 1959 (2)*

Taber, H. B. 16: v WI 1968 (1); *v E 1968 (1); v SA 1966 (5) 1969 (4); v In 1969 (5)*

Tallon, D. 21: v E 1946 (5) 1950 (5); v In 1947 (5); *v E 1948 (4) 1953 (1); v NZ 1945 (1)*

Taylor, J. M. 20: v E 1920 (5) 1924 (5); *v E 1921 (5) 1926 (3); v SA 1921 (2)*

Taylor, M. A. 96: v E 1990 (5) 1994 (5); v SA 1993 (3) 1997 (3); v WI 1988 (2) 1992 (4) 1996 (5); v NZ 1989 (1) 1993 (3) 1997 (3); v In 1991 (5); v P 1989 (3) 1995 (3); v SL 1989 (2) 1995 (3); *v E 1989 (6) 1993 (6) 1997 (6); v SA 1993 (3) 1996 (3); v WI 1990 (5) 1994 (4); v NZ 1989 (1) 1992 (3); v In 1996 (1) 1997 (3); v P 1994 (3); v SL 1992 (3)*

Taylor, P. L. 13: v E 1986 (1) 1987 (1); v WI 1988 (2); v In 1991 (2); v P 1989 (2); v SL 1987 (1); *v WI 1990 (1); v NZ 1989 (1); v P 1988 (2)*

Thomas, G. 8: v E 1965 (3); *v WI 1964 (5)*

Thoms, G. R. 1: v WI 1951

Thomson, A. L. 4: v E 1970 (4)

Thomson, J. R. 51: v E 1974 (5) 1979 (1) 1982 (4); v WI 1975 (6) 1979 (1) 1981 (2); v In 1977 (5); v P 1972 (1) 1976 (1) 1981 (3); *v E 1975 (4) 1977 (5) 1985 (2); v WI 1977 (5); v NZ 1981 (3); v P 1982 (3)*

Thomson, N. F. D. 2: v E 1876 (2)

Toohey, P. M. 15: v E 1978 (5) 1979 (1); v WI 1979 (1); v In 1977 (5); *v WI 1977 (3)*

Toshack, E. R. H. 12: v E 1946 (5); v In 1947 (2); *v E 1948 (4); v NZ 1945 (1)*

Travers, J. P. F. 1: v E 1901

Tribe, G. E. 3: v E 1946 (3)

Trott, A. E. 3: v E 1894 (3)

Trott, G. H. S. 24: v E 1891 (3) 1894 (5) 1897 (5); *v E 1888 (3) 1890 (2) 1893 (3) 1896 (3)*

Trumble, H. 32: v E 1894 (1) 1897 (5) 1901 (5) 1903 (4); *v E 1890 (2) 1893 (3) 1896 (3) 1899 (5) 1902 (3); v SA 1902 (1)*

Trumble, J. W. 7: v E 1884 (4); *v E 1886 (3)*

Trumper, V. T. 48: v E 1901 (5) 1903 (5) 1907 (5) 1911 (5); v SA 1910 (5); *v E 1899 (5) 1902 (5) 1905 (5) 1909 (5); v SA 1902 (3)*

Turner, A. 14: v WI 1975 (6); v P 1976 (3); *v E 1975 (3); v NZ 1976 (2)*

Turner, C. T. B. 17: v E 1886 (2) 1887 (1) 1891 (3) 1894 (3); *v E 1888 (3) 1890 (2) 1893 (3)*

Veivers, T. R. 21: v E 1965 (4); v SA 1963 (3); v P 1964 (1); *v E 1964 (5); v SA 1966 (4); v In 1964 (3); v P 1964 (1)*

Veletta, M. R. J. 8: v E 1987 (1); v WI 1988 (2); v NZ 1987 (3); v P 1989 (1); v SL 1987 (1)

Waite, M. G. 2: *v E 1938 (2)*

Walker, M. H. N. 34: v E 1974 (6) 1976 (1); v WI 1975 (3); v NZ 1973 (1); v P 1972 (2) 1976 (2); *v E 1975 (4) 1977 (5); v WI 1972 (5); v NZ 1973 (3) 1976 (2)*

Wall, T. W. 18: v E 1928 (1) 1932 (4); v SA 1931 (3); v WI 1930 (1); *v E 1930 (5) 1934 (4)*

Walters, F. H. 1: v E 1884

Walters, K. D. 74: v E 1965 (5) 1970 (6) 1974 (6) 1976 (1); v WI 1968 (4); v NZ 1973 (3) 1980 (3); v In 1967 (2) 1980 (3); v P 1972 (1) 1976 (3); *v E 1968 (5) 1972 (4) 1975 (4) 1977 (5); v SA 1969 (4); v WI 1972 (5); v NZ 1973 (3) 1976 (2); v In 1969 (5)*

Ward, F. A. 4: v E 1936 (3); *v E 1938 (1)*

Warne, S. K. 67: v E 1994 (5); v SA 1993 (3) 1997 (3); v WI 1992 (4) 1996 (5); v NZ 1993 (3) 1997 (3); v In 1991 (2); v P 1995 (3); v SL 1995 (3); *v E 1993 (6) 1997 (6); v SA 1993 (3) 1996 (3); v WI 1994 (4); v NZ 1992 (3); v In 1997 (3); v P 1994 (3); v SL 1992 (2)*

Watkins, J. R. 1: v P 1972

Watson, G. D. 5: *v E 1972 (2); v SA 1966 (3)*

Watson, W. J. 4: v E 1954 (1); *v WI 1954 (3)*

Waugh, M. E. 78: v E 1990 (2) 1994 (5); v SA 1993 (3) 1997 (3); v WI 1992 (5) 1996 (5); v NZ
    1993 (3) 1997 (3); v In 1991 (4); v P 1995 (3); v SL 1995 (3); *v E 1993 (6) 1997 (6); v SA
    1993 (3) 1996 (3); v WI 1990 (5) 1994 (4); v NZ 1992 (2); v In 1996 (1) 1997 (3); v P 1994 (3);
    v SL 1992 (3)*

Waugh, S. R. 103: v E 1986 (5) 1987 (1) 1990 (3) 1994 (5); v SA 1993 (1) 1997 (3); v WI 1988 (5)
    1992 (5) 1996 (4); v NZ 1987 (3) 1989 (1) 1993 (3) 1997 (3); v In 1985 (2); v P 1989 (3)
    1995 (3); v SL 1987 (1) 1989 (2) 1995 (2); *v E 1989 (6) 1993 (6) 1997 (6); v SA 1993 (3)
    1996 (3); v WI 1990 (2) 1994 (4); v NZ 1985 (3) 1989 (1) 1992 (3); v In 1986 (3) 1996 (1)
    1997 (2); v P 1988 (3) 1994 (2)*

Wellham, D. M. 6: v E 1986 (1); v WI 1981 (1); v P 1981 (2); *v E 1981 (1) 1985 (1)*

Wessels, K. C. 24: v E 1982 (4); v WI 1984 (5); v NZ 1985 (1); v P 1983 (5); *v E 1985 (6); v WI
    1983 (2); v SL 1982 (1)*

Whatmore, D. F. 7: v P 1978 (2); *v In 1979 (5)*

Whitney, M. R. 12: v WI 1988 (1) 1992 (1); v In 1991 (3); *v E 1981 (2); v WI
    1990 (2); v SL 1992 (2)*

Whitty, W. J. 14: v E 1911 (2); v SA 1910 (5); *v E 1909 (1) 1912 (3); v SA 1912 (3)*

Wiener, J. M. 6: v E 1979 (2); v WI 1979 (2); *v P 1979 (2)*

Wilson, J. W. 1: *v In 1956*

Wilson, P. 1: *v In 1997*

Wood, G. M. 59: v E 1978 (6) 1982 (1); v WI 1981 (3) 1984 (5) 1988 (3); v NZ 1980 (3); v In
    1977 (1) 1980 (3); v P 1978 (1) 1981 (3); *v E 1980 (1) 1981 (6) 1985 (5); v WI 1977 (5) 1983 (1);
    v NZ 1981 (3); v In 1979 (2); v P 1982 (3) 1988 (3); v SL 1982 (1)*

Woodcock, A. J. 1: *v NZ 1973*

Woodfull, W. M. 35: v E 1928 (5) 1932 (5); v SA 1931 (5); v WI 1930 (5); *v E 1926 (5) 1930 (5)
    1934 (5)*

Woods, S. M. J. 3: *v E 1888 (3)*

Woolley, R. D. 2: *v WI 1983 (1); v SL 1982 (1)*

Worrall, J. 11: v E 1884 (1) 1887 (1) 1894 (1) 1897 (1); *v E 1888 (3) 1899 (4)*

Wright, K. J. 10: v E 1978 (2); v P 1978 (2); *v In 1979 (6)*

Yallop, G. N. 39: v E 1978 (6); v WI 1975 (3) 1984 (1); v In 1977 (1); v P 1978 (1) 1981 (1)
    1983 (5); *v E 1980 (1) 1981 (6); v WI 1977 (4); v In 1979 (6); v P 1979 (3); v SL 1982 (1)*

Yardley, B. 33: v E 1978 (4) 1982 (5); v WI 1981 (3); v In 1977 (1) 1980 (2); v P 1978 (1) 1981 (3);
    v WI 1977 (5); v NZ 1981 (3); v In 1979 (3); v P 1982 (2); v SL 1982 (1)

Young, S. 1: *v E 1997*

Zoehrer, T. J. 10: v E 1986 (4); *v NZ 1985 (3); v In 1986 (3)*

SOUTH AFRICA

Number of Test cricketers: 271

Ackerman, H. D. 4: v P 1997 (2); v SL 1997 (2)

Adams, P. R. 19: v E 1995 (2); v A 1996 (2); v In 1996 (2); v P 1997 (1); v SL 1997 (2); *v E
    1998 (4); v A 1997 (1); v In 1996 (3); v P 1997 (2)*

Adcock, N. A. T. 26: v E 1956 (5); v A 1957 (5); v NZ 1953 (5) 1961 (2); *v E 1955 (4) 1960 (5)*

Anderson, J. H. 1: v A 1902

Ashley, W. H. 1: v E 1888

Bacher, A. 12: v A 1966 (5) 1969 (4); *v E 1965 (3)*

Bacher, A. M. 16: v A 1996 (2); v In 1996 (3); v P 1997 (3); v SL 1997 (1); *v E 1998 (1); v A
    1997 (3); v P 1997 (3)*

Balaskas, X. C. 9: v E 1930 (2) 1938 (1); v A 1935 (3); *v E 1935 (1); v NZ 1931 (2)*

Barlow, E. J. 30: v E 1964 (5); v A 1966 (5) 1969 (4); v NZ 1961 (5); *v E 1965 (3); v A 1963 (5);
    v NZ 1963 (3)*

Baumgartner, H. V. 1: v E 1913

Beaumont, R. 5: v E 1913 (2); *v E 1912 (1); v A 1912 (2)*

Begbie, D. W. 5: v E 1948 (3); v A 1949 (2)

Bell, A. J. 16: v E 1930 (3); *v E 1929 (3) 1935 (3); v A 1931 (5); v NZ 1931 (2)*

Bisset, M. 3: v E 1898 (2) 1909 (1)

Bissett, G. F. 4: v E 1927 (4)

Blanckenberg, J. M. 18: v E 1913 (5) 1922 (5); v A 1921 (3); *v E 1924 (5)*

Bland, K. C. 21: v E 1964 (5); v A 1966 (1); v NZ 1961 (5); *v E 1965 (3); v A 1963 (4); v NZ 1963 (3)*

Bock, E. G. 1: v A 1935

Bond, G. E. 1: v E 1938

Bosch, T. 1: *v WI 1991*

Botten, J. T. 3: *v E 1965 (3)*

Boucher, M. V. 11: v P 1997 (3); v SL 1997 (2); *v E 1998 (5); v P 1997 (1)*

Brann, W. H. 3: v E 1922 (3)

Briscoe, A. W. 2: v E 1938 (1); v A 1935 (1)

Bromfield, H. D. 9: v E 1964 (3); v NZ 1961 (5); *v E 1965 (1)*

Brown, L. S. 2: *v A 1931 (1); v NZ 1931 (1)*

Burger, C. G. de V. 2: v A 1957 (2)

Burke, S. F. 2: v E 1964 (1); v NZ 1961 (1)

Buys, I. D. 1: v E 1922

Cameron, H. B. 26: v E 1927 (5) 1930 (5); *v E 1929 (4) 1935 (5); v A 1931 (5); v NZ 1931 (2)*

Campbell, T. 5: v E 1909 (4); *v E 1912 (1)*

Carlstein, P. R. 8: v A 1957 (1); *v E 1960 (5); v A 1963 (2)*

Carter, C. P. 10: v E 1913 (2); v A 1921 (3); *v E 1912 (2) 1924 (3)*

Catterall, R. H. 24: v E 1922 (5) 1927 (5) 1930 (4); *v E 1924 (5) 1929 (5)*

Chapman, H. W. 2: v E 1913 (1); v A 1921 (1)

Cheetham, J. E. 24: v E 1948 (1); v A 1949 (3); v NZ 1953 (5); *v E 1951 (5) 1955 (3); v A 1952 (5); v NZ 1952 (2)*

Chevalier, G. A. 1: v A 1969

Christy, J. A. J. 10: v E 1930 (1); *v E 1929 (2); v A 1931 (5); v NZ 1931 (2)*

Chubb, G. W. A. 5: *v E 1951 (5)*

Cochran, J. A. K. 1: v E 1930

Coen, S. K. 2: v E 1927 (2)

Commaille, J. M. M. 12: v E 1909 (5) 1927 (2); *v E 1924 (5)*

Commins, J. B. 3: v NZ 1994 (2); v P 1994 (1)

Conyngham, D. P. 1: v E 1922

Cook, F. J. 1: v E 1895

Cook, S. J. 3: v In 1992 (2); *v SL 1993 (1)*

Cooper, A. H. C. 1: v E 1913

Cox, J. L. 3: v E 1913 (3)

Cripps, G. 1: v E 1891

Crisp, R. J. 9: v A 1935 (4); *v E 1935 (5)*

Cronje, W. J. 51: v E 1995 (5); v A 1993 (3) 1996 (3); v NZ 1994 (3); v In 1992 (3) 1996 (3); v P 1994 (1) 1997 (2); v SL 1997 (2); *v E 1994 (3) 1998 (5); v A 1993 (3) 1997 (3); v WI 1991 (1); v NZ 1994 (1); v In 1996 (3); v P 1997 (3); v SL 1993 (3); v Z 1995 (1)*

Cullinan, D. J. 40: v E 1995 (5); v A 1996 (3); v NZ 1994 (3); v In 1992 (1) 1996 (3); v P 1994 (1) 1997 (1); v SL 1997 (2); *v E 1994 (1) 1998 (5); v A 1993 (3) 1997 (1); v NZ 1994 (1); v In 1996 (3); v P 1997 (3); v SL 1993 (3); v Z 1995 (1)*

Curnow, S. H. 7: v E 1930 (3); *v A 1931 (4)*

Dalton, E. L. 15: v E 1930 (1) 1938 (4); v A 1935 (1); *v E 1929 (1) 1935 (4); v A 1931 (1); v NZ 1931 (2)*

Davies, E. Q. 5: v E 1938 (3); v A 1935 (2)

Dawson, O. C. 9: v E 1948 (4); *v E 1947 (5)*

Deane, H. G. 17: v E 1927 (5) 1930 (2); *v E 1924 (5) 1929 (5)*

de Villiers, P. S. 18: v A 1993 (3); v NZ 1994 (3); v P 1994 (1) 1997 (2); *v E 1994 (3); v A 1993 (3); v NZ 1994 (1); v In 1996 (2)*

Dixon, C. D. 1: v E 1913

Donald, A. A. 47: v E 1995 (5); v A 1993 (3) 1996 (3); v In 1992 (4) 1996 (3); v P 1994 (1) 1997 (3); v SL 1997 (2); *v E 1994 (3) 1998 (5); v A 1993 (3) 1997 (2); v WI 1991 (1); v NZ 1994 (1); v In 1996 (2); v P 1997 (2); v SL 1993 (3); v Z 1995 (1)*

Dower, R. R. 1: v E 1898

Draper, R. G. 2: v A 1949 (2)
Duckworth, C. A. R. 2: v E 1956 (2)
Dumbrill, R. 5: v A 1966 (2); *v E 1965 (3)*
Duminy, J. P. 3: v E 1927 (2); *v E 1929 (1)*
Dunell, O. R. 2: v E 1888 (2)
Du Preez, J. H. 2: v A 1966 (2)
Du Toit, J. F. 1: v E 1891
Dyer, D. V. 3: *v E 1947 (3)*

Eksteen, C. E. 6: v E 1995 (1); v NZ 1994 (2); v P 1994 (1); *v NZ 1994 (1); v SL 1993 (1)*
Elgie, M. K. 3: v NZ 1961 (3)
Elworthy, S. 1: *v E 1998*
Endean, W. R. 28: v E 1956 (5); v A 1957 (5); v NZ 1953 (5); *v E 1951 (1) 1955 (5); v A 1952 (5); v NZ 1952 (2)*

Farrer, W. S. 6: v NZ 1961 (3); *v NZ 1963 (3)*
Faulkner, G. A. 25: v E 1905 (5) 1909 (5); *v E 1907 (3) 1912 (3) 1924 (1); v A 1910 (5) 1912 (3)*
Fellows-Smith, J. P. 4: *v E 1960 (4)*
Fichardt, C. G. 2: v E 1891 (1) 1895 (1)
Finlason, C. E. 1: v E 1888
Floquet, C. E. 1: v E 1909
Francis, H. H. 2: v E 1898 (2)
Francois, C. M. 5: v E 1922 (5)
Frank, C. N. 3: v A 1921 (3)
Frank, W. H. B. 1: v E 1895
Fuller, E. R. H. 7: v A 1957 (1); *v E 1955 (2); v A 1952 (2); v NZ 1952 (2)*
Fullerton, G. M. 7: v A 1949 (2); *v E 1947 (2) 1951 (3)*
Funston, K. J. 18: v E 1956 (3); v A 1957 (5); v NZ 1953 (3); *v A 1952 (5); v NZ 1952 (2)*

Gamsy, D. 2: v A 1969 (2)
Gibbs, H. H. 7: v A 1996 (3); v In 1996 (1); v P 1997 (1); *v A 1997 (2); v In 1996 (2)*
Gleeson, R. A. 1: v E 1895
Glover, G. K. 1: v E 1895
Goddard, T. L. 41: v E 1956 (5) 1964 (5); v A 1957 (5) 1966 (5) 1969 (3); *v E 1955 (5) 1960 (5); v A 1963 (5); v NZ 1963 (3)*
Gordon, N. 5: v E 1938 (5)
Graham, R. 2: v E 1898 (2)
Grieveson, R. E. 2: v E 1938 (2)
Griffin, G. M. 2: *v E 1960 (2)*

Hall, A. E. 7: v E 1922 (4) 1927 (2) 1930 (1)
Hall, G. G. 1: v E 1964
Halliwell, E. A. 8: v E 1891 (1) 1895 (3) 1898 (1); v A 1902 (3)
Halse, C. G. 3: *v A 1963 (3)*
Hands, P. A. M. 7: v E 1913 (5); v A 1921 (1); *v E 1924 (1)*
Hands, R. H. M. 1: v E 1913
Hanley, M. A. 1: v E 1948
Harris, T. A. 3: v E 1948 (1); *v E 1947 (2)*
Hartigan, G. P. D. 5: v E 1913 (3); *v E 1912 (1); v A 1912 (1)*
Harvey, R. L. 2: v A 1935 (2)
Hathorn, C. M. H. 12: v E 1905 (5); v A 1902 (3); *v E 1907 (3); v A 1910 (1)*
Hearne, F. 4: v E 1891 (1) 1895 (3)
Hearne, G. A. L. 3: v E 1922 (2); *v E 1924 (1)*
Heine, P. S. 14: v E 1956 (5); v A 1957 (4); v NZ 1961 (1); *v E 1955 (4)*
Henry, O. 3: v In 1992 (3)
Hime, C. F. W. 1: v E 1895
Hudson, A. C. 35: v E 1995 (5); v A 1993 (3) 1996 (1); v NZ 1994 (2); v In 1992 (4) 1996 (1); v P 1997 (3); *v E 1994 (2); v A 1993 (3); v WI 1991 (1); v NZ 1994 (1); v In 1996 (3); v SL 1993 (3); v Z 1995 (1)*
Hutchinson, P. 2: v E 1888 (2)

Ironside, D. E. J. 3: v NZ 1953 (3)
Irvine, B. L. 4: v A 1969 (4)

Jack, S. D. 2: v NZ 1994 (2)
Johnson, C. L. 1: v E 1895

Kallis, J. H. 19: v E 1995 (2); v A 1996 (3); v P 1997 (3); v SL 1997 (2); *v E 1998 (5); v A 1997 (3); v P 1997 (1)*
Keith, H. J. 8: v E 1956 (3); *v E 1955 (4); v A 1952 (1)*
Kempis, G. A. 1: v E 1888
Kirsten, G. 45: v E 1995 (5); v A 1993 (3) 1996 (3); v NZ 1994 (3); v In 1996 (3); v P 1994 (1) 1997 (3); v SL 1997 (2); *v E 1994 (3) 1998 (5); v A 1993 (3) 1997 (3); v NZ 1994 (1); v In 1996 (3); v P 1997 (3); v Z 1995 (1)*
Kirsten, P. N. 12: v A 1993 (3); v In 1992 (4); *v E 1994 (3); v A 1993 (1); v WI 1991 (1)*
Klusener, L. 16: v A 1996 (2); v In 1996 (3); v P 1997 (2); *v E 1998 (3); v A 1997 (2); v In 1996 (2); v P 1997 (2)*
Kotze, J. J. 3: v A 1902 (2); *v E 1907 (1)*
Kuiper, A. P. 1: *v WI 1991*
Kuys, F. 1: v E 1898

Lance, H. R. 13: v A 1966 (5) 1969 (3); v NZ 1961 (2); *v E 1965 (3)*
Langton, A. B. C. 15: v E 1938 (5); v A 1935 (5); *v E 1935 (5)*
Lawrence, G. B. 5: v NZ 1961 (5)
le Roux, F. L. 1: v E 1913
Lewis, P. T. 1: v E 1913
Liebenberg, G. F. J. 5: v SL 1997 (1); *v E 1998 (4)*
Lindsay, D. T. 19: v E 1964 (3); v A 1966 (5) 1969 (2); *v E 1965 (3); v A 1963 (3); v NZ 1963 (3)*
Lindsay, J. D. 3: *v E 1947 (3)*
Lindsay, N. V. 1: v A 1921
Ling, W. V. S. 6: v E 1922 (3); v A 1921 (3)
Llewellyn, C. B. 15: v E 1895 (1) 1898 (1); v A 1902 (3); *v E 1912 (3); v A 1910 (5) 1912 (2)*
Lundie, E. B. 1: v E 1913

Macaulay, M. J. 1: v E 1964
McCarthy, C. N. 15: v E 1948 (5); v A 1949 (5); *v E 1951 (5)*
McGlew, D. J. 34: v E 1956 (1); v A 1957 (5); v NZ 1953 (5) 1961 (5); *v E 1951 (2) 1955 (5) 1960 (5); v A 1952 (4); v NZ 1952 (5)*
McKinnon, A. H. 8: v E 1964 (2); v A 1966 (2); v NZ 1961 (1); *v E 1960 (1) 1965 (2)*
McLean, R. A. 40: v E 1956 (5) 1964 (2); v A 1957 (4); v NZ 1953 (4) 1961 (5); *v E 1951 (3) 1955 (5) 1960 (5); v A 1952 (5); v NZ 1952 (2)*
McMillan, B. M. 38: v E 1995 (5); v A 1993 (3) 1996 (2); v NZ 1994 (3); v In 1992 (4) 1996 (3); v P 1994 (1); *v E 1994 (3) 1998 (1); v A 1993 (1) 1997 (3); v In 1996 (3); v P 1997 (3); v SL 1993 (2); v Z 1995 (1)*
McMillan, Q. 13: v E 1930 (5); *v E 1929 (2); v A 1931 (4); v NZ 1931 (2)*
Mann, N. B. F. 19: v E 1948 (5); v A 1949 (5); *v E 1947 (5) 1951 (4)*
Mansell, P. N. F. 13: *v E 1951 (2) 1955 (4); v A 1952 (5); v NZ 1952 (2)*
Markham, L. A. 1: v E 1948
Marx, W. F. E. 3: v A 1921 (3)
Matthews, C. R. 18: v E 1995 (3); v A 1993 (3); v NZ 1994 (2); v In 1992 (3); *v E 1994 (3); v A 1993 (2); v NZ 1994 (1); v Z 1995 (1)*
Meintjes, D. J. 2: v E 1922 (2)
Melle, M. G. 7: v A 1949 (2); *v E 1951 (1); v A 1952 (4)*
Melville, A. 11: v E 1938 (5) 1948 (1); *v E 1947 (5)*
Middleton, J. 6: v E 1895 (2) 1898 (2); v A 1902 (2)
Mills, C. 1: v E 1891
Milton, W. H. 3: v E 1888 (2) 1891 (1)
Mitchell, B. 42: v E 1930 (5) 1938 (5) 1948 (5); v A 1935 (5); *v E 1929 (5) 1935 (5) 1947 (5); v A 1931 (5); v NZ 1931 (2)*
Mitchell, F. 3: *v E 1912 (1); v A 1912 (2)*
Morkel, D. P. B. 16: v E 1927 (5); *v E 1929 (5); v A 1931 (5); v NZ 1931 (1)*
Murray, A. R. A. 10: v NZ 1953 (4); *v A 1952 (4); v NZ 1952 (2)*

Nel, J. D. 6: v A 1949 (5) 1957 (1)
Newberry, C. 4: v E 1913 (4)
Newson, E. S. 3: v E 1930 (1) 1938 (2)
Nicholson, F. 4: v A 1935 (4)
Nicolson, J. F. W. 3: v E 1927 (3)
Norton, N. O. 1: v E 1909
Nourse, A. D. 34: v E 1938 (5) 1948 (5); v A 1935 (5) 1949 (5); *v E 1935 (4) 1947 (5) 1951 (5)*
Nourse, A. W. 45: v E 1905 (5) 1909 (5) 1913 (5) 1922 (5); v A 1902 (3) 1921 (3); *v E 1907 (3) 1912 (3) 1924 (5); v A 1910 (5) 1912 (3)*
Ntini, M. 4: v SL 1997 (2); *v E 1998 (2)*
Nupen, E. P. 17: v E 1922 (4) 1927 (5) 1930 (3); v A 1921 (2) 1935 (1); *v E 1924 (2)*

Ochse, A. E. 2: v E 1888 (2)
Ochse, A. L. 3: v E 1927 (1); *v E 1929 (2)*
O'Linn, S. 7: v NZ 1961 (2); *v E 1960 (5)*
Owen-Smith, H. G. 5: *v E 1929 (5)*

Palm, A. W. 1: v E 1927
Parker, G. M. 2: *v E 1924 (2)*
Parkin, D. C. 1: v E 1891
Partridge, J. T. 11: v E 1964 (3); *v A 1963 (5); v NZ 1963 (3)*
Pearse, O. C. 3: *v A 1910 (3)*
Pegler, S. J. 16: v E 1909 (1); *v E 1912 (3) 1924 (5); v A 1910 (4) 1912 (3)*
Pithey, A. J. 17: v E 1956 (3) 1964 (5); *v E 1960 (2); v A 1963 (4); v NZ 1963 (3)*
Pithey, D. B. 8: v A 1966 (2); *v A 1963 (3); v NZ 1963 (3)*
Plimsoll, J. B. 1: *v E 1947*
Pollock, P. M. 28: v E 1964 (5); v A 1966 (5) 1969 (4); v NZ 1961 (3); *v E 1965 (3); v A 1963 (5); v NZ 1963 (3)*
Pollock, R. G. 23: v E 1964 (5); v A 1966 (5) 1969 (4); *v E 1965 (3); v A 1963 (5); v NZ 1963 (1)*
Pollock, S. M. 25: v E 1995 (1); v A 1996 (2); v In 1996 (3); v P 1997 (3); v SL 1997 (2); *v E 1998 (4); v A 1997 (3); v P 1997 (3)*
Poore, R. M. 3: v E 1895 (3)
Pothecary, J. E. 3: *v E 1960 (3)*
Powell, A. W. 1: v E 1898
Prince, C. F. H. 1: v E 1898
Pringle, M. W. 4: v E 1995 (1); v In 1992 (2); *v WI 1991 (1)*
Procter, M. J. 7: v A 1966 (3) 1969 (4)
Promnitz, H. L. E. 2: v E 1927 (2)

Quinn, N. A. 12: v E 1930 (1); *v E 1929 (4); v A 1931 (5); v NZ 1931 (2)*

Reid, N. 1: v A 1921
Rhodes, J. N. 36: v E 1995 (5); v A 1993 (3) 1996 (1); v NZ 1994 (3); v In 1992 (4); v P 1994 (1); *v E 1994 (3) 1998 (5); v A 1993 (3) 1997 (1); v NZ 1994 (1); v In 1996 (1); v P 1997 (1); v SL 1993 (3); v Z 1995 (1)*
Richards, A. R. 1: v E 1895
Richards, B. A. 4: v A 1969 (4)
Richards, W. H. 1: v E 1888
Richardson, D. J. 42: v E 1995 (5); v A 1993 (3) 1996 (3); v NZ 1994 (3); v In 1992 (4) 1996 (3); v P 1994 (1); *v E 1994 (3); v A 1993 (3) 1997 (3); v WI 1991 (1); v NZ 1994 (1); v In 1996 (3); v P 1997 (2); v SL 1993 (3); v Z 1995 (1)*
Robertson, J. B. 3: v A 1935 (3)
Rose-Innes, A. 2: v E 1888 (2)
Routledge, T. W. 4: v E 1891 (1) 1895 (3)
Rowan, A. M. B. 15: v E 1948 (5); *v E 1947 (5) 1951 (5)*
Rowan, E. A. B. 26: v E 1938 (4) 1948 (4); v A 1935 (3) 1949 (5); *v E 1935 (5) 1951 (5)*
Rowe, G. A. 5: v E 1895 (2) 1898 (2); v A 1902 (1)
Rushmere, M. W. 1: *v WI 1991*

Samuelson, S. V. 1: v E 1909
Schultz, B. N. 9: v E 1995 (1); v A 1996 (1); v In 1992 (2); *v P 1997 (1); v SL 1993 (3); v Z 1995 (1)*

Schwarz, R. O. 20: v E 1905 (5) 1909 (4); *v E 1907 (3) 1912 (1); v A 1910 (5) 1912 (2)*
Seccull, A. W. 1: v E 1895
Seymour, M. A. 7: v E 1964 (2); v A 1969 (1); *v A 1963 (4)*
Shalders, W. A. 12: v E 1898 (1) 1905 (5); v A 1902 (3); *v E 1907 (3)*
Shepstone, G. H. 2: v E 1895 (1) 1898 (1)
Sherwell, P. W. 13: v E 1905 (5); *v E 1907 (3); v A 1910 (5)*
Siedle, I. J. 18: v E 1927 (1) 1930 (5); v A 1935 (5); *v E 1929 (3) 1935 (4)*
Sinclair, J. H. 25: v E 1895 (3) 1898 (2) 1905 (5) 1909 (4); v A 1902 (3); *v E 1907 (3); v A 1910 (5)*
Smith, C. J. E. 3: v A 1902 (3)
Smith, F. W. 3: v E 1888 (2) 1895 (1)
Smith, V. I. 9: v A 1949 (3) 1957 (1); *v E 1947 (4) 1955 (1)*
Snell, R. P. 5: v NZ 1994 (1); *v A 1993 (1); v WI 1991 (1); v SL 1993 (2)*
Snooke, S. D. 1: *v E 1907*
Snooke, S. J. 26: v E 1905 (5) 1909 (5) 1922 (5); *v E 1907 (3) 1912 (3); v A 1910 (5) 1912 (2)*
Solomon, W. R. 1: v E 1898
Stewart, R. B. 1: v E 1888
Steyn, P. J. R. 3: v NZ 1994 (1); v P 1994 (1); *v NZ 1994 (1)*
Stricker, L. A. 13: v E 1909 (4); *v E 1912 (2); v A 1910 (5) 1912 (2)*
Susskind, M. J. 5: *v E 1924 (5)*
Symcox, P. L. 17: v A 1996 (1); v P 1997 (1); *v A 1993 (2) 1997 (3); v In 1996 (3); v P 1997 (3); v SL 1993 (3); v Z 1995 (1)*

Taberer, H. M. 1: v A 1902
Tancred, A. B. 2: v E 1888 (2)
Tancred, L. J. 14: v E 1905 (5) 1913 (1); v A 1902 (3); *v E 1907 (1) 1912 (2); v A 1912 (2)*
Tancred, V. M. 1: v E 1898
Tapscott, G. L. 1: v E 1913
Tapscott, L. E. 2: v E 1922 (2)
Tayfield, H. J. 37: v E 1956 (5); v A 1949 (5) 1957 (5); v NZ 1953 (5); *v E 1955 (5) 1960 (5); v A 1952 (5); v NZ 1952 (2)*
Taylor, A. I. 1: v E 1956
Taylor, D. 2: v E 1913 (2)
Taylor, H. W. 42: v E 1913 (5) 1922 (5) 1927 (5) 1930 (4); v A 1921 (3); *v E 1912 (3) 1924 (5) 1929 (3); v A 1912 (3) 1931 (5); v NZ 1931 (1)*
Theunissen, N. H. 1: v E 1888
Thornton, P. G. 1: v A 1902
Tomlinson, D. S. 1: *v E 1935*
Traicos, A. J. 3: v A 1969 (3)
Trimborn, P. H. J. 4: v A 1966 (3) 1969 (1)
Tuckett, L. 9: v E 1948 (4); *v E 1947 (5)*
Tuckett, L. R. 1: v E 1913
Twentyman-Jones, P. S. 1: v A 1902

van der Bijl, P. G. V. 5: v E 1938 (5)
Van der Merwe, E. A. 2: v A 1935 (1); *v E 1929 (1)*
Van der Merwe, P. L. 15: v E 1964 (2); v A 1966 (5); *v E 1965 (3); v A 1963 (3); v NZ 1963 (2)*
Van Ryneveld, C. B. 19: v E 1956 (5); v A 1957 (4); v NZ 1953 (5); *v E 1951 (5)*
Varnals, G. D. 3: v E 1964 (3)
Viljoen, K. G. 27: v E 1930 (3) 1938 (4) 1948 (2); v A 1935 (4); *v E 1935 (4) 1947 (5); v A 1931 (4); v NZ 1931 (1)*
Vincent, C. L. 25: v E 1927 (5) 1930 (5); *v E 1929 (4) 1935 (4); v A 1931 (5); v NZ 1931 (2)*
Vintcent, C. H. 3: v E 1888 (2) 1891 (1)
Vogler, A. E. E. 15: v E 1905 (5) 1909 (5); *v E 1907 (3); v A 1910 (2)*

Wade, H. F. 10: v A 1935 (5); *v E 1935 (5)*
Wade, W. W. 11: v E 1938 (3) 1948 (5); v A 1949 (3)
Waite, J. H. B. 50: v E 1956 (5) 1964 (2); v A 1957 (5); v NZ 1953 (5) 1961 (5); *v E 1951 (4) 1955 (5) 1960 (5); v A 1952 (5) 1963 (4); v NZ 1952 (2) 1963 (3)*
Walter, K. A. 2: v NZ 1961 (2)
Ward, T. A. 23: v E 1913 (5) 1922 (5); v A 1921 (3); *v E 1912 (2) 1924 (5); v A 1912 (3)*
Watkins, J. C. 15: v E 1956 (2); v A 1949 (3); v NZ 1953 (3); *v A 1952 (5); v NZ 1952 (2)*

Wesley, C. 3: *v E 1960 (3)*
Wessels, K. C. 16: v A 1993 (3); v In 1992 (4); *v E 1994 (3); v A 1993 (2); v WI 1991 (1); SL 1993 (3)*
Westcott, R. J. 5: v A 1957 (2); v NZ 1953 (3)
White, G. C. 17: v E 1905 (5) 1909 (4); *v E 1907 (3) 1912 (2); v A 1912 (3)*
Willoughby, J. T. 2: v E 1895 (2)
Wimble, C. S. 1: v E 1891
Winslow, P. L. 5: v A 1949 (2); *v E 1955 (3)*
Wynne, O. E. 6: v E 1948 (3); v A 1949 (3)

Zulch, J. W. 16: v E 1909 (5) 1913 (3); v A 1921 (3); *v A 1910 (5)*

WEST INDIES

Number of Test cricketers: 221

Achong, E. 6: v E 1929 (1) 1934 (2); *v E 1933 (3)*
Adams, J. C. 33: v E 1993 (5) 1997 (4); v A 1994 (4); v SA 1991 (1); v NZ 1995 (2); *v E 1995 (4); v A 1992 (3) 1996 (5); v NZ 1994 (2); v In 1994 (3)*
Alexander, F. C. M. 25: v E 1959 (5); v P 1957 (5); *v E 1957 (2); v A 1960 (5); v In 1958 (5); v P 1958 (3)*
Ali, Imtiaz 1: v In 1975
Ali, Inshan 12: v E 1973 (2); v A 1972 (3); v In 1970 (1); v P 1976 (1); v NZ 1971 (3); *v E 1973 (1); v A 1975 (1)*
Allan, D. W. 5: v A 1964 (1); v In 1961 (2); *v E 1966 (2)*
Allen, I. B. A. 2: *v E 1991 (2)*
Ambrose, C. E. L. 80: v E 1989 (3) 1993 (5) 1997 (6); v A 1990 (5) 1994 (4); v SA 1991 (1); v NZ 1995 (2); v In 1988 (4) 1996 (5); v P 1987 (3) 1992 (3); v SL 1996 (2); *v E 1988 (5) 1991 (5) 1995 (5); v A 1988 (5) 1992 (5) 1996 (4); v NZ 1994 (2); v P 1990 (3) 1997 (2); v SL 1993 (1)*
Arthurton, K. L. T. 33: v E 1993 (5); v A 1994 (3); v SA 1991 (1); v In 1988 (4); v P 1992 (3); *v E 1988 (1) 1995 (5); v A 1992 (5); v NZ 1994 (2); v In 1994 (3); v SL 1993 (1)*
Asgarali, N. 2: *v E 1957 (2)*
Atkinson, D. St E. 22: v E 1953 (4); v A 1954 (4); v P 1957 (1); *v E 1957 (2); v A 1951 (2); v NZ 1951 (1) 1955 (4); v In 1948 (4)*
Atkinson, E. St E. 8: v P 1957 (3); *v In 1958 (3); v P 1958 (2)*
Austin, R. A. 2: v A 1977 (2)

Bacchus, S. F. A. F. 19: v A 1977 (2); *v E 1980 (5); v A 1981 (2); v In 1978 (6); v P 1980 (4)*
Baichan, L. 3: *v A 1975 (1); v P 1974 (2)*
Baptiste, E. A. E. 10: v E 1989 (1); v A 1983 (3); *v E 1984 (5); v In 1983 (1)*
Barrett, A. G. 6: v E 1973 (2); v In 1970 (2); *v In 1974 (2)*
Barrow, I. 11: v E 1929 (1) 1934 (1); *v E 1933 (3) 1939 (1); v A 1930 (5)*
Bartlett, E. L. 5: *v E 1928 (1); v A 1930 (4)*
Benjamin, K. C. G. 26: v E 1993 (5) 1997 (2); v A 1994 (4); v SA 1991 (1); *v E 1995 (5); v A 1992 (1) 1996 (3); v NZ 1994 (2); v In 1994 (3)*
Benjamin, W. K. M. 21: v E 1993 (5); v A 1994 (4); v In 1988 (1); v P 1987 (3) 1992 (2); *v E 1988 (3); v NZ 1994 (1); v In 1987 (1); v SL 1993 (1)*
Best, C. A. 8: v E 1985 (3) 1989 (3); *v P 1990 (2)*
Betancourt, N. 1: v E 1929
Binns, A. P. 5: v A 1954 (1); v In 1952 (1); *v NZ 1955 (3)*
Birkett, L. S. 4: *v A 1930 (4)*
Bishop, I. R. 43: v E 1989 (4) 1997 (3); v NZ 1995 (2); v In 1988 (4) 1996 (4); v P 1992 (2); v SL 1996 (2); *v E 1991 (6); v A 1992 (5) 1996 (5); v P 1990 (3) 1997 (3)*
Boyce, K. D. 21: v E 1973 (4); v A 1972 (4); v In 1970 (1); *v E 1973 (3); v A 1975 (4); v In 1974 (3); v P 1974 (2)*
Browne, C. O. 13: v A 1994 (1); v NZ 1995 (2); v In 1996 (3); v SL 1996 (2); *v E 1995 (2); v A 1996 (3)*
Browne, C. R. 4: v E 1929 (2); *v E 1928 (2)*

Butcher, B. F. 44: v E 1959 (2) 1967 (5); v A 1964 (5); *v E 1963 (5) 1966 (5) 1969 (3); v A 1968 (5); v NZ 1968 (3); v In 1958 (5) 1966 (3); v P 1958 (3)*

Butler, L. 1: v A 1954

Butts, C. G. 7: v NZ 1984 (1); *v NZ 1986 (1); v In 1987 (3); v P 1986 (2)*

Bynoe, M. R. 4: *v In 1966 (3); v P 1958 (1)*

Camacho, G. S. 11: v E 1967 (5); v In 1970 (2); *v E 1969 (2); v A 1968 (2)*

Cameron, F. J. 5: *v In 1948 (5)*

Cameron, J. H. 2: *v E 1939 (2)*

Campbell, S. L. 30: v E 1997 (4); v A 1994 (1); v NZ 1995 (2); v In 1996 (5); v SL 1996 (2); *v E 1995 (6); v A 1996 (5); v NZ 1994 (2); v P 1997 (3)*

Carew, G. M. 4: v E 1934 (1) 1947 (2); *v In 1948 (1)*

Carew, M. C. 19: v E 1967 (1); v NZ 1971 (3); v In 1970 (3); *v E 1963 (2) 1966 (1) 1969 (1); v A 1968 (5); v NZ 1968 (3)*

Challenor, G. 3: *v E 1928 (3)*

Chanderpaul, S. 30: v E 1993 (4) 1997 (6); v NZ 1995 (2); v In 1996 (5); *v E 1995 (2); v A 1996 (5); v NZ 1994 (2); v In 1994 (1); v P 1997 (3)*

Chang, H. S. 1: *v In 1978*

Christiani, C. M. 4: v E 1934 (4)

Christiani, R. J. 22: v E 1947 (4) 1953 (1); v In 1952 (2); *v E 1950 (4); v A 1951 (5); v NZ 1951 (1); v In 1948 (5)*

Clarke, C. B. 3: *v E 1939 (3)*

Clarke, S. T. 11: v A 1977 (1); *v A 1981 (1); v In 1978 (5); v P 1980 (4)*

Constantine, L. N. 18: v E 1929 (3) 1934 (3); *v E 1928 (3) 1933 (1) 1939 (3); v A 1930 (5)*

Croft, C. E. H. 27: v E 1980 (4); v A 1977 (2); v P 1976 (5); *v E 1980 (3); v A 1979 (3) 1981 (3); v NZ 1979 (3); v P 1980 (4)*

Cuffy, C. E. 3: *v A 1996 (1); v In 1994 (2)*

Cummins, A. C. 5: v P 1992 (2); *v A 1992 (1); v In 1994 (2)*

Da Costa, O. C. 5: v E 1929 (1) 1934 (1); *v E 1933 (3)*

Daniel, W. W. 10: v A 1983 (2); v In 1975 (1); *v E 1976 (4); v In 1983 (3)*

Davis, B. A. 4: v A 1964 (4)

Davis, C. A. 15: v A 1972 (2); v NZ 1971 (5); v In 1970 (4); *v E 1969 (3); v A 1968 (1)*

Davis, W. W. 15: v A 1983 (1); v NZ 1984 (2); v In 1982 (1); *v E 1984 (1); v In 1983 (6) 1987 (4)*

De Caires, F. I. 3: v E 1929 (3)

Depeiza, C. C. 5: v A 1954 (3); *v NZ 1955 (2)*

Dewdney, T. 9: v A 1954 (2); v P 1957 (3); *v E 1957 (1); v NZ 1955 (3)*

Dhanraj, R. 4: v NZ 1995 (1); *v E 1995 (1); v NZ 1994 (1); v In 1994 (1)*

Dillon, M. 3: v In 1996 (2); *v P 1997 (1)*

Dowe, U. G. 4: v A 1972 (1); v NZ 1971 (1); v In 1970 (2)

Dujon, P. J. L. 81: v E 1985 (4) 1989 (4); v A 1983 (5) 1990 (5); v NZ 1984 (4); v In 1982 (5) 1988 (4); v P 1987 (3); *v E 1984 (5) 1988 (5) 1991 (5); v A 1981 (3) 1984 (5) 1988 (5); v NZ 1986 (3); v In 1983 (6) 1987 (4); v P 1986 (3) 1990 (3)*

Edwards, R. M. 5: *v A 1968 (2); v NZ 1968 (3)*

Ferguson, W. 8: v E 1947 (4) 1953 (1); *v In 1948 (3)*

Fernandes, M. P. 2: v E 1929 (1); *v E 1928 (1)*

Findlay, T. M. 10: v A 1972 (1); v NZ 1971 (5); v In 1970 (2); *v E 1969 (2)*

Foster, M. L. C. 14: v E 1973 (1); v A 1972 (4) 1977 (1); v NZ 1971 (3); v In 1970 (2); v P 1976 (1); *v E 1969 (1) 1973 (1)*

Francis, G. N. 10: v E 1929 (1); *v E 1928 (3) 1933 (1); v A 1930 (5)*

Frederick, M. 1: v E 1953

Fredericks, R. C. 59: v E 1973 (5); v A 1972 (5); v NZ 1971 (5); v In 1970 (4) 1975 (4); v P 1976 (5); *v E 1969 (3) 1973 (3) 1976 (5); v A 1968 (4) 1975 (6); v NZ 1968 (3); v In 1974 (5); v P 1974 (2)*

Fuller, R. L. 1: v E 1934

Furlonge, H. A. 3: v A 1954 (1); *v NZ 1955 (2)*

Ganteaume, A. G. 1: v E 1947

Garner, J. 58: v E 1980 (4) 1985 (5); v A 1977 (2) 1983 (5); v NZ 1984 (4); v In 1982 (4); v P 1976 (5); *v E 1980 (5) 1984 (5); v A 1979 (3) 1981 (3) 1984 (5); v NZ 1979 (3) 1986 (2); v P 1980 (3)*

Gaskin, B. B. M. 2: v E 1947 (2)

Gibbs, G. L. 1: v A 1954

Gibbs, L. R. 79: v E 1967 (5) 1973 (5); v A 1964 (5) 1972 (5); v NZ 1971 (2); v In 1961 (5) 1970 (1); v P 1957 (4); *v E 1963 (5) 1966 (5) 1969 (3) 1973 (3); v A 1960 (3) 1968 (5) 1975 (6); v NZ 1968 (3); v In 1958 (1) 1966 (3) 1974 (5); v P 1958 (3) 1974 (2)*

Gibson, O. D. 1: *v E 1995*

Gilchrist, R. 13: v P 1957 (5); *v E 1957 (4); v In 1958 (4)*

Gladstone, G. 1: v E 1929

Goddard, J. D. C. 27: v E 1947 (4); *v E 1950 (4) 1957 (5); v A 1951 (4); v NZ 1951 (2) 1955 (3); v In 1948 (5)*

Gomes, H. A. 60: v E 1980 (4) 1985 (5); v A 1977 (3) 1983 (2); v NZ 1984 (4); v In 1982 (5); *v E 1976 (2) 1984 (5); v A 1981 (3) 1984 (5); v NZ 1986 (3); v In 1978 (6) 1983 (6); v P 1980 (4) 1986 (3)*

Gomez, G. E. 29: v E 1947 (4) 1953 (4); v In 1952 (4); *v E 1939 (2) 1950 (4); v A 1951 (5); v NZ 1951 (1); v In 1948 (5)*

Grant, G. C. 12: v E 1934 (4); *v E 1933 (3); v A 1930 (5)*

Grant, R. S. 7: v E 1934 (4); *v E 1939 (3)*

Gray, A. H. 5: *v NZ 1986 (2); v P 1986 (3)*

Greenidge, A. E. 6: v A 1977 (2); *v In 1978 (4)*

Greenidge, C. G. 108: v E 1980 (4) 1985 (5) 1989 (4); v A 1977 (2) 1983 (5) 1990 (5); v NZ 1984 (4); v In 1982 (5) 1988 (4); v P 1976 (5) 1987 (3); *v E 1976 (5) 1980 (5) 1984 (5) 1988 (4); v A 1975 (2) 1979 (3) 1981 (2) 1984 (5) 1988 (5); v NZ 1979 (3) 1986 (3); v In 1974 (5) 1983 (6) 1987 (3); v P 1986 (3) 1990 (3)*

Greenidge, G. A. 5: v A 1972 (3); v NZ 1971 (2)

Grell, M. G. 1: v E 1929

Griffith, A. F. G. 1: *v A 1996*

Griffith, C. C. 28: v E 1959 (1) 1967 (4); v A 1964 (5); *v E 1963 (5) 1966 (5); v A 1968 (3); v NZ 1968 (2); v In 1966 (3)*

Griffith, H. C. 13: v E 1929 (3); *v E 1928 (3) 1933 (2); v A 1930 (5)*

Guillen, S. C. 5: *v A 1951 (3); v NZ 1951 (2)*

Hall, W. W. 48: v E 1959 (5) 1967 (4); v A 1964 (5); v In 1961 (5); *v E 1963 (5) 1966 (5); v A 1960 (5) 1968 (2); v NZ 1968 (1); v In 1958 (5) 1966 (3); v P 1958 (3)*

Harper, R. A. 25: v E 1985 (2); v A 1983 (4); v NZ 1984 (1); *v E 1984 (5) 1988 (3); v A 1984 (2) 1988 (1); v In 1983 (2) 1987 (1); v P 1986 (3); v SL 1993 (1)*

Haynes, D. L. 116: v E 1980 (4) 1985 (5) 1989 (4) 1993 (4); v A 1977 (2) 1983 (5) 1990 (5); v SA 1991 (1); v NZ 1984 (4); v In 1982 (5) 1988 (4); v P 1987 (3) 1992 (3); *v E 1980 (5) 1984 (5) 1988 (4) 1991 (5); v A 1979 (3) 1981 (3) 1984 (5) 1988 (5) 1992 (5); v NZ 1979 (3) 1986 (3); v In 1983 (6) 1987 (4); v P 1980 (4) 1986 (3) 1990 (3); v SL 1993 (1)*

Headley, G. A. 22: v E 1929 (4) 1934 (4) 1947 (1) 1953 (1); *v E 1933 (3) 1939 (3); v A 1930 (5); v In 1948 (1)*

Headley, R. G. A. 2: *v E 1973 (2)*

Hendriks, J. L. 20: v A 1964 (4); v In 1961 (1); *v E 1966 (3) 1969 (1); v A 1968 (5); v NZ 1968 (3); v In 1966 (3)*

Hoad, E. L. G. 4: v E 1929 (1); *v E 1928 (1) 1933 (2)*

Holder, R. I. C. 10: v E 1997 (2); v In 1996 (5); v SL 1996 (2); *v P 1997 (1)*

Holder, V. A. 40: v E 1973 (1); v A 1972 (3) 1977 (3); v NZ 1971 (4); v In 1970 (3) 1975 (1); v P 1976 (1); *v E 1969 (3) 1973 (2) 1976 (4); v A 1975 (3); v In 1974 (4) 1978 (6); v P 1974 (2)*

Holding, M. A. 60: v E 1980 (4) 1985 (4); v A 1983 (3); v NZ 1984 (3); v In 1975 (4) 1982 (5); *v E 1976 (4) 1980 (5) 1984 (4); v A 1975 (3) 1979 (3) 1981 (3) 1984 (3); v NZ 1979 (3) 1986 (1); v In 1983 (6)*

Holford, D. A. J. 24: v E 1967 (4); v NZ 1971 (5); v In 1970 (1) 1975 (3); v P 1976 (1); *v E 1966 (5); v A 1968 (2); v NZ 1968 (3); v In 1966 (1)*

Holt, J. K. 17: v E 1953 (5); v A 1954 (4); v In 1958 (5); v P 1958 (2)

Hooper, C. L. 73: v E 1989 (3) 1997 (6); v A 1990 (5) 1994 (4); v In 1996 (5); v P 1987 (3) 1992 (5); v SL 1996 (2); *v E 1988 (5) 1991 (5) 1995 (5); v A 1988 (5) 1992 (4) 1996 (5); v In 1987 (3) 1994 (3); v P 1990 (3) 1997 (3); v SL 1993 (1)*

Howard, A. B. 1: v NZ 1971
Hunte, C. C. 44: v E 1959 (5); v A 1964 (5); v In 1961 (5); v P 1957 (5); *v E 1963 (5) 1966 (5); v A 1960 (5); v In 1958 (5) 1966 (3); v P 1958 (1)*
Hunte, E. A. C. 3: v E 1929 (3)
Hylton, L. G. 6: v E 1934 (4); *v E 1939 (2)*

Johnson, H. H. H. 3: v E 1947 (1); *v E 1950 (2)*
Johnson, T. F. 1: *v E 1950*
Jones, C. M. 4: v E 1929 (1) 1934 (3)
Jones, P. E. 9: v E 1947 (1); *v E 1950 (2); v A 1951 (1); v In 1948 (5)*
Julien, B. D. 24: v E 1973 (5); v In 1975 (4); v P 1976 (1); *v E 1973 (3) 1976 (2); v A 1975 (3); v In 1974 (4); v P 1974 (2)*
Jumadeen, R. R. 12: v A 1972 (1) 1977 (2); v NZ 1971 (1); v In 1975 (4); v P 1976 (1); *v E 1976 (1); v In 1978 (2)*

Kallicharran, A. I. 66: v E 1973 (5); v A 1972 (5) 1977 (5); v NZ 1971 (2); v In 1975 (4); v P 1976 (5); *v E 1973 (3) 1976 (3) 1980 (5); v A 1975 (6) 1979 (3); v NZ 1979 (3); v In 1974 (5) 1978 (6); v P 1974 (2) 1980 (4)*
Kanhai, R. B. 79: v E 1959 (5) 1967 (5) 1973 (5); v A 1964 (5) 1972 (5); v In 1961 (5) 1970 (5); v P 1957 (5); *v E 1957 (5) 1963 (5) 1966 (5) 1973 (3); v A 1960 (5) 1968 (5); v In 1958 (5) 1966 (3); v P 1958 (5)*
Kentish, E. S. M. 2: v E 1947 (1) 1953 (1)
King, C. L. 9: v P 1976 (1); *v E 1976 (3) 1980 (1); v A 1979 (1); v NZ 1979 (3)*
King, F. M. 14: v E 1953 (3); v A 1954 (4); v In 1952 (5); *v NZ 1955 (2)*
King, L. A. 2: v E 1967 (1); v In 1961 (1)

Lambert, C. B. 3: v E 1997 (2); *v E 1991 (1)*
Lara, B. C. 54: v E 1993 (5) 1997 (6); v A 1994 (4); v SA 1991 (1); v NZ 1995 (2); v In 1996 (5); v P 1992 (3); v SL 1996 (2); *v E 1995 (6); v A 1992 (3) 1996 (5); v NZ 1994 (2); v In 1994 (3); v P 1990 (1) 1997 (3); v SL 1993 (1)*
Lashley, P. D. 4: *v E 1966 (2); v A 1960 (2)*
Legall, R. 4: v In 1952 (4)
Lewis, D. M. 3: v In 1970 (3)
Lewis, R. N. 1: *v P 1997*
Lloyd, C. H. 110: v E 1967 (5) 1973 (5) 1980 (4); v A 1972 (3) 1977 (2) 1983 (4); v NZ 1971 (2); v In 1970 (5) 1975 (4) 1982 (5); v P 1976 (5); *v E 1969 (3) 1973 (3) 1976 (5) 1980 (4) 1984 (5); v A 1968 (4) 1975 (6) 1979 (2) 1981 (3) 1984 (5); v NZ 1968 (3) 1979 (3); v In 1966 (3) 1974 (5) 1983 (6); v P 1974 (2) 1980 (4)*
Logie, A. L. 52: v E 1989 (5); v A 1983 (1) 1990 (5); v NZ 1984 (4); v In 1982 (5) 1988 (4); v P 1987 (3); *v E 1988 (5) 1991 (4); v A 1988 (5); v NZ 1986 (3); v In 1983 (3) 1987 (4); v P 1990 (3)*

McLean, N. A. M. 4: v E 1997 (4)
McMorris, E. D. A. St J. 13: v E 1959 (4); v In 1961 (4); v P 1957 (1); *v E 1963 (2) 1966 (2)*
McWatt, C. A. 6: v E 1953 (5); v A 1954 (1)
Madray, I. S. 2: v P 1957 (2)
Marshall, M. D. 81: v E 1980 (1) 1985 (5) 1989 (2); v A 1983 (4) 1990 (5); v NZ 1984 (4); v In 1982 (5) 1988 (3); v P 1987 (2); *v E 1980 (4) 1984 (4) 1988 (5) 1991 (5); v A 1984 (5) 1988 (5); v NZ 1986 (3); v In 1978 (3) 1983 (6); v P 1980 (4) 1986 (3) 1990 (3)*
Marshall, N. E. 1: v A 1954
Marshall, R. E. 4: *v A 1951 (2); v NZ 1951 (2)*
Martin, F. R. 9: v E 1929 (1); *v E 1928 (3); v A 1930 (5)*
Martindale, E. A. 10: v E 1934 (4); *v E 1933 (3) 1939 (3)*
Mattis, E. H. 4: v E 1980 (4)
Mendonca, I. L. 2: v In 1961 (2)
Merry, C. A. 2: *v E 1933 (2)*
Miller, R. 1: v In 1952
Moodie, G. H. 1: v E 1934
Moseley, E. A. 2: v E 1989 (2)
Murray, D. A. 19: v E 1980 (4); v A 1977 (3); *v A 1981 (2); v In 1978 (6); v P 1980 (4)*

Murray, D. L. 62: v E 1967 (5) 1973 (5); v A 1972 (4) 1977 (2); v In 1975 (4); v P 1976 (5); *v E 1963 (5) 1973 (3) 1976 (5) 1980 (5); v A 1975 (6) 1979 (3); v NZ 1979 (3); v In 1974 (5); v P 1974 (2)*

Murray, J. R. 29: v E 1993 (5) 1997 (1); v A 1994 (3); v In 1996 (2); v P 1992 (3); *v E 1995 (4); v A 1992 (3) 1996 (2); v NZ 1994 (2); v In 1994 (3); v SL 1993 (1)*

Nanan, R. 1: *v P 1980*

Neblett, J. M. 1: v E 1934

Noreiga, J. M. 4: v In 1970 (4)

Nunes, R. K. 4: v E 1929 (1); *v E 1928 (3)*

Nurse, S. M. 29: v E 1959 (1) 1967 (5); v A 1964 (4); v In 1961 (1); *v E 1966 (5); v A 1960 (3) 1968 (5); v NZ 1968 (3); v In 1966 (2)*

Padmore, A. L. 2: v In 1975 (1); *v E 1976 (1)*

Pairaudeau, B. H. 13: v E 1953 (2); v In 1952 (5); *v E 1957 (2); v NZ 1955 (4)*

Parry, D. R. 12: v A 1977 (5); *v NZ 1979 (1); v In 1978 (6)*

Passailaigue, C. C. 1: v E 1929

Patterson, B. P. 28: v E 1985 (5) 1989 (1); v A 1990 (5); v SA 1991 (1); v P 1987 (1); *v E 1988 (2) 1991 (3); v A 1988 (4) 1992 (1); v In 1987 (4); v P 1986 (1)*

Payne, T. R. O. 1: v E 1985

Phillip, N. 9: v A 1977 (3); *v In 1978 (6)*

Pierre, L. R. 1: v E 1947

Rae, A. F. 15: v In 1952 (2); *v E 1950 (4); v A 1951 (3); v NZ 1951 (1); v In 1948 (5)*

Ramadhin, S. 43: v E 1953 (5) 1959 (4); v A 1954 (4); v In 1952 (4); *v E 1950 (4) 1957 (5); v A 1951 (5) 1960 (2); v NZ 1951 (2) 1955 (4); v In 1958 (2); v P 1958 (2)*

Ramnarine, D. 2: v E 1997 (2)

Reifer, F. L. 2: v SL 1996 (2)

Richards, I. V. A. 121: v E 1980 (4) 1985 (5) 1989 (3); v A 1984 (3) 1983 (5) 1990 (5); v NZ 1984 (4); v In 1975 (4) 1982 (5) 1988 (4); v P 1976 (5) 1987 (2); *v E 1976 (4) 1980 (5) 1984 (5) 1988 (5) 1991 (5); v A 1975 (6) 1979 (3) 1981 (3) 1984 (5) 1988 (5); v NZ 1986 (3); v In 1974 (5) 1983 (6) 1987 (4); v P 1974 (2) 1980 (4) 1986 (3)*

Richardson, R. B. 86: v E 1985 (5) 1989 (4) 1993 (4); v A 1983 (5) 1990 (5) 1994 (4); v SA 1991 (1); v NZ 1984 (4); v In 1988 (4); v P 1987 (3) 1992 (3); *v E 1988 (3) 1991 (5) 1995 (6); v A 1984 (5) 1988 (5) 1992 (5); v NZ 1986 (3); v In 1983 (1) 1987 (4); v P 1986 (3) 1990 (3); v SL 1993 (1)*

Rickards, K. R. 2: v E 1947 (1); *v A 1951 (1)*

Roach, C. A. 16: v E 1929 (4) 1934 (1); *v E 1928 (3) 1933 (3); v A 1930 (5)*

Roberts, A. M. E. 47: v E 1973 (1) 1980 (3); v A 1977 (2); v In 1975 (2) 1982 (5); v P 1976 (5); *v E 1976 (5) 1980 (3); v A 1975 (5) 1979 (3) 1981 (2); v NZ 1979 (2); v In 1974 (5) 1983 (2); v P 1974 (2)*

Roberts, A. T. 1: *v NZ 1955*

Rodriguez, W. V. 5: v E 1967 (1); v A 1964 (1); v In 1961 (2); *v E 1963 (1)*

Rose, F. A. 10: v E 1997 (1); v In 1996 (5); v SL 1996 (2); *v P 1997 (2)*

Rowe, L. G. 30: v E 1973 (5); v A 1972 (3); v NZ 1971 (4); v In 1975 (4); *v E 1976 (2); v A 1975 (6) 1979 (3); v NZ 1979 (3)*

St Hill, E. L. 2: v E 1929 (2)

St Hill, W. H. 3: v E 1929 (1); *v E 1928 (2)*

Samuels, R. G. 6: v NZ 1995 (2); *v A 1996 (4)*

Scarlett, R. O. 3: v E 1959 (3)

Scott, A. P. H. 1: v In 1952

Scott, O. C. 8: v E 1929 (1); *v E 1928 (2); v A 1930 (5)*

Sealey, B. J. 1: *v E 1933*

Sealy, J. E. D. 11: v E 1929 (2) 1934 (4); *v E 1939 (3); v A 1930 (2)*

Shepherd, J. N. 5: v In 1970 (2); *v E 1969 (3)*

Shillingford, G. C. 7: v NZ 1971 (2); v In 1970 (3); *v E 1969 (2)*

Shillingford, I. T. 4: v A 1977 (1); *v P 1976 (3)*

Shivnarine, S. 8: v A 1977 (3); *v In 1978 (5)*

Simmons, P. V. 26: v E 1993 (2); v SA 1991 (1); v NZ 1995 (2); v P 1987 (1) 1992 (3); *v E 1991 (5); v A 1992 (5) 1996 (1); v In 1987 (1) 1994 (3); v P 1997 (1); v SL 1993 (1)*

Singh, C. K. 2: v E 1959 (2)

Small, J. A. 3: v E 1929 (1); *v E 1928 (2)*

Small, M. A. 2: v A 1983 (1); *v E 1984 (1)*

Smith, C. W. 5: v In 1961 (1); *v A 1960 (4)*

Smith, O. G. 26: v A 1954 (4); v P 1957 (5); *v E 1957 (5); v NZ 1955 (4); v In 1958 (5); v P 1958 (3)*

Sobers, G. S. 93: v E 1953 (1) 1959 (5) 1967 (5) 1973 (4); v A 1954 (4) 1964 (5); v NZ 1971 (5); v In 1961 (5) 1970 (5); v P 1957 (5); *v E 1957 (5) 1963 (5) 1966 (5) 1969 (5) 1973 (3); v A 1960 (5) 1968 (5); v NZ 1955 (4) 1968 (3); v In 1958 (5) 1966 (3); v P 1958 (3)*

Solomon, J. S. 27: v E 1959 (2); v A 1964 (4); v In 1961 (4); *v E 1963 (5); v A 1960 (5); v In 1958 (4); v P 1958 (3)*

Stayers, S. C. 4: v In 1961 (4)

Stollmeyer, J. B. 32: v E 1947 (2) 1953 (5); v A 1954 (2); v In 1952 (5); *v E 1939 (3) 1950 (4); v A 1951 (5); v NZ 1951 (2); v In 1948 (4)*

Stollmeyer, V. H. 1: *v E 1939*

Taylor, J. 3: v P 1957 (1); *v In 1958 (1); v P 1958 (1)*

Thompson, P. I. C. 2: v NZ 1995 (1); *v A 1996 (1)*

Trim, J. 4: v E 1947 (1); *v A 1951 (1); v In 1948 (2)*

Valentine, A. L. 36: v E 1953 (3); v A 1954 (3); v In 1952 (5) 1961 (2); v P 1957 (1); *v E 1950 (4) 1957 (2); v A 1951 (5) 1960 (5); v NZ 1951 (2) 1955 (4)*

Valentine, V. A. 2: *v E 1933 (2)*

Walcott, C. L. 44: v E 1947 (4) 1953 (5) 1959 (2); v A 1954 (5); v In 1952 (5); v P 1957 (4); *v E 1950 (4) 1957 (5); v A 1951 (3); v NZ 1951 (2); v In 1948 (5)*

Walcott, L. A. 1: v E 1929

Wallace, P. A. 3: v E 1997 (2); *v P 1997 (1)*

Walsh, C. A. 102: v E 1985 (1) 1989 (3) 1993 (5) 1997 (6); v A 1990 (5) 1994 (4); v SA 1991 (1); v NZ 1984 (1) 1995 (2); v In 1988 (4) 1996 (4); v P 1987 (3) 1992 (3); v SL 1996 (2); *v E 1988 (5) 1991 (5) 1995 (6); v A 1984 (5) 1988 (5) 1992 (5) 1996 (5); v NZ 1986 (3) 1994 (2); v In 1987 (4) 1994 (3); v P 1986 (3) 1990 (3) 1997 (3); v SL 1993 (1)*

Watson, C. 7: v E 1959 (5); v In 1961 (1); *v A 1960 (1)*

Weekes, E. D. 48: v E 1947 (4) 1953 (4); v A 1954 (5); v In 1952 (5); v P 1957 (5); *v E 1950 (4) 1957 (5); v A 1951 (5); v NZ 1951 (2) 1955 (4); v In 1948 (5)*

Weekes, K. H. 2: *v E 1939 (2)*

White, W. A. 2: v A 1964 (2)

Wight, C. V. 2: v E 1929 (1); *v E 1928 (1)*

Wight, G. L. 1: v In 1952

Wiles, C. A. 1: *v E 1933*

Willett, E. T. 5: v A 1972 (3); *v In 1974 (2)*

Williams, A. B. 7: v A 1977 (3); *v In 1978 (4)*

Williams, D. 11: v E 1997 (5); v SA 1991 (1); *v A 1992 (2); v P 1997 (3)*

Williams, E. A. V. 4: v E 1947 (3); *v E 1939 (1)*

Williams, S. C. 26: v E 1993 (1) 1997 (4); v A 1994 (4); v In 1996 (5); v SL 1996 (2); *v E 1995 (2); v NZ 1994 (2); v In 1994 (3); v P 1997 (3)*

Wishart, K. L. 1: v E 1934

Worrell, F. M. M. 51: v E 1947 (3) 1953 (4) 1959 (4); v A 1954 (4); v In 1952 (5) 1961 (5); *v E 1950 (4) 1957 (5) 1963 (5); v A 1951 (5) 1960 (5); v NZ 1951 (2)*

NEW ZEALAND

Number of Test cricketers: 205

Alabaster, J. C. 21: v E 1962 (2); v WI 1955 (1); v In 1967 (4); *v E 1958 (2); v SA 1961 (5); v WI 1971 (2); v In 1955 (4); v P 1955 (1)*

Allcott, C. F. W. 6: v E 1929 (2); v SA 1931 (1); *v E 1931 (3)*

Allott, G. I. 6: v E 1996 (2); v Z 1995 (2); *v A 1997 (2)*

Anderson, R. W. 9: v E 1977 (3); *v E 1978 (3); v P 1976 (3)*

Anderson, W. M. 1: v A 1945
Andrews, B. 2: *v A 1973 (2)*
Astle, N. J. 21: v E 1996 (3); v SL 1996 (2); v Z 1995 (2) 1997 (2); *v A 1997 (3); v WI 1995 (2); v P 1996 (2); v SL 1997 (3); v Z 1997 (2)*

Badcock, F. T. 7: v E 1929 (3) 1932 (3); v SA 1931 (2)
Barber, R. T. 1: v WI 1955
Bartlett, G. A. 10: v E 1965 (2); v In 1967 (2); v P 1964 (1); *v SA 1961 (5)*
Barton, P. T. 7: v E 1962 (3); *v SA 1961 (4)*
Beard, D. D. 4: v WI 1951 (2) 1955 (2)
Beck, J. E. F. 8: v WI 1955 (4); *v SA 1953 (4)*
Bell, W. 2: *v SA 1953 (2)*
Bilby, G. P. 2: v E 1965 (2)
Blain, T. E. 11: v A 1992 (2); v P 1993 (3); *v E 1986 (1); v A 1993 (3); v In 1988 (2)*
Blair, R. W. 19: v E 1954 (1) 1958 (2) 1962 (2); v SA 1952 (2) 1963 (3); v WI 1955 (2); *v E 1958 (3); v SA 1953 (4)*
Blunt, R. C. 9: v E 1929 (4); v SA 1931 (2); *v E 1931 (3)*
Bolton, B. A. 2: v E 1958 (2)
Boock, S. L. 30: v E 1977 (3) 1983 (2) 1987 (1); v WI 1979 (3) 1986 (2); v P 1978 (3) 1984 (2) 1988 (1); *v E 1978 (3); v A 1985 (1); v WI 1984 (3); v P 1984 (3); v SL 1983 (3)*
Bracewell, B. P. 6: v P 1978 (1) 1984 (1); *v E 1978 (3); v A 1980 (1)*
Bracewell, J. G. 41: v E 1987 (3); v A 1985 (2) 1989 (1); v WI 1986 (3); v In 1980 (1) 1989 (2); v P 1988 (2); *v E 1983 (4) 1986 (3) 1990 (3); v A 1980 (3) 1985 (2) 1987 (3); v WI 1984 (1); v In 1988 (3); v P 1984 (2); v SL 1983 (2) 1986 (1)*
Bradburn, G. E. 5: v SL 1990 (1); *v P 1990 (3); v SL 1992 (1)*
Bradburn, W. P. 2: v SA 1963 (2)
Brown, V. R. 2: *v A 1985 (2)*
Burgess, M. G. 50: v E 1970 (1) 1977 (3); v A 1973 (1) 1976 (2); v WI 1968 (2); v In 1967 (4) 1975 (3); v P 1972 (3) 1978 (3); *v E 1969 (2) 1973 (3) 1978 (3); v A 1980 (3); v WI 1971 (5); v In 1969 (3) 1976 (3); v P 1969 (3) 1976 (3)*
Burke, C. 1: v A 1945
Burtt, T. B. 10: v E 1946 (1) 1950 (2); v SA 1952 (1); v WI 1951 (2); *v E 1949 (4)*
Butterfield, L. A. 1: v A 1945

Cairns, B. L. 43: v E 1974 (1) 1977 (1) 1983 (1); v A 1976 (1) 1981 (3); v WI 1979 (3); v In 1975 (1) 1980 (3); v P 1978 (3) 1984 (3); v SL 1982 (2); *v E 1978 (2) 1983 (4); v A 1973 (1) 1980 (3) 1985 (1); v WI 1984 (2); v In 1976 (2); v P 1976 (2); v SL 1983 (2)*
Cairns, C. L. 33: v E 1991 (3) 1996 (3); v A 1992 (2); v P 1993 (1) 1995 (1); v SL 1990 (1) 1996 (2); v Z 1995 (2) 1997 (2); *v A 1989 (1) 1993 (2) 1997 (3); v In 1995 (3); v P 1996 (2); v SL 1997 (3); v Z 1997 (2)*
Cameron, F. J. 19: v E 1962 (3); v SA 1963 (3); v P 1964 (3); *v E 1965 (2); v SA 1961 (5); v In 1964 (1); v P 1964 (2)*
Cave, H. B. 19: v E 1954 (2); v WI 1955 (3); *v E 1949 (4) 1958 (2); v In 1955 (5); v P 1955 (3)*
Chapple, M. E. 14: v E 1954 (1) 1965 (1); v SA 1952 (1) 1963 (3); v WI 1955 (1); *v SA 1953 (5) 1961 (2)*
Chatfield, E. J. 43: v E 1974 (1) 1977 (1) 1983 (3) 1987 (3); v A 1976 (2) 1981 (1) 1985 (3); v WI 1986 (3); v P 1984 (3) 1988 (2); v SL 1982 (2); *v E 1983 (3) 1986 (1); v A 1985 (2) 1987 (2); v WI 1984 (4); v In 1988 (3); v P 1984 (1); v SL 1983 (2) 1986 (1)*
Cleverley, D. C. 2: v SA 1931 (1); v A 1945 (1)
Collinge, R. O. 35: v E 1970 (2) 1974 (2) 1977 (3); v A 1973 (3); v In 1967 (2) 1975 (3); v P 1964 (3) 1972 (2); *v E 1965 (3) 1969 (1) 1973 (3) 1978 (1); v In 1964 (2) 1976 (1); v P 1964 (2) 1976 (2)*
Colquhoun, I. A. 2: v E 1954 (2)
Coney, J. V. 52: v E 1983 (3); v A 1973 (2) 1981 (3) 1985 (3); v WI 1979 (3) 1986 (3); v In 1980 (3); v P 1978 (3) 1984 (3); v SL 1982 (2); *v E 1983 (4) 1986 (3); v A 1973 (2) 1980 (2) 1985 (3); v WI 1984 (4); v P 1984 (3); v SL 1983 (3)*
Congdon, B. E. 61: v E 1965 (3) 1970 (2) 1974 (2) 1977 (3); v A 1973 (3) 1976 (2); v WI 1968 (3); v In 1967 (4) 1975 (3); v P 1964 (3) 1972 (3); *v E 1965 (3) 1969 (3) 1973 (3) 1978 (3); v A 1973 (3); v WI 1971 (5); v In 1964 (3) 1969 (3); v P 1964 (1) 1969 (3)*
Cowie, J. 9: v E 1946 (1); v A 1945 (1); *v E 1937 (3) 1949 (4)*
Cresswell, G. F. 3: v E 1950 (2); *v E 1949 (1)*

Cromb, I. B. 5: v SA 1931 (2); *v E 1931 (3)*

Crowe, J. J. 39: v E 1983 (3) 1987 (2); v A 1989 (1); v WI 1986 (3); v P 1984 (3) 1988 (2); v SL 1982 (2); *v E 1983 (2) 1986 (3); v A 1985 (3) 1987 (3) 1989 (1); v WI 1984 (4); v P 1984 (3); v SL 1983 (3) 1986 (1)*

Crowe, M. D. 77: v E 1983 (3) 1987 (3) 1991 (3); v A 1981 (3) 1985 (3) 1992 (3); v WI 1986 (1); v WI 1986 (3); v In 1989 (3); v P 1984 (3) 1988 (2); v SL 1990 (2); *v E 1983 (4) 1986 (3) 1990 (3) 1994 (3); v A 1985 (3) 1987 (3) 1989 (1) 1993 (1); v SA 1994 (3); v WI 1984 (4); v In 1995 (3); v P 1984 (3) 1990 (3); v SL 1983 (3) 1986 (1) 1992 (2); v Z 1992 (2)*

Cunis, R. S. 20: v E 1965 (3) 1970 (2); v SA 1963 (1); v WI 1968 (3); *v E 1969 (1); v WI 1971 (5); v In 1969 (3); v P 1969 (2)*

D'Arcy, J. W. 5: *v E 1958 (5)*

Davis, H. T. 5: v E 1996 (1); v SL 1996 (2); *v E 1994 (1); v Z 1997 (1)*

de Groen, R. P. 5: v P 1993 (2); *v A 1993 (2); v SA 1994 (1)*

Dempster, C. S. 10: v E 1929 (4) 1932 (2); v SA 1931 (2); *v E 1931 (2)*

Dempster, E. W. 5: v SA 1952 (1); *v SA 1953 (4)*

Dick, A. E. 17: v E 1962 (3); v SA 1963 (2); v P 1964 (2); *v E 1965 (2); v SA 1961 (5); v P 1964 (3)*

Dickinson, G. R. 3: v E 1929 (2); v SA 1931 (1)

Donnelly, M. P. 7: *v E 1937 (3) 1949 (4)*

Doull, S. B. 24: v E 1996 (3); v WI 1994 (3); v P 1993 (3); v SL 1996 (2); v Z 1997 (2); *v A 1993 (2) 1997 (3); v SA 1994 (3); v P 1996 (2); v SL 1997 (1); v Z 1992 (1)*

Dowling, G. T. 39: v E 1962 (3) 1970 (3); v SA 1963 (1); v WI 1968 (3); v In 1967 (4); v P 1964 (2); *v E 1965 (3) 1969 (3); v SA 1961 (4); v WI 1971 (2); v In 1964 (4) 1969 (3); v P 1964 (2) 1969 (3)*

Dunning, J. A. 4: v E 1932 (1); *v E 1937 (3)*

Edgar, B. A. 39: v E 1983 (3); v A 1981 (3) 1985 (3); v WI 1979 (3); v In 1980 (3); v P 1978 (3); v SL 1982 (2); *v E 1978 (3) 1983 (4) 1986 (3); v A 1980 (3) 1985 (3); v P 1984 (3)*

Edwards, G. N. 8: v E 1977 (1); v A 1976 (2); v In 1980 (3); *v E 1978 (2)*

Emery, R. W. G. 2: v WI 1951 (2)

Fisher, F. E. 1: v SA 1952

Fleming, S. P. 37: v E 1996 (3); v SA 1994 (1); v WI 1994 (2); v In 1993 (1); v P 1995 (1); v SL 1994 (2) 1996 (2); v Z 1995 (2) 1997 (2); *v E 1994 (3); v A 1997 (3); SA 1994 (3); v WI 1995 (2); v In 1995 (3); v P 1996 (2); v SL 1997 (3); v Z 1997 (2)*

Foley, H. 1: v E 1929

Franklin, T. J. 21: v E 1987 (3); v A 1985 (1) 1989 (1); v In 1989 (3); v SL 1990 (3); *v E 1983 (1) 1990 (3); v In 1988 (3); v P 1990 (3)*

Freeman, D. L. 2: v E 1932 (2)

Gallichan, N. 1: *v E 1937*

Gedye, S. G. 4: v SA 1963 (3); v P 1964 (1)

Germon, L. K. 12: v E 1996 (2); v P 1995 (1); v Z 1995 (2); *v WI 1995 (2); v In 1995 (3); v P 1996 (2)*

Gillespie, S. R. 1: v A 1985

Gray, E. J. 10: *v E 1983 (2) 1986 (3); v A 1987 (1); v In 1988 (1); v P 1984 (2); v SL 1986 (1)*

Greatbatch, M. J. 41: v E 1987 (2) 1991 (1); v A 1989 (1) 1992 (3); v In 1989 (3) 1993 (1); v P 1988 (1) 1992 (1) 1993 (3); v SL 1990 (3); v Z 1995 (2); *v E 1990 (3) 1994 (1); v A 1989 (1) 1993 (3); v In 1988 (3) 1995 (3); v P 1990 (3) 1996 (2); v Z 1992 (2)*

Guillen, S. C. 3: v WI 1955 (3)

Guy, J. W. 12: v E 1958 (2); v WI 1955 (2); *v SA 1961 (2); v In 1955 (5); v P 1955 (1)*

Hadlee, D. R. 26: v E 1974 (2) 1977 (1); v A 1973 (3) 1976 (3); v In 1975 (3); v P 1972 (2); *v E 1969 (2) 1973 (3); v A 1973 (3); v In 1969 (3); v P 1969 (3)*

Hadlee, R. J. 86: v E 1977 (3) 1983 (3) 1987 (1); v A 1973 (2) 1976 (2) 1981 (3) 1985 (3) 1989 (1); v WI 1979 (3) 1986 (3); v In 1975 (2) 1980 (3) 1989 (3); v P 1972 (1) 1978 (3) 1984 (3) 1988 (2); v SL 1982 (2); *v E 1973 (1) 1978 (3) 1983 (4) 1986 (3) 1990 (3); v A 1973 (3) 1980 (3) 1985 (3) 1987 (3); v WI 1984 (4); v In 1976 (3) 1988 (3); v P 1976 (3); v SL 1983 (3) 1986 (1)*

Hadlee, W. A. 11: v E 1946 (1) 1950 (2); v A 1945 (1); *v E 1937 (3) 1949 (4)*

Harford, N. S. 8: *v E 1958 (4); v In 1955 (2); v P 1955 (2)*

Harford, R. I. 3: v In 1967 (3)

Harris, C. Z. 14: v A 1992 (1); v P 1992 (1); *v A 1993 (1) 1997 (1); v WI 1995 (2); v P 1996 (2); v SL 1992 (2) 1997 (2); v Z 1997 (2)*
Harris, P. G. Z. 9: v P 1964 (1); *v SA 1961 (5); v In 1955 (1); v P 1955 (2)*
Harris, R. M. 2: v E 1958 (2)
Hart, M. N. 14: v SA 1994 (1); v WI 1994 (2); v In 1993 (1); v P 1993 (2); *v E 1994 (3); v SA 1994 (3); v In 1995 (2)*
Hartland, B. R. 9: v E 1991 (3); v In 1993 (1); v P 1992 (1) 1993 (1); *v E 1994 (1); v SL 1992 (2)*
Haslam, M. J. 4: *v In 1995 (2); v Z 1992 (2)*
Hastings, B. F. 31: v E 1974 (2); v A 1973 (3); v WI 1968 (3); v In 1975 (1); v P 1972 (3); *v E 1969 (3) 1973 (3); v A 1973 (3); v WI 1971 (5); v In 1969 (2); v P 1969 (3)*
Hayes, J. A. 15: v E 1950 (2) 1954 (1); v WI 1951 (2); *v E 1958 (4); v In 1955 (5); v P 1955 (1)*
Henderson, M. 1: v E 1929
Horne, M. J. 11: v E 1996 (1); v SL 1996 (2); v Z 1997 (2); *v A 1997 (1); v SL 1997 (3); v Z 1997 (2)*
Horne, P. A. 4: v WI 1986 (1); *v A 1987 (1); v P 1990 (1); v SL 1986 (1)*
Hough, K. W. 2: v E 1958 (2)
Howarth, G. P. 47: v E 1974 (2) 1977 (3) 1983 (3); v A 1976 (2) 1981 (3); v WI 1979 (3); v In 1980 (3); v P 1978 (3) 1984 (3); v SL 1982 (2); *v E 1978 (3) 1983 (4); v A 1980 (2); v WI 1984 (4); v In 1976 (2); v P 1976 (2); v SL 1983 (3)*
Howarth, H. J. 30: v E 1970 (2) 1974 (2); v A 1973 (3) 1976 (2); v In 1975 (3); v P 1972 (3); *v E 1969 (3) 1973 (2); v WI 1971 (5); v In 1969 (3); v P 1969 (3)*

James, K. C. 11: v E 1929 (4) 1932 (2); v SA 1931 (2); *v E 1931 (3)*
Jarvis, T. W. 13: v E 1965 (1); v P 1972 (3); *v WI 1971 (4); v In 1964 (2); v P 1964 (3)*
Jones, A. H. 39: v E 1987 (1) 1991 (3); v A 1989 (1) 1992 (3); v In 1989 (3); v P 1988 (2) 1992 (1) 1993 (3); v SL 1990 (2); *v E 1990 (3); v A 1987 (3) 1993 (3); v In 1988 (3); v SL 1986 (1) 1992 (2); v Z 1992 (2)*

Kennedy, R. J. 4: v Z 1995 (2); *v WI 1995 (2)*
Kerr, J. L. 7: v E 1932 (2); v SA 1931 (1); *v E 1931 (2) 1937 (2)*
Kuggeleijn, C. M. 2: *v In 1988 (2)*

Larsen, G. R. 8: v SA 1994 (1); v P 1995 (1); v SL 1994 (2); v Z 1995 (1); *v E 1994 (1); v WI 1995 (2)*
Latham, R. T. 4: v E 1991 (1); v P 1992 (1); *v Z 1992 (1)*
Lees, W. K. 21: v E 1977 (2); v A 1976 (1); v WI 1979 (3); v P 1978 (3); v SL 1982 (2); *v E 1983 (2); v A 1980 (2); v In 1976 (3); v P 1976 (3)*
Leggat, I. B. 1: *v SA 1953*
Leggat, J. G. 9: v E 1954 (1); v SA 1952 (1); v WI 1951 (1) 1955 (1); *v In 1955 (3); v P 1955 (2)*
Lissette, A. F. 2: v WI 1955 (2)
Loveridge, G. R. 1: v Z 1995
Lowry, T. C. 7: v E 1929 (4); *v E 1931 (3)*

McEwan, P. E. 4: v WI 1979 (1); *v A 1980 (2); v P 1984 (1)*
MacGibbon, A. R. 26: v E 1950 (2) 1954 (2); v SA 1952 (1); v WI 1955 (1); *v E 1958 (5); v SA 1953 (5); v In 1955 (5); v P 1955 (3)*
McGirr, H. M. 2: v E 1929 (2)
McGregor, S. N. 25: v E 1954 (2) 1958 (2); v SA 1963 (3); v WI 1955 (4); v P 1964 (2); *v SA 1961 (5); v In 1955 (4); v P 1955 (3)*
McLeod, E. G. 1: v E 1929
McMahon T. G. 5: v WI 1955 (1); *v In 1955 (3); v P 1955 (1)*
McMillan, C. D. 8: v Z 1997 (2); *v A 1997 (3); v SL 1997 (3)*
McRae, D. A. N. 1: v A 1945
Matheson, A. M. 2: v E 1929 (1); *v E 1931 (1)*
Meale, T. 2: *v E 1958 (2)*
Merritt, W. E. 6: v E 1929 (4); *v E 1931 (2)*
Meuli, E. M. 1: v SA 1952
Milburn, B. D. 3: v WI 1968 (3)
Miller, L. S. M. 13: v SA 1952 (2); v WI 1955 (3); *v E 1958 (4); v SA 1953 (4)*
Mills, J. E. 7: v E 1929 (3) 1932 (1); *v E 1931 (3)*

Moir, A. M. 17: v E 1950 (2) 1954 (2) 1958 (2); v SA 1952 (1); v WI 1951 (2) 1955 (1); *v E 1958 (2); v In 1955 (2); v P 1955 (3)*

Moloney D. A. R. 3: *v E 1937 (3)*

Mooney, F. L. H. 14: v E 1950 (2); v SA 1952 (2); v WI 1951 (2); *v E 1949 (3); v SA 1953 (5)*

Morgan, R. W. 20: v E 1965 (2) 1970 (2); v WI 1968 (1); v P 1964 (2); *v E 1965 (3); v WI 1971 (3); v In 1964 (4); v P 1964 (3)*

Morrison, B. D. 1: v E 1962

Morrison, D. K. 48: v E 1987 (3) 1991 (3) 1996 (1); v A 1989 (1) 1992 (3); v SA 1994 (1); v WI 1994 (1); v In 1989 (1) 1993 (1); v P 1988 (1) 1992 (1) 1993 (2) 1995 (1); v SL 1990 (3) 1994 (1); *v E 1990 (3); v A 1987 (3) 1989 (1) 1993 (3); v SA 1994 (2); v WI 1995 (2); v In 1988 (1) 1995 (3); v P 1990 (3)*

Morrison, J. F. M. 17: v E 1974 (2); v A 1973 (3) 1981 (3); v In 1975 (3); *v A 1973 (3); v In 1976 (1); v P 1976 (2)*

Motz, R. C. 32: v E 1962 (2) 1965 (3); v SA 1963 (2); v WI 1968 (3); v In 1967 (4); v P 1964 (3); *v E 1965 (3) 1969 (3); v SA 1961 (5); v In 1964 (3); v P 1964 (1)*

Murray, B. A. G. 13: v E 1970 (1); v In 1967 (4); *v E 1969 (2); v In 1969 (3); v P 1969 (3)*

Murray, D. J. 8: v SA 1994 (1); v WI 1994 (2); v SL 1994 (2); *v SA 1994 (3)*

Nash, D. J. 16: v SA 1994 (1); v WI 1994 (1); v In 1993 (1); v P 1995 (1); v SL 1994 (1); v Z 1997 (2); *v E 1994 (3); v SA 1994 (1); v In 1995 (3); v SL 1992 (1); v Z 1992 (1)*

Newman J. 3: v E 1932 (2); v SA 1931 (1)

O'Connor, S. B. 6: v Z 1997 (1); *v A 1997 (2); v SL 1997 (1); v Z 1997 (2)*

O'Sullivan, D. R. 11: v In 1975 (1); v P 1972 (1); *v A 1973 (3); v In 1976 (3); v P 1976 (3)*

Overton, G. W. F. 3: *v SA 1953 (3)*

Owens, M. B. 8: v A 1992 (2); v P 1992 (1) 1993 (1); *v E 1994 (2); v SL 1992 (2)*

Page, M. L. 14: v E 1929 (4) 1932 (2); v SA 1931 (2); *v E 1931 (3) 1937 (3)*

Parker, J. M. 36: v E 1974 (2) 1977 (3); v A 1973 (3) 1976 (2); v WI 1979 (3); v In 1975 (3); v P 1972 (1) 1978 (2); *v E 1973 (3) 1978 (2); v A 1973 (3) 1980 (3); v In 1976 (3); v P 1976 (3)*

Parker, N. M. 3: *v In 1976 (2); v P 1976 (1)*

Parore, A. C. 44: v E 1991 (1) 1996 (3); v A 1992 (1); v SA 1994 (1); v WI 1994 (2); v In 1993 (1); v P 1992 (1) 1995 (1); v SL 1994 (1) 1996 (2); v Z 1995 (2) 1997 (2); *v E 1990 (1) 1994 (3); v A 1997 (3); v SA 1994 (3); v WI 1995 (1); v In 1995 (3); v P 1996 (2); v SL 1992 (2) 1997 (3); v Z 1992 (2) 1997 (2)*

Patel, D. N. 37: v E 1991 (3) 1996 (2); v A 1992 (3); v SA 1994 (1); v WI 1986 (3); v P 1988 (1) 1992 (1) 1990 (2) 1994 (3); v SL 1990 (2) 1994 (1) 1996 (2); v Z 1995 (2); *v A 1987 (3) 1989 (1) 1993 (3); v WI 1995 (1); v P 1990 (3) 1996 (2); v Z 1992 (2)*

Petherick, P. J. 6: v A 1976 (1); *v In 1976 (3); v P 1976 (2)*

Petrie, E. C. 14: v E 1958 (2) 1965 (3); *v E 1958 (5); v In 1955 (2); v P 1955 (3)*

Playle, W. R. 8: v E 1962 (3); *v E 1958 (5)*

Pocock, B. A. 15: v E 1996 (3); v P 1993 (2); v SL 1996 (2); *v E 1994 (1); v A 1993 (3) 1997 (2); v Z 1997 (2)*

Pollard, V. 32: v E 1965 (3) 1970 (1); v WI 1968 (3); v In 1967 (4); v P 1972 (1); *v E 1965 (3) 1969 (3) 1973 (3); v In 1964 (4) 1969 (1); v P 1964 (3) 1969 (3)*

Poore, M. B. 14: v E 1954 (1); v SA 1952 (1); *v SA 1953 (5); v In 1955 (4); v P 1955 (3)*

Priest, M. W. 3: v Z 1997 (1); *v E 1990 (1); v SL 1997 (1)*

Pringle, C. 14: v E 1991 (1); v In 1993 (1); v P 1993 (1); v SL 1990 (2) 1994 (1); *v E 1994 (2); v SA 1994 (2); v P 1990 (3); v SL 1992 (1)*

Puna, N. 3: v E 1965 (3)

Rabone, G. O. 12: v E 1954 (2); v SA 1952 (1); v WI 1951 (2); *v E 1949 (4); v SA 1953 (3)*

Redmond, R. E. 1: v P 1972

Reid, J. F. 19: v A 1985 (3); v In 1980 (3); v P 1978 (1) 1984 (3); *v A 1985 (3); v P 1984 (3); v SL 1983 (3)*

Reid, J. R. 58: v E 1950 (2) 1954 (2) 1958 (2) 1962 (3); v SA 1952 (2) 1963 (3); v WI 1951 (2) 1955 (4); v P 1964 (3); *v E 1949 (2) 1958 (5) 1965 (3); v SA 1953 (5) 1961 (5); v In 1955 (5) 1964 (4); v P 1955 (3) 1964 (3)*

Roberts, A. D. G. 7: *v In 1975 (2); v In 1976 (3); v P 1976 (2)*

Roberts, A. W. 5: v E 1929 (1); v SA 1931 (2); *v E 1937 (2)*

Robertson, G. K. 1: v A 1985

Rowe, C. G. 1: v A 1945

Rutherford, K. R. 56: v E 1987 (2) 1991 (2); v A 1985 (3) 1989 (1) 1992 (3); v SA 1994 (1); v WI 1986 (2) 1994 (2); v In 1989 (3) 1993 (1); v P 1992 (1) 1993 (3); v SL 1990 (3) 1994 (2); *v E 1986 (1) 1990 (2) 1994 (3); v A 1987 (1) 1993 (3); v SA 1994 (3); v WI 1984 (4); v In 1988 (2); v P 1990 (3); v SL 1986 (1) 1992 (2); v Z 1992 (2)*

Scott, R. H. 1: v E 1946

Scott, V. J. 10: v E 1946 (1) 1950 (1); v A 1945 (1); v WI 1951 (2); *v E 1949 (4)*

Sewell, D. G. 1: *v Z 1997*

Shrimpton, M. J. F. 10: v E 1962 (2) 1965 (3) 1970 (2); v SA 1963 (1); *v A 1973 (2)*

Sinclair, B. W. 21: v E 1962 (3) 1965 (3); v SA 1963 (3); v In 1967 (2); v P 1964 (2); *v E 1965 (3); v In 1964 (2); v P 1964 (3)*

Sinclair, I. M. 2: v WI 1955 (2)

Smith, F. B. 4: v E 1946 (1); v WI 1951 (1); *v E 1949 (2)*

Smith, H. D. 1: v E 1932

Smith, I. D. S. 63: v E 1983 (3) 1987 (3) 1991 (2); v A 1981 (3) 1985 (3) 1989 (1); v WI 1986 (3); v In 1983 (3) 1989 (3); v P 1984 (3) 1988 (2); v SL 1990 (3); *v E 1983 (2) 1986 (2) 1990 (2); v A 1980 (1) 1985 (3) 1987 (3) 1989 (1); v WI 1984 (4); v In 1988 (3); v P 1984 (3) 1990 (3); v SL 1983 (3) 1986 (1)*

Snedden, C. A. 1: v E 1946

Snedden, M. C. 25: v E 1983 (1) 1987 (2); v A 1981 (3) 1989 (1); v WI 1986 (1); v In 1980 (3) 1989 (3); v SL 1982 (2); *v E 1983 (1) 1990 (3); v A 1985 (1) 1987 (1) 1989 (1); v In 1988 (1); v SL 1986 (1)*

Sparling, J. T. 11: v E 1958 (2) 1962 (1); v SA 1963 (2); *v E 1958 (3); v SA 1961 (3)*

Spearman, C. M. 8: v P 1995 (1); v Z 1995 (2); *v WI 1995 (2); v SL 1997 (1); v Z 1997 (2)*

Stirling, D. A. 6: *v E 1986 (2); v WI 1984 (1); v P 1984 (3)*

Su'a, M. L. 13: v E 1991 (2); v A 1992 (2); v WI 1994 (1); v P 1992 (1); v SL 1994 (1); *v A 1993 (2); v SL 1992 (2); v Z 1992 (2)*

Sutcliffe, B. 42: v E 1946 (1) 1950 (2) 1954 (2) 1958 (2); v SA 1952 (2); v WI 1951 (2) 1955 (2); *v E 1949 (4) 1958 (4) 1965 (1); v SA 1953 (5); v In 1955 (5) 1964 (4); v P 1955 (3) 1964 (3)*

Taylor, B. R. 30: v E 1965 (1); v WI 1968 (2); v In 1967 (3); v P 1972 (3); *v E 1965 (2) 1969 (2) 1973 (3); v WI 1971 (4); v In 1964 (3) 1969 (2); v P 1964 (3) 1969 (1)*

Taylor, D. D. 3: v E 1946 (1); v WI 1955 (2)

Thomson, K. 2: v In 1967 (2)

Thomson, S. A. 19: v E 1991 (1); v WI 1994 (2); v In 1989 (1) 1993 (1); v P 1993 (3); v SL 1990 (2) 1994 (1); *v E 1994 (3); v SA 1994 (3); v In 1995 (2)*

Tindill, E. W. T. 5: v E 1946 (1); v A 1945 (1); *v E 1937 (3)*

Troup, G. B. 15: v A 1981 (2) 1985 (2); v WI 1979 (2); v In 1980 (2); v P 1978 (2); *v A 1980 (2); v WI 1984 (1); v In 1976 (1)*

Truscott, P. B. 1: v P 1964

Turner, G. M. 41: v E 1970 (2) 1974 (2); v A 1973 (3) 1976 (2); v WI 1968 (3); v In 1975 (3); v P 1972 (3); v SL 1982 (2); *v E 1969 (2) 1973 (3); v A 1973 (2); v WI 1971 (5); v In 1969 (3) 1976 (3); v P 1969 (1) 1976 (2)*

Twose, R. G. 8: v P 1995 (1); v Z 1995 (2); *v A 1997 (1); v WI 1995 (2); v In 1995 (2)*

Vance, R. H. 4: v E 1987 (1); v P 1988 (2); *v A 1989 (1)*

Vaughan, J. T. C. 6: v E 1996 (1); *v WI 1995 (2); v P 1996 (2); v SL 1992 (1)*

Vettori, D. L. 14: v E 1996 (2); v SL 1996 (2); v Z 1997 (2); *v A 1997 (3); v SL 1997 (3); v Z 1997 (2)*

Vivian, G. E. 5: *v WI 1971 (4); v In 1964 (1)*

Vivian, H. G. 7: v E 1932 (1); v SA 1931 (1); *v E 1931 (2) 1937 (3)*

Wadsworth, K. J. 33: v E 1970 (2) 1974 (2); v A 1973 (3); v In 1975 (3); v P 1972 (3); *v E 1969 (3) 1973 (3); v A 1973 (3); v WI 1971 (5); v In 1969 (3); v P 1969 (3)*

Wallace, W. M. 13: v E 1946 (1) 1950 (2); v A 1945 (1); v SA 1952 (2); *v E 1937 (3) 1949 (4)*

Walmsley, K. P. 2: v SL 1994 (2)

Ward, J. T. 8: v SA 1963 (1); v In 1967 (1); v P 1964 (1); *v E 1965 (1); v In 1964 (4)*

Watson, W. 15: v E 1991 (1); v A 1992 (2); v SL 1990 (1); *v E 1986 (2); v A 1989 (1) 1993 (1); v P 1990 (3); v Z 1992 (2)*

Watt, L. 1: v E 1954
Webb, M. G. 3: v E 1970 (1); v A 1973 (1); *v WI 1971 (1)*
Webb, P. N. 2: v WI 1979 (2)
Weir, G. L. 11: v E 1929 (3) 1932 (2); v SA 1931 (2); *v E 1931 (3) 1937 (1)*
White, D. J. 2: *v P 1990 (2)*
Whitelaw, P. E. 2: v E 1932 (2)
Wiseman, P. J. 3: *v SL 1997 (3)*
Wright, J. G. 82: v E 1977 (3) 1983 (3) 1987 (3) 1991 (3); v A 1981 (3) 1985 (2) 1989 (1) 1992 (3); v WI 1979 (3) 1986 (3); v In 1980 (3) 1989 (3); v P 1978 (3) 1984 (3)1988 (2); v SL 1982 (2) 1990 (3); *v E 1978 (2) 1983 (3) 1986 (3) 1990 (3); v A 1980 (3) 1985 (3) 1987 (3) 1989 (1); v WI 1984 (4); v In 1988 (3); v P 1984 (3); v SL 1983 (3) 1992 (2)*

Young, B. A. 33: v E 1996 (3); v SA 1994 (1); v WI 1994 (2); v In 1993 (1); v P 1993 (3) 1995 (1); v SL 1994 (2) 1996 (2); v Z 1997 (2); *v E 1994 (3); v A 1993 (1) 1997 (3); v SA 1994 (3); v In 1995 (1); v P 1996 (2); v SL 1997 (3)*
Yuile, B. W. 17: v E 1962 (2); v WI 1968 (3); v In 1967 (1); v P 1964 (3); *v E 1965 (1); v In 1964 (3) 1969 (1); v P 1964 (1) 1969 (2)*

INDIA

Number of Test cricketers: 215

Abid Ali, S. 29: v E 1972 (4); v A 1969 (1); v WI 1974 (2); v NZ 1969 (3); *v E 1971 (3) 1974 (3); v A 1967 (4); v WI 1970 (5); v NZ 1967 (4)*
Adhikari, H. R. 21: v E 1951 (3); v A 1956 (2); v WI 1948 (5) 1958 (1); v P 1952 (2); *v E 1952 (3); v A 1947 (5)*
Amarnath, L. 24: v E 1933 (3) 1951 (3); v WI 1948 (5); v P 1952 (5); *v E 1946 (3); v A 1947 (5)*
Amarnath, M. 69: v E 1976 (2) 1984 (5); v A 1969 (1) 1979 (1) 1986 (3); v WI 1978 (2) 1983 (3) 1987 (3); v NZ 1976 (3); v P 1983 (2) 1986 (5); v SL 1986 (2); *v E 1979 (2) 1986 (2); v A 1977 (5) 1985 (3); v WI 1975 (4) 1982 (5); v NZ 1975 (3); v P 1978 (3) 1982 (6) 1984 (2); v SL 1985 (2)*
Amarnath, S. 10: v E 1976 (2): *v WI 1975 (2); v NZ 1975 (3); v P 1978 (3)*
Amar Singh 7: v E 1933 (3); *v E 1932 (1) 1936 (3)*
Amir Elahi 1: *v A 1947*
Amre, P. K. 11: v E 1992 (3); v Z 1992 (1); *v SA 1992 (4); v SL 1993 (3)*
Ankola, S. A. 1: *v P 1989*
Apte, A. L. 1: *v E 1959*
Apte, M. L. 7: v P 1952 (2); *v WI 1952 (5)*
Arshad Ayub 13: v WI 1987 (4); v NZ 1988 (3); *v WI 1988 (4); v P 1989 (2)*
Arun, B. 2: v SL 1986 (2)
Arun Lal 16: v WI 1987 (4); v NZ 1988 (3); v P 1986 (1); v SL 1982 (1); *v WI 1988 (4); v P 1982 (3)*
Azad, K. 7: v E 1981 (3); v WI 1983 (2); v P 1983 (1); *v NZ 1980 (1)*
Azharuddin, M. 91: v E 1984 (3) 1992 (3); v A 1986 (3) 1996 (1) 1997 (3); v SA 1996 (3); v WI 1987 (3) 1994 (3); v NZ 1988 (3) 1995 (3); v P 1986 (5); v SL 1986 (1) 1990 (1) 1993 (3) 1997 (3); v Z 1992 (1); *v E 1986 (3) 1990 (3) 1996 (3); v A 1985 (3) 1991 (5); v SA 1992 (4) 1996 (3); v WI 1988 (3) 1996 (5); v NZ 1989 (3) 1993 (1); v P 1989 (4); v SL 1985 (3) 1993 (3) 1997 (2); v Z 1992 (1)*

Baig, A. A. 10: v A 1959 (3); v WI 1966 (2); v P 1960 (3); *v E 1959 (2)*
Banerjee, S. A. 1: v WI 1948
Banerjee, S. N. 1: v WI 1948
Banerjee, S. T. 1: *v A 1991*
Baqa Jilani, M. 1: *v E 1936*
Bedi, B. S. 67: v E 1972 (5) 1976 (5); v A 1969 (5); v WI 1966 (2) 1974 (4) 1978 (3); v NZ 1969 (3) 1976 (3); *v E 1967 (3) 1971 (3) 1974 (3) 1979 (3); v A 1967 (2) 1977 (5); v WI 1970 (5) 1975 (4); v NZ 1967 (4) 1975 (2); v P 1978 (3)*
Bhandari, P. 3: v A 1956 (1); v NZ 1955 (1); *v P 1954 (1)*
Bhat, A. R. 2: v WI 1983 (1); v P 1983 (1)

Binny, R. M. H. 27: v E 1979 (1); v WI 1983 (6); v P 1979 (6) 1983 (2) 1986 (3); *v E 1986 (3); v A 1980 (1) 1985 (2); v NZ 1980 (1); v P 1984 (1); v SL 1985 (1)*
Borde, C. G. 55: v E 1961 (5) 1963 (5); v A 1959 (5) 1964 (3) 1969 (1); v WI 1958 (4) 1966 (3); v NZ 1964 (4); v P 1960 (5); *v E 1959 (4) 1967 (3); v A 1967 (4); v WI 1961 (5); v NZ 1967 (4)*

Chandrasekhar, B. S. 58: v E 1963 (4) 1972 (5) 1976 (5); v A 1964 (2); v WI 1966 (3) 1974 (4) 1978 (4); v NZ 1964 (2) 1976 (3); *v E 1967 (3) 1971 (3) 1974 (2) 1979 (1); v A 1967 (2) 1977(5); v WI 1975 (4); v NZ 1975 (3); v P 1978 (3)*
Chauhan, C. P. S. 40: v E 1972 (2); v A 1969 (1) 1979 (6); v WI 1978 (6); v NZ 1969 (2); v P 1979 (6); *v E 1979 (4); v A 1977 (4) 1980 (3); v NZ 1980 (3); v P 1978 (3)*
Chauhan, R. K. 21: v E 1992 (3); v A 1997 (2); v WI 1994 (2); v NZ 1995 (2); v SL 1993 (3) 1997 (3); v Z 1992 (1); *v NZ 1993 (1); v SL 1993 (3) 1997 (1)*
Chowdhury, N. R. 2: v E 1951 (1); v WI 1948 (1)
Colah, S. H. M. 2: v E 1933 (1); *v E 1932 (1)*
Contractor, N. J. 31: v E 1961 (5); v A 1956 (1) 1959 (5); v WI 1958 (5); v NZ 1955 (4); v P 1960 (5); *v E 1959 (4); v WI 1961 (2)*

Dani, H. T. 1: v P 1952
Desai, R. B. 28: v E 1961 (4) 1963 (2); v A 1959 (3); v WI 1958 (1); v NZ 1964 (3); v P 1960 (5); *v E 1959 (5); v A 1967 (1); v WI 1961 (3); v NZ 1967 (1)*
Dilawar Hussain 3: v E 1933 (2); *v E 1936 (1)*
Divecha, R. V. 5: v E 1951 (2); v P 1952 (1); *v E 1952 (2)*
Doshi, D. R. 33: v E 1979 (1) 1981 (6); v A 1979 (6); v P 1979 (6) 1983 (1); v SL 1982 (1); *v E 1982 (3); v A 1980 (3); v NZ 1980 (2); v P 1982 (4)*
Dravid, R. 22: v A 1996 (1) 1997 (3); v SA 1996 (3); v SL 1997 (3); *v E 1996 (2); v SA 1996 (3); v WI 1996 (5); v SL 1997 (2)*
Durani, S. A. 29: v E 1961 (5) 1963 (5) 1972 (3); v A 1959 (1) 1964 (3); v WI 1966 (1); v NZ 1964 (3); *v WI 1961 (5) 1970 (3)*

Engineer, F. M. 46: v E 1961 (4) 1972 (5); v A 1969 (5); v WI 1966 (1) 1974 (5); v NZ 1964 (4) 1969 (2); *v E 1967 (3) 1971 (3) 1974 (3); v A 1967 (4); v WI 1961 (3); v NZ 1967 (4)*

Gadkari, C. V. 6: *v WI 1952 (3); v P 1954 (3)*
Gaekwad, A. D. 40: v E 1976 (4) 1984 (3); v WI 1974 (3) 1978 (5) 1983 (6); v NZ 1976 (3); v P 1983 (3); *v E 1979 (2); v A 1977 (1); v WI 1975 (3) 1982 (5); v P 1984 (2)*
Gaekwad, D. K. 11: v WI 1958 (1); v P 1952 (2) 1960 (1); *v E 1952 (1) 1959 (4); v WI 1952 (2)*
Gaekwad, H. G. 1: v P 1952
Gandotra, A. 2: v A 1969 (1); v NZ 1969 (1)
Ganesh, D. 4: *v SA 1996 (2); v WI 1996 (2)*
Ganguly, S. C. 20: v A 1996 (1) 1997 (3); v SA 1996 (2); v SL 1997 (3); *v E 1996 (2); v SA 1996 (3); v WI 1996 (4); v SL 1997 (2)*
Gavaskar, S. M. 125: v E 1972 (5) 1976 (5) 1979 (1) 1981 (6) 1984 (5); v A 1979 (6) 1986 (3); v WI 1974 (2) 1978 (6) 1983 (6); v NZ 1976 (3); v P 1979 (6) 1983 (3) 1986 (4); v SL 1982 (1) 1986 (3); *v E 1971 (3) 1974 (3) 1979 (4) 1982 (3) 1986 (3); v A 1977 (5) 1980 (3) 1985 (3); v WI 1970 (4) 1975 (4) 1982 (5); v NZ 1975 (3) 1980 (3); v P 1978 (3) 1982 (6) 1984 (2); v SL 1985 (3)*
Ghavri, K. D. 39: v E 1976 (3) 1979 (1); v A 1979 (6); v WI 1974 (3) 1978 (6); v NZ 1976 (2); v P 1979 (6); *v E 1979 (4); v A 1977 (3) 1980 (3); v NZ 1980 (1); v P 1978 (1)*
Ghorpade, J. M. 8: v A 1956 (1); v WI 1958 (1); v NZ 1955 (1); *v E 1959 (3); v WI 1952 (2)*
Ghulam Ahmed 22: v E 1951 (2); v A 1956 (2); v WI 1948 (1) 1958 (2); v NZ 1955 (1); v P 1952 (1); *v E 1952 (4); v P 1954 (4)*
Gopalan, M. J. 1: v E 1933
Gopinath, C. D. 8: v E 1951 (3); v A 1959 (1); v P 1952 (1); *v E 1952 (1); v P 1954 (2)*
Guard, G. M. 2: v A 1959 (1); v WI 1958 (1)
Guha, S. 4: v A 1969 (3); *v E 1967 (1)*
Gul Mahomed 8: v P 1952 (2); *v E 1946 (1); v A 1947 (5)*
Gupte, B. P. 3: v E 1963 (1); v NZ 1964 (1); v P 1960 (1)
Gupte, S. P. 36: v E 1951 (1) 1961 (2); v A 1956 (3); v WI 1958 (5); v NZ 1955 (5); v P 1952 (2) 1960 (5); *v E 1959 (5); v WI 1952 (5); v P 1954 (5)*
Gursharan Singh 1: *v NZ 1989*

Hafeez, A. 3: *v E 1946 (3)*

Hanumant Singh 14: v E 1963 (2); v A 1964 (3); v WI 1966 (2); v NZ 1964 (4) 1969 (1); *v E 1967 (2)*

Harbhajan Singh 1: v A 1997

Hardikar, M. S. 2: v WI 1958 (2)

Harvinder Singh 2: v A 1997 (2)

Hazare, V. S. 30: v E 1951 (5); v WI 1948 (5); v P 1952 (3); *v E 1946 (3) 1952 (4); v A 1947 (5); v WI 1952 (5)*

Hindlekar, D. D. 4: *v E 1936 (1) 1946 (3)*

Hirwani, N. D. 17: v SA 1996 (2); v WI 1987 (1); v NZ 1988 (3) 1995 (1); v SL 1990 (1); *v E 1990 (3); v WI 1988 (3); v NZ 1989 (3)*

Ibrahim, K. C. 4: v WI 1948 (4)

Indrajitsinhji, K. S. 4: v A 1964 (3); v NZ 1969 (1)

Irani, J. K. 2: *v A 1947 (2)*

Jadeja, A. 11: v NZ 1995 (3); *v E 1996 (2); v SA 1992 (3); v WI 1996 (2); v SL 1997 (1)*

Jahangir Khan, M. 4: *v E 1932 (1) 1936 (3)*

Jai, L. P. 1: v E 1933

Jaisimha, M. L. 39: v E 1961 (5) 1963 (5); v A 1959 (1) 1964 (3); v WI 1966 (2); v NZ 1964 (4) 1969 (1); v P 1960 (4); *v E 1959 (1); v A 1967 (2); v WI 1961 (4) 1970 (3); v NZ 1967 (4)*

Jamshedji, R. J. 1: v E 1933

Jayantilal, K. 1: *v WI 1970*

Johnson, D. J. 2: v A 1996 (1); *v SA 1996 (1)*

Joshi, P. G. 12: v E 1951 (2); v A 1959 (1); v WI 1958 (1); v P 1952 (1) 1960 (1); *v E 1959 (3); v WI 1952 (3)*

Joshi, S. B. 9: v A 1996 (1); v SA 1996 (3); *v E 1996 (1); v WI 1996 (4)*

Kambli, V. G. 17: v E 1992 (3); v WI 1994 (3); v NZ 1995 (3); v SL 1993 (3); v Z 1992 (1); *v NZ 1993 (1); v SL 1993 (3)*

Kanitkar, H. S. 2: v WI 1974 (2)

Kapil Dev 131: v E 1979 (1) 1981 (6) 1984 (4) 1992 (3); v A 1979 (6) 1986 (3); v WI 1978 (6) 1983 (6) 1987 (4); v NZ 1988 (3); v P 1979 (6) 1983 (3) 1986 (5); v SL 1982 (1) 1986 (3) 1990 (1) 1993 (3); v Z 1992 (1); *v E 1979 (4) 1982 (3) 1986 (3) 1990 (3); v A 1980 (3) 1985 (3) 1991 (3); v NZ 1980 (3) 1989 (3) 1993 (1); v P 1978 (3) 1982 (6) 1984 (2) 1989 (4); v SL 1985 (3) 1993 (3); v Z 1992 (1)*

Kapoor, A. R. 4: v A 1996 (1); v SA 1996 (1); v WI 1994 (1); v NZ 1995 (1)

Kardar, A. H. (*see* Hafeez)

Kenny, R. B. 5: v A 1959 (4); v WI 1958 (1)

Kirmani, S. M. H. 88: v E 1976 (5) 1979 (1) 1981 (6) 1984 (5); v A 1979 (6); v WI 1978 (6) 1983 (6); v NZ 1976 (3); v P 1979 (6) 1983 (3); v SL 1982 (1); *v E 1982 (3); v A 1977 (5) 1980 (3) 1985 (3); v WI 1975 (4) 1982 (5); v NZ 1975 (3) 1980 (3); v P 1978 (3) 1982 (6) 1984 (2)*

Kischenchand, G. 5: v P 1952 (1); *v A 1947 (4)*

Kripal Singh, A. G. 14: v E 1961 (3) 1963 (2); v A 1956 (2) 1964 (1); v WI 1958 (1); v NZ 1955 (4); *v E 1959 (1)*

Krishnamurthy, P. 5: *v WI 1970 (5)*

Kulkarni, N. M. 2: v SL 1997 (1); *v SL 1997 (1)*

Kulkarni, R. R. 3: v A 1986 (1); v P 1986 (2)

Kulkarni, U. N. 4: *v A 1967 (3); v WI 1967 (1)*

Kumar, V. V. 2: v E 1961 (1); v P 1960 (1)

Kumble, A. 46: v E 1992 (3); v A 1996 (1) 1997 (3); v SA 1996 (3); v WI 1994 (3); v NZ 1995 (3); v SL 1993 (3) 1997 (3); v Z 1992 (1); *v E 1990 (1) 1996 (3); v SA 1992 (4) 1996 (3); v WI 1996 (5); v NZ 1993 (1); v SL 1993 (3) 1997 (2); v Z 1992 (1)*

Kunderan, B. K. 18: v E 1961 (1) 1963 (5); v A 1959 (3); v WI 1966 (2); v NZ 1964 (1); v P 1960 (2); *v E 1967 (2); v WI 1961 (2)*

Kuruvilla, A. 10: v SL 1997 (3); *v WI 1996 (5); v SL 1997 (2)*

Lall Singh 1: *v E 1932*

Lamba, R. 4: v WI 1987 (1); v SL 1986 (3)

Laxman, V. V. S. 10: v A 1997 (2); v SA 1996 (2); *v SA 1996 (2); v WI 1996 (4)*

Madan Lal 39: v E 1976 (2) 1981 (6); v WI 1974 (2) 1983 (3); v NZ 1976 (1); v P 1983 (3); v SL 1982 (1); *v E 1974 (2) 1982 (3) 1986 (1); v A 1977 (2); v WI 1975 (4) 1982 (2); v NZ 1975 (3); v P 1982 (3) 1984 (1)*

Maka, E. S. 2: v P 1952 (1); *v WI 1952 (1)*

Malhotra, A. 7: v E 1981 (2) 1984 (1); v WI 1983 (3); *v E 1982 (1)*

Maninder Singh 35: v A 1986 (3); v WI 1983 (4) 1987 (3); v P 1986 (4); v SL 1986 (3); v Z 1992 (1); *v E 1986 (3); v WI 1982 (3); v P 1982 (5) 1984 (1) 1989 (3); v SL 1985 (2)*

Manjrekar, S. V. 37: v SA 1996 (1); v WI 1987 (1) 1994 (1); v NZ 1995 (1); v SL 1990 (1) 1993 (3); *v E 1990 (3) 1996 (2); v A 1991 (5); v SA 1992 (4); v WI 1988 (4); v NZ 1989 (3) 1993 (1); v P 1989 (4); v Z 1992 (1)*

Manjrekar, V. L. 55: v E 1951 (2) 1961 (5) 1963 (4); v A 1956 (3) 1964 (3); v WI 1958 (4); v NZ 1955 (3) 1964 (1); v P 1952 (3) 1960 (5); *v E 1952 (4) 1959 (2); v WI 1952 (4) 1961 (5); v P 1954 (5)*

Mankad, A. V. 22: v E 1976 (1); v A 1969 (5); v WI 1974 (1); v NZ 1969 (2) 1976 (3); *v E 1971 (3) 1974 (1); v A 1977 (3); v WI 1970 (3)*

Mankad, V. 44: v E 1951 (5); v A 1956 (3); v WI 1948 (5) 1958 (2); v NZ 1955 (4); v P 1952 (4); *v E 1946 (3) 1952 (3); v A 1947 (5); v WI 1952 (5); v P 1954 (5)*

Mansur Ali Khan (*see* Pataudi)

Mantri, M. K. 4: v E 1951 (1); *v E 1952 (2); v P 1954 (1)*

Meherhomji, K. R. 1: *v E 1936*

Mehra, V. L. 8: v E 1961 (1) 1963 (2); v NZ 1955 (2); *v WI 1961 (3)*

Merchant, V. M. 10: v E 1933 (3) 1951 (1); *v E 1936 (3) 1946 (3)*

Mhambrey, P. L. 2: *v E 1996 (2)*

Milkha Singh, A. G. 4: v E 1961 (1); v A 1959 (1); v P 1960 (2)

Modi, R. S. 10: v E 1951 (1); v WI 1948 (5); v P 1952 (1); *v E 1946 (3)*

Mohanty, D. S. 2: v SL 1997 (1); *v SL 1997 (1)*

Mongia, N. R. 33: v A 1996 (1) 1997 (3); v SA 1996 (3); v WI 1994 (3); v NZ 1995 (3); v SL 1993 (3) 1997 (3); *v E 1996 (3); v SA 1996 (3); v WI 1996 (5); v NZ 1993 (1); v SL 1997 (2)*

More, K. S. 49: v E 1992 (3); v A 1986 (2); v WI 1987 (4); v NZ 1988 (3); v P 1986 (5); v SL 1986 (3) 1990 (1); *v E 1986 (3) 1990 (3); v A 1991 (3); v SA 1992 (4); v WI 1988 (4); v NZ 1989 (3); v P 1989 (4); v SL 1993 (3); v Z 1992 (1)*

Muddiah, V. M. 2: v A 1959 (1); v P 1960 (1)

Mushtaq Ali, S. 11: v E 1933 (2) 1951 (1); v WI 1948 (3); *v E 1936 (3) 1946 (2)*

Nadkarni, R. G. 41: v E 1961 (1) 1963 (5); v A 1959 (5) 1964 (3); v WI 1958 (1) 1966 (1); v NZ 1955 (1) 1964 (4); v P 1960 (4); *v E 1959 (4); v A 1967 (3); v WI 1961 (5); v NZ 1967 (4)*

Naik, S. S. 3: v WI 1974 (2); *v E 1974 (1)*

Naoomal Jeoomal 3: v E 1933 (2); *v E 1932 (1)*

Narasimha Rao, M. V. 4: v A 1979 (2); v WI 1978 (2)

Navle, J. G. 2: v E 1933 (1); *v E 1932 (1)*

Nayak, S. V. 2: *v E 1982 (2)*

Nayudu, C. K. 7: v E 1933 (3); *v E 1932 (1) 1936 (3)*

Nayudu, C. S. 11: v E 1933 (2) 1951 (1); *v E 1936 (2) 1946 (2); v A 1947 (4)*

Nazir Ali, S. 2: v E 1933 (1); *v E 1932 (1)*

Nissar, Mahomed 6: v E 1933 (2); *v E 1932 (1) 1936 (3)*

Nyalchand, S. 1: v P 1952

Pai, A. M. 1: v NZ 1969

Palia, P. E. 2: *v E 1932 (1) 1936 (1)*

Pandit, C. S. 5: v A 1986 (2); *v E 1986 (1); v A 1991 (2)*

Parkar, G. A. 1: *v E 1982*

Parkar, R. D. 2: v E 1972 (2)

Parsana, D. D. 2: v WI 1978 (2)

Patankar, C. T. 1: v NZ 1955

Pataudi sen., Nawab of, 3: *v E 1946 (3)*

Pataudi jun., Nawab of (now Mansur Ali Khan) 46: v E 1961 (3) 1963 (5) 1972 (3); v A 1964 (3) 1969 (5); v WI 1966 (3) 1974 (4); v NZ 1964 (4) 1969 (3); *v E 1967 (3); v A 1967 (3); v WI 1961 (3); v NZ 1967 (4)*

Patel, B. P. 21: v E 1976 (5); v WI 1974 (3); v NZ 1976 (3); *v E 1974 (2); v A 1977 (2); v WI 1975 (3); v NZ 1975 (3)*

Patel, J. M. 7: v A 1956 (2) 1959 (3); v NZ 1955 (1); *v P 1954 (1)*

Patel, R. 1: v NZ 1988

Patiala, Yuvraj of, 1: v E 1933

Patil, S. M. 29: v E 1979 (1) 1981 (4) 1984 (2); v WI 1983 (2); v P 1979 (2) 1983 (3); v SL 1982 (1); *v E 1982 (2); v A 1980 (3); v NZ 1980 (3); v P 1982 (4) 1984 (2)*

Patil, S. R. 1: v NZ 1955

Phadkar, D. G. 31: v E 1951 (4); v A 1956 (1); v WI 1948 (4) 1958 (1); v NZ 1955 (4); v P 1952 (2); *v E 1952 (4); v A 1947 (4); v WI 1952 (4); v P 1954 (3)*

Prabhakar, M. 39: v E 1984 (2) 1992 (3); v WI 1994 (3); v NZ 1995 (3); v SL 1990 (1) 1993 (3); v Z 1992 (1); *v E 1990 (3); v A 1991 (5); v SA 1992 (4); v NZ 1989 (3); v P 1989 (4); v SL 1993 (3); v Z 1992 (1)*

Prasad, B. K. V. 18: v A 1996 (1); v SA 1996 (3); v SL 1997 (1); *v E 1996 (3); v SA 1996 (3); v WI 1996 (5); v SL 1997 (2)*

Prasanna, E. A. S. 49: v E 1961 (1) 1972 (3) 1976 (4); v A 1969 (5); v WI 1966 (1) 1974 (5); v NZ 1969 (3); *v E 1967 (3) 1974 (2); v A 1967 (4) 1977 (4); v WI 1961 (1) 1970 (3) 1975 (1); v NZ 1967 (4) 1975 (3); v P 1978 (2)*

Punjabi, P. H. 5: *v P 1954 (5)*

Rai Singh, K. 1: *v A 1947*

Rajinder Pal 1: v E 1963

Rajindernath, V. 1: v P 1952

Rajput, L. S. 2: *v SL 1985 (2)*

Raju, S. L. V. 27: v E 1992 (3); v A 1997 (3); v WI 1994 (3); v NZ 1995 (2); v SL 1990 (1) 1993 (3); *v E 1996 (1); v A 1991 (4); v SA 1992 (2); v NZ 1989 (2) 1993 (1); v SL 1993 (1); v Z 1992 (1)*

Raman, W. V. 11: v SA 1996 (1); v WI 1987 (1); v NZ 1988 (1); *v SA 1992 (1) 1996 (2); v WI 1988 (1); v NZ 1989 (3); v Z 1992 (1)*

Ramaswami, C. 2: *v E 1936 (2)*

Ramchand, G. S. 33: v A 1956 (3) 1959 (5); v WI 1958 (3); v NZ 1955 (5); v P 1952 (3); *v E 1952 (4); v WI 1952 (5); v P 1954 (5)*

Ramji, L. 1: v E 1933

Rangachari, C. R. 4: v WI 1948 (2); *v A 1947 (2)*

Rangnekar, K. M. 3: *v A 1947 (3)*

Ranjane, V. B. 7: v E 1961 (3) 1963 (1); v A 1964 (1); v WI 1958 (1); *v WI 1961 (1)*

Rathore, V. 6: v A 1996 (1); *v E 1996 (3); v SA 1996 (2)*

Razdan, V. 2: *v P 1989 (2)*

Reddy, B. 4: *v E 1979 (4)*

Rege, M. R. 1: v WI 1948

Roy, A. 4: v A 1969 (2); v NZ 1969 (2)

Roy, Pankaj 43: v E 1951 (5); v A 1956 (3) 1959 (5); v WI 1958 (5); v NZ 1955 (3); v P 1952 (3) 1960 (1); *v E 1952 (4) 1959 (5); v WI 1952 (4); v P 1954 (5)*

Roy, Pranab 2: v E 1981 (2)

Sandhu, B. S. 8: v WI 1983 (1); *v WI 1982 (4); v P 1982 (3)*

Sardesai, D. N. 30: v E 1961 (1) 1963 (5) 1972 (1); v A 1964 (3) 1969 (1); v WI 1966 (2); v NZ 1964 (3); *v E 1967 (1) 1971 (3); v A 1967 (2); v WI 1961 (3) 1970 (5)*

Sarwate, C. T. 9: v E 1951 (1); v WI 1948 (2); *v E 1946 (1); v A 1947 (5)*

Saxena, R. C. 1: *v E 1967*

Sekar, T. A. P. 2: *v P 1982 (2)*

Sen, P. 14: v E 1951 (2); v WI 1948 (5); v P 1952 (2); *v E 1952 (2); v A 1947 (3)*

Sen Gupta, A. K. 1: v WI 1958

Sharma, Ajay 1: v WI 1987

Sharma, Chetan 23: v E 1984 (3); v A 1986 (2); v WI 1987 (3); v SL 1986 (2); *v E 1986 (2); v A 1985 (2); v WI 1988 (4); v P 1984 (2); v SL 1985 (3)*

Sharma, Gopal 5: v E 1984 (1); v P 1986 (2); v SL 1990 (1); *v SL 1985 (1)*

Sharma, P. 5: v E 1976 (2); v WI 1974 (2); *v WI 1975 (1)*

Sharma, Sanjeev 2: v NZ 1988 (1); *v E 1990 (1)*

Shastri, R. J. 80: v E 1981 (6) 1984 (5); v A 1986 (2); v WI 1983 (6) 1987 (4); v NZ 1988 (3); v P 1983 (2) 1986 (5); v SL 1986 (3) 1990 (1); *v E 1982 (3) 1986 (3) 1990 (3); v A 1985 (3) 1991 (3); v SA 1992 (3); v WI 1982 (5) 1988 (4); v NZ 1980 (3); v P 1982 (2) 1984 (2) 1989 (4); v SL 1985 (3); v Z 1992 (1)*

Shinde, S. G. 7: v E 1951 (3); v WI 1948 (1); *v E 1946 (1) 1952 (2)*

Shodhan, R. H. 3: v P 1952 (1); *v WI 1952 (2)*

Shukla, R. C. 1: v SL 1982

Sidhu, N. S. 48: v E 1992 (3); v A 1997 (3); v WI 1983 (2) 1994 (3); v NZ 1988 (3) 1995 (2); v SL 1993 (3) 1997 (3); v Z 1992 (1); *v E 1990 (3); v A 1991 (3); v WI 1988 (4) 1996 (4); v NZ 1989 (1) 1993 (1); v P 1989 (4); v SL 1993 (3) 1997 (2)*

Sivaramakrishnan, L. 9: v E 1984 (5); *v A 1985 (2); v WI 1982 (1); v SL 1985 (1)*

Sohoni, S. W. 4: v E 1951 (1); *v E 1946 (2); v A 1947 (1)*

Solkar, E. D. 27: v E 1972 (5) 1976 (1); v A 1969 (4); v WI 1974 (4); v NZ 1969 (1); *v E 1971 (3) 1974 (2); v WI 1970 (5) 1975 (1)*

Sood, M. M. 1: v A 1959

Srikkanth, K. 43: v E 1981 (4) 1984 (2); v A 1986 (3); v WI 1987 (4); v NZ 1988 (3); v P 1986 (5); v SL 1986 (3); *v E 1986 (3); v A 1985 (3) 1991 (4); v P 1982 (2) 1989 (4); v SL 1985 (3)*

Srinath, J. 32: v E 1992 (2); v SA 1996 (3); v WI 1994 (3); v NZ 1995 (3); v SL 1997 (3); *v E 1996 (3); v A 1991 (5); v SA 1992 (3) 1996 (3); v NZ 1993 (1); v SL 1993 (2); v Z 1992 (1)*

Srinivasan, T. E. 1: *v NZ 1980*

Subramanya, V. 9: v NZ 1966 (2); v NZ 1964 (1); *v E 1967 (2); v A 1967 (2); v NZ 1967 (2)*

Sunderram, G. 2: v NZ 1955 (2)

Surendranath, R. 11: v A 1959 (2); v WI 1958 (2); v P 1960 (2); *v E 1959 (5)*

Surti, R. F. 26: v E 1963 (1); v A 1964 (2) 1969 (1); v WI 1966 (2); v NZ 1964 (1) 1969 (2); v P 1960 (2); *v E 1967 (2); v A 1967 (4); v WI 1961 (5); v NZ 1967 (4)*

Swamy, V. N. 1: v NZ 1955

Tamhane, N. S. 21: v A 1956 (3) 1959 (1); v WI 1958 (4); v NZ 1955 (4); v P 1960 (2); *v E 1959 (2); v P 1954 (5)*

Tarapore, K. K. 1: v WI 1948

Tendulkar, S. R. 61: v E 1992 (3); v A 1996 (1) 1997 (3); v SA 1996 (3); v WI 1994 (3); v NZ 1995 (3); v SL 1990 (1) 1993 (3) 1997 (3); v Z 1992 (1); *v E 1990 (3) 1996 (3); v A 1991 (5); v SA 1992 (4) 1996 (3); v WI 1996 (5); v NZ 1989 (3) 1993 (1); v P 1989 (4); v SL 1993 (3) 1997 (3); v Z 1992 (1)*

Umrigar, P. R. 59: v E 1951 (5) 1961 (4); v A 1956 (3) 1959 (3); v WI 1948 (1) 1958 (5); v NZ 1955 (5); v P 1952 (5) 1960 (5); *v E 1952 (4) 1959 (4); v WI 1952 (5) 1961 (5); v P 1954 (5)*

Vengsarkar, D. B. 116: v E 1976 (1) 1979 (1) 1981 (6) 1984 (5); v A 1979 (6) 1986 (2); v WI 1978 (6) 1983 (5) 1987 (3); v NZ 1988 (3); v P 1979 (5) 1983 (1) 1986 (5); v SL 1982 (1) 1986 (3) 1990 (1); *v E 1979 (4) 1982 (3) 1986 (3) 1990 (3); v A 1977 (5) 1980 (3) 1985 (3) 1991 (5); v WI 1975 (2) 1982 (5) 1988 (4); v NZ 1975 (3) 1980 (3) 1989 (2); v P 1978 (3) 1982 (6) 1984 (2); v SL 1985 (3)*

Venkataraghavan, S. 57: v E 1972 (2) 1976 (1); v A 1969 (5) 1979 (3); v WI 1966 (2) 1974 (2) 1978 (6); v NZ 1964 (4) 1969 (2) 1976 (3); v P 1983 (2); *v E 1967 (1) 1971 (3) 1974 (2) 1979 (4); v A 1977 (1); v WI 1970 (5) 1975 (3) 1982 (5); v NZ 1975 (1)*

Venkataramana, M. 1: *v WI 1988*

Viswanath, G. R. 91: v E 1972 (5) 1976 (5) 1979 (1) 1981 (6); v A 1969 (4) 1979 (6); v WI 1974 (5) 1978 (6); v NZ 1976 (3); v P 1979 (6); v SL 1982 (1); *v E 1971 (3) 1974 (3) 1979 (4) 1982 (3); v A 1977 (5) 1980 (3); v WI 1970 (3) 1975 (4); v NZ 1975 (3) 1980 (3); v P 1978 (3) 1982 (6)*

Viswanath, S. 3: *v SL 1985 (3)*

Vizianagram, Maharaj Kumar of, Sir Vijay A. 3: *v E 1936 (3)*

Wadekar, A. L. 37: v E 1972 (5); v A 1969 (5); v WI 1966 (2); v NZ 1969 (3); *v E 1967 (3) 1971 (3) 1974 (3); v A 1967 (4); v WI 1970 (5); v NZ 1967 (4)*

Wassan, A. S. 4: *v E 1990 (1); v NZ 1989 (3)*

Wazir Ali, S. 7: v E 1933 (3); *v E 1932 (1) 1936 (3)*

Yadav, N. S. 35: v E 1979 (1) 1981 (1) 1984 (4); v A 1979 (5) 1986 (3); v WI 1983 (3); v P 1979 (5) 1986 (4); v SL 1986 (2); *v A 1980 (2) 1985 (3); v NZ 1980 (1); v P 1984 (1)*

Yadav, V. S. 1: v Z 1992

Yajurvindra Singh 4: v E 1976 (2); v A 1979 (1); *v E 1979 (1)*

Yashpal Sharma 37: v E 1979 (1) 1981 (2); v A 1979 (6); v WI 1983 (1); v P 1979 (6) 1983 (3); v SL 1982 (1); *v E 1979 (3) 1982 (3); v A 1980 (3); v WI 1982 (5); v NZ 1980 (1); v P 1982 (2)*

Yograj Singh 1: *v NZ 1980*

Note: Hafeez, on going later to Oxford University, took his correct name, Kardar.

PAKISTAN

Number of Test cricketers: 152

Aamer Malik 14: v E 1987 (2); v A 1988 (1) 1994 (1); v WI 1990 (1); v In 1989 (4); *v A 1989 (2); v WI 1987 (1); v NZ 1988 (2)*

Aamir Nazir 6: v SL 1995 (1); *v SA 1994 (1); v WI 1992 (1); v NZ 1993 (1); v Z 1994 (2)*

Aamir Sohail 41: v A 1994 (3); v SA 1997 (1); v WI 1997 (3); v SL 1995 (3); v Z 1993 (3) 1996 (2); *v E 1992 (5) 1996 (2); v A 1995 (3); v SA 1994 (1) 1997 (3); v WI 1992 (2); v NZ 1992 (1) 1993 (3) 1995 (1); v SL 1994 (2); v Z 1994 (3)*

Abdul Kadir 4: v A 1964 (1); *v A 1964 (1); v NZ 1964 (2)*

Abdul Qadir 67: v E 1977 (3) 1983 (3) 1987 (3); v A 1982 (3) 1988 (3); v WI 1980 (2) 1986 (3) 1990 (2); v NZ 1984 (3) 1990 (2); v In 1982 (5) 1984 (1) 1989 (4); v SL 1985 (3); *v E 1982 (3) 1987 (4); v A 1983 (5); v WI 1987 (3); v NZ 1984 (2) 1988 (2); v In 1979 (3) 1986 (3); v SL 1985 (2)*

Afaq Hussain 2: v E 1961 (1); *v A 1964 (1)*

Aftab Baloch 2: v WI 1974 (1); v NZ 1969 (1)

Aftab Gul 6: v E 1968 (2); v NZ 1969 (1); *v E 1971 (3)*

Agha Saadat Ali 1: v NZ 1955

Agha Zahid 1: v WI 1974

Akram Raza 9: v A 1994 (2); v WI 1990 (1); v In 1989 (1); v SL 1991 (1); *v NZ 1993 (2); v SL 1994 (1); v Z 1994 (1)*

Ali Hussain Rizvi 1: v SA 1997

Alim-ud-Din 25: v E 1961 (2); v A 1956 (1) 1959 (1); v WI 1958 (1); v NZ 1955 (3); v In 1954 (5); *v E 1954 (3) 1962 (3); v WI 1957 (5); v In 1960 (1)*

Ali Naqvi 5: v SA 1997 (3); *v Z 1997 (2)*

Amir Elahi 5: *v In 1952 (5)*

Anil Dalpat 9: v E 1983 (3); v NZ 1984 (3); *v NZ 1984 (3)*

Anwar Hussain 4: *v In 1952 (4)*

Anwar Khan 1: *v In 1978*

Aqib Javed 21: v A 1994 (1); v NZ 1990 (3); v SL 1991 (3) 1995 (3); *v E 1992 (5); v A 1989 (1); v SA 1994 (1); v NZ 1988 (1) 1992 (1); v Z 1994 (2)*

Arif Butt 3: *v A 1964 (1); v NZ 1964 (2)*

Arshad Khan 1: v WI 1997

Ashfaq Ahmed 1: v Z 1993

Ashraf Ali 8: v E 1987 (3); v In 1984 (2); v SL 1981 (2) 1985 (1)

Asif Iqbal 58: v E 1968 (3) 1972 (3); v A 1964 (1); v WI 1974 (2); v NZ 1964 (3) 1969 (3) 1976 (3); v In 1978 (3); *v E 1967 (3) 1971 (3) 1974 (3); v A 1964 (1) 1972 (3) 1976 (3) 1978 (2); v WI 1976 (5); v NZ 1964 (3) 1972 (3) 1978 (2); v In 1979 (6)*

Asif Masood 16: v E 1968 (2) 1972 (1); v WI 1974 (2); v NZ 1969 (1); *v E 1971 (3) 1974 (3); v A 1972 (3) 1976 (1)*

Asif Mujtaba 25: v E 1987 (1); v WI 1986 (2); v Z 1993 (3); *v E 1992 (5) 1996 (2); v SA 1994 (1); v WI 1992 (3); v NZ 1992 (1) 1993 (2); v SL 1994 (2) 1996 (2); v Z 1994 (1)*

Ata-ur-Rehman 13: v SL 1995 (1); v Z 1993 (3); *v E 1992 (1) 1996 (2); v WI 1992 (3); v NZ 1993 (2) 1995 (1)*

Atif Rauf 1: *v NZ 1993*

Azam Khan 1: v Z 1996

Azeem Hafeez 18: v E 1983 (2); v NZ 1984 (3); v In 1984 (2); *v A 1983 (5); v NZ 1984 (3); v In 1983 (3)*

Azhar Khan 1: v A 1979

Azhar Mahmood 11: v SA 1997 (3); v WI 1997 (3); *v SA 1997 (3); v Z 1997 (2)*

Azmat Rana 1: v A 1979

Basit Ali 19: v A 1994 (2); v SL 1995 (1); v Z 1993 (3); *v A 1995 (3); v WI 1992 (3); v NZ 1993 (3) 1995 (1); v SL 1994 (2); v Z 1994 (1)*

Burki, J. 25: v E 1961 (3); v A 1964 (1); v NZ 1964 (3) 1969 (1); *v E 1962 (5) 1967 (3); v A 1964 (1); v NZ 1964 (3); v In 1960 (5)*

D'Souza, A. 6: v E 1961 (2); v WI 1958 (1); *v E 1962 (3)*

Ehtesham-ud-Din 5: v A 1979 (1); *v E 1982 (1); v In 1979 (3)*

Farooq Hamid 1: *v A 1964*
Farrukh Zaman 1: v NZ 1976
Fazal Mahmood 34: v E 1961 (1); v A 1956 (1) 1959 (2); v WI 1958 (3); v NZ 1955 (2); v In 1954 (4); *v E 1954 (4) 1962 (2); v WI 1957 (5); v In 1952 (5) 1960 (5)*
Fazl-e-Akbar 1: *v SA 1997*

Ghazali, M. E. Z. 2: *v E 1954 (2)*
Ghulam Abbas 1: *v E 1967*
Gul Mohomed 1: v A 1956

Hanif Mohammad 55: v E 1961 (3) 1968 (3); v A 1956 (1) 1959 (3) 1964 (1); v WI 1958 (1); v NZ 1955 (3) 1964 (3) 1969 (1); v In 1954 (5); *v E 1954 (4) 1962 (5) 1967 (3); v A 1964 (1); v WI 1957 (5); v NZ 1964 (3); v In 1952 (5) 1960 (5)*
Haroon Rashid 23: v E 1977 (3); v A 1979 (2) 1982 (3); v In 1982 (1); v SL 1981 (2); *v E 1978 (3) 1982 (1); v A 1976 (1) 1978 (1); v WI 1976 (5); v NZ 1978 (1)*
Hasan Raza 1: v Z 1996
Haseeb Ahsan 12: v E 1961 (2); v A 1959 (1); v WI 1958 (1); *v WI 1957 (3); v In 1960 (5)*

Ibadulla, K. 4: v A 1964 (1); *v E 1967 (2); v NZ 1964 (1)*
Ijaz Ahmed, sen. 46: v E 1987 (3); v A 1988 (3) 1994 (1); v SA 1997 (3); v WI 1990 (3) 1997 (3); v NZ 1996 (2); v Z 1996 (2); *v E 1987 (4) 1996 (3); v A 1989 (3) 1995 (2); v SA 1994 (1) 1997 (3); v WI 1987 (2); v NZ 1995 (1); v In 1986 (1); v SL 1996 (2); v Z 1994 (3) 1997 (1)*
Ijaz Ahmed, jun. 2: v SL 1995 (2)
Ijaz Butt 8: v A 1959 (2); v WI 1958 (3); *v E 1962 (3)*
Ijaz Faqih 5: v WI 1980 (1); *v A 1981 (1); v WI 1987 (2); v In 1986 (1)*
Imran Khan 88: v A 1979 (2) 1982 (3); v WI 1980 (4) 1986 (3) 1990 (3); v NZ 1976 (3); v In 1978 (3) 1982 (6) 1989 (4); v SL 1981 (1) 1985 (3) 1991 (3); *v E 1971 (1) 1974 (3) 1982 (3) 1987 (5); v A 1976 (3) 1978 (2) 1981 (3) 1983 (2) 1989 (3); v WI 1976 (5) 1987 (3); v NZ 1978 (2) 1988 (2); v In 1979 (5) 1986 (5); v SL 1985 (3)*
Imtiaz Ahmed 41: v E 1961 (3); v A 1956 (1) 1959 (3); v WI 1958 (3); v NZ 1955 (3); v In 1954 (5); *v E 1954 (4) 1962 (4); v WI 1957 (5); v In 1952 (5) 1960 (5)*
Intikhab Alam 47: v E 1961 (2) 1968 (3) 1972 (3); v A 1959 (1) 1964 (1); v WI 1974 (2); v NZ 1964 (3) 1969 (3) 1976 (3); *v E 1962 (3) 1967 (3) 1971 (3) 1974 (3); v A 1964 (1) 1972 (3); v WI 1976 (1); v NZ 1964 (3) 1972 (3); v In 1960 (3)*
Inzamam-ul-Haq 47: v A 1994 (3); v SA 1997 (3); v WI 1997 (3); v NZ 1996 (2); v SL 1995 (3); v Z 1993 (3); *v E 1992 (4) 1996 (3); v A 1995 (3); v SA 1994 (1) 1997 (2); v WI 1992 (3); v NZ 1992 (1) 1993 (3) 1995 (1); v SL 1994 (2) 1996 (2); v Z 1994 (3) 1997 (2)*
Iqbal Qasim 50: v E 1977 (3) 1987 (3); v A 1979 (3) 1982 (2) 1988 (3); v WI 1980 (4); v NZ 1984 (3); v In 1978 (3) 1982 (2); v SL 1981 (3); *v E 1978 (3); v A 1976 (3) 1981 (2); v WI 1976 (2); v NZ 1984 (1); v In 1979 (6) 1983 (1) 1986 (3)*
Israr Ali 4: v A 1959 (2); *v In 1952 (2)*

Jalal-ud-Din 6: v A 1982 (1); v In 1982 (2) 1984 (2); v SL 1985 (1)
Javed Akhtar 1: *v E 1962*
Javed Miandad 124: v E 1977 (3) 1987 (3); v A 1979 (3) 1982 (3) 1988 (3); v WI 1980 (4) 1986 (3) 1990 (2); v NZ 1976 (3) 1984 (3) 1990 (3); v In 1978 (3) 1982 (6) 1984 (2) 1989 (4); v SL 1981 (3) 1985 (3) 1991 (3); v Z 1993 (3); *v E 1978 (3) 1982 (3) 1987 (5) 1992 (5); v A 1976 (3) 1978 (2) 1981 (3) 1983 (5) 1989 (3); v WI 1976 (1) 1987 (3) 1992 (3); v NZ 1978 (3) 1984 (3) 1988 (2) 1992 (1); v In 1979 (6) 1983 (3) 1986 (4); v SL 1985 (3)*

Kabir Khan 4: *v SA 1994 (1); v SL 1994 (1); v Z 1994 (2)*
Kardar, A. H. 23: v A 1956 (1); v NZ 1955 (3); v In 1954 (5); *v E 1954 (4); v WI 1957 (5); v In 1952 (5)*
Khalid Hassan 1: *v E 1954*
Khalid Wazir 2: *v E 1954 (2)*
Khan Mohammad 13: v A 1956 (1); v NZ 1955 (3); v In 1954 (4); *v E 1954 (2); v WI 1957 (2); v In 1952 (1)*

Liaqat Ali 5: v E 1977 (2); v WI 1974 (1); *v E 1978 (2)*

Mahmood Hussain 27: v E 1961 (1); v WI 1958 (3); v NZ 1955 (1); v In 1954 (5); *v E 1954* (2)
1962 (3); v WI 1957 (3); v In 1952 (4) 1960 (5)

Majid Khan 63: v E 1968 (3) 1972 (3); v A 1964 (1) 1979 (3); v WI 1974 (2) 1980 (4); v NZ
1964 (3) 1976 (3); v In 1978 (3) 1982 (1); v SL 1981 (1); *v E 1967 (3) 1971 (2) 1974 (3)*
1982 (1); v A 1972 (3) 1976 (3) 1978 (2) 1981 (3); v WI 1976 (5); v NZ 1972 (3) 1978 (2); v In
1979 (6)

Mansoor Akhtar 19: v A 1982 (3); v WI 1980 (2); v In 1982 (3); v SL 1981 (1); *v E 1982 (3)*
1987 (5); v A 1981 (1) 1989 (1)

Manzoor Elahi 6: v NZ 1984 (1); v In 1984 (1); *v In 1986 (2); v Z 1994 (2)*

Maqsood Ahmed 16: v NZ 1955 (2); v In 1954 (5); *v E 1954 (4); v In 1952 (5)*

Masood Anwar 1: v WI 1990

Mathias, Wallis 21: v E 1961 (1); v A 1956 (1) 1959 (2); v WI 1958 (3); v NZ 1955 (1); *v E*
1962 (3); v WI 1957 (5); v In 1960 (5)

Miran Bux 2: v In 1954 (2)

Mohammad Akram 6: v NZ 1996 (1); v SL 1995 (2); *v E 1996 (1); v A 1995 (2)*

Mohammad Aslam 1: *v E 1954*

Mohammad Farooq 7: v NZ 1964 (3); *v E 1962 (2); v In 1960 (2)*

Mohammad Hussain 1: v Z 1996 (1)

Mohammad Ilyas 10: v E 1968 (2); v NZ 1964 (3); *v E 1967 (1); v A 1964 (1); v NZ 1964 (3)*

Mohammad Munaf 4: v E 1961 (2); v A 1959 (2)

Mohammad Nazir 14: v E 1972 (1); v WI 1980 (4); v NZ 1969 (3); *v A 1983 (3); v In 1983 (3)*

Mohammad Ramzan 1: v SA 1997

Mohammad Wasim 10: v SA 1997 (2); v WI 1997 (3); v NZ 1996 (2); *v SA 1997 (2); v Z 1997 (1)*

Mohammad Zahid 3: v NZ 1996 (1); *v SL 1996 (2)*

Mohsin Kamal 9: v E 1983 (1); v A 1994 (2); v SL 1985 (1); *v E 1987 (4); v SL 1985 (1)*

Mohsin Khan 48: v E 1977 (1) 1983 (3); v A 1982 (3); v WI 1986 (3); v NZ 1984 (2); v In 1982 (6)
1984 (2); v SL 1981 (2) 1985 (2); *v E 1978 (3) 1982 (3); v A 1978 (1) 1981 (2) 1983 (5); v NZ*
1978 (1) 1984 (3); v In 1983 (3); v SL 1985 (3)

Moin Khan 37: v A 1994 (1); v SA 1997 (3); v WI 1990 (2) 1997 (3); v NZ 1996 (2); v SL 1991 (3)
1995 (3); v Z 1996 (2); *v E 1992 (4) 1996 (2); v A 1995 (2); v SA 1994 (1) 1997 (3); v WI*
1992 (2); v SL 1996 (2); v Z 1997 (2)

Mudassar Nazar 76: v E 1977 (3) 1983 (1) 1987 (3); v A 1979 (3) 1982 (3) 1988 (3); v WI 1986 (2);
v NZ 1984 (3); v In 1978 (2) 1982 (6) 1984 (2); v SL 1981 (1) 1985 (3) ; *v E 1978 (3) 1982 (3)*
1987 (5); v A 1976 (1) 1978 (1) 1981 (3) 1983 (5); v WI 1987 (3); v NZ 1978 (1) 1984 (3)
1988 (2); v In 1979 (5) 1983 (3); v SL 1985 (3)

Mufasir-ul-Haq 1: *v NZ 1964*

Munir Malik 3: v A 1959 (1); *v E 1962 (2)*

Mushtaq Ahmed 38: v A 1994 (3); v SA 1997 (3); v WI 1990 (2) 1997 (3); v NZ 1996 (2); v Z
1993 (2); *v E 1992 (5) 1996 (3); v A 1989 (1) 1995 (2); v SA 1997 (3); v WI 1992 (1); v NZ*
1992 (1) 1993 (1) 1995 (1); v SL 1994 (2) 1996 (2); v Z 1997 (1)

Mushtaq Mohammad 57: v E 1961 (3) 1968 (3) 1972 (3); v WI 1958 (1) 1974 (2); v NZ 1969 (2)
1976 (3); v In 1978 (3); *v E 1962 (5) 1967 (3) 1971 (3) 1974 (3); v A 1972 (3) 1976 (3) 1978 (2);*
v WI 1976 (5); v NZ 1972 (2) 1978 (3); v In 1960 (5)

Nadeem Abbasi 3: v In 1989 (3)

Nadeem Ghauri 1: *v A 1989*

Nadeem Khan 1: *v WI 1992*

Nasim-ul-Ghani 29: v E 1961 (2); v A 1959 (2) 1964 (1); v WI 1958 (3); *v E 1962 (5) 1967 (2); v A*
1964 (1) 1972 (1); v WI 1957 (5); v NZ 1964 (3); v In 1960 (4)

Naushad Ali 6: v NZ 1964 (3); *v NZ 1964 (3)*

Naved Anjum 2: v NZ 1990 (1); v In 1989 (1)

Nazar Mohammad 5: v In 1952 (5)

Nazir Junior (*see* Mohammad Nazir)

Niaz Ahmed 2: v E 1968 (1); *v E 1967 (1)*

Pervez Sajjad 19: v E 1968 (1) 1972 (2); v A 1964 (1); v NZ 1964 (3) 1969 (3); *v E 1971 (3); v NZ*
1964 (3) 1972 (3)

Qasim Omar 26: v E 1983 (3); v WI 1986 (3); v NZ 1984 (3); v In 1984 (2); v SL 1985 (3); *v A*
1983 (5); v NZ 1984 (3); v In 1983 (1); v SL 1985 (3)

Ramiz Raja 57: v E 1983 (2) 1987 (3); v A 1988 (3); v WI 1986 (3) 1990 (2); v NZ 1990 (3); v In 1989 (4); v SL 1985 (1) 1991 (3) 1995 (3); *v E 1987 (2) 1992 (5); v A 1989 (2) 1995 (3); v WI 1987 (3) 1992 (3); v NZ 1992 (1) 1995 (1); v In 1986 (5); v SL 1985 (3) 1996 (2)*

Rashid Khan 4: v SL 1981 (2); *v A 1983 (1); v NZ 1984 (1)*

Rashid Latif 22: v A 1994 (2); v Z 1993 (3); *v E 1992 (1) 1996 (1); v A 1995 (1); v SA 1997 (1); v WI 1992 (1); v NZ 1992 (1) 1993 (3) 1995 (1); v SL 1994 (2); v Z 1994 (3) 1997 (2)*

Rehman, S. F. 1: *v WI 1957*

Rizwan-uz-Zaman 11: v WI 1986 (1); v SL 1981 (2); *v A 1981 (1); v NZ 1988 (2); v In 1986 (5)*

Sadiq Mohammad 41: v E 1972 (3) 1977 (2); v WI 1974 (1) 1980 (3); v NZ 1969 (3) 1976 (3); v In 1978 (1); *v E 1971 (3) 1974 (3) 1978 (3); v A 1972 (3) 1976 (2); v WI 1976 (5); v NZ 1972 (3); v In 1979 (3)*

Saeed Ahmed 41: v E 1961 (3) 1968 (3); v A 1959 (3) 1964 (1); v WI 1958 (3); v NZ 1964 (3); *v E 1962 (5) 1967 (3) 1971 (1); v A 1964 (1) 1972 (2); v WI 1957 (5); v NZ 1964 (3); v In 1960 (5)*

Saeed Anwar 32: v A 1994 (3); v SA 1997 (3); v WI 1990 (1) 1997 (3); v NZ 1996 (2); v SL 1995 (2); v Z 1996 (2); *v E 1996 (3); v SA 1994 (1) 1997 (3); v NZ 1993 (3); v SL 1994 (2); v Z 1994 (2) 1997 (2)*

Salah-ud-Din 5: v E 1968 (1); v NZ 1964 (3) 1969 (1)

Saleem Jaffer 14: v E 1987 (1); v A 1988 (2); v WI 1986 (3); v NZ 1990 (2); v In 1989 (3); v SL 1991 (2); *v WI 1987 (1); v NZ 1988 (2); v In 1986 (2)*

Salim Altaf 21: v E 1972 (3); v NZ 1969 (2); v In 1978 (1); *v E 1967 (2) 1971 (2); v A 1972 (3) 1976 (2); v WI 1976 (3); v NZ 1972 (3)*

Salim Elahi 4: *v A 1995 (2); v SL 1996 (2)*

Salim Malik 96: v E 1983 (3) 1987 (3); v A 1988 (3) 1994 (3); v WI 1986 (1) 1990 (3); v NZ 1984 (3) 1990 (3) 1996 (2); v In 1982 (6) 1984 (2) 1989 (4); v SL 1981 (2) 1985 (3) 1991 (3); v Z 1996 (2); *v E 1987 (5) 1992 (5) 1996 (3); v A 1983 (3) 1989 (1) 1995 (2); v SA 1994 (1); v WI 1987 (3); v NZ 1984 (3) 1988 (2) 1992 (1) 1993 (3) 1995 (1); v In 1983 (2) 1986 (5); v SL 1985 (3) 1994 (2) 1996 (2); v Z 1994 (3)*

Salim Yousuf 32: v A 1988 (3); v WI 1986 (3) 1990 (1); v NZ 1990 (3); v In 1989 (1); v SL 1981 (1) 1985 (2); *v E 1987 (5); v A 1989 (2); v NZ 1988 (2); v In 1986 (5)*

Saqlain Mushtaq 15: v SA 1997 (3); v WI 1997 (1); v NZ 1996 (1); v SL 1995 (2); v Z 1996 (2); *v A 1995 (2); v SA 1997 (1); v SL 1996 (2); v Z 1997 (1)*

Sarfraz Nawaz 55: v E 1968 (1) 1972 (2) 1977 (2) 1983 (3); v A 1979 (3); v WI 1974 (2) 1980 (2); v NZ 1976 (3); v In 1978 (3) 1982 (6); *v E 1974 (3) 1978 (2) 1982 (1); v A 1972 (2) 1976 (2) 1978 (2) 1981 (3) 1983 (3); v WI 1976 (4); v NZ 1972 (3) 1978 (3)*

Shadab Kabir 3: v Z 1996 (1); *v E 1996 (2)*

Shafiq Ahmed 6: v E 1977 (3); v WI 1980 (2); *v E 1974 (1)*

Shafqat Rana 5: v E 1968 (2); v A 1964 (1); v NZ 1969 (2)

Shahid Israr 1: v NZ 1976

Shahid Mahboob 1: v In 1989

Shahid Mahmood 1: *v E 1962*

Shahid Nazir 7: v WI 1997 (1); v NZ 1996 (2); v Z 1996 (2); *v SL 1996 (2)*

Shahid Saeed 1: v In 1989

Shakeel Ahmed 3: *v WI 1992 (1); v Z 1994 (2)*

Sharpe, D. 3: v A 1959 (3)

Shoaib Akhtar 5: v WI 1997 (1); *v SA 1997 (3); v Z 1997 (1)*

Shoaib Mohammad 45: v E 1983 (1) 1987 (1); v A 1988 (3); v WI 1990 (3); v NZ 1984 (1) 1990 (3); v In 1989 (4); v SL 1985 (1) 1991 (3) 1995 (3); v Z 1993 (3); *v E 1987 (4) 1992 (1); v A 1989 (3); v WI 1987 (3); v NZ 1984 (1) 1988 (2); v In 1983 (2) 1986 (3)*

Shuja-ud-Din 19: v E 1961 (2); v A 1959 (3); v WI 1958 (3); v NZ 1955 (3); v In 1954 (5); *v E 1954 (3)*

Sikander Bakht 26: v E 1977 (2); v WI 1980 (1); v NZ 1976 (1); v In 1978 (2) 1982 (1); *v E 1978 (3) 1982 (2); v A 1978 (2) 1981 (3); v WI 1976 (1); v NZ 1978 (3); v In 1979 (5)*

Tahir Naqqash 15: v A 1982 (3); v In 1982 (2); v SL 1981 (3); *v E 1982 (2); v A 1983 (1); v NZ 1984 (1); v In 1983 (3)*

Talat Ali 10: v E 1972 (3); *v E 1978 (2); v A 1972 (1); v NZ 1972 (1) 1978 (3)*

Taslim Arif 6: v A 1979 (3); v WI 1980 (2); *v In 1979 (1)*

Tauseef Ahmed 34: v E 1983 (2) 1987 (2); v A 1979 (3) 1988 (3); v WI 1986 (3); v NZ 1984 (1) 1990 (2); v In 1984 (1); v SL 1981 (3) 1985 (1); v Z 1993 (1); *v E 1987 (2); v A 1989 (3); v NZ 1988 (1); v In 1986 (4); v SL 1985 (2)*

Waqar Hassan 21: v A 1956 (1) 1959 (1); v WI 1958 (1); v NZ 1955 (3); v In 1954 (5); *v E 1954 (4); v WI 1957 (1); v In 1952 (5)*

Waqar Younis 53: v A 1994 (2); v SA 1997 (2); v WI 1990 (3) 1997 (2); v NZ 1990 (3) 1996 (1); v In 1989 (2); v SL 1991 (3) 1995 (1); v Z 1993 (3) 1996 (2); *v E 1992 (5) 1996 (3); v A 1989 (3) 1995 (3); v SA 1997 (3); v WI 1992 (3); v NZ 1992 (1) 1993 (3) 1995 (1); v SL 1994 (2); v Z 1997 (2)*

Wasim Akram 79: v E 1987 (2); v A 1994 (2); v SA 1997 (2); v WI 1986 (2) 1990 (3) 1997 (3); v NZ 1990 (2); v In 1989 (4); v SL 1985 (3) 1991 (3) 1995 (2); v Z 1993 (2) 1996 (2); *v E 1987 (5) 1992 (4) 1996 (3); v A 1989 (3) 1995 (3); v SA 1994 (1) 1997 (1); v WI 1987 (3) 1992 (3); v NZ 1984 (2) 1992 (1) 1993 (3) 1995 (1); v In 1986 (5); v SL 1985 (3) 1994 (2); v Z 1994 (3) 1997 (1)*

Wasim Bari 81: v E 1968 (3) 1972 (3) 1977 (3); v A 1982 (3); v WI 1974 (2) 1980 (2); v NZ 1969 (3) 1976 (2); v In 1978 (3) 1982 (6); *v E 1967 (3) 1971 (3) 1974 (3) 1978 (3) 1982 (3); v A 1972 (3) 1976 (3) 1978 (2) 1981 (3) 1983 (5); v WI 1976 (5); v NZ 1972 (3) 1978 (3); v In 1979 (6) 1983 (3)*

Wasim Raja 57: v E 1972 (1) 1977 (3) 1983 (3); v A 1979 (3); v WI 1974 (2) 1980 (4); v NZ 1976 (1) 1984 (1); v In 1982 (1) 1984 (1); v SL 1981 (3); *v E 1974 (2) 1978 (3) 1982 (1); v A 1978 (1) 1981 (3) 1983 (2); v WI 1976 (5); v NZ 1972 (3) 1978 (3) 1984 (2); v In 1979 (6) 1983 (3)*

Wazir Mohammad 20: v A 1956 (1) 1959 (1); v WI 1958 (1); v NZ 1955 (2); v In 1954 (5); *v E 1954 (2); v WI 1957 (5); v In 1952 (1)*

Younis Ahmed 4: v NZ 1969 (2); *v In 1986 (2)*
Yousuf Youhana 3: *v SA 1997 (1); v Z 1997 (2)*

Zaheer Abbas 78: v E 1972 (2) 1983 (3); v A 1979 (2) 1982 (3); v WI 1974 (2) 1980 (3); v NZ 1969 (1) 1976 (3) 1984 (3); v In 1978 (3) 1982 (6) 1984 (3); v SL 1981 (1) 1985 (2); *v E 1971 (3) 1974 (3) 1982 (3); v A 1972 (3) 1976 (3) 1978 (2) 1981 (2) 1983 (5); v WI 1976 (3); v NZ 1972 (3) 1978 (2) 1984 (2); v In 1979 (5) 1983 (3)*

Zahid Fazal 9: v A 1994 (2); v WI 1990 (3); v SL 1991 (3) 1995 (1)
Zahoor Elahi 2: v NZ 1996 (2)
Zakir Khan 2: v In 1989 (1); *v SL 1985 (1)*
Zulfiqar Ahmed 9: v A 1956 (1); v NZ 1955 (3); *v E 1954 (2); v In 1952 (3)*
Zulqarnain 3: *v SL 1985 (3)*

SRI LANKA

Number of Test cricketers: 73

Ahangama, F. S. 3: v In 1985 (3)
Amalean, K. N. 2: v P 1985 (1); *v A 1987 (1)*
Amerasinghe, A. M. J. G. 2: v NZ 1983 (2)
Anurasiri, S. D. 18: v A 1992 (3); v WI 1993 (1); v NZ 1986 (1) 1992 (2); v P 1985 (2); v Z 1997 (1); *v E 1991 (1); v In 1986 (1) 1993 (3); v P 1991 (3)*
Arnold, R. P. 3: v P 1996 (2); *v WI 1996 (1)*
Atapattu, M. S. 20: v A 1992 (1); v NZ 1997 (3); v In 1997 (2); v P 1996 (2); v Z 1997 (2); *v E 1998 (1); v SA 1997 (2); v WI 1996 (1); v NZ 1996 (1); v In 1990 (1) 1993 (1) 1997 (3)*

Bandara, C. M. 1: v NZ 1997
Bandaratilleke, M. R. C. N. 3: v NZ 1997 (3)

Dassanayake, P. B. 11: v SA 1993 (3); v WI 1993 (1); v P 1994 (2); *v In 1993 (3); v Z 1994 (2)*
de Alwis, R. G. 11: v A 1982 (1); v NZ 1983 (2); v P 1985 (2); *v A 1987 (1); v NZ 1982 (1); v In 1986 (3)*
de Mel, A. L. F. 17: v E 1981 (1); v A 1982 (1); v In 1985 (3); v P 1985 (3); *v E 1984 (1); v In 1982 (1) 1986 (1); v P 1981 (3) 1985 (3)*
de Silva, A. M. 3: v E 1992 (1); v In 1993 (2)

de Silva, D. S. 12: v E 1981 (1); v A 1982 (1); v NZ 1983 (3); *v E 1984 (1); v NZ 1982 (2); v In 1982 (1); v P 1981 (3)*

de Silva, E. A. R. 10: v In 1985 (1); v P 1985 (1); *v A 1989 (2); v NZ 1990 (3); v In 1986 (3)*

de Silva, G. R. A. 4: v E 1981 (1); *v In 1982 (1); v P 1981 (2)*

de Silva, K. S. C. 6: v In 1997 (1); v P 1996 (1); *v WI 1996 (2); v NZ 1996 (1); v In 1997 (1)*

de Silva, P. A. 74: v E 1992 (1); v A 1992 (3); v SA 1993 (3); v WI 1993 (1); v NZ 1992 (2) 1997 (3); v In 1985 (3) 1993 (3) 1997 (2); v P 1985 (3) 1994 (2) 1996 (2); v Z 1996 (2) 1997 (2); *v E 1984 (1) 1988 (1) 1991 (1) 1998 (1); v A 1987 (1) 1989 (2) 1995 (3); v SA 1997 (2); v WI 1996 (2); v NZ 1990 (3) 1994 (2) 1996 (2); v In 1986 (3) 1990 (1) 1993 (3) 1997 (3); v P 1985 (3) 1991 (3) 1995 (2); v Z 1994 (3)*

de Silva, S. K. L. 3: *v In 1997 (3)*

Dharmasena, H. D. P. K. 20: v SA 1993 (2); v NZ 1997 (2); v P 1994 (2) 1996 (1); v Z 1996 (1); *v E 1998 (1); v A 1995 (2); v WI 1996 (2); v NZ 1996 (1); v In 1997 (2); v P 1995 (2); v Z 1994 (2)*

Dias, R. L. 20: v E 1981 (1); v A 1982 (1); v NZ 1983 (2) 1986 (1); v In 1985 (3); v P 1985 (1); *v E 1984 (1); v In 1982 (1) 1986 (3); v P 1981 (3) 1985 (3)*

Dunusinghe, C. I. 5: *v NZ 1994 (2); v P 1995 (3)*

Fernando, E. R. N. S. 5: v A 1982 (1); v NZ 1983 (2); *v NZ 1982 (2)*

Goonatillake, H. M. 5: v E 1981 (1); *v In 1982 (1); v P 1981 (3)*

Gunasekera, Y. 2: *v NZ 1982 (2)*

Guneratne, R. P. W. 1: v A 1982

Gurusinha, A. P. 41: v E 1992 (1); v A 1992 (3); v SA 1993 (1); v NZ 1986 (1) 1992 (2); v In 1993 (3); v P 1985 (2) 1994 (1); v Z 1996 (2); *v E 1991 (1); v A 1989 (2) 1995 (3); v NZ 1990 (3) 1994 (2); v In 1986 (3) 1990 (1); v P 1985 (1) 1991 (3) 1995 (3); v Z 1994 (3)*

Hathurusinghe, U. C. 24: v E 1992 (1); v A 1992 (3); v SA 1993 (3); v NZ 1992 (2); v In 1993 (3); *v E 1991 (1); v A 1995 (3); v NZ 1990 (2); v P 1991 (3) 1995 (3)*

Jayasekera, R. S. A. 1: *v P 1981*

Jayasuriya S. T. 38: v E 1992 (1); v A 1992 (2); v SA 1993 (2); v WI 1993 (1); v NZ 1997 (3); v In 1993 (1) 1997 (2); v P 1994 (1) 1996 (2); v Z 1996 (2) 1997 (2); *v E 1991 (1) 1998 (1); v A 1995 (1); v SA 1997 (2); v WI 1996 (2); v NZ 1990 (2) 1996 (2); v In 1993 (1) 1997 (3); v P 1991 (3); v Z 1994 (1)*

Jayawardene, D. P. M. D. 6: v NZ 1997 (3); v In 1997 (2); *v E 1998 (1)*

Jeganathan, S. 2: *v NZ 1982 (2)*

John, V. B. 6: v NZ 1983 (3); *v E 1984 (1); v NZ 1982 (2)*

Jurangpathy, B. R. 2: v In 1985 (1); *v In 1986 (1)*

Kalpage, R. S. 10: v SA 1993 (1); v WI 1993 (1); v NZ 1997 (1); v In 1993 (1); v P 1994 (1) 1996 (1); *v In 1993 (3); v Z 1994 (1)*

Kaluperuma, L. W. 2: v E 1981 (1); *v P 1981 (1)*

Kaluperuma, S. M. S. 4: v NZ 1983 (3); *v A 1987 (1)*

Kaluwitharana, R. S. 24: v A 1992 (2); v NZ 1997 (3); v In 1993 (1) 1997 (2); v NZ 1996 (2); v Z 1996 (2) 1997 (2); *v E 1998 (1); A 1995 (3); v SA 1997 (2); v WI 1996 (2); v NZ 1996 (2)*

Kuruppu, D. S. B. P. 4: v NZ 1986 (1); *v E 1988 (1) 1991 (1); v A 1987 (1)*

Kuruppuarachchi, A. K. 2: v NZ 1986 (1); v P 1985 (1)

Labrooy, G. F. 9: *v E 1988 (1); v A 1987 (1) 1989 (2); v NZ 1990 (3); v In 1986 (1) 1990 (1)*

Liyanage, D. K. 8: v A 1992 (2); v SA 1993 (1); v NZ 1992 (2); v In 1993 (2); *v In 1993 (1)*

Madugalle, R. S. 21: v E 1981 (1); v A 1982 (1); v NZ 1983 (3) 1986 (1); v In 1985 (3); *v E 1984 (1) 1988 (1); v A 1987 (1); v NZ 1982 (2); v In 1982 (1); v P 1981 (3) 1985 (3)*

Madurasinghe, A. W. R. 3: v A 1992 (1); *v E 1988 (1); v In 1990 (1)*

Mahanama, R. S. 52: v E 1992 (1); v A 1992 (3); v SA 1993 (3); v WI 1993 (1); v NZ 1986 (1) 1992 (2); v In 1993 (3) 1997 (2); v P 1985 (2) 1994 (2); v Z 1996 (2) 1997 (2); *v E 1991 (1); v A 1987 (1) 1989 (2) 1995 (2); v SA 1997 (2); v WI 1996 (2); v NZ 1990 (1) 1996 (2); v In 1990 (1) 1993 (3) 1997 (3); v P 1991 (2) 1995 (3); v Z 1994 (3)*

Mendis, L. R. D. 24: v E 1981 (1); v A 1982 (1); v NZ 1983 (3) 1986 (1); v In 1985 (3); v P 1985 (3); *v E 1984 (1) 1988 (1); v In 1982 (1) 1986 (3); v P 1981 (3) 1985 (3)*

Muralitharan, M. 42: v E 1992 (1); v A 1992 (2); v SA 1993 (3); v WI 1993 (1); v NZ 1992 (1) 1997 (3); v In 1993 (2) 1997 (2); v P 1994 (1) 1996 (1); v Z 1996 (2) 1997 (2); *v E 1998 (1); v A 1995 (2); v SA 1997 (2); v WI 1996 (2); v NZ 1994 (2) 1996 (2); v In 1993 (3) 1997 (2); v P 1995 (3); v Z 1994 (2)*

Perera, A. S. A. 1: *v E 1998*

Pushpakumara, K. R. 18: v In 1997 (2); v P 1994 (1); v Z 1996 (1) 1997 (2); *v A 1995 (1); v SA 1997 (2); v WI 1996 (2); v NZ 1994 (2); v In 1997 (2); v P 1995 (1); v Z 1994 (2)*

Ramanayake, C. P. H. 18: v E 1992 (1); v A 1992 (3); v SA 1993 (2); v NZ 1992 (1); v In 1993 (1); *v E 1988 (1) 1991 (1); v A 1987 (1) 1989 (2); v NZ 1990 (3); v P 1991 (2)*

Ranasinghe, A. N. 2: *v In 1982 (1); v P 1981 (1)*

Ranatunga, A. 82: v E 1981 (1) 1992 (1); v A 1982 (1) 1992 (3); v SA 1993 (3); v WI 1993 (1); v NZ 1983 (3) 1986 (1) 1992 (2) 1997 (3); v In 1985 (3) 1993 (3) 1997 (2); v P 1985 (3) 1994 (2) 1996 (2); v Z 1996 (2) 1997 (2); *v E 1984 (1) 1988 (1) 1998 (1); v A 1987 (1) 1989 (2) 1995 (2); v SA 1997 (2); v WI 1996 (2); v NZ 1990 (3) 1994 (2) 1996 (2); v In 1982 (1) 1986 (3) 1990 (1) 1993 (3) 1997 (3); v P 1981 (2) 1985 (3) 1991 (3) 1995 (3); v Z 1994 (3)*

Ranatunga, D. 2: *v A 1989 (2)*

Ranatunga, S. 9: v P 1994 (1); *v A 1995 (1); v WI 1996 (1); v NZ 1994 (2); v P 1995 (1); v Z 1994 (3)*

Ratnayake, R. J. 23: v A 1982 (1); v NZ 1983 (1) 1986 (1); v In 1985 (3); v P 1985 (1); *v E 1991 (1); v A 1989 (1); v NZ 1982 (2) 1990 (3); v In 1986 (2) 1990 (1); v P 1985 (3) 1991 (3)*

Ratnayeke, J. R. 22: v NZ 1983 (2) 1986 (1); v P 1985 (3); *v E 1984 (1) 1988 (1); v A 1987 (1) 1989 (2); v NZ 1982 (2); v In 1982 (1) 1986 (3); v P 1981 (2) 1985 (3)*

Samarasekera, M. A. R. 4: *v E 1988 (1); v A 1989 (1); v In 1990 (1); v P 1991 (1)*

Samaraweera, D. P. 7: v WI 1993 (1); v P 1994 (1); *v NZ 1994 (2); v In 1993 (3)*

Senanayake, C. P. 3: *v NZ 1990 (3)*

Silva, K. J. 7: v In 1997 (1); v P 1996 (1); v Z 1996 (2) 1997 (2); *v A 1995 (1); v In 1997 (1)*

Silva, S. A. R. 9: v In 1985 (3); v P 1985 (1); *v E 1984 (1) 1988 (1); v NZ 1982 (1); v P 1985 (2)*

Tillekeratne, H. P. 53: v E 1992 (1); v A 1992 (1); v SA 1993 (3); v WI 1993 (1); v NZ 1992 (2) 1997 (3); v In 1993 (3); v P 1994 (2) 1996 (2); v Z 1996 (2) 1997 (2); *v E 1991 (1) 1998 (1); v A 1989 (1) 1995 (3); v SA 1997 (2); v WI 1996 (1); v NZ 1990 (3) 1994 (2) 1996 (2); v In 1990 (1) 1993 (3) 1997 (3); v P 1991 (3) 1995 (3); v Z 1994 (3)*

Vaas, W. P. U. J. C. 26: v In 1997 (2); v P 1994 (1) 1996 (2); v Z 1996 (2) 1997 (2); *v A 1995 (3); v SA 1997 (1); v NZ 1994 (2) 1996 (2); v In 1997 (3); v P 1995 (3); v Z 1994 (3)*

Warnapura, B. 4: v E 1981 (1); *v In 1982 (1); v P 1981 (2)*

Warnaweera, K. P. J. 10: v E 1992 (1); v NZ 1992 (2); v In 1993 (3); v P 1985 (1) 1994 (1); *v NZ 1990 (1); v In 1990 (1)*

Weerasinghe, C. D. U. S. 1: v In 1985

Wettimuny, M. D. 2: *v NZ 1982 (2)*

Wettimuny, S. 23: v E 1981 (1); v A 1982 (1); v NZ 1983 (3); v In 1985 (3); v P 1985 (3); *v E 1984 (1); v NZ 1982 (2); v In 1986 (3); v P 1981 (3) 1985 (3)*

Wickremasinghe, A. G. D. 3: v NZ 1992 (2); *v A 1989 (1)*

Wickremasinghe, G. P. 31: v A 1992 (1); v SA 1993 (2); v WI 1993 (1); v NZ 1997 (3); v In 1993 (2); v P 1994 (1); *v E 1998 (1); v A 1995 (3); v SA 1997 (2); v NZ 1994 (2) 1996 (1); v In 1993 (3) 1997 (1); v P 1991 (3) 1995 (3); v Z 1994 (2)*

Wijegunawardene, K. I. W. 2: *v E 1991 (1); v P 1991 (1)*

Wijesuriya, R. G. C. E. 4: *v P 1981 (1) 1985 (3)*

Wijetunge, P. K. 1: v SA 1993

Zoysa, D. N. T. 4: v P 1996 (1); *v SA 1997 (1); v NZ 1996 (2)*

ZIMBABWE

Number of Test cricketers: 39

Arnott, K. J. 4: v NZ 1992 (2); v In 1992 (1); *v In 1992 (1)*

Brain, D. H. 9: v NZ 1992 (1); v P 1994 (3); v SL 1994 (2); *v In 1992 (1); v P 1993 (2)*

Brandes, E. A. 9: v E 1996 (1); v NZ 1992 (1); v In 1992 (1); *v NZ 1995 (2); v In 1992 (1); v P 1993 (3)*

Briant, G. A. 1: *v In 1992*

Bruk-Jackson, G. K. 2: *v P 1993 (2)*

Burmester, M. G. 3: v NZ 1992 (2); v In 1992 (1)

Butchart, I. P. 1: v P 1994

Campbell, A. D. R. 30: v E 1996 (2); v SA 1995 (1); v NZ 1992 (2) 1997 (2); v In 1992 (1); v P 1994 (3) 1997 (2); v SL 1994 (3); *v NZ 1995 (2) 1997 (2); v In 1992 (1); v P 1993 (3) 1996 (2); v SL 1996 (2) 1997 (2)*

Carlisle, S. V. 6: v E 1996 (1); v P 1994 (3); *v NZ 1995 (2)*

Crocker, G. J. 3: v NZ 1992 (2); v In 1992 (1)

Dekker, M. H. 14: v E 1996 (1); v SA 1995 (1); v P 1994 (2); v SL 1994 (3); *v P 1993 (3) 1996 (2); v SL 1996 (2)*

Evans, C. N. 1: *v SL 1996*

Flower, A. 30: v E 1996 (2); v SA 1995 (1); v NZ 1992 (2) 1997 (2); v In 1992 (1); v P 1994 (3) 1997 (2); v SL 1994 (3); *v NZ 1995 (2) 1997 (2); v In 1992 (1); v P 1993 (3) 1996 (2); v SL 1996 (2) 1997 (2)*

Flower, G. W. 30: v E 1996 (2); v SA 1995 (1); v NZ 1992 (2) 1997 (2); v In 1992 (1); v P 1994 (3) 1997 (2); v SL 1994 (3); *v NZ 1995 (2) 1997 (2); v In 1992 (1); v P 1993 (3) 1996 (2); v SL 1996 (2) 1997 (2)*

Goodwin, M. W. 6: v P 1997 (2); *v NZ 1997 (2); v SL 1997 (2)*

Houghton, D. L. 22: v E 1996 (2); v SA 1995 (1); v NZ 1992 (2) 1997 (2); v In 1992 (1); v P 1994 (3); v SL 1994 (3); *v NZ 1995 (2); v In 1992 (1); v P 1993 (3) 1996 (2)*

Huckle, A. G. 6: v NZ 1997 (2); v P 1997 (1); *v NZ 1997 (2); v SL 1997 (1)*

James, W. R. 4: v SL 1994 (3); *v P 1993 (1)*

Jarvis, M. P. 5: v NZ 1992 (1); v In 1992 (1); v SL 1994 (3)

Lock, A. C. I. 1: v SA 1995

Madondo, T. N. 2: v P 1997 (2)

Matambanadzo, E. 2: v NZ 1997 (1); *v P 1996 (1)*

Mbangwa, M. 6: v P 1997 (2); *v NZ 1997 (2); v P 1996 (1); v SL 1997 (1)*

Olonga, H. K. 7: v E 1996 (2); v P 1994 (1); *v NZ 1995 (1); v P 1996 (1); v SL 1996 (2)*

Peall, S. G. 4: v SL 1994 (2); *v P 1993 (2)*

Pycroft, A. J. 3: v NZ 1992 (2); v In 1992 (1)

Ranchod, U. 1: *v In 1992*

Rennie, G. J. 7: v NZ 1997 (2); v P 1997 (1); *v NZ 1997 (2); v SL 1997 (2)*

Rennie, J. A. 4: v NZ 1997 (1); v SL 1994 (1); *v P 1993 (2)*

Shah, A. H. 3: v NZ 1992 (1); *v In 1992 (1); v SL 1996 (1)*

Strang, B. C. 13: v E 1996 (1); v SA 1995 (1); v NZ 1997 (2); v P 1994 (2) 1997 (1); *v NZ 1995 (2); v P 1996 (2); v SL 1996 (1) 1997 (1)*

Strang, P. A. 20: v E 1996 (1); v SA 1995 (1); v NZ 1997 (2); v P 1994 (3) 1997 (1); v SL 1994 (1); *v NZ 1995 (2) 1997 (2); v P 1996 (2); v SL 1996 (2) 1997 (2)*

Streak, H. H. 23: v E 1996 (1); v SA 1995 (1); v NZ 1997 (2); v P 1994 (3) 1997 (1); v SL 1994 (3); *v NZ 1995 (2) 1997 (2); v P 1993 (3); v SL 1996 (1) 1997 (2)*

Traicos, A. J. 4: v NZ 1992 (2); v In 1992 (1); *v In 1992 (1)*

Viljoen, D. P. 1: v P 1997

Waller, A. C. 2: v E 1996 (2)

Whittall, A. R. 8: v P 1997 (1); *v NZ 1997 (2); v P 1996 (1); v SL 1996 (2) 1997 (2)*

Whittall, G. J. 25: v E 1996 (2); v SA 1995 (1); v NZ 1997 (2); v P 1994 (3) 1997 (2); v SL 1994 (3); *v NZ 1995 (2) 1997 (2); v P 1993 (3) 1996 (2); v SL 1996 (2) 1997 (1)*

Wishart, C. B. 8: v SA 1995 (1); *v NZ 1995 (1); v P 1996 (2); v SL 1996 (2) 1997 (2)*

TWO COUNTRIES

Fourteen cricketers have appeared for two countries in Test matches, namely:

Amir Elahi, *India and Pakistan.*
J. J. Ferris, *Australia and England.*
S. C. Guillen, *West Indies and NZ.*
Gul Mahomed, *India and Pakistan.*
F. Hearne, *England and South Africa.*
A. H. Kardar, *India and Pakistan.*
W. E. Midwinter, *England and Australia.*

F. Mitchell, *England and South Africa.*
W. L. Murdoch, *Australia and England.*
Nawab of Pataudi, sen., *England and India.*
A. J. Traicos, *South Africa and Zimbabwe.*
A. E. Trott, *Australia and England.*
K. C. Wessels, *Australia and South Africa.*
S. M. J. Woods, *Australia and England*

ENGLAND v REST OF THE WORLD

In 1970, owing to the cancellation of the South African tour to England, a series of matches was arranged, with the trappings of a full Test series, between England and the Rest of the World. It was played for the Guinness Trophy.

The following were awarded England caps for playing against the Rest of the World in that series, although the five matches played are now generally considered not to have rated as full Tests: D. L. Amiss (1), G. Boycott (2), D. J. Brown (2), M. C. Cowdrey (4), M. H. Denness (1), B. L. D'Oliveira (4), J. H. Edrich (2), K. W. R. Fletcher (4), A. W. Greig (3), R. Illingworth (5), A. Jones (1), A. P. E. Knott (5), P. Lever (1), B. W. Luckhurst (5), C. M. Old (2), P. J. Sharpe (1), K. Shuttleworth (1), J. A. Snow (5), D. L. Underwood (3), A. Ward (1), D. Wilson (2).

The following players represented the Rest of the World: E. J. Barlow (5), F. M. Engineer (2), L. R. Gibbs (4), Intikhab Alam (5), R. B. Kanhai (5), C. H. Lloyd (5), G. D. McKenzie (3), D. L. Murray (3), Mushtaq Mohammad (2), P. M. Pollock (1), R. G. Pollock (5), M. J. Procter (5), B. A. Richards (5), G. S. Sobers (5).

LIMITED-OVERS INTERNATIONAL CRICKETERS

The following players have appeared for Test-playing countries in limited-overs internationals but had not represented their countries in Test matches by August 20, 1998:

England C. J. Adams, I. D. Austin, A. D. Brown, D. R. Brown, M. V. Fleming, I. J. Gould, G. W. Humpage, T. E. Jesty, G. D. Lloyd, J. D. Love, M. A. Lynch, D. L. Maddy, M. J. Smith, N. M. K. Smith, S. D. Udal, C. M. Wells.

Australia G. A. Bishop, M. J. Di Venuto, A. C. Gilchrist, S. F. Graf, I. J. Harvey, S. Lee, R. J. McCurdy, K. H. MacLeay, J. P. Maher, G. D. Porter, J. D. Siddons, A. M. Stuart, G. S. Trimble, B. E. Young, A. K. Zesers.

South Africa N. Boje, R. E. Bryson, D. J. Callaghan, D. N. Crookes, L. J. Koen, S. J. Palframan, C. E. B. Rice, M. J. R. Rindel, D. B. Rundle, T. G. Shaw, E. O. Simons, E. L. R. Stewart, R. Telemachus, C. J. P. G. van Zyl, M. Yachad.

West Indies H. A. G. Anthony, B. St A. Browne, V. C. Drakes, R. S. Gabriel, R. C. Haynes, R. D. Jacobs, N. C. McGarrell, M. R. Pydanna, C. M. Tuckett, L. R. Williams.

New Zealand B. R. Blair, P. G. Coman, M. W. Douglas, B. G. Hadlee, R. T. Hart, R. L. Hayes, L. G. Howell, B. J. McKechnie, E. B. McSweeney, J. P. Millmow, A. J. Penn, R. G. Petrie, R. B. Reid, S. J. Roberts, L. W. Stott, R. J. Webb, J. W. Wilson.

India A. B. Agarkar, S. V. Bahutule, A. C. Bedade, Bhupinder Singh, sen., G. Bose, V. B. Chandrasekhar, U. Chatterjee, N. Chopra, N. A. David, P. Dharmani, R. S. Ghai, H. H. Kanitkar, S. S. Karim, S. C. Khanna, G. K. Khoda, S. P. Mukherjee, J. V. Paranjpe, A. K. Patel, M. S. K. Prasad, Randhir Singh, R. Sanghvi, R. P. Singh, R. R. Singh†, H. S. Sodhi, S. Somasunder, Sudhakar Rao, P. S. Vaidya.

Pakistan Aamer Hameed, Aamer Hanif, Abdur Razzaq, Akhtar Sarfraz, Arshad Pervez, Ghulam Ali, Haafiz Shahid, Hasan Jamil, Iqbal Sikandar, Irfan Bhatti, Javed Qadir, Mahmood Hamid, Mansoor Rana, Manzoor Akhtar, Maqsood Rana, Masood Iqbal, Moin-ul-Atiq, Mujahid Jamshed, Naeem Ahmed, Naeem Ashraf, Naseer Malik, Parvez Mir, Saadat Ali, Saeed Azad, Sajid Ali, Sajjad Akbar, Salim Pervez, Shahid Afridi†, Shahid Anwar, Shakil Khan, Sohail Fazal, Tanvir Mehdi, Wasim Haider, Zafar Iqbal, Zahid Ahmed.

Sri Lanka U. D. U. Chandana, D. L. S. de Silva, G. N. de Silva, E. R. Fernando, T. L. Fernando, U. N. K. Fernando, J. C. Gamage, F. R. M. Goonatillake, D. A. Gunawardane, A. A. W. Gunawardene, P. D. Heyn, S. A. Jayasinghe, S. H. U. Karnain, C. Mendis, A. M. N. Munasinghe, M. N. Nawaz, A. R. M. Opatha, S. P. Pasqual, K. G. Perera, H. S. M. Pieris, S. K. Ranasinghe, N. Ranatunga, N. L. K. Ratnayake, A. P. B. Tennekoon, M. H. Tissera, K. E. A. Upashantha, D. M. Vonhagt, A. P. Weerakkody, S. R. de S. Wettimuny, R. P. A. H. Wickremaratne.

Zimbabwe G. B. Brent, R. D. Brown, K. M. Curran, S. G. Davies, K. G. Duers, E. A. Essop-Adam, D. A. G. Fletcher, J. G. Heron, V. R. Hogg, G. C. Martin, M. A. Meman, G. A. Paterson, G. E. Peckover, P. W. E. Rawson.

† Shahid Afridi and R. R. Singh both made their Test debuts in October 1998, after the deadline for this section, having played in 66 and 60 limited-overs internationals, respectively. They broke the previous record for limited-overs internationals before Test debut, 55 by G. R. Larsen of New Zealand.

PRESIDENTS OF MCC SINCE 1946

1946 General Sir Ronald Adam, Bart	1970-71 Sir Cyril Hawker
1947 Captain Lord Cornwallis	1971-72 F. R. Brown
1948 Brig.-Gen. The Earl of Gowrie	1972-73 A. M. Crawley
1949 HRH The Duke of Edinburgh	1973-74 Lord Caccia
1950 Sir Pelham Warner	1974-75 HRH The Duke of Edinburgh
1951-52 W. Findlay	1975-76 C. G. A. Paris
1952-53 The Duke of Beaufort	1976-77 W. H. Webster
1953-54 The Earl of Rosebery	1977-78 D. G. Clark
1954-55 Viscount Cobham	1978-79 C. H. Palmer
1955-56 Field Marshal Earl Alexander of Tunis	1979-80 S. C. Griffith
	1980-81 P. B. H. May
1956-57 Viscount Monckton of Brenchley	1981-82 G. H. G. Doggart
1957-58 The Duke of Norfolk	1982-83 Sir Anthony Tuke
1958-59 Marshal of the RAF Viscount Portal of Hungerford	1983-84 A. H. A. Dibbs
	1984-85 F. G. Mann
1959-60 H. S. Altham	1985-86 J. G. W. Davies
1960-61 Sir Hubert Ashton	1986-87 M. C. Cowdrey
1961-62 Col. Sir William Worsley, Bart	1987-88 J. J. Warr
1962-63 Lt-Col. Lord Nugent	1988-89 Field Marshal The Lord Bramall
1963-64 G. O. B. Allen	1989-90 The Hon. Sir Denys Roberts
1964-65 R. H. Twining	1990-91 The Rt Hon. The Lord Griffiths
1965-66 Lt-Gen. Sir Oliver Leese, Bart	1991-92 M. E. L. Melluish
1966-67 Sir Alec Douglas-Home	1992-94 D. R. W. Silk
1967-68 A. E. R. Gilligan	1994-96 The Hon. Sir Oliver Popplewell
1968-69 R. Aird	1996-98 A. C. D. Ingleby-Mackenzie
1969-70 M. J. C. Allom	1998- A. R. Lewis

Since 1951, Presidents of MCC have taken office on October 1. Previously they took office immediately after the annual general meeting at the start of the season. Since 1992, Presidents have been eligible for two consecutive years of office.

BIRTHS AND DEATHS OF PAST CRICKETERS

Details of current first-class players are no longer listed in this section but may be found in the Register of Players on pages 162-180.

The qualifications for inclusion are as follows:

   1. All players who have appeared in a Test match and are no longer playing first-class cricket.

   2. All players who have appeared in a one-day international for a Test-match playing country and are no longer playing first-class cricket.

   3. County players who appeared in 200 or more first-class matches during their careers, or 100 after the Second World War, and are no longer playing first-class cricket.

   4. English county captains who captained their county in three seasons or more since 1890 and are no longer playing first-class cricket.

   5. All *Wisden* Cricketers of the Year who are no longer playing first-class cricket, including the Public Schoolboys chosen for the 1918 and 1919 Almanacks. Cricketers of the Year are identified by the italic notation *CY* and year of appearance. A list of the Cricketers of the Year from 1889 to 1999 appears on pages 181-183.

   6. Players or personalities not otherwise qualified who are thought to be of sufficient interest to merit inclusion.

Key to abbreviations and symbols

CU – Cambridge University, OU – Oxford University.

Australian states: NSW – New South Wales, Qld – Queensland, S. Aust. – South Australia, Tas. – Tasmania, Vic. – Victoria, W. Aust. – Western Australia.

Indian teams: Eur. – Europeans, Guj. – Gujarat, H'bad – Hyderabad, H. Pradesh – Himachal Pradesh, Ind. Rlwys – Indian Railways, Ind. Serv. – Indian Services, J/K – Jammu and Kashmir, Karn. – Karnataka (Mysore to 1972-73), M. Pradesh – Madhya Pradesh (Central India [C. Ind.] to 1939-40, Holkar to 1954-55, Madhya Bharat to 1956-57), M'tra – Maharashtra, Naw. – Nawanagar, Raja. – Rajasthan, S'tra – Saurashtra (West India [W. Ind.] to 1945-46, Kathiawar to 1949-50), S. Punjab – Southern Punjab (Patiala to 1958-59, Punjab since 1968-69), TC – Travancore-Cochin (Kerala since 1956-57), TN – Tamil Nadu (Madras to 1959-60), U. Pradesh – Uttar Pradesh (United Provinces [U. Prov.] to 1948-49), Vidarbha (CP & Berar to 1949-50, Madhya Pradesh to 1956-57).

New Zealand provinces: Auck. – Auckland, Cant. – Canterbury, C. Dist. – Central Districts, N. Dist. – Northern Districts, Wgtn – Wellington.

Pakistani teams: ADBP – Agricultural Development Bank of Pakistan, B'pur – Bahawalpur, Customs – Pakistan Customs, F'bad – Faisalabad, HBFC – House Building Finance Corporation, HBL – Habib Bank Ltd, I'bad – Islamabad, IDBP – Industrial Development Bank of Pakistan, Kar. – Karachi, KRL – Khan Research Laboratories, MCB – Muslim Commercial Bank, NBP – National Bank of Pakistan, NWFP – North-West Frontier Province, PACO – Pakistan Automobile Corporation, Pak. Rlwys – Pakistan Railways, Pak. Us – Pakistan Universities, PIA – Pakistan International Airlines, PNSC – Pakistan National Shipping Corporation, PWD – Public Works Department, R'pindi – Rawalpindi, UBL – United Bank Ltd, WAPDA – Water and Power Development Authority.

South African provinces: E. Prov. – Eastern Province, E. Tvl – Eastern Transvaal (Easterns since 1995-96), Griq. W. – Griqualand West, N. Tvl – Northern Transvaal, NE Tvl – North-Eastern Transvaal, OFS – Orange Free State (Free State [FS] since 1995-96), Rhod. – Rhodesia, Tvl – Transvaal (Gauteng since 1997-98), W. Prov. – Western Province, W. Tvl – Western Transvaal (North West since 1995-96).

Sri Lankan teams: Ant. – Antonians, Bloom. – Bloomfield Cricket and Athletic Club, BRC – Burgher Recreation Club, CCC – Colombo Cricket Club, Mor. – Moratuwa Sports Club, NCC – Nondescripts Cricket Club, Pan. – Panadura Sports Club, Seb. – Sebastianites, SLAF – Air Force, SSC – Sinhalese Sports Club, TU – Tamil Union Cricket and Athletic Club, Under-23 – Board Under-23 XI, WPC – Western Province (City), WPN – Western Province (North), WPS – Western Province (South).

West Indies islands: B'dos – Barbados, BG – British Guiana (Guyana since 1966), Comb. Is. – Combined Islands, Jam. – Jamaica, T/T – Trinidad & Tobago.

Zimbabwean teams: Mash. – Mashonaland, Mat. – Matabeleland, MCD – Mashonaland Country Districts, Under-24 – Mashonaland Under-24, Zimb. – Zimbabwe.

* *Denotes Test player.* ** *Denotes appeared for two countries. There is a list of Test players country by country from page 63.*
† *Denotes also played for team under its previous name.*

Aamer Hameed (Pak. Us, Lahore, Punjab & OU) b Oct. 18, 1954

Abberley, R. N. (Warwicks) b April 22, 1944

*a'Beckett, E. L. (Vic.) b Aug. 11, 1907, d June 2, 1989

*Abdul Kadir (Kar. & NBP) b May 10, 1944

*Abdul Qadir (HBL, Lahore & Punjab) b Sept. 15, 1955

*Abel, R. (Surrey; *CY 1890*) b Nov. 30, 1857, d Dec. 10, 1936

*Abid Ali, S. (H'bad) b Sept. 9, 1941

Abrahams, J. (Lancs) b July 21, 1952

*Absolom, C. A. (CU & Kent) b June 7, 1846, d July 30, 1889

Acfield, D. L. (CU & Essex) b July 24, 1947

*Achong, E. (T/T) b Feb. 16, 1904, d Aug. 29, 1986

Ackerman, H. M. (Border, NE Tvl, Northants, Natal & W. Prov.) b April 28, 1947

Adams, P. W. (Cheltenham & Sussex; *CY 1919*) b Sept. 5, 1900, d Sept. 28, 1962

*Adcock, N. A. T. (Tvl & Natal; *CY 1961*) b March 8, 1931

*Adhikari, H. R. (Guj., Baroda & Ind. Serv.) b July 31, 1919

*Afaq Hussain (Kar., Pak Us, PIA & PWD) b Dec. 31, 1939

Afford, J. A. (Notts) b May 12, 1964

*Aftab Baloch (PWD, Kar., Sind, NBP & PIA) b April 1, 1953

*Aftab Gul (Punjab U., Pak. Us & Lahore) b March 31, 1946

*Agha Saadat Ali (Pak. Us, Punjab, B'pur & Lahore) b June 21, 1929, d Oct. 26, 1995

*Agha Zahid (Pak Us, Punjab, Lahore & HBL) b Jan. 7, 1953

*Agnew, J. P. (Leics; *CY 1988;* broadcaster) b April 4, 1960

*Ahangama, F. S. (SSC) b Sept. 14, 1959

Aird, R. (CU & Hants; Sec. MCC 1953-62, Pres. MCC 1968-69) b May 4, 1902, d Aug. 16, 1986

Aislabie, B. (Surrey, Hants, Kent & Sussex; Sec. MCC 1822-42) b Jan. 14, 1774, d June 2, 1842

Aitchison, Rev. J. K. (Scotland) b May 26, 1920, d Feb. 13, 1994

*Alabaster, J. C. (Otago) b July 11, 1930

Alcock, C. W. (Sec. Surrey CCC 1872-1907; Editor *Cricket* 1882-1907) b Dec. 2, 1842, d Feb. 26, 1907

Alderman, A. E. (Derbys) b Oct. 30, 1907, d June 4, 1990

*Alderman, T. M. (W. Aust., Kent & Glos; *CY 1982*) b June 12, 1956

*Alexander, F. C. M. (CU & Jam.) b Nov. 2, 1928

*Alexander, G. (Vic.) b April 22, 1851, d Nov. 6, 1930

*Alexander, H. H. (Vic.) b June 9, 1905, d April 15, 1993

Alikhan, R. I. (Sussex, PIA, Surrey & PNSC) b Dec. 28, 1962

*Alim-ud-Din (Rajputana, Guj., Sind, B'pur, Kar. & PWD) b Dec. 15, 1930

*Allan, D. W. (B'dos) b Nov. 5, 1937

*Allan, F. E. (Vic.) b Dec. 2, 1849, d Feb. 9, 1917

Allan, J. M. (OU, Kent, Warwicks & Scotland) b April 2, 1932

*Allan, P. J. (Qld) b Dec. 31, 1935

*Allcott, C. F. W. (Auck.) b Oct. 7, 1896, d Nov. 19, 1973

*Allen, B. O. (CU & Glos) b Oct. 13, 1911, d May 1, 1981

*Allen, D. A. (Glos) b Oct. 29, 1935

*Allen, Sir George O. B. (CU & Middx; Pres. MCC 1963-64) b July 31, 1902, d Nov. 29, 1989

*Allen, I. B. A. (Windwards) b Oct. 6, 1965

Allen, M. H. J. (Northants & Derbys) b Jan. 7, 1933, d Oct. 6, 1995

*Allen, R. C. (NSW) b July 2, 1858, d May 2, 1952

Alletson, E. B. (Notts) b March 6, 1884, d July 5, 1963

Alley, W. E. (NSW & Som; Test umpire; *CY 1962*) b Feb. 3, 1919

*Allom, M. J. C. (CU & Surrey; Pres. MCC 1969-70) b March 23, 1906, d April 8, 1995

*Allott, P. J. W. (Lancs & Wgtn) b Sept. 14, 1956

Altham, H. S. CBE (OU, Surrey & Hants; historian; Pres. MCC 1959-60) b Nov. 30, 1888, d March 11, 1965

*Amalean, K. N. (SL) b April 7, 1965

*Amarnath, Lala (N. B.) (N. Ind., S. Punjab, Guj., Patiala, U. Pradesh & Ind. Rlwys) b Sept. 11, 1911

*Amarnath, M. (Punjab & Delhi; *CY 1984*) b Sept. 24, 1950

*Amarnath, S. (Punjab & Delhi) b Dec. 30, 1948

*Amar Singh, L. (Patiala, W. Ind. & Naw.) b Dec. 4, 1910, d May 20, 1940

*Amerasinghe, A. M. J. G. (Nomads & Ant.) b Feb. 2, 1954

*Ames, L. E. G. CBE (Kent; *CY 1929*) b Dec. 3, 1905, d Feb. 26, 1990

**Amir Elahi (Baroda, N. Ind., S. Punjab & B'pur) b Sept. 1, 1908, d Dec. 28, 1980

*Amiss, D. L. MBE (Warwicks; *CY 1975*) b April 7, 1943

Anderson, I. S. (Derbys & Boland) b April 24, 1960

*Anderson, J. H. (W. Prov.) b April 26, 1874, d March 11, 1926

*Anderson, R. W. (Cant., N. Dist., Otago & C. Dist.) b Oct. 2, 1948

*Anderson, W. M. (Cant.) b Oct. 8, 1919, d Dec. 21, 1979

*Andrew, K. V. (Northants) b Dec. 15, 1929

Andrew, S. J. W. (Hants & Essex) b Jan. 27, 1966

*Andrews, B. (Cant., C. Dist. & Otago) b April 4, 1945

*Andrews, T. J. E. (NSW) b Aug. 26, 1890, d Jan. 28, 1970

Andrews, W. H. R. (Som) b April 14, 1908, d Jan. 9, 1989

Angell, F. L. (Som) b June 29, 1922

*Anil Dalpat (Kar. & PIA) b Sept. 20, 1963

*Ankola, S. A. (M'tra & †Mumbai) b March 1, 1968

Anthony, H. A. G. (Leewards & Glam) b Jan 16, 1971

*Anwar Hussain (N. Ind., Bombay, Sind & Kar.) b July 16, 1920

*Anwar Khan (Kar., Sind & NBP) b Dec. 24, 1955

*Appleyard, R. (Yorks; *CY 1952*) b June 27, 1924

*Apte, A. L. (Ind. Us, Bombay & Raja.) b Oct. 24, 1934

*Apte, M. L. (Bombay & Bengal) b Oct. 5, 1932

*Archer, A. G. (Worcs) b Dec. 6, 1871, d July 15, 1935

*Archer, K. A. (Qld) b Jan. 17, 1928

*Archer, R. G. (Qld) b Oct. 25, 1933

*Arif Butt (Lahore & Pak. Rlwys) b May 17, 1944

Arlott, John OBE (Writer & broadcaster) b Feb. 25, 1914, d Dec. 14, 1991

*Armitage, T. (Yorks) b April 25, 1848, d Sept. 21, 1922

Armstrong, N. F. (Leics) b Dec. 22, 1892, d Jan. 19, 1990

*Armstrong, W. W. (Vic.; *CY 1903*) b May 22, 1879, d July 13, 1947

Arnold, A. P. (Cant. & Northants) b Oct. 16, 1926

*Arnold, E. G. (Worcs) b Nov. 7, 1876, d Oct. 25, 1942

*Arnold, G. G. (Surrey & Sussex; *CY 1972*) b Sept. 3, 1944

*Arnold, J. (Hants) b Nov. 30, 1907, d April 4, 1984

*Arnott, K. J. (MCD) b March 8, 1961

Arnott, T. (Glam) b Feb. 16, 1902, d Feb. 2, 1975

*Arshad Ayub (H'bad) b Aug. 2, 1958

Arshad Pervez (Sargodha, Lahore, Pak. Us, Servis Ind., HBL & Punjab) b Oct. 1, 1952

*Arun, B. (TN) b Dec. 14, 1962

*Arun Lal (Delhi & Bengal) b Aug. 1 1955

*Asgarali, N. (T/T) b Dec. 28, 1920

Ashdown, W. H. (Kent) b Dec. 27, 1898, d Sept. 15, 1979

*Ashley, W. H. (W. Prov.) b Feb. 10, 1862, d July 14, 1930

*Ashraf Ali (Lahore, Income Tax, Pak. Us, Pak. Rlwys & UBL) b April 22, 1958

Ashton, C. T. (CU & Essex) b Feb. 19, 1901, d Oct. 31, 1942

Ashton, G. (CU & Worcs) b Sept. 27, 1896, d Feb. 6, 1981

Ashton, Sir Hubert (CU & Essex; *CY 1922*; Pres. MCC 1960-61) b Feb. 13, 1898, d June 17, 1979

Asif Din, M. (Warwicks) b Sept. 21, 1960

*Asif Iqbal (H'bad, Kar., Kent, PIA & NBP; *CY 1968*) b June 6, 1943

*Asif Masood (Lahore, Punjab U. & PIA) b Jan. 23, 1946

Aslett, D. G. (Kent) b Feb. 12, 1958

*Astill, W. E. (Leics; *CY 1933*) b March 1, 1888, d Feb. 10, 1948

*Athey, C. W. J. (Yorks, Glos & Sussex) b Sept. 27, 1957

Atkinson, C. R. M. CBE (Som) b July 23, 1931, d June 25, 1991

*Atkinson, D. St E. (B'dos & T/T) b Aug. 9, 1926

*Atkinson, E. St E. (B'dos) b Nov. 6, 1927, d May 29, 1998

Atkinson, G. (Som & Lancs) b March 29, 1938

*Attewell, W. (Notts; *CY 1892*) b June 12, 1861, d June 11, 1927

Austin, Sir Harold B. G. (B'dos) b July 15, 1877, d July 27, 1943

*Austin, R. A. (Jam.) b Sept. 5, 1954

Avery, A. V. (Essex) b Dec. 19, 1914, d May 10, 1997

Aylward, James (Hants & All-England) b 1741, *buried* Dec. 27, 1827

*Azad, K. (Delhi) b Jan. 2, 1959

*Azeem Hafeez (Kar., Allied Bank & PIA) b July 29, 1963

*Azhar Khan (Lahore, Punjab, Pak. Us, PIA & HBL) b Sept. 7, 1955

*Azmat Rana (B'pur, PIA, Punjab, Lahore & MCB) b Nov. 3, 1951

*Bacchus, S. F. A. F. (Guyana, W. Prov. & Border) b Jan. 31, 1954

*Bacher, Dr A. (Tvl; Managing Director UCBSA) b May 24, 1942

*Badcock, C. L. (Tas. & S. Aust.) b April 10, 1914, d Dec. 13, 1982

*Badcock, F. T. (Wgtn & Otago) b Aug. 9, 1897, d Sept. 19, 1982

Baggallay, R. R. C. (Derbys) b May 4, 1884, d Dec. 12, 1975

*Baichan, L. (Guyana) b May 12, 1946

*Baig, A. A. (H'bad, OU & Som) b March 19, 1939

Bailey, J. (Hants) b April 6, 1908, d Feb. 9, 1988

Bailey, J. A. (Essex & OU; Sec. MCC 1974-87) b June 22, 1930

*Bailey, T. E. CBE (Essex & CU; *CY 1950*) b Dec. 3, 1923

Baillie, A. W. (Sec. MCC 1858-63) b June 22, 1830, d May 10, 1867

Bainbridge, H. W. (Surrey, CU & Warwicks) b Oct. 29, 1862, d March 3, 1940

Bainbridge, P. (Glos & Durham; *CY 1986*) b April 16, 1958

*Bairstow, D. L. (Yorks & Griq. W.) b Sept. 1, 1951, d Jan. 5, 1998

Baker, C. S. (Warwicks) b Jan. 5, 1883, d Dec. 16, 1976

Baker, G. R. (Yorks & Lancs) b April 18, 1862, d Dec. 6, 1938

*Bakewell, A. H. (Northants; *CY 1934*) b Nov. 2, 1908, d Jan. 23, 1983

*Balaskas, X. C. (Griq. W., Border, W. Prov., Tvl & NE Tvl) b Oct. 15, 1910, d May 12, 1994

*Balderstone, J. C. (Yorks & Leics) b Nov. 16, 1940

Baldry, D. O. (Middx & Hants) b Dec. 26, 1931

*Banerjee, S. A. (Bengal & Bihar) b Nov. 1, 1919, d Sept. 14, 1992

*Banerjee, S. N. (Bengal, Naw., Bihar & M. Pradesh) b Oct. 3, 1911, d Oct. 14, 1980

*Bannerman, A. C. (NSW) b March 22, 1854, d Sept. 19, 1924

*Bannerman, Charles (NSW) b July 23, 1851, d Aug. 20, 1930

Bannister, J. D. (Warwicks) b Aug. 23, 1930

*Baqa Jilani, M. (N. Ind.) b July 20, 1911, d July 2, 1941

*Barber, R. T. (Wgton & C. Dist.) b June 3, 1925

*Barber, R. W. (Lancs, CU & Warwicks; *CY 1967*) b Sept. 26, 1935

*Barber, W. (Yorks) b April 18, 1901, d Sept. 10, 1968

Barclay, J. R. T. (Sussex & OFS) b Jan. 22, 1954

*Bardsley, W. (NSW; *CY 1910*) b Dec. 6, 1882, d Jan. 20, 1954

Barker, G. (Essex) b July 6, 1931

Barling, T. H. (Surrey) b Sept. 1, 1906, d Jan. 2, 1993

*Barlow, E. J. (Tvl, E. Prov., W. Prov., Derbys & Boland) b Aug. 12, 1940

*Barlow, G. D. (Middx) b March 26, 1950

*Barlow, R. G. (Lancs) b May 28, 1851, d July 31, 1919

Barnard, H. M. (Hants) b July 18, 1933

*Barnes, S. F. (Warwicks & Lancs; *CY 1910*) b April 19, 1873, d Dec. 26, 1967

*Barnes, S. G. (NSW) b June 5, 1916, d Dec. 16, 1973

*Barnes, W. (Notts; *CY 1890*) b May 27, 1852, d March 24, 1899

*Barnett, B. A. (Vic.) b March 23, 1908, d June 29, 1979

*Barnett, C. J. (Glos; *CY 1937*) b July 3, 1910, d May 28, 1993

Baroda, Maharaja of (Manager, Ind. in Eng. 1959) b April 2, 1930, d Sept. 1, 1988

*Barratt, F. (Notts) b April 12, 1894, d Jan. 29, 1947

*Barrett, A. G. (Jam.) b April 5, 1942

*Barrett, Dr J. E. (Vic.) b Oct. 15, 1866, d Feb. 6, 1916

Barrick, D. W. (Northants) b April 28, 1926

*Barrington, K. F. (Surrey; *CY 1960*) b Nov. 24, 1930, d March 14, 1981

Barron, W. (Lancs & Northants) b Oct. 26, 1917

*Barrow, I. (Jam.) b Jan. 6, 1911, d April 2, 1979

*Bartlett, E. L. (B'dos) b March 10, 1906, d Dec. 21, 1976

*Bartlett, G. A. (C. Dist. & Cant.) b Feb. 3, 1941

Bartlett, H. T. (CU, Surrey & Sussex; *CY 1939*) b Oct. 7, 1914, d June 26, 1988

Bartley, T. J. (Test umpire) b March 19, 1908, d April 2, 1964

Barton, M. R. (OU & Surrey) b Oct. 14, 1914

*Barton, P. T. (Wgtn) b Oct. 9, 1935

*Barton, V. A. (Kent & Hants) b Oct. 6, 1867, d March 23, 1906

Barwick, S. R. (Glam) b Sept. 6, 1960

Base, S. J. (W. Prov., Glam, Derbys, Boland & Border) b Jan. 2, 1960

Bates, D. L. (Sussex) b May 10, 1933

Bates, L. A. (Warwicks) b March 20, 1895, d March 11, 1971

*Bates, W. (Yorks) b Nov. 19, 1855, d Jan. 8, 1900

Bates, W. E. (Yorks & Glam) b March 5, 1884, d Jan. 17, 1957

*Baumgartner, H. V. (OFS & Tvl) b Nov. 17, 1883, d April 8, 1938

Bear, M. J. (Essex & Cant.) b Feb. 23, 1934

*Beard, D. D. (C. Dist. & N. Dist.) b Jan. 14, 1920, d July 15, 1982

*Beard, G. R. (NSW) b Aug. 19, 1950

Beauclerk, Lord Frederick (Middx, Surrey & MCC) b May 8, 1773, d April 22, 1850

*Beaumont, R. (Tvl) b Feb. 4, 1884, d May 25, 1958

*Beck, J. E. F. (Wgtn) b Aug. 1, 1934

*Bedi, B. S. (N. Punjab, Delhi & Northants) b Sept. 25, 1946

*Bedser, Sir Alec V. (Surrey; *CY 1947*) b July 4, 1918

Bedser, E. A. (Surrey) b July 4, 1918

Beet, G. (Derbys; Test umpire) b April 24, 1886, d Dec. 13, 1946

*Begbie, D. W. (Tvl) b Dec. 12, 1914

Beldham, W. (Hambledon & Surrey) b Feb. 5, 1766, d Feb. 20, 1862

*Bell, A. J. (W. Prov. & Rhod.) b April 15, 1906, d Aug. 1, 1985

Bell, R. V. (Middx & Sussex) b Jan. 7, 1931, d Oct. 26, 1989

*Bell, W. (Cant.) b Sept. 5, 1931

Bellamy, B. W. (Northants) b April 22, 1891, d Dec. 22, 1985

*Benaud, J. (NSW) b May 11, 1944

*Benaud, R. OBE (NSW; *CY 1962*; broadcaster) b Oct. 6, 1930

*Benjamin, W. K. M. (Leewards, Leics & Hants) b Dec. 31, 1964

Bencraft, Sir H. W. Russell (Hants) b March 4, 1858, d Dec. 25, 1943

Bennett, D. (Middx) b Dec. 18, 1933

*Bennett, M. J. (NSW) b Oct. 6, 1956

*Benson, M. R. (Kent) b July 6, 1958

Berry, L. G. (Leics) b April 28, 1906, d Feb. 5, 1985

*Berry, R. (Lancs, Worcs & Derbys) b Jan. 29, 1926

Berry, Scyld (Writer) b April 28, 1954

*Best, C. A. (B'dos & W. Prov.) b May 14, 1959

Bestwick, W. (Derbys) b Feb. 24, 1875, d May 2, 1938

*Betancourt, N. (T/T) b June 4, 1887, d Oct. 12, 1947

Bhalekar, R. B. (M'tra) b Feb. 17, 1952

*Bhandari, P. (Delhi & Bengal) b Nov. 27, 1935

*Bhat, A. R. (Karn.) b April 16, 1958

Bhupinder Singh (Punjab) b April 1, 1965

Bick, D. A. (Middx) b Feb. 22, 1936, d Jan. 13, 1992

Bicknell, D. J. (Surrey) b June 24, 1967

*Bilby, G. P. (Wgtn) b May 7, 1941

*Binks, J. G. (Yorks; *CY 1969*) b Oct. 5, 1935

*Binns, A. P. (Jam.) b July 24, 1929

*Binny, R. M. H. (Karn.) b July 19, 1955

Birch, J. D. (Notts) b June 18, 1955

Bird, H. D. MBE (Yorks & Leics; Test umpire) b April 19, 1933

*Bird, M. C. (Lancs & Surrey) b March 25, 1888, d Dec. 9, 1933

Bird, R. E. (Worcs) b April 4, 1915, d Feb. 20, 1985

*Birkenshaw, J. (Yorks, Leics & Worcs) b Nov. 13, 1940

*Birkett, L. S. (B'dos, BG & T/T) b April 14, 1904, d Jan. 16, 1998

Bishop, G. A. (S. Aust.) b Feb. 25, 1960

*Bisset, Sir Murray (M.) (W. Prov.) b April 14, 1876, d Oct. 24, 1931

*Bissett, G. F. (Griq. W., W. Prov. & Tvl) b Nov. 5, 1905, d Nov. 14, 1965

Bissex, M. (Glos) b Sept. 28, 1944

*Blackham, J. McC. (Vic; *CY 1891*) b May 11, 1854, d Dec. 28, 1932

*Blackie, D. D. (Vic.) b April 5, 1882, d April 18, 1955

*Blain, T. E. (C. Dist.) b Feb. 17, 1962

Blair, B. R. (Otago) b Dec. 27, 1957

*Blair, R. W. (Wgtn & C. Dist.) b June 23, 1932

*Blanckenberg, J. M. (W. Prov. & Natal) b Dec. 31, 1892, dead

*Bland, K. C. (Rhod., E. Prov. & OFS; *CY 1966*) b April 5, 1938

Blenkiron, W. (Warwicks) b July 21, 1942

*Bligh, Hon. Ivo (I. F. W.) (8th Earl of Darnley) (CU & Kent; Pres. MCC 1900) b March 13, 1859, d April 10, 1927

Blofeld, H. C. (CU; writer & broadcaster) b Sept. 23, 1939

*Blunt, R. C. MBE (Cant. & Otago; *CY 1928*) b Nov. 3, 1900, d June 22, 1966

*Blythe, C. (Kent; *CY 1904*) b May 30, 1879, d Nov. 8, 1917

*Board, J. H. (Glos) b Feb. 23, 1867, d April 15, 1924

*Bock, E. G. (Griq. W., Tvl & W. Prov.) b Sept. 17, 1908, d Sept. 5, 1961

*Bolton, B. A. (Cant. & Wgtn) b May 31, 1935

*Bolus, J. B. (Yorks, Notts & Derbys) b Jan. 31, 1934

*Bond, G. E. (W. Prov.) b April 5, 1909, d Aug. 27, 1965

Bond, J. D. (Lancs & Notts; *CY 1971*) b May 6, 1932

*Bonnor, G. J. (Vic. & NSW) b Feb. 25, 1855, d June 27, 1912

*Boock, S. L. (Otago & Cant.) b Sept. 20, 1951

Boon, T. J. (Leics) b Nov. 1, 1961

*Booth, B. C. MBE (NSW) b Oct. 19, 1933

Booth, B. J. (Lancs & Leics) b Dec. 3, 1935

Booth, C. (CU & Hants) b May 11, 1842, d July 14, 1926

*Booth, M. W. (Yorks; *CY 1914*) b Dec. 10, 1886, d July 1, 1916

Booth, R. (Yorks & Worcs) b Oct. 1, 1926

*Borde, C. G. (Baroda & M'tra) b July 21, 1933

*Border, A. R. (NSW, Glos, Qld & Essex; *CY 1982*) b July 27, 1955

Bore, M. K. (Yorks & Notts) b June 2, 1947

Borrington, A. J. (Derbys) b Dec. 8, 1948

*Bosanquet, B. J. T. (OU & Middx; *CY 1905*) b Oct. 13, 1877, d Oct. 12, 1936

Bose, G. (Bengal) b May 20, 1947

Boshier, B. S. (Leics) b March 6, 1932

*Botham, I. T. OBE (Som, Worcs, Durham & Qld; *CY 1978*) b Nov. 24, 1955

*Botten, J. T. (NE Tvl & N. Tvl) b June 21, 1938

Boucher, J. C. (Ireland) b Dec. 22, 1910, d Dec. 25, 1995

Bowden, J. (Derbys) b Oct. 8, 1884, d March 1, 1958

*Bowden, M. P. (Surrey & Tvl) b Nov. 1, 1865, d Feb. 19, 1892

Bowell, A. (Hants) b April 27, 1880, d Aug. 28, 1957

*Bowes, W. E. (Yorks; *CY 1932*) b July 25, 1908, d Sept. 5, 1987

*Bowley, E. H. (Sussex & Auck.; *CY 1930*) b June 6, 1890, d July 9, 1974

Bowley, F. L. (Worcs) b Nov. 9 1873, d May 31, 1943

Box, T. (Sussex) b Feb. 7, 1808, d July 12, 1876

*Boyce, K. D. (B'dos & Essex; *CY 1974*) b Oct. 11, 1943, d Oct. 11, 1996

*Boycott, G. OBE (Yorks & N. Tvl; *CY 1965*) b Oct. 21, 1940

Boyd-Moss, R. J. (CU & Northants) b Dec. 16, 1959

Boyes, G. S. (Hants) b March 31, 1899, d Feb. 11, 1973

*Boyle, H. F. (Vic.) b Dec. 10, 1847, d Nov. 21, 1907

*Bracewell, B. P. (C. Dist., Otago & N. Dist.) b Sept. 14, 1959

*Bracewell, J. G. (Otago & Auck.) b April 15, 1958

*Bradburn, W. P. (N. Dist.) b Nov. 24, 1938

*Bradley, W. M. (Kent) b Jan. 2, 1875, d June 19, 1944

*Bradman, Sir Donald G. (NSW & S. Aust.; *CY 1931*) b Aug. 27, 1908

Brain, B. M. (Worcs & Glos) b Sept. 13, 1940

*Brain, D. H. (Mash.) b Oct. 4, 1964

Brann, G. (Sussex) b April 23, 1865, d June 14, 1954

*Brann, W. H. (E. Prov.) b April 4, 1899, d Sept. 22, 1953

Brassington, A. J. (Glos) b Aug. 9, 1954

*Braund, L. C. (Surrey & Som; *CY 1902*) b Oct. 18, 1875, d Dec. 23, 1955

Bray, C. (Essex) b April 6, 1898, d Sept. 12, 1993

Brayshaw, I. J. (W. Aust.) b Jan. 14, 1942

Breakwell, D. (Northants & Som) b July 2, 1948

*Brearley, J. M. OBE (CU & Middx; *CY 1977*) b April 28, 1942

*Brearley, W. (Lancs; *CY 1909*) b March 11, 1876, d Jan. 13, 1937

*Brennan, D. V. (Yorks) b Feb. 10, 1920, d Jan. 9, 1985

*Briant, G. A. (Mash.) b April 11, 1969

Bridges, J. J. (Som) b June 28, 1887, d Sept. 26, 1966

Brierley, T. L. (Glam, Lancs & Canada) b June 15, 1910, d Jan. 7, 1989

Briers, N. E. (Leics; *CY 1993*) b Jan. 15, 1955

*Briggs, John (Lancs; *CY 1889*) b Oct. 3, 1862, d Jan. 11, 1902

*Bright, R. J. (Vic.) b July 13, 1954

*Briscoe, A. W. (Tvl) b Feb. 6, 1911, d April 22, 1941

*Broad, B. C. (Glos & Notts) b Sept. 29, 1957

Broadbent, R. G. (Worcs) b June 21, 1924, d April 26, 1993

*Brockwell, W. (Surrey & Kimberley; *CY 1895*) b Jan. 21, 1865, d June 30, 1935

Broderick, V. (Northants) b Aug. 17, 1920

*Bromfield, H. D. (W. Prov.) b June 26, 1932

*Bromley, E. H. (W. Aust. & Vic.) b Sept. 2, 1912, d Feb. 1, 1967

*Bromley-Davenport, H. R. (CU, Eur., & Middx) b Aug. 18, 1870, d May 23, 1954

*Brookes, D. (Northants; *CY 1957*) b Oct. 29, 1915

Brookes, Wilfrid H. (Editor of *Wisden* 1936-39) b Dec. 5, 1894, d May 28, 1955

*Brown, A. (Kent) b Oct. 17, 1935

Brown, A. D. (Surrey) b Feb. 11, 1970

Brown, A. S. (Glos) b June 24, 1936

*Brown, D. J. (Warwicks) b Jan. 30, 1942

*Brown, F. R. MBE (CU, Surrey & Northants; *CY 1933*; Pres. MCC 1971-72) b Dec. 16, 1910, d July 24, 1991

*Brown, G. (Hants) b Oct. 6, 1887, d Dec. 3, 1964

Brown, J. MBE (Scotland) b Sept. 24, 1931

*Brown, J. T. (Yorks; *CY 1895*) b Aug. 20, 1869, d Nov. 4, 1904

*Brown, L. S. (Tvl, NE Tvl & Rhod.) b Nov. 24, 1910, d Sept. 1, 1983

Brown, R. D. (Mash.) b March 11, 1951

Brown, S. M. (Middx) b Dec. 8, 1917, d Dec. 28, 1987

*Brown, V. R. (Cant. & Auck.) b Nov. 3, 1959

*Brown, W. A. (NSW & Qld; *CY 1939*) b July 31, 1912

Brown, W. C. (Northants) b Nov. 13, 1900, d Jan. 20, 1986

Browne, B. St A. (Guyana) b Sept. 16, 1967

*Browne, C. R. (B'dos & BG) b Oct. 8, 1890, d Jan. 12, 1964

*Bruce, W. (Vic.) b May 22, 1864, d Aug. 3, 1925

*Bruk-Jackson, G. K. (MCD) b April 25, 1969

Bryan, G. J. CBE (Kent) b Dec. 29, 1902, d April 4, 1991

Bryan, J. L. (CU & Kent; *CY 1922*) b May 26, 1896, d April 23, 1985

Bryan, R. T. (Kent) b July 30, 1898, d July 27, 1970

*Buckenham, C. P. (Essex) b Jan. 16, 1876, d Feb. 23, 1937

Bucknor, S. A. (Test umpire) b May 31, 1946

Buckston, R. H. R. (Derbys) b Oct. 10, 1908, d May 16, 1967

Budd, E. H. (Middx & All-England) b Feb. 23, 1785, d March 29, 1875

Budd, W. L. (Hants; Test umpire) b Oct. 25, 1913, d Aug. 23, 1986

Bull, F. G. (Essex; *CY 1898*) b April 2, 1875, d Sept. 16, 1910

Buller, J. S. MBE (Yorks & Worcs; Test umpire) b Aug. 23, 1909, d Aug. 7, 1970

Burden, M. D. (Hants) b Oct. 4, 1930, d Nov. 9, 1987

*Burge, P. J. (Qld; *CY 1965;* ICC referee) b May 17, 1932

*Burger, C. G. de V. (Natal) b July 12, 1935

Burgess, G. I. (Som) b May 5, 1943

*Burgess, M. G. (Auck.) b July 17, 1944

*Burke, C. (Auck.) b March 22, 1914, d Aug. 4, 1997

*Burke, J. W. (NSW; *CY 1957*) b June 12, 1930, d Feb. 2, 1979

*Burke, S. F. (NE Tvl & OFS) b March 11, 1934

*Burki, Javed (Pak. Us, OU, Punjab, Lahore, Kar., R'pindi & NWFP; ICC referee) b May 8, 1938

*Burmester, M. G. (Mash.) b Jan. 24, 1968

*Burn, K. E. (Tas.) b Sept. 17, 1862, d July 20, 1956

Burns, N. D. (Essex, W. Prov., Som) b Sept. 19, 1965

Burns, W. B. (Worcs) b Aug. 29, 1883, d July 7, 1916

Burnup, C. J. (CU & Kent; *CY 1903*) b Nov. 21, 1875, d April 5, 1960

Burrough, H. D. (Som) b Feb. 6, 1909, d April 9, 1994

Burrows, R. D. (Worcs) b June 6, 1871, d Feb. 12, 1943

Burton, D. C. F. (Yorks) b Sept. 13, 1887, d Sept. 24, 1971

*Burton, F. J. (Vic. & NSW) b Nov. 2, 1865, d Aug. 25, 1929

*Burtt, T. B. (Cant.) b Jan. 22, 1915, d May 24, 1988

Buse, H. T. F. (Som) b Aug. 5, 1910, d Feb. 23, 1992

Buss, A. (Sussex) b Sept. 1, 1939

Buss, M. A. (Sussex & OFS) b Jan. 24, 1944

*Butchart, I. P. (MCD) b May 9, 1960

*Butcher, B. F. (Guyana; *CY 1970*) b Sept. 3, 1933

Butcher, I. P. (Leics & Glos) b July 1, 1962

*Butcher, R. O. (Middx, B'dos & Tas.) b Oct. 14, 1953

*Butler, H. J. (Notts) b March 12, 1913, d July 17, 1991

*Butler, L. (T/T) b Feb. 9, 1929

*Butt, H. R. (Sussex) b Dec. 27, 1865, d Dec. 21, 1928

*Butterfield, L. A. (Cant.) b Aug. 29, 1913

*Butts, C. G. (Guyana) b July 8, 1957

Buxton, I. R. (Derbys) b April 17, 1938

*Buys, I. D. (W. Prov.) b Feb. 3, 1895, dead

*Bynoe, M. R. (B'dos) b Feb. 23, 1941

Byrne, J. F. (Warwicks) b June 19, 1871, d May 10, 1954

Cadman, S. (Derbys) b Jan. 29, 1877, d May 6, 1952

Caesar, Julius (Surrey & All-England) b March 25, 1830, d March 6, 1878

Caffyn, W. (Surrey & NSW) b Feb. 2, 1828, d Aug. 28, 1919

Caine, C. Stewart (Editor of *Wisden* 1926-33) b Oct. 28, 1861, d April 15, 1933

*Cairns, B. L. (C. Dist., Otago & N. Dist.) b Oct. 10, 1949

Calder, H. L. (Cranleigh; *CY 1918*) b Jan. 24, 1901, d Sept. 15, 1995

*Callaway, S. T. (NSW & Cant.) b Feb. 6, 1868, d Nov. 25, 1923

*Callen, I. W. (Vic. & Boland) b May 2, 1955

*Calthorpe, Hon. F. S. Gough- (CU, Sussex & Warwicks) b May 27, 1892, d Nov. 19, 1935

*Camacho, G. S. (Guyana; Chief Exec. WICB) b Oct. 15, 1945

*Cameron, F. J. (Jam.) b June 22, 1923, d Feb. 1995

*Cameron, F. J. MBE (Otago) b June 1, 1932

*Cameron, H. B. (Tvl, E. Prov. & W. Prov.; *CY 1936*) b July 5, 1905, d Nov. 2, 1935

*Cameron, J. H. (CU, Jam. & Som) b April 8, 1914

*Campbell, G. D. (Tas.) b March 10, 1964

*Campbell, T. (Tvl) b Feb. 9, 1882, d Oct. 5, 1924

Cannings, V. H. D. (Warwicks & Hants) b April 3, 1919

Cardus, Sir Neville (Writer) b April 3, 1888, d Feb. 27, 1975

*Carew, G. M. (B'dos) b June 4, 1910, d Dec. 9, 1974

*Carew, M. C. (T/T) b Sept. 15, 1937

*Carkeek, W. (Vic.) b Oct. 17, 1878, d Feb. 20, 1937

*Carlisle, S. V. (Zimb. U-24) b May 10, 1972

*Carlson, P. H. (Qld) b Aug. 8, 1951

*Carlstein, P. R. (OFS, Tvl, Natal & Rhod.) b Oct. 28, 1938

Carpenter, D. (Glos) b Sept. 12, 1935

Carpenter, H. A. (Essex) b July 12, 1869, d Dec. 12, 1933

Carpenter, R. (Cambs & Utd England XI) b Nov. 18, 1830, d July 13, 1901

*Carr, A. W. (Notts; *CY 1923*) b May 21, 1893, d Feb. 7, 1963

*Carr, D. B. OBE (OU & Derbys; *CY 1960*; Sec. TCCB 1974-86) b Dec. 28, 1926

*Carr, D. W. (Kent; *CY 1910*) b March 17, 1872, d March 23, 1950

Carr, J. D. (OU & Middx) b June 15, 1963

Carrick, P. (Yorks & E. Prov.) b July 16, 1952

*Carter, C. P. (Natal & Tvl) b April 23, 1881, d Nov. 8, 1952

*Carter, H. (NSW) b March 15, 1878, d June 8, 1948

Carter, R. G. M. (Worcs) b July 11, 1937

*Cartwright, T. W. (Warwicks, Som & Glam) b July 22, 1935

Case, C. C. C. (Som) b Sept. 7, 1895, d Nov. 11, 1969

Cass, G. R. (Essex, Worcs & Tas.) b April 23, 1940

Catt, A. W. (Kent & W. Prov.) b Oct. 2, 1933

*Catterall, R. H. (Tvl, Rhod., Natal & OFS; *CY 1925*) b July 10, 1900, d Jan. 3, 1961

*Cave, H. B. (Wgtn & C. Dist.) b Oct. 10, 1922, d Sept. 15, 1989

Chalk, F. G. H. (OU & Kent) b Sept. 7, 1910, d Feb. 17, 1943

*Challenor, G. (B'dos) b June 28, 1888, d July 30, 1947

Chamberlain, W. R. F. (Northants; Chairman TCCB 1990-94) b April 13, 1925

*Chandrasekhar, B. S. (†Karn.; *CY 1972*) b May 17, 1945

*Chang, H. S. (Jam.) b July 22, 1952

Chaplin, H. P. (Sussex & Eur.) b March 1, 1883, d March 6, 1970

*Chapman, A. P. F. (Uppingham, OU & Kent; *CY 1919*) b Sept. 3, 1900, d Sept. 16, 1961

*Chapman, H. W. (Natal) b June 30, 1890, d Dec. 1, 1941

Chapman, J. (Derbys) b March 11, 1877, d Aug. 12, 1956

*Chappell, G. S. MBE (S. Aust., Som & Qld; *CY 1973*) b Aug. 7, 1948

*Chappell, I. M. (S. Aust. & Lancs; *CY 1976*; broadcaster) b Sept. 26, 1943

*Chappell, T. M. (S. Aust., W. Aust. & NSW) b Oct. 21, 1952

*Chapple, M. E. (Cant. & C. Dist.) b July 25, 1930, d July 31, 1985

Charlesworth, C. (Warwicks) b Feb. 12, 1875, d June 15, 1953

*Charlton, P. C. (NSW) b April 9, 1867, d Sept. 30, 1954

*Charlwood, H. R. J. (Sussex) b Dec. 19, 1846, d June 6, 1888

*Chatfield, E. J. MBE (Wgtn) b July 3, 1950

*Chatterton, W. (Derbys) b Dec. 27, 1861, d March 19, 1913

*Chauhan, C. P. S. (M'tra & Delhi) b July 21, 1947

*Cheetham, J. E. (W. Prov.) b May 26, 1920, d Aug. 21, 1980

Chester, F. (Worcs; Test umpire) b Jan. 20, 1895, d April 8, 1957

*Chevalier, G. A. (W. Prov.) b March 9, 1937

*Childs, J. H. (Glos & Essex; *CY 1987*) b Aug. 15, 1951

*Chipperfield, A. G. (NSW) b Nov. 17, 1905, d July 29, 1987

Chisholm, R. H. E. (Scotland) b May 22, 1927

*Chowdhury, N. R. (Bihar & Bengal) b May 23, 1923, d Dec. 14, 1979

*Christiani, C. M. (BG) b Oct. 28, 1913, d April 4, 1938

*Christiani, R. J. (BG) b July 19, 1920

*Christopherson, S. (Kent; Pres. MCC 1939-45) b Nov. 11, 1861, d April 6, 1949

*Christy, J. A. J. (Tvl & Qld) b Dec. 12, 1904, d Feb. 1, 1971

*Chubb, G. W. A. (Border & Tvl) b April 12, 1911, d Aug. 28, 1982

Clark, D. G. (Kent; Pres. MCC 1977-78) b Jan. 27, 1919

Clark, E. A. (Middx) b April 15, 1937

*Clark, E. W. (Northants) b Aug. 9, 1902, d April 28, 1982

Clark, T. H. (Surrey) b Oct. 5, 1924, d June 14, 1981.

*Clark, W. M. (W. Aust.) b Sept. 19, 1953

*Clarke, Dr C. B. OBE (B'dos, Northants & Essex) b April 7, 1918, d Oct. 14, 1993

Clarke, R. W. (Northants) b April 22, 1924, d Aug. 3, 1981

*Clarke, S. T. (B'dos, Surrey, Tvl, OFS & N. Tvl) b Dec. 11, 1954

Clarke, William (Notts; founded All-England XI & Trent Bridge ground) b Dec. 24, 1798, d Aug. 25, 1856

Clarkson, A. (Yorks & Som) b Sept. 5, 1939

*Clay, J. C. (Glam) b March 18, 1898, d Aug. 12, 1973

Clay, J. D. (Notts) b Oct. 15, 1924

Clayton, G. (Lancs & Som) b Feb. 3, 1938

*Cleverley, D. C. (Auck.) b Dec. 23, 1909

Clift, Patrick B. (Rhod., Leics & Natal) b July 14, 1953, d Sept. 2, 1996

Clift, Phil B. (Glam) b Sept. 3, 1918

Clinton, G. S. (Kent, Surrey & Zimb.-Rhod.) b May 5, 1953

*Close, D. B. CBE (Yorks & Som; *CY 1964*) b Feb. 24, 1931

Cobb, R. A. (Leics & N. Tvl) b May 18, 1961

Cobham, 10th Visct (Hon. C. J. Lyttelton) (Worcs; Pres. MCC 1954) b Aug. 8, 1909, d March 20, 1977

*Cochrane, J. A. K. (Tvl & Griq. W.) b July 15, 1909, d June 15, 1987

Coe, S. (Leics) b June 3, 1873, d Nov. 4, 1955

*Coen, S. K. (OFS, W. Prov., Tvl & Border) b Oct. 14, 1902, d Jan. 28, 1967

*Colah, S. M. H. (Bombay, W. Ind. & Naw.) b Sept. 22, 1902, d Sept. 11, 1950

Colchin, Robert ("Long Robin") (Kent & All-England) b Nov. 1713, d April 1750

*Coldwell, L. J. (Worcs) b Jan. 10, 1933, d Aug. 6, 1996

*Colley, D. J. (NSW) b March 15, 1947

*Collinge, R. O. (C. Dist., Wgtn & N. Dist.) b April 2, 1946

Collins, A. E. J. (Clifton Coll. & Royal Engineers) b Aug. 18, 1885, d Nov. 11, 1914

Collins, G. C. (Kent) b Sept. 21, 1889, d Jan. 23, 1949

*Collins, H. L. (NSW) b Jan. 21, 1888, d May 28, 1959

Collins, R. (Lancs) b March 10, 1934

*Colquhoun, I. A. (C. Dist.) b June 8, 1924

Coman, P. G. (Cant.) b April 13, 1943

*Commaille, J. M. M. (W. Prov., Natal, OFS & Griq. W.) b Feb. 21, 1883, d July 28, 1956

*Compton, D. C. S. CBE (Middx & Holkar; *CY 1939*) b May 23, 1918, d April 23, 1997

Compton, L. H. (Middx) b Sept. 12, 1912, d Dec. 27, 1984

*Coney, J. V. MBE (Wgtn; *CY 1984*) b June 21, 1952

*Congdon, B. E. OBE (C. Dist., Wgtn, Otago & Cant.; *CY 1974*) b Feb. 11, 1938

*Coningham, A. (NSW & Qld) b July 14, 1863, d June 13, 1939

*Connolly, A. N. (Vic. & Middx) b June 29, 1939

Constable, B. (Surrey) b Feb. 19, 1921, d May 15, 1997

Constant, D. J. (Kent & Leics; Test umpire) b Nov. 9, 1941

*Constantine, L. N. (later Baron Constantine of Maraval and Nelson) (T/T & B'dos; *CY 1940*) b Sept. 21, 1902, d July 1, 1971

Constantine, L. S. (T/T) b May 25, 1874, d Jan. 5, 1942

*Contractor, N. J. (Guj. & Ind. Rlwys) b March 7, 1934

*Conyngham, D. P. (Natal, Tvl & W. Prov.) b May 10, 1897, d July 7, 1979

*Cook, C. (Glos) b Aug. 23, 1921, d Sept. 4, 1996

*Cook, F. J. (E. Prov.) b 1870, d Nov. 30, 1914

*Cook, G. (Northants & E. Prov.) b Oct. 9, 1951

Cook, L. W. (Lancs) b March 28, 1885, d Dec. 2, 1933

*Cook, N. G. B. (Leics & Northants) b June 17, 1956

*Cook, S. J. (Tvl & Som; *CY 1990*) b July 31, 1953

Cook, T. E. R. (Sussex) b Jan. 5, 1901, d Jan. 15, 1950

*Cooper, A. H. C. (Tvl) b Sept. 2, 1893, d July 18, 1963

*Cooper, B. B. (Middx, Kent & Vic.) b March 15, 1844, d Aug. 7, 1914

Cooper, E. (Worcs) b Nov. 30, 1915, d Oct. 29, 1968

Cooper, F. S. Ashley- (Historian) b March 17, 1877, d Jan. 31, 1932

Cooper, G. C. (Sussex) b Sept. 2, 1936

Cooper, K. E. (Notts & Glos) b Dec. 27, 1957

*Cooper, W. H. (Vic.) b Sept. 11, 1849, d April 5, 1939

Cooray, B. C. (Test umpire) b May 15, 1941

*Cope, G. A. (Yorks) b Feb. 23, 1947

*Copson, W. H. (Derbys; *CY 1937*) b April 27, 1908, d Sept. 14, 1971

Cordle, A. E. (Glam) b Sept. 21, 1940

*Corling, G. E. (NSW) b July 13, 1941

Cornford, J. H. (Sussex) b Dec. 9, 1911, d June 17, 1985

*Cornford, W. L. (Sussex) b Dec. 25, 1900, d Feb. 6, 1964

Cornwallis, W. S. (later 2nd Baron) (Kent) b March 14, 1892, d Jan. 4, 1982

Corrall, P. (Leics) b July 16, 1906, d Feb. 1994

Corran, A. J. (OU & Notts) b Nov. 25, 1936

*Cosier, G. J. (Vic., S. Aust. & Qld) b April 25, 1953

Cottam, J. T. (NSW) b Sept. 5, 1867, d Jan. 30, 1897

*Cottam, R. M. H. (Hants & Northants) b Oct. 16, 1944

*Cotter, A. (NSW) b Dec. 3, 1884, d Oct. 31, 1917

Cotton, J. (Notts & Leics) b Nov. 7, 1940

*Coulthard, G. (Vic.; Test umpire) b Aug. 1, 1856, d Oct. 22, 1883

*Coventry, Hon. C. J. (Worcs) b Feb. 26, 1867, d June 2, 1929

*Cowans, N. G. (Middx & Hants) b April 17, 1961

*Cowdrey, C. S. (Kent & Glam) b Oct. 20, 1957

Cowdrey, G. R. (Kent) b June 27, 1964

*Cowdrey, M. C. (later Baron Cowdrey of Tonbridge) (OU & Kent; *CY 1956*; Pres. MCC 1986-87) b Dec. 24, 1932

Cowie, D. B. (Test umpire) b Dec. 2, 1946

*Cowie, J. OBE (Auck.) b March 30, 1912, d June 3, 1994

Cowley, N. G. (Hants & Glam) b March 1, 1953

*Cowper, R. M. (Vic. & W. Aust.) b Oct. 5, 1940

Cox, A. L. (Northants) b July 22, 1907, d Nov. 13, 1986

Cox, G., jun. (Sussex) b Aug. 23, 1911, d March 30, 1985

Cox, G., sen. (Sussex) b Nov. 29, 1873, d March 24, 1949

*Cox, J. L. (Natal) b June 28, 1886, d July 4, 1971

*Coxon, A. (Yorks) b Jan. 18, 1916

Cozier, Tony (Writer & broadcaster) b July 10, 1940

*Craig, I. D. (NSW) b June 12, 1935

Cranfield, L. M. (Glos) b Aug. 29, 1909, d Nov. 18, 1993

Cranmer, P. (Warwicks & Eur.) b Sept. 10, 1914, d May 29, 1994

*Cranston, J. (Glos) b Jan. 9, 1859, d Dec. 10, 1904

Cranston, K. (Lancs) b Oct. 20, 1917

*Crapp, J. F. (Glos; Test umpire) b Oct. 14, 1912, d Feb. 15, 1981

*Crawford, J. N. (Surrey, S. Aust., Wgtn & Otago; *CY 1907*) b Dec. 1, 1886, d May 2, 1963

*Crawford, P. (NSW) b Aug. 3, 1933

Crawford, V. F. S. (Surrey & Leics) b April 11, 1879, d Aug. 21, 1922

Crawley, A. M. MBE (OU & Kent; Pres. MCC 1972-73) b April 10, 1908, d Nov. 3, 1993

Cray, S. J. (Essex) b May 29, 1921

Creese, W. L. (Hants) b Dec. 27, 1907, d March 9, 1974

*Cresswell, G. F. (Wgtn & C. Dist.) b March 22, 1915, d Jan. 10, 1966

Cripps, G. (W. Prov.) b Oct. 19, 1865, d July 27, 1943

*Crisp, R. J. (Rhod., W. Prov. & Worcs) b May 28, 1911, d March 3, 1994

*Crocker, G. J. (MCD) b May 16, 1962

*Croft, C. E. H. (Guyana & Lancs) b March 15, 1953

*Cromb, I. B. (Cant.) b June 25, 1905, d March 6, 1984

Croom, A. J. (Warwicks) b May 23, 1896, d Aug. 16, 1947

*Crowe, J. J. (S. Aust. & Auck.) b Sept. 14, 1958

*Crowe, M. D. MBE (Auck., C. Dist., Som & Wgtn; *CY 1985*) b Sept. 22, 1962

Crump, B. S. (Northants) b April 25, 1938

Cuffe, J. A. (NSW & Worcs) b June 26, 1880, d May 16, 1931

Cumbes, J. (Lancs, Surrey, Worcs & Warwicks) b May 4, 1944

*Cummins, A. C. (B'dos & Durham) b May 7, 1966

*Cunis, R. S. (Auck. & N. Dist.) b Jan. 5, 1941

*Curnow, S. H. (Tvl) b Dec. 16, 1907, d July 28, 1986

Curtis, T. S. (Worcs & CU) b Jan. 15, 1960

Cutmore, J. A. (Essex) b Dec. 28, 1898, d Nov. 30, 1985

*Cuttell, W. R. (Lancs; *CY 1898*) b Sept. 13, 1864, d Dec. 9, 1929

*Da Costa, O. C. (Jam.) b Sept. 11, 1907, d Oct. 1, 1936

Dacre, C. C. (Auck. & Glos) b May 15, 1899, d Nov. 2, 1975

Daft, H. B. (Notts) b April 5, 1866, d Jan. 12, 1945

Daft, Richard (Notts & All-England) b Nov. 2, 1835, d July 18, 1900

Dalmeny, Lord (later 6th Earl of Rosebery) (Middx, Surrey & Scotland) b Jan. 8, 1882, d May 30, 1974

Dalmiya, J. (President ICC 1997-) b May 30, 1940

*Dalton, E. L. (Natal) b Dec. 2, 1906, d June 3, 1981

*Dani, H. T. (M'tra & Ind. Serv.) b May 24, 1933

*Daniel, W. W. (B'dos, Middx & W. Aust.) b Jan. 16, 1956

*D'Arcy, J. W. (Cant., Wgtn & Otago) b April 23, 1936

Dare, R. (Hants) b Nov. 26, 1921

*Darling, J. (S. Aust.; *CY 1900*) b Nov. 21, 1870, d Jan. 2, 1946

*Darling, L. S. (Vic.) b Aug. 14, 1909, d June 24, 1992

*Darling, W. M. (S. Aust.) b May 1, 1957

Davey, J. (Glos) b Sept. 4, 1944

*Davidson, A. K. OBE (NSW; *CY 1962*) b June 14, 1929

Davidson, G. (Derbys) b June 29, 1866, d Feb. 8, 1899

Davies, Dai (Glam; Test umpire) b Aug. 26, 1896, d July 16, 1976

Davies, Emrys (Glam; Test umpire) b June 27, 1904, d Nov. 10, 1975

*Davies, E. Q. (E. Prov., Tvl & NE Tvl) b Aug. 26, 1909, d Nov. 11, 1976

Davies, H. G. (Glam) b April 23, 1912, d Sept. 4, 1993

Davies, J. G. W. OBE (CU & Kent; Pres. MCC 1985-86) b Sept. 10, 1911, d Nov. 5, 1992

Davies, S. G. (Mat.) b May 12, 1977

Davies, T. (Glam) b Oct. 25, 1960

*Davis, B. A. (T/T & Glam) b May 2, 1940

*Davis, C. A. (T/T) b Jan. 1, 1944

Davis, E. (Northants) b March 8, 1922

*Davis, I. C. (NSW & Qld) b June 25, 1953
Davis, P. (Northants) b May 24, 1915
Davis, R. C. (Glam) b Jan. 1, 1946
Davis, R. P. (Kent, Warwicks & Glos) b March 18, 1966
*Davis, S. P. (Vic.) b Nov. 8, 1959
*Davis, W. W. (Windwards, Glam, Tas., Northants & Wgtn) b Sept. 18, 1958
Davison, B. F. (Rhod., Leics, Tas. & Glos) b Dec. 21, 1946
Davison, I. J. (Notts) b Oct. 4, 1937
Dawkes, G. O. (Leics & Derbys) b July 19, 1920
*Dawson, E. W. (CU & Leics) b Feb. 13, 1904, d June 4, 1979
*Dawson, O. C. (Natal & Border) b Sept. 1, 1919
Day, A. P. (Kent; *CY 1910*) b April 10, 1885, d Jan. 22, 1969
*de Alwis, R. G. (SSC) b Feb. 15, 1959
*Dean, H. (Lancs) b Aug. 13, 1884, d March 12, 1957
Dean, J., sen. (Sussex) b Jan. 4, 1816, d Dec. 25, 1881
*Deane, H. G. (Natal & Tvl) b July 21, 1895, d Oct. 21, 1939
*De Caires, F. I. (BG) b May 12, 1909, d Feb. 2, 1959
*De Courcy, J. H. (NSW) b April 18, 1927
*de Groen, R. P. (Auck. & N. Dist.) b Aug. 5, 1962
*Dekker, M. H. (Mat.) b Dec. 5, 1969
*Dell, A. R. (Qld) b Aug. 6, 1947
*de Mel, A. L. F. (SL) b May 9, 1959
*Dempster, C. S. (Wgtn, Leics, Scotland & Warwicks; *CY 1932*) b Nov. 15, 1903, d Feb. 14, 1974
*Dempster, E. W. (Wgtn) b Jan. 25, 1925
*Denness, M. H. (Scotland, Kent & Essex; *CY 1975;* ICC referee) b Dec. 1, 1940
Dennett, G. (Glos) b April 27, 1880, d Sept. 14, 1937
Denning, P. W. (Som) b Dec. 16, 1949
Dennis, F. (Yorks) b June 11, 1907
Dennis, S. J. (Yorks, OFS & Glam) b Oct. 18, 1960
*Denton, D. (Yorks; *CY 1906*) b July 4, 1874, d Feb. 16, 1950
Deodhar, D. B. (M'tra) b Jan. 14, 1892, d Aug. 24, 1993
*Depeiza, C. C. (B'dos) b Oct. 10, 1928, d Nov. 10, 1995
*Desai, R. B. (Bombay) b June 20, 1939, d April 27, 1998
*de Silva, A. M. (CCC) b Dec. 3, 1963
de Silva, D. L. S. (SL) b Nov. 17, 1956, d April 12, 1980
*de Silva, D. S. (Bloom.) b June 11, 1942
*de Silva, E. A. R. (NCC & Galle) b March 28, 1956
de Silva, G. N. (SL) b March 12, 1955

*de Silva, G. R. A. (SL) b Dec. 12, 1952
de Smidt, R. W. (W. Prov.; *believed to be longest-lived first-class cricketer*) b Nov. 24, 1883, d Aug. 3, 1986
De Trafford, C. E. (Lancs & Leics) b May 21, 1864, d Nov. 11, 1951
Devereux, L. N. (Middx, Worcs & Glam) b Oct. 20, 1931
*Dewdney, C. T. (Jam.) b Oct. 23, 1933
*Dewes, J. G. (CU & Middx) b Oct. 11, 1926
Dews, G. (Worcs) b June 5, 1921
*Dexter, E. R. (CU & Sussex; *CY 1961*) b May 15, 1935
*Dias, R. L. (CCC) b Oct. 18, 1952
*Dick, A. E. (Otago & Wgtn) b Oct. 10, 1936
*Dickinson, G. R. (Otago) b March 11, 1903, d March 17, 1978
*Dilawar Hussain (C. Ind. and U. Prov.) b March 19, 1907, d Aug. 26, 1967
*Dilley, G. R. (Kent, Natal & Worcs) b May 18, 1959
Dillon, E. W. (Kent & OU) b Feb. 15, 1881, d April 20, 1941
*Dipper, A. E. (Glos) b Nov. 9, 1885, d Nov. 7, 1945
*Divecha, R. V. (Bombay, OU, Northants, Vidarbha & S'tra) b Oct. 18, 1927
Diver, A. J. D. (Cambs., Middx, Notts & All-England) b June 6, 1824, d March 25, 1876
Diver, E. J. (Surrey & Warwicks) b March 20, 1861, d Dec. 27, 1924
Dixon, A. L. (Kent) b Nov. 27, 1933
*Dixon, C. D. (Tvl) b Feb. 12, 1891, d Sept. 9, 1969
Dixon, J. A. (Notts) b May 27, 1861, d June 8, 1931
Dodds, T. C. (Essex) b May 29, 1919
*Doggart, G. H. G. OBE (CU & Sussex; Pres. MCC 1981-82) b July 18, 1925
*D'Oliveira, B. L. OBE (Worcs; *CY 1967*) b Oct. 4, 1931
D'Oliveira, D. B. (Worcs) b Oct. 19, 1960
*Dollery, H. E. (Warwicks & Wgtn; *CY 1952*) b Oct. 14, 1914, d Jan. 20, 1987
*Dolphin, A. (Yorks) b Dec. 24, 1885, d Oct. 23, 1942
*Donnan, H. (NSW) b Nov. 12, 1864, d Aug. 13, 1956
*Donnelly, M. P. (Wgtn, Cant., OU, Middx & Warwicks; *CY 1948*) b Oct. 17, 1917
*Dooland, B. (S. Aust. & Notts; *CY 1955*) b Nov. 1, 1923, d Sept. 8, 1980
Dorrinton, W. (Kent & All-England) b April 29, 1809, d Nov. 8, 1848
Dorset, 3rd Duke of (Kent) b March 24, 1745, d July 19, 1799
*Doshi, D. R. (Bengal, Notts, Warwicks & S'tra) b Dec. 22, 1947
*Douglas, J. W. H. T. (Essex; *CY 1915*) b Sept. 3, 1882, d Dec. 19, 1930

Dovey, R. R. (Kent) b July 18, 1920, d Dec. 27, 1974

*Dowe, U. G. (Jam.) b March 29, 1949

*Dower, R. R. (E. Prov.) b June 4, 1876, d Sept. 15, 1964

*Dowling, G. T. OBE (Cant.; ICC referee) b March 4, 1937

*Downton, P. R. (Kent & Middx) b April 4, 1957

*Draper, R. G. (E. Prov. & Griq. W.) b Dec. 24, 1926

Dredge, C. H. (Som) b Aug. 4, 1954

*Druce, N. F. (CU & Surrey; *CY 1898*) b Jan. 1, 1875, d Oct. 27, 1954

Drybrough, C. D. (OU & Middx) b Aug. 31, 1938

*D'Souza, A. (Kar., Peshawar & PIA) b Jan. 17, 1939

*Ducat, A. (Surrey; *CY 1920*) b Feb. 16, 1886, d July 23, 1942

*Duckworth, C. A. R. (Natal & Rhod.) b March 22, 1933

*Duckworth, G. (Lancs; *CY 1929*) b May 9, 1901, d Jan. 5, 1966

Dudleston, B. (Leics, Glos & Rhod.; Test umpire) b July 16, 1945

Duers, K. G. (Mash.) b June 30, 1960

*Duff, R. A. (NSW) b Aug. 17, 1878, d Dec. 13, 1911

*Dujon, P. J. L. (Jam.; *CY 1989*) b May 28, 1956

*Duleepsinhji, K. S. (CU & Sussex; *CY 1930*) b June 13, 1905, d Dec. 5, 1959

*Dumbrill, R. (Natal & Tvl) b Nov. 19, 1938

*Duminy, J. P. (OU, W. Prov. & Tvl) b Dec. 16, 1897, d Jan. 31, 1980

*Duncan, J. R. F. (Qld & Vic.) b March 25, 1944

*Dunell, O. R. (E. Prov.) b July 15, 1856, d Oct. 21, 1929

Dunne, R. S. (Otago; Test umpire) b April 22, 1943

*Dunning, J. A. (Otago & OU) b Feb. 6, 1903, d June 24, 1971

*Dunusinghe, C. I. (Ant. & NCC) b Oct. 19, 1970

*Du Preez, J. H. (Rhod. & Zimb.) b Nov. 14, 1942

*Durani, S. A. (S'tra, Guj. & Raja.) b Dec. 11, 1934

*Durston, F. J. (Middx) b July 11, 1893, d April 8, 1965

*Du Toit, J. F. (SA) b April 5, 1868, d July 10, 1909

*Dye, J. C. J. (Kent, Northants & E. Prov.) b July 24, 1942

*Dyer, D. V. (Natal) b May 2, 1914, d June 18, 1990

*Dyer, G. C. (NSW) b March 16, 1959

*Dymock, G. (Qld) b July 21, 1945

Dyson, A. H. (Glam) b July 10, 1905, d June 7, 1978

Dyson, Jack (Lancs) b July 8, 1934

*Dyson, John (NSW) b June 11, 1954

*Eady, C. J. (Tas.) b Oct. 29, 1870, d Dec. 20, 1945

Eagar, E. D. R. (OU, Glos & Hants) b Dec. 8, 1917, d Sept. 13, 1977

Ealham, A. G. E. (Kent) b Aug. 30, 1944

East, D. E. (Essex) b July 27, 1959

East, R. E. (Essex) b June 20, 1947

Eastman, L. C. (Essex & Otago) b June 3, 1897, d April 17, 1941

*Eastwood, K. H. (Vic.) b Nov. 23, 1935

Ebeling, H. I. MBE (Vic.) b Jan. 1, 1905, d Jan. 12, 1980

Ebrahim, Ahmed (ICC referee) b Dec. 2, 1937

Eckersley, P. T. (Lancs) b July 2, 1904, d Aug. 13, 1940

*Edgar, B. A. (Wgtn) b Nov. 23, 1956

Edinburgh, HRH Duke of (Pres. MCC 1948-49, 1974-75) b June 10, 1921

Edmeades, B. E. A. (Essex) b Sept. 17, 1941

*Edmonds, P. H. (CU, Middx & E. Prov.) b March 8, 1951

Edrich, B. R. (Kent & Glam) b Aug. 18, 1922

Edrich, E. H. (Lancs) b March 27, 1914, d July 9, 1993

Edrich, G. A. (Lancs) b July 13, 1918

*Edrich, J. H. MBE (Surrey; *CY 1966*) b June 21, 1937

*Edrich, W. J. (Middx; *CY 1940*) b March 26, 1916, d April 24, 1986

*Edwards, G. N. (C. Dist.) b May 27, 1955

*Edwards, J. D. (Vic.) b June 12, 1862, d July 31, 1911

Edwards, M. J. (CU & Surrey) b March 1, 1940

*Edwards, R. (W. Aust. & NSW) b Dec. 1, 1942

*Edwards, R. M. (B'dos) b June 3, 1940

*Edwards, W. J. (W. Aust.) b Dec. 23, 1949

*Ehtesham-ud-Din (Lahore, Punjab, PIA, NBP & UBL) b Sept. 4, 1950

*Elgie, M. K. (Natal) b March 6, 1933

Elliott, C. S. MBE (Derbys; Test umpire) b April 24, 1912

Elliott, Harold (Lancs; Test umpire) b June 15, 1904, d April 15, 1969

Elliott, Harry (Derbys) b Nov. 2, 1891, d Feb. 2, 1976

*Ellison, R. M. (Kent & Tas.; *CY 1986*) b Sept. 21, 1959

*Emburey, J. E. (Middx, W. Prov. & Northants; *CY 1984*) b Aug. 20, 1952

*Emery, R. W. G. (Auck. & Cant.) b March 28, 1915, d Dec. 18, 1982

*Emery, S. H. (NSW) b Oct. 16, 1885, d Jan. 7, 1967

*Emmett, G. M. (Glos) b Dec. 2, 1912, d Dec. 18, 1976

*Emmett, T. (Yorks) b Sept. 3, 1841, d June 30, 1904

*Endean, W. R. (Tvl) b May 31, 1924

*Engineer, F. M. (Bombay & Lancs) b Feb. 25, 1938

Enthoven, H. J. (CU & Middx) b June 4, 1903, d June 29, 1975

Essop-Adam, E. A. (Mash.) b Nov. 16, 1968

*Evans, A. J. (OU, Hants & Kent) b May 1, 1889, d Sept. 18, 1960

Evans, D. G. L. (Glam; Test umpire) b July 27, 1933, d March 25, 1990

*Evans, E. (NSW) b March 26, 1849, d July 2, 1921

*Evans, T. G. CBE (Kent; CY 1951) b Aug. 18, 1920

Evershed, Sir Sydney H. (Derbys) b Jan. 13, 1861, d March 7, 1937

Every, T. (Glam) b Dec. 19, 1909, d Jan. 20, 1990

Eyre, T. J. P. (Derbys) b Oct. 17, 1939

*Fagg, A. E. (Kent; Test umpire) b June 18, 1915, d Sept. 13, 1977

*Fairfax, A. G. (NSW) b June 16, 1906, d May 17, 1955

Fairservice, W. J. (Kent) b May 16, 1881, d June 26, 1971

Fane, F. L. (OU & Essex) b April 27, 1875, d Nov. 27, 1960

*Farnes, K. (CU & Essex; CY 1939) b July 8, 1911, d Oct. 20, 1941

*Farooq Hamid (Lahore & PIA) b March 3, 1945

*Farrer, W. S. (Border) b Dec. 8, 1936

*Farrimond, W. (Lancs) b May 23, 1903, d Nov. 14, 1979

*Farrukh Zaman (Peshawar, NWFP, Punjab & MCB) b April 2, 1956

*Faulkner, G. A. (Tvl) b Dec. 17, 1881, d Sept. 10, 1930

*Favell, L. E. MBE (S. Aust.) b Oct. 6, 1929, d June 14, 1987

*Fazal Mahmood (N. Ind., Punjab & Lahore; CY 1955) b Feb. 18, 1927

Fearnley, C. D. (Worcs; bat-maker) b April 12, 1944

Featherstone, N. G. (Tvl, N. Tvl, Middx & Glam) b Aug. 20, 1949

'Felix', N. (Wanostrocht) (Kent, Surrey & All-England) b Oct. 4, 1804, d Sept. 3, 1876

*Fellows-Smith, J. P. (OU, Tvl & Northants) b Feb. 3, 1932

Feltham, M. A. (Surrey & Middx) b June 26, 1963

Felton, N. A. (Som & Northants) b Oct. 24, 1960

*Fender, P. G. H. (Sussex & Surrey; CY 1915) b Aug. 22, 1892, d June 15, 1985

*Ferguson, W. (T/T) b Dec. 14, 1917, d Feb. 23, 1961

Ferguson, W. H. BEM (Scorer) b June 6, 1880, d Sept. 22, 1957

*Fernandes, M. P. (BG) b Aug. 12, 1897, d May 8, 1981

Fernando, E. R. (SL) b Feb. 22, 1944

*Fernando, E. R. N. S. (SLAF) b Dec. 19, 1955

Fernando, T. L. (Colts & BRC) b Dec. 27, 1962

Ferreira, A. M. (N. Tvl & Warwicks) b April 13, 1955

**Ferris, J. J. (NSW, Glos & S. Aust.; CY 1889) b May 21, 1867, d Nov. 21, 1900

*Fichardt, C. G. (OFS) b March 20, 1870, d May 30, 1923

Fiddling, K. (Yorks & Northants) b Oct. 13, 1917, d June 19, 1992

Field, F. E. (Warwicks) b Sept. 23, 1874, d Aug. 25, 1934

*Fielder, A. (Kent; CY 1907) b July 19, 1877, d Aug. 30, 1949

*Findlay, T. M. MBE (Comb. Is. & Windwards) b Oct. 19, 1943

Findlay, W. (OU & Lancs; Sec. Surrey CCC 1907-19; Sec. MCC 1926-36) b June 22, 1880, d June 19, 1953

*Fingleton, J. H. OBE (NSW; writer) b April 28, 1908, d Nov. 22, 1981

*Finlason, C. E. (Tvl & Griq. W.) b Feb. 19, 1860, d July 31, 1917

Finney, R. J. (Derbys) b Aug. 2, 1960

Firth, Canon J. D'E. E. (Winchester, OU & Notts; CY 1918) b Jan. 21, 1900, d Sept. 21, 1957

Firth, J. (Yorks & Leics) b June 27, 1917, d Sept. 7, 1981

*Fisher, F. E. (Wgtn & C. Dist.) b July 28, 1924, d June 19, 1996

*Fishlock, L. B. (Surrey; CY 1947) b Jan. 2, 1907, d June 26, 1986

Fishwick, T. S. (Warwicks) b July 24, 1876, d Feb. 21, 1950

Fitzgerald, R. A. (CU & Middx; Sec. MCC 1863-76) b Oct. 1, 1834, d Oct. 28, 1881

Fitzroy-Newdegate, Hon. J. M. (Northants) b March 20, 1897, d May 7, 1976

*Flavell, J. A. (Worcs; CY 1965) b May 15, 1929

*Fleetwood-Smith, L. O'B. (Vic.) b March 30, 1908, d March 16, 1971

Fletcher, D. A. G. (Rhod. & Zimb.) b Sept. 27, 1948

Fletcher, D. G. W. (Surrey) b July 6, 1924

*Fletcher, K. W. R. OBE (Essex; CY 1974) b May 20, 1944

Fletcher, S. D. (Yorks & Lancs) b June 8, 1964

*Floquet, C. E. (Tvl) b Nov. 3, 1884, d Nov. 22, 1963

*Flowers, W. (Notts) b Dec. 7, 1856, d Nov. 1, 1926

*Foley, H. (Wgtn) b Jan. 28, 1906, d Oct. 16, 1948

Folley, I. (Lancs & Derbys) b Jan. 9, 1963, d Aug. 30, 1993

Forbes, C. (Notts) b Aug. 9, 1936

*Ford, F. G. J. (CU & Middx) b Dec. 14, 1866, d Feb. 7, 1940

Fordham, A. (Northants) b Nov. 9, 1964

Foreman, D. J. (W. Prov. & Sussex) b Feb. 1, 1933

*Foster, F. R. (Warwicks; *CY 1912*) b Jan. 31, 1889, d May 3, 1958

Foster, G. N. (OU, Worcs & Kent) b Oct. 16, 1884, d Aug. 11, 1971

*Foster, H. K. (OU & Worcs; *CY 1911*) b Oct. 30, 1873, d June 23, 1950

Foster, M. K. (Worcs) b Jan. 1, 1889, d Dec. 3, 1940

*Foster, M. L. C. (Jam.) b May 9, 1943

*Foster, N. A. (Essex & Tvl; *CY 1988*) b May 6, 1962

*Foster, R. E. (OU & Worcs; *CY 1901*) b April 16, 1878, d May 13, 1914

*Fothergill, A. J. (Som) b Aug. 26, 1854, d Aug. 1, 1932

*Fowke, G. H. S. (Leics) b Oct. 14, 1880, d June 24, 1946

*Fowler, G. (Lancs & Durham) b April 20, 1957

*Francis, B. C. (NSW & Essex) b Feb. 18, 1948

Francis, D. A. (Glam) b Nov. 29, 1953

*Francis, G. N. (B'dos) b Dec. 11, 1897, d Jan. 7, 1942

*Francis, H. H. (Glos & W. Prov.) b May 26, 1868, d Jan. 7, 1936

Francis, K. T. (Test umpire) b Oct. 15, 1949

Francke, F. M. (SL & Qld) b March 29, 1941

*Francois, C. M. (Griq. W.) b June 20, 1897, d May 26, 1944

*Frank, C. N. (Tvl) b Jan. 27, 1891, d Dec. 25, 1961

*Frank, W. H. B. (SA) b Nov. 23, 1872, d Feb. 16, 1945

*Franklin, T. J. (Auck.) b March 18, 1962

*Frederick, M. (B'dos, Derbys & Jam.) b May 6, 1927

*Fredericks, R. C. (†Guyana & Glam; *CY 1974*) b Nov. 11, 1942

*Freeman, A. P. (Kent; *CY 1923*) b May 17, 1888, d Jan. 28, 1965

*Freeman, D. L. (Wgtn) b Sept. 8, 1914, d May 31, 1994

*Freeman, E. W. (S. Aust.) b July 13, 1944

Freeman, J. R. (Essex) b Sept. 3, 1883, d Aug. 8, 1958

*Freer, F. W. (Vic.) b Dec. 4, 1915, d Nov. 2 1998

*French, B. N. (Notts) b Aug. 13, 1959

Frost, G. (Notts) b Jan. 15, 1947

*Fry, C. B. (OU, Sussex & Hants; *CY 1895*) b April 25, 1872, d Sept. 7, 1956

*Fuller, E. R. H. (W. Prov.) b Aug. 2, 1931

*Fuller, R. L. (Jam.) b Jan. 30, 1913, d May 3, 1987

*Fullerton, G. M. (Tvl) b Dec. 8, 1922

*Funston, K. J. (NE Tvl, OFS & Tvl) b Dec. 3, 1925

*Furlonge, H. A. (T/T) b June 19, 1934

Gabriel, R. S. (T/T) b June 5, 1952

*Gadkari, C. V. (M'tra & Ind. Serv.) b Feb. 3, 1928, d Jan. 11, 1998

*Gaekwad, A. D. (Baroda) b Sept. 23, 1952

*Gaekwad, D. K. (Baroda) b Oct. 27, 1928

*Gaekwad, H. G. (†M. Pradesh) b Aug. 29, 1923

Gale, R. A. (Middx) b Dec. 10, 1933

*Gallichan, N. (Wgtn) b June 3, 1906, d March 25, 1969

Gamage, J. C. (Galle) b April 17, 1964

*Gamsy, D. (Natal) b Feb. 17, 1940

*Gandotra, A. (Delhi & Bengal) b Nov. 24, 1948

*Gannon, J. B. (W. Aust.) b Feb. 8, 1947

*Ganteaume, A. G. (T/T) b Jan. 22, 1921

Gard, T. (Som) b June 2, 1957

Gardiner, Howard (ICC referee) b Jan. 1, 1944

Gardner, F. C. (Warwicks) b June 4, 1922, d Jan. 12, 1979

Gardner, L. R. (Leics) b Feb. 23, 1934

Garland-Wells, H. M. (OU & Surrey) b Nov. 14, 1907, d May 28, 1993

Garlick, R. G. (Lancs & Northants) b April 11, 1917, d May 16, 1988

*Garner, J. MBE (B'dos, Som & S. Aust.; *CY 1980*) b Dec. 16, 1952

Garnham, M. A. (Glos, Leics & Essex) b Aug. 20, 1960

*Garrett, T. W. (NSW) b July 26, 1858, d Aug. 6, 1943

*Gaskin, B. B. M. (BG) b March 21, 1908, d May 1, 1979

*Gaunt, R. A. (W. Aust. & Vic.) b Feb. 26, 1934

*Gavaskar, S. M. (Bombay & Som; *CY 1980*) b July 10, 1949

*Gay, L. H. (CU, Hants & Som) b March 24, 1871, d Nov. 1, 1949

*Geary, G. (Leics; *CY 1927*) b July 9, 1893, d March 6, 1981

Gedye, S. G. (Auck.) b May 2, 1929

*Gehrs, D. R. A. (S. Aust.) b Nov. 29, 1880, d June 25, 1953

Ghai, R. S. (Punjab) b June 12, 1960

*Ghavri, K. D. (S'tra & Bombay) b Feb. 28, 1951

*Ghazali, M. E. Z. (M'tra & Pak. Serv.) b June 15, 1924

*Ghorpade, J. M. (Baroda) b Oct. 2, 1930, d March 29, 1978

*Ghulam Abbas (Kar., NBP & PIA) b May 1, 1947

*Ghulam Ahmed (H'bad) b July 4, 1922, d Oct. 28, 1998

*Gibb, P. A. (CU, Scotland, Yorks & Essex) b July 11, 1913, d Dec. 7, 1977

Gibbons, H. H. (Worcs) b Oct. 10, 1904, d Feb. 16, 1973

*Gibbs, G. L. (BG) b Dec. 27, 1925, d Feb. 21, 1979

*Gibbs, L. R. (†Guyana, S. Aust. & Warwicks; *CY 1972*) b Sept. 29, 1934

Gibbs, P. J. K. (OU & Derbys) b Aug. 17, 1944

Gibson, C. H. (Eton, CU & Sussex; *CY 1918*) b Aug. 23, 1900, d Dec. 31, 1976

Gibson, D. (Surrey) b May 1, 1936

*Giffen, G. (S. Aust.; *CY 1894*) b March 27, 1859, d Nov. 29, 1927

*Giffen, W. F. (S. Aust.) b Sept. 20, 1861, d June 29, 1949

*Gifford, N. MBE (Worcs & Warwicks; *CY 1975*) b March 30, 1940

*Gilbert, D. R. (NSW, Tas. & Glos) b Dec. 29, 1960

*Gilchrist, R. (Jam. & H'bad) b June 28, 1934

Giles, R. J. (Notts) b Oct. 17, 1919

Gilhouley, K. (Yorks & Notts) b Aug. 8, 1934

*Gillespie, S. R. (Auck.) b March 2, 1957

Gilliat, R. M. C. (OU & Hants) b May 20, 1944

*Gilligan, A. E. R. (CU, Surrey & Sussex; *CY 1924;* Pres. MCC 1967-68) b Dec. 23, 1894, d Sept. 5, 1976

*Gilligan, A. H. H. (Sussex) b June 29, 1896, d May 5, 1978

Gilligan, F. W. (OU & Essex) b Sept. 20, 1893, d May 4, 1960

Gillingham, Canon F. H. (Essex) b Sept. 6, 1875, d April 1, 1953

*Gilmour, G. J. (NSW) b June 26, 1951

*Gimblett, H. (Som; *CY 1953*) b Oct. 19, 1914, d March 30, 1978

*Gladstone, G. (*see* Marais, G. G.)

*Gladwin, Cliff (Derbys) b April 3, 1916, d April 10, 1988

*Gleeson, J. W. (NSW & E. Prov.) b March 14, 1938

*Gleeson, R. A. (E. Prov.) b Dec. 6, 1873, d Sept. 27, 1919

Glover, A. C. S. (Warwicks) b April 19, 1872, d May 22, 1949

*Glover, G. K. (Kimberley & Griq. W.) b May 13, 1870, d Nov. 15, 1938

*Goddard, J. D. C. OBE (B'dos) b April 21, 1919, d Aug. 26, 1987

*Goddard, T. L. (Natal & NE Tvl) b Aug. 1, 1931

*Goddard, T. W. (Glos; *CY 1938*) b Oct. 1, 1900, d May 22, 1966

Goel, R. (Patiala & Haryana) b Sept. 29, 1942

*Gomes, H. A. (T/T & Middx; *CY 1985*) b July 13, 1953

*Gomez, G. E. (T/T) b Oct. 10, 1919, d Aug. 6, 1996

*Gooch, G. A. OBE (Essex & W. Prov.; *CY 1980*) b July 23, 1953

Goodwin, K. (Lancs) b June 25, 1938

Goodwin, T. J. (Leics) b Jan. 22, 1929

Goonatillake, F. R. M. de S. (SL) b Aug. 15, 1951

*Goonatillake, H. M. (SL) b Aug. 16, 1952

Goonesena, G. (Ceylon, Notts, CU & NSW) b Feb. 16, 1931

*Gopalan, M. J. (Madras) b June 6, 1909

*Gopinath, C. D. (Madras) b March 1, 1930

*Gordon, N. (Tvl) b Aug. 6, 1911

Gore, A. C. (Eton & Army; *CY 1919*) b May 14, 1900, d June 7, 1990

Gould, I. J. (Middx, Auck. & Sussex) b Aug. 19, 1957

*Gover, A. R. MBE (Surrey; *CY 1937; oldest surviving CY and oldest living Test cricketer at end of 1998*) b Feb. 29, 1908

*Gower, D. I. OBE (Leics & Hants; *CY 1979*) b April 1, 1957

Grace, C. B. (London County; son of W. G.) b March 1882, d June 6, 1938

*Grace, Dr E. M. (Glos; brother of W. G.) b Nov. 28, 1841, d May 20, 1911

*Grace, G. F. (Glos; brother of W. G.) b Dec. 13, 1850, d Sept. 22, 1880

Grace, Dr Henry (Glos; brother of W. G.) b Jan. 31, 1833, d Nov. 15, 1895

Grace, Dr H. M. (father of W. G.) b Feb. 21, 1808, d Dec. 23, 1871

Grace, Mrs H. M. (mother of W. G.) b July 18, 1812, d July 25, 1884

*Grace, Dr W. G. (Glos; *CY 1896*) b July 18, 1848, d Oct. 23, 1915

Grace, W. G., jun. (CU & Glos; son of W. G.) b July 6, 1874, d March 2, 1905

Graf, S. F. (Vic., W. Aust. & Hants) b May 19, 1957

*Graham, H. (Vic. & Otago) b Nov. 22, 1870, d Feb. 7, 1911

Graham, J. N. (Kent) b May 8, 1943

*Graham, R. (W. Prov.) b Sept. 16, 1877, d April 21, 1946

*Grant, G. C. (CU, T/T & Rhod.) b May 9, 1907, d Oct. 26, 1978

*Grant, R. S. (CU & T/T) b Dec. 15, 1909, d Oct. 18, 1977

Graveney, D. A. (Glos, Som & Durham) b Jan. 2, 1953

Graveney, J. K. (Glos) b Dec. 16, 1924

*Graveney, T. W. OBE (Glos, Worcs & Qld; *CY 1953*) b June 16, 1927

Graves, P. J. (Sussex & OFS) b May 19, 1946

*Gray, A. H. (T/T, Surrey & W. Tvl) b May 23, 1963

*Gray, E. J. (Wgtn) b Nov. 18, 1954

Gray, J. R. (Hants) b May 19, 1926

Gray, L. H. (Middx) b Dec. 15, 1915, d Jan. 3, 1983

Green, A. M. (Sussex & OFS) b May 28, 1960

Green, D. M. (OU, Lancs & Glos; *CY 1969*) b Nov. 10, 1939

Green, Major L. (Lancs) b Feb. 1, 1890, d March 2, 1963

*Greenhough, T. (Lancs) b Nov. 9, 1931

*Greenidge, A. E. (B'dos) b Aug. 20, 1956

*Greenidge, C. G. MBE (Hants & B'dos; *CY 1977*) b May 1, 1951

*Greenidge, G. A. (B'dos & Sussex) b May 26, 1948

Greensmith, W. T. (Essex) b Aug. 16, 1930

*Greenwood, A. (Yorks) b Aug. 20, 1847, d Feb. 12, 1889

Greetham, C. (Som) b Aug. 28, 1936

*Gregory, D. W. (NSW; first Australian captain) b April 15, 1845, d Aug. 4, 1919

*Gregory, E. J. (NSW) b May 29, 1839, d April 22, 1899

*Gregory, J. M. (NSW; *CY 1922*) b Aug. 14, 1895, d Aug. 7, 1973

*Gregory, R. G. (Vic.) b Feb. 28, 1916, d June 10, 1942

Gregory, R. J. (Surrey) b Aug. 26, 1902, d Oct. 6, 1973

*Gregory, S. E. (NSW; *CY 1897*) b April 14, 1870, d Aug. 1, 1929

*Greig, A. W. (Border, E. Prov. & Sussex; *CY 1975*) b Oct. 6, 1946

*Greig, I. A. (CU, Border, Sussex & Surrey) b Dec. 8, 1955

*Grell, M. G. (T/T) b Dec. 18, 1899, d Jan. 11, 1976

*Grieve, B. A. F. (Eng.) b May 28, 1864, d Nov. 19, 1917

Grieves, K. J. (NSW & Lancs) b Aug. 27, 1925, d Jan. 3, 1992

*Grieveson, R. E. OBE (Tvl) b Aug. 24, 1909, d July 24, 1998

*Griffin, G. M. (Natal & Rhod.) b June 12, 1939

*Griffith, C. C. (B'dos; *CY 1964*) b Dec. 14, 1938

Griffith, G. ("Ben") (Surrey & Utd England XI) b Dec. 20, 1833, d May 3, 1879

*Griffith, H. C. (B'dos) b Dec. 1, 1893, d March 18, 1980

Griffith, M. G. (CU & Sussex) b Nov. 25, 1943

*Griffith, S. C. CBE (CU, Surrey & Sussex; Sec. MCC 1962-74; Pres. MCC 1979-80) b June 16, 1914, d April 7, 1993

Griffiths, B. J. (Northants) b June 13, 1949

*Grimmett, C. V. (Wgtn, Vic., & S. Aust.; *CY 1931*) b Dec. 25, 1891, d May 2, 1980

*Groube, T. U. (Vic.) b Sept. 2, 1857, d Aug. 5, 1927

*Grout, A. T. W. (Qld) b March 30, 1927, d Nov. 9, 1968

Grove, C. W. (Warwicks & Worcs) b Dec. 16, 1912, d Feb. 15, 1982

Grundy, James (Notts & Utd England XI) b March 5, 1824, d Nov. 24, 1873

*Guard, G. M. (Bombay & Guj.) b Dec. 12, 1925, d March 13, 1978

*Guest, C. E. J. (Vic. & W. Aust.) b Oct. 7, 1937

*Guha, S. (Bengal) b Jan. 31, 1946

**Guillen, S. C. (T/T & Cant.) b Sept. 24, 1924

**Gul Mahomed (N. Ind., Baroda, H'bad, Punjab & Lahore) b Oct. 15, 1921, d May 8, 1992

*Gunasekera, Y. (SL) b Nov. 8, 1957

*Guneratne, R. P. W. (Nomads) b Jan. 26, 1962

*Gunn, G. (Notts; *CY 1914*) b June 13, 1879, d June 29, 1958

Gunn, G. V. (Notts) b June 21, 1905, d Oct. 14, 1957

*Gunn, J. (Notts; *CY 1904*) b July 19, 1876, d Aug. 21, 1963

*Gunn, W. (Notts; *CY 1890*) b Dec. 4, 1858, d Jan. 29, 1921

*Gupte, B. P. (Bombay, Bengal & Ind. Rlwys) b Aug. 30, 1934

*Gupte, S. P. (Bombay, Bengal, Raja. & T/T) b Dec. 11, 1929

*Gursharan Singh (Punjab) b March 8, 1963

*Gurusinha, A. P. (SSC & NCC) b Sept. 16, 1966

*Guy, J. W. (C. Dist., Wgtn, Northants, Cant., Otago & N. Dist.) b Aug. 29, 1934

Haafiz Shahid (WAPDA) b April 10, 1963

Hadlee, B. G. (Cant.) b Dec. 14, 1941

*Hadlee, D. R. (Cant.) b Jan. 6, 1948

*Hadlee, Sir Richard J. (Cant., Notts & Tas.; *CY 1982*) b July 3, 1951

*Hadlee, W. A. CBE (Cant. & Otago) b June 4, 1915

*Hafeez, A. (*see* Kardar)

*Haig, N. E. (Middx) b Dec. 12, 1887, d Oct. 27, 1966

*Haigh, S. (Yorks; *CY 1901*) b March 19, 1871, d Feb. 27, 1921

Hair, D. B. (Test umpire) b Sept. 30, 1952

Halfyard, D. J. (Kent & Notts) b April 3, 1931, d Aug. 23, 1996

*Hall, A. E. (Tvl & Lancs) b Jan. 23, 1896, d Jan. 1, 1964

*Hall, G. G. (NE Tvl & E. Prov.) b May 24, 1938, d June 26, 1987

Hall, I. W. (Derbys) b Dec. 27, 1939

Hall, L. (Yorks; *CY 1890*) b Nov. 1, 1852, d Nov. 19, 1915

*Hall, W. W. (B'dos, T/T & Qld) b Sept. 12, 1937

Hallam, A. W. (Lancs & Notts; *CY 1908*) b Nov. 12, 1869, d July 24, 1940

Hallam, M. R. (Leics) b Sept. 10, 1931

Halliday, H. (Yorks) b Feb. 9, 1920, d Aug. 27, 1967

*Halliwell, E. A. (Tvl & Middx; *CY 1905*) b Sept. 7, 1864, d Oct. 2, 1919

*Hallows, C. (Lancs; *CY 1928*) b April 4, 1895, d Nov. 10, 1972

Hallows, J. (Lancs; *CY 1905*) b Nov. 14, 1873, d May 20, 1910

*Halse, C. G. (Natal) b Feb. 28, 1935

Hamence, R. A. (S. Aust.) b Nov. 25, 1915

Hamer, A. (Yorks & Derbys) b Dec. 8, 1916, d Nov. 3, 1993

Hammond, H. E. (Sussex) b Nov. 7, 1907, d June 16, 1985

*Hammond, J. R. (S. Aust.) b April 19, 1950

*Hammond, W. R. (Glos; *CY 1928*) b June 19, 1903, d July 1, 1965

*Hampshire, J. H. (Yorks, Derbys & Tas.; Test umpire) b Feb. 10, 1941

*Hands, P. A. M. (W. Prov.) b March 18, 1890, d April 27, 1951

*Hands, R. H. M. (W. Prov.) b July 26, 1888, d April 20, 1918

*Hanif Mohammad (B'pur, Kar. & PIA; *CY 1968*) b Dec. 21, 1934

Hanley, M. A. (Border & W. Prov.) b Nov. 10, 1918

*Hanumant Singh (M. Pradesh & Raja.; ICC referee) b March 29, 1939

Hardie, B. R. (Scotland & Essex) b Jan. 14, 1950

*Hardikar, M. S. (Bombay) b Feb. 8, 1936, d Feb. 4, 1995

*Hardinge, H. T. W. (Kent; *CY 1915*) b Feb. 25, 1886, d May 8, 1965

*Hardstaff, J. (Notts; Test umpire) b Nov. 9, 1882, d April 2, 1947

*Hardstaff, J., jun. (Notts & Auck.; *CY 1938*) b July 3, 1911, d Jan. 1, 1990

Hardy, J. J. E. (Hants, Som, W. Prov. & Glos) b Oct. 2, 1960

*Harford, N. S. (C. Dist. & Auck.) b Aug. 30, 1930, d March 30, 1981

*Harford, R. I. (Auck.) b May 30, 1936

Hargreave, S. (Warwicks) b Sept. 22, 1875, d Jan. 1, 1929

Harman, R. (Surrey) b Dec. 28, 1941

*Haroon Rashid (Kar., Sind, NBP, PIA & UBL) b March 25, 1953

*Harper, R. A. (Guyana & Northants) b March 17, 1963

*Harris, 4th Lord (OU & Kent; Pres. MCC 1895) b Feb. 3, 1851, d March 24, 1932

Harris, C. B. (Notts) b Dec. 6, 1907, d Aug. 8, 1954

Harris, David (Hants & All-England) b 1755, d May 19, 1803

*Harris, J. H. (Som; umpire) b Feb. 13, 1936

Harris, M. J. (Middx, Notts, E. Prov. & Wgtn) b May 25, 1944

*Harris, P. G. Z. (Cant.) b July 18, 1927, d Dec. 1, 1991

*Harris, R. M. (Auck.) b July 27, 1933

*Harris, T. A. (Griq. W. & Tvl) b Aug. 27, 1916, d March 7, 1993

Harrison, L. (Hants) b June 8, 1922

*Harry, J. (Vic.) b Aug. 1, 1857, d Oct. 27, 1919

Hart, R. T. (C. Dist. & Wgtn) b Nov. 7, 1961

*Hartigan, G. P. D. (Border) b Dec. 30, 1884, d Jan. 7, 1955

*Hartigan, R. J. (NSW & Qld) b Dec. 12, 1879, d June 7, 1958

*Hartkopf, A. E. V. (Vic.) b Dec. 28, 1889, d May 20, 1968

*Hartland, B. R. (Cant.) b Oct. 22, 1966

Hartley, A. (Lancs; *CY 1911*) b April 11, 1879, d Oct. 9, 1918

*Hartley, J. C. (OU & Sussex) b Nov. 15, 1874, d March 8, 1963

Hartley, S. N. (Yorks & OFS) b March 18, 1956

Harvey, J. F. (Derbys) b Sept. 27, 1939

*Harvey, M. R. (Vic.) b April 29, 1918, d March 20, 1995

Harvey, P. F. (Notts) b Jan. 15, 1923

Harvey, R. L. (Natal) b Sept. 14, 1911

*Harvey, R. N. MBE (Vic. & NSW; *CY 1954*) b Oct. 8, 1928

Hasan Jamil (Kalat, Kar., Pak. Us & PIA) b July 25, 1952

*Haseeb Ahsan (Peshawar, Pak. Us, Kar. & PIA) b July 15, 1939

Hassan, B. (Notts) b March 24, 1944

*Hassett, A. L. MBE (Vic.; *CY 1949*) b Aug. 28, 1913, d June 16, 1993

*Hastings, B. F. (Wgtn, C. Dist. & Cant.) b March 23, 1940

*Hathorn, C. M. H. (Tvl) b April 7, 1878, d May 17, 1920

*Hawke, 7th Lord (CU & Yorks; *CY 1909*; Pres. MCC 1914-18) b Aug. 16, 1860, d Oct. 10, 1938

*Hawke, N. J. N. (W. Aust., S. Aust. & Tas.) b June 27, 1939

Hawkins, D. G. (Glos) b May 18, 1935

*Hayes, E. G. (Surrey & Leics; *CY 1907*) b Nov. 6, 1876, d Dec. 2, 1953

*Hayes, F. C. (Lancs) b Dec. 6, 1946

*Hayes, J. A. (Auck. & Cant.) b Jan. 11, 1927

Hayes, R. L. (N. Dist.) b May 9, 1971

Haygarth, A. (Sussex; Historian) b Aug. 4, 1825, d May 1, 1903

Hayhurst, A. N. (Lancs, Som & Derbys) b Nov. 23, 1962

*Haynes, D. L. (B'dos, Middx & W. Prov.; *CY 1991*) b Feb. 15, 1956

Haynes, R. C. (Jam.) b Nov. 11, 1964

Hayward, T. (Cambs. & All-England) b March 21, 1835, d July 21, 1876

*Hayward, T. W. (Surrey; *CY 1895*) b March 29, 1871, d July 19, 1939

*Hazare, V. S. (M'tra, C. Ind. & Baroda) b March 11, 1915

Hazell, H. L. (Som) b Sept. 30, 1909, d March 31, 1990

Hazlerigg, Sir A. G. Bt (later 1st Lord) (Leics) b Nov. 17, 1878, d May 25, 1949

Hazlitt, G. R. (Vic. & NSW) b Sept. 4, 1888, d Oct. 30, 1915

*Headley, G. A. MBE (Jam.; *CY 1934*) b May 30, 1909, d Nov. 30, 1983

*Headley, R. G. A. (Worcs & Jam.) b June 29, 1939

Heane, G. F. H. (Notts) b Jan. 2, 1904, d Oct. 24, 1969

Heap, J. S. (Lancs) b Aug. 12, 1882, d Jan. 30, 1951

Hearn, P. (Kent) b Nov. 18, 1925

*Hearne, A. (Kent; *CY 1894*) b July 22, 1863, d May 16, 1952

**Hearne, F. (Kent & W. Prov.) b Nov. 23, 1858, d July 14, 1949

*Hearne, G. A. L. (W. Prov.) b March 27, 1888, d Nov. 13, 1978

*Hearne, G. G. (Kent) b July 7, 1856, d Feb. 13, 1932

*Hearne, J. T. (Middx; *CY 1892*) b May 3, 1867, d April 17, 1944

*Hearne, J. W. (Middx; *CY 1912*) b Feb. 11, 1891, d Sept. 14, 1965

Hearne, T. (Middx) b Sept. 4, 1826, d May 13, 1900

Heath, G. E. M. (Hants) b Feb. 20, 1913

Heath, M. (Hants) b March 9, 1934

Hedges, B. (Glam) b Nov. 10, 1927

Hedges, L. P. (Tonbridge, OU, Kent & Glos; *CY 1919*) b July 13, 1900, d Jan. 12, 1933

*Heine, P. S. (NE Tvl, OFS & Tvl) b June 28, 1928

*Hemmings, E. E. (Warwicks, Notts & Sussex) b Feb. 20, 1949

Hemsley, E. J. O. (Worcs) b Sept. 1, 1943

*Henderson, M. (Wgtn) b Aug. 2, 1895, d June 17, 1970

Henderson, R. (Surrey; *CY 1890*) b March 30, 1865, d Jan. 29, 1931

*Hendren, E. H. (Middx; *CY 1920*) b Feb. 5, 1889, d Oct. 4, 1962

*Hendrick, M. (Derbys & Notts; *CY 1978*) b Oct. 22, 1948

*Hendriks, J. L. (Jam.; ICC referee) b Dec. 21, 1933

*Hendry, H. L. (NSW & Vic.) b May 24, 1895, d Dec. 16, 1988

*Henry, O. (W. Prov., Boland, OFS & Scotland) b Jan. 23, 1952

Herman, O. W. (Hants) b Sept. 18, 1907, d June 24, 1987

Herman, R. S. (Middx, Border, Griq. W. & Hants) b Nov. 30, 1946

Heron, J. G. (Zimb.) b Nov. 8, 1948

*Heseltine, C. (Hants) b Nov. 26, 1869, d June 13, 1944

Hever, N. G. (Middx & Glam) b Dec. 17, 1924, d Sept. 11, 1987

Hewett, H. T. (OU & Som; *CY 1893*) b May 25, 1864, d March 4, 1921.

Heyhoe-Flint, Rachael (England Women) b June 11, 1939

Heyn, P. D. (SL) b June 26, 1945

*Hibbert, P. A. (Vic.) b July 23, 1952

Hide, M. E. (Molly) (England Women) b Oct 24, 1913, d Sept. 10, 1995

*Higgs, J. D. (Vic.) b July 11, 1950

*Higgs, K. (Lancs & Leics; *CY 1968*) b Jan. 14, 1937

Hignell, A. J. (CU & Glos) b Sept. 4, 1955

*Hilditch, A. M. J. (NSW & S. Aust.) b May 20, 1956

Hill, Alan (Derbys & OFS) b June 29, 1950

*Hill, Allen (Yorks) b Nov. 14, 1843, d Aug. 29, 1910

*Hill, A. J. L. (CU & Hants) b July 26, 1871, d Sept. 6, 1950

*Hill, C. (S. Aust.; *CY 1900*) b March 18, 1877, d Sept. 5, 1945

Hill, E. (Som) b July 9, 1923

Hill, G. (Hants) b April 15, 1913

*Hill, J. C. (Vic.) b June 25, 1923, d Aug. 11, 1974

Hill, M. (Notts, Derbys & Som) b Sept. 14, 1935

Hill, N. W. (Notts) b Aug. 22, 1935

Hill, W. A. (Warwicks) b April 27, 1910, d Aug. 11, 1995

Hill-Wood, Sir Samuel H. (Derbys) b March 21, 1872, d Jan. 4, 1949

Hillyer, W. R. (Kent & Surrey) b March 5, 1813, d Jan. 8, 1861

Hilton, C. (Lancs & Essex) b Sept. 26, 1937

*Hilton, M. J. (Lancs; *CY 1957*) b Aug. 2, 1928, d July 8, 1990

*Hime, C. F. W. (Natal) b Oct. 24, 1869, d Dec. 6, 1940

*Hindlekar, D. D. (Bombay) b Jan. 1, 1909, d March 30, 1949

Hinks, S. G. (Kent & Glos) b Oct. 12, 1960

Hipkin, A. B. (Essex) b Aug. 8, 1900, d Feb. 11, 1957

*Hirst, G. H. (Yorks; *CY 1901*) b Sept. 7, 1871, d May 10, 1954

*Hitch, J. W. (Surrey; *CY 1914*) b May 7, 1886, d July 7, 1965

Hitchcock, R. E. (Cant. & Warwicks) b Nov. 28, 1929

*Hoad, E. L. G. (B'dos) b Jan. 29, 1896, d March 5, 1986

*Hoare, D. E. (W. Aust.) b Oct. 19, 1934

*Hobbs, Sir John B. "Jack" (Surrey; *CY 1909, special portrait 1926*) b Dec. 16, 1882, d Dec. 21, 1963

*Hobbs, R. N. S. (Essex & Glam) b May 8, 1942

*Hodges, J. (Vic.) b Aug. 11, 1855, death unknown

Hodgson, A. (Northants) b Oct. 27, 1951

Hodgson, G. D. (Glos) b Oct. 22, 1966

*Hogan, T. G. (W. Aust.) b Sept. 23, 1956

*Hogg, R. M. (S. Aust.) b March 5, 1951

Hogg, V. R. (Zimb.) b July 3, 1952

*Hohns, T. V. (Qld) b Jan. 23, 1954

*Holder, J. W. (Hants; Test umpire) b March 19, 1945

*Holder, V. A. (B'dos, Worcs & OFS) b Oct. 8, 1945

*Holding, M. A. (Jam., Lancs, Derbys, Tas. & Cant.; *CY 1977*) b Feb. 16, 1954

*Hole, G. B. (NSW & S. Aust.) b Jan. 6, 1931, d Feb. 14, 1990

*Holford, D. A. J. (B'dos & T/T) b April 16, 1940

Holland, F. C. (Surrey) b Feb. 10, 1876, d Feb. 5, 1957

*Holland, R. G. (NSW & Wgtn) b Oct. 19, 1946

*Hollies, W. E. (Warwicks; *CY 1955*) b June 5, 1912, d April 16, 1981

Holmes, Gp Capt. A. J. (Sussex) b June 30, 1899, d May 21, 1950

*Holmes, E. R. T. (OU & Surrey; *CY 1936*) b Aug. 21, 1905, d Aug. 16, 1960

Holmes, G. C. (Glam) b Sept. 16, 1958

*Holmes, P. (Yorks; *CY 1920*) b Nov. 25, 1886, d Sept. 3, 1971

Holt, A. G. (Hants) b April 8, 1911, d July 28, 1994

*Holt, J. K., jun. (Jam.) b Aug. 12, 1923, d July 2, 1997

Home of the Hirsel, Lord (Middx; Pres. MCC 1966-67) b July 2, 1903, d Oct. 9, 1995

*Hone, L. (MCC) b Jan. 30, 1853, d Dec. 31, 1896

Hooker, R. W. (Middx) b Feb. 22, 1935

*Hookes, D. W. (S. Aust.) b May 3, 1955

*Hopkins, A. J. (NSW) b May 3, 1874, d April 25, 1931

Hopkins, J. A. (Glam & E. Prov.) b June 16, 1953

Hopkins, V. (Glos) b Jan. 21, 1911, d Aug. 6, 1984

*Hopwood, J. L. (Lancs) b Oct. 30, 1903, d June 15, 1985

*Horan, T. P. (Vic.) b March 8, 1854, d April 16, 1916

*Hordern, Dr H. V. (NSW & Philadelphia) b Feb. 10, 1884, d June 17, 1938

Hornby, A. H. (CU & Lancs) b July 29, 1877, d Sept. 6, 1952

*Hornby, A. N. (Lancs) b Feb. 10, 1847, d Dec. 17, 1925

*Horne, P. A. (Auck.) b Jan. 21, 1960

Horner, N. F. (Yorks & Warwicks) b May 10, 1926

*Hornibrook, P. M. (Qld) b July 27, 1899, d Aug. 25, 1976

Horsfall, R. (Essex & Glam) b June 26, 1920, d Aug. 25, 1981

Horton, H. (Worcs & Hants) b April 18, 1923, d Nov. 2, 1998

*Horton, M. J. (Worcs & N. Dist.) b April 21, 1934

*Hough, K. W. (Auck.) b Oct. 24, 1928

*Howard, A. B. (B'dos) b Aug. 27, 1946

*Howard, N. D. (Lancs) b May 18, 1925, d May 31, 1979

Howard, Major R. (Lancs; MCC Team Manager) b April 17, 1890, d Sept. 10, 1967

*Howarth, G. P. OBE (Auck., Surrey & N. Dist.) b March 29, 1951

*Howarth, H. J. (Auck.) b Dec. 25, 1943

*Howell, H. (Warwicks) b Nov. 29, 1890, d July 9, 1932

*Howell, W. P. (NSW) b Dec. 29, 1869, d July 14, 1940

*Howorth, R. (Worcs) b April 26, 1909, d April 2, 1980

Hubble, J. C. (Kent) b Feb. 10, 1881, d Feb. 26, 1965

Huggins, H. J. (Glos) b March 15, 1877, d Nov. 20, 1942

Hughes, D. P. (Lancs & Tas.; *CY 1988*) b May 13, 1947

*Hughes, K. J. (W. Aust. & Natal; *CY 1981*) b Jan. 26, 1954

*Hughes, M. G. (Vic. & Essex; *CY 1994*) b Nov. 23, 1961

Hughes, S. P. (Middx, N. Tvl & Durham) b Dec. 20, 1959

Huish, F. H. (Kent) b Nov. 15, 1869, d March 16, 1957

Hulme, J. H. A. (Middx) b Aug. 26, 1904, d Sept. 26, 1991

Humpage, G. W. (Warwicks & OFS; *CY 1985*) b April 24, 1954

Humphrey, T. (Surrey) b Jan. 16, 1839, d Sept. 3, 1878

Humphreys, E. (Kent & Cant.) b Aug. 24, 1881, d Nov. 6, 1949

Humphreys, W. A. (Sussex & Hants) b Oct. 28, 1849, d March 23, 1924

Humphries, D. J. (Leics & Worcs) b Aug. 6, 1953

*Humphries, J. (Derbys) b May 19, 1876, d May 7, 1946

Hunt, A. V. (Scotland & Bermuda) b Oct. 1, 1910

Hunt, G. E. (Som) b Sept. 30, 1896, d Jan. 22, 1959

*Hunt, W. A. (NSW) b Aug. 26, 1908, d Dec. 30, 1983

*Hunte, C. C. (B'dos; *CY 1964*) b May 9, 1932

*Hunte, E. A. C. (T/T) b Oct. 3, 1905, d June 26, 1967

Hunter, D. (Yorks) b Feb. 23, 1860, d Jan. 11, 1927

*Hunter, J. (Yorks) b Aug. 3, 1855, d Jan. 4, 1891

*Hurst, A. G. (Vic.) b July 15, 1950

Hurst, R. J. (Middx) b Dec. 29, 1933, d Feb. 10, 1996

*Hurwood, A. (Qld) b June 17, 1902, d Sept. 26, 1982

*Hutchings, K. L. (Kent; *CY 1907*) b Dec. 7, 1882, d Sept. 3, 1916

Hutchinson, J. M. (Derbys; *believed to be oldest living county cricketer at end 1998*) b Nov. 29, 1896

*Hutchinson, P. (SA) b Jan. 26, 1862, d Sept. 30, 1925

*Hutton, Sir Leonard (Yorks; *CY 1938*) b June 23, 1916, d Sept. 6, 1990

*Hutton, R. A. (CU, Yorks & Tvl) b Sept. 6, 1942

*Hylton, L. G. (Jam.) b March 29, 1905, d May 17, 1955

*Ibadulla, K. (Punjab, Warwicks, Tas. & Otago) b Dec. 20, 1935

*Ibrahim, K. C. (Bombay) b Jan. 26, 1919

Iddison, R. (Yorks & Lancs) b Sept. 15, 1834, d March 19, 1890

*Iddon, J. (Lancs) b Jan. 8, 1902, d April 17, 1946

*Ijaz Butt (Pak. Us, Punjab, Lahore, R'pindi & Multan) b March 10, 1938

*Ijaz Faqih (Kar., Sind, PWD & MCB) b March 24, 1956

*Ikin, J. T. (Lancs) b March 7, 1918, d Sept. 15, 1984

*Illingworth, R. CBE (Yorks & Leics; *CY 1960*) b June 8, 1932

*Imran Khan (Lahore, Dawood, Worcs, OU, PIA, Sussex & NSW; *CY 1983*) b Nov. 25, 1952

*Imtiaz Ahmed (N. Ind., Comb. Us, NWFP, Pak. Servs, Peshawar & PAF) b Jan. 5, 1928

*Imtiaz Ali (T/T) b July 28, 1954

Inchmore, J. D. (Worcs & N. Tvl) b Feb. 22, 1949

*Indrajitsinhji, K. S. (S'tra & Delhi) b June 15, 1937

Ingle, R. A. (Som) b Nov. 5, 1903, d Dec. 19, 1992

Ingleby-Mackenzie, A. C. D. (Hants; Pres. MCC 1996-98) b Sept. 15, 1933

Inman, C. C. (Ceylon & Leics) b Jan. 29, 1936

*Inshan Ali (T/T) b Sept. 25, 1949, d June 24, 1995

*Insole, D. J. CBE (CU & Essex; *CY 1956*) b April 18, 1926

*Intikhab Alam (Kar., PIA, Surrey, PWD, Sind, Punjab) b Dec. 28, 1941

*Inverarity, R. J. (W. Aust. & S. Aust.) b Jan. 31, 1944

*Iqbal Qasim (Kar., Sind & NBP) b Aug. 6, 1953

*Irani, J. K. (Sind) b Aug. 18, 1923, d Feb. 25, 1982

*Iredale, F. A. (NSW) b June 19, 1867, d April 15, 1926

Iremonger, J. (Notts; *CY 1903*) b March 5, 1876, d March 25, 1956

*Ironmonger, H. (Qld & Vic.) b April 7, 1882, d June 1, 1971

*Ironside, D. E. J. (Tvl) b May 2, 1925

*Irvine, B. L. (W. Prov., Natal, Essex & Tvl) b March 9, 1944

*Israr Ali (S. Punjab, B'pur & Multan) b May 1, 1927

*Iverson, J. B. (Vic.) b July 27, 1915, d Oct. 24, 1973

*Jack, S. D. (Tvl) b Aug. 4, 1970

*Jackman, R. D. (Surrey, W. Prov. & Rhod.; *CY 1981*) b Aug. 13, 1945

*Jackson, A. A. (NSW) b Sept. 5, 1909, d Feb. 16, 1933

Jackson, A. B. (Derbys) b Aug. 21, 1933

*Jackson, Rt Hon. Sir F. Stanley (CU & Yorks; *CY 1894*; Pres. MCC 1921) b Nov. 21, 1870, d March 9, 1947

Jackson, G. R. (Derbys) b June 23, 1896, d Feb. 21, 1966

*Jackson, H. L. (Derbys; *CY 1959*) b April 5, 1921

Jackson, J. (Notts & All-England) b May 21, 1833, d Nov. 4, 1901

Jackson, P. F. (Worcs) b May 11, 1911

Jackson, V. E. (NSW & Leics) b Oct. 25, 1916, d Jan. 30, 1965

*Jahangir Khan (N. Ind. & CU) b Feb. 1, 1910, d July 23, 1988

*Jai, L. P. (Bombay) b April 1, 1902, d Jan. 29, 1968

*Jaisimha, M. L. (H'bad) b March 3, 1939

Jakeman, F. (Yorks & Northants) b Jan. 10, 1920, d May 18, 1986

*Jalal-ud-Din (PWD, Kar., IDBP & Allied Bank) b June 12, 1959

James, A. E. (Sussex) b Aug. 7, 1924

James, C. L. R. (Writer) b Jan. 4, 1901, d May 31, 1989

*James, K. C. (Wgtn & Northants) b March 12, 1904, d Aug. 21, 1976

*James, W. R. (Mat.) b Aug. 27, 1965

Jameson, J. A. (Warwicks) b June 30, 1941

*Jamshedji, R. J. (Bombay) b Nov. 18, 1892, d April 5, 1976

*Jardine, D. R. (OU & Surrey; *CY 1928*) b Oct. 23, 1900, d June 18, 1958

*Jarman, B. N. (S. Aust.; ICC referee) b Feb. 17, 1936

*Jarvis, A. H. (S. Aust.) b Oct. 19, 1860, d Nov. 15, 1933

Jarvis, K. B. S. (Kent & Glos) b April 23, 1953

*Jarvis, M. P. (Mash.) b Dec. 6, 1955

*Jarvis, T. W. (Auck. & Cant.) b July 29, 1944

*Javed Akhtar (R'pindi & Pak. Serv.; Test umpire) b Nov. 21, 1940

*Javed Miandad (Kar., Sind, Sussex, HBL & Glam; *CY 1982*) b June 12, 1957

*Jayantilal, K. (H'bad) b Jan. 13, 1948

*Jayasekera, R. S. A. (SL) b Dec. 7, 1957

Jayasinghe, S. (Ceylon & Leics) b Jan. 19, 1931

Jayasinghe, S. A. (SL) b July 15, 1955, d April 20, 1995

Jeeves, P. (Warwicks) b March 5, 1888, d July 22, 1916

Jefferies, S. T. (W. Prov., Derbys, Lancs, Hants & Boland) b Dec. 8, 1959

*Jeganathan, S. (SL) b July 11, 1951, d May 14, 1996

*Jenkins, R. O. (Worcs; *CY 1950*) b Nov. 24, 1918, d July 21, 1995

*Jenner, T. J. (W. Aust. & S. Aust.) b Sept. 8, 1944

*Jennings, C. B. (S. Aust.) b June 5, 1884, d June 20, 1950

Jennings, R. V. (Tvl & N. Tvl) b Aug. 9, 1954

Jephson, D. L. A. (CU & Surrey) b Feb. 23, 1871, d Jan. 19, 1926

Jepson, A. (Notts; Test umpire) b July 12, 1915, d July 17, 1997

*Jessop, G. L. (CU & Glos; *CY 1898*) b May 19, 1874, d May 11, 1955

Jesty, T. E. (Hants, Border, Griq. W., Cant., Surrey & Lancs; *CY 1983*) b June 2, 1948

Jewell, Major M. F. S. (Worcs & Sussex) b Sept. 15, 1885, d May 28, 1978

*John, V. B. (SL) b May 27, 1960

*Johnson, C. L. (Tvl) b 1871, d May 31, 1908

Johnson, G. W. (Kent & Tvl) b Nov. 8, 1946

*Johnson, H. H. H. (Jam.) b July 17, 1910, d June 24, 1987

Johnson, H. L. (Derbys) b Nov. 8, 1927

*Johnson, I. W. OBE (Vic.) b Dec. 8, 1917, d Oct. 9, 1998

Johnson, L. A. (Northants) b Aug. 12, 1936

*Johnson, L. J. (Qld) b March 18, 1919, d April 20, 1977

Johnson, P. R. (CU & Som) b Aug. 5, 1880, d July 1, 1959

*Johnson, T. F. (T/T) b Jan. 10, 1917, d April 5, 1985

Johnston, Brian A. CBE (Broadcaster) b June 24, 1912, d Jan. 5, 1994

*Johnston, W. A. (Vic.; *CY 1949*) b Feb. 26, 1922

Jones, A. MBE (Glam, W. Aust., N. Tvl & Natal; *CY 1978*) b Nov. 4, 1938

Jones, A. A. (Sussex, Som, Middx, Glam, N. Tvl & OFS) b Dec. 9, 1947

*Jones, A. H. (Wgtn & C. Dist.) b May 9, 1959

Jones, A. L. (Glam) b June 1, 1957

Jones, A. N. (Sussex, Border & Som) b July 22, 1961

*Jones, A. O. (Notts & CU; *CY 1900*) b Aug. 16, 1872, d Dec. 21, 1914

*Jones, C. M. (BG) b Nov. 3, 1902, d Dec. 10, 1959

*Jones, Ernest (S. Aust. & W. Aust.) b Sept. 30, 1869, d Nov. 23, 1943

Jones, E. C. (Glam) b Dec. 14, 1911, d April 14, 1989

Jones, E. W. (Glam) b June 25, 1942

*Jones, I. J. (Glam) b Dec. 10, 1941

Jones, K. V. (Middx) b March 28, 1942

*Jones, P. E. (T/T) b June 6, 1917, d Nov. 21, 1991

Jones, P. H. (Kent) b June 19, 1935

*Jones, S. P. (NSW, Qld & Auck.) b Aug. 1, 1861, d July 14, 1951

Jones, W. E. (Glam) b Oct. 31, 1916, d July 25, 1996

Jordon, R. C. (Vic.) b Feb. 17, 1937

*Joshi, P. G. (M'tra) b Oct. 27, 1926, d Jan. 8, 1987

Joshi, U. C. (S'tra, Ind. Rlwys, Guj. & Sussex) b Dec. 23, 1944

*Joslin, L. R. (Vic.) b Dec. 13, 1947

Julian, A. (Leics) b Aug. 23, 1936

*Julien, B. D. (T/T & Kent) b March 13, 1950

*Jumadeen, R. R. (T/T) b April 12, 1948

*Jupp, H. (Surrey) b Nov. 19, 1841, d April 8, 1889

*Jupp, V. W. C. (Sussex & Northants; *CY 1928*) b March 27, 1891, d July 9, 1960

*Jurangpathy, B. R. (CCC) b June 25, 1967

*Kallicharran, A. I. (Guyana, Warwicks, Qld, Tvl & OFS; *CY 1983*) b March 21, 1949

*Kaluperuma, L. W. (SL) b May 25, 1949

*Kaluperuma, S. M. S. (SL) b Oct. 22, 1961

*Kanhai, R. B. (†Guyana, T/T, W. Aust., Warwicks & Tas.; *CY 1964*) b Dec. 26, 1935

*Kanitkar, H. S. (M'tra) b Dec. 8, 1942

*Kapil Dev (Haryana, Northants & Worcs; *CY 1983*) b Jan. 6, 1959

**Kardar, A. H. (formerly Abdul Hafeez) (N. Ind., OU, Warwicks & Pak. Serv.) b Jan. 17, 1925, d April 21, 1996

Karnain, S. H. U. (NCC & Moors) b Aug. 11, 1962

*Keeton, W. W. (Notts; *CY 1940*) b April 30, 1905, d Oct. 10, 1980

*Keith, H. J. (Natal) b Oct. 25, 1927, d Nov. 17, 1997

*Kelleway, C. (NSW) b April 25, 1886, d Nov. 16, 1944

*Kelly, J. J. (NSW; *CY 1903*) b May 10, 1867, d Aug. 14, 1938

Kelly, J. M. (Lancs & Derbys) b March 19, 1922, d Nov. 13, 1979

*Kelly, T. J. D. (Vic.) b May 3, 1844, d July 20, 1893

*Kempis, G. A. (Natal) b Aug. 4, 1865, d May 19, 1890

*Kendall, T. (Vic. & Tas.) b Aug. 24, 1851, d Aug. 17, 1924

Kennedy, A. (Lancs) b Nov. 4, 1949

*Kennedy, A. S. (Hants; *CY 1933*) b Jan. 24, 1891, d Nov. 15, 1959

*Kenny, R. B. (Bombay & Bengal) b Sept. 29, 1930, d Nov. 21, 1985

*Kent, M. F. (Qld) b Nov. 23, 1953

*Kentish, E. S. M. (Jam. & OU) b Nov. 21, 1916

*Kenyon, D. (Worcs; *CY 1963*) b May 15, 1924, d Nov. 12, 1996

Kenyon, M. N. (Lancs) b Dec. 25, 1886, d Nov. 21, 1960

*Kerr, J. L. (Cant.) b Dec. 28, 1910

*Kerr, R. B. (Qld) b June 16, 1961

Key, Sir Kingsmill J. (Surrey & OU) b Oct. 11, 1864, d Aug. 9, 1932

*Khalid Hassan (Punjab & Lahore) b July 14, 1937

*Khalid Wazir (Pak.) b April 27, 1936

*Khan Mohammad (N. Ind., Pak. Us, Som, B'pur, Sind, Kar. & Lahore) b Jan. 1, 1928

Khanna, S. C. (Delhi) b June 3, 1956

Killick, E. H. (Sussex) b Jan. 17, 1875, d Sept. 29, 1948

*Killick, Rev. E. T. (CU & Middx) b May 9, 1907, d May 18, 1953

Kilner, N. (Yorks & Warwicks) b July 21, 1895, d April 28, 1979

*Kilner, R. (Yorks; *CY 1924*) b Oct. 17, 1890, d April 5, 1928

King, B. P. (Worcs & Lancs) b April 22, 1915, d March 31, 1970

*King, C. L. (B'dos, Glam, Worcs & Natal) b June 11, 1951

*King, F. M. (B'dos) b Dec. 14, 1926, d Dec. 23, 1990

King, J. B. (Philadelphia) b Oct. 19, 1873, d Oct. 17, 1965

*King, J. H. (Leics) b April 16, 1871, d Nov. 18, 1946

*King, L. A. (Jam. & Bengal) b Feb. 27, 1939, d July 9, 1998

*Kinneir, S. P. (Warwicks; *CY 1912*) b May 13, 1871, d Oct. 16, 1928

*Kippax, A. F. (NSW) b May 25, 1897, d Sept. 4, 1972

Kirby, D. (CU & Leics) b Jan. 18, 1939

*Kirmani, S. M. H. (†Karn.) b Dec. 29, 1949

*Kirsten, P. N. (W. Prov., Sussex, Derbys & Border) b May 14, 1955

*Kischenchand, G. (W. Ind., Guj. & Baroda) b April 14, 1925, d April 16, 1997

Kitchen, M. J. (Som; Test umpire) b Aug. 1, 1940

Kline, L. F. (Vic.) b Sept. 29, 1934

*Knight, A. E. (Leics; *CY 1904*) b Oct. 8, 1872, d April 25, 1946

*Knight, B. R. (Essex & Leics) b Feb. 18, 1938

*Knight, D. J. (OU & Surrey; *CY 1915*) b May 12, 1894, d Jan. 5, 1960

Knight, R. D. V. (CU, Surrey, Glos & Sussex; Sec. MCC 1994-   ) b Sept. 6, 1946

Knight, W. H. (Editor of *Wisden* 1870-79) b Nov. 29, 1812, d Aug. 16, 1879

*Knott, A. P. E. (Kent & Tas.; *CY 1970*) b April 9, 1946

Knott, C. J. (Hants) b Nov. 26, 1914

Knowles, J. (Notts) b March 25, 1910

*Knox, N. A. (Surrey; *CY 1907*) b Oct. 10, 1884, d March 3, 1935

Koertzen, R. E. (Test umpire) b March 26, 1949

Kortright, C. J. (Essex) b Jan. 9, 1871, d Dec. 12, 1952

*Kotze, J. J. (Tvl & W. Prov.) b Aug. 7, 1879, d July 7, 1931

*Kripal Singh, A. G. (Madras & H'bad) b Aug. 6, 1933, d July 23, 1987

*Krishnamurthy, P. (H'bad) b July 12, 1947

*Kuggeleijn, C. M. (N. Distr.) b May 10, 1956

*Kulkarni, R. R. (Bombay) b Sept. 25, 1962

*Kulkarni, U. N. (Bombay) b March 7, 1942

*Kumar, V. V. (†TN) b June 22, 1935

*Kunderan, B. K. (Ind. Rlwys & Mysore) b Oct. 2, 1939

*Kuruppu, D. S. B. P. (BRC) b Jan. 5, 1962

*Kuruppuarachchi, A. K. (NCC) b Nov. 1, 1964

*Kuys, F. (W. Prov.) b March 21, 1870, d Sept. 12, 1953

Kynaston, R. (Middx; Sec. MCC 1846-58) b Nov. 5, 1805, d June 21, 1874

*Labrooy, G. F. (CCC) b June 7, 1964

Lacey, Sir Francis E. (CU & Hants; Sec. MCC 1898-1926) b Oct. 19, 1859, d May 26, 1946

*Laird, B. M. (W. Aust.) b Nov. 21, 1950

*Laker, J. C. (Surrey, Auck. & Essex; *CY 1952*) b Feb. 9, 1922, d April 23, 1986

*Lall Singh (S. Punjab) b Dec. 16, 1909, d Nov. 19, 1985
*Lamb, A. J. (W. Prov., Northants & OFS; *CY 1981*) b June 20, 1954
Lamb, Hon. T. M. (OU, Middx & Northants; Chief Exec. ECB, 1997-   ) b March 24, 1953
*Lamba, R. (Delhi) b Jan. 2, 1960, d Feb. 23, 1998
Lambert, G. E. (Glos & Som) b May 11, 1918, d Oct. 31, 1991
Lambert, R. H. (Ireland) b July 18, 1874, d March 24, 1956
Lambert, Wm (Surrey) b 1779, d April 19, 1851
*Lance, H. R. (NE Tvl & Tvl) b June 6, 1940
Langdon, T. (Glos) b Jan. 8, 1879, d Nov. 30, 1944
Langford, B. A. (Som) b Dec. 17, 1935
*Langley, G. R. A. (S. Aust.; *CY 1957*) b Sept. 14, 1919
*Langridge, James (Sussex; *CY 1932*) b July 10, 1906, d Sept. 10, 1966
Langridge, John MBE (Sussex; Test umpire; *CY 1950*) b Feb. 10, 1910
Langridge, R. J. (Sussex) b April 13, 1939
*Langton, A. B. C. (Tvl) b March 2, 1912, d Nov. 27, 1942
*Larkins, W. (Northants, E. Prov. & Durham) b Nov. 22, 1953
*Larter, J. D. F. (Northants) b April 24, 1940
*Larwood, H. MBE (Notts; *CY 1927*) b Nov. 14, 1904, d July 22, 1995
*Lashley, P. D. (B'dos) b Feb. 11, 1937
Latchman, H. C. (Middx & Notts) b July 26, 1943
*Latham, R. T. (Cant.) b June 12, 1961
*Laughlin, T. J. (Vic.) b Jan. 30, 1951
Laver, F. (Vic.) b Dec. 7, 1869, d Sept. 24, 1919
Lavis, G. (Glam) b Aug. 17, 1908, d July 29, 1956
*Lawrence, D. V. (Glos) b Jan. 28, 1964
*Lawrence, G. B. (Rhod. & Natal) b March 31, 1932
Lawrence, J. (Som) b March 29, 1914, d Dec. 10, 1988
*Lawry, W. M. (Vic.; *CY 1962*) b Feb. 11, 1937
*Lawson, G. F. (NSW & Lancs) b Dec. 7, 1957
Lawton, A. E. (Derbys & Lancs) b March 31, 1879, d Dec. 25, 1955
Leach, G. (Sussex) b July 18, 1881, d Jan. 10, 1945
Leadbeater, B. (Yorks) b Aug. 14, 1943
*Leadbeater, E. (Yorks & Warwicks) b Aug. 15, 1927
Leary, S. E. (Kent) b April 30, 1933, d Aug. 21, 1988
Lee, C. (Yorks & Derbys) b March 17, 1924
Lee, F. S. (Middx & Som; Test umpire) b July 24, 1905, d March 30, 1982

Lee, G. M. (Notts & Derbys) b June 7, 1887, d Feb. 29, 1976
*Lee, H. W. (Middx) b Oct. 26, 1890, d April 21, 1981
Lee, J. W. (Middx & Som) b Feb. 1, 1904, d June 20, 1944
Lee, P. G. (Northants & Lancs; *CY 1976*) b Aug. 27, 1945
*Lee, P. K. (S. Aust.) b Sept. 15, 1904, d Aug. 9, 1980
*Lees, W. K. MBE (Otago) b March 19, 1952
*Lees, W. S. (Surrey; *CY 1906*) b Dec. 25, 1875, d Sept. 10, 1924
Lefebvre, R. P. (Holland, Som, Cant. & Glam) b Feb. 7, 1963
*Legall, R. (B'dos & T/T) b Dec. 1, 1925
*Leggat, I. B. (C. Dist.) b June 7, 1930
*Leggat, J. G. (Cant.) b May 27, 1926, d March 9, 1973
*Legge, G. B. (OU & Kent) b Jan. 26, 1903, d Nov. 21, 1940
Lenham, L. J. (Sussex) b May 24, 1936
Lenham, N. J. (Sussex) b Dec. 17, 1965
*le Roux, F. L. (Tvl & E. Prov.) b Feb. 5, 1882, d Sept. 22, 1963
le Roux, G. S. (W. Prov. & Sussex) b Sept. 4, 1955
*Leslie, C. F. H. (OU & Middx) b Dec. 8, 1861, d Feb. 12, 1921
Lester, E. (Yorks) b Feb. 18, 1923
Lester, G. (Leics) b Dec. 27, 1915, d Jan. 26, 1998
Lester, Dr J. A. (Philadelphia) b Aug. 1, 1871, d Sept. 3, 1969
*Lever, J. K. MBE (Essex & Natal; *CY 1979*) b Feb. 24, 1949
*Lever, P. (Lancs & Tas.) b Sept. 17, 1940
*Leveson Gower, Sir H. D. G. (OU & Surrey) b May 8, 1873, d Feb. 1, 1954
*Levett, W. H. V. (Kent) b Jan. 25, 1908, d Nov. 30, 1995
*Lewis, A. R. (Glam & CU; Pres. MCC 1998-   ; writer & broadcaster) b July 6, 1938
Lewis, A. E. (Som) b Jan. 20, 1877, d Feb. 22, 1956
Lewis, C. BEM (Kent) b July 27, 1908, d April 26, 1993
*Lewis, D. M. (Jam.) b Feb. 21, 1946
Lewis, E. J. (Glam & Sussex) b Jan. 31, 1942
*Lewis, P. T. (W. Prov.) b Oct. 2, 1884, d Jan. 30, 1976
*Leyland, M. (Yorks; *CY 1929*) b July 20, 1900, d Jan. 1, 1967
*Liaqat Ali (Kar., Sind, HBL & PIA) b May 21, 1955
Lightfoot, A. (Northants) b Jan. 8, 1936
*Lillee, D. K. MBE (W. Aust., Tas. & Northants; *CY 1973*) b July 18, 1949
*Lilley, A. A. (Warwicks; *CY 1897*) b Nov. 28, 1866, d Nov. 17, 1929
Lilley, A. W. (Essex) b May 8, 1959

Lilley, B. (Notts) b Feb. 11, 1895, d Aug. 4, 1950

Lillywhite, Fred (Sussex; Editor of *Lillywhite's Guide to Cricketers*) b July 23, 1829, d Sept. 15, 1866

Lillywhite, F. W. ("William") (Sussex) b June 13, 1792, d Aug. 21, 1854

*Lillywhite, James, jun. (Sussex) b Feb. 23, 1842, d Oct. 25, 1929

*Lindsay, D. T. (NE Tvl, N. Tvl & Tvl) b Sept. 4, 1939

*Lindsay, J. D. (Tvl & NE Tvl) b Sept. 8, 1909, d Aug. 31, 1990

*Lindsay, N. V. (Tvl & OFS) b July 30, 1886, d Feb. 2, 1976

*Lindwall, R. R. MBE (NSW & Qld; *CY 1949*) b Oct. 3, 1921, d June 22, 1996

*Ling, W. V. S. (Griq. W. & E. Prov.) b Oct. 3, 1891, d Sept. 26, 1960

*Lissette, A. F. (Auck. & N. Dist.) b Nov. 6, 1919, d Jan. 24, 1973

Lister, W. H. L. (CU & Lancs) b Oct. 7, 1911, d July 29, 1998

Livingston, L. (NSW & Northants) b May 3, 1920, d Jan. 16, 1998

Livingstone, D. A. (Hants) b Sept. 21, 1933, d Sept. 8, 1988

Livsey, W. H. (Hants) b Sept. 23, 1893, d Sept. 12, 1978

*Llewellyn, C. B. (Natal & Hants; *CY 1911*) b Sept. 26, 1876, d June 7, 1964

Llewellyn, M. J. (Glam) b Nov. 27, 1953

Lloyd, B. J. (Glam) b Sept. 6, 1953

*Lloyd, C. H. OBE (†Guyana & Lancs; *CY 1971*) b Aug. 31, 1944

*Lloyd, D. (Lancs) b March 18, 1947

*Lloyd, T. A. (Warwicks & OFS) b Nov. 5, 1956

Lloyds, J. W. (Som, OFS & Glos) b Nov. 17, 1954

*Loader, P. J. (Surrey & W. Aust.; *CY 1958*) b Oct. 25, 1929

Lobb, B. (Warwicks & Som) b Jan. 11, 1931

*Lock, G. A. R. (Surrey, W. Aust. & Leics; *CY 1954*) b July 5, 1929, d March 29, 1995

Lock, H. C. (Surrey; first TCCB pitch inspector) b May 8, 1903, d May 19, 1978

Lockwood, Ephraim (Yorks) b April 4, 1845, d Dec. 19, 1921

*Lockwood, W. H. (Notts & Surrey; *CY 1899*) b March 25, 1868, d April 26, 1932

Lockyer, T. (Surrey & All-England) b Nov. 1, 1826, d Dec. 22, 1869

Logan, J. D., jun. (SA) b June 24, 1880, d Jan. 3, 1960

*Logie, A. L. (T/T) b Sept. 28, 1960

*Lohmann, G. A. (Surrey, W. Prov. & Tvl; *CY 1889*) b June 2, 1865, d Dec. 1, 1901

Lomax, J. G. (Lancs & Som) b May 5, 1925, d May 21, 1992

Long, A. (Surrey & Sussex) b Dec. 18, 1940

Longrigg, E. F. (Som & CU) b April 16, 1906, d July 23, 1974

Lord, Thomas (Middx; founder of Lord's) b Nov. 23, 1755, d Jan. 13, 1832

*Love, H. S. B. (NSW & Vic.) b Aug. 10, 1895, d July 22, 1969

Love, J. D. (Yorks) b April 22, 1955

*Lowry, T. C. (Wgtn, CU & Som) b Feb. 17, 1898, d July 20, 1976

*Lowson, F. A. (Yorks) b July 1, 1925, d Sept. 8, 1984

*Loxton, S. J. E. (Vic.) b March 29, 1921

*Lucas, A. P. (CU, Surrey, Middx & Essex) b Feb. 20, 1857, d Oct. 12, 1923

Luckes, W. T. (Som) b Jan. 1, 1901, d Oct. 27, 1982

*Luckhurst, B. W. (Kent; *CY 1971*) b Feb. 5, 1939

Lumb, R. G. (Yorks) b Feb. 27, 1950

*Lundie, E. B. (E. Prov., W. Prov. & Tvl) b March 15, 1888, d Sept. 12, 1917

Lupton, A. W. (Yorks) b Feb. 23, 1879, d April 14, 1944

Lynch, M. A. (Surrey, Glos & Guyana) b May 21, 1958

Lyon, B. H. (OU & Glos; *CY 1931*) b Jan. 19, 1902, d June 22, 1970

Lyon, M. D. (CU & Som) b April 22, 1898, d Feb. 17, 1964

*Lyons, J. J. (S. Aust.) b May 21, 1863, d July 21, 1927

*Lyttelton, Hon. Alfred (CU & Middx; Pres. MCC 1898) b Feb. 7, 1857, d July 5, 1913

Lyttelton, Rev. Hon. C. F. (CU & Worcs) b Jan. 26, 1887, d Oct. 3, 1931

Lyttelton, Hon. C. G. (CU) b Oct. 27, 1842, d June 9, 1922

Lyttelton, Hon. C. J. (*see* 10th Visct Cobham)

*McAlister, P. A. (Vic.) b July 11, 1869, d May 10, 1938

*Macartney, C. G. (NSW & Otago; *CY 1922*) b June 27, 1886, d Sept. 9, 1958

*Macaulay, G. G. (Yorks; *CY 1924*) b Dec. 7, 1897, d Dec. 13, 1940

*Macaulay, M. J. (Tvl, W. Prov., OFS, NE Tvl & E. Prov.) b April 1939

*MacBryan, J. C. W. (CU & Som; *CY 1925*) b July 22, 1892, d July 14, 1983

*McCabe, S. J. (NSW; *CY 1935*) b July 16, 1910, d Aug. 25, 1968

*McCarthy, C. N. (Natal & CU) b March 24, 1929

McConnon, J. E. (Glam) b June 21, 1922

*McCool, C. L. (NSW, Qld & Som) b Dec. 9, 1916, d April 5, 1986

McCorkell, N. (Hants) b March 23, 1912

*McCormick, E. L. (Vic.) b May 16, 1906, d June 28, 1991

*McCosker, R. B. (NSW; *CY 1976*) b Dec. 11, 1946

McCurdy, R. J. (Vic., Derbys, S. Aust., E. Prov. & Natal) b Dec. 30, 1959

*McDermott, C. J. (Qld; *CY 1986*) b April 14, 1965

*McDonald, C. C. (Vic.) b Nov. 17, 1928

*McDonald, E. A. (Tas., Vic. & Lancs; *CY 1922*) b Jan. 6, 1891, d July 22, 1937

*McDonnell, P. S. (Vic., NSW & Qld) b Nov. 13, 1858, d Sept. 24, 1896

McEwan, K. S. (E. Prov., W. Prov., Essex & W. Aust.; *CY 1978*) b July 16, 1952

*McEwan, P. E. (Cant.) b Dec. 19, 1953

*McGahey, C. P. (Essex; *CY 1902*) b Feb. 12, 1871, d Jan. 10, 1935

*MacGibbon, A. R. (Cant.) b Aug. 28, 1924

McGilvray, A. D. (NSW; broadcaster) b Dec. 6, 1909, d July 16, 1996

*McGirr, H. M. (Wgtn) b Nov. 5, 1891, d April 14, 1964

*McGlew, D. J. (Natal; *CY 1956*) b March 11, 1929, d June 9, 1998

*MacGregor, G. (CU & Middx; *CY 1891*) b Aug. 31, 1869, d Aug. 20, 1919

*McGregor, S. N. (Otago) b Dec. 18, 1931

*McIlwraith, J. (Vic.) b Sept. 7, 1857, d July 5, 1938

*McIntyre, A. J. (Surrey; *CY 1958*) b May 14, 1918

*Mackay, K. D. MBE (Qld) b Oct. 24, 1925, d June 13, 1982

McKechnie, B. J. (Otago) b Nov. 6, 1953

*McKenzie, G. D. (W. Aust. & Leics; *CY 1965*) b June 24, 1941

*McKibbin, T. R. (NSW) b Dec. 10, 1870, d Dec. 15, 1939

*McKinnon, A. H. (E. Prov. & Tvl) b Aug. 20, 1932, d Dec. 1, 1983

*MacKinnon, F. A. (CU & Kent; *believed to be longest-lived Test cricketer*) b April 9, 1848, d Feb. 27, 1947

*MacLaren, A. C. (Lancs; *CY 1895*) b Dec. 1, 1871, d Nov. 17, 1944

*McLaren, J. W. (Qld) b Dec. 24, 1887, d Nov. 17, 1921

MacLaurin of Knebworth, Lord (Chairman ECB 1997–) b March 30, 1937

*Maclean, J. A. (Qld) b April 27, 1946

*McLean, R. A. (Natal; *CY 1961*) b July 9, 1930

MacLeay, K. H. (W. Aust. & Som) b April 2, 1959

*McLeod, C. E. (Vic.) b Oct. 24, 1869, d Nov. 26, 1918

*McLeod, E. G. (Auck. & Wgtn) b Oct. 14, 1900, d Sept. 14, 1989

*McLeod, R. W. (Vic.) b Jan. 19, 1868, d June 14, 1907

McMahon, J. W. (Surrey & Som) b Dec. 28, 1919

McMahon, T. G. (Wgtn) b Nov. 8, 1929

*McMaster, J. E. P. (Eng.) b March 16, 1861, d June 7, 1929

*McMillan, Q. (Tvl) b June 23, 1904, d July 3, 1948

*McMorris, E. D. A. (Jam.) b April 4, 1935

*McRae, D. A. N. (Cant.) b Dec. 25, 1912, d Aug. 10, 1986

*McShane, P. G. (Vic.) b 1857, d Dec. 11, 1903

McSweeney, E. B. (C. Dist. & Wgtn) b March 8, 1957

McVicker, N. M. (Warwicks & Leics) b Nov. 4, 1940

*McWatt, C. A. (BG) b Feb. 1, 1922, d July 12, 1997

*Madan Lal (Punjab & Delhi) b March 20, 1951

*Maddocks, L. V. (Vic. & Tas.) b May 24, 1926

*Madray, I. S. (BG) b July 2, 1934

*Madugalle, R. S. (NCC; ICC referee) b April 22, 1959

*Maguire, J. N. (Qld, E. Prov. & Leics) b Sept. 15, 1956

Maher, B. J. M. (Derbys) b Feb. 11, 1958

*Mahmood Hussain (Pak. Us, Punjab, Kar., E. Pak. & NTB) b April 2, 1932, d Dec. 25, 1991

*Mailey, A. A. (NSW; writer) b Jan. 3, 1886, d Dec. 31, 1967

*Majid Khan (Lahore, Pak. Us, CU, Glam, PIA, Qld, Punjab; *CY 1970*) b Sept. 28, 1946

*Maka, E. S. (Bombay) b March 5, 1922, dead

*Makepeace, H. (Lancs) b Aug. 22, 1881, d Dec. 19, 1952

*Malhotra, A. (Haryana, Bengal & Delhi) b Jan. 26, 1957

*Mallender, N. A. (Northants, Otago & Som) b Aug. 13, 1961

*Mallett, A. A. (S. Aust.) b July 13, 1945

*Malone, M. F. (W. Aust. & Lancs) b Oct. 9, 1950

*Maninder Singh (Delhi) b June 13, 1965

*Manjrekar, V. L. (Bombay, Bengal, Andhra, U. Pradesh, Raja. & M'tra) b Sept. 26, 1931, d Oct. 18, 1983

*Mankad, A. V. (Bombay) b Oct. 12, 1946

*Mankad, V. (M. H.) (W. Ind., Naw., M'tra, Guj., Bengal, Bombay & Raja.; *CY 1947*) b April 12, 1917, d Aug. 21, 1978

*Mann, A. L. (W. Aust.) b Nov. 8, 1945

*Mann, F. G. CBE (CU & Middx; Pres. MCC 1984-85) b Sept. 6, 1917

*Mann, F. T. (CU & Middx) b March 3, 1888, d Oct. 6, 1964

*Mann, N. B. F. (Natal & E. Prov.) b Dec. 28, 1920, d July 31, 1952

Manning, J. S. (S. Aust. & Northants) b June 11, 1924, d May 5, 1988

Manning, T. E. (Northants) b Sept. 2, 1884, d Nov. 22, 1975

*Mansell, P. N. F. MBE (Rhod.) b March 16, 1920, d May 9, 1995

*Mansoor Akhtar (Kar., UBL & Sind) b Dec. 25, 1957

Mansur Ali Khan (*see* Pataudi, Mansur Ali, Nawab of)

*Mantri, M. K. (Bombay & M'tra) b Sept. 1, 1921

*Maqsood Ahmed (S. Punjab, R'pindi & Kar.) b March 26, 1925, d Jan. 4, 1999

*Marais, G. G. ("G. Gladstone") (Jam.) b Jan. 14, 1901, d May 19, 1978

Marchant, F. (Kent & CU) b May 22, 1864, d April 13, 1946

*Markham, L. A. (Natal) b Sept. 12, 1924

*Marks, V. J. (OU, Som & W. Aust.; writer) b June 25, 1955

Marlar, R. G. (CU & Sussex; writer) b Jan. 2, 1931

Marlow, F. W. (Sussex) b Oct. 8, 1867, d Aug. 7, 1952

Marner, P. T. (Lancs & Leics) b March 31, 1936

*Marr, A. P. (NSW) b March 28, 1962, d March 15, 1940

*Marriott, C. S. (CU, Lancs & Kent) b Sept. 14, 1895, d Oct. 13, 1966

Marsden, Tom (Eng.) b 1805, d Feb. 27, 1843

*Marsh, G. R. (W. Aust.) b Dec. 31, 1958

*Marsh, R. W. MBE (W. Aust.; *CY 1982*) b Nov. 11, 1947

Marshal, Alan (Qld & Surrey; *CY 1909*) b June 12, 1883, d July 23, 1915

*Marshall, M. D. (B'dos, Hants & Natal; *CY 1983*) b April 18, 1958

*Marshall, N. E. (B'dos & T/T) b Feb. 27, 1924

*Marshall, R. E. (B'dos & Hants; *CY 1959*) b April 25, 1930, d Oct. 27, 1992

Marsham, C. H. B. (OU & Kent) b Feb. 10, 1879, d July 19, 1928

Martin, E. J. (Notts) b Aug. 17, 1925

*Martin, F. (Kent; *CY 1892*) b Oct. 12, 1861, d Dec. 13, 1921

*Martin, F. R. (Jam.) b Oct. 12, 1893, d Nov. 23, 1967

*Martin, J. W. (NSW & S. Aust.) b July 28, 1931, d July 16, 1992

*Martin, J. W. (Kent) b Feb. 16, 1917, d Jan. 4, 1987

Martin, S. H. (Worcs, Natal & Rhod.) b Jan. 11, 1909, d Feb. 17, 1988

*Martindale, E. A. (B'dos) b Nov. 25, 1909, d March 17, 1972

Martin-Jenkins, Christopher (Writer & broadcaster) b Jan. 20, 1945

*Marx, W. F. E. (Tvl) b July 4, 1895, d June 2, 1974

*Mason, J. R. (Kent; *CY 1898*) b March 26, 1874, d Oct. 15, 1958

*Masood Anwar (UBL, Multan & F'bad) b Dec. 12, 1967

Masood Iqbal (Lahore, Punjab U., Pak. Us & HBL) b April 17, 1952

*Massie, H. H. (NSW) b April 11, 1854, d Oct. 12, 1938

*Massie, R. A. L. (W. Aust.; *CY 1973*) b April 14, 1947

*Matheson, A. M. (Auck.) b Feb. 27, 1906, d Dec. 31, 1985

*Mathias, Wallis (Sind, Kar. & NBP) b Feb. 4, 1935, d Sept. 1, 1994

*Matthews, A. D. G. (Northants & Glam) b May 3, 1904, d July 29, 1977

*Matthews, C. D. (W. Aust. & Lancs) b Sept. 22, 1962

*Matthews, T. J. (Vic.) b April 3, 1884, d Oct. 14, 1943

*Mattis, E. H. (Jam.) b April 11, 1957

*May, P. B. H. CBE (CU & Surrey; *CY 1952*; Pres. MCC 1980-81) b Dec. 31, 1929, d Dec. 27, 1994

*May, T. B. A. (S. Aust.) b Jan. 26, 1962

Mayer, J. H. (Warwicks) b March 2, 1902, d Sept. 6, 1981

Maynard, C. (Warwicks & Lancs) b April 8, 1958

*Mayne, E. R. (S. Aust. & Vict.) b July 2, 1882, d Oct. 26, 1961

*Mayne, L. C. (W. Aust.) b Jan. 23, 1942

*Mead, C. P. (Hants; *CY 1912*) b March 9, 1887, d March 26, 1958

*Mead, W. (Essex; *CY 1904*) b March 25, 1868, d March 18, 1954

Meads, E. A. (Notts) b Aug. 17, 1916

*Meale, T. (Wgtn) b Nov. 11, 1928

*Meckiff, I. (Vic.) b Jan. 6, 1935

Medlycott, K. T. (Surrey & N. Tvl) b May 12, 1965

*Meherhomji, K. R. (W. Ind. & Bombay) b Aug. 9, 1911, d Feb. 10, 1982

*Mehra, V. L. (E. Punjab, Ind. Rlwys & Delhi) b March 12, 1938

*Meintjes, D. J. (Tvl) b June 9, 1890, d July 17, 1979

*Melle, M. G. (Tvl & W. Prov.) b June 3, 1930

*Melville, A. (OU, Sussex, Natal & Tvl; *CY 1948*) b May 19, 1910, d April 18, 1983

Meman, M. A. (Zimb.) b June 26, 1952

Mendis, G. D. (Sussex & Lancs) b April 20, 1955

*Mendis, L. R. D. (SSC) b Aug. 25, 1952

Mendis, M. C. (Colts) b Dec. 28, 1968

*Mendonca, I. L. (BG) b July 13, 1934

Mercer, J. (Sussex, Glam & Northants; *CY 1927*) b April 22, 1895, d Aug. 31, 1987

*Merchant, V. M. (Bombay; *CY 1937*) b Oct. 12, 1911, d Oct. 27, 1987

*Merritt, W. E. (Cant. & Northants) b Aug. 18, 1908, d June 9, 1977

*Merry, C. A. (T/T) b Jan. 20, 1911, d April 19, 1964

Metcalfe, A. A. (Yorks & Notts) b Dec. 25, 1963

Metson, C. P. (Middx & Glam) b July 2, 1963

*Meuleman, K. D. (Vic. & W. Aust.) b Sept. 5, 1923

*Meuli, E. M. (C. Dist.) b Feb. 20, 1926

Meyer, B. J. (Glos; Test umpire) b Aug. 21, 1932

Meyer, R. J. O. OBE (CU, Som & W. Ind.) b March 15, 1905, d March 9, 1991

Mian Mohammed Saeed (N. India, Patiala & S. Punjab) b Aug. 31, 1910, d Aug. 23, 1979

*Middleton, J. (W. Prov.) b Sept. 30, 1865, d Dec. 23, 1913

Middleton, T. C. (Hants) b Feb. 1, 1964

**Midwinter, W. E. (Vic. & Glos) b June 19, 1851, d Dec. 3, 1890

*Milburn, B. D. (Otago) b Nov. 24, 1943

*Milburn, C. (Northants & W. Aust.; *CY 1967*) b Oct. 23, 1941, d Feb. 28, 1990

*Milkha Singh, A. G. (Madras) b Dec. 31, 1941

*Miller, A. M. (Eng.) b Oct. 19, 1869, d June 26, 1959

Miller, F. P. (Surrey) b July 29, 1828, d Nov. 22, 1875

*Miller, G. (Derbys, Natal & Essex) b Sept. 8, 1952

*Miller, K. R. MBE (Vic., NSW & Notts; *CY 1954*) b Nov. 28, 1919

*Miller, L. S. M. (C. Dist. & Wgtn) b March 31, 1923, d Dec. 17, 1996

Miller, R. (Warwicks) b Jan. 6, 1941, d May 7, 1996

*Miller, R. C. (Jam.) b Dec. 24, 1924

*Milligan, F. W. (Yorks) b March 19, 1870, d March 31, 1900

*Millman, G. (Notts) b Oct. 2, 1934

Millmow, J. P. (Wgtn) b Sept. 22, 1967

*Mills, C. H. (Surrey, Kimberley & W. Prov.) b Nov. 26, 1867, d July 26, 1948

*Mills, J. E. (Auck.) b Sept. 3, 1905, d Dec. 11, 1972

Mills, P. T. (Glos) b May 7, 1879, d Dec. 8, 1950

*Milton, C. A. (Glos; *CY 1959*) b March 10, 1928

*Milton, Sir William H. (W. Prov.) b Dec. 3, 1854, d March 6, 1930

*Minnett, R. B. (NSW) b June 13, 1888, d Oct. 21, 1955

Minshull, John (scorer of first recorded century) b *circa* 1741, d Oct. 1793

*Miran Bux (Pak. Serv., Punjab & R'pindi) b April 20, 1907, d Feb. 8, 1991

*Misson, F. M. (NSW) b Nov. 19, 1938

*Mitchell, A. (Yorks) b Sept. 13, 1902, d Dec. 25, 1976

*Mitchell, B. (Tvl; *CY 1936*) b Jan. 8, 1909, d July 2, 1995

**Mitchell, F. (CU, Yorks & Tvl; *CY 1902*) b Aug. 13, 1872, d Oct. 11, 1935

*Mitchell, T. B. (Derbys) b Sept. 4, 1902, d Jan. 27, 1996

*Mitchell-Innes, N. S. (OU & Som) b Sept. 7, 1914

Mitchley, C. J. (Tvl; Test umpire) b July 4, 1938

*Modi, R. S. (Bombay) b Nov. 11, 1924, d May 17, 1996

*Mohammad Aslam (N. Ind. & Pak. Rlwys) b Jan. 5, 1920

*Mohammad Farooq (Kar.) b April 8, 1938

*Mohammad Ilyas (Lahore & PIA) b March 19, 1946

*Mohammad Munaf (Sind, E. Pak., Kar. & PIA) b Nov. 2, 1935

*Mohammad Nazir (Pak. Rlwys) b March 8, 1946

*Mohammad Zahid (PIA) b Aug. 2, 1976

*Mohsin Kamal (Lahore, Allied Bank & PNSC) b June 16, 1963

*Mohsin Khan (Pak. Rlwys, Kar., Sind, Pak. Us & HBL) b March 15, 1955

*Moir, A. M. (Otago) b July 17, 1919

*Mold, A. (Lancs; *CY 1892*) b May 27, 1863, d April 29, 1921

Moles, A. J. (Warwicks & Griq. W.) b Feb. 12, 1961

*Moloney, D. A. R. (Wgtn, Otago & Cant.) b Aug. 11, 1910, d July 15, 1942

*Moodie, G. H. (Jam.) b Nov. 25, 1915

*Moon, L. J. (CU & Middx) b Feb. 9, 1878, d Nov. 23, 1916

*Mooney, F. L. H. (Wgtn) b May 26, 1921

Moore, H. I. (Notts) b Feb. 28, 1941

Moore, R. H. (Hants) b Nov. 14, 1913

Moorhouse, R. (Yorks) b Sept. 7, 1866, d Jan. 7, 1921

Morgan, D. C. (Derbys) b Feb. 26, 1929

*Morgan, R. W. (Auck.) b Feb. 12, 1941

*Morkel, D. P. B. (W. Prov.) b Jan. 25, 1906, d Oct. 6, 1980

Morley, F. (Notts) b Dec. 16, 1850, d Sept. 28, 1884

*Moroney, J. (NSW) b July 24, 1917

*Morris, A. R. MBE (NSW; *CY 1949*) b Jan. 19, 1922

*Morris, H. (Glam) b Oct. 5, 1963

Morris, H. M. (Essex & CU) b April 16, 1898, d Nov. 18, 1984

*Morris, S. (Vic.) b June 22, 1855, d Sept. 20, 1931

*Morrison, B. D. (Wgtn) b Dec. 17, 1933

*Morrison, D. K. (Auck. & Lancs) b Feb. 3, 1966

*Morrison, J. F. M. (C. Dist. & Wgtn) b Aug. 27, 1947

Mortensen, O. H. (Denmark & Derbys) b Jan. 29, 1958

*Mortimore, J. B. (Glos) b May 14, 1933

Mortlock, W. (Surrey & Utd Eng. XI) b July 18, 1832, d Jan. 23, 1884

Morton, A., jun. (Derbys) b May 7, 1883, d Dec. 19, 1935

*Moseley, E. A. (B'dos, Glam, E. Prov. & N. Tvl) b Jan. 5, 1958

Moseley, H. R. (B'dos & Som) b May 28, 1948

Moses, H. (NSW) b Feb. 13, 1858, d Dec. 7, 1938

*Moss, A. E. (Middx) b Nov. 14, 1930

*Moss, J. K. (Vic.) b June 29, 1947

*Motz, R. C. (Cant.; *CY 1966*) b Jan. 12, 1940

*Moule, W. H. (Vic.) b Jan. 31, 1858, d Aug. 24, 1939

*Moxon, M. D. (Yorks & Griq. W.; *CY 1993*) b May 4, 1960

*Mudassar Nazar (Lahore, Punjab, Pak. Us, HBL, PIA & UBL) b April 6, 1956

*Muddiah, V. M. (Mysore & Ind. Servs) b June 8, 1929

*Mufasir-ul-Haq (Kar., Dacca, PWD, E. Pak. & NBP) b Aug. 16, 1944, d July 27, 1983

Mukherjee, S. P. (Bengal) b Oct. 5, 1964

Muncer, B. L. (Glam & Middx) b Oct. 23, 1913, d Jan. 18, 1982

Munden, V. S. (Leics) b Jan. 2, 1928

*Munir Malik (Punjab, R'pindi, Pak. Serv. & Kar.) b July 10, 1934

**Murdoch, W. L. (NSW & Sussex) b Oct. 18, 1854, d Feb. 18, 1911

*Murray, A. R. A. (E. Prov.) b April 30, 1922, d April 17, 1995

*Murray, B. A. G. (Wgtn) b Sept. 18, 1940

*Murray, D. A. (B'dos) b Sept. 29, 1950

*Murray, D. L. (T/T, CU, Notts & Warwicks) b May 20, 1943

*Murray, J. T. MBE (Middx; *CY 1967*) b April 1, 1935

Murray-Wood, W. (OU & Kent) b June 30, 1917, d Dec. 21, 1968

Murrell, H. R. (Kent & Middx) b Nov. 19, 1879, d Aug. 15, 1952

*Musgrove, H. (Vic.) b Nov. 27, 1860, d Nov. 2, 1931

*Mushtaq Ali, S. (C. Ind., Guj., †M. Pradesh & U. Pradesh) b Dec. 17, 1914

*Mushtaq Mohammad (Kar., Northants & PIA; *CY 1963*) b Nov. 22, 1943

Mynn, Alfred (Kent & All-Eng.) b Jan. 19, 1807, d Nov. 1, 1861

*Nadkarni, R. G. (M'tra & Bombay) b April 4, 1932

Naeem Ahmed, (Kar., Pak Us, NBP, UBL & PIA) b Sept. 20, 1952

*Nagel, L. E. (Vic.) b March 6, 1905, d Nov. 23, 1971

*Naik, S. S. (Bombay) b Feb. 21, 1945

*Nanan, R. (T/T) b May 29, 1953

*Naoomal Jeoomal, M. (N. Ind. & Sind) b April 17, 1904, d July 18, 1980

*Narasimha Rao, M. V. (H'bad) b Aug. 11, 1954

Naseer Malik (Khairpair & NBP) b Feb. 1, 1950

*Nash, L. J. (Tas. & Vic.) b May 2, 1910, d July 24, 1986

Nash, M. A. (Glam) b May 9, 1945

*Nasim-ul-Ghani (Kar., Pak. Us, Dacca, E. Pak., PWD & NBP) b May 14, 1941

*Naushad Ali (Kar., E. Pak., R'pindi, Peshawar, NWFP, Punjab & Pak. Serv.) b Oct. 1, 1943

*Navle, J. G. (Rajputna, C. Ind., Holkar & Gwalior) b Dec. 7, 1902, d Sept. 7, 1979

*Nayak, S. V. (Bombay) b Oct. 20, 1954

*Nayudu, Col. C. K. (C. Ind., Andhra, U. Pradesh & Holkar; *CY 1933*) b Oct. 31, 1895, d Nov. 14, 1967

*Nayudu, C. S. (C. Ind., Holkar, Baroda, Bengal, Andhra & U. Pradesh) b April 18, 1914

*Nazar Mohammad (N. Ind. & Punjab) b March 5, 1921, d July 12, 1996

*Nazir Ali, S. (S. Punjab & Sussex) b June 8, 1906, d Feb. 18, 1975

Neale, P. A. (Worcs; *CY 1989*) b June 5, 1954

Neale, W. L. (Glos) b March 3, 1904, d Oct. 26, 1955

*Neblett, J. M. (B'dos & BG) b Nov. 13, 1901, d March 28, 1959

Needham, A. (Surrey & Middx) b March 23, 1957

*Nel, J. D. (W. Prov.) b July 10, 1928

Nelson, R. P. (Middx, CU & Northants) b Aug. 7, 1912, d Oct. 29, 1940

*Newberry, C. (Tvl) b 1889, d Aug. 1, 1916

Newell, M. (Notts) b Feb. 25, 1965

*Newham, W. (Sussex) b Dec. 12, 1860, d June 26, 1944

Newland, Richard (Sussex) b *circa* 1718, d May 29, 1791

*Newman, Sir Jack (Wgtn & Cant.) b July 3, 1902, d Sept. 23, 1996

Newman, J. A. (Hants & Cant.) b Nov. 12, 1884, d Dec. 21, 1973

Newman, P. G. (Derbys) b Jan. 10, 1959

*Newson, E. S. OBE (Tvl & Rhod.) b Dec. 2, 1910, d April 24, 1988

Newstead, J. T. (Yorks; *CY 1909*) b Sept. 8, 1877, d March 25, 1952

Newton, A. E. (OU & Som) b Sept. 12, 1862, d Sept. 15, 1952

*Niaz Ahmed (Dacca, E. Pak., PWD & Pak. Rlwys) b Nov. 11, 1945

Nicholas, M. C. J. (Hants) b Sept. 29, 1957

Nicholls, D. (Kent) b Dec. 8, 1943

Nicholls, E. A. (Test umpire) b Dec. 10, 1947

Nicholls, R. B. (Glos) b Dec. 4, 1933, d July 21, 1994

*Nichols, M. S. (Essex; *CY 1934*) b Oct. 6, 1900, d Jan. 26, 1961

Nicholson, A. G. (Yorks) b June 25, 1938, d Nov. 4, 1985

*Nicholson, F. (Griq. W.) b Sept. 17, 1909, d July 30, 1982

*Nicolson, J. F. W. (Natal & OU) b July 19, 1899, d Dec. 13, 1935

*Nissar, Mahomed (Patiala, S. Punjab & U. Pradesh) b Aug. 1, 1910, d March 11, 1963

*Nitschke, H. C. (S. Aust.) b April 14, 1905, d Sept. 29, 1982

*Noble, M. A. (NSW; *CY 1900*) b Jan. 28, 1873, d June 22, 1940

*Noblet, G. (S. Aust.) b Sept. 14, 1916

*Noreiga, J. M. (T/T) b April 15, 1936

Norman, M. E. J. C. (Northants & Leics) b Jan. 19, 1933

*Norton, N. O. (W. Prov. & Border) b May 11, 1881, d June 27, 1968

*Nothling, O. E. (NSW & Qld) b Aug. 1, 1900, d Sept. 26, 1965

*Nourse, A. D. ("Dudley") (Natal; *CY 1948*) b Nov. 12, 1910, d Aug. 14, 1981

*Nourse, A. W. ("Dave") (Natal, Tvl & W. Prov.) b Jan. 26, 1878, d July 8, 1948

*Nunes, R. K. (Jam.) b June 7, 1894, d July 22, 1958

*Nupen, E. P. (Tvl) b Jan. 1, 1902, d Jan. 29, 1977

*Nurse, S. M. (B'dos; *CY 1967*) b Nov. 10, 1933

Nutter, A. E. (Lancs & Northants) b June 28, 1913, d June 3, 1996

*Nyalchand, S. (W. Ind., Kathiawar, Guj., & S'tra) b Sept. 14, 1919, d Jan. 3, 1997

Nyren, John (Hants) b Dec. 15, 1764, d June 28, 1837

Nyren, Richard (Hants & Sussex; Proprietor Bat & Ball Inn, Broadhalfpenny Down) b 1734, d April 25, 1797

Oakes, C. (Sussex) b Aug. 10, 1912

Oakes, J. (Sussex) b March 3, 1916, d July 4, 1997

*Oakman, A. S. M. (Sussex) b April 20, 1930

Oates, T. W. (Notts) b Aug. 9, 1875, d June 18, 1949

Oates, W. F. (Yorks & Derbys) b June 11, 1929

*O'Brien, L. P. J. (Vic.) b July 2, 1907, d March 13, 1997

*O'Brien, Sir Timothy C. (OU & Middx) b Nov. 5, 1861, d Dec. 9, 1948

*Ochse, A. E. (Tvl) b March 11, 1870, d April 11, 1918

*Ochse, A. L. (E. Prov.) b Oct. 11, 1899, d May 5, 1949

*O'Connor, J. (Essex) b Nov. 6, 1897, d Feb. 22, 1977

*O'Connor, J. D. A. (NSW & S. Aust.) b Sept. 9, 1875, d Aug. 23, 1941

*O'Donnell, S. P. (Vic.) b Jan. 26, 1963

*Ogilvie, A. D. (Qld) b June 3, 1951

O'Gorman, T. J. G. (Derbys) b May 15, 1967

*O'Keeffe, K. J. (NSW & Som) b Nov. 25, 1949

*Old, C. M. (Yorks, Warwicks & N. Tvl; *CY 1979*) b Dec. 22, 1948

*Oldfield, N. (Lancs & Northants; Test umpire) b May 5, 1911, d April 19, 1996

Oldfield, W. A. MBE (NSW; *CY 1927*) b Sept. 9, 1894, d Aug. 10, 1976

Oldham, S. (Yorks & Derbys) b July 26, 1948

Oldroyd, E. (Yorks) b Oct. 1, 1888, d Dec. 27, 1964

*O'Linn, S. (Kent, W. Prov. & Tvl) b May 5, 1927

Oliver, L. (Derbys) b Oct. 18, 1886, d Jan. 22, 1948

*O'Neill, N. C. (NSW; *CY 1962*) b Feb. 19, 1937

Ontong, R. C. (Border, Tvl, N. Tvl & Glam) b Sept. 9, 1955

Opatha, A. R. M. (SL) b Aug. 5, 1947

Orchard, D. L. (Natal; Test umpire) b June 24, 1948

Ord, J. S. (Warwicks) b July 12, 1912

*O'Reilly, W. J. OBE (NSW; *CY 1935*) b Dec. 20, 1905, d Oct. 6, 1992

Ormrod, J. A. (Worcs & Lancs) b Dec. 22, 1942

Oscroft, W. (Notts) b Dec. 16, 1843, d Oct. 10, 1905

O'Shaughnessy, S. J. (Lancs & Worcs) b Sept. 9, 1961

Oslear, D. O. (Test umpire) b March 3, 1929

*O'Sullivan, D. R. (C. Dist. & Hants) b Nov. 16, 1944

Outschoorn, L. (Worcs) b Sept. 26, 1918, d Jan. 9, 1994

*Overton, G. W. F. (Otago) b June 8, 1919, d Sept. 7, 1993

Owen, H. G. P. (CU & Essex) b May 19, 1859, d Oct. 20, 1912

*Owens, M. B. (Cant.) b Nov. 11, 1969

*Owen-Smith, H. G. (W. Prov., OU & Middx; *CY 1930*) b Feb. 18, 1909, d Feb. 28, 1990

Owen-Thomas, D. R. (CU & Surrey) b Sept. 20, 1948

*Oxenham, R. K. (Qld) b July 28, 1891, d Aug. 16, 1939

*Padgett, D. E. V. (Yorks) b July 20, 1934

*Padmore, A. L. (B'dos) b Dec. 17, 1946

Page, J. C. T. (Kent) b May 20, 1930, d Dec. 14, 1990

Page, M. H. (Derbys) b June 17, 1941

*Page, M. L. (Cant.) b May 8, 1902, d Feb. 13, 1987

*Pai, A. M. (Bombay) b April 28, 1945

*Paine, G. A. E. (Middx & Warwicks; *CY 1935*) b June 11, 1908, d March 30, 1978

*Pairaudeau, B. H. (BG & N. Dist.) b April 14, 1931

*Palairet, L. C. H. (OU & Som; *CY 1893*) b May 27, 1870, d March 27, 1933

Palairet, R. C. N. (OU & Som) b June 25, 1871, d Feb. 11, 1955

*Palia, P. E. (Parsis, Madras, U. Prov., Bombay, Mysore & Bengal) b Sept. 5, 1910, d Sept. 9, 1981

*Palm, A. W. (W. Prov.) b June 8, 1901, d Aug. 17, 1966

*Palmer, C. H. CBE (Worcs & Leics; Pres. MCC 1978-79) b May 15, 1919

*Palmer, G. E. (Vic. & Tas.) b Feb. 22, 1859, d Aug. 22, 1910

*Palmer, K. E. (Som; Test umpire) b April 22, 1937

Palmer, R. (Som; Test umpire) b July 12, 1942

Pardon, Charles F. (Editor of *Wisden* 1887-90) b March 28, 1850, d April 18, 1890

Pardon, Sydney H. (Editor of *Wisden* 1891-1925) b Sept. 23, 1855, d Nov. 20, 1925

*Parfitt, P. H. (Middx; *CY1963*) b Dec. 8, 1936

Paris, C. G. A. (Hants; Pres. MCC 1975-76) b Aug. 20, 1911, d April 4, 1998

Parish, R. J. (Aust. Administrator) b May 7, 1916

*Park, Dr R. L. (Vic.) b July 30, 1892, d Jan. 23, 1947

*Parkar, G. A. (Bombay) b Oct. 24, 1955

*Parkar, R. D. (Bombay) b Oct. 31, 1946

Parkar, Z. (Bombay) b Nov. 22, 1957

*Parker, C. W. L. (Glos; *CY 1923*) b Oct. 14, 1882, d July 11, 1959

*Parker, G. M. (SA) b May 27, 1899, d May 1, 1969

Parker, J. F. (Surrey) b April 23, 1913, d Jan. 27, 1983

*Parker, J. M. (N. Dist. & Worcs) b Feb. 21, 1951

*Parker, N. M. (Otago & Cant.) b Aug. 28, 1948

*Parker, P. W. G. (CU, Sussex, Natal & Durham) b Jan. 15, 1956

*Parkhouse, W. G. A. (Glam) b Oct. 12, 1925

*Parkin, C. H. (Yorks & Lancs; *CY 1924*) b Feb. 18, 1886, d June 15, 1943

*Parkin, D. C. (E. Prov., Tvl & Griq. W.) b Feb. 20, 1873, d March 20, 1936

Parks, H. W. (Sussex) b July 18, 1906, d May 7, 1984

*Parks, J. H. (Sussex & Cant.; *CY 1938*) b May 12, 1903, d Nov. 21, 1980

*Parks, J. M. (Sussex & Som; *CY 1968*) b Oct. 21, 1931

Parks, R. J. (Hants & Kent) b June 15, 1959

Parr, George (Notts & All-England) b May 22, 1826, d June 23, 1891

*Parry, D. R. (Comb. Is. & Leewards) b Dec. 22, 1954

*Parsana, D. D. (S'tra, Ind. Rlwys & Guj.) b Dec. 2, 1947

Parsons, A. B. D. (CU & Surrey) b Sept. 20, 1933

Parsons, G. J. (Leics, Warwicks, Boland, Griq. W. & OFS) b Oct. 17, 1959

Parsons, Canon J. H. (Warwicks) b May 30, 1890, d Feb. 2, 1981

*Partridge, J. T. (Rhod.) b Dec. 9, 1932, d June 7, 1988

Partridge, N. E. (Malvern, CU & Warwicks; *CY 1919*) b Aug. 10, 1900, d March 10, 1982

Partridge, R. J. (Northants) b Feb. 11, 1912, d Feb. 1, 1997

Parvez Mir (R'pindi, Lahore, Punjab, Pak. Us, Derbys, HBL & Glam) b Sept. 24, 1953

*Pascoe, L. S. (NSW) b Feb. 13, 1950

Pasqual, S. P. (SL) b Oct. 15, 1961

*Passailaigue, C. C. (Jam.) b Aug. 1902, d Jan. 7, 1972

*Patankar, C. T. (Bombay) b Nov. 24, 1930

**Pataudi, Iftiqar Ali, Nawab of (OU, Worcs, Patiala, N. Ind. & S. Punjab; *CY 1932*) b March 16, 1910, d Jan. 5, 1952

*Pataudi, Mansur Ali, Nawab of (Sussex, OU, Delhi & H'bad; *CY 1968*) b Jan. 5, 1941

*Patel, A. K. (S'tra) b March 6, 1957

*Patel, B. P. (Karn.) b Nov. 24, 1952

*Patel, D. N. (Worcs & Auck.) b Oct. 25, 1958

*Patel, J. M. (Guj.) b Nov. 26, 1924, d Dec. 12, 1992

*Patel, R. G. M. (Baroda) b June 1, 1964

Paterson, G. A. (Zimb.) b June 9, 1960

*Patiala, Maharaja of (N. Ind., Patiala & S. Punjab) b Jan. 17, 1913, d June 17, 1974

*Patil, S. M. (Bombay & M. Pradesh) b Aug. 18, 1956

*Patil, S. R. (M'tra) b Oct. 10, 1933

*Patterson, B. P. (Jam., Tas. & Lancs) b Sept. 15, 1961

Patterson, W. H. (OU & Kent) b March 11, 1859, d May 3, 1946

*Payne, T. R. O. (B'dos) b Feb. 13, 1957

*Paynter, E. (Lancs; *CY 1938*) b Nov. 5, 1901, d Feb. 5, 1979

Payton, W. R. D. (Notts) b Feb. 13, 1882, d May 2, 1943

Peach, H. A. (Surrey) b Oct. 6, 1890, d Oct. 8, 1961

*Peall, S. G. (MCD) b Sept. 2, 1969

Pearce, T. N. (Essex) b Nov. 3, 1905, d April 10, 1994

*Pearse, O. C. (Natal) b Oct. 10, 1884, d May 7, 1953

Pearson, F. (Worcs & Auck.) b Sept. 23, 1880, d Nov. 10, 1963

*Peate, E. (Yorks) b March 2, 1855, d March 11, 1900

Peckover, G. E. (Zimb.) b June 2, 1955

*Peebles, I. A. R. (OU, Middx & Scotland; writer; *CY 1931*) b Jan. 20, 1908, d Feb. 28, 1980

*Peel, R. (Yorks; *CY 1889*) b Feb. 12, 1857, d Aug. 12, 1941

*Pegler, S. J. (Tvl) b July 28, 1888, d Sept. 10, 1972

*Pellew, C. E. (S. Aust.) b Sept. 21, 1893, d May 9, 1981

Penn, C. (Kent) b June 19, 1963

*Penn, F. (Kent) b March 7, 1851, d Dec. 26, 1916

Pepper, C. G. (NSW & Aust. Serv.; umpire) b Sept. 15, 1916, d March 24, 1993

Perkins, H. (CU & Cambs; Sec. MCC 1876-97) b Dec. 10, 1832, d May 6, 1916

*Perks, R. T. D. (Worcs) b Oct. 4, 1911, d Nov. 22, 1977

Perrin, P. A. (Essex; *CY 1905*) b May 26, 1876, d Nov. 20, 1945

Perryman, S. P. (Warwicks & Worcs) b Oct. 22, 1955

*Pervez Sajjad (Lahore, PIA & Kar.) b Aug. 30, 1942

*Petherick, P. J. (Otago & Wgtn) b Sept. 25, 1942

*Petrie, E. C. (Auck. & N. Dist.) b May 22, 1927

Pettiford, J. (NSW & Kent) b Nov. 29, 1919, d Oct. 11, 1964

*Phadkar, D. G. (M'tra, Bombay, Bengal & Ind. Rlwys) b Dec. 10, 1925, d March 17, 1985

Phebey, A. H. (Kent) b Oct. 1, 1924, d June 28, 1998

Phelan, P. J. (Essex) b Feb. 9, 1938

*Philipson, H. (OU & Middx) b June 8, 1866, d Dec. 4, 1935

*Phillip, N. (Comb. Is., Windwards & Essex) b June 12, 1948

Phillips, H. (Sussex) b Oct. 14, 1844, d July 3, 1919

Phillips, R. B. (NSW & Qld) b May 23, 1954

*Phillips, W. B. (S. Aust.) b March 1, 1958

*Phillips, W. N. (Vic.) b Nov. 7, 1962

Phillipson, C. P. (Sussex) b Feb. 10, 1952

Phillipson, W. E. (Lancs; Test umpire) b Dec. 3, 1910, d Aug. 24, 1991

*Philpott, P. I. (NSW) b Nov. 21, 1934

Pick, R. A. (Notts & Wgtn) b Nov. 19, 1963

Pieris, H. S. M. (SL) b Feb. 16, 1946

*Pierre, L. R. (T/T) b June 5, 1921, d April 14, 1989

*Pigott, A. C. S. (Sussex, Wgtn & Surrey) b June 4, 1958

Pilch, Fuller (Norfolk & Kent) b March 17, 1804, d May 1, 1870

Pilling, H. (Lancs) b Feb. 23, 1943

*Pilling, R. (Lancs; *CY 1891*) b July 5, 1855, d March 28, 1891

*Pithey, A. J. (Rhod. & W. Prov.) b July 17, 1933

*Pithey, D. B. (Rhod., OU, Northants, W. Prov., Natal & Tvl) b Oct. 4, 1936

*Place, W. (Lancs) b Dec. 7, 1914

Platt, R. K. (Yorks & Northants) b Dec. 21, 1932

*Playle, W. R. (Auck. & W. Aust.) b Dec. 1, 1938

Pleass, J. E. (Glam) b May 21, 1923

Plews, N. T. (Test umpire) b Sept. 5, 1934

*Plimsoll, J. B. (W. Prov. & Natal) b Oct. 27, 1917

Pocock, N. E. J. (Hants) b Dec. 15, 1951

*Pocock, P. I. (Surrey & N. Tvl) b Sept. 24, 1946

*Pollard, R. (Lancs) b June 19, 1912, d Dec. 16, 1985

*Pollard, V. (C. Dist. & Cant.) b Sept. 7, 1945

*Pollock, P. M. (E. Prov.; *CY 1966*) b June 30, 1941

*Pollock, R. G. (E. Prov. & Tvl; *CY 1966*) b Feb. 27, 1944

*Ponsford, W. H. MBE (Vic.; *CY 1935*) b Oct. 19, 1900, d April 6, 1991

Pont, K. R. (Essex) b Jan. 16, 1953

*Poole, C. J. (Notts) b March 13, 1921, d Feb. 11, 1996

Pooley, E. (Surrey & first England tour) b Feb. 13, 1838, d July 18, 1907

*Poore, M. B. (Cant.) b June 1, 1930

*Poore, Brig-Gen. R. M. (Hants & SA; *CY 1900*) b March 20, 1866, d July 14, 1938

*Pope, A. V. (Derbys) b Aug. 15, 1909, d May 11, 1996

*Pope, G. H. (Derbys) b Jan. 27, 1911, d Oct. 29, 1993

*Pope, Dr R. J. (NSW) b Feb. 18, 1864, d July 27, 1952

*Popplewell, N. F. M. (CU & Som) b Aug. 8, 1957

Popplewell, Hon. Sir Oliver B. (CU; Pres. MCC 1994-96) b Aug. 15, 1927

*Porter, G. D. (W. Aust.) b March 18, 1955

Pothecary, A. E. (Hants) b March 1, 1906, d May 21, 1991

*Pothecary, J. E. (W. Prov.) b Dec. 6, 1933

Potter, L. (Kent, Griq. W., Leics & OFS) b Nov. 7, 1962

*Pougher, A. D. (Leics) b April 19, 1865, d May 20, 1926

*Powell, A. W. (Griq. W.) b July 18, 1873, d Sept. 11, 1948

*Prabhakar, M. (Delhi & Durham) b April 15, 1963

*Prasanna, E. A. S. (†Karn.) b May 22, 1940

Prentice, F. T. (Leics) b April 22, 1912, d July 10, 1978

Pressdee, J. S. (Glam & NE Tvl) b June 19, 1933

Preston, Hubert (Editor of *Wisden* 1944-51)
  b Dec. 16, 1868, d Aug. 6, 1960
Preston, K. C. (Essex) b Aug. 22, 1925
Preston, Norman (Editor of *Wisden* 1952-80)
  b March 18, 1903, d March 6, 1980
Pretlove, J. F. (CU & Kent) b Nov. 23, 1932
*Price, J. S. E. (Middx) b July 22, 1937
*Price, W. F. (Middx; Test umpire) b April 25,
  1902, d Jan. 13, 1969
*Prideaux, R. M. (CU, Kent, Northants, Sussex
  & OFS) b July 31, 1939
Pridgeon, A. P. (Worcs) b Feb. 22, 1954
*Prince, C. F. H. (W. Prov., Border & E. Prov.)
  b Sept. 11, 1874, d Feb. 2, 1949
*Pringle, D. R. (CU & Essex) b Sept. 18, 1958
Pritchard, T. L. (Wgtn, Warwicks & Kent) b
  March 10, 1917
*Procter, M. J. (Glos, Natal, W. Prov., Rhod.
  & OFS; *CY 1970*) b Sept. 15, 1946
Prodger, J. M. (Kent) b Sept. 1, 1935
*Promnitz, H. L. E. (Border, Griq. W. & OFS)
  b Feb. 23, 1904, d Sept. 7, 1983
*Pullar, G. (Lancs & Glos; *CY 1960*) b Aug.
  1, 1935
*Puna, N. (N. Dist.) b Oct. 28, 1929, d June
  7, 1996
*Punjabi, P. H. (Sind & Guj.) b Sept. 20, 1921
*Pycroft, J. A. (Zimb.) b June 6, 1956
Pydanna, M. R. (Guyana) b Jan. 27, 1950

*Qasim Omar (Kar. & MCB) b Feb. 9, 1957
Quaife, B. W. (Warwicks & Worcs) b Nov.
  24, 1899, d Nov. 28, 1984
Quaife, Walter (Sussex & Warwicks) b April
  1, 1864, d Jan. 18, 1943
*Quaife, William (W. G.) (Warwicks & Griq.
  W.; *CY 1902*) b March 17, 1872, d Oct.
  13, 1951
*Quinn, N. A. (Griq. W. & Tvl) b Feb. 21,
  1908, d Aug. 5, 1934

*Rabone, G. O. (Wgtn & Auck.) b Nov. 6,
  1921
*Rackemann, C. G. (Qld & Surrey) b June 3,
  1960
Radcliffe, Sir Everard J. Bt (Yorks) b Jan. 27,
  1884, d Nov. 23, 1969
*Radford, N. V. (Lancs, Tvl & Worcs; *CY
  1986*) b June 7, 1957
*Radley, C. T. (Middx; *CY 1979*) b May 13,
  1944
*Rae, A. F. (Jam.) b Sept. 30, 1922
Raees Mohammad (Kar.) b Dec. 24, 1932
*Rai Singh, K. (S. Punjab & Ind. Serv.) b Feb.
  24, 1922
Rait Kerr, Col. R. S. (Eur.; Sec. MCC 1936-
  52) b April 13, 1891, d April 2, 1961
Rajadurai, B. E. A. (SSC) b Aug. 24, 1965

*Rajindernath, V. (N. Ind., U. Prov., S. Punjab,
  Bihar & E. Punjab) b Jan. 7, 1928, d Nov.
  22, 1989
*Rajinder Pal (Delhi, S. Punjab & Punjab) b
  Nov. 18, 1937
Ralph, L. H. R. (Essex) b May 22, 1920
*Ramadhin, S. (T/T & Lancs; *CY 1951*) b May
  1, 1929
*Ramaswami, C. (Madras) b June 18, 1896,
  presumed dead.
Ramaswamy, V. K. (Test umpire) b April 26,
  1946
*Ramchand, G. S. (Sind, Bombay & Raja.) b
  July 26, 1927
*Ramji, L. (W. Ind.) b Oct. 2, 1902, d Dec.
  20, 1948
*Ranasinghe, A. N. (BRC) b Oct. 13, 1956, d
  Nov. 9, 1998
Ranasinghe, S. K. (SL) b July 4, 1962
*Ranatunga, D. (SSC) b Oct. 12, 1962
*Randall, D. W. (Notts; *CY 1980*) b Feb. 24,
  1951
Randhir Singh (Orissa & Bihar) b Aug. 16,
  1957
*Rangachari, C. R. (Madras) b April 14, 1916,
  d Oct. 9, 1993
*Rangnekar, K. M. (M'tra, Bombay & †M.
  Pradesh) b June 27, 1917, d Oct. 11, 1984
*Ranjane, V. B. (M'tra & Ind. Rlwys) b July
  22, 1937
*Ranjitsinhji, K. S., (later H. H. the Jam Sahib
  of Nawanagar) (CU & Sussex; *CY 1897*) b
  Sept. 10, 1872, d April 2, 1933
*Ransford, V. S. (Vic.; *CY 1910*) b March 20,
  1885, d March 19, 1958
*Rashid Khan (PWD, Kar. & PIA) b Dec. 15,
  1959
Ratnayake, N. L. K. (SSC) b Nov. 22, 1968
*Ratnayake, R. J. (NCC) b Jan. 2, 1964
*Ratnayeke, J. R. (NCC) b May 2, 1960
Rawlin, J. T. (Yorks & Middx) b Nov. 10,
  1856, d Jan. 19, 1924
Rawson, P. W. E. (Zimb. & Natal) b May 25,
  1957
Rayment, A. W. H. (Hants) b May 29, 1928
*Razdan, V. (Delhi) b Aug. 25, 1969
*Read, H. D. (Surrey & Essex) b Jan. 28, 1910
*Read, J. M. (Surrey; *CY 1890*) b Feb. 9, 1859,
  d Feb. 17, 1929
*Read, W. W. (Surrey; *CY 1893*) b Nov. 23,
  1855, d Jan. 6, 1907
*Reddy, B. (TN) b Nov. 12, 1954
*Redmond, R. E. (Wgtn & Auck.) b Dec. 29,
  1944
*Redpath, I. R. MBE (Vic.) b May 11, 1941
Reed, B. L. (Hants) b Sept. 17, 1937
*Reedman, J. C. (S. Aust.) b Oct. 9, 1865, d
  March 25, 1924
Rees, A. (Glam) b Feb. 17, 1938
*Reeve, D. A. OBE (Sussex & Warwicks; *CY
  1996*) b April 2, 1963

Reeves, W. (Essex; Test umpire) b Jan. 22, 1875, d March 22, 1944

*Rege, M. R. (M'tra) b March 18, 1924

*Rehman, S. F. (Punjab, Pak. Us & Lahore) b June 11, 1935

*Reid, B. A. (W. Aust.) b March 14, 1963

*Reid, J. F. (Auck.) b March 3, 1956

*Reid, J. R. OBE (Wgtn & Otago; *CY 1959*; ICC referee) b June 3, 1928

*Reid, N. (W. Prov.) b Dec. 26, 1890, d June 6, 1947

Reid, R. B. (Wgtn & Auck.) b Dec. 3, 1958

Reidy, B. W. (Lancs) b Sept. 18, 1953

*Relf, A. E. (Sussex & Auck.; *CY 1914*) b June 26, 1874, d March 26, 1937

Relf, R. R. (Sussex) b Sept. 1, 1883, d April 28, 1965

*Renneburg, D. A. (NSW) b Sept. 23, 1942

Revill, A. C. (Derbys & Leics) b March 27, 1923, d July 6, 1998

Reynolds, B. L. (Northants) b June 10, 1932

Rhodes, A. E. G. (Derbys; Test umpire) b Oct. 10, 1916, d Oct. 18, 1983

*Rhodes, H. J. (Derbys) b July 22, 1936

*Rhodes, W. (Yorks; *CY 1899*) b Oct. 29, 1877, d July 8, 1973

Rice, C. E. B. (Tvl & Notts; *CY 1981*) b July 23, 1949

Rice, J. M. (Hants) b Oct. 23, 1949

*Richards, A. R. (W. Prov.) b Dec. 14, 1867, d Jan. 9, 1904

*Richards, B. A. (Natal, Glos, Hants & S. Aust.; *CY 1969*) b July 21, 1945

*Richards, C. J. (Surrey & OFS) b Aug. 10, 1958

Richards, D. L. (Chief Exec. ICC 1993-) b July 28, 1946

Richards, G. (Glam) b Nov. 29, 1951

*Richards, Sir Vivian (I. V. A.) OBE (Comb. Is., Leewards, Som, Qld & Glam; *CY 1977*) b March 7, 1952

*Richards, W. H. (SA) b March 26, 1862, d Jan. 4, 1903

*Richardson, A. J. (S. Aust.) b July 24, 1888, d Dec. 23, 1973

Richardson, A. W. (Derbys) b March 4, 1907, d July 29, 1983

*Richardson, D. W. (Worcs) b Nov. 3, 1934

*Richardson, P. E. (Worcs & Kent; *CY 1957*) b July 4, 1931

*Richardson, T. (Surrey & Som; *CY 1897*) b Aug. 11, 1870, d July 2, 1912

*Richardson, V. Y. (S. Aust.) b Sept. 7, 1894, d Oct. 29, 1969

Riches, N. V. H. (Glam) b June 9, 1883, d Nov. 6, 1975

*Richmond, T. L. (Notts) b June 23, 1890, d Dec. 29, 1957

*Rickards, K. R. (Jam. & Essex) b Aug. 23, 1923, d Aug. 21, 1995

Riddington, A. (Leics) b Dec. 22, 1911, d Feb. 25, 1998

*Ridgway, F. (Kent) b Aug. 10, 1923

*Rigg, K. E. (Vic.) b May 21, 1906, d Feb. 28, 1995

Ring, D. T. (Vic.) b Oct. 14, 1918

Ritchie, G. M. (Qld) b Jan. 23, 1960

Rixon, S. J. (NSW) b Feb. 25, 1954

*Roach, C. A. (T/T) b March 13, 1904, d April 16, 1988

*Roberts, A. D. G. (N. Dist.) b May 6, 1947, d Oct. 26, 1989

*Roberts, A. M. E. CBE (Comb. Is., Leewards, Hants, NSW & Leics; *CY 1975*) b Jan. 29, 1951

*Roberts, A. T. (Windwards & T/T) b Sept. 18, 1937, d July 24, 1996

*Roberts, A. W. (Cant. & Otago) b Aug. 20, 1909, d May 13, 1978

Roberts, B. (Tvl & Derbys) b May 30, 1962

Roberts, F. G. (Glos) b April 1, 1862, d April 7, 1936

Roberts, S. J. (Cant.) b March 22, 1965

Roberts, W. B. (Lancs & Victory Tests) b Sept. 27, 1914, d Aug. 24, 1951

*Robertson, G. K. (C. Dist.) b July 15, 1960

*Robertson, J. B. (W. Prov.) b June 5, 1906, d July 5, 1985

*Robertson, J. D. (Middx; *CY 1948*) b Feb. 22, 1917, d Oct. 12, 1996

*Robertson, W. R. (Vic.) b Oct. 6, 1861, d June 24, 1938

Robertson-Glasgow, R. C. (OU & Som; writer) b July 15, 1901, d March 4, 1965

Robins, D. H. (Warwicks) b June 26, 1914

*Robins, R. W. V. (CU & Middx; *CY 1930*) b June 3, 1906, d Dec. 12, 1968

Robinson, D. C. (Glos & Essex) b April 20, 1884, d July 29, 1963

Robinson, E. (Yorks) b Nov. 16, 1883, d Nov. 17, 1969

Robinson, E. P. (Yorks & Som) b Aug. 10, 1911, d Nov. 10, 1998

Robinson, Sir Foster G. (Glos) b Sept. 19, 1880, d Oct. 31, 1967

Robinson, I. D. (Test umpire) b March 11, 1947

Robinson, P. E. (Yorks & Leics) b Aug. 3, 1963

Robinson, P. J. (Worcs & Som) b Feb. 9, 1943

*Robinson, R. D. (Vic.) b June 8, 1946

*Robinson, R. H. (NSW, S. Aust. & Otago) b March 26, 1914, d Aug. 10, 1965

Robson, C. (Hants) b June 20, 1859, d Sept. 27, 1943

Robson, E. (Som) b May 1, 1870, d May 23, 1924

*Rodriguez, W. V. (T/T) b June 25, 1934

Roe, B. (Som) b Jan. 27, 1939

Roebuck, P. M. (CU & Som; *CY 1988*) b March 6, 1956

Rogers, N. H. (Hants) b March 9, 1918

Rogers, S. S. (Eur. & Som) b March 18, 1923, d Nov. 6, 1969

Romaines, P. W. (Northants, Glos & Griq. W.) b Dec. 25, 1955

*Roope, G. R. J. (Surrey & Griq. W.) b July 12, 1946

*Root, C. F. (Derbys & Worcs) b April 16, 1890, d Jan. 20, 1954

*Rorke, G. F. (NSW) b June 27, 1938

*Rose, B. C. (Som; *CY 1980*) b June 4, 1950

*Rose-Innes, A. (Kimberley & Tvl) b Feb. 16, 1868, d Nov. 22, 1946

Rotherham, G. A. (Rugby, CU, Warwicks & Wgtn.; *CY 1918*) b May 28, 1899, d Jan. 31, 1985

Rouse, S. J. (Warwicks) b Jan. 20, 1949

*Routledge, T. W. (W. Prov. & Tvl) b April 18, 1867, d May 9, 1927

*Rowan, A. M. B. (Tvl) b Feb. 7, 1921, d Feb. 21, 1998

*Rowan, E. A. B. (Tvl; *CY 1952*) b July 20, 1909, d April 30, 1993

Rowbotham, J. (Yorks; Test umpire) b July 8, 1831, d Dec. 22, 1899

*Rowe, C. G. (Wgtn & C. Dist.) b June 30, 1915, d June 9, 1995

Rowe, C. J. C. (Kent & Glam) b Nov. 11, 1951

Rowe, E. J. (Notts) b July 21, 1920, d Dec. 17, 1989

*Rowe, G. A. (W. Prov.) b June 15, 1874, d Jan. 8, 1950

*Rowe, L. G. (Jam. & Derbys) b Jan. 8, 1949

*Roy, A. (Bengal) b June 5, 1945, d Sept. 19, 1997

*Roy, Pankaj (Bengal) b May 31, 1928

*Roy, Pranab (Bengal) b Feb. 10, 1957

*Royle, Rev. V. P. F. A. (OU & Lancs) b Jan. 29, 1854, d May 21, 1929

Rumsey, F. E. (Worcs, Som & Derbys) b Dec. 4, 1935

Rundle, D. B. (W. Prov.) b Sept. 25, 1965

Rushby, T. (Surrey) b Sept. 6, 1880, d July 13, 1962

*Russell, A. C. (Essex; *CY 1923*) b Oct. 7, 1887, d March 23, 1961

Russell, P. E. (Derbys) b May 9, 1944

Russell, S. E. J. (Middx & Glos) b Oct. 4, 1937, d June 18, 1994

*Russell, W. E. (Middx) b July 3, 1936

*Rutherford, J. W. (W. Aust.) b Sept. 25, 1929

Ryan, F. (Hants & Glam) b Nov. 14, 1888, d Jan. 5, 1954

Ryan, M. (Yorks) b June 23, 1933

*Ryder, J. (Vic.) b Aug. 8, 1889, d April 3, 1977

Saadat Ali (Lahore, UBL & HBFC) b Feb. 6, 1955

*Sadiq Mohammad (Kar., PIA, Tas., Essex, Glos & UBL) b May 3, 1945

*Saeed Ahmed (Punjab, Pak. Us, Lahore, PIA, Kar., PWD & Sind) b Oct. 1, 1937

*Saggers, R. A. (NSW) b May 15, 1917, d March 17, 1987

Sainsbury, P. J. (Hants; *CY 1974*) b June 13, 1934

*St Hill, E. L. (T/T) b March 9, 1904, d May 21, 1957

*St Hill, W. H. (T/T) b July 6, 1893, d *circa* 1957

*Salah-ud-Din (Kar., PIA & Pak. Us) b Feb. 14, 1947

*Saleem Altaf (Lahore & PIA) b April 19, 1944

*Saleem Jaffer (Kar. & UBL) b Nov. 19, 1962

Salim Badar (Test umpire) b May 16, 1953

Salim Pervez (NBP) b Sept. 9, 1947

*Salim Yousuf (Sind, Kar., IDBP, Allied Bank & Customs) b Dec. 7, 1959

Samaranayake, A. D. A. (SL) b Feb. 25, 1962

*Samarasekera, M. A. R. (CCC) b Aug. 5, 1961

Sampson, H. (Yorks & All-England) b March 13, 1813, d March 29, 1885

*Samuelson, S. V. (Natal) b Nov. 21, 1883, d Nov. 18, 1958

*Sandham, A. (Surrey; *CY 1923*) b July 6, 1890, d April 20, 1982

Sandhu, B. S. (Bombay) b Aug. 3, 1956

Santall, F. R. (Warwicks) b July 12, 1903, d Nov. 3, 1950

Santall, S. (Warwicks) b June 10, 1873, d March 19, 1957

*Sardesai, D. N. (Bombay) b Aug. 8, 1940

*Sarfraz Nawaz (Lahore, Punjab, Northants, Pak. Rlwys & UBL) b Dec. 1, 1948

*Sarwate, C. T. (CP & B, M'tra, Bombay & †M. Pradesh) b June 22, 1920

*Saunders, J. V. (Vic. & Wgtn) b March 21, 1876, d Dec. 21, 1927

Savage, J. S. (Leics & Lancs) b March 3, 1929

Savill, L. A. (Essex) b June 30, 1935

Saville, G. J. (Essex) b Feb. 5, 1944

Saxelby, K. (Notts) b Feb. 23, 1959

*Saxena, R. C. (Delhi & Bihar) b Sept. 20, 1944

Sayer, D. M. (OU & Kent) b Sept. 19, 1936

*Scarlett, R. O. (Jam.) b Aug. 15, 1934

*Schultz, S. S. (CU & Lancs) b Aug. 29, 1857, d Dec. 18, 1937

*Schwarz, R. O. (Middx & Natal; *CY 1908*) b May 4, 1875, d Nov. 18, 1918

*Scott, A. P. H. (Jam.) b July 29, 1934

Scott, C. J. (Glos) b May 1, 1919, d Nov. 22, 1992

Scott, C. W. (Notts & Durham) b Jan. 23, 1964

*Scott, H. J. H. (Vic.) b Dec. 26, 1858, d Sept. 23, 1910

Scott, M. E. (Northants) b May 8, 1936

*Scott, O. C. (Jam.) b Aug. 14, 1893, d June 15, 1961

*Scott, R. H. (Cant.) b March 6, 1917

Scott, S. W. (Middx; *CY 1893*) b March 24, 1854, d Dec. 8, 1933

*Scott, V. J. (Auck.) b July 31, 1916, d Aug. 2, 1980

*Scotton, W. H. (Notts) b Jan. 15, 1856, d July 9, 1893

*Sealey, B. J. (T/T) b Aug. 12, 1899, d Sept. 12, 1963

*Sealy, J. E. D. (B'dos & T/T) b Sept. 11, 1912, d Jan. 3, 1982

*Seccull, A. W. (Kimberley, W. Prov. & Tvl) b Sept. 14, 1868, d July 20, 1945

*Sekar, T. A. P. (TN) b March 28, 1955

*Selby, J. (Notts) b July 1, 1849, d March 11, 1894

Sellers, A. B. MBE (Yorks; *CY 1940*) b March 5, 1907, d Feb. 20, 1981

*Sellers, R. H. D. (S. Aust.) b Aug. 20, 1940

*Selvey, M. W. W. (CU, Surrey, Middx, Glam & OFS; writer) b April 25, 1948

*Sen, P. (Bengal) b May 31, 1926, d Jan. 27, 1970

*Sen Gupta, A. K. (Ind. Serv.) b Aug. 3, 1939

*Senanayake, C. P. (CCC) b Dec. 19, 1962

*Serjeant, C. S. (W. Aust.) b Nov. 1, 1951

Seymour, James (Kent) b Oct. 25, 1879, d Sept. 30, 1930

*Seymour, M. A. (W. Prov.) b June 5, 1936

*Shackleton, D. (Hants; *CY 1959*) b Aug. 12, 1924

*Shafiq Ahmed (Lahore, Punjab, NBP & UBL) b March 28, 1949

*Shafqat Rana (Lahore & PIA) b Aug. 10, 1943

*Shah, A. H. (Mash.) b Aug. 7, 1959

*Shahid Israr (Kar. & Sind) b March 1, 1950

*Shahid Mahmoud (Kar., Pak. Us & PWD) b March 17, 1939

*Shahid Saeed (HBFC, Lahore & PACO) b Jan. 6, 1966

*Shalders, W. A. (Griq. W. & Tvl) b Feb. 12, 1880, d March 18, 1917

*Sharma, Chetan (Haryana & Bengal) b Jan. 3, 1966

*Sharma, Gopal (U. Pradesh) b Aug. 3, 1960

*Sharma, P. (Raja.) b Aug. 5, 1948

Sharma, Sanjeev (Delhi & H. Pradesh) b Aug. 25, 1965

Sharp, G. (Northants; Test umpire) b March 12, 1950

Sharp, H. P. (Middx) b Oct. 6, 1917, d Jan. 15, 1995

*Sharp, J. (Lancs) b Feb. 15, 1878, d Jan. 28, 1938

Sharp, K. (Yorks & Griq. W.) b April 6, 1959

*Sharpe, D. (Punjab, Pak. Rlwys, Lahore & S. Aust.) b Aug. 3, 1937

*Sharpe, J. W. (Surrey & Notts; *CY 1892*) b Dec. 9, 1866, d June 19, 1936

*Sharpe, P. J. (Yorks & Derbys; *CY 1963*) b Dec. 27, 1936

*Shastri, R. J. (Bombay & Glam) b May 27, 1962

*Shaw, Alfred (Notts & Sussex) b Aug. 29, 1842, d Jan. 16, 1907

Shaw, T. G. (E. Prov.) b July 5, 1959

*Sheahan, A. P. (Vic.) b Sept. 30, 1946

Sheffield, J. R. (Essex & Wgtn) b Nov. 19, 1906, d Nov. 16, 1997

*Shepherd, B. K. (W. Aust.) b April 23, 1937

Shepherd, D. J. (Glam; *CY 1970*) b Aug. 12, 1927

Shepherd, D. R. MBE (Glos; Test umpire) b Dec. 27, 1940

*Shepherd, J. N. (B'dos, Kent, Rhod. & Glos; *CY 1979*) b Nov. 9, 1943

Shepherd, T. F. (Surrey) b Dec. 5, 1889, d Feb. 13, 1957

*Sheppard, Rt Rev. D. S. (Bishop of Liverpool; later Baron Sheppard) (CU & Sussex; *CY 1953*) b March 6, 1929

*Shepstone, G. H. (Tvl) b April 9, 1876, d July 3, 1940

*Sherwell, P. W. (Tvl) b Aug. 17, 1880, d April 17, 1948

*Sherwin, M. (Notts; *CY 1891*) b Feb. 26, 1851, d July 3, 1910

Shields, J. (Leics) b Feb. 1, 1882, d May 11, 1960

*Shillingford, G. C. (Comb. Is. & Windwards) b Sept. 25, 1944

*Shillingford, I. T. (Comb. Is. & Windwards) b April 18, 1944

*Shinde, S. G. (Baroda, M'tra & Bombay) b Aug. 18, 1923, d June 22, 1955

Shipman, A. W. (Leics) b March 7, 1901, d Dec. 12, 1979

Shirreff, A. C. (CU, Hants, Kent & Som) b Feb. 12, 1919

*Shivnarine, S. (Guyana) b May 13, 1952

*Shodhan, R. H. (Guj. & Baroda) b Oct. 18, 1928

*Shrewsbury, A. (Notts; *CY 1890*) b April 11, 1856, d May 19, 1903

*Shrimpton, M. J. F. (C. Dist. & N. Dist.) b June 23, 1940

*Shuja-ud-Din, Col. (N. Ind., Pak. Us, Pak. Serv., B'pur & R'pindi) b April 10, 1930

*Shukla, R. C. (Bihar & Delhi) b Feb. 4, 1948

*Shuter, J. (Kent & Surrey) b Feb. 9, 1855, d July 5, 1920

*Shuttleworth, K. (Lancs & Leics) b Nov. 13, 1944

Sibbles, F. M. (Lancs) b March 15, 1904, d July 20, 1973

*Sidebottom, A. (Yorks & OFS) b April 1, 1954

Sidwell, T. E. (Leics) b Jan. 30, 1888, d Dec. 8, 1958

*Siedle, I. J. (Natal) b Jan. 11, 1903, d Aug. 24, 1982

*Sievers, M. W. (Vic.) b April 13, 1912, d May 10, 1968

*Sikander Bakht (PWD, PIA, Sind, Kar. & UBL) b Aug. 25, 1957

Silk, D. R. W. CBE (CU & Som; Pres. MCC 1992-94; Chairman TCCB 1994-96) b Oct. 8, 1931

*Silva, S. A. R. (NCC) b Dec. 12, 1960

Sime, W. A. MBE (OU & Notts) b Feb. 8, 1909, d May 5, 1983

Simmons, J. MBE (Lancs & Tas.; *CY 1985*) b March 28, 1941

*Simpson, R. B. (NSW & W. Aust.; *CY 1965*) b Feb. 3, 1936

*Simpson, R. T. (Sind & Notts; *CY 1950*) b Feb. 27, 1920

*Simpson-Hayward, G. H. (Worcs) b June 7, 1875, d Oct. 2, 1936

Sims, Sir Arthur (Cant.) b July 22, 1877, d April 27, 1969

*Sims, J. M. (Middx) b May 13, 1903, d April 27, 1973

*Sinclair, B. W. (Wgtn) b Oct. 23, 1936

*Sinclair, I. M. (Cant.) b June 1, 1933

*Sinclair, J. H. (Tvl) b Oct. 16, 1876, d Feb. 23, 1913

*Sincock, D. J. (S. Aust.) b Feb. 1, 1942

*Sinfield, R. A. (Glos) b Dec. 24, 1900, d March 17, 1988

*Singh, Charan K. (T/T) b Nov. 27, 1935

Singh, R. P. (U. Pradesh) b Jan. 6, 1963

Singleton, A. P. (OU, Worcs & Rhod.) b Aug. 5, 1914

Skelding, A. (Leics; umpire) b Sept. 5, 1886, d April 17, 1960

*Slack, W. N. (Middx & Windwards) b Dec. 12, 1954, d Jan. 15, 1989

*Slade, D. N. F. (Worcs) b Aug. 24, 1940

Slater, A. G. (Derbys) b Nov. 22, 1890, d July 22, 1949

*Slater, K. N. (W. Aust.) b March 12, 1935

*Sleep, P. R. (S. Aust.) b May 4, 1957

*Slight, J. (Vic.) b Oct. 20, 1855, d Dec. 9, 1930

Slocombe, P. A. (Som) b Sept. 6, 1954

*Smailes, T. F. (Yorks) b March 27, 1910, d Dec. 1, 1970

Smales, K. (Yorks & Notts) b Sept. 15, 1927

*Small, G. C. (Warwicks & S. Aust.) b Oct. 18, 1961

Small, John, sen. (Hants & All-England) b April 19, 1737, d Dec. 31, 1826

*Small, J. A. (T/T) b Nov. 3, 1892, d April 26, 1958

*Small, M. A. (B'dos) b Feb. 12, 1964

Smart, C. C. (Warwicks & Glam) b July 23, 1898, d May 21, 1975

Smart, J. A. (Warwicks) b April 12, 1891, d Oct. 3, 1979

Smedley, M. J. (Notts) b Oct. 28, 1941

*Smith, A. C. CBE (OU & Warwicks; Chief Exec. TCCB 1987-96; ICC referee) b Oct. 25, 1936

*Smith, Sir C. Aubrey (CU, Sussex & Tvl) b July 21, 1863, d Dec. 20, 1948

*Smith, C. I. J. (Middx; *CY 1935*) b Aug. 25, 1906, d Feb. 9, 1979

*Smith, C. J. E. (Tvl) b Dec. 25, 1872, d March 27, 1947

*Smith, C. L. (Natal, Glam & Hants; *CY 1984*) b Oct. 15, 1958

Smith, C. L. A. (Sussex) b Jan. 1, 1879, d Nov. 22, 1949

Smith, C. S. (later Sir Colin Stansfield-) (CU & Lancs) b Oct. 1, 1932

*Smith, C. W. (B'dos; ICC referee) b July 29, 1933

*Smith, Denis (Derbys; *CY 1936*) b Jan. 24, 1907, d Sept. 12, 1979

*Smith, D. B. M. (Vic.) b Sept. 14, 1884, d July 29, 1963

Smith, D. H. K. (Derbys & OFS) b June 29, 1940

*Smith, D. M. (Surrey, Worcs & Sussex) b Jan. 9, 1956

*Smith, D. R. (Glos) b Oct. 5, 1934

*Smith, D. V. (Sussex) b June 14, 1923

Smith, Edwin (Derbys) b Jan. 2, 1934

Smith, Ernest (OU & Yorks) b Oct. 19, 1869, d April 9, 1945

*Smith, E. J. (Warwicks) b Feb. 6, 1886, d Aug. 31, 1979

*Smith, F. B. (Cant.) b March 13, 1922, d July 6, 1997

*Smith, F. W. (Tvl) b unknown, d April 17, 1914, aged 53

Smith, G. J. (Essex) b April 2, 1935

*Smith, Harry (Glos) b May 21, 1890, d Nov. 12, 1937

Smith, H. A. (Leics) b March 29, 1901, d Aug. 7, 1948

*Smith, H. D. (Otago & Cant.) b Jan. 8, 1913, d Jan. 25, 1986

*Smith, I. D. S. MBE (C. Dist. & Auck.) b Feb. 28, 1957

Smith, K. D. (Warwicks) b July 9, 1956

Smith, M. J. (Middx) b Jan. 4, 1942

*Smith, M. J. K. OBE (Leics, OU & Warwicks; *CY 1960*) b June 30, 1933

Smith, N. (Yorks & Essex) b April 1, 1949

*Smith, O. G. ("Collie") (Jam.; *CY 1958*) b May 5, 1933, d Sept. 9, 1959

Smith, P. A. (Warwicks) b April 5, 1964

Smith, Ray (Essex) b Aug. 10, 1914, d Feb. 21, 1996

Smith, Roy (Som) b April 14, 1930

Smith, R. C. (Leics) b Aug. 3, 1935

*Smith, S. B. (NSW & Tvl) b Oct. 18, 1961

*Smith, S. G. (T/T, Northants & Auck.; *CY 1915*) b Jan. 15, 1881, d Oct. 25, 1963

*Smith, T. P. B. (Essex; *CY 1947*) b Oct. 30, 1908, d Aug. 4, 1967

*Smith, V. I. (Natal) b Feb. 23, 1925

Smith, W. A. (Surrey) b Sept. 15, 1937

Smith, W. C. (Surrey; *CY 1911*) b Oct. 4, 1877, d July 16, 1946

*Smithson, G. A. (Yorks & Leics) b Nov. 1, 1926, d Sept. 6, 1970

*Snedden, C. A. (Auck.) b Jan. 7, 1918, d May 19, 1993

*Snedden, M. C. (Auck.) b Nov. 23, 1958

Snellgrove, K. L. (Lancs) b Nov. 12, 1941

*Snooke, S. D. (W. Prov. & Tvl) b Nov. 11, 1878, d April 6, 1959

*Snooke, S. J. (Border, W. Prov. & Tvl) b Feb. 1, 1881, d Aug. 14, 1966

*Snow, J. A. (Sussex; *CY 1973*) b Oct. 13, 1941

*Sobers, Sir Garfield S. (B'dos, S. Aust. & Notts; *CY 1964*) b July 28, 1936

Sohail Fazal (HBL) b Nov. 11, 1967

*Sohoni, S. W. (M'tra, Baroda & Bombay) b March 5, 1918, d May 19, 1993

*Solkar, E. D. (Bombay & Sussex) b March 18, 1948

*Solomon, J. S. (BG) b Aug. 26, 1930

*Solomon, W. R. (Tvl & E. Prov.) b April 23, 1872, d July 12, 1964

*Sood, M. M. (Delhi) b July 6, 1939

*Southern, J. W. (Hants) b Sept. 2, 1952

*Southerton, James (Surrey, Hants & Sussex) b Nov. 16, 1827, d June 16, 1880

Southerton, S. J. (Editor of *Wisden* 1934-35) b July 7, 1874, d March 12, 1935

*Sparling, J. T. (Auck.) b July 24, 1938

Spencer, C. T. (Leics) b Aug. 18, 1931

Spencer, J. (CU & Sussex) b Oct. 6, 1949

Spencer, T. W. OBE (Kent; Test umpire) b March 22, 1914

Sperry, J. (Leics) b March 19, 1910, d April 21, 1997

*Spofforth, F. R. (NSW & Vic.) b Sept. 9, 1853, d June 4, 1926

*Spooner, R. H. (Lancs; *CY 1905*) b Oct. 21, 1880, d Oct. 2, 1961

*Spooner, R. T. (Warwicks) b Dec. 30, 1919, d Dec. 20, 1997

Springall, J. D. (Notts) b Sept. 19, 1932

Sprot, E. M. (Hants) b Feb. 4, 1872, d Oct. 8, 1945

Squires, H. S. (Surrey) b Feb. 22, 1909, d Jan. 24, 1950

*Srikkanth, K. (TN) b Dec. 21, 1959

*Srinivasan, T. E. (TN) b Oct. 26, 1950

*Stackpole, K. R. MBE (Vic.; *CY 1973*) b July 10, 1940

Standen, J. A. (Worcs) b May 30, 1935

*Stanyforth, Lt.-Col. R. T. (Yorks) b May 30, 1892, d Feb. 20, 1964

Staples, A. (Notts) b Feb. 4, 1899, d Sept. 9, 1965

*Staples, S. J. (Notts; *CY 1929*) b Sept. 18, 1892, d June 4, 1950

*Statham, J. B. CBE (Lancs; *CY 1955*) b June 17, 1930

*Stayers, S. C. (†Guyana & Bombay) b June 9, 1937

Stead, B. (Yorks, Essex, Notts & N. Tvl) b June 21, 1939, d April 15, 1980

*Steel, A. G. (CU & Lancs; Pres. MCC 1902) b Sept. 24, 1858, d June 15, 1914

*Steele, D. S. OBE (Northants & Derbys; *CY 1976*) b Sept. 29, 1941

Steele, J. F. (Leics, Natal & Glam) b July 23, 1946

Stephens, E. J. (Glos) b March 23, 1909, d April 3, 1983

Stephenson, F. D. (B'dos, Glos, Tas., Notts, Sussex & †FS; *CY 1989*) b April 8, 1959

Stephenson, G. R. (Derbys & Hants) b Nov. 19, 1942

Stephenson, H. H. (Surrey & All-England) b May 3, 1832, d Dec. 17, 1896

Stephenson, H. W. (Som) b July 18, 1920

Stephenson, Lt.-Col. J. R. CBE (Sec. MCC 1987-93) b Feb. 25, 1931

Stephenson, Lt.-Col. J. W. A. (Essex, Worcs, Army, Europeans & Victory Tests) b Aug. 1, 1907, d May 20, 1982

Stevens, Edward ("Lumpy") (Hants) b *circa* 1735, d Sept. 7, 1819

*Stevens, G. B. (S. Aust.) b Feb. 29, 1932

*Stevens, G. T. S. (UCS, OU & Middx; *CY 1918*) b Jan. 7, 1901, d Sept. 19, 1970

*Stevenson, G. B. (Yorks & Northants) b Dec. 16, 1955

Stevenson, K. (Derbys & Hants) b Oct. 6, 1950

*Stewart, M. J. OBE (Surrey; *CY 1958*) b Sept. 16, 1932

*Stewart, R. B. (SA) b Sept. 3, 1856, d Sept. 12, 1913

Stewart, W. J. (Warwicks & Northants) b Oct. 31, 1934

*Stirling, D. A. (C. Dist.) b Oct. 5, 1961

Stocks, F. W. (Notts) b Nov. 6, 1918, d Feb. 23, 1996

*Stoddart, A. E. (Middx; *CY 1893*) b March 11, 1863, d April 3, 1915

*Stollmeyer, J. B. (T/T) b April 11, 1921, d Sept. 10, 1989

*Stollmeyer, V. H. (T/T) b Jan. 24, 1916

Stone, J. (Hants & Glam) b Nov. 29, 1876, d Nov. 15, 1942

Storer, H. jun. (Derbys) b Feb. 2, 1898, d Sept. 1, 1967

*Storer, W. (Derbys; *CY 1899*) b Jan. 25, 1867, d Feb. 28, 1912

Storey, S. J. (Surrey & Sussex) b Jan. 6, 1941

Stott, L. W. (Auck.) b Dec. 8, 1946

Stott, W. B. (Yorks) b July 18, 1934

Stovold, A. W. (Glos & OFS) b March 19, 1953

*Street, G. B. (Sussex) b Dec. 6, 1889, d April 24, 1924

*Stricker, L. A. (Tvl) b May 26, 1884, d Feb. 5, 1960

*Strudwick, H. (Surrey; *CY 1912*) b Jan. 28, 1880, d Feb. 14, 1970

*Studd, C. T. (CU & Middx) b Dec. 2, 1860, d July 16, 1931

*Studd, G. B. (CU & Middx) b Oct. 20, 1859, d Feb. 13, 1945

Studd, Sir J. E. Kynaston (Middx & CU; Pres. MCC 1930) b July 26, 1858, d Jan. 14, 1944

*Su'a, M. L. (N. Dist. & Auck.) b Nov. 7, 1966

*Subba Row, R. CBE (CU, Surrey & Northants; *CY 1961*; ICC referee) b Jan. 29, 1932

*Subramanya, V. (Mysore) b July 16, 1936

Sudhakar Rao, R. (Karn.) b Aug. 8, 1952

Sueter, T. (Hants & Surrey) b *circa* 1749, d Feb. 17, 1827

*Sugg, F. H. (Yorks, Derbys & Lancs; *CY 1890*) b Jan. 11, 1862, d May 29, 1933

Sullivan, J. (Lancs) b Feb. 5, 1945

Sully, H. (Som & Northants) b Nov. 1, 1939

*Sunderram, G. (Bombay & Raja.) b March 29, 1930

*Surendranath, R. (Ind. Serv.) b Jan. 4, 1937

Surridge, W. S. (Surrey; *CY 1953*) b Sept. 3, 1917, d April 13, 1992

*Surti, R. F. (Guj., Raja., & Qld) b May 25, 1936

*Susskind, M. J. (CU, Middx & Tvl) b June 8, 1891, d July 9, 1957

*Sutcliffe, B. MBE (Auck., Otago & N. Dist.; *CY 1950*) b Nov. 17, 1923

*Sutcliffe, H. (Yorks; *CY 1920*) b Nov. 24, 1894, d Jan. 22, 1978

Sutcliffe, W. H. H. (Yorks) b Oct. 10, 1926, d Sept. 16, 1998

Suttle, K. G. (Sussex) b Aug. 25, 1928

*Swamy, V. N. (Ind. Serv.) b May 23, 1924, d May 1, 1983

Swanton, E. W. CBE (Middx; writer & broadcaster) b Feb. 11, 1907

Swarbrook, F. W. (Derbys, Griq. W. & OFS) b Dec. 17, 1950

Swart, P. D. (Rhod., W. Prov., Glam & Boland) b April 27, 1946

*Swetman, R. (Surrey, Notts & Glos) b Oct. 25, 1933

Sydenham, D. A. D. (Surrey) b April 6, 1934

*Taber, H. B. (NSW) b April 29, 1940

*Taberer, H. M. (OU & Natal) b Oct. 7, 1870, d June 5, 1932

*Tahir Naqqash (Servis Ind., MCB, Punjab & Lahore) b July 6, 1959

*Talat Ali (Lahore, PIA & UBL; ICC referee) b May 29, 1950

*Tallon, D. (Qld; *CY 1949*) b Feb. 17, 1916, d Sept. 7, 1984

*Tamhane, N. S. (Bombay) b Aug. 4, 1931

*Tancred, A. B. (Kimberley, Griq. W. & Tvl) b Aug. 20, 1865, d Nov. 23, 1911

*Tancred, L. J. (Tvl) b Oct. 7, 1876, d July 28, 1934

*Tancred, V. M. (Tvl) b July 7, 1875, d June 3, 1904

Tanvir Mehdi (Lahore & UBL) b Nov. 7, 1972

*Tapscott, G. L. (Griq. W.) b Nov. 7, 1889, d Dec. 13, 1940

*Tapscott, L. E. (Griq. W.) b March 18, 1894, d July 7, 1934

*Tarapore, K. K. (Bombay) b Dec. 17, 1910, d June 15, 1986

Tarbox, C. V. (Worcs) b July 2, 1891, d June 15, 1978

Tarrant, F. A. (Vic., Middx & Patiala; *CY 1908*) b Dec. 11, 1880, d Jan. 29, 1951

Tarrant, G. F. (Cambs. & All-England) b Dec. 7, 1838, d July 2, 1870

*Taslim Arif (Kar., Sind & NBP) b May 1, 1954

*Tate, F. W. (Sussex) b July 24, 1867, d Feb. 24, 1943

*Tate, M. W. (Sussex; *CY 1924*) b May 30, 1895, d May 18, 1956

*Tattersall, R. (Lancs) b Aug. 17, 1922

Tavaré, C. J. (OU, Kent & Som) b Oct. 27, 1954

*Tayfield, H. J. (Natal, Rhod. & Tvl; *CY 1956*) b Jan. 30, 1929, d Feb. 25, 1994

*Taylor, A. I. (Tvl) b July 25, 1925

Taylor, B. (Essex; *CY 1972*) b June 19, 1932

*Taylor, B. R. (Cant. & Wgtn) b July 12, 1943

Taylor, C. G. (CU & Sussex) b Nov. 21, 1816, d Sept. 10, 1869

*Taylor, Daniel (Natal) b Jan. 9, 1887, d Jan. 24, 1957

*Taylor, D. D. (Auck. & Warwicks) b March 2, 1923, d Dec. 5, 1980

Taylor, D. J. S. (Surrey, Som & Griq. W.) b Nov. 12, 1942

*Taylor, H. W. (Natal, Tvl & W. Prov.; *CY 1925*) b May 5, 1889, d Feb. 8, 1973

*Taylor, J. (T/T) b Jan. 3, 1932

*Taylor, J. M. (NSW) b Oct. 10, 1895, d May 12, 1971

*Taylor, K. (Yorks & Auck.) b Aug. 21, 1935

*Taylor, L. B. (Leics & Natal) b Oct. 25, 1953

Taylor, M. N. S. (Notts & Hants) b Nov. 12, 1942

*Taylor, P. L. (NSW & Qld) b Aug. 22, 1956

Taylor, R. M. (Essex) b Nov. 30, 1909, d Jan. 7, 1984

*Taylor, R. W. MBE (Derbys; *CY 1977*) b July 17, 1941

Taylor, T. L. (CU & Yorks; *CY 1901*) b May 25, 1878, d March 16, 1960

Tennekoon, A. P. B. (SL) b Oct. 29, 1946

*Tennyson, 3rd Lord (Hon. L. H.) (Hants; *CY 1914*) b Nov. 7, 1889, d June 6, 1951

*Terry, V. P. (Hants) b Jan. 14, 1959

*Theunissen, N. H. (W. Prov.) b May 4, 1867, d Nov. 9, 1929

Thomas, A. E. (Northants) b June 7, 1893, d March 21, 1965

Thomas, D. J. (Surrey, N. Tvl, Natal & Glos) b June 30, 1959

*Thomas, G. (NSW) b March 21, 1938

*Thomas, J. G. (Glam, Border, E. Prov. & Northants) b Aug. 12, 1960

Thompson, A. (Middx) b April 17, 1916

*Thompson, G. J. (Northants; Test umpire; *CY 1906*) b Oct. 27, 1877, d March 3, 1943

Thompson, R. G. (Warwicks) b Sept. 26, 1932

*Thoms, G. R. (Vic.) b March 22, 1927

*Thomson, A. L. (Vic.) b Dec. 2, 1945

*Thomson, J. R. (NSW, Qld & Middx) b Aug. 16, 1950

*Thomson, K. (Cant.) b Feb. 26, 1941

*Thomson, N. F. D. (NSW) b May 29, 1839, d Sept. 2, 1896

*Thomson, N. I. (Sussex) b Jan. 23, 1929

*Thomson, S. A. (N. Dist.) b Jan. 27, 1969

Thornton, C. I. (CU, Kent & Middx) b March 20, 1850, d Dec. 10, 1929

*Thornton, Dr P. G. (Yorks, Middx & SA) b Dec. 24, 1867, d Jan. 31, 1939

*Thurlow, H. M. (Qld) b Jan. 10, 1903, d Dec. 3, 1975

Tiffin, R. B. (Test umpire) b June 4, 1959

Timms, B. S. V. (Hants & Warwicks) b Dec. 17, 1940

Timms, J. E. (Northants) b Nov. 3, 1906, d May 18, 1980

Tindall, R. A. E. (Surrey) b Sept. 23, 1935

*Tindill, E. W. T. (Wgtn) b Dec. 18, 1910

Tissera, M. H. (SL) b March 23, 1939

*Titmus, F. J. MBE (Middx, Surrey & OFS; *CY 1963*) b Nov. 24, 1932

Todd, L. J. (Kent) b June 19, 1907, d Aug. 20, 1967

Todd, P. A. (Notts & Glam) b March 12, 1953

*Tolchard, R. W. (Leics) b June 15, 1946

Tomlins, K. P. (Middx & Glos) b Oct. 23, 1957

Tomlinson, D. S. (Rhod. & Border) b Sept. 4, 1910, d July 11, 1993

Tompkin, M. (Leics) b Feb. 17, 1919, d Sept. 27, 1956

*Toohey, P. M. (NSW) b April 20, 1954

Topley, T. D. (Surrey, Essex & Griq. W.) b Feb. 25, 1964

Toshack, E. R. H. (NSW) b Dec. 15, 1914

Townsend, A. (Warwicks) b March 26, 1921

Townsend, A. F. (Derbys) b March 29, 1912, d Feb. 25, 1994

*Townsend, C. L. (Glos; *CY 1899*) b Nov. 7, 1876, d Oct. 17, 1958

*Townsend, D. C. H. (OU) b April 20, 1912, d Jan. 27, 1997

*Townsend, L. F. (Derbys & Auck.; *CY 1934*) b June 8, 1903, d Feb. 17, 1993

**Traicos, A. J. (Rhod. & Mash.) b May 17, 1947

*Travers, J. P. F. (S. Aust.) b Jan. 10, 1871, d Sept. 15, 1942

*Tremlett, M. F. (Som & C. Dist.) b July 5, 1923, d July 30, 1984

Tremlett, T. M. (Hants) b July 26, 1956

*Tribe, G. E. (Vic. & Northants; *CY 1955*) b Oct. 4, 1920

*Trim, J. (BG) b Jan. 25, 1915, d Nov. 12, 1960

Trimble, G. S. (Qld) b Jan. 1, 1963

*Trimborn, P. H. J. (Natal) b May 18, 1940

**Trott, A. E. (Vic., Middx & Hawkes Bay; *CY 1899*) b Feb. 6, 1873, d July 30, 1914

*Trott, G. H. S. (Vic.; *CY 1894*) b Aug. 5, 1866, d Nov. 10, 1917

Troughton, L. H. W. (Kent) b May 17, 1879, d Aug. 31, 1933

Troup, G. B. (Auck.) b Oct. 3, 1952

*Trueman, F. S. OBE (Yorks; *CY 1953*) b Feb. 6, 1931

*Trumble, H. (Vic.; *CY 1897*) b May 12, 1867, d Aug. 14, 1938

*Trumble, J. W. (Vic.) b Sept. 16, 1863, d Aug. 17, 1944

*Trumper, V. T. (NSW; *CY 1903*) b Nov. 2, 1877, d June 28, 1915

*Truscott, P. B. (Wgtn) b Aug. 14, 1941

*Tuckett, L. (OFS) b Feb. 6, 1919

*Tuckett, L. R. (Natal & OFS) b April 19, 1885, d April 8, 1963

Tufnell, N. C. (CU & Surrey) b June 13, 1887, d Aug. 3, 1951

Tunnicliffe, C. J. (Derbys) b Aug. 11, 1951

Tunnicliffe, J. (Yorks; *CY 1901*) b Aug. 26, 1866, d July 11, 1948

*Turnbull, M. J. (CU & Glam; *CY 1931*) b March 16, 1906, d Aug. 5, 1944

*Turner, A. (NSW) b July 23, 1950

Turner, C. (Yorks) b Jan. 11, 1902, d Nov. 19, 1968

*Turner, C. T. B. (NSW; *CY 1889*) b Nov. 16, 1862, d Jan. 1, 1944

Turner, D. R. (Hants & W. Prov.) b Feb. 5, 1949

Turner, F. M. MBE (Leics) b Aug. 8, 1934

*Turner, G. M. (Otago, N. Dist. & Worcs; *CY 1971*) b May 26, 1947

Turner, S. (Essex & Natal) b July 18, 1943

*Twentyman-Jones, P. S. (W. Prov.) b Sept. 13, 1876, d March 8, 1954

*Tyldesley, E. (Lancs; *CY 1920*) b Feb. 5, 1889, d May 5, 1962

*Tyldesley, J. T. (Lancs; *CY 1902*) b Nov. 22, 1873, d Nov. 27, 1930

*Tyldesley, R. K. (Lancs; *CY 1925*) b March 11, 1897, d Sept. 17, 1943

*Tylecote, E. F. S. (OU & Kent) b June 23, 1849, d March 15, 1938

*Tyler, E. J. (Som) b Oct. 13, 1864, d Jan. 25, 1917

*Tyson, F. H. (Northants; *CY 1956*) b June 6, 1930

Ufton, D. G. (Kent) b May 31, 1928

*Ulyett, G. (Yorks) b Oct. 21, 1851, d June 18, 1898

*Umrigar, P. R. (Bombay & Guj.) b March 28, 1926

*Underwood, D. L. MBE (Kent; *CY 1969*) b June 8, 1945

Vaidya, P. S. (Bengal) b Sept. 23, 1967

*Valentine, A. L. (Jam.; *CY 1951*) b April 29, 1930

*Valentine, B. H. (CU & Kent) b Jan. 17, 1908, d Feb. 2, 1983

*Valentine, V. A. (Jam.) b April 4, 1908, d July 6, 1972

*Vance, R. H. (Wgtn) b March 31, 1955

*van der Bijl, P. G. (W. Prov. & OU) b Oct. 21, 1907, d Feb. 16, 1973

van der Bijl, V. A. P. (Natal, Middx & Tvl; *CY 1981*) b March 19, 1948

*Van der Merwe, E. A. (Tvl) b Nov. 9, 1904, d Feb. 26, 1971

*Van der Merwe, P. L. (W. Prov. & E. Prov.; ICC referee) b March 14, 1937

van Geloven, J. (Yorks & Leics) b Jan. 4, 1934

*Van Ryneveld, C. B. (W. Prov. & OU) b March 19, 1928

van Zyl, C. J. P. G. (OFS & Glam) b Oct. 1, 1961

*Varnals, G. D. (E. Prov., Tvl & Natal) b July 24, 1935

*Vaughan, J. T. C. (Auck.) b Aug. 30, 1967

*Veivers, T. R. (Qld) b April 6, 1937

*Veletta, M. R. J. (W. Aust.) b Oct. 30, 1963

*Vengsarkar, D. B. (Bombay; *CY 1987*) b April 6, 1956

*Venkataraghavan, S. (†TN & Derbys; Test umpire) b April 21, 1946

*Verity, H. (Yorks; *CY 1932*) b May 18, 1905, d July 31, 1943

*Vernon, G. F. (Middx) b June 20, 1856, d Aug. 10, 1902

Vials, G. A. T. (Northants) b March 18, 1887, d April 26, 1974

Vigar, F. H. (Essex) b July 7, 1917

*Viljoen, K. G. (Griq. W., OFS & Tvl) b May 14, 1910, d Jan. 21, 1974

*Vincent, C. L. (Tvl) b Feb. 16, 1902, d Aug. 24, 1968

*Vine, J. (Sussex; *CY 1906*) b May 15, 1875, d April 25, 1946

*Vintcent, C. H. (Tvl & Griq. W.) b Sept. 2, 1866, d Sept. 28, 1943

Virgin, R. T. (Som, Northants & W. Prov.; *CY 1971*) b Aug. 26, 1939

*Viswanath, G. R. (†Karn.; ICC referee) b Feb. 12, 1949

*Viswanath, S. (Karn.) b Nov. 29, 1962

*Vivian, G. E. (Auck.) b Feb. 28, 1946

*Vivian, H. G. (Auck.) b Nov. 4, 1912, d Aug. 12, 1983

*Vizianagram, Maharaj Kumar of, Sir Vijay A., (U. Prov.) b Dec. 28, 1905, d Dec. 2, 1965

*Voce, W. (Notts; *CY 1933*) b Aug. 8, 1909, d June 6, 1984

*Vogler, A. E. E. (Middx, Natal, Tvl & E. Prov.; *CY 1908*) b Nov. 28, 1876, d Aug. 9, 1946

Vonhagt, D. M. (Moors) b March 31, 1965

*Waddington, A. (Yorks) b Feb. 4, 1893, d Oct. 28, 1959

*Wade, H. F. (Natal) b Sept. 14, 1905, d Nov. 23, 1980

Wade, T. H. (Essex) b Nov. 24, 1910, d July 25, 1987

Wade, W. W. (Natal) b June 18, 1914

*Wadekar, A. L. (Bombay) b April 1, 1941

*Wadsworth, K. J. (C. Dist. & Cant.) b Nov. 30, 1946, d Aug. 19, 1976

*Wainwright, E. (Yorks; *CY 1894*) b April 8, 1865, d Oct. 28, 1919

*Waite, J. H. B. (E. Prov. & Tvl) b Jan. 19, 1930

*Waite, M. G. (S. Aust.) b Jan. 7, 1911, d Dec. 16, 1985

*Walcott, Sir Clyde L. (B'dos & BG; *CY 1958*) b Jan. 17, 1926

*Walcott, L. A. (B'dos) b Jan. 18, 1894, d Feb. 27, 1984

Walden, F. (Northants; Test umpire) b March 1, 1888, d May 3, 1949

Walker, C. (Yorks & Hants) b June 27, 1919, d Dec. 3, 1992

Walker, I. D. (Middx) b Jan. 8, 1844, d July 6, 1898

*Walker, M. H. N. (Vic.) b Sept. 12, 1948

Walker, P. M. (Glam, Tvl & W. Prov.) b Feb. 17, 1936

Walker, V. E. (Middx) b April 20, 1837, d Jan. 3, 1906

Walker, W. (Notts) b Nov. 24, 1892, d Dec. 3, 1991

*Wall, T. W. (S. Aust.) b May 13, 1904, d March 25, 1981

*Wallace, W. M. (Auck.) b Dec. 19, 1916

*Waller, A. C. (Mash.) b Sept. 25, 1959

Waller, C. E. (Surrey & Sussex) b Oct. 3, 1948

Walsh, J. E. (NSW & Leics) b Dec. 4, 1912, d May 20, 1980

*Walter, K. A. (Tvl) b Nov. 5, 1939

*Walters, C. F. (Glam & Worcs; *CY 1934*) b Aug. 28, 1905, d Dec. 23, 1992

*Walters, F. H. (Vic. & NSW) b Feb. 9, 1860, d June 1, 1922

*Walters, K. D. MBE (NSW) b Dec. 21, 1945

*Waqar Hassan (Pak. Us, Punjab, Pak. Serv. & Kar.) b Sept. 12, 1932

*Ward, Alan (Derbys, Leics & Border) b Aug. 10, 1947

*Ward, Albert (Yorks & Lancs; *CY 1890*) b Nov. 21, 1865, d Jan. 6, 1939

Ward, B. (Essex) b Feb. 28, 1944

Ward, D. (Glam) b Aug. 30, 1934

Ward, D. M. (Surrey) b Feb. 10, 1961

*Ward, F. A. (S. Aust.) b Feb. 23, 1906, d March 25, 1974

*Ward, J. T. (Cant.) b March 11, 1937

*Ward, T. A. (Tvl) b Aug. 2, 1887, d Feb. 16, 1936

Ward, William (MCC & Hants) b July 24, 1787, d June 30, 1849

*Wardle, J. H. (Yorks; *CY 1954*) b Jan. 8, 1923, d July 23, 1985

*Warnapura, B. (SL) b March 1, 1953

*Warnaweera, K. P. J. (Galle & Singha) b Nov. 23, 1960

Warner, A. E. (Worcs & Derbys) b May 12, 1959

*Warner, Sir Pelham F. (OU & Middx; *CY 1904, special portrait 1921;* Pres. MCC 1950-51) b Oct. 2, 1873, d Jan. 30, 1963

*Warr, J. J. (CU & Middx; Pres. MCC 1987-88) b July 16, 1927

*Warren, A. R. (Derbys) b April 2, 1875, d Sept. 3, 1951

*Washbrook, C. CBE (Lancs; *CY 1947*) b Dec. 6, 1914

*Wasim Bari (Kar., PIA & Sind) b March 23, 1948

Wasim Haider (PIA & F'bad) b June 6, 1967

*Wasim Raja (Lahore, Sargodha, Pak. Us, PIA, Punjab & NBP) b July 3, 1952

Wass, T. G. (Notts; *CY 1908*) b Dec. 26, 1873, d Oct. 27, 1953

Wassell, A. (Hants) b April 15, 1940

*Watkins, A. J. (Glam) b April 21, 1922

*Watkins, J. C. (Natal) b April 10, 1923

*Watkins, J. R. (NSW) b April 16, 1943

Watson, A. (Lancs) b Nov. 4, 1844, d Oct. 26, 1920

*Watson, C. (Jam. & Delhi) b July 1, 1938

Watson, F. (Lancs) b Sept. 17, 1898, d Feb. 1, 1976

*Watson, G. D. (Vic., W. Aust. & NSW) b March 8, 1945

Watson, G. S. (Kent & Leics) b April 10, 1907, d April 1, 1974

*Watson, W. (Yorks & Leics; *CY 1954*) b March 7, 1920

*Watson, W. (Auck.) b Aug. 31, 1965

*Watson, W. J. (NSW) b Jan. 31, 1931

Watt, A. E. (Kent) b June 19, 1907, d Feb. 3, 1974

*Watt, L. (Otago) b Sept. 17, 1924, d Nov. 15, 1996

Watts, E. A. (Surrey) b Aug. 1, 1911, d May 2, 1982

Watts, P. D. (Northants & Notts) b March 31, 1938

Watts, P. J. (Northants) b June 16, 1940

*Wazir, Ali, S. (C. Ind., S. Punjab & Patiala) b Sept. 15, 1903, d June 17, 1950

*Wazir Mohammad (B'pur & Kar.) b Dec. 22, 1929

*Webb, M. G. (Otago & Cant.) b June 22, 1947

*Webb, P. N. (Auck.) b July 14, 1957

Webb, R. J. (Otago) b Sept. 15, 1952

Webb, R. T. (Sussex) b July 11, 1922

*Webbe, A. J. (OU & Middx) b Jan. 16, 1855, d Feb. 19, 1941

Webber, Roy (Statistician) b July 23, 1914, d Nov. 14, 1962

*Weekes, Sir Everton D. (B'dos; *CY 1951*) b Feb. 26, 1925

*Weekes, K. H. (Jam.) b Jan. 24, 1912, d Feb. 9, 1998

Weeks, R. T. (Warwicks) b April 30, 1930

Weerakkody, A. P. (NCC) b Oct. 1, 1970

*Weerasinghe, C. D. U. S. (TU & NCC) b March 1, 1968

Weigall, G. J. V. (CU & Kent) b Oct. 19, 1870, d May 17, 1944

*Weir, G. L. (Auck.) b June 2, 1908

*Wellard, A. W. (Som; *CY 1936*) b April 8, 1902, d Dec. 31, 1980

*Wellham, D. M. (NSW, Tas. & Qld) b March 13, 1959

Wells, B. D. (Glos & Notts) b July 27, 1930

Wells, C. M. (Sussex, Border, W. Prov. & Derbys) b March 3, 1960

Wells, W. (Northants) b March 14, 1881, d March 18, 1939

Wenman, E. G. (Kent & England) b Aug. 18, 1803, d Dec. 31, 1879

Wensley, A. F. (Sussex, Auck., Naw. & Eur.) b May 23, 1898, d June 17, 1970

*Wesley, C. (Natal) b Sept. 5, 1937

West, G. H. (Editor of *Wisden* 1880-86) b 1851, d Oct. 6, 1896

*Westcott, R. J. (W. Prov.) b Sept. 19, 1927

Weston, M. J. (Worcs) b April 8, 1959

*Wettimuny, M. D. (SL) b June 11, 1951

*Wettimuny, S. (SL; *CY 1985;* ICC referee) b Aug. 12, 1956

Wettimuny, S. R. de S. (SL) b Feb. 7, 1949

*Wharton, A. (Lancs & Leics) b April 30, 1923, d Aug. 26, 1993

*Whatmore, D. F. (Vic.) b March 16, 1954

Wheatley, O. S. CBE (CU, Warwicks & Glam; *CY 1969*) b May 28, 1935

Whitaker, Haddon OBE (Editor of *Wisden* 1940-43) b Aug. 30, 1908, d Jan. 5, 1982

White, A. F. T. (CU, Warwicks & Worcs) b Sept. 5, 1915, d March 16, 1993

White, Sir Archibald W. 4th Bt (Yorks) b Oct. 14, 1877, d Dec. 16, 1945

*White, D. J. (N. Dist.) b June 26, 1961

*White, D. W. (Hants & Glam) b Dec. 14, 1935

*White, G. C. (Tvl) b Feb. 5, 1882, d Oct. 17, 1918

*White, J. C. (Som; *CY 1929*) b Feb. 19, 1891, d May 2, 1961

White, Hon. L. R. (5th Lord Annaly) (Middx & Victory Test) b March 15, 1927, d Sept. 30, 1990

White, R. A. (Middx & Notts) b Oct. 6, 1936

White, R. C. (CU, Glos & Tvl) b Jan. 29, 1941

*White, W. A. (B'dos) b Nov. 20, 1938

Whitehead, A. G. T. (Som; Test umpire) b Oct. 28, 1940

Whitehead, H. (Leics) b Sept. 19, 1874, d Sept. 14, 1944

Whitehouse, J. (Warwicks) b April 8, 1949

*Whitelaw, P. E. (Auck.) b Feb. 10, 1910, d Aug. 28, 1988

Whiteside, J. P. (Lancs & Leics) b June 11, 1861, d March 8, 1946

Whitfield, E. W. (Surrey & Northants) b May 31, 1911, d Aug. 10, 1996

Whitington, R. S. (S. Aust. & Victory Tests; writer) b June 30, 1912, d March 13, 1984

*Whitney, M. R. (NSW & Glos) b Feb. 24, 1959

Whittaker, G. J. (Surrey) b May 29, 1916, d April 20, 1997

Whitticase, P. (Leics) b March 15, 1965

Whittingham, N. B. (Notts) b Oct. 22, 1940

*Whitty, W. J. (S. Aust.) b Aug. 15, 1886, d Jan. 30, 1974

*Whysall, W. W. (Notts; *CY 1925*) b Oct. 31, 1887, d Nov. 11, 1930

*Wickremasinghe, A. G. D. (NCC) b Dec. 27, 1965

*Wiener, J. M. (Vic.) b May 1, 1955

*Wight, C. V. (BG) b July 28, 1902, d Oct. 4, 1969

*Wight, G. L. (BG) b May 28, 1929

Wight, P. B. (BG, Som & Cant.) b June 25, 1930

*Wijegunawardene, K. I. W. (CCC) b Nov. 23, 1964

*Wijesuriya, R. G. C. E. (Mor. & Colts) b Feb. 18, 1960

Wilcox, D. R. (Essex & CU) b June 4, 1910, d Feb. 6, 1953

Wild, D. J. (Northants) b Nov. 28, 1962

*Wiles, C. A. (B'dos & T/T) b Aug. 11, 1892, d Nov. 4, 1957

Wilkins, C. P. (Derbys, Border, E. Prov. & Natal) b July 31, 1944

Wilkinson, C. T. A. (Surrey) b Oct. 4, 1884, d Dec. 16, 1970

*Wilkinson, L. L. (Lancs) b Nov. 5, 1916

Willatt, G. L. (CU, Notts & Derbys) b May 7, 1918

Willett, E. T. (Comb. Is. & Leewards) b May 1, 1953

Willett, M. D. (Surrey) b April 21, 1933

Willey, P. (Northants, E. Prov. & Leics; Test umpire) b Dec. 6, 1949

*Williams, A. B. (Jam.) b Nov. 21, 1949

Williams, D. L. (Glam) b Nov. 20, 1946

*Williams, E. A. V. (B'dos) b April 10, 1914, d April 13, 1997

Williams, R. G. (Northants) b Aug. 10, 1957

*Willis, R. G. D. MBE (Surrey, Warwicks & N. Tvl; *CY 1978*) b May 30, 1949

*Willoughby, J. T. (SA) b Nov. 7, 1874, d March 11, 1952

Willsher, E. (Kent & All-England) b Nov. 22, 1828, d Oct. 7, 1885

Wilson, A. (Lancs) b April 24, 1921

Wilson, A. E. (Middx & Glos) b May 18, 1910

Wilson, Rev. C. E. M. (CU & Yorks) b May 15, 1875, d Feb. 8, 1944

*Wilson, D. (Yorks) b Aug. 7, 1937

Wilson, E. R. (Betty) (Australia Women) b Nov. 21, 1921

*Wilson, E. R. (CU & Yorks) b March 25, 1879, d July 21, 1957

Wilson, G. (CU & Yorks) b Aug. 21, 1895, d Nov. 29, 1960

Wilson, H. L. (Sussex) b June 27, 1881, d March 15, 1937

Wilson, J. V. (Yorks; *CY 1961*) b Jan. 17, 1921

Wilson, J. W. (Otago) b Oct. 24, 1973

*Wilson, J. W. (Vic. & S. Aust.) b Aug. 20, 1921, d Oct. 13, 1985

Wilson, R. C. (Kent) b Feb. 18, 1928

*Wimble, C. S. (Tvl) b April 22, 1861, d Jan. 28, 1930

Windows, A. R. (Glos & CU) b Sept. 25, 1942

Winfield, H. M. (Notts) b June 13, 1933

Winrow, H. F. (Notts) b Jan. 17, 1916, d Aug. 19, 1973

*Winslow, P. L. (Sussex, Tvl & Rhod.) b May 21, 1929

Wisden, John (Sussex; founder John Wisden & Co and *Wisden's Cricketers' Almanack; special portrait 1913*) b Sept. 5, 1826, d April 5, 1884

*Wishart, K. L. (BG) b Nov. 28, 1908, d Oct. 18, 1972

Wolton, A. V. (Warwicks) b June 12, 1919, d Sept. 9, 1990

*Wood, A. (Yorks; *CY 1939*) b Aug. 25, 1898, d April 1, 1973

*Wood, B. (Yorks, Lancs, Derbys & E. Prov.) b Dec. 26, 1942

Wood, C. J. B. (Leics) b Nov. 21, 1875, d June 5, 1960

Wood, D. J. (Sussex) b May 19, 1914, d March 12, 1989

*Wood, G. E. C. (CU & Kent) b Aug. 22, 1893, d March 18, 1971

*Wood, G. M. (W. Aust.) b Nov. 6, 1956

*Wood, H. (Kent & Surrey; *CY 1891*) b Dec. 14, 1854, d April 30, 1919

*Wood, R. (Lancs & Vic.) b March 7, 1860, d Jan. 6, 1915

*Woodcock, A. J. (S. Aust.) b Feb. 27, 1948

Woodcock, John C. OBE (Writer; Editor of *Wisden* 1981-86) b Aug. 7, 1926

*Woodfull, W. M. OBE (Vic.; *CY 1927*) b Aug. 22, 1897, d Aug. 11, 1965

Woodhead, F. G. (Notts) b Oct. 30, 1912, d May 24, 1991

**Woods, S. M. J. (CU & Som; *CY 1889*) b April 13, 1867, d April 30, 1931

*Wooller, W. (CU & Glam) b Nov. 20, 1912, d March 10, 1997

Woolley, C. N. (Glos & Northants) b May 5, 1886, d Nov. 3, 1962

*Woolley, F. E. (Kent; *CY 1911*) b May 27, 1887, d Oct. 18, 1978

*Woolley, R. D. (Tas.) b Sept. 16, 1954

*Woolmer, R. A. (Kent, Natal & W. Prov.; *CY 1976*) b May 14, 1948

*Worrall, J. (Vic.) b June 21, 1861, d Nov. 17, 1937

*Worrell, Sir Frank M. M. (B'dos & Jam.; *CY 1951*) b Aug. 1, 1924, d March 13, 1967

Worsley, D. R. (OU & Lancs) b July 18, 1941

*Worthington, T. S. (Derbys; *CY 1937*) b Aug. 21, 1905, d Aug. 31, 1973

Wrathall, H. (Glos) b Feb. 1, 1869, d June 1, 1944

Wright, A. C. (Kent) b April 4, 1895, d May 26, 1959

*Wright, C. W. (CU & Notts) b May 27, 1863, d Jan. 10, 1936

*Wright, D. V. P. (Kent; *CY 1940*) b Aug. 21, 1914, d Nov. 13, 1998

Wright, Graeme A. (Editor of *Wisden* 1987-92) b April 23, 1943

*Wright, J. G. MBE (N. Dist., Derbys, Cant. & Auck.) b July 5, 1954

*Wright, K. J. (W. Aust. & S. Aust.) b Dec. 27, 1953

Wright, L. G. (Derbys; *CY 1906*) b June 15, 1862, d Jan. 11, 1953

Wright, W. (Notts & Kent) b Feb. 29, 1856, d March 22, 1940

*Wyatt, R. E. S. (Warwicks & Worcs; *CY 1930*) b May 2, 1901, d April 20, 1995

*Wynne, O. E. (Tvl & W. Prov.) b June 1, 1919, d July 13, 1975

*Wynyard, E. G. (Hants) b April 1, 1861, d Oct. 30, 1936

Yachad, M. (Tvl) b Nov. 17, 1960

*Yadav, N. S. (H'bad) b Jan. 26, 1957

*Yajurvindra Singh (M'tra & S'tra) b Aug. 1, 1952

*Yallop, G. N. (Vic.) b Oct. 7, 1952

*Yardley, B. (W. Aust.) b Sept. 5, 1947

*Yardley, N. W. D. (CU & Yorks; *CY 1948*) b March 19, 1915, d Oct. 4, 1989

Yardley, T. J. (Worcs & Northants) b Oct. 27, 1946

Yarnold, H. (Worcs) b July 6, 1917, d Aug. 13, 1974

*Yashpal Sharma (Punjab) b Aug. 11, 1954

Yawar Saeed (Som & Punjab) b Jan. 22, 1935

*Yograj Singh (Haryana & Punjab) b March 25, 1958

Young, A. (Som) b Nov. 6, 1890, d April 2, 1936

Young, D. M. (Worcs & Glos) b April 15, 1924, d June 18, 1993

Young, H. I. (Essex) b Feb. 5, 1876, d Dec. 12, 1964

*Young, J. A. (Middx) b Oct. 14, 1912, d Feb. 5, 1993

*Young, R. A. (CU & Sussex) b Sept. 16, 1885, d July 1, 1968

*Younis Ahmed (Lahore, Kar., Surrey, PIA, S. Aust., Worcs & Glam) b Oct. 20, 1947

*Yuile, B. W. (C. Dist.) b Oct. 29, 1941

*Zaheer Abbas (Kar., Glos, PWD, Dawood Ind., Sind & PIA; *CY 1972*) b July 24, 1947

*Zakir Khan (Sind, Peshawar & ADBP) b April 3, 1963

Zesers, A. K. (S. Aust.) b March 11, 1967

*Zoehrer, T. J. (W. Aust.) b Sept. 25, 1961

*Zulch, J. W. (Tvl) b Jan. 2, 1886, d May 19, 1924

*Zulfiqar Ahmed (B'pur & PIA) b Nov. 22, 1926

*Zulqarnain (Pak. Rlwys, Lahore, HBFC & PACO) b May 25, 1962

REGISTER OF CURRENT PLAYERS

The qualifications for inclusion are as follows:

1. All players who appeared in Tests or one-day internationals for a Test-playing country in 1997-98 or 1998.

2. All players who appeared in the County Championship in 1998.

3. All players who appeared in the Sheffield Shield, Supersport Series, President's Cup, Shell Conference and Duleep Trophy in 1997-98.

4. All players who appeared in first-class domestic cricket in 1997-98, who have also played in Tests or one-day international cricket.

5. All players who appeared in one-day internationals for Bangladesh and Kenya in 1997-98.

Notes: The forename by which the player is known is underlined if it is not his first name.

Teams are those played for in 1997-98 and/or 1998, or the last domestic team for which that player appeared.

Countries are those for which players are qualified.

The country of birth is given if it is not the one for which a player is qualified. It is also given to differentiate between nations in the Leeward and Windward Islands, and where it is essential for clarity.

* *Denotes Test player.*

	Team	Country	Born	Birthplace
Aamir Hanif	Karachi/Allied Bank	P	4.10.71	*Karachi*
* **Aamer Malik**	PIA	P	3.1.63	*Mandi Bahauddin*
* **Aamir Nazir**	Gujranwala/Allied Bank	P	2.1.71	*Lahore*
* **Aamir Sohail**	Allied Bank	P	14.9.66	*Lahore*
Abbas Ali Syed	Madhya Pradesh	I	20.2.76	*Indore*
Abdur Razzaq	Lahore/KRL	P	2.12.79	*Lahore*
Abrahams Shafiek	Eastern Province	SA	4.3.68	*Port Elizabeth*
Abrahim Zahir Ahmed	Griqualand West	SA	5.6.72	*Robertson*
* **Ackerman** Hylton Deon	Western Province	SA	14.2.73	*Cape Town*
Adam Shaun Michael	Natal	SA	13.9.79	*Durban*
Adams Christopher John	Sussex	E	6.5.70	*Whitwell*
Adams Fabian Alex	Leeward Islands	WI	7.1.75	*The Valley, Anguilla*
* **Adams** James Clive	Jamaica	WI	9.1.68	*Port Maria*
* **Adams** Paul Regan	Western Province	SA	20.1.77	*Cape Town*
Adcock Nathan Tennyson	South Australia	A	22.4.78	*Adelaide*
Afzaal Usman	Nottinghamshire	E	9.6.77	*Rawalpindi, Pakistan*
Agarkar Ajit Bhalchandra	Mumbai	I	4.12.77	*Bombay*
Akhtar Sarfraz	Peshawar/National Bank	P	20.2.76	*Peshawar*
Akram Khan	Bangladesh	B	1.11.68	*Chittagong*
* **Akram Raza**	Faisalabad/Habib Bank	P	22.11.64	*Lahore*
Albanie James Daniel	Boland	SA	1.5.68	*Touwsrivier*
Aldred Paul	Derbyshire	E	4.2.69	*Chellaston*
* **Ali Hussain Rizvi**	Karachi/Customs	P	6.1.74	*Karachi*
* **Ali Naqvi**	Karachi	P	19.3.77	*Lahore*
Alley Phillip John Sydney	New South Wales	A	26.7.70	*Orange*
Alleyne Mark Wayne	Gloucestershire	E	23.5.68	*Tottenham*
* **Allott** Geoffrey Ian	Canterbury	NZ	24.12.71	*Christchurch*
Altree Darren Anthony	Warwickshire	E	30.9.74	*Rugby*
* **Ambrose** Curtly Elconn Lynwall	Leeward Islands	WI	21.9.63	*Swetes Village, Antigua*
Amin Rupesh Mahesh	Surrey	E	20.8.77	*London*
Amin-ul-Islam	Bangladesh	B	2.2.68	*Dhaka*
Amm Philip Geoffrey	Border	SA	2.4.64	*Grahamstown*
* **Amre** Pravin Kalyan	Rajasthan	I	14.8.68	*Bombay*
Angara Joseph Oduol	Kenya	K	8.11.71	*Nairobi*
Angel Jo	Western Australia	A	22.4.68	*Mount Lawley*
Anis-ur-Rehman	Bangladesh	B	1.3.71	*Dhaka*
* **Anurasiri** Sangarange Don	Panadura	SL	25.2.66	*Panadura*

	Team	Country	Born	Birthplace
* **Aqib Javed**	Allied Bank	P	5.8.72	*Sheikhupura*
Archer Graeme Francis	Nottinghamshire	E	26.9.70	*Carlisle*
Arnberger Jason Lee	Victoria	A	18.11.72	*Penrith*
* **Arnold** Russel Premakumaran	Nondescripts	SL	25.10.73	*Colombo*
* **Arshad Khan**	Peshawar/Allied Bank	P	22.3.71	*Peshawar*
Arthur John Michael	Griqualand West	SA	17.5.68	*Johannesburg*
* **Arthurton** Keith Lloyd Thomas	Leeward Islands	WI	21.2.65	*Charlestown, Nevis*
* **Ashfaq Ahmed**	PIA	P	6.6.73	*Lahore*
Asif Karim	Kenya	K	15.12.63	*Mombasa*
* **Asif Mujtaba**	Karachi/PIA	P	4.11.67	*Karachi*
Astle Nathan John	Canterbury	NZ	15.9.71	*Christchurch*
* **Atapattu** Marvan Samson	Sinhalese	SL	22.11.70	*Kalutara*
* **Ata-ur-Rehman**	Lahore/Allied Bank	P	28.3.75	*Lahore*
Ather Ali Khan	Bangladesh	B	10.2.62	*Dhaka*
* **Atherton** Michael Andrew	Lancashire	E	23.3.68	*Manchester*
* **Atif Rauf**	Islamabad/ADBP	P	3.3.64	*Lahore*
Atkinson Mark Neville	Tasmania	A	11.2.69	*Sydney*
Atkinson Mark Peter	Western Australia	A	27.11.70	*Bentley*
Austin Ian David	Lancashire	E	30.5.66	*Haslingden*
Aymes Adrian Nigel	Hampshire	E	4.6.64	*Southampton*
* **Azam Khan**	Karachi/Customs	P	1.3.69	*Karachi*
* **Azhar Mahmood**	Islamabad	P	28.2.75	*Rawalpindi*
* **Azharuddin** Mohammad	Hyderabad	I	8.2.63	*Hyderabad*
* **Bacher** Adam Marc	Gauteng	SA	29.10.73	*Johannesburg*
Badani Hemang Kamal	Tamil Nadu	I	14.11.76	*Madras*
Badenhorst Alan	Eastern Province	SA	10.7.70	*Cape Town*
Bahutule Sairaj Vasant	Mumbai	I	6.1.73	*Bombay*
Bailey Mark David	Northern Districts	NZ	26.11.70	*Hamilton*
* **Bailey** Robert John	Northamptonshire	E	28.10.63	*Biddulph*
Bailey Tobin Michael Barnaby	Northamptonshire	E	28.8.76	*Kettering*
Baker Robert Michael	Western Australia	A	24.7.75	*Osborne Park*
Bakkes Herman Charles	Free State	SA	24.12.69	*Port Elizabeth*
Ball Martyn Charles John	Gloucestershire	E	26.4.70	*Bristol*
Balliram Anil	Trinidad & Tobago	WI	27.2.74	*Trinidad*
Bandara Charitha Malinga	Kalutara	SL	31.12.79	*Kalutara*
Bandaratilleke Mapa Rallage Chandima Niroshan	Tamil Union	SL	16.5.75	*Colombo*
* **Banerjee** Subroto Tara	Bengal	I	13.2.69	*Patna*
Bangar Sanjay Bapusaheb	Railways	I	11.10.72	*Beed*
* **Baptiste** Eldine Ashworth Elderfield	Eastern Province	WI	12.3.60	*Liberta, Antigua*
Barnard Pieter Hendrik	Griqualand West	SA	8.5.70	*Nelspruit*
Barnes Aaron Craig	Auckland	NZ	21.12.71	*Turangi*
* **Barnett** Kim John	Derbyshire	E	17.7.60	*Stoke-on-Trent*
Basdeo Amarnath	Trinidad & Tobago	WI	13.4.77	*Trinidad*
* **Basit Ali**	Karachi	P	13.12.70	*Karachi*
Bastow Jonathan Edward	Natal	SA	12.2.74	*Pietermaritzburg*
Bates Justin Jonathan	Sussex	E	9.4.76	*Farnborough, Hants*
Bates Richard Terry	Nottinghamshire	E	17.6.72	*Stamford*
Batson Nathan Evan	Worcestershire	E	24.7.78	*Basildon*
Batt Christopher James	Middlesex	E	22.9.76	*Taplow*
Batty Jonathan Neil	Surrey	E	18.4.74	*Chesterfield*
Beamish Michael Gwynne	Eastern Province	SA	30.7.69	*King William's Town*
Bedade Atul Chandrakant	Baroda	I	24.9.66	*Bombay*
Bell Matthew David	Wellington	NZ	25.2.77	*Dunedin*
Benfield Mark Rowland	Gauteng	SA	3.12.76	*Potgietersrus*
* **Benjamin** Joseph Emmanuel	Surrey	E	2.2.61	*Christ Church, St Kitts*
* **Benjamin** Kenneth Charlie Griffith	Leeward Islands	WI	8.4.67	*St John's, Antigua*
Benkenstein Dale Martin	Natal	SA	9.6.74	*Salisbury, Rhodesia*
Berry Darren Shane	Victoria	A	10.12.69	*Melbourne*

	Team	Country	Born	Birthplace
Betts Melvyn Morris	Durham	E	26.3.75	Sacriston
Beukes Jonathan	Free State	SA	15.3.79	Kimberley
* **Bevan** Michael Gwyl	New South Wales/Sussex	A	8.5.70	Belconnen
* **Bichel** Andrew John	Queensland	A	27.8.70	Laidley
* **Bicknell** Martin Paul	Surrey	E	14.1.69	Guildford
Birrell Adrian Victor	Eastern Province	SA	8.12.60	Grahamstown
* **Bishop** Ian Raphael	Trinidad & Tobago	WI	24.10.67	Port-of-Spain
Blackwell Ian David	Derbyshire	E	10.6.78	Chesterfield
* **Blakey** Richard John	Yorkshire	E	15.1.67	Huddersfield
Blanchett Ian Neale	Middlesex	E	2.10.75	Melbourne, Australia
* **Blewett** Gregory Scott	South Australia	A	29.10.71	Adelaide
Bloomfield Timothy Francis	Middlesex	E	31.5.73	Ashford, Middlesex
Boje Nico	Free State	SA	20.3.73	Bloemfontein
Bond Shane Edward	Canterbury	NZ	7.6.75	Christchurch
* **Boon** David Clarence	Tasmania/Durham	A	29.12.60	Launceston
* **Bosch** Tertius	Natal	SA	14.3.66	Vereeniging
Bosman Lungile Loots	Griqualand West	SA	14.4.77	Kimberley
Bossenger Wendell	Griqualand West	SA	23.10.76	Cape Town
Botha Anthony Greyvensteyn	Natal B	SA	17.11.76	Pretoria
Botha Peterus Johannes	Border	SA	28.9.66	Vereeniging
* **Botha** Mark Verdon	Border	SA	3.12.76	East London
Bowen Mark Nicholas	Nottinghamshire	E	6.12.67	Redcar
Bowler Peter Duncan	Somerset	E	30.7.63	Plymouth
* **Bradburn** Grant Eric	Northern Districts	NZ	26.5.66	Hamilton
Bradfield Carl Crispin	Eastern Province	SA	18.1.75	Grahamstown
Bradshaw Ian David Russell	Barbados	WI	9.7.74	Barbados
* **Brandes** Eddo Andre	Mashonaland	Z	5.3.63	Port Shepstone, SA
Breese Gareth Rohan	Jamaica	WI	9.1.76	Montego Bay
Brent Gary Bazil	Mashonaland	Z	13.1.76	Sinoia
Brimson Matthew Thomas	Leicestershire	E	1.12.70	Plumstead
Brooker Finley Clint	Griqualand West	SA	26.12.72	Kimberley
Brown Alistair Duncan	Surrey	E	11.2.70	Beckenham
Brown Douglas Robert	Warwickshire	E	29.10.69	Stirling, Scotland
Brown Jason Fred	Northamptonshire	E	10.10.74	Newcastle-under-Lyme
Brown Keith Robert	Middlesex	E	18.3.63	Edmonton
* **Brown** Simon John Emmerson	Durham	E	29.6.69	Cleadon
* **Browne** Courtney Oswald	Barbados	WI	7.12.70	London, England
* **Bruk-Jackson** Glen Keith	Mashonaland	Z	25.4.69	Salisbury
Bruyns Mark Lloyd	Natal	SA	8.11.73	Pietermaritzburg
Bryan Henderson Ricardo	Barbados/Griqualand West	WI	21.3.70	Barbados
Bryson Rudi Edwin	Northerns	SA	25.7.68	Springs
Bulbeck Matthew Paul Leonard	Somerset	E	8.11.79	Taunton
Bulfin Carl Edward	Central Districts	NZ	19.8.73	Blenheim
Burns Michael	Somerset	E	2.6.69	Barrow-in-Furness
* **Butcher** Alan Raymond	Surrey	E	7.1.54	Croydon
Butcher Gary Paul	Glamorgan	E	11.3.75	Clapham
* **Butcher** Mark Alan	Surrey	E	23.8.72	Croydon
Byas David	Yorkshire	E	26.8.63	Kilham
* **Caddick** Andrew Richard	Somerset	E	21.11.68	Christchurch, NZ
* **Cairns** Christopher Lance	Canterbury	NZ	13.6.70	Picton
Callaghan David John	Eastern Province	SA	1.2.65	Queenstown
* **Campbell** Alistair Douglas Ross	Mashonaland	Z	23.9.72	Salisbury
Campbell Ryan John	Western Australia	A	7.2.72	Osborne Park
* **Campbell** Sherwin Legay	Barbados	WI	1.11.70	Bridgetown
* **Capel** David John	Northamptonshire	E	6.2.63	Northampton
Carpenter James Robert	Sussex	E	20.10.75	Birkenhead
Cary Sean Ross	Western Australia	A	10.3.71	Subiaco
Cassar Matthew Edward	Derbyshire	E	16.10.72	Sydney, Australia
Catterall Duncan Neil	Worcestershire	A	17.9.78	Preston

	Team	Country	Born	Birthplace
Chandana Umagiliya Durage Upul	Tamil Union	SL	7.5.72	Galle
* **Chanderpaul** Shivnarine	Guyana	WI	18.8.74	Unity Village
Chandler Philip John Barry	Wellington	NZ	6.7.72	Wellington
Chandrasekhar Vakkadai Biksheswaran	Goa	I	21.8.61	Madras
Chapman Robert James	Worcestershire	E	28.7.72	Nottingham
Chapman Steven	Durham	E	2.10.71	Crook
Chapple Glen	Lancashire	E	23.1.74	Skipton
Chatterjee Utpal	Bengal	I	13.7.64	Calcutta
* **Chauhan** Rajesh Kumar	Madhya Pradesh	I	19.12.66	Ranchi
Chee Quee Richard	New South Wales	A	4.1.71	Camperdown
Cherry Daniel David	Glamorgan	E	7.2.80	Newport, S. Wales
Chilton Mark James	Lancashire	E	2.10.76	Sheffield
Chopra Akash	Delhi	I	19.9.77	Agra
Chopra Nikhil	Delhi	I	26.12.73	Allahabad
Chudasama Dipak	Kenya	K	20.5.63	Mombasa
Church Matthew John	Gloucestershire	E	26.7.72	Guildford
Cilliers Sarel Arnold	Free State	SA	6.6.71	Klerksdorp
Clark Stuart Rupert	New South Wales	A	28.4.75	Carringbah
Clarke Vincent Paul	Derbyshire	E	11.11.71	Liverpool
Clough Gareth David	Yorkshire	E	23.5.78	Leeds
Coley Andre Nicolo	Jamaica	WI	22.9.74	Kingston
Collingwood Paul David	Durham	E	26.5.76	Shotley Bridge
Collins Pedro Tyrone	Barbados	WI	12.8.76	Boscobelle
* **Commins** John Brian	Western Province	SA	19.2.65	East London
Connor Cardigan Adolphus	Hampshire	E	24.3.61	The Valley, Anguilla
* **Cook** Simon Hewitt	New South Wales	A	29.1.72	Hastings
Cork Dominic Gerald	Derbyshire	E	7.8.71	Newcastle-under-Lyme
Cosker Dean Andrew	Glamorgan	E	7.1.78	Weymouth
Cottey Phillip Anthony	Glamorgan	E	2.6.66	Swansea
Cousins Darren Mark	Essex	E	24.9.71	Cambridge
Cowan Ashley Preston	Essex	E	7.5.75	Hitchin
Cox Jamie	Tasmania	A	15.10.69	Burnie
Crafton Alton Laurie	Windward Islands	WI	17.12.69	St Lucia
Craig Shawn Andrew Jacob	Victoria	A	23.6.73	Carlton
Craven Christiaan Frans	Free State	SA	6.12.70	Dundee
* **Crawley** John Paul	Lancashire	E	21.9.71	Maldon
Creevey Brendan Neville	Queensland	A	18.2.70	Charleville
* **Croft** Robert Damien Bale	Glamorgan	E	25.5.70	Morriston
* **Cronje** Wessel Johannes (Hansie)	Free State	SA	25.9.69	Bloemfontein
Crookes Derek Norman	Gauteng	SA	5.3.69	Mariannhill
Crowe Carl Daniel	Leicestershire	E	25.11.75	Leicester
Croy Martyn Gilbert	Otago	NZ	23.1.74	Hamilton
* **Cuffy** Cameron Eustace	Windward Islands	WI	8.2.70	South Rivers, St Vincent
* **Cullinan** Daryll John	Gauteng	SA	4.3.67	Kimberley
Cumming Craig Derek	Canterbury	NZ	31.8.75	Timaru
Cunliffe Robert John	Gloucestershire	E	8.11.73	Oxford
Curran Kevin Malcolm	Northamptonshire/Boland	E	7.9.59	Rusape, Rhodesia
Dahiya Vijay	Delhi	I	10.5.73	Delhi
Dakin Jonathan Michael	Leicestershire	E	28.2.73	Hitchin
* **Dale** Adam Craig	Queensland	A	30.12.68	Ivanhoe
Dale Adrian	Glamorgan	E	24.10.68	Germiston, South Africa
Daley James Arthur	Durham	E	24.9.73	Sunderland
Darlington Kevin Godfrey	Guyana	WI	26.4.72	Guyana
Das Shiv Sunder	Orissa	I	5.11.77	Bhubaneshwar
* **Dassanayake** Pubudu Bathiya	Bloomfield	SL	11.7.70	Kandy
David Noel Arthur	Hyderabad	I	26.2.71	Hyderabad
Davids Faiek	Western Province	SA	1.9.64	Cape Town
Davies Andrew Philip	Glamorgan	E	7.11.76	Neath

	Team	Country	Born	Birthplace
Davies Christopher James	South Australia	A	15.11.78	Adelaide
Davies Michael Kenton	Northamptonshire	E	17.7.76	Ashby-de-la-Zouch
Davis Casper Andre	Windward Islands	WI	14.3.66	St Vincent
* **Davis** Heath Te-Ihi-O-Te-Rangi	Wellington	NZ	30.11.71	Lower Hutt
Davis Mark Jeffrey Gronow	Northerns	SA	10.10.71	Port Elizabeth
Davison John Michael	Victoria	A	9.5.70	Campbell River, Canada
Davison Rodney John	New South Wales	A	26.6.69	Kogarah
Dawes Joseph Henry	Queensland	A	29.8.70	Herston
Dawood Ismail	Glamorgan	E	23.7.76	Dewsbury
Dawson Alan Charles	Western Province	SA	27.11.69	Cape Town
Dawson Robert Ian	Gloucestershire	E	29.3.70	Exmouth
Dean Kevin James	Derbyshire	E	16.10.75	Derby
de Bruyn Pierre	Northerns	SA	31.3.77	Pretoria
de Bruyn Zander	Gauteng	SA	5.7.75	Johannesburg
* **DeFreitas** Phillip Anthony Jason	Derbyshire	E	18.2.66	Scotts Head, Dominica
De Groot Nicholas Alexander	Guyana	WI	22.10.75	Guyana
de la Pena Jason Michael	Kent	E	16.9.72	London
de Nobrega Justin	Western Province	SA	14.7.79	Cape Town
* **de Silva** Karunakalage Sajeewa Chanaka	Nondescripts	SL	11.1.71	Kalutara
* **de Silva** Pinnaduwage <u>Aravinda</u>	Nondescripts	SL	17.10.65	Colombo
* **de Silva** Sanjeewa Kumara <u>Lanka</u>	Kurunegala Youth	SL	29.7.75	Kurunegala
* **de Villiers** Petrus Stephanus	Northerns	SA	13.10.64	Vereeniging
de Vos Dirk Johannes Jacobus	Northerns	SA	15.6.75	Pretoria
* **Dhanraj** Rajindra	Trinidad & Tobago	WI	6.2.69	Barrackpore
Dharmani Pankaj	Punjab	I	27.9.74	Delhi
* **Dharmasena** Handunnettige Deepthi Priyantha <u>Kumar</u>	Bloomfield	SL	24.4.71	Colombo
Dighton Michael Gray	Western Australia	A	24.7.76	Toowoomba
* **Dillon** Mervyn	Trinidad & Tobago	WI	5.6.74	Toco
Dippenaar Hendrik Human	Free State	SA	14.6.77	Kimberley
Di Venuto Michael James	Tasmania	A	12.12.73	Hobart
Dixon Troy James	Queensland	A	22.12.69	Geelong
* **Dodemaide** Anthony Ian Christopher	Victoria	A	5.10.63	Williamstown
* **Donald** Allan Anthony	Free State	SA	20.10.66	Bloemfontein
Douglas Mark William	Central Districts	NZ	20.10.68	Nelson
* **Doull** Simon Blair	Northern Districts	NZ	6.8.69	Pukekohe
Dowlin Travis Montague	Guyana	WI	24.2.77	Georgetown
Dowman Mathew Peter	Nottinghamshire	E	10.5.74	Grantham
Drakes Vasbert Conniel	Barbados/Border	WI	5.8.69	St James
* **Dravid** Rahul	Karnataka	I	11.1.73	Indore
Drew Bryan John	Boland	SA	23.1.71	Durban
Driver Ryan Craig	Worcestershire	E	30.4.79	Truro
Dros Gerald	Northerns	SA	2.4.73	Pretoria
Drum Christopher James	Auckland	NZ	10.7.74	Auckland
Dry Willem Moolman	Griqualand West	SA	9.1.71	Vryburg
Dumas Vernon	Windward Islands	WI	79	Dominica
Dutch Keith Philip	Middlesex	E	21.3.73	Harrow
Dutta Gautam	Assam	I	28.10.73	Gauhati
* **Ealham** Mark Alan	Kent	E	27.8.69	Willesborough
Ecclestone Simon Charles	Somerset	E	16.7.71	Great Dunmow
Edmond Michael Denis	Warwickshire	E	30.7.69	Barrow-in-Furness
Edwards Alexander David	Sussex	E	2.8.75	Cuckfield
Eime Andrew Barry	South Australia	A	3.7.71	North Adelaide
* **Eksteen** Clive Edward	Gauteng	SA	2.12.66	Johannesburg
* **Elliott** Matthew Thomas Gray	Victoria	A	28.9.71	Chelsea
* **Elworthy** Steven	Northerns	SA	23.2.65	Bulawayo, Rhodesia
* **Emery** Philip Allen	New South Wales	A	25.6.64	St Ives

	Team	Country	Born	Birthplace
Emslie Peter Arthur Norman	Border	SA	21.10.68	*Grahamstown*
Enam-ul-Haque	Bangladesh	B	27.2.67	*Comilla*
English Cedric Vaughan	Griqualand West	SA	13.9.73	*Kimberley*
Eugene John	Windward Islands	WI	16.8.70	*St Lucia*
Evans Alun Wyn	Glamorgan	E	20.8.75	*Glanamman*
* **Evans** Craig Neil	Mashonaland	Z	29.11.69	*Salisbury*
Evans Kevin Paul	Nottinghamshire	E	10.9.63	*Calverton*
* **Fairbrother** Neil Harvey	Lancashire	E	9.9.63	*Warrington*
Faull Martin Peter	South Australia	A	10.5.68	*Darwin*
* **Fazl-e-Akbar**	Peshawar/ADBP	P	20.10.80	*Peshawar*
Fellows Gary Matthew	Yorkshire	E	30.7.78	*Halifax*
Fernando Ungamandalige <u>Nisal</u> Kumudusiri	Sinhalese	SL	10.3.70	*Colombo*
Ferreira Evert Johann	Boland	SA	29.4.76	*Pretoria*
Ferreira Lloyd Douglas	Western Province	SA	6.5.74	*Johannesburg*
Ferreira Quentin	Eastern Province	SA	28.12.72	*East London*
Fisher Ian Douglas	Yorkshire	E	31.5.76	*Bradford*
Fitzgerald David Andrew	South Australia	A	30.11.72	*Osborne Park*
Flanagan Ian Nicholas	Essex	E	5.6.80	*Colchester*
Flegler Shawn Leonard	Victoria	A	23.3.72	*Darwin*
* **Fleming** Damien William	Victoria	A	24.4.70	*Bentley*
Fleming Matthew Valentine	Kent	E	12.12.64	*Macclesfield*
* **Fleming** Stephen Paul	Canterbury	NZ	1.4.73	*Christchurch*
* **Flintoff** Andrew	Lancashire	E	6.12.77	*Preston*
* **Flower** Andrew	Mashonaland	Z	28.4.68	*Cape Town, SA*
* **Flower** Grant William	Mashonaland	Z	20.12.70	*Salisbury*
Foley Geoffrey Ian	Queensland	A	11.10.67	*Jandowae*
Follett David	Northamptonshire	E	14.10.68	*Newcastle-under-Lyme*
Forde Keith Adrian	Natal	SA	12.7.69	*Pietermaritzburg*
Foster Michael James	Durham	E	17.9.72	*Leeds*
Fourie Brenden Craig	Border	SA	13.4.70	*East London*
Francis Nigel Bernard	Trinidad & Tobago	WI	6.9.71	*Trinidad*
Franks Paul John	Nottinghamshire	E	3.2.79	*Mansfield*
* **Fraser** Angus Robert Charles	Middlesex	E	8.8.65	*Billinge*
Freedman David Andrew	New South Wales	A	19.6.64	*Sydney*
Frost Tony	Warwickshire	E	17.11.75	*Stoke-on-Trent*
Fulton David Paul	Kent	E	15.11.71	*Lewisham*
Furlong Campbell James Marie	Central Districts	NZ	16.6.74	*Napier*
Gaffaney Christopher Blair	Otago	NZ	30.11.75	*Dunedin*
Gain Douglas Robert	Gauteng	SA	29.12.76	*Johannesburg*
Gale Aaron James	Otago	NZ	8.4.70	*Balclutha*
* **Gallian** Jason Edward Riche	Nottinghamshire	E	25.6.71	*Sydney, Australia*
Gandhe Pritam Vithal	Vidarbha	I	6.8.71	*Nagpur*
Gandhi Devang	Bengal	I	6.9.71	*Bhavnagar*
Ganesh Doddanarasiah	Karnataka	I	30.6.73	*Bangalore*
Ganga Daren	Trinidad & Tobago	WI	14.1.79	*Barrackpore*
* **Ganguly** Sourav Chandidas	Bengal	I	8.7.72	*Calcutta*
Gardiner Grant Bruce	Victoria	A	26.2.65	*Melbourne*
Garnaut Matthew Stuart	Western Australia	A	7.11.73	*Subiaco*
Garrick Leon Vivian	Jamaica	WI	11.11.76	*St Ann*
* **Gatting** Michael William	Middlesex	E	6.6.57	*Kingsbury*
Gavaskar Rohan Sunil	Bengal	I	20.2.76	*Kanpur*
George Mulligan Frank	Western Province	SA	10.9.76	*Cape Town*
George Shane Peter	South Australia	A	20.10.70	*Adelaide*
* **Germon** Lee Kenneth	Canterbury	NZ	4.11.68	*Christchurch*
Geyer Kevin James	New South Wales	A	11.10.73	*Bathurst*
Ghulam Ali	Karachi/PIA	P	8.9.66	*Karachi*
* **Gibbs** Herschelle Herman	Western Province	SA	23.2.74	*Cape Town*

	Team	Country	Born	Birthplace
* **Gibson** Ottis Delroy	Barbados	WI	16.3.69	Sion Hill
Giddins Edward Simon Hunter	Warwickshire	E	20.7.71	Eastbourne
Gidley Martyn Ian	Griqualand West	SA	30.9.68	Leicester, England
Gie Noel Addison	Nottinghamshire	E	12.4.77	Pretoria, South Africa
Gilchrist Adam Craig	Western Australia	A	14.11.71	Bellingen
Gilder Gary Michael	Natal	SA	6.7.74	Salisbury, Rhodesia
* **Giles** Ashley Fraser	Warwickshire	E	19.3.73	Chertsey
Gillespie Jason Neil	South Australia	A	19.4.75	Darlinghurst
Glassock Craig Anthony	New South Wales	A	29.11.73	Mona Vale
Goodchild David John	Middlesex	E	17.9.76	Harrow
* **Goodwin** Murray William	Mashonaland A	Z	11.12.72	Salisbury, Rhodesia
* **Gough** Darren	Yorkshire	E	18.9.70	Barnsley
Gough Michael Andrew	Durham	E	18.12.79	Hartlepool
Grace Graham Vernon	Eastern Province	SA	16.8.75	Salisbury
Graham Hattian	Barbados	WI		
Grainger Chad	Boland	SA	23.9.72	Johannesburg
Grayson Adrian Paul	Essex	E	31.3.71	Ripon
* **Greatbatch** Mark John	Central Districts	NZ	11.12.63	Auckland
Green Richard James	Lancashire	E	13.3.76	Warrington
* **Griffith** Adrian Frank Gordon	Barbados	WI	19.11.71	Barbados
Griffiths Steven Paul	Derbyshire	E	31.5.73	Hertford
Grove Jamie Oliver	Essex	E	3.7.79	Bury St Edmunds
Gunawardene Aruna Alwis Wijesiri	Sinhalese	SL	31.3.69	Colombo
Gunawardene Dihan Avishka	Nondescripts	SL	26.5.77	Colombo
Habib Aftab	Leicestershire	E	7.2.72	Reading
Habib-ul-Bashar	Bangladesh	B	17.8.72	Kushtia
Hafeez Abdul	Worcestershire	E	21.3.77	Birmingham
Haldipur Nikhil	Bengal	I	19.12.77	Calcutta
Hall Andrew James	Gauteng	SA	31.7.75	Johannesburg
Hamilton Gavin Mark	Yorkshire	E	16.9.74	Broxburn, Scotland
Hammond George Matthew	Border	SA	27.3.76	Vryburg
Hancock Timothy Harold Coulter	Gloucestershire	E	20.4.72	Reading
Haniff Azeemul	Guyana	WI	24.10.77	Guyana
Haniff Zaheer Abbass	Guyana	WI	13.4.74	Guyana
* **Harbhajan Singh**	Punjab	I	3.7.80	Jullundur
Harden Richard John	Somerset	E	16.8.65	Bridgwater
Harmison Stephen James	Durham	E	23.10.78	Ashington
Harper Laurence Damien	Victoria	A	10.12.70	Deniliquin
Harper Peter Quinton	Victoria	A	11.12.77	Burwood
Harrigan Lanville Allonie	Leeward Islands	WI	26.9.67	Anguilla
Harris Andrew James	Derbyshire	E	26.6.73	Ashton-under-Lyne
* **Harris** Chris Zinzan	Canterbury	NZ	20.11.69	Christchurch
Harrity Mark Andrew	South Australia	A	9.3.74	Semaphore
* **Hart** Matthew Norman	Northern Districts	NZ	16.5.72	Hamilton
Hart Robert Garry	Northern Districts	NZ	2.12.74	Hamilton
Hartley Peter John	Hampshire	E	18.4.60	Keighley
Harvey Ian Joseph	Victoria	A	10.4.72	Wonthaggi
Harvey Kade Murray	Western Australia	A	7.10.75	Subiaco
Harvey Mark Edward	Lancashire	E	26.6.74	Burnley
* **Harvinder Singh**	Punjab	I	23.12.77	Amritsar
* **Hasan Raza**	Karachi/Customs	P	11.3.82	Karachi
Hasib-ul-Hassan	Bangladesh	B	3.6.77	Dhaka
* **Haslam** Mark James	Auckland	NZ	26.9.72	Bury, England
* **Hathurusinghe** Upul Chandika	Moors	SL	13.9.68	Colombo
* **Hayden** Matthew Lawrence	Queensland	A	29.10.71	Kingaroy
Haynes Gavin Richard	Worcestershire	E	29.9.69	Stourbridge
Hayward Mornantau	Eastern Province	SA	6.3.77	Uitenhage
* **Headley** Dean Warren	Kent	E	27.1.70	Stourbridge

	Team	Country	Born	Birthplace
* **Healy** Ian Andrew	Queensland	A	30.4.64	*Spring Hill*
Hearle Philip Kenyon	Boland	SA	31.5.78	*Johannesburg*
Hegg Warren Kevin	Lancashire	E	23.2.68	*Whitefield*
Hemp David Lloyd	Warwickshire	E	8.11.70	*Hamilton, Bermuda*
Henderson Claude William	Boland	SA	14.6.72	*Worcester*
Henderson James Michael	Boland	SA	6.8.75	*Worcester*
Hewitt James Peter	Middlesex	E	26.2.76	*Southwark*
Hewson Dominic Robert	Gloucestershire	E	3.10.74	*Cheltenham*
Hibbert Andrew James Edward	Essex	E	17.12.74	*Harold Wood*
* **Hick** Graeme Ashley	Worcestershire	E	23.5.66	*Salisbury, Rhodesia*
Hills Dene Fleetwood	Tasmania	A	27.8.70	*Wynyard*
Hinds Wavell Wayne	Jamaica	WI	7.9.76	*Kingston*
* **Hirwani** Narendra Deepchand	Madhya Pradesh	I	18.10.68	*Gorakhpur*
Hitesh Modi	Kenya	K	13.10.71	*Kisumu*
Hodge Bradley John	Victoria	A	29.12.74	*Sandringham*
Hodgson Timothy Philip	Essex	E	27.3.75	*Guildford*
Hogg George Bradley	Western Australia	A	6.2.71	*Narrogin*
Hoggard Matthew James	Yorkshire	E	31.12.76	*Leeds*
* **Holder** Roland Irwin Christopher	Barbados	WI	22.12.67	*Port-of-Spain, Trinidad*
* **Hollioake** Adam John	Surrey	E	5.9.71	*Melbourne, Australia*
* **Hollioake** Benjamin Caine	Surrey	E	11.11.77	*Melbourne, Australia*
Holloway Piran Charles Laity	Somerset	E	1.10.70	*Helston*
Hook Benjamin James	South Australia	A	5.3.73	*Kingswood*
* **Hooper** Carl Llewellyn	Guyana/Kent	WI	15.12.66	*Georgetown*
Hopkins Gareth James	Northern Districts	NZ	24.11.76	*Lower Hutt*
* **Horne** Matthew Jeffery	Otago	NZ	5.2.70	*Takapuna*
Hotter Stephen John	Wellington	NZ	2.12.69	*New Plymouth*
Houghton David Laud	Mashonaland	Z	23.6.57	*Bulawayo*
House William John	Kent/Cambridge U.	E	16.3.76	*Sheffield*
Howell Ian Lester	Border	SA	20.5.58	*Port Elizabeth*
Howell Llorne Gregory	Central Districts	NZ	8.7.72	*Napier*
Hoyte Ricardo Lawrence	Barbados	WI	15.10.69	*Bridgetown*
* **Huckle** Adam George	Matabeleland	Z	21.9.71	*Bulawayo*
* **Hudson** Andrew Charles	Natal	SA	17.3.65	*Eshowe*
Humphries Shaun	Sussex	E	11.1.73	*Horsham*
* **Hussain** Nasser	Essex	E	28.3.68	*Madras, India*
Hussey Michael Edward	Western Australia	A	27.5.75	*Morley*
Hutchison Paul James	Tasmania	A	17.2.68	*Glen Innes*
Hutchison Paul Michael	Yorkshire	E	9.6.77	*Leeds*
Hyam Barry James	Essex	E	9.9.75	*Romford*
* **Igglesden** Alan Paul	Kent	E	8.10.64	*Farnborough, Kent*
* **Ijaz Ahmed**, sen.	Habib Bank	P	20.9.68	*Sialkot*
* **Ijaz Ahmed**, jun.	Faisalabad/Allied Bank	P	2.2.69	*Lyallpur*
* **Illingworth** Richard Keith	Worcestershire	E	23.8.63	*Bradford*
* **Ilott** Mark Christopher	Essex	E	27.8.70	*Watford*
Ingram Keith	Gauteng	SA	11.5.77	*Cape Town*
Innes Kevin John	Northamptonshire	E	24.9.75	*Wellingborough*
Inness Mathew William Hunter	Victoria	A	13.11.78	*East Melbourne*
* **Inzamam-ul-Haq**	Faisalabad	P	3.3.70	*Multan*
Iqbal Sikandar	Karachi	P	19.12.58	*Karachi*
* **Irani** Ronald Charles	Essex	E	26.10.71	*Leigh*
Irfan Bhatti	Rawalpindi	P	28.9.64	*Peshawar*
Irish Lesroy	Leeward Islands	WI		*Montserrat*
Jackson Kenneth Charles	Boland	SA	16.8.64	*Kitwe, Zambia*
Jackson Paul William	Queensland	A	1.11.61	*East Melbourne*
Jacobs Ridley Detamore	Leeward Islands	WI	26.11.67	*Antigua*
Jacobs Stefan	Gauteng	SA	11.3.66	*Virginia*
* **Jadeja** Ajaysinhji	Haryana	I	1.2.71	*Jamnagar*

	Team	Country	Born	Birthplace
Jahangir Alam	Bangladesh	B	5.3.73	Narayangonj
James Kevan David	Hampshire	E	18.3.61	Lambeth
* **James** Stephen Peter	Glamorgan	E	7.9.67	Lydney
* **Jarvis** Paul William	Sussex	E	29.6.65	Redcar
Javed Omar	Bangladesh	B	25.11.76	Dhaka
Javed Qadir	Karachi/PIA	P	25.8.76	Karachi
* **Jayasuriya** Sanath Teran	Bloomfield	SL	30.6.69	Matara
* **Jayawardene** Denagamage Proboth Mahela De Silva	Sinhalese	SL	27.5.77	Colombo
Jefferson Mark Robin	Wellington	NZ	28.6.76	Oamaru
Jitender Singh	Haryana	I	10.1.76	Rohtak
Johnson Benjamin Andrew	South Australia	A	1.8.73	Naracoorte
* **Johnson** David Jude	Karnataka	I	16.10.71	Arasikere
Johnson Neil Clarkson	Natal	SA	24.1.70	Salisbury, Rhodesia
Johnson Paul	Nottinghamshire	E	24.4.65	Newark
Johnson Richard Leonard	Middlesex	E	29.12.74	Chertsey
Jonas Glenn Ralph	Wellington	NZ	13.8.70	Carterton
* **Jones** Dean Mervyn	Victoria	A	24.3.61	Coburg
Jones Philip Steffan	Somerset	E	9.2.74	Llanelli
Jones Richard Andrew	Auckland	NZ	22.10.73	Auckland
Jones Simon Philip	Glamorgan	E	25.12.78	Swansea
Jordaan Deon	Northerns	SA	3.12.70	Bloemfontein
Joseph David Rolston Emmanuel	Leeward Islands	WI	15.11.69	Antigua
Joseph Dawnley Alister	Windward Islands	WI	20.8.66	Stubbs, St Vincent
Joseph Sylvester Cleofoster	Leeward Islands	WI	5.9.78	St John's, Antigua
* **Joshi** Sunil Bandacharya	Karnataka	I	6.6.69	Gadag
Joubert Pierre	Northerns	SA	2.5.78	Pretoria
* **Julian** Brendon Paul	Western Australia	A	10.8.70	Hamilton, New Zealand
* **Kabir Khan**	Peshawar/Habib Bank	P	12.4.74	Peshawar
Kahler Lance Warren	Queensland	A	27.6.77	Crow's Nest
* **Kallis** Jacques Henry	Western Province	SA	16.10.75	Cape Town
* **Kalpage** Ruwan Senani	Bloomfield	SL	19.2.70	Kandy
* **Kaluwitharana** Romesh Shantha	Colts	SL	24.11.69	Colombo
* **Kambli** Vinod Ganpat	Mumbai	I	18.1.72	Bombay
Kanitkar Hrishikesh Hemant	Maharashtra	I	14.11.74	Poona
* **Kapoor** Aashish Rakesh	Punjab	I	25.3.71	Madras
Karim Syed Saba	Bengal	I	14.11.67	Patna
Kartik Murali	Railways	I	11.9.76	Madras
* **Kasprowicz** Michael Scott	Queensland	A	10.2.72	South Brisbane
Katich Simon Mathew	Western Australia	A	21.8.75	Middle Swan
Keech Matthew	Hampshire	E	21.10.70	Hampstead
Keedy Gary	Lancashire	E	27.11.74	Wakefield
Kelton Matthew David	South Australia	A	9.4.74	Woodville South
Kemp Justin Miles	Eastern Province	SA	2.10.77	Queenstown
Kendall William Salwey	Hampshire	E	18.12.73	Wimbledon
* **Kennedy** Robert John	Otago	NZ	3.6.72	Dunedin
Kennis Gregor John	Somerset	E	9.3.74	Yokohama, Japan
Kenway Derek Anthony	Hampshire	E	12.6.78	Fareham
Kettleborough Richard Allan	Middlesex	E	15.3.73	Sheffield
Key Robert William Trevor	Kent	E	12.5.79	East Dulwich
Khaled Mahmud	Bangladesh	B	26.7.71	Dhaka
Khaled Masud	Bangladesh	B	8.2.76	Rajshahi
Khan Amer Ali	Sussex	E	5.11.69	Lahore, Pakistan
Khan Wasim Gulzar	Sussex	E	26.2.71	Birmingham
Khoda Gagan Kishanlal	Rajasthan	I	24.10.74	Barmer
Khurasia Amay Ramsevak	Madhya Pradesh	I	18.5.72	Jabalpur
Kidwell Errol Wayne	Gauteng	SA	6.6.75	Vereeniging
Killeen Neil	Durham	E	17.10.75	Shotley Bridge

	Team	Country	Born	Birthplace
King Reon Dane	Guyana	WI	6.10.75	*Guyana*
* **Kirsten** Gary	Western Province	SA	23.11.67	*Cape Town*
Kirsten Paul	Western Province	SA	30.10.69	*Cape Town*
Kirtley Robert <u>James</u>	Sussex	E	10.1.75	*Eastbourne*
Klusener Lance	Natal	SA	4.9.71	*Durban*
* **Knight** Nicholas Verity	Warwickshire	E	28.11.69	*Watford*
Knott James Alan	Surrey	E	14.6.75	*Canterbury*
Koen Louis Johannes	Eastern Province	SA	28.3.67	*Paarl*
Koenig Sven Gaetan	Gauteng	SA	9.12.73	*Durban*
Kotak Shitanshu Hargovindbhai	Saurashtra	I	19.10.72	*Rajkot*
Krikken Karl Matthew	Derbyshire	E	9.4.69	*Bolton*
Kruis Gideon Jacobus	Griqualand West	SA	9.5.74	*Pretoria*
* **Kuiper** Adrian Paul	Boland	SA	24.8.59	*Johannesburg*
* **Kulkarni** Nilesh Moreshwar	Mumbai	I	3.4.73	*Dombivili*
* **Kumble** Anil	Karnataka	I	17.10.70	*Bangalore*
* **Kuruvilla** Abey	Mumbai	I	8.8.68	*Mannar*
Lacey Simon James	Derbyshire	E	9.3.75	*Nottingham*
Lake Anthony	Leeward Islands	WI		
* **Lamba** Raman	Delhi	I	2.1.60	*Meerut*
Died February 23, 1998				
* **Lambert** Clayton Benjamin	Guyana	WI	10.2.62	*New Amsterdam*
Lampitt Stuart Richard	Worcestershire	E	29.7.66	*Wolverhampton*
Laney Jason Scott	Hampshire	E	27.4.73	*Winchester*
* **Langer** Justin Lee	W. Australia/Middlesex	A	21.11.70	*Perth*
Langeveldt Charl Kenneth	Boland	SA	17.12.74	*Stellenbosch*
* **Lara** Brian Charles	T & T/Warwickshire	WI	2.5.69	*Santa Cruz*
Larsen Gavin Rolf	Wellington	NZ	27.9.62	*Wellington*
* **Lathwell** Mark Nicholas	Somerset	E	26.12.71	*Bletchley*
Lavender Mark Philip	Western Australia	A	28.8.67	*Madras, India*
Law Danny Richard	Essex	E	15.7.75	*London*
* **Law** Stuart Grant	Queensland/Essex	A	18.10.68	*Herston*
Law Wayne Lincoln	Glamorgan	E	4.9.78	*Swansea*
Lawson Robert Arthur	Otago	NZ	14.9.74	*Otago*
* **Laxman** Vangipurappu Venkata Sai	Hyderabad	I	1.11.74	*Hyderabad*
Leatherdale David Antony	Worcestershire	E	26.11.67	*Bradford*
Lee Brett	New South Wales	A	8.11.76	*Wollongong*
Lee Shane	New South Wales	A	8.8.73	*Wollongong*
* **Lehmann** Darren Scott	South Australia/Yorkshire	A	5.2.70	*Gawler*
* **Lewis** Clairmonte <u>Christopher</u>	Leicestershire	E	14.2.68	*Georgetown, Guyana*
Lewis Jonathan	Gloucestershire	E	26.8.75	*Aylesbury*
Lewis Jonathan James Benjamin	Durham	E	21.5.70	*Isleworth*
* **Lewis** Rawl Nicholas	Windward Islands	WI	5.9.74	*Grenada*
Lewry Jason David	Sussex	E	2.4.71	*Worthing*
* **Liebenberg** Gerhardus Frederick Johannes	Free State	SA	7.4.72	*Upington*
Light Craig	Griqualand West	SA	23.9.72	*Randburg*
* **Liyanage** Dulip Kapila	Colts	SL	6.6.72	*Kalutara*
Llong Nigel James	Kent	E	11.2.69	*Ashford, Kent*
Lloyd Graham David	Lancashire	E	1.7.69	*Accrington*
* **Lock** Alan <u>Charles</u> Ingram	Mashonaland	Z	10.9.62	*Marondellas*
Love Geoff Terry	Eastern Province	SA	19.9.76	*Port Elizabeth*
Love Martin Lloyd	Queensland	A	30.3.74	*Mundubbera*
Lovell Roderick St Orbin	Guyana	WI	23.5.72	*Guyana*
* **Loveridge** Greg Riaka	Cambridge U.	NZ	15.1.75	*Palmerston North*
Loye Malachy Bernard	Northamptonshire	E	27.9.72	*Northampton*
Lugsden Steven	Durham	E	10.7.76	*Gateshead*

	Team	Country	Born	Birthplace
* McCague Martin John	Kent	E	24.5.69	Larne, Northern Ireland
McGarrell Neil Christopher	Guyana	WI	12.7.72	Guyana
* MacGill Stuart Charles Glyndwr	New South Wales	A	25.2.71	Mount Lawley
McGrath Anthony	Yorkshire	E	6.10.75	Bradford
* McGrath Glenn Donald	New South Wales	A	9.2.70	Dubbo
McIntyre Peter Edward	South Australia	A	27.4.66	Gisborne
McKenzie Neil Douglas	Gauteng	SA	24.11.75	Johannesburg
McKeown Patrick Christopher	Lancashire	E	1.6.76	Liverpool
Mackey Jonathan Brian	Boland	SA	1.6.77	Durban
* McLean Nixon Alexei McNamara	Windward Islands/Hants	WI	20.7.73	St Vincent
* McMillan Brian Mervin	Western Province	SA	22.12.63	Welkom
* McMillan Craig Douglas	Canterbury	NZ	13.9.76	Christchurch
Macmillan Gregor Innes	Gloucestershire	E	7.8.69	Guildford
McNamara Bradley Edward	New South Wales	A	30.12.65	Sydney
MacQueen Robert Bruce	Natal	SA	6.9.77	Durban
Maddy Darren Lee	Leicestershire	E	23.5.74	Leicester
Madhukar Nekkanti	Andhra	I	18.5.76	Vijayawada
* Madondo Trevor Nyasha	Matabeleland	Z	22.11.76	Mount Darwin
* Madurasinghe Arachchige Wijaysiri Ranjith	Kurunegala Youth	SL	30.1.61	Kurunegala
Mafiz-ur-Rahman	Bangladesh	B	10.11.78	Madaripur
* Mahanama Roshan Siriwardene	Bloomfield	SL	31.5.66	Colombo
Maharab Hossain	Bangladesh	B	22.9.78	Dhaka
Maher James Patrick	Queensland	A	27.2.74	Innisfail
Mahmood Hamid	Karachi/PIA	P	19.1.69	Karachi
Makalima Dumisa	Border	SA	29.12.80	King William's Town
* Malcolm Devon Eugene	Northamptonshire	E	22.2.63	Kingston, Jamaica
Manack Hussein Ahmed	Gauteng	SA	10.4.68	Pretoria
* Manjrekar Sanjay Vijay	Mumbai	I	12.7.65	Mangalore
Mansoor Rana	Lahore/ADBP	P	27.12.62	Lahore
Manzoor Akhtar	Karachi/Allied Bank	P	16.4.68	Karachi
* Manzoor Elahi	ADBP	P	15.4.63	Sahiwal
Maqsood Rana	Lahore/National Bank	P	1.8.72	Lahore
Maron Ryan	Western Province	SA	24.2.75	Cape Town
Marquet Joshua Phillip	Tasmania	A	3.12.69	Melbourne
Marsh Daniel James	Tasmania	A	14.6.73	Subiaco
Marsh Steven Andrew	Kent	E	27.1.61	London
Marshall Dave Kerwin	Barbados	WI	24.5.72	Barbados
Marshall Roy Ashworth	Windward Islands	WI	1.4.65	St Joseph, Dominica
Martin Gary Christopher	Mashonaland	Z	30.5.66	Marandellas
Martin Jacob Joseph	Baroda	I	11.5.72	Baroda
Martin Kenroy	Windward Islands	WI		St Vincent
Martin Neil Donald	Middlesex	E	19.8.79	Enfield
* Martin Peter James	Lancashire	E	15.11.68	Accrington
Martin-Jenkins Robin Simon Christopher	Sussex	E	28.10.75	Guildford
* Martyn Damien Richard	Western Australia	A	21.10.71	Darwin
Maru Rajesh Jamandass	Hampshire	E	28.10.62	Nairobi, Kenya
Mascarenhas Adrian Dimitri	Hampshire	E	30.10.77	London
Masikazana Lulama	Eastern Province	SA	6.2.73	Port Elizabeth
Mason Matthew Sean	Western Australia	A	20.3.74	Claremont
Mason Timothy James	Leicestershire	E	12.4.75	Leicester
* Matambanadzo Everton	Mashonaland	Z	13.4.76	Salisbury
* Matthews Craig Russell	Western Province	SA	15.2.65	Cape Town
* Matthews Gregory Richard John	New South Wales	A	15.12.59	Newcastle
May Michael Robert	Derbyshire	E	22.7.71	Chesterfield
* Maynard Matthew Peter	Glamorgan/Otago	E	21.3.66	Oldham
* Mbangwa Mpumelelo	Matabeleland	Z	26.6.76	Plumtree
Mehta Bhavin Niranjan	Gujarat	I	17.1.69	Ahmedabad
Mendis Chaminda	Colts	SL	28.12.68	Galle

	Team	Country	Born	Birthplace
* **Mhambrey** Paras Laxmikant	Mumbai	I	20.6.72	*Bombay*
Middlebrook James Daniel	Yorkshire	E	13.5.77	*Leeds*
Miller Colin Reid	Tasmania	A	6.2.64	*Footscray*
Millns David James	Leicestershire	E	27.2.65	*Clipstone*
Mills Jason Martin	Auckland	NZ	12.8.69	*Auckland*
Minagall Matthew John Peter	South Australia	A	13.11.71	*Adelaide*
Minhas Mithun	Delhi	I	12.9.77	*Jammu*
Minhaz-ul-Abedin	Bangladesh	B	25.9.65	*Chittagong*
Mitchell Ian	Border	SA	14.12.77	*Johannesburg*
Mitchum Junie	Leeward Islands	WI	22.11.73	*St Kitts*
* **Mohammad Akram**	Rawalpindi/Allied Bank	P	10.9.74	*Islamabad*
* **Mohammad Hussain**	Lahore	P	8.10.76	*Lahore*
Mohammad Rafiq	Bangladesh	B	15.5.70	*Dhaka*
* **Mohammad Ramzan**	Faisalabad/Customs	P	25.12.70	*Lyallpur*
Mohammad Sheikh	Kenya	K		
* **Mohammad Wasim**	Rawalpindi/ADBP	P	8.8.77	*Rawalpindi*
* **Mohanty** Debasis Sarbeswar	Orissa	I	20.7.76	*Bhubaneshwar*
* **Moin Khan**	PIA	P	23.9.71	*Rawalpindi*
Moin-ul-Atiq	Peshawar/Habib Bank	P	5.8.64	*Karachi*
* **Mongia** Nayan Ramlal	Baroda	I	19.12.69	*Baroda*
Montgomerie Richard Robert	Northamptonshire	E	3.7.71	*Rugby*
* **Moody** Thomas Masson	W. Australia/Worcs	A	2.10.65	*Adelaide*
Moores Peter	Sussex	E	18.12.62	*Macclesfield*
* **More** Kiran Shankar	Baroda	I	4.9.62	*Baroda*
Morgan Grant	Northerns	SA	19.5.71	*Port Elizabeth*
Morgan McNeil Junior	Windward Islands	WI	18.10.70	*St Vincent*
Morris Alexander Corfield	Hampshire	E	4.10.76	*Barnsley*
* **Morris** John Edward	Durham	E	1.4.64	*Crewe*
Morris Robin Francis	Orissa	I	6.11.76	*Bombay*
Morris Zachary Clegg	Hampshire	E	4.9.78	*Barnsley*
Morshed Ali Khan	Bangladesh	B	14.5.72	*Fareedpur*
Mott Matthew Peter	Queensland	A	3.10.73	*Charleville*
Mpitsang Victor Phenyo	Free State	SA	28.3.80	*Kimberley*
Mudgal Manoj Sitaram	Uttar Pradesh	I	18.10.72	*Meerut*
Mujahid Jamshed	Gujranwala/Habib Bank	P	1.12.71	*Muredke*
Mulder Bret	Western Australia	A	6.2.64	*Subiaco*
* **Mullally** Alan David	Leicestershire	E	12.7.69	*Southend-on-Sea*
Muller Scott Andrew	Queensland	A	11.7.71	*Herston*
Munasinghe Arachchige <u>Manjula</u> Nishantha	Sinhalese	SL	10.12.71	*Colombo*
* **Munton** Timothy Alan	Warwickshire	E	30.7.65	*Melton Mowbray*
* **Muralitharan** Muttiah	Tamil Union	SL	17.4.72	*Kandy*
Murphy Brian Andrew	Western Province	SA	1.12.76	*Salisbury*
Murphy Brian Samuel	Jamaica	WI	7.4.73	*Jamaica*
* **Murray** Darrin James	Canterbury	NZ	4.9.67	*Christchurch*
* **Murray** Junior Randalph	Windward Islands	WI	20.1.68	*St Georges, Grenada*
* **Mushtaq Ahmed**	Somerset	P	28.6.70	*Sahiwal*
Muzumdar Amol Anil	Mumbai	I	11.11.74	*Bombay*
* **Nadeem Abbasi**	Rawalpindi/KRL	P	15.4.64	*Rawalpindi*
* **Nadeem Ghauri**	Habib Bank	P	12.10.62	*Lahore*
* **Nadeem Khan**	Karachi/PIA	P	10.12.69	*Rawalpindi*
Naeem Ashraf	Lahore/National Bank	P	10.11.72	*Lahore*
Nagamootoo Mahendra Veeren	Guyana	WI	9.10.75	*Guyana*
Nagamootoo Vishal	Guyana	WI	7.1.77	*Guyana*
Naim-ur-Rahman	Bangladesh	B	19.9.74	*Dhaka*
Napier Graham Richard	Essex	E	6.1.80	*Colchester*
Nash David Charles	Middlesex	E	19.11.78	*Chertsey*
* **Nash** Dion Joseph	Northern Districts	NZ	20.11.71	*Auckland*
* **Naved Anjum**	Habib Bank	P	27.7.63	*Lahore*

	Team	Country	Born	Birthplace
Nawaz Mohamed Naveed	Bloomfield	SL	20.9.73	Colombo
Nevin Christopher John	Wellington	NZ	3.8.75	Dunedin
Newell Keith	Sussex	E	25.3.72	Crawley
Newell Mark	Sussex	E	19.12.73	Crawley
Newman Anwell Noel	Boland	SA	10.12.66	Stellenbosch
* **Newport** Philip John	Worcestershire	E	11.10.62	High Wycombe
Nielsen Timothy John	South Australia	A	5.5.68	Forest Gate, England
Nixon Paul Andrew	Leicestershire	E	21.10.70	Carlisle
Noon Wayne Michael	Nottinghamshire	E	5.2.71	Grimsby
* **Ntini** Makhaya	Border	SA	6.7.77	Zwelitsha
* **O'Connor** Shayne Barry	Otago	NZ	15.11.73	Hastings
Odoyo Thomas	Kenya	K	12.5.78	Nairobi
Odumbe Maurice Omondi	Kenya	K	15.6.69	Nairobi
Oldroyd Bradley John	Western Australia	A	5.11.73	Bentley
* **Olonga** Henry Khaaba	Matabeleland	Z	3.7.76	Lusaka, Zambia
Ontong Justin Lee	Boland	SA	4.1.80	Paarl
Onyango Lameck	Kenya	K	22.9.73	Nairobi
Oram Andrew Richard	Nottinghamshire	E	7.3.75	Northampton
Ormond James	Leicestershire	E	20.8.77	Walsgrave
Ostler Dominic Piers	Warwickshire	E	15.7.70	Solihull
Otieno Kennedy	Kenya	K	11.3.72	Nairobi
Palframan Steven John	Boland	SA	12.5.70	East London
Pandey Sanjay	Madhya Pradesh	I	14.12.76	Bhopal
* **Pandit** Chandrakant Sitaram	Madhya Pradesh	I	30.9.61	Bombay
Pangarker Hassan	Western Province	SA	31.8.68	Cape Town
Paranjpe Jatin Vasudeo	Mumbai	I	17.4.72	Bombay
Parida Kulamani Shankar	Railways	I	9.3.77	Cuttack
Parillon Joseph	Windward Islands	WI		Dominica
Parker Bradley	Yorkshire	E	30.1.66	Mirfield
Parker Geoffrey Ross	South Australia	A	31.8.68	Malvern
Parkin Owen Thomas	Glamorgan	E	24.9.72	Coventry
Parlane Michael Edward	Northern Districts	NZ	22.7.72	Pukekohe
* **Parore** Adam Craig	Auckland	NZ	23.1.71	Auckland
Parsons Keith Alan	Somerset	E	2.5.73	Taunton
* **Patel** Minal Mahesh	Kent	E	7.7.70	Bombay, India
Pathak Amit	Andhra	I	30.11.72	Vishakhapatnam
Payne Dean Geoffrey	Western Province	SA	13.1.69	Cape Town
Peirce Michael Toby Edward	Sussex	E	14.6.73	Maidenhead
Penberthy Anthony Leonard	Northamptonshire	E	1.9.69	Troon, Cornwall
Penn Andrew Jonathan	Central Districts	NZ	27.7.74	Wanganui
Penney Trevor Lionel	Warwicks/Mashonaland A	E	12.6.68	Salisbury, Rhodesia
* **Perera** Anhettige Suresh Asanka	Sinhalese	SL	16.2.78	Colombo
Perera Kahawelage Gamini	Antonians	SL	22.5.64	Colombo
Perry Nehemiah Odolphus	Jamaica	WI	16.6.68	Jamaica
Persad Mukesh	Trinidad & Tobago	WI	1.5.70	Trinidad
Peters Stephen David	Essex	E	10.12.78	Harold Wood
Petrie Richard George	Wellington	NZ	23.8.67	Christchurch
Phillip Warrington Dexter	Leeward Islands	WI	23.7.68	Nevis
Phillips Ben James	Kent	E	30.9.74	Lewisham
Phillips Nicholas Charles	Durham	E	10.5.74	Pembury
Pickering Kelby Sinclair	South Australia	A	3.1.76	Lameroo
Pienaar Roy Francois	Northern Transvaal	SA	17.7.61	Johannesburg
Pierson Adrian Roger Kirshaw	Somerset	E	21.7.63	Enfield, Middlesex
Piper Keith John	Warwickshire	E	18.12.69	Leicester
Player Bradley Thomas	Western Province	SA	18.1.67	Benoni
* **Pocock** Blair Andrew	Auckland	NZ	18.6.71	Papakura
Pollard Paul Raymond	Nottinghamshire	E	24.9.68	Nottingham
* **Pollock** Shaun Maclean	Natal	SA	16.7.73	Port Elizabeth

	Team	Country	Born	Birthplace
* **Ponting** Ricky Thomas	Tasmania	A	19.12.74	Launceston
Pope Steven Charles	Border	SA	15.11.72	East London
Pope Uzzah	Windward Islands	WI	3.1.71	St Vincent
Pothas Nic	Gauteng	SA	18.11.73	Johannesburg
Powell Kirk Howard	Jamaica	WI	17.6.72	Kingston
Powell Michael James	Warwickshire	E	5.4.75	Bolton
Powell Michael John	Glamorgan	E	3.2.77	Abergavenny
Powell Ricardo	Jamaica	WI	16.12.78	St Elizabeth
Powell Ronald Malcolm	Leeward Islands	WI	5.3.68	Nevis
Powell Tony Orlando	Jamaica	WI	22.12.72	Jamaica
* **Prasad** Bapu Krishnarao Venkatesh	Karnataka	I	5.8.69	Bangalore
Prasad Mannava Sri Kanth	Andhra	I	24.4.75	Guntur
Pratt Andrew	Durham	E	4.3.75	Helmington Row
Pretorius Dewald	Free State	SA	6.12.77	Pretoria
Prichard Paul John	Essex	E	7.1.65	Billericay
* **Priest** Mark Wellings	Canterbury	NZ	12.8.61	Greymouth
Prince Ashwell Gavin	Western Province	SA	28.5.77	Port Elizabeth
Pringle Meyrick Wayne	Eastern Province	SA	22.6.66	Adelaide
Pushpakumara Karuppiahyage Ravindra	Nondescripts	SL	21.7.75	Panadura
Quinn Whitmoore Kenneth Lyndon	Leeward Islands	WI	30.5.71	All Saints, Antigua
Radley Philip Johannes Lourens	Free State	SA	7.2.69	Bloemfontein
Ragoonath Suruj	Trinidad & Tobago	WI	22.3.68	Trinidad
Rajab Ali	Kenya	K	19.11.65	Nairobi
* **Rajput** Lalchand Sitaram	Vidarbha	I	18.12.61	Bombay
* **Raju** Sagi Lakshmi Venkatapathy	Hyderabad	I	9.7.69	Hyderabad
* **Raman** Woorkeri Venkat	Tamil Nadu	I	23.5.65	Madras
* **Ramanayake** Champaka Priyadarshana Hewage	Tamil Union	SL	8.1.65	Colombo
* **Ramiz** Raja	Allied Bank	P	14.8.62	Lyallpur
* **Ramnarine** Dinanath	Trinidad & Tobago	WI	4.6.75	Trinidad
Rampersad Denis	Trinidad & Tobago	WI	22.9.74	Trinidad
* **Ramprakash** Mark Ravin	Middlesex	E	5.9.69	Bushey
* **Ranatunga** Arjuna	Sinhalese	SL	1.12.63	Colombo
Ranatunga Nishantha	Colts	SL	22.1.66	Gampaha
Ranatunga Sanjeeva	Sinhalese	SL	25.4.69	Colombo
Ranchod Ujesh	Mashonaland	Z	17.5.69	Salisbury
Rao Kashireddi Var Prasad	Bihar	I	21.11.65	Jamshedpur
Rao Rajesh Krishnakant	Sussex	E	9.12.74	Park Royal
* **Rashid** Latif	Karachi/Allied Bank	P	14.10.68	Karachi
Ratcliffe Jason David	Surrey	E	19.6.69	Solihull
* **Rathore** Vikram	Punjab	I	26.3.69	Jullundur
Raul Sanjay	Orissa	I	6.10.76	Cuttack
Ravindu Shah	Kenya	K		
Rawnsley Matthew James	Worcestershire	E	8.6.76	Birmingham
Read Christopher Mark Wells	Nottinghamshire	E	10.8.78	Paignton
Reid Winston Emmerson	Barbados	WI	29.9.62	Bank Hall
* **Reifer** Floyd Lamonte	Barbados	WI	23.7.72	Parish Land
* **Reiffel** Paul Ronald	Victoria	A	19.4.66	Box Hill
* **Rennie** Gavin James	Mashonaland	Z	12.1.76	Fort Victoria
* **Rennie** John Alexander	Matabeleland	Z	29.7.70	Fort Victoria
Renshaw Simon John	Hampshire	E	6.3.74	Bebington
* **Rhodes** Jonathan Neil	Natal	SA	27.7.69	Pietermaritzburg
* **Rhodes** Steven John	Worcestershire	E	17.6.64	Bradford
Richards Corey John	New South Wales	A	25.8.75	Camden
Richards O'Neil Rohan	Jamaica	WI	7.12.76	St Catherine
* **Richardson** David John	Eastern Province	SA	16.9.59	Johannesburg
Richardson Mark Hunter	Otago	NZ	11.6.71	Hastings

	Team	Country	Born	Birthplace
* **Richardson** Richard Benjamin	Windward Islands	WI	12.1.62	Five Islands, Antigua
Ridgway Mark William	Tasmania	A	21.5.63	Warragul
Ridgway Paul Mathew	Lancashire	E	13.2.77	Airedale
Rindel Michael John Raymond	Northerns	SA	9.2.63	Durban
Ripley David	Northamptonshire	E	13.9.66	Leeds
* **Rizwan-uz-Zaman**	PIA	P	4.9.61	Karachi
Roberts David James	Northamptonshire	E	29.12.76	Truro
Roberts Glenn Martin	Derbyshire	E	4.11.73	Huddersfield
Roberts Kevin Joseph	New South Wales	A	25.7.72	North Sydney
Roberts Lincoln Abraham	Trinidad & Tobago	WI	4.9.74	Tobago
Robertson Ashley Peter Scott	Victoria	A	9.3.72	Footscray
* **Robertson** Gavin Ron	New South Wales	A	28.5.66	Sydney
Robinson Darren David John	Essex	E	2.3.73	Braintree
Robinson Mark Andrew	Sussex	E	23.11.66	Hull
* **Robinson** Robert <u>Timothy</u>	Nottinghamshire	E	21.11.58	Sutton-in-Ashfield
Roe Garth Anthony	Griqualand West	SA	9.7.73	Port Elizabeth
Rollins Adrian Stewart	Derbyshire	E	8.2.72	Barking
Rollins Robert John	Essex	E	30.1.74	Plaistow
Rollock Terry Euclyn	Barbados	WI	25.9.69	Barbados
* **Rose** Franklyn Albert	Jamaica/Northants	WI	1.2.72	St Ann's Bay
Rose Graham David	Somerset	E	12.4.64	Tottenham
Roseberry Michael Anthony	Durham	E	28.11.66	Sunderland
Rowell Gregory John	Queensland	A	1.9.66	Lindfield
Rummans Graeme Clifford	New South Wales	A	13.12.76	Camperdown
Rushmere Mark Weir	Eastern Province	SA	7.1.65	Port Elizabeth
Russell Robert Charles	Gloucestershire	E	15.8.63	Stroud
Rutherford Kenneth Robert	Gauteng	NZ	26.10.65	Dunedin
* **Saeed Anwar**	ADBP	P	6.9.68	Karachi
Saeed Azad	Karachi/National Bank	P	14.8.66	Karachi
Saggers Martin John	Durham	E	23.5.72	King's Lynn
Saif-ul-Islam	Bangladesh	B	14.4.69	Mymensingh
Saikia Subhrajit	Assam	I	9.12.75	Dibrugarh
Sajid Ali	Bahawalpur/National Bank	P	1.7.63	Karachi
Sajjad Akbar	Lahore	P	1.3.61	Lahore
Saker David James	Victoria	A	29.5.66	Oakleigh
Sales David John	Northamptonshire	E	3.12.77	Carshalton
* **Salim Elahi**	Lahore/Habib Bank	P	21.11.76	Sahiwal
* **Salim Malik**	Habib Bank	P	16.4.63	Lahore
* **Salisbury** Ian David Kenneth	Surrey	E	21.1.70	Northampton
Samant Vinayak Radhakrishna	Assam	I	25.10.72	Bombay
Samaraweera Dulip Prasanna	Colts	SL	12.2.72	Colombo
* **Samuels** Robert George	Jamaica	WI	13.3.71	Jamaica
Sanghvi Rahul	Delhi	I	3.9.74	Surat
Sanuar Hossain	Bangladesh	B	5.8.73	Mymensingh
* **Saqlain Mushtaq**	Islamabad/PIA/Surrey	P	27.11.76	Lahore
Sarkar Arindam	Bengal	I	12.8.73	Calcutta
Sarwan Ramnaresh	Guyana	WI	23.6.80	Guyana
Schofield Christopher Paul	Lancashire	E	6.10.78	Rochdale
Schultz Brett Nolan	Western Province	SA	26.8.70	East London
Scott Darren Anthony	Kent	E	26.8.72	Canterbury
Scuderi Joseph Charles	South Australia	A	24.12.68	Ingham
Seccombe Wade Anthony	Queensland	A	30.10.71	Murgon
Searle Jason Paul	Durham	E	16.5.76	Bath
Semple Keith Fitzpatrick	Guyana	WI	21.8.70	Georgetown
Sewell David Graham	Otago	NZ	20.10.77	Christchurch
Seymore Andre Johan	Gauteng	SA	16.2.75	Rustenburg
* **Shadab Kabir**	Karachi	P	12.11.77	Karachi
Shadford Darren James	Lancashire	E	4.3.75	Oldham
Shafiuddin Ahmed	Bangladesh	B	1.6.73	Dhaka

	Team	Country	Born	Birthplace
Shah Owais Alam	Middlesex	E	22.10.78	Karachi, Pakistan
Shahid Nadeem	Surrey	E	23.4.69	Karachi, Pakistan
Shahid Afridi	Karachi/Habib Bank	P	1.3.80	Khyber Agency
Shahid Anwar	Lahore/National Bank	P	5.7.68	Multan
* **Shahid** Mahboob	Karachi	P	25.8.62	Karachi
* **Shahid** Nazir	Faisalabad/Habib Bank	P	4.12.77	Faisalabad
Shahriar Hossain	Bangladesh	B	1.6.76	Narayangonj
* **Shakeel** Ahmed	Gujranwala/Habib Bank	P	12.11.71	Daska
Shakeel Khan	Habib Bank	P	28.5.68	Lahore
Shamshad Rizwan	Uttar Pradesh	I	19.11.72	Aligarh
Sharath Sridharan	Tamil Nadu	I	31.10.72	Madras
Sharif-ul-Haq	Bangladesh	B		Mymensingh
* **Sharma** Ajay	Delhi	I	3.4.64	Delhi
Shaw Adrian David	Glamorgan	E	17.2.72	Neath
Sheikh Mohamed Avez	Warwickshire	E	2.7.73	Birmingham
Sheikh Salahuddin	Bangladesh	B	10.2.69	Khulna
Sheriyar Alamgir	Worcestershire	E	15.11.73	Birmingham
Shine Kevin James	Somerset	E	22.2.69	Bracknell
* **Shoaib** Akhtar	Rawalpindi/ADBP	P	13.8.75	Rawalpindi
* **Shoaib** Mohammad	Karachi/PIA	P	8.1.61	Karachi
Siddons James Darren	South Australia	A	25.4.64	Robinvale
Sidebottom Ryan Jay	Yorkshire	E	15.6.78	Huddersfield
Sidhu Navjot Singh	Punjab	I	20.10.63	Patiala
* **Silva** Kelaniyage Jayantha	Sinhalese	SL	2.6.73	Kalutara
* **Silverwood** Christopher Eric Wilfred	Yorkshire	E	5.3.75	Pontefract
* **Simmons** Philip Verant	T & T/Leicestershire	WI	18.4.63	Arima
Simons Eric Owen	Western Province	SA	9.3.62	Cape Town
Sinclair Mathew Stuart	Central Districts	NZ	9.11.75	Katherine, Australia
Singh Anurag	Warwicks/Camb. U.	E	9.9.75	Kanpur, India
Singh Rabindra Ramanarayan	Tamil Nadu	I	14.9.63	Princes Town, Trinidad
Singh Robin	Delhi	I	1.1.70	Delhi
* **Sivaramakrishnan** Laxman	Tamil Nadu	I	31.12.65	Madras
* **Slater** Michael Jonathon	New South Wales/Derbys	A	21.2.70	Wagga Wagga
Smit Willem Johannes	Free State	SA	1.8.74	Calvinia
* **Smith** Andrew Michael	Gloucestershire	E	1.10.67	Dewsbury
Smith Benjamin Francis	Leicestershire	E	3.4.72	Corby
Smith Dennis James	Northerns	SA	26.11.71	Durban
Smith Edward Thomas	Kent/Cambridge U.	E	19.7.77	Pembury
Smith Gregory James	Northerns	SA	30.10.71	Pretoria
Smith Neil Michael Knight	Warwickshire	E	27.7.67	Birmingham
Smith Richard Andrew Mortimer	Trinidad & Tobago	WI	17.7.71	Trinidad
* **Smith** Robin Arnold	Hampshire	E	13.9.63	Durban, South Africa
Smith Trevor Mark	Derbyshire	E	18.1.77	Derby
* **Snell** Richard Peter	Gauteng	SA	12.9.68	Durban
Solanki Vikram Singh	Worcestershire	E	1.4.76	Udaipur, India
Somasunder Sujith	Karnataka	I	2.12.72	Bangalore
Speak Nicholas Jason	Durham	E	21.11.66	Manchester
* **Spearman** Craig Murray	Central Districts	NZ	4.7.72	Auckland
Speight Martin Peter	Durham	E	24.10.67	Walsall
Spendlove Benjamin Lee	Derbyshire	E	4.11.78	Belper
* **Srinath** Javagal	Karnataka	I	31.8.69	Mysore
Stead Gary Raymond	Canterbury	NZ	9.1.72	Christchurch
Stemp Richard David	Yorkshire	E	11.12.67	Birmingham
Stephenson John Patrick	Hampshire	E	14.3.65	Stebbing
* **Stewart** Alec James	Surrey	E	8.4.63	Merton
Stewart Errol Leslie Rae	Natal	SA	30.7.69	Durban
Stewart James	Western Australia	A	22.8.70	East Fremantle
* **Steyn** Philippus Jeremia Rudolf	Northerns	SA	30.6.67	Kimberley
Storey Keith Graham	Natal	SA	25.1.69	Salisbury, Rhodesia

	Team	Country	Born	Birthplace
* **Strang** Bryan Colin	Mashonaland	Z	9.6.72	Bulawayo
* **Strang** Paul Andrew	Mashonaland/Notts	Z	28.7.70	Bulawayo
Strauss Andrew John	Middlesex	E	2.3.77	Johannesburg, SA
* **Streak** Heath Hilton	Matabeleland	Z	16.3.74	Bulawayo
Strydom Morné	Griqualand West	SA	20.2.74	Port Elizabeth
Strydom Pieter Coenraad	Border	SA	10.6.69	Somerset East
Stuart Anthony Mark	New South Wales	A	2.1.70	Newcastle
Stuart Colin Ellsworth Laurie	Guyana	WI	28.9.73	Guyana
* **Such** Peter Mark	Essex	E	12.6.64	Helensburgh, Scotland
Sugden Craig Brian	Natal	SA	7.3.74	Durban
Suji Anthony	Kenya	K	5.2.76	
Suji Martin	Kenya	K	2.6.71	Nairobi
Sukhbir Singh	Baroda	I	3.1.74	Gurudaspur
Sutcliffe Iain John	Leicestershire	E	20.12.74	Leeds
Sutton Luke David	Somerset	E	4.10.76	Keynsham
Swain Brett Andrew	South Australia	A	14.2.74	Stirling
Swanepoel Adriaan Johannes	Griqualand West	SA	19.3.72	Kimberley
Swann Alec James	Northamptonshire	E	26.10.76	Northampton
Swann Graeme Peter	Northamptonshire	E	24.3.79	Northampton
Sylvester John Anthony Rodney	Windward Islands	WI	6.10.69	Grenada
* **Symcox** Patrick Leonard	Natal	SA	14.4.60	Kimberley
Symington Marc Joseph	Durham	E	10.1.80	Newcastle-upon-Tyne
Symonds Andrew	Queensland	A	9.6.75	Birmingham, England
Tait Alex Ross	Northern Districts	NZ	13.6.72	Paparoa
Taljard Dion	Border	SA	7.1.70	East London
Targett Benjamin Stuart	Tasmania	A	27.12.72	Paddington
Tariq-ur-Rehman	Bihar	I	22.2.74	Darbanga
Tatton Craig Ross	Natal	SA	29.1.75	Bulawayo
* **Tauseef Ahmed**	Customs	P	10.5.60	Karachi
* **Taylor** Jonathan Paul	Northamptonshire	E	8.8.64	Ashby-de-la-Zouch
* **Taylor** Mark Anthony	New South Wales	A	27.10.64	Leeton
Taylor Neil Royston	Sussex	E	21.7.59	Orpington
Telemachus Roger	Boland	SA	27.3.73	Stellenbosch
* **Tendulkar** Sachin Ramesh	Mumbai	I	24.4.73	Bombay
Terbrugge David John	Gauteng	SA	31.1.77	Ladysmith
Thomas Stuart Darren	Glamorgan	E	25.1.75	Morriston
Thompson Julian Barton DeCourcy	Kent	E	28.10.68	Cape Town, SA
* **Thompson** Patterson Ian Chesterfield	Barbados	WI	26.9.71	Barbados
Thompson Scott Michael	New South Wales	A	4.5.72	Bankstown
Thorpe Graham Paul	Surrey	E	1.8.69	Farnham
Tikolo Stephen Ogomji	Kenya	K	25.6.71	Nairobi
* **Tillekeratne** Hashan Prasantha	Nondescripts	SL	14.7.67	Colombo
Titchard Stephen Paul	Lancashire	E	17.12.67	Warrington
Tolley Christopher Mark	Nottinghamshire	E	30.12.67	Kidderminster
Trainor Nicholas James	Gloucestershire	E	29.6.75	Gateshead
Trescothick Marcus Edward	Somerset	E	25.12.75	Keynsham
Tucker Rodney James	Tasmania	A	28.8.64	Auburn
Tuckett Carl McArthur	Leeward Islands	WI	18.5.70	Nevis
Tudor Alex Jeremy	Surrey	E	23.10.77	Kensington
* **Tufnell** Philip Charles Roderick	Middlesex	E	29.4.66	Barnet
Turner Robert Julian	Somerset	E	25.11.67	Malvern
Tweats Timothy Andrew	Derbyshire	E	18.4.74	Stoke-on-Trent
* **Twose** Roger Graham	Wellington	NZ	17.4.68	Torquay, England
Udal Shaun David	Hampshire	E	18.3.69	Farnborough, Hants
Upashantha Kalutarage Eric Amila	Colts	SL	10.6.72	Kurunegala

	Team	Country	Born	Birthplace
* **Vaas** Warnakulasooriya Patabendige Ushantha Joseph <u>Chaminda</u>	Colts	SL	27.1.74	*Mattumagala*
Vadher Alpesh	Kenya	K	7.9.74	
van der Merwe Casparus Cornelius	Border	SA	11.7.73	*Johannesburg*
van Jaarsveld Martin	Northerns	SA	18.6.74	*Klerksdorp*
van Troost Adrianus Petrus	Somerset	Hol	2.10.72	*Schiedam, Netherlands*
van Wyk Morne Nico	Free State	SA	20.3.79	*Bloemfontein*
Vaughan Jeffrey Mark	South Australia	A	26.3.74	*Blacktown*
Vaughan Michael Paul	Yorkshire	E	29.10.74	*Manchester*
Veenstra Ross Edward	Gauteng	SA	22.4.72	*Estcourt*
* **Venkataramana** Margashayam	Tamil Nadu	I	24.4.66	*Secunderabad*
Venter Jacobus Francois	Free State	SA	1.10.69	*Bloemfontein*
Ventura Mario Dimitri	Jamaica	WI	21.4.74	*Jamaica*
* **Vettori** Daniel Luca	Northern Districts	NZ	27.1.79	*Auckland*
* **Viljoen** Dirk Peter	Mashonaland	Z	11.3.77	*Salisbury*
Vimpani Graeme Ronald	Victoria	A	27.1.72	*Herston*
Volsteedt Andre Kenne	Free State	SA	6.5.75	*Bloemfontein*
Vorster Christiaan Jakobus	Free State	SA	17.8.76	*Paarl*
Wagh Mark Anant	Warwicks/Oxford U.	E	20.10.76	*Birmingham*
Waldron Horace Ricardo	Barbados	WI	22.9.71	*Barbados*
Walker Alan	Durham	E	7.7.62	*Emley*
Walker Matthew David John	Central Districts	NZ	17.1.77	*Opunake*
Walker Matthew Jonathan	Kent	E	2.1.74	*Gravesend*
* **Wallace** Philo Alphonso	Barbados	WI	2.8.70	*Around-the-town*
* **Walmsley** Kerry Peter	Auckland	NZ	23.8.73	*Dunedin*
Walsh Christopher David	Kent	E	6.11.75	*Pembury*
* **Walsh** Courtney Andrew	Jamaica/Gloucestershire	WI	30.10.62	*Kingston*
* **Waqar Younis**	Multan/Glamorgan	P	16.11.71	*Vehari*
Ward Ian James	Surrey	E	30.9.72	*Plymouth*
Ward Trevor Robert	Kent	E	18.1.68	*Farningham*
* **Warne** Shane Keith	Victoria	A	13.9.69	*Ferntree Gully*
Warren Russell John	Northamptonshire	E	10.9.71	*Northampton*
* **Wasim Akram**	Lahore/PIA/Lancashire	P	3.6.66	*Lahore*
Wasim Jaffer	Mumbai	I	16.2.78	*Bombay*
* **Wassan** Atul Satish	Delhi	I	23.3.68	*Delhi*
Watkin Steven Llewellyn	Glamorgan	E	15.9.64	*Maesteg*
* **Watkinson** Michael	Lancashire	E	1.8.61	*Westhoughton*
Watson Douglas James	Natal	SA	15.5.73	*Pietermaritzburg*
Watt Balthazar Michael	Windward Islands	WI	12.4.75	*Dominica*
* **Waugh** Mark Edward	New South Wales	A	2.6.65	*Sydney*
* **Waugh** Stephen Rodger	New South Wales	A	2.6.65	*Sydney*
Webber Darren Scott	South Australia	A	18.8.71	*Barnside*
Weekes Paul Nicholas	Middlesex	E	8.7.69	*Hackney*
Welch Graeme	Warwickshire	E	21.3.72	*Durham*
* **Wells** Alan Peter	Kent	E	2.10.61	*Newhaven*
Wells Vincent John	Leicestershire	E	6.8.65	*Dartford*
Welton Guy Edward	Nottinghamshire	E	4.5.78	*Grimsby*
* **Wessels** Kepler Christoffel	Eastern Province	SA	14.9.57	*Bloemfontein*
Weston Robin Michael Swann	Derbyshire	E	7.6.75	*Durham*
Weston William <u>Philip</u> Christopher	Worcestershire	E	16.6.73	*Durham*
Wharf Alexander George	Nottinghamshire	E	4.6.75	*Bradford*
Whiley Matthew Jeffrey Allen	Nottinghamshire	E	6.5.80	*Nottingham*
* **Whitaker** John James	Leicestershire	E	5.5.62	*Skipton*
Whitaker Paul Robert	Hampshire	E	28.6.73	*Keighley*
White Brad Middleton	Border	SA	15.5.70	*Johannesburg*
* **White** Craig	Yorkshire	E	16.12.69	*Morley*
White Giles William	Hampshire	E	23.3.72	*Barnstaple*
* **Whittall** Andrew Richard	Matabeleland	Z	28.3.73	*Mutare*
* **Whittall** Guy James	Matabeleland	Z	5.9.72	*Chipinga*

	Team	Country	Born	Birthplace
Wiblin Wayne	Border	SA	13.2.69	Grahamstown
Wickremaratne Ranasinghe Pattikirikoralalage Aruna Hemantha	Sinhalese	SL	21.2.71	Colombo
* **Wickremasinghe** Gallage Pramodya	Sinhalese	SL	14.8.71	Matara
Wiggill Justin Victor	Boland	SA	22.6.75	East London
Wigney Bradley Neil	South Australia	A	30.6.65	Leongatha
* **Wijetunge** Piyal Kashyapa	Moors	SL	6.8.71	Badulla
Wilkinson Louis Johannes	Free State	SA	19.11.66	Vereeniging
Williams Brad Andrew	Victoria	A	20.11.74	Frankston
* **Williams** David	Trinidad & Tobago	WI	4.11.63	San Fernando
Williams Henry Smith	Boland	SA	11.6.67	Stellenbosch
Williams Laurie Rohan	Jamaica	WI	12.12.68	Jamaica
* **Williams** Neil FitzGerald	Essex	E	2.7.62	Hope Well, St Vincent
Williams Richard Charles James	Gloucestershire	E	8.8.69	Southmead
* **Williams** Stuart Clayton	Leeward Islands	WI	12.8.69	Government Road, Nevis
Williamson Dominic	Leicestershire	E	15.11.75	Durham
Willis Simon Charles	Kent	E	19.3.74	London
Willoughby Charl Myles	Boland	SA	3.12.74	Cape Town
Wilson Daniel Graeme	Essex	E	18.2.77	London
Wilson Elliott James	Worcestershire	E	3.11.76	London
* **Wilson** Paul	South Australia	A	12.1.72	Newcastle
Wilton Nicholas James	Sussex	E	23.9.78	Pembury
Windows Matthew Guy Norman	Gloucestershire	E	5.4.73	Bristol
* **Wiseman** Paul John	Otago	NZ	4.5.70	Auckland
* **Wishart** Craig Brian	Mashonaland	Z	9.1.74	Salisbury
Wisneski Warren Anthony	Canterbury	NZ	19.2.69	New Plymouth
Wong Kenneth Arthur	Guyana	WI	22.5.73	Guyana
Wood John	Durham	E	22.7.70	Crofton
Wood Matthew James	Yorkshire	E	6.4.77	Huddersfield
Wood Nathan Theodore	Lancashire	E	4.10.74	Thornhill Edge
Wright Anthony John	Gloucestershire	E	27.6.62	Stevenage
Wright Carl	Jamaica	WI	17.9.77	St Elizabeth
Wright Damien Geoffrey	Tasmania	A	25.7.75	Casino
Wylie Andrew Robert	Boland	SA	31.12.71	Pietermaritzburg
Yadav Jyoti Prasad	Uttar Pradesh	I	26.9.77	Allahabad
* **Yadav** Vijay Singh	Haryana	I	14.3.67	Gonda
Yates Gary	Lancashire	E	20.9.67	Ashton-under-Lyne
Young Bradley Evan	South Australia	A	23.2.73	Semaphore
* **Young** Bryan Andrew	Northern Districts	NZ	3.11.64	Whangarei
* **Young** Shaun	Tasmania/Glos	A	13.6.70	Burnie
* **Yousuf** Youhana	Lahore/WAPDA	P	27.8.74	Lahore
Zafar Iqbal	Karachi/Nat. Bank	P	6.3.69	Karachi
Zahid Ahmed	PIA	P	15.11.61	Karachi
* **Zahid Fazal**	Gujranwala/PIA	P	10.11.73	Sialkot
Zahir Shah	Natal	P	12.11.73	Rawalpindi
* **Zahoor Elahi**	Lahore/ADBP	P	1.3.71	Sahiwal
Zakir Hassan	Bangladesh	B	1.12.72	Mymensingh
Zakir Hussain	Railways	I	26.1.76	Bikaner
* **Zoysa** Demuni Nuwan Tharanga	Sinhalese	SL	13.5.78	Colombo

WISDEN'S CRICKETERS OF THE YEAR, 1889-1999

1889	*Six Great Bowlers of the Year:* J. Briggs, J. J. Ferris, G. A. Lohmann, R. Peel, C. T. B. Turner, S. M. J. Woods.
1890	*Nine Great Batsmen of the Year:* R. Abel, W. Barnes, W. Gunn, L. Hall, R. Henderson, J. M. Read, A. Shrewsbury, F. H. Sugg, A. Ward.
1891	*Five Great Wicket-Keepers:* J. McC. Blackham, G. MacGregor, R. Pilling, M. Sherwin, H. Wood.
1892	*Five Great Bowlers:* W. Attewell, J. T. Hearne, F. Martin, A. W. Mold, J. W. Sharpe.
1893	*Five Batsmen of the Year:* H. T. Hewett, L. C. H. Palairet, W. W. Read, S. W. Scott, A. E. Stoddart.
1894	*Five All-Round Cricketers:* G. Giffen, A. Hearne, F. S. Jackson, G. H. S. Trott, E. Wainwright.
1895	*Five Young Batsmen of the Season:* W. Brockwell, J. T. Brown, C. B. Fry, T. W. Hayward, A. C. MacLaren.
1896	W. G. Grace.
1897	*Five Cricketers of the Season:* S. E. Gregory, A. A. Lilley, K. S. Ranjitsinhji, T. Richardson, H. Trumble.
1898	*Five Cricketers of the Year:* F. G. Bull, W. R. Cuttell, N. F. Druce, G. L. Jessop, J. R. Mason.
1899	*Five Great Players of the Season:* W. H. Lockwood, W. Rhodes, W. Storer, C. L. Townsend, A. E. Trott.
1900	*Five Cricketers of the Season:* J. Darling, C. Hill, A. O. Jones, M. A. Noble, Major R. M. Poore.
1901	*Mr R. E. Foster and Four Yorkshiremen:* R. E. Foster, S. Haigh, G. H. Hirst, T. L. Taylor, J. Tunnicliffe.
1902	L. C. Braund, C. P. McGahey, F. Mitchell, W. G. Quaife, J. T. Tyldesley.
1903	W. W. Armstrong, C. J. Burnup, J. Iremonger, J. J. Kelly, V. T. Trumper.
1904	C. Blythe, J. Gunn, A. E. Knight, W. Mead, P. F. Warner.
1905	B. J. T. Bosanquet, E. A. Halliwell, J. Hallows, P. A. Perrin, R. H. Spooner.
1906	D. Denton, W. S. Lees, G. J. Thompson, J. Vine, L. G. Wright.
1907	J. N. Crawford, A. Fielder, E. G. Hayes, K. L. Hutchings, N. A. Knox.
1908	A. W. Hallam, R. O. Schwarz, F. A. Tarrant, A. E. E. Vogler, T. G. Wass.
1909	*Lord Hawke and Four Cricketers of the Year:* W. Brearley, Lord Hawke, J. B. Hobbs, A. Marshal, J. T. Newstead.
1910	W. Bardsley, S. F. Barnes, D. W. Carr, A. P. Day, V. S. Ransford.
1911	H. K. Foster, A. Hartley, C. B. Llewellyn, W. C. Smith, F. E. Woolley.
1912	*Five Members of the MCC's Team in Australia:* F. R. Foster, J. W. Hearne, S. P. Kinneir, C. P. Mead, H. Strudwick.
1913	John Wisden: Personal Recollections.
1914	M. W. Booth, G. Gunn, J. W. Hitch, A. E. Relf, Hon. L. H. Tennyson.
1915	J. W. H. T. Douglas, P. G. H. Fender, H. T. W. Hardinge, D. J. Knight, S. G. Smith.
1916-17	No portraits appeared.
1918	*School Bowlers of the Year:* H. L. Calder, J. E. D'E. Firth, C. H. Gibson, G. A. Rotherham, G. T. S. Stevens.
1919	*Five Public School Cricketers of the Year:* P. W. Adams, A. P. F. Chapman, A. C. Gore, L. P. Hedges, N. E. Partridge.
1920	*Five Batsmen of the Year:* A. Ducat, E. H. Hendren, P. Holmes, H. Sutcliffe, E. Tyldesley.
1921	P. F. Warner.
1922	H. Ashton, J. L. Bryan, J. M. Gregory, C. G. Macartney, E. A. McDonald.
1923	A. W. Carr, A. P. Freeman, C. W. L. Parker, A. C. Russell, A. Sandham.
1924	*Five Bowlers of the Year:* A. E. R. Gilligan, R. Kilner, G. G. Macaulay, C. H. Parkin, M. W. Tate.
1925	R. H. Catterall, J. C. W. MacBryan, H. W. Taylor, R. K. Tyldesley, W. W. Whysall.
1926	J. B. Hobbs.

1927   G. Geary, H. Larwood, J. Mercer, W. A. Oldfield, W. M. Woodfull.
1928   R. C. Blunt, C. Hallows, W. R. Hammond, D. R. Jardine, V. W. C. Jupp.
1929   L. E. G. Ames, G. Duckworth, M. Leyland, S. J. Staples, J. C. White.
1930   E. H. Bowley, K. S. Duleepsinhji, H. G. Owen-Smith, R. W. V. Robins, R. E. S. Wyatt.
1931   D. G. Bradman, C. V. Grimmett, B. H. Lyon, I. A. R. Peebles, M. J. Turnbull.
1932   W. E. Bowes, C. S. Dempster, James Langridge, Nawab of Pataudi sen., H. Verity.
1933   W. E. Astill, F. R. Brown, A. S. Kennedy, C. K. Nayudu, W. Voce.
1934   A. H. Bakewell, G. A. Headley, M. S. Nichols, L. F. Townsend, C. F. Walters.
1935   S. J. McCabe, W. J. O'Reilly, G. A. E. Paine, W. H. Ponsford, C. I. J. Smith.
1936   H. B. Cameron, E. R. T. Holmes, B. Mitchell, D. Smith, A. W. Wellard.
1937   C. J. Barnett, W. H. Copson, A. R. Gover, V. M. Merchant, T. S. Worthington.
1938   T. W. J. Goddard, J. Hardstaff jun., L. Hutton, J. H. Parks, E. Paynter.
1939   H. T. Bartlett, W. A. Brown, D. C. S. Compton, K. Farnes, A. Wood.
1940   L. N. Constantine, W. J. Edrich, W. W. Keeton, A. B. Sellers, D. V. P. Wright.
1941-46 No portraits appeared.
1947   A. V. Bedser, L. B. Fishlock, V. (M. H.) Mankad, T. P. B. Smith, C. Washbrook.
1948   M. P. Donnelly, A. Melville, A. D. Nourse, J. D. Robertson, N. W. D. Yardley.
1949   A. L. Hassett, W. A. Johnston, R. R. Lindwall, A. R. Morris, D. Tallon.
1950   T. E. Bailey, R. O. Jenkins, John Langridge, R. T. Simpson, B. Sutcliffe.
1951   T. G. Evans, S. Ramadhin, A. L. Valentine, E. D. Weekes, F. M. M. Worrell.
1952   R. Appleyard, H. E. Dollery, J. C. Laker, P. B. H. May, E. A. B. Rowan.
1953   H. Gimblett, T. W. Graveney, D. S. Sheppard, W. S. Surridge, F. S. Trueman.
1954   R. N. Harvey, G. A. R. Lock, K. R. Miller, J. H. Wardle, W. Watson.
1955   B. Dooland, Fazal Mahmood, W. E. Hollies, J. B. Statham, G. E. Tribe.
1956   M. C. Cowdrey, D. J. Insole, D. J. McGlew, H. J. Tayfield, F. H. Tyson.
1957   D. Brookes, J. W. Burke, M. J. Hilton, G. R. A. Langley, P. E. Richardson.
1958   P. J. Loader, A. J. McIntyre, O. G. Smith, M. J. Stewart, C. L. Walcott.
1959   H. L. Jackson, R. E. Marshall, C. A. Milton, J. R. Reid, D. Shackleton.
1960   K. F. Barrington, D. B. Carr, R. Illingworth, G. Pullar, M. J. K. Smith.
1961   N. A. T. Adcock, E. R. Dexter, R. A. McLean, R. Subba Row, J. V. Wilson.
1962   W. E. Alley, R. Benaud, A. K. Davidson, W. M. Lawry, C. C. O'Neill.
1963   D. Kenyon, Mushtaq Mohammad, P. H. Parfitt, P. J. Sharpe, F. J. Titmus.
1964   D. B. Close, C. C. Griffith, C. C. Hunte, R. B. Kanhai, G. S. Sobers.
1965   G. Boycott, P. J. Burge, J. A. Flavell, G. D. McKenzie, R. B. Simpson.
1966   K. C. Bland, J. H. Edrich, R. C. Motz, P. M. Pollock, R. G. Pollock.
1967   R. W. Barber, B. L. D'Oliveira, C. Milburn, J. T. Murray, S. M. Nurse.
1968   Asif Iqbal, Hanif Mohammad, K. Higgs, J. M. Parks, Nawab of Pataudi jun.
1969   J. G. Binks, D. M. Green, B. A. Richards, D. L. Underwood, O. S. Wheatley.
1970   B. F. Butcher, A. P. E. Knott, Majid Khan, M. J. Procter, J. Shepherd.
1971   J. D. Bond, C. H. Lloyd, B. W. Luckhurst, G. M. Turner, R. T. Virgin.
1972   G. G. Arnold, B. S. Chandrasekhar, L. R. Gibbs, B. Taylor, Zaheer Abbas.
1973   G. S. Chappell, D. K. Lillee, R. A. L. Massie, J. A. Snow, K. R. Stackpole.
1974   K. D. Boyce, B. E. Congdon, K. W. R. Fletcher, R. C. Fredericks, P. J. Sainsbury.
1975   D. L. Amiss, M. H. Denness, N. Gifford, A. W. Greig, A. M. E. Roberts.
1976   I. M. Chappell, P. G. Lee, R. B. McCosker, D. S. Steele, A. Woolmer.
1977   J. M. Brearley, C. G. Greenidge, M. A. Holding, I. V. A. Richards, R. W. Taylor.
1978   I. T. Botham, M. Hendrick, A. Jones, K. S. McEwan, R. G. D. Willis.
1979   D. I. Gower, J. K. Lever, C. M. Old, C. T. Radley, J. N. Shepherd.
1980   J. Garner, S. M. Gavaskar, G. A. Gooch, D. W. Randall, B. C. Rose.
1981   K. J. Hughes, R. D. Jackman, A. J. Lamb, C. E. B. Rice, V. A. P. van der Bijl.
1982   T. M. Alderman, A. R. Border, R. J. Hadlee, Javed Miandad, R. W. Marsh.
1983   Imran Khan, T. E. Jesty, A. I. Kallicharran, Kapil Dev, M. D. Marshall.
1984   M. Amarnath, J. V. Coney, J. E. Emburey, M. W. Gatting, C. L. Smith.
1985   M. D. Crowe, H. A. Gomes, G. W. Humpage, J. Simmons, S. Wettimuny.
1986   P. Bainbridge, R. M. Ellison, C. J. McDermott, N. V. Radford, R. T. Robinson.
1987   J. H. Childs, G. A. Hick, D. B. Vengsarkar, C. A. Walsh, J. J. Whitaker.
1988   J. P. Agnew, N. A. Foster, D. P. Hughes, P. M. Roebuck, Salim Malik.
1989   K. J. Barnett, P. J. L. Dujon, P. A. Neale, F. D. Stephenson, S. R. Waugh.

1990	S. J. Cook, D. M. Jones, R. C. Russell, R. A. Smith, M. A. Taylor.
1991	M. A. Atherton, M. Azharuddin, A. R. Butcher, D. L. Haynes, M. E. Waugh.
1992	C. E. L. Ambrose, P. A. J. DeFreitas, A. A. Donald, R. B. Richardson, Waqar Younis.
1993	N. E. Briers, M. D. Moxon, I. D. K. Salisbury, A. J. Stewart, Wasim Akram.
1994	D. C. Boon, I. A. Healy, M. G. Hughes, S. K. Warne, S. L. Watkin.
1995	B. C. Lara, D. E. Malcolm, T. A. Munton, S. J. Rhodes, K. C. Wessels.
1996	D. G. Cork, P. A. de Silva, A. R. C. Fraser, A. Kumble, D. A. Reeve.
1997	S. T. Jayasuriya, Mushtaq Ahmed, Saeed Anwar, P. V. Simmons, S. R. Tendulkar.
1998	M. T. G. Elliott, S. G. Law, G. D. McGrath, M. P. Maynard, G. P. Thorpe.
1999	I. D. Austin, D. Gough, M. Muralitharan, A. Ranatunga, J. N. Rhodes.

CRICKETERS OF THE YEAR: AN ANALYSIS

The five players selected to be Cricketers of the Year for 1999 bring the number chosen since selection began in 1889 to 502. They have been chosen from 36 different teams as follows:

Derbyshire	13	Northants	13	Cambridge Univ.	10	Cheltenham College	1
Essex	22	Nottinghamshire	25	Australians	62	Cranleigh School	1
Glamorgan	10	Somerset	16	South Africans	20	Eton College	2
Gloucestershire	15	Surrey	45	West Indians	23	Malvern College	1
Hampshire	14	Sussex	20	New Zealanders	7	Rugby School	1
Kent	25	Warwickshire	19	Indians	11	Tonbridge School	1
Lancashire	31	Worcestershire	14	Pakistanis	10	Univ. Coll. School	1
Leicestershire	8	Yorkshire	39	Sri Lankans	4	Uppingham School	1
Middlesex	25	Oxford Univ.	6	Staffordshire	1	Winchester College	1

Durham and the Zimbabweans have as yet had no team members chosen as Cricketers of the Year.

Notes: Schoolboys were chosen in 1918 and 1919 when first-class cricket was suspended due to war. The total of sides comes to 518 because 16 players played regularly for two teams (England excluded) in the year for which they were chosen. John Wisden, listed as a Sussex player, retired 50 years before his posthumous selection.

Types of Players

Of the 502 Cricketers of the Year, 255 are best classified as batsmen, 144 as bowlers, 71 as all-rounders and 32 as wicket-keepers.

Nationalities

At the time they were chosen, 323 players (64.34 per cent) were qualified to play for England, 71 for Australia, 36 West Indies, 30 South Africa, 13 Pakistan, 12 India, 11 New Zealand, 5 Sri Lanka and 1 Zimbabwe.

N.B. Nationalities and teams are not necessarily identical.

Ages

On April 1 in the year of selection

Youngest: 17 years 67 days H. L. Calder, 1918. The youngest first-class cricketer was Mushtaq Mohammad, 19 years 130 days in 1963.

Oldest: 48 years 228 days Lord Hawke, 1909. (This excludes John Wisden, whose portrait appeared 87 years after his birth and 29 years after his death.)

An analysis of post-war Cricketers of the Year may be found in Wisden *1998, page 174.*

Research: Robert Brooke

PART FOUR: RECORDS

CRICKET RECORDS

First-class and limited-overs records by PHILIP BAILEY
Test match records by BILL FRINDALL

Records in the England v Australia section (pages 261-272) have been updated to include the 1998-99 Ashes series. These figures are NOT included elsewhere. The deadline for other sections is the end of the 1998 season in England.

Updated Test records can be found on Wisden's web site, www.wisden.com

Unless otherwise stated, all records apply only to first-class cricket. This is traditionally considered to have started in 1815, after the Napoleonic War.

* Denotes not out or an unbroken partnership.

(A), (SA), (WI), (NZ), (I), (P), (SL) or (Z) indicates either the nationality of the player, or the country in which the record was made.

FIRST-CLASS RECORDS

BATTING RECORDS

BOWLING RECORDS

ALL-ROUND RECORDS

WICKET-KEEPING RECORDS

FIELDING RECORDS

TEAM RECORDS

TEST MATCH RECORDS

BATTING RECORDS

BOWLING RECORDS

ALL-ROUND RECORDS

WICKET-KEEPING RECORDS

FIELDING RECORDS

TEAM RECORDS

PLAYERS

CAPTAINCY

UMPIRING

TEST SERIES

LIMITED-OVERS INTERNATIONAL RECORDS

MISCELLANEOUS

FIRST-CLASS RECORDS

BATTING RECORDS

HIGHEST INDIVIDUAL SCORES

501*	B. C. Lara	Warwickshire v Durham at Birmingham	1994
499	Hanif Mohammad	Karachi v Bahawalpur at Karachi.	1958-59
452*	D. G. Bradman	NSW v Queensland at Sydney.	1929-30
443*	B. B. Nimbalkar	Maharashtra v Kathiawar at Poona	1948-49
437	W. H. Ponsford	Victoria v Queensland at Melbourne	1927-28
429	W. H. Ponsford	Victoria v Tasmania at Melbourne	1922-23

428	Aftab Baloch	Sind v Baluchistan at Karachi	1973-74
424	A. C. MacLaren	Lancashire v Somerset at Taunton	1895
405*	G. A. Hick	Worcestershire v Somerset at Taunton	1988
385	B. Sutcliffe	Otago v Canterbury at Christchurch	1952-53
383	C. W. Gregory	NSW v Queensland at Brisbane	1906-07
377	S. V. Manjrekar	Bombay v Hyderabad at Bombay	1990-91
375	B. C. Lara	West Indies v England at St John's	1993-94
369	D. G. Bradman	South Australia v Tasmania at Adelaide	1935-36
366	N. H. Fairbrother	Lancashire v Surrey at The Oval	1990
366	M. V. Sridhar	Hyderabad v Andhra at Secunderabad	1993-94
365*	C. Hill	South Australia v NSW at Adelaide	1900-01
365*	G. S. Sobers	West Indies v Pakistan at Kingston	1957-58
364	L. Hutton	England v Australia at The Oval	1938
359*	V. M. Merchant	Bombay v Maharashtra at Bombay	1943-44
359	R. B. Simpson	NSW v Queensland at Brisbane	1963-64
357*	R. Abel	Surrey v Somerset at The Oval	1899
357	D. G. Bradman	South Australia v Victoria at Melbourne	1935-36
356	B. A. Richards	South Australia v Western Australia at Perth	1970-71
355*	G. R. Marsh	Western Australia v South Australia at Perth	1989-90
355	B. Sutcliffe	Otago v Auckland at Dunedin	1949-50
352	W. H. Ponsford	Victoria v NSW at Melbourne	1926-27
350	Rashid Israr	Habib Bank v National Bank at Lahore	1976-77
345	C. G. Macartney	Australians v Nottinghamshire at Nottingham	1921
344*	G. A. Headley	Jamaica v Lord Tennyson's XI at Kingston	1931-32
344	W. G. Grace	MCC v Kent at Canterbury	1876
343*	P. A. Perrin	Essex v Derbyshire at Chesterfield	1904
341	G. H. Hirst	Yorkshire v Leicestershire at Leicester	1905
340*	D. G. Bradman	NSW v Victoria at Sydney	1928-29
340	S. M. Gavaskar	Bombay v Bengal at Bombay	1981-82
340	S. T. Jayasuriya	Sri Lanka v India at Colombo	1997-98
338*	R. C. Blunt	Otago v Canterbury at Christchurch	1931-32
338	W. W. Read	Surrey v Oxford University at The Oval	1888
337*	Pervez Akhtar	Railways v Dera Ismail Khan at Lahore	1964-65
337*	D. J. Cullinan	Transvaal v Northern Transvaal at Johannesburg	1993-94
337†	Hanif Mohammad	Pakistan v West Indies at Bridgetown	1957-58
336*	W. R. Hammond	England v New Zealand at Auckland	1932-33
336	W. H. Ponsford	Victoria v South Australia at Melbourne	1927-28
334	D. G. Bradman	Australia v England at Leeds	1930
333	K. S. Duleepsinhji	Sussex v Northamptonshire at Hove	1930
333	G. A. Gooch	England v India at Lord's	1990
332	W. H. Ashdown	Kent v Essex at Brentwood	1934
331*	J. D. Robertson	Middlesex v Worcestershire at Worcester	1949
325*	H. L. Hendry	Victoria v New Zealanders at Melbourne	1925-26
325	A. Sandham	England v West Indies at Kingston	1929-30
325	C. L. Badcock	South Australia v Victoria at Adelaide	1935-36
324*	D. M. Jones	Victoria v South Australia at Melbourne	1994-95
324	J. B. Stollmeyer	Trinidad v British Guiana at Port-of-Spain	1946-47
324	Waheed Mirza	Karachi Whites v Quetta at Karachi	1976-77
323	A. L. Wadekar	Bombay v Mysore at Bombay	1966-67
322*	M. B. Loye	Northamptonshire v Glamorgan at Northampton	1998
322	E. Paynter	Lancashire v Sussex at Hove	1937
322	I. V. A. Richards	Somerset v Warwickshire at Taunton	1985
321	W. L. Murdoch	NSW v Victoria at Sydney	1881-82
320	R. Lamba	North Zone v West Zone at Bhilai	1987-88
319	Gul Mahomed	Baroda v Holkar at Baroda	1946-47
318*	W. G. Grace	Gloucestershire v Yorkshire at Cheltenham	1876
317	W. R. Hammond	Gloucestershire v Nottinghamshire at Gloucester . . .	1936
317	K. R. Rutherford	New Zealanders v D. B. Close's XI at Scarborough . .	1986
316*	J. B. Hobbs	Surrey v Middlesex at Lord's	1926
316*	V. S. Hazare	Maharashtra v Baroda at Poona	1939-40
316	R. H. Moore	Hampshire v Warwickshire at Bournemouth	1937

315*	T. W. Hayward	Surrey v Lancashire at The Oval	1898
315*	P. Holmes	Yorkshire v Middlesex at Lord's	1925
315*	A. F. Kippax	NSW v Queensland at Sydney	1927-28
314*	C. L. Walcott	Barbados v Trinidad at Port-of-Spain	1945-46
314*	Wasim Jaffer	Mumbai v Saurashtra at Rajkot	1996-97
313*	S. J. Cook	Somerset v Glamorgan at Cardiff	1990
313	H. Sutcliffe	Yorkshire v Essex at Leyton	1932
313	W. V. Raman§	Tamil Nadu v Goa at Panjim	1988-89
312*	W. W. Keeton	Nottinghamshire v Middlesex at The Oval‡	1939
312*	J. M. Brearley	MCC Under-25 v North Zone at Peshawar	1966-67
312	R. Lamba	Delhi v Himachal Pradesh at Delhi	1994-95
312	J. E. R. Gallian	Lancashire v Derbyshire at Manchester	1996
311*	G. M. Turner	Worcestershire v Warwickshire at Worcester	1982
311	J. T. Brown	Yorkshire v Sussex at Sheffield	1897
311	R. B. Simpson	Australia v England at Manchester	1964
311	Javed Miandad	Karachi Whites v National Bank at Karachi	1974-75
310*	J. H. Edrich	England v New Zealand at Leeds	1965
310	H. Gimblett	Somerset v Sussex at Eastbourne	1948
309	V. S. Hazare	The Rest v Hindus at Bombay	1943-44
308*	F. M. M. Worrell	Barbados v Trinidad at Bridgetown	1943-44
307*	T. N. Lazard	Boland v W. Province at Worcester, Cape Province . .	1993-94
307	M. C. Cowdrey	MCC v South Australia at Adelaide	1962-63
307	R. M. Cowper	Australia v England at Melbourne	1965-66
306*	A. Ducat	Surrey v Oxford University at The Oval	1919
306*	E. A. B. Rowan	Transvaal v Natal at Johannesburg	1939-40
306*	D. W. Hookes	South Australia v Tasmania at Adelaide	1986-87
305*	F. E. Woolley	MCC v Tasmania at Hobart	1911-12
305*	F. R. Foster	Warwickshire v Worcestershire at Dudley	1914
305*	W. H. Ashdown	Kent v Derbyshire at Dover	1935
304*	A. W. Nourse	Natal v Transvaal at Johannesburg	1919-20
304*	P. H. Tarilton	Barbados v Trinidad at Bridgetown	1919-20
304*	E. D. Weekes	West Indians v Cambridge University at Cambridge	1950
304	R. M. Poore	Hampshire v Somerset at Taunton	1899
304	D. G. Bradman	Australia v England at Leeds	1934
303*	W. W. Armstrong	Australians v Somerset at Bath	1905
303*	Mushtaq Mohammad	Karachi Blues v Karachi University at Karachi . . .	1967-68
303*	Abdul Azeem	Hyderabad v Tamil Nadu at Hyderabad	1986-87
303*	S. Chanderpaul	Guyana v Jamaica at Kingston	1995-96
303*	G. A. Hick	Worcestershire v Hampshire at Southampton	1997
302*	P. Holmes	Yorkshire v Hampshire at Portsmouth	1920
302*	W. R. Hammond	Gloucestershire v Glamorgan at Bristol	1934
302*	Arjan Kripal Singh§	Tamil Nadu v Goa at Panjim	1988-89
302	W. R. Hammond	Gloucestershire v Glamorgan at Newport	1939
302	L. G. Rowe	West Indies v England at Bridgetown	1973-74
301*	E. H. Hendren	Middlesex v Worcestershire at Dudley	1933
301*	V. V. S. Laxman	Hyderabad v Bihar at Jamshedpur	1997-98
301	W. G. Grace	Gloucestershire v Sussex at Bristol	1896
300*	V. T. Trumper	Australians v Sussex at Hove	1899
300*	F. B. Watson	Lancashire v Surrey at Manchester	1928
300*	Imtiaz Ahmed	PM's XI v Commonwealth XI at Bombay	1950-51
300	J. T. Brown	Yorkshire v Derbyshire at Chesterfield	1898
300	D. C. S. Compton	MCC v N. E. Transvaal at Benoni	1948-49
300	R. Subba Row	Northamptonshire v Surrey at The Oval	1958
300	Ramiz Raja	Allied Bank v Habib Bank at Lahore	1994-95

† *Hanif Mohammad batted for 16 hours 10 minutes, the longest innings in first-class cricket.*
‡ *Played at The Oval because Lord's was required for Eton v Harrow.*
§ *In the same innings, a unique occurrence.*

Note: M. A. Taylor scored 334* for Australia v Pakistan at Peshawar in 1998-99, after the deadline
for this section.

DOUBLE-HUNDRED ON DEBUT

227	T. Marsden	Sheffield & Leicester v Nottingham at Sheffield	1826
207	N. F. Callaway†	New South Wales v Queensland at Sydney	1914-15
240	W. F. E. Marx	Transvaal v Griqualand West at Johannesburg	1920-21
200*	A. Maynard	Trinidad v MCC at Port-of-Spain	1934-35
232*	S. J. E. Loxton	Victoria v Queensland at Melbourne	1946-47
215*	G. H. G. Doggart	Cambridge University v Lancashire at Cambridge	1948
202	J. Hallebone	Victoria v Tasmania at Melbourne	1951-52
230	G. R. Viswanath	Mysore v Andhra at Vijayawada	1967-68
260	A. A. Muzumdar	Bombay v Haryana at Faridabad	1993-94
209*	A. Pandey	Madhya Pradesh v Uttar Pradesh at Bhilai	1995-96
210*	D. J. Sales	Northants v Worcestershire at Kidderminster	1996
200*	M. J. Powell	Glamorgan v Oxford University at Oxford	1997

† *In his only first-class innings. He was killed in action in France in 1917.*

TWO SEPARATE HUNDREDS ON DEBUT

148	and 111	A. R. Morris	New South Wales v Queensland at Sydney	1940-41
152	and 102*	N. J. Contractor	Gujarat v Baroda at Baroda	1952-53
132*	and 110	Aamer Malik	Lahore "A" v Railways at Lahore	1979-80

HUNDRED ON DEBUT IN ENGLAND

This does not include players who have previously appeared in first-class cricket outside the British Isles. The following have achieved the feat since 1990. For fuller lists please see earlier *Wisdens*.

116*	J. J. B. Lewis	Essex v Surrey at The Oval	1990
117	J. D. Glendenen	Durham v Oxford University at Oxford	1992
109	J. R. Wileman	Nottinghamshire v Cambridge University at Nottingham. .	1992
123	A. J. Hollioake†	Surrey v Derbyshire at Ilkeston	1993
101	E. T. Smith	Cambridge University v Glamorgan at Cambridge	1996
110	S. D. Peters	Essex v Cambridge University at Cambridge	1996
210*	D. J. Sales†	Northamptonshire v Worcestershire at Kidderminster . . .	1996
200*	M. J. Powell	Glamorgan v Oxford University at Oxford	1997

† *In his second innings.*

TWO DOUBLE-HUNDREDS IN A MATCH

A. E. Fagg	244	202*	Kent v Essex at Colchester	1938

TRIPLE-HUNDRED AND HUNDRED IN A MATCH

G. A. Gooch	333	123	England v India at Lord's	1990

DOUBLE-HUNDRED AND HUNDRED IN A MATCH

C. B. Fry	125	229	Sussex v Surrey at Hove	1900
W. W. Armstrong	157*	245	Victoria v South Australia at Melbourne . . .	1920-21
H. T. W. Hardinge . . .	207	102*	Kent v Surrey at Blackheath	1921
C. P. Mead	113	224	Hampshire v Sussex at Horsham	1921
K. S. Duleepsinhji . . .	115	246	Sussex v Kent at Hastings	1929

D. G. Bradman	124	225	Woodfull's XI v Ryder's XI at Sydney	1929-30
B. Sutcliffe	243	100*	New Zealanders v Essex at Southend	1949
M. R. Hallam	210*	157	Leicestershire v Glamorgan at Leicester	1959
M. R. Hallam	203*	143*	Leicestershire v Sussex at Worthing	1961
Hanumant Singh	109	213*	Rajasthan v Bombay at Bombay	1966-67
Salah-ud-Din	256	102*	Karachi v East Pakistan at Karachi	1968-69
K. D. Walters	242	103	Australia v West Indies at Sydney	1968-69
S. M. Gavaskar	124	220	India v West Indies at Port-of-Spain	1970-71
L. G. Rowe	214	100*	West Indies v New Zealand at Kingston	1971-72
G. S. Chappell	247*	133	Australia v New Zealand at Wellington	1973-74
L. Baichan	216*	102	Berbice v Demerara at Georgetown	1973-74
Zaheer Abbas	216*	156*	Gloucestershire v Surrey at The Oval	1976
Zaheer Abbas	230*	104*	Gloucestershire v Kent at Canterbury	1976
Zaheer Abbas	205*	108*	Gloucestershire v Sussex at Cheltenham	1977
Saadat Ali	141	222	Income Tax v Multan at Multan	1977-78
Talat Ali	214*	104	PIA v Punjab at Lahore	1978-79
Shafiq Ahmad	129	217*	National Bank v MCB at Karachi	1978-79
D. W. Randall	209	146	Nottinghamshire v Middlesex at Nottingham	1979
Zaheer Abbas	215*	150*	Gloucestershire v Somerset at Bath	1981
Qasim Omar	210*	110	MCB v Lahore at Lahore	1982-83
A. I. Kallicharran	200*	117*	Warwickshire v Northants at Birmingham	1984
Rizwan-uz-Zaman	139	217*	PIA v PACO at Lahore	1989-90
G. A. Hick	252*	100*	Worcestershire v Glamorgan at Abergavenny	1990
N. R. Taylor	204	142	Kent v Surrey at Canterbury	1990
N. R. Taylor	111	203*	Kent v Sussex at Hove	1991
W. V. Raman	226	120	Tamil Nadu v Haryana at Faridabad	1991-92
A. J. Lamb	209	107	Northants v Warwicks at Northampton	1992
G. A. Gooch	101	205	Essex v Worcestershire at Worcester	1994
P. A. de Silva	255	116	Kent v Derbyshire at Maidstone	1995
M. C. Mendis	111	200*	Colts CC v Singha SC at Colombo	1995-96
A. M. Bacher	210	112*	Transvaal v Griqualand West at Kimberley	1996-97
H. H. Gibbs	200*	171	South Africans v India A at Nagpur	1996-97
M. L. Hayden	235*	119	Hampshire v Warwickshire at Southampton	1997

TWO SEPARATE HUNDREDS IN A MATCH

Eight times: Zaheer Abbas.

Seven times: W. R. Hammond.

Six times: J. B. Hobbs, G. M. Turner.

Five times: C. B. Fry, G. A. Gooch.

Four times: D. G. Bradman, G. S. Chappell, J. H. Edrich, L. B. Fishlock, T. W. Graveney, C. G. Greenidge, H. T. W. Hardinge, E. H. Hendren, Javed Miandad, G. L. Jessop, H. Morris, P. A. Perrin, B. Sutcliffe, H. Sutcliffe.

Three times: Agha Zahid, L. E. G. Ames, Basit Ali, G. Boycott, I. M. Chappell, D. C. S. Compton, S. J. Cook, M. C. Cowdrey, D. Denton, P. A. de Silva, K. S. Duleepsinhji, R. E. Foster, R. C. Frederricks, S. M. Gavaskar, W. G. Grace, G. Gunn, M. R. Hallam, Hanif Mohammad, M. J. Harris, M. L. Hayden, T. W. Hayward, V. S. Hazare, G. A. Hick, D. W. Hookes, L. Hutton, A. Jones, D. M. Jones, P. N. Kirsten, R. B. McCosker, P. B. H. May, C. P. Mead, T. M. Moody, M. H. Parmar, R. T. Ponting, M. R. Ramprakash, Rizwan-uz-Zaman, R. T. Robinson, A. C. Russell, Sadiq Mohammad, J. T. Tyldesley, K. C. Wessels.

Notes: W. Lambert scored 107 and 157 for Sussex v Epsom at Lord's in 1817, and it was not until W. G. Grace made 130 and 102* for South of the Thames v North of the Thames at Canterbury in 1868 that the feat was repeated.

C. J. B. Wood, 107* and 117* for Leicestershire v Yorkshire at Bradford in 1911, and S. J. Cook, 120* and 131* for Somerset v Nottinghamshire at Nottingham in 1989, are alone in carrying their bats and scoring hundreds in each innings.

FOUR HUNDREDS OR MORE IN SUCCESSION

Six in succession: D. G. Bradman 1938-39; C. B. Fry 1901; M. J. Procter 1970-71.

Five in succession: B. C. Lara 1993-94/1994; E. D. Weekes 1955-56.

Four in succession: C. W. J. Athey 1987; M. Azharuddin 1984-85; M. G. Bevan 1990-91; A. R. Border 1985; D. G. Bradman 1931-32, 1948/1948-49; D. C. S. Compton 1946-47; N. J. Contractor 1957-58; S. J. Cook 1989; K. S. Duleepsinhji 1931; C. B. Fry 1911; C. G. Greenidge 1986; W. R. Hammond 1936-37, 1945/1946; H. T. W. Hardinge 1913; T. W. Hayward 1906; G. A. Hick 1998; J. B. Hobbs 1920, 1925; D. W. Hookes 1976-77; Ijaz Ahmed, jun. 1994-95; R. S. Kaluwitharana 1996-97; P. N. Kirsten 1976-77; J. G. Langridge 1949; C. G. Macartney 1921; K. S. McEwan 1977; P. B. H. May 1956-57; V. M. Merchant 1941-42; A. Mitchell 1933; Nawab of Pataudi sen. 1931; Rizwan-uz-Zaman 1989-90; L. G. Rowe 1971-72; Pankaj Roy 1962-63; Sadiq Mohammad 1976; Saeed Ahmed 1961-62; M. V. Sridhar 1990-91/1991-92; H. Sutcliffe 1931, 1939; S. R. Tendulkar 1994-95; E. Tyldesley 1926; W. W. Whysall 1930; F. E. Woolley 1929; Zaheer Abbas 1970-71, 1982-83.

Notes: T. W. Hayward (Surrey v Nottinghamshire and Leicestershire) and D. W. Hookes (South Australia v Queensland and New South Wales) are the only players listed above to score two hundreds in two successive matches. Hayward scored his in six days, June 4-9, 1906.

The most fifties in consecutive innings is ten – by E. Tyldesley in 1926, by D. G. Bradman in the 1947-48 and 1948 seasons and by R. S. Kaluwitharana in 1994-95.

MOST HUNDREDS IN A SEASON

Eighteen: D. C. S. Compton 1947.
Sixteen: J. B. Hobbs 1925.
Fifteen: W. R. Hammond 1938.
Fourteen: H. Sutcliffe 1932.
Thirteen: G. Boycott 1971, D. G. Bradman 1938, C. B. Fry 1901, W. R. Hammond 1933 and 1937, T. W. Hayward 1906, E. H. Hendren 1923, 1927 and 1928, C. P. Mead 1928, H. Sutcliffe 1928 and 1931.

Since 1969 (excluding G. Boycott – above)

Twelve: G. A. Gooch 1990.
Eleven: S. J. Cook 1991, Zaheer Abbas 1976.
Ten: G. A. Hick 1988, H. Morris 1990, M. R. Ramprakash 1995, G. M. Turner 1970, Zaheer Abbas 1981.

MOST DOUBLE-HUNDREDS IN A SEASON

Six: D. G. Bradman 1930.
Five: K. S. Ranjitsinhji 1900; E. D. Weekes 1950.
Four: Arun Lal 1986-87; C. B. Fry 1901; W. R. Hammond 1933, 1934; E. H. Hendren 1929-30; V. M. Merchant 1944-45; G. M. Turner 1971-72.
Three: L. E. G. Ames 1933; Arshad Pervez 1977-78; D. G. Bradman 1930-31, 1931-32, 1934, 1935-36, 1936-37, 1938, 1939-40; W. J. Edrich 1947; C. B. Fry 1903, 1904; M. W. Gatting 1994; G. A. Gooch 1994; W. R. Hammond 1928, 1928-29, 1932-33, 1938; J. Hardstaff jun. 1937, 1947; V. S. Hazare 1943-44; E. H. Hendren 1925; J. B. Hobbs 1914, 1926; L. Hutton 1949; D. M. Jones 1991-92; A. I. Kallicharran 1982; V. G. Kambli 1992-93; P. N. Kirsten 1980; R. S. Modi 1944-45; Nawab of Pataudi sen. 1933; W. H. Ponsford 1927-28, 1934; W. V. Raman 1988-89; M. R. Ramprakash 1995; K. S. Ranjitsinhji 1901; I. V. A. Richards 1977; R. B. Simpson 1963-64; P. R. Umrigar 1952, 1959; F. B. Watson 1928.

MOST HUNDREDS IN A CAREER

(35 or more)

		100s	Total Inns	100th 100 Season	Inns	400+	300+	200+
1	J. B. Hobbs	197	1,315	1923	821	0	1	16
2	E. H. Hendren	170	1,300	1928-29	740	0	1	22
3	W. R. Hammond	167	1,005	1935	679	0	4	36
4	C. P. Mead	153	1,340	1927	892	0	0	13
5	G. Boycott	151	1,014	1977	645	0	0	10
6	H. Sutcliffe	149	1,088	1932	700	0	1	17
7	F. E. Woolley	145	1,532	1929	1,031	0	1	9
8	L. Hutton	129	814	1951	619	0	1	11
9	G. A. Gooch	128	988	1992-93	820	0	1	13
10	W. G. Grace	126	1,493	1895	1,113	0	3	13
11	D. C. S. Compton	123	839	1952	552	0	1	9
12	T. W. Graveney	122	1,223	1964	940	0	0	7
13	D. G. Bradman	117	338	1947-48	295	1	6	37
14	I. V. A. Richards	114	796	1988-89	658	0	1	10
15	Zaheer Abbas	108	768	1982-83	658	0	0	10
16	A. Sandham	107	1,000	1935	871	0	1	11
	M. C. Cowdrey	107	1,130	1973	1,035	0	1	3
18	T. W. Hayward	104	1,138	1913	1,076	0	1	8
19	**G. A. Hick**	**103**	**595**	**1998**	**574**	**1**	**1**	**11**
	G. M. Turner	103	792	1982	779	0	1	10
	J. H. Edrich	103	979	1977	945	0	1	4
22	L. E. G. Ames	102	951	1950	915	0	0	9
	E. Tyldesley	102	961	1934	919	0	0	7
	D. L. Amiss	102	1,139	1986	1,081	0	0	3

E. H. Hendren, D. G. Bradman and I. V. A. Richards scored their 100th hundreds in Australia; G. A. Gooch scored his in India. His record includes his century in South Africa in 1981-82, which is no longer accepted by ICC. Zaheer Abbas scored his 100th in Pakistan. Zaheer Abbas and G. Boycott did so in Test matches.

Most double-hundreds scored by batsmen not included in the above list:

Sixteen: C. B. Fry. **Fourteen:** C. G. Greenidge, K. S. Ranjitsinhji. **Thirteen:** W. H. Ponsford (including two 400s and two 300s), J. T. Tyldesley. **Twelve:** P. Holmes, Javed Miandad, R. B. Simpson. **Eleven:** J. W. Hearne, V. M. Merchant. **Ten:** S. M. Gavaskar, J. Hardstaff, jun., V. S. Hazare, A. Shrewsbury, R. T. Simpson.

J. W. Hearne 96	J. G. Langridge 76	**D. C. Boon 67**
C. B. Fry 94	C. Washbrook 76	R. N. Harvey 67
M. W. Gatting 94	H. T. W. Hardinge 75	P. Holmes 67
C. G. Greenidge 92	R. Abel 74	J. D. Robertson 67
A. J. Lamb 89	S. J. S. Chappell 74	**M. E. Waugh 67**
A. I. Kallicharran 87	D. Kenyon 74	P. A. Perrin 66
W. J. Edrich 86	K. S. McEwan 74	**K. C. Wessels 66**
G. S. Sobers 86	Majid Khan 73	S. J. Cook 64
J. T. Tyldesley 86	Mushtaq Mohammad . . . 72	R. G. Pollock 64
P. B. H. May 85	J. O'Connor 72	R. T. Simpson 64
R. E. S. Wyatt 85	W. G. Quaife 72	K. W. R. Fletcher . . . 63
J. Hardstaff, jun 83	K. S. Ranjitsinhji 72	**T. M. Moody 63**
R. B. Kanhai 83	D. Brookes 71	**R. T. Robinson 63**
S. M. Gavaskar 81	M. D. Crowe 71	G. Gunn 62
Javed Miandad 80	A. C. Russell 71	D. L. Haynes 61
M. Leyland 80	A. R. Border 70	V. S. Hazare 60
B. A. Richards 80	D. Denton 69	G. H. Hirst 60
C. H. Lloyd 79	M. J. K. Smith 69	R. B. Simpson 60
K. F. Barrington 76	R. E. Marshall 68	P. F. Warner 60

I. M. Chappell 59
A. L. Hassett 59
W. Larkins 59
A. Shrewsbury 59
J. G. Wright 59
A. E. Fagg 58
P. H. Parfitt 58
W. Rhodes 58
P. N. Kirsten 57
L. B. Fishlock 56
A. Jones 56
C. A. Milton 56
R. A. Smith **56**
C. W. J. Athey 55
C. Hallows 55
Hanif Mohammad 55
D. M. Jones **55**
D. B. Vengsarkar 55
W. Watson 55
D. J. Insole 54
W. W. Keeton 54
W. Bardsley 53
K. J. Barnett **53**
B. F. Davison 53
A. E. Dipper 53
D. I. Gower 53
G. L. Jessop 53
H. Morris 53
James Seymour 53
Shafiq Ahmad 53
E. H. Bowley 52
D. B. Close 52
A. Ducat 52
D. W. Randall 52
E. R. Dexter 51
J. M. Parks 51
W. W. Whysall 51
M. Azharuddin 50
B. C. Broad 50
G. Cox, jun. 50
H. E. Dollery 50
K. S. Duleepsinhji 50
J. Gimblett 50
W. M. Lawry 50
Sadiq Mohammad 50
F. B. Watson 50
C. G. Macartney 49
M. J. Stewart 49
K. G. Suttle 49
P. R. Umrigar 49
W. M. Woodfull 49
C. J. Barnett 48
M. R. Benson 48
W. Gunn 48
E. G. Hayes 48
B. W. Luckhurst 48
M. J. Procter 48
C. E. B. Rice 48
C. J. Tavaré 48

C. L. Hooper 47
A. C. MacLaren 47
J. E. Morris **47**
P. W. G. Parker 47
W. H. Ponsford 47
C. L. Smith 47
S. R. Waugh **47**
M. A. Atherton **46**
A. R. Butcher **46**
J. Iddon 46
A. R. Morris 46
C. T. Radley 46
Younis Ahmed 46
W. W. Armstrong 45
Asif Iqbal 45
L. G. Berry 45
J. M. Brearley 45
A. W. Carr 45
C. Hill 45
M. D. Moxon 45
N. C. O'Neill 45
E. Paynter 45
Rev. D. S. Sheppard 45
N. R. Taylor **45**
K. D. Walters 45
H. H. Gibbons 44
V. M. Merchant 44
A. Mitchell 44
M. R. Ramprakash **44**
P. E. Richardson 44
B. Sutcliffe 44
G. R. Viswanath 44
A. P. Wells **44**
P. Willey 44
R. J. Bailey **43**
E. J. Barlow 43
T. S. Curtis 43
B. L. D'Oliveira 43
J. H. Hampshire 43
A. F. Kippax 43
J. W. H. Makepeace 43
M. P. Maynard **43**
James Langridge 42
Mudassar Nazar 42
H. W. Parks 42
T. F. Shepherd 42
A. J. Stewart **42**
V. T. Trumper 42
M. J. Harris 41
G. D. Mendis 41
K. R. Miller 41
A. D. Nourse 41
J. H. Parks 41
R. M. Prideaux 41
G. Pullar 41
W. E. Russell 41
Salim Malik **41**
N. H. Fairbrother **40**
R. C. Fredericks 40

J. Gunn 40
M. J. Smith 40
M. A. Taylor **40**
C. L. Walcott 40
D. M. Young 40
Arshad Pervez 39
W. H. Ashdown 39
Asif Mujtaba **39**
J. B. Bolus 39
W. A. Brown 39
R. J. Gregory 39
M. A. Lynch 39
W. R. D. Payton 39
J. R. Reid 39
F. M. M. Worrell 39
I. T. Botham 38
F. L. Bowley 38
P. J. Burge 38
J. F. Crapp 38
N. Hussain **38**
D. Lloyd 38
V. L. Manjrekar 38
A. W. Nourse 38
N. Oldfield 38
Rev. J. H. Parsons 38
W. W. Read 38
Rizwan-uz-Zaman **38**
J. Sharp 38
V. P. Terry 38
L. J. Todd 38
J. J. Whitaker **38**
M. G. Bevan **37**
G. Brown 37
G. Cook 37
P. A. de Silva **37**
G. M. Emmett 37
H. W. Lee 37
M. A. Noble 37
B. P. Patel 37
R. B. Richardson **37**
H. S. Squires 37
R. T. Virgin 37
C. J. B. Wood 37
N. F. Armstrong 36
G. Fowler 36
P. Johnson **36**
M. C. J. Nicholas 36
E. Oldroyd 36
W. Place 36
A. L. Wadekar 36
E. D. Weekes 36
C. S. Dempster 35
S. P. James **35**
D. R. Jardine 35
T. E. Jesty 35
Ajay Sharma **35**
B. H. Valentine 35
G. M. Wood 35

Bold type denotes those who played in 1997-98 and 1998 seasons.

3,000 RUNS IN A SEASON

	Season	I	NO	R	HS	100s	Avge
D. C. S. Compton	1947	50	8	3,816	246	18	90.85
W. J. Edrich	1947	52	8	3,539	267*	12	80.43
T. W. Hayward	1906	61	8	3,518	219	13	66.37
L. Hutton	1949	56	6	3,429	269*	12	68.58
F. E. Woolley	1928	59	4	3,352	198	12	60.94
H. Sutcliffe	1932	52	7	3,336	313	14	74.13
W. R. Hammond	1933	54	5	3,323	264	13	67.81
E. H. Hendren	1928	54	7	3,311	209*	13	70.44
R. Abel	1901	68	8	3,309	247	7	55.15
W. R. Hammond	1937	55	5	3,252	217	13	65.04
M. J. K. Smith	1959	67	11	3,245	200*	8	57.94
E. H. Hendren	1933	65	9	3,186	301*	11	56.89
C. P. Mead	1921	52	6	3,179	280*	10	69.10
T. W. Hayward	1904	63	5	3,170	203	11	54.65
K. S. Ranjitsinhji	1899	58	8	3,159	197	8	63.18
C. B. Fry	1901	43	3	3,147	244	13	78.67
K. S. Ranjitsinhji	1900	40	5	3,065	275	11	87.57
L. E. G. Ames	1933	57	5	3,058	295	9	58.80
J. T. Tyldesley	1901	60	5	3,041	221	9	55.29
C. P. Mead	1928	50	10	3,027	180	13	75.67
J. B. Hobbs	1925	48	5	3,024	266*	16	70.32
E. Tyldesley	1928	48	10	3,024	242	10	79.57
W. E. Alley	1961	64	11	3,019	221*	11	56.96
W. R. Hammond	1938	42	2	3,011	271	15	75.27
E. H. Hendren	1923	51	12	3,010	200*	13	77.17
H. Sutcliffe	1931	42	11	3,006	230	13	96.96
J. H. Parks	1937	63	4	3,003	168	11	50.89
H. Sutcliffe	1928	44	5	3,002	228	13	76.97

Notes: W. G. Grace scored 2,739 runs in 1871 – the first batsman to reach 2,000 runs in a season. He made ten hundreds and twice exceeded 200, with an average of 78.25 in all first-class matches.

The highest aggregate in a season since the reduction of County Championship matches in 1969 is 2,755 by S. J. Cook (42 innings) in 1991.

2,000 RUNS IN A SEASON

Since Reduction of Championship Matches in 1969

Five times: G. A. Gooch 2,746 (1990), 2,559 (1984), 2,324 (1988), 2,208 (1985), 2,023 (1993).

Three times: D. L. Amiss 2,239 (1984), 2,110 (1976), 2,030 (1978); S. J. Cook 2,755 (1991), 2,608 (1990), 2,241 (1989); M. W. Gatting 2,257 (1984), 2,057 (1991), 2,000 (1992); G. A. Hick 2,713 (1988), 2,347 (1990), 2,004 (1986); G. M. Turner 2,416 (1973), 2,379 (1970), 2,101 (1981).

Twice: G. Boycott 2,503 (1971), 2,051 (1970); J. H. Edrich 2,238 (1969), 2,031 (1971); A. I. Kallicharran 2,301 (1984), 2,120 (1982); Zaheer Abbas 2,554 (1976), 2,306 (1981).

Once: M. Azharuddin 2,016 (1991); J. B. Bolus 2,143 (1970); P. D. Bowler 2,044 (1992); B. C. Broad 2,226 (1990); A. R. Butcher 2,116 (1990); C. G. Greenidge 2,035 (1986); M. J. Harris 2,238 (1971); D. L. Haynes 2,346 (1990); Javed Miandad 2,083 (1981); A. J. Lamb 2,049 (1981); B. C. Lara 2,066 (1994); K. S. McEwan 2,176 (1983); Majid Khan 2,074 (1972); A. A. Metcalfe 2,047 (1990); H. Morris 2,276 (1990); M. R. Ramprakash 2,258 (1995); D. W. Randall 2,151 (1979); I. V. A. Richards 2,161 (1977); R. T. Robinson 2,032 (1984); M. A. Roseberry 2,044 (1992); C. L. Smith 2,000 (1985); R. T. Virgin 2,223 (1970); D. M. Ward 2,072 (1990); M. E. Waugh 2,072 (1990).

1,000 RUNS IN A SEASON MOST TIMES

(Includes Overseas Tours and Seasons)

28 times: W. G. Grace 2,000 (6); F. E. Woolley 3,000 (1), 2,000 (12).

27 times: M. C. Cowdrey 2,000 (2); C. P. Mead 3,000 (2), 2,000 (9).

26 times: G. Boycott 2,000 (3); J. B. Hobbs 3,000 (1), 2,000 (16).

25 times: E. H. Hendren 3,000 (3), 2,000 (12).

24 times: D. L. Amiss 2,000 (3); W. G. Quaife 2,000 (1); H. Sutcliffe 3,000 (3), 2,000 (12).

23 times: A. Jones.

22 times: T. W. Graveney 2,000 (7); W. R. Hammond 3,000 (3), 2,000 (9).

21 times: D. Denton 2,000 (5); J. H. Edrich 2,000 (6); G. A. Gooch 2,000 (5); W. Rhodes 2,000 (2).

20 times: D. B. Close; K. W. R. Fletcher; M. W. Gatting 2,000 (3); G. Gunn; T. W. Hayward 3,000 (2), 2,000 (8); James Langridge 2,000 (1); J. M. Parks 2,000 (3); A. Sandham 2,000 (8); M. J. K. Smith 3,000 (1), 2,000 (5); C. Washbrook 2,000 (2).

19 times: J. W. Hearne 2,000 (4); G. H. Hirst 2,000 (3); D. Kenyon 2,000 (7); E. Tyldesley 3,000 (1), 2,000 (5); J. T. Tyldesley 3,000 (1), 2,000 (4).

18 times: L. G. Berry 2,000 (1); H. T. W. Hardinge 2,000 (5); R. E. Marshall 2,000 (6); P. A. Perrin; G. M. Turner 2,000 (3); R. E. S. Wyatt 2,000 (5).

17 times: L. E. G. Ames 3,000 (1), 2,000 (5); T. E. Bailey 2,000 (1); D. Brookes 2,000 (6); D. C. S. Compton 3,000 (1), 2,000 (2); C. G. Greenidge 2,000 (1); L. Hutton 3,000 (1), 2,000 (8); J. G. Langridge 2,000 (11); M. Leyland 2,000 (3); I. V. A. Richards 2,000 (1); K. G. Suttle 2,000 (1); Zaheer Abbas 2,000 (2).

16 times: D. G. Bradman 2,000 (4); D. E. Davies 2,000 (1); E. G. Hayes 2,000 (2); C. A. Milton 2,000 (1); J. O'Connor 2,000 (4); C. T. Radley; James Seymour 2,000 (1); C. J. Tavaré.

15 times: G. Barker; K. J. Barnett; K. F. Barrington 2,000 (3); E. H. Bowley 2,000 (4); M. H. Denness; A. E. Dipper 2,000 (5); H. E. Dollery 2,000 (2); W. J. Edrich 3,000 (1), 2,000 (8); J. H. Hampshire; G. A. Hick 2,000 (3); P. Holmes 2,000 (7); Mushtaq Mohammad; R. B. Nicholls 2,000 (1); P. H. Parfitt 2,000 (3); W. G. A. Parkhouse 2,000 (1); B. A. Richards 2,000 (1); J. D. Robertson 2,000 (9); G. S. Sobers; M. J. Stewart 2,000 (1).

Notes: F. E. Woolley reached 1,000 runs in 28 consecutive seasons (1907-1938), C. P. Mead in 27 (1906-1936).

Outside England, 1,000 runs in a season has been reached most times by D. G. Bradman (in 12 seasons in Australia).

Three batsmen have scored 1,000 runs in a season in each of four different countries: G. S. Sobers in West Indies, England, India and Australia; M. C. Cowdrey and G. Boycott in England, South Africa, West Indies and Australia.

HIGHEST AGGREGATES OUTSIDE ENGLAND

	Season	I	NO	R	HS	100s	Avge
In Australia							
D. G. Bradman	1928-29	24	6	1,690	340*	7	93.88
In South Africa							
J. R. Reid	1961-62	30	2	1,915	203	7	68.39
In West Indies							
E. H. Hendren	1929-30	18	5	1,765	254*	6	135.76
In New Zealand							
M. D. Crowe	1986-87	21	3	1,676	175*	8	93.11
In India							
C. G. Borde	1964-65	28	3	1,604	168	6	64.16
In Pakistan							
Saadat Ali	1983-84	27	1	1,649	208	4	63.42

	Season	I	NO	R	HS	100s	Avge
In Sri Lanka							
R. P. Arnold	1995-96	24	3	1,475	217*	5	70.23
In Zimbabwe							
G. W. Flower..............	1994-95	20	3	983	201*	4	57.82

Note: In more than one country, the following aggregates of over 2,000 runs have been recorded:

M. Amarnath (P/I/WI)	1982-83	34	6	2,234	207	9	79.78
J. R. Reid (SA/A/NZ)	1961-62	40	2	2,188	203	7	57.57
S. M. Gavaskar (I/P)	1978-79	30	6	2,121	205	10	88.37
R. B. Simpson (I/P/A/WI).	1964-65	34	4	2,063	201	8	68.76

LEADING BATSMEN IN AN ENGLISH SEASON

(Qualification: 8 completed innings)

Season	Leading scorer	Runs	Avge	Top of averages	Runs	Avge
1946	D. C. S. Compton . . .	2,403	61.61	W. R. Hammond	1,783	84.90
1947	D. C. S. Compton . . .	3,816	90.85	D. C. S. Compton . . .	3,816	90.85
1948	L. Hutton	2,654	64.73	D. G. Bradman	2,428	89.92
1949	L. Hutton	3,429	68.58	J. Hardstaff.	2,251	72.61
1950	R. T. Simpson	2,576	62.82	E. Weekes	2,310	79.65
1951	J. D. Robertson	2,917	56.09	P. B. H. May	2,339	68.79
1952	L. Hutton	2,567	61.11	D. S. Sheppard	2,262	64.62
1953	W. J. Edrich	2,557	47.35	R. N. Harvey	2,040	65.80
1954	D. Kenyon	2,636	51.68	D. C. S. Compton . . .	1,524	58.61
1955	D. J. Insole	2,427	42.57	D. J. McGlew	1,871	58.46
1956	T. W. Graveney	2,397	49.93	K. Mackay	1,103	52.52
1957	T. W. Graveney	2,361	49.18	P. B. H. May	2,347	61.76
1958	P. B. H. May	2,231	63.74	P. B. H. May	2,231	63.74
1959	M. J. K. Smith	3,245	57.94	V. L. Manjrekar.	755	68.63
1960	M. J. K. Smith	2,551	45.55	R. Subba Row.	1,503	55.66
1961	W. E. Alley	3,019	56.96	W. M. Lawry	2,019	61.18
1962	J. H. Edrich	2,482	51.70	R. T. Simpson	867	54.18
1963	J. B. Bolus	2,190	41.32	G. S. Sobers	1,333	47.60
1964	T. W. Graveney	2,385	54.20	K. F. Barrington	1,872	62.40
1965	J. H. Edrich	2,319	62.67	M. C. Cowdrey	2,093	63.42
1966	A. R. Lewis	2,198	41.47	G. S. Sobers	1,349	61.31
1967	C. A. Milton	2,089	46.42	K. F. Barrington	2,059	68.63
1968	B. A. Richards	2,395	47.90	G. Boycott	1,487	64.65
1969	J. H. Edrich	2,238	69.93	J. H. Edrich	2,238	69.93
1970	G. M. Turner	2,379	61.00	G. S. Sobers	1,742	75.73
1971	G. Boycott	2,503	100.12	G. Boycott	2,503	100.12
1972	Majid Khan	2,074	61.00	G. Boycott	1,230	72.35
1973	G. M. Turner	2,416	67.11	G. M. Turner	2,416	67.11
1974	R. T. Virgin	1,936	56.94	C. H. Lloyd	1,458	63.39
1975	G. Boycott	1,915	73.65	R. B. Kanhai	1,073	82.53
1976	Zaheer Abbas.	2,554	75.11	Zaheer Abbas	2,554	75.11
1977	I. V. A. Richards	2,161	65.48	G. Boycott	1,701	68.04
1978	D. L. Amiss.	2,030	53.42	C. E. B. Rice	1,871	66.82
1979	K. C. Wessels	1,800	52.94	G. Boycott	1,538	102.53
1980	P. N. Kirsten	1,895	63.16	A. J. Lamb.	1,797	66.55
1981	Zaheer Abbas.	2,306	88.69	Zaheer Abbas	2,306	88.69
1982	A. I. Kallicharran	2,120	66.25	G. M. Turner	1,171	90.07
1983	K. S. McEwan	2,176	64.00	I. V. A. Richards	1,204	75.25
1984	G. A. Gooch	2,559	67.34	C. G. Greenidge	1,069	82.23
1985	G. A. Gooch	2,208	71.22	I. V. A. Richards	1,836	76.50
1986	C. G. Greenidge	2,035	67.83	C. G. Greenidge	2,035	67.83

Season	Leading scorer	Runs	Avge	Top of averages	Runs	Avge
1987	G. A. Hick	1,879	52.19	M. D. Crowe	1,627	67.79
1988	G. A. Hick	2,713	77.51	R. A. Harper	622	77.75
1989	S. J. Cook	2,241	60.56	D. M. Jones	1,510	88.82
1990	G. A. Gooch	2,746	101.70	G. A. Gooch	2,746	101.70
1991	S. J. Cook	2,755	81.02	C. L. Hooper	1,501	93.81
1992	{ P. D. Bowler	2,044	65.93	Salim Malik	1,184	78.93
	{ M. A. Roseberry . . .	2,044	56.77			
1993	G. A. Gooch	2,023	63.21	D. C. Boon	1,437	75.63
1994	B. C. Lara	2,066	89.82	J. D. Carr	1,543	90.76
1995	M. R. Ramprakash . .	2,258	77.86	M. R. Ramprakash . .	2,258	77.86
1996	G. A. Gooch	1,944	67.03	S. C. Ganguly	762	95.25
1997	S. P. James	1,775	68.26	G. A. Hick	1,524	69.27
1998	J. P. Crawley	1,851	74.04	J. P. Crawley	1,851	74.04

Notes: The highest average recorded in an English season was 115.66 (2,429 runs, 26 innings) by D. G. Bradman in 1938.

In 1953 W. A. Johnston averaged 102.00 from 17 innings, 16 not out.

25,000 RUNS IN A CAREER

Dates in italics denote the first half of an overseas season; i.e. *1945* denotes the 1945-46 season.

		Career	R	I	NO	HS	100s	Avge
1	J. B. Hobbs	1905-34	61,237	1,315	106	316*	197	50.65
2	F. E. Woolley	1906-38	58,969	1,532	85	305*	145	40.75
3	E. H. Hendren	1907-38	57,611	1,300	166	301*	170	50.80
4	C. P. Mead	1905-36	55,061	1,340	185	280*	153	47.67
5	W. G. Grace	1865-1908	54,896	1,493	105	344	126	39.55
6	W. R. Hammond	1920-51	50,551	1,005	104	336*	167	56.10
7	H. Sutcliffe	1919-45	50,138	1,088	123	313	149	51.95
8	G. Boycott	1962-86	48,426	1,014	162	261*	151	56.83
9	T. W. Graveney	1948-*71*	47,793	1,223	159	258	122	44.91
10	G. A. Gooch	1973-*97*	44,841	988	75	333	128	49.11
11	T. W. Hayward	1893-1914	43,551	1,138	96	315*	104	41.79
12	D. L. Amiss	1960-87	43,423	1,139	126	262*	102	42.86
13	M. C. Cowdrey	1950-76	42,719	1,130	134	307	107	42.89
14	A. Sandham	1911-37	41,284	1,000	79	325	107	44.82
15	L. Hutton	1934-60	40,140	814	91	364	129	55.51
16	M. J. K. Smith	1951-75	39,832	1,091	139	204	69	41.84
17	W. Rhodes	1898-1930	39,802	1,528	237	267*	58	30.83
18	J. H. Edrich	1956-78	39,790	979	104	310*	103	45.47
19	R. E. S. Wyatt	1923-57	39,405	1,141	157	232	85	40.04
20	D. C. S. Compton . . .	1936-64	38,942	839	88	300	123	51.85
21	E. Tyldesley	1909-36	38,874	961	106	256*	102	45.46
22	J. T. Tyldesley	1895-1923	37,897	994	62	295*	86	40.66
23	K. W. R. Fletcher	1962-88	37,665	1,167	170	228*	63	37.77
24	C. G. Greenidge	1970-92	37,354	889	75	273*	92	45.88
25	J. W. Hearne	1909-36	37,252	1,025	116	285*	96	40.98
26	L. E. G. Ames	1926-*51*	37,248	951	95	295	102	43.51
27	D. Kenyon	1946-67	37,002	1,159	59	259	74	33.63
28	W. J. Edrich	1934-58	36,965	964	92	267*	86	42.39
29	J. M. Parks	1949-76	36,673	1,227	172	205*	51	34.76
30	**M. W. Gatting . . . . .**	**1975-98**	**36,549**	**861**	**123**	**258**	**94**	**49.52**
31	D. Denton	1894-1920	36,479	1,163	70	221	69	33.37
32	G. H. Hirst	1891-1929	36,323	1,215	151	341	60	34.13
33	I. V. A. Richards	*1971*-93	36,212	796	63	322	114	49.40
34	A. Jones	1957-83	36,049	1,168	72	204*	56	32.89
35	W. G. Quaife	1894-1928	36,012	1,203	185	255*	72	35.37
36	R. E. Marshall	*1945*-72	35,725	1,053	59	228*	68	35.94

		Career	R	I	NO	HS	100s	Avge
37	G. Gunn	1902-32	35,208	1,061	82	220	62	35.96
38	D. B. Close	1949-86	34,994	1,225	173	198	52	33.26
39	Zaheer Abbas.	*1965-86*	34,843	768	92	274	108	51.54
40	J. G. Langridge	1928-55	34,380	984	66	250*	76	37.45
41	G. M. Turner	*1964-82*	34,346	792	101	311*	103	49.70
42	C. Washbrook	1933-64	34,101	906	107	251*	76	42.67
43	M. Leyland	1920-48	33,660	932	101	263	80	40.50
44	H. T. W. Hardinge . .	1902-33	33,519	1,021	103	263*	75	36.51
45	R. Abel.	1881-1904	33,124	1,007	73	357*	74	35.46
46	A. I. Kallicharran . .	*1966-90*	32,650	834	86	243*	87	43.64
47	A. J. Lamb	*1972-95*	32,502	772	108	294	89	48.94
48	C. A. Milton	1948-74	32,150	1,078	125	170	56	33.73
49	J. D. Robertson	1937-59	31,914	897	46	331*	67	37.50
50	J. Hardstaff, jun. . . .	1930-55	31,847	812	94	266	83	44.35
51	James Langridge	1924-53	31,716	1,058	157	167	42	35.20
52	K. F. Barrington . . .	1953-68	31,714	831	136	256	76	45.63
53	C. H. Lloyd.	*1963-86*	31,232	730	96	242*	79	49.26
54	Mushtaq Mohammad .	*1956-85*	31,091	843	104	303*	72	42.07
55	C. B. Fry	1892-*1921*	30,886	658	43	258*	94	50.22
56	D. Brookes	1934-59	30,874	925	70	257	71	36.10
57	P. Holmes	1913-35	30,573	810	84	315*	67	42.11
58	R. T. Simpson	*1944*-63	30,546	852	55	259	64	38.32
59	{ L. G. Berry	1924-51	30,225	1,056	57	232	45	30.25
	{ K. G. Suttle	1949-71	30,225	1,064	92	204*	49	31.09
61	**G. A. Hick . . . . . .**	***1983-98***	**29,777**	**595**	**59**	**405***	**103**	**55.55**
62	P. A. Perrin	1896-1928	29,709	918	91	343*	66	35.92
63	P. F. Warner	1894-1929	29,028	875	75	244	60	36.28
64	R. B. Kanhai	*1954-81*	28,774	669	82	256	83	49.01
65	J. O'Connor	1921-39	28,764	903	79	248	72	34.90
66	Javed Miandad.	*1973-93*	28,647	631	95	311	80	53.44
67	T. E. Bailey.	1945-67	28,641	1,072	215	205	28	33.42
68	D. W. Randall	1972-93	28,456	827	81	237	52	38.14
69	E. H. Bowley.	1912-34	28,378	859	47	283	52	34.94
70	B. A. Richards	*1964-82*	28,358	576	58	356	80	54.74
71	G. S. Sobers	*1952-74*	28,315	609	93	365*	86	54.87
72	A. E. Dipper	1908-32	28,075	865	69	252*	53	35.27
73	D. G. Bradman	*1927-48*	28,067	338	43	452*	117	95.14
74	J. H. Hampshire	1961-84	28,059	924	112	183*	43	34.55
75	P. B. H. May	1948-63	27,592	618	77	285*	85	51.00
76	B. F. Davison	*1967-87*	27,453	766	79	189	53	39.96
77	Majid Khan.	*1961-84*	27,444	700	62	241	73	43.01
78	A. C. Russell	1908-30	27,358	717	59	273	71	41.57
79	E. G. Hayes	1896-1926	27,318	896	48	276	48	32.21
80	A. E. Fagg	1932-57	27,291	803	46	269*	58	36.05
81	James Seymour	1900-26	27,237	911	62	218*	53	32.08
82	W. Larkins	1972-95	27,142	842	54	252	59	34.44
83	A. R. Border	*1976-95*	27,131	625	97	205	70	51.38
84	**R. T. Robinson . . . .**	**1978-98**	**27,046**	**717**	**84**	**220***	**63**	**42.72**
85	P. H. Parfitt	1956-*73*	26,924	845	104	200*	58	36.33
86	G. L. Jessop	1894-1914	26,698	855	37	286	53	32.63
87	K. S. McEwan	*1972-91*	26,628	705	67	218	74	41.73
88	D. E. Davies	1924-54	26,564	1,032	80	287*	32	27.90
89	A. Shrewsbury	1875-1902	26,505	813	90	267	59	36.65
90	M. J. Stewart	1954-72	26,492	898	93	227*	49	32.90
91	C. T. Radley	1964-87	26,441	880	134	200	46	35.44
92	D. I. Gower	1975-93	26,339	727	70	228	53	40.08
93	C. E. B. Rice.	*1969-93*	26,331	766	123	246	48	40.95
94	Younis Ahmed	*1961-86*	26,073	762	118	221*	46	40.48
95	P. E. Richardson . . .	1949-65	26,055	794	41	185	44	34.60
96	D. L. Haynes	1976-96	26,030	639	72	255*	61	45.90

		Career	R	I	NO	HS	100s	Avge
97	M. H. Denness.....	1959-80	25,886	838	65	195	33	33.48
98	S. M. Gavaskar....	1966-87	25,834	563	61	340	81	51.46
99	J. W. H. Makepeace .	1906-30	25,799	778	66	203	43	36.23
100	W. Gunn.........	1880-1904	25,691	850	72	273	48	33.02
101	W. Watson........	1939-64	25,670	753	109	257	55	39.86
102	G. Brown	1908-33	25,649	1,012	52	232*	37	26.71
103	J. H. Emmett	1936-59	25,602	865	50	188	37	31.41
104	J. B. Bolus	1956-75	25,598	833	81	202*	39	34.03
105	**K. J. Barnett**	**1979-98**	**25,556**	**702**	**68**	**239***	**53**	**40.30**
106	W. E. Russell.....	1956-72	25,525	796	64	193	41	34.87
107	C. W. J. Athey.....	1976-97	25,453	784	71	184	55	35.69
108	C. J. Barnett	1927-53	25,389	821	45	259	48	32.71
109	L. B. Fishlock	1931-52	25,376	699	54	253	56	39.34
110	D. J. Insole	1947-63	25,241	743	72	219*	54	37.61
111	J. M. Brearley ...	1961-83	25,185	768	102	312*	45	37.81
112	J. Vine	1896-1922	25,171	920	79	202	34	29.92
113	R. M. Prideaux	1958-74	25,136	808	75	202*	41	34.29
114	J. H. King........	1895-1925	25,122	988	69	227*	34	27.33
115	J. G. Wright	1975-92	25,073	636	44	192	59	42.35

Bold type denotes those who played in 1997-98 and 1998 seasons.

Note: Some works of reference provide career figures which differ from those in this list, owing to the exclusion or inclusion of matches recognised or not recognised as first-class by *Wisden*.

Current Players with 20,000 Runs

	Career	R	I	NO	HS	100s	Avge
K. C. Wessels	1973-97	24,392	527	50	254	66	51.13
A. R. Butcher	1972-98	22,667	684	60	216*	46	36.32
R. A. Smith..........	1980-98	22,498	593	80	209*	56	43.85
D. C. Boon	1978-98	22,314	543	50	227	67	45.26
A. J. Stewart	1981-98	21,466	590	65	271*	42	40.88
M. E. Waugh.........	1985-97	20,925	443	56	229*	67	54.06
A. P. Wells	1981-98	20,312	594	79	253*	44	39.44
T. M. Moody..........	1985-98	20,143	465	41	272	63	47.50

CAREER AVERAGE OVER 50

(Qualification: 10,000 runs)

Avge		Career	I	NO	R	HS	100s
95.14	D. G. Bradman	1927-48	338	43	28,067	452*	117
71.22	V. M. Merchant	1929-51	229	43	13,248	359*	44
65.18	W. H. Ponsford	1920-34	235	23	13,819	437	47
64.99	W. M. Woodfull	1921-34	245	39	13,388	284	49
60.11	**S. R. Tendulkar**	**1988-97**	**207**	**21**	**11,181**	**204***	**34**
58.24	A. L. Hassett	1932-53	322	32	16,890	232	59
58.19	V. S. Hazare	1934-66	365	45	18,621	316*	60
57.22	A. F. Kippax	1918-35	256	33	12,762	315*	43
56.83	G. Boycott	1962-86	1,014	162	48,426	261*	151
56.55	C. L. Walcott	1941-63	238	29	11,820	314*	40
56.37	K. S. Ranjitsinhji	1893-1920	500	62	24,692	285*	72
56.22	R. B. Simpson	1952-77	436	62	21,029	359	60
56.10	W. R. Hammond	1920-51	1,005	104	50,551	336*	167
56.02	M. D. Crowe	1979-95	412	62	19,608	299	71
55.55	**G. A. Hick**	**1983-98**	**595**	**59**	**29,777**	**405***	**103**
55.51	L. Hutton	1934-60	814	91	40,140	364	129
55.34	E. D. Weekes	1944-64	241	24	12,010	304*	36

Avge		Career	I	NO	R	HS	100s
55.11	**S. V. Manjrekar**	**1984-97**	**217**	**31**	**10,252**	**377**	**31**
54.87	G. S. Sobers	1952-74	609	93	28,315	365*	86
54.74	B. A. Richards	1964-82	576	58	28,358	356	80
54.67	R. G. Pollock	1960-86	437	54	20,940	274	64
54.24	F. M. M. Worrell	1941-64	326	49	15,025	308*	39
54.17	**M. L. Hayden**	**1991-98**	**216**	**23**	**10,455**	**235***	**33**
54.06	**M. E. Waugh**	**1985-97**	**443**	**56**	**20,925**	**229***	**67**
53.78	R. M. Cowper	1959-69	228	31	10,595	307	26
53.67	A. R. Morris	1940-63	250	15	12,614	290	46
53.44	Javed Miandad	1973-93	631	95	28,647	311	80
53.13	**M. G. Bevan**	**1989-98**	**259**	**44**	**11,423**	**203***	**37**
52.86	D. B. Vengsarkar	1975-91	390	52	17,868	284	55
52.32	Hanif Mohammad	1951-75	371	45	17,059	499	55
52.27	P. R. Umrigar	1944-67	350	41	16,154	252*	49
52.20	G. S. Chappell	1966-83	542	72	24,535	247*	74
52.01	**D. S. Lehmann**	**1987-98**	**228**	**11**	**11,288**	**255**	**33**
51.98	**M. Azharuddin**	**1981-97**	**313**	**34**	**14,504**	**226**	**50**
51.95	H. Sutcliffe	1919-45	1,088	123	50,138	313	149
51.94	**S. R. Waugh**	**1984-98**	**385**	**65**	**16,623**	**216***	**47**
51.85	**D. M. Jones**	**1981-97**	**415**	**45**	**19,188**	**324***	**55**
51.85	D. C. S. Compton	1936-64	839	88	38,942	300	123
51.54	Zaheer Abbas	1965-86	768	92	34,843	274	108
51.53	A. D. Nourse	1931-52	269	27	12,472	260*	41
51.46	S. M. Gavaskar	1966-87	563	61	25,834	340	81
51.44	W. A. Brown	1932-49	284	15	13,838	265*	39
51.38	A. R. Border	1976-95	625	97	27,131	205	70
51.13	**K. C. Wessels**	**1973-97**	**527**	**50**	**24,392**	**254**	**66**
51.12	**Asif Mujtaba**	**1984-97**	**330**	**65**	**13,549**	**208**	**39**
51.11	**B. C. Lara**	**1987-98**	**255**	**7**	**12,676**	**501***	**34**
51.00	P. B. H. May	1948-63	618	77	27,592	285*	85
50.95	N. C. O'Neill	1955-67	306	34	13,859	284	45
50.93	R. N. Harvey	1946-62	461	35	21,699	231*	67
50.90	W. M. Lawry	1955-71	417	49	18,734	266	50
50.90	A. V. Mankad	1963-82	326	71	12,980	265	31
50.80	E. H. Hendren	1907-38	1,300	166	57,611	301*	170
50.65	J. B. Hobbs	1905-34	1,315	106	61,237	316*	197
50.58	S. J. Cook	1972-94	475	57	21,143	313*	64
50.51	**J. P. Crawley**	**1990-98**	**288**	**29**	**13,083**	**286**	**30**
50.22	C. B. Fry	1892-1921	658	43	30,886	258*	94
50.01	Shafiq Ahmad	1967-90	449	58	19,555	217*	53

Note: G. A. Headley (1927-1954) scored 9,921 runs, average 69.86.

Bold type denotes those who played in 1997-98 and 1998 seasons.

FASTEST FIFTIES

Minutes			
11	C. I. J. Smith (66)	Middlesex v Gloucestershire at Bristol	1938
14	S. J. Pegler (50)	South Africans v Tasmania at Launceston	1910-11
14	F. T. Mann (53)	Middlesex v Nottinghamshire at Lord's	1921
14	H. B. Cameron (56)	Transvaal v Orange Free State at Johannesburg. . .	1934-35
14	C. I. J. Smith (52)	Middlesex v Kent at Maidstone	1935

Note: The following fastest fifties were scored in contrived circumstances when runs were given from full tosses and long hops to expedite a declaration: C. C. Inman (8 minutes), Leicestershire v Nottinghamshire at Nottingham, 1965; G. Chapple (10 minutes), Lancashire v Glamorgan at Manchester, 1993; T. M. Moody (11 minutes), Warwickshire v Glamorgan at Swansea, 1990; A. J. Stewart (14 minutes), Surrey v Kent at Dartford, 1986; M. P. Maynard (14 minutes), Glamorgan v Yorkshire at Cardiff, 1987.

FASTEST HUNDREDS

Minutes

35	P. G. H. Fender (113*)	Surrey v Northamptonshire at Northampton	1920
40	G. L. Jessop (101)	Gloucestershire v Yorkshire at Harrogate	1897
40	Ahsan-ul-Haq (100*)	Muslims v Sikhs at Lahore	1923-24
42	G. L. Jessop (191)	Gentlemen of South v Players of South at Hastings	1907
43	A. H. Hornby (106)	Lancashire v Somerset at Manchester	1905
43	D. W. Hookes (107)	South Australia v Victoria at Adelaide	1982-83
44	R. N. S. Hobbs (100)	Essex v Australians at Chelmsford	1975

Notes: The fastest recorded authentic hundred in terms of balls received was scored off 34 balls by D. W. Hookes (above).

Research of the scorebook has shown that P. G. H. Fender scored his hundred from between 40 and 46 balls. He contributed 113 to an unfinished sixth-wicket partnership of 171 in 42 minutes with H. A. Peach.

E. B. Alletson (Nottinghamshire) scored 189 out of 227 runs in 90 minutes against Sussex at Hove in 1911. It has been estimated that his last 139 runs took 37 minutes.

The following fast hundreds were scored in contrived circumstances when runs were given from full tosses and long hops to expedite a declaration: G. Chapple (21 minutes), Lancashire v Glamorgan at Manchester, 1993; T. M. Moody (26 minutes), Warwickshire v Glamorgan at Swansea, 1990; S. J. O'Shaughnessy (35 minutes), Lancashire v Leicestershire at Manchester, 1983; C. M. Old (37 minutes), Yorkshire v Warwickshire at Birmingham, 1977; N. F. M. Popplewell (41 minutes), Somerset v Gloucestershire at Bath, 1983.

FASTEST DOUBLE-HUNDREDS

Minutes

113	R. J. Shastri (200*)	Bombay v Baroda at Bombay	1984-85
120	G. L. Jessop (286)	Gloucestershire v Sussex at Hove	1903
120	C. H. Lloyd (201*)	West Indians v Glamorgan at Swansea	1976
130	G. L. Jessop (234)	Gloucestershire v Somerset at Bristol	1905
131	V. T. Trumper (293)	Australians v Canterbury at Christchurch	1913-14

FASTEST TRIPLE-HUNDREDS

Minutes

181	D. C. S. Compton (300)	MCC v N. E. Transvaal at Benoni	1948-49
205	F. E. Woolley (305*)	MCC v Tasmania at Hobart	1911-12
205	C. G. Macartney (345)	Australians v Nottinghamshire at Nottingham	1921
213	D. G. Bradman (369)	South Australia v Tasmania at Adelaide	1935-36

300 RUNS IN ONE DAY

390*	B. C. Lara	Warwickshire v Durham at Birmingham	1994
345	C. G. Macartney	Australians v Nottinghamshire at Nottingham	1921
334	W. H. Ponsford	Victoria v New South Wales at Melbourne	1926-27
333	K. S. Duleepsinhji	Sussex v Northamptonshire at Hove	1930
331*	J. D. Robertson	Middlesex v Worcestershire at Worcester	1949
325*	B. A. Richards	S. Australia v W. Australia at Perth	1970-71
322†	E. Paynter	Lancashire v Sussex at Hove	1937
322	I. V. A. Richards	Somerset v Warwickshire at Taunton	1985
318	C. W. Gregory	New South Wales v Queensland at Brisbane	1906-07
317	K. R. Rutherford	New Zealanders v D. B. Close's XI at Scarborough	1986

316†	R. H. Moore	Hampshire v Warwickshire at Bournemouth	1937
315*	R. C. Blunt	Otago v Canterbury at Christchurch	1931-32
312*	J. M. Brearley	MCC Under-25 v North Zone at Peshawar	1966-67
311*	G. M. Turner	Worcestershire v Warwickshire at Worcester	1982
311*	N. H. Fairbrother	Lancashire v Surrey at The Oval	1990
309*	D. G. Bradman	Australia v England at Leeds	1930
307*	W. H. Ashdown	Kent v Essex at Brentwood	1934
306*	A. Ducat	Surrey v Oxford University at The Oval	1919
305*	F. R. Foster	Warwickshire v Worcestershire at Dudley	1914

† E. Paynter's 322 and R. H. Moore's 316 were scored on the same day: July 28, 1937.

These scores do not necessarily represent the complete innings. See pages 188-190.

1,000 RUNS IN MAY

	Runs	Avge
W. G. Grace, May 9 to May 30, 1895 (22 days):	1,016	112.88
13, 103, 18, 25, 288, 52, 257, 73*, 18, 169		
Grace was within two months of completing his 47th year.		
W. R. Hammond, May 7 to May 31, 1927 (25 days):	1,042	74.42
27, 135, 108, 128, 17, 11, 99, 187, 4, 30, 83, 7, 192, 14		
Hammond scored his 1,000th run on May 28, thus equalling		
Grace's record of 22 days.		
C. Hallows, May 5 to May 31, 1928 (27 days):	1,000	125.00
100, 101, 51*, 123, 101*, 22, 74, 104, 58, 34*, 232		

1,000 RUNS IN APRIL AND MAY

	Runs	Avge
T. W. Hayward, April 16 to May 31, 1900:	1,074	97.63
120*, 55, 108, 131*, 55, 193, 120, 5, 6, 3, 40, 146, 92		
D. G. Bradman, April 30 to May 31, 1930:	1,001	143.00
236, 185*, 78, 9, 48*, 66, 4, 44, 252*, 32, 47*		
On April 30 Bradman was 75 not out.		
D. G. Bradman, April 30 to May 31, 1938:	1,056	150.85
258, 58, 137, 278, 2, 143, 145*, 5, 30*		
Bradman scored 258 on April 30, and his 1,000th run on May 27.		
W. J. Edrich, April 30 to May 31, 1938:	1,010	84.16
104, 37, 115, 63, 20*, 182, 71, 31, 53*, 45, 15, 245, 0, 9, 20*		
Edrich was 21 not out on April 30. All his runs were scored at Lord's.		
G. M. Turner, April 24 to May 31, 1973:	1,018	78.30
41, 151*, 143, 85, 7, 8, 17*, 81, 13, 53, 44, 153*, 3, 2, 66*, 30, 10*, 111		
G. A. Hick, April 17 to May 29, 1988:	1,019	101.90
61, 37, 212, 86, 14, 405*, 8, 11, 6, 7, 172		
Hick scored a record 410 runs in April, and his 1,000th run on May 28.		

1,000 RUNS IN TWO SEPARATE MONTHS

Only four batsmen, C. B. Fry, K. S. Ranjitsinhji, H. Sutcliffe and L. Hutton, have scored over 1,000 runs in each of two months in the same season. L. Hutton, by scoring 1,294 in June 1949, made more runs in a single month than anyone else. He also made 1,050 in August 1949.

MOST RUNS SCORED OFF ONE OVER

(All instances refer to six-ball overs)

36	G. S. Sobers	off M. A. Nash, Nottinghamshire v Glamorgan at Swansea (six sixes)	1968
36	R. J. Shastri	off Tilak Raj, Bombay v Baroda at Bombay (six sixes)	1984-85
34	E. B. Alletson	off E. H. Killick, Nottinghamshire v Sussex at Hove (46604446; including two no-balls)	1911
34	F. C. Hayes	off M. A. Nash, Lancashire v Glamorgan at Swansea (646666)	1977
34†	A. Flintoff	off A. J. Tudor, Lancashire v Surrey at Manchester (64444660; including two no-balls)	1998
32	I. T. Botham	off I. R. Snook, England XI v Central Districts at Palmerston North (466666)	1983-84
32	P. W. G. Parker	off A. I. Kallicharran, Sussex v Warwickshire at Birmingham (466664)	1982
32	I. R. Redpath	off N. Rosendorff, Australians v Orange Free State at Bloemfontein (666644)	1969-70
32	C. C. Smart	off G. Hill, Glamorgan v Hampshire at Cardiff (664664)	1935

† *Altogether 38 runs were scored off this over, the two no-balls counting for two extra runs each under ECB regulations.*

Notes: The following instances have been excluded from the above table because of the bowlers' compliance: 34 – M. P. Maynard off S. A. Marsh, Glamorgan v Kent at Swansea, 1992; 34 – G. Chapple off P. A. Cottey, Lancashire v Glamorgan at Manchester, 1993; 34 – F. B. Touzel off F. J. J. Viljoen, Western Province B v Griqualand West at Kimberley, 1993-94; 32 – C. C. Inman off N. W. Hill, Leicestershire v Nottinghamshire at Nottingham, 1965; 32 – T. E. Jesty off R. J. Boyd-Moss, Hampshire v Northamptonshire at Southampton, 1984; 32 – M. A. Ealham off G. D. Hodgson, Kent v Gloucestershire at Bristol, 1992; 32 – G. Chapple off P. A. Cottey, Lancashire v Glamorgan at Manchester, 1993. Chapple's 34 and 32 came off successive overs from Cottey.

There were 35 runs off an over received by A. T. Reinholds off H. T. Davis, Auckland v Wellington at Auckland 1995-96, but this included six no-balls (counting as two runs each), four byes and only 19 off the bat.

The greatest number of runs scored off an eight-ball over is 34 (40446664) by R. M. Edwards off M. C. Carew, Governor-General's XI v West Indians at Auckland, 1968-69.

In a Shell Trophy match against Canterbury at Christchurch in 1989-90, R. H. Vance (Wellington), acting on the instructions of his captain, deliberately conceded 77 runs in an over of full tosses which contained 17 no-balls and, owing to the umpire's understandable miscalculation, only five legitimate deliveries.

MOST SIXES IN AN INNINGS

16	A. Symonds (254*)	Gloucestershire v Glamorgan at Abergavenny	1995
15	J. R. Reid (296)	Wellington v Northern Districts at Wellington	1962-63
14	Shakti Singh (128)	Himachal Pradesh v Haryana at Dharmsala	1990-91
13	Majid Khan (147*)	Pakistanis v Glamorgan at Swansea	1967
13	C. G. Greenidge (273*)	D. H. Robins' XI v Pakistanis at Eastbourne	1974
13	C. G. Greenidge (259)	Hampshire v Sussex at Southampton	1975
13	G. W. Humpage (254)	Warwickshire v Lancashire at Southport	1982
13	R. J. Shastri (200*)	Bombay v Baroda at Bombay	1984-85
12	Gulfraz Khan (207)	Railways v Universities at Lahore	1976-77
12	I. T. Botham (138*)	Somerset v Warwickshire at Birmingham	1985
12	R. A. Harper (234)	Northamptonshire v Gloucestershire at Northampton	1986
12	D. M. Jones (248)	Australians v Warwickshire at Birmingham	1989
12	U. N. K. Fernando (160)	Sinhalese SC v Sebastianites C and AC at Colombo	1990-91
12	D. N. Patel (204)	Auckland v Northern Districts at Auckland	1991-92
12	W. V. Raman (206)	Tamil Nadu v Kerala at Madras	1991-92

12	G. D. Lloyd (241)	Lancashire v Essex at Chelmsford	1996
12	Wasim Akram (257*)	Pakistan v Zimbabwe at Sheikhupura	1996-97
11	C. K. Nayudu (153)	Hindus v MCC at Bombay	1926-27
11	C. J. Barnett (194)	Gloucestershire v Somerset at Bath.	1934
11	R. Benaud (135)	Australians v T. N. Pearce's XI at Scarborough.	1953
11	R. Bora (126)	Assam v Tripura at Gauhati.	1987-88
11	G. A. Hick (405*)	Worcestershire v Somerset at Taunton	1988
11	A. S. Jayasinghe (183)	Tamil Union v Burgher RC at Colombo	1996-97

Note: F. B. Touzel (128*) hit 13 sixes for Western Province B v Griqualand West in contrived circumstances at Kimberley in 1993-94.

MOST SIXES IN A MATCH

20	A. Symonds (254*, 76)	Gloucestershire v Glamorgan at Abergavenny	1995
17	W. J. Stewart (155, 125)	Warwickshire v Lancashire at Blackpool	1959

MOST SIXES IN A SEASON

80	I. T. Botham	1985		49	I. V. A. Richards	1985
66	A. W. Wellard	1935		48	A. W. Carr.	1925
57	A. W. Wellard	1936		48	J. H. Edrich	1965
57	A. W. Wellard	1938		48	A. Symonds	1995
51	A. W. Wellard	1933				

MOST BOUNDARIES IN AN INNINGS

	4s/6s			
72	62/10	B. C. Lara (501*)	Warwickshire v Durham at Birmingham.	1994
68	68/–	P. A. Perrin (343*)	Essex v Derbyshire at Chesterfield	1904
65	64/1	A. C. MacLaren (424)	Lancashire v Somerset at Taunton	1895
64	64/–	Hanif Mohammad (499)	Karachi v Bahawalpur at Karachi	1958-59
57	52/5	J. H. Edrich (310*)	England v New Zealand at Leeds	1965
55	55/–	C. W. Gregory (383)	NSW v Queensland at Brisbane	1906-07
55	51/3†	S. V. Manjrekar (377)	Bombay v Hyderabad at Bombay	1990-91
55	53/2	G. R. Marsh (355*)	W. Australia v S. Australia at Perth. . . .	1989-90
54	53/1	G. H. Hirst (341)	Yorkshire v Leicestershire at Leicester . . .	1905
53	53/–	A. W. Nourse (304*)	Natal v Transvaal at Johannesburg	1919-20
53	45/8	K. R. Rutherford (317)	New Zealanders v D. B. Close's XI at Scarborough	1986
52	47/5	N. H. Fairbrother (366)	Lancashire v Surrey at The Oval	1990
51	51/–	W. G. Grace (344)	MCC v Kent at Canterbury	1876
51	47/4	C. G. Macartney (345)	Australians v Notts at Nottingham	1921
51	50/1	B. B. Nimbalkar (443*)	Maharashtra v Kathiawar at Poona	1948-49
50	46/4	D. G. Bradman (369)	S. Australia v Tasmania at Adelaide . . .	1935-36
50	47/–‡	A. Ducat (306*)	Surrey v Oxford U. at The Oval.	1919
50	35/15	J. R. Reid (296)	Wellington v N. Districts at Wellington .	1962-63
50	42/8	I. V. A. Richards (322)	Somerset v Warwickshire at Taunton . . .	1985

† *Plus one five.*
‡ *Plus three fives.*

PARTNERSHIPS OVER 500

577	V. S. Hazare (288) and Gul Mahomed (319), fourth wicket, Baroda v Holkar at Baroda	1946-47
576	S. T. Jayasuriya (340) and R. S. Mahanama (225), second wicket, Sri Lanka v India at Colombo	1997-98
574*	F. M. M. Worrell (255*) and C. L. Walcott (314*), fourth wicket, Barbados v Trinidad at Port-of-Spain	1945-46
561	Waheed Mirza (324) and Mansoor Akhtar (224*), first wicket, Karachi Whites v Quetta at Karachi	1976-77
555	P. Holmes (224*) and H. Sutcliffe (313), first wicket, Yorkshire v Essex at Leyton	1932
554	J. T. Brown (300) and J. Tunnicliffe (243), first wicket, Yorkshire v Derbyshire at Chesterfield	1898
502*	F. M. M. Worrell (308*) and J. D. C. Goddard (218*), fourth wicket, Barbados v Trinidad at Bridgetown	1943-44

HIGHEST PARTNERSHIPS FOR EACH WICKET

The following lists include all stands above 400; otherwise the top ten for each wicket.

First Wicket

561	Waheed Mirza and Mansoor Akhtar, Karachi Whites v Quetta at Karachi	1976-77
555	P. Holmes and H. Sutcliffe, Yorkshire v Essex at Leyton	1932
554	J. T. Brown and J. Tunnicliffe, Yorkshire v Derbyshire at Chesterfield	1898
490	E. H. Bowley and J. G. Langridge, Sussex v Middlesex at Hove	1933
464	R. Sehgal and R. Lamba, Delhi v Himachal Pradesh at Delhi	1994-95
459	Wasim Jaffer and S. K. Kulkarni, Mumbai v Saurashtra at Rajkot	1996-97
456	E. R. Mayne and W. H. Ponsford, Victoria v Queensland at Melbourne	1923-24
451*	S. Desai and R. M. H. Binny, Karnataka v Kerala at Chikmagalur.	1977-78
431	M. R. J. Veletta and G. R. Marsh, Western Australia v South Australia at Perth.	1989-90
428	J. B. Hobbs and A. Sandham, Surrey v Oxford University at The Oval.	1926
424	I. J. Siedle and J. F. W. Nicolson, Natal v Orange Free State at Bloemfontein .	1926-27
421	S. M. Gavaskar and G. A. Parkar, Bombay v Bengal at Bombay.	1981-82
418	Kamal Najamuddin and Khalid Alvi, Karachi v Railways at Karachi	1980-81
413	V. Mankad and Pankaj Roy, India v New Zealand at Madras	1955-56
405	C. P. S. Chauhan and M. S. Gupte, Maharashtra v Vidarbha at Poona	1972-73

Second Wicket

576	S. T. Jayasuriya and R. S. Mahanama, Sri Lanka v India at Colombo.	1997-98
475	Zahir Alam and L. S. Rajput, Assam v Tripura at Gauhati	1991-92
465*	J. A. Jameson and R. B. Kanhai, Warwicks v Gloucestershire at Birmingham . .	1974
455	K. V. Bhandarkar and B. B. Nimbalkar, Maharashtra v Kathiawar at Poona. . .	1948-49
451	W. H. Ponsford and D. G. Bradman, Australia v England at The Oval	1934
446	C. C. Hunte and G. S. Sobers, West Indies v Pakistan at Kingston	1957-58
429*	J. G. Dewes and G. H. G. Doggart, Cambridge U. v Essex at Cambridge	1949
426	Arshad Pervez and Mohsin Khan, Habib Bank v Income Tax at Lahore	1977-78
417†	K. J. Barnett and T. A. Tweats, Derbyshire v Yorkshire at Derby	1997
415	A. Jadeja and S. V. Manjrekar, Indians v Bowl XI at Springs	1992-93
403	G. A. Gooch and P. J. Prichard, Essex v Leicestershire at Chelmsford	1990

Third Wicket

467	A. H. Jones and M. D. Crowe, New Zealand v Sri Lanka at Wellington	1990-91
456	Khalid Irtiza and Aslam Ali, United Bank v Multan at Karachi	1975-76
451	Mudassar Nazar and Javed Miandad, Pakistan v India at Hyderabad	1982-83
445	P. E. Whitelaw and W. N. Carson, Auckland v Otago at Dunedin	1936-37
438*†	G. A. Hick and T. M. Moody, Worcestershire v Hampshire at Southampton . . .	1997
434	J. B. Stollmeyer and G. E. Gomez, Trinidad v British Guiana at Port-of-Spain.	1946-47
424*	W. J. Edrich and D. C. S. Compton, Middlesex v Somerset at Lord's.	1948
413	D. J. Bicknell and D. M. Ward, Surrey v Kent at Canterbury	1990
410*	R. S. Modi and L. Amarnath, India in England v The Rest at Calcutta	1946-47
405	A. Jadeja and A. S. Kaypee, Haryana v Services at Faridabad.	1991-92

Fourth Wicket

577	V. S. Hazare and Gul Mahomed, Baroda v Holkar at Baroda	1946-47
574*	C. L. Walcott and F. M. M. Worrell, Barbados v Trinidad at Port-of-Spain .	1945-46
502*	F. M. M. Worrell and J. D. C. Goddard, Barbados v Trinidad at Bridgetown . .	1943-44
470	A. I. Kallicharran and G. W. Humpage, Warwicks v Lancs at Southport	1982
462*	D. W. Hookes and W. B. Phillips, South Australia v Tasmania at Adelaide . . .	1986-87
448	R. Abel and T. W. Hayward, Surrey v Yorkshire at The Oval	1899
436	S. Abbas Ali and P. K. Dwevedi, Madhya Pradesh v Railways at Indore.	1997-98
425*†	A. Dale and I. V. A. Richards, Glamorgan v Middlesex at Cardiff	1993
424	I. S. Lee and S. O. Quin, Victoria v Tasmania at Melbourne	1933-34
411	P. B. H. May and M. C. Cowdrey, England v West Indies at Birmingham. . . .	1957
410	G. Abraham and P. Balan Pandit, Kerala v Andhra at Palghat	1959-60
402	W. Watson and T. W. Graveney, MCC v British Guiana at Georgetown	1953-54
402	R. B. Kanhai and K. Ibadulla, Warwicks v Notts at Nottingham	1968

Fifth Wicket

464*†	M. E. Waugh and S. R. Waugh, New South Wales v Western Australia at Perth	1990-91
405	S. G. Barnes and D. G. Bradman, Australia v England at Sydney	1946-47
401†	M. B. Loye and D. Ripley, Northamptonshire v Glamorgan at Northampton . .	1998
397	W. Bardsley and C. Kelleway, New South Wales v South Australia at Sydney .	1920-21
393	E. G. Arnold and W. B. Burns, Worcestershire v Warwickshire at Birmingham.	1909
391	A. Malhotra and S. Dogra, Delhi v Services at Delhi	1995-96
385	S. R. Waugh and S. G. Blewett, Australia v South Africa at Johannesburg. . . .	1996-97
360	U. M. Merchant and M. N. Raiji, Bombay v Hyderabad at Bombay.	1947-48
355	Altaf Shah and Tariq Bashir, HBFC v Multan at Multan	1976-77
355	A. J. Lamb and J. J. Strydom, OFS v Eastern Province at Bloemfontein.	1987-88

Sixth Wicket

487*	G. A. Headley and C. C. Passailaigue, Jamaica v Lord Tennyson's XI at Kingston	1931-32
428	W. W. Armstrong and M. A. Noble, Australians v Sussex at Hove.	1902
411	R. M. Poore and E. G. Wynyard, Hampshire v Somerset at Taunton	1899
376	R. Subba Row and A. Lightfoot, Northamptonshire v Surrey at The Oval	1958
371	M. V. Merchant and R. S. Modi, Bombay v Maharashtra at Bombay	1943-44
356	W. V. Raman and A. Kripal Singh, Tamil Nadu v Goa at Panjim.	1988-89
353	Salah-ud-Din and Zaheer Abbas, Karachi v East Pakistan at Karachi	1968-69
346	J. H. W. Fingleton and D. G. Bradman, Australia v England at Melbourne . . .	1936-37
337†	R. R. Montgomerie and D. J. Capel, Northamptonshire v Kent at Canterbury. .	1995
332	N. G. Marks and G. Thomas, New South Wales v South Australia at Sydney .	1958-59

Seventh Wicket

460	Bhupinder Singh, jun. and P. Dharmani, Punjab v Delhi at Delhi.	1994-95
347	D. St E. Atkinson and C. C. Depeiza, West Indies v Australia at Bridgetown. .	1954-55
344	K. S. Ranjitsinhji and W. Newham, Sussex v Essex at Leyton	1902
340	K. J. Key and H. Philipson, Oxford University v Middlesex at Chiswick Park .	1887
336	F. C. W. Newman and C. R. N. Maxwell, Sir J. Cahn's XI v Leicestershire at Nottingham.	1935
335	C. W. Andrews and E. C. Bensted, Queensland v New South Wales at Sydney	1934-35
325	G. Brown and C. H. Abercrombie, Hampshire v Essex at Leyton	1913
323	E. H. Hendren and L. F. Townsend, MCC v Barbados at Bridgetown	1929-30
308	Waqar Hassan and Imtiaz Ahmed, Pakistan v New Zealand at Lahore	1955-56
301	C. C. Lewis and B. N. French, Nottinghamshire v Durham at Chester-le-Street	1993

Eighth Wicket

433	V. T. Trumper and A. Sims, A. Sims' Aust. XI v Canterbury at Christchurch .	1913-14
313	Wasim Akram and Saqlain Mushtaq, Pakistan v Zimbabwe at Sheikhupura . . .	1996-97
292	R. Peel and Lord Hawke, Yorkshire v Warwickshire at Birmingham.	1896
270	V. T. Trumper and E. P. Barbour, New South Wales v Victoria at Sydney	1912-13
263	D. R. Wilcox and R. M. Taylor, Essex v Warwickshire at Southend . .	1946
255	E. A. V. Williams and E. A. Martindale, Barbados v Trinidad at Bridgetown . .	1935-36
249*	Shaukat Mirza and Akram Raza, Habib Bank v PNSC at Lahore.	1993-94
246	L. E. G. Ames and G. O. B. Allen, England v New Zealand at Lord's	1931
243	R. J. Hartigan and C. Hill, Australia v England at Adelaide	1907-08
242*	T. J. Zoehrer and K. H. MacLeay, W. Australia v New South Wales at Perth . .	1990-91

Ninth Wicket

283	J. Chapman and A. Warren, Derbyshire v Warwickshire at Blackwell	1910
268	J. B. Commins and N. Boje, South Africa A v Mashonaland at Harare	1994-95
251	J. W. H. T. Douglas and S. N. Hare, Essex v Derbyshire at Leyton	1921
245	V. S. Hazare and N. D. Nagarwalla, Maharashtra v Baroda at Poona	1939-40
244*	Arshad Ayub and M. V. Ramanamurthy, Hyderabad v Bihar at Hyderabad . .	1986-87
239	H. B. Cave and I. B. Leggat, Central Districts v Otago at Dunedin	1952-53
232	C. Hill and E. Walkley, South Australia v New South Wales at Adelaide.	1900-01
231	P. Sen and J. Mitter, Bengal v Bihar at Jamshedpur	1950-51
230	D. A. Livingstone and A. T. Castell, Hampshire v Surrey at Southampton	1962
226	C. Kelleway and W. A. Oldfield, New South Wales v Victoria at Melbourne . .	1925-26

Tenth Wicket

307	A. F. Kippax and J. E. H. Hooker, New South Wales v Victoria at Melbourne .	1928-29
249	C. T. Sarwate and S. N. Banerjee, Indians v Surrey at The Oval	1946
235	F. E. Woolley and A. Fielder, Kent v Worcestershire at Stourbridge	1909
233	Ajay Sharma and Maninder Singh, Delhi v Bombay at Bombay	1991-92
230	R. W. Nicholls and W. Roche, Middlesex v Kent at Lord's	1899
228	R. Illingworth and K. Higgs, Leicestershire v Northamptonshire at Leicester . .	1977
218	F. H. Vigar and T. P. B. Smith, Essex v Derbyshire at Chesterfield	1947
211	M. Ellis and T. J. Hastings, Victoria v South Australia at Melbourne	1902-03
196*	Nadim Yousuf and Maqsood Kundi, MCB v National Bank at Lahore	1981-82
192	H. A. W. Bowell and W. H. Livsey, Hampshire v Worcs at Bournemouth	1921

† *Partnerships affected by ECB or ACB regulations governing no-balls and wides.*

UNUSUAL DISMISSALS

Handled the Ball

J. Grundy	MCC v Kent at Lord's	1857
G. Bennett	Kent v Sussex at Hove	1872
W. H. Scotton	Smokers v Non-Smokers at East Melbourne	1886-87
C. W. Wright	Nottinghamshire v Gloucestershire at Bristol	1893
E. Jones	South Australia v Victoria at Melbourne	1894-95
A. W. Nourse	South Africans v Sussex at Hove	1907
E. T. Benson	MCC v Auckland at Auckland	1929-30
A. W. Gilbertson	Otago v Auckland at Auckland	1952-53
W. R. Endean	South Africa v England at Cape Town	1956-57
P. J. Burge	Queensland v New South Wales at Sydney	1958-59
Dildar Awan	Services v Lahore at Lahore	1959-60
M. Mehra	Railways v Delhi at Delhi	1959-60
Mahmood-ul-Hasan	Karachi University v Railways-Quetta at Karachi	1960-61
Ali Raza	Karachi Greens v Hyderabad at Karachi	1961-62
Mohammad Yusuf	Rawalpindi v Peshawar at Peshawar	1962-63
A. Rees	Glamorgan v Middlesex at Lord's	1965
Pervez Akhtar	Multan v Karachi Greens at Sahiwal	1971-72
Javed Mirza	Railways v Punjab at Lahore	1972-73
R. G. Pollock	Eastern Province v Western Province at Cape Town	1973-74
C. I. Dey	Northern Transvaal v Orange Free State at Bloemfontein	1973-74
Nasir Valika	Karachi Whites v National Bank at Karachi	1974-75
Haji Yousuf	National Bank v Railways at Lahore	1974-75
Masood-ul-Hasan	PIA v National Bank B at Lyallpur	1975-76
D. K. Pearse	Natal v Western Province at Cape Town	1978-79
A. M. J. Hilditch	Australia v Pakistan at Perth	1978-79
Musleh-ud-Din	Railways v Lahore at Lahore	1979-80
Jalal-ud-Din	IDBP v Habib Bank at Bahawalpur	1981-82
Mohsin Khan	Pakistan v Australia at Karachi	1982-83
D. L. Haynes	West Indies v India at Bombay	1983-84
K. Azad	Delhi v Punjab at Amritsar	1983-84
Athar A. Khan	Allied Bank v HBFC at Sialkot	1983-84
A. N. Pandya	Saurashtra v Baroda at Baroda	1984-85
G. L. Linton	Barbados v Windward Islands at Bridgetown	1985-86
R. B. Gartrell	Tasmania v Victoria at Melbourne	1986-87
R. Nayyar	Himachal Pradesh v Punjab at Una	1988-89
R. Weerawardene	Moratuwa v Nomads SC at Colombo	1988-89
A. M. Kane	Vidarbha v Railways at Nagpur	1989-90
P. Bali	Jammu and Kashmir v Services at Delhi	1991-92
M. J. Davis	Northern Transvaal B v OFS B at Bloemfontein	1991-92
J. T. C. Vaughan	Emerging Players v England XI at Hamilton	1991-92
G. A. Gooch	England v Australia at Manchester	1993
A. C. Waller	Mashonaland CD v Mashonaland Under-24 at Harare	1994-95
K. M. Krikken	Derbyshire v Indians at Derby	1996

Obstructing the Field

C. A. Absolom	Cambridge University v Surrey at The Oval	1868
T. Straw	Worcestershire v Warwickshire at Worcester	1899
T. Straw	Worcestershire v Warwickshire at Birmingham	1901
J. P. Whiteside	Leicestershire v Lancashire at Leicester	1901
L. Hutton	England v South Africa at The Oval	1951
J. A. Hayes	Canterbury v Central Districts at Christchurch	1954-55
D. D. Deshpande	Madhya Pradesh v Uttar Pradesh at Benares	1956-57
K. Ibadulla	Warwickshire v Hampshire at Coventry	1963
Qaiser Khan	Dera Ismail Khan v Railways at Lahore	1964-65
Ijaz Ahmed	Lahore Greens v Lahore Blues at Lahore	1973-74
Qasim Feroze	Bahawalpur v Universities at Lahore	1974-75
T. Quirk	Northern Transvaal v Border at East London	1978-79

Mahmood Rashid	United Bank v Muslim Commercial Bank at Bahawalpur		1981-82
Arshad Ali	Sukkur v Quetta at Quetta		1983-84
H. R. Wasu	Vidarbha v Rajasthan at Akola		1984-85
Khalid Javed	Railways v Lahore at Lahore		1985-86
C. Binduhewa	Singha SC v Sinhalese SC at Colombo		1990-91
S. J. Kalyani	Bengal v Orissa at Calcutta		1994-95

Hit the Ball Twice

G. Rawlins	Sheffield v Nottingham at Nottingham	1827
H. E. Bull	MCC v Oxford University at Lord's	1864
H. R. J. Charlwood	Sussex v Surrey at Hove	1872
R. G. Barlow	North v South at Lord's	1878
P. S. Wimble	Transvaal v Griqualand West at Kimberley	1892-93
G. B. Nicholls	Somerset v Gloucestershire at Bristol	1896
A. A. Lilley	Warwickshire v Yorkshire at Birmingham	1897
J. H. King	Leicestershire v Surrey at The Oval	1906
A. P. Binns	Jamaica v British Guiana at Georgetown	1956-57
K. Bhavanna	Andhra v Mysore at Guntur	1963-64
Zaheer Abbas	PIA A v Karachi Blues at Karachi	1969-70
Anwar Miandad	IDBP v United Bank at Lahore	1979-80
Anwar Iqbal	Hyderabad v Sukkur at Hyderabad	1983-84
Iqtidar Ali	Allied Bank v Muslim Commercial Bank at Lahore	1983-84
Aziz Malik	Lahore Division v Faisalabad at Sialkot	1984-85
Javed Mohammad	Multan v Karachi Whites at Sahiwal	1986-87
Shahid Pervez	Jammu and Kashmir v Punjab at Srinagar	1986-87

Timed Out

H. Yadav	Tripura v Orissa at Cuttack	1997-98

BOWLING RECORDS

TEN WICKETS IN AN INNINGS

	O	M	R		
E. Hinkly (Kent)				v England at Lord's	1848
*J. Wisden (North)				v South at Lord's	1850
V. E. Walker (England)	43	17	74	v Surrey at The Oval	1859
V. E. Walker (Middlesex)	44.2	5	104	v Lancashire at Manchester	1865
G. Wootton (All England)	31.3	9	54	v Yorkshire at Sheffield	1865
W. Hickton (Lancashire)	36.2	19	46	v Hampshire at Manchester	1870
S. E. Butler (Oxford)	24.1	11	38	v Cambridge at Lord's	1871
James Lillywhite (South)	60.2	22	129	v North at Canterbury	1872
A. Shaw (MCC)	36.2	8	73	v North at Lord's	1874
E. Barratt (Players)	29	11	43	v Australians at The Oval	1878
G. Giffen (Australian XI)	26	10	66	v The Rest at Sydney	1883-84
W. G. Grace (MCC)	36.2	17	49	v Oxford University at Oxford	1886
G. Burton (Middlesex)	52.3	25	59	v Surrey at The Oval	1888
†A. E. Moss (Canterbury)	21.3	10	28	v Wellington at Christchurch	1889-90
S. M. J. Woods (Cambridge U.)	31	6	69	v Thornton's XI at Cambridge	1890
T. Richardson (Surrey)	15.3	3	45	v Essex at The Oval	1894
H. Pickett (Essex)	27	11	32	v Leicestershire at Leyton	1895
E. J. Tyler (Somerset)	34.3	15	49	v Surrey at Taunton	1895
W. P. Howell (Australians)	23.2	14	28	v Surrey at The Oval	1899
C. H. G. Bland (Sussex)	25.2	10	48	v Kent at Tonbridge	1899
J. Briggs (Lancashire)	28.5	7	55	v Worcestershire at Manchester	1900
A. E. Trott (Middlesex)	14.2	5	42	v Somerset at Taunton	1900
A. Fielder (Players)	24.5	1	90	v Gentlemen at Lord's	1906
E. G. Dennett (Gloucestershire)	19.4	7	40	v Essex at Bristol	1906

	O	M	R		
A. E. E. Vogler (E. Province) ...	12	2	26	v Griqualand W. at Johannesburg	1906-07
C. Blythe (Kent)	16	7	30	v Northants at Northampton ..	1907
A. Drake (Yorkshire)	8.5	0	35	v Somerset at Weston-s-Mare ..	1914
W. Bestwick (Derbyshire)	19	2	40	v Glamorgan at Cardiff	1921
A. A. Mailey (Australians)	28.4	5	66	v Gloucestershire at Cheltenham	1921
C. W. L. Parker (Glos.)	40.3	13	79	v Somerset at Bristol	1921
T. Rushby (Surrey)	17.5	4	43	v Somerset at Taunton	1921
J. C. White (Somerset)	42.2	11	76	v Worcestershire at Worcester ..	1921
G. C. Collins (Kent)	19.3	4	65	v Nottinghamshire at Dover ...	1922
H. Howell (Warwickshire)	25.1	5	51	v Yorkshire at Birmingham ...	1923
A. S. Kennedy (Players)	22.4	10	37	v Gentlemen at The Oval	1927
G. O. B. Allen (Middlesex)	25.3	10	40	v Lancashire at Lord's	1929
A. P. Freeman (Kent)	42	9	131	v Lancashire at Maidstone ...	1929
G. Geary (Leicestershire)	16.2	8	18	v Glamorgan at Pontypridd ...	1929
C. V. Grimmett (Australians) ...	22.3	8	37	v Yorkshire at Sheffield	1930
A. P. Freeman (Kent)	30.4	8	53	v Essex at Southend	1930
H. Verity (Yorkshire)	18.4	6	36	v Warwickshire at Leeds	1931
A. P. Freeman (Kent)	36.1	9	79	v Lancashire at Manchester ...	1931
V. W. C. Jupp (Northants)	39	6	127	v Kent at Tunbridge Wells ...	1932
H. Verity (Yorkshire)	19.4	16	10	v Nottinghamshire at Leeds ...	1932
T. W. Wall (South Australia) ...	12.4	2	36	v New South Wales at Sydney..	1932-33
T. B. Mitchell (Derbyshire)	19.1	4	64	v Leicestershire at Leicester ...	1935
J. Mercer (Glamorgan)	26	10	51	v Worcestershire at Worcester ..	1936
T. W. J. Goddard (Glos.)	28.4	4	113	v Worcestershire at Cheltenham .	1937
T. F. Smailes (Yorkshire)	17.1	5	47	v Derbyshire at Sheffield	1939
E. A. Watts (Surrey)	24.1	8	67	v Warwickshire at Birmingham .	1939
*W. E. Hollies (Warwickshire) ..	20.4	4	49	v Notts at Birmingham	1946
J. M. Sims (East)	18.4	2	90	v West at Kingston	1948
T. E. Bailey (Essex)	39.4	9	90	v Lancashire at Clacton	1949
J. K. Graveney (Glos.)	18.4	2	66	v Derbyshire at Chesterfield ...	1949
R. Berry (Lancashire)	36.2	9	102	v Worcestershire at Blackpool ...	1953
S. P. Gupte (President's XI)	24.2	7	78	v Combined XI at Bombay ...	1954-57
J. C. Laker (Surrey)	46	18	88	v Australians at The Oval	1956
J. C. Laker (England)	51.2	23	53	v Australia at Manchester	1956
G. A. R. Lock (Surrey)	29.1	18	54	v Kent at Blackheath	1956
K. Smales (Nottinghamshire)	41.3	20	66	v Gloucestershire at Stroud	1956
P. M. Chatterjee (Bengal)	19	11	20	v Assam at Jorhat	1956-57
J. D. Bannister (Warwickshire) ..	23.3	11	41	v Comb. Services at Birmingham‡	1959
A. J. G. Pearson (Cambridge U.) .	30.3	8	78	v Leics at Loughborough	1961
N. I. Thomson (Sussex)	34.2	19	49	v Warwickshire at Worthing ...	1964
P. J. Allan (Queensland)	15.6	3	61	v Victoria at Melbourne	1965-66
I. J. Brayshaw (W. Australia) ...	17.6	4	44	v Victoria at Perth........	1967-68
Shahid Mahmood (Karachi Whites)	25	5	58	v Khairpur at Karachi	1969-70
E. E. Hemmings (International XI)	49.3	14	175	v West Indies XI at Kingston ...	1982-83
P. Sunderam (Rajasthan)	22	5	78	v Vidarbha at Jodhpur	1985-86
S. T. Jefferies (W. Province)	22.5	7	59	v Orange Free State at Cape Town	1987-88
Imran Adil (Bahawalpur).......	22.5	3	92	v Faisalabad at Faisalabad.....	1989-90
G. P. Wickremasinghe (Sinhalese SC)	19.2	5	41	v Kalutara at Colombo	1991-92
R. L. Johnson (Middlesex)	18.5	6	45	v Derbyshire at Derby	1994
Naeem Akhtar (Rawalpindi B) ...	21.3	10	28	v Peshawar at Peshawar	1995-96

Note: The following instances were achieved in 12-a-side matches:

	O	M	R		
E. M. Grace (MCC)..........	32.2	7	69	v Gents of Kent at Canterbury..	1862
W. G. Grace (MCC)..........	46.1	15	92	v Kent at Canterbury	1873
†D. C. S. Hinds (A. B. St Hill's XII)	19.1	6	36	v Trinidad at Port-of-Spain	1900-01

* *J. Wisden and W. E. Hollies achieved the feat without the direct assistance of a fielder. Wisden's ten were all bowled; Hollies bowled seven and had three lbw.*

† *On debut in first-class cricket.* ‡ *Mitchells & Butlers Ground.*

OUTSTANDING ANALYSES

	O	M	R	W		
H. Verity (Yorkshire)	19.4	16	10	10	v Nottinghamshire at Leeds . .	1932
G. Elliott (Victoria)	19	17	2	9	v Tasmania at Launceston . .	1857-58
Ahad Khan (Railways)	6.3	4	7	9	v Dera Ismail Khan at Lahore	1964-65
J. C. Laker (England)	14	12	2	8	v The Rest at Bradford	1950
D. Shackleton (Hampshire) . .	11.1	7	4	8	v Somerset at Weston-s-Mare	1955
E. Peate (Yorkshire)	16	11	5	8	v Surrey at Holbeck	1883
F. R. Spofforth (Australians) . .	8.3	6	3	7	v England XI at Birmingham .	1884
W. A. Henderson (North-Eastern					v Orange Free State at Bloem-	
Transvaal)	9.3	7	4	7	fontein	1937-38
Rajinder Goel (Haryana)	7	4	4	7	v Jammu and Kashmir at	
					Chandigarh	1977-78
V. I. Smith (South Africans). . .	4.5	3	1	6	v Derbyshire at Derby	1947
S. Costick (Victoria)	21.1	20	1	6	v Tasmania at Melbourne. . . .	1868-69
Israr Ali (Bahawalpur)	11	10	1	6	v Dacca U. at Bahawalpur . .	1957-58
A. D. Pougher (MCC)	3	3	0	5	v Australians at Lord's	1896
G. R. Cox (Sussex)	6	6	0	5	v Somerset at Weston-s-Mare .	1921
R. K. Tyldesley (Lancashire) . .	5	5	0	5	v Leicestershire at Manchester	1924
P. T. Mills (Gloucestershire). . .	6.4	6	0	5	v Somerset at Bristol	1928

MOST WICKETS IN A MATCH

19-90	J. C. Laker	England v Australia at Manchester	1956
17-48	C. Blythe	Kent v Northamptonshire at Northampton	1907
17-50	C. T. B. Turner	Australians v England XI at Hastings	1888
17-54	W. P. Howell	Australians v Western Province at Cape Town	1902-03
17-56	C. W. L. Parker	Gloucestershire v Essex at Gloucester	1925
17-67	A. P. Freeman	Kent v Sussex at Hove	1922
17-89	W. G. Grace	Gloucestershire v Nottinghamshire at Cheltenham . . .	1877
17-89	F. C. L. Matthews	Nottinghamshire v Northants at Nottingham	1923
17-91	H. Dean	Lancashire v Yorkshire at Liverpool	1913
17-91	H. Verity	Yorkshire v Essex at Leyton	1933
17-92	A. P. Freeman	Kent v Warwickshire at Folkestone	1932
17-103	W. Mycroft	Derbyshire v Hampshire at Southampton	1876
17-106	G. R. Cox	Sussex v Warwickshire at Horsham	1926
17-106	T. W. J. Goddard	Gloucestershire v Kent at Bristol	1939
17-119	W. Mead	Essex v Hampshire at Southampton	1895
17-137	W. Brearley	Lancashire v Somerset at Manchester.	1905
17-159	S. F. Barnes	England v South Africa at Johannesburg	1913-14
17-201	G. Giffen	South Australia v Victoria at Adelaide	1885-86
17-212	J. C. Clay	Glamorgan v Worcestershire at Swansea.	1937

SIXTEEN OR MORE WICKETS IN A DAY

17-48	C. Blythe	Kent v Northamptonshire at Northampton	1907
17-91	H. Verity	Yorkshire v Essex at Leyton	1933
17-106	T. W. J. Goddard	Gloucestershire v Kent at Bristol	1939
16-38	T. Emmett	Yorkshire v Cambridgeshire at Hunslet.	1869
16-52	J. Southerton	South v North at Lord's	1875
16-69	T. G. Wass	Nottinghamshire v Lancashire at Liverpool	1906
16-38	A. E. E. Vogler	E. Province v Griqualand West at Johannesburg	1906-07
16-103	T. G. Wass	Nottinghamshire v Essex at Nottingham	1908
16-83	J. C. White	Somerset v Worcestershire at Bath	1919

FOUR WICKETS WITH CONSECUTIVE BALLS

J. Wells	Kent v Sussex at Brighton	1862
G. Ulyett	Lord Harris's XI v New South Wales at Sydney	1878-79
G. Nash	Lancashire v Somerset at Manchester	1882
J. B. Hide	Sussex v MCC and Ground at Lord's	1890
F. J. Shacklock	Nottinghamshire v Somerset at Nottingham	1893
A. D. Downes	Otago v Auckland at Dunedin	1893-94
F. Martin	MCC and Ground v Derbyshire at Lord's	1895
A. W. Mold	Lancashire v Nottinghamshire at Nottingham	1895
W. Brearley†	Lancashire v Somerset at Manchester	1905
S. Haigh	MCC v Army XI at Pretoria	1905-06
A. E. Trott‡	Middlesex v Somerset at Lord's	1907
F. A. Tarrant	Middlesex v Gloucestershire at Bristol	1907
A. Drake	Yorkshire v Derbyshire at Chesterfield	1914
S. G. Smith	Northamptonshire v Warwickshire at Birmingham	1914
H. A. Peach	Surrey v Sussex at The Oval	1924
A. F. Borland	Natal v Griqualand West at Kimberley	1926-27
J. E. H. Hooker†	New South Wales v Victoria at Sydney	1928-29
R. K. Tyldesley†	Lancashire v Derbyshire at Derby	1929
R. J. Crisp	Western Province v Griqualand West at Johannesburg ...	1931-32
R. J. Crisp	Western Province v Natal at Durban	1933-34
A. R. Gover	Surrey v Worcestershire at Worcester	1935
W. H. Copson	Derbyshire v Warwickshire at Derby	1937
W. A. Henderson	N.E. Transvaal v Orange Free State at Bloemfontein	1937-38
F. Ridgway	Kent v Derbyshire at Folkestone	1951
A. K. Walker§	Nottinghamshire v Leicestershire at Leicester	1956
S. N. Mohol	President's XI v Combined XI at Poona	1965-66
P. I. Pocock	Surrey v Sussex at Eastbourne	1972
S. S. Saini†	Delhi v Himachal Pradesh at Delhi	1988-89
D. Dias	W. Province (Suburbs) v Central Province at Colombo ...	1990-91
Ali Gauhar	Karachi Blues v United Bank at Peshawar	1994-95
K. D. James**	Hampshire v Indians at Southampton	1996

† *Not all in the same innings.*

‡ *Trott achieved another hat-trick in the same innings of this, his benefit match.*

§ *Having bowled Firth with the last ball of the first innings, Walker achieved a unique feat by dismissing Lester, Tompkin and Smithson with the first three balls of the second.*

** *James also scored a century, a unique double.*

Notes: In their match with England at The Oval in 1863, Surrey lost four wickets in the course of a four-ball over from G. Bennett.

Sussex lost five wickets in the course of the final (six-ball) over of their match with Surrey at Eastbourne in 1972. P. I. Pocock, who had taken three wickets in his previous over, captured four more, taking in all seven wickets with 11 balls, a feat unique in first-class matches. (The eighth wicket fell to a run-out.)

HAT-TRICKS

Double Hat-Trick

Besides Trott's performance, which is given in the preceding section, the following instances are recorded of players having performed the hat-trick twice in the same match, Rao doing so in the same innings.

A. Shaw	Nottinghamshire v Gloucestershire at Nottingham	1884
T. J. Matthews	Australia v South Africa at Manchester	1912
C. W. L. Parker	Gloucestershire v Middlesex at Bristol	1924
R. O. Jenkins	Worcestershire v Surrey at Worcester	1949
J. S. Rao	Services v Northern Punjab at Amritsar	1963-64
Amin Lakhani	Combined XI v Indians at Multan	1978-79

Five Wickets in Six Balls

W. H. Copson	Derbyshire v Warwickshire at Derby.................	1937
W. A. Henderson	N.E. Transvaal v Orange Free State at Bloemfontein	1937-38
P. I. Pocock	Surrey v Sussex at Eastbourne.....................	1972

Most Hat-Tricks

Seven times: D. V. P. Wright.

Six times: T. W. J. Goddard, C. W. L. Parker.

Five times: S. Haigh, V. W. C. Jupp, A. E. G. Rhodes, F. A. Tarrant.

Four times: R. G. Barlow, A. P. Freeman, J. T. Hearne, J. C. Laker, G. A. R. Lock, G. G. Macaulay, T. J. Matthews, M. J. Procter, T. Richardson, F. R. Spofforth, F. S. Trueman.

Three times: W. M. Bradley, H. J. Butler, S. T. Clarke, W. H. Copson, R. J. Crisp, J. W. H. T. Douglas, J. A. Flavell, G. Giffen, D. W. Headley, K. Higgs, A. Hill, W. A. Humphreys, R. D. Jackman, R. O. Jenkins, A. S. Kennedy, W. H. Lockwood, E. A. McDonald, T. L. Pritchard, J. S. Rao, A. Shaw, J. B. Statham, M. W. Tate, H. Trumble, D. Wilson, G. A. Wilson.

Twice (current players only): D. G. Cork, A. Kumble.

Hat-Trick on Debut

H. Hay	South Australia v Lord Hawke's XI at Unley, Adelaide	1902-03
H. A. Sedgwick ...	Yorkshire v Worcestershire at Hull..................	1906
J. C. Treanor	New South Wales v Queensland at Brisbane............	1954-55
V. B. Ranjane.....	Maharashtra v Saurashtra at Poona	1956-57
N. Frederick......	Ceylon v Madras at Colombo	1963-64
J. S. Rao	Services v Jammu and Kashmir at Delhi	1963-64
Mehboodullah ...	Uttar Pradesh v Madhya Pradesh at Lucknow..........	1971-72
R. O. Estwick	Barbados v Guyana at Bridgetown	1982-83
S. A. Ankola	Maharashtra v Gujarat at Poona	1988-89
J. Srinath........	Karnataka v Hyderabad at Secunderabad	1989-90
S. P. Mukherjee ...	Bengal v Hyderabad at Secunderabad	1989-90

Notes: R. R. Phillips (Border) took a hat-trick in his first over in first-class cricket (v Eastern Province at Port Elizabeth, 1939-40) having previously played in four matches without bowling.

J. S. Rao took two more hat-tricks in his next match.

250 WICKETS IN A SEASON

	Season	O	M	R	W	Avge
A. P. Freeman............	1928	1,976.1	423	5,489	304	18.05
A. P. Freeman............	1933	2,039	651	4,549	298	15.26
T. Richardson	1895‡	1,690.1	463	4,170	290	14.37
C. T. B. Turner...........	1888†	2,427.2	1,127	3,307	283	11.68
A. P. Freeman............	1931	1,618	360	4,307	276	15.60
A. P. Freeman............	1930	1,914.3	472	4,632	275	16.84
T. Richardson	1897‡	1,603.4	495	3,945	273	14.45
A. P. Freeman............	1929	1,670.5	381	4,879	267	18.27
W. Rhodes	1900	1,553	455	3,606	261	13.81
J. T. Hearne	1896	2,003.1	818	3,670	257	14.28
A. P. Freeman............	1932	1,565.5	404	4,149	253	16.39
W. Rhodes	1901	1,565	505	3,797	251	15.12

† *Indicates 4-ball overs;* ‡ *5-ball overs.*

Notes: In four consecutive seasons (1928-31), A. P. Freeman took 1,122 wickets, and in eight consecutive seasons (1928-35), 2,090 wickets. In each of these eight seasons he took over 200 wickets.

T. Richardson took 1,005 wickets in four consecutive seasons (1894-97).

In 1896, J. T. Hearne took his 100th wicket as early as June 12. In 1931, C. W. L. Parker did the same and A. P. Freeman obtained his 100th wicket a day later.

LEADING BOWLERS IN AN ENGLISH SEASON

(Qualification: 10 wickets in 10 innings)

Season	Leading wicket-taker	Wkts	Avge	Top of averages	Wkts	Avge
1946	W. E. Hollies	184	15.60	A. Booth	111	11.61
1947	T. W. J. Goddard	238	17.30	J. C. Clay	65	16.44
1948	J. E. Walsh	174	19.56	J. C. Clay	41	14.17
1949	R. O. Jenkins	183	21.19	T. W. J. Goddard	160	19.18
1950	R. Tattersall	193	13.59	R. Tattersall	193	13.59
1951	R. Appleyard	200	14.14	R. Appleyard	200	14.14
1952	J. H. Wardle	177	19.54	F. S. Trueman	61	13.78
1953	B. Dooland	172	16.58	C. J. Knott	38	13.71
1954	B. Dooland	196	15.48	J. B. Statham	92	14.13
1955	G. A. R. Lock	216	14.49	R. Appleyard	85	13.01
1956	D. J. Shepherd	177	15.36	G. A. R. Lock	155	12.46
1957	G. A. R. Lock	212	12.02	G. A. R. Lock	212	12.02
1958	G. A. R. Lock	170	12.08	H. L. Jackson	143	10.99
1959	D. Shackleton	148	21.55	J. B. Statham	139	15.01
1960	F. S. Trueman	175	13.98	J. B. Statham	135	12.31
1961	J. A. Flavell	171	17.79	J. A. Flavell	171	17.79
1962	D. Shackleton	172	20.15	C. Cook	58	17.13
1963	D. Shackleton	146	16.75	C. C. Griffith	119	12.83
1964	D. Shackleton	142	20.40	J. A. Standen	64	13.00
1965	D. Shackleton	144	16.08	H. J. Rhodes	119	11.04
1966	D. L. Underwood	157	13.80	D. L. Underwood	157	13.80
1967	T. W. Cartwright	147	15.52	D. L. Underwood	136	12.39
1968	R. Illingworth	131	14.36	O. S. Wheatley	82	12.95
1969	R. M. H. Cottam	109	21.04	A. Ward	69	14.82
1970	D. J. Shepherd	106	19.16	Majid Khan	11	18.81
1971	L. R. Gibbs	131	18.89	G. G. Arnold	83	17.12
1972	T. W. Cartwright	98	18.64	I. M. Chappell	10	10.60
	B. Stead	98	20.38			
1973	B. S. Bedi	105	17.94	T. W. Cartwright	89	15.84
1974	A. M. E. Roberts	119	13.62	A. M. E. Roberts	119	13.62
1975	P. G. Lee	112	18.45	A. M. E. Roberts	57	15.80
1976	G. A. Cope	93	24.13	M. A. Holding	55	14.38
1977	M. J. Procter	109	18.04	R. A. Woolmer	19	15.21
1978	D. L. Underwood	110	14.49	D. L. Underwood	110	14.49
1979	D. L. Underwood	106	14.85	J. Garner	55	13.83
	J. K. Lever	106	17.30			
1980	R. D. Jackman	121	15.40	J. Garner	49	13.93
1981	R. J. Hadlee	105	14.89	R. J. Hadlee	105	14.89
1982	M. D. Marshall	134	15.73	R. J. Hadlee	61	14.57
1983	J. K. Lever	106	16.28	Imran Khan	12	7.16
	D. L. Underwood	106	19.28			
1984	R. J. Hadlee	117	14.05	R. J. Hadlee	117	14.05
1985	N. V. Radford	101	24.68	R. M. Ellison	65	17.20
1986	C. A. Walsh	118	18.17	M. D. Marshall	100	15.08
1987	N. V. Radford	109	20.81	R. J. Hadlee	97	12.64
1988	F. D. Stephenson	125	18.31	M. D. Marshall	42	13.16
1989	D. R. Pringle	94	18.64	T. M. Alderman	70	15.64
	S. L. Watkin	94	25.09			
1990	N. A. Foster	94	26.61	I. R. Bishop	59	19.05
1991	Waqar Younis	113	14.65	Waqar Younis	113	14.65
1992	C. A. Walsh	92	15.96	C. A. Walsh	92	15.96
1993	S. L. Watkin	92	22.80	Wasim Akram	59	19.27
1994	M. M. Patel	90	22.86	C. E. L. Ambrose	77	14.45
1995	A. Kumble	105	20.40	A. A. Donald	89	16.07
1996	C. A. Walsh	85	16.84	C. E. L. Ambrose	43	16.67
1997	A. M. Smith	83	17.63	A. A. Donald	60	15.63
1998	C. A. Walsh	106	17.31	V. J. Wells	36	14.27

100 WICKETS IN A SEASON

Since Reduction of Championship Matches in 1969

Five times: D. L. Underwood 110 (1978), 106 (1979), 106 (1983), 102 (1971), 101 (1969).

Four times: J. K. Lever 116 (1984), 106 (1978), 106 (1979), 106 (1983).

Twice: B. S. Bedi 112 (1974), 105 (1973); T. W. Cartwright 108 (1969), 104 (1971); N. A. Foster 105 (1986), 102 (1991); N. Gifford 105 (1970), 104 (1983); R. J. Hadlee 117 (1984), 105 (1981); P. G. Lee 112 (1975), 101 (1973); M. D. Marshall 134 (1982), 100 (1986); M. J. Procter 109 (1977), 108 (1969); N. V. Radford 109 (1987), 101 (1985); F. J. Titmus 105 (1970), 104 (1971); C. A. Walsh 118 (1986), 106 (1998).

Once: J. P. Agnew 101 (1987); I. T. Botham 100 (1978); A. R. Caddick 105 (1998); K. E. Cooper 101 (1988); R. M. H. Cottam 109 (1969); D. R. Doshi 101 (1980); J. E. Emburey 103 (1983); L. R. Gibbs 131 (1971); R. N. S. Hobbs 102 (1970); Intikhab Alam 104 (1971); R. D. Jackman 121 (1980); A. Kumble 105 (1995); A. M. E. Roberts 119 (1974); P. J. Sainsbury 107 (1971); Sarfraz Nawaz 101 (1975); M. W. W. Selvey 101 (1978); D. J. Shepherd 106 (1970); F. D. Stephenson 125 (1988); Waqar Younis 113 (1991); D. Wilson 102 (1969).

100 WICKETS IN A SEASON MOST TIMES

(Includes Overseas Tours and Seasons)

23 times: W. Rhodes 200 wkts (3).

20 times: D. Shackleton (In successive seasons – 1949 to 1968 inclusive).

17 times: A. P. Freeman 300 wkts (1), 200 wkts (7).

16 times: T. W. J. Goddard 200 wkts (4), C. W. L. Parker 200 wkts (5), R. T. D. Perks, F. J. Titmus.

15 times: J. T. Hearne 200 wkts (3), G. H. Hirst 200 wkts (1), A. S. Kennedy 200 wkts (1).

14 times: C. Blythe 200 wkts (1), W. E. Hollies, G. A. R. Lock 200 wkts (2), M. W. Tate 200 wkts (3), J. C. White.

13 times: J. B. Statham.

12 times: J. Briggs, E. G. Dennett 200 wkts (1), C. Gladwin, D. J. Shepherd, N. I. Thomson, F. S. Trueman.

11 times: A. V. Bedser, G. Geary, S. Haigh, J. C. Laker, M. S. Nichols, A. E. Relf.

10 times: W. Attewell, W. G. Grace, R. Illingworth, H. L. Jackson, V. W. C. Jupp, G. G. Macaulay 200 wkts (1), W. Mead, T. B. Mitchell, T. Richardson 200 wkts (3), J. Southerton 200 wkts (1), R. K. Tyldesley, D. L. Underwood, J. H. Wardle, T. G. Wass, D. V. P. Wright.

100 WICKETS IN A SEASON OUTSIDE ENGLAND

W		Season	Country	R	Avge
116	M. W. Tate	1926-27	India/Ceylon	1,599	13.78
107	Ijaz Faqih	1985-86	Pakistan	1,719	16.06
106	C. T. B. Turner	1887-88	Australia	1,441	13.59
106	R. Benaud	1957-58	South Africa	2,056	19.39
105	Murtaza Hussain	1995-96	Pakistan	1,882	17.92
104	S. F. Barnes	1913-14	South Africa	1,117	10.74
104	Sajjad Akbar	1989-90	Pakistan	2,328	22.38
103	Abdul Qadir	1982-83	Pakistan	2,367	22.98

1,500 WICKETS IN A CAREER

Dates in italics denote the first half of an overseas season; i.e. *1970* denotes the 1970-71 season.

		Career	W	R	Avge
1	W. Rhodes	1898-1930	4,187	69,993	16.71
2	A. P. Freeman	1914-36	3,776	69,577	18.42
3	C. W. L. Parker	1903-35	3,278	63,817	19.46
4	J. T. Hearne	1888-1923	3,061	54,352	17.75
5	T. W. J. Goddard	1922-52	2,979	59,116	19.84
6	W. G. Grace	1865-1908	2,876	51,545	17.92
7	A. S. Kennedy	1907-36	2,874	61,034	21.23
8	D. Shackleton	1948-69	2,857	53,303	18.65
9	G. A. R. Lock	1946-*70*	2,844	54,709	19.23
10	F. J. Titmus	1949-82	2,830	63,313	22.37
11	M. W. Tate	1912-37	2,784	50,571	18.16
12	G. H. Hirst	1891-1929	2,739	51,282	18.72
13	C. Blythe	1899-1914	2,506	42,136	16.81
14	D. L. Underwood	1963-87	2,465	49,993	20.28
15	W. E. Astill	1906-39	2,431	57,783	23.76
16	J. C. White	1909-37	2,356	43,759	18.57
17	W. E. Hollies	1932-57	2,323	48,656	20.94
18	F. S. Trueman	1949-69	2,304	42,154	18.29
19	J. B. Statham	1950-68	2,260	36,999	16.37
20	R. T. D. Perks	1930-55	2,233	53,770	24.07
21	J. Briggs	1879-1900	2,221	35,431	15.95
22	D. J. Shepherd	1950-72	2,218	47,302	21.32
23	E. G. Dennett	1903-26	2,147	42,571	19.82
24	T. Richardson	1892-1905	2,104	38,794	18.43
25	T. E. Bailey	1945-67	2,082	48,170	23.13
26	R. Illingworth	1951-83	2,072	42,023	20.28
27	{ N. Gifford	1960-88	2,068	48,731	23.56
	{ F. E. Woolley	1906-38	2,068	41,066	19.85
29	G. Geary	1912-38	2,063	41,339	20.03
30	D. V. P. Wright	1932-57	2,056	49,307	23.98
31	J. A. Newman	1906-30	2,032	51,111	25.15
32	†A. Shaw	1864-97	2,027	24,580	12.12
33	S. Haigh	1895-1913	2,012	32,091	15.94
34	H. Verity	1930-39	1,956	29,146	14.90
35	W. Attewell	1881-1900	1,951	29,896	15.32
36	J. C. Laker	1946-*64*	1,944	35,791	18.41
37	A. V. Bedser	1939-60	1,924	39,279	20.41
38	W. Mead	1892-1913	1,916	36,388	18.99
39	A. E. Relf	1900-21	1,897	39,724	20.94
40	P. G. H. Fender	1910-36	1,894	47,458	25.05
41	J. W. H. T. Douglas	1901-30	1,893	44,159	23.32
42	J. H. Wardle	1946-67	1,846	35,027	18.97
43	G. R. Cox	1895-1928	1,843	42,136	22.86
44	G. A. Lohmann	1884-97	1,841	25,295	13.73
45	J. W. Hearne	1909-36	1,839	44,926	24.42
46	G. G. Macaulay	1920-35	1,837	32,440	17.65
47	M. S. Nichols	1924-39	1,833	39,666	21.63
48	J. B. Mortimore	1950-75	1,807	41,904	23.18
49	C. Cook	1946-64	1,782	36,578	20.52
50	R. Peel	1882-99	1,752	28,442	16.23
51	H. L. Jackson	1947-63	1,733	30,101	17.36
52	J. K. Lever	1967-89	1,722	41,772	24.25
53	T. P. B. Smith	1929-52	1,697	45,059	26.55
54	J. Southerton	1854-79	1,681	24,290	14.44
55	A. E. Trott	*1892*-1911	1,674	35,317	21.09
56	A. W. Mold	1889-1901	1,673	26,010	15.54

		Career	W	R	Avge
57	T. G. Wass	1896-1920	1,666	34,092	20.46
58	V. W. C. Jupp	1909-38	1,658	38,166	23.01
59	C. Gladwin	1939-58	1,653	30,265	18.30
60	M. D. Marshall	1977-95	1,651	31,548	19.10
61	W. E. Bowes	1928-47	1,639	27,470	16.76
62	**C. A. Walsh . . . .**	*1981-98*	**1,621**	**35,551**	**21.93**
63	A. W. Wellard	1927-50	1,614	39,302	24.35
64	J. E. Emburey	1973-97	1,608	41,958	26.09
65	P. I. Pocock	1964-86	1,607	42,648	26.53
66	N. I. Thomson	1952-72	1,597	32,867	20.58
67 {	J. Mercer	1919-47	1,591	37,210	23.38
	G. J. Thompson	1897-1922	1,591	30,058	18.89
69	J. M. Sims	1929-53	1,581	39,401	24.92
70 {	T. Emmett	1866-88	1,571	21,314	13.56
	Intikhab Alam	1957-82	1,571	43,474	27.67
72	B. S. Bedi	1961-81	1,560	33,843	21.69
73	W. Voce	1927-52	1,558	35,961	23.08
74	A. R. Gover	1928-48	1,555	36,753	23.63
75 {	T. W. Cartwright	1952-77	1,536	29,357	19.11
	K. Higgs	1958-86	1,536	36,267	23.61
77	James Langridge	1924-53	1,530	34,524	22.56
78	J. A. Flavell	1949-67	1,529	32,847	21.48
79	E. E. Hemmings	1966-95	1,515	44,403	29.30
80 {	C. F. Root	1910-33	1,512	31,933	21.11
	F. A. Tarrant	1898-1936	1,512	26,450	17.49
82	R. K. Tyldesley	1919-35	1,509	25,980	17.21

Bold type denotes those who played in 1997-98 and 1998 seasons.

† *The figures for A. Shaw exclude one wicket for which no analysis is available.*

Note: Some works of reference provide career figures which differ from those in this list, owing to the exclusion or inclusion of matches recognised or not recognised as first-class by *Wisden*.

Current Player with 1,000 Wickets

	Career	W	R	Avge
A. A. Donald	*1985-98*	1,043	23,137	22.18

ALL-ROUND RECORDS

HUNDRED RUNS AND TEN WICKETS IN AN INNINGS

V. E. Walker, England v Surrey at The Oval; 20*, 108, ten for 74, and four for 17 . .	1859
W. G. Grace, MCC v Oxford University at Oxford; 104, two for 60, and ten for 49 . .	1886

Note: E. M. Grace, for MCC v Gentlemen of Kent in a 12-a-side match at Canterbury in 1862, scored 192* and took five for 77 and ten for 69.

TWO HUNDRED RUNS AND SIXTEEN WICKETS

G. Giffen, South Australia v Victoria at Adelaide; 271, nine for 96, and seven for 70 . . 1891-92

HUNDRED IN EACH INNINGS AND FIVE WICKETS TWICE

G. H. Hirst, Yorkshire v Somerset at Bath; 111, 117*, six for 70, and five for 45 . . . 1906

HUNDRED IN EACH INNINGS AND TEN WICKETS

W. G. Grace, MCC v Kent at Canterbury (12-a-side); 123, five for 82 and six for 47 including a hat-trick	1874
B. J. T. Bosanquet, Middlesex v Sussex at Lord's; 103, 100*, three for 75, and eight for 53	1905
F. D. Stephenson, Nottinghamshire v Yorkshire at Nottingham; 111, 117, four for 105, and seven for 117	1988

HUNDRED AND FOUR WICKETS WITH CONSECUTIVE BALLS

K. D. James, Hampshire v Indians at Southampton; 103 and five for 74 including four wickets with consecutive balls.	1996

HUNDRED AND HAT-TRICK

W. G. Grace, MCC v Kent at Canterbury (12-a-side)	1874
G. Giffen, Australians v Lancashire at Manchester	1884
W. E. Roller, Surrey v Sussex at The Oval. *Unique instance of 200 and hat-trick*	1885
W. B. Burns, Worcestershire v Gloucestershire at Worcester	1913
V. W. C. Jupp, Sussex v Essex at Colchester	1921
R. E. S. Wyatt, MCC v Ceylon at Colombo	1926-27
L. N. Constantine, West Indians v Northamptonshire at Northampton	1928
D. E. Davies, Glamorgan v Leicestershire at Leicester	1937
V. M. Merchant, Dr C. R. Pereira's XI v Sir Homi Mehta's XI at Bombay	1946-47
M. J. Procter, Gloucestershire v Essex at Westcliff-on-Sea	1972
M. J. Procter, Gloucestershire v Leicestershire at Bristol	1979

SEASON DOUBLES

2,000 Runs and 200 Wickets

1906   G. H. Hirst   2,385 runs and 208 wickets

3,000 Runs and 100 Wickets

1937   J. H. Parks   3,003 runs and 101 wickets

2,000 Runs and 100 Wickets

	Season	R	W		Season	R	W
W. G. Grace	1873	2,139	106	F. E. Woolley	1914	2,272	125
W. G. Grace	1876	2,622	130	J. W. Hearne	1920	2,148	142
C. L. Townsend	1899	2,440	101	V. W. C. Jupp	1921	2,169	121
G. L. Jessop	1900	2,210	104	F. E. Woolley	1921	2,101	167
G. H. Hirst	1904	2,501	132	F. E. Woolley	1922	2,022	163
G. H. Hirst	1905	2,266	110	F. E. Woolley	1923	2,091	101
W. Rhodes	1909	2,094	141	L. F. Townsend	1933	2,268	100
W. Rhodes	1911	2,261	117	D. E. Davies	1937	2,012	103
F. A. Tarrant	1911	2,030	111	James Langridge	1937	2,082	101
J. W. Hearne	1913	2,036	124	T. E. Bailey	1959	2,011	100
J. W. Hearne	1914	2,116	123				

1,000 Runs and 200 Wickets

	Season	R	W		Season	R	W
A. E. Trott	1899	1,175	239	M. W. Tate	1923	1,168	219
A. E. Trott	1900	1,337	211	M. W. Tate	1924	1,419	205
A. S. Kennedy	1922	1,129	205	M. W. Tate	1925	1,290	228

1,000 Runs and 100 Wickets

Sixteen times: W. Rhodes.
Fourteen times: G. H. Hirst.
Ten times: V. W. C. Jupp.
Nine times: W. E. Astill.
Eight times: T. E. Bailey, W. G. Grace, M. S. Nichols, A. E. Relf, F. A. Tarrant, M. W. Tate†, F. J. Titmus, F. E. Woolley.
Seven times: G. E. Tribe.

† *M. W. Tate also scored 1,193 runs and took 116 wickets for MCC in first-class matches on the 1926-27 MCC tour of India and Ceylon.*

Note: R. J. Hadlee (1984) and F. D. Stephenson (1988) are the only players to perform the feat since the reduction of County Championship matches. A complete list of those performing the feat before then will be found on page 202 of the 1982 *Wisden*.

Wicket-Keeper's Double

	Season	R	D
L. E. G. Ames	1928	1,919	122
L. E. G. Ames	1929	1,795	128
L. E. G. Ames	1932	2,482	104
J. T. Murray	1957	1,025	104

20,000 RUNS AND 2,000 WICKETS IN A CAREER

	Career	R	Avge	W	Avge	Doubles
W. E. Astill	1906-39	22,731	22.55	2,431	23.76	9
T. E. Bailey	1945-67	28,641	33.42	2,082	23.13	8
W. G. Grace	1865-1908	54,896	39.55	2,876	17.92	8
G. H. Hirst	1891-1929	36,323	34.13	2,739	18.72	14
R. Illingworth	1951-83	24,134	28.06	2,072	20.28	6
W. Rhodes	1898-1930	39,802	30.83	4,187	16.71	16
M. W. Tate	1912-37	21,717	25.01	2,784	18.16	8†
F. J. Titmus	1949-82	21,588	23.11	2,830	22.37	8
F. E. Woolley	1906-38	58,969	40.75	2,068	19.85	8

† *Plus one double overseas (see above).*

WICKET-KEEPING RECORDS

MOST DISMISSALS IN AN INNINGS

9 (8ct, 1st)	Tahir Rashid	Habib Bank v PACO at Gujranwala	1992-93
9 (7ct, 2st)	W. R. James*	Matabeleland v Mashonaland CD at Bulawayo	1995-96
8 (all ct)	A. T. W. Grout	Queensland v Western Australia at Brisbane	1959-60

8 (all ct)†	D. E. East	Essex v Somerset at Taunton	1985
8 (all ct)	S. A. Marsh‡	Kent v Middlesex at Lord's	1991
8 (6ct, 2st)	T. J. Zoehrer	Australians v Surrey at The Oval	1993
8 (7ct, 1st)	D. S. Berry	Victoria v South Australia at Melbourne	1996-97
7 (4ct, 3st)	E. J. Smith	Warwickshire v Derbyshire at Birmingham	1926
7 (6ct, 1st)	W. Farrimond	Lancashire v Kent at Manchester	1930
7 (all ct)	W. F. F. Price	Middlesex v Yorkshire at Lord's	1937
7 (3ct, 4st)	D. Tallon	Queensland v Victoria at Brisbane	1938-39
7 (all ct)	R. A. Saggers	New South Wales v Combined XI at Brisbane	1940-41
7 (1ct, 6st)	H. Yarnold	Worcestershire v Scotland at Dundee	1951
7 (4ct, 3st)	J. Brown	Scotland v Ireland at Dublin	1957
7 (6ct, 1st)	N. Kirsten	Border v Rhodesia at East London	1959-60
7 (all ct)	M. S. Smith	Natal v Border at East London	1959-60
7 (all ct)	K. V. Andrew	Northamptonshire v Lancashire at Manchester	1962
7 (all ct)	A. Long	Surrey v Sussex at Hove	1964
7 (all ct)	R. M. Schofield	Central Districts v Wellington at Wellington	1964-65
7 (all ct)	R. W. Taylor	Derbyshire v Glamorgan at Derby	1966
7 (6ct, 1st)	H. B. Taber	New South Wales v South Australia at Adelaide . . .	1968-69
7 (6ct, 1st)	E. W. Jones	Glamorgan v Cambridge University at Cambridge . .	1970
7 (6ct, 1st)	S. Benjamin	Central Zone v North Zone at Bombay	1973-74
7 (all ct)	R. W. Taylor	Derbyshire v Yorkshire at Chesterfield	1975
7 (6ct, 1st)	Shahid Israr	Karachi Whites v Quetta at Karachi	1976-77
7 (4ct, 3st)	Wasim Bari	PIA v Sind at Lahore	1977-78
7 (all ct)	J. A. Maclean	Queensland v Victoria at Melbourne	1977-78
7 (5ct, 2st)	Taslim Arif	National Bank v Punjab at Lahore	1978-79
7 (all ct)	Wasim Bari	Pakistan v New Zealand at Auckland	1978-79
7 (all ct)	R. W. Taylor	England v India at Bombay	1979-80
7 (all ct)	D. L. Bairstow	Yorkshire v Derbyshire at Scarborough	1982
7 (6ct, 1st)	R. B. Phillips	Queensland v New Zealanders at Bundaberg	1982-83
7 (3ct, 4st)	Masood Iqbal	Habib Bank v Lahore at Lahore	1982-83
7 (3ct, 4st)	Arif-ud-Din	United Bank v PACO at Sahiwal	1983-84
7 (6ct, 1st)	R. J. East	OFS v Western Province B at Cape Town	1984-85
7 (all ct)	B. A. Young	Northern Districts v Canterbury at Christchurch	1986-87
7 (all ct)	D. J. Richardson	Eastern Province v OFS at Bloemfontein	1988-89
7 (6ct, 1st)	Dildar Malik	Multan v Faisalabad at Sahiwal	1988-89
7 (all ct)	W. K. Hegg	Lancashire v Derbyshire at Chesterfield	1989
7 (all ct)	Imran Zia	Bahawalpur v Faisalabad at Faisalabad	1989-90
7 (all ct)	I. D. S. Smith	New Zealand v Sri Lanka at Hamilton	1990-91
7 (all ct)	J. F. Holyman	Tasmania v Western Australia at Hobart	1990-91
7 (all ct)	P. J. L. Radley	OFS v Western Province at Cape Town	1990-91
7 (all ct)	C. P. Metson	Glamorgan v Derbyshire at Chesterfield	1991
7 (all ct)	H. M. de Vos	W. Transvaal v E. Transvaal at Potchefstroom	1993-94
7 (all ct)	P. Kirsten	Griqualand West v W. Transvaal at Potchefstroom . .	1993-94
7 (6ct, 1st)	S. A. Marsh	Kent v Durham at Canterbury	1994
7 (all ct)	K. J. Piper	Warwickshire v Essex at Birmingham	1994
7 (6ct, 1st)	K. J. Piper	Warwickshire v Derbyshire at Chesterfield	1994
7 (all ct)	H. H. Devapriya	Colts CC v Sinhalese SC at Colombo	1995-96
7 (all ct)	D. J. R. Campbell	Mashonaland CD v Matabeleland at Bulawayo	1995-96
7 (all ct)	A. C. Gilchrist	Western Australia v South Australia at Perth	1995-96
7 (all ct)	C. W. Scott	Durham v Yorkshire at Chester-le-Street	1996
7 (all ct)	Zahid Umar	WAPDA v Habib Bank at Sheikhupura	1997-98
7 (all ct)	K. S. M. Iyer	Vidarbha v Uttar Pradesh at Allahabad	1997-98

* *W. R. James also scored 99 and 99 not out.*
† *The first eight wickets to fall.*
‡ *S. A. Marsh also scored 108 not out.*

WICKET-KEEPERS' HAT-TRICKS

W. H. Brain, Gloucestershire v Somerset at Cheltenham, 1893 – three stumpings off successive balls from C. L. Townsend.

G. O. Dawkes, Derbyshire v Worcestershire at Kidderminster, 1958 – three catches off successive balls from H. L. Jackson.

R. C. Russell, Gloucestershire v Surrey at The Oval, 1986 – three catches off successive balls from C. A. Walsh and D. V. Lawrence (2).

MOST DISMISSALS IN A MATCH

13 (11ct, 2st)	W. R. James*	Matabeleland v Mashonaland CD at Bulawayo ..	1995-96
12 (8ct, 4st)	E. Pooley	Surrey v Sussex at The Oval	1868
12 (9ct, 3st)	D. Tallon	Queensland v New South Wales at Sydney	1938-39
12 (9ct, 3st)	H. B. Taber	New South Wales v South Australia at Adelaide. .	1968-69
11 (all ct)	A. Long	Surrey v Sussex at Hove	1964
11 (all ct)	R. W. Marsh	Western Australia v Victoria at Perth	1975-76
11 (all ct)	D. L. Bairstow	Yorkshire v Derbyshire at Scarborough.	1982
11 (all ct)	W. K. Hegg	Lancashire v Derbyshire at Chesterfield	1989
11 (all ct)	A. J. Stewart	Surrey v Leicestershire at Leicester	1989
11 (all ct)	T. J. Nielsen	South Australia v Western Australia at Perth	1990-91
11 (10ct, 1st)	I. A. Healy	Australians v N. Transvaal at Verwoerdburg . . .	1993-94
11 (10ct, 1st)	K. J. Piper	Warwickshire v Derbyshire at Chesterfield	1994
11 (all ct)	D. S. Berry	Victoria v Pakistanis at Melbourne	1995-96
11 (10ct, 1st)	W. A. Seccombe	Queensland v Western Australia at Brisbane	1995-96
11 (all ct)	R. C. Russell	England v South Africa (Second Test) at Johannesburg	1995-96
11 (10ct, 1st)	D. S. Berry	Victoria v South Australia at Melbourne	1996-97
11 (all ct)	Wasim Yousufi	Peshawar v Bahawalpur at Peshawar	1997-98

* W. R. James also scored 99 and 99 not out.

MOST DISMISSALS IN A SEASON

128 (79ct, 49st)	L. E. G. Ames	1929		104 (82ct, 22st)	J. T. Murray	1957
122 (70ct, 52st)	L. E. G. Ames	1928		102 (69ct, 33st)	F. H. Huish	1913
110 (63ct, 47st)	H. Yarnold	1949		102 (95ct, 7st)	J. T. Murray	1960
107 (77ct, 30st)	G. Duckworth	1928		101 (62ct, 39st)	F. H. Huish	1911
107 (96ct, 11st)	J. G. Binks	1960		101 (85ct, 16st)	R. Booth	1960
104 (40ct, 64st)	L. E. G. Ames	1932		100 (91ct, 9st)	R. Booth	1964

MOST DISMISSALS IN A CAREER

Dates in italics denote the first half of an overseas season; i.e. *1914* denotes the 1914-15 season.

		Career	M	Ct	St	Total
1	R. W. Taylor	1960-88	639	1,473	176	1,649
2	J. T. Murray	1952-75	635	1,270	257	1,527
3	H. Strudwick	1902-27	675	1,242	255	1,497
4	A. P. E. Knott	1964-85	511	1,211	133	1,344
5	F. H. Huish	1895-*1914*.	497	933	377	1,310
6	B. Taylor	1949-73	572	1,083	211	1,294
7	D. Hunter	1889-*1909*.	548	906	347	1,253
8	H. R. Butt	1890-1912	550	953	275	1,228

		Career	M	Ct	St	Total
9	J. H. Board	1891-*1914*	525	852	355	1,207
10	H. Elliott	1920-47	532	904	302	1,206
11	J. M. Parks	1949-76	739	1,088	93	1,181
12	R. Booth	1951-70	468	948	178	1,126
13	L. E. G. Ames	1926-51	593	703	418†	1,121
14	D. L. Bairstow	1970-90	459	961	138	1,099
15	G. Duckworth	1923-47	504	753	343	1,096
16	**R. C. Russell**	**1981-98**	**392**	**972**	**111**	**1,083**
17	H. W. Stephenson	1948-64	462	748	334	1,082
18	J. G. Binks	1955-75	502	895	176	1,071
19	T. G. Evans	1939-69	465	816	250	1,066
20	A. Long	1960-80	452	922	124	1,046
21	G. O. Dawkes	1937-61	482	895	148	1,043
22	R. W. Tolchard	1965-83	483	912	125	1,037
23	W. L. Cornford	1921-47	496	675	342	1,017

Bold type denotes those who played in 1997-98 and 1998 seasons.

† *Record.*

Current Players with 500 Dismissals

	Career	M	Ct	St	Total
S. J. Rhodes	1981-98	346	864	110	974
S. A. Marsh	1982-98	276	660	54	714
I. A. Healy	*1986-97*	202	613	55	668
W. K. Hegg	1986-98	238	570	66	636
R. J. Blakey	1985-98	275	586	48	634
D. Ripley	1984-98	264	555	75	630
D. J. Richardson	*1977-97*	200	579	40	619
P. Moores	1983-98	231	502	44	546

FIELDING RECORDS

(Excluding wicket-keepers)

MOST CATCHES IN AN INNINGS

7	M. J. Stewart	Surrey v Northamptonshire at Northampton	1957
7	A. S. Brown	Gloucestershire v Nottinghamshire at Nottingham	1966

MOST CATCHES IN A MATCH

10	W. R. Hammond†	Gloucestershire v Surrey at Cheltenham	1928
8	W. B. Burns	Worcestershire v Yorkshire at Bradford	1907
8	F. G. Travers	Europeans v Parsees at Bombay	1923-24
8	A. H. Bakewell	Northamptonshire v Essex at Leyton	1928
8	W. R. Hammond	Gloucestershire v Worcestershire at Cheltenham	1932
8	K. J. Grieves	Lancashire v Sussex at Manchester	1951
8	C. A. Milton	Gloucestershire v Sussex at Hove	1952
8	G. A. R. Lock	Surrey v Warwickshire at The Oval	1957
8	J. M. Prodger	Kent v Gloucestershire at Cheltenham	1961
8	P. M. Walker	Glamorgan v Derbyshire at Swansea	1970
8	Masood Anwar	Rawalpindi v Lahore Division at Rawalpindi	1983-84
8	M. C. J. Ball	Gloucestershire v Yorkshire at Cheltenham	1994
8	J. D. Carr	Middlesex v Warwickshire at Birmingham	1995

† *Hammond also scored a hundred in each innings.*

MOST CATCHES IN A SEASON

78	W. R. Hammond	1928		69	P. M. Walker	1960
77	M. J. Stewart	1957		66	J. Tunnicliffe	1895
73	P. M. Walker	1961		65	W. R. Hammond	1925
71	P. J. Sharpe	1962		65	P. M. Walker	1959
70	J. Tunnicliffe	1901		65	D. W. Richardson	1961
69	J. G. Langridge	1955				

Note: The most catches by a fielder since the reduction of County Championship matches in 1969 is 49 by C. J. Tavaré in 1978.

MOST CATCHES IN A CAREER

Dates in italics denote the first half of an overseas season; i.e. *1970* denotes the 1970-71 season.

1,018	F. E. Woolley (1906-38)		784	J. G. Langridge (1928-55)
887	W. G. Grace (1865-1908)		764	W. Rhodes (1898-1930)
830	G. A. R. Lock (1946-*70*)		758	C. A. Milton (1948-74)
819	W. R. Hammond (1920-51)		754	E. H. Hendren (1907-38)
813	D. B. Close (1949-86)			

Most Catches by Current Players

493	M. W. Gatting (1975-98)	441	G. A. Hick (*1983*-98)

TEAM RECORDS

HIGHEST TOTALS

1,107	Victoria v New South Wales at Melbourne	1926-27
1,059	Victoria v Tasmania at Melbourne	1922-23
952-6 dec.	Sri Lanka v India at Colombo	1997-98
951-7 dec.	Sind v Baluchistan at Karachi	1973-74
944-6 dec.	Hyderabad v Andhra at Secunderabad	1993-94
918	New South Wales v South Australia at Sydney	1900-01
912-8 dec.	Holkar v Mysore at Indore	1945-46
912-6 dec.†	Tamil Nadu v Goa at Panjim	1988-89
910-6 dec.	Railways v Dera Ismail Khan at Lahore	1964-65
903-7 dec.	England v Australia at The Oval	1938
887	Yorkshire v Warwickshire at Birmingham	1896
868†	North Zone v West Zone at Bhilai	1987-88
863	Lancashire v Surrey at The Oval	1990
855-6 dec.†	Bombay v Hyderabad at Bombay	1990-91
849	England v West Indies at Kingston	1929-30
843	Australians v Oxford & Cambridge U P & P at Portsmouth	1893
839	New South Wales v Tasmania at Sydney	1898-99
826-4	Maharashtra v Kathiawar at Poona	1948-49
824	Lahore Greens v Bahawalpur at Lahore	1965-66
821-7 dec.	South Australia v Queensland at Adelaide	1939-40
815	New South Wales v Victoria at Sydney	1908-09
811	Surrey v Somerset at The Oval	1899
810-4 dec.	Warwickshire v Durham at Birmingham	1994

807	New South Wales v South Australia at Adelaide	1899-1900
805	New South Wales v Victoria at Melbourne	1905-06
803-4 dec.	Kent v Essex at Brentwood	1934
803	Non-Smokers v Smokers at East Melbourne	1886-87
802-8 dec.	Karachi Blues v Lahore City at Peshawar	1994-95
802	New South Wales v South Australia at Sydney	1920-21
801	Lancashire v Somerset at Taunton	1895
798	Maharashtra v Northern India at Poona	1940-41
793	Victoria v Queensland at Melbourne	1927-28
791-6 dec.	Karnataka v Bengal at Calcutta	1990-91
790-3 dec.	West Indies v Pakistan at Kingston	1957-58
786	New South Wales v South Australia at Adelaide	1922-23
784	Baroda v Holkar at Baroda	1946-47
783-8 dec.	Hyderabad v Bihar at Secunderabad	1986-87
781-7 dec.	Northamptonshire v Nottinghamshire at Northampton	1995
780-8	Punjab v Delhi at Delhi	1994-95
777	Canterbury v Otago at Christchurch	1996-97
775	New South Wales v Victoria at Sydney	1881-82

† *Tamil Nadu's total of 912-6 dec. included 52 penalty runs from their opponents' failure to meet the required bowling rate. North Zone's total of 868 included 68, and Bombay's total of 855-6 dec. included 48.*

LOWEST TOTALS

12	Oxford University v MCC and Ground at Oxford	†1877
12	Northamptonshire v Gloucestershire at Gloucester	1907
13	Auckland v Canterbury at Auckland	1877-78
13	Nottinghamshire v Yorkshire at Nottingham	1901
14	Surrey v Essex at Chelmsford	1983
15	MCC v Surrey at Lord's	1839
15	Victoria v MCC at Melbourne	†1903-04
15	Northamptonshire v Yorkshire at Northampton	†1908
15	Hampshire v Warwickshire at Birmingham	1922
	Following on, Hampshire scored 521 and won by 155 runs.	
16	MCC and Ground v Surrey at Lord's	1872
16	Derbyshire v Nottinghamshire at Nottingham	1879
16	Surrey v Nottinghamshire at The Oval	1880
16	Warwickshire v Kent at Tonbridge	1913
16	Trinidad v Barbados at Bridgetown	1942-43
16	Border v Natal at East London (first innings)	1959-60
17	Gentlemen of Kent v Gentlemen of England at Lord's	1850
17	Gloucestershire v Australians at Cheltenham	1896
18	The Bs v England at Lord's	1831
18	Kent v Sussex at Gravesend	†1867
18	Tasmania v Victoria at Melbourne	1868-69
18	Australians v MCC and Ground at Lord's	†1896
18	Border v Natal at East London (second innings)	1959-60
19	Sussex v Surrey at Godalming	1830
19	Sussex v Nottinghamshire at Hove	†1873
19	MCC and Ground v Australians at Lord's	1878
19	Wellington v Nelson at Nelson	1885-86

† *Signifies that one man was absent.*

Notes: At Lord's in 1810, The Bs, with one man absent, were dismissed by England for 6.

On November 17, 1998, National Bank of Pakistan were reported to have been bowled out for 20 by Pakistan Customs at Karachi, the fifth score of 20 in first-class history, and the lowest total since 1983.

LOWEST TOTAL IN A MATCH

34 (16 and 18) Border v Natal at East London 1959-60
42 (27 and 15) Northamptonshire v Yorkshire at Northampton 1908

Note: Northamptonshire batted one man short in each innings.

HIGHEST MATCH AGGREGATES

2,376 for 37 wickets Maharashtra v Bombay at Poona 1948-49
2,078 for 40 wickets Bombay v Holkar at Bombay 1944-45
1,981 for 35 wickets England v South Africa at Durban 1938-39
1,945 for 18 wickets Canterbury v Wellington at Christchurch 1994-95
1,929 for 39 wickets New South Wales v South Australia at Sydney 1925-26
1,911 for 34 wickets New South Wales v Victoria at Sydney 1908-09
1,905 for 40 wickets Otago v Wellington at Dunedin 1923-24

In Britain

1,808 for 20 wickets Sussex v Essex at Hove 1993
1,723 for 31 wickets England v Australia at Leeds 1948
1,706 for 23 wickets Hampshire v Warwickshire at Southampton 1997
1,650 for 19 wickets Surrey v Lancashire at The Oval 1990
1,642 for 29 wickets Nottinghamshire v Kent at Nottingham 1995
1,641 for 16 wickets Glamorgan v Worcestershire at Abergavenny 1990
1,614 for 30 wickets England v India at Manchester 1990
1,606 for 34 wickets Somerset v Derbyshire at Taunton 1996
1,603 for 28 wickets England v India at Lord's 1990
1,601 for 29 wickets England v Australia at Lord's 1930
1,601 for 35 wickets Kent v Surrey at Canterbury 1995

LOWEST AGGREGATE IN A COMPLETED MATCH

105 for 31 wickets MCC v Australians at Lord's 1878

Note: The lowest aggregate since 1900 is 157 for 22 wickets, Surrey v Worcestershire at The Oval, 1954.

HIGHEST FOURTH-INNINGS TOTALS

(Unless otherwise stated, the side making the runs won the match.)

654-5 England v South Africa at Durban 1938-39
       After being set 696 to win. The match was left drawn on the tenth day.
604   Maharashtra (*set 959 to win*) v Bombay at Poona 1948-49
576-8 Trinidad (*set 672 to win*) v Barbados at Port-of-Spain 1945-46
572   New South Wales (*set 593 to win*) v South Australia at Sydney 1907-08
529-9 Combined XI (*set 579 to win*) v South Africans at Perth 1963-64
518   Victoria (*set 753 to win*) v Queensland at Brisbane 1926-27
507-7 Cambridge University v MCC and Ground at Lord's 1896
506-6 South Australia v Queensland at Adelaide 1991-92
502-6 Middlesex v Nottinghamshire at Nottingham 1925
502-8 Players v Gentlemen at Lord's 1900
500-7 South African Universities v Western Province at Stellenbosch 1978-79

LARGEST VICTORIES

Largest Innings Victories

Inns and 851 runs:	Railways (910-6 dec.) v Dera Ismail Khan (Lahore)	1964-65
Inns and 666 runs:	Victoria (1,059) v Tasmania (Melbourne)	1922-23
Inns and 656 runs:	Victoria (1,107) v New South Wales (Melbourne)	1926-27
Inns and 605 runs:	New South Wales (918) v South Australia (Sydney)	1900-01
Inns and 579 runs:	England (903-7 dec.) v Australia (The Oval)	1938
Inns and 575 runs:	Sind (951-7 dec.) v Baluchistan (Karachi)	1973-74
Inns and 527 runs:	New South Wales (713) v South Australia (Adelaide)	1908-09
Inns and 517 runs:	Australians (675) v Nottinghamshire (Nottingham)	1921

Largest Victories by Runs Margin

685 runs:	New South Wales (235 and 761-8 dec.) v Queensland (Sydney)	1929-30
675 runs:	England (521 and 342-8 dec.) v Australia (Brisbane)	1928-29
638 runs:	New South Wales (304 and 770) v South Australia (Adelaide)	1920-21
609 runs:	Muslim Commercial Bank (575 and 282-0 dec.) v WAPDA (Lahore)	1977-78
585 runs:	Sargodha (336 and 416) v Lahore Municipal Corporation (Faisalabad)	1978-79
573 runs:	Sinhalese SC (395-7 dec. and 350-2 dec.) v Sebastianites C and AC (Colombo)	1990-91
571 runs:	Victoria (304 and 649) v South Australia (Adelaide)	1926-27
562 runs:	Australia (701 and 327) v England (The Oval)	1934

Victory Without Losing a Wicket

Lancashire (166-0 dec. and 66-0) beat Leicestershire by ten wickets (Manchester)	1956
Karachi A (277-0 dec.) beat Sind A by an innings and 77 runs (Karachi)	1957-58
Railways (236-0 dec. and 16-0) beat Jammu and Kashmir by ten wickets (Srinagar)	1960-61
Karnataka (451-0 dec.) beat Kerala by an innings and 186 runs (Chikmagalur)	1977-78

TIED MATCHES

Since 1948 a tie has been recognised only when the scores are level with all the wickets down in the fourth innings.

The following are the instances since then:

D. G. Bradman's XI v A. L. Hassett's XI at Melbourne	1948-49
Hampshire v Kent at Southampton	1950
Sussex v Warwickshire at Hove	1952
Essex v Lancashire at Brentwood	1952
Northamptonshire v Middlesex at Peterborough	1953
Yorkshire v Leicestershire at Huddersfield	1954
Sussex v Hampshire at Eastbourne	1955
Victoria v New South Wales at Melbourne	1956-57
T. N. Pearce's XI v New Zealanders at Scarborough	1958
Essex v Gloucestershire at Leyton	1959
Australia v West Indies (First Test) at Brisbane	1960-61
Bahawalpur v Lahore B at Bahawalpur	1961-62
Hampshire v Middlesex at Portsmouth	1967
England XI v England Under-25 XI at Scarborough	1968
Yorkshire v Middlesex at Bradford	1973
Sussex v Essex at Hove	1974
South Australia v Queensland at Adelaide	1976-77
Central Districts v England XI at New Plymouth	1977-78
Victoria v New Zealanders at Melbourne	1982-83

Muslim Commercial Bank v Railways at Sialkot........................	1983-84
Sussex v Kent at Hastings..	1984
Northamptonshire v Kent at Northampton	1984
Eastern Province B v Boland at Albany SC, Port Elizabeth	1985-86
Natal B v Eastern Province B at Pietermaritzburg	1985-86
India v Australia (First Test) at Madras	1986-87
Gloucestershire v Derbyshire at Bristol	1987
Bahawalpur v Peshawar at Bahawalpur	1988-89
Wellington v Canterbury at Wellington	1988-89
Sussex v Kent at Hove...	†1991
Nottinghamshire v Worcestershire at Nottingham	1993

† *Sussex (436) scored the highest total to tie a first-class match.*

MATCHES BEGUN AND FINISHED ON FIRST DAY

Since World War II.

Derbyshire v Somerset at Chesterfield, June 11	1947
Lancashire v Sussex at Manchester, July 12	1950
Surrey v Warwickshire at The Oval, May 16	1953
Somerset v Lancashire at Bath, June 6 (H. F. T. Buse's benefit)...............	1953
Kent v Worcestershire at Tunbridge Wells, June 15	1960

TEST MATCH RECORDS

Note: This section covers all Tests up to August 31, 1998.

BATTING RECORDS

HIGHEST INDIVIDUAL INNINGS

375	B. C. Lara	West Indies v England at St John's	1993-94
365*	G. S. Sobers	West Indies v Pakistan at Kingston	1957-58
364	L. Hutton	England v Australia at The Oval	1938
340	S. T. Jayasuriya	Sri Lanka v India at Colombo (RPS).	1997-98
337	Hanif Mohammad	Pakistan v West Indies at Bridgetown	1957-58
336*	W. R. Hammond	England v New Zealand at Auckland.	1932-33
334	D. G. Bradman	Australia v England at Leeds	1930
333	G. A. Gooch	England v India at Lord's	1990
325	A. Sandham	England v West Indies at Kingston	1929-30
311	R. B. Simpson	Australia v England at Manchester	1964
310*	J. H. Edrich	England v New Zealand at Leeds	1965
307	R. M. Cowper	Australia v England at Melbourne.	1965-66
304	D. G. Bradman	Australia v England at Leeds	1934
302	L. G. Rowe.	West Indies v England at Bridgetown	1973-74
299*	D. G. Bradman	Australia v South Africa at Adelaide	1931-32
299	M. D. Crowe.	New Zealand v Sri Lanka at Wellington	1990-91
291	I. V. A. Richards	West Indies v England at The Oval	1976
287	R. E. Foster	England v Australia at Sydney	1903-04
285*	P. B. H. May.	England v West Indies at Birmingham	1957
280*	Javed Miandad.	Pakistan v India at Hyderabad	1982-83
278	D. C. S. Compton . . .	England v Pakistan at Nottingham.	1954
277	B. C. Lara	West Indies v Australia at Sydney	1992-93
274	R. G. Pollock	South Africa v Australia at Durban	1969-70
274	Zaheer Abbas	Pakistan v England at Birmingham	1971
271	Javed Miandad.	Pakistan v New Zealand at Auckland	1988-89
270*	G. A. Headley	West Indies v England at Kingston	1934-35
270	D. G. Bradman	Australia v England at Melbourne.	1936-37
268	G. N. Yallop	Australia v Pakistan at Melbourne.	1983-84
267*	B. A. Young	New Zealand v Sri Lanka at Dunedin	1996-97
267	P. A. de Silva	Sri Lanka v New Zealand at Wellington	1990-91
266	W. H. Ponsford	Australia v England at The Oval	1934
266	D. L. Houghton	Zimbabwe v Sri Lanka at Bulawayo	1994-95
262*	D. L. Amiss	England v West Indies at Kingston	1973-74
261	F. M. M. Worrell	West Indies v England at Nottingham	1950
260	C. C. Hunte	West Indies v Pakistan at Kingston	1957-58
260	Javed Miandad.	Pakistan v England at The Oval	1987
259	G. M. Turner.	New Zealand v West Indies at Georgetown	1971-72
258	T. W. Graveney	England v West Indies at Nottingham	1957
258	S. M. Nurse	West Indies v New Zealand at Christchurch	1968-69
257*	Wasim Akram	Pakistan v Zimbabwe at Sheikhupura.	1996-97
256	R. B. Kanhai	West Indies v India at Calcutta.	1958-59
256	K. F. Barrington.	England v Australia at Manchester	1964
255*	D. J. McGlew	South Africa v New Zealand at Wellington	1952-53
254	D. G. Bradman	Australia v England at Lord's.	1930
251	W. R. Hammond	England v Australia at Sydney	1928-29
250	K. D. Walters	Australia v New Zealand at Christchurch	1976-77
250	S. F. A. F. Bacchus. . .	West Indies v India at Kanpur	1978-79

The highest individual innings for India is:

236*	S. M. Gavaskar	India v West Indies at Madras	1983-84

Note: M. A. Taylor scored 334* for Australia v Pakistan at Peshawar in 1998-99, after the deadline for this section.

HUNDRED ON TEST DEBUT

C. Bannerman (165*)	Australia v England at Melbourne	1876-77
W. G. Grace (152)	England v Australia at The Oval	1880
H. Graham (107)	Australia v England at Lord's	1893
†K. S. Ranjitsinhji (154*) . . .	England v Australia at Manchester	1896
†P. F. Warner (132*)	England v South Africa at Johannesburg	1898-99
†R. A. Duff (104)	Australia v England at Melbourne	1901-02
R. E. Foster (287)	England v Australia at Sydney	1903-04
G. Gunn (119).	England v Australia at Sydney	1907-08
†R. J. Hartigan (116)	Australia v England at Adelaide	1907-08
†H. L. Collins (104).	Australia v England at Sydney	1920-21
W. H. Ponsford (110)	Australia v England at Sydney	1924-25
A. A. Jackson (164)	Australia v England at Adelaide	1928-29
†G. A. Headley (176).	West Indies v England at Bridgetown	1929-30
J. E. Mills (117)	New Zealand v England at Wellington.	1929-30
Nawab of Pataudi sen. (102) .	England v Australia at Sydney	1932-33
B. H. Valentine (136)	England v India at Bombay.	1933-34
†L. Amarnath (118)	India v England at Bombay.	1933-34
†P. A. Gibb (106)	England v South Africa at Johannesburg	1938-39
S. C. Griffith (140).	England v West Indies at Port-of-Spain	1947-48
A. G. Ganteaume (112). . . .	West Indies v England at Port-of-Spain	1947-48
†J. W. Burke (101*)	Australia v England at Adelaide	1950-51
P. B. H. May (138)	England v South Africa at Leeds	1951
R. H. Shodhan (110)	India v Pakistan at Calcutta.	1952-53
B. H. Pairaudeau (115)	West Indies v India at Port-of-Spain	1952-53
†O. G. Smith (104)	West Indies v Australia at Kingston	1954-55
A. G. Kripal Singh (100*). . .	India v New Zealand at Hyderabad.	1955-56
C. C. Hunte (142)	West Indies v Pakistan at Bridgetown	1957-58
C. A. Milton (104*)	England v New Zealand at Leeds.	1958
†A. A. Baig (112)	India v England at Manchester.	1959
Hanumant Singh (105)	India v England at Delhi.	1963-64
Khalid Ibadulla (166)	Pakistan v Australia at Karachi	1964-65
B. R. Taylor (105)	New Zealand v India at Calcutta	1964-65
K. D. Walters (155)	Australia v England at Brisbane	1965-66
J. H. Hampshire (107)	England v West Indies at Lord's.	1969
†G. R. Viswanath (137)	India v Australia at Kanpur	1969-70
G. S. Chappell (108)	Australia v England at Perth	1970-71
‡L. G. Rowe (214, 100*) . . .	West Indies v New Zealand at Kingston	1971-72
A. I. Kallicharran (100*). . .	West Indies v New Zealand at Georgetown	1971-72
R. E. Redmond (107)	New Zealand v Pakistan at Auckland	1972-73
†F. C. Hayes (106*)	England v West Indies at The Oval.	1973
†C. G. Greenidge (107)	West Indies v India at Bangalore	1974-75
†L. Baichan (105*)	West Indies v Pakistan at Lahore	1974-75
G. J. Cosier (109)	Australia v West Indies at Melbourne	1975-76
S. Amarnath (124)	India v New Zealand at Auckland	1975-76
Javed Miandad (163)	Pakistan v New Zealand at Lahore	1976-77
†A. B. Williams (100)	West Indies v Australia at Georgetown	1977-78
†D. M. Wellham (103)	Australia v England at The Oval	1981
†Salim Malik (100*)	Pakistan v Sri Lanka at Karachi	1981-82
K. C. Wessels (162)	Australia v England at Brisbane	1982-83
W. B. Phillips (159)	Australia v Pakistan at Perth	1983-84
§M. Azharuddin (110)	India v England at Calcutta	1984-85
D. S. B. P. Kuruppu (201*) . .	Sri Lanka v New Zealand at Colombo (CCC). .	1986-87
†M. J. Greatbatch (107*) . . .	New Zealand v England at Auckland	1987-88
M. E. Waugh (138)	Australia v England at Adelaide	1990-91
A. C. Hudson (163)	South Africa v West Indies at Bridgetown	1991-92
R. S. Kaluwitharana (132*) .	Sri Lanka v Australia at Colombo (SSC)	1992-93
D. L. Houghton (121).	Zimbabwe v India at Harare	1992-93
P. K. Amre (103).	India v South Africa at Durban	1992-93

†G. P. Thorpe (114*)	England v Australia at Nottingham	1993
G. S. Blewett (102*)	Australia v England at Adelaide	1994-95
S. C. Ganguly (131)	India v England at Lord's	1996
†Mohammad Wasim (109*) . .	Pakistan v New Zealand at Lahore	1996-97
Ali Naqvi (115)	Pakistan v South Africa at Rawalpindi	1997-98
Azhar Mahmood (128*)	Pakistan v South Africa at Rawalpindi	1997-98

   † *In his second innings of the match.*
   ‡ *L. G. Rowe is the only batsman to score a hundred in each innings on debut.*
   § *M. Azharuddin is the only batsman to score hundreds in each of his first three Tests.*

Notes: L. Amarnath and S. Amarnath were father and son.
   Ali Naqvi and Azhar Mahmood achieved the feat in the same innings.

300 RUNS IN FIRST TEST

314	L. G. Rowe (214, 100*)	West Indies v New Zealand at Kingston	1971-72
306	R. E. Foster (287, 19)	England v Australia at Sydney	1903-04

TWO SEPARATE HUNDREDS IN A TEST

   Three times: S. M. Gavaskar.
   Twice in one series: C. L. Walcott v Australia (1954-55).
   Twice: †A. R. Border; G. S. Chappell; ‡P. A. de Silva; G. A. Headley; H. Sutcliffe.
   Once: W. Bardsley; D. G. Bradman; I. M. Chappell; D. C. S. Compton; G. W. Flower; G. A. Gooch; C. G. Greenidge; A. P. Gurusinha; W. R. Hammond; Hanif Mohammad; V. S. Hazare; G. P. Howarth; Javed Miandad; A. H. Jones; D. M. Jones; R. B. Kanhai; G. Kirsten; A. Melville; L. R. D. Mendis; B. Mitchell; J. Moroney; A. R. Morris; E. Paynter; §L. G. Rowe; A. C. Russell; R. B. Simpson; G. S. Sobers; A. J. Stewart; G. M. Turner; K. D. Walters; S. R. Waugh; E. D. Weekes.

   † *A. R. Border scored 150* and 153 against Pakistan in 1979-80 to become the first to score 150 in each innings of a Test match.*
   ‡ *P. A. de Silva scored 138* and 103* against Pakistan in 1996-97 to become the first to score two not out hundreds in a Test match.*
   § *L. G. Rowe's two hundreds were on his Test debut.*

TRIPLE-HUNDRED AND HUNDRED IN SAME TEST

G. A. Gooch (England)	333 and 123 v India at Lord's	1990

   The only instance in first-class cricket.

DOUBLE-HUNDRED AND HUNDRED IN SAME TEST

K. D. Walters (Australia)	242 and 103 v West Indies at Sydney	1968-69
S. M. Gavaskar (India)	124 and 220 v West Indies at Port-of-Spain	1970-71
†L. G. Rowe (West Indies)	214 and 100* v New Zealand at Kingston	1971-72
G. S. Chappell (Australia)	247* and 133 v New Zealand at Wellington	1973-74

   † *On Test debut.*

MOST RUNS IN A SERIES

	T	I	NO	R	HS	100s	Avge		
D. G. Bradman.	5	7	0	974	334	4	139.14	A v E	1930
W. R. Hammond. . . .	5	9	1	905	251	4	113.12	E v A	1928-29
M. A. Taylor	6	11	1	839	219	2	83.90	A v E	1989
R. N. Harvey.	5	9	0	834	205	4	92.66	A v SA	1952-53
I. V. A. Richards . . .	4	7	0	829	291	3	118.42	WI v E	1976
C. L. Walcott.	5	10	0	827	155	5	82.70	WI v A	1954-55
G. S. Sobers.	5	8	2	824	365*	3	137.33	WI v P	1957-58
D. G. Bradman.	5	9	0	810	270	3	90.00	A v E	1936-37
D. G. Bradman.	5	5	1	806	299*	4	201.50	A v SA	1931-32
B. C. Lara.	5	8	0	798	375	2	99.75	WI v E	1993-94
E. D. Weekes.	5	7	0	779	194	4	111.28	WI v I	1948-49
†S. M. Gavaskar. . . .	4	8	3	774	220	4	154.80	I v WI	1970-71
B. C. Lara.	6	10	1	765	179	3	85.00	WI v E	1995
Mudassar Nazar	6	8	2	761	231	4	126.83	P v I	1982-83
D. G. Bradman.	5	8	0	758	304	2	94.75	A v E	1934
D. C. S. Compton. . .	5	8	0	753	208	4	94.12	E v SA	1947
‡G. A. Gooch	3	6	0	752	333	3	125.33	E v I	1990

† *Gavaskar's aggregate was achieved in his first Test series.*

‡ *G. A. Gooch is alone in scoring 1,000 runs in Test cricket during an English season with 1,058 runs in 11 innings against New Zealand and India in 1990.*

MOST RUNS IN A CALENDAR YEAR

	T	I	NO	R	HS	100s	Avge	Year
I. V. A. Richards (WI)	11	19	0	1,710	291	7	90.00	1976
S. M. Gavaskar (I)	18	27	1	1,555	221	5	59.80	1979
G. R. Viswanath (I).	17	26	3	1,388	179	5	60.34	1979
R. B. Simpson (A)	14	26	3	1,381	311	3	60.04	1964
D. L. Amiss (E)	13	22	2	1,379	262*	5	68.95	1974
S. M. Gavaskar (I)	18	32	4	1,310	236*	5	46.78	1983
S. T. Jayasuriya (SL)	11	19	0	1,271	340	3	66.89	1997
G. A. Gooch (E).	9	17	1	1,264	333	4	79.00	1990
D. C. Boon (A)	16	25	5	1,241	164*	4	62.05	1993
B. C. Lara (WI)	20	20	2	1,222	179	4	67.88	1995
P. A. de Silva (SL)	11	19	3	1,220	168	7	76.25	1997
M. A. Taylor (A)	11	20	1	1,219	219	4	64.15	1989†

† *The year of his debut.*

Notes: M. Amarnath reached 1,000 runs in 1983 on May 3.

The only batsman to score 1,000 runs in a year before World War II was C. Hill of Australia: 1,061 in 1902.

MOST RUNS IN A CAREER

(Qualification: 2,500 runs)

ENGLAND

		T	I	NO	R	HS	100s	Avge
1	G. A. Gooch	118	215	6	8,900	333	20	42.58
2	D. I. Gower.	117	204	18	8,231	215	18	44.25
3	G. Boycott	108	193	23	8,114	246*	22	47.72
4	M. C. Cowdrey	114	188	15	7,624	182	22	44.06
5	W. R. Hammond.	85	140	16	7,249	336*	22	58.45

		T	I	NO	R	HS	100s	Avge
6	L. Hutton	79	138	15	6,971	364	19	56.67
7	K. F. Barrington	82	131	15	6,806	256	20	58.67
8	**M. A. Atherton**	**84**	**155**	**6**	**5,935**	**185***	**12**	**39.83**
9	D. C. S. Compton	78	131	15	5,807	278	17	50.06
10	**A. J. Stewart**	**81**	**146**	**10**	**5,652**	**190**	**11**	**41.55**
11	J. B. Hobbs	61	102	7	5,410	211	15	56.94
12	I. T. Botham	102	161	6	5,200	208	14	33.54
13	J. H. Edrich	77	127	9	5,138	310*	12	43.54
14	T. W. Graveney	79	123	13	4,882	258	11	44.38
15	A. J. Lamb	79	139	10	4,656	142	14	36.09
16	H. Sutcliffe	54	84	9	4,555	194	16	60.73
17	P. B. H. May	66	106	9	4,537	285*	13	46.77
18	E. R. Dexter	62	102	8	4,502	205	9	47.89
19	M. W. Gatting	79	138	14	4,409	207	10	35.55
20	A. P. E. Knott	95	149	15	4,389	135	5	32.75
21	R. A. Smith	62	112	15	4,236	175	9	43.67
22	D. L. Amiss	50	88	10	3,612	262*	11	46.30
23	A. W. Greig	58	93	4	3,599	148	8	40.43
24	E. H. Hendren	51	83	9	3,525	205*	7	47.63
25	**G. P. Thorpe**	**52**	**95**	**11**	**3,366**	**138**	**6**	**40.07**
26	F. E. Woolley	64	98	7	3,283	154	5	36.07
27	K. W. R. Fletcher	59	96	14	3,272	216	7	39.90
28	**G. A. Hick**	**49**	**85**	**6**	**2,788**	**178**	**5**	**35.29**
28	M. Leyland	41	65	5	2,764	187	9	46.06
30	C. Washbrook	37	66	6	2,569	195	6	42.81

AUSTRALIA

		T	I	NO	R	HS	100s	Avge
1	A. R. Border	156	265	44	11,174	205	27	50.56
2	D. C. Boon	107	190	20	7,422	200	21	43.65
3	G. S. Chappell	87	151	19	7,110	247*	24	53.86
4	D. G. Bradman	52	80	10	6,996	334	29	99.94
5	**M. A. Taylor**	**96**	**171**	**12**	**6,784**	**219**	**18**	**42.66**
6	**S. R. Waugh**	**103**	**162**	**29**	**6,480**	**200**	**14**	**48.72**
7	R. N. Harvey	79	137	10	6,149	205	21	48.41
8	K. D. Walters	74	125	14	5,357	250	15	48.26
9	I. M. Chappell	75	136	10	5,345	196	14	42.42
10	W. M. Lawry	67	123	12	5,234	210	13	47.15
11	**M. E. Waugh**	**78**	**128**	**7**	**5,219**	**153***	**14**	**43.13**
12	R. B. Simpson	62	111	7	4,869	311	10	46.81
13	I. R. Redpath	66	120	11	4,737	171	8	43.45
14	K. J. Hughes	70	124	6	4,415	213	9	37.41
15	**I. A. Healy**	**103**	**157**	**21**	**3,906**	**161***	**3**	**28.72**
16	R. W. Marsh	96	150	13	3,633	132	3	26.51
17	D. M. Jones	52	89	11	3,631	216	11	46.55
18	A. R. Morris	46	79	3	3,533	206	12	46.48
19	C. Hill	49	89	2	3,412	191	7	39.21
20	G. M. Wood	59	112	6	3,374	172	9	31.83
21	V. T. Trumper	48	89	8	3,163	214*	8	39.04
22	C. C. McDonald	47	83	4	3,107	170	5	39.32
23	A. L. Hassett	43	69	3	3,073	198*	10	46.56
24	K. R. Miller	55	87	7	2,958	147	7	36.97
25	W. W. Armstrong	50	84	10	2,863	159*	6	38.68
26	G. R. Marsh	50	93	7	2,854	138	4	33.18
27	**M. J. Slater**	**37**	**65**	**3**	**2,817**	**219**	**7**	**45.43**
28	K. R. Stackpole	43	80	5	2,807	207	7	37.42
29	N. C. O'Neill	42	69	8	2,779	181	6	45.55
30	G. N. Yallop	39	70	3	2,756	268	8	41.13
31	S. J. McCabe	39	62	5	2,748	232	6	48.21

SOUTH AFRICA

		T	I	NO	R	HS	100s	Avge
1	B. Mitchell............	42	80	9	3,471	189*	8	48.88
2	**W. J. Cronje**.........	**51**	**88**	**9**	**3,079**	**135**	**6**	**38.97**
3	A. D. Nourse..........	34	62	7	2,960	231	9	53.81
4	H. W. Taylor..........	42	76	4	2,936	176	7	40.77
5	**G. Kirsten**..........	**45**	**81**	**7**	**2,895**	**210**	**7**	**39.12**
6 {	E. J. Barlow..........	30	57	2	2,516	201	6	45.74
	T. L. Goddard.........	41	78	5	2,516	112	1	34.46

K. C. Wessels scored 2,788 runs in 40 Tests: 1,761 (average 42.95) in 24 Tests for Australia, and 1,027 (average 38.03) in 16 Tests for South Africa.

WEST INDIES

		T	I	NO	R	HS	100s	Avge
1	I. V. A. Richards........	121	182	12	8,540	291	24	50.23
2	G. S. Sobers...........	93	160	21	8,032	365*	26	57.78
3	C. G. Greenidge.........	108	185	16	7,558	226	19	44.72
4	C. H. Lloyd...........	110	175	14	7,515	242*	19	46.67
5	D. L. Haynes..........	116	202	25	7,487	184	18	42.29
6	R. B. Kanhai..........	79	137	6	6,227	256	15	47.53
7	R. B. Richardson.......	86	146	12	5,949	194	16	44.39
8	**B. C. Lara**..........	**54**	**91**	**3**	**4,550**	**375**	**10**	**51.70**
9	E. D. Weekes..........	48	81	5	4,455	207	15	58.61
10	A. I. Kallicharran......	66	109	10	4,399	187	12	44.43
11	R. C. Fredericks........	59	109	7	4,334	169	8	42.49
12	F. M. M. Worrell.......	51	87	9	3,860	261	9	49.48
13	**C. L. Hooper**.........	**73**	**122**	**13**	**3,826**	**178***	**9**	**35.10**
14	C. L. Walcott.........	44	74	7	3,798	220	15	56.68
15	P. J. L. Dujon.........	81	115	11	3,322	139	5	31.94
16	C. C. Hunte...........	44	78	6	3,245	260	8	45.06
17	H. A. Gomes...........	60	91	11	3,171	143	9	39.63
18	B. F. Butcher..........	44	78	6	3,104	209*	7	43.11
19	S. M. Nurse...........	29	54	2	2,523	258	6	47.60

NEW ZEALAND

		T	I	NO	R	HS	100s	Avge
1	M. D. Crowe..........	77	131	11	5,444	299	17	45.36
2	J. G. Wright	82	148	7	5,334	185	12	37.82
3	B. E. Congdon.........	61	114	7	3,448	176	7	32.22
4	J. R. Reid...........	58	108	5	3,428	142	6	33.28
5	R. J. Hadlee	86	134	19	3,124	151*	2	27.16
6	G. M. Turner..........	41	73	6	2,991	259	7	44.64
7	A. H. Jones..........	39	74	8	2,922	186	7	44.27
8	B. Sutcliffe	42	76	8	2,727	230*	5	40.10
9	M. G. Burgess.........	50	92	6	2,684	119*	5	31.20
10	J. V. Coney	52	85	14	2,668	174*	3	37.57
11	G. P. Howarth.........	47	83	5	2,531	147	6	32.44

INDIA

		T	I	NO	R	HS	100s	Avge
1	S. M. Gavaskar	125	214	16	10,122	236*	34	51.12
2	D. B. Vengsarkar	116	185	22	6,868	166	17	42.13
3	G. R. Viswanath	91	155	10	6,080	222	14	41.93
4	**M. Azharuddin**	**91**	**132**	**8**	**5,697**	**199**	**20**	**45.94**
5	Kapil Dev	131	184	15	5,248	163	8	31.05
6	**S. R. Tendulkar**	**61**	**92**	**9**	**4,552**	**179**	**16**	**54.84**
7	M. Amarnath	69	113	10	4,378	138	11	42.50
8	R. J. Shastri	80	121	14	3,830	206	11	35.79
9	P. R. Umrigar	59	94	8	3,631	223	12	42.22
10	V. L. Manjrekar	55	92	10	3,208	189*	7	39.12
11	**N. S. Sidhu**	**48**	**72**	**2**	**3,148**	**201**	**9**	**44.97**
12	C. G. Borde	55	97	11	3,061	177*	5	35.59
13	Nawab of Pataudi jun.	46	83	3	2,793	203*	6	34.91
14	S. M. H. Kirmani	88	124	22	2,759	102	2	27.04
15	F. M. Engineer	46	87	3	2,611	121	2	31.08

PAKISTAN

		T	I	NO	R	HS	100s	Avge
1	Javed Miandad	124	189	21	8,832	280*	23	52.57
2	Salim Malik	96	142	21	5,528	237	15	45.68
3	Zaheer Abbas	78	124	11	5,062	274	12	44.79
4	Mudassar Nazar	76	116	8	4,114	231	10	38.09
5	Majid Khan	63	106	5	3,931	167	8	38.92
6	Hanif Mohammad	55	97	8	3,915	337	12	43.98
7	Imran Khan	88	126	25	3,807	136	6	37.69
8	Mushtaq Mohammad	57	100	7	3,643	201	10	39.17
9	Asif Iqbal	58	99	7	3,575	175	11	38.85
10	**Inzamam-ul-Haq**	**47**	**77**	**9**	**2,998**	**177**	**6**	**44.08**
11	Saeed Ahmed	41	78	4	2,991	172	5	40.41
12	Ramiz Raja	57	94	5	2,833	122	2	31.83
13	Wasim Raja	57	92	14	2,821	125	4	36.16
14	Mohsin Khan	48	79	6	2,709	200	7	37.10
15	Shoaib Mohammad	45	68	7	2,705	203*	7	44.34
16	Sadiq Mohammad	41	74	2	2,579	166	5	35.81
17	**Aamir Sohail**	**41**	**72**	**3**	**2,554**	**205**	**4**	**37.01**

SRI LANKA

		T	I	NO	R	HS	100s	Avge
1	P. A. de Silva	74	128	9	5,129	267	17	43.10
2	A. Ranatunga	82	138	8	4,595	135*	4	35.34
3	H. P. Tillekeratne	53	87	13	2,879	126*	6	38.90
4	S. T. Jayasuriya	38	64	7	2,612	340	5	45.82
5	R. S. Mahanama	52	89	1	2,576	225	4	29.27

ZIMBABWE: The highest aggregate is 1,991, average 38.28, by **G. W. Flower** in 30 Tests.

Bold type denotes those who played Test cricket in 1997-98 and 1998 seasons.

HIGHEST CAREER AVERAGES

(Qualification: 20 innings)

Avge		T	I	NO	R	HS	100s
99.94	D. G. Bradman (A)	52	80	10	6,996	334	29
60.97	R. G. Pollock (SA)	23	41	4	2,256	274	7
60.83	G. A. Headley (WI)	22	40	4	2,190	270*	10
60.73	H. Sutcliffe (E)	54	84	9	4,555	194	16
59.23	E. Paynter (E)	20	31	5	1,540	243	4
58.67	K. F. Barrington (E)	82	131	15	6,806	256	20
58.61	E. D. Weekes (WI)	48	81	5	4,455	207	15
58.45	W. R. Hammond (E)	85	140	16	7,249	336*	22
57.78	G. S. Sobers (WI)	93	160	21	8,032	365*	26
56.94	J. B. Hobbs (E)	61	102	7	5,410	211	15
56.68	C. L. Walcott (WI)	44	74	7	3,798	220	15
56.67	L. Hutton (E)	79	138	15	6,971	364	19
55.00	E. Tyldesley (E)	14	20	2	990	122	3
54.84	**S. R. Tendulkar (I)**	**61**	**92**	**9**	**4,552**	**179**	**16**
54.20	C. A. Davis (WI)	15	29	5	1,301	183	4
54.20	V. G. Kambli (I)	17	21	1	1,084	227	4
53.86	G. S. Chappell (A)	87	151	19	7,110	247*	24
53.81	A. D. Nourse (SA)	34	62	7	2,960	231	9
52.57	Javed Miandad (P)	124	189	21	8,832	280*	23
51.70	**B. C. Lara (WI)**	**54**	**91**	**3**	**4,550**	**375**	**10**
51.62	J. Ryder (A)	20	32	5	1,394	201*	3
51.34	**R. Dravid (I)**	**22**	**35**	**3**	**1,643**	**148**	**1**
51.31	**J. C. Adams (WI)**	**33**	**52**	**11**	**2,104**	**208***	**5**
51.13	**S. C. Ganguly (I)**	**20**	**31**	**2**	**1,483**	**173**	**5**
51.12	S. M. Gavaskar (I)	125	214	16	10,122	236*	34
50.56	A. R. Border (A)	156	265	44	11,174	205	27
50.23	I. V. A. Richards (WI)	121	182	12	8,540	291	24
50.06	D. C. S. Compton (E)	78	131	15	5,807	278	17

Bold type denotes those who played Test cricket in 1997-98 and 1998 seasons.

MOST HUNDREDS

	Total	200+	Inns	E	A	SA	WI	NZ	I	P	SL	Z
									Opponents			
S. M. Gavaskar (I) . .	34	4	214	4	8	–	13	2	–	5	2	–
D. G. Bradman (A) . . .	29	12	80	19	–	4	2	–	4	–	–	–
A. R. Border (A) . . .	27	2	265	8	–	0	3	5	4	6	1	–
G. S. Sobers (WI) . . .	26	2	160	10	4	–	–	1	8	3	–	–
G. S. Chappell (A) . . .	24	4	151	9	–	5	3	1	6	0	–	–
I. V. A. Richards (WI)	24	3	182	8	5	–	–	1	8	2	–	–
Javed Miandad (P) . . .	23	6	189	2	6	–	2	7	5	–	1	–
G. Boycott (E)	22	1	193	–	7	1	5	2	4	3	–	–
M. C. Cowdrey (E) . .	22	0	188	–	5	3	6	2	3	3	–	–
W. R. Hammond (E) . .	22	7	140	–	9	6	1	4	2	–	–	–
D. C. Boon (A)	21	1	190	7	–	–	3	3	6	1	1	–
R. N. Harvey (A) . . .	21	2	137	6	–	8	3	–	4	0	–	–
M. Azharuddin (I) . .	**20**	**0**	**132**	**6**	**2**	**3**	**0**	**1**	**–**	**3**	**5**	**0**
K. F. Barrington (E) . .	20	1	131	–	5	2	3	3	3	4	–	–
G. A. Gooch (E)	20	2	215	–	4	–	5	4	5	1	1	–

Notes: The most hundreds for New Zealand is 17 by M. D. Crowe in 131 innings, for Sri Lanka 17 by **P. A. de Silva** in 128 innings, for South Africa 9 by A. D. Nourse in 62 innings and for Zimbabwe 5 by **A. Flower** in 53 innings and by **G. W. Flower** in 54 innings.

The most double-hundreds by batsmen not qualifying for the above list is four by C. G. Greenidge (West Indies), L. Hutton (England) and Zaheer Abbas (Pakistan).

Bold type denotes those who played Test cricket in 1997-98 and 1998 seasons. Dashes indicate that a player did not play against the country concerned.

CARRYING BAT THROUGH TEST INNINGS

(Figures in brackets show side's total)

A. B. Tancred	26* (47)	South Africa v England at Cape Town	1888-89
J. E. Barrett	67* (176)	Australia v England at Lord's	1890
R. Abel	132* (307)	England v Australia at Sydney	1891-92
P. F. Warner	132* (237)	England v South Africa at Johannesburg	1898-99
W. W. Armstrong	159* (309)	Australia v South Africa at Johannesburg	1902-03
J. W. Zulch	43* (103)	South Africa v England at Cape Town	1909-10
W. Bardsley	193* (383)	Australia v England at Lord's	1926
W. M. Woodfull	30* (66)‡	Australia v England at Brisbane	1928-29
W. M. Woodfull	73* (193)†	Australia v England at Adelaide	1932-33
W. A. Brown	206* (422)	Australia v England at Lord's	1938
L. Hutton	202* (344)	England v West Indies at The Oval	1950
L. Hutton	156* (272)	England v Australia at Adelaide	1950-51
Nazar Mohammad§	124* (331)	Pakistan v India at Lucknow	1952-53
F. M. M. Worrell	191* (372)	West Indies v England at Nottingham	1957
T. L. Goddard	56* (99)	South Africa v Australia at Cape Town	1957-58
D. J. McGlew	127* (292)	South Africa v New Zealand at Durban	1961-62
C. C. Hunte	60* (131)	West Indies v Australia at Port-of-Spain	1964-65
G. M. Turner	43* (131)	New Zealand v England at Lord's	1969
W. M. Lawry	49* (107)	Australia v India at Delhi	1969-70
W. M. Lawry	60* (116)†	Australia v England at Sydney	1970-71
G. M. Turner	223* (386)	New Zealand v West Indies at Kingston	1971-72
I. R. Redpath	159* (346)	Australia v New Zealand at Auckland	1973-74
G. Boycott	99* (215)	England v Australia at Perth	1979-80
S. M. Gavaskar	127* (286)	India v Pakistan at Faisalabad	1982-83
Mudassar Nazar§	152* (323)	Pakistan v India at Lahore	1982-83
S. Wettimuny	63* (144)	Sri Lanka v New Zealand at Christchurch	1982-83
D. C. Boon	58* (103)	Australia v New Zealand at Auckland	1985-86
D. L. Haynes	88* (211)	West Indies v Pakistan at Karachi	1986-87
G. A. Gooch	154* (252)	England v West Indies at Leeds	1991
D. L. Haynes	75* (176)	West Indies v England at The Oval	1991
A. J. Stewart	69* (175)	England v Pakistan at Lord's	1992
D. L. Haynes	143* (382)	West Indies v Pakistan at Port-of-Spain	1992-93
M. H. Dekker	68* (187)	Zimbabwe v Pakistan at Rawalpindi	1993-94
M. A. Atherton	94* (228)	England v New Zealand at Christchurch	1996-97
G. Kirsten	100* (239)	South Africa v Pakistan at Faisalabad	1997-98
M. A. Taylor	169* (350)	Australia v South Africa at Adelaide	1997-98
G. W. Flower	156* (321)	Zimbabwe v Pakistan at Bulawayo	1997-98

† *One man absent.*   ‡ *Two men absent.*   § *Father and son.*

Notes: G. M. Turner (223*) holds the record for the highest score by a player carrying his bat through a Test innings. He is also the youngest player to do so, being 22 years 63 days old when he first achieved the feat (1969).

D. L. Haynes, who is alone in achieving this feat on three occasions, also opened the batting and was last man out in each innings for West Indies v New Zealand at Dunedin, 1979-80.

FASTEST FIFTIES

Minutes

28	J. T. Brown	England v Australia at Melbourne	1894-95
29	S. A. Durani	India v England at Kanpur.	1963-64
30	E. A. V. Williams . . .	West Indies v England at Bridgetown	1947-48
30	B. R. Taylor	New Zealand v West Indies at Auckland	1968-69
33	C. A. Roach	West Indies v England at The Oval	1933
34	C. R. Browne	West Indies v England at Georgetown	1929-30

The fastest fifties in terms of balls received (where recorded) are:

Balls

30	Kapil Dev	India v Pakistan at Karachi (2nd Test)	1982-83
31	W. J. Cronje	South Africa v Sri Lanka at Centurion	1997-98
32	I. V. A. Richards . . .	West Indies v India at Kingston	1982-83
32	I. T. Botham	England v New Zealand at The Oval	1986
33	R. C. Fredericks	West Indies v Australia at Perth	1975-76
33	Kapil Dev	India v Pakistan at Karachi	1978-79
33	Kapil Dev	India v England at Manchester	1982
33	A. J. Lamb	England v New Zealand at Auckland	1991-92

FASTEST HUNDREDS

Minutes

70	J. M. Gregory	Australia v South Africa at Johannesburg	1921-22
75	G. L. Jessop	England v Australia at The Oval	1902
78	R. Benaud	Australia v West Indies at Kingston	1954-55
80	J. H. Sinclair	South Africa v Australia at Cape Town	1902-03
81	I. V. A. Richards . . .	West Indies v England at St John's	1985-86
86	B. R. Taylor	New Zealand v West Indies at Auckland	1968-69

The fastest hundreds in terms of balls received (where recorded) are:

Balls

56	I. V. A. Richards . . .	West Indies v England at St John's	1985-86
67	J. M. Gregory	Australia v South Africa at Johannesburg	1921-22
71	R. C. Fredericks	West Indies v Australia at Perth	1975-76
74	Majid Khan	Pakistan v New Zealand at Karachi	1976-77
74	Kapil Dev	India v Sri Lanka at Kanpur	1986-87
74	M. Azharuddin	India v South Africa at Calcutta	1996-97
76	G. L. Jessop	England v Australia at The Oval	1902

FASTEST DOUBLE-HUNDREDS

Minutes

214	D. G. Bradman	Australia v England at Leeds	1930
223	S. J. McCabe	Australia v England at Nottingham	1938
226	V. T. Trumper	Australia v South Africa at Adelaide	1910-11
234	D. G. Bradman	Australia v England at Lord's	1930
240	W. R. Hammond . . .	England v New Zealand at Auckland	1932-33
241	S. E. Gregory	Australia v England at Sydney	1894-95
245	D. C. S. Compton . . .	England v Pakistan at Nottingham.	1954

The fastest double-hundreds in terms of balls received (where recorded) are:

Balls

220	I. T. Botham	England v India at The Oval	1982
232	C. G. Greenidge	West Indies v England at Lord's	1984
240	C. H. Lloyd	West Indies v India at Bombay	1974-75
241	Zaheer Abbas	Pakistan v India at Lahore	1982-83
242	D. G. Bradman	Australia v England at The Oval.	1934
242	I. V. A. Richards . . .	West Indies v Australia at Melbourne	1984-85

FASTEST TRIPLE-HUNDREDS

Minutes
288	W. R. Hammond	England v New Zealand at Auckland.........	1932-33
336	D. G. Bradman	Australia v England at Leeds...............	1930

MOST RUNS IN A DAY BY A BATSMAN

309	D. G. Bradman	Australia v England at Leeds...............	1930
295	W. R. Hammond	England v New Zealand at Auckland.........	1932-33
273	D. C. S. Compton	England v Pakistan at Nottingham..........	1954
271	D. G. Bradman	Australia v England at Leeds...............	1934

SLOWEST INDIVIDUAL BATTING

2* in 81 minutes	P. C. R. Tufnell, England v India at Bombay...........	1992-93
3* in 100 minutes	J. T. Murray, England v Australia at Sydney	1962-63
5 in 102 minutes	Nawab of Pataudi jun., India v England at Bombay......	1972-73
6 in 106 minutes	D. R. Martyn, Australia v South Africa at Sydney.......	1993-94
7 in 123 minutes	G. Miller, England v Australia at Melbourne	1978-79
9 in 132 minutes	R. K. Chauhan, India v Sri Lanka at Ahmedabad	1993-94
10* in 133 minutes	T. G. Evans, England v Australia at Adelaide	1946-47
14* in 165 minutes	D. K. Morrison, New Zealand v England at Auckland	1996-97
18 in 194 minutes	W. R. Playle, New Zealand v England at Leeds	1958
19 in 217 minutes	M. D. Crowe, New Zealand v Sri Lanka at Moratuwa	1983-84
25 in 242 minutes	D. K. Morrison, New Zealand v Pakistan at Faisalabad ...	1990-91
29* in 277 minutes	R. C. Russell, England v South Africa at Johannesburg ...	1995-96
35 in 332 minutes	C. J. Tavaré, England v India at Madras	1981-82
60 in 390 minutes	D. N. Sardesai, India v West Indies at Bridgetown	1961-62
62 in 408 minutes	Ramiz Raja, Pakistan v West Indies at Karachi.........	1986-87
68 in 458 minutes	T. E. Bailey, England v Australia at Brisbane	1958-59
99 in 505 minutes	M. L. Jaisimha, India v Pakistan at Kanpur...........	1960-61
105 in 575 minutes	D. J. McGlew, South Africa v Australia at Durban	1957-58
114 in 591 minutes	Mudassar Nazar, Pakistan v England at Lahore.........	1977-78
163 in 720 minutes	Shoaib Mohammad, Pakistan v New Zealand at Wellington .	1988-89
201* in 777 minutes	D. S. B. P. Kuruppu, Sri Lanka v New Zealand at Colombo (CCC)..	1986-87
337 in 970 minutes	Hanif Mohammad, Pakistan v West Indies at Bridgetown ...	1957-58

Note: The longest any batsman in all first-class innings has taken to score his first run is 97 minutes by T. G. Evans for England against Australia at Adelaide, 1946-47.

SLOWEST HUNDREDS

557 minutes	Mudassar Nazar, Pakistan v England at Lahore..............	1977-78
545 minutes	D. J. McGlew, South Africa v Australia at Durban.............	1957-58
535 minutes	A. P. Gurusinha, Sri Lanka v Zimbabwe at Harare.............	1994-95
516 minutes	J. J. Crowe, New Zealand v Sri Lanka at Colombo (CCC)	1986-87
500 minutes	S. V. Manjrekar, India v Zimbabwe at Harare	1992-93
488 minutes	P. E. Richardson, England v South Africa at Johannesburg	1956-57

Notes: The slowest hundred for any Test in England is 458 minutes (329 balls) by K. W. R. Fletcher, England v Pakistan, The Oval, 1974.

The slowest double-hundred in a Test was scored in 777 minutes (548 balls) by D. S. B. P. Kuruppu for Sri Lanka v New Zealand at Colombo (CCC), 1986-87, on his debut. It is also the slowest-ever first-class double-hundred.

MOST DUCKS

C. A. Walsh (West Indies) 29; D. K. Morrison (New Zealand) 24; B. S. Chandrasekhar (India) 23.

PARTNERSHIPS OVER 400

576	for 2nd	S. T. Jayasuriya (340)/R. S. Mahanama (225).	SL v I	Colombo (RPS)	1997-98
467	for 3rd	A. H. Jones (186)/M. D. Crowe (299).	NZ v SL	Wellington	1990-91
451	for 2nd	W. H. Ponsford (266)/D. G. Bradman (244).	A v E	The Oval	1934
451	for 3rd	Mudassar Nazar (231)/Javed Miandad (280*).	P v I	Hyderabad	1982-83
446	for 2nd	C. C. Hunte (260)/G. S. Sobers (365*).	WI v P	Kingston	1957-58
413	for 1st	V. Mankad (231)/Pankaj Roy (173).	I v NZ	Madras	1955-56
411	for 4th	P. B. H. May (285*)/M. C. Cowdrey (154).	E v WI	Birmingham	1957
405	for 5th	S. G. Barnes (234)/D. G. Bradman (234).	A v E	Sydney	1946-47

Note: 415 runs were scored for the third wicket for India v England at Madras in 1981-82 between D. B. Vengsarkar (retired hurt), G. R. Viswanath and Yashpal Sharma.

HIGHEST PARTNERSHIPS FOR EACH WICKET

The following lists include all stands above 300; otherwise the top ten for each wicket.

First Wicket

413	V. Mankad (231)/Pankaj Roy (173)	I v NZ	Madras	1955-56
387	G. M. Turner (259)/T. W. Jarvis (182)	NZ v WI	Georgetown	1971-72
382	W. M. Lawry (210)/R. B. Simpson (201)	A v WI	Bridgetown	1964-65
359	L. Hutton (158)/C. Washbrook (195)	E v SA	Johannesburg	1948-49
329	G. R. Marsh (138)/M. A. Taylor (219)	A v E	Nottingham	1989
323	J. B. Hobbs (178)/W. Rhodes (179)	E v A	Melbourne	1911-12
298	C. G. Greenidge (149)/D. L. Haynes (167)	WI v E	St John's	1989-90
298	Aamir Sohail (160)/Ijaz Ahmed, sen. (151)	P v WI	Karachi	1997-98
296	C. G. Greenidge (154*)/D. L. Haynes (136)	WI v I	St John's	1982-83
290	G. Pullar (175)/M. C. Cowdrey (155)	E v SA	The Oval	1960

Second Wicket

576	S. T. Jayasuriya (340)/R. S. Mahanama (225)	SL v I	Colombo (RPS)	1997-98
451	W. H. Ponsford (266)/D. G. Bradman (244)	A v E	The Oval	1934
446	C. C. Hunte (260)/G. S. Sobers (365*)	WI v P	Kingston	1957-58
382	L. Hutton (364)/M. Leyland (187)	E v A	The Oval	1938
369	J. H. Edrich (310*)/K. F. Barrington (163)	E v NZ	Leeds	1965
351	G. A. Gooch (196)/D. I. Gower (157)	E v A	The Oval	1985
344*	S. M. Gavaskar (182*)/D. B. Vengsarkar (157*). . .	I v WI	Calcutta	1978-79
331	R. T. Robinson (148)/D. I. Gower (215)	E v A	Birmingham	1985
301	A. R. Morris (182)/D. G. Bradman (173*)	A v E	Leeds	1948
298	W. M. Lawry (205)/I. M. Chappell (165)	A v WI	Melbourne	1968-69

Third Wicket

467	A. H. Jones (186)/M. D. Crowe (299)	NZ v SL	Wellington	1990-91
451	Mudassar Nazar (231)/Javed Miandad (280*). . . .	P v I	Hyderabad	1982-83
397	Qasim Omar (206)/Javed Miandad (203*)	P v SL	Faisalabad	1985-86
370	W. J. Edrich (189)/D. C. S. Compton (208).	E v SA	Lord's	1947
341	E. J. Barlow (201)/R. G. Pollock (175).	SA v A	Adelaide	1963-64
338	E. D. Weekes (206)/F. M. M. Worrell (142)	WI v E	Port-of-Spain	1953-54
323	Aamir Sohail (160)/Inzamam-ul-Haq (177)	P v WI	Rawalpindi	1997-98
319	A. Melville (189)/A. D. Nourse (149)	SA v E	Nottingham	1947
316†	G. R. Viswanath (222)/Yashpal Sharma (140)	I v E	Madras	1981-82
308	R. B. Richardson (154)/I. V. A. Richards (178) . . .	WI v A	St John's	1983-84
308	G. A. Gooch (333)/A. J. Lamb (139)	E v I	Lord's	1990
303	I. V. A. Richards (232)/A. I. Kallicharran (97) . . .	WI v E	Nottingham	1976
303	M. A. Atherton (135)/R. A. Smith (175)	E v WI	St John's	1993-94

† *415 runs were scored for this wicket in two separate partnerships; D. B. Vengsarkar retired hurt when he and Viswanath had added 99 runs.*

Fourth Wicket

411	P. B. H. May (285*)/M. C. Cowdrey (154)	E v WI	Birmingham	1957
399	G. S. Sobers (226)/F. M. M. Worrell (197*)	WI v E	Bridgetown	1959-60
388	W. H. Ponsford (181)/D. G. Bradman (304)	A v E	Leeds	1934
350	Mushtaq Mohammad (201)/Asif Iqbal (175)	P v NZ	Dunedin	1972-73
336	W. M. Lawry (151)/K. D. Walters (242)	A v WI	Sydney	1968-69
322	Javed Miandad (153*)/Salim Malik (165)	P v E	Birmingham	1992
288	N. Hussain (207)/G. P. Thorpe (138)	E v A	Birmingham	1997
287	Javed Miandad (126)/Zaheer Abbas (168)	P v I	Faisalabad	1982-83
283	F. M. M. Worrell (261)/E. D. Weekes (129)	WI v E	Nottingham	1950
269	G. W. Flower (201*)/A. Flower (156)	Z v P	Harare	1994-95

Fifth Wicket

405	S. G. Barnes (234)/D. G. Bradman (234)	A v E	Sydney	1946-47
385	S. R. Waugh (160)/G. S. Blewett (214)	A v SA	Johannesburg	1996-97
332*	A. R. Border (200*)/S. R. Waugh (157*)	A v E	Leeds	1993
281	Javed Miandad (163)/Asif Iqbal (166)	P v NZ	Lahore	1976-77
277*	M. W. Goodwin (166*)/A. Flower (100*)	Z v P	Bulawayo	1997-98
268	M. T. G. Elliott (199)/R. T. Ponting (127)	A v E	Leeds	1997
265	S. M. Nurse (137)/G. S. Sobers (174)	WI v E	Leeds	1966
258	Salim Malik (140)/Inzamam-ul-Haq (135*)	P v NZ	Wellington	1993-94
254	K. W. R. Fletcher (113)/A. W. Greig (148)	E v I	Bombay	1972-73
242	W. R. Hammond (227)/L. E. G. Ames (103)	E v NZ	Christchurch	1932-33

Sixth Wicket

346	J. H. Fingleton (136)/D. G. Bradman (270)	A v E	Melbourne	1936-37
298*	D. B. Vengsarkar (164*)/R. J. Shastri (121*)	I v A	Bombay	1986-87
274*	G. S. Sobers (163*)/D. A. J. Holford (105*)	WI v E	Lord's	1966
272	M. Azharuddin (199)/Kapil Dev (163)	I v SL	Kanpur	1986-87
260*	D. M. Jones (118*)/S. R. Waugh (134*)	A v SL	Hobart	1989-90
254	C. A. Davis (183)/G. S. Sobers (142)	WI v NZ	Bridgetown	1971-72
250	C. H. Lloyd (242*)/D. L. Murray (91)	WI v I	Bombay	1974-75
246*	J. J. Crowe (120*)/R. J. Hadlee (151*)	NZ v SL	Colombo (CCC)	1986-87
240	P. H. Parfitt (131*)/B. R. Knight (125)	E v NZ	Auckland	1962-63
232	I. T. Botham (138)/D. W. Randall (164)	E v NZ	Wellington	1983-84

Seventh Wicket

347	D. St E. Atkinson (219)/C. C. Depeiza (122)	WI v A	Bridgetown	1954-55
308	Waqar Hassan (189)/Imtiaz Ahmed (209)	P v NZ	Lahore	1955-56
246	D. J. McGlew (255*)/A. R. A. Murray (109)	SA v NZ	Wellington	1952-53
235	R. J. Shastri (142)/S. M. H. Kirmani (102)	I v E	Bombay	1984-85
221	D. T. Lindsay (182)/P. L. van der Merwe (76)	SA v A	Johannesburg	1966-67
217	K. D. Walters (250)/G. J. Gilmour (101)	A v NZ	Christchurch	1976-77
197	M. J. K. Smith (96)/J. M. Parks (101*)	E v WI	Port-of-Spain	1959-60
186	D. N. Sardesai (150)/E. D. Solkar (65)	I v WI	Bridgetown	1970-71
186	W. K. Lees (152)/R. J. Hadlee (87)	NZ v P	Karachi	1976-77
185	G. N. Yallop (268)/G. R. J. Matthews (75)	A v P	Melbourne	1983-84

Eighth Wicket

313	Wasim Akram (257*)/Saqlain Mushtaq (79)	P v Z	Sheikhupura	1996-97
246	L. E. G. Ames (137)/G. O. B. Allen (122)	E v NZ	Lord's	1931
243	R. J. Hartigan (116)/C. Hill (160)	A v E	Adelaide	1907-08
217	T. W. Graveney (165)/J. T. Murray (112)	E v WI	The Oval	1966
173	C. E. Pellew (116)/J. M. Gregory (100)	A v E	Melbourne	1920-21

168	R. Illingworth (107)/P. Lever (88*)	E v I	Manchester	1971
161	M. Azharuddin (109)/A. Kumble (88).	I v SA	Calcutta	1996-97
154	G. J. Bonnor (128)/S. P. Jones (40)	A v E	Sydney	1884-85
154	C. W. Wright (71)/H. R. Bromley-Davenport (84). .	E v SA	Johannesburg	1895-96
154	D. Tallon (92)/R. R. Lindwall (100).	A v E	Melbourne	1946-47

Ninth Wicket

195	M. V. Boucher (78)/P. L. Symcox (108)	SA v P	Johannesburg	1997-98
190	Asif Iqbal (146)/Intikhab Alam (51).	P v E	The Oval	1967
163*	M. C. Cowdrey (128*)/A. C. Smith (69*)	E v NZ	Wellington	1962-63
161	C. H. Lloyd (161*)/A. M. E. Roberts (68)	WI v I	Calcutta	1983-84
161	Zaheer Abbas (82*)/Sarfraz Nawaz (90)	P v E	Lahore	1983-84
154	S. E. Gregory (201)/J. McC. Blackham (74)	A v E	Sydney	1894-95
151	W. H. Scotton (90)/W. W. Read (117)	E v A	The Oval	1884
150	E. A. E. Baptiste (87*)/M. A. Holding (69).	WI v E	Birmingham	1984
149	P. G. Joshi (52*)/R. B. Desai (85).	I v P	Bombay	1960-61
147	Mohammad Wasim (192)/Mushtaq Ahmed (57) . .	P v Z	Harare	1997-98

Tenth Wicket

151	B. F. Hastings (110)/R. O. Collinge (68*)	NZ v P	Auckland	1972-73
151	Azhar Mahmood (128*)/Mushtaq Ahmed (59) . . .	P v SA	Rawalpindi	1997-98
133	Wasim Raja (71)/Wasim Bari (60*)	P v WI	Bridgetown	1976-77
130	R. E. Foster (287)/W. Rhodes (40*).	E v A	Sydney	1903-04
128	K. Higgs (63)/J. A. Snow (59*)	E v WI	The Oval	1966
127	J. M. Taylor (108)/A. A. Mailey (46*)	A v E	Sydney	1924-25
124	J. G. Bracewell (83*)/S. L. Boock (37)	NZ v A	Sydney	1985-86
120	R. A. Duff (104)/W. W. Armstrong (45*)	A v E	Melbourne	1901-02
117*	P. Willey (100*)/R. G. D. Willis (24*)	E v WI	The Oval	1980
109	H. R. Adhikari (81*)/Ghulam Ahmed (50).	I v P	Delhi	1952-53

BOWLING RECORDS

MOST WICKETS IN AN INNINGS

10-53	J. C. Laker	England v Australia at Manchester	1956
9-28	G. A. Lohmann	England v South Africa at Johannesburg	1895-96
9-37	J. C. Laker	England v Australia at Manchester	1956
9-52	R. J. Hadlee	New Zealand v Australia at Brisbane	1985-86
9-56	Abdul Qadir	Pakistan v England at Lahore	1987-88
9-57	D. E. Malcolm	England v South Africa at The Oval	1994
9-65	M. Muralitharan . . .	Sri Lanka v England at The Oval	1998
9-69	J. M. Patel	India v Australia at Kanpur	1959-60
9-83	Kapil Dev	India v West Indies at Ahmedabad	1983-84
9-86	Sarfraz Nawaz	Pakistan v Australia at Melbourne	1978-79
9-95	J. M. Noreiga	West Indies v India at Port-of-Spain	1970-71
9-102	S. P. Gupte	India v West Indies at Kanpur	1958-59
9-103	S. F. Barnes	England v South Africa at Johannesburg	1913-14
9-113	H. J. Tayfield	South Africa v England at Johannesburg	1956-57
9-121	A. A. Mailey	Australia v England at Melbourne	1920-21

8-7	G. A. Lohmann	England v South Africa at Port Elizabeth	1895-96
8-11	J. Briggs	England v South Africa at Cape Town	1888-89
8-29	S. F. Barnes	England v South Africa at The Oval	1912
8-29	C. E. H. Croft	West Indies v Pakistan at Port-of-Spain	1976-77
8-31	F. Laver	Australia v England at Manchester	1909
8-31	F. S. Trueman	England v India at Manchester	1952
8-34	I. T. Botham	England v Pakistan at Lord's	1978
8-35	G. A. Lohmann	England v Australia at Sydney	1886-87
8-38	L. R. Gibbs	West Indies v India at Bridgetown	1961-62
8-38	G. D. McGrath	Australia v England at Lord's	1997
8-43†	A. E. Trott	Australia v England at Adelaide	1894-95
8-43	H. Verity	England v Australia at Lord's	1934
8-43	R. G. D. Willis	England v Australia at Leeds	1981
8-45	C. E. L. Ambrose	West Indies v England at Bridgetown	1989-90
8-51	D. L. Underwood	England v Pakistan at Lord's	1974
8-52	V. Mankad	India v Pakistan at Delhi	1952-53
8-53	G. B. Lawrence	South Africa v New Zealand at Johannesburg	1961-62
8-53†	R. A. L. Massie	Australia v England at Lord's	1972
8-53	A. R. C. Fraser	England v West Indies at Port-of-Spain	1997-98
8-55	V. Mankad	India v England at Madras	1951-52
8-56	S. F. Barnes	England v South Africa at Johannesburg	1913-14
8-58	G. A. Lohmann	England v Australia at Sydney	1891-92
8-58	Imran Khan	Pakistan v Sri Lanka at Lahore	1981-82
8-59	C. Blythe	England v South Africa at Leeds	1907
8-59	A. A. Mallett	Australia v Pakistan at Adelaide	1972-73
8-60	Imran Khan	Pakistan v India at Karachi	1982-83
8-61†	N. D. Hirwani	India v West Indies at Madras	1987-88
8-64†	L. Klusener	South Africa v India at Calcutta	1996-97
8-65	H. Trumble	Australia v England at The Oval	1902
8-68	W. Rhodes	England v Australia at Melbourne	1903-04
8-69	H. J. Tayfield	South Africa v England at Durban	1956-57
8-69	Sikander Bakht	Pakistan v India at Delhi	1979-80
8-70	S. J. Snooke	South Africa v England at Johannesburg	1905-06
8-71	G. D. McKenzie	Australia v West Indies at Melbourne	1968-69
8-71	S. K. Warne	Australia v England at Brisbane	1994-95
8-71	A. A. Donald	South Africa v Zimbabwe at Harare	1995-96
8-72	S. Venkataraghavan	India v New Zealand at Delhi	1964-65
8-75†	N. D. Hirwani	India v West Indies at Madras	1987-88
8-75	A. R. C. Fraser	England v West Indies at Bridgetown	1993-94
8-76	E. A. S. Prasanna	India v New Zealand at Auckland	1975-76
8-79	B. S. Chandrasekhar	India v England at Delhi	1972-73
8-81	L. C. Braund	England v Australia at Melbourne	1903-04
8-83	J. R. Ratnayeke	Sri Lanka v Pakistan at Sialkot	1985-86
8-84†	R. A. L. Massie	Australia v England at Lord's	1972
8-85	Kapil Dev	India v Pakistan at Lahore	1982-83
8-86	A. W. Greig	England v West Indies at Port-of-Spain	1973-74
8-87	M. G. Hughes	Australia v West Indies at Perth	1988-89
8-92	M. A. Holding	West Indies v England at The Oval	1976
8-94	T. Richardson	England v Australia at Sydney	1897-98
8-97	C. J. McDermott	Australia v England at Perth	1990-91
8-103	I. T. Botham	England v West Indies at Lord's	1984
8-104†	A. L. Valentine	West Indies v England at Manchester	1950
8-106	Kapil Dev	India v Australia at Adelaide	1985-86
8-107	B. J. T. Bosanquet	England v Australia at Nottingham	1905
8-107	N. A. Foster	England v Pakistan at Leeds	1987
8-112	G. F. Lawson	Australia v West Indies at Adelaide	1984-85
8-126	J. C. White	England v Australia at Adelaide	1928-29
8-141	C. J. McDermott	Australia v England at Manchester	1985
8-143	M. H. N. Walker	Australia v England at Melbourne	1974-75

† *On Test debut.*

Note: The best for Zimbabwe is 6-90 by H. H. Streak against Pakistan at Harare in 1994-95.

OUTSTANDING ANALYSES

	O	M	R	W		
J. C. Laker (E)	51.2	23	53	10	v Australia at Manchester........	1956
G. A. Lohmann (E)	14.2	6	28	9	v South Africa at Johannesburg....	1895-96
J. C. Laker (E)	16.4	4	37	9	v Australia at Manchester........	1956
G. A. Lohmann (E)	9.4	5	7	8	v South Africa at Port Elizabeth....	1895-96
J. Briggs (E)	14.2	5	11	8	v South Africa at Cape Town.....	1888-89
J. Briggs (E)	19.1	11	17	7	v South Africa at Cape Town.....	1888-89
M. A. Noble (A)	7.4	2	17	7	v England at Melbourne	1901-02
W. Rhodes (E)	11	3	17	7	v Australia at Birmingham	1902
A. E. R. Gilligan (E)	6.3	4	7	6	v South Africa at Birmingham	1924
S. Haigh (E)	11.4	6	11	6	v South Africa at Cape Town	1898-99
D. L. Underwood (E)	11.6	7	12	6	v New Zealand at Christchurch....	1970-71
S. L. V. Raju (I)	17.5	13	12	6	v Sri Lanka at Chandigarh	1990-91
H. J. Tayfield (SA)	14	7	13	6	v New Zealand at Johannesburg ...	1953-54
C. T. B. Turner (A)	18	11	15	6	v England at Sydney...........	1886-87
M. H. N. Walker (A)	16	8	15	6	v Pakistan at Sydney..........	1972-73
E. R. H. Toshack (A)	2.3	1	2	5	v India at Brisbane	1947-48
H. Ironmonger (A)	7.2	5	6	5	v South Africa at Melbourne	1931-32
T. B. A. May (A)	6.5	3	9	5	v West Indies at Adelaide	1992-93
Pervez Sajjad (P)	12	8	5	4	v New Zealand at Rawalpindi	1964-65
K. Higgs (E)	9	7	5	4	v New Zealand at Christchurch ..	1965-66
P. H. Edmonds (E)	8	6	6	4	v Pakistan at Lord's	1978
J. C. White (E)	6.3	2	7	4	v Australia at Brisbane	1928-29
J. H. Wardle (E)	5	2	7	4	v Australia at Manchester	1953
R. Appleyard (E)	6	3	7	4	v New Zealand at Auckland	1954-55
R. Benaud (A)	3.4	3	0	3	v India at Delhi	1959-60

MOST WICKETS IN A MATCH

19-90	J. C. Laker	England v Australia at Manchester	1956
17-159	S. F. Barnes......	England v South Africa at Johannesburg	1913-14
16-136†	N. D. Hirwani	India v West Indies at Madras	1987-88
16-137†	R. A. L. Massie ...	Australia v England at Lord's	1972
16-220	M. Muralitharan ...	Sri Lanka v England at The Oval	1998
15-28	J. Briggs	England v South Africa at Cape Town.........	1888-89
15-45	G. A. Lohmann ...	England v South Africa at Port Elizabeth.......	1895-96
15-99	C. Blythe	England v South Africa at Leeds	1907
15-104	H. Verity........	England v Australia at Lord's	1934
15-123	R. J. Hadlee......	New Zealand v Australia at Brisbane	1985-86
15-124	W. Rhodes.......	England v Australia at Melbourne...........	1903-04
14-90	F. R. Spofforth	Australia v England at The Oval	1882
14-99	A. V. Bedser	England v Australia at Nottingham	1953
14-102	W. Bates	England v Australia at Melbourne...........	1882-83
14-116	Imran Khan	Pakistan v Sri Lanka at Lahore	1981-82
14-124	J. M. Patel......	India v Australia at Kanpur	1959-60
14-144	S. F. Barnes......	England v South Africa at Durban	1913-14
14-149	M. A. Holding	West Indies v England at The Oval	1976
14-199	C. V. Grimmett....	Australia v South Africa at Adelaide	1931-32

† *On Test debut.*

Notes: The best for South Africa is 13-165 by H. J. Tayfield against Australia at Melbourne, 1952-53, and for Zimbabwe 11-255 by A. G. Huckle v New Zealand at Bulawayo, 1997-98.

MOST WICKETS IN A SERIES

	T	R	W	Avge		
S. F. Barnes	4	536	49	10.93	England v South Africa . . .	1913-14
J. C. Laker	5	442	46	9.60	England v Australia	1956
C. V. Grimmett	5	642	44	14.59	Australia v South Africa . .	1935-36
T. M. Alderman	6	893	42	21.26	Australia v England	1981
R. M. Hogg	6	527	41	12.85	Australia v England	1978-79
T. M. Alderman	6	712	41	17.36	Australia v England	1989
Imran Khan.	6	558	40	13.95	Pakistan v India	1982-83
A. V. Bedser	5	682	39	17.48	England v Australia	1953
D. K. Lillee	6	870	39	22.30	Australia v England	1981
M. W. Tate	5	881	38	23.18	England v Australia	1924-25
W. J. Whitty	5	632	37	17.08	Australia v South Africa . .	1910-11
H. J. Tayfield	5	636	37	17.18	South Africa v England . . .	1956-57
A. E. E. Vogler	5	783	36	21.75	South Africa v England . . .	1909-10
A. A. Mailey.	5	946	36	26.27	Australia v England	1920-21
G. D. McGrath	6	701	36	19.47	Australia v England	1997
G. A. Lohmann	3	203	35	5.80	England v South Africa . . .	1895-96
B. S. Chandrasekhar	5	662	35	18.91	India v England	1972-73
M. D. Marshall	5	443	35	12.65	West Indies v England . . .	1988

Notes: The most for New Zealand is 33 by R. J. Hadlee against Australia in 1985-86, for Sri Lanka 20 by R. J. Ratnayake against India in 1985-86, and for Zimbabwe 22 by H. H. Streak against Pakistan in 1994-95.

MOST WICKETS IN A CALENDAR YEAR

	T	R	W	Avge	5W/i	10W/m	Year
D. K. Lillee (A).	13	1,781	85	20.95	5	2	1981
J. Garner (WI).	15	1,604	77	20.83	4	–	1984
Kapil Dev (I)	18	1,739	75	23.18	5	1	1983
Kapil Dev (I)	18	1,720	74	23.24	5	–	1979
M. D. Marshall (WI) . . .	13	1,471	73	20.15	9	1	1984
S. K. Warne (A)	16	1,697	72	23.56	2	–	1993
G. D. McKenzie (A). . . .	14	1,737	71	24.46	4	1	1964
S. K. Warne (A)	10	1,274	70	18.20	6	2	1994

MOST WICKETS IN A CAREER

(Qualification: 100 wickets)

ENGLAND

		T	Balls	R	W	Avge	5W/i	10W/m
1	I. T. Botham.	102	21,815	10,878	383	28.40	27	4
2	R. G. D. Willis	90	17,357	8,190	325	25.20	16	—
3	F. S. Trueman.	67	15,178	6,625	307	21.57	17	3
4	D. L. Underwood . . .	86	21,862	7,674	297	25.83	17	6
5	J. B. Statham	70	16,056	6,261	252	24.84	9	1
6	A. V. Bedser	51	15,918	5,876	236	24.89	15	5
7	J. A. Snow.	49	12,021	5,387	202	26.66	8	1
8	J. C. Laker	46	12,027	4,101	193	21.24	9	3
9	S. F. Barnes	27	7,873	3,106	189	16.43	24	7
10	G. A. R. Lock	49	13,147	4,451	174	25.58	9	3

		T	Balls	R	W	Avge	5W/i	10W/m
11	**A. R. C. Fraser**	**44**	**10,462**	**4,607**	**173**	**26.63**	**13**	**2**
12	M. W. Tate	39	12,523	4,055	155	26.16	7	1
13	F. J. Titmus	53	15,118	4,931	153	32.22	7	—
14	J. E. Emburey......	64	15,391	5,646	147	38.40	6	—
15	H. Verity	40	11,173	3,510	144	24.37	5	2
16	C. M. Old	46	8,858	4,020	143	28.11	4	—
17	A. W. Greig.......	58	9,802	4,541	141	32.20	6	2
18	P. A. J. DeFreitas ..	44	9,838	4,700	140	33.57	4	—
19	G. R. Dilley.......	41	8,192	4,107	138	29.76	6	—
20	T. E. Bailey	61	9,712	3,856	132	29.21	5	1
21	D. E. Malcolm	40	8,480	4,748	128	37.09	5	2
22	W. Rhodes........	58	8,231	3,425	127	26.96	6	1
23	P. H. Edmonds	51	12,028	4,273	125	34.18	2	—
24 {	D. A. Allen	39	11,297	3,779	122	30.97	4	—
	R. Illingworth.....	61	11,934	3,807	122	31.20	3	—
26	J. Briggs	33	5,332	2,095	118	17.75	9	4
27	G. G. Arnold	34	7,650	3,254	115	28.29	6	—
28	G. A. Lohmann	18	3,821	1,205	112	10.75	9	5
29	D. V. P. Wright.....	34	8,135	4,224	108	39.11	6	1
30	**D. Gough**	**26**	**5,487**	**2,891**	**104**	**27.79**	**4**	—
31	J. H. Wardle.......	28	6,597	2,080	102	20.39	5	1
32	R. Peel	20	5,216	1,715	101	16.98	5	1
33	C. Blythe........	19	4,546	1,863	100	18.63	9	4
34	**P. C. R. Tufnell**	**34**	**9,230**	**3,636**	**100**	**36.36**	**5**	**2**

AUSTRALIA

		T	Balls	R	W	Avge	5W/i	10W/m
1	D. K. Lillee	70	18,467	8,493	355	23.92	23	7
2	**S. K. Warne**	**67**	**19,791**	**7,756**	**313**	**24.77**	**14**	**4**
3	C. J. McDermott....	71	16,586	8,332	291	28.63	14	2
4	R. Benaud	63	19,108	6,704	248	27.03	16	1
5	G. D. McKenzie	60	17,681	7,328	246	29.78	16	3
6	R. R. Lindwall	61	13,650	5,251	228	23.03	12	—
7	C. V. Grimmett....	37	14,513	5,231	216	24.21	21	7
8	M. G. Hughes	53	12,285	6,017	212	28.38	7	1
9	J. R. Thomson	51	10,535	5,601	200	28.00	8	—
10	A. K. Davidson	44	11,587	3,819	186	20.53	14	2
11	G. F. Lawson	46	11,118	5,501	180	30.56	11	2
12 {	K. R. Miller.......	55	10,461	3,906	170	22.97	7	1
	T. M. Alderman ..	41	10,181	4,616	170	27.15	14	1
14	**G. D. McGrath**	**37**	**8,849**	**3,900**	**166**	**23.49**	**9**	—
15	W. A. Johnston	40	11,048	3,826	160	23.91	7	—
16	W. J. O'Reilly	27	10,024	3,254	144	22.59	11	3
17	H. Trumble	32	8,099	3,072	141	21.78	9	3
18	M. H. N. Walker...	34	10,094	3,792	138	27.47	6	—
19	A. A. Mallett	38	9,990	3,940	132	29.84	6	1
20	B. Yardley	33	8,909	3,986	126	31.63	6	1
21	R. M. Hogg	38	7,633	3,503	123	28.47	6	2
22	M. A. Noble	42	7,159	3,025	121	25.00	9	2
23	B. A. Reid.......	27	6,244	2,784	113	24.63	5	2
24	I. W. Johnson	45	8,780	3,182	109	29.19	3	—
25	**P. R. Reiffel**	**35**	**6,403**	**2,804**	**104**	**26.96**	**5**	—
26	G. Giffen.........	31	6,457	2,791	103	27.09	7	1
27	A. N. Connolly.....	29	7,818	2,981	102	29.22	4	—
28	C. T. B. Turner.....	17	5,179	1,670	101	16.53	11	2

SOUTH AFRICA

		T	Balls	R	W	Avge	5W/i	10W/m
1	**A. A. Donald**	47	**11,005**	**5,233**	237	22.08	15	2
2	H. J. Tayfield	37	13,568	4,405	170	25.91	14	2
3	T. L. Goddard	41	11,736	3,226	123	26.22	5	—
4	P. M. Pollock	28	6,522	2,806	116	24.18	9	1
5	N. A. T. Adcock	26	6,391	2,195	104	21.10	5	

WEST INDIES

		T	Balls	R	W	Avge	5W/i	10W/m
1	M. D. Marshall	81	17,584	7,876	376	20.94	22	4
2	**C. A. Walsh**	102	**22,026**	**9,668**	375	25.78	15	2
3	**C. E. L. Ambrose**	80	**17,988**	**7,133**	337	21.16	20	3
4	L. R. Gibbs	79	27,115	8,989	309	29.09	18	2
5	J. Garner	58	13,169	5,433	259	20.97	7	—
6	M. A. Holding	60	12,680	5,898	249	23.68	13	2
7	G. S. Sobers	93	21,599	7,999	235	34.03	6	—
8	A. M. E. Roberts	47	11,136	5,174	202	25.61	11	2
9	W. W. Hall	48	10,421	5,066	192	26.38	9	1
10	**I. R. Bishop**	43	**8,407**	**3,909**	161	24.27	**6**	
11	S. Ramadhin	43	13,939	4,579	158	28.98	10	1
12	A. L. Valentine	36	12,953	4,215	139	30.32	8	2
13	C. E. H. Croft	27	6,165	2,913	125	23.30	3	—
14	V. A. Holder	40	9,095	3,627	109	33.27	3	

NEW ZEALAND

		T	Balls	R	W	Avge	5W/i	10W/m
1	R. J. Hadlee	86	21,918	9,612	431	22.29	36	9
2	D. K. Morrison	48	10,064	5,549	160	34.68	10	—
3	B. L. Cairns	43	10,628	4,280	130	32.92	6	1
4	E. J. Chatfield	43	10,360	3,958	123	32.17	3	1
5	R. O. Collinge	35	7,689	3,392	116	29.24	3	—
6	B. R. Taylor	30	6,334	2,953	111	26.60	4	—
7	**C. L. Cairns**	33	**6,019**	**3,294**	**103**	31.98	5	—
8	J. G. Bracewell	41	8,403	3,653	102	35.81	4	1
9	R. C. Motz	32	7,034	3,148	100	31.48	5	—

INDIA

		T	Balls	R	W	Avge	5W/i	10W/m
1	Kapil Dev	131	27,740	12,867	434	29.64	23	2
2	B. S. Bedi	67	21,364	7,637	266	28.71	14	1
3	B. S. Chandrasekhar	58	15,963	7,199	242	29.74	16	2
4	**A. Kumble**	46	**13,990**	**5,603**	197	28.44	11	**1**
5	E. A. S. Prasanna	49	14,353	5,742	189	30.38	10	2
6	V. Mankad	44	14,686	5,236	162	32.32	8	2
7	S. Venkataraghavan	57	14,877	5,634	156	36.11	3	1
8	R. J. Shastri	80	15,751	6,185	151	40.96	2	—
9	S. P. Gupte	36	11,284	4,403	149	29.55	12	1
10	D. R. Doshi	33	9,322	3,502	114	30.71	6	—
11	{ K. D. Ghavri	39	7,042	3,656	109	33.54	4	—
	{ **J. Srinath**	32	**7,222**	**3,410**	109	31.28	**2**	—
13	N. S. Yadav	35	8,349	3,580	102	35.09	3	—

PAKISTAN

		T	Balls	R	W	Avge	5W/i	10W/m
1	Imran Khan	88	19,458	8,258	362	22.81	23	6
2	**Wasim Akram**	**79**	**17,922**	**7,706**	**341**	**22.59**	**21**	**4**
3	**Waqar Younis**	**53**	**10,798**	**5,748**	**267**	**21.52**	**21**	**5**
4	Abdul Qadir.	67	17,126	7,742	236	32.80	15	5
5	Sarfraz Nawaz	55	13,927	5,798	177	32.75	4	1
6	Iqbal Qasim	50	13,019	4,807	171	28.11	8	2
7	**Mushtaq Ahmed**	**38**	**9,544**	**4,426**	**160**	**27.66**	**10**	**3**
8	Fazal Mahmood	34	9,834	3,434	139	24.70	13	4
9	Intikhab Alam	47	10,474	4,494	125	35.95	5	2

SRI LANKA

		T	Balls	R	W	Avge	5W/i	10W/m
1	**M. Muralitharan** . . .	**42**	**13,041**	**5,464**	**203**	**26.91**	**16**	**2**

ZIMBABWE: The highest aggregate is 94 wickets, average 24.84, by **H. H. Streak** in 23 Tests.

Bold type denotes those who played Test cricket in 1997-98 and 1998 seasons.

WICKET WITH FIRST BALL IN TEST CRICKET

	Batsman dismissed			
A. Coningham	A. C. MacLaren	A v E	Melbourne	1894-95
W. M. Bradley	F. Laver	E v A	Manchester.	1899
E. G. Arnold	V. T. Trumper	E v A	Sydney	1903-04
G. G. Macaulay	G. A. L. Hearne	E v SA	Cape Town.	1922-23
M. W. Tate	M. J. Susskind	E v SA	Birmingham	1924
M. Henderson	E. W. Dawson	NZ v E	Christchurch	1929-30
H. D. Smith	E. Paynter	NZ v E	Christchurch	1932-33
T. F. Johnson	W. W. Keeton	WI v E	The Oval	1939
R. Howorth	D. V. Dyer	E v SA	The Oval	1947
Intikhab Alam	C. C. McDonald	P v A	Karachi	1959-60
R. K. Illingworth	P. V. Simmons	E v WI	Nottingham	1991
N. M. Kulkarni	M. S. Atapattu	I v SL	Colombo (RPS). .	1997-98

HAT-TRICKS

F. R. Spofforth	Australia v England at Melbourne	1878-79
W. Bates.	England v Australia at Melbourne	1882-83
J. Briggs.	England v Australia at Sydney	1891-92
G. A. Lohmann	England v South Africa at Port Elizabeth	1895-96
J. T. Hearne	England v Australia at Leeds.	1899
H. Trumble	Australia v England at Melbourne	1901-02
H. Trumble	Australia v England at Melbourne	1903-04
T. J. Matthews†	} Australia v South Africa at Manchester	1912
T. J. Matthews		
M. J. C. Allom‡.	England v New Zealand at Christchurch	1929-30
T. W. J. Goddard	England v South Africa at Johannesburg	1938-39
P. J. Loader	England v West Indies at Leeds.	1957
L. F. Kline	Australia v South Africa at Cape Town	1957-58

W. W. Hall	West Indies v Pakistan at Lahore	1958-59
G. M. Griffin	South Africa v England at Lord's	1960
L. R. Gibbs.	West Indies v Australia at Adelaide	1960-61
P. J. Petherick‡	New Zealand v Pakistan at Lahore	1976-77
C. A. Walsh§.	West Indies v Australia at Brisbane	1988-89
M. G. Hughes§	Australia v West Indies at Perth	1988-89
D. W. Fleming‡	Australia v Pakistan at Rawalpindi	1994-95
S. K. Warne	Australia v England at Melbourne	1994-95
D. G. Cork	England v West Indies at Manchester	1995

     † *T. J. Matthews did the hat-trick in each innings of the same match.*

     ‡ *On Test debut.*

     § *Not all in the same innings.*

Note: D. Gough took a hat-trick for England v Australia at Sydney in 1998-99, after the deadline for this section.

FOUR WICKETS IN FIVE BALLS

M. J. C. Allom	England v New Zealand at Christchurch	1929-30
	On debut, in his eighth over: W-WWW	
C. M. Old	England v Pakistan at Birmingham.	1978
	Sequence interrupted by a no-ball: WW-WW	
Wasim Akram	Pakistan v West Indies at Lahore (*WW-WW*)	1990-91

MOST BALLS BOWLED IN A TEST

S. Ramadhin (West Indies) sent down 774 balls in 129 overs against England at Birmingham, 1957. It was the most delivered by any bowler in a Test, beating H. Verity's 766 for England against South Africa at Durban, 1938-39. In this match Ramadhin also bowled the most balls (588) in any single first-class innings, including Tests.

ALL-ROUND RECORDS

100 RUNS AND FIVE WICKETS IN AN INNINGS

England

A. W. Greig	148	6-164	v West Indies	Bridgetown	1973-74
I. T. Botham	103	5-73	v New Zealand	Christchurch	1977-78
I. T. Botham	108	8-34	v Pakistan	Lord's	1978
I. T. Botham	114	6-58 } 7-48 }	v India	Bombay	1979-80
I. T. Botham	149*	6-95	v Australia	Leeds	1981
I. T. Botham	138	5-59	v New Zealand	Wellington	1983-84

Australia

C. Kelleway	114	5-33	v South Africa	Manchester	1912
J. M. Gregory	100	7-69	v England	Melbourne	1920-21
K. R. Miller	109	6-107	v West Indies	Kingston	1954-55
R. Benaud	100	5-84	v South Africa	Johannesburg	1957-58

South Africa

| J. H. Sinclair | 106 | 6-26 | v England | Cape Town | 1898-99 |
| G. A. Faulkner | 123 | 5-120 | v England | Johannesburg | 1909-10 |

West Indies

D. St E. Atkinson	219	5-56	v Australia	Bridgetown	1954-55
O. G. Smith	100	5-90	v India	Delhi	1958-59
G. S. Sobers	104	5-63	v India	Kingston	1961-62
G. S. Sobers	174	5-41	v England	Leeds	1966

New Zealand

| B. R. Taylor† | 105 | 5-86 | v India | Calcutta | 1964-65 |

India

| V. Mankad | 184 | 5-196 | v England | Lord's | 1952 |
| P. R. Umrigar | 172* | 5-107 | v West Indies | Port-of-Spain | 1961-62 |

Pakistan

Mushtaq Mohammad	201	5-49	v New Zealand	Dunedin	1972-73
Mushtaq Mohammad	121	5-28	v West Indies	Port-of-Spain	1976-77
Imran Khan	117	6-98 } 5-82 }	v India	Faisalabad	1982-83
Wasim Akram	123	5-100	v Australia	Adelaide	1989-90

Zimbabwe

| P. A. Strang | 106* | 5-212 | v Pakistan | Sheikhupura | 1996-97 |

† *On debut.*

100 RUNS AND FIVE DISMISSALS IN AN INNINGS

D. T. Lindsay	182	6ct	SA v A	Johannesburg	1966-67
I. D. S. Smith	113*	4ct, 1st	NZ v E	Auckland	1983-84
S. A. R. Silva	111	5ct	SL v I	Colombo (PSS)	1985-86

100 RUNS AND TEN WICKETS IN A TEST

A. K. Davidson	44 80	5-135 } 6-87 }	A v WI	Brisbane	1960-61
I. T. Botham	114	6-58 } 7-48 }	E v I	Bombay	1979-80
Imran Khan	117	6-98 } 5-82 }	P v I	Faisalabad	1982-83

1,000 RUNS AND 100 WICKETS IN A CAREER

	Tests	Runs	Wkts	Tests for Double
England				
T. E. Bailey	61	2,290	132	47
†I. T. Botham	102	5,200	383	21
J. E. Emburey	64	1,713	147	46
A. W. Greig	58	3,599	141	37
R. Illingworth	61	1,836	122	47
W. Rhodes	58	2,325	127	44
M. W. Tate	39	1,198	155	33
F. J. Titmus	53	1,449	153	40

	Tests	Runs	Wkts	Tests for Double
Australia				
R. Benaud	63	2,201	248	32
A. K. Davidson	44	1,328	186	34
G. Giffen	31	1,238	103	30
M. G. Hughes	53	1,032	212	52
I. W. Johnson	45	1,000	109	45
R. R. Lindwall	61	1,502	228	38
K. R. Miller	55	2,958	170	33
M. A. Noble	42	1,997	121	27
S. K. Warne	**67**	**1,230**	**313**	**58**
South Africa				
T. L. Goddard	41	2,516	123	36
West Indies				
C. E. L. Ambrose	**80**	**1,188**	**337**	**69**
M. D. Marshall	81	1,810	376	49
†G. S. Sobers	93	8,032	235	48
New Zealand				
J. G. Bracewell	41	1,001	102	41
C. L. Cairns	**33**	**1,442**	**103**	**33**
R. J. Hadlee	86	3,124	431	28
India				
Kapil Dev	131	5,248	434	25
V. Mankad	44	2,109	162	23
R. J. Shastri	80	3,830	151	44
Pakistan				
Abdul Qadir	67	1,029	236	62
Imran Khan	88	3,807	362	30
Intikhab Alam	47	1,493	125	41
Sarfraz Nawaz	55	1,045	177	55
Wasim Akram	**79**	**2,018**	**341**	**45**

Bold type denotes those who played Test cricket in 1997-98 and 1998 seasons.

† I. T. Botham (120 catches) and G. S. Sobers (109) are the only players to have achieved the treble of 1,000 runs, 100 wickets and 100 catches.

WICKET-KEEPING RECORDS

Most Dismissals in an Innings

7 (all ct)	Wasim Bari	Pakistan v New Zealand at Auckland	1978-79
7 (all ct)	R. W. Taylor	England v India at Bombay	1979-80
7 (all ct)	I. D. S. Smith	New Zealand v Sri Lanka at Hamilton	1990-91
6 (all ct)	A. T. W. Grout	Australia v South Africa at Johannesburg . . .	1957-58
6 (all ct)	D. T. Lindsay	South Africa v Australia at Johannesburg . . .	1966-67
6 (all ct)	J. T. Murray	England v India at Lord's	1967
6 (5ct, 1st)	S. M. H. Kirmani . . .	India v New Zealand at Christchurch	1975-76
6 (all ct)	R. W. Marsh	Australia v England at Brisbane	1982-83
6 (all ct)	S. A. R. Silva	Sri Lanka v India at Colombo (SSC)	1985-86
6 (all ct)	R. C. Russell	England v Australia at Melbourne	1990-91
6 (all ct)	R. C. Russell	England v South Africa at Johannesburg . . .	1995-96
6 (all ct)	I. A. Healy	Australia v England at Birmingham	1997
6 (all ct)	A. J. Stewart	England v Australia at Manchester	1997
6 (all ct)	M. V. Boucher	South Africa v Pakistan at Port Elizabeth . . .	1997-98
6 (all ct)	Rashid Latif	Pakistan v Zimbabwe at Bulawayo	1997-98
6 (all ct)	M. V. Boucher	South Africa v Sri Lanka at Cape Town . . .	1997-98

Note: The most stumpings in an innings is 5 by K. S. More for India v West Indies at Madras in 1987-88.

Most Dismissals in a Test

11 (all ct)	R. C. Russell	England v South Africa at Johannesburg . . .	1995-96
10 (all ct)	R. W. Taylor	England v India at Bombay.	1979-80
9 (8ct, 1st)	G. R. A. Langley . . .	Australia v England at Lord's	1956
9 (all ct)	D. A. Murray.	West Indies v Australia at Melbourne	1981-82
9 (all ct)	R. W. Marsh	Australia v England at Brisbane	1982-83
9 (all ct)	S. A. R. Silva	Sri Lanka v India at Colombo (SSC)	1985-86
9 (8ct, 1st)	S. A. R. Silva	Sri Lanka v India at Colombo (PSS)	1985-86
9 (all ct)	D. J. Richardson. . . .	South Africa v India at Port Elizabeth	1992-93
9 (all ct)	Rashid Latif	Pakistan v New Zealand at Auckland	1993-94
9 (all ct)	I. A. Healy	Australia v England at Brisbane	1994-95
9 (all ct)	C. O. Browne	West Indies v England at Nottingham	1995
9 (7ct, 2st)	R. C. Russell	England v South Africa at Port Elizabeth	1995-96
9 (8ct, 1st)	M. V. Boucher	South Africa v Pakistan at Port Elizabeth . . .	1997-98

Notes: S. A. R. Silva made 18 dismissals in two successive Tests.

The most stumpings in a match is 6 by K. S. More for India v West Indies at Madras in 1987-88.

J. J. Kelly (8ct) for Australia v England in 1901-02 and L. E. G. Ames (6ct, 2st) for England v West Indies in 1933 were the only wicket-keepers to make eight dismissals in a Test before World War II.

Most Dismissals in a Series

(Played in 5 Tests unless otherwise stated)

28 (all ct)	R. W. Marsh	Australia v England	1982-83
27 (25ct, 2st)	R. C. Russell	England v South Africa	1995-96
27 (25ct, 2st)	I. A. Healy	Australia v England (6 Tests).	1997
26 (23ct, 3st)	J. H. B. Waite	South Africa v New Zealand	1961-62
26 (all ct)	R. W. Marsh	Australia v West Indies (6 Tests)	1975-76
26 (21ct, 5st)	I. A. Healy	Australia v England (6 Tests).	1993
26 (25ct, 1st)	M. V. Boucher	South Africa v England	1998
25 (23ct, 2st)	I. A. Healy	Australia v England	1994-95

Notes: S. A. R. Silva made 22 dismissals (21ct, 1st) in three Tests for Sri Lanka v India in 1985-86.

H. Strudwick, with 21 (15ct, 6st) for England v South Africa in 1913-14, was the only wicket-keeper to make as many as 20 dismissals in a series before World War II.

Most Dismissals in a Career

		T	Ct	St	Total
1	R. W. Marsh (Australia)	96	343	12	355
2	**I. A. Healy (Australia)**	**103**	**328**	**25**	**353**
3	P. J. L. Dujon (West Indies)	81	267	5	272
4	A. P. E. Knott (England).	95	250	19	269
5	Wasim Bari (Pakistan)	81	201	27	228
6	T. G. Evans (England)	91	173	46	219
7	S. M. H. Kirmani (India)	88	160	38	198
8	D. L. Murray (West Indies).	62	181	8	189
9	A. T. W. Grout (Australia).	51	163	24	187
10	I. D. S. Smith (New Zealand)	63	168	8	176
11	R. W. Taylor (England).	57	167	7	174
12	**R. C. Russell (England)**	**54**	**153**	**12**	**165**
13	**D. J. Richardson (South Africa)**.	**42**	**150**	**2**	**152**
14	**A. J. Stewart (England)**	**81**	**144**	**7**	**151**

		T	Ct	St	Total
15	J. H. B. Waite (South Africa)	50	124	17	141
16	K. S. More (India)	49	110	20	130
	W. A. S. Oldfield (Australia)	54	78	52	130
18	J. M. Parks (England)	46	103	11	114
19	Salim Yousuf (Pakistan)	32	91	13	104

Notes: The records for P. J. L. Dujon and J. M. Parks each include two catches taken when not keeping wicket in two and three Tests respectively. A. J. Stewart's record includes 33 catches taken in 46 Tests when not keeping wicket.

I. A. Healy passed R. W. Marsh's total of 355 dismissals in 1998-99, after the deadline for this section.

The most wicket-keeping dismissals for other countries are Sri Lanka 58 (**R. S. Kaluwitharana** 47ct, 11st in 24 Tests) and Zimbabwe 71 (**A. Flower** 66ct, 5st in 26 Tests as wicket-keeper).

Bold type denotes those who played Test cricket in 1997-98 and 1998 seasons.

FIELDING RECORDS

(Excluding wicket-keepers)

Most Catches in an Innings

5	V. Y. Richardson	Australia v South Africa at Durban	1935-36
5	Yajurvindra Singh	India v England at Bangalore	1976-77
5	M. Azharuddin	India v Pakistan at Karachi	1989-90
5	K. Srikkanth	India v Australia at Perth	1991-92
5	S. P. Fleming	New Zealand v Zimbabwe at Harare	1997-98

Most Catches in a Test

7	G. S. Chappell	Australia v England at Perth	1974-75
7	Yajurvindra Singh	India v England at Bangalore	1976-77
7	H. P. Tillekeratne	Sri Lanka v New Zealand at Colombo (SSC)	1992-93
7	S. P. Fleming	New Zealand v Zimbabwe at Harare	1997-98
6	A. Shrewsbury	England v Australia at Sydney	1887-88
6	A. E. E. Vogler	South Africa v England at Durban	1909-10
6	F. E. Woolley	England v Australia at Sydney	1911-12
6	J. M. Gregory	Australia v England at Sydney	1920-21
6	B. Mitchell	South Africa v Australia at Melbourne	1931-32
6	V. Y. Richardson	Australia v South Africa at Durban	1935-36
6	R. N. Harvey	Australia v England at Sydney	1962-63
6	M. C. Cowdrey	England v West Indies at Lord's	1963
6	E. D. Solkar	India v West Indies at Port-of-Spain	1970-71
6	G. S. Sobers	West Indies v England at Lord's	1973
6	I. M. Chappell	Australia v New Zealand at Adelaide	1973-74
6	A. W. Greig	England v Pakistan at Leeds	1974
6	D. F. Whatmore	Australia v India at Kanpur	1979-80
6	A. J. Lamb	England v New Zealand at Lord's	1983
6	G. A. Hick	England v Pakistan at Leeds	1992
6	B. A. Young	New Zealand v Pakistan at Auckland	1993-94
6	J. C. Adams	West Indies v England at Kingston	1993-94
6	S. P. Fleming	New Zealand v Australia at Brisbane	1997-98

Most Catches in a Series

15	J. M. Gregory	Australia v England	1920-21
14	G. S. Chappell	Australia v England (6 Tests)	1974-75
13	R. B. Simpson	Australia v South Africa	1957-58
13	R. B. Simpson	Australia v West Indies	1960-61
13	B. C. Lara	West Indies v England (6 Tests)	1997-98

Most Catches in a Career

A. R. Border (Australia)	156	W. R. Hammond (England)	110
M. A. Taylor (Australia)	**144**	G. S. Sobers (West Indies)	109
G. S. Chappell (Australia)	122	S. M. Gavaskar (India)	108
I. V. A. Richards (West Indies)	122	I. M. Chappell (Australia)	105
I. T. Botham (England)	120	G. A. Gooch (England)	103
M. C. Cowdrey (England)	120	**M. Azharuddin (India)**	**101**
R. B. Simpson (Australia)	110		

Notes: M. A. Taylor passed A. R. Border's total of 156 catches in 1998-99, after the deadline for this section.

The most catches in the field for other countries are South Africa 56 (B. Mitchell); New Zealand 71 (M. D. Crowe); Pakistan 93 (Javed Miandad); Sri Lanka 56 (**R. S. Mahanama**); Zimbabwe 29 (**A. D. R. Campbell**).

Bold type denotes those who played Test cricket in 1997-98 and 1998 seasons.

TEAM RECORDS

HIGHEST INNINGS TOTALS

952-6 dec.	Sri Lanka v India at Colombo (RPS)	1997-98
903-7 dec.	England v Australia at The Oval	1938
849	England v West Indies at Kingston	1929-30
790-3 dec.	West Indies v Pakistan at Kingston	1957-58
758-8 dec.	Australia v West Indies at Kingston	1954-55
729-6 dec.	Australia v England at Lord's	1930
708	Pakistan v England at The Oval	1987
701	Australia v England at The Oval	1934
699-5	Pakistan v India at Lahore	1989-90
695	Australia v England at The Oval	1930
692-8 dec.	West Indies v England at The Oval	1995
687-8 dec.	West Indies v England at The Oval	1976
681-8 dec.	West Indies v England at Port-of-Spain	1953-54
676-7	India v Sri Lanka at Kanpur	1986-87
674-6	Pakistan v India at Faisalabad	1984-85
674	Australia v India at Adelaide	1947-48
671-4	New Zealand v Sri Lanka at Wellington	1990-91
668	Australia v West Indies at Bridgetown	1954-55
660-5 dec.	West Indies v New Zealand at Wellington	1994-95

The highest innings for the countries not mentioned above are:

622-9 dec.	South Africa v Australia at Durban	1969-70
544-4 dec.	Zimbabwe v Pakistan at Harare	1994-95

HIGHEST FOURTH-INNINGS TOTALS

To win

406-4	India (needing 403) v West Indies at Port-of-Spain	1975-76
404-3	Australia (needing 404) v England at Leeds.	1948
362-7	Australia (needing 359) v West Indies at Georgetown	1977-78
348-5	West Indies (needing 345) v New Zealand at Auckland	1968-69
344-1	West Indies (needing 342) v England at Lord's	1984

To tie

347	India v Australia at Madras.	1986-87

To draw

654-5	England (needing 696 to win) v South Africa at Durban	1938-39
429-8	India (needing 438 to win) v England at The Oval	1979
423-7	South Africa (needing 451 to win) v England at The Oval	1947
408-5	West Indies (needing 836 to win) v England at Kingston	1929-30

To lose

445	India (lost by 47 runs) v Australia at Adelaide	1977-78
440	New Zealand (lost by 38 runs) v England at Nottingham	1973
417	England (lost by 45 runs) v Australia at Melbourne.	1976-77
411	England (lost by 193 runs) v Australia at Sydney	1924-25
402	Australia (lost by 103 runs) v England at Manchester.	1981

MOST RUNS IN A DAY (BOTH SIDES)

588	England (398-6), India (190-0) at Manchester (2nd day).	1936
522	England (503-2), South Africa (19-0) at Lord's (2nd day).	1924
508	England (221-2), South Africa (287-6) at The Oval (3rd day)	1935

MOST RUNS IN A DAY (ONE SIDE)

503	England (503-2) v South Africa at Lord's (2nd day).	1924
494	Australia (494-6) v South Africa at Sydney (1st day).	1910-11
475	Australia (475-2) v England at The Oval (1st day).	1934
471	England (471-8) v India at The Oval (1st day)	1936
458	Australia (458-3) v England at Leeds (1st day).	1930
455	Australia (455-1) v England at Leeds (2nd day)	1934

MOST WICKETS IN A DAY

27	England (18-3 to 53 all out and 62) v Australia (60) at Lord's (2nd day)	1888
25	Australia (112 and 48-5) v England (61) at Melbourne (1st day)	1901-02

HIGHEST MATCH AGGREGATES

Runs	Wkts			Days played
1,981	35	South Africa v England at Durban	1938-39	10†
1,815	34	West Indies v England at Kingston	1929-30	9‡
1,764	39	Australia v West Indies at Adelaide	1968-69	5
1,753	40	Australia v England at Adelaide	1920-21	6
1,723	31	England v Australia at Leeds.	1948	5
1,661	36	West Indies v Australia at Bridgetown.	1954-55	6

† *No play on one day.*   ‡ *No play on two days.*

LOWEST INNINGS TOTALS

26	New Zealand v England at Auckland	1954-55
30	South Africa v England at Port Elizabeth	1895-96
30	South Africa v England at Birmingham	1924
35	South Africa v England at Cape Town	1898-99
36	Australia v England at Birmingham	1902
36	South Africa v Australia at Melbourne	1931-32
42	Australia v England at Sydney	1887-88
42	New Zealand v Australia at Wellington	1945-46
42†	India v England at Lord's	1974
43	South Africa v England at Cape Town	1888-89
44	Australia v England at The Oval	1896
45	England v Australia at Sydney	1886-87
45	South Africa v Australia at Melbourne	1931-32
46	England v West Indies at Port-of-Spain	1993-94
47	South Africa v England at Cape Town	1888-89
47	New Zealand v England at Lord's	1958

The lowest innings for the countries not mentioned above are:

53	West Indies v Pakistan at Faisalabad	1986-87
62	Pakistan v Australia at Perth	1981-82
71	Sri Lanka v Pakistan at Kandy	1994-95
127	Zimbabwe v Sri Lanka at Colombo (RPS)	1996-97

† *Batted one man short.*

FEWEST RUNS IN A FULL DAY'S PLAY

95 At Karachi, October 11, 1956. Australia 80 all out; Pakistan 15 for two (first day, 5½ hours).

104 At Karachi, December 8, 1959. Pakistan 0 for no wicket to 104 for five v Australia (fourth day, 5½ hours).

106 At Brisbane, December 9, 1958. England 92 for two to 198 all out v Australia (fourth day, 5 hours). *England were dismissed five minutes before the close of play, leaving no time for Australia to start their second innings.*

112 At Karachi, October 15, 1956. Australia 138 for six to 187 all out; Pakistan 63 for one (fourth day, 5½ hours).

115 At Karachi, September 19, 1988. Australia 116 for seven to 165 all out and 66 for five following on v Pakistan (fourth day, 5½ hours).

117 At Madras, October 19, 1956. India 117 for five v Australia (first day, 5½ hours).

117 At Colombo (SSC), March 21, 1984. New Zealand 6 for no wicket to 123 for four (fifth day, 5 hours 47 minutes).

In England

151 At Lord's, August 26, 1978. England 175 for two to 289 all out; New Zealand 37 for seven (third day, 6 hours).

158 At Manchester, July 6, 1998. England 211 for two to 369 for nine v South Africa (fifth day, 6 hours).

159 At Leeds, July 10, 1971. Pakistan 208 for four to 350 all out; England 17 for one (third day, 6 hours).

LOWEST MATCH AGGREGATES

(For a completed match)

Runs	Wkts			Days played
234	29	Australia v South Africa at Melbourne	1931-32	3†
291	40	England v Australia at Lord's	1888	2
295	28	New Zealand v Australia at Wellington	1945-46	2
309	29	West Indies v England at Bridgetown	1934-35	3
323	30	England v Australia at Manchester	1888	2

† *No play on one day.*

PLAYERS

YOUNGEST TEST PLAYERS

Years	Days			
14	227†	Hasan Raza	Pakistan v Zimbabwe at Faisalabad	1996-97
15	124	Mushtaq Mohammad	Pakistan v West Indies at Lahore	1958-59
16	189	Aqib Javed	Pakistan v New Zealand at Wellington . .	1988-89
16	205	S. R. Tendulkar	India v Pakistan at Karachi	1989-90
16	221	Aftab Baloch	Pakistan v New Zealand at Dacca	1969-70
16	248	Nasim-ul-Ghani	Pakistan v West Indies at Bridgetown . . .	1957-58
16	352	Khalid Hassan	Pakistan v England at Nottingham	1954
17	5	Zahid Fazal	Pakistan v West Indies at Karachi	1990-91
17	69	Ata-ur-Rehman	Pakistan v England at Birmingham	1992
17	118	L. Sivaramakrishnan	India v West Indies at St John's	1982-83
17	122	J. E. D. Sealy	West Indies v England at Bridgetown . . .	1929-30
17	129	Fazl-e-Akbar	Pakistan v South Africa at Durban	1997-98
17	189	C. D. U. S. Weerasinghe . .	Sri Lanka v India at Colombo (PSS) . . .	1985-86
17	193	Maninder Singh	India v Pakistan at Karachi	1982-83
17	239	I. D. Craig	Australia v South Africa at Melbourne . .	1952-53
17	245	G. S. Sobers	West Indies v England at Kingston	1953-54
17	265	V. L. Mehra	India v New Zealand at Bombay	1955-56
17	265	Harbhajan Singh	India v Australia at Bangalore	1997-98
17	300	Hanif Mohammad	Pakistan v India at Delhi	1952-53
17	341	Intikhab Alam	Pakistan v Australia at Karachi	1959-60
17	364	Waqar Younis	Pakistan v India at Karachi	1989-90

† *Hasan Raza's age is in dispute and has been rejected by the Pakistan Cricket Board.*

Note: The youngest Test players for countries not mentioned above are: England – D. B. Close, 18 years 149 days, v New Zealand at Manchester, 1949; New Zealand – D. L. Vettori, 18 years 10 days, v England at Wellington, 1996-97; South Africa – P. R. Adams, 18 years 340 days v England at Port Elizabeth, 1995-96; Zimbabwe – H. R. Olonga, 18 years 212 days, v Pakistan at Harare, 1994-95.

OLDEST PLAYERS ON TEST DEBUT

Years	Days			
49	119	J. Southerton	England v Australia at Melbourne	1876-77
47	284	Miran Bux	Pakistan v India at Lahore	1954-55
46	253	D. D. Blackie	Australia v England at Sydney	1928-29
46	237	H. Ironmonger	Australia v England at Brisbane	1928-29
42	242	N. Betancourt	West Indies v England at Port-of-Spain . .	1929-30
41	337	E. R. Wilson	England v Australia at Sydney	1920-21
41	27	R. J. D. Jamshedji	India v England at Bombay	1933-34
40	345	C. A. Wiles	West Indies v England at Manchester . . .	1933
40	295	O. Henry	South Africa v India at Durban	1992-93
40	216	S. P. Kinneir	England v Australia at Sydney	1911-12
40	110	H. W. Lee	England v South Africa at Johannesburg . .	1930-31
40	56	G. W. A. Chubb	South Africa v England at Nottingham . .	1951
40	37	C. Ramaswami	India v England at Manchester	1936

Note: The oldest Test player on debut for New Zealand was H. M. McGirr, 38 years 101 days, v England at Auckland, 1929-30; for Sri Lanka, D. S. de Silva, 39 years 251 days, v England at Colombo (PSS), 1981-82; for Zimbabwe, A. C. Waller, 37 years 84 days, v England at Bulawayo, 1996-97. A. J. Traicos was 45 years 154 days old when he made his debut for Zimbabwe (v India at Harare, 1992-93) having played three Tests for South Africa in 1969-70.

OLDEST TEST PLAYERS

(Age on final day of their last Test match)

Years	Days			
52	165	W. Rhodes	England v West Indies at Kingston	1929-30
50	327	H. Ironmonger	Australia v England at Sydney	1932-33
50	320	W. G. Grace	England v Australia at Nottingham	1899
50	303	G. Gunn	England v West Indies at Kingston	1929-30
49	139	J. Southerton	England v Australia at Melbourne	1876-77
47	302	Miran Bux	Pakistan v India at Peshawar	1954-55
47	249	J. B. Hobbs	England v Australia at The Oval	1930
47	87	F. E. Woolley.	England v Australia at The Oval	1934
46	309	D. D. Blackie	Australia v England at Adelaide	1928-29
46	206	A. W. Nourse.	South Africa v England at The Oval . . .	1924
46	202	H. Strudwick	England v Australia at The Oval	1926
46	41	E. H. Hendren	England v West Indies at Kingston	1934-35
45	304	A. J. Traicos	Zimbabwe v India at Delhi	1992-93
45	245	G. O. B. Allen	England v West Indies at Kingston	1947-48
45	215	P. Holmes	England v India at Lord's	1932
45	140	D. B. Close	England v West Indies at Manchester. . .	1976

MOST TEST APPEARANCES

156	A. R. Border (Australia)		114	M. C. Cowdrey (England)
131	Kapil Dev (India)		110	C. H. Lloyd (West Indies)
125	S. M. Gavaskar (India)		108	G. Boycott (England)
124	Javed Miandad (Pakistan)		108	C. G. Greenidge (West Indies)
121	I. V. A. Richards (West Indies)		107	D. C. Boon (Australia)
118	G. A. Gooch (England)		**103**	**I. A. Healy (Australia)**
117	D. I. Gower (England)		**103**	**S. R. Waugh (Australia)**
116	D. L. Haynes (West Indies)		102	I. T. Botham (England)
116	D. B. Vengsarkar (India)		**102**	**C. A. Walsh (West Indies)**

Note: M. A. Taylor played his 100th Test in 1998-99, after the deadline for this section.

The most appearances for New Zealand is 86 by R. J. Hadlee, for South Africa 51 by W. J. Cronje, for Sri Lanka 82 by **A. Ranatunga** and for Zimbabwe 30 by **A. D. R. Campbell, A. Flower** and **G. W. Flower**.

Bold type denotes those who played Test cricket in 1997-98 and 1998 seasons.

MOST CONSECUTIVE TEST APPEARANCES

153	A. R. Border (Australia).	March 1979 to March 1994
106	S. M. Gavaskar (India).	January 1975 to February 1987
87	G. R. Viswanath (India).	March 1971 to February 1983
85	G. S. Sobers (West Indies)	April 1955 to April 1972
72	D. L. Haynes (West Indies)	December 1979 to June 1988
71	I. M. Chappell (Australia).	January 1966 to February 1976
66	Kapil Dev (India)	October 1978 to December 1984
65	I. T. Botham (England).	February 1978 to March 1984
65	Kapil Dev (India)	January 1985 to March 1994
65	A. P. E. Knott (England).	March 1971 to August 1977

The most consecutive Test appearances for the countries not mentioned on the previous page are:

58†	J. R. Reid (New Zealand)	July 1949 to July 1965
53	Javed Miandad (Pakistan)	December 1977 to January 1984
45†	A. W. Nourse (South Africa)	October 1902 to August 1924
35	P. A. de Silva (Sri Lanka)	February 1988 to March 1995

The most for Zimbabwe is 30 (as previous page).

† Indicates complete Test career.

CAPTAINCY

MOST TESTS AS CAPTAIN

	P	W	L	D		P	W	L	D
A. R. Border (A)	93	32	22	38*	G. S. Sobers (WI)	39	9	10	20
C. H. Lloyd (WI)	74	36	12	26	**W. J. Cronje (SA)**	**36**	**15**	**10**	**11**
A. Ranatunga (SL)	**55**	**12**	**19**	**24**	G. A. Gooch (E)	34	10	12	12
M. A. Atherton (E)	**52**	**13**	**19**	**20**	Javed Miandad (P)	34	14	6	14
I. V. A. Richards (WI)	50	27	8	15	Kapil Dev (I)	34	4	7	22*
G. S. Chappell (A)	48	21	13	14	J. R. Reid (NZ)	34	3	18	13
Imran Khan (P)	48	14	8	26	D. I. Gower (E)	32	5	18	9
S. M. Gavaskar (I)	47	9	8	30	J. M. Brearley (E)	31	18	4	9
M. A. Taylor (A)	**42**	**22**	**12**	**8**	R. Illingworth (E)	31	12	5	14
P. B. H. May (E)	41	20	10	11	I. M. Chappell (A)	30	15	5	10
M. Azharuddin (I)	**40**	**13**	**10**	**17**	E. R. Dexter (E)	30	9	7	14
Nawab of Pataudi jun. (I)	40	9	19	12	G. P. Howarth (NZ)	30	11	7	12
R. B. Simpson (A)	39	12	12	15					

* One match tied.

Most Tests as captain of Zimbabwe:

	P	W	L	D
A. D. R. Campbell	14	1	7	6

Notes: A. R. Border captained Australia in 93 consecutive Tests.

W. W. Armstrong (Australia) captained his country in the most Tests without being defeated: ten matches with eight wins and two draws.

I. T. Botham (England) captained his country in the most Tests without ever winning: 12 matches with eight draws and four defeats.

Bold type denotes those who were captains in 1997-98 and 1998 seasons.

UMPIRING

MOST TEST MATCHES

		First Test	Last Test
66	H. D. Bird (England)	1973	1996
48	F. Chester (England)	1924	1955
42	C. S. Elliott (England)	1957	1974
42	**D. R. Shepherd (England)**	**1985**	**1998**
37	S. A. Bucknor (West Indies)	**1988-89**	**1997-98**
36	D. J. Constant (England)	1971	1988
36	**S. G. Randell (Australia)**	**1984-85**	**1997-98**
34	Khizar Hayat (Pakistan)	1979-80	1996-97
33	J. S. Buller (England)	1956	1969
33	A. R. Crafter (Australia)	1978-79	1991-92
32	R. W. Crockett (Australia)	1901-02	1924-25
31	D. Sang Hue (West Indies)	1961-62	1980-81

Bold type indicates an umpire who stood in 1997-98 or 1998 seasons.

SUMMARY OF ALL TEST MATCHES

To August 31, 1998

	Opponents	Tests	E	A	SA	WI	NZ	I	P	SL	Z	Tied	Drawn
England	Australia	291	92	114	–	–	–	–	–	–	–	–	85
	South Africa	115	49	–	21	–	–	–	–	–	–	–	45
	West Indies	121	28	–	–	51	–	–	–	–	–	–	42
	New Zealand	78	36	–	–	–	4	–	–	–	–	–	38
	India	84	32	–	–	–	–	14	–	–	–	–	38
	Pakistan	55	14	–	–	–	–	–	9	–	–	–	32
	Sri Lanka	6	3	–	–	–	–	–	–	2	–	–	1
	Zimbabwe	2	0	–	–	–	–	–	–	–	0	–	2
Australia	South Africa	65	–	34	14	–	–	–	–	–	–	–	17
	West Indies	86	–	35	–	29	–	–	–	–	–	1	21
	New Zealand	35	–	15	–	–	7	–	–	–	–	–	13
	India	54	–	25	–	–	–	11	–	–	–	1	17
	Pakistan	40	–	14	–	–	–	–	11	–	–	–	15
	Sri Lanka	10	–	7	–	–	–	–	–	0	–	–	3
South Africa	West Indies	1	–	–	0	1	–	–	–	–	–	–	0
	New Zealand	21	–	–	12	–	3	–	–	–	–	–	6
	India	10	–	–	4	–	–	2	–	–	–	–	4
	Pakistan	7	–	–	3	–	–	–	1	–	–	–	3
	Sri Lanka	5	–	–	3	–	–	–	–	0	–	–	2
	Zimbabwe	1	–	–	1	–	–	–	–	–	0	–	0
West Indies	New Zealand	28	–	–	–	10	4	–	–	–	–	–	14
	India	70	–	–	–	28	–	7	–	–	–	–	35
	Pakistan	34	–	–	–	12	–	–	10	–	–	–	12
	Sri Lanka	3	–	–	–	1	–	–	–	0	–	–	2
New Zealand	India	35	–	–	–	–	6	13	–	–	–	–	16
	Pakistan	39	–	–	–	–	5	–	18	–	–	–	16
	Sri Lanka	18	–	–	–	–	7	–	–	4	–	–	7
	Zimbabwe	8	–	–	–	–	3	–	–	–	0	–	5
India	Pakistan	44	–	–	–	–	–	4	7	–	–	–	33
	Sri Lanka	19	–	–	–	–	–	7	–	1	–	–	11
	Zimbabwe	2	–	–	–	–	–	1	–	–	0	–	1
Pakistan	Sri Lanka	19	–	–	–	–	–	–	9	3	–	–	7
	Zimbabwe	10	–	–	–	–	–	–	6	–	1	–	3
Sri Lanka	Zimbabwe	7	–	–	–	–	–	–	–	4	0	–	3
		1,423	254	244	58	132	39	59	71	14	1	2	549

	Tests	Won	Lost	Drawn	Tied	Toss Won
England	752	254	215	283	–	368
Australia	581	244	164	171	2	289
South Africa	225	58	90	77	–	109
West Indies	343	132	84	126	1	179
New Zealand	262	39	108	115	–	133
India	318	59	103	155	1	164
Pakistan	248	71	56	121	–	120
Sri Lanka	87	14	37	36	–	42
Zimbabwe	30	1	15	14	–	19

ENGLAND v AUSTRALIA

This section has been updated to include the 1998-99 Ashes series, which is not included elsewhere in Cricket Records.

		Captains					
Season	England		Australia	T	E	A	D
1876-77	James Lillywhite		D. W. Gregory	2	1	1	0
1878-79	Lord Harris		D. W. Gregory	1	0	1	0
1880	Lord Harris		W. L. Murdoch	1	1	0	0
1881-82	A. Shaw		W. L. Murdoch	4	0	2	2
1882	A. N. Hornby		W. L. Murdoch	1	0	1	0

THE ASHES

Season	Captains England	Australia	T	E	A	D	Held by
1882-83	Hon. Ivo Bligh	W. L. Murdoch	4*	2	2	0	E
1884	Lord Harris[1]	W. L. Murdoch	3	1	0	2	E
1884-85	A. Shrewsbury	T. P. Horan[2]	5	3	2	0	E
1886	A. G. Steel	H. J. H. Scott	3	3	0	0	E
1886-87	A. Shrewsbury	P. S. McDonnell	2	2	0	0	E
1887-88	W. W. Read	P. S. McDonnell	1	1	0	0	E
1888	W. G. Grace[3]	P. S. McDonnell	3	2	1	0	E
1890†	W. G. Grace	W. L. Murdoch	2	2	0	0	E
1891-92	W. G. Grace	J. McC. Blackham	3	1	2	0	A
1893	W. G. Grace[4]	J. McC. Blackham	3	1	0	2	E
1894-95	A. E. Stoddart	G. Giffen[5]	5	3	2	0	E
1896	W. G. Grace	G. H. S. Trott	3	2	1	0	E
1897-98	A. E. Stoddart[6]	G. H. S. Trott	5	1	4	0	A
1899	A. C. MacLaren[7]	J. Darling	5	0	1	4	A
1901-02	A. C. MacLaren	J. Darling[8]	5	1	4	0	A
1902	A. C. MacLaren	J. Darling	5	1	2	2	A
1903-04	P. F. Warner	M. A. Noble	5	3	2	0	E
1905	Hon. F. S. Jackson	J. Darling	5	2	0	3	E
1907-08	A. O. Jones[9]	M. A. Noble	5	1	4	0	A
1909	A. C. MacLaren	M. A. Noble	5	1	2	2	A
1911-12	J. W. H. T. Douglas	C. Hill	5	4	1	0	E
1912	C. B. Fry	S. E. Gregory	3	1	0	2	E
1920-21	J. W. H. T. Douglas	W. W. Armstrong	5	0	5	0	A
1921	Hon. L. H. Tennyson[10]	W. W. Armstrong	5	0	3	2	A
1924-25	A. E. R. Gilligan	H. L. Collins	5	1	4	0	A
1926	A. W. Carr[11]	H. L. Collins[12]	5	1	0	4	E
1928-29	A. P. F. Chapman[13]	J. Ryder	5	4	1	0	E
1930	A. P. F. Chapman[14]	W. M. Woodfull	5	1	2	2	A
1932-33	D. R. Jardine	W. M. Woodfull	5	4	1	0	E
1934	R. E. S. Wyatt[15]	W. M. Woodfull	5	1	2	2	A
1936-37	G. O. B. Allen	D. G. Bradman	5	2	3	0	A
1938†	W. R. Hammond	D. G. Bradman	4	1	1	2	A
1946-47	W. R. Hammond[16]	D. G. Bradman	5	0	3	2	A
1948	N. W. D. Yardley	D. G. Bradman	5	0	4	1	A
1950-51	F. R. Brown	A. L. Hassett	5	1	4	0	A
1953	L. Hutton	A. L. Hassett	5	1	0	4	E
1954-55	L. Hutton	I. W. Johnson[17]	5	3	1	1	E
1956	P. B. H. May	I. W. Johnson	5	2	1	2	E
1958-59	P. B. H. May	R. Benaud	5	0	4	1	A
1961	P. B. H. May[18]	R. Benaud[19]	5	1	2	2	A
1962-63	E. R. Dexter	R. Benaud	5	1	1	3	A
1964	E. R. Dexter	R. B. Simpson	5	0	1	4	A
1965-66	M. J. K. Smith	R. B. Simpson[20]	5	1	1	3	A
1968	M. C. Cowdrey[21]	W. M. Lawry[22]	5	1	1	3	A
1970-71†	R. Illingworth	W. M. Lawry[23]	6	2	0	4	E
1972	R. Illingworth	I. M. Chappell	5	2	2	1	E
1974-75	M. H. Denness[24]	I. M. Chappell	6	1	4	1	A
1975	A. W. Greig[25]	I. M. Chappell	4	0	1	3	A
1976-77‡	A. W. Greig	G. S. Chappell	1	0	1	0	—
1977	J. M. Brearley	G. S. Chappell	5	3	0	2	E
1978-79	J. M. Brearley	G. N. Yallop	6	5	1	0	E
1979-80‡	J. M. Brearley	G. S. Chappell	3	0	3	0	—
1980‡	I. T. Botham	G. S. Chappell	1	0	0	1	—
1981	J. M. Brearley[26]	K. J. Hughes	6	3	1	2	E

Captains

Season	England	Australia	T	E	A	D	Held by
1982-83	R. G. D. Willis	G. S. Chappell	5	1	2	2	A
1985	D. I. Gower	A. R. Border	6	3	1	2	E
1986-87	M. W. Gatting	A. R. Border	5	2	1	2	E
1987-88‡	M. W. Gatting	A. R. Border	1	0	0	1	—
1989	D. I. Gower	A. R. Border	6	0	4	2	A
1990-91	G. A. Gooch[27]	A. R. Border	5	0	3	2	A
1993	G. A. Gooch[28]	A. R. Border	6	1	4	1	A
1994-95	M. A. Atherton	M. A. Taylor	5	1	3	1	A
1997	M. A. Atherton	M. A. Taylor	6	2	3	1	A
1998-99	A. J. Stewart	M. A. Taylor	5	1	3	1	A

		T	E	A	D
In Australia		155	53	76	26
In England		141	40	41	60
Totals		296	93	117	86

* The Ashes were awarded in 1882-83 after a series of three matches which England won 2-1. A fourth match was played and this was won by Australia.

† The matches at Manchester in 1890 and 1938 and at Melbourne (Third Test) in 1970-71 were abandoned without a ball being bowled and are excluded.

‡ The Ashes were not at stake in these series.

Notes: The following deputised for the official touring captain or were appointed by the home authority for only a minor proportion of the series:

[1]A. N. Hornby (First). [2]W. L. Murdoch (First), H. H. Massie (Third), J. McC. Blackham (Fourth). [3]A. G. Steel (First). [4]A. E. Stoddart (First). [5]J. McC. Blackham (First). [6]A. C. MacLaren (First, Second and Fifth). [7]W. G. Grace (First). [8]H. Trumble (Fourth and Fifth). [9]F. L. Fane (First, Second and Third). [10]J. W. H. T. Douglas (First and Second). [11]A. P. F. Chapman (Fifth). [12]W. Bardsley (Third and Fourth). [13]J. C. White (Fifth). [14]R. E. S. Wyatt (Fifth). [15]C. F. Walters (First). [16]N. W. D. Yardley (Fifth). [17]A. R. Morris (Second). [18]M. C. Cowdrey (First and Second). [19]R. N. Harvey (Second). [20]B. C. Booth (First and Third). [21]T. W. Graveney (Fourth). [22]B. N. Jarman (Fourth). [23]I. M. Chappell (Seventh). [24]J. H. Edrich (Fourth). [25]M. H. Denness (First). [26]I. T. Botham (First and Second). [27]A. J. Lamb (First). [28]M. Atherton (Fifth and Sixth).

HIGHEST INNINGS TOTALS

For England in England: 903-7 dec. at The Oval	1938
in Australia: 636 at Sydney	1928-29
For Australia in England: 729-6 dec. at Lord's	1930
in Australia: 659-8 dec. at Sydney	1946-47

LOWEST INNINGS TOTALS

For England in England: 52 at The Oval	1948
in Australia: 45 at Sydney	1886-87
For Australia in England: 36 at Birmingham	1902
in Australia: 42 at Sydney	1887-88

INDIVIDUAL HUNDREDS

For England (206)

R. Abel (1)
132*‡	Sydney	1891-92

L. E. G. Ames (1)
120	Lord's	1934

M. A. Atherton (1)
105	Sydney	1990-91

R. W. Barber (1)
185	Sydney	1965-66

W. Barnes (1)
134	Adelaide . . .	1884-85

C. J. Barnett (2)
129	Adelaide . . .	1936-37
126	Nottingham .	1938

K. F. Barrington (5)
132*	Adelaide . . .	1962-63
101	Sydney	1962-63
256	Manchester. .	1964
102	Adelaide . . .	1965-66
115	Melbourne . .	1965-66

I. T. Botham (4)
119*	Melbourne . .	1979-80
149*	Leeds	1981
118	Manchester. .	1981
138	Brisbane . . .	1986-87

G. Boycott (7)
113	The Oval . . .	1964
142*	Sydney	1970-71
119*	Adelaide . . .	1970-71
107	Nottingham .	1977
191	Leeds	1977
128*	Lord's	1980
137	The Oval . . .	1981

L. C. Braund (2)
103*	Adelaide . . .	1901-02
102	Sydney	1903-04

J. Briggs (1)
121	Melbourne . .	1884-85

B. C. Broad (4)
162	Perth.	1986-87
116	Adelaide . . .	1986-87
112	Melbourne . .	1986-87
139	Sydney	1987-88

J. T. Brown (1)
140	Melbourne . .	1894-95

M. A. Butcher (1)
116	Brisbane . . .	1998-99

A. P. F. Chapman (1)
121	Lord's	1930

D. C. S. Compton (5)
102†	Nottingham .	1938
147 103* }	Adelaide . . .	1946-47
184	Nottingham .	1948
145*	Manchester. .	1948

M. C. Cowdrey (5)
102	Melbourne . .	1954-55
100*	Sydney	1958-59

M. H. Denness (1)
188	Melbourne . .	1974-75

E. R. Dexter (2)
180	Birmingham .	1961
174	Manchester. .	1964

B. L. D'Oliveira (2)
158	The Oval . . .	1968
117	Melbourne . .	1970-71

K. S. Duleepsinhji (1)
173†	Lord's	1930

J. H. Edrich (7)
120†	Lord's	1964
109	Melbourne . .	1965-66
103	Sydney	1965-66
164	The Oval . . .	1968
115*	Perth.	1970-71
130	Adelaide . . .	1970-71
175	Lord's	1975

W. J. Edrich (2)
119	Sydney	1946-47
111	Leeds	1948

K. W. R. Fletcher (1)
146	Melbourne . .	1974-75

R. E. Foster (1)
287†	Sydney	1903-04

C. B. Fry (1)
144	The Oval . . .	1905

M. W. Gatting (4)
160	Manchester. .	1985
100*	Birmingham .	1985
100	Adelaide . . .	1986-87
117	Adelaide . . .	1994-95

G. A. Gooch (4)
196	The Oval . . .	1985
117	Adelaide . . .	1990-91
133	Manchester. .	1993
120	Nottingham .	1993

D. I. Gower (9)
102	Perth.	1978-79
114	Adelaide . . .	1982-83
166	Nottingham .	1985
215	Birmingham .	1985
157	The Oval . . .	1985
136	Perth.	1986-87
106	Lord's	1989
100	Melbourne . .	1990-91
123	Sydney	1990-91

W. G. Grace (2)
152†	The Oval . . .	1880
170	The Oval . . .	1886

T. W. Graveney (1)
111	Sydney	1954-55

A. W. Greig (1)
110	Brisbane . . .	1974-75

G. Gunn (2)
119†	Sydney	1907-08
122*	Sydney	1907-08

W. Gunn (1)
102*	Manchester. .	1893

W. R. Hammond (9)
251	Sydney	1928-29
200	Melbourne . .	1928-29
119* 177 }	Adelaide . . .	1928-29
113	Leeds	1930
112	Sydney	1932-33
101	Sydney	1932-33
231*	Sydney	1936-37
240	Lord's	1938

J. Hardstaff jun. (1)
169*	The Oval . . .	1938

T. W. Hayward (2)
130	Manchester. .	1899
137	The Oval . . .	1899

J. W. Hearne (1)
114	Melbourne . .	1911-12

E. H. Hendren (3)
127*	Lord's	1926
169	Brisbane . . .	1928-29
132	Manchester. .	1934

J. B. Hobbs (12)
126*	Melbourne . .	1911-12
187	Adelaide . . .	1911-12
178	Melbourne . .	1911-12
107	Lord's	1912
122	Melbourne . .	1920-21
123	Adelaide . . .	1920-21
115	Sydney	1924-25
154	Melbourne . .	1924-25
119	Adelaide . . .	1924-25
119	Lord's	1926
100	The Oval . . .	1926
142	Melbourne . .	1928-29

N. Hussain (2)
207	Birmingham .	1997
105	Leeds	1997

K. L. Hutchings (1)
126	Melbourne . .	1907-08

L. Hutton (5)
100†	Nottingham .	1938
364	The Oval . . .	1938
122*	Sydney	1946-47
156*‡	Adelaide . . .	1950-51
145	Lord's	1953

Hon. F. S. Jackson (5)
103	The Oval . . .	1893
118	The Oval . . .	1899
128	Manchester. .	1902
144*	Leeds	1905
113	Manchester. .	1905

G. L. Jessop (1)

104	The Oval...	1902

A. P. E. Knott (2)

106*	Adelaide ...	1974-75
135	Nottingham .	1977

A. J. Lamb (1)

125	Leeds	1989

M. Leyland (7)

137†	Melbourne ..	1928-29
109	Lord's.....	1934
153	Manchester..	1934
110	The Oval...	1934
126	Brisbane ...	1936-37
111*	Melbourne ..	1936-37
187	The Oval...	1938

B. W. Luckhurst (2)

131	Perth......	1970-71
109	Melbourne ..	1970-71

A. C. MacLaren (5)

120	Melbourne ..	1894-95
109	Sydney	1897-98
124	Adelaide ...	1897-98
116	Sydney	1901-02
140	Nottingham .	1905

J. W. H. Makepeace (1)

117	Melbourne ..	1920-21

P. B. H. May (3)

104	Sydney	1954-55
101	Leeds	1956
113	Melbourne ..	1958-59

C. P. Mead (1)

182*	The Oval...	1921

Nawab of Pataudi sen. (1)

102†	Sydney	1932-33

E. Paynter (1)

216*	Nottingham .	1938

D. W. Randall (3)

174†	Melbourne ..	1976-77
150	Sydney	1978-79
115	Perth......	1982-83

K. S. Ranjitsinhji (2)

154*†	Manchester..	1896
175	Sydney	1897-98

W. W. Read (1)

117	The Oval...	1884

W. Rhodes (1)

179	Melbourne ..	1911-12

C. J. Richards (1)

133	Perth......	1986-87

P. E. Richardson (1)

104	Manchester..	1956

R. T. Robinson (2)

175†	Leeds	1985
148	Birmingham.	1985

A. C. Russell (3)

135*	Adelaide ...	1920-21
101	Manchester..	1921
102*	The Oval...	1921

R. C. Russell (1)

128*	Manchester..	1989

J. Sharp (1)

105	The Oval...	1909

Rev. D. S. Sheppard (2)

113	Manchester..	1956
113	Melbourne ..	1962-63

A. Shrewsbury (3)

105*	Melbourne ..	1884-85
164	Lord's.....	1886
106	Lord's.....	1893

R. T. Simpson (1)

156*	Melbourne ..	1950-51

R. A. Smith (2)

143	Manchester..	1989
101	Nottingham .	1989

A. G. Steel (2)

135*	Sydney	1882-83
148	Lord's.....	1884

A. J. Stewart (1)

107	Melbourne ..	1998-99

A. E. Stoddart (2)

134	Adelaide ...	1891-92
173	Melbourne ..	1894-95

R. Subba Row (2)

112†	Birmingham.	1961
137	The Oval...	1961

H. Sutcliffe (8)

115†	Sydney	1924-25
176 }	Melbourne ..	1924-25
127 }		1924-25
143	Melbourne ..	1924-25
161	The Oval...	1926
135	Melbourne ..	1928-29
161	The Oval...	1930
194	Sydney	1932-33

G. P. Thorpe (3)

114*†	Nottingham .	1993
123	Perth......	1994-95
138	Birmingham.	1997

J. T. Tyldesley (3)

138	Birmingham.	1902
100	Leeds	1905
112*	The Oval...	1905

G. Ulyett (1)

149	Melbourne ..	1881-82

A. Ward (1)

117	Sydney	1894-95

C. Washbrook (2)

112	Melbourne ..	1946-47
143	Leeds	1948

W. Watson (1)

109†	Lord's.....	1953

F. E. Woolley (2)

133*	Sydney	1911-12
123	Sydney	1924-25

R. A. Woolmer (3)

149	The Oval...	1975
120	Lord's.....	1977
137	Manchester..	1977

† *Signifies hundred on first appearance in England–Australia Tests.*
‡ *Carried his bat.*

For Australia (247)

W. W. Armstrong (4)

133*	Melbourne ..	1907-08
158	Sydney	1920-21
121	Adelaide ...	1920-21
123*	Melbourne ..	1920-21

C. L. Badcock (1)

118	Melbourne ..	1936-37

C. Bannerman (1)

165*†	Melbourne ..	1876-77

W. Bardsley (3)

136 }	The Oval...	1909
130 }		1909
193*‡	Lord's.....	1926

S. G. Barnes (2)

234	Sydney	1946-47
141	Lord's.....	1948

G. S. Blewett (3)

102*†	Adelaide ...	1994-95
115	Perth......	1994-95
125	Birmingham.	1997

G. J. Bonnor (1)

128	Sydney	1884-85

D. C. Boon (7)

103	Adelaide ...	1986-87
184*	Sydney	1987-88
121	Adelaide ...	1990-91
164*	Lord's.....	1993
101	Nottingham .	1993
107	Leeds	1993
131	Melbourne ..	1994-95

B. C. Booth (2)

112	Brisbane ...	1962-63
103	Melbourne ..	1962-63

A. R. Border (8)

115	Perth......	1979-80
123*	Manchester..	1981
106*	The Oval...	1981
196	Lord's.....	1985
146*	Manchester..	1985
125	Perth......	1986-87
100*	Adelaide ...	1986-87
200*	Leeds	1993

D. G. Bradman (19)

112	Melbourne ..	1928-29
123	Melbourne ..	1928-29

131	Nottingham .	1930
254	Lord's.....	1930
334	Leeds	1930
232	The Oval...	1930
103*	Melbourne ..	1932-33
304	Leeds	1934
244	The Oval...	1934
270	Melbourne ..	1936-37
212	Adelaide ...	1936-37
169	Melbourne ..	1936-37
144*	Nottingham .	1938
102*	Lord's.....	1938
103	Leeds	1938
187	Brisbane ...	1946-47
234	Sydney	1946-47
138	Nottingham .	1948
173*	Leeds	1948

W. A. Brown (3)

105	Lord's.....	1934
133	Nottingham .	1938
206*‡	Lord's.....	1938

P. J. Burge (4)

181	The Oval...	1961
103	Sydney	1962-63
160	Leeds	1964
120	Melbourne ..	1965-66

J. W. Burke (1)

101*†	Adelaide ...	1950-51

G. S. Chappell (9)

108†	Perth......	1970-71
131	Lord's.....	1972
113	The Oval...	1972
144	Sydney	1974-75
102	Melbourne ..	1974-75
112	Manchester..	1977
114	Melbourne ..	1979-80
117	Perth......	1982-83
115	Adelaide ...	1982-83

I. M. Chappell (4)

111	Melbourne ..	1970-71
104	Adelaide ...	1970-71
118	The Oval...	1972
192	The Oval...	1975

H. L. Collins (3)

104†	Sydney	1920-21
162	Adelaide ...	1920-21
114	Sydney	1924-25

R. M. Cowper (1)

307	Melbourne ..	1965-66

J. Darling (3)

101	Sydney	1897-98
178	Adelaide ...	1897-98
160	Sydney	1897-98

R. A. Duff (2)

104†	Melbourne ..	1901-02
146	The Oval...	1905

J. Dyson (1)

102	Leeds	1981

R. Edwards (2)

170*	Nottingham .	1972
115	Perth......	1974-75

M. T. G. Elliott (2)

112	Lord's.....	1997
199	Leeds	1997

J. H. Fingleton (2)

100	Brisbane ...	1936-37
136	Melbourne ..	1936-37

G. Giffen (1)

161	Sydney	1894-95

H. Graham (2)

107†	Lord's.....	1893
105	Sydney	1894-95

J. M. Gregory (1)

100	Melbourne ..	1920-21

S. E. Gregory (4)

201	Sydney	1894-95
103	Lord's.....	1896
117	The Oval...	1899
112	Adelaide ...	1903-04

R. J. Hartigan (1)

116†	Adelaide ...	1907-08

R. N. Harvey (6)

112†	Leeds	1948
122	Manchester..	1953
162	Brisbane ...	1954-55
167	Melbourne ..	1958-59
114	Birmingham .	1961
154	Adelaide ...	1962-63

A. L. Hassett (4)

128	Brisbane ...	1946-47
137	Nottingham .	1948
115	Nottingham .	1953
104	Lord's.....	1953

I. A. Healy (2)

102*	Manchester..	1993
134	Brisbane ...	1998-99

H. L. Hendry (1)

112	Sydney	1928-29

A. M. J. Hilditch (1)

119	Leeds	1985

C. Hill (4)

188	Melbourne ..	1897-98
135	Lord's.....	1899
119	Sheffield ..	1902
160	Adelaide ...	1907-08

T. P. Horan (1)

124	Melbourne ..	1881-82

K. J. Hughes (3)

129	Brisbane ...	1978-79
117	Lord's.....	1980
137	Sydney	1982-83

F. A. Iredale (2)

140	Adelaide ...	1894-95
108	Manchester.	1896

A. A. Jackson (1)

164†	Adelaide ...	1928-29

D. M. Jones (3)

184*	Sydney	1986-87
157	Birmingham .	1989
122	The Oval...	1989

C. Kelleway (1)

147	Adelaide ...	1920-21

A. F. Kippax (1)

100	Melbourne ..	1928-29

J. L. Langer (1)

179*	Adelaide ...	1998-99

W. M. Lawry (7)

130	Lord's.....	1961
102	Manchester.	1961
106	Manchester.	1964
166	Brisbane ...	1965-66
119	Adelaide ...	1965-66
108	Melbourne ..	1965-66
135	The Oval...	1968

R. R. Lindwall (1)

100	Melbourne ..	1946-47

J. J. Lyons (1)

134	Sydney	1891-92

C. G. Macartney (5)

170	Sydney	1920-21
115	Leeds	1921
133*	Lord's.....	1926
151	Leeds	1926
109	Manchester.	1926

S. J. McCabe (4)

187*	Sydney	1932-33
137	Manchester.	1934
112	Melbourne ..	1936-37
232	Nottingham .	1938

C. L. McCool (1)

104*	Melbourne ..	1946-47

R. B. McCosker (2)

127	The Oval...	1975
107	Nottingham .	1977

C. C. McDonald (2)

170	Adelaide ...	1958-59
133	Melbourne ..	1958-59

P. S. McDonnell (3)

147	Sydney	1881-82
103	The Oval...	1884
124	Adelaide ...	1884-85

C. E. McLeod (1)

112	Melbourne ..	1897-98

G. R. Marsh (2)

110†	Brisbane ...	1986-87
138	Nottingham .	1989

R. W. Marsh (1)

110*	Melbourne ..	1976-77

G. R. J. Matthews (1)

128	Sydney	1990-91

K. R. Miller (3)

141*	Adelaide ...	1946-47
145*	Sydney	1950-51
109	Lord's.....	1953

A. R. Morris (8)

155	Melbourne ..	1946-47
122 } 124* }	Adelaide ...	1946-47
105	Lord's.....	1948
182	Leeds	1948
196	The Oval...	1948
206	Adelaide ...	1950-51
153	Brisbane ...	1954-55

W. L. Murdoch (2)			
153*	The Oval...		1880
211	The Oval...		1884
M. A. Noble (1)			
133	Sydney		1903-04
N. C. O'Neill (2)			
117	The Oval ...		1961
100	Adelaide ...		1962-63
C. E. Pellew (2)			
116	Melbourne .		1920-21
104	Adelaide ...		1920-21
W. H. Ponsford (5)			
110†	Sydney		1924-25
128	Melbourne .		1924-25
110	The Oval ...		1930
181	Leeds		1934
266	The Oval ...		1934
R. T. Ponting (1)			
127†	Leeds		1997
V. S. Ransford (1)			
143*	Lord's.....		1909
I. R. Redpath (2)			
171	Perth.....		1970-71
105	Sydney		1974-75
A. J. Richardson (1)			
100	Leeds		1926
V. Y. Richardson (1)			
138	Melbourne .		1924-25
G. M. Ritchie (1)			
146	Nottingham .		1985
J. Ryder (2)			
201*	Adelaide ...		1924-25
112	Melbourne .		1928-29
H. J. H. Scott (1)			
102	The Oval...		1884

R. B. Simpson (2)			
311	Manchester..		1964
225	Adelaide ...		1965-66
M. J. Slater (7)			
152	Lord's.....		1993
176	Brisbane ...		1994-95
103	Sydney		1994-95
124	Perth......		1994-95
113	Brisbane ...		1998-99
103	Adelaide ...		1998-99
123	Sydney		1998-99
K. R. Stackpole (3)			
207	Brisbane ...		1970-71
136	Adelaide ...		1970-71
114	Nottingham .		1972
J. M. Taylor (1)			
108	Sydney		1924-25
M. A. Taylor (6)			
136†	Leeds		1989
219	Nottingham .		1989
124	Manchester..		1993
111	Lord's.....		1993
113	Sydney		1994-95
129	Birmingham .		1997
G. H. S. Trott (1)			
143	Lord's.....		1896
V. T. Trumper (6)			
135*	Lord's.....		1899
104	Manchester..		1902
185*	Sydney		1903-04
113	Adelaide ...		1903-04
166	Sydney		1907-08
113	Sydney		1911-12
K. D. Walters (4)			
155†	Brisbane ...		1965-66

115	Melbourne .		1965-66
112	Brisbane ...		1970-71
103	Perth......		1974-75
M. E. Waugh (4)			
138†	Adelaide ...		1990-91
137	Birmingham .		1993
140	Brisbane ...		1994-95
121	Sydney		1998-99
S. R. Waugh (7)			
177*	Leeds		1989
152*	Lord's.....		1989
157*	Leeds		1993
108 } 116 }	Manchester..		1997
112	Brisbane ...		1998-99
122*	Melbourne ..		1998-99
D. M. Wellham (1)			
103†	The Oval...		1981
K. C. Wessels (1)			
162†	Brisbane ...		1982-83
G. M. Wood (3)			
100	Melbourne .		1978-79
112	Lord's.....		1980
172	Nottingham .		1985
W. M. Woodfull (6)			
141	Leeds		1926
117	Manchester..		1926
111	Sydney		1928-29
107	Melbourne .		1928-29
102	Melbourne .		1928-29
155	Lord's.....		1930
G. N. Yallop (3)			
102†	Brisbane ...		1978-79
121	Sydney		1978-79
114	Manchester..		1981

† *Signifies hundred on first appearance in England–Australia Tests.*
‡ *Carried his bat.*

RECORD PARTNERSHIPS FOR EACH WICKET

For England

323 for 1st	J. B. Hobbs and W. Rhodes at Melbourne	1911-12
382 for 2nd†	L. Hutton and M. Leyland at The Oval.................	1938
262 for 3rd	W. R. Hammond and D. R. Jardine at Adelaide	1928-29
288 for 4th	N. Hussain and G. P. Thorpe at Birmingham	1997
206 for 5th	E. Paynter and D. C. S. Compton at Nottingham	1938
215 for 6th	{ L. Hutton and J. Hardstaff jun. at The Oval..........	1938
	{ G. Boycott and A. P. E. Knott at Nottingham.........	1977
143 for 7th	F. E. Woolley and J. Vine at Sydney.................	1911-12
124 for 8th	E. H. Hendren and H. Larwood at Brisbane	1928-29
151 for 9th	W. H. Scotton and W. W. Read at The Oval	1884
130 for 10th†	R. E. Foster and W. Rhodes at Sydney	1903-04

For Australia

329 for 1st	G. R. Marsh and M. A. Taylor at Nottingham	1989
451 for 2nd†	W. H. Ponsford and D. G. Bradman at The Oval	1934
276 for 3rd	D. G. Bradman and A. L. Hassett at Brisbane	1946-47
388 for 4th†	W. H. Ponsford and D. G. Bradman at Leeds	1934
405 for 5th†‡	S. G. Barnes and D. G. Bradman at Sydney	1946-47
346 for 6th†	J. H. Fingleton and D. G. Bradman at Melbourne	1936-37
165 for 7th	C. Hill and H. Trumble at Melbourne	1897-98
243 for 8th†	R. J. Hartigan and C. Hill at Adelaide	1907-08
154 for 9th†	S. E. Gregory and J. McC. Blackham at Sydney	1894-95
127 for 10th†	J. M. Taylor and A. A. Mailey at Sydney	1924-25

† *Denotes record partnership against all countries.*
‡ *Record fifth-wicket partnership in first-class cricket.*

MOST RUNS IN A SERIES

England in England	732 (average 81.33)	D. I. Gower	1985
England in Australia	905 (average 113.12)	W. R. Hammond	1928-29
Australia in England	974 (average 139.14)	D. G. Bradman	1930
Australia in Australia	810 (average 90.00)	D. G. Bradman	1936-37

TEN WICKETS OR MORE IN A MATCH

For England (37)

13-163 (6-42, 7-121)	S. F. Barnes, Melbourne	1901-02
14-102 (7-28, 7-74)	W. Bates, Melbourne	1882-83
10-105 (5-46, 5-59)	A. V. Bedser, Melbourne	1950-51
14-99 (7-55, 7-44)	A. V. Bedser, Nottingham	1953
11-102 (6-44, 5-58)	C. Blythe, Birmingham	1909
11-176 (6-78, 5-98)	I. T. Botham, Perth	1979-80
10-253 (6-125, 4-128)	I. T. Botham, The Oval	1981
11-74 (5-29, 6-45)	J. Briggs, Lord's	1886
12-136 (6-49, 6-87)	J. Briggs, Adelaide	1891-92
10-148 (5-34, 5-114)	J. Briggs, The Oval	1893
10-104 (6-77, 4-27)†	R. M. Ellison, Birmingham	1985
10-179 (5-102, 5-77)†	K. Farnes, Nottingham	1934
10-60 (6-41, 4-19)	J. T. Hearne, The Oval	1896
11-113 (5-58, 6-55)	J. C. Laker, Leeds	1956
19-90 (9-37, 10-53)	J. C. Laker, Manchester	1956
10-124 (5-96, 5-28)	H. Larwood, Sydney	1932-33
11-76 (6-48, 5-28)	W. H. Lockwood, Manchester	1902
12-104 (7-36, 5-68)	G. A. Lohmann, The Oval	1886
10-87 (8-35, 2-52)	G. A. Lohmann, Sydney	1886-87
10-142 (8-58, 2-84)	G. A. Lohmann, Sydney	1891-92
12-102 (6-50, 6-52)†	F. Martin, The Oval	1890
11-68 (7-31, 4-37)	R. Peel, Manchester	1888
15-124 (7-56, 8-68)	W. Rhodes, Melbourne	1903-04
10-156 (5-49, 5-107)†	T. Richardson, Manchester	1893
11-173 (6-39, 5-134)	T. Richardson, Lord's	1896
13-244 (7-168, 6-76)	T. Richardson, Manchester	1896
10-204 (8-94, 2-110)	T. Richardson, Sydney	1897-98

11-228 (6-130, 5-98)†	M. W. Tate, Sydney	1924-25
11-88 (5-58, 6-30)	F. S. Trueman, Leeds	1961
11-93 (7-66, 4-27)	P. C. R. Tufnell, The Oval	1997
10-130 (4-45, 6-85)	F. H. Tyson, Sydney	1954-55
10-82 (4-37, 6-45)	D. L. Underwood, Leeds	1972
11-215 (7-113, 4-102)	D. L. Underwood, Adelaide	1974-75
15-104 (7-61, 8-43)	H. Verity, Lord's	1934
10-57 (6-41, 4-16)	W. Voce, Brisbane	1936-37
13-256 (5-130, 8-126)	J. C. White, Adelaide	1928-29
10-49 (5-29, 5-20)	F. E. Woolley, The Oval	1912

For Australia (40)

10-151 (5-107, 5-44)	T. M. Alderman, Leeds	1989
10-239 (4-129, 6-110)	L. O'B. Fleetwood-Smith, Adelaide	1936-37
10-160 (4-88, 6-72)	G. Giffen, Sydney	1891-92
11-82 (5-45, 6-37)†	C. V. Grimmett, Sydney	1924-25
10-201 (5-107, 5-94)	C. V. Grimmett, Nottingham	1930
10-122 (5-65, 5-57)	R. M. Hogg, Perth	1978-79
10-66 (5-30, 5-36)	R. M. Hogg, Melbourne	1978-79
12-175 (5-85, 7-90)†	H. V. Hordern, Sydney	1911-12
10-161 (5-95, 5-66)	H. V. Hordern, Sydney	1911-12
10-164 (7-88, 3-76)	E. Jones, Lord's	1899
11-134 (6-47, 5-87)	G. F. Lawson, Brisbane	1982-83
10-181 (5-58, 5-123)	D. K. Lillee, The Oval	1972
11-165 (6-26, 5-139)	D. K. Lillee, Melbourne	1976-77
11-138 (6-60, 5-78)	D. K. Lillee, Melbourne	1979-80
11-159 (7-89, 4-70)	D. K. Lillee, The Oval	1981
11-85 (7-58, 4-27)	C. G. Macartney, Leeds	1909
11-157 (8-97, 3-60)	C. J. McDermott, Perth	1990-91
12-107 (5-57, 7-50)	S. C. G. MacGill, Sydney	1998-99
10-302 (5-160, 5-142)	A. A. Mailey, Adelaide	1920-21
13-236 (4-115, 9-121)	A. A. Mailey, Melbourne	1920-21
16-137 (8-84, 8-53)†	R. A. L. Massie, Lord's	1972
10-152 (5-72, 5-80)	K. R. Miller, Lord's	1956
13-77 (7-17, 6-60)	M. A. Noble, Melbourne	1901-02
11-103 (5-51, 6-52)	M. A. Noble, Sheffield	1902
10-129 (5-63, 5-66)	W. J. O'Reilly, Melbourne	1932-33
11-129 (4-75, 7-54)	W. J. O'Reilly, Nottingham	1934
10-122 (5-66, 5-56)	W. J. O'Reilly, Leeds	1938
11-165 (7-68, 4-97)	G. E. Palmer, Sydney	1881-82
10-126 (7-65, 3-61)	G. E. Palmer, Melbourne	1882-83
13-148 (6-97, 7-51)	B. A. Reid, Melbourne	1990-91
13-110 (6-48, 7-62)	F. R. Spofforth, Melbourne	1878-79
14-90 (7-46, 7-44)	F. R. Spofforth, The Oval	1882
11-117 (4-73, 7-44)	F. R. Spofforth, Sydney	1882-83
10-144 (4-54, 6-90)	F. R. Spofforth, Sydney	1884-85
12-89 (6-59, 6-30)	H. Trumble, The Oval	1896
10-128 (4-75, 6-53)	H. Trumble, Manchester	1902
12-173 (8-65, 4-108)	H. Trumble, The Oval	1902
12-87 (5-44, 7-43)	C. T. B. Turner, Sydney	1887-88
10-63 (5-27, 5-36)	C. T. B. Turner, Lord's	1888
11-110 (3-39, 8-71)	S. K. Warne, Brisbane	1994-95

† *Signifies ten wickets or more on first appearance in England–Australia Tests.*

Note: J. Briggs, J. C. Laker, T. Richardson in 1896, R. M. Hogg, A. A. Mailey, H. Trumble and C. T. B. Turner took ten wickets or more in successive Tests. J. Briggs was omitted, however, from the England team for the first Test match in 1893.

MOST WICKETS IN A SERIES

England in England	46 (average 9.60)	J. C. Laker	1956
England in Australia	38 (average 23.18)	M. W. Tate	1924-25
Australia in England	42 (average 21.26)	T. M. Alderman (6 Tests) .	1981
Australia in Australia	41 (average 12.85)	R. M. Hogg (6 Tests)	1978-79

WICKET-KEEPING – MOST DISMISSALS

	M	*Ct*	*St*	*Total*
†R. W. Marsh (Australia)	42	141	7	148
I. A. Healy (Australia)	33	123	12	135
A. P. E. Knott (England)	34	97	8	105
†W. A. Oldfield (Australia)	38	59	31	90
A. A. Lilley (England)	32	65	19	84
A. T. W. Grout (Australia)	22	69	7	76
T. G. Evans (England)	31	63	12	75

† The number of catches by R. W. Marsh (141) and stumpings by W. A. Oldfield (31) are respective records in England–Australia Tests.

SCORERS OF OVER 2,000 RUNS

	T		*I*		*NO*		*R*		*HS*		*Avge*
D. G. Bradman	37	..	63	..	7	..	5,028	..	334	..	89.78
J. B. Hobbs	41	..	71	..	4	..	3,636	..	187	..	54.26
A. R. Border	47	..	82	..	19	..	3,548	..	200*	..	56.31
D. I. Gower	42	..	77	..	4	..	3,269	..	215	..	44.78
G. Boycott	38	..	71	..	9	..	2,945	..	191	..	47.50
W. R. Hammond	33	..	58	..	3	..	2,852	..	251	..	51.85
H. Sutcliffe	27	..	46	..	5	..	2,741	..	194	..	66.85
C. Hill	41	..	76	..	1	..	2,660	..	188	..	35.46
J. H. Edrich	32	..	57	..	3	..	2,644	..	175	..	48.96
G. A. Gooch	42	..	79	..	0	..	2,632	..	196	..	33.31
G. S. Chappell	35	..	65	..	8	..	2,619	..	144	..	45.94
S. R. Waugh	37	..	60	..	16	..	2,574	..	177*	..	58.50
M. A. Taylor	33	..	61	..	2	..	2,496	..	219	..	42.30
M. C. Cowdrey	43	..	75	..	4	..	2,433	..	113	..	34.26
L. Hutton	27	..	49	..	6	..	2,428	..	364	..	56.46
R. N. Harvey	37	..	68	..	5	..	2,416	..	167	..	38.34
V. T. Trumper	40	..	74	..	5	..	2,263	..	185*	..	32.79
D. C. Boon	31	..	57	..	8	..	2,237	..	184	..	45.65
W. M. Lawry	29	..	51	..	5	..	2,233	..	166	..	48.54
S. E. Gregory	52	..	92	..	7	..	2,193	..	201	..	25.80
W. W. Armstrong	42	..	71	..	9	..	2,172	..	158	..	35.03
I. M. Chappell	30	..	56	..	4	..	2,138	..	192	..	41.11
K. F. Barrington	23	..	39	..	6	..	2,111	..	256	..	63.96
A. R. Morris	24	..	43	..	2	..	2,080	..	206	..	50.73

BOWLERS WITH 100 WICKETS

	T		Balls		R		W		5W/i		Avge
D. K. Lillee	29	..	8,516	..	3,507	..	167	..	11	..	21.00
I. T. Botham	36	..	8,479	..	4,093	..	148	..	9	..	27.65
H. Trumble	31	..	7,895	..	2,945	..	141	..	9	..	20.88
R. G. D. Willis	35	..	7,294	..	3,346	..	128	..	7	..	26.14
M. A. Noble	39	..	6,845	..	2,860	..	115	..	9	..	24.86
R. R. Lindwall	29	..	6,728	..	2,559	..	114	..	6	..	22.44
W. Rhodes	41	..	5,791	..	2,616	..	109	..	6	..	24.00
S. F. Barnes	20	..	5,749	..	2,288	..	106	..	12	..	21.58
C. V. Grimmett	22	..	9,224	..	3,439	..	106	..	11	..	32.44
D. L. Underwood	29	..	8,000	..	2,770	..	105	..	4	..	26.38
A. V. Bedser	21	..	7,065	..	2,859	..	104	..	7	..	27.49
G. Giffen	31	..	6,457	..	2,791	..	103	..	7	..	27.09
W. J. O'Reilly	19	..	7,864	..	2,587	..	102	..	8	..	25.36
R. Peel	20	..	5,216	..	1,715	..	101	..	5	..	16.98
C. T. B. Turner	17	..	5,195	..	1,670	..	101	..	11	..	16.53
T. M. Alderman	17	..	4,717	..	2,117	..	100	..	11	..	21.17
J. R. Thomson	21	..	4,951	..	2,418	..	100	..	5	..	24.18

RESULTS ON EACH GROUND

In England

THE OVAL (32)

England (15)   1880, 1886, 1888, 1890, 1893, 1896, 1902, 1912, 1926, 1938, 1953, 1968, 1985, 1993, 1997.
Australia (5)   1882, 1930, 1934, 1948, 1972.
Drawn (12)   1884, 1899, 1905, 1909, 1921, 1956, 1961, 1964, 1975, 1977, 1981, 1989.

MANCHESTER (27)

England (7)   1886, 1888, 1905, 1956, 1972, 1977, 1981.
Australia (7)   1896, 1902, 1961, 1968, 1989, 1993, 1997.
Drawn (13)   1884, 1893, 1899, 1909, 1912, 1921, 1926, 1930, 1934, 1948, 1953, 1964, 1985.

The scheduled matches in 1890 and 1938 were abandoned without a ball bowled and are excluded.

LORD'S (31)

England (5)   1884, 1886, 1890, 1896, 1934.
Australia (12)   1888, 1899, 1909, 1921, 1930, 1948, 1956, 1961, 1972, 1985, 1989, 1993.
Drawn (14)   1893, 1902, 1905, 1912, 1926, 1938, 1953, 1964, 1968, 1975, 1977, 1980, 1981, 1997.

NOTTINGHAM (18)

England (3)   1905, 1930, 1977.
Australia (6)   1921, 1934, 1948, 1981, 1989, 1997.
Drawn (9)   1899, 1926, 1938, 1953, 1956, 1964, 1972, 1985, 1993.

LEEDS (22)

England (6)   1956, 1961, 1972, 1977, 1981, 1985.
Australia (8)   1909, 1921, 1938, 1948, 1964, 1989, 1993, 1997.
Drawn (8)   1899, 1905, 1926, 1930, 1934, 1953, 1968, 1975.

BIRMINGHAM (10)

England (4)	1909, 1981, 1985, 1997.
Australia (2)	1975, 1993.
Drawn (4)	1902, 1961, 1968, 1989.

SHEFFIELD (1)

Australia (1)	1902.

In Australia

MELBOURNE (51)

England (19)	*1876, 1882, 1884(2), 1894(2), 1903, 1907, 1911(2), 1924, 1928, 1950, 1954, 1962, 1974, 1982, 1986, 1998.*
Australia (25)	*1876, 1878, 1882, 1891, 1897(2), 1901(2), 1903, 1907, 1920(2), 1924, 1928, 1932, 1936(2), 1950, 1958(2), 1976, 1978, 1979, 1990, 1994.*
Drawn (7)	*1881(2), 1946, 1965(2), 1970, 1974.*

One scheduled match in 1970-71 was abandoned without a ball bowled and is excluded.

SYDNEY (51)

England (20)	*1882, 1886(2), 1887, 1894, 1897, 1901, 1903(2), 1911, 1928, 1932(2), 1936, 1954, 1965, 1970(2), 1978(2).*
Australia (24)	*1881(2), 1882, 1884(2), 1891, 1894, 1897, 1901, 1907(2), 1911, 1920(2), 1924(2), 1946(2), 1950, 1962, 1974, 1979, 1986, 1998.*
Drawn (7)	*1954, 1958, 1962, 1982, 1987, 1990, 1994.*

ADELAIDE (27)

England (8)	*1884, 1891, 1911, 1928, 1932, 1954, 1978, 1994.*
Australia (14)	*1894, 1897, 1901, 1903, 1907, 1920, 1924, 1936, 1950, 1958, 1965, 1974, 1982, 1998.*
Drawn (5)	*1946, 1962, 1970, 1986, 1990.*

BRISBANE Exhibition Ground (1)

England (1)	*1928.*

BRISBANE Woolloongabba (16)

England (4)	*1932, 1936, 1978, 1986.*
Australia (8)	*1946, 1950, 1954, 1958, 1974, 1982, 1990, 1994.*
Drawn (4)	*1962, 1965, 1970, 1998.*

PERTH (9)

England (1)	*1978.*
Australia (5)	*1974, 1979, 1990, 1994, 1998.*
Drawn (3)	*1970, 1982, 1986.*

For Tests in Australia the first year of the season is given in italics; i.e. *1876* denotes the 1876-77 season.

ENGLAND v SOUTH AFRICA

Captains

Season	England	South Africa	T	E	SA	D
1888-89	C. A. Smith[1]	O. R. Dunell[2]	2	2	0	0
1891-92	W. W. Read	W. H. Milton	1	1	0	0
1895-96	Lord Hawke[3]	E. A. Halliwell[4]	3	3	0	0
1898-99	Lord Hawke	M. Bisset	2	2	0	0
1905-06	P. F. Warner	P. W. Sherwell	5	1	4	0
1907	R. E. Foster	P. W. Sherwell	3	1	0	2
1909-10	H. D. G. Leveson Gower[5]	S. J. Snooke	5	2	3	0
1912	C. B. Fry	F. Mitchell[6]	3	3	0	0
1913-14	J. W. H. T. Douglas	H. W. Taylor	5	4	0	1
1922-23	F. T. Mann	H. W. Taylor	5	2	1	2
1924	A. E. R. Gilligan[7]	H. W. Taylor	5	3	0	2
1927-28	R. T. Stanyforth[8]	H. G. Deane	5	2	2	1
1929	J. C. White[9]	H. G. Deane	5	2	0	3
1930-31	A. P. F. Chapman	H. G. Deane[10]	5	0	1	4
1935	R. E. S. Wyatt	H. F. Wade	5	0	1	4
1938-39	W. R. Hammond	A. Melville	5	1	0	4
1947	N. W. D. Yardley	A. Melville	5	3	0	2
1948-49	F. G. Mann	A. D. Nourse	5	2	0	3
1951	F. R. Brown	A. D. Nourse	5	3	1	1
1955	P. B. H. May	J. E. Cheetham[11]	5	3	2	0
1956-57	P. B. H. May	C. B. van Ryneveld[12]	5	2	2	1
1960	M. C. Cowdrey	D. J. McGlew	5	3	0	2
1964-65	M. J. K. Smith	T. L. Goddard	5	1	0	4
1965	M. J. K. Smith	P. L. van der Merwe	3	0	1	2
1994	M. A. Atherton	K. C. Wessels	3	1	1	1
1995-96	M. A. Atherton	W. J. Cronje	5	0	1	4
1998	A. J. Stewart	W. J. Cronje	5	2	1	2
	In South Africa.....................		63	25	14	24
	In England........................		52	24	7	21
	Totals		115	49	21	45

Notes: The following deputised for the official touring captain or were appointed by the home authority for only a minor proportion of the series:

[1]M. P. Bowden (Second). [2]W. H. Milton (Second). [3]Sir T. C. O'Brien (First). [4]A. R. Richards (Third). [5]F. L. Fane (Fourth and Fifth). [6]L. J. Tancred (Second and Third). [7]J. W. H. T. Douglas (Fourth). [8]G. T. S. Stevens (Fifth). [9]A. W. Carr (Fourth and Fifth). [10]E. P. Nupen (First), H. B. Cameron (Fourth and Fifth). [11]D. J. McGlew (Third and Fourth). [12]D. J. McGlew (Second).

HIGHEST INNINGS TOTALS

For England in England: 554-8 dec. at Lord's............................ 1947
           in South Africa: 654-5 at Durban 1938-39

For South Africa in England: 552-5 dec. at Manchester 1998
           in South Africa: 530 at Durban 1938-39

LOWEST INNINGS TOTALS

For England in England: 76 at Leeds	1907
in South Africa: 92 at Cape Town......................	1898-99
For South Africa in England: 30 at Birmingham	1924
in South Africa: 30 at Port Elizabeth	1895-96

INDIVIDUAL HUNDREDS

For England (94)

R. Abel (1)
120　Cape Town . 1888-89

L. E. G. Ames (2)
148*　The Oval...　1935
115　Cape Town . 1938-39

M. A. Atherton (2)
185*　Johannesburg 1995-96
103　Birmingham .　1998

K. F. Barrington (2)
148*　Durban 1964-65
121　Johannesburg 1964-65

G. Boycott (1)
117　Port Elizabeth 1964-65

L. C. Braund (1)
104†　Lord's.....　1907

M. A. Butcher (1)
116　Leeds .....　1998

D. C. S. Compton (7)
163†　Nottingham .　1947
208　Lord's.....　1947
115　Manchester. .　1947
113　The Oval....　1947
114　Johannesburg 1948-49
112　Nottingham .　1951
158　Manchester. .　1955

M. C. Cowdrey (3)
101　Cape Town . 1956-57
155　The Oval...　1960
105　Johannesburg .　1965

D. Denton (1)
104　Johannesburg 1909-10

E. R. Dexter (1)
172　Johannesburg 1964-65

J. W. H. T. Douglas (1)
119†　Durban 1913-14

W. J. Edrich (3)
219　Durban 1938-39
189　Lord's.....　1947
191　Manchester. .　1947

F. L. Fane (1)
143　Johannesburg 1905-06

C. B. Fry (1)
129　The Oval...　1907

P. A. Gibb (2)
106†　Johannesburg 1938-39
120　Durban 1938-39

W. R. Hammond (6)
138*　Birmingham .　1929
101*　The Oval...　1929

136*　Durban 1930-31
181　Cape Town . 1938-39
120　Durban 1938-39
140　Durban 1938-39

T. W. Hayward (1)
122　Johannesburg 1895-96

E. H. Hendren (2)
132　Leeds .....　1924
142　The Oval...　1924

G. A. Hick (2)
110　Leeds .....　1994
141　Centurion...　1995-96

A. J. L. Hill (1)
124　Cape Town . 1895-96

J. B. Hobbs (2)
187　Cape Town . 1909-10
211　Lord's.....　1924

N. Hussain (1)
105　Lord's.....　1998

L. Hutton (4)
100　Leeds .....　1947
158　Johannesburg 1948-49
123　Johannesburg 1948-49
100　Leeds .....　1951

D. J. Insole (1)
110*　Durban 1956-57

M. Leyland (2)
102　Lord's.....　1929
161　The Oval...　1935

F. G. Mann (1)
136*　Port Elizabeth 1948-49

P. B. H. May (3)
138†　Leeds .....　1951
112　Lord's.....　1955
117　Manchester. .　1955

C. P. Mead (3)
102　Johannesburg 1913-14
117　Port Elizabeth 1913-14
181　Durban 1922-23

P. H. Parfitt (1)
122*　Johannesburg 1964-65

J. M. Parks (1)
108*　Durban 1964-65

E. Paynter (2)
117*⎱ †Johannesburg 1938-39
100 ⎰
243　Durban 1938-39

G. Pullar (1)
175　The Oval...　1960

W. Rhodes (1)
152　Johannesburg 1913-14

P. E. Richardson (1)
117†　Johannesburg 1956-57

R. W. V. Robins (1)
108　Manchester. .　1935

A. C. Russell (2)
140 ⎱
111 ⎰ Durban 1922-23

R. T. Simpson (1)
137　Nottingham .　1951

M. J. K. Smith (1)
121　Cape Town . 1964-65

R. H. Spooner (1)
119†　Lord's.....　1912

A. J. Stewart (1)
164　Manchester. .　1998

H. Sutcliffe (6)
122　Lord's.....　1924
102　Johannesburg 1927-28
114　Birmingham .　1929
100　Lord's.....　1929
104 ⎱
109* ⎰ The Oval....　1929

M. W. Tate (1)
100*　Lord's.....　1929

E. Tyldesley (2)
122　Johannesburg 1927-28
100　Durban 1927-28

J. T. Tyldesley (1)
112　Cape Town . 1898-99

B. H. Valentine (1)
112　Cape Town . 1938-39

P. F. Warner (1)
132*†‡Johannesburg 1898-99

C. Washbrook (1)
195　Johannesburg 1948-49

A. J. Watkins (1)
111　Johannesburg 1948-49

H. Wood (1)
134*　Cape Town . 1891-92

F. E. Woolley (3)
115*　Johannesburg 1922-23
134*　Lord's.....　1924
154　Manchester. .　1929

R. E. S. Wyatt (2)
113　Manchester. .　1929
149　Nottingham .　1935

For South Africa (66)

E. J. Barlow (1)	100 Durban 1956-57	**E. A. B. Rowan** (2)
138 Cape Town . 1964-65	109 Manchester. . 1960	156* Johannesburg 1948-49
K. C. Bland (2)	**B. M. McMillan** (1)	236 Leeds 1951
144* Johannesburg 1964-65	100* Johannesburg 1995-96	**P. W. Sherwell** (1)
127 The Oval... 1965	**A. Melville** (4)	115 Lord's 1907
R. H. Catterall (3)	103 Durban 1938-39	**I. J. Siedle** (1)
120 Birmingham . 1924	189 } Nottingham . 1947	141 Cape Town . 1930-31
120 Lord's 1924	104* }	**J. H. Sinclair** (1)
119 Durban .. 1927-28	117 Lord's 1947	106 Cape Town . 1898-99
W. J. Cronje (1)	**B. Mitchell** (7)	**H. W. Taylor** (7)
126 Nottingham . 1998	123 Cape Town . 1930-31	109 Durban 1913-14
E. L. Dalton (2)	164* Lord's 1935	176 Johannesburg 1922-23
117 The Oval... 1935	128 The Oval... 1935	101 Johannesburg 1922-23
102 Johannesburg 1938-39	109 Durban 1938-39	102 Durban 1922-23
W. R. Endean (1)	120 } The Oval ... 1947	101 Johannesburg 1927-28
116* Leeds 1955	189 }	121 The Oval ... 1929
G. A. Faulkner (1)	120 Cape Town . 1948-49	117 Cape Town . 1930-31
123 Johannesburg 1909-10	**A. D. Nourse** (7)	**P. G. V. van der Bijl** (1)
T. L. Goddard (1)	120 Cape Town . 1938-39	125 Durban 1938-39
112 Johannesburg 1964-65	103 Durban 1938-39	**K. G. Viljoen** (1)
C. M. H. Hathorn (1)	149 Nottingham . 1947	124 Manchester. . 1935
102 Johannesburg 1905-06	115 Manchester. . 1947	**W. W. Wade** (1)
J. H. Kallis (1)	112 Cape Town . 1948-49	125 Port Elizabeth 1948-49
132 Manchester. . 1998	129* Johannesburg 1948-49	**J. H. B. Waite** (1)
G. Kirsten (2)	208 Nottingham . 1951	113 Manchester. . 1955
110 Johannesburg 1995-96	**H. G. Owen-Smith** (1)	**K. C. Wessels** (1)
210 Manchester. . 1998	129 Leeds 1929	105† Lord's 1994
P. N. Kirsten (1)	**A. J. Pithey** (1)	**G. C. White** (2)
104 Leeds 1994	154 Cape Town . 1964-65	147 Johannesburg 1905-06
D. J. McGlew (2)	**R. G. Pollock** (2)	118 Durban 1909-10
104* Manchester. . 1955	137 Port Elizabeth 1964-65	**P. L. Winslow** (1)
133 Leeds 1955	125 Nottingham . 1965	108 Manchester. . 1955
R. A. McLean (3)	**J. N. Rhodes** (1)	
142 Lord's 1955	117 Lord's 1998	

† *Signifies hundred on first appearance in England–South Africa Tests. K. C. Wessels had earlier scored 162 on his Test debut for Australia against England at Brisbane in 1982-83.*

‡ *P. F. Warner carried his bat through the second innings.*

Notes: A. Melville's four hundreds were made in successive Test innings.

H. Wood scored the only hundred of his career in a Test match.

RECORD PARTNERSHIPS FOR EACH WICKET

For England

359	for 1st†	L. Hutton and C. Washbrook at Johannesburg	1948-49
280	for 2nd	P. A. Gibb and W. J. Edrich at Durban	1938-39
370	for 3rd†	W. J. Edrich and D. C. S. Compton at Lord's	1947
197	for 4th	W. R. Hammond and L. E. G. Ames at Cape Town	1938-39
237	for 5th	D. C. S. Compton and N. W. D. Yardley at Nottingham	1947
206*	for 6th	K. F. Barrington and J. M. Parks at Durban	1964-65
115	for 7th	J. W. H. T. Douglas and M. C. Bird at Durban	1913-14
154	for 8th	C. W. Wright and H. R. Bromley-Davenport at Johannesburg	1895-96
71	for 9th	H. Wood and J. T. Hearne at Cape Town	1891-92
92	for 10th	A. C. Russell and A. E. R. Gilligan at Durban	1922-23

For South Africa

260	for 1st†	B. Mitchell and I. J. Siedle at Cape Town	1930-31
238	for 2nd†	G. Kirsten and J. H. Kallis at Manchester	1998
319	for 3rd	A. Melville and A. D. Nourse at Nottingham	1947
214	for 4th†	H. W. Taylor and H. G. Deane at The Oval	1929
184	for 5th†	W. J. Cronje and J. N. Rhodes at Lord's	1998
171	for 6th	J. H. B. Waite and P. L. Winslow at Manchester	1955
123	for 7th	H. G. Deane and E. P. Nupen at Durban	1927-28
109*	for 8th	B. Mitchell and L. Tuckett at The Oval	1947
137	for 9th	E. L. Dalton and A. B. C. Langton at The Oval	1935
103	for 10th†	H. G. Owen-Smith and A. J. Bell at Leeds	1929

† Denotes record partnership against all countries.

MOST RUNS IN A SERIES

England in England	753 (average 94.12)	D. C. S. Compton	1947
England in South Africa	653 (average 81.62)	E. Paynter	1938-39
South Africa in England	621 (average 69.00)	A. D. Nourse	1947
South Africa in South Africa	582 (average 64.66)	H. W. Taylor	1922-23

TEN WICKETS OR MORE IN A MATCH

For England (25)

11-110 (5-25, 6-85)†	S. F. Barnes, Lord's	1912
10-115 (6-52, 4-63)	S. F. Barnes, Leeds	1912
13-57 (5-28, 8-29)	S. F. Barnes, The Oval	1912
10-105 (5-57, 5-48)	S. F. Barnes, Durban	1913-14
17-159 (8-56, 9-103)	S. F. Barnes, Johannesburg	1913-14
14-144 (7-56, 7-88)	S. F. Barnes, Durban	1913-14
12-112 (7-58, 5-54)	A. V. Bedser, Manchester	1951
11-118 (6-68, 5-50)	C. Blythe, Cape Town	1905-06
15-99 (8-59, 7-40)	C. Blythe, Leeds	1907
10-104 (7-46, 3-58)	C. Blythe, Cape Town	1909-10
15-28 (7-17, 8-11)	J. Briggs, Cape Town	1888-89
13-91 (6-54, 7-37)†	J. J. Ferris, Cape Town	1891-92
10-122 (5-60, 5-62)	A. R. C. Fraser, Nottingham	1998
10-207 (7-115, 3-92)	A. P. Freeman, Leeds	1929
12-171 (7-71, 5-100)	A. P. Freeman, Manchester	1929
12-130 (7-70, 5-60)	G. Geary, Johannesburg	1927-28
11-90 (6-7, 5-83)	A. E. R. Gilligan, Birmingham	1924
10-119 (4-64, 6-55)	J. C. Laker, The Oval	1951
15-45 (7-38, 8-7)†	G. A. Lohmann, Port Elizabeth	1895-96
12-71 (9-28, 3-43)	G. A. Lohmann, Johannesburg	1895-96
10-138 (1-81, 9-57)	D. E. Malcolm, The Oval	1994
11-97 (6-63, 5-34)	J. B. Statham, Lord's	1960
12-101 (7-52, 5-49)	R. Tattersall, Lord's	1951
12-89 (5-53, 7-36)	J. H. Wardle, Cape Town	1956-57
10-175 (5-95, 5-80)	D. V. P. Wright, Lord's	1947

For South Africa (6)

11-112 (4-49, 7-63)†	A. E. Hall, Cape Town	1922-23
11-150 (5-63, 6-87)	E. P. Nupen, Johannesburg	1930-31
10-87 (5-53, 5-34)	P. M. Pollock, Nottingham	1965

12-127 (4-57, 8-70)	S. J. Snooke, Johannesburg	1905-06
13-192 (4-79, 9-113)	H. J. Tayfield, Johannesburg	1956-57
12-181 (5-87, 7-94)	A. E. E. Vogler, Johannesburg	1909-10

† *Signifies ten wickets or more on first appearance in England–South Africa Tests.*

Note: S. F. Barnes took ten wickets or more in his first five Tests v South Africa and in six of his seven Tests v South Africa. A. P. Freeman and G. A. Lohmann took ten wickets or more in successive matches.

MOST WICKETS IN A SERIES

England in England	34 (average 8.29)	S. F. Barnes	1912
England in South Africa	49 (average 10.93)	S. F. Barnes	1913-14
South Africa in England	33 (average 19.78)	A. A. Donald	1998
South Africa in South Africa	37 (average 17.18)	H. J. Tayfield	1956-57

ENGLAND v WEST INDIES

Captains

Season	England	West Indies	T	E	WI	D
1928	A. P. F. Chapman	R. K. Nunes	3	3	0	0
1929-30	Hon. F. S. G. Calthorpe	E. L. G. Hoad[1]	4	1	1	2
1933	D. R. Jardine[2]	G. C. Grant	3	2	0	1
1934-35	R. E. S. Wyatt	G. C. Grant	4	1	2	1
1939	W. R. Hammond	R. S. Grant	3	1	0	2
1947-48	G. O. B. Allen[3]	J. D. C. Goddard[4]	4	0	2	2
1950	N. W. D. Yardley[5]	J. D. C. Goddard	4	1	3	0
1953-54	L. Hutton	J. B. Stollmeyer	5	2	2	1
1957	P. B. H. May	J. D. C. Goddard	5	3	0	2
1959-60	P. B. H. May[6]	F. C. M. Alexander	5	1	0	4

THE WISDEN TROPHY

Captains

Season	England	West Indies	T	E	WI	D	Held by
1963	E. R. Dexter	F. M. M. Worrell	5	1	3	1	WI
1966	M. C. Cowdrey[7]	G. S. Sobers	5	1	3	1	WI
1967-68	M. C. Cowdrey	G. S. Sobers	5	1	0	4	E
1969	R. Illingworth	G. S. Sobers	3	2	0	1	E
1973	R. Illingworth	R. B. Kanhai	3	0	2	1	WI
1973-74	M. H. Denness	R. B. Kanhai	5	1	1	3	WI
1976	A. W. Greig	C. H. Lloyd	5	0	3	2	WI
1980	I. T. Botham	C. H. Lloyd	5	0	1	4	WI
1980-81†	I. T. Botham	C. H. Lloyd	4	0	2	2	WI
1984	D. I. Gower	C. H. Lloyd	5	0	5	0	WI
1985-86	D. I. Gower	I. V. A. Richards	5	0	5	0	WI
1988	J. E. Emburey[9]	I. V. A. Richards	5	0	4	1	WI
1989-90‡	G. A. Gooch[10]	I. V. A. Richards[11]	4	1	2	1	WI
1991	G. A. Gooch	I. V. A. Richards	5	2	2	1	WI
1993-94	M. A. Atherton	R. B. Richardson[12]	5	1	3	1	WI
1995	M. A. Atherton	R. B. Richardson	6	2	2	2	WI
1997-98	M. A. Atherton	B. C. Lara	6	1	3	2	WI

In England			65	18	28	19
In West Indies			56	10	23	23
Totals			121	28	51	42

† *The Second Test, at Georgetown, was cancelled owing to political pressure and is excluded.*
‡ *The Second Test, at Georgetown, was abandoned without a ball being bowled and is excluded.*

Notes: The following deputised for the official touring captain or were appointed by the home authority for only a minor proportion of the series:

¹N. Betancourt (Second), M. P. Fernandes (Third), R. K. Nunes (Fourth). ²R. E. S. Wyatt (Third). ³K. Cranston (First). ⁴G. A. Headley (First), G. E. Gomez (Second). ⁵F. R. Brown (Fourth). ⁶M. C. Cowdrey (Fourth and Fifth). ⁷M. J. K. Smith (First), D. B. Close (Fifth). ⁸I. V. A. Richards (Fifth). ⁹M. W. Gatting (First), C. S. Cowdrey (Fourth), G. A. Gooch (Fifth). ¹⁰A. J. Lamb (Fourth and Fifth). ¹¹D. L. Haynes (Third). ¹²C. A. Walsh (Fifth).

HIGHEST INNINGS TOTALS

For England in England: 619-6 dec. at Nottingham 1957
in West Indies: 849 at Kingston 1929-30

For West Indies in England: 692-8 dec. at The Oval 1995
in West Indies: 681-8 dec. at Port-of-Spain 1953-54

LOWEST INNINGS TOTALS

For England in England: 71 at Manchester 1976
in West Indies: 46 at Port-of-Spain 1993-94

For West Indies in England: 86 at The Oval 1957
in West Indies: 102 at Bridgetown 1934-35

INDIVIDUAL HUNDREDS

For England (98)

L. E. G. Ames (3)	**M. C. Cowdrey (6)**	109 Nottingham . 1966
105 Port-of-Spain 1929-30	154† Birmingham . 1957	165 The Oval. . . 1966
149 Kingston . . . 1929-30	152 Lord's 1957	118 Port-of-Spain 1967-68
126 Kingston . . . 1934-35	114 Kingston . . . 1959-60	**A. W. Greig (3)**
D. L. Amiss (4)	119 Port-of-Spain 1959-60	148 Bridgetown . 1973-74
174 Port-of-Spain 1973-74	101 Kingston . . . 1967-68	121 Georgetown . 1973-74
262* Kingston . . . 1973-74	148 Port-of-Spain 1967-68	116 Leeds 1976
118 Georgetown . 1973-74	**E. R. Dexter (2)**	**S. C. Griffith (1)**
203 The Oval. . . 1976	136*† Bridgetown . 1959-60	140† Port-of-Spain 1947-48
M. A. Atherton (3)	110 Georgetown . 1959-60	**W. R. Hammond (1)**
144 Georgetown . 1993-94	**J. H. Edrich (1)**	138 The Oval. . . 1939
135 St John's . . 1993-94	146 Bridgetown . 1967-68	**J. H. Hampshire (1)**
113 Nottingham . 1995	**T. G. Evans (1)**	107† Lord's 1969
A. H. Bakewell (1)	104 Manchester. . 1950	**F. C. Hayes (1)**
107† The Oval. . . 1933	**K. W. R. Fletcher (1)**	106*† The Oval. . . 1973
K. F. Barrington (3)	129* Bridgetown . 1973-74	**E. H. Hendren (2)**
128† Bridgetown . 1959-60	**G. Fowler (1)**	205* Port-of-Spain 1929-30
121 Port-of-Spain 1959-60	106 Lord's 1984	123 Georgetown . 1929-30
143 Port-of-Spain 1967-68	**G. A. Gooch (5)**	**G. A. Hick (1)**
G. Boycott (5)	123 Lord's 1980	118* Nottingham . 1995
116 Georgetown . 1967-68	116 Bridgetown . 1980-81	**J. B. Hobbs (1)**
128 Manchester. . 1969	153 Kingston . . . 1980-81	159 The Oval. . . 1928
106 Lord's 1969	146 Nottingham . 1988	**N. Hussain (1)**
112 Port-of-Spain 1973-74	154*‡ Leeds 1991	106 St John's . . . 1997-98
104* St John's . . 1980-81	**D. I. Gower (1)**	**L. Hutton (5)**
D. C. S. Compton (2)	154* Kingston . . . 1980-81	196† Lord's 1939
120† Lord's 1939	**T. W. Graveney (5)**	165* The Oval. . . 1939
133 Port-of-Spain 1953-54	258 Nottingham . 1957	202*‡ The Oval. . . 1950
	164 The Oval. . . 1957	169 Georgetown . 1953-54
		205 Kingston . . . 1953-54

R. Illingworth (1)

113	Lord's	1969

D. R. Jardine (1)

127	Manchester. .	1933

A. P. E. Knott (1)

116	Leeds	1976

A. J. Lamb (6)

110	Lord's	1984
100	Leeds	1984
100*	Manchester. .	1984
113	Lord's	1988
132	Kingston . . .	1989-90
119	Bridgetown .	1989-90

P. B. H. May (3)

135	Port-of-Spain	1953-54
285*	Birmingham .	1957
104	Nottingham .	1957

C. Milburn (1)

126*	Lord's	1966

J. T. Murray (1)

112†	The Oval . . .	1966

J. M. Parks (1)

101*†	Port-of-Spain	1959-60

W. Place (1)

107	Kingston . . .	1947-48

M. R. Ramprakash (1)

154	Bridgetown .	1997-98

P. E. Richardson (2)

126	Nottingham .	1957
107	The Oval . . .	1957

J. D. Robertson (1)

133	Port-of-Spain	1947-48

A. Sandham (2)

152†	Bridgetown .	1929-30
325	Kingston . . .	1929-30

M. J. K. Smith (1)

108	Port-of-Spain	1959-60

R. A. Smith (3)

148*	Lord's	1991
109	The Oval . . .	1991
175	St John's . . .	1993-94

D. S. Steele (1)

106†	Nottingham .	1976

A. J. Stewart (2)

118	} Bridgetown .	1993-94
143		

R. Subba Row (1)

100†	Georgetown .	1959-60

G. P. Thorpe (1)

103	Bridgetown .	1997-98

E. Tyldesley (1)

122†	Lord's	1928

C. Washbrook (2)

114†	Lord's	1950
102	Nottingham .	1950

W. Watson (1)

116†	Kingston . . .	1953-54

P. Willey (2)

100*	The Oval . . .	1980
102*	St John's . . .	1980-81

For West Indies (110)

J. C. Adams (1)

137	Georgetown .	1993-94

K. L. T. Arthurton (1)

126	Kingston . . .	1993-94

I. Barrow (1)

105	Manchester. .	1933

C. A. Best (1)

164	Bridgetown .	1989-90

B. F. Butcher (2)

133	Lord's	1963
209*	Nottingham .	1966

G. M. Carew (1)

107	Port-of-Spain	1947-48

S. Chanderpaul (1)

118	Georgetown .	1997-98

C. A. Davis (1)

103	Lord's	1969

P. J. L. Dujon (1)

101	Manchester. .	1984

R. C. Fredericks (3)

150	Birmingham .	1973
138	Lord's	1976
109	Leeds	1976

A. G. Ganteaume (1)

112†	Port-of-Spain	1947-48

H. A. Gomes (2)

143	Birmingham .	1984
104*	Leeds	1984

C. G. Greenidge (7)

134	} Manchester. .	1976
101		
115	Leeds	1976
214*	Lord's	1984
223	Manchester. .	1984
103	Lord's	1988
149	St John's . . .	1989-90

D. L. Haynes (5)

184	Lord's	1980
125	The Oval . . .	1984
131	St John's . . .	1985-86
109	Bridgetown .	1989-90
167	St John's . . .	1989-90

G. A. Headley (8)

176†	Bridgetown .	1929-30
114	} Georgetown .	1929-30
112		
223	Kingston . . .	1929-30
169*	Manchester. .	1933
270*	Kingston . . .	1934-35
106	} Lord's	1939
107		

D. A. J. Holford (1)

105*	Lord's	1966

J. K. Holt (1)

166	Bridgetown .	1953-54

C. L. Hooper (3)

111	Lord's	1991
127	The Oval . . .	1995
108*	St John's . . .	1997-98

C. C. Hunte (3)

182	Manchester. .	1963
108*	The Oval . . .	1963
135	Manchester. .	1966

B. D. Julien (1)

121	Lord's	1973

A. I. Kallicharran (2)

158	Port-of-Spain	1973-74
119	Bridgetown .	1973-74

R. B. Kanhai (5)

110	Port-of-Spain	1959-60
104	The Oval . . .	1966
153	Port-of-Spain	1967-68

150	Georgetown .	1967-68
157	Lord's	1973

C. B. Lambert (1)

104	St John's . . .	1997-98

B. C. Lara (5)

167	Georgetown .	1993-94
375	St John's . . .	1993-94
145	Manchester. .	1995
152	Nottingham .	1995
179	The Oval . . .	1995

C. H. Lloyd (5)

118*	Port-of-Spain	1967-68
113*	Bridgetown .	1967-68
132	The Oval . . .	1973
101	Manchester. .	1980
100	Bridgetown .	1980-81

S. M. Nurse (2)

137	Leeds	1966
136	Port-of-Spain	1967-68

A. F. Rae (2)

106	Lord's	1950
109	The Oval . . .	1950

I. V. A. Richards (8)

232†	Nottingham .	1976
135	Manchester. .	1976
291	The Oval . . .	1976
145	Lord's	1980
182*	Bridgetown .	1980-81
114	St John's . . .	1980-81
117	Birmingham .	1984
110*	St John's . . .	1985-86

R. B. Richardson (4)

102	Port-of-Spain	1985-86
160	Bridgetown .	1985-86
104	Birmingham .	1991
121	The Oval . . .	1991

C. A. Roach (2)			145	Georgetown .	1959-60	**E. D. Weekes** (3)
122	Bridgetown .	1929-30	102	Leeds	1963	141	Kingston . . .	1947-48
209	Georgetown .	1929-30	161	Manchester. .	1966	129	Nottingham .	1950
L. G. Rowe (3)			163*	Lord's	1966	206	Port-of-Spain	1953-54
120	Kingston . . .	1973-74	174	Leeds	1966	**K. H. Weekes** (1)
302	Bridgetown .	1973-74	113*	Kingston . . .	1967-68	137	The Oval. . .	1939
123	Port-of-Spain	1973-74	152	Georgetown .	1967-68	**F. M. M. Worrell** (6)
O. G. Smith (2)			150*	Lord's	1973	131*	Georgetown .	1947-48
161†	Birmingham .	1957	**C. L. Walcott** (4)			261	Nottingham .	1950
168	Nottingham .	1957	168*	Lord's	1950	138	The Oval. . .	1950
G. S. Sobers (10)			220	Bridgetown .	1953-54	167	Port-of-Spain	1953-54
226	Bridgetown .	1959-60	124	Port-of-Spain	1953-54	191*‡	Nottingham .	1957
147	Kingston . . .	1959-60	116	Kingston . . .	1953-54	197*	Bridgetown .	1959-60

† *Signifies hundred on first appearance in England–West Indies Tests. S. C. Griffith provides the only instance for England of a player hitting his maiden century in first-class cricket in his first Test.*

‡ *Carried his bat.*

RECORD PARTNERSHIPS FOR EACH WICKET

For England

212	for 1st	C. Washbrook and R. T. Simpson at Nottingham	1950
266	for 2nd	P. E. Richardson and T. W. Graveney at Nottingham	1957
303	for 3rd	M. A. Atherton and R. A. Smith at St John's	1993-94
411	for 4th†	P. B. H. May and M. C. Cowdrey at Birmingham	1957
150	for 5th	A. J. Stewart and G. P. Thorpe at Bridgetown	1993-94
205	for 6th	M. R. Ramprakash and G. P. Thorpe at Bridgetown	1997-98
197	for 7th†	M. J. K. Smith and J. M. Parks at Port-of-Spain	1959-60
217	for 8th	T. W. Graveney and J. T. Murray at The Oval	1966
109	for 9th	G. A. R. Lock and P. I. Pocock at Georgetown	1967-68
128	for 10th	K. Higgs and J. A. Snow at The Oval	1966

For West Indies

298	for 1st†	C. G. Greenidge and D. L. Haynes at St John's	1989-90
287*	for 2nd	C. G. Greenidge and H. A. Gomes at Lord's	1984
338	for 3rd†	E. D. Weekes and F. M. M. Worrell at Port-of-Spain	1953-54
399	for 4th†	G. S. Sobers and F. M. M. Worrell at Bridgetown	1959-60
265	for 5th†	S. M. Nurse and G. S. Sobers at Leeds	1966
274*	for 6th†	G. S. Sobers and D. A. J. Holford at Lord's	1966
155*	for 7th‡	G. S. Sobers and B. D. Julien at Lord's	1973
99	for 8th	C. A. McWatt and J. K. Holt at Georgetown	1953-54
150	for 9th	E. A. E. Baptiste and M. A. Holding at Birmingham	1984
70	for 10th	I. R. Bishop and D. Ramnarine at Georgetown	1997-98

† *Denotes record partnership against all countries.*

‡ *231 runs were added for this wicket in two separate partnerships: G. S. Sobers retired ill and was replaced by K. D. Boyce when 155 had been added.*

TEN WICKETS OR MORE IN A MATCH

For England (12)

11-98 (7-44, 4-54)	T. E. Bailey, Lord's.	1957
11-110 (8-53, 3-57)	A. R. C. Fraser, Port-of-Spain	1997-98
10-93 (5-54, 5-39)	A. P. Freeman, Manchester	1928
13-156 (8-86, 5-70)	A. W. Greig, Port-of-Spain	1973-74

11-48 (5-28, 6-20)	G. A. R. Lock, The Oval	1957
10-137 (4-60, 6-77)	D. E. Malcolm, Port-of-Spain	1989-90
11-96 (5-37, 6-59)†	C. S. Marriott, The Oval	1933
10-142 (4-82, 6-60)	J. A. Snow, Georgetown	1967-68
10-195 (5-105, 5-90)†	G. T. S. Stevens, Bridgetown	1929-30
11-152 (6-100, 5-52)	F. S. Trueman, Lord's	1963
12-119 (5-75, 7-44)	F. S. Trueman, Birmingham	1963
11-149 (4-79, 7-70)	W. Voce, Port-of-Spain	1929-30

For West Indies (14)

10-127 (2-82, 8-45)	C. E. L. Ambrose, Bridgetown	1989-90
11-84 (5-60, 6-24)	C. E. L. Ambrose, Port-of-Spain	1993-94
10-174 (5-105, 5-69)	K. C. G. Benjamin, Nottingham	1995
11-147 (5-70, 6-77)†	K. D. Boyce, The Oval	1973
11-229 (5-137, 6-92)	W. Ferguson, Port-of-Spain	1947-48
11-157 (5-59, 6-98)†	L. R. Gibbs, Manchester	1963
10-106 (5-37, 5-69)	L. R. Gibbs, Manchester	1966
14-149 (8-92, 6-57)	M. A. Holding, The Oval	1976
10-96 (5-41, 5-55)†	H. H. H. Johnson, Kingston	1947-48
10-92 (6-32, 4-60)	M. D. Marshall, Lord's	1988
11-152 (5-66, 6-86)	S. Ramadhin, Lord's	1950
10-123 (5-60, 5-63)	A. M. E. Roberts, Lord's	1976
11-204 (8-104, 3-100)†	A. L. Valentine, Manchester	1950
10-160 (4-121, 6-39)	A. L. Valentine, The Oval	1950

† *Signifies ten wickets or more on first appearance in England–West Indies Tests.*

Note: F. S. Trueman took ten wickets or more in successive matches.

ENGLAND v NEW ZEALAND

Captains

Season	England	New Zealand	T	E	NZ	D
1929-30	A. H. H. Gilligan	T. C. Lowry	4	1	0	3
1931	D. R. Jardine	T. C. Lowry	3	1	0	2
1932-33	D. R. Jardine[1]	M. L. Page	2	0	0	2
1937	R. W. V. Robins	M. L. Page	3	1	0	2
1946-47	W. R. Hammond	W. A. Hadlee	1	0	0	1
1949	F. G. Mann[2]	W. A. Hadlee	4	0	0	4
1950-51	F. R. Brown	W. A. Hadlee	2	1	0	1
1954-55	L. Hutton	G. O. Rabone	2	2	0	0
1958	P. B. H. May	J. R. Reid	5	4	0	1
1958-59	P. B. H. May	J. R. Reid	2	1	0	1
1962-63	E. R. Dexter	J. R. Reid	3	3	0	0
1965	M. J. K. Smith	J. R. Reid	3	3	0	0
1965-66	M. J. K. Smith	B. W. Sinclair[3]	3	0	0	3
1969	R. Illingworth	G. T. Dowling	3	2	0	1
1970-71	R. Illingworth	G. T. Dowling	2	1	0	1
1973	R. Illingworth	B. E. Congdon	3	2	0	1
1974-75	M. H. Denness	B. E. Congdon	2	1	0	1
1977-78	G. Boycott	M. G. Burgess	3	1	1	1
1978	J. M. Brearley	M. G. Burgess	3	3	0	0
1983	R. G. D. Willis	G. P. Howarth	4	3	1	0
1983-84	R. G. D. Willis	G. P. Howarth	3	0	1	2
1986	M. W. Gatting	J. V. Coney	3	0	1	2
1987-88	M. W. Gatting	J. J. Crowe[4]	3	0	0	3
1990	G. A. Gooch	J. G. Wright	3	1	0	2

Season	England	New Zealand	T	E	NZ	D
1991-92	G. A. Gooch	M. D. Crowe	3	2	0	1
1994	M. A. Atherton	K. R. Rutherford	3	1	0	2
1996-97	M. A. Atherton	L. K. Germon⁵	3	2	0	1
	In New Zealand		38	15	2	21
	In England		40	21	2	17
	Totals		78	36	4	38

Notes: The following deputised for the official touring captain or were appointed by the home authority for only a minor proportion of the series:
¹R. E. S. Wyatt (Second). ²F. R. Brown (Third and Fourth). ³M. E. Chapple (First). ⁴J. G. Wright (Third). ⁵S. P. Fleming (Third).

HIGHEST INNINGS TOTALS

For England in England: 567-8 dec. at Nottingham 1994
          in New Zealand: 593-6 dec. at Auckland 1974-75

For New Zealand in England: 551-9 dec. at Lord's 1973
          in New Zealand: 537 at Wellington 1983-84

LOWEST INNINGS TOTALS

For England in England: 158 at Birmingham 1990
          in New Zealand: 64 at Wellington. 1977-78

For New Zealand in England: 47 at Lord's. 1958
          in New Zealand: 26 at Auckland 1954-55

INDIVIDUAL HUNDREDS

For England (83)

G. O. B. Allen (1)			**T. E. Bailey** (1)			**G. Boycott** (2)		

G. O. B. Allen (1)
122† Lord's 1931

L. E. G. Ames (2)
137† Lord's 1931
103 Christchurch . 1932-33

D. L. Amiss (2)
138*† Nottingham . 1973
164* Christchurch . 1974-75

M. A. Atherton (4)
151† Nottingham . 1990
101 Nottingham . 1994
111 Manchester. . 1994
118 Christchurch . 1996-97

T. E. Bailey (1)
134* Christchurch . 1950-51

K. F. Barrington (3)
126† Auckland. . . 1962-63
137 Birmingham . 1965
163 Leeds 1965

I. T. Botham (3)
103 Christchurch . 1977-78
103 Nottingham . 1983
138 Wellington. . 1983-84

E. H. Bowley (1)
109 Auckland. . . 1929-30

G. Boycott (2)
115 Leeds 1973
131 Nottingham . 1978

B. C. Broad (1)
114† Christchurch . 1987-88

D. C. S. Compton (2)
114 Leeds 1949
116 Lord's. 1949

M. C. Cowdrey (2)
128* Wellington . . 1962-63
119 Lord's 1965

M. H. Denness (1)
181 Auckland. . . 1974-75

E. R. Dexter (1)
141   Christchurch. 1958-59
B. L. D'Oliveira (1)
100   Christchurch. 1970-71
K. S. Duleepsinhji (2)
117   Auckland . . . 1929-30
109   The Oval . . . 1931
J. H. Edrich (3)
310*† Leeds 1965
115   Lord's 1969
155   Nottingham . 1969
W. J. Edrich (1)
100   The Oval . . . 1949
K. W. R. Fletcher (2)
178   Lord's 1973
216   Auckland . 1974-75
G. Fowler (1)
105† The Oval . . . 1983
M. W. Gatting (1)
121   The Oval . . . 1986
G. A. Gooch (4)
183   Lord's 1986
154   Birmingham . 1990
114   Auckland . . 1991-92
210   Nottingham . 1994
D. I. Gower (4)
111† The Oval . . . 1978
112* Leeds 1983
108   Lord's 1983
131   The Oval . . . 1986

A. W. Greig (1)
139† Nottingham .   1973
W. R. Hammond (4)
100* The Oval . . . 1931
227   Christchurch. 1932-33
336* Auckland. . . 1932-33
140   Lord's. 1937
J. Hardstaff jun. (2)
114† Leeds 1937
103   The Oval . . . 1937
L. Hutton (3)
100   Manchester. .   1937
101   Leeds 1949
206   The Oval . . . 1949
B. R. Knight (1)
125† Auckland . . . 1962-63
A. P. E. Knott (1)
101   Auckland . . . 1970-71
A. J. Lamb (3)
102*† The Oval . . . 1983
137* Nottingham .   1983
142   Wellington . . 1991-92
G. B. Legge (1)
196   Auckland . . . 1929-30
P. B. H. May (3)
113* Leeds 1958
101   Manchester. .   1958
124* Auckland . . 1958-59
C. A. Milton (1)
104*† Leeds 1958

P. H. Parfitt (1)
131*† Auckland. . . 1962-63
C. T. Radley (1)
158   Auckland . . . 1977-78
D. W. Randall (2)
164   Wellington . . 1983-84
104   Auckland . . . 1983-84
P. E. Richardson (1)
100† Birmingham .   1958
J. D. Robertson (1)
121† Lord's 1949
P. J. Sharpe (1)
111   Nottingham .   1969
R. T. Simpson (1)
103† Manchester. .   1949
A. J. Stewart (4)
148   Christchurch. 1991-92
107   Wellington . . 1991-92
119   Lord's 1994
173   Auckland . . . 1996-97
H. Sutcliffe (2)
117† The Oval . . . 1931
109* Manchester. .   1931
C. J. Tavaré (1)
109† The Oval . . . 1983
G. P. Thorpe (2)
119† Auckland . . . 1996-97
108   Wellington . . 1996-97
C. Washbrook (1)
103* Leeds 1949

For New Zealand (40)

N. J. Astle (1)
102*† Auckland . . . 1996-97
J. G. Bracewell (1)
110   Nottingham .   1986
M. G. Burgess (2)
104   Auckland . . . 1970-71
105   Lord's 1973
J. V. Coney (1)
174* Wellington . . 1983-84
B. E. Congdon (3)
104   Christchurch. 1965-66
176   Nottingham .   1973
175   Lord's 1973
J. J. Crowe (1)
128   Auckland . . . 1983-84
M. D. Crowe (5)
100   Wellington . . 1983-84
106   Lord's 1986
143   Wellington . . 1987-88
142   Lord's 1994
115   Manchester. .   1994
C. S. Dempster (2)
136   Wellington . . 1929-30

120   Lord's 1931
M. P. Donnelly (1)
206   Lord's 1949
S. P. Fleming (1)
129   Auckland . . . 1996-97
T. J. Franklin (1)
101   Lord's 1990
M. J. Greatbatch (1)
107*† Auckland . . . 1987-88
W. A. Hadlee (1)
116   Christchurch. 1946-47
G. P. Howarth (3)
122 }
102 } Auckland . . 1977-78
123   Lord's 1978
A. H. Jones (1)
143   Wellington . . 1991-92
J. E. Mills (1)
117† Wellington . . 1929-30
M. L. Page (1)
104   Lord's 1931

J. M. Parker (1)
121   Auckland . . . 1974-75
V. Pollard (2)
116   Nottingham .   1973
105* Lord's 1973
J. R. Reid (1)
100   Christchurch. 1962-63
K. R. Rutherford (1)
107* Wellington . . 1987-88
B. W. Sinclair (1)
114   Auckland . . . 1965-66
I. D. S. Smith (1)
113* Auckland . . . 1983-84
B. Sutcliffe (2)
101   Manchester.   1949
116   Christchurch. 1950-51
J. G. Wright (4)
130   Auckland . . . 1983-84
119   The Oval . . . 1986
103   Auckland . . . 1987-88
116   Wellington . . 1991-92

† *Signifies hundred on first appearance in England–New Zealand Tests.*

RECORD PARTNERSHIPS FOR EACH WICKET

For England

223	for 1st	G. Fowler and C. J. Tavaré at The Oval	1983
369	for 2nd	J. H. Edrich and K. F. Barrington at Leeds	1965
245	for 3rd	J. Hardstaff jun. and W. R. Hammond at Lord's	1937
266	for 4th	M. H. Denness and K. W. R. Fletcher at Auckland	1974-75
242	for 5th	W. R. Hammond and L. E. G. Ames at Christchurch	1932-33
240	for 6th†	P. H. Parfitt and B. R. Knight at Auckland.	1962-63
149	for 7th	A. P. E. Knott and P. Lever at Auckland	1970-71
246	for 8th†	L. E. G. Ames and G. O. B. Allen at Lord's	1931
163*	for 9th†	M. C. Cowdrey and A. C. Smith at Wellington	1962-63
59	for 10th	A. P. E. Knott and N. Gifford at Nottingham	1973

For New Zealand

276	for 1st	C. S. Dempster and J. E. Mills at Wellington	1929-30
241	for 2nd†	J. G. Wright and A. H. Jones at Wellington	1991-92
210	for 3rd	B. A. Edgar and M. D. Crowe at Lord's	1986
155	for 4th	M. D. Crowe and M. J. Greatbatch at Wellington	1987-88
180	for 5th	M. D. Crowe and S. A. Thomson at Lord's	1994
141	for 6th	M. D. Crowe and A. C. Parore at Manchester	1994
117	for 7th	D. N. Patel and C. L. Cairns at Christchurch	1991-92
104	for 8th	D. A. R. Moloney and A. W. Roberts at Lord's	1937
118	for 9th	J. V. Coney and B. L. Cairns at Wellington	1983-84
106*	for 10th	N. J. Astle and D. K. Morrison at Auckland.	1996-97

† *Denotes record partnership against all countries.*

TEN WICKETS OR MORE IN A MATCH

For England (8)

11-140 (6-101, 5-39)	I. T. Botham, Lord's	1978
10-149 (5-98, 5-51)	A. W. Greig, Auckland	1974-75
11-65 (4-14, 7-51)	G. A. R. Lock, Leeds	1958
11-84 (5-31, 6-53)	G. A. R. Lock, Christchurch	1958-59
11-147 (4-100, 7-47)†	P. C. R. Tufnell, Christchurch	1991-92
11-70 (4-38, 7-32)†	D. L. Underwood, Lord's	1969
12-101 (6-41, 6-60)	D. L. Underwood, The Oval	1969
12-97 (6-12, 6-85)	D. L. Underwood, Christchurch	1970-71

For New Zealand (5)

10-144 (7-74, 3-70)	B. L. Cairns, Leeds	1983
10-140 (4-73, 6-67)	J. Cowie, Manchester	1937
10-100 (4-74, 6-26)	R. J. Hadlee, Wellington	1977-78
10-140 (6-80, 4-60)	R. J. Hadlee, Nottingham	1986
11-169 (6-76, 5-93)	D. J. Nash, Lord's	1994

† *Signifies ten wickets or more on first appearance in England–New Zealand Tests.*

Note: D. L. Underwood took 12 wickets in successive matches against New Zealand in 1969 and 1970-71.

HAT-TRICK AND FOUR WICKETS IN FIVE BALLS

M. J. C. Allom, in his first Test match, v New Zealand at Christchurch in 1929-30, dismissed C. S. Dempster, T. C. Lowry, K. C. James, and F. T. Badcock to take four wickets in five balls (w-www).

ENGLAND v INDIA

Captains

Season	England	India	T	E	I	D
1932	D. R. Jardine	C. K. Nayudu	1	1	0	0
1933-34	D. R. Jardine	C. K. Nayudu	3	2	0	1
1936	G. O. B. Allen	Maharaj of Vizianagram	3	2	0	1
1946	W. R. Hammond	Nawab of Pataudi sen.	3	1	0	2
1951-52	N. D. Howard¹	V. S. Hazare	5	1	1	3
1952	L. Hutton	V. S. Hazare	4	3	0	1
1959	P. B. H. May²	D. K. Gaekwad³	5	5	0	0
1961-62	E. R. Dexter	N. J. Contractor	5	0	2	3
1963-64	M. J. K. Smith	Nawab of Pataudi jun.	5	0	0	5
1967	D. B. Close	Nawab of Pataudi jun.	3	3	0	0
1971	R. Illingworth	A. L. Wadekar	3	0	1	2
1972-73	A. R. Lewis	A. L. Wadekar	5	1	2	2
1974	M. H. Denness	A. L. Wadekar	3	3	0	0
1976-77	A. W. Greig	B. S. Bedi	5	3	1	1
1979	J. M. Brearley	S. Venkataraghavan	4	1	0	3
1979-80	J. M. Brearley	G. R. Viswanath	1	1	0	0
1981-82	K. W. R. Fletcher	S. M. Gavaskar	6	0	1	5
1982	R. G. D. Willis	S. M. Gavaskar	3	1	0	2
1984-85	D. I. Gower	S. M. Gavaskar	5	2	1	2
1986	M. W. Gatting⁴	Kapil Dev	3	0	2	1
1990	G. A. Gooch	M. Azharuddin	3	1	0	2
1992-93	G. A. Gooch⁵	M. Azharuddin	3	0	3	0
1996	M. A. Atherton	M. Azharuddin	3	1	0	2
	In England		41	22	3	16
	In India		43	10	11	22
	Totals.		84	32	14	38

Notes: The 1932 Indian touring team was captained by the Maharaj of Porbandar but he did not play in the Test match.

The following deputised for the official touring captain or were appointed by the home authority for only a minor proportion of the series:
¹D. B. Carr (Fifth). ²M. C. Cowdrey (Fourth and Fifth). ³Pankaj Roy (Second). ⁴D. I. Gower (First). ⁵A. J. Stewart (Second).

HIGHEST INNINGS TOTALS

For England in England: 653-4 dec. at Lord's.	1990
in India: 652-7 dec. at Madras	1984-85
For India in England: 606-9 dec. at The Oval.	1990
in India: 591 at Bombay	1992-93

LOWEST INNINGS TOTALS

For England in England: 101 at The Oval	1971
in India: 102 at Bombay	1981-82
For India in England: 42 at Lord's	1974
in India: 83 at Madras	1976-77

INDIVIDUAL HUNDREDS

For England (76)

D. L. Amiss (2)
188	Lord's	1974
179	Delhi	1976-77

M. A. Atherton (2)
131	Manchester. .	1990
160	Nottingham .	1996

K. F. Barrington (3)
151*	Bombay. . . .	1961-62
172	Kanpur	1961-62
113*	Delhi	1961-62

I. T. Botham (5)
137	Leeds	1979
114	Bombay. . . .	1979-80
142	Kanpur	1981-82
128	Manchester. .	1982
208	The Oval. . .	1982

G. Boycott (4)
246*†	Leeds	1967
155	Birmingham .	1979
125	The Oval . . .	1979
105	Delhi	1981-82

M. C. Cowdrey (3)
160	Leeds	1959
107	Calcutta. . . .	1963-64
151	Delhi	1963-64

M. H. Denness (2)
118	Lord's	1974
100	Birmingham .	1974

E. R. Dexter (1)
126*	Kanpur	1961-62

B. L. D'Oliveira (1)
109†	Leeds	1967

J. H. Edrich (1)
100*	Manchester. .	1974

T. G. Evans (1)
104	Lord's	1952

K. W. R. Fletcher (2)
113	Bombay. . . .	1972-73
123*	Manchester. .	1974

G. Fowler (1)
201	Madras	1984-85

M. W. Gatting (3)
136	Bombay. . . .	1984-85
207	Madras	1984-85
183*	Birmingham .	1986

G. A. Gooch (5)
127	Madras	1981-82
114	Lord's	1986
333 }	Lord's	1990
123 }		
116	Manchester. .	1990

D. I. Gower (2)
200*†	Birmingham .	1979
157*	The Oval . . .	1990

T. W. Graveney (2)
175†	Bombay. . . .	1951-52
151	Lord's	1967

A. W. Greig (3)
148	Bombay. . . .	1972-73
106	Lord's	1974
103	Calcutta. . . .	1976-77

W. R. Hammond (2)
167	Manchester. .	1936
217	The Oval. . .	1936

J. Hardstaff jun. (1)
205*	Lord's	1946

G. A. Hick (1)
178	Bombay. . . .	1992-93

N. Hussain (2)
128†	Birmingham .	1996
107*	Nottingham .	1996

L. Hutton (2)
150	Lord's	1952
104	Manchester. .	1952

R. Illingworth (1)
107	Manchester. .	1971

B. R. Knight (1)
127	Kanpur	1963-64

A. J. Lamb (3)
107	The Oval . . .	1982

139 Lord's 1990
109 Manchester. . 1990

A. R. Lewis (1)
125	Kanpur	1972-73

C. C. Lewis (1)
117	Madras	1992-93

D. Lloyd (1)
214*	Birmingham .	1974

B. W. Luckhurst (1)
101	Manchester. .	1971

P. B. H. May (1)
106	Nottingham .	1959

P. H. Parfitt (1)
121	Kanpur	1963-64

G. Pullar (2)
131	Manchester. .	1959
119	Kanpur	1961-62

D. W. Randall (1)
126	Lord's	1982

R. T. Robinson (1)
160	Delhi	1984-85

R. C. Russell (1)
124	Lord's	1996

D. S. Sheppard (1)
119	The Oval . . .	1952

M. J. K. Smith (1)
100†	Manchester. .	1959

R. A. Smith (2)
100*†	Lord's	1990
121*	Manchester. .	1990

C. J. Tavaré (1)
149	Delhi	1981-82

B. H. Valentine (1)
136†	Bombay. . . .	1933-34

C. F. Walters (1)
102	Madras	1933-34

A. J. Watkins (1)
137*†	Delhi	1951-52

T. S. Worthington (1)
128	The Oval. . .	1936

For India (64)

L. Amarnath (1)
118†	Bombay. . . .	1933-34

M. Azharuddin (6)
110†	Calcutta. . . .	1984-85
105	Madras	1984-85
122	Kanpur	1984-85
121	Lord's	1990
179	Manchester. .	1990
182	Calcutta. . . .	1992-93

A. A. Baig (1)
112†	Manchester. .	1959

F. M. Engineer (1)
121	Bombay. . . .	1972-73

S. C. Ganguly (2)
131†	Lord's	1996
136	Nottingham .	1996

S. M. Gavaskar (4)
101	Manchester. .	1974
108	Bombay. . . .	1976-77
221	The Oval . . .	1979
172	Bangalore . .	1981-82

Hanumant Singh (1)
105†	Delhi	1963-64

V. S. Hazare (2)
164*	Delhi	1951-52
155	Bombay. . . .	1951-52

M. L. Jaisimha (2)
127	Delhi	1961-62
129	Calcutta. . . .	1963-64

V. G. Kambli (1)
224	Bombay. . . .	1992-93

Kapil Dev (2)
116	Kanpur	1981-82
110	The Oval . . .	1990

S. M. H. Kirmani (1)
102	Bombay. . . .	1984-85

B. K. Kunderan (2)
192	Madras	1963-64
100	Delhi	1963-64

V. L. Manjrekar (3)	**S. M. Patil** (1)	**P. R. Umrigar** (3)
133 Leeds 1952	129* Manchester. . 1982	130* Madras 1951-52
189* Delhi 1961-62	**D. G. Phadkar** (1)	118 Manchester. . 1959
108 Madras 1963-64	115 Calcutta. . . . 1951-52	147* Kanpur 1961-62
V. Mankad (1)	**Pankaj Roy** (2)	**D. B. Vengsarkar** (5)
184 Lord's 1952	140 Bombay. . . . 1951-52	103 Lord's. 1979
V. M. Merchant (3)	111 Madras 1951-52	157 Lord's. 1982
114 Manchester. . 1936	**R. J. Shastri** (4)	137 Kanpur 1984-85
128 The Oval . . . 1946	142 Bombay 1984-85	126* Lord's 1986
154 Delhi 1951-52	111 Calcutta. . . . 1984-85	102* Leeds 1986
Mushtaq Ali (1)	100 Lord's 1990	**G. R. Viswanath** (4)
112 Manchester. . 1936	187 The Oval . . . 1990	113 Bombay. . . . 1972-73
R. G. Nadkarni (1)	**N. S. Sidhu** (1)	113 Lord's 1979
122* Kanpur 1963-64	106 Madras 1992-93	107 Delhi 1981-82
Nawab of Pataudi jun. (3)	**S. R. Tendulkar** (4)	222 Madras 1981-82
103 Madras 1961-62	119* Manchester. . 1990	**Yashpal Sharma** (1)
203* Delhi 1963-64	165 Madras 1992-93	140 Madras 1981-82
148 Leeds 1967	122 Birmingham . . 1996	
	177 Nottingham . . 1996	

† *Signifies hundred on first appearance in England–India Tests.*

Notes: G. A. Gooch's match aggregate of 456 (333 and 123) for England at Lord's in 1990 is the record in Test matches and provides the only instance of a batsman scoring a triple-hundred and a hundred in the same first-class match. His 333 is the highest innings in any match at Lord's.

M. Azharuddin scored hundreds in each of his first three Tests.

RECORD PARTNERSHIPS FOR EACH WICKET

For England

225 for 1st	G. A. Gooch and M. A. Atherton at Manchester	1990
241 for 2nd	G. Fowler and M. W. Gatting at Madras	1984-85
308 for 3rd	G. A. Gooch and A. J. Lamb at Lord's	1990
266 for 4th	W. R. Hammond and T. S. Worthington at The Oval	1936
254 for 5th†	K. W. R. Fletcher and A. W. Greig at Bombay	1972-73
171 for 6th	I. T. Botham and R. W. Taylor at Bombay	1979-80
125 for 7th	D. W. Randall and P. H. Edmonds at Lord's	1982
168 for 8th	R. Illingworth and P. Lever at Manchester	1971
83 for 9th	K. W. R. Fletcher and N. Gifford at Madras	1972-73
70 for 10th	P. J. W. Allott and R. G. D. Willis at Lord's	1982

For India

213 for 1st	S. M. Gavaskar and C. P. S. Chauhan at The Oval	1979
192 for 2nd	F. M. Engineer and A. L. Wadekar at Bombay	1972-73
316 for 3rd†‡	G. R. Viswanath and Yashpal Sharma at Madras	1981-82
222 for 4th†	V. S. Hazare and V. L. Manjrekar at Leeds	1952
214 for 5th†	M. Azharuddin and R. J. Shastri at Calcutta.	1984-85
130 for 6th	S. M. H. Kirmani and Kapil Dev at The Oval	1982
235 for 7th†	R. J. Shastri and S. M. H. Kirmani at Bombay	1984-85
128 for 8th	R. J. Shastri and S. M. H. Kirmani at Delhi	1981-82
104 for 9th	R. J. Shastri and Madan Lal at Delhi	1981-82
51 for 10th	{ R. G. Nadkarni and B. S. Chandrasekhar at Calcutta	1963-64
	{ S. M. H. Kirmani and Chetan Sharma at Madras	1984-85

† *Denotes record partnership against all countries.*

‡ *415 runs were added between the fall of the 2nd and 3rd wickets: D. B. Vengsarkar retired hurt when he and Viswanath had added 99 runs.*

TEN WICKETS OR MORE IN A MATCH

For England (7)

10-78 (5-35, 5-43)†	G. O. B. Allen, Lord's	1936
11-145 (7-49, 4-96)†	A. V. Bedser, Lord's	1946
11-93 (4-41, 7-52)	A. V. Bedser, Manchester	1946
13-106 (6-58, 7-48)	I. T. Botham, Bombay	1979-80
11-163 (6-104, 5-59)†	N. A. Foster, Madras	1984-85
10-70 (7-46, 3-24)†	J. K. Lever, Delhi	1976-77
11-153 (7-49, 4-104)	H. Verity, Madras	1933-34

For India (4)

10-177 (6-105, 4-72)	S. A. Durani, Madras	1961-62
12-108 (8-55, 4-53)	V. Mankad, Madras	1951-52
10-188 (4-130, 6-58)	Chetan Sharma, Birmingham	1986
12-181 (6-64, 6-117)†	L. Sivaramakrishnan, Bombay	1984-85

† *Signifies ten wickets or more on first appearance in England–India Tests.*

Note: A. V. Bedser took 11 wickets in a match in each of the first two Tests of his career.

ENGLAND v PAKISTAN

Captains

Season	England	Pakistan	T	E	P	D
1954	L. Hutton[1]	A. H. Kardar	4	1	1	2
1961-62	E. R. Dexter	Imtiaz Ahmed	3	1	0	2
1962	E. R. Dexter[2]	Javed Burki	5	4	0	1
1967	D. B. Close	Hanif Mohammad	3	2	0	1
1968-69	M. C. Cowdrey	Saeed Ahmed	3	0	0	3
1971	R. Illingworth	Intikhab Alam	3	1	0	2
1972-73	A. R. Lewis	Majid Khan	3	0	0	3
1974	M. H. Denness	Intikhab Alam	3	0	0	3
1977-78	J. M. Brearley[3]	Wasim Bari	3	0	0	3
1978	J. M. Brearley	Wasim Bari	3	2	0	1
1982	R. G. D. Willis[4]	Imran Khan	3	2	1	0
1983-84	R. G. D. Willis[5]	Zaheer Abbas	3	0	1	2
1987	M. W. Gatting	Imran Khan	5	0	1	4
1987-88	M. W. Gatting	Javed Miandad	3	0	1	2
1992	G. A. Gooch	Javed Miandad	5	1	2	2
1996	M. A. Atherton	Wasim Akram	3	0	2	1
	In England		37	13	7	17
	In Pakistan		18	1	2	15
	Totals		55	14	9	32

Notes: The following deputised for the official touring captain or were appointed by the home authority for only a minor proportion of the series:
[1]D. S. Sheppard (Second and Third). [2]M. C. Cowdrey (Third). [3]G. Boycott (Third). [4]D. I. Gower (Second). [5]D. I. Gower (Second and Third).

HIGHEST INNINGS TOTALS

For England in England: 558-6 dec. at Nottingham		1954
in Pakistan: 546-8 dec. at Faisalabad		1983-84
For Pakistan in England: 708 at The Oval		1987
in Pakistan: 569-9 dec. at Hyderabad		1972-73

LOWEST INNINGS TOTALS

For England in England: 130 at The Oval 1954
         in Pakistan: 130 at Lahore.. 1987-88

For Pakistan in England: 87 at Lord's 1954
         in Pakistan: 191 at Faisalabad 1987-88

INDIVIDUAL HUNDREDS

For England (47)

D. L. Amiss (3)
112 Lahore 1972-73
158 Hyderabad.. 1972-73
183 The Oval... 1974
C. W. J. Athey (1)
123 Lord's..... 1987
K. F. Barrington (4)
139† Lahore 1961-62
148 Lord's..... 1967
109* Nottingham . 1967
142 The Oval.. 1967
I. T. Botham (2)
100† Birmingham . 1978
108 Lord's..... 1978
G. Boycott (3)
121* Lord's..... 1971
112 Leeds 1971
100* Hyderabad.. 1977-78
B. C. Broad (1)
116 Faisalabad . 1987-88
D. C. S. Compton (1)
278 Nottingham . 1954
M. C. Cowdrey (3)
159† Birmingham . 1962
182 The Oval... 1962
100 Lahore 1968-69

J. P. Crawley (1)
106 The Oval... 1996
E. R. Dexter (2)
205 Karachi 1961-62
172 The Oval... 1962
B. L. D'Oliveira (1)
114* Dacca 1968-69
K. W. R. Fletcher (1)
122 The Oval... 1974
M. W. Gatting (2)
124 Birmingham . 1987
150* The Oval... 1987
G. A. Gooch (1)
135 Leeds 1992
D. I. Gower (2)
152 Faisalabad .. 1983-84
173* Lahore 1983-84
T. W. Graveney (3)
153 Lord's..... 1962
114 Nottingham . 1962
105 Karachi 1968-69
N. V. Knight (1)
113 Leeds 1996
A. P. E. Knott (1)
116 Birmingham . 1971

B. W. Luckhurst (1)
108*† Birmingham . 1971
C. Milburn (1)
139 Karachi 1968-69
P. H. Parfitt (4)
111 Karachi 1961-62
101* Birmingham . 1962
119 Leeds 1962
101* Nottingham . 1962
G. Pullar (1)
165 Dacca 1961-62
C. T. Radley (1)
106† Birmingham . 1978
D. W. Randall (1)
105 Birmingham . 1982
R. T. Robinson (1)
166† Manchester.. 1987
R. T. Simpson (1)
101 Nottingham . 1954
R. A. Smith (1)
127† Birmingham . 1992
A. J. Stewart (2)
190† Birmingham . 1992
170 Leeds 1996

For Pakistan (38)

Aamir Sohail (1)
205 Manchester.. 1992
Alim-ud-Din (1)
109 Karachi 1961-62
Asif Iqbal (3)
146 The Oval... 1967
104* Birmingham . 1971
102 Lahore 1972-73
Hanif Mohammad (3)
111 ⎫
104 ⎬ Dacca 1961-62
187* Lord's..... 1967
Haroon Rashid (2)
122† Lahore 1977-78
108 Hyderabad.. 1977-78

Ijaz Ahmed, sen. (1)
141 Leeds 1996
Imran Khan (1)
118 The Oval... 1987
Intikhab Alam (1)
138 Hyderabad.. 1972-73
Inzamam-ul-Haq (1)
148 Lord's..... 1996
Javed Burki (3)
138† Lahore 1961-62
140 Dacca 1961-62
101 Lord's..... 1962
Javed Miandad (2)
260 The Oval... 1987
153* Birmingham . 1992

Mohsin Khan (2)
200 Lord's..... 1982
104 Lahore 1983-84
Moin Khan (1)
105 Leeds 1996
Mudassar Nazar (3)
114† Lahore 1977-78
124 Birmingham . 1987
120 Lahore 1987-88
Mushtaq Mohammad (3)
100* Nottingham . 1962
100 Birmingham . 1971
157 Hyderabad.. 1972-73
Nasim-ul-Ghani (1)
101 Lord's..... 1962

Sadiq Mohammad (1)	102	The Oval . . .	1987	**Zaheer Abbas** (2)
119 Lahore 1972-73	165	Birmingham .	1992	274† Birmingham .	1971
Saeed Anwar (1)	100*	The Oval . . .	1996	240 The Oval . . .	1974
176 The Oval . . . 1996			
Salim Malik (4)	**Wasim Raja** (1)		
116 Faisalabad . . 1983-84	112	Faisalabad . . 1983-84	

† *Signifies hundred on first appearance in England–Pakistan Tests.*

Note: Three batsmen — Majid Khan, Mushtaq Mohammad and D. L. Amiss — were dismissed for 99 at Karachi, 1972-73: the only instance in Test matches.

RECORD PARTNERSHIPS FOR EACH WICKET

For England

198	for 1st	G. Pullar and R. W. Barber at Dacca	1961-62
248	for 2nd	M. C. Cowdrey and E. R. Dexter at The Oval	1962
227	for 3rd	A. J. Stewart and R. A. Smith at Birmingham	1992
188	for 4th	E. R. Dexter and P. H. Parfitt at Karachi	1961-62
192	for 5th	D. C. S. Compton and T. E. Bailey at Nottingham	1954
153*	for 6th	P. H. Parfitt and D. A. Allen at Birmingham	1962
167	for 7th	D. I. Gower and V. J. Marks at Faisalabad	1983-84
99	for 8th	P. H. Parfitt and D. A. Allen at Leeds	1962
76	for 9th	T. W. Graveney and F. S. Trueman at Lord's	1962
79	for 10th	R. W. Taylor and R. G. D. Willis at Birmingham	1982

For Pakistan

173	for 1st	Mohsin Khan and Shoaib Mohammad at Lahore	1983-84
291	for 2nd†	Zaheer Abbas and Mushtaq Mohammad at Birmingham	1971
180	for 3rd	Mudassar Nazar and Haroon Rashid at Lahore	1977-78
322	for 4th	Javed Miandad and Salim Malik at Birmingham	1992
197	for 5th	Javed Burki and Nasim-ul-Ghani at Lord's	1962
145	for 6th	Mushtaq Mohammad and Intikhab Alam at Hyderabad	1972-73
112	for 7th	Asif Mujtaba and Moin Khan at Leeds	1996
130	for 8th	Hanif Mohammad and Asif Iqbal at Lord's	1967
190	for 9th†	Asif Iqbal and Intikhab Alam at The Oval	1967
62	for 10th	Sarfraz Nawaz and Asif Masood at Leeds	1974

† *Denotes record partnership against all countries.*

TEN WICKETS OR MORE IN A MATCH

For England (2)

11-83 (6-65, 5-18)†	N. G. B. Cook, Karachi	1983-84
13-71 (5-20, 8-51)	D. L. Underwood, Lord's	1974

For Pakistan (6)

10-194 (5-84, 5-110)	Abdul Qadir, Lahore	1983-84
10-211 (7-96, 3-115)	Abdul Qadir, The Oval	1987
13-101 (9-56, 4-45)	Abdul Qadir, Lahore	1987-88
10-186 (5-88, 5-98)	Abdul Qadir, Karachi	1987-88
12-99 (6-53, 6-46)	Fazal Mahmood, The Oval	1954
10-77 (3-37, 7-40)	Imran Khan, Leeds	1987

† *Signifies ten wickets or more on first appearance in England–Pakistan Tests.*

FOUR WICKETS IN FIVE BALLS

C. M. Old, v Pakistan at Birmingham in 1978, dismissed Wasim Raja, Wasim Bari, Iqbal Qasim and Sikander Bakht to take four wickets in five balls (ww-ww).

ENGLAND v SRI LANKA

Captains

Season	England	Sri Lanka	T	E	SL	D
1981-82	K. W. R. Fletcher	B. Warnapura	1	1	0	0
1984	D. I. Gower	L. R. D. Mendis	1	0	0	1
1988	G. A. Gooch	R. S. Madugalle	1	1	0	0
1991	G. A. Gooch	P. A. de Silva	1	1	0	0
1992-93	A. J. Stewart	A. Ranatunga	1	0	1	0
1998	A. J. Stewart	A. Ranatunga	1	0	1	0
	In England		4	2	1	1
	In Sri Lanka		2	1	1	0
	Totals.		6	3	2	1

HIGHEST INNINGS TOTALS

For England in England: 445 at The Oval 1998
            in Sri Lanka: 380 at Colombo (SSC). 1992-93

For Sri Lanka in England: 591 at The Oval 1998
            in Sri Lanka: 469 at Colombo (SSC). 1992-93

LOWEST INNINGS TOTALS

For England in England: 181 at The Oval 1998
            in Sri Lanka: 223 at Colombo (PSS). 1981-82

For Sri Lanka in England: 194 at Lord's 1988
            in Sri Lanka: 175 at Colombo (PSS). 1981-82

INDIVIDUAL HUNDREDS

For England (6)

J. P. Crawley (1)		G. A. Hick (1)		R. A. Smith (1)	
156*† The Oval . . .	1998	107 The Oval . . .	1998	128 Colombo (SSC)	1992-93
G. A. Gooch (1)		A. J. Lamb (1)		A. J. Stewart (1)	
174 Lord's	1991	107† Lord's	1984	113*† Lord's	1991

For Sri Lanka (5)

P. A. de Silva (1)		L. R. D. Mendis (1)		S. Wettimuny (1)	
152 The Oval . . .	1998	111 Lord's	1984	190 Lord's	1984
S. T. Jayasuriya (1)		S. A. R. Silva (1)			
213 The Oval . . .	1998	102*† Lord's	1984		

† *Signifies hundred on first appearance in England–Sri Lanka Tests.*

RECORD PARTNERSHIPS FOR EACH WICKET

For England

78 for 1st	G. A. Gooch and H. Morris at Lord's	1991
139 for 2nd	G. A. Gooch and A. J. Stewart at Lord's	1991
112 for 3rd	R. A. Smith and G. A. Hick at Colombo (SSC)	1992-93
128 for 4th	G. A. Hick and M. R. Ramprakash at The Oval	1998
40 for 5th	A. J. Stewart and I. T. Botham at Lord's	1991
87 for 6th	A. J. Lamb and R. M. Ellison at Lord's	1984
63 for 7th	A. J. Stewart and R. C. Russell at Lord's	1991

20 for 8th	J. E. Emburey and P. W. Jarvis at Colombo (SSC)	. . . .	1992-93
37 for 9th	P. J. Newport and N. A. Foster at Lord's	. . . .	1988
89 for 10th	J. P. Crawley and A. R. C. Fraser at The Oval	. . . .	1998

For Sri Lanka

99 for 1st	R. S. Mahanama and U. C. Hathurusinghe at Colombo (SSC)	. . . . .	1992-93
83 for 2nd	B. Warnapura and R. L. Dias at Colombo (PSS)	. . . .	1981-82
243 for 3rd†	S. T. Jayasuriya and P. A. de Silva at The Oval	. . . .	1998
148 for 4th	S. Wettimuny and A. Ranatunga at Lord's	. . . .	1984
150 for 5th†	S. Wettimuny and L. R. D. Mendis at Lord's	. . . .	1984
138 for 6th	S. A. R. Silva and L. R. D. Mendis at Lord's	. . . .	1984
74 for 7th	U. C. Hathurusinghe and R. J. Ratnayake at Lord's	. . . .	1991
29 for 8th	R. J. Ratnayake and C. P. H. Ramanayake at Lord's	. . . .	1991
83 for 9th†	H. P. Tillekeratne and M. Muralitharan at Colombo (SSC)	. . . . .	1992-93
64 for 10th†	J. R. Ratnayeke and G. F. Labrooy at Lord's	. . . .	1988

† *Denotes record partnership against all countries.*

TEN WICKETS OR MORE IN A MATCH

For Sri Lanka (1)

16-220 (7-155, 9-65)	M. Muralitharan at The Oval	. . . .	1998

Note: The best match figures by an England bowler are 8-95 (5-28, 3-67) by D. L. Underwood at Colombo (PSS), 1981-82.

ENGLAND v ZIMBABWE

		Captains					
Season	*England*		*Zimbabwe*	*T*	*E*	*Z*	*D*
1996-97	M. A. Atherton		A. D. R. Campbell	2	0	0	2

HIGHEST INNINGS TOTALS

For England: 406 at Bulawayo	. . . .	1996-97
For Zimbabwe: 376 at Bulawayo	. . . .	1996-97

INDIVIDUAL HUNDREDS

For England (3)

J. P. Crawley (1)	**N. Hussain (1)**	**A. J. Stewart (1)**
112† Bulawayo . . 1996-97	113† Bulawayo . . 1996-97	101* Harare. 1996-97

For Zimbabwe (1)

A. Flower (1)
112† Bulawayo . . 1996-97

† *Signifies hundred on first appearance in England–Zimbabwe Tests.*

HUNDRED PARTNERSHIPS

For England

137 for 2nd	N. V. Knight and A. J. Stewart at Bulawayo	. . . .	1996-97
106* for 4th	A. J. Stewart and G. P. Thorpe at Harare	. . . .	1996-97
148 for 5th	N. Hussain and J. P. Crawley at Bulawayo	. . . .	1996-97

For Zimbabwe

127 for 2nd	G. W. Flower and A. D. R. Campbell at Bulawayo	. . . .	1996-97

BEST MATCH BOWLING ANALYSES

For England

6-137 (2-76, 4-61)†   P. C. R. Tufnell, Bulawayo...................... 1996-97

For Zimbabwe

7-186 (5-123, 2-63)†   P. A. Strang, Bulawayo 1996-97

† *Signifies on first appearance in England–Zimbabwe Tests.*

AUSTRALIA v SOUTH AFRICA

Captains

Season	Australia	South Africa	T	A	SA	D
1902-03S	J. Darling	H. M. Taberer[1]	3	2	0	1
1910-11A	C. Hill	P. W. Sherwell	5	4	1	0
1912E	S. E. Gregory	F. Mitchell[2]	3	2	0	1
1921-22S	H. L. Collins	H. W. Taylor	3	1	0	2
1931-32A	W. M. Woodfull	H. B. Cameron	5	5	0	0
1935-36S	V. Y. Richardson	H. F. Wade	5	4	0	1
1949-50S	A. L. Hassett	A. D. Nourse	5	4	0	1
1952-53A	A. L. Hassett	J. E. Cheetham	5	2	2	1
1957-58S	I. D. Craig	C. B. van Ryneveld[3]	5	3	0	2
1963-64A	R. B. Simpson[4]	T. L. Goddard	5	1	1	3
1966-67S	R. B. Simpson	P. L. van der Merwe	5	1	3	1
1969-70S	W. M. Lawry	A. Bacher	4	0	4	0
1993-94A	A. R. Border	K. C. Wessels[5]	3	1	1	1
1993-94S	A. R. Border	K. C. Wessels	3	1	1	1
1996-97S	M. A. Taylor	W. J. Cronje	3	2	1	0
1997-98A	M. A. Taylor	W. J. Cronje	3	1	0	2
	In South Africa		36	18	9	9
	In Australia		26	14	5	7
	In England		3	2	0	1
	Totals		65	34	14	17

S Played in South Africa.   A Played in Australia.   E Played in England.

Notes: The following deputised for the official touring captain or were appointed by the home authority for only a minor proportion of the series:
[1]J. H. Anderson (Second), E. A. Halliwell (Third). [2]L. J. Tancred (Third). [3]D. J. McGlew (First).
[4]R. Benaud (First). [5]W. J. Cronje (Third).

HIGHEST INNINGS TOTALS

For Australia in Australia: 578 at Melbourne 1910-11
in South Africa: 628-8 dec. at Johannesburg.................. 1996-97

For South Africa in Australia: 595 at Adelaide 1963-64
in South Africa: 622-9 dec. at Durban 1969-70

LOWEST INNINGS TOTALS

For Australia in Australia: 111 at Sydney............................ 1993-94
in South Africa: 75 at Durban 1949-50

For South Africa in Australia: 36† at Melbourne 1931-32
in South Africa: 85‡ at Johannesburg 1902-03
85‡ at Cape Town..................... 1902-03

† *Scored 45 in the second innings giving the smallest aggregate of 81 (12 extras) in Test cricket.*
‡ *In successive innings.*

INDIVIDUAL HUNDREDS

For Australia (65)

W. W. Armstrong (2)
159*‡ Johannesburg 1902-03
132   Melbourne . . 1910-11
W. Bardsley (3)
132† Sydney 1910-11
121   Manchester. . 1912
164   Lord's 1912
R. Benaud (2)
122   Johannesburg 1957-58
100   Johannesburg 1957-58
G. S. Blewett (1)
214† Johannesburg 1996-97
B. C. Booth (2)
169† Brisbane . . . 1963-64
102* Sydney 1963-64
D. G. Bradman (4)
226† Brisbane . . . 1931-32
112   Sydney 1931-32
167   Melbourne . . 1931-32
299* Adelaide . . . 1931-32
W. A. Brown (1)
121   Cape Town . 1935-36
J. W. Burke (1)
189   Cape Town . 1957-58
A. G. Chipperfield (1)
109† Durban 1935-36
H. L. Collins (1)
203   Johannesburg 1921-22
J. H. Fingleton (3)
112   Cape Town . 1935-36
108   Johannesburg 1935-36
118   Durban 1935-36

J. M. Gregory (1)
119   Johannesburg 1921-22
R. N. Harvey (8)
178   Cape Town . 1949-50
151* Durban 1949-50
100   Johannesburg 1949-50
116   Port Elizabeth 1949-50
109   Brisbane . . . 1952-53
190   Sydney 1952-53
116   Adelaide . . . 1952-53
205   Melbourne . . 1952-53
A. L. Hassett (3)
112† Johannesburg 1949-50
167   Port Elizabeth 1949-50
163   Adelaide . . . 1952-53
C. Hill (3)
142† Johannesburg 1902-03
191   Sydney 1910-11
100   Melbourne . . 1910-11
C. Kelleway (2)
114   Manchester. . 1912
102   Lord's 1912
W. M. Lawry (1)
157   Melbourne . . 1963-64
S. J. E. Loxton (1)
101† Johannesburg 1949-50
C. G. Macartney (2)
137   Sydney 1910-11
116   Durban 1921-22
S. J. McCabe (2)
149   Durban 1935-36
189* Johannesburg 1935-36
C. C. McDonald (1)
154   Adelaide . . . 1952-53

J. Moroney (2)
118 }
101*} Johannesburg 1949-50
A. R. Morris (2)
111   Johannesburg 1949-50
157   Port Elizabeth 1949-50
R. T. Ponting (1)
105† Melbourne . . 1997-98
K. E. Rigg (1)
127† Sydney 1931-32
J. Ryder (1)
142   Cape Town . 1921-22
R. B. Simpson (1)
153   Cape Town . 1966-67
K. R. Stackpole (1)
134   Cape Town . 1966-67
M. A. Taylor (2)
170† Melbourne . . 1993-94
169*‡ Adelaide . . . 1997-98
V. T. Trumper (2)
159   Melbourne . . 1910-11
214* Adelaide . . . 1910-11
M. E. Waugh (4)
113* Durban 1993-94
116   Port Elizabeth 1996-97
100   Sydney 1997-98
115* Adelaide . . . 1997-98
S. R. Waugh (2)
164† Adelaide . . . 1993-94
160   Johannesburg 1996-97
W. M. Woodfull (1)
161   Melbourne . . 1931-32

For South Africa (40)

E. J. Barlow (5)
114† Brisbane . . . 1963-64
109   Melbourne . . 1963-64
201   Adelaide . . . 1963-64
127   Cape Town . 1969-70
110   Johannesburg 1969-70
K. C. Bland (1)
126   Sydney 1963-64
W. J. Cronje (1)
122   Johannesburg 1993-94
W. R. Endean (1)
162* Melbourne . . 1952-53
G. A. Faulkner (3)
204   Melbourne . . 1910-11
115   Adelaide . . . 1910-11
122* Manchester. . 1912

C. N. Frank (1)
152   Johannesburg 1921-22
A. C. Hudson (1)
102   Cape Town . 1993-94
B. L. Irvine (1)
102   Port Elizabeth 1969-70
J. H. Kallis (1)
101   Melbourne . . 1997-98
G. Kirsten (1)
108* Adelaide . . . 1997-98
D. T. Lindsay (3)
182   Johannesburg 1966-67
137   Durban 1966-67
131   Johannesburg 1966-67
D. J. McGlew (2)
108   Johannesburg 1957-58

105   Durban 1957-58
A. D. Nourse (2)
231   Johannesburg 1935-36
114   Cape Town . 1949-50
A. W. Nourse (1)
111   Johannesburg 1921-22
R. G. Pollock (5)
122   Sydney 1963-64
175   Adelaide . . . 1963-64
209   Cape Town . 1966-67
105   Port Elizabeth 1966-67
274   Durban 1969-70
B. A. Richards (2)
140   Durban 1969-70
126   Port Elizabeth 1969-70

E. A. B. Rowan (1)		**S. J. Snooke** (1)		134	Durban 1957-58
143 Durban 1949-50		103 Adelaide . . . 1910-11		**J. W. Zulch** (2)	
J. H. Sinclair (2)		**K. G. Viljoen** (1)		105	Adelaide . . . 1910-11
101 Johannesburg 1902-03		111 Melbourne . . 1931-32		150	Sydney 1910-11
104 Cape Town . 1902-03		**J. H. B. Waite** (2)			
		115 Johannesburg 1957-58			

† *Signifies hundred on first appearance in Australia–South Africa Tests.*
‡ *Carried his bat.*

RECORD PARTNERSHIPS FOR EACH WICKET

For Australia

233 for 1st	J. H. Fingleton and W. A. Brown at Cape Town	1935-36
275 for 2nd	C. C. McDonald and A. L. Hassett at Adelaide	1952-53
242 for 3rd	C. Kelleway and W. Bardsley at Lord's	1912
169 for 4th	M. A. Taylor and M. E. Waugh at Melbourne	1993-94
385 for 5th	S. R. Waugh and G. S. Blewett at Johannesburg	1996-97
108 for 6th	S. R. Waugh and I. A. Healy at Cape Town	1993-94
160 for 7th	R. Benaud and G. D. McKenzie at Sydney	1963-64
83 for 8th	A. G. Chipperfield and C. V. Grimmett at Durban	1935-36
78 for 9th {	D. G. Bradman and W. J. O'Reilly at Adelaide	1931-32
{	K. D. Mackay and I. Meckiff at Johannesburg	1957-58
82 for 10th	V. S. Ransford and W. J. Whitty at Melbourne	1910-11

For South Africa

176 for 1st	D. J. McGlew and T. L. Goddard at Johannesburg	1957-58
173 for 2nd	L. J. Tancred and C. B. Llewellyn at Johannesburg	1902-03
341 for 3rd†	E. J. Barlow and R. G. Pollock at Adelaide	1963-64
206 for 4th	C. N. Frank and A. W. Nourse at Johannesburg	1921-22
129 for 5th	J. H. B. Waite and W. R. Endean at Johannesburg	1957-58
200 for 6th†	R. G. Pollock and H. R. Lance at Durban	1969-70
221 for 7th	D. T. Lindsay and P. L. van der Merwe at Johannesburg	1966-67
124 for 8th	A. W. Nourse and E. A. Halliwell at Johannesburg	1902-03
85 for 9th	R. G. Pollock and P. M. Pollock at Cape Town	1966-67
74 for 10th	B. M. McMillan and P. L. Symcox at Adelaide	1997-98

† *Denotes record partnership against all countries.*

TEN WICKETS OR MORE IN A MATCH

For Australia (7)

14-199 (7-116, 7-83)	C. V. Grimmett, Adelaide	1931-32
10-88 (5-32, 5-56)	C. V. Grimmett, Cape Town	1935-36
10-110 (3-70, 7-40)	C. V. Grimmett, Johannesburg	1935-36
13-173 (7-100, 6-73)	C. V. Grimmett, Durban	1935-36
11-24 (5-6, 6-18)	H. Ironmonger, Melbourne	1931-32
12-128 (7-56, 5-72)	S. K. Warne, Sydney	1993-94
11-109 (5-75, 6-34)	S. K. Warne, Sydney	1997-98

For South Africa (3)

10-123 (4-80, 6-43)	P. S. de Villiers, Sydney	1993-94
10-116 (5-43, 5-73)	C. B. Llewellyn, Johannesburg	1902-03
13-165 (6-84, 7-81)	H. J. Tayfield, Melbourne	1952-53

Note: C. V. Grimmett took ten wickets or more in three consecutive matches in 1935-36.

AUSTRALIA v WEST INDIES

Captains

Season	Australia	West Indies	T	A	WI	T	D
1930-31A	W. M. Woodfull	G. C. Grant	5	4	1	0	0
1951-52A	A. L. Hassett[1]	J. D. C. Goddard[2]	5	4	1	0	0
1954-55W	I. W. Johnson	D. St E. Atkinson[3]	5	3	0	0	2

THE FRANK WORRELL TROPHY

Captains

Season	Australia	West Indies	T	A	WI	T	D	Held by
1960-61*A*	R. Benaud	F. M. M. Worrell	5	2	1	1	1	A
1964-65*W*	R. B. Simpson	G. S. Sobers	5	1	2	0	2	WI
1968-69*A*	W. M. Lawry	G. S. Sobers	5	3	1	0	1	A
1972-73*W*	I. M. Chappell	R. B. Kanhai	5	2	0	0	3	A
1975-76*A*	G. S. Chappell	C. H. Lloyd	6	5	1	0	0	A
1977-78*W*	R. B. Simpson	A. I. Kallicharran[4]	5	1	3	0	1	WI
1979-80*A*	G. S. Chappell	C. H. Lloyd[5]	3	0	2	0	1	WI
1981-82*A*	G. S. Chappell	C. H. Lloyd	3	1	1	0	1	WI
1983-84*W*	K. J. Hughes	C. H. Lloyd[6]	5	0	3	0	2	WI
1984-85*A*	A. R. Border[7]	C. H. Lloyd	5	1	3	0	1	WI
1988-89*A*	A. R. Border	I. V. A. Richards	5	1	3	0	1	WI
1990-91*W*	A. R. Border	I. V. A. Richards	5	1	2	0	2	WI
1992-93*A*	A. R. Border	R. B. Richardson	5	1	2	0	2	WI
1994-95*W*	M. A. Taylor	R. B. Richardson	4	2	1	0	1	A
1996-97*A*	M. A. Taylor	C. A. Walsh	5	3	2	0	0	A

	T	A	WI	T	D
In Australia.	52	25	18	1	8
In West Indies.	34	10	11	0	13
Totals	86	35	29	1	21

A Played in Australia.   W Played in West Indies.

Notes: The following deputised for the official touring captain or were appointed by the home authority for only a minor proportion of the series:
[1]A. R. Morris (Third). [2]J. B. Stollmeyer (Fifth). [3]J. B. Stollmeyer (Second and Third). [4]C. H. Lloyd (First and Second). [5]D. L. Murray (First). [6]I. V. A. Richards (Second). [7]K. J. Hughes (First and Second).

HIGHEST INNINGS TOTALS

For Australia in Australia: 619 at Sydney	1968-69
in West Indies: 758-8 dec. at Kingston	1954-55
For West Indies in Australia: 616 at Adelaide	1968-69
in West Indies: 573 at Bridgetown	1964-65

LOWEST INNINGS TOTALS

For Australia in Australia: 76 at Perth	1984-85
in West Indies: 90 at Port-of-Spain	1977-78
For West Indies in Australia: 78 at Sydney	1951-52
in West Indies: 109 at Georgetown	1972-73

INDIVIDUAL HUNDREDS

For Australia (78)

R. G. Archer (1)
128 Kingston . . . 1954-55

R. Benaud (1)
121 Kingston . . . 1954-55

D. C. Boon (3)
149   Sydney 1988-89
109* Kingston . . . 1990-91
111   Brisbane . . . 1992-93

B. C. Booth (1)
117 Port-of-Spain 1964-65

A. R. Border (3)
126 Adelaide . . . 1981-82

100* Port-of-Spain 1983-84
110   Melbourne . . 1992-93

D. G. Bradman (2)
223 Brisbane . . . 1930-31
152 Melbourne . . 1930-31

G. S. Chappell (5)
106   Bridgetown . . 1972-73
123 } ‡Brisbane . . 1975-76
109* }
182* Sydney 1975-76
124   Brisbane . . . 1979-80

I. M. Chappell (5)
117† Brisbane . . . 1968-69
165   Melbourne . . 1968-69
106* Bridgetown . 1972-73
109   Georgetown . . 1972-73
156   Perth. 1975-76

G. J. Cosier (1)
109† Melbourne . . 1975-76

R. M. Cowper (2)
143   Port-of-Spain 1964-65
102   Bridgetown . 1964-65

J. Dyson (1)
127*† Sydney 1981-82
R. N. Harvey (3)
133 Brisbane ... 1954-55
133 Port-of-Spain 1954-55
204 Kingston ... 1954-55
A. L. Hassett (2)
132 Sydney 1951-52
102 Melbourne .. 1951-52
M. L. Hayden (1)
125 Adelaide ... 1996-97
I. A. Healy (1)
161* Brisbane ... 1996-97
A. M. J. Hilditch (1)
113† Melbourne .. 1984-85
K. J. Hughes (2)
130*† Brisbane ... 1979-80
100* Melbourne .. 1981-82
D. M. Jones (1)
216 Adelaide ... 1988-89
A. F. Kippax (1)
146† Adelaide ... 1930-31
W. M. Lawry (4)
210 Bridgetown . 1964-65
105 Brisbane ... 1968-69
205 Melbourne .. 1968-69
151 Sydney 1968-69
R. R. Lindwall (1)
118 Bridgetown . 1954-55

R. B. McCosker (1)
109* Melbourne .. 1975-76
C. C. McDonald (2)
110 Port-of-Spain 1954-55
127 Kingston ... 1954-55
K. R. Miller (4)
129 Sydney 1951-52
147 Kingston ... 1954-55
137 Bridgetown . 1954-55
109 Kingston ... 1954-55
A. R. Morris (1)
111 Port-of-Spain 1954-55
N. C. O'Neill (1)
181† Brisbane ... 1960-61
W. B. Phillips (1)
120 Bridgetown . 1983-84
W. H. Ponsford (2)
183 Sydney 1930-31
109 Brisbane ... 1930-31
I. R. Redpath (4)
132 Sydney 1968-69
102 Melbourne .. 1975-76
103 Adelaide ... 1975-76
101 Melbourne .. 1975-76
C. S. Serjeant (1)
124 Georgetown . 1977-78
R. B. Simpson (1)
201 Bridgetown . 1964-65

K. R. Stackpole (1)
142 Kingston ... 1972-73
M. A. Taylor (1)
144 St John's ... 1990-91
P. M. Toohey (1)
122 Kingston ... 1977-78
A. Turner (1)
136 Adelaide ... 1975-76
K. D. Walters (6)
118 Sydney 1968-69
110 Adelaide ... 1968-69
242 ⎫
103 ⎬ Sydney ... 1968-69
102* Bridgetown . 1972-73
112 Port-of-Spain 1972-73
M. E. Waugh (3)
139* St John's ... 1990-91
112 Melbourne .. 1992-93
126 Kingston ... 1994-95
S. R. Waugh (2)
100 Sydney 1992-93
200 Kingston ... 1994-95
K. C. Wessels (1)
173 Sydney 1984-85
G. M. Wood (2)
126 Georgetown . 1977-78
111 Perth...... 1988-89

For West Indies (81)

F. C. M. Alexander (1)
108 Sydney 1960-61
K. L. T. Arthurton (1)
157*† Brisbane ... 1992-93
D. St E. Atkinson (1)
219 Bridgetown . 1954-55
B. F. Butcher (3)
117 Port-of-Spain 1964-65
101 Sydney 1968-69
118 Adelaide ... 1968-69
S. L. Campbell (1)
113 Brisbane ... 1996-97
C. C. Depeiza (1)
122 Bridgetown . 1954-55
P. J. L. Dujon (2)
130 Port-of-Spain 1983-84
139 Perth...... 1984-85
M. L. C. Foster (1)
125† Kingston ... 1972-73
R. C. Fredericks (1)
169 Perth...... 1975-76
H. A. Gomes (6)
101† Georgetown . 1977-78
115 Kingston ... 1977-78
126 Sydney 1981-82
124* Adelaide ... 1981-82
127 Perth...... 1984-85
120* Adelaide ... 1984-85

C. G. Greenidge (4)
120* Georgetown . 1983-84
127 Kingston ... 1983-84
104 Adelaide ... 1988-89
226 Bridgetown . 1990-91
D. L. Haynes (5)
103* Georgetown . 1983-84
145 Bridgetown . 1983-84
100 Perth...... 1988-89
143 Sydney 1988-89
111 Georgetown . 1990-91
G. A. Headley (2)
102* Brisbane ... 1930-31
105 Sydney 1930-31
C. L. Hooper (1)
102 Brisbane ... 1996-97
C. C. Hunte (1)
110 Melbourne .. 1960-61
A. I. Kallicharran (4)
101 Brisbane ... 1975-76
127 Port-of-Spain 1977-78
126 Kingston ... 1977-78
106 Adelaide ... 1979-80
R. B. Kanhai (5)
117 ⎫
115 ⎬ Adelaide ... 1960-61
129 Bridgetown . 1964-65
121 Port-of-Spain 1964-65
105 Bridgetown . 1972-73

B. C. Lara (2)
277 Sydney 1992-93
132 Perth...... 1996-97
C. H. Lloyd (6)
129† Brisbane ... 1968-69
178 Georgetown . 1972-73
149 Perth...... 1975-76
102 Melbourne .. 1975-76
121 Adelaide ... 1979-80
114 Brisbane ... 1984-85
F. R. Martin (1)
123* Sydney 1930-31
S. M. Nurse (2)
201 Bridgetown . 1964-65
137 Sydney 1968-69
I. V. A. Richards (5)
101 Adelaide ... 1975-76
140 Brisbane ... 1979-80
178 St John's ... 1983-84
208 Melbourne .. 1984-85
146 Perth...... 1988-89
R. B. Richardson (9)
131* Bridgetown . 1983-84
154 St John's ... 1983-84
138 Brisbane ... 1984-85
122 Melbourne .. 1988-89
106 Adelaide ... 1988-89
104* Kingston ... 1990-91

182	Georgetown .	1990-91	**G. S. Sobers** (4)
109	Sydney	1992-93	132 Brisbane . . . 1960-61
100	Kingston . . .	1994-95	168 Sydney 1960-61

L. G. Rowe (1)
107 Brisbane . . . 1975-76
P. V. Simmons (1)
110 Melbourne . . 1992-93
O. G. Smith (1)
104† Kingston . . . 1954-55

110 Adelaide . . . 1968-69
113 Sydney 1968-69
J. B. Stollmeyer (1)
104 Sydney 1951-52
C. L. Walcott (5)
108 Kingston . . . 1954-55

126 ⎫ Port-of-Spain 1954-55
110 ⎭
155 ⎫ Kingston . . . 1954-55
110 ⎭
E. D. Weekes (1)
139 Port-of-Spain 1954-55
A. B. Williams (1)
100† Georgetown . 1977-78
F. M. M. Worrell (1)
108 Melbourne . . 1951-52

† *Signifies hundred on first appearance in Australia–West Indies Tests.*
‡ *G. S. Chappell is the only player to score hundreds in both innings of his first Test as captain.*

Note: F. C. M. Alexander and C. C. Depeiza scored the only hundreds of their first-class careers in a Test match.

RECORD PARTNERSHIPS FOR EACH WICKET

For Australia

382 for 1st†	W. M. Lawry and R. B. Simpson at Bridgetown		1964-65
298 for 2nd	W. M. Lawry and I. M. Chappell at Melbourne		1968-69
295 for 3rd†	C. C. McDonald and R. N. Harvey at Kingston		1954-55
336 for 4th	W. M. Lawry and K. D. Walters at Sydney		1968-69
220 for 5th	K. R. Miller and R. G. Archer at Kingston		1954-55
206 for 6th	K. R. Miller and R. G. Archer at Bridgetown		1954-55
134 for 7th	A. K. Davidson and R. Benaud at Brisbane		1960-61
137 for 8th	R. Benaud and I. W. Johnson at Kingston		1954-55
114 for 9th	D. M. Jones and M. G. Hughes at Adelaide		1988-89
97 for 10th	T. G. Hogan and R. M. Hogg at Georgetown		1983-84

For West Indies

250* for 1st	C. G. Greenidge and D. L. Haynes at Georgetown		1983-84
297 for 2nd	D. L. Haynes and R. B. Richardson at Georgetown		1990-91
308 for 3rd	R. B. Richardson and I. V. A. Richards at St John's		1983-84
198 for 4th	L. G. Rowe and A. I. Kallicharran at Brisbane		1975-76
210 for 5th	R. B. Kanhai and M. L. C. Foster at Kingston		1972-73
165 for 6th	R. B. Kanhai and D. L. Murray at Bridgetown		1972-73
347 for 7th†	D. St E. Atkinson and C. C. Depeiza at Bridgetown		1954-55
87 for 8th	P. J. L. Dujon and C. E. L. Ambrose at Port-of-Spain		1990-91
122 for 9th	D. A. J. Holford and J. L. Hendriks at Adelaide		1968-69
56 for 10th	J. Garner and C. E. H. Croft at Brisbane		1979-80

† *Denotes record partnership against all countries.*

TEN WICKETS OR MORE IN A MATCH

For Australia (12)

10-113 (4-31, 6-82)	M. G. Bevan, Adelaide	1996-97
11-96 (7-46, 4-50)	A. R. Border, Sydney	1988-89
11-222 (5-135, 6-87)†	A. K. Davidson, Brisbane	1960-61
11-183 (7-87, 4-96)†	C. V. Grimmett, Adelaide	1930-31
10-115 (6-72, 4-43)	N. J. N. Hawke, Georgetown	1964-65
10-144 (6-54, 4-90)	R. G. Holland, Sydney	1984-85
13-217 (5-130, 8-87)	M. G. Hughes, Perth	1988-89
11-79 (7-23, 4-56)	H. Ironmonger, Melbourne	1930-31
11-181 (8-112, 3-69)	G. F. Lawson, Adelaide	1984-85
10-127 (7-83, 3-44)	D. K. Lillee, Melbourne	1981-82
10-159 (8-71, 2-88)	G. D. McKenzie, Melbourne	1968-69
10-185 (3-87, 7-98)	B. Yardley, Sydney	1981-82

For West Indies (4)

10-120 (6-74, 4-46)	C. E. L. Ambrose, Adelaide	1992-93
10-113 (7-55, 3-58)	G. E. Gomez, Sydney	1951-52
11-107 (5-45, 6-62)	M. A. Holding, Melbourne	1981-82
10-107 (5-69, 5-38)	M. D. Marshall, Adelaide	1984-85

† *Signifies ten wickets or more on first appearance in Australia–West Indies Tests.*

AUSTRALIA v NEW ZEALAND

Season	Australia	*Captains* New Zealand	T	A	NZ	D
1945-46N	W. A. Brown	W. A. Hadlee	1	1	0	0
1973-74A	I. M. Chappell	B. E. Congdon	3	2	0	1
1973-74N	I. M. Chappell	B. E. Congdon	3	1	1	1
1976-77N	G. S. Chappell	G. M. Turner	2	1	0	1
1980-81A	G. S. Chappell	G. P. Howarth[1]	3	2	0	1
1981-82N	G. S. Chappell	G. P. Howarth	3	1	1	1

TRANS-TASMAN TROPHY

Season	Australia	*Captains* New Zealand	T	A	NZ	D	Held by
1985-86A	A. R. Border	J. V. Coney	3	1	2	0	NZ
1985-86N	A. R. Border	J. V. Coney	3	0	1	2	NZ
1987-88A	A. R. Border	J. J. Crowe	3	1	0	2	A
1989-90A	A. R. Border	J. G. Wright	1	0	0	1	A
1989-90N	A. R. Border	J. G. Wright	1	0	1	0	NZ
1992-93N	A. R. Border	M. D. Crowe	3	1	1	1	NZ
1993-94A	A. R. Border	M. D. Crowe[2]	3	2	0	1	A
1997-98A	M. A. Taylor	S. P. Fleming	3	2	0	1	A
	In Australia		19	10	2	7	
	In New Zealand		16	5	5	6	
	Totals......................		35	15	7	13	

A Played in Australia.   N Played in New Zealand.

Note: The following deputised for the official touring captain: [1]M. G. Burgess (Second). [2]K. R. Rutherford (Second and Third).

HIGHEST INNINGS TOTALS

For Australia in Australia: 607-6 dec. at Brisbane		1993-94
in New Zealand: 552 at Christchurch		1976-77
For New Zealand in Australia: 553-7 dec. at Brisbane		1985-86
in New Zealand: 484 at Wellington		1973-74

LOWEST INNINGS TOTALS

For Australia in Australia: 162 at Sydney...............................		1973-74
in New Zealand: 103 at Auckland		1985-86
For New Zealand in Australia: 121 at Perth		1980-81
in New Zealand: 42 at Wellington		1945-46

INDIVIDUAL HUNDREDS

For Australia (32)

D. C. Boon (3)		**M. T. G. Elliott** (1)	
143	Brisbane . . 1987-88	114	Hobart 1997-98
200	Perth. 1989-90	**G. J. Gilmour** (1)	
106	Hobart 1993-94	101	Christchurch . 1976-77
A. R. Border (5)		**I. A. Healy** (1)	
152*	Brisbane . . 1985-86	113*	Perth 1993-94
140 ⎱	Christchurch. 1985-86	**G. R. Marsh** (1)	
114* ⎰		118	Auckland . . . 1985-86
205	Adelaide . . . 1987-88	**R. W. Marsh** (1)	
105	Brisbane . . . 1993-94	132	Adelaide . . . 1973-74
G. S. Chappell (3)		**G. R. J. Matthews** (2)	
247* ⎱	Wellington . . 1973-74	115†	Brisbane . . . 1985-86
133 ⎰		130	Wellington . . 1985-86
176	Christchurch . 1981-82	**I. R. Redpath** (1)	
I. M. Chappell (2)		159*‡	Auckland . . . 1973-74
145 ⎱	Wellington . . 1973-74	**M. J. Slater** (1)	
121 ⎰		168	Hobart 1993-94

K. R. Stackpole (1)		
122†	Melbourne . .	1973-74
M. A. Taylor (2)		
142*	Perth.	1993-94
112	Brisbane . . .	1997-98
K. D. Walters (3)		
104*	Auckland . . .	1973-74
250	Christchurch.	1976-77
107	Melbourne . .	1980-81
M. E. Waugh (1)		
111	Hobart	1993-94
S. R. Waugh (1)		
147*	Brisbane . . .	1993-94
G. M. Wood (2)		
111†	Brisbane . . .	1980-81
100	Auckland . . .	1981-82

For New Zealand (20)

J. V. Coney (1)		**M. J. Greatbatch** (1)	
101*	Wellington . . 1985-86	146*†	Perth. 1989-90
B. E. Congdon (2)		**B. F. Hastings** (1)	
132	Wellington . . 1973-74	101	Wellington . . 1973-74
107*	Christchurch . 1976-77	**M. J. Horne** (1)	
M. D. Crowe (3)		133†	Hobart. 1997-98
188	Brisbane . . . 1985-86	**A. H. Jones** (2)	
137	Christchurch . 1985-86	150	Adelaide . . . 1987-88
137	Adelaide . . . 1987-88	143	Perth 1993-94
B. A. Edgar (1)		**J. F. M. Morrison** (1)	
161	Auckland . . . 1981-82	117	Sydney 1973-74

J. M. Parker (1)		
108	Sydney	1973-74
J. F. Reid (1)		
108†	Brisbane . . .	1985-86
K. R. Rutherford (1)		
102	Christchurch.	1992-93
G. M. Turner (2)		
101 ⎱	Christchurch.	1973-74
110* ⎰		
J. G. Wright (2)		
141	Christchurch.	1981-82
117*	Wellington . .	1989-90

    † *Signifies hundred on first appearance in Australia–New Zealand Tests.*
    ‡ *Carried his bat.*

Notes: G. S. and I. M. Chappell at Wellington in 1973-74 provide the only instance in Test matches of brothers both scoring a hundred in each innings and in the same Test.

RECORD PARTNERSHIPS FOR EACH WICKET

For Australia

198 for 1st	M. J. Slater and M. A. Taylor at Perth	1993-94
235 for 2nd	M. J. Slater and D. C. Boon at Hobart	1993-94
264 for 3rd	I. M. Chappell and G. S. Chappell at Wellington	1973-74
153 for 4th	M. E. Waugh and S. R. Waugh at Perth	1997-98
213 for 5th	G. M. Ritchie and G. R. J. Matthews at Wellington	1985-86
197 for 6th	A. R. Border and G. R. J. Matthews at Brisbane.	1985-86
217 for 7th†	K. D. Walters and G. J. Gilmour at Christchurch	1976-77
93 for 8th	G. J. Gilmour and K. J. O'Keeffe at Auckland	1976-77
69 for 9th	I. A. Healy and C. J. McDermott at Perth	1993-94
60 for 10th	K. D. Walters and J. D. Higgs at Melbourne	1980-81

For New Zealand

111	for 1st	M. J. Greatbatch and J. G. Wright at Wellington.............	1992-93
132	for 2nd	M. J. Horne and A. C. Parore at Hobart	1997-98
224	for 3rd	J. F. Reid and M. D. Crowe at Brisbane	1985-86
229	for 4th	B. E. Congdon and B. F. Hastings at Wellington...........	1973-74
88	for 5th	J. V. Coney and M. G. Burgess at Perth	1980-81
109	for 6th	K. R. Rutherford and J. V. Coney at Wellington	1985-86
132*	for 7th	J. V. Coney and R. J. Hadlee at Wellington	1985-86
88*	for 8th	M. J. Greatbatch and M. C. Snedden at Perth.............	1989-90
73	for 9th	H. J. Howarth and D. R. Hadlee at Christchurch...........	1976-77
124	for 10th	J. G. Bracewell and S. L. Boock at Sydney	1985-86

† *Denotes record partnership against all countries.*

TEN WICKETS OR MORE IN A MATCH

For Australia (2)

| 10-174 (6-106, 4-68) | R. G. Holland, Sydney........................... | 1985-86 |
| 11-123 (5-51, 6-72) | D. K. Lillee, Auckland .... | 1976-77 |

For New Zealand (4)

10-106 (4-74, 6-32)	J. G. Bracewell, Auckland	1985-86
15-123 (9-52, 6-71)	R. J. Hadlee, Brisbane.........................	1985-86
11-155 (5-65, 6-90)	R. J. Hadlee, Perth	1985-86
10-176 (5-109, 5-67)	R. J. Hadlee, Melbourne	1987-88

AUSTRALIA v INDIA

Captains

Season	Australia	India	T	A	I	T	D
1947-48A	D. G. Bradman	L. Amarnath	5	4	0	0	1
1956-57I	I. W. Johnson[1]	P. R. Umrigar	3	2	0	0	1
1959-60I	R. Benaud	G. S. Ramchand	5	2	1	0	2
1964-65I	R. B. Simpson	Nawab of Pataudi jun.	3	1	1	0	1
1967-68A	R. B. Simpson[2]	Nawab of Pataudi jun.[3]	4	4	0	0	0
1969-70I	W. M. Lawry	Nawab of Pataudi jun.	5	3	1	0	1
1977-78A	R. B. Simpson	B. S. Bedi	5	3	2	0	0
1979-80I	K. J. Hughes	S. M. Gavaskar	6	0	2	0	4
1980-81A	G. S. Chappell	S. M. Gavaskar	3	1	1	0	1
1985-86A	A. R. Border	Kapil Dev	3	0	0	0	3
1986-87I	A. R. Border	Kapil Dev	3	0	0	1	2
1991-92A	A. R. Border	M. Azharuddin	5	4	0	0	1
1996-97I	M. A. Taylor	S. R. Tendulkar	1	0	1	0	0
1997-98I	M. A. Taylor	M. Azharuddin	3	1	2	0	0
	In Australia....................		25	16	3	0	6
	In India		29	9	8	1	11
	Totals		54	25	11	1	17

A Played in Australia. I Played in India.

Notes: The following deputised for the official touring captain or were appointed by the home authority for only a minor proportion of the series:
[1]R. R. Lindwall (Second). [2]W. M. Lawry (Third and Fourth). [3]C. G. Borde (First).

HIGHEST INNINGS TOTALS

For Australia in Australia: 674 at Adelaide 1947-48
              in India: 574-7 dec. at Madras 1986-87

For India in Australia: 600-4 dec. at Sydney 1985-86
          in India: 633-5 dec. at Calcutta 1997-98

LOWEST INNINGS TOTALS

For Australia in Australia: 83 at Melbourne 1980-81
          in India: 105 at Kanpur 1959-60

For India in Australia: 58 at Brisbane 1947-48
          in India: 135 at Delhi 1959-60

INDIVIDUAL HUNDREDS

For Australia (53)

S. G. Barnes (1)	**R. M. Cowper** (2)	**A. R. Morris** (1)
112 Adelaide . . . 1947-48	108 Adelaide . . . 1967-68	100* Melbourne . . 1947-48
D. C. Boon (6)	165 Sydney . . . 1967-68	**N. C. O'Neill** (2)
123† Adelaide . . . 1985-86	**L. E. Favell** (1)	163 Bombay. . . . 1959-60
131 Sydney . . . 1985-86	101 Madras . . . 1959-60	113 Calcutta. . . . 1959-60
122 Madras . . . 1986-87	**R. N. Harvey** (4)	**G. M. Ritchie** (1)
129* Sydney 1991-92	153 Melbourne . . 1947-48	128† Adelaide . . . 1985-86
135 Adelaide . . . 1991-92	140 Bombay. . . 1956-57	**A. P. Sheahan** (1)
107 Perth. 1991-92	114 Delhi 1959-60	114 Kanpur 1969-70
A. R. Border (4)	102 Bombay. . . 1959-60	**R. B. Simpson** (4)
162† Madras 1979-80	**A. L. Hassett** (1)	103 Adelaide . . . 1967-68
124 Melbourne . . 1980-81	198* Adelaide . . . 1947-48	109 Melbourne . . 1967-68
163 Melbourne . . 1985-86	**K. J. Hughes** (2)	176 Perth. 1977-78
106 Madras 1986-87	100 Madras . . . 1979-80	100 Adelaide . . . 1977-78
D. G. Bradman (4)	213 Adelaide . . . 1980-81	**K. R. Stackpole** (1)
185† Brisbane . . . 1947-48	**D. M. Jones** (2)	103† Bombay. . . . 1969-70
132 ⎱ Melbourne . . 1947-48	210† Madras 1986-87	**M. A. Taylor** (2)
127 ⎰	150* Perth. 1991-92	100 Adelaide . . . 1991-92
201 Adelaide . . . 1947-48	**W. M. Lawry** (1)	102* Bangalore . . 1997-98
J. W. Burke (1)	100 Melbourne . . 1967-68	**K. D. Walters** (1)
161 Bombay. . . 1956-57	**A. L. Mann** (1)	102 Madras . . . 1969-70
G. S. Chappell (1)	105 Perth. 1977-78	**M. E. Waugh** (1)
204† Sydney 1980-81	**G. R. Marsh** (1)	153* Bangalore . . 1997-98
I. M. Chappell (2)	101 Bombay. . . 1986-87	**G. M. Wood** (1)
151 Melbourne . . 1967-68	**G. R. J. Matthews** (1)	125 Adelaide . . . 1980-81
138 Delhi 1969-70	100* Melbourne . . 1985-86	**G. N. Yallop** (2)
	T. M. Moody (1)	121† Adelaide . . . 1977-78
	101† Perth. 1991-92	167 Calcutta. . . . 1979-80

For India (39)

M. Amarnath (2)			**M. L. Jaisimha** (1)		**R. J. Shastri** (2)	
100	Perth....	1977-78	101	Brisbane ... 1967-68	121*	Bombay.... 1986-87
138	Sydney ...	1985-86	**Kapil Dev** (1)		206	Sydney 1991-92
M. Azharuddin (2)			119	Madras ... 1986-87	**K. Srikkanth** (1)	
106	Adelaide ...	1991-92	**S. M. H. Kirmani** (1)		116	Sydney 1985-86
163*	Calcutta....	1997-98	101*	Bombay.... 1979-80	**S. R. Tendulkar** (4)	
N. J. Contractor (1)			**V. Mankad** (2)		148*	Sydney 1991-92
108	Bombay....	1959-60	116	Melbourne .. 1947-48	114	Perth.... 1991-92
S. M. Gavaskar (8)			111	Melbourne .. 1947-48	155*	Chennai.... 1997-98
113†	Brisbane ...	1977-78	**N. R. Mongia** (1)		177	Bangalore .. 1997-98
127	Perth....	1977-78	152†	Delhi 1996-97	**D. B. Vengsarkar** (2)	
118	Melbourne ..	1977-78	**Nawab of Pataudi jun.** (1)		112	Bangalore .. 1979-80
115	Delhi	1979-80	128*†	Madras ... 1964-65	164*	Bombay.... 1986-87
123	Bombay....	1979-80	**S. M. Patil** (1)		**G. R. Viswanath** (4)	
166*	Adelaide ...	1985-86	174	Adelaide ... 1980-81	137†	Kanpur 1969-70
172	Sydney ...	1985-86	**D. G. Phadkar** (1)		161*	Bangalore .. 1979-80
103	Bombay....	1986-87	123	Adelaide ... 1947-48	131	Delhi 1979-80
V. S. Hazare (2)			**G. S. Ramchand** (1)		114	Melbourne .. 1980-81
116	Adelaide ...	1947-48	109	Bombay.... 1956-57	**Yashpal Sharma** (1)	
145					100*	Delhi 1979-80

† *Signifies hundred on first appearance in Australia–India Tests.*

RECORD PARTNERSHIPS FOR EACH WICKET

For Australia

217	for 1st	D. C. Boon and G. R. Marsh at Sydney	1985-86
236	for 2nd	S. G. Barnes and D. G. Bradman at Adelaide...............	1947-48
222	for 3rd	A. R. Border and K. J. Hughes at Madras................	1979-80
178	for 4th	D. M. Jones and A. R. Border at Madras	1986-87
223*	for 5th	A. R. Morris and D. G. Bradman at Melbourne............	1947-48
151	for 6th	T. R. Veivers and B. N. Jarman at Bombay	1964-65
66	for 7th	G. R. J. Matthews and R. J. Bright at Melbourne	1985-86
73	for 8th	T. R. Veivers and G. D. McKenzie at Madras	1964-65
96	for 9th	I. A. Healy and G. R. Robertson at Chennai	1997-98
77	for 10th	A. R. Border and D. R. Gilbert at Melbourne	1985-86

For India

192	for 1st	S. M. Gavaskar and C. P. S. Chauhan at Bombay	1979-80
224	for 2nd	S. M. Gavaskar and M. Amarnath at Sydney	1985-86
159	for 3rd	S. M. Gavaskar and G. R. Viswanath at Delhi	1979-80
159	for 4th	D. B. Vengsarkar and G. R. Viswanath at Bangalore	1979-80
196	for 5th	R. J. Shastri and S. R. Tendulkar at Sydney..............	1991-92
298*	for 6th†	D. B. Vengsarkar and R. J. Shastri at Bombay	1986-87
132	for 7th	V. S. Hazare and H. R. Adhikari at Adelaide	1947-48
127	for 8th	S. M. H. Kirmani and K. D. Ghavri at Bombay	1979-80
81	for 9th	S. R. Tendulkar and K. S. More at Perth	1991-92
94	for 10th	S. M. Gavaskar and N. S. Yadav at Adelaide	1985-86

† *Denotes record partnership against all countries.*

TEN WICKETS OR MORE IN A MATCH

For Australia (11)

11-105 (6-52, 5-53)	R. Benaud, Calcutta	1956-57
12-124 (5-31, 7-93)	A. K. Davidson, Kanpur	1959-60

12-166 (5-99, 7-67)	G. Dymock, Kanpur	1979-80
10-168 (5-76, 5-92)	C. J. McDermott, Adelaide	1991-92
10-91 (6-58, 4-33)†	G. D. McKenzie, Madras	1964-65
10-151 (7-66, 3-85)	G. D. McKenzie, Melbourne	1967-68
10-144 (5-91, 5-53)	A. A. Mallett, Madras	1969-70
10-249 (5-103, 5-146)	G. R. J. Matthews, Madras	1986-87
12-126 (6-66, 6-60)	B. A. Reid, Melbourne	1991-92
11-31 (5-2, 6-29)†	E. R. H. Toshack, Brisbane	1947-48
11-95 (4-68, 7-27)	M. R. Whitney, Perth	1991-92

For India (6)

10-194 (5-89, 5-105)	B. S. Bedi, Perth	1977-78
12-104 (6-52, 6-52)	B. S. Chandrasekhar, Melbourne	1977-78
10-130 (7-49, 3-81)	Ghulam Ahmed, Calcutta	1956-57
11-122 (5-31, 6-91)	R. G. Nadkarni, Madras	1964-65
14-124 (9-69, 5-55)	J. M. Patel, Kanpur	1959-60
10-174 (4-100, 6-74)	E. A. S. Prasanna, Madras	1969-70

† *Signifies ten wickets or more on first appearance in Australia–India Tests.*

AUSTRALIA v PAKISTAN

		Captains				
Season	Australia	Pakistan	T	A	P	D
1956-57P	I. W. Johnson	A. H. Kardar	1	0	1	0
1959-60P	R. Benaud	Fazal Mahmood[1]	3	2	0	1
1964-65P	R. B. Simpson	Hanif Mohammad	1	0	0	1
1964-65A	R. B. Simpson	Hanif Mohammad	1	0	0	1
1972-73A	I. M. Chappell	Intikhab Alam	3	3	0	0
1976-77A	G. S. Chappell	Mushtaq Mohammad	3	1	1	1
1978-79A	G. N. Yallop[2]	Mushtaq Mohammad	2	1	1	0
1979-80P	G. S. Chappell	Javed Miandad	3	0	1	2
1981-82A	G. S. Chappell	Javed Miandad	3	2	1	0
1982-83P	K. J. Hughes	Imran Khan	3	0	3	0
1983-84A	K. J. Hughes	Imran Khan[3]	5	2	0	3
1988-89P	A. R. Border	Javed Miandad	3	0	1	2
1989-90A	A. R. Border	Imran Khan	3	1	0	2
1994-95P	M. A. Taylor	Salim Malik	3	0	1	2
1995-96A	M. A. Taylor	Wasim Akram	3	2	1	0
	In Pakistan		17	2	7	8
	In Australia		23	12	4	7
	Totals		40	14	11	15

A Played in Australia.   P Played in Pakistan.

Notes: The following deputised for the official touring captain or were appointed by the home authority for only a minor proportion of the series:
[1]Imtiaz Ahmed (Second). [2]K. J. Hughes (Second). [3]Zaheer Abbas (First, Second and Third).

HIGHEST INNINGS TOTALS

For Australia in Australia: 585 at Adelaide	1972-73
in Pakistan: 617 at Faisalabad	1979-80
For Pakistan in Australia: 624 at Adelaide	1983-84
in Pakistan: 537 at Rawalpindi	1994-95

LOWEST INNINGS TOTALS

For Australia in Australia: 125 at Melbourne 1981-82
             in Pakistan: 80 at Karachi. 1956-57

For Pakistan in Australia: 62 at Perth 1981-82
             in Pakistan: 134 at Dacca 1959-60

INDIVIDUAL HUNDREDS

For Australia (42)

J. Benaud (1)
142   Melbourne . . 1972-73
D. C. Boon (1)
114*   Karachi 1994-95
A. R. Border (6)
105†   Melbourne . . 1978-79
150* ⎫
153 ⎭ Lahore 1979-80
118   Brisbane . . . 1983-84
117*   Adelaide . . . 1983-84
113*   Faisalabad . . 1988-89
G. S. Chappell (6)
116*   Melbourne . . 1972-73
121   Melbourne . . 1976-77
235   Faisalabad . . 1979-80
201   Brisbane . . . 1981-82
150*   Brisbane . . . 1983-84
182   Sydney 1983-84
I. M. Chappell (1)
196   Adelaide . . . 1972-73
G. J. Cosier (1)
168   Melbourne . . 1976-77

I. C. Davis (1)
105†   Adelaide . . . 1976-77
K. J. Hughes (2)
106   Perth. 1981-82
106   Adelaide . . . 1983-84
D. M. Jones (2)
116 ⎫
121* ⎭ Adelaide . . . 1989-90
R. B. McCosker (1)
105   Melbourne . . 1976-77
R. W. Marsh (1)
118†   Adelaide . . . 1972-73
N. C. O'Neill (1)
134   Lahore 1959-60
W. B. Phillips (1)
159†   Perth. 1983-84
I. R. Redpath (1)
135   Melbourne . . 1972-73
G. M. Ritchie (1)
106*   Faisalabad . . 1982-83
A. P. Sheahan (1)
127   Melbourne . . 1972-73

R. B. Simpson (2)
153 ⎫
115 ⎭ †Karachi 1964-65
M. J. Slater (1)
110   Rawalpindi. . 1994-95
M. A. Taylor (3)
101†   Melbourne . . 1989-90
101*   Sydney 1989-90
123   Hobart 1995-96
K. D. Walters (1)
107   Adelaide . . . 1976-77
M. E. Waugh (1)
116   Sydney 1995-96
S. R. Waugh (1)
112*   Brisbane . . . 1995-96
K. C. Wessels (1)
179   Adelaide . . . 1983-84
G. M. Wood (1)
100   Melbourne . . 1981-82
G. N. Yallop (3)
172   Faisalabad . . 1979-80
141   Perth. 1983-84
268   Melbourne . . 1983-84

For Pakistan (36)

Aamir Sohail (1)
105   Lahore 1994-95
Asif Iqbal (3)
152*   Adelaide . . . 1976-77
120   Sydney 1976-77
134*   Perth. 1978-79
Hanif Mohammad (2)
101*   Karachi . . . 1959-60
104   Melbourne . . 1964-65
Ijaz Ahmed, sen. (3)
122   Faisalabad . . 1988-89
121   Melbourne . . 1989-90
137   Sydney 1995-96
Imran Khan (1)
136   Adelaide . . . 1989-90
Javed Miandad (6)
129*   Perth. 1978-79
106*   Faisalabad . . 1979-80
138   Lahore 1982-83

131   Adelaide . . . 1983-84
211   Karachi 1988-89
107   Faisalabad . . 1988-89
Khalid Ibadulla (1)
166†   Karachi . . . 1964-65
Majid Khan (3)
158   Melbourne . . 1972-73
108   Melbourne . . 1978-79
110*   Lahore 1979-80
Mansoor Akhtar (1)
111   Faisalabad . . 1982-83
Mohsin Khan (3)
135   Lahore 1982-83
149   Adelaide . . . 1983-84
152   Melbourne . . 1983-84
Moin Khan (1)
115*† Lahore 1994-95

Mushtaq Mohammad (1)
121   Sydney 1972-73
Qasim Omar (1)
113   Adelaide . . . 1983-84
Sadiq Mohammad (2)
137   Melbourne . . 1972-73
105   Melbourne . . 1976-77
Saeed Ahmed (1)
166   Lahore 1959-60
Salim Malik (2)
237   Rawalpindi. . 1994-95
143   Lahore 1994-95
Taslim Arif (1)
210*   Faisalabad . . 1979-80
Wasim Akram (1)
123   Adelaide . . . 1989-90
Zaheer Abbas (2)
101   Adelaide . . . 1976-77
126   Faisalabad . . 1982-83

† *Signifies hundred on first appearance in Australia–Pakistan Tests.*

RECORD PARTNERSHIPS FOR EACH WICKET

For Australia

176 for 1st	M. A. Taylor and M. J. Slater at Rawalpindi	1994-95
259 for 2nd	W. B. Phillips and G. N. Yallop at Perth	1983-84
203 for 3rd	G. N. Yallop and K. J. Hughes at Melbourne	1983-84
217 for 4th	G. S. Chappell and G. N. Yallop at Faisalabad	1979-80
171 for 5th	{ G. S. Chappell and G. J. Cosier at Melbourne	1976-77
	{ A. R. Border and G. S. Chappell at Brisbane	1983-84
139 for 6th	R. M. Cowper and T. R. Veivers at Melbourne	1964-65
185 for 7th	G. N. Yallop and G. R. J. Matthews at Melbourne	1983-84
117 for 8th	G. J. Cosier and K. J. O'Keeffe at Melbourne	1976-77
83 for 9th	J. R. Watkins and R. A. L. Massie at Sydney	1972-73
52 for 10th	{ D. K. Lillee and M. H. N. Walker at Sydney	1976-77
	{ G. F. Lawson and T. M. Alderman at Lahore	1982-83

For Pakistan

249 for 1st	Khalid Ibadulla and Abdul Kadir at Karachi	1964-65
233 for 2nd	Mohsin Khan and Qasim Omar at Adelaide	1983-84
223* for 3rd	Taslim Arif and Javed Miandad at Faisalabad	1979-80
155 for 4th	Mansoor Akhtar and Zaheer Abbas at Faisalabad	1982-83
186 for 5th	Javed Miandad and Salim Malik at Adelaide	1983-84
196 for 6th	Salim Malik and Aamir Sohail at Lahore	1994-95
104 for 7th	Intikhab Alam and Wasim Bari at Adelaide	1972-73
111 for 8th	Majid Khan and Imran Khan at Lahore	1979-80
56 for 9th	Intikhab Alam and Afaq Hussain at Melbourne	1964-65
87 for 10th	Asif Iqbal and Iqbal Qasim at Adelaide	1976-77

TEN WICKETS OR MORE IN A MATCH

For Australia (4)

10-111 (7-87, 3-24)†	R. J. Bright, Karachi	1979-80
10-135 (6-82, 4-53)	D. K. Lillee, Melbourne	1976-77
11-118 (5-32, 6-86)†	C. G. Rackemann, Perth	1983-84
11-77 (7-23, 4-54)	S. K. Warne, Brisbane	1995-96

For Pakistan (6)

11-218 (4-76, 7-142)	Abdul Qadir, Faisalabad	1982-83
13-114 (6-34, 7-80)†	Fazal Mahmood, Karachi	1956-57
12-165 (6-102, 6-63)	Imran Khan, Sydney	1976-77
11-118 (4-69, 7-49)	Iqbal Qasim, Karachi	1979-80
11-125 (2-39, 9-86)	Sarfraz Nawaz, Melbourne	1978-79
11-160 (6-62, 5-98)†	Wasim Akram, Melbourne	1989-90

† Signifies ten wickets or more on first appearance in Australia–Pakistan Tests.

AUSTRALIA v SRI LANKA

Captains

Season	Australia	Sri Lanka	T	A	SL	D
1982-83S	G. S. Chappell	L. R. D. Mendis	1	1	0	0
1987-88A	A. R. Border	R. S. Madugalle	1	1	0	0
1989-90A	A. R. Border	A. Ranatunga	2	1	0	1
1992-93S	A. R. Border	A. Ranatunga	3	1	0	2
1995-96A	M. A. Taylor	A. Ranatunga[1]	3	3	0	0
	In Australia..................		6	5	0	1
	In Sri Lanka		4	2	0	2
	Totals......................		10	7	0	3

A Played in Australia.   S Played in Sri Lanka.

Note: The following deputised for the official touring captain:
[1]P. A. de Silva (Third).

HIGHEST INNINGS TOTALS

For Australia in Australia: 617-5 dec. at Perth............................. 1995-96
     in Sri Lanka: 514-4 dec. at Kandy 1982-83

For Sri Lanka in Australia: 418 in Brisbane 1989-90
     in Sri Lanka: 547-8 dec. at Colombo (SSC) 1992-93

LOWEST INNINGS TOTALS

For Australia in Australia: 224 at Hobart.................................. 1989-90
     in Sri Lanka: 247 at Colombo (KS) 1992-93

For Sri Lanka in Australia: 153 at Perth 1987-88
     in Sri Lanka: 164 at Colombo (SSC)..................... 1992-93

INDIVIDUAL HUNDREDS

For Australia (15)

D. C. Boon (1)
110 Melbourne . . 1995-96
A. R. Border (1)
106 Moratuwa . . 1992-93
D. W. Hookes (1)
143*† Kandy..... 1982-83
D. M. Jones (3)
102† Perth...... 1987-88
118* Hobart..... 1989-90

100* Colombo (KS) 1992-93
T. M. Moody (1)
106† Brisbane . . . 1989-90
M. J. Slater (1)
219† Perth...... 1995-96
M. A. Taylor (2)
164† Brisbane . . . 1989-90
108 Hobart. 1989-90

M. E. Waugh (1)
111 Perth...... 1995-96
S. R. Waugh (3)
134* Hobart. 1989-90
131* Melbourne . . 1995-96
170 Adelaide . . . 1995-96
K. C. Wessels (1)
141† Kandy..... 1982-83

For Sri Lanka (7)

P. A. de Silva (1)
167 Brisbane . . . 1989-90
A. P. Gurusinha (2)
137 Colombo (SSC) 1992-93
143 Melbourne . . 1995-96

S. T. Jayasuriya (1)
112 Adelaide . . . 1995-96
R. S. Kaluwitharana (1)
132*† Colombo (SSC) 1992-93

A. Ranatunga (1)
127 Colombo (SSC) 1992-93
H. P. Tillekeratne (1)
119 Perth...... 1995-96

† *Signifies hundred on first appearance in Australia–Sri Lanka Tests.*

RECORD PARTNERSHIPS FOR EACH WICKET

For Australia

228	for 1st	M. J. Slater and M. A. Taylor at Perth	1995-96
170	for 2nd	K. C. Wessels and G. N. Yallop at Kandy	1982-83
158	for 3rd	T. M. Moody and A. R. Border at Brisbane	1989-90
163	for 4th	M. A. Taylor and A. R. Border at Hobart	1989-90
155*	for 5th	D. W. Hookes and A. R. Border at Kandy	1982-83
260*	for 6th	D. M. Jones and S. R. Waugh at Hobart	1989-90
129	for 7th	G. R. J. Matthews and I. A. Healy at Moratuwa	1992-93
56	for 8th	G. R. J. Matthews and C. J. McDermott at Colombo (SSC)	1992-93
45	for 9th	I. A. Healy and S. K. Warne at Colombo (SSC)	1992-93
49	for 10th	I. A. Healy and M. R. Whitney at Colombo (SSC)	1992-93

For Sri Lanka

110	for 1st	R. S. Mahanama and U. C. Hathurusinghe at Colombo (KS)	1992-93
92	for 2nd	R. S. Mahanama and A. P. Gurusinha at Colombo (SSC)	1992-93
125	for 3rd	S. T. Jayasuriya and S. Ranatunga at Adelaide	1995-96
230	for 4th	A. P. Gurusinha and A. Ranatunga at Colombo (SSC)	1992-93
116	for 5th	H. P. Tillekeratne and A. Ranatunga at Moratuwa	1992-93
96	for 6th	A. P. Gurusinha and R. S. Kaluwitharana at Colombo (SSC)	1992-93
144	for 7th†	P. A. de Silva and J. R. Ratnayeke at Brisbane	1989-90
33	for 8th	A. Ranatunga and C. P. H. Ramanayake at Perth	1987-88
46	for 9th	H. D. P. K. Dharmasena and G. P. Wickremasinghe at Perth	1995-96
27	for 10th	P. A. de Silva and C. P. H. Ramanayake at Brisbane	1989-90

† *Denotes record partnership against all countries.*

BEST MATCH BOWLING ANALYSES

For Australia

8-156 (3-68, 5-88)	M. G. Hughes, Hobart	1989-90

For Sri Lanka

8-157 (5-82, 3-75)	C. P. H. Ramanayake, Moratuwa	1992-93

SOUTH AFRICA v WEST INDIES

Season	South Africa	*Captains* West Indies	T	SA	WI	D
1991-92W	K. C. Wessels	R. B. Richardson	1	0	1	0

W Played in West Indies.

HIGHEST INNINGS TOTALS

For South Africa: 345 at Bridgetown 1991-92

For West Indies: 283 at Bridgetown 1991-92

INDIVIDUAL HUNDREDS

For South Africa (1)

A. C. Hudson (1)

163† Bridgetown . 1991-92

Highest score for West Indies: 79* at Bridgetown 1991-92 by J. C. Adams.

† *Signifies hundred on first appearance in South Africa–West Indies Tests.*

HIGHEST PARTNERSHIPS

For South Africa

125 for 2nd   A. C. Hudson and K. C. Wessels at Bridgetown   1991-92

For West Indies

99 for 1st   D. L. Haynes and P. V. Simmons at Bridgetown   1991-92

BEST MATCH BOWLING ANALYSES

For South Africa

8-158 (4-84, 4-74)   R. P. Snell, Bridgetown   1991-92

For West Indies

8-81 (2-47, 6-34)   C. E. L. Ambrose, Bridgetown.   1991-92

SOUTH AFRICA v NEW ZEALAND

Captains

Season	South Africa	New Zealand	T	SA	NZ	D
1931-32*N*	H. B. Cameron	M. L. Page	2	2	0	0
1952-53*N*	J. E. Cheetham	W. M. Wallace	2	1	0	1
1953-54*S*	J. E. Cheetham	G. O. Rabone[1]	5	4	0	1
1961-62*S*	D. J. McGlew	J. R. Reid	5	2	2	1
1963-64*N*	T. L. Goddard	J. R. Reid	3	0	0	3
1994-95*S*	W. J. Cronje	K. R. Rutherford	3	2	1	0
1994-95*N*	W. J. Cronje	K. R. Rutherford	1	1	0	0
In New Zealand			8	4	0	4
In South Africa			13	8	3	2
Totals.			21	12	3	6

N Played in New Zealand.   S Played in South Africa.

Note: The following deputised for the official touring captain:
   [1]B. Sutcliffe (Fourth and Fifth).

HIGHEST INNINGS TOTALS

For South Africa in South Africa: 464 at Johannesburg   1961-62
in New Zealand: 524-8 at Wellington   1952-53

For New Zealand in South Africa: 505 at Cape Town   1953-54
in New Zealand: 364 at Wellington   1931-32

LOWEST INNINGS TOTALS

For South Africa in South Africa: 148 at Johannesburg 1953-54
                in New Zealand: 223 at Dunedin 1963-64

For New Zealand in South Africa: 79 at Johannesburg 1953-54
                in New Zealand: 138 at Dunedin 1963-64

INDIVIDUAL HUNDREDS

For South Africa (14)

X. C. Balaskas (1)
122* Wellington . . 1931-32
J. A. J. Christy (1)
103† Christchurch . 1931-32
W. J. Cronje (2)
112   Cape Town .   1994-95
101   Auckland . . . 1994-95
W. R. Endean (1)
116   Auckland . . . 1952-53

D. J. McGlew (3)
255*† Wellington . . 1952-53
127*‡ Durban 1961-62
120   Johannesburg 1961-62
R. A. McLean (2)
101   Durban 1953-54
113   Cape Town .   1961-62
B. Mitchell (1)
113† Christchurch . 1931-32

A. R. A. Murray (1)
109† Wellington . . 1952-53
D. J. Richardson (1)
109   Cape Town .   1994-95
J. H. B. Waite (1)
101   Johannesburg 1961-62

For New Zealand (7)

P. T. Barton (1)
109   Port Elizabeth 1961-62
P. G. Z. Harris (1)
101   Cape Town .   1961-62

G. O. Rabone (1)
107   Durban 1953-54
J. R. Reid (2)
135   Cape Town .   1953-54
142   Johannesburg 1961-62

B. W. Sinclair (1)
138   Auckland . . . 1963-64
H. G. Vivian (1)
100† Wellington . . 1931-32

† *Signifies hundred on first appearance in South Africa–New Zealand Tests.*
‡ *Carried his bat.*

RECORD PARTNERSHIPS FOR EACH WICKET

For South Africa

196 for 1st	J. A. J. Christy and B. Mitchell at Christchurch	1931-32
97 for 2nd	G. Kirsten and J. B. Commins at Durban	1994-95
112 for 3rd	D. J. McGlew and R. A. McLean at Johannesburg	1961-62
135 for 4th	K. J. Funston and R. A. McLean at Durban	1953-54
130 for 5th	W. R. Endean and J. E. Cheetham at Auckland	1952-53
83 for 6th	K. C. Bland and D. T. Lindsay at Auckland	1963-64
246 for 7th†	D. J. McGlew and A. R. A. Murray at Wellington	1952-53
95 for 8th	J. E. Cheetham and H. J. Tayfield at Cape Town	1953-54
60 for 9th	P. M. Pollock and N. A. T. Adcock at Port Elizabeth	1961-62
47 for 10th	D. J. McGlew and H. D. Bromfield at Port Elizabeth	1961-62

For New Zealand

126 for 1st	G. O. Rabone and M. E. Chapple at Cape Town	1953-54
72 for 2nd	D. J. Murray and S. P. Fleming at Johannesburg	1994-95
94 for 3rd	M. B. Poore and B. Sutcliffe at Cape Town	1953-54
171 for 4th	B. W. Sinclair and S. N. McGregor at Auckland	1963-64
174 for 5th	J. R. Reid and J. E. F. Beck at Cape Town	1953-54
100 for 6th	H. G. Vivian and F. T. Badcock at Wellington	1931-32
84 for 7th	J. R. Reid and G. A. Bartlett at Johannesburg	1961-62
74 for 8th	S. A. Thomson and D. J. Nash at Johannesburg	1994-95
69 for 9th	C. F. W. Allcott and I. B. Cromb at Wellington	1931-32
57 for 10th	S. B. Doull and R. P. de Groen at Johannesburg	1994-95

† *Denotes record partnership against all countries.*

TEN WICKETS OR MORE IN A MATCH

For South Africa (1)

11-196 (6-128, 5-68)†   S. F. Burke, Cape Town.......................... 1961-62

   † *Signifies ten wickets or more on first appearance in South Africa–New Zealand Tests.*

Note: The best match figures by a New Zealand bowler are 8-134 (3-57, 5-77), M. N. Hart at Johannesburg, 1994-95.

SOUTH AFRICA v INDIA

Season	South Africa	*Captains* India	T	SA	I	D
1992-93*S*	K. C. Wessels	M. Azharuddin	4	1	0	3
1996-97*I*	W. J. Cronje	S. R. Tendulkar	3	1	2	0
1996-97*S*	W. J. Cronje	S. R. Tendulkar	3	2	0	1
	In South Africa		7	3	0	4
	In India		3	1	2	0
	Totals.....................		10	4	2	4

S Played in South Africa.   I Played in India.

HIGHEST INNINGS TOTALS

For South Africa in South Africa: 529-7 dec. at Cape Town 1996-97
                 in India: 428 at Calcutta 1996-97

For India in South Africa: 410 at Johannesburg....................... 1996-97
           in India: 400-7 dec. at Kanpur 1996-97

LOWEST INNINGS TOTALS

For South Africa in South Africa: 235 at Durban 1996-97
                 in India: 105 at Ahmedabad........................ 1996-97

For India in South Africa: 66 at Durban 1996-97
           in India: 137 at Calcutta 1996-97

INDIVIDUAL HUNDREDS

For South Africa (10)

W. J. Cronje (1)
135   Port Elizabeth 1992-93

D. J. Cullinan (2)
153*   Calcutta.... 1996-97
122*   Johannesburg 1996-97

A. C. Hudson (1)
146   Calcutta.... 1996-97

G. Kirsten (3)
102
133 } Calcutta.... 1996-97
103   Cape Town . 1996-97

L. Klusener (1)
102*   Cape Town . 1996-97

B. M. McMillan (1)
103*   Cape Town . 1996-97

K. C. Wessels (1)
118†   Durban 1992-93

For India (8)

P. K. Amre (1)	163* Kanpur 1996-97	**Kapil Dev** (1)
103† Durban 1992-93	115 Cape Town . 1996-97	129 Port Elizabeth 1992-93
M. Azharuddin (3)	**R. Dravid** (1)	**S. R. Tendulkar** (2)
109 Calcutta.... 1996-97	148 Johannesburg 1996-97	111 Johannesburg 1992-93
		169 Cape Town . 1996-97

† *Signifies hundred on first appearance in South Africa–India Tests.*

RECORD PARTNERSHIPS FOR EACH WICKET

For South Africa

236	for 1st	A. C. Hudson and G. Kirsten at Calcutta	1996-97
212	for 2nd	G. Kirsten and D. J. Cullinan at Calcutta	1996-97
114	for 3rd	G. Kirsten and D. J. Cullinan at Cape Town	1996-97
94	for 4th	A. C. Hudson and D. J. Cullinan at Cape Town	1996-97
99	for 5th	D. J. Cullinan and J. N. Rhodes at Cape Town.	1992-93
112	for 6th	B. M. McMillan and S. M. Pollock at Johannesburg	1996-97
101*	for 7th	B. M. McMillan and S. M. Pollock at Cape Town	1996-97
147*	for 8th†	B. M. McMillan and L. Klusener at Cape Town	1996-97
60	for 9th	P. S. de Villiers and A. A. Donald at Ahmedabad	1996-97
74	for 10th	B. M. McMillan and A. A. Donald at Durban	1996-97

For India

90	for 1st	V. Rathore and N. R. Mongia at Johannesburg	1996-97
85	for 2nd	M. Prabhakar and S. V. Manjrekar at Cape Town	1992-93
54	for 3rd	R. Dravid and S. R. Tendulkar at Johannesburg	1996-97
145	for 4th	R. Dravid and S. C. Ganguly at Johannesburg	1996-97
87	for 5th	M. Azharuddin and P. K. Amre at Durban	1992-93
222	for 6th	S. R. Tendulkar and M. Azharuddin at Cape Town	1996-97
76	for 7th	R. Dravid and J. Srinath at Johannesburg	1996-97
161	for 8th†	M. Azharuddin and A. Kumble at Calcutta	1996-97
77	for 9th	Kapil Dev and A. Kumble at Port Elizabeth	1992-93
19	for 10th	S. R. Tendulkar and D. Ganesh at Cape Town	1996-97

† *Denotes record partnership against all countries.*

TEN WICKETS OR MORE IN A MATCH

For South Africa (1)

12-139 (5-55, 7-84)	A. A. Donald, Port Elizabeth	1992-93

For India (1)

10-153 (5-60, 5-93)	B. K. V. Prasad, Durban	1996-97

SOUTH AFRICA v PAKISTAN

		Captains				
Season	South Africa	Pakistan	T	SA	P	D
1994-95S	W. J. Cronje	Salim Malik	1	1	0	0
1997-98P	W. J. Cronje	Saeed Anwar	3	1	0	2
1997-98S	W. J. Cronje[1]	Rashid Latif[2]	3	1	1	1
	In South Africa		4	2	1	1
	In Pakistan		3	1	0	2
	Totals.		7	3	1	3

S Played in South Africa.   P Played in Pakistan.

Notes: The following deputised for the official touring captain or were appointed by the home authority for only a minor proportion of the series:
[1]G. Kirsten (First). [2]Aamir Sohail (First and Second).

HIGHEST INNINGS TOTALS

For South Africa: 460 at Johannesburg   1994-95

For Pakistan: 456 at Rawalpindi.   1997-98

LOWEST INNINGS TOTALS

For South Africa: 214 at Faisalabad   1997-98

For Pakistan: 92 at Faisalabad.   1997-98

INDIVIDUAL HUNDREDS

For South Africa (3)

G. Kirsten (1)
100*‡ Faisalabad . . 1997-98

B. M. McMillan (1)
113† Johannesburg 1994-95

P. L. Symcox (1)
108   Johannesburg 1997-98

For Pakistan (5)

Ali Naqvi (1)
115† Rawalpindi. . 1997-98

Azhar Mahmood (3)
128*† Rawalpindi. . 1997-98
136   Johannesburg 1997-98
132   Durban 1997-98

Saeed Anwar (1)
118   Durban 1997-98

† Signifies hundred on first appearance in South Africa–Pakistan Tests.
‡ Carried his bat.

RECORD PARTNERSHIPS FOR EACH WICKET

For South Africa

135 for 1st	G. Kirsten and A. M. Bacher at Sheikhupura	1997-98
114 for 2nd	G. Kirsten and J. H. Kallis at Rawalpindi	1997-98
83 for 3rd	J. H. Kallis and H. D. Ackerman at Durban	1997-98
79 for 4th	G. Kirsten and W. J. Cronje at Johannesburg	1994-95
43 for 5th	P. L. Symcox and W. J. Cronje at Faisalabad	1997-98
157 for 6th	J. N. Rhodes and B. M. McMillan at Johannesburg	1994-95
106 for 7th	S. M. Pollock and D. J. Richardson at Rawalpindi	1997-98
124 for 8th	G. Kirsten and P. L. Symcox at Faisalabad	1997-98
195 for 9th†	M. V. Boucher and P. L. Symcox at Johannesburg.	1997-98
71 for 10th	P. S. de Villiers and A. A. Donald at Johannesburg	1994-95

For Pakistan

101 for 1st	Saeed Anwar and Aamir Sohail at Durban	1997-98
69 for 2nd	Ali Naqvi and Mohammad Ramzan at Rawalpindi.	1997-98
72 for 3rd	Ijaz Ahmed, sen. and Mohammad Wasim at Johannesburg	1997-98
93 for 4th	Asif Mujtaba and Inzamam-ul-Haq at Johannesburg.	1994-95
44 for 5th	Ali Naqvi and Mohammad Wasim at Rawalpindi	1997-98
144 for 6th	Inzamam-ul-Haq and Moin Khan at Faisalabad	1997-98
35 for 7th	Salim Malik and Wasim Akram at Johannesburg.	1994-95
40 for 8th	Inzamam-ul-Haq and Kabir Khan at Johannesburg.	1994-95
80 for 9th	Azhar Mahmood and Shoaib Akhtar at Durban	1997-98
151 for 10th†	Azhar Mahmood and Mushtaq Ahmed at Rawalpindi.	1997-98

† *Denotes record partnership against all countries.*

TEN WICKETS OR MORE IN A MATCH

For South Africa (1)

10-108 (6-81, 4-27)†	P. S. de Villiers, Johannesburg.	1994-95

For Pakistan (1)

10-133 (6-78, 4-55)	Waqar Younis, Port Elizabeth	1997-98

† *Signifies ten wickets or more on first appearance in South Africa–Pakistan Tests.*

SOUTH AFRICA v SRI LANKA

Season	South Africa	*Captains*	Sri Lanka	T	SA	SL	D
1993-94*SL*	K. C. Wessels		A. Ranatunga	3	1	0	2
1997-98*SA*	W. J. Cronje		A. Ranatunga	2	2	0	0
	In South Africa			2	2	0	0
	In Sri Lanka			3	1	0	2
	Totals.			5	3	0	2

SA Played in South Africa.   SL Played in Sri Lanka.

HIGHEST INNINGS TOTALS

For South Africa: 495 at Colombo (SSC) 1993-94

For Sri Lanka: 331 at Moratuwa. 1993-94

LOWEST INNINGS TOTALS

For South Africa: 200 at Centurion 1997-98

For Sri Lanka: 119 at Colombo (SSC) 1993-94

INDIVIDUAL HUNDREDS

For South Africa (5)

W. J. Cronje (1)	**D. J. Cullinan** (3)	**J. N. Rhodes** (1)
122 Colombo (SSC) 1993-94	102 Colombo (PSS) 1993-94	101*† Moratuwa . . 1993-94
	113 Cape Town . 1997-98	
	103 Centurion. . . 1997-98	

For Sri Lanka (1)

A. Ranatunga (1)
131†   Moratuwa . . 1993-94

† *Signifies hundred on first appearance in South Africa–Sri Lanka Tests.*

HUNDRED PARTNERSHIPS

For South Africa

137 for 1st	K. C. Wessels and A. C. Hudson at Colombo (SSC)	1993-94
104 for 1st	K. C. Wessels and A. C. Hudson at Moratuwa	1993-94
116 for 3rd	J. H. Kallis and D. J. Cullinan at Cape Town.	1997-98
105 for 3rd	W. J. Cronje and D. J. Cullinan at Colombo (SSC)	1993-94
116 for 4th	G. Kirsten and W. J. Cronje at Centurion	1997-98
122 for 6th	D. J. Cullinan and D. J. Richardson at Colombo (PSS)	1993-94

For Sri Lanka

129 for 3rd	M. S. Atapattu and P. A. de Silva at Cape Town.	1997-98
118 for 4th	R. S. Mahanama and A. Ranatunga at Centurion.	1997-98
101 for 4th	P. A. de Silva and A. Ranatunga at Colombo (PSS)	1993-94
121 for 5th	P. A. de Silva and A. Ranatunga at Moratuwa	1993-94
103 for 6th	A. Ranatunga and H. P. Tillekeratne at Moratuwa	1993-94

BEST MATCH BOWLING ANALYSES

For South Africa

9-106 (5-48, 4-58)   B. N. Schultz, Colombo (SSC)...................... 1993-94

For Sri Lanka

8-157 (5-63, 3-94)   M. Muralitharan, Centurion 1997-98

SOUTH AFRICA v ZIMBABWE

Season	South Africa	*Captains* Zimbabwe	T	SA	Z	D
1995-96Z	W. J. Cronje	A. Flower	1	1	0	0

Z Played in Zimbabwe.

HIGHEST INNINGS TOTALS

For South Africa: 346 at Harare..................................... 1995-96

For Zimbabwe: 283 at Harare 1995-96

INDIVIDUAL HUNDREDS

For South Africa (1)

A. C. Hudson (1)
135†   Harare..... 1995-96

Highest score for Zimbabwe: 63 by A. Flower at Harare 1995-96.

† *Signifies hundred on first appearance in South Africa–Zimbabwe Tests.*

HUNDRED PARTNERSHIP

For South Africa

101 for 6th   A. C. Hudson and B. M. McMillan at Harare................ 1995-96

Note: The highest partnership for Zimbabwe is 97 for the 5th wicket between A. Flower and G. J. Whittall at Harare, 1995-96.

TEN WICKETS OR MORE IN A MATCH

For South Africa (1)

11-113 (3-42, 8-71)†   A. A. Donald, Harare   1995-96

Note: The best match figures for Zimbabwe are 5-105 (3-68, 2-37) by A. C. I. Lock at Harare, 1995-96.

† *Signifies ten wickets or more on first appearance in South Africa–Zimbabwe Tests.*

WEST INDIES v NEW ZEALAND

		Captains				
Season	West Indies	New Zealand	T	WI	NZ	D
1951-52N	J. D. C. Goddard	B. Sutcliffe	2	1	0	1
1955-56N	D. St E. Atkinson	J. R. Reid[1]	4	3	1	0
1968-69N	G. S. Sobers	G. T. Dowling	3	1	1	1
1971-72W	G. S. Sobers	G. T. Dowling[2]	5	0	0	5
1979-80N	C. H. Lloyd	G. P. Howarth	3	0	1	2
1984-85W	I. V. A. Richards	G. P. Howarth	4	2	0	2
1986-87N	I. V. A. Richards	J. V. Coney	3	1	1	1
1994-95N	C. A. Walsh	K. R. Rutherford	2	1	0	1
1995-96W	C. A. Walsh	L. K. Germon	2	1	0	1
	In New Zealand		17	7	4	6
	In West Indies		11	3	0	8
	Totals		28	10	4	14

N Played in New Zealand.   W Played in West Indies.

Notes: The following deputised for the official touring captain or were appointed by the home authority for only a minor proportion of the series:
[1]H. B. Cave (First). [2]B. E. Congdon (Third, Fourth and Fifth).

HIGHEST INNINGS TOTALS

For West Indies in West Indies: 564-8 at Bridgetown   1971-72
        in New Zealand: 660-5 dec. at Wellington   1994-95

For New Zealand in West Indies: 543-3 dec. at Georgetown   1971-72
        in New Zealand: 460 at Christchurch   1979-80

LOWEST INNINGS TOTALS

For West Indies in West Indies: 133 at Bridgetown   1971-72
        in New Zealand: 77 at Auckland   1955-56

For New Zealand in West Indies: 94 at Bridgetown   1984-85
        in New Zealand: 74 at Dunedin   1955-56

INDIVIDUAL HUNDREDS

By West Indies (31)

J. C. Adams (2)			121	Wellington	1986-87
151	Wellington	1994-95	**A. I. Kallicharran** (2)		
208*	St John's	1995-96	100*†	Georgetown	1971-72
S. L. Campbell (1)			101	Port-of-Spain	1971-72
208	Bridgetown	1995-96	**C. L. King** (1)		
M. C. Carew (1)			100*	Christchurch	1979-80
109†	Auckland	1968-69	**B. C. Lara** (1)		
C. A. Davis (1)			147	Wellington	1994-95
183	Bridgetown	1971-72	**J. R. Murray** (1)		
R. C. Fredericks (1)			101*	Wellington	1994-95
163	Kingston	1971-72	**S. M. Nurse** (2)		
C. G. Greenidge (2)			168†	Auckland	1968-69
100	Port-of-Spain	1984-85	258	Christchurch	1968-69
213	Auckland	1986-87	**I. V. A. Richards** (1)		
D. L. Haynes (3)			105	Bridgetown	1984-85
105†	Dunedin	1979-80	**R. B. Richardson** (1)		
122	Christchurch	1979-80	185	Georgetown	1984-85

L. G. Rowe (3)		
214	†Kingston	1971-72
100*	†Kingston	1971-72
100	Christchurch	1979-80
R. G. Samuels (1)		
125	St John's	1995-96
G. S. Sobers (1)		
142	Bridgetown	1971-72
J. B. Stollmeyer (1)		
152	Auckland	1951-52
C. L. Walcott (1)		
115	Auckland	1951-52
E. D. Weekes (3)		
123	Dunedin	1955-56
103	Christchurch	1955-56
156	Wellington	1955-56
F. M. M. Worrell (1)		
100	Auckland	1951-52

By New Zealand (20)

N. J. Astle (2)			119	Wellington	1986-87
125†	Bridgetown	1995-96	104	Auckland	1986-87
103	St John's	1995-96	**B. A. Edgar** (1)		
M. G. Burgess (1)			127	Auckland	1979-80
101	Kingston	1971-72	**R. J. Hadlee** (1)		
B. E. Congdon (2)			103	Christchurch	1979-80
166*	Port-of-Spain	1971-72	**B. F. Hastings** (2)		
126	Bridgetown	1971-72	117*	Christchurch	1968-69
J. J. Crowe (1)			105	Bridgetown	1971-72
112	Kingston	1984-85	**G. P. Howarth** (1)		
M. D. Crowe (3)			147	Christchurch	1979-80
188	Georgetown	1984-85			

T. W. Jarvis (1)		
182	Georgetown	1971-72
A. C. Parore (1)		
100*†	Christchurch	1994-95
B. R. Taylor (1)		
124†	Auckland	1968-69
G. M. Turner (2)		
223*‡	Kingston	1971-72
259	Georgetown	1971-72
J. G. Wright (1)		
138	Wellington	1986-87

† *Signifies hundred on first appearance in West Indies–New Zealand Tests.*
‡ *Carried his bat.*

Notes: E. D. Weekes in 1955-56 made three hundreds in consecutive innings.

L. G. Rowe and A. I. Kallicharran each scored hundreds in their first two innings in Test cricket, Rowe being the only batsman to do so in his first match.

RECORD PARTNERSHIPS FOR EACH WICKET

For West Indies

225 for 1st	C. G. Greenidge and D. L. Haynes at Christchurch	1979-80
269 for 2nd	R. C. Fredericks and L. G. Rowe at Kingston	1971-72
221 for 3rd	B. C. Lara and J. C. Adams at Wellington	1994-95
162 for 4th	{ E. D. Weekes and O. G. Smith at Dunedin	1955-56
	{ C. G. Greenidge and A. I. Kallicharran at Christchurch	1979-80
189 for 5th	F. M. M. Worrell and C. L. Walcott at Auckland	1951-52
254 for 6th	C. A. Davis and G. S. Sobers at Bridgetown	1971-72
143 for 7th	D. St E. Atkinson and J. D. C. Goddard at Christchurch	1955-56
83 for 8th	I. V. A. Richards and M. D. Marshall at Bridgetown	1984-85
70 for 9th	M. D. Marshall and J. Garner at Bridgetown	1984-85
31 for 10th	T. M. Findlay and G. C. Shillingford at Bridgetown	1971-72

For New Zealand

387	for 1st†	G. M. Turner and T. W. Jarvis at Georgetown	1971-72
210	for 2nd	G. P. Howarth and J. J. Crowe at Kingston	1984-85
241	for 3rd	J. G. Wright and M. D. Crowe at Wellington	1986-87
175	for 4th	B. E. Congdon and B. F. Hastings at Bridgetown	1971-72
144	for 5th	N. J. Astle and J. T. C. Vaughan at Bridgetown	1995-96
220	for 6th	G. M. Turner and K. J. Wadsworth at Kingston	1971-72
143	for 7th	M. D. Crowe and I. D. S. Smith at Georgetown	1984-85
136	for 8th†	B. E. Congdon and R. S. Cunis at Port-of-Spain	1971-72
62*	for 9th	V. Pollard and R. S. Cunis at Auckland	1968-69
45	for 10th	D. K. Morrison and R. J. Kennedy at Bridgetown	1995-96

† *Denotes record partnership against all countries.*

TEN WICKETS OR MORE IN A MATCH

For West Indies (2)

11-120 (4-40, 7-80)	M. D. Marshall, Bridgetown	1984-85
13-55 (7-37, 6-18)	C. A. Walsh, Wellington	1994-95

For New Zealand (3)

10-124 (4-51, 6-73)†	E. J. Chatfield, Port-of-Spain	1984-85
11-102 (5-34, 6-68)†	R. J. Hadlee, Dunedin	1979-80
10-166 (4-71, 6-95)	G. B. Troup, Auckland	1979-80

† *Signifies ten wickets or more on first appearance in West Indies–New Zealand Tests.*

WEST INDIES v INDIA

	Captains					
Season	*West Indies*	*India*	*T*	*WI*	*I*	*D*
1948-49*I*	J. D. C. Goddard	L. Amarnath	5	1	0	4
1952-53*W*	J. B. Stollmeyer	V. S. Hazare	5	1	0	4
1958-59*I*	F. C. M. Alexander	Ghulam Ahmed[1]	5	3	0	2
1961-62*W*	F. M. M. Worrell	N. J. Contractor[2]	5	5	0	0
1966-67*I*	G. S. Sobers	Nawab of Pataudi jun.	3	2	0	1
1970-71*W*	G. S. Sobers	A. L. Wadekar	5	0	1	4
1974-75*I*	C. H. Lloyd	Nawab of Pataudi jun.[3]	5	3	2	0
1975-76*W*	C. H. Lloyd	B. S. Bedi	4	2	1	1
1978-79*I*	A. I. Kallicharran	S. M. Gavaskar	6	0	1	5
1982-83*W*	C. H. Lloyd	Kapil Dev	5	2	0	3
1983-84*I*	C. H. Lloyd	Kapil Dev	6	3	0	3
1987-88*I*	I. V. A. Richards	D. B. Vengsarkar[4]	4	1	1	2
1988-89*W*	I. V. A. Richards	D. B. Vengsarkar	4	3	0	1
1994-95*I*	C. A. Walsh	M. Azharuddin	3	1	1	1
1996-97*W*	C. A. Walsh[5]	S. R. Tendulkar	5	1	0	4
	In India		37	14	5	18
	In West Indies		33	14	2	17
	Totals		70	28	7	35

I Played in India. W Played in West Indies.

Notes: The following deputised for the official touring captain or were appointed by the home authority for only a minor proportion of the series: [1]P. R. Umrigar (First), V. Mankad (Fourth), H. R. Adhikari (Fifth). [2]Nawab of Pataudi jun. (Third, Fourth and Fifth). [3]S. Venkataraghavan (Second). [4]R. J. Shastri (Fourth). [5]B. C. Lara (Third).

HIGHEST INNINGS TOTALS

For West Indies in West Indies: 631-8 dec. at Kingston	1961-62
in India: 644-8 dec. at Delhi	1958-59
For India in West Indies: 469-7 at Port-of-Spain	1982-83
in India: 644-7 dec. at Kanpur	1978-79

LOWEST INNINGS TOTALS

For West Indies in West Indies: 140 at Bridgetown	1996-97
in India: 127 at Delhi	1987-88
For India in West Indies: 81 at Bridgetown	1996-97
in India: 75 at Delhi	1987-88

INDIVIDUAL HUNDREDS

For West Indies (82)

J. C. Adams (2)
125*   Nagpur   1994-95
174*   Mohali   1994-95

S. F. A. F. Bacchus (1)
250   Kanpur   1978-79

B. F. Butcher (2)
103   Calcutta . . .   1958-59
142   Madras   1958-59

S. Chanderpaul (1)
137*   Bridgetown .   1996-97

R. J. Christiani (1)
107†   Delhi   1948-49

C. A. Davis (2)
125*   Georgetown .   1970-71
105   Port-of-Spain   1970-71

P. J. L. Dujon (1)
110   St John's . .   1982-83

R. C. Fredericks (2)
100   Calcutta . . .   1974-75
104   Bombay . . .   1974-75

H. A. Gomes (1)
123   Port-of-Spain   1982-83

G. E. Gomez (1)
101†   Delhi   1948-49

C. G. Greenidge (5)
107†   Bangalore . .   1974-75
154*   St John's . .   1982-83
194   Kanpur   1983-84
141   Calcutta . . .   1987-88
117   Bridgetown .   1988-89

D. L. Haynes (2)
136   St John's . .   1982-83
112*   Bridgetown .   1988-89

J. K. Holt (1)
123   Delhi   1958-59

C. L. Hooper (2)
100*   Calcutta . . .   1987-88
129   Kingston . . .   1996-97

C. C. Hunte (1)
101   Bombay . . .   1966-67

A. I. Kallicharran (3)
124†   Bangalore . .   1974-75
103*   Port-of-Spain   1975-76
187   Bombay . . .   1978-79

R. B. Kanhai (4)
256   Calcutta   1958-59
138   Kingston . . .   1961-62
139   Port-of-Spain   1961-62
158*   Kingston . . .   1970-71

B. C. Lara (1)
103   St John's . .   1996-97

C. H. Lloyd (7)
163   Bangalore . .   1974-75
242*   Bombay   1974-75
102   Bridgetown .   1975-76
143   Port-of-Spain   1982-83
106   St John's . .   1982-83
103   Delhi   1983-84
161*   Calcutta . . .   1983-84

A. L. Logie (2)
130   Bridgetown .   1982-83
101   Calcutta   1987-88

E. D. A. McMorris (1)
125†   Kingston . . .   1961-62

B. H. Pairaudeau (1)
115†   Port-of-Spain   1952-53

A. F. Rae (2)
104   Bombay   1948-49
109   Madras   1948-49

I. V. A. Richards (8)
192*   Delhi   1974-75
142   Bridgetown .   1975-76
130   Port-of-Spain   1975-76
177   Port-of-Spain   1975-76
109   Georgetown .   1982-83
120   Bombay   1983-84
109*   Delhi   1987-88
110   Kingston . . .   1988-89

R. B. Richardson (2)
194   Georgetown .   1988-89
156   Kingston . . .   1988-89

O. G. Smith (1)
100   Delhi   1958-59

G. S. Sobers (8)
142*†   Bombay   1958-59
198   Kanpur   1958-59
106*   Calcutta . . .   1958-59
153   Kingston . . .   1961-62
104   Kingston . . .   1961-62
108*   Georgetown .   1970-71
178*   Bridgetown .   1970-71
132   Port-of-Spain   1970-71

J. S. Solomon (1)
100*   Delhi   1958-59

J. B. Stollmeyer (2)
160   Madras   1948-49
104*   Port-of-Spain   1952-53

C. L. Walcott (4)
152†   Delhi   1948-49
108   Calcutta   1948-49
125   Georgetown .   1952-53
118   Kingston . . .   1952-53

E. D. Weekes (7)
128†   Delhi   1948-49
194   Bombay   1948-49
162 }   Calcutta   1948-49
101 }
207   Port-of-Spain   1952-53
161   Port-of-Spain   1952-53
109   Kingston . . .   1952-53

A. B. Williams (1)
111   Calcutta . . .   1978-79

S. C. Williams (1)
128   Port-of-Spain   1996-97

F. M. M. Worrell (1)
237   Kingston . . .   1952-53

For India (59)

H. R. Adhikari (1)			120	Delhi	1978-79	150	Bridgetown .	1970-71	
114*†	Delhi	1948-49	147*	Georgetown .	1982-83	**R. J. Shastri** (2)			
M. Amarnath (3)			121	Delhi	1983-84	102	St John's . . .	1982-83	
101*	Kanpur	1978-79	236*	Madras	1983-84	107	Bridgetown .	1988-89	
117	Port-of-Spain	1982-83	**V. S. Hazare** (2)			**N. S. Sidhu** (3)			
116	St John's . . .	1982-83	134*	Bombay. . . .	1948-49	116	Kingston . . .	1988-89	
M. L. Apte (1)			122	Bombay. . . .	1948-49	107	Nagpur	1994-95	
163*	Port-of-Spain	1952-53	**Kapil Dev** (3)			201	Port-of-Spain	1996-97	
C. G. Borde (3)			126*	Delhi	1978-79	**E. D. Solkar** (1)			
109	Delhi	1958-59	100*	Port-of-Spain	1982-83	102	Bombay. . . .	1974-75	
121	Bombay. . . .	1966-67	109	Madras	1987-88	**S. R. Tendulkar** (1)			
125	Madras	1966-67	**S. V. Manjrekar** (1)			179	Nagpur	1994-95	
S. A. Durani (1)			108	Bridgetown .	1988-89	**P. R. Umrigar** (3)			
104	Port-of-Spain	1961-62	**V. L. Manjrekar** (1)			130	Port-of-Spain	1952-53	
F. M. Engineer (1)			118	Kingston . . .	1952-53	117	Kingston . . .	1952-53	
109	Madras	1966-67	**R. S. Modi** (1)			172*	Port-of-Spain	1961-62	
A. D. Gaekwad (1)			112	Bombay. . . .	1948-49	**D. B. Vengsarkar** (6)			
102	Kanpur	1978-79	**Mushtaq Ali** (1)			157*	Calcutta. . . .	1978-79	
S. M. Gavaskar (13)			106†	Calcutta. . . .	1948-49	109	Delhi	1978-79	
116	Georgetown .	1970-71	**B. P. Patel** (1)			159	Delhi	1983-84	
117*	Bridgetown .	1970-71	115*	Port-of-Spain	1975-76	100	Bombay. . . .	1983-84	
124 }	Port-of-Spain	1970-71	**M. Prabhakar** (1)			102	Delhi	1987-88	
220 }			120	Mohali	1994-95	102*	Calcutta. . . .	1987-88	
156	Port-of-Spain	1975-76	**Pankaj Roy** (1)			**G. R. Viswanath** (4)			
102	Port-of-Spain	1975-76	150	Kingston . . .	1952-53	139	Calcutta. . . .	1974-75	
205	Bombay. . . .	1978-79	**D. N. Sardesai** (3)			112	Port-of-Spain	1975-76	
107 }	Calcutta. . . .	1978-79	212	Kingston . . .	1970-71	124	Madras	1978-79	
182* }			112	Port-of-Spain	1970-71	179	Kanpur	1978-79	

† *Signifies hundred on first appearance in West Indies–India Tests.*

RECORD PARTNERSHIPS FOR EACH WICKET

For West Indies

296	for 1st	C. G. Greenidge and D. L. Haynes at St John's	1982-83
255	for 2nd	E. D. A. McMorris and R. B. Kanhai at Kingston	1961-62
220	for 3rd	I. V. A. Richards and A. I. Kallicharran at Bridgetown	1975-76
267	for 4th	C. L. Walcott and G. E. Gomez at Delhi	1948-49
219	for 5th	E. D. Weekes and B. H. Pairaudeau at Port-of-Spain	1952-53
250	for 6th	C. H. Lloyd and D. L. Murray at Bombay	1974-75
130	for 7th	C. G. Greenidge and M. D. Marshall at Kanpur	1983-84
124	for 8th†	I. V. A. Richards and K. D. Boyce at Delhi	1974-75
161	for 9th†	C. H. Lloyd and A. M. E. Roberts at Calcutta	1983-84
98*	for 10th	F. M. M. Worrell and W. W. Hall at Port-of-Spain	1961-62

For India

153	for 1st	S. M. Gavaskar and C. P. S. Chauhan at Bombay	1978-79
344*	for 2nd†	S. M. Gavaskar and D. B. Vengsarkar at Calcutta	1978-79
177	for 3rd	N. S. Sidhu and S. R. Tendulkar at Nagpur	1994-95
172	for 4th	G. R. Viswanath and A. D. Gaekwad at Kanpur	1978-79
204	for 5th	S. M. Gavaskar and B. P. Patel at Port-of-Spain	1975-76
170	for 6th	S. M. Gavaskar and R. J. Shastri at Madras	1983-84
186	for 7th	D. N. Sardesai and E. D. Solkar at Bridgetown	1970-71
107	for 8th	Yashpal Sharma and B. S. Sandhu at Kingston	1982-83
143*	for 9th	S. M. Gavaskar and S. M. H. Kirmani at Madras	1983-84
64	for 10th	J. Srinath and S. L. V. Raju at Mohali	1994-95

† *Denotes record partnership against all countries.*

TEN WICKETS OR MORE IN A MATCH

For West Indies (4)

11-126 (6-50, 5-76)	W. W. Hall, Kanpur	1958-59
11-89 (5-34, 6-55)	M. D. Marshall, Port-of-Spain	1988-89
12-121 (7-64, 5-57)	A. M. E. Roberts, Madras	1974-75
10-101 (6-62, 4-39)	C. A. Walsh, Kingston	1988-89

For India (4)

11-235 (7-157, 4-78)†	B. S. Chandrasekhar, Bombay	1966-67
10-223 (9-102, 1-121)	S. P. Gupte, Kanpur	1958-59
16-136 (8-61, 8-75)†	N. D. Hirwani, Madras	1987-88
10-135 (1-52, 9-83)	Kapil Dev, Ahmedabad	1983-84

† *Signifies ten wickets or more on first appearance in West Indies–India Tests.*

WEST INDIES v PAKISTAN

	Captains					
Season	West Indies	Pakistan	T	WI	P	D
1957-58W	F. C. M. Alexander	A. H. Kardar	5	3	1	1
1958-59P	F. C. M. Alexander	Fazal Mahmood	3	1	2	0
1974-75P	C. H. Lloyd	Intikhab Alam	2	0	0	2
1976-77W	C. H. Lloyd	Mushtaq Mohammad	5	2	1	2
1980-81P	C. H. Lloyd	Javed Miandad	4	1	0	3
1986-87P	I. V. A. Richards	Imran Khan	3	1	1	1
1987-88W	I. V. A. Richards[1]	Imran Khan	3	1	1	1
1990-91P	D. L. Haynes	Imran Khan	3	1	1	1
1992-93W	R. B. Richardson	Wasim Akram	3	2	0	1
1997-98P	C. A. Walsh	Wasim Akram	3	0	3	0
	In West Indies		16	8	3	5
	In Pakistan		18	4	7	7
	Totals		34	12	10	12

P Played in Pakistan. W Played in West Indies.

Note: The following was appointed by the home authority for only a minor proportion of the series:

[1]C. G. Greenidge (First).

HIGHEST INNINGS TOTALS

For West Indies in West Indies: 790-3 dec. at Kingston	1957-58
in Pakistan: 493 at Karachi	1974-75
For Pakistan in West Indies: 657-8 dec. at Bridgetown	1957-58
in Pakistan: 471 at Rawalpindi	1997-98

LOWEST INNINGS TOTALS

For West Indies in West Indies: 127 at Port-of-Spain	1992-93
in Pakistan: 53 at Faisalabad	1986-87
For Pakistan in West Indies: 106 at Bridgetown	1957-58
in Pakistan: 77 at Lahore	1986-87

INDIVIDUAL HUNDREDS

For West Indies (25)

L. Baichan (1)
105*† Lahore 1974-75

P. J. L. Dujon (1)
106* Port-of-Spain 1987-88

R. C. Fredericks (1)
120 Port-of-Spain 1976-77

C. G. Greenidge (1)
100 Kingston . . . 1976-77

D. L. Haynes (3)
117 Karachi 1990-91
143*‡ Port-of-Spain 1992-93
125 Bridgetown . 1992-93

C. L. Hooper (3)
134 Lahore 1990-91

178* St John's . . . 1992-93
106 Karachi 1997-98

C. C. Hunte (3)
142† Bridgetown . 1957-58
260 Kingston . . . 1957-58
114 Georgetown . 1957-58

B. D. Julien (1)
101 Karachi 1974-75

A. I. Kallicharran (1)
115 Karachi 1974-75

R. B. Kanhai (1)
217 Lahore 1958-59

C. H. Lloyd (1)
157 Bridgetown . 1976-77

I. V. A. Richards (2)
120* Multan 1980-81
123 Port-of-Spain 1987-88

I. T. Shillingford (1)
120 Georgetown . 1976-77

G. S. Sobers (3)
365* Kingston . . . 1957-58
125 ⎫
109*⎭ Georgetown . 1957-58

C. L. Walcott (1)
145 Georgetown . 1957-58

E. D. Weekes (1)
197† Bridgetown . 1957-58

For Pakistan (22)

Aamir Sohail (2)
160 Rawalpindi. . 1997-98
160 Karachi 1997-98

Asif Iqbal (1)
135 Kingston . . . 1976-77

Hanif Mohammad (2)
337† Bridgetown . 1957-58
103 Karachi 1958-59

Ijaz Ahmed, sen. (1)
151 Karachi 1997-98

Imtiaz Ahmed (1)
122 Kingston . . . 1957-58

Imran Khan (1)
123 Lahore 1980-81

Inzamam-ul-Haq (2)
123 St John's . . . 1992-93
177 Rawalpindi. . 1997-98

Javed Miandad (2)
114 Georgetown . 1987-88
102 Port-of-Spain 1987-88

Majid Khan (2)
100 Karachi 1974-75
167 Georgetown . 1976-77

Mushtaq Mohammad (2)
123 Lahore 1974-75

121 Port-of-Spain 1976-77

Saeed Ahmed (1)
150 Georgetown . 1957-58

Salim Malik (1)
102 Karachi 1990-91

Wasim Raja (2)
107* Karachi 1974-75
117* Bridgetown . 1976-77

Wazir Mohammad (2)
106 Kingston . . . 1957-58
189 Port-of-Spain 1957-58

† *Signifies hundred on first appearance in West Indies–Pakistan Tests.*
‡ *Carried his bat.*

RECORD PARTNERSHIPS FOR EACH WICKET

For West Indies

182	for 1st	R. C. Fredericks and C. G. Greenidge at Kingston	1976-77
446	for 2nd†	C. C. Hunte and G. S. Sobers at Kingston.	1957-58
169	for 3rd	D. L. Haynes and B. C. Lara at Port-of-Spain	1992-93
188*	for 4th	G. S. Sobers and C. L. Walcott at Kingston.	1957-58
185	for 5th	E. D. Weekes and O. G. Smith at Bridgetown	1957-58
151	for 6th	C. H. Lloyd and C. L. Murray at Bridgetown	1976-77
70	for 7th	C. H. Lloyd and J. Garner at Bridgetown	1976-77
60	for 8th	C. H. Hooper and A. C. Cummins at St John's.	1992-93
61*	for 9th	P. J. L. Dujon and W. K. M. Benjamin at Bridgetown	1987-88
106	for 10th†	C. L. Hooper and C. A. Walsh at St John's	1992-93

For Pakistan

298	for 1st†	Aamir Sohail and Ijaz Ahmed, sen. at Karachi	1997-98
178	for 2nd	Hanif Mohammad and Saeed Ahmed at Karachi	1958-59
323	for 3rd	Aamir Sohail and Inzamam-ul-Haq at Rawalpindi	1997-98
174	for 4th	Shoaib Mohammad and Salim Malik at Karachi	1990-91

88	for 5th	Basit Ali and Inzamam-ul-Haq at St John's	1992-93
166	for 6th	Wazir Mohammad and A. H. Kardar at Kingston	1957-58
128	for 7th[1]	Wasim Raja and Wasim Bari at Karachi	1974-75
94	for 8th	Salim Malik and Salim Yousuf at Port-of-Spain	1987-88
96	for 9th	Inzamam-ul-Haq and Nadeem Khan at St John's.	1992-93
133	for 10th	Wasim Raja and Wasim Bari at Bridgetown	1976-77

† *Denotes record partnership against all countries.*
[1]*Although the seventh wicket added 168 runs against West Indies at Lahore in 1980-81, this comprised two partnerships with Imran Khan adding 72* with Abdul Qadir (retired hurt) and a further 96 with Sarfraz Nawaz.*

TEN WICKETS OR MORE IN A MATCH

For Pakistan (3)

12-100 (6-34, 6-66)	Fazal Mahmood, Dacca	1958-59
11-121 (7-80, 4-41)	Imran Khan, Georgetown	1987-88
10-106 (5-35, 5-71)	Mushtaq Ahmed, Peshawar	1997-98

Note: The best match figures for West Indies are 9-95 (8-29, 1-66) by C. E. H. Croft at Port-of-Spain, 1976-77.

WEST INDIES v SRI LANKA

		Captains				
Season	*West Indies*	*Sri Lanka*	*T*	*WI*	*SL*	*D*
1993-94S	R. B. Richardson	A. Ranatunga	1	0	0	1
1996-97W	C. A. Walsh	A. Ranatunga	2	1	0	1
	In West Indies		2	1	0	1
	In Sri Lanka		1	0	0	1
	Totals.		3	1	0	2

W Played in West Indies. S Played in Sri Lanka.

HIGHEST INNINGS TOTALS

For West Indies: 343 at St Vincent	1996-97
For Sri Lanka: 233-8 at St Vincent.	1996-97

LOWEST INNINGS TOTALS

For West Indies: 147 at St Vincent	1996-97
For Sri Lanka: 152 at St John's.	1996-97

INDIVIDUAL HUNDREDS
For West Indies (1)

B. C. Lara (1)
115   St Vincent . . 1996-97

Highest score for Sri Lanka: 90 by S. T. Jayasuriya at St Vincent   1996-97

HUNDRED PARTNERSHIPS
For West Indies

160 for 1st   S. L. Campbell and S. C. Williams at St John's   1996-97

For Sri Lanka

110 for 4th   S. T. Jayasuriya and A. Ranatunga at St John's.   1996-97

BEST MATCH BOWLING ANALYSES
For West Indies

8-78 (5-37, 3-41)   C. E. L. Ambrose, St John's   1996-97

For Sri Lanka

8-106 (5-34, 3-72)   M. Muralitharan, St John's   1996-97

NEW ZEALAND v INDIA

Season	New Zealand	*Captains* India	T	NZ	I	D
1955-56*I*	H. B. Cave	P. R. Umrigar[1]	5	0	2	3
1964-65*I*	J. R. Reid	Nawab of Pataudi jun.	4	0	1	3
1967-68*N*	G. T. Dowling[2]	Nawab of Pataudi jun.	4	1	3	0
1969-70*I*	G. T. Dowling	Nawab of Pataudi jun.	3	1	1	1
1975-76*N*	G. M. Turner	B. S. Bedi	3	1	1	1
1976-77*I*	G. M. Turner	B. S. Bedi	3	0	2	1
1980-81*N*	G. P. Howarth	S. M. Gavaskar	3	1	0	2
1988-89*I*	J. G. Wright	D. B. Vengsarkar	3	1	2	0
1989-90*N*	J. G. Wright	M. Azharuddin	3	1	0	2
1993-94*N*	K. R. Rutherford	M. Azharuddin	1	0	0	1
1995-96*I*	L. K. Germon	M. Azharuddin	3	0	1	2
	In India		21	2	9	10
	In New Zealand		14	4	4	6
	Totals.		35	6	13	16

I Played in India. N Played in New Zealand.

Notes: The following deputised for the official touring captain or were appointed by the home authority for a minor proportion of the series:
[1]Ghulam Ahmed (First). [2]B. W. Sinclair (First). [3]S. M. Gavaskar (First).

HIGHEST INNINGS TOTALS

For New Zealand in New Zealand: 502 at Christchurch 1967-68
in India: 462-9 dec. at Calcutta 1964-65

For India in New Zealand: 482 at Auckland 1989-90
in India: 537-3 dec. at Madras 1955-56

LOWEST INNINGS TOTALS

For New Zealand in New Zealand: 100 at Wellington 1980-81
in India: 124 at Hyderabad 1988-89

For India in New Zealand: 81 at Wellington 1975-76
in India: 88 at Bombay 1964-65

INDIVIDUAL HUNDREDS

For New Zealand (21)

M. D. Crowe (1)
113   Auckland . . . 1989-90
G. T. Dowling (3)
129   Bombay. . . . 1964-65
143   Dunedin . . . 1967-68
239   Christchurch . 1967-68
J. W. Guy (1)
102† Hyderabad . . 1955-56
G. P. Howarth (1)
137* Wellington . . 1980-81
A. H. Jones (1)
170* Auckland . . . 1989-90

J. M. Parker (1)
104   Bombay. . . . 1976-77
J. F. Reid (1)
123* Christchurch . 1980-81
J. R. Reid (2)
119* Delhi 1955-56
120   Calcutta. . . . 1955-56
I. D. S. Smith (1)
173   Auckland . . . 1989-90
B. Sutcliffe (3)
137*† Hyderabad . . 1955-56

230* Delhi 1955-56
151* Calcutta. . . . 1964-65
B. R. Taylor (1)
105† Calcutta. . . . 1964-65
G. M. Turner (2)
117   Christchurch . 1975-76
113   Kanpur 1976-77
J. G. Wright (3)
110   Auckland . . . 1980-81
185   Christchurch . 1989-90
113* Napier. 1989-90

For India (22)

S. Amarnath (1)
124† Auckland . . . 1975-76
M. Azharuddin (1)
192   Auckland . . . 1989-90
C. G. Borde (1)
109   Bombay. . . . 1964-65
S. M. Gavaskar (2)
116† Auckland . . . 1975-76
119   Bombay. . . . 1976-77
A. G. Kripal Singh (1)
100*† Hyderabad . . 1955-56
V. L. Manjrekar (3)
118† Hyderabad . . 1955-56

177   Delhi 1955-56
102* Madras 1964-65
V. Mankad (2)
223   Bombay. . . . 1955-56
231   Madras 1955-56
Nawab of Pataudi jun. (2)
153   Calcutta. . . . 1964-65
113   Delhi 1964-65
G. S. Ramchand (1)
106* Calcutta. . . . 1955-56
Pankaj Roy (2)
100   Calcutta. . . . 1955-56
173   Madras 1955-56

D. N. Sardesai (2)
200* Bombay. . . . 1964-65
106   Delhi 1964-65
N. S. Sidhu (1)
116† Bangalore . . 1988-89
P. R. Umrigar (1)
223† Hyderabad . . 1955-56
G. R. Viswanath (1)
103* Kanpur 1976-77
A. L. Wadekar (1)
143   Wellington . . 1967-68

† *Signifies hundred on first appearance in New Zealand–India Tests. B. R. Taylor provides the only instance for New Zealand of a player scoring his maiden hundred in first-class cricket in his first Test.*

RECORD PARTNERSHIPS FOR EACH WICKET

For New Zealand

149	for 1st	T. J. Franklin and J. G. Wright at Napier	1989-90
155	for 2nd	G. T. Dowling and B. E. Congdon at Dunedin	1967-68
222*	for 3rd	B. Sutcliffe and J. R. Reid at Delhi	1955-56
125	for 4th	J. G. Wright and M. J. Greatbatch at Christchurch	1989-90
119	for 5th	G. T. Dowling and K. Thomson at Christchurch	1967-68
87	for 6th	J. W. Guy and A. R. MacGibbon at Hyderabad	1955-56
163	for 7th	B. Sutcliffe and B. R. Taylor at Calcutta	1964-65
103	for 8th	R. J. Hadlee and I. D. S. Smith at Auckland	1989-90
136	for 9th†	I. D. S. Smith and M. C. Snedden at Auckland	1989-90
61	for 10th	J. T. Ward and R. O. Collinge at Madras.	1964-65

For India

413	for 1st†	V. Mankad and Pankaj Roy at Madras	1955-56
204	for 2nd	S. M. Gavaskar and S. Amarnath at Auckland	1975-76
238	for 3rd	P. R. Umrigar and V. L. Manjrekar at Hyderabad	1955-56
171	for 4th	P. R. Umrigar and A. G. Kripal Singh at Hyderabad	1955-56
127	for 5th	V. L. Manjrekar and G. S. Ramchand at Delhi	1955-56
193*	for 6th	D. N. Sardesai and Hanumant Singh at Bombay	1964-65
128	for 7th	S. R. Tendulkar and K. S. More at Napier	1989-90
143	for 8th	R. G. Nadkarni and F. M. Engineer at Madras	1964-65
105	for 9th	{ S. M. H. Kirmani and B. S. Bedi at Bombay	1976-77
		{ S. M. H. Kirmani and N. S. Yadav at Auckland	1980-81
57	for 10th	R. B. Desai and B. S. Bedi at Dunedin	1967-68

† *Denotes record partnership against all countries.*

TEN WICKETS OR MORE IN A MATCH

For New Zealand (2)

11-58 (4-35, 7-23)	R. J. Hadlee, Wellington	1975-76
10-88 (6-49, 4-39)	R. J. Hadlee, Bombay	1988-89

For India (2)

11-140 (3-64, 8-76)	E. A. S. Prasanna, Auckland	1975-76
12-152 (8-72, 4-80)	S. Venkataraghavan, Delhi	1964-65

NEW ZEALAND v PAKISTAN

Captains

Season	New Zealand	Pakistan	T	NZ	P	D
1955-56*P*	H. B. Cave	A. H. Kardar	3	0	2	1
1964-65*N*	J. R. Reid	Hanif Mohammad	3	0	0	3
1964-65*P*	J. R. Reid	Hanif Mohammad	3	0	2	1
1969-70*P*	G. T. Dowling	Intikhab Alam	3	1	0	2
1972-73*N*	B. E. Congdon	Intikhab Alam	3	0	1	2
1976-77*P*	G. M. Turner[1]	Mushtaq Mohammad	3	0	2	1
1978-79*N*	M. G. Burgess	Mushtaq Mohammad	3	0	1	2
1984-85*P*	J. V. Coney	Zaheer Abbas	3	0	2	1

		Captains				
Season	*New Zealand*	*Pakistan*	*T*	*NZ*	*P*	*D*
1984-85N	G. P. Howarth	Javed Miandad	3	2	0	1
1988-89N†	J. G. Wright	Imran Khan	2	0	0	2
1990-91P	M. D. Crowe	Javed Miandad	3	0	3	0
1992-93N	K. R. Rutherford	Javed Miandad	1	0	1	0
1993-94N	K. R. Rutherford	Salim Malik	3	1	2	0
1995-96N	L. K. Germon	Wasim Akram	1	0	1	0
1996-97P	L. K. Germon	Saeed Anwar	2	1	1	0
	In Pakistan		20	2	12	6
	In New Zealand		19	3	6	10
	Totals		39	5	18	16

N Played in New Zealand.   P Played in Pakistan.

† *The First Test at Dunedin was abandoned without a ball being bowled and is excluded.*

Note: The following deputised for the official touring captain:
¹J. M. Parker (Third).

HIGHEST INNINGS TOTALS

For New Zealand in New Zealand: 492 at Wellington   1984-85
in Pakistan: 482-6 dec. at Lahore   1964-65

For Pakistan in New Zealand: 616-5 dec. at Auckland   1988-89
in Pakistan: 565-9 dec. at Karachi   1976-77

LOWEST INNINGS TOTALS

For New Zealand in New Zealand: 93 at Hamilton   1992-93
in Pakistan: 70 at Dacca   1955-56

For Pakistan in New Zealand: 169 at Auckland   1984-85
in Pakistan: 102 at Faisalabad   1990-91

INDIVIDUAL HUNDREDS

For New Zealand (21)

M. G. Burgess (2)
119* Dacca 1969-70
111   Lahore 1976-77
J. V. Coney (1)
111* Dunedin . . . 1984-85
M. D. Crowe (2)
174   Wellington . . 1988-89
108* Lahore 1990-91
B. A. Edgar (1)
129† Christchurch . 1978-79
M. J. Greatbatch (1)
133   Hamilton . . . 1992-93
B. F. Hastings (1)
110   Auckland . . . 1972-73

G. P. Howarth (1)
114   Napier 1978-79
W. K. Lees (1)
152   Karachi 1976-77
S. N. McGregor (1)
111   Lahore 1955-56
R. E. Redmond (1)
107† Auckland . . . 1972-73
J. F. Reid (3)
106   Hyderabad . . 1984-85
148   Wellington . . 1984-85
158* Auckland . . . 1984-85
J. R. Reid (1)
128   Karachi 1964-65

B. W. Sinclair (1)
130   Lahore 1964-65
S. A. Thomson (1)
120* Christchurch . 1993-94
G. M. Turner (1)
110† Dacca 1969-70
J. G. Wright (1)
107   Karachi 1984-85
B. A. Young (1)
120   Christchurch . 1993-94

For Pakistan (41)

Asif Iqbal (3)		160* Christchurch. 1978-79	103* Hyderabad . . 1976-77
175 Dunedin . . . 1972-73	104 } Hyderabad . . 1984-85	**Saeed Ahmed (1)**
166 Lahore 1976-77	103* }	172 Karachi . . . 1964-65
104 Napier. 1978-79	118 Wellington . . 1988-89	**Saeed Anwar (2)**
Basit Ali (1)	271 Auckland. . . 1988-89	169 Wellington . . 1993-94
103 Christchurch. 1993-94	**Majid Khan (3)**	149 Rawalpindi. . 1996-97
Hanif Mohammad (3)	110 Auckland. . . 1972-73	**Salim Malik (2)**
103 Dacca 1955-56	112 Karachi 1976-77	119* Karachi . . . 1984-85
100* Christchurch. 1964-65	119* Napier. . . . 1978-79	140 Wellington . . 1993-94
203* Lahore 1964-65	**Mohammad Ilyas (1)**	**Shoaib Mohammad (5)**
Ijaz Ahmed, sen. (2)	126 Karachi 1964-65	163 Wellington . . 1988-89
103 Christchurch. 1995-96	**Mohammad Wasim (1)**	112 Auckland. . . 1988-89
125 Rawalpindi. . 1996-97	109*† Lahore 1996-97	203* Karachi . . . 1990-91
Imtiaz Ahmed (1)	**Mudassar Nazar (1)**	105 Lahore 1990-91
209 Lahore 1955-56	106 Hyderabad . . 1984-85	142 Faisalabad . . 1990-91
Inzamam-ul-Haq (1)	**Mushtaq Mohammad (3)**	**Waqar Hassan (1)**
135* Wellington . . 1993-94	201 Dunedin . . . 1972-73	189 Lahore 1955-56
Javed Miandad (7)	101 Hyderabad . . 1976-77	**Zaheer Abbas (1)**
163† Lahore 1976-77	107 Karachi 1976-77	135 Auckland. . . 1978-79
206 Karachi 1976-77	**Sadiq Mohammad (2)**	
	166 Wellington . . 1972-73	

† *Signifies hundred on first appearance in New Zealand–Pakistan Tests.*

Notes: Mushtaq and Sadiq Mohammad, at Hyderabad in 1976-77, provide the fourth instance in Test matches, after the Chappells (thrice), of brothers each scoring hundreds in the same innings.

RECORD PARTNERSHIPS FOR EACH WICKET

For New Zealand

159 for 1st	R. E. Redmond and G. M. Turner at Auckland.	1972-73
195 for 2nd	J. G. Wright and G. P. Howarth at Napier	1978-79
178 for 3rd	B. W. Sinclair and J. R. Reid at Lahore	1964-65
128 for 4th	B. F. Hastings and M. G. Burgess at Wellington	1972-73
183 for 5th††	M. G. Burgess and R. W. Anderson at Lahore	1976-77
145 for 6th	J. F. Reid and R. J. Hadlee at Wellington	1984-85
186 for 7th†	W. K. Lees and R. J. Hadlee at Karachi	1976-77
100 for 8th	B. W. Yuile and D. R. Hadlee at Karachi	1969-70
96 for 9th	M. G. Burgess and R. S. Cunis at Dacca	1969-70
151 for 10th†	B. F. Hastings and R. O. Collinge at Auckland	1972-73

For Pakistan

172 for 1st	Ramiz Raja and Shoaib Mohammad at Karachi	1990-91
262 for 2nd	Saeed Anwar and Ijaz Ahmed, sen. at Rawalpindi.	1996-97
248 for 3rd	Shoaib Mohammad and Javed Miandad at Auckland	1988-89
350 for 4th†	Mushtaq Mohammad and Asif Iqbal at Dunedin	1972-73
281 for 5th†	Javed Miandad and Asif Iqbal at Lahore	1976-77
217 for 6th†	Hanif Mohammad and Majid Khan at Lahore	1964-65
308 for 7th†	Waqar Hassan and Imtiaz Ahmed at Lahore.	1955-56
89 for 8th	Anil Dalpat and Iqbal Qasim at Karachi	1984-85
52 for 9th	Intikhab Alam and Arif Butt at Auckland	1964-65
65 for 10th	Salah-ud-Din and Mohammad Farooq at Rawalpindi	1964-65

† *Denotes record partnership against all countries.*

TEN WICKETS OR MORE IN A MATCH

For New Zealand (1)

11-152 (7-52, 4-100)   C. Pringle, Faisalabad   1990-91

For Pakistan (10)

10-182 (5-91, 5-91)	Intikhab Alam, Dacca	1969-70
11-130 (7-52, 4-78)	Intikhab Alam, Dunedin	1972-73
11-130 (4-64, 7-66)†	Mohammad Zahid, Rawalpindi	1996-97
10-171 (3-115, 7-56)	Mushtaq Ahmed, Christchurch.	1995-96
10-143 (4-59, 6-84)	Mushtaq Ahmed, Lahore	1996-97
10-106 (3-20, 7-86)	Waqar Younis, Lahore	1990-91
12-130 (7-76, 5-54)	Waqar Younis, Faisalabad.	1990-91
10-128 (5-56, 5-72)	Wasim Akram, Dunedin	1984-85
11-179 (4-60, 7-119)	Wasim Akram, Wellington	1993-94
11-79 (5-37, 6-42)†	Zulfiqar Ahmed, Karachi	1955-56

† *Signifies ten wickets or more on first appearance in New Zealand–Pakistan Tests.*

Note: Waqar Younis's performances were in successive matches.

NEW ZEALAND v SRI LANKA

		Captains				
Season	New Zealand	Sri Lanka	T	NZ	SL	D
1982-83N	G. P. Howarth	D. S. de Silva	2	2	0	0
1983-84S	G. P. Howarth	L. R. D. Mendis	3	2	0	1
1986-87S†	J. J. Crowe	L. R. D. Mendis	1	0	0	1
1990-91N	M. D. Crowe[1]	A. Ranatunga	3	0	0	3
1992-93S	M. D. Crowe	A. Ranatunga	2	0	1	1
1994-95N	K. R. Rutherford	A. Ranatunga	2	0	1	1
1996-97N	S. P. Fleming	A. Ranatunga	2	2	0	0
1997-98S	S. P. Fleming	A. Ranatunga	3	1	2	0
	In New Zealand		9	4	1	4
	In Sri Lanka		9	3	3	3
	Totals.		18	7	4	7

N Played in New Zealand.   S Played in Sri Lanka.

† *The Second and Third Tests were cancelled owing to civil disturbances.*

Note: The following was appointed by the home authority for only a minor proportion of the series:

[1]I. D. S. Smith (Third).

HIGHEST INNINGS TOTALS

For New Zealand in New Zealand: 671-4 at Wellington		1990-91
in Sri Lanka: 459 at Colombo (CCC)		1983-84
For Sri Lanka in New Zealand: 497 at Wellington.		1990-91
in Sri Lanka: 397-9 dec. at Colombo (CCC).		1986-87

LOWEST INNINGS TOTALS

For New Zealand in New Zealand: 109 at Napier		1994-95
in Sri Lanka: 102 at Colombo (SSC)		1992-93
For Sri Lanka in New Zealand: 93 at Wellington		1982-83
in Sri Lanka: 97 at Kandy.		1986-87

INDIVIDUAL HUNDREDS

For New Zealand (13)

J. J. Crowe (1)
120* Colombo (CCC) 1986-87
M. D. Crowe (2)
299 Wellington . . 1990-91
107 Colombo (SSC) 1992-93
S. P. Fleming (1)
174* Colombo (RPS) 1997-98
R. J. Hadlee (1)
151* Colombo (CCC) 1986-87

A. H. Jones (3)
186 Wellington . . 1990-91
122 } Hamilton . . . 1990-91
100* }
C. D. McMillan (1)
142† Colombo (RPS) 1997-98
J. F. Reid (1)
180 Colombo (CCC) 1983-84

K. R. Rutherford (1)
105 Moratuwa . . 1992-93
J. G. Wright (1)
101 Hamilton . . . 1990-91
B. A. Young (1)
267* Dunedin . . . 1996-97

For Sri Lanka (12)

P. A. de Silva (2)
267† Wellington . . 1990-91
123 Auckland . . 1990-91
R. L. Dias (1)
108† Colombo (SSC) 1983-84
A. P. Gurusinha (3)
119 } Hamilton . . . 1990-91
102 }

127 Dunedin . . . 1994-95
D. P. M. D. Jayawardene (1)
167 Galle. 1997-98
R. S. Kaluwitharana (1)
103† Dunedin . . . 1996-97
D. S. B. P. Kuruppu (1)
201*† Colombo (CCC) 1986-87

R. S. Mahanama (2)
153 Moratuwa . . 1992-93
109 Colombo (SSC) 1992-93
H. P. Tillekeratne (1)
108 Dunedin . . . 1994-95

† *Signifies hundred on first appearance in New Zealand–Sri Lanka Tests.*

Note: A. P. Gurusinha and A. H. Jones at Hamilton in 1990-91 provided the second instance of a player on each side hitting two separate hundreds in a Test match.

RECORD PARTNERSHIPS FOR EACH WICKET

For New Zealand

161	for 1st	T. J. Franklin and J. G. Wright at Hamilton		1990-91
140	for 2nd	B. A. Young and M. J. Horne at Dunedin		1996-97
467	for 3rd†‡	A. H. Jones and M. D. Crowe at Wellington		1990-91
240	for 4th	S. P. Fleming and C. D. McMillan at Colombo (RPS)		1997-98
151	for 5th	K. R. Rutherford and C. Z. Harris at Moratuwa		1992-93
246*	for 6th†	J. J. Crowe and R. J. Hadlee at Colombo (CCC)		1986-87
47	for 7th	D. N. Patel and M. L. Su'a at Dunedin		1994-95
79	for 8th	J. V. Coney and W. K. Lees at Christchurch		1982-83
43	for 9th	A. C. Parore and P. J. Wiseman at Galle		1997-98
52	for 10th	W. K. Lees and E. J. Chatfield at Christchurch		1982-83

For Sri Lanka

102	for 1st	R. S. Mahanama and U. C. Hathurusinghe at Colombo (SSC)		1992-93
138	for 2nd	R. S. Mahanama and A. P. Gurusinha at Moratuwa		1992-93
159*	for 3rd[1]	S. Wettimuny and R. L. Dias at Colombo (SSC).		1983-84
192	for 4th	A. P. Gurusinha and H. P. Tillekeratne at Dunedin		1994-95
130	for 5th	R. S. Madugalle and D. S. de Silva at Wellington		1982-83
109*	for 6th[2]	R. S. Madugalle and A. Ranatunga at Colombo (CCC).		1983-84
137	for 7th	R. S. Kaluwitharana and W. P. U. J. C. Vaas at Dunedin		1996-97
73	for 8th	H. P. Tillekeratne and G. P. Wickremasinghe at Dunedin		1996-97
31	for 9th	{ G. F. Labrooy and R. J. Ratnayake at Auckland		1990-91
		{ S. T. Jayasuriya and R. J. Ratnayake at Auckland		1990-91
71	for 10th	R. S. Kaluwitharana and M. Muralitharan at Colombo (SSC)		1997-98

† *Denotes record partnership against all countries.*

‡ *Record third-wicket partnership in first-class cricket.*

[1] *163 runs were added for this wicket in two separate partnerships: S. Wettimuny retired hurt and was replaced by J. R. Ratnayeke when 159 had been added.*

[2] *119 runs were added for this wicket in two separate partnerships: R. S. Madugalle retired hurt and was replaced by D. S. de Silva when 109 had been added.*

TEN WICKETS OR MORE IN A MATCH

For New Zealand (1)

10-102 (5-73, 5-29) R. J. Hadlee, Colombo (CCC). 1983-84

For Sri Lanka (1)

10-90 (5-47, 5-43)† W. P. U. J. C. Vaas, Napier 1994-95

† *Signifies ten wickets or more on first appearance in New Zealand–Sri Lanka Tests.*

NEW ZEALAND v ZIMBABWE

	Captains					
Season	New Zealand	Zimbabwe	T	NZ	Z	D
1992-93Z	M. D. Crowe	D. L. Houghton	2	1	0	1
1995-96N	L. K. Germon	A. Flower	2	0	0	2
1997-98Z	S. P. Fleming	A. D. R. Campbell	2	0	0	2
1997-98N	S. P. Fleming	A. D. R. Campbell	2	2	0	0
	In New Zealand		4	2	0	2
	In Zimbabwe		4	1	0	3
	Totals		8	3	0	5

N Played in New Zealand. Z Played in Zimbabwe.

HIGHEST INNINGS TOTALS

For New Zealand in New Zealand: 460 at Auckland 1997-98
                    in Zimbabwe: 403 at Bulawayo 1997-98

For Zimbabwe in New Zealand: 326 at Auckland 1995-96
                in Zimbabwe: 461 at Bulawayo 1997-98

LOWEST INNINGS TOTALS

For New Zealand in New Zealand: 251 at Auckland 1995-96
                    in Zimbabwe: 207 at Harare 1997-98

For Zimbabwe in New Zealand: 170 at Auckland 1997-98
                in Zimbabwe: 137 at Harare 1992-93

INDIVIDUAL HUNDREDS

For New Zealand (7)

N. J. Astle (1)	**M. J. Horne** (1)	**C. M. Spearman** (1)
114 Auckland . . . 1997-98	157 Auckland . . . 1997-98	112 Auckland . . . 1995-96
C. L. Cairns (1)	**R. T. Latham** (1)	
120 Auckland . . . 1995-96	119† Bulawayo . . 1992-93	
M. D. Crowe (1)	**C. D. McMillan** (1)	
140 Harare 1992-93	139† Wellington . . 1997-98	

For Zimbabwe (5)

K. J. Arnott (1)	**D. L. Houghton** (1)
101*† Bulawayo . . 1992-93	104* Auckland . . . 1995-96
G. W. Flower (2)	
104	**G. J. Whittall** (1)
151 } Harare 1997-98	203* Bulawayo . . 1997-98

† *Signifies hundred on first appearance in New Zealand–Zimbabwe Tests.*

RECORD PARTNERSHIPS FOR EACH WICKET

For New Zealand

214	for 1st	C. M. Spearman and R. G. Twose at Auckland..............	1995-96
127	for 2nd	R. T. Latham and A. H. Jones at Bulawayo.................	1992-93
71	for 3rd	A. H. Jones and M. D. Crowe at Bulawayo................	1992-93
243	for 4th†	M. J. Horne and N. J. Astle at Auckland...................	1997-98
166	for 5th	A. C. Parore and C. L. Cairns at Auckland................	1995-96
82*	for 6th	A. C. Parore and L. K. Germon at Hamilton	1995-96
108	for 7th	C. D. McMillan and D. J. Nash at Wellington	1997-98
112	for 8th	C. Z. Harris and D. L. Vettori at Bulawayo...............	1997-98
18	for 9th	D. L. Vettori and S. B. O'Connor at Bulawayo............	1997-98
27	for 10th	C. D. McMillan and S. B. Doull at Auckland..............	1997-98

For Zimbabwe

156	for 1st††	G. J. Rennie and G. W. Flower at Harare	1997-98
107	for 2nd	K. J. Arnott and A. D. R. Campbell at Harare	1992-93
70	for 3rd	A. Flower and G. J. Whittall at Bulawayo.................	1997-98
88	for 4th	D. L. Houghton and A. Flower at Auckland................	1995-96
78	for 5th	G. J. Whittall and D. L. Houghton at Bulawayo	1997-98
70	for 6th	D. L. Houghton and A. Flower at Bulawayo	1992-93
91	for 7th	G. J. Whittall and P. A. Strang at Hamilton	1995-96
94	for 8th†	A. D. R. Campbell and H. H. Streak at Wellington	1997-98
46	for 9th	G. J. Crocker and M. G. Burmester at Harare.............	1992-93
40	for 10th	G. J. Whittall and E. Matambanadzo at Bulawayo..........	1997-98

† *Denotes record partnership against all countries.*

TEN WICKETS OR MORE IN A MATCH

For Zimbabwe (1)

11-255 (6-109, 5-146)	A. G. Huckle, Bulawayo	1997-98

Note: The best match figures for New Zealand are 8-85 (4-35, 4-50) by S. B. Doull at Auckland, 1997-98.

INDIA v PAKISTAN

Captains

Season	India	Pakistan	T	I	P	D
1952-53*I*	L. Amarnath	A. H. Kardar	5	2	1	2
1954-55*P*	V. Mankad	A. H. Kardar	5	0	0	5
1960-61*I*	N. J. Contractor	Fazal Mahmood	5	0	0	5
1978-79*P*	B. S. Bedi	Mushtaq Mohammad	3	0	2	1
1979-80*I*	S. M. Gavaskar	Asif Iqbal[1]	6	2	0	4
1982-83*P*	S. M. Gavaskar	Imran Khan	6	0	3	3
1983-84*I*	Kapil Dev	Zaheer Abbas	3	0	0	3
1984-85*P*	S. M. Gavaskar	Zaheer Abbas	2	0	0	2
1986-87*I*	Kapil Dev	Imran Khan	5	0	1	4
1989-90*P*	K. Srikkanth	Imran Khan	4	0	0	4
	In India		24	4	2	18
	In Pakistan		20	0	5	15
	Totals..................		44	4	7	33

I Played in India. P Played in Pakistan.

Note: The following was appointed by the home authority for only a minor proportion of the series:

[1]G. R. Viswanath (Sixth).

HIGHEST INNINGS TOTALS

For India in India: 539-9 dec. at Madras 1960-61
        in Pakistan: 509 at Lahore 1989-90

For Pakistan in India: 487-9 dec. at Madras 1986-87
        in Pakistan: 699-5 at Lahore 1989-90

LOWEST INNINGS TOTALS

For India in India: 106 at Lucknow 1952-53
        in Pakistan: 145 at Karachi 1954-55

For Pakistan in India: 116 at Bangalore 1986-87
        in Pakistan: 158 at Dacca 1954-55

INDIVIDUAL HUNDREDS

For India (31)

M. Amarnath (4)
109* Lahore 1982-83
120   Lahore 1982-83
103* Karachi 1982-83
101* Lahore 1984-85
M. Azharuddin (3)
141   Calcutta. . . . 1986-87
110   Jaipur 1986-87
109   Faisalabad . . 1989-90
C. G. Borde (1)
177* Madras 1960-61
A. D. Gaekwad (1)
201   Jullundur . . . 1983-84
S. M. Gavaskar (5)
111 } Karachi 1978-79
137 }
166   Madras 1979-80
127*‡ Faisalabad . . 1982-83
103* Bangalore . . . 1983-84
V. S. Hazare (1)
146* Bombay. . . . 1952-53
S. V. Manjrekar (2)
113*† Karachi 1989-90
218   Lahore 1989-90
S. M. Patil (1)
127   Faisalabad . . 1984-85
R. J. Shastri (3)
128   Karachi 1982-83
139   Faisalabad . . 1984-85
125   Jaipur 1986-87
R. H. Shodhan (1)
110† Calcutta 1952-53
K. Srikkanth (1)
123   Madras 1986-87
P. R. Umrigar (5)
102   Bombay. . . . 1952-53
108   Peshawar . . . 1954-55
115   Kanpur 1960-61
117   Madras 1960-61
112   Delhi 1960-61
D. B. Vengsarkar (2)
146* Delhi 1979-80
109   Ahmedabad . 1986-87
G. R. Viswanath (1)
145† Faisalabad . . 1978-79

For Pakistan (41)

Aamer Malik (2)
117   Faisalabad . . 1989-90
113   Lahore 1989-90
Alim-ud-Din (1)
103* Karachi 1954-55
Asif Iqbal (1)
104† Faisalabad . . 1978-79
Hanif Mohammad (2)
142   Bahawalpur . 1954-55
160   Bombay. . . . 1960-61
Ijaz Faqih (1)
105† Ahmedabad . 1986-87
Imtiaz Ahmed (1)
135   Madras 1960-61
Imran Khan (3)
117   Faisalabad . . 1982-83
135* Madras 1986-87
109* Karachi 1989-90
Javed Miandad (5)
154*† Faisalabad . . 1978-79
100   Karachi 1978-79
126   Faisalabad . . 1982-83
280* Hyderabad . . 1982-83
145   Lahore 1989-90
Mohsin Khan (1)
101*† Lahore 1982-83
Mudassar Nazar (6)
126   Bangalore . . . 1979-80
119   Karachi 1982-83
231   Hyderabad . . 1982-83
152*‡ Lahore 1982-83
152   Karachi 1982-83
199   Faisalabad . . 1984-85
Mushtaq Mohammad (1)
101   Delhi 1960-61
Nazar Mohammad (1)
124*‡ Lucknow . . . 1952-53
Qasim Omar (1)
210   Faisalabad . . 1984-85
Ramiz Raja (1)
114   Jaipur 1986-87
Saeed Ahmed (2)
121† Bombay. . . . 1960-61
103   Madras 1960-61
Salim Malik (3)
107   Faisalabad . . 1982-83
102* Faisalabad . . 1984-85
102* Karachi 1989-90
Shoaib Mohammad (2)
101   Madras 1986-87
203* Lahore 1989-90
Wasim Raja (1)
125   Jullundur . . . 1983-84
Zaheer Abbas (6)
176† Faisalabad . . 1978-79
235* Lahore 1978-79
215   Lahore 1982-83
186   Karachi 1982-83
168   Faisalabad . . 1982-83
168* Lahore 1984-85

† *Signifies hundred on first appearance in India–Pakistan Tests.*
‡ *Carried his bat.*

RECORD PARTNERSHIPS FOR EACH WICKET

For India

200 for 1st	S. M. Gavaskar and K. Srikkanth at Madras	1986-87
135 for 2nd	N. S. Sidhu and S. V. Manjrekar at Karachi	1989-90
190 for 3rd	M. Amarnath and Yashpal Sharma at Lahore	1982-83
186 for 4th	S. V. Manjrekar and R. J. Shastri at Lahore	1989-90
200 for 5th	S. M. Patil and R. J. Shastri at Faisalabad	1984-85
143 for 6th	M. Azharuddin and Kapil Dev at Calcutta	1986-87
155 for 7th	R. M. H. Binny and Madan Lal at Bangalore	1983-84
122 for 8th	S. M. H. Kirmani and Madan Lal at Faisalabad	1982-83
149 for 9th†	P. G. Joshi and R. B. Desai at Bombay	1960-61
109 for 10th†	H. R. Adhikari and Ghulam Ahmed at Delhi	1952-53

For Pakistan

162 for 1st	Hanif Mohammad and Imtiaz Ahmed at Madras	1960-61
250 for 2nd	Mudassar Nazar and Qasim Omar at Faisalabad	1984-85
451 for 3rd†	Mudassar Nazar and Javed Miandad at Hyderabad	1982-83
287 for 4th	Javed Miandad and Zaheer Abbas at Faisalabad	1982-83
213 for 5th	Zaheer Abbas and Mudassar Nazar at Karachi	1982-83
207 for 6th	Salim Malik and Imran Khan at Faisalabad	1982-83
154 for 7th	Imran Khan and Ijaz Faqih at Ahmedabad	1986-87
112 for 8th	Imran Khan and Wasim Akram at Madras	1986-87
60 for 9th	Wasim Bari and Iqbal Qasim at Bangalore	1979-80
104 for 10th	Zulfiqar Ahmed and Amir Elahi at Madras	1952-53

† *Denotes record partnership against all countries.*

TEN WICKETS OR MORE IN A MATCH

For India (3)

11-146 (4-90, 7-56)	Kapil Dev, Madras	1979-80
10-126 (7-27, 3-99)	Maninder Singh, Bangalore	1986-87
13-131 (8-52, 5-79)†	V. Mankad, Delhi	1952-53

For Pakistan (5)

12-94 (5-52, 7-42)	Fazal Mahmood, Lucknow	1952-53
11-79 (3-19, 8-60)	Imran Khan, Karachi	1982-83
11-180 (6-98, 5-82)	Imran Khan, Faisalabad	1982-83
10-175 (4-135, 6-40)	Iqbal Qasim, Bombay	1979-80
11-190 (8-69, 3-121)	Sikander Bakht, Delhi	1979-80

† *Signifies ten wickets or more on first appearance in India–Pakistan Tests.*

INDIA v SRI LANKA

		Captains				
Season	*India*	*Sri Lanka*	*T*	*I*	*SL*	*D*
1982-83*I*	S. M. Gavaskar	B. Warnapura	1	0	0	1
1985-86*S*	Kapil Dev	L. R. D. Mendis	3	0	1	2
1986-87*I*	Kapil Dev	L. R. D. Mendis	3	2	0	1
1990-91*I*	M. Azharuddin	A. Ranatunga	1	1	0	0
1993-94*S*	M. Azharuddin	A. Ranatunga	3	1	0	2
1993-94*I*	M. Azharuddin	A. Ranatunga	3	3	0	0
1997-98*S*	S. R. Tendulkar	A. Ranatunga	2	0	0	2
1997-98*I*	S. R. Tendulkar	A. Ranatunga	3	0	0	3
	In India		11	6	0	5
	In Sri Lanka		8	1	1	6
	Totals		19	7	1	11

I Played in India. S Played in Sri Lanka.

HIGHEST INNINGS TOTALS

For India in India: 676-7 at Kanpur 1986-87
　　　　in Sri Lanka: 537-8 dec. at Colombo (RPS) 1997-98

For Sri Lanka in India: 420 at Kanpur 1986-87
　　　　in Sri Lanka: 952-6 dec. at Colombo (RPS) 1997-98

LOWEST INNINGS TOTALS

For India in India: 288 at Chandigarh............................ 1990-91
　　　　in Sri Lanka: 198 at Colombo (PSS)..................... 1985-86

For Sri Lanka in India: 82 at Chandigarh......................... 1990-91
　　　　in Sri Lanka: 198 at Kandy............................. 1985-86

INDIVIDUAL HUNDREDS

For India (27)

M. Amarnath (2)
116*　Kandy..... 1985-86
131　　Nagpur .. 1986-87

M. Azharuddin (5)
199　　Kanpur ... 1986-87
108　　Bangalore .. 1993-94
152　　Ahmedabad . 1993-94
126　　Colombo (RPS) 1997-98
108*　Colombo (SSC) 1997-98

S. C. Ganguly (3)
147　　Colombo (SSC) 1997-98
109　　Mohali 1997-98
173　　Mumbai.. 1997-98

S. M. Gavaskar (2)
155†　Madras 1982-83
176　　Kanpur .. 1986-87

V. G. Kambli (2)
125　　Colombo (SSC) 1993-94
120　　Colombo (PSS) 1993-94

Kapil Dev (1)
163　　Kanpur 1986-87

S. M. Patil (1)
114*†　Madras ... 1982-83

N. S. Sidhu (4)
104　　Colombo (SSC) 1993-94

124　　Lucknow ... 1993-94
111　　Colombo (RPS) 1997-98
131　　Mohali 1997-98

S. R. Tendulkar (5)
104*　Colombo (SSC) 1993-94
142　　Lucknow ... 1993-94
143　　Colombo (RPS) 1997-98
139　　Colombo (SSC) 1997-98
148　　Mumbai.... 1997-98

D. B. Vengsarkar (2)
153　　Nagpur ... 1986-87
166　　Cuttack 1986-87

For Sri Lanka (17)

M. S. Atapattu (1)
108　　Mohali 1997-98

P. A. de Silva (5)
148　　Colombo (PSS) 1993-94
126　　Colombo (RPS) 1997-98
146 }　Colombo (SSC) 1997-98
120 }
110*　Mohali 1997-98

R. L. Dias (1)
106　　Kandy.... 1985-86

S. T. Jayasuriya (2)
340　　Colombo (RPS) 1997-98
199　　Colombo (SSC) 1997-98

R. S. Madugalle (1)
103　　Colombo (SSC) 1985-86

R. S. Mahanama (2)
151　　Colombo (RPS) 1993-94

225　　Colombo (RPS) 1997-98

L. R. D. Mendis (3)
105 }†Madras 1982-83
105 }
124　　Kandy..... 1985-86

A. Ranatunga (1)
111　　Colombo (SSC) 1985-86

S. A. R. Silva (1)
111　　Colombo (PSS) 1985-86

† *Signifies hundred on first appearance in India–Sri Lanka Tests.*

RECORD PARTNERSHIPS FOR EACH WICKET

For India

171	for 1st	M. Prabhakar and N. S. Sidhu at Colombo (SSC)..............	1993-94
173	for 2nd	S. M. Gavaskar and D. B. Vengsarkar at Madras	1982-83
173	for 3rd	M. Amarnath and D. B. Vengsarkar at Nagpur	1986-87
256	for 4th	S. C. Ganguly and S. R. Tendulkar at Mumbai...............	1997-98
150	for 5th	S. R. Tendulkar and S. C. Ganguly at Colombo (SSC).	1997-98
272	for 6th	M. Azharuddin and Kapil Dev at Kanpur...................	1986-87
78*	for 7th	S. M. Patil and Madan Lal at Madras.....................	1982-83
70	for 8th	Kapil Dev and L. Sivaramakrishnan at Colombo (PSS)	1985-86
89	for 9th	S. C. Ganguly and A. Kuruvilla at Mohali..................	1997-98
29	for 10th	Kapil Dev and Chetan Sharma at Colombo (PSS)	1985-86

For Sri Lanka

159 for 1st†	S. Wettimuny and J. R. Ratnayeke at Kanpur	1986-87
576 for 2nd†	S. T. Jayasuriya and R. S. Mahanama at Colombo (RPS)	1997-98
218 for 3rd	S. T. Jayasuriya and P. A. de Silva at Colombo (SSC)	1997-98
216 for 4th	R. L. Dias and L. R. D. Mendis at Kandy	1985-86
144 for 5th	R. S. Madugalle and A. Ranatunga at Colombo (SSC)	1985-86
103 for 6th	P. A. de Silva and H. D. P. K. Dharmasena at Mohali	1997-98
77 for 7th	R. S. Madugalle and D. S. de Silva at Madras	1982-83
48 for 8th	P. A. de Silva and M. Muralitharan at Colombo (SSC)	1997-98
60 for 9th	H. P. Tillekeratne and A. W. R. Madurasinghe at Chandigarh	1990-91
44 for 10th	R. J. Ratnayake and E. A. R. de Silva at Nagpur	1986-87

† *Denotes record partnership against all countries.*

TEN WICKETS OR MORE IN A MATCH

For India (3)

11-128 (4-69, 7-59)	A. Kumble, Lucknow	1993-94
10-107 (3-56, 7-51)	Maninder Singh, Nagpur	1986-87
11-125 (5-38, 6-87)	S. L. V. Raju, Ahmedabad	1993-94

Note: The best match figures for Sri Lanka are 9-125 (4-76, 5-49) by R. J. Ratnayake at Colombo (PSS), 1985-86.

INDIA v ZIMBABWE

		Captains				
Season	India	Zimbabwe	T	I	Z	D
1992-93Z	M. Azharuddin	D. L. Houghton	1	0	0	1
1992-93I	M. Azharuddin	D. L. Houghton	1	1	0	0
	In India		1	1	0	0
	In Zimbabwe		1	0	0	1
	Totals		2	1	0	1

I Played in India.   Z Played in Zimbabwe.

HIGHEST INNINGS TOTALS

For India: 536-7 dec. at Delhi 1992-93

For Zimbabwe: 456 at Harare 1992-93

INDIVIDUAL HUNDREDS

For India (2)

V. G. Kambli (1)	**S. V. Manjrekar** (1)
227† Delhi 1992-93	104† Harare 1992-93

For Zimbabwe (2)

A. Flower (1)	**D. L. Houghton** (1)
115 Delhi 1992-93	121† Harare 1992-93

† *Signifies hundred on first appearance in India–Zimbabwe Tests.*

HUNDRED PARTNERSHIPS

For India

107 for 2nd	N. S. Sidhu and V. G. Kambli at Delhi.....................	1992-93
137 for 3rd	V. G. Kambli and S. R. Tendulkar at Delhi	1992-93
107 for 4th	V. G. Kambli and M. Azharuddin at Delhi.................	1992-93

For Zimbabwe

100 for 1st	K. J. Arnott and G. W. Flower at Harare...................	1992-93
192 for 4th	G. W. Flower and A. Flower at Delhi......................	1992-93
165 for 6th†	D. L. Houghton and A. Flower at Harare	1992-93

† *Denotes record partnership against all countries.*

BEST MATCH BOWLING ANALYSES

For India

8-160 (3-90, 5-70)	A. Kumble, Delhi............................	1992-93

For Zimbabwe

5-86 (5-86)	A. J. Traicos, Harare........................	1992-93

PAKISTAN v SRI LANKA

Season	Pakistan	Captains Sri Lanka	T	P	SL	D
1981-82*P*	Javed Miandad	B. Warnapura[1]	3	2	0	1
1985-86*P*	Javed Miandad	L. R. D. Mendis	3	2	0	1
1985-86*S*	Imran Khan	L. R. D. Mendis	3	1	1	1
1991-92*P*	Imran Khan	P. A. de Silva	3	1	0	2
1994-95*S*†	Salim Malik	A. Ranatunga	2	2	0	0
1995-96*P*	Ramiz Raja	A. Ranatunga	3	1	2	0
1996-97*S*	Ramiz Raja	A. Ranatunga	2	0	0	2
	In Pakistan		12	6	2	4
	In Sri Lanka		7	3	1	3
	Totals.....................		19	9	3	7

P Played in Pakistan. S Played in Sri Lanka.

† *One Test was cancelled owing to the threat of civil disturbances following a general election.*

Note: The following deputised for the official touring captain:
[1] L. R. D. Mendis (Second).

HIGHEST INNINGS TOTALS

For Pakistan in Pakistan: 555-3 at Faisalabad.........................		1985-86
in Sri Lanka: 390 at Colombo (PSS).....................		1994-95
For Sri Lanka in Pakistan: 479 at Faisalabad		1985-86
in Sri Lanka: 423-8 dec. at Colombo (RPS)		1996-97

LOWEST INNINGS TOTALS

For Pakistan in Pakistan: 209 at Faisalabad		1995-96
in Sri Lanka: 132 at Colombo (CCC)		1985-86

For Sri Lanka in Pakistan: 149 at Karachi 1981-82
in Sri Lanka: 71 at Kandy................................. 1994-95

INDIVIDUAL HUNDREDS

For Pakistan (13)

Haroon Rashid (1)	**Mohsin Khan (1)**	**Saeed Anwar (1)**
153† Karachi.... 1981-82	129 Lahore.... 1981-82	136† Colombo (PSS) 1994-95
Ijaz Ahmed, sen. (1)	**Moin Khan (1)**	**Salim Malik (3)**
113† Colombo (RPS) 1996-97	117* Sialkot.... 1995-96	100*† Karachi.... 1981-82
Inzamam-ul-Haq (1)	**Qasim Omar (1)**	101 Sialkot.... 1991-92
100* Kandy..... 1994-95	206† Faisalabad .. 1985-86	155 Colombo (SSC) 1996-97
Javed Miandad (1)	**Ramiz Raja (1)**	**Zaheer Abbas (1)**
203* Faisalabad .. 1985-86	122 Colombo (PSS) 1985-86	134† Lahore.... 1981-82

For Sri Lanka (14)

P. A. de Silva (7)	**R. L. Dias (1)**	**H. P. Tillekeratne (2)**
122† Faisalabad .. 1985-86	109 Lahore.... 1981-82	115 Faisalabad .. 1995-96
105 Karachi.... 1985-86	**A. P. Gurusinha (1)**	103 Colombo (RPS) 1996-97
127 Colombo (PSS) 1994-95	116* Colombo (PSS) 1985-86	**S. Wettimuny (1)**
105 Faisalabad .. 1995-96	**S. T. Jayasuriya (1)**	157 Faisalabad .. 1981-82
168 Colombo (RPS) 1996-97	113 Colombo (SSC) 1996-97	
138*} Colombo (SSC) 1996-97	**A. Ranatunga (1)**	
103*}	135* Colombo (PSS) 1985-86	

† Signifies hundred on first appearance in Pakistan–Sri Lanka Tests.

RECORD PARTNERSHIPS FOR EACH WICKET

For Pakistan

128 for 1st {	Ramiz Raja and Shoaib Mohammad at Sialkot	1991-92
	Saeed Anwar and Aamir Sohail at Colombo (PSS)	1994-95
151 for 2nd	Mohsin Khan and Majid Khan at Lahore................	1981-82
397 for 3rd	Qasim Omar and Javed Miandad at Faisalabad............	1985-86
162 for 4th	Salim Malik and Javed Miandad at Karachi..............	1981-82
132 for 5th	Salim Malik and Imran Khan at Sialkot...............	1991-92
100 for 6th	Zaheer Abbas and Imran Khan at Lahore...............	1981-82
104 for 7th	Haroon Rashid and Tahir Naqqash at Karachi............	1981-82
38 for 8th	Saqlain Mushtaq and Mushtaq Ahmed at Colombo (RPS).......	1996-97
127 for 9th	Haroon Rashid and Rashid Khan at Karachi	1981-82
65 for 10th	Moin Khan and Aamir Nazir at Sialkot................	1995-96

For Sri Lanka

157 for 1st	S. T. Jayasuriya and R. P. Arnold at Colombo (SSC)..........	1996-97
217 for 2nd	S. Wettimuny and R. L. Dias at Faisalabad	1981-82
176 for 3rd	U. C. Hathurusinghe and P. A. de Silva at Faisalabad	1995-96
240* for 4th†	A. P. Gurusinha and A. Ranatunga at Colombo (PSS)	1985-86
125 for 5th	A. Ranatunga and H. P. Tillekeratne at Peshawar	1995-96
121 for 6th	A. Ranatunga and P. A. de Silva at Faisalabad	1985-86
131 for 7th	H. P. Tillekeratne and R. S. Kalpage at Kandy	1994-95
76 for 8th†	P. A. de Silva and W. P. U. J. C. Vaas at Colombo (SSC).......	1996-97
52 for 9th	P. A. de Silva and R. J. Ratnayake at Faisalabad.........	1985-86
36 for 10th	R. J. Ratnayake and R. G. C. E. Wijesuriya at Faisalabad.	1985-86

† Denotes record partnership against all countries.

TEN WICKETS OR MORE IN A MATCH

For Pakistan (2)

14-116 (8-58, 6-58)	Imran Khan, Lahore	1981-82
11-119 (6-34, 5-85)	Waqar Younis, Kandy	1994-95

Note: The best match figures by a Sri Lankan bowler are 9-162 (4-103, 5-59), D. S. de Silva at Faisalabad, 1981-82.

PAKISTAN v ZIMBABWE

		Captains				
Season	Pakistan	Zimbabwe	T	P	Z	D
1993-94P	Wasim Akram[1]	A. Flower	3	2	0	1
1994-95Z	Salim Malik	A. Flower	3	2	1	0
1996-97P	Wasim Akram	A. D. R. Campbell	2	1	0	1
1997-98Z	Rashid Latif	A. D. R. Campbell	2	1	0	1
	In Pakistan		5	3	0	2
	In Zimbabwe		5	3	1	1
	Totals		10	6	1	3

P Played in Pakistan. Z Played in Zimbabwe.

Note: The following was appointed by the home authority for only a minor proportion of the series:

[1]Waqar Younis (First).

HIGHEST INNINGS TOTALS

For Pakistan in Pakistan: 553 at Sheikhupura		1996-97
in Zimbabwe: 354 at Harare		1997-98
For Zimbabwe in Pakistan: 375 at Sheikhupura		1996-97
in Zimbabwe: 544-4 dec. at Harare		1994-95

LOWEST INNINGS TOTALS

For Pakistan in Pakistan: 147 at Lahore		1993-94
in Zimbabwe: 158 at Harare		1994-95
For Zimbabwe in Pakistan: 133 at Faisalabad		1996-97
in Zimbabwe: 139 at Harare		1994-95

INDIVIDUAL HUNDREDS

For Pakistan (3)

Inzamam-ul-Haq (1)		**Mohammad Wasim** (1)		**Wasim Akram** (1)	
101 Harare	1994-95	192† Harare	1997-98	257* Sheikhupura .	1996-97

For Zimbabwe (8)

A. Flower (2)		110 Sheikhupura .	1996-97	**P. A. Strang** (1)	
156 Harare	1994-95	156*‡ Bulawayo . .	1997-98	106* Sheikhupura .	1996-97
100* Bulawayo . .	1997-98	**M. W. Goodwin** (1)		**G. J. Whittall** (1)	
G. W. Flower (3)		166*† Bulawayo . .	1997-98	113* Harare	1994-95
201* Harare	1994-95				

† Signifies hundred on first appearance in Pakistan–Zimbabwe Tests.
‡ Carried his bat.

RECORD PARTNERSHIPS FOR EACH WICKET

For Pakistan

95	for 1st	Aamir Sohail and Shoaib Mohammad at Karachi (DS).........	1993-94
118*	for 2nd	Shoaib Mohammad and Asif Mujtaba at Lahore..............	1993-94
83	for 3rd	Shoaib Mohammad and Javed Miandad at Karachi (DS).......	1993-94
116	for 4th	Inzamam-ul-Haq and Ijaz Ahmed, sen. at Harare............	1994-95
110	for 5th	Yousuf Youhana and Moin Khan at Bulawayo	1997-98
96	for 6th	Inzamam-ul-Haq and Rashid Latif at Harare...............	1994-95
120	for 7th	Ijaz Ahmed, sen. and Inzamam-ul-Haq at Harare...........	1994-95
313	for 8th†	Wasim Akram and Saqlain Mushtaq at Sheikhupura	1996-97
147	for 9th	Mohammad Wasim and Mushtaq Ahmed at Harare	1997-98
27	for 10th	Inzamam-ul-Haq and Aamir Nazir at Harare................	1994-95

For Zimbabwe

47	for 1st	G. W. Flower and G. J. Rennie at Harare	1997-98
135	for 2nd†	M. H. Dekker and A. D. R. Campbell at Rawalpindi.........	1993-94
84	for 3rd	G. W. Flower and D. L. Houghton at Sheikhupura	1996-97
269	for 4th†	G. W. Flower and A. Flower at Bulawayo	1994-95
277*	for 5th†	M. W. Goodwin and A. Flower at Bulawayo	1997-98
72	for 6th	M. H. Dekker and G. J. Whittall at Rawalpindi	1993-94
131	for 7th†	G. W. Flower and P. A. Strang at Sheikhupura	1996-97
110	for 8th†	G. J. Whittall and B. C. Strang at Harare	1997-98
87	for 9th†	P. A. Strang and B. C. Strang at Sheikhupura.............	1996-97
29	for 10th	E. A. Brandes and S. G. Peall at Rawalpindi	1993-94

† *Denotes record partnership against all countries.*

TEN WICKETS OR MORE IN A MATCH

For Pakistan (2)

13-135 (7-91, 6-44)†	Waqar Younis, Karachi (DS)	1993-94
10-106 (6-48, 4-58)	Wasim Akram, Faisalabad.........................	1996-97

Note: The best match figures for Zimbabwe are 9-105 (6-90, 3-15) by H. H. Streak at Harare, 1994-95.

† *Signifies ten wickets or more on first appearance in Pakistan–Zimbabwe Tests.*

SRI LANKA v ZIMBABWE

		Captains				
Season	Sri Lanka	Zimbabwe	T	SL	Z	D
1994-95Z	A. Ranatunga	A. Flower	3	0	0	3
1996-97S	A. Ranatunga	A. D. R. Campbell	2	2	0	0
1997-98S	A. Ranatunga	A. D. R. Campbell	2	2	0	0
In Sri Lanka			4	4	0	0
In Zimbabwe.................			3	0	0	3
Totals......................			7	4	0	3

S Played in Sri Lanka.   Z Played in Zimbabwe.

HIGHEST INNINGS TOTALS

For Sri Lanka: 469-9 dec. at Kandy....................................		1997-98
For Zimbabwe: 462-9 dec. at Bulawayo.................................		1994-95

LOWEST INNINGS TOTALS

For Sri Lanka: 218 at Bulawayo 1994-95
For Zimbabwe: 127 at Colombo (RPS) 1996-97

INDIVIDUAL HUNDREDS

For Sri Lanka (7)

M. S. Atapattu (1)		**A. P. Gurusinha** (1)		100* Bulawayo .. 1994-95
223† Kandy..... 1997-98	128† Harare..... 1994-95	**H. P. Tillekeratne** (2)
P. A. de Silva (1)	**S. Ranatunga** (2)	116 Harare..... 1994-95
143* Colombo (SSC) 1997-98	118† Harare..... 1994-95	126* Colombo (SSC) 1996-97

For Zimbabwe (3)

A. Flower (1)	**D. L. Houghton** (2)
105* Colombo (SSC) 1997-98	266 Bulawayo .. 1994-95
	142 Harare..... 1994-95

† *Signifies hundred on first appearance in Sri Lanka–Zimbabwe Tests.*

HUNDRED PARTNERSHIPS

For Sri Lanka

217	for 2nd†	A. P. Gurusinha and S. Ranatunga at Harare	1994-95
140	for 3rd	M. S. Atapattu and P. A. de Silva at Kandy.................	1997-98
105	for 3rd	S. T. Jayasuriya and P. A. de Silva at Colombo (SSC)..........	1997-98
114	for 5th	A. P. Gurusinha and H. P. Tillekeratne at Colombo (SSC)	1996-97
189*	for 6th†	P. A. de Silva and A. Ranatunga at Colombo (SSC)	1997-98
143	for 6th	A. Ranatunga and R. S. Kaluwitharana at Colombo (RPS)	1996-97

For Zimbabwe

113 for 1st	G. W. Flower and M. H. Dekker at Harare	1994-95
194 for 3rd†	A. D. R. Campbell and D. L. Houghton at Harare	1994-95
121 for 4th	D. L. Houghton and A. Flower at Bulawayo	1994-95
100 for 6th	D. L. Houghton and W. R. James at Bulawayo...............	1994-95

† *Denotes record partnership against all countries.*

TEN WICKETS OR MORE IN A MATCH

For Sri Lanka (1)

12-117 (5-23, 7-94)   M. Muralitharan, Kandy....................... 1997-98

Note: The best match figures for Zimbabwe are 6-112 (2-28, 4-84) by H. H. Streak at Colombo (SSC), 1997-98.

TEST MATCH GROUNDS

In Chronological Sequence

City and Ground	First Test Match		Tests
1 Melbourne, Melbourne Cricket Ground	March 15, 1877	A v E	90
2 London, Kennington Oval	September 6, 1880	E v A	81
3 Sydney, Sydney Cricket Ground (No. 1)	February 17, 1882	A v E	84
4 Manchester, Old Trafford	July 11, 1884	E v A	64

	City and Ground	*First Test Match*		*Tests*
5	London, Lord's	July 21, 1884	E v A	97
6	Adelaide, Adelaide Oval	December 12, 1884	A v E	56
7	Port Elizabeth, St George's Park	March 12, 1889	SA v E	16
8	Cape Town, Newlands	March 25, 1889	SA v E	30
9	Johannesburg, Old Wanderers	March 2, 1896	SA v E	22
	Now the site of Johannesburg Railway Station.			
10	Nottingham, Trent Bridge	June 1, 1899	E v A	46
11	Leeds, Headingley	June 29, 1899	E v A	60
12	Birmingham, Edgbaston	May 29, 1902	E v A	34
13	Sheffield, Bramall Lane	July 3, 1902	E v A	1
	Sheffield United Football Club have built a stand over the cricket pitch.			
14	Durban, Lord's	January 21, 1910	SA v E	4
	Ground destroyed and built on.			
15	Durban, Kingsmead	January 18, 1923	SA v E	25
16	Brisbane, Exhibition Ground	November 30, 1928	A v E	2
	No longer used for cricket.			
17	Christchurch, Lancaster Park	January 10, 1930	NZ v E	35
18	Bridgetown, Kensington Oval	January 11, 1930	WI v E	34
19	Wellington, Basin Reserve	January 24, 1930	NZ v E	32
20	Port-of-Spain, Queen's Park Oval	February 1, 1930	WI v E	47
21	Auckland, Eden Park	February 17, 1930	NZ v E	40
22	Georgetown, Bourda	February 21, 1930	WI v E	25
23	Kingston, Sabina Park	April 3, 1930	WI v E	33
24	Brisbane, Woolloongabba	November 27, 1931	A v SA	40
25	Bombay, Gymkhana Ground	December 15, 1933	I v E	1
	No longer used for first-class cricket.			
26	Calcutta, Eden Gardens	January 5, 1934	I v E	29
27	Madras (*now Chennai*),			
	Chepauk (Chidambaram Stadium)	February 10, 1934	I v E	23
28	Delhi, Feroz Shah Kotla	November 10, 1948	I v WI	24
29	Bombay, Brabourne Stadium	December 9, 1948	I v WI	17
	Rarely used for first-class cricket.			
30	Johannesburg, Ellis Park	December 27, 1948	SA v E	6
	Mainly a rugby stadium, no longer used for cricket.			
31	Kanpur, Green Park (Modi Stadium)	January 12, 1952	I v E	17
32	Lucknow, University Ground	October 25, 1952	I v P	1
	Ground destroyed, now partly under a river bed.			
33	Dacca, Dacca Stadium	January 1, 1955	P v I	7
	Ceased staging Tests after East Pakistan seceded and became Bangladesh.			
34	Bahawalpur, Dring (now Bahawal) Stadium	January 15, 1955	P v I	1
	Still used for first-class cricket.			
35	Lahore, Lawrence Gardens (Bagh-i-Jinnah)	January 29, 1955	P v I	3
	Still used for club and occasional first-class matches.			
36	Peshawar, Services Ground	February 13, 1955	P v I	1
	Superseded by new stadium.			
37	Karachi, National Stadium	February 26, 1955	P v I	32
38	Dunedin, Carisbrook	March 11, 1955	NZ v E	10
39	Hyderabad, Fateh Maidan			
	(Lal Bahadur Stadium)	November 19, 1955	I v NZ	3
40	Madras, Corporation Stadium	January 6, 1956	I v NZ	9
	Superseded by rebuilt Chepauk Stadium.			
41	Johannesburg, Wanderers	December 24, 1956	SA v E	19
42	Lahore, Gaddafi Stadium	November 21, 1959	P v A	28
43	Rawalpindi, Pindi Club Ground	March 27, 1965	P v NZ	1
	Superseded by new stadium.			
44	Nagpur, Vidarbha C.A. Ground	October 3, 1969	I v NZ	5
45	Perth, Western Australian C.A. Ground	December 11, 1970	A v E	25
46	Hyderabad, Niaz Stadium	March 16, 1973	P v E	5

City and Ground	First Test Match	Tests
47 Bangalore, Karnataka State C.A. Ground (Chinnaswamy Stadium)	November 22, 1974	I v WI	12
48 Bombay (*now Mumbai*), Wankhede Stadium	January 23, 1975	I v WI	16
49 Faisalabad, Iqbal Stadium	October 16, 1978	P v I	19
50 Napier, McLean Park	February 16, 1979	NZ v P	3
51 Multan, Ibn-e-Qasim Bagh Stadium	December 30, 1980	P v WI	1
52 St John's (Antigua), Recreation Ground	March 27, 1981	WI v E	13
53 Colombo, P. Saravanamuttu Stadium	February 17, 1982	SL v E	6
54 Kandy, Asgiriya Stadium	April 22, 1983	SL v A	7
55 Jullundur, Burlton Park	September 24, 1983	I v P	1
56 Ahmedabad, Gujarat Stadium	November 12, 1983	I v WI	4
57 Colombo, Sinhalese Sports Club Ground	March 16, 1984	SL v NZ	12
58 Colombo, Colombo Cricket Club Ground	March 24, 1984	SL v NZ	3
59 Sialkot, Jinnah Stadium	October 27, 1985	P v SL	4
60 Cuttack, Barabati Stadium	January 4, 1987	I v SL	2
61 Jaipur, Sawai Mansingh Stadium	February 21, 1987	I v P	1
62 Hobart, Bellerive Oval	December 16, 1989	A v SL	4
63 Chandigarh, Sector 16 Stadium	November 23, 1990	I v SL	1
Superseded by Mohali ground.			
64 Hamilton, Seddon Park	February 22, 1991	NZ v SL	5
Ground also known under various sponsors' names.			
65 Gujranwala, Municipal Stadium	December 20, 1991	P v SL	1
66 Colombo, R. Premadasa (Khettarama) Stadium	August 28, 1992	SL v A	5
67 Moratuwa, Tyronne Fernando Stadium	September 8, 1992	SL v A	4
68 Harare, Harare Sports Club	October 18, 1992	Z v I	10
69 Bulawayo, Bulawayo Athletic Club	November 1, 1992	Z v NZ	1
Superseded by Queens Sports Club ground.			
70 Karachi, Defence Stadium	December 1, 1993	P v Z	1
71 Rawalpindi, Rawalpindi Cricket Stadium	December 9, 1993	P v Z	5
72 Lucknow, K. D. "Babu" Singh Stadium	January 18, 1994	I v SL	1
73 Bulawayo, Queens Sports Club	October 20, 1994	Z v SL	5
74 Mohali, Punjab Cricket Association Stadium	December 10, 1994	I v WI	2
75 Peshawar, Arbab Niaz Stadium	September 8, 1995	P v SL	2
76 Centurion (*formerly Verwoerdburg*), Centurion Park	November 16, 1995	SA v E	3
77 Sheikhupura, Municipal Stadium	October 17, 1996	P v Z	2
78 St Vincent, Arnos Vale	June 20, 1997	WI v SL	1
79 Galle, International Stadium	June 3, 1998	SL v NZ	1

FAMILIES IN TEST CRICKET

GRANDFATHER, FATHER AND SON

G. A. Headley (West Indies, 22 Tests, 1929-30–1953-54), R. G. A. Headley (West Indies, 2 Tests, 1973) and D. W. Headley (England, 10 Tests, 1997–1998).

FATHERS AND SONS

England

A. R. Butcher (1 Test, 1979) and M. A. Butcher (14 Tests, 1997–1998).
M. C. Cowdrey (114 Tests, 1954-55–1974-75) and C. S. Cowdrey (6 Tests, 1984-85–1988).
J. Hardstaff (5 Tests, 1907-08) and J. Hardstaff jun. (23 Tests, 1935–1948).
L. Hutton (79 Tests, 1937–1954-55) and R. A. Hutton (5 Tests, 1971).
F. T. Mann (5 Tests, 1922-23) and F. G. Mann (7 Tests, 1948-49–1949).
J. H. Parks (1 Test, 1937) and J. M. Parks (46 Tests, 1954–1967-68).
M. J. Stewart (8 Tests, 1962–1963-64) and A. J. Stewart (81 Tests, 1989-90–1998).
F. W. Tate (1 Test, 1902) and M. W. Tate (39 Tests, 1924–1935).
C. L. Townsend (2 Tests, 1899) and D. C. H. Townsend (3 Tests, 1934-35).

Australia

E. J. Gregory (1 Test, 1876-77) and S. E. Gregory (58 Tests, 1890–1912).

South Africa

F. Hearne (4 Tests, 1891-92–1895-96) and G. A. L. Hearne (3 Tests, 1922-23–1924).
  F. Hearne also played 2 Tests for England in 1888-89.

J. D. Lindsay (3 Tests, 1947) and D. T. Lindsay (19 Tests, 1963-64–1969-70).

A. W. Nourse (45 Tests, 1902-03–1924) and A. D. Nourse (34 Tests, 1935–1951).

P. M. Pollock (28 Tests, 1961-62–1969-70) and S. M. Pollock (25 Tests, 1995-96–1998).

L. R. Tuckett (1 Test, 1913-14) and L. Tuckett (9 Tests, 1947–1948-49).

West Indies

O. C. Scott (8 Tests, 1928–1930-31) and A. P. H. Scott (1 Test, 1952-53).

New Zealand

W. M. Anderson (1 Test, 1945-46) and R. W. Anderson (9 Tests, 1976-77–1978).

W. P. Bradburn (2 Tests, 1963-64) and G. E. Bradburn (4 Tests, 1990-91).

B. L. Cairns (43 Tests, 1973-74–1985-86) and C. L. Cairns (33 Tests, 1989-90–1997-98).

W. A. Hadlee (11 Tests, 1937–1950-51) and D. R. Hadlee (26 Tests, 1969–1977-78); R. J. Hadlee
  (86 Tests, 1972-73–1990).

P. G. Z. Harris (9 Tests, 1955-56–1964-65) and C. Z. Harris (14 Tests, 1993-94–1997-98).

H. G. Vivian (7 Tests, 1931–1937) and G. E. Vivian (5 Tests, 1964-65–1971-72).

India

L. Amarnath (24 Tests, 1933-34–1952-53) and M. Amarnath (69 Tests, 1969-70–1987-88);
S. Amarnath (10 Tests, 1975-76–1978-79).

D. K. Gaekwad (11 Tests, 1952–1960-61) and A. D. Gaekwad (40 Tests, 1974-75–1984-85).

Nawab of Pataudi (Iftikhar Ali Khan) (3 Tests, 1946) and Nawab of Pataudi (Mansur Ali Khan)
  (46 Tests, 1961-62–1974-75).
  Nawab of Pataudi sen. also played 3 Tests for England, 1932-33–1934.

V. L. Manjrekar (55 Tests, 1951-52–1964-65) and S. V. Manjrekar (37 Tests, 1987-88–1996-97).

V. Mankad (44 Tests, 1946–1958-59) and A. V. Mankad (22 Tests, 1969-70–1977-78).

Pankaj Roy (43 Tests, 1951-52–1960-61) and Pranab Roy (2 Tests, 1981-82).

India and Pakistan

M. Jahangir Khan (4 Tests, 1932–1936) and Majid Khan (63 Tests, 1964-65–1982-83).

S. Wazir Ali (7 Tests, 1932–1936) and Khalid Wazir (2 Tests, 1954).

Pakistan

Hanif Mohammad (55 Tests, 1954–1969-70) and Shoaib Mohammad (45 Tests, 1983-84–1995-96).

Nazar Mohammad (5 Tests, 1952-53) and Mudassar Nazar (76 Tests, 1976-77–1988-89).

GRANDFATHER AND GRANDSONS

Australia

V. Y. Richardson (19 Tests, 1924-25–1935-36) and G. S. Chappell (87 Tests, 1970-71–1983-84);
  I. M. Chappell (75 Tests, 1964-65–1979-80); T. M. Chappell (3 Tests, 1981).

GREAT-GRANDFATHER AND GREAT-GRANDSON

Australia

W. H. Cooper (2 Tests, 1881-82 and 1884-85) and A. P. Sheahan (31 Tests, 1967-68–1973-74).

BROTHERS IN SAME TEST TEAM

England
E. M., G. F. and W. G. Grace: 1 Test, 1880; C. T. and G. B. Studd: 4 Tests, 1882-83; A. and
G. G. Hearne: 1 Test, 1891-92. *F. Hearne, their brother, played in this match for South Africa*;
D. W. and P. E. Richardson: 1 Test, 1957; A. J. and B. C. Hollioake: 1 Test, 1997.

Australia
E. J. and D. W. Gregory: 1 Test, 1876-77; C. and A. C. Bannerman: 1 Test, 1878-79; G. and
W. F. Giffen: 2 Tests, 1891-92; G. H. S. and A. E. Trott: 3 Tests, 1894-95; I. M. and G. S.
Chappell: 43 Tests, 1970-71–1979-80; S. R. and M. E. Waugh: 60 Tests, 1990-91–1997-98 – the
only instance of twins appearing together.

South Africa
S. J. and S. D. Snooke: 1 Test, 1907; D. and H. W. Taylor: 2 Tests, 1913-14; R. H. M. and
P. A. M. Hands: 1 Test, 1913-14; E. A. B. and A. M. B. Rowan: 9 Tests, 1948-49–1951;
P. M. and R. G. Pollock: 23 Tests, 1963-64–1969-70; A. J. and D. B. Pithey: 5 Tests, 1963-64;
P. N. and G. Kirsten (half-brothers): 7 Tests, 1993-94–1994.

West Indies
G. C. and R. S. Grant: 4 Tests, 1934-35; J. B. and V. H. Stollmeyer: 1 Test, 1939; D. St E. and
E. St E. Atkinson: 1 Test, 1957-58.

New Zealand
D. R. and R. J. Hadlee: 10 Tests, 1973–1977-78; H. J. and G. P. Howarth: 4 Tests, 1974-75–
1976-77; J. M. and N. M. Parker: 3 Tests, 1976-77; B. P. and J. G. Bracewell: 1 Test, 1980-81;
J. J. and M. D. Crowe: 34 Tests, 1983–1989-90.

India
S. Wazir Ali and S. Nazir Ali: 2 Tests, 1932–1933-34; L. Ramji and Amar Singh: 1 Test,
1933-34; C. K. and C. S. Nayudu: 4 Tests, 1933-34–1936; A. G. Kripal Singh and A. G. Milkha
Singh: 1 Test, 1961-62; S. and M. Amarnath: 8 Tests, 1975-76–1978-79.

Pakistan
Wazir and Hanif Mohammad: 18 Tests, 1952-53–1959-60; Wazir and Mushtaq Mohammad:
1 Test, 1958-59; Hanif and Mushtaq Mohammad: 19 Tests, 1960-61–1969-70; Hanif, Mushtaq
and Sadiq Mohammad: 1 Test, 1969-70; Mushtaq and Sadiq Mohammad: 26 Tests, 1969-70–
1978-79; Wasim and Ramiz Raja: 2 Tests, 1983-84.

Sri Lanka
M. D. and S. Wettimuny: 2 Tests, 1982-83; A. and D. Ranatunga: 2 Tests, 1989-90; A. and
S. Ranatunga: 8 Tests, 1994-95–1996-97.

Zimbabwe
A. and G. W. Flower: 30 Tests, 1992-93–1997-98; J. A. and G. J. Rennie: 1 Test, 1997-98;
P. A. and B. C. Strang: 12 Tests, 1994-95–1997-98.

LIMITED-OVERS INTERNATIONAL RECORDS

Note: This section covers all limited-overs internationals up to August 20, 1998.

Limited-overs international matches do not have first-class status.

SUMMARY OF ALL LIMITED-OVERS INTERNATIONALS

1970-71 to 1998

Team	Opponents	Matches	E	A	SA	WI	NZ	I	P	SL	Z	Ass	Tied	NR
England	Australia	60	29	29	–	–	–	–	–	–	–	–	1	1
	South Africa	16	6	–	10	–	–	–	–	–	–	–	–	–
	West Indies	58	25	–	–	31	–	–	–	–	–	–	–	2
	New Zealand	47	23	–	–	–	20	–	–	–	–	–	1	3
	India	33	19	–	–	–	–	13	–	–	–	–	–	1
	Pakistan	41	26	–	–	–	–	–	14	–	–	–	–	1
	Sri Lanka	14	9	–	–	–	–	–	–	5	–	–	–	–
	Zimbabwe	6	1	–	–	–	–	–	–	–	5	–	–	–
	Associates	4	4	–	–	–	–	–	–	–	–	0	–	–
Australia	South Africa	37	–	18	19	–	–	–	–	–	–	–	–	–
	West Indies	84	–	33	–	49	–	–	–	–	–	–	1	1
	New Zealand	73	–	51	–	–	20	–	–	–	–	–	–	2
	India	53	–	29	–	–	–	21	–	–	–	–	–	3
	Pakistan	46	–	22	–	–	–	–	21	–	–	–	1	2
	Sri Lanka	35	–	22	–	–	–	–	–	11	–	–	–	2
	Zimbabwe	11	–	10	–	–	–	–	–	–	1	–	–	–
	Associates	3	–	3	–	–	–	–	–	–	–	0	–	–
South Africa	West Indies	10	–	–	5	5	–	–	–	–	–	–	–	–
	New Zealand	12	–	–	7	–	5	–	–	–	–	–	–	–
	India	27	–	–	18	–	–	8	–	–	–	–	–	1
	Pakistan	21	–	–	14	–	–	–	7	–	–	–	–	–
	Sri Lanka	14	–	–	7	–	–	–	–	6	–	–	–	1
	Zimbabwe	7	–	–	6	–	–	–	–	–	0	–	–	1
	Associates	3	–	–	3	–	–	–	–	–	–	0	–	–
West Indies	New Zealand	24	–	–	–	18	4	–	–	–	–	–	–	2
	India	56	–	–	–	36	–	19	–	–	–	–	1	–
	Pakistan	83	–	–	–	55	–	–	26	–	–	–	2	–
	Sri Lanka	29	–	–	–	20	–	–	–	8	–	–	–	1
	Zimbabwe	5	–	–	–	5	–	–	–	–	0	–	–	–
	Associates	1	–	–	–	0	–	–	–	–	–	1*	–	–
New Zealand	India	46	–	–	–	–	19	25	–	–	–	–	–	2
	Pakistan	48	–	–	–	–	18	–	28	–	–	–	1	1
	Sri Lanka	39	–	–	–	–	24	–	–	12	–	–	1	2
	Zimbabwe	16	–	–	–	–	12	–	–	–	3	–	1	–
	Associates	4	–	–	–	–	4	–	–	–	–	0	–	–
India	Pakistan	66	–	–	–	–	–	24	38	–	–	–	–	4
	Sri Lanka	55	–	–	–	–	–	28	–	22	–	–	–	5
	Zimbabwe	18	–	–	–	–	–	14	–	–	2	–	2	–
	Associates	13	–	–	–	–	–	12	–	–	–	1†	–	–
Pakistan	Sri Lanka	71	–	–	–	–	–	–	46	23	–	–	–	2
	Zimbabwe	16	–	–	–	–	–	–	14	–	1	–	1	–
	Associates	10	–	–	–	–	–	–	10	–	–	0	–	–
Sri Lanka	Zimbabwe	13	–	–	–	–	–	–	–	11	2	–	–	–
	Associates	7	–	–	–	–	–	–	–	7	–	0	–	–
Zimbabwe	Associates	8	–	–	–	–	–	–	–	–	7	0	–	1
Associate	Associates	5	–	–	–	–	–	–	–	–	–	5‡	–	–
		1,348	142	217	89	219	126	164	204	105	21	7	13	41

* *Kenya beat West Indies in the 1996 World Cup.*
† *Kenya beat India at Gwalior, 1997-98.*
‡ *United Arab Emirates beat Holland in the 1996 World Cup. Bangladesh met Kenya four times in 1997-98: Bangladesh won 1, Kenya won 3.*

Note: Current Associate Members of ICC who have played one-day internationals are Bangladesh, Canada, East Africa, Holland, Kenya and United Arab Emirates. Sri Lanka and Zimbabwe also played one-day internationals before being given Test status; these are not included among the Associates' results.

RESULTS SUMMARY OF ALL LIMITED-OVERS INTERNATIONALS

1970-71 to 1998 (1,348 matches)

	Matches	Won	Lost	Tied	No Result	% Won (excl. NR)
West Indies	350	219	121	4	6	63.66
South Africa	147	89	55	–	3	61.80
Australia	402	217	171	3	11	55.49
England	279	142	127	2	8	52.39
Pakistan	402	204	183	5	10	52.04
India	367	164	184	3	16	46.72
New Zealand	309	126	167	4	12	42.42
Sri Lanka	277	105	158	1	13	39.77
Kenya	20	5	14	–	1	26.31
Zimbabwe	100	21	73	4	2	21.42
United Arab Emirates	7	1	6	–	–	14.28
Bangladesh	25	1	24	–	–	4.00
Canada	3	–	3	–	–	–
East Africa	3	–	3	–	–	–
Holland	5	–	5	–	–	–

Note: ICC has ruled that matches abandoned and started again should now count as official internationals in their own right, contrary to its previous ruling.

MOST RUNS

	M	I	NO	R	HS	100s	Avge
D. L. Haynes (West Indies)....	238	237	28	8,648	152*	17	41.37
M. Azharuddin (India).......	291	268	51	8,285	153*	6	38.17
P. A. de Silva (Sri Lanka).....	241	234	24	7,684	145	11	36.59
Javed Miandad (Pakistan).....	233	218	41	7,381	119*	8	41.70
S. R. Tendulkar (India).......	196	189	17	7,070	143	17	41.10
Salim Malik (Pakistan).......	268	242	37	6,883	102	5	33.57
A. Ranatunga (Sri Lanka) .	244	230	45	6,872	131*	4	37.14
I. V. A. Richards (West Indies) .	187	167	24	6,721	189*	11	47.00
A. R. Border (Australia)......	273	252	39	6,524	127*	3	30.62
R. B. Richardson (West Indies) .	224	217	30	6,249	122	5	33.41
D. M. Jones (Australia)	164	161	25	6,068	145	7	44.61
D. C. Boon (Australia).......	181	177	16	5,964	122	5	37.04
Ramiz Raja (Pakistan).......	198	197	15	5,841	119*	9	32.09
S. R. Waugh (Australia)......	245	222	44	5,639	102*	1	31.67
Saeed Anwar (Pakistan)	153	151	14	5,551	194	15	40.51
B. C. Lara (West Indies)	130	128	12	5,448	169	12	46.96
M. E. Waugh (Australia)......	158	153	12	5,385	130	11	38.19
Ijaz Ahmed, sen. (Pakistan)....	204	187	25	5,171	139*	7	31.91
C. G. Greenidge (West Indies)..	128	127	13	5,134	133*	11	45.03
Inzamam-ul-Haq (Pakistan)....	163	153	21	5,084	137*	5	38.51
R. S. Mahanama (Sri Lanka)..	195	180	22	4,841	119*	4	30.63
M. D. Crowe (New Zealand)...	143	140	18	4,704	107*	4	38.55
S. T. Jayasuriya (Sri Lanka) ...	164	156	6	4,359	151*	7	29.06
G. R. Marsh (Australia)	117	115	9	4,357	126*	9	39.97
G. A. Gooch (England)	125	122	6	4,290	142	8	36.98

	M	I	NO	R	HS	100s	Avge
Aamir Sohail (Pakistan)	137	136	4	4,286	134	5	32.46
N. S. Sidhu (India)	131	122	8	4,267	134*	6	37.42
W. J. Cronje (South Africa)	142	132	23	4,262	112	2	39.10
C. L. Hooper (West Indies)	167	151	35	4,174	113*	5	35.98
K. Srikkanth (India)	146	145	4	4,092	123	4	29.02
A. J. Lamb (England)	122	118	16	4,010	118	4	39.31

Leading aggregate for Zimbabwe:

	M	I	NO	R	HS	100s	Avge
G. W. Flower	78	76	3	2,647	112	2	36.26

HIGHEST INDIVIDUAL SCORES

194	Saeed Anwar	Pakistan v India at Chennai	1996-97
189*	I. V. A. Richards	West Indies v England at Manchester	1984
188*	G. Kirsten	South Africa v UAE at Rawalpindi	1995-96
181	I. V. A. Richards	West Indies v Sri Lanka at Karachi	1987-88
175*	Kapil Dev	India v Zimbabwe at Tunbridge Wells	1983
171*	G. M. Turner	New Zealand v East Africa at Birmingham	1975
169*	D. J. Callaghan	South Africa v New Zealand at Verwoerdburg	1994-95
169	B. C. Lara	West Indies v Sri Lanka at Sharjah	1995-96
167*	R. A. Smith	England v Australia at Birmingham	1993
161	A. C. Hudson	South Africa v Holland at Rawalpindi	1995-96
158	D. I. Gower	England v New Zealand at Brisbane	1982-83
153*	I. V. A. Richards	West Indies v Australia at Melbourne	1979-80
153*	M. Azharuddin	India v Zimbabwe at Cuttack	1997-98
153	B. C. Lara	West Indies v Pakistan at Sharjah	1993-94
152*	D. L. Haynes	West Indies v India at Georgetown	1988-89
151*	S. T. Jayasuriya	Sri Lanka v India at Mumbai	1996-97

Highest individual scores for other Test-playing countries:

145	D. M. Jones	Australia v England at Brisbane	1990-91
145	R. T. Ponting	Australia v Zimbabwe at Delhi	1997-98
142	D. L. Houghton	Zimbabwe v New Zealand at Hyderabad, India	1987-88

MOST HUNDREDS

Total		*Opponents*									
		E	A	SA	WI	NZ	I	P	SL	Z	Ass
17	D. L. Haynes (West Indies)	2	6	0	–	2	2	4	1	0	–
17	S. R. Tendulkar (India)	0	4	1	1	2	–	2	4	1	2
15	Saeed Anwar (Pakistan)	0	1	0	2	2	3	–	6	1	0
12	B. C. Lara (West Indies)	1	2	2	–	2	0	4	1	0	0
11	P. A. de Silva (Sri Lanka)	0	2	0	0	0	3	3	–	2	1
11	C. G. Greenidge (West Indies)	0	1	–	–	3	3	2	1	1	–
11	I. V. A. Richards (West Indies)	3	3	–	–	1	3	0	1	0	–
11	M. E. Waugh (Australia)	1	–	2	1	3	1	1	1	0	1
9	G. R. Marsh (Australia)	1	–	0	2	2	3	1	0	0	–
9	Ramiz Raja (Pakistan)	1	0	0	2	3	0	–	3	0	0
8	G. A. Gooch (England)	–	4	0	1	1	1	1	0	0	0
8	Javed Miandad (Pakistan)	1	0	1	1	0	3	–	2	0	0
8	G. Kirsten (South Africa)	1	2	–	0	1	2	1	0	0	1
7	D. I. Gower (England)	–	2	–	0	3	0	1	1	–	0
7	Ijaz Ahmed, sen. (Pakistan)	0	0	2	0	0	2	–	1	1	1
7	S. T. Jayasuriya (Sri Lanka)	0	0	0	0	1	2	2	–	1	1
7	D. M. Jones (Australia)	3	–	0	0	2	0	1	1	0	0
7	Zaheer Abbas (Pakistan)	0	2	–	0	1	3	–	1	–	0

Note: Ass = Associate Members.

HIGHEST PARTNERSHIP FOR EACH WICKET

252	for 1st	S. C. Ganguly and S. R. Tendulkar	I v SL	Colombo (RPS)	1997-98
263	for 2nd	Aamir Sohail and Inzamam-ul-Haq	P v NZ	Sharjah	1993-94
230	for 3rd	Saeed Anwar and Ijaz Ahmed, sen.	P v I	Dhaka	1997-98
275*	for 4th	M. Azharuddin and A. Jadeja	I v Z	Cuttack	1997-98
223	for 5th	M. Azharuddin and A. Jadeja	I v SL	Colombo (RPS)	1997-98
154	for 6th	R. B. Richardson and P. J. L. Dujon	WI v P	Sharjah	1991-92
119	for 7th	T. Odoyo and A. Suji	K v Z	Nairobi (Aga Khan)	1997-98
119	for 8th	P. R. Reiffel and S. K. Warne	A v SA	Port Elizabeth	1993-94
126*	for 9th	Kapil Dev and S. M. H. Kirmani	I v Z	Tunbridge Wells	1983
106*	for 10th	I. V. A. Richards and M. A. Holding	WI v E	Manchester	1984

MOST WICKETS

	M	Balls	R	W	BB	4W/i	Avge
Wasim Akram (Pakistan)	247	12,764	8,116	356	5-15	20	22.79
Waqar Younis (Pakistan)	171	8,513	6,496	281	6-26	20	23.11
Kapil Dev (India)	225	11,202	6,945	253	5-43	4	27.45
C. E. L. Ambrose (West Indies) . .	151	8,051	4,720	204	5-17	10	23.13
C. A. Walsh (West Indies)	185	9,772	6,312	204	5-1	6	30.94
C. J. McDermott (Australia)	138	7,461	5,018	203	5-44	5	24.71
A. Kumble (India)	146	7,867	5,373	199	6-12	7	27.00
S. R. Waugh (Australia)	245	8,331	6,285	184	4-33	3	34.15
A. A. Donald (South Africa).	107	5,706	3,863	182	6-23	9	21.22
Imran Khan (Pakistan)	175	7,461	4,845	182	6-14	4	26.62
J. Srinath (India)	135	6,991	4,996	179	5-23	5	27.91
Aqib Javed (Pakistan)	157	7,730	5,531	177	7-37	6	31.24
R. J. Hadlee (New Zealand)	115	6,182	3,407	158	5-25	6	21.56
M. D. Marshall (West Indies)	136	7,175	4,233	157	4-18	6	26.96
M. Prabhakar (India).	130	6,360	4,535	157	5-33	6	28.88
Saqlain Mushtaq (Pakistan)	79	4,133	2,964	155	5-29	10	19.12
S. K. Warne (Australia)	96	5,397	3,704	150	5-32	10	24.69
C. L. Hooper (West Indies)	167	6,853	4,934	148	4-34	2	33.33
J. Garner (West Indies)	98	5,330	2,752	146	5-31	5	18.84
I. T. Botham (England)	116	6,271	4,139	145	4-31	3	28.54
S. T. Jayasuriya (Sri Lanka)	164	5,902	4,802	144	6-29	6	32.34
Mushtaq Ahmed (Pakistan).	130	6,723	4,842	144	5-36	3	33.62
M. A. Holding (West Indies)	102	5,473	3,034	142	5-26	6	21.36
E. J. Chatfield (New Zealand)	114	6,065	3,618	140	5-34	4	25.84
M. Muralitharan (Sri Lanka).	99	5,393	3,793	135	5-23	5	28.09
Abdul Qadir (Pakistan)	104	5,100	3,453	132	5-44	6	26.15
R. J. Shastri (India)	150	6,613	4,650	129	5-15	3	36.04
D. K. Morrison (New Zealand) . . .	96	4,586	3,470	126	5-34	3	27.53
I. R. Bishop (West Indies)	84	4,332	3,127	118	5-25	9	26.50
I. V. A. Richards (West Indies) . . .	187	5,644	4,228	118	6-41	3	35.83
P. A. J. DeFreitas (England)	103	5,712	3,775	115	4-35	1	32.82
M. C. Snedden (New Zealand) . . .	93	4,525	3,237	114	4-34	1	28.39
B. K. V. Prasad (India)	93	4,607	3,642	113	4-17	3	32.23
C. Z. Harris (New Zealand)	113	5,317	3,753	112	5-42	1	33.50
Mudassar Nazar (Pakistan).	122	4,855	3,432	111	5-28	2	30.91
W. P. U. J. C. Vaas (Sri Lanka) . .	89	4,207	2,841	111	4-20	3	25.59
S. P. O'Donnell (Australia).	87	4,350	3,102	108	5-13	6	28.72
D. K. Lillee (Australia)	63	3,593	2,145	103	5-34	6	20.82
C. Pringle (New Zealand)	64	3,314	2,455	103	5-45	3	23.83
W. K. M. Benjamin (West Indies) .	85	4,442	3,079	100	5-22	1	30.79
R. A. Harper (West Indies).	105	5,175	3,431	100	4-40	3	34.31

Leading aggregate for Zimbabwe:

	M	Balls	R	W	BB	4W/i	Avge
H. H. Streak	58	2,959	2,171	71	5-32	4	30.57

BEST ANALYSES

7-37	Aqib Javed	Pakistan v India at Sharjah	1991-92
7-51	W. W. Davis	West Indies v Australia at Leeds	1983
6-12	A. Kumble	India v West Indies at Calcutta	1993-94
6-14	G. J. Gilmour	Australia v England at Leeds	1975
6-14	Imran Khan	Pakistan v India at Sharjah	1984-85
6-15	C. E. H. Croft	West Indies v England at St Vincent	1980-81
6-20	B. C. Strang	Zimbabwe v Bangladesh at Nairobi (Aga Khan)	1997-98
6-23	A. A. Donald	South Africa v Kenya at Nairobi (Gymkhana)	1996-97
6-26	Waqar Younis	Pakistan v Sri Lanka at Sharjah	1989-90
6-29	B. P. Patterson	West Indies v India at Nagpur	1987-88
6-29	S. T. Jayasuriya	Sri Lanka v England at Moratuwa	1992-93
6-30	Waqar Younis	Pakistan v New Zealand at Auckland	1993-94
6-39	K. H. MacLeay	Australia v India at Nottingham	1983
6-41	I. V. A. Richards	West Indies v India at Delhi	1989-90
6-44	Waqar Younis	Pakistan v New Zealand at Sharjah	1996-97
6-49	L. Klusener	South Africa v Sri Lanka at Lahore	1997-98
6-50	A. H. Gray	West Indies v Australia at Port-of-Spain	1990-91

Best analyses for other Test-playing countries:

5-20	V. J. Marks	England v New Zealand at Wellington	1983-84
5-22	M. N. Hart	New Zealand v West Indies at Margao	1994-95

HAT-TRICKS

Jalal-ud-Din	Pakistan v Australia at Hyderabad	1982-83
B. A. Reid	Australia v New Zealand at Sydney	1985-86
Chetan Sharma	India v New Zealand at Nagpur	1987-88
Wasim Akram	Pakistan v West Indies at Sharjah	1989-90
Wasim Akram	Pakistan v Australia at Sharjah	1989-90
Kapil Dev	India v Sri Lanka at Calcutta	1990-91
Aqib Javed	Pakistan v India at Sharjah	1991-92
D. K. Morrison	New Zealand v India at Napier	1993-94
Waqar Younis	Pakistan v New Zealand at East London	1994-95
Saqlain Mushtaq†	Pakistan v Zimbabwe at Peshawar	1996-97
E. A. Brandes	Zimbabwe v England at Harare	1996-97
A. M. Stuart	Australia v Pakistan at Melbourne	1996-97

† *Four wickets in five balls.*

MOST DISMISSALS IN AN INNINGS

5 (all ct)	R. W. Marsh	Australia v England at Leeds	1981
5 (all ct)	R. G. de Alwis	Sri Lanka v Australia at Colombo (PSS)	1982-83
5 (all ct)	S. M. H. Kirmani	India v Zimbabwe at Leicester	1983
5 (3ct, 2st)	S. Viswanath	India v England at Sydney	1984-85
5 (3ct, 2st)	K. S. More	India v New Zealand at Sharjah	1987-88
5 (all ct)	H. P. Tillekeratne	Sri Lanka v Pakistan at Sharjah	1990-91
5 (3ct, 2st)	N. R. Mongia	India v New Zealand at Auckland	1993-94
5 (3ct, 2st)	A. C. Parore	New Zealand v West Indies at Margao	1994-95
5 (all ct)	D. J. Richardson	South Africa v Pakistan at Johannesburg	1994-95
5 (all ct)	Moin Khan	Pakistan v Zimbabwe at Harare	1994-95
5 (4ct, 1st)	R. S. Kaluwitharana	Sri Lanka v Pakistan at Sharjah	1994-95
5 (all ct)	D. J. Richardson	South Africa v Zimbabwe at Harare	1995-96
5 (all ct)	A. Flower	Zimbabwe v South Africa at Harare	1995-96
5 (all ct)	C. O. Browne	West Indies v Sri Lanka at Brisbane	1995-96
5 (4 ct, 1 st)	J. C. Adams	West Indies v Kenya at Pune	1995-96
5 (4 ct, 1 st)	Rashid Latif	Pakistan v New Zealand at Lahore	1995-96
5 (3 ct, 2 st)	N. R. Mongia	India v Pakistan at Toronto	1996-97
5 (all ct)	A. Flower	Zimbabwe v England at Harare	1996-97
5 (4 ct, 1 st)	R. D. Jacobs	West Indies v England at St Vincent	1997-98

MOST DISMISSALS IN A CAREER

	M	Ct	St	Total
I. A. Healy (Australia)	168	195	39	234
P. J. L. Dujon (West Indies)	169	183	21	204
D. J. Richardson (South Africa)	122	148	17	165
Moin Khan (Pakistan)	106	92	36	128
R. W. Marsh (Australia)	92	120	4	124
Rashid Latif (Pakistan)	101	94	28	122
N. R. Mongia (India)	103	81	36	117
R. S. Kaluwitharana (Sri Lanka)	96	62	42	104
Salim Yousuf (Pakistan)	86	81	22	103
A. J. Stewart (England)	105	92	11	103

MOST CATCHES IN AN INNINGS

(Excluding wicket-keepers)

5	J. N. Rhodes	South Africa v West Indies at Bombay	1993-94
4	Salim Malik	Pakistan v New Zealand at Sialkot	1984-85
4	S. M. Gavaskar	India v Pakistan at Sharjah	1984-85
4	R. B. Richardson	West Indies v England at Birmingham	1991
4	K. C. Wessels	South Africa v West Indies at Kingston	1991-92
4	M. A. Taylor	Australia v West Indies at Sydney	1992-93
4	C. L. Hooper	West Indies v Pakistan at Durban	1992-93
4	K. R. Rutherford	New Zealand v India at Napier	1994-95
4	P. V. Simmons	West Indies v Sri Lanka at Sharjah	1995-96
4	M. Azharuddin	India v Pakistan at Toronto	1997-98
4	S. R. Tendulkar	India v Pakistan at Dhaka	1997-98

Note: While fielding as substitute, J. G. Bracewell held 4 catches for New Zealand v Australia at Adelaide, 1980-81.

MOST CATCHES IN A CAREER

	M	Ct
M. Azharuddin (India)	291	140
A. R. Border (Australia)	273	127
I. V. A. Richards (West Indies)	187	101
R. S. Mahanama (Sri Lanka)	195	100
S. R. Waugh (Australia)	245	84
C. L. Hooper (West Indies)	167	81
Ijaz Ahmed, sen. (Pakistan)	204	77
Salim Malik (Pakistan)	268	76
R. B. Richardson (West Indies)	224	75
P. A. de Silva (Sri Lanka)	241	74
Kapil Dev (India)	225	71

1,000 RUNS AND 100 WICKETS

	M	R	W
I. T. Botham (England)	116	2,113	145
R. J. Hadlee (New Zealand)	115	1,751	158
C. Z. Harris (New Zealand)	113	2,064	112
C. L. Hooper (West Indies)	167	4,174	148
Imran Khan (Pakistan).	175	3,709	182
S. T. Jayasuriya (Sri Lanka)	164	4,359	144
Kapil Dev (India).	225	3,783	253
Mudassar Nazar (Pakistan)	122	2,653	111
S. P. O'Donnell (Australia).	87	1,242	108
M. Prabhakar (India).	130	1,858	157
I. V. A. Richards (West Indies)	187	6,721	118
R. J. Shastri (India).	150	3,108	129
Wasim Akram (Pakistan)	247	2,384	356
S. R. Waugh (Australia).	245	5,639	184

1,000 RUNS AND 100 DISMISSALS

	M	R	W
P. J. L. Dujon (West Indies)	169	1,945	204
I. A. Healy (Australia).	168	1,764	234
R. S. Kaluwitharana (Sri Lanka)	96	1,537	104
R. W. Marsh (Australia).	92	1,225	124
Moin Khan (Pakistan)	106	1,448	128
A. J. Stewart (England)	105	3,013	103

TEAM RECORDS

HIGHEST INNINGS TOTALS

398-5	(50 overs)	Sri Lanka v Kenya at Kandy	1995-96
371-9	(50 overs)	Pakistan v Sri Lanka at Nairobi (Gymkhana).	1996-97
363-7	(55 overs)	England v Pakistan at Nottingham.	1992
360-4	(50 overs)	West Indies v Sri Lanka at Karachi	1987-88
349-9	(50 overs)	Sri Lanka v Pakistan at Singapore	1995-96
348-8	(50 overs)	New Zealand v India at Nagpur	1995-96
347-3	(50 overs)	Kenya v Bangladesh at Nairobi (Gymkhana)	1997-98
339-4	(50 overs)	Sri Lanka v Pakistan at Mohali.	1996-97
338-4	(50 overs)	New Zealand v Bangladesh at Sharjah	1989-90
338-5	(60 overs)	Pakistan v Sri Lanka at Swansea.	1983
334-4	(60 overs)	England v India at Lord's	1975
333-7	(50 overs)	West Indies v Sri Lanka at Sharjah	1995-96
333-8	(45 overs)	West Indies v India at Jamshedpur	1983-84
333-9	(60 overs)	England v Sri Lanka at Taunton	1983
332-3	(50 overs)	Australia v Sri Lanka at Sharjah	1989-90
330-6	(60 overs)	Pakistan v Sri Lanka at Nottingham	1975

Highest totals by other Test-playing countries:

328-3	(50 overs)	South Africa v Holland at Rawalpindi	1995-96
316-7	(47.5 overs)	India v Pakistan at Dhaka	1997-98
312-4	(50 overs)	Zimbabwe v Sri Lanka at New Plymouth	1991-92

HIGHEST TOTALS BATTING SECOND

329	(49.3 overs)	Sri Lanka v West Indies at Sharjah	1995-96
		(Lost by 4 runs)	
316-7	(47.5 overs)	India v Pakistan at Dhaka	1997-98
		(Won by 3 wickets)	
315	(49.4 overs)	Pakistan v Sri Lanka at Singapore	1995-96
		(Lost by 34 runs)	
313-7	(49.2 overs)	Sri Lanka v Zimbabwe at New Plymouth	1991-92
		(Won by 3 wickets)	
301	(49.3 overs)	Sri Lanka v India at Colombo (RPS)	1997-98
		(Lost by 6 runs)	
300-7	(50 overs)	India v Sri Lanka at Colombo (RPS)	1997-98
		(Lost by 2 runs)	
300-6	(48 overs)	Pakistan v Sri Lanka at Kimberley	1997-98
		(Won by 4 wickets)	

HIGHEST MATCH AGGREGATES

664-19	(99.4 overs)	Pakistan v Sri Lanka at Singapore	1995-96
662-17	(99.3 overs)	Sri Lanka v West Indies at Sharjah	1995-96
660-19	(99.5 overs)	Pakistan v Sri Lanka at Nairobi (Gymkhana)	1996-97
652-12	(100 overs)	Sri Lanka v Kenya at Kandy	1995-96
630-12	(95.5 overs)	Pakistan v India at Dhaka	1997-98
626-14	(120 overs)	Pakistan v Sri Lanka at Swansea	1983
625-11	(99.2 overs)	Sri Lanka v Zimbabwe at New Plymouth	1991-92

LOWEST INNINGS TOTALS

43	(19.5 overs)	Pakistan v West Indies at Cape Town	1992-93
45	(40.3 overs)	Canada v England at Manchester	1979
55	(28.3 overs)	Sri Lanka v West Indies at Sharjah	1986-87
63	(25.5 overs)	India v Australia at Sydney	1980-81
64	(35.5 overs)	New Zealand v Pakistan at Sharjah	1985-86
69	(28 overs)	South Africa v Australia at Sydney	1993-94
70	(25.2 overs)	Australia v England at Birmingham	1977
70	(26.3 overs)	Australia v New Zealand at Adelaide	1985-86

Note: This section does not take into account those matches in which the number of overs was reduced.

Lowest totals by other Test-playing countries:

87	(29.3 overs)	West Indies v Australia at Sydney	1992-93
93	(36.2 overs)	England v Australia at Leeds	1975
94	(31.4 overs)	Zimbabwe v Pakistan at Sharjah	1996-97

LARGEST VICTORIES

232 runs	Australia (323-2 in 50 overs) v Sri Lanka (91 in 35.5 overs) at Adelaide .	1984-85
206 runs	New Zealand (276-7 in 50 overs) v Australia (70 in 26.3 overs) at Adelaide	1985-86
202 runs	England (334-4 in 60 overs) v India (132-3 in 60 overs) at Lord's	1975

By ten wickets: There have been ten instances of victory by ten wickets.

TIED MATCHES

West Indies 222-5 (50 overs) v Australia 222-9 (50 overs) at Melbourne 1983-84
England 226-5 (55 overs) v Australia 226-8 (55 overs) at Nottingham. 1989
West Indies 186-5 (39 overs) v Pakistan 186-9 (39 overs) at Lahore 1991-92
India 126 (47.4 overs) v West Indies 126 (41 overs) at Perth 1991-92
Australia 228-7 (50 overs) v Pakistan 228-9 (50 overs) at Hobart 1992-93
Pakistan 244-6 (50 overs) v West Indies 244-5 (50 overs) at Georgetown 1992-93
India 248-5 (50 overs) v Zimbabwe 248 (50 overs) at Indore 1993-94
Pakistan 161-9 (50 overs) v New Zealand 161 (49.4 overs) at Auckland 1993-94
Zimbabwe 219-9 (50 overs) v Pakistan 219 (49.5 overs) at Harare 1994-95
New Zealand 169-8 (50 overs) v Sri Lanka 169 (48 overs) at Sharjah 1996-97
Zimbabwe 236-8 (50 overs) v India 236 (49.5 overs) at Paarl 1996-97
New Zealand 237 (49.4 overs) v England 237-8 (50 overs) at Napier 1996-97
Zimbabwe 233-8 (50 overs) v New Zealand 233-9 (50 overs) at Bulawayo 1997-98

MOST APPEARANCES

(200 or more)

	Total	E	A	SA	WI	NZ	I	P	SL	Z	Ass
M. Azharuddin (I)	291	22	41	26	42	33	–	52	49	16	10
A. R. Border (A)	273	43	–	15	61	52	38	34	23	5	2
Salim Malik (P)	268	24	24	16	45	42	45	–	53	13	6
Wasim Akram (P)	247	25	29	16	54	26	34	–	41	16	6
S. R. Waugh (A)	245	26	–	35	39	49	39	28	20	7	2
A. Ranatunga (SL)	244	12	28	14	22	34	51	65	–	12	6
P. A. de Silva (SL)	241	10	29	14	25	30	49	65	–	12	7
D. L. Haynes (WI)	238	35	64	8	–	13	36	65	14	3	–
Javed Miandad (P)	233	27	35	3	64	24	35	–	35	6	4
Kapil Dev (I)	225	23	41	13	42	29	–	32	34	9	2
R. B. Richardson (WI) . .	224	35	51	9	–	11	32	61	21	3	1
Ijaz Ahmed, sen. (P) . . .	204	17	23	17	36	23	37	–	36	10	5

Note: M. Azharuddin became the first player to appear in 300 one-day internationals in October 1998, after the deadline for this section.

Most appearances for other Test-playing countries:

J. G. Wright (NZ)	149	30	42	–	11	–	21	18	24	2	1
W. J. Cronje (SA)	142	16	37	–	9	12	25	20	13	7	3
G. A. Gooch (E)	125	–	32	1	32	16	17	16	7	3	1
A. Flower (Z)	88	6	7	7	3	14	14	16	13	–	8

WORLD CUP

World Cup records can be found on pages 59-61.

CAPTAINCY

LIMITED-OVERS INTERNATIONAL CAPTAINS

England (279 matches; 21 captains)

G. A. Gooch 50; M. A. Atherton 43; M. W. Gatting 37; R. G. D. Willis 29; J. M. Brearley 25; D. I. Gower 24; M. H. Denness 12; A. J. Hollioake 12; A. J. Stewart 10; I. T. Botham 9; K. W. R. Fletcher 5; J. E. Emburey 4; A. J. Lamb 4; D. B. Close 3; R. Illingworth 3; G. Boycott 2; N. Gifford 2; A. W. Greig 2; J. H. Edrich 1; N. Hussain 1; A. P. E. Knott 1.

Australia (402 matches; 14 captains)

A. R. Border 178; M. A. Taylor 67; G. S. Chappell 49; K. J. Hughes 49; S. R. Waugh 26; I. M. Chappell 11; I. A. Healy 8; G. R. Marsh 4; G. N. Yallop 4; R. B. Simpson 2; R. J. Bright 1; D. W. Hookes 1; W. M. Lawry 1; S. K. Warne 1.

South Africa (147 matches; 3 captains)

W. J. Cronje 92; K. C. Wessels 52; C. E. B. Rice 3.

West Indies (350 matches; 13 captains)

I. V. A. Richards 108; R. B. Richardson 87; C. H. Lloyd 81; C. A. Walsh 43; C. G. Greenidge 8; D. L. Haynes 7; B. C. Lara 7; M. A. Holding 2; R. B. Kanhai 2; D. L. Murray 2; P. J. L. Dujon 1; C. L. Hooper 1; A. I. Kallicharran 1.

New Zealand (309 matches; 13 captains)

G. P. Howarth 60; M. D. Crowe 44; K. R. Rutherford 37; L. K. Germon 36; S. P. Fleming 33; J. G. Wright 31; J. V. Coney 25; J. J. Crowe 16; M. G. Burgess 8; G. M. Turner 8; B. E. Congdon 6; G. R. Larsen 3; A. H. Jones 2.

India (367 matches; 14 captains)

M. Azharuddin 142; Kapil Dev 74; S. R. Tendulkar 54; S. M. Gavaskar 37; D. B. Vengsarkar 18; K. Srikkanth 13; R. J. Shastri 11; S. Venkataraghavan 7; B. S. Bedi 4; A. Jadeja 2; A. L. Wadekar 2; M. Amarnath 1; S. M. H. Kirmani 1; G. R. Viswanath 1.

Pakistan (402 matches; 18 captains)

Imran Khan 139; Wasim Akram 72; Javed Miandad 62; Salim Malik 34; Ramiz Raja 22; Rashid Latif 13; Zaheer Abbas 13; Aamir Sohail 10; Saeed Anwar 8; Asif Iqbal 6; Abdul Qadir 5; Wasim Bari 5; Mushtaq Mohammad 4; Intikhab Alam 3; Majid Khan 2; Moin Khan 2; Sarfraz Nawaz 1; Waqar Younis 1.

Sri Lanka (277 matches; 10 captains)

A. Ranatunga 168; L. R. D. Mendis 61; P. A. de Silva 18; R. S. Madugalle 13; B. Warnapura 8; A. P. B. Tennekoon 4; R. S. Mahanama 2; D. S. de Silva 1; S. T. Jayasuriya 1; J. R. Ratnayeke 1.

Zimbabwe (100 matches; 5 captains)

A. D. R. Campbell 43; A. Flower 28; D. L. Houghton 17; D. A. G. Fletcher 6; A. J. Traicos 6.

Associate Members (63 matches; 11 captains)

Akram Khan (Bangladesh) 15; Asif Karim (Kenya) 11; M. O. Odumbe (Kenya) 9; Gazi Ashraf (Bangladesh) 7; Sultan M. Zarawani (UAE) 7; S. W. Lubbers (Holland) 4; B. M. Mauricette (Canada) 3; Harilal R. Shah (East Africa) 3; Minhaz-ul-Abedin (Bangladesh) 2; Amin-ul-Islam (Bangladesh) 1; R. P. Lefebvre (Holland) 1.

MISCELLANEOUS

LARGE ATTENDANCES

Test Series

943,000	Australia v England (5 Tests)	1936-37
In England		
549,650	England v Australia (5 Tests)	1953

Test Matches

†350,534	Australia v England, Melbourne (Third Test)	1936-37
325,000+	India v England, Calcutta (Second Test)	1972-73
In England		
158,000+	England v Australia, Leeds (Fourth Test)	1948
137,915	England v Australia, Lord's (Second Test)	1953

Test Match Day

90,800	Australia v West Indies, Melbourne (Fifth Test, 2nd day)	1960-61

Other First-Class Matches in England

93,000	England v Australia, Lord's (Fourth Victory Match, 3 days)	1945
80,000+	Surrey v Yorkshire, The Oval (3 days)	1906
78,792	Yorkshire v Lancashire, Leeds (3 days)	1904
76,617	Lancashire v Yorkshire, Manchester (3 days)	1926

Limited-Overs Internationals

‡100,000	India v South Africa, Calcutta	1993-94
‡100,000	India v West Indies, Calcutta	1993-94
‡100,000	India v West Indies, Calcutta	1994-95
‡100,000	India v Sri Lanka, Calcutta (World Cup semi-final)	1995-96
‡90,000	India v Pakistan, Calcutta	1986-87
‡90,000	India v South Africa, Calcutta	1991-92
87,182	England v Pakistan, Melbourne (World Cup final)	1991-92
86,133	Australia v West Indies, Melbourne	1983-84

  † *Although no official figures are available, the attendance at the Fourth Test between India and England at Calcutta, 1981-82, was thought to have exceeded this figure.*

  ‡ *No official attendance figures were issued for these games, but capacity is believed to have reached 100,000 following rebuilding in 1993.*

LORD'S CRICKET GROUND

Lord's and the Marylebone Cricket Club were founded in 1787. The Club has enjoyed an uninterrupted career since that date, but there have been three grounds known as Lord's. The first (1787-1810) was situated where Dorset Square now is; the second (1809-13), at North Bank, had to be abandoned owing to the cutting of the Regent's Canal; and the third, opened in 1814, is the present one at St John's Wood. It was not until 1866 that the freehold of Lord's was secured by MCC. The present pavilion was erected in 1890 at a cost of £21,000.

HIGHEST INDIVIDUAL SCORES MADE AT LORD'S

333	G. A. Gooch	England v India	1990
316*	J. B. Hobbs	Surrey v Middlesex	1926
315*	P. Holmes	Yorkshire v Middlesex	1925

Note: The longest innings in a first-class match at Lord's was played by S. Wettimuny (636 minutes, 190 runs) for Sri Lanka v England, 1984.

HIGHEST TOTALS AT LORD'S

First-Class Matches

729-6 dec.	Australia v England	1930
665	West Indians v Middlesex	1939
653-4 dec.	England v India	1990
652-8 dec.	West Indies v England	1973

Minor Match

735-9 dec.	MCC and Ground v Wiltshire	1888

BIGGEST HIT AT LORD'S

The only known instance of a batsman hitting a ball over the present pavilion at Lord's occurred when A. E. Trott, appearing for MCC against Australians on July 31, August 1, 2, 1899, drove M. A. Noble so far and high that the ball struck a chimney pot and fell behind the building.

MINOR CRICKET

HIGHEST INDIVIDUAL SCORES

628*	A. E. J. Collins, Clark's House v North Town at Clifton College.	
	(A Junior House match. His innings of 6 hours 50 minutes was spread over four afternoons.)	1899
566	C. J. Eady, Break-o'-Day v Wellington at Hobart	1901-02
515	D. R. Havewalla, B.B. and C.I. Rly v St Xavier's at Bombay	1933-34
506*	J. C. Sharp, Melbourne GS v Geelong College at Melbourne	1914-15
502*	Chaman Lal, Mehandra Coll., Patiala v Government Coll., Rupar at Patiala . . .	1956-57
485	A. E. Stoddart, Hampstead v Stoics at Hampstead.	1886
475*	Mohammad Iqbal, Muslim Model HS v Islamia HS, Sialkot at Lahore	1958-59
466*	G. T. S. Stevens, Beta v Lambda (University College School House match) at Neasden.	1919
459	J. A. Prout, Wesley College v Geelong College at Geelong.	1908-09

Note: The highest score in a Minor County match is 323* by F. E. Lacey for Hampshire v Norfolk at Southampton in 1887; the highest in the Minor Counties Championship is 282 by E. Garnett for Berkshire v Wiltshire at Reading in 1908.

HIGHEST PARTNERSHIP

664* for 3rd	V. G. Kambli and S. R. Tendulkar, Sharadashram Vidyamandir School v St Xavier's High School at Bombay.	1987-88

RECORD HIT

The Rev. W. Fellows, while at practice on the Christ Church ground at Oxford in 1856, drove a ball bowled by Charles Rogers 175 yards from hit to pitch.

THROWING THE CRICKET BALL

140 yards 2 feet, Robert Percival, on the Durham Sands racecourse, Co. Durham . . . c1882
140 yards 9 inches, Ross Mackenzie, at Toronto 1872
140 yards, "King Billy" the Aborigine, at Clermont, Queensland 1872

Note: Extensive research by David Rayvern Allen has shown that these traditional records are probably authentic, if not necessarily wholly accurate. Modern competitions have failed to produce similar distances although Ian Pont, the Essex all-rounder who also played baseball, was reported to have thrown 138 yards in Cape Town in 1981. There have been speculative reports attributing throws of 150 yards or more to figures as diverse as the South African Test player Colin Bland, the Latvian javelin thrower Janis Lusis, who won a gold medal for the Soviet Union in the 1968 Olympics, and the British sprinter Charley Ransome. The definitive record is still awaited.

COUNTY CHAMPIONSHIP

MOST APPEARANCES

762	W. Rhodes.	Yorkshire	1898-1930
707	F. E. Woolley.	Kent	1906-38
668	C. P. Mead	Hampshire	1906-36
617	N. Gifford	Worcestershire (484), Warwickshire (133). . .	1960-88
611	W. G. Quaife	Warwickshire	1895-1928
601	G. H. Hirst	Yorkshire	1891-1921

MOST CONSECUTIVE APPEARANCES

423	K. G. Suttle	Sussex	1954-69
412	J. G. Binks.	Yorkshire	1955-69

Notes: J. Vine made 417 consecutive appearances for Sussex in all first-class matches (399 of them in the Championship) between July 1900 and September 1914.

J. G. Binks did not miss a Championship match for Yorkshire between making his debut in June 1955 and retiring at the end of the 1969 season.

UMPIRES

MOST COUNTY CHAMPIONSHIP APPEARANCES

569	T. W. Spencer	1950-1980
533	F. Chester	1922-1955
516	H. G. Baldwin	1932-1962
481	P. B. Wight	1966-1995
457	A. Skelding	1931-1958

MOST SEASONS ON FIRST-CLASS LIST

31	T. W. Spencer	1950-1980
30	**D. J. Constant**	**1969-1998**
30	P. B. Wight	1966-1995
29	**H. D. Bird**	**1970-1998**
29	**A. G. T. Whitehead**	**1970-1998**
28	F. Chester	1922-1955
27	**R. Julian**	**1972-1998**
27	J. Moss	1899-1929
27	**K. E. Palmer**	**1972-1998**
26	W. A. J. West	1896-1925
25	H. G. Baldwin	1932-1962
25	A. Jepson	1960-1984
25	J. G. Langridge	1956-1980
25	B. J. Meyer	1973-1997

Bold type denotes umpires who stood in the 1998 season.

WOMEN'S TEST MATCH RECORDS

Amended by MARION COLLIN to the end of the 1998 season in England

HIGHEST INDIVIDUAL SCORES

204	K. E. Flavell	New Zealand v England at Scarborough	1996
200	J. Broadbent	Australia v England at Guildford	1998
193	D. A. Annetts	Australia v England at Collingham	1987
190	S. Agarwal	India v England at Worcester	1986
189	E. A. Snowball	England v New Zealand at Christchurch	1934-35
179	R. Heyhoe-Flint	England v Australia at The Oval	1976
176*	K. L. Rolton	Australia v England at Worcester	1998

MOST RUNS IN A CAREER

1,935	J. A. Brittin (England)	1,110	S. Agarwal (India)
1,594	R. Heyhoe-Flint (England)	1,078	E. Bakewell (England)
1,301	D. A. Hockley (New Zealand)	1,007	M. E. Maclagan (England)
1,164	C. A. Hodges (England)		

BEST ANALYSES

8-53	N. David	India v England at Jamshedpur	1995-96
7-6	M. B. Duggan .	England v Australia at Melbourne	1957-58
7-7	E. R. Wilson . .	Australia v England at Melbourne	1957-58
7-10	M. E. Maclagan	England v Australia at Brisbane	1934-35
7-18	A. Palmer	Australia v England at Brisbane	1934-35

MOST WICKETS IN A MATCH

11-16	E. R. Wilson	Australia v England at Melbourne	1957-58
11-63	J. Greenwood . . .	England v West Indies at Canterbury	1979

MOST WICKETS IN A CAREER

77	M. B. Duggan (England)	57	R. H. Thompson (Australia)
68	E. R. Wilson (Australia)	55	J. Lord (New Zealand)
60	M. E. Maclagan (England)	50	E. Bakewell (England)

MOST DISMISSALS IN AN INNINGS

8 (6ct, 2st)	L. Nye	England v New Zealand at New Plymouth	1991-92
6 (2ct, 4st)	B. Brentnall . . .	New Zealand v South Africa at Johannesburg . . .	1971-72

HIGHEST INNINGS TOTALS

569-6 dec.	Australia v England at Guildford	1998
525	Australia v India at Ahmedabad	1983-84
517-8	New Zealand v England at Scarborough	1996
503-5 dec.	England v New Zealand at Christchurch	1934-35

LOWEST INNINGS TOTALS

35	England v Australia at Melbourne	1957-58
38	Australia v England at Melbourne	1957-58
44	New Zealand v England at Christchurch	1934-35
47	Australia v England at Brisbane	1934-35

PART FIVE: ENGLISH CRICKET IN 1998

FEATURES OF 1998

Double-Hundreds (19)

322*†‡	M. B. Loye	Northamptonshire v Glamorgan at Northampton.
241	M. W. Gatting	Middlesex v Essex at Southgate.
239	J. P. Crawley	Lancashire v Hampshire at Manchester.
233*	J. L. Langer	Middlesex v Somerset at Lord's.
227†	S. P. James	Glamorgan v Northamptonshire at Northampton.
226	B. C. Lara	Warwickshire v Middlesex at Lord's.
220*	T. H. C. Hancock	Gloucestershire v Nottinghamshire at Nottingham.
213	S. T. Jayasuriya	Sri Lanka v England (Only Test) at The Oval.
212*	G. D. Lloyd	Lancashire v Derbyshire at Manchester.
210§	G. Kirsten	South Africa v England (Third Test) at Manchester.
209‖	R. P. Arnold	Sri Lankans v Somerset at Taunton.
209†	D. Ripley	Northamptonshire v Glamorgan at Northampton.
207	D. P. Fulton	Kent v Yorkshire at Maidstone.
205*§	G. Kirsten	South Africans v British Universities at Cambridge.
204	B. F. Smith	Leicestershire v Surrey at The Oval.
203	C. L. Hooper	Kent v Lancashire at Canterbury.
200*	D. J. Cullinan	South Africans v Durham at Chester-le-Street.
200*	M. J. Wood	Yorkshire v Warwickshire at Leeds.
200	D. S. Lehmann	Yorkshire v Worcestershire at Worcester.

† M. B. Loye and D. Ripley scored double-hundreds in the same innings; S. P. James also scored his in that match.

‡ County record.

§ G. Kirsten scored two double-hundreds, in successive innings.

‖ R. P. Arnold scored 209 on his first-class debut in England.

Three or More Hundreds in Successive Innings

J. P. Crawley (Lancashire)	108 v Worcestershire at Lytham
	124 and 136 v Glamorgan at Colwyn Bay.
G. A. Hick (Worcestershire)	166 v Middlesex at Uxbridge
	104 and 132 v Sussex at Worcester
	119 v Surrey at The Oval.

Hundred in Each Innings of a Match

C. J. Adams	135	105	Sussex v Essex at Chelmsford.
J. P. Crawley	124	136	Lancashire v Glamorgan at Colwyn Bay.
G. A. Hick	104	132	Worcestershire v Sussex at Worcester.
G. Kirsten	125	131*	South Africans v Gloucestershire at Bristol.
M. R. Ramprakash	122	108	Middlesex v Worcestershire at Uxbridge.

Fastest Hundreds

A. D. Brown	72 balls	Surrey v Northamptonshire at The Oval.
C. L. Hooper	72 balls	Kent v Worcestershire at Canterbury.

Hundred Before Lunch

V. S. Solanki	11* to 119*	Worcestershire v Derbyshire at Derby (3rd day).
Wasim Akram	28* to 150*	Lancashire v Nottinghamshire at Nottingham (3rd day).

Carrying Bat Through Completed Innings

M. A. Butcher	109*	Surrey (245) v Somerset at Taunton.
J. E. R. Gallian	113*	Nottinghamshire (243†) v Hampshire at Portsmouth.
N. V. Knight	67*	Warwickshire (129) v Somerset at Taunton.
	130*	Warwickshire (297†) v Yorkshire at Leeds.
J. J. B. Lewis	70*	Durham (158†) v Lancashire at Chester-le-Street.
M. J. Powell	70*	Warwickshire (130) v Nottinghamshire at Birmingham.
W. P. C. Weston	91*	Worcestershire (212) v Northamptonshire at Worcester.

† *One batsman absent.*

First to 1,000 Runs

J. L. Langer (Middlesex) on June 27.

2,000 Runs

No batsman scored 2,000 runs. The highest aggregate was 1,851 by J. P. Crawley (Lancashire).

Most Runs off One Over

34 (64444660)   A. Flintoff off A. J. Tudor, Lancashire v Surrey at Manchester.

The over included two no-balls, each counting for two extra runs under ECB regulations, making 38 conceded in all.

Notable Partnerships

First Wicket
372† M. W. Gatting/J. L. Langer, Middlesex v Essex at Southgate.
272 M. J. Powell/N. V. Knight, Warwickshire v Sussex at Hove.

Second Wicket
296 R. J. Bailey/M. B. Loye, Northamptonshire v Derbyshire at Northampton.
276* J. L. Langer/M. R. Ramprakash, Middlesex v Glamorgan at Lord's.
261 J. P. Crawley/N. H. Fairbrother, Lancashire v Hampshire at Manchester.
257* G. Kirsten/J. H. Kallis, South Africans v British Universities at Cambridge.

Fourth Wicket
254 K. J. Barnett/M. E. Cassar, Derbyshire v Sussex at Horsham.

Fifth Wicket
401‡ M. B. Loye/D. Ripley, Northamptonshire v Glamorgan at Northampton.
322† B. F. Smith/P. V. Simmons, Leicestershire v Nottinghamshire at Worksop.
252 B. F. Smith/A. Habib, Leicestershire v Surrey at The Oval.
229 M. R. Ramprakash/P. N. Weekes, Middlesex v Leicestershire at Leicester.

Sixth Wicket
193† D. C. Boon/P. D. Collingwood, Durham v Warwickshire at Birmingham.

Seventh Wicket
110† P. D. Collingwood/M. J. Foster, Durham v Nottinghamshire at Nottingham.

Tenth Wicket
123 D. W. Headley/M. M. Patel, Kent v Hampshire at Canterbury.
109 D. J. Millns/M. T. Brimson, Leicestershire v Warwickshire at Birmingham.
102 M. J. Foster/S. J. Harmison, Durham v Kent at Canterbury.
102 A. P. Cowan/P. M. Such, Essex v Leicestershire at Leicester.

* *Unbroken partnership.* † *County record for that wicket.* ‡ *National record for that wicket.*

Eight or More Wickets in an Innings (4)

9-65	M. Muralitharan	Sri Lanka v England (Only Test) at The Oval.
8-55	C. White	Yorkshire v Gloucestershire at Gloucester.
8-64	A. R. Caddick	Somerset v Worcestershire at Taunton.
8-65	Saqlain Mushtaq	Surrey v Derbyshire at The Oval.

Twelve or More Wickets in a Match (3)

16-220	M. Muralitharan	Sri Lanka v England (Only Test) at The Oval.
12-133	K. J. Dean	Derbyshire v Somerset at Taunton.
12-153	C. A. Walsh	Gloucestershire v Warwickshire at Bristol.

Hat-Tricks

K. J. Dean	Derbyshire v Kent at Derby.
D. R. Law	Essex v Durham at Chester-le-Street.
J. D. Lewry	Sussex v Gloucestershire at Cheltenham.
C. White	Yorkshire v Gloucestershire at Gloucester.

100 Wickets

106 C. A. Walsh (Gloucestershire)   105 A. R. Caddick (Somerset)

Caddick reached the mark first, on September 11.

Outstanding Innings Analysis

8-6-4-4 . . . . M. T. Brimson   Leicestershire v Glamorgan at Cardiff.

Most Overs Bowled in a Match

113.5-41-220-16 . . . M. Muralitharan   Sri Lanka v England (Only Test) at The Oval.

Six Wicket-Keeping Dismissals in an Innings

6 ct	W. K. Hegg	Lancashire v Worcestershire at Lytham.
6 ct	B. J. Hyam	Essex v Yorkshire at Scarborough.
6 ct	K. J. Piper	Warwickshire v Sussex at Hove.

Six Catches in an Innings in the Field

6 ct . . . . G. P. Thorpe   Surrey v Kent at The Oval.

Thorpe took seven catches in the match.

Match Double (100 Runs and 10 Wickets)

G. M. Hamilton . . . . 79, 70; 5-69, 5-43   Yorkshire v Glamorgan at Cardiff.

No Byes Conceded in Total of 500 or More

C. M. W. Read . . . . . Nottinghamshire v Leicestershire (505-6 dec.) at Worksop.
A. J. Stewart . . . . . . Surrey v Leicestershire (585-6 dec.) at The Oval.

Highest Innings Totals

712†	Northamptonshire v Glamorgan at Northampton.
627-6 dec.	Worcestershire v Middlesex at Uxbridge.
608-6 dec.	Northamptonshire v Derbyshire at Northampton.
593	Derbyshire v Sussex at Horsham.
591	Sri Lanka v England (Only Test) at The Oval.
591	Surrey v Hampshire at Southampton.
585-6 dec.	Leicestershire v Surrey at The Oval.
580-9 dec.	Kent v Yorkshire at Maidstone.
564	Gloucestershire v Essex at Colchester.
563†	Glamorgan v Northamptonshire at Northampton.
552-5 dec.	South Africa v England (Third Test) at Manchester.

† *Glamorgan scored 563 and Northamptonshire 712 in the same match.*

Lowest Innings Totals

54	Sri Lankans v Glamorgan at Cardiff.
61	Nottinghamshire v Leicestershire at Worksop.
65†	Essex v Derbyshire at Derby.
70†	Derbyshire v Essex at Derby.
72	Middlesex v Gloucestershire at Lord's.
72	Sussex v Northamptonshire at Northampton.
74	Durham v Yorkshire at Chester-le-Street.
74	Somerset v Leicestershire at Leicester.

† *Essex and Derbyshire bowled each other out for 70 and 65 respectively on the first day of their match.*

Match Aggregate of 1,400 Runs

Runs	Wkts	
1,491	30	Northamptonshire v Glamorgan at Northampton.

Most Extras in an Innings

	b	l-b	w	n-b	
69	3	8	0	58	Durham (286) v South Africans at Chester-le-Street.
69	15	18	2	34	Middlesex (437) v Hampshire at Southampton.
65	4	22	5	34	Leicestershire (362) v Sri Lankans at Leicester.

Under ECB regulations (Test matches excluded), two extras were scored for every no-ball in addition to any runs scored off that ball, and two extras were also scored for every wide. There were 25 further instances of 50 or more extras in an innings.

Career Aggregate Milestones

25,000 runs	K. J. Barnett.
20,000 runs	T. M. Moody, A. P. Wells.
15,000 runs	K. M. Curran, P. J. Prichard, M. R. Ramprakash.
10,000 runs	K. R. Brown, P. A. Cottey, W. J. Cronje, D. J. Cullinan, A. Ranatunga.
500 wickets	A. R. Caddick, D. Gough, M. C. Ilott, C. C. Lewis.

FIRST-CLASS AVERAGES, 1998

BATTING

(Qualification: 8 completed innings)

* Signifies not out.   † *Denotes a left-handed batsman.*

		M	I	NO	R	HS	100s	50s	Avge	Ct/St
1	J. P. Crawley (*Lancs*)	18	28	3	1,851	239	8	5	74.04	7
2	W. J. Cronje (*South Africans*)	11	12	2	704	195	2	4	70.40	6
3	D. J. Cullinan (*South Africans*)	12	17	4	900	200*	2	6	69.23	9
4	†G. Kirsten (*South Africans*)	12	19	5	892	210	4	2	63.71	8
5	†J. L. Langer (*Middx*)	15	28	5	1,448	233*	4	6	62.95	12
6	B. F. Smith (*Leics*)	19	24	4	1,240	204	4	4	62.00	13
7	†D. S. Lehmann (*Yorks*)	10	16	0	969	200	3	4	60.56	4
8	M. B. Loye (*Northants*)	15	22	2	1,198	322*	4	4	59.90	7
9	A. Habib (*Leics*)	19	22	5	952	198	3	3	56.00	12
10	J. H. Kallis (*South Africans*)	10	14	3	612	132	2	3	55.63	9
11	†M. G. Bevan (*Sussex*)	12	19	2	935	149*	3	4	55.00	10
12	†N. H. Fairbrother (*Lancs*)	12	17	2	759	138	3	3	50.60	11
13	S. P. James (*Glam*)	15	28	1	1,339	227	4	5	49.59	9
14	A. D. Brown (*Surrey*)	15	22	1	1,036	155	4	6	49.33	20
15	†S. T. Jayasuriya (*Sri Lankans*)	5	9	1	382	213	1	0	47.75	4
16	K. J. Barnett (*Derbys*)	17	32	6	1,229	162	1	7	47.26	8
17	M. J. Wood (*Yorks*)	19	29	6	1,080	200*	4	4	46.95	17
18	G. F. J. Liebenberg (*South Africans*)	10	17	3	642	104*	1	5	45.85	11
19	C. L. Hooper (*Kent*)	15	28	1	1,215	203	6	1	45.00	15
20	†N. V. Knight (*Warwicks*)	15	26	2	1,069	192	4	4	44.54	18
21	M. W. Gatting (*Middx*)	17	29	3	1,139	241	2	7	43.80	19
22	A. J. Stewart (*Surrey*)	14	24	2	963	164	1	5	43.77	41
23	G. A. Hick (*Worcs*)	17	30	0	1,304	166	7	2	43.46	24
24	M. G. N. Windows (*Glos*)	16	29	2	1,173	151	4	5	43.44	13
25	J. N. Rhodes (*South Africans*)	11	14	1	562	123	2	3	43.23	4
26	†P. N. Weekes (*Middx*)	16	26	5	903	139	1	5	43.00	20
27	M. R. Ramprakash (*Middx*)	15	26	3	979	128*	4	2	42.56	10
28	W. S. Kendall (*Hants*)	8	11	3	340	78*	0	2	42.50	8
29	T. M. Moody (*Worcs*)	13	23	2	886	132	2	4	42.19	10
30	C. J. Adams (*Sussex*)	18	29	1	1,174	170	4	4	41.92	30
31	G. W. White (*Hants*)	19	31	2	1,211	156	4	5	41.75	12
32	N. M. K. Smith (*Warwicks*)	18	29	5	1,002	147	2	6	41.75	2
33	M. P. Vaughan (*Yorks*)	19	31	3	1,161	177	2	5	41.46	10
34	†M. A. Butcher (*Surrey*)	16	26	1	1,024	116	3	6	40.96	11
	D. C. Boon (*Durham*)	16	29	4	1,024	139*	3	5	40.96	12
36	S. G. Law (*Essex*)	14	26	2	982	165	2	3	40.91	19
37	D. Ripley (*Northants*)	17	22	2	805	209	1	5	40.25	30/1
38	†A. L. Penberthy (*Northants*)	14	21	2	755	128	2	4	39.73	14
39	†B. C. Lara (*Warwicks*)	15	26	0	1,033	226	3	3	39.73	15
40	M. A. Atherton (*Lancs*)	13	24	2	874	152	2	3	39.72	9
41	†H. P. Tillekeratne (*Sri Lankans*)	6	9	1	317	120	1	1	39.62	5
42	C. White (*Yorks*)	10	15	3	475	104*	1	4	39.58	16
43	G. D. Lloyd (*Lancs*)	15	22	1	831	212*	2	3	39.57	11
44	O. A. Shah (*Middx*)	15	23	3	786	140	2	4	39.30	10
45	P. Johnson (*Notts*)	15	26	1	976	139	2	4	39.04	14
46	†R. P. Arnold (*Sri Lankans*)	5	9	1	312	209	1	0	39.00	1
47	M. W. Alleyne (*Glos*)	18	33	2	1,189	137	3	6	38.35	24
48	T. H. C. Hancock (*Glos*)	18	34	2	1,227	220*	2	7	38.34	16
49	†P. A. Nixon (*Leics*)	19	21	4	638	101*	2	1	37.52	41/5
50	R. A. Smith (*Hants*)	17	25	2	853	138	3	2	37.08	10
51	W. L. Law (*Glam*)	9	14	2	444	131	1	2	37.00	4

		M	I	NO	R	HS	100s	50s	Avge	Ct/St
52	W. K. Hegg (*Lancs*)	15	21	4	628	85	0	6	36.94	34/3
53	V. J. Wells (*Leics*)	17	25	2	836	171	3	3	36.34	10
54	A. Singh (*CU & Warwicks*)	10	12	0	434	117	1	2	36.16	2
55	N. Shahid (*Surrey*)	12	22	3	683	126*	2	3	35.94	13
56	A. N. Aymes (*Hants*)	18	27	6	754	133	2	3	35.90	53/2
57	S. J. Rhodes (*Worcs*)	18	33	5	1,000	104*	1	6	35.71	43/2
58	M. J. Slater (*Derbys*)	14	24	0	848	185	1	3	35.33	9
59	M. J. Powell (*Glam*)	16	27	3	840	106	1	5	35.00	10
60	P. A. Cottey (*Glam*)	19	32	3	1,012	123	2	5	34.89	20
61	J. E. Morris (*Durham*)	13	24	2	767	163	3	1	34.86	5
62	R. T. Robinson (*Notts*)	11	18	2	553	114	1	4	34.56	6
63	R. J. Bailey (*Northants*)	16	24	2	759	188	1	2	34.50	10
64	G. P. Swann (*Northants*)	14	18	2	548	111	1	2	34.25	7
65	A. J. Hollioake (*Surrey*)	15	22	2	684	112	1	4	34.20	15
66	†K. D. James (*Hants*)	18	26	9	570	57	0	3	33.52	6
67	D. A. Leatherdale (*Worcs*)	18	32	2	1,001	137	2	4	33.36	9
68	C. C. Lewis (*Leics*)	13	14	3	367	71*	0	4	33.36	10
69	G. R. Haynes (*Worcs*)	12	21	5	532	86	0	4	33.25	2
70	M. A. Wagh (*OU & Warwicks*)	14	23	2	686	126	2	3	32.66	6
71	A. S. Rollins (*Derbys*)	10	19	0	618	107	1	4	32.52	11
72	T. Frost (*Warwicks*)	8	14	2	389	111*	1	1	32.41	22
73	R. C. Irani (*Essex*)	18	33	2	1,001	127*	2	2	32.29	6
74	K. M. Curran (*Northants*)	18	26	4	709	90*	0	6	32.22	23
75	A. Dale (*Glam*)	19	33	1	1,028	92	0	9	32.12	7
76	†G. M. Hamilton (*Yorks*)	15	19	1	578	79	0	6	32.11	3
77	J. D. Ratcliffe (*Surrey*)	9	15	1	449	100	1	2	32.07	2
78	B. W. Byrne (*OU*)	8	12	4	256	69*	0	1	32.00	4
79	K. Newell (*Sussex*)	11	19	6	414	84	0	3	31.84	7
80	D. P. Fulton (*Kent*)	17	31	1	954	207	1	7	31.80	21
81	†I. J. Sutcliffe (*Leics*)	19	26	4	698	167	1	2	31.72	11
82	J. A. Daley (*Durham*)	12	22	2	634	157	1	3	31.70	5
83	R. M. S. Weston (*Derbys*)	9	17	0	537	97	0	4	31.58	5
84	R. K. Illingworth (*Worcs*)	15	21	6	473	84	0	3	31.53	5
85	†M. E. Trescothick (*Somerset*)	18	29	2	847	98	0	6	31.37	20
86	†Wasim Akram (*Lancs*)	13	18	1	531	155	1	1	31.23	8
87	†D. Byas (*Yorks*)	18	28	1	842	116	4	3	31.18	20
88	†I. J. Ward (*Surrey*)	10	19	2	529	81*	0	5	31.11	9
89	N. Hussain (*Essex*)	10	19	0	591	105	1	4	31.10	9
90	S. D. Udal (*Hants*)	14	18	5	404	62	0	1	31.07	9
91	†P. R. Whitaker (*Hants*)	7	11	1	309	74	0	2	30.90	7
92	P. D. Collingwood (*Durham*)	19	33	6	833	105	1	5	30.85	16
93	A. F. Giles (*Warwicks*)	21	21	5	489	83	0	3	30.56	7
94	K. R. Brown (*Middx*)	17	25	6	576	59*	0	2	30.31	41/5
95	M. N. Lathwell (*Somerset*)	12	19	0	574	106	1	5	30.21	7
96	D. R. Brown (*Warwicks*)	16	27	4	691	81*	0	5	30.04	9
97 {	M. Newell (*Sussex*)	10	14	1	386	135*	2	0	29.69	6
	A. W. Evans (*Glam*)	8	14	1	386	125	1	1	29.69	7
99	J. P. Stephenson (*Hants*)	16	24	1	681	114	2	4	29.60	14
100	†W. P. C. Weston (*Worcs*)	17	31	3	829	95	0	5	29.60	9
101	D. P. M. D. Jayawardene (*Sri Lankans*)	6	10	1	266	90	0	2	29.55	7
102	R. S. C. Martin-Jenkins (*Sussex*)	8	13	1	353	78	0	2	29.41	3
103	†W. J. House (*CU & Kent*)	8	11	0	322	65	0	3	29.27	3
104	M. Watkinson (*Lancs*)	10	12	1	318	87	0	2	28.90	6
105	†W. G. Khan (*Sussex*)	18	30	1	837	125	1	6	28.86	5
106	M. P. Maynard (*Glam*)	17	29	2	776	99	0	5	28.74	21
107	†N. T. Wood (*Lancs*)	12	19	3	457	80*	0	2	28.56	1
108	V. S. Solanki (*Worcs*)	19	36	1	999	170	2	4	28.54	28
109	†R. A. Kettleborough (*Middx*)	12	22	4	512	92*	0	3	28.44	7
110	M. A. Gough (*Durham*)	10	18	0	508	123	1	2	28.22	12
111	G. F. Archer (*Notts*)	13	23	0	647	107	1	5	28.13	23

		M	I	NO	R	HS	100s	50s	Avge	Ct/St
112	A. D. Mascarenhas (*Hants*)	17	25	2	645	89	0	6	28.04	11
113	R. J. Turner (*Somerset*).	14	22	2	558	105	1	2	27.90	43
114	A. P. Wells (*Kent*)	15	26	1	684	95	0	5	27.36	3
115	M. E. Cassar (*Derbys*)	17	31	5	708	121	1	5	27.23	4
116	J. E. R. Gallian (*Notts*)	14	25	3	592	113*	1	3	26.90	8
117	M. A. Roseberry (*Durham*)	6	11	0	295	97	0	2	26.81	2
118	M. J. Foster (*Durham*)	8	13	1	321	76*	0	2	26.75	2
119	R. W. T. Key (*Kent*).	13	23	0	612	115	2	1	26.60	11
120	M. Burns (*Somerset*)	10	17	0	450	96	0	3	26.47	16/1
121	N. J. Speak (*Durham*)	15	27	2	658	77*	0	6	26.32	9
122	P. D. Bowler (*Somerset*)	18	32	2	789	104	2	3	26.30	18
123	†M. J. Walker (*Kent*).	8	14	1	341	68	0	2	26.23	6
124	†G. P. Thorpe (*Surrey*)	9	13	1	314	114	1	1	26.16	10
125	G. P. Butcher (*Glam*)	9	14	2	311	85	0	2	25.91	5
126	†D. L. Hemp (*Warwicks*)	15	26	1	646	102	1	4	25.84	16
127	S. A. Marsh (*Kent*)	16	28	4	620	92	0	5	25.83	42/4
128	A. R. K. Pierson (*Somerset*)	13	20	3	438	108*	1	1	25.76	6
129	†U. Afzaal (*Notts*).	17	30	3	686	109*	2	4	25.40	7
130	G. D. Rose (*Somerset*)	17	26	2	606	76	0	4	25.25	3
131	J. A. M. Molins (*OU & Ireland*) . . .	8	12	0	302	73	0	3	25.16	2
132	C. M. W. Read (*Notts*)	13	22	6	401	76	0	2	25.06	39/3
133	†P. C. L. Holloway (*Somerset*).	16	28	3	624	123	1	1	24.96	7
134	D. J. Goodchild (*Middx*)	7	14	1	324	105	1	1	24.92	1
135	E. T. Smith (*CU & Kent*)	11	18	1	422	58	0	1	24.82	1
136	M. P. Speight (*Durham*)	17	29	4	614	97*	0	4	24.56	58/3
137	A. McGrath (*Yorks*)	17	28	3	612	63*	0	3	24.48	5
138	P. V. Simmons (*Leics*)	17	19	0	464	194	1	2	24.42	23
139	M. J. Powell (*Warwicks*)	13	22	1	511	132	1	3	24.33	13
140	A. Flintoff (*Lancs*)	17	25	0	608	124	1	3	24.32	23
141	M. A. Ealham (*Kent*)	12	22	3	461	121	1	2	24.26	2
142	†M. T. E. Peirce (*Sussex*)	19	32	1	744	96	0	5	24.00	7
143	M. Keech (*Hants*)	12	14	0	335	70	0	3	23.92	12
144	C. E. W. Silverwood (*Yorks*)	13	13	3	239	57*	0	1	23.90	2
145	D. L. Maddy (*Leics*)	18	26	2	569	162	2	0	23.70	17
146	†G. M. Roberts (*Derbys*)	8	13	3	237	44	0	0	23.70	7
147	M. C. J. Ball (*Glos*)	18	30	5	592	67*	0	3	23.68	22
148	M. V. Fleming (*Kent*)	17	30	4	612	51	0	1	23.53	9
149	D. R. Hewson (*Glos*)	12	22	3	447	78*	0	3	23.52	4
150	T. L. Penney (*Warwicks*)	9	16	2	329	53*	0	1	23.50	5
151	M. V. Boucher (*South Africans*)	11	10	1	211	46	0	0	23.44	43/1
152	†I. D. Austin (*Lancs*)	13	17	4	304	64	0	2	23.38	7
153	†I. N. Flanagan (*Essex*)	6	11	0	254	61	0	2	23.09	9
154	S. D. Peters (*Essex*)	13	23	2	484	64	0	3	23.04	7
155	J. J. B. Lewis (*Durham*)	15	28	1	622	72	0	4	23.03	10
156	S. R. Lampitt (*Worcs*)	18	28	7	481	48	0	0	22.90	8
157	R. D. B. Croft (*Glam*)	13	22	7	343	63*	0	1	22.86	9
158	A. M. Smith (*Glos*)	18	30	13	384	61	0	2	22.58	5
159	B. Parker (*Yorks*)	8	10	2	180	41	0	0	22.50	3
160	†S. D. Thomas (*Glam*)	18	26	3	507	74	0	3	22.04	10
161	{ D. G. Cork (*Derbys*)	16	27	4	506	102*	1	3	22.00	11
	{ C. M. Tolley (*Notts*)	11	19	2	374	78	0	2	22.00	5
163	†A. C. Morris (*Hants*)	12	15	5	219	51	0	1	21.90	6
164	†J. P. Taylor (*Northants*)	15	20	3	371	58	0	3	21.82	5
165	P. A. J. DeFreitas (*Derbys*)	14	23	3	435	87	0	2	21.75	6
166	†P. J. Franks (*Notts*)	12	20	2	390	66*	0	1	21.66	6
167	M. P. Bicknell (*Surrey*)	17	21	1	433	81	0	1	21.65	5
168	R. J. Blakey (*Yorks*)	17	23	2	448	67*	0	3	21.33	69/2
169	D. C. Nash (*Middx*)	14	19	0	404	114	1	1	21.26	8/1
170	P. J. Newport (*Worcs*)	13	16	3	270	56	0	1	20.76	4
171	M. J. McCague (*Kent*)	10	15	7	166	38	0	0	20.75	8

		M	I	NO	R	HS	100s	50s	Avge	Ct/St
172	J. N. Batty (*Surrey*)	16	19	2	351	63	0	2	20.64	39/6
173	R. R. Montgomerie (*Northants*)	10	16	3	268	54	0	1	20.61	4
174	B. C. Hollioake (*Surrey*)	17	26	3	469	60	0	2	20.39	8
175	R. K. Rao (*Sussex*)	10	17	1	325	76	0	2	20.31	0
176	†R. C. Russell (*Glos*)	16	28	2	527	63*	0	2	20.26	56
177	M. M. Patel (*Kent*)	14	20	5	303	58*	0	0	20.20	7
178	{ R. J. Kirtley (*Sussex*)	18	26	10	320	59	0	1	20.00	2
	{ P. A. Strang (*Notts*)	13	18	3	300	48	0	0	20.00	19
180	K. M. Krikken (*Derbys*)	17	27	5	439	83	0	3	19.95	36/2
181	M. R. May (*Derbys*)	13	24	0	473	101	1	1	19.70	4
182	I. D. K. Salisbury (*Surrey*)	15	18	2	314	61	0	3	19.62	8
183	†M. P. Dowman (*Notts*)	13	24	1	451	63	0	2	19.60	7
184	G. I. Macmillan (*Glos*)	5	9	0	176	53	0	2	19.55	4
185	G. Welch (*Warwicks*)	12	18	1	332	54	0	1	19.52	6
186	B. L. Spendlove (*Derbys*)	10	19	1	350	49	0	0	19.44	4
187	†K. J. Dean (*Derbys*)	15	21	13	154	27*	0	0	19.25	1
188	D. P. Ostler (*Warwicks*)	6	10	1	173	133*	1	0	19.22	7
189	D. Gough (*Yorks*)	11	15	1	269	89	0	2	19.21	1
190	B. J. Hyam (*Essex*)	10	19	3	307	47*	0	0	19.18	32/2
191	A. R. Caddick (*Somerset*)	17	25	8	322	37	0	0	18.94	5
192	T. R. Ward (*Kent*)	12	22	0	416	94	0	1	18.90	8
193	G. Chapple (*Lancs*)	14	18	3	282	69	0	1	18.80	7
194	D. R. Law (*Essex*)	14	25	0	466	65	0	3	18.64	10
195	T. A. Tweats (*Derbys*)	9	18	0	332	161	1	0	18.44	8
196	†T. P. Hodgson (*Essex*)	7	13	0	236	54	0	1	18.15	4
197	D. D. J. Robinson (*Essex*)	14	25	0	446	85	0	1	17.84	11
198	A. Hafeez (*Worcs*)	10	18	1	303	55	0	1	17.82	6
199	M. N. Bowen (*Notts*)	10	13	5	142	32	0	0	17.75	2
200	I. Dawood (*Glam*)	7	12	1	194	40	0	0	17.63	19/1
201	Saqlain Mushtaq (*Surrey*)	12	15	5	176	45*	0	0	17.60	7
202	A. P. Cowan (*Essex*)	8	13	0	228	94	0	2	17.53	4
203	D. J. Sales (*Northants*)	14	21	1	346	60	0	2	17.30	10
204	A. J. Wright (*Glos*)	11	20	0	345	57	0	1	17.25	5
205	J. S. Laney (*Hants*)	8	13	0	224	101	1	1	17.23	10
206	N. F. Williams (*Essex*)	9	16	6	171	36	0	0	17.10	2
207	G. E. Welton (*Notts*)	5	9	0	152	55	0	1	16.88	3
208	A. J. Tudor (*Surrey*)	10	13	3	167	48	0	0	16.70	3
209	K. A. Parsons (*Somerset*)	14	23	1	367	101*	1	1	16.68	16
210	D. W. Headley (*Kent*)	14	21	5	265	81	0	1	16.56	5
211	A. D. Shaw (*Glam*)	11	16	1	248	71	0	2	16.53	26
212	A. P. Grayson (*Essex*)	17	31	0	509	59	0	4	16.41	9
213	†J. A. G. Fulton (*OU*)	8	12	1	180	78	0	1	16.36	4
214	D. R. Lockhart (*OU & Scotland*)	9	15	0	241	46	0	0	16.06	7
215	N. A. Gie (*Notts*)	4	8	0	128	50	0	1	16.00	3
216	†P. M. Hutchison (*Yorks*)	17	16	8	127	30	0	0	15.87	4
217	R. J. Harden (*Somerset*)	12	21	2	301	63	0	2	15.84	15
218	†J. P. Hewitt (*Middx*)	15	19	2	268	53	0	1	15.76	5
219	K. J. Piper (*Warwicks*)	13	23	5	283	44*	0	0	15.72	29/3
220	R. J. Cunliffe (*Glos*)	12	22	0	339	53	0	2	15.40	14
221	P. J. Martin (*Lancs*)	14	15	5	154	26	0	0	15.40	3
222	Mushtaq Ahmed (*Somerset*)	6	9	1	121	37	0	0	15.12	1
223	G. R. Loveridge (*CU*)	7	9	1	118	41	0	0	14.75	0
224	A. J. Swann (*Northants*)	11	17	0	250	85	0	1	14.70	6
225	A. D. Mullally (*Leics*)	15	11	2	132	38*	0	0	14.66	3
226	†N. A. M. McLean (*Hants*)	16	22	2	288	43	0	0	14.40	5
227	M. T. Brimson (*Leics*)	18	14	6	115	54*	0	1	14.37	3
228	R. J. Rollins (*Essex*)	8	12	0	171	42	0	0	14.25	13
229	†I. D. Blackwell (*Derbys*)	11	18	0	254	57	0	2	14.11	6
230	J. D. Middlebrook (*Yorks*)	8	12	2	139	41	0	0	13.90	7
231	†J. R. Carpenter (*Sussex*)	9	16	0	222	65	0	1	13.87	3

		M	I	NO	R	HS	100s	50s	Avge	Ct/St
232	N. J. Trainor (*Glos*)	4	8	0	109	52	0	1	13.62	4
233	S. Humphries (*Sussex*)	14	22	1	286	66	0	1	13.61	25
234	R. I. Dawson (*Glos*)	8	15	2	177	46	0	0	13.61	3
235	J. Lewis (*Glos*)	18	31	2	390	54*	0	1	13.44	5
236	R. L. Johnson (*Middx*)	14	21	3	242	43	0	0	13.44	5
237	P. J. Prichard (*Essex*)	10	18	0	237	24	0	0	13.16	7
238	R. J. Chapman (*Worcs*)	11	16	8	102	43*	0	0	12.75	2
239	†C. J. Batt (*Middx*)	9	14	2	150	43	0	0	12.50	1
240	S. J. Harmison (*Durham*)	14	22	4	223	36	0	0	12.38	3
241	P. J. Hartley (*Hants*)	13	16	3	160	29	0	0	12.30	3
242	M. M. Betts (*Durham*)	12	18	7	135	29*	0	0	12.27	3
243	B. J. Phillips (*Kent*)	11	17	0	203	54	0	1	11.94	1
244	†M. C. Ilott (*Essex*)	17	30	4	307	38	0	0	11.80	3
245	J. Wood (*Durham*)	17	26	4	236	37	0	0	10.72	3
246	†T. M. Smith (*Derbys*)	7	10	1	94	29	0	0	10.44	0
247	D. E. Malcolm (*Northants*)	14	16	5	114	42	0	0	10.36	3
248	E. J. Wilson (*Worcs*)	5	10	0	101	27	0	0	10.10	1
249	K. P. Evans (*Notts*)	9	13	0	129	36	0	0	9.92	3
250	N. C. Phillips (*Durham*)	17	25	2	227	35	0	0	9.86	8
251	P. C. R. Tufnell (*Middx*)	17	22	6	155	24	0	0	9.68	2
252	A. R. C. Fraser (*Middx*)	14	19	5	134	32	0	0	9.57	1
253	O. T. Parkin (*Glam*)	11	13	4	85	24*	0	0	9.44	2
254	F. A. Rose (*Northants*)	14	17	2	133	21	0	0	8.86	0
255	C. A. Walsh (*Glos*)	17	23	10	111	25	0	0	8.53	4
256	T. A. Munton (*Warwicks*)	9	12	2	72	20	0	0	7.20	0
257	M. J. Rawnsley (*Worcs*)	6	8	0	55	21	0	0	6.87	7
258	D. A. Cosker (*Glam*)	15	21	3	123	37	0	0	6.83	11
259	†J. D. Lewry (*Sussex*)	17	23	0	132	24	0	0	5.73	1
260	R. J. Warren (*Northants*)	5	8	0	30	11	0	0	3.75	7
261	A. R. Oram (*Notts*)	11	19	8	39	13	0	0	3.54	0
262	M. A. Robinson (*Sussex*)	16	21	8	40	7	0	0	3.07	1
263	E. S. H. Giddins (*Warwicks*)	18	23	8	43	11*	0	0	2.86	4

BOWLING

(Qualification: 10 wickets in 10 innings)

		Style	O	M	R	W	BB	5W/i	Avge
1	V. J. Wells (*Leics*)	RM	199.1	66	514	36	5-18	1	14.27
2	C. White (*Yorks*)	RFM	147.1	36	391	25	8-55	2	15.64
3	T. H. C. Hancock (*Glos*)	RM	68	16	214	13	3-5	0	16.46
4	C. A. Walsh (*Glos*)	RF	633	162	1,835	106	6-36	7	17.31
5	Saqlain Mushtaq (*Surrey*)	OB/LB	475	136	1,119	63	8-65	3	17.76
6	A. D. Mullally (*Leics*)	LFM	448.5	156	1,128	60	7-55	3	18.80
7	M. P. L. Bulbeck (*Somerset*)	LM	154.4	28	609	32	4-40	0	19.03
8	T. A. Munton (*Warwicks*)	RM	278.5	72	708	37	7-66	3	19.13
9	D. A. Leatherdale (*Worcs*)	RM	111.4	22	416	21	5-20	1	19.80
10	A. R. Caddick (*Somerset*)	RFM	687.2	156	2,082	105	8-64	10	19.82
11	R. S. C. Martin-Jenkins (*Sussex*) . .	RM	141.5	43	437	22	7-54	1	19.86
12	A. R. C. Fraser (*Middx*)	RFM	480.3	120	1,224	61	6-23	4	20.06
13	A. A. Donald (*South Africans*)	RF	302.2	89	785	39	6-56	5	20.12
14	A. C. Morris (*Hants*)	RM	314	64	1,012	50	4-30	0	20.24
15	G. M. Hamilton (*Yorks*)	RFM	415	105	1,212	59	7-50	4	20.54
16	M. P. Bicknell (*Surrey*)	RFM	494.1	141	1,340	65	5-27	2	20.61
17	M. J. Foster (*Durham*)	RM	113	23	351	17	4-41	0	20.64

		Style	O	M	R	W	BB	5W/i	Avge
18	A. M. Smith (*Glos*)	LFM	522.3	139	1,440	68	6-32	4	21.17
19	K. J. Dean (*Derbys*)	LFM	465.3	96	1,572	74	6-63	5	21.24
20	P. V. Simmons (*Leics*)	RM	170.5	44	491	23	7-49	1	21.34
21	Wasim Akram (*Lancs*)	LF	335.5	75	1,025	48	5-56	1	21.35
22	G. Chapple (*Lancs*)	RFM	313	58	942	44	5-49	1	21.40
23	D. W. Headley (*Kent*)	RFM	410.2	88	1,175	54	6-71	4	21.75
24	M. J. Hoggard (*Yorks*)	RF	258	51	895	41	5-57	1	21.82
25	S. L. Watkin (*Glam*)	RFM	370.4	104	917	42	5-30	1	21.83
26	J. F. Brown (*Northants*)	OB	280.2	68	726	33	6-53	4	22.00
27	M. M. Betts (*Durham*)	RFM	363	81	1,061	48	6-83	4	22.10
28	P. J. Martin (*Lancs*)	RFM	388	94	1,062	48	4-21	0	22.12
29	O. T. Parkin (*Glam*)	RFM	300.3	99	757	34	5-24	2	22.26
30	J. D. Lewry (*Sussex*)	LFM	461.3	112	1,409	62	6-72	3	22.72
31	T. M. Smith (*Derbys*)	RFM	150.3	42	484	21	6-32	2	23.04
32	M. C. Ilott (*Essex*)	LFM	506.5	138	1,345	58	6-20	2	23.18
33	C. E. W. Silverwood (*Yorks*)	RFM	390.1	99	1,123	48	5-13	3	23.39
34	E. S. H. Giddins (*Warwicks*)	RFM	668.2	161	2,006	84	6-79	5	23.88
35	D. J. Millns (*Leics*)	RFM	243.3	55	817	34	4-60	0	24.02
36	P. M. Hutchison (*Yorks*)	LFM	474.3	119	1,432	59	7-31	3	24.27
37	J. Lewis (*Glos*)	RM	462.1	108	1,447	59	6-48	3	24.52
38	S. D. Thomas (*Glam*)	RFM	544.1	94	1,749	71	5-84	3	24.63
39	S. M. Pollock (*South Africans*)	RF	266.5	87	594	24	5-53	1	24.75
40	J. P. Taylor (*Northants*)	LFM	436.5	105	1,337	54	4-31	0	24.75
41	P. J. Newport (*Worcs*)	RM	335.1	117	893	36	4-44	0	24.80
42	C. C. Lewis (*Leics*)	RFM	266.4	53	972	39	6-60	2	24.92
43	B. C. Hollioake (*Surrey*)	RFM	275.4	51	908	36	4-28	0	25.22
44	N. A. M. McLean (*Hants*)	RF	518.5	105	1,575	62	6-101	2	25.40
45	D. Gough (*Yorks*)	RF	340.3	65	1,067	42	6-42	2	25.40
46	A. J. Tudor (*Surrey*)	RF	184.2	34	737	29	5-43	1	25.41
47	A. Dale (*Glam*)	RM	249.3	46	794	31	5-25	1	25.61
48	M. A. Ealham (*Kent*)	RM	242.4	83	593	23	5-23	3	25.78
49	I. D. K. Salisbury (*Surrey*)	LBG	387.5	109	958	37	7-65	2	25.89
50	P. A. J. DeFreitas (*Derbys*)	RM/OB	482.4	114	1,363	52	5-38	2	26.21
51	P. J. Franks (*Notts*)	RFM	404.2	87	1,375	52	6-63	4	26.44
52	M. V. Fleming (*Kent*)	RM	404.4	115	1,008	38	4-24	0	26.52
53	S. R. Lampitt (*Worcs*)	RM	416	97	1,330	50	5-33	4	26.60
54	M. A. Robinson (*Sussex*)	RM	416.1	107	1,126	42	4-72	0	26.80
55	G. D. Rose (*Somerset*)	RFM	480.3	132	1,399	52	5-48	2	26.90
56	G. R. Haynes (*Worcs*)	RM	227.5	61	705	26	6-50	2	27.11
57	I. D. Austin (*Lancs*)	RM	345.4	80	978	36	4-21	0	27.16
58	K. P. Evans (*Notts*)	RFM	273	73	735	27	5-92	2	27.22
59	M. T. Brimson (*Leics*)	SLA	369.5	129	901	33	4-4	0	27.30
60	F. A. Rose (*Northants*)	RFM	373.2	59	1,367	50	7-39	3	27.34
61	R. L. Johnson (*Middx*)	RFM	377.2	77	1,369	50	7-86	1	27.38
62	A. P. Davies (*Glam*)	RFM	135.5	41	390	14	2-22	0	27.85
63	M. J. McCague (*Kent*)	RF	235.1	45	758	27	4-40	0	28.07
64	M. N. Bowen (*Notts*)	RFM	309.1	76	875	31	7-73	1	28.22
65	C. M. Tolley (*Notts*)	LM	324.3	76	960	34	7-45	3	28.23
66	R. J. Kirtley (*Sussex*)	RFM	490.4	116	1,532	54	7-29	3	28.37
67	J. E. Benjamin (*Surrey*)	RFM	189.1	42	626	22	6-35	1	28.45
68	A. F. Giles (*Warwicks*)	SLA	459.3	154	1,025	36	5-48	1	28.47
69	R. J. Chapman (*Worcs*)	RFM	246.1	44	943	33	6-105	1	28.57
70	D. G. Cork (*Derbys*)	RFM	545	111	1,618	56	6-119	3	28.89
71	G. P. Butcher (*Glam*)	RM	152.4	24	551	19	4-14	0	29.00
72	M. J. Rawnsley (*Worcs*)	SLA	172.1	46	497	17	6-44	2	29.23
73	T. M. Moody (*Worcs*)	RM	251.1	73	790	27	5-64	1	29.25
74	Mushtaq Ahmed (*Somerset*)	LBG	136	40	411	14	3-26	0	29.35

		Style	O	M	R	W	BB	5W/i	Avge
75	D. R. Brown (*Warwicks*)	RFM	438.2	93	1,489	50	5-40	2	29.78
76	T. F. Bloomfield (*Middx*)	RFM	168.5	27	660	22	5-67	2	30.00
77	G. P. Swann (*Northants*)	OB	199.4	41	666	22	5-29	1	30.27
78	L. Klusener (*South Africans*)	RF	156	38	424	14	4-66	0	30.28
79	S. J. Harmison (*Durham*)	RFM	455.5	93	1,545	51	5-70	1	30.29
80	M. Ntini (*South Africans*)	RF	184.3	48	578	19	4-72	0	30.42
81	C. L. Hooper (*Kent*)	OB	386.2	104	957	31	7-93	1	30.87
82	J. Wood (*Durham*)	RFM	572.5	113	1,916	62	5-52	2	30.90
83	M. A. Butcher (*Surrey*)	RM	119.4	29	340	11	4-41	0	30.90
84	A. R. Oram (*Notts*)	RFM	305.5	75	969	31	4-37	0	31.25
85	G. Keedy (*Lancs*)	SLA	182.3	43	563	18	5-35	1	31.27
86	C. J. Batt (*Middx*)	LFM	201.5	23	846	27	6-101	2	31.33
87	J. P. Stephenson (*Hants*)	RM	286.4	71	770	24	4-29	1	32.08
88	J. D. Middlebrook (*Yorks*)	OB	164.1	45	422	13	3-20	0	32.46
89	N. F. Williams (*Essex*)	RFM	246.5	47	849	26	4-42	0	32.65
90	P. A. Strang (*Notts*)	LBG	353.3	105	983	30	5-166	1	32.76
91	M. M. Patel (*Kent*)	SLA	418.3	102	1,123	34	5-73	1	33.02
92	J. H. Kallis (*South Africans*)	RFM	226.1	79	529	16	4-24	0	33.06
93	M. P. Dowman (*Notts*)	RM	139	31	397	12	2-10	0	33.08
94	D. E. Malcolm (*Northants*)	RF	334	48	1,331	40	6-54	2	33.27
95	A. D. Mascarenhas (*Hants*)	RM	280.5	58	1,000	30	4-31	0	33.33
96	P. J. Hartley (*Hants*)	RM	353.5	66	1,109	33	4-42	0	33.60
97	J. P. Hewitt (*Middx*)	RFM	377.3	64	1,378	41	6-71	2	33.60
98	M. Watkinson (*Lancs*)	RM/OB	175.4	22	607	18	5-45	1	33.72
99	D. P. Mather (*OU*)	LM	168.5	32	574	17	6-74	1	33.76
100	K. D. James (*Hants*)	LM	340	70	1,083	32	4-22	0	33.84
101	R. C. Irani (*Essex*)	RFM	443.5	104	1,392	41	5-47	1	33.95
102	M. W. Alleyne (*Glos*)	RM	284.1	82	818	24	4-63	0	34.08
103	S. D. Udal (*Hants*)	OB	191.2	44	549	16	4-37	0	34.31
104	M. G. Bevan (*Sussex*)	SLC	175.4	27	653	19	3-36	0	34.36
105	M. C. J. Ball (*Glos*)	OB	433	108	1,173	34	4-26	0	34.50
106	D. A. Cosker (*Glam*)	SLA	483.5	127	1,265	36	6-140	1	35.13
107	D. R. Law (*Essex*)	RFM	247.5	44	1,045	29	5-46	1	36.03
108	R. D. Stemp (*Yorks*)	SLA	409	141	1,001	27	5-191	1	37.07
109	I. D. Blackwell (*Derbys*)	SLA	156.2	32	524	14	5-115	1	37.42
110	M. E. Trescothick (*Somerset*)	RM	193.3	45	654	17	4-82	0	38.47
111	A. P. Grayson (*Essex*)	SLA	248.2	59	734	19	3-13	0	38.63
112	P. M. Such (*Essex*)	OB	527	129	1,479	38	5-73	2	38.92
113	P. R. Adams (*South Africans*)	SLC	281.2	79	666	17	4-63	0	39.17
114	G. Welch (*Warwicks*)	RFM	314.5	68	996	25	4-94	0	39.84
115	N. M. K. Smith (*Warwicks*)	OB	329.3	84	957	24	5-128	1	39.87
116	A. Sheriyar (*Worcs*)	LFM	286.1	69	962	24	5-81	1	40.08
117	A. R. K. Pierson (*Somerset*)	OB	258.1	53	842	21	5-117	1	40.09
118	P. C. R. Tufnell (*Middx*)	SLA	631.5	162	1,602	39	4-24	0	41.07
119	M. Hayward (*South Africans*)	RFM	121	20	518	12	3-34	0	43.16
120	N. C. Phillips (*Durham*)	OB	425.4	101	1,216	28	5-56	1	43.42
121	P. D. Collingwood (*Durham*)	RM	200.1	53	582	13	3-89	0	44.76
122	A. P. Cowan (*Essex*)	RFM	238.3	54	859	19	3-18	0	45.21
123	P. Aldred (*Derbys*)	RFM	181.4	38	556	12	3-30	0	46.33
124	G. R. Loveridge (*CU*)	LBG	204	34	655	13	5-59	1	50.38
125	B. W. Byrne (*OU*)	OB	174.1	31	583	11	3-103	0	53.00
126	P. N. Weekes (*Middx*)	OB	237	37	702	13	3-113	0	54.00
127	B. J. Phillips (*Kent*)	RFM	294	55	928	17	3-66	0	54.58
128	R. D. B. Croft (*Glam*)	OB	453.5	117	1,144	20	4-76	0	57.20
129	M. E. Cassar (*Derbys*)	RM	157	29	614	10	3-26	0	61.40
130	R. K. Illingworth (*Worcs*)	SLA	305	81	853	13	3-28	0	65.61

The following bowlers took ten wickets but bowled in fewer than ten innings:

	Style	O	M	R	W	BB	5W/i	Avge
A. C. Dale (*Australia A*)	RM	83.5	30	183	18	6-43	1	10.16
M. Muralitharan (*Sri Lankans*)	OB	226.3	77	463	34	9-65	5	13.61
J. Ormond (*Leics*)	RFM	133.3	51	311	19	6-33	2	16.36
P. L. Symcox (*South Africans*)	OB	92.3	26	207	12	5-60	1	17.25
J. J. Bates (*Sussex*)	OB	102.5	24	273	14	5-67	2	19.50
G. Yates (*Lancs*)	OB	131.3	26	432	18	4-64	0	24.00
S. Elworthy (*South Africans*)	RFM	127	31	415	16	4-71	0	25.93
A. P. van Troost (*Somerset*)	RF	118	24	415	15	4-18	0	27.66
N. Killeen (*Durham*)	RFM	101.2	25	349	12	5-49	1	29.08
C. P. Schofield (*Lancs*)	LBG	79.4	9	299	10	4-56	0	29.90
J. B. D. Thompson (*Kent*)	RM	95.4	20	335	11	4-52	0	30.45
G. P. Wickremasinghe (*Sri Lankans*)	RFM	135.1	26	397	13	4-69	0	30.53
D. Follett (*Northants*)	RFM	103	17	325	10	3-48	0	32.50
Waqar Younis (*Glam*)	RF	100.1	13	397	12	3-147	0	33.08
D. J. Eadie (*OU*)	RFM	113.5	19	434	13	2-34	0	33.38

BOWLING STYLES

LB	Leg-breaks (1)
LBG	Leg-breaks and googlies (5)
LF	Left-arm fast (1)
LFM	Left-arm fast-medium (9)
LM	Left-arm medium (4)
OB	Off-breaks (20)
RF	Right-arm fast (13)
RFM	Right-arm fast-medium (51)
RM	Right-arm medium (31)
SLA	Slow left-arm (11)
SLC	Slow left-arm chinaman (2)

Note: The total comes to 148, because Saqlain Mushtaq, P. A. J. DeFreitas and M. Watkinson have two styles of bowling.

Fourteen players (Donald, Gough, Hoggard, Klusener, McCague, McLean, Malcolm, Ntini, Pollock, Tudor, van Troost, Walsh, Waqar and Wasim) have been designated as fast bowlers in the 1998 season after consultation with a panel of senior players, coaches and umpires.

PETER SMITH MEMORIAL AWARD, 1998

The Peter Smith Memorial Award, given by the Cricket Writers' Club in memory of its former chairman for services to the presentation of cricket to the public, was won in 1998 by Angus Fraser. The award was instituted in 1992. Previous winnes were David Gower, John Woodcock, Brian Lara, Mark Taylor, the Sri Lankan 1996 World Cup squad and Dickie Bird.

RIDLEY WICKET

The Ridley Wicket, a silver stump, was awarded to Andrew Caddick, the first bowler to reach 100 first-class wickets in 1998. He received £1,000.

INDIVIDUAL SCORES OF 100 AND OVER

There were 228 three-figure innings in 187 first-class matches in 1998, 35 fewer than in 1997 when 196 matches were played. Of these, 19 were double-hundreds, compared with 17 in 1997. The list includes 178 hundreds hit in the County Championship, compared with 196 in 1997.

* *Signifies not out.*

J. P. Crawley (8)
109	Lancs v Northants, Northampton
108	Lancs v Worcs, Lytham
124 136	Lancs v Glam, Colwyn Bay
180	Lancs v Yorks, Leeds
156*	England v Sri Lanka, The Oval
100	Lancs v Derbys, Manchester
239	Lancs v Hants, Manchester

G. A. Hick (7)
124	Worcs v Oxford U., Oxford
166	Worcs v Middx, Uxbridge
104 132	Worcs v Sussex, Worcester
119	Worcs v Surrey, The Oval
107	England v Sri Lanka, The Oval
110	Worcs v Somerset, Taunton

C. L. Hooper (6)
203	Kent v Lancs, Canterbury
122	Kent v Notts, Canterbury
100	Kent v Essex, Southend
111	Kent v Glos, Bristol
154	Kent v Worcs, Canterbury
157*	Kent v Northants, Northampton

C. J. Adams (4)
135 105	Sussex v Essex, Chelmsford
102	Sussex v Somerset, Hove
170	Sussex v Middx, Hove

A. D. Brown (4)
100	Surrey v Northants, The Oval
155	Surrey v Hants, Southampton
100	Surrey v Glam, Swansea
132	Surrey v Derbys, The Oval

D. Byas (4)
101	Yorks v Somerset, Leeds
103	Yorks v Derbys, Leeds
116	Yorks v Leics, Leeds
101	Yorks v Lancs, Leeds

S. P. James (4)
227	Glam v Northants, Northampton
152	Glam v Worcs, Cardiff
121	Glam v Notts, Nottingham
147	Glam v Essex, Chelmsford

G. Kirsten (4)
125 131*	South Africans v Glos, Bristol
205*	South Africans v British Universities, Cambridge
210	South Africa v England, Manchester

N. V. Knight (4)
109	Warwicks v Derbys, Derby
159	Warwicks v Sussex, Hove
192	Warwicks v Lancs, Birmingham
130*	Warwicks v Yorks, Leeds

J. L. Langer (4)
233*	Middx v Somerset, Lord's
118	Middx v Worcs, Uxbridge
153*	Middx v Glam, Lord's
166	Middx v Essex, Southgate

M. B. Loye (4)
322*	Northants v Glam, Northampton
149	Northants v Lancs, Northampton
157	Northants v Derbys, Northampton
103	Northants v Notts, Nottingham

T. M. Moody (4)
132	Worcs v Middx, Uxbridge
104*	Worcs v Glam, Cardiff
107*	Worcs v Lancs, Lytham
112	Worcs v Notts, Kidderminster

M. R. Ramprakash (4)
122 108	Middx v Worcs, Uxbridge
128*	Middx v Glam, Lord's
110	Middx v Leics, Leicester

B. F. Smith (4)
121*	Leics v Glos, Bristol
153	Leics v Northants, Leicester
159	Leics v Notts, Worksop
204	Leics v Surrey, The Oval

G. W. White (4)
150	Hants v Oxford U., Oxford
101	Hants v Somerset, Taunton
156	Hants v Sri Lankans, Southampton
106	Hants v Middx, Southampton

M. G. N. Windows (4)
100* Glos v Yorks, Gloucester
143 Glos v Derbys, Chesterfield
103 Glos v Kent, Bristol
151 Glos v Essex, Colchester

M. J. Wood (4)
103 Yorks v Derbys, Leeds
108 Yorks v Hants, Leeds
200* Yorks v Warwicks, Leeds
118* Yorks v Sussex, Hove

M. W. Alleyne (3)
109 Glos v South Africans, Bristol
137 Glos v Warwicks, Bristol
116 Glos v Somerset, Bristol

M. G. Bevan (3)
127 Sussex v Derbys, Horsham
149* Sussex v Leics, Leicester
146* Sussex v Somerset, Hove

D. C. Boon (3)
107 Durham v Warwicks, Birmingham
139* Durham v Yorks, Chester-le-Street
106 Durham v Glam, Chester-le-Street

M. A. Butcher (3)
106 Surrey v Hants, Southampton
109* Surrey v Somerset, Taunton
116 England v South Africa, Leeds

N. H. Fairbrother (3)
126 Lancs v Essex, Chelmsford
138 Lancs v Durham, Chester-le-Street
103* Lancs v Hants, Manchester

A. Habib (3)
112 Leics v Hants, Leicester
198 Leics v Northants, Leicester
114 Leics v Surrey, The Oval

B. C. Lara (3)
226 Warwicks v Middx, Lord's
158 Warwicks v Northants, Northampton
144 Warwicks v Worcs, Worcester

D. S. Lehmann (3)
136 Yorks v Kent, Maidstone
131 Yorks v Notts, Scarborough
200 Yorks v Worcs, Worcester

J. E. Morris (3)
110* Durham v Cambridge U., Cambridge
163 Durham v Glam, Chester-le-Street
140* Durham v Surrey, Chester-le-Street

R. A. Smith (3)
104* Hants v Derbys, Basingstoke
134 Hants v Durham, Southampton
138 Hants v Essex, Portsmouth

V. J. Wells (3)
120 Leics v Glos, Bristol
144 Leics v Yorks, Leeds
171 Leics v Essex, Leicester

U. Afzaal (2)
109* Notts v Derbys, Derby
103* Notts v Northants, Nottingham

M. A. Atherton (2)
152 Lancs v Kent, Canterbury
103 England v South Africa, Birmingham

A. N. Aymes (2)
133 Hants v Leics, Leicester
120 Hants v Glam, Southampton

P. D. Bowler (2)
104 Somerset v Hants, Taunton
101 Somerset v Sussex, Hove

P. A. Cottey (2)
113 Glam v Northants, Northampton
123 Glam v Durham, Chester-le-Street

W. J. Cronje (2)
195 South Africans v Derbys, Derby
126 South Africa v England, Nottingham

D. J. Cullinan (2)
200* South Africans v Durham, Chester-le-Street
157 South Africans v Essex, Chelmsford

M. W. Gatting (2)
241 Middx v Essex, Southgate
103* Middx v Yorks, Lord's

T. H. C. Hancock (2)
135 Glos v Essex, Colchester
220* Glos v Notts, Nottingham

D. F. Hills (2)
118 Australia A v Scotland, Edinburgh
110 Australia A v Scotland, Linlithgow

R. C. Irani (2)
127* Essex v Somerset, Bath
104 Essex v Middx, Southgate

P. Johnson (2)
105 Notts v Northants, Nottingham
139 Notts v Worcs, Kidderminster

J. H. Kallis (2)
106* South Africans v British Universities, Cambridge
132 South Africa v England, Manchester

R. W. T. Key (2)
101 Kent v Durham, Canterbury
115 Kent v Notts, Canterbury

S. G. Law (2)
106   Essex v Notts, Ilford
165   Essex v Northants, Chelmsford

D. A. Leatherdale (2)
134*   Worcs v Oxford U., Oxford
137   Worcs v Middx, Uxbridge

G. D. Lloyd (2)
104   Lancs v Durham, Chester-le-Street
212*   Lancs v Derbys, Manchester

D. L. Maddy (2)
162   Leics v Durham, Darlington
107   Leics v Somerset, Leicester

M. Newell (2)
135*   Sussex v Derbys, Horsham
118   Sussex v Somerset, Hove

P. A. Nixon (2)
101*   Leics v Glam, Cardiff
101*   Leics v Surrey, The Oval

A. L. Penberthy (2)
102*   Northants v Middx, Northampton
128   Northants v Warwicks, Northampton

J. N. Rhodes (2)
123   South Africans v Glos, Bristol
117   South Africa v England, Lord's

O. A. Shah (2)
140   Middx v Yorks, Lord's
116   Middx v Derbys, Derby

N. Shahid (2)
124   Surrey v Worcs, The Oval
126*   Surrey v Lancs, Manchester

N. M. K. Smith (2)
113   Warwicks v Durham, Birmingham
147   Warwicks v Somerset, Taunton

V. S. Solanki (2)
155   Worcs v Sussex, Worcester
170   Worcs v Derbys, Derby

J. P. Stephenson (2)
114   Hants v Glos, Southampton
105   Hants v Middx, Southampton

M. P. Vaughan (2)
177   Yorks v Durham, Chester-le-Street
107   Yorks v Middx, Lord's

M. A. Wagh (2)
126   Oxford U. v Kent, Canterbury
119   Warwicks v Worcs, Worcester

The following each played one three-figure innings:

G. F. Archer, 107, Notts v Glam, Nottingham; R. P. Arnold, 209, Sri Lankans v Somerset, Taunton; M. S. Atapattu, 114, Sri Lankans v Middx, Lord's.

R. J. Bailey, 188, Northants v Derbys, Northampton; K. J. Barnett, 162, Derbys v Sussex, Horsham.

M. E. Cassar, 121, Derbys v Sussex, Horsham; P. D. Collingwood, 105, Durham v Warwicks, Birmingham; D. G. Cork, 102*, Derbys v Sussex, Horsham.

J. A. Daley, 157, Durham v Derbys, Derby; P. A. de Silva, 152, Sri Lanka v England, The Oval; M. J. Di Venuto, 138, Australia A v Scotland, Edinburgh.

M. A. Ealham, 121, Kent v Yorks, Maidstone; A. W. Evans, 125, Glam v Cambridge U., Cambridge.

A. Flintoff, 124, Lancs v Northants, Northampton; T. Frost, 111*, Warwicks v Oxford U., Oxford; D. P. Fulton, 207, Kent v Yorks, Maidstone.

J. E. R. Gallian, 113*, Notts v Hants, Portsmouth; D. J. Goodchild, 105, Middx v Sri Lankans, Lord's; M. A. Gough, 123, Durham v Cambridge U., Cambridge.

U. C. Hathurusinghe, 108*, Sri Lankans v Hants, Southampton; M. L. Hayden, 123, Australia A v Scotland, Linlithgow; D. L. Hemp, 102, Warwicks v Leics, Birmingham; A. J. Hollioake, 112, Surrey v Glos, Cheltenham; P. C. L. Holloway, 123, Somerset v Surrey, Taunton; N. Hussain, 105, England v South Africa, Lord's; M. E. Hussey, 125*, Australia A v Ireland, Rathmines; S. Hutton, 100, Durham v Cambridge U., Cambridge.

S. T. Jayasuriya, 213, Sri Lanka v England, The Oval.

W. G. Khan, 125, Sussex v Derbys, Horsham.

J. S. Laney, 101, Hants v Oxford U., Oxford; M. N. Lathwell, 106, Somerset v Kent, Canterbury; W. L. Law, 131, Glam v Lancs, Colwyn Bay; G. F. J. Liebenberg, 104*, South Africans v Durham, Chester-le-Street.

M. R. May, 101, Derbys v South Africans, Derby; I. Mohammed, 136, Cambridge U. v Yorks, Leeds.

D. C. Nash, 114, Middx v Somerset, Lord's.

D. P. Ostler, 133*, Warwicks v Oxford U., Oxford.

K. A. Parsons, 101*, Somerset v Sri Lankans, Taunton; A. R. K. Pierson, 108*, Somerset v Sussex, Hove; M. J. Powell, 132, Warwicks v Sussex, Hove; M. J. Powell, 106, Glam v Northants, Northampton.

A. Ranatunga, 110, Sri Lankans v Leics, Leicester; J. D. Ratcliffe, 100, Surrey v Worcs, The Oval; S. J. Rhodes, 104*, Worcs v Glam, Cardiff; D. Ripley, 209, Northants v Glam, Northampton; R. T. Robinson, 114, Notts v Yorks, Scarborough; A. S. Rollins, 107, Derbys v Glos, Chesterfield.

P. V. Simmons, 194, Leics v Notts, Worksop; A. Singh, 117, Cambridge U. v Oxford U., Lord's; M. J. Slater, 185, Derbys v South Africans, Derby; A. J. Stewart, 164, England v South Africa, Manchester; I. J. Sutcliffe, 167, Leics v Middx, Leicester; G. P. Swann, 111, Northants v Leics, Leicester.

G. P. Thorpe, 114, Surrey v Warwicks, The Oval; H. P. Tillekeratne, 120, Sri Lankans v Leics, Leicester; R. J. Turner, 105, Somerset v Sussex, Hove; T. A. Tweats, 161, Derbys v Notts, Derby.

Wasim Akram, 155, Lancs v Notts, Nottingham; P. N. Weekes, 139, Middx v Leics, Leicester; C. White, 104*, Yorks v Surrey, Leeds.

TEN WICKETS IN A MATCH

There were 21 instances of bowlers taking ten or more wickets in a match in first-class cricket in 1998, nine fewer than in 1997. The list includes 16 in the County Championship. Two bowlers achieved the feat in the same match, when E. S. H. Giddins took 11 wickets for Warwickshire and C. A. Walsh 12 wickets for Gloucestershire at Bristol.

A. R. Caddick (3)
10-165, Somerset v Durham, Taunton; 11-111, Somerset v Worcs, Taunton; 10-101, Somerset v Kent, Canterbury.

Saqlain Mushtaq (3)
11-157, Surrey v Worcs, The Oval; 11-104, Surrey v Sussex, The Oval; 11-107, Surrey v Derbys, The Oval.

G. M. Hamilton (2)
10-112, Yorks v Glam, Cardiff; 11-72, Yorks v Surrey, Leeds.

M. Muralitharan (2)
10-94, Sri Lankans v Glam, Cardiff; 16-220, Sri Lanka v England, The Oval.

C. A. Walsh (2)
12-153, Glos v Warwicks, Bristol; 10-86, Glos v Northants, Bristol.

The following each took ten wickets in a match on one occasion:

J. F. Brown, 11-102, Northants v Somerset, Taunton.
K. J. Dean, 12-133, Derbys v Somerset, Taunton.
A. R. C. Fraser, 10-122, England v South Africa, Nottingham.
E. S. H. Giddins, 11-164, Warwicks v Glos, Bristol.
R. J. Kirtley, 10-88, Sussex v Notts, Nottingham.
D. P. Mather, 10-139, Oxford U. v Cambridge U., Lord's; A. D. Mullally, 11-89, Leics v Notts, Worksop.
M. J. Rawnsley, 11-116, Worcs v Oxford U., Oxford; F. A. Rose, 11-90, Northants v Worcs, Worcester.

THE SOUTH AFRICANS IN ENGLAND, 1998

Review by TIM de LISLE

It is a requirement of thriller writing that the hero should be taken almost to the point of no return. At the end of the second act, he (or she) will ideally be clinging to a precipice, in a hurricane, by one finger, while the baddie takes leisurely aim, from a sheltered vantage point, with an automatic weapon. This is precisely the position in which the England cricket team found themselves on July 5–6, 1998.

They had followed one follow-on, at Lord's, with another, graver, one at Old Trafford: in reply to South Africa's 552 for five declared, they had scraped 183 all out – a third of the runs, for twice as many wickets. Sent in again by Hansie Cronje, England were soon 11 for two. "In terms of competing," chairman of selectors David Graveney admitted, "we're just not there." The players were not the only ones who were not there: Old Trafford was nowhere near full. The football World Cup was still raging and, even with England knocked out, the back pages belonged to men in shorts. It wasn't just the cricket team that appeared to be in mortal danger, but English cricket. An SOS went out: Save our Summer, perhaps even Save our Sport.

That second wicket brought together Alec Stewart and Mike Atherton, the new captain and his predecessor. When playing for pride, no one comes prouder than these two. They pooled all their dissimilar skills and similar experience to add 226, the highest of their nine century partnerships. Atherton stayed six hours, Stewart seven, and, with one fast bowler absent (Shaun Pollock) and another injured (Lance Klusener), England's supporters began to hope. But then both Atherton and Stewart were caught on the long-leg boundary – captain hook following ex-captain hook. Two more wickets fell immediately. With four left, and only Mark Ramprakash to shield the tail, England were still half a day from safety.

Cometh the three hours, cometh the man. Robert Croft, wicketless all summer and virtually runless for a year, chose this moment to stand up and be counted, to fend off the straight ones and dig out the yorkers, to punch the wide ones through the covers and waft only at anything that was too good for him to get a touch. When Ramprakash was out, there were still nearly two hours to go, but Darren Gough, Croft's soul mate and fellow under-achiever with the bat, also rose to the occasion. At twenty to six, Gough fell to Allan Donald, and the precipice beckoned again: England were still two runs behind. Donald thudded a yorker into Angus Fraser's lower shin. If umpire Cowie's finger had gone up, England could not have won the series. The finger stayed down. Fraser survived 13 balls, and even laid a bat on one of them. Stewart, who had apparently started the recovery with a dressing-room speech on Sunday morning, reserved his most stirring rhetoric for the media: "I'd rather be one down than two down."

To say that England never looked back would be overstating the case, but the corner had been turned. Their in-house psychologist, Steve Bull, noted that the result, on paper "a losing draw", felt like a victory. The next Test, at Trent Bridge, was just as dramatic. Croft was left out, but Gough took

THE SOUTH AFRICAN TOURING PARTY

[*Patrick Eagar*]

Standing: P. R. Adams, A. M. Bacher, M. V. Boucher, L. Klusener, M. Hayward, S. M. Pollock, P. L. Symcox, G. F. J. Liebenberg, J. H. Kallis, M. Ntini, C. J. P. G. van Zyl (*assistant coach*). *Seated*: J. N. Rhodes, D. J. Cullinan, A. A. Donald, S. K. Reddy (*manager*), W. J. Cronje (*captain*), G. Rajah, G Kirsten, R. A. Woolmer (*coach*), B. M. McMillan.

five wickets and Fraser ten, to leave England needing 247 to win. Donald hurled himself at Atherton like a man who had taken 24 wickets in the series and had just worked out that he could still finish on the losing side. An irresistible force met an immovable object, and the consequence was one of the great duels in Test history. Atherton was plainly out, caught behind off his glove, for 27, but was not given. Donald pressed even harder on the accelerator. The two men exchanged world-class stares. Eventually, Atherton escaped to the other end, and Donald induced a snick from Nasser Hussain. Mark Boucher, the young wicket-keeper who had made a habit of fumbling only when it didn't matter, dropped the catch. Donald let out a great wounded roar, of the kind normally heard only by tourists *to* South Africa. Within five minutes, he had composed himself to the extent of trotting up from fine leg in mid-over to give Boucher a forgiving pat on the backside. If ever a visiting cricketer deserved to win a Test series, this man did.

Atherton went on to 98 not out, depriving himself of a hundred, happy to let Stewart turn a slow march into a waltz. It was 1-1, but the tide was with England. In the Fifth Test at Headingley, as if to emphasise how well-matched they were, the teams held a sort of collapsing competition, assisted by a trigger-happy umpire from Pakistan named Javed Akhtar. South Africa were left to chase 219 in five sessions; they needed only a good start, but after an hour Gough and Fraser had them reeling at 27 for five.

Jonty Rhodes, not far behind Donald in the Men Who Did Not Deserve To Lose stakes, mounted a counter-attack, putting together a stand with Brian McMillan that lasted two and a half hours. By the close, South Africa required only 34 to win with two wickets left. It was then that Donald, whose work with the ball was done, finally put a foot wrong. With the England bowlers weary, the South Africans could have benefited from the extra half-hour. But they failed to ask for it before the umpires called time.

England came out on Monday morning charged up like a mobile phone. Fraser lured Donald into the edge that Donald had not been able to lure him into five weeks earlier. Finally, just before 11.30 a.m., Gough had Makhaya Ntini leg-before. It was the tenth lbw in the match and the eighth to be given against South Africa, but that counted for no more in the heat of the moment than it would in the cold print of the scorebook. England had won a big series for the first time since Australia in 1986-87, when Atherton had yet to play first-class cricket. Joy was unconfined, or confined only to the extent that the market for cricket had shrivelled during the years of drought.

The prize that had eluded Atherton, through the longest captaincy stint in England's history, had gone to Stewart at the first time of asking. This was not necessarily an indictment. To a degree, Stewart was reaping what Atherton (once best-known for having earth in his pocket) had sown: a tougher team, better-drilled, still brittle and inconsistent, but no pushovers. What Stewart added was a spark, a dynamism, an old-fashioned directness. By making him wicket-keeper as well as captain and No. 4 batsman, the selectors were asking for trouble, and it was revealing that he passed 50 only after the two follow-ons, when he had had a proper rest. But the decision did help him to impose himself, because it made him the hub of the team as well as its driver. At 35, Stewart was, by his own admission, a much better captain than he had been as a young man at Surrey, trying to cement his Test place. He gave more interviews, more willingly, than any captain in England's history, and carried his good PR out on to the field, showing far more fluency in body language than Atherton or Graham Gooch. The tone was set in the First Test, when he led a charge to set up a target of 290 on the last day. Rain swept away both sides' chances, but Stewart had at least thrown down the gauntlet, as perhaps only a wicket-keeper/captain can.

Around him, Team England continued to grow like grass in this damp summer. Two appointments had a clear impact on the field. Steve Bull had meetings with the players on the long Tuesday afternoons, two days before a Test, and earned some of the credit for Fraser's second comeback of the year. Halfway through the series, Fraser's bowling had fallen back in line with his facial expression – tired and unemotional. Then Bull said something that possibly no one had ever dared say to the old metronome: why not try a few variations? (Interesting that this came from the psychologist. Perhaps the coach was too busy discussing Jung with the batsmen.) The difference was marginal, but it was enough to propel Fraser from six wickets in the first three Tests to 18 in the last two. England also hired a fast-bowling coach, Bob Cottam, who got Dominic Cork's out-swinger working again, and knocked some consistency into the attack.

Good generals need luck, and Stewart had more of it in a month than his predecessor was granted in five years. Above all, he had what Atherton had been denied for the previous year: runs from Atherton himself. There was media talk of not even selecting him: Darren Maddy of Leicestershire was being written up as the new Atherton. Stewart would have none of it. All the same, Atherton walked out to bat on the first morning of the series with the odds stacked against him. The toss had been lost, the Edgbaston pitch was green, the air was dank, his partner was the unproven Mark Butcher, and they had to see off two top-class bowlers on their home-from-home ground. He played and missed a few times, as anyone would have in the conditions, but his balance was back and he despatched the loose balls to the square boundaries with such authority that Stewart addressed him a couple of times as Skipper. At the close, he was on 103 out of 249 for one. All summer, he batted, and looked – and wrote, in his *Sunday Telegraph* column – like a man released from prison.

And then there was the umpiring, which became the most talked-about aspect of the series. The South African papers seethed at the injustice of it. It was certainly true that fortune favoured England in the last two Tests, and umpire Steve Dunne's little shake of the head when Atherton gloved Donald may well have been critical. But in a series as tight as this, you can pinpoint almost anything as having made the difference: a survey by Lawrence Booth in *Wisden Cricket Monthly* suggested that England had actually lost more wickets to contentious decisions than South Africa had, by ten to seven – and, where there is doubt, the umpire is more at fault if he raises the finger than if he keeps it down. It was just that all seven of the controversial South African dismissals occurred in the last two Tests. In the end-of-series interviews, which lasted longer than the final day's play, the South Africans had ample opportunity to complain about the umpiring, and didn't. Donald had made a few remarks after Trent Bridge, but only after Mervyn Kitchen himself had been quoted as owning up to his error, which made the fine slapped on Donald look silly.

What was not in dispute was that the umpiring had been too erratic for comfort. Again and again, television viewers knew beyond reasonable doubt there had been a miscarriage of justice. It was clear that something would have to be done. Since the viewers could not suddenly be offered less information, the umpires were going to have to be offered more.

Perhaps it was not just diplomacy that prevented Cronje from complaining, but a sneaking realisation that he had let the series slip through his fingers. He was a formidable captain in nearly every way – commanding, mature beyond his 28 years, clear-thinking, and the most consistent batsman on either side, with five major contributions in successive innings. But his strategy was narrow and too often defensive. He gave Jacques Kallis, a speedy but green fourth seamer, 30 overs per Test, with instructions to bowl eight inches outside off. The idea was to bore England into submission. It worked spectacularly well at Lord's but, in the other Tests, Kallis collected only six wickets for 274 in 134 overs. The ploy failed to stop Atherton and Stewart scoring at something like their normal rates, 34 and 51 respectively per 100 balls. It put the brakes on Hussain and Ramprakash, who out-tortoised Atherton with 32 and 30 respectively, but they gutsed it out and England were never made to pay for their sedateness.

South Africa, by contrast, had one great opportunity to pile up a crushing total, when they batted first on a belter at Old Trafford. To say that they blew it would be unkind, since they cruised to 552 for five. But that was just the problem – they cruised. Gary Kirsten took 525 balls to make 210. Daryll Cullinan, a more natural talent, needed 235 balls for his 75. Cronje felt unable to declare until nearly noon on Saturday. It was his team's bad luck that a second fast bowler went lame, but they had contributed to it in a way that would be hard to imagine from, say, a recent Australian side. In the field, as England teetered on the brink, Cronje seldom had a third slip, and a couple of edges duly went there. He was apt to handle his team as if they were the underdogs, and in the end they were.

We should not be too hard on him. South Africa are a team of limited resources, shrewdly exploited by Bob Woolmer, and unlimited grit, personified by Cronje himself, intense, brooding, thunder-browed. They may have been simply too tired. The South African board, so enlightened in many ways, seems incapable of turning down an invitation. Rare is the triangular or quadrangular tournament that does not include South Africa. Probably the only person who has done more touring than Cronje in the past few years is Bob Dylan. How many roads must a man walk down, before you give him a break?

Many things are out of a captain's hands and one of them is his strike bowlers' radar. Nine times out of ten, Donald and Pollock would have skittled England on that first day of the series. Instead, they sprayed the ball around like a couple of Englishmen. While Atherton found his old self at one end, Mark Butcher found his feet at the other, coming solidly forward to spank the half-volleys, rocking back to cut the long-hops. Butcher came on so rapidly that England barely noticed the absence of Graham Thorpe, restricted by a bad back to 63 runs in the series. Injury also kept Butcher out of two Tests, yet he was the find of the summer. He and Atherton added 435 runs in six opening partnerships, while South Africa's openers scraped 104 from eight. And Butcher's maiden hundred arrived when it was most needed, in the first innings at Headingley, where the next highest score was Cork's 24.

South Africa's main supplier of timely runs was Rhodes. He had some tuition in footwork from Graeme Pollock and his batting was as twinkle-toed as his fielding. He arrived in a crisis at both Edgbaston (125 for four) and Lord's (46 for four), though you would never have known it from the way he danced to scores of 95 and 117. Edgbaston was a rearguard action but, at Lord's, once Rhodes had broken the shackles, South Africa set the pace. Their total of 360 was enough to push England's batsmen back into their old ways. Donald and Pollock came back strongly from their Edgbaston embarrassment, as Glenn McGrath had a year earlier, and England capitulated to 110 all out. As Atherton, Hussain and Stewart did their best to play catch-up, Cronje played sit-back, or "aggressive containment" as Woolmer oxymoronically called it. Their fast bowlers outdid England's for discipline as well as pace (South Africa had five of the six men in the series who averaged more than 80 mph on the new public speedometer, and the sixth, Gough, missed this match). England's second innings lasted 120 overs, 12 more than South Africa's first, but they made 96 fewer runs. The visitors, rising to the Lord's occasion as visitors usually do, had simply bowled to their field: or rather to their star fielder. Lord's wheeled out its new Hover Cover, but no mere piece of state-of-the-art equipment could hover like South Africa's cover.

In a squad that was short on charisma, Rhodes alone had the ability to light up some of the less glamorous tour fixtures. Donald and Pollock were handled so carefully by the management that they bowled only 106 first-class overs between them outside the Tests. The explosive Klusener went home early with a bad ankle, the exuberant Pat Symcox failed to get a Test, and the agreeably aggressive McMillan was virtually pensioned off: he suffered the indignity of being left out of the side while Gerry Liebenberg, an opener of exceptional haplessness, was repeatedly included. In selection, as in most areas, the teams were well matched: the England selectors did well to persist with Butcher and rehabilitate Cork, but they too had their Liebenbergs. Graeme Hick, recalled on the strength of his hundredth hundred, stuttered to his umpteenth Test flop. Their spinners sent down 153 overs for a single wicket. Ian Salisbury's new-found accuracy evaporated in the face of a calculated onslaught from Cronje, who had seen too much of Shane Warne to take an English leg-spinner seriously. For the second summer running, England's various No. 7s were united only by their inefficacy. After three Tests, Mark Ealham and Cork, bowlers who were supposed to be able to bat, gave way to Andy Flintoff, a batsman of beefy promise preferred to John Crawley on the grounds that he could bowl. He took one wicket and made 17 runs, to take the grand total of the designated No. 7s to 48 runs and three wickets.

Unlike any previous tourists to England, South Africa had to play two one-day tournaments on top of five Tests. The first was the final Texaco Trophy, in which they had little trouble ending England's four-year run of victories. England were captained for the first time at home by Adam Hollioake, who had done badly in the West Indies but well enough in Sharjah to be preferred to Stewart. Compared with South Africa (and most other countries), his team were hugely inexperienced, and they showed it by buckling in the second match at Old Trafford when they were in sight of levelling the series. They then won an irrelevant match in some style.

Three months later came the Triangular Tournament, the first in England since 1912, and a good workout for England against two teams that lead the world in one-day cricket (and are both in England's World Cup group). The tournament was too compressed to gather much momentum (the administrators will not make that mistake again), but it had its moments. One was when England's 12th man, Fraser, shuffled round the Tavern boundary at Lord's with a drink for Alan Mullally, and got a standing ovation which made him the most acclaimed waiter since Manuel in *Fawlty Towers*.

That was a comment on England's series. A comment on South Africa came a few weeks later, when several of them were in Kuala Lumpur, winning gold medals in the Commonwealth Games. Next, they were winning the Mini World Cup in Dhaka. They are not quite the best team in the world, but they may be the most resilient.

Tim de Lisle is editor of Wisden Cricket Monthly.

SOUTH AFRICAN TOURING PARTY

W. J. Cronje (Free State) (*captain*), G. Kirsten (Western Province) (*vice-captain*), P. R. Adams (Western Province), A. M. Bacher (Gauteng), M. V. Boucher (Border), D. J. Cullinan (Gauteng), A. A. Donald (Free State), M. Hayward (Eastern Province), J. H. Kallis (Western Province), L. Klusener (Natal), G. F. J. Liebenberg (Free State), B. M. McMillan (Western Province), M. Ntini (Border), S. M. Pollock (Natal), J. N. Rhodes (Natal), P. L. Symcox (Natal), R. Telemachus (Boland).

Telemachus was injured in practice on the second playing day of the tour and returned home; he was replaced by S. Elworthy (Northerns). Later, M. J. R. Rindel (Northerns) joined the party when Bacher and Klusener also returned home injured.

Manager: S. K. Reddy.   *Coach:* R. A. Woolmer.

SOUTH AFRICAN TOUR RESULTS

Test matches – Played 5: Won 1, Lost 2, Drawn 2.
First-class matches – Played 12: Won 3, Lost 2, Drawn 7.
Wins – England, Worcestershire, Gloucestershire.
Losses – England (2).
Draws – England (2), Sussex, British Universities, Durham, Derbyshire, Essex.
One-day internationals – Played 5: Won 3, Lost 2. *Wins* – England (3). *Losses* – England, Sri Lanka.
Other non-first-class matches – Played 10: Won 8, Lost 1, No result 1. *Wins* – Duke of Norfolk's XI, Kent, Minor Counties, Nottinghamshire, Northamptonshire, Holland, Ireland, Essex. *Loss* – First-Class Counties XI. *No result* – Ireland.

TEST MATCH AVERAGES

ENGLAND – BATTING

	T	I	NO	R	HS	100s	50s	Avge	Ct
M. A. Butcher	3	6	0	338	116	1	2	56.33	1
M. A. Atherton	5	10	1	493	103	1	3	54.77	2
A. J. Stewart	5	10	1	465	164	1	1	51.66	23
R. D. B. Croft	3	6	4	90	37*	0	0	45.00	1
N. Hussain	5	10	0	347	105	1	2	34.70	2
M. R. Ramprakash . . .	5	9	1	249	67*	0	1	31.12	5
D. G. Cork	5	9	1	99	36	0	0	12.37	2
G. P. Thorpe	3	6	0	63	43	0	0	10.50	0
D. Gough	4	6	1	43	16*	0	0	8.60	0
A. R. C. Fraser	5	8	2	39	17	0	0	6.50	0
M. A. Ealham	2	4	0	24	8	0	0	6.00	0

Played in two Tests: A. Flintoff 17, 0, 0 (1 ct); G. A. Hick 6, 2, 1 (3 ct); I. D. K. Salisbury 23, 0, 4 (2 ct). Played in one Test: A. F. Giles 16*, 1; D. W. Headley 2, 1; S. P. James 10, 0; N. V. Knight 11, 1.

* Signifies not out.

BOWLING

	O	M	R	W	BB	5W/i	Avge
A. R. C. Fraser	203.3	55	492	24	5-42	3	20.50
D. Gough	130.5	26	388	17	6-42	1	22.82
D. G. Cork	174.4	29	573	18	6-119	2	31.83

Also bowled: M. A. Butcher 14–5–37–0; R. D. B. Croft 87–20–211–0; M. A. Ealham 38–10–105–2; A. Flintoff 35–4–112–1; A. F. Giles 36–7–106–1; D. W. Headley 22–2–69–2; M. R. Ramprakash 5–0–17–0; I. D. K. Salisbury 25–3–106–0.

SOUTH AFRICA – BATTING

	T	I	NO	R	HS	100s	50s	Avge	Ct/St
W. J. Cronje	5	7	1	401	126	1	4	66.83	4
J. N. Rhodes	5	7	0	367	117	1	2	52.42	1
J. H. Kallis	5	7	0	294	132	1	1	42.00	7
D. J. Cullinan	5	8	1	287	78	0	3	41.00	3
G. Kirsten	5	8	1	257	210	1	0	36.71	4
S. M. Pollock	4	6	1	146	50	0	1	29.20	3
M. V. Boucher	5	6	0	84	35	0	0	14.00	25/1
G. F. J. Liebenberg . . .	4	6	0	59	21	0	0	9.83	1
A. A. Donald	5	6	3	29	7*	0	0	9.66	1
P. R. Adams	4	4	1	10	6*	0	0	3.33	0

Played in three Tests: L. Klusener 57, 34, 17* (2 ct). Played in two Tests: M. Ntini 4*, 0 (1 ct). Played in one Test: A. M. Bacher 22 (1 ct); S. Elworthy 48, 10; B. M. McMillan 7, 54 (2 ct).

* Signifies not out.

BOWLING

	O	M	R	W	BB	5W/i	Avge
A. A. Donald	243.2	69	653	33	6-88	4	19.78
S. M. Pollock	219.5	72	464	18	5-53	1	25.77
J. H. Kallis	158.1	65	306	11	4-24	0	27.81
P. R. Adams	180.1	58	388	13	4-63	0	29.84
M. Ntini	81	27	210	6	4-72	0	35.00
L. Klusener	90	25	217	6	3-27	0	36.16

Also bowled: W. J. Cronje 29–10–65–0; D. J. Cullinan 2–0–2–0; S. Elworthy 31–9–79–1; B. M. McMillan 20–0–46–0.

SOUTH AFRICAN TOUR AVERAGES – FIRST-CLASS MATCHES

BATTING

	M	I	NO	R	HS	100s	50s	Avge	Ct/St
W. J. Cronje	11	12	2	704	195	2	4	70.40	6
D. J. Cullinan	12	17	4	900	200*	2	6	69.23	9
L. Klusener	5	5	2	207	73*	0	2	69.00	4
G. Kirsten.	12	19	5	892	210	4	2	63.71	8
J. H. Kallis	10	14	3	612	132	2	3	55.63	9
G. F. J. Liebenberg. . .	10	17	3	642	104*	1	5	45.85	11
J. N. Rhodes	11	14	1	562	123	2	3	43.23	4
S. M. Pollock	6	8	2	187	50	0	1	31.16	3
M. V. Boucher.	11	10	1	211	46	0	0	23.44	43/1
B. M. McMillan.	6	6	0	119	54	0	1	19.83	8
P. R. Adams	7	6	2	60	27	0	0	15.00	0
A. A. Donald	7	6	3	29	7*	0	0	9.66	1

Played in seven matches: M. Ntini 4*, 0 (2 ct). Played in six matches: M. Hayward 46, 4* (3 ct). Played in five matches: S. Elworthy 48, 10 (2 ct). Played in four matches: P. L. Symcox 21* (2 ct). Played in two matches: A. M. Bacher 43*, 22 (2 ct).

* *Signifies not out.*

BOWLING

	O	M	R	W	BB	5W/i	Avge
P. L. Symcox.	92.3	26	207	12	5-60	1	17.25
A. A. Donald	302.2	89	785	39	6-56	5	20.12
S. M. Pollock	266.5	87	594	24	5-53	1	24.75
S. Elworthy	127	31	415	16	4-71	0	25.93
B. M. McMillan.	85.5	26	210	8	3-38	0	26.25
L. Klusener	156	38	424	14	4-66	0	30.28
M. Ntini	184.3	48	578	19	4-72	0	30.42
J. H. Kallis	226.1	79	529	16	4-24	0	33.06
P. R. Adams	281.2	79	666	17	4-63	0	39.17
M. Hayward	121	20	518	12	3-34	0	43.16

Also bowled: W. J. Cronje 42.1–16–97–1; D. J. Cullinan 27–6–97–0.

Note: Matches in this section which were not first-class are signified by a dagger.

WORCESTERSHIRE v SOUTH AFRICANS

At Worcester, May 14, 15, 16. South Africans won by 89 runs. Toss: South Africans.

A devastating spell from Donald launched the South African tour in winning fashion: Worcestershire, chasing 279, subsided from 125 for one to 189 all out. Donald, who had struggled to find his rhythm earlier, blew away the batting with a spell of six for 24 in 13 overs. Even so, there were only four balls remaining when Adams claimed the final wicket. On the opening day, Newport had bowled well without luck, in ideal conditions for swing. But Kallis and Liebenberg, whose 98 took up 74 overs, put on 162 for the second wicket to form the bedrock of the South African innings. Hick declared the county's reply 59 behind, before tea on the second day, after a fluent 69 from Leatherdale. Then Kallis's second seventy of the game set up a target of 4.5 runs per over. Worcestershire started briskly, and Hick scored a good-looking 58 off 70 balls. Then Donald moved into top gear to provide a taster for the Test series. On the second day, another South African pace bowler ended his tour before it had started: Roger Telemachus, who was not playing, dislocated his shoulder in practice. He had to fly home, and Steve Elworthy reinforced the party.

Close of play: First day, Worcestershire 31-1 (W. P. C. Weston 8*, G. A. Hick 23*); Second day, South Africans 107-2 (J. H. Kallis 44*, D. J. Cullinan 8*).

South Africans

G. Kirsten c Rawnsley b Newport	1	– (2) b Rawnsley	51
G. F. J. Liebenberg c Rawnsley b Hick	98	– (1) c Rhodes b Newport	0
J. H. Kallis b Sheriyar	75	– c Hick b Lampitt	74
D. J. Cullinan not out	67	– lbw b Newport	9
*W. J. Cronje run out	29	– (8) not out	5
J. N. Rhodes (did not bat)		– (5) c Hick b Newport	10
†M. V. Boucher (did not bat)		– (6) not out	34
L. Klusener (did not bat)		– (7) c Newport b Hick	26
B 2, l-b 5, n-b 10	17	B 2, l-b 2, n-b 6	10

1/2 2/164 (4 wkts dec.) 287　　1/0 2/85 3/113 (6 wkts dec.) 219
3/228 4/287　　　　　　　　　　4/131 5/160 6/202

P. R. Adams, A. A. Donald and M. Hayward did not bat.

Bowling: First Innings—Newport 15.1–6–43–1; Sheriyar 20–6–47–1; Lampitt 15–6–26–0; Haynes 12–2–24–0; Leatherdale 4–2–12–0; Rawnsley 15–0–85–0; Hick 11–1–43–1. *Second Innings*—Newport 16–9–30–3; Sheriyar 16–3–57–0; Haynes 6–2–13–0; Lampitt 9–3–22–1; Rawnsley 16–2–55–1; Ellis 6–1–26–0; Hick 4–0–12–1.

Worcestershire

W. P. C. Weston b Klusener	18	– c Cronje b Donald	48
V. S. Solanki lbw b Klusener	0	– lbw b Cronje	34
*G. A. Hick c Liebenberg b Klusener	33	– c Boucher b Klusener	58
G. R. Haynes c Klusener b Kallis	25	– c Rhodes b Donald	1
D. A. Leatherdale b Klusener	69	– c Liebenberg b Donald	3
†S. J. Rhodes c Cullinan b Adams	45	– b Donald	3
S. R. Lampitt not out	20	– lbw b Donald	11
S. W. K. Ellis not out	0	– b Klusener	0
P. J. Newport (did not bat)		– c Cullinan b Adams	9
M. J. Rawnsley (did not bat)		– b Klusener	0
A. Sheriyar (did not bat)		– not out	5
B 4, l-b 6, w 2, n-b 6	18	B 5, l-b 9, w 1, n-b 2	17

1/4 2/47 3/54 (6 wkts dec.) 228　　1/69 2/125 3/134 4/146 5/152　　189
4/120 5/175 6/221　　　　　　　　　6/154 7/168 8/171 9/171

Bowling: First Innings—Donald 18–7–39–0; Klusener 17–4–66–4; Adams 12.5–3–36–1; Hayward 9–1–47–0; Kallis 13–2–30–1. *Second Innings*—Donald 18.4–8–56–6; Klusener 16–3–51–2; Adams 16.2–8–28–1; Cronje 7–4–13–1; Hayward 4–0–27–0.

Umpires: D. R. Shepherd and P. Willey.

†DUKE OF NORFOLK'S XI v SOUTH AFRICANS

At Arundel, May 17. South Africans won by 61 runs. Toss: South Africans.

Before a crowd of 7,000, Bacher and Kirsten opened with a century stand, and the middle order pushed on to set a target of almost six an over. The home side also made a decent start, reaching 70 without loss, but most of their later batsmen crumbled. The exceptions were Hugh Morris, the ECB's technical director, who had emerged from retirement to score 54, and Western Australian Matthew Mason, who made up for expensive bowling by hitting an unbeaten 34.

South Africans

A. M. Bacher c Morris b Mason	44	S. M. Pollock b Thomas	3
G. Kirsten c Thomas b Whittall	71	†M. V. Boucher not out	8
L. Klusener c Solanki b Sheriyar	24	B 1, l-b 13, w 13	27
D. J. Cullinan c Sheriyar b Mason	42		—
*W. J. Cronje c Morris b Sheriyar	33	1/100 2/137 3/167 (7 wkts, 50 overs)	295
J. N. Rhodes c Mason b Sheriyar	35	4/220 5/263	
B. M. McMillan not out	8	6/278 7/287	

P. L. Symcox and M. Ntini did not bat.

Bowling: Sheriyar 10–1–45–3; Thomas 10–0–55–1; Mason 10–0–72–2; Whittall 10–0–54–1; Adams 10–0–55–0.

Duke of Norfolk's XI

W. P. C. Weston c Cronje b Klusener	40	S. D. Thomas run out	8
D. L. Haynes lbw b McMillan	29	M. S. Mason not out	34
J. C. Adams b Symcox	20	A. Sheriyar st Boucher b Bacher	0
A. J. Lamb c Cullinan b Symcox	19	L-b 5, w 11, n-b 7	23
V. S. Solanki lbw b McMillan	5		—
*H. Morris c Ntini b Bacher	54	1/70 2/94 3/107 (48.2 overs)	234
†S. J. Rhodes b Pollock	1	4/115 5/146 6/149	
A. R. Whittall c Rhodes b Pollock	1	7/151 8/178 9/234	

Bowling: Pollock 8–0–26–2; Ntini 9–1–44–0; McMillan 7–0–38–2; Klusener 8–0–29–1; Symcox 10–0–43–2; Cullinan 4–0–33–0; Bacher 2.2–0–16–2.

Umpires: I. Farrell and G. Sharp.

†KENT v SOUTH AFRICANS

At Canterbury, May 19. South Africans won by 98 runs. Toss: Kent.

The tourists continued preparations for their one-day series with England by completing their third win in four days. The South African batsmen scored swiftly: Cronje hit 64 in 45 balls and took 18 runs off one over from Patel. Only Igglesden could slow them down, and he was rewarded with four wickets, while his team-mate McCague failed to strike on his comeback from a month off injured. Kent stumbled from 65 for no wicket to 192 all out, with five overs to spare. Their 19-year-old opener Key was the best batsman in a weakened side.

South Africans

G. Kirsten lbw b Igglesden	13	†M. V. Boucher b Igglesden	0
G. F. J. Liebenberg lbw b Cowdrey	72		
J. H. Kallis c Fulton b Patel	61	L-b 7, w 6	13
D. J. Cullinan b Igglesden	48		
*W. J. Cronje b Key b Patel	64	1/40 2/155 3/156 (7 wkts, 50 overs)	290
J. N. Rhodes b Igglesden	16	4/266 5/273	
S. M. Pollock not out	3	6/290 7/290	

L. Klusener, P. L. Symcox and A. A. Donald did not bat.

Bowling: Igglesden 10–0–40–4; McCague 10–1–51–0; Thompson 10–0–69–0; Llong 5–0–26–0; Cowdrey 6–0–31–1; Patel 9–0–66–2.

Kent

D. P. Fulton c Symcox b Donald	16	J. B. D. Thompson not out		3
R. W. T. Key b Symcox	54	M. J. McCague c Liebenberg b Cullinan		11
*T. R. Ward c Boucher b Cronje	1	A. P. Igglesden c Boucher b Pollock		1
M. J. Walker c Boucher b Donald	15	B 1, l-b 9, w 5, n-b 2		17
N. J. Llong b Symcox	31			
G. R. Cowdrey b Kallis	26	1/65 2/68 3/97	(44.4 overs)	192
†S. C. Willis b Klusener b Symcox	14	4/97 5/142 6/169		
M. M. Patel c Cronje b Pollock	3	7/172 8/177 9/190		

Bowling: Pollock 7.4–1–15–2; Klusener 8–0–40–0; Donald 8–0–28–2; Cronje 6–1–31–1; Symcox 10–1–41–3; Kallis 4–0–15–1; Cullinan 1–0–12–1.

Umpires: J. H. Hampshire and R. Julian.

†ENGLAND v SOUTH AFRICA

First One-Day International

At The Oval, May 21. South Africa won by three wickets. Toss: South Africa. International debuts: C. J. Adams, D. L. Maddy.

Twice England held the advantage, and twice they let it slip, condemning one-day captain Adam Hollioake to his fifth defeat in a row. They started strongly, as Knight supervised two half-century stands and lifted the score to 155 for two after 36 overs. But, when he became the first England batsman of the summer to fall victim to Rhodes's electrifying fielding, England suffered a mid-innings crisis: four wickets fell for six runs. A total of 223 was short of substance, but South Africa were to experience difficulties of their own. After Kallis had announced himself with a stylish 62, Cronje took the total to 175 before his powerful drive was brilliantly snaffled by Hussain at mid-wicket; then Pollock was bowled next ball. Rhodes, though, was commanding. His pull for six off Croft swung the pendulum back towards South Africa, and his stand of 39 with Klusener set up victory with eight balls to spare. England had included Hussain at 24 hours' notice as cover for the injured Thorpe; of the 14-man squad, Alistair Brown, Fraser and Fleming were omitted.

Man of the Match: J. H. Kallis.   *Attendance:* 16,139; *receipts* £512,304.

England

N. V. Knight run out	64	R. D. B. Croft not out		7
†A. J. Stewart b Donald	27	D. Gough not out		0
C. J. Adams c Boucher b Kallis	25	L-b 7, w 12, n-b 2		21
N. Hussain c Boucher b Donald	27			
D. L. Maddy lbw b Symcox	1	1/58 (2) 2/109 (3)	(9 wkts, 50 overs)	223
*A. J. Hollioake c Symcox b Klusener	32	3/155 (1) 4/158 (5)		
M. A. Ealham run out	1	5/160 (4) 6/161 (7)		
C. C. Lewis run out	16	7/201 (8) 8/209 (9)		
A. F. Giles c Boucher b Cronje	2	9/220 (6)	Score at 15 overs: 60-1	

Bowling: Pollock 10–1–45–0; Klusener 8–1–33–1; Donald 10–2–45–2; Cronje 8–1–26–1; Kallis 4–0–24–1; Symcox 10–0–43–1.

South Africa

G. Kirsten c Adams b Gough	4	†M. V. Boucher not out		2
G. F. J. Liebenberg b Giles	30			
J. H. Kallis c Holliioake b Croft	62	B 4, l-b 2, w 2, n-b 1		9
D. J. Cullinan run out	16			
*W. J. Cronje c Hussain b Croft	40	1/4 (1) 2/76 (2)	(7 wkts, 48.4 overs)	224
J. N. Rhodes not out	39	3/105 (4) 4/134 (5)		
S. M. Pollock b Croft	0	5/175 (5) 6/175 (7)		
L. Klusener lbw b Giles	22	7/214 (8)	Score at 15 overs: 73-1	

P. L. Symcox and A. A. Donald did not bat.

Bowling: Gough 10–1–38–1; Lewis 8.4–1–46–0; Ealham 10–0–38–0; Giles 9–0–37–2; Croft 10–0–51–3; Holliioake 1–0–8–0.

Umpires: J. C. Balderstone and P. Willey.

†ENGLAND v SOUTH AFRICA

Second One-Day International

At Manchester, May 23. South Africa won by 32 runs. Toss: England.

In the previous match, Gough had taken a wicket with his second ball after a ten-month lay-off from international cricket. Now he claimed four as South Africa were bowled out for 226. It was not a strong total, but would have been far weaker without Klusener, who made 55 not out from 49 balls after he came to the crease at 143 for six. When England batted, their top scorer again attempted a sharp single to Rhodes and again regretted it. This time it was Stewart, who kept on running back to the pavilion when Boucher flicked off the bails. The TV replay, however, showed that the ball was actually lodged in his armpit at the time; Boucher himself was probably too winded either to appeal or call Stewart back. In any case, Pollock quickly followed up with a perfect in-swinger to remove Hollioake for 46, and the all-rounders packing England's tail failed to live up to their billing. Donald, who bowled with fire and accuracy, finished with three for 32.

Man of the Match: L. Klusener.   *Attendance:* 19,133; *receipts* £580,932.

South Africa

G. F. J. Liebenberg lbw b Ealham	39	P. L. Symcox b Gough		2
G. Kirsten c Adams b Gough	2	A. A. Donald not out		6
J. H. Kallis c Stewart b Gough	9	B 2, l-b 6, w 3, n-b 3		14
D. J. Cullinan lbw b Ealham	14			
*W. J. Cronje c Stewart b Lewis	35	1/6 (2) 2/24 (3)	(9 wkts, 50 overs)	226
J. N. Rhodes lbw b Croft	41	3/42 (4) 4/103 (5)		
S. M. Pollock lbw b Croft	3	5/130 (1) 6/143 (7)		
L. Klusener not out	55	7/166 (6) 8/189 (9)		
†M. V. Boucher b Gough	6	9/200 (10)	Score at 15 overs: 56-3	

Bowling: Gough 10–0–35–4; Lewis 10–1–42–1; Ealham 10–0–34–2; Fleming 8–0–51–0; Croft 10–0–43–2; Hollioake 2–0–13–0.

England

N. V. Knight c Boucher b Donald	34	R. D. B. Croft run out		7
A. D. Brown c Rhodes b Klusener	13	D. Gough c Rhodes b Donald		2
†A. J. Stewart run out	52	L-b 2, w 7		9
N. Hussain c Boucher b Donald	1			
C. J. Adams lbw b Symcox	3	1/30 (2) 2/77 (1) 3/83 (4)	(46.4 overs)	194
*A. J. Hollioake lbw b Pollock	46	4/90 (5) 5/143 (3)		
M. A. Ealham b Cullinan	12	6/169 (6) 7/169 (7)		
M. V. Fleming c Kallis b Cullinan	5	8/182 (8) 9/190 (10)		
C. C. Lewis not out	10	10/194 (11)	Score at 15 overs: 77-2	

Bowling: Pollock 8–0–28–1; Klusener 9–0–58–1; Symcox 10–0–34–1; Donald 8.4–0–32–3; Cullinan 9–0–30–2; Kallis 2–0–10–0.

Umpires: R. Julian and D. R. Shepherd.

†ENGLAND v SOUTH AFRICA

Third One-Day International

At Leeds, May 24. England won by seven wickets. Toss: South Africa.

Now that the series was lost, England produced their best one-day form, sweeping to victory with 15 overs in hand. Fraser made his first international appearance of the summer, and his figures of two for 23 from ten overs were instrumental in limiting South Africa to 205 for eight. Pollock made 60 towards the end, but the extra runs that he and Boucher eked out proved irrelevant in the face of a spectacular opening partnership of 114 between Brown and Knight, followed by a more sedate unbroken 58-run stand between Stewart and Hussain. Brown, showing fast hands and a superb eye, reached 50 in 31 balls: only Chris Old, who needed 30 balls against India, at Lord's in 1975, has bettered that for England. Brown's fifty was the fastest in any Texaco Trophy game (beating Graeme Hick, 34 balls against Pakistan, at Trent Bridge in 1992), and it would remain so: Texaco had announced that after 15 seasons, this, their 53rd sponsored one-day international, would be their last.

Man of the Match: A. D. Brown.   *Men of the Series:* D. Gough and J. N. Rhodes.
Attendance: 13,809; *receipts* £384,578.

South Africa

G. Kirsten b Fraser	19
G. F. J. Liebenberg lbw b Ealham	13
J. H. Kallis run out	1
D. J. Cullinan run out	13
*W. J. Cronje c Stewart b Ealham	35
J. N. Rhodes c Stewart b Ealham	6
S. M. Pollock b Fleming	60
L. Klusener c Stewart b Fraser	14

A. A. Donald did not bat.

†M. V. Boucher not out 26
P. L. Symcox not out 1
L-b 9, w 5, n-b 3 17
—
(8 wkts, 50 overs) 205

1/26 (1) 2/29 (3)
3/57 (4) 4/68 (2)
5/78 (6) 6/118 (5)
7/146 (8) 8/198 (7)   Score at 15 overs: 36-2

Bowling: Gough 10–2–57–0; Fraser 10–1–23–2; Fleming 10–1–41–1; Ealham 10–0–44–3; Croft 10–0–31–0.

England

N. V. Knight c Rhodes b Donald	51
A. D. Brown run out	59
M. V. Fleming b Donald	18
†A. J. Stewart not out	26
N. Hussain not out	33
B 4, l-b 2, w 3, n-b 10	19

1/114 (2) 2/139 (1)   (3 wkts, 35 overs) 206
3/148 (3)   Score at 15 overs: 113-0

D. L. Maddy, *A. J. Hollioake, M. A. Ealham, R. D. B. Croft, D. Gough and A. R. C. Fraser did not bat.

Bowling: Pollock 7–1–34–0; Klusener 6–0–45–0; Donald 7–0–35–2; Symcox 9–1–51–0; Cronje 6–0–35–0.

Umpires: J. H. Hampshire and G. Sharp.   Series referee: Javed Burki (Pakistan).

†MINOR COUNTIES v SOUTH AFRICANS

At Stone, May 27. South Africans won by 94 runs. Toss: Minor Counties.

The South Africans built a large total through McMillan, who made 79 in his second innings of the tour, and Cronje, who hit 58 from 38 balls, with four sixes. Then Hayward grabbed three wickets for eight in 17 balls, reducing Minor Counties to 46 for three. They would have lost even more heavily but for the gift of 49 extras; no-balls, with 34, were only just beaten to the top score of the innings by Mark Humphries, the Staffordshire wicket-keeper. He hit out for 39, sharing a last-wicket stand of 40 with Richardson. It seemed possible that this would be the traditional Minor Counties team's last fixture against a touring Test side, because of the ECB's reforms of non-first-class cricket.

South Africans

A. M. Bacher b Richardson	15
G. F. J. Liebenberg c Dean b Thomas	15
D. J. Cullinan b Fielding	26
B. M. McMillan c Potter b Oakes	79
†M. V. Boucher c Ward b Potter	1
J. H. Kallis lbw b Richardson	55
*W. J. Cronje b Thomas	58

M. Hayward and M. Ntini did not bat.

S. Elworthy not out 12
P. R. Adams not out 3
L-b 6, w 7, n-b 6 19
—
(7 wkts, 50 overs) 283

1/30 2/41 3/111
4/114 5/170
6/256 7/278

Bowling: Thomas 10–1–74–2; Richardson 10–2–49–2; Oakes 10–0–44–1; Fielding 10–0–50–1; Potter 10–0–60–1.

Minor Counties

L. Potter lbw b Hayward	15	S. Oakes b Hayward	6
S. J. Dean c Boucher b Hayward	10	P. A. Thomas lbw b Hayward	0
N. R. Gaywood c Boucher b Ntini	26	A. Richardson not out	6
D. M. Ward lbw b Hayward	0	L-b 8, w 7, n-b 34	49
*I. Cockbain c Liebenberg b Elworthy	16		
R. G. Hignett b Elworthy	21	1/28 2/46 3/46	(43.5 overs) 189
†M. I. Humphries b Ntini	39	4/75 5/114 6/120	
J. M. Fielding st Boucher b Adams	1	7/133 8/149 9/149	

Bowling: Elworthy 8–0–33–2; Hayward 10–1–36–5; Ntini 7.5–1–29–2; McMillan 6–0–26–0; Adams 10–0–45–1; Bacher 2–0–12–0.

Umpires: C. S. Kelly and M. P. Moran.

GLOUCESTERSHIRE v SOUTH AFRICANS

At Bristol, May 29, 30, 31, June 1. South Africans won by 167 runs. Toss: South Africans.

Acting-captain Kirsten was intent on batting practice, after an indifferent one-day series, and succeeded with hundreds in both innings. His first, four hours in the making, was also the first for the South Africans against Gloucestershire since Ken Viljoen's at Cheltenham in 1935. The home captain, Alleyne, responded in kind. Anchoring the first innings, he shared century partnerships with Windows and Williams, and batted six hours for 109. Alleyne declared 13 behind and, on resuming, Kirsten and Rhodes both scored centuries: Rhodes was especially entertaining. The third declaration set Gloucestershire 302 in 68 overs on the final day. Earlier, the tourists had bowled too short. They analysed their mistakes, and bowled the county out inside 32 overs, including five wickets in seven overs during the final session. The South Africans might have won even more heavily had they not conceded 58 extras in the first innings, the most Gloucestershire have ever received.

Close of play: First day, South Africans 337-7 (L. Klusener 33*, M. Hayward 33*); Second day, Gloucestershire 265-6 (M. W. Alleyne 70*, R. C. J. Williams 4*); Third day, South Africans 200-3 (G. Kirsten 104*, J. N. Rhodes 68*).

South Africans

G. F. J. Liebenberg c Ball b Alleyne	22	– c Alleyne b Lewis	1
*G. Kirsten c Alleyne b Ball	125	– not out	131
J. H. Kallis c Williams b Alleyne	7	– (6) not out	2
D. J. Cullinan b Smith	20	– c Windows b Hancock	4
J. N. Rhodes st Williams b Ball	59	– c Williams b Averis	123
B. M. McMillan c Hancock b Ball	3	– (3) c Windows b Averis	21
†M. V. Boucher c Macmillan b Alleyne	20		
L. Klusener not out	73		
M. Hayward c Cunliffe b Alleyne	46		
P. R. Adams not out	23		
L-b 4, w 2, n-b 12	18	L-b 2, n-b 4	6

1/48 2/72 3/112 4/208	(8 wkts dec.) 416	1/9 2/80	(4 wkts dec.) 288
5/226 6/259 7/265 8/377		3/105 4/281	

M. Ntini did not bat.

Bowling: *First Innings*—Smith 22–3–75–1; Lewis 21–2–91–0; Averis 17–3–87–0; Alleyne 26–9–63–4; Ball 28–10–65–3; Hancock 8–1–24–0; Windows 1–0–7–0. *Second Innings*—Smith 11–4–29–0; Lewis 16–1–79–1; Averis 18–7–40–2; Ball 15–3–66–0; Alleyne 10–3–37–0; Hancock 7–1–35–1.

Gloucestershire

G. I. Macmillan c and b Hayward	52	– c Hayward b Klusener	3
T. H. C. Hancock c Boucher b Kallis	11	– c Cullinan b Hayward	35
D. R. Hewson run out	19	– lbw b Klusener	0
*M. W. Alleyne c Boucher b Kallis	109	– b Ntini	4
M. G. N. Windows c Boucher b McMillan	68	– c Liebenberg b Ntini	22
R. J. Cunliffe c Boucher b McMillan	0	– b Hayward	3
M. C. J. Ball b McMillan	2	– run out	1
†R. C. J. Williams c Klusener b Hayward	67	– c Liebenberg b Hayward	0
J. Lewis c Ntini b Adams	11	– c Kirsten b McMillan	23
J. M. M. Averis not out	6	– c Liebenberg b Ntini	0
A. M. Smith not out	0	– not out	31
B 12, l-b 8, w 4, n-b 34	58	L-b 4, n-b 8	12

1/65 2/69 3/122 4/249 5/257 (9 wkts dec.) 403   1/24 2/26 3/50 4/50 5/57   134
6/261 7/367 8/386 9/398   6/72 7/72 8/84 9/86

Bowling: *First Innings*—Hayward 15–4–78–2; Klusener 26–5–67–0; Kallis 26–5–79–2; Ntini 13–1–51–0; McMillan 19–9–38–3; Adams 28–6–66–1; Cullinan 1–0–4–0. *Second Innings*—Klusener 7–1–23–2; Hayward 11–2–34–3; Ntini 8–3–43–3; Kallis 1–0–4–0; McMillan 3.5–1–14–1; Adams 1–0–12–0.

Umpires: K. J. Lyons and N. T. Plews.

ENGLAND v SOUTH AFRICA

First Cornhill Test

At Birmingham, June 4, 5, 6, 7, 8. Drawn. Toss: South Africa.

For the second time in three Tests, rain denied England the chance of a victory, but their competitive and spirited display allowed new captain Alec Stewart to hope for better things to come. His batsmen were rewarded for their positive approach, while his bowlers willingly accepted the extra workload forced upon them when Gough broke a finger.

In everything but the result, England's performance echoed the corresponding Test in 1997, when national expectations were raised by Australia's comprehensive defeat. Even the loud, jingoistic and often drunken support, welcomed by the players but causing consternation among more serious cricket watchers, was much the same. Atherton, shorn of the responsibilities of captaincy, revelled in a return to the ranks with his first Test century in over a year, Cork marked his comeback with five wickets and Fraser continued his consistent Caribbean form to claim his 150th Test wicket.

England fielded seven of the team which lost the final Test at Antigua in March. Tufnell, Caddick and Russell were dropped and Headley was left out of the final eleven. Cork and Gough returned after injury, Croft was the solitary spinner, after playing just one Test in the West Indies, and Ealham was chosen for his first Test for 11 months. South Africa opted to play Rhodes in their middle order and Klusener to strengthen the seam bowling, excluding McMillan from their final line-up.

Cronje chose to give his formidable attack first use of Edgbaston's traditionally bowler-friendly surface. With Donald and Pollock both used to exploiting local conditions for Warwickshire, it was a toss Stewart had not wanted to lose. Yet, by the close of the first day, England had overcome a nervy, tense start to reach an imposing 249 for one, thanks to a 179-run opening stand between Atherton and Butcher. They enjoyed an inordinate amount of luck – Atherton estimated Pollock had beaten the bat "about 30 times" – and Butcher was very fortunate to get the benefit of the doubt from umpire Tiffin after a strong lbw appeal when he was 11. By the time Adams finally made the breakthrough, they had built the best opening stand in any Edgbaston Test, and England's best in a home Test since Atherton and Graham Gooch put on 225 against India at Manchester eight years earlier.

THE ENGLAND TEAM FOR THE EDGBASTON TEST

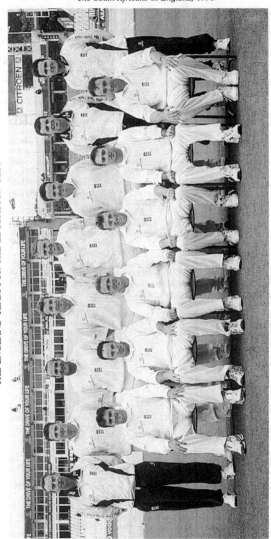

[*Patrick Eagar*

Standing: D. Lloyd (*coach*), D. Gough, M. A. Butcher, R. D. B. Croft, D. G. Cork, M. A. Ealham, W. P. Morton (*physiotherapist*), D. Riddle (*fitness trainer*).
Seated: M. R. Ramprakash, N. Hussain, A. J. Stewart (*captain*), M. A. Atherton, G. P. Thorpe, A. R. C. Fraser.

On Butcher's demise, Stewart promoted himself to No. 3, as next batsman Hussain was answering a call of nature. Fittingly, that meant he was there when Atherton celebrated his first century in 24 Test innings. Even the unconventional manner in which Atherton brought up his hundred – an edge through the slips for four – failed to diminish his relief, signalled by a kiss of the England badge on his helmet. Atherton's six-hour innings ended without addition early the following morning, but he had galvanised England, who surged on to an imposing 462. There was a price, however: Gough, batting in fading light towards the close of the second day, was hit by a short delivery from Donald. Despite two examinations by Wayne Morton, England's physiotherapist, he continued to the end of the innings, but a hospital visit revealed a broken right index finger, which kept him out until the Third Test.

Cork and Fraser, forced to shoulder most of the workload in Gough's absence, epitomised England's wholehearted display. They bowled 67 overs and claimed nine wickets between them, dismissing South Africa for 343 to earn a 119-run advantage. Cork not only marked his return to the Test arena after 16 months by taking five for 93, but also recommended Derbyshire team-mate Ben Spendlove as Gough's fielding replacement. Spendlove claimed two catches close to the wicket – though he later spoiled the effect by dropping Rhodes on 64. Had he held the catch, South Africa would have been 248 for seven, still 15 short of saving the follow-on. Rhodes exploited his reprieve by hitting a lusty 95, before becoming Fraser's 150th Test victim, and shared a determined 104-run partnership with Klusener, which steered South Africa to comparative safety. Even their positive batting was eclipsed by England's adventurous second-innings strategy; they flayed the ball with the freedom of a one-day run-chase, trying to score quickly enough to give their tired attack time to force victory on the final day. At the close, they led by 289 with two wickets left.

However, as in Barbados three months earlier, when another promising position was washed out on the last day, heavy rain with the forecast of more to come forced the captains to agree no further play would be possible during the afternoon. England were left pondering lost opportunities, with South Africa thankful for their reprieve. – MYLES HODGSON.

Man of the Match: M. A. Atherton.   *Attendance:* 62,238; *receipts* £1,458,980.

Close of play: First day, England 249-1 (M. A. Atherton 103*, A. J. Stewart 28*); Second day, England 462; Third day, South Africa 192-5 (J. N. Rhodes 36*, S. M. Pollock 0*); Fourth day, England 170-8 (R. D. B. Croft 1*).

England

M. A. Butcher c Kallis b Adams	77	– lbw b Pollock	11
M. A. Atherton c Boucher b Donald	103	– b Klusener	43
*†A. J. Stewart c Cullinan b Klusener	49	– (4) b Donald	28
N. Hussain lbw b Adams	35	– (3) lbw b Donald	0
G. P. Thorpe b Pollock	10	– b Klusener	43
M. R. Ramprakash b Donald	49	– c Kallis b Adams	11
M. A. Ealham b Adams	5	– c Pollock b Klusener	7
D. G. Cork c Pollock b Donald	36	– st Boucher b Adams	2
R. D. B. Croft c Boucher b Donald	19	– not out	1
D. Gough not out	16		
A. R. C. Fraser c Cronje b Pollock	9		
B 18, l-b 26, w 8, n-b 2	54	B 10, l-b 6, w 8	24

1/179 (1) 2/249 (2) 3/309 (3) 4/309 (4)   462   1/24 (1) 2/31 (3)   (8 wkts) 170
5/329 (5) 6/356 (7) 7/411 (6)   3/80 (4) 4/148 (5) 5/153 (2)
8/430 (8) 9/437 (9) 10/462 (11)   6/167 (6) 7/167 (7) 8/170 (8)

Bowling: *First Innings*—Donald 35–9–95–4; Pollock 42–12–92–2; Klusener 31–7–74–1; Cronje 11–3–28–0; Adams 42–10–83–3; Kallis 20–7–46–0. *Second Innings*—Donald 10–1–48–2; Pollock 12–2–43–1; Klusener 11–4–27–3; Adams 12.1–3–36–2.

South Africa

G. Kirsten c Butcher b Cork	12
G. F. J. Liebenberg c sub (B. L. Spendlove) b Cork	3
J. H. Kallis c Stewart b Cork	61
D. J. Cullinan b Fraser	78
*W. J. Cronje c sub (B. L. Spendlove) b Cork	1
J. N. Rhodes c Stewart b Fraser	95
S. M. Pollock c Croft b Fraser	16
†M. V. Boucher c Stewart b Fraser	0

L. Klusener c Stewart b Ealham	57
A. A. Donald c and b Cork	7
P. R. Adams not out	6
L-b 5, n-b 2	7

1/6 (2) 2/38 (1) 3/119 (3)
4/125 (5) 5/191 (4) 6/211 (7)
7/224 (8) 8/328 (6)
9/328 (9) 10/343 (10)   343

Bowling: Fraser 34–6–103–4; Cork 32.3–7–93–5; Ealham 23–8–55–1; Croft 27–3–85–0; Butcher 1–0–2–0.

Umpires: R. B. Tiffin (Zimbabwe) and D. R. Shepherd. Referee: Javed Burki (Pakistan).

†NOTTINGHAMSHIRE v SOUTH AFRICANS

At Nottingham, June 10. South Africans won by 22 runs. Toss: Nottinghamshire.

Pollock dominated the South African innings, hitting out for 87 from 59 balls before he finally fell in the last over. He struck five sixes and four fours, adding 109 in 15 overs with McMillan. The only home bowler able to restrain the scoring-rate was Dowman, who conceded barely two an over. When Nottinghamshire replied, Afzaal and Robinson kept them going with a third-wicket stand of 129, while Pollard scored 56 in 50 balls. But apart from Extras, which contributed 50, no one else passed ten, as Symcox picked up four wickets.

South Africans

A. M. Bacher c Read b Dowman	39
G. F. J. Liebenberg c Robinson b Evans	13
J. H. Kallis b Hindson	52
*W. J. Cronje c Hindson b Dowman	15
B. M. McMillan b Franks	62
S. M. Pollock c Read b Franks	87

†M. V. Boucher not out	2
P. L. Symcox not out	0
B 1, l-b 7, w 6	14

1/25 2/65 3/94   (6 wkts, 50 overs) 284
4/146 5/255 6/284

S. Elworthy, M. Hayward and M. Ntini did not bat.

Bowling: Evans 9–0–72–1; Franks 8–0–45–2; Wharf 7–0–41–0; Dowman 10–1–21–2; Hindson 9–0–53–1; Afzaal 7–0–44–0.

Nottinghamshire

M. P. Dowman b Symcox	10
U. Afzaal c Hayward b Symcox	74
G. E. Welton b Pollock	0
*R. T. Robinson c McMillan b Symcox	50
P. R. Pollard not out	56
N. A. Gie lbw b Symcox	8
P. J. Franks b Elworthy	7
A. G. Wharf c McMillan b Elworthy	0

†C. M. W. Read c Pollock b McMillan	5
K. P. Evans not out	2
B 6, l-b 9, w 13, n-b 22	50

1/19 2/21 3/150   (8 wkts, 50 overs) 262
4/170 5/187 6/208
7/208 8/222

J. E. Hindson did not bat.

Bowling: Pollock 7–1–18–1; Elworthy 10–1–58–2; Symcox 10–0–43–4; Hayward 10–0–50–0; Ntini 8–0–37–0; McMillan 4–0–26–1; Bacher 1–0–15–0.

Umpires: J. H. Harris and A. A. Jones.

SUSSEX v SOUTH AFRICANS

At Arundel, June 12, 13, 14. Drawn. Toss: Sussex. First-class debut: M. R. Strong.

Having played only one fixture there before, in 1960, South Africa returned to Arundel for the second time on this tour. But rain ruined the match: no play was possible on the second day and only 43.3 overs on the third. Both sides settled for batting practice on a desperately slow pitch. Khan, who was bowled by a no-ball on nought, grafted his way to fifty, but only Adams played with any freedom, before falling to the persevering Hayward. When the South Africans finally replied, Bacher and Kirsten batted themselves into form ahead of the Lord's Test. Michael Strong, a bustling seamer from Cuckfield, worked up a lively pace on first-class debut and Rao, recently tutored by Shane Warne's mentor, Terry Jenner, bowled some tidy leg-spin. The South Africans had arrived late from Brighton on the first day after the tyres of their coach were let down. The vandalism did not seem to be aimed at the tourists, but at Manchester United, the coach's usual passengers. Further damage occurred a few hours later, during the lunch interval: Donald, practising in the middle, bowled some wild deliveries which eluded assistant coach Corrie van Zyl's baseball glove. One spectator was hit in the face, and another had her potato salad splattered.

Close of play: First day, Sussex 252-5 (R. K. Rao 1*, A. D. Edwards 4*); Second day, No play.

Sussex

M. T. E. Peirce c McMillan b Elworthy .	5	†S. Humphries c Boucher b Ntini	14
W. G. Khan c McMillan b Ntini	50	P. W. Jarvis c Boucher b Ntini	3
M. Newell c Rhodes b Symcox.	48	M. R. Strong not out	2
*C. J. Adams b Hayward.	41	B 4, l-b 7, n-b 28	39
J. R. Carpenter lbw b Elworthy	29		
K. Newell retired hurt.	37		277
R. K. Rao c Bacher b Elworthy	5	1/22 2/118 3/129	
A. D. Edwards c Boucher b Elworthy . .	4	4/175 5/235 6/252	
		7/261 8/270 9/277	

K. Newell retired hurt at 242.

Bowling: Elworthy 26–10–71–4; Hayward 20–6–43–1; Ntini 18.3–3–53–3; McMillan 12–4–26–0; Symcox 17–4–43–1; Cullinan 5–0–30–0.

South Africans

A. M. Bacher not out	43
G. Kirsten not out	51
L-b 2	2
(no wkt)	96

D. J. Cullinan, B. M. McMillan, *W. J. Cronje, J. N. Rhodes, †M. V. Boucher, P. L. Symcox, M. Hayward, S. Elworthy and M. Ntini did not bat.

Bowling: Strong 11–2–41–0; Jarvis 12–2–21–0; Rao 7–1–17–0; Edwards 6–0–15–0.

Umpires: H. D. Bird and J. F. Steele.

ENGLAND v SOUTH AFRICA

Second Cornhill Test

At Lord's, June 18, 19, 20, 21. South Africa won by ten wickets. Toss: England. Test debut: S. P. James.

South Africa exploited ideal conditions for pace bowling to take a 1-0 lead in the series. With the ball swinging in the air, and movement off the seam accentuated by the Lord's slope, England's batsmen, with the exception of Stewart and Hussain on Sunday morning, had few answers to the potency of Donald and Pollock. Both teams lost their four first-innings wickets before reaching 50; South Africa fought back with their highest-ever fifth-wicket partnership, while England went to pieces.

[*Patrick Eagar*

Home, James: Donald celebrates as England's newcomer departs.

England had two changes forced on them by injury; Headley replaced Gough, and Steve James of Glamorgan received a late call-up when Butcher bruised his thumb. Stewart recovered from a back spasm in time to play. South Africa brought in Bacher for Liebenberg, though it was to be his last appearance of the tour, as he damaged his shoulder in the field.

Rain delayed play until 1.30 p.m. on the opening day, when there were three further interruptions. The damp conditions persuaded Stewart to field first. It appeared an astute decision as Cork's aggressive out-swing quickly reduced South Africa to 46 for four. The dismissal of Kallis indicated the problems: he was beaten twice in succession by balls that left him, then bowled by a delivery which held its line to clip the off stump.

But without Gough, England lacked the cutting edge to consolidate their advantage once Cork tired. Even so, South Africa's eventual recovery was built on suspect foundations. Rhodes had made only ten when he offered a shoulder-high catch to third slip, which Atherton could only parry. In the following over, Atherton did catch Rhodes, only for England's celebrations to be cut short by the call of no-ball from umpire Sharp. From tentative beginnings, Rhodes flourished as he dominated a stand of 184, a South African fifth-wicket record, with Cronje. In the First Test at Edgbaston, Rhodes had driven fluently, so England adopted a shorter length – only to discover that he was a more than adequate cutter of the ball. In all, Rhodes batted for two minutes short of five hours while compiling his second Test century, nearly five years after his first. He struck 14 fours and a six before finally edging the persistent Fraser into Stewart's gloves. With Cronje making 81 and useful contributions from Boucher and Klusener, South Africa got to 360, a total at least a hundred higher than might have been expected.

England started their reply on the second evening, with the speedometer recording Donald as bowling consistently at around 90 miles an hour. By the close, they were in serious danger at 40 for three. James, making his debut aged 30 (having been ignored when he was really on form in 1997) struck two handsome fours but then nudged a short rising delivery down the leg side to Boucher. Atherton had already been held at slip off Pollock, who also brought the ball back sharply for Stewart to fall lbw.

Saturday morning saw a steady procession of England batsmen returning to the pavilion, their defences breached by fast bowling of the highest quality, backed by agile fielding. Hussain was taken by Boucher diving in front of slip, and Thorpe was brilliantly caught off the middle of the bat by Bacher at short leg. Ramprakash, who could muster only one scoring shot in his first 80 minutes at the crease, was caught off a delivery from Donald that bounced and appeared to brush his elbow on its way through to Boucher. Ramprakash's subsequent display of dissent (he altered his course to tell umpire Hair: "You're messing with my career, Darrell") earned him a suspended one-match ban and an £850 fine. England were bowled out inside 47 overs. For only the fourth time in their Test history, Extras contributed England's highest score: 20, with Hussain's 15 the next best.

EXTRAS AS TOP SCORER IN TEST INNINGS

Extras	Total		
17	58	South Africa v England at Lord's	1912
11	30	South Africa v England at Birmingham	1924
20	97	New Zealand v England at Nottingham	1973
25	126	England v West Indies at Manchester	1976
46	227	England v Pakistan at Lord's	1982
36	200	Australia v West Indies at St John's	1983-84
59	315	England v West Indies at Port-of-Spain	1985-86
38	160	New Zealand v Pakistan at Lahore	1990-91
53	248	Australia v West Indies at Georgetown	1990-91
22	93	New Zealand v Pakistan at Hamilton	1992-93
22	114	India v West Indies at Mohali	1994-95
20	**110**	**England v South Africa at Lord's**	**1998**

[Research: Gordon Vince

When the follow-on was enforced on the third afternoon, James soon edged an out-swinger to second slip. But, as the bowling was beginning to tire, England at last provided some resistance, in a 94-run partnership between Atherton and Hussain. Their work, however, was unstitched when, with the close of play approaching, Atherton rashly swept Adams to square leg, where Kallis pulled off a fine overhead catch.

The prospect of an England escape existed only while Hussain and Stewart were adding 116 for the fourth wicket. Hussain completed his seventh Test century shortly after lunch on Sunday. But, when Stewart was caught behind off Kallis, England produced a horrendous collapse. Five more wickets fell for the addition of only 11 runs as Kallis, the fourth member of the South African seam attack, recorded Test-best figures of four for 24. Only a defiant last-wicket stand between Fraser and Croft averted an innings defeat. A Test which had begun with a bright symbol for English cricket, as the Duke of Edinburgh officially opened the new Grand Stand, ended in crushing defeat, seven balls after tea on the fourth day. – GRAHAM OTWAY.

Man of the Match: J. N. Rhodes.   *Attendance:* 106,070; *receipts* £2,992,071.
Close of play: First day, South Africa 135-4 (W. J. Cronje 38*, J. N. Rhodes 47*); Second day, England 40-3 (N. Hussain 10*, D. W. Headley 0*); Third day, England 105-2 (N. Hussain 52*, D. W. Headley 1*).

South Africa

A. M. Bacher c Stewart b Cork	22		
G. Kirsten b Cork	4	– (1) not out	9
J. H. Kallis b Cork	0		
D. J. Cullinan c Stewart b Cork	16	– (2) not out	5
*W. J. Cronje c Ramprakash b Ealham	81		
J. N. Rhodes c Stewart b Fraser	117		
S. M. Pollock c Hussain b Cork	14		
†M. V. Boucher c Stewart b Headley	35		
L. Klusener b Headley	34		
A. A. Donald not out	7		
P. R. Adams c Stewart b Cork	3		
B 1, l-b 20, n-b 6	27	N-b 1	1

1/8 (2) 2/16 (3) 3/43 (1) 4/46 (4)   360   (no wkt) 15
5/230 (5) 6/273 (7) 7/283 (6)
8/340 (9) 9/353 (8) 10/360 (11)

Bowling: *First Innings*—Fraser 31–8–78–1; Cork 31.1–5–119–6; Headley 22–2–69–2; Ealham 15–2–50–1. *Second Innings*—Fraser 1–0–10–0; Cork 0.1–0–5–0.

England

S. P. James c Boucher b Donald	10	– (2) c Kallis b Pollock	0
M. A. Atherton c Kirsten b Pollock	0	– (1) c Kallis b Adams	44
N. Hussain c Boucher b Donald	15	– lbw b Klusener	105
*†A. J. Stewart lbw b Pollock	14	– (5) c Boucher b Kallis	56
D. W. Headley c Boucher b Donald	2	– (4) c Cronje b Adams	1
G. P. Thorpe c Bacher b Kallis	10	– lbw b Kallis	0
M. R. Ramprakash c Boucher b Donald	12	– b Klusener	0
M. A. Ealham run out	8	– b Kallis	4
D. G. Cork c Klusener b Pollock	12	– c Boucher b Kallis	2
R. D. B. Croft not out	6	– not out	16
A. R. C. Fraser c Boucher b Donald	1	– c Pollock b Adams	17
B 8, l-b 10, n-b 2	20	B 1, l-b 6, w 5, n-b 7	19

1/15 (2) 2/15 (1) 3/40 (4) 4/48 (3)   110   1/8 (2) 2/102 (1) 3/106 (4)   264
5/49 (5) 6/64 (6) 7/74 (8)   4/222 (5) 5/224 (6) 6/224 (3)
8/97 (7) 9/109 (9) 10/110 (11)   7/225 (7) 8/228 (9)
                                      9/233 (8) 10/264 (11)

Bowling: *First Innings*—Donald 15.3–5–32–5; Pollock 18–5–42–3; Klusener 8–5–10–0; Kallis 5–3–8–1. *Second Innings*—Donald 24–6–82–0; Pollock 27–16–29–1; Klusener 23–5–54–2; Kallis 19–9–24–4; Adams 23–7–62–3; Cronje 4–2–6–0.

Umpires: D. B. Hair (Australia) and G. Sharp.   Referee: Javed Burki (Pakistan).

BRITISH UNIVERSITIES v SOUTH AFRICANS

At Cambridge, June 24, 25, 26. Drawn. Toss: South Africans. First-class debuts: B. L. Hutton, D. Leather.

So unequal was the contest that the South Africans scored 535 runs for one wicket, and that was a run-out. On the opening day, Kirsten batted 348 minutes and 333 balls for 205 not out, including 22 fours, the fourth double-century of his career. He gave one chance, a possible stumping off Loveridge, on 180, and shared stands of 137 with Liebenberg and 257 with Kallis. In reply, the Universities folded for 199, with Symcox claiming four wickets. Only Singh, the Cambridge captain, fought back against the second-string South African attack, hitting 64 in what was his first first-class innings of the summer, thanks to bad weather and his law finals. The tourists preferred more batting practice to enforcing the follow-on. But rain permitted only 37 overs on the final day, during which Ntini broke Smith's finger, which was to put him out of the Varsity Match. The debutants included Ben Hutton, son of Richard and grandson of Sir Leonard.

Close of play: First day, British Universities 14-1 (E. T. Smith 4*, M. J. Chilton 6*); Second day, South Africans 130-0 (G. F. J. Liebenberg 56*, D. J. Cullinan 72*).

South Africans

G. Kirsten not out	205			
G. F. J. Liebenberg run out	52	– (1) not out	64	
J. H. Kallis not out	106			
D. J. Cullinan (did not bat)		– (2) not out	75	
B 7, l-b 4, w 3, n-b 17	31	L-b 1, w 1	2	

1/137	(1 wkt dec.) 394	(no wkt dec.) 141

B. M. McMillan, *W. J. Cronje, †M. V. Boucher, P. L. Symcox, S. Elworthy, M. Hayward and M. Ntini did not bat.

Bowling: *First Innings*—Leather 6–0–38–0; Francis 14–3–49–0; Hutton 8–0–32–0; Davies 31–3–101–0; Loveridge 28–3–112–0; Wagh 11–1–29–0; Chilton 4–0–19–0; House 1–0–3–0. *Second Innings*—Francis 8–2–24–0; Leather 4–1–6–0; Loveridge 15–0–58–0; Chilton 2–1–5–0; Davies 12–3–37–0; Wagh 1–1–0–0; Hutton 2–0–10–0.

British Universities

M. A. Wagh (*Oxford*) lbw b Elworthy	0	– not out	24
E. T. Smith (*Cambridge*) c Cullinan b Elworthy	13	– retired hurt	17
M. J. Chilton (*Durham*) c Boucher b Hayward	21	– c McMillan b Elworthy	12
*A. Singh (*Cambridge*) c Elworthy b Symcox	64	– c McMillan b Elworthy	7
W. J. House (*Cambridge*) b Symcox	9	– c Symcox b Ntini	28
G. R. Loveridge (*Cambridge*) c and b Hayward	11	– not out	4
†T. M. B. Bailey (*Loughborough*) c Boucher b McMillan	3		
B. L. Hutton (*Durham*) c Boucher b Elworthy	10		
D. Leather (*Loughborough*) c McMillan b Symcox	0		
M. K. Davies (*Loughborough*) c Kirsten b Symcox	16		
S. R. G. Francis (*Durham*) not out	6		
B 4, l-b 14, n-b 28	46	B 4, l-b 5, n-b 8	17

1/2 2/37 3/47 4/79 5/127	199	1/41 2/51 3/103 (3 wkts) 109
6/162 7/162 8/163 9/187		

In the second innings E. T. Smith retired hurt at 25.

Bowling: *First Innings*—Elworthy 13–1–62–3; Hayward 14–3–65–2; Symcox 13.4–3–28–4; Ntini 6–2–9–0; McMillan 9–5–17–1. *Second Innings*—Elworthy 8–2–31–2; Ntini 8–2–28–1; Symcox 6–0–18–0; Hayward 5–2–9–0; Cullinan 6–2–14–0.

Umpires: G. I. Burgess and N. G. Cowley.

†NORTHAMPTONSHIRE v SOUTH AFRICANS

At Northampton, June 28. South Africans won by 98 runs (D/L method). Toss: South Africans. Taking full advantage of his promotion to open, Klusener batted Northamptonshire out of a rain-affected match with an unbeaten 142 from 132 balls. He hit 19 fours, and added 185 at seven an over with Cronje, whose run-a-ball 77 featured a spectacular six into the new Indoor Cricket Centre off Malcolm, the tourists' tormentor at The Oval four years earlier. The weather intervened during the South African innings and Northamptonshire were left to chase a revised target of 287 in 45 overs. They never looked like achieving it, although Warren gained some useful practice.

South Africans

G. Kirsten c Sales b Follett	33
L. Klusener not out	142
J. H. Kallis c Warren b Penberthy	2
*W. J. Cronje c Walton b Taylor	77
B 2, l-b 7, w 10, n-b 2	21

1/75 2/90 3/275   (3 wkts, 45 overs) 275

†G. F. J. Liebenberg, B. M. McMillan, J. N. Rhodes, S. M. Pollock, P. R. Adams, A. A. Donald and M. Ntini did not bat.

Bowling: Taylor 9–1–51–1; Malcolm 9–0–53–0; Penberthy 9–0–40–1; Follett 9–0–68–1; Snape 4–0–29–0; Curran 5–0–25–0.

Northamptonshire

†R. J. Warren c Kallis b Adams	81	J. P. Taylor b Ntini	1
R. J. Bailey run out	30	D. Follett not out	9
M. B. Loye c Donald b Ntini	19		
D. J. Sales c Kallis b Adams	4	L-b 2, w 8, n-b 24	34
A. L. Penberthy run out	7		
T. C. Walton c Liebenberg b Ntini	0	1/80 2/113 3/135 (8 wkts, 45 overs) 189	
*K. M. Curran not out	4	4/161 5/161 6/174	
J. N. Snape run out	0	7/174 8/178	

D. E. Malcolm did not bat.

Bowling: Donald 6–0–28–0; Pollock 6–1–17–0; McMillan 6–1–19–0; Klusener 6–0–45–0; Adams 9–1–36–2; Ntini 9–0–32–3; Cronje 2–0–7–0; Rhodes 1–0–3–0.

Umpires: P. Carrick and R. A. White.

ENGLAND v SOUTH AFRICA

Third Cornhill Test

At Manchester, July 2, 3, 4, 5, 6. Drawn. Toss: South Africa. Test debut: A. F. Giles.

Having been totally outplayed at Lord's, England did produce a display of old-fashioned guts to avoid going down the same hole at Old Trafford. They had to follow on in successive Tests for the first time since India in 1992-93 and were only secure from defeat when less than three overs remained on the final evening. But it was a Dunkirk-style evacuation of the kind much beloved of English cricket followers which kept England in with a chance of winning the series. Their last pair had been at the crease for a nerve-wracking 19 minutes and their aggregate score was level with South Africa. For England, the recriminations were smothered by the relief. But they had come very close to defeat on a pitch almost devoid of bounce and totally devoid of pace. At Lord's, they had at least succumbed on a surface which encouraged the South African fast bowlers.

England named two spinners, including new cap Ashley Giles of Warwickshire, for the first time in the series. With Gough fit again and Knight preferred to James, they had three changes; Headley and Ealham were also dropped, and Ben Hollioake was omitted from the 12. South Africa made two forced changes: Bacher's shoulder had not recovered since Lord's, so Liebenberg returned, and they rested Pollock, who had a thigh strain, giving Ntini his first overseas Test.

The pitch produced some turn on the first day, but helped the slow bowlers less and less as the match progressed. Winning the toss allowed South Africa to grind out a big total on the first two days, constructing an invincible position and ensuring that England's spinners would not have a fourth innings to bowl in. In retrospect, they must have wished that they had got England in on the second evening rather than an hour into the third morning. Had they scored more quickly, there would have been time to bundle England out twice. But in the end, they failed to win because they ran out of bowlers in England's second innings. Donald bowled himself to a standstill, battling his suspect left ankle, Klusener managed only three overs and Kallis gave up in the final hour when his hamstring caved in.

LONGEST INNINGS BY SOUTH AFRICANS

Hrs	Mins	Runs			
11	27	214	P. G. Amm	Eastern Province v Transvaal at Port Elizabeth . .	1988-89
10	56	337*	D. J. Cullinan	Transvaal v Northern Transvaal at Johannesburg .	1993-94
10	**50**	**210**	**G. Kirsten**	**South Africa v England at Manchester**	**1998**
10	33	141	G. F. J. Liebenberg	Orange Free State v E. Province at Bloemfontein	1994-95
10	16	307*	T. N. Lazard	Boland v Western Province at Worcester (SA). . .	1993-94

[*Source:* Wisden Book of Cricket Records *(Fourth edition)*

South Africa's total of 552 for five, their highest against England, was built around a 238-run partnership between Kirsten and Kallis – a South African second-wicket Test record and their best for any wicket since isolation. Kirsten's 210 was his maiden Test double-century but his second in successive first-class innings. He batted ten hours and 50 minutes, the longest Test innings by a South African; even Bruce Mitchell and Jackie McGlew never matched this for stickability. Kirsten hit 24 fours and a six in 525 balls. Kallis scored a Test-best 132, in just under six hours, and even the normally free-flowing Cullinan took five hours over 75. England checked the scoring-rate efficiently, but it seemed too early to go on the defensive on the first afternoon, when South Africa were hardly rollicking along at 59 for one from 31 overs.

England's reply was a repeat of their Lord's nightmare. They were not helped by Thorpe's recurrent back injury, which made him a passenger. But the South Africans got far more out of the pitch than England had, even though their efforts extracted a terrible price in injuries by the finish. Only Atherton and Stewart did not seem out of their depth against the magnificent Donald, who set up the kill. The left-arm spinner Adams cashed in with four wickets, his best figures against England.

Even with Klusener unable to share the new ball, England collapsed to 11 for two following on. Another four-day defeat beckoned. But then Atherton and Stewart combined in a courageous stand. They almost matched Kirsten and Kallis, putting on 226, and they were under infinitely more pressure. Stewart even took control of the attack on Sunday afternoon, when they added 121 between lunch and tea. When they were still together at the close, with the deficit down to 158, England began to hope the game could be saved. But Atherton perished an hour into the final day, and Stewart half an hour after lunch, both hooking. Stewart's defiant 164, lasting seven hours, was an astonishing performance from someone carrying so much responsibility.

[*Patrick Eagar*

Driving on: Kirsten on the long road to 210.

Donald knew he represented the difference between victory and the draw, and was at his best as he swept through the remaining middle order. Then England found an unlikely hero in Croft, who made up for three wicketless Tests by keeping his end intact for more than three hours. Gough supported him for 78 minutes, but England were still two short of making South Africa bat again when last man Fraser arrived, with 7.1 of the statutory final 15 overs remaining. When Croft levelled the scores, two more overs – for a change of innings – were knocked off the requirement. Donald bowled a superb final over to Fraser, whose heart must have missed a beat at a loud appeal for lbw last ball. There was some debate about the relevant regulation, which had just been altered. But it was clear that if a wicket had fallen during the next over, South Africa would not have had time to bat; Croft played out a maiden against Adams, but England were already safe.

Poor crowds, especially on the first day, when 11,200 spectators took up barely half the ground's capacity, prompted much discussion of cricket's apparently fading appeal, especially in the midst of the frenzy of World Cup soccer in France. The ECB issued a press release arguing, on the basis of 15-year attendance patterns, that the figure was just below average. Following near-pantomime scenes at Edgbaston, Lancashire had introduced stricter rules on bringing alcohol into the ground and on "fancy dress which might obstruct the view". Some thought this had put the crowds off. Others thought a little English success was all that was required. – MICHAEL OWEN-SMITH.

Man of the Match: J. H. Kallis.   *Attendance:* 50,953; receipts £1,105,594.

Close of play: First day, South Africa 237-1 (G. Kirsten 98*, J. H. Kallis 117*); Second day, South Africa 487-4 (W. J. Cronje 27*, J. N. Rhodes 12*); Third day, England 162-8 (A. F. Giles 1*, D. Gough 0*); Fourth day, England 211-2 (M. A. Atherton 81*, A. J. Stewart 114*).

South Africa

G. Kirsten c Stewart b Fraser 210	L. Klusener not out 17
G. F. J. Liebenberg b Gough 16	B 4, l-b 10, w 1, n-b 6 21
J. H. Kallis b Gough 132	
D. J. Cullinan b Giles 75	1/25 (2) 2/263 (3) (5 wkts dec.) 552
*W. J. Cronje not out 69	3/439 (1) 4/457 (4)
J. N. Rhodes c Cork b Gough 12	5/490 (6)

†M. V. Boucher, A. A. Donald, P. R. Adams and M. Ntini did not bat.

Bowling: Gough 37–5–116–3; Cork 35.5–7–109–0; Fraser 35–11–87–1; Croft 51–14–103–0; Giles 36–7–106–1; Ramprakash 5–0–17–0.

England

N. V. Knight c Boucher b Donald	11	– c Boucher b Donald 1
M. A. Atherton c Boucher b Ntini	41	– c Ntini b Kallis 89
N. Hussain c Boucher b Donald	4	– b Kallis 5
*†A. J. Stewart b Kallis	40	– c Klusener b Donald 164
M. R. Ramprakash c Boucher b Adams	30	– lbw b Donald 34
D. G. Cork c Cronje b Adams	6	– (7) b Adams 1
R. D. B. Croft b Ntini	11	– (8) not out 37
G. P. Thorpe lbw b Adams	0	– (6) b Donald 0
A. F. Giles not out	16	– c sub (B. M. McMillan) b Donald . 1
D. Gough c Donald b Adams	6	– c Kirsten b Donald 12
A. R. C. Fraser lbw b Kallis	0	– not out 0
B 5, l-b 12, n-b 1	18	B 20, l-b 2, w 1, n-b 2 . . . 25

1/26 (1) 2/34 (3) 3/94 (2) 4/108 (4)   183   1/4 (1) 2/11 (3) 3/237 (2)   (9 wkts) 369
5/136 (6) 6/155 (7) 7/156 (8)   4/293 (4) 5/293 (6)
8/161 (5) 9/179 (10) 10/183 (11)   6/296 (7) 7/323 (5)
                                                 8/329 (9) 9/367 (10)

Bowling: *First Innings*—Donald 13–3–28–2; Klusener 14–4–37–0; Ntini 16–7–28–2; Adams 31–10–63–4; Kallis 8.1–3–10–2. *Second Innings*—Donald 40–14–88–6; Kallis 41–19–71–2; Ntini 29–11–67–0; Adams 51–22–90–1; Klusener 3–0–15–0; Cronje 6–3–15–0; Cullinan 1–0–1–0.

Umpires: D. B. Cowie (New Zealand) and P. Willey.   Referee: Javed Burki (Pakistan).

†At Amstelveen, July 8. South Africans won by 83 runs. Toss: South Africans. South Africans 248 for six (50 overs) (G. Kirsten 123 not out, M. V. Boucher 52; T. B. M. de Leede three for 56); Holland 165 (49.5 overs) (Extras 46; M. Hayward three for 29).

†At Downpatrick, July 10. No result. Toss: Ireland. South Africans 333 for nine (50 overs) (J. N. Rhodes 39, S. M. Pollock 116 not out, M. V. Boucher 79, Extras 34; G. Cooke four for 60); Ireland 72 for two (16.3 overs) (Extras 32).
The South Africans returned to Ireland for the first time since 1951.

†At Castle Avenue, Dublin, July 12. South Africans won by 63 runs. Toss: South Africans. South Africans 289 for five (50 overs) (G. Kirsten 47, D. J. Cullinan 117 not out, W. J. Cronje 74; M. Dwyer three for 50); Ireland 226 for nine (50 overs) (A. R. Dunlop 101 not out, Extras 39; S. Elworthy three for 40).
Irish captain Angus Dunlop scored only the second century by Ireland against a Test touring team, and the first since T. G. McVeagh's 102 not out in 1928, when they beat West Indies.

DURHAM v SOUTH AFRICANS

At Chester-le-Street, July 14, 15, 16. Drawn. Toss: Durham.

The tourists pulled in more than 8,000 spectators over three days, but there was not much to entertain them after a double-hundred by Cullinan, the first at the Riverside. On a pitch with pace and bounce, Cullinan played beautifully to reach his first hundred off 193 balls, then brutally to score his second in 81. He hit 37 fours in 338 minutes, and added 232 with Liebenberg, who had returned after being hit on the finger. When Durham batted, Extras was easily their highest contributor, with 69; Hayward bowled 15 no-balls, which counted for 30 runs. The next highest score was Gough's 39, taking three and a quarter hours. Symcox claimed five wickets, varying his flight cleverly. Careless strokes saw the South Africans slip to 35 for four on resuming; Liebenberg restored order with a workmanlike hundred, but there was little sign of urgency from anyone. The declaration set Durham 287 from 51 overs, but neither side got close to victory.

Close of play: First day, Durham 10-0 (J. J. B. Lewis 3*, M. A. Gough 6*); Second day, South Africans 49-4 (G. F. J. Liebenberg 25*, W. J. Cronje 11*).

South Africans

G. Kirsten b Betts	13	– (2) b Betts		5
G. F. J. Liebenberg b Collingwood	85	– (1) not out		104
D. J. Cullinan not out	200	– b Harmison		1
*W. J. Cronje c Gough b Betts	33	– (6) lbw b Wood		41
J. N. Rhodes not out	0	– (4) c Harmison b Betts		1
B. M. McMillan (did not bat)		– (5) lbw b Phillips		5
†M. V. Boucher (did not bat)		– c Wood b Harmison		27
P. L. Symcox (did not bat)		– not out		21
B 4, l-b 5, w 2, n-b 20	31	L-b 3, n-b 2		5
1/45 2/115 3/347 (3 wkts dec.)	362	1/15 2/18 3/21 (6 wkts dec.)		210
		4/35 5/111 6/168		

M. Hayward, S. Elworthy and A. A. Donald did not bat.

In the first innings G. F. J. Liebenberg, when 1, retired hurt at 10 and resumed at 115.

Bowling: *First Innings*—Betts 18-4-77-2; Harmison 20-5-82-0; Wood 21-4-86-0; Phillips 14-2-48-0; Collingwood 20.1-6-54-1; Gough 2-0-6-0. *Second Innings*—Betts 14-1-40-2; Harmison 20-3-63-2; Phillips 12-0-65-1; Wood 8-1-30-1; Collingwood 10-5-9-0.

Durham

J. J. B. Lewis c Elworthy b McMillan	29	– c McMillan b Hayward		15
M. A. Gough run out	39	– lbw b Elworthy		17
N. J. Speak b Symcox	16	– lbw b Elworthy		4
J. A. Daley c Boucher b Elworthy	25	– lbw b McMillan		8
*D. C. Boon c Liebenberg b Symcox	31	– not out		40
P. D. Collingwood c Boucher b McMillan	12	– not out		4
†M. P. Speight b Elworthy	33			
N. C. Phillips c Kirsten b Symcox	2			
M. M. Betts c Liebenberg b Symcox	10			
J. Wood not out	11			
S. J. Harmison c Cullinan b Symcox	9			
B 3, l-b 8, n-b 58	69	L-b 3, n-b 16		19
1/58 2/100 3/149 4/152 5/182	286	1/22 2/31 3/55 4/92 (4 wkts)		107
6/218 7/232 8/262 9/262				

In the second innings M. A. Gough, when 1, retired hurt at 5 and resumed at 55.

Bowling: *First Innings*—Donald 16-5-31-0; Elworthy 21-5-86-2; Cronje 1-1-0-0; McMillan 12-5-31-2; Hayward 12-1-67-0; Symcox 25.5-6-60-5. *Second Innings*—Donald 7-4-6-0; Elworthy 11-1-37-2; Hayward 8-1-33-1; McMillan 6-2-17-1; Symcox 7-4-11-0.

Umpires: J. W. Holder and V. A. Holder.

DERBYSHIRE v SOUTH AFRICANS

At Derby, July 18, 19, 20. Drawn. Toss: Derbyshire.

Slater and Cronje both came close to double-centuries with imposing innings. But in establishing a lead of 116, the South Africans limited the possibilities, and Derbyshire batted out the third day. Krikken was the only capped player in their side, and they began poorly against Pollock, who was proving his fitness for the Trent Bridge Test, and Ntini. The tail offered more support to Slater, who was ninth out after hitting a six and 28 fours from 206 balls. In that time, he passed Derbyshire's best in a tour game, John Wright's 164 against the Pakistanis in 1978. Cullinan, a less-than-happy Derbyshire player in 1995, missed the hundred he wanted when he became one of Smith's five victims, but Cronje dealt fiercely with a limited attack, striking four sixes and 23 fours in 200 balls. May, whose 101 took his average against all touring teams to 75, and Cassar made sure Derbyshire avoided trouble.

Close of play: First day, South Africans 88-2 (G. F. J. Liebenberg 43*, D. J. Cullinan 17*); Second day, Derbyshire 57-0 (M. J. Slater 28*, M. R. May 24*).

Derbyshire

M. J. Slater c Boucher b Ntini	185	– c Boucher b Adams	63
M. R. May c Kirsten b Pollock	0	– c Boucher b Ntini	101
R. M. S. Weston c Kallis b Ntini	10	– lbw b Kallis	3
M. E. Cassar c Cullinan b Pollock	1	– not out	91
T. A. Tweats b Hayward	10	– run out	27
B. L. Spendlove c Boucher b Hayward	0	– not out	32
*†K. M. Krikken c Rhodes b Kallis	7		
G. M. Roberts b Pollock	40		
P. Aldred c Liebenberg b Hayward	15		
K. J. Dean not out	27		
T. M. Smith c Boucher b Ntini	13		
B 9, l-b 3, w 1, n-b 16	29	B 3, l-b 9, n-b 8	20

1/3 2/36 3/39 4/77 5/81   337   1/141 2/160   (4 wkts) 337
6/94 7/163 8/233 9/319   3/199 4/264

Bowling: *First Innings*—Pollock 15-3-58-3; Ntini 18-5-61-3; Hayward 12-0-74-3; Kallis 13-2-67-1; Adams 15-0-65-0. *Second Innings*—Pollock 16-8-35-0; Ntini 17-1-69-1; Cronje 5.1-1-19-0; Hayward 11-0-41-0; Adams 28-4-71-1; Kallis 15-5-43-1; Cullinan 13-4-47-0.

South Africans

G. Kirsten b Smith	0	P. R. Adams c Krikken b Dean	27
G. F. J. Liebenberg b Dean	47	M. Hayward not out	4
J. H. Kallis c Slater b Smith	25		
D. J. Cullinan c Krikken b Smith	80	L-b 3, w 1, n-b 6	10
*W. J. Cronje b Dean	195		
J. N. Rhodes c Spendlove b Smith	0	1/0 2/43 3/99 (9 wkts dec.) 453
S. M. Pollock b Cassar	19	4/237 5/241 6/277
†M. V. Boucher c Weston b Smith	46	7/369 8/434 9/453

M. Ntini did not bat.

Bowling: Smith 26-6-88-5; Dean 24.1-4-86-3; Cassar 20-3-90-1; Roberts 16-0-100-0; Aldred 17-4-86-0.

Umpires: B. Dudleston and J. H. Harris.

ENGLAND v SOUTH AFRICA

Fourth Cornhill Test

At Nottingham, July 23, 24, 25, 26, 27. England won by eight wickets. Toss: England. Test debuts: A. Flintoff; S. Elworthy.

This was the match English cricket desperately needed. In a summer of endless televised sport, previous Tests had been heavily overshadowed by the football World

Cup, fuelling talk of a game in crisis. Now, though, a window in the sporting calendar gave Test cricket the chance to hog the limelight. It grabbed the opportunity, producing a spectacle that, for passion and controversy, was every bit the equal of a penalty shoot-out. The drama mounted steadily until the fourth afternoon when, with England chasing 247 for victory, Atherton and Donald, two giants of the modern game, fought out a titanic battle. One of the largest fifth-day crowds for many years, 11,000, then saw Stewart exuberantly lead his team to an emphatic victory – his first as Test captain. The win set the series alight: one-all with one to play. As Atherton hit the winning runs, the Headingley switchboard was besieged by requests for tickets for the final Test. Amid the euphoria, talk of a crisis evaporated.

The day before the game, Sir Garry Sobers had opened the elegant £7.2 million Radcliffe Road stand. Some claimed that, by blocking the breeze from the Trent, it encouraged swing. With two wickets in the last two Tests, Fraser was rumoured to be making way for left-armer Alan Mullally, who might have been better able to take advantage. But Fraser survived, repaying his selection with ten wickets. Hick, in for the injured Thorpe, and Salisbury, replacing Giles, were given the opportunity to resuscitate flagging Test careers. Butcher returned after a hand injury and 20-year-old Andrew Flintoff – recently in the headlines for walloping 34 in an over – made his debut. South Africa recalled Pollock, back to full fitness, and gave Steve Elworthy, 13 years Flintoff's senior, his first Test; Klusener had gone home with an ankle injury and Ntini had a bad heel.

The pitch was green enough for Croft, Manchester's batting hero (but without a wicket in three Tests), to be left out. Critics believed Stewart's decision to bowl was coloured more by fear of Donald and Pollock than faith in his attack. He vehemently denied this, later claiming that fielding first was a major factor in the victory. Nevertheless, the English bowlers struggled to find the predicted swing. Gough had pace enough to force Liebenberg and Kirsten into false shots, Fraser had his trademark accuracy and Flintoff youthful enthusiasm. But runs flowed steadily; wickets fell slowly. Cronje, in his 50th Test, and Kallis put on a stylish 79 before Flintoff claimed a notable first Test scalp – his eighth in first-class cricket – with one that jagged back at Kallis. But by then Cronje had demolished Salisbury's confidence in a calculated assault; after an initial maiden, Salisbury's next eight overs cost 57. South Africa moved from 100 to 150 in just 49 balls.

Shortly after Cronje had reached his sixth Test hundred – his first in 29 matches – South Africa were well set at 292 for five. Before the close, though, Fraser found enough lift and movement with the new ball to remove Pollock, for a lively 50, and Boucher. When Cronje was caught at second slip next morning, Fraser had taken five in a Test innings for the 11th time. But there was still enough loose bowling around for Elworthy to hit 48 from 52 balls.

In the hands of the South Africans, the ball noticeably swung and seamed, but Atherton and Butcher went for their shots, going on to their third century partnership. After failures by James and Knight, Butcher emphasised his value as Atherton's opening partner, with an innings of great aplomb. A century seemed to be his but, in the first of several debatable decisions, umpire Dunne ruled him lbw to Donald, bowling round the wicket from wide of the stumps. The middle order stuttered, though Flintoff's 17 was a cameo of power and impetuousness. But Ramprakash doggedly hung around for four and a half hours to reduce the deficit to 38.

South Africa made a poor start to their second innings and, for once, the tail could not rescue them. Cullinan and Cronje, who became the second South African, after Bruce Mitchell, to score 3,000 Test runs, took the total from 21 to 119. Thereafter, batsmen departed to poor shots or to questionable decisions from umpire Kitchen. Kallis and Rhodes were both aggrieved when deemed to have edged Cork to Stewart. Rhodes left shaking his head in incredulity. On the fourth morning, with Gough nursing an injured toe, Fraser bowled an 11-over spell, relentlessly hitting the ideal line and length and ultimately collecting another five wickets. Cork, rediscovering his swing, took four, all caught behind.

[*Patrick Eagar*

The one that got away: the fielders are jubilant, but Atherton is given not out.

England's target was 247 in a day and a half, a total which, amazingly, they had not reached in the fourth innings to win a home Test since The Oval in 1902. Donald began at a furious pace, frequently registering 88 m.p.h. or more. But only Butcher got out. Atherton and Hussain fought on, punishing the rare loose ball. Then came a passage of play to rank with the greatest cricketing duels. Cronje, desperate for a wicket, brought back Donald. With England 82 for one, Atherton, on 27, gloved the umpteenth vicious short delivery to Boucher. The celebrations were loud, but short-lived. The batsman stood his ground; umpire Dunne was similarly unmoved. Donald was first incredulous, then livid. The next ball shot off the inside edge to the boundary. The bowler, now incandescent, snarled at Atherton, who stared impassively back. Channelling all his fury into an unremittingly hostile spell, Donald refused to let the pressure drop. Physically bruised but mentally resilient, Atherton was relishing the battle. Hussain, when 23, having weathered much of the same storm, was eventually beaten; but to Donald's utter disbelief, Boucher dropped the catch. At the close, England, on 108 for one, were within sight of victory.

By lunch on the last day, England needed 57. Then Donald belatedly got the wicket he deserved when Kallis pulled off a spectacular catch at second slip to dismiss Hussain. Stewart signalled his intentions by sweeping his first ball, from Adams, for four. His uncompromising approach – he hit another eight boundaries from his next 33 balls – left Atherton stranded on 98. Stewart offered him the chance of a century but Atherton said that victory, rather than a personal landmark, was the aim. Soon after the end of the game, the two teams, Donald and Atherton included, were sharing a beer. – HUGH CHEVALLIER.

Man of the Match: A. R. C. Fraser.   *Attendance:* 49,820; *receipts* £1,313,041.
Close of play: First day, South Africa 302-7 (W. J. Cronje 113*, S. Elworthy 0*); Second day, England 202-4 (M. R. Ramprakash 4*, I. D. K. Salisbury 1*); Third day, South Africa 92-3 (D. J. Cullinan 41*, W. J. Cronje 32*); Fourth day, England 108-1 (M. A. Atherton 43*, N. Hussain 25*).

South Africa

G. Kirsten b Gough	7	– lbw b Fraser	6
G. F. J. Liebenberg c Stewart b Gough	13	– lbw b Gough	0
J. H. Kallis c Stewart b Flintoff	47	– c Stewart b Cork	11
D. J. Cullinan c Ramprakash b Fraser	30	– c Ramprakash b Fraser	56
*W. J. Cronje c Hick b Fraser	126	– c Stewart b Cork	67
J. N. Rhodes lbw b Fraser	24	– c Stewart b Cork	2
S. M. Pollock c Stewart b Fraser	50	– c Stewart b Cork	7
†M. V. Boucher lbw b Fraser	4	– c Hussain b Fraser	35
S. Elworthy c Ramprakash b Gough	48	– lbw b Fraser	10
A. A. Donald not out	4	– not out	7
P. R. Adams c Hick b Gough	0	– c Stewart b Fraser	1
B 9, l-b 3, n-b 9	21	B 1, l-b 4, w 1	6

1/21 (2) 2/26 (1) 3/68 (4) 4/147 (3)   374   1/3 (2) 2/17 (3) 3/21 (1)   208
5/196 (6) 6/292 (7) 7/302 (8)   4/119 (4) 5/122 (6) 6/136 (7)
8/325 (5) 9/374 (9) 10/374 (11)   7/189 (5) 8/193 (8)
                                       9/200 (9) 10/208 (11)

Bowling: *First Innings*—Gough 30.2–4–116–4; Cork 17–2–65–0; Fraser 26–7–60–5; Flintoff 17–2–52–1; Salisbury 9–1–57–0; Butcher 4–1–12–0. *Second Innings*—Gough 16–4–56–1; Fraser 28.3–6–62–5; Cork 20–4–60–4; Flintoff 6–1–16–0; Salisbury 5–2–9–0.

England

M. A. Butcher lbw b Donald	75	– c Boucher b Pollock	22
M. A. Atherton c Boucher b Donald	58	– not out	98
N. Hussain lbw b Elworthy	22	– c Kallis b Donald	58
*†A. J. Stewart c Kirsten b Kallis	19	– not out	45
M. R. Ramprakash not out	67		
I. D. K. Salisbury b Donald	23		
G. A. Hick b Donald	6		
A. Flintoff c Boucher b Kallis	17		
D. G. Cork c Boucher b Pollock	6		
D. Gough c Boucher b Donald	2		
A. R. C. Fraser lbw b Pollock	7		
B 7, l-b 13, w 1, n-b 13	34	B 2, l-b 11, w 2, n-b 9	24

1/145 (2) 2/150 (1) 3/191 (4) 4/199 (3)   336   1/40 (1) 2/192 (3)   (2 wkts) 247
5/244 (6) 6/254 (7) 7/285 (8)
8/302 (9) 9/307 (10) 10/336 (11)

Bowling: *First Innings*—Donald 33–8–109–5; Pollock 35.5–12–75–2; Elworthy 22–8–41–1; Kallis 28–9–60–2; Adams 9–2–31–0. *Second Innings*—Donald 23–8–56–1; Pollock 26–3–79–1; Adams 12–4–23–0; Kallis 13.5–5–26–0; Elworthy 9–1–38–0; Cronje 4–1–12–0.

Umpires: R. S. Dunne (New Zealand) and M. J. Kitchen.
Referee: A. M. Ebrahim (Zimbabwe).

†ESSEX v SOUTH AFRICANS

At Chelmsford, July 29. South Africans won by 177 runs. Toss: South Africans.

A weak Essex team were no match for the tourists, who were able to boost their morale after their defeat at Nottingham by scoring at more than six an over. Kirsten batted throughout, hitting an unbeaten 141 from 132 balls, with 15 fours and a six. He shared productive stands with Mike Rindel, drafted in from league cricket to help fill the gaps caused by injury, and Rhodes. None of the home batsmen could resist for long; they were dismissed with more than 18 overs remaining.

South Africans

G. Kirsten not out	141	†M. V. Boucher not out		11
M. J. R. Rindel b Such	50			
B. M. McMillan c Hyam b Such	6	L-b 8, w 8, n-b 2		18
S. M. Pollock c Hyam b Such	9			
J. N. Rhodes c Such b Cousins	69	1/97 2/115 3/139	(5 wkts, 50 overs)	310
J. H. Kallis c Wilson b Cowan	6	4/263 5/280		

*W. J. Cronje, S. Elworthy, P. L. Symcox and M. Ntini did not bat.

Bowling: Cowan 10–1–63–1; Cousins 10–1–79–1; Wilson 7–0–56–0; Such 10–1–31–3; Grayson 10–0–54–0; Hibbert 3–0–19–0.

Essex

*P. J. Prichard c Rhodes b McMillan	20	A. P. Cowan c Rhodes b Symcox		16
D. D. J. Robinson lbw b Elworthy	0	D. M. Cousins c Rindel b Symcox		1
T. P. Hodgson c McMillan b Pollock	14	P. M. Such not out		0
A. P. Grayson c and b Elworthy	1	B 2, l-b 6, w 4, n-b 6		18
A. J. E. Hibbert b Symcox	9			
D. R. Law c Elworthy b Symcox	3	1/1 2/44 3/45	(31.4 overs)	133
D. G. Wilson c McMillan b Pollock	24	4/47 5/50 6/77		
†B. J. Hyam c McMillan b Symcox	27	7/91 8/119 9/127		

Bowling: Pollock 8–0–25–2; Elworthy 7–3–20–2; McMillan 6–0–27–1; Symcox 8.4–1–40–5; Ntini 2–0–13–0.

Umpires: M. J. Harris and B. Leadbeater.

ESSEX v SOUTH AFRICANS

At Chelmsford, July 31, August 1, 2. Drawn. Toss: Essex.

Three full sessions were washed out during the last two days, despite the fire brigade's attempts to assist the ground staff in mopping up. Again, Essex's injury list meant their team was far from full-strength, with only five regulars, whereas South Africa fielded eight players from the Test which ended four days earlier. Liebenberg managed to save his place for Leeds by scoring 96. Though his average in the Test series was in single figures, it was over 70 in other first-class tour matches. He added 217 with Cullinan, who was dropped at slip on nought, but then batted freely for four and a half hours and struck 15 fours and two sixes in his 157. Essex's batsmen found the going tough; Hodgson was their top scorer, with 46.

Close of play: First day, Essex 13-0 (D. D. J. Robinson 6*, I. N. Flanagan 3*); Second day, Essex 102-3 (T. P. Hodgson 33*, A. P. Grayson 0*).

South Africans

G. Kirsten b Irani	43	– not out	10
†G. F. J. Liebenberg c Hodgson b Grayson	96	– not out	14
D. J. Cullinan lbw b Ilott	157		
B. M. McMillan lbw b Wilson	29		
J. H. Kallis not out	29		
J. N. Rhodes c Hyam b Ilott	2		
S. M. Pollock not out	22		
B 3, l-b 9, n-b 16	28	B 2, l-b 1	3
1/62 2/279 3/331 4/353 5/360	(5 wkts dec.) 406	(no wkt)	27

*W. J. Cronje, P. L. Symcox, S. Elworthy and M. Ntini did not bat.

Bowling: *First Innings*—Ilott 16–4–48–2; Williams 15–2–79–0; Irani 12–2–44–1; Wilson 13–2–68–1; Such 23–0–76–0; Grayson 14–1–60–1; Hibbert 5–1–19–0. *Second Innings*—Ilott 4–3–4–0; Williams 4–0–7–0; Wilson 2–0–8–0; Such 1–0–5–0.

Essex

D. D. J. Robinson b Ntini	17	M. C. Ilott c Liebenberg b Elworthy	26
I. N. Flanagan c Kallis b Pollock	6	N. F. Williams run out	10
T. P. Hodgson b Pollock	46	P. M. Such not out	0
R. C. Irani c and b Symcox	33		
*A. P. Grayson c Liebenberg b Pollock	2	B 5, l-b 2, w 2, n-b 12	21
A. J. E. Hibbert lbw b Ntini	13		
†B. J. Hyam c Cronje b Symcox	38		215
D. G. Wilson b Elworthy	3		

1/22 2/49 3/92 4/111 5/120
6/157 7/173 8/173 9/199

Bowling: Pollock 16–4–37–3; Elworthy 17–3–49–2; Ntini 15–4–54–2; McMillan 4–0–21–0; Symcox 23–9–47–2.

Umpires: D. J. Constant and M. J. Harris.

ENGLAND v SOUTH AFRICA

Fifth Cornhill Test

At Leeds, August 6, 7, 8, 9, 10. England won by 23 runs. Toss: England.

At the end of an epic Test, the hardest-to-please audience in the cricketing world gathered, thousands strong, beneath Headingley's balcony to watch the England players dousing themselves with champagne. The game's rulers, pausing in their planning for an uncertain future, could be forgiven for joining the faintly delirious rejoicing. On the way to winning their first major series for nearly 12 years, England had, it seemed, conquered the public cynicism bred during an era in which humiliation followed hope as routinely as day turned into night.

Almost six weeks earlier, on the first day of the Third Test, Old Trafford had been half-empty. Yet, on the last day here, around 10,000 turned up for what, it transpired, was a mere half-hour's cricket. Admittedly, Headingley threw open its gates and, in these parts, getting summat for nowt still has its appeal. But four days of gripping, finely balanced, hand-to-hand combat had created an unmissable climax. In an atmosphere that changed by the second from deathly silence to roaring expectation, South Africa, 185 for eight overnight, set out to get 34 to win. They never looked like making it. In the sixth over, Fraser lured Donald into waving a catch to Stewart. In the next over, last man Ntini was hit on the pad by Gough and Pakistani umpire Javed Akhtar made the last and easiest of the decisions that had brought him four days of painful notoriety.

Resentment over umpiring mistakes lingered on from the previous Test. Even while the South Africans were having their pre-match net, Donald was fined half his match fee (about £550) for claiming in a radio interview that umpire Mervyn Kitchen "made a few shockers" at Trent Bridge. Referee Ahmed Ebrahim, a judge of the Zimbabwe Supreme Court, considered an immediate one-match ban, but instead suspended it for a year.

That allowed South Africa to field an all-pace attack, to drop left-arm spinner Adams, give 34-year-old McMillan his first Test of the series and restore Ntini in place of Elworthy. England stayed with the same eleven. This time off-spinner Croft was not even called up, but Salisbury was included ahead of pace bowler Mullally, a misjudgment that might have had far more serious consequences. The theory was that Salisbury's wrist-spin might be useful in the last innings. In fact, it was irrelevant throughout. The wicket was slow and two-paced, and the bounce grew ever less predictable.

The highly hyped return bout between Atherton and Donald never got beyond them promising a good, clean fight. Atherton stayed 18 overs, but faced only six balls from

Donald before he was caught at slip, setting Ntini on his way to Test-best figures of four for 72. By then, Butcher had decided on bold action, which brought him a maiden Test century and, ultimately, the match award. England's faith in him encouraged Butcher to play the brave, opportunistic, less-than-perfect style that comes naturally to him. He struck 18 fours in his 116, some of them apparently hit for sheer pleasure without a thought for survival. By coincidence, his father made a comeback for Surrey the same day. Alan Butcher froze in his only Test. Mark was determined never to follow suit.

When he swung once too often at Pollock and edged into his stumps, England went into steep decline and raging controversy. They lost their last six for 34 – a feat they repeated exactly in the second innings – and left the television cameras re-examining several dismissals with slow-motion, magnification and something approaching paranoia. Did the ball brush Hussain's thumb on the way to wicket-keeper Boucher? Did Boucher take Ramprakash's edge on the half volley? Did Flintoff's bat make any contact when the ball flew to Liebenberg at short leg? Sometimes, even the camera could not believe its own eye.

The only unarguable fact was that England's 230 was inadequate. South Africa were not able to exploit that because, yet again, Fraser bowled with intelligence and impeccable accuracy. He took five wickets for the third successive Test innings, giving South Africa their obligatory bad start by removing Kirsten and Liebenberg for only 36. Slowly, the middle order rebuilt, with a mixture of grit and good luck. Though Ramprakash took a spine-twisting catch to get Kallis for 40, England dropped three easier ones in 22 balls. Cronje was put down by Hussain at slip, Rhodes by Ramprakash at square leg and Hick at slip. Inevitably, Fraser cleared up the mess by having Cronje leg-before for a four-hour 57. Fraser can never be as tired as he looks, but he was close to exhaustion when he drove himself into a last-hour effort to take three in 11 balls.

A lead of only 22 disappointed South Africa, but the bounce was becoming more eccentric and their slender advantage looked priceless on the third morning, when Atherton was leg-before to Donald's first ball. Had Hussain not chosen this moment to play what was mentally the toughest and physically the most courageous innings of his Test career, England would have been finished. Donald and Pollock, tearing at the innings like lions fighting over a fresh kill, shared the ten wickets. But Hussain stayed the rest of that day and when, on the next, he pushed Pollock's slower ball to mid-off, he had been there seven hours. He was six short of a century and walked off, head down, wiping away the tears, oblivious to the standing ovation.

Donald demolished the rest of the innings, leaving South Africa to aim for 219. On another day and another ground, it would have been well within their scope. Here, though, the crowd was hostile and the opposition rampant. Within 15 overs, they were 27 for five. Gough, so often unbalanced by Headingley's adulation, was this time inspired. He got three of those five for only ten. It took the bouncy Rhodes and the bearlike McMillan to cool the temperature. They reached 144 for five before McMillan, who made 54 in two and a half hours, top-edged his swing at Cork and lobbed a catch to Stewart. Minutes later, Rhodes's superb 85 was over and Gough was celebrating his 100th Test wicket, as were the zealots on the Western Terrace. With their alcohol rationed by an anti-hooligan campaign, they had got steadily drunk on success.

Many of them were there next morning when Gough finished off South Africa to collect his best Test analysis, six for 42. Stewart, having led England positively and sometimes adventurously in his first series as captain, was not slow to realise that this new, precious rapport with the public had to be preserved. The presentation ceremony was droning on when he cut it short, demanded the Cornhill Trophy and brandished it, Cup Final fashion, before the crowd. They had waited long enough. – PETER JOHNSON.

Man of the Match: M. A. Butcher.   *Men of the Series:* England – M. A. Atherton; South Africa – A. A. Donald.   *Attendance:* 60,035; receipts £1,102,334.

Close of play: First day, South Africa 9-0 (G. Kirsten 4*, G. F. J. Liebenberg 4*); Second day, England 2-0 (M. A. Butcher 0*, M. A. Atherton 1*); Third day, England 206-4 (N. Hussain 83*, I. D. K. Salisbury 4*); Fourth day, South Africa 185-8 (S. M. Pollock 24*, A. A. Donald 2*).

England

M. A. Butcher b Pollock	116	– c McMillan b Pollock	37
M. A. Atherton c Kallis b Ntini	16	– lbw b Donald	1
N. Hussain c Boucher b Pollock	9	– c Cronje b Pollock	94
*†A. J. Stewart c Kallis b Donald	15	– c Boucher b Pollock	35
M. R. Ramprakash c Boucher b Donald	21	– lbw b Pollock	25
G. A. Hick c Rhodes b Ntini	2	– (7) c Kirsten b Donald	1
A. Flintoff c Liebenberg b Pollock	0	– (8) c Boucher b Donald	0
D. G. Cork not out	24	– (9) c Boucher b Donald	10
I. D. K. Salisbury b Ntini	0	– (6) c Boucher b Pollock	4
D. Gough c McMillan b Ntini	2	– c Cullinan b Donald	5
A. R. C. Fraser c Cullinan b Donald	4	– not out	1
B 4, l-b 5, w 2, n-b 10	21	B 14, l-b 1, w 2, n-b 10	27
	230		**240**

1/45 (2) 2/83 (3) 3/110 (4) 4/181 (5)   230   1/2 (2) 2/81 (1) 3/143 (4)   240
5/196 (1) 6/196 (6) 7/198 (6)   4/200 (5) 5/206 (6) 6/207 (7)
8/200 (9) 9/213 (10) 10/230 (11)   7/207 (8) 8/229 (3)
                                     9/235 (9) 10/240 (10)

Bowling: *First Innings*—Donald 20.3–6–44–3; Pollock 24–8–51–3; Ntini 21–5–72–4; Kallis 9–4–30–0; McMillan 9–0–24–0. *Second Innings*—Pollock 35–14–53–5; Donald 29.2–9–71–5; McMillan 11–0–22–0; Ntini 15–4–43–0; Kallis 15–6–31–0; Cullinan 1–0–1–0; Cronje 4–1–4–0.

South Africa

G. Kirsten lbw b Fraser	6	– c Atherton b Gough	3
G. F. J. Liebenberg c Hick b Fraser	21	– lbw b Gough	6
J. H. Kallis c Ramprakash b Cork	40	– lbw b Fraser	3
D. J. Cullinan c Stewart b Gough	27	– lbw b Gough	0
*W. J. Cronje lbw b Fraser	57	– c Stewart b Fraser	0
J. N. Rhodes c Stewart b Gough	32	– c Flintoff b Gough	85
B. M. McMillan c Salisbury b Cork	7	– c Stewart b Cork	54
S. M. Pollock c Salisbury b Fraser	31	– not out	28
†M. V. Boucher c Atherton b Gough	6	– lbw b Gough	4
A. A. Donald lbw b Fraser	0	– c Stewart b Fraser	4
M. Ntini not out	4	– lbw b Gough	0
L-b 20, n-b 1	21	L-b 6, n-b 2	8
	252		**195**

1/17 (1) 2/36 (2) 3/83 (4) 4/120 (3)   252   1/9 (2) 2/12 (1) 3/12 (3)   195
5/163 (6) 6/184 (7) 7/237 (5)   4/12 (5) 5/27 (4) 6/144 (7)
8/242 (8) 9/242 (10) 10/252 (9)   7/167 (6) 8/175 (9)
                                     9/194 (10) 10/195 (11)

Bowling: *First Innings*—Gough 24.3–7–58–3; Fraser 25–9–42–5; Cork 21–3–72–2; Flintoff 8–1–31–0; Salisbury 3–0–6–0; Butcher 9–4–23–0. *Second Innings*—Gough 23–6–42–6; Fraser 23–8–50–3; Cork 17–1–50–1; Flintoff 4–0–13–0; Salisbury 8–0–34–0.

Umpires: Javed Akhtar (Pakistan) and P. Willey. Referee: A. M. Ebrahim (Zimbabwe).

†FIRST-CLASS COUNTIES SELECT XI v SOUTH AFRICANS

At Leeds, August 12. First-Class Counties Select XI won by five runs (D/L method). Toss: South Africans.

The South Africans returned to the scene of their Test defeat two days earlier, for a one-day match in preparation for the triangular tournament with England and Sri Lanka. But their fortunes did not improve. A Select XI drawn from five counties – all wearing their own coloured Sunday League kit – won a narrow victory. Knight and Brown put on 139 for the first wicket and, in the closing stages, Hollioake and Alleyne ran up 113 at nine an over. Then Bicknell reduced the South Africans to 55 for four. Rhodes, however, almost turned the match round. He hit 90 from 72 balls, with 12 fours, and added 127 in 15 overs with Pollock. But despite levelling the scores, they fell just short of their target, revised because the Select XI's innings had been interrupted by rain. Some consolation came with the news that the tourists were to receive full bonuses as if they had won the Test series, in recognition of their gruelling summer.

First-Class Counties Select XI

N. V. Knight c and b Symcox	45		M. W. Alleyne not out		37
A. D. Brown c Kirsten b Symcox	79		L-b 3, w 8, n-b 22		33
B. C. Holhoake not out	70				
*M. P. Maynard lbw b Kallis	15		1/139 2/146 3/166	(3 wkts, 43 overs)	279

A. P. Grayson, R. C. Irani, A. F. Giles, †K. J. Piper, M. P. Bicknell and E. S. H. Giddins did not bat.

Bowling: Pollock 8–0–41–0; Elworthy 7–0–58–0; Hayward 8–0–63–0; Symcox 9–1–56–2; Kallis 9–1–37–1; Cronje 2–0–21–0.

South Africans

G. Kirsten b Bicknell	0		†M. V. Boucher c Grayson b Holhoake		10
M. J. R. Rindel lbw b Giddins	5		S. Elworthy not out		4
J. H. Kallis b Giles	44		M. Hayward run out		0
D. J. Cullinan c Piper b Bicknell	15		L-b 7, w 12, n-b 6		25
*W. J. Cronje c Grayson b Bicknell	10				
J. N. Rhodes b Holhoake	90		1/7 2/7 3/32	(42.5 overs)	279
S. M. Pollock b Giddins	59		4/55 5/108 6/235		
P. L. Symcox b Giddins	17		7/257 8/268 9/278		

Bowling: Bicknell 9–1–36–3; Giddins 9–0–53–3; Alleyne 6–0–43–0; Irani 4–0–25–0; Giles 6–0–46–1; Grayson 2–0–21–0; Holhoake 6.5–0–48–2.

Umpires: A. Clarkson and A. A. Jones.

South Africa's matches v Sri Lanka and England in the Emirates Triangular Tournament (August 14–18) may be found in that section.

ENGLAND'S INTERNATIONAL SCHEDULE

Home		Away	
1999	WORLD CUP	1999-2000	Tests and one-day internationals in South Africa and Zimbabwe
	Tests v New Zealand		
2000	Tests and one-day internationals v West Indies and Zimbabwe	2000-01	Tests and one-day internationals in Pakistan and Sri Lanka
2001	Tests and one-day internationals v Australia	2001-02	Tests and one-day internationals in India and New Zealand
2002	Tests and one-day internationals v India and Sri Lanka	2002-03	Tests and one-day internationals in Australia
2003	Tests and one-day internationals v South Africa and New Zealand		WORLD CUP in South Africa
2004	Tests and one-day internationals v Pakistan and Zimbabwe	2003-04	Tests and one-day internationals in the West Indies
2005	Tests and one-day internationals v Australia		

All fixtures subject to confirmation.

ENGLAND PLAYER OF THE YEAR

The Cornhill Insurance England Player of the Year Award was won in June 1998 by Graham Thorpe of Surrey.

THE SRI LANKANS IN ENGLAND, 1998

Review by DAVID HOPPS

The Sri Lankans could regard their short tour of England as an unmitigated success. Not only did they win both their sole Test match and the one-day triangular series against England and South Africa, they drew large crowds eager to witness a zestful approach which had become more widely appreciated since their victory in the 1996 World Cup. The English authorities, who had routinely sought to justify the sparse number of matches against Sri Lanka since their elevation to Test status on economic grounds, confirmed a three-Test tour of the island in 2000-01, with a lengthier Sri Lankan visit to England provisionally scheduled for 2002. The gesture was not before time.

In the wake of a Test series against South Africa of growing and ultimately exhausting intensity, Sri Lanka's exhilarating cricket ensured that the summer finished with a joyous release of tension. The batting, primarily of Sanath Jayasuriya and Aravinda de Silva, and the unique bowling style of Muttiah Muralitharan, whose 16 wickets in the Oval Test confirmed him as the finest off-spinner in the world, made a particular impact. Muralitharan's match figures at The Oval of 16 for 220 represented the fifth-best Test bowling return in history, but it was not achieved without controversy. David Lloyd, the England coach, had reopened the debate about the legality of Muralitharan's bowling action by expressing his reservations to the International Cricket Council after the Emirates tournament. Then, inadvisedly and insensitively, with England on the brink of defeat in the Test, he implied to the media that he still regarded him as a chucker. Muralitharan had been called for throwing in Australia nearly three years earlier, most notoriously by the Australian umpire, Darrell Hair, during the Boxing Day Test at Melbourne. But his action was later passed as legitimate by ICC after the study of comprehensive video footage as well as medical submissions concerning a hereditary deformity which prevents him entirely straightening his elbow.

It was not surprising that Lloyd, as England coach, should take such a subjective view of matters; an emotional style had proved a vital facet of his success as a dressing-room motivator. His insinuations, nevertheless, were unfortunate, ill-considered and perhaps even a trifle xenophobic. An over-critical ECB response then produced wild tabloid speculation that Lloyd might be sacked for little more than a nod and a wink. Lloyd received a severe reprimand – his second in two years in the job – and briefly considered resigning. He left for the Ashes tour knowing that another misjudgment would cost him his job.

For Arjuna Ranatunga, the Sri Lankan captain, the tour of England was a personal triumph. Ranatunga, who had made his debut against England in Sri Lanka's inaugural Test 16 years earlier, was contemplating retirement after the 1999 World Cup in England. He arrived for what would therefore be his last Test in the country nearly two stones lighter than usual.

THE SRI LANKAN TOURING PARTY

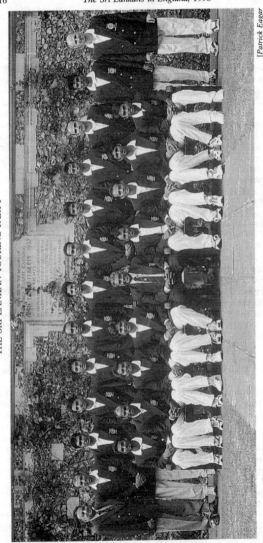

[*Patrick Eagar*

Standing: A. Wahab (*liaison officer*), U. C. Hathurusinghe, D. P. M. D. Jayawardene, H. P. W. Jayawardene, M. R. C. N. Bandaratilleke, M. S. Villavarayen, H. D. P. K. Dharmasena, K. R. Pushpakumara, A. S. A. Perera, R. P. Arnold, M. S. Atapattu, U. D. U. Chandana, A. Kountari (*physiotherapist*). *Seated*: M. Muralitharan, S. T. Jayasuriya, R. L. Dias (*coach*), A. Ranatunga (*captain*), E. R. Fernando (*manager*), P. A. de Silva, H. P. Tillekeratne, G. P. Wickremasinghe, R. S. Kaluwitharana.

Even for such a deft and cunning captain, the absence through injury of two pace bowlers, Chaminda Vaas and Nuwan Zoysa, threatened to cause insurmountable problems. Muralitharan, at times, was a one-man attack, taking 34 first-class wickets at 13.61, and attracting overtures from several English counties; in September, he signed for Lancashire. Pramodya Wickremasinghe was the only other Sri Lankan to take even ten first-class wickets on tour, although the 20-year-old Suresh Perera at times displayed enterprise and a fair turn of pace.

Sri Lanka's batting initially malfunctioned as they took time to come to terms with a damp English summer. Against Somerset at Taunton, they followed on 236 behind, only to come close to winning the game as Russel Arnold hit an elegant and orthodox double-century, his one convincing innings of the tour. Against Glamorgan at Cardiff, even worse followed; the Sri Lankans were routed on a damp pitch of indifferent bounce for 54 in only 21.5 overs. As Ranjit Fernando, their gracious and personable tour manager, remarked a few weeks later: "That made us sit back and think." Centuries for two old heads, Ranatunga and Hashan Tillekeratne, steadied matters with victory against Leicestershire, before a series of limited-overs victories ensured that Sri Lanka arrived at the triangular series in fine heart.

Their opening victory against South Africa at Trent Bridge regained the ascendancy against the one country to dominate them in the limited-overs format since they became world champions. Although England then defeated them at Lord's, Sri Lanka took the trophy on the same ground four days later, driven ahead by a controlled unbeaten century by Marvan Atapattu.

Whatever the occasion – Test, one-day jamboree, or the first afternoon of a county match – the Sri Lankan batsman remained true to type, gambolling along at around four runs per over. Their fielding was inconsistent, their seam bowling weak, but, as long as they retain an ability to produce high-class spinners (and their colleges are not exactly overflowing with them at the moment), they will remain competitive. Perhaps we may even hope for the day when all English commentators, on radio and TV alike, will wake up to their responsibilities and learn how to pronounce their names.

SRI LANKAN TOURING PARTY

A. Ranatunga (Sinhalese SC) (*captain*), P. A. de Silva (Nondescripts CC) (*vice-captain*), R. P. Arnold (Nondescripts CC), M. S. Atapattu (Sinhalese SC), M. R. C. N. Bandaratilleke (Tamil Union), U. D. U. Chandana (Tamil Union), H. D. P. K. Dharmasena (Bloomfield C and AC), U. C. Hathurusinghe (Moors SC), S. T. Jayasuriya (Bloomfield C and AC), D. P. M. D. Jayawardene (Sinhalese SC), H. P. W. Jayawardene, R. S. Kaluwitharana (Colts CC), M. Muralitharan (Tamil Union), A. S. A. Perera (Sinhalese SC), K. R. Pushpakumara (Nondescripts CC), H. P. Tillekeratne (Nondescripts CC), M. S. Villavarayen (Tamil Union), G. P. Wickremasinghe (Sinhalese SC).

W. P. U. J. C. Vaas (Colts CC) later reinforced the party.

Manager: E. R. Fernando.   *Coach:* R. L. Dias.

SRI LANKAN TOUR RESULTS

Test match – Played 1: Won 1.
First-class matches – Played 6: Won 3, Lost 1, Drawn 2.
Wins – England, Leicestershire, Hampshire.
Loss – Glamorgan.
Draws – Somerset, Middlesex.
One-day internationals – Played 3: Won 2, Lost 1. *Wins* – South Africa, England. *Loss* – England.
Other non-first-class matches – Played 5: Won 5. Abandoned 1. *Wins* – Worcestershire, ECB XI,
   Northamptonshire (2), Kent. *Abandoned* – Hampshire.

SRI LANKAN TOUR AVERAGES – FIRST-CLASS MATCHES

BATTING

	M	I	NO	R	HS	100s	50s	Avge	Ct/St
M. S. Atapattu	4	7	1	316	114	1	2	52.66	1
U. C. Hathurusinghe	5	8	3	255	108*	1	1	51.00	4
S. T. Jayasuriya	5	9	1	382	213	1	0	47.75	4
A. Ranatunga	3	4	0	181	110	1	0	45.25	0
H. P. Tillekeratne	6	9	1	317	120	1	1	39.62	5
R. P. Arnold	5	9	1	312	209	1	0	39.00	1
R. S. Kaluwitharana	3	4	0	152	73	0	1	38.00	11/2
D. P. M. D. Jayawardene .	6	10	1	266	90	0	2	29.55	7
U. D. U. Chandana	2	4	1	78	34	0	0	26.00	0
M. Muralitharan	3	4	2	47	30	0	0	23.50	1
H. D. P. K. Dharmasena . .	3	4	1	68	45*	0	0	22.66	3
M. S. Villavarayen	4	4	0	39	32	0	0	9.75	1
G. P. Wickremasinghe . . .	4	4	0	24	18	0	0	8.00	0

Played in three matches: H. P. W. Jayawardene 0, 0, 25 (8 ct); A. S. A. Perera 26, 10, 43*;
K. R. Pushpakumara 8*, 0, 7*. Played in two matches: M. R. C. N. Bandaratilleke 11; P. A.
de Silva 1, 152.

* *Signifies not out.*

BOWLING

	O	M	R	W	BB	5W/i	Avge
M. Muralitharan	226.3	77	463	34	9-65	5	13.61
G. P. Wickremasinghe	135.1	26	397	13	4-69	0	30.53
M. S. Villavarayen	86.4	18	276	9	4-36	0	30.66
K. R. Pushpakumara	57	7	224	6	3-52	0	37.33
A. S. A. Perera	129.5	31	343	7	2-60	0	49.00
U. C. Hathurusinghe	114	23	358	6	3-64	0	59.66

Also bowled: R. P. Arnold 7–2–15–1; M. S. Atapattu 1–0–4–0; M. R. C. N. Bandaratilleke
26–3–107–1; U. D. U. Chandana 36.2–6–129–4; P. A. de Silva 19.3–6–30–1; H. D. P. K.
Dharmasena 112.3–31–258–3; S. T. Jayasuriya 66–19–144–3; D. P. M. D. Jayawardene 14–1–66–0;
H. P. Tillekeratne 3–0–16–0.

Note: Matches in this section which were not first-class are signified by a dagger.

†HAMPSHIRE v SRI LANKANS

At Southampton, July 12. Abandoned.

SOMERSET v SRI LANKANS

At Taunton, July 14, 15, 16. Drawn. Toss: Somerset.

The Sri Lankans' opening match swung from one extreme to another. In the first half, they were hit hard by Somerset's batsmen, then hustled out by a second-string attack. But when Sri Lanka followed on, Arnold hit a handsome double-hundred, and they even had a sniff of victory. Both sides omitted key players, with Sri Lankan captain Ranatunga among the absentees. On a cool first day, Parsons hit an attractive century and Trescothick, restored to open, just missed one. The Sri Lankans lost two men that evening, including Jayasuriya, given out for treading on his stumps, though he indicated that the wind might have blown off the bails. In humid weather next day, they struggled against the moving ball and were all out 236 behind. When Arnold resumed, Somerset thought he was caught on 31, but the umpire ruled it had not carried. Amid the confusion, he ran a single, and Atapattu was out next ball. Arnold went on to bat 327 minutes and 270 balls, hitting 37 fours. The Sri Lankans declared to set Somerset 248 in 37 overs; Bowler scored swiftly, but they were seven down by the close.

Close of play: First day, Sri Lankans 8-2 (M. S. Atapattu 0*, M. R. C. N. Bandaratilleke 1*); Second day, Sri Lankans 243-3 (R. P. Arnold 115*, H. P. Tillekeratne 51*).

Somerset

*P. D. Bowler c Kaluwitharana b Wickremasinghe .	27	– run out 66
M. E. Trescothick b Dharmasena	95	– (6) run out 26
R. J. Harden c Kaluwitharana b Wickremasinghe	8	– c Dharmasena b Villavarayen 0
M. N. Lathwell c Kaluwitharana b Wickremasinghe	56	– c Jayawardene b Villavarayen 5
K. A. Parsons not out	101	– c Villavarayen b Hathurusinghe . . 25
M. Burns b Bandaratilleke	13	– (2) c Dharmasena b Wickremasinghe 13
A. R. K. Pierson c Tillekeratne b Wickremasinghe	39	– st Kaluwitharana b Dharmasena . . 3
†L. D. Sutton not out	3	– not out 16
P. S. Jones (did not bat)		– not out 8
B 2, l-b 10, w 2, n-b 10	24	L-b 13, n-b 2 15

1/47 2/65 3/183 4/201   (6 wkts dec.) 366   1/27 2/29 3/39 4/94   (7 wkts) 177
5/229 6/355   5/139 6/146 7/155

M. P. L. Bulbeck and B. J. Trott did not bat.

Bowling: *First Innings*—Wickremasinghe 24.1–5–69–4; Villavarayen 15–3–78–0; Hathurusinghe 18–4–76–0; Dharmasena 23–1–66–1; Bandaratilleke 12–1–53–1; Jayawardene 2–0–6–0; Jayasuriya 2–0–6–0. *Second Innings*—Wickremasinghe 9–0–25–1; Villavarayen 8–0–35–2; Hathurusinghe 6–0–32–1; Bandaratilleke 4–0–26–0; Dharmasena 5–0–17–1; Jayasuriya 3–0–19–0; Atapattu 1–0–4–0; Tillekeratne 1–0–6–0.

Sri Lankans

*S. T. Jayasuriya hit wkt b Bulbeck	0	– lbw b Bulbeck	4
M. S. Atapattu lbw b Bulbeck	7	– c Burns b Bulbeck	53
R. P. Arnold c Parsons b Jones	2	– c Harden b Trescothick	209
M. R. C. N. Bandaratilleke c Sutton b Bulbeck	11		
D. P. M. D. Jayawardene b Trott	3	– (4) c Sutton b Parsons	9
H. P. Tillekeratne not out	38	– (5) b Bulbeck	82
†R. S. Kaluwitharana b Trott	21	– (6) c Parsons b Trescothick	33
U. C. Hathurusinghe c Harden b Jones	4	– (7) not out	34
H. D. P. K. Dharmasena c Sutton b Trescothick	10	– (8) not out	45
G. P. Wickremasinghe c Trescothick b Parsons	18		
M. S. Villavarayen c Sutton b Parsons	5		
L-b 11	11	B 4, l-b 4, w 6	14

1/4 2/7 3/25 4/26 5/30	130	1/8 2/93 3/127	(6 wkts dec.) 483
6/58 7/65 8/102 9/121		4/326 5/395 6/408	

Bowling: *First Innings*—Bulbeck 11–4–20–3; Jones 12–3–32–2; Trott 8–2–16–2; Trescothick 11–4–25–1; Parsons 10.4–3–26–2. *Second Innings*—Bulbeck 19–1–104–3; Jones 20–2–84–0; Burns 6–1–44–0; Trott 9–2–40–0; Pierson 15–3–54–0; Trescothick 20–3–83–2; Parsons 11–4–29–1; Bowler 9–3–25–0; Harden 4–1–12–0.

Umpires: B. Dudleston and R. Palmer.

GLAMORGAN v SRI LANKANS

At Cardiff, July 18, 19. Glamorgan won by five wickets. Toss: Sri Lankans.

Glamorgan's two-day victory earned them an £11,000 bonus from Vodafone; it was their first first-class win against a touring Test team since the Pakistanis in 1971, and their first ever against the Sri Lankans. The tourists never recovered from being dismissed for 54 inside 22 overs, the lowest total ever recorded by a Test side against Glamorgan. Only Atapattu reached double figures as Dale and Thomas shared eight wickets with their swing and seam. It was the performance of batsmen struggling with alien conditions. Arjuna Ranatunga insisted: "We will improve." Maynard led Glamorgan's reply, falling one short of his century to set up a lead of 170. The Sri Lankans were batting again by the close; pitch consultant Harry Brind was called in as 22 wickets had fallen, but recommended no action over a strip suffering from prolonged wet weather. The tourists did better this time – Atapattu was also caught behind for 99 – but were again undone by Dale, who took four for two in 19 balls, giving him a match analysis of nine for 45. Glamorgan needed only 53, but struggled against Muralitharan, who obtained considerable turn, taking five wickets and ten in the match. This was to prove more significant for the future of the tour than the Sri Lankans' earlier embarrassment.

Close of play: First day, Sri Lankans 35-2 (M. S. Atapattu 19*, A. Ranatunga 11*).

Sri Lankans

M. S. Atapattu lbw b Thomas	19	– c Dawood b Thomas	99
R. P. Arnold c Maynard b Watkin	3	– b Watkin	1
D. P. M. D. Jayawardene c Law b Davies	0	– lbw b Watkin	4
*A. Ranatunga lbw b Dale	6	– c Cottey b Dale	14
H. P. Tillekeratne lbw b Dale	2	– c Powell b Cosker	36
U. C. Hathurusinghe c Dawood b Dale	7	– lbw b Dale	15
U. D. U. Chandana lbw b Thomas	1	– c Davies b Croft	33
†H. P. W. Jayawardene c Dawood b Thomas	0	– lbw b Dale	0
M. S. Villavarayen b Thomas	0	– lbw b Dale	2
K. R. Pushpakumara not out	8	– (11) c Cosker b Dale	0
M. Muralitharan b Dale	6	– (10) not out	4
B 1, l-b 1	2	B 1, l-b 5, n-b 8	14

1/9 2/10 3/24 4/32 5/32	54	1/1 2/9 3/48 4/150 5/166	222
6/34 7/38 8/38 9/48		6/205 7/205 8/217 9/222	

Bowling: *First Innings*—Watkin 7–2–13–1; Davies 5–2–9–1; Dale 5.5–1–20–4; Thomas 4–1–10–4. *Second Innings*—Watkin 17–6–38–2; Davies 6–2–12–0; Thomas 15–1–52–1; Croft 14–6–38–1; Dale 10.3–2–25–5; Cosker 16–5–51–1.

Glamorgan

*M. P. Maynard c H. P. W. Jayawardene				
b Villavarayen .	99	– b Muralitharan		5
W. L. Law c Hathurusinghe b Muralitharan . . .	28	– (7) not out		1
A. Dale lbw b Chandana	0	– c D. P. M. D. Jayawardene		
		b Muralitharan .	0	
M. J. Powell b Chandana	2	– lbw b Muralitharan	7	
P. A. Cottey lbw b Muralitharan	27	– not out	9	
R. D. B. Croft c H. P. W. Jayawardene				
b Chandana .	24	– lbw b Muralitharan	7	
†I. Dawood b Muralitharan	4	– (2) b Muralitharan	22	
S. D. Thomas c D. P. M. D. Jayawardene				
b Muralitharan .	15			
A. P. Davies b Chandana	1			
D. A. Cosker b Muralitharan	0			
S. L. Watkin not out	0			
L-b 10, n-b 14	24	N-b 2		2

1/110 2/111 3/121 4/175 5/177   224   `1/18 2/18 3/35   (5 wkts) 53
6/198 7/210 8/214 9/215   4/40 5/48

Bowling: *First Innings*—Pushpakumara 10–1–57–0; Villavarayen 6–1–25–1; Muralitharan 27.4–7–77–5; Chandana 20–5–45–4; Hathurusinghe 3–0–10–0. *Second Innings*—Pushpakumara 2–0–9–0; Villavarayen 3–1–5–0; Muralitharan 7–0–17–5; Chandana 5.2–0–22–0.

Umpires: M. J. Kitchen and P. Willey.

LEICESTERSHIRE v SRI LANKANS

At Leicester, July 24, 25, 26, 27. Sri Lankans won by nine wickets. Toss: Leicestershire.

The Sri Lankans found their winning touch at last, though Leicestershire made them work hard for victory on the final day. The county rested four regulars before their NatWest quarter-final, while Ormond was injured and Millns able to bowl only one first-innings over, owing to twisting his ankle. Choosing to bat on a newly relaid pitch, they sank to 81 for six. But, with Dakin supervising the tail, the last four added 164. Dakin went on to claim the Sri Lankans' first three wickets, within 16 balls. Then Ranatunga and Tillekeratne exploited the weak attack to hit fine centuries, establishing a lead of 264. Stand-in captain Smith led a more determined second-innings effort, though Muralitharan took his haul of wickets to 18 in two matches. Leicestershire managed to prolong the match into the final session, but the Sri Lankans knocked off a target of 99 with 15 overs to spare.

Close of play: First day, Sri Lankans 51-0 (S. T. Jayasuriya 16*, R. P. Arnold 27*); Second day, Sri Lankans 442-7 (H. P. Tillekeratne 91*, G. P. Wickremasinghe 6*); Third day, Leicestershire 234-5 (P. A. Nixon 24*, J. M. Dakin 19*).

Leicestershire

D. L. Maddy c H. P. W. Jayawardene b Perera .	26	– c D. P. M. D. Jayawardene
		b Muralitharan . 29
I. J. Sutcliffe c Hathurusinghe b Wickremasinghe	17	– b Muralitharan 15
D. I. Stevens b Hathurusinghe	1	– lbw b Muralitharan 2
*B. F. Smith c Jayasuriya b Hathurusinghe	0	– c Arnold b de Silva 75
A. Habib c H. P. W. Jayawardene		
b Hathurusinghe .	0	– lbw b Muralitharan 23
†P. A. Nixon lbw b Perera	20	– b Perera 38
J. M. Dakin c H. P. W. Jayawardene		
b Muralitharan .	79	– c Tillekeratne b Wickremasinghe . 42
D. Williamson c Jayasuriya b Wickremasinghe	20	– lbw b Wickremasinghe. 34
D. J. Millns not out	46	– c D. P. M. D. Jayawardene
		b Muralitharan . 14
C. D. Crowe c H. P. W. Jayawardene		
b Muralitharan .	2	– lbw b Perera 23
M. T. Brimson c Jayasuriya b Muralitharan . . .	1	– not out 2
L-b 8, w 9, n-b 16	33	B 4, l-b 22, w 5, n-b 34 . . 65

1/40 2/45 3/45 4/51 5/59   245   1/53 2/59 3/64 4/148 5/203   362
6/81 7/149 8/228 9/233   6/267 7/288 8/315 9/351

Bowling: *First Innings*—Wickremasinghe 17–4–54–2; Perera 17–4–60–2; Hathurusinghe 27–7–64–3; Muralitharan 23–8–41–3; D. P. M. D. Jayawardene 3–0–18–0. *Second Innings*—Wickremasinghe 30–7–99–2; Perera 25.5–5–77–2; Hathurusinghe 10–3–21–0; Muralitharan 55–21–108–5; Jayasuriya 4–1–6–0; Arnold 3–0–11–0; de Silva 9–3–14–1.

Sri Lankans

S. T. Jayasuriya c Nixon b Dakin	36	– c Williamson b Crowe. 30
R. P. Arnold lbw b Dakin	33	– not out 44
D. P. M. D. Jayawardene c Nixon b Williamson	48	– not out 21
P. A. de Silva c Nixon b Dakin	1	
*A. Ranatunga c Maddy b Brimson	110	
H. P. Tillekeratne lbw b Williamson	120	
U. C. Hathurusinghe lbw b Dakin	60	
†H. P. W. Jayawardene b Williamson	25	
G. P. Wickremasinghe c Nixon b Brimson	6	
A. S. A. Perera c Williamson b Crowe	26	
M. Muralitharan not out	7	
B 5, l-b 19, w 1, n-b 12	37	L-b 2, n-b 2 4

1/70 2/83 3/89 4/226 5/267   509   1/53   (1 wkt) 99
6/386 7/426 8/447 9/501

Bowling: *First Innings*—Dakin 38–6–110–4; Millns 1–0–14–0; Williamson 28–6–110–3; Crowe 33.4–3–120–1; Brimson 22–3–84–2; Maddy 10–2–47–0. *Second Innings*—Millns 10–2–49–0; Dakin 5–0–21–0; Crowe 7–2–20–1; Brimson 2.5–0–7–0.

Umpires: N. T. Plews and J. F. Steele.

†WORCESTERSHIRE v SRI LANKANS

At Worcester, July 28. Sri Lankans won by seven wickets. Toss: Worcestershire.

A late addition to the tourists' schedule brought them another win, this one against a county at full strength. Still, it was Worcestershire's youngest player, 21-year-old Elliott Wilson, who helped Hick to build a strong position in a stand of 104. Hick advanced to 111 from 109 balls, with eight fours and four sixes; he was caught in the deep looking for another. When Moody was lbw next ball, the Sri Lankans were able to impose a brake. No one, however, could put a brake on Jayasuriya and Atapattu, who added 92 in ten overs. De Silva followed up with a more stately 73, completing victory with 16 balls to spare.

Worcestershire

W. P. C. Weston c Ranatunga	S. R. Lampitt b Chandana 13
b Pushpakumara . 15	†S. J. Rhodes not out 7
E. J. Wilson c Kaluwitharana b Chandana 61	
G. A. Hick c Atapattu b Dharmasena . . . 111	L-b 15, w 23, n-b 4 42
V. S. Solanki b Hathurusinghe 7	
*T. M. Moody lbw b Dharmasena 10	1/50 2/154 3/204 (6 wkts, 50 overs) 279
D. A. Leatherdale not out 13	4/243 5/243 6/265

R. K. Illingworth, P. J. Newport and R. J. Chapman did not bat.

Bowling: Pushpakumara 7–0–40–1; Perera 7–0–28–0; Hathurusinghe 10–0–51–1; Dharmasena 10–0–46–2; Jayasuriya 8–0–42–0; Chandana 8–0–57–2.

Sri Lankans

S. T. Jayasuriya c Wilson b Leatherdale . 60	*A. Ranatunga not out 25
†R. S. Kaluwitharana c Hick b Newport . 19	L-b 16, w 12, n-b 8 36
M. S. Atapattu c Rhodes b Newport . . . 68	
P. A. de Silva not out 73	1/37 2/129 3/216 (3 wkts, 47.2 overs) 281

D. P. M. D. Jayawardene, U. C. Hathurusinghe, H. D. P. K. Dharmasena, U. D. U. Chandana, A. S. A. Perera and K. R. Pushpakumara did not bat.

Bowling: Newport 10–1–33–2; Chapman 9.2–0–61–0; Lampitt 10–0–62–0; Leatherdale 8–0–56–1; Illingworth 8–0–43–0; Hick 2–0–10–0.

Umpires: K. J. Lyons and A. G. T. Whitehead.

MIDDLESEX v SRI LANKANS

At Lord's, July 31, August 1, 2, 3. Drawn. Toss: Sri Lankans.

The Sri Lankans' first visit to Lord's on this trip was something of an anticlimax, with more than two sessions lost to bad light and rain, small crowds and little urgency on either side as the match faded into a draw. Goodchild, at least, must have enjoyed it; he followed up an unbeaten 83 against Yorkshire with a maiden hundred, in only his fifth first-class innings. With Muralitharan rested, Goodchild was able to show application and solid method. Atapattu replied with his own century, as the Sri Lankans batted rather more smartly – they scored 111 more runs than the county in four fewer overs. Middlesex cleared their arrears on the third evening, but the weather cost 40 overs on the final day. Only the Sri Lankans could win, but Brown – dropped with 18 overs to go, when his side's lead was barely 100 – held out to reach safety.

Close of play: First day, Middlesex 282-8 (C. J. Batt 3*, P. C. R. Tufnell 5*); Second day, Sri Lankans 214-4 (D. P. M. D. Jayawardene 38*, H. P. Tillekeratne 1*); Third day, Middlesex 123-3 (P. N. Weekes 22*, R. L. Johnson 4*).

Middlesex

D. J. Goodchild run out 105	– lbw b Pushpakumara	6
R. A. Kettleborough b Villavarayen 9	– c Kaluwitharana b Villavarayen . . .	38
D. C. Nash lbw b Villavarayen 1	– lbw b Pushpakumara	42
P. N. Weekes c Kaluwitharana b Pushpakumara . 43	– c Dharmasena b Hathurusinghe . . .	49
J. L. Langer c Kaluwitharana b Villavarayen . . . 43	– (6) c Kaluwitharana	
	b Pushpakumara .	12
*†K. R. Brown b Dharmasena 25	– (7) not out	40
K. P. Dutch b Pushpakumara 0	– (8) b Hathurusinghe	8
R. L. Johnson c Kaluwitharana b Pushpakumara . 8	– (5) b Perera	4
C. J. Batt lbw b Perera 11	– not out	18
P. C. R. Tufnell c Hathurusinghe b Villavarayen 24		
T. F. Bloomfield not out 2		
L-b 7, w 4, n-b 31 42	B 2, l-b 4, n-b 8	14

1/32 2/40 3/129 4/202 5/250	313	1/27 2/88 3/114 4/123 (7 wkts) 231
6/261 7/261 8/277 9/309		5/142 6/181 7/201

Bowling: *First Innings*—Perera 21–6–46–1; Pushpakumara 23–1–93–3; Hathurusinghe 17–4–54–0; Villavarayen 18.4–7–36–4; Dharmasena 30–8–74–1; Jayasuriya 4–1–3–0. *Second Innings*—Perera 15–4–34–1; Pushpakumara 18–5–52–3; Dharmasena 17–6–34–0; Villavarayen 15–1–43–1; Hathurusinghe 22–3–62–2.

Sri Lankans

*S. T. Jayasuriya c Dutch b Batt	24	U. C. Hathurusinghe lbw b Batt	20
M. S. Atapattu c Brown b Tufnell	114	A. S. A. Perera c Weekes b Bloomfield	10
R. P. Arnold c Weekes b Batt	20	M. S. Villavarayen b Batt	32
D. P. M. D. Jayawardene c Nash		K. R. Pushpakumara not out	7
b Bloomfield	79	B 8, l-b 14, w 2, n-b 10	34
H. D. P. K. Dharmasena lbw b Tufnell	0		
H. P. Tillekeratne c Kettleborough		1/56 2/127 3/211	424
b Tufnell	11	4/211 5/237 6/334	
†R. S. Kaluwitharana c Langer b Johnson	73	7/354 8/377 9/397	

Bowling: Bloomfield 22–2–74–2; Batt 22.5–1–103–4; Johnson 22–5–72–1; Tufnell 24–4–90–3; Goodchild 6–0–20–0; Dutch 13–4–43–0.

Umpires: P. Adams and B. Leadbeater.

†ECB XI v SRI LANKANS

At Lakenham, August 5. Sri Lankans won by eight wickets. Toss: Sri Lankans.

While most of his senior colleagues took the day off, de Silva took complete charge of this match, against an ECB team drawn from the Minor Counties and Second Elevens. He took three wickets for 12 in his ten overs; after the ECB openers had fought their way to 48, the rest of the innings was completely tied up by Sri Lankan spin. Then de Silva scored 53 at more than a run a ball to hurry his side to victory.

ECB XI

N. R. Gaywood c Chandana		J. M. Fielding st H. P. W. Jayawardene	
b Bandaratilleke	29	b de Silva	10
*M. J. Roberts c and b Bandaratilleke	14	B. C. Usher lbw b de Silva	0
S. Foster c and b Chandana	32	K. A. Arnold b Chandana	0
J. D. Robinson c H. P. W. Jayawardene		A. Richardson not out	5
b de Silva	0	L-b 2, w 4, n-b 8	14
D. R. Clarke st H. P. W. Jayawardene			
b Chandana	22	1/48 2/48 3/49 (9 wkts, 50 overs)	141
R. G. Halsall lbw b Arnold	1	4/98 5/99 6/113	
†S. N. V. Waterton not out	14	7/130 8/130 9/132	

Bowling: Villavarayen 4–1–17–0; Perera 4–0–23–0; de Silva 10–4–12–3; Bandaratilleke 9–1–19–2; Arnold 10–2–31–1; Chandana 10–2–25–3; D. P. M. D. Jayawardene 3–0–12–0.

Sri Lankans

M. S. Atapattu c Clarke b Foster	23
R. P. Arnold c Clarke b Richardson	31
*P. A. de Silva not out	53
H. P. Tillekeratne not out	20
L-b 10, w 3, n-b 4	17

1/60 2/64 (2 wkts, 28.1 overs) 144

D. P. M. D. Jayawardene, U. C. Hathurusinghe, M. R. C. N. Bandaratilleke, M. S. Villavarayen, †H. P. W. Jayawardene, A. S. A. Perera and U. D. U. Chandana did not bat.

Bowling: Arnold 5–1–26–0; Richardson 8–1–26–1; Foster 6–0–24–1; Fielding 6–0–34–0; Usher 3.1–0–24–0.

Umpires: T. E. Jesty and R. Julian.

†NORTHAMPTONSHIRE v SRI LANKANS

At Northampton, August 7. Sri Lankans won by one wicket. Toss: Sri Lankans.

The Sri Lankans' casual approach nearly cost them the match. They collapsed from 196 for four, with 12 overs remaining, to 227 for nine, with the scores level, once Ranatunga had holed out after hitting 69 from 72 balls. It was then left to Muralitharan to edge the winning boundary off Bailey. Northamptonshire were rescued from the depths of 60 for five by Sales and Snape, who shared an unbroken stand worth 167 at six an over. The final two overs, from Wickremasinghe and Jayasuriya, yielded 30 runs. But Jayasuriya then began the Sri Lankan reply with a typical flourish, scoring 31 from 27 deliveries.

Northamptonshire

M. B. Loye st Kaluwitharana b Muralitharan	29	T. C. Walton lbw b Dharmasena		0
R. J. Bailey c Jayasuriya b Pushpakumara	0	J. N. Snape not out		78
*K. M. Curran b Muralitharan	14	B 1, l-b 2, w 7		10
D. J. Sales not out	91			
A. L. Penberthy b Dharmasena	5	1/1 2/41 3/49 (5 wkts, 50 overs)		227
		4/60 5/60		

†D. Ripley, J. P. Taylor, D. Follett and D. E. Malcolm did not bat.

Bowling: Wickremasinghe 9–0–51–0; Pushpakumara 5.1–1–9–1; de Silva 3.5–0–26–0; Muralitharan 10–1–37–2; Dharmasena 10–1–27–2; Chandana 6–0–28–0; Jayasuriya 6–0–46–0.

Sri Lankans

S. T. Jayasuriya lbw b Malcolm	31	G. P. Wickremasinghe run out		1
†R. S. Kaluwitharana c Sales b Penberthy	28	M. Muralitharan not out		4
M. S. Atapattu st Ripley b Snape	28	K. R. Pushpakumara not out		0
P. A. de Silva c Taylor b Curran	26	L-b 9, w 7		16
*A. Ranatunga c Follett b Penberthy	69			
H. P. Tillekeratne b Follett	17	1/47 2/74 3/117 (9 wkts, 47.5 overs)		231
U. D. U. Chandana b Follett	0	4/129 5/196 6/196		
H. D. P. K. Dharmasena lbw b Taylor	11	7/223 8/227 9/227		

Bowling: Malcolm 10–2–47–1; Taylor 10–0–45–1; Follett 10–0–51–2; Penberthy 4–0–26–2; Snape 10–0–38–1; Curran 3–1–11–1; Bailey 0.5–0–4–0.

Umpires: D. J. Constant and K. Shuttleworth.

†NORTHAMPTONSHIRE v SRI LANKANS

At Northampton, August 9. Sri Lankans won by 16 runs. Toss: Sri Lankans.

Led by Jayasuriya, the Sri Lankan batsmen enjoyed themselves against a below-strength county attack. Jayasuriya struck 16 fours in 116 balls, sharing century stands with Kaluwitharana and de Silva. Northamptonshire were undaunted, however, and Penberthy, who scored 71 in 64 balls, gave them a chance. But the task proved just too great; Jayasuriya rounded off his day by bowling Taylor with the first ball of the final over. The match had been switched to Northampton from Milton Keynes due to lack of sponsorship.

Sri Lankans

S. T. Jayasuriya c Curran b Snape	119	G. P. Wickremasinghe c T. M. B. Bailey b Follett		1
†R. S. Kaluwitharana st T. M. B. Bailey b Swann	49	A. S. A. Perera not out		5
P. A. de Silva c Loye b Taylor	60	L-b 7, w 10		17
*A. Ranatunga c Curran b R. J. Bailey	33			
M. S. Atapattu c Snape b Taylor	15	1/100 2/235 3/252 (6 wkts, 50 overs)		308
D. P. M. D. Jayawardene not out	9	4/284 5/297 6/300		

U. C. Hathurusinghe, H. D. P. K. Dharmasena and M. R. C. N. Bandaratilleke did not bat.

Bowling: Taylor 10–1–50–2; Follett 8–0–48–1; Penberthy 4–0–33–0; Curran 1–0–15–0; Snape 10–0–50–1; Swann 10–0–55–1; R. J. Bailey 7–0–50–1.

Northamptonshire

M. B. Loye b Bandaratilleke	59
*K. M. Curran c Kaluwitharana b Wickremasinghe	12
R. J. Bailey c Kaluwitharana b Wickremasinghe	3
D. J. Sales c Ranatunga b Bandaratilleke	44
J. N. Snape b Dharmasena	1
A. L. Penberthy run out	71
T. C. Walton c Atapattu b Perera	42
G. P. Swann run out	2
†T. M. B. Bailey b Wickremasinghe	9
J. P. Taylor b Jayasuriya	13
D. Follett not out	10
B 1, l-b 16, w 9	26

1/19 2/37 3/121   (49.1 overs) 292
4/124 5/140 6/240
7/248 8/265 9/282

Bowling: Wickremasinghe 7–0–42–3; Perera 10–1–47–1; Hathurusinghe 2–0–18–0; Dharmasena 9–0–59–1; Bandaratilleke 8–0–41–2; de Silva 9–0–37–0; Jayasuriya 4.1–0–31–1.

Umpires: J. W. Lloyds and D. R. Shepherd.

†KENT v SRI LANKANS

At Canterbury, August 11. Sri Lankans won by eight wickets. Toss: Kent.

Umpires Holder and Jesty stopped the original game after only 23 balls, in which the Sri Lankans reached 20 without loss, deeming the pitch "too dangerous" to continue. Jayasuriya was hit on the hands four times by lifting deliveries from Headley and Igglesden. Jayasuriya was left not out five, and Kaluwitharana not out nine. A new match, reduced from 50 to 45 overs a side, was played on the pitch just used for a Sunday League game. The ECB announced an immediate enquiry and pitch consultant Harry Brind visited the ground the following day. In the rearranged match, Kent batted first, though only Ealham made much impression. Then a 128-run stand between Atapattu and former Canterbury favourite de Silva saw the Sri Lankans home with more than 11 overs to spare. Jayasuriya did not play this time, nursing damaged hands and wrist in advance of the triangular tournament. Graham Cowdrey did appear, in his last match for Kent before retirement; he had made his debut, also against the Sri Lankans, 14 years earlier to the day.

Kent

R. W. T. Key run out	34
E. T. Smith run out	6
D. P. Fulton c Tillekeratne b Arnold	11
M. A. Ealham c de Silva b Dharmasena	40
C. L. Hooper c Atapattu b Perera	15
M. V. Fleming c Tillekeratne b Muralitharan	10
G. R. Cowdrey run out	18
*†S. A. Marsh not out	10
J. B. D. Thompson c Kaluwitharana b Muralitharan	0
D. W. Headley not out	5
B 5, l-b 6, w 12, n-b 4	27

A. P. Igglesden did not bat.

1/33 2/62 3/67   (8 wkts, 45 overs) 176
4/115 5/130 6/154
7/163 8/163

Bowling: Perera 7–1–45–1; Villavarayen 6–1–9–0; de Silva 7–0–19–0; Dharmasena 9–0–38–1; Muralitharan 9–1–21–2; Arnold 7–0–33–1.

Sri Lankans

R. P. Arnold run out	9
†R. S. Kaluwitharana b Headley	27
M. S. Atapattu not out	53
*P. A. de Silva not out	66
B 1, l-b 3, w 8, n-b 12	24

1/47 2/51   (2 wkts, 33.4 overs) 179

H. P. Tillekeratne, D. P. M. D. Jayawardene, U. C. Hathurusinghe, H. D. P. K. Dharmasena, M. Muralitharan, A. S. A. Perera and M. S. Villavarayen did not bat.

Bowling: Headley 7–2–14–1; Igglesden 4–0–30–0; Thompson 7–1–39–0; Hooper 9–0–48–0; Ealham 3–0–23–0; Fleming 2.4–0–17–0; Cowdrey 1–0–4–0.

Umpires: V. A. Holder and T. E. Jesty.

Sri Lanka's matches v South Africa and England in the Emirates Triangular Tournament (August 14–20) may be found in that section.

HAMPSHIRE v SRI LANKANS

At Southampton, August 22, 23, 24. Sri Lankans won by five wickets. Toss: Sri Lankans.

One more first-class match gave the Sri Lankans a last chance to settle the remaining places in their Test side. Two opening batsmen will remember it for different reasons. Hampshire's White batted all but five minutes of the first day for a career-best 156, including 23 fours. Sri Lankan Arnold, in contrast, was out twice for nought in 75 minutes, both times to Morris, facing a total of nine balls. Rain washed out the second day, forcing Smith to declare overnight. Arnold was caught at mid-off as the Sri Lankans fell away to 39 for four. Then Jayasuriya also declared, and Hampshire forfeited an innings, leaving the Sri Lankans 82 overs to get 309. This time, Arnold was lbw, but other Test contenders made the most of an easing pitch and brightening skies to win with 17 balls to spare. Hathurusinghe's century was not quite enough to earn him a place at The Oval, but Mahela Jayawardene's 90 saw him through.

Close of play: First day, Hampshire 347-8 (A. C. Morris 35*, R. J. Maru 0*); Second day, No play.

Hampshire

G. W. White c Tillekeratne b Arnold	156	†M. Garaway c Hathurusinghe	
D. A. Kenway lbw b Wickremasinghe	38	b Jayasuriya	19
W. S. Kendall c H. P. W. Jayawardene		A. C. Morris not out	35
b Wickremasinghe	59	R. J. Maru not out	0
*R. A. Smith run out	11	B 2, l-b 3, n-b 10	15
M. Keech b Jayasuriya	3		
A. D. Mascarenhas b Jayasuriya	0	1/77 2/195 3/208	(8 wkts dec.) 347
K. D. James c H. P. W. Jayawardene		4/213 5/213 6/232	
b Villavarayen	11	7/291 8/343	

S. R. G. Francis did not bat.

Bowling: Pushpakumara 4–0–13–0; Wickremasinghe 21–6–53–2; Villavarayen 21–5–54–1; Hathurusinghe 11–2–39–0; Bandaratilleke 10–2–28–0; Chandana 11–1–62–0; Jayasuriya 14–3–42–3; D. P. M. D. Jayawardene 7–1–37–0; Arnold 4–2–4–1; Tillekeratne 2–0–10–0.

Hampshire forfeited their second innings.

Sri Lankans

*S. T. Jayasuriya c James b Francis	11	– c Keech b James		40
R. P. Arnold c James b Morris	0	– lbw b Morris		0
D. P. M. D. Jayawardene c Kendall b Francis	3	– c Maru b Francis		90
H. P. Tillekeratne c Keech b Morris	5	– (5) c Keech b Francis		23
U. C. Hathurusinghe not out	7	– (4) not out		108
U. D. U. Chandana not out	10	– c Kendall b White		34
G. P. Wickremasinghe (did not bat)		– not out		0
L-b 3	3	B 4, l-b 2, n-b 8		14
1/1 2/6 3/21 4/21	(4 wkts dec.) 39	1/9 2/70 3/178	(5 wkts) 309	
		4/246 5/304		

†H. P. W. Jayawardene, M. R. C. N. Bandaratilleke, K. R. Pushpakumara and M. S. Villavarayen did not bat.

Bowling: *First Innings*—Morris 6–1–15–2; Francis 6–2–21–2. *Second Innings*—Morris 12–2–53–1; Francis 15–1–47–2; Mascarenhas 14–0–66–0; James 20–3–78–1; Maru 17–4–55–0; White 1.1–1–4–1.

Umpires: J. C. Balderstone and N. A. Mallender.

ENGLAND v SRI LANKA

Cornhill Test Match

At The Oval, August 27, 28, 29, 30, 31. Sri Lanka won by ten wickets. Toss: Sri Lanka. Test debut: A. S. A. Perera.

Only three weeks after a Test series victory against South Africa had encouraged talk that English cricket was embarking upon a more successful era, the unique bowling talents of the Sri Lankan off-spinner, Muralitharan, brought England back down to earth in the final Test of the summer. Muralitharan, the hill-country Tamil and son of a biscuit manufacturer, born with a deformity of the elbow joint and a highly manoeuvrable wrist, produced one of the most phenomenal bowling displays in Test history as Sri Lanka won by ten wickets inside the final hour. Muralitharan's 16 for 220 was the fifth-best match analysis in Test history; his nine for 65 in England's second innings was seventh on the all-time list. On the way, he passed 200 Test wickets in his 42nd Test. Among spinners, only Clarrie Grimmett had reached 200 in fewer Tests; another Australian, Shane Warne, also took 42. Many who observed Muralitharan's prodigious performance wondered whether, given continued fitness, he could become the greatest Test wicket-taker in history.

England had long identified Muralitharan as Sri Lanka's prime bowling threat (indeed, Sri Lanka's captain, Ranatunga, had no compunction in referring to him as his only real asset), and the nature of the Oval surface strengthened that conviction. Slow and largely unresponsive to the seamers, the pitch negated the England trio of Gough, Fraser and Cork that had been central to the defeat of South Africa. Salisbury's leg-spin, seemingly fraught with anxiety, also failed to impress. That left the only battle between Muralitharan, his own exhaustion and the tortuous resistance of the England batsmen. Muralitharan's unorthodox action, angled in from wide of the crease, achieved turn and dip from the outset, and provided an engrossing spectacle, even against batsmen largely committed to survival. As long as ICC remains satisfied by its legitimacy, it is an unorthodox action that we are privileged to witness. Evidence suggested that only a small minority of spectators at The Oval had much sympathy with England's coach, David Lloyd, when he hinted at his unhappiness with Muralitharan's methods on the fourth evening. Lloyd's remark that "I have my opinions that I have made known to the authorities" brought an official protest to the ECB from the Board of Control for Cricket in Sri Lanka, and led to Lloyd receiving a severe reprimand.

Rarely has a Test innings encouraged more misleading conclusions than England's first. England took not far short of two days to make 445 and were assumed, at the very least, to be safe from defeat: they weren't. Hick's computerised, indeed colourless, century on the first day had been greeted as making his selection for the winter's Ashes series inevitable; thanks to Crawley's subsequent 156, a crisper, more appealing affair, it didn't. And, thirdly, the widespread condemnation of Ranatunga, for putting England in to bat, had to be gradually re-addressed. Ranatunga later crowed that he had wanted Muralitharan to have a rest in between innings, a points-scoring explanation which required us to believe that, had Sri Lanka batted first, they would have automatically made England follow on.

Atherton withdrew late on Wednesday, because of back trouble, and England awarded a second cap to James – who was allowed to rush home to Cardiff between the first and second days to attend the birth of his daughter. With Hussain also out with a groin injury, Crawley was recalled, and Ben Holliake replaced Flintoff. Hick's fifth Test hundred therefore came in the rarified atmosphere of No. 3. A sound innings against a limited attack proved little as to how he might fare in more pressurised circumstances. By tea on the second day, Hick had been overshadowed: Crawley, on his return, drove expansively, played purposefully off his legs and curbed Muralitharan's growing threat.

[*Patrick Eagar*

The gate is open: Crawley is bowled, and England are doomed.

Both batted for around five and a half hours; Crawley (who might have gone to a return catch by Muralitharan before scoring – it was called a no-ball) allowed himself the liberty of a relaxed last-wicket frolic with Fraser. But there was an unavoidable sense of tour applications being penned at the crease.

None of this could match the entertainment in store on the third day. Sri Lanka, 79 for one overnight, danced to 446 for three. Jayasuriya, who had suffered a lean Test year since taking 340 off India in Colombo, stroked 213 in 346 minutes from 278 balls, with 33 fours and a six. De Silva, habitually pulling good-length balls, collected a hundred, which made him the first Sri Lankan to pass 5,000 Test runs. Together, they added 243, breaking their own record for Sri Lanka's third wicket. Even though England fought back staunchly on Sunday, when six wickets fell for 86, debutant Suresh Perera and Muralitharan put on 59 to extend Sri Lanka's lead to 146.

Muralitharan had two wickets by the close, including Hick for a duck. Next day, Ramprakash's run-out of his captain, Stewart, proved significant. Perhaps it cost England the game; just as possibly, it robbed Muralitharan of the opportunity of joining Jim Laker as only the second bowler to take all ten wickets in a Test innings. Crawley was bowled on the stroke of lunch, attempting an extravagant drive; Hollioake fell first ball immediately afterwards. Only when Gough, who reined himself in for almost two and a half hours, joined Ramprakash did England suggest they might achieve a draw, to match that at Old Trafford earlier in the summer. It was marvellous cat-and-mouse – Ramprakash cleverly protecting Gough from Muralitharan, the bowler regularly switching ends to try to get at him. Finally, Ramprakash's hair-shirt defiance, more than four hours for 42, ended when he pushed to short leg. Gough was bowled behind his legs, sweeping. All that remained was for Sri Lanka to score 36 to win, and for Muralitharan to retrieve the match ball and assert once again that he was doing no wrong. – DAVID HOPPS.

Man of the Match: M. Muralitharan.   *Attendance:* 70,688; *receipts* £1,404,250.

Close of play: First day, England 228-4 (G. A. Hick 107*, J. P. Crawley 10*); Second day, Sri Lanka 79-1 (S. T. Jayasuriya 59*, D. P. M. D. Jayawardene 4*); Third day, Sri Lanka 446-3 (P. A. de Silva 125*, A. Ranatunga 50*); Fourth day, England 54-2 (S. P. James 20*, A. J. Stewart 15*).

England

M. A. Butcher c Jayasuriya b Wickremasinghe	10	– st Kaluwitharana b Muralitharan	15
S. P. James c and b Muralitharan	36	– c Jayawardene b Muralitharan	25
G. A. Hick c Kaluwitharana b Wickremasinghe	107	– lbw b Muralitharan	0
*†A. J. Stewart c Tillekeratne b Perera	2	– run out	32
M. R. Ramprakash c Jayawardene b Muralitharan	53	– c Tillekeratne b Muralitharan	42
J. P. Crawley not out	156	– b Muralitharan	14
B. C. Hollioake c Atapattu b Muralitharan	14	– lbw b Muralitharan	0
D. G. Cork b Muralitharan	6	– c Kaluwitharana b Muralitharan	8
I. D. K. Salisbury b Muralitharan	2	– lbw b Muralitharan	0
D. Gough c Kaluwitharana b Muralitharan	4	– b Muralitharan	15
A. R. C. Fraser b Muralitharan	32	– not out	0
B 1, l-b 11, w 2, n-b 9	23	B 7, l-b 8, w 1, n-b 14	30

1/16 (1) 2/78 (2) 3/81 (4) 4/209 (5)   445   1/25 (1) 2/25 (3) 3/78 (2)   181
5/230 (6) 6/277 (7) 7/333 (8)   4/93 (4) 5/116 (6) 6/116 (7)
8/343 (9) 9/356 (10) 10/445 (11)   7/127 (8) 8/127 (9)
                                                            9/180 (5) 10/181 (10)

Bowling: *First Innings*—Wickremasinghe 30–4–81–2; Perera 40–10–104–1; Dharmasena 18–3–55–0; Muralitharan 59.3–14–155–7; Jayasuriya 11–0–38–0. *Second Innings*—Wickremasinghe 4–0–16–0; Perera 11–2–22–0; Muralitharan 54.2–27–65–9; Dharmasena 19.3–13–12–0; Jayasuriya 28–14–30–0; de Silva 10.3–3–16–0; Jayawardene 2–0–5–0.

Sri Lanka

S. T. Jayasuriya c Stewart b Hollioake	213	– not out	24
M. S. Atapattu lbw b Cork	15	– not out	9
D. P. M. D. Jayawardene c Hollioake b Fraser	9		
P. A. de Silva c Stewart b Hollioake	152		
*A. Ranatunga lbw b Gough	51		
H. P. Tillekeratne lbw b Gough	0		
†R. S. Kaluwitharana c Crawley b Cork	25		
H. D. P. K. Dharmasena lbw b Fraser	13		
A. S. A. Perera not out	43		
G. P. Wickremasinghe b Fraser	0		
M. Muralitharan c Stewart b Salisbury	30		
B 15, l-b 20, w 1, n-b 4	40	L-b 4	4

1/53 (2) 2/85 (3) 3/328 (1) 4/450 (5)   591   (no wkt) 37
5/450 (6) 6/488 (7) 7/504 (4)
8/526 (8) 9/532 (10) 10/591 (11)

Bowling: *First Innings*—Gough 30–5–102–2; Fraser 23–3–95–3; Hollioake 26–2–105–2; Cork 36–5–128–2; Salisbury 25.5–7–86–1; Ramprakash 5–0–24–0; Butcher 11–2–16–0. *Second Innings*—Fraser 2–0–19–0; Cork 2–0–3–0; Hollioake 1–0–11–0.

Umpires: E. A. Nicholls (West Indies) and D. R. Shepherd.
Referee: A. M. Ebrahim (Zimbabwe).

CEAT CRICKETER OF THE YEAR

The third CEAT International Cricketer of the Year was Sanath Jayasuriya of Sri Lanka. Judges Sunil Gavaskar, Clive Lloyd and Ian Chappell have devised a system awarding points for performances in Tests and limited-overs internationals. The judges make monthly assessments and add the CEAT Efficiency Quotient. In 1997-98, Jayasuriya tied on points with Sachin Tendulkar of India, but the judges ruled that the award should go to Jayasuriya. Previous winners were Brian Lara of West Indies and Venkatesh Prasad of India. The 1997-98 team award was given to Australia.

EMIRATES TRIANGULAR TOURNAMENT, 1998

For the first time, England adopted the idea of a triangular one-day international tournament, a format beloved of all the other major cricketing countries. It was a harbinger of the future, though it was partly a negative result of the ECB's bizarre refusal to accept the Sri Lankans as a serious power and drawcard; the South Africans had already been given a traditional one-day series in May, and the administrators seemed reluctant to let them go. Sri Lanka responded in their now-familiar fashion by winning the tournament.

There had been some trouble even finding a sponsor. Texaco, England's one-day sponsors since 1984, had withdrawn from the role earlier in the summer. Eventually, Emirates Airlines, who had already signed up for the 1999 World Cup, took advantage of what was believed to be a cut-price offer and stepped in. Their PR people were somewhat startled when a plan to photograph their stewardesses with the England team in front of the Lord's pavilion was vetoed, as being in breach of MCC's regulations banning the use of the pavilion in adverts.

The event was popular enough overall to encourage the ECB to repeat it at greater length in future. The week produced some of the kindest weather of a poor summer. There was an encouraging turn-out to watch the meeting of the visiting teams at Trent Bridge; England's two preliminary matches drew full houses; and, though the final was not sold out (England's supporters were hardly likely to gamble on their team's success and buy tickets in advance), large queues built up during the morning.

However, the conservative format – just one preliminary match against each opponent – predictably resulted in an outcome familiar to anyone who has ever played the child's game, scissors-paper-stone. Everyone beat someone else, and the finalists were decided on net run-rate. South Africa, dispirited after losing the Test series, looked as though they would rather be elsewhere. They soon had their wish, but did have a consolatory win at Edgbaston, after England had secured their passage to the final.

England turned away from their policy of having separate Test and one-day captains. Alec Stewart took charge while his county captain, Adam Hollioake, was reduced to the ranks, his reputation blotted by defeats in the series against West Indies and South Africa, and a decline in his own form. The selectors generally showed more enthusiasm for their proven high-class five-day players, rather than the utility men who had served them well enough on the slow surface of Sharjah in December.

Everyone was now absorbing the message that the 1999 World Cup, played early in an English season, would produce very different conditions from those in the subcontinent three years earlier, and that the slam-bang pinch-hitters, so successful then, might have to show bowlers a great deal more respect. For now, though, Sri Lanka's approach worked splendidly yet again, and English crowds were at last able to enjoy the quality of their cricketers.

Note: Matches in this section were not first-class.

SOUTH AFRICA v SRI LANKA

At Nottingham, August 14. Sri Lanka won by 57 runs. Toss: South Africa.

Four days after the crushing disappointment of losing the Leeds Test, South Africa understandably failed to raise their game for this addendum to their tour. Chasing 259, they lost Kirsten in the first over and quickly slid to 66 for five, the first three to Wickremasinghe. Symcox, promoted to No. 5 (but appearing eccentrically with 77 on his numbered shirt), made the most of his chance after a tour in the shadows, and put on 100 with Rhodes, who batted 49 balls for his 54. But when Symcox holed out, the innings crumpled. The South Africans had been on the receiving end of the Sri Lankans' traditional blazing start: 79 in the first ten overs. Forty-three of these came off Elworthy, who conceded 11 extras, including all four variants, in one over. To restore order, Donald had to come on much earlier than their strategists had planned. He helped prevent a run-riot, but Ranatunga nursed the later order successfully enough. He ran his singles more gingerly than ever because of a knee injury, and did not take the field. Instead of a maker's name, Ranatunga's bat had the words "Sam's Chicken and Ribs" on it; ICC forced him to amend this to "Sam's" in subsequent games. A good-size crowd, with no partisan concern, watched everything benignly.

Man of the Match: G. P. Wickremasinghe.	*Attendance:* 7,505; *receipts* £200,612.

Sri Lanka

S. T. Jayasuriya c Boucher b Donald	36
†R. S. Kaluwitharana c Cronje b Kallis	33
M. S. Atapattu st Boucher b Symcox	40
P. A. de Silva c Kirsten b Donald	12
*A. Ranatunga run out	58
D. P. M. D. Jayawardene c Boucher b Cronje	5
U. C. Hathurusinghe lbw b Cronje	14
G. P. Wickremasinghe b Pollock	8
H. D. P. K. Dharmasena c Boucher b Pollock	9
A. S. A. Perera not out	0
M. Muralitharan c Elworthy b Pollock	4
B 4, l-b 12, w 16, n-b 7	39
	258

1/85 (2) 2/88 (1) 3/102 (4) (47.5 overs) 258
4/182 (3) 5/192 (6)
6/224 (7) 7/235 (8)
8/252 (9) 9/254 (5)
10/258 (11)	Score at 15 overs: 102-3

Bowling: Pollock 8.5–0–54–3; Elworthy 5–0–43–0; Donald 8–0–40–2; Kallis 7–0–22–1; Rindel 2–0–12–0; Symcox 9–1–42–1; Cronje 8–0–29–2.

South Africa

G. Kirsten b Wickremasinghe	0
M. J. R. Rindel c sub (U. D. U. Chandana) b Wickremasinghe	18
J. H. Kallis c Atapattu b Wickremasinghe	6
D. J. Cullinan b Perera	2
P. L. Symcox c sub (U. D. U. Chandana) b Dharmasena	58
*W. J. Cronje lbw b Muralitharan	21
J. N. Rhodes c Hathurusinghe b Dharmasena	54
S. M. Pollock not out	11
†M. V. Boucher run out	2
S. Elworthy b Jayasuriya	0
A. A. Donald b Dharmasena	12
L-b 7, w 10	17
	201

1/0 (1) 2/8 (3) 3/30 (2) (49 overs) 201
4/32 (4) 5/66 (6)
6/166 (7) 7/175 (5)
8/178 (9) 9/178 (10)
10/201 (11)	Score at 15 overs: 41-4

Bowling: Wickremasinghe 7–2–20–3; Perera 7–0–22–1; Hathurusinghe 6–1–33–0; Muralitharan 10–1–42–1; Dharmasena 10–0–41–3; Jayasuriya 9–0–36–1.

Umpires: B. Dudleston and P. Willey.

ENGLAND v SRI LANKA

At Lord's, August 16. England won by 36 runs. Toss: Sri Lanka. International debut: I. D. Austin.

England maintained the momentum of their Test series win against South Africa six days earlier and, on a perfect Lord's day, pleased a packed house with a convincing bowling performance. The white ball swung even in the fine weather, imposing unfamiliar constraints on the Sri Lankans' blistering batting. England had anticipated this by preferring specialists to bits-and-pieces men in their squad. Included – but left out here – were Atherton and Fraser, plus the slow left-armer Giles; Ealham was also picked, but withdrew through injury and was replaced, unexpectedly, by the burly 32-year-old Lancastrian Ian Austin, regarded by many as the epitome of the cheerful county journeyman. Austin had been pulled off the field at Headingley in the midst of the Roses match. But the star of this game was Hick, who had added to his air of mystery by failing yet again in the Tests. Here, with no one round the bat, he played with complete authority. Stands with Stewart and Hussain gave England the basis for a decent score, but the later batsmen failed totally. Sri Lanka immediately ran into trouble with Gough, Martin and Mullally all achieved clear-air turbulence; there was a regular clatter of wickets, and England were never threatened. On the day, they also outfielded Sri Lanka – who dropped five catches. However, the calculators showed that Sri Lanka's net run-rate had already secured their return four days later for the final.

Man of the Match: G. A. Hick.	*Attendance:* 25,001; *receipts:* £853,526.

England

N. V. Knight c Atapattu		
b Wickremasinghe .	17	P. J. Martin run out 3
A. D. Brown c Atapattu		D. Gough not out. 1
b Wickremasinghe .	12	A. D. Mullally b Perera 1
*†A. J. Stewart b Jayasuriya	51	L-b 11, w 12 23
G. A. Hick run out	86	
N. Hussain b Dharmasena	39	1/14 (2) 2/56 (1) 3/132 (3) (49.3 overs) 247
A. J. Hollioake b Jayasuriya.	16	4/223 (5) 5/224 (4)
R. D. B. Croft c Kaluwitharana b Perera	3	6/228 (6) 7/233 (7)
I. D. Austin b Jayasuriya.	8	8/241 (9) 9/244 (8)
		10/247 (11) Score at 15 overs: 87-2

Bowling: Wickremasinghe 7–0–33–2; Perera 9.3–0–48–2; Hathurusinghe 3–0–23–0; Dharmasena 10–0–54–1; Muralitharan 10–0–42–0; Jayasuriya 10–0–36–3.

Sri Lanka

S. T. Jayasuriya c Knight b Gough	11	G. P. Wickremasinghe b Gough 18
†R. S. Kaluwitharana c Stewart b Martin	2	M. Muralitharan b Austin 18
M. S. Atapattu lbw b Gough	6	B 1, l-b 13, w 10, n-b 6 30
P. A. de Silva lbw b Austin	33	
R. P. Arnold b Mullally.	3	1/13 (2) 2/17 (1) 3/28 (3) (49.3 overs) 211
*A. Ranatunga b Croft	33	4/49 (5) 5/83 (4)
U. C. Hathurusinghe c Stewart b Mullally	7	6/97 (7) 7/126 (6)
H. D. P. K. Dharmasena not out	33	8/159 (9) 9/189 (10)
A. S. A. Perera c Brown b Hollioake. . .	17	10/211 (11) Score at 15 overs: 67-4

Bowling: Gough 10–0–51–3; Martin 8–0–34–1; Mullally 8–1–20–2; Austin 8.3–0–37–2; Croft 10–0–37–1; Hollioake 5–0–18–1.

Umpires: M. J. Kitchen and K. E. Palmer.

ENGLAND v SOUTH AFRICA

At Birmingham, August 18. South Africa won by 14 runs. Toss: South Africa. International debut: M. Hayward.

The South Africans achieved a consolation victory to end their unsuccessful tour, but failed to reach the final of this competition, an outcome that may not have displeased all their weary players: the plane home was an attractive alternative. During the change of innings, England became aware that the contortions of net run-rate meant that their "real" target was 198. Subconsciously, at least, they settled for that and resumed their old habits of defeat. South Africa had surprisingly opted to bat on a cloudy morning, thus handing England control of the mathematics. Demob-happy, Cullinan played one of his best innings of the tour – 70 off 73 balls – and received late support from Symcox. Dropped by Hollioake on three, Symcox smashed four sixes in 39 balls. England began with all their new-found confidence, and Knight and Hick put on 113. But with a place in the final assured, their batting again fell away wretchedly.

Man of the Match: P. L. Symcox.   *Attendance*: 19,225; *receipts* £579,705.

South Africa

G. Kirsten c Stewart b Gough	7	†M. V. Boucher not out. 3
M. J. R. Rindel lbw b Gough.	10	
D. J. Cullinan b Gough	70	L-b 9, w 5, n-b 2 16
J. N. Rhodes c Stewart b Mullally.	15	
*W. J. Cronje lbw b Croft	31	1/20 (2) 2/25 (1) (7 wkts, 50 overs) 244
J. H. Kallis b Austin	19	3/73 (4) 4/140 (3)
S. M. Pollock not out	22	5/160 (5) 6/172 (6)
P. L. Symcox b Mullally	51	7/241 (8) Score at 15 overs: 76-3

A. A. Donald and M. Hayward did not bat.

Bowling: Gough .10–1–43–3; Martin 9–0–47–0; Austin 10–0–41–1; Mullally 9–0–33–2; Hollioake 2–0–22–0; Croft 10–0–49–1.

England

N. V. Knight b Symcox	74	P. J. Martin c Cronje b Donald	1
A. D. Brown run out	0	A. D. Mullally not out	1
*†A. J. Stewart c Rhodes b Pollock	27	L-b 7, w 11, n-b 1	19
G. A. Hick c Symcox b Cronje	64		
N. Hussain c and b Cronje	1	1/7 (2) 2/48 (3) 3/161 (4) (48.5 overs) 230	
A. J. Hollioake b Symcox	10	4/170 (5) 5/186 (1)	
R. D. B. Croft c Rhodes b Rindel	8	6/193 (6) 7/208 (7)	
I. D. Austin b Donald	10	8/213 (8) 9/217 (10)	
D. Gough lbw b Pollock	15	10/230 (9) Score at 15 overs: 73-2	

Bowling: Donald 9–1–41–2; Pollock 8.5–0–36–2; Kallis 4–0–24–0; Hayward 4–0–35–0; Symcox 10–0–36–2; Cronje 10–0–43–2; Rindel 3–0–8–1.

Umpires: J. W. Holder and G. Sharp.

QUALIFYING TABLE

	Played	Won	Lost	Points	Net run-rate
England	2	1	1	2	0.22
Sri Lanka	2	1	1	2	0.21
South Africa	2	1	1	2	–0.43

England and Sri Lanka reached the final ahead of South Africa on net run-rate, all three teams having won one of their head-to-head matches. Net run-rate was calculated by subtracting runs conceded per over from runs scored per over.

FINAL

ENGLAND v SRI LANKA

At Lord's, August 20. Sri Lanka won by five wickets. Toss: England.

Sri Lanka won their fifth multilateral one-day tournament in the 29 months since their World Cup triumph, after England's middle and late order collapsed in the most spectacular fashion yet. Knight and Atherton delighted Lord's with an opening stand of 132 in the first 25 overs; in the second 25, England lost eight for 124. This represented the first triumph in England for Muralitharan, the Sri Lankan off-spinner who would achieve even greater success just over a week later. He took five for 34, which beat Joel Garner's five for 38 in the 1979 World Cup final as the best figures in a one-day international at Lord's. Muralitharan first stifled the openers' scoring-rate, then worked through the innings, turning and flighting the ball far more than most slow bowlers dare in one-day cricket. The Sri Lankan batsmen had few problems. Gough, to a huge roar, followed two wides by bowling Jayasuriya for a duck with his second legitimate ball. But Atapattu and Kaluwitharana, two men with little reputation in England, showed the breadth of Sri Lanka's batting by adding 138 in 27 overs. Atapattu was in devastating form. It was England's turn to look ragged in the field; their morale was not helped by bowling which, Gough aside, looked wholly innocuous.

Man of the Match: M. Muralitharan.   *Attendance:* 25,266; *receipts* £818,050.
Man of the Series: M. S. Atapattu.

England

N. V. Knight c and b Muralitharan	94	I. D. Austin not out	11
M. A. Atherton c Ranatunga b Muralitharan	64	D. Gough b Perera	0
*†A. J. Stewart c Kaluwitharana b Muralitharan	18	P. J. Martin not out	1
G. A. Hick b Chandana	14	B 4, l-b 5, w 10	19
A. D. Brown b Muralitharan	18	1/132 (2) 2/170 (3) (8 wkts, 50 overs) 256	
N. Hussain lbw b Muralitharan	0	3/191 (4) 4/218 (1)	
R. D. B. Croft c Kaluwitharana b Perera	17	5/218 (6) 6/223 (5)	
		7/246 (7) 8/246 (9) Score at 15 overs: 83-0	

A. D. Mullally did not bat.

Bowling: Wickremasinghe 5–0–29–0; Perera 9–0–44–2; Dharmasena 9–0–47–0; Muralitharan 10–0–34–5; de Silva 2–0–10–0; Jayasuriya 8–0–45–0; Chandana 7–0–38–1.

Sri Lanka

S. T. Jayasuriya b Gough	0	H. P. Tillekeratne not out	10
†R. S. Kaluwitharana c Hick b Croft	68	L-b 7, w 6	13
M. S. Atapattu not out	132		
P. A. de Silva c Brown b Gough	34	1/2 (1) 2/140 (2) (5 wkts, 47.1 overs) 260	
*A. Ranatunga c Knight b Martin	1	3/210 (4) 4/224 (5)	
U. D. U. Chandana c Knight b Croft	2	5/233 (6) Score at 15 overs: 82-1	

H. D. P. K. Dharmasena, G. P. Wickremasinghe, A. S. A. Perera and M. Muralitharan did not bat.

Bowling: Gough 10–0–50–2; Martin 10–1–60–1; Mullally 10–0–37–0; Austin 10–1–48–0; Croft 7–0–54–2; Hick 0.1–0–4–0.

Umpires: D. J. Constant and D. R. Shepherd.   Series referee: A. M. Ebrahim.

ONE-DAY INTERNATIONAL RESULTS, 1997-98

	P	W	L	T	NR	% W (excl. NR)
South Africa	27	21	6	0	0	77.77
Sri Lanka	32	20	10	0	2	66.66
Australia	25	14	11	0	0	56.00
India	48	23	19	0	6	54.76
West Indies	12	6	6	0	0	50.00
England	15	7	8	0	0	46.66
Pakistan	32	12	18	0	2	40.00
New Zealand	28	10	15	1	2	38.46
Kenya	11	4	7	0	0	36.36
Zimbabwe	23	8	14	1	0	34.78
Bangladesh	13	1	12	0	0	7.69

Note: Matches abandoned without a ball bowled are excluded.

BRITANNIC ASSURANCE
COUNTY CHAMPIONSHIP, 1998

Ben Smith

As the argument over two-division cricket intensified, a so-called unfashionable county – the sort expected to be in the lower division – won the County Championship for the third year running. In 1997 it was Glamorgan; in 1998, as in 1996, it was Leicestershire. They became the first team in 24 years to complete a season, surging through with a sensational late run in which – one washed-out match excluded – they scored 190 points out of the last 192.

One team had dominated the table almost all summer, but it was not Leicestershire: Surrey had taken the lead in May and were not headed until September 4, despite sometimes losing up to four players to England. However, they lost the advantage after a bad defeat at Headingley, and came to the final game nine points behind Leicestershire. By coincidence, the top two were playing each other at The Oval.

BRITANNIC ASSURANCE CHAMPIONSHIP

					Bonus Points		
Win = 16 pts Draw = 3 pts	Played	Won	Lost	Drawn	Batting	Bowling	Points
1 – Leicestershire (10)	17	11	0	6	47	51	292
2 – Lancashire (11)	17	11	1	5	30	56	277
3 – Yorkshire (6)	17	9	3	5	47	63	269
4 – Gloucestershire (7)	17	11	5	1	23	65	267
5 – Surrey (8)	17	10	5	2	38	57	261
6 – Hampshire (14)	17	6	5	6	27	61	202
7 – Sussex (18)	17	6	7	4	30	63	201
8 – Warwickshire (4)	17	6	8	3	35	60	200
9 – Somerset (12)	17	6	7	4	30	54	192
10 – Derbyshire (16)	17	6	7	4	28	55	191
11 – Kent (2)	17	5	5	7	18	59	178
12 – Glamorgan (1)	17	4	6	7	36	55	176†
13 – Worcestershire (3)	17	4	6	7	32	59	176†
14 – Durham (17)	17	3	9	5	30	65	158
15 – Northamptonshire (15)	17	4	5	8	31	52	146*
16 – Nottinghamshire (13)	17	3	10	4	20	60	140
17 – Middlesex (4)	17	2	9	6	28	52	130
18 – Essex (8)	17	2	11	4	16	58	118

1997 positions are shown in brackets.

* Northamptonshire had 25 points deducted as a penalty for a substandard pitch at Northampton.

† Glamorgan finished above Worcestershire by virtue of taking more wickets over the season.

See (i) on page 438.

But the showdown turned into a walkover: Surrey's all-stars were made to suffer by an unsung batsman with the uncharismatic name of Ben Smith. Leicestershire won by an innings and 211, with Smith scoring a double-century. Surrey not merely missed out on the title; they were stunned to find themselves out of the top four – and the prize money.

Leicestershire won thanks to a remarkable team effort: their captain James Whitaker was absent injured throughout, and their overseas player Phil Simmons – the dominant figure in 1996 – struggled for form. They were challenged to the last, not only by Surrey but also by Lancashire, who, like Leicestershire, won their last six matches. Having won two one-day competitions, they entertained hopes of a treble. But the Championship, which has not gone to Old Trafford (shared titles excepted) since 1934, eluded them yet again, and they settled for being runners-up.

Yorkshire were also beneficiaries of the Surrey collapse. They won their last five, and came third, their best placing since 1975, thanks mainly to a strong hand of young seam bowlers which enabled them to overcome Darren Gough's regular absences with England. With 35-year-old Courtney Walsh passing 100 wickets, Gloucestershire came fourth. As so often, Cheltenham was vital, and produced two home wins, including a thrilling two-wicket victory over Surrey, who were 130 ahead on first innings. Had Surrey won that, they would have been unstoppable.

The two most unexpected sides of the season were Hampshire and Sussex. Under new captain Robin Smith, Hampshire rose eight places to sixth, having finished in the bottom six for the previous six seasons. And Sussex, last of all following their internal turmoil in 1997, went up 11 places to seventh. All these counties were rewarded with places in the 1999 Super Cup, a one-day competition reserved for the top eight in the Championship. The last place went to Warwickshire, who were relieved to scrape in, but were thoroughly disappointed with a season under Brian Lara's captaincy.

They were followed by Somerset, up three places to ninth: Andrew Caddick took 105 wickets, but received little support from the batsmen. Derbyshire played cricket rather than politics, at least until the season ended, and climbed six positions to tenth. The top three in 1997 were all below them. Kent went from second to 11th and Worcestershire third to 13th. In between were the champions Glamorgan who, after their one wonderful year, ran into familiar problems of injuries and bad weather, and slithered down to 12th, finishing ahead of Worcestershire on a technicality.

The one cheerful side at this end of the table were Durham. For them, 14th represented the best season of their seven as a first-class county. It did not quite fulfil the hopes of midsummer: the longest day dawned with Durham in second place. But they escaped the ignominy of being asked to play a first-class county as their first game in the 1999 NatWest, a punishment now reserved for the bottom four.

Northamptonshire (docked 25 points for an unsuitable pitch) were unchanged in 15th, though that was about the only thing that did not change at Northampton. They were unable to field a settled team, and in the autumn quickly sacked both manager John Emburey and captain Kevin Curran.

Before the season, no one could have predicted the bottom three – counties who between them had won 13 of the last 20 Championships. Nottinghamshire lost their last four games and came 16th; and Middlesex lost their last five (their worst run since 1933) to be 17th, their worst position ever. These two also parted company with their managers, Alan Ormrod and John Buchanan. Most stunning of all, Essex were last, for the first time since 1950. They lost their last six games (their worst run ever) and failed to take any of the last five into a final day. Here the captain, Paul Prichard, paid the penalty, even though he had carried off the Benson and Hedges Cup in mid-season.

Of the 153 Championship matches, 44 were drawn, down by a third on 1997. Of the 109 games with a result, more than half – 55 – were over inside three days, and five of these inside two.

Pre-season betting (William Hill) 9-2 Warwickshire; 13-2 Kent and LEICESTERSHIRE; 7-1 Essex; 15-2 Middlesex; 8-1 Surrey; 9-1 Glamorgan; 11-1 Yorkshire; 12-1 Lancashire and Worcestershire; 25-1 Derbyshire and Northamptonshire; 28-1 Gloucestershire; 33-1 Nottinghamshire and Somerset; 50-1 Hampshire and Sussex; 200-1 Durham.

Leaders: from April 27 Yorkshire; May 16 Surrey; September 4 Leicestershire. Leicestershire became champions on September 19.

Bottom place: from April 27 Leicestershire; May 17 Hampshire; June 6 Essex; June 20 Nottinghamshire; July 4 Northamptonshire; July 26 Essex.

Prize money

First (Leicestershire)	£100,000
Second (Lancashire)	£45,000
Third (Yorkshire)	£22,000
Fourth (Gloucestershire)	£15,000
Winners of each match	£2,000

Scoring of Points

(*a*) For a win, 16 points plus any points scored in the first innings.

(*b*) In a tie, each side scores eight points, plus any points scored in the first innings.

(*c*) In a drawn match, each side scores three points, plus any points scored in the first innings (see also paragraph (*f*)).

(*d*) If the scores are equal in a drawn match, the side batting in the fourth innings scores eight points, plus any points scored in the first innings, and the opposing side scores three points plus any points scored in the first innings.

(*e*) First-innings points (awarded only for performances in the first 120 overs of each first innings and retained whatever the result of the match).

   (i) A maximum of four batting points to be available: 200 to 249 runs – 1 point; 250 to 299 runs – 2 points; 300 to 349 runs – 3 points; 350 runs or over – 4 points.

   (ii) A maximum of four bowling points to be available: 3 or 4 wickets taken – 1 point; 5 or 6 wickets taken – 2 points; 7 or 8 wickets taken – 3 points; 9 or 10 wickets taken – 4 points.

(*f*) If play starts when less than eight hours' playing time remains and a one-innings match is played, no first-innings points shall be scored. The side winning on the one innings scores 12 points. In a tie, each side scores six points. In a drawn match, each side scores three points. If the scores are equal in a drawn match, the side batting in the second innings scores six points and the opposing side scores three points.

(*g*) If a match is abandoned without a ball being bowled, each side scores three points.

(*h*) A county which is adjudged to have prepared a pitch unsuitable for four-day first-class cricket shall be liable to have 25 points deducted. In addition, a penalty of 10 or 15 points may in certain circumstances be imposed on a county in respect of a poor pitch.

(*i*) The side which has the highest aggregate of points shall be the Champion County. Should any sides in the Championship table be equal on points, the following tie-breakers will be applied in the order stated: most wins, fewest losses, team achieving most points in head-to-head contests between teams level on points, most wickets taken, most runs scored.

In 1999, 12 points were due to be awarded for a win, and four for a draw.

Under ECB playing conditions, two extras were scored for every no-ball and wide bowled whether scored off or not. Any runs scored off the bat were credited to the batsman, while byes and leg-byes were counted as no-balls or wides, as appropriate, in accordance with Law 24.9, in addition to the initial penalty.

DATES OF FORMATION OF FIRST-CLASS COUNTIES

County	First known organisation	Original date	Present Club Reorganisation, if substantial	First-class status from
Derbyshire	1870	1870	—	1871
Durham.	1874	1882	1991	1992
Essex	By 1790	1876	—	1895
Glamorgan.	1861	1888	—	1921
Gloucestershire	1863	1871	—	1870
Hampshire	1849	1863	1879	1864
Kent.	1842	1859	1870	1864
Lancashire	1864	1864	—	1865
Leicestershire	By 1820	1879	—	1895
Middlesex	1863	1864	—	1864
Northamptonshire . .	1820†	1878	—	1905
Nottinghamshire . . .	1841	1841	1866	1864
Somerset	1864	1875	—	1882
Surrey.	1845	1845	—	1864
Sussex	1836	1839	1857	1864
Warwickshire	1826	1882	—	1895
Worcestershire	1844	1865	—	1899
Yorkshire.	1861	1863	1891	1864

Note: Derbyshire lost first-class status from 1888 to 1894, Hampshire between 1886 and 1894 and Somerset between 1886 and 1890.

† *Town club.*

CONSTITUTION OF COUNTY CHAMPIONSHIP

At least four possible dates have been given for the start of county cricket in England. The first, patchy, references began in 1825. The earliest mention in any cricket publication is in 1864 and eight counties have come to be regarded as first-class from that date, including Cambridgeshire, who dropped out after 1871. For many years, the County Championship was considered to have started in 1873, when regulations governing qualification first applied; indeed, a special commemorative stamp was issued by the Post Office in 1973. However, the Championship was not formally organised until 1890 and before then champions were proclaimed by the press; sometimes publications differed in their views and no definitive list of champions can start before that date. Eight teams contested the 1890 competition – Gloucestershire, Kent, Lancashire, Middlesex, Nottinghamshire, Surrey, Sussex and Yorkshire. Somerset joined in the following year, and in 1895 the Championship began to acquire something of its modern shape when Derbyshire, Essex, Hampshire, Leicestershire and Warwickshire were added. At that point MCC officially recognised the competition's existence. Worcestershire, Northamptonshire and Glamorgan were admitted to the Championship in 1899, 1905 and 1921 respectively and are regarded as first-class from these dates. An invitation in 1921 to Buckinghamshire to enter the Championship was declined, owing to the lack of necessary playing facilities, and an application by Devon in 1948 was unsuccessful. Durham were admitted to the Championship in 1992 and were granted first-class status prior to their pre-season tour of Zimbabwe.

COUNTY CHAMPIONS

The title of champion county is unreliable before 1890. In 1963, *Wisden* formally accepted the list of champions "most generally selected" by contemporaries, as researched by the late Rowland Bowen (See *Wisden* 1959, pp 91-98). This appears to be the most accurate available list but has no official status. The county champions from 1864 to 1890 were, according to Bowen:

1864 Surrey; 1865 Nottinghamshire; 1866 Middlesex; 1867 Yorkshire; 1868 Nottinghamshire;
1869 Nottinghamshire and Yorkshire; 1870 Yorkshire; 1871 Nottinghamshire; 1872 Nottinghamshire; 1873 Gloucestershire and Nottinghamshire; 1874 Gloucestershire; 1875 Nottinghamshire;
1876 Gloucestershire; 1877 Gloucestershire; 1878 undecided; 1879 Lancashire and Nottinghamshire; 1880 Nottinghamshire; 1881 Lancashire; 1882 Lancashire and Nottinghamshire; 1883
Nottinghamshire; 1884 Nottinghamshire; 1885 Nottinghamshire; 1886 Nottinghamshire; 1887
Surrey; 1888 Surrey; 1889 Lancashire, Nottinghamshire and Surrey.

Official champions					
1890	Surrey	1928	Lancashire	1967	Yorkshire
1891	Surrey	1929	Nottinghamshire	1968	Yorkshire
1892	Surrey	1930	Lancashire	1969	Glamorgan
1893	Yorkshire	1931	Yorkshire	1970	Kent
1894	Surrey	1932	Yorkshire	1971	Surrey
1895	Surrey	1933	Yorkshire	1972	Warwickshire
1896	Yorkshire	1934	Lancashire	1973	Hampshire
1897	Lancashire	1935	Yorkshire	1974	Worcestershire
1898	Yorkshire	1936	Derbyshire	1975	Leicestershire
1899	Surrey	1937	Yorkshire	1976	Middlesex
1900	Yorkshire	1938	Yorkshire	1977 {	Middlesex
1901	Yorkshire	1939	Yorkshire		Kent
1902	Yorkshire	1946	Yorkshire	1978	Kent
1903	Middlesex	1947	Middlesex	1979	Essex
1904	Lancashire	1948	Glamorgan	1980	Middlesex
1905	Yorkshire	1949 {	Middlesex	1981	Nottinghamshire
1906	Kent		Yorkshire	1982	Middlesex
1907	Nottinghamshire	1950 {	Lancashire	1983	Essex
1908	Yorkshire		Surrey	1984	Essex
1909	Kent	1951	Warwickshire	1985	Middlesex
1910	Kent	1952	Surrey	1986	Essex
1911	Warwickshire	1953	Surrey	1987	Nottinghamshire
1912	Yorkshire	1954	Surrey	1988	Worcestershire
1913	Kent	1955	Surrey	1989	Worcestershire
1914	Surrey	1956	Surrey	1990	Middlesex
1919	Yorkshire	1957	Surrey	1991	Essex
1920	Middlesex	1958	Surrey	1992	Essex
1921	Middlesex	1959	Yorkshire	1993	Middlesex
1922	Yorkshire	1960	Yorkshire	1994	Warwickshire
1923	Yorkshire	1961	Hampshire	1995	Warwickshire
1924	Yorkshire	1962	Yorkshire	1996	Leicestershire
1925	Yorkshire	1963	Yorkshire	1997	Glamorgan
1926	Lancashire	1964	Worcestershire	1998	Leicestershire
1927	Lancashire	1965	Worcestershire		
		1966	Yorkshire		

Notes: Since the championship was constituted in 1890 it has been won outright as follows: Yorkshire
29 times, Surrey 15, Middlesex 10, Lancashire 7, Essex and Kent 6, Warwickshire and Worcestershire
5, Nottinghamshire 4, Glamorgan and Leicestershire 3, Hampshire 2, Derbyshire 1.

   The title has been shared three times since 1890, involving Middlesex twice, Kent, Lancashire,
Surrey and Yorkshire.

Wooden Spoons: Since the major expansion of the Championship from nine teams to 14 in
1895, the counties have finished outright bottom as follows: Derbyshire, Northamptonshire and
Somerset 11; Glamorgan 9; Nottinghamshire 8; Leicestershire and Sussex 7; Gloucestershire and
Worcestershire 6; Hampshire 5; Durham and Warwickshire 3; Essex and Kent 2; Yorkshire 1.
Lancashire, Middlesex and Surrey have never finished bottom. Leicestershire have also shared
bottom place twice, once with Hampshire and once with Somerset.

   From 1977 to 1983 the Championship was sponsored by Schweppes and from 1994 to 1998
by Britannic Assurance.

COUNTY CHAMPIONSHIP – FINAL POSITIONS, 1890-1998

	Derbyshire	Essex	Glamorgan	Gloucestershire	Hampshire	Kent	Lancashire	Leicestershire	Middlesex	Northamptonshire	Nottinghamshire	Somerset	Surrey	Sussex	Warwickshire	Worcestershire	Yorkshire
1890	—	—	—	6	—	3	2	—	7	—	5	—	1	8	—	—	3
1891	—	—	—	9	—	5	2	—	3	—	4	5	1	7	—	—	8
1892	—	—	—	7	—	7	4	—	5	—	2	3	1	9	—	—	6
1893	—	—	—	9	—	4	2	—	3	—	6	8	5	7	—	—	1
1894	—	—	—	9	—	4	4	—	3	—	7	6	1	8	—	—	2
1895	5	9	—	4	10	14	2	12	6	—	12	8	1	11	6	—	3
1896	7	5	—	10	8	9	2	13	3	—	6	11	4	14	12	—	1
1897	14	3	—	5	9	12	1	13	8	—	10	11	2	6	7	—	4
1898	9	5	—	3	12	7	6	13	2	—	8	13	4	9	9	—	1
1899	15	6	—	9	10	8	4	13	2	—	10	13	1	5	7	12	3
1900	13	10	—	7	15	3	2	14	7	—	5	11	7	3	6	12	1
1901	15	10	—	14	7	7	3	12	2	—	9	12	6	4	5	11	1
1902	10	13	—	14	15	7	5	11	12	—	3	7	4	2	6	9	1
1903	12	8	—	13	14	8	4	14	1	—	5	10	11	2	7	6	3
1904	10	14	—	9	15	3	1	7	4	—	5	12	11	6	7	13	2
1905	14	12	—	8	16	6	2	5	11	13	10	15	4	3	7	8	1
1906	16	7	—	9	8	1	4	15	11	11	5	11	3	10	6	14	2
1907	16	7	—	10	12	8	6	11	5	15	1	14	4	13	9	2	2
1908	14	11	—	10	9	2	7	13	4	15	8	16	3	5	12	6	1
1909	15	14	—	16	8	1	2	13	6	7	10	11	5	4	12	8	3
1910	15	11	—	12	6	1	4	10	3	9	5	16	2	7	14	13	8
1911	14	6	—	12	11	2	4	13	5	3	10	8	16	5	1	9	7
1912	12	15	—	11	6	3	4	13	5	2	8	14	7	10	9	16	1
1913	13	15	—	9	10	1	8	14	6	4	5	16	3	7	11	12	2
1914	12	8	—	16	5	3	11	13	2	9	10	15	1	6	7	14	4
1919	9	14	—	8	7	2	5	9	13	12	3	5	4	11	15	—	1
1920	16	9	—	8	11	5	2	13	1	14	7	10	3	6	12	15	4
1921	12	15	17	7	6	4	5	11	1	13	8	10	2	9	16	14	3
1922	11	8	16	13	6	4	5	14	7	15	2	10	3	9	12	17	1
1923	10	13	16	11	7	5	3	14	8	17	2	9	4	6	12	15	1
1924	17	15	13	6	12	5	4	11	2	16	6	8	3	10	9	14	1
1925	14	7	17	10	9	5	3	12	6	11	4	15	2	13	8	16	1
1926	11	9	8	15	7	3	1	13	6	16	4	14	5	10	12	17	2
1927	5	8	15	12	13	4	1	7	9	16	2	14	6	10	11	17	3
1928	10	16	15	5	12	2	1	9	8	13	3	14	6	7	11	17	4
1929	7	12	17	4	11	8	2	9	6	13	1	15	10	4	14	16	2
1930	9	6	11	2	13	5	1	12	16	17	4	13	8	7	15	10	3
1931	7	10	15	2	12	3	6	16	11	17	5	13	8	4	9	14	1
1932	10	14	15	13	8	3	6	12	10	16	4	7	5	2	9	17	1
1933	6	4	16	10	14	3	5	17	12	13	8	11	9	2	7	15	1
1934	3	8	13	7	14	5	1	12	10	17	9	15	11	2	4	16	5
1935	2	9	13	15	16	10	4	6	3	17	5	14	11	7	8	12	1
1936	1	9	16	4	10	8	11	15	2	17	5	7	6	14	13	12	3
1937	3	6	7	4	14	12	9	16	2	17	10	13	8	5	11	15	1
1938	5	6	16	10	14	9	4	15	2	17	12	7	3	8	13	11	1
1939	9	4	13	3	15	5	6	17	2	16	12	14	8	10	11	7	1
1946	15	8	6	5	10	6	3	11	2	16	13	4	11	17	14	8	1
1947	5	11	9	2	16	4	3	14	1	17	11	11	6	9	15	7	7

	Derbyshire	Durham	Essex	Glamorgan	Gloucestershire	Hampshire	Kent	Lancashire	Leicestershire	Middlesex	Northamptonshire	Nottinghamshire	Somerset	Surrey	Sussex	Warwickshire	Worcestershire	Yorkshire
1948	6	—	13	1	8	9	15	5	11	3	17	14	12	2	16	7	10	4
1949	15	—	9	8	7	16	13	11	17	1	6	11	9	5	13	4	3	1
1950	5	—	17	11	7	12	9	1	16	14	10	15	7	1	13	4	6	3
1951	11	—	8	5	12	9	16	3	15	7	13	17	14	6	10	1	4	2
1952	4	—	10	7	9	12	15	3	6	5	8	16	17	1	13	10	14	2
1953	6	—	12	10	6	14	16	3	3	5	11	8	17	1	2	9	15	12
1954	3	—	15	4	13	14	11	10	16	7	7	5	17	1	9	6	11	2
1955	8	—	14	16	12	3	13	9	6	5	7	11	17	1	4	9	15	2
1956	12	—	11	13	3	6	16	2	17	5	4	8	15	1	9	14	9	7
1957	4	—	5	9	12	13	14	6	17	7	2	15	8	1	9	11	16	3
1958	5	—	6	15	14	2	8	7	12	10	4	17	3	1	13	16	9	11
1959	7	—	9	6	2	8	13	5	16	10	11	17	12	3	15	4	14	1
1960	5	—	6	11	8	12	10	2	17	3	9	16	14	7	4	15	13	1
1961	7	—	6	14	5	1	11	13	9	3	16	17	10	15	8	12	4	2
1962	7	—	9	14	4	10	11	16	17	13	8	15	6	5	12	3	2	1
1963	17	—	12	2	8	10	13	15	16	6	7	9	3	11	4	4	14	1
1964	12	—	10	11	17	12	7	14	16	6	3	15	8	4	9	2	1	5
1965	9	—	15	3	10	12	5	13	14	6	2	17	7	8	16	11	1	4
1966	9	—	16	14	15	11	4	12	8	12	5	17	3	7	10	6	2	1
1967	6	—	15	14	17	12	2	11	2	7	9	15	8	4	13	10	5	1
1968	8	—	14	3	16	5	2	6	9	10	13	4	12	15	17	11	7	1
1969	16	—	6	1	2	5	10	15	14	11	9	8	17	3	7	4	12	13
1970	7	—	12	2	17	10	1	3	15	16	14	11	13	5	9	7	6	4
1971	17	—	10	16	8	9	4	3	5	6	14	12	7	1	11	2	15	13
1972	17	—	5	13	3	9	2	15	6	8	4	14	11	12	16	1	7	10
1973	16	—	8	11	5	1	4	12	9	13	3	17	10	2	15	7	6	14
1974	17	—	12	16	14	2	10	8	4	6	3	15	5	7	13	9	1	11
1975	15	—	7	9	16	3	5	4	1	11	8	13	12	6	17	14	10	2
1976	15	—	6	17	3	12	14	16	4	1	2	13	7	9	10	5	11	8
1977	7	—	6	14	3	11	1	16	5	1	9	17	4	14	8	10	13	12
1978	14	—	2	13	10	8	1	12	6	3	17	7	5	16	9	11	15	4
1979	16	—	1	17	10	12	5	13	6	14	11	9	8	3	4	15	2	7
1980	9	—	8	13	7	10	17	16	15	1	12	3	5	2	4	14	11	6
1981	12	—	5	14	13	7	9	16	8	4	15	1	3	6	2	17	11	10
1982	11	—	7	16	15	3	13	12	2	1	9	4	6	5	8	17	14	10
1983	9	—	1	15	12	3	7	12	4	6	14	10	8	11	5	16	5	17
1984	12	—	1	13	17	15	5	16	4	3	11	2	7	8	6	9	10	14
1985	13	—	4	12	3	2	9	14	16	1	10	8	17	6	7	15	5	11
1986	11	—	1	17	2	6	8	15	7	12	9	4	16	3	14	12	5	10
1987	6	—	12	13	10	5	14	2	3	16	7	1	11	4	17	15	9	8
1988	14	—	3	17	10	15	2	9	8	7	12	5	11	4	16	6	1	13
1989	6	—	2	17	9	6	15	4	13	3	5	11	14	12	10	8	1	16
1990	12	—	2	8	13	3	16	6	7	1	11	13	15	9	17	5	4	10
1991	3	—	1	12	13	9	6	8	16	15	10	4	17	5	11	2	6	14
1992	5	18	1	14	10	15	2	12	8	11	3	4	9	13	7	6	17	16
1993	15	18	11	3	17	13	8	13	9	1	4	7	5	6	10	16	2	12
1994	17	16	6	18	12	13	9	10	2	4	5	3	11	7	8	1	15	13
1995	14	17	5	16	6	13	18	4	7	2	3	11	9	12	15	1	10	8
1996	2	18	5	10	13	14	4	15	1	9	16	17	11	3	12	8	7	6
1997	16	17	8	1	7	14	2	11	10	4	15	13	12	8	18	4	3	6
1998	10	14	18	12	4	6	11	2	1	17	15	16	9	5	7	8	13	3

MATCH RESULTS, 1864-1998

County	Years of Play	Played	Won	Lost	Tied	Drawn
Derbyshire	1871-87; 1895-1998	2,258	562	825	1	870
Durham	1992-1998	123	17	72	0	34
Essex	1895-1998	2,220	641	649	5	925
Glamorgan	1921-1998	1,755	388	597	0	770
Gloucestershire	1870-1998	2,494	743	923	2	826
Hampshire	1864-85; 1895-1998	2,329	606	802	4	917
Kent	1864-1998	2,618	947	789	5	877
Lancashire	1865-1998	2,696	1,001	563	3	1,129
Leicestershire	1895-1998	2,187	497	798	1	891
Middlesex	1864-1998	2,398	896	607	5	890
Northamptonshire	1905-1998	1,955	480	681	3	791
Nottinghamshire	1864-1998	2,527	764	675	1	1,087
Somerset	1882-85; 1891-1998	2,228	528	895	3	802
Surrey	1864-1998	2,775	1,096	620	4	1,055
Sussex	1864-1998	2,667	741	925	6	995
Warwickshire	1895-1998	2,200	601	642	1	956
Worcestershire	1899-1998	2,142	537	741	2	862
Yorkshire	1864-1998	2,795	1,241	482	2	1,070
Cambridgeshire	1864-69; 1871	19	8	8	0	3
		20,193	12,294	12,294	24	7,875

Notes: Matches abandoned without a ball bowled are wholly excluded.

Counties participated in the years shown, except that there were no matches in the years 1915-18 and 1940-45; Hampshire did not play inter-county matches in 1868-69, 1871-74 and 1879; Worcestershire did not take part in the Championship in 1919.

SUMMARY OF RESULTS, 1998

	Derbyshire	Durham	Essex	Glamorgan	Gloucestershire	Hampshire	Kent	Lancashire	Leicestershire	Middlesex	Northamptonshire	Nottinghamshire	Somerset	Surrey	Sussex	Warwickshire	Worcestershire	Yorkshire
Derbyshire	—	**D**	**W**	*D*	*D*	*L*	**D**	*L*	**L**	**W**	*L*	**W**	**W**	*L*	*W*	**L**	**W**	*L*
Durham	*D*	—	**W**	**D**	*L*	*D*	*L*	**L**	**L**	**W**	**D**	**W**	*L*	**L**	*L*	*D*	*L*	**L**
Essex	*L*	*L*	—	**L**	**L**	*L*	**L**	*L*	*L*	*D*	**L**	**D**	**W**	**D**	**D**	*W*	*L*	*L*
Glamorgan	**D**	*D*	**W**	—	*W*	**L**	**D**	**D**	*L*	**L**	*D*	**W**	**W**	**L**	*L*	**D**	*D*	**L**
Gloucestershire	*D*	**W**	**W**	**L**	—	*W*	**W**	*L*	**L**	**W**	**W**	**W**	*L*	**W**	**W**	**W**	*L*	**W**
Hampshire	**W**	**D**	**W**	**W**	*D*	—	*W*	*L*	*L*	*L*	**W**	*D*	**W**	**D**	*L*	**W**	*L*	*D*
Kent	*D*	**W**	**W**	*D*	*L*	**W**	—	*D*	*D*	**W**	*D*	**W**	*L*	*L*	*L*	*L*	**D**	**D**
Lancashire	**W**	**W**	**W**	*D*	**W**	**W**	*D*	—	**D**	**D**	*D*	**W**	**W**	**W**	*L*	*W*	**W**	**W**
Leicestershire	*W*	*W*	**W**	*W*	**W**	*D*	*D*	**D**	—	**W**	**W**	*W*	**W**	*D*	*W*	**D**	*D*	*D*
Middlesex	*L*	**L**	**D**	**W**	*L*	*L*	*L*	*L*	*D*	—	*D*	*L*	**W**	*L*	**L**	**D**	**D**	*D*
Northamptonshire	**W**	*D*	**W**	**D**	*L*	*D*	**D**	**D**	*L*	**D**	—	*D*	*L*	**W**	*L*	*L*	**W**	**W**
Nottinghamshire	*L*	**L**	**D**	*L*	**L**	*L*	*L*	**L**	**W**	**D**	—	*D*	**L**	*L*	**W**	**W**	*D*	**W**
Somerset	**L**	**W**	**L**	*L*	**W**	**D**	**W**	*L*	*L*	*L*	**W**	**D**	—	**W**	*D*	**W**	**D**	*L*
Surrey	**W**	**W**	*D*	**W**	*L*	**W**	*L*	**W**	**D**	**W**	*D*	**W**	*L*	—	**W**	**W**	**W**	*L*
Sussex	**L**	**W**	*D*	**W**	*L*	**L**	**W**	**W**	*D*	**W**	*L*	**W**	**D**	*L*	—	*L*	**D**	*L*
Warwickshire	**W**	**D**	**L**	**D**	*L*	**W**	**W**	**L**	*L*	*D*	**W**	*L*	*L*	**W**	*W*	—	**W**	*L*
Worcestershire	*L*	**W**	**W**	*D*	**W**	**D**	**D**	*L*	*L*	*D*	**W**	**D**	*L*	**D**	**L**	*L*	—	**L**
Yorkshire	**W**	*W*	**W**	*W*	*L*	**L**	*D*	*D*	**L**	*D*	*D*	*L*	**D**	**W**	**W**	**W**	*W*	—

Home games in bold, away games in italics. W = Won, L = Lost, D = Drawn.

BRITANNIC ASSURANCE CHAMPIONSHIP
STATISTICS FOR 1998

County	For			Against		
	Runs	Wickets	Avge	Runs	Wickets	Avge
Derbyshire	7,314	279	26.21	7,342	237	30.97
Durham	7,296	283	25.78	7,734	246	31.43
Essex	6,781	300	22.60	8,235	243	33.88
Glamorgan	7,570	253	29.92	8,032	264	30.42
Gloucestershire . . .	7,594	283	26.83	6,685	304	21.99
Hampshire	7,126	234	30.45	7,918	249	31.79
Kent	7,765	280	27.73	7,253	235	30.86
Lancashire	8,041	221	36.38	7,400	258	28.68
Leicestershire	6,628	175	37.87	5,900	258	22.86
Middlesex	7,818	244	32.04	7,927	230	34.46
Northamptonshire .	6,912	235	29.41	6,988	231	30.25
Nottinghamshire . .	6,801	270	25.18	7,492	243	30.83
Somerset	6,700	263	25.47	7,158	264	27.11
Surrey	7,393	230	32.14	6,533	276	23.67
Sussex	7,056	269	26.23	7,155	239	29.93
Warwickshire	7,915	273	28.99	7,581	262	28.93
Worcestershire . . .	8,316	272	30.57	7,580	243	31.19
Yorkshire	7,616	217	35.09	7,729	299	25.84
	132,642	4,581	28.95	132,642	4,581	28.95

OVERS BOWLED AND RUNS SCORED IN THE
BRITANNIC ASSURANCE CHAMPIONSHIP, 1998

County	Over-rate per hour	Run-rate/ 100 balls
Derbyshire (10)	16.13	55.99
*Durham (14)	15.70	49.38
*Essex (18)	15.59	48.45
Glamorgan (12)	16.22	57.59
†Gloucestershire (4)	15.14	54.24
†Hampshire (6)	15.36	51.14
Kent (11)	16.06	52.54
*Lancashire (2)	15.88	59.06
*Leicestershire (1)	15.71	57.36
†Middlesex (17)	15.41	50.97
*Northamptonshire (15)	15.66	54.96
*Nottinghamshire (16)	15.66	50.34
‡Somerset (9)	14.94	49.46
†Surrey (5)	15.19	57.97
Sussex (7)	16.05	46.07
*Warwickshire (8)	15.86	57.26
†Worcestershire (13)	15.47	52.80
*Yorkshire (3)	15.74	53.19
1998 average rate	15.65	52.98

1998 Championship positions are shown in brackets.
* £4,000 fine.   † £6,000 fine.   ‡ £8,000 fine.

ECB COUNTY PITCHES TABLE

First-Class Matches and Under-19 Tests

		Points	Matches	Average in 1998	Average in 1997
1	Hampshire (13)............	105	10	5.25	4.39
2	Somerset (1).............	114	11	5.18	5.18
3	Leicestershire (6)	92	9	5.11	4.67
4	Gloucestershire (12)........	101	10	5.05	4.40
5	Oxford University (–)	58	6	4.83	4.44
6	Cambridge University (–).....	48	5	4.80	4.42
7	Surrey (2)	86	9	4.78	4.95
8	Nottinghamshire (10)........	94	10	4.70	4.50
9 {	Derbyshire (9)	93	10	4.65	4.55
	Essex (4)...............	93	10	4.65	4.82
11	Sussex (7)	92	10	4.60	4.61
12	Durham (8)	82	9	4.56	4.56
13	Middlesex (16)...........	98	11	4.45	4.29
14	Worcestershire (13)	97	11	4.41	4.39
15	Warwickshire (17).........	79	9	4.39	4.20
16	Lancashire (10)...........	76	9	4.22	4.50
17	Yorkshire (15)	92	11	4.18	4.32
18	Kent (5)	81	10	4.05	4.73
19	Glamorgan (18)	71	9	3.94	4.00
20	Northamptonshire (3).......	61	8	3.81	4.83

One-Day Matches

		Points	Matches	Average in 1998	Average in 1997
1	Oxford University (–)	32	3	5.33	5.00
2	Gloucestershire (8)	126	12	5.25	4.79
3	Essex (6=).............	110	11	5.00	4.82
4	Surrey (4=)	147	15	4.90	4.83
5	Hampshire (10)...........	127	13	4.88	4.71
6	Nottinghamshire (12).......	133	14	4.75	4.68
7	Kent (11)...............	142	15	4.73	4.69
8	Leicestershire (1)	136	15	4.53	5.14
9	Worcestershire (9)	90	10	4.50	4.75
10	Warwickshire (6=).........	116	13	4.46	4.82
11	Somerset (2)	98	11	4.45	5.09
12	Middlesex (17)	167	19	4.39	4.15
13	Glamorgan (18)	96	11	4.36	4.04
14 {	Durham (16)	94	11	4.27	4.40
	Sussex (4=).............	94	11	4.27	4.83
16	Derbyshire (3)	84	10	4.20	4.85
17	Northamptonshire (14).......	99	12	4.13	4.58
18	Yorkshire (15)	124	16	3.88	4.42
19	Lancashire (13)...........	98	13	3.77	4.64
	Cambridge University (–)	–			5.25

In both tables 1997 positions are shown in brackets. Each umpire marks the pitch on the following scale: 6 – very good; 5 – good; 4 – above average; 3 – below average; 2 – poor; 1 – unfit.

The tables, based on information provided by the ECB, cover all major matches, including Tests and Under-19 internationals, played on grounds under the county's jurisdiction. Middlesex pitches at Lord's are the responsibility of MCC. The ECB points out that the tables are not a direct assessment of the groundsmen's ability. Marks may be affected by many factors including weather, soil conditions and the resources available.

DERBYSHIRE

Kevin Dean

President: J. W. Moss

Chairman: G. T. Bowring

Chairman, Cricket Committee:

Secretary/General Manager: J. Smedley

Captain: D. G. Cork

Head Groundsman: B. Marsh

Scorer: S. W. Tacey

Winters can be more interesting than summers for observers of Derbyshire. In 1998-99, they manufactured another period of strife, culminating in the resignation of chairman Vic Brownett five days before a heated annual general meeting in January. The problems began in October, when captain Dominic Cork issued a statement criticising the cricket committee for acting against his wishes. Cork declared he would not continue if Harold Rhodes, the former England bowler and a member of the committee, and Andy Hayhurst, director of coaching and development, retained an influence over decisions about senior staff.

Hayhurst had already been eased away from direct involvement with the first team, but Cork wanted Kim Barnett, the former captain, installed as player-coach. Barnett, experienced in Derbyshire politics, represented Cork in his absence (he was in England's Ashes tour party) and there was impasse for the best part of four months. The committee, while keen for Cork to continue as captain, did not feel inclined to give him control of who sat where in the committee room or who was employed. The unresolved questions were how much power Cork had been promised on his appointment, and whether these promises were made known to all parties.

Cork had specific objections about the retention of two players, and the signing of two more from the Derbyshire League. Brownett said he supported Cork's views on this (although he had chaired the relevant meeting). But he then resigned, citing the effect of the dispute on his business and personal life, leaving a new chairman, Trevor Bowring, to try to resolve the situation. Members forced an extraordinary meeting, due to be held before the start of the 1999 season. Some thought this action was belated: Derbyshire had suffered a steady drain of talented players since 1993. Meanwhile, Barnett and Cork both asked to be released, and in February Barnett was. This seemed to mark the end of one of the county's most distinguished modern careers.

The dispute was especially unwelcome because it distracted the club from development of the Grandstand, which was purchased from Wolverhampton and Dudley Breweries in May. This helped seal the county's decision to centralise all matches at Derby and end county cricket at Queens Park, Chesterfield, one of the most attractive of all venues, after exactly 100 years.

The winter turmoil was even sadder because, after their disastrous decline in 1997 following the Dean Jones saga, the team had done better than expected under Cork in 1998. The emergence of Kevin Dean as a match-winning bowler was a key factor. Derbyshire won six Championship matches, climbing six places, and reached the NatWest Trophy final. Even if they were outplayed at Lord's, their right to be there was established by excellent away victories over Surrey and, in a tense semi-final, Leicestershire. It was the more encouraging because two important players, Chris Adams and Devon Malcolm, were with new counties. Taking into account the extent of injuries to experienced players, the supporters would have settled for less.

Michael Slater, engaged as overseas player because of doubts about Saeed Anwar's availability throughout the season, broke a hand in the opening match and missed the next month. Andrew Harris did not play after mid-May because of a stress fracture of the back, and disc trouble ruled out opening batsman Adrian Rollins for two months. Startlingly, he returned for the NatWest final with no preparation. Tim Tweats, expected to replace Adams at No. 3, started with 161 against Nottinghamshire, but his form declined so sharply that he was dropped in July. His erosion of confidence was difficult to understand, but the gap was filled in the second half of the season by Robin Weston who, having been released by Durham, eagerly accepted a chance to develop his career.

Cork made a good start as captain, seizing his opportunities to beat Nottinghamshire in the opening game. His early form, including a century in the victory over Sussex at Horsham, led to him being recalled by England. That gave extra responsibility to Karl Krikken, the vice-captain. Krikken suffered a nasty facial injury at Basingstoke, and Slater led Derbyshire to their victory over Essex, a match in which Barnett reached 25,000 first-class runs. Barnett was again Derbyshire's most reliable batsman, and completed 1,000 runs for the 15th time in 20 seasons.

Despite a splendid 185 against the South Africans, Slater passed 50 only twice in the Championship, often being dismissed when apparently well set. He made such a good impression, however, that Derbyshire were eager to re-engage him, watching in some frustration as he enjoyed a fine winter for Australia. Matthew Cassar scored a maiden century at Horsham, and his 134 at Northampton was the highest Sunday League innings of the season. At his best, Cassar is genuinely exciting, but he remains an uncertain starter.

Dean, left-arm over the wicket at a lively pace, became steadily more of a force and reached his peak with 12 for 133 at Taunton. Phillip DeFreitas, given more work because of Cork's frequent absence, bowled with great skill and heart as well as producing the occasional explosive innings. Trevor Smith showed promise as a seam bowler and took eight Essex wickets in only his second Championship match.

There were even flickers in the spin department, seldom a Derbyshire strength: Ian Blackwell has all-round talent, but must continue the search for consistency. Frailties in Derbyshire's approach were sometimes exposed, but heavy defeats failed to dampen their optimism. If only they could concentrate on playing cricket. – GERALD MORTIMER.

DERBYSHIRE 1998

[Bill Smith]

Back row: I. D. Blackwell, S. D. Stubbings, T. A. Tweats, V. P. Clarke, T. M. Smith, K. J. Dean, J. D. Brown (*youth coach*). *Middle row:* A. N. Hayhurst (*director of cricket*), M. R. May, S. J. Lacey, B. L. Spendlove, G. M. Roberts, M. E. Cassar, S. P. Griffiths, P. Aldred, A. M. Brown, A. E. Brentnall (*physiotherapist*), S. W. Tacey (*scorer*). *Front row:* A. S. Rollins, K. J. Barnett, K. M. Krikken, D. G. Cork (*captain*), P. A. J. DeFreitas, A. J. Harris, J. Smedley (*secretary/general manager*). *Inset:* M. J. Slater.

DERBYSHIRE RESULTS

All first-class matches – Played 18: Won 6, Lost 7, Drawn 5. Abandoned 1.

County Championship matches – Played 17: Won 6, Lost 7, Drawn 4.

Competition placings – Britannic Assurance County Championship, 10th;
NatWest Trophy, finalists; Benson and Hedges Cup, 4th in Group B;
AXA League, 15th.

COUNTY CHAMPIONSHIP AVERAGES
BATTING

Cap		M	I	NO	R	HS	100s	50s	Avge	Ct/St
1982	K. J. Barnett	17	32	6	1,229	162	1	7	47.26	8
	R. M. S. Weston . . .	8	15	0	524	97	0	4	34.93	4
1995	A. S. Rollins	10	19	0	618	107	1	4	32.52	11
1993	D. G. Cork	10	16	3	393	102*	1	3	30.23	9
1998	M. J. Slater§	13	22	0	600	99	0	2	27.27	8
	M. E. Cassar	16	29	4	616	121	1	4	24.64	4
	G. M. Roberts . . .	7	12	3	197	44	0	0	21.88	7
1994	P. A. J. DeFreitas . .	14	23	3	435	87	0	2	21.75	6
1992	K. M. Krikken	16	26	5	432	83	0	3	20.57	34/2
	B. L. Spendlove† . . .	9	17	0	318	49	0	0	18.70	3
	T. A. Tweats	8	16	0	295	161	1	0	18.43	8
	M. R. May†	12	22	0	372	54	0	1	16.90	4
	P. Aldred†	6	8	3	80	37*	0	0	16.00	6
1998	K. J. Dean†	14	20	12	127	25*	0	0	15.87	1
	I. D. Blackwell† . . .	11	18	0	254	57	0	2	14.11	6
	T. M. Smith†	6	9	1	81	29	0	0	10.12	0
	V. P. Clarke	4	7	0	67	26	0	0	9.57	4

Also batted: S. P. Griffiths (1 match) 12, 3 (5 ct); A. J. Harris (cap 1996) (2 matches) 4, 0, 5;
S. J. Lacey (3 matches) 11, 0, 17 (1 ct).

* Signifies not out. † *Born in Derbyshire.* § *Overseas player.*

BOWLING

	O	M	R	W	BB	5W/i	Avge
K. J. Dean	441.2	92	1,486	71	6-63	5	20.92
T. M. Smith	124.3	36	396	16	6-32	1	24.75
D. G. Cork	332.2	77	914	36	5-72	1	25.38
P. A. J. DeFreitas	482.4	114	1,363	52	5-38	3	26.21
I. D. Blackwell	156.2	32	524	14	5-115	1	37.42
P. Aldred	164.4	34	470	12	3-30	0	39.16

Also bowled: K. J. Barnett 54–10–148–4; M. E. Cassar 137–26–524–9; V. P. Clarke 41–4–173–2;
A. J. Harris 32–3–136–4; S. J. Lacey 88–19–274–4; M. R. May 3–0–51–0; G. M. Roberts
169–27–629–9; T. A. Tweats 3–0–29–0.

COUNTY RECORDS

Highest score for:	274	G. Davidson v Lancashire at Manchester	1896
Highest score against:	343*	P. A. Perrin (Essex) at Chesterfield	1904
Best bowling for:	10-40	W. Bestwick v Glamorgan at Cardiff	1921
Best bowling against:	10-45	R. L. Johnson (Middlesex) at Derby	1994
Highest total for:	645	v Hampshire at Derby	1898
Highest total against:	662	by Yorkshire at Chesterfield	1898
Lowest total for:	16	v Nottinghamshire at Nottingham	1879
Lowest total against:	23	by Hampshire at Burton upon Trent	1958

DERBYSHIRE v NOTTINGHAMSHIRE

At Derby, April 17, 18, 19, 20. Derbyshire won by six wickets. Derbyshire 24 pts, Nottinghamshire 2 pts. Toss: Nottinghamshire. County debuts: M. J. Slater; J. E. R. Gallian, A. G. Wharf.

The bad news for Derbyshire was that Slater broke a bone in his left hand when knocking up a slip chance on the first morning. But even then the ball rebounded to Tweats to dismiss Johnson. And other than that, Cork's first match as captain could hardly have gone better. Remorseless seam bowling turned Nottinghamshire's first innings into a procession. Then Tweats, who ended 1997 with 189 against Yorkshire, marked the new season – and his 24th birthday – with 161, including 21 fours, as Derbyshire led by 270. Nottinghamshire were soon struggling again, but rain interruptions, coupled with a determined partnership between Afzaal and Tolley, raised their hopes of survival. They added 108 before Tolley pulled a calf muscle in reaching 50 and retired hurt. Although Afzaal completed an assured maiden century, Cork was quick to exploit the breach in the defences; the last five wickets fell for 15. Needing 43 from six overs, Derbyshire lost three wickets in the first seven balls. DeFreitas and Barnett then restored sanity, and the victory came with a ball to spare.

Close of play: First day, Derbyshire 115-1 (T. A. Tweats 48*, I. D. Blackwell 20*); Second day, Derbyshire 358-6 (K. M. Krikken 72*, P. A. J. DeFreitas 11*); Third day, Nottinghamshire 104-4 (R. T. Robinson 9*, U. Afzaal 4*).

Nottinghamshire

M. P. Dowman lbw b Aldred	19	– c Krikken b DeFreitas	4
P. R. Pollard lbw b DeFreitas	12	– c and b DeFreitas	0
J. E. R. Gallian c Tweats b Cork	2	– c Dean b Aldred	26
*P. Johnson c Tweats b Dean	13	– c Krikken b Dean	49
R. T. Robinson c Slater b Aldred	5	– lbw b Dean	41
U. Afzaal b Aldred	0	– not out	109
C. M. Tolley lbw b Dean	9	– c sub b DeFreitas	51
A. G. Wharf lbw b Dean	2	– lbw b Cork	3
†W. M. Noon c Krikken b Cork	6	– b Cork	0
K. P. Evans c Krikken b Cork	28	– c and b DeFreitas	0
M. N. Bowen not out	2	– c Cassar b Cork	5
L-b 2, w 2, n-b 16	20	B 1, l-b 3, n-b 20	24

1/19 2/28 3/56 4/61 5/61   118   1/3 2/12 3/89 4/95 5/173   312
6/64 7/67 8/74 9/97   6/297 7/297 8/298 9/311

Bonus points – Derbyshire 4.

In the second innings C. M. Tolley, when 50, retired hurt at 281 and resumed at 311.

Bowling: *First Innings*—DeFreitas 10.4–4–12–1; Cork 12.4–4–45–3; Dean 11–4–29–3; Aldred 14–2–30–3. *Second Innings*—DeFreitas 35.2–8–89–4; Cork 26–3–93–3; Dean 22–8–70–2; Aldred 22–8–41–1; Cassar 3–2–4–0; Blackwell 5–1–11–0.

Derbyshire

A. S. Rollins c Dowman b Bowen	44	– (2) run out	0
T. A. Tweats c Noon b Evans	161	– (5) run out	2
I. D. Blackwell c Noon b Evans	53	– b Evans	0
K. J. Barnett lbw b Tolley	0	– (6) not out	8
M. E. Cassar c Gallian b Evans	5		
*D. G. Cork c Tolley b Wharf	6	– (1) b Bowen	1
†K. M. Krikken c Johnson b Evans	83		
P. A. J. DeFreitas c Afzaal b Evans	13	– (4) not out	32
P. Aldred b Bowen	14		
K. J. Dean not out	1		
M. J. Slater absent hurt			
L-b 6, n-b 2	8		

1/78 2/165 3/168 4/179 5/194   388   1/1 2/1 3/1 4/10   (4 wkts) 43
6/336 7/360 8/378 9/388

Bonus points – Derbyshire 4, Nottinghamshire 2 (Score at 120 overs: 353-6).

Bowling: *First Innings*—Bowen 39–10–109–2; Wharf 20–3–71–1; Evans 32.1–8–92–5; Tolley 22–5–72–1; Gallian 15–5–37–0; Dowman 1–0–1–0. *Second Innings*—Bowen 3–0–13–1; Evans 2.5–0–30–1.

Umpires: J. C. Balderstone and M. J. Harris.

At Leeds, April 23, 24, 25, 27. DERBYSHIRE lost to YORKSHIRE by 111 runs.

DERBYSHIRE v WARWICKSHIRE

At Derby, May 13, 14. Warwickshire won by an innings and 61 runs. Warwickshire 23 pts, Derbyshire 4 pts. Toss: Warwickshire.

Derbyshire were all out by lunch on the first day, batted for only 88 overs in two innings, and lost by an innings inside two days. At no stage did a recovery seem possible. With hazy conditions assisting swing, and the pitch encouraging seam, Brown took five for 18 in his first eight overs. Warwickshire's batsmen were given a much easier time, and Knight settled to play a mature innings, adding 130 with Hemp at almost four an over. His century was unhurried and, until Lara drove loosely at DeFreitas to begin a slide that saw five wickets fall for 25, the bowlers struggled. Warwickshire gave a further twist to the knife when Welch and Frost added 85 for the ninth wicket. Derbyshire's batsmen fared little better at the second attempt, making an innings defeat – their first by Warwickshire since 1913 – inevitable.

Close of play: First day, Warwickshire 253-8 (G. Welch 13*, T. Frost 2*).

Derbyshire

A. S. Rollins c Frost b Brown	4	– b Giddins 0
T. A. Tweats c Frost b Brown	2	– c Welch b Brown 14
B. L. Spendlove b Brown	16	– c Knight b Brown 6
K. J. Barnett c Knight b Welch	20	– c Hemp b Giddins 39
V. P. Clarke c Frost b Brown	2	– c Frost b Welch 26
†K. M. Krikken c Frost b Brown	5	– c Frost b Welch 2
*D. G. Cork b Giddins	8	– not out 32
I. D. Blackwell c Ostler b Welch	0	– b Giles 3
P. A. J. DeFreitas not out	30	– b Giddins 9
P. Aldred c Lara b Giddins	0	– c Hemp b Giles 6
A. J. Harris b Giddins	0	– b Giddins 5
L-b 1, w 2, n-b 8	11	B 13, l-b 10, w 2, n-b 6 .. 31
	98	**173**

1/4 2/11 3/30 4/32 5/44   98   1/0 2/24 3/25 4/80 5/90   173
6/54 7/54 8/96 9/96   6/121 7/124 8/141 9/154

Bonus points – Warwickshire 4.

Bowling: *First Innings*—Giddins 11.5–3–35–3; Brown 14–2–40–5; Welch 6–0–22–2. *Second Innings*—Giddins 20.1–6–62–4; Brown 12–3–45–2; Welch 8–4–17–2; Giles 16–7–26–2.

Warwickshire

M. J. Powell c Krikken b Cork	0	G. Welch c Clarke b Blackwell	54
N. V. Knight c Krikken b DeFreitas	109	†T. Frost c sub b DeFreitas	33
D. L. Hemp c Spendlove b Aldred	59	E. S. H. Giddins not out	0
*B. C. Lara c Krikken b DeFreitas	23		
D. P. Ostler c Tweats b Aldred	1	B 8, l-b 9, n-b 32	49
D. R. Brown c Clarke b Harris	0		
N. M. K. Smith c Cork b Harris	3	1/8 2/138 3/179 4/186 5/189	332
A. F. Giles b Aldred	1	6/199 7/204 8/247 9/332	

Bonus points – Warwickshire 3, Derbyshire 4.

Bowling: Cork 24–3–81–1; DeFreitas 29.2–7–91–3; Harris 12–0–53–2; Aldred 27–4–69–3; Clarke 4–0–10–0; Blackwell 3–1–11–1.

Umpires: J. H. Harris and T. E. Jesty.

At Horsham, May 21, 22, 23, 24. DERBYSHIRE beat SUSSEX by seven wickets.

DERBYSHIRE v LEICESTERSHIRE

At Chesterfield, May 29, 30, 31. Leicestershire won by 38 runs. Leicestershire 21 pts, Derbyshire 4 pts. Toss: Leicestershire.

On a fast, bouncy pitch, Leicestershire's flying start proved crucial. They reached 131 for two by lunch, but from then on the bowlers dominated, with 19 wickets falling on the second day. Ormond, returning to the team after surgery to his back, took five as Derbyshire fell 69 short on first innings. Wells and Maddy began the second innings with a determined stand of 76 but the other partnerships mustered only another 110, all the wickets falling to Dean and DeFreitas. Derbyshire's target was 256 against a weakened attack – a groin strain limited Ormond to five overs – and, while Barnett was there, they had a chance. But batting was never easy, least of all against Mullally, who bowled consistently well. As wickets fell, Derbyshire exchanged patience for rashness. The presence of England coach David Lloyd fuelled speculation that Maddy would make his Test debut, though in the event it was Cork who was selected, having followed a century against Sussex with his best Championship bowling since September 1995.

Close of play: First day, Derbyshire 71-2 (T. A. Tweats 22*, P. Aldred 1*); Second day, Derbyshire 43-1 (A. S. Rollins 20*, K. J. Dean 0*).

Leicestershire

D. L. Maddy c Aldred b DeFreitas	7	– (2) c Rollins b Dean	40
V. J. Wells c Aldred b Dean	27	– (1) c Aldred b Dean	64
I. J. Sutcliffe c Krikken b Aldred	82	– lbw b Dean	6
B. F. Smith lbw b Cork	25	– c Slater b DeFreitas	11
P. V. Simmons lbw b Cork	10	– (6) lbw b DeFreitas	1
A. Habib not out	39	– (5) c Tweats b Dean	33
†P. A. Nixon lbw b Cork	20	– c Krikken b DeFreitas	0
*C. C. Lewis c Aldred b Cork	0	– lbw b DeFreitas	0
J. Ormond b Cork	0	– b DeFreitas	9
A. D. Mullally c Rollins b DeFreitas	0	– c Aldred b Dean	14
M. T. Brimson b DeFreitas	3	– not out	0
L-b 7, w 2, n-b 24	33	L-b 6, n-b 2	8

1/34 2/69 3/158 4/172 5/174   246   1/76 2/86 3/115 4/125 5/128   186
6/229 7/235 8/235 9/240   6/132 7/132 8/154 9/173

Bonus points – Leicestershire 1, Derbyshire 4.

Bowling: First Innings—Cork 28–7–72–5; DeFreitas 25.1–3–81–3; Aldred 17–4–42–1; Dean 12–0–44–1. *Second Innings*—Cork 22–5–60–0; DeFreitas 24–10–38–5; Aldred 7–2–25–0; Dean 16.2–3–57–5.

Derbyshire

M. J. Slater c Smith b Ormond	24	– (2) lbw b Ormond	13
A. S. Rollins c Brimson b Ormond	0	– (1) c Wells b Mullally	44
T. A. Tweats c Habib b Lewis	26	– (4) c Sutcliffe b Wells	13
P. Aldred b Mullally	7	– (11) not out	10
K. J. Barnett b Mullally	30	– c Lewis b Brimson	57
M. R. May b Lewis	16	– c and b Wells	22
M. E. Cassar b Lewis	0	– c Wells b Mullally	9
†K. M. Krikken c Maddy b Ormond	5	– c Nixon b Mullally	0
*D. G. Cork c Maddy b Ormond	8	– c Lewis b Brimson	8
P. A. J. DeFreitas c Habib b Ormond	19	– c Simmons b Mullally	6
K. J. Dean not out	0	– (3) c Nixon b Wells	12
B 12, l-b 8, w 6, n-b 16	42	B 1, l-b 7, w 3, n-b 12	23

1/14 2/63 3/89 4/89 5/120   177   1/38 2/76 3/96 4/101 5/182   217
6/120 7/125 8/155 9/177   6/182 7/182 8/195 9/201

Bonus points – Leicestershire 4.

Bowling: *First Innings*—Mullally 14–3–51–2; Ormond 14.1–6–50–5; Lewis 12–2–56–3. *Second Innings*—Lewis 19–4–76–0; Ormond 5–0–22–1; Mullally 23.5–9–57–4; Brimson 12–7–24–2; Wells 13–7–19–3; Maddy 2–1–11–0.

Umpires: M. J. Harris and J. W. Holder.

DERBYSHIRE v GLOUCESTERSHIRE

At Chesterfield, June 3, 4, 5, 6. Drawn. Derbyshire 7 pts, Gloucestershire 11 pts. Toss: Gloucestershire.

For the second match at Queen's Park, the pitch was considerably slower. After a blank first day, Gloucestershire steadily built a formidable total of 459, with Windows scoring his second consecutive Championship century. Despite Russell's curious passivity – eight runs in 18 overs – Gloucestershire added quick runs on the third morning. Lewis reached a maiden fifty from only 37 balls, and then went on to claim six for 48, his best bowling figures. Needing 310 to avoid the follow-on, Derbyshire were nought for two after three balls from Walsh and, despite seventies from Barnett and Cassar, Alleyne was able to put them in again. This time, Rollins drove and pulled powerfully for his first century of the season, and May's doggedness helped to ensure a draw. There was, however, gloom surrounding the future of one of county cricket's best-loved venues. The festival arranged to celebrate the centenary of Derbyshire's first visit to Queen's Park had been a financial failure, with poor attendances and limited interest from sponsors, and the club said they intended to examine the viability of playing at Chesterfield. "It is an expensive way to enjoy the view," said secretary John Smedley.

Close of play: First day, No play; Second day, Gloucestershire 329–5 (M. G. N. Windows 99*, R. C. Russell 1*); Third day, Derbyshire 281–9 (M. E. Cassar 65*, K. J. Dean 0*).

Gloucestershire

G. I. Macmillan c Lacey b DeFreitas	2	J. Lewis not out	54
T. H. C. Hancock c Rollins b Barnett	94	A. M. Smith not out	17
A. J. Wright c Tweats b Dean	17		
*M. W. Alleyne b Barnett	43	L-b 6, n-b 16	22
M. G. N. Windows run out	143		
D. R. Hewson b Aldred	52	1/16 2/59 3/170 (8 wkts dec.) 459	
†R. C. Russell b Dean	8	4/175 5/325 6/373	
M. C. J. Ball c Krikken b Dean	7	7/381 8/402	

C. A. Walsh did not bat.

Bonus points – Gloucestershire 4, Derbyshire 2 (Score at 120 overs: 357–5).

Bowling: DeFreitas 33–7–74–1; Dean 32–4–123–3; Aldred 31–3–117–1; Cassar 10.3–1–58–0; Lacey 10–0–51–0; Barnett 20–7–30–2.

Derbyshire

M. J. Slater c Smith b Walsh	0	– (2) c Russell b Lewis	31
A. S. Rollins lbw b Lewis	34	– (1) c Smith b Lewis	107
T. A. Tweats c Russell b Walsh	0	– c Russell b Alleyne	0
K. J. Barnett b Alleyne	74	– c Russell b Walsh	28
M. R. May lbw b Lewis	11	– c Russell b Alleyne	54
M. E. Cassar not out	78	– not out	22
*†K. M. Krikken lbw b Lewis	60	– not out	12
P. A. J. DeFreitas c Russell b Lewis	0		
S. J. Lacey c Ball b Smith	0		
P. Aldred b Lewis	3		
K. J. Dean c Ball b Lewis	1		
L-b 4, w 2, n-b 28	34	B 3, l-b 15, n-b 28	46

1/0 2/0 3/105 4/137 5/143   295   1/73 2/74 3/158   (5 wkts dec.) 300
6/255 7/261 8/270 9/279   4/244 5/266

Bonus points – Derbyshire 2, Gloucestershire 4.

Bowling: *First Innings*—Walsh 20–3–76–2; Smith 17–2–59–1; Lewis 21.3–7–48–6; Ball 7–2–45–0; Alleyne 13–2–63–1. *Second Innings*—Walsh 12–0–87–1; Smith 6–1–31–0; Alleyne 11–2–39–2; Lewis 17–2–61–2; Ball 20–2–50–0; Macmillan 5–2–14–0.

Umpires: B. Dudleston and A. A. Jones.

At Cambridge, June 10, 11, 12. CAMBRIDGE UNIVERSITY v DERBYSHIRE. Abandoned.

At Basingstoke, June 17, 18, 19, 20. DERBYSHIRE lost to HAMPSHIRE by five wickets.

DERBYSHIRE v ESSEX

At Derby, July 1, 2, 3. Derbyshire won by 181 runs. Derbyshire 20 pts, Essex 4 pts. Toss: Derbyshire.

Derbyshire's third win over Essex in 51 Championship games since 1962 had seemed unlikely when they were reduced to 18 for six on the first morning. It seemed a grim reward for breaking a sequence of eight lost Championship tosses. A magnificent victory arrived, however, a little over 48 hours later – in Slater's first match as captain. Although 23 wickets fell on the first day, the umpires could find nothing wrong with the pitch. Instead, lavish swing, movement off the seam and inappropriate strokes accounted for the hectic proceedings. Ilott found conditions more congenial than at Southgate the previous week, when Middlesex ran up 488 for two; he claimed six wickets. Derbyshire's 70 was then the lowest total of the season, but only until tea, as Essex were dismissed for five less by DeFreitas and Dean. Derbyshire's second innings was more measured, and the last two wickets added 106. Then Trevor Smith, a 21-year-old seamer from Sandiacre playing his second Championship match, took Essex's first six wickets, before Dean ended with four in 14 balls. On the opening day, Barnett completed 25,000 first-class runs, having scored his first against Essex in 1979, while Such, playing his eighth first-class innings of the season, was dismissed for the first time, having totalled 16.

Close of play: First day, Derbyshire 112-3 (K. J. Barnett 27*, M. E. Cassar 37*); Second day, Essex 92-4 (A. P. Grayson 30*, P. M. Such 0*).

Derbyshire

A. S. Rollins c Robinson b Ilott	1	– (2) c Hyam b Cowan	12
*M. J. Slater c Hyam b Cowan	0	– (1) lbw b Ilott	24
T. A. Tweats b Cowan	0	– c S. G. Law b Cowan	5
K. J. Barnett c Hyam b Ilott	16	– lbw b Cowan	48
M. E. Cassar b Ilott	0	– c Grayson b D. R. Law	58
B. L. Spendlove c Hyam b Ilott	0	– c S. G. Law b Ilott	45
P. A. J. DeFreitas lbw b Ilott	4	– b D. R. Law	2
†S. P. Griffiths b Irani	12	– b Such	3
G. M. Roberts b Cowan	30	– c S. G. Law b Grayson	44
T. M. Smith c Grayson b Ilott	1	– (11) c and b Such	29
K. J. Dean not out	1	– (10) not out	25
L-b 5	5	L-b 6, w 8, n-b 10	24

1/2 2/2 3/18 4/18 5/18   70   1/30 2/46 3/47 4/142 5/176   319
6/18 7/29 8/57 9/64   6/178 7/191 8/213 9/266

Bonus points – Essex 4.

Bowling: *First Innings*—Ilott 13–5–20–6; Cowan 9.3–4–18–3; Irani 7–2–19–1; Such 4–1–8–0. *Second Innings*—Ilott 25–8–68–2; Cowan 25.4–4–107–3; D. R. Law 16–2–58–2; Irani 8–2–30–0; Such 11.5–4–28–2; Grayson 10–4–22–1.

Essex

*P. J. Prichard c Roberts b Dean	9	– c Rollins b Smith	21
D. D. J. Robinson c Griffiths b Dean	0	– c Griffiths b Smith	7
A. P. Grayson c Rollins b DeFreitas	6	– c Barnett b Smith	33
S. G. Law c Griffiths b Dean	4	– c Roberts b Smith	8
R. C. Irani c Cassar b DeFreitas	26	– lbw b Smith	18
S. D. Peters c Griffiths b Dean	5	– (7) lbw b Smith	2
†B. J. Hyam c Tweats b DeFreitas	5	– (8) lbw b Dean	11
D. R. Law lbw b Smith	3	– (9) c Rollins b Dean	0
A. P. Cowan lbw b Smith	0	– (10) b Dean	14
M. C. Ilott not out	4	– (11) lbw b Dean	0
P. M. Such b DeFreitas	2	– (6) not out	19
L-b 1	1	L-b 4, n-b 6	10

1/6 2/15 3/15 4/19 5/29   65   1/30 2/31 3/39 4/84 5/95   143
6/55 7/58 8/58 9/62   6/99 7/125 8/125 9/143

Bonus points – Derbyshire 4.

Bowling: *First Innings*—DeFreitas 16.2–6–19–4; Dean 10–2–39–4; Smith 6–3–6–2. *Second Innings*—DeFreitas 27–12–60–0; Dean 9.3–1–27–4; Smith 21–10–32–6; Roberts 7–2–20–0.

Umpires: R. Julian and D. R. Shepherd.

At Derby, July 18, 19, 20. DERBYSHIRE drew with SOUTH AFRICANS (See South African tour section).

At Northampton, July 22, 23, 24. DERBYSHIRE lost to NORTHAMPTONSHIRE by an innings and 94 runs.

DERBYSHIRE v KENT

At Derby, July 30, 31, August 1, 3. Drawn. Derbyshire 9 pts, Kent 7 pts. Toss: Kent.

Dean, who along with Slater was awarded his county cap during the Sunday game, performed the hat-trick in Kent's second innings by dismissing Smith, Hooper and Llong. It was the third time a Derbyshire player had dismissed Hooper during a hat-trick: Cork had done it twice, for the county in 1994, and for England against West Indies the following year. Weather ruined the match: it wiped out the first day and allowed only 38 balls on the last, washing away Derbyshire's hopes of victory. Kent wasted a good start, as DeFreitas and Dean shared the wickets, while Derbyshire relied on Weston for substance. He was denied a maiden century by a fine catch by Llong at extra cover. But Roberts helped extend the lead to 95, and Kent lost half their side before clearing it.

Close of play: First day, No play; Second day, Derbyshire 159-5 (R. M. S. Weston 58*, D. G. Cork 6*); Third day, Kent 104-5 (M. A. Ealham 45*, M. V. Fleming 6*).

Kent

D. P. Fulton c Clarke b Dean	28	– c Clarke b Cork	0
E. T. Smith lbw b Dean	34	– c DeFreitas b Dean	10
T. R. Ward c Slater b Dean	0	– lbw b Cork	34
C. L. Hooper c Krikken b Dean	26	– lbw b Dean	0
N. J. Llong lbw b DeFreitas	4	– c Krikken b Dean	0
M. A. Ealham c Cork b DeFreitas	1	– not out	61
M. V. Fleming c Roberts b DeFreitas	26	– not out	15
*†S. A. Marsh lbw b DeFreitas	4		
J. B. D. Thompson retired hurt	8		
D. W. Headley not out	3		
M. J. McCague b DeFreitas	6		
L-b 5, n-b 20	25	L-b 3, n-b 6	9
	165	(5 wkts)	**129**

1/70 2/70 3/85 4/90 5/100
6/104 7/111 8/154 9/165

1/0 2/26 3/26
4/26 5/78

Bonus points – Derbyshire 4.

In the first innings J. B. D. Thompson retired hurt at 154-7.

Bowling: *First Innings*—Cork 10-2-39-0; DeFreitas 18.2-3-55-5; Dean 12-2-52-4; Roberts 3-0-14-0. *Second Innings*—Cork 13-2-27-2; Dean 13.2-1-47-3; DeFreitas 5-2-18-0; Clarke 9-1-32-0; Roberts 4-2-20-0.

Derbyshire

M. J. Slater c Marsh b Ealham	34	P. A. J. DeFreitas c Ward b Fleming	9
M. R. May b Ealham	19	G. M. Roberts b Headley	38
R. M. S. Weston c Llong b Headley	97	K. J. Dean not out	4
K. J. Barnett c Marsh b Headley	21	B 4, l-b 9, n-b 4	17
M. E. Cassar b Headley	4		
V. P. Clarke c Ealham b Headley	4	1/44 2/79 3/121	**260**
*D. G. Cork lbw b Thompson	11	4/143 5/147 6/166	
†K. M. Krikken b Marsh b Thompson	2	7/172 8/189 9/247	

Bonus points – Derbyshire 2, Kent 4.

Bowling: McCague 13-2-35-0; Headley 28.2-6-64-5; Fleming 17-4-56-1; Ealham 16-3-36-2; Hooper 6-2-14-0; Thompson 21-7-42-2.

Umpires: T. E. Jesty and D. R. Shepherd.

At The Oval, August 6, 7, 8. DERBYSHIRE lost to SURREY by 226 runs.

DERBYSHIRE v WORCESTERSHIRE

At Derby, August 14, 15, 16. Derbyshire won by 28 runs. Derbyshire 22 pts, Worcestershire 4 pts. Toss: Worcestershire.

Worcestershire suffered their fourth consecutive Championship defeat, their worst sequence since 1986. But they came close to winning a fluctuating match, which exposed flaws of technique against swing. This was especially true when 23 wickets fell on the second day. The umpires notified the ECB but exonerated the pitch; the batsmen were not so blameless. Robin Weston continued his good form when Derbyshire were put in, but his brother Philip was an early victim as Worcestershire lost three quick wickets to DeFreitas, and never recovered. Krikken, who decided not to enforce the follow-on, hoped to rest his bowlers as well as stretch the lead, but Derbyshire's second innings was frenetic, and they were back in the field to capture three wickets on the second evening. They also dropped Solanki and Moody. Solanki struck the ball wonderfully in a career-best 170 and, profiting from two further escapes, threatened to win the game until he was caught on the extra-cover boundary. He hit a six and 31 fours from 188 balls.

Close of play: First day, Derbyshire 280; Second day, Worcestershire 53-3 (V. S. Solanki 11*, T. M. Moody 10*).

Derbyshire

M. J. Slater c Rhodes b Newport	23	– c Solanki b Newport	32
M. R. May lbw b Lampitt	24	– c Rhodes b Newport	21
R. M. S. Weston lbw b Lampitt	84	– run out	0
K. J. Barnett c Weston b Lampitt	21	– c Rhodes b Moody	0
M. E. Cassar c Solanki b Lampitt	11	– b Newport	0
B. L. Spendlove c Solanki b Moody	16	– (9) c Weston b Moody	45
I. D. Blackwell c Rhodes b Lampitt	0	– (6) lbw b Moody	23
*†K. M. Krikken c Wilson b Moody	27	– b Newport	19
P. A. J. DeFreitas c Weston b Chapman	21	– (7) lbw b Moody	8
K. J. Dean not out	10	– not out	10
T. M. Smith lbw b Chapman	23	– c Solanki b Moody	5
B 1, l-b 7, n-b 12	20	L-b 5	5

1/34 2/87 3/157 4/174 5/181	**280**
6/181 7/212 8/241 9/245	

1/54 2/54 3/54 4/54 5/57	**168**
6/72 7/87 8/137 9/158	

Bonus points – Derbyshire 2, Worcestershire 4.

Bowling: *First Innings*—Newport 14–5–35–1; Chapman 13.4–1–63–2; Moody 13–0–68–2; Lampitt 16–7–33–5; Rawnsley 22–7–53–0; Weston 2–0–20–0. *Second Innings*—Newport 17–6–44–4; Chapman 5–0–40–0; Moody 11.1–2–64–5; Lampitt 5–1–15–0.

Worcestershire

W. P. C. Weston lbw b DeFreitas	3	– lbw b DeFreitas	7
E. J. Wilson c Slater b DeFreitas	0	– c Blackwell b DeFreitas	12
N. E. Batson lbw b Dean	5	– b DeFreitas	3
V. S. Solanki c Krikken b DeFreitas	9	– c Weston b DeFreitas	170
*T. M. Moody c Krikken b Dean	12	– lbw b Dean	31
D. A. Leatherdale lbw b Smith	16	– lbw b Dean	26
†S. J. Rhodes b Cassar	34	– c Barnett b Dean	0
S. R. Lampitt not out	10	– lbw b Dean	2
P. J. Newport c DeFreitas b Smith	1	– c May b DeFreitas	31
M. J. Rawnsley c Blackwell b Dean	7	– lbw b Dean	6
R. J. Chapman lbw b Dean	6	– not out	0
B 1	1	B 2, l-b 10, w 2, n-b 14	28

1/1 2/4 3/8 4/26 5/30	**104**
6/66 7/80 8/87 9/98	

1/19 2/24 3/29 4/112 5/212	**316**
6/218 7/226 8/305 9/316	

Bonus points – Derbyshire 4.

Bowling: *First Innings*—DeFreitas 13–8–10–3; Dean 15.5–2–52–4; Smith 9–3–27–2; Cassar 6–2–14–1. *Second Innings*—DeFreitas 21.1–4–95–5; Dean 25–5–90–5; Smith 13–3–58–0; Cassar 5–0–40–0; Blackwell 6–1–21–0.

Umpires: R. Julian and N. T. Plews.

At Taunton, August 19, 20, 21. DERBYSHIRE beat SOMERSET by 72 runs.

DERBYSHIRE v DURHAM

At Derby, August 26, 27, 28, 29. Drawn. Derbyshire 5 pts, Durham 10 pts. Toss: Durham. Championship debut: M. J. Symington.

After a blank first day, Durham dominated the match, but they were thwarted by bad light in the final session. With all five bulbs shining, Boon could not use his seam bowlers, and Derbyshire clung on to draw. Fifties from Slater and Blackwell could not conceal Derbyshire's batting frailties, and Durham built a lead of 229. Roseberry and Daley, without a Championship half-century between them for more than two years, added 204 in 77 overs, one short of Durham's third-wicket record. Roseberry just missed his first Championship century for Durham, but Daley constructed an excellent innings and was only two short of his career-best. Barnett completed 1,000 runs for the 15th time and also narrowly failed to achieve another milestone: two more would have brought him a full set of centuries against the other counties. Derbyshire needed the determination of their tail to hold out, as Phillips took five wickets for the first time.

Close of play: First day, No play; Second day, Durham 82-2 (M. A. Roseberry 20*, J. A. Daley 24*); Third day, Derbyshire 27-1 (K. J. Barnett 10*, G. M. Roberts 7*).

Derbyshire

M. J. Slater lbw b Symington	54	– c Boon b Killeen	9
K. J. Barnett b Killeen	11	– c Killeen b Phillips	98
R. M. S. Weston b Killeen	2	– (4) c Lewis b Phillips	45
M. E. Cassar b Wood	14	– (5) c Morris b Phillips	9
M. R. May c Speight b Phillips	24	– (6) b Collingwood	24
B. L. Spendlove c Speight b Symington	1	– (7) c Killeen b Wood	15
*†K. M. Krikken lbw b Wood	5	– (8) lbw b Phillips	5
I. D. Blackwell c Collingwood b Phillips	57	– (9) lbw b Phillips	5
G. M. Roberts c Speight b Wood	1	– (3) c Speight b Wood	28
K. J. Dean not out	12	– not out	5
T. M. Smith c Speight b Symington	22	– not out	0
L-b 2	2	B 12, l-b 10, n-b 4	26

1/16 2/18 3/82 4/82 5/83   205   1/17 2/66 3/187   (9 wkts) 269
6/92 7/164 8/171 9/171   4/202 5/203 6/224
                                   7/231 8/239 9/265

Bonus points – Derbyshire 1, Durham 4.

Bowling: First Innings—Wood 24–4–58–3; Killeen 18–6–53–2; Symington 15.2–3–55–3; Phillips 12–3–37–2. *Second Innings*—Wood 25–5–74–2; Killeen 18–3–64–1; Phillips 38–19–56–5; Symington 8–2–32–0; Collingwood 9–4–19–1; Boon 5–3–2–0.

Durham

J. J. B. Lewis c Slater b Roberts	26	†M. P. Speight not out	52
J. E. Morris b Smith	4	N. C. Phillips not out	21
M. A. Roseberry b Dean	97	B 6, l-b 13, w 16, n-b 2	37
J. A. Daley st Krikken b Roberts	157		
*D. C. Boon b Roberts	40	1/16 2/46 3/250 (6 wkts dec.) 434	
P. D. Collingwood b Roberts	0	4/338 5/341 6/344	

M. J. Symington, J. Wood and N. Killeen did not bat.

Bonus points – Durham 3, Derbyshire 1 (Score at 120 overs: 328-3).

Bowling: Dean 29–9–76–1; Smith 23–6–90–1; Roberts 31–9–105–4; Blackwell 30–7–98–0; Cassar 19–7–46–0.

Umpires: G. I. Burgess and A. Clarkson.

At Manchester, September 1, 2, 3. DERBYSHIRE lost to LANCASHIRE by an innings and eight runs.

At Cardiff, September 9, 10, 11, 12. DERBYSHIRE drew with GLAMORGAN.

DERBYSHIRE v MIDDLESEX

At Derby, September 17, 18, 19, 20. Derbyshire won by four wickets. Derbyshire 24 pts, Middlesex 4 pts. Toss: Derbyshire.

Mike Gatting was warmly saluted by the Derby crowd in his final match before retirement, but was unable to sign off with a victory. Instead, Middlesex were beaten for the fifth Championship match running, equalling their worst-ever sequence. He had the consolation of being applauded to and from the crease in both innings and, with Brown, who was also retiring, received a farewell presentation from Derbyshire. Gatting fell cheaply in a shapeless Middlesex first innings, and

Derbyshire took a lead of 188, owing much to Rollins, who had been greatly missed during two months out with a back injury. Another collapse, in a season with all too many for Middlesex, briefly threatened. But Gatting had no intention of finishing that way; he bowed out on the third morning with one last half-century, taking his career aggregate to 36,549 first-class runs at 49.52. Though he was lbw to the first ball after lunch, causing some wry smiles, a classy and disciplined century by Shah, coupled with a near-miss by Weekes, enabled Middlesex to set a target of 167. Dean rounded off a fine season with another six wickets. Derbyshire were then labouring, but Gatting's last chance of glory was lost when he dropped Barnett, who combined with Krikken to see them through. The last time Middlesex lost five in a row was at the end of the 1933 season; the only other occurrences were in 1877 and 1888. They could break the record at the start of 1999. Including Sunday League games, this was their ninth consecutive defeat.

Close of play: First day, Derbyshire 135-3 (A. S. Rollins 85*, B. L. Spendlove 24*); Second day, Middlesex 38-2 (A. J. Strauss 12*, O. A. Shah 14*); Third day, Middlesex 346-9 (J. P. Hewitt 5*, A. R. C. Fraser 0*).

Middlesex

D. J. Goodchild c Barnett b Smith	10	– c Blackwell b Cork	8
R. A. Kettleborough lbw b Cassar	30	– lbw b Dean	1
A. J. Strauss b Cork	8	– lbw b Dean	13
O. A. Shah c Rollins b Cork	28	– lbw b Cork	116
M. W. Gatting lbw b Dean	8	– lbw b Cork	62
P. N. Weekes lbw b Cork	0	– c Cork b Dean	96
*†K. R. Brown not out	27	– c Spendlove b Cork	6
R. L. Johnson b Smith	43	– c Cork b Dean	9
J. P. Hewitt b Cassar	1	– lbw b Dean	9
A. R. C. Fraser c Cork b Smith	0	– (11) not out	0
P. C. R. Tufnell c Krikken b Smith	11	– (10) c Barnett b Dean	10
B 1, l-b 8, w 2, n-b 18	29	B 4, l-b 12, w 4, n-b 4	24
	195		**354**

1/21 2/43 3/98 4/100 5/100
6/118 7/177 8/178 9/181

1/8 2/10 3/40 4/143 5/297
6/313 7/329 8/329 9/345

Bonus points – Derbyshire 4.

Bowling: *First Innings*—Cork 18–6–32–3; Dean 19–6–67–1; Smith 16.3–4–60–4; Cassar 9–1–27–2. *Second Innings*—Cork 38–10–97–4; Dean 33.3–8–97–6; Cassar 14–2–58–0; Blackwell 1–0–2–0; Smith 20–4–63–0; Barnett 9–3–21–0.

Derbyshire

A. S. Rollins c Brown b Johnson	91	– (7) b Weekes	13
M. R. May b Fraser	10	– c Brown b Fraser	3
R. M. S. Weston run out	0	– b Johnson	22
M. E. Cassar c Kettleborough b Johnson	7	– c Brown b Johnson	25
B. L. Spendlove c Tufnell b Hewitt	30	– (1) c Shah b Hewitt	11
K. J. Barnett c Weekes b Hewitt	44	– (5) not out	49
I. D. Blackwell c Gatting b Hewitt	29		
*D. G. Cork c Brown b Gatting	51	– (6) c Strauss b Weekes	0
†K. M. Krikken c Kettleborough b Tufnell	58	– (8) not out	27
K. J. Dean not out	21		
T. M. Smith c Hewitt b Tufnell	0		
B 12, l-b 14, w 6, n-b 10	42	B 2, l-b 7, n-b 8	17
	383	(6 wkts)	**167**

1/39 2/39 3/67 4/141 5/164
6/223 7/265 8/317 9/375

1/17 2/17 3/66
4/71 5/71 6/103

Bonus points – Derbyshire 4, Middlesex 4.

Bowling: *First Innings*—Fraser 26–7–78–1; Hewitt 28–4–95–3; Johnson 14–0–82–2; Tufnell 19–4–34–2; Kettleborough 14–1–54–0; Weekes 4–1–5–0; Gatting 5–1–9–1. *Second Innings*—Fraser 12.4–4–13–1; Hewitt 7–1–32–1; Johnson 12–3–37–2; Tufnell 26–11–55–0; Weekes 12.4–3–21–2.

Umpires: A. G. T. Whitehead and P. Willey.

Steve Harmison

DURHAM

Patrons: Sir Donald Bradman and A. W. Austin
President: H. J. Banks
Chairman: J. D. Robson
Cricket Executive: G. Cook
Chief Executive: M. Candlish
Coach: N. Gifford
Captain: D. C. Boon
Head Groundsman: T. Flintoft
Scorer: B. Hunt

Second in the table in early June and 14th at the final curtain represented a season of unprecedented heights for Durham, who had not finished higher than 16th before. They also reached the Benson and Hedges quarter-finals for the first time and earned their first England A stripes through young pace bowlers Melvyn Betts and Steve Harmison.

They would have settled for this at the start of the season, when it was learned that Simon Brown, usually the spearhead of their attack, had a cruciate ligament injury. Having made a successful outing against Cambridge University, he was risked in the Benson and Hedges quarter-final; after negotiating his ten overs, he broke down in the field and an operation sidelined him for the rest of the season. But what might have been a devastating blow was hardly felt until late in the season because of the remarkable emergence of the lanky 19-year-old Harmison and the improved form and fitness of John Wood, who took 61 Championship wickets.

Hampered by a back injury, Harmison had spent 1997 playing for Ashington Seconds as a batsman. But he worked hard through the winter; Durham quietly awarded him a one-year contract just before the start of the season, then pitched him into the opening match at Edgbaston. Using his 6ft 3in to great effect, he proved deceptively quick, achieved steep bounce and bowled a deadly yorker. Early on, Harmison was second only to Betts as the country's leading wicket-taker. Betts impressed most in the Championship victory over Middlesex at Lord's, taking nine wickets in the match and hitting a six over mid-wicket off Phil Tufnell, followed by a three to clinch a one-wicket win with ten balls remaining. It was quite possibly the highlight of Durham's first-class existence: David Boon was said to have leapt on to another player's back in the dressing-room. An hour later, he was telling the press: "We should not get carried away by this."

He was right, of course. The three teams Durham had beaten in the previous four matches all finished below them in the table and, after a clear opportunity to beat Northamptonshire in the next game was ruined by the rain, the bubble was burst by Yorkshire. There were to be no more Championship wins, and Durham also slid down the Sunday League, to finish 17th for the second successive season.

The team never had the same balance once the only genuine all-rounder, Mike Foster, was hit by injury. This coincided with runs drying up for Paul Collingwood, who began with a high-class hundred at Edgbaston and was averaging over 50 in early June. Betts also began to struggle, initially because of an Achilles problem, before a torn groin muscle ended his season in mid-August. But the real weakness again lay with the batting, where only Boon provided any consistency. Jon Lewis had a disappointing season after his remarkable debut with Durham in 1997, while John Morris, Nick Speak and Mike Roseberry all gave glimpses of former glories without dispelling the impression that even the immediate future should lie with younger players.

After being overlooked by Boon for a season and a half, Jimmy Daley was granted an extended run in the second half of the summer, and his 157 at Derby earned him second place in the county averages. The danger of his departure, which had so angered members 12 months previously, still lingered. But he signed a new two-year contract in September, saying: "The team spirit here is fantastic. I can't see it being better anywhere else."

Everyone spoke highly of Boon in that respect, and he was persuaded to extend his two-year stay by one more season. Morris handed over the vice-captaincy to Speak for 1999, when he becomes the first player to have a benefit. Martin Speight improved with bat and gloves, his 61 victims behind the stumps – many of them from athletic catches – beating the Durham record of 56 set by Chris Scott in 1994. But there was little improvement on the spin-bowling front. Nicky Phillips, signed from Sussex, took 23 wickets in 15 Championship matches at 45.08. He was preferred from the outset to his fellow off-spinner James Boiling, who announced in early May that he would be retiring at the end of the season and was ignored thereafter. There were no opportunities for David Cox, whose frustration boiled over in July, when there was an off-field incident which prompted his early release. Also released were Stewart Hutton, Jason Searle, Steve Lugsden, Martin Saggers, Colin Campbell and Alan Walker, who was to be kept on in a management role after spending the season as second-team captain.

The clear-out came as no surprise. Graham Gooch had been taken on in a consultancy role and in his first month stressed the need for only the best of Durham's playing staff of 26 to be retained, creating more chances for youngsters. Harmison apart, the brightest of those proved to be Michael Gough, whose single-minded approach earned him a lengthy run at the top of the order before England Under-19 duties intervened. Two local all-rounders, Marc Symington and left-arm spinner Steve Chapman, made their Championship debuts and were offered contracts.

During 1998, Durham decided to fall into line with the other 17 counties in giving county caps as a reward. Previously, they had given caps to all playing staff. But, in the spring, they announced that the traditional hierarchy, under which capped cricketers are more highly paid, would provide security for their more experienced players and an incentive for the rest. Ten players were duly upgraded at a dinner in September, to celebrate the end of a season which tailed off alarmingly but still left much cause for optimism. – TIM WELLOCK.

462

DURHAM 1998

[Bill Smith]

Standing: P. Forster (*Second Eleven scorer*), S. J. Harmison, J. P. Searle, M. J. Saggers, N. Killeen, M. A. Gough, J. Wood, C. L. Campbell, S. Lugsden, P. D. Collingwood, J. J. B. Lewis, M. M. Betts, J. A. Graham, N. C. Phillips, A. Pratt, N. Gifford (*coach*). *Seated:* D. M. Cox, J. A. Daley, M. J. Foster, M. P. Speight, N. J. Speak, M. A. Roseberry, D. C. Boon (*captain*), J. E. Morris, S. J. E. Brown, J. Boiling, A. Walker, S. Hutton.

DURHAM RESULTS

All first-class matches – Played 19: Won 4, Lost 9, Drawn 6.

County Championship matches – Played 17: Won 3, Lost 9, Drawn 5.

*Competition placings – Britannic Assurance County Championship, 14th;
NatWest Trophy, 2nd round; Benson and Hedges Cup, q-f;
AXA League, 17th.*

COUNTY CHAMPIONSHIP AVERAGES
BATTING

Cap		M	I	NO	R	HS	100s	50s	Avge	Ct/St
1998	D. C. Boon§	15	27	3	953	139*	3	5	39.70	12
	J. A. Daley†	10	19	2	554	157	1	1	32.58	4
1998	P. D. Collingwood† .	17	30	4	793	105	1	5	30.50	16
1998	J. E. Morris	12	23	1	657	163	2	1	29.86	5
1998	N. J. Speak	14	25	2	638	77*	0	6	27.73	9
1998	M. A. Roseberry† . .	6	11	0	295	97	0	2	26.81	2
	M. J. Foster	8	13	1	321	76*	0	2	26.75	2
1998	M. P. Speight	16	28	4	581	97*	0	4	24.20	58/3
1998	J. J. B. Lewis	14	26	1	578	72	0	4	23.12	10
	M. A. Gough†	8	15	0	329	62	0	2	21.93	9
	S. J. Harmison	13	21	4	214	36	0	0	12.58	1
1998	M. M. Betts†	11	17	7	125	29*	0	0	12.50	3
	M. J. Saggers	2	4	2	25	10	0	0	12.50	1
	N. C. Phillips	15	24	2	225	35	0	0	10.22	6
1998	J. Wood	16	25	3	225	37	0	0	10.22	2
	S. Lugsden†	3	5	2	15	8*	0	0	5.00	1

Also batted: S. Chapman† (1 match) 2, 11; N. Killeen† (2 matches) 12, 0 (2 ct); A. Pratt† (1 match) 0, 34 (2 ct); J. P. Searle (1 match) 0, 0 (1 ct); A. Walker (1 match) 3*, 2*. M. J. Symington (1 match) did not bat.

* Signifies not out.   † Born in Durham.   § Overseas player.

BOWLING

	O	M	R	W	BB	5W/i	Avge
M. J. Foster	113	23	351	17	4-41	0	20.64
M. M. Betts	331	76	944	44	6-83	4	21.45
N. Killeen	76.2	19	275	10	5-49	1	27.50
S. J. Harmison.	415.5	85	1,400	49	5-70	1	28.57
J. Wood	543.5	108	1,800	61	5-52	2	29.50
P. D. Collingwood . . .	170	42	519	12	3-89	0	43.25
N. C. Phillips	360.4	78	1,037	23	5-56	1	45.08

Also bowled: D. C. Boon 27.4–8–107–1; S. Chapman 29–6–79–0; M. A. Gough 24.2–4–109–1; J. J. B. Lewis 8–0–73–1; S. Lugsden 72.2–6–325–8; M. J. Saggers 58.2–14–149–7; J. P. Searle 20.4–4–92–3; N. J. Speak 2–0–13–0; M. J. Symington 23.2–5–87–3; A. Walker 23.5–5–51–1.

COUNTY RECORDS

Highest score for:	210*	J. J. B. Lewis v Oxford University at Oxford . . .	1997
Highest score against:	501*	B. C. Lara (Warwickshire) at Birmingham	1994
Best bowling for:	9-64	M. M. Betts v Northamptonshire at Northampton .	1997
Best bowling against:	8-22	D. Follett (Middlesex) at Lord's	1996
Highest total for:	625-6 dec.	v Derbyshire at Chesterfield	1994
Highest total against:	810-4 dec.	by Warwickshire at Birmingham	1994
Lowest total for:	67	v Middlesex at Lord's	1996
Lowest total against:	73	by Oxford University at Oxford	1994

At Birmingham, April 17, 18, 20, 21. DURHAM drew with WARWICKSHIRE.

DURHAM v GLOUCESTERSHIRE

At Chester-le-Street, April 23, 24, 25, 27. Gloucestershire won by 46 runs. Gloucestershire 22 pts, Durham 4 pts. Toss: Gloucestershire.

After a first-day washout, an interesting contest evolved: Durham went into the last 16 overs needing 76, with four wickets left. But Walsh had the last word, as always looked likely, and finished with six for 42. When play finally started on the second day, 19-year-old Steve Harmison took four for 21 in his opening 12-over spell, on his way to a first five-wicket haul. Harmison, 6 ft 3 in and lean, from the traditional Northumberland sporting town of Ashington, surprised good batsmen with his pace and bounce. Gloucestershire were 78 for five, but Russell led a recovery almost strong enough to make Durham follow on; they were still 12 short of the target when Harmison came in at No. 11. He fearlessly took on Walsh to make the runs, and then wreaked havoc with the ball again. The visitors lost six for 34 in 13 overs on the final morning. Dawson and Ball led a revival before the declaration set Durham 248 in 74 overs. Walsh quickly had them in trouble but, while Speak was making a well-paced 74, they had a chance of victory.

Close of play: First day, No play; Second day, Gloucestershire 182-6 (R. C. Russell 39*, M. C. J. Ball 19*); Third day, Gloucestershire 32-0 (N. J. Trainor 17*, R. J. Cunliffe 13*).

Gloucestershire

N. J. Trainor c Boon b Harmison	20	– c Speight b Harmison	17
R. J. Cunliffe c Speight b Harmison	17	– c Speight b Wood	24
T. H. C. Hancock lbw b Harmison	5	– b Harmison	7
A. J. Wright lbw b Wood	9	– c Boon b Wood	0
R. I. Dawson b Harmison	1	– not out	23
*M. W. Alleyne run out	51	– b Harmison	0
†R. C. Russell lbw b Harmison	60	– lbw b Wood	2
M. C. J. Ball c Speight b Collingwood	42	– not out	22
J. Lewis not out	44		
A. M. Smith c Boon b Walker	6		
C. A. Walsh run out	0		
B 3, l-b 5, w 2, n-b 22	32	B 2, l-b 4, n-b 2	8

1/29 2/45 3/48 4/52 5/78   287   1/33 2/47 3/47   (6 wkts dec.) 103
6/137 7/216 8/259 9/284   4/53 5/53 6/66

Bonus points – Gloucestershire 2, Durham 4.

Bowling: *First Innings*—Wood 34-5-101-1; Harmison 36-13-70-5; Walker 23.5-5-51-1; Phillips 13-1-34-0; Collingwood 8-3-23-1. *Second Innings*—Wood 16-2-54-3; Harmison 14-3-32-3; Phillips 2-0-7-0; Boon 1-0-4-0.

Durham

J. J. B. Lewis lbw b Smith	7	– lbw b Walsh	0
M. A. Roseberry b Lewis	23	– lbw b Walsh	9
J. E. Morris c Trainor b Smith	3	– c Hancock b Walsh	12
N. J. Speak c Walsh b Lewis	16	– b Ball	74
*D. C. Boon b Walsh	37	– lbw b Lewis	5
†M. P. Speight c Smith b Alleyne	3	– lbw b Walsh	29
P. D. Collingwood c Cunliffe b Ball	3	– c Cunliffe b Ball	10
N. C. Phillips c Alleyne b Walsh	0	– b Walsh	35
J. Wood c Hancock b Ball	1	– b Ball	7
A. Walker not out	3	– not out	2
S. J. Harmison b Ball	12	– c Russell b Walsh	1
L-b 9, w 2, n-b 24	35	L-b 3, n-b 14	17

1/17 2/31 3/59 4/70 5/88   143   1/0 2/16 3/25 4/42 5/115   201
6/106 7/119 8/124 9/126   6/132 7/189 8/189 9/198

Bonus points – Gloucestershire 4.

Bowling: *First Innings*—Walsh 19–5–50–2; Smith 12–3–33–2; Lewis 10–2–24–2; Alleyne 4–1–13–1; Ball 9.2–6–14–3. *Second Innings*—Walsh 18.5–6–42–6; Smith 15–2–52–0; Ball 20–5–53–3; Lewis 14–2–46–1; Dawson 1–0–5–0.

Umpires: R. A. White and P. Willey.

DURHAM v ESSEX

At Chester-le-Street, May 13, 14, 15, 16. Durham won by 95 runs. Durham 22 pts, Essex 4 pts. Toss: Durham. First-class debut: M. A. Gough. Championship debut: D. G. Wilson.

Injuries gave an unexpected opportunity to 18-year-old Michael Gough, from Hartlepool, who seized the chance by batting for 283 minutes to make 62 in his maiden first-class innings. He reinforced a reputation gained with England Under-19 for single-minded obduracy, and only Hussain, with 63 in Essex's second innings, outscored him. Essex, also weakened by injury, trailed by 91, and it took a hat-trick from Danny Law to get them into the game. The first two victims, Foster and Phillips, were caught by Stuart Law at second slip and the third, Betts, was lbw. This reduced Durham to 177 for eight in their second innings, but the tail added another 70 and a target of 339 proved beyond Essex's reach. They began the last day needing 145, with four wickets standing, but Betts bowled superbly to finish them off before lunch. It was a deserved reward for the captaincy of Speak, deputising for an injured Boon, who switched his fielders and bowlers around very thoughtfully. This ended a run of four Essex Championship wins over Durham.

Close of play: First day, Essex 0-0 (D. D. J. Robinson 0*, A. P. Grayson 0*); Second day, Durham 104-3 (N. J. Speak 41*, P. D. Collingwood 0*); Third day, Essex 194-6 (R. J. Rollins 26*, D. R. Law 1*).

Durham

M. A. Roseberry c Robinson b Irani	26	– (6) c S. G. Law b D. R. Law		20
M. A. Gough lbw b Ilott	62	– (1) lbw b Irani		16
J. A. Daley c S. G. Law b Irani	8	– lbw b Williams		26
*N. J. Speak b Ilott	41	– lbw b D. R. Law		41
P. D. Collingwood c Peters b D. R. Law	26	– c Grayson b Williams		42
†M. P. Speight b Wilson	30	– (2) c Hussain b Williams		10
M. J. Foster c Robinson b Williams	21	– c S. G. Law b D. R. Law		11
N. C. Phillips b Ilott	12	– c S. G. Law b D. R. Law		0
M. M. Betts b Williams	3	– lbw b D. R. Law		0
J. Wood lbw b Ilott	4	– c Rollins b Irani		37
S. J. Harmison not out	4	– not out		28
L-b 11, w 2, n-b 26	39	B 2, l-b 8, w 2, n-b 4		16

1/49 2/63 3/134 4/170 5/208	276	1/12 2/33 3/98 4/104 5/153	247
6/223 7/245 8/263 9/269		6/177 7/177 8/177 9/204	

Bonus points – Durham 2, Essex 4.

Bowling: *First Innings*—Ilott 23.1–8–49–4; Williams 21–4–72–2; Irani 22–8–50–2; D. R. Law 16–2–51–1; Wilson 7–2–22–1; Grayson 11–3–21–0. *Second Innings*—Ilott 17–2–61–0; Williams 20–5–46–3; D. R. Law 17–6–46–5; Irani 11.1–1–44–2; Wilson 3–0–16–0; Grayson 8–2–24–0.

Essex

D. D. J. Robinson c Speight b Foster	11	– c Collingwood b Wood	15
A. P. Grayson b Betts	8	– c Speight b Betts	10
*N. Hussain run out	12	– c Collingwood b Wood	63
S. G. Law c Speight b Phillips	18	– b Betts	12
R. C. Irani c Speak b Harmison	29	– lbw b Harmison	3
S. D. Peters c Speight b Wood	16	– c Gough b Betts	35
†R. J. Rollins c Gough b Wood	1	– c Daley b Betts	41
D. R. Law c Roseberry b Wood	25	– b Betts	7
D. G. Wilson c Collingwood b Betts	14	– not out	14
M. C. Ilott c Speight b Harmison	8	– lbw b Betts	1
N. F. Williams not out	12	– lbw b Phillips	11
B 3, l-b 6, w 12, n-b 10	31	B 9, l-b 8, w 10, n-b 4	31

1/23 2/41 3/47 4/75 5/112   185   1/25 2/58 3/87 4/94 5/139   243
6/115 7/120 8/161 9/167   6/184 7/214 8/219 9/221

Bonus points – Durham 4.

Bowling: *First Innings*—Betts 17–8–30–2; Harmison 17.4–3–47–2; Wood 16–4–54–3; Foster 10–1–29–1; Phillips 6–2–16–1. *Second Innings*—Betts 28–6–83–6; Harmison 22–4–71–1; Foster 10–4–18–0; Wood 16–6–31–2; Phillips 9.4–1–23–1.

Umpires: A. A. Jones and K. E. Palmer.

At Cambridge, May 18, 19, 20. DURHAM beat CAMBRIDGE UNIVERSITY by 95 runs.

At Canterbury, May 21, 22, 23. DURHAM lost to KENT by an innings and 27 runs.

At Nottingham, May 29, 30, 31. DURHAM beat NOTTINGHAMSHIRE by eight wickets.

At Lord's, June 3, 4, 5, 6. DURHAM beat MIDDLESEX by one wicket.

DURHAM v NORTHAMPTONSHIRE

At Chester-le-Street, June 11, 12, 13, 15. Drawn. Durham 8 pts, Northamptonshire 4 pts. Toss: Durham.

Poor weather made it difficult to judge the success of an experimental 12.30 start on the first two days, although it did allow more play than would otherwise have been possible on the opening day, when a wet outfield delayed the start until 5 p.m. But after a tea interval taken at 5.56, more than an hour was lost on the second evening, and there was only an hour's cricket on the third day before the match was washed out. Despite that, five bonus points lifted Durham into second place in the Championship, their highest-ever position. When play did occur, movement off the seam allowed Wood to take his first five-wicket haul for four years. Only 211 runs were scored in 83 overs on the second day, but Speight and Collingwood added 81 in an hour on Saturday.

Close of play: First day, Northamptonshire 120-6 (A. L. Penberthy 20*, G. P. Swann 20*); Second day, Durham 168-4 (P. D. Collingwood 13*, M. P. Speight 24*); Third day, Durham 249-4 (P. D. Collingwood 50*, M. P. Speight 66*).

Northamptonshire

R. J. Warren lbw b Wood	1		D. Follett c Speight b Wood	7
A. J. Swann c Speight b Harmison	30		F. A. Rose c Betts b Wood	12
M. B. Loye b Betts	6		D. E. Malcolm not out	2
R. J. Bailey b Wood	10			
*K. M. Curran b Wood	8		B 1, l-b 6, w 10, n-b 10	27
A. L. Penberthy c Speak b Betts	20			
†D. Ripley lbw b Foster	9			163
G. P. Swann c Speight b Betts	31			

1/1 2/8 3/55 4/59 5/69
6/81 7/123 8/146 9/160

Bonus points – Durham 4.

Bowling: Betts 22-7-33-3; Wood 19.2-3-52-5; Harmison 16-2-49-1; Foster 4-0-17-1; Phillips 2-1-5-0.

Durham

J. J. B. Lewis c Curran b Rose	39		†M. P. Speight not out	66
M. A. Gough c sub b Malcolm	9			
N. J. Speak c Ripley b Follett	31		B 2, l-b 8, n-b 8	18
*D. C. Boon c Follett b Malcolm	36			
P. D. Collingwood not out	50		1/21 2/68 3/117 4/154	(4 wkts) 249

M. J. Foster, N. C. Phillips, M. M. Betts, J. Wood and S. J. Harmison did not bat.

Bonus points – Durham 1, Northamptonshire 1.

Bowling: Malcolm 22-8-66-2; Rose 14.3-2-55-1; Follett 17-3-51-1; Curran 5-0-19-0; Penberthy 7-1-10-0; G. P. Swann 11-2-38-0.

Umpires: J. W. Holder and N. T. Plews.

DURHAM v YORKSHIRE

At Chester-le-Street, June 17, 18, 19. Yorkshire won by nine wickets. Yorkshire 23 pts, Durham 7 pts. Toss: Yorkshire.

Durham's excellent run came to an abrupt halt on the third day of this match. Yorkshire began it 102 behind with only two first-innings wickets left. But after reducing the deficit to 18, they dismissed Durham for 74 and reached their target inside 19 overs. The astonishing turnaround came on a pitch described by Yorkshire's Australian, Lehmann, as the best he had seen in England. It was sparked by two questionable decisions, however: Lewis was caught behind although a replay on Tyne-Tees TV suggested the ball hit his calf, then next ball Speak was given lbw when very well forward. The impressive Hutchison took both wickets and, after he had Boon palpably lbw with another in-swinger, Durham capsized. All the wickets fell to left-armers. Durham thus recorded the lowest total at the Riverside ground on the same day that Vaughan completed the highest individual innings there. He scored 177 before being last out, and was on the field throughout the match. Boon had made an unbeaten hundred on the first two days, his biggest yet for Durham, and a better indicator of the pitch's quality than the disaster that followed.

Close of play: First day, Durham 311-7 (D. C. Boon 120*, M. M. Betts 14*); Second day, Yorkshire 235-8 (M. P. Vaughan 118*, R. J. Sidebottom 1*).

Durham

J. J. B. Lewis lbw b Hutchison	22	– c Blakey b Hutchison	8
M. A. Gough c Wood b Hoggard	0	– lbw b Stemp	9
N. J. Speak c Blakey b Hutchison	57	– lbw b Hutchison	0
*D. C. Boon not out	139	– lbw b Hutchison	8
P. D. Collingwood b Hutchison	0	– c Byas b Sidebottom	13
†M. P. Speight c Blakey b Stemp	41	– c Byas b Sidebottom	4
M. J. Foster c Sidebottom b Hamilton	35	– c Hoggard b Sidebottom	2
N. C. Phillips lbw b Sidebottom	4	– c Hamilton b Stemp	5
M. M. Betts b Hoggard	18	– not out	6
J. Wood c Byas b Hamilton	2	– c Blakey b Stemp	4
S. J. Harmison run out	0	– c McGrath b Stemp	10
L-b 15, n-b 4	19	B 2, l-b 1, w 2	5
	337		**74**

1/13 2/35 3/104 4/112 5/205
6/250 7/273 8/323 9/336

1/16 2/16 3/26 4/30 5/39
6/47 7/54 8/54 9/60

Bonus points – Durham 3, Yorkshire 4.

Bowling: *First Innings*—Hoggard 22–5–79–2; Hutchison 24.1–5–55–3; Hamilton 20.3–4–58–2; Sidebottom 17–4–58–1; Stemp 25–6–60–1; Lehmann 5–0–12–0. *Second Innings*—Hutchison 10–4–22–3; Hoggard 1–0–10–0; Stemp 21–17–13–4; Sidebottom 9–3–13–3; Hamilton 3–0–13–0.

Yorkshire

A. McGrath c Speight b Harmison	31	– c Wood b Phillips	33
M. P. Vaughan b Foster	177	– not out	36
*D. Byas b Harmison	3	– not out	18
D. S. Lehmann st Speight b Phillips	6		
M. J. Wood lbw b Phillips	1		
†R. J. Blakey c Collingwood b Betts	14		
G. M. Hamilton c Lewis b Phillips	19		
R. D. Stemp b Phillips	8		
P. M. Hutchison c Gough b Betts	5		
R. J. Sidebottom c Gough b Harmison	8		
M. J. Hoggard not out	13		
B 2, l-b 8, n-b 24	34	N-b 6	6
	319	(1 wkt)	**93**

1/62 2/76 3/87 4/97 5/140
6/171 7/193 8/222 9/274

1/48

Bonus points – Yorkshire 3, Durham 4 (Score at 120 overs: 317-9).

Bowling: *First Innings*—Betts 27–4–79–2; Wood 13–2–46–0; Phillips 52–13–89–4; Harmison 22–4–76–3; Foster 5.2–1–15–1; Speak 1–0–4–0. *Second Innings*—Betts 4–0–23–0; Harmison 6–0–42–0; Phillips 5.4–0–14–1; Wood 3–1–14–0.

Umpires: G. I. Burgess and T. E. Jesty.

DURHAM v LEICESTERSHIRE

At Darlington, July 1, 2, 3. Leicestershire won by an innings and 103 runs. Leicestershire 24 pts, Durham 3 pts. Toss: Leicestershire.

Leicestershire, who set off two points behind Durham, leapfrogged above them into second place with their eighth win in eight meetings since Durham gained first-class status. Maddy, who had scored only 162 in 11 Championship innings in 1998 despite a glut of Benson and Hedges runs, doubled that in one go, easily passing his previous Championship best of 103. On a slow pitch, he waited for the loose ball and hit 25 fours, driving immaculately. Maddy added 209 with

Habib, who lost little by comparison, until the weather warmed up on the second afternoon: at this point, the ball began to swing, and both were bowled. It was swing and seam that undid Durham. Simmons took seven for 49, beating his previous best analysis, also against Durham; four of the wickets came in nine balls. Wells removed three of the top four in the second innings and then Crowe, playing his second first-class match after a three-year gap, picked up three wickets in two overs with his well-flighted off-breaks. Durham surrendered with a day to spare.

Close of play: First day, Leicestershire 247-4 (D. L. Maddy 115*, A. Habib 46*); Second day, Durham 102-5 (J. A. Daley 22*, M. P. Speight 3*).

Leicestershire

V. J. Wells c Morris b Wood	11	
D. L. Maddy b Betts	162	
I. J. Sutcliffe b Harmison	13	
B. F. Smith c Harmison b Wood	47	
P. V. Simmons c Speight b Betts	0	
A. Habib b Wood	96	
†P. A. Nixon b Wood	1	
*C. C. Lewis lbw b Wood	9	

C. D. Crowe c Speight b Betts	2
A. D. Mullally not out	38
M. T. Brimson c Phillips b Harmison . .	4
B 8, l-b 9, w 2, n-b 12	31

1/27 2/41 3/122 4/131 5/340   414
6/351 7/354 8/357 9/385

Bonus points – Leicestershire 4, Durham 3 (Score at 120 overs: 355-7).

Bowling: Betts 41–11–98–3; Wood 33–11–104–5; Harmison 28.2–4–107–2; Collingwood 16–5–40–0; Phillips 13–2–48–0.

Durham

J. J. B. Lewis lbw b Lewis	0	– c Smith b Wells	16
J. E. Morris lbw b Simmons	9	– lbw b Wells	0
N. J. Speak b Simmons	30	– c Crowe b Simmons	25
*D. C. Boon b Wells	9	– c Lewis b Wells	22
P. D. Collingwood b Simmons	10	– b Mullally	8
J. A. Daley c Nixon b Simmons	30	– not out	42
†M. P. Speight b Mullally	16	– c Sutcliffe b Crowe	11
N. C. Phillips not out	4	– b Crowe	0
M. M. Betts b Simmons	0	– c Sutcliffe b Crowe	0
J. Wood lbw b Simmons	0	– st Nixon b Brimson	36
S. J. Harmison c Habib b Simmons	4	– c Habib b Brimson	4
L-b 6, n-b 16	22	L-b 5, w 2, n-b 6	13

1/0 2/40 3/49 4/61 5/69   134   1/4 2/25 3/50 4/59 5/84   177
6/126 7/126 8/126 9/126   6/97 7/97 8/97 9/155

Bonus points – Leicestershire 4.

Bowling: *First Innings*—Lewis 9–2–29–1; Mullally 22–10–33–1; Wells 10–3–15–1; Simmons 19.2–4–49–7; Brimson 2–2–0–0; Crowe 1–0–2–0. *Second Innings*—Lewis 9–1–24–0; Wells 12–5–30–3; Brimson 6.4–2–21–2; Mullally 11–3–28–1; Simmons 6–1–20–1; Crowe 13–2–49–3.

Umpires: B. Dudleston and V. A. Holder.

At Chester-le-Street, July 14, 15, 16. DURHAM drew with SOUTH AFRICANS (See South African tour section).

At Taunton, July 22, 23, 24. DURHAM lost to SOMERSET by ten wickets.

At Southampton, July 30, 31, August 1, 3. DURHAM drew with HAMPSHIRE.

At Eastbourne, August 5, 6, 7. DURHAM lost to SUSSEX by an innings and 81 runs.

DURHAM v GLAMORGAN

At Chester-le-Street, August 14, 15, 16, 17. Drawn. Durham 11 pts, Glamorgan 9 pts. Toss: Durham. Championship debut: S. P. Jones.

A flat pitch and two depleted attacks resulted in stalemate. Morris overtook Wayne Larkins as Durham's leading century-maker, advancing to his 11th hundred on the final day. But a two-fingered gesture on reaching the landmark landed him in hot water. He explained he had been signalling to a friend who bet him £20 he would not make a century, not to the crowd who had barracked him the previous day. The club ruled that, whatever Morris's reason, it was offensive, and "appropriate disciplinary action" was taken. Earlier, Durham's hopes of victory – raised after a Boon hundred – were badly hit when Betts tore a groin muscle delivering his fourth ball. With Cottey cutting merrily on his way to 123, Glamorgan hurried to a lead of 90, reasoning that, without Betts, Durham were unlikely to set a target. But Glamorgan's attack was also below strength, and they were unable to press home their advantage. Their understudies included Simon Jones, 19-year-old son of England bowler Jeff Jones, who, unlike his father, bowls right-arm.

Close of play: First day, Durham 269-4 (D. C. Boon 86*, P. D. Collingwood 8*); Second day, Glamorgan 259-4 (P. A. Cottey 68*, M. J. Powell 21*); Third day, Durham 128-0 (J. J. B. Lewis 53*, J. E. Morris 68*).

Durham

J. J. B. Lewis c Cottey b Thomas	34	– b Thomas	54
J. E. Morris c Powell b Thomas	27	– st Dawood b Cosker	163
N. J. Speak c Jones b Davies	59	– c Dawood b Dale	25
J. A. Daley c Dawood b Dale	20	– c Dawood b Jones	22
*D. C. Boon b Davies	106	– not out	62
P. D. Collingwood c Dawood b Thomas	20	– c Dawood b Cosker	11
†M. P. Speight c Dawood b Cosker	40	– c Cottey b Cosker	0
N. C. Phillips c Thomas b Cosker	8	– c Cosker b Cottey	21
J. Wood c Cosker b Thomas	6	– not out	6
M. M. Betts not out	11		
S. Lugsden b Thomas	4		
B 15, l-b 13, w 15, n-b 18	61	B 4, l-b 9, n-b 8	21

1/76 2/81 3/112 4/240 5/307   396   1/130 2/237 3/267   (7 wkts dec.) 385
6/333 7/362 8/378 9/380   4/280 5/297
                                 6/301 7/372

Bonus points – Durham 4, Glamorgan 2 (Score at 120 overs: 352-6).

Bowling: *First Innings*—Jones 21–3–74–0; Davies 23–9–61–2; Dale 24.5–5–52–1; Thomas 30.1–2–107–5; Cosker 43–15–69–2; Law 1–0–5–0. *Second Innings*—Thomas 18.4–4–41–1; Davies 18–4–72–0; Dale 13–2–33–1; Jones 18–2–61–1; Cosker 49–16–124–3; Maynard 2–0–12–0; Law 5–0–14–0; Cottey 5–0–15–1.

Glamorgan

S. P. James c Speak b Lugsden	42	A. P. Davies run out	5
W. L. Law b Wood	0	D. A. Cosker c Speight b Collingwood	1
A. Dale b Collingwood	34	S. P. Jones not out	0
*M. P. Maynard b Lugsden	79		
P. A. Cottey c Speight b Collingwood	123	B 5, l-b 10, w 6, n-b 8	29
M. J. Powell c Collingwood b Phillips	67		
†I. Dawood c Collingwood b Wood	32	1/2 2/83 3/85 4/217 5/338	486
S. D. Thomas c Speight b Wood	74	6/388 7/451 8/467 9/480	

Bonus points – Glamorgan 4, Durham 4.

Bowling: Betts 0.4–0–1–0; Lugsden 29.2–0–151–2; Wood 30.4–1–143–3; Collingwood 29–8–89–3; Phillips 21–0–78–1; Speak 1–0–9–0.

Umpires: A. Clarkson and R. A. White.

DURHAM v LANCASHIRE

At Chester-le-Street, August 19, 20, 21. Lancashire won by 350 runs. Lancashire 20 pts, Durham 4 pts. Toss: Lancashire. Championship debut: A. Pratt.

On a quick and bouncy pitch, the first day brought 377 runs for 20 wickets. Killeen had Lancashire rocking at 43 for five, and took a career-best five for 49, but Wasim Akram turned the tables. He scored 68 and made decisive early inroads into both Durham innings – despite a bruised toe; 21-year-old Paul Ridgway helped by making 35, his first first-class runs, and taking three wickets. Durham were held together for 40 overs by Lewis, who carried his bat for the second time (Speak was unable to bat, having strained his groin diving to catch Hegg.) When the pitch eased on the second day, Fairbrother and Lloyd raced to hundreds and Wasim hit 63 more to leave a target of 473. Wicket-keeper Andrew Pratt, deputising for the injured Speight, top-scored with 34 in his first Championship match, but Lancashire wrapped up victory after lunch on the third day. It was a match of motoring problems: a six by Wasim broke a reporter's headlight, while the Toyota Lexus belonging to former England footballer John Barnes, who was training with Newcastle United nearby, stopped play for eight minutes; the sun was glinting off the windscreen.

Close of play: First day, Lancashire 23-1 (N. T. Wood 5*, G. Chapple 0*); Second day, Lancashire 434.

Lancashire

N. T. Wood c Pratt b Wood	14	– (2) c Pratt b Collingwood	48
J. P. Crawley b Killeen	4	– (1) b Killeen	14
N. H. Fairbrother b Killeen	0	– (4) c Lewis b Collingwood	138
A. Flintoff b Wood	2	– (5) lbw b Wood	0
G. D. Lloyd c Collingwood b Lugsden	15	– (6) c Searle b Lugsden	104
†W. K. Hegg c Speak b Killeen	12	– (7) c Lewis b Killeen	21
*Wasim Akram c Lewis b Wood	68	– (8) c Wood b Searle	63
G. Yates b Killeen	5	– (9) b Searle	14
G. Chapple b Lugsden	15	– (3) c Lugsden b Wood	12
P. M. Ridgway c Morris b Killeen	35	– c Lewis b Searle	4
G. Keedy not out	5	– not out	4
B 10, l-b 9, n-b 2	21	B 1, l-b 11	12
	196		**434**

1/16 2/16 3/21 4/30 5/43   1/19 2/42 3/214 4/217 5/225
6/69 7/80 8/111 9/178   6/266 7/394 8/422 9/428

Bowling: *First Innings*—Wood 20-4-70-3; Killeen 15.2-4-49-5; Lugsden 8-1-45-2; Collingwood 4-0-13-0. *Second Innings*—Wood 28-3-81-2; Killeen 25-6-109-2; Collingwood 24-1-78-2; Lugsden 13-0-62-1; Searle 20.4-4-92-3.

Durham

J. J. B. Lewis not out	70	– lbw b Wasim Akram	0
J. E. Morris lbw b Wasim Akram	12	– b Wasim Akram	4
J. A. Daley b Wasim Akram	0	– w b Wasim Akram	13
*D. C. Boon c Flintoff b Wasim Akram	3	– lbw b Ridgway	20
P. D. Collingwood c Hegg b Ridgway	36	– b Wasim Akram	25
†A. Pratt c Hegg b Ridgway	0	– c Hegg b Chapple	34
J. Wood c Flintoff b Ridgway	10	– not out	8
N. Killeen b Chapple	12	– b Chapple	0
J. P. Searle lbw b Chapple	0	– lbw b Wasim Akram	0
S. Lugsden b Chapple	0	– b Chapple	0
N. J. Speak absent hurt		– absent hurt	
L-b 3, w 8, n-b 4	15	L-b 6, w 2, n-b 10	18
	158		**122**

1/25 2/29 3/35 4/107 5/107   1/0 2/4 3/26 4/42 5/102
6/121 7/148 8/152 9/158   6/116 7/116 8/119 9/122

Bonus points – Lancashire 4.

Bowling: *First Innings*—Wasim Akram 12–3–39–3; Chapple 10–0–37–3; Ridgway 10–1–51–3; Flintoff 4–0–17–0; Keedy 4–0–11–0. *Second Innings*—Wasim Akram 16–5–40–4; Chapple 12.4–3–26–4; Ridgway 8–1–32–1; Flintoff 4–1–12–0; Keedy 2–1–2–0; Yates 1–0–4–0.

Umpires: B. Dudleston and R. Julian.

At Derby, August 26, 27, 28, 29. DURHAM drew with DERBYSHIRE.

DURHAM v SURREY

At Chester-le-Street, September 9, 10, 11, 12. Surrey won by 121 runs. Surrey 20 pts, Durham 6 pts. Toss: Surrey.

Surrey had to win to stay in the title race: victory left them nine points behind Leicestershire as they headed for a showdown at The Oval. But there were some tricky negotiations after half the playing time was lost in the first three days. Surrey's bowling and fielding grew ragged as Morris progressed serenely from 32 to 126 in 40 overs on the third day, and Durham held the aces on the final morning. When play began, 55 minutes late, they batted on for one over and were donated a second batting point, guaranteeing their highest Championship finish, before declaring 70 behind. Surrey then plundered 142 from 15.4 overs of declaration bowling, in which Lewis claimed a maiden first-class wicket. Durham's target was 213 in 61 overs. But, after sweating under the covers, the pitch offered generous movement off the seam, which Benjamin exploited superbly. Durham collapsed from 20 without loss to 58 for nine as he grabbed six for 35 in 17 overs. Three of those fell to edged catches, two were lbw, while Roseberry was bowled by an absolute beauty.

Close of play: First day, Durham 32-0 (J. J. B. Lewis 6*, J. E. Morris 13*); Second day, Durham 72-1 (J. E. Morris 32*, M. J. Saggers 0*); Third day, Durham 231-3 (J. E. Morris 126*, J. A. Daley 18*).

Surrey

M. A. Butcher lbw b Wood	12	– st Speight b Lewis	60
A. J. Stewart c Boon b Saggers	17	– not out	63
N. Shahid c Boon b Harmison	20	– not out	16
B. C. Hollioake c Daley b Collingwood	34		
A. D. Brown c Speight b Wood	51		
*A. J. Hollioake c Speight b Wood	67		
†J. N. Batty b Wood	2		
M. P. Bicknell c Lewis b Phillips	39		
I. D. K. Salisbury c Collingwood b Harmison	20		
Saqlain Mushtaq not out	1		
J. E. Benjamin c Morris b Phillips	6		
B 4, l-b 12, w 8, n-b 30	54	L-b 1, n-b 2	3

1/20 2/54 3/74 4/156 5/168   323   1/88   (1 wkt dec.) 142
6/181 7/276 8/310 9/314

Bonus points – Surrey 3, Durham 4.

Bowling: *First Innings*—Wood 25–5–87–4; Harmison 15–2–89–2; Saggers 19–5–54–1; Collingwood 10–3–36–1; Phillips 12.1–1–41–2. *Second Innings*—Lewis 8–0–73–1; Boon 7.4–0–68–0.

Durham

J. J. B. Lewis c Batty b Benjamin	13	– lbw b Bicknell	10
J. E. Morris not out	140	– c Stewart b Benjamin	7
M. A. Roseberry b Butcher	8	– b Benjamin	9
M. J. Saggers c Batty b B. C. Hollioake	10	– (10) lbw b Benjamin	0
J. A. Daley not out	19	– (4) b Bicknell	0
*D. C. Boon (did not bat)		– (5) c Batty b Benjamin	10
†M. P. Speight (did not bat)		– (6) c Stewart b Benjamin	1
P. D. Collingwood (did not bat)		– (7) c A. J. Hollioake b Butcher	1
N. C. Phillips (did not bat)		– (8) lbw b Benjamin	3
J. Wood (did not bat)		– (9) b B. C. Hollioake	33
S. J. Harmison (did not bat)		– not out	6
B 12, l-b 8, w 2, n-b 41	63	L-b 7, n-b 4	11

1/51 2/129 3/169   (3 wkts dec.) 253   1/20 2/26 3/26 4/40 5/42   91
                                                 6/45 7/49 8/58 9/58

Bonus points – Durham 2, Surrey 1.

In the first innings M. A. Roseberry, when 3, retired hurt at 72 and resumed at 129.

Bowling: *First Innings*—Bicknell 20–6–54–0; B. C. Hollioake 10–2–45–1; Saqlain Mushtaq 4–1–12–0; Benjamin 10–1–46–1; A. J. Hollioake 7–3–18–0; Butcher 12–3–36–1; Batty 1–0–22–0. *Second Innings*—Bicknell 12–3–30–2; Benjamin 17–5–35–6; Butcher 7–1–11–1; B. C. Hollioake 1.5–0–8–1.

Umpires: D. J. Constant and G. Sharp.

At Worcester, September 17, 18, 19, 20. DURHAM lost to WORCESTERSHIRE by 155 runs.

DURHAM'S RECORD AGAINST EACH COUNTY IN THE CHAMPIONSHIP, 1992-98

	Played	Won	Lost	Drawn
Derbyshire	7	3	1	3
Essex	7	2	5	0
Glamorgan	8	3	3	2
Gloucestershire	7	1	3	3
Hampshire	7	1	0	6
Kent	8	1	5	2
Lancashire	7	0	6	1
Leicestershire	8	0	8	0
Middlesex	7	1	4	2
Northamptonshire	7	1	3	3
Nottinghamshire	7	2	2	3
Somerset	8	1	6	1
Surrey	7	0	7	0
Sussex	7	0	6	1
Warwickshire	7	1	3	3
Worcestershire	7	0	4	3
Yorkshire	7	0	6	1
Total	123	17	72	34

Notes: Durham played two fixtures each against Glamorgan, Hampshire, Kent, Leicestershire and Somerset in 1992, before the reduction of the County Championship.

Their match with Hampshire in 1997 was abandoned without a ball bowled.

Ronnie Irani

ESSEX

President: D. J. Insole
Chairman: D. L. Acfield
Chairman, Cricket Committee: G. J. Saville
Secretary/General Manager: P. J. Edwards
Captain: 1998 – P. J. Prichard
1999 – N. Hussain
Cricket Consultant: K. W. R. Fletcher
Head Groundsman: S. Kerrison
Scorer: C. F. Driver

A traumatic summer ended with Paul Prichard resigning the captaincy, after the county had finished bottom of the Championship for only the second time. Whether he was given a gentle shove was unclear. Rumours persisted that some senior players were dissatisfied with Prichard's leadership, although the public pronouncement that he wished to concentrate on rediscovering his form and fitness was valid.

Prichard missed seven Championship matches with shin splints, but when he could play scored only 237 runs at an average of 13.16 – horrendous statistics for someone of his talent. Yet he led from the front magnificently as Essex lifted the last Benson and Hedges Cup, crushing Leicestershire at Lord's in July. Prichard scored a superb 92 and was named man of the match.

From then onwards it was all downhill, and the season ended with six successive Championship defeats – the worst sequence in Essex history. The Cup win and third place in the Sunday League meant it was not a wholly disastrous summer. But these successes could not disguise glaring deficiencies and pathetic displays at four-day level – or, to be more precise, over three days. Essex were so lacking in belief and resilience that they failed to take any of their last five matches into the final day.

There were a number of reasons for the shambolic Championship showing. Injuries deprived them of several key players: Ashley Cowan, for example, played in only eight games because of a troublesome shoulder. Meanwhile, Nasser Hussain spent most of the summer on England duty. Essex lacked the strength in depth to compensate, though it would be unfair to blame the enforced introduction of inexperienced youngsters for the embarrassing performances. An accusing finger should be pointed at more senior players, the batsmen especially. Stuart Law left it until the final match, when he scored 165 against Northamptonshire, to produce the sort of form which destroyed attacks in his previous two seasons. His aggregate of 982 was exactly 500 down on 1997, but still represented a rich harvest compared with others.

Darren Robinson, who greeted the season with three successive one-day centuries, topped fifty only once in 13 Championship games, and averaged 17.87; Paul Grayson undercut that at 16.90. With Prichard also failing to contribute, it was small wonder that Essex went through the season without ever recording a maximum four batting points and finished with a pitiful total of 16. They lost 11 Championship matches, their worst showing since 1964, when they played 28 games not 17.

One player who stood out from the rest was Ronnie Irani, who consistently performed with an enthusiasm and determination conspicuous by its absence elsewhere. At least he looked purposeful rather than funereal when striding to the middle. Irani was the only Essex player to reach 1,000 first-class runs. Even so, he would have been disappointed not to have collected many more: he was dismissed in the thirties or forties 11 times. With the ball, too, Irani was a yard quicker than in 1997, and took 75 wickets in all cricket. Danny Law, whose high spot was a hat-trick against Durham in May, was more productive than in the previous year with both bat and ball, but his Championship form still fell short of expectations. Stephen Peters scored twin half-centuries against Nottinghamshire in June, but afterwards flattered to deceive. He was often a victim of his own impetuosity, and in his last 13 innings was out in single figures eight times, passing 30 only once.

With Cowan injured and Peter Such, like other spinners in 1998, toiling away on unhelpful pitches, it was seamer Mark Ilott who emerged as the leading wicket-taker by some distance. He had 56 Championship victims, and 93 in all cricket.

Several youngsters thrust into action discovered that there is a wide gulf between Second Eleven and first-class cricket. Among the more successful were left-handed batsman Ian Flanagan and fast bowler Jamie Grove, who marked his debut against Surrey by removing the Hollioake brothers, Adam and Ben, in the same over. But one of the major disappointments was the decline of Robert Rollins, regarded as one of the country's most promising wicket-keepers three summers earlier. Not only was his glovework often untidy, his batting lacked sparkle and conviction. A knee injury cost Rollins his place after eight matches, and he was unable to regain it when pronounced fit. That was because Barry Hyam seized his opportunity, proving less error-prone and more resolute with the bat.

Following Prichard's abdication, Hussain found himself at the helm. He is widely acknowledged to possess a shrewd tactical brain, but international calls were expected to keep him away for lengthy spells. With no vice-captain appointed, it was uncertain who would take over in Hussain's absence, though Stuart Law, who agreed to return for a fourth year, seemed a likely candidate. Several players were dispensed with, the most notable being Neil Williams, whose appearances since joining from Middlesex in 1995 had been intermittent. Others released were pace bowler Darren Cousins, all-rounder Danny Wilson and batsman Andrew Hibbert – a trio who rarely figured at senior level. – NIGEL FULLER.

476

ESSEX 1998

[Bill Smith]

Standing: J. Davis (*physiotherapist*), J. H. Childs (*Second Eleven coach*), R. J. Rollins, D. M. Cousins, D. R. Law, A. P. Cowan, N. F. Williams, D. D. J. Robinson, G. G. Arnold (*bowling coach*). *Seated:* P. M. Such, M. C. Ilott, N. Hussain, P. J. Prichard (*captain*), S. G. Law, R. C. Irani, A. P. Grayson, K. W. R. Fletcher (*cricket consultant*).

ESSEX RESULTS

All first-class matches – Played 18: Won 2, Lost 11, Drawn 5.

County Championship matches – Played 17: Won 2, Lost 11, Drawn 4.

Competition placings – Britannic Assurance County Championship, 18th; NatWest Trophy, 2nd round; Benson and Hedges Cup, winners; AXA League, 3rd.

COUNTY CHAMPIONSHIP AVERAGES
BATTING

Cap		M	I	NO	R	HS	100s	50s	Avge	Ct/St
1996	S. G. Law§	14	26	2	982	165	1	3	40.91	19
1994	R. C. Irani	17	32	2	968	127*	2	2	32.26	6
1989	N. Hussain	5	9	0	244	68	0	2	27.11	7
	I. N. Flanagan† . . .	5	10	0	248	61	0	2	24.80	9
	S. D. Peters†	13	23	2	484	64	0	3	23.04	7
1991	P. M. Such	15	24	17	133	25	0	0	19.00	5
	D. R. Law	14	25	0	466	65	0	3	18.64	10
	A. J. E. Hibbert† . . .	2	4	0	72	47	0	0	18.00	2
	B. J. Hyam†	9	18	3	269	47*	0	0	17.93	31/2
1996	N. F. Williams	8	15	6	161	36	0	0	17.88	2
1997	D. D. J. Robinson† .	13	24	0	429	85	0	1	17.87	11
1997	A. P. Cowan	8	13	0	228	94	0	0	17.53	4
1996	A. P. Grayson	16	30	0	507	59	0	4	16.90	9
	T. P. Hodgson	6	12	0	190	54	0	1	15.83	4
	J. O. Grove	4	7	1	88	33	0	0	14.66	0
1995	R. J. Rollins†	8	12	0	171	42	0	0	14.25	13
1986	P. J. Prichard†	10	18	0	237	24	0	0	13.16	7
1993	M. C. Ilott†	16	29	4	281	38	0	0	11.24	3

Also batted: D. M. Cousins (1 match) 8, 6; G. R. Napier† (2 matches) 4, 7, 4; D. G. Wilson† (1 match) 14, 14*.

* Signifies not out. † Born in Essex. § Overseas player.

BOWLING

	O	M	R	W	BB	5W/i	Avge
M. C. Ilott	486.5	131	1,293	56	6-20	2	23.08
N. F. Williams	227.5	45	763	26	4-42	0	29.34
R. C. Irani	431.5	102	1,348	40	5-47	1	33.70
D. R. Law	247.5	34	1,045	29	5-46	1	36.03
P. M. Such	503	129	1,398	38	5-73	2	36.78
A. P. Grayson	234.2	58	674	18	3-13	0	37.44
A. P. Cowan	238.3	54	859	19	3-18	0	45.21

Also bowled: D. M. Cousins 15–5–52–1; I. N. Flanagan 1–0–1–0; J. O. Grove 74.1–8–347–9; A. J. E. Hibbert 11.3–3–29–3; G. R. Napier 17–4–72–2; D. G. Wilson 10–2–38–1.

COUNTY RECORDS

Highest score for:	343*	P. A. Perrin v Derbyshire at Chesterfield	1904
Highest score against:	332	W. H. Ashdown (Kent) at Brentwood	1934
Best bowling for:	10-32	H. Pickett v Leicestershire at Leyton	1895
Best bowling against:	10-40	E. G. Dennett (Gloucestershire) at Bristol	1906
Highest total for:	761-6 dec.	v Leicestershire at Chelmsford	1990
Highest total against:	803-4 dec.	by Kent at Brentwood	1934
Lowest total for:	30	v Yorkshire at Leyton	1901
Lowest total against:	14	by Surrey at Chelmsford	1983

At Worcester, April 17, 18, 20, 21. ESSEX lost to WORCESTERSHIRE by six wickets.

ESSEX v SUSSEX

At Chelmsford, April 23, 24, 25, 27. Drawn. Essex 9 pts, Sussex 11 pts. Toss: Essex.

The Sussex captain Chris Adams became the third player in cricket history to score a century in each innings for two counties – following C. B. Fry of Sussex and Hampshire, and Alan Butcher of Surrey and Glamorgan. He had achieved the feat for Derbyshire in both 1995 and 1996. Having led his new county to victory in his opening match, Adams now dominated the Essex bowling with a succession of superbly timed drives. His first-innings 135 came from 196 deliveries and included 84 in boundaries, while he needed just 122 balls for his later 105, which contained four sixes and ten fours. At the start of the second day, Hussain assumed the Essex captaincy when Prichard was diagnosed as suffering from shin splints. Night-watchman Cowan and Robinson shared the batting honours before Essex fell 70 runs adrift on first innings. But frequent interruptions for bad light and rain prevented the match developing into a contest.

Close of play: First day, Sussex 186-4 (C. J. Adams 86*, K. Newell 2*); Second day, Essex 49-1 (D. D. J. Robinson 22*, A. P. Cowan 7*); Third day, Sussex 7-1 (M. T. E. Peirce 4*, C. J. Adams 3*).

Sussex

N. R. Taylor lbw b Irani	35			
M. T. E. Peirce c Law b Napier	20	– c Hussain b Irani		45
*C. J. Adams c Hussain b Irani	135	– b Irani		105
J. R. Carpenter b Such	19	– lbw b Irani		9
R. K. Rao c Rollins b Grayson	12	– (1) lbw b Cowan		0
K. Newell b Williams	13	– (5) not out		1
†P. Moores b Such	36	– (6) not out		0
P. W. Jarvis c sub b Williams	39			
A. A. Khan c Rollins b Napier	5			
R. J. Kirtley not out	12			
J. D. Lewry c Hussain b Cowan	18			
B 4, l-b 7, n-b 14	25	B 4, l-b 3, n-b 6		13

1/52 2/60 3/130 4/172 5/231   369   1/4 2/135 3/168 4/173   (4 wkts) 173
6/254 7/294 8/303 9/334

Bonus points – Sussex 4, Essex 4.

Bowling: *First Innings*—Cowan 21.4–6–67–1; Williams 22–7–71–2; Napier 14–3–59–2; Irani 23–7–66–2; Such 23–6–81–2; Grayson 9–4–14–1. *Second Innings*—Cowan 6–2–32–1; Williams 10–1–38–0; Napier 3–1–13–0; Such 5–0–33–0; Irani 11–2–24–3; Grayson 10–2–26–0.

Essex

D. D. J. Robinson c Kirtley b Jarvis	85	N. F. Williams lbw b Jarvis		0
A. P. Grayson lbw b Jarvis	17	*P. J. Prichard b Newell		15
A. P. Cowan b Khan	66	P. M. Such not out		6
N. Hussain c Moores b Khan	1			
S. G. Law c Jarvis b Newell	43	B 1, l-b 7, n-b 6		14
R. C. Irani c Khan b Newell	47			
†R. J. Rollins c Moores b Kirtley	1	1/39 2/154 3/166 4/224 5/224		299
G. R. Napier lbw b Kirtley	4	6/237 7/247 8/248 9/276		

Bonus points – Essex 2, Sussex 4.

Bowling: Kirtley 25–5–90–2; Jarvis 20–1–67–3; Khan 20–4–69–2; Lewry 9–2–42–0; Newell 8.4–1–23–3.

Umpires: J. H. Harris and R. Palmer.

At Chester-le-Street, May 13, 14, 15, 16. ESSEX lost to DURHAM by 95 runs.

ESSEX v LANCASHIRE

At Chelmsford, May 21, 22, 23, 24. Lancashire won by seven wickets. Lancashire 23 pts, Essex 5 pts. Toss: Lancashire. Championship debut: A. J. E. Hibbert.

Lancashire secured a comfortable win – their first of the season – within an hour on the final morning. Fittingly, Chapple, who had set them on the road with five wickets and three catches in the first innings, was there at the end. The pattern for Essex's injury-stricken season was set when they went into the match with five uncapped players. But Lancashire were without Martin and Austin, and the rawest Essex recruit, 23-year-old Andrew Hibbert, had no trouble translating some of his Second Eleven form into county cricket. After losing three quick wickets on a cloudy second morning, Lancashire raced ahead when the sun came out, thanks to a dazzling innings by Fairbrother, who hit 20 fours, mostly off the back foot through the off side, in 227 balls. Teenagers Flanagan and Peters confirmed their promise in the Essex second innings, but it was another Lancashire old-stager, Watkinson, who worked his way through the batting, and gave his team a straightforward target.

Close of play: First day, Lancashire 36-0 (N. T. Wood 13*, M. A. Atherton 16*); Second day, Essex 48-0 (D. D. J. Robinson 17*, I. N. Flanagan 24*); Third day, Lancashire 107-3 (J. P. Crawley 23*, G. Chapple 0*).

Essex

D. D. J. Robinson lbw b Chapple	32	– c sub b Chapple	26
I. N. Flanagan lbw b Chapple	0	– lbw b Watkinson	44
S. D. Peters c Flintoff b Chapple	0	– c sub b Chapple	45
*S. G. Law c Watkinson b Flintoff	55	– c Hegg b Green	49
R. C. Irani b Chapple	4	– c Hegg b Chapple	2
A. J. E. Hibbert c Chapple b Watkinson	47	– b Watkinson	6
†R. J. Rollins c Hegg b Chapple	23	– lbw b Watkinson	4
D. R. Law c Chapple b Shadford	13	– st Hegg b Watkinson	17
M. C. Ilott c Chapple b Watkinson	24	– b Flintoff	14
N. F. Williams not out	11	– not out	5
D. M. Cousins b Wasim Akram	8	– b Watkinson	6
B 2, l-b 15, n-b 8	25	B 9, l-b 9, w 8	26
	242		**244**

1/0 2/0 3/91 4/99 5/99   1/67 2/118 3/167 4/169 5/193
6/139 7/160 8/221 9/222   6/195 7/200 8/227 9/237

Bonus points – Essex 1, Lancashire 4.

Bowling: *First Innings*—Wasim Akram 16.5–2–49–1; Chapple 18–2–49–5; Shadford 18–1–56–1; Green 14–4–41–0; Flintoff 8–3–18–1; Watkinson 7–3–12–2. *Second Innings*—Wasim Akram 7.1–2–21–0; Chapple 20–5–59–3; Shadford 12.5–3–34–0; Watkinson 24.5–6–45–5; Green 21–7–57–1; Flintoff 4–0–10–1.

Lancashire

N. T. Wood c Rollins b Ilott	14	– c Irani b Williams	32
M. A. Atherton c Rollins b Ilott	20	– c Rollins b Williams	13
J. P. Crawley b Irani	1	– not out	64
N. H. Fairbrother c Flanagan b Williams	126		
A. Flintoff c Flanagan b Cousins	29	– (4) c Williams b Ilott	37
M. Watkinson c Robinson b D. R. Law	40		
*Wasim Akram lbw b D. R. Law	0		
†W. K. Hegg c Hibbert b D. R. Law	0		
G. Chapple c Flanagan b D. R. Law	31	– (5) not out	23
R. J. Green b Ilott	14		
D. J. Shadford not out	13		
L-b 8, w 12, n-b 6	26	B 1, l-b 1, n-b 4	6
	314		**(3 wkts) 175**

1/40 2/41 3/43 4/100 5/179   1/34 2/57 3/106
6/181 7/181 8/284 9/284

Bonus points – Lancashire 3, Essex 4.

Bowling: *First Innings*—Ilott 23.4–8–49–3; Williams 20–5–58–1; Cousins 15–5–52–1; Irani 22–6–64–1; D. R. Law 22–6–70–4; Hibbert 5–1–13–0. *Second Innings*—Ilott 14–7–37–1; D. R. Law 9–2–56–0; Williams 10–2–50–2; Irani 6.1–1–29–0; Flanagan 1–0–1–0.

Umpires: J. W. Lloyds and R. A. White.

ESSEX v NOTTINGHAMSHIRE

At Ilford, June 3, 4, 5, 6. Drawn. Essex 10 pts, Nottinghamshire 9 pts. Toss: Nottinghamshire.

An unbeaten half-century from 19-year-old Peters, his second of the match, guided Essex to safety. They were unable to make any impression on a target of 300 in 74 overs and, once Stuart Law was out, their only ambition was a draw. Johnson, returning after a shoulder injury, dominated the early stages, but fell five short of his century to a magnificent diving catch by Irani, racing from third man to backward point. Despite a terrible start in which they lost two wickets in Franks's second over, Essex came close to first-innings equality thanks to Law's first hundred of the summer. He was assisted by Flanagan, who hit a maiden fifty on the eve of his 18th birthday. At tea on the third day, the Nottinghamshire second innings was delayed for half an hour when an 85-year-old spectator suffered a suspected stroke. The ambulance had to be escorted round the square to park on the outfield. Archer then hit a sharp 69 to prepare for the declaration; he had caused an earlier medical alert by hitting a spectator on the head with a first-innings six. Law took six catches in the match, all at slip.

Close of play: First day, Nottinghamshire 288-7 (C. M. W. Read 12*, P. A. Strang 2*); Second day, Essex 230-7 (S. D. Peters 20*); Third day, Nottinghamshire 173-4 (G. F. Archer 60*, N. A. Gie 16*).

Nottinghamshire

M. P. Dowman c Robinson b Ilott	48	– lbw b Irani	12
R. T. Robinson c S. G. Law b Ilott	3	– c and b Such	54
U. Afzaal c S. G. Law b Irani	31	– c S. G. Law b Such	4
*P. Johnson c Irani b Ilott	95	– c and b Such	17
G. F. Archer c S. G. Law b Cowan	63	– c S. G. Law b Ilott	69
N. A. Gie b Such	12	– lbw b Cowan	18
P. J. Franks c Rollins b Such	3	– c Cowan b Such	34
†C. M. W. Read b Ilott	27	– c Flanagan b Irani	28
P. A. Strang c Rollins b Irani	30	– c Cowan b Such	14
M. N. Bowen c S. G. Law b Irani	0	– not out	8
A. R. Oram not out	2	– not out	0
B 4, l-b 10, w 12, n-b 2	28	B 1, l-b 8, n-b 12	21

1/5 2/78 3/106 4/226 5/259   **342**   1/22 2/51 3/71   (9 wkts dec.) **279**
6/269 7/276 8/318 9/318   4/124 5/180 6/198
                                               7/252 8/271 9/271

Bonus points – Nottinghamshire 3, Essex 4.

Bowling: *First Innings*—Ilott 21.1–5–62–4; Cowan 28–9–73–1; D. R. Law 10–2–42–0; Irani 22–8–66–3; Such 23–5–70–2; Grayson 6–3–15–0. *Second Innings*—Ilott 18–6–33–1; Cowan 15–5–70–1; Irani 10–1–50–2; Such 32–11–73–5; Grayson 9.2–1–44–0.

Essex

D. D. J. Robinson lbw b Franks	3	– c Strang b Oram	0
I. N. Flanagan c and b Strang	57	– c Robinson b Strang	33
A. P. Grayson c Archer b Franks	0	– c Read b Oram	3
*S. G. Law c Franks b Afzaal	106	– lbw b Bowen	22
R. C. Irani c Read b Bowen	7	– c Archer b Franks	27
S. D. Peters c Archer b Oram	64	– not out	53
†R. J. Rollins c Johnson b Oram	12	– c Dowman b Strang	13
D. R. Law b Franks	19	– c Gie b Bowen	22
A. P. Cowan c Read b Oram	1	– c Robinson b Strang	1
M. C. Ilott c Read b Dowman	38	– not out	0
P. M. Such not out	3		
L-b 10, n-b 2	12	B 9, l-b 15	24

1/5 2/5 3/157 4/173 5/181	322	1/14 2/34 3/70 (8 wkts) 198
6/206 7/230 8/233 9/316		4/70 5/125 6/148
		7/196 8/197

Bonus points – Essex 3, Nottinghamshire 3 (Score at 120 overs: 306-8).

Bowling: *First Innings*—Bowen 27-9-71-1; Franks 26-10-57-3; Oram 29-8-89-3; Strang 36-13-84-1; Afzaal 5-2-11-1; Dowman 1-1-0-1. *Second Innings*—Oram 13.5-5-27-2; Franks 14-3-61-1; Strang 28-14-41-3; Bowen 11-3-28-2; Afzaal 5.5-1-11-0; Dowman 2-0-6-0.

Umpires: A. Clarkson and R. Palmer.

ESSEX v SURREY

At Chelmsford, June 11, 12, 13, 15. Drawn. Essex 8 pts, Surrey 11 pts. Toss: Essex. First-class debut: J. O. Grove.

Rain, which curtailed the final day by around three hours, rescued Essex as they struggled to avoid an innings defeat. When play resumed, Surrey had 73 balls to take the last six wickets, but they called off the attempt after five overs without a breakthrough. The brittleness of the Essex batting was clearly exposed in their first innings, and it fell to 18-year-old Jamie Grove, hitting the joint top score on his debut, to steer them to a solitary batting point, still 170 in arrears. But he had been selected as a fast bowler, and he showed promise, pace and some good fortune to capture three wickets, including both Hollioakes within three balls. The middle order had put Surrey back in control after a poor start, and last man Saqlain Mushtaq took full advantage of a tired and wayward attack to plunder an undefeated 45 from 40 balls – his highest innings for Surrey. The draw left the two counties where they started: at opposite ends of the table. Umpire Kitchen caused a stir on the first morning by sternly enforcing a new ECB regulation instructing that "the strict limited-over wide interpretation" should be applied when bowlers used leg-side bowling as a negative tactic. He called two wides against Grayson, brought on to bowl slow left-arm over-the-wicket at a time when Surrey had been racing along.

Close of play: First day, Surrey 127-4 (A. D. Brown 17*, A. J. Hollioake 27*); Second day, Essex 120-6 (S. D. Peters 7*, D. R. Law 9*); Third day, Essex 151-8 (S. D. Peters 21*, J. O. Grove 2*).

Surrey

M. A. Butcher b Ilott	1	A. J. Tudor c Robinson b Grayson	17
J. D. Ratcliffe b D. R. Law	25	M. P. Bicknell b Grove	13
A. J. Stewart lbw b Ilott	20	Saqlain Mushtaq not out	45
G. P. Thorpe b D. R. Law	14	B 4, l-b 20, w 6, n-b 16	46
A. D. Brown lbw b Ilott	79		
*A. J. Hollioake c Irani b Grove	59	1/5 2/35 3/59	373
B. C. Hollioake c Such b Grove	2	4/66 5/197 6/199	
†J. N. Batty c Grayson b Ilott	52	7/248 8/288 9/310	

Bonus points – Surrey 4, Essex 4.

Bowling: Grove 14-1-74-3; Ilott 21.5-3-64-4; D. R. Law 17-1-91-2; Irani 15-2-72-0; Grayson 11-3-30-1; Such 9-0-18-0.

Essex

D. D. J. Robinson c Stewart b Bicknell	23	– c Butcher b Bicknell	5
A. P. Grayson c Saqlain Mushtaq b Tudor	8	– b Bicknell	1
*N. Hussain c Brown b B. C. Hollioake	25	– b Bicknell	0
S. G. Law c Ratcliffe b B. C. Hollioake	31	– not out	29
R. C. Irani c Stewart b B. C. Hollioake	0	– c Butcher b Tudor	13
S. D. Peters lbw b Saqlain Mushtaq	33	– not out	17
†R. J. Rollins lbw b Saqlain Mushtaq	1		
D. R. Law c Batty b Bicknell	9		
M. C. Ilott c Stewart b Bicknell	5		
J. O. Grove b Tudor	33		
P. M. Such not out	1		
B 4, l-b 6, w 2, n-b 22	34	B 2, w 2, n-b 6	10

1/16 2/48 3/84 4/86 5/99   203   1/5 2/5 3/26 4/49   (4 wkts) 75
6/102 7/123 8/149 9/171

Bonus points – Essex 1, Surrey 4.

Bowling: *First Innings*—Bicknell 24–6–68–3; Tudor 12.3–2–49–2; B. C. Hollioake 10–2–21–3; Saqlain Mushtaq 19–5–42–2; Butcher 4–1–13–0. *Second Innings*—Bicknell 11–3–26–3; Tudor 10–0–47–1.

Umpires: M. J. Kitchen and B. Leadbeater.

At Bath, June 17, 18, 19, 20. ESSEX beat SOMERSET by one wicket.

At Southgate, June 26, 27, 28, 29. ESSEX drew with MIDDLESEX.

At Derby, July 1, 2, 3. ESSEX lost to DERBYSHIRE by 181 runs.

ESSEX v KENT

At Southend, July 15, 16, 17, 18. Kent won by two wickets. Kent 23 pts, Essex 5 pts. Toss: Essex.

Essex, fresh from victory in the Benson and Hedges Cup final, were left to reflect on the deficiencies of their batsmen at the four-day game as they suffered their fifth Championship defeat of the season. Their leading strokeplayers all perished in the forties when looking well set. Hooper, by contrast, overcame a slow pitch to record his fourth Championship century against Essex in as many matches, playing with a freedom alien to the other batsmen. A second inept batting display by Essex left the modest target of 155 for Kent, who contrived to make heavy weather of it. Fulton, however, demonstrating the value of concentration with his second fifty of the match, did enough for Kent to limp home.

Close of play: First day, Kent 8-0 (D. P. Fulton 5*, R. W. T. Key 3*); Second day, Kent 313-7 (M. V. Fleming 35*, D. W. Headley 0*); Third day, Essex 223.

Essex

*P. J. Prichard lbw b McCague	15	– c Key b McCague	7
A. P. Grayson lbw b Ealham	6	– c Fleming b Ealham	6
N. Hussain c Hooper b Fleming	48	– lbw b Ealham	12
S. G. Law c Marsh b Fleming	47	– lbw b Fleming	38
R. C. Irani c Hooper b Patel	47	– c Hooper b Ealham	2
S. D. Peters c Ward b Hooper	9	– b Fleming	19
D. R. Law c Hooper b Ealham	18	– lbw b Ealham	52
†B. J. Hyam not out	47	– b Ealham	25
M. C. Ilott c Fulton b McCague	15	– b McCague	3
N. F. Williams c Marsh b Patel	2	– c Key b Fleming	36
P. M. Such c Key b McCague	25	– not out	9
B 6, l-b 4, n-b 6	16	B 4, l-b 10	14

1/23 2/27 3/113 4/134 5/163   295   1/7 2/21 3/34 4/38 5/82   223
6/196 7/206 8/231 9/248   6/87 7/159 8/168 9/188

Bonus points – Essex 2, Kent 4.

Bowling: *First Innings*—Headley 17–2–53–0; McCague 18.2–5–78–3; Ealham 15–4–42–2; Patel 20–5–42–2; Fleming 14–5–30–2; Hooper 10–2–40–1. *Second Innings*—Headley 16–3–36–0; McCague 13–1–33–2; Ealham 24–9–45–5; Patel 17–4–56–0; Fleming 10.3–2–28–3; Hooper 4–0–11–0.

Kent

D. P. Fulton c Hyam b Williams	50	– st Hyam b Such	59
R. W. T. Key c Hyam b Ilott	6	– lbw b Ilott	5
T. R. Ward c S. G. Law b Such	32	– c S. G. Law b Irani	7
C. L. Hooper c Peters b Grayson	100	– c Prichard b Such	9
A. P. Wells c Irani b Such	30	– (8) lbw b Grayson	20
M. A. Ealham b Williams	28	– (5) c Hussain b Irani	8
M. V. Fleming c Prichard b Ilott	44	– (6) b Such	15
*†S. A. Marsh b Ilott	9	– (7) c Grayson b Ilott	16
D. W. Headley b Such	24	– not out	2
M. M. Patel lbw b Ilott	0		
M. J. McCague not out	16	– (10) not out	6
B 4, l-b 9, n-b 12	25	B 2, l-b 4, n-b 2	8

1/17 2/80 3/125 4/201 5/241   364   1/13 2/25 3/50 4/65   (8 wkts) 155
6/288 7/311 8/329 9/344   5/88 6/113 7/145 8/147

Bonus points – Kent 3, Essex 3 (Score at 120 overs: 335-8).

Bowling: *First Innings*—Ilott 35–9–91–4; Williams 27–4–67–2; Irani 15–6–30–0; Such 29.1–10–101–3; D. R. Law 7–0–38–0; Grayson 14–6–24–1. *Second Innings*—Ilott 13–4–28–2; Williams 2–0–6–0; Such 26–8–67–3; Irani 7–0–24–2; Grayson 8.4–2–24–1.

Umpires: G. I. Burgess and R. A. White.

At Birmingham, July 23, 24, 25. ESSEX beat WARWICKSHIRE by two wickets.

At Chelmsford, July 29. ESSEX lost to SOUTH AFRICANS by 177 runs (See South African tour section).

At Chelmsford, July 31, August 1, 2. ESSEX drew with SOUTH AFRICANS (See South African tour section).

ESSEX v GLAMORGAN

At Chelmsford, August 5, 6, 7, 8. Glamorgan won by 216 runs. Glamorgan 22 pts, Essex 6 pts. Toss: Glamorgan.

A below-strength Essex were swept away with embarrassing ease. After an even first innings, Glamorgan took command on the third day, when James and Dale put on 169, with James scoring a polished 147. This confirmed the friendly nature of the pitch and left Essex to score exactly 400. They failed to get even halfway against a varied six-man attack, all of whom got at least one wicket. The game had started with a robust run-a-ball 68 from 19-year-old Wayne Law. With Dale, he gave Glamorgan a solid start, but the middle order fell away against Such. Then Irani, playing despite a cracked finger, was able to help Grayson lead Essex temporarily back into the contest.

Close of play: First day, Essex 23-1 (D. D. J. Robinson 10*, T. P. Hodgson 4*); Second day, Glamorgan 20-1 (S. P. James 12*, D. A. Cosker 0*); Third day, Essex 41-2 (D. D. J. Robinson 18*, M. C. Ilott 1*).

Glamorgan

S. P. James c Hyam b Williams	11	– b Grayson	147
W. L. Law b Such	68	– c Hyam b Williams	8
A. Dale c Hyam b Williams	73	– (4) c Hodgson b Williams	82
*M. P. Maynard c Robinson b Such	30	– (5) c Flanagan b Grayson	29
P. A. Cottey c Grayson b Such	2	– (6) not out	38
R. D. B. Croft c Flanagan b Such	4		
†I. Dawood c Flanagan b Williams	6	– not out	9
S. D. Thomas c Law b Williams	6		
A. P. Davies c Williams b Such	34		
D. A. Cosker c Hodgson b Law	7	– (3) b Grayson	37
O. T. Parkin not out	24		
B 2, l-b 9, w 4, n-b 8	23	B 1, l-b 3, w 8, n-b 9	21

1/21 2/106 3/172 4/174 5/200   288   1/13 2/121 3/290 (5 wkts dec.) 371
6/202 7/211 8/214 9/230   4/294 5/341

Bonus points – Glamorgan 2, Essex 4.

Bowling: *First Innings*—Ilott 10–2–30–0; Williams 13–3–42–4; Irani 15–2–59–0; Such 39.2–12–110–5; Law 14–3–36–1. *Second Innings*—Williams 17–0–77–2; Irani 19–1–74–0; Such 25–1–90–0; Ilott 9–2–28–0; Grayson 16–0–69–3; Law 5–0–29–0.

Essex

D. D. J. Robinson lbw b Parkin	14	– c Dale b Davies	24
I. N. Flanagan lbw b Parkin	5	– c Dawood b Parkin	0
T. P. Hodgson c James b Cosker	35	– c Maynard b Thomas	17
R. C. Irani c Cosker b Croft	51	– (5) c sub b Cosker	31
*A. P. Grayson c and b Cosker	59	– (6) c Maynard b Croft	3
S. D. Peters c Cottey b Davies	20	– (7) c Maynard b Cosker	47
D. R. Law c Croft b Davies	0	– (8) lbw b Dale	0
†B. J. Hyam c Dawood b Thomas	5	– (9) c Croft b Thomas	11
M. C. Ilott c Thomas b Cosker	22	– (4) b Dale	13
N. F. Williams c Parkin b Thomas	13	– lbw b Davies	25
P. M. Such not out	2	– not out	3
B 11, l-b 7, w 4, n-b 2	24	B 2, l-b 3, w 2, n-b 2	9

1/7 2/34 3/114 4/126 5/164   260   1/1 2/38 3/49 4/91 5/96   183
6/164 7/204 8/241 9/244   6/97 7/97 8/112 9/167

Bonus points – Essex 2, Glamorgan 4.

Bowling: *First Innings*—Parkin 15–4–29–2; Thomas 13.5–2–44–2; Croft 34–8–84–1; Davies 12–6–25–2; Cosker 37–13–60–3. *Second Innings*—Parkin 10–4–27–1; Davies 12–4–28–2; Thomas 18–9–38–2; Croft 23–7–37–1; Cosker 19.4–9–31–2; Dale 9–3–17–2.

Umpires: G. I. Burgess and J. H. Hampshire.

At Portsmouth, August 14, 15, 16. ESSEX lost to HAMPSHIRE by an innings and 111 runs.

ESSEX v GLOUCESTERSHIRE

At Colchester, August 19, 20, 21. Gloucestershire won by an innings and 281 runs. Gloucestershire 24 pts, Essex 2 pts. Toss: Gloucestershire.

On the ground where Essex have won so many vital Championship games over the past two decades, they succumbed to a humiliating defeat. It was Gloucestershire's biggest-ever innings victory (surpassing an innings and 268 against Somerset in 1885), and Essex's third-heaviest defeat. The only worse matches in their history were very famous ones: when the Australians scored 721 against them in 1948 (lost by an innings and 451) and when Holmes and Sutcliffe put on their record 555 for Yorkshire in 1932 (an innings and 313). For Essex, this one will simply be best forgotten. They surrendered meekly on a pitch giving the bowlers minimal help. First Gloucestershire made their highest score against them, 564, with 135 from Hancock and 151 from Windows, his fourth century of a productive summer. Hancock followed with a telling intervention as a bowler, taking three wickets in a three-over spell, after Walsh and Smith had, unusually, gone wicketless. Essex followed on 388 behind, and off-spinner Ball opened the bowling. This time Walsh, bowling second change, did join in and, along with Hancock, they sent Essex crashing just after lunch on the third day.

Close of play: First day, Gloucestershire 401-5 (M. G. N. Windows 69*, R. C. Russell 6*); Second day, Essex 16-0 (D. D. J. Robinson 9*, I. N. Flanagan 4*).

Gloucestershire

R. J. Cunliffe c Hyam b Grove	7	J. Lewis c Flanagan b Such	4
T. H. C. Hancock c and b Law	135	A. M. Smith not out	6
D. R. Hewson c Hyam b Grove	44	C. A. Walsh c Robinson b Such	7
*M. W. Alleyne c Peters b Law	47		
M. G. N. Windows c Law b Grayson	151	B 15, l-b 18, w 2, n-b 22	57
R. I. Dawson b Ilott	46		—
†R. C. Russell c Ilott b Law	28	1/21 2/144 3/253 4/258 5/382	564
M. C. J. Ball c Hodgson b Grayson	32	6/448 7/536 8/546 9/552	

Bonus points – Gloucestershire 4, Essex 2 (Score at 120 overs: 474-6).

Bowling: Ilott 22-1-81-1; Grove 27-4-119-2; Irani 16-5-39-0; Law 17-0-77-3; Such 48.4-7-168-2; Grayson 15-4-47-2.

Essex

D. D. J. Robinson c Alleyne b Lewis	16	– lbw b Walsh	40
I. N. Flanagan c Ball b Hancock	29	– c Dawson b Walsh	6
T. P. Hodgson c Russell b Lewis	5	– c Russell b Hancock	4
R. C. Irani c Ball b Lewis	36	– c and b Hancock	1
*A. P. Grayson b Hancock	0	– b Ball	28
S. D. Peters c Walsh b Hancock	1	– b Ball	3
D. R. Law c Alleyne b Ball	3	– c Cunliffe b Ball	0
†B. J. Hyam c Alleyne b Ball	33	– c Windows b Walsh	3
M. C. Ilott not out	35	– c Walsh b Ball	3
J. O. Grove lbw b Dawson	3	– c Windows b Walsh	1
P. M. Such b Dawson	8	– not out	0
L-b 3, w 2, n-b 2	7	B 5, l-b 1, n-b 12	18
1/21 2/37 3/61 4/61 5/67	176	1/19 2/28 3/34 4/79 5/85	107
6/70 7/106 8/157 9/166		6/85 7/92 8/101 9/107	

Bonus points – Gloucestershire 4.

Bowling: *First Innings*—Walsh 11-2-40-0; Smith 9-2-14-0; Lewis 11-1-51-3; Ball 13-4-29-2; Hancock 3-1-5-3; Dawson 5.4-0-34-2. *Second Innings*—Ball 11.1-4-26-4; Dawson 2-0-7-0; Smith 7-5-9-0; Walsh 12-4-18-4; Hancock 9-4-24-2; Lewis 5-0-17-0.

Umpires: A. Clarkson and M. J. Kitchen.

At Scarborough, August 26, 27, 28. ESSEX lost to YORKSHIRE by one wicket.

At Leicester, September 9, 10, 11. ESSEX lost to LEICESTERSHIRE by an innings and 99 runs.

ESSEX v NORTHAMPTONSHIRE

At Chelmsford, September 17, 18, 19. Northamptonshire won by seven wickets. Northamptonshire 22 pts, Essex 6 pts. Toss: Northamptonshire.

Essex took the wooden spoon for only the second time – the first was in 1950 – after their sixth consecutive defeat, and their fifth inside three days. This was their longest-ever losing sequence; they had been beaten five times in a row on seven occasions, most recently in 1964. Northamptonshire's victory spared them the possible indignity of finishing bottom themselves after they were docked 25 points for an unsuitable pitch against Sussex. It looked a serious possibility during the first five sessions. Law produced his highest score of the season: his 165, with 21 fours and a six, kept Essex afloat on the first day, during which Peters suffered a fractured cheekbone when struck by a ball from Rose. Next day, the bowlers gave Essex their first first-innings lead of 1998. But that evening, Essex collapsed to 50 for five – effectively six, because of Peters. Taylor did the damage in a devastating spell of four for two in 14 deliveries. Malcolm mopped up in the morning to leave Northamptonshire a simple target of 117. As the players left the field, several of the Essex team applauded the members, thanking them for their continued patience.

Close of play: First day, Northamptonshire 57-1 (R. J. Bailey 9*, A. L. Penberthy 35*); Second day, Essex 50-5 (B. J. Hyam 9*, M. C. Ilott 0*).

Essex

*P. J. Prichard b Taylor	5	– c Curran b Taylor	11
S. D. Peters c Sales b G. P. Swann	19	– absent hurt	
T. P. Hodgson c G. P. Swann b Rose	1	– (2) c Curran b Taylor	9
S. G. Law c Curran b Rose	165	– (3) c T. M. B. Bailey b Taylor	2
R. C. Irani b Malcolm	11	– (4) c Sales b Brown	16
A. P. Grayson c G. P. Swann b Brown	46	– (5) lbw b Taylor	0
†B. J. Hyam c Sales b G. P. Swann	0	– (6) c A. J. Swann b Malcolm	12
M. C. Ilott c Curran b G. P. Swann	3	– (7) c G. P. Swann b Malcolm	8
A. P. Cowan b G. P. Swann	1	– (8) c T. M. B. Bailey b Malcolm	3
J. O. Grove c sub b Rose	14	– (9) not out	25
P. M. Such not out	2	– (10) c sub b Malcolm	0
B 4, l-b 2, n-b 10	16	B 5, l-b 2, n-b 2	9

1/7 2/12 3/77 4/191 5/192　　　　　　283　　1/18 2/21 3/32 4/32 5/50　　　　95
6/204 7/206 8/218 9/271　　　　　　　　　　6/55 7/62 8/81 9/95

Bonus points – Essex 2, Northamptonshire 4.

In the first innings S. D. Peters, when 19, retired hurt at 49 and resumed at 206.

Bowling: *First Innings*—Rose 14.3–1–50–3; Taylor 14–2–58–1; Malcolm 12–0–63–1; Penberthy 7–3–15–0; Brown 19–6–44–1; G. P. Swann 16–1–47–4. *Second Innings*—Malcolm 15.2–1–48–4; Taylor 16–5–31–4; Brown 5–2–4–1; G. P. Swann 4–1–5–0.

Northamptonshire

R. J. Bailey c Hyam b Ilott	19	– c sub b Such	46
A. J. Swann b Cowan	0	– st Hyam b Such	40
A. L. Penberthy lbw b Grove	50	– c Ilott b Such	15
*K. M. Curran lbw b Ilott	0	– not out	9
D. J. Sales c Prichard b Cowan	53	– not out	0
G. P. Swann c sub b Such	20		
†T. M. B. Bailey c Hyam b Such	12		
J. P. Taylor run out	58		
F. A. Rose c Cowan b Such	2		
J. F. Brown not out	4		
D. E. Malcolm b Cowan	8		
B 12, l-b 4, w 2, n-b 18	36	B 2, l-b 4, n-b 4	10

1/6 2/78 3/82 4/82 5/156   262   1/70 2/111 3/112   (3 wkts) 120
6/170 7/230 8/234 9/253

Bonus points – Northamptonshire 2, Essex 4.

Bowling: *First Innings*—Ilott 17–6–41–2; Cowan 22–7–57–3; Irani 13–4–34–0; Such 34–13–53–3; Grayson 1–0–2–0; Grove 10–2–59–1. *Second Innings*—Ilott 5–1–19–0; Cowan 11–1–37–0; Irani 3–1–10–0; Such 10–0–29–3; Grove 5.4–0–19–0.

Umpires: B. Dudleston and G. Sharp.

BIGGEST FALLS IN THE COUNTY CHAMPIONSHIP

15 places	Gloucestershire	second to 17th	1970
	Glamorgan	third to 18th	1994
14 places	Glamorgan	second to 16th	1971
	Middlesex	first to 15th	1991
13 places	Middlesex	first equal to 14th	1950
	Leicestershire	third equal to 16th	1954
	Kent	second to 15th	1989
	Worcestershire	second to 15th	1994
	Northamptonshire	third to 16th	1996
	Middlesex	fourth to 17th	1998

COUNTY BENEFITS AWARDED FOR 1999

Durham	J. E. Morris.		Northamptonshire	K. M. Curran.
Essex	N. Hussain.		Nottinghamshire	M. Newell.
Gloucestershire	M. W. Alleyne.		Somerset	A. R. Caddick.
Hampshire	K. D. James.		Surrey	D. J. Bicknell.
Kent	T. R. Ward.		Sussex	N. J. Lenham.
Lancashire	W. K. Hegg.		Warwickshire	A. A. Donald.
Leicestershire	D. J. Millns.		Worcestershire	G. A. Hick.
Middlesex	P. C. R. Tufnell.			

No benefit was awarded by Derbyshire, Glamorgan or Yorkshire.

GLAMORGAN

Michael Powell

Patron: HRH The Prince of Wales
President: G. Craven
Chairman: G. Elias, QC
Chairman, Cricket Committee: H. D. Davies
Secretary: M. J. Fatkin
Captain: M. P. Maynard
First Eleven Coach: 1998 – J. Derrick
                          1999 – D. A. G. Fletcher
Grounds Supervisor: L. A. Smith
Scorer: B. T. Denning

Few counties could have suffered quite as much from injuries in one season as Glamorgan did in 1998, and it was scarcely surprising that they were unable to sustain a challenge for the Championship they won the previous year. After relying on only 14 players in 1997, Glamorgan were without Waqar Younis for all but four Championship games, and were forced to use nine different opening combinations, three wicket-keepers and, on occasion, six uncapped players.

They had known they would be without Hugh Morris, who had retired at the end of the previous summer, but to lose Waqar, who bowled barely 100 Championship overs, was a huge blow. He was suffering from a degenerative condition of the elbow, and returned home disappointed and dejected at not fulfilling his two-year contract. Matthew Maynard was out for a month with a groin injury, Steve Watkin missed five Championship games, and Robert Croft played only nine, due to Test calls and a knee injury. Both Maynard and Croft needed operations after the season.

Despite their injuries, Glamorgan should have finished higher than 12th. In May, they allowed Northamptonshire, who resumed 391 behind with more than two days remaining, to score 712 in their second innings. In June, playing Worcestershire, they failed by 14 to score the 26 runs needed from the last three overs with six wickets in hand. And as the season drew to a close in September, they subsided against Sussex while chasing a target of 146.

The daunting run of injuries did present opportunities to younger players, who justified their selection with some impressive performances. Michael Powell, who began his first-class career in 1997 with an undefeated double-century against Oxford University, became a first-team regular and, after reaching a rapid maiden Championship century at Northampton, he blossomed throughout the season with his positive strokeplay. Wayne Law, a 19-year-old batsman from Llanelli who scored a memorable 131 against Lancashire in only his second Championship game, had a refreshing – almost carefree – approach to batting. This might lead to his downfall on occasions, but should provide much entertainment.

Given Morris's retirement and Maynard's miserable form, Steve James shouldered the responsibilities of senior batsman. Though he could not quite touch his heights of the previous two seasons, in each of which he passed 1,700 runs, he responded with four centuries and five fifties, and his aggregate of 1,339 first-class runs was exceeded only by John Crawley and Australian Justin Langer. This time, James's consistency earned him two England caps, against South Africa at Lord's and Sri Lanka at The Oval. Adrian Dale made a useful job of filling the No. 3 position. He passed 1,000 runs for the season in the final game against Somerset – as did Tony Cottey, who also played some outstanding one-day innings. But, in November, Cottey announced that he was moving to Sussex, who offered him a five-year contract against Glamorgan's two.

Maynard failed to reach 1,000 runs for only the second time in 13 seasons. He also failed, for the first time since his debut in 1985, to score a first-class century or, indeed, one in any cricket. His best score was 99 against the Sri Lankans, who suffered their only first-class defeat when they were bowled out for 54 at Cardiff, Wales doing far better than England. Dale and Darren Thomas were the destroyers. Thomas, who in Watkin's absence became Glamorgan's main bowler, ended his most successful season with 71 wickets and created a county record in the Sunday League by taking seven for 16 against Surrey. His all-round contribution – he scored 507 first-class runs at No. 8 – was rewarded with selection for the England A tour.

Owen Parkin made the most of his opportunities in Waqar's absence to take 34 first-class wickets and, with Andrew Davies emerging as a capable new-ball bowler – dismissing Nick Knight three times on successive days – the club had plenty of promising young seamers. While they prospered during a wet summer, Robert Croft and Dean Cosker's hopes for dry, turning pitches went unrealised. Both spinners endured unrewarding seasons and took only 56 first-class wickets between them; rarely were they given the chance to bowl on anything resembling a turner. Of the other young players tried, Simon Jones, son of former England fast bowler Jeff, has undoubted pace but needs harnessing, while Daniel Cherry, an 18-year-old left-hander from Tonbridge School, made his Championship debut against Derbyshire. Mark Wallace, only 16, kept wicket for the England Under-19 side and should soon challenge Adrian Shaw and Ismail Dawood, who competed for the first-team place in 1998.

Glamorgan failed to make an impact in either of the cup competitions. But after a poor start in the Sunday League, they rallied to win six of their last eight games and narrowly failed to qualify for the top division of the new National League. Off the field, there were obvious signs of progress. Following the purchase of Sophia Gardens in 1997, the club embarked upon the first stages of a multi-million pound development. New offices and an indoor school were expected to be in use at the start of 1999, in time for the World Cup. There were other hints of a better year ahead. Duncan Fletcher, who coached them to the Championship in 1997, agreed to return after missing 1998. And the county did well to secure Jacques Kallis, the South African all-rounder, as replacement for Waqar. – EDWARD BEVAN.

490

GLAMORGAN 1998

Back row: S. C. B. Tomlinson, B. M. Morgan, W. L. Law, M. J. Powell, S. P. Jones, A. P. Davies, I. Dawood, I. D. Thomas. *Middle row:* G. N. Lewis (*Second Eleven scorer*), D. O. Conway (*physiotherapist*), D. A. Cosker, G. P. Butcher, A. D. Shaw, O. T. Parkin, A. W. Evans, J. R. A. Williams (*youth coach*), B. T. Denning (*First Eleven scorer*). *Front row:* A. Jones (*director of coaching*), A. Dale, S. P. James, P. A. Cottey, M. P. Maynard (*captain*), S. L. Watkin, R. D. B. Croft, S. D. Thomas, J. Derrick (*First Eleven coach*). *Inset:* Waqar Younis.

[*Bill Smith*]

GLAMORGAN RESULTS

All first-class matches – Played 19: Won 6, Lost 6, Drawn 7.

County Championship matches – Played 17: Won 4, Lost 6, Drawn 7.

Competition placings – Britannic Assurance County Championship, 12th; NatWest Trophy, 2nd round; Benson and Hedges Cup, 3rd in Group D; AXA League, 10th.

COUNTY CHAMPIONSHIP AVERAGES
BATTING

Cap		M	I	NO	R	HS	100s	50s	Avge	Ct/St
1992	S. P. James........	13	24	1	1,268	227	4	5	55.13	9
	W. L. Law.......	7	11	1	414	131	1	2	41.40	2
	M. J. Powell†.....	14	23	2	783	106	1	5	37.28	8
1989	S. L. Watkin†.....	12	15	12	107	25*	0	0	35.66	4
1992	P. A. Cottey†.....	17	28	2	901	123	2	4	34.65	17
1992	A. Dale........	17	30	1	969	92	0	8	33.41	7
1987	M. P. Maynard....	16	27	2	672	94	0	4	26.88	20
1997	S. D. Thomas†....	17	25	3	492	74	0	3	22.36	10
	A. W. Evans†.....	7	13	1	261	87	0	1	21.75	5
1992	R. D. B. Croft†...	9	14	3	222	63*	0	1	20.18	8
	I. Dawood.......	6	10	1	168	40	0	0	18.66	16/1
	G. P. Butcher....	8	12	1	186	85	0	1	16.90	4
	A. P. Davies†.....	4	5	1	54	34	0	0	13.50	0
	A. D. Shaw†.....	10	15	1	177	51	0	1	12.64	24
	O. T. Parkin.....	10	13	4	85	24*	0	0	9.44	2
	D. A. Cosker§....	13	3	2	123	37	0	0	7.23	10
1997	Waqar Younis§....	4	6	0	39	15	0	0	6.50	1

Also batted: D. D. Cherry† (1 match) 11; S. P. Jones† (2 matches) 0*, 0*, 2* (1 ct).

* Signifies not out.   *† Born in Wales.*   *§ Overseas player.*

BOWLING

	O	M	R	W	BB	5W/i	Avge
S. L. Watkin.......	346.4	96	866	39	5-30	1	22.20
O. T. Parkin.......	276.3	92	699	31	5-24	2	22.54
S. D. Thomas......	525.1	92	1,687	66	5-84	3	25.56
A. P. Davies......	124.5	37	369	13	2-22	0	28.38
G. P. Butcher.......	132	18	494	15	4-22	0	32.93
Waqar Younis......	100.1	13	397	12	3-147	0	33.08
A. Dale.........	217.1	38	696	21	3-23	0	33.14
D. A. Cosker.......	429.5	114	1,126	32	6-140	1	35.18
R. D. B. Croft......	352.5	91	895	19	4-76	0	47.10

Also bowled: P. A. Cottey 40–9–92–3; S. P. Jones 63–8–261–5; W. L. Law 14–1–50–1; M. P. Maynard 5.4–0–46–0; M. J. Powell 0.2–0–8–0; A. D. Shaw 1–0–7–0.

COUNTY RECORDS

Highest score for:	287*	D. E. Davies v Gloucestershire at Newport.....	1939
Highest score against:	322*	M. B. Loye (Northamptonshire) at Northampton..	1998
Best bowling for:	10-51	J. Mercer v Worcestershire at Worcester......	1936
Best bowling against:	10-18	G. Geary (Leicestershire) at Pontypridd.......	1929
Highest total for:	597-8 dec.	v Durham at Cardiff.....................	1997
Highest total against:	712	by Northamptonshire at Northampton.........	1998
Lowest total for:	22	v Lancashire at Liverpool.................	1924
Lowest total against:	33	by Leicestershire at Ebbw Vale.............	1965

At Bristol, April 17, 18, 20. GLAMORGAN beat GLOUCESTERSHIRE by 141 runs.

GLAMORGAN v KENT

At Cardiff, April 23, 24, 25, 27. Drawn. Glamorgan 7 pts, Kent 4 pts. Toss: Glamorgan.

The enticing prospect of a game between the 1997 county champions and runners-up was sabotaged by the weather. The first day was washed out and another three sessions were lost during the next two. When play did start, Kent slipped to 21 for three, but a 94-run partnership between Fulton and Wells saved them from collapse. On the closing day, Fulton scored a second fifty and an enterprising declaration left Glamorgan to score 246 from 60 overs. They needed someone to play a long innings; Dale might have done it, but once he fell for 54, no one else threatened apart from Croft, who remained undefeated on 42. Glamorgan lost their eighth wicket in the final over but held out for the draw.

Close of play: First day, No play; Second day, Kent 91-3 (D. P. Fulton 55*, A. P. Wells 24*); Third day, Glamorgan 63-3 (M. P. Maynard 34*, D. A. Cosker 0*).

Kent

D. P. Fulton lbw b Butcher	61	– not out	71
M. J. Walker lbw b Watkin	0	– b Thomas	8
T. R. Ward lbw b Butcher	11	– b Dale	10
C. L. Hooper c Maynard b Watkin	1	– lbw b Dale	4
A. P. Wells lbw b Croft	46		
M. A. Ealham c Maynard b Butcher	0	– (5) not out	45
M. V. Fleming b Thomas	12		
*†S. A. Marsh c Shaw b Thomas	10		
B. J. Phillips b Cosker	9		
D. W. Headley b Thomas	5		
A. P. Igglesden not out	3		
L-b 4, w 2, n-b 2	8	N-b 4	4

1/3 2/20 3/21 4/115 5/115   166   1/26 2/45 3/57   (3 wkts dec.) 142
6/135 7/141 8/147 9/155

Bonus points – Glamorgan 4.

Bowling: First Innings—Watkin 17–7–31–2; Thomas 21–8–46–3; Butcher 14–4–35–3; Croft 24–8–33–1; Cosker 7.5–1–17–1. *Second Innings*—Watkin 7–2–21–0; Thomas 6–1–20–1; Butcher 3–0–14–0; Dale 5–2–13–2; Cosker 8–0–39–0; Croft 5–0–12–0; Maynard 1–0–16–0; Shaw 1–0–7–0.

Glamorgan

S. P. James lbw b Headley	2	– lbw b Headley	18
A. W. Evans lbw b Fleming	20	– c Fulton b Phillips	17
A. Dale c Walker b Headley	0	– c Fleming b Headley	54
*M. P. Maynard not out	34	– c Marsh b Fleming	9
D. A. Cosker not out	0	– (10) not out	0
P. A. Cottey (did not bat)		– (5) c Headley b Hooper	27
G. P. Butcher (did not bat)		– (6) b Hooper	16
R. D. B. Croft (did not bat)		– (7) not out	42
†A. D. Shaw (did not bat)		– (8) c Headley b Fleming	15
S. D. Thomas (did not bat)		– (9) b Headley	1
B 1, n-b 6	7	B 5, l-b 4, n-b 4	13

1/6 2/10 3/56   (3 wkts dec.) 63   1/30 2/47 3/83   (8 wkts) 212
                                            4/117 5/146 6/154
                                            7/201 8/212

S. L. Watkin did not bat.

Bonus point – Kent 1.

Bowling: *First Innings*—Headley 6–3–7–2; Igglesden 5–0–18–0; Ealham 6–3–8–0; Phillips 4–0–21–0; Hooper 5–4–1–0; Fleming 4–1–7–1. *Second Innings*—Headley 16.5–1–56–3; Igglesden 5–0–27–0; Ealham 9–2–30–0; Phillips 10–0–37–1; Hooper 11–4–29–2; Fleming 8–2–24–2.

Umpires: H. D. Bird and J. W. Holder.

At Cambridge, May 13, 14, 15. GLAMORGAN beat CAMBRIDGE UNIVERSITY by 171 runs.

At Northampton, May 21, 22, 23, 24. GLAMORGAN drew with NORTHAMPTONSHIRE.

At Lord's, May 29, 30, June 1, 2. GLAMORGAN lost to MIDDLESEX by nine wickets.

At Southampton, June 3, 4, 5, 6. GLAMORGAN lost to HAMPSHIRE by nine wickets.

GLAMORGAN v WORCESTERSHIRE

At Cardiff, June 11, 12, 13, 15. Drawn. Glamorgan 9 pts, Worcestershire 9 pts. Toss: Glamorgan.
Glamorgan's hopes of a second Championship win were thwarted when Leatherdale took four for three in nine balls. James, who scored a masterly 152, and Cottey were apparently guiding them towards victory; they had added 69 in ten overs and needed another 26 from the last three. Then Leatherdale had Cottey caught at short extra cover, trapped Powell with his next ball, and in the following over dismissed Croft and James. Glamorgan's run-chase had suffered an earlier blow when Maynard was unluckily run out – a drive by James was deflected on to the non-striker's stumps. On the first day, Worcestershire had been let off the hook when Rhodes was dropped at third slip off Thomas, on five. That would have been 72 for six. Rhodes went on to the tenth century of his career and added 114 for the ninth wicket with Newport. Glamorgan took a narrow lead, despite a career-best five for 59 from Haynes; Moody then set up a target of 282 from 58 overs by scoring a hundred himself.
Close of play: First day, Worcestershire 241-8 (S. J. Rhodes 81*, P. J. Newport 49*); Second day, Glamorgan 288-9 (S. D. Thomas 69*); Third day, Worcestershire 127-4 (T. M. Moody 3*, D. A. Leatherdale 10*).

Worcestershire

V. S. Solanki lbw b Waqar Younis	1	– c Shaw b Watkin	32
A. Hafeez c Shaw b Watkin	42	– lbw b Waqar Younis	1
G. A. Hick c Powell b Thomas	13	– c Shaw b Waqar Younis	66
G. R. Haynes c Shaw b Waqar Younis	3	– c Powell b Croft	8
*T. M. Moody c Shaw b Thomas	0	– not out	104
D. A. Leatherdale lbw b Butcher	30	– c James b Croft	54
†S. J. Rhodes not out	104	– b Butcher	4
S. R. Lampitt lbw b Thomas	6	– lbw b Croft	2
R. K. Illingworth b Thomas	6	– not out	13
P. J. Newport c Butcher b Thomas	56		
A. Sheriyar c Butcher b Watkin	0		
L-b 8, w 2, n-b 2	12	L-b 6, w 2, n-b 4	12

1/2 2/43 3/54 4/59 5/63	273	1/13 2/74 3/113	(7 wkts dec.) 296
6/120 7/141 8/155 9/269		4/115 5/221	
		6/246 7/271	

Bonus points – Worcestershire 2, Glamorgan 4.

Bowling: *First Innings*—Waqar Younis 15.1–5–36–2; Watkin 25.4–9–48–2; Thomas 27–4–92–5; Croft 15–3–43–0; Butcher 8–1–37–1; Dale 3.5–0–9–0. *Second Innings*—Waqar Younis 15–3–68–2; Watkin 10–4–27–1; Croft 35.2–7–119–3; Dale 6–0–27–0; Butcher 9–0–49–1.

Glamorgan

S. P. James b Haynes	43	– c Solanki b Leatherdale	152
†A. D. Shaw c Solanki b Moody	34	– b Sheriyar	2
A. Dale c sub b Haynes	8	– c Rhodes b Solanki	35
*M. P. Maynard lbw b Haynes	8	– (5) run out	20
P. A. Cottey c sub b Moody	0	– (6) c Moody b Leatherdale	29
M. J. Powell lbw b Newport	40	– (7) lbw b Leatherdale	0
G. P. Butcher c Hick b Haynes	9	– (9) not out	0
R. D. B. Croft c Hick b Illingworth	35	– c Newport b Leatherdale	3
S. D. Thomas not out	69	– (10) not out	0
Waqar Younis c Hafeez b Haynes	4	– (4) c Hafeez b Solanki	15
B 8, l-b 15, n-b 15	38	B 1, l-b 3, w 8	12

1/86 2/92 3/105 4/108 5/110 (9 wkts dec.) 288	1/36 2/117 3/159 (8 wkts) 268
6/150 7/169 8/269 9/288	4/187 5/256 6/256
	7/266 8/268

S. L. Watkin did not bat.

Bonus points – Glamorgan 2, Worcestershire 4.

Bowling: *First Innings*—Newport 11–2–39–1; Sheriyar 15–4–52–0; Haynes 25.3–9–59–5; Moody 21–6–66–2; Illingworth 14–8–27–1; Leatherdale 4–0–22–0. *Second Innings*—Newport 7–2–19–0; Sheriyar 12–0–72–1; Haynes 3–0–20–0; Lampitt 6–0–17–0; Illingworth 18–2–84–0; Solanki 9–0–36–2; Leatherdale 3–0–16–4.

Umpires: J. C. Balderstone and J. H. Hampshire.

GLAMORGAN v LEICESTERSHIRE

At Cardiff, June 17, 18, 19, 20. Leicestershire won by 140 runs. Leicestershire 19 pts, Glamorgan 4 pts. Toss: Leicestershire. Championship debut: W. L. Law.

Glamorgan, missing Croft, James – gaining his first England cap – and Watkin, suffered their third Championship defeat, one more than in the whole of the previous summer. Nixon became the fourth wicket-keeper to score a Championship hundred against Glamorgan in 1998. His partnership of 107 with Lewis rescued Leicestershire after a faltering start. But with rain having washed out all but 45 overs of the first two days, the captains agreed that Glamorgan should chase 285 on the final day. Rain delayed them for another 45 minutes, after which they subsided to 32 for three against Mullally and Lewis, swinging the ball in the heavy atmosphere. Maynard and Cottey resisted, putting on 68 for the fourth wicket. But, after they left, the tail surrendered to the left-arm spin of Brimson, who claimed four for four from eight overs.

Close of play: First day, Leicestershire 133-5 (A. Habib 22*, P. A. Nixon 15*); Second day, No play; Third day, Leicestershire 66-2 dec.

Leicestershire

V. J. Wells c Dale b Waqar Younis	6	– c Shaw b Parkin	11
D. L. Maddy c Cosker b Thomas	40	– not out	31
I. J. Sutcliffe c Shaw b Waqar Younis	0	– c Thomas b Waqar Younis	1
B. F. Smith c Maynard b Butcher	24	– not out	20
P. V. Simmons c Powell b Thomas	16		
A. Habib b Parkin	27		
†P. A. Nixon not out	101		
*C. C. Lewis c Cottey b Cosker	50		
J. M. Dakin c Dale b Law	3		
A. D. Mullally run out	0		
M. T. Brimson c Law b Cosker	5		
B 4, l-b 12, n-b 4	20	L-b 1, n-b 2	3

1/8 2/8 3/73 4/73 5/102 292	1/17 2/18 (2 wkts dec.) 66
6/146 7/253 8/274 9/276	

Bonus points – Leicestershire 2, Glamorgan 4.

Bowling: *First Innings*—Waqar Younis 14–2–36–2; Parkin 17–7–27–1; Cosker 20.3–3–53–2; Thomas 22–5–71–2; Butcher 14–2–58–1; Law 8–1–31–1. *Second Innings*—Waqar Younis 6–0–30–1; Parkin 5–1–15–1; Cosker 4–1–5–0; Butcher 2–0–12–0; Cottey 2–0–3–0.

Glamorgan

W. L. Law not out	21	– c Wells b Mullally	25
A. Dale b Mullally	11	– c Simmons b Lewis	5
M. J. Powell c Nixon b Wells	23	– c Nixon b Lewis	0
*M. P. Maynard lbw b Wells	0	– run out	32
P. A. Cottey not out	9	– c Dakin b Mullally	41
G. P. Butcher (did not bat)		– lbw b Lewis	4
†A. D. Shaw (did not bat)		– c Sutcliffe b Brimson	4
S. D. Thomas (did not bat)		– lbw b Brimson	9
Waqar Younis (did not bat)		– c Lewis b Brimson	8
D. A. Cosker (did not bat)		– not out	1
O. T. Parkin (did not bat)		– b Brimson	0
B 1, l-b 1, n-b 8	10	B 4, l-b 7, n-b 4	15

1/23 2/63 3/63   (3 wkts dec.) 74   1/30 2/32 3/32 4/100 5/107   144
                                                        6/119 7/119 8/137 9/144

Bonus point – Leicestershire 1.

Bowling: *First Innings*—Mullally 6–3–12–1; Lewis 5–2–17–0; Dakin 8–3–14–0; Simmons 3–2–11–0; Wells 6–0–18–2; Brimson 1–1–0–0. *Second Innings*—Mullally 18–7–47–2; Lewis 15–5–47–3; Wells 8–3–23–0; Dakin 5–1–12–0; Brimson 8–6–4–4.

Umpires: A. Clarkson and D. R. Shepherd.

At Nottingham, June 26, 27, 28, 29. GLAMORGAN beat NOTTINGHAMSHIRE by 46 runs.

GLAMORGAN v SURREY

At Swansea, July 1, 2, 3. Surrey won by six wickets. Surrey 20 pts, Glamorgan 4 pts. Toss: Glamorgan.

The contest between the champions and the leaders was evenly balanced until Salisbury recorded seven for 65, his best figures for Surrey, in Glamorgan's second innings. Salisbury, recovering from a groin injury, had not been in the original team, and was brought in only when Surrey concluded the pitch would turn. His intervention left them 211 to win, and a decisive century from Brown, with five sixes, settled the match with a day to spare. Brown put on 156 with Ward, the patient understudy to Surrey's Test batsmen, who scored his fifth fifty in four Championship matches. Salisbury was not even called on in the first innings when Hollioake returned career-best figures of his own, and Surrey led by only two. Maynard, who had promoted himself to opener, scored his second fifty of the game and Glamorgan were well placed when Salisbury came on and engineered a collapse of nine wickets for 104.

Close of play: First day, Surrey 113-6 (J. N. Batty 1*, M. P. Bicknell 3*); Second day, Glamorgan 170-6 (A. D. Shaw 16*, S. D. Thomas 12*).

Glamorgan

Batsman	First Innings		Second Innings	
S. P. James	lbw b Bicknell	9	lbw b Bicknell	7
*M. P. Maynard	c Batty b Bicknell	65	c Ratcliffe b Salisbury	71
A. Dale	b Hollioake	1	c Brown b Saqlain Mushtaq	29
M. J. Powell	c Tudor b Hollioake	0	b Salisbury	4
P. A. Cottey	lbw b Hollioake	3	st Batty b Salisbury	4
G. P. Butcher	c Brown b Saqlain Mushtaq	4	c Brown b Salisbury	4
†A. D. Shaw	lbw b Bicknell	27	c Brown b Salisbury	21
S. D. Thomas	c Salisbury b Hollioake	22	c Hollioake b Saqlain Mushtaq	18
D. A. Cosker	lbw b Hollioake	2	c Saqlain Mushtaq b Salisbury	12
S. L. Watkin	not out	10	b Salisbury	13
O. T. Parkin	c Ward b Saqlain Mushtaq	3	not out	6
Extras	B 5, l-b 14, w 6, n-b 26	51	B 8, l-b 7, n-b 8	23
		197		**212**

1/40 2/51 3/51 4/61 5/100 6/135 7/156 8/180 9/180

1/30 2/108 3/121 4/129 5/137 6/144 7/178 8/182 9/203

Bonus points – Surrey 4.

Bowling: *First Innings*—Bicknell 22–7–53–3; Tudor 4–1–25–0; Hollioake 22–5–62–5; Saqlain Mushtaq 18.1–5–38–2. *Second Innings*—Bicknell 9–3–16–1; Tudor 4–0–14–0; Saqlain Mushtaq 36–9–85–2; Hollioake 8–3–17–0; Salisbury 30.2–7–65–7.

Surrey

Batsman	First Innings		Second Innings	
J. D. Ratcliffe	b Watkin	0	b Cosker	14
I. J. Ward	run out	50	not out	79
N. Shahid	c Shaw b Watkin	14	c Dale b Cosker	17
*A. J. Hollioake	b Parkin	7	lbw b Thomas	0
A. D. Brown	b Thomas	24	lbw b Cottey	100
J. A. Knott	lbw b Cosker	5	not out	0
†J. N. Batty	c James b Thomas	30		
M. P. Bicknell	b Parkin	13		
I. D. K. Salisbury	lbw b Thomas	11		
A. J. Tudor	not out	9		
Saqlain Mushtaq	b Parkin	25		
Extras	B 1, l-b 2, w 2, n-b 6	11	B 2, n-b 2	4
		199	(4 wkts)	**214**

1/0 2/14 3/31 4/79 5/106 6/107 7/128 8/158 9/167

1/25 2/51 3/52 4/208

Bonus points – Glamorgan 4.

Bowling: *First Innings*—Watkin 13–2–40–2; Parkin 17.4–4–50–3; Thomas 19–3–47–3; Cosker 19–4–47–1; Butcher 3–0–12–0. *Second Innings*—Watkin 11–4–20–0; Parkin 7–1–16–0; Cosker 30–7–101–2; Thomas 15–3–28–1; Dale 6.2–0–32–0; Cottey 6–1–15–1.

Umpires: H. D. Bird and R. A. White.

At Cardiff, July 18, 19. GLAMORGAN beat SRI LANKANS by five wickets (See Sri Lankan tour section).

GLAMORGAN v LANCASHIRE

At Colwyn Bay, July 22, 23, 24, 25. Drawn. Glamorgan 11 pts, Lancashire 10 pts. Toss: Lancashire. First-class debut: C. P. Schofield.

Lancashire lost an opportunity to press home their Championship challenge when Wasim Akram decided to prolong their second innings rather than set Glamorgan a target on the last day. Wasim claimed that Maynard should have declared behind to make up for bad weather, instead of pushing on to a 17-run first-innings lead. But Lancashire suffered, as did the public. At one stage, they had been 254 ahead with 41 overs left and, with the pitch turning, Glamorgan might have been hard pressed to survive that long; both Maynard and Wayne Law were injured. It was scant reward for Crawley, who dominated the match with two centuries, following a century in his previous

GLAMORGAN'S YOUNGEST CENTURY-MAKERS

Years	Days		
18	214	M. J. Llewellyn, 112* v Cambridge University at Swansea	1972
19	159	M. P. Maynard, 102 v Yorkshire at Swansea	1985
19	288	S. P. James, 106 v Oxford University at Oxford.	1987
19	**323**	**W. L. Law, 131 v Lancashire at Colwyn Bay**	**1998**
20	122	M. J. Powell, 200* v Oxford University at Oxford	1997
20	161	M. J. L. Turnbull, 106* v Worcestershire at Cardiff (Arms Park).	1926
20	280	H. Morris, 114* v Yorkshire at Cardiff (Sophia Gardens).	1984
20	289	G. C. Holmes, 100 v Gloucestershire at Bristol	1979
20	320	C. F. Walters, 116 v Warwickshire at Swansea.	1926

Research: Andrew Hignell

Championship innings at Lytham a week earlier. In the first innings, he was upstaged by Law, Glamorgan's teenage opener from Llanelli, who made 131 in only his second Championship match. He became the county's second-youngest Championship centurion, behind only Maynard, and showed something of his captain's fearlessness, hitting the last two balls before lunch for four and six, and playing throughout with aggression and skill.

Close of play: First day, Lancashire 213-4 (J. P. Crawley 75*, M. Watkinson 2*); Second day, Glamorgan 60-0 (W. L. Law 37*, I. Dawood 14*); Third day, Lancashire 42-1 (P. C. McKeown 21*, J. P. Crawley 8*).

Lancashire

P. C. McKeown lbw b Dale	20	– c Powell b Croft.	31
N. T. Wood c and b Watkin	37	– lbw b Watkin	13
J. P. Crawley c Parkin b Croft	124	– c Cottey b Croft.	136
M. J. Chilton b Thomas	13	– b Cottey	47
G. D. Lloyd c Thomas b Croft	50	– c Thomas b Cosker	73
M. Watkinson lbw b Watkin	3	– c Cottey b Cosker	8
†W. K. Hegg b Croft	25	– c Maynard b Cosker	10
*Wasim Akram c Maynard b Parkin	43	– c and b Croft.	0
I. D. Austin c Watkin b Croft.	3	– c Cottey b Cosker	2
P. J. Martin c Croft b Parkin	26	– (11) lbw b Cosker	4
C. P. Schofield not out	1	– (10) not out.	4
B 1, l-b 10, n-b 10	21	B 2, l-b 2, n-b 2	6

1/48 2/85 3/113 4/192 5/214	366	1/31 2/76 3/229 4/239 5/271	334
6/249 7/336 8/336 9/343		6/289 7/290 8/303 9/330	

Bonus points – Lancashire 4, Glamorgan 4.

Bowling: *First Innings*—Watkin 22–11–49–2; Parkin 20.2–9–76–2; Thomas 26–7–76–1; Cosker 13–3–48–0; Dale 9–2–30–1; Croft 27–7–76–4. *Second Innings*—Watkin 7–1–20–1; Parkin 2–0–8–0; Croft 44–14–139–3; Thomas 6–1–23–0; Cosker 34–8–140–6; Cottey 1–1–0–0.

Glamorgan

W. L. Law b Austin	131			
†I. Dawood c Hegg b Martin	14	– c Austin b Schofield	19
A. Dale c Crawley b Austin	73	– (1) c Austin b Watkinson	23
M. J. Powell lbw b Austin	88	– (3) not out	25
P. A. Cottey lbw b Austin	0	– (4) c Austin b Schofield	28
R. D. B. Croft c Hegg b Watkinson	18	– (5) not out	1
S. D. Thomas c Wasim Akram b Watkinson	12		
D. A. Cosker b Wasim Akram	24		
S. L. Watkin not out	4		
B 1, l-b 10, n-b 8	19	L-b 2, n-b 2	4

1/61 2/222 3/233 4/233   (8 wkts dec.) 383   1/39 2/43 3/78   (3 wkts) 100
5/282 6/302 7/377 8/383

*M. P. Maynard and O. T. Parkin did not bat.

Bonus points – Glamorgan 4, Lancashire 3.

Bowling: *First Innings*—Wasim Akram 12–1–39–1; Martin 17–2–71–1; Schofield 29–0–139–0; Austin 16.5–6–33–4; Watkinson 26–4–74–2; Chilton 3–1–16–0. *Second Innings*—Austin 4–0–19–0; Chilton 5–1–8–0; Schofield 11–3–44–2; Watkinson 9–2–27–1.

Umpires: D. J. Constant and B. Dudleston.

At Birmingham, July 30, 31, August 1, 2. GLAMORGAN drew with WARWICKSHIRE.

At Chelmsford, August 5, 6, 7, 8. GLAMORGAN beat ESSEX by 216 runs.

At Chester-le-Street, August 14, 15, 16, 17. GLAMORGAN drew with DURHAM.

GLAMORGAN v YORKSHIRE

At Cardiff, August 20, 21, 22. Yorkshire won by 114 runs. Yorkshire 23 pts, Glamorgan 6 pts. Toss: Glamorgan. First-class debut: G. D. Clough.

Yorkshire's visit to Wales was dominated by a Scotsman. Gavin Hamilton, torn between the certainty of playing for Scotland and the possibility of England, gave some indication that his decision might matter with a tremendous all-round display. He made the top two scores of the match, 79 and 70, and took five wickets in each innings, for figures of ten for 112 in the match. But no one else got anything like as much life and movement as he did; he led Yorkshire to victory despite the absence of Gough, Silverwood and Hutchison from their attack. Hamilton enabled them to recover from a terrible start – they were 88 for six – after they had been put in on a green pitch. Helped mainly by Sidebottom, he guided Yorkshire towards 300 in the first innings and then his bowling secured a first-innings lead of 40. Glamorgan were set 337, and had a slim chance after Dale and Powell led them to 186 for four, but Hamilton finished them off.

Close of play: First day, Glamorgan 161-4 (A. Dale 30*, P. A. Cottey 12*); Second day, Yorkshire 272-7 (G. M. Hamilton 64*).

Yorkshire

*D. Byas lbw b Jones	25	– c Dawood b Thomas	2
M. P. Vaughan lbw b Parkin	0	– c Dale b Parkin	12
M. J. Wood c Cottey b Thomas	0	– b Thomas	62
D. S. Lehmann c Cosker b Dale	29	– lbw b Jones	24
A. McGrath lbw b Dale	10	– c Cottey b Thomas	9
†R. J. Blakey c Dawood b Jones	0	– c Maynard b Parkin	18
G. M. Hamilton c Cottey b Cosker	79	– b Parkin	70
J. D. Middlebrook lbw b Jones	26	– c Dawood b Thomas	30
G. D. Clough b Cosker	33	– b Parkin	1
R. J. Sidebottom run out	54	– not out	9
M. J. Hoggard not out	0	– lbw b Jones	2
B 4, l-b 17, w 2, n-b 27	50	B 12, l-b 27, w 10, n-b 8	57

1/1 2/16 3/49 4/79 5/82   306   1/23 2/27 3/65 4/85 5/136   296
6/88 7/169 8/233 9/286   6/196 7/272 8/275 9/290

Bonus points – Yorkshire 3, Glamorgan 4.

Bowling: *First Innings*—Parkin 16.5-3-59-1; Thomas 18-1-70-1; Dale 12-4-48-2; Jones 14-0-94-3; Cosker 13-5-14-2. *Second Innings*—Parkin 25.4-7-67-5; Thomas 25-4-72-4; Dale 13-1-49-0; Jones 10-3-32-1; Maynard 2-0-13-0; Cosker 11-4-24-0.

Glamorgan

S. P. James b Hamilton	31	– c Middlebrook b Hoggard	7
W. L. Law b Hamilton	57	– lbw b Sidebottom	9
A. Dale lbw b Sidebottom	31	– c Clough b Middlebrook	67
*M. P. Maynard lbw b Hoggard	5	– c Blakey b Hamilton	29
D. A. Cosker b Sidebottom	1	– (9) b Lehmann	0
P. A. Cottey c Blakey b Hamilton	42	– (5) c McGrath b Hamilton	0
M. J. Powell lbw b Hoggard	43	– (6) c Byas b Middlebrook	54
†I. Dawood lbw b Hamilton	0	– (7) c Middlebrook b Hamilton	29
S. D. Thomas c Blakey b Hoggard	9	– (8) c Hoggard b Hamilton	3
O. T. Parkin b Hamilton	9	– b Hamilton	0
S. P. Jones not out	0	– not out	2
B 4, l-b 8, w 4, n-b 22	38	B 5, l-b 7, w 2, n-b 8	22

1/104 2/113 3/130 4/145 5/178   266   1/14 2/22 3/84 4/88 5/186   222
6/212 7/212 8/245 9/266   6/197 7/206 8/220 9/220

Bonus points – Glamorgan 2, Yorkshire 4.

Bowling: *First Innings*—Sidebottom 17-0-75-2; Hoggard 20-1-92-3; Hamilton 15.5-1-69-5; Clough 2-0-11-0; Middlebrook 3-0-7-0. *Second Innings*—Hoggard 18-4-55-1; Sidebottom 13-3-55-1; Hamilton 15-5-43-5; Middlebrook 8-3-31-2; McGrath 4-0-26-0; Lehmann 0.4-0-0-1.

Umpires: J. H. Harris and A. G. T. Whitehead.

At Hove, August 31, September 1, 2, 3. GLAMORGAN lost to SUSSEX by 18 runs.

GLAMORGAN v DERBYSHIRE

At Cardiff, September 9, 10, 11, 12. Drawn. Glamorgan 5 pts, Derbyshire 7 pts. Toss: Derbyshire. First-class debut: D. D. Cherry.

The game was called off on the final morning after rain had reduced the contest to little more than a day's cricket. When play began on the first afternoon, Cork decided to bowl, and Glamorgan were dismissed by the close. Conditions encouraged the seamers, but there was also some undistinguished batting: the last wicket put on 23, the highest stand of the innings. Derbyshire subsided to 64 for five, but Barnett and Cork fought back with an unbroken partnership of 135, and were in control when the weather closed in. Daniel Cherry, an 18-year-old left-handed batsman who had just left Tonbridge School, made his first-class debut for Glamorgan.

Close of play: First day, Glamorgan 114; Second day, Derbyshire 181-5 (K. J. Barnett 72*, D. G. Cork 50*); Third day, Derbyshire 199-5 (K. J. Barnett 75*, D. G. Cork 64*).

Glamorgan

W. L. Law b Cassar	25	D. A. Cosker b Cork	9
A. W. Evans lbw b Cork	14	S. L. Watkin not out	8
A. Dale b Smith	1	O. T. Parkin c Krikken b Cassar	15
*†M. P. Maynard run out	8		
P. A. Cottey c Barnett b Dean	4	L-b 5, n-b 6	11
M. J. Powell b Cork	0		
D. D. Cherry c Krikken b Dean	11	1/14 2/28 3/28 4/28 5/37	114
S. D. Thomas b Cassar	8	6/53 7/69 8/91 9/91	

Bonus points – Derbyshire 4.

W. L. Law, when 5, retired hurt at 5 and resumed at 53.

Bowling: Cork 17–6–29–3; Dean 14–1–37–2; Smith 8–3–17–1; Cassar 8.2–2–26–3.

Derbyshire

M. J. Slater lbw b Parkin	14	K. J. Barnett not out	75
A. S. Rollins c Evans b Parkin	9	*D. G. Cork not out	64
M. R. May c Maynard b Watkin	3	B 4, l-b 7	11
M. E. Cassar c Maynard b Watkin	4		
B. L. Spendlove lbw b Dale	19	1/17 2/26 3/26 4/32 5/64 (5 wkts)	199

†K. M. Krikken, I. D. Blackwell, K. J. Dean and T. M. Smith did not bat.

Bonus points – Glamorgan 2.

Bowling: Watkin 18.1–3–43–2; Parkin 17–5–44–2; Dale 13–2–40–1; Thomas 12–1–48–0; Cosker 5–1–13–0.

Umpires: B. Leadbeater and J. W. Lloyds.

GLAMORGAN v SOMERSET

At Cardiff, September 17, 18, 19, 20. Glamorgan won by 298 runs. Glamorgan 21 pts, Somerset 4 pts. Toss: Glamorgan.

The circumstances could not compare with the final match of 1997, when Glamorgan crushed Somerset to win the title, but they at least managed to end their unhappy 1998 in style, winning before lunch on the final day to record their highest-ever margin of victory by runs in the Championship. It was their fourth Championship win against Somerset in succession. The pitch had to be reported after the first day, because 17 wickets fell, but the umpires were unconcerned and blamed "funny batting". This came mainly from Somerset, who had a day's respite because of rain, but then fell to 133 all out, 113 behind. They were left to score 392 for victory, but collapsed on the final morning when Parkin and Watkin shared five wickets in the first ten overs. Somerset's failure knocked them down from eighth to ninth place and thus out of the 1999 Super Cup.

Close of play: First day, Somerset 80-7 (G. D. Rose 4*, A. R. K. Pierson 0*); Second day, No play; Third day, Somerset 31-1 (M. E. Trescothick 13*, A. P. van Troost 0*).

Glamorgan

S. P. James c Pierson b van Troost	1	b Caddick	54
A. W. Evans c Turner b van Troost	2	run out	13
A. Dale c Trescothick b Caddick	60	c Burns b Pierson	12
*M. P. Maynard lbw b van Troost	11	c Parsons b Pierson	23
P. A. Cottey b Pierson	64	c Caddick b Pierson	37
M. J. Powell b Pierson	49	c Burns b Pierson	37
†I. Dawood lbw b Pierson	12	c Lathwell b Rose	40
S. D. Thomas not out	28	c Turner b Rose	1
D. A. Cosker b Pierson	0	c Burns b Pierson	3
S. L. Watkin b Caddick	7	not out	25
O. T. Parkin c Turner b Caddick	0	not out	11
B 3, l-b 7, n-b 2	12	B 4, l-b 6, w 4, n-b 8	22

1/3 2/8 3/24 4/145 5/145   246   1/29 2/51 3/106   (9 wkts dec.) 278
6/174 7/221 8/221 9/244   4/120 5/179 6/208
                                 7/209 8/215 9/252

Bonus points – Glamorgan 1, Somerset 4.

Bowling: *First Innings*—Caddick 21.1–5–56–3; van Troost 9–1–49–3; Pierson 29–2–94–4; Rose 5–1–19–0; Bowler 7–1–18–0. *Second Innings*—Caddick 15–3–53–1; van Troost 3–0–15–0; Rose 20–3–62–2; Pierson 28–4–117–5; Parsons 4–1–21–0.

Somerset

*P. D. Bowler lbw b Thomas	15	(9) c Thomas b Parkin	2
P. C. L. Holloway lbw b Watkin	10	(1) c and b Cosker	16
M. E. Trescothick c Cottey b Cosker	26	(2) c Dawood b Parkin	17
M. N. Lathwell c Maynard b Cosker	2	c Dawood b Watkin	1
M. Burns lbw b Thomas	16	(6) c Maynard b Watkin	9
K. A. Parsons c Cottey b Cosker	4	(7) c Maynard b Parkin	0
†R. J. Turner b Dale	2	(8) lbw b Cosker	10
G. D. Rose not out	28	(5) lbw b Parkin	0
A. R. K. Pierson lbw b Thomas	0	(10) not out	11
A. R. Caddick c Dawood b Thomas	25	(11) c Watkin b Cosker	7
A. P. van Troost run out	0	(3) b Parkin	10
B 2, l-b 3	5	L-b 10	10

1/13 2/34 3/41 4/58 5/72   133   1/25 2/42 3/47 4/48 5/57   93
6/76 7/76 8/81 9/125   6/59 7/59 8/64 9/83

Bonus points – Glamorgan 4.

Bowling: *First Innings*—Watkin 8–1–15–1; Parkin 5–1–15–0; Cosker 20.4–8–38–3; Thomas 16–3–56–4; Dale 2–1–4–1. *Second Innings*—Watkin 12–5–29–2; Parkin 10–1–24–5; Cosker 6.1–0–25–3; Dale 1–0–1–0; Cottey 1–1–0–0; Thomas 3–1–4–0.

Umpires: A. A. Jones and R. Palmer.

CRICKET SOCIETY AWARDS, 1998

Paul Franks of Nottinghamshire won the Cricket Society's Most Promising Young Cricketer Award. The A. A. Thomson Fielding Prize, for the best schoolboy fielder, went to John Snashall of Cavendish School. The Sir John Hobbs Memorial Prize, for the outstanding under-16 schoolboy, was won by Nicky Peng of the Royal Grammar School, Newcastle. Wetherell awards went to Gavin Hamilton of Yorkshire as the leading all-rounder in the first-class game and Darren Thomas of Glamorgan as the outstanding young all-rounder, with the schools award going to Joe Porter of St John's, Leatherhead.

GLOUCESTERSHIRE

Matt Windows

Patron: Lord Vestey
President: N. P. Walters
Chairman: J. C. Higson
Chief Executive: C. L. Sexstone
Captain: M. W. Alleyne
Director of Coaching: A. W. Stovold
First Eleven Coach: J. G. Bracewell
Head Groundsman: D. Bridle
Scorer: K. T. Gerrish

For the second year running, Gloucestershire shaped up as if they might win their first Championship since it took official form in 1890. No county won more games than their 11 but, as so often, they lost their chance in the final weeks. Still, fourth place was three up on 1997.

Gloucestershire debated long whether to go for a top overseas batsman or turn again to the pace and knowledge of Courtney Walsh. They took the right decision: Walsh, arguably the most durable overseas player any county has had in modern times, had a magnificent year. He finished with 106 wickets, the highest return for any county since the Championship was reduced to 17 matches a side in 1993. With the back-up of Mike Smith and a fast-improving Jon Lewis, who bowled himself to his county cap, Gloucestershire took 65 bowling points; no county managed more. For Walsh, it was a last hurrah. Negotiations over a new contract broke down acrimoniously in midwinter, and it was clear that the long love affair was over.

The batting was a different story from the bowling. Although three batsmen – Matt Windows, Mark Alleyne and Tim Hancock – reached 1,000 runs, in a season when only 27 did so in all, Gloucestershire's total of 23 batting points was the fourth lowest in the table. They never had the luxury of a settled top four, and too often their lower-order batsmen had to rescue them. In a wet summer which offered him little as a spin bowler, Martyn Ball justified his place with the bat.

Gloucestershire's new coach, John Bracewell, arrived from New Zealand on a two-year contract saying he would like a long look at the English game before taking decisions. But early home defeats by Glamorgan and Leicestershire soon forced him into action. As well as trying to lead the dressing-room towards a new attitude, Bracewell divided their season into mini-leagues of three matches a time, and challenged the players to finish on top of each group. The idea took root. Another of Bracewell's innovations was less well-received: he had the team out for a "warm-down" run at the close of play, when their thoughts were more for a quiet drink at the bar. Team spirit, though, soared quickly, and Alleyne, cheery and unflappable, moulded a team largely unfancied outside their own shire into a winning combination. There was great delight when he was called into England's one-day squad during the winter.

Coach and captain could look back on two major breakthroughs among the batsmen. Windows ended with 1,173 first-class runs and an average of 43.44. In his early years, he had been looked upon as an opener, but Bracewell quickly realised he was more comfortable in the middle order. Windows was capped, as was Hancock, seven years after his first game. Hancock's summers have had their disappointments, but he ended this one with a double-century – and his wedding. The caps showed the faith the new regime has in its present players; extended contracts were also on offer, and signed.

At 35, Jack Russell was given one to the end of 2002. Since he also renounced international cricket in the autumn, his long-term deputy Reggie Williams was left looking, once more, for a county able to offer regular first-team cricket. Behind the stumps, Russell passed another milestone – he has now held more catches for Gloucestershire than anyone else – but never quite emerged from the shadow of his horrendous tour of the West Indies. His batting, less eccentric in style, lacked its old panache: his Championship average of 47.57 in 1997 sank to 20.26. But Russell's influence on the team remained strong, as did his support for Alleyne.

After a mixed start, the season peaked in July, when three successive wins – over Hampshire at Southampton, then Sussex and a weakened Surrey, Championship leaders at the time, at Cheltenham – saw Gloucestershire go second in the table. On each occasion, they overcame the handicap of losing the toss. But in August, their otherwise triumphant progress was interrupted by defeats at the hands of Lancashire and Somerset. Losing to Somerset effectively ended the dream of the Championship pennant, despite another run of three victories in September.

In the one-day game, Gloucestershire have been consistent under-achievers, although they will be lining up in the higher division of the National League and – thanks to their Championship form – the Super Cup. Sixth place in the Sunday League owed everything to a farcical win over Somerset in a rain-affected floodlit game at Bristol. The match would never have been completed but for a capacity crowd, drawn by the novelty of night cricket, and a TV contract. In the Benson and Hedges Cup, Gloucestershire somehow lost to British Universities, despite a record fourth-wicket stand of 207 by Russell and Tony Wright, and in the NatWest they went out at home to Surrey in the second round.

The season ended the Gloucestershire career of Philip August, a popular cricket secretary and former chief executive, who was made redundant after a dozen years with the county. It also saw the end of fast bowler David Lawrence's attempt to revive his career after his terrible knee injury in New Zealand six years earlier, while former captain Tony Wright announced his retirement, and moved into coaching. There was structural change too, as the Jessop Tavern, home of cheap drink and enthusiastic support, was pulled down. A stand costing £500,000 has gone up in its place. Grants have met half the cost; now the county have to fill it. – GRAHAM RUSSELL.

504

GLOUCESTERSHIRE 1998

[Bill Smith]

Back row: R. J. Cunliffe, T. H. C. Hancock, M. A. Coombes, J. M. M. Averis, R. I. Dawson, D. R. Hewson, M. G. N. Windows. *Middle row:* K. T. Gerrish (*First Eleven scorer*), R. C. J. Williams, K. P. Sheeraz, P. S. Lazenbury, M. J. Cawdron, J. Lewis, M. J. Church, N. J. Trainor, B. W. Gannon. *Front row:* J. G. Bracewell (*First Eleven coach*), M. C. J. Ball, D. V. Lawrence, M. W. Alleyne (*captain*), J. C. Higson (*chairman*), R. C. Russell, A. J. Wright, A. M. Smith, A. W. Stovold (*director of coaching*). *Inset:* C. A. Walsh.

GLOUCESTERSHIRE RESULTS

All first-class matches – Played 18: Won 11, Lost 6, Drawn 1.

County Championship matches – Played 17: Won 11, Lost 5, Drawn 1.

Competition placings – Britannic Assurance County Championship, 4th;
NatWest Trophy, 2nd round; Benson and Hedges Cup, 4th in Group C;
AXA League, 6th.

COUNTY CHAMPIONSHIP AVERAGES
BATTING

Cap		M	I	NO	R	HS	100s	50s	Avge	Ct
1998	M. G. N. Windows†	15	27	2	1,083	151	4	4	43.32	11
1998	T. H. C. Hancock	17	32	2	1,181	220*	2	7	39.36	15
1990	M. W. Alleyne	17	31	2	1,076	137	2	6	37.10	22
1996	M. C. J. Ball†	17	28	5	589	67*	0	3	25.60	21
	D. R. Hewson†	11	20	3	428	78*	0	3	25.17	4
1995	A. M. Smith	17	28	11	353	61	0	2	20.76	5
1985	R. C. Russell†	16	28	2	527	63*	0	2	20.26	56
	G. I. Macmillan	4	7	0	121	53	0	1	17.28	3
1987	A. J. Wright	11	20	0	345	57	0	1	17.25	5
	R. J. Cunliffe	11	20	0	336	53	0	2	16.80	13
	N. J. Trainor	4	8	0	109	52	0	1	13.62	4
	R. I. Dawson	8	15	2	177	46	0	0	13.61	3
1998	J. Lewis	17	29	2	356	54*	0	1	13.18	5
	M. J. Church	4	7	0	85	30	0	0	12.14	5
1985	C. A. Walsh§	17	23	10	111	25	0	0	8.53	4

Also batted: R. C. J. Williams† (cap 1996) (1 match) 5 (1 ct).

* *Signifies not out.*   † *Born in Gloucestershire.*   § *Overseas player.*

BOWLING

	O	M	R	W	BB	5W/i	Avge
T. H. C. Hancock	53	14	155	12	3-5	0	12.91
C. A. Walsh	633	162	1,835	106	6-36	7	17.31
A. M. Smith	489.3	132	1,336	67	6-32	4	19.94
J. Lewis	425.1	105	1,277	58	6-48	3	22.01
M. C. J. Ball	390	95	1,042	31	4-26	0	33.61
M. W. Alleyne	248.1	70	718	20	3-16	0	35.90

Also bowled: R. I. Dawson 14.3–0–67–5; D. R. Hewson 3–1–7–1; G. I. Macmillan 5–2–14–0.

COUNTY RECORDS

Highest score for:	318*	W. G. Grace v Yorkshire at Cheltenham	1876
Highest score against:	296	A. O. Jones (Nottinghamshire) at Nottingham	1903
Best bowling for:	10-40	E. G. Dennett v Essex at Bristol	1906
Best bowling against:	{10-66	A. A. Mailey (Australians) at Cheltenham	1921
	{10-66	K. Smales (Nottinghamshire) at Stroud	1956
Highest total for:	653-6 dec.	v Glamorgan at Bristol	1928
Highest total against:	774-7 dec.	by Australians at Bristol	1948
Lowest total for:	17	v Australians at Cheltenham	1896
Lowest total against:	12	by Northamptonshire at Gloucester	1907

GLOUCESTERSHIRE v GLAMORGAN

At Bristol, April 17, 18, 20. Glamorgan won by 141 runs. Glamorgan 21 pts, Gloucestershire 4 pts. Toss: Gloucestershire.

Glamorgan began the defence of their title with a comprehensive win after dismissing Gloucestershire for 89 inside 30 overs. But that followed an even swifter collapse of their own. When the third day finally started at three o'clock, they were 106 for one; 80 balls later they were all out for 138. They were undone by the unexpected figure of Lewis. The return of Walsh (complete with handwarmers for a chilly English spring) had relegated Lewis to first change, but he responded by striding into the cold wind and taking six for 11 in 38 balls. Rather surprisingly put in, Glamorgan led by 92 on first innings. James then stretched that lead before the collapse, and Gloucestershire finally needed 231. It was virtually over when Thomas and Watkin reduced them to 27 for five. Allowing for stoppages, the game lasted only two days; 19 wickets fell in three hours at the end. The umpires did not report the pitch, and blamed the batsmen. Glamorgan's captain, Maynard, thought both sides were rusty.

Close of play: First day, Glamorgan 204-7 (A. Dale 59*, S. D. Thomas 12*); Second day, Glamorgan 106-1 (S. P. James 62*, A. Dale 31*).

Glamorgan

S. P. James c Russell b Lewis	27	– c Wright b Walsh	76
A. W. Evans c Wright b Alleyne	27	– b Smith	1
A. Dale lbw b Smith	75	– c Wright b Walsh	31
*M. P. Maynard lbw b Walsh	9	– c Russell b Lewis	0
P. A. Cottey lbw b Alleyne	15	– c Wright b Lewis	0
G. P. Butcher run out	23	– b Lewis	4
R. D. B. Croft c Hancock b Lewis	4	– b Lewis	0
†A. D. Shaw lbw b Lewis	4	– c Cunliffe b Lewis	0
S. D. Thomas c Ball b Smith	19	– c Alleyne b Lewis	11
D. A. Cosker b Walsh	0	– lbw b Walsh	0
S. L. Watkin not out	5	– not out	0
L-b 6, w 4, n-b 18	28	L-b 11, n-b 4	15

1/64 2/64 3/94 4/123 5/160   236   1/8 2/106 3/107 4/113 5/125   138
6/166 7/178 8/219 9/220   6/125 7/125 8/133 9/138

Bonus points – Glamorgan 1, Gloucestershire 4.

Bowling: *First Innings*—Walsh 20–3–58–2; Smith 22.2–3–79–2; Lewis 19–5–52–3; Alleyne 14–6–35–2; Ball 2–0–6–0. *Second Innings*—Walsh 17–6–42–3; Smith 7–2–16–1; Lewis 14.2–4–49–6; Alleyne 5–0–14–0; Ball 5–2–6–0.

Gloucestershire

N. J. Trainor c Shaw b Watkin	11	– c James b Watkin	7
R. J. Cunliffe c Croft b Thomas	19	– b Thomas	3
T. H. C. Hancock lbw b Butcher	13	– c Thomas b Watkin	6
A. J. Wright lbw b Watkin	24	– lbw b Thomas	3
R. I. Dawson lbw b Watkin	5	– lbw b Thomas	4
*M. W. Alleyne c James b Watkin	0	– c Shaw b Butcher	32
†R. C. Russell c Butcher b Thomas	31	– c Watkin b Butcher	11
M. C. J. Ball b Croft	0	– c sub b Thomas	15
J. Lewis c Thomas b Croft	25	– c James b Butcher	0
A. M. Smith not out	2	– c Butcher b Thomas	0
C. A. Walsh c Butcher b Croft	0	– not out	4
B 2, l-b 6, w 2, n-b 4	14	L-b 2, w 2	4

1/20 2/33 3/67 4/83 5/83   144   1/10 2/10 3/13 4/19 5/27   89
6/84 7/85 8/137 9/143   6/46 7/75 8/83 9/85

Bonus points – Glamorgan 4.

Bowling: *First Innings*—Watkin 17–5–53–4; Thomas 16–5–30–2; Butcher 9–2–17–1; Croft 13.3–2–36–3. *Second Innings*—Watkin 12–2–28–2; Thomas 9–2–37–4; Butcher 8.3–3–22–4.

Umpires: V. A. Holder and N. T. Plews.

At Chester-le-Street, April 23, 24, 25, 27. GLOUCESTERSHIRE beat DURHAM by 46 runs.

GLOUCESTERSHIRE v LEICESTERSHIRE

At Bristol, May 13, 14, 15. Leicestershire won by nine wickets. Leicestershire 24 pts, Gloucestershire 4 pts. Toss: Leicestershire.

By the end of the opening day, Gloucestershire had discovered what a bad toss they had lost. First, they were bowled out for 134 by Chris Lewis and Mullally; with an aggressive assault on the off stump, and moving the ball away, Lewis took six for 60. Then Wells raced to a 103-ball century. He hit a six and 19 fours in his 120, and put on 153 in 30 overs with Ben Smith. Leicestershire already led by 111 at the close, and next day extended that to 217. Smith went on to bat six and a quarter hours for 121 not out. At 18 for three, Gloucestershire faced a two-day defeat. But Alleyne and Windows restored a little home pride with a battling century stand, and the lower order hit out gamely to avoid the innings defeat. Gloucestershire coach John Bracewell said he was looking for similar determination from the recognised batsmen.

Close of play: First day, Leicestershire 245-5 (B. F. Smith 81*, P. A. Nixon 13*); Second day, Gloucestershire 146-6 (J. Lewis 11*, R. C. Russell 0*).

Gloucestershire

R. J. Cunliffe lbw b Mullally	0	– lbw b Lewis	8
T. H. C. Hancock lbw b Mullally	19	– c Maddy b Millns	4
A. J. Wright c Simmons b Lewis	3	– lbw b Millns	2
*M. W. Alleyne c Simmons b Mullally	27	– b Maddy	56
M. G. N. Windows b Lewis	9	– b Mullally	38
M. J. Church c Maddy b Lewis	30	– (7) lbw b Mullally	5
†R. C. Russell c Simmons b Mullally	15	– (8) c Nixon b Mullally	14
M. C. J. Ball c Maddy b Lewis	0	– (9) b Lewis	44
J. Lewis c Simmons b Lewis	2	– (6) b Mullally	22
A. M. Smith b Lewis	6	– c Millns b Simmons	14
C. A. Walsh not out	4	– not out	11
B 9, l-b 2, n-b 8	19	B 2, l-b 11, w 6, n-b 22	41

1/0 2/17 3/25 4/46 5/94   134   1/10 2/18 3/18 4/130 5/134   259
6/106 7/116 8/118 9/124   6/139 7/168 8/189 9/227

Bonus points – Leicestershire 4.

Bowling: *First Innings*—Mullally 14–7–33–4; Lewis 16.3–3–60–6; Millns 7–1–25–0; Wells 4–2–5–0. *Second Innings*—Mullally 24–10–54–4; Millns 15–3–44–2; Lewis 22.2–5–85–2; Wells 6–2–13–0; Brimson 7–2–15–0; Simmons 7–1–26–1; Maddy 5–2–9–1.

Leicestershire

V. J. Wells b Smith	120	– b Walsh	12
D. L. Maddy c Russell b Smith	0	– not out	24
I. J. Sutcliffe c Ball b Smith	2	– not out	4
B. F. Smith not out	121		
P. V. Simmons c Russell b Lewis	0		
A. Habib c Russell b Smith	5		
†P. A. Nixon c Alleyne b Lewis	24		
*C. C. Lewis lbw b Lewis	22		
D. J. Millns b Alleyne	14		
A. D. Mullally b Walsh	10		
M. T. Brimson lbw b Smith	2		
B 1, l-b 10, w 6, n-b 14	31	L-b 2, n-b 2	4

1/8 2/24 3/177 4/188 5/201   351   1/27   (1 wkt) 44
6/270 7/304 8/328 9/346

Bonus points – Leicestershire 4, Gloucestershire 4.

Bowling: *First Innings*—Walsh 26–1–131–1; Smith 24.1–7–66–5; Lewis 22–4–67–3; Alleyne 15–5–51–1; Ball 16–5–25–0. *Second Innings*—Ball 2.1–0–10–0; Walsh 6–1–24–1; Smith 4–1–8–0.

Umpires: J. H. Hampshire and M. J. Harris.

GLOUCESTERSHIRE v YORKSHIRE

At Gloucester, May 21, 22, 23, 24. Gloucestershire won by 300 runs. Gloucestershire 23 pts, Yorkshire 4 pts. Toss: Gloucestershire. Championship debut: M. J. Hoggard.

Former Leicestershire batsman and Oxford captain Gregor Macmillan made an electrifying first-class debut for Gloucestershire, starting the game by crashing 53 off 39 balls. His half-century was the rallying point his new county needed to set them on the road to a massive victory. And Yorkshire captain Byas noted ruefully that he has never been on the winning side against them – he missed the last win in 1987. His team did fight back from the initial onslaught. White, bowling straight and extracting bounce, took five for one in ten balls, including a hat-trick (Alleyne, Ball and Lewis), and ended with a career-best eight for 55. But this was a pitch full of runs, and Russell and Smith hit back, putting on 114 for the ninth wicket to take Gloucestershire past 300. Smith hit 14 fours in a career-best 61, and then removed the Yorkshire openers. Night-watchman Hutchison clung on through three and three-quarter hours as his side crumbled. Alleyne waived the follow-on, instead knocking up 55 in 83 balls in a century stand with Wright. They passed 300 again thanks to Windows, looking far more comfortable down the order than he had as an opener, scoring a hundred full of pleasant, well-timed drives. Yorkshire were left 514 behind, with more than a day to spare. And, for once, the traditional Gloucester Festival rain did not come to anyone's rescue.

Close of play: First day, Yorkshire 16-1 (M. P. Vaughan 6*, P. M. Hutchison 1*); Second day, Gloucestershire 158-4 (M. G. N. Windows 18*, M. J. Church 19*); Third day, Yorkshire 136-5 (M. J. Wood 4*, R. J. Blakey 0*).

Gloucestershire

G. I. Macmillan c Blakey b White	53	– c Wood b Hutchison	0
T. H. C. Hancock c Blakey b Hutchison	49	– c Blakey b Hoggard	4
A. J. Wright lbw b White	44	– c and b White	57
*M. W. Alleyne b White	19	– c Byas b Vaughan	55
M. G. N. Windows b White	20	– not out	100
M. J. Church lbw b White	0	– c White b Hoggard	23
†R. C. Russell not out	63	– c and b Hamilton	37
M. C. J. Ball lbw b White	0	– c Blakey b Stemp	6
J. Lewis b White	0	– c Stemp b Hoggard	5
A. M. Smith c Vaughan b White	61	– not out	24
C. A. Walsh c Hutchison b Stemp	9		
B 4, l-b 3, n-b 4	11	B 13, l-b 2, w 2	17

1/75 2/146 3/162 4/196 5/196	329	1/0 2/4 3/118 (8 wkts dec.) 328
6/199 7/199 8/199 9/313		4/132 5/178 6/251
		7/262 8/277

Bonus points – Gloucestershire 3, Yorkshire 4.

Bowling: *First Innings*—Hoggard 15–2–69–0; Hutchison 24–5–102–1; White 22–9–55–8; Hamilton 11–0–37–0; Stemp 18.1–6–49–1; Vaughan 2–0–10–0. *Second Innings*—Hutchison 15–2–43–1; Hoggard 13–2–43–3; White 16.2–3–50–1; Hamilton 14–2–56–1; Stemp 17–5–41–1; Vaughan 15–1–80–1.

Yorkshire

A. McGrath lbw b Smith	6	– c Russell b Smith	16
M. P. Vaughan b Smith	10	– lbw b Smith	4
P. M. Hutchison not out	23	– (10) not out	1
*D. Byas c Church b Walsh	2	– (3) run out	15
D. S. Lehmann b Alleyne	41	– (4) c Alleyne b Ball	69
C. White c Russell b Lewis	24	– (5) c Church b Walsh	19
M. J. Wood lbw b Lewis	0	– (6) c Hancock b Smith	25
†R. J. Blakey c Russell b Walsh	14	– (7) c Windows b Ball	34
G. M. Hamilton b Walsh	0	– (8) c Hancock b Ball	9
R. D. Stemp b Ball	6	– (9) b Walsh	9
M. J. Hoggard b Ball	1	– lbw b Ball	0
B 2, l-b 6, w 2, n-b 6	16	L-b 1, n-b 12	13

1/9 2/20 3/23 4/78 5/112	143	1/18 2/41 3/56 4/130 5/132	214
6/112 7/134 8/134 9/141		6/192 7/202 8/203 9/213	

Bonus points – Gloucestershire 4.

Bowling: *First Innings*—Walsh 19–10–30–3; Smith 13–8–15–2; Alleyne 7–0–19–1; Lewis 10–0–58–2; Ball 13.4–9–13–2. *Second Innings*—Walsh 16–3–55–2; Smith 16–2–55–3; Ball 26.4–6–72–4; Lewis 5–1–22–0; Alleyne 5–1–9–0.

Umpires: R. Palmer and A. G. T. Whitehead.

At Bristol, May 29, 30, 31, June 1. GLOUCESTERSHIRE lost to SOUTH AFRICANS by 167 runs (See South African tour section).

At Chesterfield, June 3, 4, 5, 6. GLOUCESTERSHIRE drew with DERBYSHIRE.

GLOUCESTERSHIRE v WARWICKSHIRE

At Bristol, June 11, 12, 13, 15. Gloucestershire won by 170 runs. Gloucestershire 20 pts, Warwickshire 4 pts. Toss: Gloucestershire.

Two fast bowlers dominated this match: Giddins and Walsh took 23 wickets between them. Walsh just outdid Giddins, 12–11, and emerged victorious as Warwickshire crashed to a third successive defeat, their worst sequence since 1993. An experimental noon start did little for the first-day attendance, and apparently achieved even less for Gloucestershire as they were rolled over by Giddins before 4.30. This set up a fascinating hour-long duel between Walsh, the former West Indies captain, and his successor Lara, who fought off everything Walsh could hurl at him only to be caught behind off Mike Smith. Warwickshire eked out a first-innings lead of six. Giddins whipped through the early Gloucestershire batting a second time, but this time was countered by Alleyne, who produced a tour de force. He was masterly both in his strokeplay and his ability to control the strike, as Smith helped him add 105 for the ninth wicket. This broke Warwickshire's spirit. They were left with a target of 302 and, after a damp Saturday, crashed a second time to Walsh. Lara himself fell to Smith again, third ball. He admitted that his own form was "terrible" and that the team's morale was low.

Close of play: First day, Warwickshire 127-6 (K. J. Piper 13*, G. Welch 16*); Second day, Gloucestershire 295-9 (M. W. Alleyne 127*); Third day, Warwickshire 44-2 (N. V. Knight 8*, A. F. Giles 18*).

Gloucestershire

G. I. Macmillan b Giddins	0	– lbw b Giddins	11
T. H. C. Hancock c Knight b Giddins	62	– c Knight b Giddins	9
A. J. Wright b Brown	30	– b Giddins	2
*M. W. Alleyne b Welch	33	– b Giddins	137
M. G. N. Windows lbw b Giddins	0	– c Powell b Giles	38
D. R. Hewson not out	27	– c Piper b Giles	0
†R. C. Russell b Giddins	1	– c Powell b Giles	11
M. C. J. Ball c Giles b Welch	6	– c Welch b Giles	6
J. Lewis c Piper b Giddins	0	– c Piper b Giddins	10
A. M. Smith c Brown b Giddins	0	– c Knight b Brown	41
C. A. Walsh c Powell b Welch	1	– not out	0
L-b 7, w 2, n-b 12	21	L-b 20, w 12, n-b 10	42
	181		**307**

1/0 2/104 3/104 4/104 5/159   181   1/24 2/25 3/26 4/113 5/123   307
6/162 7/173 8/180 9/180   6/151 7/163 8/190 9/295

Bonus points – Warwickshire 4.

Bowling: *First Innings*—Giddins 23–3–79–6; Brown 17–4–50–1; Welch 15.3–5–45–3. *Second Innings*—Giddins 27.4–3–85–5; Brown 18–3–83–1; Welch 10–0–39–0; Giles 24–6–60–4; Smith 4–1–17–0; Hemp 1–0–3–0.

Warwickshire

M. J. Powell c Wright b Walsh	3	– c Russell b Walsh	4
N. V. Knight lbw b Walsh	8	– b Smith	15
D. L. Hemp c Ball b Smith	9	– c Macmillan b Walsh	12
*B. C. Lara c Russell b Smith	16	– (5) lbw b Smith	0
T. L. Penney b Lewis	19	– (6) c Ball b Smith	9
D. R. Brown b Alleyne	23	– (7) c Lewis b Walsh	39
†K. J. Piper b Walsh	14	– (8) c Windows b Walsh	6
G. Welch not out	40	– (9) b Walsh	12
N. M. K. Smith b Walsh	30	– (10) b Walsh	0
A. F. Giles c Russell b Walsh	0	– (4) b Smith	27
E. S. H. Giddins b Walsh	0	– not out	4
B 1, l-b 12, n-b 12	25	L-b 1, n-b 2	3
	187		**131**

1/4 2/19 3/31 4/56 5/96   187   1/8 2/24 3/56 4/56 5/66   131
6/100 7/128 8/181 9/187   6/77 7/88 8/108 9/108

Bonus points – Gloucestershire 4.

Bowling: *First Innings*—Walsh 24.2–6–88–6; Smith 20–4–46–2; Lewis 11–5–22–1; Alleyne 10–5–18–1. *Second Innings*—Walsh 18.3–3–65–6; Lewis 7–0–11–0; Smith 14–4–54–4.

Umpires: A. Clarkson and V. A. Holder.

At Worcester, June 17, 18, 19, 20. GLOUCESTERSHIRE lost to WORCESTERSHIRE by five wickets.

At Southampton, July 1, 2, 3, 4. GLOUCESTERSHIRE beat HAMPSHIRE by two wickets.

GLOUCESTERSHIRE v SUSSEX

At Cheltenham, July 14, 15, 16. Gloucestershire won by seven wickets. Gloucestershire 21 pts, Sussex 4 pts. Toss: Sussex.

Gloucestershire gained their first batting point in four matches – and eventually won a low-scoring game comfortably. They took a first-innings lead of 47, thanks to 76 from Hancock and an eighth-wicket stand of 48 between Ball and Russell. Walsh had become the first bowler to 50 Championship wickets, but it was Smith, with four in the second innings, who kept Gloucestershire's target to 116. They began disastrously when Lewry bowled Trainor and Hewson with his first two deliveries, giving him an unusual hat-trick, since he had ended Gloucestershire's first innings by bowling Smith. But Windows, who hit 13 boundaries, and Alleyne saw Gloucestershire home with an unbeaten partnership of 89, the highest of the match. Adams was left waiting for his luck to turn: he added just seven runs, including a duck, to the pair he had made at Cheltenham the previous year for Derbyshire.

Close of play: First day, Gloucestershire 94-3 (T. H. C. Hancock 60*, J. Lewis 1*); Second day, Sussex 118-6 (M. T. E. Peirce 57*, S. Humphries 8*).

Sussex

M. T. E. Peirce b Smith	5	– c Russell b Smith	59
W. G. Khan b Walsh	59	– c Russell b Smith	9
M. Newell b Smith	0	– c Russell b Walsh	12
*C. J. Adams b Lewis	0	– c Church b Smith	7
M. G. Bevan c Russell b Lewis	47	– c Alleyne b Ball	0
N. R. Taylor c Russell b Smith	6	– c Hewson b Lewis	10
R. S. C. Martin-Jenkins c Windows b Walsh	40	– c Russell b Lewis	4
†S. Humphries b Lewis	0	– lbw b Smith	12
R. J. Kirtley b Walsh	16	– not out	17
J. D. Lewry c Russell b Ball	0	– lbw b Ball	16
M. A. Robinson not out	6	– c Windows b Lewis	1
L-b 2, n-b 10	12	L-b 9, w 4, n-b 2	15
	191		**162**

1/11 2/23 3/38 4/89 5/100   1/10 2/57 3/70 4/71 5/96
6/140 7/140 8/176 9/177   6/100 7/121 8/126 9/155

Bonus points – Gloucestershire 4.

Bowling: *First Innings*—Walsh 21.1–3–52–3; Smith 18–10–30–3; Lewis 15–3–42–3; Alleyne 12–2–46–0; Ball 6–1–19–1. *Second Innings*—Walsh 22–8–46–1; Smith 19–9–31–4; Lewis 15.1–6–39–3; Alleyne 9–6–3–0; Ball 12.4–34–2.

Gloucestershire

N. J. Trainor lbw b Lewry	2	– b Lewry	0
T. H. C. Hancock c Humphries b Kirtley	76	– lbw b Lewry	16
D. R. Hewson c Humphries b Martin-Jenkins	13	– b Lewry	0
*M. W. Alleyne c Adams b Bevan	17	– not out	27
J. Lewis c Humphries b Robinson	22		
M. G. N. Windows lbw b Robinson	14	– (5) not out	60
M. J. Church b Bevan	22		
†R. C. Russell b Taylor b Martin-Jenkins	25		
M. C. J. Ball b Lewry	33		
A. M. Smith b Lewry	4		
C. A. Walsh not out	6		
B 1, l-b 1, n-b 2	4	B 4, l-b 7, w 2, n-b 2	15
	238		**(3 wkts) 118**

1/12 2/50 3/89 4/116 5/141   1/0 2/0 3/29
6/170 7/170 8/218 9/232

Bonus points – Gloucestershire 1, Sussex 4.

Bowling: *First Innings*—Lewry 19.5–3–73–3; Kirtley 17–4–53–1; Martin-Jenkins 19–9–56–2; Robinson 14–6–27–2; Bevan 8–0–27–2. *Second Innings*—Lewry 10–4–18–3; Kirtley 7–0–25–0; Martin-Jenkins 2–0–20–0; Bevan 4–0–24–0; Robinson 3.1–1–20–0.

Umpires: D. J. Constant and T. E. Jesty.

GLOUCESTERSHIRE v SURREY

At Cheltenham, July 22, 23, 24. Gloucestershire won by two wickets. Gloucestershire 20 pts, Surrey 6 pts. Toss: Surrey.

To rapturous applause from a 3,000-strong crowd, Gloucestershire moved into second place in the table, just 18 points behind their victims. Surrey had looked set for a victory that would have given them an overwhelming lead. They gained a first-innings advantage of 130 and had Gloucestershire on the run at 163 for six as they chased 266 for victory. But now it was Surrey's turn to suffer: Cunliffe was dropped twice in a powerful half-century; Windows battled to 60, and Ball, badly missed at square leg with just 12 runs needed, inched the team towards one of their most compelling Cheltenham wins. Adam Hollioake had started the game by putting an end to a run of low scores despite the opposition of Smith, making good use of heavy cloud cover and a bouncy pitch. And Surrey took full command when Bicknell and Saqlain Mushtaq engineered a dramatic collapse: the last six Gloucestershire first-innings wickets fell for one run. Walsh kept the game alive by thundering in to take four wickets in four overs. Then his team-mates played their part with the bat. Earlier, Russell had equalled Barrie Meyer's county record for catches: 708.

Close of play: First day, Surrey 256-6 (A. J. Hollioake 100*, J. N. Batty 0*); Second day, Surrey 111-5 (B. C. Hollioake 23*, Saqlain Mushtaq 6*).

Surrey

J. D. Ratcliffe c Lewis b Walsh	38	– c Church b Walsh	8
I. J. Ward c Russell b Smith	0	– c Russell b Smith	8
N. Shahid lbw b Smith	12	– lbw b Lewis	14
*A. J. Hollioake c Ball b Smith	112	– c Alleyne b Walsh	30
A. D. Brown c Lewis b Walsh	22	– c Church b Alleyne	13
B. C. Hollioake c Ball b Smith	19	– c Hewson b Walsh	27
J. A. Knott c Russell b Hancock	35	– (8) not out	4
†J. N. Batty b Smith	14	– (9) lbw b Walsh	6
M. P. Bicknell c Windows b Walsh	5	– (10) c Russell b Walsh	0
A. J. Tudor b Smith	0	– (11) lbw b Smith	0
Saqlain Mushtaq not out	4	– (7) c Ball b Walsh	10
B 4, l-b 7, w 2, n-b 23	36	L-b 5, n-b 10	15

1/2 2/44 3/77 4/109 5/138   297   1/16 2/16 3/39 4/62 5/94   135
6/253 7/284 8/293 9/293   6/115 7/129 8/130 9/134

Bonus points – Surrey 2, Gloucestershire 4.

Bowling: *First Innings*—Walsh 21–6–57–3; Smith 19.5–2–66–6; Lewis 15–2–69–0; Alleyne 9–1–53–0; Ball 11–1–37–0; Hancock 2–1–4–1. *Second Innings*—Walsh 14–1–47–6; Smith 14.4–3–43–2; Lewis 6–1–16–1; Alleyne 5–0–24–1.

Gloucestershire

R. J. Cunliffe lbw b Saqlain Mushtaq	16	– b B. C. Hollioake	53
T. H. C. Hancock b B. C. Hollioake	37	– b Saqlain Mushtaq	13
D. R. Hewson c Batty b Bicknell	52	– b Shahid b Saqlain Mushtaq	0
*M. W. Alleyne c A. J. Hollioake b Saqlain Mushtaq	1	– (6) c Shahid b Bicknell	27
M. G. N. Windows c Saqlain Mushtaq b Bicknell	23	– b Batty b Saqlain Mushtaq	60
M. J. Church lbw b Saqlain Mushtaq	5	– (7) lbw b Bicknell	0
†R. C. Russell lbw b Bicknell	0	– (4) lbw b Bicknell	9
M. C. J. Ball not out	0	– not out	48
J. Lewis c Brown b Saqlain Mushtaq	0	– lbw b Tudor	1
A. M. Smith c Batty b Bicknell	1	– not out	9
C. A. Walsh lbw b Bicknell	0		
L-b 14, n-b 18	32	B 14, l-b 10, n-b 22	46

1/53 2/89 3/90 4/145 5/166   167   1/44 2/44 3/67   (8 wkts) 266
6/166 7/166 8/166 9/167   4/100 5/161 6/163
                            7/242 8/245

Bonus points – Surrey 4.

Bowling: *First Innings*—Bicknell 14–5–34–5; Tudor 11–3–23–0; Saqlain Mushtaq 24–5–84–4; B. C. Holloake 8–3–12–1. *Second Innings*—Bicknell 21–2–81–3; Tudor 13.5–4–27–1; Saqlain Mushtaq 38–12–94–3; B. C. Holloake 12–1–35–1; A. J. Holloake 2–1–5–0.

Umpires: M. J. Harris and R. A. White.

At Manchester, August 5, 6, 7. GLOUCESTERSHIRE lost to LANCASHIRE by an innings and 35 runs.

GLOUCESTERSHIRE v KENT

At Bristol, August 14, 15, 16, 17. Gloucestershire won by 138 runs. Gloucestershire 20 pts, Kent 4 pts. Toss: Kent.

Seven overs had already been lost to rain after tea on the final day, when, with drizzle still in the air, Smith had McCague caught behind to give Gloucestershire their seventh Championship win. Despite 17 wickets falling on the first day, umpire Sharp saw nothing wrong: "The pitch had pace and bounce," he said, "but it was consistent." The batting from both sides had been appalling, though Gloucestershire made amends in the second innings. Windows, who had been given his cap on the opening day, hit his third Championship hundred of the season, and put on 185 for the fourth wicket with Alleyne to take the game out of Kent's reach. Requiring 436 to win, they started the final day on 83 for two – after Russell had completed his 800th dismissal for Gloucestershire – and maybe had an outside chance while Hooper was there. He scored his fourth century of the season but, on a hunch, Alleyne brought on Hewson, who had been bowling very slow-medium in the nets, and Hooper played too soon at his third delivery in first-class cricket.

Close of play: First day, Kent 94-7 (S. A. Marsh 20*, B. J. Phillips 14*); Second day, Gloucestershire 212-3 (M. W. Alleyne 42*, M. G. N. Windows 40*); Third day, Kent 83-2 (T. R. Ward 20*, B. J. Phillips 0*).

Gloucestershire

R. J. Cunliffe b Phillips	32	– b Fleming	40
T. H. C. Hancock c Hooper b Thompson	0	– c Marsh b McCague	63
D. R. Hewson c Hooper b Thompson	0	– c Fulton b McCague	9
*M. W. Alleyne c Fleming b Thompson	55	– c Marsh b McCague	83
M. G. N. Windows c Marsh b McCague	11	– c Marsh b Thompson	103
R. I. Dawson c Fulton b Fleming	5	– c Marsh b Thompson	12
†R. C. Russell b McCague	14	– c Marsh b Fleming	41
M. C. J. Ball b Thompson	0	– b Thompson	6
J. Lewis c Phillips b McCague	2	– c Wells b Hooper	13
A. M. Smith not out	1	– not out	28
C. A. Walsh b McCague	2	– c Walsh b Thompson	25
B 8, l-b 2, w 2, n-b 8	20	B 10, l-b 7, w 2, n-b 14	33

1/2 2/4 3/48 4/78 5/87   142   1/84 2/120 3/129 4/314 5/338   456
6/114 7/115 8/122 9/140   6/343 7/369 8/393 9/401

Bonus points – Kent 4.

Bowling: *First Innings*—McCague 16.5–3–41–4; Thompson 14–4–52–4; Phillips 7–1–18–1; Fleming 9–3–21–1. *Second Innings*—McCague 22–5–69–3; Thompson 23.4–5–82–4; Phillips 23–3–89–0; Fleming 31–6–81–2; Hooper 44–8–118–1.

Kent

D. P. Fulton c Alleyne b Walsh	18	– c Alleyne b Smith	9
E. T. Smith lbw b Smith	3	– c Russell b Lewis	49
T. R. Ward b Walsh	0	– lbw b Lewis	29
C. L. Hooper c and b Alleyne	13	– (5) c Hancock b Hewson	111
A. P. Wells c Russell b Walsh	12	– (6) c Cunliffe b Ball	7
C. D. Walsh c Cunliffe b Alleyne	0	– (7) c Windows b Walsh	10
M. V. Fleming run out	3	– (8) c and b Hancock	22
*†S. A. Marsh lbw b Lewis	60	– (9) not out	15
B. J. Phillips c Russell b Alleyne	34	– (4) lbw b Hancock	14
J. B. D. Thompson b Walsh	4	– lbw b Walsh	5
M. J. McCague not out	0	– c Russell b Smith	5
B 2, w 2, n-b 12	16	B 2, l-b 5, n-b 14	21

1/16 2/19 3/30 4/40 5/40   163   1/48 2/77 3/101 4/114 5/146   297
6/46 7/55 8/138 9/153   6/191 7/256 8/268 9/278

Bonus points – Gloucestershire 4.

Bowling: *First Innings*—Walsh 23–5–77–4; Alleyne 9–4–16–3; Lewis 12.4–7–21–1. *Second Innings*—Walsh 25–11–62–2; Smith 21–5–60–2; Lewis 15–3–38–2; Hewson 3–1–7–1; Ball 28–6–92–1; Hancock 7–1–25–2; Dawson 1–0–6–0.

Umpires: G. Sharp and J. F. Steele.

At Colchester, August 19, 20, 21. GLOUCESTERSHIRE beat ESSEX by an innings and 281 runs.

GLOUCESTERSHIRE v SOMERSET

At Bristol, August 27, 28, 29, 30. Somerset won by five wickets. Somerset 24 pts, Gloucestershire 7 pts. Toss: Somerset.

Gloucestershire's bid for the title was left in tatters after they were outplayed by Somerset and, in particular, Caddick, who bowled magnificently. Bowler chose to field first, which looked dubious as Gloucestershire strode to 355, with Alleyne staying five hours for 116. But Somerset took the lead, thanks to Burns and Trescothick, who both narrowly missed hundreds having been dropped early on. After Caddick and Rose despatched Gloucestershire's second innings, Somerset were left to score 164 to win. They were struggling when three batsmen were lbw in seven balls and they had to fight for every run, especially against Walsh. But Holloway battled through successfully, spending more than four and a half hours over 58.

Close of play: First day, Gloucestershire 311-7 (M. C. J. Ball 21*, J. Lewis 0*); Second day, Somerset 269-5 (M. Burns 83*, R. J. Turner 23*); Third day, Gloucestershire 187-6 (A. J. Wright 31*, M. C. J. Ball 28*).

Gloucestershire

R. J. Cunliffe c Turner b Caddick	0	– b van Troost	3
T. H. C. Hancock b van Troost	65	– c Parsons b van Troost	73
†R. C. Russell b Caddick	12	– c Trescothick b Caddick	3
*M. W. Alleyne c Turner b van Troost	116	– c Bowler b Rose	15
M. G. N. Windows b Pierson	39	– c Parsons b Pierson	6
R. I. Dawson c Parsons b Pierson	27	– c Turner b Caddick	5
A. J. Wright c Burns b Caddick	14	– c Parsons b Caddick	36
M. C. J. Ball c and b Caddick	58	– c Parsons b Caddick	45
J. Lewis b Caddick	2	– c Trescothick b Rose	1
A. M. Smith b van Troost	0	– not out	1
C. A. Walsh not out	1	– lbw b Rose	1
B 1, l-b 8, w 2, n-b 10	21	B 4, l-b 5, w 2, n-b 4	15

1/0 2/65 3/100 4/183 5/239   355   1/21 2/34 3/53 4/76 5/83   204
6/279 7/303 8/322 9/325   6/130 7/192 8/199 9/201

Bonus points – Gloucestershire 4, Somerset 4.

Bowling: *First Innings*—Caddick 36.2–9–97–5; van Troost 24–5–73–3; Rose 22–4–63–0; Pierson 26–5–87–2; Parsons 5–2–18–0; Burns 2–0–8–0. *Second Innings*—Caddick 25–4–66–4; van Troost 13–3–41–2; Rose 14.3–3–34–3; Pierson 16–2–52–1; Bowler 1–0–2–0.

Somerset

*P. D. Bowler c Alleyne b Walsh	7	– lbw b Walsh	6
P. C. L. Holloway c Russell b Lewis	36	– not out	58
M. E. Trescothick c Russell b Walsh	92	– lbw b Walsh	0
G. J. Kennis lbw b Lewis	4	– lbw b Walsh	0
K. A. Parsons c Russell b Smith	2	– c Alleyne b Walsh	25
M. Burns b Walsh	96	– c Lewis b Ball	31
†R. J. Turner c Ball b Alleyne	36	– not out	36
G. D. Rose c Russell b Lewis	28		
A. R. K. Pierson c Russell b Smith	25		
A. R. Caddick not out	27		
A. P. van Troost b Walsh	8		
B 8, l-b 11, n-b 16	35	L-b 6, n-b 2	8

1/10 2/105 3/113 4/116 5/191   396   1/20 2/20 3/21   (5 wkts) 164
6/298 7/300 8/359 9/377   4/62 5/112

Bonus points – Somerset 4, Gloucestershire 3 (Score at 120 overs: 363-8).

Bowling: *First Innings*—Walsh 33.1–12–80–4; Smith 25–5–79–2; Lewis 26–4–110–3; Ball 19–4–59–0; Alleyne 22–9–41–1; Hancock 3–1–8–0. *Second Innings*—Walsh 22–6–36–3; Smith 8–0–34–1; Lewis 14–3–28–0; Ball 23–3–47–1; Alleyne 5.1–1–13–0.

Umpires: K. J. Lyons and G. Sharp.

GLOUCESTERSHIRE v NORTHAMPTONSHIRE

At Bristol, September 1, 2. Gloucestershire won by ten wickets. Gloucestershire 21 pts, Northamptonshire 4 pts. Toss: Gloucestershire.

This was a miserable performance by Northamptonshire. They were bowled out twice inside two days for a combined total of 218; in both innings the highest contribution came from Extras. Walsh and Smith exploited the damp pitch perfectly, gaining movement and late swing; both recorded their best figures for the season. The pitch was greener than usual, but Northamptonshire's lack of resistance owed more to poor concentration than to the surface. Only Penberthy and Sales hinted at respectability, putting on 63 in the first innings, after the top three batsmen had failed to score. For Gloucestershire, Cunliffe returned to form with a fifty graced with fine off-drives. He shared a stand of 78 with Windows, who had that day been included in England A's winter tour party. Windows also received a cheque for £1,000 when the county's sponsors named him player of the year.

Close of play: First day, Gloucestershire 150-5 (A. J. Wright 9*, R. C. Russell 8*).

Northamptonshire

R. R. Montgomerie lbw b Smith	0	– c Alleyne b Smith	2
A. J. Swann b Walsh	0	– lbw b Smith	10
M. B. Loye lbw b Smith	0	– c Russell b Walsh	12
A. L. Penberthy lbw b Hancock	30	– c Ball b Smith	6
D. J. Sales lbw b Walsh	25	– lbw b Smith	0
*K. M. Curran b Walsh	7	– c Dawson b Walsh	0
†D. Ripley c Cunliffe b Lewis	4	– b Walsh	17
J. P. Taylor b Walsh	6	– c Cunliffe b Smith	4
F. A. Rose not out	13	– b Smith	18
D. Follett b Walsh	0	– b Walsh	0
J. F. Brown c Ball b Walsh	2	– not out	3
B 10, l-b 2, n-b 24	36	B 8, l-b 5, n-b 10	23

1/1 2/1 3/1 4/64 5/80   123   1/11 2/24 3/44 4/46 5/48   95
6/97 7/97 8/119 9/119   6/48 7/58 8/84 9/92

Bonus points – Gloucestershire 4.

Bowling: *First Innings*—Walsh 17.4–8–36–6; Smith 10–6–9–2; Alleyne 6–1–19–0; Lewis 12–3–40–1; Hancock 3–1–7–1. *Second Innings*—Walsh 12.4–2–50–4; Smith 12–3–32–6.

Gloucestershire

R. I. Dawson c Penberthy b Rose	2	– not out 4
T. H. C. Hancock c Penberthy b Taylor	7	– not out 3
R. J. Cunliffe b Follett	53	
*M. W. Alleyne b Follett	18	
M. G. N. Windows b Follett	35	
A. J. Wright lbw b Taylor	25	
†R. C. Russell b Rose	26	
M. C. J. Ball c Ripley b Rose	0	
J. Lewis c Ripley b Taylor	5	
A. M. Smith c Follett b Rose	5	
C. A. Walsh not out	6	
B 4, l-b 6, n-b 18	28	N-b 2 2

1/4 2/12 3/49 4/127 5/132   210   (no wkt) 9
6/177 7/178 8/191 9/195

Bonus points – Gloucestershire 1, Northamptonshire 4.

Bowling: *First Innings*—Rose 23.5–8–63–4; Taylor 23–7–55–3; Follett 17–3–48–3; Curran 2–0–13–0; Brown 5–1–21–0. *Second Innings*—Rose 1.5–0–7–0; Follett 1–0–2–0.

Umpires: J. W. Holder and J. F. Steele.

At Lord's, September 9, 10, 11. GLOUCESTERSHIRE beat MIDDLESEX by 96 runs.

At Nottingham, September 17, 18, 19, 20. GLOUCESTERSHIRE beat NOTTINGHAMSHIRE by 189 runs.

GROUNDSMEN OF THE YEAR

Nigel Gray of Hampshire was named the ECB's Groundsman of the Year, with Geoff Swift of Cheltenham College winning the award for county out-grounds.

COUNTY CAPS AWARDED IN 1998

Derbyshire........	K. J. Dean, M. J. Slater.
Durham	M. M. Betts, D. C. Boon, S. J. E. Brown, P. D. Collingwood, J. J. B. Lewis, J. E. Morris, M. A. Roseberry, N. J. Speak, M. P. Speight, J. Wood.
Gloucestershire.....	T. H. C. Hancock, J. Lewis, M. G. N. Windows.
Hampshire........	P. J. Hartley, N. A. M. McLean, A. D. Mascarenhas, G. W. White.
Kent............	D. P. Fulton.
Lancashire.......	A. Flintoff.
Leicestershire......	M. T. Brimson, A. Habib.
Middlesex	J. P. Hewitt, J. L. Langer.
Nottinghamshire	M. P. Dowman, J. E. R. Gallian.
Surrey	J. D. Ratcliffe, I. D. K. Salisbury, Saqlain Mushtaq, N. Shahid.
Sussex	C. J. Adams, M. G. Bevan, R. J. Kirtley.
Warwickshire......	E. S. H. Giddins.
Worcestershire	V. S. Solanki.
Yorkshire	G. M. Hamilton, P. M. Hutchison.

No caps were awarded by Essex, Glamorgan, Northamptonshire or Somerset. For the first time, Durham awarded caps on merit, rather than giving them to all playing staff.

HAMPSHIRE

Patron: Lord Denning
President: W. J. Weld
Chairman: B. G. Ford
Chairman, Cricket Committee: D. J. Robinson
Chief Executive: A. F. Baker
Captain: R. A. Smith
Director of Cricket: T. M. Tremlett
Coach: M. D. Marshall
Head Groundsman: N. Gray
Scorer: V. H Isaacs

Adrian Aymes

By far the most significant announcement concerning Hampshire in 1998 was the news that the County Ground had been sold to developers for £5.5 million. Hampshire have now finally committed themselves to leave Northlands Road, their headquarters for more than a century, in October 2000, for a £16 million purpose-built stadium already taking shape near the M27 at West End. Before the season began, the fear among Hampshire's dwindling number of members (at little more than 4,000 the lowest since the early 1950s) was that they would not have a team worthy of such palatial surroundings when first-class cricket was played there in 2001.

But after five seasons of decline since Hampshire last won a trophy, the slide was halted in 1998. Whether it has been stopped permanently or temporarily remains to be seen. But there was a marked respite in Robin Smith's first season as captain, in which all expectations – modest ones, it has to be said – were exceeded. Hampshire reached the semi-finals of the NatWest Trophy, while they came sixth in the Championship and eighth in the Sunday League. None of this seemed likely in mid-May, when Hampshire finished bottom of their Benson and Hedges group, below British Universities, and were crushed so overwhelmingly by Surrey in the Championship (by an innings and 184 runs) that it was hard to predict anything other than a drawer full of wooden spoons. Along the way, West Indian fast bowler Nixon McLean, the third-choice overseas player, was dropped for the Benson and Hedges match at Bristol because he was struggling to come to terms with an English length and line.

But as McLean improved, so did Hampshire, even if he did not cut a swathe through batting orders in quite the same way as previous Caribbean imports Andy Roberts and Malcolm Marshall. Had Queenslanders Michael Kasprowicz or Andy Bichel been available, McLean would not have been a Hampshire player at all, but he answered a late emergency call to sample his first season in county cricket. Under the watchful guidance of his mentor, Marshall, he became consistently the quickest bowler on the circuit. His total of 62 first-class wickets may have been 44 less than another West Indian, Courtney Walsh, produced for Gloucestershire; but his presence gave

Hampshire an edge they had been lacking since Marshall's retirement. It was no coincidence that Hampshire gleaned 61 out of a possible 68 bowling bonus points in the Championship. For the first time in years, there was a capacity to bowl out the opposition twice, which they did six times.

Hampshire's other seamers all benefited from having the ever-willing McLean bowling from the other end. Alex Morris, 21, one of three players recruited from Yorkshire, capped a highly promising first season at Hampshire by reaching 50 first-class wickets. But the club's main spinner, Shaun Udal, in common with most of his type, found few pitches to suit him.

Had the batting matched the bowling, Hampshire might have done even better, but they averaged well under two batting points a game. Only Giles White reached 1,000 first-class runs, and had a season of steady personal improvement; no others matched his progress. Jason Laney, of whom so much was and is expected, had a summer best forgotten, while Matthew Keech and Will Kendall did not make the expected leap forward. Even Smith, with three centuries in 853 first-class runs, was unable to find the consistency which might have recaptured the England selectors' waning interest. Early in the season, Adrian Aymes, promoted to bat at No. 5, hinted at providing stability. But he could not build on an excellent start which included centuries against Leicestershire and Glamorgan, though his keeping was always of a high standard; he was unfortunate to miss selection for the Ashes tour.

The bonuses for Hampshire were the advances made by young all-rounders Morris and Dimitri Mascarenhas, and the unexpected but welcome run in the NatWest Trophy. The reliable Cardigan Connor, now mostly restricted to limited-overs cricket by his bad knee, inspired a second-round victory over the holders Essex, while Aymes and White made sure of a quarter-final win at Middlesex's expense. If the semi-final defeat by Lancashire was an anticlimax, it has to be remembered that, in the first round, Hampshire was nought for three against Dorset.

Smith's first year of captaincy in succession to John Stephenson was an eventful one. Once he had become aware that he needed to do more than lead by example, he and Marshall generated a team spirit second to none, another reason why Hampshire confounded their critics. However, his desire to consult not just one but several of his team-mates regularly during play, and a reticence to set attacking fields to tailenders mystified spectators at times. If Hampshire are to build on their success they will need to improve the batting and bring down the average age. Connor, his ailing knees testimony to 15 years' unstinting toil and 614 wickets in the Hampshire cause, will not easily be replaced. At the end of the season, left-arm spinner Raj Maru, who joined Hampshire in the same season as Connor, 1984, retired with 504 wickets, moving into coaching. His contribution to Hampshire was underestimated, and as a slip fielder there were few better. – PAT SYMES.

519

HAMPSHIRE 1998

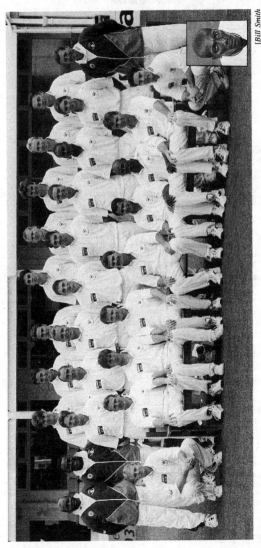

[*Bill Smith*]

Back row: J. S. Laney, G. W. White, N. J. Makin, S. R. G. Francis, R. R. Dibden, H. J. H. Loudon, W. S. Kendall, D. A. Kenway. *Middle row*: M. D. Marshall (*First Eleven coach*), D. L. Haynes (*batting coach*), M. Keech, P. J. Hartley, T. M. Hansen, S. J. Renshaw, L. Savident, A. C. Morris, A. D. Mascarenhas, Z. C. Morris, T. M. Tremlett (*director of cricket*). *Front row*: P. R. Whitaker, A. N. Aymes, K. D. James, S. D. Udal, R. A. Smith (*captain*), R. J. Maru, C. A. Connor, J. P. Stephenson, M. Garaway. *Inset*: N. A. M. McLean.

HAMPSHIRE RESULTS

All first-class matches – Played 19: Won 6, Lost 6, Drawn 7.

County Championship matches – Played 17: Won 6, Lost 5, Drawn 6.

*Competition placings – Britannic Assurance County Championship, 6th;
NatWest Trophy, s-f; Benson and Hedges Cup, 6th in Group C;
AXA League, 8th.*

COUNTY CHAMPIONSHIP AVERAGES
BATTING

Cap		M	I	NO	R	HS	100s	50s	Avge	Ct/St
1985	R. A. Smith	15	23	5	841	138	3	2	40.04	10
1991	A. N. Aymes†	17	26	5	741	133	2	3	35.28	52/2
	W. S. Kendall	6	9	2	245	78*	0	1	35.00	6
1989	K. D. James	17	25	9	559	57	0	3	34.93	4
1998	G. W. White	17	29	2	905	106	2	5	33.51	12
1992	S. D. Udal†	13	18	5	404	62	0	1	31.07	9
1995	J. P. Stephenson . . .	15	23	1	681	114	2	4	30.95	14
	P. R. Whitaker	7	11	1	309	74	0	2	30.90	7
1998	A. D. Mascarenhas . .	16	24	2	645	89	0	6	29.31	11
	M. Keech	10	12	0	262	67	0	2	21.83	9
	D. A. Kenway†	2	4	0	80	57	0	1	20.00	1
	A. C. Morris	11	14	4	184	51	0	1	18.40	6
1998	N. A. M. McLean§ . .	16	22	2	288	43	0	0	14.40	5
1998	P. J. Hartley	12	16	3	160	29	0	0	12.30	3
	J. S. Laney†	7	12	0	123	67	0	1	10.25	8

Also batted: C. A. Connor (cap 1988) (3 matches) 0*; R. J. Maru (cap 1986) (1 match) 13, 14 (1 ct); Z. C. Morris (1 match) 0, 10; S. J. Renshaw (1 match) 10*.

* Signifies not out.   † Born in Hampshire.   § Overseas player.

BOWLING

	O	M	R	W	BB	5W/i	Avge
A. C. Morris	296	61	944	47	4-30	0	20.08
N. A. M. McLean . . .	518.5	105	1,575	62	6-101	2	25.40
A. D. Mascarenhas . . .	266.5	58	934	30	4-31	0	31.13
K. D. James	320	67	1,005	31	4-22	0	32.41
J. P. Stephenson	271.4	66	735	22	4-29	0	33.40
P. J. Hartley	348.5	65	1,102	31	4-42	0	35.54
S. D. Udal	176.2	34	542	13	4-37	0	41.69

Also bowled: A. N. Aymes 11–0–166–2; C. A. Connor 35–5–122–2; W. S. Kendall 4–0–16–0; D. A. Kenway 2–0–17–0; J. S. Laney 2–0–14–0; R. J. Maru 31–5–112–2; Z. C. Morris 1–0–5–0; S. J. Renshaw 6–1–9–1; R. A. Smith 21–1–197–2; P. R. Whitaker 6–1–15–1; G. W. White 11–1–47–0.

COUNTY RECORDS

Highest score for:	316	R. H. Moore v Warwickshire at Bournemouth . . .	1937
Highest score against:	303*	G. A. Hick (Worcestershire) at Southampton	1997
Best bowling for:	9-25	R. M. H. Cottam v Lancashire at Manchester . . .	1965
Best bowling against:	10-46	W. Hickton (Lancashire) at Manchester	1870
Highest total for:	672-7 dec.	v Somerset at Taunton	1899
Highest total against:	742	by Surrey at The Oval	1909
Lowest total for:	15	v Warwickshire at Birmingham	1922
Lowest total against:	23	by Yorkshire at Middlesbrough	1965

At Oxford, April 17, 18, 20. HAMPSHIRE drew with OXFORD UNIVERSITY.

HAMPSHIRE v NORTHAMPTONSHIRE

At Southampton, April 23, 24, 25, 27. Drawn. Hampshire 5 pts, Northamptonshire 5 pts. Toss: Hampshire. County debut: F. A. Rose.

Rain allowed only one hour during the first three days, but the last day was dry and Hampshire helped set up a contest by feeding Northamptonshire declaration runs at 13 an over. The batsmen took 105 off Smith's gentle occasional leg-spin, while wicket-keeper Aymes rejoiced in a career-best two for 135 – both caught and bowled. Two forfeitures left Hampshire to score 276 in 76 overs. But Northamptonshire's new fast bowling recruits, Malcolm and West Indian Test player Franklyn Rose, reduced them to 54 for five. Keech was joined by the reliable James in a stand of 96, until Malcolm broke through again. It needed Aymes in the more familiar role of stubborn batsman to ensure the draw; he and No. 10 Renshaw held out for five overs.

Close of play: First day, No play; Second day, Northamptonshire 35-2 (M. B. Loye 10*, J. P. Taylor 0*); Third day, No play.

Northamptonshire

R. R. Montgomerie c James b Renshaw	3	*K. M. Curran not out		58
A. J. Swann lbw b Stephenson	19			
M. B. Loye c and b Aymes	77	L-b 1, n-b 2		3
J. P. Taylor c Aymes b Smith	58			
R. J. Bailey not out	53	1/3 2/32 3/152	(5 wkts dec.)	275
D. J. Sales c and b Aymes	4	4/168 5/172		

†D. Ripley, G. P. Swann, D. E. Malcolm and F. A. Rose did not bat.

Bonus points – Northamptonshire 2, Hampshire 2.

Bowling: Connor 5–0–15–0; Renshaw 6–1–9–1; James 3–1–8–0; Stephenson 2–1–2–1; Aymes 9–0–135–2; Smith 9–0–105–1.

Northamptonshire forfeited their second innings.

Hampshire

Hampshire forfeited their first innings.

J. S. Laney b Malcolm	9	S. D. Udal b Malcolm		0
G. W. White c Ripley b Malcolm	0	S. J. Renshaw not out		10
*R. A. Smith b Malcolm	7			
M. Keech c A. J. Swann b Bailey	67	L-b 4, n-b 15		19
W. S. Kendall c Loye b Rose	1			
J. P. Stephenson c Ripley b Rose	11	1/7 2/12 3/23	(8 wkts)	193
K. D. James c Ripley b Malcolm	54	4/26 5/54 6/150		
†A. N. Aymes not out	15	7/171 8/171		

C. A. Connor did not bat.

Bowling: Malcolm 21–4–60–5; Rose 18.5–4–57–2; Taylor 15–5–38–0; Curran 6–1–18–0; G. P. Swann 13–5–12–0; Bailey 2–1–4–1.

Umpires: J. W. Lloyds and N. T. Plews.

HAMPSHIRE v SURREY

At Southampton, May 13, 14, 15. Surrey won by an innings and 184 runs. Surrey 24 pts, Hampshire 2 pts. Toss: Surrey. Championship debut: N. A. M. McLean.

A week after the County Ground was sold for £5 million, there was a reminder of what batsmen will be missing after 2000, when Nigel Gray's sublime surfaces are given up for housing. At least, the reminder was there while Surrey were amassing 591: Butcher and Stewart opened with a stand of 118, while Brown – who hit 155 in 147 balls – and Batty added 187 for the sixth wicket. When Hampshire batted, it was a different story, however. Tudor's pace and the spin of Saqlain Mushtaq and Salisbury sliced through a frail top order, and only Mascarenhas resisted for long. Hampshire followed on 402 behind, and provided only sporadic defiance once Bicknell had broken through. The merciful end came five balls after tea on the third day as McLean heaved across the line at Saqlain. Stephenson's absence for most of the match with a viral infection was small excuse for Hampshire: the big gap between the sides, in class and expectation, looked obvious.

Close of play: First day, Surrey 434-5 (A. D. Brown 111*, J. N. Batty 51*); Second day, Hampshire 9-2 (P. J. Hartley 6*).

Surrey

M. A. Butcher c Aymes b McLean	106		I. D. K. Salisbury c Aymes b Mascarenhas		7
A. J. Stewart lbw b James	59		A. J. Tudor b Hartley		48
G. P. Thorpe c Aymes b Mascarenhas	32		M. P. Bicknell c Smith b Udal		38
*A. J. Holloake c Mascarenhas b McLean	30		Saqlain Mushtaq not out		0
A. D. Brown lbw b McLean	155		B 5, l-b 13, w 14, n-b 8		40
B. C. Holloake c Aymes b McLean	13				—
†J. N. Batty lbw b Mascarenhas	63		1/118 2/176 3/247 4/269 5/295		591
			6/482 7/500 8/500 9/591		

Bonus points – Surrey 4, Hampshire 2 (Score at 120 overs: 494-6).

Bowling: McLean 29-4-107-4; Hartley 28-0-107-1; Stephenson 5-1-23-0; James 27-8-104-1; Mascarenhas 25-4-119-3; Udal 27.2-3-94-1; Laney 2-0-14-0; White 1-0-5-0.

Hampshire

G. W. White b Saqlain Mushtaq	23	– c Stewart b Bicknell	1
J. S. Laney lbw b Tudor	2	– c Batty b Tudor	0
K. D. James b Salisbury	18	– (4) lbw b Bicknell	1
*R. A. Smith c Batty b Salisbury	29	– (5) c B. C. Holloake b Salisbury	42
M. Keech b Saqlain Mushtaq	1	– (6) c Stewart b Bicknell	31
A. D. Mascarenhas not out	60	– (7) c Thorpe b Tudor	13
†A. N. Aymes c A. J. Holloake b Saqlain Mushtaq	1	– (8) not out	30
S. D. Udal c Saqlain Mushtaq b Tudor	20	– (9) run out	30
P. J. Hartley c Thorpe b Tudor	6	– (3) c Brown b Tudor	18
N. A. M. McLean c Butcher b Tudor	0	– b Saqlain Mushtaq	15
J. P. Stephenson absent ill		– absent ill	
B 1, l-b 6, w 4, n-b 18	29	B 8, l-b 7, w 4, n-b 18	37
1/4 2/54 3/66 4/67 5/119	189	1/1 2/9 3/24 4/56 5/96	218
6/134 7/175 8/189 9/189		6/126 7/140 8/202 9/218	

Bonus points – Surrey 4.

Bowling: *First Innings*—Bicknell 7-3-22-0; Tudor 8-3-32-4; B. C. Holloake 4-1-15-0; Saqlain Mushtaq 20-5-62-3; Salisbury 15-3-51-2. *Second Innings*—Tudor 16-4-53-3; Bicknell 15-6-43-3; Saqlain Mushtaq 24.5-8-57-1; Salisbury 19-6-43-1; B. C. Holloake 3-0-7-0.

Umpires: A. Clarkson and R. Julian.

At Leicester, May 21, 22, 23, 24. HAMPSHIRE drew with LEICESTERSHIRE.

HAMPSHIRE v GLAMORGAN

At Southampton, June 3, 4, 5, 6. Hampshire won by nine wickets. Hampshire 23 pts, Glamorgan 4 pts. Toss: Hampshire.

Smith's first victory as Hampshire captain provided a timely fillip to morale. It came at the expense of the defending champions and lifted them from the foot of the table. Winning the toss was his first major contribution: Glamorgan struggled to make runs in overcast conditions against McLean and Mascarenhas. Their own attack was weakened by the absence of Waqar

Younis and Croft. First Smith scored a four-hour 84, then Aymes's second century in consecutive matches stabilised the middle order, enabled Hampshire to build a first-innings lead of 202 and carried him past 5,000 first-class runs on his 34th birthday. Glamorgan never looked like saving the match once Hartley had removed three top-order batsmen, although Evans, with a maiden Championship half-century, and Butcher delayed the end until the final afternoon. Left 38 overs to get 84, Hampshire completed their task with 14.5 overs to spare. Whitaker made the winning hit to follow an aggressive first-innings 74.

Close of play: First day, Hampshire 0-1 (G. W. White 0*, R. A. Smith 0*); Second day, Hampshire 247-5 (A. N. Aymes 48*, P. R. Whitaker 39*); Third day, Glamorgan 127-5 (A. W. Evans 55*, O. T. Parkin 0*).

Glamorgan

S. P. James lbw b James	34	– lbw b Hartley	20
A. W. Evans b McLean	10	– c Aymes b Stephenson	87
A. Dale c Aymes b Mascarenhas	92	– c Whitaker b Hartley	0
*M. P. Maynard c Aymes b Mascarenhas	7	– c Aymes b James	5
P. A. Cottey b McLean	14	– c Whitaker b Hartley	17
M. J. Powell c Smith b Hartley	52	– c Hartley b Whitaker	20
G. P. Butcher c Aymes b McLean	5	– (8) c Aymes b Hartley	85
†A. D. Shaw lbw b James	7	– (9) c Mascarenhas b Stephenson	3
S. D. Thomas c Aymes b Mascarenhas	11	– (10) c White b Mascarenhas	18
S. L. Watkin not out	12	– (11) not out	2
O. T. Parkin b Mascarenhas	13	– (7) b McLean	3
B 4, l-b 2, n-b 6	12	L-b 7, n-b 18	25
	269		285

1/23 2/60 3/83 4/112 5/201   269
6/218 7/230 8/244 9/245

1/52 2/52 3/65 4/84 5/124   285
6/141 7/191 8/211 9/254

Bonus points – Glamorgan 2, Hampshire 4.

Bowling: *First Innings*—McLean 19–5–42–3; Hartley 18–3–65–1; Mascarenhas 21–5–68–4; James 21–2–75–2; Udal 7–2–13–0. *Second Innings*—McLean 22.2–87–1; Hartley 21.1–2–77–4; James 19–5–51–1; Mascarenhas 9–2–31–1; Udal 4–0–8–0; Whitaker 2–0–2–1; Stephenson 15–7–22–2.

Hampshire

G. W. White c Thomas b Watkin	56	– not out	27
J. P. Stephenson lbw b Parkin	0	– c Maynard b Watkin	21
*R. A. Smith c Shaw b Watkin	84		
M. Keech c Shaw b Butcher	4		
†A. N. Aymes c Shaw b Dale	120		
A. D. Mascarenhas lbw b Butcher	0		
P. R. Whitaker c Shaw b Parkin	74	– (3) not out	25
K. D. James run out	36		
S. D. Udal not out	42		
N. A. M. McLean c Powell b Dale	11		
P. J. Hartley c Evans b Watkin	18		
B 1, l-b 15, w 4, n-b 6	26	B 5, l-b 2, n-b 4	11
	471	(1 wkt)	84

1/0 2/139 3/157 4/161 5/163   471
6/308 7/387 8/425 9/449

1/43   (1 wkt) 84

Bonus points – Hampshire 3, Glamorgan 2 (Score at 120 overs: 300-5).

Bowling: *First Innings*—Watkin 37–9–106–3; Parkin 34–16–47–2; Thomas 34–7–106–0; Butcher 26–3–86–2; Dale 17–1–72–2; Cottey 16–2–38–0. *Second Innings*—Watkin 8–0–28–1; Parkin 8–2–21–0; Thomas 4–0–14–0; Butcher 3.1–0–14–0.

Umpires: T. E. Jesty and K. E. Palmer.

At Leeds, June 11, 12, 13, 15. HAMPSHIRE drew with YORKSHIRE.

HAMPSHIRE v DERBYSHIRE

At Basingstoke, June 17, 18, 19, 20. Hampshire won by five wickets. Hampshire 21 pts, Derbyshire 5 pts. Toss: Hampshire.

There were two minor curiosities to savour on Hampshire's annual visit to May's Bounty; Smith used seven bowlers in the first 23 overs of another rain-affected match, and the winning runs came from a no-ball by Dean that went for four byes and thus counted, under ECB regulations, as six no-balls. In between, there was plenty to frustrate the best efforts of the Basingstoke Cricket Club ground staff and volunteers, as a quarter of the first day and the whole of the second were washed out. Rollins was in pugnacious form in Derbyshire's first innings, while Roberts and Aldred helped to ensure maximum batting points with a later flurry. Smith replied with a century on the third day, but some bargaining was necessary to contrive a result; Hampshire were set 281 on an easing wicket. Stephenson's early belligerence – he hit 14 boundaries in his 75 – made the target look generous, and the in-form Aymes made sure of victory.

Close of play: First day, Derbyshire 245-6 (K. M. Krikken 25*, G. M. Roberts 0*); Second day, No play; Third day, Hampshire 210-4 (R. A. Smith 104*, A. D. Mascarenhas 0*).

Derbyshire

A. S. Rollins c Stephenson b Hartley	89	– c Stephenson b Connor	9
M. J. Slater lbw b Stephenson	47	– c Smith b Connor	14
T. A. Tweats lbw b Stephenson	9	– b Smith	44
K. J. Barnett b Stephenson	43	– not out	44
M. E. Cassar c Stephenson b James	10	– not out	24
*†K. M. Krikken c Udal b McLean	29		
P. A. J. DeFreitas c and b James	2		
G. M. Roberts b Udal	35		
P. Aldred not out	37		
S. J. Lacey c and b Udal	17		
K. J. Dean c White b Udal	5		
L-b 9, w 4, n-b 14	27	L-b 1, n-b 4	5

1/92 2/116 3/178 4/208 5/228   350   1/19 2/28 3/106   (3 wkts dec.) 140
6/244 7/257 8/306 9/332

Bonus points – Derbyshire 4, Hampshire 4.

Bowling: *First Innings*—McLean 18–3–56–1; Hartley 25–4–85–1; Udal 11.3–3–25–3; James 7–2–31–2; Connor 8–0–41–0; Stephenson 28–6–75–3; Mascarenhas 12.5–5–28–0. *Second Innings*—McLean 6–1–15–0; Connor 6–1–23–2; Smith 9–1–63–1; White 8–1–38–0.

Hampshire

G. W. White b Aldred	16	– c Tweats b Dean	7
J. P. Stephenson c Krikken b Dean	1	– c Roberts b Lacey	75
K. D. James c Tweats b Lacey	24		
*R. A. Smith not out	104	– c sub b DeFreitas	17
†A. N. Aymes c Aldred b DeFreitas	40	– not out	61
A. D. Mascarenhas not out	0	– b Aldred	51
P. R. Whitaker (did not bat)		– (3) b Roberts	45
S. D. Udal (did not bat)		– (7) not out	2
B 11, l-b 2, w 4, n-b 8	25	B 6, l-b 9, n-b 8	23

1/4 2/35 3/77 4/210   (4 wkts dec.) 210   1/17 2/111 3/150   (5 wkts) 281
4/152 5/266

C. A. Connor, P. J. Hartley and N. A. M. McLean did not bat.

Bonus points – Hampshire 1, Derbyshire 1.

Bowling: *First Innings*—DeFreitas 22–8–54–1; Dean 11–5–17–1; Aldred 10–1–25–1; Lacey 18–5–53–1; Roberts 14–0–48–0. *Second Innings*—DeFreitas 13–2–50–1; Dean 10.3–1–51–1; Aldred 6–1–44–1; Lacey 13–2–48–1; Roberts 17–2–65–1; Barnett 2–0–8–0.

Umpires: V. A. Holder and B. Leadbeater.

At Taunton, June 26, 27, 28, 29. HAMPSHIRE drew with SOMERSET.

HAMPSHIRE v GLOUCESTERSHIRE

At Southampton, July 1, 2, 3, 4. Gloucestershire won by two wickets. Gloucestershire 20 pts, Hampshire 4 pts. Toss: Hampshire. First-class debut: Z. C. Morris.

Dominic Hewson batted four hours for an unbeaten 78 as Gloucestershire recorded the highest total of the match to win. In pursuit of 331 on an increasingly docile pitch, Gloucestershire had stumbled to 112 for five after losing three wickets in the first eight overs of the last day. But Hewson received crucial support from the other later-order batsmen, especially Ball, who rushed to 54, and Hampshire ran out of ideas. Stephenson had scored his first century of the season to give them what looked like a winning position after both sides failed in the first innings, Hampshire crumpling to 27 for five soon after the start. Zac Morris, the former England Under-19 left-arm spinner, made his first-class debut, joining his brother Alex in the team, but damaged his knee while fielding and could bowl only one over.

Close of play: First day, Gloucestershire 91-4 (T. H. C. Hancock 51*, D. R. Hewson 14*); Second day, Hampshire 156-1 (J. P. Stephenson 87*, P. R. Whitaker 40*); Third day, Gloucestershire 83-2 (N. J. Trainor 31*, A. J. Wright 6*).

Hampshire

G. W. White c Russell b Lewis	10	– c Hancock b Alleyne	22
J. P. Stephenson c Russell b Walsh	4	– c Trainor b Ball	114
P. R. Whitaker c Trainor b Smith	0	– c Russell b Walsh	40
*R. A. Smith c Russell b Lewis	8	– b Walsh	4
†A. N. Aymes b Walsh	3	– lbw b Smith	22
A. D. Mascarenhas c Russell b Alleyne	10	– c Russell b Walsh	3
M. Keech c Russell b Lewis	25	– lbw b Walsh	2
K. D. James c Hewson b Ball	57	– not out	29
A. C. Morris not out	33	– lbw b Smith	10
N. A. M. McLean run out	18	– c Hewson b Ball	43
Z. C. Morris c Trainor b Walsh	0	– b Smith	10
L-b 6, n-b 10	16	B 4, l-b 9, w 2, n-b 8	23

1/5 2/6 3/22 4/25 5/27   184   1/60 2/156 3/166 4/208 5/216   322
6/47 7/76 8/149 9/182   6/218 7/218 8/241 9/303

Bonus points – Gloucestershire 4.

Bowling: *First Innings*—Walsh 16.2–5–39–3; Smith 20–9–38–1; Lewis 12–4–29–3; Alleyne 10–3–27–1; Ball 8–1–36–1; Hancock 2–0–9–0. *Second Innings*—Walsh 33–8–90–4; Smith 21.3–4–59–3; Lewis 25–14–27–0; Alleyne 16–8–20–1; Ball 40–10–108–2; Hancock 6–2–5–0.

Gloucestershire

N. J. Trainor c White b McLean	0	– run out	52
T. H. C. Hancock c Keech b A. C. Morris	65	– c Stephenson b McLean	41
A. J. Wright lbw b Stephenson	13	– (4) c Whitaker b A. C. Morris	7
*M. W. Alleyne c Whitaker b McLean	1	– (5) b McLean	2
M. G. N. Windows b McLean	1	– (6) lbw b A. C. Morris	38
D. R. Hewson lbw b Stephenson	38	– (7) not out	78
†R. C. Russell c Aymes b James	1	– (3) lbw b McLean	0
M. C. J. Ball c Mascarenhas b McLean	25	– b Stephenson	54
J. Lewis c White b Mascarenhas	18	– c Mascarenhas b McLean	27
A. M. Smith c Stephenson b Mascarenhas	0	– not out	4
C. A. Walsh not out	0		
L-b 14	14	B 10, l-b 8, w 6, n-b 6	30

1/0 2/36 3/43 4/49 5/115   176   1/71 2/71 3/86 4/91   (8 wkts) 333
6/120 7/146 8/176 9/176   5/112 6/173 7/249 8/323

Bonus points – Hampshire 4.

Bowling: *First Innings*—McLean 20.5–5–39–4; A. C. Morris 12–4–25–1; Stephenson 17–2–46–2; Mascarenhas 5–1–19–2; James 10–2–28–1; Z. C. Morris 1–0–5–0. *Second Innings*—McLean 28.3–11–71–4; A. C. Morris 22–3–78–2; Stephenson 24–7–58–1; James 16–3–65–0; Mascarenhas 11–1–35–0; Whitaker 3–1–8–0.

Umpires: G. I. Burgess and R. Palmer.

At Southampton, July 12. HAMPSHIRE v SRI LANKANS. Abandoned (See Sri Lankan tour section).

At Birmingham, July 15, 16, 17. HAMPSHIRE lost to WARWICKSHIRE by 225 runs.

HAMPSHIRE v NOTTINGHAMSHIRE

At Portsmouth, July 22, 23, 24. Hampshire won by seven wickets. Hampshire 23 pts, Nottinghamshire 4 pts. Toss: Hampshire.

Hampshire secured their third victory of the season before tea on the third day. Acting-captain Udal made Nottinghamshire bat first on a drying pitch that initially offered plenty of help to the seamers. He was rewarded when they were all out for 128 and, as the wicket got easier, so did Hampshire's task. Even so, they lurched to 54 for five before Mascarenhas, making a career-best 89, and Laney, with his first Championship fifty of the season, helped build a first-innings lead of 173. Gallian and Johnson wiped out the arrears in a third-wicket stand of 139 but, when Johnson edged Mascarenhas into his stumps, the rest of the batting quickly folded. Gallian stood alone and carried his bat – Robinson had broken his left wrist facing his first ball from McLean on the opening day and was unable to bat. Alex Morris finished with match figures of seven for 61, leaving Hampshire only 71 to win.

Close of play: First day, Hampshire 108-5 (J. S. Laney 49*, A. D. Mascarenhas 28*); Second day, Nottinghamshire 140-2 (J. E. R. Gallian 81*, P. Johnson 37*).

Nottinghamshire

M. P. Dowman c Whitaker b McLean	16	– c Laney b Hartley	1
J. E. R. Gallian b McLean	15	– not out	113
U. Afzaal c Aymes b Hartley	15	– lbw b Morris	18
R. T. Robinson retired hurt	0	– absent hurt	
*P. Johnson b Morris	18	– (4) b Mascarenhas	66
G. F. Archer c Laney b Stephenson	16	– (5) c Laney b Hartley	7
P. J. Franks c Udal b Morris	23	– (6) c Aymes b Morris	22
†C. M. W. Read lbw b McLean	5	– (7) c Stephenson b Morris	6
P. A. Strang c Morris b McLean	4	– (8) c Morris b McLean	0
K. P. Evans c Aymes b Morris	4	– (9) c Whitaker b Morris	0
M. N. Bowen not out	3	– (10) c Laney b McLean	2
L-b 1, w 8	9	L-b 2, w 4, n-b 2	8

1/31 2/38 3/59 4/75 5/93   128   1/3 2/41 3/180 4/187 5/223   243
6/99 7/119 8/122 9/128   6/233 7/238 8/238 9/243

Bonus points – Hampshire 4.

In the first innings R. T. Robinson retired hurt at 38-2.

Bowling: *First Innings*—McLean 14–4–45–4; Hartley 10–2–41–1; Mascarenhas 6–1–11–0; Morris 8.2–1–26–3; Stephenson 2–1–4–1; Udal 1–1–0–0. *Second Innings*—McLean 15.5–1–65–2; Hartley 16–2–38–2; Stephenson 7–1–18–0; Udal 7–1–15–0; Morris 12–2–35–4; James 12–2–34–0; Mascarenhas 7–1–36–1.

Hampshire

J. S. Laney c Read b Evans	67	– c Read b Evans	0
J. P. Stephenson c Evans b Franks	11	– c Evans b Bowen	6
G. W. White lbw b Bowen	11	– c Read b Bowen	16
K. D. James run out	0	– not out	29
†A. N. Aymes b Johnson b Bowen	0	– not out	19
P. R. Whitaker b Evans	0		
A. D. Mascarenhas c Read b Franks	89		
*S. D. Udal lbw b Bowen	35		
A. C. Morris not out	15		
N. A. M. McLean c Franks b Strang	36		
P. J. Hartley c Archer b Strang	16		
L-b 11, n-b 10	21	L-b 3	3

1/19 2/44 3/50 4/53 5/54   301   1/0 2/12 3/27   (3 wkts) 73
6/157 7/224 8/234 9/275

Bonus points – Hampshire 3, Nottinghamshire 4.

Bowling: *First Innings*—Franks 24–4–99–2; Evans 27–9–74–2; Bowen 19–2–64–3; Strang 16.2–6–41–2; Dowman 3–0–12–0. *Second Innings*—Evans 8–1–23–1; Bowen 9–4–32–2; Strang 3–1–6–0; Afzaal 1.2–0–9–0.

Umpires: J. H. Hampshire and D. R. Shepherd.

HAMPSHIRE v DURHAM

At Southampton, July 30, 31, August 1, 3. Drawn. Hampshire 11 pts, Durham 8 pts. Toss: Hampshire.

Hampshire remained the only county never to have beaten Durham, thwarted by the weather and a determined last-wicket stand. Durham went into the last day in a seemingly impossible position, only 95 ahead and with the last pair at the crease. But rain prevented a start until 2 p.m., and then Speight and Lugsden held out against the wayward pace of McLean and everything else Hampshire could muster for a further 21 overs (after four the previous day) until more rain prompted Durham celebrations and Hampshire embarrassment. It left Speight three short of what would have been a maiden century for Durham. He intelligently shielded Lugsden, in his first game of the season, from the strike; Lugsden contributed three to the unbroken partnership of 61. Hampshire's supremacy had been established by four for 30 from Alex Morris in Durham's first innings and 134 from Smith, a powerful reminder of his England pomp.

Close of play: First day, Hampshire 47-1 (J. P. Stephenson 19*, A. C. Morris 2*); Second day, Durham 4-0 (J. E. Morris 3*, M. A. Gough 1*); Third day, Durham 288-9 (M. P. Speight 55*, S. Lugsden 1*).

Durham

J. E. Morris c Aymes b Stephenson	48	– c White b James	50
M. A. Gough b Morris	11	– c Aymes b Hartley	20
N. J. Speak b James	11	– lbw b Hartley	2
J. A. Daley c Laney b Morris	36	– c Aymes b James	33
*D. C. Boon c Mascarenhas b Morris	12	– st Aymes b Udal	54
P. D. Collingwood c Smith b Mascarenhas	14	– c Aymes b Udal	39
†M. P. Speight run out	18	– not out	97
M. J. Foster b Mascarenhas	2	– c Aymes b McLean	14
J. Wood c Laney b James	5	– b McLean	0
M. M. Betts c McLean b Morris	20	– c McLean b Udal	2
S. Lugsden not out	8	– not out	3
B 1, l-b 9, n-b 8	18	B 5, l-b 11, n-b 2	18

1/25 2/66 3/98 4/123 5/138   203   1/36 2/38 3/93   (9 wkts) 332
6/148 7/156 8/173 9/187   4/114 5/196 6/221
                            7/262 8/268 9/271

Bonus points – Durham 1, Hampshire 4.

Bowling: *First Innings*—McLean 22–3–62–0; Hartley 10–3–20–0; Morris 13.4–4–30–4; James 12–2–35–2; Stephenson 10–3–17–1; Mascarenhas 13–3–29–2. *Second Innings*—McLean 27–4–61–2; Morris 19–4–49–0; Hartley 22–7–56–2; Udal 19–1–80–3; Stephenson 14.4–4–36–0; James 9–3–17–2; Mascarenhas 6–1–17–0.

Hampshire

J. S. Laney c Lugsden	20	S. D. Udal c Collingwood b Wood	8
J. P. Stephenson c Speight b Lugsden . .	40	N. A. M. McLean c Gough b Wood . . .	0
A. C. Morris c Speight b Betts	3	P. J. Hartley b Wood	6
G. W. White c Gough b Betts	18		
*R. A. Smith c Speight b Betts	134	L-b 13, w 9, n-b 4	26
†A. N. Aymes c Speight b Lugsden	54		
A. D. Mascarenhas b Collingwood	47	1/44 2/58 3/90 4/112 5/271	396
K. D. James not out	40	6/292 7/346 8/366 9/366	

Bonus points – Hampshire 4, Durham 4.

Bowling: Betts 27–3–74–3; Wood 26.2–2–106–3; Lugsden 22–5–67–3; Foster 3–0–22–0; Collingwood 18–8–47–1; Gough 16–4–67–0.

Umpires: R. Palmer and G. Sharp.

At Canterbury, August 5, 6, 7. HAMPSHIRE lost to KENT by 292 runs.

HAMPSHIRE v ESSEX

At Portsmouth, August 14, 15, 16. Hampshire won by an innings and 111 runs. Hampshire 24 pts, Essex 3 pts. Toss: Hampshire.

Essex slumped to their seventh defeat of the season an hour after lunch on the third day. They failed to cope with the loss of several key players, though their cricket consultant Keith Fletcher blamed the pitch, arguing that the United Services Ground was unsuitable for four-day cricket. But after Essex had quickly collapsed to McLean and Hartley, Hampshire managed 490, and came within one run of creating a county record – never had six of their batsmen reached fifty in the same innings. Five had already reached the mark – Smith went on to 138 – and James was 49 not out when last man Hartley was caught at long-on. Hartley atoned for his lack of statistical reverence by taking seven for 132 in the match, though it was Morris, continuing his good form with four for 39, who overcame what resistance Essex offered in the second innings.

Close of play: First day, Hampshire 191-3 (R. A. Smith 78*, A. N. Aymes 11*); Second day, Essex 50-2 (D. D. J. Robinson 26*, R. C. Irani 14*).

Essex

D. D. J. Robinson c Kendall b McLean	0	– lbw b Hartley.	36
A. J. E. Hibbert c Aymes b Morris	17	– run out	2
T. P. Hodgson c Keech b McLean	16	– b McLean	2
R. C. Irani b Hartley b McLean	34	– c Mascarenhas b Morris	35
*A. P. Grayson lbw b Hartley.	16	– b Hartley.	5
G. R. Napier lbw b Hartley	7	– lbw b Hartley.	4
D. R. Law c Keech b Hartley.	16	– c Stephenson b McLean	48
†B. J. Hyam c Aymes b McLean	0	– c Keech b Morris	31
M. C. Ilott c Aymes b McLean	14	– c Aymes b Morris	23
N. F. Williams c Mascarenhas b Hartley	8	– not out	27
P. M. Such not out	2	– c Aymes b Morris	10
B 4, l-b 6, w 2, n-b 4	16	L-b 7, w 4, n-b 4	15
1/0 2/26 3/49 4/85 5/99	141	1/3 2/7 3/81 4/93 5/93	238
6/113 7/117 8/117 9/135		6/97 7/152 8/201 9/202	

Bonus points – Hampshire 4.

Bowling: *First Innings*—McLean 15.4–3–37–5; Hartley 16–3–42–4; Stephenson 5–2–18–0; Morris 6–2–17–1; James 3–0–17–0. *Second Innings*—McLean 19–3–69–2; Hartley 25–6–90–3; Stephenson 9–1–30–0; Morris 13–1–39–4; Mascarenhas 1–0–3–0.

Hampshire

G. W. White lbw b Law	58	A. C. Morris c Hyam b Ilott	51
J. P. Stephenson c Hyam b Williams	2	N. A. M. McLean c Law b Hibbert	6
W. S. Kendall lbw b Ilott	20	P. J. Hartley c Law b Hibbert	0
*R. A. Smith c Hibbert b Williams	138	B 2, l-b 5, w 2, n-b 32	41
†A. N. Aymes c Hyam b Irani	11		
M. Keech c Grayson b Irani	61	1/14 2/67 3/147	490
A. D. Mascarenhas b Hibbert	53	4/204 5/278 6/370	
K. D. James not out	49	7/395 8/479 9/489	

Bonus points – Hampshire 4, Essex 3 (Score at 120 overs: 423-7).

Bowling: Ilott 32–13–70–2; Williams 23–5–85–2; Such 22–4–75–0; Irani 23–2–92–2; Law 17–1–92–1; Grayson 13–2–53–0; Hibbert 6.3–2–16–3.

Umpires: J. H. Harris and J. W. Lloyds.

At Southampton, August 22, 23, 24. HAMPSHIRE lost to SRI LANKANS by five wickets (See Sri Lankan tour section).

At Hove, August 26, 27, 28. HAMPSHIRE beat SUSSEX by nine wickets.

HAMPSHIRE v MIDDLESEX

At Southampton, August 31, September 1, 2, 3. Hampshire won by seven wickets. Hampshire 21 pts, Middlesex 8 pts. Toss: Hampshire. First-class debut: A. J. Strauss.

Phil Tufnell will not remember this match fondly. During the course of Hampshire's third successive Championship victory, he discovered he had been ignored by England for the winter tours, and was then stung twice by wasps. Rain then forced Middlesex to surrender a dominant position. Andrew Strauss, South African-born, Durham-educated, marked his first-class debut with a cultured 83 for Middlesex, and Johnson took three wickets in five balls – just too late, after Hampshire had avoided the follow-on. When rain intervened at lunch on the third day, Middlesex were 231 ahead with eight second-innings wickets standing. The next day, they were fed quick runs for a declaration, which left Hampshire 67 overs to get 300. White followed his first-innings century with a capable 47, then Stephenson, scoring a belligerent 105, and Kendall completed the job. For the third time in 1998, Hampshire increased their record for extras conceded: Middlesex's first innings included 69, despite a £2 club fine for each no-ball. Middlesex were almost as prodigal, and the match total reached 195.

Close of play: First day, Middlesex 357-5 (K. R. Brown 37*, K. P. Dutch 16*); Second day, Hampshire 291-9 (K. D. James 13*, P. J. Hartley 0*); Third day, Middlesex 105-2 (R. A. Kettleborough 31*, M. W. Gatting 33*).

Middlesex

D. J. Goodchild lbw b James	16	– b Hartley	5
R. A. Kettleborough c Aymes b James	60	– not out	62
A. J. Strauss c Kendall b McLean	83	– c Aymes b Morris	12
M. W. Gatting c Keech b Mascarenhas	77	– retired hurt	33
P. N. Weekes c Aymes b Hartley	17	– not out	29
*†K. R. Brown c Aymes b James	53		
K. P. Dutch c Keech b McLean	16		
C. J. Batt b Morris	15		
J. P. Hewitt b Morris	1		
R. L. Johnson c Smith b Morris	23		
P. C. R. Tufnell not out	7		
B 15, l-b 18, w 2, n-b 34	69	B 16, l-b 4, w 8, n-b 4	32

1/56 2/155 3/240 4/289 5/311   437   1/19 2/41   (2 wkts dec.) 173
6/357 7/396 8/401 9/410

Bonus points – Middlesex 4, Hampshire 2 (Score at 120 overs: 396-6).

In the second innings M. W. Gatting retired hurt at 105.

Bowling: *First Innings*—McLean 30–6–67–2; Hartley 21–6–67–1; James 24–7–64–3; Morris 24.1–2–106–3; Mascarenhas 19–5–53–1; Stephenson 13–3–47–0. *Second Innings*—McLean 9–3–19–0; Hartley 7–2–19–1; James 5–1–21–0; Morris 6–1–31–1; Stephenson 1–0–3–0; Smith 3–0–29–0; Aymes 2–0–31–0.

Hampshire

G. W. White lbw b Batt	106	– c Goodchild b Weekes	47
J. P. Stephenson c Gatting b Batt	0	– c Strauss b Tufnell	105
W. S. Kendall c Brown b Johnson	29	– not out	78
*R. A. Smith st Brown b Tufnell	7	– (5) not out	21
†A. N. Aymes b Batt	16		
M. Keech c Brown b Hewitt	11		
A. D. Mascarenhas c Brown b Johnson	63		
K. D. James not out	17		
A. C. Morris c Dutch b Johnson	0		
N. A. M. McLean b Johnson	0	– (4) c Johnson b Tufnell	10
P. J. Hartley c Weekes b Tufnell	8		
B 8, l-b 7, w 9, n-b 30	54	B 6, l-b 4, w 18, n-b 12	40

1/6 2/64 3/85 4/110 5/124   311   1/141 2/231 3/259   (3 wkts) 301
6/243 7/290 8/290 9/290

Bonus points – Hampshire 3, Middlesex 4.

Bowling: *First Innings*—Hewitt 18–2–82–1; Batt 16–1–60–3; Johnson 17–4–75–4; Tufnell 24–4–79–2. *Second Innings*—Hewitt 13–0–79–0; Batt 5–0–35–0; Johnson 11–2–42–0; Tufnell 21–2–80–2; Weekes 10.5–3–42–1; Dutch 3–0–13–0.

Umpires: B. Dudleston and R. A. White.

At Worcester, September 9, 10, 11, 12. HAMPSHIRE drew with WORCESTERSHIRE.

At Manchester, September 17, 18, 19, 20. HAMPSHIRE lost to LANCASHIRE by 161 runs.

KENT

Patron: HRH The Duke of Kent
President: J. F. Pretlove
Chairman: D. S. Kemp
Chairman, Cricket Committee: D. G. Ufton
Secretary: 1998 – S. T. W. Anderson
　　　　　1999 – P. Millman
Captain 1998 – S. A. Marsh
　　　　　1999 – M. V. Fleming
Coach: J. G. Wright
Cricket Administrator: Ms L. Walters
Head Groundsman: M. Grantham
Scorer: J. C. Foley

Carl Hooper

For a county expected to mount a real challenge for honours, 1998 proved a big disappointment. Having been runners-up in three competitions the year before, Kent not only lacked the killer instinct to go one better, but regularly found themselves outplayed. They came 11th in the County Championship, after touching fourth in three different months; they still looked capable of a top-five finish when they beat Hampshire in three days in early August. However, that was as good as it got: the remaining five games produced two hard-earned draws and three defeats. There was a casualty from all this: Steve Marsh lost the captaincy after two full seasons and Matthew Fleming was appointed for 1999.

Kent were unlucky in the Sunday League, with three games washed out when they were in a good position. Sussex were struggling at 50 for four when rain halted proceedings at Tunbridge Wells in June. A week later, Leicestershire had reached 25 for five before a downpour at Grace Road, and in August Worcestershire got 16 for two on the board before, yet again, rain intervened. So those matches gave Kent six rather than a potential 12 points; instead of being runners-up again, they had to settle for fifth spot and a place in the top division of the new National League. The Benson and Hedges Cup saw them beaten in the quarter-final by Leicestershire, while a hundred from Brian Lara, and another brittle batting display, added up to a second-round exit at Warwickshire's hands in the NatWest Trophy. Since Kent's last one-day win at Edgbaston, in 1988, they have lost ten matches there, with one no-result.

A lack of consistent performers with both bat and ball explained Kent's lack of success. Carl Hooper proved he was still a world-class performer on his day, with several vintage innings, but there was a succession of single-figure scores in between. He seemed weighed down by the burden of being Kent's only real match-winner. A double-hundred in their draw against Lancashire in May whetted the appetite of Kent's supporters, and his hundred against Nottinghamshire in June was arguably the best of his six centuries: he tore into a depleted visiting attack, producing a dazzling array of shots. Kent won that match, and beat Essex when he scored 100. But another century, against Gloucestershire at Bristol, failed to save Kent from defeat. In his next two matches, he registered hundreds against Worcestershire and Northamptonshire, both matches being drawn, before saying his farewells after a three-day defeat by Somerset in early September. Because of the World Cup in 1999 and West Indies' tour in 2000, Hooper would not be returning in the foreseeable future. His biggest regret was that he had failed to win a trophy in his five seasons with the county – he missed Kent's Sunday League win in 1995.

Hooper was the only Kent player to pass one thousand runs for the season, totalling 1,215 at 45.00; David Fulton, capped during the Canterbury Festival, was on course to join him, but lost form in the closing weeks and finished on 954. His best innings came at Maidstone in July, where he batted ten and a half hours to make 207 and deny Yorkshire victory. Trevor Ward suffered one of his leanest seasons, and was eventually dropped. He scored only 416 first-class runs, averaging 18.90. Alan Wells also struggled for consistency and was sidelined for a month, after chipping a bone in his ankle playing football in a warm-down session at Southend. Mark Ealham missed seven Championship matches through England calls and a rib injury.

The most encouraging development was the form of youngster Robert Key. Given his chance to claim a regular first-team place, Key celebrated his first Championship hundred aged 19 years and ten days, earned another call-up for England Under-19 and was rewarded with selection for England A's tour of Zimbabwe and South Africa. Key opened with Fulton until Ed Smith returned from Cambridge, with a first-class honours degree in history and a lot of expectations for his cricketing future. Overall, the county's batting was fragile, earning only 18 bonus points. They were dismissed twice for 86, by Surrey and Somerset, the lowest points of their season – both matches ended in innings defeats. Dean Headley shouldered the job of front-line seamer with great enthusiasm. Required for only one Test by England, he collected 52 wickets; Fleming was the next most successful with 38.

Graham Cowdrey failed to get into the Championship side in what proved to be his final year on the staff. He made his last appearance against the Sri Lankans. It meant that, in 1999, the famous cricketing family name would be absent from Kent's staff for the first time since 1950. Alan Igglesden also decided to retire after his testimonial year. His recent career had been blighted by injury and illness and he accepted medical advice to step down, though he was disappointed not to make a farewell playing appearance at the St Lawrence Ground. Igglesden hoped to stay in the game in a coaching capacity. Left-arm spinner Eddie Stanford was released after making only five first-class appearances since his debut in 1995.

Another departure was secretary Stuart Anderson, who retired after eight years at the helm. He was succeeded by Paul Millman, an England squash international who had a spell as assistant secretary at Middlesex earlier in his career. He is a former managing director of Merrydown Cider, sponsors of Sussex. – ANDREW GIDLEY.

533

KENT 1998

Standing: D. W. Headley, B. J. Phillips, D. D. Masters, R. W. T. Key, J. B. D. Thompson, S. C. Willis, M. J. Walker, M. A. Ealham, A. P. Wells, J. B. Hockley, E. J. Stanford, D. P. Fulton. *Seated:* M. McJennett (*sponsor*), N. J. Llong, M. M. Patel, M. V. Fleming, G. R. Cowdrey, S. A. Marsh (*captain*), T. R. Ward, A. P. Igglesden, M. J. McCague, J. Neame (*sponsor*). *Insets:* C. L. Hooper, E. T. Smith, C. D. Walsh, W. J. House.

[*Bill Smith*]

KENT RESULTS

All first-class matches – Played 18: Won 5, Lost 6, Drawn 7.

County Championship matches – Played 17: Won 5, Lost 5, Drawn 7.

*Competition placings – Britannic Assurance County Championship, 11th;
NatWest Trophy, 2nd round; Benson and Hedges Cup, q-f;
AXA League, 5th.*

COUNTY CHAMPIONSHIP AVERAGES

BATTING

Cap		M	I	NO	R	HS	100s	50s	Avge	Ct/St
1992	C. L. Hooper§.	15	28	1	1,215	203	6	1	45.00	15
1998	D. P. Fulton	17	31	1	954	207	1	7	31.80	21
1992	M. A. Ealham†	10	18	3	437	121	1	2	29.13	2
1997	A. P. Wells	15	26	1	684	95	0	5	27.36	3
	R. W. T. Key	13	23	0	612	115	2	1	26.60	11
1986	S. A. Marsh	16	28	4	620	92	0	5	25.83	42/4
	M. J. Walker†	7	12	0	276	68	0	2	23.00	5
	E. T. Smith†	7	14	0	321	58	0	1	22.92	1
1990	M. V. Fleming	16	29	4	571	51	0	1	22.84	9
1994	M. M. Patel	13	19	5	303	58*	0	2	21.64	7
1992	M. J. McCague	10	15	7	166	38	0	0	20.75	8
1989	T. R. Ward†	12	22	0	416	94	0	1	18.90	8
1993	D. W. Headley	13	19	5	262	81	0	1	18.71	5
	B. J. Phillips.	10	16	0	193	54	0	1	12.06	1
	J. B. D. Thompson. .	3	5	3	24	8*	0	0	12.00	0
	C. D. Walsh†	2	4	0	38	20	0	0	9.50	1
1989	A. P. Igglesden† . . .	3	4	3	8	4*	0	0	8.00	2

Also batted: J. M. de la Pena (1 match) 0*; W. J. House (1 match) 5, 0 (1 ct); N. J. Llong†
(cap 1993) (1 match) 4, 0 (1 ct); D. A. Scott† (1 match) 3*, 2*; S. C. Willis (1 match) 0* (1 ct).

* Signifies not out.   † Born in Kent.   § Overseas player.

BOWLING

	O	M	R	W	BB	5W/i	Avge
D. W. Headley.	388.2	86	1,106	52	6-71	4	21.26
J. B. D. Thompson . .	76.4	17	251	11	4-52	0	22.81
M. A. Ealham	204.4	73	488	21	5-23	3	23.23
M. V. Fleming	404.4	115	1,008	38	4-24	0	26.52
M. J. McCague	235.1	45	758	27	4-40	0	28.07
C. L. Hooper.	386.2	104	957	31	7-93	1	30.87
M. M. Patel	387.3	96	1,015	29	5-73	1	35.00
B. J. Phillips.	275	53	839	13	3-66	0	64.53

Also bowled: J. M. de la Pena 33–2–126–3; A. P. Igglesden 70–13–202–2; R. W. T. Key
1–0–1–0; D. A. Scott 41–13–103–1; M. J. Walker 12–0–51–0; T. R. Ward 2–0–4–0.

COUNTY RECORDS

Highest score for:	332	W. H. Ashdown v Essex at Brentwood	1934
Highest score against:	344	W. G. Grace (MCC) at Canterbury	1876
Best bowling for:	10-30	C. Blythe v Northamptonshire at Northampton. . .	1907
Best bowling against:	10-48	C. H. G. Bland (Sussex) at Tonbridge	1899
Highest total for:	803-4 dec.	v Essex at Brentwood	1934
Highest total against:	676	by Australians at Canterbury.	1921
Lowest total for:	18	v Sussex at Gravesend	1867
Lowest total against:	16	by Warwickshire at Tonbridge	1913

KENT v MIDDLESEX

At Canterbury, April 17, 18, 20, 21. Kent won by four wickets. Kent 20 pts, Middlesex 1 pt. Toss: Kent. First-class debut: R. W. T. Key. County debuts: R. A. Kettleborough, J. L. Langer.

Fleming hooked Fraser for six in the penultimate over to secure a Kent victory with eight balls to spare. He finished matters in typical quickfire fashion, belting 40 from 44 balls. The Easter downpours before the match allowed just seven overs in the first two days and forced captains Marsh and Ramprakash into contrivance: Kent were given a target of 252 in 60 overs. England Under-19 batsman Robert Key made his debut for Kent but went quickly, along with opening partner Fulton. Walker, fighting back after a poor season in 1997 and looking slimmer as well, piled on the runs with Wells before Fleming finished things off.

Close of play: First day, No play; Second day, Middlesex 11-0 (R. A. Kettleborough 6*, J. L. Langer 5*); Third day, Middlesex 146-5 (O. A. Shah 15*, K. R. Brown 0*).

Middlesex

R. A. Kettleborough c Fulton b Fleming	27	– not out	11
J. L. Langer c Fulton b Fleming	44	– not out	12
*M. R. Ramprakash c Marsh b Headley	25		
M. W. Gatting c Fleming b Phillips	5		
O. A. Shah lbw b Fleming	40		
D. C. Nash lbw b Phillips	10		
†K. R. Brown lbw b Headley	17		
R. L. Johnson lbw b Phillips	1		
J. P. Hewitt c and b Patel	3		
A. R. C. Fraser st Marsh b Patel	6		
T. F. Bloomfield not out	8		
L-b 10, w 8, n-b 24	42		

1/73 2/82 3/116 4/124 5/144   228   (no wkt dec.) 23
6/183 7/184 8/209 9/215

Bonus points – Middlesex 1, Kent 4.

Bowling: *First Innings*—McCague 12–3–42–0; Headley 22–6–50–2; Patel 10.1–2–12–2; Phillips 21–8–66–3; Ealham 11–4–16–0; Fleming 13–5–32–3. *Second Innings*—Walker 3–0–16–0; Patel 2–0–7–0.

Kent

Kent forfeited their first innings.

D. P. Fulton c Brown b Hewitt	4	*†S. A. Marsh c and b Johnson	7
R. W. T. Key b Bloomfield	15	M. J. McCague not out	6
M. J. Walker c Kettleborough b Johnson	68	L-b 9, w 6, n-b 6	21
A. P. Wells b Fraser	77		
M. A. Ealham c Johnson b Hewitt	15	1/5 2/36 3/127	(6 wkts) 253
M. V. Fleming not out	40	4/171 5/208 6/223	

M. M. Patel, B. J. Phillips and D. W. Headley did not bat.

Bowling: Fraser 19.4–1–79–1; Hewitt 14–3–49–2; Bloomfield 6–1–29–1; Johnson 14–2–71–2; Ramprakash 5–1–16–0.

Umpires: J. H. Harris and R. Julian.

At Cardiff, April 23, 24, 25, 27. KENT drew with GLAMORGAN.

KENT v LANCASHIRE

At Canterbury, May 13, 14, 15, 16. Drawn. Kent 5 pts, Lancashire 10 pts. Toss: Kent.

A match of two contrasting centuries – one slow but of immense significance, the other fast and furious – ended in a tame draw, Lancashire declining the challenge to score 259 in 50 overs. Atherton, who had resigned the England captaincy in March, scored his first hundred in 21 innings and the 45th of his first-class career. He went on to pass 150 for the ninth time, staying 466 minutes, and sharing important stands with Flintoff, Watkinson and Hegg. It was a timely return to form, reassuring the selectors of his talents when there was talk of him being dropped for the First Test. Hooper, one of the West Indians who helped end Atherton's reign, announced his return to county cricket even more eloquently. Back with Kent after a one-season absence, he led a spirited fightback after they had begun their second innings 259 behind. He hit 203 in 282 minutes, from just 220 balls, including 23 fours and six sixes. Marsh added a 44-ball unbeaten fifty as Kent's second innings made amends for the first, when only Ealham, playing with real determination, had coped with the overcast conditions.

Close of play: First day, Lancashire 90-3 (M. A. Atherton 42*); Second day, Lancashire 419-8 (W. K. Hegg 51*, P. J. Martin 2*); Third day, Kent 343-3 (C. L. Hooper 147*, A. P. Wells 13*).

Kent

D. P. Fulton c Hegg b Flintoff	25	– lbw b Martin	96
R. W. T. Key c Fairbrother b Martin	7	– c Hegg b Martin	41
T. R. Ward b Wasim Akram	19	– c Flintoff b Watkinson	19
C. L. Hooper c Watkinson b Martin	4	– c Fairbrother b Watkinson	203
A. P. Wells c Atherton b Austin	20	– c Atherton b Martin	35
M. A. Ealham c Wasim Akram b Keedy	73	– b Keedy	22
M. V. Fleming c Martin b Austin	7	– b Watkinson	2
*†S. A. Marsh c Fairbrother b Martin	12	– not out	50
B. J. Phillips c Flintoff b Watkinson	7	– c Wood b Keedy	4
D. W. Headley b Keedy	10	– run out	0
M. M. Patel not out	6	– b Watkinson	5
B 1, l-b 4, n-b 4	9	B 11, l-b 19, w 6, n-b 4	40
	186		**517**

1/12 2/21 3/28 4/61 5/65 6/73 7/103 8/167 9/177

1/86 2/124 3/257 4/399 5/444 6/451 7/465 8/498 9/506

Bonus points – Lancashire 4.

Bowling: First Innings—Wasim Akram 19–5–45–1; Martin 16–4–37–3; Austin 15–1–56–2; Flintoff 7–4–13–1; Watkinson 6–1–17–1; Keedy 10–6–13–2. *Second Innings*—Wasim Akram 14–1–51–0; Martin 31–5–74–3; Austin 26–6–104–0; Keedy 36–7–134–2; Watkinson 23.5–1–94–4; Flintoff 7–0–30–0.

Lancashire

N. T. Wood c Marsh b Hooper	27	– c Hooper b Headley	12
M. A. Atherton c Hooper b Fleming	152	– lbw b Headley	2
J. P. Crawley c Marsh b Patel	0	– not out	45
N. H. Fairbrother b Hooper	16	– not out	52
A. Flintoff b Hooper	42		
M. Watkinson c Fleming b Phillips	87		
†W. K. Hegg c Fulton b Headley	64		
*Wasim Akram c Fulton b Fleming	7		
I. D. Austin b Patel	7		
P. J. Martin c Marsh b Headley	11		
G. Keedy not out	4		
B 13, l-b 9, w 2, n-b 4	28	B 7, l-b 1, w 2, n-b 4	14
	445	(2 wkts)	**125**

1/62 2/65 3/90 4/180 5/301 6/386 7/394 8/417 9/440

1/15 2/24

Bonus points – Lancashire 3, Kent 2 (Score at 120 overs: 345-5).

Bowling: *First Innings*—Headley 33.3–4–105–2; Phillips 19–6–59–1; Fleming 19–3–51–2; Ealham 18–9–36–0; Hooper 38–9–92–3; Patel 30–8–80–2. *Second Innings*—Headley 8–6–3–2; Phillips 5–0–16–0; Fleming 2–0–9–0; Patel 17–4–40–0; Hooper 14–6–26–0; Ealham 3–0–22–0; Key 1–0–1–0.

Umpires: G. I. Burgess and A. G. T. Whitehead.

At Canterbury, May 19. KENT lost to SOUTH AFRICANS by 98 runs (See South African tour section).

KENT v DURHAM

At Canterbury, May 21, 22, 23. Kent won by an innings and 27 runs. Kent 24 pts, Durham 4 pts. Toss: Kent.

Durham lost in only two and a half days despite irritating Kent twice with last-wicket stands. Although the pitch offered sharp turn and bounce throughout, their inexperienced attack was unable to take advantage and Kent piled up a first-innings lead of 266. It would have been much higher but for Foster and Harmison, who came together at 127 for nine and put on 102, one short of Durham's record. Kent soon forgot their annoyance as 19-year-old Key became their fourth-youngest century-maker. He mixed fiery aggression with a cool temperament, and was especially strong on the cut and pull. This was followed by a stand of 150 between Wells and Marsh,

---

KENT'S YOUNGEST CENTURY-MAKERS

Years	Days		
17	247	G. J. Bryan, 124 v Nottinghamshire at Nottingham	1920
18	225	S. H. Day, 101* v Gloucestershire at Cheltenham	1897
18	337	A. E. Fagg, 111 v Somerset at Taunton	1934
19	**10**	**R. W. T. Key, 101 v Durham at Canterbury**	**1998**
19	22	F. E. Woolley, 116 v Hampshire at Tonbridge	1906

---

both of whom were out in the nineties. It was Marsh's fiftieth first-class score between 50 and 100. When Durham went in again, they were wrecked by a ferocious spell of fast bowling from Headley, who upstaged Patel, the main first-innings destroyer, and took six for 71, his best Championship return in two years. Once again Harmison put most of the specialist bats to shame: this time he added 43 with Betts.

Close of play: First day, Kent 117-0 (D. P. Fulton 45*, R. W. T. Key 55*); Second day, Durham 30-1 (J. J. B. Lewis 19*, N. C. Phillips 5*).

Durham

J. J. B. Lewis c Fulton b Headley	7	– st Marsh b Patel	72
M. A. Gough c Patel b Hooper	31	– c Fulton b Headley	2
*J. E. Morris c McCague b Patel	28	– (7) c Fulton b Headley	32
N. J. Speak c Patel b Hooper	0	– lbw b Headley	0
P. D. Collingwood c Hooper b Patel	18	– b Headley	0
†M. P. Speight c Igglesden b Headley	7	– c Headley b McCague	18
M. J. Foster not out	76	– (8) c McCague b Patel	39
N. C. Phillips c Marsh b Patel	1	– (3) c McCague b Headley	5
M. M. Betts lbw b Headley	0	– not out	12
J. Wood c Ward b Patel	0	– c McCague b Headley	0
S. J. Harmison b Patel	36	– c Walker b Headley	30
B 4, l-b 7, w 6, n-b 8	25	B 7, l-b 6, n-b 16	29

1/9 2/77 3/77 4/89 5/108   229   1/15 2/63 3/63 4/77 5/116   239
6/108 7/119 8/122 9/127   6/124 7/190 8/196 9/196

Bonus points – Durham 1, Kent 4.

Bowling: *First Innings*—Igglesden 12–3–31–0; Headley 18–5–49–3; McCague 10–1–44–0; Hooper 11–4–21–2; Patel 22.2–5–73–5. *Second Innings*—Headley 19–4–71–6; McCague 12–1–58–1; Hooper 1–1–0–0; Igglesden 7–0–30–0; Patel 15.2–1–67–3.

Kent

D. P. Fulton c Collingwood b Wood	... 65	M. M. Patel lbw b Gough	....	24
R. W. T. Key b Harmison	 101	M. J. McCague b Phillips	....	0
T. R. Ward c Speight b Betts	 19	A. P. Igglesden not out	....	1
C. L. Hooper c Speight b Harmison	... 1			
A. P. Wells b Foster	 95	B 4, l-b 16, w 16, n-b 17	....	53
M. J. Walker b Harmison	 13			
*†S. A. Marsh c Speight b Foster	 92	1/168 2/207 3/209 4/216 5/252		495
D. W. Headley st Speight b Phillips	... 31	6/402 7/454 8/477 9/477		

Bonus points – Kent 4, Durham 3 (Score at 120 overs: 473-7).

Bowling: Betts 27–7–86–1; Harmison 22–3–91–3; Wood 22–2–87–1; Phillips 26–3–97–2; Foster 20–2–75–2; Gough 7.2–0–39–1.

Umpires: D. J. Constant and J. F. Steele.

At The Oval, May 29, 30, 31. KENT lost to SURREY by an innings and 30 runs.

KENT v SUSSEX

At Tunbridge Wells, June 3, 4, 5, 6. Sussex won by 75 runs. Sussex 20 pts, Kent 5 pts. Toss: Kent.

A spell of four for eight in 33 balls from Kirtley consigned Kent to their second successive Championship defeat. Set a target of 282 from 84 overs, they were always struggling, and lost their last four wickets – all to Kirtley, who made light of a jarred knee – for 24. Kent had Sussex in trouble on the first day at 84 for seven, but Kirtley came to the rescue then as well, putting on 102 for the eighth wicket with Humphries; both made their highest first-class scores. One Kent bowler had special reason for annoyance: a falling branch broke Patel's car windscreen. Kent started better but their last five wickets went down for just 36, and they led by only 22. Adams, returning to his confident early-season form, and Wasim Khan provided enough runs for Sussex to declare. The turning point of the run-chase was the dismissal of Hooper. After that, Kent fell away, and Sussex continued their unexpected early challenge at the top of the table.

Close of play: First day, Kent 0-0 (D. P. Fulton 0*, R. W. T. Key 0*); Second day, Sussex 46-0 (M. T. E. Peirce 17*, W. G. Khan 25*); Third day, Sussex 265-5 (K. Newell 27*, A. D. Edwards 4*).

Sussex

M. T. E. Peirce c Marsh b Fleming	 11	– c Marsh b Phillips	 23
W. G. Khan c Marsh b Fleming	 12	– st Marsh b Patel	 72
*C. J. Adams c Igglesden b Phillips	 12	– c Patel b Fleming	 84
M. G. Bevan c Ward b Phillips	 6	– b Patel	 25
J. R. Carpenter b Hooper	 1	– b Patel	 0
K. Newell c Marsh b Igglesden	 16	– not out	 40
A. D. Edwards lbw b Igglesden	 16	– lbw b Fleming	 4
†S. Humphries run out	 66	– c Hooper b Fleming	 3
R. J. Kirtley c Key b Fleming	 24	– not out	 18
J. D. Lewry c Walker b Fleming	 1		
M. A. Robinson not out	 0		
L-b 14, w 16	 30	B 5, l-b 19, w 10	 34

1/26 2/43 3/53 4/56 5/56	189
6/79 7/84 8/186 9/187	

1/62 2/200 3/202	(7 wkts dec.) 303
4/209 5/252	
6/265 7/271	

Bonus points – Kent 4.

Bowling: *First Innings*—Igglesden 24–9–36–2; Phillips 25–4–72–2; Fleming 23.3–14–24–4; Hooper 26–12–30–1; Patel 8–3–9–0; Walker 2–0–4–0. *Second Innings*—Phillips 15–1–38–1; Igglesden 17–1–60–0; Fleming 33–10–76–3; Hooper 23–7–48–0; Patel 28–9–57–3.

Kent

D. P. Fulton lbw b Lewry	4	– c Humphries b Robinson	37
R. W. T. Key lbw b Lewry	45	– c Humphries b Edwards	17
T. R. Ward lbw b Lewry	27	– c Adams b Robinson	8
C. L. Hooper lbw b Robinson	7	– c Bevan b Edwards	49
A. P. Wells c Bevan b Robinson	0	– run out	4
M. J. Walker b Newell	45	– c Newell b Bevan	21
M. V. Fleming c Adams b Bevan	19	– not out	41
*†S. A. Marsh c Humphries b Bevan	1	– c Edwards b Kirtley	6
B. J. Phillips b Bevan	2	– c Edwards b Kirtley	2
M. M. Patel b Lewry	17	– c Bevan b Kirtley	8
A. P. Igglesden not out	4	– b Kirtley	0
B 8, l-b 8, w 2, n-b 22	40	L-b 4, w 5, n-b 4	13

1/10 2/63 3/74 4/78 5/138   211   1/37 2/61 3/98 4/123 5/123   206
6/175 7/179 8/181 9/184   6/170 7/182 8/188 9/206

Bonus points – Kent 1, Sussex 4.

Bowling: *First Innings*—Lewry 23–8–55–4; Kirtley 13–5–32–0; Edwards 5–0–20–0; Robinson 19–5–47–2; Newell 12–8–5–1; Bevan 13–3–36–3. *Second Innings*—Lewry 9–1–32–0; Kirtley 10.3–4–19–4; Edwards 15–3–60–2; Robinson 16–5–34–2; Bevan 11–1–57–1.

Umpires: J. W. Holder and B. Leadbeater.

At Leicester, June 11, 12, 13, 15. KENT drew with LEICESTERSHIRE.

KENT v NOTTINGHAMSHIRE

At Canterbury, June 17, 18, 19, 20. Kent won by three wickets. Kent 22 pts, Nottinghamshire 7 pts. Toss: Kent. County debut: J. M. de la Pena.

Strang had an unhappy return to Kent, for whom he performed so well in 1997, when his leg-spin was hit lustily by Hooper, his predecessor and successor as the county's overseas player. Hooper struck a match-winning century and sent Nottinghamshire to the bottom of the table. Set 334 in 58 overs, Kent got there with 15 balls to spare as Hooper, despite eight single-figure scores in his previous 11 innings, showed utter disdain for Nottinghamshire's depleted attack. He scored 122 from 97 balls and, with Wells, added 134 in 21 overs. He was particularly severe on Strang, whom he hit for five leg-side sixes, including one that struck the ice-cream van. With Dowman and Oram unable to bowl, Strang went for seven an over – though he also picked up his only five-wicket return of the season. Earlier, Gallian had celebrated his return to fitness with two half-centuries, just missing his maiden hundred for Nottinghamshire when he fell to Kent's unexpected selection, medium-pacer Jason de la Pena, formerly of Gloucestershire and Surrey. Gallian enabled Nottinghamshire to take a narrow first-innings lead, despite another century for Kent from Key.

Close of play: First day, Nottinghamshire 184-2 (J. E. R. Gallian 74*, R. T. Robinson 56*); Second day, Kent 156-7 (R. W. T. Key 59*, B. J. Phillips 0*); Third day, Nottinghamshire 152-1 (J. E. R. Gallian 78*, R. T. Robinson 64*).

Nottinghamshire

M. P. Dowman b McCague	12	– retired hurt	1
J. E. R. Gallian lbw b de la Pena	92	– lbw b Phillips	80
U. Afzaal lbw b Fleming	18	– c Marsh b McCague	4
R. T. Robinson run out	58	– c Key b Fleming	76
*P. Johnson c Ward b Fleming	46	– c Fulton b Phillips	16
G. F. Archer c Walker b de la Pena	1	– b de la Pena	51
P. J. Franks lbw b Fleming	3	– not out	66
†C. M. W. Read c Marsh b Fleming	8	– not out	4
P. A. Strang not out	23		
M. N. Bowen c Ward b Phillips	16		
A. R. Oram run out	1		
L-b 13, w 10, n-b 8	31	L-b 1, w 4, n-b 4	9

1/24 2/54 3/186 4/235 5/243   309   1/14 2/154 3/174   (5 wkts dec.) 307
6/258 7/259 8/272 9/303   4/194 5/286

Bonus points – Nottinghamshire 3, Kent 4.

In the second innings M. P. Dowman retired hurt at 2.

Bowling: *First Innings*—McCague 29–7–69–1; Phillips 22–3–73–1; de la Pena 21–2–54–2; Fleming 19–4–49–4; Hooper 18–4–51–0. *Second Innings*—McCague 19–4–70–1; Phillips 20–3–56–2; Fleming 18.4–6–46–1; de la Pena 12–0–72–1; Hooper 15–2–37–0; Walker 4–0–21–0; Ward 2–0–4–0.

Kent

D. P. Fulton c Read b Franks	14	– c Robinson b Franks	20
R. W. T. Key c Strang b Oram	115	– c and b Strang	45
M. J. Walker c Robinson b Franks	0	– (7) c and b Strang	1
C. L. Hooper c Read b Franks	7	– st Read b Afzaal	122
A. P. Wells c Archer b Bowen	2	– not out	78
T. R. Ward c Afzaal b Dowman	40	– c Dowman b Strang	3
M. V. Fleming c Afzaal b Dowman	6	– (3) lbw b Strang	16
*†S. A. Marsh b Strang	21	– c Robinson b Strang	1
B. J. Phillips c and b Bowen	23		
M. J. McCague c Read b Franks	38	– (9) not out	25
J. M. de la Pena not out	0		
L-b 1, w 2, n-b 14	17	B 10, l-b 9, n-b 4	23

1/17 2/19 3/29 4/38 5/90   283   1/39 2/74 3/113 4/247   (7 wkts) 334
6/112 7/152 8/228 9/283   5/278 6/281 7/283

Bonus points – Kent 2, Nottinghamshire 4.

Bowling: *First Innings*—Oram 17.1–2–67–1; Franks 27.5–4–104–4; Bowen 24.1–5–66–2; Dowman 7–4–10–2; Strang 25–13–30–1; Afzaal 2–0–5–0. *Second Innings*—Bowen 8–0–63–0; Franks 9–2–40–1; Strang 23–1–166–5; Afzaal 14.3–1–41–1; Dowman 1–0–5–0.

Umpires: D. J. Constant and K. E. Palmer.

KENT v OXFORD UNIVERSITY

At Canterbury, June 27, 28, 29. Oxford University won by three wickets. Toss: Oxford University. First-class debuts: J. B. Hockley, D. A. Scott.

For the second season running, Oxford offered some justification for their first-class status by defeating a county. They scrambled a leg-bye off the last ball to reach the generous target of 241 set by acting-captain Fleming. Kent turned out something close to a second team, with only three capped players, and they failed to bowl or field well enough to save the game; rain, which interrupted play for more than two hours, looked far more likely to affect the result. The crucial innings was played by Wagh, who scored Oxford's only century of the season: a career-best 126 from 128 balls, including 17 fours and a six. Mutual declarations set up the finish after constant trouble with the weather, but the contrivance was not for the benefit of spectators: attendance throughout was notably thin.

Close of play: First day, Kent 169-7 (S. C. Willis 15*, J. B. D. Thompson 13*); Second day, Oxford University 108-4 (B. W. Byrne 37*, J. A. Claughton 8*).

Kent

C. D. Walsh c Wagh b Eadie	4	– lbw b Mather 0
J. B. Hockley lbw b Mather	21	– b Garland 9
M. J. Walker c Claughton b Garland	31	– not out 34
*M. V. Fleming c Lockhart b Byrne	41	
N. J. Llong c Lockhart b Eadie	16	– (4) not out 12
B. J. Phillips run out	10	
†S. C. Willis b Wagh	58	
M. M. Patel c Molins b Garland	0	
J. B. D. Thompson not out	65	
D. A. Scott not out	17	
B 2, l-b 10, w 6, n-b 10	28	W 2 2

1/5 2/51 3/77 4/110 5/138   (8 wkts dec.) 291   1/0 2/26   (2 wkts dec.) 57
6/144 7/144 8/234

J. M. de la Pena did not bat.

Bowling: *First Innings*—Mather 20–3–67–1; Eadie 17–2–67–2; Garland 16–3–64–2; Byrne 18–1–68–1; Wagh 10–3–13–1. *Second Innings*—Mather 6–3–18–1; Garland 5–0–30–1; Eadie 0.5–0–9–0.

Oxford University

D. R. Lockhart c Walker b Patel	12	– (2) lbw b Patel 21
J. A. M. Molins b Phillips	20	– (1) b Phillips 5
M. A. Wagh c Llong b Phillips	0	– st Willis b Patel 126
B. W. Byrne not out	37	– run out 17
*J. A. G. Fulton run out	14	– c Willis b Patel 14
J. A. Claughton not out	8	– (7) st Willis b Patel 7
D. J. Eadie (did not bat)		– (6) c Willis b Phillips 4
R. Garland (did not bat)		– not out 15
N. G. Pirihi (did not bat)		– not out 14
L-b 7, w 2, n-b 8	17	B 1, l-b 11, n-b 6 18

1/28 2/36 3/36 4/95   (4 wkts dec.) 108   1/7 2/89 3/137 4/163   (7 wkts) 241
5/179 6/209 7/210

†J. P. B. Barnes and D. P. Mather did not bat.

Bowling: *First Innings*—Thompson 8–1–33–0; Phillips 8–1–36–2; Patel 14–3–27–1; de la Pena 2–2–0–0; Scott 3–1–5–0. *Second Innings*—Thompson 11–2–51–0; Phillips 11–1–53–2; de la Pena 7–2–28–0; Patel 17–3–81–4; Scott 4–0–16–0.

Umpires: A. A. Jones and K. Shuttleworth.

KENT v YORKSHIRE

At Maidstone, July 1, 2, 3, 4. Drawn. Kent 6 pts, Yorkshire 11 pts. Toss: Yorkshire.

Kent batted for two days to save a match they looked likely to lose in three. Their hero was Fulton, who left his past Championship form far behind by batting ten hours 23 minutes for 207. He faced 505 balls and hit 19 fours. It was not very entertaining, but it turned the match into a statistician's delight. Fulton's innings and the total of 580 were both Kent records against Yorkshire.

He shared two huge stands: 172 with Ward and 210 with Ealham. After giving up their hopes of victory, Yorkshire diverted themselves by trying to bowl the quickest over ever. This involved Lehmann bowling off a two-step run, and the batsmen quickly prodding the ball back. It worked fine until there was a misfield off the fifth ball. The fielders also had an ice-lolly break. Yorkshire had passed 400 thanks to the Australian Lehmann and the Scot Hamilton, who put on 174, the biggest stand ever for the county by two non-Yorkshiremen. Kent then collapsed inexplicably to 99 for nine and, though the last pair put on 66, they still followed on 258 behind.

Close of play: First day, Yorkshire 292-5 (D. S. Lehmann 120*, G. M. Hamilton 68*); Second day, Kent 165; Third day, Kent 332-4 (D. P. Fulton 142*, M. A. Ealham 24*).

Yorkshire

A. McGrath lbw b Fleming	28	C. E. W. Silverwood not out	57
M. P. Vaughan c Marsh b Fleming	33	R. D. Stemp not out	43
*D. Byas c Fulton b Hooper	7		
D. S. Lehmann c Fulton b McCague	136	B 10, l-b 2, w 6, n-b 8	26
M. J. Wood c Marsh b McCague	17		
†R. J. Blakey lbw b Ealham	3	1/62 2/71 3/81 4/118 (7 wkts dec.)	423
G. M. Hamilton b McCague	73	5/135 6/309 7/314	

P. M. Hutchison and R. J. Sidebottom did not bat.

Bonus points – Yorkshire 4, Kent 3 (Score at 120 overs: 368-7).

Bowling: McCague 21–2–77–3; Phillips 19–6–58–0; Ealham 27–6–86–1; Fleming 31–10–76–2; Hooper 23–4–80–1; Patel 10–1–34–0.

Kent

D. P. Fulton b Stemp	21	– st Blakey b Lehmann	207
R. W. T. Key lbw b Hutchison	6	– lbw b Stemp	23
T. R. Ward lbw b Silverwood	9	– c McGrath b Stemp	94
C. L. Hooper c Hamilton b Silverwood	0	– lbw b Stemp	24
A. P. Wells b Hutchison	1	– c Lehmann b Stemp	8
M. A. Ealham c Blakey b Hutchison	0	– c Wood b Lehmann	121
M. V. Fleming lbw b Sidebottom	49	– c Byas b Stemp	2
*†S. A. Marsh b Hamilton	2	– not out	56
B. J. Phillips c Byas b Hamilton	28	– c Wood b Lehmann	3
M. J. McCague lbw b Sidebottom	0	– (11) not out	18
M. M. Patel not out	36	– (10) c and b Lehmann	1
B 11, l-b 2	13	B 4, l-b 6, w 6, n-b 8	23

1/10 2/23 3/23 4/30 5/30	165	1/47 2/219 3/267 (9 wkts dec.)	580
6/67 7/74 8/99 9/99		4/277 5/487 6/495	
		7/517 8/525 9/529	

Bonus points – Yorkshire 4.

Bowling: *First Innings*—Silverwood 15–4–39–2; Hutchison 11–1–41–3; Stemp 13.3–3–29–2; Hamilton 11–4–26–1; Sidebottom 6–1–17–2. *Second Innings*—Silverwood 32–7–92–0; Hutchison 21–2–73–0; Hamilton 26–6–63–0; Stemp 71–27–191–5; Sidebottom 15–2–61–0; Vaughan 26–11–49–0; Lehmann 26–10–42–4.

Umpires: J. H. Hampshire and J. W. Lloyds.

At Southend, July 15, 16, 17, 18. KENT beat ESSEX by two wickets.

At Derby, July 30, 31, August 1, 3. KENT drew with DERBYSHIRE.

KENT v HAMPSHIRE

At Canterbury, August 5, 6, 7. Kent won by 292 runs. Kent 24 pts, Hampshire 4 pts. Toss: Kent.

After the match, captain Marsh hailed this emphatic victory as Kent's best performance of the season. It completed a successful Canterbury festival, on and off the pitch. They were indebted, as so often, to the lower order: after a struggle to 172 for seven, their last three wickets produced 219 runs. Fleming began the recovery with his only half-century of 1998, before Headley and Patel put on 123, Kent's highest last-wicket stand against Hampshire. They also benefited from 54 extras, a Hampshire record which fell twice more before the end of the season. Robin Smith hit an aggressive 72, taking him past 15,000 runs for his county, but that was the only highlight of Hampshire's reply. Kent were able to build on a lead of 218 to leave a target of 446. The dismissal of Smith, to a brilliant catch by House at cover point, heralded the end, and Kent wrapped up victory with a day to spare, as McCague bowled with hostility and accuracy. Guests booked into the festival marquees for the final day were entertained by a regimental band instead.

Close of play: First day, Kent 391; Second day, Kent 86-3 (R. W. T. Key 33*, C. L. Hooper 5*).

Kent

D. P. Fulton lbw b Morris	54	– lbw b Hartley	2
E. T. Smith c Aymes b Hartley	0	– c Stephenson b Udal	44
R. W. T. Key c Aymes b McLean	34	– lbw b Hartley	33
C. L. Hooper lbw b Morris	36	– (5) b McLean	12
W. J. House c and b Morris	5	– (4) c Stephenson b Udal	0
M. A. Ealham c White b James	11	– c Udal b Hartley	10
M. V. Fleming c Stephenson b Morris	51	– c White b Stephenson	21
*†S. A. Marsh c Aymes b Stephenson	0	– st Aymes b Udal	47
D. W. Headley c Aymes b James	81	– not out	10
M. J. McCague b James	7	– c Smith b Udal	26
M. M. Patel not out	58	– lbw b Mascarenhas	6
B 6, l-b 10, w 14, n-b 24	54	B 4, l-b 10, n-b 2	16

1/12 2/86 3/128 4/134 5/157   391   1/9 2/80 3/80 4/87 5/107   227
6/171 7/172 8/257 9/268   6/107 7/184 8/186 9/218

Bonus points – Kent 4, Hampshire 4.

Bowling: *First Innings*—McLean 19–5–65–1; Hartley 17–1–54–1; Stephenson 16–4–56–1; Udal 11–2–39–0; James 16.2–2–66–3; Morris 18–2–72–4; Mascarenhas 6–0–23–0. *Second Innings*—McLean 11–1–29–1; Hartley 13–3–21–3; Udal 11–3–37–4; Morris 10–2–36–0; Mascarenhas 10–4–30–1; Stephenson 17–3–58–1; James 3–2–2–0.

Hampshire

J. S. Laney c Fulton b Headley	4	– c Marsh b Patel	12
J. P. Stephenson c Ealham b McCague	21	– c Marsh b McCague	4
G. W. White lbw b Headley	13	– c Marsh b Headley	19
*R. A. Smith c McCague b Hooper	72	– c House b Hooper	1
†A. N. Aymes c Patel b Hooper	29	– c McCague b Hooper	8
A. D. Mascarenhas c Marsh b McCague	4	– c Fulton b Hooper	16
K. D. James c Hooper b Headley	8	– b Key b Hooper	12
S. D. Udal c Marsh b McCague	2	– (9) not out	25
A. C. Morris not out	2	– (8) b McCague	22
N. A. M. McLean c Fulton b Hooper	4	– c Marsh b McCague	10
P. J. Hartley c McCague b Hooper	0	– c Marsh b McCague	0
B 3, l-b 3, n-b 8	14	B 10, l-b 8, n-b 6	24

1/16 2/34 3/67 4/143 5/156   173   1/18 2/48 3/48 4/56 5/61   153
6/156 7/159 8/168 9/173   6/83 7/92 8/131 9/151

Bonus points – Kent 4.

Bowling: *First Innings*—Headley 12–4–42–3; McCague 13–4–33–3; Ealham 7–2–23–0; Patel 4–1–14–0; Fleming 8–1–41–0; Hooper 14.4–9–14–4. *Second Innings*—Headley 9–4–9–1; McCague 13–2–40–4; Fleming 7–4–3–0; Hooper 21–12–29–4; Patel 22–7–54–1.

Umpires: A. A. Jones and N. T. Plews.

At Canterbury, August 11. KENT lost to SRI LANKANS by eight wickets (See Sri Lankan tour section).

At Bristol, August 14, 15, 16, 17. KENT lost to GLOUCESTERSHIRE by 138 runs.

KENT v WORCESTERSHIRE

At Canterbury, August 19, 20, 21, 22. Drawn. Kent 9 pts, Worcestershire 10 pts. Toss: Worcestershire.

Kent's tailenders again stole the honours and saved a game. Things looked bleak at 127 for seven halfway through the final afternoon; but then Phillips and Headley fought back with an eighth-wicket stand of 51, followed by 66 from Phillips and Patel, who both hit fifties. At 51 for four in their second innings, Worcestershire's lead had been a slender 67 before their middle order, led by Rhodes, batted Kent out of the game. On the second day, Hooper had scored his second century in successive Championship innings and equalled the quickest hundred of the season – 72 balls by Alistair Brown. His second fifty came from 28 balls, with eight fours and two sixes. Before that, Smith and Wells were both caught by Worcestershire coach Bill Athey, appearing as a substitute.

Close of play: First day, Worcestershire 281-6 (S. J. Rhodes 33*, S. R. Lampitt 22*); Second day, Kent 323-7 (S. A. Marsh 46*, D. W. Headley 1*); Third day, Worcestershire 300-6 (S. J. Rhodes 86*, S. R. Lampitt 0*).

Worcestershire

W. P. C. Weston c Smith b Patel	60	– c Marsh b Hooper		23
E. J. Wilson c Fulton b Thompson	14	– c Hooper b Fleming		13
*T. M. Moody run out	41	– (5) st Marsh b Patel		59
V. S. Solanki b Headley	15	– lbw b Headley		0
A. Hafeez c Marsh b Patel	31	– (3) c Key b Headley		1
D. A. Leatherdale c Marsh b Headley	24	– b Fleming		79
†S. J. Rhodes c Fulton b Patel	42	– lbw b Headley		95
S. R. Lampitt c Fulton b Headley	22	– not out		9
R. K. Illingworth lbw b Hooper	42	– run out		6
M. J. Rawnsley lbw b Patel	21			
R. J. Chapman not out	0			
B 15, l-b 5, w 2, n-b 26	48	B 10, l-b 10, w 2, n-b 26. .		48

1/40 2/104 3/143 4/171 5/226   360   1/31 2/43 3/43   (8 wkts dec.) 333
6/228 7/282 8/316 9/356   4/51 5/147 6/299
                             7/316 8/333

Bonus points – Worcestershire 3, Kent 3 (Score at 120 overs: 330-8).

Bowling: *First Innings*—Headley 30–7–84–3; Thompson 18–1–75–1; Phillips 20–1–65–0; Fleming 15–4–36–0; Patel 40–16–55–4; Hooper 4–0–25–1. *Second Innings*—Headley 16–2–56–3; Phillips 16–5–46–0; Fleming 9–1–32–2; Hooper 23–4–87–1; Patel 38.4–9–92–1.

Kent

D. P. Fulton c Moody b Chapman	17	– c Solanki b Illingworth	15
E. T. Smith c sub b Chapman	21	– b Chapman	10
R. W. T. Key c Rhodes b Moody	9	– lbw b Moody	4
C. L. Hooper c Solanki b Rawnsley	154	– c Leatherdale b Moody	33
A. P. Wells c sub b Lampitt	9	– c Solanki b Moody	8
M. V. Fleming c Solanki b Rawnsley	42	– c Rhodes b Chapman	33
*†S. A. Marsh c Illingworth b Chapman	48	– lbw b Chapman	10
B. J. Phillips b Lampitt	0	– b Moody	54
D. W. Headley b Chapman	17	– c Hafeez b Rawnsley	20
M. M. Patel c Wilson b Lampitt	0	– not out	55
J. B. D. Thompson not out	2	– not out	5
B 1, l-b 10, w 6, n-b 8	25	B 3, l-b 2, w 4, n-b 14	23
	344	**(9 wkts)**	**270**

1/43 2/56 3/98 4/125 5/261

6/288 7/306 8/336 9/336

1/27 2/30 3/46

4/71 5/84 6/120

7/127 8/178 9/244

Bonus points – Kent 3, Worcestershire 4.

Bowling: *First Innings*—Chapman 20.1–3–79–4; Leatherdale 6–0–38–0; Moody 19–4–66–1; Lampitt 17–4–55–3; Rawnsley 13–0–74–2; Illingworth 9–2–21–0. *Second Innings*—Chapman 17–3–67–3; Leatherdale 8–2–9–0; Moody 24–8–63–4; Illingworth 12–3–41–1; Lampitt 15–4–63–0; Rawnsley 11–7–22–1.

Umpires: V. A. Holder and J. W. Lloyds.

At Northampton, August 26, 27, 28, 29. KENT drew with NORTHAMPTONSHIRE.

KENT v SOMERSET

At Canterbury, September 9, 10, 11. Somerset won by an innings and 46 runs. Somerset 23 pts, Kent 4 pts. Toss: Somerset.

To the delight of his team-mates, Andrew Caddick took his 100th first-class wicket of the season as Somerset crushed Kent in three days. Caddick, the first English-qualified bowler to reach the landmark since Neil Foster in 1991, could not have wished for a better scalp: he had Hooper, believed to be playing his last Championship innings for Kent, caught in the gully. Somerset also had the bonus of a hundred from Lathwell, his first in two seasons, after he had missed four games out of five through injury. That set up a first-innings lead of 256 after Kent were 86 all out for the second time in 1998. The batsmen had no answer to Caddick or van Troost, who produced one of his most focused performances. Kent followed on and subsided again, a little more slowly. Caddick finished with match figures of ten for 101. Ian Botham was the last Somerset player to pass 100 in a season, in 1978, but Caddick was the first bowler to take 100 for Somerset since Tom Cartwright in 1971 and the first to take 100 in the Championship for them since Brian Langford in 1966.

Close of play: First day, Somerset 233-6 (R. J. Turner 3*, A. R. K. Pierson 0*); Second day, Kent 17-1 (R. W. T. Key 4*, B. J. Phillips 0*).

Somerset

*P. D. Bowler b Fleming	17	M. P. L. Bulbeck b Headley	29
P. C. L. Holloway c Fleming b Headley	5	A. R. Caddick b Headley	4
M. E. Trescothick c Fleming b Phillips	7	A. P. van Troost not out	4
M. N. Lathwell c Hooper b Headley	106	B 6, l-b 13, w 4, n-b 10	33
M. Burns b Fleming	69		
†R. J. Turner c Patel b Headley	51		**342**
G. D. Rose c Key b Headley	0	1/16 2/29 3/65 4/229 5/231	
A. R. K. Pierson b Fleming	17	6/233 7/274 8/331 9/335	

Bonus points – Somerset 3, Kent 4.

Bowling: Phillips 22–3–69–1; Headley 33.4–7–97–6; Fleming 33–10–83–3; Hooper 11–2–31–0; Patel 10–1–33–0; Walker 3–0–10–0.

Kent

D. P. Fulton c Holloway b van Troost	5	– c Turner b Caddick	0
R. W. T. Key c Lathwell b Caddick	5	– b Caddick	56
B. J. Phillips c Lathwell b van Troost	4	– (9) c Bowler b van Troost	2
E. T. Smith lbw b Caddick	0	– (3) c Pierson b Rose	34
A. P. Wells b Caddick	0	– (4) lbw b Bulbeck	3
M. J. Walker b van Troost	11	– (5) c Holloway b Caddick	39
C. L. Hooper lbw b van Troost	8	– (6) c Burns b Caddick	14
M. V. Fleming not out	25	– (7) c Burns b van Troost	1
*†S. A. Marsh b Caddick	0	– (8) c Turner b Caddick	27
D. W. Headley b Caddick	0	– c Burns b Rose	7
M. M. Patel c Trescothick b Bulbeck	8	– not out	6
L-b 8, n-b 12	20	L-b 11, w 2, n-b 8	21

1/9 2/21 3/26 4/26 5/29   86   1/0 2/70 3/83 4/141 5/160   210
6/37 7/48 8/57 9/61   6/167 7/167 8/178 9/200

Bonus points – Somerset 4.

Bowling: *First Innings*—Caddick 14–3–40–5; van Troost 11–5–18–4; Bulbeck 2.4–0–20–1. *Second Innings*—Caddick 23.5–4–61–5; Rose 13–4–36–2; van Troost 16–3–74–2; Bulbeck 6–0–28–1.

Umpires: J. H. Hampshire and M. J. Kitchen.

At Birmingham, September 17, 18, 19, 20. KENT lost to WARWICKSHIRE by 186 runs.

YOUNG CRICKETER OF THE YEAR

(Elected by the Cricket Writers' Club)

1950	R. Tattersall	1975	A. Kennedy
1951	P. B. H. May	1976	G. Miller
1952	F. S. Trueman	1977	I. T. Botham
1953	M. C. Cowdrey	1978	D. I. Gower
1954	P. J. Loader	1979	P. W. G. Parker
1955	K. F. Barrington	1980	G. R. Dilley
1956	B. Taylor	1981	M. W. Gatting
1957	M. J. Stewart	1982	N. G. Cowans
1958	A. C. D. Ingleby-Mackenzie	1983	N. A. Foster
1959	G. Pullar	1984	R. J. Bailey
1960	D. A. Allen	1985	D. V. Lawrence
1961	P. H. Parfitt	1986	{ A. A. Metcalfe
1962	P. J. Sharpe		{ J. J. Whitaker
1963	G. Boycott	1987	R. J. Blakey
1964	J. M. Brearley	1988	M. P. Maynard
1965	A. P. E. Knott	1989	N. Hussain
1966	D. L. Underwood	1990	M. A. Atherton
1967	A. W. Greig	1991	M. R. Ramprakash
1968	R. M. H. Cottam	1992	I. D. K. Salisbury
1969	A. Ward	1993	M. N. Lathwell
1970	C. M. Old	1994	J. P. Crawley
1971	J. Whitehouse	1995	A. Symonds
1972	D. R. Owen-Thomas	1996	C. E. W. Silverwood
1973	M. Hendrick	1997	B. C. Hollioake
1974	P. H. Edmonds	1998	A. Flintoff

An additional award, in memory of Norman Preston, Editor of *Wisden* from 1951 to 1980, was made to C. W. J. Athey in 1980.

John Crawley

LANCASHIRE

Patron: HM The Queen
President: Sir Patrick Russell
Chairman: J. Simmons
Chairman, Cricket Committee: G. Ogden
Chief Executive: J. Cumbes
Cricket Secretary: D. M. R. Edmundson
Captain: 1998 – Wasim Akram
　　　　 1999 – J. P. Crawley
Head Coach: D. F. Whatmore
Head Groundsman: P. Marron
Scorer: A. West

Again, frustratingly again, there were no Championship celebrations. But Lancashire could lay claim to the unofficial title of Team of the Year, having carried off the NatWest Trophy and the Sunday League, and come close to the most desired component of the treble. Old Trafford was definitely the place to be, on a glorious Sunday morning in September, when captain Wasim Akram waved goodbye to the crowd gathered under the dressing-room balcony. Although Lancashire's Championship bid had just ended in anti-climax – Leicestershire's triumph at The Oval the previous day left them trailing – there were emotional scenes as the fans paid tribute to their team and to Wasim, in his first and only season as captain. Leaving the club after ten years, he had to fight to clear himself of the match-fixing allegations engulfing cricket in Pakistan, but at least he had a rousing send-off.

Wasim was departing reluctantly. He wanted to return in 1999, but Lancashire, who had earlier been led to believe he would not be available, had already lined up Sri Lankan spinner Muttiah Muralitharan – who destroyed England in the Oval Test – as their overseas player. The signing was announced in September, the day after Lancashire completed their double. However, in the New Year, the deal was cast into doubt by the Sri Lankan authorities, anxious to protect their star bowler. Lancashire also agreed a new two-year contract for their coach, Dav Whatmore. John Crawley was promoted from vice-captain to captain. A memorable summer was quickly pushed into the background.

But what a summer it was. Lancashire went into it better prepared than ever before, thanks to the introduction of 12-month player contracts – an innovation which should be examined by other counties. It enabled them to work as a squad through the winter; they emerged stronger, physically and mentally, and much closer. And they knew that one player would provide that extra gleam of inspiration to transform all their hard work into silverware. Wasim's entrance as captain was eagerly awaited.

Yet the catalyst for so much of their success proved to be an England discard. Dropped from the Test team halfway through the winter tour of the West Indies, Crawley returned home to enjoy the most prolific season of his career, with 1,681 Championship runs, a wonderful comeback century for

England against Sri Lanka, and 849 runs in one-day matches, which had
much to do with Lancashire's double triumph. He hit eight first-class centuries,
three in successive innings, and finally 239 in the game against Hampshire
just before he was proclaimed Lancashire's new captain. Crawley headed the
national first-class averages with 1,851 runs at 74.04. He deputised as wicket-
keeper in place of the injured Warren Hegg in two first-class matches, as
captain for Wasim in four, and, when Lancashire adjusted their batting order,
he switched uncomplainingly between No. 3 and opener. Whatmore described
him as the team's "bridge", and he was voted the Lancashire members' player
of the year.

The tall, lean Crawley was the outstanding figure, but many others hit high
notes, and five played for England; Andy Flintoff joined Mike Atherton and
Crawley in playing Tests, while Peter Martin was picked for one-day
internationals, as was Ian Austin, called up at short notice. Remarkably, 22
players were used in the Championship. Only Crawley passed 1,000 runs and
no one took 50 wickets, underlining that Lancashire's was a genuine team –
or squad – achievement.

Led out by Crawley, Lancashire lost the first Championship game of the
season in a contrived finish at Hove. They never lost another. Their feat of
winning the last six matches and claiming runners-up spot replicated their
performance in 1987, the last time they finished so high. That time, they won
ten of their 24 fixtures; this time, they won 11 of 17, as many as champions
Leicestershire. Rain continued to plague them – costing three days in each
of the games against Middlesex and Leicestershire at Old Trafford – but they
proved masters of contrivance. That should not detract from their overall
performance. Lancashire grabbed their chances in such matches, but still had
to play well, and later, in improving weather, they steamrollered the opposition.

The seam attack of Wasim, Martin, Austin and Glen Chapple was a potent
force, notching up 176 wickets between them, although the best individual
analysis of that group was a mere five for 49. Spin had little chance in 1998,
but 19-year-old leg-spinner Chris Schofield captured eight wickets in his
second game and off-spinner Gary Yates totted up 18 in his four appearances.
Hegg's improved batting – 628 runs at 36.94 – won him a place in the Ashes
squad and Test caps at Melbourne and Sydney.

Despite all this, Lancashire again had to rely on their prowess in one-day
competitions to augment the honours list. They suffered very rare lapses in
limited-overs games – a Benson and Hedges quarter-final knockout by Surrey,
and only two Sunday League defeats. Victory over Derbyshire in a one-sided,
rain-affected NatWest final fell a little flat, but should not mask the fact that
Lancashire were deserving winners, having beaten five first-class counties to
claim the trophy. Jack Simmons, in his first full season as chairman, had tears
in his eyes at Lord's, and again when the team clinched their third double of
the 1990s. "I never cried when I was a player," he said. But this was a summer
which tugged at the emotions of most at Old Trafford. – COLIN EVANS.

549

LANCASHIRE 1998

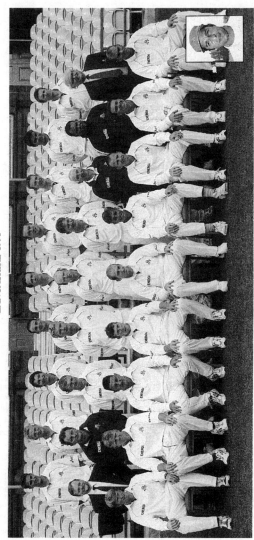

[*Bill Smith*]

Back row: M. J. Chilton, R. J. Green, M. E. Harvey, J. J. Haynes, P. C. McKeown, P. M. Ridgway, C. P. Schofield, D. J. Shadford, N. T. Wood.
Middle row: D. White (*Second Eleven scorer*), P. R. Sleep (*Second Eleven captain/coach*), G. Keedy, A. Flintoff, S. P. Titchard, G. Yates, L. G. Brown
(*physiotherapist*), D. F. Whatmore (*coach*), A. West (*First Eleven scorer*). *Front row*: G. Chapple, P. J. Martin, I. D. Austin, M. A. Atherton, J. P. Crawley,
M. Watkinson, N. H. Fairbrother, W. K. Hegg, G. D. Lloyd. *Inset*: Wasim Akram (*captain*).

LANCASHIRE RESULTS

All first-class matches – Played 17: Won 11, Lost 1, Drawn 5.

County Championship matches – Played 17: Won 11, Lost 1, Drawn 5.

*Competition placings – Britannic Assurance County Championship, 2nd;
NatWest Trophy, winners; Benson and Hedges Cup, q-f;
AXA League, winners.*

COUNTY CHAMPIONSHIP AVERAGES

BATTING

Cap		M	I	NO	R	HS	100s	50s	Avge	Ct/St
1994	J. P. Crawley	17	26	2	1,681	239	7	5	70.04	6
1985	N. H. Fairbrother† . .	12	17	2	759	138	3	3	50.60	11
1992	G. D. Lloyd†	15	22	1	831	212*	2	3	39.57	11
1989	W. K. Hegg†	15	21	4	628	85	0	6	36.94	34/3
1994	G. Yates†	4	6	1	174	55	0	1	34.80	2
	M. J. Chilton	2	4	0	125	47	0	0	31.25	0
1989	Wasim Akram§	13	18	1	531	155	1	2	31.23	8
1989	M. A. Atherton† . . .	8	14	1	381	152	1	0	29.30	7
1987	M. Watkinson†	10	12	1	318	87	0	2	28.90	6
	N. T. Wood	12	19	3	457	80*	0	2	28.56	1
1998	A. Flintoff†	15	22	0	591	124	1	3	26.86	22
	P. C. McKeown† . . .	5	7	0	186	42	0	0	26.57	6
1990	I. D. Austin†	13	17	4	304	64	0	2	23.38	7
1994	G. Chapple	14	18	3	282	69	0	1	18.80	7
1994	P. J. Martin†	14	15	5	154	26	0	0	15.40	3
	G. Keedy	7	10	5	44	13	0	0	8.80	2

Also batted: R. J. Green† (6 matches) 14, 0*, 0 (1 ct); M. E. Harvey† (1 match) 0, 0*; P. M. Ridgway (1 match) 35, 4; C. P. Schofield† (2 matches) 1*, 4*, 0 (1 ct); D. J. Shadford† (1 match) 13*. S. P. Titchard† (cap 1995) (1 match) did not bat.

Note: In the match v Yorkshire at Leeds, I. D. Austin, called up for a one-day international, was replaced by R. J. Green.

* *Signifies not out.*   † *Born in Lancashire.*   § *Overseas player.*

BOWLING

	O	M	R	W	BB	5W/i	Avge
Wasim Akram	335.5	75	1,025	48	5-56	1	21.35
G. Chapple	313	58	942	44	5-49	1	21.40
P. J. Martin	388	94	1,062	48	4-21	0	22.12
G. Yates	131.3	26	432	18	4-64	0	24.00
I. D. Austin	345.4	80	978	36	4-21	0	27.16
C. P. Schofield	79.4	9	299	10	4-56	0	29.90
G. Keedy	182.3	43	563	18	5-35	1	31.27
M. Watkinson	175.4	22	607	18	5-45	1	33.72

Also bowled: M. J. Chilton 8–2–24–0; J. P. Crawley 1–0–21–0; A. Flintoff 104–25–317–6; R. J. Green 126–28–424–4; M. E. Harvey 5–0–48–0; G. D. Lloyd 7.3–1–49–0; P. M. Ridgway 18–2–83–4; D. J. Shadford 30.5–4–90–1; N. T. Wood 5.1–0–80–0.

COUNTY RECORDS

Highest score for:	424	A. C. MacLaren v Somerset at Taunton	1895
Highest score against:	315*	T. W. Hayward (Surrey) at The Oval	1898
Best bowling for:	10-46	W. Hickton v Hampshire at Manchester	1870
Best bowling against:	10-40	G. O. B. Allen (Middlesex) at Lord's	1929
Highest total for:	863	v Surrey at The Oval	1990
Highest total against:	707-9 dec.	by Surrey at The Oval	1990
Lowest total for:	25	v Derbyshire at Manchester	1871
Lowest total against:	22	by Glamorgan at Liverpool	1924

At Hove, April 17, 18, 19, 20. LANCASHIRE lost to SUSSEX by two wickets.

LANCASHIRE v MIDDLESEX

At Manchester, April 23, 24, 25, 27. Drawn. Lancashire 4 pts, Middlesex 4 pts. Toss: Lancashire.

Lancashire's first home game of the season was a washout. Play was possible only on Saturday, the third day, when Middlesex were put in and reached 205 for four on a slowish, seaming pitch. Langer scored his maiden fifty for the county. Lancashire supporters had to wait until June 11 for their next home Championship match: with the ECB's blessing, the club's fixtures had been arranged so they could stage a money-spinning rock concert at Old Trafford featuring Elton John and Billy Joel. In the event even that was cancelled, when Joel fell ill.

Close of play: First day, No play; Second day, No play; Third day, Middlesex 205-4 (O. A. Shah 64*, P. N. Weekes 21*).

Middlesex

R. A. Kettleborough c Hegg b Austin . .	20	P. N. Weekes not out 21
J. L. Langer c and b Watkinson	68	
*M. R. Ramprakash c Flintoff b Martin .	10	B 2, l-b 4, n-b 4 10
O. A. Shah not out	64	—
D. C. Nash b Green	12	1/29 2/90 3/120 4/161 (4 wkts) 205

†K. R. Brown, R. L. Johnson, J. P. Hewitt, A. R. C. Fraser and P. C. R. Tufnell did not bat.

Bonus points – Middlesex 1, Lancashire 1.

Bowling: Martin 13–2–42–1; Austin 17–3–41–1; Chapple 20–7–43–0; Green 13–4–37–1; Watkinson 10–0–30–1; Flintoff 6–5–6–0.

Lancashire

N. T. Wood, S. P. Titchard, *J. P. Crawley, I. D. Austin, G. D. Lloyd, A. Flintoff, M. Watkinson, †W. K. Hegg, G. Chapple, P. J. Martin and R. J. Green.

Umpires: J. H. Hampshire and A. G. T. Whitehead.

At Canterbury, May 13, 14, 15, 16. LANCASHIRE drew with KENT.

At Chelmsford, May 21, 22, 23, 24. LANCASHIRE beat ESSEX by seven wickets.

At Northampton, June 3, 4, 5, 6. LANCASHIRE drew with NORTHAMPTONSHIRE.

LANCASHIRE v SOMERSET

At Manchester, June 11, 12, 13, 15. Lancashire won by nine runs. Lancashire 22 pts, Somerset 5 pts. Toss: Lancashire.

An entertaining match twisted and turned its way to a pulsating finish: Trescothick and Rose took Somerset to the verge of victory with an eighth-wicket stand of 102. Needing 271, Somerset had stumbled to 123 for seven, but Trescothick looked capable of snatching a remarkable win, helped by 28 in no-balls and two dropped chances. He celebrated his second escape by pulling Martin for six. But Rose had already gone, and he ran out of partners. The pitch encouraged both batsmen and bowlers prepared to make an effort. Crawley scored 72 and 44, despite just having lost half a stone through gastroenteritis. In between, Bowler batted diligently over four and a quarter hours, ending a worrying sequence of failures. Caddick and Martin, hoping to impress England's selectors, bowled well, and no one grafted harder than Wasim Akram, who collected seven for 147 from 50.3 overs. But neither side could hold the advantage until Lancashire took four cheap wickets when Somerset resumed on the third evening.

Close of play: First day, Somerset 37-0 (P. D. Bowler 10*, P. C. L. Holloway 22*); Second day, Lancashire 139-4 (G. D. Lloyd 36*, G. Chapple 2*); Third day, Somerset 47-4 (P. C. L. Holloway 14*, S. C. Ecclestone 0*).

Lancashire

P. C. McKeown c Turner b Mushtaq Ahmed . . .	39	– (2) c Turner b Caddick	23
M. A. Atherton b Rose	0	– (1) c Bowler b Mushtaq Ahmed . . .	28
J. P. Crawley c Trescothick b Rose	72	– c Turner b Bulbeck	44
A. Flintoff b Trescothick	18	– c Turner b Rose	1
G. D. Lloyd c Harden b Trescothick	0	– c Ecclestone b Bulbeck	47
M. Watkinson lbw b Rose	19	– (7) lbw b Caddick	17
*Wasim Akram c Turner b Caddick	32	– (8) b Bowler b Caddick	4
†W. K. Hegg not out	54	– (9) not out	23
I. D. Austin c Turner b Caddick	0	– (10) b Caddick	0
G. Chapple c Harden b Caddick	0	– (6) c Turner b Caddick	26
P. J. Martin c Harden b Caddick	18	– b Rose	3
L-b 7, n-b 8	15	L-b 14, w 2, n-b 4	20

1/18 2/92 3/115 4/115 5/144　　　　　　267　　1/37 2/71 3/84 4/128 5/161　　　　236
6/155 7/210 8/210 9/222　　　　　　　　　　　6/200 7/204 8/209 9/209

Bonus points – Lancashire 2, Somerset 4.

Bowling: First Innings—Caddick 22.2–8–67–4; Rose 22–7–60–3; Bulbeck 8–2–39–0; Trescothick 19–5–65–2; Mushtaq Ahmed 12–8–29–1. *Second Innings*—Caddick 29–5–80–5; Rose 26–6–68–2; Trescothick 3–0–11–0; Mushtaq Ahmed 9–0–38–1; Bulbeck 6–1–25–2.

Somerset

*P. D. Bowler lbw b Chapple	63	– c Watkinson b Wasim Akram	7
P. C. L. Holloway c Hegg b Martin	36	– c Atherton b Chapple	47
R. J. Harden b Martin	0	– c Hegg b Wasim Akram	6
M. N. Lathwell lbw b Chapple	4	– c Hegg b Chapple	5
S. C. Ecclestone c Flintoff b Martin	23	– (6) c Hegg b Austin	11
†R. J. Turner b Martin	0	– (7) c McKeown b Martin	7
M. E. Trescothick c Atherton b Wasim Akram	13	– (8) not out	73
G. D. Rose c Flintoff b Wasim Akram	47	– (9) b Wasim Akram	56
Mushtaq Ahmed c Flintoff b Chapple	0	– (10) c Chapple b Martin	1
A. R. Caddick b Wasim Akram	21	– (11) c Hegg b Wasim Akram	2
M. P. L. Bulbeck not out	1	– (5) b Chapple	0
B 5, l-b 6, n-b 14	25	B 5, l-b 5, w 8, n-b 28 . . .	46

1/52 2/52 3/67 4/112 5/112　　　　　　233　　1/8 2/20 3/35 4/43 5/84　　　　　　261
6/139 7/186 8/190 9/226　　　　　　　　　　　6/101 7/123 8/225 9/236

Bonus points – Somerset 1, Lancashire 4.

Bowling: First Innings—Wasim Akram 20.2–7–42–3; Martin 20–3–66–4; Austin 20–5–53–0; Chapple 15–5–42–3; Flintoff 5–0–19–0. *Second Innings*—Wasim Akram 30.1–6–100–4; Martin 25–4–63–2; Chapple 16–4–47–3; Austin 11–4–25–1; Watkinson 2–0–11–0.

Umpires: A. A. Jones and R. Julian.

LANCASHIRE v SURREY

At Manchester, June 18, 19, 20, 21. Lancashire won by six wickets. Lancashire 20 pts, Surrey 3 pts. Toss: Lancashire.

This will go down in history as Flintoff's match, or perhaps just Flintoff's over. In a battle between two of English cricket's highest-rated young players, he crashed 34 in an over from his former England Under-19 team-mate Tudor. Since Tudor also bowled two no-balls, the over cost him 38, the most expensive in first-class history – excluding only the bizarre 77-run over at Christchurch in 1989-90, when Robert Vance was bowling deliberate no-balls to try and contrive a finish. It happened on Sunday afternoon, as Lancashire closed on their victory target of 250 in 53 overs. Flintoff hit 64444660; the first and fifth deliveries were no-balls. All the hits were on the leg side. Flintoff missed the last ball to lose his chance of passing Garry Sobers and Ravi Shastri's 36 off an over. He was out for 61 off 24 balls with Lancashire just short of victory. Yet Tudor had taken five for 43 in the first innings. "He was bowling very fast," said Surrey captain Adam Hollioake. "Anyone who says there is no young talent in English cricket should come and watch these two guys." It was a spectacular end to a match of fits and starts. The first day and most of the third were lost to rain, but 16 wickets fell on the second. Shahid hit a hundred off joke bowling to set up the finish. Crawley (who kept wicket because Hegg was injured) and Wood did the groundwork. Then Flintoff took wing.

Close of play: First day, No play; Second day, Lancashire 111-6 (M. Watkinson 26*, Wasim Akram 4*); Third day, Lancashire 151-7 (Wasim Akram 23*, G. Chapple 0*).

Surrey

J. D. Ratcliffe c Watkinson b Martin	11	– lbw b Chapple	33
I. J. Ward b Wasim Akram	1	– not out	81
N. Shahid lbw b Wasim Akram	0	– not out	126
*A. J. Hollioake c Wasim Akram b Martin	22		
A. D. Brown c Flintoff b Martin	26		
B. C. Hollioake b Wasim Akram	7		
†J. N. Batty b Wasim Akram	5		
A. J. Tudor c Wasim Akram b Green	1		
M. P. Bicknell c Crawley b Chapple	41		
J. E. Benjamin run out	15		
R. M. Amin not out	0		
B 1, l-b 4, w 6, n-b 6	17	B 2, l-b 6, w 2, n-b 4	14

1/13 2/13 3/16 4/64 5/67   146   1/69   (1 wkt dec.) 254
6/73 7/82 8/94 9/134

Bonus points – Lancashire 4.

Bowling: First Innings—Wasim Akram 19-6-42-4; Martin 17-5-35-3; Green 9-1-32-1; Chapple 8.1-1-32-1. *Second Innings*—Wasim Akram 5-1-11-0; Martin 7-1-24-0; Green 6-0-23-0; Chapple 4-2-8-1; Watkinson 6-0-23-0; Lloyd 6-1-29-0; Wood 5.1-0-80-0; Harvey 5-0-48-0.

Lancashire

P. C. McKeown c Batty b Tudor	42	– b Benjamin	10
N. T. Wood c Tudor b Benjamin	5	– not out	80
†J. P. Crawley c Ward b Benjamin	3	– st Batty b Amin	78
A. Flintoff c Batty b Tudor	0	– c Ward b Bicknell	61
G. D. Lloyd b Tudor	21	– c B. C. Hollioake b Bicknell	1
M. E. Harvey lbw b Tudor	0	– not out	0
M. Watkinson c A. J. Hollioake b Tudor	42		
*Wasim Akram not out	23		
G. Chapple not out	0		
L-b 9, n-b 6	15	L-b 6, w 6, n-b 8	20

1/16 2/30 3/31 4/69   (7 wkts dec.) 151   1/15 2/151 3/239 4/246   (4 wkts) 250
5/69 6/106 7/149

P. J. Martin and R. J. Green did not bat.

Bonus points – Surrey 3.

Bowling: First Innings—Bicknell 14-6-39-0; Benjamin 12.5-1-37-2; Tudor 16-6-43-5; A. J. Hollioake 6-2-17-0; Amin 3-1-6-0. *Second Innings*—Bicknell 14-3-65-2; Benjamin 11-2-35-1; Tudor 11-1-82-0; B. C. Hollioake 2-0-13-0; Amin 6-0-45-1; A. J. Hollioake 0.2-0-4-0.

Umpires: J. H. Hampshire and J. H. Harris.

At Birmingham, June 26, 27, 28, 29. LANCASHIRE beat WARWICKSHIRE by four wickets.

LANCASHIRE v WORCESTERSHIRE

At Lytham, July 14, 15, 16, 17. Lancashire won by two wickets. Lancashire 23 pts, Worcestershire 8 pts. Toss: Worcestershire.

With a large and enthusiastic crowd cheering every single, Austin saw Lancashire to a nerve-tingling victory: their fifth win out of six. Lancashire had been set 281, and Crawley took command with a stylish 108. He fell after tea, and a sudden downpour, which cost five overs, threatened to end their chances; they made it, though, with seven balls to spare. It seemed Lancashire might come a cropper when six dropped catches and tail-end resistance enabled Worcestershire to reach 350 in their first innings. Lancashire's problems were compounded by the loss of Fairbrother, who twisted an ankle treading on the ball. But they recovered well, reduced the deficit to 43 and had Worcestershire in trouble before Moody moved to an impressive 93 on the third day. He completed his century against declaration bowling.

Close of play: First day, Worcestershire 261-7 (S. R. Lampitt 12*); Second day, Lancashire 195-5 (Wasim Akram 34*, W. K. Hegg 12*); Third day, Worcestershire 196-6 (T. M. Moody 93*, S. R. Lampitt 17*).

Worcestershire

W. P. C. Weston c Hegg b Martin	21	– c Flintoff b Austin	36
A. Hafeez c Flintoff b Austin	14	– c Atherton b Martin	5
G. A. Hick c Hegg b Flintoff	34	– lbw b Chapple	8
V. S. Solanki c Hegg b Austin	87	– c Hegg b Chapple	2
*T. M. Moody c Hegg b Flintoff	11	– not out	107
D. A. Leatherdale c Fairbrother b Flintoff	0	– c Crawley b Chapple	0
†S. J. Rhodes c Hegg b Martin	44	– c Hegg b Austin	13
S. R. Lampitt lbw b Wasim Akram	36	– not out	38
R. K. Illingworth c Hegg b Austin	50		
P. J. Newport b Wasim Akram	4		
R. J. Chapman not out	1		
B 10, l-b 12, w 22, n-b 4	48	B 5, l-b 3, w 2, n-b 18	28

1/35 2/55 3/100 4/128 5/142   350   1/18 2/43 3/55   (6 wkts dec.) 237
6/221 7/261 8/316 9/326   4/69 5/76 6/128

Bonus points – Worcestershire 4, Lancashire 4.

Bowling: *First Innings*—Wasim Akram 26–5–77–2; Martin 20–6–58–2; Austin 31–9–82–3; Chapple 15–2–45–0; Flintoff 14–2–51–3; Watkinson 3–1–15–0. *Second Innings*—Wasim Akram 13–4–35–0; Martin 18–2–44–1; Chapple 12–2–39–3; Austin 14–2–39–2; Flintoff 6–2–16–0; Watkinson 6–2–15–0; Lloyd 1.3–0–20–0; Crawley 1–0–21–0.

Lancashire

M. A. Atherton c Weston b Chapman	3	– (2) c Moody b Lampitt	22
J. P. Crawley c Hick b Illingworth	39	– (1) b Newport	108
A. Flintoff c Solanki b Newport	15	– c Rhodes b Lampitt	8
G. D. Lloyd c Rhodes b Lampitt	27	– c and b Leatherdale	18
M. Watkinson lbw b Leatherdale	55	– c Moody b Newport	22
*Wasim Akram c Hick b Lampitt	38	– b Newport	0
†W. K. Hegg c Weston b Newport	54	– c Hick b Lampitt	37
I. D. Austin not out	59	– not out	44
G. Chapple c Rhodes b Newport	0	– c Solanki b Leatherdale	10
P. J. Martin c Hick b Chapman	3	– not out	2
N. H. Fairbrother absent hurt			
L-b 12, n-b 2	14	B 2, w 2, n-b 6	10

1/3 2/22 3/65 4/118 5/158   307   1/75 2/93 3/127 4/174   (8 wkts) 281
6/199 7/276 8/276 9/307   5/174 6/193 7/259 8/279

Bonus points – Lancashire 3, Worcestershire 4.

Bowling: *First Innings*—Newport 18–6–53–3; Chapman 12.4–6–31–2; Lampitt 19–5–55–2; Moody 24–10–54–0; Leatherdale 14–1–56–1; Illingworth 18–7–42–1; Solanki 2–1–4–0. *Second Innings*—Newport 17–4–61–3; Chapman 11–3–56–0; Lampitt 11–1–56–3; Moody 6–2–27–0; Leatherdale 6.5–0–36–2; Illingworth 14–2–39–0; Solanki 2–1–4–0.

Umpires: H. D. Bird and A. Clarkson.

At Colwyn Bay, July 22, 23, 24, 25. LANCASHIRE drew with GLAMORGAN.

LANCASHIRE v LEICESTERSHIRE

At Manchester, July 30, 31, August 1, 3. Drawn. Lancashire 6 pts, Leicestershire 4 pts. Toss: Lancashire.

Play was possible only on the second day – and that after the morning had been lost. But the cricket, if brief, was intriguing. Lancashire removed both openers for ducks, then failed to drive home that advantage, while Leicestershire showed the doggedness which was to win the Championship: Habib and Nixon led a fightback from 82 for five. The omens looked doubtful for them during this match, as their rivals Surrey were in the dry at The Oval, slaughtering Sussex. And their vice-captain, Lewis, was fined after he was left off a 37-strong list of World Cup possibles issued by the England selectors: he called the decision "crap".

Close of play: First day, No play; Second day, Leicestershire 218-7 (P. A. Nixon 42*, C. D. Crowe 29*); Third day, No play.

Leicestershire

V. J. Wells lbw b Wasim Akram	0	D. J. Millns lbw b Wasim Akram	9	
D. L. Maddy c Hegg b Martin	0	C. D. Crowe not out	29	
I. J. Sutcliffe c and b Martin	32			
B. F. Smith hit wkt b Wasim Akram	19	B 2, l-b 11, w 4, n-b 8	25	
*P. V. Simmons c Hegg b Chapple	6			
A. Habib c McKeown b Martin	56	1/0 2/0 3/37 4/49	(7 wkts) 218	
†P. A. Nixon not out	42	5/82 6/155 7/173		

M. T. Brimson and A. D. Mullally did not bat.

Bonus points – Leicestershire 1, Lancashire 3.

Bowling: Wasim Akram 16–4–58–3; Martin 15–3–41–3; Austin 14–3–35–0; Chapple 11–2–28–1; Flintoff 6–2–27–0; Watkinson 4–0–16–0.

Lancashire

P. C. McKeown, N. T. Wood, J. P. Crawley, G. D. Lloyd, A. Flintoff, M. Watkinson, †W. K. Hegg, *Wasim Akram, I. D. Austin, G. Chapple and P. J. Martin.

Umpires: G. I. Burgess and P. Willey.

LANCASHIRE v GLOUCESTERSHIRE

At Manchester, August 5, 6, 7. Lancashire won by an innings and 35 runs. Lancashire 23 pts, Gloucestershire 3 pts. Toss: Lancashire.

Old Trafford devotees had waited a long time to see an effective Lancashire leg-spinner, and 19-year-old Chris Schofield from Littleborough, making his first home appearance after a debut at Colwyn Bay, gave them great encouragement. He picked up eight wickets in the match, though England Under-19 duties and injury made it his last county game of the season. There were also eight wickets for his partner, the off-spinner Yates, playing his first Championship match of 1998. On a dry, turning pitch which put Walsh and company out of business, they collected all but two of the 12 wickets Gloucestershire lost on the second day, when they tumbled to 158 and then 11 for two following on. The rout was completed next day, despite a defiant stand of 83 – a county tenth-wicket record against Lancashire – from Ball and Lewis. Earlier, Yates had played his part with the bat, too. All of Lancashire's upper order made starts, but only Yates and fellow tailender Chapple went on to fifties, helping to add 124 for the last three wickets.

Close of play: First day, Lancashire 269-7 (G. Yates 30*, G. Chapple 6*); Second day, Gloucestershire 11-2 (C. A. Walsh 0*, A. M. Smith 0*).

Lancashire

P. C. McKeown c Hancock b Ball	21		G. Chapple c Alleyne b Dawson	69
N. T. Wood c Smith b Ball	24		P. J. Martin not out	19
J. P. Crawley c Lewis b Alleyne	43		C. P. Schofield lbw b Dawson	0
N. H. Fairbrother lbw b Ball	35			
G. D. Lloyd c Dawson b Hancock	26		B 8, l-b 11	19
†W. K. Hegg c Hancock b Walsh	26			—
*Wasim Akram lbw b Dawson	37			386
G. Yates b Lewis	55		1/39 2/49 3/119 4/145 5/180	
			6/212 7/262 8/316 9/386	

Bonus points – Lancashire 3, Gloucestershire 3 (Score at 120 overs: 316-7).

Bowling: Walsh 24–10–33–1; Smith 14–3–44–0; Ball 52–10–153–3; Lewis 18–7–35–1; Alleyne 17–3–59–1; Hancock 10–2–28–1; Dawson 4.5–0–15–3.

Gloucestershire

R. J. Cunliffe b Yates	20	– (2) b Schofield	6
T. H. C. Hancock b Wasim Akram	0	– (1) c Hegg b Yates	2
D. R. Hewson c McKeown b Yates	37	– (5) c Chapple b Martin	1
*M. W. Alleyne c Wasim Akram b Schofield	30	– (6) c Hegg b Schofield	14
M. G. N. Windows b Yates	21	– (7) c McKeown b Yates	12
R. I. Dawson b Wasim Akram	0	– (8) c Crawley b Yates	10
†R. C. Russell lbw b Schofield	11	– (9) b Schofield	8
M. C. J. Ball lbw b Schofield	9	– (10) not out	40
J. Lewis st Hegg b Yates	0	– (11) c Schofield b Yates	35
A. M. Smith not out	2	– (4) c McKeown b Schofield	31
C. A. Walsh c Yates b Schofield	6	– (3) c McKeown b Martin	0
B 8, l-b 6, n-b 8	22	B 10, l-b 10, n-b 14	34
	—		—
1/0 2/40 3/65 4/111 5/116	158	1/3 2/11 3/11 4/27 5/78	193
6/127 7/142 8/150 9/152		6/83 7/95 8/110 9/110	

Bonus points – Lancashire 4.

Bowling: *First Innings*—Yates 26–5–64–4; Wasim Akram 10–3–20–2; Martin 5–3–3–0; Chapple 4–3–1–0; Schofield 16.4–3–56–4. *Second Innings*—Schofield 23–3–60–4; Yates 21.3–3–91–4; Martin 5–3–5–2; Wasim Akram 4–0–17–0.

Umpires: J. C. Balderstone and B. Leadbeater.

At Leeds, August 14, 15, 16, 17. LANCASHIRE beat YORKSHIRE by 59 runs.

At Chester-le-Street, August 19, 20, 21. LANCASHIRE beat DURHAM by 350 runs.

LANCASHIRE v DERBYSHIRE

At Manchester, September 1, 2, 3. Lancashire won by an innings and eight runs. Lancashire 24 pts, Derbyshire 6 pts. Toss: Lancashire.

Audacious batting and potent pace bowling hurried Lancashire to a breathtaking victory, squeezed into two days after a first-day washout. It meant a leisurely drive south on the scheduled fourth day, before they met Derbyshire again in the NatWest final, and also kept them in touch with the Championship leaders and their dream of the treble. The frenetic pace of a match which generated 966 runs and 30 wickets inside 222 overs was set in the first over, when Wasim Akram conceded 17. By the close, Lancashire's innings was in full swing: Fairbrother lit the fuse with 48 off 31 balls. Crawley accelerated to his seventh century of the summer, completed in 134 balls next morning, while Lloyd gorged himself with an unbeaten 212 in 299 minutes and 227 balls, including 21 fours and five sixes. He hit 28 – two sixes and four fours – in one over from left-arm spinner Blackwell. Cork did his utmost, bowling well, shocking Austin with a spectacular run-out, and scoring a defiant 50. But Derbyshire were overpowered.

Close of play: First day, No play; Second day, Lancashire 214-2 (J. P. Crawley 96*, G. D. Lloyd 56*).

Derbyshire

K. J. Barnett c Flintoff b Martin	28	– c Fairbrother b Wasim Akram	25
M. R. May c Fairbrother b Martin	4	– b Wasim Akram	11
R. M. S. Weston lbw b Austin	18	– lbw b Chapple	40
M. E. Cassar c and b Chapple	70	– c Wasim Akram b Martin	4
B. L. Spendlove c Atherton b Chapple	0	– c sub b Austin	9
*D. G. Cork lbw b Wasim Akram	23	– lbw b Martin	50
V. P. Clarke lbw b Wasim Akram	7	– c and b Wasim Akram	11
P. A. J. DeFreitas c Lloyd b Austin	69	– c Hegg b Martin	12
†K. M. Krikken c Hegg b Martin	22	– not out	7
I. D. Blackwell b Wasim Akram	6	– b Wasim Akram	0
G. M. Roberts not out	0	– b Martin	0
B 4, l-b 6, w 8, n-b 16	34	L-b 5, n-b 24	29

1/44 2/55 3/75 4/80 5/132   281   1/51 2/58 3/63 4/85 5/163   198
6/154 7/201 8/249 9/271   6/163 7/191 8/191 9/191

Bonus points – Derbyshire 2, Lancashire 4.

Bowling: *First Innings*—Wasim Akram 18–7–60–3; Martin 15–1–70–3; Austin 13.2–5–50–2; Chapple 12–0–37–2; Flintoff 4–0–19–0; Keedy 9–2–35–0. *Second Innings*—Wasim Akram 16–2–66–4; Martin 16–4–45–4; Austin 10–2–26–1; Keedy 8–1–38–0; Chapple 5–0–18–1.

Lancashire

M. A. Atherton b DeFreitas	4	G. Chapple c Blackwell b Roberts	42
J. P. Crawley c Krikken b Cork	100	P. J. Martin b Clarke	2
N. H. Fairbrother c Krikken b Cork	48	G. Keedy b Cassar	7
G. D. Lloyd not out	212		
A. Flintoff c Weston b DeFreitas	14	B 5, l-b 4, w 8, n-b 6	23
†W. K. Hegg c Weston b Cassar	19		
*Wasim Akram c Roberts b Cassar	13		487
I. D. Austin run out	3		

1/13 2/75 3/218 4/247 5/276
6/302 7/305 8/445 9/452

Bonus points – Lancashire 4, Derbyshire 4.

Bowling: Cork 19–3–57–2; DeFreitas 17–3–68–2; Blackwell 10–1–87–0; Cassar 13.1–0–65–3; Roberts 21–3–124–1; Clarke 15–1–77–1.

Umpires: M. J. Kitchen and R. Palmer.

At Nottingham, September 11, 12, 13. LANCASHIRE beat NOTTINGHAMSHIRE by 289 runs.

LANCASHIRE v HAMPSHIRE

At Manchester, September 17, 18, 19, 20. Lancashire won by 161 runs. Lancashire 20 pts, Hampshire 4 pts. Toss: Lancashire.

The setting sun, dazzling the batsmen at the Warwick Road End, twice ended play early; it seemed to symbolise the setting of Lancashire's Championship hopes for another year. Their chances of overtaking Leicestershire shrank when they were bowled out for 185, their lowest total of 1998. Fifteen wickets fell on the opening day, but there was no need to contact the ECB, who had adopted the precaution of sending an observer to approve the pitch before the game. Next day, after Hampshire's dismissal 13 runs behind, the Lancashire batsmen proved the pitch's worth. Though it was rapidly becoming clear that they were fighting only for second place in the Championship, the match turned into the coronation of Crawley. He scored his eighth century of the season, and his seventh in the Championship – the most for Lancashire since Winston Place and Cyril Washbrook in 1947 – and converted it into the fourth double-hundred of his career. In all, he batted for 293 minutes and 264 balls, hitting eight sixes and 27 fours, epitomising his move to a more aggressive style. Crawley finished with 1,851 first-class runs, over 400 more than the next highest aggregate, and easily headed the national averages. Against a weakened attack – McLean and Morris were injured – he and Fairbrother, who chivvied his way to another hundred, added 261 to put Lancashire into an impregnable position. It was a pity that the glare of the sun prevented them from finishing off Hampshire before a large Saturday crowd. Only two wickets were needed on Sunday morning, but a decent number of spectators turned up to witness Lancashire's 11th Championship win, hear the farewell speech of captain Wasim Akram, and witness Crawley's appointment as his successor, before enjoying a picnic lunch.

Close of play: First day, Hampshire 74-5 (A. D. Mascarenhas 18*, K. D. James 0*); Second day, Lancashire 296-1 (J. P. Crawley 211*, N. H. Fairbrother 47*); Third day, Hampshire 232-8 (S. D. Udal 8*, R. J. Maru 4*).

Lancashire

M. A. Atherton c Maru b Mascarenhas	45	– (2) c sub b Maru	28
J. P. Crawley c Aymes b Mascarenhas	15	– (1) b James	239
N. H. Fairbrother c Kendall b James	16	– not out	103
G. D. Lloyd c Kendall b Morris	0	– c Mascarenhas b Maru	45
A. Flintoff c Kendall b Morris	1	– c and b Udal	4
†W. K. Hegg c Aymes b Morris	4	– not out	11
I. D. Austin c Aymes b James	27		
*Wasim Akram c Smith b James	13		
G. Yates c Smith b James	37		
P. J. Martin c Udal b Morris	13		
G. Keedy not out	0		
L-b 12, n-b 2	14	B 7, l-b 8, w 2, n-b 2	19

1/26 2/50 3/54 4/60 5/82   185   1/94 2/355   (4 wkts dec.) 449
6/90 7/119 8/142 9/176   3/416 4/421

Bonus points – Hampshire 4.

Bowling: *First Innings*—McLean 17–4–27–0; Morris 21–7–57–4; James 13.1–5–22–4; Mascarenhas 14–3–56–2; Maru 3–0–11–0. *Second Innings*—Udal 28–4–105–1; James 23–2–88–1; McLean 4–1–8–0; Mascarenhas 16–3–95–0; Kendall 4–0–16–0; Maru 28–5–101–2; White 2–0–4–0; Kenway 2–0–17–0.

Hampshire

G. W. White c Fairbrother b Martin	1	– lbw b Martin	12
D. A. Kenway b Wasim Akram	4	– lbw b Keedy	57
W. S. Kendall b Austin	33	– b Wasim Akram	31
*R. A. Smith lbw b Wasim Akram	2	– b Yates	47
†A. N. Aymes c Hegg b Wasim Akram	2	– lbw b Martin	8
A. D. Mascarenhas c Lloyd b Keedy	21	– c Austin b Yates	26
K. D. James b Wasim Akram	39	– c Lloyd b Austin	3
S. D. Udal not out	33	– c Austin b Keedy	43
A. C. Morris b Austin	0	– c Crawley b Wasim Akram	0
N. A. M. McLean c Lloyd b Austin	2	– (11) not out	24
R. J. Maru c and b Austin	13	– (10) st Hegg b Yates	14
B 9, l-b 3, n-b 10	22	B 4, l-b 8, w 2, n-b 22	36

1/9 2/11 3/15 4/23 5/74   172   1/27 2/112 3/118 4/149 5/189   301
6/77 7/146 8/147 9/149   6/210 7/212 8/223 9/259

Bonus points – Lancashire 4.

Bowling: *First Innings*—Wasim Akram 18–5–37–4; Martin 16–8–30–1; Austin 17.4–3–50–4; Yates 4–1–11–0; Flintoff 3–0–13–0; Keedy 7–2–19–1. *Second Innings*—Wasim Akram 16–3–62–2; Martin 14–4–56–2; Keedy 18.1–3–57–2; Yates 20–3–86–3; Austin 12–3–28–1.

Umpires: J. W. Holder and J. F. Steele.

UNBEATEN CHAMPIONSHIP SEASONS

		P	W	L	D	A	Position
1900	Yorkshire	28	16	0	12	0	1
1904	Lancashire	26	16	0	10	0	1
1907	Nottinghamshire	19	15	0	4	1	1
1908	Yorkshire	28	16	0	12	0	1
1925	Yorkshire	32	21	0	11	0	1
1926	Yorkshire	31	14	0	17	1	2
1928	Lancashire	30	15	0	15	0	1
1928	Yorkshire	26	8	0	18	0	4
1930	Lancashire	28	10	0	18	0	1
1969	Glamorgan	24	11	0	13	0	1
1972	Warwickshire	20	9	0	11	0	1
1973	Hampshire	20	10	0	10	0	1
1974	Lancashire	20	5	0	15	0	8
1998	Leicestershire	17	11	0	6	0	1

Note: Seasons before the formal constitution of the Championship in 1890 are excluded.

WOMBWELL CRICKET LOVERS' SOCIETY AWARDS, 1998

John Crawley of Lancashire was voted Cricketer of the Year by members of the Wombwell Cricket Lovers' Society. Other award-winners were: C. B. Fry Young Cricketer of the Year – Gavin Hamilton; Brian Sellers Captain of the Year – Alec Stewart; Arthur Wood Wicket-keeper of the Year – Richard Blakey; Denis Compton Memorial Award for Flair – Jonty Rhodes; J. M. Kilburn Cricket Writer of the Year – Mark Nicholas; Jack Fingleton Cricket Commentator of the Year – Richie Benaud; Ted Umbers Services to Yorkshire Cricket – Derek Hodgson.

LEICESTERSHIRE

President: B. A. F. Smith

Chairman: R. Goadby

Chairman, Cricket Committee: P. R. Haywood

Chief Executive: D. G. Collier

Captain: J. J. Whitaker

Cricket Manager: J. Birkenshaw

Head Groundsman: S. Wright

Scorer: G. A. York

Aftab Habib

After Leicestershire's second County Championship in three years, a journalist friend said: "Done well your boys, haven't they? Leicestershire, though ... Not *really* that good, are they?" I enquired how many times he had watched them. "Well, er, none actually," he said sheepishly.

This attitude is not unusual. Leicestershire are never mentioned in the same breath as the counties that play on a Test ground. Because the team is short of "stars" and Grace Road does not boast a tree in the outfield, or a cathedral on its doorstep, while fans still eat in the run-down Meet and the crowds are among the lowest on the circuit, Leicestershire are deemed unfashionable. Even the Saatchi brothers would struggle to improve their image.

But in 1998 Leicestershire proved their 1996 win was no fluke. They are a good team – not great, because the Championship is not a great competition. But their record now shows they can play a bit. They became only the fourth side since the war to win the title unbeaten, having lost just one game in each of the previous two seasons. Their last home Championship defeat was by Lancashire, in August 1995.

There were still disappointments. Only two players, Alan Mullally and Darren Maddy, were selected for England tours, and Leicestershire's 13-year drought in one-day cricket continued. They finished fourth in the Sunday League; they reached the Benson and Hedges final, only to be hammered in a rain-affected match by Essex, and then the semi-finals of the NatWest, where they snatched defeat from victory against Derbyshire.

But ultimately, Leicestershire were compensated by their third Championship triumph – the second in three years under the captaincy of James Whitaker. This time, Whitaker did not face a single ball in the competition, because of a knee injury that required two operations. He did, however, play every ball his team faced, bowl every ball they bowled and catch every catch. Once back on his feet, Whitaker did not miss a match and often paced the boundary, smoking nervily. At the Lord's final, he was ejected from the field as he tried to encourage his players. This selfless fostering of team spirit was one of the factors behind Leicestershire's success. Another was

Birkenshaw's ability to spot good – and good-natured – players, such as Vince Wells and Aftab Habib, languishing in another county's second team and to help them blossom. They made a potent partnership: Birkenshaw with his coaching and analysis, Whitaker with his encouragement and a stream of buzz words like "energy" and "externalise". But their bond was tested to the full at Worksop in August. Until then, Whitaker had resisted interfering with the running of the side by acting-captain Chris Lewis. But he dropped both Lewis and fast bowler David Millns when they arrived late for practice. Birkenshaw backed him all the way.

Leicestershire probably made a mistake in appointing Lewis as Whitaker's stand-in instead of West Indian Phil Simmons, their first lieutenant in 1996. It was asking a lot of Lewis, in his first season back at Grace Road after his years of wandering. The decision also hurt Simmons. It cannot be coincidence that, at Worksop, Simmons finally discovered the form sadly missing until then; he scored 194, after his previous 14 innings totalled 120.

It was Simmons who coined the phrase "there is no I in this team", illustrating that the 1998 Championship was more of a team effort than that in 1996, when Simmons himself played a huge part. Only one batsman, Ben Smith, scored 1,000 runs, and only one bowler, Mullally, took 50 wickets. But everyone chipped in. Confirmed as acting-captain (a job he had already taken on when Lewis was injured), Simmons led Leicestershire to a title that seemed a long shot at the end of June. Of their first eight games, they had won just three, hampered by appalling weather: they lost the equivalent of 17 days to rain, only five less than in the whole of the previous record-breaking damp summer. But the weather smiled on them in the run-in, and Leicestershire won eight of their last nine games. In that time, excluding a rain-wrecked draw with Lancashire, they dropped just two points out of 192: all the more remarkable that they finished with fewer bowling points than any other county.

Two of those eight wins were particularly significant. Against Northamptonshire in July, they successfully chased an unbelievable 204 in 20 overs, thanks to Wells and Lewis, in what became his last match as captain; Wells scored 58 and Lewis 71, both off 33 balls. Then, in early September, they beat Warwickshire just after tea on the last day, under threat from rain which never arrived. With Surrey losing to Yorkshire, Leicestershire went top for the first time, with two matches to go. But the most satisfying victory was the one over Surrey in the final game, which clinched the title. There was a touch of irony here. In 1996, Leicestershire's only defeat had been inflicted by Surrey. This time, Leicestershire beat them by an innings and 211 runs. Appropriately, the win was set up by a double-hundred from Smith and a century from Habib, their best batsmen of the season, and some devastating fast bowling by Millns and Mullally, who reduced Surrey to eight for four. Surrey captain Adam Hollioake, whose team had led the table for most of the season, graciously said Leicestershire were the best Championship side he had faced.

The title was effectively settled when Wells, who epitomises the modern Leicestershire, trapped Ian Salisbury lbw to earn the seventh bonus point. Wells called it the highlight of his career; and Whitaker, tears in his eyes, hobbled on to congratulate his men. – CHRIS GODDARD.

LEICESTERSHIRE 1998

[*Bill Smith*]

Back row: T. J. Mason, D. I. Stevens, J. Ormond, A. S. Wright. *Middle row:* M. T. Brimson, C. D. Crowe, S. P. Kirby, J. M. Dakin, A. Habib, P. E. Robinson, D. Williamson. *Front row:* V. J. Wells, P. A. Nixon, C. C. Lewis, B. F. Smith, J. Birkenshaw (*cricket manager*), J. J. Whitaker (*captain*), A. D. Mullally, D. J. Millns, I. J. Sutcliffe, D. L. Maddy. *Inset:* P. V. Simmons.

LEICESTERSHIRE RESULTS

All first-class matches – Played 19: Won 11, Lost 1, Drawn 7.

County Championship matches – Played 17: Won 11, Drawn 6.

Competition placings – Britannic Assurance County Championship, winners;
NatWest Trophy, s-f; Benson and Hedges Cup, finalists;
AXA League, 4th.

COUNTY CHAMPIONSHIP AVERAGES
BATTING

Cap		M	I	NO	R	HS	100s	50s	Avge	Ct/St
1995	B. F. Smith.	17	22	4	1,165	204	4	3	64.72	13
1998	A. Habib	17	20	5	929	198	3	3	61.93	12
1991	D. J. Millns	10	8	3	229	99	0	1	45.80	4
1994	P. A. Nixon	17	19	4	580	101*	2	1	38.66	37/5
1994	V. J. Wells	16	24	1	826	171	3	3	35.91	10
1990	C. C. Lewis	12	14	3	367	71*	0	4	33.36	10
1997	I. J. Sutcliffe.	17	23	3	659	167	1	2	32.95	11
1994	P. V. Simmons§. . . .	17	19	0	464	194	1	2	24.42	23
1996	D. L. Maddy†.	16	23	2	512	162	2	0	24.38	16
	C. D. Crowe†.	5	4	1	63	29*	0	0	21.00	3
1998	M. T. Brimson	16	12	5	112	54*	0	1	16.00	3
1993	A. D. Mullally	15	11	2	132	38*	0	0	14.66	3
	J. Ormond	5	5	0	15	9	0	0	3.00	0
	J. M. Dakin	5	4	0	7	4	0	0	1.75	2

Also batted: D. Williamson (1 match) 41* (1 ct). T. J. Mason† (1 match) did not bat.

* Signifies not out.   † Born in Leicestershire.   § Overseas player.

BOWLING

	O	M	R	W	BB	5W/i	Avge
V. J. Wells	199.1	66	514	36	5-18	1	14.27
J. Ormond.	133.3	51	311	19	6-33	2	16.36
A. D. Mullally.	448.5	156	1,128	60	7-55	3	18.80
P. V. Simmons	170.5	44	491	23	7-49	1	21.34
D. J. Millns.	232.3	53	754	34	4-60	0	22.17
C. C. Lewis.	266.4	53	972	39	6-60	2	24.92
M. T. Brimson	345	126	810	31	4-4	0	26.12

Also bowled: C. D. Crowe 21–5–61–4; J. M. Dakin 89–25–243–4; A. Habib 4–0–15–0;
D. L. Maddy 24–7–83–2; T. J. Mason 45.2–9–139–0; B. F. Smith 5–0–11–0; I. J. Sutcliffe
9–0–51–1; D. Williamson 23–4–73–1.

COUNTY RECORDS

Highest score for:	261	P. V. Simmons v Northamptonshire at Leicester . .	1994
Highest score against:	341	G. H. Hirst (Yorkshire) at Leicester	1905
Best bowling for:	10-18	G. Geary v Glamorgan at Pontypridd	1929
Best bowling against:	10-32	H. Pickett (Essex) at Leyton.	1895
Highest total for:	701-4 dec.	v Worcestershire at Worcester.	1906
Highest total against:	761-6 dec.	by Essex at Chelmsford.	1990
Lowest total for:	25	v Kent at Leicester	1912
Lowest total against:	{ 24	by Glamorgan at Leicester	1971
	24	by Oxford University at Oxford	1985

At Cambridge, April 17, 18, 19. LEICESTERSHIRE drew with CAMBRIDGE UNIVERSITY.

LEICESTERSHIRE v WORCESTERSHIRE

At Leicester, April 23, 24, 25, 27. Drawn. Leicestershire 3 pts, Worcestershire 3 pts. Toss: Leicestershire.

The big black cloud that followed Leicestershire around in 1997, robbing them of a third of the season, reappeared. The first three days of their opening Championship match were washed out, resulting in a one-innings game for 12 points, with no bonuses, on the final day. It gave Moody just enough time to get back from Sharjah, where he had been playing for Australia; he arrived on the fourth morning, though his deputy, Hick, went out for the toss. Leicestershire also changed their scheduled captain: by the time the game began, Whitaker was injured, so Lewis took over in his first Championship match for his old county after six years of wandering. But the match ended in a draw after Worcestershire, having lost four wickets cheaply, decided they had little chance of setting a target and batted out the day. On a fairly lifeless pitch, Weston and Leatherdale saw them through in a stand of 167.

Close of play: First day, No play; Second day, No play; Third day, No play.

Worcestershire

W. P. C. Weston c Simmons b Brimson .	77	S. R. Lampitt not out	0
V. S. Solanki c Maddy b Millns	0	R. K. Illingworth not out	2
G. A. Hick c Nixon b Millns	10		
G. R. Haynes c Simmons b Lewis.	16	B 2, l-b 11, w 9, n-b 29	51
*T. M. Moody c Smith b Lewis	0		—
D. A. Leatherdale c Lewis b Brimson . .	99	1/4 2/26 3/68 4/78 (7 wkts) 268
†S. J. Rhodes c Simmons b Brimson . . .	13	5/245 6/259 7/266

P. J. Newport and A. Sheriyar did not bat.

Bowling: Mullally 17–8–43–0; Millns 17–6–72–2; Lewis 5–1–23–2; Brimson 20–10–21–3; Dakin 15–5–42–0; Maddy 1–1–0–0; Sutcliffe 6–0–34–0; Habib 4–0–15–0; Smith 2–0–5–0.

Leicestershire

D. L. Maddy, I. J. Sutcliffe, J. M. Dakin, A. Habib, P. V. Simmons, B. F. Smith, *C. C. Lewis, †P. A. Nixon, D. J. Millns, A. D. Mullally and M. T. Brimson.

Umpires: G. I. Burgess and D. J. Constant.

At Bristol, May 13, 14, 15. LEICESTERSHIRE beat GLOUCESTERSHIRE by nine wickets.

LEICESTERSHIRE v HAMPSHIRE

At Leicester, May 21, 22, 23, 24. Drawn. Leicestershire 8 pts, Hampshire 9 pts. Toss: Hampshire.

Leicestershire supporters greeted another dull finale with slow hand-clapping as the visitors batted out the final day. Hampshire had taken a first-innings lead of 56 after Simmons declared behind, and they offered to set a target. Leicestershire preferred to try bowling them out, but failed on a flat pitch and with three top bowlers missing. After losing six wickets for 77, Hampshire shut up shop. Earlier, Aymes scored a career-best 133, while Mullally took five wickets, and Habib responded with a century. He managed to keep out the pace of West Indian McLean, who claimed all the other wickets which fell, to return career-best figures of six for 101.

Close of play: First day, Hampshire 276-6 (A. N. Aymes 116*, S. D. Udal 12*); Second day, Leicestershire 122-5 (A. Habib 27*, P. A. Nixon 0*); Third day, Hampshire 58-3 (M. Keech 32*, P. J. Hartley 0*).

Hampshire

G. W. White c Nixon b Wells	14	– c Sutcliffe b Brimson	21
J. S. Laney c Williamson b Mullally	8	– b Mullally	0
*R. A. Smith c Simmons b Mullally	40	– lbw b Dakin	3
M. Keech c Simmons b Dakin	4	– c Simmons b Dakin	33
†A. N. Aymes b Wells	133	– (6) b Mullally	4
A. D. Mascarenhas c Nixon b Williamson	46	– (7) b Dakin	63
K. D. James c Brimson b Mullally	20	– (8) not out	55
S. D. Udal c Nixon b Mullally	44	– (9) lbw b Sutcliffe	62
N. A. M. McLean c Smith b Wells	6	– (10) not out	17
P. J. Hartley c Nixon b Mullally	21	– (5) c Simmons b Mullally	5
C. A. Connor not out	0		
B 4, l-b 9, w 6, n-b 6	25	B 5, l-b 4, w 2, n-b 2	13

1/17 2/52 3/65 4/85 5/199	361	1/3 2/10 3/54	(8 wkts dec.) 276
6/259 7/324 8/334 9/340		4/64 5/68 6/77	
		7/151 8/252	

Bonus points – Hampshire 3, Leicestershire 2 (Score at 120 overs: 303-6).

Bowling: *First Innings*—Mullally 36.5–15–72–5; Simmons 7–0–22–0; Dakin 14–4–58–1; Wells 16–8–34–3; Mason 20.2–5–67–0; Brimson 22.4–9–36–0; Williamson 20–4–59–1. *Second Innings*—Mullally 20–8–45–3; Dakin 25–8–38–3; Brimson 28–9–68–1; Wells 5–2–7–0; Mason 25–4–72–0; Williamson 3–0–14–0; Sutcliffe 3–0–17–1; Smith 3–0–6–0.

Leicestershire

V. J. Wells c Keech b McLean	15		D. Williamson not out	41
I. J. Sutcliffe lbw b McLean	17			
B. F. Smith b McLean	40		B 11, l-b 15, w 6, n-b 16	48
A. Habib c Hartley b Mascarenhas	112			
*P. V. Simmons b McLean	1		1/38 2/55 3/104	(7 wkts dec.) 305
J. M. Dakin b McLean	0		4/112 5/122	
†P. A. Nixon lbw b McLean	31		6/199 7/305	

T. J. Mason, A. D. Mullally and M. T. Brimson did not bat.

Bonus points – Leicestershire 3, Hampshire 3.

Bowling: McLean 28–6–101–6; Hartley 17–4–45–0; Connor 16–4–43–0; James 15–1–50–0; Mascarenhas 11–1–31–1; Udal 2–0–9–0.

Umpires: H. D. Bird and J. H. Harris.

At Chesterfield, May 29, 30, 31. LEICESTERSHIRE beat DERBYSHIRE by 38 runs.

At Leeds, June 3, 4, 5, 6. LEICESTERSHIRE drew with YORKSHIRE.

LEICESTERSHIRE v KENT

At Leicester, June 11, 12, 13, 15. Drawn. Leicestershire 6 pts, Kent 7 pts. Toss: Kent.

Rain continued to hold Grace Road in thrall. The first and last days were washed out and only 31 balls were possible on the third. On the second, however, 16 wickets fell for only 212 runs. Ealham took his first five Championship wickets of the season as Leicestershire were bowled out for 103 on a pitch of somewhat variable bounce, though that did not justify the poor batting. Kent just inched past that by the close. Leicestershire had now lost more than six days' play out of 12 in home Championship matches; it might have been even worse without a newly installed £25,000 drainage system.

Close of play: First day, No play; Second day, Kent 109-6 (M. A. Ealham 12*); Third day, Kent 120-7 (M. A. Ealham 17*, S. C. Willis 0*).

Leicestershire

V. J. Wells b Headley	6	J. Ormond c Wells b Ealham		0
D. L. Maddy b McCague	2	A. D. Mullally c Ward b Ealham		0
I. J. Sutcliffe run out	20	M. T. Brimson not out		1
B. F. Smith c Key b Ealham	6			
P. V. Simmons c McCague b Fleming	17	B 6, l-b 2, w 2, n-b 2		12
A. Habib b Ealham	23			—
†P. A. Nixon c Ward b McCague	8	1/6 2/14 3/30 4/37 5/66		103
*C. C. Lewis c Willis b Ealham	8	6/88 7/94 8/100 9/100		

Bonus points – Kent 4.

Bowling: Headley 13–4–29–1; McCague 14–4–34–2; Ealham 18.4–10–23–5; Fleming 6–2–9–1.

Kent

D. P. Fulton lbw b Brimson	44	M. V. Fleming c Smith b Mullally		6
R. W. T. Key b Lewis	19	†S. C. Willis not out		0
*T. R. Ward lbw b Lewis	2			
C. L. Hooper c Simmons b Mullally	0	B 1, l-b 4, w 2, n-b 10		17
A. P. Wells c Habib b Mullally	14			—
M. A. Ealham not out	17	1/41 2/45 3/56 4/74	(7 wkts)	120
D. W. Headley lbw b Mullally	1	5/105 6/109 7/119		

M. M. Patel and M. J. McCague did not bat.

Bonus points – Leicestershire 3.

Bowling: Mullally 18–5–45–4; Ormond 15–9–18–0; Lewis 14–1–40–2; Wells 3–1–4–0; Brimson 5–3–8–1.

Umpires: T. E. Jesty and A. G. T. Whitehead.

At Cardiff, June 17, 18, 19, 20. LEICESTERSHIRE beat GLAMORGAN by 140 runs.

LEICESTERSHIRE v SUSSEX

At Leicester, June 26, 27, 28, 29. Drawn. Leicestershire 9 pts, Sussex 10 pts. Toss: Sussex.

Leicestershire's fourth successive home draw ended in stony silence. What crowd there was voted with their feet, driven away by boredom, the lure of the soccer World Cup, and the late finish. This was the second of three matches starting at mid-day but the plan to attract people leaving work fell flat, only a dozen witnessing the bitter end. Leicestershire manager Jack Birkenshaw reckoned the number might be down to two next time, after a meaningless last day when the captains could not settle on a target for Sussex. Trailing by 233, Sussex favoured a declaration, a forfeit and a day-long run-chase; Leicestershire offered 280. A possible compromise of 250 was not agreed. Anything less was giving it away, said Birkenshaw. Only 19 overs were played on the first two days but, on the third, Lewis and Nixon rescued Leicestershire in a seventh-wicket stand of 93. Then Millns, returning after two months off with an ear infection, struck twice, reducing Sussex to 56 for four. On the dead last day, Bevan scored an unbeaten 149, his highest yet for Sussex, without breaking sweat. It proved how flat the pitch was.

Close of play: First day, Leicestershire 42-0 (V. J. Wells 19*, D. L. Maddy 15*); Second day, Leicestershire 44-1 (V. J. Wells 20*, I. J. Sutcliffe 1*); Third day, Sussex 56-4 (M. G. Bevan 16*, N. R. Taylor 5*).

Leicestershire

V. J. Wells c Humphries b Kirtley	26	– not out	6
D. L. Maddy c Humphries b Kirtley	15	– lbw b Lewry	0
I. J. Sutcliffe lbw b Bevan	38	– not out	0
B. F. Smith c Humphries b Kirtley	2		
P. V. Simmons lbw b Kirtley	0		
A. Habib c Humphries b Bevan	20		
†P. A. Nixon hit wkt b Jarvis	45		
*C. C. Lewis c and b Jarvis	63		
D. J. Millns not out	26		
A. D. Mullally c Adams b Kirtley	16		
M. T. Brimson c Jarvis b Bevan	14		
B 6, l-b 12, w 2, n-b 4	24		

1/43 2/68 3/70 4/74 5/112   289   1/2   (1 wkt)   6
6/121 7/214 8/233 9/265

Bonus points – Leicestershire 2, Sussex 4.

Bowling: *First Innings*—Lewry 19–7–59–0; Kirtley 27–5–83–5; Robinson 20–7–33–0; Jarvis 15–2–52–2; Bevan 15–4–44–3. *Second Innings*—Kirtley 2–0–6–0; Lewry 1–1–0–1.

Sussex

M. T. E. Peirce hit wkt b Mullally	0	R. J. Kirtley c Sutcliffe b Millns	27	
W. G. Khan lbw b Millns	0	J. D. Lewry c Mullally b Brimson	4	
M. Newell lbw b Wells	18	M. A. Robinson st Nixon b Brimson	0	
*C. J. Adams b Millns	10			
M. G. Bevan not out	149	B 4, l-b 5, n-b 22	31	
N. R. Taylor c Nixon b Millns	51			
P. W. Jarvis c Nixon b Lewis	12	1/0 2/0 3/28 4/43 5/132	302	
†S. Humphries b Lewis	0	6/166 7/168 8/286 9/299		

Bonus points – Sussex 3, Leicestershire 4.

Bowling: Mullally 28–11–56–1; Millns 25–6–68–4; Brimson 20–5–72–2; Wells 11–1–48–1; Lewis 12–4–49–2.

Umpires: J. C. Balderstone and K. E. Palmer.

At Darlington, July 1, 2, 3. LEICESTERSHIRE beat DURHAM by an innings and 103 runs.

LEICESTERSHIRE v NORTHAMPTONSHIRE

At Leicester, July 14, 15, 16, 17. Leicestershire won by four wickets. Leicestershire 24 pts, Northamptonshire 7 pts. Toss: Northamptonshire.

After Northamptonshire's tail had held out until after tea on the final day, and with the crowd drifting away, Leicestershire embarked on one of the most remarkable run-chases in Championship history. That they attempted to make 204 in 20 overs, even on a good pitch, was daring; that they won by four wickets with five balls to spare was outrageous. Northamptonshire coach John Emburey said he had "never seen anything like it in all my years". "You could try that a thousand times and only pull it off once," said Leicestershire's acting-captain Chris Lewis. Leicestershire were inspired first by Wells, who thrashed 58 off 32 balls, and then by Lewis, whose unbeaten

71 contained four sixes and five fours, and came off 33 deliveries. Opening with Malcolm, and employing a normal field, Curran obviously felt the target was beyond his opponents. But Wells hit Malcolm for 16 – and out of the attack – before taking 18 off the second over from Rose. After three overs, the score was 47, and Northamptonshire had packed the boundary. Lewis maintained the momentum by cracking 27 off seven balls in the 15th and 16th overs; enraged, Rose threatened to run him out as he backed up, only to be restrained by Curran, his captain.

FASTEST RUN-CHASES IN FIRST-CLASS CRICKET

Score	Runs per Ball			Result
204-6	**1.77**	**Leicestershire v Northamptonshire at Leicester** .	**1998**	**Won**
218-3	1.61	Madhya Pradesh v Vidarbha at Nagpur	1991-92	Won
219-2	1.56	Kent v Gloucestershire at Dover.	1937	Won
208-6	1.50	East Zone v North Zone at Pune	1993-94	Drawn
206-7	1.43	South Australia v Victoria at Adelaide	1982-83	Drawn
		David Hookes reached 100 off 34 balls		
279-1	1.32	Nottinghamshire v Leicestershire at Nottingham . .	1949	Won
207-7	1.28	Northamptonshire v Warwickshire at Birmingham .	1987	Drawn

Only totals over 200 included.

Main source: Wisden Book of Cricket Records *(Fourth edition)*

Curran himself was later criticised for sticking with his fast bowlers. The outcome was poor reward for Northamptonshire's 19-year-old all-rounder, Swann. He had shown marvellous potential and had seemingly kept his side in the game with innings of 92 and 111, his maiden century, batting No. 8 both times. Smith and Habib gave Leicestershire the original advantage with a fourth-wicket stand of 249 (which they would surpass at The Oval in September). Habib batted almost nine hours and hit 27 fours before being run out two short of a double-century.

Close of play: First day, Leicestershire 41-3 (B. F. Smith 28*, A. Habib 3*); Second day, Leicestershire 407-7 (A. Habib 156*, D. J. Millns 16*); Third day, Northamptonshire 161-6 (D. Ripley 14*, G. P. Swann 14*).

Northamptonshire

R. J. Warren b Mullally.	5	– c Nixon b Mullally	2
R. J. Bailey c Simmons b Mullally	5	– c Lewis b Millns	29
M. B. Loye c Wells b Maddy	76	– c Lewis b Brimson	19
D. J. Sales b Mullally.	5	– c Smith b Mullally	10
*K. M. Curran b Wells	18	– c Sutcliffe b Mullally	18
A. L. Penberthy c Habib b Mullally	18	– c Nixon b Millns	17
†D. Ripley c Nixon b Mullally	10	– c Simmons b Lewis	32
G. P. Swann c Nixon b Millns	92	– c Sutcliffe b Brimson	111
J. P. Taylor c Nixon b Lewis	41	– lbw b Mullally	56
F. A. Rose b Brimson	1	– c Mullally b Brimson	5
D. E. Malcolm not out	14	– not out	4
B 4, l-b 3, n-b 30	37	B 1, l-b 23, w 4, n-b 34 . .	62

1/11 2/14 3/28 4/69 5/110	322	1/12 2/63 3/81 4/89 5/117	365
6/124 7/235 8/274 9/275		6/128 7/205 8/347 9/361	

Bonus points – Northamptonshire 3, Leicestershire 4.

Bowling: *First Innings*—Mullally 18-3–62–5; Millns 19-4–61–1; Wells 11-2–45–1; Lewis 14.5–1–73–1; Brimson 16-5–55–1; Maddy 3-0–19–1. *Second Innings*—Mullally 27.1–9–48–4; Millns 28-4–83–2; Lewis 23-3–82–1; Wells 4-1–8–0; Brimson 51-23–88–3; Simmons 6-1–17–0; Maddy 3-0–15–0.

Leicestershire

V. J. Wells lbw b Rose	1	– c Malcolm b Taylor	58
D. L. Maddy c Penberthy b Malcolm	3	– run out	15
I. J. Sutcliffe c Ripley b Malcolm	1	– (7) b Rose	12
B. F. Smith c Ripley b Taylor	153	– lbw b Rose	6
A. Habib run out	198	– (8) not out	7
†P. A. Nixon c Ripley b Rose	27	– run out	2
P. V. Simmons b Rose	7	– (3) c Penberthy b Rose	25
*C. C. Lewis c Bailey b Rose	8	– (5) not out	71
D. J. Millns c Taylor b Rose	20		
A. D. Mullally c Warren b Taylor	0		
M. T. Brimson not out	18		
B 12, l-b 12, w 2, n-b 22	48	B 4, n-b 4	8

1/1 2/2 3/29 4/278 5/356   484   1/60 2/98 3/99   (6 wkts) 204
6/364 7/376 8/418 9/418   4/114 5/118 6/167

Bonus points – Leicestershire 4, Northamptonshire 4 (Score at 120 overs: 427-9).

Bowling: *First Innings*—Malcolm 25–2–113–2; Rose 28.2–1–123–5; Curran 10–3–22–0; Taylor 34–9–75–2; Swann 13–2–56–0; Penberthy 15–2–50–0; Bailey 11–2–21–0. *Second Innings*—Malcolm 1–0–16–0; Rose 9.1–0–93–3; Taylor 9–0–91–1.

Umpires: B. Leadbeater and A. G. T. Whitehead.

At Leicester, July 24, 25, 26, 27. LEICESTERSHIRE lost to SRI LANKANS by nine wickets (See Sri Lankan tour section).

At Manchester, July 30, 31, August 1, 3. LEICESTERSHIRE drew with LANCASHIRE.

LEICESTERSHIRE v SOMERSET

At Leicester, August 5, 6. Leicestershire won by an innings and 85 runs. Leicestershire 22 pts, Somerset 4 pts. Toss: Somerset. Championship debut: L. J. Sutton.

Leicestershire kept in sight of leaders Surrey after Somerset capitulated twice – for 74 and 112. The match ended just before tea on the second day, but the bonus of two days off was soured by the consequent loss of revenue, with a promising holiday-time Friday and Saturday ahead. Although 17 wickets fell on the first day, the umpires said the pitch was one of the best they had seen all year. Umpire Julian added: "Leicestershire need shooting if they don't make 300 on it." They failed, but 271 proved more than enough. Somerset were undone in the first innings by Ormond, who, having delivered just 205 Championship balls in an injury-stricken season, bowled beautifully to take a career-best six for 33. He improved his match figures to nine for 62 in the second, when Wells started the collapse by dismissing three of Somerset's top five. Leicestershire's batting was indebted to Maddy, with his second first-class century of the season, and to Smith.

Close of play: First day, Leicestershire 238-7 (D. L. Maddy 97*, C. D. Crowe 12*).

Somerset

*P. D. Bowler c Habib b Ormond	17	– c Maddy b Millns	5
P. C. L. Holloway c Nixon b Wells	7	– c Nixon b Wells	8
M. E. Trescothick c Smith b Wells	16	– c Nixon b Wells	14
R. J. Harden c Nixon b Ormond	0	– c Crowe b Millns	25
K. A. Parsons c Smith b Wells	5	– b Wells	2
M. Burns b Ormond	7	– c Millns b Ormond	5
G. D. Rose lbw b Ormond	8	– c Wells b Simmons	4
A. R. K. Pierson c Crowe b Simmons	7	– not out	3
†L. D. Sutton b Ormond	0	– c Millns b Brimson	5
A. R. Caddick c Nixon b Ormond	2	– c Maddy b Ormond	31
P. S. Jones not out	1	– c Wells b Ormond	0
W 2, n-b 2	4	N-b 10	10

1/20 2/26 3/26 4/35 5/46	74	1/10 2/33 3/34 4/36 5/51	112
6/52 7/69 8/69 9/71	6/66 7/72 8/79 9/112

Bonus points – Leicestershire 4.

Bowling: *First Innings*—Millns 6–3–8–0; Ormond 11.4–2–33–6; Wells 9–1–30–3; Simmons 2–0–3–1. *Second Innings*—Millns 12–0–46–2; Ormond 16.4–8–29–3; Wells 8–3–12–3; Crowe 1–0–2–0; Simmons 5–3–6–1; Brimson 8–3–17–1.

Leicestershire

V. J. Wells c Bowler b Caddick	5	C. D. Crowe c Sutton b Caddick	26
D. L. Maddy c Caddick b Rose	107	J. Ormond c Holloway b Rose	5
I. J. Sutcliffe c Harden b Caddick	17	M. T. Brimson not out	0
B. F. Smith lbw b Caddick	67		
*P. V. Simmons c Trescothick b Caddick	16	L-b 8, n-b 12	20
A. Habib c Caddick	8		
†P. A. Nixon c Burns b Rose	0	1/24 2/50 3/146 4/182 5/194	271
D. J. Millns c Harden b Caddick	0	6/195 7/206 8/262 9/267	

Bonus points – Leicestershire 2, Somerset 4.

Bowling: Caddick 32–5–96–7; Rose 25.5–6–62–3; Trescothick 7–2–29–0; Jones 8–2–24–0; Parsons 6–1–31–0; Pierson 4–1–11–0; Bowler 1–0–10–0.

Umpires: V. A. Holder and R. Julian.

LEICESTERSHIRE v MIDDLESEX

At Leicester, August 19, 20, 21, 22. Leicestershire won by eight wickets. Leicestershire 24 pts, Middlesex 6 pts. Toss: Middlesex.

Leicestershire maintained their encouraging form with another comfortable win. Their victory, on a featherbed, without either the injured Lewis or Mullally (on England duty) said as much about their self-belief as it did about the problems faced by a Middlesex side lacking Fraser. Wells had a fine match, scoring 67 and taking six wickets, including a six-ball spell of three for one in the first innings, to go top of the national bowling averages and leave Middlesex on 20 for four. Centuries from Ramprakash – his fourth of the season – and Weekes, dropped three times, repaired the damage; together, they added 229. But Sutcliffe stole the show with a career-best 167 in four hours and 13 minutes, which contained a six and 24 fours. In the second innings, Millns took the first two wickets in two balls and, despite some middle-order resistance, victory came just after tea on the final day.

Close of play: First day, Middlesex 293-8 (K. R. Brown 14*, R. L. Johnson 0*); Second day, Leicestershire 377-5 (A. Habib 68*, P. A. Nixon 23*); Third day, Middlesex 153-6 (P. N. Weekes 10*, K. R. Brown 4*).

Middlesex

D. J. Goodchild b Ormond	0	– c Dakin b Millns	0
J. L. Langer c Nixon b Wells	10	– b Simmons	44
*M. R. Ramprakash c Nixon b Simmons	110	– lbw b Millns	0
M. W. Gatting lbw b Wells	0	– c Simmons b Wells	73
O. A. Shah b Wells	2	– lbw b Wells	11
P. N. Weekes b Ormond	139	– run out	49
†K. R. Brown c Smith b Millns	19	– (8) lbw b Ormond	20
J. P. Hewitt b Millns	0	– (9) c Maddy b Wells	1
C. J. Batt b Millns	5	– (7) c Nixon b Brimson	0
R. L. Johnson c Maddy b Millns	4	– not out	23
P. C. R. Tufnell not out	4	– c Habib b Millns	6
B 5, l-b 3, n-b 6	14	B 2, l-b 12, n-b 4	18

1/1 2/18 3/18 4/20 5/249   307   1/0 2/0 3/96 4/134 5/143   245
6/280 7/283 8/291 9/301   6/144 7/188 8/199 9/233

Bonus points – Middlesex 3, Leicestershire 4.

Bowling: *First Innings*—Millns 25.3–7–65–4; Ormond 26–11–56–2; Wells 14–6–27–3; Simmons 22–6–56–1; Dakin 15–2–46–0; Brimson 12–5–38–0; Maddy 4–2–11–0. *Second Innings*—Millns 16.3–3–49–3; Ormond 21–5–46–1; Wells 14–3–42–3; Simmons 24–6–42–1; Brimson 24–5–52–1; Dakin 1–1–0–0.

Leicestershire

V. J. Wells c Ramprakash b Johnson	67	– c Gatting b Hewitt	8
D. L. Maddy c Ramprakash b Hewitt	1	– c Gatting b Johnson	9
I. J. Sutcliffe c Brown b Hewitt	167	– not out	40
B. F. Smith lbw b Tufnell	9	– not out	39
*P. V. Simmons c and b Johnson	0		
A. Habib c Brown b Johnson	84		
†P. A. Nixon c Langer b Hewitt	34		
J. M. Dakin c Shah b Hewitt	4		
D. J. Millns not out	24		
J. Ormond run out	1		
M. T. Brimson b Johnson	7		
B 3, l-b 25, n-b 26	54	L-b 3, n-b 2	5

1/18 2/174 3/183 4/188 5/303   452   1/13 2/19   (2 wkts) 101
6/405 7/409 8/421 9/437

Bonus points – Leicestershire 4, Middlesex 3 (Score at 120 overs: 436-8).

Bowling: *First Innings*—Batt 11–1–72–0; Hewitt 26–2–85–4; Johnson 31.2–6–129–4; Goodchild 1–0–9–0; Tufnell 37–8–76–1; Weekes 16–2–49–0; Ramprakash 4–1–4–0. *Second Innings*—Johnson 6–1–33–1; Hewitt 5–1–16–1; Weekes 11–3–24–0; Tufnell 10–3–16–0; Ramprakash 1–0–9–0.

Umpires: R. Palmer and R. A. White.

At Worksop, August 26, 27, 28. LEICESTERSHIRE beat NOTTINGHAMSHIRE by an innings and 223 runs.

At Birmingham, September 1, 2, 3, 4. LEICESTERSHIRE beat WARWICKSHIRE by 73 runs.

LEICESTERSHIRE v ESSEX

At Leicester, September 9, 10, 11. Leicestershire won by an innings and 99 runs. Leicestershire 24 pts, Essex 4 pts. Toss: Essex.

Leicestershire took revenge for their humiliation in the Benson and Hedges final, beating Essex by an innings in two days and one session. But, more importantly, they strengthened their position at the top of the Championship table; their fifth successive win meant that they went to The Oval, nine points ahead, for the final shoot-out with Surrey. By contrast, Essex, who had been bottom of the table since the end of July, suffered a fifth successive defeat. Performing without confidence, they were rolled over for 95 and 201. Only a defiant, but ultimately futile, last-wicket stand of 102 between Cowan and Such, a county record against Leicestershire, restored any measure of pride. Cowan showed the batsmen how it should have been done, hitting a career-best 94 off 81 balls, with a six and 15 fours. On the opening two days, Wells had set up Leicestershire's victory with an outstanding innings of 171, after they had been inserted on a green pitch. He then added three cheap wickets as the seamers ran riot. This completed a third successive season for Leicestershire without a home defeat in the Championship. Their last was against Lancashire in August 1995.

Close of play: First day, Leicestershire 301-6 (V. J. Wells 140*, C. C. Lewis 2*); Second day, Essex 58-4 (T. P. Hodgson 11*, M. C. Ilott 2*).

Leicestershire

V. J. Wells c Ilott b Grove 171	D. J. Millns not out 37
D. L. Maddy c Hyam b Cowan 7	C. D. Crowe c Peters b Grove 6
I. J. Sutcliffe c Hyam b Cowan 39	A. D. Mullally lbw b Grove 0
B. F. Smith lbw b Irani 1	
*P. V. Simmons c Cowan b Irani 61	B 3, l-b 6, n-b 16 25
A. Habib c Hyam b Irani 8	
†P. A. Nixon b Such 26	1/18 2/126 3/129 4/247 5/263 395
C. C. Lewis lbw b Ilott 14	6/299 7/314 8/371 9/395

Bonus points – Leicestershire 4, Essex 4.

Bowling: Ilott 25–7–68–1; Cowan 19–4–79–2; Irani 23–6–80–3; Grove 17.3–1–76–3; Such 19–4–63–1; Grayson 4–0–20–0.

Essex

*P. J. Prichard b Lewis 18	– b Lewis	1
S. D. Peters c Wells b Mullally 2	– c Lewis b Millns	8
T. P. Hodgson c Simmons b Wells 20	– c Nixon b Lewis	14
S. G. Law b Mullally 7	– c Maddy b Millns	0
R. C. Irani c Simmons b Lewis 11	– c Simmons b Crowe	27
A. P. Grayson b Millns 11	– (7) lbw b Lewis	6
†B. J. Hyam b Millns 1	– (8) b Mullally	0
M. C. Ilott c Sutcliffe b Millns 0	– (6) c Maddy b Mullally	2
A. P. Cowan b Wells 4	– c Nixon b Millns	94
J. O. Grove c Mullally b Wells 12	– b Lewis	0
P. M. Such not out 0	– not out	24
B 1, l-b 6, n-b 2 9	B 2, l-b 11, n-b 12	25

1/7 2/31 3/38 4/49 5/76	95	1/1 2/23 3/25 4/56 5/61 201
6/76 7/76 8/81 9/81		6/65 7/65 8/97 9/99

Bonus points – Leicestershire 4.

Bowling: *First Innings*—Mullally 11–4–23–2; Lewis 11–4–40–2; Millns 7–5–8–3; Wells 6.4–2–17–3. *Second Innings*—Mullally 15–2–45–2; Lewis 20–5–72–4; Millns 10.3–1–62–3; Wells 4–3–1–0; Crowe 5–3–5–1; Simmons 4–3–3–0.

Umpires: J. W. Holder and A. A. Jones.

At The Oval, September 17, 18, 19. LEICESTERSHIRE beat SURREY by an innings and 211 runs.

Justin Langer

MIDDLESEX

Patron: HRH The Duke of Edinburgh
President: M. P. Murray
Chairman: A. E. Moss
Chairman, Cricket Committee: A. J. T. Miller
Secretary: V. J. Codrington
Captain: M. R. Ramprakash
First-team Coach (1998): J. M. Buchanan
Director of Coaching (1999): M. W. Gatting
Club Coach: I. J. Gould
Scorer: M. J. Smith

Middlesex had a dreadful season, culminating in five consecutive defeats and their worst-ever Championship placing – 17th. Nor was there much consolation on the one-day front, where an inept performance in the NatWest quarter-final was the abiding memory. Even veteran Middlesex watchers, who remember the barren period before the Brearley era, could not recall so many embarrassing displays. An August Saturday at Hove, when Middlesex were bowled out twice in less than two sessions, was the nadir.

The club secretary received a good many letters from disgruntled members, and there was a move to call an EGM to propose a vote of no confidence in the cricket committee. In the event, cricket committee chairman Bob Gale had already retired, after nine years; another former opening batsman, Andrew Miller, inherited the post. Mike Gatting, who retired as a player in September, was appointed director of coaching, responsible for all teams from Under-17 level upwards. He was given a particular brief to ensure that petty organisational details were no longer a distraction for the captain.

After such a year, it was tempting to find a scapegoat. First-team coach John Buchanan, recruited from Queensland to bring a fresh approach, was the popular choice. The fact that he was not asked to return was seen by some as an indictment. According to Gale, however, Buchanan's appointment was always intended to last only one or two years, depending on how soon Gatting moved into coaching, and the decision not to invite him back for a second year should not be interpreted to mean that the committee were unhappy. Buchanan certainly spared no effort, recording every ball bowled on video and introducing some energetic and entertaining pre-match drills. The problem appeared to be his feeling that players should devote more time to match preparation, and his desire for more responsibility in areas traditionally left to the captain. In 1999, that responsibility devolved to Gatting. Buchanan obviously wanted to stay on; in August, he said the committee had left him to decide. A month later, he said he would not be returning, and implied that it was not his choice.

If Middlesex's awful year was not the coach's fault, how much blame should be attached to the captain? For two reasons, Mark Ramprakash did not appear the ideal man for the job. It is always difficult for a county to be led by an often-absent Test player. Ramprakash played only nine Championship matches – just two at Lord's. In addition, his England place was not assured, the sort of distraction an inexperienced captain can do without. Keith Brown was a dedicated vice-captain and, in a couple of one-day games, Western Australian Justin Langer led the side with great enthusiasm. Langer's run-scoring, particularly in May and June, gave Middlesex's season a decent start. He was the first batsman in the country to reach 1,000 first-class runs, and finished with 1,448, second only to John Crawley. Apart from him, only Gatting scored 1,000 for Middlesex. Langer's predecessor, South African all-rounder Jacques Kallis, was missed for his bowling, however; the seam attack often lacked penetration. Richard Johnson managed 50 first-class wickets, but James Hewitt fell away disappointingly after being capped in June.

It was in mid-June that it all seemed to go wrong. Middlesex had suffered only one defeat in the first five Championship matches, and were joint fifth in the table, while they headed the Sunday League. But an exciting match against Durham went the wrong way, and then the team seemed to forget how to win. They remained stuck on two victories and went down to nine defeats. In one-day cricket, the collapse was even more spectacular; they lost six of their last seven League fixtures and finished 12th, well out of the National League's higher division. There was an improvement in the Benson and Hedges Cup – they won all four group matches – but it ended in a disappointing quarter-final defeat by Essex. They won a thrilling victory over Durham in the NatWest second round, but the loss to Hampshire in the quarter-final was as shoddy a performance as they gave all year.

By the end of the season, the general dressing-room discontent had completely undermined the team's cohesiveness, and in the autumn Angus Fraser said he was considering leaving for another county. This would have been seen as not just the loss of a body, but a blow to the club's soul. In the New Year, though, Fraser relented.

There were other reasons for optimism. The emergence of young batsmen David Goodchild and Andy Strauss, and left-arm seamer Chris Batt, was encouraging; another seamer, Tim Bloomfield, made progress, while Johnson and Paul Weekes, who scored 903 runs, rediscovered their form. David Nash and Keith Dutch made some useful contributions. Many thought the high praise lavished on Owais Shah meant that a little humility had to be added to his undoubted talent; being dropped at Guildford seemed to help – centuries against Yorkshire and Derbyshire followed. Hewitt's return to form, with six Sussex wickets for 71, was the one bright spot in the Hove disaster. The decision to release Jason Pooley was sad and, with the batting so unreliable, it seemed strange that he was not given a Championship run.

The season ended at Derby with the farewell appearances of two Middlesex heroes, Gatting and Brown. Gatting had completed 1,000 runs for the 19th time in his 24 seasons with the county, taking him to 36,549 runs in all, though his two centuries in 1998 still left him six short of the hundred mark. Brown had made his debut in 1984, and passed 10,000 runs during 1998; he had taken 466 catches, with 33 stumpings. He had accepted a job as sports master at a school near Exeter; Gatting took on the task of trying to restore the glory years at Middlesex as coach. – NORMAN DE MESQUITA.

MIDDLESEX 1998

Back row: A. J. Strauss, R. A. Kettleborough, J. L. Langer, S. J. Cook, I. N. Blanchett, U. B. A. Rashid, D. C. Nash, J. M. Buchanan (*First Eleven coach*).
Middle row: I. J. Gould (*Second Eleven coach*), S. G. M. Shepard (*physiotherapist*), O. A. Shah, B. L. Hutton, T. F. Bloomfield, J. P. Hewitt, A. W. Laraman,
D. J. Goodchild, K. P. Dutch, N. D. Martin, J. K. Maunders, A. Jones (*Second Eleven scorer*). *Front row*: R. L. Johnson, J. C. Pooley, P. C. R. Tufnell,
K. R. Brown, M. R. Ramprakash (*captain*), M. W. Gatting, A. R. C. Fraser, P. N. Weekes. *Insets*: C. J. Batt, M. J. Smith (*First Eleven scorer*).

[*Bill Smith*]

MIDDLESEX RESULTS

All first-class matches – Played 19: Won 2, Lost 9, Drawn 8.

County Championship matches – Played 17: Won 2, Lost 9, Drawn 6.

*Competition placings – Britannic Assurance County Championship, 17th;
NatWest Trophy, q-f; Benson and Hedges Cup, q-f;
AXA League, 12th.*

COUNTY CHAMPIONSHIP AVERAGES
BATTING

Cap		M	I	NO	R	HS	100s	50s	Avge	Ct/St
1998	J. L. Langer§	14	26	5	1,393	233*	4	6	66.33	11
1990	M. R. Ramprakash. .	9	15	2	635	128*	4	4	48.84	5
1977	M. W. Gatting† . . .	16	28	3	1,077	241	2	6	43.08	18
1993	P. N. Weekes	15	24	5	811	139	1	5	42.68	18
	O. A. Shah	14	22	2	707	140	2	3	35.35	10
1990	K. R. Brown†	16	23	5	511	59*	0	2	28.38	40/5
	A. J. Strauss	3	6	0	146	83	0	1	24.33	3
	R. A. Kettleborough .	10	19	3	373	62*	0	2	23.31	6
	D. C. Nash.	12	17	0	361	114	1	1	21.23	7/1
	D. J. Goodchild† . . .	6	12	1	213	83*	0	2	19.36	1
1998	J. P. Hewitt	15	19	2	268	53	0	1	15.76	5
1995	R. L. Johnson	13	19	3	230	43	0	0	14.37	5
	C. J. Batt	7	12	1	121	43	0	0	11.00	1
1988	A. R. C. Fraser	8	9	2	63	30	0	0	9.00	1
1990	P. C. R. Tufnell	16	21	6	131	19	0	0	8.73	2
	T. F. Bloomfield . . .	7	9	4	35	20*	0	0	7.00	0
	I. N. Blanchett	3	4	0	25	18	0	0	6.25	1

Also batted: K. P. Dutch† (2 matches) 11, 6, 16 (1 ct). N. D. Martin† (1 match) did not bat.

* Signifies not out. *† Born in Middlesex.* *§ Overseas player.*

BOWLING

	O	M	R	W	BB	5W/i	Avge
A. R. C. Fraser	252	64	618	34	6-23	1	18.17
R. L. Johnson	355.2	72	1,297	49	7-86	1	26.46
T. F. Bloomfield.	146.5	25	586	20	5-67	2	29.30
J. P. Hewitt	377.3	64	1,378	41	6-71	2	33.60
C. J. Batt	170	21	712	19	6-101	2	37.47
P. C. R. Tufnell	607.5	158	1,512	36	4-24	0	42.00
P. N. Weekes.	237	37	702	13	3-113	0	54.00

Also bowled: I. N. Blanchett 78–9–285–5; K. P. Dutch 27–7–63–1; M. W. Gatting 5–1–9–1;
D. J. Goodchild 11–1–42–0; R. A. Kettleborough 23–1–89–0; J. L. Langer 13–5–34–1; N. D.
Martin 12–1–61–0; D. C. Nash 0.1–0–0–0; M. R. Ramprakash 42.2–8–112–5; O. A. Shah
17.5–1–79–1.

COUNTY RECORDS

Highest score for:	331*	J. D. Robertson v Worcestershire at Worcester . . .	1949
Highest score against:	316*	J. B. Hobbs (Surrey) at Lord's	1926
Best bowling for:	10-40	G. O. B. Allen v Lancashire at Lord's	1929
Best bowling against:	9-38	R. C. Robertson-Glasgow (Somerset) at Lord's . .	1924
Highest total for:	642-3 dec.	v Hampshire at Southampton	1923
Highest total against:	665	by West Indians at Lord's	1939
Lowest total for:	20	v MCC at Lord's	1864
Lowest total against: {	31	by Gloucestershire at Bristol	1924
	31	by Glamorgan at Cardiff	1997

At Canterbury, April 17, 18, 20, 21. MIDDLESEX lost to KENT by four wickets.

At Manchester, April 23, 24, 25, 27. MIDDLESEX drew with LANCASHIRE.

MIDDLESEX v SOMERSET

At Lord's, May 13, 14, 15, 16. Middlesex won by 211 runs. Middlesex 21 pts, Somerset 6 pts.
Toss: Middlesex.

Australian Justin Langer scored an unbeaten 233 to help his new county to a resounding win.
He batted for 533 minutes and faced 369 balls, hitting 33 fours and a six. This was Langer's fifth
double-century, and he was concentrating as hard at the finish as at the start. He was swiftly
rewarded with his county cap. But local talent also prospered: Nash made a career-best 114 in a
stand of 222 with Langer, after Johnson had picked up seven wickets. On the first morning,
Middlesex slumped to 73 for six, Caddick and Rose exploiting extravagant lateral movement,
before the lower order staged a stout rearguard action. Somerset still took a 49-run lead, thanks
to a beautifully judged 91 from Lathwell. But, by the time Langer was done, they faced a target
of 402. A spell of four for four in 25 balls by Fraser left Somerset on 49 for six; Lathwell, batting
another three hours, denied Middlesex until shortly after lunch on the last day.

Close of play: First day, Somerset 157-5 (M. N. Lathwell 52*, K. J. Shine 1*); Second day,
Middlesex 151-3 (J. L. Langer 80*, D. C. Nash 25*); Third day, Somerset 50-6 (M. N. Lathwell
8*, M. E. Trescothick 0*).

Middlesex

R. A. Kettleborough c Parsons b Caddick	31	– c Turner b Caddick	19
J. L. Langer c Trescothick b Shine	5	– not out	233
M. W. Gatting c Harden b Rose	22	– b Caddick	20
O. A. Shah c Turner b Rose	0	– lbw b Caddick	0
D. C. Nash c Harden b Rose	0	– c Burns b Trescothick	114
*†K. R. Brown c Trescothick b Caddick	1	– not out	45
P. N. Weekes c Bowler b Mushtaq Ahmed	42		
R. L. Johnson c Lathwell b Caddick	27		
J. P. Hewitt c Bowler b Mushtaq Ahmed	47		
A. R. C. Fraser c Turner b Caddick	6		
P. C. R. Tufnell not out	0		
L-b 5, w 4, n-b 14	23	B 1, l-b 10, n-b 8	19

1/8 2/55 3/57 4/63 5/70	204	1/42 2/101	(4 wkts dec.) 450
6/73 7/121 8/165 9/202		3/109 4/331	

Bonus points – Middlesex 1, Somerset 4.

Bowling: *First Innings*—Caddick 20.5–3–74–4; Shine 10–1–37–1; Rose 15–4–43–3; Trescothick
2–0–19–0; Mushtaq Ahmed 6–1–26–2. *Second Innings*—Caddick 33–6–118–3; Shine 20.2–2–86–0;
Rose 25.5–5–94–0; Mushtaq Ahmed 30–8–76–0; Trescothick 16–2–36–1; Parsons 6–0–29–0.

Somerset

*P. D. Bowler c Brown b Fraser	19	– c Gatting b Fraser	21
M. Burns lbw b Johnson	4	– c Langer b Hewitt	8
K. A. Parsons c Langer b Johnson	3	– c Shah b Johnson	4
R. J. Harden b Johnson	63	– lbw b Fraser	2
M. N. Lathwell c Brown b Johnson	91	– c Nash b Hewitt	88
†R. J. Turner c Nash b Johnson	0	– c Nash b Fraser	1
K. J. Shine b Johnson	9	– c Kettleborough b Fraser	2
M. E. Trescothick c Brown b Fraser	1	– c Hewitt b Johnson	3
G. D. Rose c Weekes b Fraser	16	– c Kettleborough b Tufnell	16
Mushtaq Ahmed not out	22	– c Weekes b Tufnell	12
A. R. Caddick c Brown b Johnson	0	– not out	15
B 5, l-b 2, w 8, n-b 10	25	B 4, l-b 10, n-b 4	18

1/31 2/33 3/45 4/142 5/152   253   1/12 2/31 3/38 4/39 5/47   190
6/166 7/167 8/206 9/253   6/49 7/56 8/97 9/133

Bonus points — Somerset 2, Middlesex 4.

Bowling: *First Innings*—Fraser 21–5–51–3; Hewitt 20–4–74–0; Johnson 23–4–86–7; Tufnell 11–2–18–0; Shah 2–0–12–0; Weekes 2–0–5–0. *Second Innings*—Fraser 17–3–39–4; Hewitt 9–0–41–2; Johnson 17–4–48–2; Tufnell 13–2–34–2; Weekes 6–2–14–0.

Umpires: D. J. Constant and J. W. Lloyds.

MIDDLESEX v WORCESTERSHIRE

At Uxbridge, May 21, 22, 23, 24. Drawn. Middlesex 9 pts, Worcestershire 10 pts. Toss: Worcestershire. First-class debut: I. N. Blanchett.

Uxbridge once again broke bowlers' hearts, and the match produced 1,389 runs for just 21 wickets. Though Worcestershire made Middlesex follow on, they never looked like bowling them out again. They had, however, ended a unique boast: alone of the 18 counties, Middlesex had never conceded a 600-run total to another county. Nottinghamshire's 596 at Trent Bridge in 1887 had stood as the record against them in the Championship for 111 years. (There had been three higher non-Championship totals.) Worcestershire reached 627 before declaring. The only doubt

HIGHEST TOTALS AGAINST MIDDLESEX

665	by West Indians at Lord's	1939
627-6 dec.	**by Worcestershire at Uxbridge**	**1998**
612	by Oxford University at Prince's	1876
603-5 dec.	by Rest of England at The Oval	1920
596	by Nottinghamshire at Nottingham	1887

on the first day was when, not if, Hick would complete his 98th hundred. He did it during a stand of 222 in 45 overs with Moody, who also had three figures by the close. Leatherdale became the third centurion next day, but Worcestershire had used up 162 overs, and a scoring-rate below four an over was too slow on such an easy pitch and a small ground. Langer and Ramprakash advanced to 203 for one and, although Middlesex were all out 238 behind, only three and a half sessions remained. Ramprakash made a second century (for the third time, and the second time at Uxbridge). Langer also reached a hundred, having missed out by three in the first innings.

Close of play: First day, Worcestershire 435-4 (T. M. Moody 132*, D. A. Leatherdale 16*); Second day, Middlesex 154-1 (J. L. Langer 69*, M. R. Ramprakash 65*); Third day, Middlesex 67-0 (R. A. Kettleborough 23*, J. L. Langer 37*).

Worcestershire

W. P. C. Weston b Hewitt	21	†S. J. Rhodes not out		67
V. S. Solanki b Hewitt	78			
G. A. Hick c Weekes b Blanchett	166	B 1, l-b 7, w 2, n-b 16		26
G. R. Haynes lbw b Tufnell	0			
*T. M. Moody lbw b Johnson	132	1/35 2/168 3/171	(6 wkts dec.)	627
D. A. Leatherdale b Shah	137	4/393 5/436 6/627		

S. R. Lampitt, R. K. Illingworth, P. J. Newport and A. Sheriyar did not bat.

Bonus points – Worcestershire 4, Middlesex 2 (Score at 120 overs: 470-5).

Bowling: Hewitt 27–5–105–2; Johnson 29–7–105–1; Blanchett 28–1–125–1; Kettleborough 4–0–16–0; Tufnell 40–4–136–1; Weekes 25–0–86–0; Shah 8.5–0–46–1.

Middlesex

R. A. Kettleborough lbw b Newport	5	– lbw b Newport	24
J. L. Langer c Rhodes b Moody	97	– b Haynes	118
*M. R. Ramprakash st Rhodes b Solanki	122	– c Hick b Solanki	108
M. W. Gatting lbw b Haynes	39	– not out	83
O. A. Shah c Weston b Haynes	17	– run out	20
†D. C. Nash lbw b Newport	15	– b Illingworth	0
P. N. Weekes st Rhodes b Solanki	11	– not out	0
R. L. Johnson lbw b Sheriyar	2		
J. P. Hewitt c Rhodes b Sheriyar	25		
I. N. Blanchett c sub b Sheriyar	18		
P. C. R. Tufnell not out	10		
B 6, l-b 16, n-b 6	28	B 2, l-b 6, w 2, n-b 10	20
1/28 2/203 3/261 4/299 5/299	389	1/76 2/201 3/313 (5 wkts dec.)	373
6/322 7/328 8/338 9/366		4/372 5/373	

Bonus points – Middlesex 4, Worcestershire 3 (Score at 120 overs: 356-8).

Bowling: *First Innings*—Newport 25–10–54–2; Sheriyar 23.3–7–75–3; Lampitt 6–0–34–0; Illingworth 28–4–75–0; Hick 5–0–20–0; Solanki 21–7–55–2; Moody 7–2–25–1; Haynes 13–4–29–2. *Second Innings*—Newport 11–3–32–1; Haynes 13–6–31–1; Moody 4–1–12–0; Solanki 24–7–77–1; Illingworth 29–8–69–1; Lampitt 11–0–56–0; Sheriyar 5–0–26–0; Hick 14–0–62–0.

Umpires: M. J. Harris and T. E. Jesty.

MIDDLESEX v GLAMORGAN

At Lord's, May 29, 30, 31, June 1. Middlesex won by nine wickets. Middlesex 22 pts, Glamorgan 7 pts. Toss: Middlesex.

Langer's third century in successive matches and Ramprakash's third in four innings, which completed his set against all the other counties, secured a comfortable win after Middlesex were set 313 in just over a day. The decision to insert Glamorgan – on a pitch already used for a one-day match – seemed odd. Though Shaw fell without a run on the board, a first-day 293 for five suggested the batting side was on top. But, next morning, Fraser and Hewitt removed the last five in just 37 balls. In reply, Middlesex struggled to 97 for five, even though Waqar Younis had bowled just three overs before withdrawing with a painful elbow; only Nash resisted the persevering Watkin. Then Powell led the way in pushing Glamorgan's lead past 300. But luck was with Middlesex. Langer survived two chances and Ramprakash one, and both might have been run out. Instead, with Waqar still absent, they added 276 to win with an hour to spare. Glamorgan's dismal Lord's run continued: their last Championship victory over Middlesex there was in 1954, and by the end of the season they had gone – uniquely – through 36 years of knockout finals without winning one.

Close of play: First day, Glamorgan 293-5 (P. A. Cottey 73*, R. D. B. Croft 18*); Second day, Middlesex 250-9 (D. C. Nash 75*, P. C. R. Tufnell 4*); Third day, Middlesex 6-0 (J. L. Langer 2*, R. A. Kettleborough 4*).

Glamorgan

S. P. James c Shah b Hewitt	79	– c Brown b Ramprakash	45
†A. D. Shaw lbw b Hewitt	0	– st Brown b Tufnell	51
A. Dale b Ramprakash	38	– c Langer b Blanchett	1
*M. P. Maynard c Hewitt b Fraser	25	– lbw b Tufnell	10
P. A. Cottey c Gatting b Hewitt	81	– b Fraser	7
M. J. Powell c Brown b Ramprakash	43	– not out	79
R. D. B. Croft c Brown b Fraser	18	– c Langer b Fraser	1
S. D. Thomas lbw b Hewitt	3	– b Ramprakash	25
Waqar Younis lbw b Hewitt	1	– lbw b Fraser	9
D. A. Cosker c Brown b Fraser	0	– b Blanchett	12
S. L. Watkin not out	0	– c Kettleborough b Ramprakash	6
B 1, l-b 7, n-b 12	20	L-b 6, w 6, n-b 2	14

1/0 2/107 3/137 4/151 5/237   308   1/96 2/97 3/118 4/122 5/134   260
6/293 7/300 8/307 9/308   6/144 7/194 8/208 9/247

Bonus points – Glamorgan 3, Middlesex 4.

Bowling: *First Innings*—Fraser 26.1–7–66–3; Hewitt 24–5–69–5; Blanchett 15–1–56–0; Tufnell 31–6–76–0; Ramprakash 14–2–33–2. *Second Innings*—Fraser 19–5–47–3; Hewitt 11–1–49–0; Tufnell 36–13–88–2; Blanchett 12–1–38–2; Ramprakash 12.2–3–32–3.

Middlesex

J. L. Langer lbw b Watkin	35	– not out	153
R. A. Kettleborough c Shaw b Watkin	19	– c Maynard b Watkin	17
*M. R. Ramprakash c Croft b Watkin	3	– not out	128
M. W. Gatting b Thomas	12		
O. A. Shah c Croft b Thomas	15		
D. C. Nash c Maynard b Watkin	76		
†K. R. Brown lbw b Watkin	17		
J. P. Hewitt c Cottey b Cosker	24		
I. N. Blanchett lbw b Croft	0		
A. R. C. Fraser b Thomas	30		
P. C. R. Tufnell not out	7		
B 5, l-b 9, w 2, n-b 2	18	L-b 14, w 2	16

1/40 2/52 3/63 4/82 5/97   256   1/38   (1 wkt) 314
6/127 7/179 8/180 9/231

Bonus points – Middlesex 2, Glamorgan 4.

Bowling: *First Innings*—Waqar Younis 3–0–26–0; Watkin 21.5–7–30–5; Thomas 19–1–56–3; Croft 38–6–91–1; Dale 2–0–3–0; Cosker 18–2–36–1; Cottey 1–1–0–0. *Second Innings*—Watkin 18–5–49–1; Thomas 16–3–69–0; Croft 26–7–65–0; Cosker 16–1–73–0; Dale 12–3–36–0; Powell 0.2–0–8–0.

Umpires: G. I. Burgess and V. A. Holder.

MIDDLESEX v DURHAM

At Lord's, June 3, 4, 5, 6. Durham won by one wicket. Durham 23 pts, Middlesex 7 pts. Toss: Durham.

Durham's third Championship win of 1998, and their first ever over Middlesex, brought a day of sustained excitement to a thrilling conclusion. With two overs left, Durham's last pair batting, and nine runs needed, any result was possible. But Betts hoisted Tufnell into the upper tier of the new Grand Stand and next ball ran three with Harmison. Betts, the country's leading wicket-taker, and the rising star Harmison had also claimed 16 wickets between them. Middlesex limped to 175 for six on the opening day, before Weekes and Hewitt rallied them in a stand of 143. Durham kept the deficit down to 23, despite five wickets from Bloomfield, and then had Middlesex's upper order in trouble again. Their eventual target was 240 from 76 overs, which looked unlikely at 11 for two. A flurry of wickets after lunch, including Gough for a valiant 56, left them 149 for six and made Middlesex favourites. Both runs and wickets kept coming, and tension mounted until Betts's final heroics. It was Durham's second win on a Test ground in a week, after a six-year blank at all six venues.

Close of play: First day, Middlesex 175-6 (P. N. Weekes 4*, J. P. Hewitt 7*); Second day, Durham 172-2 (J. J. B. Lewis 60*, D. C. Boon 62*); Third day, Middlesex 139-6 (P. N. Weekes 11*, J. P. Hewitt 14*).

Middlesex

J. L. Langer c Collingwood b Betts	35	– (2) c Phillips b Betts		1
R. A. Kettleborough c Speak b Wood	18	– (1) lbw b Betts		0
M. W. Gatting lbw b Foster	13	– b Foster		66
O. A. Shah b Betts	47	– b Betts		14
D. C. Nash c Speight b Harmison	26	– c Speight b Harmison		10
*†K. R. Brown c Gough b Betts	3	– lbw b Harmison		5
P. N. Weekes not out	93	– not out		51
J. P. Hewitt c Boon b Harmison	53	– c Gough b Harmison		19
I. N. Blanchett c Speight b Harmison	7	– c Speight b Betts		19
P. C. R. Tufnell c Speight b Harmison	6	– c Speight b Wood		19
T. F. Bloomfield c Speak b Betts	0	– lbw b Betts		0
B 5, l-b 9, w 2, n-b 18	34	B 8, l-b 5, n-b 17		30
	335			**216**

1/30 2/56 3/120 4/139 5/161   335   1/0 2/5 3/29 4/78 5/90   216
6/163 7/306 8/314 9/330   6/118 7/151 8/158 9/213

Bonus points – Middlesex 3, Durham 4.

Bowling: *First Innings*—Betts 29–6–83–4; Wood 23–5–89–1; Foster 8–2–18–1; Harmison 26–3–88–4; Collingwood 8–2–26–0; Phillips 13–5–17–0. *Second Innings*—Betts 19–4–52–5; Wood 9–3–20–1; Harmison 20–4–57–3; Phillips 12–1–52–0; Foster 7–2–22–1.

Durham

J. J. B. Lewis c Brown b Bloomfield	68	– c Weekes b Hewitt		8
M. A. Gough lbw b Bloomfield	38	– c Gatting b Tufnell		56
N. J. Speak c Brown b Bloomfield	0	– c Nash b Bloomfield		0
*D. C. Boon c Gatting b Hewitt	68	– st Nash b Tufnell		21
P. D. Collingwood c Weekes b Hewitt	66	– b Bloomfield		33
†M. P. Speight c Nash b Bloomfield	2	– lbw b Bloomfield		17
M. J. Foster c Langer b Hewitt	6	– c Blanchett b Weekes		27
N. C. Phillips c Langer b Blanchett	16	– b Hewitt		28
M. M. Betts c Brown b Blanchett	0	– not out		29
J. Wood not out	26	– c Shah b Tufnell		4
S. J. Harmison c Brown b Bloomfield	3	– not out		0
L-b 5, w 4, n-b 10	19	B 2, l-b 11, w 2, n-b 2		17
	312	(9 wkts)		**240**

1/58 2/58 3/180 4/202 5/207   312   1/10 2/11 3/50   (9 wkts) 240
6/214 7/267 8/273 9/299   4/111 5/137 6/149
   7/191 8/219 9/228

Bonus points – Durham 3, Middlesex 4.

Bowling: *First Innings*—Bloomfield 22.5–0–98–5; Hewitt 26–7–82–3; Blanchett 20–6–52–2; Tufnell 25–11–29–0; Shah 1–0–3–0; Weekes 10–0–43–0. *Second Innings*—Hewitt 18–0–59–2; Bloomfield 16–3–43–3; Tufnell 30.2–11–89–3; Weekes 7–0–22–1; Blanchett 3–0–14–0.

Umpires: J. C. Balderstone and M. J. Kitchen.

At Oxford, June 13, 15, 16. MIDDLESEX drew with OXFORD UNIVERSITY.

At Northampton, June 17, 18, 19, 20. MIDDLESEX drew with NORTHAMPTONSHIRE.

MIDDLESEX v ESSEX

At Southgate, June 26, 27, 28, 29. Drawn. Middlesex 8 pts, Essex 3 pts. Toss: Middlesex.

Away from Lord's, Middlesex served up another belting pitch. As first-class cricket returned to the Walker Ground after 139 years, Gatting and Langer celebrated with 372 for the first wicket, a county record. Gatting scored his 93rd century, converting it into his tenth double. He batted for 520 minutes and 426 balls and hit 30 fours. On the way, he became Middlesex's second heaviest scorer, overtaking J. W. Hearne's 27,612; Patsy Hendren's 40,302 looked unattainable. Meanwhile, Langer was the first batsman to reach 1,000 for the season. At least half the first two days were washed away, and the teams agreed a formula which left Essex chasing 338 on the final day, and produced a tremendous finish. Middlesex dismissed their top three for a combined total of eight runs. But, with Irani playing anchor, Stuart Law regained the initiative, which was maintained by Peters and Danny Law, who struck five sixes. With 24 needed from 27 balls, a fine catch by Shah removed Cowan; next ball, Irani spoiled his second hundred in successive matches with a rash reverse sweep. The last pair played out the final four overs. Despite rain and bitter cold, the venue – a rural idyll less than a mile from the Piccadilly Line – was much liked by spectators, and there seemed every chance Middlesex would return.

Close of play: First day, Middlesex 174-0 (M. W. Gatting 93*, J. L. Langer 72*); Second day, Middlesex 373-1 (M. W. Gatting 180*, M. R. Ramprakash 0*); Third day, Essex 151-3 dec.

Middlesex

M. W. Gatting c Prichard b D. R. Law	. .	241
J. L. Langer c Rollins b Irani	. . . .	166
*M. R. Ramprakash not out	. . . .	43
O. A. Shah not out	. . . .	1
B 6, l-b 11, w 7, n-b 13	. . . . . .	37

1/372 2/485   (2 wkts dec.) 488

D. C. Nash, P. N. Weekes, †K. R. Brown, T. F. Bloomfield, J. P. Hewitt, A. R. C. Fraser and P. C. R. Tufnell did not bat.

Bonus points – Middlesex 4 (Score at 120 overs: 416-1).

Bowling: Ilott 24–3–85–0; Cowan 28–3–93–0; D. R. Law 18–2–63–1; Irani 21–3–74–1; Such 26–6–78–0; Grayson 22–1–78–0.

Middlesex forfeited their second innings.

Essex

*P. J. Prichard c Brown b Fraser	23	– b Fraser	2
D. D. J. Robinson c Gatting b Hewitt	5	– c Brown b Fraser	3
A. P. Grayson c Ramprakash b Weekes	54	– b Bloomfield	3
S. G. Law not out	48	– c Hewitt b Weekes	62
R. C. Irani not out	8	– b Weekes	104
S. D. Peters (did not bat)		– c Gatting b Tufnell	59
†R. J. Rollins (did not bat)		– b Tufnell	2
D. R. Law (did not bat)		– c Weekes b Tufnell	62
A. P. Cowan (did not bat)		– c Shah b Weekes	5
P. M. Such (did not bat)		– not out	1
M. C. Ilott (did not bat)		– not out	0
L-b 1, n-b 12	13	B 1, l-b 7, w 2, n-b 2	12

1/11 2/37 3/134   (3 wkts dec.) 151   1/2 2/5 3/31   (9 wkts) 315
                                                4/88 5/172 6/186
                                                7/290 8/314 9/314

Bonus point – Middlesex 1.

Bowling: *First Innings*—Hewitt 6–2–8–1; Bloomfield 12–0–56–0; Fraser 11–5–19–1; Weekes 9–0–24–1; Tufnell 14–1–43–0; Ramprakash 1–1–0–0; Nash 0.1–0–0–0. *Second Innings*—Fraser 20–5–45–2; Hewitt 7–2–9–0; Weekes 30–3–113–3; Bloomfield 8–3–20–1; Ramprakash 5–0–18–0; Tufnell 34–9–102–3.

Umpires: N. T. Plews and J. F. Steele.

At Nottingham, July 1, 2, 3. MIDDLESEX lost to NOTTINGHAMSHIRE by an innings and 92 runs.

At Guildford, July 15, 16, 17. MIDDLESEX lost to SURREY by 280 runs.

MIDDLESEX v YORKSHIRE

At Lord's, July 22, 23, 24, 25. Drawn. Middlesex 10 pts, Yorkshire 7 pts. Toss: Middlesex. Championship debut: J. D. Middlebrook.

After dreadful performances at Trent Bridge and Guildford, Middlesex were relieved to regain respectability, and might have won. But, not for the first time, they were unable to bowl the opposition out in the fourth innings. Shah, left out of the last match after bagging his second pair of the season, responded by showing that he can add application to his talent, and spent 372 minutes making 140 to put Middlesex in control. A century from Vaughan and 72 from Hamilton at No. 9 allowed Yorkshire to avoid the follow-on, but an unbroken stand of 197 between Gatting and Goodchild meant Middlesex continued to dictate terms. Brown declared after Gatting reached his hundred in 112 balls: his 94th and last before his retirement from regular county cricket, and his eighth against Yorkshire. The target was 321 in 79 overs, and Lehmann, dropped by his fellow-Australian Langer at slip first ball, gave Yorkshire a chance of victory, but his dismissal heralded a slide from 250 for four to 261 for eight. When a leg-bye took Extras to fifty, this was given the full treatment on the electronic scoreboard, prompting applause.

Close of play: First day, Middlesex 278-4 (O. A. Shah 96*, P. N. Weekes 36*); Second day, Yorkshire 90-2 (M. P. Vaughan 56*, P. M. Hutchison 0*); Third day, Middlesex 105-1 (D. J. Goodchild 35*, M. W. Gatting 56*).

Middlesex

D. J. Goodchild lbw b Silverwood	0	– not out	83
J. L. Langer lbw b Stemp	63	– c Blakey b Hutchison	9
M. W. Gatting b Stemp	22	– not out	103
O. A. Shah lbw b Hamilton	140		
*†K. R. Brown c Byas b Middlebrook	40		
P. N. Weekes c Byas b Silverwood	67		
D. C. Nash st Blakey b Middlebrook	23		
J. P. Hewitt c Blakey b Silverwood	5		
R. L. Johnson c Vaughan b Stemp	17		
C. J. Batt not out	23		
P. C. R. Tufnell b Hutchison	14		
B 9, l-b 13, w 2, n-b 10	34	B 6, l-b 4, n-b 2	12

1/0 2/67 3/108 4/183 5/344   448   1/10   (1 wkt dec.) 207
6/387 7/387 8/396 9/422

Bonus points – Middlesex 3, Yorkshire 1 (Score at 120 overs: 313-4).

Bowling: *First Innings*—Silverwood 34–13–62–3; Hutchison 24.3–3–93–1; Hamilton 28–9–71–1; Stemp 43–7–117–3; Middlebrook 33–15–64–2; McGrath 3–1–12–0; Lehmann 4–2–7–0. *Second Innings*—Silverwood 6–1–16–0; Hutchison 10–1–37–1; Hamilton 8–2–40–0; Stemp 10.3–0–57–0; Middlebrook 4–0–18–0; McGrath 3–0–18–0; Lehmann 1–0–11–0.

Yorkshire

*D. Byas b Tufnell	9	– c Brown b Johnson	12
M. P. Vaughan c Gatting b Tufnell	107	– b Tufnell	29
M. J. Wood c Nash b Weekes	14	– b Johnson	8
P. M. Hutchison c Langer b Johnson	1		
D. S. Lehmann c Weekes b Johnson	6	– (4) c Brown b Weekes	93
A. McGrath lbw b Tufnell	15	– (5) c Shah b Tufnell	37
†R. J. Blakey run out	65	– (6) c Hewitt b Tufnell	25
J. D. Middlebrook b Johnson	0	– lbw b Tufnell	0
G. M. Hamilton st Brown b Tufnell	72	– (7) lbw b Weekes	4
C. E. W. Silverwood b Johnson	4	– (9) not out	18
R. D. Stemp not out	0	– (10) not out	0
B 4, l-b 6, n-b 32	42	B 11, l-b 18, w 6, n-b 24	59

1/41 2/86 3/106 4/114 5/153   335   1/44 2/60 3/90   (8 wkts) 285
6/214 7/215 8/323 9/335   4/194 5/250 6/260
                                                     7/261 8/261

Bonus points – Yorkshire 3, Middlesex 4.

Bowling: *First Innings*—Batt 18–5–60–0; Hewitt 17–1–80–0; Tufnell 35.3–10–65–4; Johnson 24–8–72–4; Weekes 16–4–47–1; Langer 1–0–1–0. *Second Innings*—Johnson 15.5–3–58–2; Batt 5–0–27–0; Tufnell 36–13–77–4; Weekes 12–1–45–2; Hewitt 10–1–49–0.

Umpires: J. W. Holder and G. Sharp.

At Lord's, July 31, August 1, 2, 3. MIDDLESEX drew with SRI LANKANS (See Sri Lankan tour section).

MIDDLESEX v WARWICKSHIRE

At Lord's, August 5, 6, 7, 8. Drawn. Middlesex 8 pts, Warwickshire 11 pts. Toss: Warwickshire.
    After 14 months and 39 innings without a first-class century, Lara returned to form with a vengeance. He came in on the first morning with Warwickshire 38 for two and was in complete command all day. Lara was out quickly on the second morning but by then he had 226, a record for Warwickshire against Middlesex. It took 341 minutes and 281 balls, with 33 fours and a six. It was still not enough to bring victory. Munton, bowling superbly to take seven for 66 in his second match back after injury, forced Middlesex to follow on. But the bowlers tired, and left their batsmen only 24 overs to reach a target of 205. Lara took 25 off an over from Bloomfield – hitting the first three deliveries for six, and the fourth, a no-ball, for four – and reached 51 in 30 balls, with three fours and four sixes. But he fell at 83 and, although Warwickshire charged to 101 for three after ten overs, they lost too many wickets to sustain the pace.
    Close of play: First day, Warwickshire 372-5 (B. C. Lara 224*, N. M. K. Smith 33*); Second day, Middlesex 194-4 (P. N. Weekes 56*, K. R. Brown 21*); Third day, Middlesex 157-2 (M. W. Gatting 20*, C. J. Batt 1*).

Warwickshire

M. J. Powell c Weekes b Batt	8	– (7) c Brown b Tufnell	0
N. V. Knight b Batt	36	– (1) st Brown b Tufnell	28
M. A. Wagh b Johnson	2	– (6) c Gatting b Tufnell	1
*B. C. Lara lbw b Johnson	226	– (3) c Gatting b Johnson	51
A. Singh c Shah b Johnson	41	– (4) c Batt b Johnson	14
†K. J. Piper b Tufnell	0	– (9) not out	7
N. M. K. Smith c Weekes b Tufnell	61	– (2) b Bloomfield	4
G. Welch c Gatting b Bloomfield	6	– c Nash b Tufnell	1
A. F. Giles c Brown b Bloomfield	29	– (5) c sub b Johnson	13
T. A. Munton c Langer b Johnson	20	– not out	4
E. S. H. Giddins not out	6		
B 4, l-b 21, n-b 6	31	B 8, l-b 5, w 6, n-b 8	27

1/29 2/38 3/100 4/256 5/261   466   1/6 2/83 3/101 4/115   (8 wkts) 150
6/381 7/398 8/415 9/445   5/125 6/130 7/131 8/134

Bonus points – Warwickshire 4, Middlesex 3 (Score at 120 overs: 430-8).

Bowling: *First Innings*—Bloomfield 22-6-101-2; Batt 21-2-88-2; Johnson 26.2-7-60-4; Goodchild 7-1-20-0; Tufnell 35-6-93-2; Weekes 12-1-53-0; Langer 4-1-17-0; Shah 2-0-9-0. *Second Innings*—Batt 3-0-24-0; Bloomfield 4-0-53-1; Johnson 8.5-2-32-3; Tufnell 7-1-24-4; Weekes 1-0-4-0.

Middlesex

D. J. Goodchild run out	14	– c Piper b Giddins	73
J. L. Langer lbw b Munton	33	– b Giles	55
M. W. Gatting b Munton	11	– c Knight b Welch	91
O. A. Shah lbw b Giddins	52	– (5) c Singh b Wagh	52
P. N. Weekes c Knight b Munton	89	– (6) lbw b Welch	0
*†K. R. Brown lbw b Welch	26	– (7) not out	37
D. C. Nash b Munton	23	– (8) lbw b Wagh	2
R. L. Johnson c Powell b Munton	17	– (9) c sub b Wagh	2
C. J. Batt b Munton	6	– (4) lbw b Giles	43
P. C. R. Tufnell b Munton	0	– c Powell b Wagh	0
T. F. Bloomfield not out	3	– b Munton	0
L-b 12, n-b 11	23	B 7, l-b 9, n-b 2	18

1/38 2/60 3/61 4/132 5/199   297   1/130 2/156 3/243 4/293 5/293   373
6/254 7/279 8/282 9/282   6/356 7/360 8/372 9/372

Bonus points – Middlesex 2, Warwickshire 4.

Bowling: *First Innings*—Giddins 26-10-55-1; Welch 19-5-52-1; Smith 16-3-37-0; Munton 28-9-66-7; Giles 28-7-56-0; Wagh 3-0-19-0. *Second Innings*—Giddins 16-4-46-1; Munton 20-3-46-1; Welch 26-5-91-2; Powell 2-0-9-0; Giles 40-14-94-2; Wagh 6-3-11-4; Smith 16-5-44-0; Lara 2-0-16-0.

Umpires: J. H. Harris and J. F. Steele.

At Hove, August 14, 15. MIDDLESEX lost to SUSSEX by an innings and 160 runs.

At Leicester, August 19, 20, 21, 22. MIDDLESEX lost to LEICESTERSHIRE by eight wickets.

At Southampton, August 31, September 1, 2, 3. MIDDLESEX lost to HAMPSHIRE by seven wickets.

MIDDLESEX v GLOUCESTERSHIRE

At Lord's, September 9, 10, 11. Gloucestershire won by 96 runs. Gloucestershire 21 pts, Middlesex 4 pts. Toss: Middlesex.

Mike Gatting was applauded from the field after his last innings at Lord's before retirement. But the circumstances were far removed from almost everything he had known in his 24-year Middlesex career. Gatting was out for two, and Middlesex, needing a modest 169, were bowled out by the Gloucestershire seamers for 72 for their fourth successive defeat, leaving a first wooden spoon still a possibility. Both sides were dismissed for two-figure totals on the last day, and Peter Roebuck, in the *Daily Telegraph*, called it "the worst day's batting I have seen in county cricket". Gloucestershire had gained a first-innings lead of 80, thanks to a recovery led by Ball and a last-wicket stand of 52. Middlesex started well, but collapsed when Walsh and Smith shared four wickets in ten balls. Fraser put them back in the game with six for 23, but the batsmen let him down badly. Tufnell, with 16, was top-scorer in the Middlesex second innings, which said it all.

Close of play: First day, Gloucestershire 232-9 (M. C. J. Ball 67*, C. A. Walsh 14*); Second day, Gloucestershire 49-4 (M. W. Alleyne 26*, A. M. Smith 0*).

Gloucestershire

R. J. Cunliffe b Fraser	26	– lbw b Johnson	4
T. H. C. Hancock b Fraser	23	– lbw b Fraser	15
D. R. Hewson c Shah b Johnson	5	– c Weekes b Johnson	0
*M. W. Alleyne b Johnson	6	– lbw b Fraser	27
M. G. N. Windows lbw b Johnson	0	– (7) c Weekes b Fraser	3
R. I. Dawson b Johnson	31	– (8) b Hewitt	2
†R. C. Russell c Brown b Hewitt	40	– (9) c Strauss b Fraser	3
M. C. J. Ball not out	67	– (6) b Fraser	0
J. Lewis c Weekes b Hewitt	0	– (5) lbw b Hewitt	4
A. M. Smith c Brown b Hewitt	0	– (6) c sub b Fraser	29
C. A. Walsh lbw b Fraser	20	– not out	0
L-b 8, w 12	20	L-b 1	1
	238		**88**

1/50 2/53 3/60 4/60 5/67   1/17 2/19 3/22 4/37 5/58
6/132 7/186 8/186 9/186   6/78 7/83 8/87 9/87

Bonus points – Gloucestershire 1, Middlesex 4.

Bowling: *First Innings*—Fraser 25.4–7–48–3; Hewitt 22–5–61–3; Johnson 23–6–56–4; Tufnell 12–3–42–0; Kettleborough 5–0–19–0; Weekes 1–0–4–0. *Second Innings*—Fraser 13.2–4–23–6; Hewitt 7–3–14–2; Johnson 8–0–50–2.

Middlesex

A. J. Strauss lbw b Lewis	24	– c Cunliffe b Walsh	6
R. A. Kettleborough c Alleyne b Smith	0	– c Russell b Smith	11
*M. R. Ramprakash b Walsh	10	– (6) c Russell b Lewis	8
M. W. Gatting c Alleyne b Walsh	35	– (7) lbw b Walsh	2
O. A. Shah c Russell b Walsh	36	– (3) c Cunliffe b Walsh	4
P. N. Weekes c Alleyne b Smith	21	– (4) c Windows b Smith	5
†K. R. Brown c Ball b Smith	9	– (5) c Russell b Smith	0
J. P. Hewitt c Ball b Smith	0	– (9) not out	3
R. L. Johnson not out	9	– (8) c Smith b Walsh	4
A. R. C. Fraser lbw b Smith	0	– c Hancock b Lewis	0
P. C. R. Tufnell c Alleyne b Walsh	1	– c Ball b Lewis	16
L-b 5, n-b 8	13	L-b 1, w 2, n-b 10	13
	158		**72**

1/0 2/23 3/57 4/109 5/120   1/8 2/12 3/28 4/28 5/33
6/146 7/146 8/147 9/147   6/49 7/53 8/55 9/56

Bonus points – Gloucestershire 4.

Bowling: *First Innings*—Walsh 19.2–5–41–4; Smith 15–5–40–5; Lewis 11–2–35–1; Alleyne 9–0–31–0; Ball 3–1–6–0. *Second Innings*—Walsh 10–3–22–4; Smith 10–2–17–3; Lewis 9.2–2–32–3.

Umpires: K. E. Palmer and D. R. Shepherd.

At Derby, September 17, 18, 19, 20. MIDDLESEX lost to DERBYSHIRE by four wickets.

Mike Gatting makes his way towards the pavilion in his last match at Lord's before retiring.

David Ripley

NORTHAMPTONSHIRE

Patrons: The Earl of Dalkeith and
The Earl Spencer
President: A. P. Arnold
Chairman: L. A. Wilson
Chairman, Cricket Committee: R. T. Virgin
Chief Executive: S. P. Coverdale
Captain: 1998 – K. M. Curran
1999 – M. L. Hayden
Director of Cricket: 1998 – J. E. Emburey
1999 – R. M. Carter
Head Groundsman: D. Bates
Scorer: A. C. Kingston

Not since the grim years immediately before and after the Second World War have Northamptonshire endured such a joyless and chaotic season. The only other serious contender – 1978, when they finished bottom of the Championship – at least saw Sunday League performances improve and, crucially, Allan Lamb announce his arrival on the county scene. Twenty years on, with the exception of Mal Loye's form in the first part of the summer and the emergence of Graeme Swann as an all-rounder of enormous potential, there was precious little to cheer the faithful.

The club's response was swift and drastic. By the first week of October both Kevin Curran, who inherited the captaincy from Rob Bailey the previous autumn, and director of cricket John Emburey, with a year of his contract outstanding, had been relieved of their posts. Curran's reign was thus the shortest of any official captain at Wantage Road since Roy Virgin failed to see out the season in 1975. It was ironic that Virgin should chair the cricket sub-committee which dismissed Curran. The former coach Bob Carter, who had left the club in 1995 to go to New Zealand, agreed to return as director of cricket, one of the few decisions well received by supporters. A much lower-profile figure than Emburey, Carter is highly regarded by those who know him for his quiet skills and attention to detail. Matthew Hayden of Queensland was signed as both overseas player and captain.

The results left little room for argument. Northamptonshire finished 15th in the Championship, the same as in 1997, but fell four places to 13th in the Sunday League. Early exits from both the Benson and Hedges Cup, in which the side's only victory came against the Minor Counties, and the NatWest Trophy, Gloucestershire inflicting a first-round defeat at Bristol, completed the sorry picture.

The third of Northamptonshire's four Championship victories, over Sussex in September, provided further damning evidence of the flawed thinking that blighted the summer. Emburey's decision to play on a pitch marked "poor" for a Sunday League game ten days earlier, and not renovated in the interim, was intended to give Northamptonshire's talented young slow bowlers an opportunity to shine; they did so, securing a win by 136 runs, only to have their efforts negated immediately by a 25-point penalty.

On too many other occasions, Curran's men were conclusively outgunned. Successive matches in July saw them capitulate inside two days at Worcester – depriving Supporters' Club members of any Championship cricket on their annual weekend jaunt – and then allow Leicestershire to achieve a seemingly impossible target of 204 in 20 overs. Devon Malcolm's solitary over in the débâcle at Grace Road cost 16 runs. It was probably the low point of the year for Malcolm, the former England fast bowler whose capture during the winter so delighted Northamptonshire. He claimed 25 wickets in his first five Championship games, but only ten in the next eight.

Franklyn Rose, signed in April to replace the injured Australian Paul Reiffel, and the reliable Paul Taylor proved more successful, both reaching 50 Championship wickets, although the most heartening returns came from the two off-spinners, Jason Brown and Graeme Swann. The 19-year-old Swann was a refreshing presence, exuding breezy confidence while others around him appeared careworn and unsure of themselves. His efforts with both bat – including a maiden century at Leicester – and ball earned him the Frank Rudd Trophy as Northamptonshire's outstanding young cricketer of 1998.

Morale was high in May, when Loye and David Ripley set a host of records in a 401-run partnership against Glamorgan, the biggest stand for the fifth wicket in England. Loye's unbeaten 322, Northamptonshire's highest-ever score, began a remarkable sequence which saw him amass 981 runs in nine Championship innings to the end of July. But his form dipped in the closing weeks and he missed the last two matches through a recurring back problem. Despite securing a place on the England A tour, leading the national run-scorers' list in the Sunday League with 650 (another Northamptonshire record), and being named the club's player of the year, Loye ended the summer unsettled and considering a move to another county. Happily, he announced in November that he would stay, a decision helped by Carter's appointment. Ripley was again a pillar of the side, as batsman and keeper, while Tony Penberthy, having waited nine years for his first Championship century, scored two in as many months, suggesting he may have finally made a top-order place his own. That he bowled only 65 first-class overs was just one more mystery in a season replete with them.

Neither Bailey nor Curran prospered consistently, while Richard Montgomerie (who was released in September and promptly signed for Sussex), Alec Swann, David Sales and Russell Warren were all disappointing. The nine different opening combinations tried in the Championship yielded just three stands over 35.

The success of the Second Eleven, coached by Nick Cook, in winning both the Championship and AON Trophy engendered a little optimism, particularly the late-season contributions of batsman Mark Powell and seam bowlers Richard Logan and Dale Iniff. Another positive development was David Capel's appointment to the new post of director of excellence, to work with the county's young cricketers. He had been jettisoned from the playing staff in July, thus ending an 18-year career.

Capel and his colleagues will have Northampton's new £1.7 million Indoor Cricket Centre at their disposal as they bring on the next generation. The effects are awaited keenly, for supporters are unlikely to accept with equanimity too many more wasted weekends in Worcester. – ANDREW RADD.

NORTHAMPTONSHIRE 1998

[Bill Smith]

Back row: A. M. Dobson, R. J. Logan, J. A. R. Blain, G. P. Swann, S. A. J. Boswell, A. J. Swann, D. Follett, D. J. Roberts, K. J. Innes. *Middle row:* K. A. Russell (*physiotherapist*), J. N. Snape, D. J. Sales, A. L. Penberthy, R. J. Warren, A. E. Malcolm, M. B. Loye, R. R. Montgomerie, T. C. Walton, J. F. Brown, N. A. Foster (*development coach*). *Front row:* J. P. Taylor, N. G. B. Cook (*Second Eleven captain/coach*), D. J. Capel, K. M. Curran (*captain*), J. E. Emburey (*director of cricket*), R. J. Bailey, D. Ripley. *Insets:* M. K. Davies, F. A. Rose.

NORTHAMPTONSHIRE RESULTS

All first-class matches – Played 18: Won 4, Lost 5, Drawn 9.

County Championship matches – Played 17: Won 4, Lost 5, Drawn 8.

*Competition placings – Britannic Assurance County Championship, 15th;
NatWest Trophy, 1st round; Benson and Hedges Cup, 5th in Group A;
AXA League, 13th.*

COUNTY CHAMPIONSHIP AVERAGES
BATTING

Cap		M	I	NO	R	HS	100s	50s	Avge	Ct/St
1994	M. B. Loye†	14	21	2	1,184	322*	4	4	62.31	7
1987	D. Ripley	16	22	2	805	209	1	5	40.25	30/1
1994	A. L. Penberthy	13	21	2	755	128	2	4	39.73	14
1985	R. J. Bailey	16	24	2	759	188	1	2	34.50	10
	G. P. Swann†	13	18	2	548	111	1	2	34.25	7
1992	K. M. Curran	17	25	3	668	90*	0	6	30.36	23
1992	J. P. Taylor	15	20	3	371	58	0	3	21.82	5
	D. J. Sales	13	20	1	337	60	0	2	17.73	10
1995	R. R. Montgomerie .	9	15	2	222	54	0	1	17.07	4
	A. J. Swann†	10	16	0	249	85	0	1	15.56	6
	D. E. Malcolm	14	16	5	114	42	0	0	10.36	3
	F. A. Rose§	14	17	2	133	21	0	0	8.86	0
1995	R. J. Warren†	5	8	0	30	11	0	0	3.75	7
	J. F. Brown	8	11	5	18	6*	0	0	3.00	1
	D. Follett	5	7	1	13	7	0	0	2.16	2

Also batted: T. M. B. Bailey† (1 match) 12 (2 ct); M. K. Davies (1 match) 3*, 4; K. J. Innes†
(1 match) 6, 31 (2 ct); D. J. Roberts (1 match) 39, 0 (3 ct). D. J. Capel† (cap 1986) (1 match)
did not bat.

* Signifies not out. † Born in Northamptonshire. § Overseas player.

BOWLING

	O	M	R	W	BB	5W/i	Avge
J. F. Brown	280.2	68	726	33	6-53	4	22.00
J. P. Taylor	436.5	105	1,337	54	4-31	0	24.75
F. A. Rose	373.2	59	1,367	50	7-39	3	27.34
G. P. Swann	199.4	41	666	22	5-29	1	30.27
D. Follett	103	17	325	10	3-48	0	32.50
D. E. Malcolm	334	48	1,331	40	6-54	2	33.27

Also bowled: R. J. Bailey 66–14–178–6; D. J. Capel 13–1–66–1; K. M. Curran 78–20–265–2;
M. K. Davies 39–17–54–7; M. B. Loye 2–0–42–0; A. L. Penberthy 65–13–204–0; D. J. Sales
11–2–36–1; A. J. Swann 6.3–0–59–0.

COUNTY RECORDS

Highest score for:	322*	M. B. Loye v Glamorgan at Northampton	1998
Highest score against:	333	K. S. Duleepsinhji (Sussex) at Hove	1930
Best bowling for:	10-127	V. W. C. Jupp v Kent at Tunbridge Wells	1932
Best bowling against:	10-30	C. Blythe (Kent) at Northampton	1907
Highest total for:	781-7 dec.	v Nottinghamshire at Northampton	1995
Highest total against:	670-9 dec.	by Sussex at Hove	1921
Lowest total for:	12	v Gloucestershire at Gloucester	1907
Lowest total against:	33	by Lancashire at Northampton	1977

At Cambridge, April 14, 15, 16. NORTHAMPTONSHIRE drew with CAMBRIDGE UNIVERSITY.

At The Oval, April 17, 18, 20, 21. NORTHAMPTONSHIRE drew with SURREY.

At Southampton, April 23, 24, 25, 27. NORTHAMPTONSHIRE drew with HAMPSHIRE.

NORTHAMPTONSHIRE v YORKSHIRE

At Northampton, May 13, 14, 15. Northamptonshire won by eight wickets. Northamptonshire 23 pts, Yorkshire 4 pts. Toss: Yorkshire.

Byas's surprising decision to bat in hazy conditions, ideal for swing bowling, had a significant bearing on the outcome. Malcolm claimed four wickets – including his 800th in first-class cricket when he bowled McGrath – in the space of 24 balls on the first morning. Then Sales, batting with uncharacteristic restraint for nearly three hours, and Graeme Swann, who fell one run short of a maiden fifty, guided Northamptonshire to a lead of 184. Yorkshire were in danger of losing by an innings as Swann, flighting his off-breaks skilfully, made inroads with a spell of three for two in ten deliveries. But Blakey added 83 in 20 overs with Gough and a further 69 with Silverwood before Malcolm mopped up. Northamptonshire still completed victory half an hour after lunch on the third day.

Close of play: First day, Northamptonshire 158-4 (D. J. Sales 28*, D. Ripley 14*); Second day, Yorkshire 147-7 (R. J. Blakey 4*, D. Gough 10*).

Yorkshire

A. McGrath b Malcolm	0	– c Bailey b Rose	26
M. P. Vaughan c Curran b Malcolm	17	– c Ripley b Taylor	13
*D. Byas lbw b Malcolm	5	– lbw b Malcolm	34
M. J. Wood lbw b Malcolm	0	– c A. J. Swann b Taylor	3
D. S. Lehmann c Bailey b Taylor	5	– c Curran b G. P. Swann	27
C. White c Montgomerie b Taylor	42	– lbw b G. P. Swann	10
†R. J. Blakey b Malcolm	0	– (8) b Malcolm	49
D. Gough lbw b Rose	3	– (9) c Curran b Taylor	58
C. E. W. Silverwood c Curran b Malcolm	40	– (10) c Bailey b Malcolm	34
R. D. Stemp c G. P. Swann b Taylor	14	– (11) not out	1
P. M. Hutchison not out	8	– (7) lbw b G. P. Swann	4
L-b 8, w 2, n-b 4	14	B 1, l-b 14, n-b 14	29

1/0 2/24 3/24 4/25 5/41   148   1/33 2/57 3/75 4/102 5/125   288
6/46 7/54 8/96 9/132   6/132 7/135 8/218 9/287

Bonus points – Northamptonshire 4.

Bowling: *First Innings*—Malcolm 18–4–54–6; Rose 10–1–36–1; Taylor 16–5–50–3. *Second Innings*—Malcolm 22.3–2–87–3; Rose 26–7–73–1; G. P. Swann 22–4–69–3; Taylor 14–4–37–3; Curran 1–0–1–0; Bailey 1–0–6–0.

Northamptonshire

R. R. Montgomerie lbw b Hutchison	22	– not out	49
A. J. Swann c Blakey b Hutchison	5	– lbw b White	1
M. B. Loye lbw b White	28	– c sub b Stemp	4
R. J. Bailey c Blakey b Gough	35	– not out	46
D. J. Sales b White	60		
†D. Ripley c Blakey b White	35		
*K. M. Curran c Stemp b White	2		
G. P. Swann c White b Silverwood	49		
F. A. Rose lbw b Gough	10		
J. P. Taylor not out	32		
D. E. Malcolm b White	0		
B 6, l-b 12, w 6, n-b 30	54	B 2, l-b 1, n-b 2	5

1/29 2/40 3/93 4/121 5/206   332   1/23 2/28   (2 wkts) 105
6/220 7/223 8/248 9/319

Bonus points – Northamptonshire 3, Yorkshire 4.

Bowling: *First Innings*—Gough 28–5–82–2; Silverwood 27–6–84–1; Hutchison 25–6–68–2; White 20.3–4–46–5; Stemp 8–1–34–0. *Second Innings*—Gough 5–1–16–0; Silverwood 4–0–9–0; Hutchison 4–0–16–0; Stemp 4–0–27–1; White 4–2–10–1; Vaughan 4–1–24–0; Lehmann 0.2–0–0–0.

Umpires: J. F. Steele and R. A. White.

NORTHAMPTONSHIRE v GLAMORGAN

At Northampton, May 21, 22, 23, 24. Drawn. Northamptonshire 6 pts, Glamorgan 11 pts. Toss: Glamorgan.

Just after 3 p.m. on the final afternoon, Malachy Loye cut Steve Watkin for four to record the highest score by a Northamptonshire player, surpassing Raman Subba Row's 300 against Surrey at The Oval in 1958. His achievement was watched by his father and a few hundred other faithful supporters; at Wembley, 40,000 Northampton Town fans had just seen their team start the Division Two play-off final against Grimsby, which finished less happily for them. Loye's unbeaten 322, which came from 534 balls, included 49 fours and lasted 648 minutes, was one of several records set on a bland pitch that rendered bowlers of both sides impotent. His partnership of 401 in 92 overs with Ripley was a county record for any wicket and the best for the fifth wicket in first-class cricket in England, exceeding the 393 hit by William Burns and Ted Arnold for Worcestershire against Warwickshire at Edgbaston in 1909. Ripley batted 335 minutes, faced 266 balls and hit a seven, a six and 34 fours. The home side's 712 also replaced Cambridge University's 703 for nine, made 108 years earlier, as the highest second-innings total scored in England. Northamptonshire had looked set for a hefty defeat after a poor batting performance on the first day allowed Glamorgan to build a huge lead. James struck 36 fours in six and a quarter hours and 312 balls,

HIGHEST SECOND-INNINGS SCORES IN FIRST-CLASS CRICKET

452*	D. G. Bradman, New South Wales v Queensland at Sydney	1929-30
344	W. G. Grace, MCC v Kent at Canterbury	1876
338*	R. C. Blunt, Otago v Canterbury at Christchurch	1931-32
337	Hanif Mohammad, Pakistan v West Indies at Bridgetown	1957-58
322*	**M. B. Loye, Northamptonshire v Glamorgan at Northampton**	**1998**
314*	C. L. Walcott, Barbados v Trinidad at Port-of-Spain	1945-46
309	V. S. Hazare, The Rest v Hindus at Bombay	1943-44

IN COUNTY CHAMPIONSHIP

322*	**M. B. Loye, Northamptonshire v Glamorgan at Northampton**	**1998**
287*	Emrys Davies, Glamorgan v Gloucestershire at Newport	1939
285*	K. S. Ranjitsinhji, Sussex v Somerset at Taunton	1901
280*	C. P. Mead, Hampshire v Nottinghamshire at Southampton	1921
280*	E. H. Bowley, Sussex v Gloucestershire at Hove	1929

HIGHEST SECOND-INNINGS TOTALS IN FIRST-CLASS CRICKET

770	New South Wales v South Australia at Adelaide	1920-21
764	Bombay v Holkar at Bombay.	1944-45
761-8 dec.	New South Wales v Queensland at Sydney.	1929-30
726-7 dec.	Barbados v Trinidad at Bridgetown	1926-27
724	Victoria v South Australia at Melbourne.	1920-21
714-8 dec.	Bombay v Maharashtra at Poona	1948-49
712	**Northamptonshire v Glamorgan at Northampton**	**1998**
703-9 dec.	Cambridge University v Sussex at Hove.	1890

IN COUNTY CHAMPIONSHIP

712	**Northamptonshire v Glamorgan at Northampton**	**1998**
636-6 dec.	Northamptonshire v Essex at Chelmsford	1990
634-7 dec.	Middlesex v Essex at Chelmsford	1983
630	Somerset v Yorkshire at Leeds	1901
613-6 dec.	Surrey v Essex at The Oval.	1990

Research: Robert Brooke

but fell one run short of Roy Fredericks's county record against Northamptonshire. Powell helped him add 186 in 38 overs before Cottey pressed home the advantage ruthlessly. When Loye and Ripley came together on the third afternoon at 142 for four, the home team were still 249 adrift. They proceeded to save the match – and make history. Subba Row promptly sent Loye a congratulatory fax, warning him to expect another record-breaker in 40 years' time.

Close of play: First day, Glamorgan 204-2 (S. P. James 123*, M. J. Powell 7*); Second day, Northamptonshire 0-0 (R. R. Montgomerie 0*, A. J. Swann 0*); Third day, Northamptonshire 411-4 (M. B. Loye 201*, D. Ripley 148*).

[Mick Cheney

Subba Row and Loye: Northamptonshire's old record holder and the new.

Northamptonshire

R. R. Montgomerie c Shaw b Watkin	1	– lbw b Watkin	2
A. J. Swann c Powell b Waqar Younis	5	– lbw b Waqar Younis	2
M. B. Loye lbw b Thomas	29	– not out	322
R. J. Bailey c Cosker b Waqar Younis	4	– (10) c Shaw b Dale	32
D. J. Sales c Evans b Thomas	0	– (4) c Evans b Watkin	22
*K. M. Curran c James b Dale	54	– (5) lbw b Waqar Younis	21
†D. Ripley b Watkin	59	– (6) c Waqar Younis b Cottey	209
G. P. Swann lbw b Butcher	4	– (7) c Cosker b Thomas	17
J. P. Taylor b Watkin	0	– (8) c James b Waqar Younis	0
F. A. Rose not out	3	– (9) c and b Thomas	10
D. E. Malcolm b Butcher	2	– c Dale b Thomas	42
L-b 5, w 4, n-b 2	11	B 12, l-b 5, w 6, n-b 10	33
	172		**712**

1/1 2/9 3/21 4/29 5/45   1/5 2/15 3/72 4/142 5/543
6/135 7/165 8/165 9/169   6/562 7/565 8/584 9/663

Bonus points – Glamorgan 4.

Bowling: *First Innings*—Waqar Younis 12–1–54–2; Watkin 15–5–30–3; Thomas 7–0–27–2; Butcher 7.2–2–22–2; Dale 9–2–25–1; Cosker 1–0–9–0. *Second Innings*—Waqar Younis 35–2–147–3; Watkin 34–5–131–2; Thomas 31.5–3–154–3; Butcher 17–1–79–0; Cosker 39–12–107–0; Dale 11–0–63–1; Cottey 6–2–14–1.

Glamorgan

S. P. James c Ripley b G. P. Swann	227	– not out	10
A. W. Evans b Malcolm	10	– not out	25
A. Dale b Malcolm	45		
M. J. Powell c G. P. Swann b Sales	106		
*P. A. Cottey c Curran b Taylor	113		
G. P. Butcher c Ripley b Rose	1		
†A. D. Shaw c A. J. Swann b Malcolm	0		
Waqar Younis c Taylor b Rose	2		
S. D. Thomas b Taylor	17		
D. A. Cosker c Ripley b Taylor	3		
S. L. Watkin not out	1		
B 6, l-b 16, w 2, n-b 14	38	B 4, l-b 1, n-b 4	9
	563	(no wkt)	**44**

1/25 2/169 3/355 4/447 5/454
6/469 7/478 8/524 9/544

Bonus points – Glamorgan 4, Northamptonshire 3 (Score at 120 overs: 541-8).

Bowling: *First Innings*—Malcolm 28–3–144–3; Rose 28–3–130–2; Taylor 25.5–1–105–3; Curran 5–3–24–0; G. P. Swann 24–3–98–1; Bailey 1–1–0–0; Sales 9–2–28–1; A. J. Swann 3–0–12–0. *Second Innings*—Rose 4–1–15–0; Taylor 2–0–20–0; A. J. Swann 1–0–4–0.

Umpires: N. G. Cowley and B. Leadbeater.

NORTHAMPTONSHIRE v LANCASHIRE

At Northampton, June 3, 4, 5, 6. Drawn. Northamptonshire 10 pts, Lancashire 8 pts. Toss: Northamptonshire.

Having fought back well from a first-innings deficit of 102, Lancashire were understandably reluctant to set a generous target on an easy pitch. Crawley's cautious last-day declaration left Northamptonshire to make 337 in 66 overs. Once Loye had departed in the last over before tea, they never seriously threatened. His fluent 88-ball 71, following a first-innings hundred, took his tally in three Championship innings to 542. Loye had shared century partnerships with Penberthy and Ripley to put Northamptonshire in control after Lancashire struggled on a rain-shortened first day. But Crawley and Flintoff responded positively, taking advantage of wayward fast bowling to add 166 in 33 overs. Flintoff drove with great power and flair in a career-best 124; Crawley's innings was more circumspect but just as valuable.

Close of play: First day, Lancashire 152-8 (I. D. Austin 12*, P. J. Martin 1*); Second day, Northamptonshire 248-5 (M. B. Loye 119*, D. Ripley 22*); Third day, Lancashire 311-3 (A. Flintoff 124*, G. D. Lloyd 20*).

Lancashire

N. T. Wood lbw b Rose	3	– b Rose	5
*J. P. Crawley c Warren b Rose	22	– c Curran b Swann	109
N. H. Fairbrother c Bailey b Taylor	7	– b Taylor	37
A. Flintoff c Curran b Rose	46	– lbw b Taylor	124
G. D. Lloyd c Ripley b Malcolm	8	– c Ripley b Malcolm	49
M. Watkinson lbw b Malcolm	0	– lbw b Malcolm	20
†W. K. Hegg c Malcolm b Rose	22	– not out	56
I. D. Austin lbw b Taylor	64	– lbw b Malcolm	0
G. Chapple c Loye b Rose	4	– b Malcolm	7
P. J. Martin b Malcolm	17	– not out	7
R. J. Green not out	0		
B 4, l-b 2, w 9, n-b 22	37	B 2, l-b 20, n-b 2	24

1/13 2/24 3/46 4/68 5/68	230	1/11 2/96 3/262 (8 wkts dec.) 438
6/125 7/136 8/146 9/230		4/312 5/362 6/379
		7/379 8/405

Bonus points – Lancashire 1, Northamptonshire 4.

Bowling: First Innings—Malcolm 15.1–2–52–3; Rose 24–4–89–5; Taylor 13–2–49–2; Curran 7–2–22–0; Penberthy 4–0–12–0. *Second Innings*—Malcolm 25–0–145–4; Rose 16–0–66–1; Taylor 18–3–61–2; Swann 21–2–80–1; Curran 5–2–17–0; Bailey 1–0–6–0; Penberthy 8–1–41–0.

Northamptonshire

R. R. Montgomerie c Flintoff b Chapple	6	– lbw b Austin	21
R. J. Warren lbw b Martin	11	– lbw b Chapple	4
M. B. Loye c Flintoff b Martin	149	– lbw b Austin	71
R. J. Bailey b Austin	19	– c Flintoff b Green	31
*K. M. Curran c Martin b Austin	4	– not out	90
A. L. Penberthy b Martin	47	– c and b Watkinson	15
†D. Ripley b Austin	56	– b Martin	24
G. P. Swann b Martin	12	– not out	4
J. P. Taylor c Lloyd b Chapple	4		
F. A. Rose c Green b Chapple	0		
D. E. Malcolm not out	0		
B 5, l-b 17, n-b 2	24	B 4, l-b 4, n-b 6	14

1/25 2/25 3/64 4/73 5/178	332	1/6 2/41 3/124 (6 wkts) 274
6/304 7/321 8/328 9/329		4/140 5/201 6/260

Bonus points – Northamptonshire 3, Lancashire 4.

Bowling: First Innings—Martin 28–7–56–4; Chapple 22.1–1–92–3; Austin 22–6–58–3; Green 18–6–52–0; Watkinson 7–1–25–0; Flintoff 12–3–27–0. *Second Innings*—Martin 16–2–72–1; Chapple 5–0–12–1; Austin 16–5–38–2; Watkinson 16–0–103–1; Green 10–0–41–1.

Umpires: M. J. Harris and G. Sharp.

At Chester-le-Street, June 11, 12, 13, 15. NORTHAMPTONSHIRE drew with DURHAM.

NORTHAMPTONSHIRE v MIDDLESEX

At Northampton, June 17, 18, 19, 20. Drawn. Northamptonshire 7 pts, Middlesex 7 pts. Toss: Middlesex. Championship debut: N. D. Martin.

Northamptonshire had a brief glimpse of victory on the final afternoon but could not press home their advantage. Middlesex, set 286 in 54 overs, collapsed to 87 for five with 25 overs remaining, and Langer resting after Rose had struck him on the head. But Brown and Hewitt prevented any further alarms and a halt was called two overs early. Play did not begin until the third day when Northamptonshire made a bad start against the lively Bloomfield, who went on to career-best figures of five for 67. The middle order turned things round and Penberthy recorded a maiden Championship century nine years after his debut. The fourth morning was lost to rain, and three and a half overs of joke bowling were necessary to make the run-chase possible. Langer helped himself to a 15-ball 55.

Close of play: First day, No play; Second day, No play; Third day, Northamptonshire 366.

Northamptonshire

R. J. Warren b Bloomfield	3		D. Follett c Gatting b Hewitt		0
A. J. Swann b Bloomfield	1		F. A. Rose c Brown b Bloomfield		12
M. B. Loye c Brown b Hewitt	78		D. E. Malcolm b Weekes		14
R. J. Bailey b Hewitt	10				
*K. M. Curran b Bloomfield	61		B 1, l-b 6, w 6, n-b 18		31
A. L. Penberthy not out	102				—
†D. Ripley c Brown b Bloomfield	51		1/3 2/4 3/50 4/138 5/193		366
G. P. Swann st Brown b Langer	3		6/266 7/279 8/298 9/351		

Bonus points – Northamptonshire 4, Middlesex 4.

Bowling: Hewitt 27–6–109–3; Bloomfield 21–5–67–5; Martin 12–1–61–0; Tufnell 23–4–72–0; Weekes 11.3–3–31–1; Shah 4–1–9–0; Langer 5–3–10–1.

Northamptonshire forfeited their second innings.

Middlesex

J. L. Langer not out	55		– retired hurt	3
R. A. Kettleborough not out	18		– lbw b Malcolm	0
M. W. Gatting (did not bat)			– c Warren b Follett	17
O. A. Shah (did not bat)			– c Warren b Malcolm	48
D. C. Nash (did not bat)			– c Bailey b G. P. Swann	0
P. N. Weekes (did not bat)			– b Follett	10
*†K. R. Brown (did not bat)			– not out	27
J. P. Hewitt (did not bat)			– not out	30
W 2, n-b 6	8		L-b 8, n-b 4	12

(no wkt dec.) 81   1/7 2/49 3/52   (5 wkts) 147
4/73 5/87

N. D. Martin, T. F. Bloomfield and P. C. R. Tufnell did not bat.

In the second innings J. L. Langer retired hurt at 3.

Bowling: *First Innings*—Loye 2–0–42–0; A. J. Swann 1.3–0–39–0. *Second Innings*—Malcolm 19–4–42–2; Rose 14–3–35–0; Follett 8–1–35–2; G. P. Swann 11–5–27–1.

Umpires: A. A. Jones and R. Palmer.

At Northampton, June 28. NORTHAMPTONSHIRE lost to SOUTH AFRICANS by 98 runs (D/L method) (See South African tour section).

At Worcester, July 1, 2. NORTHAMPTONSHIRE lost to WORCESTERSHIRE by 157 runs.

At Leicester, July 14, 15, 16, 17. NORTHAMPTONSHIRE lost to LEICESTERSHIRE by four wickets.

NORTHAMPTONSHIRE v DERBYSHIRE

At Northampton, July 22, 23, 24. Northamptonshire won by an innings and 94 runs. Northamptonshire 24 pts, Derbyshire 2 pts. Toss: Northamptonshire.

Northamptonshire climbed off the bottom against their favourite opposition: they recorded their seventh successive Championship victory over Derbyshire, winning with a day to spare after a ruthlessly efficient batting performance. Bailey, in a stay of just under seven hours, made his only hundred of the summer and his highest since June 1993, adding 296 in 80 overs for the second wicket with Loye, who became the second player – and the first Englishman – to pass 1,000 first-class runs in the season. One of Loye's three straight sixes off Roberts hit a spectator on the head. The partnership was an all-wicket county record against Derbyshire. Swann, who hit 91 in 75 balls, and Penberthy piled on a further 149 to enable Northamptonshire to pass 600 for the second time in 1998 and the fifth time in the 1990s, though the total had eluded them in their first 75 seasons in county cricket. Derbyshire then subsided after a promising start, losing their last six wickets for 34 on the third day. Barnett and Cassar resisted when they followed on but the two off-spinners, Swann and Brown, worked their way through the rest.

Close of play: First day, Northamptonshire 335-2 (R. J. Bailey 149*, K. M. Curran 18*); Second day, Derbyshire 161-4 (M. E. Cassar 14*, K. J. Dean 2*).

Northamptonshire

R. R. Montgomerie c Spendlove b DeFreitas .	2	G. P. Swann c Cassar b Roberts	91
R. J. Bailey lbw b Dean	188	†D. Ripley lbw b Barnett.	29
M. B. Loye c Krikken b DeFreitas	157	B 1, l-b 9, w 2, n-b 2	14
*K. M. Curran b DeFreitas	59		
A. L. Penberthy not out	68	1/2 2/298 3/416 (6 wkts dec.) 608
		4/418 5/567 6/608	

J. P. Taylor, F. A. Rose, D. E. Malcolm and J. F. Brown did not bat.

Bonus points – Northamptonshire 4, Derbyshire 1 (Score at 120 overs: 446-4).

Bowling: DeFreitas 36–3–117–3; Dean 29–3–121–1; Smith 8–0–43–0; Roberts 43–4–161–1; Barnett 13–0–59–1; Cassar 17–2–97–0.

Derbyshire

M. J. Slater c Loye b Taylor	27	– lbw b Malcolm	46
M. R. May lbw b Taylor	32	– b Rose	0
R. M. S. Weston c Curran b Swann	51	– lbw b Swann	33
K. J. Barnett c Loye b Rose	24	– c Ripley b Brown	68
M. E. Cassar c Curran b Brown	38	– c Bailey b Swann	60
K. J. Dean b Rose	8	– (10) not out	0
B. L. Spendlove c Ripley b Rose	1	– (6) c Penberthy b Brown	28
*†K. M. Krikken c Montgomerie b Brown . . .	7	– (7) hit wkt b Swann	9
P. A. J. DeFreitas c Penberthy b Brown	19	– (8) c Penberthy b Swann	27
G. M. Roberts not out	6	– (9) lbw b Brown	5
T. M. Smith c Penberthy b Swann	1	– lbw b Brown	0
B 1, l-b 6, n-b 4	11	B 4, l-b 5, n-b 4	13

1/45 2/88 3/124 4/157 5/191   225   1/14 2/70 3/122 4/187 5/233   289
6/191 7/199 8/199 9/220   6/251 7/261 8/273 9/289

Bonus points – Derbyshire 1, Northamptonshire 4.

Bowling: *First Innings*—Rose 17–2–53–3; Taylor 21–5–54–2; Malcolm 8–2–26–0; Brown 28–5–78–3; Swann 7.3–4–6–2; Curran 2–1–1–0. *Second Innings*—Malcolm 11–2–38–1; Rose 8–0–47–1; Taylor 10–1–42–0; Brown 21.4–4–62–4; Swann 23–4–91–4.

Umpires: J. C. Balderstone and J. W. Lloyds.

At Nottingham, July 30, 31, August 1, 3. NORTHAMPTONSHIRE drew with NOTTINGHAM-SHIRE.

At Northampton, August 7. NORTHAMPTONSHIRE lost to SRI LANKANS by one wicket (See Sri Lankan tour section).

At Northampton, August 9. NORTHAMPTONSHIRE lost to SRI LANKANS by 16 runs (See Sri Lankan tour section).

At Taunton, August 14, 15, 16. NORTHAMPTONSHIRE lost to SOMERSET by two wickets.

NORTHAMPTONSHIRE v WARWICKSHIRE

At Northampton, August 19, 20, 21. Warwickshire won by four wickets. Warwickshire 24 pts, Northamptonshire 7 pts. Toss: Northamptonshire.

Warwickshire stuttered to their modest target of 122 late on the third evening after collapsing to 94 for six, as Taylor and Follett bowled with spirit on a wearing pitch. They had claimed a valuable first-innings lead of 93, thanks to Lara, who hit five sixes and 18 fours in his 154-ball 158, and made Northamptonshire pay for dropping him on 18 and 71. He added 145 in 28 overs with Singh, before Smith pressed home the advantage. Curran sent in Taylor to open and Follett at No. 3, but both night-watchmen fell in the first over to Giddins who, with Munton, bowled Warwickshire into a winning position. Northamptonshire's first innings was dominated by Penberthy. Opening the batting for the first time in the Championship, he hit a career-best 128. Together with Ripley, he put on 195, having joined forces at 52 for four. But the last five wickets tumbled for 14 as Northamptonshire squandered a promising position.

Close of play: First day, Warwickshire 17-1 (M. J. Powell 4*, K. J. Piper 9*); Second day, Northamptonshire 0-2 (A. L. Penberthy 0*, R. J. Bailey 0*).

Northamptonshire

A. L. Penberthy c Powell b Smith	128	– (2) c Piper b Munton	45
R. J. Bailey c Piper b Brown	0	– (4) lbw b Munton	35
M. B. Loye c Lara b Brown	1	– (5) b Giddins	1
*K. M. Curran c Penney b Brown	17	– (6) c Powell b Munton	17
D. J. Sales lbw b Brown	4	– (7) c Hemp b Giddins	40
†D. Ripley c Piper b Munton	98	– (8) c Penney b Wagh	48
G. P. Swann b Giddins	32	– (9) b Munton	13
J. P. Taylor not out	4	– (1) c Piper b Giddins	0
D. Follett c Piper b Giddins	0	– (3) lbw b Giddins	0
J. F. Brown b Smith	0	– not out	0
D. E. Malcolm b Giddins	8	– b Munton	0
B 13, l-b 8, n-b 6	27	B 2, l-b 5, w 2, n-b 6	15

1/10 2/18 3/44 4/52 5/247	319	1/0 2/0 3/77 4/84 5/90	214
6/305 7/307 8/307 9/308		6/114 7/183 8/212 9/214

Bonus points – Northamptonshire 3, Warwickshire 4.

Bowling: *First Innings*—Giddins 23–8–56–3; Brown 17–2–68–4; Munton 18–4–48–1; Smith 28–9–86–2; Wagh 10–4–36–0; Lara 1–0–4–0. *Second Innings*—Giddins 21–6–52–4; Brown 19–2–65–0; Munton 16.1–3–41–5; Smith 16–5–41–0; Wagh 2–0–8–1.

Warwickshire

M. J. Powell lbw b Taylor	11				
M. A. Wagh b Taylor	3	– lbw b Taylor	5
†K. J. Piper c Ripley b Taylor	34	– (1) not out	7
D. L. Hemp c Sales b Brown	31	– (3) lbw b Taylor	31
*B. C. Lara c Ripley b Brown	158	– (6) lbw b Taylor	7
A. Singh c Taylor b Brown	56	– (4) lbw b Follett	4
T. L. Penney not out	26	– (5) c Ripley b Follett	13
N. M. K. Smith c Loye b Brown	56	– (7) c Sales b Taylor	11
D. R. Brown c sub b Bailey	6	– (8) not out	28
T. A. Munton c Penberthy b Brown	0		
E. S. H. Giddins c Taylor b Bailey	3		
B 8, l-b 16, n-b 4	28	L-b 10, n-b 6	16

1/8 2/33 3/75 4/171 5/316   412   1/7 2/21 3/67   (6 wkts) 122
6/317 7/395 8/408 9/409   4/71 5/85 6/94

Bonus points – Warwickshire 4, Northamptonshire 4.

In the second innings K. J. Piper, when 0, retired hurt at 9 and resumed at 94.

Bowling: *First Innings*—Malcolm 13–2–55–0; Taylor 18–3–74–3; Follett 18–1–83–0; Brown 37–7–114–5; Swann 8–2–17–0; Curran 3–0–25–0; Bailey 7–0–20–2. *Second Innings*—Taylor 12–2–58–4; Follett 9–0–40–2; Brown 2.4–0–14–0.

Umpires: J. H. Hampshire and K. E. Palmer.

NORTHAMPTONSHIRE v KENT

At Northampton, August 26, 27, 28, 29. Drawn. Northamptonshire 11 pts, Kent 6 pts. Toss: Kent.

Northamptonshire appeared on course for a comfortable victory when Kent slipped to 114 for five on the final morning, still 59 runs away from making their opponents bat again. But Hooper and Wells came to the rescue, adding 176 in 51 overs. Hooper was unbeaten at the close, having hit four sixes and 16 fours in a delightful exhibition of strokeplay which blended power and touch in equal measure. Wells also held Kent together in their first innings while the other batsmen struggled against the seamers. Bailey and Swann then provided Northamptonshire with their best start of the season, compiling 166 in 59 overs. Penberthy followed up with another useful half-century, and only some lively fast bowling from Headley prevented a huge score.

Close of play: First day, Kent 83-4 (A. P. Wells 19*, C. D. Walsh 14*); Second day, Northamptonshire 153-0 (R. J. Bailey 75*, A. J. Swann 66*); Third day, Kent 64-2 (E. T. Smith 15*, B. J. Phillips 0*).

Kent

D. P. Fulton b Rose	0	– lbw b Taylor	20
E. T. Smith lbw b Taylor	1	– c Ripley b Taylor	33
T. R. Ward c Ripley b Rose	13	– lbw b Bailey	23
C. L. Hooper c Ripley b Rose	22	– (7) not out	157
A. P. Wells c Curran b Taylor	79	– (6) b Brown	77
C. D. Walsh c Swann b Taylor	20	– (5) b Rose	8
M. V. Fleming c Curran b Taylor	2	– (8) c Curran b Brown	8
*†S. A. Marsh c Bailey b Brown	33	– (9) not out	15
B. J. Phillips b Follett	2	– (4) b Follett	5
D. W. Headley not out	12		
M. M. Patel c Curran b Rose	0		
B 4, l-b 8, w 4, n-b 18	34	B 12, l-b 7, n-b 12	31

1/0 2/8 3/28 4/45 5/110   218   1/33 2/63 3/71   (7 wkts dec.) 377
6/112 7/189 8/194 9/215   4/94 5/114
                          6/290 7/340

Bonus points – Kent 1, Northamptonshire 4.

Bowling: *First Innings*—Rose 20.3–2–75–4; Taylor 25–4–71–4; Brown 15–3–41–1; Follett 10–5–19–1. *Second Innings*—Rose 15–2–51–1; Taylor 13–5–30–2; Brown 43–8–148–2; Bailey 11–1–52–1; Follett 23–4–47–1; Penberthy 6–0–26–0; Swann 1–0–4–0.

Northamptonshire

R. J. Bailey lbw b Headley	79	F. A. Rose c Fulton b Hooper	19
A. J. Swann lbw b Headley	85	D. Follett not out	6
M. B. Loye c Fleming b Patel	38	J. F. Brown c Headley b Hooper	1
*K. M. Curran b Headley	3		
A. L. Penberthy b Headley	61	B 2, l-b 14, w 8, n-b 12	36
D. J. Sales lbw b Headley	22		
†D. Ripley c Headley b Hooper	20	1/166 2/189 3/193 4/261 5/322	391
J. P. Taylor c Marsh b Fleming	21	6/327 7/360 8/380 9/388	

Bonus points – Northamptonshire 4, Kent 2 (Score at 120 overs: 352-6).

Bowling: Headley 31–5–79–5; Phillips 27–9–56–0; Fleming 37–11–87–1; Hooper 24.3–1–80–3; Patel 15–1–73–1.

Umpires: J. H. Harris and P. Willey.

At Bristol, September 1, 2. NORTHAMPTONSHIRE lost to GLOUCESTERSHIRE by ten wickets.

NORTHAMPTONSHIRE v SUSSEX

At Northampton, September 9, 10, 11. Northamptonshire won by 136 runs. Northamptonshire 20 pts, Sussex 4 pts. Toss: Northamptonshire.

Northamptonshire's satisfaction at notching their third Championship victory of the season lasted only as long as it took for a fax to arrive from the ECB, confirming that the county had been deducted 25 points for an unfit pitch. A panel, led by former England captain Mike Denness, was called in by the Board's consultant, Harry Brind, on the second day, and delivered a detailed and damning report on a strip which "displayed uneven bounce and turned excessively early in the match". The same pitch had been marked "poor" by the umpires when it was used for an

TEAMS PENALISED FOR UNSUITABLE PITCHES

The home county had 25 points deducted in each case.

Essex*	v Yorkshire at Southend	1989
Nottinghamshire	v Derbyshire at Nottingham	1989
Derbyshire	v Middlesex at Derby	1990
Lancashire	v Middlesex at Manchester	1994
Northamptonshire	v Sussex at Northampton	1998

* Essex would have been county champions but for this deduction.

AXA League match ten days earlier, and no serious attempt at renovation was made in the intervening period. Northamptonshire's three spinners all bagged five-wicket hauls, in ideal conditions, with career-best figures for Davies and Graeme Swann, and also for Bates of Sussex. The only batsman to prosper was Northamptonshire captain Curran, who hit the highest two scores of the game, as if trying to silence the swelling chorus of condemnation. Swann finished the match with four full sessions to spare, taking the last five wickets in eight overs.

Close of play: First day, Northamptonshire 102-6 (K. M. Curran 21*, G. P. Swann 13*); Second day, Northamptonshire 104-4 (K. M. Curran 37*, K. J. Innes 31*).

Northamptonshire

R. J. Bailey c Peirce b Kirtley	9	– c Humphries b Kirtley	4
A. J. Swann lbw b Edwards	9	– c Peirce b Bates	12
A. L. Penberthy c Adams b Bates	12	– b Bates	11
*K. M. Curran c Martin-Jenkins b Bates	60	– lbw b Bates	46
D. J. Sales lbw b Bates	13	– lbw b Bates	0
K. J. Innes b Robinson	6	– b Robinson	31
†D. Ripley b Robinson	5	– run out	5
G. P. Swann c and b Bates	26	– lbw b Robinson	12
J. P. Taylor c Newell b Kirtley	7	– c Humphries b Kirtley	22
M. K. Davies not out	3	– c Newell b Bates	4
J. F. Brown b Kirtley	2	– not out	0
B 4, l-b 4, n-b 18	26	B 4, l-b 10, n-b 4	18

1/14 2/34 3/36 4/54 5/69   178   1/4 2/28 3/31 4/35 5/104   165
6/81 7/142 8/165 9/175   6/113 7/131 8/135 9/163

Bonus points – Sussex 4.

Bowling: *First Innings*—Kirtley 15–2–48–3; Edwards 5–0–19–1; Bates 28–4–69–4; Robinson 19–9–34–2. *Second Innings*—Kirtley 7–4–9–2; Edwards 3–0–8–0; Bates 23.5–7–67–5; Robinson 14–6–32–2; Rao 12–2–35–0.

Sussex

M. T. E. Peirce b Davies	9	– b Taylor	1
W. G. Khan lbw b Davies	0	– b Davies	28
*C. J. Adams lbw b Davies	13	– run out	14
R. K. Rao c Sales b Brown	15	– c Penberthy b Taylor	0
K. Newell b Brown	3	– c Ripley b Davies	14
R. S. C. Martin-Jenkins b Brown	10	– lbw b G. P. Swann	20
A. D. Edwards c Brown b Davies	6	– lbw b G. P. Swann	4
†S. Humphries c Innes b Davies	0	– c Penberthy b G. P. Swann	17
J. J. Bates b Brown	4	– b G. P. Swann	4
R. J. Kirtley not out	2	– c Innes b G. P. Swann	12
M. A. Robinson c G. P. Swann b Brown	0	– not out	4
B 1, l-b 7, w 2	10	B 5, l-b 12	17

1/4 2/19 3/35 4/48 5/49   72   1/2 2/23 3/23 4/59 5/82   135
6/66 7/66 8/66 9/72   6/94 7/105 8/111 9/127

Bonus points – Northamptonshire 4.

Bowling: *First Innings*—Taylor 7–2–20–0; Penberthy 2–1–2–0; Davies 19–10–19–5; Brown 15.5–3–23–5. *Second Innings*—Taylor 6–2–10–2; Penberthy 3–1–17–0; Davies 20–7–35–2; Brown 13–5–27–0; G. P. Swann 13.1–5–29–5.

Umpires: T. E. Jesty and R. A. White.

At Chelmsford, September 17, 18, 19. NORTHAMPTONSHIRE beat ESSEX by seven wickets.

NOTTINGHAMSHIRE

Paul Franks

President: K. A. Taylor
Chairmen: A. Wheelhouse/J. R. Cope
Chairman, Cricket Committee: S. Foster
Chief Executive: M. Arthur
Secretary: B. Robson
Captains: 1998 – P. Johnson/J. E. R. Gallian
1999 – J. E. R. Gallian
Cricket Manager: 1998 – J. A. Ormrod
1999 – C. E. B. Rice
Head Groundsman: S. Birks
Scorer: G. Stringfellow

Nottinghamshire's greatest desire is to recapture the glory days of Clive Rice's captaincy. After a season which yet again fell well below expectations and plunged into a steep decline, Alan Ormrod lost his job as cricket manager, which he had held since 1994. Everyone agreed that there was only one man for the job, the inspirational leader who had lifted Nottinghamshire out of the doldrums two decades ago.

Initially, Rice offered little encouragement. He said it was two years too early, given his circumstances at home in South Africa. Nottinghamshire were determined, however, to get their man. When they dangled a financial carrot that was too good to resist, he reorganised his other commitments and accepted.

That news lifted some of the gloom from Trent Bridge. Nottinghamshire's dismal home form had been their biggest stumbling block; a quarter-final appearance in the NatWest Trophy was the brightest spot of the season. Losing the first six home games in the Sunday League wrecked their hopes of qualifying for the top division of the new National League, and embarrassing defeats in the last four Championship matches, all of them at home, saw them slip to 16th. In total, 17 of 23 home games ended in defeat, and the exciting one-wicket victory over Somerset in the NatWest Trophy was one of only four home wins.

There had been good grounds for optimism back in April: three quality signings, Jason Gallian, Paul Strang and Chris Read, had joined a young squad that had shown promise in 1997. But it took barely 48 overs on the opening day of the season, at a bleak and blustery Derby, for their high hopes to be blown away, when they were bowled out for 118. It was a grim struggle from then on, leaving three victims in its trail.

Paul Johnson was the first, his patience running out after waiting so long for Nottinghamshire's fortunes to change. He decided to hand over the captaincy to Gallian when the last hope of success disappeared in the NatWest. Johnson's resignation was quickly followed by the departure of bowling coach Eddie Hemmings. Finally, Ormrod paid the price for poor results. His dismissal came as concern rose about Nottinghamshire's lack of fight, a problem highlighted when they were dismissed for 61 by Leicestershire, and suffered one of the heaviest defeats in their history. The last 56 Championship matches of Ormrod's reign produced only eight wins. While he maintained he was leaving a promising squad, he blamed the senior batsmen for failing to deliver.

He had a case. Inconsistent batting was again the root of Nottinghamshire's problems. Though Johnson looked more like his old self after shedding the captaincy, reaching 976 runs, no other batsman got anywhere near that. Tim Robinson missed the last two months of the season with a broken wrist, when he was running into form, and Gallian was hit by injury early on. But Mathew Dowman failed to build on his success in 1997, Graeme Archer had just one purple patch and Paul Pollard's early struggles led to his release (he moved on to Worcestershire). The real enigma was Usman Afzaal, who went from one extreme to another; he was probably a little over-exposed after being handed the problem No. 3 spot.

Gallian must have wondered what he had let himself in for when he left Lancashire, especially when the chance to build a captain–manager partnership with Ormrod, the man who had brought him from Australia to England in the first place, was snatched away. Extra responsibility was, of course, something Gallian was seeking when he moved to Trent Bridge, but he did not expect it so soon. The burden weighed on his shoulders, and his form declined dramatically. Of the other new faces, Strang failed to repeat his success of the previous season with Kent, although the wet summer did not help. But Read suggested he could be a future England wicket-keeper – he took over when Wayne Noon broke a finger at Edgbaston – and also played some capable innings.

Read was one member of the younger generation to emerge with credit; another was Paul Franks, whose 52 Championship wickets made him the leading bowler by far. Franks spearheaded a steady seam department, which rarely allowed the batsmen to get on top; Andy Oram overcame fitness problems, and Chris Tolley confirmed he was a useful signing. The spin picture was not so bright. Apart from Strang's difficulties, slow left-armer Jimmy Hindson was released; he had struggled for three seasons, after being the county's leading wicket-taker in 1995. In November, Richard Stemp was signed from Yorkshire.

A season which Nottinghamshire will want to forget had at least one happy moment. There was the opening of the magnificent £7.2 million Radcliffe Road Stand and Trent Bridge Cricket Centre, much admired during England's victory in the Fourth Test. But in August the club mourned the death of their highly respected chairman, Alan Wheelhouse, which put the problems on the field into perspective. – NICK LUCY.

NOTTINGHAMSHIRE 1998

[Bill Smith]

Back row: S. J. Randall, L. N. P. Walker, U. Afzaal, P. J. Franks, J. P. Hart, A. R. Oram, G. E. Welton, N. A. Gie, C. M. W. Read. Middle row: S. A. Ball (physiotherapist), C. M. Tolley, G. F. Archer, R. T. Bates, M. N. Bowen, A. G. Wharf, J. E. Hindson, W. M. Noon, M. P. Dowman. Front row: E. E. Hemmings (coach), J. E. R. Gallian, K. P. Evans, R. T. Robinson, J. A. Ormrod (cricket manager), P. Johnson (captain), P. A. Strang, P. R. Pollard, M. Newell.

NOTTINGHAMSHIRE RESULTS

All first-class matches – Played 17: Won 3, Lost 10, Drawn 4.

County Championship matches – Played 17: Won 3, Lost 10, Drawn 4.

*Competition placings – Britannic Assurance County Championship, 16th;
NatWest Trophy, q-f; Benson and Hedges Cup, 4th in Group A;
AXA League, 11th.*

COUNTY CHAMPIONSHIP AVERAGES

BATTING

Cap		M	I	NO	R	HS	100s	50s	Avge	Ct/St
1986	P. Johnson†	15	26	1	976	139	2	4	39.04	14
1983	R. T. Robinson† . . .	11	18	2	553	114	1	4	34.56	6
1995	G. F. Archer	13	23	0	647	107	1	5	28.13	23
1998	J. E. R. Gallian	14	25	3	592	113*	1	3	26.90	8
	U. Afzaal	17	30	3	686	109*	2	4	25.40	7
	C. M. W. Read	13	22	6	401	76	0	2	25.06	39/3
1997	C. M. Tolley	11	19	2	374	78	0	2	22.00	5
	P. J. Franks†	12	20	2	390	66*	0	2	21.66	6
	P. A. Strang§	13	18	3	300	48	0	0	20.00	19
1998	M. P. Dowman	13	24	1	451	63	0	2	19.60	7
1997	M. N. Bowen	10	13	5	142	32	0	0	17.75	2
1992	P. R. Pollard†	4	7	0	121	69	0	1	17.28	3
	G. E. Welton	5	9	0	152	55	0	1	16.88	3
	N. A. Gie.	4	8	0	128	50	0	1	16.00	3
1990	K. P. Evans†	9	13	0	129	36	0	0	9.92	3
	R. T. Bates.	2	4	2	17	7	0	0	8.50	7
1995	W. M. Noon	4	5	1	22	16*	0	0	5.50	9
	A. R. Oram	11	19	8	39	13	0	0	3.54	0
	A. G. Wharf	5	6	1	8	3	0	0	1.60	6

Also batted: M. J. A. Whiley† (1 match) 0, 0*.

* Signifies not out.   † Born in Nottinghamshire.   § Overseas player.

BOWLING

	O	M	R	W	BB	5W/i	Avge
P. J. Franks	404.2	87	1,375	52	6-63	4	26.44
K. P. Evans	273	73	735	27 ,	5-92	2	27.22
M. N. Bowen	309.1	76	875	31	7-73	1	28.22
C. M. Tolley	324.3	76	960	34	7-45	3	28.23
A. R. Oram	305.5	75	969	31	4-37	0	31.25
P. A. Strang	353.3	105	983	30	5-166	1	32.76
M. P. Dowman	139	31	397	12	2-10	0	33.08

Also bowled: U. Afzaal 75.4–9–292–7; R. T. Bates 21–2–98–0; J. E. R. Gallian 47.1–13–103–2;
A. G. Wharf 83.1–14–333–9; M. J. A. Whiley 29–4–124–1.

COUNTY RECORDS

Highest score for:	312*	W. W. Keeton v Middlesex at The Oval	1939
Highest score against:	345	C. G. Macartney (Australians) at Nottingham . . .	1921
Best bowling for:	10-66	K. Smales v Gloucestershire at Stroud	1956
Best bowling against:	10-10	H. Verity (Yorkshire) at Leeds	1932
Highest total for:	739-7 dec.	v Leicestershire at Nottingham	1903
Highest total against:	781-7 dec.	by Northamptonshire at Northampton	1995
Lowest total for:	13	v Yorkshire at Nottingham	1901
Lowest total against:	{ 16	by Derbyshire at Nottingham	1879
	16	by Surrey at The Oval	1880

At Derby, April 17, 18, 19, 20. NOTTINGHAMSHIRE lost to DERBYSHIRE by six wickets.

At Taunton, April 23, 24, 25, 27. NOTTINGHAMSHIRE drew with SOMERSET.

NOTTINGHAMSHIRE v SUSSEX

At Nottingham, May 13, 14, 15. Sussex won by four wickets. Sussex 23 pts, Nottinghamshire 6 pts. Toss: Sussex. Championship debut: S. Humphries.

Kirtley swung the ball with devastating effect to set up Sussex's first victory over Nottinghamshire since 1977. It almost slipped away on the third afternoon; after reaching 52 without loss, chasing a modest 74, Sussex suddenly lost six wickets, but they edged nervously home. Despite a shaky start, Nottinghamshire had the better of the first day; Johnson hit 68 off 75 balls, and two Sussex wickets fell without a run on the board. But Peirce held firm for five and a half hours, with Carpenter helping him add 147. Though he missed his hundred, Peirce guided his team to a 49-run lead. Then Kirtley snatched three wickets on the second evening, which became six for three in 39 balls when he continued his trail of destruction next morning. Nottinghamshire slumped to 23 for seven. Gallian, using a runner because of a torn groin muscle, and Strang added 83, but Kirtley mopped up to finish with a career-best seven for 29, and ten for 88 in the match.

Close of play: First day, Sussex 49-3 (M. T. E. Peirce 22*, R. J. Kirtley 1*); Second day, Nottinghamshire 11-3 (M. P. Dowman 7*).

Nottinghamshire

P. R. Pollard lbw b Lewry	24	– lbw b Kirtley	0
M. P. Dowman c Newell b Kirtley	1	– lbw b Kirtley	7
J. E. R. Gallian c Adams b Kirtley	3	– (7) b Lewry	33
*P. Johnson c Khan b Kirtley	68	– (5) b Lewry	7
R. T. Robinson c Humphries b Lewry	31	– (4) c Jarvis b Kirtley	0
U. Afzaal c Humphries b Bevan	22	– lbw b Kirtley	0
†W. M. Noon c Bevan b Robinson	0	– (8) c Adams b Kirtley	0
P. A. Strang b Lewry	48	– (9) b Lewry	48
A. G. Wharf lbw b Bevan	0	– (3) c Adams b Kirtley	0
M. N. Bowen c Humphries b Lewry	25	– not out	8
A. R. Oram not out	2	– b Kirtley	4
L-b 7, w 22, n-b 22	51	L-b 9, n-b 6	15
	275		**122**

1/4 2/16 3/96 4/120 5/165 6/166 7/211 8/211 9/268 **275**

1/1 2/1 3/11 4/14 5/14 6/22 7/23 8/106 9/111 **122**

Bonus points – Nottinghamshire 2, Sussex 4.

Bowling: *First Innings*—Lewry 18.3–3–57–4; Kirtley 19–5–59–3; Jarvis 18–3–59–0; Robinson 14–0–60–1; Bevan 6–1–28–2; Peirce 1–0–5–0. *Second Innings*—Lewry 13–6–32–3; Kirtley 14.3–6–29–7; Jarvis 6–0–35–0; Robinson 4–0–17–0.

Sussex

M. T. E. Peirce lbw b Dowman	96	– c Pollard b Wharf	21
W. G. Khan c Wharf b Oram	0	– c Wharf b Strang	27
*C. J. Adams run out	0	– (4) c Noon b Wharf	4
M. G. Bevan lbw b Bowen	18	– (5) b Strang	7
R. J. Kirtley b Strang	6		
J. R. Carpenter run out	65	– lbw b Wharf	1
K. Newell b Dowman	48	– not out	4
†S. Humphries c Noon b Bowen	19	– (3) lbw b Strang	2
P. W. Jarvis lbw b Strang	25	– (8) not out	1
J. D. Lewry b Bowen	0		
M. A. Robinson not out	3		
B 3, l-b 13, w 10, n-b 18	44	L-b 1, w 4, n-b 2	7

1/0 2/0 3/47 4/61 5/208   324   1/52 2/52 3/58   (6 wkts) 74
6/223 7/283 8/311 9/312   4/58 5/59 6/69

Bonus points – Sussex 3, Nottinghamshire 4 (Score at 120 overs: 324-9).

Bowling: *First Innings*—Bowen 30.5–7–79–3; Oram 24–6–61–1; Wharf 18–3–61–0; Strang 29.3–10–74–2; Gallian 1.1–1–0–0; Dowman 18–5–33–2. *Second Innings*—Bowen 6–1–11–0; Oram 4–0–11–0; Strang 10–2–26–3; Wharf 8–3–25–3.

Umpires: V. A. Holder and R. Palmer.

At Birmingham, May 21, 22, 23, 24. NOTTINGHAMSHIRE beat WARWICKSHIRE by six wickets.

NOTTINGHAMSHIRE v DURHAM

At Nottingham, May 29, 30, 31. Durham won by eight wickets. Durham 22 pts, Nottinghamshire 5 pts. Toss: Durham. Championship debut: C. M. W. Read.

Durham won their first away Championship match since Swansea in 1995, and their first ever on a Test ground. The three-day victory carried them to third place in the table. On the first day, when the new Radcliffe Road Stand was "topped out", Betts took five wickets to dismiss the home side for 211. More than half of that came from Franks, with 66 in two hours, and Extras. But Nottinghamshire, captained by the Zimbabwean Strang because Johnson had a bad shoulder, hit back to reduce Durham to 98 for six. The match turned again when the belligerent Foster joined Collingwood in a stand of 110, a county seventh-wicket record. The game was evenly balanced when last man Harmison came in, with Durham five ahead. But Collingwood, whose first fifty took four hours, skilfully manipulated the strike, racing to 97 in the next half-hour, and making the lead 58. Foster removed both Robinson and Archer, just when they looked threatening, and ensured that Durham's target was only 167. They lost two early wickets then coasted.

Close of play: First day, Durham 67-4 (P. D. Collingwood 3*, J. Wood 2*); Second day, Nottinghamshire 144-4 (N. A. Gie 12*, M. N. Bowen 5*).

Nottinghamshire

M. P. Dowman c Speak b Harmison	13	– c Speak b Wood	8
R. T. Robinson b Wood	0	– c Speight b Foster	64
U. Afzaal c Collingwood b Betts	25	– lbw b Wood	0
G. F. Archer b Foster	11	– b Foster	44
N. A. Gie b Betts	20	– c Lewis b Foster	20
C. M. Tolley lbw b Foster	7	– (7) c Phillips b Foster	6
P. J. Franks c Speight b Betts	66	– (8) c Foster b Wood	4
†C. M. W. Read lbw b Betts	0	– (9) not out	16
*P. A. Strang c and b Betts	13	– (10) c Phillips b Betts	10
M. N. Bowen not out	9	– (6) c Speight b Betts	32
A. R. Oram c Speight b Wood	1	– c Speight b Harmison	1
B 9, l-b 3, w 20, n-b 14	46	B 1, l-b 1, w 13, n-b 4	19

1/8 2/24 3/64 4/68 5/85   211   1/15 2/15 3/108 4/131 5/152   224
6/179 7/179 8/199 9/206   6/168 7/183 8/202 9/216

Bonus points – Nottinghamshire 1, Durham 4.

Bowling: *First Innings*—Betts 21–7–59–5; Wood 16.3–5–50–2; Harmison 16–5–57–1; Foster 9–4–26–2; Phillips 4–0–7–0. *Second Innings*—Betts 22–5–71–2; Wood 21–5–62–3; Harmison 9.1–3–29–1; Phillips 5–1–16–0; Foster 15–3–41–4; Gough 1–0–3–0.

Durham

J. J. B. Lewis lbw b Franks	15	– c Franks b Oram	8
M. A. Gough c Archer b Tolley	23	– lbw b Strang	21
N. J. Speak c Archer b Tolley	16	– not out	77
*D. C. Boon lbw b Strang	4	– not out	54
P. D. Collingwood not out	97		
J. Wood lbw b Franks	16		
†M. P. Speight c Archer b Oram	0		
M. J. Foster c and b Tolley	68		
N. C. Phillips c Bowen b Tolley	4		
M. M. Betts lbw b Tolley	0		
S. J. Harmison lbw b Strang	3		
B 1, l-b 12, w 10	23	L-b 7	7

1/23 2/55 3/60 4/64 5/91   269   1/28 2/47   (2 wkts) 167
6/98 7/208 8/216 9/216

Bonus points – Durham 2, Nottinghamshire 4.

Bowling: *First Innings*—Bowen 21–8–45–0; Franks 19–4–73–2; Dowman 6–1–21–0; Oram 18–8–52–1; Tolley 25–10–48–5; Strang 7.3–3–17–2. *Second Innings*—Oram 10–2–35–1; Franks 11–1–32–0; Tolley 5–0–17–0; Strang 13.2–4–37–1; Bowen 7–1–20–0; Dowman 4–0–19–0.

Umpires: J. H. Hampshire and P. Willey.

At Ilford, June 3, 4, 5, 6. NOTTINGHAMSHIRE drew with ESSEX.

At Nottingham, June 10. NOTTINGHAMSHIRE lost to SOUTH AFRICANS by 22 runs (See South African tour section).

At Canterbury, June 17, 18, 19, 20. NOTTINGHAMSHIRE lost to KENT by three wickets.

NOTTINGHAMSHIRE v GLAMORGAN

At Nottingham, June 26, 27, 28, 29. Glamorgan won by 46 runs. Glamorgan 20 pts, Nottinghamshire 3 pts. Toss: Glamorgan.

Rain permitted only nine overs on the first two days, and Maynard questioned the standard of the covering; the edges of the square were saturated, causing long delays. Despite the hold-ups, Glamorgan completed their first Championship win since April. Sunday started badly for James, who learned he was being dropped by England after a single Test. A fax followed from his friend Atherton, urging him to keep his chin up, and he responded with his third hundred of the season, exploiting two lives to bat three and a half hours. Two declarations and a forfeiture left Nottinghamshire to chase 321 on the last day. Afzaal batted defiantly, but they never looked like winning until Archer cut loose, hitting his first century since September 1996. It was all in vain; he was last out with eight overs to go.

Close of play: First day, No play; Second day, Glamorgan 45-1 (S. P. James 21*, M. J. Powell 0*); Third day, Nottinghamshire 31-2 dec.

Glamorgan

S. P. James c Read b Evans	121	
A. Dale c Archer b Oram	22	
M. J. Powell c Read b Evans	7	
*M. P. Maynard c Johnson b Oram	2	
P. A. Cottey c Johnson b Dowman	37	
†A. D. Shaw c Johnson b Tolley	6	
G. P. Butcher c Archer b Dowman	31	
R. D. B. Croft not out	63	

S. D. Thomas c sub b Afzaal	41
S. L. Watkin not out	2
B 5, l-b 8, n-b 6	19
	—
1/45 2/52 3/89 (8 wkts dec.)	351
4/170 5/205 6/212	
7/274 8/347	

O. T. Parkin did not bat.

Bonus points – Glamorgan 4, Nottinghamshire 3.

Bowling: Oram 13–5–40–2; Bowen 17–2–66–0; Evans 21–2–84–2; Tolley 25–5–77–1; Dowman 19–7–42–2; Afzaal 6–1–29–1.

Glamorgan forfeited their second innings.

Nottinghamshire

M. P. Dowman c Maynard b Watkin	4	– c Shaw b Parkin	10
J. E. R. Gallian not out	13	– lbw b Watkin	3
U. Afzaal lbw b Dale	1	– lbw b Dale	51
R. T. Robinson not out	13	– c Maynard b Thomas	12
*P. Johnson (did not bat)		– c James b Parkin	40
G. F. Archer (did not bat)		– c Croft b Thomas	107
C. M. Tolley (did not bat)		– c Shaw b Thomas	1
†C. M. W. Read (did not bat)		– c Cottey b Thomas	14
K. P. Evans (did not bat)		– run out	1
M. N. Bowen (did not bat)		– c Cottey b Parkin	14
A. R. Oram (did not bat)		– not out	0
		B 8, l-b 1, w 4, n-b 8	21

		—	
1/4 2/8	(2 wkts dec.) 31	1/3 2/17 3/57 4/103 5/155	274
		6/161 7/216 8/224 9/264	

Bowling: *First Innings*—Watkin 3–1–8–1; Parkin 3–3–0–0; Dale 2–0–11–1; Cottey 2–1–7–0; Maynard 0.4–0–5–0. *Second Innings*—Watkin 18–4–43–1; Parkin 21–8–60–3; Butcher 8–0–37–0; Thomas 20–4–78–4; Dale 8–1–22–1; Croft 13–4–25–0.

Umpires: J. W. Lloyds and P. Willey.

NOTTINGHAMSHIRE v MIDDLESEX

At Nottingham, July 1, 2, 3. Nottinghamshire won by an innings and 92 runs. Nottinghamshire 23 pts, Middlesex 3 pts. Toss: Middlesex. Championship debut: C. J. Batt.

Nottinghamshire pulled themselves off the bottom of the table with a second win. Their bowlers had a difficult first morning; Gatting and Langer cruised to 97, continuing their record-breaking form from their last match. Then, just before lunch, Tolley grabbed three wickets in seven balls. It changed the complexion of the innings – Middlesex collapsed without a batting point. But Championship newcomer Chris Batt, a left-arm seamer previously with Sussex, hit back with three wickets in 11 balls before the close. Nottinghamshire could have followed in their visitors' footsteps. Afzaal, however, played a disciplined six-hour innings – with only 42 scoring strokes in his 251 balls – to wear down the Middlesex bowlers. Read profited, hitting 12 fours in a lively maiden fifty, before becoming one of Batt's six victims. Middlesex trailed by 215, and lost night-watchman Johnson in four balls on the second evening. Next day, they subsided tamely as Franks took five wickets for the first time to claim a match haul of eight for 96.

Close of play: First day, Nottinghamshire 119-3 (U. Afzaal 3*, K. P. Evans 9*); Second day, Middlesex 0-1 (J. L. Langer 0*).

Middlesex

M. W. Gatting c Franks b Tolley	32	– (3) c Johnson b Franks	4
J. L. Langer b Franks	74	– lbw b Evans	29
O. A. Shah c Read b Tolley	0	– (4) c Wharf b Franks	0
P. N. Weekes c Archer b Tolley	0	– (5) c Read b Tolley	25
D. C. Nash c Johnson b Tolley	15	– (6) c Strang b Evans	10
*†K. R. Brown c Gallian b Franks	22	– (7) c Read b Wharf	9
J. P. Hewitt b Strang	22	– (8) c Gallian b Franks	19
R. L. Johnson c Gallian b Franks	0	– (1) c Wharf b Franks	0
C. J. Batt b Strang	6	– c Afzaal b Franks	7
P. C. R. Tufnell not out	0	– b Wharf	8
T. F. Bloomfield run out	0	– not out	3
B 3, l-b 8, w 2, n-b 14	27	L-b 1, n-b 8	9

1/97 2/101 3/101 4/131 5/151   198   1/0 2/8 3/8 4/44 5/70   123
6/188 7/188 8/193 9/198   6/72 7/94 8/106 9/119

Bonus points – Nottinghamshire 4.

Bowling: *First Innings*—Franks 15–5–38–3; Wharf 9–2–40–0; Evans 20–8–43–0; Tolley 18–7–51–4; Strang 7.2–3–15–2. *Second Innings*—Franks 14–3–58–5; Wharf 8.1–1–27–2; Tolley 8–0–23–1; Evans 10–6–8–2; Strang 1–0–6–0.

Nottinghamshire

R. T. Robinson c Gatting b Batt	35	†C. M. W. Read c Brown b Batt	76
J. E. R. Gallian c Weekes b Batt	52	P. A. Strang b Batt	40
U. Afzaal c Shah b Johnson	73	A. G. Wharf not out	1
*P. Johnson lbw b Batt	0		
K. P. Evans lbw b Bloomfield	22	B 3, l-b 26, w 4, n-b 10	43
G. F. Archer c Weekes b Johnson	51		
C. M. Tolley c Brown b Batt	15	1/105 2/108 3/108 4/141 5/227	413
P. J. Franks lbw b Weekes	5	6/266 7/285 8/304 9/400	

Bonus points – Nottinghamshire 3, Middlesex 3 (Score at 120 overs: 340-8).

Bowling: Hewitt 18–6–60–0; Bloomfield 23–6–74–1; Johnson 27–5–89–2; Batt 29–6–101–6; Tufnell 21–9–43–0; Weekes 16–6–17–1; Langer 1–1–0–0.

Umpires: A. Clarkson and J. W. Holder.

At Scarborough, July 15, 16, 17, 18. NOTTINGHAMSHIRE drew with YORKSHIRE.

At Portsmouth, July 22, 23, 24. NOTTINGHAMSHIRE lost to HAMPSHIRE by seven wickets.

NOTTINGHAMSHIRE v NORTHAMPTONSHIRE

At Nottingham, July 30, 31, August 1, 3. Drawn. Nottinghamshire 11 pts, Northamptonshire 8 pts. Toss: Nottinghamshire.

The match began with the accession of Gallian to the Nottinghamshire captaincy. But rain had delayed the start and stymied the county's plans for a public announcement, so the news spread only after careful observers of the scorecard noted that he had been given the asterisk. Johnson, his predecessor, had resigned the day before, blaming the pressure of the job for his poor form. His last official duty was to present Gallian with his cap. The last day was rained off as well; even so, it was a batsman's match. Loye continued his splendid run with his fourth century of the season, and deserved better support from Northamptonshire's lower order, who let 323 for five slip to 346 all out. Johnson then eloquently proved his point by hitting only his third hundred since his appointment as captain nearly three years before. Freed of inhibitions, he reached 100 from 98 balls, and he put on 170 with Afzaal. Gallian, aware of the grim weather forecast, put batting points before the contrivance of a run-chase, and Nottinghamshire ended the third day a meaningless 34 ahead.

Close of play: First day, Northamptonshire 129-2 (J. P. Taylor 9*, M. B. Loye 4*); Second day, Nottinghamshire 56-0 (G. E. Welton 20*, J. E. R. Gallian 25*); Third day, Nottinghamshire 380-5 (U. Afzaal 103*, C. M. Tolley 20*).

Northamptonshire

R. R. Montgomerie c Strang b Evans...	54	F. A. Rose c sub b Strang		7
R. J. Bailey c Strang b Bowen	42	D. E. Malcolm c Dowman b Evans		0
J. P. Taylor c Welton b Strang	20	J. F. Brown c Archer b Strang		0
M. B. Loye c Johnson b Dowman	103			
*K. M. Curran c Strang b Tolley	15	L-b 3, n-b 22		25
A. L. Penberthy b Strang	49			—
D. J. Sales c Strang b Evans	20	1/114 2/114 3/158 4/206 5/286		346
†D. Ripley not out	11	6/323 7/327 8/335 9/336		

Bonus points – Northamptonshire 3, Nottinghamshire 4.

Bowling: Evans 31–6–88–3; Bowen 15–2–54–1; Tolley 26–7–61–1; Strang 30.5–4–92–4; Dowman 14–1–31–1; Afzaal 3–1–17–0.

Nottinghamshire

G. E. Welton b Taylor	55	C. M. Tolley not out		20
*J. E. R. Gallian lbw b Taylor	25			
U. Afzaal not out	103	B 5, l-b 13, n-b 22		40
P. Johnson lbw b Taylor	105			—
M. P. Dowman c Ripley b Bailey	20	1/66 2/123 3/293	(5 wkts)	380
G. F. Archer c Loye b Taylor	12	4/323 5/349		

†C. M. W. Read, P. A. Strang, K. P. Evans and M. N. Bowen did not bat.

Bonus points – Nottinghamshire 4, Northamptonshire 2.

Bowling: Malcolm 21–2–93–0; Rose 24–5–105–0; Taylor 30.1–13–62–4; Curran 4–1–13–0; Brown 14–2–48–0; Penberthy 7–2–21–0; Sales 2–0–8–0; Bailey 5–1–12–1.

Umpires: V. A. Holder and A. A. Jones.

At Kidderminster, August 5, 6, 7, 8. NOTTINGHAMSHIRE beat WORCESTERSHIRE by 90 runs.

NOTTINGHAMSHIRE v SURREY

At Nottingham, August 19, 20, 21. Surrey won by seven wickets. Surrey 22 pts, Nottinghamshire 5 pts. Toss: Surrey.

Surrey consolidated their position at the top of the table with a convincing win over a fragile Nottinghamshire, who had prepared a well-grassed pitch to counter the threat of Saqlain Mushtaq and Salisbury. The ploy backfired when the Surrey seamers took full advantage of the conditions and threatened to wrap up victory in two days. Asked to bat, Nottinghamshire stumbled to 92 for six before England A wicket-keeper Read rescued them with a mature, unbeaten 66. Then Butcher and Shahid, the only other batsmen to reach fifty, looked to have put Surrey in total command at 245 for five – until the remaining wickets fell for 25. But a deficit of 57 assumed huge proportions as Nottinghamshire collapsed again. When bad light ended play six overs early on the second day, they were 22 ahead with seven down; more rain and some belated resistance delayed Surrey's victory until just after lunch on the third. Hollioake took a career-best four for 28.

Close of play: First day, Surrey 84-2 (M. A. Butcher 38*, B. C. Hollioake 18*); Second day, Nottinghamshire 79-7 (C. M. W. Read 3*, P. A. Strang 1*).

Nottinghamshire

G. E. Welton c Batty b Benjamin	7	– c Batty b Hollioake 15
*J. E. R. Gallian c Butcher b Hollioake	23	– lbw b Bicknell 17
U. Afzaal c Batty b Benjamin	8	– c Batty b Bicknell 0
P. Johnson c Batty b Benjamin	8	– lbw b Hollioake 14
G. F. Archer c Butcher b Bicknell	37	– b Bicknell 0
C. M. Tolley c Hollioake b Bicknell	4	– lbw b Benjamin 17
P. J. Franks c Butcher b Hollioake	8	– b Hollioake 0
†C. M. W. Read not out	66	– not out 10
P. A. Strang run out	18	– c Shahid b Hollioake 5
K. P. Evans c Shahid b Saqlain Mushtaq	6	– c Shahid b Saqlain Mushtaq 19
A. R. Oram b Hollioake	13	– b Benjamin 0
L-b 3, w 2, n-b 10	15	B 8, l-b 12, n-b 8 28

1/15 2/39 3/47 4/51 5/65   213   1/25 2/25 3/44 4/47 5/59   125
6/92 7/112 8/157 9/173   6/65 7/77 8/88 9/124

Bonus points – Nottinghamshire 1, Surrey 4.

Bowling: *First Innings*—Bicknell 25–8–64–2; Benjamin 15.3–5–45–3; Hollioake 15.3–5–45–3; Saqlain Mushtaq 10–3–30–1; Butcher 4–1–12–0. *Second Innings*—Bicknell 17–6–51–3; Benjamin 10.2–4–21–2; Hollioake 13–7–28–4; Saqlain Mushtaq 4–1–5–1.

Surrey

*M. A. Butcher b Evans	77	– c Read b Franks 8
I. J. Ward c Archer b Oram	25	– c Strang b Franks 2
J. D. Ratcliffe c Strang b Franks	1	– not out 23
B. C. Hollioake b Oram	34	– c Evans b Strang 26
N. Shahid c Read b Tolley	64	– not out 9
J. A. Knott lbw b Evans	0	
†J. N. Batty run out	31	
M. P. Bicknell c Read b Oram	9	
I. D. K. Salisbury c Read b Franks	0	
Saqlain Mushtaq c Read b Oram	8	
J. E. Benjamin not out	1	
B 1, l-b 5, n-b 14	20	L-b 4 4

1/36 2/37 3/130 4/160 5/160   270   1/10 2/17 3/55   (3 wkts) 72
6/245 7/256 8/259 9/269

Bonus points – Surrey 2, Nottinghamshire 4.

Bowling: *First Innings*—Franks 24–6–81–2; Evans 21–7–53–2; Oram 21–6–37–4; Tolley 21–8–55–1; Strang 17–7–38–0. *Second Innings*—Oram 5–0–22–0; Franks 4–0–12–2; Afzaal 4–0–19–0; Strang 3.4–0–15–1.

Umpires: H. D. Bird and T. E. Jesty.

NOTTINGHAMSHIRE v LEICESTERSHIRE

At Worksop, August 26, 27, 28. Leicestershire won by an innings and 223 runs. Leicestershire 24 pts, Nottinghamshire 1 pt. Toss: Leicestershire.

An extraordinary match was overshadowed by a strange piece of Leicestershire internal politics, in which Lewis and Millns were dropped after they had been late for training the previous day. With coach Jack Birkenshaw away due to a bereavement, Leicestershire got into a public relations tangle and tried to pretend, implausibly, they had been dropped for tactical reasons. Rumours then spread that the two had been in a punch-up. If the decision had been tactical, it would have been vindicated: Leicestershire surged to an overwhelming win. After rain and a waterlogged pitch had delayed play until 4 p.m., Mullally and Wells moved the ball around so much that, by the close, they had shot out Nottinghamshire for the lowest Championship total of the season. Harry Brind, the ECB's pitches consultant, was summoned but, in the sunshine of the second afternoon, Smith and Simmons, the acting-captain, showed the true nature of the pitch with a partnership of 322, a county fifth-wicket record. In a lean summer, Simmons's previous highest score had been 25; now, he hit 30 fours and a towering six on to the bowling green in his 250-ball 194. Smith struck 21 fours and a six in his 159. Mullally then took a timely career-best seven for 55 to give him match figures of 11 for 89 and cement his place on the Ashes tour. Afzaal and Welton collected pairs as Nottinghamshire crashed to their heaviest defeat for four years.

Close of play: First day, Leicestershire 27-1 (I. J. Sutcliffe 6*, M. T. Brimson 4*); Second day, Leicestershire 457-5 (B. F. Smith 158*, A. Habib 7*).

Nottinghamshire

G. E. Welton c Mullally	0	– (7) c Maddy b Mullally	0
*J. E. R. Gallian c Maddy b Ormond	4	– (1) c Simmons b Mullally	14
U. Afzaal b Mullally	0	– c Smith b Mullally	0
P. R. Pollard lbw b Mullally	6	– (2) run out	69
G. F. Archer b Wells	10	– (4) c Smith b Mullally	23
M. P. Dowman b Mullally	0	– (5) c Habib b Brimson	52
C. M. Tolley c Habib b Wells	12	– (6) lbw b Mullally	25
†C. M. W. Read lbw b Wells	10	– b Mullally	0
P. A. Strang c Habib b Wells	8	– b Mullally	8
R. T. Bates lbw b Wells	7	– not out	5
A. R. Oram not out	2	– st Nixon b Brimson	1
W 2	2	B 8, l-b 4, n-b 12	24

1/0 2/2 3/12 4/12 5/12   61   1/26 2/26 3/65 4/167 5/198   221
6/28 7/39 8/51 9/52   6/198 7/200 8/209 9/220

Bonus points – Leicestershire 4.

Bowling: *First Innings*—Mullally 12–2–34–4; Ormond 9–5–9–1; Wells 8.3–4–18–5. *Second Innings*—Mullally 26–10–55–7; Ormond 15–5–48–0; Wells 8–3–31–0; Brimson 22.4–5–63–2; Crowe 1–0–3–0; Simmons 8–6–9–0.

Leicestershire

D. L. Maddy c Read b Oram	11	A. Habib not out	33
I. J. Sutcliffe b Strang	60	†P. A. Nixon not out	19
M. T. Brimson lbw b Oram	4	L-b 9, w 4, n-b 9	22
V. J. Wells c Read b Tolley	3		
B. F. Smith lbw b Strang	159	1/18 2/32 3/35 (6 wkts dec.) 505	
*P. V. Simmons lbw b Dowman	194	4/127 5/449 6/461	

C. D. Crowe, A. D. Mullally and J. Ormond did not bat.

Bonus points – Leicestershire 4, Nottinghamshire 1 (Score at 120 overs: 445-4).

Bowling: Oram 30–4–114–2; Tolley 34–7–110–1; Dowman 11–2–48–1; Strang 33–6–104–2; Gallian 3–1–7–0; Bates 14–1–64–0; Afzaal 10–0–49–0.

Umpires: M. J. Kitchen and J. F. Steele.

NOTTINGHAMSHIRE v LANCASHIRE

At Nottingham, September 11, 12, 13. Lancashire won by 289 runs. Lancashire 21 pts, Nottinghamshire 4 pts. Toss: Nottinghamshire.

Nottinghamshire sacked cricket manager Alan Ormrod after another heavy defeat, but they were unlucky to come across Wasim Akram at his most devastating. On the third day, he followed his highest innings for Lancashire – and his first Championship hundred for five years – with his best bowling of the summer. Nottinghamshire had begun encouragingly and, if Gallian had held his old team-mate Fairbrother at slip on 34, things might have been different. As it was, Lancashire enjoyed a first-innings lead of 103, but struggled to build on it. Franks even gave Nottinghamshire a fighting chance by reducing Lancashire to 144 for seven. But then came Wasim's heroics. Off the field, he was fighting for his reputation, after accusations of match-fixing from Pakistan; on it, he smashed five sixes and 14 fours as he hit 122. These came out of 147 runs off the bat on the third morning and, with Keedy (contribution: four), he shared a stand of 97 for the last wicket. Only Johnson and Franks coped with Wasim the bowler. Lancashire's fifth victory in a row left them 11 points behind Leicestershire and two behind Surrey with one to play.

Close of play: First day, Nottinghamshire 61-4 (G. F. Archer 18*, C. M. Tolley 3*); Second day, Lancashire 193-7 (Wasim Akram 28*, G. Chapple 20*).

Lancashire

J. P. Crawley c Archer b Evans	44	– (2) c Read b Tolley	58
M. J. Chilton c Archer b Tolley	28	– (1) c Gallian b Franks	37
N. H. Fairbrother b Franks	88	– lbw b Tolley	4
G. D. Lloyd lbw b Tolley	13	– c Read b Franks	2
A. Flintoff c Read b Tolley	9	– c Read b Franks	23
†W. K. Hegg c Welton b Tolley	7	– c Read b Franks	0
*Wasim Akram c Archer b Tolley	0	– (8) c Johnson b Oram	155
I. D. Austin c Archer b Oram	1	– (7) b Franks	9
G. Chapple b Oram	2	– b Franks	29
P. J. Martin not out	4	– c Johnson b Gallian	11
G. Keedy c Read b Tolley	2	– not out	4
L-b 6, w 4, n-b 10	20	L-b 9, w 2, n-b 14	25
	218		**357**

1/64 2/94 3/127 4/147 5/175   218
6/175 7/182 8/212 9/213

1/86 2/94 3/97 4/110 5/114   357
6/137 7/144 8/212 9/260

Bonus points – Lancashire 1, Nottinghamshire 4.

Bowling: *First Innings*—Franks 13-4-35-1; Oram 16-2-63-2; Evans 20-8-40-1; Tolley 22.5-5-74-6. *Second Innings*—Evans 4-3-1-0; Franks 24-4-99-6; Oram 19.2-1-107-1; Tolley 31-4-88-2; Gallian 11-3-19-1; Bates 7-1-34-0.

Nottinghamshire

G. E. Welton lbw b Martin	7	– c Fairbrother b Wasim Akram	6
*J. E. R. Gallian c Flintoff b Martin	3	– lbw b Wasim Akram	0
U. Afzaal c Hegg b Wasim Akram	1	– c Fairbrother b Martin	4
P. Johnson lbw b Austin	19	– b Wasim Akram	90
G. F. Archer c Hegg b Chapple	20	– b Austin	8
C. M. Tolley lbw b Martin	27	– c Flintoff b Chapple	8
P. J. Franks c Flintoff b Austin	13	– c Keedy b Austin	30
†C. M. W. Read b Austin	4	– b Wasim Akram	4
K. P. Evans c Fairbrother b Martin	4	– b Wasim Akram	0
R. T. Bates not out	4	– c Wasim Akram b Austin	1
A. R. Oram b Austin	1	– not out	0
B 8, l-b 2, n-b 2	12	B 2, l-b 8, n-b 10	20
	115		**171**

1/10 2/11 3/17 4/57 5/71   115
6/100 7/102 8/109 9/113

1/5 2/12 3/26 4/37 5/52   171
6/142 7/164 8/164 9/169

Bonus points – Lancashire 4.

Bowling: *First Innings*—Wasim Akram 9-2-23-1; Martin 10-1-21-4; Chapple 10-3-40-1; Austin 11.2-3-21-4. *Second Innings*—Wasim Akram 13.2-1-56-5; Martin 9-6-11-1; Austin 16-4-54-3; Chapple 7-1-33-1; Flintoff 3-0-7-0.

Umpires: M. J. Harris and N. T. Plews.

NOTTINGHAMSHIRE v GLOUCESTERSHIRE

At Nottingham, September 17, 18, 19, 20. Gloucestershire won by 189 runs. Gloucestershire 23 pts, Nottinghamshire 5 pts. Toss: Gloucestershire.

Gloucestershire clinched fourth place in the Championship – their highest since 1986 – when they condemned Nottinghamshire to their fourth successive defeat. It was a momentous match for Walsh, who became the second bowler to take 100 first-class wickets in the season. And, though no one then knew it, this would mark the end of his epic career with Gloucestershire. He ended 1998 with 106 wickets, one ahead of Andrew Caddick; Walsh had passed a hundred once before, also in 1986. Now he claimed a match return of nine for 154, including his seventh five-wicket haul of the summer. He shared the limelight with Hancock who, after Gloucestershire had established a lead of 70, put the game out of Nottinghamshire's reach with his maiden double-century, which lasted 383 minutes and 315 balls and included 28 fours. Facing a target of 482, Tolley hit a defiant 78, his highest score for Nottinghamshire, but Walsh was altogether too good for his side, whose season had ended atrociously. With four home games left, they were equal ninth; they lost all four by convincing margins, and finished 16th. Afzaal's performance epitomised his team's: four of his last eight innings were ducks, the other four were single figures.

Close of play: First day, Nottinghamshire 42-2 (J. E. R. Gallian 16*); Second day, Gloucestershire 74-2 (T. H. C. Hancock 40*, A. M. Smith 0*); Third day, Nottinghamshire 105-2 (M. P. Dowman 45*, P. Johnson 31*).

Gloucestershire

R. J. Cunliffe b Oram	5	b Oram	0
T. H. C. Hancock c Read b Oram	1	not out	220
D. R. Hewson c Archer b Whiley	39	lbw b Afzaal	28
*M. W. Alleyne c Gie b Gallian	72	(5) c Archer b Afzaal	22
M. G. N. Windows b Dowman	63	(6) c and b Franks	52
A. J. Wright c sub b Oram	10	(8) st Read b Afzaal	0
†R. C. Russell c Read b Franks	38	(9) not out	15
M. C. J. Ball c and b Franks	15		
J. Lewis c Gie b Franks	40	(7) st Read b Afzaal	3
A. M. Smith not out	6	(4) c Tolley b Oram	55
C. A. Walsh c Dowman b Tolley	4		
L-b 4, n-b 22	26	L-b 2, n-b 14	16
	319	**(7 wkts dec.)**	**411**

1/6 2/11 3/130 4/146 5/171
6/225 7/258 8/295 9/314

1/0 2/73 3/149
4/218 5/363
6/376 7/376

Bonus points – Gloucestershire 3, Nottinghamshire 4.

Bowling: *First Innings*—Franks 20-1-89-3; Oram 14.4-4-55-3; Tolley 15.4-4-57-1; Whiley 15-1-66-1; Gallian 7-1-14-1; Dowman 8-2-34-1. *Second Innings*—Oram 21.5-5-56-2; Franks 15-0-92-1; Whiley 14-3-58-0; Dowman 9-1-27-0; Afzaal 24-3-101-4; Tolley 13-2-53-0; Gallian 5-0-22-0.

Nottinghamshire

*J. E. R. Gallian b Ball	33	c Russell b Lewis	17
U. Afzaal lbw b Smith	0	c Russell b Walsh	7
M. P. Dowman lbw b Smith	23	c Cunliffe b Lewis	49
G. F. Archer c Cunliffe b Walsh	15	(5) b Walsh	52
N. A. Gie lbw b Ball	50	(6) c Russell b Walsh	2
C. M. Tolley c Cunliffe b Walsh	30	(7) c Russell b Lewis	78
P. Johnson b Walsh	0	(4) b Walsh	33
P. J. Franks c Hancock	32	c Russell b Walsh	0
†C. M. W. Read not out	46	b Lewis	41
A. R. Oram b Walsh	4	c Alleyne b Lewis	3
M. J. A. Whiley c Ball b Hancock	0	not out	0
B 2, w 2, n-b 12	16	B 2, l-b 2, n-b 6	10
	249		**292**

1/0 2/42 3/61 4/98 5/151
6/152 7/163 8/225 9/244

1/15 2/40 3/109 4/127 5/135
6/224 7/224 8/287 9/291

Bonus points – Nottinghamshire 1, Gloucestershire 4.

Bowling: *First Innings*—Walsh 25-8-72-4; Smith 18-7-34-2; Ball 29-7-54-2; Lewis 12-1-56-0; Alleyne 7-2-16-0; Hancock 4-0-15-2. *Second Innings*—Walsh 25-4-82-5; Smith 17-5-46-0; Ball 11-2-35-0; Lewis 19.1-4-66-5; Hancock 4-1-25-0; Alleyne 8-2-34-0.

Umpires: J. H. Harris and B. Leadbeater.

SOMERSET

Andy Caddick

Patron: P. C. Ondaatje
President: M. F. Hill
Chairman: R. Parsons
Chairman, Cricket Committee: B. C. Rose
Chief Executive: P. W. Anderson
Captain: 1998 – P. D. Bowler
        1999 – J. Cox
Coach: D. A. Reeve
Head Groundsman: P. Frost
Scorer: D. A. Oldam

Andy Caddick of Somerset and Gloucestershire's Courtney Walsh, just up the M5, were by some distance the best fast bowlers in the 1998 County Championship. Caddick narrowly pipped Walsh to 100 first-class wickets (though he finished with 105 to Walsh's 106) and was the first to achieve the target for Somerset since Tom Cartwright in 1971. He had never bowled better or with more relish. The lift could be disconcerting, the line was tight, and there was always enough movement off the seam to keep the slips busy. More significantly, he looked relaxed, as well as penetrative. West Country members groaned in disbelief when his name was omitted from the Ashes list.

Caddick produced some marvellous marathon bowling stints and re-peatedly had the opposition in trouble, so that it is surprising his county won only six Championship matches and finished ninth – just missing qualification for the Super Cup. Yet Somerset too often stumbled through the season, lacking a vigorous competitive edge and giving away their own wickets in a flurry of frailties that mocked their theoretical strength. The batsmen were the primary culprits.

Marcus Trescothick got nearest 1,000 first-class runs, with 847, at least showing some improvement on his inexplicable recession since 1994. But there was a painful paucity of backbone in the higher order. The captain, Peter Bowler, took a worrying time to get going and dropped himself for some of the one-day games in June. He did still score two hundreds, and provided disciplined defiance, notably in the win over Northamptonshire.

Mark Lathwell did not play until mid-May and too occasionally demonstrated his exquisitely instinctive batsmanship. Richard Harden was often in turmoil; Piran Holloway continued to dig in during crises, but his aggregate of 624 was disappointing. There were timely innings, though not enough, from Mike Burns and Rob Turner. Keith Parsons was one of several who failed to build on his undoubted promise. Adrian Pierson found little in the summer's strips for his off-breaks, but did graft for his maiden century, at Hove.

Pondering on the experiences of Somerset's slow bowlers brings us with some sadness to Pakistani leg-spinner Mushtaq Ahmed, who turned up at Taunton in 1993 to create an immediate *frisson*. Here was a magician and an incorrigible entertainer, a cheerful personality who never wanted to let go of the ball. In 1998, Mushtaq played just six Championship games, took 14 wickets, and looked almost jaded. He was no longer beating the bat, no longer visibly chuckling, as he used to when he varied his deliveries at will. The troublesome knee was a burden. He had worries at home over his wife's confinement and was given compassionate leave. He was hardly seen in Taunton, and it was increasingly evident that his career with Somerset was over. Opposing batsmen may have got wiser to his supple wrist and tweaking fingers, but the lack of a fit, enthusiastic Mushtaq upset the team's balance and strategy. Jamie Cox of Tasmania was signed as both overseas player and captain for 1999.

Other injuries also worked against Somerset. Kevin Shine managed only three Championship matches. Simon Ecclestone was forced to retire, victim of a recurrent knee problem. His regular absence was a crucial factor in the county's indeterminate season. Ecclestone brought added power (especially power) and technique to the high order; he was a left-hander whose sturdy strokeplay delighted spectators. On occasions he stood in as captain and it seemed right that he should be groomed for the job on a permanent basis. Such departures as his and Mushtaq's left Somerset with too many unscheduled gaps; the fringe players were not accomplished or confident enough to take over. The vibes from the county academy were highly encouraging, though new talent needed time to mature.

Matthew Bulbeck came from the academy, however, and his emergence, as a left-arm swing bowler who could only get better, was among the most positive signs in a year of misplaced optimism and sluggish technical development. He topped the county bowling averages and appeared a genuine prospect for 1999. Again, Graham Rose bowled effectively and carved runs usefully, even if less profitably than in his previous season. He remained a valued all-rounder. Andre van Troost remained an enigma. Much time and tuition has been invested in him; towards the end of the season, he came back with a consciously revised run-up and action. The pace, the bounce, the intermittent unplayable ball were there, along with added control. The jury was still out, though. Paul Jarvis, moving from Sussex, augmented the county's bowling resources for 1999.

Somerset made no significant impact in the limited-overs matches, finishing 14th in the Sunday League and making early exits in the knockouts. The mental blockage, a palpable "freezing" when the pressure was on, refused to go away. It was something Dermot Reeve, the coach, had hoped to put right. He admitted he was not satisfied with the way the team had played; nor, he said with some candour, had he found the transition from Warwickshire captain to Somerset coach as easy as he had expected. Reeve had planned to make a partial comeback in one-day matches but, after a handful of games, found he was not fit enough.

He emphasised that there was nothing wrong with team spirit. At the county's lower points, spectators became restive, wondering whether Reeve – so used to success at Edgbaston – would want to stay for long. But he insisted that his dedication to Somerset cricket was as intense as ever. A halfway position in the final table was hardly one of abject failure. Ultimately, however, it reflected the inadequacies of a side which searched in vain for fibre and consistency in its batting. – DAVID FOOT.

SOMERSET 1998

[Bill Smith]

Back row: J. P. Tucker, B. J. Trott, A. R. K. Pierson, M. P. L. Bulbeck, P. M. Warren. *Middle row:* D. Veness (*physiotherapist*), P. C. L. Holloway, L. D. Sutton, M. E. Trescothick, J. I. D. Kerr, A. P. van Troost, K. J. Shine, K. A. Parsons, M. Burns, P. Wishart (*bowling coach*), C. M. Wells (*Second Eleven coach*), R. J. Turner, A. R. Caddick, D. A. Reeve (*First Eleven coach*), R. Parsons (*chairman*), P. D. Bowler (*captain*), S. C. Ecclestone, G. D. Rose, R. J. Harden. *Insets:* Mushtaq Ahmed, M. N. Lathwell, N. R. Boulton.

SOMERSET RESULTS

All first-class matches – Played 18: Won 6, Lost 7, Drawn 5.

County Championship matches – Played 17: Won 6, Lost 7, Drawn 4.

Competition placings – Britannic Assurance County Championship, 9th; NatWest Trophy, 2nd round; Benson and Hedges Cup, 3rd in Group C; AXA League, 14th.

COUNTY CHAMPIONSHIP AVERAGES
BATTING

Cap		M	I	NO	R	HS	100s	50s	Avge	Ct/St
1992	M. N. Lathwell	11	17	0	513	106	1	4	30.17	7
	M. E. Trescothick† . .	17	27	2	726	98	0	5	29.04	19
	M. Burns	9	15	0	424	96	0	3	28.26	15/1
	M. P. L. Bulbeck† . .	7	11	6	141	35	0	0	28.20	2
1994	R. J. Turner	14	22	2	558	105	1	2	27.90	43
1997	S. C. Ecclestone . . .	5	7	0	186	94	0	1	26.57	4
	A. R. K. Pierson . . .	12	18	3	396	108*	1	1	26.40	6
1988	G. D. Rose	17	26	2	606	76	0	4	25.25	3
1997	P. C. L. Holloway . .	16	28	3	624	123	1	1	24.96	7
1995	P. D. Bowler	17	30	2	696	104	2	3	24.85	18
1992	A. R. Caddick	17	25	8	322	37	0	0	18.94	5
1989	R. J. Harden†	11	19	2	293	63	0	2	17.23	13
1993	Mushtaq Ahmed§. . .	6	9	1	121	37	0	0	15.12	1
1997	K. J. Shine	3	5	2	44	18	0	0	14.66	0
	G. J. Kennis	3	6	0	71	49	0	0	11.83	5
	P. S. Jones	3	4	2	23	22*	0	0	11.50	0
	K. A. Parsons†	13	21	0	241	58	0	1	11.47	14
1997	A. P. van Troost . . .	5	7	1	61	23	0	0	10.16	-

Also batted: L. D. Sutton† (1 match) 0, 5 (1 ct).

* *Signifies not out.*   † *Born in Somerset.*   § *Overseas player.*

BOWLING

	O	M	R	W	BB	5W/i	Avge
M. P. L. Bulbeck	124.4	23	485	26	4-40	0	18.65
A. R. Caddick	687.2	156	2,082	105	8-64	10	19.82
G. D. Rose	480.3	132	1,399	52	5-48	2	26.90
A. P. van Troost	118	24	415	15	4-18	0	27.66
Mushtaq Ahmed	136	40	411	14	3-26	0	29.35
A. R. K. Pierson	243.1	50	788	21	5-117	1	37.52
M. E. Trescothick	162.3	38	546	14	4-82	0	39.00

Also bowled: P. D. Bowler 22.5-4-71-4; M. Burns 2-0-8-0; P. S. Jones 42.5-11-129-2; K. A. Parsons 107.4-27-357-5; K. J. Shine 57.4-10-216-4.

COUNTY RECORDS

Highest score for:	322	I. V. A. Richards v Warwickshire at Taunton	1985
Highest score against:	424	A. C. MacLaren (Lancashire) at Taunton	1895
Best bowling for:	10-49	E. J. Tyler v Surrey at Taunton	1895
Best bowling against:	10-35	A. Drake (Yorkshire) at Weston-super-Mare	1914
Highest total for:	675-9 dec.	v Hampshire at Bath	1924
Highest total against:	811	by Surrey at The Oval	1899
Lowest total for:	25	v Gloucestershire at Bristol	1947
Lowest total against:	22	by Gloucestershire at Bristol	1920

At Leeds, April 17, 18, 20, 21. SOMERSET lost to YORKSHIRE by 215 runs.

SOMERSET v NOTTINGHAMSHIRE

At Taunton, April 23, 24, 25, 27. Drawn. Somerset 5 pts, Nottinghamshire 7 pts. Toss: Nottinghamshire.

There was no play on the first day and only intermittent evidence of it afterwards, even though both sides forfeited an innings in a vain attempt to produce a result. On the final day, when just 15 overs were possible, Nottinghamshire were uneasily placed on 16 for two, facing a target of 256. When Somerset batted, three of the early order went without scoring, while Harden did his best to steady the innings. Between the showers, two players stood out. Pierson, the tall off-spinner signed from Leicestershire – to the surprise of some at Grace Road – drove pleasantly on his way to 71, his highest first-class score. There were also career-best figures for the Nottinghamshire seamer, Bowen. He had a wicket in his opening over and his first spell of nine overs brought him four for ten. He removed Holloway and Ecclestone with successive balls and, with a confident lbw appeal against Turner, narrowly missed a hat-trick.

Close of play: First day, No play; Second day, Somerset 94-5 (R. J. Turner 20*, A. R. K. Pierson 2*); Third day, Somerset 213-8 (A. R. K. Pierson 67*, A. R. Caddick 6*).

Somerset

*P. D. Bowler c Dowman b Bowen	0	M. E. Trescothick lbw b Wharf	6
P. C. L. Holloway c Pollard b Bowen	22	A. R. Caddick not out	26
K. A. Parsons c Wharf b Bowen	0	K. J. Shine lbw b Bowen	18
R. J. Harden c Noon b Bowen	36		
S. C. Ecclestone c Pollard b Bowen	0	L-b 2, w 2, n-b 20	24
†R. J. Turner b Bowen	45		
A. R. K. Pierson c Gallian b Wharf	71	1/6 2/6 3/39 4/39 5/89	255
G. D. Rose c Gallian b Wharf	7	6/160 7/169 8/179 9/232	

Bonus points – Somerset 2, Nottinghamshire 4.

Bowling: Bowen 27.4–8–73–7; Franks 17–4–63–0; Wharf 16–1–93–3; Strang 8–3–20–0; Gallian 5–2–4–0.

Somerset forfeited their second innings.

Nottinghamshire

Nottinghamshire forfeited their first innings.

P. R. Pollard lbw b Caddick	10
M. P. Dowman lbw b Rose	4
J. E. R. Gallian not out	0
*P. Johnson not out	0
N-b 2	2

1/16 2/16   (2 wkts) 16

R. T. Robinson, U. Afzaal, P. A. Strang, †W. M. Noon, P. J. Franks, A. G. Wharf and M. N. Bowen did not bat.

Bowling: Caddick 5–3–7–1; Rose 4–2–9–1.

Umpires: T. E. Jesty and M. J. Kitchen.

At Lord's, May 13, 14, 15, 16. SOMERSET lost to MIDDLESEX by 211 runs.

SOMERSET v SURREY

At Taunton, May 21, 22, 23, 24. Somerset won by 165 runs. Somerset 20 pts, Surrey 5 pts.
Toss: Surrey. First-class debut: M. P. L. Bulbeck.

Surrey were missing four batsmen on England duty, but that should not detract from a fine Somerset performance, especially from 18-year-old Matthew Bulbeck on debut. Born in Taunton, he has progressed through Somerset's cricket academy. Never remotely overawed, Bulbeck claimed six well-deserved wickets with his left-arm swing and in two undefeated innings hit 45 valuable runs. The win was a notable recovery for Somerset, saved from ignominy in their first innings by the tail after the top seven all fell for single figures. Then, in the second innings, a resolute hundred from Holloway, with Turner and Rose strong in support, swung the balance. Surrey needed 411, and Butcher, standing in as captain, did his best to sustain the suspense, carrying his bat for a chanceless century. But, once the opening partnership had been broken, his was a forlorn gesture. The green pitch had seamed early on and Bicknell returned impressive figures in the first innings; later it was Salisbury's turn, with challenging spin. For Somerset, Caddick bowled more than 60 overs, but gained scant reward for continually beating the bat.

Close of play: First day, Surrey 156-7 (J. N. Batty 25*, I. D. K. Salisbury 17*); Second day, Somerset 259-4 (P. C. L. Holloway 110*, R. J. Turner 74*); Third day, Surrey 92-1 (M. A. Butcher 45*, I. J. Ward 5*).

Somerset

*P. D. Bowler lbw b Bicknell	9	– lbw b Benjamin	9
P. C. L. Holloway c Batty b Benjamin	5	– b Salisbury	123
M. E. Trescothick lbw b Bicknell	9	– lbw b Benjamin	4
M. N. Lathwell c and b Bicknell	2	– c Batty b Benjamin	0
K. A. Parsons c Batty b Hollioake	9	– lbw b Tudor	28
†R. J. Turner c Shahid b Hollioake	7	– b Salisbury	88
M. Burns c Shahid b Tudor	5	– b Salisbury	40
G. D. Rose lbw b Benjamin	15	– c Benjamin b Salisbury	76
A. R. Caddick c Batty b Hollioake	30	– c Bicknell b Shahid	37
M. P. L. Bulbeck not out	27	– not out	18
A. P. van Troost c Knott b Bicknell	23	– c and b Salisbury	0
L-b 7, n-b 28	35	B 12, l-b 7, w 11, n-b 22	52
	176		**475**

1/22 2/24 3/34 4/39 5/56   176   1/9 2/21 3/27 4/72 5/286   475
6/65 7/65 8/113 9/129   6/297 7/388 8/435 9/473

Bonus points – Surrey 4.

Bowling: *First Innings*—Bicknell 10.3–2–14–4; Benjamin 13–1–69–2; Hollioake 11–1–55–3; Tudor 3–0–31–1. *Second Innings*—Bicknell 25–7–77–0; Benjamin 23–7–71–3; Tudor 20.4–80–1; Butcher 8–3–20–0; Hollioake 23–2–85–0; Salisbury 47.2–9–98–5; Ratcliffe 2–1–4–0; Knott 1–0–2–0; Shahid 6–0–19–1.

Surrey

*M. A. Butcher b Bulbeck	28	– not out	109
J. D. Ratcliffe c Bulbeck b Rose	0	– c Parsons b Rose	33
I. J. Ward b Trescothick	14	– c Turner b Bulbeck	5
N. Shahid lbw b Trescothick	6	– lbw b Bulbeck	0
B. C. Hollioake lbw b Rose	37	– lbw b Trescothick	28
J. A. Knott c Turner b Bulbeck	12	– lbw b Rose	4
†J. N. Batty lbw b Rose	39	– c Parsons b Caddick	5
A. J. Tudor c Lathwell b Bulbeck	1	– lbw b Bulbeck	9
I. D. K. Salisbury c Lathwell b Caddick	51	– b Caddick	10
M. P. Bicknell b Bulbeck	6	– c Holloway b van Troost	23
J. E. Benjamin not out	18	– b Caddick	1
L-b 9, n-b 20	29	L-b 6, w 2, n-b 10	18
	241		**245**

1/0 2/44 3/52 4/62 5/96   241   1/85 2/92 3/92 4/140 5/145   245
6/124 7/127 8/177 9/212   6/163 7/182 8/203 9/244

Bonus points – Surrey 1, Somerset 4.

Bowling: *First Innings*—Caddick 28.4–8–73–2; Rose 25–11–51–3; Trescothick 12–2–34–2; van Troost 8–1–22–0; Bulbeck 11–0–52–3. *Second Innings*—Caddick 31.4–5–91–3; van Troost 4–0–30–1; Trescothick 13–3–52–1; Bulbeck 22–7–48–3; Rose 12–5–18–2.

Umpires: J. W. Holder and V. A. Holder.

SOMERSET v WARWICKSHIRE

At Taunton, June 3, 4, 5. Somerset won by eight wickets. Somerset 24 pts, Warwickshire 4 pts. Toss: Warwickshire.

Somerset won in comfort with a day to spare after enforcing the follow-on. The margin would have been even bigger, but for a thumping last-innings from Smith, who hit 147 off 133 balls when an innings defeat looked certain for Warwickshire. It did little to console his captain, Lara, whose wretched run continued. He began by dropping two slip catches before the left-handers, Ecclestone and Trescothick, recaptured their form and took Somerset to 364. Lara responded by creaming five fours; what was meant to be his sixth caused his downfall. Bulbeck, supporting fine swing and seam from Caddick and Rose, built on his reputation with a spell of three for two, and Warwickshire were all out 235 behind, with Knight carrying his bat. Second time around, he went quickly; Lara, who struggled to get the strike, stayed 114 minutes rather than 35, but came out with the same score as in the first innings, 21; and even Smith's heroics were nowhere near enough.

Close of play: First day, Somerset 253-5 (M. E. Trescothick 84*, M. P. L. Bulbeck 7*); Second day, Warwickshire 53-3 (B. C. Lara 11*, K. J. Piper 5*).

Somerset

*P. D. Bowler lbw b Brown	9	– c Giddins b Giles	10
P. C. L. Holloway b Giddins	2	– not out	22
R. J. Harden c Piper b Brown	13	– (4) not out	4
M. N. Lathwell c Brown b Giddins	18		
S. C. Ecclestone c Lara b Hemp	94		
†R. J. Turner not out	33		
M. E. Trescothick lbw b Smith	98		
M. P. L. Bulbeck st Piper b Giles	35		
G. D. Rose b Giles	11		
Mushtaq Ahmed c Penney b Giddins	14	– (3) b Giles	21
A. R. Caddick b Brown	7		
B 6, l-b 8, n-b 16	30	B 8, l-b 1, n-b 4	13

1/5 2/19 3/38 4/52 5/242	364	1/26 2/50	(2 wkts) 70
6/279 7/307 8/337 9/355			

Bonus points – Somerset 4, Warwickshire 4.

In the first innings R. J. Turner, when 0, retired hurt at 52-4 and resumed at 279.

Bowling: *First Innings*—Giddins 25–4–79–3; Brown 22.5–5–79–3; Welch 15–6–48–0; Smith 25–6–71–1; Giles 19–3–68–2; Hemp 2–0–5–1. *Second Innings*—Giddins 3–0–9–0; Brown 8–2–21–0; Giles 7–2–30–2; Smith 1.5–1–1–0.

Warwickshire

M. J. Powell b Caddick	2	– lbw b Caddick	2
N. V. Knight not out	67	– lbw b Caddick	5
D. L. Hemp b Rose	11	– c Bowler b Caddick	25
*B. C. Lara c Trescothick b Rose	21	– c Turner b Bulbeck	21
T. L. Penney lbw b Bulbeck	0	– (6) c Harden b Mushtaq Ahmed	36
D. R. Brown lbw b Bulbeck	0	– (7) b Bulbeck	0
†K. J. Piper lbw b Caddick	1	– (5) c Turner b Caddick	19
N. M. K. Smith b Caddick	4	– (9) b Bowler b Mushtaq Ahmed	147
A. F. Giles lbw b Bulbeck	1	– (10) c Ecclestone b Mushtaq Ahmed	28
G. Welch c Turner b Rose	19	– (8) b Bulbeck	0
E. S. H. Giddins b Rose	0	– not out	0
L-b 1, n-b 2	3	B 2, l-b 9, w 2, n-b 8	21

1/8 2/35 3/65 4/66 5/68	129	1/11 2/20 3/43 4/82 5/82	304
6/79 7/83 8/84 9/129		6/82 7/84 8/193 9/283	

Bonus points – Somerset 4.

Bowling: *First Innings*—Caddick 14–2–58–3; Mushtaq Ahmed 11–6–20–0; Rose 9.4–3–25–4; Bulbeck 8–2–10–3; Trescothick 7–4–15–0. *Second Innings*—Rose 18–5–68–0; Caddick 29–10–79–4; Mushtaq Ahmed 15.2–3–63–3; Bulbeck 16–4–70–3; Trescothick 3–1–13–0.

Umpires: R. A. White and P. Willey.

At Manchester, June 11, 12, 13, 15. SOMERSET lost to LANCASHIRE by nine runs.

SOMERSET v ESSEX

At Bath, June 17, 18, 19, 20. Essex won by one wicket. Essex 20 pts, Somerset 1 pt. Toss: Essex.

There was no sign of joyful festival cricket until the final day, when Essex overcame a poor start to win what turned into a thriller. Their hero was Irani, with a powerful, intelligent 127 not out. There had been little play on the first two days and it was agreed that Essex, forfeiting an innings, would chase 300 on the last. To fulfil their half of the bargain, Somerset crawled to 68 from almost 40 overs, leaving the third-day crowd confused and uneasy. Initially, Essex's attempt, on a damp pitch and against a side strong on pace and swing, looked unimpressive at 84 for five. And 24 were still wanted when the ninth wicket fell and Such came in. But a man who was once one of cricket's most jittery rabbits has acquired professional phlegm: he faced 14 balls calmly while Irani thrashed the winning runs. As the rain fell on the second day, Somerset dressing-room high spirits spilled out on to the field: Mushtaq Ahmed was manhandled on to the pitch and tied to a chair; it was said to be revenge for his own practical jokes.

Close of play: First day, Somerset 45-0 (P. D. Bowler 17*, P. C. L. Holloway 4*); Second day, Somerset 98-1 (P. C. L. Holloway 25*, R. J. Harden 2*); Third day, Somerset 68-6 (M. P. L. Bulbeck 0*, G. D. Rose 0*).

Somerset

*P. D. Bowler lbw b Cowan		35	– lbw b Ilott	1
P. C. L. Holloway c Rollins b Ilott		35	– lbw b Such	25
R. J. Harden lbw b Ilott		2	– c Rollins b Grayson	9
M. N. Lathwell c Peters b Such		16	– b Grayson	0
S. C. Ecclestone lbw b D. R. Law		14		
†R. J. Turner c Peters b Ilott		22	– c Rollins b D. R. Law	4
M. E. Trescothick b Grayson		32	– (5) c S. G. Law b Grayson	11
G. D. Rose c and b Grayson		15	– not out	0
Mushtaq Ahmed c Peters b Such		11		
A. R. Caddick not out		2		
M. P. L. Bulbeck b Such		1	– (7) not out	0
B 5, l-b 7, w 2, n-b 32		46	B 1, l-b 3, n-b 14	18

1/89 2/98 3/115 4/128 5/162	231	1/8 2/41 3/51	(6 wkts dec.) 68
6/170 7/213 8/228 9/228		4/51 5/55 6/67	

Bonus points – Somerset 1, Essex 4.

Bowling: *First Innings*—Ilott 22–10–27–3; Cowan 17–5–67–1; Irani 19–4–35–0; Such 26.5–10–38–3; D. R. Law 6–1–29–1; Grayson 7–2–23–2. *Second Innings*—Ilott 6–1–14–1; Cowan 5–0–22–0; Grayson 14–8–13–3; Such 10–5–8–1; D. R. Law 4.1–1–7–1.

Essex

Essex forfeited their first innings.

*P. J. Prichard lbw b Rose	3	A. P. Cowan c Turner b Rose	0
D. D. J. Robinson lbw b Rose	7	M. C. Ilott b Rose	0
A. P. Grayson c Bowler b Rose	23	P. M. Such not out	1
S. G. Law c Lathwell b Caddick	33	B 3, l-b 4, n-b 10	17
R. C. Irani not out	127		
S. D. Peters c Ecclestone b Bulbeck	1	1/3 2/29 3/36	(9 wkts) 300
†R. J. Rollins lbw b Mushtaq Ahmed	42	4/77 5/84 6/160	
D. R. Law c Harden b Caddick	46	7/273 8/276 9/276	

Bowling: Caddick 26.1–5–126–2; Rose 20–4–48–5; Bulbeck 11–0–56–1; Trescothick 5–1–15–0; Mushtaq Ahmed 9–2–48–1.

Umpires: M. J. Harris and A. G. T. Whitehead.

SOMERSET v HAMPSHIRE

At Taunton, June 26, 27, 28, 29. Drawn. Somerset 9 pts, Hampshire 11 pts. Toss: Somerset. County debut: A. C. Morris.

No match could have lived up to the opening of this one. After three legitimate balls, bowled by McLean, the score was 17 for one. This included a single off a no-ball plus three separate wides. Under ECB regulations, these all counted for two plus any runs scored, and two of the wides evaded Aymes and crashed to the boundary, thus counting six. Then McLean found his direction and, after a dot ball, yorked Holloway. Bowler saw out this over and went on to make his first hundred of a hitherto unproductive summer. White, who played one game for Somerset in 1991, then matched him with a century of his own, and shared a stand of 119 with Stephenson. But there had been no play on the first day and nothing until mid-afternoon on the last, and the game merely became a quest for bonus points.

Close of play: First day, No play; Second day, Somerset 243-4 (P. D. Bowler 85*, R. J. Turner 0*); Third day, Hampshire 259-2 (P. R. Whitaker 63*, R. A. Smith 12*).

Somerset

*P. D. Bowler c White b Morris	104	A. R. K. Pierson c Aymes b Mascarenhas	20
P. C. L. Holloway b McLean	0	Mushtaq Ahmed c McLean b James	3
R. J. Harden c White b McLean	4	A. R. Caddick not out	8
M. N. Lathwell c Morris b Mascarenhas	76		
K. A. Parsons lbw b James	58	L-b 2, w 18, n-b 4	24
†R. J. Turner c McLean b Mascarenhas	40		
M. E. Trescothick c White b Morris	9	1/17 2/21 3/151 4/243 5/284	378
G. D. Rose c Udal b Mascarenhas	32	6/314 7/326 8/357 9/360	

Bonus points – Somerset 4, Hampshire 4.

Bowling: McLean 20–2–92–2; Morris 20–1–90–2; James 11–1–43–2; Stephenson 17–2–48–0; Mascarenhas 19.2–3–55–4; Whitaker 1–0–5–0; Udal 13–3–43–0.

Hampshire

G. W. White c Bowler b Mushtaq Ahmed	101	K. D. James not out	22
J. P. Stephenson c Turner b Parsons	67		
P. R. Whitaker c Pierson b Caddick	72		
*R. A. Smith c Trescothick b Pierson	21	L-b 8, n-b 15	23
†A. N. Aymes not out	41		
A. D. Mascarenhas c Trescothick b Pierson	3	1/119 2/235 3/281	(5 wkts dec.) 350
		4/281 5/287	

M. Keech, S. D. Udal, A. C. Morris and N. A. M. McLean did not bat.

Bonus points – Hampshire 4, Somerset 2.

Bowling: Mushtaq Ahmed 20–6–57–1; Pierson 31–9–80–2; Caddick 24–4–91–1; Rose 16.3–6–56–0; Parsons 7–0–26–1; Trescothick 8–3–28–0; Bowler 2–1–4–0.

Umpires: D. J. Constant and J. W. Holder.

At Hove, July 1, 2, 3, 4. SOMERSET drew with SUSSEX.

At Taunton, July 14, 15, 16. SOMERSET drew with SRI LANKANS (See Sri Lankan tour section).

SOMERSET v DURHAM

At Taunton, July 22, 23, 24. Somerset won by ten wickets. Somerset 23 pts, Durham 6 pts. Toss: Durham.

After two even days, Somerset dominated the third to win a match of careless batting and untidy fielding. A glassy pitch favoured the ball but offered little excuse for some embarrassing mistakes. Morris should have been run out early on the first day when Lathwell, at the stumps, fumbled an accurate throw from Holloway. And in Somerset's innings, Collingwood put down a simple slip catch off Pierson; determined to redeem his lapse, he hurled at the wickets and conceded four overthrows. That drop helped Somerset to fight back and take a 59-run lead, after Harmison, Durham's promising 19-year-old fast bowler, had struck to leave them 174 for seven. For Somerset, Caddick bowled consistently and picked up ten; he turned the match in the second innings, when Durham succumbed in less than 39 overs. Then Bowler and Holloway, so obdurate the previous day, reached their target at express speed. The match ended on a ludicrous – if technically correct – note: tea was taken with Somerset needing two for victory. Twenty minutes later, Bowler hit the next ball for four.

Close of play: First day, Durham 168-3 (N. J. Speak 43*, D. C. Boon 52*); Second day, Somerset 228-8 (A. R. K. Pierson 10*, Mushtaq Ahmed 14*).

Durham

J. J. B. Lewis b Caddick	19	– lbw b Rose	0
J. E. Morris c Pierson b Parsons	30	– c Parsons b Rose	9
N. J. Speak b Caddick	51	– c and b Caddick	10
J. A. Daley c Trescothick b Bulbeck	2	– c Mushtaq Ahmed b Caddick	36
*D. C. Boon c Burns b Caddick	73	– b Caddick	0
P. D. Collingwood c Parsons b Mushtaq Ahmed	16	– c Trescothick b Caddick	1
†M. P. Speight c Burns b Bulbeck	10	– c Pierson b Caddick	9
M. J. Foster c Bulbeck b Caddick	15	– st Burns b Mushtaq Ahmed	5
N. C. Phillips b Caddick	6	– c Rose b Mushtaq Ahmed	5
M. M. Betts not out	8	– not out	20
S. J. Harmison b Mushtaq Ahmed	0	– c Rose b Mushtaq Ahmed	18
B 13, l-b 8, n-b 14	35	B 4, l-b 3, n-b 8	15

1/34 2/74 3/81 4/192 5/201   259   1/10 2/13 3/31 4/31 5/37   128
6/225 7/242 8/253 9/259   6/76 7/83 8/83 9/94

Bonus points – Durham 2, Somerset 4.

Bowling: *First Innings*—Caddick 31–3–116–5; Rose 19–6–51–0; Parsons 9–6–4–1; Bulbeck 11–2–30–2; Pierson 1–0–4–0; Mushtaq Ahmed 14–4–28–2; Trescothick 2–1–5–0. *Second Innings*—Caddick 17–4–49–5; Rose 11–4–35–2; Mushtaq Ahmed 9.4–2–26–3; Pierson 1–0–11–0.

Somerset

*P. D. Bowler c Speight b Harmison	12	– not out 44
P. C. L. Holloway c Foster b Betts	42	– not out 25
M. E. Trescothick c Speak b Harmison	25	
M. N. Lathwell c Speight b Harmison	4	
K. A. Parsons c Boon b Foster	4	
†M. Burns c Speight b Betts	43	
G. D. Rose b Harmison	22	
A. R. K. Pierson c Speight b Foster	43	
M. P. L. Bulbeck c Daley b Foster	23	
Mushtaq Ahmed c Daley b Foster	37	
A. R. Caddick not out	31	
B 12, l-b 2, w 8, n-b 10	32	L-b 1, n-b 2 3
	318	(no wkt) 72

1/17 2/51 3/55 4/60 5/141
6/174 7/174 8/214 9/262

Bonus points – Somerset 3, Durham 4.

Bowling: *First Innings*—Betts 25–6–80–2; Harmison 28–6–98–4; Foster 17.4–3–48–4; Collingwood 7–1–22–0; Phillips 12–2–56–0. *Second Innings*—Harmison 4–0–29–0; Betts 2–0–11–0; Foster 4–1–20–0; Phillips 2.1–0–11–0.

Umpires: J. H. Harris and B. Leadbeater.

At Leicester, August 5, 6. SOMERSET lost to LEICESTERSHIRE by an innings and 85 runs.

SOMERSET v NORTHAMPTONSHIRE

At Taunton, August 14, 15, 16. Somerset won by two wickets. Somerset 20 pts, Northamptonshire 4 pts. Toss: Northamptonshire. County debut: G. J. Kennis.

There was never much between the teams and a Somerset defeat was possible up until the moment they scraped a tense third-day victory by two wickets. Certainly, Brown, Northamptonshire's 23-year-old off-spinner, kept good line and length in a tally of 11 for 102, and did not deserve to be on the losing side. Before the pitch turned from seam to spin, Caddick (for the fourth consecutive innings) and Graham Rose each took five wickets as Northamptonshire struggled against the moving ball. Somerset fared even worse, though Bowler doggedly stayed to limit the deficit to eight. Curran batted well a second time, while Caddick picked up four more wickets, including his 500th in first-class cricket, leaving a target of 214. The game boiled down to whether Somerset could counter the turning ball. It developed into an absorbing contest, with Brown's six wickets, a career-best, not quite enough. As in the first innings, Bowler's discipline made the difference.

Close of play: First day, Somerset 135-6 (P. D. Bowler 53*, G. D. Rose 9*); Second day, Somerset 29-1 (P. C. L. Holloway 4*, A. R. K. Pierson 9*).

Northamptonshire

R. R. Montgomerie lbw b Rose	15	– c Kennis b Caddick	3
R. J. Bailey c Parsons b Caddick	1	– c Parsons b Pierson	17
M. B. Loye c Trescothick b Rose	13	– c Bowler b Caddick	0
*K. M. Curran c Holloway b Caddick	41	– c Burns b Caddick	44
A. L. Penberthy c Kennis b Caddick	0	– lbw b Pierson	53
D. J. Sales c Bowler b Rose	41	– c Burns b Caddick	9
†D. Ripley c Trescothick b Caddick	6	– not out	54
J. P. Taylor c Kennis b Rose	22	– c and b Bowler	5
F. A. Rose lbw b Rose	21	– lbw b Bowler	0
J. F. Brown not out	6	– lbw b Pierson	0
D. E. Malcolm c Burns b Caddick	12	– c Rose b Bowler	7
B 4, l-b 3, n-b 2	9	B 4, l-b 7, n-b 2	13

1/3 2/23 3/32 4/33 5/100   187   1/6 2/6 3/42 4/105 5/115   205
6/120 7/128 8/163 9/168   6/166 7/171 8/173 9/178

Bonus points – Somerset 4.

Bowling: *First Innings*—Caddick 21.2–5–70–5; Jones 4–2–11–0; Rose 18–4–57–5; Pierson 7–2–26–0; Parsons 6–2–16–0. *Second Innings*—Caddick 17–5–45–4; Rose 10–2–30–0; Jones 8–2–30–0; Bowler 7.5–0–25–3.

Somerset

*P. D. Bowler c Malcolm b Brown	78	– (6) not out	41
P. C. L. Holloway c Loye b Rose	8	– c Ripley b Bailey	27
M. E. Trescothick c Sales b Taylor	22	– (4) c Curran b Brown	30
R. J. Harden c Curran b Brown	5	– (5) c Curran b Brown	3
G. J. Kennis c Penberthy b Taylor	3	– (1) c Curran b Taylor	15
K. A. Parsons b Brown	10	– (7) c Bailey b Brown	22
†M. Burns c Sales b Brown	20	– (8) lbw b Brown	18
G. D. Rose c Taylor b Rose	18	– (9) c Montgomerie b Brown	15
A. R. K. Pierson lbw b Brown	3	– (3) c Penberthy b Brown	9
A. R. Caddick not out	7	– not out	7
P. S. Jones b Taylor	0		
B 1, l-b 2, n-b 2	5	B 10, l-b 17	27

1/16 2/52 3/66 4/69 5/92   179   1/17 2/34 3/89 4/96   (8 wkts) 214
6/124 7/156 8/171 9/172   5/100 6/144 7/164 8/204

Bonus points – Northamptonshire 4.

Bowling: *First Innings*—Malcolm 9–1–37–0; Rose 20–3–45–2; Taylor 19–6–32–3; Curran 4–1–13–0; Brown 20–4–49–5. *Second Innings*—Rose 2–0–9–0; Taylor 15–3–48–1; Brown 41.1–18–53–6; Malcolm 7–3–20–0; Bailey 27–8–57–1.

Umpires: H. D. Bird and D. R. Shepherd.

SOMERSET v DERBYSHIRE

At Taunton, August 19, 20, 21. Derbyshire won by 72 runs. Derbyshire 22 pts, Somerset 4 pts. Toss: Derbyshire.

This was a match for left-arm swing bowlers. Dean recorded career-best figures of six for 70 in the first innings, improved upon them with six for 63 in the second, and helped Derbyshire to their fifth Championship win. For Somerset, Bulbeck took three in ten balls at the start of Derbyshire's second innings, and seven in the game. On a blameless pitch, too many wickets were sacrificed wantonly: 15 on the first day, 20 on the second. Derbyshire, in one-day style, blazed to 290 all out in 66 overs on the opening day. Weston led the way, with teenagers Spendlove and

Blackwell not far behind. Somerset's recruit from Surrey, Gregor Kennis, scored in more sedate fashion as they saved the follow-on. Somerset were then allowed to bowl themselves back into contention, facing a final target of 249 and ample time to score them. But technical flaws were again too apparent; Trescothick alone seemed likely to sort out the strange tempo, and find the elusive runs.

Close of play: First day, Somerset 96-5 (G. J. Kennis 37*, A. R. K. Pierson 0*); Second day, Somerset 93-5 (M. E. Trescothick 43*, R. J. Turner 2*).

Derbyshire

M. J. Slater c Turner b Caddick	15	– c Turner b Bulbeck	48
M. R. May lbw b Bulbeck	14	– lbw b Bulbeck	14
R. M. S. Weston c Kennis b Caddick	73	– c Turner b Bulbeck	6
K. J. Barnett lbw b Rose	30	– c Turner b Bulbeck	0
M. E. Cassar c Turner b Rose	4	– c Turner b Caddick	10
B. L. Spendlove c Bowler b Pierson	49	– c and b Caddick	27
I. D. Blackwell b Bulbeck	44	– c Holloway b Caddick	4
*D. G. Cork b Bulbeck	0	– lbw b Rose	8
†K. M. Krikken not out	10	– b Caddick	1
P. A. J. DeFreitas c Kennis b Rose	32	– not out	12
K. J. Dean c Trescothick b Rose	1	– b Caddick	1
L-b 8, n-b 10	18	L-b 6, n-b 2	8

1/26 2/51 3/124 4/132 5/172   290   1/45 2/51 3/51 4/80 5/84   139
6/246 7/246 8/250 9/287   6/93 7/119 8/125 9/131

Bonus points – Derbyshire 2, Somerset 4.

Bowling: *First Innings*—Caddick 21–6–72–2; Rose 16.5–1–75–4; Bulbeck 12–2–67–3; Parsons 13–0–60–0; Pierson 3–1–8–1. *Second Innings*—Caddick 16.2–3–49–5; Rose 7–1–44–1; Bulbeck 11–3–40–4.

Somerset

*P. D. Bowler c Cork b Dean	5	– c May b Cork	21
P. C. L. Holloway b Cork	6	– c Krikken b Cork	8
M. E. Trescothick c Krikken b Cork	0	– c Krikken b Dean	60
M. N. Lathwell b Dean	11	– c Slater b Dean	2
G. J. Kennis lbw b Dean	49	– c Blackwell b Dean	0
K. A. Parsons c Krikken b Dean	30	– c Weston b Dean	8
A. R. K. Pierson c Krikken b Dean	15	– (10) c Krikken b Cork	7
†R. J. Turner b DeFreitas	21	– (7) c Cork b Dean	27
G. D. Rose c Slater b DeFreitas	29	– b Blackwell	23
A. R. Caddick lbw b Dean	0	– (8) lbw b Dean	2
M. P. L. Bulbeck not out	0	– not out	7
B 4, l-b 1, n-b 10	15	L-b 7, n-b 4	11

1/7 2/10 3/11 4/31 5/90   181   1/31 2/38 3/60 4/60 5/78   176
6/123 7/140 8/166 9/181   6/128 7/130 8/143 9/150

Bonus points – Derbyshire 4.

Bowling: *First Innings*—Cork 16–5–32–2; Dean 22.1–6–70–6; DeFreitas 11–2–46–2; Cassar 4–1–14–0; Blackwell 4–1–14–0. *Second Innings*—Cork 24–6–68–3; Dean 21–6–63–6; DeFreitas 12–4–33–0; Blackwell 2.4–0–5–1.

Umpires: J. F. Steele and P. Willey.

At Bristol, August 27, 28, 29, 30. SOMERSET beat GLOUCESTERSHIRE by five wickets.

SOMERSET v WORCESTERSHIRE

At Taunton, September 1, 2, 3, 4. Drawn. Somerset 9 pts, Worcestershire 8 pts. Toss: Worcestershire. First-class debut: D. N. Catterall.

The ironies were as heavy as the rainclouds which ruined any chance of a result. Caddick and Hick had just been overlooked for the Ashes tour and they responded with a vigorous eloquence. Bowling as well as at any time in his exceptional season, Caddick took eight for 64 in Worcestershire's first innings. On the ground where he scored his undefeated 405 ten years earlier, Hick took an hour to score his first run; he was eventually out for 44, caught at point by his opposing captain, Bowler, who had arrived late at the ground after sitting a law exam. In the second innings, Hick composed a good-looking hundred, the 103rd of his career, off just 118 balls. A few days later, both Caddick and Hick, together with Phil Tufnell, were named as official standby players for the Australian tour.

Close of play: First day, Somerset 33-1 (A. R. K. Pierson 6*, M. E. Trescothick 6*); Second day, Somerset 135-6 (M. Burns 15*, R. J. Turner 4*); Third day, Worcestershire 230-6 (S. R. Lampitt 30*, G. R. Haynes 23*).

Worcestershire

W. P. C. Weston c Trescothick b Caddick	8	– c Pierson b Caddick	3
A. Hafeez c Trescothick b Caddick	4	– b Caddick	1
*G. A. Hick c Bowler b Caddick	44	– c Burns b Rose	110
V. S. Solanki lbw b Caddick	47	– c Parsons b Rose	38
D. A. Leatherdale c Caddick	27	– lbw b Parsons	16
†S. J. Rhodes c Bowler b Caddick	0	– lbw b Caddick	0
S. R. Lampitt lbw b Jones	11	– not out	41
G. R. Haynes c Turner b Caddick	56	– not out	36
R. K. Illingworth not out	16		
D. N. Catterall c Harden b Caddick	0		
R. J. Chapman c Turner b Jones	0		
L-b 5, n-b 6	11	L-b 5, n-b 4	9

1/12 2/13 3/102 4/109 5/109   224   1/4 2/15 3/113   (6 wkts) 254
6/131 7/188 8/217 9/217   4/164 5/165 6/175

Bonus points – Worcestershire 1, Somerset 4.

Bowling: *First Innings*—Caddick 31–13–64–8; Rose 22–10–62–0; Jones 12.5–2–25–2; Trescothick 9–2–28–0; Parsons 2–0–8–0; Pierson 10–1–32–0. *Second Innings*—Caddick 19–6–47–3; Jones 10–3–39–0; Trescothick 3–0–14–0; Rose 11–2–48–2; Pierson 13.1–4–47–0; Parsons 15–4–46–1; Bowler 1–0–8–0.

Somerset

A. R. K. Pierson c Weston b Haynes	6	G. D. Rose c Hick b Chapman	52
P. C. L. Holloway b Haynes	8	A. R. Caddick b Hafeez b Leatherdale	24
M. E. Trescothick c Solanki b Lampitt	38	P. S. Jones not out	22
*P. D. Bowler c Lampitt b Haynes	4		
R. J. Harden c Hick b Haynes	22	L-b 7, w 16, n-b 6	29
K. A. Parsons lbw b Chapman	21		
M. Burns run out	53	1/20 2/33 3/41 4/78 5/115	283
†R. J. Turner lbw b Lampitt	4	6/115 7/137 8/188 9/204	

Bonus points – Somerset 2, Worcestershire 4.

Bowling: Chapman 20.4–4–81–2; Haynes 24–7–74–4; Lampitt 20–5–54–2; Illingworth 5–2–17–0; Catterall 13–2–31–0; Leatherdale 6–1–19–1.

Umpires: J. C. Balderstone and G. I. Burgess.

At Canterbury, September 9, 10, 11. SOMERSET beat KENT by an innings and 46 runs.

At Cardiff, September 17, 18, 19, 20. SOMERSET lost to GLAMORGAN by 298 runs.

SURREY

Martin Bicknell

Patron: HM The Queen
President: M. J. Stewart
Chairman: M. J. Soper
Chief Executive: P. C. J. Sheldon
Captain: A. J. Hollioake
Cricket Manager: K. T. Medlycott
Director of Cricket Development: M. J. Edwards
Head Groundsman: P. D. Brind
Scorer: K. R. Booth

When the going got tough, Surrey were found wanting. Their whole season boiled down to one game: at home to Leicestershire, who had steadily gained ground on them, to discover which was the best side. By the time it was over, Surrey were left in no doubt as to where they stood – out of the money and a long way short of being champion county. Though they won ten matches, and led the table from May to the start of September, fifth place was an accurate reflection of their year.

Of their five Championship defeats, four were at the hands of the sides which finished above them; the last, against the eventual winners Leicestershire, was the most emphatic. They had under-performed earlier in the season, against Somerset, against Lancashire and, especially, against Yorkshire, but nothing had prepared anyone for the wretched show they put up against a team that everyone had been calling a bits-and-pieces side. In the end, it was Surrey who were shredded – by an innings and 211 runs.

The Championship would have been a remarkable achievement. Surrey were without their dependable opener Darren Bicknell, who took most of the summer to recover from a back operation. International calls deprived them of more key personnel, notably Alec Stewart, Mark Butcher, Graham Thorpe (who then dropped out with another back injury), and, during the one-day series, Alistair Brown and Adam Hollioake.

For long spells, they rose above their handicaps. Their squad system held firm, and the stand-ins – Jason Ratcliffe, Nadeem Shahid, James Knott, Ian Ward and, latterly, Joey Benjamin – did more than anyone could have hoped; they kept Surrey on top of the Championship until, ironically, after the final Test match. But the return of most of their England men coincided with a poor showing against Yorkshire. And they would have done far better to have remained loyal to one of the lesser players rather than bring back a half-fit Thorpe for the final game.

The weather hit everyone, restricting the harvest of bonus points. Surrey, though, missed out without any help from the climate. They achieved maximum points with the bat in just half a dozen matches; on five occasions, they were bowled out for less than 200 runs in the first innings and got none. Only Brown passed 1,000 runs for the county and at a hugely respectable average of 49.33; no one else was remotely near. Butcher reached the mark courtesy of his England form – Stewart was 37 short. There were just 11 hundreds in the Championship, four of those by Brown.

The bowling was the key to Surrey's apparent superiority for so much of the summer, and the Pakistan off-spinner Saqlain Mushtaq must take pride of place, despite the noble efforts of Martin Bicknell.

Saqlain played in five fewer matches than Bicknell, Surrey's only ever-present, but his bowling, at times unreadable, brought him 63 wickets, compared with Bicknell's 65. In three games (all at The Oval), he finished with 11-wicket returns, all match-winning performances. His departure before the showdown with Leicestershire, for yet another meaningless money-spinning one-day international tournament, was particularly galling; when Saqlain had been signed, it was implied that Pakistan would not call on him if Surrey were in contention for the Championship. The World Cup and the probability of further call-ups by Pakistan threw his return in 1999 into doubt.

Another blow to Surrey's cause was the stress fracture of the foot suffered by improving fast bowler Alex Tudor, who took 29 wickets in the ten games he did play, and showed enough promise to earn a place on the Ashes tour, and a Test debut in Perth. Ian Salisbury's fall-off in form, as well as an injury, also hit hard. On the soft pitches of early summer, when it was least expected, he was bowling as well as he ever has, especially in tandem with Saqlain. But his unsuccessful return to Test cricket and subsequent loss of confidence left Surrey in still more of a mess. It was again up to the old faithful, Bicknell, who had not done so badly with the bat either, to lead the way.

The Benson and Hedges Cup semi-final was the earliest manifestation of Leicestershire as Surrey's nemesis, ending a run of 13 consecutive wins in the tournament. The NatWest Trophy quarter-final tie at home to Derbyshire was a woeful display. Wickets, and thus the game, were cast away wilfully. But nothing could match the depths to which Surrey sank in the Sunday League. Regardless of the fact that the final half of the season was used to try out new players, there could be no justification for their incompetent showing. They finished bottom, for only the second time, and it was all they deserved: they won just one game before September. Thanks to the unseasonable weather, they sometimes fell foul of the Duckworth/Lewis method. But there is so much talent in the squad that excuses are absurd. – DAVID LLEWELLYN.

SURREY 1998

[*Bill Smith*]

Back row: J. N. Batty, M. A. V. Bell, R. M. Amin, M. W. Patterson, I. J. Ward. *Middle row:* A. R. Butcher (*assistant coach*), D. J. Naylor (*physiotherapist*), N. Shahid, B. C. Hollioake, A. J. Tudor, J. D. Ratcliffe, I. D. K. Salisbury, J. A. Knott, K. R. Booth (*scorer*), K. T. Medlycott (*cricket manager*). *Front row:* A. D. Brown, J. E. Benjamin, M. P. Bicknell, A. J. Stewart, A. J. Hollioake (*captain*), D. J. Bicknell, G. P. Thorpe, M. A. Butcher. *Inset:* Saqlain Mushtaq.

SURREY RESULTS

All first-class matches – Played 17: Won 10, Lost 5, Drawn 2.

County Championship matches – Played 17: Won 10, Lost 5, Drawn 2.

Competition placings – Britannic Assurance County Championship, 5th;
NatWest Trophy, q-f; Benson and Hedges Cup, s-f;
AXA League, 18th.

COUNTY CHAMPIONSHIP AVERAGES
BATTING

Cap		M	I	NO	R	HS	100s	50s	Avge	Ct/St
1994	A. D. Brown.	15	22	1	1,036	155	4	6	49.33	20
1985	A. J. Stewart†	8	12	1	464	96	0	4	42.18	15
1991	G. P. Thorpe†	6	7	1	251	114	1	1	41.83	10
1996	M. A. Butcher†	12	18	1	661	109*	2	4	38.88	10
1998	N. Shahid	12	22	3	683	126*	2	3	35.94	13
1995	A. J. Hollioake	15	22	2	684	112	1	4	34.20	15
1998	J. D. Ratcliffe.	9	15	1	449	100	1	2	32.07	2
	I. J. Ward.	10	19	2	529	81*	0	5	31.11	9
1998	I. D. K. Salisbury . . .	12	13	2	285	61	0	3	25.90	6
	B. C. Hollioake. . . .	16	24	3	455	60	0	2	21.66	7
1989	M. P. Bicknell†	17	21	1	433	81	0	1	21.65	5
	J. N. Batty	16	19	2	351	63	0	2	20.64	39/6
1998	Saqlain Mushtaq§ . . .	12	15	5	176	45*	0	0	17.60	7
	J. A. Knott	5	9	3	103	41*	0	0	17.16	1
	A. J. Tudor.	10	13	3	167	48	0	0	16.70	3
1993	J. E. Benjamin	8	9	3	57	18*	0	0	9.50	1
	R. M. Amin†	3	4	2	14	12	0	0	7.00	0

Also batted: A. R. Butcher† (cap 1975) (1 match) 22, 12.

* Signifies not out. † *Born in Surrey.* § *Overseas player.*

BOWLING

	O	M	R	W	BB	5W/i	Avge
Saqlain Mushtaq. . . .	475	136	1,119	63	8-65	3	17.76
M. P. Bicknell	494.1	141	1,340	65	5-27	2	20.61
I. D. K. Salisbury . . .	337	99	766	36	7-65	2	21.27
B. C. Hollioake	248.4	49	792	34	4-28	0	23.29
A. J. Tudor	184.2	34	737	29	5-43	1	25.41
M. A. Butcher	94.4	22	287	11	4-41	0	26.09
J. E. Benjamin	189.1	42	626	22	6-35	1	28.45

Also bowled: R. M. Amin 59–9–176–3; J. N. Batty 1–0–22–0; A. D. Brown 2–1–2–0; A. J. Hollioake 92.5–29–247–8; J. A. Knott 1–0–2–0; J. D. Ratcliffe 2–1–4–0; N. Shahid 16–1–66–2.

COUNTY RECORDS

Highest score for:	357*	R. Abel v Somerset at The Oval.	1899
Highest score against:	366	N. H. Fairbrother (Lancashire) at The Oval	1990
Best bowling for:	10-43	T. Rushby v Somerset at Taunton	1921
Best bowling against:	10-28	W. P. Howell (Australians) at The Oval	1899
Highest total for:	811	v Somerset at The Oval	1899
Highest total against:	863	by Lancashire at The Oval	1990
Lowest total for:	14	v Essex at Chelmsford	1983
Lowest total against:	16	by MCC at Lord's	1872

SURREY v NORTHAMPTONSHIRE

At The Oval, April 17, 18, 20, 21. Drawn. Surrey 7 pts, Northamptonshire 5 pts. Toss: Northamptonshire. Championship debut: G. P. Swann. County debut: D. E. Malcolm.

A match that lost more than two days to rain descended into farce when a squabble between the captains prevented a positive conclusion. The saving grace was a whirlwind century from Brown as Surrey thrashed their way to maximum batting points. In pique, Curran then declared at two down, denying them any bowling points, whereupon Adam Hollioake, at 5.11 p.m. on the final afternoon, enforced the follow-on. Negotiations between the captains on an acceptable target had broken down earlier in the day. Brown's hundred came off 72 deliveries, the fastest in the Championship for almost two years; he scored more than half his runs off England Under-19 off-spinner Graeme Swann, on his Championship debut. In all, Brown hit six sixes and ten ones, and shared a fourth-wicket stand of 155 with Thorpe. Shortly before the game ended, Adam Hollioake left the field with blood pouring from a wound; Salisbury, attempting a run-out, struck him on the head with his throw. The Swanns became the first brothers to play together for Northamptonshire since Peter and Jim Watts in 1966.

Close of play: First day, No play; Second day, Surrey 88-1 (J. D. Ratcliffe 39*, N. Shahid 14*); Third day, No play.

Surrey

M. A. Butcher c G. P. Swann b Taylor	29		B. C. Hollioake not out		10
J. D. Ratcliffe c A. J. Swann b Malcolm	61				
N. Shahid st Ripley b G. P. Swann	58		B 4, l-b 11, w 8		23
G. P. Thorpe not out	63				—
A. D. Brown c Montgomerie b Capel	100		1/67 2/135 3/170	(5 wkts dec.)	351
*A. J. Hollioake b Taylor	7		4/325 5/339		

†J. N. Batty, I. D. K. Salisbury, M. P. Bicknell and J. E. Benjamin did not bat.

Bonus points – Surrey 4, Northamptonshire 2.

Bowling: Malcolm 23–5–72–1; Taylor 27–4–90–2; Curran 8–3–17–0; Capel 13–1–66–1; G. P. Swann 13–1–91–1.

Northamptonshire

R. R. Montgomerie c Brown b B. C. Hollioake	13	– not out		29
A. J. Swann c Batty b B. C. Hollioake	29	– c A. J. Hollioake b B. C. Hollioake		1
M. B. Loye not out	0			
G. P. Swann (did not bat)		– (3) not out		14
N-b 2	2	N-b 2		2
				—
1/35 2/44	(2 wkts dec.) 44	1/7	(1 wkt)	46

D. J. Sales, R. J. Bailey, *K. M. Curran, D. J. Capel, †D. Ripley, J. P. Taylor and D. E. Malcolm did not bat.

Bowling: *First Innings*—Bicknell 5–3–7–0; Benjamin 6–0–17–0; Salisbury 5–2–14–0; B. C. Hollioake 3.2–1–6–2. *Second Innings*—B. C. Hollioake 4–0–17–1; Salisbury 6–1–13–0; Shahid 3–0–16–0.

Umpires: G. I. Burgess and B. Dudleston.

SURREY v WARWICKSHIRE

At The Oval, April 23, 24, 25, 27. Surrey won by an innings and 49 runs. Surrey 24 pts, Warwickshire 3 pts. Toss: Surrey.

Warwickshire began as Championship favourites, but collapsed twice and lost by an innings to a confident Surrey. After looking fragile against Durham, their top order fared little better when, though experimental opener Ostler finally got off the mark – just – in his fourth innings of the season. No one seemed to know how to cope with the leg-spin of Salisbury or the seam of

Bicknell. When they batted, Surrey were given the perfect start by Butcher and Warwickshire old boy Ratcliffe, who shared a 172-run opening stand. Thorpe capitalised on this with his 32nd first-class hundred, allowing Hollioake to declare 198 ahead on first innings. A back spasm then prevented Knight from batting until fifth wicket down and makeshift opener Piper was not up to the job. Lara and Hemp gave fleeting hope of a recovery but, when Lara fell to Butcher's tempting slow-medium pace for the second time, the game was effectively over. Bicknell returned his 28th five-wicket haul. This continued Warwickshire's dismal run at The Oval, where they had not won in the Championship since 1975. It was their sixth successive defeat on the ground, and five of those were by an innings.

Close of play: First day, Warwickshire 102-4 (T. L. Penney 17*, D. R. Brown 15*); Second day, Surrey 162-0 (M. A. Butcher 70*, J. D. Ratcliffe 85*); Third day, Surrey 405-6 (A. J. Hollioake 9*, J. N. Batty 6*).

Warwickshire

N. V. Knight lbw b Butcher	27	– (7) lbw b Bicknell	6
D. P. Ostler b Bicknell	0	– (1) c Batty b Benjamin	9
*B. C. Lara c Salisbury b Butcher	38	– c Batty b Butcher	57
D. L. Hemp c A. J. Hollioake b B. C. Hollioake	2	– lbw b Bicknell	37
T. L. Penney b Salisbury	46	– c Thorpe b Bicknell	2
D. R. Brown lbw b Butcher	60	– c Salisbury b Bicknell	4
N. M. K. Smith b Salisbury	10	– (9) c Shahid b Salisbury	0
†K. J. Piper c B. C. Hollioake b Salisbury	0	– (2) lbw b Bicknell	4
G. Welch c Brown b Bicknell	12	– (8) b Salisbury	16
T. A. Munton c Butcher b Salisbury	2	– b A. J. Hollioake	5
E. S. H. Giddins not out	0	– not out	4
L-b 4, n-b 4	10	L-b 5	5
	207		**149**

1/1 2/59 3/62 4/82 5/176   1/9 2/21 3/100 4/109 5/110
6/182 7/182 8/195 9/207   6/120 7/127 8/130 9/137

Bonus points – Warwickshire 1, Surrey 4.

Bowling: *First Innings*—Bicknell 21–5–55–2; Benjamin 14–5–48–0; B. C. Hollioake 14–1–52–1; Butcher 13–4–39–3; A. J. Hollioake 1–1–0–0; Salisbury 11.3–7–7–4. *Second Innings*—Bicknell 20–6–27–5; Benjamin 12–4–36–1; B. C. Hollioake 5–0–18–0; Butcher 6–0–30–1; Salisbury 21–12–30–2; A. J. Hollioake 1.3–0–3–1.

Surrey

M. A. Butcher c Hemp b Brown	72	B. C. Hollioake b Smith	0
J. D. Ratcliffe c sub b Smith	93	†J. N. Batty not out	6
N. Shahid c Brown b Smith	90	B 9, l-b 2, n-b 4	15
G. P. Thorpe c Penney b Smith	114		
A. D. Brown c Brown b Smith	6		**(6 wkts dec.) 405**
*A. J. Hollioake not out	9		

1/172 2/178 3/368
4/388 5/394 6/394

I. D. K. Salisbury, M. P. Bicknell and J. E. Benjamin did not bat.

Bonus points – Surrey 4, Warwickshire 2.

Bowling: Giddins 21–1–72–0; Brown 18–3–67–1; Munton 16–2–46–0; Welch 14–2–51–0; Smith 26.4–2–128–5; Hemp 6–0–30–0.

Umpires: J. C. Balderstone and D. R. Shepherd.

At Southampton, May 13, 14, 15. SURREY beat HAMPSHIRE by an innings and 184 runs.

At Taunton, May 21, 22, 23, 24. SURREY lost to SOMERSET by 165 runs.

SURREY v KENT

At The Oval, May 29, 30, 31. Surrey won by an innings and 30 runs. Surrey 23 pts, Kent 4 pts. Toss: Surrey.

By the end of the first day, Hooper had spun his way to six wickets. The next morning he added another, to record career-best figures of seven for 93. It was a sign of things to come. The pitch had already been used for a one-day international and the Benson and Hedges quarter-final; there was little doubt that, whatever Hooper could manage, Saqlain Mushtaq and Salisbury could do better. They finished with 13 victims between them, and both were awarded their county caps. Kent were duly rolled over for 86 at their first attempt. Thorpe's sharp reflexes and safe hands earned him six catches in the innings, all at slip – one short of the world record for a fielder. Following on, Hooper gave the consummate demonstration of how to play spin, using his head, hands and feet in perfect co-ordination. But even he succumbed eventually, top-edging an intended sweep off Saqlain. No other Kent batsman could match him as they subsided early on the third day.

Close of play: First day, Surrey 314-9 (I. D. K. Salisbury 48*, M. P. Bicknell 0*); Second day, Kent 195-8 (D. W. Headley 5*, M. M. Patel 6*).

Surrey

M. A. Butcher c Marsh b Hooper	51	Saqlain Mushtaq lbw b Headley	9
A. J. Stewart c Hooper b Patel	86	A. J. Tudor lbw b Headley	6
G. P. Thorpe c Patel b Hooper	26	M. P. Bicknell b Hooper	14
*A. J. Hollioake b Hooper	32		
A. D. Brown b Hooper	0	B 11, l-b 10, n-b 4	25
B. C. Hollioake c and b Hooper	4		
†J. N. Batty c Marsh b Hooper	33	1/142 2/142 3/193 4/193 5/205	342
I. D. K. Salisbury not out	56	6/212 7/284 8/296 9/314	

Bonus points – Surrey 3, Kent 4 (Score at 120 overs: 335-9).

Bowling: Headley 17–5–40–2; McCague 9–1–35–0; Ealham 11–5–16–0; Patel 43–10–129–1; Fleming 4–2–8–0; Hooper 39.1–7–93–7.

Kent

D. P. Fulton c Thorpe b Tudor	3	– c Stewart b Bicknell	0
R. W. T. Key lbw b Bicknell	10	– c Batty b Tudor	0
T. R. Ward c Thorpe b Salisbury	9	– c A. J. Hollioake b Bicknell	21
C. L. Hooper lbw b Bicknell	4	– c Batty b Saqlain Mushtaq	94
A. P. Wells lbw b Saqlain Mushtaq	24	– c Thorpe b Salisbury	24
M. A. Ealham c Thorpe b Salisbury	5	– c Butcher b Salisbury	7
M. V. Fleming c Thorpe b Salisbury	10	– c Saqlain Mushtaq b Salisbury	22
*†S. A. Marsh c Thorpe b Saqlain Mushtaq	1	– b Saqlain Mushtaq	3
D. W. Headley not out	3	– b Saqlain Mushtaq	5
M. M. Patel c Thorpe b Saqlain Mushtaq	0	– c Butcher b Saqlain Mushtaq	24
M. J. McCague run out	0	– not out	13
B 9, l-b 2, n-b 6	17	B 2, l-b 1, w 2, n-b 8	13
1/17 2/17 3/21 4/61 5/61	86	1/0 2/2 3/50 4/113 5/131	226
6/75 7/76 8/84 9/85		6/163 7/167 8/189 9/195	

Bonus points – Surrey 4.

Bowling: *First Innings*—Bicknell 10–5–26–2; Tudor 6–1–18–1; Saqlain Mushtaq 14–6–18–3; Salisbury 11.4–4–13–3. *Second Innings*—Bicknell 7–1–15–2; Tudor 3–0–26–1; Saqlain Mushtaq 24.5–6–100–4; Salisbury 24–6–75–3; B. C. Hollioake 2–0–7–0.

Umpires: B. Dudleston and R. Palmer.

SURREY v WORCESTERSHIRE

At The Oval, June 3, 4, 5, 6. Surrey won by 79 runs. Surrey 23 pts, Worcestershire 5 pts. Toss: Surrey.

Hick continued his remarkable run with a fourth hundred in consecutive innings. His 101st first-class century was a slow one – it took him 264 balls to reach three figures. It was his sixth against Surrey. Hick's achievements were overshadowed, though, by a bold piece of captaincy by Adam Hollioake. Surrey could not afford to lose their momentum at the head of the Championship table, but had three top-line batsmen on England duty. With the match dribbling towards a draw, Hollioake declared at lunch on the final day, leaving Worcestershire, although no target had been agreed, 67 overs to make 266. For a while nothing happened. Then Saqlain Mushtaq struck. He finished with a career-best seven for 41, and Hollioake's spirit of adventure was well rewarded. Earlier, the Surrey reserves had produced some fine batting: Ratcliffe and Shahid each hit a hundred, and Ward two fifties, including a career-best 64. An experiment with noon starts was not an obvious success.

Close of play: First day, Surrey 193-3 (N. Shahid 12*, A. D. Brown 4*); Second day, Worcestershire 104-2 (G. A. Hick 40*, G. R. Haynes 6*); Third day, Worcestershire 366-9 (R. K. Illingworth 45*, A. Sheriyar 11*).

Surrey

J. D. Ratcliffe c Illingworth	100	– c Newport b Sheriyar	9
I. J. Ward lbw b Illingworth	64	– c Leatherdale	58
N. Shahid c Newport b Haynes	124	– c Rhodes b Newport	9
*A. J. Hollioake lbw b Illingworth	0	– lbw b Leatherdale	47
A. D. Brown c Moody b Sheriyar	72	– not out	0
B. C. Hollioake lbw b Haynes	51	– not out	1
A. J. Tudor b Haynes	26		
I. D. K. Salisbury not out	28		
M. P. Bicknell not out	7		
B 3, l-b 13, n-b 14	30	B 2, l-b 2, w 2	6

1/164 2/183 3/183 4/336   (7 wkts dec.) 502   1/15 2/35   (4 wkts dec.) 130
5/440 6/442 7/487   3/128 4/129

†J. N. Batty and Saqlain Mushtaq did not bat.

Bonus points – Surrey 4, Worcestershire 2 (Score at 120 overs: 440-5).

Bowling: *First Innings*—Newport 21–9–42–0; Sheriyar 22–2–118–1; Moody 13–4–60–0; Lampitt 19–5–68–0; Illingworth 30–8–90–3; Haynes 12.4–4–46–3; Solanki 10–1–44–0; Leatherdale 1–0–8–0; Hick 3–0–10–0. *Second Innings*—Newport 5–1–15–1; Sheriyar 6–1–31–1; Illingworth 8–1–43–0; Lampitt 4–0–25–0; Leatherdale 3–0–12–2.

Worcestershire

V. S. Solanki c B. C. Hollioake b Tudor	0	– b Tudor	4
A. Hafeez c A. J. Hollioake b Saqlain Mushtaq	33	– c Shahid b Saqlain Mushtaq	30
G. A. Hick b Bicknell	119	– lbw b Saqlain Mushtaq	22
G. R. Haynes c Ward b Bicknell	14	– c Brown b Saqlain Mushtaq	9
*T. M. Moody c Shahid b Salisbury	22	– c Batty b Salisbury	62
D. A. Leatherdale c A. J. Hollioake b Saqlain Mushtaq	9	– c Brown b Saqlain Mushtaq	9
†S. J. Rhodes b Saqlain Mushtaq	0	– b Saqlain Mushtaq	1
S. R. Lampitt b Tudor	43	– c Brown b Saqlain Mushtaq	7
R. K. Illingworth not out	45	– lbw b Saqlain Mushtaq	7
P. J. Newport c A. J. Hollioake b Saqlain Mushtaq	18	– c Shahid b Salisbury	19
A. Sheriyar c Batty b Bicknell	11	– not out	0
B 3, l-b 22, w 2, n-b 26	53	B 4, l-b 2, n-b 10	16

1/5 2/72 3/113 4/144 5/155   367   1/7 2/51 3/73 4/74 5/92   186
6/155 7/270 8/284 9/329   6/98 7/128 8/160 9/168

Bonus points – Worcestershire 3, Surrey 3 (Score at 120 overs: 311-8).

Bowling: *First Innings*—Bicknell 24.4–7–61–3; Tudor 11–0–61–2; Saqlain Mushtaq 60–17–116–4; Salisbury 50–19–100–1; A. J. Hollioake 1–0–4–0. *Second Innings*—Bicknell 6–3–19–0; Tudor 8–0–39–1; Saqlain Mushtaq 28–11–41–7; Salisbury 24.5–6–81–2.

Umpires: J. W. Lloyds and A. G. T. Whitehead.

At Chelmsford, June 11, 12, 13, 15. SURREY drew with ESSEX.

At Manchester, June 18, 19, 20, 21. SURREY lost to LANCASHIRE by six wickets.

At Swansea, July 1, 2, 3. SURREY beat GLAMORGAN by six wickets.

SURREY v MIDDLESEX

At Guildford, July 15, 16, 17. Surrey won by 280 runs. Surrey 20 pts, Middlesex 4 pts. Toss: Surrey.

The opening day of Middlesex's first-ever visit to Guildford saw the fall of 20 wickets, including those of three England captains for nought. But there was no question of the pitch being condemned; though the ball swung and seamed, the main explanation was poor batting. Having led by only 35, Surrey were able to pass 400 in their second innings and set up their heaviest victory in terms of runs over their metropolitan rivals. The Browns – Alistair of Surrey and Keith of Middlesex – were the only batsmen to perform consistently well. They top-scored in each innings and Alistair showed application which belied his reputation as a one-day player. Adam Hollioake and Salisbury joined him in making fifties in the second innings. Middlesex, needing 456 to win, then capitulated, mainly to Salisbury, who made his case for a return to Test cricket with four for 43. The scorecard entry "Batty b Batt" created much cheerful speculation about future combinations, perhaps involving Ball of Gloucestershire.

Close of play: First day, Middlesex 115; Second day, Surrey 335-8 (I. D. K. Salisbury 24*).

Surrey

M. A. Butcher c Tunnell b Fraser	0	– c Ramprakash b Batt 10
I. J. Ward c Brown b Batt	35	– c Brown b Fraser 39
A. J. Stewart b Batt	0	– lbw b Batt 46
*A. J. Hollioake lbw b Fraser	0	– c Gatting b Johnson 59
A. D. Brown c Weekes b Tunnell	51	– lbw b Johnson 79
B. C. Hollioake lbw b Batt	6	– c Langer b Dutch 12
†J. N. Batty b Batt	0	– lbw b Tunnell 5
M. P. Bicknell lbw b Fraser	6	– c Johnson b Fraser 26
I. D. K. Salisbury lbw b Fraser	31	– c Langer b Johnson 61
A. J. Tudor not out	1	– c Fraser b Tunnell 41
Saqlain Mushtaq c Ramprakash b Fraser	0	– not out 0
L-b 14, w 4, n-b 2	20	B 9, l-b 19, w 6, n-b 8 42

1/0 2/7 3/7 4/92 5/101   150
6/101 7/108 8/139 9/150

1/21 2/92 3/155 4/204 5/222   420
6/233 7/271 8/335 9/418

Bonus points – Middlesex 4.

Bowling: *First Innings*—Fraser 16.1–6–34–4; Batt 15–3–51–5; Johnson 6–0–24–0; Tunnell 18–10–24–1; Dutch 2–0–3–0. *Second Innings*—Fraser 25–5–76–2; Batt 27–1–109–2; Johnson 21–1–85–3; Tunnell 27–5–59–2; Dutch 22–7–47–1; Weekes 4–1–10–0; Langer 2–0–6–0.

Middlesex

M. W. Gatting b Bicknell	0	– b Bicknell	0
J. L. Langer lbw b Bicknell	14	– c Bicknell b Tudor	20
*M. R. Ramprakash c Batty b Tudor	13	– c Tudor b Bicknell	16
P. N. Weekes c B. C. Hollioake b Tudor	5	– c A. J. Hollioake b Tudor	7
D. C. Nash b Bicknell	0	– c Brown b Salisbury	25
†K. R. Brown lbw b Tudor	30	– not out	59
K. P. Dutch c Stewart b B. C. Hollioake	11	– c Stewart b Saqlain Mushtaq	6
R. L. Johnson c Salisbury b Saqlain Mushtaq	11	– st Batty b Salisbury	8
C. J. Batt lbw b Saqlain Mushtaq	0	– lbw b Salisbury	5
A. R. C. Fraser not out	11	– c Ward b Salisbury	10
P. C. R. Tufnell c A. J. Hollioake b Tudor	2	– st Batty b Saqlain Mushtaq	8
B 4, l-b 4, w 4, n-b 6	18	B 2, l-b 5, w 2, n-b 2	11

1/10 2/35 3/41 4/41 5/47   115   1/0 2/24 3/46 4/48 5/88   175
6/73 7/96 8/96 9/106   6/101 7/121 8/139 9/165

Bonus points – Surrey 4.

Bowling: *First Innings*—Bicknell 12–2–25–3; Tudor 14–2–47–4; B. C. Hollioake 7–2–12–1; A. J. Hollioake 3–1–8–0; Saqlain Mushtaq 6–1–15–2. *Second Innings*—Bicknell 14–5–33–2; Tudor 10–3–31–2; B. C. Hollioake 5–3–8–0; A. J. Hollioake 1–0–1–0; Saqlain Mushtaq 15.5–1–52–2; Salisbury 18–4–43–4.

Umpires: J. W. Lloyds and K. E. Palmer.

At Cheltenham, July 22, 23, 24. SURREY lost to GLOUCESTERSHIRE by two wickets.

SURREY v SUSSEX

At The Oval, July 30, 31, August 1. Surrey won by an innings and 69 runs. Surrey 24 pts, Sussex 4 pts. Toss: Sussex.

On the pitch used earlier in the week for their NatWest quarter-final, Surrey cruised to victory, thanks largely to off-spinner Saqlain Mushtaq. After a promising start, Sussex lost all ten first-innings wickets while adding 32, a collapse which included a spell of seven for 17 in 65 balls – and four for none in seven – by Saqlain, who finished with what was (for a week) a career-best seven for 30. Next, it was the batsmen's turn to confirm Surrey's superiority; helped by dropped catches, Stewart and the in-form Brown narrowly missed hundreds. Brown was one of five victims for Sussex's own off-spinner, Bates. When Sussex batted again, Saqlain was not quite as potent as before but still tricky enough to pick up his second haul of 11 wickets in the season. Adams, who showed fight lacking in his colleagues, was left stranded on 99.

Close of play: First day, Surrey 112-2 (A. J. Stewart 63*, A. J. Hollioake 3*); Second day, Sussex 59-4 (C. J. Adams 20*, R. J. Kirtley 4*).

Sussex

M. T. E. Peirce c Batty b B. C. Hollioake	54	– c Brown b Saqlain Mushtaq	29
W. G. Khan c Batty b Bicknell	41	– lbw b Bicknell	0
M. Newell c Stewart b Bicknell	0	– c A. J. Hollioake b Bicknell	0
*C. J. Adams c Brown b Saqlain Mushtaq	0	– not out	99
M. G. Bevan c Batty b Bicknell	5	– c Brown b Saqlain Mushtaq	1
R. K. Rao c B. C. Hollioake b Saqlain Mushtaq	1	– (7) c A. J. Hollioake b Bicknell	6
†S. Humphries c Butcher b Saqlain Mushtaq	7	– (8) c Ward b Saqlain Mushtaq	5
J. J. Bates lbw b Saqlain Mushtaq	0	– (9) lbw b Salisbury	7
R. J. Kirtley c Stewart b Bicknell	1	– (6) b Bicknell	5
J. D. Lewry b Saqlain Mushtaq	0	– lbw b Saqlain Mushtaq	0
M. A. Robinson not out	2	– c Brown b Salisbury	4
B 5, l-b 3, n-b 6	14	L-b 6, w 2, n-b 6	14
	125		**170**

1/93 2/93 3/96 4/114 5/114
6/121 7/121 8/122 9/122

1/1 2/17 3/53 4/55 5/72
6/108 7/117 8/134 9/141

Bonus points – Surrey 4.

Bowling: *First Innings*—Bicknell 14–4–35–2; Tudor 3–0–9–0; B. C. Hollioake 15–3–43–1; Saqlain Mushtaq 19.2–10–30–7. *Second Innings*—Bicknell 15–4–45–4; B. C. Hollioake 3–1–11–0; Saqlain Mushtaq 35–10–74–4; A. J. Hollioake 6–3–12–0; Salisbury 17.2–7–22–2.

Surrey

M. A. Butcher c Humphries b Lewry	34	I. D. K. Salisbury lbw b Bates	8
I. J. Ward c Newell b Lewry	4	Saqlain Mushtaq lbw b Lewry	40
A. J. Stewart lbw b Robinson	96	A. J. Tudor not out	8
*A. J. Hollioake c and b Bates	28		
A. D. Brown c Lewry b Bates	94	B 3, l-b 4, w 4, n-b 4	15
B. C. Hollioake c Newell b Bates	1		
†J. N. Batty c Bevan b Bates	1	1/7 2/99 3/168 4/186 5/191	**364**
M. P. Bicknell b Kirtley	35	6/193 7/308 8/308 9/325	

Bonus points – Surrey 4, Sussex 4.

Bowling: Lewry 14.2–3–65–3; Kirtley 24–3–105–1; Bates 33–7–100–5; Robinson 22–3–57–1; Bevan 9–2–30–0.

Umpires: J. C. Balderstone and R. Julian.

SURREY v DERBYSHIRE

At The Oval, August 6, 7, 8. Surrey won by 226 runs. Surrey 23 pts, Derbyshire 4 pts. Toss: Surrey.

Surrey, hit by injuries, Test calls and their decision to suspend Ratcliffe for one match for disciplinary reasons, called on 44-year-old Alan Butcher, now the Second Eleven coach, to play his first game for the club for 12 years. Butcher contributed 22 and 12 to Surrey's victory, and began his first innings while son Mark was on his way to a maiden Test hundred at Headingley. Greeted by a doff of the panama from umpire Kitchen, he drove his first ball through the covers for four. Once again, however, it was Saqlain Mushtaq's match. Making good use of his mystery ball – a leg-break delivered with an off-break action – he took 11 wickets for the third time in the season, including, for the second match running, career-best figures, this time eight for 65. Brown's fourth Championship hundred of 1998 had been the centrepiece of Surrey's first innings, when left-arm spinner Blackwell also claimed the best figures of his career: five for 115. Hollioake's decision not to enforce the follow-on spared his bowlers from flogging away in draining heat, though Bicknell used the respite to score 81, at No. 9, leaving Derbyshire with a target of 433. They succumbed with a day to spare.

Close of play: First day, Derbyshire 46-2 (R. M. S. Weston 15*, K. J. Barnett 8*); Second day, Surrey 148-7 (J. A. Knott 21*, M. P. Bicknell 20*).

Surrey

I. J. Ward b Blackwell	26	– c Krikken b Dean	7
†J. N. Batty c Barnett b DeFreitas	21	– c Barnett b DeFreitas	21
N. Shahid b Blackwell	6	– b Blackwell	27
*A. J. Hollioake c Krikken b Blackwell	36	– c May b Blackwell	25
A. D. Brown c Roberts b Blackwell	132	– c May b Dean	11
B. C. Hollioake c Blackwell b Clarke	16	– c DeFreitas b Blackwell	4
J. A. Knott b Blackwell	2	– not out	41
A. R. Butcher lbw b Dean	22	– c Roberts b Blackwell	12
M. P. Bicknell c Barnett b Dean	32	– st Krikken b Roberts	81
Saqlain Mushtaq c Krikken b Dean	31	– c Krikken b Roberts	0
R. M. Amin not out	2		
L-b 5, n-b 2	7	L-b 5, w 4	9

1/29 2/52 3/57 4/148 5/189   333   1/13 2/38 3/72   (9 wkts dec.) 238
6/198 7/238 8/287 9/322   4/89 5/91 6/101
                                    7/123 8/238 9/238

Bonus points – Surrey 3, Derbyshire 4.

Bowling: *First Innings*—DeFreitas 13–2–50–1; Dean 10–1–34–3; Blackwell 33–6–115–5; Cassar 5–0–28–0; Roberts 14–1–51–0; Clarke 11–2–50–1. *Second Innings*—DeFreitas 13–5–26–1; Dean 20–2–70–2; Blackwell 38–9–94–4; Clarke 2–0–4–0; Roberts 15–4–39–2.

Derbyshire

M. J. Slater c Saqlain Mushtaq b B. C. Hollioake	7	– c and b Saqlain Mushtaq	99
M. R. May b Bicknell	1	– c Shahid b Saqlain Mushtaq	43
R. M. S. Weston st Batty b Saqlain Mushtaq	37	– c Batty b Saqlain Mushtaq	16
K. J. Barnett b Bicknell	13	– c Ward b Amin	18
M. E. Cassar b B. C. Hollioake	4	– c Ward b Saqlain Mushtaq	9
I. D. Blackwell c Bicknell b B. C. Hollioake	10	– st Batty b Saqlain Mushtaq	2
*†K. M. Krikken c Shahid b Saqlain Mushtaq	11	– lbw b Saqlain Mushtaq	0
P. A. J. DeFreitas lbw b B. C. Hollioake	4	– c Batty b Amin	6
V. P. Clarke b Bicknell	16	– b Saqlain Mushtaq	1
G. M. Roberts b Saqlain Mushtaq	8	– not out	2
K. J. Dean not out	0	– lbw b Saqlain Mushtaq	2
B 1, l-b 8, n-b 19	28	B 2, l-b 6	8

1/11 2/13 3/62 4/80 5/94   139   1/93 2/127 3/160   206
6/96 7/103 8/119 9/139   4/171 5/181 6/181
                                    7/192 8/193 9/202

Bonus points – Surrey 4.

Bowling: *First Innings*—Bicknell 17–3–48–3; B. C. Hollioake 11–4–36–4; Saqlain Mushtaq 24.3–9–42–3; Amin 1–0–4–0; A. J. Hollioake 1–1–0–0. *Second Innings*—Bicknell 12–2–47–0; B. C. Hollioake 11–0–41–0; Saqlain Mushtaq 27.3–4–65–8; A. J. Hollioake 2–0–13–0; Amin 10–0–32–2.

Umpires: M. J. Kitchen and R. Palmer.

At Nottingham, August 19, 20, 21. SURREY beat NOTTINGHAMSHIRE by seven wickets.

At Leeds, September 1, 2, 3, 4. SURREY lost to YORKSHIRE by 164 runs.

At Chester-le-Street, September 9, 10, 11, 12. SURREY beat DURHAM by 121 runs.

SURREY v LEICESTERSHIRE

At The Oval, September 17, 18, 19. Leicestershire won by an innings and 211 runs. Leicestershire 24 pts, Surrey 2 pts. Toss: Leicestershire.

Leicestershire won the 1998 County Championship, their second in three years, in devastating fashion with a massive victory over the team who had led the table right through from May until September. It was their sixth successive win, and the fifth in a row producing maximum points. Surrey and Lancashire started the final round of matches with a chance of overhauling them, but Leicestershire's form made them unstoppable. Surrey, in contrast, were embarrassing and they were duly punished: having been first or second all season, they finished fifth in the final table. On a dry, grassless pitch, Surrey desperately missed their match-winning off-spinner Saqlain Mushtaq, withdrawn by Pakistan. After they lost a crucial toss, however, other factors came into play: the failure of their attack, an injury to Bicknell, inept batting and sloppy fielding all coincided with some fine Leicestershire cricket. Smith and Habib transformed Leicestershire's innings with a stand of 252, following one of 249 in July, an all-wicket county record against Surrey. Smith batted eight hours for a maiden double-hundred, from 417 balls, containing 21 fours, a six and a seven. A third century, from Nixon, allowed Simmons to declare at 585. Four overs later, Surrey had lost their top three for ducks, including Thorpe, returning after injury for his first game in 11 weeks. At 13 for four at the end of the second day, their faint hopes were dead; with the exception of Adam Hollioake in both innings, and brother Ben, in the first, there was little further resistance. Now that a Surrey victory could be discounted, the title would be Leicestershire's provided they took a third bowling point. And when Salisbury was seventh out before noon on the third morning, Leicestershire had effectively sealed the title. When they followed on, Surrey fared only a little better. Sky TV broadcast the match live; after a season of poor attendances at Grace Road, Leicestershire at last gained some of the publicity their cricket deserved.

Close of play: First day, Leicestershire 349-4 (B. F. Smith 137*, A. Habib 114*); Second day, Surrey 13-4 (A. J. Stewart 7*, A. J. Hollioake 3*).

Leicestershire

V. J. Wells c Salisbury b B. C. Hollioake	24	C. C. Lewis not out	54
D. L. Maddy c Stewart b Bicknell	7		
I. J. Sutcliffe c Brown b Benjamin	18	L-b 14, w 14, n-b 14	42
B. F. Smith c Brown b Shahid	204		
*P. V. Simmons b B. C. Hollioake	21		(6 wkts dec.) 585
A. Habib c Stewart b B. C. Hollioake	114	1/11 2/44	
†P. A. Nixon not out	101	3/74 4/102	
		5/354 6/480	

D. J. Millns, A. D. Mullally and M. T. Brimson did not bat.

Bonus points – Leicestershire 4, Surrey 2 (Score at 120 overs: 409-5).

Bowling: Bicknell 13-4-49-1; Benjamin 27-5-95-1; B. C. Hollioake 27-3-106-3; Butcher 16-3-59-0; Salisbury 36-6-111-0; A. J. Hollioake 13-2-29-0; Amin 39-8-89-0; Shahid 7-1-31-1; Brown 2-1-2-0.

Surrey

M. A. Butcher c Maddy b Mullally	0	– c Wells b Millns	24
N. Shahid c Nixon b Millns	0	– (3) b Simmons	34
G. P. Thorpe lbw b Mullally	0	– (4) run out	2
†A. J. Stewart b Lewis	33	– (5) c Nixon b Simmons	16
A. D. Brown lbw b Millns	3	– (6) st Nixon b Brimson	12
*A. J. Hollioake c Nixon b Lewis	40	– (7) not out	54
B. C. Hollioake not out	46	– (2) c Millns b Mullally	17
I. D. K. Salisbury lbw b Wells	1	– lbw b Simmons	1
M. P. Bicknell c Nixon b Wells	0	– c sub b Brimson	31
J. E. Benjamin b Brimson	12	– b Millns	0
R. M. Amin c Nixon b Simmons	0	– st Nixon b Brimson	12
B 4, l-b 3, n-b 4	11	L-b 11, w 4, n-b 10	25

1/0 2/0 3/0 4/8 5/79	146	1/47 2/53 3/56 4/85 5/106	228
6/80 7/85 8/85 9/133		6/122 7/123 8/194 9/195	

Bonus points – Leicestershire 4.

Bowling: *First Innings*—Mullally 10–4–26–2; Millns 9–3–36–2; Wells 6–2–11–2; Lewis 6–1–12–2; Brimson 6–1–33–1; Simmons 6–1–21–1. *Second Innings*—Mullally 20–9–54–1; Lewis 4–0–19–0; Millns 13–5–32–2; Brimson 21.4–6–62–3; Simmons 14–3–50–3.

Umpires: J. H. Hampshire and K. E. Palmer.

DATES OF WINNING COUNTY CHAMPIONSHIP

The dates on which the County Championship has been settled since 1979 are as follows:

			Final margin
1979	Essex	August 21	77 pts
1980	Middlesex	September 2	13 pts
1981	Nottinghamshire	September 14	2 pts
1982	Middlesex	September 11	39 pts
1983	Essex	September 13	16 pts
1984	Essex	September 11	14 pts
1985	Middlesex	September 17	18 pts
1986	Essex	September 10	28 pts
1987	Nottinghamshire	September 14	4 pts
1988	Worcestershire	September 16	1 pt
1989	Worcestershire	August 31	6 pts
1990	Middlesex	September 20	31 pts
1991	Essex	September 19	13 pts
1992	Essex	September 3	41 pts
1993	Middlesex	August 30	36 pts
1994	Warwickshire	September 2	42 pts
1995	Warwickshire	September 16	32 pts
1996	Leicestershire	September 21	27 pts
1997	Glamorgan	September 20	4 pts
1998	Leicestershire	September 19	15 pts

Note: The earliest date on which the Championship has been won since it was expanded in 1895 was August 12, 1910, by Kent.

WALTER LAWRENCE TROPHY

The Walter Lawrence Trophy, sponsored by EDS, for the fastest first-class century in 1998 was shared by Alistair Brown of Surrey, who reached 100 in 72 balls against Northamptonshire, and Carl Hooper of Kent, who took the same number of balls against Worcestershire. Each batsman received £1,000.

Jason Lewry

SUSSEX

President: The Duke of Richmond and Gordon

Chairman: D. G. Trangmar

Chief Executive: A. C. S. Pigott

General Manager: D. R. Gilbert

Captain: C. J. Adams

Cricket Manager and Senior Coach: P. Moores

Head Groundsman: P. Eaton

Scorer: L. V. Chandler

A final place of seventh in the County Championship was no mean feat, considering that Sussex had propped up the rest the previous year. The new regime – installed at Hove after the revolution of early 1997 – said their first priority was to finish in the top eight, and qualify for the new Super Cup. They achieved this, and chief executive Tony Pigott admitted they could not have hoped for better. "If someone had offered me at the end of 1997 that we would be seventh in the Championship the next year, I would have laughed," he said.

One-day results were less pleasing. Sussex had finished bottom of the Sunday League, as well as the Championship, the previous season, and rose only two places in 1998, completing six wins. They flopped again in the Benson and Hedges Cup, while their hopes in the NatWest Trophy were ended by eventual winners Lancashire in the first round.

The acquisition of a new captain, Chris Adams, from Derbyshire, and the Australian left-hander Michael Bevan as overseas player considerably strengthened the batting, although Bevan's departure for the Commonwealth Games exposed a weakness in the final three Championship games. He also missed the first two, again through international duties, but in the 12 matches he did play scored 935 first-class runs at 55. Adams was the only batsman to reach 1,000, averaging 42. Opening batsmen Wasim Khan, signed from Warwickshire, and Toby Peirce both passed 700 runs, though their form tailed off in the closing matches. Sussex were keen to put their top players on long contracts, and Adams indicated that an extension of his existing deal would probably keep him at Hove for the rest of his career. Bevan's contract was extended by two years, tying him to Sussex until 2001.

The county accumulated 63 bowling bonus points out of a possible 68 – only Gloucestershire and Durham managed more. Much of the credit must go to Jason Lewry and James Kirtley, who formed a highly effective new-ball attack. It was a particularly happy season for Lewry, the left-arm swing bowler who had missed 1997 after an operation on his lower back. This time, he missed only one Championship game, took 62 wickets at 22.72, and was picked for the England A tour. Kirtley was close behind him, with 54 wickets, and Mark Robinson claimed 42 with some consistent and disciplined bowling. Additional support came from Robin Martin-Jenkins, who underlined his all-round promise in a thrilling 18-run win over Glamorgan at the start of September. He claimed match figures of nine for 119 and scored 78, both career-bests.

Though the seamers flourished, Sussex were in need of a specialist slow bowler. Leg-spinner Amer Khan did not get a look in after three early Championship games. Often, Bevan provided the spin option with his left-arm chinamen, while Rajesh Rao's leg-breaks were occasionally pressed into service; Sussex hoped he could develop this side of his game.

Pigott had stressed at the start of the season that the team rebuilding programme was some way from completion, and the year saw several retirements and departures, as well as new signings. Neil Taylor, who had headed the Sussex averages after joining from Kent in 1997, ended a 19-year career in which he had scored 19,031 first-class runs. He missed five games early on, with knee trouble, and lost his place to Rao after a brief return in June. Former Test bowler Paul Jarvis found the success of the seam attack made him surplus to requirements; he appeared in only four Championship games. He had played five seasons for Sussex since leaving Yorkshire, and taken 133 wickets, despite injury problems; feeling he still had something to offer, he fixed up a move to Somerset. The Newell brothers, Keith and Mark, could not command regular places and rejected one-year contracts. Amer Khan and fellow-spinner Richard Davis also departed.

In the autumn, Sussex made several acquisitions to fill these gaps. They invited Richard Montgomerie, leaving Northamptonshire after eight seasons, to bolster the top of the batting order, and then captured Tony Cottey, the 32-year-old Glamorgan vice-captain, as their List One signing, on a five-year contract. Spinner Umer Rashid joined from Middlesex.

Wicket-keeper Shaun Humphries finally got his chance in his sixth season on the staff. He had played only four first-class matches since his debut in 1993, but took his place in the team when Peter Moores announced his retirement in early May. Moores, who had made 546 dismissals in 16 seasons (two of them with Worcestershire), captained Sussex the previous year, but had already begun to move into coaching. He decided to concentrate on that side of his career, and was eventually appointed cricket manager and coach. A restructuring of the administration team also saw Australian Dave Gilbert switch from director of cricket to general manager.

Sussex's push to attract more spectators and raise their profile continued. They staged two more day/night Sunday League matches at Hove, though a third, against Glamorgan in early September, was cancelled because of lack of sponsorship. But Pigott sees floodlit cricket as part of the future of the game, and obtained permission to install eight permanent towers, 100 feet high. They might not be very permanent, however. The club stressed to members at their AGM that they wanted to be at the forefront of any discussions for a new multi-sport site in the county; they were encouraged by the way supporters accepted that there were difficulties about redeveloping Hove, their home since 1872. – ANDY ARLIDGE.

SUSSEX 1998

[Bill Smith]

Back row: N. J. Wilton, A. D. Edwards, J. R. Carpenter, R. S. C. Martin-Jenkins, G. R. Haywood, R. K. Rao, G. R. A. Campbell, A. A. Khan. Middle row: J. J. Bates. M. T. E. Peirce, W. G. Khan, K. Newell, M. Newell, R. J. Kirtley, S. Humphries, M. R. Strong, T. Wright (physiotherapist). Front row: N. R. Taylor, J. D. Lewry, P. Moores, C. J. Adams (captain), K. Greenfield, P. W. Jarvis, M. A. Robinson. Insets: M. G. Bevan, R. P. Davis.

SUSSEX RESULTS

All first-class matches – Played 19: Won 6, Lost 7, Drawn 6.

County Championship matches – Played 17: Won 6, Lost 7, Drawn 4.

*Competition placings – Britannic Assurance County Championship, 7th;
NatWest Trophy, 1st round; Benson and Hedges Cup, 4th in Group D;
AXA League, 16th.*

COUNTY CHAMPIONSHIP AVERAGES

BATTING

Cap		M	I	NO	R	HS	100s	50s	Avge	Ct
1998	M. G. Bevan§	12	19	2	935	149*	3	4	55.00	10
1998	C. J. Adams	16	27	1	1,116	170	4	4	42.92	30
	M. Newell†	8	12	1	338	135*	2	0	30.72	6
	R. S. C. Martin-Jenkins	8	13	1	353	78	0	2	29.41	3
	W. G. Khan	16	28	1	775	125	1	5	28.70	5
	M. T. E. Peirce	17	30	1	725	96	0	5	25.00	7
	K. Newell†	9	17	4	325	84	0	2	25.00	7
	N. J. Wilton	2	4	2	46	19*	0	0	23.00	5
1997	N. R. Taylor	5	7	0	153	51	0	1	21.85	4
1994	P. W. Jarvis	4	6	1	107	39	0	0	21.40	4
	R. K. Rao	9	16	1	320	76	0	2	21.33	0
1998	R. J. Kirtley†	17	26	10	320	59	0	1	20.00	2
	S. Humphries†	13	21	1	272	66	0	1	13.60	25
	J. R. Carpenter	8	15	0	193	65	0	1	12.86	3
	A. A. Khan	3	4	0	41	23	0	0	10.25	4
	J. J. Bates	4	7	0	54	38	0	0	7.71	4
1996	J. D. Lewry†	16	23	0	132	24	0	0	5.73	1
	A. D. Edwards†	3	6	0	26	10	0	0	4.33	3
1997	M. A. Robinson	15	21	8	40	7	0	0	3.07	1

Also batted: P. Moores (cap 1989) (2 matches) 20*, 36, 0* (2 ct).

* *Signifies not out.* † *Born in Sussex.* § *Overseas player.*

BOWLING

	O	M	R	W	BB	5W/i	Avge
J. J. Bates	102.5	24	273	14	5-67	2	19.50
R. S. C. Martin-Jenkins .	141.5	43	437	22	7-54	1	19.86
J. D. Lewry	461.3	112	1,409	62	6-72	3	22.72
M. A. Robinson	416.1	107	1,126	42	4-72	0	26.80
R. J. Kirtley	490.4	116	1,532	54	7-29	3	28.37
M. G. Bevan	175.4	27	653	19	3-36	0	34.36

Also bowled: C. J. Adams 30.5–5–109–0; A. D. Edwards 53–9–198–3; P. W. Jarvis 96–11–347–7; A. A. Khan 116–25–389–6; W. G. Khan 1.5–0–7–0; K. Newell 65.4–22–190–5; M. Newell 2–0–15–0; M. T. E. Peirce 43–18–99–1; R. K. Rao 27–2–119–1.

COUNTY RECORDS

Highest score for:	333	K. S. Duleepsinhji v Northamptonshire at Hove . .	1930
Highest score against:	322	E. Paynter (Lancashire) at Hove	1937
Best bowling for:	10-48	C. H. G. Bland v Kent at Tonbridge	1899
Best bowling against:	9-11	A. P. Freeman (Kent) at Hove	1922
Highest total for:	705-8 dec.	v Surrey at Hastings	1902
Highest total against:	726	by Nottinghamshire at Nottingham	1895
Lowest total for:	{ 19	v Surrey at Godalming	1830
	19	v Nottinghamshire at Hove	1873
Lowest total against:	18	by Kent at Gravesend	1867

At Oxford, April 14, 15, 16. SUSSEX drew with OXFORD UNIVERSITY.

SUSSEX v LANCASHIRE

At Hove, April 17, 18, 19, 20. Sussex won by two wickets. Sussex 20 pts, Lancashire 3 pts. Toss: Sussex.

A match blighted by cold and rain ended in joy for Adams, the new Sussex captain, who led his team to victory – their first win at Hove since June 1996 – with two balls to spare. Two declarations left them a generous target of 260 in 87 overs. Adams and Wasim Khan, another new import, put on 62, before Lancashire removed half the side for 121. Then Newell and Martin-Jenkins added 106 in 26 overs. Martin-Jenkins's career-best 63, following some impressive bowling, ensured Sussex were well set: 12 needed from 12 overs with three wickets remaining. Then came more rain, leaving Sussex 12 balls to reach their target. Keedy immediately heightened the tension by bowling Lewry and, with three balls left, all four results were possible. But Kirtley swept Keedy for four to secure victory. Earlier, Lewry celebrated his return to action after 20 months out with back trouble by removing Atherton for a duck in his first innings after resigning the England captaincy.

Close of play: First day, Lancashire 23-1 (N. T. Wood 11*, J. P. Crawley 8*); Second day, Lancashire 201-6 (A. Flintoff 57*, W. K. Hegg 32*); Third day, Sussex 75-4 (R. K. Rao 2*, K. Newell 0*).

Lancashire

M. A. Atherton lbw b Lewry	0	– (2) not out 33
N. T. Wood c Martin-Jenkins b Lewry	11	– (1) not out 32
*J. P. Crawley b Martin-Jenkins	49	
N. H. Fairbrother c Taylor b Lewry	8	
G. D. Lloyd c Khan b Martin-Jenkins	20	
A. Flintoff c Newell b Kirtley	68	
I. D. Austin c Taylor b Robinson	1	
†W. K. Hegg c Newell b Robinson	59	
G. Chapple c Taylor b Martin-Jenkins	7	
P. J. Martin not out	14	
G. Keedy b Robinson	4	
B 1, l-b 6, w 2, n-b 16	25	L-b 1, n-b 2 3

1/5 2/23 3/52 4/96 5/105 **266**   (no wkt dec.) **68**
6/106 7/222 8/244 9/250

Bonus points – Lancashire 2, Sussex 4.

Bowling: *First Innings*—Lewry 25–5–78–3; Kirtley 23–7–66–1; Robinson 24.2–6–73–3; Martin-Jenkins 19–7–42–3. *Second Innings*—Adams 4–0–36–0; Rao 3–0–31–0.

Sussex

W. G. Khan lbw b Chapple	10	– c Lloyd b Keedy 40
M. T. E. Peirce c and b Austin	30	– c Fairbrother b Martin ... 1
*C. J. Adams c Atherton b Martin	5	– c Flintoff b Chapple 39
N. R. Taylor lbw b Austin	21	– c Lloyd b Austin 16
R. K. Rao not out	2	– c Lloyd b Martin 6
K. Newell not out	0	– b Keedy 52
R. S. C. Martin-Jenkins (did not bat)		– b Keedy 63
†P. Moores (did not bat)		– not out 20
J. D. Lewry (did not bat)		– b Keedy 2
R. J. Kirtley (did not bat)		– not out 4
L-b 5, w 2	7	L-b 7, n-b 10 17

1/13 2/24 3/64 4/75   (4 wkts dec.) **75**   1/1 2/63 3/82 4/89   (8 wkts) **260**
5/121 6/227 7/248 8/256

M. A. Robinson did not bat.

Bonus point – Lancashire 1.

Bowling: *First Innings*—Martin 9–5–18–1; Chapple 10–2–33–1; Austin 9.3–3–19–2. *Second Innings*—Martin 25–9–61–2; Austin 18–2–57–1; Chapple 15–1–65–1; Flintoff 4–1–12–0; Keedy 15.4–2–58–4.

Umpires: M. J. Kitchen and D. R. Shepherd.

At Chelmsford, April 23, 24, 25, 27. SUSSEX drew with ESSEX.

At Nottingham, May 13, 14, 15. SUSSEX beat NOTTINGHAMSHIRE by four wickets.

SUSSEX v DERBYSHIRE

At Horsham, May 21, 22, 23, 24. Derbyshire won by seven wickets. Derbyshire 24 pts, Sussex 6 pts. Toss: Sussex.

Despite spirited resistance from the Sussex batsmen, Derbyshire won a high-scoring match – which included six centuries – in front of healthy crowds to defeat Sussex for the fifth time in six years. The prospect of Adams facing the county he acrimoniously left the previous season was dashed by his selection for England's one-day side, though he returned to admit graciously that the better side won. Mark Newell – in the team as Adams's replacement after recovering from shin splints – followed his maiden hundred in the last Championship match of 1997 with another in his first of 1998. His unbeaten 135 underpinned Sussex's first innings, though Barnett and Cassar, sharing a partnership of 254, and then Cork all made hundreds in reply; Cassar's was a maiden century. Derbyshire batted well into the third day to set up a winning position. Wasim Khan and Bevan made their first centuries for their new county but, when they departed, DeFreitas, bowling off-spin, and Blackwell finished off the innings. Derbyshire reached their target with 50 balls to spare.

Close of play: First day, Sussex 315-9 (M. Newell 129*, R. J. Kirtley 14*); Second day, Derbyshire 366-5 (K. J. Dean 3*, K. M. Krikken 0*); Third day, Sussex 167-2 (W. G. Khan 80*, M. G. Bevan 54*).

Sussex

M. T. E. Peirce c Krikken b DeFreitas	18	– b Dean	12
W. G. Khan c Slater b Dean	70	– c Rollins b Barnett	125
M. Newell not out	135	– lbw b Cork	7
*M. G. Bevan lbw b Dean	5	– b Lacey	127
J. R. Carpenter lbw b DeFreitas	1	– c Cork b DeFreitas	19
K. Newell c Rollins b Cork	13	– c Rollins b DeFreitas	16
†S. Humphries b Cork	0	– c Rollins b Blackwell	16
P. W. Jarvis lbw b DeFreitas	22	– c Cassar b Lacey	8
A. A. Khan lbw b Cork	23	– lbw b Blackwell	4
J. D. Lewry c Krikken b Cork	0	– c Cork b Blackwell	2
R. J. Kirtley run out	17	– not out	1
B 1, l-b 10, w 2, n-b 8	21	B 4, l-b 13, w 4, n-b 16	37
	—		—
	325		374

1/33 2/143 3/157 4/158 5/198   325
6/198 7/228 8/272 9/280

1/42 2/63 3/255 4/303 5/325   374
6/333 7/350 8/363 9/365

Bonus points – Sussex 3, Derbyshire 4.

Bowling: *First Innings*—Cork 28–9–77–4; DeFreitas 23–1–74–3; Dean 26.1–8–90–2; Lacey 12–3–33–0; Cassar 19–6–35–0; Blackwell 4–2–5–0. *Second Innings*—Cork 14–5–30–1; DeFreitas 32–4–101–2; Dean 17–4–63–1; Lacey 35–9–89–2; Blackwell 11.4–2–38–3; Cassar 4–0–12–0; Barnett 7–0–24–1.

Derbyshire

M. J. Slater b Lewry	0	– (2) c Peirce b Bevan	39
A. S. Rollins c A. A. Khan b Jarvis	58	– (1) c Bevan b A. A. Khan	37
T. A. Tweats c Carpenter b Lewry	11	– c Bevan b A. A. Khan	0
K. J. Barnett c M. Newell b Lewry	162	– not out	12
M. E. Cassar c A. A. Khan b Lewry	121	– not out	13
K. J. Dean c Bevan b A. A. Khan	8		
†K. M. Krikken lbw b Lewry	12		
*D. G. Cork not out	102		
P. A. J. DeFreitas c K. Newell b A. A. Khan	87		
I. D. Blackwell b Lewry	1		
S. J. Lacey b Jarvis	11		
B 2, l-b 16, n-b 2	20	B 4, l-b 2	6

1/4 2/40 3/106 4/360 5/365   **593**   1/76 2/82 3/82   (3 wkts) 107
6/373 7/385 8/514 9/533

Bonus points – Derbyshire 4, Sussex 3 (Score at 120 overs: 406-7).

Bowling: *First Innings*—Lewry 36–12–72–6; Kirtley 20–3–98–0; A. A. Khan 59–12–185–2; Jarvis 34–5–118–2; Bevan 12–0–66–0; K. Newell 10–3–23–0; Peirce 1–0–13–0. *Second Innings*—Lewry 7–2–21–0; Jarvis 3–0–16–0; A. A. Khan 8–1–24–2; Bevan 7.4–0–40–1.

Umpires: A. Clarkson and N. T. Plews.

At Worcester, May 29, 30, 31, June 1. SUSSEX drew with WORCESTERSHIRE.

At Tunbridge Wells, June 3, 4, 5, 6. SUSSEX beat KENT by 75 runs.

At Arundel, June 12, 13, 14. SUSSEX drew with SOUTH AFRICANS (See South African tour section).

SUSSEX v WARWICKSHIRE

At Hove, June 17, 18, 19, 20. Warwickshire won by an innings and 32 runs. Warwickshire 23 pts, Sussex 1 pt. Toss: Sussex.

Warwickshire bounced back after three successive defeats to win with ten minutes to spare when Robinson was smartly caught by Powell at short leg; Sussex's last pair, threatening an unlikely escape, had held out for 17 overs. Warwickshire had cashed in on Adams's surprise decision to field first when Powell, scoring a maiden hundred, and Knight shared an opening stand of 272. They batted into the third day in the hope of an innings victory. Lara failed again with the bat – out second ball – but his gamble paid off. In the Sussex reply, Giddins, returning to old haunts 22 months after being sacked, took three wickets; only Peirce, with a typically dogged 64, showed the required determination. Others followed his example when they followed on, but the ball was turning appreciably, and, once Smith had broken an entertaining partnership of 118 between Adams and Bevan, Warwickshire were on course for victory.

Close of play: First day, Warwickshire 276-1 (N. V. Knight 115*, D. L. Hemp 0*); Second day, Warwickshire 489-8 (T. L. Penney 53*, A. F. Giles 21*); Third day, Sussex 49-1 (M. T. E. Peirce 30*, M. Newell 7*).

Warwickshire

M. J. Powell c Carpenter b Robinson	132		N. M. K. Smith c Newell b Lewry	14
N. V. Knight b Lewry	159		A. F. Giles b Lewry	22
D. L. Hemp c Humphries b Bevan	19			
*B. C. Lara lbw b Lewry	0		B 10, l-b 27, w 2, n-b 10	49
T. L. Penney not out	53			
D. R. Brown c Edwards b Peirce	8		1/272 2/342 3/342	(9 wkts. dec.) 490
†K. J. Piper c Adams b Bevan	7		4/348 5/361 6/382	
G. Welch c Kirtley b Bevan	27		7/422 8/453 9/490	

E. S. H. Giddins did not bat.

Bonus points – Warwickshire 3, Sussex 1 (Score at 120 overs: 343-3).

Bowling: Lewry 35.1–7–89–4; Kirtley 38–8–81–0; Robinson 33–5–85–1; Edwards 25–6–91–0; Bevan 27–3–83–3; Adams 3–0–8–0; Peirce 9–2–16–1.

Sussex

M. T. E. Peirce c Piper b Brown	64	– c Lara b Smith	46
W. G. Khan c Piper b Giddins	8	– c Piper b Welch	5
M. Newell b Brown	24	– c Knight b Giddins	11
*C. J. Adams c Piper b Giddins	22	– b Smith	79
M. G. Bevan lbw b Giddins	2	– c Knight b Giles	71
J. R. Carpenter c Piper b Welch	9	– c Welch b Giles	1
A. D. Edwards c Piper b Welch	0	– run out	2
†S. Humphries c Piper b Giles	17	– c Brown b Smith	17
R. J. Kirtley not out	7	– not out	15
J. D. Lewry b Giles	0	– c Hemp b Giddins	11
M. A. Robinson lbw b Brown	1	– c Powell b Smith	7
L-b 6, w 6, n-b 6	18	B 1, l-b 4, n-b 16	21

1/21 2/81 3/105 4/107 5/119	172	1/31 2/53 3/89 4/207 5/208	286
6/125 7/162 8/164 9/165		6/217 7/248 8/248 9/261	

Bonus points – Warwickshire 4.

Bowling: *First Innings*—Giddins 14–5–34–3; Brown 14.5–3–40–3; Welch 12–3–26–2; Smith 19–6–32–0; Giles 17–6–34–2. *Second Innings*—Giddins 21.5–3–64–2; Brown 17–5–35–0; Welch 15–4–63–1; Giles 41–25–47–2; Smith 35–9–72–4.

Umpires: M. J. Kitchen and J. W. Lloyds.

At Leicester, June 26, 27, 28, 29. SUSSEX drew with LEICESTERSHIRE.

SUSSEX v SOMERSET

At Hove, July 1, 2, 3, 4. Drawn. Sussex 11 pts, Somerset 7 pts. Toss: Somerset.

Bevan scored an unbeaten hundred for the second successive game, and was one of six centuries in a match that always looked destined for dreary stalemate; any life in the desperately slow pitch was rolled out of it after the opening day. Turner rescued Somerset after Kirtley, celebrating the award of his county cap on the first morning, had made early inroads. Then Adams played the most attractive innings of the match, and together with Newell and Bevan took Sussex to a lead of 163. But Sussex could not score quickly enough on the third day to give themselves time to bowl out Somerset again. Bowler defied them grimly for four sessions and night-watchman Pierson batted through the final day for his maiden first-class century, though by then Adams had resorted to bowling himself and, for the first time in first-class cricket, Newell. Sussex experimented with the playing hours for the second successive match, though they tried a 12.30 start rather than 1 p.m.: it still backfired, with most spectators filing away long before the 8 p.m. close.

Close of play: First day, Sussex 23-0 (M. T. E. Peirce 3*, W. G. Khan 15*); Second day, Sussex 326-3 (M. Newell 104*, M. G. Bevan 71*); Third day, Somerset 92-1 (P. D. Bowler 49*, A. R. K. Pierson 8*).

Somerset

*P. D. Bowler lbw b Robinson	18	– c Humphries b Robinson	101
P. C. L. Holloway b Kirtley	10	– b Robinson	27
R. J. Harden b Kirtley	0	– (4) not out	56
M. N. Lathwell c Newell b Kirtley	87		
K. A. Parsons c Humphries b Lewry	1		
†R. J. Turner b Robinson	105		
M. E. Trescothick not out	67		
G. D. Rose b Lewry	7		
A. R. K. Pierson b Lewry	4	– (3) not out	108
A. R. Caddick lbw b Lewry	0		
A. P. van Troost c Adams b Lewry	16		
B 1, l-b 6, w 2, n-b 6	15	L-b 3, w 4, n-b 8	15

1/32 2/33 3/36 4/46 5/227   330   1/70 2/175   (2 wkts dec.) 307
6/245 7/266 8/278 9/278

Bonus points – Somerset 3, Sussex 4.

Bowling: *First Innings*—Lewry 21.4–2–89–5; Kirtley 20–2–81–3; Robinson 16–4–46–2; Martin-Jenkins 17–4–56–0; Bevan 11–1–51–0. *Second Innings*—Lewry 20–5–32–0; Kirtley 22–7–59–0; Robinson 19–8–37–2; Bevan 23–2–72–0; Martin-Jenkins 19–11–30–0; Peirce 24–14–33–0; Adams 11–2–26–0; Newell 2–0–15–0.

Sussex

M. T. E. Peirce run out	3	R. J. Kirtley b Rose	11
W. G. Khan c Turner b Rose	19	J. D. Lewry b Caddick	9
M. Newell c Harden b Rose	118	M. A. Robinson lbw b Caddick	0
*C. J. Adams b Pierson	102		
M. G. Bevan not out	146	B 1, l-b 8, w 2, n-b 27	38
N. R. Taylor b Trescothick	14		
R. S. C. Martin-Jenkins lbw b Pierson	28		493
†S. Humphries c Turner b Bowler	5		

1/27 2/30 3/195 4/356 5/380
6/430 7/441 8/468 9/493

Bonus points – Sussex 4, Somerset 1 (Score at 120 overs: 359-4).

Bowling: Caddick 39.4–11–107–2; van Troost 30–6–93–0; Rose 35–11–75–3; Trescothick 21–2–76–1; Pierson 25–8–88–2; Parsons 10–2–41–0; Bowler 3–2–4–1.

Umpires: J. H. Harris and N. T. Plews.

At Cheltenham, July 14, 15, 16. SUSSEX lost to GLOUCESTERSHIRE by seven wickets.

At The Oval, July 30, 31, August 1. SUSSEX lost to SURREY by an innings and 69 runs.

SUSSEX v DURHAM

At Eastbourne, August 5, 6, 7. Sussex won by an innings and 81 runs. Sussex 24 pts, Durham 3 pts. Toss: Sussex. First-class debut: S. Chapman.

Sussex were on top from the moment they took first use of a flat Saffrons strip against a Durham side badly missing the injured Betts, and they comfortably made their Championship record against them six wins out of seven. Slow left-armer Steve Chapman, called up from club cricket with Bishop Auckland, and the rest of the Durham attack could do little as Khan and Bevan led the scoring. Kirtley, playing his first Championship match on his home ground, made a maiden fifty on the second morning to prolong Durham's agony. The pitch looked a different proposition when

Durham batted. Only Speight, against his old county, resisted; Lewry, swinging the ball both ways, and Robinson ensured they were soon following on 262 behind. Wickets again fell quickly, though Collingwood dug in, and Speight supported him until he was freakishly caught at silly point. Peirce took evasive action, but the ball lodged between his forearm and hip. Understandably, Durham went quietly after that, with Kirtley maintaining an excellent line in very hot weather.

Close of play: First day, Sussex 335-7 (J. J. Bates 6*, R. J. Kirtley 7*); Second day, Durham 116-5 (P. D. Collingwood 29*, M. P. Speight 15*).

Sussex

M. T. E. Peirce c Gough b Harmison	16	R. J. Kirtley c Collingwood b Wood		59
W. G. Khan b Wood	91	M. A. Robinson not out		3
M. Newell lbw b Harmison	7	J. D. Lewry b Harmison		24
*C. J. Adams c Speight b Harmison	56			
M. G. Bevan b Wood	95	B 10, l-b 9, w 8, n-b 14		41
R. K. Rao run out	18			
†S. Humphries c Speight b Collingwood	12	1/39 2/49 3/166 4/214 5/277		460
J. J. Bates c Speight b Wood	38	6/322 7/322 8/430 9/431		

Bonus points — Sussex 4, Durham 3 (Score at 120 overs: 375-7).

Bowling: Wood 37–12–107–4; Harmison 39.4–13–94–4; Collingwood 25–5–80–1; Chapman 29–6–79–0; Phillips 23–7–81–0.

Durham

J. E. Morris lbw b Lewry	15	– c Newell b Kirtley		8
M. A. Gough b Lewry	5	– lbw b Lewry		26
N. J. Speak lbw b Robinson	7	– c Adams b Robinson		7
J. A. Daley b Robinson	16	– lbw b Robinson		18
*D. C. Boon b Lewry	20	– lbw b Robinson		5
P. D. Collingwood c Adams b Robinson	29	– not out		56
†M. P. Speight not out	60	– c Peirce b Bevan		19
S. Chapman lbw b Lewry	2	– lbw b Lewry		11
N. C. Phillips b Kirtley	9	– b Kirtley		9
J. Wood c Bates b Kirtley	12	– b Kirtley		1
S. J. Harmison lbw b Bevan	12	– b Kirtley		0
L-b 3, n-b 8	11	B 5, l-b 4, w 2, n-b 10		21
1/17 2/22 3/38 4/51 5/81	198	1/9 2/23 3/57 4/63 5/73		181
6/121 7/140 8/161 9/181		6/107 7/140 8/175 9/181		

Bonus points – Sussex 4.

Bowling: *First Innings*—Lewry 30–12–63–4; Kirtley 22–7–54–2; Robinson 21–9–47–3; Bates 11–4–28–0; Bevan 3–2–3–1. *Second Innings*—Lewry 16–5–44–2; Kirtley 17.2–6–41–4; Robinson 15–5–21–3; Adams 7–2–21–0; Bevan 12–4–37–1; Bates 5–1–8–0.

Umpires: H. D. Bird and M. J. Harris.

SUSSEX v MIDDLESEX

At Hove, August 14, 15. Sussex won by an innings and 160 runs. Sussex 24 pts, Middlesex 4 pts. Toss: Sussex.

Sussex bowled Middlesex out twice in a day to inflict a crushing two-day defeat. The pitch had more grass than usual but did little untoward. Adams certainly enjoyed it when he delighted a large crowd with his highest score yet for Sussex: 170, with 27 fours, mainly from powerful drives and wristy cuts. Only when Hewitt returned to cut a swathe through the tail did Middlesex, who badly missed Fraser, have any control. Lewry got to work on a fragile Middlesex line-up and probably sealed his place on the A tour when he yorked Gatting, one of the selectors, first ball. Swinging the ball with good control, he took five for 43, including his 50th wicket of the summer. Middlesex were soon following on. Ramprakash showed brief defiance before Kirtley and Lewry finished off his dispirited side; the last five wickets went in 17 balls.

Close of play: First day, Sussex 371-7 (S. Humphries 13*, R. J. Kirtley 5*).

Sussex

M. T. E. Peirce lbw b Batt	20		R. J. Kirtley not out		12
W. G. Khan lbw b Hewitt	13		M. A. Robinson lbw b Hewitt		0
M. Newell c Weekes b Bloomfield	6		J. D. Lewry b Hewitt		5
*C. J. Adams c Brown b Hewitt	170				
M. G. Bevan c Gatting b Tufnell	35		L-b 14, n-b 38		52
R. K. Rao run out	54				
R. S. C. Martin-Jenkins lbw b Hewitt	5		1/56 2/58 3/154 4/306 5/306		392
†S. Humphries c Brown b Hewitt	20		6/320 7/353 8/386 9/386		

Bonus points – Sussex 4, Middlesex 4.

Bowling: Johnson 21–7–63–0; Batt 20–2–85–1; Bloomfield 12–1–45–1; Hewitt 17.3–3–71–6; Tufnell 22–6–58–1; Weekes 20–4–43–0; Goodchild 3–0–13–0.

Middlesex

D. J. Goodchild lbw b Lewry	0	– b Kirtley	4
J. L. Langer c Humphries b Lewry	13	– lbw b Kirtley	4
*M. R. Ramprakash b Martin-Jenkins	3	– b Martin-Jenkins	36
M. W. Gatting b Lewry	0	– c Bevan b Kirtley	6
P. N. Weekes lbw b Kirtley	31	– c Adams b Kirtley	3
†K. R. Brown lbw b Lewry	18	– c Humphries b Martin-Jenkins	21
J. P. Hewitt b Robinson	0	– c Humphries b Lewry	6
C. J. Batt lbw b Kirtley	18	– c Adams b Lewry	0
R. L. Johnson b Lewry	30	– not out	0
P. C. R. Tufnell c Adams b Martin-Jenkins	1	– c Humphries b Lewry	0
T. F. Bloomfield not out	20	– b Martin-Jenkins	1
B 1, l-b 2, n-b 12	15	L-b 1, w 4, n-b 4	9
1/0 2/17 3/17 4/17 5/56	142	1/8 2/17 3/29 4/35 5/68	90
6/57 7/81 8/102 9/103		6/85 7/89 8/89 9/89	

Bonus points – Sussex 4.

Bowling: *First Innings*—Lewry 15–4–43–5; Kirtley 14–4–49–2; Martin-Jenkins 10–2–26–2; Robinson 9–2–21–1. *Second Innings*—Lewry 7–2–20–3; Kirtley 7–0–29–4; Robinson 7–1–18–0; Martin-Jenkins 6.1–0–22–3.

Umpires: J. H. Hampshire and V. A. Holder.

SUSSEX v HAMPSHIRE

At Hove, August 26, 27, 28. Hampshire won by nine wickets. Hampshire 21 pts, Sussex 4 pts. Toss: Sussex.

Hampshire gained their first away victory in nearly 15 months after Sussex produced one of their worst bowling performances of the season. The game was evenly poised until the fourth innings. Hampshire needed 209 to win; after a low-scoring contest on a greentop, it was expected to be close. Instead, White eased them to a nine-wicket win with a day and a half to spare. In his last match before leaving for the Commonwealth Games, Bevan had top-scored in both innings for Sussex, and he might have given them the lead but for a commanding 84 by Stephenson. Hampshire also had to cope with a plague of no-balls and wides from McLean – Sussex scored only 432 in two innings, and 94 came from Extras. McLean shortened his run-up – and finished with seven for 87 in the match. Adams admitted his side had been outplayed, and blamed the negotiation of contracts during the game for distracting his squad.

Close of play: First day, Hampshire 97-3 (J. P. Stephenson 59*, A. N. Aymes 1*); Second day, Sussex 200-6 (R. S. C. Martin-Jenkins 6*, R. J. Kirtley 3*).

Sussex

M. T. E. Peirce c Kendall b McLean	10	– lbw b Mascarenhas	24
W. G. Khan c Morris b McLean	2	– c Aymes b James	11
J. R. Carpenter lbw b James	2	– c Aymes b Hartley	13
*C. J. Adams c Aymes b McLean	8	– lbw b Mascarenhas	8
M. G. Bevan lbw b Mascarenhas	58	– c Aymes b McLean	42
R. K. Rao c Stephenson b Mascarenhas	31	– c Keech b McLean	40
R. S. C. Martin-Jenkins c Aymes b Morris	2	– lbw b McLean	22
R. J. Kirtley lbw b Morris	1	– c Aymes b Morris	12
†N. J. Wilton not out	19	– not out	11
M. A. Robinson b Morris	0	– b McLean	2
J. D. Lewry b James	20	– b Morris	0
B 4, l-b 10, w 10, n-b 10	34	B 2, l-b 15, w 21, n-b 22	60
	187		245

1/3 2/22 3/24 4/50 5/132
6/143 7/143 8/144 9/144

1/28 2/73 3/81 4/87 5/190
6/191 7/230 8/232 9/240

Bonus points – Hampshire 4.

Bowling: *First Innings*—McLean 14–3–41–3; Hartley 10–2–23–0; James 11.3–3–24–2; Morris 12–4–33–3; Stephenson 8–1–28–0; Mascarenhas 8–2–24–2. *Second Innings*—McLean 23–9–46–4; Hartley 11–3–43–1; James 8–2–28–1; Morris 18–7–46–2; Mascarenhas 9–2–45–2; Stephenson 7–2–20–0.

Hampshire

G. W. White c Wilton b Kirtley	13	– not out	95
J. P. Stephenson lbw b Lewry	84	– c Khan b Martin-Jenkins	50
W. S. Kendall c Peirce b Martin-Jenkins	4	– not out	49
*R. A. Smith c Adams b Robinson	14		
†A. N. Aymes c Adams b Kirtley	1		
M. Keech c Bevan b Robinson	18		
A. D. Mascarenhas c Wilton b Martin-Jenkins	15		
K. D. James not out	14		
A. C. Morris b Lewry	2		
N. A. M. McLean c Carpenter b Lewry	10		
P. J. Hartley c Adams b Kirtley	17		
B 2, l-b 6, w 6, n-b 18	32	B 1, l-b 2, n-b 12	15
	224	(1 wkt)	209

1/44 2/49 3/89 4/108 5/137
6/167 7/169 8/175 9/191

1/92

Bonus points – Hampshire 1, Sussex 4.

Bowling: *First Innings*—Lewry 16–4–64–3; Kirtley 16.2–4–63–3; Martin-Jenkins 11–4–31–2; Robinson 14–3–58–2. *Second Innings*—Lewry 9–1–36–0; Kirtley 8–0–49–0; Robinson 10–2–40–0; Rao 8–0–33–0; Martin-Jenkins 8–1–35–1; Adams 2.5–0–13–0.

Umpires: B. Dudleston and A. G. T. Whitehead.

SUSSEX v GLAMORGAN

At Hove, August 31, September 1, 2, 3. Sussex won by 18 runs. Sussex 22 pts, Glamorgan 8 pts. Toss: Sussex.

All-rounder Robin Martin-Jenkins celebrated the offer of an improved contract by producing career-best performances with both bat and ball as Sussex won a contest of fluctuating fortunes. Glamorgan looked clear favourites as they set off on the final morning needing just 146. But Martin-Jenkins, who took the new ball only because Lewry had injured his shoulder, ripped through their batting in two inspired spells either side of lunch and ended with seven for 54. Supported by some superb close catching, notably from Adams, he reaped the rewards of pitching the ball up, although poor shot selection hastened Glamorgan's downfall. Martin-Jenkins had scored 78 in the first innings, which he dominated along with Newell. Maynard and Cottey then displayed the most fluent batting of the game before Glamorgan's weakened attack took advantage of favourable conditions and poor batting to set up what briefly looked like a winning position. Glamorgan had still not won a Championship match at Hove since 1975.

Close of play: First day, Sussex 313-8 (N. J. Wilton 3*); Second day, Sussex 0-0 (M. T. E. Peirce 0*, W. G. Khan 0*); Third day, Sussex 163-9 (M. A. Robinson 2*, J. D. Lewry 2*).

Sussex

M. T. E. Peirce c Law b Parkin	0	– c Dale b Croft	11
W. G. Khan lbw b Parkin	3	– b Croft	9
J. R. Carpenter c Shaw b Davies	0	– lbw b Parkin	20
*C. J. Adams run out	43	– c sub b Davies	47
R. K. Rao c Shaw b Davies	76	– b Davies	8
K. Newell c Powell b Dale	84	– c sub b Thomas	11
R. S. C. Martin-Jenkins c Shaw b Thomas	78	– b Dale	30
R. J. Kirtley b Thomas	6	– lbw b Dale	0
†N. J. Wilton c Evans b Thomas	16	– b Dale	0
J. D. Lewry c Shaw b Thomas	4	– (11) b Thomas	2
M. A. Robinson not out	2	– (10) not out	4
B 8, l-b 6, w 2, n-b 4	20	B 2, l-b 11	13
	332		**166**

1/2 2/3 3/23 4/90 5/187   332   1/22 2/31 3/85 4/99 5/110   166
6/255 7/292 8/313 9/329   6/122 7/158 8/158 9/161

Bonus points – Sussex 3, Glamorgan 4.

Bowling: *First Innings*—Parkin 28-9-88-2; Davies 21-5-68-2; Thomas 28.3-5-63-4; Dale 20-5-51-1; Croft 16-6-48-0. *Second Innings*—Parkin 14-7-26-1; Davies 11-3-22-2; Croft 13-4-34-2; Thomas 14-2-48-2; Dale 10-3-23-3.

Glamorgan

W. L. Law c Adams b Robinson	45	– lbw b Martin-Jenkins	25
A. W. Evans lbw b Martin-Jenkins	26	– c Peirce b Martin-Jenkins	9
A. Dale c Wilton b Lewry	18	– c Adams b Martin-Jenkins	37
*M. P. Maynard run out	94	– c Adams b Martin-Jenkins	0
P. A. Cottey c Khan b Martin-Jenkins	91	– lbw b Robinson	1
M. J. Powell c Robinson b Lewry	23	– c Khan b Robinson	5
R. D. B. Croft c Adams b Robinson	15	– c Adams b Martin-Jenkins	0
S. D. Thomas c Wilton b Robinson	0	– c Wilton b Martin-Jenkins	23
A. P. Davies not out	0	– b Martin-Jenkins	4
O. T. Parkin not out	0	– (11) c sub b Robinson	1
†A. D. Shaw (did not bat)		– (10) not out	3
B 4, l-b 3, w 2, n-b 32	41	L-b 5, w 2, n-b 12	19
	353		**127**

1/85 2/85 3/134 4/236   (8 wkts. dec.) 353   1/20 2/41 3/41 4/42 5/62   127
5/311 6/351 7/351 8/353   6/65 7/105 8/115 9/126

Bonus points – Glamorgan 4, Sussex 3.

Bowling: *First Innings*—Lewry 22-2-86-2; Kirtley 21-2-71-0; Robinson 16-2-69-3; Martin-Jenkins 14.4-3-65-2; Newell 6-0-36-0; Rao 3-0-19-0. *Second Innings*—Kirtley 6-2-35-0; Martin-Jenkins 16-2-54-7; Robinson 12.3-2-33-3.

Umpires: R. Julian and K. E. Palmer.

At Northampton, September 9, 10, 11. SUSSEX lost to NORTHAMPTONSHIRE by 136 runs.

SUSSEX v YORKSHIRE

At Hove, September 17, 18, 19. Yorkshire won by ten wickets. Yorkshire 22 pts, Sussex 4 pts. Toss: Yorkshire.

Yorkshire completed a comprehensive victory over a tired-looking Sussex midway through the third afternoon. It was their fifth win in a row, their best Championship sequence since Ray

Illingworth bowled them to victory over Leicestershire in July 1967. They could not quite match the glories of those days, but still finished third in the table, their highest since 1975. And there was some satisfaction for Sussex, who hung on to seventh place, and thus qualified for the inaugural Super Cup, having come bottom in 1997. On another grassy Hove wicket, Yorkshire took control when Sussex, 111 for two on the first day, lost their last eight wickets for 18, and the last six for three; Hutchison took five for one in 13 balls, and finished with a career-best seven for 31. Yorkshire also began badly, but Wood coped well with the swinging ball, reached his fourth century of the season and saw Yorkshire to a lead of 123. Sussex looked brittle without Bevan's calming influence. Adams played the shot of the match – a swatted six over mid-wicket off Silverwood – but was out next ball. On the opening day, bowlers had taken two wickets in two balls four times, but there was no hat-trick.

Close of play: First day, Yorkshire 159-7 (M. J. Wood 59*, C. E. W. Silverwood 12*); Second day, Sussex 91-4 (W. G. Khan 43*, R. S. C. Martin-Jenkins 1*).

Sussex

M. T. E. Peirce lbw b Hoggard	44	– c White b Hutchison	0
W. G. Khan c Wood b Hutchison	10	– b Hoggard	49
*C. J. Adams c Blakey b Hutchison	18	– b Silverwood	27
R. K. Rao c White b Hoggard	42	– b Silverwood	9
K. Newell c Blakey b Hoggard	0	– b Silverwood	2
R. S. C. Martin-Jenkins c Blakey b Hutchison	7	– not out	44
†S. Humphries not out	2	– lbw b Hoggard	9
J. J. Bates lbw b Hutchison	1	– c Byas b Hoggard	0
R. J. Kirtley lbw b Hutchison	0	– c White b Hoggard	2
J. D. Lewry b Hutchison	0	– b Hamilton	9
M. A. Robinson b Hutchison	0	– b Hamilton	1
L-b 1, n-b 4	5	B 1, l-b 7, n-b 10	18
	129		**170**

1/16 2/36 3/111 4/111 5/126 　　　　129
6/128 7/129 8/129 9/129

1/1 2/46 3/76 4/90 5/121 　　　　170
6/137 7/137 8/149 9/164

Bonus points – Yorkshire 4.

Bowling: *First Innings*—Silverwood 8–2–25–0; Hutchison 13.4–4–31–7; Hamilton 9–0–36–0; Middlebrook 2–0–6–0; Hoggard 10–2–27–3; McGrath 1–0–3–0. *Second Innings*—Silverwood 13–4–31–3; Hutchison 17–5–55–1; Hoggard 16–4–50–4; Hamilton 11.1–4–16–2; Middlebrook 5–3–10–0; McGrath 1–1–0–0.

Yorkshire

C. White lbw b Kirtley	7	– not out	46
M. P. Vaughan c Bates b Kirtley	11	– not out	1
M. J. Wood not out	118		
*D. Byas b Kirtley	2		
A. McGrath b Kirtley	42		
†R. J. Blakey c Humphries b Robinson	5		
G. M. Hamilton b Robinson	0		
J. D. Middlebrook c Martin-Jenkins b Kirtley	5		
C. E. W. Silverwood c Adams b Robinson	37		
P. M. Hutchison b Rao	6		
M. J. Hoggard c Adams b Robinson	1		
B 4, l-b 4, w 2, n-b 8	18	W 4	4
	252	(no wkt)	**51**

1/14 2/23 3/25 4/101 5/122 　　　　252
6/122 7/145 8/216 9/245

(no wkt) 51

Bonus points – Yorkshire 2, Sussex 4.

Bowling: *First Innings*—Lewry 24–5–73–0; Kirtley 35–13–80–5; Robinson 30.5–6–72–4; Newell 3–1–12–0; Adams 3–1–5–0; Bates 2–1–1–0; Rao 1–0–1–1. *Second Innings*—Lewry 2–0–11–0; Kirtley 3–1–10–0; Newell 3–1–23–0; Khan 1.5–0–7–0.

Umpires: G. I. Burgess and M. J. Harris.

WARWICKSHIRE

Ed Giddins

President: The Earl of Aylesford
Chairman: M. J. K. Smith
Chairman, Cricket Committee: J. Whitehouse
Chief Executive: D. L. Amiss
Captain: 1998 – B. C. Lara
1999 – N. M. K. Smith
Director of Coaching: P. A. Neale
Head Groundsman: S. J. Rouse
Scorer: D. Wainwright

Rarely in recent years have Warwickshire ended a season wanting to forget it; they did in 1998. Second place in the Sunday League was the only redeeming feature of a campaign sullied by a public fine and reprimand for captain Brian Lara. A substantial minority of the membership had expressed reservations about Lara's appointment, despite his record-breaking feats for the club in 1994. But the committee believed the responsibility of captaincy would prevent the time-keeping lapses which marred that stay. In May, however, after a trip home to Trinidad, Lara caught a later plane than arranged, without the club's permission. He arrived too late for a Sunday game at Taunton, where the team crumbled for 96; Lara was fined £2,000.

For the choice to work, Lara needed another outstanding season. Nobody expected a repeat of 1994, when he scored 2,066 in 25 innings, with nine hundreds, including the world record 501 not out. But both Lara and the club hoped for more than they got – 1,033, precisely half his previous aggregate, in one more innings. Poor home pitches showed up his technical deficiencies; he did not score a hundred in 39 first-class innings between June 1997 and August 1998. Then, a double-hundred at Lord's started a run of three centuries in as many matches. But Lara's lack of form until the final quarter of the season – he missed the last two games – was at the heart of a general batting slump.

Lara and coach Phil Neale never forged a relationship to match the Reeve–Woolmer axis that won the treble in 1994. The team lost the knack of squeezing victory from difficult situations, and finished eighth in the Championship; they were beaten eight times, having lost only 11 matches in the previous four seasons.

Warwickshire failed to qualify for the Benson and Hedges knockout stages, despite winning four group games, when they failed to spot Lancashire coming up on the rails. In their final match, they reduced Nottinghamshire to 66 for five, and should have had an unbeatable net run-rate. But they relaxed so much that they won by only five runs. The NatWest quarter-final at Leicester was an embarrassment, the top order collapsing to Alan Mullally's spell of five for 18 – including Lara, caught off a reckless drive.

The Sunday League was the one competition in which Warwickshire threatened. They lost only two of their first ten matches, but then suffered

three successive defeats, all at home in mid-week games under floodlights.
Three defeats – costing 12 points – was the precise margin between Warwickshire's second place and the winners, Lancashire. The club staged four day/
night games, and submitted a planning application for permanent floodlights.
But they had not consulted local residents. Strong protests meant that the
application was deferred, and the committee had another fence to mend.

Back on the field, Lara's struggles had a domino effect on other batsmen,
such as Dominic Ostler, David Hemp and Trevor Penney. All three were
dropped at some stage. Injury prevented a farewell appearance from Andy
Moles, leaving Nick Knight to hold the top order together – with a little help
from youngsters Tony Frost, Michael Powell, Mark Wagh and Anurag Singh.

Both Knight and Neil Smith reached 1,000 first-class runs for the county
for the first time; Smith's final average of 41.75 made it incomprehensible
that he had been dropped to No. 8 or 9, often behind Keith Piper. Piper's
wicket-keeping was sometimes brilliant, but he reached double figures only
eight times. Graeme Welch missed six Championship games through injury,
all-rounder Dougie Brown missed two and, with the lower-middle order
juggled around for no good reason, the side lost its stability.

Brown and left-arm spinner Ashley Giles were less prolific than in 1997
but, with Knight, were taken to Bangladesh in England's one-day international
squad. Giles had played his first Test, alongside Knight, at Old Trafford –
where he was unfairly criticised for taking only one wicket in unfriendly
conditions. Tim Munton, who had missed much of the season through injury,
regained fitness in time to take 36 wickets in the last seven matches.

Injuries, loss of form and international call-ups for Knight and Giles meant
that only Smith and Ed Giddins played in every Championship match. Fast
bowler Giddins, released by Sussex and banned during 1997 because of drug
offences, was magnificent. He promised members "60 or 70 wickets to help
you forget my previous problems"; he delivered 84, combining technique
with astute thinking. He swung the ball both ways, and many of his wickets
were carefully planned. Only Andrew Caddick bowled more than his 644
Championship overs. Giddins refused to be affected by whispers about his
action, particularly the bouncer. Chairman of selectors David Graveney
emphasised that his omission from England's squads – he was widely touted
before each Test – had nothing to do with such talk. That only increased the
mystery of why he was overlooked.

The committee's first priority in restoring confidence after the travails of
1998 was to choose the right captain. In October, the appointment of Neil
Smith, son of the county's former captain and present chairman M. J. K.,
was an overdue recognition of a shrewd cricketing brain. He had much to
do; in 1999, Warwickshire expected to lose two or three players, including
vice-captain Knight, for several weeks during the World Cup. With Allan
Donald expected to return after that, however, there was reason for hope,
especially if he could form a successful partnership with Giddins, backed
up by a fully fit Munton. But batsmen – most of them – needed tighter
guidelines on technique. – JACK BANNISTER.

WARWICKSHIRE 1998

[Bill Smith]

Back row: S. Westergaard, M. J. Powell, D. A. Altree, M. A. Sheikh, B. W. O'Connell. *Middle row*: M. D. Edmond, T. Frost, E. S. H. Giddins, D. R. Brown, A. F. Giles, D. L. Hemp, G. Welch, S. Nottingham (*physiotherapist*), A. E. Davis (*scorer*). *Front row*: R. N. Abberley (*head coach*). K. J. Piper, T. L. Penney, N. M. K. Smith, N. V. Knight, B. C. Lara (*captain*), P. A. Neale (*director of coaching*), T. A. Munton, G. C. Small, A. J. Moles, D. P. Ostler. *Insets*: A. Singh, M. A. Wagh.

WARWICKSHIRE RESULTS

All first-class matches – Played 18: Won 6, Lost 8, Drawn 4.

County Championship matches – Played 17: Won 6, Lost 8, Drawn 3.

Competition placings – Britannic Assurance County Championship, 8th;
NatWest Trophy, q-f; Benson and Hedges Cup, 3rd in Group A;
AXA League, 2nd.

COUNTY CHAMPIONSHIP AVERAGES
BATTING

Cap		M	I	NO	R	HS	100s	50s	Avge	Ct/St
1995	N. V. Knight	14	24	2	1,057	192	4	4	48.04	18
1993	N. M. K. Smith† . . .	17	28	4	959	147	2	6	39.95	2
1994	B. C. Lara§	15	26	0	1,033	226	3	3	39.73	15
1996	A. F. Giles	13	19	4	472	83	0	3	31.46	7
1995	D. R. Brown	15	26	4	658	81*	0	5	29.90	7
	A. Singh	5	7	0	185	56	0	1	26.42	2
	M. A. Wagh†	8	15	0	391	119	1	2	26.06	4
1997	D. L. Hemp	14	24	0	578	102	1	3	24.08	15
	M. J. Powell	12	20	1	455	132	1	3	23.94	12
1994	T. L. Penney	9	16	2	329	53*	0	1	23.50	5
	T. Frost	7	13	1	278	50	0	1	23.16	19
1997	G. Welch	11	17	1	323	54	0	1	20.18	6
	M. D. Edmond	2	4	1	48	32	0	0	16.00	1
1992	K. J. Piper	13	23	5	283	44*	0	0	15.72	29/3
1989	T. A. Munton	8	12	2	72	20	0	0	7.20	0
1991	D. P. Ostler†	5	8	0	38	18	0	0	4.75	4
1998	E. S. H. Giddins . . .	17	23	8	43	11*	0	0	2.86	4

Also batted: D. A. Altree† (1 match) 2*, 0; M. A. Sheikh† (1 match) 1, 25.

* Signifies not out.   † Born in Warwickshire.   § Overseas player.

BOWLING

	O	M	R	W	BB	5W/i	Avge
T. A. Munton	265.1	66	691	36	7-66	3	19.19
E. S. H. Giddins	644.2	151	1,952	83	6-79	5	23.51
A. F. Giles	423.3	147	919	35	5-48	1	26.25
D. R. Brown	430.2	92	1,458	50	5-40	2	29.16
N. M. K. Smith	299.3	72	914	21	5-128	1	43.52
G. Welch	295.3	65	961	22	4-94	0	43.68

Also bowled: D. A. Altree 13–4–34–0; M. D. Edmond 20–5–52–1; T. Frost 1–0–6–0; D. L. Hemp 13–0–51–2; N. V. Knight 1.5–0–15–0; B. C. Lara 5–0–44–0; M. J. Powell 7–0–30–0; M. A. Sheikh 27–7–56–3; M. A. Wagh 33–9–95–7.

COUNTY RECORDS

Highest score for:	501*	B. C. Lara v Durham at Birmingham	1994
Highest score against:	322	I. V. A. Richards (Somerset) at Taunton	1985
Best bowling for:	10-41	J. D. Bannister v Combined Services at Birmingham . .	1959
Best bowling against:	10-36	H. Verity (Yorkshire) at Leeds	1931
Highest total for:	810-4 dec.	v Durham at Birmingham	1994
Highest total against:	887	by Yorkshire at Birmingham	1896
Lowest total for:	16	v Kent at Tonbridge	1913
Lowest total against:	15	by Hampshire at Birmingham	1922

WARWICKSHIRE v DURHAM

At Birmingham, April 17, 18, 20, 21. Drawn. Warwickshire 10 pts, Durham 10 pts. Toss: Durham. County debuts: E. S. H. Giddins; N. C. Phillips.

There were three centuries in this match, but none of them attracted as much attention as one duck. Last time he faced Durham on this ground, Lara scored his world-record 501 not out. Returning as captain, he was caught behind off Wood after eight balls, and he was dismissed the same way for 13 in the second innings. "He's just a batsman like everybody else," said Wood. Warwickshire were 115 for five when Smith arrived to score an ebullient 113 – his third first-class hundred. Next, it was the turn of Giddins, who had joined Warwickshire from Sussex during a 20-month ban for drug use. He began to repay them when his fifth ball claimed a wicket; he was to finish with six, including his former team-mate Phillips, another Sussex émigré. Durham looked bad at 45 for five, but Boon and Collingwood, scoring his first Championship hundred, united to add 193, a county sixth-wicket record. Warwickshire led by only 31 and, when they subsided to 99 for six, Durham scented victory. Again Smith rallied them, almost reaching another century. The target was 219 on the final day and rain spoiled a potentially good finish; five Durham wickets were down but Speak was batting well.

Close of play: First day, Durham 17-1 (M. A. Roseberry 1*, J. E. Morris 14*); Second day, Durham 292-7 (P. D. Collingwood 105*, M. M. Betts 0*); Third day, Warwickshire 187.

Warwickshire

D. P. Ostler b Betts	0	– b Betts	0
N. V. Knight b Wood	6	– b Harmison	12
*B. C. Lara c Speight b Wood	0	– c Speight b Wood	13
D. L. Hemp c Lewis b Phillips	52	– b Harmison	6
T. L. Penney b Betts	35	– c Roseberry b Wood	3
D. R. Brown c Speight b Harmison	32	– b Wood	27
N. M. K. Smith b Betts	113	– b Collingwood	90
†T. Frost c Phillips b Harmison	21	– b Harmison	5
M. D. Edmond c and b Betts	32	– c Speight b Phillips	13
E. S. H. Giddins c Morris b Betts	7	– not out	0
D. A. Altree not out	2	– lbw b Collingwood	0
B 7, l-b 13, w 8, n-b 8	36	B 2, l-b 4, w 8, n-b 4	18

1/0 2/7 3/24 4/115 5/115   **336**   1/6 2/33 3/41 4/41 5/46   **187**
6/247 7/277 8/322 9/329   6/99 7/134 8/187 9/187

Bonus points – Warwickshire 3, Durham 4.

Bowling: *First Innings*—Betts 17.2–2–66–5; Wood 17–2–65–2; Harmison 19–4–76–2; Collingwood 8–1–33–0; Phillips 15–2–76–1. *Second Innings*—Betts 2–0–15–1; Wood 21–3–74–3; Harmison 17–3–74–3; Collingwood 4–1–13–2; Phillips 1–0–5–1.

Durham

J. J. B. Lewis b Giddins	0	– c Lara b Brown	19
M. A. Roseberry c Knight b Brown	10	– lbw b Giddins	2
J. E. Morris b Giddins	17	– c Lara b Brown	5
N. J. Speak b Brown	8	– not out	50
*D. C. Boon lbw b Giddins	107	– b Edmond	2
†M. P. Speight c Lara b Brown	0	– c Frost b Brown	3
P. D. Collingwood lbw b Giddins	105	– not out	0
N. C. Phillips c Frost b Giddins	23		
M. M. Betts not out	2		
J. Wood c Frost b Brown	2		
S. J. Harmison c Frost b Giddins	7		
B 3, l-b 9, w 4, n-b 8	24	B 1, l-b 6, n-b 2	9

1/0 2/28 3/30 4/41 5/45   **305**   1/5 2/26 3/34   **(5 wkts) 90**
6/238 7/288 8/293 9/298   4/49 5/90

Bonus points – Durham 3, Warwickshire 4.

Bowling: *First Innings*—Giddins 31.2–5–89–6; Brown 28–8–89–4; Altree 11–2–34–0; Edmond 10–1–32–0; Smith 16–2–49–0. *Second Innings*—Giddins 14–5–47–1; Brown 12.1–7–23–3; Altree 2–2–0–0; Edmond 7–3–13–1.

Umpires: K. E. Palmer and A. G. T. Whitehead.

At The Oval, April 23, 24, 25, 27. WARWICKSHIRE lost to SURREY by an innings and 49 runs.

At Derby, May 13, 14. WARWICKSHIRE beat DERBYSHIRE by an innings and 61 runs.

At Oxford, May 18, 19, 20. WARWICKSHIRE drew with OXFORD UNIVERSITY.

WARWICKSHIRE v NOTTINGHAMSHIRE

At Birmingham, May 21, 22, 23, 24. Nottinghamshire won by six wickets. Nottinghamshire 21 pts, Warwickshire 4 pts. Toss: Nottinghamshire.

Nottinghamshire's first Championship win was Warwickshire's first home defeat since September 1996. But it was their second defeat in four games in 1998, and the tinkle of alarm bells was turning into a crescendo. One home player did enhance his reputation: Powell became the first man to carry his bat for Warwickshire for ten years, and the first uncapped player to do so since Fred Gardner in 1949, improving his career-best in both innings. On the opening day, his best support came from Extras, with 17, as the seamers overwhelmed his colleagues. A green pitch did not help batsmen, and Noon retired when a rising ball from Brown broke his finger (Johnson took over the gloves). Conditions were put in perspective as Nottinghamshire took a lead of 88, and again when Lara – finding Championship form at last – scored 80 off 97 balls. But Warwickshire collapsed a second time, losing seven wickets for 48, which left the visitors to score 193. Dowman and Afzaal ensured victory, though Giddins had time to take his match haul to seven.

Close of play: First day, Nottinghamshire 71-2 (M. P. Dowman 28*, P. Johnson 24*); Second day, Warwickshire 159-2 (M. J. Powell 52*, B. C. Lara 54*); Third day, Nottinghamshire 66-1 (M. P. Dowman 29*, U. Afzaal 21*).

Warwickshire

M. J. Powell not out	70	– c Johnson b Oram	73
†T. Frost c Strang b Franks	13	– c Johnson b Dowman	40
D. L. Hemp lbw b Franks	0	– c Johnson b Bowen	4
*B. C. Lara c Strang b Bowen	2	– c Afzaal b Franks	80
D. P. Ostler c Noon b Oram	6	– lbw b Oram	18
D. R. Brown c Noon b Bowen	6	– c Afzaal b Dowman	1
N. M. K. Smith b Bowen	0	– c sub b Oram	0
G. Welch c Dowman b Bowen	14	– c Robinson b Bowen	12
M. A. Sheikh c Noon b Oram	1	– c Afzaal b Tolley	25
M. D. Edmond c Noon b Franks	0	– not out	3
E. S. H. Giddins c Tolley b Oram	1	– b Bowen	0
B 6, l-b 9, w 2	17	B 7, l-b 13, w 2, n-b 2	24
	130		**280**

1/29 2/29 3/36 4/47 5/56   6/62 7/94 8/100 9/101

1/59 2/80 3/196 4/232 5/235   6/235 7/235 8/277 9/278

Bonus points – Nottinghamshire 4.

Bowling: *First Innings*—Franks 19–6–39–3; Oram 17.2–6–36–3; Bowen 16–6–22–4; Tolley 3–0–17–0; Strang 2–1–1–0. *Second Innings*—Franks 19–2–64–1; Oram 24–11–35–3; Bowen 28.3–8–59–3; Dowman 14–5–45–2; Tolley 8–1–46–1; Strang 3–1–11–0.

Nottinghamshire

M. P. Dowman c Brown b Giddins	44	– c Lara b Sheikh	63
R. T. Robinson b Brown	11	– c Frost b Giddins	8
U. Afzaal c Welch b Brown	0	– not out	73
*P. Johnson c Frost b Sheikh	45	– c Ostler b Giddins	17
N. A. Gie c Lara b Sheikh	1	– c Welch b Giddins	5
C. M. Tolley c Frost b Giddins	12	– not out	3
P. J. Franks lbw b Brown	33		
†W. M. Noon retired hurt	16		
P. A. Strang not out	18		
M. N. Bowen b Giddins	18		
A. R. Oram b Giddins	0		
B 2, l-b 4, n-b 14	20	B 2, l-b 6, n-b 16	24

1/28 2/32 3/106 4/108 5/118   218   1/21 2/133 3/174 4/186   (4 wkts) 193
6/130 7/171 8/216 9/218

Bonus points – Nottinghamshire 1, Warwickshire 4.

In the first innings W. M. Noon retired hurt at 186.

Bowling: *First Innings*—Giddins 22.4–9–47–4; Brown 23–6–77–3; Welch 20–3–63–0; Sheikh 10–2–18–2; Edmond 3–1–7–0. *Second Innings*—Giddins 25.4–5–74–3; Brown 13–4–19–0; Welch 10–3–26–0; Smith 8–2–16–0; Sheikh 17.5–5–38–1; Hemp 3–0–12–0.

Umpires: G. I. Burgess and A. A. Jones.

At Taunton, June 3, 4, 5. WARWICKSHIRE lost to SOMERSET by eight wickets.

At Bristol, June 11, 12, 13, 15. WARWICKSHIRE lost to GLOUCESTERSHIRE by 170 runs.

At Hove, June 17, 18, 19, 20. WARWICKSHIRE beat SUSSEX by an innings and 32 runs.

WARWICKSHIRE v LANCASHIRE

At Birmingham, June 26, 27, 28, 29. Lancashire won by four wickets. Lancashire 18 pts, Warwickshire 4 pts. Toss: Warwickshire.

The first two days were lost to rain, compelling last-day contrivance. But Warwickshire generously agreed to hand out 39 runs in 23 balls on the final morning, giving Lancashire what became 96 overs to score 336. Their task grew even easier when Giddins went off with flu. Wood anchored the innings, which took off after tea when Fairbrother, using a runner, and Flintoff cut loose. Flintoff enhanced his growing reputation, following up his big hitting against Surrey with 70 off 95 balls, striking eight fours and two sixes. Though he eventually fell to Brown – whose marathon spell claimed five out of the six wickets – Austin hit the winning six with nine balls to spare. It was Lancashire's fourth win out of five, moving them into second place, and Warwickshire's fifth defeat of the season. The previous day, Knight, just called up by England, had scored a career-best 192 in six and a half hours. He shared two century stands, with Powell and Brown, but ran out his captain, Lara, whose wretched patch continued.

Close of play: First day, No play; Second day, No play; Third day, Warwickshire 374-5 (D. R. Brown 51*, K. J. Piper 5*).

Warwickshire

M. J. Powell c Crawley b Chapple	53	†K. J. Piper not out	5
N. V. Knight c sub b Chapple	192		
D. L. Hemp b Chapple	7	B 4, l-b 10, n-b 4	18
*B. C. Lara run out	25		
T. L. Penney b Watkinson	23	1/109 2/131 3/202 (5 wkts dec.) 374	
D. R. Brown not out	51	4/258 5/364	

G. Welch, N. M. K. Smith, A. F. Giles and E. S. H. Giddins did not bat.

Bonus points – Warwickshire 4, Lancashire 2.

Bowling: Martin 21–4–59–0; Chapple 21–3–74–3; Austin 21–2–62–0; Green 14–3–53–0; Watkinson 25–1–100–1; Flintoff 2–0–12–0.

Warwickshire forfeited their second innings.

Lancashire

N. T. Wood not out	14	– c sub b Giles	79
I. D. Austin not out	23	– (7) not out	12
M. A. Atherton (did not bat)	–	(2) lbw b Brown	31
*†J. P. Crawley (did not bat)	–	(3) c Piper b Brown	34
N. H. Fairbrother (did not bat)	–	(4) c Hemp b Brown	54
A. Flintoff (did not bat)	–	(5) c Giles b Brown	70
G. D. Lloyd (did not bat)	–	(6) c Piper b Brown	30
M. Watkinson (did not bat)	–	not out	5
N-b 2	2	B 4, l-b 7, w 2, n-b 10	23
	(no wkt dec.) 39	1/75 2/139 3/184 (6 wkts) 338	
		4/254 5/319 6/320	

R. J. Green, G. Chapple and P. J. Martin did not bat.

Bowling: *First Innings*—Lara 2–0–24–0; Knight 1.5–0–15–0. *Second Innings*—Giddins 13–2–53–0; Welch 11–2–50–0; Brown 27.3–5–125–5; Smith 13–3–31–0; Giles 30–8–68–1.

Umpires: G. Sharp and D. R. Shepherd.

WARWICKSHIRE v HAMPSHIRE

At Birmingham, July 15, 16, 17. Warwickshire won by 225 runs. Warwickshire 24 pts, Hampshire 5 pts. Toss: Warwickshire.

Warwickshire owed their first home win of the season to the batting of their bowlers. Hampshire quickly took control on the first day, but consistent scoring from the lower order, including half-centuries from Smith and Giles, took Warwickshire's total from 100 for five to 367. On a sub-standard pitch, that gave them an advantage they rammed home over the next two days. Giles reduced Hampshire to 158 for eight, though first Morris and then a last-wicket stand of 51 between Hartley and Udal staved off the follow-on. As the surface grew ever more worn, no Warwickshire batsman got to 30 in their second innings, when Morris underlined his all-round ability with another three wickets. Even so, Hampshire needed 306 to win. They were all out for 80; Giles took four for nine, and nine for 57 in the match.

Close of play: First day, Warwickshire 356-9 (A. F. Giles 68*, E. S. H. Giddins 11*); Second day, Warwickshire 24-0 (M. J. Powell 17*, T. Frost 7*).

Warwickshire

M. J. Powell c Aymes b McLean	0	– c Stephenson b James	27
T. Frost b Hartley	13	– c James b Morris	22
D. L. Hemp b McLean	4	– c Mascarenhas b Hartley	8
*B. C. Lara c Mascarenhas b Morris	35	– c Laney b McLean	22
T. L. Penney lbw b Hartley	20	– c Aymes b Morris	14
D. R. Brown c Udal b Stephenson	51	– c Laney b Stephenson	25
†K. J. Piper c Udal b Stephenson	44	– lbw b Morris	7
G. Welch b Morris	38	– lbw b Stephenson	8
N. M. K. Smith c Whitaker b Morris	51	– not out	27
A. F. Giles c and b Morris	75	– c and b McLean	8
E. S. H. Giddins not out	11	– c Stephenson b Hartley	0
B 5, l-b 16, w 2, n-b 2	25	B 5, l-b 8, w 4, n-b 2	19
	367		**187**

1/10 2/18 3/18 4/63 5/100   367
6/169 7/184 8/254 9/291

1/42 2/59 3/59 4/92 5/124   187
6/136 7/139 8/155 9/186

Bonus points – Warwickshire 4, Hampshire 4.

Bowling: *First Innings*—McLean 21–4–71–2; Hartley 23–5–94–2; Mascarenhas 12–3–31–0; Morris 16.5–2–75–4; Udal 10–3–30–0; James 4–0–22–0; Stephenson 12–5–23–2. *Second Innings*—McLean 15–5–53–2; Hartley 15.4–4–41–2; Morris 14–5–27–3; James 10–2–23–1; Mascarenhas 2–0–10–0; Stephenson 8–1–20–2.

Hampshire

J. S. Laney lbw b Brown	1	– b Giddins	0
J. P. Stephenson b Brown	4	– retired hurt	12
G. W. White lbw b Giles	79	– c Lara b Giles	22
P. R. Whitaker lbw b Welch	15	– c Piper b Giddins	0
†A. N. Aymes lbw b Giddins	28	– lbw b Brown	5
K. D. James c Welch b Giles	0	– lbw b Smith	12
A. D. Mascarenhas c and b Giles	14	– c Lara b Giles	0
A. C. Morris b Hemp	46	– b Giles	0
N. A. M. McLean c Penney b Giles	4	– (10) c Giddins b Giles	20
P. J. Hartley b Giles	29	– (11) not out	3
*S. D. Udal not out	17	– (9) c Hemp b Smith	4
L-b 8, n-b 4	12	L-b 2	2
	249		**80**

1/8 2/21 3/42 4/134 5/134   249
6/134 7/154 8/158 9/198

1/0 2/19 3/24 4/43 5/43   80
6/51 7/55 8/64 9/80

Bonus points – Hampshire 1, Warwickshire 4.

In the second innings J. P. Stephenson retired hurt at 13.

Bowling: *First Innings*—Giddins 25–7–45–1; Brown 23–5–74–2; Welch 15–3–44–1; Smith 10–3–29–0; Giles 22–8–48–5; Hemp 1–0–1–1. *Second Innings*—Giddins 9–5–24–2; Brown 8–2–18–1; Welch 8–3–11–0; Giles 6.2–4–9–4; Smith 2–0–16–2.

Umpires: R. Julian and J. F. Steele.

WARWICKSHIRE v ESSEX

At Birmingham, July 23, 24, 25. Essex won by two wickets. Essex 20 pts, Warwickshire 4 pts. Toss: Warwickshire.

Lara and his team left the field to boos from the members after Warwickshire lost an incident-packed match inside three days. The opening day saw 21 wickets fall, but Lord's took no action; it was swing that accounted for most batsmen. Night-watchman Giles coped with the conditions next time round, though, and hit his second fifty in successive matches. Smith joined in to help set Essex 332, a mammoth task. Irani batted well for 69, but it was Danny Law, with a 65 that included 22 off one over from Smith, who won the game for Essex. Warwickshire's sixth defeat in ten starts inevitably spelled criticism for Lara, but his captaincy was blameless, and he was unlucky that Brown could take little part after breaking a knuckle. Lara's batting remained a more legitimate concern: his average was now 22.29 in 17 Championship innings. Despite their victory, Essex slipped to the bottom of the table, where they would remain.

Close of play: First day, Warwickshire 23-1 (N. V. Knight 6*, A. F. Giles 8*); Second day, Essex 75-1 (I. N. Flanagan 49*, M. C. Ilott 1*).

Warwickshire

M. J. Powell lbw b Ilott	0	– c Grayson b Ilott	5
N. V. Knight c Irani b D. R. Law	34	– c Hyam b Such	29
M. A. Wagh c Hyam b Ilott	0	– (4) c Prichard b Such	7
*B. C. Lara lbw b Williams	0	– (5) c D. R. Law b Williams	26
T. Frost c Hyam b Ilott	5	– (6) c Prichard b D. R. Law	23
D. R. Brown b Irani	26	– (11) not out	1
†K. J. Piper c D. R. Law b Williams	37	– b D. R. Law	20
G. Welch c D. R. Law b Williams	29	– lbw b Such	26
N. M. K. Smith not out	43	– c Prichard b Ilott	47
A. F. Giles c Hyam b Irani	4	– (3) c Flanagan b Williams	63
E. S. H. Giddins c D. R. Law b Irani	1	– (10) b Williams	1
B 1, l-b 2, n-b 8	11	B 4, l-b 16, n-b 12	32

1/0 2/6 3/9 4/20 5/70   **190**   1/6 2/88 3/106 4/147 5/154   **280**
6/139 7/140 8/161 9/173   6/184 7/221 8/236 9/237

Bonus points – Essex 4.

In the first innings D. R. Brown, when 26, retired hurt at 76 and resumed at 173.

Bowling: *First Innings*—Ilott 13-2-36-3; Williams 15-3-57-3; D. R. Law 11-0-45-1; Irani 13.4-2-49-3. *Second Innings*—Ilott 18.2-4-64-2; Williams 19-5-68-3; Such 23-6-62-3; Irani 11-3-30-0; D. R. Law 9-2-36-2.

Essex

*P. J. Prichard c Smith b Giddins	7	– c and b Giddins	18
I. N. Flanagan b Giddins	13	– c Lara b Welch	61
S. D. Peters c sub b Giddins	0	– (4) b Smith	26
R. C. Irani c Piper b Welch	39	– (5) c Lara b Giles	69
A. P. Grayson b Welch	1	– (6) lbw b Wagh	33
S. G. Law c Powell b Giles	8	– (7) c Lara b Giddins	14
D. R. Law c Piper b Giles	10	– (8) c Knight b Wagh	65
†B. J. Hyam not out	20	– (9) not out	19
M. C. Ilott c sub b Welch	17	– (3) c Piper b Giddins	8
N. F. Williams b Giddins	0	– not out	4
P. M. Such lbw b Giles	12		
B 1, l-b 5, n-b 6	12	B 1, l-b 4, n-b 10	15

1/20 2/20 3/27 4/38 5/75   **139**   1/71 2/85 3/115   (8 wkts) **332**
6/84 7/86 8/111 9/120   4/146 5/226 6/226
                                               7/246 8/320

Bonus points – Warwickshire 4.

Bowling: *First Innings*—Giddins 12-1-37-4; Welch 18-3-69-3; Giles 7.1-1-27-3. *Second Innings*—Giddins 34-8-102-3; Welch 36-5-121-1; Giles 40-23-42-1; Smith 10-3-46-1; Wagh 9-1-16-2.

Umpires: H. D. Bird and T. E. Jesty.

WARWICKSHIRE v GLAMORGAN

At Birmingham, July 30, 31, August 1, 2. Drawn. Warwickshire 7 pts, Glamorgan 7 pts. Toss: Warwickshire.

Despite the loss of a day and a half, mutual declarations set up an exciting finale: both teams glimpsed victory – but ultimately had to settle for a draw. Munton, who missed the 1997 season and much of this one with a back injury, made the most of a disrupted opening day to take his first Championship wickets since September 1996. After Cottey and Thomas steered Glamorgan towards 300, more rain meant it was the last morning before Lara declared, 180 behind. Maynard set Warwickshire a generous 290 in 75 overs. Thomas took five wickets, compensating for the loss of Watkin to injury, but it was Cosker's left-arm spin that induced a rash shot from Lara. Smith, who had inexplicably been batting at No. 8 or 9, despite his fine form, now came in at No. 6 and hit another half-century. At 172 for five, Warwickshire were well placed; at 233 for eight, Glamorgan were pressing for victory, but Smith and Munton saw out the last eight overs. Both sides fielded a Michael J. Powell.

Close of play: First day, Glamorgan 159-4 (P. A. Cottey 35*, R. D. B. Croft 18*); Second day, Warwickshire 76-1 (N. V. Knight 37*, M. A. Wagh 25*); Third day, Warwickshire 135-4 (T. Frost 7*, K. J. Piper 3*).

Glamorgan

S. P. James c Powell b Munton	53	– lbw b Munton	52
*M. P. Maynard c Powell b Welch	20	– not out	47
A. Dale b Welch	3	– not out	8
M. J. Powell lbw b Munton	18		
P. A. Cottey b Welch	74		
R. D. B. Croft c Giles b Welch	18		
†I. Dawood c Lara b Munton	7		
S. D. Thomas c Wagh b Smith	64		
A. P. Davies c Wagh b Giddins	11		
D. A. Cosker c Piper b Giddins	11		
S. L. Watkin not out	12		
B 4, l-b 10, w 8, n-b 2	24	N-b 2	2
	315	**(1 wkt dec.)**	**109**

1/33 2/55 3/84 4/111 5/161   315   1/86   (1 wkt dec.) 109
6/196 7/223 8/290 9/292

Bonus points – Glamorgan 3, Warwickshire 4.

Bowling: First Innings—Welch 32–8–94–4; Giddins 33.3–3–110–2; Munton 21–8–41–3; Giles 15–3–31–0; Smith 10–3–25–1. *Second Innings*—Welch 5–1–29–0; Giddins 4–0–42–0; Powell 5–0–21–0; Munton 4–0–11–1; Frost 1–0–6–0.

Warwickshire

M. J. Powell c Maynard b Watkin	9	– lbw b Thomas	21
N. V. Knight c Cottey b Davies	52	– b Davies	0
M. A. Wagh lbw b Thomas	39	– lbw b Thomas	34
*B. C. Lara c Cosker b Thomas	15	– c Cosker	22
T. Frost not out	7	– c Dawood b Thomas	22
†K. J. Piper not out	3	– (7) lbw b Thomas	21
N. M. K. Smith (did not bat)		– (6) not out	72
G. Welch (did not bat)		– c Dawood b Davies	9
A. F. Giles (did not bat)		– b Thomas	23
T. A. Munton (did not bat)		– not out	4
B 1, l-b 5, w 2, n-b 2	10	L-b 9, w 8, n-b 8	25
	(4 wkts dec.) 135	**(8 wkts)**	**253**

1/20 2/98 3/110 4/123   (4 wkts dec.) 135   1/3 2/63 3/72 4/112   (8 wkts) 253
5/134 6/172 7/190 8/233

E. S. H. Giddins did not bat.

Bonus point – Glamorgan 1.

Bowling: *First Innings*—Watkin 12–4–17–1; Davies 13–5–47–1; Dale 6–1–21–0; Thomas 9.5–0–38–2; Croft 3–1–5–0; Cosker 1–0–1–0. *Second Innings*—Davies 14.5–1–46–2; Thomas 20–1–84–5; Croft 23–7–48–0; Dale 3–0–14–0; Cosker 14–1–52–1.

Umpires: J. W. Holder and A. G. T. Whitehead.

At Lord's, August 5, 6, 7, 8. WARWICKSHIRE drew with MIDDLESEX.

At Northampton, August 19, 20, 21. WARWICKSHIRE beat NORTHAMPTONSHIRE by four wickets.

At Worcester, August 26, 27, 28. WARWICKSHIRE beat WORCESTERSHIRE by an innings and 116 runs.

WARWICKSHIRE v LEICESTERSHIRE

At Birmingham, September 1, 2, 3, 4. Leicestershire won by 73 runs. Leicestershire 24 pts, Warwickshire 6 pts. Toss: Leicestershire.

A trademark team effort took Leicestershire to a victory that lifted them to the top of the table for the first time in 1998. Ben Smith was the only frontline batsman to prosper as they struggled to 203 for eight. But Millns made 99 and shared a last-wicket partnership of 109 with Brimson, who reached a maiden first-class fifty. Lewis, like Millns, had missed the previous game for disciplinary reasons, and he too enjoyed a successful return, taking five for 76 as Leicestershire gained a lead of 113. The two miscreants brought Lara's indifferent season to an unhappy conclusion, each trapping him lbw without playing a stroke. Smith then beat his first-innings 86 by one to go past 1,000 first-class runs for the season – 672 had come from his last ten Championship innings – and leave Warwickshire 405 for victory. Thanks to Hemp, who scored his first hundred in 15 months, they made a good attempt. His innings lasted 125 balls, with 18 fours and a six, but he had insufficient support. The total of 1,287 runs was the highest in 159 games between the counties.

Close of play: First day, Leicestershire 190-6 (B. F. Smith 82*, C. C. Lewis 5*); Second day, Warwickshire 157-6 (D. R. Brown 24*); Third day, Warwickshire 46-0 (N. V. Knight 5*, M. A. Wagh 37*).

Leicestershire

V. J. Wells c Piper b Brown	2	– b Giddins	15
D. L. Maddy lbw b Giddins	9	– c Piper b Giddins	19
I. J. Sutcliffe c Brown b Munton	24	– st Piper b Giles	36
B. F. Smith lbw b Giddins	86	– lbw b Munton	87
*P. V. Simmons c Piper b Munton	0	– c Hemp b Munton	68
A. Habib c Knight b Brown	29	– not out	16
†P. A. Nixon c Knight b Munton	24	– st Piper b Smith	12
C. C. Lewis lbw b Munton	13	– not out	20
D. J. Millns c Piper b Giddins	99		
A. D. Mullally c Smith b Brown	26		
M. T. Brimson not out	54		
B 1, l-b 4, w 2, n-b 16	23	B 8, l-b 8, w 2	18

1/11 2/21 3/47 4/53 5/124   389   1/26 2/51 3/127   (6 wkts dec.) 291
6/177 7/203 8/203 9/280   4/227 5/246 6/265

Bonus points – Leicestershire 4, Warwickshire 4.

Bowling: *First Innings*—Giddins 30.4–6–124–3; Brown 26–1–129–3; Munton 29–4–90–4; Giles 15–5–25–0; Smith 6–2–16–0. *Second Innings*—Giddins 12–3–50–2; Munton 20–2–74–2; Brown 7–1–35–0; Giles 20–0–92–1; Smith 4–0–24–1.

Warwickshire

N. V. Knight c Nixon b Lewis	5	– c Wells b Lewis	6
M. A. Wagh c Nixon b Lewis	33	– b Millns	60
D. L. Hemp c Smith b Lewis	0	– c Nixon b Simmons	102
*B. C. Lara lbw b Lewis	26	– (5) lbw b Millns	5
A. Singh c Lewis b Simmons	37	– (4) c Simmons b Millns	0
D. R. Brown c Smith b Lewis	75	– c Lewis b Millns	39
T. A. Munton c Sutcliffe b Simmons	5	– (10) c Sutcliffe b Brimson	11
N. M. K. Smith c and b Simmons	13	– (7) b Mullally	41
†K. J. Piper b Brimson	0	– (8) not out	44
A. F. Giles not out	34	– (9) c Habib b Lewis	0
E. S. H. Giddins c Nixon b Simmons	0	– b Simmons	0
B 1, l-b 4, w 8, n-b 35	48	B 1, l-b 4, w 4, n-b 14	23

1/11 2/13 3/70 4/87 5/149   276   1/53 2/87 3/87 4/93 5/181   331
6/157 7/219 8/220 9/271   6/244 7/286 8/293 9/330

Bonus points – Warwickshire 2, Leicestershire 4.

Bowling: *First Innings*—Mullally 17–1–77–0; Lewis 18–2–76–5; Millns 8–1–35–0; Wells 3–1–10–0; Brimson 10–4–19–1; Simmons 10.3–2–54–4. *Second Innings*—Mullally 19–3–75–1; Lewis 17–5–51–2; Wells 6–1–36–0; Brimson 17–5–54–1; Simmons 10–0–50–2; Millns 14–1–60–4.

Umpires: J. W. Lloyds and G. Sharp.

At Leeds, September 9, 10, 11, 12. WARWICKSHIRE lost to YORKSHIRE by an innings and 27 runs.

WARWICKSHIRE v KENT

At Birmingham, September 17, 18, 19, 20. Warwickshire won by 186 runs. Warwickshire 23 pts, Kent 4 pts. Toss: Warwickshire. Championship debut: D. A. Scott.

Both teams had started the season with high expectations but, as they began their last match, minus their West Indian stars, the Championship was being decided elsewhere. The sole issue at stake here was qualification for the 1999 Super Cup. Warwickshire's convincing victory at least achieved that, but for Kent, defeat brought a gloomy end to a disappointing campaign. Knight moved past 1,000 Championship runs for the first time as he and Wagh shared an opening stand of 101. Warwickshire went on to 323, far too much for a Kent side whose feeble efforts explained why they had collected only 18 batting points. Walker and Marsh just avoided the follow-on as Giddins took his fifth five-wicket haul of 1998. Forceful Warwickshire batting extended the lead and, once Neil Smith had passed his 1,000 runs, Knight set a target of 389. The Smiths had the best of the fourth innings; Ed doggedly scored his only fifty of the season while Neil picked up four wickets.

Close of play: First day, Warwickshire 317-7 (A. F. Giles 26*, D. P. Ostler 0*); Second day, Kent 186-7 (S. A. Marsh 51*, D. W. Headley 5*); Third day, Kent 18-1 (E. T. Smith 6*, D. P. Fulton 5*).

Warwickshire

*N. V. Knight c Key b Ealham	68	– c Marsh b Headley	0
M. A. Wagh c Wells b Patel	65	– c Marsh b Ealham	22
D. L. Hemp c Fleming b Headley	12	– b Scott	74
M. J. Powell b Patel	13	– c Key b Headley	22
†T. Frost run out	24	– b Patel	50
D. R. Brown c Marsh b Patel	35	– not out	81
N. M. K. Smith c Marsh b Ealham	59	– not out	10
A. F. Giles not out	28		
D. P. Ostler c Walker b Ealham	4		
T. A. Munton lbw b Ealham	0		
E. S. H. Giddins b Ealham	0		
B 8, l-b 3, w 2, n-b 2	15	L-b 3	3

1/101 2/137 3/162 4/172 5/222   **323**   1/0 2/47 3/107   (5 wkts dec.) **262**
6/252 7/311 8/321 9/323   4/127 5/220

Bonus points – Warwickshire 3, Kent 4.

Bowling: *First Innings*—Headley 22–6–98–1; Ealham 23–12–49–5; Fleming 18–3–61–0; Scott 23–8–55–0; Patel 26–9–49–3. *Second Innings*—Headley 20–2–78–2; Ealham 16–4–56–1; Fleming 15–2–38–0; Scott 18–5–48–1; Patel 9–0–39–1.

Kent

R. W. T. Key c Knight b Brown	11	– b Munton	5
E. T. Smith c Frost b Giddins	24	– c Giles b Smith	58
D. P. Fulton c Frost b Giddins	0	– c Knight b Giddins	5
A. P. Wells c Frost b Brown	11	– c Hemp b Giddins	0
M. J. Walker c Wagh b Munton	57	– c Frost b Smith	13
M. A. Ealham c Powell b Brown	8	– c Knight b Smith	5
M. V. Fleming c sub b Giddins	10	– c Frost b Giles	21
*†S. A. Marsh c Frost b Munton	57	– c Ostler b Smith	17
D. W. Headley c Knight b Munton	5	– c Giles b Giddins	26
M. M. Patel c Ostler b Giddins	1	– c Hemp b Giles	48
D. A. Scott not out	3	– not out	2
B 2, l-b 8	10	L-b 2	2

1/32 2/32 3/48 4/49 5/89   **197**   1/5 2/18 3/28 4/49 5/59   **202**
6/103 7/148 8/186 9/192   6/98 7/121 8/126 9/192

Bonus points – Warwickshire 4.

Bowling: *First Innings*—Giddins 30.2–14–61–5; Munton 25–11–46–2; Brown 14–6–33–3; Giles 18–5–47–0. *Second Innings*—Giddins 13.2–4–44–3; Munton 7–3–19–1; Giles 23–9–36–2; Smith 26–6–92–4; Brown 3–1–9–0.

Umpires: J. C. Balderstone and A. Clarkson.

6673

WORCESTERSHIRE

Patron: The Duke of Westminster
President: R. Booth
Chairman: J. W. Elliott
Chairman, Cricket Committee: M. J. Horton
Secretary: The Rev. M. D. Vockins
Captain: T. M. Moody
Coach: C. W. J. Athey
Head Groundsman: R. McLaren

David Leatherdale

Worcestershire experienced their most unproductive season for years, failing to make an impact in any competition. They had looked forward to the 1998 campaign with great optimism, after finishing third in the County Championship the previous year. The management were looking for the final pieces in the jigsaw and, during the winter, thought they had secured one by signing Devon Malcolm from Derbyshire. But Malcolm opted for Northamptonshire, where he was not a success. His decision in itself, though, was depressing. Once again, Worcestershire were left without the genuine cutting edge they had lacked since the days of Graham Dilley.

The nadir of the season was a NatWest Trophy exit at the hands of Scotland. Before that, Worcestershire maintained their reputation as slow starters when they failed to qualify for the knockout stages of the Benson and Hedges Cup for the third year running. In the Championship, by contrast, Worcestershire began with a victory and, by early July, when they beat Northamptonshire in two days, stood in eighth position, only 39 points behind leaders Surrey with a match in hand. But that was followed by four successive defeats, their worst run since 1986, and they won only once more, in the final game against Durham.

A morsel of comfort came in the last Sunday game of the season: victory over Hampshire pushed them into the top half of the table and a place in the First Division of the National League for 1999.

The happiest moment of the season occurred when Graeme Hick became the 24th player – and the second youngest – to complete a hundred hundreds, with his second century of the home match against Sussex at the end of May. Hick's early-season form, which brought him four hundreds in successive innings, earned him a Test recall after a two-year absence. But he could not deliver against South Africa. A century against Sri Lanka at The Oval was not enough to put him in the original winter Ashes party, though he was called up later to cover for injuries.

Overall, Worcestershire's sharp decline can be put down to a combination of injuries, which exposed their lack of strength in depth, and the failure of several stalwarts to live up to past achievements. Stuart Lampitt, Phil Newport and Richard Illingworth – three players associated with the successful years of the 1980s and early 1990s – were all left out at various junctures. Time seemed to have caught up with Newport. On his day, he remained one of the best swing bowlers in England. But he had become increasingly injury-prone and missed a considerable chunk of his benefit year. His new-ball partner, Alamgir Sheriyar, initially looked as if he would carry on the form which brought him 62 wickets in 1997: he claimed eight in the opening match against Essex. But he failed to sustain that, and injuries sidelined him during the second half of the season. With the promising Maneer Mirza ruled out by a back problem, the county's attack often looked threadbare.

Illingworth was understood to be less than happy at being passed over for the vice-captaincy – Hick inherited the post from Steve Rhodes – while the wet summer meant his left-arm spin gathered only 13 wickets in 15 games, his lowest return in 17 seasons at New Road.

It was fortunate that all-rounder Lampitt rallied to finish with a respectable 50 first-class wickets. But the major plus in that department was the emergence of pace bowler Bobby Chapman. The son of former Nottingham Forest footballer Sammy Chapman, he had moved to Worcestershire from Trent Bridge in 1997, and now thrived on his longest run of first-class cricket, collecting 33 wickets.

The top-order batting lacked consistency and experience, and was badly exposed when Hick became unavailable through international commitments. Phil Weston was cast as senior opener, after the retirement of Tim Curtis, but did not register a single century. He suffered from not having a regular opening partner: Reuben Spiring, who had been earmarked to fill that role, missed the entire season with a knee injury. The county hoped that Paul Pollard, signed from Nottinghamshire in the autumn, would help. With Gavin Haynes also succumbing to a knee injury for several weeks, Worcestershire had to throw in untried youngsters such as Abdul Hafeez, Elliott Wilson and Ryan Driver.

All this placed a huge responsibility on the shoulders of the county's Australian captain, Tom Moody. Despite scoring four centuries, he was less prolific than before. He signed a one-year contract for 1999, but it seemed likely to be his last season in England. Vikram Solanki advanced, earning his county cap and a place on the England A tour. He played several exciting innings, scored 999 runs and showed no fear at the wicket, but needed greater consistency.

It was two players who often found themselves repairing the damage from early collapses who could look back on 1998 with most satisfaction. David Leatherdale passed 1,000 runs in a season for the first time, and his medium-pace bowling saw him placed ninth in the national averages, with 21 wickets at 19.80. Rhodes also had a fine year – completing 1,000 runs for the second time when he usually batted at No. 7 was no mean achievement. Any marginal decline in his wicket-keeping skills was counterbalanced by his continuing infectious enthusiasm for the game.

In the winter, Worcestershire stepped up their efforts to strengthen the squad. With Hick and Moody likely to be missing until June, because of the World Cup, an experienced middle-order batsman was high on the agenda. But the priority, as it had been the previous year, was to find a strike bowler. – JOHN CURTIS.

WORCESTERSHIRE 1998

[Bill Smith]

Back row: A. Hafeez, D. N. Catterall, E. J. Wilson, R. C. Driver, D. Patel. *Middle row:* R. J. Chapman, M. J. Rawnsley, K. R. Spiring, D. A. Leatherdale, W. P. C. Weston, A. Sheriyar, V. S. Solanki, S. W. K. Ellis, M. M. Mirza, J. Rees *(physiotherapist)*. *Front row:* The Rev. M. D. Vockins *(secretary)*, D. B. D'Oliveira, S. R. Lampitt, R. K. Illingworth, G. A. Hick, J. W. Elliott *(chairman)*, S. J. Rhodes, P. J. Newport, G. R. Haynes, C. W. J. Athey *(coach)*. *Insets:* T. M. Moody *(captain)*, N. E. Batson. J. E. Chadd *(chairman, cricket sub-committee)*.

Worcestershire in 1998

WORCESTERSHIRE RESULTS

All first-class matches – Played 19: Won 5, Lost 7, Drawn 7.

County Championship matches – Played 17: Won 4, Lost 6, Drawn 7.

Competition placings – Britannic Assurance County Championship, 13th; NatWest Trophy, 1st round; Benson and Hedges Cup, 3rd in Group B; AXA League, 7th.

COUNTY CHAMPIONSHIP AVERAGES
BATTING

Cap		M	I	NO	R	HS	100s	50s	Avge	Ct/St
1986	G. A. Hick	12	22	0	973	166	5	1	44.22	19
1991	T. M. Moody§	13	23	2	886	132	4	2	42.19	10
1986	S. J. Rhodes	17	31	5	952	104*	1	6	36.61	42/2
1994	G. R. Haynes†	11	19	5	506	86	0	4	36.14	2
1986	R. K. Illingworth . . .	15	21	6	473	84	0	3	31.53	5
1995	W. P. C. Weston . . .	15	27	2	731	95	0	5	29.24	9
1994	D. A. Leatherdale . . .	16	29	1	795	137	1	3	28.39	8
1998	V. S. Solanki	17	32	0	904	170	2	3	28.25	26
1989	S. R. Lampitt	16	26	6	450	48	0	0	22.50	5
1986	P. J. Newport	12	15	3	261	56	0	1	21.75	3
	A. Hafeez	9	17	0	270	55	0	1	15.88	5
	R. J. Chapman	10	16	8	102	43*	0	0	12.75	2
1997	A. Sheriyar	10	9	3	61	20	0	0	10.16	1
	E. J. Wilson	5	10	0	101	27	0	0	10.10	3
	N. E. Batson	3	6	0	50	18	0	0	8.33	0
	M. J. Rawnsley	4	7	0	55	21	0	0	7.85	4

Also batted: D. N. Catterall (1 match) 0; R. C. Driver (1 match) 5, 0.

* Signifies not out. † Born in Worcestershire. § Overseas player.

BOWLING

	O	M	R	W	BB	5W/i	Avge
D. A. Leatherdale	107.4	20	404	21	5-20	1	19.23
P. J. Newport	304	102	820	32	4-44	0	25.62
G. R. Haynes	209.5	57	668	26	6-50	2	25.69
S. R. Lampitt	375	81	1,253	48	5-33	4	26.10
R. J. Chapman	233.1	41	914	33	6-105	1	27.69
T. M. Moody	251.4	73	790	27	5-64	1	29.25
A. Sheriyar	237.1	54	837	23	5-85	1	36.39
R. K. Illingworth	305	81	853	13	3-28	0	65.61

Also bowled: D. N. Catterall 13–2–31–0; G. A. Hick 45–6–152–1; M. J. Rawnsley 88.4–28–241–5; V. S. Solanki 96–19–350–7; W. P. C. Weston 2–0–20–0.

COUNTY RECORDS

Highest score for:	405*	G. A. Hick v Somerset at Taunton	1988
Highest score against:	331*	J. D. Robertson (Middlesex) at Worcester	1949
Best bowling for:	9-23	C. F. Root v Lancashire at Worcester	1931
Best bowling against:	10-51	J. Mercer (Glamorgan) at Worcester	1936
Highest total for:	670-7 dec.	v Somerset at Worcester	1995
Highest total against:	701-4 dec.	by Leicestershire at Worcester	1906
Lowest total for:	24	v Yorkshire at Huddersfield	1903
Lowest total against:	30	by Hampshire at Worcester	1903

WORCESTERSHIRE v ESSEX

At Worcester, April 17, 18, 20, 21. Worcestershire won by six wickets. Worcestershire 23 pts, Essex 4 pts. Toss: Worcestershire. First-class debut: A. Hafeez.

Despite all five lamps on the scoreboard shining in the gloom, Worcestershire, led by Hick for the first time in a Championship match, reached an improbable target – 122 from 15 overs – with three balls to spare. Solanki hit a 26-ball 53, including five sixes, which proved decisive against a depleted Essex attack; Ilott was unable to bowl in the second innings, while Cowan limped off the field with a back spasm after conceding 19 runs in the first over. On a slow pitch and in freezing conditions – umpire Hampshire resorted to white ski hat and mittens on the first day – Essex squandered a century stand between Hussain and Stuart Law, and lost their last five wickets for 14. Weston ground out 95 in over six hours to ensure a healthy lead of 189. Essex seemed safe, though, at 221 for three just after an early lunch on the last day. Sheriyar thought otherwise, and a burst of four for nought in 12 balls paved the way for Solanki's big-hitting finale. Play had started on time on the first day despite dreadful Severn floods only a week earlier, New Road for once escaping quite lightly.

Close of play: First day, Worcestershire 49-1 (W. P. C. Weston 20*, G. A. Hick 15*); Second day, Worcestershire 320-6 (S. J. Rhodes 28*, S. R. Lampitt 8*); Third day, Essex 148-3 (S. G. Law 30*, R. C. Irani 20*).

Essex

*P. J. Prichard c Rhodes b Sheriyar	14	– b Lampitt	24
D. D. J. Robinson lbw b Sheriyar	0	– lbw b Lampitt	35
N. Hussain c Rhodes b Sheriyar	68	– c Rhodes b Newport	15
S. G. Law c Hick b Newport	45	– c Rhodes b Sheriyar	87
R. C. Irani b Lampitt	41	– c Lampitt b Sheriyar	37
A. P. Grayson lbw b Newport	53	– b Sheriyar	0
†R. J. Rollins lbw b Illingworth	8	– c Sheriyar b Illingworth	23
D. R. Law c Leatherdale b Illingworth	1	– c Solanki b Sheriyar	0
M. C. Ilott b Sheriyar	4	– c Hick b Lampitt	11
A. P. Cowan b Illingworth	2	– c Haynes b Lampitt	37
P. M. Such not out	0	– not out	2
L-b 9, n-b 12	21	B 1, l-b 12, n-b 26	39
	257		**310**

1/4 2/15 3/128 4/150 5/210   257
6/243 7/251 8/253 9/257

1/58 2/87 3/108 4/221 5/221   310
6/226 7/226 8/259 9/279

Bonus points – Essex 2, Worcestershire 4.

Bowling: First Innings—Newport 19-6-52-2; Sheriyar 18.2-2-60-4; Lampitt 15-1-66-1; Haynes 5-0-26-0; Leatherdale 3-1-16-0; Illingworth 16-7-28-3. *Second Innings*—Newport 22-8-45-1; Sheriyar 24-6-80-4; Lampitt 23-5-61-4; Haynes 17-3-69-0; Leatherdale 3-0-14-0; Illingworth 10-5-13-1; Hick 8-3-15-0.

Worcestershire

W. P. C. Weston c Rollins b Grayson	95		
V. S. Solanki lbw b Ilott	6	– (1) c D. R. Law b Irani	53
*G. A. Hick lbw b Ilott	15	– (2) c Hussain b Irani	25
G. R. Haynes b Cowan	86	– (3) not out	26
D. A. Leatherdale c Such b Grayson	21	– (4) lbw b Irani	7
A. Hafeez c Robinson b Grayson	15		
†S. J. Rhodes c Rollins b D. R. Law	66	– (6) not out	5
S. R. Lampitt lbw b Irani	16	– (5) c and b Irani	0
R. K. Illingworth c Hussain b Cowan	61		
P. J. Newport c Robinson b Cowan	14		
A. Sheriyar not out	2		
B 1, l-b 18, w 2, n-b 28	49	W 2, n-b 4	6
	446	**(4 wkts)**	**122**

1/11 2/57 3/228 4/263 5/274   446
6/297 7/345 8/396 9/439

1/47 2/103 3/114 4/114   (4 wkts) 122

Bonus points – Worcestershire 3, Essex 2 (Score at 120 overs: 320-6).

Bowling: *First Innings*—Ilott 20.4–7–50–2; Cowan 30.2–4–118–3; Irani 30–10–64–1; Such 36–12–63–0; D. R. Law 14–2–78–1; Grayson 31.2–9–54–3. *Second Innings*—Cowan 1–0–19–0; Irani 6.3–0–38–4; D. R. Law 1–0–11–0; Grayson 3–0–30–0; Such 3–0–24–0.

Umpires: J. H. Hampshire and J. F. Steele.

At Leicester, April 23, 24, 25, 27. WORCESTERSHIRE drew with LEICESTERSHIRE.

At Oxford, May 11, 12, 13. WORCESTERSHIRE beat OXFORD UNIVERSITY by 115 runs.

At Worcester, May 14, 15, 16. WORCESTERSHIRE lost to SOUTH AFRICANS by 89 runs (See South African tour section).

At Uxbridge, May 21, 22, 23, 24. WORCESTERSHIRE drew with MIDDLESEX.

WORCESTERSHIRE v SUSSEX

At Worcester, May 29, 30, 31, June 1. Drawn. Worcestershire 11 pts, Sussex 9 pts. Toss: Worcestershire.

At 3.29 p.m. on the third afternoon, Graeme Hick, aged 32 years and eight days and playing his 574th first-class innings, flicked Robinson to mid-wicket. The two runs took him to his second hundred of the match (which he had achieved twice before) and his third in successive innings. It was also the 100th of his career, a feat managed by just 23 others. Only one (Wally Hammond, by a fortnight) did it at a younger age, and only two (Bradman, 295, and Compton, 552) did it in fewer innings. Hick had announced his wish to reach the milestone either at New Road or in a Test. His exclusion from the squad for the First Test – announced that morning – may have spurred him on to seize the first opportunity in front of his home crowd. Worcestershire president Tom Graveney, who had scored his own 100th hundred on this ground in 1964, walked out to the middle with a bottle of champagne and two glasses on a silver salver to toast the occasion. There had been less ceremony when Solanki, the batsman at the other end, reached his first Championship century two balls earlier, though it was, perhaps, the classier of the two innings. He and Hick put on 243 to help set a daunting target of 419. But after Sussex got to an unhurried 123 without loss, a lunchtime downpour ended any possibility of a last-afternoon run-chase. Hick's 99th hundred had illuminated the first day, and on the second Sussex were soon in trouble at 33 for three. Moody then bowled Bevan, on 19, only to discover it was a no-ball. The escape was vital; Bevan went on to 96 and shared in a stand of 100 with Carpenter. Lampitt took five for 56, but Worcestershire's hopes of a decisive lead were thwarted.

Close of play: First day, Worcestershire 353-9 (S. R. Lampitt 31*, A. Sheriyar 0*); Second day, Worcestershire 24-0 (W. P. C. Weston 9*, V. S. Solanki 14*); Third day, Sussex 35-0 (M. T. E. Peirce 10*, W. G. Khan 13*).

Worcestershire

W. P. C. Weston c Adams b Lewry	14	– c Adams b Robinson	21
V. S. Solanki c Humphries b Kirtley	28	– b Robinson	155
G. A. Hick c Adams b Robinson	104	– c Peirce b Newell	132
G. R. Haynes c Adams b Lewry	20	– not out	8
*T. M. Moody c Adams b Kirtley	48		
D. A. Leatherdale c A. A. Khan b Bevan	39		
†S. J. Rhodes lbw b Lewry	28		
S. R. Lampitt not out	31		
R. K. Illingworth b Lewry	0		
P. J. Newport lbw b Bevan	13		
A. Sheriyar not out	0		
B 4, l-b 4, w 6, n-b 14	28	B 5, l-b 9, w 2, n-b 11	27

1/32 2/73 3/134 4/224 5/256   (9 wkts dec.) 353   1/58 2/301 3/343   (3 wkts dec.) 343
6/293 7/321 8/321 9/353

Bonus points – Worcestershire 4, Sussex 4.

Bowling: *First Innings*—Lewry 24–5–104–4; Kirtley 20–5–47–2; Robinson 24–6–68–1; A. A. Khan 10–4–43–0; Newell 13–4–35–0; Bevan 13–4–48–2. *Second Innings*—Lewry 15–1–51–0; Kirtley 17–2–61–0; Robinson 19.2–4–77–0; Newell 10–4–33–1; A. A. Khan 19–4–68–0; Bevan 1–0–7–0; Peirce 8–2–32–0.

Sussex

M. T. E. Peirce lbw b Newport	2	– not out	51
W. G. Khan run out	9	– not out	53
C. J. Adams c Solanki b Newport	9		
*M. G. Bevan lbw b Lampitt	96		
J. R. Carpenter c Rhodes b Moody	33		
K. Newell c Leatherdale b Illingworth	8		
†S. Humphries c Hick b Lampitt	43		
A. A. Khan lbw b Lampitt	9		
R. J. Kirtley not out	22		
J. D. Lewry c Rhodes b Lampitt	5		
M. A. Robinson b Lampitt	0		
L-b 2, n-b 40	42	B 1, l-b 8, n-b 10	19

1/2 2/16 3/33 4/133 5/179   278   (no wkt) 123
6/179 7/191 8/270 9/278

Bonus points – Sussex 2, Worcestershire 4.

Bowling: *First Innings*—Newport 20–5–65–2; Sheriyar 18–6–66–0; Lampitt 18.2–4–56–5; Moody 20–9–48–1; Haynes 9–5–24–0; Illingworth 9–3–17–1. *Second Innings*—Newport 10–4–32–0; Sheriyar 13–6–22–0; Illingworth 13–2–25–0; Lampitt 9–3–16–0; Haynes 4–2–9–0; Moody 6–3–10–0.

Umpires: A. A. Jones and G. Sharp.

At The Oval, June 3, 4, 5, 6. WORCESTERSHIRE lost to SURREY by 79 runs.

At Cardiff, June 11, 12, 13, 15. WORCESTERSHIRE drew with GLAMORGAN.

WORCESTERSHIRE v GLOUCESTERSHIRE

At Worcester, June 17, 18, 19, 20. Worcestershire won by five wickets. Worcestershire 20 pts, Gloucestershire 3 pts. Toss: Worcestershire.

Abdul Hafeez belted his maiden first-class fifty from 35 balls to help Worcestershire achieve their target of 208 from 40 overs with six deliveries to spare. Only 50 minutes' play was possible on the first two days, but on the third 18 wickets fell in humid conditions. Leatherdale took five for 20, his best figures, and restricted Gloucestershire to 188. A stand of 85 between Wright and Windows had given the innings some stability, but the last seven wickets fell for 35. Then it was Walsh's turn to take five wickets as Worcestershire subsided to 89 for eight. Reciprocal declarations gave Worcestershire a handsome opportunity. Hafeez and Weston responded with a stand of 80 in 15 overs and the middle order eased them home.

Close of play: First day, Gloucestershire 37-0 (G. I. Macmillan 20*, T. H. C. Hancock 15*); Second day, No play; Third day, Worcestershire 111-8 (D. A. Leatherdale 25*, P. J. Newport 15*).

Gloucestershire

G. I. Macmillan c Rhodes b Moody	25	– c and b Haynes	30
T. H. C. Hancock c Rhodes b Lampitt	29	– c and b Lampitt	25
A. J. Wright c Rhodes b Leatherdale	36	– run out	13
*M. W. Alleyne b Lampitt	0	– not out	43
M. G. N. Windows c Solanki b Moody	43	– c Lampitt b Leatherdale	0
D. R. Hewson lbw b Leatherdale	0	– (7) not out	5
M. C. J. Ball b Leatherdale	9		
†R. C. J. Williams c Rhodes b Leatherdale	5		
J. Lewis c Moody b Leatherdale	14	– (6) c Weston b Lampitt	3
A. M. Smith b Moody	0		
C. A. Walsh not out	4		
L-b 3, n-b 20	23	L-b 14, n-b 8	22

1/56 2/68 3/68 4/153 5/153   188   1/71 2/71 3/91   (5 wkts dec.) 141
6/157 7/170 8/177 9/178   4/95 5/108

Bonus points – Worcestershire 4.

Bowling: *First Innings*—Newport 12–1–46–0; Sheriyar 4–0–18–0; Lampitt 11–2–36–2; Moody 16–6–42–3; Haynes 6–2–16–0; Illingworth 3–0–7–0; Leatherdale 9.5–4–20–5. *Second Innings*—Newport 5–0–37–0; Haynes 8–1–38–1; Lampitt 8–0–31–2; Leatherdale 5–0–21–1.

Worcestershire

W. P. C. Weston c Windows b Walsh	6	– c Ball b Lewis	25
A. Hafeez c Windows b Lewis	0	– c Hancock b Alleyne	55
*T. M. Moody b Walsh	1	– c Macmillan b Smith	45
V. S. Solanki c Williams b Alleyne	24	– c Alleyne b Walsh	40
G. R. Haynes c Ball b Alleyne	21	– (6) not out	20
D. A. Leatherdale not out	30	– (5) c Hancock b Smith	14
†S. J. Rhodes c Macmillan b Walsh	14	– not out	10
S. R. Lampitt c Hancock b Walsh	1		
R. K. Illingworth c Ball b Walsh	0		
P. J. Newport not out	19		
L-b 2, n-b 4	6	N-b 2	2

1/2 2/3 3/12 4/49 5/56   (8 wkts dec.) 122   1/80 2/80 3/145   (5 wkts) 211
6/81 7/89 8/89   4/173 5/191

A. Sheriyar did not bat.

Bonus points – Gloucestershire 3.

Bowling: *First Innings*—Walsh 17–4–44–5; Lewis 15–5–27–1; Smith 11–3–33–0; Alleyne 11–4–16–2. *Second Innings*—Walsh 12–0–63–1; Smith 10–0–57–2; Ball 2–0–13–0; Lewis 6–1–39–1; Alleyne 9–2–39–1.

Umpires: H. D. Bird and P. Willey.

WORCESTERSHIRE v NORTHAMPTONSHIRE

At Worcester, July 1, 2. Worcestershire won by 157 runs. Worcestershire 20 pts, Northamptonshire 4 pts. Toss: Worcestershire.

Weston earned Worcestershire a two-day victory when he was the only batsman to prosper in overcast conditions ideal for swing and pace. Twenty-one wickets fell on the first day, and initially Rose's career-best seven for 39 looked to have put Northamptonshire on top. But Moody and Leatherdale, more gentle but equally testing, bowled them out 22 behind. While others continued to struggle, and Rose took his match haul to 11 for 90, Weston carried his bat for the second time in his career, in a chanceless innings of nearly five hours. When he ran out of partners, Northamptonshire needed 235 from seven sessions. Newport wrecked their start with an opening spell of three for three, Moody demolished the middle order and Chapman completed the rout in the 40th over – all out for 77. This second successive victory lifted Worcestershire to eighth place, 39 points behind leaders Surrey with a game in hand, but proved the high point of their season; they did not win again until the final match. It was Northamptonshire's first defeat, although they were already bottom.

Close of play: First day, Worcestershire 52-1 (W. P. C. Weston 23*).

Worcestershire

W. P. C. Weston c Roberts b Rose	12	– not out		91
A. Hafeez c Roberts b Taylor	4	– c Warren b Taylor		23
G. A. Hick c Curran b Rose	38	– lbw b Taylor		0
V. S. Solanki c Roberts b Curran	8	– c Ripley b Rose		3
*T. M. Moody c Ripley b Rose	8	– c Bailey b Malcolm		33
D. A. Leatherdale c Ripley b Rose	12	– c Warren b Malcolm		1
†S. J. Rhodes c Warren b Rose	12	– b Malcolm		5
R. K. Illingworth not out	23	– c Sales b Rose		28
P. J. Newport c Ripley b Rose	3	– lbw b Curran		6
A. Sheriyar c Sales b Rose	6	– c Penberthy b Rose		8
R. J. Chapman run out	0	– b Rose		0
B 1, l-b 5, n-b 4	10	L-b 6, w 2, n-b 6		14

1/10 2/50 3/63 4/67 5/85   136   1/52 2/52 3/57 4/106 5/121   212
6/92 7/105 8/111 9/125   6/135 7/180 8/197 9/212

Bonus points – Northamptonshire 4.

Bowling: *First Innings*—Malcolm 6–0–33–0; Taylor 15.5–3–33–1; Rose 16.5–5–39–7; Curran 6–0–25–1. *Second Innings*—Rose 17.5–5–51–4; Taylor 18–9–43–2; Malcolm 12–1–67–3; Penberthy 6–2–10–0; Curran 10–3–35–1.

Northamptonshire

R. J. Warren c Hick b Sheriyar	3	– (2) lbw b Newport		1
D. J. Roberts c Leatherdale	39	– (1) b Newport		0
R. J. Bailey c Solanki b Moody	21	– c Rhodes b Moody		24
D. J. Sales c Solanki b Leatherdale	4	– lbw b Newport		5
*K. M. Curran c Hick b Moody	4	– c Solanki b Moody		12
A. L. Penberthy lbw b Leatherdale	6	– c Weston b Moody		2
†D. Ripley c Hafeez b Moody	18	– c Moody b Chapman		5
G. P. Swann c Moody b Leatherdale	5	– c Hick b Chapman		12
J. P. Taylor c Hick b Newport	4	– not out		7
F. A. Rose c Illingworth b Moody	0	– c Rhodes b Chapman		0
D. E. Malcolm not out	1	– c Solanki b Chapman		0
L-b 1, w 6, n-b 2	9	L-b 3, w 4, n-b 2		9

1/7 2/67 3/67 4/71 5/84   114   1/0 2/1 3/21 4/43 5/47   77
6/89 7/103 8/109 9/113   6/58 7/58 8/71 9/71

Bonus points – Worcestershire 4.

Bowling: *First Innings*—Newport 10–2–29–1; Sheriyar 7–1–17–1; Chapman 4–1–23–0; Moody 15–8–20–4; Leatherdale 8–3–24–4. *Second Innings*—Newport 9–7–3–3; Sheriyar 13–1–38–0; Chapman 6.1–4–9–4; Moody 11–3–24–3.

Umpires: M. J. Kitchen and K. E. Palmer.

At Lytham, July 14, 15, 16, 17. WORCESTERSHIRE lost to LANCASHIRE by two wickets.

At Worcester, July 28. WORCESTERSHIRE lost to SRI LANKANS by seven wickets (See Sri Lankan tour section).

WORCESTERSHIRE v YORKSHIRE

At Worcester, July 30, 31, August 1, 3. Yorkshire won by an innings and 160 runs. Yorkshire 24 pts, Worcestershire 4 pts. Toss: Yorkshire. First-class debut: E. J. Wilson.

Yorkshire outplayed Worcestershire from the moment they won the toss, and only the weather ever threatened to deny them. Lehmann shrugged off a knee injury on the first morning and advanced to his fifth double-hundred – his first for Yorkshire – which occupied 269 balls and 315 minutes and contained 28 fours and two sixes. On a dry pitch, he shared a stand of 236 with Wood. Although Yorkshire later lost six wickets for 49, left-armer Hutchison maintained their supremacy. Openers Weston and debutant Elliott Wilson, a 21-year-old recruit from Durham University, put on 58, but Hutchison triggered a collapse; only Yorkshire grit from Rhodes and Illingworth earned Worcestershire a single batting point. Following on 254 behind, they quickly lost their opening pair. But rain prevented play on the final day until 2.30 p.m. Yorkshire need not have worried: the last eight wickets went down very rapidly. Gough provided the breakthrough – three for eight in 15 balls – and was admirably backed up by Hamilton.

Close of play: First day, Yorkshire 398-4 (A. McGrath 45*, P. M. Hutchison 0*); Second day, Worcestershire 145-7 (S. J. Rhodes 21*, R. K. Illingworth 5*); Third day, Worcestershire 19-2 (S. R. Lampitt 8*, G. A. Hick 4*).

Yorkshire

*D. Byas c Hick b Lampitt	13		D. Gough c Rhodes b Lampitt	6
M. P. Vaughan lbw b Chapman	23		J. D. Middlebrook not out	3
M. J. Wood c Rhodes b Hick	94		R. D. Stemp not out	6
D. S. Lehmann c Rhodes b Newport	200		B 5, l-b 9, w 2, n-b 16	32
A. McGrath lbw b Chapman	50			
P. M. Hutchison b Newport	4		1/39 2/43 3/279	(9 wkts dec.) 455
†R. J. Blakey b Newport	0		4/395 5/407 6/407	
G. M. Hamilton lbw b Lampitt	24		7/420 8/443 9/444	

Bonus points – Yorkshire 4, Worcestershire 3 (Score at 120 overs: 443-7).

Bowling: Newport 22–8–58–3; Chapman 23–3–81–2; Lampitt 23–3–73–3; Leatherdale 5–0–31–0; Illingworth 25–5–83–0; Solanki 10–1–46–0; Hick 15–3–45–1; Moody 6–0–24–0.

Worcestershire

W. P. C. Weston lbw b Hutchison	23	– c Blakey b Hamilton	4
E. J. Wilson c Vaughan b Hutchison	25	– lbw b Gough	3
G. A. Hick c Gough b Hutchison	8	– (4) c Middlebrook b Gough	12
V. S. Solanki lbw b Hamilton	9	– (5) c Blakey b Gough	0
*T. M. Moody c Wood b Hamilton	9	– (6) c Lehmann b Gough	8
D. A. Leatherdale b Gough	4	– (7) lbw b Hamilton	30
†S. J. Rhodes b Middlebrook	45	– (8) c Blakey b Hamilton	0
S. R. Lampitt c Blakey b Middlebrook	8	– (3) c Blakey b Stemp	24
R. K. Illingworth c Blakey b Hamilton	25	– c Middlebrook b Hamilton	0
P. J. Newport not out	2	– lbw b Gough	4
R. J. Chapman c Wood b Middlebrook	1	– not out	5
B 19, l-b 11, w 2, n-b 10	42	L-b 4	4

1/58 2/58 3/77 4/87 5/90   201   1/7 2/7 3/32 4/32 5/40   94
6/96 7/125 8/198 9/198   6/80 7/80 8/84 9/86

Bonus points – Worcestershire 1, Yorkshire 4.

Bowling: *First Innings*—Gough 22–4–60–1; Hutchison 21–7–54–3; Hamilton 12–4–20–3; Stemp 7–2–17–0; Middlebrook 12.2–4–20–3. *Second Innings*—Gough 11.5–2–36–5; Hamilton 14–5–17–4; Middlebrook 4–0–15–0; Hutchison 5–1–19–0; Stemp 9–6–3–1.

Umpires: B. Dudleston and J. F. Steele.

WORCESTERSHIRE v NOTTINGHAMSHIRE

At Kidderminster, August 5, 6, 7, 8. Nottinghamshire won by 90 runs. Nottinghamshire 20 pts, Worcestershire 6 pts. Toss: Nottinghamshire. First-class debut: N. E. Batson.

After dominating for two days, Worcestershire were undone by their former all-rounder, Kidderminster-born Tolley, who achieved career-best figures of seven for 45. It was Nottinghamshire's first-ever win at Chester Road – they had lost on all their previous five visits. A sixth defeat loomed on the opening day, when fine swing bowling and undistinguished batting saw them dismissed for 164. Worcestershire also found it hard going, but Moody scored his fifth century at Kidderminster to earn a first-innings lead of 125, despite six for 63 from Franks, his best return yet. There was another career-best analysis – six for 105 – by Chapman, once of Nottinghamshire, in the next innings. But crucially, Newport was unable to bowl much because of a bad knee. Johnson took advantage to score his second hundred in three innings since relinquishing the captaincy. He shared century stands with Afzaal and Tolley, and left a target of 277. Tolley then exposed Worcestershire's Hick-less batting and, once Moody had departed for a duck, Nottinghamshire's win became inevitable.

Close of play: First day, Worcestershire 123-4 (T. M. Moody 41*, D. A. Leatherdale 35*); Second day, Nottinghamshire 100-2 (U. Afzaal 19*, P. Johnson 13*); Third day, Worcestershire 29-2 (W. P. C. Weston 13*, M. J. Rawnsley 0*).

Nottinghamshire

G. E. Welton c Leatherdale b Moody	18	– lbw b Lampitt	44
*J. E. R. Gallian c Leatherdale b Chapman	14	– b Leatherdale	6
U. Afzaal c Moody b Lampitt	10	– c Rhodes b Chapman	34
P. Johnson c Leatherdale b Chapman	43	– lbw b Chapman	139
G. F. Archer c Solanki b Rawnsley	27	– c Moody b Chapman	1
C. M. Tolley b Newport	1	– c Solanki b Newport	48
P. J. Franks c Rhodes b Newport	0	– c Rawnsley b Chapman	19
†C. M. W. Read run out	13	– lbw b Newport	17
P. A. Strang c Solanki b Lampitt	11	– c Rhodes b Chapman	0
K. P. Evans c Solanki b Rawnsley	6	– c Rhodes b Chapman	36
A. R. Oram not out	0	– not out	4
L-b 1, n-b 20	21	L-b 12, w 4, n-b 37	53

1/28 2/41 3/87 4/103 5/112   164   1/24 2/65 3/176 4/178 5/300   401
6/112 7/135 8/154 9/164   6/327 7/333 8/333 9/377

Bonus points – Worcestershire 4.

Bowling: *First Innings*—Newport 14–6–25–2; Chapman 14–3–52–2; Lampitt 15–7–35–2; Moody 5–0–23–1; Rawnsley 6.4–2–14–2; Leatherdale 3–1–14–0. *Second Innings*—Chapman 31.5–6–105–6; Leatherdale 19–7–48–1; Moody 12–3–40–0; Lampitt 21–2–84–1; Rawnsley 29–11–50–0; Solanki 3–0–28–0; Newport 15–7–34–2.

Worcestershire

W. P. C. Weston c Archer b Franks	4	– c Archer b Evans 29
E. J. Wilson lbw b Evans	4	– b Tolley 1
N. E. Batson c Archer b Tolley	15	– c Read b Tolley 4
V. S. Solanki c Strang b Franks	0	– (5) c Strang b Tolley........ 0
*T. M. Moody c Read b Strang	112	– (6) c Read b Tolley.......... 0
D. A. Leatherdale c Strang b Franks	36	– (7) c Read b Evans.......... 19
†S. J. Rhodes c Read b Franks	44	– (8) c Strang b Franks 19
S. R. Lampitt c and b Tolley	20	– (9) lbw b Tolley............ 24
P. J. Newport c Strang b Franks	26	– (10) not out............... 45
M. J. Rawnsley c Gallian b Franks	1	– (4) b Tolley................ 5
R. J. Chapman not out	0	– c Welton b Tolley........... 5
L-b 7, n-b 20	27	B 4, l-b 5, w 2, n-b 24 ... 35

1/6 2/14 3/22 4/51 5/128   289   1/4 2/20 3/48 4/50 5/54   186
6/240 7/240 8/287 9/289   6/79 7/86 8/110 9/134

Bonus points – Worcestershire 2, Nottinghamshire 4.

Bowling: *First Innings*—Franks 30–13–63–6; Evans 28–8–52–1; Tolley 25.4–4–66–2; Oram 9–0–45–0; Strang 16–4–56–1. *Second Innings*—Franks 21–2–69–1; Tolley 21.2–7–45–7; Strang 8–3–19–0; Evans 9–2–27–2; Oram 2–0–17–0.

Umpires: G. Sharp and R. A. White.

At Derby, August 14, 15, 16. WORCESTERSHIRE lost to DERBYSHIRE by 28 runs.

At Canterbury, August 19, 20, 21, 22. WORCESTERSHIRE drew with KENT.

WORCESTERSHIRE v WARWICKSHIRE

At Worcester, August 26, 27, 28. Warwickshire won by an innings and 116 runs. Warwickshire 24 pts, Worcestershire 4 pts. Toss: Worcestershire.

Warwickshire achieved their first victory at New Road for 18 years with a day and a half to spare. Moody, in his final appearance before departing for the Commonwealth Games, put Warwickshire in, but by the end of the first day the scoreboard stood at 476 for five. It was not necessarily a blunder – Lara would also have fielded – but a weak attack was unmercifully exposed. Openers Knight and Wagh, with his second Championship century, put on 158 before Lara made hay with 144 in three hours. After scoring only 416 in 19 first-class innings, Lara had plundered 586 from five, belatedly passing 1,000 runs. Then Giddins and Munton demolished an inexperienced home top order, only Rhodes resisting long. Worcestershire followed on 308 behind, and five wickets tumbled for 29 on the second evening. Only an eighth-wicket stand of 134 between Rhodes and Lampitt – a county record against Warwickshire – delayed the inevitable next day, as Munton and Giddins split the wickets between them.

Close of play: First day, Warwickshire 476-5 (B. C. Lara 141*, N. M. K. Smith 36*); Second day, Worcestershire 29-5 (N. E. Batson 1*, D. A. Leatherdale 1*).

Warwickshire

N. V. Knight c Rhodes b Lampitt	63	A. F. Giles not out	29
M. A. Wagh c Rhodes b Haynes	119	T. A. Munton lbw b Lampitt	12
D. L. Hemp b Illingworth	28	E. S. H. Giddins c Solanki b Lampitt	5
*B. C. Lara c Wilson b Chapman	144		
A. Singh c Rhodes b Chapman	33	B 2, l-b 22, w 4, n-b 30	58
D. R. Brown c and b Chapman	3		
N. M. K. Smith c Illingworth b Lampitt	47	1/158 2/218 3/286 4/360 5/370	544
†K. J. Piper c Leatherdale b Lampitt	3	6/479 7/488 8/501 9/536	

Bonus points – Warwickshire 4, Worcestershire 3 (Score at 120 overs: 536-8).

Bowling: Chapman 33–2–138–3; Haynes 19–2–106–1; Moody 18–2–54–0; Lampitt 27.3–2–120–5; Illingworth 23–4–98–1; Solanki 2–0–4–0.

Worcestershire

W. P. C. Weston c Hemp b Giddins	19	– lbw b Giddins	0
E. J. Wilson lbw b Giddins	27	– b Munton	2
V. S. Solanki c Knight b Giddins	1	– (4) lbw b Munton	3
N. E. Batson b Munton	18	– (6) c Hemp b Giddins	5
D. A. Leatherdale lbw b Munton	0	– (7) c Hemp b Munton	11
†S. J. Rhodes b Brown	54	– (8) lbw b Munton	79
*T. M. Moody c Hemp b Brown	22	– (3) c Piper b Munton	19
G. R. Haynes c Singh b Giles	31	– (10) not out	14
S. R. Lampitt c Hemp b Giles	9	– lbw b Giddins	48
R. K. Illingworth not out	31	– (5) lbw b Giddins	3
R. J. Chapman lbw b Brown	12	– c Wagh b Giddins	1
B 4, l-b 2, w 2, n-b 4	12	L-b 3, n-b 4	7
1/24 2/30 3/65 4/67 5/67	236	1/0 2/2 3/10 4/23 5/27	192
6/125 7/177 8/183 9/207		6/43 7/43 8/177 9/191	

Bonus points – Worcestershire 1, Warwickshire 4.

Bowling: *First Innings*—Giddins 14–2–55–3; Brown 23.5–3–73–3; Munton 9–0–26–2; Smith 5–1–34–0; Giles 13–3–37–2; Wagh 3–1–5–0. *Second Innings*—Giddins 27.2–6–87–5; Munton 19–7–43–5; Brown 13–1–51–0; Giles 5–2–8–0.

Umpires: M. J. Harris and B. Leadbeater.

At Taunton, September 1, 2, 3, 4. WORCESTERSHIRE drew with SOMERSET.

WORCESTERSHIRE v HAMPSHIRE

At Worcester, September 9, 10, 11, 12. Drawn. Worcestershire 8 pts, Hampshire 7 pts. Toss: Hampshire.

Rain, which had already ravaged proceedings, washed out the final day. On a slow, seaming pitch with low bounce, nine of the 24 wickets to fall were lbw. The first of them came in a three-wicket blast from McLean, which put Worcestershire on the back foot on a first day of only 24 overs. They were dismissed for 212 and Hampshire reached 65 without loss. But Haynes collected a career-best six for 50 to earn Worcestershire an unexpected lead of 34. They seemed to have wasted that at 65 for four, but an unbroken stand of 79 between Weston and Rhodes increased their advantage to 178 before the rains returned. Earlier in the innings, Leatherdale completed 1,000 first-class runs for the first time, ten years after his debut.

Close of play: First day, Worcestershire 80-4 (D. A. Leatherdale 16*, R. K. Illingworth 4*); Second day, Hampshire 77-2 (J. P. Stephenson 36*, R. A. Smith 6*); Third day, Worcestershire 144-4 (W. P. C. Weston 57*, S. J. Rhodes 34*).

Worcestershire

W. P. C. Weston b McLean	22	– not out	57
A. Hafeez b McLean	6	– lbw b McLean	5
*G. A. Hick lbw b McLean	6	– c Aymes b McLean	5
V. S. Solanki c and b Stephenson	17	– c White b James	6
D. A. Leatherdale lbw b Morris	21	– b McLean	24
R. K. Illingworth c Mascarenhas b McLean	27		
†S. J. Rhodes c Aymes b Stephenson	34	– (6) not out	34
S. R. Lampitt c Keech b Stephenson	6		
G. R. Haynes lbw b Stephenson	14		
A. Sheriyar c James b Morris	20		
R. J. Chapman not out	19		
L-b 14, w 4, n-b 2	20	B 1, l-b 6, w 2, n-b 4	13
	212	**(4 wkts)**	**144**

1/15 2/35 3/38 4/66 5/89
6/133 7/153 8/158 9/187

1/13 2/21 3/32 4/65

Bonus points – Worcestershire 1, Hampshire 4.

Bowling: *First Innings*—McLean 21–1–82–4; Morris 16–4–47–2; James 11–2–25–0; Udal 1–0–1–0; Stephenson 12–3–29–4; Mascarenhas 3–0–14–0. *Second Innings*—McLean 11–3–37–3; Morris 14–4–25–0; James 10–3–15–1; Mascarenhas 9–3–40–0; Stephenson 7–2–17–0; Udal 3–1–3–0.

Hampshire

G. W. White lbw b Haynes	30		S. D. Udal c Illingworth b Haynes	15
J. P. Stephenson lbw b Haynes	47		A. C. Morris not out	0
W. S. Kendall lbw b Haynes	0		N. A. M. McLean c Chapman b Haynes	11
*R. A. Smith lbw b Sheriyar	33			
†A. N. Aymes c Rhodes b Haynes	0		B 4, l-b 2, n-b 8	14
M. Keech lbw b Sheriyar	5			—
A. D. Mascarenhas c Rhodes b Lampitt	14		1/65 2/65 3/102 4/102 5/107	**178**
K. D. James b Sheriyar	9		6/136 7/136 8/167 9/167	

Bonus points – Worcestershire 4.

Bowling: Sheriyar 20–8–48–3; Chapman 8–1–29–0; Lampitt 21–7–45–1; Haynes 22.4–6–50–6.

Umpires: A. Clarkson and A. G. T. Whitehead.

WORCESTERSHIRE v DURHAM

At Worcester, September 17, 18, 19, 20. Worcestershire won by 155 runs. Worcestershire 23 pts, Durham 7 pts. Toss: Worcestershire. First-class debut: R. C. Driver.

Worcestershire finally ended a dismal run of eight Championship matches without a win, thanks to a last-day revival. They seemed doomed at 122 for six in their second innings – only 90 ahead. But Illingworth and Chapman shared a determined stand of 108, and Durham's eventual target was 281. Lampitt then completed the turnaround with five wickets, lifting his aggregate for the season to 50, as Durham collapsed. Worcestershire introduced 19-year-old Cornishman Ryan Driver, part of their sixth different opening combination of the campaign. But he managed only five, and the batsmen struggled until Rhodes and Haynes rallied the innings. Durham closed the second day on 248 for four – only 62 behind – after Roseberry and Daley had ground out 128 together. Sheriyar, however, restricted their lead to 32 with his only five-wicket haul of an injury-hit year. That looked like being enough, as Worcestershire's top order floundered again, until the late switch of fortunes. Boon and Rhodes both completed 1,000 runs at the last gasp.

Close of play: First day, Worcestershire 310; Second day, Durham 248-4 (D. C. Boon 21*, P. D. Collingwood 9*); Third day, Worcestershire 184-6 (G. R. Haynes 48*, R. K. Illingworth 17*).

Worcestershire

W. P. C. Weston b Saggers	15	– c Collingwood b Phillips	35
R. C. Driver c Boon b Harmison	5	– c Speight b Wood	0
*G. A. Hick c Saggers b Harmison	23	– c Speight b Harmison	13
V. S. Solanki lbw b Wood	46	– c Boon b Saggers	22
†S. J. Rhodes c Boon b Saggers	72	– c Collingwood b Saggers	14
S. R. Lampitt lbw b Saggers	17	– lbw b Boon	19
G. R. Haynes c Speight b Harmison	72	– lbw b Wood	52
R. K. Illingworth c Boon b Wood	4	– c Lewis b Saggers	84
M. J. Rawnsley c and b Phillips	15	– lbw b Wood	0
R. J. Chapman not out	9	– not out	43
A. Sheriyar c Speight b Harmison	14		
L-b 6, w 6, n-b 6	18	B 4, l-b 18, w 2, n-b 6	30

1/22 2/39 3/61 4/132 5/188 310
6/201 7/223 8/262 9/284

1/1 2/28 3/64 (9 wkts dec.) 312
4/88 5/104 6/122
7/194 8/204 9/312

Bonus points – Worcestershire 3, Durham 4.

Bowling: *First Innings*—Wood 23–8–74–2; Harmison 23–2–88–4; Saggers 25–7–47–3; Phillips 32–8–95–1. *Second Innings*—Wood 25–5–97–3; Harmison 15–4–36–1; Saggers 14.2–2–48–3; Phillips 29–6–76–1; Boon 14–5–33–1.

Durham

J. J. B. Lewis c Rhodes b Haynes	38	– c Hick b Lampitt	25
J. E. Morris c Lampitt b Sheriyar	21	– c Hick b Chapman	13
M. A. Roseberry b Sheriyar	87	– c Rawnsley b Chapman	4
J. A. Daley c Rhodes b Sheriyar	60	– c Rawnsley b Solanki	16
*D. C. Boon lbw b Lampitt	35	– c sub b Chapman	1
P. D. Collingwood c Rawnsley b Lampitt	56	– lbw b Lampitt	8
†M. P. Speight c Solanki b Sheriyar	18	– c Rhodes b Lampitt	0
N. C. Phillips c Rhodes b Haynes	1	– c Rhodes b Lampitt	5
J. Wood lbw b Haynes	4	– c Illingworth b Solanki	1
M. J. Saggers not out	6	– not out	9
S. J. Harmison b Sheriyar	0	– c Rhodes b Lampitt	36
L-b 6, n-b 10	16	B 1, l-b 2, n-b 4	7

1/47 2/67 3/195 4/234 5/267 342
6/295 7/296 8/300 9/341

1/22 2/44 3/48 4/51 5/60 125
6/62 7/76 8/78 9/81

Bonus points – Durham 3, Worcestershire 4.

Bowling: *First Innings*—Sheriyar 30.2–10–85–5; Chapman 4–0–34–0; Haynes 25–6–65–3; Lampitt 23–9–60–2; Illingworth 21–8–34–0; Rawnsley 7–1–28–0; Solanki 8–1–30–0. *Second Innings*—Sheriyar 6–0–29–0; Chapman 9–2–26–3; Lampitt 11.1–4–39–5; Haynes 3–0–6–0; Solanki 5–0–22–2.

Umpires: T. E. Jesty and D. R. Shepherd.

PROFESSIONAL CRICKETERS' ASSOCIATION AWARDS

The Professional Cricketers' Association chose Mal Loye of Northamptonshire as the winner of the Reg Hayter Cup for Player of the Year in 1998. The John Arlott Cup for Young Player of the Year went to Andy Flintoff of Lancashire. Graeme Hick of Worcestershire won the Slazenger Sheer Instinct Individual Performance Award, for his 100th first-class hundred in May. Ray Julian was awarded the Umpires' Cup. Dickie Bird was given the Waterford Crystal PCA Special Merit Award for his achievements in the game. The PCA in the Community Award, introduced for the first time in 1998, went to Tony Moody of Lambeth Borough Council Cricket Association.

YORKSHIRE

Gavin Hamilton

Patron: HRH The Duchess of Kent

President: Sir Lawrence Byford

Chairman: K. H. Moss

Chairman of Cricket Committee: R. K. Platt

Chief Executive: C. D. Hassell

Captain: D. Byas

Head Groundsman: A. W. Fogarty

Scorer: J. T. Potter

A rousing start and a storming finish made this Yorkshire's most successful first-class season in years. And there was the promise of even better to come from a young and enthusiastic squad, with a battery of talented fast bowlers. A ten-wicket win at Hove in the last match gave Yorkshire their fifth consecutive Championship victory, a sequence they had not equalled since 1967, and third place in the table was their highest since coming second in 1975.

Yorkshire reached the Benson and Hedges semi-finals after winning all of their group games, but their hopes of going on to Lord's were dashed; they were unable to raise their game above the mediocre against a determined Essex, and were well beaten. Their NatWest Trophy advance was halted in the second round by Lancashire and, after five wins from their first six Sunday League games had lifted them to the top of the table, they fell away to ninth. That was sufficient, however, to make it into the top division of the new National League in 1999. With a place, also, in the Super Cup knockout, they entered the reorganised English season among the elite.

A fear that Yorkshire would be short of fast bowlers proved to be unfounded. So well did their youngsters develop that the county was able to overcome a double handicap. They were unable to use Craig White as a bowler when he succumbed to a bad back, after the first five matches had brought him 25 wickets, and Darren Gough was frequently absent on Test duties. Indeed, Gough's pulled hamstring, incurred while playing for England against Sri Lanka, saved Yorkshire from an awkward poser: which in-form bowler to drop to accommodate him for the last three matches?

Much of the work fell to left-arm swing bowler Paul Hutchison, who missed only one Championship match, with a broken thumb. After his sensational breakthrough in August 1997, he settled into a regular pattern of wicket-taking, though without any spectacular returns, until well into the season.

Hutchison led the way with 57 Championship wickets, one ahead of Gavin Hamilton, whose all-round form was a revelation. Doubt about whether Hamilton was good enough evaporated as, in three successive matches, he improved on his career-best analysis; it finally settled at seven for 50 as he claimed 11 wickets against Surrey. His batting also progressed beyond recognition; he scored five seventies. It seemed clear that Hamilton would soon play international cricket, the only question being for whom. New ICC rules have made it easier for him to hang fire, and hope to be selected for England in the World Cup, but fall back on a certain place with his native Scotland otherwise.

While Hamilton impressed with his utter determination, Matthew Hoggard secured a regular place with bowling which became ever faster, more accurate and more hostile. Tall, with a sturdy frame and a smooth, well-controlled run-up, he bagged 31 wickets in the last six matches.

If Hoggard was the bowling find of the season, then 21-year-old Matthew Wood was the batting discovery. He began with one first-class match behind him, but went on to join Michael Vaughan as the only Yorkshire batsmen to complete 1,000 first-class runs.

Wood showed an amazing fondness for Headingley, following up a fifty in the opening match against Somerset with a maiden hundred in the next, against Derbyshire. He added a high-class century off Hampshire, before signing off from the ground with an unbeaten 200 against Warwickshire. Just to show he had learned to travel, he concluded with 118 not out at Hove. Cool and composed, Wood seemed unaffected by pressure. Most of his boundaries came from well-timed ground strokes. But, when bowlers tried to unsettle him with short-pitched stuff, he could deal with it ruthlessly.

Captain David Byas constantly encouraged his younger players, and showed his faith in them, with little outward concern at Gough's absences or the unexpected loss of White. His batting also thrived at Headingley, where he hit four centuries in the season, a ground record, though elsewhere he made less impact. Darren Lehmann, restricted to ten matches by Australian calls early and late on, and by a back injury in the middle, once again entertained on a lavish scale, looking like a world-class batsman. Because of his likely inclusion in Australia's World Cup squad, Yorkshire chose his South Australian team-mate Greg Blewett as their overseas player for 1999, with Lehmann returning on a two-year contract in 2000.

Only Leicestershire could match Yorkshire's tally of 47 batting bonus points – which was something of a surprise, because the openers rarely provided solid starts. Anthony McGrath's poor form caused him to drop down the order and then lose his place, and there was also weakness in the middle. It was often the tailenders who squeezed out the third or fourth batting point.

It was a disappointing time for spinners. Richard Stemp only occasionally found pitches which suited him, and eventually moved to Nottinghamshire. His left-arm understudy, Ian Fisher, did not advance his claims, but James Middlebrook demonstrated he could push through his off-spinners with commendable accuracy – as well as batting pretty well and showing a safe pair of hands in the field. The reliable Richard Blakey was the country's leading wicket-keeper, with 69 catches and two stumpings.

Yorkshire made definite progress during the season, even if they could not quite translate it into their first trophy since 1987. And, with none of their players yet over the hill, they had the vigour and resources to take those extra few steps to the top of the ladder. – DAVID WARNER.

YORKSHIRE 1998

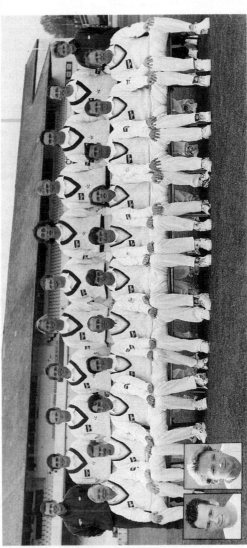

[Bill Smith]

Standing: W. P. Morton (*physiotherapist*), M. J. Wood, B. Parker, I. D. Fisher, P. M. Hutchison, A. McGrath, R. J. Sidebottom, M. J. Hoggard, G. M. Hamilton, C. A. Chapman, C. A. Becker (*physiotherapist*). *Seated:* D. E. V. Padgett (*Second Eleven coach*), R. D. Stemp, C. E. W. Silverwood, M. P. Vaughan, D. S. Lehmann, D. Byas (*captain*), M. D. Moxon (*director of coaching*), R. J. Blakey, D. Gough, C. White, S. Oldham (*cricket development manager*). *Insets:* J. D. Middlebrook, G. M. Fellows.

YORKSHIRE RESULTS

All first-class matches – Played 19: Won 9, Lost 3, Drawn 7.

County Championship matches – Played 17: Won 9, Lost 3, Drawn 5.

*Competition placings – Britannic Assurance County Championship, 3rd;
NatWest Trophy, 2nd round; Benson and Hedges Cup, s-f;
AXA League, 9th.*

COUNTY CHAMPIONSHIP AVERAGES

BATTING

Cap		M	I	NO	R	HS	100s	50s	Avge	Ct/St
1997	D. S. Lehmann§ . . .	10	16	0	969	200	3	4	60.56	4
	M. J. Wood†	17	25	3	991	200*	4	4	45.04	15
	R. J. Sidebottom† . .	4	4	2	84	54	0	1	42.00	2
1995	M. P. Vaughan	17	28	3	1,022	177	2	3	40.88	6
1993	C. White†	8	12	3	356	104*	1	1	39.55	13
1998	G. M. Hamilton. . . .	14	18	1	572	79	0	4	33.64	3
1991	D. Byas†	17	26	1	810	116	4	3	32.40	20
1993	D. Gough†	5	6	0	186	89	0	2	31.00	1
	B. Parker†	6	7	1	154	41	0	1	25.66	2
1996	C. E. W. Silverwood†	12	13	3	239	57*	0	1	23.90	2
	A. McGrath†	15	24	1	518	63*	0	2	22.52	5
1987	R. J. Blakey†	17	23	2	448	67*	0	3	21.33	69/2
1998	P. M. Hutchison† . . .	16	16	8	127	30	0	0	15.87	3
1996	R. D. Stemp	11	15	8	107	43*	0	0	15.28	5
	J. D. Middlebrook† . .	7	11	2	132	41	0	0	14.66	7
	M. J. Hoggard†	8	10	3	35	13*	0	0	5.00	3

Also batted: G. D. Clough† (1 match) 33, 1 (1 ct); G. M. Fellows† (1 match) 3, 18. I. D. Fisher† (1 match) did not bat.

* Signifies not out. † Born in Yorkshire. § Overseas player.

BOWLING

	O	M	R	W	BB	5W/i	Avge
C. White.	124.1	30	337	25	8-55	2	13.48
G. M. Hamilton	387	91	1,143	56	7-50	4	20.41
M. J. Hoggard	227	46	805	36	5-57	1	22.36
C. E. W. Silverwood. .	376.1	97	1,085	46	5-13	3	23.58
P. M. Hutchison	460.3	115	1,397	57	7-31	3	24.50
D. Gough	156.4	27	523	21	5-36	1	24.90
J. D. Middlebrook . . .	136.2	41	338	11	3-20	0	30.72
R. D. Stemp	360	121	922	26	5-191	1	35.46

Also bowled: G. D. Clough 2–0–11–0; G. M. Fellows 3–0–21–0; I. D. Fisher 3–1–3–0; D. S. Lehmann 57–16–124–6; A. McGrath 36–8–135–3; R. J. Sidebottom 93–17–322–9; M. P. Vaughan 67–19–216–2.

COUNTY RECORDS

Highest score for:	341	G. H. Hirst v Leicestershire at Leicester	1905
Highest score against:	318*	W. G. Grace (Gloucestershire) at Cheltenham . . .	1876
Best bowling for:	10-10	H. Verity v Nottinghamshire at Leeds	1932
Best bowling against:	10-37	C. V. Grimmett (Australians) at Sheffield	1930
Highest total for:	887	v Warwickshire at Birmingham	1896
Highest total against:	681-7 dec.	by Leicestershire at Bradford	1996
Lowest total for:	23	v Hampshire at Middlesbrough	1965
Lowest total against:	13	by Nottinghamshire at Nottingham	1901

YORKSHIRE v SOMERSET

At Leeds, April 17, 18, 20, 21. Yorkshire won by 215 runs. Yorkshire 23 pts, Somerset 4 pts.
Toss: Somerset. Championship debut: M. J. Wood. County debut: A. R. K. Pierson.

Yorkshire had complained to Lord's about being allocated two home fixtures in April, fearing bad weather would put them at a disadvantage. But, although conditions were grim for this match, not a ball was lost to rain or bad light, and Yorkshire outplayed opponents who had no luck whatsoever. Holloway was ill with flu; Rose also succumbed after gamely helping to avoid the follow-on; and Ecclestone collapsed with his old knee injury on the last morning, later resuming with a runner. Caddick bowled splendidly without reward on the first morning and it took a gritty century from Byas to guide Yorkshire to a commanding 383. He was assisted by Vaughan and Wood, who made 52 on his Championship debut, but the innings gained later impetus from Gough, who produced one of his occasional blasts, hitting his last 65 runs off 61 balls. Yorkshire's four-pronged pace attack never allowed Somerset to settle in either innings; a target of 351 was forgotten when they sank to 43 for five on the third evening, and it was all over before lunch next day.

Close of play: First day, Yorkshire 253-7 (R. J. Blakey 1*, D. Gough 0*); Second day, Somerset 160-7 (G. D. Rose 28*, A. R. K. Pierson 17*); Third day, Somerset 46-5 (S. C. Ecclestone 16*, M. E. Trescothick 0*).

Yorkshire

A. McGrath lbw b Rose	0	– c sub b Caddick	3
M. P. Vaughan b Trescothick	46	– c sub b Pierson	37
*D. Byas c Turner b Rose	101	– c Trescothick b Shine	52
M. J. Wood lbw b Parsons	52	– c Turner b Trescothick	22
C. White c Turner b Trescothick	23	– lbw b Trescothick	8
B. Parker c Harden b Trescothick	12	– c Harden b Caddick	41
R. D. Stemp c Turner b Trescothick	0	– (10) not out	1
†R. J. Blakey c Turner b Shine	20	– (7) c Turner b Caddick	13
D. Gough c Holloway b Parsons	89	– (8) c Bowler b Caddick	0
C. E. W. Silverwood c Ecclestone b Shine	5	– (9) c Trescothick b Shine	0
P. M. Hutchison not out	0		
B 4, l-b 13, w 6, n-b 12	35	B 1, l-b 10, w 6, n-b 10 . .	27

1/1 2/82 3/212 4/226 5/250   383   1/11 2/105 3/121   (9 wkts dec.) 204
6/252 7/253 8/363 9/381   4/145 5/146 6/195
                                   7/195 8/202 9/204

Bonus points – Yorkshire 3, Somerset 1 (Score at 120 overs: 316-7).

Bowling: *First Innings*—Caddick 32–6–97–0; Rose 29.2–11–71–2; Parsons 20.4–9–43–2; Shine 16.4–6–40–2; Pierson 15–3–33–0; Trescothick 22–7–82–4. *Second Innings*—Shine 11–1–53–1; Caddick 11–2–33–4; Rose 7–1–35–0; Pierson 12–3–34–1; Trescothick 10.3–3–24–3; Parsons 4–0–14–0.

Somerset

*P. D. Bowler c Blakey b Gough	13	– lbw b Gough	3
P. C. L. Holloway c Blakey b Silverwood	0	– (8) b White	6
K. A. Parsons lbw b Hutchison	4	– (2) c McGrath b Silverwood	1
R. J. Harden c Stemp b Silverwood	39	– (3) c White b Silverwood	4
S. C. Ecclestone b Silverwood	21	– (4) lbw b White	23
†R. J. Turner c Blakey b Gough	3	– (5) c Blakey b Hutchison	16
M. E. Trescothick c Blakey b Hutchison	27	– c and b White	26
G. D. Rose c Wood b Stemp	62	– (9) c Parker b Gough	19
A. R. K. Pierson c Blakey b White	47	– (6) c and b Hutchison	0
A. R. Caddick b Gough	7	– c Blakey b White	0
K. J. Shine not out	0	– not out	15
B 1, l-b 5, n-b 8	14	B 1, l-b 11, n-b 10	22

1/12 2/18 3/41 4/76 5/82   237   1/4 2/8 3/8 4/43 5/43   135
6/101 7/136 8/224 9/237   6/84 7/91 8/119 9/120

Bonus points – Somerset 1, Yorkshire 4.

In the second innings S. C. Ecclestone, when 16, retired hurt at 46 and resumed at 91.

Bowling: *First Innings*—Gough 18.4–5–48–3; Silverwood 21–5–52–3; Hutchison 15–5–35–2; White 12–3–28–1; Stemp 21–8–42–1; Vaughan 7–2–13–0; McGrath 3–0–13–0. *Second Innings*—Gough 14–3–61–2; Silverwood 10–4–34–2; Hutchison 10–5–15–2; White 12.2–5–13–4.

Umpires: A. Clarkson and B. Leadbeater.

YORKSHIRE v DERBYSHIRE

At Leeds, April 23, 24, 25, 27. Yorkshire won by 111 runs. Yorkshire 22 pts, Derbyshire 2 pts. Toss: Yorkshire.

Byas scored his second hundred in successive matches while leading Yorkshire to a second victory and first place in the embryonic Championship table. He put on 230 with Wood, who scored a maiden century. Together, they made up for time lost to the weather, setting up a declaration on the third day at 352 for five. Although this match was expected to produce a keen battle between Gough and Cork, it was Silverwood who took the fast bowling honours as he quickly ran through five Derbyshire wickets. Barnett helped stage a recovery, but it came as an unpleasant surprise to spectators enjoying "proper" cricket when Derbyshire were allowed to declare at 136 without following on and May, bowling three overs for 51, fed Yorkshire runs. Derbyshire were set 322 in 91 overs. With Silverwood again to the fore, they soon subsided, despite a second fifty from Barnett.

Close of play: First day, Yorkshire 5-0 (A. McGrath 0*, M. P. Vaughan 3*); Second day, Yorkshire 157-2 (D. Byas 21*, M. J. Wood 22*); Third day, Yorkshire 87-0 (A. McGrath 56*, M. P. Vaughan 29*).

Yorkshire

A. McGrath c DeFreitas b Harris	42	– not out	63
M. P. Vaughan lbw b Harris	33	– not out	36
*D. Byas b Aldred	103		
M. J. Wood c Krikken b DeFreitas	103		
C. White not out	9		
B. Parker lbw b DeFreitas	0		
†R. J. Blakey not out	3		
B 1, l-b 10, w 8, n-b 40	59	W 2, n-b 4	6

1/79 2/96 3/326 4/332 5/335 (5 wkts dec.) 352 (no wkt dec.) 105

D. Gough, C. E. W. Silverwood, P. M. Hutchison and I. D. Fisher did not bat.

Bonus points – Yorkshire 4, Derbyshire 2.

Bowling: *First Innings*—DeFreitas 33–6–102–2; Cork 19–1–60–0; Harris 18–3–73–2; Aldred 30.4–9–77–1; Blackwell 8–1–23–0; Barnett 3–0–6–0. *Second Innings*—Cork 3.4–0–15–0; Harris 2–0–10–0; May 3–0–51–0; Tweats 3–0–29–0.

Derbyshire

A. S. Rollins lbw b Silverwood	3	– c Wood b White	63
M. R. May lbw b Silverwood	22	– c Blakey b Silverwood	0
T. A. Tweats b Silverwood	3	– c Blakey b Silverwood	5
K. J. Barnett not out	55	– c White b Silverwood	68
M. E. Cassar b Silverwood	0	– lbw b White	0
I. D. Blackwell b Silverwood	14	– c Blakey b White	3
†K. M. Krikken not out	14	– lbw b Gough	0
*D. G. Cork (did not bat)		– lbw b Silverwood	21
P. A. J. DeFreitas (did not bat)		– c Blakey b Hutchison	12
P. Aldred (did not bat)		– not out	3
A. J. Harris (did not bat)		– b Gough	4
L-b 1, n-b 21	22	B 4, l-b 7, n-b 20	31

1/15 2/34 3/49 4/57 5/91 (5 wkts dec.) 136   1/4 2/26 3/136 4/136 5/140   210
6/143 7/174 8/203 9/205

Bonus points – Yorkshire 2.

Bowling: *First Innings*—Gough 9–2–49–0; Silverwood 11–1–38–5; Hutchison 8–1–31–0; White 3–0–14–0; Fisher 3–1–3–0. *Second Innings*—Gough 10–1–46–2; Silverwood 12–4–42–4; Hutchison 10–2–44–1; Vaughan 7–3–18–0; White 13–1–49–3.

Umpires: K. E. Palmer and G. Sharp.

At Northampton, May 13, 14, 15. YORKSHIRE lost to NORTHAMPTONSHIRE by eight wickets.

At Gloucester, May 21, 22, 23, 24. YORKSHIRE lost to GLOUCESTERSHIRE by 300 runs.

At Oxford, May 29, 30, June 1. YORKSHIRE drew with OXFORD UNIVERSITY.

YORKSHIRE v LEICESTERSHIRE

At Leeds, June 3, 4, 5, 6. Drawn. Yorkshire 9 pts, Leicestershire 8 pts. Toss: Yorkshire.

Given their early-season worries, it was ironic that Yorkshire were to suffer far more from bad weather in June and this match was ruined by blank first and last days. Leicestershire were put in and Wells, who hit a maiden double-hundred on his previous visit to Yorkshire, was in prime form again. He scored 144 with 19 fours and a six – assisted by poor new-ball bowling in helpful conditions, and a life on 44 when Byas dropped him at second slip. Nixon, whose first 26 runs came from three sixes and two fours, also helped Leicestershire to maximum batting points. Their hopes of bowling Yorkshire out soon vanished: Lehmann was missing his first Championship match through injury since joining Yorkshire in 1997, but it hardly mattered as Byas scored his third century in three matches at Headingley, and was well supported by Vaughan and Wood. He declared as soon as he was out, conceding a first-innings lead of 80. Leicestershire increased this to 158, before the rain came again.

Close of play: First day, No play; Second day, Yorkshire 25-0 (A. McGrath 8*, M. P. Vaughan 11*); Third day, Leicestershire 78-2 (B. F. Smith 35*, A. Habib 11*).

Leicestershire

V. J. Wells b Stemp	144	– c Blakey b White	24
D. L. Maddy b Hutchison	0	– lbw b Hutchison	3
I. J. Sutcliffe c Wood b Hamilton	30		
B. F. Smith c Blakey b Hamilton	4	– (3) not out	35
A. Habib c White b Stemp	10	– (4) not out	11
P. V. Simmons c Wood b Hamilton	21		
†P. A. Nixon lbw b Vaughan	63		
J. M. Dakin c Blakey b White	0		
*C. C. Lewis c Stemp b Silverwood	35		
A. D. Mullally not out	28		
L-b 4, w 6, n-b 8	18	B 4, l-b 1	5

1/4 2/65 3/89 4/116 5/169 (9 wkts dec.) 353   1/12 2/43 (2 wkts) 78
6/259 7/260 8/307 9/353

M. T. Brimson did not bat.

Bonus points – Leicestershire 4, Yorkshire 4.

Bowling: *First Innings*—Silverwood 17.3–3–83–1; Hutchison 16–5–52–1; Hamilton 19–2–67–3; White 18–3–61–1; Stemp 18–6–64–2; Vaughan 6–1–22–1. *Second Innings*—Silverwood 5–0–30–0; Hutchison 7–4–17–1; White 3–0–11–1; Hamilton 4–2–7–0; Stemp 3–2–8–0.

Yorkshire

A. McGrath c Maddy b Lewis		8
M. P. Vaughan lbw b Brimson		77
*D. Byas c and b Brimson		116
M. J. Wood not out		52
L-b 6, n-b 14		20

1/30 2/144 3/273   (3 wkts dec.) 273

C. White, B. Parker, †R. J. Blakey, G. M. Hamilton, C. E. W. Silverwood, R. D. Stemp and P. M. Hutchison did not bat.

Bonus points – Yorkshire 2, Leicestershire 1.

Bowling: Mullally 21–10–53–0; Simmons 17–5–52–0; Lewis 14–2–41–1; Brimson 24.2–8–60–2; Wells 3–0–10–0; Dakin 6–1–33–0; Maddy 6–1–18–0.

Umpires: D. J. Constant and R. Julian.

YORKSHIRE v HAMPSHIRE

At Leeds, June 11, 12, 13, 15. Drawn. Yorkshire 10 pts, Hampshire 7 pts. Toss: Yorkshire.

The loss of the third day to rain helped Hampshire hold out for a draw after following on. On the opening day, Yorkshire enjoyed an innings of great maturity from 21-year-old Wood, whose hundred was his second of the season at Headingley, in addition to two fifties. He tamed McLean's aggression by hitting him for four fours in an over. Hampshire's innings had a sensational start, when Silverwood – about to be named in England's Test squad – produced a dynamic spell of three wickets for one run. With Hutchison also striking, they went in to lunch at three for four. That became 50 for eight before a blast of 33 from 19 balls by McLean pushed Hampshire to a modest 104. During the innings, a blow from Udal caused the ball to be lost for about a minute in a spectator's half-zipped bag. Following on, Hampshire stiffened their resolve: White scored a fine 67, and the final fightback was orchestrated by Aymes, who took root for almost four hours to wipe out the deficit.

Close of play: First day, Yorkshire 242-3 (M. J. Wood 103*, B. Parker 12*); Second day, Hampshire 109-3 (D. A. Kenway 19*, A. N. Aymes 8*); Third day, No play.

Yorkshire

A. McGrath b Hartley	14	R. D. Stemp c White b Mascarenhas		0
M. P. Vaughan c Aymes b Udal	86	P. M. Hutchison not out		13
*D. Byas c Kenway b Stephenson	11	R. J. Sidebottom not out		13
M. J. Wood b Mascarenhas	108	L-b 17, w 4, n-b 6		27
B. Parker b Mascarenhas	41			
†R. J. Blakey c Aymes b Mascarenhas	4	1/23 2/52 3/174	(9 wkts dec.)	327
G. M. Hamilton c Smith b James	0	4/269 5/284 6/285		
C. E. W. Silverwood c Smith b James	10	7/289 8/289 9/299		

Bonus points – Yorkshire 3, Hampshire 4.

Bowling: McLean 19–3–81–0; Hartley 23–3–74–1; James 16.4–4–47–2; Stephenson 15–4–37–1; Mascarenhas 12.3–5–31–4; Udal 20.3–7–40–1.

Hampshire

G. W. White c Stemp b Silverwood	0	– b Hutchison	67
J. P. Stephenson c Parker b Hutchison	2	– lbw b Hutchison	0
*R. A. Smith lbw b Silverwood	0	– b Hamilton	13
D. A. Kenway lbw b Silverwood	0	– c Blakey b Silverwood	19
†A. N. Aymes lbw b Silverwood	17	– lbw b Stemp	73
A. D. Mascarenhas c Blakey b Silverwood	0	– c Blakey b Stemp	34
P. R. Whitaker b Hamilton	6	– b Hutchison	32
K. D. James lbw b Hamilton	4	– not out	7
S. D. Udal lbw b Hutchison	18	– lbw b Silverwood	4
N. A. M. McLean c Sidebottom b Hutchison	33	– c and b Silverwood	8
P. J. Hartley not out	8	– not out	5
B 2, l-b 6, w 6, n-b 2	16	B 1, l-b 5, n-b 4	10

1/0 2/2 3/2 4/2 5/22		104
6/23 7/29 8/50 9/86		

1/2 2/47 3/93		(9 wkts) 272
4/113 5/172 6/235		
7/250 8/255 9/265		

Bonus points – Yorkshire 4.

Bowling: *First Innings*—Silverwood 10–3–13–5; Hutchison 9.1–2–49–3; Sidebottom 6–3–13–0; Hamilton 6–1–21–2. *Second Innings*—Silverwood 28–8–87–3; Hutchison 20.3–11–22–3; Hamilton 21–3–63–1; Stemp 34–13–64–2; Sidebottom 10–1–30–0.

Umpires: M. J. Harris and P. Willey.

At Chester-le-Street, June 17, 18, 19. YORKSHIRE beat DURHAM by nine wickets.

YORKSHIRE v CAMBRIDGE UNIVERSITY

At Leeds, June 27, 28, 29. Drawn. Toss: Yorkshire. First-class debuts: J. D. Middlebrook, R. Wilkinson.

Promoted to open because Ed Smith was injured, Cambridge's Imraan Mohammed responded with a sweetly timed maiden century – against a full-strength Yorkshire attack, as Gough had returned to try out the finger he broke in the First Test. Imraan's hundred came 22 years after his father, Pakistan Test player Sadiq, hit 107 at Headingley for Gloucestershire. The first day was washed out, and on the third Cambridge lost the initiative through negative tactics, batting on instead of declaring. Some spectators assumed both teams had forfeited innings to set up a run-chase, and were puzzled when Yorkshire walked off at 94 for one. Cambridge did then skip an innings, so Yorkshire resumed needing 273 from 58 overs. But they were troubled for a while by some excellent leg-spin from Loveridge, who had already played a Test for New Zealand.

Close of play: First day, No play; Second day, Cambridge University 331-7 (A. N. Janisch 6*, M. J. Birks 6*).

Cambridge University

J. P. Pyemont b Silverwood	11	†M. J. Birks c White b Silverwood	6
I. Mohammed c Parker b Wilkinson	136	P. J. Moffat c Chapman b Middlebrook	4
Q. J. Hughes c Hutchison b Gough	38	J. P. Lowe not out	1
*A. Singh b Vaughan	30	B 12, l-b 8, w 6, n-b 6	32
W. J. House lbw b Gough	51		
G. R. Loveridge c Vaughan b Hutchison	30	1/40 2/135 3/196	366
B. J. Collins c Chapman b Hutchison	4	4/256 5/307 6/319	
A. N. Janisch b Middlebrook	23	7/319 8/337 9/357	

Bowling: Gough 23–7–54–2; Hutchison 14–4–35–2; Silverwood 14–2–38–2; White 15–3–43–0; Middlebrook 27.5–4–84–2; Wilkinson 15–3–35–1; McGrath 5–2–23–0; Vaughan 9–2–34–1.

Cambridge University forfeited their second innings.

Yorkshire

A. McGrath not out	51	– c Collins b Loveridge	28
*M. P. Vaughan b Moffat	11		
M. J. Wood not out	25	– (7) not out	30
C. White (did not bat)		– (2) b Lowe	2
B. Parker (did not bat)		– (3) lbw b Loveridge	18
J. D. Middlebrook (did not bat)		– (4) b Loveridge	7
R. Wilkinson (did not bat)		– (5) st Birks b Loveridge	9
D. Gough (did not bat)		– (6) c Hughes b Mohammed	21
†C. A. Chapman (did not bat)		– (8) not out	7
B 2, l-b 3, w 2	7	L-b 9	9

1/20	(1 wkt dec.) 94	1/4 2/50 3/51 (6 wkts) 131
		4/72 5/73 6/122

C. E. W. Silverwood and P. M. Hutchison did not bat.

Bowling: *First Innings*—Lowe 5–0–18–0; Moffat 11–6–17–1; Janisch 4–3–6–0; House 2–0–6–0; Loveridge 4–3–1–0; Singh 2–0–21–0; Pyemont 2–0–20–0. *Second Innings*—Moffat 4–0–6–0; Lowe 8–1–23–1; Loveridge 18–6–47–4; Janisch 9–3–17–0; Hughes 4–0–16–0; Mohammed 6–1–13–1.

Umpires: M. R. Benson and T. E. Jesty.

At Maidstone, July 1, 2, 3, 4. YORKSHIRE drew with KENT.

YORKSHIRE v NOTTINGHAMSHIRE

At Scarborough, July 15, 16, 17, 18. Drawn. Yorkshire 11 pts, Nottinghamshire 7 pts. Toss: Yorkshire.

Yorkshire looked on course for victory before rain washed out much of the last two days. Put in to bat, Nottinghamshire struggled except during a third-wicket stand of 161 between Robinson and Afzaal. Robinson, dropped at first slip on eight, overcame his early unease against Gough to record his sixth first-class century against Yorkshire, and his 63rd in all. Lehmann then made his first Championship hundred in Yorkshire, following the five he had scored outside the county since joining them in 1997. Heavy morning rain and a broken-down waterhog delayed play until after tea on the third day. Yorkshire batted on to reach 406, before Gough reduced Nottinghamshire to 37 for two. But on the final day just five overs were possible before 3.45 p.m., though Yorkshire insisted on playing on to the bitter end before accepting the stalemate.

Close of play: First day, Yorkshire 43-1 (M. P. Vaughan 19*, P. M. Hutchison 0*); Second day, Yorkshire 358-7 (R. J. Blakey 15*, D. Gough 6*); Third day, Nottinghamshire 37-2 (M. P. Dowman 13*, R. T. Robinson 11*).

Nottinghamshire

M. P. Dowman lbw b Gough	4	– (2) lbw b Silverwood	36
J. E. R. Gallian b Silverwood	0	– (1) c Blakey b Gough	4
U. Afzaal c Blakey b Gough	71	– c Vaughan b Gough	4
R. T. Robinson c McGrath b Hamilton	114	– c Blakey b Silverwood	28
*P. Johnson lbw b Gough	5	– c Wood b Stemp	23
G. F. Archer c Blakey b Hamilton	10	– c Byas b Hutchison	12
P. J. Franks b Hamilton	0	– not out	29
†C. M. W. Read lbw b Hutchison	5	– not out	1
P. A. Strang not out	2		
A. G. Wharf c Blakey b Hamilton	2		
K. P. Evans c Blakey b Gough	3		
B 2, l-b 10, w 2, n-b 4	18	B 4, l-b 5, n-b 14	23

1/4 2/10 3/171 4/183 5/204   234   1/4 2/8 3/74   (6 wkts) 160
6/204 7/213 8/227 9/229   4/83 5/113 6/143

Bonus points – Nottinghamshire 1, Yorkshire 4.

Bowling: *First Innings*—Gough 20.1–3–72–4; Silverwood 17–7–28–1; Hutchison 16–1–58–1; Hamilton 20–3–59–4; McGrath 3–2–4–0; Stemp 3–2–1–0. *Second Innings*—Gough 18–1–53–2; Silverwood 20–4–55–2; Hutchison 9–2–21–1; Hamilton 8–4–20–0; Stemp 3.5–2–2–1.

Yorkshire

A. McGrath lbw b Evans	14	D. Gough c Read b Franks	30
M. P. Vaughan b Evans	41	C. E. W. Silverwood b Franks	22
P. M. Hutchison c Wharf b Evans	11	R. D. Stemp not out	0
*D. Byas c Archer b Evans	54		
D. S. Lehmann c Read b Evans	131	L-b 16, w 2, n-b 20	38
M. J. Wood b Franks	26		
†R. J. Blakey c Read b Franks	16	1/41 2/77 3/92 4/207 5/306	406
G. M. Hamilton b Franks	23	6/310 7/350 8/359 9/397	

Bonus points – Yorkshire 4, Nottinghamshire 3 (Score at 120 overs: 357-7).

Bowling: Franks 38.3–9–107–5; Evans 39–5–120–5; Wharf 4–1–16–0; Strang 32–6–84–0; Dowman 21–2–63–0.

Umpires: J. C. Balderstone and N. T. Plews.

At Lord's, July 22, 23, 24, 25. YORKSHIRE drew with MIDDLESEX.

At Worcester, July 30, 31, August 1, 3. YORKSHIRE beat WORCESTERSHIRE by an innings and 160 runs.

YORKSHIRE v LANCASHIRE

At Leeds, August 14, 15, 16, 17. Lancashire won by 59 runs. Lancashire 22 pts, Yorkshire 7 pts. Toss: Lancashire.

A Roses match with the teams in an old-fashioned position – both in the top six – began in a thoroughly untraditional way when Lancashire scored 82 in the first 11 overs and reached 200 immediately after lunch. It was enough to set them on the path to victory. There was another feature that would have bemused old-timers: for the first time in any Championship fixture, 12 different players batted for Lancashire. Austin left the game at lunchtime on the second day when he was called into England's one-day squad instead of the injured Mark Ealham. This meant that Green, who was already on the field as substitute for the injured Wasim Akram, was allowed to play a full part as a replacement for Austin, under ECB regulations. There were precedents for this, but on previous occasions the player replaced had always gone before batting. Austin would have left the ground sooner than he did, but he was selected for a random drugs test and apparently had problems providing a sample. He had scored 49, one of several useful support acts for a

HIGHEST SCORES FOR LANCASHIRE IN ROSES MATCHES

225	G. D. Lloyd at Leeds†	1997
200*	R. H. Spooner at Manchester	1910
181	C. H. Lloyd at Manchester	1972
180	A. Ward at Manchester	1892
180	**J. P. Crawley at Leeds**	**1998**
178	E. Tyldesley at Sheffield	1922
170	C. Washbrook at Leeds	1948

† In non-Championship match.

magnificent performance by Crawley, who scored 180 off 293 balls in five and a half hours. It was the best score for Lancashire in a Championship match in Yorkshire. The team went on to 484, their highest total in Yorkshire. Byas led a strong reply, until he was caught by Lancashire coach Dav Whatmore, as substitute. He declared 27 behind, and Hutchison soon reduced Lancashire to 22 for four. But Crawley stayed firm, with Hegg, and Yorkshire had to chase 243 off 60 overs. They succumbed to the spinners, led – to make matters even worse – by their own former player, Wakefield-born Keedy.

Close of play: First day, Lancashire 455-8 (G. Yates 29*); Second day, Yorkshire 264-4 (A. McGrath 28*, P. M. Hutchison 0*); Third day, Lancashire 109-4 (J. P. Crawley 53*, W. K. Hegg 41*).

Lancashire

N. T. Wood c Byas b Hutchison	7	– (2) c Blakey b Hutchison	0
J. P. Crawley c Blakey b Hutchison	180	– (1) c Blakey b Hutchison	56
N. H. Fairbrother c Blakey b McGrath	27	– c Middlebrook b Hutchison	0
A. Flintoff c Vaughan b Hoggard	16	– c Byas b Hutchison	3
G. D. Lloyd c Wood b Hutchison	56	– b Hutchison	2
†W. K. Hegg lbw b McGrath	39	– lbw b Hoggard	85
*Wasim Akram b Middlebrook	14	– b Lehmann	21
I. D. Austin c Hoggard b Middlebrook	49	– absent	
G. Yates not out	37	– (8) b Stemp	26
G. Chapple c Blakey b Hoggard	4	– (9) not out	1
G. Keedy c Blakey b Hoggard	13	– c Blakey b Hoggard	1
R. J. Green (did not bat)		– (10) lbw b Hoggard	0
B 8, l-b 8, n-b 26	42	B 6, l-b 2, n-b 12	20

1/21 2/109 3/129 4/209 5/285	484	1/2 2/2 3/12 4/22 5/117	215
6/328 7/384 8/455 9/462		6/159 7/209 8/209 9/211	

Bonus points – Lancashire 4, Yorkshire 4.

Bowling: *First Innings*—Hoggard 23–0–122–3; Hutchison 23–4–88–3; Hamilton 18–4–71–0; McGrath 6–1–33–2; Stemp 13–2–60–0; Middlebrook 24–5–74–2; Lehmann 8–3–20–0. *Second Innings*—Hoggard 10–1–41–3; Hutchison 13–2–39–5; Hamilton 8–1–36–0; Stemp 17–6–43–1; Middlebrook 13–2–27–0; Lehmann 8–1–21–1.

Yorkshire

*D. Byas c sub b Yates	101	– c Lloyd b Yates	27
M. P. Vaughan c Yates b Keedy	45	– lbw b Wasim Akram	15
M. J. Wood c Hegg b Chapple	5	– b Keedy	44
D. S. Lehmann c Flintoff b Yates	71	– lbw b Keedy	7
A. McGrath lbw b Chapple	40	– c Lloyd b Keedy	24
P. M. Hutchison b Chapple	5	– (11) not out	10
†R. J. Blakey not out	67	– (6) lbw b Yates	2
G. M. Hamilton c Flintoff b Keedy	56	– (7) c Keedy b Yates	11
J. D. Middlebrook c Lloyd b Yates	41	– (8) c Chapple b Yates	1
R. D. Stemp not out	5	– (9) b Keedy	14
M. J. Hoggard (did not bat)		– (10) lbw b Keedy	0
L-b 11, n-b 10	21	B 17, l-b 4, w 7	28

1/82 2/93 3/210 4/260 (8 wkts dec.) 457   1/32 2/69 3/90 4/126 5/145   183
5/273 6/284 7/378 8/450   6/145 7/156 8/173 9/173

Bonus points – Yorkshire 3, Lancashire 2 (Score at 120 overs: 323-6).

Bowling: *First Innings*—Chapple 32–9–59–3; Austin 10–3–28–0; Flintoff 5–2–8–0; Keedy 50–12–161–2; Yates 41–12–107–3; Green 20–3–83–0. *Second Innings*—Wasim Akram 5–0–30–1; Green 1–0–5–0; Chapple 8–0–23–0; Keedy 22.4–7–35–5; Yates 18–2–69–4.

Umpires: J. W. Holder and A. A. Jones.

At Cardiff, August 20, 21, 22. YORKSHIRE beat GLAMORGAN by 114 runs.

YORKSHIRE v ESSEX

At Scarborough, August 26, 27, 28. Yorkshire won by one wicket. Yorkshire 23 pts, Essex 5 pts. Toss: Yorkshire.

Chasing 148, Yorkshire stumbled to their first one-wicket win in 19 years in a game without forfeitures; the previous occasion had also been against Essex at Scarborough. They slumped to 81 for eight in the face of splendid swing bowling from Ilott and Irani, but a recovery by Hamilton and Hutchison brought an enthralling finish. The pair, who had received their caps on the first day, put on 61 before Hutchison was out, but last man Hoggard kept his cool to hit the winning boundary through the covers. Hamilton remained unbeaten on 41, though he had been dropped when the score was 113. Both he and Hoggard had earlier completed career-best bowling returns. In Yorkshire's first innings, Lehmann had reached 99 off 96 balls with 18 fours and a six, slashed square over cover point, but then froze as he lost sight of a dipping full toss from Danny Law; the ball hit his stumps via his foot.

Close of play: First day, Yorkshire 40-1 (M. P. Vaughan 20*); Second day, Essex 97-3 (T. P. Hodgson 40*, R. C. Irani 25*).

Essex

*P. J. Prichard c Wood b Hoggard	20	– c Blakey b Hoggard	24
D. D. J. Robinson c Byas b Hamilton	42	– b Hutchison	0
T. P. Hodgson lbw b Middlebrook	13	– lbw b Hamilton	54
S. G. Law c Blakey b McGrath	47	– c Blakey b Hoggard	2
R. C. Irani c Blakey b Hoggard	22	– c Middlebrook b Hoggard	43
A. P. Grayson b Hamilton	11	– lbw b Silverwood	57
D. R. Law b Hamilton	6	– lbw b Silverwood	29
†B. J. Hyam c Byas b Hamilton	14	– b Hoggard	22
M. C. Ilott lbw b Hamilton	3	– b Silverwood	3
N. F. Williams not out	7	– c Lehmann b Hoggard	0
P. M. Such c Blakey b Hamilton	0	– not out	1
B 1, l-b 4, w 6, n-b 4	15	L-b 14, n-b 12	26

1/37 2/75 3/82 4/130 5/162   **200**   1/0 2/45 3/47 4/125 5/151   **261**
6/170 7/176 8/191 9/196   6/195 7/240 8/254 9/255

Bonus points – Essex 1, Yorkshire 4.

Bowling: *First Innings*—Silverwood 14–4–37–0; Hutchison 15–3–51–0; Hoggard 15–7–32–2; Hamilton 18.4–4–50–6; Middlebrook 3–1–10–1; McGrath 8–3–13–1; Lehmann 1–0–2–0. *Second Innings*—Silverwood 23–5–70–3; Hutchison 10–2–36–1; Hoggard 20–5–57–5; Hamilton 10–2–33–1; McGrath 4–0–13–0; Middlebrook 7–0–29–0; Lehmann 3–0–9–0.

Yorkshire

*D. Byas c Hyam b Irani	12	– c Hyam b Ilott	0
M. P. Vaughan c Robinson b Irani	71	– c S. G. Law b Irani	8
M. J. Wood c S. G. Law b Irani	1	– b Ilott	1
D. S. Lehmann b D. R. Law	99	– c Hyam b Irani	25
A. McGrath c Hyam b Ilott	0	– lbw b Ilott	7
†R. J. Blakey c Hyam b Irani	51	– lbw b Ilott	6
G. M. Hamilton c Hyam b D. R. Law	13	– not out	41
J. D. Middlebrook c Hyam b Ilott	20	– lbw b Irani	5
C. E. W. Silverwood c Hyam b Ilott	0	– lbw b Ilott	5
P. M. Hutchison not out	6	– lbw b D. R. Law	30
M. J. Hoggard b Irani	5	– not out	6
B 8, l-b 9, w 2, n-b 17	36	B 10, l-b 2, n-b 4	16

1/40 2/42 3/200 4/203 5/219   **314**   1/0 2/10 3/24 4/31 5/51   (9 wkts) **150**
6/253 7/289 8/297 9/308   6/51 7/68 8/81 9/142

Bonus points – Yorkshire 3, Essex 4.

Bowling: *First Innings*—Ilott 20–4–64–3; Williams 8.5–1–26–0; D. R. Law 14–1–75–2; Irani 21.2–9–47–5; Such 17.1–4–58–0; Grayson 7–1–27–0. *Second Innings*—Ilott 18–3–54–5; Irani 18–4–55–3; Grayson 4–1–14–0; D. R. Law 3.4–0–15–1.

Umpires: D. J. Constant and V. A. Holder.

YORKSHIRE v SURREY

At Leeds, September 1, 2, 3, 4. Yorkshire won by 164 runs. Yorkshire 22 pts, Surrey 4 pts. Toss: Surrey. First-class debut: G. M. Fellows.

On a green pitch, and after a blank first day, Surrey lost the match and, with it, their position at the top of the table, which they had held since mid-May. White, having been out of Championship cricket for three months with a back injury, returned as a batsman. Opening in both innings, he first scored a patient 55, and then set up a declaration by hitting his first hundred for a year. Hamilton took seven for 50 to improve his career-best figures for the third game in a row. He went on to complete his best-ever match analysis, 11 for 72, when he added four more wickets to skittle Surrey a second time; Silverwood claimed five. Only Ben Hollioake, with a ferocious 60, showed any fight, as Surrey made little impression on their target of 300.

Close of play: First day, No play; Second day, Surrey 17-0 (M. A. Butcher 10*, I. J. Ward 3*); Third day, Yorkshire 151-4 (C. White 82*).

Yorkshire

C. White c Brown b B. C. Hollioake	55	– not out	104
M. P. Vaughan lbw b Butcher	23	– c Batty b Butcher	8
M. J. Wood c Stewart b Bicknell	15	– c Batty b B. C. Hollioake	20
*D. Byas lbw b Butcher	52	– c Batty b B. C. Hollioake	6
G. M. Fellows c Batty b B. C. Hollioake	3	– c Ward b Bicknell	18
B. Parker lbw b A. J. Hollioake	32	– not out	20
†R. J. Blakey c Batty b A. J. Hollioake	10		
G. M. Hamilton b Butcher	0		
C. E. W. Silverwood not out	7		
M. J. Hoggard c Bicknell b Butcher	7		
P. M. Hutchison not out	0		
B 6, l-b 12, w 8, n-b 20	46	B 1, l-b 15, n-b 4	20

1/42 2/69 3/150 4/156 5/214   (9 wkts dec.) 250   1/46 2/107   (4 wkts dec.) 196
6/234 7/234 8/234 9/247   3/123 4/151

Bonus points – Yorkshire 2, Surrey 4.

Bowling: *First Innings*—Bicknell 26–7–59–1; Benjamin 13–4–43–0;. Saqlain Mushtaq 20–7–39–0; B. C. Hollioake 14–5–31–2; Butcher 14.4–4–41–4; A. J. Hollioake 8–5–19–2. *Second Innings*—Bicknell 17–4–52–1; Benjamin 4–1–14–0; B. C. Hollioake 14–2–35–2; Butcher 10–2–26–1; A. J. Hollioake 10–2–35–0; Saqlain Mushtaq 2–0–18–0.

Surrey

M. A. Butcher lbw b Hamilton	40	– lbw b Silverwood	0
I. J. Ward lbw b Hoggard	26	– c Vaughan b Silverwood	5
N. Shahid c White b Hamilton	7	– lbw b Hamilton	30
A. J. Stewart lbw b Hamilton	13	– c White b Hamilton	15
A. D. Brown c Blakey b Hamilton	6	– c Blakey b Hoggard	0
*A. J. Hollioake c Blakey b Hoggard	16	– c Silverwood b Hamilton	4
B. C. Hollioake c White b Hamilton	0	– b Hamilton	60
†J. N. Batty not out	8	– lbw b Silverwood	9
M. P. Bicknell c Byas b Hamilton	6	– b Silverwood	8
Saqlain Mushtaq b Hoggard	2	– c Hutchison b Silverwood	1
J. E. Benjamin lbw b Hamilton	3	– not out	1
B 10, l-b 4, w 2, n-b 4	20	B 2	2

1/80 2/86 3/88 4/98 5/125   147   1/0 2/11 3/47 4/50 5/52   135
6/125 7/125 8/131 9/140   6/63 7/117 8/133 9/133

Bonus points – Yorkshire 4.

Bowling: *First Innings*—Silverwood 9–2–41–0; Hutchison 11–3–24–0; Hamilton 17.1–4–50–7; Hoggard 15–6–18–3. *Second Innings*—Silverwood 14.4–6–30–5; Hutchison 8–1–34–0; Hamilton 14–7–22–4; Hoggard 11–3–26–1; Fellows 3–0–21–0.

Umpires: A. Clarkson and N. T. Plews.

YORKSHIRE v WARWICKSHIRE

At Leeds, September 9, 10, 11, 12. Yorkshire won by an innings and 27 runs. Yorkshire 24 pts, Warwickshire 2 pts. Toss: Yorkshire.

A battery of photographers saw Yorkshire crush Warwickshire, but the focus of their attention was Dickie Bird, officiating in his final first-class game. So it came as no surprise when a sudden downpour flooded the ground half an hour before the scheduled start, allowing only 44 balls in the day. Next morning, Yorkshire recovered from early setbacks, thanks to an unbeaten double-century from Wood, the third hundred of his debut Championship season. He batted for 411 minutes and 339 balls, hitting 23 fours. Then Warwickshire, a man short, lost their last seven wickets for 27. Silverwood and Hutchison required only 141 deliveries to wrap up the innings for 84. In Warwickshire's follow-on, Knight batted superbly and, together with Giles, frustrated Yorkshire until the final afternoon, putting on 122 for the eighth wicket before Giles went for 83. Knight was left carrying his bat for 130 when Giddins became a victim of an lbw decision from Bird – generally regarded as a rarity – to end the game. True to form, there had earlier been a Dickie-type incident: he was unable to see how many lamps were glowing to indicate bad light because of a blinding low sun.

Close of play: First day, Yorkshire 20-0 (C. White 5*, M. P. Vaughan 14*); Second day, Yorkshire 311-5 (M. J. Wood 160*, G. M. Hamilton 31*); Third day, Warwickshire 190-7 (N. V. Knight 103*, A. F. Giles 3*).

Yorkshire

C. White b Munton	9	G. M. Hamilton c Giddins b Brown	78
M. P. Vaughan b Giddins	23	J. D. Middlebrook not out	1
M. J. Wood not out	200	B 15, l-b 15, n-b 2	32
*D. Byas lbw b Munton	28		
B. Parker c Giles b Brown	8	1/29 2/41 3/85	(6 wkts dec.) 408
†R. J. Blakey b Brown	29	4/116 5/253 6/395	

C. E. W. Silverwood, P. M. Hutchison and M. J. Hoggard did not bat.

Bonus points – Yorkshire 4, Warwickshire 2 (Score at 120 overs: 391-5).

Bowling: Giddins 39–10–133–1; Brown 31.1–8–110–3; Munton 33–10–94–2; Giles 17–6–34–0; Smith 2–0–7–0.

Warwickshire

*N. V. Knight c Middlebrook b Hutchison	0	– not out	130
M. A. Wagh c Blakey b Silverwood	1	– b Hutchison	0
D. L. Hemp b Hutchison	16	– c Byas b Hamilton	29
T. L. Penney c Blakey b Silverwood	17	– c Blakey b Hamilton	13
D. R. Brown c Byas b Hutchison	18	– c Blakey b Middlebrook	19
N. M. K. Smith c Byas b Hutchison	4	– b Hoggard	2
†K. J. Piper lbw b Silverwood	0	– b Hoggard	0
A. F. Giles not out	4	– (9) b Hamilton	83
T. A. Munton c Wood b Hutchison	1	– (8) c Blakey b Hoggard	8
E. S. H. Giddins c Byas b Hutchison	0	– lbw b Hamilton	0
A. Singh absent hurt		– absent hurt	
B 4, l-b 15, w 2, n-b 2	23	B 9, l-b 4	13

1/11 2/15 3/57 4/61 5/76	84	1/4 2/61 3/115 4/152 5/159	297
6/79 7/79 8/80 9/84		6/159 7/175 8/297 9/297	

Bonus points – Yorkshire 4.

Bowling: *First Innings*—Silverwood 12–1–40–3; Hutchison 11.3–6–25–6. *Second Innings*—Silverwood 13–3–47–0; Hutchison 23–10–47–1; Hamilton 24.4–8–79–4; Hoggard 18–4–84–3; Middlebrook 18–8–27–1.

Umpires: H. D. Bird and R. Julian.

At Hove, September 17, 18, 19. YORKSHIRE beat SUSSEX by ten wickets.

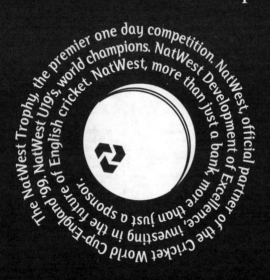

NATWEST TROPHY, 1998

Peter Martin

Lancashire reasserted their reputation as the kings of one-day county cricket when they won their 11th Lord's final, and their seventh in the 36 seasons of the Gillette/NatWest. They did it in overwhelming fashion, beating Derbyshire by nine wickets.

It was the 12th win out of 13 for the team batting second, a sequence that had already persuaded the ECB to bring the 1999 final forward a week, into late August rather than early September, in the hope of finding fairer conditions. Because rain delayed the start until teatime, it was Lancashire who had to bat in the morning – Sunday morning – and Derbyshire's batsmen made an excellent start against wayward bowling. But they collapsed amazingly: from 70 for nought to 81 for seven against Ian Austin and Peter Martin, and then to 108 all out. Lancashire knocked off the runs very easily; Austin was the man of the match.

One of the early favourites thus finished as winners of a competition that produced several surprises, including a victory for one of the minor teams for the first time in seven years. Since Hertfordshire's 1991 win came in a bowl-out, it was the first fair-and-square one since 1988. The successful team were Scotland who, after 15 consecutive defeats, put paid to Worcestershire. There were also uneasy moments for Hampshire – reduced to nought for three by Dorset – and Warwickshire, whose bowlers found it unexpectedly hard to subdue Ireland.

Scotland were well beaten in the second round by Derbyshire, who themselves went on to score surprising away wins over Surrey and Leicestershire. Hampshire were the other unfancied team to do well, beating Middlesex at Lord's before going down easily to Lancashire in the semi-final at a packed Northlands Road.

The NatWest is to change in 1999, with all the Minor Counties and Huntingdonshire taking part, plus the English county Board XIs, and four national sides: Denmark, Holland, Ireland and Scotland. These 42 teams will battle for 14 places alongside the Championship teams in the third round, making a Lancashire v Lancashire final at least a theoretical possibility.

Prize money

£47,000 for winners: LANCASHIRE.
£23,500 for runners-up: DERBYSHIRE.
£11,750 for losing semi-finalists: HAMPSHIRE, LEICESTERSHIRE.
£5,750 for losing quarter-finalists: MIDDLESEX, NOTTINGHAMSHIRE, SURREY, WARWICKSHIRE.

Man of the Match award winners received £1,250 in the final, £475 in the semi-finals, £425 in the quarter-finals, £375 in the second round and £300 in the first round. The prize money was increased from £122,700 in the 1997 tournament to £128,700.

FIRST ROUND

CHESHIRE v ESSEX

At Chester, June 24. Essex won by ten wickets. Toss: Essex.

Grant Flower, the Zimbabwean Test opener drafted in for the occasion, headed Cheshire's list of batting failures, and Extras scored almost three times more than any individual. Irani and Such were close to unplayable in damp conditions, and Prichard and Robinson then steered the holders effortlessly into the next round; it was their first ten-wicket win in this competition.

Man of the Match: R. C. Irani.

Cheshire

P. R. J. Bryson lbw b Ilott	0	†S. Bramhall c Hussain b Such	2
G. W. Flower c Rollins b Cowan	8	S. W. Hampson c Irani b Such	0
J. D. Bean c Hussain b Cowan	9	A. J. Murphy c Rollins b Ilott	10
*I. Cockbain lbw b Irani	4	B 8, l-b 10, w 10, n-b 6	34
S. C. Wundke c Prichard b Irani	10		
R. G. Hignett c S. G. Law b Irani	3	1/0 2/17 3/23 (36.5 overs) 92
N. D. Cross run out	0	4/54 5/62 6/65
S. A. Stoneman not out	12	7/68 8/70 9/76

Bowling: Ilott 8.5–2–23–2; Cowan 6–0–16–2; S. G. Law 3–1–12–0; Irani 10–4–13–3; Such 9–3–10–2.

Essex

*P. J. Prichard not out	55
D. D. J. Robinson not out	37
W 2, n-b 2	4

(no wkt, 24.5 overs) 96

N. Hussain, S. G. Law, R. C. Irani, A. P. Grayson, †R. J. Rollins, D. R. Law, A. P. Cowan, M. C. Ilott and P. M. Such did not bat.

Bowling: Murphy 7–1–22–0; Stoneman 6–0–27–0; Hampson 7–1–32–0; Wundke 3.5–0–15–0; Flower 1–1–0–0.

Umpires: J. D. Bond and R. Julian.

DERBYSHIRE v CUMBERLAND

At Derby, June 24. Derbyshire won by 64 runs. Toss: Cumberland.

David Pennett, who spent five seasons on Nottinghamshire's staff, reduced the home team to 15 for two before an undefeated 90 from Cassar, making his NatWest debut, guided Derbyshire to a demanding score. Cumberland also lost early wickets and, despite a spirited innings from Dutton, never threatened.

Man of the Match: M. E. Cassar.

Derbyshire

K. J. Barnett b Dagnall	33	*D. G. Cork not out	25
M. J. Slater b Pennett	0		
T. A. Tweats lbw b Pennett	5	L-b 5, w 5, n-b 2	12
†A. S. Rollins c Dutton b Sharp	58		
M. E. Cassar not out	90	1/4 2/15 3/65 (5 wkts, 60 overs) 266
B. L. Spendlove run out	43	4/121 5/188

V. P. Clarke, P. A. J. DeFreitas, G. M. Roberts and K. J. Dean did not bat.

Bowling: Pennett 12–5–44–2; Sharp 12–3–63–1; Fielding 12–2–40–0; Dagnall 9–0–37–1; Kippax 9–0–34–0; Beech 6–0–43–0.

Cumberland

A. D. Mawson c Rollins b Cork	4	C. E. Dagnall c Rollins b Dean	4
D. J. Pearson b Roberts	24	D. B. Pennett b Cork	1
A. A. Metcalfe lbw b Dean	9	M. A. Sharp b DeFreitas	17
S. T. Knox b Clarke	27	B 1, l-b 8, w 6, n-b 8	23
*†S. M. Dutton not out	68		
P. Beech lbw b Cork	18	1/6 2/22 3/66 (56.4 overs)	202
S. A. J. Kippax b Dean	3	4/86 5/133 6/138	
J. M. Fielding c Barnett b Cork	4	7/155 8/173 9/174	

Bowling: Cork 12–1–46–4; DeFreitas 10.4–1–43–1; Dean 12–1–49–3; Roberts 12–3–30–1; Clarke 10–1–25–1.

Umpires: J. C. Balderstone and M. K. Reed.

DEVON v YORKSHIRE

At Exmouth, June 24. Yorkshire won by nine wickets. Toss: Devon.

After rain delayed the start, the Devon captain Peter Roebuck chose to bat. He concluded the day by writing the match report in the *Daily Telegraph*. Batting first, he said, "seemed like a good idea at the time". Only Roebuck and another former Somerset player, Folland, reached double figures as Hutchison swung the ball sharply, and all the bowlers drew movement from the damp pitch. Yorkshire knocked off the 81 they needed in 69 minutes, losing Byas to Australian Test leg-spinner MacGill.

Man of the Match: P. M. Hutchison.

Devon

N. R. Gaywood c Blakey b Hutchison	5	K. Donohue c Blakey b Sidebottom	4
G. T. J. Townsend c McGrath b Hutchison	8	A. C. Cottam b Sidebottom	0
N. A. Folland lbw b Hamilton	15	S. C. G. MacGill c Blakey b Sidebottom	0
K. A. O. Barrett c Byas b Hamilton	3	I. E. Bishop not out	1
A. J. Pugh lbw b Hutchison	4	B 2, l-b 4, w 7, n-b 2	15
*P. M. Roebuck c Byas b Silverwood	22		
†A. K. Hele c Byas b Hamilton	3	1/10 2/26 3/36 4/43 5/52 (28.3 overs)	80
		6/56 7/76 8/76 9/76	

Bowling: Silverwood 6.3–1–14–1; Hutchison 12–4–18–3; Sidebottom 4–1–15–3; Hamilton 6–0–27–3.

Yorkshire

*D. Byas lbw b MacGill	14
M. P. Vaughan not out	38
M. J. Wood not out	25
W 2, n-b 2	4

1/22 (1 wkt, 20.2 overs) 81

A. McGrath, D. S. Lehmann, B. Parker, †R. J. Blakey, G. M. Hamilton, C. E. W. Silverwood, P. M. Hutchison and R. J. Sidebottom did not bat.

Bowling: Donohue 5–0–23–0; Bishop 7–0–27–0; MacGill 8–1–29–1; Cottam 0.2–0–2–0.

Umpires: N. A. Mallender and R. Palmer.

DORSET v HAMPSHIRE

At Bournemouth, June 24, 25. Hampshire won by 161 runs. Toss: Hampshire.

Six years after their last home game on the ground, Hampshire returned to Dean Park and suffered one of their worst starts ever: by the fourth over, they were nought for three. But Smith, sharing a stand of 179 with Aymes, steadied the ship. His undefeated 144 made him the first player to score eight NatWest centuries (he had shared the old record of seven with his brother Chris), and the third to pass 2,000 runs. It later earned him his ninth match award, equalling Graham Gooch's record. Despite the game's early promise, it ceased to be a contest once Hampshire had passed 200. Hardy – formerly Smith's county colleague and now his business partner – hung around for a while, but, after play spilled over on to the second day, Dorset collapsed to Udal and Stephenson.

Man of the Match: R. A. Smith.

Close of play: Dorset 51-3 (13 overs) (J. J. E. Hardy 20*, M. Swarbrick 5*).

Hampshire

G. W. White lbw b Shackleton	0	A. D. Mascarenhas not out		30
J. P. Stephenson c Lamb b Forshaw	0			
*R. A. Smith not out	144	L-b 6, w 19, n-b 10		35
P. R. Whitaker c and b Forshaw	0			—
†A. N. Aymes b Scott	73	1/0 2/0 3/0	(5 wkts, 60 overs)	315
N. A. M. McLean c Rintoul b Pyman	33	4/179 5/244		

M. Keech, S. D. Udal, K. D. James and C. A. Connor did not bat.

Bowling: Shackleton 12–6–18–1; Forshaw 9–2–59–2; Pike 12–3–36–0; Scott 10–0–89–1; Pyman 12–0–81–1; Ferreira 3–0–26–0.

Dorset

*J. J. E. Hardy lbw b Stephenson	45	V. J. Pike c White b Udal		11
L. D. Ferreira c Aymes b McLean	7	S. M. Forshaw b Udal		0
T. W. Richings b Connor	14	J. H. Shackleton c Aymes b Udal		2
S. W. D. Rintoul lbw b Connor	0	L-b 5, w 15, n-b 2		22
M. Swarbrick b Stephenson	24			—
R. J. Scott c James b Udal	14	1/23 2/44 3/44	(45.3 overs)	154
†T. C. Z. Lamb not out	15	4/101 5/120 6/130		
R. A. Pyman b James	0	7/131 8/144 9/146		

Bowling: McLean 6–0–35–1; Connor 8–2–28–2; Mascarenhas 4–0–21–0; James 6–2–13–0; Stephenson 12–1–25–3; Udal 8.3–2–20–4; Whitaker 1–0–7–0.

Umpires: J. H. Harris and K. J. Lyons.

GLAMORGAN v BEDFORDSHIRE

At Cardiff, June 24, 25. Glamorgan won by 148 runs. Toss: Bedfordshire.

Half-centuries from three of Glamorgan's top order took them to their highest 60-over score, surpassing their 345 for two against Durham in 1991. After Croft had fallen for nought, James and Dale shared a stand of 123. Sher and Fantham proved particularly expensive: their combined total of 23 overs cost 159. The Bedfordshire bowlers made some amends, however, with the bat: the last three wickets added 119 runs, allowing their team to reach their highest total in the competition as well.

Man of the Match: A. Dale.

Close of play: Bedfordshire 73-3 (19 overs) (D. R. Clarke 17*).

Glamorgan

S. P. James c Sandford b Dalton	65	S. D. Thomas not out		28
R. D. B. Croft lbw b Hughes	0			
A. Dale b Sher	89	B 5, l-b 17, w 12, n-b 6		40
*M. P. Maynard lbw b Roberts	32			
P. A. Cottey c Larkins b Hughes	68	1/1 2/124 3/181	(7 wkts, 60 overs)	373
M. J. Powell b Sher	4	4/227 5/242		
†A. D. Shaw c Sher b White	47	6/310 7/373		

Waqar Younis, S. L. Watkin and O. T. Parkin did not bat.

Bowling: Hughes 10–0–60–2; White 9–2–35–1; Roberts 8–0–55–1; Sher 11–0–77–2; Dalton 10–1–42–1; Fantham 12–0–82–0.

Bedfordshire

A. R. Roberts c Shaw b Watkin	11	I. J. Fantham c Thomas b Croft		32
W. Larkins c and b Thomas	3	†G. D. Sandford c Parkin b Croft		26
D. R. Clarke c Maynard b Waqar Younis	17	M. R. White b Thomas		0
J. P. Hughes b Croft	30	L-b 8, w 14, n-b 8		30
D. J. M. Mercer lbw b Waqar Younis	0			
*P. D. B. Hoare c Shaw b Waqar Younis	17	1/14 2/27 3/73	(54.3 overs)	225
R. N. Dalton c Shaw b Waqar Younis	12	4/75 5/76 6/91		
Z. A. Sher not out	47	7/106 8/171 9/222		

Bowling: Waqar Younis 12–2–46–4; Watkin 12–2–44–1; Thomas 8.3–1–31–2; Parkin 10–0–34–0; Croft 12–1–62–3.

Umpires: M. J. Kitchen and A. G. T. Whitehead.

GLOUCESTERSHIRE v NORTHAMPTONSHIRE

At Bristol, June 24, 25. Gloucestershire won by 20 runs. Toss: Northamptonshire.

Tim Hancock hit 60, his highest NatWest score, and then claimed three wickets in as many overs to secure his first match award and a Gloucestershire victory in one of the two all-first-class county ties. He fielded superbly as well. When play eventually started at 3.30 p.m., Hancock and Hewson put on a gritty 99 for the first wicket. The middle order filled in to ensure a reasonable target of 267. At 119 for two in the 35th over, Northamptonshire were on track. But after Curran smacked a catch to mid-off, they slid to 161 for six. Despite one big straight six from Rose, the tail could not quite cope with a rate of seven an over.

Man of the Match: T. H. C. Hancock.

Close of play: Northamptonshire 6-0 (3 overs) (R. J. Warren 0*, R. J. Bailey 4*).

Gloucestershire

D. R. Hewson c Curran b Rose	45	J. Lewis not out		2
T. H. C. Hancock c Walton b Malcolm	60	A. M. Smith not out		6
A. J. Wright c Bailey b Taylor	28			
*M. W. Alleyne c Rose b Malcolm	23	B 1, l-b 6, w 6, n-b 2		15
M. G. N. Windows b Snape	25			
R. I. Dawson b Taylor	35	1/99 2/139 3/141	(8 wkts, 60 overs)	266
†R. C. Russell c Warren b Rose	27	4/180 5/189 6/250		
M. C. J. Ball b Rose	0	7/250 8/260		

C. A. Walsh did not bat.

Bowling: Malcolm 12–0–55–2; Taylor 12–2–54–2; Rose 12–1–43–3; Penberthy 8–1–33–0; Curran 5–0–27–0; Snape 11–1–47–1.

Northamptonshire

†R. J. Warren c Russell b Smith	7		F. A. Rose run out	19
R. J. Bailey run out	13		J. P. Taylor not out	3
M. B. Loye c Walsh b Hancock	40		D. E. Malcolm b Walsh	1
*K. M. Curran c Smith b Hancock	53		L-b 11, w 5, n-b 2	18
A. L. Penberthy c Russell b Hancock	0			
D. J. Sales c Russell b Walsh	42		1/24 2/26 3/119 (57.5 overs)	246
T. C. Walton c Hancock b Alleyne	15		4/119 5/130 6/161	
J. N. Snape c Smith b Alleyne	35		7/210 8/239 9/243	

Bowling: Smith 11–1–25–1; Walsh 11.5–1–32–2; Lewis 11–2–43–0; Alleyne 12–1–62–2; Ball 6–0–43–0; Hancock 6–0–30–3.

Umpires: A. Clarkson and G. Sharp.

KENT v CAMBRIDGESHIRE

At Canterbury, June 24. Kent won by eight wickets. Toss: Cambridgeshire.

Tight bowling from the Kent attack prevented Cambridgeshire from building a defensible total. Looking healthy at 59 for one, they were scuppered by the brisk medium-pace of Phillips, making his NatWest debut. Kent strolled to victory with more than 22 overs to spare.

Man of the Match: B. J. Phillips.

Cambridgeshire

J. S. G. Norman c Ward b McCague	7		T. S. Smith lbw b Ealham	1
N. T. Gadsby c Phillips b Hooper	23		D. F. Ralfs c Headley b Fleming	8
S. A. Kellett c Headley b Phillips	20			
S. Mohammad c Hooper b Phillips	4		L-b 9, w 8, n-b 4	21
N. Mohammad run out	35			
B. T. P. Donelan c Ward b Phillips	1		1/21 2/59 3/59 (9 wkts, 60 overs)	153
J. P. T. Latham c Willis b Headley	12		4/65 5/71 6/121	
*A. Akhtar not out	21		7/122 8/127 9/153	

†C. D. Durant did not bat.

Bowling: Headley 12–3–23–1; McCague 12–4–28–1; Ealham 12–1–34–1; Phillips 7–2–14–3; Hooper 12–1–29–1; Fleming 5–0–16–1.

Kent

D. P. Fulton c Durant b Ralfs	13
R. W. T. Key st Durant b Akhtar	18
*T. R. Ward not out	61
A. P. Wells not out	53
B 1, l-b 4, w 2, n-b 2	9
1/34 2/34 (2 wkts, 37.2 overs)	154

C. L. Hooper, M. A. Ealham, †S. C. Willis, B. J. Phillips, M. V. Fleming, M. J. McCague and D. W. Headley did not bat.

Bowling: Akhtar 8–1–27–1; Ralfs 9–2–26–1; Latham 4–0–16–0; Smith 6–1–20–0; Donelan 7–0–37–0; N. Mohammad 3.2–0–23–0.

Umpires: P. Adams and B. Dudleston.

LANCASHIRE v SUSSEX

At Manchester, June 24, 25. Lancashire won by 48 runs. Toss: Sussex.

On a lively pitch that encouraged the seamers, Lancashire exacted revenge on Sussex for their 1997 second-round defeat. Lancashire squandered the promising position of 134 for one, and were all out with eight overs unused. But they were rescued by Martin. Well supported by his fellow-seamers, he removed five Sussex batsmen for 30. Newell and Jarvis managed to save face, but there was no way back from 33 for six.

Man of the Match: P. J. Martin.

Close of play: Sussex 11-2 (5 overs) (R. J. Kirtley 5*).

Lancashire

M. A. Atherton c Humphries b Lewry	53	G. Chapple c Adams b Jarvis		1
A. Flintoff c Jarvis b Robinson	35	P. J. Martin c Khan b Lewry		12
*†J. P. Crawley c Bevan b Lewry	32	R. J. Green c Humphries b Bevan		0
N. H. Fairbrother c Bevan b Lewry	7	L-b 4, w 17, n-b 4		25
G. D. Lloyd not out	29			
M. Watkinson lbw b Jarvis	7	1/56 2/134 3/139	(51.3 overs)	210
I. D. Austin b Kirtley	2	4/143 5/157 6/168		
G. Yates b Kirtley	7	7/178 8/180 9/210		

Bowling: Lewry 12–0–42–4; Kirtley 9–1–38–2; Robinson 10–2–36–1; Jarvis 10–0–50–2; Bevan 10.3–0–40–1.

Sussex

M. T. E. Peirce b Austin	1	†S. Humphries c Crawley b Chapple		10
W. G. Khan c Atherton b Martin	2	J. D. Lewry b Martin		9
R. J. Kirtley c Fairbrother b Martin	6	M. A. Robinson b Watkinson b Martin		4
M. Newell not out	63	L-b 10, w 14		24
M. G. Bevan c Crawley b Austin	8			
N. R. Taylor c Crawley b Martin	1	1/4 2/11 3/13	(54.5 overs)	162
*C. J. Adams c Flintoff b Green	1	4/29 5/32 6/33		
P. W. Jarvis b Yates	33	7/99 8/129 9/155		

Bowling: Martin 11.5–2–30–5; Austin 10–2–29–2; Green 11–2–35–1; Chapple 10–0–30–1; Flintoff 5–0–9–0; Yates 7–2–19–1.

Umpires: M. J. Harris and K. E. Palmer.

LEICESTERSHIRE v STAFFORDSHIRE

At Leicester, June 24. Leicestershire won by six wickets. Toss: Leicestershire.

Simmons emerged from a run of poor form when he struck an unbeaten century – including 15 fours and a six – from 124 balls. Although the next highest contribution came from Extras, Leicestershire had little trouble surpassing 189, in which Lewis had taken competition-best figures of five for 19.

Man of the Match: P. V. Simmons.

Staffordshire

*S. J. Dean c Wells b Lewis	1	D. J. P. Boden c Nixon b Lewis		8
I. W. E. Stokes c Nixon b Mullally	4	A. Richardson b Lewis		3
L. Potter b Brimson	22	S. D. Horsfall c Nixon b Lewis		2
P. E. Wellings b Williamson	20	L-b 17, w 13, n-b 8		38
M. V. Steele c Maddy b Williamson	24			
R. P. Harvey b Mullally	32	1/5 2/21 3/78	(59.4 overs)	189
D. R. Womble c Nixon b Lewis	20	4/82 5/127 6/159		
†M. I. Humphries not out	15	7/161 8/177 9/187		

Bowling: Mullally 12–2–40–2; Lewis 9.4–3–19–5; Simmons 9–2–27–0; Wells 7–1–23–0; Williamson 11–1–34–2; Brimson 11–1–29–1.

Leicestershire

P. V. Simmons not out	107	†P. A. Nixon not out.		5
I. J. Sutcliffe c Dean b Horsfall	10	L-b 8, w 19, n-b 10.		37
B. F. Smith st Humphries b Potter.	30			—
A. Habib c Potter b Richardson	1	1/39 2/146	(4 wkts, 37.5 overs)	192
V. J. Wells c Humphries b Potter	2	3/150 4/167		

D. L. Maddy, *C. C. Lewis, D. Williamson, A. D. Mullally and M. T. Brimson did not bat.

Bowling: Richardson 12–2–48–1; Horsfall 6–1–28–1; Boden 5.5–0–45–0; Womble 4–0–39–0; Potter 9–2–20–2; Harvey 1–0–4–0.

Umpires: J. H. Hampshire and N. T. Plews.

MIDDLESEX v HEREFORDSHIRE

At Lord's, June 24. Middlesex won by seven wickets. Toss: Middlesex.

Fifties from Sylvester and Hall enabled Herefordshire, in only their third NatWest tie, to muster a respectable 213. It was never enough to pose problems for Middlesex, however, for whom Langer hit an undefeated 114 from 137 balls. He shared a partnership of 130 with Shah, after Radford, the former Worcestershire and England bowler, had a hand in the first two wickets.

Man of the Match: J. L. Langer.

Herefordshire

H. V. Patel lbw b Fraser	2	*K. E. Cooper not out		12
J. P. J. Sylvester b Ramprakash	53	R. J. Harding not out		2
C. W. Boroughs b Bloomfield	22			
S. J. Price b Dutch	13	L-b 17, w 8, n-b 6		31
D. A. Graham c Dutch b Ramprakash	8			—
M. P. Briers c Brown b Dutch	0	1/2 2/42 3/82	(8 wkts, 60 overs)	213
†R. Hall b Johnson	53	4/97 5/98 6/145		
N. V. Radford c Brown b Johnson	17	7/192 8/209		

P. J. Humphries did not bat.

Bowling: Fraser 10–1–25–1; Hewitt 8–0–31–0; Johnson 9–3–25–2; Bloomfield 10–2–35–1; Dutch 10–0–30–2; Ramprakash 7–1–24–2; Weekes 6–0–26–0.

Middlesex

M. W. Gatting lbw b Radford.	4	P. N. Weekes not out		18
J. L. Langer not out	114			
*M. R. Ramprakash c Radford b Boroughs	17	L-b 8, w 11, n-b 6		25
O. A. Shah c Harding b Humphries	37	1/18 2/52 3/182	(3 wkts, 45.4 overs)	215

†K. R. Brown, K. P. Dutch, R. L. Johnson, J. P. Hewitt, A. R. C. Fraser and T. F. Bloomfield did not bat.

Bowling: Radford 7–0–24–1; Humphries 12–1–63–1; Boroughs 11–0–40–1; Cooper 11.4–0–53–0; Harding 4–0–27–0.

Umpires: M. R. Benson and V. A. Holder.

NORFOLK v DURHAM

At Lakenham, June 24. Durham won by eight wickets. Toss: Durham.

David Thomas and his nephew, Mark, who hit 26 off 19 balls, dragged Norfolk towards a respectable total after a slow start. Phillips conceded only 16 off his 12 overs. Chasing 199, Durham faltered, losing two early wickets and Roseberry to a foot injury. But they were steadied by Speak and Boon, whose unbroken stand of 145 ensured a comfortable win.

Man of the Match: N. C. Phillips.

Norfolk

C. Amos c Speight b Wood	2	P. J. Bradshaw not out	2
C. J. Rogers c Speight b Collingwood	30	G. L. Bailey not out	2
M. R. Tipping run out	12		
S. C. Goldsmith c Speight b Phillips	8	L-b 11, w 12, n-b 18	41
D. R. Thomas b Killeen	59		
P. J. Harwood st Speight b Phillips	1	1/8 2/60 3/62 (8 wkts, 60 overs)	198
*P. G. Newman lbw b Wood	15	4/86 5/92 6/124	
M. W. Thomas run out	26	7/181 8/196	

†M. K. L. Boyden did not bat.

Bowling: Betts 12–1–43–0; Wood 12–0–40–2; Killeen 12–2–63–1; Phillips 12–4–16–2; Collingwood 12–1–25–1.

Durham

J. J. B. Lewis c Boyden b Bradshaw	15	*D. C. Boon not out	80
M. A. Roseberry retired hurt	23	B 1, l-b 1, w 7, n-b 4	13
J. E. Morris c Amos b Goldsmith	11		
N. J. Speak not out	57	1/34 2/54 (2 wkts, 54.1 overs)	199

P. D. Collingwood, †M. P. Speight, N. C. Phillips, M. M. Betts, N. Killeen and J. Wood did not bat.

M. A. Roseberry retired hurt at 51.

Bowling: Newman 8–2–27–0; Bradshaw 9–4–19–1; Goldsmith 12–2–42–1; M. W. Thomas 11.1–1–40–0; Bailey 5–0–25–0; D. R. Thomas 4–0–17–0; Rogers 5–0–27–0.

Umpires: B. Leadbeater and J. W. Lloyds.

SCOTLAND v WORCESTERSHIRE

At Raeburn Place, Edinburgh, June 24. Scotland won by four runs. Toss: Worcestershire.

Scotland's cricketers did their bit to restore national sporting pride after the football team's exit from the World Cup the previous evening. Patterson and Allingham laid the foundations of a healthy score in a second-wicket stand of 118; Parsons and Stanger made sure it was achieved, despite a slow pitch. Needing 245, Worcestershire subsided from 65 for one to 98 for six, thanks to a spell of hostile seam bowling by Craig Wright, who finished with five for 23. A belated revival by Lampitt and Haynes threatened to rob Scotland, but Lampitt, needing five off the last ball, was bowled. It was the first time an amateur side had beaten a first-class county in the NatWest – bowl-outs aside – since Cheshire scraped home against Northamptonshire in 1988.

Man of the Match: C. M. Wright.

Scotland

B. M. W. Patterson b Lampitt	71	I. M. Stanger not out	23
B. G. Lockie c Rhodes b Newport	10	C. M. Wright not out	5
M. J. D. Allingham b Lampitt	54	L-b 12, w 2, n-b 6	20
*G. Salmond run out	27		
R. A. Parsons c Leatherdale b Moody	30	1/25 2/143 3/160 (6 wkts, 60 overs)	244
J. G. Williamson c Leatherdale b Moody	4	4/180 5/189 6/227	

†A. G. Davies, P. D. Steindl and Asim Butt did not bat.

Bowling: Newport 11–1–46–1; Haynes 8–2–10–0; Lampitt 12–1–44–2; Moody 12–3–55–2; Illingworth 12–0–48–0; Leatherdale 5–0–29–0.

Worcestershire

W. P. C. Weston c Parsons b Steindl	...	6	†S. J. Rhodes c Asim Butt b Williamson	6
A. Hafeez c Stanger b Wright	....	33	R. K. Illingworth not out	0
G. A. Hick c Davies b Wright	....	29		
*T. M. Moody c Davies b Wright	.....	4	B 5, l-b 7, w 8, n-b 10 30	
D. A. Leatherdale c Davies b Wright	...	3		
V. S. Solanki c Davies b Wright	......	1	1/32 2/65 3/73 (9 wkts, 60 overs) 240	
S. R. Lampitt b Williamson	....	54	4/87 5/89 6/98	
G. R. Haynes b Allingham	....	74	7/229 8/236 9/240	

P. J. Newport did not bat.

Bowling: Asim Butt 12–2–43–0; Steindl 9–1–36–1; Wright 12–5–23–5; Stanger 7–0–36–0; Allingham 11–0–43–1; Williamson 9–0–47–2.

Umpires: P. Carrick and T. E. Jesty.

SOMERSET v HOLLAND

At Taunton, June 24. Somerset won by ten wickets. Toss: Somerset.

In his second match as Somerset captain, Mushtaq Ahmed managed to win an important toss and then exploited it by claiming five Dutch wickets for 26, his best figures in the NatWest. Batting first in overcast conditions on a desperately slow pitch, Holland struggled to 117 in almost 50 overs. In complete contrast, Burns and Holloway set off at a cracking pace, and Holland were crushed with more than 42 overs to spare; it was Somerset's first ten-wicket victory in the competition.

Man of the Match: Mushtaq Ahmed.

Holland

R. R. Bradley c Lathwell			†J. Smits c Burns b Rose	1
	b Mushtaq Ahmed .	31	K. A. Khan c Lathwell b Mushtaq Ahmed	11
B. Zuiderent c Turner b Jones	....	12	L. Bouter not out	0
D. B. Bakker c Mushtaq Ahmed b Jones		5		
K. J. van Noortwijk b Mushtaq Ahmed .		6	L-b 5, w 9, n-b 6 20	
*T. B. M. de Leede c Harden b Caddick		15		
C. R. Miller lbw b Mushtaq Ahmed	..	4	1/18 2/42 3/54 (49.2 overs) 117	
D. A. Rijkens lbw b Rose	....	12	4/62 5/68 6/87	
R. P. Lefebvre b Mushtaq Ahmed	.....	0	7/92 8/106 9/117	

Bowling: Caddick 10–4–15–1; Rose 8.2–4–5–2; Jones 8–1–36–2; Trescothick 6–0–15–0; Mushtaq Ahmed 12–4–26–5; Parsons 5–1–15–0.

Somerset

M. Burns not out	....	84
P. C. L. Holloway not out	....	28
L-b 6, w 2	....	8

(no wkt, 17.4 overs) 120

R. J. Harden, M. N. Lathwell, †R. J. Turner, M. E. Trescothick, G. D. Rose, K. A. Parsons, *Mushtaq Ahmed, A. R. Caddick and P. S. Jones did not bat.

Bowling: Lefebvre 4–0–22–0; Khan 4–1–24–0; Miller 5–0–35–0; Bouter 4.4–0–33–0.

Umpires: J. W. Holder and D. R. Shepherd.

SURREY v BUCKINGHAMSHIRE

At The Oval, June 24. Surrey won by 132 runs. Toss: Buckinghamshire.

Surrey, who took the field as favourites to win the trophy, strolled to an easy victory. Their total was sizeable, but not as huge as looked likely while Stewart, who scored 97 from 106 balls, and Ratcliffe were putting on 161 for the first wicket. An experienced attack, including three former first-class players – Bovill, Harrison and Scriven – ensured that the total did not become too embarrassing, but it was well out of Buckinghamshire's reach.

Man of the Match: A. J. Stewart.

Surrey

J. D. Ratcliffe c Sawyer b Scriven	....	71	M. P. Bicknell not out	....	20
†A. J. Stewart b Scriven	....	97	A. J. Tudor run out	....	1
G. P. Thorpe b Bovill	....	17	J. E. Benjamin not out	....	5
A. D. Brown lbw b Scriven	....	0	L-b 3, w 4, n-b 2	....	9
*A. J. Hollioake st Burns b Cole	.....	34			
I. J. Ward c Burns b Bovill	....	16	1/161 2/180 3/180	(9 wkts, 60 overs)	315
B. C. Hollioake b Bovill	....	33	4/204 5/235 6/255		
N. Shahid c Sawyer b Cole	....	12	7/283 8/295 9/303		

Bowling: Sullivan 2–0–24–0; Thomas 10–1–43–0; Harrison 12–0–44–0; Rindell 4–0–19–0; Scriven 12–0–61–3; Cole 8–0–57–2; Bovill 12–0–64–3.

Buckinghamshire

*J. C. Harrison c Stewart b Shahid	....	34	A. W. Thomas c Bicknell b Tudor	.....	8
M. J. Rindell c A. J. Hollioake			J. N. B. Bovill lbw b Tudor	....	0
b Bicknell	.	46	M. E. Sullivan not out	....	14
R. P. Lane c Stewart b B. C. Hollioake	.	29	L-b 9, w 4, n-b 10	....	23
†N. D. Burns c Bicknell b Shahid	.....	2			
P. R. Sawyer c Stewart b B. C. Hollioake		9	1/83 2/104 3/124	(43.3 overs)	183
R. B. Hurd lbw b Tudor	....	15	4/126 5/134 6/137		
T. J. A. Scriven lbw b Shahid	....	3	7/140 8/154 9/154		
A. P. Cole c Stewart b Tudor	....	0			

Bowling: Bicknell 8–0–33–1; Benjamin 7–1–33–0; Tudor 10.3–1–39–4; B. C. Hollioake 7–0–28–2; Shahid 9–1–30–3; A. J. Hollioake 2–0–11–0.

Umpires: A. A. Jones and J. F. Steele.

WALES v NOTTINGHAMSHIRE

At Colwyn Bay, June 24, 25. Nottinghamshire won by 89 runs. Toss: Wales.

Play started almost five hours late, and disciplined bowling and sharp fielding restricted Nottinghamshire to 258. Steve Barwick, for 16 years a mainstay of the Glamorgan attack, led the way with two for 45 from his 12 overs, and his team-mates all went for less than five an over. Gallian, who put on 100 for the first wicket with Dowman, top-scored with 63. In reply, Steffan Jenkins hit a dogged 44 but, apart from one over in which Jenkins hit Dowman for 15, Wales could not raise the scoring-rate enough.

Man of the Match: J. E. R. Gallian.

Close of play: Wales 27-0 (11 overs) (A. J. Jones 7*, M. J. Newbold 18*).

Nottinghamshire

M. P. Dowman b M. Davies	....	37	P. A. Strang b Barr	....	15
J. E. R. Gallian b Barwick	....	63	†C. M. W. Read not out	....	6
R. T. Robinson c Jones b Towse	.....	46	L-b 4, w 10, n-b 2	....	16
*P. Johnson c Clitheroe b Barwick	...	40			
G. F. Archer st Clitheroe b J. Davies	...	8	1/100 2/112 3/167	(7 wkts, 60 overs)	258
C. M. Tolley run out	....	1	4/187 5/193		
P. J. Franks not out	....	26	6/227 7/249		

K. P. Evans and R. T. Bates did not bat.

Bowling: Towse 12–2–50–1; J. Davies 12–2–53–1; Barr 12–0–50–1; Barwick 12–0–45–2; M. Davies 12–0–56–1.

Wales

A. J. Jones b Tolley	25	A. J. L. Barr run out		3
M. J. Newbold b Strang	30	S. R. Barwick c Tolley b Evans		5
S. H. G. Jenkins st Read b Strang	44	J. Davies not out		0
D. J. Lovell b Tolley	8	B 1, l-b 4, w 9		14
K. M. Bell c Dowman b Bates	3			—
*†R. I. Clitheroe b Bates	4	1/51 2/63 3/83	(9 wkts, 60 overs)	169
M. Davies c Johnson b Dowman	6	4/91 5/101 6/111		
A. D. Towse not out	27	7/154 8/160 9/168		

Bowling: Tolley 8–1–16–2; Evans 10–2–19–1; Bates 12–2–32–2; Strang 12–2–33–2; Franks 5–0–20–0; Dowman 12–2–40–1; Johnson 1–0–4–0.

Umpires: H. D. Bird and K. Shuttleworth.

WARWICKSHIRE v IRELAND

At Birmingham, June 24, 25. Warwickshire won by 41 runs. Toss: Ireland.

Ireland briefly threatened to overhaul the 302 scored by Warwickshire, finalists in five of the last nine seasons. At 164 for two, with 20 overs remaining, the required seven an over was possible. But once 19-year-old Ed Joyce had fallen for 73, the innings lost momentum. On the previous day, Knight had hit an unbeaten 143 from 183 balls; Lara's wretched form continued with another duck.

Man of the Match: N. V. Knight.

Close of play: Ireland 16-0 (11 overs) (W. K. McCallan 12*, E. C. Joyce 3*).

Warwickshire

N. V. Knight not out	143	A. F. Giles not out		3
N. M. K. Smith c Dunlop b McCallan	52			
*B. C. Lara b McCallan	0	L-b 13, w 7, n-b 2		22
D. P. Ostler c Davy b Gillespie	30			—
T. L. Penney c Rutherford b Gillespie	7	1/96 2/100 3/157	(5 wkts, 60 overs)	302
D. L. Hemp c Rutherford b Heasley	45	4/184 5/291		

G. Welch, †K. J. Piper, G. C. Small and T. A. Munton did not bat.

Bowling: Cooke 12–0–56–0; Eagleson 12–1–53–0; Davy 8–1–53–0; Heasley 11–0–55–1; McCallan 12–1–45–2; Gillespie 5–0–27–2.

Ireland

W. K. McCallan b Munton	32	†A. T. Rutherford lbw b Giles		0
E. C. Joyce st Piper b Smith	73	J. O. Davy not out		2
S. G. Smyth c Piper b Hemp	19			
D. Heasley b Giles	36	B 8, l-b 12, w 9, n-b 5		34
A. D. Patterson c Piper b Smith	0			—
*A. R. Dunlop not out	44	1/51 2/99 3/182	(8 wkts, 60 overs)	261
P. G. Gillespie c Penney b Giles	20	4/183 5/190 6/233		
R. L. Eagleson b Giles	1	7/240 8/240		

G. Cooke did not bat.

Bowling: Welch 8–2–8–0; Small 9–2–19–0; Smith 11–0–60–2; Munton 12–1–79–1; Hemp 7–1–40–1; Giles 12–1–29–4; Ostler 1–0–6–0.

Umpires: D. J. Constant and R. A. White.

SECOND ROUND

GLAMORGAN v LEICESTERSHIRE

At Cardiff, July 8. Leicestershire won by five wickets. Toss: Glamorgan.

Welsh hopes of a quarter-final place were dashed by a 132-run partnership from Habib and Wells, who rescued Leicestershire from a precarious 42 for four. Their attack conceded 20 wides, but otherwise bowled steadily on a slow pitch and restricted Glamorgan to just four boundaries in the first 40 overs. Only Maynard, with a measured 66, made a score as Glamorgan were dismissed with an over remaining. When Leicestershire batted, Maynard was in the thick of it again, pulling off an astonishing left-handed catch to remove Maddy – one of three wickets in nine balls for Watkin. Glamorgan's 188 began to seem a challenging total. But neither Wells nor Habib gave a chance until Habib played on to Thomas 15 short of victory.

Man of the Match: V. J. Wells.

Glamorgan

S. P. James c Nixon b Mullally	14	D. A. Cosker not out		4
†A. D. Shaw lbw b Mullally	1	S. L. Watkin b Williamson		0
A. Dale c Simmons b Wells	26	O. T. Parkin b Mullally		2
*M. P. Maynard c Smith b Williamson	66	L-b 2, w 20, n-b 4		26
P. A. Cottey lbw b Wells	8			
M. J. Powell c Nixon b Williamson	11	1/2 2/24 3/79	(59 overs)	188
R. D. B. Croft c Sutcliffe b Williamson	19	4/93 5/123 6/159		
S. D. Thomas c Maddy b Williamson	11	7/180 8/184 9/185		

Bowling: Mullally 12–3–33–3; Lewis 6–0–19–0; Wells 12–0–42–2; Simmons 6–0–23–0; Brimson 12–2–32–0; Williamson 11–1–37–5.

Leicestershire

D. L. Maddy c Maynard b Watkin	5	†P. A. Nixon not out		11
I. J. Sutcliffe b Thomas	29			
B. F. Smith c Shaw b Watkin	0			
P. V. Simmons lbw b Watkin	4	L-b 6, w 14, n-b 2		22
V. J. Wells not out	51			
A. Habib b Thomas	67	1/28 2/28 3/32	(5 wkts, 55.2 overs)	189
		4/42 5/174		

*C. C. Lewis, D. Williamson, A. D. Mullally and M. T. Brimson did not bat.

Bowling: Watkin 12–2–25–3; Parkin 9–1–40–0; Croft 12–2–34–0; Thomas 12–1–41–2; Cosker 5.2–0–20–0; Dale 5–1–23–0.

Umpires: A. Clarkson and J. H. Harris.

GLOUCESTERSHIRE v SURREY

At Bristol, July 8. Surrey won by 52 runs. Toss: Surrey.

Surrey won a match of two top-order collapses through their greater powers of recovery. Adam Hollioake and Stewart shared a crucial partnership of 156 after Smith had reduced them to 20 for four. Smith had taken three for seven, and Walsh conceded only six runs in six overs. But Alleyne committed a strategic blunder when he took his opening pair out of the attack. It was another 38 overs before the next wicket fell, when Hollioake, having made a competition-best 88, holed out to deep mid-off. He and Stewart were the only batsmen to reach double figures. On a good surface, 216 was attainable, but Gloucestershire failed even more miserably. Their first five wickets mustered just 45; Alleyne and Russell rallied them briefly, but Surrey's spinners ensured a comfortable victory. "We froze," said Alleyne. During the match, Russell pulled level with Alan Knott on 65 NatWest dismissals; only Bob Taylor, on 66, remained ahead.

Man of the Match: A. J. Hollioake.

Surrey

J. D. Ratcliffe lbw b Smith	8	I. D. K. Salisbury c Russell b Lewis	4	
I. J. Ward run out	1	Saqlain Mushtaq c Windows b Smith	6	
†A. J. Stewart c Alleyne b Walsh	89	J. E. Benjamin not out	0	
N. Shahid c Russell b Smith	0	L-b 4, w 7	11	
A. D. Brown lbw b Smith	0			
*A. J. Hollioake c Lewis b Alleyne	88	1/10 2/12 3/12	(59.1 overs) 215	
B. C. Hollioake c Hewson b Ball	7	4/20 5/176 6/186		
M. P. Bicknell run out	1	7/190 8/202 9/215		

Bowling: Smith 12–1–46–4; Walsh 11.1–2–25–1; Lewis 8–0–42–1; Alleyne 12–1–35–1; Ball 12–1–46–1; Hancock 4–0–17–0.

Gloucestershire

D. R. Hewson b Benjamin	12	M. C. J. Ball b Saqlain Mushtaq	12	
T. H. C. Hancock c Stewart b Bicknell	10	J. Lewis b Saqlain Mushtaq	1	
A. J. Wright c A. J. Hollioake b Bicknell	5	A. M. Smith b Salisbury	1	
*M. W. Alleyne lbw b Bicknell	39	C. A. Walsh b Salisbury	17	
M. G. N. Windows c Stewart b B. C. Hollioake	4	B 2, l-b 4, w 5, n-b 2	13	
R. I. Dawson b B. C. Hollioake	0	1/24 2/24 3/36 4/45 5/45	(55 overs) 163	
†R. C. Russell not out	49	6/95 7/121 8/127 9/130		

Bowling: Bicknell 10–1–24–3; Benjamin 7–1–19–1; Saqlain Mushtaq 11–0–24–2; B. C. Hollioake 12–0–39–2; A. J. Hollioake 9–0–23–0; Salisbury 6–0–28–2.

Umpires: R. Julian and N. T. Plews.

HAMPSHIRE v ESSEX

At Southampton, July 8. Hampshire won by three wickets. Toss: Hampshire.

The outcome was all but decided in the first five balls: Connor, 37 years old and handicapped by a persistent bad knee, left Essex, the holders, reeling at two for three. Forced to bat first on a drying wicket, Essex were unable to recover. They fell to 32 for six, as McLean took two wickets and Connor a fourth. Danny Law then mixed defence with some judicious hitting. But a target of 130 never looked like a challenge – until Hampshire, without the injured Smith, threw away a good start and subsided to 50 for four. Aymes and James, two more of Hampshire's thirty-somethings, put them in sight of a laboured victory and they finally overcame their nerves to end Essex's hopes of reaching their fourth Lord's final out of five.

Man of the Match: C. A. Connor.

Essex

*P. J. Prichard b Connor	0	M. C. Ilott lbw b Stephenson	8	
A. P. Grayson c Stephenson b McLean	13	A. P. Cowan b Stephenson	9	
N. Hussain c White b Connor	0	P. M. Such not out	3	
S. G. Law c Aymes b Connor	2	L-b 10, w 12, n-b 4	26	
R. C. Irani c Laney b McLean	5			
S. D. Peters b Connor	6	1/0 2/0 3/2	(41.4 overs) 129	
†R. J. Rollins c Aymes b Hartley	10	4/17 5/32 6/32		
D. R. Law c Udal b Hartley	47	7/79 8/95 9/114		

Bowling: Connor 8–3–13–4; McLean 10–0–33–2; Hartley 10.4–1–33–2; James 6–2–25–0; Stephenson 7–1–15–2.

Hampshire

J. S. Laney c Rollins b Irani	24	*S. D. Udal c Irani b Cowan	12
J. P. Stephenson c S. G. Law b Irani	10	N. A. M. McLean not out	4
G. W. White c Hussain b Irani	3	W 5, n-b 18	23
†A. N. Aymes c Peters b Irani	18		
P. R. Whitaker lbw b Cowan	1	1/33 2/42 3/49 (7 wkts, 41.1 overs)	132
K. D. James c Rollins b Ilott	24	4/50 5/99	
A. D. Mascarenhas not out	13	6/100 7/124	

P. J. Hartley and C. A. Connor did not bat.

Bowling: Ilott 12–5–20–1; Cowan 8.1–2–44–2; Irani 12–2–41–4; Such 6–1–12–0; D. R. Law 3–0–15–0.

Umpires: D. J. Constant and M. J. Kitchen.

LANCASHIRE v YORKSHIRE

At Manchester, July 8. Lancashire won by three wickets. Toss: Yorkshire.

Fairbrother knuckled down to score 76 not out from 165 balls and steered Lancashire to a tense victory in a low-scoring Roses contest, in which their big-match experience was significant. The game was played on the slow pitch that had seen England hold out for an epic draw two days earlier, and batting was never easy; Austin's trademark accuracy enabled him to concede just 12 runs from his 12 overs. With wickets falling steadily, Yorkshire were forced to rely on their bowlers for their runs. Hamilton and Gough, their two top scorers, came together at 82 for six to add 57. When it was his turn to bowl, Gough induced a Lancashire wobble – 132 for three became 133 for six – but Fairbrother weathered the storm and nicked the match award from him.

Man of the Match: N. H. Fairbrother.

Yorkshire

*D. Byas b Wasim Akram	11	C. E. W. Silverwood not out	12
M. P. Vaughan b Wasim Akram	8	R. D. Stemp b Martin	0
D. S. Lehmann run out	1	P. M. Hutchison not out	4
A. McGrath lbw b Wasim Akram	25	L-b 5, w 5, n-b 14	24
B. Parker b Austin	2		
†R. J. Blakey b Watkinson	10	1/16 2/19 3/32 (9 wkts, 60 overs)	178
G. M. Hamilton b Austin	39	4/42 5/60 6/82	
D. Gough lbw b Martin	42	7/139 8/165 9/165	

Bowling: Wasim Akram 12–0–50–3; Martin 12–2–37–2; Austin 12–8–12–2; Yates 12–2–39–0; Watkinson 12–1–35–1.

Lancashire

M. A. Atherton c Blakey b Silverwood	0	†W. K. Hegg b Gough	15
A. Flintoff c Byas b Gough	12	I. D. Austin not out	2
J. P. Crawley c Lehmann b Silverwood	10	L-b 7, w 13, n-b 4	24
N. H. Fairbrother not out	76		
G. D. Lloyd c Byas b Gough	40	1/2 2/16 3/32 (7 wkts, 57 overs)	179
M. Watkinson b Gough	0	4/132 5/132	
*Wasim Akram c Hamilton b Lehmann	0	6/133 7/172	

G. Yates and P. J. Martin did not bat.

Bowling: Gough 12–1–50–4; Silverwood 12–1–23–2; Hutchison 2–0–6–0; Hamilton 8–2–14–0; Stemp 10–1–37–0; Vaughan 6–2–28–0; Lehmann 7–2–14–1.

Umpires: R. A. White and A. G. T. Whitehead.

MIDDLESEX v DURHAM

At Southgate, July 8. Middlesex won by two wickets. Toss: Middlesex.

Defying a hopeless position, Middlesex gained an improbable win thanks to the tail holding their nerve while the bowlers lost theirs. On a pitch that never encouraged quick scoring, Durham's 240, built around a painstaking 73 from Speak, looked enough, especially when none of Middlesex's specialist batsmen was able to force the pace. The Durham bowlers began well, with Saggers the best. Middlesex slumped to 62 for four, then 129 for seven in the 44th over. But Dutch, making amends for his expensive bowling, and Johnson rose to the task, lashing 66 together in just seven overs. Dutch hit 49 off 53 balls and Johnson 45 from 27.

Man of the Match: R. L. Johnson.

Durham

J. J. B. Lewis lbw b A. R. C. Fraser	18		J. Wood not out	8
J. E. Morris c A. R. C. Fraser b Johnson	23		N. Killeen not out	1
N. J. Speak b A. G. J. Fraser	73			
*D. C. Boon c Johnson b Weekes	29		L-b 8, w 4, n-b 6	18
P. D. Collingwood b A. R. C. Fraser	23			
†M. P. Speight b Dutch	32		1/27 2/51 3/111 (8 wkts, 60 overs)	240
N. C. Phillips run out	1		4/168 5/188 6/192	
M. M. Betts c Ramprakash b Johnson	14		7/227 8/233	

M. J. Saggers did not bat.

Bowling: A. R. C. Fraser 12–2–39–2; Johnson 12–2–38–2; A. G. J. Fraser 12–2–39–1; Dutch 12–0–67–1; Weekes 12–0–49–1.

Middlesex

M. W. Gatting b Saggers	17		A. G. J. Fraser b Killeen	18
J. L. Langer c Speight b Betts	47		R. L. Johnson not out	45
*M. R. Ramprakash c Betts b Saggers	9			
O. A. Shah run out	0		B 1, l-b 12, w 6, n-b 2	21
P. N. Weekes b Killeen	4			
†K. R. Brown lbw b Betts	26		1/34 2/54 3/54 (8 wkts, 58.4 overs)	244
J. C. Pooley run out	8		4/62 5/110 6/121	
K. P. Dutch not out	49		7/129 8/178	

A. R. C. Fraser did not bat.

Bowling: Betts 12–2–45–2; Wood 11–1–44–0; Saggers 9.4–1–42–2; Killeen 12–0–46–2; Phillips 11–0–43–0; Collingwood 3–0–11–0.

Umpires: K. E. Palmer and D. R. Shepherd.

NOTTINGHAMSHIRE v SOMERSET

At Nottingham, July 8. Nottinghamshire won by one wicket. Toss: Somerset.

Tolley struck a crucial 77 to wrest the initiative from Somerset and set up a thrilling finish, Nottinghamshire eventually scrambling home with one wicket and three balls to spare. It was a magnificent result in an otherwise bleak season for them. Somerset had amassed a respectable total thanks to 61 from Harden. Chasing 256, Nottinghamshire were in trouble at 103 for five. Tolley, dropped twice early on, then began to chance his arm. He gained valuable support from Strang and Franks and, although Caddick took two wickets with the last two balls of the 59th over, did enough to ensure a home win.

Man of the Match: C. M. Tolley.

Somerset

M. Burns c Dowman b Tolley	29	A. R. K. Pierson b Franks		9
†P. C. L. Holloway c Gallian b Franks. .	22	Mushtaq Ahmed not out		8
R. J. Harden c Evans b Dowman	61	A. R. Caddick not out.		2
M. N. Lathwell c and b Bates	6		B 1, l-b 6, w 1, n-b 2	10
*P. D. Bowler c Gallian b Strang	43			
K. A. Parsons c Strang b Evans	42	1/48 2/56 3/73	(9 wkts, 60 overs)	255
M. E. Trescothick c Evans.	22	4/162 5/177 6/230		
G. D. Rose c Gallian b Franks	1	7/233 8/236 9/249		

Bowling: Evans 10–0–51–2; Franks 9–1–40–3; Tolley 12–3–26–1; Bates 12–0–47–1; Strang 11–0–61–1; Dowman 6–1–23–1.

Nottinghamshire

M. P. Dowman lbw b Caddick	6	†C. M. W. Read b Caddick		8
J. E. R. Gallian c Burns		K. P. Evans not out		2
b Mushtaq Ahmed	50	R. T. Bates not out.		0
R. T. Robinson lbw b Trescothick	11			
*P. Johnson c Bowler b Trescothick	15		B 1, l-b 8, w 5, n-b 9	23
G. F. Archer b Mushtaq Ahmed	0			
C. M. Tolley c Harden b Caddick	77	1/8 2/37 3/65	(9 wkts, 59.3 overs)	256
P. A. Strang c Bowler b Caddick	40	4/74 5/103 6/171		
P. J. Franks run out	24	7/234 8/254 9/254		

Bowling: Caddick 12–2–63–4; Rose 11.3–2–60–0; Trescothick 9–1–49–2; Mushtaq Ahmed 12–2–23–2; Pierson 11–0–32–0; Parsons 4–0–20–0.

Umpires: G. I. Burgess and B. Dudleston.

SCOTLAND v DERBYSHIRE

At Raeburn Place, Edinburgh, July 8. Derbyshire won by seven wickets. Toss: Derbyshire. County debut: R. M. S. Weston.

A dour innings of 44 from Stanger allowed Scotland to salvage self-respect, but could only delay the inevitable defeat. Stanger began his fightback with the score on three for four, after left-armer Dean had removed three batsmen for ducks. Things got worse – 19 for six – before they got better; but the gentler pace of Barnett and Clarke let the pressure slip slightly, and runs began to trickle from the bat. Stanger stayed 49 overs to guide Scotland past three figures. Even on a pitch of variable bounce and considerable movement, a total of 113 was inadequate, and Derbyshire managed it with few alarms. Robin Weston hit an assured 43 not out for his new county; he was released by Durham in 1997.

Man of the Match: K. J. Dean.

Scotland

S. T. Crawley c Slater b Cork	2	P. D. Steindl run out.		18
B. M. W. Patterson c Barnett b Dean. .	0	K. L. P. Sheridan lbw b Clarke		3
†D. R. Lockhart c Clarke b Dean	0	Asim Butt not out		9
M. J. Smith c Krikken b Dean	0			
*G. Salmond run out	12		L-b 8, w 5, n-b 2	15
I. M. Stanger c Dean b Clarke	44			
C. M. Wright lbw b Cork	0	1/3 2/3 3/3 4/3 5/18	(52.4 overs)	113
J. G. Williamson st Krikken b Barnett . .	10	6/19 7/45 8/89 9/95		

Bowling: Cork 12–4–28–2; Dean 10–5–13–3; Clarke 11.4–1–29–2; Barnett 9–1–24–1; Roberts 10–4–11–0.

Derbyshire

M. J. Slater b Asim Butt	0	*D. G. Cork not out	2
K. J. Barnett b Sheridan	49	L-b 3, w 4, n-b 2	9
R. M. S. Weston not out	43		
M. E. Cassar c Salmond b Stanger	11	1/4 2/89 3/104 (3 wkts, 39.2 overs)	114

B. L. Spendlove, T. A. Tweats, V. P. Clarke, †K. M. Krikken, G. M. Roberts and K. J. Dean did not bat.

Bowling: Asim Butt 10–3–18–1; Wright 8–2–26–0; Steindl 6–0–17–0; Sheridan 8–2–24–1; Stanger 7.2–0–26–1.

Umpires: J. H. Hampshire and B. Leadbeater.

WARWICKSHIRE v KENT

At Birmingham, July 8. Warwickshire won by 167 runs. Toss: Kent.

The highlight of Warwickshire's easy win was a magnificent 133 from Lara, his first century in the NatWest. Out of form for most of the season, he was lucky to survive a testing early spell from Headley. But a calculated assault on Hooper, his West Indies team-mate, yielded 25 in two overs. It was enough for Lara to get his eye in, and thereafter he ran amok. His fifty came from 83 balls; his next 83 from another 75. He was fourth out at 240, leaving Penney enough time to take the total beyond 300, and the game effectively beyond Kent. Welch clinched the win by removing four of their top five. These two teams had now met in this competition seven times in 11 seasons; it was Warwickshire's sixth successive victory, the last five of them coming at Edgbaston.

Man of the Match: B. C. Lara.

Warwickshire

N. V. Knight c Wells b Headley	13	A. F. Giles c Willis b Hooper	5
N. M. K. Smith b Headley	1		
*B. C. Lara c Ealham b Fleming	133	L-b 15, w 15, n-b 4	34
D. L. Hemp c Willis b Ealham	59		—
T. L. Penney not out	45	1/8 2/28 3/197 (6 wkts, 60 overs)	303
D. R. Brown run out	13	4/240 5/286 6/303	

G. Welch, †K. J. Piper, G. C. Small and E. S. H. Giddins did not bat.

Bowling: Headley 12–2–48–2; McCague 10–0–45–0; Ealham 9–0–22–1; Fleming 12–1–60–1; Hooper 9–0–60–1; Phillips 8–1–53–0.

Kent

D. P. Fulton c Knight b Welch	2	M. J. McCague b Giles	19
R. W. T. Key b Brown	6	B. J. Phillips not out	9
*T. R. Ward c Lara b Welch	9	D. W. Headley c Piper b Small	2
C. L. Hooper lbw b Welch	38	L-b 8, w 5	13
A. P. Wells c Giddins b Welch	24		—
M. A. Ealham c Piper b Giddins	6	1/6 2/20 3/26 (42.1 overs)	136
M. V. Fleming b Giddins	5	4/81 5/90 6/98	
†S. C. Willis c Small b Giles	3	7/102 8/114 9/131	

Bowling: Welch 12–2–31–4; Giddins 10–2–23–2; Brown 5–1–5–1; Small 8.1–0–40–1; Smith 3–0–11–0; Giles 4–0–18–2.

Umpires: J. C. Balderstone and R. Palmer.

QUARTER-FINALS

LANCASHIRE v NOTTINGHAMSHIRE

At Manchester, July 28. Lancashire won by six wickets. Toss: Lancashire.

Atherton, having batted England to victory at Trent Bridge the previous day, found enough reserves of stamina to produce a patient 76 from 130 balls and guide Lancashire to a six-wicket win. Nottinghamshire's innings had begun well: Gallian, Atherton's former county opening partner, marked his return to Old Trafford with a solid 83. He shared a century stand with Dowman, but both departed to fine catches by Chilton at backward point. And, with Chapple taking five for 57, Nottinghamshire's innings never fulfilled its early promise. Chilton, playing because Fairbrother was injured, then helped Atherton lay the foundations for victory with an opening partnership of 96. Consistent batting down the order saw Lancashire home with 13 balls to spare after they had been docked two overs for a slow bowling rate.

Man of the Match: M. A. Atherton.

Nottinghamshire

J. E. R. Gallian c Chilton b Chapple	83	†C. M. W. Read not out	7
U. Afzaal b Chapple	13	K. P. Evans run out	15
M. P. Dowman c Chilton		R. T. Bates not out	0
b Wasim Akram	47		
*P. Johnson c Hegg b Chapple	13	B 1, l-b 6, w 14, n-b 6	27
G. F. Archer c Hegg b Chapple	12		
C. M. Tolley c Crawley b Chapple	13	1/45 2/145 3/164 (9 wkts, 60 overs) 249
P. J. Franks run out	8	4/181 5/201 6/206
P. A. Strang c Wasim Akram b Martin	11	7/218 8/227 9/248

Bowling: Wasim Akram 11–0–43–1; Martin 11–0–52–1; Austin 12–1–31–0; Chapple 12–0–57–5; Yates 12–0–48–0; Flintoff 2–0–11–0.

Lancashire

M. J. Chilton b Strang	41	*Wasim Akram not out	37
M. A. Atherton c Read b Evans	76	B 3, l-b 9, w 5, n-b 8	25
J. P. Crawley c Johnson b Bates	20		
A. Flintoff c Bates b Tolley	27	1/96 2/136 (4 wkts, 55.5 overs) 255
G. D. Lloyd not out	29	3/174 4/193

†W. K. Hegg, G. Yates, I. D. Austin, G. Chapple and P. J. Martin did not bat.

Bowling: Evans 11–1–40–1; Franks 11–0–51–0; Bates 10.5–0–68–1; Tolley 11–2–50–1; Strang 12–2–34–1.

Umpires: H. D. Bird and G. I. Burgess.

LEICESTERSHIRE v WARWICKSHIRE

At Leicester, July 28. Leicestershire won by eight wickets. Toss: Leicestershire.

Warwickshire's hopes were crushed by a devastating spell from Mullally, who took a competition-best five for 18. On a greenish pitch and under heavy skies, he bowled beautifully, finding movement off the seam and extravagant swing. Lewis gave him sterling support and, thanks to superb catching and poor batting, Warwickshire found themselves 36 for seven, still three short of the NatWest's worst, set by Ireland at Hove in 1985. An erratic first over by Simmons, including five wides and two no-balls, decreased the pressure, and helped Piper and Welch concoct a partnership of 52. But Warwickshire succumbed for below 100 for the first time in the competition; this left Nottinghamshire as the only first-class county never dismissed for double figures. Sutcliffe and Smith eased Leicestershire towards their second semi-final of 1998. As Lara left the field, he was jeered and heckled by some angry Warwickshire fans.

Man of the Match: A. D. Mullally.

Warwickshire

N. V. Knight c Lewis b Mullally	0	†K. J. Piper lbw b Lewis	19
N. M. K. Smith b Mullally	4	M. A. Sheikh c Nixon b Wells	5
*B. C. Lara c Nixon b Mullally	14	E. S. H. Giddins not out	0
D. L. Hemp c Simmons b Lewis	0		
T. L. Penney c Simmons b Lewis	1	L-b 1, w 14, n-b 6	21
D. P. Ostler c Lewis b Mullally	7		
A. F. Giles c Lewis b Mullally	2	1/1 2/15 3/16 4/19 5/26 (36 overs) 98
G. Welch c Maddy b Wells	25	6/29 7/36 8/88 9/96

Bowling: Mullally 12–3–18–5; Lewis 10–1–25–3; Simmons 5–0–32–0; Wells 6–1–18–2; Williamson 3–1–4–0.

Leicestershire

D. L. Maddy b Giddins	1
I. J. Sutcliffe not out	39
B. F. Smith c Penney b Giddins	30
P. V. Simmons not out	16
L-b 2, w 13	15

1/2 2/45   (2 wkts, 36.2 overs) 101

V. J. Wells, A. Habib, †P. A. Nixon, *C. C. Lewis, D. Williamson, A. D. Mullally and T. J. Mason did not bat.

Bowling: Giddins 9–3–19–2; Welch 9–3–20–0; Sheikh 11–2–38–0; Hemp 1–0–3–0; Giles 6.2–1–19–0.

Umpires: T. E. Jesty and J. W. Lloyds.

MIDDLESEX v HAMPSHIRE

At Lord's, July 28. Hampshire won by 144 runs. Toss: Middlesex.

Accomplished batting by Hampshire took them into the semi-finals for the first time in seven years and ruled out a grand finale to Gatting's career. Middlesex never got into gear: they were sloppy in the field, and the bowling fell apart towards the end. Although Fraser was his usual self, Johnson was hit for 18 from one over and Langer 36 from three, as Hampshire added 112 from their last ten. Aymes equalled his highest NatWest score, set five weeks earlier, and Mascarenhas and McLean joined in happily. By the 18th over, Middlesex were 65 for five. Langer and Dutch then put on 70, but it was a lost cause. Work on the construction of the new media centre was halted when the din threatened play.

Man of the Match: A. N. Aymes.

Hampshire

J. S. Laney c Gatting b Fraser	47	N. A. M. McLean not out	16
J. P. Stephenson st Brown b Dutch	21		
*R. A. Smith b Batt	7	L-b 12, w 11, n-b 10	33
G. W. White c Brown b Langer	69		
†A. N. Aymes not out	73	1/70 2/82 3/98 (5 wkts, 60 overs) 295
A. D. Mascarenhas c Dutch b Weekes	29	4/238 5/276

K. D. James, S. D. Udal, P. J. Hartley and C. A. Connor did not bat.

Bowling: Fraser 12–3–25–1; Bloomfield 7–0–45–0; Batt 8–0–37–1; Langer 5–0–45–1; Dutch 12–0–38–1; Johnson 9–0–56–0; Weekes 7–0–37–1.

Middlesex

M. W. Gatting lbw b Connor	14	C. J. Batt run out	0
J. L. Langer c Udal b Mascarenhas	57	A. R. C. Fraser not out	3
*M. R. Ramprakash lbw b McLean	5	T. F. Bloomfield b McLean	0
O. A. Shah c Aymes b Connor	7	L-b 5, w 6, n-b 2	13
P. N. Weekes lbw b Hartley	9		
†K. R. Brown c Aymes b Hartley	4	1/16 2/22 3/36	(42.4 overs) 151
K. P. Dutch c Mascarenhas b Udal	35	4/52 5/65 6/135	
R. L. Johnson c and b Udal	4	7/146 8/146 9/151	

Bowling: Connor 7–1–29–2; McLean 7.4–1–23–2; Hartley 7–0–18–2; Mascarenhas 12–0–37–1; Stephenson 4–0–28–0; Udal 5–1–11–2.

Umpires: A. A. Jones and P. Willey.

SURREY v DERBYSHIRE

At The Oval, July 28. Derbyshire won by five wickets. Toss: Surrey.

Derbyshire won a convincing victory to overcome the favourites – and their delaying tactics, perceived by some as blatant gamesmanship. Surrey's illustrious top order failed to deliver, none of them reaching 30: Stewart and Butcher, perhaps, could blame the exertions of their Test victory at Trent Bridge the previous day. It needed a gutsy innings from a bowler, Bicknell, to set Derbyshire even the moderate target of 218. Slater and Barnett then shared an opening stand of 162, a county record, until Barnett was run out by a direct hit from Brown. The innings lost momentum briefly as Surrey began time-wasting – one over from off-spinner Saqlain Mushtaq took five minutes – but Krikken calmed Derbyshire's nerves by hitting successive balls to the mid-wicket boundary.

Man of the Match: K. J. Barnett.

Surrey

M. A. Butcher c Krikken b Cork	8	M. P. Bicknell not out	48
I. J. Ward run out	27	I. D. K. Salisbury not out	34
†A. J. Stewart c Cork b Dean	3	L-b 7, w 9, n-b 14	30
J. D. Ratcliffe c Spendlove b DeFreitas	11		
A. D. Brown lbw b Barnett	29	1/17 2/26 3/41	(7 wkts, 60 overs) 217
*A. J. Hollioake c Cork b Barnett	9	4/89 5/102	
B. C. Hollioake c Weston b Dean	18	6/109 7/139	

Saqlain Mushtaq and J. E. Benjamin did not bat.

Bowling: Cork 12–4–32–1; Dean 12–1–38–2; DeFreitas 12–1–55–1; Clarke 12–1–27–0; Barnett 12–1–58–2.

Derbyshire

M. J. Slater c Butcher b Saqlain Mushtaq	82	†K. M. Krikken not out	8
K. J. Barnett run out	60		
R. M. S. Weston lbw b Bicknell	2	L-b 7, w 15, n-b 8	30
M. E. Cassar c Stewart b B. C. Hollioake	11		
B. L. Spendlove c Stewart b Salisbury	14	1/162 2/170 3/174	(5 wkts, 54.5 overs) 218
*D. G. Cork not out	11	4/188 5/210	

P. A. J. DeFreitas, V. P. Clarke, G. M. Roberts and K. J. Dean did not bat.

Bowling: Bicknell 12–0–56–1; Benjamin 7–0–36–0; Saqlain Mushtaq 12–3–33–1; B. C. Hollioake 7–0–32–1; A. J. Hollioake 6–0–24–0; Salisbury 10.5–2–30–1.

Umpires: V. A. Holder and J. F. Steele.

SEMI-FINALS

HAMPSHIRE v LANCASHIRE

At Southampton, August 11. Lancashire won by 43 runs. Toss: Hampshire.

The match was more one-sided than the winning margin suggests. Pursuing a target of 253, Hampshire were reduced to 28 for five in the 17th over by the pace and movement of the Lancashire attack, and the capacity 4,500-strong crowd were deprived of a contest. James and Mascarenhas prevented a rout, adding 104, a county sixth-wicket record, but for all their valour it was an irrelevance. Austin accounted for them both in a miserly three for 25. Earlier, there were three wickets apiece for Mascarenhas and for Connor, who had been on crutches the previous day after his hip seized up; only painkillers kept him going. Their determination saw Lancashire spiral from a prosperous 164 for one to lose their last nine for 88. Crawley, carefully compiling 79, and Fairbrother, with a less inhibited 58 (ended by a spectacular catch at short cover), had put on 116 for the second wicket, also a county record.

Man of the Match: A. D. Mascarenhas.

Lancashire

M. A. Atherton c Aymes b James	17	G. Yates b Connor	6	
*J. P. Crawley c Udal b Mascarenhas	79	G. Chapple run out	6	
N. H. Fairbrother c Stephenson b Hartley	58	P. J. Martin not out	5	
A. Flintoff c Aymes b Mascarenhas	8	B 1, l-b 8, w 12, n-b 6	27	
G. D. Lloyd c White b McLean	10			
M. Watkinson c White b Mascarenhas	7	1/48 2/164 3/176	(60 overs)	252
†W. K. Hegg c James b Connor	28	4/188 5/198 6/200		
I. D. Austin c Connor	1	7/209 8/219 9/244		

Bowling: Connor 12–2–31–3; McLean 12–1–50–1; Hartley 8–0–35–1; James 7–0–24–1; Stephenson 5–0–30–0; Udal 8–0–45–0; Mascarenhas 8–0–28–3.

Hampshire

J. S. Laney b Austin	1	S. D. Udal not out	11	
J. P. Stephenson lbw b Martin	5	P. J. Hartley lbw b Chapple	0	
G. W. White c Hegg b Flintoff	8	C. A. Connor not out	2	
*R. A. Smith c Hegg b Martin	1	L-b 3, w 12, n-b 2	17	
†A. N. Aymes c Hegg b Chapple	3			
A. D. Mascarenhas c Chapple b Austin	73	1/8 2/10 3/13	(9 wkts, 60 overs)	209
K. D. James c and b Austin	52	4/23 5/28 6/132		
N. A. M. McLean c Flintoff b Martin	36	7/176 8/203 9/205		

Bowling: Martin 11–1–54–3; Austin 12–3–25–3; Chapple 8–2–39–2; Flintoff 5–1–18–1; Yates 12–0–31–0; Watkinson 12–0–39–0.

Umpires: J. C. Balderstone and J. W. Holder.

LEICESTERSHIRE v DERBYSHIRE

At Leicester, August 12. Derbyshire won by three runs. Toss: Leicestershire.

Leicestershire could hardly believe their failure to reach a second Lord's final of the season. Cruising to victory at 243 for three, needing just 56 off 11 overs, they did a Devon Loch in sight of the finishing line to lose by three runs. The crucial wicket was that of Simmons, who had a big heave at Cork and was bowled ten short of his century, ending a 97-run stand with Habib. Dean and Barnett, with his slow seamers, then bowled so well that Leicestershire lost vital momentum. They needed 11 off the last over, ten if they did not lose a wicket, and three off the last ball, which Nixon missed. The bowler was the former Leicestershire player Clarke, who looked far cooler under pressure than many better-known participants. It was an astonishing comeback for Derbyshire, whose batsmen had fought well after being 58 for three. There were fifties from two youngsters, Weston and Spendlove, backed up by the experienced Cork and DeFreitas.

Man of the Match: D. G. Cork.

Derbyshire

M. J. Slater c Nixon b Williamson	....	30	I. D. Blackwell run out	4
K. J. Barnett c Simmons b Ormond	....	8	V. P. Clarke not out	10
R. M. S. Weston c Smith b Mullally	...	56	L-b 14, w 17	31
M. E. Cassar b Wells		0		
B. L. Spendlove b Simmons	....	58	1/21 2/56 3/58 (7 wkts, 60 overs)	298
*D. G. Cork not out	....	61	4/178 5/182	
P. A. J. DeFreitas b Maddy	....	40	6/257 7/280	

†K. M. Krikken and K. J. Dean did not bat.

Bowling: Mullally 12–1–34–1; Ormond 10–1–58–1; Williamson 11–2–68–1; Wells 12–0–45–1; Brimson 7–0–26–0; Simmons 6–0–35–1; Maddy 2–0–18–1.

Leicestershire

V. J. Wells run out	....	3	†P. A. Nixon not out	6
D. L. Maddy c Clarke b DeFreitas	....	30	D. Williamson not out	19
B. F. Smith c and b Dean	....	60	L-b 6, w 10, n-b 6	22
P. V. Simmons b Cork	....	90		
A. Habib run out	....	56	1/8 2/53 3/146 (6 wkts, 60 overs)	295
*C. C. Lewis c Clarke b Dean	....	9	4/243 5/268 6/269	

J. Ormond, A. D. Mullally and M. T. Brimson did not bat.

Bowling: Cork 12–0–47–1; Dean 12–1–63–2; DeFreitas 12–0–65–1; Clarke 10–0–48–0; Barnett 8–0–33–0; Blackwell 6–0–33–0.

Umpires: N. T. Plews and D. R. Shepherd.

FINAL

DERBYSHIRE v LANCASHIRE

At Lord's, September 5, 6. Lancashire won by nine wickets. Toss: Lancashire.

Lancashire won what was arguably the most one-sided final in the history of a competition that specialises in them. Rain prevented any play before 4.30 p.m., but even so the game was concluded, in front of a sparse crowd, by Sunday lunch. Lancashire lost just one wicket in attaining their target of 109. Only 67 overs were bowled in the match. This is nothing new; the 1996 final was the shortest on record until 1997, and this was shorter still. The 1999 final is scheduled to be held a week earlier, on the August Bank Holiday weekend.

Lancashire were overwhelming favourites and might still have won whatever. But the winners have batted second in 12 of the past 13 finals and the damage, to Derbyshire's morale if nothing else, had been done when Wasim Akram won the toss. Early autumn dankness and the time the pitch had spent under cover always made it likely that seam would hold sway over bat from the start, even though Derbyshire's terrible collapse eventually gave them the advantage of bowling in morning conditions.

The surprise was that Lancashire, with all their experience of such occasions, allowed Derbyshire a dream start. The new-ball bowling of Wasim Akram and Martin was uncontrollably tense and wild, and the openers had 70 on the board after 18 overs. Slater, who had flown to Brisbane the previous week and returned specifically for the final, had just taken ten off two balls from Chapple – a six driven over extra cover and a four pulled through mid-wicket – and expectation had been turned upside down.

For Derbyshire, that was as good as it got. Their nemesis, in the rotund, metronomic form of Austin, was already operating at the Pavilion End. He and Martin, visibly more relaxed in his second spell, were moving the ball wickedly. Austin had Slater lbw for 34, to precipitate an astounding collapse that saw four wickets fall for one run and, ten runs later, another three for none: 70 for nought became 81 for seven. In a six-over spell, Martin took four for seven. But

Austin hardly bowled a bad ball and his figures of three for 14 from ten overs were distorted by
four overthrows: he won the match award from David Gower. As Wasim strained for the *coup
de grâce* on the Sunday morning, some lusty blows from Clarke hauled Derbyshire past 100, but
their total of 108 was the lowest by a team batting first in the final. Lancashire themselves had
scored the previous worst, 118 against Kent in 1974.

To steal a miraculous victory, Derbyshire needed instant wickets to instil doubt in the batsmen.
They should have had one in the first over when Atherton was dropped at slip, and had to wait
until the tenth before Cork eventually got his man, removing Atherton's off stump with a superb
delivery. Crawley, with a confident, untroubled fifty that included 11 fours, and Fairbrother, playing
his tenth Lord's final, saw Lancashire home with an unbroken stand of 81. – MIKE SELVEY.

Man of the Match: I. D. Austin.   *Attendance*: 24,023: *receipts* £801,401.

Close of play: Derbyshire 92-7 (32.1 overs) (D. G. Cork 4*, K. M. Krikken 1*).

Derbyshire

M. J. Slater lbw b Austin 34	V. P. Clarke b Wasim Akram 13
K. J. Barnett b Martin. 23	K. J. Dean not out 0
A. S. Rollins c Flintoff b Martin 1	
R. M. S. Weston b Austin 0	L-b 5, w 7, n-b 8 20
M. E. Cassar c Chapple b Austin 6	
B. L. Spendlove lbw b Martin 4	1/70 (1) 2/70 (2) 3/71 (4) (36.4 overs) 108
*D. G. Cork c Hegg b Wasim Akram . . 5	4/71 (3) 5/81 (6) 6/81 (5)
P. A. J. DeFreitas lbw b Martin 0	7/81 (8) 8/94 (7)
†K. M. Krikken c Hegg b Flintoff 2	9/102 (9) 10/108 (10)

Bowling: Wasim Akram 8.4–1–39–2; Martin 9–2–19–4; Chapple 6–0–27–0; Austin 10–5–14–3;
Flintoff 3–1–4–1.

Lancashire

M. A. Atherton b Cork 10	
J. P. Crawley not out 53	
N. H. Fairbrother not out. 38	
L-b 2, w 4, n-b 2 8	

1/28 (1)   (1 wkt, 30.2 overs) 109

G. D. Lloyd, A. Flintoff, *Wasim Akram, †W. K. Hegg, I. D. Austin, G. Yates, G. Chapple and
P. J. Martin did not bat.

Bowling: Cork 10.2–4–24–1; Dean 5–0–38–0; DeFreitas 9–3–13–0; Cassar 6–0–32–0.

Umpires: K. E. Palmer and G. Sharp.

MOST APPEARANCES IN A LORD'S FINAL

	NatWest Trophy/ Gillette Cup	Benson and Hedges Cup	Total	First and most recent appearances
N. H. Fairbrother (Lancashire).	4	6	10	1984-1998
D. L. Underwood (Kent)	5	5	10	1967-1986
D. P. Hughes (Lancashire)	7	2	9	1970-1990
M. Watkinson (Lancashire).	3	6	9	1986-1996
M. A. Atherton (Lancashire). . .	3	5	8	1990-1998
I. D. Austin (Lancashire). . . .	3	5	8	1990-1998
J. E. Emburey (Middlesex)†	5	3	8	1977-1996
W. K. Hegg (Lancashire)	3	5	8	1990-1998
A. J. Lamb (Northamptonshire). .	6	2	8	1979-1995
J. Simmons (Lancashire)	7	1	8	1970-1986

† *Includes one appearance for Northamptonshire.*

NATWEST TROPHY RECORDS

(Including Gillette Cup, 1963-80)

65-over games in 1963; 60-over games 1964-98, to be reduced to 50 overs in 1999.

Batting

Highest individual scores: 206, A. I. Kallicharran, Warwickshire v Oxfordshire, Birmingham, 1984; 201, V. J. Wells, Leicestershire v Berkshire, Leicester, 1996; 180*, T. M. Moody, Worcestershire v Surrey, The Oval, 1994; 177, C. G Greenidge, Hampshire v Glamorgan, Southampton, 1975; 177, A. J. Wright, Gloucestershire v Scotland, Bristol, 1997; 172*, G. A. Hick, Worcestershire v Devon, Worcester, 1987; 165*, V. P. Terry, Hampshire v Berkshire, Southampton, 1985; 162*, C. J. Tavaré, Somerset v Devon, Torquay, 1990; 162*, I. V. A. Richards, Glamorgan v Oxfordshire, Swansea, 1993.

Most runs: 2,547, G. A. Gooch; 2,148, M. W. Gatting; 2,106, R. A. Smith; 1,998, A. J. Lamb; 1,950, D. L. Amiss.

Fastest hundred: G. D. Rose off 36 balls, Somerset v Devon, Torquay, 1990.

Most hundreds: 8, R. A. Smith; 7, C. L. Smith; 6, G. A. Gooch; 5, D. I. Gower, I. V. A. Richards and G. M. Turner.

Highest totals: 413 for four, Somerset v Devon, Torquay, 1990; 406 for five, Leicestershire v Berkshire, Leicester, 1996; 404 for three, Worcestershire v Devon, Worcester, 1987; 392 for five, Warwickshire v Oxfordshire, Birmingham, 1984; 386 for five, Essex v Wiltshire, Chelmsford, 1988; 384 for six, Kent v Berkshire, Finchampstead, 1994; 384 for nine, Sussex v Ireland, Belfast, 1996; 373 for seven, Glamorgan v Bedfordshire, Cardiff, 1998; 372 for five, Lancashire v Gloucestershire, Manchester, 1990; 371 for four, Hampshire v Glamorgan, Southampton, 1975. *In the final:* 322 for five, Warwickshire v Sussex, Lord's, 1993.

Highest total by a minor county: 305 for nine, Durham v Glamorgan, Darlington, 1991.

Highest total by a side batting first and losing: 327 for eight (60 overs), Derbyshire v Sussex, Derby, 1997. *In the final:* 321 for six (60 overs), Sussex v Warwickshire, 1993.

Highest totals by a side batting second: 350 (59.5 overs), Surrey lost to Worcestershire, The Oval, 1994; 339 for nine (60 overs), Somerset lost to Warwickshire, Birmingham, 1995; 329 for five (59.2 overs), Sussex beat Derbyshire, Derby, 1997; 326 for nine (60 overs), Hampshire lost to Leicestershire, Leicester, 1987; 322 for five (60 overs), Warwickshire beat Sussex, Lord's, 1993 (*in the final*); 319 for nine (59.5 overs), Essex beat Lancashire, Chelmsford, 1992.

Lowest completed totals: 39 (26.4 overs), Ireland v Sussex, Hove, 1985; 41 (20 overs), Cambridgeshire v Buckinghamshire, Cambridge, 1972; 41 (19.4 overs), Middlesex v Essex, Westcliff, 1972; 41 (36.1 overs), Shropshire v Essex, Wellington, 1974. *In the final:* 57 (27.2 overs), Essex v Lancashire, 1996.

Lowest total by a side batting first and winning: 98 (56.2 overs), Worcestershire v Durham, Chester-le-Street, 1968.

Shortest innings: 10.1 overs (60 for one), Worcestershire v Lancashire, Worcester, 1963.

Matches rearranged on a reduced number of overs are excluded from the above.

Record partnerships for each wicket

311	for 1st	A. J. Wright and N. J. Trainor, Gloucestershire v Scotland at Bristol	1997
286	for 2nd	I. S. Anderson and A. Hill, Derbyshire v Cornwall at Derby	1986
309*	for 3rd	T. S. Curtis and T. M. Moody, Worcestershire v Surrey at The Oval . .	1994
234*	for 4th	D. Lloyd and C. H. Lloyd, Lancashire v Gloucestershire at Manchester .	1978
166	for 5th	M. A. Lynch and G. R. J. Roope, Surrey v Durham at The Oval	1982
178	for 6th	J. P. Crawley and I. D. Austin, Lancashire v Sussex at Hove	1997

160*	for 7th	C. J. Richards and I. R. Payne, Surrey v Lincolnshire at Sleaford	....	1983
112	for 8th	A. L. Penberthy and J. E. Emburey, Northamptonshire v Lancashire at Manchester		1996
87	for 9th	M. A. Nash and A. E. Cordle, Glamorgan v Lincolnshire at Swansea	..	1974
81	for 10th	S. Turner and R. E. East, Essex v Yorkshire at Leeds	....	1982

Bowling

Most wickets: 81, G. G. Arnold; 80, C. A. Connor; 79, J. Simmons.

Best bowling (12 overs unless stated): eight for 21 (10.1 overs), M. A. Holding, Derbyshire v Sussex, Hove, 1988; eight for 31 (11.1 overs), D. L. Underwood, Kent v Scotland, Edinburgh, 1987; seven for 15, A. L. Dixon, Kent v Surrey, The Oval, 1967; seven for 15 (9.3 overs), R. P. Lefebvre, Somerset v Devon, Torquay, 1990; seven for 19, N. V. Radford, Worcestershire v Bedfordshire, Bedford, 1991; seven for 27 (9.5 overs), D. Gough, Yorkshire v Ireland, Leeds, 1997; seven for 30, P. J. Sainsbury, Hampshire v Norfolk, Southampton, 1965; seven for 32, S. P. Davis, Durham v Lancashire, Chester-le-Street, 1983; seven for 33, R. D. Jackman, Surrey v Yorkshire, Harrogate, 1970; seven for 35 (10.1 overs), D. E. Malcolm, Derbyshire v Northamptonshire, Derby, 1997; seven for 37, N. A. Mallender, Northamptonshire v Worcestershire, Northampton, 1984. *In the final:* six for 18 (6.2 overs), G. Chapple, Lancashire v Essex, 1996.

Most economical analysis: 12–9–3–1, J. Simmons, Lancashire v Suffolk, Bury St Edmunds, 1985.

Most expensive analysis: 12–0–107–2, C. C. Lovell, Cornwall v Warwickshire, St Austell, 1996.

Hat-tricks (11): J. D. F. Larter, Northamptonshire v Sussex, Northampton, 1963; D. A. D. Sydenham, Surrey v Cheshire, Hoylake, 1964; R. N. S. Hobbs, Essex v Middlesex, Lord's, 1968; N. M. McVicker, Warwickshire v Lincolnshire, Birmingham, 1971; G. S. le Roux, Sussex v Ireland, Hove, 1985; M. Jean-Jacques, Derbyshire v Nottinghamshire, Derby, 1987; J. F. M. O'Brien, Cheshire v Derbyshire, Chester, 1988; R. A. Pick, Nottinghamshire v Scotland, Nottingham, 1995; J. E. Emburey, Northamptonshire v Cheshire, Northampton, 1996; A. R. Caddick, Somerset v Gloucestershire, Taunton, 1996; D. Gough, Yorkshire v Ireland, Leeds, 1997.

Four wickets in five balls: D. A. D. Sydenham, Surrey v Cheshire, Hoylake, 1964.

Wicket-keeping and Fielding

Most dismissals: 66 (58 ct, 8 st), R. W. Taylor; 65 (59 ct, 6 st), A. P. E. Knott, and (56 ct, 9 st), R. C. Russell.

Most dismissals in an innings: 7 (all ct), A. J. Stewart, Surrey v Glamorgan, Swansea, 1994.

Most catches by a fielder: 27, J. Simmons; 26, M. W. Gatting and G. A. Gooch; 25, G. Cook; 24, P. J. Sharpe.

Most catches by a fielder in an innings: 4 – A. S. Brown, Gloucestershire v Middlesex, Bristol, 1963; G. Cook, Northamptonshire v Glamorgan, Northampton, 1972; C. G. Greenidge, Hampshire v Cheshire, Southampton, 1981; D. C. Jackson, Durham v Northamptonshire, Darlington, 1984; T. S. Smith, Hertfordshire v Somerset, St Albans, 1984; H. Morris, Glamorgan v Scotland, Edinburgh, 1988; C. C. Lewis, Nottinghamshire v Worcestershire, Nottingham, 1992.

Results

Largest victories in runs: Somerset by 346 runs v Devon, Torquay, 1990; Sussex by 304 runs v Ireland, Belfast, 1996; Worcestershire by 299 runs v Devon, Worcester, 1987; Essex by 291 runs v Wiltshire, Chelmsford, 1988; Sussex by 244 runs v Ireland, Hove, 1985; Lancashire by 241 runs v Gloucestershire, Manchester, 1990.

Victories by ten wickets (17): By Essex, Glamorgan, Hampshire (twice), Middlesex, Northamptonshire, Nottinghamshire, Somerset, Surrey, Sussex (twice), Warwickshire (twice), Yorkshire (four times).

Earliest finishes: both at 2.20 p.m. Worcestershire beat Lancashire by nine wickets at Worcester, 1963; Essex beat Middlesex by eight wickets at Westcliff, 1972.

Scores level (10): Nottinghamshire 215, Somerset 215 for nine at Taunton, 1964; Surrey 196, Sussex 196 for eight at The Oval, 1970; Somerset 287 for six, Essex 287 at Taunton, 1978; Surrey 195 for seven, Essex 195 at Chelmsford, 1980; Essex 149, Derbyshire 149 for eight at Derby, 1981; Northamptonshire 235 for nine, Derbyshire 235 for six at Lord's, 1981 (*in the final*); Middlesex 222 for nine, Somerset 222 for eight at Lord's, 1983; Hampshire 224 for eight, Essex 224 for seven at Southampton, 1985; Essex 307 for six, Hampshire 307 for five at Chelmsford, 1990; Hampshire 204 for nine, Leicestershire 204 for nine at Leicester, 1995. *Note:* Under the rules the side which lost fewer wickets won; at Leicester in 1995, Leicestershire won by virtue of their higher total after 30 overs.

Match Awards

Most awards: 9, G. A. Gooch and R. A. Smith; 8, C. H. Lloyd and C. L. Smith.

WINNERS 1963-98

Gillette Cup

		Man of the Match
1963	SUSSEX* beat Worcestershire by 14 runs.	N. Gifford†
1964	SUSSEX beat Warwickshire* by eight wickets.	N. I. Thomson
1965	YORKSHIRE beat Surrey* by 175 runs.	G. Boycott
1966	WARWICKSHIRE* beat Worcestershire by five wickets.	R. W. Barber
1967	KENT* beat Somerset by 32 runs.	M. H. Denness
1968	WARWICKSHIRE beat Sussex* by four wickets.	A. C. Smith
1969	YORKSHIRE beat Derbyshire* by 69 runs.	B. Leadbeater
1970	LANCASHIRE* beat Sussex by six wickets.	H. Pilling
1971	LANCASHIRE* beat Kent by 24 runs.	Asif Iqbal†
1972	LANCASHIRE* beat Warwickshire by four wickets.	C. H. Lloyd
1973	GLOUCESTERSHIRE* beat Sussex by 40 runs.	A. S. Brown
1974	KENT* beat Lancashire by four wickets.	A. P. E. Knott
1975	LANCASHIRE* beat Middlesex by seven wickets.	C. H. Lloyd
1976	NORTHAMPTONSHIRE* beat Lancashire by four wickets.	P. Willey
1977	MIDDLESEX* beat Glamorgan by five wickets.	C. T. Radley
1978	SUSSEX* beat Somerset by five wickets.	P. W. G. Parker
1979	SOMERSET beat Northamptonshire* by 45 runs.	I. V. A. Richards
1980	MIDDLESEX* beat Surrey by seven wickets.	J. M. Brearley

NatWest Trophy

1981	DERBYSHIRE* beat Northamptonshire by losing fewer wickets with the scores level.	G. Cook†
1982	SURREY* beat Warwickshire by nine wickets.	D. J. Thomas
1983	SOMERSET beat Kent* by 24 runs.	V. J. Marks
1984	MIDDLESEX beat Kent* by four wickets.	C. T. Radley
1985	ESSEX beat Nottinghamshire* by one run.	B. R. Hardie
1986	SUSSEX* beat Lancashire by seven wickets.	D. A. Reeve
1987	NOTTINGHAMSHIRE* beat Northamptonshire by three wickets.	R. J. Hadlee
1988	MIDDLESEX* beat Worcestershire by three wickets.	M. R. Ramprakash
1989	WARWICKSHIRE beat Middlesex* by four wickets.	D. A. Reeve
1990	LANCASHIRE* beat Northamptonshire by seven wickets.	P. A. J. DeFreitas
1991	HAMPSHIRE* beat Surrey by four wickets.	R. A. Smith
1992	NORTHAMPTONSHIRE* beat Leicestershire by eight wickets.	A. Fordham
1993	WARWICKSHIRE* beat Sussex by five wickets.	Asif Din
1994	WORCESTERSHIRE* beat Warwickshire by eight wickets.	T. M. Moody

1995	WARWICKSHIRE beat Northamptonshire* by four wickets.	D. A. Reeve
1996	LANCASHIRE beat Essex* by 129 runs.	G. Chapple
1997	ESSEX* beat Warwickshire by nine wickets.	S. G. Law
1998	LANCASHIRE* beat Derbyshire by nine wickets.	I. D. Austin

* *Won toss.*   † *On losing side.*

TEAM RECORDS 1963-98

	Rounds reached				Matches		
	W	F	SF	QF	P	W	L
Derbyshire.	1	3	4	13	75*	40	35
Durham	0	0	0	1	41	13	28
Essex	2	3	6	15	81	47	34
Glamorgan	0	1	4	14	76	40	36
Gloucestershire.	1	1	5	14	74	39	35
Hampshire.	1	1	9	21	92	57	35
Kent.	2	5	7	14	82	48	34
Lancashire.	7	10	15	20	103	74	29
Leicestershire.	0	1	4	15	75	39	36
Middlesex	4	6	13	20	98	66	32
Northamptonshire . . .	2	7	10	19	91	57	34
Nottinghamshire	1	2	3	13	76	41	35
Somerset.	2	4	9	17	86	52	34
Surrey	1	4	10	21	91*	56	35
Sussex	4	8	13	19	93	61	32
Warwickshire	5	10	16	21	104	73	31
Worcestershire	1	4	10	14	81	46	35
Yorkshire	2	2	6	16	77	43	34

* Derbyshire and Surrey totals each include a bowling contest after their first-round matches were abandoned in 1991; Derbyshire lost to Hertfordshire and Surrey beat Oxfordshire.

MINOR COUNTY RECORDS

From 1964 to 1979 the previous season's top five Minor Counties were invited to take part in the competition. In 1980 these were joined by Ireland, and in 1983 the competition was expanded to embrace 13 Minor Counties, Ireland and Scotland. The number of Minor Counties dropped to 12 in 1992 when Durham attained first-class status, and 11 in 1995 when Holland were admitted to the competition.

Between 1964 and 1991 Durham qualified 21 times, including 15 years in succession from 1977-91. They reached the second round a record six times.

Including the 1998 tournament, Staffordshire have qualified most among the remaining Minor Counties, 20 times, followed by Devon 19, Cambridgeshire, Hertfordshire and Oxfordshire 18, Berkshire, Buckinghamshire, Cheshire and Norfolk 17, Suffolk 16, Shropshire 13, Bedfordshire, Cumberland, Dorset, Lincolnshire and Wiltshire 12, Northumberland 8, Cornwall 7, Herefordshire and Wales Minor Counties 3. Only Hertfordshire have reached the quarter-finals, beating Berkshire and then Essex in 1976.

In 1999, the competition was reformed and two preliminary rounds introduced, in which 42 teams were to compete for the right to join the first-class counties in the third round. They are all 20 Minor Counties (including Wales), plus Huntingdonshire, the first-class county Boards XIs (excluding Glamorgan, who are covered by Wales) and the national teams of Denmark, Holland, Ireland and Scotland.

Wins by a minor team over a first-class county (9): Durham v Yorkshire (by five wickets), Harrogate, 1973; Lincolnshire v Glamorgan (by six wickets), Swansea, 1974; Hertfordshire v Essex (by 33 runs), 2nd round, Hitchin, 1976; Shropshire v Yorkshire (by 37 runs), Telford, 1984; Durham v Derbyshire (by seven wickets), Derby, 1985; Buckinghamshire v Somerset (by seven runs), High Wycombe, 1987; Cheshire v Northamptonshire (by one wicket), Chester, 1988; Hertfordshire v Derbyshire (2-1 in a bowling contest after the match was abandoned), Bishop's Stortford, 1991; Scotland v Worcestershire (by four runs), Edinburgh, 1998.

BENSON AND HEDGES CUP, 1998

Darren Maddy

Twenty-six years after it began by providing Leicestershire with their first major trophy, the Benson and Hedges Cup ended by giving the county one of the most embarrassing days in their history. Symmetry suggested the tournament ought to fade away with another Leicestershire triumph. Reality was that they capitulated to a horrible defeat. They were bowled out for 76, and Paul Prichard, the Essex captain, held a trophy aloft for the second successive Lord's final: Essex had won the NatWest the previous September.

The result was especially harsh on the Leicestershire opener Darren Maddy, who had dominated the rest of the 1998 competition in unprecedented fashion. Maddy hit 629 runs, beating Graham Gooch's one-season record of 591, at an average of 125.80, and won five Gold Awards. In the final, he held firm while the other batting specialists were swept away, but was then sixth out for five.

Overall, it was a dismal end to a tournament that had started to outlive its usefulness. Rain prevented a one-day finish and the teams had to return on the Sunday. This is always an anticlimax but, with the football World Cup final taking place that night, the restarted game had extra trouble competing for public attention. Leicestershire had already returned 2,000 tickets, providing further evidence that two Lord's finals a season had diminished the novelty value for the followers of many counties.

Leicestershire's presence had been a surprise, as they had been obliged to play their semi-final against Surrey, the 1997 winners and warm favourites. But Surrey's sequence of 13 consecutive victories in the tournament was ended by Maddy. Many of the other games were routine in a damp, cool spring, but some of the competition's perennial losers had their consolations. Durham reached the quarter-finals for the first time, after failing in their six previous seasons; the British Universities beat Gloucestershire and came close against Somerset; Scotland also had moments of encouragement.

With increasing concern being voiced about the amount of one-day cricket on the fixture list, this competition – labour-intensive for the players while attracting small crowds in the early stages – was ripe for the chop, especially as tobacco sponsorship was becoming unacceptable to politicians and many members of the public. However, it was a popular event with administrators, as Benson and Hedges, with few alternative advertising outlets, were uncomplainingly loyal sponsors. And it will leave the memories of some crackingly exciting fixtures over the years.

Prize money

£43,000 for winners: ESSEX.
£22,000 for runners-up: LEICESTERSHIRE.
£11,000 for losing semi-finalists: SURREY, YORKSHIRE.
£5,500 for losing quarter-finalists: DURHAM, KENT, LANCASHIRE, MIDDLESEX.

There was also £850 each for the winners of group matches. Gold Award winners received £950 in the final, £450 in the semi-finals, £400 in the quarter-finals and £275 in the group matches. The prize money was increased from £160,750 in the 1997 tournament to £168,700; the total sponsorship rose from £824,457 to £859,986.

FINAL GROUP TABLES

	Played	Won	Lost	No result	Points	Net run-rate
Group A						
LEICESTERSHIRE	5	4	1	0	8	23.32
LANCASHIRE	5	4	1	0	8	17.31
Warwickshire	5	4	1	0	8	16.35
Nottinghamshire	5	2	3	0	4	1.51
Northamptonshire	5	1	4	0	2	−10.40
Minor Counties	5	0	5	0	0	−50.57
Group B						
YORKSHIRE	4	4	0	0	8	13.13
DURHAM	4	3	1	0	6	−1.42
Worcestershire	4	2	2	0	4	3.66
Derbyshire	4	1	3	0	2	−3.27
Scotland	4	0	4	0	0	−10.51
Group C						
SURREY	5	5	0	0	10	13.16
KENT	5	3	1	1	7	14.17
Somerset	5	2	2	1	5	−0.43
Gloucestershire.	5	2	3	0	4	2.89
British Universities	5	1	4	0	2	−13.26
Hampshire	5	1	4	0	2	−15.56
Group D						
MIDDLESEX	4	4	0	0	8	3.71
ESSEX	4	2	1	1	5	19.48
Glamorgan	4	1	2	1	3	10.33
Sussex	4	1	2	1	3	−1.53
Ireland	4	0	3	1	1	−33.29

Net run-rate was calculated by subtracting runs conceded per 100 balls from runs scored per 100 balls, revising figures in shortened matches and discounting those not played to a result.

GROUP A

The Minor Counties' squad for the competition was: S. J. Dean (Staffordshire) (*captain*), R. N. Dalton (Bedfordshire), M. A. Fell (Lincolnshire), J. M. Fielding (Cumberland), N. R. Gaywood (Devon), S. C. Goldsmith (Norfolk), R. G. Hignett (Cheshire), A. J. Jones (Wales), P. G. Newman (Norfolk), P. J. Nicholson (Northumberland), S. Oakes (Lincolnshire), D. B. Pennett (Cumberland), L. Potter (Staffordshire), A. Richardson (Staffordshire), A. R. Roberts (Bedfordshire), C. J. Rogers (Norfolk), M. A. Sharp (Cumberland), D. M. Ward (Hertfordshire).

LANCASHIRE v WARWICKSHIRE

At Manchester, April 29. Warwickshire won by 50 runs. Toss: Warwickshire.

Lancashire, who until April 1997 went five years without losing a cup-tie at Old Trafford, lost their third out of five. At 108 for one, chasing Warwickshire's modest 234, they seemed well set. Then Lara, switching his bowlers idiosyncratically but effectively, engineered the removal of Watkinson and Crawley after they had put on 82 for the second wicket. Giles followed his highest innings in the tournament with his best bowling.

Gold Award: A. F. Giles.

Warwickshire

N. V. Knight b Chapple	33	†K. J. Piper not out	13
N. M. K. Smith c Wasim Akram b Martin	18	G. C. Small not out	2
D. L. Hemp c Hegg b Martin	55		
*B. C. Lara lbw b Austin	13	L-b 4, w 11, n-b 6	21
T. L. Penney c Atherton b Chapple	17		
D. R. Brown b Wasim Akram	9	1/34 2/76 3/102 (8 wkts, 50 overs)	234
A. F. Giles c Watkinson b Wasim Akram	37	4/134 5/152 6/173	
G. Welch c Martin b Chapple	16	7/199 8/225	

E. S. H. Giddins did not bat.

Bowling: Wasim Akram 10–1–35–2; Martin 10–0–60–2; Chapple 10–0–40–3; Austin 10–0–51–1; Yates 10–0–44–0.

Lancashire

M. A. Atherton c Piper b Giddins	11	G. Yates not out	5
M. Watkinson b Giddins	34	G. Chapple c Giles b Giddins	3
J. P. Crawley lbw b Smith	54	P. J. Martin b Giles	4
A. Flintoff lbw b Small	1	L-b 14, w 6	20
G. D. Lloyd c Brown b Small	16		
*Wasim Akram c Giddins b Giles	31	1/26 2/108 3/110 (45.1 overs)	184
†W. K. Hegg c Piper b Smith	0	4/128 5/132 6/134	
I. D. Austin st Piper b Giles	5	7/159 8/172 9/179	

Bowling: Giddins 10–1–35–3; Brown 7–0–32–0; Giles 7.1–2–22–3; Small 10–0–39–2; Smith 10–0–35–2; Welch 1–0–7–0.

Umpires: V. A. Holder and G. Sharp.

MINOR COUNTIES v NORTHAMPTONSHIRE

At Luton, April 29. Northamptonshire won by five wickets. Toss: Northamptonshire.

Neither side found batting easy on a slow pitch but, by the time Minor Counties had slumped to 27 for five, the result was beyond doubt. Rose, making his debut in the competition, took five for 14, a county record, while Malcolm's first 30 balls yielded just one run. Newman, once of Derbyshire, made Northamptonshire sweat at 39 for four, but Curran and Penberthy led the way home.

Gold Award: F. A. Rose.

Minor Counties

*S. J. Dean c Curran b Rose	0	†P. J. Nicholson run out	15
C. J. Rogers c Capel b Rose	1	D. B. Pennett not out	26
L. Potter b Penberthy	10	A. Richardson c Curran b Rose	1
D. M. Ward b Rose	0	L-b 4, w 6, n-b 2	12
M. A. Fell c Ripley b Rose	6		
A. R. Roberts c Ripley b Snape	25	1/1 2/4 3/4 (49.1 overs)	103
R. N. Dalton b Curran	0	4/13 5/27 6/32	
P. G. Newman lbw b Swann	7	7/55 8/62 9/88	

Bowling: Malcolm 10–5–18–0; Rose 9.1–3–14–5; Curran 7–2–10–1; Penberthy 6–0–18–1; Capel 2–0–2–0; Snape 9–1–23–1; Swann 6–0–14–1.

Northamptonshire

F. A. Rose c Potter b Newman	15	M. B. Loye not out	3
D. J. Capel c Potter b Newman	10		
J. N. Snape c Roberts b Newman	1	B 2, w 7	9
*K. M. Curran c Roberts b Richardson	28		
R. J. Bailey b Pennett	4	1/18 2/26 3/26 (5 wkts, 32.2 overs) 104	
A. L. Penberthy not out	34	4/39 5/91	

R. R. Montgomerie, G. P. Swann, †D. Ripley and D. E. Malcolm did not bat.

Bowling: Newman 8–2–19–3; Pennett 10–2–30–1; Potter 5–1–13–0; Richardson 6–1–16–1; Dalton 3.2–0–24–0.

Umpires: R. Palmer and J. F. Steele.

LEICESTERSHIRE v LANCASHIRE

At Leicester, May 1. Lancashire won by two wickets. Toss: Lancashire.

Maddy did his best to ensure selection for the one-day internationals against South Africa, but his unbeaten 136 was not enough to stave off defeat. He and Smith put on 206 – a county second-wicket record – on a pitch made for batting. In Lancashire's reply, interrupted by several showers, Crawley and Fairbrother shared a stand of 156 and, despite a mid-innings wobble, Hegg steered them home in gathering gloom.

Gold Award: D. L. Maddy.

Leicestershire

D. L. Maddy not out	136
I. J. Sutcliffe c Hegg b Martin	4
B. F. Smith lbw b Yates	90
P. V. Simmons not out	25
B 1, l-b 11, w 14, n-b 2	28
1/13 2/219 (2 wkts, 50 overs) 283	

A. Habib, *C. C. Lewis, †P. A. Nixon, D. J. Millns, D. Williamson, A. D. Mullally and J. M. Dakin did not bat.

Bowling: Wasim Akram 10–0–46–0; Martin 10–0–48–1; Chapple 10–1–54–0; Austin 9–0–59–0; Yates 9–0–45–1; Flintoff 2–0–19–0.

Lancashire

M. A. Atherton c Nixon b Mullally	12	G. Yates c Sutcliffe b Dakin	9
A. Flintoff c Habib b Simmons	23	G. Chapple not out	1
J. P. Crawley b Lewis	88	B 1, l-b 11, w 13, n-b 4	29
N. H. Fairbrother b Mullally	68		
G. D. Lloyd lbw b Simmons	16	1/30 2/47 3/203 (8 wkts, 49.3 overs) 287	
*Wasim Akram c Smith b Lewis	4	4/214 5/218 6/248	
I. D. Austin c Sutcliffe b Dakin	12	7/248 8/268	
†W. K. Hegg not out	25		

P. J. Martin did not bat.

Bowling: Mullally 10–1–39–2; Millns 6–0–30–0; Lewis 10–0–48–2; Simmons 7–0–41–1; Dakin 9.3–0–68–3; Williamson 4–0–29–0; Maddy 3–0–20–0.

Umpires: K. E. Palmer and J. F. Steele.

NOTTINGHAMSHIRE v MINOR COUNTIES

At Nottingham, May 1. Nottinghamshire won by nine wickets. Toss: Nottinghamshire.

Ward, formerly of Surrey, and Pennett, once of Nottinghamshire, did their best for Minor Counties against a weak attack. But Gallian, with his first fifty for his new county, and Afzaal shared an unbroken stand of 131 and strolled to victory with almost 16 overs remaining.

Gold Award: J. E. R. Gallian.

Minor Counties

*S. J. Dean b Bowen	14
C. J. Rogers c Gallian b Oram	4
D. M. Ward b Dowman	33
M. A. Fell lbw b Bowen	0
A. R. Roberts c Noon b Dowman	16
R. N. Dalton lbw b Bates	3
†P. J. Nicholson run out	10

P. G. Newman not out	26
D. B. Pennett not out	39
L-b 8, w 8	16

1/12 2/33 3/33　　　(7 wkts, 50 overs) 161
4/69 5/78
6/87 7/95

M. A. Sharp and A. Richardson did not bat.

Bowling: Bowen 10–2–40–2; Oram 10–2–43–1; Strang 10–2–18–0; Dowman 6–0–18–2; Gallian 5–0–16–0; Bates 9–0–18–1.

Nottinghamshire

P. R. Pollard b Newman	22
U. Afzaal not out	54
J. E. R. Gallian not out	74
L-b 1, w 11	12

1/31　　　　　(1 wkt, 34.1 overs) 162

*P. Johnson, R. T. Robinson, M. P. Dowman, P. A. Strang, †W. M. Noon, R. T. Bates, A. R. Oram and M. N. Bowen did not bat.

Bowling: Newman 8–0–27–1; Sharp 7–1–39–0; Pennett 7–1–33–0; Richardson 5–0–22–0; Roberts 6–0–31–0; Dalton 1.1–0–9–0.

Umpires: G. I. Burgess and R. Julian.

WARWICKSHIRE v NORTHAMPTONSHIRE

At Birmingham, May 1. Warwickshire won by 71 runs. Toss: Warwickshire.

Lara, striking his first one-day century for Warwickshire, led them to an easy victory. His 89-ball 101 bristled with confidence, though it also included the occasional rash shot. The only bowler to contain the flow of runs was his West Indian team-mate Rose. Giddins, finding swing at a brisk pace, ensured that Northamptonshire never threatened – he dismissed both openers and conceded only 11 in seven overs.

Gold Award: B. C. Lara.

Warwickshire

N. V. Knight b Malcolm	21
N. M. K. Smith c Ripley b Malcolm	0
D. L. Hemp c Snape b Taylor	18
*B. C. Lara b Snape	101
T. L. Penney c Ripley b Rose	10
D. R. Brown c Penberthy b Rose	52
A. F. Giles c Taylor b Penberthy	4
G. Welch c Bailey b Rose	2

†K. J. Piper not out	12
G. C. Small b Taylor	19
E. S. H. Giddins not out	4
L-b 7, w 8, n-b 2	17

1/1 2/46 3/62　　　(9 wkts, 50 overs) 260
4/114 5/207 6/220
7/223 8/225 9/256

Bowling: Malcolm 10–0–50–2; Taylor 10–1–57–2; Penberthy 10–0–42–1; Rose 10–0–31–3; Curran 5–0–37–0; Snape 5–0–36–1.

Northamptonshire

D. J. Capel b Giddins	17	†D. Ripley not out		25
R. R. Montgomerie c Knight b Giddins	9	J. P. Taylor b Welch		11
R. J. Bailey c Piper b Smith	30	D. E. Malcolm b Giles		16
*K. M. Curran c Hemp b Brown	15	L-b 9, w 5		14
A. L. Penberthy c Penney b Smith	43			—
F. A. Rose c Brown b Giles	0	1/27 2/30 3/63	(48.1 overs)	189
D. J. Sales c Knight b Welch	6	4/100 5/101 6/127		
J. N. Snape c Brown b Welch	3	7/133 8/138 9/153		

Bowling: Giddins 7–3–11–2; Small 8–0–34–0; Welch 10–1–37–3; Brown 8–0–40–1; Smith 7–0–18–2; Giles 8.1–0–40–2.

Umpires: D. J. Constant and A. A. Jones.

NOTTINGHAMSHIRE v LEICESTERSHIRE

At Nottingham, May 2. Leicestershire won by eight wickets. Toss: Leicestershire.

For Lewis, this was a triumphant return to one of his old haunts. He commanded his forces with great skill and, even before wickets began falling, runs were at a premium. Nottinghamshire then tumbled from 104 without loss after 30 overs to 196 for eight. Sutcliffe, scoring his maiden century in the competition, shared an unbroken partnership of 143 with Simmons to see Leicestershire to an emphatic win.

Gold Award: I. J. Sutcliffe.

Nottinghamshire

P. R. Pollard st Nixon b Brimson	50	R. T. Bates run out		8
U. Afzaal c Nixon b Mullally	78	M. N. Bowen not out		1
*P. Johnson run out	5			
J. E. R. Gallian c Nixon b Lewis	5	L-b 4, w 7		11
R. T. Robinson c Nixon b Lewis	17			—
P. A. Strang c Simmons b Millns	0	1/104 2/110 3/123	(8 wkts, 50 overs)	196
A. G. Wharf b Maddy	9	4/164 5/165 6/165		
†W. M. Noon not out	12	7/177 8/194		

A. R. Oram did not bat.

Bowling: Mullally 10–4–17–1; Millns 10–2–37–1; Dakin 9–1–42–0; Lewis 10–0–42–2; Brimson 10–0–43–1; Maddy 1–0–11–1.

Leicestershire

D. L. Maddy c Pollard b Oram	3
I. J. Sutcliffe not out	105
B. F. Smith lbw b Strang	24
P. V. Simmons not out	48
B 8, l-b 3, w 7	18

1/14 2/55   (2 wkts, 45.1 overs) 198

A. Habib, *C. C. Lewis, †P. A. Nixon, D. J. Millns, M. T. Brimson, J. M. Dakin and A. D. Mullally did not bat.

Bowling: Oram 9–3–19–1; Bowen 6.1–0–39–0; Wharf 10–0–48–0; Strang 10–1–31–1; Bates 6–0–30–0; Gallian 4–0–20–0.

Umpires: G. Sharp and A. G. T. Whitehead.

LEICESTERSHIRE v WARWICKSHIRE

At Leicester, May 4. Leicestershire won by three wickets. Toss: Warwickshire.

A whirlwind 89 from 75 balls from Simmons gave Leicestershire victory after they had been in trouble due to the profligacy of their bowlers. They gave away 53 extras, then a competition record, including 11 wides bowled by Mullally and ten by Millns, who produced five of them in one over. For Warwickshire, Penney and Brown added 116 for the fifth wicket, but 263 was not enough to defend them from Simmons's assault.

Gold Award: P. V. Simmons.

Warwickshire

N. V. Knight lbw b Mullally	12	A. F. Giles b Simmons		1
N. M. K. Smith c Wells b Millns	1	G. Welch not out		1
D. L. Hemp c Habib b Mason	29	L-b 11, w 34, n-b 8		53
*B. C. Lara c and b Mason	49			—
T. L. Penney not out	57	1/6 2/46 3/121	(6 wkts, 50 overs)	263
D. R. Brown c Simmons b Mullally	60	4/134 5/250 6/254		

†K. J. Piper, E. S. H. Giddins and T. A. Munton did not bat.

Bowling: Mullally 9–0–42–2; Millns 4–0–27–1; Lewis 8–1–38–0; Simmons 10–0–60–1; Mason 10–0–44–2; Wells 9–1–41–0.

Leicestershire

D. L. Maddy c Piper b Smith	32	†P. A. Nixon not out		36
I. J. Sutcliffe c Lara b Smith	50	D. J. Millns not out		3
B. F. Smith st Piper b Smith	11	B 4, l-b 6, w 11, n-b 2		23
P. V. Simmons c Penney b Giles	89			—
V. J. Wells b Giles	19	1/87 2/92 3/105	(7 wkts, 49.3 overs)	269
A. Habib b Giles	6	4/178 5/197		
*C. C. Lewis run out	0	6/197 7/243		

T. J. Mason and A. D. Mullally did not bat.

Bowling: Giddins 10–0–54–0; Munton 10–0–49–0; Brown 8–0–34–0; Giles 10–1–65–3; Smith 7.3–0–36–3; Welch 4–0–21–0.

Umpires: M. J. Kitchen and N. T. Plews.

NORTHAMPTONSHIRE v NOTTINGHAMSHIRE

At Northampton, May 4. Nottinghamshire won by 35 runs. Toss: Northamptonshire.

After two successive fifties, Afzaal might have felt aggrieved to be replaced by the more aggressive Archer. The decision was vindicated, though; Archer hit 70 from 71 balls, with Rose his main victim. Northamptonshire never managed to keep up with the required rate, despite a combative 71 by Curran.

Gold Award: G. F. Archer.

Nottinghamshire

P. R. Pollard b Taylor	13	P. A. Strang not out		23
M. P. Dowman c Curran b Penberthy	29			
J. E. R. Gallian c Ripley b Penberthy	27	L-b 11, w 6, n-b 4		21
*P. Johnson c Sales b Rose	69			—
R. T. Robinson b Penberthy	11	1/26 2/60 3/85	(7 wkts, 50 overs)	272
G. F. Archer b Rose	70	4/128 5/200		
A. G. Wharf c and b Malcolm	9	6/215 7/272		

†W. M. Noon, A. R. Oram and M. N. Bowen did not bat.

Bowling: Malcolm 10–0–39–1; Taylor 10–0–65–1; Penberthy 10–1–22–3; Rose 10–0–72–2; Snape 10–0–63–0.

Northamptonshire

D. J. Capel c Archer b Bowen	10	†D. Ripley c Wharf b Oram	13
M. B. Loye b Strang	41	J. P. Taylor run out	1
D. J. Sales c Oram b Wharf	26	D. E. Malcolm not out	0
*K. M. Curran c Robinson b Strang	71	B 2, l-b 6, w 5, n-b 4	17
R. J. Bailey lbw b Gallian	18		
A. L. Penberthy c Dowman b Strang	19	1/12 2/80 3/84	(47.4 overs) 237
J. N. Snape c sub b Wharf	19	4/137 5/173 6/219	
F. A. Rose lbw b Strang	2	7/221 8/221 9/236	

Bowling: Bowen 8–0–35–1; Oram 8.4–1–40–1; Strang 10–1–49–4; Wharf 10–0–49–2; Gallian 9–0–49–1; Dowman 2–0–7–0.

Umpires: V. A. Holder and K. E. Palmer.

MINOR COUNTIES v LANCASHIRE

At Lakenham, May 5. Lancashire won by seven wickets. Toss: Lancashire.

Minor Counties scored a mere 52, the second-lowest total in 27 seasons of Benson and Hedges cricket, to lose a one-sided match by three o'clock, despite a lengthy rain interruption. The entire match lasted barely 40 overs. Chapple won the Gold Award for his remarkable figures of five for seven.

Gold Award: G. Chapple.

Minor Counties

*S. J. Dean c Flintoff b Martin	9	J. M. Fielding b Chapple	2
C. J. Rogers c Atherton b Austin	11	M. A. Sharp c Flintoff b Wasim Akram	1
A. J. Jones lbw b Martin	1	A. Richardson not out	1
S. C. Goldsmith c Atherton b Chapple	8	L-b 3, w 6	9
M. A. Fell c Atherton b Austin	2		
P. G. Newman lbw b Chapple	3	1/18 2/24 3/31	(26.5 overs) 52
†P. J. Nicholson lbw b Chapple	0	4/34 5/40 6/41	
D. B. Pennett c Martin b Chapple	5	7/42 8/50 9/50	

Bowling: Wasim Akram 4.5–1–3–1; Martin 8–1–20–2; Austin 9–1–19–2; Chapple 5–2–7–5.

Lancashire

M. A. Atherton not out	28	G. D. Lloyd not out	0
A. Flintoff c Nicholson b Newman	0	W 3	3
J. P. Crawley c Rogers b Sharp	17		
N. H. Fairbrother c Dean b Sharp	5	1/2 2/22 3/28	(3 wkts, 13.4 overs) 53

*Wasim Akram, †W. K. Hegg, I. D. Austin, G. Chapple, G. Yates and P. J. Martin did not bat.

Bowling: Newman 6–2–18–1; Sharp 6.4–2–25–2; Richardson 1–0–10–0.

Umpires: T. E. Jesty and A. A. Jones.

MINOR COUNTIES v WARWICKSHIRE

At Lakenham, May 6. Warwickshire won by six wickets. Toss: Warwickshire.

A total of 111 was not spectacular but, after the previous day's fiasco, reaching three figures was a relief for Minor Counties. Andrew Jones (son of former Glamorgan opener Alan) and Jonathan Fielding built enough of a target for Lara to have to bat – which is what the spectators had really come to see. He obliged with a breezy 30 not out from 27 balls. But Warwickshire's most successful player was Hemp, his first bowl in this competition bringing him four for 32.

Gold Award: D. L. Hemp.

Minor Counties

*S. J. Dean b Giddins	1	D. B. Pennett b Hemp	0	
C. J. Rogers c Piper b Brown	7	J. M. Fielding lbw b Hemp	26	
A. J. Jones c Giddins b Hemp	30	M. A. Sharp not out	14	
S. C. Goldsmith b Giddins	1	B l-b 5, w 13, n-b 2	20	
M. A. Fell c Piper b Welch	1			
R. G. Hignett c and b Welch	4	1/7 2/10 3/16	(47.1 overs)	111
P. G. Newman lbw b Welch	0	4/24 5/41 6/41		
†P. J. Nicholson c Piper b Hemp	7	7/55 8/68 9/70		

Bowling: Giddins 10–3–14–2; Brown 10–2–21–1; Welch 9–2–20–3; Small 10–0–19–0; Hemp 8.1–0–32–4.

Warwickshire

N. V. Knight c Goldsmith b Sharp	17	T. L. Penney not out	5	
N. M. K. Smith c Nicholson b Goldsmith	13	B 1, l-b 2, n-b 2	5	
D. L. Hemp c Sharp b Pennett	34			
A. F. Giles c Dean b Goldsmith	8	1/31 2/33	(4 wkts, 24 overs)	112
*B. C. Lara not out	30	3/49 4/89		

D. R. Brown, G. Welch, †K. J. Piper, G. C. Small and E. S. H. Giddins did not bat.

Bowling: Newman 4–0–19–0; Sharp 7–0–21–1; Goldsmith 7–2–22–2; Pennett 5–0–43–1; Fielding 1–0–4–0.

Umpires: A. Clarkson and P. Willey.

NORTHAMPTONSHIRE v LEICESTERSHIRE

At Northampton, May 6. Leicestershire won by eight wickets. Toss: Northamptonshire.

Maddy and Sutcliffe, both century-makers in earlier games, added further fifties as Leicestershire rattled up 123 for the first wicket. After that, it was plain sailing to overhaul a total of 198.

Gold Award: D. L. Maddy.

Northamptonshire

D. J. Capel lbw b Lewis	9	†D. Ripley not out	16	
M. B. Loye c Nixon b Mullally	0	F. A. Rose c Wells b Mason	2	
D. J. Sales c Lewis b Mullally	4	D. E. Malcolm not out	0	
*K. M. Curran b Wells	26	B 4, l-b 6, w 8	18	
R. J. Bailey c Nixon b Wells	35			
A. L. Penberthy b Mason	62	1/1 2/12 3/26	(9 wkts, 50 overs)	198
T. C. Walton c Habib b Mason	26	4/55 5/95 6/151		
J. N. Snape c Nixon b Mullally	0	7/155 8/191 9/193		

Bowling: Mullally 10–2–34–3; Lewis 6–2–15–1; Wells 10–3–28–2; Millns 8–0–34–0; Simmons 7–0–36–0; Mason 9–0–41–3.

Leicestershire

D. L. Maddy c Ripley b Malcolm	89	
I. J. Sutcliffe c Walton b Capel	55	
B. F. Smith not out	27	
P. V. Simmons not out	10	
B 4, l-b 7, w 3, n-b 4	18	

1/123 2/179   (2 wkts, 39.2 overs) 199

V. J. Wells, A. Habib, *C. C. Lewis, †P. A. Nixon, D. J. Millns, T. J. Mason and A. D. Mullally did not bat.

Bowling: Malcolm 10–2–42–1; Rose 6–2–28–0; Penberthy 6.2–0–43–0; Curran 5–0–20–0; Capel 6–0–28–1; Snape 6–0–27–0.

Umpires: J. W. Holder and T. E. Jesty.

NOTTINGHAMSHIRE v LANCASHIRE

At Nottingham, May 7. Lancashire won by 58 runs. Toss: Nottinghamshire.

A breathtaking late onslaught from Wasim Akram put the match beyond Nottinghamshire's reach, despite game innings from Dowman and Gallian, facing his old county for the first time. Wasim, though, was imperious: he struck 89, his best score in the competition, in only 43 balls, with six sixes and eight fours. In the final two overs, which went for 52 in all, he moved from 43 to 89 in just ten balls. He scored 26 (624446) off the 49th over, bowled by Wharf, and 20 (6662) off the last four balls of the innings, from Oram.

Gold Award: Wasim Akram.

Lancashire

M. A. Atherton lbw b Bowen	1	†W. K. Hegg not out		36
A. Flintoff c Oram b Wharf	46			
J. P. Crawley c Dowman b Oram	81	B 1, l-b 6, w 3		10
N. H. Fairbrother c Strang b Gallian	11			
G. D. Lloyd run out	24	1/4 2/95 3/125	(5 wkts, 50 overs)	298
*Wasim Akram not out	89	4/166 5/175		

I. D. Austin, G. Yates, G. Chapple and P. J. Martin did not bat.

Bowling: Oram 10–0–67–1; Bowen 10–1–41–1; Wharf 10–0–81–1; Gallian 10–0–55–1; Strang 10–1–47–0.

Nottinghamshire

P. R. Pollard c Hegg b Wasim Akram	31	†W. M. Noon b Wasim Akram		0
M. P. Dowman c Crawley b Chapple	82	M. N. Bowen b Austin		9
J. E. R. Gallian c Wasim Akram b Yates	41	A. R. Oram not out		1
*P. Johnson c Chapple b Yates	17			
R. T. Robinson c Wasim Akram		L-b 10, w 3, n-b 4		17
b Chapple	8			
G. F. Archer b Austin	16	1/51 2/147 3/177	(48.1 overs)	240
A. G. Wharf c Lloyd b Chapple	10	4/188 5/189 6/203		
P. A. Strang c Atherton b Martin	8	7/217 8/225 9/225		

Bowling: Martin 10–0–53–1; Austin 9.1–0–33–2; Wasim Akram 9–1–50–2; Yates 10–0–48–2; Chapple 10–0–46–3.

Umpires: R. Julian and J. W. Lloyds.

LEICESTERSHIRE v MINOR COUNTIES

At Leicester, May 8. Leicestershire won by 256 runs. Toss: Leicestershire.

Records aplenty were set in this mismatch. Leicestershire ran up their highest – and the competition's second-highest – total, as well as winning by the second-highest margin. (Both total and margin were records for the 50-over format, introduced in 1996.) Three individuals also enjoyed memorable days: Maddy scored 151 from 125 balls to win his third Gold Award of the season, Wells took six for 25, his best figures in any competition, and Cumberland's Sharp bowled his ten overs for just 29 runs, when none of his colleagues could manage less than seven an over.

Gold Award: D. L. Maddy.

Leicestershire

D. L. Maddy c Oakes b Fielding	151	*C. C. Lewis not out		55
I. J. Sutcliffe c Nicholson b Sharp	19	†P. A. Nixon not out		23
B. F. Smith c Rogers b Pennett	7	B 1, l-b 13, w 6, n-b 8		28
P. V. Simmons c Goldsmith b Fielding	37			
V. J. Wells c Fielding b Pennett	18	1/66 2/85 3/175	(6 wkts, 50 overs)	382
J. M. Dakin b Pennett	44	4/236 5/279 6/324		

D. J. Millns, T. J. Mason and A. D. Mullally did not bat.

Bowling: Sharp 10–3–29–1; Oakes 10–0–96–0; Goldsmith 10–0–70–0; Pennett 10–0–97–3; Fielding 10–0–76–2.

Minor Counties

*S. J. Dean lbw b Lewis	28		J. M. Fielding b Wells	0
D. M. Ward b Simmons	27		S. Oakes b Wells	5
C. J. Rogers c Nixon b Wells	11		M. A. Sharp not out	0
A. J. Jones c Nixon b Lewis	0		B 1, l-b 5, w 10, n-b 10	26
N. R. Gaywood c Nixon b Simmons	14			
S. C. Goldsmith c Maddy b Wells	11		1/56 2/85 3/87	(29 overs) 126
†P. J. Nicholson lbw b Wells	3		4/89 5/115 6/116	
D. B. Pennett c sub b Wells	1		7/117 8/118 9/121	

Bowling: Mullally 2–0–16–0; Millns 2–0–24–0; Simmons 7–0–27–2; Lewis 8–1–28–2; Wells 10–2–25–6.

Umpires: J. W. Lloyds and K. E. Palmer.

LANCASHIRE v NORTHAMPTONSHIRE

At Manchester, May 9. Lancashire won by 71 runs. Toss: Northamptonshire.

To qualify, Lancashire had to win convincingly and hope that Warwickshire either lost to Nottinghamshire or let their net run-rate slip. Atherton's wretched form continued, but Flintoff held the innings together with a classy run-a-ball 92 and Hegg hit a spirited 44. Northamptonshire, without Curran and Malcolm, and with no hope of qualification, capitulated. Meanwhile, news from Edgbaston confirmed that Lancashire's efforts had borne fruit.

Gold Award: A. Flintoff.

Lancashire

M. A. Atherton c Ripley b Rose	0		G. Yates c Capel b Rose	16
A. Flintoff c Sales b Penberthy	92		G. Chapple not out	2
J. P. Crawley c Loye b Snape	21			
N. H. Fairbrother b Penberthy	14		L-b 3, w 4, n-b 12	19
G. D. Lloyd lbw b Snape	38			
*Wasim Akram c Rose b Snape	8		1/2 2/80 3/111	(8 wkts, 50 overs) 258
†W. K. Hegg not out	44		4/169 5/187 6/205	
I. D. Austin c Snape b Capel	4		7/218 8/247	

P. J. Martin did not bat.

Bowling: Rose 10–0–59–2; Taylor 10–2–48–0; Capel 7–0–33–1; Snape 9–0–44–3; Penberthy 10–0–40–2; Innes 4–0–31–0.

Northamptonshire

M. B. Loye c Chapple b Austin	25		*†D. Ripley run out	4
D. J. Capel c Hegg b Austin	10		F. A. Rose b Flintoff	1
D. J. Sales b Yates	16		J. P. Taylor b Yates	14
R. J. Bailey lbw b Martin	1		B 2, l-b 11, w 13	26
A. L. Penberthy not out	56			
T. C. Walton c Hegg b Wasim Akram	2		1/31 2/47 3/48	(41 overs) 187
J. N. Snape lbw b Wasim Akram	31		4/64 5/74 6/136	
K. J. Innes lbw b Chapple	1		7/147 8/157 9/164	

Bowling: Martin 8–2–32–1; Austin 7–0–21–2; Wasim Akram 8–1–20–2; Yates 9–0–47–2; Chapple 6–0–42–1; Flintoff 3–0–12–1.

Umpires: V. A. Holder and M. J. Kitchen.

WARWICKSHIRE v NOTTINGHAMSHIRE

At Birmingham, May 9. Warwickshire won by five runs. Toss: Warwickshire.

Lara was accused of naive captaincy as Warwickshire missed out on the quarter-finals. At the start, they enjoyed a net run-rate of 20.24 to Lancashire's 15.62. And when Nottinghamshire, in pursuit of a modest 229, were languishing at 66 for five, Warwickshire's progress seemed safe. But then Lara chose to bowl his two spinners, Smith and Giles, and the runs flowed. Gie, batting with assurance beyond his 21 years, and Noon put on 121 in 24 overs. If Lara realised the effect on his team's chances, he did not show it. Giles eventually removed both batsmen, and Nottinghamshire fell six short, but Warwickshire's victory was a hollow one: Lancashire went through instead.

Gold Award: N. A. Gie.

Warwickshire

N. V. Knight lbw b Evans	10	†K. J. Piper b Evans		12
N. M. K. Smith c Strang b Evans	0	G. C. Small not out		5
D. L. Hemp c Wharf b Dowman	50	E. S. H. Giddins not out		1
*B. C. Lara c Noon b Strang	49	L-b 11, w 10, n-b 4		25
T. L. Penney c Pollard b Evans	49			
D. R. Brown b Wharf	24	1/1 2/43 3/116	(9 wkts, 50 overs)	228
A. F. Giles c and b Oram	1	4/141 5/197 6/200		
G. Welch run out	2	7/205 8/215 9/227		

Bowling: Oram 10–2–46–1; Evans 10–0–27–4; Wharf 10–0–54–1; Gallian 3–0–25–0; Strang 10–0–43–1; Dowman 7–0–22–1.

Nottinghamshire

P. R. Pollard b Welch	1	P. A. Strang not out		6
M. P. Dowman c Piper b Welch	28	K. P. Evans not out		2
J. E. R. Gallian c Piper b Welch	0			
G. F. Archer c Giles b Brown	25	B 7, l-b 11, w 7		25
N. A. Gie c and b Giles	70			
*P. Johnson c Piper b Giddins	0	1/2 2/9 3/52	(8 wkts, 50 overs)	223
†W. M. Noon b Giles	46	4/65 5/66 6/187		
A. G. Wharf c Penney b Giles	20	7/200 8/220		

A. R. Oram did not bat.

Bowling: Welch 10–2–25–3; Brown 10–0–36–1; Giddins 8–0–40–1; Small 4–0–18–0; Smith 8–1–35–0; Giles 10–0–51–3.

Umpires: B. Dudleston and B. Leadbeater.

GROUP B

DERBYSHIRE v DURHAM

At Derby, April 28. Durham won by six runs. Toss: Durham.

Durham continued their encouraging start to the season in a match reduced to 36 overs a side by overnight rain. They were largely indebted to Collingwood's 30 from 18 balls at the end of the innings, and to Betts, who bowled Barnett when Derbyshire's reply was belatedly gathering momentum.

Gold Award: P. D. Collingwood.

Durham

J. J. B. Lewis b Cork	47	P. D. Collingwood not out		30
M. J. Foster b DeFreitas	9	J. Boiling not out		1
J. E. Morris c Blackwell b Harris	21	B 1, l-b 10, w 4, n-b 8		23
*D. C. Boon c Barnett b Clarke	31			—
N. J. Speak b Harris	19	1/25 2/62 3/122	(6 wkts, 36 overs)	185
†M. P. Speight c Harris b Clarke	4	4/128 5/140 6/182		

M. M. Betts, J. Wood and S. J. Harmison did not bat.

Bowling: DeFreitas 6–0–25–1; Cork 8–0–42–1; Harris 7–0–32–2; Aldred 7–0–30–0; Clarke 7–0–38–2; Barnett 1–0–7–0.

Derbyshire

*D. G. Cork c Speight b Betts	25	P. A. J. DeFreitas not out		19
A. S. Rollins c Morris b Wood	14	I. D. Blackwell not out		2
T. A. Tweats run out	3	B 2, l-b 10, w 11		23
K. J. Barnett b Betts	38			—
S. D. Stubbings b Foster	7	1/46 2/47 3/57	(6 wkts, 36 overs)	179
V. P. Clarke run out	48	4/75 5/140 6/166		

†K. M. Krikken, P. Aldred and A. J. Harris did not bat.

Bowling: Betts 8–1–28–2; Harmison 6–0–36–0; Wood 7–1–22–1; Foster 7–0–37–1; Boiling 4–0–22–0; Collingwood 4–0–22–0.

Umpires: D. J. Constant and J. H. Hampshire.

YORKSHIRE v WORCESTERSHIRE

At Leeds, April 28. Yorkshire won by five wickets (D/L method). Toss: Worcestershire.

Worcestershire's lacklustre batting and inspired seam bowling by Hamilton left Yorkshire a modest target, which rain revised to 116 from 35 overs. Hamilton, who last played in this competition for Scotland in 1994, bowled Moody and took three more wickets within ten balls. At 64 for eight, Worcestershire were heading for their lowest one-day total, but Leatherdale and Newport helped to double the score. After a poor start, Lehmann and White made sure for Yorkshire, and they won with 15 balls to spare.

Gold Award: G. M. Hamilton.

Worcestershire

W. P. C. Weston run out	12	R. K. Illingworth c Byas b Hamilton		0
V. S. Solanki c Parker b Silverwood	10	P. J. Newport not out		28
G. A. Hick c Byas b Gough	3	A. Sheriyar b Hutchison		8
*T. M. Moody b Hamilton	9	B 6, l-b 6, w 5, n-b 6		23
G. R. Haynes c Blakey b Hutchison	4			—
D. A. Leatherdale lbw b Gough	25	1/17 2/23 3/32	(35.5 overs)	128
S. R. Lampitt c Byas b Hamilton	4	4/51 5/58 6/62		
†S. J. Rhodes c Blakey b Hamilton	2	7/64 8/64 9/109		

Bowling: Silverwood 8–2–16–1; Gough 8–1–32–2; Hamilton 8–0–33–4; Hutchison 4.5–2–9–2; White 7–1–26–0.

Yorkshire

A. McGrath lbw b Moody	22	†R. J. Blakey not out		2
M. P. Vaughan c Solanki b Haynes	3	L-b 1, w 7, n-b 2		10
*D. Byas lbw b Haynes	5			—
D. S. Lehmann c Illingworth b Moody	31	1/5 2/17 3/57	(5 wkts, 32.3 overs)	119
C. White c Solanki b Lampitt	27	4/90 5/98		
B. Parker not out	19			

D. Gough, C. E. W. Silverwood, G. M. Hamilton and P. M. Hutchison did not bat.

Bowling: Newport 7–1–15–0; Haynes 6–1–20–2; Moody 7–3–24–2; Lampitt 6–0–30–1; Sheriyar 2–0–16–0; Leatherdale 4.3–0–13–0.

Umpires: V. A. Holder and R. A. White.

WORCESTERSHIRE v DERBYSHIRE

At Worcester, May 1. Worcestershire won by one wicket. Toss: Worcestershire.

Sheriyar belted his first ball – the last of the game – for four to win a topsy-turvy match. Victory seemed improbable when Worcestershire needed 31 from three overs, with three wickets standing, but Rhodes kept his cool with an unbeaten 37. DeFreitas – who had hit 51 off 42 balls – was unable to bowl at the end, having complained of dizzy spells.

Gold Award: S. J. Rhodes.

Derbyshire

*D. G. Cork c Haynes b Newport	35	S. D. Stubbings c Lampitt b Moody	1
I. D. Blackwell b Sheriyar	17	P. A. J. DeFreitas not out	51
T. A. Tweats c Weston b Newport	9	L-b 4, w 16, n-b 2	22
K. J. Barnett c Leatherdale b Illingworth	23		
A. S. Rollins not out	70	1/27 2/73 3/73 (7 wkts, 50 overs)	229
V. P. Clarke run out	0	4/126 5/126	
†K. M. Krikken c Rhodes b Moody	1	6/130 7/134	

P. Aldred and A. J. Harris did not bat.

Bowling: Newport 7–1–26–2; Haynes 6–0–26–0; Sheriyar 7–0–24–1; Lampitt 10–0–46–0; Moody 8–1–51–2; Illingworth 10–1–29–1; Leatherdale 2–0–23–0.

Worcestershire

W. P. C. Weston c Harris b DeFreitas	10	R. K. Illingworth lbw b Aldred	11
V. S. Solanki c Harris b DeFreitas	5	P. J. Newport run out	5
G. A. Hick c and b Barnett	57	A. Sheriyar not out	4
*T. M. Moody b Harris	29	B 4, l-b 5, w 3	12
G. R. Haynes c Cork b Clarke	35		
D. A. Leatherdale c and b Barnett	4	1/15 2/15 3/75 (9 wkts, 50 overs)	231
S. R. Lampitt c Cork b Harris	22	4/144 5/150 6/150	
†S. J. Rhodes not out	37	7/195 8/221 9/227	

Bowling: DeFreitas 7–0–28–2; Cork 10–2–44–0; Harris 10–0–59–2; Aldred 8–0–40–1; Clarke 9–0–31–1; Barnett 6–0–20–2.

Umpires: J. W. Holder and R. A. White.

SCOTLAND v YORKSHIRE

At Linlithgow, May 2. Yorkshire won by three wickets. Toss: Yorkshire.

To the discomfort of his compatriots, Scottish-born Hamilton, playing his second Cup match for Yorkshire, returned to his home ground to help send Scotland to defeat. He took two quick wickets, and conceded just 13 in his seven overs. Despite the slow wicket, 169 should not have worried the visiting batsmen, but it did. An upset was distinctly possible when Yorkshire were 79 for five, with three wickets for the left-arm swing of Asim Butt, formerly of Lahore, making his debut for Scotland after four years' residence. But Blakey and Gough held firm.

Gold Award: Asim Butt.

Scotland

B. M. W. Patterson c Lehmann		C. M. Wright c Fisher b White	1
b Hamilton .	13	Asim Butt not out	2
B. G. Lockie b Lehmann	48		
M. J. Smith c Silverwood b Hamilton	21	B 1, l-b 7, w 6, n-b 6	20
*G. Salmond b Gough	15		
J. G. Williamson c Gough b Lehmann	5	1/28 2/60 3/104 (7 wkts, 50 overs) 168
†A. G. Davies c McGrath b Fisher	13	4/120 5/120
J. E. Brinkley not out	30	6/144 7/156

K. Thomson and N. R. Dyer did not bat.

Bowling: Silverwood 3–0–22–0; Gough 10–2–39–1; Hamilton 7–2–13–2; White 6–2–18–1; Fisher 8–1–26–1; Vaughan 10–2–25–0; Lehmann 6–0–17–2.

Yorkshire

A. McGrath lbw b Asim Butt	0	D. Gough lbw b Thomson	30
M. P. Vaughan b Brinkley	5	G. M. Hamilton not out	1
*D. Byas c Salmond b Dyer	43	L-b 1, w 9, n-b 2	12
D. S. Lehmann c Davies b Asim Butt	23		
C. White lbw b Asim Butt	0	1/6 2/32 3/74 (7 wkts, 46.5 overs) 172
B. Parker c Davies b Wright	15	4/78 5/79
†R. J. Blakey not out	43	6/111 7/160

I. D. Fisher and C. E. W. Silverwood did not bat.

Bowling: Brinkley 10–3–26–1; Thomson 9–3–35–1; Asim Butt 10–1–42–3; Williamson 2–0–10–0; Dyer 10–1–30–1; Wright 5.5–0–28–1.

Umpires: A. Clarkson and J. H. Hampshire.

DERBYSHIRE v YORKSHIRE

At Derby, May 4. Yorkshire won by 36 runs. Toss: Derbyshire.

Yorkshire's Australian left-hander Lehmann proved far too good for the home attack, batting just 94 balls and bringing up his hundred with a six off Cork. For Derbyshire, Barnett scored a measured 56 and DeFreitas a swift 42. But Silverwood and White – whose four for 29 was his best in this competition – gave Yorkshire their third successive victory, and condemned Derbyshire to their third successive defeat.

Gold Award: D. S. Lehmann.

Yorkshire

A. McGrath st Krikken b Aldred	55	D. Gough c Blackwell b Dean	0
M. P. Vaughan c Krikken b Cork	8	G. M. Hamilton not out	16
*D. Byas c Cork b Aldred	26	L-b 4, w 16, n-b 10	30
D. S. Lehmann not out	102		
C. White c Clarke b Cork	5	1/14 2/75 3/139 (7 wkts, 50 overs) 271
B. Parker b Aldred	19	4/152 5/197
†R. J. Blakey b Dean	10	6/229 7/230

C. E. W. Silverwood and P. M. Hutchison did not bat.

Bowling: DeFreitas 10–0–44–0; Cork 10–0–42–2; Dean 10–0–62–2; Aldred 10–0–53–3; Clarke 10–0–66–0.

Derbyshire

*D. G. Cork b Silverwood	5	†K. M. Krikken b White	0
I. D. Blackwell c Parker b White	27	P. Aldred not out	24
A. S. Rollins lbw b Silverwood	3	K. J. Dean not out	14
K. J. Barnett c McGrath b Silverwood	56	L-b 5, w 10, n-b 8	23
V. P. Clarke b White	2		
T. A. Tweats c McGrath b Vaughan	28	1/19 2/29 3/56	(9 wkts, 50 overs) 235
P. A. J. DeFreitas lbw b Hamilton	42	4/58 5/116 6/167	
B. L. Spendlove c McGrath b White	11	7/187 8/187 9/199	

Bowling: Silverwood 10–0–59–3; Gough 10–1–42–0; White 10–0–29–4; Hutchison 6–1–13–0; Hamilton 8–0–57–1; Lehmann 3–0–11–0; Vaughan 3–0–19–1.

Umpires: R. Julian and A. G. T. Whitehead.

WORCESTERSHIRE v SCOTLAND

At Worcester, May 4. Worcestershire won by six wickets. Toss: Scotland.

Moody combined four for 24 with a run-a-ball fifty, to earn him a seventh Gold Award and his side a comfortable victory. None of the Scottish batsmen played a dominant innings and Worcestershire's target was a modest 141. That seemed a little steeper at two for two, but Hick and Moody, as so often, ended the county's anxieties.

Gold Award: T. M. Moody.

Scotland

B. M. W. Patterson st Rhodes b Illingworth	33	Asim Butt lbw b Moody	0
B. G. Lockie b Haynes	0	K. Thomson lbw b Moody	3
R. A. Parsons b Newport	18	N. R. Dyer not out	0
*J. G. Williamson b Newport	0		
M. J. D. Allingham c Rhodes b Lampitt	22	L-b 2, w 5, n-b 4	11
†A. G. Davies c Solanki b Illingworth	35	1/0 2/37 3/39	(47.1 overs) 140
J. E. Brinkley c Rhodes b Moody	7	4/73 5/81 6/97	
C. M. Wright c Haynes b Moody	11	7/131 8/131 9/140	

Bowling: Newport 10–3–18–2; Haynes 4–0–17–1; Sheriyar 5–1–15–0; Lampitt 8–2–29–1; Illingworth 7.1–0–21–2; Moody 8–1–24–4; Leatherdale 5–0–14–0.

Worcestershire

W. P. C. Weston c Davies b Asim Butt	1	D. A. Leatherdale not out	1
V. S. Solanki lbw b Brinkley	1	L-b 2, w 10	12
G. A. Hick not out	61		
*T. M. Moody b Dyer	51	1/2 2/2	(4 wkts, 27.3 overs) 141
G. R. Haynes c Davies b Asim Butt	14	3/83 4/139	

†S. J. Rhodes, S. R. Lampitt, R. K. Illingworth, P. J. Newport and A. Sheriyar did not bat.

Bowling: Asim Butt 6.3–1–20–2; Brinkley 9–1–32–1; Wright 2–0–22–0; Thomson 4–0–25–0; Dyer 6–0–40–1.

Umpires: G. I. Burgess and J. H. Harris.

DURHAM v SCOTLAND

At Chester-le-Street, May 6. Durham won by two wickets. Toss: Scotland.

Only a determined knock of 55 by Speight allowed Durham to avoid serious embarrassment. Had Scotland been able to start with greater urgency – Lockie battled 40 overs for his 54 – things might have ended otherwise. Lockhart speeded matters up with 75, though the only other significant contribution was 49 from Extras.

Gold Award: D. R. Lockhart.

Scotland

B. M. W. Patterson lbw b Betts	6	M. J. D. Allingham not out	4
B. G. Lockie c Speight b Wood	54	†A. G. Davies not out	1
D. R. Lockhart b Wood	75	L-b 23, w 19, n-b 7	49
R. A. Parsons c Speight b Killeen	15		
J. E. Brinkley run out	1	1/26 2/135 3/194 (6 wkts, 50 overs)	210
*G. Salmond b Killeen	5	4/195 5/195 6/209	

C. M. Wright, Asim Butt and N. R. Dyer did not bat.

Bowling: Betts 10–2–32–1; Wood 10–1–30–2; Killeen 10–0–64–2; Foster 10–2–26–0; Boiling 10–0–35–0.

Durham

J. J. B. Lewis run out	38	M. M. Betts not out	10
M. A. Roseberry run out	11	N. Killeen not out	0
N. J. Speak c Lockhart b Dyer	13		
*D. C. Boon c Davies b Allingham	8	B 3, l-b 5, w 11, n-b 8	27
P. D. Collingwood c Wright b Allingham	16		
†M. P. Speight c Salmond b Brinkley	55	1/36 2/78 3/79 (8 wkts, 48.3 overs)	213
M. J. Foster b Wright	35	4/96 5/120 6/203	
J. Boiling lbw b Wright	0	7/203 8/205	

J. Wood did not bat.

Bowling: Asim Butt 10–1–52–0; Brinkley 9.3–0–46–1; Wright 9–2–43–2; Dyer 10–0–21–1; Allingham 10–0–43–2.

Umpires: N. T. Plews and R. A. White.

DURHAM v WORCESTERSHIRE

At Chester-le-Street, May 7. Durham won by two wickets. Toss: Worcestershire.

Durham qualified for the quarter-finals for the first time through their third successive win. In an upside-down sort of match, the bowlers were always in control – even with the bat. Illingworth and Sheriyar put on 48 for Worcestershire's tenth wicket while Betts and Killeen shared an unbroken ninth-wicket stand of 50 to win. To reinforce the point, Foster, who had taken three top-order wickets, hit the only fifty of the game. There was one other landmark in Worcestershire's final Benson and Hedges match; on catching Speight, Rhodes became only the second wicket-keeper, after the late David Bairstow, to make 100 dismissals in the competition.

Gold Award: M. J. Foster.

Worcestershire

W. P. C. Weston lbw b Betts	10	R. K. Illingworth not out	35
V. S. Solanki c Boiling b Foster	25	P. J. Newport c Boon b Killeen	0
G. A. Hick c Speight b Wood	7	A. Sheriyar b Betts	15
*T. M. Moody b Foster	7	L-b 17, w 4, n-b 4	25
G. R. Haynes c Wood b Foster	16		
D. A. Leatherdale run out	1	1/24 2/40 3/58 (49.1 overs)	161
S. R. Lampitt b Boiling	9	4/61 5/63 6/90	
†S. J. Rhodes b Killeen	11	7/90 8/111 9/113	

Bowling: Betts 9.1–2–26–2; Killeen 10–3–28–2; Foster 10–0–26–3; Wood 10–2–30–1; Boiling 10–0–34–1.

Durham

M. A. Roseberry c Weston b Newport	7	M. M. Betts not out	20
M. J. Foster b Leatherdale	54	N. Killeen not out	24
J. E. Morris c Leatherdale b Newport	0		
N. J. Speak b Hick b Sheriyar	2	L-b 4, w 3, n-b 22	29
*D. C. Boon c Rhodes b Newport	1		
J. J. B. Lewis b Newport	4	1/17 2/17 3/34 (8 wkts, 40.5 overs)	162
†M. P. Speight c Rhodes b Lampitt	12	4/35 5/50 6/81	
J. Boiling b Leatherdale	9	7/111 8/112	

J. Wood did not bat.

Bowling: Newport 10–1–36–4; Sheriyar 10–1–47–1; Lampitt 5–0–28–1; Moody 8–0–28–0; Illingworth 3–2–1–0; Leatherdale 4.5–1–18–2.

Umpires: N. T. Plews and G. Sharp.

SCOTLAND v DERBYSHIRE

At Forfar, May 8. Derbyshire won by three wickets. Toss: Derbyshire.

Neither team had won yet, and twice the Scots had glimpses of a famous victory, but ultimately the professionals' nerve was the stronger. Defending a total of 174 – which featured four run-outs – Scotland bowled and fielded with huge commitment to reduce Derbyshire to 116 for seven. But Tweats and Krikken pulled them through.

Gold Award: T. A. Tweats.

Scotland

B. M. W. Patterson c Spendlove b Harris	9	S. Gourlay run out	24
B. G. Lockie b Clarke	51	C. M. Wright c DeFreitas b Harris	9
*D. R. Lockhart lbw b Clarke	24	N. R. Dyer not out	0
R. A. Parsons lbw b Barnett	4	B 1, l-b 8, w 12	21
J. G. Williamson run out	20		
M. J. D. Allingham lbw b Aldred	12	1/26 2/84 3/100 (49.4 overs)	174
J. E. Brinkley run out	0	4/108 5/137 6/137	
†A. G. Davies run out	0	7/137 8/141 9/174	

Bowling: DeFreitas 4–0–18–0; Harris 8.4–2–22–2; Aldred 10–0–38–1; Cork 9–0–30–0; Barnett 10–2–35–1; Clarke 8–2–22–2.

Derbyshire

*D. G. Cork c Davies b Wright	14	T. A. Tweats not out	42
I. D. Blackwell c Davies b Wright	0	†K. M. Krikken not out	22
A. S. Rollins lbw b Brinkley	16	L-b 1, w 11, n-b 8	20
K. J. Barnett c and b Gourlay	37		
P. A. J. DeFreitas c Davies b Williamson	7	1/0 2/24 3/43 (7 wkts, 49 overs)	177
V. P. Clarke b Williamson	14	4/57 5/79	
B. L. Spendlove lbw b Dyer	5	6/94 7/116	

P. Aldred and A. J. Harris did not bat.

Bowling: Brinkley 10–2–31–1; Wright 10–2–37–2; Allingham 7–0–24–0; Williamson 10–0–45–2; Dyer 8–0–25–1; Gourlay 4–0–14–1.

Umpires: H. D. Bird and M. J. Harris.

YORKSHIRE v DURHAM

At Leeds, May 9. Yorkshire won by eight wickets. Toss: Durham.

After three wins, Durham came back to earth with a bump. The Yorkshire seamers found assistance in a pitch of variable pace, and only Lewis offered serious resistance. The wicket seemed calmer later, and Byas and Lehmann, whose unbeaten 65 came from 63 balls, easily maintained Yorkshire's 100 per cent record in the group.

Gold Award: J. J. B. Lewis.

Durham

M. A. Roseberry c Blakey b Gough	...	1	M. M. Betts c White b Gough	11
M. J. Foster c Gough b Hutchison	...	18	N. Killeen b Silverwood	1
*J. E. Morris c Blakey b Hutchison	...	19	J. Wood not out	2
N. J. Speak c Blakey b Silverwood	...	23	B 1, l-b 6, w 4, n-b 8	19
J. J. B. Lewis c Gough b Hamilton	...	67		
†M. P. Speight b Silverwood	...	0	1/3 2/32 3/48	(49.2 overs) 172
J. A. Daley c Lehmann b Hutchison	...	7	4/116 5/120 6/148	
J. Boiling b Gough	...	4	7/150 8/165 9/170	

Bowling: Silverwood 10–1–38–3; Gough 9.2–1–27–3; Hutchison 5–0–14–3; Hamilton 10–2–33–1; White 10–1–31–0; Vaughan 5–0–22–0.

Yorkshire

A. McGrath c Speight b Wood	...	35
M. P. Vaughan lbw b Betts	...	13
*D. Byas not out	...	52
D. S. Lehmann not out	...	65
L-b 3, w 5, n-b 2	...	10
1/38 2/75	(2 wkts, 34.1 overs)	175

C. White, B. Parker, †R. J. Blakey, D. Gough, G. M. Hamilton, C. E. W. Silverwood and P. M. Hutchison did not bat.

Bowling: Wood 7.1–1–43–1; Betts 10–1–51–1; Killeen 7–0–35–0; Foster 6–1–20–0; Boiling 4–0–23–0.

Umpires: J. W. Holder and J. W. Lloyds.

GROUP C

The British Universities' squad for the competition was: A. Singh (Cambridge) (*captain*), T. M. B. Bailey (Loughborough), M. J. Chilton (Durham), M. K. Davies (Loughborough), W. J. House (Cambridge), B. L. Hutton (Durham), J. R. G. Lawrence (Durham), D. Leather (Loughborough), G. R. Loveridge (Cambridge), R. S. C. Martin-Jenkins (Durham), J. P. Pyemont (Cambridge), A. J. Strauss (Durham), L. D. Sutton (Durham).

HAMPSHIRE v SURREY

At Southampton, April 28. Surrey won by 48 runs. Toss: Hampshire.

Cup holders Surrey began their campaign with a straightforward victory over Hampshire, who had not beaten them in this competition since 1986. The customary lightning start from Surrey's openers – Brown made 43 out of 69 in 12 overs – was an ideal base for Thorpe and Butcher, and three bowlers cost 60 or more. Once White and Smith were separated, Hampshire's reply fizzled out; Salisbury's leg-spin proved too much for the lower-middle order.

Gold Award: M. A. Butcher.

Surrey

A. D. Brown c Smith b Mascarenhas	...	43	I. D. K. Salisbury not out	6
†A. J. Stewart b Mascarenhas	...	19	M. P. Bicknell not out	8
B. C. Hollioake c Aymes b Hartley	...	13		
G. P. Thorpe c Aymes b Renshaw	...	48	L-b 17, w 10	27
M. A. Butcher c Aymes b Hartley	...	67		
*A. J. Hollioake c McLean b Mascarenhas	16		1/69 2/70 3/86	(8 wkts, 50 overs) 267
J. D. Ratcliffe c Laney b Mascarenhas	..	4	4/181 5/212 6/220	
N. Shahid c Keech b Hartley	...	16	7/252 8/254	

J. E. Benjamin did not bat.

Bowling: Renshaw 10–0–69–1; McLean 10–0–61–0; Hartley 10–0–32–3; Mascarenhas 10–0–28–4; Udal 10–0–60–0.

Hampshire

S. D. Udal c Ratcliffe b Bicknell	13	†A. N. Aymes not out	18
J. S. Laney c and b Bicknell	12	N. A. M. McLean lbw b B. C. Hollioake	2
G. W. White c B. C. Hollioake b Bicknell	47	S. J. Renshaw b B. C. Hollioake	23
*R. A. Smith b A. J. Hollioake	45	L-b 9, w 9, n-b 3	21
M. Keech lbw b Bicknell	16		—
P. J. Hartley st Stewart b Salisbury	3	1/30 2/38 3/116 (48.4 overs)	219
A. D. Mascarenhas b Salisbury	14	4/137 5/143 6/149	
W. S. Kendall lbw b Salisbury	5	7/169 8/172 9/177	

Bowling: Bicknell 10–1–38–4; Benjamin 7–0–26–0; B. C. Hollioake 9.4–0–56–2; Butcher 5–0–19–0; A. J. Hollioake 7–0–39–1; Salisbury 10–1–32–3.

Umpires: A. A. Jones and M. J. Kitchen.

SOMERSET v KENT

At Taunton, April 28. No result (abandoned).

SOMERSET v BRITISH UNIVERSITIES

At Taunton, April 30. Somerset won by two wickets. Toss: Somerset.

The Universities came close again on this ground, nine years after nearly knocking Somerset out in a quarter-final. An elegant unbeaten 46 from Chilton enabled the students to set a healthy target in a match reduced to 20 overs. Burns and Rose sped Somerset towards their goal and had reached 98 for one from 12 overs, when Greg Loveridge, a leg-spinner who played one Test for New Zealand in 1995-96, broke through. He and Northamptonshire slow left-armer Davies took three wickets each to accelerate the collapse: seven wickets fell for 21 before Pierson and Reeve – the old master in these situations – scrambled the county home.

Gold Award: M. Burns.

British Universities

*A. Singh b Caddick	8	†T. M. B. Bailey run out	2
G. R. Loveridge c Harden b Caddick	8	D. Leather not out	12
M. J. Chilton not out	46	B 1, l-b 4, w 3, n-b 2	10
J. P. Pyemont b Trescothick	25		—
W. J. House c Turner b Trescothick	9	1/14 2/24 3/71 (6 wkts, 20 overs)	127
R. S. C. Martin-Jenkins c Reeve b Burns	7	4/83 5/98 6/108	

B. L. Hutton, M. K. Davies and J. R. G. Lawrence did not bat.

Bowling: Rose 4–0–26–0; Caddick 4–0–25–2; Trescothick 4–0–20–2; Reeve 4–0–21–0; Burns 2–0–15–1; Parsons 2–0–15–0.

Somerset

M. Burns b Loveridge	55	D. A. Reeve not out	2
S. C. Ecclestone run out	0	A. R. K. Pierson not out	8
G. D. Rose b Loveridge	38		
†R. J. Turner c Pyemont b Loveridge	0	L-b 4, w 7, n-b 2	13
R. J. Harden b Davies	0		—
*P. D. Bowler lbw b Martin-Jenkins	12	1/0 2/98 3/98 (8 wkts, 19 overs)	130
K. A. Parsons st Bailey b Davies	1	4/100 5/100 6/113	
M. E. Trescothick st Bailey b Davies	1	7/119 8/119	

A. R. Caddick did not bat.

Bowling: Martin-Jenkins 4–0–20–1; Leather 2–0–16–0; Lawrence 4–0–42–0; Chilton 1–0–9–0; Loveridge 4–1–28–3; Davies 4–1–11–3.

Umpires: B. Dudleston and D. R. Shepherd.

SURREY v GLOUCESTERSHIRE

At The Oval, April 30. Surrey won by seven wickets. Toss: Surrey.

For the third successive year, these two teams met on the last day of April: for the third successive year, Surrey triumphed by reaching a target of over 260. Gloucestershire's total was built around a wily 83 by Russell, batting at No. 3, and Cunliffe, whose 58 followed centuries in this fixture in 1996 and 1997. But Brown, who hit three sixes in his 68-ball 74, and Thorpe made a respectable score seem thoroughly inadequate.

Gold Award: A. D. Brown.

Gloucestershire

N. J. Trainor c Thorpe b Benjamin	6		M. C. J. Ball c A. J. Hollioake		
R. J. Cunliffe b Butcher	58		b B. C. Hollioake	6
†R. C. Russell c Butcher			J. Lewis not out	9
b B. C. Hollioake	83		L-b 6, w 9	15
A. J. Wright c A. J. Hollioake b Benjamin	33				
R. I. Dawson b B. C. Hollioake	29		1/7 2/103 3/180	(7 wkts, 50 overs) 266
*M. W. Alleyne not out	24		4/219 5/226	
T. H. C. Hancock st Stewart b Salisbury	3		6/236 7/247	

A. M. Smith and C. A. Walsh did not bat.

Bowling: Bicknell 8–1–39–0; Benjamin 10–3–54–2; B. C. Hollioake 9–0–62–3; Butcher 8–1–30–1; A. J. Hollioake 5–0–21–0; Salisbury 10–0–54–1.

Surrey

A. D. Brown c Walsh b Hancock	74		*A. J. Hollioake not out	23
†A. J. Stewart b Ball	39		L-b 5, w 2, n-b 2	9
G. P. Thorpe c Wright b Smith	85				
M. A. Butcher not out	40		1/88 2/152 3/239	(3 wkts, 47.3 overs) 270

B. C. Hollioake, N. Shahid, J. D. Ratcliffe, I. D. K. Salisbury, M. P. Bicknell and J. E. Benjamin did not bat.

Bowling: Lewis 9–0–69–0; Smith 10–0–49–1; Walsh 9.3–0–55–0; Ball 10–0–46–1; Alleyne 7–0–39–0; Hancock 2–0–7–1.

Umpires: H. D. Bird and A. G. T. Whitehead.

BRITISH UNIVERSITIES v HAMPSHIRE

At Oxford, May 1. Hampshire won by three wickets. Toss: Hampshire.

Martin-Jenkins and Leather rescued the Universities after they had subsided to 100 for six but, on an easy pitch, 209 was never likely to be enough. Hampshire's struggle for victory said more about their lack of confidence than the students' bowling. Only Keech and, at the end, Mascarenhas, who scored an undefeated 52 from 48 balls, made serious contributions.

Gold Award: R. S. C. Martin-Jenkins.

British Universities

*A. Singh lbw b Renshaw	17		D. Leather not out	42
J. P. Pyemont b Renshaw	11		J. R. G. Lawrence not out	4
M. J. Chilton c Laney b Hartley	3				
G. R. Loveridge c and b James	22		L-b 12, w 20, n-b 2	34
W. J. House c James b Udal	24				
L. D. Sutton lbw b James	4		1/31 2/36 3/46	(8 wkts, 50 overs) 209
R. S. C. Martin-Jenkins run out	39		4/92 5/96 6/100	
†T. M. B. Bailey run out	9		7/129 8/177	

M. K. Davies did not bat.

Bowling: McLean 10–2–18–0; Renshaw 10–0–51–2; Hartley 10–1–45–1; Mascarenhas 2–0–9–0; Udal 10–1–33–1; James 8–0–41–2.

Hampshire

S. D. Udal c Bailey b Martin-Jenkins ..	10	†A. N. Aymes run out	. . . .	5
J. S. Laney c Bailey b Martin-Jenkins ..	8	S. J. Renshaw not out	. . . .	2
G. W. White c Pyemont b Leather	11	L-b 4, w 19	. . . .	23
*R. A. Smith run out	13			—
M. Keech c Lawrence b Chilton	74	1/14 2/31 3/31	(7 wkts, 48.5 overs)	212
K. D. James st Bailey b Chilton	14	4/78 5/127		
A. D. Mascarenhas not out	52	6/163 7/190		

P. J. Hartley and N. A. M. McLean did not bat.

Bowling: Martin-Jenkins 9.5–1–34–2; Leather 9–2–38–1; Loveridge 10–0–43–0; Chilton 10–1–38–2; Davies 7–1–34–0; Lawrence 2–0–11–0; House 1–0–10–0.

Umpires: H. D. Bird and R. Palmer.

KENT v GLOUCESTERSHIRE

At Canterbury, May 2. Kent won by three wickets. Toss: Kent.

Gloucestershire made a confident start but subsided from 81 for nought to 98 for four within five overs. In Kent's reply, Walker and Ealham received support from most of the top order, although no single batsman dominated, and the winning run came from the last ball of a rain-shortened game.

Gold Award: M. A. Ealham.

Gloucestershire

R. J. Cunliffe c Hooper b Ealham	20	J. Lewis c Wells b Fleming	. . . .	1
T. H. C. Hancock b Fleming	56	A. M. Smith not out	. . . .	9
†R. C. Russell c Marsh b Ealham	12	C. A. Walsh not out	. . . .	16
A. J. Wright hit wkt b Hooper	3	B 1, l-b 13, w 8, n-b 2	24
R. I. Dawson c Marsh b Igglesden	25			—
*M. W. Alleyne c Hooper b Ealham . . .	9	1/81 2/83 3/98	(9 wkts, 43 overs)	195
M. G. N. Windows b Headley	17	4/98 5/111 6/150		
M. C. J. Ball c Marsh b Igglesden	3	7/156 8/158 9/159		

Bowling: Headley 8–0–33–1; Igglesden 8–1–41–2; Hooper 9–0–39–1; Ealham 9–0–30–3; Fleming 7–0–20–2; Phillips 2–0–18–0.

Kent

T. R. Ward c Russell b Walsh	13	*†S. A. Marsh not out	. . . .	3
M. J. Walker b Hancock	57	B. J. Phillips not out	. . . .	1
C. L. Hooper c Russell b Lewis	20	L-b 5, w 11, n-b 6	22
A. P. Wells b Walsh	22			—
M. A. Ealham c Russell b Smith	32	1/19 2/71 3/126	(7 wkts, 43 overs)	196
G. R. Cowdrey c Russell b Walsh	12	4/130 5/163		
M. V. Fleming c Cunliffe b Smith	14	6/183 7/194		

D. W. Headley and A. P. Igglesden did not bat.

Bowling: Walsh 9–1–36–3; Smith 9–0–53–2; Lewis 9–0–34–1; Alleyne 8–0–33–0; Ball 4–0–18–0; Hancock 4–0–17–1.

Umpires: M. J. Harris and M. J. Kitchen.

GLOUCESTERSHIRE v SOMERSET

At Bristol, May 4. Gloucestershire won by 26 runs. Toss: Somerset.

The ferocity of Lewis's batting swung the game for Gloucestershire. With the four front-line bowlers having completed their allocation, Bowler was forced to use back-up men at the end of the innings. Lewis clubbed 33 from 13 balls; the last four overs cost 51. Trescothick and Reeve tried to salvage something for Somerset, but there was no way back from 110 for seven.

Gold Award: J. Lewis.

Gloucestershire

R. J. Cunliffe b Reeve	31		J. Lewis not out	33
T. H. C. Hancock b Rose	4		M. J. Cawdron not out	5
†R. C. Russell c Turner b Trescothick	17		L-b 12, w 5, n-b 4	21
A. J. Wright run out	44			
R. I. Dawson lbw b Mushtaq Ahmed	31		1/16 2/55 3/63 (7 wkts, 50 overs) 234	
*M. W. Alleyne c Parsons b Caddick	24		4/125 5/163	
M. G. N. Windows c Parsons b Burns	24		6/177 7/219	

A. M. Smith and C. A. Walsh did not bat.

Bowling: Caddick 10–0–33–1; Rose 10–1–35–1; Trescothick 7–0–40–1; Reeve 10–1–29–1; Mushtaq Ahmed 10–1–50–1; Parsons 2–0–20–0; Burns 1–0–15–1.

Somerset

*P. D. Bowler b Smith	13		D. A. Reeve b Lewis	26
M. Burns c Wright b Cawdron	25		A. R. Caddick c Alleyne b Hancock	10
P. C. L. Holloway c Russell b Smith	0		Mushtaq Ahmed not out	6
R. J. Harden c Russell b Lewis	8		B 1, l-b 10, w 3, n-b 2	16
G. D. Rose b Alleyne	31			
†R. J. Turner c and b Alleyne	18		1/28 2/36 3/51 (48 overs) 208	
K. A. Parsons b Walsh	6		4/56 5/99 6/110	
M. E. Trescothick c Russell b Hancock	49		7/110 8/171 9/186	

Bowling: Walsh 9–2–39–1; Smith 10–4–17–2; Lewis 9–0–49–2; Cawdron 6–0–27–1; Alleyne 10–0–42–2; Hancock 4–0–23–2.

Umpires: D. J. Constant and B. Leadbeater.

SURREY v BRITISH UNIVERSITIES

At The Oval, May 4. Surrey won by 105 runs. Toss: Surrey.

Surrey won the match at a canter, but it was the versatility of Durham University's Mark Chilton that stayed in the memory. Bowling a gentle medium-pace, he claimed four wickets, took three catches and won his second Gold Award (his first came in the students' victory over Sussex in 1997). Of Surrey's long list of internationals, Thorpe and Hollioake senior both scored half-centuries, but the county were dismissed inside 50 overs. Chilton could not reproduce his form with the bat, however, and the students went down honourably but convincingly.

Gold Award: M. J. Chilton.

Surrey

A. D. Brown c House b Leather	30		I. D. K. Salisbury c Chilton	
†A. J. Stewart c Loveridge			b Martin-Jenkins	12
b Martin-Jenkins	19		M. P. Bicknell not out	10
B. C. Hollioake lbw b Chilton	32		Saqlain Mushtaq st Bailey b Hutton	6
G. P. Thorpe c Chilton b Hutton	58		B 4, l-b 5, w 8, n-b 2	19
M. A. Butcher run out	13			
*A. J. Hollioake c and b Chilton	55		1/27 2/67 3/95 (49.1 overs) 263	
N. Shahid c sub b Chilton	4		4/124 5/196 6/201	
J. D. Ratcliffe c Loveridge b Chilton	5		7/215 8/242 9/249	

Bowling: Martin-Jenkins 8–0–46–2; Leather 10–0–56–1; Loveridge 6–1–39–0; Chilton 10–0–28–4; Davies 6–0–42–0; Hutton 9.1–0–43–2.

British Universities

*A. Singh lbw b Bicknell	4	D. Leather st Stewart b Salisbury	2
J. P. Pyemont run out	22	B. L. Hutton c Saqlain Mushtaq	
M. J. Chilton b B. C. Hollioake	9	b B. C. Hollioake	4
G. R. Loveridge c Ratcliffe		M. K. Davies c Stewart	
b Saqlain Mushtaq	31	b B. C. Hollioake	1
W. J. House c Saqlain Mushtaq			
b A. J. Hollioake	30	B 3, l-b 8, w 9, n-b 4	24
L. D. Sutton lbw b A. J. Hollioake	17		—
R. S. C. Martin-Jenkins st Stewart		1/5 2/23 3/74	(43.3 overs) 158
b Salisbury	2	4/92 5/120 6/133	
†T. M. B. Bailey not out	12	7/134 8/150 9/156	

Bowling: Bicknell 8–0–30–1; B. C. Hollioake 8.3–3–23–3; Saqlain Mushtaq 7–2–16–1; Butcher 3–0–19–0; Salisbury 10–2–38–2; A. J. Hollioake 7–1–21–2.

Umpires: J. W. Holder and P. Willey.

SOMERSET v HAMPSHIRE

At Taunton, May 5. Somerset won by five wickets. Toss: Hampshire.

A questionable decision to bat and pedestrian scoring helped to ensure Hampshire's early exit. Only the last man, McLean, took the attack to the bowlers; he smashed 28 from nine deliveries, including three sixes and two fours from the final over, bowled by Caddick. More typical of the innings was Rose's analysis of two for ten from eight overs. Stephenson's medium-pace slowed Somerset's progress, but the result was inevitable.

Gold Award: G. D. Rose.

Hampshire

G. W. White b Rose	0	†A. N. Aymes run out	0
J. S. Laney c Trescothick b Rose	6	P. J. Hartley c Reeve b Mushtaq Ahmed	20
*R. A. Smith b Mushtaq Ahmed	20	N. A. M. McLean not out	28
M. Keech b Pierson	29		
A. D. Mascarenhas c Trescothick		L-b 1, w 1, n-b 6	8
b Pierson	15		—
J. P. Stephenson c Burns b Trescothick	5	1/0 2/19 3/39	(9 wkts, 50 overs) 169
S. D. Udal c Pierson b Trescothick	5	4/77 5/80 6/88	
K. D. James not out	33	7/93 8/95 9/132	

Bowling: Rose 8–2–10–2; Caddick 10–1–60–0; Mushtaq Ahmed 9–0–33–2; Reeve 6–0–18–0; Trescothick 9–0–28–2; Pierson 8–1–19–2.

Somerset

*P. D. Bowler c Aymes b Udal	41	M. E. Trescothick not out	9
M. Burns c and b McLean	0		
R. J. Harden lbw b James	39	L-b 7, w 11, n-b 2	20
G. D. Rose lbw b Stephenson	14		—
†R. J. Turner lbw b Stephenson	15	1/1 2/64 3/101	(5 wkts, 43.3 overs) 170
K. A. Parsons not out	32	4/111 5/133	

D. A. Reeve, A. R. Caddick, A. R. K. Pierson and Mushtaq Ahmed did not bat.

Bowling: McLean 8.3–0–54–1; Hartley 8–2–24–0; James 10–1–41–1; Stephenson 10–2–18–2; Udal 4–0–15–1; Mascarenhas 3–0–11–0.

Umpires: D. R. Shepherd and J. F. Steele.

GLOUCESTERSHIRE v BRITISH UNIVERSITIES

At Bristol, May 6. British Universities won by seven runs. Toss: Gloucestershire.

Russell and Wright shared the first double-century fourth-wicket stand in the competition's 27 years, but Gloucestershire still suffered the biggest shock of the 1998 tournament. They were beaten by Will House, of Kent and Cambridge, who first hit a blistering 64 off 44 balls to ensure a challenging target. Then he broke the partnership by getting Wright caught for 93, and raced through the middle order. The students generally outclassed the opposition with their fielding and spirit, and Russell's highest one-day score was in vain. This success followed the Universities' victory over Sussex in 1997.

Gold Award: W. J. House.

British Universities

*A. Singh c Russell b Alleyne	56	A. J. Strauss not out	18
J. P. Pyemont lbw b Lewis	5		
M. J. Chilton c Alleyne b Ball	54	B 2, l-b 10, w 14, n-b 6	32
G. R. Loveridge c Ball b Walsh	26		—
W. J. House c Alleyne b Lewis	64	1/7 2/103 3/148 (5 wkts, 50 overs) 279	
L. D. Sutton not out	24	4/192 5/241	

†T. M. B. Bailey, R. S. C. Martin-Jenkins, B. L. Hutton and M. K. Davies did not bat.

Bowling: Walsh 10–1–36–1; Lewis 10–1–60–2; Smith 10–0–57–0; Alleyne 7–0–34–1; Ball 10–0–49–1; Hancock 3–0–31–0.

Gloucestershire

R. J. Cunliffe b Hutton	1	M. G. N. Windows c Hutton b House	6
T. H. C. Hancock c House b Martin-Jenkins	16	M. C. J. Ball c Loveridge b Martin-Jenkins	2
†R. C. Russell not out	119	C. A. Walsh c Loveridge b House	0
*M. W. Alleyne c Chilton b Martin-Jenkins	1	L-b 4, w 20, n-b 4	28
A. J. Wright c Singh b House	93		—
J. Lewis c Pyemont b House	4	1/12 2/28 3/29 (9 wkts, 50 overs) 272	
R. I. Dawson lbw b House	2	4/236 5/240 6/246	
		7/260 8/264 9/272	

A. M. Smith did not bat.

Bowling: Martin-Jenkins 10–3–39–3; Hutton 7–0–27–1; Davies 10–0–51–0; Chilton 8–0–59–0; House 9–0–58–5; Loveridge 6–0–34–0.

Umpires: J. F. Steele and A. G. T. Whitehead.

KENT v SURREY

At Canterbury, May 6. Surrey won by four wickets. Toss: Surrey.

Marsh clobbered 24 off the last over, bowled by Saqlain Mushtaq, to set a respectable target, but the Surrey top order easily knocked off the runs and beat Kent, as they had in the 1997 final. Brown and Stewart scored at almost eight an over to lay the ideal foundation for Thorpe to make an unbeaten 85. The margin of victory would have been greater, but for two controversial decisions to dismiss Stewart and Adam Hollioake. Stewart was out when Patel took a return catch between his elbows, although replays suggested he took it on the bounce. Hollioake was stumped when a leg-side wide rebounded on to the stumps from the keeper's shoulder, although many thought the batsman's foot was grounded. The third umpire was available, but John Harris did not call on him in either case. Mindful of their public roles, the captains of the England Test and one-day sides – both appointed the previous day – departed without demur.

Gold Award: G. P. Thorpe.

Kent

T. R. Ward c Brown b Benjamin	51	M. M. Patel st Stewart	
M. J. Walker run out	2	b Saqlain Mushtaq	7
C. L. Hooper run out	69	D. W. Headley c and b A. J. Hollioake	1
A. P. Wells run out	6	A. P. Igglesden not out	0
M. A. Ealham c and b Salisbury	56	L-b 11, w 5, n-b 6	22
G. R. Cowdrey lbw b Salisbury	3		
M. V. Fleming c Butcher		1/14 2/92 3/111 (9 wkts, 50 overs)	260
b B. C. Hollioake	4	4/202 5/204 6/211	
*†S. A. Marsh not out	37	7/212 8/231 9/236	

Bowling: Bicknell 8–1–32–0; Benjamin 10–2–37–1; B. C. Hollioake 5–0–38–1; Saqlain Mushtaq 10–0–66–1; Salisbury 10–0–36–2; A. J. Hollioake 7–0–40–1.

Surrey

A. D. Brown c Wells b Hooper	46	B. C. Hollioake c and b Headley	2
†A. J. Stewart c and b Patel	40	M. P. Bicknell not out	14
G. P. Thorpe not out	85	L-b 10, w 8, n-b 6	24
*A. J. Hollioake st Marsh b Fleming	44		
M. A. Butcher c Marsh b Fleming	6	1/93 2/102 3/200 (6 wkts, 47 overs)	261
J. D. Ratcliffe lbw b Patel	0	4/218 5/219 6/222	

J. E. Benjamin, I. D. K. Salisbury and Saqlain Mushtaq did not bat.

Bowling: Headley 9–0–59–1; Igglesden 6–0–38–0; Fleming 8–0–37–2; Patel 10–0–59–2; Hooper 7–1–26–1; Ealham 7–1–32–0.

Umpires: J. C. Balderstone and J. H. Harris.

HAMPSHIRE v KENT

At Southampton, May 7. Kent won by 125 runs. Toss: Hampshire.

Wells hit his first Benson and Hedges century and won his first Gold Award in 17 seasons to set up an easy victory. On a pitch of variable pace that rewarded the seam bowlers, he and Ward saw Kent to a total of 246 that always looked too much for a struggling Hampshire. Headley and Phillips both struck early to leave them sinking at 33 for five.

Gold Award: A. P. Wells.

Kent

T. R. Ward b James	60	M. V. Fleming c White b Stephenson	5
M. J. Walker c Stephenson b Hartley	7	*†S. A. Marsh not out	17
C. L. Hooper lbw b James	14	L-b 9, w 13	22
A. P. Wells not out	111		
M. A. Ealham c Udal b Stephenson	4	1/12 2/40 3/152 (6 wkts, 50 overs)	246
G. R. Cowdrey c Aymes b Hartley	6	4/161 5/183 6/193	

B. J. Phillips, D. W. Headley and M. M. Patel did not bat.

Bowling: McLean 9–0–65–0; Hartley 10–3–37–2; James 10–0–28–2; Stephenson 10–0–51–2; Udal 8–0–34–0; Mascarenhas 3–0–22–0.

Hampshire

G. W. White lbw b Phillips	1	S. D. Udal c Hooper b Headley	4
J. P. Stephenson c Fleming b Headley	15	P. J. Hartley c Marsh b Hooper	4
*R. A. Smith c Marsh b Headley	1	N. A. M. McLean c Walker b Fleming	1
M. Keech c Marsh b Phillips	1	L-b 7, w 2, n-b 4	13
J. S. Laney c Hooper b Phillips	6		
†A. N. Aymes not out	46	1/18 2/21 3/22 (37.4 overs)	121
K. D. James c Phillips b Fleming	24	4/22 5/33 6/73	
A. D. Mascarenhas b Hooper	5	7/81 8/100 9/105	

Bowling: Headley 10–2–33–3; Phillips 8–2–13–3; Patel 5–0–21–0; Hooper 10–0–28–2; Fleming 4.4–0–19–2.

Umpires: G. I. Burgess and D. R. Shepherd.

Benson and Hedges Cup, 1998 759

SURREY v SOMERSET

At The Oval, May 8. Surrey won by nine runs. Toss: Surrey. County debut: M. A. V. Bell.

Surrey won their 12th successive Benson and Hedges match and ensured a home tie in the quarter-finals, though it was unexpectedly close. Their reliable batting again set a stiff target, Stewart compiling his fourth century in the competition and Ben Hollioake striking 91 from 98 balls; together they added 185 in 34 overs. In the style of their opponents, Reeve and Burns charged out of the blocks – the first wicket fell at 158, with 21 overs remaining. But as Somerset began the last three overs needing another 21, they had just two wickets in hand, and fell short.

Gold Award: B. C. Hollioake.

Surrey

A. D. Brown c Rose b Caddick	19	J. D. Ratcliffe lbw b Caddick	9	
†A. J. Stewart c Caddick b Trescothick	108	I. D. K. Salisbury not out	7	
B. C. Hollioake lbw b Trescothick	91	B 1, l-b 14, w 9	24	
M. A. Butcher b Reeve	15			
*A. J. Hollioake b Trescothick	10	1/40 2/225 3/240	(6 wkts, 50 overs) 296	
N. Shahid not out	13	4/255 5/263 6/281		

M. P. Bicknell, M. A. V. Bell and J. E. Benjamin did not bat.

Bowling: Caddick 10–1–42–2; Rose 10–1–49–0; Reeve 10–0–64–1; Trescothick 10–0–46–3; Mushtaq Ahmed 3–0–36–0; Pierson 6–0–35–0; Parsons 1–0–9–0.

Somerset

D. A. Reeve c Bicknell b A. J. Hollioake	60	A. R. Caddick b B. C. Hollioake	0	
M. Burns b Salisbury	95	Mushtaq Ahmed c Butcher b Bicknell	26	
M. E. Trescothick b Salisbury	25	A. R. K. Pierson not out	2	
*P. D. Bowler lbw b B. C. Hollioake	19			
R. J. Harden b B. C. Hollioake	0	L-b 11, w 7, n-b 8	26	
G. D. Rose c Shahid b Bicknell	14			
†R. J. Turner c A. J. Hollioake b Bicknell	8	1/158 2/189 3/200	(48.5 overs) 287	
K. A. Parsons c and b A. J. Hollioake	12	4/201 5/232 6/242		
		7/250 8/250 9/278		

Bowling: Bell 4–0–25–0; B. C. Hollioake 10–0–62–3; Bicknell 9.5–0–51–3; Benjamin 6–0–43–0; Salisbury 10–0–51–2; A. J. Hollioake 9–0–44–2.

Umpires: R. Palmer and P. Willey.

BRITISH UNIVERSITIES v KENT

At Oxford, May 9. Kent won by six wickets. Toss: British Universities.

Only a crushing defeat could have prevented Kent from qualifying for the quarter-finals for the 19th time in 27 attempts. Chilton and Sutton added 98 for the students' fifth wicket, but 204 was insufficient to test a team of Kent's one-day strengths. They wobbled mid-innings, but England all-rounders Fleming and Ealham saw them to a comfortable win. Fleming's century won him his seventh Gold Award.

Gold Award: M. V. Fleming.

British Universities

*A. Singh c Marsh b Phillips	9	†T. M. B. Bailey lbw b Ealham	0	
J. P. Pyemont lbw b Igglesden	11	B. L. Hutton b Ealham	0	
M. J. Chilton st Marsh b Patel	56	M. K. Davies not out	2	
G. R. Loveridge c Marsh b Phillips	0	L-b 16, w 4, n-b 2	22	
W. J. House c Fleming b Igglesden	10			
L. D. Sutton b Phillips	60	1/19 2/29 3/30	(48.3 overs) 204	
A. J. Strauss c Marsh b Ealham	29	4/45 5/143 6/176		
R. S. C. Martin-Jenkins b Fleming	5	7/196 8/197 9/197		

Bowling: Igglesden 9–1–34–2; Phillips 10–3–34–3; Hooper 10–1–36–0; Ealham 7.3–0–20–3; Patel 5–0–30–1; Fleming 7–0–34–1.

Kent

T. R. Ward lbw b Hutton	0	M. A. Ealham not out	50
M. J. Walker c Singh b Loveridge	32	B 1, l-b 4, w 11	16
M. V. Fleming not out	105		
C. L. Hooper lbw b Davies	0	1/1 2/91	(4 wkts, 39.5 overs) 205
G. R. Cowdrey c and b Loveridge	2	3/91 4/102	

A. P. Wells, *†S. A. Marsh, B. J. Phillips, A. P. Igglesden and M. M. Patel did not bat.

Bowling: Martin-Jenkins 9–1–60–0; Hutton 5–0–31–1; Loveridge 10–1–41–2; Davies 10–1–31–1; Chilton 4–1–23–0; House 1.5–0–14–0.

Umpires: A. Clarkson and K. E. Palmer.

GLOUCESTERSHIRE v HAMPSHIRE

At Bristol, May 9. Gloucestershire won by six wickets. Toss: Hampshire.

With neither county able to qualify, there was little at stake. Hampshire struggled on a sticky pitch, Alleyne taking three wickets as they slumped to 50 for four. Stephenson and Mascarenhas, continuing his good form, helped them to 173. Initially, Gloucestershire fared even worse, losing their fourth wicket at 47, but there the parallels stopped. Church, in his first Benson and Hedges innings, hit an undefeated 64 and Hampshire finished bottom of the group.

Gold Award: M. J. Church.

Hampshire

G. W. White run out	3	S. D. Udal not out	14
J. P. Stephenson c Wright b Ball	53	P. J. Hartley c Russell b Cawdron	8
*R. A. Smith c Williams b Alleyne	4	C. A. Connor not out	1
M. Keech c Wright b Alleyne	2	B 1, l-b 4, w 8, n-b 2	15
W. S. Kendall c Cunliffe b Alleyne	3		
A. D. Mascarenhas c Cunliffe b Cawdron	53	1/22 2/37 3/39	(9 wkts, 50 overs) 173
K. D. James c Hancock b Cawdron	10	4/50 5/104 6/139	
†A. N. Aymes c Cunliffe b Cawdron	9	7/141 8/159 9/170	

Bowling: Smith 9–3–20–0; Lewis 8–1–35–0; Alleyne 10–1–22–3; Cawdron 9–1–28–4; Ball 10–1–48–1; Hancock 4–0–15–0.

Gloucestershire

R. J. Cunliffe run out	5	M. J. Church not out	64
T. H. C. Hancock c Stephenson b Hartley	24	L-b 5, w 6, n-b 2	17
R. C. Russell c Aymes b Connor	0		
A. J. Wright not out	59	1/29 2/33	(4 wkts, 42 overs) 174
*M. W. Alleyne lbw b James	5	3/35 4/47	

M. J. Cawdron, M. C. J. Ball, J. Lewis, †R. C. J. Williams and A. M. Smith did not bat.

Bowling: Connor 10–2–40–1; Hartley 9–2–33–1; Stephenson 7–1–26–0; James 5–1–23–1; Udal 6–0–20–0; Mascarenhas 5–1–27–0.

Umpires: G. I. Burgess and J. F. Steele.

GROUP D

GLAMORGAN v ESSEX

At Cardiff, April 29. No result. Toss: Essex.

Croft opened the batting against Ilott, reviving memories of their shoving match in the Chelmsford gloom the previous August. Croft got the better of the contest here, with 77 from 64 balls, but the game was washed out.

Glamorgan

S. P. James b Ilott	71	†A. D. Shaw not out		10
R. D. B. Croft st Rollins b Grayson	77			
A. Dale run out	7	L-b 11, w 3		14
*M. P. Maynard run out	55			
P. A. Cottey c Rollins b Ilott	7	1/116 2/129 3/227	(5 wkts, 46.2 overs)	254
G. P. Butcher not out	13	4/227 5/240		

Waqar Younis, S. D. Thomas, S. L. Watkin and D. A. Cosker did not bat.

Bowling: Ilott 8.2–0–48–2; Cowan 10–0–60–0; Napier 3–0–25–0; Irani 5–0–35–0; Grayson 10–0–32–1; Such 10–0–43–0.

Essex

D. D. J. Robinson, S. G. Law, *N. Hussain, R. C. Irani, S. D. Peters, A. P. Grayson, G. R. Napier, †R. J. Rollins, M. C. Ilott, A. P. Cowan and P. M. Such.

Umpires: G. I. Burgess and N. T. Plews.

MIDDLESEX v SUSSEX

At Lord's, April 29. Middlesex won by six runs. Toss: Sussex. County debut: M. G. Bevan.

Makeshift opener Brown, scoring his first century in this competition, got help from Weekes and enabled Middlesex to set a challenging target. Ramprakash then took two wickets, including Bevan's, to follow his promising bowling on the West Indies tour. Determined batting from Newell made a game of it, but he took a leg-bye off the third ball of the final over, and could only watch as the last two batsmen fell to Weekes. It was Middlesex's first victory over a first-class county in the Benson and Hedges since May 1995.

Gold Award: K. R. Brown.

Middlesex

†K. R. Brown c Moores b Edwards	114	P. N. Weekes not out		66
J. L. Langer b Edwards	3	B 3, l-b 12, w 9, n-b 10		34
*M. R. Ramprakash c Adams b Robinson	29			
J. C. Pooley lbw b Lewry	20	1/6 2/73 3/124	(5 wkts, 50 overs)	283
O. A. Shah c Moores b Robinson	17	4/163 5/283		

D. C. Nash, R. L. Johnson, J. P. Hewitt, A. R. C. Fraser and T. F. Bloomfield did not bat.

Bowling: Lewry 10–0–42–1; Edwards 10–0–55–2; Jarvis 10–0–51–0; Robinson 10–1–55–2; Davis 5–0–32–0; Newell 5–0–33–0.

Sussex

*C. J. Adams c Brown b Fraser	54	R. P. Davis c Shah b Weekes		16
A. D. Edwards lbw b Johnson	20	J. D. Lewry b Weekes		3
K. Greenfield c Weekes b Johnson	0	M. A. Robinson b Weekes		0
M. G. Bevan b Ramprakash	36	L-b 16, w 5, n-b 4		25
J. R. Carpenter b Ramprakash	31			
K. Newell not out	62	1/74 2/78 3/79	(50 overs)	277
†P. Moores run out	14	4/145 5/163 6/197		
P. W. Jarvis b Johnson	16	7/223 8/262 9/277		

Bowling: Fraser 10–1–48–1; Hewitt 6–0–36–0; Weekes 10–0–42–3; Johnson 10–0–64–3; Bloomfield 6–0–32–0; Ramprakash 8–0–39–2.

Umpires: H. D. Bird and B. Leadbeater.

IRELAND v GLAMORGAN

At Castle Avenue, Dublin, May 1. Glamorgan won by 115 runs. Toss: Glamorgan.

Croft continued the batting form he had shown against Essex by striking another brisk fifty. Only Cottey and Waqar gave much support, though McCrum, bowling nine wides in his first six overs, aided the Welsh cause. Waqar and Croft also bowled well; the Irish never recovered from 32 for four, despite a stand of 54 between Joyce and Dunlop.

Gold Award: R. D. B. Croft.

Glamorgan

S. P. James b McCrum	13	Waqar Younis c Molins b Johnson	33
R. D. B. Croft b Johnson	67	D. A. Cosker not out	1
A. Dale c Molins b Dwyer	17	S. L. Watkin not out	0
*M. P. Maynard lbw b Heasley	10	B 1, l-b 4, w 13, n-b 10	28
P. A. Cottey c McCallan b Cooke	54		
G. P. Butcher b Dwyer	2	1/48 2/95 3/115 (9 wkts, 50 overs) 230	
†A. D. Shaw run out	2	4/150 5/161 6/169	
S. D. Thomas b Molins b Cooke	3	7/178 8/226 9/229	

Bowling: McCrum 8–0–46–1; Eagleson 7–1–30–0; Heasley 8–1–36–1; Dwyer 10–0–40–2; Johnson 10–0–40–2; Cooke 7–0–33–2.

Ireland

J. A. M. Molins run out	14	G. Cooke c Shaw b Dale	11
R. L. Eagleson lbw b Watkin	0	P. McCrum c Croft b Dale	0
†A. D. Patterson b Waqar Younis	8	M. D. Dwyer not out	0
N. C. Johnson lbw b Waqar Younis	4	L-b 2, w 14	16
E. C. Joyce st Shaw b Cosker	28		
*A. R. Dunlop lbw b Croft	26	1/6 2/28 3/28 (44 overs) 115	
W. K. McCallan st Shaw b Croft	1	4/32 5/86 6/94	
D. Heasley c sub b Cosker	7	7/94 8/105 9/108	

Bowling: Waqar Younis 7–1–22–2; Watkin 7–2–27–1; Thomas 5–0–13–0; Cosker 10–1–26–2; Croft 10–4–16–2; Dale 3–1–6–2; Cottey 2–1–3–0.

Umpires: T. E. Jesty and P. Willey.

SUSSEX v ESSEX

At Hove, May 2. Essex won by seven wickets. Toss: Essex.

On an easy pitch, 566 runs were scored for the loss of just six wickets. Sussex began slowly, but Greenfield and Bevan, whose 87 came from 71 balls, picked up the tempo. Essex, helped on their way by some wayward bowling, shrugged off the early loss of Law to make light of an exacting target. Robinson's 137 improved his best in this competition by 101 runs.

Gold Award: D. D. J. Robinson.

Sussex

*C. J. Adams c Such b Irani	29	J. R. Carpenter not out	11
A. D. Edwards b Grayson	43	B 1, l-b 10, w 7	18
K. Greenfield not out	93		
M. G. Bevan b Grayson	87	1/70 2/79 3/239 (3 wkts, 50 overs) 281	

K. Newell, †P. Moores, P. W. Jarvis, R. P. Davis, J. D. Lewry and M. A. Robinson did not bat.

Bowling: Cowan 10–1–37–0; Ilott 10–1–42–0; Napier 6–0–37–0; Irani 10–0–63–1; Grayson 6–0–44–2; Such 8–0–47–0.

Essex

D. D. J. Robinson not out	137	A. P. Grayson not out	13
S. G. Law c Adams b Lewry	0	B 2, l-b 5, w 9, n-b 16.	32
*N. Hussain b Jarvis	62		
R. C. Irani c Carpenter b Jarvis	41	1/11 2/164 3/253 (3 wkts, 48.5 overs) 285	

S. D. Peters, †R. J. Rollins, G. R. Napier, M. C. Ilott, A. P. Cowan and P. M. Such did not bat.

Bowling: Lewry 9–0–49–1; Edwards 6–0–38–0; Robinson 10–1–42–0; Jarvis 10–0–63–2; Davis 2–0–13–0; Newell 3–0–15–0; Bevan 8.5–0–58–0.

Umpires: J. C. Balderstone and V. A. Holder.

ESSEX v IRELAND

At Chelmsford, May 4. Essex won by 171 runs. Toss: Essex.

Robinson hit his third one-day century in nine days as Essex ran up 359, which was then the fifth-highest total in this competition. Valuable support came from the other front-line batsmen and Extras, which contributed 39. Ireland never attempted the run-chase.

Gold Award: D. D. J. Robinson.

Essex

D. D. J. Robinson c Dunlop b Heasley. .	114	A. P. Cowan not out	2
S. G. Law c Patterson b Eagleson	46		
*N. Hussain c Dwyer b Heasley	71	L-b 5, w 14, n-b 20.	39
R. C. Irani c Patterson b McCrum	69		
A. P. Grayson c Joyce b Heasley	16	1/86 2/219 3/316 (7 wkts, 50 overs) 359	
†R. J. Rollins st Patterson b McCrum . .	1	4/352 5/355	
S. D. Peters run out	1	6/356 7/359	

M. C. Ilott, N. F. Williams and P. M. Such did not bat.

Bowling: McCrum 10–0–60–2; Eagleson 10–1–36–1; Neely 3–0–32–0; Heasley 7–0–77–3; Dwyer 10–0–59–0; Johnson 7–0–62–0; McCallan 3–0–28–0.

Ireland

J. A. M. Molins c Hussain b Irani	9	R. L. Eagleson not out	15
W. K. McCallan b Williams	19	P. McCrum not out	1
†A. D. Patterson c Rollins b Such	10	L-b 7, w 6, n-b 2	15
N. C. Johnson b Grayson	53		
E. C. Joyce b Grayson	42	1/33 2/39 3/63 (7 wkts, 50 overs) 188	
*A. R. Dunlop c Rollins b Ilott	24	4/115 5/165	
D. Heasley c Law b Williams	0	6/168 7/181	

M. D. Dwyer and G. J. Neely did not bat.

Bowling: Ilott 9–2–26–1; Cowan 6–2–9–0; Irani 8–1–43–1; Williams 7–0–26–2; Such 10–0–39–1; Grayson 10–2–38–2.

Umpires: J. C. Balderstone and G. Sharp.

MIDDLESEX v IRELAND

At Lord's, May 5. Middlesex won by six wickets. Toss: Ireland.

After the Irish heroics in Dublin the previous year, this was a more sober affair. Ireland were without both Hansie Cronje, about to start the more serious job of captaining South Africa, and local star "Decker" Curry, who had reportedly fallen out with coach Mike Hendrick. Only Dunlop's 66-ball 59 not out threatened the county attack, which included both Angus Fraser and his younger brother, Alastair, back at Middlesex on a match-by-match basis ten years after his first spell with the club. Playing with understandable caution, the home team made unexciting but inexorable progress towards their target.

Gold Award: A. R. Dunlop.

Ireland

J. A. M. Molins b Johnson	34	R. L. Eagleson c Langer b Johnson	3
W. K. McCallan c Nash b A. G. J. Fraser	35	G. Cooke not out	4
†A. D. Patterson c Shah b Ramprakash	23	B 2, l-b 8, w 9, n-b 2	21
N. C. Johnson c Weekes b A. G. J. Fraser	0		
E. C. Joyce run out	6	1/74 2/89 3/89 (7 wkts, 50 overs) 196	
*A. R. Dunlop not out	59	4/97 5/128	
D. Heasley c A. G. J. Fraser b Johnson	11	6/144 7/167	

P. McCrum and M. D. Dwyer did not bat.

Bowling: A. R. C. Fraser 10–1–22–0; Hewitt 7–1–37–0; Johnson 10–2–37–3; A. G. J. Fraser 9–1–40–2; Weekes 9–1–35–0; Ramprakash 5–0–15–1.

Middlesex

J. L. Langer b Cooke	4	P. N. Weekes not out	4
†K. R. Brown c and b Dwyer	46	L-b 14, w 19	33
R. L. Johnson b McCrum	26		
*M. R. Ramprakash not out	55	1/23 2/86 (4 wkts, 48 overs) 199	
J. C. Pooley c McCallan b Eagleson	31	3/104 4/183	

O. A. Shah, D. C. Nash, A. G. J. Fraser, J. P. Hewitt and A. R. C. Fraser did not bat.

Bowling: Cooke 10–0–43–1; Eagleson 9–0–36–1; McCrum 10–0–49–1; Dwyer 10–2–23–1; Heasley 9–1–34–0.

Umpires: H. D. Bird and J. W. Lloyds.

SUSSEX v GLAMORGAN

At Hove, May 5. Sussex won by three runs. Toss: Glamorgan.

Thanks to the result at Lord's, Sussex's rousing victory was not enough to prevent them failing to reach the quarter-finals for the 11th time in 12 seasons. Adams and the one-day specialist Bevan led Sussex to a massive 302 despite four wickets for Waqar Younis. When he joined Cottey, Waqar also lifted Glamorgan's reply from 204 for seven to 285, but the Welsh fell agonisingly short when two wickets went down in the final over.

Gold Award: M. G. Bevan.

Sussex

M. T. E. Peirce b Waqar Younis	16	J. D. Lewry run out	13
W. G. Khan st Shaw b Cosker	33	R. J. Kirtley c Waqar Younis b Butcher	2
*C. J. Adams c Butcher b Waqar Younis	81		
M. G. Bevan not out	95	L-b 14, w 16	30
J. R. Carpenter lbw b Waqar Younis	3		
K. Newell c Shaw b Waqar Younis	5	1/21 2/139 3/162 (9 wkts, 50 overs) 302	
A. D. Edwards c Shaw b Thomas	8	4/172 5/182 6/213	
†S. Humphries lbw b Watkin	16	7/248 8/299 9/302	

M. A. Robinson did not bat.

Bowling: Waqar Younis 10–0–43–4; Watkin 10–0–71–1; Thomas 8–0–65–1; Butcher 5–0–36–1; Croft 10–0–41–0; Cosker 7–0–32–1.

Glamorgan

S. P. James c Humphries b Lewry	2	Waqar Younis b Kirtley	45
R. D. B. Croft c Adams b Robinson	59	S. L. Watkin b Edwards	5
†A. D. Shaw lbw b Lewry	25	D. A. Cosker not out	0
A. Dale b Robinson	18	L-b 2, w 5, n-b 6	13
*P. A. Cottey run out	96		
A. W. Evans lbw b Robinson	10	1/9 2/76 3/99 (49.3 overs) 299	
G. P. Butcher c Peirce b Robinson	4	4/122 5/148 6/156	
S. D. Thomas b Kirtley	22	7/204 8/285 9/299	

Bowling: Kirtley 10–0–57–2; Lewry 10–0–51–2; Edwards 7.3–0–77–1; Robinson 10–1–53–4; Bevan 10–0–40–0; Newell 2–0–19–0.

Umpires: B. Dudleston and M. J. Harris.

ESSEX v MIDDLESEX

At Chelmsford, May 7. Middlesex won by four wickets. Toss: Middlesex.

Alastair Fraser, brother of the more famous Angus, outperformed him with four wickets to steer Middlesex to victory. This was more bad luck for Hussain, who shrugged off the disappointment of being passed over for the England captaincy with an elegant century. Most of the Middlesex top order made starts only to get out, so it fell to Weekes to settle the game with a determined 37. Victory ensured a home quarter-final for Middlesex.

Gold Award: A. G. J. Fraser.

Essex

D. D. J. Robinson c Weekes		A. P. Cowan c Brown b A. R. C. Fraser .	13
b A. R. C. Fraser .	0	M. C. Ilott c and b Ramprakash	4
S. G. Law b Johnson	37	N. F. Williams not out	20
*N. Hussain c Hewitt b Ramprakash . . .	101	P. M. Such not out	8
R. C. Irani c Brown b A. G. J. Fraser . .	11	L-b 4, w 4	8
A. P. Grayson c Shah b A. G. J. Fraser .	25		—
†R. J. Rollins c Ramprakash		1/0 2/57 3/101 (9 wkts, 50 overs) 233	
b A. G. J. Fraser .	5	4/149 5/161 6/166	
S. D. Peters c Nash b A. G. J. Fraser .	1	7/197 8/199 9/219	

Bowling: A. R. C. Fraser 10–0–40–2; Hewitt 8–0–46–0; Johnson 10–0–55–1; A. G. J. Fraser 10–0–45–4; Weekes 10–1–36–0; Ramprakash 2–0–7–2.

Middlesex

†K. R. Brown c Williams b Irani	39	P. N. Weekes not out	37
J. L. Langer c Law b Ilott	12	D. C. Nash not out	9
R. L. Johnson c Such b Ilott	24	L-b 10, w 9, n-b 4	23
*M. R. Ramprakash run out	39		—
J. C. Pooley c Hussain b Williams	48	1/27 2/63 3/116 (6 wkts, 48.5 overs) 234	
O. A. Shah lbw b Grayson	3	4/140 5/148 6/198	

J. P. Hewitt, A. R. C. Fraser and A. G. J. Fraser did not bat.

Bowling: Ilott 9.5–0–45–2; Cowan 9–0–49–0; Williams 10–0–60–1; Such 4.3–1–6–0; Irani 7–0–29–1; Grayson 8.3–0–35–1.

Umpires: J. H. Hampshire and T. E. Jesty.

GLAMORGAN v MIDDLESEX

At Cardiff, May 9. Middlesex won by 19 runs. Toss: Glamorgan.

To make it to the last eight, Glamorgan needed to overhaul not just Middlesex's total but also Essex's net run-rate. Frantic calculations determined their real target was 254 from 38.5 overs. Croft – hitting his fourth consecutive fifty in the competition – and James briefly looked as though they could manage it between them. But Croft departed in the 12th over, and their middle order let them down. For Middlesex, Brown compiled his second century of the qualifying rounds.

Gold Award: K. R. Brown.

Middlesex

†K. R. Brown c Cottey b Waqar Younis	109	D. C. Nash not out		1
J. L. Langer b Croft	46			
*M. R. Ramprakash c Shaw b Dale	23			
J. C. Pooley c Cottey b Waqar Younis	44	L-b 6, w 7, n-b 2		15
O. A. Shah c Cosker b Thomas	11			
P. N. Weekes c Cottey b Thomas	4	1/117 2/158 3/215 (6 wkts, 50 overs)		253
		4/246 5/251 6/253		

R. L. Johnson, A. G. J. Fraser, A. R. C. Fraser and T. F. Bloomfield did not bat.

Bowling: Waqar Younis 10-0-45-2; Watkin 10-1-41-0; Thomas 9-0-53-2; Cosker 6-1-32-0; Croft 10-0-47-1; Dale 5-0-29-1.

Glamorgan

S. P. James c Brown b Johnson	48	Waqar Younis st Brown b Shah		37
R. D. B. Croft c Shah b Weekes	50	S. L. Watkin not out		12
S. D. Thomas c Brown b Johnson	29	D. A. Cosker c and b Shah		1
†A. D. Shaw c Langer b Weekes	1	B 1, l-b 12, w 9, n-b 8		30
A. Dale b Ramprakash	7			
*P. A. Cottey run out	5	1/83 2/142 3/145 (45.2 overs)		234
G. P. Butcher lbw b Johnson	0	4/145 5/154 6/154		
A. W. Evans run out	14	7/167 8/179 9/231		

Bowling: A. R. C. Fraser 10-0-60-0; Bloomfield 8-0-58-0; Weekes 9-1-35-2; Johnson 10-2-33-3; Ramprakash 4-1-11-1; A. G. J. Fraser 3-0-22-0; Shah 1.2-0-2-2.

Umpires: J. C. Balderstone and A. A. Jones.

IRELAND v SUSSEX

At Eglinton, May 9. No result (abandoned).

QUARTER-FINALS

LEICESTERSHIRE v KENT

At Leicester, May 27. Leicestershire won by eight wickets. Toss: Leicestershire.

On a wicket so green it was barely distinguishable from the rest of the square, Leicestershire won an important toss, going on to win the match at a canter. Young pace bowler Ormond started the rout with three wickets in ten balls and Simmons, who bowled after an injection for his damaged ribs, finished it with five for 33. The only resistance came from Hooper, with 60, closely followed by Extras which, at 55 and containing 24 wides and 20 no-balls, broke the competition record of 53, set by Leicestershire themselves in the preliminary rounds. Mullally gave away 11 of the wides. Maddy continued his remarkable Benson and Hedges form with an unbeaten 93, to see his side home with more than 12 overs to spare.

Gold Award: D. L. Maddy.

Kent

T. R. Ward c Lewis b Mullally	1	B. J. Phillips b Simmons		0
R. W. T. Key c Smith b Ormond	4	D. W. Headley c Wells b Mullally		1
M. V. Fleming c Nixon b Ormond	11	A. P. Igglesden not out		0
C. L. Hooper c Maddy b Simmons	60	B 5, l-b 6, w 24, n-b 20		55
A. P. Wells lbw b Ormond	0			
M. A. Ealham c Brimson b Simmons	21	1/8 2/24 3/30 (45.1 overs)		158
G. R. Cowdrey c Lewis b Simmons	5	4/32 5/108 6/131		
*†S. A. Marsh c and b Simmons	0	7/131 8/137 9/147		

Bowling: Mullally 10-1-26-2; Ormond 7-0-31-3; Wells 10-1-34-0; Lewis 6-0-19-0; Simmons 9.1-1-33-5; Dakin 3-0-4-0.

Leicestershire

D. L. Maddy not out	. . . .	93
I. J. Sutcliffe lbw b Ealham	. . . .	30
B. F. Smith b Ealham	. . . .	0
P. V. Simmons not out	. . . .	25
L-b 2, w 7, n-b 2	. . . .	11

1/88 2/88   **(2 wkts, 37.2 overs)** 159

V. J. Wells, *C. C. Lewis, †P. A. Nixon, J. M. Dakin, J. Ormond, A. D. Mullally and M. T. Brimson did not bat.

Bowling: Headley 7–0–23–0; Igglesden 6–0–24–0; Phillips 5.2–0–38–0; Ealham 10–2–32–2; Fleming 4–0–25–0; Hooper 5–0–15–0.

Umpires: B. Dudleston and R. A. White.

MIDDLESEX v ESSEX

At Lord's, May 27, 28. Essex won by eight runs. Toss: Middlesex.

When play finally began at 4.45 p.m., Middlesex contributed to their own downfall with an ill-judged bowling performance that included 16 wides. The teenager Peters made 58 not out from just 57 balls and was particularly severe on Blanchett, who retreated after his first over cost 12 runs. In reply next day, Middlesex were unable to cope with Cowan, who removed the top five batsmen. When Shah joined Langer, the scoring edged towards the required rate. But they both fell lbw to Cowan in the 38th over, leaving the lower order insufficient time to finish the job. The eight-run margin made the result look closer than it really was: Fraser hit the last ball of the match for six. Cowan's five for 28 was his best return in limited-overs cricket.

Gold Award: A. P. Cowan.

Close of play: Essex 232-9 (50 overs).

Essex

D. D. J. Robinson c Brown b Fraser	. . .	0	A. P. Cowan c Fraser b Hewitt	5
S. G. Law c Langer b Johnson	. . . . . .	40	M. C. Ilott c Fraser b Weekes	8
*N. Hussain c Ramprakash b Fraser	. . .	16	P. M. Such not out	7
†R. J. Rollins c Dutch b Johnson	. . . . .	28	L-b 4, w 16	20
R. C. Irani c Dutch b Weekes	. . . . . .	22		
A. P. Grayson c Brown b Dutch	. . . . .	16	1/1 2/39 3/94 **(9 wkts, 50 overs)** 232
S. D. Peters not out	. . . .	58	4/100 5/135 6/137
D. R. Law c and b Johnson	. . . .	12	7/166 8/204 9/218

Bowling: Fraser 10–0–51–2; Hewitt 10–1–47–1; Johnson 10–0–40–3; Dutch 10–0–34–1; Weekes 9–0–44–2; Blanchett 1–0–12–0.

Middlesex

†K. R. Brown c S. G. Law b Cowan	. .	11	K. P. Dutch not out	5
R. L. Johnson b Cowan	. . . .	9	A. R. C. Fraser not out	14
J. L. Langer lbw b Cowan	. . . .	71	L-b 9, w 4	13
*M. R. Ramprakash c S. G. Law b Cowan	.	14		
O. A. Shah lbw b Cowan	. . . .	43	1/10 2/23 3/51 **(7 wkts, 50 overs)** 224
J. C. Pooley c Grayson b Ilott	. . . . .	20	4/159 5/160
P. N. Weekes c Irani b S. G. Law	. . . .	24	6/202 7/207

J. P. Hewitt and I. N. Blanchett did not bat.

Bowling: Ilott 10–1–39–1; Cowan 10–0–28–5; Irani 9–0–42–0; Such 10–0–39–0; S. G. Law 8–0–50–1; Grayson 3–0–17–0.

Umpires: A. Clarkson and R. Palmer.

SURREY v LANCASHIRE

At The Oval, May 27, 28. Surrey won by five wickets. Toss: Surrey.

A fluent innings by Atherton dented the popular perception that he is not a one-day player, but was overshadowed by a fine all-round effort from cup-holders Surrey. They fielded superbly, bowled tightly and batted belligerently enough to wrap up the tie with more than four overs remaining. Saqlain Mushtaq, the Pakistan off-spinner, claimed a hat-trick to finish off Lancashire's innings; unable to capitalise on Atherton's form, they subsided from 148 for one to 203 all out. Brown and Stewart provided a solid base for Surrey and, after an overnight interruption (rain on the first day had meant a 3.30 p.m. start), took their partnership to 81. Their other England players kept up the impetus, with Ben Hollioake striking a final flurry of boundaries.

Gold Award: M. A. Atherton.

Close of play: Surrey 35-0 (8 overs) (A. D. Brown 17*, A. J. Stewart 13*).

Lancashire

M. A. Atherton lbw b Bicknell	93	G. Yates c Ratcliffe b Saqlain Mushtaq	.	7
A. Flintoff c Ratcliffe b Bicknell	11	G. Chapple c Benjamin		
J. P. Crawley st Stewart		b Saqlain Mushtaq	.	0
b Saqlain Mushtaq	44	P. J. Martin not out		0
N. H. Fairbrother run out	11			
G. D. Lloyd c Stewart b Salisbury	1			
*Wasim Akram c B. C. Hollioake				
b Salisbury	0	L-b 5, w 6, n-b 2		13
†W. K. Hegg c Stewart b A. J. Hollioake	8			
I. D. Austin c Ratcliffe		1/26 2/148 3/164	(49.4 overs)	203
b Saqlain Mushtaq	15	4/167 5/167 6/168		
		7/185 8/203 9/203		

Bowling: Bicknell 10–2–25–2; Benjamin 10–1–43–0; A. J. Hollioake 7–0–35–1; Saqlain Mushtaq 9.4–0–46–4; Salisbury 10–0–34–2; B. C. Hollioake 3–0–15–0.

Surrey

A. D. Brown b Yates	41	B. C. Hollioake not out		14
†A. J. Stewart c Flintoff b Chapple	31			
G. P. Thorpe c Hegg b Yates	15	L-b 9, w 9, n-b 2		20
J. D. Ratcliffe c Chapple b Wasim Akram	10			
M. A. Butcher c Hegg b Martin	36	1/81 2/84 3/106	(5 wkts, 45.4 overs)	206
*A. J. Hollioake not out	39	4/113 5/183		

M. P. Bicknell, I. D. K. Salisbury, Saqlain Mushtaq and J. E. Benjamin did not bat.

Bowling: Martin 10–0–54–1; Austin 8–0–39–0; Wasim Akram 9–1–31–1; Yates 10–1–35–2; Chapple 8.4–1–38–1.

Umpires: D. R. Shepherd and A. G. T. Whitehead.

YORKSHIRE v DURHAM

At Leeds, May 27. Yorkshire won by 102 runs. Toss: Durham.

After being put in, Yorkshire suffered two early blows – in the second over they were two for two, with both McGrath and Byas gone without scoring. But a glorious innings of 119 in 133 balls from Lehmann set up an easy win. He combined unorthodox and textbook shots, making Collingwood's miss at backward point – when he was 36 – a costly error. Lehmann added 184 with Vaughan for the third wicket, a competition record for Yorkshire. He was out attempting an audacious sweep from outside off stump. Durham began positively and by the 14th over had reached 61 for two, when Boon, batting with Hutton, turned down the chance to come off for bad light. Soon afterwards, both fell to Hamilton, and the innings went into swift decline.

Gold Award: D. S. Lehmann.

Yorkshire

A. McGrath c Boon b Betts	0	†R. J. Blakey not out	26
M. P. Vaughan b Phillips	70		
*D. Byas c Speight b Brown	0	B 1, l-b 7, w 11, n-b 4	23
D. S. Lehmann c Speight b Betts	119		
C. White st Speight b Phillips	13	1/0 2/2 3/186	(5 wkts, 50 overs) 269
B. Parker not out	18	4/210 5/229	

D. Gough, G. M. Hamilton, C. E. W. Silverwood and P. M. Hutchison did not bat.

Bowling: Betts 10–3–44–2; Brown 10–2–28–1; Wood 9–0–62–0; Foster 8–0–51–0; Phillips 10–0–47–2; Collingwood 3–0–29–0.

Durham

J. J. B. Lewis c White b Silverwood	12	M. M. Betts c White b Lehmann	0
S. Hutton c Blakey b Hamilton	38	J. Wood not out	10
N. J. Speak c White b Hutchison	14	S. J. E. Brown absent hurt	
*D. C. Boon c Gough b Hamilton	14		
P. D. Collingwood c Silverwood b Lehmann	39	L-b 10, w 2, n-b 2	14
†M. P. Speight lbw b Gough	11	1/19 2/47 3/88	(39 overs) 167
M. J. Foster b Vaughan	2	4/91 5/109 6/112	
N. C. Phillips b Gough	13	7/137 8/138 9/167	

Bowling: Silverwood 6–0–23–1; Gough 9–0–38–2; Hutchison 4–1–8–1; White 6–1–20–0; Hamilton 6–1–17–2; Vaughan 4–0–24–1; Lehmann 4–0–27–2.

Umpires: J. H. Harris and M. J. Harris.

SEMI-FINALS

LEICESTERSHIRE v SURREY

At Leicester, June 9. Leicestershire won by 20 runs. Toss: Surrey.

Holders Surrey finally met their match after 13 consecutive wins in the competition since April 1997. It turned out to be the one person in even more invincible form. Maddy hit his third century in seven innings; on the way, he passed Graham Gooch's competition record of 591 runs in a season. He picked up his fifth Gold Award of 1998 and helped his side into their fifth final. It meant that Leicestershire, victorious in the first final in 1972, would also contest the last. Maddy, who scored 120 from 138 balls, shared in a second-wicket partnership of 172 with Smith. Simmons later scored at more than a run a ball to take the innings past 300. It proved too much for Surrey, although Adam Hollioake – making amends for his expensive bowling – set nerves jangling in the home dressing-room with a scorching 85 before he became the last of Lewis's four illustrious victims: England Test batsmen all.

Gold Award: D. L. Maddy.

Leicestershire

D. L. Maddy not out	120	*C. C. Lewis not out	0
I. J. Sutcliffe lbw b Bicknell	6	B 2, l-b 14, w 9, n-b 14	39
B. F. Smith st Stewart b Saqlain Mushtaq	89		
P. V. Simmons b B. C. Hollioake	40	1/17 2/189	(4 wkts, 50 overs) 311
†P. A. Nixon run out	17	3/286 4/307	

V. J. Wells, A. Habib, J. Ormond, A. D. Mullally and D. Williamson did not bat.

Bowling: Benjamin 10–2–33–0; Bicknell 10–0–55–1; Saqlain Mushtaq 10–0–46–1; A. J. Hollioake 8–0–76–0; Salisbury 0.1–0–3–0; Butcher 1.5–0–22–0; B. C. Hollioake 10–1–60–1.

Surrey

A. D. Brown run out	3	Saqlain Mushtaq run out	11
†A. J. Stewart c Simmons b Lewis	21	J. E. Benjamin not out	1
B. C. Hollioake c Lewis b Ormond	63		
G. P. Thorpe c Nixon b Lewis	2	B 6, l-b 7, w 7, n-b 6	26
M. A. Butcher hit wkt b Lewis	0		—
*A. J. Hollioake b Lewis	85	1/4 2/60 3/72 (8 wkts, 50 overs)	291
J. D. Ratcliffe st Nixon b Simmons	41	4/72 5/113 6/193	
M. P. Bicknell not out	38	7/274 8/288	

I. D. K. Salisbury did not bat.

Bowling: Mullally 10–1–45–0; Ormond 10–0–58–1; Lewis 10–1–40–4; Wells 6–0–32–0; Simmons 9–0–69–1; Williamson 5–0–34–0.

Umpires: D. J. Constant and J. H. Hampshire.

YORKSHIRE v ESSEX

At Leeds, June 9. Essex won by 95 runs. Toss: Yorkshire.

Even when languishing on 33 for three, Essex still seemed confident of making it to Lord's. Hussain – despite being briefly dazed by a heavy collision with Blakey – and Irani set about repairing the damage in almost contemptuous fashion. They had put on 83 runs in only 18 overs when Irani was caught behind. But the lower order supported Hussain until he was lbw for 78, and then Danny Law and Cowan plundered the Gough-less attack with an unbroken 56 from the last six overs. Yorkshire were 29 for three inside ten overs, and they never got on terms. Grayson took three wickets against his former colleagues, who capitulated in the 43rd over.

Gold Award: N. Hussain.

Essex

D. D. J. Robinson lbw b Silverwood	0	D. R. Law not out	36
S. G. Law c Parker b Silverwood	10	A. P. Cowan not out	15
*N. Hussain lbw b Sidebottom	78	B 6, l-b 8, w 10, n-b 6	30
†R. J. Rollins c Hamilton b Hutchison	9		—
R. C. Irani c Blakey b Sidebottom	39	1/0 2/17 3/33 (7 wkts, 50 overs)	258
A. P. Grayson c McGrath b White	24	4/116 5/159	
S. D. Peters run out	17	6/189 7/202	

M. C. Ilott and P. M. Such did not bat.

Bowling: Silverwood 7–0–45–2; Hutchison 7–0–38–1; Hamilton 8–0–35–0; White 8–0–41–1; Sidebottom 10–0–42–2; Vaughan 10–0–43–0.

Yorkshire

M. P. Vaughan lbw b Cowan	0	C. E. W. Silverwood run out	6
C. White c Rollins b Ilott	7	P. M. Hutchison not out	4
*D. Byas c Peters b Ilott	13	R. J. Sidebottom st Rollins b S. G. Law	4
D. S. Lehmann c Rollins b Such	40	B 1, l-b 4, w 9, n-b 4	18
A. McGrath b Grayson	39		—
B. Parker lbw b Grayson	10	1/0 2/16 3/29 (42.4 overs)	163
†R. J. Blakey c Such b Grayson	2	4/99 5/112 6/118	
G. M. Hamilton b S. G. Law	20	7/135 8/152 9/156	

Bowling: Cowan 8–1–33–1; Ilott 6–0–22–2; Irani 7–2–21–0; Such 10–1–34–1; Grayson 8–0–32–3; S. G. Law 3.4–0–16–2.

Umpires: B. Leadbeater and P. Willey.

FINAL

ESSEX v LEICESTERSHIRE

At Lord's, July 11, 12. Essex won by 192 runs. Toss: Leicestershire.

Essex's crushing victory in the last Benson and Hedges final reflected the topsy-turvy nature of county cricket. Next to bottom in the Championship, but top of the Sunday League, they outplayed Leicestershire, second in the Championship. Essex were lucky with the weather: no sooner had they completed their innings on the first day than the rain came, and Leicestershire – who had won the toss – could not bat until late on Sunday afternoon. By then, the pitch had become ideal for seam bowling. Leicestershire were dismissed inside 28 overs for 76, the lowest total in all 27 finals, while Essex's margin of victory was the widest in terms of runs.

The Essex innings produced some compelling batting. Conditions should have favoured the bowlers early on as well but Mullally and Lewis, pitching wide of the stumps, wasted the new ball. Lewis, in particular, gave the batsmen every chance to cut and pull. After Prichard and Stuart Law had opened with 40 in ten overs, Law played Wells off his legs to mid-wicket. His batting form remained poor, but he was to play his part later.

This brought in Hussain. He and Prichard played adventurous, high-class cricket in a decisive 134-run partnership spanning 25 overs. Prichard can seldom have looked so dominating, except perhaps in the previous Lord's final when he led his team to victory in the 1997 NatWest. As a square-cutter he looked as good as Steve Waugh, and he pulled and drove with power and fluency. Hussain capitalised on the width he was given, opening the face of the bat, as he prefers, and driving square on the off side. Simmons, too, was punished for his lack of control; his first three overs cost 27.

Prichard's fifty came from 83 balls with seven fours. He then drove both Wells and Lewis over square cover for sixes, while Hussain square cut Williamson for another. With the score on 174, Prichard was eventually caught driving at cover for 92, from 113 balls, containing 11 fours and two sixes. By the time Lewis removed Hussain it was too late, even though Essex's later batsmen contributed little.

Leicestershire's downfall the following afternoon was begun by two catches at second slip – one good, the other brilliant. First Sutcliffe flashed at Cowan, Stuart Law taking it two-handed up by his ear. Next ball, Smith pushed forward and edged, probably nearer to first slip than second, but Law saw it early and dived far and low to his left, pulling off a spectacular catch, again with both hands. Simmons then had an ugly heave at a ball from Ilott that came back into him between bat and pad, and hit the outside of the off stump.

Ten for three quickly became 36 for seven, as Maddy's charmed tournament fizzled out with just five runs. The pitch helped the Essex bowlers more than it had their opponents but, once they had lost their first three wickets, the Leicestershire batsmen came and went like lambs to the slaughter. Only a few brave blows by Nixon took them past fifty. The one-sided finish and the inevitably subdued second-day atmosphere meant a disappointing end to the competition after 27 years. – HENRY BLOFELD.

Gold Award: P. J. Prichard.   *Attendance:* 22,223; *receipts* £734,081.

Close of play: Essex 268-7 (50 overs).

Essex

*P. J. Prichard c Simmons b Williamson.	92	A. P. Cowan not out	3	
S. G. Law c Mullally b Wells	6			
N. Hussain c Smith b Lewis	88	B 2, l-b 8, w 18	28	
R. C. Irani c Maddy b Mullally	32			
D. R. Law c Lewis b Williamson	1	1/40 (2) 2/174 (1) (7 wkts, 50 overs) 268		
A. P. Grayson not out	9	3/234 (3) 4/244 (5)		
†P. J. Rollins c Brimson b Mullally . . .	0	5/245 (4) 6/250 (7)		
S. D. Peters b Mullally	9	7/265 (8) Score at 15 overs: 61-1		

M. C. Ilott and P. M. Such did not bat.

Bowling: Mullally 10–1–36–3; Lewis 9–0–59–1; Wells 10–0–34–1; Simmons 9–0–67–0; Brimson 2–0–13–0; Williamson 10–0–49–2.

Leicestershire

D. L. Maddy c S. G. Law b Cowan	...	5	A. D. Mullally lbw b Irani	1
I. J. Sutcliffe c S. G. Law b Cowan	...	1	M. T. Brimson b S. G. Law	0
B. F. Smith c S. G. Law b Cowan	....	0		
P. V. Simmons b Ilott		2	L-b 8, w 17, n-b 4	29
V. J. Wells lbw b Ilott		1		
A. Habib lbw b Ilott		5	1/6 (2) 2/6 (3) 3/10 (4) (27.4 overs)	76
†P. A. Nixon not out		21	4/17 (5) 5/31 (6) 6/31 (1)	
*C. C. Lewis c Peters b Irani		0	7/36 (8) 8/67 (9)	
D. Williamson c Hussain b S. G. Law		11	9/73 (10) 10/76 (11) Score at 15 overs: 34-6	

Bowling: Ilott 8–2–10–3; Cowan 10–2–24–3; Irani 6–2–21–2; S. G. Law 3.4–0–13–2.

Umpires: R. Julian and M. J. Kitchen.

FINAL BENSON AND HEDGES CUP RECORDS

55 overs available in all games 1972-95, 50 overs in 1996-98.

Batting

Highest individual scores: 198*, G. A. Gooch, Essex v Sussex, Hove, 1982; 177, S. J. Cook, Somerset v Sussex, Hove, 1990; 173*, C. G. Greenidge, Hampshire v Minor Counties (South), Amersham, 1973; 167*, A. J. Stewart, Surrey v Somerset, The Oval, 1994; 160, A. J. Stewart, Surrey v Hampshire, The Oval, 1996; 158*, B. F. Davison, Leicestershire v Warwickshire, Coventry, 1972; 158, W. J. Cronje, Leicestershire v Lancashire, Manchester, 1995; 155*, M. D. Crowe, Somerset v Hampshire, Southampton, 1987; 155*, R. A. Smith, Hampshire v Glamorgan, Southampton, 1989; 154*, M. J. Procter, Gloucestershire v Somerset, Taunton, 1972; 154*, C. L. Smith, Hampshire v Combined Universities, Southampton, 1990; 151*, M. P. Maynard, Glamorgan v Middlesex, Lord's, 1996; 151, D. L. Maddy, Leicestershire v Minor Counties, Leicester, 1998. *In the final:* 132*, I. V. A. Richards, Somerset v Surrey, 1981. (314 hundreds were scored in the competition. The most hundreds in one season was 26 in 1996.)

Most runs: 5,176, G. A. Gooch; 2,921, M. W. Gatting; 2,761, C. J. Tavaré; 2,749, K. J. Barnett; 2,718, W. Larkins; 2,717, G. A. Hick; 2,663, D. W. Randall; 2,636, A. J. Lamb; 2,626, R. J. Bailey; 2,598, A. J. Stewart; 2,580, N. H. Fairbrother; 2,567, R. T. Robinson; 2,551, C. W. J. Athey.

Fastest hundred: M. A. Nash in 62 minutes, Glamorgan v Hampshire at Swansea, 1976.

Most hundreds: 15, G. A. Gooch; 7, G. A. Hick and W. Larkins; 6, N. R. Taylor; 5, C. G. Greenidge, A. J. Lamb and R. A. Smith.

Highest totals: 388 for seven, Essex v Scotland, Chelmsford, 1992; 382 for six, Leicestershire v Minor Counties, Leicester, 1998; 371 for six, Leicestershire v Scotland, Leicester, 1997; 369 for eight, Warwickshire v Minor Counties, Jesmond, 1996; 366 for four, Derbyshire v Combined Universities, Oxford, 1991; 359 for seven, Essex v Ireland, Chelmsford, 1998; 353 for seven, Lancashire v Nottinghamshire, Manchester, 1995; 350 for three, Essex v Oxford & Cambridge Univs, Chelmsford, 1979; 349 for seven, Somerset v Ireland, Taunton, 1997; 338 for six, Kent v Somerset, Maidstone, 1996; 333 for four, Essex v Oxford & Cambridge Univs, Chelmsford, 1985; 333 for six, Surrey v Hampshire, The Oval, 1996; 331 for five, Surrey v Hampshire, The Oval, 1990; 331 for five, Essex v British Univs, Chelmsford, 1996; 330 for four, Lancashire v Sussex, Manchester, 1991. *In the final:* 290 for six, Essex v Surrey, 1979.

Highest total by a side batting second and winning: 318 for five (54.3 overs), Lancashire v Leicestershire (312 for five), Manchester, 1995. *In the final:* 244 for six (55 overs), Yorkshire v Northamptonshire (244 for seven), 1987; 244 for seven (55 overs), Nottinghamshire v Essex (243 for seven), 1989.

Highest total by a side batting second and losing: 303 for seven (55 overs), Derbyshire v Somerset (310 for three), Taunton, 1990. *In the final:* 255 (51.4 overs), Surrey v Essex (290 for six), 1979.

Highest match aggregates: 631 for 15 wickets, Kent (338 for six) v Somerset (293 for nine), Maidstone, 1996; 630 for ten wickets, Leicestershire (312 for five) v Lancashire (318 for five), Manchester, 1995; 629 for 14 wickets, Lancashire (353 for seven) v Nottinghamshire (276 for seven), Manchester, 1995; 628 for 15 wickets, Warwickshire (312 for six) v Lancashire (316 for nine), Manchester, 1996; 626 for ten wickets, British Univs (312 for eight) v Glamorgan (314 for two), Cambridge, 1996; 615 for 11 wickets, Gloucestershire (307 for four) v Surrey (308 for seven), The Oval, 1996; 613 for ten wickets, Somerset (310 for three) v Derbyshire (303 for seven), Taunton, 1990; 610 for eight wickets, Sussex (303 for six) v Kent (307 for two), Hove, 1995; 610 for 14 wickets, Warwickshire (304 for eight) v Kent (306 for six), Canterbury, 1997.

Lowest totals: 50 in 27.2 overs, Hampshire v Yorkshire, Leeds, 1991; 52 in 26.5 overs, Minor Counties v Lancashire, Lakenham, 1998; 56 in 26.2 overs, Leicestershire v Minor Counties, Wellington, 1982; 59 in 34 overs, Oxford & Cambridge Univs v Glamorgan, Cambridge, 1983; 60 in 26 overs, Sussex v Middlesex, Hove, 1978; 61 in 25.3 overs, Essex v Lancashire, Chelmsford, 1992; 62 in 26.5 overs, Gloucestershire v Hampshire, Bristol, 1975. *In the final:* 76 in 27.4 overs, Leicestershire v Essex, 1998.

Shortest completed innings: 21.4 overs (156), Surrey v Sussex, Hove, 1988.

Record partnership for each wicket

252	for 1st	V. P. Terry and C. L. Smith, Hampshire v Combined Universities at Southampton	1990
285*	for 2nd	C. G. Greenidge and D. R. Turner, Hampshire v Minor Counties (South) at Amersham	1973
269*	for 3rd	P. M. Roebuck and M. D. Crowe, Somerset v Hampshire at Southampton	1987
207	for 4th	R. C. Russell and A. J. Wright, Gloucestershire v British Universities at Bristol	1998
160	for 5th	A. J. Lamb and D. J. Capel, Northamptonshire v Leicestershire at Northampton	1986
167*	for 6th	M. G. Bevan and R. J. Blakey, Yorkshire v Lancashire at Manchester . .	1996
149*	for 7th	J. D. Love and C. M. Old, Yorkshire v Scotland at Bradford	1981
109	for 8th	R. E. East and N. Smith, Essex v Northamptonshire at Chelmsford	1977
83	for 9th	P. G. Newman and M. A. Holding, Derbyshire v Nottinghamshire at Nottingham	1985
80*	for 10th	D. L. Bairstow and M. Johnson, Yorkshire v Derbyshire at Derby.	1981

Bowling

Most wickets: 149, J. K. Lever; 132, I. T. Botham.

Best bowling: seven for 12, W. W. Daniel, Middlesex v Minor Counties (East), Ipswich, 1978; seven for 22, J. R. Thomson, Middlesex v Hampshire, Lord's, 1981; seven for 24, Mushtaq Ahmed, Somerset v Ireland, Taunton, 1997; seven for 32, R. G. D. Willis, Warwickshire v Yorkshire, Birmingham, 1981. *In the final:* five for 13, S. T. Jefferies, Hampshire v Derbyshire, 1988.

Hat-tricks (12): G. D. McKenzie, Leicestershire v Worcestershire, Worcester, 1972; K. Higgs, Leicestershire v Surrey in the final, Lord's, 1974; A. A. Jones, Middlesex v Essex, Lord's, 1977; M. J. Procter, Gloucestershire v Hampshire, Southampton, 1977; W. Larkins, Northamptonshire v Oxford & Cambridge Univs, Northampton, 1980; E. A. Moseley, Glamorgan v Kent, Cardiff, 1981; G. C. Small, Warwickshire v Leicestershire, Leicester, 1984; N. A. Mallender, Somerset v Combined Universities, Taunton, 1987; W. K. M. Benjamin, Leicestershire v Nottinghamshire, Leicester, 1987; A. R. C. Fraser, Middlesex v Sussex, Lord's, 1988; S. M. Pollock (four in four balls), Warwickshire v Leicestershire, Birmingham, 1996; Saqlain Mushtaq, Surrey v Lancashire, The Oval, 1998.

Wicket-keeping and Fielding

Most dismissals: 122 (117 ct, 5 st), D. L. Bairstow; 100 (90 ct, 10 st), S. J. Rhodes.

Most dismissals in an innings: 8 (all ct), D. J. S. Taylor, Somerset v Oxford & Cambridge Univs, Taunton, 1982.

Most catches by a fielder: 68, G. A. Gooch; 55, C. J. Tavaré; 53, I. T. Botham.

Most catches by a fielder in an innings: 5, V. J. Marks, Oxford & Cambridge Univs v Kent, Oxford, 1976.

Results

Largest victories in runs: Essex by 272 runs v Scotland, Chelmsford, 1992; Leicestershire by 256 runs v Minor Counties, Leicester, 1998; Somerset by 233 runs v Ireland, Eglinton, 1995; Somerset by 221 runs v Ireland, Taunton, 1997; Glamorgan by 217 runs v Combined Universities, Cardiff, 1995; Essex by 214 runs v Oxford & Cambridge Univs, Chelmsford, 1979; Derbyshire by 206 runs v Combined Universities, Oxford, 1991; Warwickshire by 195 runs v Minor Counties, Jesmond, 1996.

Victories by ten wickets (19): By Derbyshire, Essex (twice), Glamorgan, Hampshire, Kent (twice), Lancashire, Leicestershire (twice), Middlesex, Northamptonshire, Somerset, Warwickshire, Worcestershire (twice), Yorkshire (three times).

Gold Awards

Most awards: 22, G. A. Gooch; 11, K. J. Barnett, M. W. Gatting, G. A. Hick, T. E. Jesty and B. Wood.

WINNERS 1972-98

		Gold Award
1972	LEICESTERSHIRE* beat Yorkshire by five wickets.	J. C. Balderstone
1973	KENT* beat Worcestershire by 39 runs.	Asif Iqbal
1974	SURREY* beat Leicestershire by 27 runs.	J. H. Edrich
1975	LEICESTERSHIRE beat Middlesex* by five wickets.	N. M. McVicker
1976	KENT* beat Worcestershire by 43 runs.	G. W. Johnson
1977	GLOUCESTERSHIRE* beat Kent by 64 runs.	A. W. Stovold
1978	KENT beat Derbyshire* by six wickets.	R. A. Woolmer
1979	ESSEX beat Surrey* by 35 runs.	G. A. Gooch
1980	NORTHAMPTONSHIRE* beat Essex by six runs.	A. J. Lamb
1981	SOMERSET* beat Surrey by seven wickets.	I. V. A. Richards
1982	SOMERSET* beat Nottinghamshire by nine wickets.	V. J. Marks
1983	MIDDLESEX beat Essex* by four wickets.	C. T. Radley
1984	LANCASHIRE* beat Warwickshire by six wickets.	J. Abrahams
1985	LEICESTERSHIRE* beat Essex by five wickets.	P. Willey
1986	MIDDLESEX beat Kent* by two runs.	J. E. Emburey
1987	YORKSHIRE* beat Northamptonshire, having taken more wickets with the scores tied.	J. D. Love
1988	HAMPSHIRE* beat Derbyshire by seven wickets.	S. T. Jefferies
1989	NOTTINGHAMSHIRE beat Essex* by three wickets.	R. T. Robinson
1990	LANCASHIRE beat Worcestershire by 69 runs.	M. Watkinson
1991	WORCESTERSHIRE beat Lancashire* by 65 runs.	G. A. Hick
1992	HAMPSHIRE beat Kent* by 41 runs.	R. A. Smith
1993	DERBYSHIRE beat Lancashire* by six runs.	D. G. Cork
1994	WARWICKSHIRE* beat Worcestershire by six wickets.	P. A. Smith
1995	LANCASHIRE beat Kent* by 35 runs.	P. A. de Silva†
1996	LANCASHIRE* beat Northamptonshire by 31 runs.	I. D. Austin
1997	SURREY beat Kent* by eight wickets.	B. C. Hollioake
1998	ESSEX beat Leicestershire* by 192 runs.	P. J. Prichard

* Won toss.　　† On losing side.

WINS BY NON-CHAMPIONSHIP TEAMS

1973	OXFORD beat Northamptonshire at Northampton by two wickets.
1975	{ OXFORD & CAMBRIDGE beat Worcestershire at Cambridge by 66 runs. { OXFORD & CAMBRIDGE beat Northamptonshire at Oxford by three wickets.
1976	OXFORD & CAMBRIDGE beat Yorkshire at Barnsley by seven wickets.
1980	MINOR COUNTIES beat Gloucestershire at Chippenham by three runs.
1981	MINOR COUNTIES beat Hampshire at Southampton by three runs.
1982	MINOR COUNTIES beat Leicestershire at Wellington by 131 runs.
1984	OXFORD & CAMBRIDGE beat Gloucestershire at Bristol by 27 runs.
1986	SCOTLAND beat Lancashire at Perth by three runs.
1987	MINOR COUNTIES beat Glamorgan at Oxford (Christ Church) by seven wickets.
1989	{ COMBINED UNIVERSITIES beat Surrey at Cambridge by nine runs. { COMBINED UNIVERSITIES beat Worcestershire at Worcester by five runs.
1990	{ COMBINED UNIVERSITIES beat Yorkshire at Leeds by two wickets. { SCOTLAND beat Northamptonshire at Northampton by two runs.
1992	MINOR COUNTIES beat Sussex at Marlow by 19 runs.
1995	MINOR COUNTIES beat Leicestershire at Leicester by 26 runs.
1997	{ IRELAND beat Middlesex at Dublin (Castle Avenue) by 46 runs. { BRITISH UNIVERSITIES beat Sussex at Cambridge by 19 runs.
1998	BRITISH UNIVERSITIES beat Gloucestershire at Bristol by seven runs.

TEAM RECORDS 1972-98

	Rounds reached					Matches			
	W	F	SF	QF	P	W	L	NR	
Derbyshire	1	3	4	9	121	63	50	8	
Durham	0	0	0	1	26	11	13	2	
Essex	2	6	9	16	136	84	48	4	
Glamorgan	0	0	1	8	114	50	59	5	
Gloucestershire	1	1	2	7	116	56	56	4	
Hampshire	2	2	5	12	125	62	58	5	
Kent	3	8	13	19	145	93	48	4	
Lancashire	4	6	10	17	140	90	43	7	
Leicestershire	3	5	8	11	131	73	51	7	
Middlesex	2	3	5	15	129	67	54	8	
Northamptonshire	1	3	6	11	123	58	57	8	
Nottinghamshire	1	2	5	13	125	71	47	7	
Somerset	2	2	8	13	127	69	55	3	
Surrey	2	4	9	13	132	77	51	4	
Sussex	0	0	1	9	115	55	58	2	
Warwickshire	1	2	7	14	129	72	50	7	
Worcestershire	1	5	8	15	131	68	59	4	
Yorkshire	1	2	7	12	124	68	49	7	
Cambridge University	0	0	0	0	8	0	8	0	
Oxford University	0	0	0	0	4	1	3	0	
Oxford & Cambridge Universities	0	0	0	0	48	4	42	2	
Combined/British Universities	0	0	0	1	47	5	41	1	
Minor Counties	0	0	0	0	75	6	65	4	
Minor Counties (North)	0	0	0	0	20	0	20	0	
Minor Counties (South)	0	0	0	0	20	0	19	1	
Minor Counties (East)	0	0	0	0	12	0	12	0	
Minor Counties (West)	0	0	0	0	12	0	12	0	
Scotland	0	0	0	0	70	2	64	4	
Ireland	0	0	0	0	17	1	14	2	

Middlesex beat Gloucestershire on the toss of a coin in their quarter-final in 1983. Derbyshire, Kent, Somerset and Warwickshire totals each include a bowling contest; Derbyshire beat Somerset and Warwickshire beat Kent when their quarter-finals, in 1993 and 1994 respectively, were abandoned.

AXA LEAGUE, 1998

Neil Fairbrother

Lancashire won the last of the old-style Sunday Leagues when they surged clear of the field in the second half of the season, taking the title for the fourth time. They lost to both the teams who were to be their closest rivals – Warwickshire and Essex – but were unbeaten after July 1 with six wins and two washouts. Their batting consistently proved itself more adaptable to the demands of 40-over cricket than anyone else's.

They clinched the title with their 250th victory in the competition's 30th season, against Hampshire at Old Trafford, 24 hours after winning the NatWest at Lord's. This particular double even eluded Warwickshire in their epic year of 1994, though Lancashire had achieved it themselves in 1970, as did Somerset in 1979 and Essex in 1985.

Lancashire ended up celebrating on a Monday afternoon, which was typical of a season that marked a transition from the old Sunday routine to a new two-division, 45-over National League due to start in 1999. Matches took place on all kinds of unexpected days of the week, partly due to eccentric scheduling and partly to accommodate the new fashion for floodlit cricket. Seven counties staged games under lights, most of which proved popular successes despite frequently bleak weather and the generally downbeat nature of the season.

Warwickshire were the boldest, with four matches, all of which attracted crowds of at least 7,000 and protests from nearby residents. While the administration counted the money, the players counted the cost of their failures: they lost three successive night games at Edgbaston in three weeks, which denied them a chance of retaining the title. Essex were on top from early July to late August. Then they lost badly at Scarborough and thereafter carried their terrible Championship form into the League, lost their final two games as well, and finished third.

In contrast, Surrey, who led the Championship for most of the season, were inexplicably awful in this event. They remained pioneers of the new-style marketing, but forgot to play properly, losing nine consecutive matches and 12 out of 13. At the very moment they lost their grip in county cricket, they recovered in this event, and won their last two, too late to avoid the wooden spoon. Surrey will thus play in the lower division of the new League in 1999, along with the other teams who finished below ninth place. These included Middlesex, who were joint leaders in July.

The season marked the end of the insurance company AXA's venture into cricket sponsorship after six years. The competition was under its third official name in three years (having been the AXA Equity & Law League in 1996 and the AXA Life League in 1997) and its eighth in all.

AXA LEAGUE

	M	W	L	T	NR	Pts	Net run-rate
1 – Lancashire (3)	17	12	2	0	3	54	12.18
2 – Warwickshire (1)	17	9	5	0	3	42	4.23
3 – Essex (7)	17	9	5	1	2	42	1.27
4 – Leicestershire (4)	17	9	6	0	2	40	15.13
5 – Kent (2)	17	8	6	0	3	38	1.19
6 – Gloucestershire (11)	17	7	6	0	4	36	−1.65
7 – Worcestershire (8).	17	7	6	1	3	36	−4.60
8 – Hampshire (15)	17	8	8	0	1	34	0.95
9 – Yorkshire (10)	17	8	8	0	1	34	−2.47
10 – Glamorgan (13)	17	7	8	0	2	32	−0.25
11 – Nottinghamshire (12). . . .	17	7	8	1	1	32	−0.67
12 – Middlesex (16)	17	7	8	0	2	32	−4.90
13 – Northamptonshire (9) . . .	17	6	7	1	3	32	2.80
14 – Somerset (6)	17	6	8	1	2	30	−0.10
15 – Derbyshire (14)	17	6	8	0	3	30	−5.10
16 – Sussex (18).	17	6	9	0	2	28	−1.84
17 – Durham (17)	17	4	9	1	3	24	−7.89
18 – Surrey (5).	17	3	12	0	2	16	−8.17

1997 positions are shown in brackets.

The top nine teams qualify for the First Division of the new National League in 1999, the bottom nine for the Second Division.

When two or more counties finished with an equal number of points, the positions were decided by a) most wins, b) higher net run-rate (runs scored per 100 balls minus runs conceded per 100 balls).

Leading run-scorers: M. B. Loye 650 (£5,000 individual award), P. Johnson 621, C. L. Hooper 583, R. I. Dawson 555, R. A. Smith 537, R. C. Irani 528, S. G. Law 487, P. V. Simmons 463, V. S. Solanki 461, D. S. Lehmann 455.

Leading wicket-takers: R. J. Kirtley 25 (£5,000 individual award), A. J. Hollioake, C. A. Walsh and D. Williamson 23, K. P. Dutch, P. J. Franks, D. W. Headley, R. C. Irani and N. A. M. McLean 22.

Most economical bowlers (runs per over, minimum 100 overs): J. E. Benjamin 3.77, M. A. Robinson 3.80, G. D. Rose 4.01, M. C. Ilott 4.42, S. D. Udal 4.54, A. R. Caddick 4.60, R. J. Kirtley 4.61, N. A. M. McLean 4.86.

Leading wicket-keepers: S. J. Rhodes 25 (19 ct, 6 st) (£2,000 individual award), W. K. Hegg 22 (19 ct, 3 st) and P. A. Nixon 22 (20 ct, 2 st), K. M. Krikken 21 (16 ct, 5 st), R. J. Blakey 20 (18 ct, 2 st).

Leading fielders: J. R. Carpenter 15, D. Byas 14, S. G. Law 12, A. P. Cowan, C. L. Hooper and S. D. Udal 9.

Prize money

£43,000 for winners: LANCASHIRE.
£22,000 for runners-up: WARWICKSHIRE.
£11,000 for third place: ESSEX.
£5,500 for fourth place: LEICESTERSHIRE.
£525 for the winners of each match, shared if tied or no result.

SUMMARY OF RESULTS, 1998

	Derbyshire	Durham	Essex	Glamorgan	Gloucestershire	Hampshire	Kent	Lancashire	Leicestershire	Middlesex	Northamptonshire	Nottinghamshire	Somerset	Surrey	Sussex	Warwickshire	Worcestershire	Yorkshire
Derbyshire	—	L	L	L	N	L	W	L	W	N	W	L	N	W	W	L	L	W
Durham	W	—	T	L	W	L	L	N	L	L	N	W	W	L	L	N	L	L
Essex	W	T	—	W	N	W	W	W	L	L	W	L	L	W	W	W	N	L
Glamorgan	W	W	L	—	N	L	L	N	L	L	W	L	W	W	W	W	L	L
Gloucestershire	N	L	N	N	—	W	L	L	W	W	L	W	W	W	W	N	L	L
Hampshire	W	W	L	W	L	—	L	L	L	W	W	L	L	W	W	L	L	N
Kent	L	W	L	W	W	W	—	L	N	W	W	L	W	L	N	L	N	W
Lancashire	W	N	L	N	W	W	W	—	W	N	W	W	W	W	N	L	W	W
Leicestershire	L	W	W	W	L	W	N	L	—	W	L	L	W	W	N	L	W	W
Middlesex	N	W	W	L	L	L	L	N	L	—	L	W	W	L	L	W	W	W
Northamptonshire	L	N	L	L	W	L	L	W	W	—	W	W	N	W	N	T	L
Nottinghamshire	W	L	W	L	L	W	L	L	W	L	L	—	T	N	L	W	L	W
Somerset	N	L	W	W	L	W	L	L	L	L	T	—	W	W	W	N	L
Surrey	L	W	L	L	L	W	L	L	W	N	N	L	—	L	L	L	L	L
Sussex	L	W	L	L	L	L	N	L	N	W	L	W	L	W	—	L	W	W
Warwickshire	W	N	L	L	N	L	W	W	W	W	N	L	L	W	W	—	W	W
Worcestershire	W	W	N	W	W	W	N	L	L	L	T	W	N	W	L	L	—	L
Yorkshire	L	W	W	W	N	L	L	L	L	W	L	W	L	W	L	L	W	—

Home games in bold, away games in italics. W = Won, L = Lost, T = Tied, N = No result.

DERBYSHIRE

DERBYSHIRE v NOTTINGHAMSHIRE

At Derby, April 21. Nottinghamshire won by two wickets. Toss: Nottinghamshire. County debut: P. A. Strang.

Strang made an immediate impact for his new county, stealing the game in a ninth-wicket partnership of 45 with Bates. It helped when Bates hit a Cork no-ball for six, scoring eight. Nottinghamshire had made unsteady progress before that; Barnett achieved his first four-wicket haul in 20 years of League cricket. Derbyshire had struggled themselves until Blackwell raced to 89 from 80 balls. Assisted by Cassar, he launched an assault which took them from 92 to 176 in the final ten overs.

Derbyshire

A. S. Rollins c Johnson b Bowen	5	†K. M. Krikken b Evans		1
*D. G. Cork b Evans	3	P. Aldred not out		5
T. A. Tweats b Bowen	2			
K. J. Barnett b Wharf	15	L-b 9, w 4		13
I. D. Blackwell c Gallian b Bowen	89			
M. E. Cassar c Dowman b Bowen	26	1/9 2/11 3/18	(8 wkts, 40 overs)	176
P. A. J. DeFreitas b Gallian	10	4/42 5/121 6/155		
V. P. Clarke not out	7	7/163 8/168		

A. J. Harris did not bat.

Bowling: Bowen 8–2–35–4; Evans 7–1–23–2; Wharf 8–0–23–1; Strang 7–0–34–0; Bates 6–0–29–0; Gallian 4–0–23–1.

Nottinghamshire

J. E. R. Gallian b Harris	24	K. P. Evans b Barnett	1
M. P. Dowman c Krikken b DeFreitas	2	R. T. Bates not out	28
*P. Johnson lbw b Clarke	47		
G. F. Archer lbw b Barnett	24	B 1, l-b 7, w 12, n-b 10	30
N. A. Gie c Krikken b Barnett	0		
A. G. Wharf run out	7	1/17 2/58 3/110 (8 wkts, 39.4 overs) 179
†W. M. Noon lbw b Barnett	2	4/110 5/110 6/116
P. A. Strang not out	14	7/124 8/134

M. N. Bowen did not bat.

Bowling: DeFreitas 4–0–20–1; Cork 8–0–48–0; Harris 8–1–28–1; Aldred 4.4–0–31–0; Clarke 7–1–19–1; Barnett 8–0–25–4.

Umpires: J. C. Balderstone and M. J. Harris.

At Leeds, April 26. DERBYSHIRE beat YORKSHIRE by five wickets (D/L method).

At Manchester, May 10. DERBYSHIRE lost to LANCASHIRE by 31 runs (D/L method).

DERBYSHIRE v WARWICKSHIRE

At Derby, May 17. Warwickshire won by 47 runs. Toss: Derbyshire.

Champions Warwickshire won their third match in succession to go joint top of the table. They appeared to be in trouble at 74 for four, but Brown helped Ostler repair the damage with a decisive stand of 109 in 18 overs. Slater scored 29 on his return after a month off with a broken hand and, while Tweats and DeFreitas were together, Derbyshire had a chance. But then Giles, just picked for England's one-day squad, engineered a collapse.

Warwickshire

N. V. Knight c Barnett b Cork	16	G. Welch not out	1
N. M. K. Smith lbw b Dean	8	G. C. Small not out	3
D. L. Hemp b Dean	6	B 1, l-b 13, w 4, n-b 2	20
*B. C. Lara c Aldred b Cork	15		
D. P. Ostler b Barnett	62	1/23 2/31 3/43 (7 wkts, 40 overs) 201
D. R. Brown c Rollins b Barnett	63	4/74 5/183
A. F. Giles c Cork	7	6/196 7/197

†T. Frost and E. S. H. Giddins did not bat.

Bowling: DeFreitas 8–0–48–0; Dean 8–1–26–2; Cork 8–0–30–3; Aldred 7–0–29–0; Clarke 3–0–19–0; Barnett 6–0–35–2.

Derbyshire

M. J. Slater lbw b Giddins	29	†K. M. Krikken lbw b Giles	4
K. J. Barnett c Frost b Giddins	1	P. Aldred not out	4
A. S. Rollins c Brown b Welch	12	K. J. Dean b Brown	1
T. A. Tweats st Frost b Giles	35	L-b 8, w 2, n-b 2	12
P. A. J. DeFreitas c Welch b Small	26		
*D. G. Cork b Giles	26	1/19 2/41 3/46 (36 overs) 154
V. P. Clarke b Small	1	4/104 5/111 6/112
I. D. Blackwell c Brown b Giles	3	7/121 8/140 9/149

Bowling: Giddins 8–0–34–2; Welch 7–0–31–1; Small 8–0–28–2; Brown 7–0–36–1; Giles 6–0–17–4.

Umpires: J. H. Harris and T. E. Jesty.

DERBYSHIRE v LEICESTERSHIRE

At Derby, May 19. Derbyshire won by seven runs. Toss: Derbyshire.

Leicestershire went down to their third successive defeat. They needed 11 off the final over but Cork held them to three. The decisive innings came from Slater, who rose above the constraints of a sluggish pitch and shared a 56-run stand with DeFreitas to redeem Derbyshire's situation after the unusual dismissal of Rollins. He advanced and missed; Nixon fumbled, but recovered to break the wicket in front of the stumps. Rollins was originally given run out by umpire Willey but a later ruling from Lord's was that, under Law 39.1, he was stumped.

Derbyshire

M. J. Slater st Nixon b Williamson	68	*D. G. Cork b Simmons	0
K. J. Barnett run out	6	†K. M. Krikken not out	15
A. S. Rollins st Nixon b Brimson	11	B 2, l-b 10, w 3, n-b 2	17
T. A. Tweats c and b Wells	4		
P. A. J. DeFreitas c Smith b Williamson	45	1/20 2/64 3/71 (6 wkts, 40 overs) 190	
M. E. Cassar not out	24	4/127 5/154 6/159	

P. Aldred, G. M. Roberts and K. J. Dean did not bat.

Bowling: Mullally 8–2–20–0; Simmons 8–0–44–1; Wells 8–0–33–1; Brimson 8–0–29–1; Williamson 6–0–34–2; Dakin 2–0–18–0.

Leicestershire

*P. V. Simmons c Cork b DeFreitas	8	D. I. Stevens b Cork	21
V. J. Wells b Cork	25	D. Williamson not out	2
B. F. Smith b Roberts	39	B 5, l-b 2, w 2, n-b 2	11
I. J. Sutcliffe b Aldred	8		
A. Habib c Rollins b Aldred	7	1/24 2/44 3/67 (7 wkts, 40 overs) 183	
†P. A. Nixon not out	50	4/80 5/120	
J. M. Dakin c Slater b Roberts	12	6/136 7/181	

M. T. Brimson and A. D. Mullally did not bat.

Bowling: DeFreitas 8–0–30–1; Dean 8–0–33–0; Cork 8–0–35–2; Aldred 8–0–38–2; Roberts 8–0–40–2.

Umpires: K. E. Palmer and P. Willey.

At Horsham, May 25. DERBYSHIRE beat SUSSEX by six wickets.

DERBYSHIRE v GLOUCESTERSHIRE

At Chesterfield, June 7. No result (abandoned).

DERBYSHIRE v MIDDLESEX

At Derby, June 14. No result (abandoned).

At Basingstoke, June 21. DERBYSHIRE lost to HAMPSHIRE by seven wickets.

DERBYSHIRE v ESSEX

At Derby, July 5. Essex won by eight wickets. Toss: Essex.

Essex went back to the top of the table with a very easy win. Derbyshire's batsmen faded away after a solid start, failing to cope with a pitch of low bounce. Grayson finished with four for 28.

Derbyshire

*M. J. Slater st Rollins b Napier	30	P. Aldred b Grayson	3
K. J. Barnett c S. G. Law b Grayson	50	T. M. Smith b Grayson	6
A. S. Rollins c Cowan b Napier	2	K. J. Dean not out	5
†M. E. Cassar c and b Napier	1	B 7, l-b 4, w 6	17
B. L. Spendlove c S. G. Law b Ilott	25		
T. A. Tweats c Cowan b Such	4	1/56 2/68 3/72	(39.5 overs) 152
V. P. Clarke lbw b Such	6	4/121 5/121 6/130	
G. M. Roberts b Grayson	3	7/135 8/137 9/141	

Bowling: Ilott 7–0–28–1; Cowan 7–0–26–0; Irani 5–0–11–0; Napier 5–0–22–3; Such 8–0–26–2; Grayson 7.5–1–28–4.

Essex

*P. J. Prichard c Smith b Roberts	26
S. G. Law not out	78
S. D. Peters lbw b Clarke	1
R. C. Irani not out	32
B 2, l-b 9, w 6	17

1/63 2/67   (2 wkts, 32.3 overs) 154

G. R. Napier, A. P. Grayson, †R. J. Rollins, D. R. Law, A. P. Cowan, M. C. Ilott and P. M. Such did not bat.

Bowling: Smith 4.3–0–31–0; Dean 4–0–16–0; Roberts 8–0–31–1; Clarke 7–0–27–1; Barnett 4–0–17–0; Aldred 5–0–21–0.

Umpires: R. Julian and D. R. Shepherd.

DERBYSHIRE v WORCESTERSHIRE

At Derby, July 12. Worcestershire won by 48 runs. Toss: Derbyshire.

Slater, struggling to make an impact for Derbyshire, raced to his first hundred in any county competition in just 87 balls with four sixes. But the pressures of chasing nearly seven an over told on their later batsmen, and eight wickets went down in only 52 balls. Worcestershire's dominating score came from an unbroken stand of 175 in 19 overs from Solanki, who scored his first one-day century, and Hick at his most imperious. His 88 came off 63 balls.

Worcestershire

*T. M. Moody st Krikken b Roberts	39
V. S. Solanki not out	120
G. A. Hick not out	88
L-b 7, w 11, n-b 6	24

1/96   (1 wkt, 40 overs) 271

D. A. Leatherdale, W. P. C. Weston, A. Hafeez, †S. J. Rhodes, S. R. Lampitt, R. K. Illingworth, R. J. Chapman and P. J. Newport did not bat.

Bowling: Cork 8–0–41–0; Dean 7–1–42–0; Aldred 4–0–56–0; Clarke 5–0–38–0; Roberts 8–0–47–1; Barnett 8–0–40–0.

Derbyshire

M. J. Slater lbw b Leatherdale	110	G. M. Roberts lbw b Lampitt	0
*D. G. Cork b Moody	38	P. Aldred b Lampitt	2
V. P. Clarke b Moody	12	K. J. Dean st Rhodes b Lampitt	2
K. J. Barnett c Lampitt b Leatherdale	39	L-b 6, w 2	8
M. E. Cassar b Leatherdale	0		
B. L. Spendlove lbw b Lampitt	3	1/100 2/118 3/179 (38.4 overs)	223
†K. M. Krikken not out	9	4/179 5/198 6/216	
R. M. S. Weston lbw b Leatherdale	0	7/216 8/217 9/219	

Bowling: Newport 6–0–34–0; Chapman 6–0–34–0; Moody 8–0–51–2; Illingworth 8–0–46–0; Leatherdale 5–1–19–4; Lampitt 5.4–0–33–4.

Umpires: H. D. Bird and D. J. Constant.

At Northampton, July 26. DERBYSHIRE beat NORTHAMPTONSHIRE by 32 runs.

DERBYSHIRE v KENT

At Derby, August 2. Derbyshire won by eight wickets. Toss: Derbyshire.

Derbyshire designated the occasion "Family Fun Day" but Kent completely failed to join in. They were quickly one for two, never properly recovered and were sent to their third successive defeat. Cassar made sure with an unbeaten 67 off 65 balls. During the tea interval, Derbyshire capped both Slater and Dean, who had taken a hat-trick the previous day.

Kent

T. R. Ward b Dean	0	B. J. Phillips b Cork	13
E. T. Smith c Krikken b Cork	1	J. B. D. Thompson not out	1
C. L. Hooper c Krikken b Cork	5		
M. A. Ealham c Slater b DeFreitas	32	B 1, l-b 7, w 2	10
N. J. Llong c Krikken b Dean	11		
M. V. Fleming c Cork b Barnett	14	1/1 2/1 3/20 (8 wkts, 40 overs)	155
W. J. House st Krikken b Roberts	38	4/35 5/57 6/98	
*†S. A. Marsh not out	30	7/114 8/145	

M. J. McCague did not bat.

Bowling: Cork 8–1–26–3; Dean 8–0–20–2; DeFreitas 8–0–24–1; Clarke 7–0–34–0; Roberts 5–0–27–1; Barnett 4–0–16–1.

Derbyshire

M. J. Slater b Ealham	12
K. J. Barnett not out	46
R. M. S. Weston c Hooper b McCague	26
M. E. Cassar not out	67
L-b 5	5

1/19 2/57 (2 wkts, 34.5 overs) 156

*D. G. Cork, P. A. J. DeFreitas, †K. M. Krikken, V. P. Clarke, G. M. Roberts, K. J. Dean and I. D. Blackwell did not bat.

Bowling: Thompson 3–0–11–0; Ealham 5–1–30–1; Hooper 8–1–27–0; McCague 5–0–23–1; Fleming 4–0–12–0; Llong 3–0–20–0; Phillips 3.5–0–17–0; House 3–0–11–0.

Umpires: T. E. Jesty and D. R. Shepherd.

At The Oval, August 5. DERBYSHIRE beat SURREY by 28 runs.

At Taunton, August 23. SOMERSET v DERBYSHIRE. No result (abandoned).

DERBYSHIRE v DURHAM

At Derby, August 30. Durham won by 22 runs. Toss: Durham.

Durham's victory – after a run of one win out of ten – helped drag Derbyshire down with them towards the lower division of the new National League. Morris and Speight put on 91 as Durham reached 217. Derbyshire's openers began smartly but the bowlers picked up wickets steadily.

Durham

*D. C. Boon c Krikken b DeFreitas	13	J. Wood b Clarke	2
M. A. Roseberry b Roberts	28	N. Killeen not out	11
P. D. Collingwood st Krikken		M. J. Saggers not out	4
b Blackwell	19		
J. E. Morris c Spendlove b Roberts	50	B 1, l-b 11, w 4, n-b 6	22
†M. P. Speight b DeFreitas	44		—
J. J. B. Lewis c Krikken b Roberts	1	1/25 2/70 3/72 (9 wkts, 40 overs) 217
J. A. Daley c Clarke b Blackwell	18	4/163 5/166 6/175
N. C. Phillips run out	5	7/192 8/195 9/206

Bowling: Dean 5–0–18–0; DeFreitas 8–0–46–2; Barnett 3–0–11–0; Clarke 8–0–53–1; Roberts 8–1–38–3; Blackwell 8–1–39–2.

Derbyshire

M. E. Cassar b Collingwood	61	*†K. M. Krikken run out	16
K. J. Barnett run out	33	G. M. Roberts b Killeen	4
R. M. S. Weston b Boon	16	K. J. Dean not out	3
S. D. Stubbings st Speight b Boon	4	L-b 8, w 1	9
P. A. J. DeFreitas c Boon b Collingwood	18		—
B. L. Spendlove lbw b Wood	20	1/86 2/114 3/120 (39 overs) 195
V. P. Clarke b Collingwood	0	4/120 5/145 6/146
I. D. Blackwell c Morris b Phillips	11	7/163 8/176 9/181

Bowling: Wood 8–0–35–1; Killeen 5–0–22–1; Phillips 6–0–35–1; Saggers 4–0–31–0; Boon 8–0–44–2; Collingwood 8–0–20–3.

Umpires: G. I. Burgess and A. Clarkson.

At Cardiff, September 13. DERBYSHIRE lost to GLAMORGAN by 56 runs.

DURHAM

At Birmingham, April 19. WARWICKSHIRE v DURHAM. No result (abandoned).

DURHAM v GLOUCESTERSHIRE

At Chester-le-Street, April 26. Durham won by two runs. Toss: Durham.

Reduced to 19 overs a side, the match produced two rapid fifties. For Durham, Morris hit a belligerent 66 off 46 balls, including three sixes; in reply, Dawson scurried to his half-century in 40. Gloucestershire were well placed halfway through their innings, but a flurry of late wickets left them just short.

Durham

M. A. Roseberry retired hurt	10		J. Boiling not out	11
M. J. Foster c Dawson b Lewis	3		N. Killeen not out	10
J. E. Morris c Cunliffe b Hancock	66			
*D. C. Boon b Hancock	20		L-b 5, w 4, n-b 4	13
†M. P. Speight c and b Hancock	0			
J. J. B. Lewis lbw b Lewis	9		1/15 2/88 3/88 (6 wkts, 19 overs)	146
P. D. Collingwood c Trainor b Walsh	4		4/116 5/124 6/126	

J. Wood and A. Walker did not bat.

M. A. Roseberry retired hurt at 15-1.

Bowling: Smith 4–0–21–0; Lewis 4–0–19–2; Ball 2–0–24–0; Walsh 4–0–34–1; Alleyne 3–0–25–0; Hancock 2–0–18–3.

Gloucestershire

N. J. Trainor c Boon b Foster	25		R. J. Cunliffe not out	8
R. I. Dawson c sub b Foster	56		C. A. Walsh not out	2
M. C. J. Ball c Boon b Collingwood	15			
†R. C. Russell c Collingwood b Wood	6		B 1, l-b 2, w 1	4
*M. W. Alleyne run out	13			
A. J. Wright c Morris b Killeen	3		1/72 2/90 3/100 (8 wkts, 19 overs)	144
T. H. C. Hancock c Walker b Killeen	4		4/105 5/112 6/116	
J. Lewis c Collingwood b Wood	8		7/133 8/133	

A. M. Smith did not bat.

Bowling: Boiling 3–0–19–0; Wood 4–0–32–2; Walker 3–0–23–0; Foster 4–0–25–2; Killeen 4–0–35–2; Collingwood 1–0–7–1.

Umpires: R. A. White and P. Willey.

At Worcester, May 3. DURHAM lost to WORCESTERSHIRE by 24 runs.

At Nottingham, May 10. DURHAM beat NOTTINGHAMSHIRE by six wickets (D/L method).

DURHAM v ESSEX

At Chester-le-Street, May 17. Tied. Toss: Durham.

These teams tied for the second time in four seasons when the reserve wicket-keeper, Andrew Pratt, batting at No. 11 in his first county innings, saved the day for Durham. Pratt scampered the runs needed to level the scores, after his team-mates had thrown away a promising position: seven wickets tumbled for 25. Earlier, deputising for the injured Speight, he had caught the first three Essex batsmen. Only Grayson made the score respectable.

Essex

D. D. J. Robinson c Pratt b Betts	20		M. C. Ilott not out	12
S. G. Law c Pratt b Foster	20		N. F. Williams run out	0
*N. Hussain c Pratt b Killeen	5		D. M. Cousins c Speak b Boiling	1
R. C. Irani lbw b Foster	17		L-b 6, w 1	7
A. P. Grayson b Betts	59			
†R. J. Rollins lbw b Foster	27		1/33 2/48 3/48 (39.4 overs)	194
S. D. Peters b Boiling	7		4/85 5/147 6/162	
D. R. Law b Wood	19		7/180 8/186 9/186	

Bowling: Wood 8–0–29–1; Betts 8–2–23–2; Killeen 8–0–45–1; Foster 8–1–34–3; Boiling 7.4–0–57–2.

Durham

M. A. Roseberry c Hussain b Ilott	11	J. Wood b Cousins	0
S. Hutton c Williams b D. R. Law	44	N. Killeen b Irani	0
J. A. Daley c Hussain b Cousins	69	†A. Pratt not out	5
*N. J. Speak c Peters b Ilott	20	B 2, l-b 13, w 10, n-b 4	29
P. D. Collingwood b Irani	2		
M. J. Foster not out	13	1/25 2/118 3/163 (9 wkts, 40 overs) 194	
J. Boiling b Irani	0	4/171 5/173 6/173	
M. M. Betts run out	1	7/178 8/183 9/188	

Bowling: Ilott 8–0–25–2; Cousins 8–0–43–2; Irani 5–0–30–3; Williams 3–0–18–0; Grayson 8–0–25–0; D. R. Law 8–0–38–1.

Umpires: A. A. Jones and K. E. Palmer.

At Canterbury, May 25. DURHAM lost to KENT by 100 runs.

At Lord's, June 7. DURHAM lost to MIDDLESEX by three wickets.

DURHAM v NORTHAMPTONSHIRE

At Chester-le-Street, June 14. No result (abandoned).

DURHAM v YORKSHIRE

At Chester-le-Street, June 21. Yorkshire won by six wickets. Toss: Durham.

A perfectly paced unbeaten 79 from Byas put Yorkshire level on points with Lancashire at the top of the League. With Lehmann offering spirited support, he saw his side to victory in the final over. Yorkshire's ploy of bowling two left-arm spinners, Stemp and Lehmann, for a full eight overs each, slowed Durham's progress, and Lewis had little help as he tried to revive the innings from 60 for four.

Durham

M. A. Roseberry c and b Lehmann	22	M. M. Betts c Lehmann b Silverwood	1
†M. P. Speight c Parker b Hutchison	16	N. Killeen b Silverwood	6
N. J. Speak b Stemp	9	M. J. Saggers not out	1
*D. C. Boon b Stemp	6	L-b 5, w 7, n-b 2	14
P. D. Collingwood c Blakey b Hamilton	23		
J. J. B. Lewis run out	61	1/26 2/46 3/60 (40 overs) 180	
M. J. Foster b Sidebottom	14	4/60 5/104 6/137	
N. C. Phillips run out	7	7/159 8/165 9/178	

Bowling: Hutchison 7–0–39–1; Silverwood 7–0–30–2; Hamilton 7–0–33–1; Stemp 8–2–19–2; Lehmann 8–0–33–1; Sidebottom 3–0–21–1.

Yorkshire

*D. Byas not out	79	†R. J. Blakey not out	25
M. P. Vaughan run out	5		
D. S. Lehmann c Roseberry b Collingwood	52	L-b 4, w 1	5
A. McGrath c Foster b Killeen	10	1/10 2/104 (4 wkts, 39.1 overs) 182	
B. Parker c Speight b Saggers	6	3/119 4/135	

G. M. Hamilton, R. D. Stemp, C. E. W. Silverwood, P. M. Hutchison and R. J. Sidebottom did not bat.

Bowling: Betts 7–0–30–0; Saggers 8–1–32–1; Killeen 7.1–1–36–1; Foster 8–0–33–0; Phillips 6–0–32–0; Collingwood 3–0–15–1.

Umpires: G. I. Burgess and T. E. Jesty.

DURHAM v LEICESTERSHIRE

At Darlington, July 5. Leicestershire won by five runs. Toss: Leicestershire.

Having dismissed Leicestershire for 174, Durham were well set for victory at 87 for one when Wells spoilt the party. He grabbed three wickets in five balls to finish with four for 18, and Durham fell short. Extras top-scored, Leicestershire continuing their season-long habit of gifting wides and no-balls.

Leicestershire

*P. V. Simmons c Phillips b Saggers . . .	23	D. Williamson run out.	1
V. J. Wells b Wood.	13	D. J. Millns c Speak b Killeen	6
B. F. Smith c and b Killeen	21	M. T. Brimson not out	1
D. L. Maddy c Boon b Saggers	9	L-b 11, w 8, n-b 2.	21
†P. A. Nixon c Speight b Killeen	33		—
A. Habib run out	24	1/30 2/64 3/67	(38.2 overs) 174
I. J. Sutcliffe lbw b Betts.	21	4/92 5/131 6/150	
J. M. Dakin c and b Phillips	1	7/157 8/159 9/172	

Bowling: Betts 7–0–26–1; Wood 8–0–42–1; Saggers 8–1–35–2; Killeen 7.2–0–33–3; Phillips 8–1–27–1.

Durham

J. E. Morris lbw b Wells	48	J. Wood b Dakin	6
†M. P. Speight b Simmons.	1	M. J. Saggers not out	8
N. J. Speak c Nixon b Dakin	33	N. Killeen c Nixon b Dakin	14
*D. C. Boon lbw b Wells	0	L-b 13, w 17, n-b 22	52
P. D. Collingwood c Habib b Wells	1		—
J. J. B. Lewis b Wells.	3	1/10 2/87 3/87	(38.2 overs) 169
N. C. Phillips b Williamson	3	4/89 5/102 6/123	
M. M. Betts c Nixon b Williamson	0	7/133 8/135 9/143	

Bowling: Millns 3–0–26–0; Simmons 6–0–46–1; Wells 8–3–18–4; Brimson 8–2–26–0; Williamson 8–0–22–2; Dakin 5.2–0–18–3.

Umpires: B. Dudleston and V. A. Holder.

At Taunton, July 26. DURHAM beat SOMERSET by six runs.

At Southampton, August 2. DURHAM lost to HAMPSHIRE by seven wickets.

At Eastbourne, August 9. DURHAM lost to SUSSEX by seven wickets.

DURHAM v LANCASHIRE

At Chester-le-Street, August 23. No result. Toss: Durham.

Asked to bat, Lancashire were under pressure from a keen Durham attack, with four wickets down before rain finished the match in the 14th over.

Lancashire

M. A. Atherton c Speight b Saggers. . . .	15	*Wasim Akram not out	0
J. P. Crawley c Collingwood b Killeen. .	7	L-b 5, w 3	8
N. H. Fairbrother not out.	5		—
G. D. Lloyd b Collingwood	8	1/22 2/29	(4 wkts, 13.2 overs) 43
A. Flintoff c Speight b Collingwood . . .	0	3/41 4/43	

†W. K. Hegg, G. Yates, I. D. Austin, G. Chapple and P. J. Martin did not bat.

Bowling: Wood 4–0–14–0; Killeen 4–1–6–1; Saggers 3–1–7–1; Collingwood 2.2–0–11–2.

Durham

J. E. Morris, *D. C. Boon, J. A. Daley, P. D. Collingwood, J. J. B. Lewis, †M. P. Speight, M. J. Symington, N. C. Phillips, M. J. Saggers, J. Wood and N. Killeen.

Umpires: B. Dudleston and R. Julian.

At Derby, August 30. DURHAM beat DERBYSHIRE by 22 runs.

DURHAM v GLAMORGAN

At Chester-le-Street, September 6. Glamorgan won by 26 runs. Toss: Durham.

Maynard, who shared an opening stand of 170 with James, passed the personal landmark of 5,000 runs in the competition. Glamorgan lost six wickets in the final five overs, but they had enough.

Glamorgan

S. P. James b Phillips	78	†I. Dawood not out		1
*M. P. Maynard c sub b Phillips	90	A. P. Davies not out		1
A. Dale c Chapman b Phillips	21	L-b 16, w 6, n-b 6		28
P. A. Cottey run out	3			
M. J. Powell b Collingwood	8	1/170 2/209 3/214	(7 wkts, 40 overs)	232
A. W. Evans c sub b Wood	1	4/214 5/225		
W. L. Law c Morris b Collingwood	1	6/227 7/229		

D. A. Cosker and O. T. Parkin did not bat.

Bowling: Wood 8–0–29–1; Killeen 4–0–22–0; Collingwood 8–0–40–2; Harmison 6–0–45–0; Chapman 6–0–35–0; Phillips 8–0–45–3.

Durham

*D. C. Boon b Parkin	76	J. Wood not out		19
M. A. Roseberry c James b Parkin	2	N. Killeen not out		21
J. E. Morris c Powell b Parkin	6			
†M. P. Speight c Davies b Cosker	28	B 4, l-b 4, w 5		13
P. D. Collingwood c Maynard b Cottey	22			
J. J. B. Lewis c Maynard b Cottey	3	1/7 2/20 3/71	(8 wkts, 40 overs)	206
S. Chapman lbw b Davies	14	4/116 5/124 6/148		
N. C. Phillips c Law b Davies	2	7/152 8/166		

S. J. Harmison did not bat.

Bowling: Parkin 8–0–25–3; Davies 8–1–46–2; Cosker 8–0–53–1; Dale 8–0–32–0; Maynard 4–0–20–0; Cottey 4–1–22–2.

Umpires: H. D. Bird and V. A. Holder.

DURHAM v SURREY

At Chester-le-Street, September 13. Surrey won by 101 runs. Toss: Surrey. First-team debut: A. M. Davies.

Surrey at last brought their normal form to the Sunday League, but a thumping win over their nearest rivals at the bottom came far too late to save them from the wooden spoon. Stewart and Butcher led the best batting performance of their League season to maintain Surrey's unique 100 per cent record against Durham in this competition. Durham quickly slid into trouble and Boon could not rescue them.

Surrey

I. J. Ward c Roseberry b Davies	22	N. Shahid b Saggers	17
B. C. Hollioake c Daley b Davies	9	†J. N. Batty not out	7
A. J. Stewart c Saggers b Chapman	58	L-b 13, w 6, n-b 2	21
M. A. Butcher not out	85		
A. D. Brown st Speight b Phillips	9	1/19 2/52 3/149 (6 wkts, 40 overs)	237
*A. J. Hollioake c Davies b Chapman	9	4/175 5/190 6/222	

I. D. K. Salisbury, M. A. V. Bell and J. E. Benjamin did not bat.

Bowling: Wood 8–1–44–0; Davies 8–0–44–2; Saggers 8–0–27–1; Chapman 8–0–57–2; Phillips 8–0–52–1.

Durham

*D. C. Boon c and b Salisbury	47	J. Wood b Salisbury	0
M. A. Roseberry c Batty		M. J. Saggers st Batty b Salisbury	0
b B. C. Hollioake	5	A. M. Davies run out	0
J. E. Morris lbw b Benjamin	0		
†M. P. Speight c Stewart b Benjamin	3	B 3, l-b 7, w 15, n-b 6	31
J. M. B. Lewis c Batty b Butcher	16		
J. A. Daley not out	30	1/11 2/17 3/22 (32.1 overs)	136
S. Chapman b Butcher	3	4/81 5/110 6/125	
N. C. Phillips run out	1	7/126 8/129 9/135	

Bowling: Benjamin 8–0–22–2; B. C. Hollioake 5–1–18–1; Bell 2–0–21–0; Butcher 6–0–34–2; A. J. Hollioake 5.1–1–16–0; Salisbury 6–0–15–3.

Umpires: D. J. Constant and G. Sharp.

ESSEX

At Worcester, April 19. WORCESTERSHIRE v ESSEX. No result (abandoned).

ESSEX v SUSSEX

At Chelmsford, April 26. Essex won by 127 runs. Toss: Sussex.

An unbroken third-wicket stand of 174 in 21 overs between Darren Robinson and Irani shut Sussex out of the contest. Robinson, having scored 85 in the Championship game, powered to 129 not out, his first one-day century; it came in his 67th innings since his debut in 1993. In a rain-reduced match, Sussex needed 7.25 an over. They never threatened.

Essex

D. D. J. Robinson not out	129
S. G. Law c Carpenter b Robinson	14
*N. Hussain b Robinson	6
R. C. Irani not out	68
W 10, n-b 4	14
1/45 2/57 (2 wkts, 32 overs)	231

S. D. Peters, D. R. Law, †R. J. Rollins, G. R. Napier, A. P. Cowan, M. C. Ilott and P. M. Such did not bat.

Bowling: Edwards 6–0–45–0; Kirtley 7–0–46–0; Robinson 7–0–28–2; Haywood 3–0–16–0; Davis 5–0–45–0; Newell 2–0–20–0; Adams 2–0–31–0.

Sussex

*C. J. Adams c Robinson b Cowan	....	18	R. P. Davis c S. G. Law b Cowan	 8
R. K. Rao lbw b Ilott	....	1	R. J. Kirtley b Cowan	 5
K. Greenfield c Ilott b Napier	....	13	M. A. Robinson not out	 1
J. R. Carpenter c Cowan b Napier	....	6	L-b 5, w 5, n-b 4	 14
K. Newell c Ilott b Napier	....	20		
G. R. Haywood b Such	....	14	1/9 2/36 3/42	(28.1 overs) 104
†P. Moores st Rollins b Such	....	3	4/53 5/79 6/87	
A. D. Edwards c Peters b Such	.....	1	7/89 8/93 9/102	

Bowling: Ilott 5–0–17–1; Cowan 6.1–1–22–3; Irani 4–0–15–0; Napier 7–1–27–3; Such 6–0–18–3.

Umpires: J. H. Harris and R. Palmer.

At Southampton, May 10. ESSEX beat HAMPSHIRE by two wickets.

At Chester-le-Street, May 17. ESSEX tied with DURHAM.

At Uxbridge, May 19. ESSEX lost to MIDDLESEX by two runs.

ESSEX v LANCASHIRE

At Chelmsford, May 25. Essex won by three wickets. Toss: Essex.

Irani propelled Essex to victory with a fine all-round performance, taking four for 32 and blasting an unbeaten 95. Atherton's diligent 70 apart, Lancashire's batting foundered against tidy bowling and spectacular fielding, in particular from Grayson, who ran round to catch Austin left-handed while blinded by the sun. Replying, Essex stumbled before Irani found just enough support to steer them home.

Lancashire

M. A. Atherton b Ilott	....	70	G. Yates not out	 12
A. Flintoff c S. G. Law b Cousins	....	17	G. Chapple b Irani	 1
*J. P. Crawley b D. R. Law	....	22	L-b 3, w 11	 14
N. H. Fairbrother b Irani	....	22		
G. D. Lloyd c S. G. Law b Ilott	......	9	1/33 2/77 3/137	(8 wkts, 40 overs) 188
†W. K. Hegg b Irani	....	18	4/147 5/168 6/174	
I. D. Austin c Grayson b Irani	....	3	7/184 8/188	

P. J. Martin and R. J. Green did not bat.

Bowling: Ilott 8–0–40–2; Cousins 8–1–28–1; Irani 8–0–32–4; D. R. Law 8–0–43–1; Grayson 8–0–42–0.

Essex

D. D. J. Robinson c Hegg b Martin	....	1	†R. J. Rollins b Chapple	 6
*S. G. Law b Austin	....	16	D. G. Wilson not out	 2
S. D. Peters lbw b Austin	....	2	B 4, l-b 4, w 11, n-b 2	 21
R. C. Irani not out	....	95		
A. P. Grayson b Green	....	15	1/3 2/8 3/31	(7 wkts, 36.1 overs) 190
D. R. Law c Fairbrother b Chapple	....	16	4/82 5/111	
G. R. Napier c Fairbrother b Flintoff	..	16	6/172 7/183	

M. C. Ilott and D. M. Cousins did not bat.

Bowling: Martin 8–0–31–1; Austin 8–2–28–2; Green 8–0–42–1; Chapple 7.1–0–40–2; Yates 4–0–32–0; Flintoff 1–0–9–1.

Umpires: J. W. Lloyds and R. A. White.

ESSEX v NORTHAMPTONSHIRE

At Ilford, May 31. Essex won by eight wickets. Toss: Essex.

Stuart Law, having failed to reach fifty in nine one-day innings in 1998, returned to form in blistering style. He hit 83 off 59 balls, peppered with flowing cover drives, to give the chase unstoppable momentum. Backed up by Robinson and Hussain, he took Essex to victory and joint top place in the League. Only late work by Bailey and Walton had given Northamptonshire a chance on a ground encouraging fast scoring.

Northamptonshire

M. B. Loye c S. G. Law b Such	28	R. J. Bailey not out	38
†R. J. Warren run out	22	T. C. Walton not out	51
J. N. Snape c Irani b Such	10	L-b 6, w 6, n-b 4	16
*K. M. Curran lbw b Such	18		
A. L. Penberthy c S. G. Law b Irani	30	1/49 2/65 3/73 (6 wkts, 40 overs)	239
D. J. Sales run out	26	4/103 5/142 6/152	

G. P. Swann, F. A. Rose and D. E. Malcolm did not bat.

Bowling: Ilott 8–0–42–0; Cowan 8–0–40–0; Irani 8–0–59–1; Such 8–0–33–3; Grayson 8–0–59–0.

Essex

D. D. J. Robinson st Warren b Snape	66	R. C. Irani not out	23
S. G. Law c Bailey b Snape	83	L-b 1, w 5	6
*N. Hussain not out	62		
		1/131 2/176 (2 wkts, 36.2 overs)	240

A. P. Grayson, S. D. Peters, †R. J. Rollins, D. R. Law, A. P. Cowan, M. C. Ilott and P. M. Such did not bat.

Bowling: Rose 5.2–0–24–0; Penberthy 7–0–56–0; Curran 3–0–35–0; Malcolm 8–0–40–0; Snape 8–0–46–2; Swann 5–0–38–0.

Umpires: A. Clarkson and D. J. Constant.

ESSEX v SURREY

At Chelmsford, June 14. Essex won by 26 runs (D/L method). Toss: Surrey.

Essex regained the joint leadership after a week off. They made the most of being asked to bat and a favourable Duckworth/Lewis ruling. Before the rain, they made effective progress to 136. Surrey were initially allotted 17 overs, but further rain, when they were 44 for five from eight, gave them a new target of 126 from 15. They returned and struggled on in steady drizzle for another three overs, one more than the minimum for a result.

Essex

D. D. J. Robinson lbw b Tudor	25	D. R. Law not out	14
S. G. Law c Batty b Tudor	30	L-b 5, w 7, n-b 4	16
*N. Hussain c Batty b Ratcliffe	30		
R. C. Irani not out	21	1/55 2/67 3/122 (3 wkts, 27 overs)	136

A. P. Grayson, S. D. Peters, †R. J. Rollins, M. C. Ilott, P. M. Such and D. M. Cousins did not bat.

Bowling: Bicknell 6–0–36–0; Benjamin 8–0–22–0; Tudor 4–0–22–2; Saqlain Mushtaq 5–0–12–0; Hollioake 3–0–24–0; Ratcliffe 1–0–15–1.

Surrey

G. P. Thorpe b Cousins	14	†J. N. Batty not out	6
A. J. Stewart c Irani b Cousins	15	M. P. Bicknell not out	2
M. A. Butcher lbw b Irani	3		
*A. J. Hollioake c S. G. Law b Irani	1	L-b 2, w 3	5
J. D. Ratcliffe c Hussain b Grayson	17		
I. J. Ward c D. R. Law b Cousins	3	1/32 2/35 3/36 (7 wkts, 11 overs) 69	
A. J. Tudor b S. G. Law	3	4/36 5/41 6/53 7/64	

Saqlain Mushtaq and J. E. Benjamin did not bat.

Bowling: Ilott 2–0–12–0; Cousins 4–0–23–3; Irani 2–0–7–2; Grayson 2–0–15–1; S. G. Law 1–0–10–1.

Umpires: M. J. Kitchen and B. Leadbeater.

At Bath, June 21. ESSEX lost to SOMERSET by seven wickets (D/L method).

At Derby, July 5. ESSEX beat DERBYSHIRE by eight wickets.

ESSEX v KENT

At Southend, July 19. Essex won by 30 runs. Toss: Kent.

Essex went clear at the top of the table, defeating Kent comprehensively to the delight of a 6,000 crowd. Stuart Law was at his most commanding, scoring 126 at more than a run a ball. He built a steady opening stand with Prichard, and then demolished the bowling with Danny Law, in a stand of 117 in 14 overs. Key and Hooper made a rapid response, but the task was too great.

Essex

*P. J. Prichard b Hooper	34	†R. J. Rollins b Ealham	1
S. G. Law b Fleming	126	A. P. Cowan not out	1
N. Hussain lbw b Hooper	0	B 1, l-b 4, w 10, n-b 6	21
R. C. Irani c Ealham b Llong	20		
D. R. Law run out	50	1/78 2/80 3/121 (7 wkts, 40 overs) 259	
A. P. Grayson not out	4	4/238 5/252	
S. D. Peters b Fleming	2	6/254 7/255	

M. C. Ilott and P. M. Such did not bat.

Bowling: Headley 6–1–28–0; Igglesden 2–0–19–0; Ealham 7–0–45–1; Fleming 8–0–49–2; Hooper 8–0–44–2; Llong 6–0–39–1; McCague 3–0–30–0.

Kent

T. R. Ward c S. G. Law b Ilott	0	*†S. A. Marsh lbw b Cowan	5
R. W. T. Key c Prichard b Ilott	62	D. W. Headley lbw b Irani	1
C. L. Hooper c Cowan b Irani	27	A. P. Igglesden not out	3
M. J. McCague c Peters b Such	12	L-b 9, w 9, n-b 6	24
N. J. Llong c Peters b Grayson	30		
M. A. Ealham c Irani b Grayson	4	1/0 2/66 3/80 (38.5 overs) 229	
M. J. Walker c S. G. Law b Ilott	47	4/145 5/145 6/162	
M. V. Fleming b Grayson	14	7/199 8/206 9/209	

Bowling: Ilott 7.5–0–43–3; Cowan 8–0–57–1; Such 8–0–45–1; Irani 7–0–35–2; Grayson 8–0–40–3.

Umpires: G. I. Burgess and R. A. White.

At Birmingham, July 21. ESSEX beat WARWICKSHIRE by 17 runs.

ESSEX v GLAMORGAN

At Chelmsford, August 9. Essex won by eight wickets. Toss: Essex.

Beaten decisively in the Championship on Saturday, Essex turned on Glamorgan to secure their seventh League win out of eight. Prichard, who was considered unfit for first-class matches, took the helm again and hit a fighting, undefeated 99. He added 143 with Irani, who had helped subdue Glamorgan earlier with a League-best four for 26.

Glamorgan

S. P. James run out.	5	A. P. Davies c Irani b Ilott.	18
*M. P. Maynard c Peters b Cowan	4	D. A. Cosker not out	6
A. Dale c Hyam b Ilott.	2		
P. A. Cottey b Irani	34	B 1, l-b 10, w 1	12
M. J. Powell c Hyam b Irani	13		
R. D. B. Croft c Cowan b Irani	0	1/12 2/15 3/18 (9 wkts, 40 overs) 172
†I. Dawood b Irani.	57	4/46 5/46 6/84
S. D. Thomas c Cowan b Such.	21	7/117 8/149 9/172

O. T. Parkin did not bat.

Bowling: Ilott 8–0–36–2; Cowan 8–0–25–1; Such 8–0–29–1; Irani 8–0–26–4; Grayson 8–0–45–0.

Essex

*P. J. Prichard not out.	99
D. D. J. Robinson b Parkin	10
S. D. Peters c Cottey b Davies	2
R. C. Irani not out	39
B 4, l-b 4, w 15	23

1/25 2/30 (2 wkts, 32.3 overs) 173

A. P. Grayson, D. R. Law, G. R. Napier, †B. J. Hyam, A. P. Cowan, M. C. Ilott and P. M. Such did not bat.

Bowling: Parkin 6.3–0–19–1; Davies 5–0–25–1; Thomas 3–0–17–0; Dale 2–0–16–0; Croft 8–0–39–0; Cosker 8–0–49–0.

Umpires: G. I. Burgess and J. H. Hampshire.

ESSEX v GLOUCESTERSHIRE

At Colchester, August 23. No result. Toss: Essex.

Dawson struck Ilott for three leg-side fours before being bowled by the 17th ball of the match. It was to be the last one, as heavy rain swept across the ground. Essex were overtaken on points by Lancashire next day.

Gloucestershire

R. I. Dawson b Ilott	13
M. C. J. Ball not out	0
L-b 1	1

1/14 (1 wkt, 2.5 overs) 14

*M. W. Alleyne, M. G. N. Windows, D. R. Hewson, †R. C. Russell, T. H. C. Hancock, M. J. Cawdron, J. Lewis, A. M. Smith and C. A. Walsh did not bat.

Bowling: Ilott 1.5–0–12–1; Cowan 1–0–1–0.

Essex

*P. J. Prichard, S. G. Law, D. D. J. Robinson, R. C. Irani, A. P. Grayson, S. D. Peters, D. R. Law, †B. J. Hyam, A. P. Cowan, M. C. Ilott and P. M. Such.

Umpires: A. Clarkson and M. J. Kitchen.

At Scarborough, August 30. ESSEX lost to YORKSHIRE by eight wickets.

ESSEX v NOTTINGHAMSHIRE

At Chelmsford, September 6. Nottinghamshire won by 51 runs. Toss: Essex.

The bad finally overwhelmed the good in Essex's two-faced season when they lost all realistic chance of winning the League. Chasing 193, they crumpled to 89 for nine. Cowan and Such – just selected for the Ashes tour – staged a spirited but meaningless fightback; many of the crowd did not even stay for the entertainment. Earlier, Such had conceded just 18 off his eight overs, but the batting of Johnson and Archer, whose 50 contained two sixes but no fours, turned out to be more significant than it had seemed at first.

Nottinghamshire

*J. E. R. Gallian c S. G. Law b Ilott	12		P. J. Franks run out	4
P. R. Pollard c Cowan b Such	23		†C. M. W. Read not out	15
P. Johnson b Grayson	31		B 1, l-b 9, w 6	16
G. F. Archer not out	50			—
M. P. Dowman run out	13		1/25 2/70 3/70 (6 wkts, 40 overs)	192
C. M. Tolley lbw b Cowan	28		4/101 5/157 6/163	

K. P. Evans, R. T. Bates and A. R. Oram did not bat.

Bowling: Ilott 8–0–32–1; Cowan 8–0–44–1; Such 8–2–18–1; Irani 8–0–47–0; Grayson 8–0–41–1.

Essex

*P. J. Prichard c and b Franks	11		A. P. Cowan not out	40
S. G. Law c Pollard b Evans	6		M. C. Ilott c Read b Franks	1
S. D. Peters c Pollard b Franks	7		P. M. Such not out	13
R. C. Irani lbw b Oram	22		L-b 9, w 7, n-b 4	20
A. P. Grayson b Bates	15			—
D. D. J. Robinson b Tolley	0		1/19 2/23 3/32 (9 wkts, 40 overs)	141
D. R. Law c Archer b Bates	5		4/57 5/59 6/81	
†B. J. Hyam c Gallian b Dowman	1		7/81 8/87 9/89	

Bowling: Evans 8–1–32–1; Franks 8–1–24–3; Tolley 5–0–22–1; Oram 8–2–22–1; Bates 7–0–21–2; Dowman 4–0–11–1.

Umpires: J. C. Balderstone and B. Dudleston.

At Leicester, September 13. ESSEX lost to LEICESTERSHIRE by 128 runs.

GLAMORGAN

At Bristol, April 19. GLOUCESTERSHIRE v GLAMORGAN. No result (abandoned).

GLAMORGAN v KENT

At Cardiff, April 26. Kent won by eight wickets. Toss: Kent.

Glamorgan were soundly beaten as Kent displayed their best one-day form. After being given a good start by James and Dale, Glamorgan lost five wickets for four as they tried to accelerate. Walker, initially playing second fiddle to Ward, batted throughout Kent's innings. Because of the reduction to 27 overs a side, no more than two bowlers should have been allowed six overs; but a third, Watkin, completed six before the regulation was remembered.

Glamorgan

S. P. James b Hooper	30	†A. D. Shaw b Phillips	1
A. Dale c Cowdrey b Phillips	37	S. L. Watkin not out	5
*M. P. Maynard c Phillips b Fleming	21		
P. A. Cottey c Ealham b Hooper	21	B 1, l-b 1, w 2	4
R. D. B. Croft not out	11		
M. J. Powell lbw b Ealham	0	1/58 2/91 3/93 (8 wkts, 27 overs)	132
G. P. Butcher b Fleming	2	4/120 5/120 6/123	
S. D. Thomas b Fleming	0	7/123 8/124	

O. T. Parkin did not bat.

Bowling: Headley 6–0–25–0; Igglesden 3–0–22–0; Ealham 5–0–19–1; Phillips 3–0–20–2; Hooper 6–0–26–2; Fleming 4–0–18–3.

Kent

T. R. Ward c Croft b Watkin	35
M. J. Walker not out	62
C. L. Hooper lbw b Parkin	18
A. P. Wells not out	8
L-b 5, w 4, n-b 2	11

1/50 2/91   (2 wkts, 23.4 overs) 134

M. A. Ealham, G. R. Cowdrey, M. V. Fleming, *†S. A. Marsh, D. W. Headley, B. J. Phillips and A. P. Igglesden did not bat.

Bowling: Watkin 6–0–35–1; Thomas 3–0–19–0; Croft 6–0–24–0; Parkin 6–0–29–1; Butcher 2.4–0–22–0.

Umpires: H. D. Bird and J. W. Holder.

At Lord's, May 3. GLAMORGAN lost to MIDDLESEX by three wickets.

GLAMORGAN v SOMERSET

At Cardiff, May 10. Somerset won by eight wickets. Toss: Glamorgan.

Croft's run of one-day successes – five fifties in five innings – came to an end, but his team's run of failures continued. Glamorgan made it 12 games since their last League win when Somerset made light work of a target of 184. Burns batted through and won the match by hitting Watkin into the pavilion for his second six.

Glamorgan

S. P. James c Reeve b Rose	9		Waqar Younis lbw b Reeve	4
R. D. B. Croft c Reeve b Rose	1		S. L. Watkin not out	0
A. Dale c Rose b Mushtaq Ahmed	39			
*P. A. Cottey b Caddick	4		L-b 11, w 5, n-b 2	18
†A. D. Shaw b Trescothick	40			
A. W. Evans b Trescothick	17		1/2 2/26 3/50 (9 wkts, 40 overs)	183
M. J. Powell run out	30		4/72 5/114 6/125	
S. D. Thomas c Trescothick b Rose	21		7/172 8/183 9/183	

D. A. Cosker did not bat.

Bowling: Reeve 6–0–24–1; Rose 8–0–33–3; Parsons 2–0–13–0; Caddick 8–1–37–1; Mushtaq Ahmed 8–0–24–1; Trescothick 5–0–23–2; Bowler 3–0–18–0.

Somerset

*P. D. Bowler run out	19
M. Burns not out	84
G. D. Rose c Cottey b Croft	41
R. J. Harden not out	32
L-b 3, w 9	12

1/56 2/124   (2 wkts, 33.2 overs) 188

M. N. Lathwell, M. E. Trescothick, K. A. Parsons, †R. J. Turner, D. A. Reeve, A. R. Caddick and Mushtaq Ahmed did not bat.

Bowling: Waqar Younis 3–0–20–0; Watkin 5.2–0–35–0; Croft 8–0–36–1; Cosker 8–0–50–0; Dale 3–0–20–0; Thomas 6–1–24–0.

Umpires: G. I. Burgess and G. Sharp.

GLAMORGAN v YORKSHIRE

At Cardiff, May 19. Yorkshire won by 37 runs. Toss: Glamorgan.

Thanks to a free-admission deal with local sponsors, a full house turned up on a fine Tuesday afternoon to watch Glamorgan endure their fourth successive League defeat and 13th successive winless game. The team, however, was much depleted. Acting-captain Cottey tried to rally the troops, and put on 75 in 11 overs with Butcher. But their hopes were crushed when Sidebottom took four wickets in his final over (WW1WW1). He finished with six for 40.

Yorkshire

M. P. Vaughan c Powell b Parkin	25		B. Parker c Parkin b Thomas	0
C. White c Cottey b Parkin	15		L-b 5, w 7	12
*D. Byas c Cottey b Waqar Younis	71			
D. S. Lehmann c Shaw b Cosker	47		1/41 2/46 3/140 (5 wkts, 40 overs)	225
A. McGrath not out	55		4/219 5/225	

†R. J. Blakey, P. M. Hutchison, G. M. Hamilton, R. D. Stemp and R. J. Sidebottom did not bat.

Bowling: Waqar Younis 8–0–49–1; Parkin 8–0–29–2; Watkin 8–1–39–0; Thomas 6–0–32–1; Dale 4–0–24–0; Cosker 6–0–47–1.

Glamorgan

†A. D. Shaw c Blakey b Sidebottom	5		S. L. Watkin not out	2
A. Dale lbw b Sidebottom	17		D. A. Cosker b Sidebottom	0
*P. A. Cottey b Sidebottom	78		O. T. Parkin b White	1
M. J. Powell c Vaughan b White	33		L-b 11, w 6, n-b 4	21
A. W. Evans c Blakey b Hamilton	3			
G. P. Butcher c Vaughan b Hamilton	27		1/21 2/33 3/95 (37.1 overs)	188
S. D. Thomas b Sidebottom	1		4/106 5/181 6/185	
Waqar Younis lbw b Sidebottom	0		7/185 8/186 9/186	

Bowling: Sidebottom 8–0–40–6; Hutchison 7–0–30–0; Stemp 5–0–31–0; White 6.1–1–17–2; Hamilton 6–0–30–2; Lehmann 3–0–19–0; Vaughan 2–0–10–0.

Umpires: J. H. Harris and D. R. Shepherd.

At Northampton, May 25. GLAMORGAN beat NORTHAMPTONSHIRE by five wickets (D/L method).

At Southampton, June 7. GLAMORGAN lost to HAMPSHIRE by 131 runs (D/L method).

GLAMORGAN v WORCESTERSHIRE

At Cardiff, June 14. Worcestershire won by seven wickets. Toss: Worcestershire.
Hick and Leatherdale made light work of a seven-an-over target in a match reduced to 19 overs a side. They put on 98 from 73 balls, with Hick on top form.

Glamorgan

*M. P. Maynard c Newport b Moody...	42	G. P. Butcher not out.............	13
R. D. B. Croft c Hafeez b Newport....	12	W. L. Law not out................	1
P. A. Cottey c Moody b Chapman....	8	L-b 1, w 1................	2
A. Dale c Illingworth b Moody.......	22		
S. P. James run out................	9	1/27 2/45 3/73 (7 wkts, 19 overs) 129		
M. J. Powell run out................	8	4/90 5/103	
†A. D. Shaw st Rhodes b Illingworth...	12	6/108 7/120	

D. A. Cosker and O. T. Parkin did not bat.

Bowling: Newport 4–0–17–1; Haynes 3–0–23–0; Chapman 2–0–18–1; Moody 4–0–32–2; Illingworth 4–0–25–1; Leatherdale 2–0–13–0.

Worcestershire

*T. M. Moody c Cosker b Croft......	10	G. R. Haynes not out.............	5
V. S. Solanki c Cottey b Parkin......	3	B 5, w 7................	12
G. A. Hick c Dale b Croft..........	65		
D. A. Leatherdale not out..........	36	1/12 2/23 3/121 (3 wkts, 18.4 overs) 131		

S. W. K. Ellis, †S. J. Rhodes, A. Hafeez, R. K. Illingworth, P. J. Newport and R. J. Chapman did not bat.

Bowling: Parkin 4–0–13–1; Croft 4–0–21–2; Cosker 3–0–30–0; Dale 4–0–30–0; Cottey 2–0–16–0; Butcher 1.4–0–16–0.

Umpires: J. C. Balderstone and J. H. Hampshire.

GLAMORGAN v LEICESTERSHIRE

At Pontypridd, June 21. Leicestershire won by 20 runs. Toss: Glamorgan. County debut: I. Dawood.
Glamorgan sank to their sixth successive home League defeat despite reducing Leicestershire to 31 for four. Lewis hit a breezy 56 to take the score past 200. Glamorgan stayed in touch through 66 in 64 balls from Maynard, but the later batsmen failed to keep up.

Leicestershire

P. V. Simmons c Law b Watkin	10	J. M. Dakin run out		19
V. J. Wells c Dawood b Thomas	13	D. Williamson b Butcher		2
B. F. Smith c Dawood b Watkin	2	L-b 5, w 12		17
D. L. Maddy c Butcher b Dale	33			
D. I. Stevens c Dawood b Thomas	0	1/18 2/21 3/31	(8 wkts, 40 overs)	202
†P. A. Nixon c Dale b Thomas	50	4/31 5/99 6/155		
*C. C. Lewis not out	56	7/190 8/202		

M. T. Brimson and A. D. Mullally did not bat.

Bowling: Watkin 8–1–20–2; Parkin 8–0–22–0; Thomas 7–0–41–3; Cosker 5–0–37–0; Dale 8–0–40–1; Butcher 4–0–37–1.

Glamorgan

W. L. Law b Wells	24	S. L. Watkin b Mullally		2
A. Dale c and b Williamson	38	D. A. Cosker not out		2
*M. P. Maynard b Mullally	66	O. T. Parkin b Lewis		2
P. A. Cottey lbw b Williamson	9	L-b 5, w 1, n-b 2		8
M. J. Powell c and b Brimson	5			
G. P. Butcher lbw b Williamson	2	1/46 2/89 3/117	(39.5 overs)	182
†I. Dawood run out	12	4/126 5/135 6/157		
S. D. Thomas run out	12	7/170 8/176 9/177		

Bowling: Mullally 7–0–21–2; Lewis 6.5–0–30–1; Simmons 6–0–35–0; Wells 5–0–24–1; Williamson 8–0–36–3; Brimson 7–0–31–1.

Umpires: A. Clarkson and D. R. Shepherd.

GLAMORGAN v SURREY

At Swansea, July 5. Glamorgan won by 107 runs. Toss: Glamorgan. First-team debut: S. C. B. Tomlinson.

Surrey had the worst day yet of their wretched season in the League when they were humiliated by Darren Thomas. Bowling at a lively pace, he took their last seven wickets for 16. These figures have been bettered only twice in the competition's 30 seasons, by Keith Boyce and Richard Hutton. Thomas took the final six wickets for four in 21 balls but gave the credit to the opening bowlers, Parkin and Watkin, for making the batsmen struggle: "When I came on, they had to go for their shots." Surrey were 77 all out and fell to their eighth consecutive League defeat. Glamorgan's win was their first at home since their previous match at St Helen's just over a year earlier.

Glamorgan

G. P. Butcher st Batty b Saqlain Mushtaq	3	D. A. Cosker c Batty b B. C. Hollioake		19
A. Dale c and b B. C. Hollioake	65	S. L. Watkin b A. J. Hollioake		2
*M. P. Maynard c Salisbury b Bicknell	1	O. T. Parkin not out		0
P. A. Cottey c Benjamin b Salisbury	28	L-b 10, w 5, n-b 6		21
M. J. Powell st Batty b Saqlain Mushtaq	30			
†I. Dawood c Shahid b B. C. Hollioake	1	1/6 2/14 3/90	(39.2 overs)	184
S. D. Thomas b Salisbury	12	4/130 5/132 6/160		
S. C. B. Tomlinson st Batty b Salisbury	2	7/160 8/171 9/180		

Bowling: Saqlain Mushtaq 8–0–34–2; Benjamin 6–1–20–0; Bicknell 5–0–14–1; Salisbury 8–0–45–3; A. J. Hollioake 4–0–15–1; Shahid 3–0–16–0; B. C. Hollioake 5.2–1–30–3.

Surrey

A. D. Brown b Thomas	30	I. D. K. Salisbury c Dawood b Thomas	1
I. J. Ward c Dawood b Parkin	0	Saqlain Mushtaq b Thomas	4
J. D. Ratcliffe b Parkin	12	J. E. Benjamin b Thomas	0
N. Shahid c Tomlinson b Parkin	3	L-b 4, w 5	9
B. C. Hollioake b Thomas	4		
*A. J. Hollioake c Watkin b Thomas	5	1/1 2/25 3/31	(25.5 overs) 77
†J. N. Batty lbw b Thomas	4	4/50 5/60 6/60	
M. P. Bicknell not out	5	7/65 8/69 9/76	

Bowling: Parkin 8–0–24–3; Watkin 6–1–16–0; Thomas 6.5–0–16–7; Tomlinson 5–0–17–0.

Umpires: H. D. Bird and R. A. White.

At Nottingham, July 12. GLAMORGAN beat NOTTINGHAMSHIRE by nine runs.

GLAMORGAN v LANCASHIRE

At Colwyn Bay, July 26. No result (abandoned).

At Birmingham, August 3. GLAMORGAN beat WARWICKSHIRE by 39 runs (D/L method).

At Chelmsford, August 9. GLAMORGAN lost to ESSEX by eight wickets.

At Hove, August 30. GLAMORGAN beat SUSSEX by 37 runs.

At Chester-le-Street, September 6. GLAMORGAN beat DURHAM by 26 runs.

GLAMORGAN v DERBYSHIRE

At Cardiff, September 13. Glamorgan won by 56 runs. Toss: Glamorgan.

Glamorgan's late charge up the table, with only one defeat in their final eight matches, just failed to give them First Division status for 1999. A fourth-wicket stand of 112 between Dale and Powell, on a slow pitch, gave the bowlers plenty to defend. After the early loss of Slater, Derbyshire were never in the hunt, despite a stubborn effort from Barnett.

Glamorgan

S. P. James c and b Clarke	24	A. W. Evans not out	9
*M. P. Maynard lbw b Dean	6	†I. Dawood not out	12
A. Dale b Clarke	82	L-b 10, w 8	18
P. A. Cottey c and b Barnett	4		
M. J. Powell b Clarke	55	1/14 2/49 3/62	(6 wkts, 40 overs) 210
S. D. Thomas c Blackwell b Cassar	0	4/174 5/181 6/182	

A. P. Davies, D. A. Cosker and O. T. Parkin did not bat.

Bowling: Cork 8–1–28–0; Dean 8–1–39–1; Clarke 8–0–47–3; Barnett 8–1–32–1; Blackwell 6–0–43–0; Cassar 2–0–11–1.

Derbyshire

M. J. Slater c Maynard b Davies	7	V. P. Clarke not out	25
K. J. Barnett c and b Cosker	41	†K. M. Krikken c Dale b Cosker	1
A. S. Rollins b Dale	5	K. J. Dean not out	16
*D. G. Cork st Dawood b Dale	15	L-b 1, w 10	11
I. D. Blackwell b Dale	2		
M. E. Cassar b Thomas	6	1/9 2/24 3/69 (9 wkts, 40 overs)	154
R. M. S. Weston c Maynard b Cosker	16	4/73 5/75 6/84	
B. L. Spendlove b Thomas	9	7/105 8/112 9/118	

Bowling: Parkin 8–2–19–0; Davies 8–1–20–1; Dale 8–0–36–3; Thomas 8–0–39–2; Cosker 8–0–39–3.

Umpires: B. Leadbeater and J. W. Lloyds.

GLOUCESTERSHIRE

GLOUCESTERSHIRE v GLAMORGAN

At Bristol, April 19. No result (abandoned).

At Chester-le-Street, April 26. GLOUCESTERSHIRE lost to DURHAM by two runs.

GLOUCESTERSHIRE v KENT

At Bristol, May 10. Kent won by six wickets. Toss: Gloucestershire.

Kent stayed top of the League with their third successive win. Ward led the chase in belligerent mood, leaving Hooper, with an unbeaten 68, to see Kent to victory.

Gloucestershire

R. J. Cunliffe b Phillips	37	M. C. J. Ball not out	21
T. H. C. Hancock b Headley	0	R. I. Dawson not out	16
†R. C. Russell c Marsh b Phillips	27	L-b 5, w 11, n-b 2	18
A. J. Wright lbw b Phillips	1		
*M. W. Alleyne b Fleming	37	1/2 2/65 3/67 (7 wkts, 40 overs)	182
M. J. Church lbw b Ealham	25	4/102 5/130	
J. Lewis b Fleming	0	6/130 7/159	

A. M. Smith and C. A. Walsh did not bat.

Bowling: Igglesden 6–0–24–0; Headley 8–1–19–1; Ealham 7–0–34–1; Phillips 7–0–31–3; Hooper 8–0–45–0; Fleming 4–0–24–2.

Kent

T. R. Ward c Smith b Alleyne	52	G. R. Cowdrey not out	10
M. J. Walker b Alleyne	20	L-b 1, w 5, n-b 4	10
C. L. Hooper not out	68		
A. P. Wells lbw b Walsh	26	1/72 2/83 (4 wkts, 38.1 overs)	186
M. A. Ealham b Ball	0	3/147 4/151	

M. V. Fleming, *†S. A. Marsh, B. J. Phillips, D. W. Headley and A. P. Igglesden did not bat.

Bowling: Smith 7.1–0–44–0; Walsh 8–1–20–1; Ball 7–0–33–1; Alleyne 8–0–43–2; Lewis 4–0–16–0; Hancock 4–0–29–0.

Umpires: J. C. Balderstone and A. A. Jones.

GLOUCESTERSHIRE v LEICESTERSHIRE

At Bristol, May 17. Gloucestershire won by four wickets. Toss: Gloucestershire.

Courtney Walsh took five for two off his last 14 balls to finish the Leicestershire innings, but Gloucestershire only just scraped home. Jon Lewis had to hit 26 off 18 balls to give them victory.

Leicestershire

P. V. Simmons c Dawson b Lewis	23	D. Williamson b Walsh	17
V. J. Wells c and b Alleyne	30	T. J. Mason b Walsh	0
B. F. Smith b Walsh	74	A. D. Mullally not out	1
*C. C. Lewis c and b Ball	16	B 4, l-b 15, w 10, n-b 2	31
D. L. Maddy c Walsh b Ball	5		
A. Habib b Walsh	7	1/65 2/67 3/106	(39 overs) 206
J. M. Dakin c Russell b Walsh	0	4/117 5/148 6/148	
†P. A. Nixon c Dawson b Alleyne	2	7/162 8/205 9/205	

Bowling: Walsh 8–0–23–5; Smith 7–0–39–0; Lewis 8–0–56–1; Alleyne 8–1–38–2; Ball 8–0–31–2.

Gloucestershire

R. J. Cunliffe retired hurt	7	M. C. J. Ball not out	9
R. I. Dawson b Mason	32	J. Lewis not out	26
*M. W. Alleyne c Nixon b Maddy	63		
A. J. Wright c Habib b Maddy	30	B 1, l-b 11, w 8, n-b 2	22
M. J. Church b Simmons	3		
†R. C. Russell b Simmons	1	1/72 2/140 3/144	(6 wkts, 39.4 overs) 207
T. H. C. Hancock c Williamson b Maddy	14	4/148 5/160 6/169	

A. M. Smith and C. A. Walsh did not bat.

R. J. Cunliffe retired hurt at 12.

Bowling: Mullally 8–0–25–0; Lewis 7.4–0–38–0; Wells 3–0–13–0; Dakin 1–0–12–0; Williamson 2–0–10–0; Mason 5–0–34–1; Simmons 8–0–29–2; Maddy 5–0–34–3.

Umpires: J. H. Hampshire and M. J. Harris.

At Nottingham, May 19. GLOUCESTERSHIRE beat NOTTINGHAMSHIRE by one run.

GLOUCESTERSHIRE v YORKSHIRE

At Gloucester, May 25. Yorkshire won by nine runs. Toss: Gloucestershire.

A hat-trick for Smith came too late to hinder Yorkshire's progress. Parker, who had hit three sixes, was his first victim – one of three men to be dismissed for 40 – followed by Hamilton and Sidebottom. Alleyne struck 88 off 94 balls, but Gloucestershire found themselves needing 16 off the last over.

Yorkshire

M. P. Vaughan c Windows b Ball	40	R. D. Stemp not out	0
C. White c and b Alleyne	35	R. J. Sidebottom lbw b Smith	0
*D. Byas c Smith b Alleyne	16	P. M. Hutchison not out	1
D. S. Lehmann c Ball b Hancock	40	L-b 6, w 4, n-b 2	12
A. McGrath lbw b Ball	11		
B. Parker c sub b Smith	40	1/60 2/87 3/118	(9 wkts, 40 overs) 215
†R. J. Blakey c Ball b Smith	12	4/149 5/151 6/180	
G. M. Hamilton c Alleyne b Smith	8	7/214 8/214 9/214	

Bowling: Lewis 7–0–56–0; Smith 8–0–29–4; Averis 5–0–29–0; Alleyne 8–0–39–2; Ball 8–0–31–2; Hancock 4–0–25–1.

Gloucestershire

R. J. Cunliffe c Blakey b Hutchison	1	J. Lewis b Hutchison	4
M. G. N. Windows b Sidebottom	11	A. M. Smith c Vaughan b Hutchison	2
*M. W. Alleyne c Hutchison b Stemp	88	J. M. M. Averis b Hutchison	0
A. J. Wright c Vaughan b Hamilton	18	L-b 7, w 5, n-b 2	14
M. J. Church b Sidebottom	6		
†R. C. Russell c Blakey b Sidebottom	3	1/12 2/18 3/66	(39.5 overs) 206
T. H. C. Hancock run out	30	4/105 5/113 6/165	
M. C. J. Ball not out	29	7/174 8/191 9/201	

Bowling: Sidebottom 8–0–28–3; Hutchison 7.5–0–34–4; Hamilton 8–0–40–1; White 8–0–34–0; Stemp 8–0–63–1.

Umpires: R. Palmer and A. G. T. Whitehead.

At Chesterfield, June 7. DERBYSHIRE v GLOUCESTERSHIRE. No result (abandoned).

GLOUCESTERSHIRE v WARWICKSHIRE

At Bristol, June 14. No result. Toss: Gloucestershire.

After choosing to bat, Gloucestershire were soon in trouble at 33 for three. They had little chance to repair the damage: a heavy storm washed out play in the 12th over.

Gloucestershire

G. I. Macmillan b Giddins	0	M. G. N. Windows not out	5
R. I. Dawson b Small	13	L-b 2, w 6	8
*M. W. Alleyne c Knight b Giddins	1		
A. J. Wright not out	22	1/7 2/11 3/33	(3 wkts, 11.4 overs) 49

T. H. C. Hancock, †R. C. Russell, M. C. J. Ball, M. J. Cawdron, A. M. Smith and C. A. Walsh did not bat.

Bowling: Brown 6–1–13–0; Giddins 4–0–20–2; Small 1.4–0–14–1.

Warwickshire

N. M. K. Smith, N. V. Knight, D. P. Ostler, *B. C. Lara, T. L. Penney, D. R. Brown, A. F. Giles, G. Welch, †K. J. Piper, G. C. Small and E. S. H. Giddins.

Umpires: A. Clarkson and V. A. Holder.

At Worcester, June 21. GLOUCESTERSHIRE lost to WORCESTERSHIRE by 13 runs.

At Southampton, July 5. GLOUCESTERSHIRE beat HAMPSHIRE by six wickets.

GLOUCESTERSHIRE v SUSSEX

At Cheltenham, July 18. Gloucestershire won by 35 runs. Toss: Sussex.

Gloucestershire marked the 150th anniversary of W. G. Grace's birth with a pre-match Victorian pageant, followed by a deserved win in front of a good crowd. Dawson was the mainstay of their innings. Bevan struggled to keep Sussex in the game but was let down by three run-outs as Gloucestershire fielded tenaciously. One of the victims was Adams, out for his fifth single-figure score at Cheltenham out of six over the past two seasons. Alleyne passed 4,000 League runs in his 146th consecutive appearance in the competition – a record, beating 145 by David Bairstow and Ken McEwan.

Gloucestershire

R. I. Dawson b Robinson	60	J. Lewis b Lewry	19
T. H. C. Hancock lbw b Kirtley	0	A. M. Smith not out	8
*M. W. Alleyne b Robinson	17	C. A. Walsh not out	1
A. J. Wright c Carpenter b Robinson	0		
M. G. N. Windows c Bevan b Rao	32	B 1, l-b 7, w 9	17
G. I. Macmillan c Kirtley b Lewry	31		
†R. C. Russell c Carpenter		1/8 2/62 3/68 (9 wkts, 40 overs) 219	
b Martin-Jenkins	20	4/96 5/129 6/173	
M. C. J. Ball c Humphries b Kirtley	14	7/179 8/209 9/209	

Bowling: Lewry 8–0–40–2; Kirtley 8–0–57–2; Martin-Jenkins 8–0–38–1; Robinson 8–0–24–3; Bevan 4–0–29–0; Rao 4–1–23–1.

Sussex

R. K. Rao run out	2	J. D. Lewry b Walsh	0
W. G. Khan c and b Alleyne	25	R. J. Kirtley not out	5
*C. J. Adams run out	5	M. A. Robinson b Smith	0
M. G. Bevan c Dawson b Walsh	78	L-b 19, w 3, n-b 2	24
M. Newell b Lewis	19		
R. S. C. Martin-Jenkins b Lewis	13	1/3 2/20 3/71 (39 overs) 184	
J. R. Carpenter run out	0	4/112 5/138 6/139	
†S. Humphries c Ball b Smith	13	7/178 8/179 9/183	

Bowling: Lewis 8–0–38–2; Smith 8–2–26–2; Walsh 7–1–28–2; Alleyne 8–0–36–1; Ball 8–0–37–0.

Umpires: D. J. Constant and T. E. Jesty.

GLOUCESTERSHIRE v NORTHAMPTONSHIRE

At Cheltenham, July 19. Northamptonshire won by 72 runs. Toss: Northamptonshire.

Gloucestershire's experiment of playing two "Sunday" matches in two days ended in defeat after six successive Championship and League wins at Cheltenham. Loye maintained his excellent form with a dashing 92 and Curran hit out purposefully against his former county. Gloucestershire quickly slipped to 43 for four, and, despite Dawson's second half-century on successive days, their challenge folded with five overs to spare.

Northamptonshire

M. B. Loye c Macmillan b Lewis	92	J. P. Taylor run out	0
†R. J. Warren lbw b Ball	32	D. Follett not out	0
*K. M. Curran run out	48	T. C. Walton b Walsh	0
A. L. Penberthy c Windows b Hancock	20	L-b 6, w 1	7
J. N. Snape c Hancock b Ball	20		
R. J. Bailey b Walsh	12	1/88 2/154 3/179 (40 overs) 250	
D. J. Sales c Lewis b Walsh	15	4/217 5/218 6/244	
F. A. Rose b Smith	4	7/250 8/250 9/250	

Bowling: Smith 8–1–27–1; Lewis 7–0–41–1; Alleyne 7–0–48–0; Walsh 8–1–42–3; Ball 7–0–51–2; Hancock 3–0–35–1.

Gloucestershire

T. H. C. Hancock c Warren b Follett	3	J. Lewis c Curran b Snape	2
R. I. Dawson lbw b Snape	75	A. M. Smith c Sales b Penberthy	14
*M. W. Alleyne b Rose	9	C. A. Walsh c Penberthy b Follett	2
A. J. Wright b Curran	0	L-b 2, w 4, n-b 2	8
M. G. N. Windows b Taylor	2		
G. I. Macmillan b Snape	14	1/6 2/34 3/36 (34.5 overs) 178	
†R. C. Russell c Bailey b Penberthy	13	4/43 5/88 6/119	
M. C. J. Ball not out	36	7/130 8/136 9/162	

Bowling: Follett 6.5–1–22–2; Rose 5–1–17–1; Taylor 5–0–19–1; Curran 5–1–31–1; Snape 6–0–39–3; Penberthy 7–0–48–2.

Umpires: R. Julian and G. Sharp.

GLOUCESTERSHIRE v SURREY

At Cheltenham, July 26. Gloucestershire won by 22 runs. Toss: Gloucestershire.

Gloucestershire completed another successful Cheltenham Festival with their fourth win out of five. Dawson scored his third successive League fifty, and Surrey were forced to chase more than a run a ball. They started terribly and were soon 26 for four, but the innings was transformed by a stand of 157 between Ratcliffe and Knott, who showed some hereditary battling qualities as he nudged the ball square of the wicket in his 98. However, Surrey's Sunday form reasserted itself, and the last five wickets fell for eight. They were all out with an over to spare, having been docked one for their slow over-rate.

Gloucestershire

G. I. Macmillan c J. N. Batty b Benjamin	13	M. C. J. Ball not out	15
R. I. Dawson b Bell	68	J. Lewis c Knott b B. C. Hollioake	2
*M. W. Alleyne c J. N. Batty b Bell	18	M. J. Cawdron not out	2
†R. C. Russell c B. C. Hollioake			
b G. J. Batty	39		
M. G. N. Windows c Ratcliffe		B 4, l-b 13, w 10, n-b 4	31
b A. J. Hollioake	59		
M. J. Church c Bell b B. C. Hollioake	4	1/36 2/78 3/129 (8 wkts, 40 overs) 261
T. H. C. Hancock c Knott		4/190 5/204 6/228
b A. J. Hollioake	10	7/240 8/247

C. A. Walsh did not bat.

Bowling: Benjamin 8–0–40–1; B. C. Hollioake 8–0–71–2; A. J. Hollioake 8–0–45–2; Bell 8–0–56–2; G. J. Batty 8–0–32–1.

Surrey

I. J. Ward c Russell b Lewis	6	G. J. Batty not out	7
A. D. Brown c Hancock b Lewis	14	M. A. V. Bell b Cawdron	0
J. D. Ratcliffe b Lewis	80	J. E. Benjamin c Russell b Cawdron	1
N. Shahid c Ball b Hancock	1	L-b 3, w 2, n-b 8	13
B. C. Hollioake lbw b Hancock	0		
J. A. Knott b Walsh	98	1/23 2/24 3/26 (38 overs) 239
*A. J. Hollioake run out	19	4/26 5/183 6/231
†J. N. Batty b Walsh	0	7/231 8/236 9/237

Bowling: Walsh 7–1–25–2; Lewis 8–1–45–3; Hancock 5–0–30–2; Cawdron 7–1–46–2; Ball 7–0–51–0; Alleyne 4–0–39–0.

Umpires: M. J. Harris and R. A. White.

At Manchester, August 9. GLOUCESTERSHIRE lost to LANCASHIRE by 71 runs.

At Colchester, August 23. ESSEX v GLOUCESTERSHIRE. No result.

GLOUCESTERSHIRE v SOMERSET

At Bristol, August 25 (day/night). Gloucestershire won by ten wickets (D/L method). Toss: Somerset.

The West Country's first floodlit League game attracted a near-capacity crowd of 7,500, generating a profit of £30,000. Local residents were less happy, complaining that supporters' cars were blocking access to their homes. Somerset started badly, but Rose organised middle-order resistance. Rain between innings gave Gloucestershire a revised target of 117 in 18 overs; after further rain, it was revised again to 67 from ten overs, the minimum needed for a result. Dawson, with some fierce blows to leg, ensured victory.

Somerset

M. Burns b Smith	7		A. R. K. Pierson c Windows b Walsh		6
M. N. Lathwell lbw b Lewis	3		A. R. Caddick not out		2
M. E. Trescothick run out	32		P. S. Jones b Walsh		1
*P. D. Bowler run out	3		L-b 9, w 6, n-b 2		17
G. D. Rose run out	59				
K. A. Parsons b Alleyne	16		1/11 2/11 3/16	(40 overs)	193
†R. J. Turner c Lewis b Alleyne	18		4/70 5/113 6/145		
J. I. D. Kerr c Williams b Lewis	29		7/152 8/189 9/189		

Bowling: Lewis 8–0–34–2; Smith 8–0–35–1; Walsh 8–1–36–2; Cawdron 6–0–26–0; Ball 4–0–20–0; Alleyne 6–0–33–2.

Gloucestershire

R. I. Dawson not out	44
M. C. J. Ball not out	18
B 1, l-b 2, n-b 2	5
(no wkt, 9.4 overs)	67

*M. W. Alleyne, M. G. N. Windows, D. R. Hewson, †R. C. J. Williams, T. H. C. Hancock, M. J. Cawdron, J. Lewis, A. M. Smith and C. A. Walsh did not bat.

Bowling: Rose 2–0–5–0; Jones 2–0–17–0; Parsons 1.4–0–7–0; Burns 2–0–25–0; Caddick 2–0–10–0.

Umpires: K. E. Palmer and R. A. White.

At Lord's, September 13. GLOUCESTERSHIRE beat MIDDLESEX by 22 runs.

HAMPSHIRE

HAMPSHIRE v NORTHAMPTONSHIRE

At Southampton, April 26. Hampshire won by three wickets. Toss: Hampshire. County debut: N. A. M. McLean.

Two West Indian Test players, Nixon McLean and Franklyn Rose, were bowling for the first time in county cricket, and both gave their new teams some encouragement. But a boisterous partnership between Keech and Mascarenhas tipped the match in Hampshire's favour. They added 90 in 11 overs, Mascarenhas scoring a maiden fifty, though three late wickets left Hampshire to scrape in with only three balls remaining.

Northamptonshire

M. B. Loye c Mascarenhas b Udal	65		F. A. Rose b McLean		0
R. R. Montgomerie c Udal b Renshaw	6		†D. Ripley run out		7
*K. M. Curran c Udal b Stephenson	16		J. P. Taylor not out		0
D. J. Capel c Laney b Renshaw	41		B 1, l-b 6, w 4		11
D. J. Sales c Mascarenhas b Renshaw	12				
R. J. Bailey b McLean	11		1/19 2/46 3/107	(40 overs)	199
A. L. Penberthy c Aymes b Hartley	9		4/144 5/146 6/165		
J. N. Snape c Smith b Renshaw	21		7/176 8/176 9/195		

Bowling: McLean 8–0–30–2; Renshaw 8–0–44–4; Hartley 8–1–24–1; Stephenson 7–0–52–1; Udal 8–0–36–1; Mascarenhas 1–0–6–0.

Hampshire

G. W. White b Penberthy	26	†A. N. Aymes c Sales b Curran	0
J. S. Laney c Ripley b Rose	3	P. J. Hartley not out	0
*R. A. Smith b Snape	33	B 1, l-b 4, w 11, n-b 14	30
M. Keech b Rose	49		
S. D. Udal c Curran b Capel	7	1/24 2/74 3/91 (7 wkts, 39.3 overs) 203	
A. D. Mascarenhas not out	55	4/106 5/196	
J. P. Stephenson c Sales b Taylor	0	6/197 7/199	

N. A. M. McLean and S. J. Renshaw did not bat.

Bowling: Taylor 8–0–46–1; Rose 8–2–32–2; Penberthy 8–0–21–0; Curran 4.3–0–33–1; Snape 7–0–36–1; Capel 4–0–30–1.

Umpires: J. W. Lloyds and N. T. Plews.

At Arundel, May 3. HAMPSHIRE beat SUSSEX by 76 runs.

HAMPSHIRE v ESSEX

At Southampton, May 10. Essex won by two wickets. Toss: Essex.

Hampshire pushed Essex hard to the finish. Their total was given backbone by Aymes, opening for the first time in the League, and Udal. Hussain responded in forthright fashion, adding 116 with Irani. Despite a late collapse, Essex edged home.

Hampshire

J. P. Stephenson b Ilott	20	K. D. James c Hussain b Grayson	12
†A. N. Aymes c Rollins b Williams	59	P. J. Hartley not out	6
*R. A. Smith c D. R. Law b Cousins	17	W 6, n-b 4	10
M. Keech c Rollins b Grayson	10		
A. D. Mascarenhas c Cousins b Williams	19	1/25 2/58 3/88 (8 wkts, 40 overs) 193	
J. S. Laney run out	11	4/119 5/144 6/145	
S. D. Udal c Rollins b Irani	29	7/165 8/193	

C. A. Connor and N. A. M. McLean did not bat.

Bowling: Ilott 8–0–42–1; Cousins 8–1–32–1; Irani 8–0–39–1; Grayson 8–0–41–2; Williams 8–0–39–2.

Essex

D. D. J. Robinson c Aymes b McLean	7	M. C. Ilott b McLean	2
S. G. Law c Laney b Connor	7	N. F. Williams not out	0
*N. Hussain c James b Stephenson	73	L-b 1, w 6	7
R. C. Irani c James b Stephenson	55		
A. P. Grayson c Udal b Stephenson	18	1/15 2/17 3/133 (8 wkts, 39.3 overs) 194	
†R. J. Rollins st Aymes b Udal	1	4/161 5/162 6/170	
S. D. Peters st Aymes b Udal	4	7/180 8/186	
D. R. Law not out	20		

D. M. Cousins did not bat.

Bowling: McLean 7–0–34–2; Connor 8–2–27–1; Hartley 6.3–1–35–0; James 3–0–22–0; Udal 7–0–37–2; Stephenson 8–0–38–3.

Umpires: N. T. Plews and P. Willey.

HAMPSHIRE v SURREY

At Southampton, May 17. Hampshire won by 75 runs. Toss: Surrey.

Emerging from a thrashing in the Championship, Hampshire easily turned the tables on Surrey. Smith and White led the way, scoring freely in a stand of 124, and the Surrey spinners failed to restore order as Keech cut loose. By contrast, probing off-spin from Udal picked up five wickets, his best League analysis, with only Shahid showing much resolve.

Hampshire

G. W. White c Salisbury		
b Saqlain Mushtaq .	58	K. D. James c Salisbury
†A. N. Aymes b Benjamin	0	b A. J. Hollioake . 3
*R. A. Smith b B. C. Hollioake	62	P. J. Hartley not out 2
A. D. Mascarenhas b B. C. Hollioake . .	0	
M. Keech b B. C. Hollioake.	42	L-b 12, w 3, n-b 2 17
P. R. Whitaker not out	24	
N. A. M. McLean run out	16	1/2 2/126 3/128 (8 wkts, 40 overs) 239
S. D. Udal c Ratcliffe b A. J. Hollioake .	15	4/141 5/180 6/198
		7/218 8/229

C. A. Connor did not bat.

Bowling: Bicknell 7–0–41–0; Benjamin 8–0–32–1; A. J. Hollioake 8–0–46–2; Saqlain Mushtaq 6–0–31–1; Salisbury 3–0–28–0; B. C. Hollioake 8–0–49–3.

Surrey

M. A. Butcher c White b McLean	13	I. D. K. Salisbury b McLean 11
A. D. Brown c Whitaker b Hartley	16	Saqlain Mushtaq lbw b Udal 0
†A. J. Stewart b James	2	J. E. Benjamin not out 1
N. Shahid c White b Udal	48	L-b 11, w 7, n-b 2 20
*A. J. Hollioake st Aymes b Udal	25	
B. C. Hollioake b Connor	16	1/40 2/43 3/43 (33.2 overs) 164
J. D. Ratcliffe c Connor b Udal	4	4/88 5/126 6/133
M. P. Bicknell c White b Udal	8	7/142 8/150 9/150

Bowling: Connor 6–0–23–1; McLean 4.2–0–29–2; James 8–0–31–1; Hartley 7–1–27–1; Udal 8–0–43–5.

Umpires: A. Clarkson and R. Julian.

At Leicester, May 25. HAMPSHIRE lost to LEICESTERSHIRE by 117 runs.

HAMPSHIRE v GLAMORGAN

At Southampton, June 7. Hampshire won by 131 runs (D/L method). Toss: Glamorgan.

In a rain-shortened game, an under-strength Glamorgan attack proved powerless to prevent Smith racing to a century, his tenth in the competition. He added 164 with White, as Hampshire scored at seven and a half an over. When Glamorgan replied, Hartley grabbed three important wickets, and they slid to defeat with a third of their overs unused. One over was lost very early in Hampshire's innings, bringing on the Duckworth/Lewis system but to negligible effect: Glamorgan officially had to overhaul a total of 249.23.

Hampshire

G. W. White c Evans b Watkin	76	P. R. Whitaker not out 17
J. P. Stephenson c Powell b Thomas . . .	7	
*R. A. Smith b Cosker	103	L-b 3, w 10, n-b 2 15
A. D. Mascarenhas b Cosker	7	
N. A. M. McLean not out	24	1/26 2/190 3/197 (5 wkts, 33 overs) 249
S. D. Udal lbw b Thomas	0	4/202 5/203

D. A. Kenway, K. D. James, †A. N. Aymes and P. J. Hartley did not bat.

Bowling: Thomas 6–0–44–2; Butcher 6–0–43–0; Cosker 7–0–52–2; Watkin 7–0–44–1; Dale 4–0–34–0; Cottey 3–0–29–0.

Glamorgan

S. P. James c White b Hartley	4	S. D. Thomas b Udal		3
*M. P. Maynard b Hartley	11	S. L. Watkin b Mascarenhas		2
A. Dale c James b McLean	25	D. A. Cosker not out		2
P. A. Cottey b Hartley	15	L-b 4, w 4, n-b 7		15
M. J. Powell c Stephenson b Mascarenhas	18			
G. P. Butcher b McLean	2	1/19 2/20 3/62	(22.1 overs)	119
†A. D. Shaw c White b Mascarenhas	16	4/64 5/67 6/96		
A. W. Evans c Mascarenhas b Udal	6	7/107 8/111 9/116		

Bowling: James 4–0–22–0; Hartley 7–0–38–3; McLean 4–0–27–2; Udal 4–0–19–2; Mascarenhas 3.1–1–9–3.

Umpires: T. E. Jesty and K. E. Palmer.

At Leeds, June 14. YORKSHIRE v HAMPSHIRE. No result.

HAMPSHIRE v DERBYSHIRE

At Basingstoke, June 21. Hampshire won by seven wickets. Toss: Hampshire.

Following his century in the Championship match, Smith continued to dominate the Derbyshire attack with an unbeaten 88. Connor had been just as impressive with the ball, which he swung effectively in helpful conditions; only Barnett stood firm.

Derbyshire

T. A. Tweats c Stephenson b Connor	5	G. M. Roberts lbw b Udal		7
M. J. Slater c Whitaker b James	7	P. Aldred b Stephenson		3
†A. S. Rollins b Connor	4	K. J. Dean not out		8
*K. J. Barnett not out	52	L-b 12, w 10		22
P. A. J. DeFreitas b Connor	0			
M. E. Cassar run out	11	1/11 2/15 3/25	(9 wkts, 40 overs)	160
V. P. Clarke c Aymes b McLean	27	4/25 5/57 6/94		
B. L. Spendlove c Smith b Udal	14	7/114 8/125 9/132		

Bowling: James 8–2–23–1; Connor 8–1–27–3; Stephenson 8–0–21–1; Mascarenhas 3–0–19–0; McLean 6–0–30–1; Udal 7–1–28–2.

Hampshire

G. W. White c Clarke b Roberts	22	A. D. Mascarenhas not out		24
J. P. Stephenson c Clarke b Dean	4	B 2, l-b 11, w 7		20
*R. A. Smith not out	88			
P. R. Whitaker c Cassar b Roberts	6	1/15 2/74 3/109	(3 wkts, 37.4 overs)	164

D. A. Kenway, S. D. Udal, K. D. James, †A. N. Aymes, C. A. Connor and N. A. M. McLean did not bat.

Bowling: Dean 7–0–34–1; DeFreitas 8–1–24–0; Clarke 8–1–29–0; Aldred 6.4–0–43–0; Roberts 8–2–21–2.

Umpires: V. A. Holder and B. Leadbeater.

HAMPSHIRE v GLOUCESTERSHIRE

At Southampton, July 5. Gloucestershire won by six wickets. Toss: Hampshire.

From an unpromising 16 for two, Dawson and Wright added 79 brisk runs to tip the match Gloucestershire's way. Hampshire's batting tailed off after Smith was well caught on the cover boundary. Connor derived some consolation, when he dismissed Alleyne, by taking his 1,000th wicket for Hampshire in all cricket.

Hampshire

G. W. White lbw b Alleyne	20	S. D. Udal lbw b Walsh	0
J. P. Stephenson c Windows b Lewis	0	K. D. James c Windows b Walsh	0
*R. A. Smith c Dawson b Alleyne	27	C. A. Connor c Russell b Walsh	0
P. R. Whitaker not out	40	L-b 7, w 16, n-b 2	25
M. Keech run out	0		
A. D. Mascarenhas c Alleyne b Hancock	7	1/16 2/61 3/68	(37.4 overs) 135
N. A. M. McLean b Smith	4	4/72 5/85 6/97	
†A. N. Aymes c Wright b Ball	12	7/135 8/135 9/135	

Bowling: Lewis 6–0–30–1; Smith 7–1–16–1; Alleyne 6–0–18–2; Walsh 6.4–0–27–3; Ball 8–0–22–1; Hancock 4–0–15–1.

Gloucestershire

T. H. C. Hancock c Aymes b McLean	10	N. J. Trainor not out	9
R. I. Dawson b Mascarenhas	46	L-b 9, w 2, n-b 2	13
*M. W. Alleyne lbw b Connor	1		
A. J. Wright run out	33	1/15 2/16	(4 wkts, 33.3 overs) 139
M. G. N. Windows not out	27	3/95 4/112	

†R. C. Russell, J. Lewis, M. C. J. Ball, A. M. Smith and C. A. Walsh did not bat.

Bowling: McLean 8–0–24–1; Connor 8–2–19–1; Stephenson 6–1–26–0; James 2.3–0–15–0; Udal 6–0–26–0; Mascarenhas 3–0–20–1.

Umpires: G. I. Burgess and R. Palmer.

At Birmingham, July 14. HAMPSHIRE beat WARWICKSHIRE by one wicket.

At Taunton, July 19. HAMPSHIRE lost to SOMERSET by three wickets.

HAMPSHIRE v NOTTINGHAMSHIRE

At Portsmouth, July 26. Nottinghamshire won by 30 runs. Toss: Hampshire.

Having restricted the early Nottinghamshire batting, Hampshire lost control when Strang and Franks lashed 45 from the innings's last four overs. Their reply started brightly, but Tolley took three wickets in eight balls.

Nottinghamshire

G. E. Welton lbw b McLean	2	P. J. Franks not out	17
J. E. R. Gallian c Aymes b Hartley	31	P. A. Strang not out	28
*P. Johnson lbw b Connor	9	L-b 13, w 8	21
G. F. Archer c Udal b Stephenson	37		
M. P. Dowman st Aymes b Udal	22	1/3 2/16 3/76	(6 wkts, 37 overs) 167
C. M. Tolley c Hartley b Stephenson	0	4/103 5/108 6/122	

†C. M. W. Read, K. P. Evans and R. T. Bates did not bat.

Bowling: Connor 6–1–21–1; McLean 6–1–24–1; Morris 5–0–19–0; Hartley 6–0–25–1; Udal 8–0–37–1; Stephenson 6–1–28–2.

Hampshire

L. Savident c Evans b Tolley	13	S. D. Udal b Franks	11
J. P. Stephenson c Archer b Bates	59	A. C. Morris not out	3
N. A. M. McLean c Bates b Tolley	3	C. A. Connor b Franks	0
G. W. White c Gallian b Tolley	0	L-b 4, w 2, n-b 4	10
*R. A. Smith lbw b Strang	1		
A. D. Mascarenhas c Archer b Bates	27	1/45 2/51 3/51	(35.4 overs) 137
P. J. Hartley c Bates b Evans	2	4/52 5/104 6/108	
†A. N. Aymes c Johnson b Franks	8	7/114 8/129 9/137	

Bowling: Evans 6–0–24–1; Franks 7.4–1–32–3; Tolley 7–1–22–3; Strang 8–1–17–1; Bates 7–0–38–2.

Umpires: J. H. Hampshire and D. R. Shepherd.

HAMPSHIRE v DURHAM

At Southampton, August 2. Hampshire won by seven wickets. Toss: Durham.

Exhilarating batting from Hampshire secured victory with 15 balls to spare. Four batsmen scored fifties, with White, capped before the start, striking 56 off 49 balls. Durham had started purposefully and, when Lewis joined Collingwood to add 88 in 14 overs, hopes were high; 229 was their best total in the League all season.

Durham

J. E. Morris c White b Connor	7	M. J. Foster not out	13
*D. C. Boon c Laney b Udal	38		
N. J. Speak b Hartley	21	B 2, l-b 4, w 7, n-b 6	19
†M. P. Speight c Udal b Stephenson	11		
P. D. Collingwood c Hartley b Udal	53	1/10 2/74 3/82	(5 wkts, 40 overs) 229
J. J. B. Lewis not out	67	4/94 5/182	

N. C. Phillips, M. M. Betts, J. Wood and N. Killeen did not bat.

Bowling: Connor 8–0–37–1; McLean 8–0–45–0; Udal 8–0–47–2; Hartley 8–0–38–1; Stephenson 5–0–34–1; Mascarenhas 3–0–22–0.

Hampshire

J. S. Laney b Betts	0	†A. N. Aymes not out	60
J. P. Stephenson c Speak b Killeen	56	L-b 4, w 4	8
*R. A. Smith b Killeen	50		
G. W. White not out	56	1/1 2/111 3/112	(3 wkts, 37.3 overs) 230

P. R. Whitaker, A. D. Mascarenhas, S. D. Udal, N. A. M. McLean, P. J. Hartley and C. A. Connor did not bat.

Bowling: Betts 7.3–0–50–1; Wood 8–0–41–0; Phillips 8–0–52–0; Killeen 7–0–29–2; Foster 3–0–29–0; Collingwood 4–0–25–0.

Umpires: R. Palmer and G. Sharp.

At Canterbury, August 9. HAMPSHIRE lost to KENT by seven wickets.

HAMPSHIRE v MIDDLESEX

At Southampton, August 30. Hampshire won by 12 runs. Toss: Hampshire.

With this win, Hampshire leap-frogged Middlesex in the table and came close to making sure of Division One status in the National League in 1999. A depleted Middlesex were struggling after losing two wickets in the first over, and they never looked like scoring 211 to win. Hampshire's own innings had faded after an opening stand of 96.

Hampshire

G. W. White lbw b Weekes	51	†A. N. Aymes not out	14
J. P. Stephenson c Weekes b Tufnell	36		
N. A. M. McLean b Johnson	25	B 1, l-b 4, w 9	14
*R. A. Smith b Dutch	34		
M. Keech not out	23	1/96 2/100 3/143 (5 wkts, 40 overs) 210	
A. D. Mascarenhas c Weekes b Dutch	13	4/169 5/187	

W. S. Kendall, S. D. Udal, C. A. Connor and P. J. Hartley did not bat.

Bowling: Hewitt 5–0–22–0; Dutch 8–0–41–2; Batt 3–1–21–0; Johnson 8–0–41–1; Tufnell 8–0–43–1; Weekes 8–0–37–1.

Middlesex

M. W. Gatting b Connor	0	R. L. Johnson c Aymes b McLean	17
R. A. Kettleborough lbw b Udal	48	J. P. Hewitt not out	13
A. J. Strauss c Aymes b Connor	4	B 4, l-b 7, w 14, n-b 6	31
*†K. R. Brown c Aymes b Mascarenhas	11		
P. N. Weekes c Keech b Udal	11	1/1 2/6 3/56 (7 wkts, 40 overs) 198	
K. P. Dutch b Connor	25	4/94 5/100	
D. J. Goodchild not out	38	6/128 7/174	

C. J. Batt and P. C. R. Tufnell did not bat.

Bowling: Connor 8–0–36–3; McLean 8–0–26–1; Mascarenhas 5–0–27–1; Hartley 7–0–35–0; Stephenson 5–0–29–0; Udal 7–1–34–2.

Umpires: J. C. Balderstone and R. A. White.

At Manchester, September 7. HAMPSHIRE lost to LANCASHIRE by 16 runs.

At Worcester, September 13. HAMPSHIRE lost to WORCESTERSHIRE by four runs.

KENT

KENT v MIDDLESEX

At Canterbury, April 19. Kent won by one run (D/L method). Toss: Kent.

The match ended in confusion with Middlesex – and most spectators – thinking it was a tie. Their captain Ramprakash complained furiously when he discovered Kent had won. Duckworth/Lewis reckoning came into force when the umpires took the players off in steady rain after 26 overs of the Kent innings. A tie was actually an impossible result: Kent's par score was calculated as 114.29. Although they were the team batting second, they were declared winners by one run, repeating the eccentric precedent set at Cardiff in 1997. They had technically won by 0.71 of a run. Had Wells not scored a single off the penultimate ball, Middlesex would have won. The highlight of the cricket itself was 94 in 79 balls from Pooley.

Middlesex

†K. R. Brown b Igglesden	10	P. N. Weekes not out	12
J. L. Langer run out	41	A. R. C. Fraser not out	0
*M. R. Ramprakash c Fulton b Headley	1	L-b 9, w 8, n-b 6	23
O. A. Shah lbw b Igglesden	1		
J. C. Pooley c Ealham b Hooper	94	1/35 2/44 3/47 (7 wkts, 40 overs) 206	
D. C. Nash b McCague	24	4/90 5/172	
R. L. Johnson lbw b McCague	0	6/172 7/206	

T. F. Bloomfield and J. P. Hewitt did not bat.

Bowling: Igglesden 8–0–24–2; Headley 8–0–30–1; Ealham 6–0–42–0; McCague 8–0–37–2; Hooper 8–0–46–1; Fleming 2–0–18–0.

Kent

D. P. Fulton c Brown b Hewitt	4	M. A. Ealham not out	2
M. J. Walker b Fraser	6	L-b 8, w 4	12
C. L. Hooper c Pooley b Johnson	45		
A. P. Wells not out	46	1/14 2/16 3/103 (3 wkts, 26 overs)	115

G. R. Cowdrey, M. V. Fleming, *†S. A. Marsh, D. W. Headley, A. P. Igglesden and M. J. McCague did not bat.

Bowling: Fraser 8–0–21–1; Hewitt 8–2–15–1; Bloomfield 5–0–38–0; Weekes 2–0–12–0; Johnson 3–0–21–1.

Umpires: J. H. Harris and R. Julian.

At Cardiff, April 26. KENT beat GLAMORGAN by eight wickets.

At Bristol, May 10. KENT beat GLOUCESTERSHIRE by six wickets.

KENT v LANCASHIRE

At Canterbury, May 17. Lancashire won by 16 runs. Toss: Lancashire.

A commanding century by Crawley, his first in the competition, provided the cornerstone of Lancashire's total, and the key to Kent's first League defeat. He formed useful partnerships with Flintoff and Fairbrother, whereas Ward, batting equally well for his own hundred, lacked convincing support. Kent's luck expired when Hooper was run out at the non-striker's end backing up.

Lancashire

A. Flintoff c Ealham b Fleming	38	†W. K. Hegg not out	19
M. Watkinson c Marsh b Headley	1	I. D. Austin not out	2
J. P. Crawley c Wells b Fleming	100	B 2, l-b 11, w 1, n-b 4	18
N. H. Fairbrother b Fleming	32		
G. D. Lloyd c Ealham b Headley	26	1/16 2/64 3/135 (6 wkts, 40 overs)	240
*Wasim Akram run out	4	4/208 5/219 6/220	

G. Yates, G. Chapple and R. J. Green did not bat.

Bowling: Igglesden 8–0–32–0; Headley 8–0–53–2; Fleming 8–0–49–3; Ealham 8–0–43–0; Hooper 8–0–50–0.

Kent

T. R. Ward c Wasim Akram b Austin	101	N. J. Llong b Austin	5
M. J. Walker c and b Chapple	9	D. W. Headley not out	6
M. V. Fleming c Lloyd b Green	20		
C. L. Hooper run out	26	L-b 9, w 5, n-b 5	19
A. P. Wells c Flintoff b Yates	28		
M. A. Ealham not out	10	1/34 2/71 3/147 (8 wkts, 40 overs)	224
G. R. Cowdrey b Austin	0	4/199 5/207 6/208	
*†S. A. Marsh b Wasim Akram	0	7/209 8/216	

A. P. Igglesden did not bat.

Bowling: Austin 8–0–29–3; Chapple 8–1–37–1; Green 8–0–52–1; Wasim Akram 8–0–38–1; Yates 8–0–59–1.

Umpires: G. I. Burgess and A. G. T. Whitehead.

KENT v DURHAM

At Canterbury, May 25. Kent won by 100 runs. Toss: Durham.

Wells and Hooper cut the Durham attack to pieces with a stand of 208 in 24 overs, and Kent raced to their highest-ever 40-over total and the best score in the League all season. Wells achieved a version of one of cricket's most cherished feats by hitting six successive sixes. He drove the last ball of an over from Phillips against the players' balcony. Then, after Hooper took a single from Lewis's first ball, Wells hit the next five over the short boundary by the lime tree. This matched Viv Richards, who had taken five sixes in an over from David Graveney at Taunton in 1977. Lewis was immediately taken off, leaving his one over (1–0–31–0) as the most expensive single-over spell in League history. Wells hit eight sixes in all. Meanwhile, Hooper broke the bowlers' hearts and, with one six, the window of a spectator's Volvo. Their stand beat the Kent third-wicket record, set by Mike Denness and Brian Luckhurst against Northamptonshire in 1976. Ealham finished off the innings with an unbeaten 54 off 30 balls. Durham's response was game but unavailing.

Kent

T. R. Ward c Daley b Wood	8	G. R. Cowdrey not out	4
R. W. T. Key c Killeen b Betts	9	B 2, l-b 6, w 14, n-b 4	26
C. L. Hooper run out	100		
A. P. Wells b Foster	118	1/19 2/30 (4 wkts, 40 overs)	319
M. A. Ealham not out	54	3/238 4/294	

M. V. Fleming, *†S. A. Marsh, B. J. Phillips, D. W. Headley and A. P. Igglesden did not bat.

Bowling: Betts 8–0–34–1; Wood 8–0–59–1; Foster 7–0–74–1; Killeen 8–0–64–0; Phillips 8–0–49–0; Lewis 1–0–31–0.

Durham

S. Hutton lbw b Igglesden	16	M. M. Betts c Fleming b Headley	0
M. J. Foster c Marsh b Headley	10	N. Killeen b Fleming	28
J. A. Daley c Marsh b Headley	3	J. Wood not out	4
†M. P. Speight c Wells b Headley	17	L-b 3, w 1, n-b 6	10
J. J. B. Lewis c Hooper b Phillips	7		
P. D. Collingwood b Hooper	62	1/19 2/23 3/45 (38.3 overs)	219
*N. J. Speak b Fleming	25	4/51 5/63 6/145	
N. C. Phillips b Fleming	37	7/155 8/156 9/209	

Bowling: Headley 7–0–36–4; Igglesden 8–0–40–1; Phillips 6–0–52–1; Fleming 6.3–0–37–3; Ealham 5–0–22–0; Hooper 6–0–29–1.

Umpires: D. J. Constant and J. F. Steele.

KENT v SUSSEX

At Tunbridge Wells, June 7. No result. Toss: Kent.

Having reduced Sussex to 50 for four, Kent were thwarted when rain ended play.

Sussex

K. Newell b Headley	14	M. T. E. Peirce not out	0
*C. J. Adams run out	14	L-b 2, w 9, n-b 4	15
M. Newell c Hooper b Headley	1		
M. G. Bevan not out	4	1/29 2/39 (4 wkts, 13.1 overs)	50
J. R. Carpenter c Marsh b Phillips	2	3/39 4/49	

A. D. Edwards, †S. Humphries, R. J. Kirtley, P. W. Jarvis and M. A. Robinson did not bat.

Bowling: Headley 5–0–11–2; Phillips 4–0–24–1; McCague 4.1–1–13–0.

Kent

R. W. T. Key, T. R. Ward, C. L. Hooper, A. P. Wells, M. J. Walker, G. R. Cowdrey, *†S. A. Marsh, M. V. Fleming, B. J. Phillips, M. J. McCague and D. W. Headley.

Umpires: J. W. Holder and B. Leadbeater.

At Leicester, June 14. LEICESTERSHIRE v KENT. No result.

KENT v NOTTINGHAMSHIRE

At Canterbury, June 21. Nottinghamshire won by nine wickets. Toss: Kent.
Initially, Kent looked capable of defending their disappointing total, as Gallian and Dowman struggled for runs. But the arrival of Johnson transformed the game. Kent's fielding wilted as he struck 78 in 59 balls.

Kent

T. R. Ward c Robinson b Franks	21	*†S. A. Marsh lbw b Evans		10
R. W. T. Key c and b Bates	50	B. J. Phillips c Johnson b Franks		0
C. L. Hooper c and b Strang	20	A. P. Igglesden not out		1
A. P. Wells c Dowman b Bates	25	B 1, l-b 7, w 5, n-b 2		15
G. R. Cowdrey c Dowman b Franks	17			
W. J. House c Dowman b Tolley	7	1/34 2/79 3/118	(38.3 overs)	177
M. V. Fleming c Read b Tolley	3	4/130 5/149 6/154		
M. J. McCague lbw b Evans	8	7/154 8/173 9/174		

Bowling: Franks 7–1–21–3; Evans 7.3–0–53–2; Strang 8–0–28–1; Tolley 8–1–27–2; Bates 8–0–40–2.

Nottinghamshire

J. E. R. Gallian not out	62
M. P. Dowman c Phillips b Fleming	21
*P. Johnson not out	78
L-b 12, w 5	17

1/60   (1 wkt, 34.1 overs) 178

G. F. Archer, R. T. Robinson, C. M. Tolley, P. J. Franks, †C. M. W. Read, P. A. Strang, K. P. Evans and R. T. Bates did not bat.

Bowling: McCague 8–0–33–0; Igglesden 8–0–21–0; Phillips 6–0–32–0; Fleming 5.1–0–28–1; Hooper 2–0–16–0; House 2–0–16–0; Cowdrey 3–0–20–0.

Umpires: D. J. Constant and K. E. Palmer.

KENT v YORKSHIRE

At Maidstone, July 5. Kent won by five wickets. Toss: Yorkshire.
Yorkshire fell off the top of the table despite reaching what was easily their highest League score of the season. A second-wicket partnership of 172 between Byas and Lehmann allowed Parker the freedom to club 38 in 21 balls. But Kent responded in kind, with Ward, at his most forceful, and Key putting on 125. Then Hooper scored 68 in 53 balls, and Kent squeezed home in the last over.

Yorkshire

*D. Byas b Fleming	86	†R. J. Blakey not out		17
M. P. Vaughan b Igglesden	7	B 2, l-b 10, w 4		16
D. S. Lehmann run out	99			—
B. Parker not out	38	1/24 2/196 3/220	(3 wkts, 40 overs)	263

M. J. Wood, G. M. Hamilton, C. E. W. Silverwood, P. M. Hutchison, R. D. Stemp and R. J. Sidebottom did not bat.

Bowling: Headley 8–0–43–0; Igglesden 5–0–24–1; Ealham 7–0–40–0; McCague 2–0–16–0; Hooper 8–0–48–0; Fleming 8–0–68–1; Cowdrey 2–0–12–0.

Kent

T. R. Ward c Wood b Stemp	85	*†S. A. Marsh not out		2
R. W. T. Key run out	55			
C. L. Hooper run out	68	L-b 14, w 10		24
A. P. Wells c Byas b Hamilton	15			—
M. A. Ealham not out	10	1/125 2/170 3/228	(5 wkts, 39.3 overs)	266
G. R. Cowdrey c Wood b Hutchison	7	4/245 5/257		

M. V. Fleming, D. W. Headley, M. J. McCague and A. P. Igglesden did not bat.

Bowling: Hutchison 8–1–29–1; Silverwood 7.3–0–37–0; Sidebottom 8–0–68–0; Stemp 8–0–57–1; Hamilton 6–0–43–1; Lehmann 2–0–18–0.

Umpires: J. H. Hampshire and J. W. Lloyds.

At Birmingham, July 12. KENT lost to WARWICKSHIRE by five wickets (D/L method).

At Southend, July 19. KENT lost to ESSEX by 30 runs.

At Derby, August 2. KENT lost to DERBYSHIRE by eight wickets.

KENT v HAMPSHIRE

At Canterbury, August 9. Kent won by seven wickets. Toss: Kent.

A defiant 65 from Mascarenhas could not repair an early collapse, when Headley and Thompson left Hampshire shattered at 19 for five. Kent were never troubled, and won with more than seven overs to spare.

Hampshire

J. S. Laney c Marsh b Headley	2	N. A. M. McLean c Marsh b Hooper		6
J. P. Stephenson c Hooper b Headley	4	P. J. Hartley not out		7
*R. A. Smith lbw b Headley	4	C. A. Connor b House		5
G. W. White c Hooper b Thompson	1	B 2, l-b 1, w 3, n-b 6		12
†A. N. Aymes lbw b Thompson	1			—
A. D. Mascarenhas b Hooper	65	1/4 2/14 3/17	(39.3 overs)	137
M. Keech c Marsh b Fleming	22	4/19 5/19 6/64		
S. D. Udal b Fleming	8	7/82 8/89 9/132		

Bowling: Headley 8–1–26–3; Thompson 8–3–16–2; McCague 8–1–42–0; Fleming 8–1–28–2; Hooper 7–0–18–2; House 0.3–0–4–1.

Kent

T. R. Ward b Hartley	30	N. J. Llong not out	35
E. T. Smith b McLean	31	L-b 4, w 7, n-b 2	13
R. W. T. Key lbw b Stephenson	3		
C. L. Hooper not out	26	1/53 2/59 3/87	(3 wkts, 32.2 overs) 138

W. J. House, M. V. Fleming, *†S. A. Marsh, M. J. McCague, D. W. Headley and J. B. D. Thompson did not bat.

Bowling: Connor 6.2–1–35–0; McLean 8–0–29–1; Hartley 6–0–21–1; Stephenson 6–2–13–1; Udal 4–0–19–0; Mascarenhas 2–0–17–0.

Umpires: A. A. Jones and N. T. Plews.

KENT v WORCESTERSHIRE

At Canterbury, August 23. No result. Toss: Worcestershire.

Worcestershire, hampered by fine bowling from Headley, who conceded only three runs in 23 balls, were already in trouble when persistent drizzle ended the match.

Worcestershire

*T. M. Moody c Marsh b Headley	1
V. S. Solanki not out	10
G. A. Hick c Llong b Phillips	0
D. A. Leatherdale not out	4
L-b 1	1
1/6 2/7 (2 wkts, 6.5 overs)	16

W. P. C. Weston, G. R. Haynes, †S. J. Rhodes, S. R. Lampitt, R. K. Illingworth, E. J. Wilson and R. J. Chapman did not bat.

Bowling: Headley 3.5–2–3–1; Phillips 3–0–12–1.

Kent

T. R. Ward, E. T. Smith, R. W. T. Key, C. L. Hooper, M. J. Walker, N. J. Llong, W. J. House, M. V. Fleming, *†S. A. Marsh, B. J. Phillips and D. W. Headley.

Umpires: V. A. Holder and J. W. Lloyds.

At Northampton, August 30. KENT beat NORTHAMPTONSHIRE by seven wickets.

At The Oval, September 6. KENT lost to SURREY by 41 runs.

KENT v SOMERSET

At Canterbury, September 13. Kent won by six wickets (D/L method). Toss: Kent.

Hooper led the run-chase that secured victory and fifth place; Kent would advance to the First Division in 1999, while Somerset missed out. Pursuing a revised target of 172 from 28 overs, Hooper and Walker added 105 from 14. Lathwell had scored more than half Somerset's runs, with 87 from 78 balls.

Somerset

M. Burns c Hooper b Headley	6	*P. D. Bowler not out	5
M. N. Lathwell c sub b Ealham	87		
M. E. Trescothick c Marsh b Headley	11	L-b 6, w 7	13
J. I. D. Kerr c sub b Ealham	18		
K. A. Parsons b Fleming	23	1/12 2/37 3/74 (7 wkts, 28 overs) 164
G. D. Rose b Ealham	1	4/136 5/151
†R. J. Turner b Fleming	0	6/152 7/164

A. R. K. Pierson, A. R. Caddick and P. S. Jones did not bat.

Bowling: Headley 7–0–22–2; Phillips 7–0–30–0; Ealham 6–0–47–3; McCague 2–0–18–0; Fleming 4–0–26–2; Hooper 2–0–15–0.

Kent

T. R. Ward lbw b Caddick	2	M. V. Fleming not out	20
R. W. T. Key b Rose	13	L-b 2, w 6, n-b 6	14
C. L. Hooper lbw b Jones	62		
M. J. Walker c Turner b Jones	50	1/9 2/36 (4 wkts, 26.4 overs) 174
M. A. Ealham not out	13	3/141 4/144

W. J. House, *†S. A. Marsh, B. J. Phillips, M. J. McCague and D. W. Headley did not bat.

Bowling: Rose 6–0–15–1; Caddick 5–0–36–1; Trescothick 4–0–37–0; Jones 5.4–0–36–2; Burns 3–0–29–0; Parsons 3–0–19–0.

Umpires: J. H. Hampshire and M. J. Kitchen.

LANCASHIRE

At Hove, April 21. LANCASHIRE beat SUSSEX by ten runs.

LANCASHIRE v MIDDLESEX

At Manchester, April 26. No result (abandoned).

LANCASHIRE v DERBYSHIRE

At Manchester, May 10. Lancashire won by 31 runs (D/L method). Toss: Derbyshire.

Atherton, now England's ex-captain and far from certain of his international place, began his rehabilitation with a welcome if scratchy 98. He was out trying to reach his century four balls from the end of the innings and was given a warm ovation. Atherton's steadiness allowed Fairbrother to play more freely. Derbyshire's cause already looked lost when the rain came. Under Duckworth/Lewis rules, they would have needed 109 for victory.

Lancashire

M. A. Atherton lbw b Harris	98	†W. K. Hegg not out	1
A. Flintoff c Barnett b Cork	0		
J. P. Crawley b Harris	31	L-b 4, w 3, n-b 2	9
N. H. Fairbrother c Cork b Harris	70		
*Wasim Akram c Spendlove b Cork	2	1/4 2/49 3/187 (5 wkts, 40 overs) 219
G. D. Lloyd not out	8	4/197 5/218

I. D. Austin, G. Yates, G. Chapple and P. J. Martin did not bat.

Bowling: DeFreitas 8–1–41–0; Cork 8–0–37–2; Aldred 6–0–43–0; Harris 8–0–36–3; Clarke 6–0–30–0; Barnett 4–0–28–0.

Derbyshire

*D. G. Cork b Austin	5	P. A. J. DeFreitas c Flintoff b Chapple	11
K. J. Barnett not out	36	L-b 5, w 2	7
A. S. Rollins b Wasim Akram	14		
T. A. Tweats st Hegg b Yates	5	1/8 2/40 3/49 4/78 (4 wkts, 20.3 overs)	78

I. D. Blackwell, V. P. Clarke, B. L. Spendlove, †K. M. Krikken, P. Aldred and A. J. Harris did not bat.

Bowling: Martin 4–0–23–0; Austin 5–0–10–1; Wasim Akram 4–0–12–1; Yates 5–0–16–1; Chapple 2.3–1–12–1.

Umpires: J. W. Holder and R. Palmer.

At Canterbury, May 17. LANCASHIRE beat KENT by 16 runs.

At Chelmsford, May 25. LANCASHIRE lost to ESSEX by three wickets.

At Northampton, June 7. LANCASHIRE beat NORTHAMPTONSHIRE by seven wickets.

LANCASHIRE v SOMERSET

At Manchester, June 14. Lancashire won by six wickets. Toss: Lancashire.

A modest Somerset total looked even more modest when Flintoff launched Lancashire's reply in flamboyant style. He hit three sixes in his 39 and, with help from Atherton and Crawley, gave the innings such momentum that they won with more than 11 overs to spare.

Somerset

M. Burns c Yates b Green	21	M. E. Trescothick not out	18
P. C. L. Holloway c Wasim Akram		A. R. Caddick run out	16
b Yates	34	P. S. Jones not out	6
G. D. Rose b Wasim Akram	9		
M. N. Lathwell c Hegg b Green	2	B 3, l-b 5, w 5	13
*S. C. Ecclestone c Martin b Yates	29		
Mushtaq Ahmed c and b Yates	6	1/44 2/69 3/73 (9 wkts, 40 overs)	163
†R. J. Turner lbw b Austin	2	4/94 5/102 6/109	
K. A. Parsons c Lloyd b Green	7	7/121 8/124 9/145	

Bowling: Martin 8–0–36–0; Austin 6–1–18–1; Green 7–0–37–3; Wasim Akram 8–1–15–1; Flintoff 3–0–14–0; Yates 8–0–35–3.

Lancashire

M. A. Atherton c Turner		*Wasim Akram not out	0
b Mushtaq Ahmed	37		
A. Flintoff c Burns b Jones	39	L-b 5, w 6, n-b 4	15
J. P. Crawley c Jones b Caddick	41		
G. D. Lloyd not out	23	1/59 2/104 (4 wkts, 28.3 overs)	166
M. Watkinson c Lathwell b Trescothick	11	3/143 4/162	

†W. K. Hegg, I. D. Austin, R. J. Green, G. Yates and P. J. Martin did not bat.

Bowling: Caddick 8–2–36–1; Rose 6–0–34–0; Jones 5–0–32–1; Trescothick 6–0–42–1; Mushtaq Ahmed 3.3–0–17–1.

Umpires: A. A. Jones and R. Julian.

LANCASHIRE v SURREY

At Manchester, June 17 (day/night). Lancashire won by four wickets (D/L method). Toss: Surrey.

Lancashire marked the first competitive floodlit fixture at Old Trafford by going top of the League. For the public, though, the threatening weather was more of a factor than the rock music, fireworks and hog roast, or the cricket. Fewer than 5,000 turned up. The club seemed to see it coming: they picked the nickname Lancashire Lightning. In reality, there was only Manchester rain. Ward and Adam Holliake had rescued Surrey with a stand of 122. After an interruption, Lancashire were given a fresh target of 132 in 22 overs. Despite three run-outs, Austin and Yates clinched victory.

Surrey

J. D. Ratcliffe lbw b Austin	6	†J. N. Batty not out 2
A. D. Brown c Lloyd b Austin	16	M. P. Bicknell not out........ 0
N. Shahid b Martin	0	B 4, l-b 7, w 9, n-b 2 22
*A. J. Holliake run out	70	
I. J. Ward c Hegg b Martin	55	1/15 2/17 3/27 (6 wkts, 39 overs) 182
B. C. Holliake b Wasim Akram	11	4/149 5/176 6/182

A. J. Tudor, R. M. Amin and J. E. Benjamin did not bat.

Bowling: Martin 7–1–31–2; Austin 8–1–30–2; Wasim Akram 8–0–23–1; Green 8–0–36–0; Yates 8–0–51–0.

Lancashire

A. Flintoff lbw b Benjamin	8	I. D. Austin not out 27
P. C. McKeown run out	14	G. Yates not out.............. 24
J. P. Crawley c B. C. Holliake		
b Benjamin .	0	L-b 1, n-b 4............ 5
G. D. Lloyd run out	29	
M. Watkinson c Brown b Benjamin	18	1/13 2/13 3/24 (6 wkts, 21.3 overs) 135
*Wasim Akram run out	10	4/57 5/77 6/85

†W. K. Hegg, R. J. Green and P. J. Martin did not bat.

Bowling: Bicknell 5–0–26–0; Benjamin 5–0–30–3; A. J. Holliake 4–0–21–0; Tudor 4–0–34–0; Ratcliffe 2.3–0–17–0; Ward 1–0–6–0.

Umpires: J. H. Hampshire and J. H. Harris.

At Birmingham, July 1. LANCASHIRE lost to WARWICKSHIRE by 27 runs.

LANCASHIRE v WORCESTERSHIRE

At Manchester, July 20 (day/night). Lancashire won by one wicket. Toss: Lancashire.

A match played on a surface of unpredictable bounce produced only three boundaries. But a crowd of 9,000 – Lancashire's best in the League for three years – saw a late-night thriller when Martin hit the winning run off the final ball at 11 p.m. For Worcestershire, only Solanki and Extras reached double figures in a game reduced to 25 overs a side. But Lancashire's batsmen found the pitch hard work too. Atherton was hit on the hand by Chapman and batted on in some pain, causing worries about his availability for the Trent Bridge Test. He was out at 39 for five, and Lancashire were in trouble. Lloyd scored a crucial 24 before the ninth wicket fell with the scores level. Rhodes took five catches.

Worcestershire

*T. M. Moody c Hegg b Flintoff	7	†S. J. Rhodes not out		5
V. S. Solanki run out	42	R. K. Illingworth b Wasim Akram		2
G. A. Hick c Atherton b Austin	0	P. J. Newport not out		1
D. A. Leatherdale c Hegg b Chapple	7	L-b 7, w 9		16
W. P. C. Weston c Crawley				—
b Wasim Akram	8	1/18 2/22 3/40	(8 wkts, 25 overs)	92
A. Hafeez c Hegg b Wasim Akram	2	4/74 5/74 6/78		
S. R. Lampitt run out	2	7/81 8/83		

R. J. Chapman did not bat.

Bowling: Martin 5–0–9–0; Austin 5–0–15–1; Flintoff 5–0–14–1; Chapple 5–1–29–1; Wasim Akram 5–0–18–3.

Lancashire

M. A. Atherton c Rhodes b Moody	17	G. Yates c Rhodes b Leatherdale		1
A. Flintoff c Leatherdale b Chapman	0	G. Chapple run out		3
J. P. Crawley c Rhodes b Newport	5	P. J. Martin not out		1
G. D. Lloyd c Moody b Illingworth	24	B 3, l-b 2, w 5, n-b 2		12
M. Watkinson c Rhodes b Moody	1			—
*Wasim Akram run out	2	1/4 2/13 3/30	(9 wkts, 25 overs)	93
†W. K. Hegg c Rhodes b Moody	17	4/32 5/39 6/74		
I. D. Austin not out	10	7/81 8/84 9/92		

Bowling: Newport 5–1–6–1; Chapman 5–1–15–1; Moody 5–0–17–3; Lampitt 5–0–20–0; Leatherdale 4–0–22–1; Illingworth 1–0–8–1.

Umpires: B. Leadbeater and N. T. Plews.

At Colwyn Bay, July 26. GLAMORGAN v LANCASHIRE. No result (abandoned).

LANCASHIRE v LEICESTERSHIRE

At Manchester, August 2. Lancashire won by 20 runs. Toss: Lancashire.

Lancashire, bowling accurately and fielding tigerishly, snatched a vital win. With ten overs remaining, Leicestershire needed 54 and had eight wickets standing, but they cracked under pressure – Martin captured three wickets in an over – and the early batsmen's work went to waste. Fairbrother, resuming after three weeks out injured, made 82 not out off 98 balls for Lancashire.

Lancashire

A. Flintoff c Simmons b Ormond	2	I. D. Austin c Smith b Simmons		1
M. A. Atherton c Mullally b Brimson	19	G. Yates not out		1
J. P. Crawley c Wells b Mullally	0	B 1, l-b 3, w 3, n-b 7		14
N. H. Fairbrother not out	82			—
G. D. Lloyd c Habib b Brimson	30	1/5 2/7 3/39	(7 wkts, 40 overs)	183
*Wasim Akram c Williamson b Simmons	24	4/97 5/142		
†W. K. Hegg b Ormond	10	6/166 7/169		

G. Chapple and P. J. Martin did not bat.

Bowling: Mullally 8–1–20–1; Ormond 7–0–17–2; Williamson 8–0–29–0; Brimson 8–0–40–2; Wells 3–0–21–0; Simmons 6–0–52–2.

Leicestershire

*P. V. Simmons b Yates.	27	J. Ormond b Wasim Akram	4
V. J. Wells b Chapple	49	A. D. Mullally c Lloyd b Austin.	2
B. F. Smith c Chapple b Wasim Akram .	35	M. T. Brimson not out	0
A. Habib b Austin	8	L-b 14, w 4, n-b 6.	24
†P. A. Nixon b Austin.	14		
D. L. Maddy b Martin	0	1/74 2/119 3/135 (39.4 overs) 163	
J. M. Dakin c Hegg b Martin	0	4/148 5/149 6/149	
D. Williamson lbw b Martin.	0	7/149 8/158 9/161	

Bowling: Martin 8–0–40–3; Austin 7.4–2–8–3; Wasim Akram 8–1–27–2; Chapple 8–1–30–1; Yates 8–0–44–1.

Umpires: G. I. Burgess and P. Willey.

LANCASHIRE v GLOUCESTERSHIRE

At Manchester, August 9. Lancashire won by 71 runs. Toss: Lancashire.

Fairbrother held Lancashire's batting together for the second week running. This time he had crucial help from Wasim Akram, who blasted 75 from 42 balls with six sixes. The attack gave little away and Gloucestershire were always behind.

Lancashire

P. C. McKeown b Lewis	20	†W. K. Hegg b Walsh.	3
M. J. Chilton c Russell b Smith	0	I. D. Austin not out	8
N. H. Fairbrother run out.	76	L-b 9, w 3, n-b 2	14
G. D. Lloyd st Russell b Ball.	12		
M. Watkinson c Dawson b Ball	14	1/2 2/39 3/64 (6 wkts, 40 overs) 222	
*Wasim Akram not out	75	4/101 5/200 6/210	

G. Yates, G. Chapple and P. J. Martin did not bat.

Bowling: Lewis 8–1–27–1; Smith 8–0–40–1; Walsh 8–0–48–1; Ball 8–0–32–2; Cawdron 4–0–19–0; Alleyne 4–0–47–0.

Gloucestershire

R. I. Dawson c Chilton b Yates.	38	J. Lewis st Hegg b Yates.	9
M. C. J. Ball c Hegg b Austin	7	A. M. Smith not out	4
*M. W. Alleyne c Hegg b Martin	0	C. A. Walsh b Martin	1
M. G. N. Windows b Austin.	4	L-b 7, w 2.	9
†R. C. Russell c Martin b Chapple	4		
D. R. Hewson c Martin b Yates	25	1/14 2/14 3/35 (33.4 overs) 151	
T. H. C. Hancock c Lloyd b Chapple. . .	49	4/45 5/66 6/110	
M. J. Cawdron st Hegg b Watkinson . .	1	7/116 8/143 9/147	

Bowling: Austin 6–1–25–2; Martin 5.4–1–18–2; Wasim Akram 3–0–11–0; Chapple 7–0–21–2; Yates 8–0–37–3; Watkinson 4–0–32–1.

Umpires: J. C. Balderstone and B. Leadbeater.

At Chester-le-Street, August 23. DURHAM v LANCASHIRE. No result.

At Leeds, August 24. LANCASHIRE beat YORKSHIRE by 101 runs.

LANCASHIRE v HAMPSHIRE

At Manchester, September 7. Lancashire won by 16 runs. Toss: Lancashire.

Wasim Akram lifted a trophy as Lancashire captain for the second day running. Just over 24 hours after his team had romped home in the delayed NatWest final, Lancashire became the last winners of the Sunday League – on a Monday afternoon. It was their fourth title, equalling Kent's record, and they still had hopes of adding the Championship and winning a treble. However, Wasim's week was to take a more sensational turn; two days later, a Pakistani judge was to recommend he should be banned on suspicion of match-fixing. The title was already a near-certainty even if they lost, and Hampshire refused to accept their role as fall guys quietly. Lancashire, without Atherton, lost early wickets before Flintoff returned to form, scoring a powerful 69 in a stand of 110 in 16 overs with Lloyd. Hampshire countered well, and were still in the game with ten overs remaining: only two wickets down and 74 to win. But the loss of Smith and Kendall, in quick succession, made it too difficult. Excluding a washout, it was Lancashire's ninth successive League win at Old Trafford, and their 250th in all since the competition started.

Lancashire

J. P. Crawley c Udal b Mascarenhas	7	G. Yates not out		4
M. J. Chilton b Hartley	20	G. Chapple b McLean		1
N. H. Fairbrother c Aymes b Stephenson	10	P. J. Martin b McLean		2
G. D. Lloyd st Aymes b Stephenson	36	L-b 8, w 7, n-b 6		21
A. Flintoff c Keech b Mascarenhas	69			
*Wasim Akram c and b Mascarenhas	9	1/25 2/48 3/50	(39.4 overs)	202
†W. K. Hegg c and b McLean	16	4/160 5/164 6/182		
I. D. Austin run out	7	7/194 8/196 9/200		

Bowling: Connor 8–1–18–0; McLean 7.4–0–39–3; Mascarenhas 6–0–24–3; Hartley 8–0–40–1; Stephenson 6–0–42–2; Udal 4–0–31–0.

Hampshire

G. W. White c Austin b Wasim Akram	27	†A. N. Aymes not out		8
J. P. Stephenson c Wasim Akram b Austin	15	S. D. Udal not out		2
*R. A. Smith c Hegg b Chapple	44	B 2, l-b 7, w 9, n-b 6		24
W. S. Kendall c Austin b Martin	44			
A. D. Mascarenhas b Martin	9	1/32 2/53 3/149	(7 wkts, 40 overs)	186
N. A. M. McLean c Chapple b Martin	3	4/156 5/162		
M. Keech b Wasim Akram	10	6/172 7/179		

C. A. Connor and P. J. Hartley did not bat.

Bowling: Austin 8–0–30–1; Martin 8–1–41–3; Chapple 8–0–29–1; Wasim Akram 8–0–34–2; Flintoff 4–0–18–0; Yates 4–0–25–0.

Umpires: D. J. Constant and P. Willey.

At Nottingham, September 9. LANCASHIRE beat NOTTINGHAMSHIRE by 52 runs.

LEICESTERSHIRE

LEICESTERSHIRE v WORCESTERSHIRE

At Leicester, April 26. Leicestershire won by 49 runs. Toss: Worcestershire.

The return of Simmons and Lewis to Leicestershire's ranks inspired the team to a solid all-round performance. Simmons, recapturing his form of 1996, hit a robust 60 off 54 balls while Lewis scored 33 and took two important wickets. Leicestershire's total of 218 looked formidable in damp conditions, and Mullally's opening spell of six overs for six runs put the game out of Worcestershire's reach.

Leicestershire

P. V. Simmons c Illingworth b Sheriyar .	60	†P. A. Nixon b Leatherdale		0
*J. J. Whitaker c Solanki b Haynes	10			
B. F. Smith ç Rhodes b Sheriyar.	40	L-b 4, w 2, n-b 6		12
C. C. Lewis run out	33			—
D. L. Maddy c Hick b Leatherdale	38	1/28 2/107 3/131	(7 wkts, 40 overs)	218
A. Habib not out	25	4/172 5/205		
J. M. Dakin lbw b Lampitt	0	6/213 7/218		

D. Williamson, A. D. Mullally and T. J. Mason did not bat.

Bowling: Newport 7–0–46–0; Haynes 6–1–32–1; Illingworth 8–0–42–0; Lampitt 7–0–42–1; Sheriyar 7–1–33–2; Leatherdale 5–0–19–2.

Worcestershire

W. P. C. Weston b Dakin.	12	R. K. Illingworth b Mullally.		2
V. S. Solanki c and b Lewis.	0	P. J. Newport not out		5
*G. A. Hick c Whitaker b Lewis.	2	A. Sheriyar not out		5
G. R. Haynes b Dakin	39	L-b 3, w 3, n-b 4		10
D. A. Leatherdale b Williamson	20			
S. R. Lampitt b Simmons	39	1/2 2/4 3/38	(9 wkts, 40 overs)	169
†S. J. Rhodes b Williamson	15	4/69 5/79 6/114		
S. W. K. Ellis c Simmons b Mullally. . .	20	7/156 8/159 9/160		

Bowling: Mullally 8–1–11–2; Lewis 6–0–31–2; Simmons 6–0–45–1; Dakin 8–2–22–2; Williamson 8–0–26–2; Mason 3–0–23–0; Maddy 1–0–8–0.

Umpires: G. I. Burgess and D. J. Constant.

At Birmingham, May 10. LEICESTERSHIRE lost to WARWICKSHIRE by 21 runs (D/L method).

At Bristol, May 17. LEICESTERSHIRE lost to GLOUCESTERSHIRE by four wickets.

At Derby, May 19. LEICESTERSHIRE lost to DERBYSHIRE by seven runs.

LEICESTERSHIRE v HAMPSHIRE

At Leicester, May 25. Leicestershire won by 117 runs. Toss: Hampshire.

Hampshire collapsed on a seaming pitch to Dakin and Wells and were bowled out for 88. Leicestershire had themselves been in trouble after losing three batsmen in Hartley's first two overs, but Wells and Nixon led a successful fightback.

Leicestershire

*P. V. Simmons c Keech b Hartley	4	D. Williamson c Aymes b McLean		13
V. J. Wells run out	45	J. Ormond not out		1
B. F. Smith c Mascarenhas b Hartley. . .	1			
D. L. Maddy b Hartley	0	B 1, l-b 6, w 8, n-b 8		23
A. Habib lbw b James	25			
†P. A. Nixon not out.	60	1/7 2/15 3/15	(8 wkts, 40 overs)	205
J. M. Dakin b McLean	15	4/80 5/101 6/128		
D. I. Stevens run out	18	7/186 8/200		

M. T. Brimson did not bat.

Bowling: Connor 8–0–45–0; Hartley 8–0–37–3; James 8–0–23–1; McLean 8–0–51–2; Udal 4–0–19–0; Mascarenhas 4–0–23–0.

Hampshire

G. W. White c Maddy b Ormond	0	P. J. Hartley b Wells		4
†A. N. Aymes c Nixon b Dakin	8	N. A. M. McLean c Nixon b Wells		0
*R. A. Smith b Dakin	1	C. A. Connor b Brimson		1
A. D. Mascarenhas c Nixon b Dakin	6	B 1, l-b 2, w 4, n-b 10		17
M. Keech c Nixon b Dakin	4			
P. R. Whitaker c Maddy b Wells	6	1/3 2/11 3/21	(30.3 overs)	88
S. D. Udal c Habib b Wells	11	4/34 5/35 6/46		
K. D. James not out	30	7/59 8/69 9/69		

Bowling: Ormond 8–1–26–1; Dakin 8–3–14–4; Wells 8–0–24–4; Brimson 6.3–0–21–1.

Umpires: H. D. Bird and J. H. Harris.

At Leeds, June 7. LEICESTERSHIRE beat YORKSHIRE by eight wickets.

LEICESTERSHIRE v KENT

At Leicester, June 14. No result. Toss: Kent.

Leicestershire, speedily reduced to 25 for five, could not cope with Headley and Ealham on a helpful pitch. Relief, and two points, came when the third interruption by rain ended play.

Leicestershire

P. V. Simmons c Marsh b Headley	4	D. I. Stevens not out		0
V. J. Wells c Marsh b Ealham	0			
B. F. Smith b Ealham	0	L-b 1, n-b 2		3
*C. C. Lewis c Marsh b Headley	13			
D. L. Maddy b Headley	0	1/4 2/4 3/10	(5 wkts, 9 overs)	25
†P. A. Nixon not out	5	4/10 5/25		

J. M. Dakin, D. Williamson, A. Habib and A. D. Mullally did not bat.

Bowling: Headley 5–1–14–3; Ealham 4–0–10–2.

Kent

R. W. T. Key, T. R. Ward, C. L. Hooper, A. P. Wells, M. A. Ealham, M. V. Fleming, G. R. Cowdrey, *†S. A. Marsh, B. J. Phillips, D. W. Headley and M. J. McCague.

Umpires: T. E. Jesty and A. G. T. Whitehead.

At Pontypridd, June 21. LEICESTERSHIRE beat GLAMORGAN by 20 runs.

At Darlington, July 5. LEICESTERSHIRE beat DURHAM by five runs.

At The Oval, July 13. LEICESTERSHIRE beat SURREY by 44 runs (D/L method).

LEICESTERSHIRE v NORTHAMPTONSHIRE

At Leicester, July 18. Northamptonshire won by five wickets. Toss: Northamptonshire.

Having won the Championship match the previous day by scoring at ten an over, Leicestershire seemed unprepared for a reinvigorated Northamptonshire. Their seam bowlers, backed by sharp fielding, held Leicestershire in check on a slow, green pitch. In reply, Loye, the League's top scorer to date, built purposefully with a brisk 47, and Penberthy saw Northamptonshire to a deserved win.

Leicestershire

P. V. Simmons c Warren b Taylor	8		J. M. Dakin c Follett b Rose	17
V. J. Wells b Follett	14		T. J. Mason lbw b Bailey	4
B. F. Smith b Follett	10			
D. L. Maddy c Rose b Taylor	1		B 2, l-b 5, w 2	9
†P. A. Nixon c Penberthy b Curran	2			
A. Habib run out	11		1/17 2/31 3/32　　(9 wkts, 40 overs)	140
*C. C. Lewis c Loye b Snape	32		4/37 5/39 6/63	
D. Williamson not out	32		7/100 8/129 9/140	

M. T. Brimson did not bat.

Bowling: Follett 8–0–29–2; Rose 4–0–20–1; Taylor 8–1–18–2; Curran 8–1–19–1; Snape 8–0–25–1; Bailey 4–0–22–1.

Northamptonshire

M. B. Loye lbw b Maddy	47		T. C. Walton not out	10
†R. J. Warren c Smith b Brimson	19			
*K. M. Curran c Simmons b Brimson	6		B 2, l-b 2, w 3, n-b 2	9
A. L. Penberthy not out	30			
J. N. Snape c Nixon b Mason	10		1/61 2/68 3/76　　(5 wkts, 38.4 overs)	144
R. J. Bailey b Brimson	13		4/88 5/127	

D. J. Sales, J. P. Taylor, F. A. Rose and D. Follett did not bat.

Bowling: Wells 8–2–14–0; Williamson 5.4–0–33–0; Mason 8–0–39–1; Brimson 8–1–23–3; Maddy 4–0–16–1; Simmons 5–1–15–0.

Umpires: B. Leadbeater and A. G. T. Whitehead.

At Manchester, August 2. LEICESTERSHIRE lost to LANCASHIRE by 20 runs.

LEICESTERSHIRE v SOMERSET

At Leicester, August 9. Leicestershire won by five runs. Toss: Somerset.

Parsons was caught at long-on as he attempted to win the match with a six off the final ball. He became the fourth victim of the day for Ormond, who had taken three middle-order wickets in eight balls. The seamers held the upper hand throughout on a slow pitch.

Leicestershire

P. V. Simmons c Parsons b Rose	0		D. Williamson not out	25
V. J. Wells c Bowler b Burns	32		T. J. Mason not out	5
B. F. Smith c Parsons b Jones	22		L-b 8, w 4, n-b 4	16
D. L. Maddy run out	7			
*C. C. Lewis c and b Rose	25		1/5 2/51 3/68　　(7 wkts, 40 overs)	165
†P. A. Nixon b Rose	19		4/72 5/115	
J. M. Dakin run out	14		6/119 7/147	

A. D. Mullally and J. Ormond did not bat.

Bowling: Parsons 8–0–23–0; Rose 8–0–35–3; Jones 7–0–29–1; Caddick 8–0–32–0; Burns 8–1–26–1; Bowler 1–0–12–0.

Somerset

*P. D. Bowler c Nixon b Mullally	5		A. R. K. Pierson run out	2
M. Burns c Nixon b Ormond	23		A. R. Caddick lbw b Dakin	0
M. E. Trescothick c Simmons b Ormond	19		P. S. Jones not out	0
M. N. Lathwell b Williamson	36		B 3, l-b 4, w 9	16
G. D. Rose c Williamson b Ormond	0			
R. J. Harden lbw b Wells	5		1/8 2/48 3/50	(40 overs) 160
K. A. Parsons c Williamson b Ormond	48		4/50 5/66 6/116	
†P. C. L. Holloway b Mullally	6		7/138 8/156 9/156	

Bowling: Mullally 8–0–36–2; Ormond 8–0–32–4; Wells 8–1–25–1; Mason 4–0–18–0; Williamson 8–0–24–1; Dakin 4–0–18–1.

Umpires: V. A. Holder and R. Julian.

LEICESTERSHIRE v SUSSEX

At Leicester, August 23. No result (abandoned).

At Nottingham, August 30. LEICESTERSHIRE lost to NOTTINGHAMSHIRE by four runs.

LEICESTERSHIRE v MIDDLESEX

At Leicester, September 6. Leicestershire won by 160 runs. Toss: Middlesex.

Inept batting from Middlesex and some incisive bowling from Ormond saw the visitors shot out for 62, the League's lowest total of the season. He had figures of 8–3–12–4, while Dakin finished off the innings with his first hat-trick. Leicestershire's total had been based on a businesslike 77 from Wells and a flamboyant unbeaten 40 from Simmons.

Leicestershire

V. J. Wells b Weekes	77		D. Williamson b Johnson	7
J. M. Dakin c Hewitt b Tufnell	29		J. Ormond not out	11
†P. A. Nixon c Gatting b Dutch	3			
A. Habib c and b Tufnell	8		B 5, l-b 8, w 3, n-b 2	18
B. F. Smith c Dutch b Johnson	3			
*P. V. Simmons not out	40		1/69 2/80 3/115	(8 wkts, 40 overs) 222
D. L. Maddy b Johnson	3		4/122 5/151 6/168	
C. C. Lewis c Hewitt b Johnson	23		7/196 8/210	

M. T. Brimson did not bat.

Bowling: Fraser 8–0–43–0; Hewitt 8–1–36–0; Tufnell 8–0–39–2; Dutch 5–0–26–1; Johnson 8–0–45–4; Weekes 3–0–20–1.

Middlesex

†K. R. Brown run out	0		J. P. Hewitt c Lewis b Dakin	7
A. J. Strauss c Nixon b Ormond	5		A. R. C. Fraser lbw b Dakin	0
*M. R. Ramprakash c Brimson b Ormond	16		P. C. R. Tufnell b Dakin	0
O. A. Shah c Smith b Lewis	3		L-b 6, w 2	8
P. N. Weekes c Simmons b Ormond	5			
M. W. Gatting b Ormond	2		1/0 2/12 3/21	(22.4 overs) 62
K. P. Dutch not out	16		4/33 5/37 6/40	
R. L. Johnson b Williamson	0		7/41 8/62 9/62	

Bowling: Ormond 8–3–12–4; Lewis 5–0–17–1; Williamson 6–2–17–1; Dakin 3.4–1–10–3.

Umpires: R. Palmer and N. T. Plews.

LEICESTERSHIRE v ESSEX

At Leicester, September 13. Leicestershire won by 128 runs. Toss: Essex.

For the fourth time in 1998, Leicestershire bowled out the opposition for under 100 in a League match. Essex, their season now disintegrating, collapsed to 91 all out after their two most experienced batsmen, Prichard and Stuart Law, had put on 45 for the first wicket. Off-spinner Mason took four for 12. Smith and Simmons had scored 94 with their fourth-wicket stand alone. Victory gave Leicestershire fourth place, one position behind Essex, who had led the table for almost two months until they ended the season with three consecutive defeats.

Leicestershire

J. M. Dakin run out	17	T. J. Mason b Ilott	11
V. J. Wells lbw b Such	29	J. Ormond not out	2
A. Habib lbw b Ilott	2	C. D. Crowe not out	4
B. F. Smith b Cowan	54	B 1, l-b 6, w 4, n-b 2	13
*P. V. Simmons c D. R. Law b Irani	56		
D. L. Maddy b Cowan	0	1/26 2/39 3/68 (9 wkts, 40 overs) 219
†P. A. Nixon c Grayson b Irani	21	4/162 5/162 6/176
D. Williamson c Cowan b Irani	10	7/197 8/204 9/215

Bowling: Cowan 8–0–32–2; Ilott 8–0–44–2; Irani 8–0–38–3; Such 8–0–55–1; Grayson 8–0–43–0.

Essex

*P. J. Prichard b Ormond	22	M. C. Ilott c Simmons b Mason	1
S. G. Law c Habib b Simmons	23	†B. J. Hyam lbw b Williamson	6
T. P. Hodgson run out	8	P. M. Such c Maddy b Mason	4
R. C. Irani c Dakin b Ormond	9	L-b 1, w 7	8
A. P. Grayson c Ormond b Mason	4		
S. D. Peters c Nixon b Mason	0	1/45 2/49 3/64 (26.1 overs) 91
D. R. Law lbw b Williamson	0	4/68 5/76 6/76
A. P. Cowan not out	2	7/76 8/77 9/86

Bowling: Ormond 8–1–36–2; Simmons 8–0–33–1; Mason 5.1–2–12–4; Williamson 5–1–9–2.

Umpires: J. W. Holder and A. A. Jones.

MIDDLESEX

At Canterbury, April 19. MIDDLESEX lost to KENT by one run (D/L method).

At Manchester, April 26. LANCASHIRE v MIDDLESEX. No result (abandoned).

MIDDLESEX v GLAMORGAN

At Lord's, May 3. Middlesex won by three wickets. Toss: Middlesex.

Middlesex, needing 45 in the last four overs, scored a remarkable win with three balls to spare. Johnson added insult to injury by striking Waqar Younis over extra cover for six in the 38th over; the game was won with a wide. Glamorgan's day had begun badly when Maynard strained a groin muscle while warming up, but they had the edge when Middlesex, chasing 219, were 89 for five.

Glamorgan

S. P. James c Dutch b Hewitt	7	Waqar Younis c Hewitt b Dutch	9
R. D. B. Croft b Johnson	50	†A. D. Shaw not out	0
A. Dale c Brown b A. R. C. Fraser	12		
*P. A. Cottey b Ramprakash	56	L-b 12, w 12	24
M. J. Powell lbw b Dutch	4		
G. P. Butcher b A. R. C. Fraser	12	1/18 2/43 3/112 (8 wkts, 40 overs) 218	
A. W. Evans not out	26	4/125 5/154 6/162	
S. D. Thomas c Langer b Dutch	18	7/198 8/217	

S. L. Watkin did not bat.

Bowling: A. R. C. Fraser 8–0–34–2; Hewitt 8–0–30–1; Johnson 8–0–54–1; A. G. J. Fraser 4–0–32–0; Dutch 8–0–46–3; Ramprakash 4–0–10–1.

Middlesex

†K. R. Brown run out	11	A. G. J. Fraser b Waqar Younis	8
J. L. Langer c Cottey b Croft	38	R. L. Johnson not out	22
*M. R. Ramprakash b Thomas	7	B 1, l-b 11, w 11	23
O. A. Shah not out	88		
J. C. Pooley lbw b Thomas	1	1/18 2/37 3/77 (7 wkts, 39.3 overs) 219	
D. C. Nash c Shaw b Thomas	0	4/89 5/89	
K. P. Dutch lbw b Dale	21	6/162 7/174	

J. P. Hewitt and A. R. C. Fraser did not bat.

Bowling: Watkin 8–0–29–0; Waqar Younis 7.3–1–41–1; Thomas 8–0–46–3; Dale 4–0–28–1; Croft 8–0–41–1; Butcher 4–0–22–0.

Umpires: M. J. Harris and A. A. Jones.

MIDDLESEX v SOMERSET

At Lord's, May 17. Middlesex won by one run. Toss: Somerset.

Somerset failed to make ten runs from the last over, bowled by Weekes. Mushtaq hit the first ball for six, but Weekes then regained control, and Caddick was run out off the last ball as he tried to get a second run for a tie. Most batsmen were unsettled on a pitch being used for the fifth day running.

Middlesex

R. L. Johnson run out	23	K. P. Dutch lbw b Mushtaq Ahmed	5
J. L. Langer run out	15	J. P. Hewitt not out	21
†D. C. Nash b Rose	1	I. N. Blanchett b Jones	7
J. C. Pooley lbw b Rose	0	B 1, l-b 7, w 11	19
O. A. Shah c Turner b Trescothick	30		
P. N. Weekes lbw b Mushtaq Ahmed	31	1/32 2/37 3/38 (9 wkts, 40 overs) 160	
*M. R. Ramprakash		4/56 5/102 6/118	
lbw b Mushtaq Ahmed	8	7/121 8/133 9/160	

A. R. C. Fraser did not bat.

Bowling: Parsons 3–0–20–0; Rose 8–0–27–2; Caddick 8–1–19–0; Jones 6–0–31–1; Trescothick 7–0–33–1; Mushtaq Ahmed 8–2–22–3.

Somerset

*P. D. Bowler c Nash b Hewitt	5	Mushtaq Ahmed run out	15
M. Burns b Fraser	1	A. R. Caddick run out	2
G. D. Rose b Fraser	0	P. S. Jones not out	0
R. J. Harden c Weekes b Johnson	52	B 4, l-b 8, w 7	19
M. N. Lathwell c and b Blanchett	31		
†R. J. Turner run out	25	1/4 2/4 3/14 (40 overs)	159
K. A. Parsons c Ramprakash b Dutch	2	4/79 5/128 6/130	
M. E. Trescothick c Shah b Weekes	7	7/135 8/157 9/158	

Bowling: Fraser 8–2–17–2; Hewitt 6–1–16–1; Johnson 8–0–34–1; Weekes 6–0–34–1; Dutch 8–0–30–1; Blanchett 4–0–16–1.

Umpires: D. J. Constant and J. W. Lloyds.

MIDDLESEX v ESSEX

At Uxbridge, May 19. Middlesex won by two wickets. Toss: Essex. County debut: J. E. Brinkley.

Middlesex pulled off their third narrow home win in a row when Essex failed to score nine off the final over. With five needed off the last two balls, Blanchett ran out Robinson from the boundary for 83 to follow his tight spell of seam bowling. On a pitch less benign than usual at Uxbridge, only Ramprakash scored well for Middlesex, and Robinson and Peters appeared to have given Essex the edge.

Middlesex

R. L. Johnson b Cousins	16	J. P. Hewitt b Ilott	1
J. L. Langer lbw b Cousins	3	I. N. Blanchett not out	9
*M. R. Ramprakash c Hussain b Wilson	57		
J. C. Pooley lbw b Cousins	4	B 1, l-b 11, w 18, n-b 2	32
O. A. Shah run out	10		
P. N. Weekes c S. G. Law b D. R. Law	20	1/20 2/32 3/47 (8 wkts, 40 overs)	200
†D. C. Nash b Irani	29	4/72 5/110 6/159	
K. P. Dutch not out	19	7/186 8/187	

N. D. Martin did not bat.

Bowling: Ilott 8–0–24–1; Cousins 8–0–29–3; Irani 8–0–39–1; D. R. Law 6–0–36–1; Brinkley 6–0–35–0; Wilson 4–0–25–1.

Essex

D. D. J. Robinson run out	83	D. G. Wilson not out	7
S. G. Law c Dutch b Hewitt	13	J. E. Brinkley not out	0
*N. Hussain c and b Martin	20	L-b 4, w 16	20
R. C. Irani lbw b Martin	0		
S. D. Peters c Pooley b Dutch	54	1/23 2/68 3/72 (7 wkts, 40 overs)	198
†R. J. Rollins c Johnson b Dutch	0	4/179 5/179	
D. R. Law c Hewitt b Johnson	1	6/182 7/197	

M. C. Ilott and D. M. Cousins did not bat.

Bowling: Hewitt 6–0–30–1; Johnson 8–0–38–1; Martin 6–0–28–2; Dutch 8–0–31–2; Blanchett 7–0–25–0; Weekes 4–0–31–0; Shah 1–0–11–0.

Umpires: B. Leadbeater and J. F. Steele.

MIDDLESEX v WORCESTERSHIRE

At Uxbridge, May 25. Middlesex won by seven wickets (D/L method). Toss: Middlesex.

On a lively pitch, Worcestershire never quite recovered from a disastrous start when Hewitt grabbed four quick wickets. Weston fought stubbornly until dismissed in curious fashion: having survived Angus Fraser's attempt to run him out, he chanced a single from the rebound, only to be thrown out at the other end by Fraser's second effort. Rain brought a recalculation of Middlesex's target, to 120 from 34 overs, but Shah was in complete control.

Worcestershire

*T. M. Moody b A. R. C. Fraser	5	R. K. Illingworth lbw b Weekes	11	
V. S. Solanki c Nash b Hewitt	4	P. J. Newport not out	9	
G. A. Hick c Nash b Hewitt	5	A. Sheriyar not out	2	
G. R. Haynes c Nash b Hewitt	3			
D. A. Leatherdale lbw b Hewitt	15	B 3, l-b 5, w 8	16	
W. P. C. Weston run out	35			
S. R. Lampitt c Nash b A. G. J. Fraser	15	1/8 2/12 3/18 (9 wkts, 40 overs) 138		
†S. J. Rhodes c Blanchett		4/25 5/43 6/68		
b A. R. C. Fraser	18	7/108 8/114 9/136		

Bowling: A. R. C. Fraser 8–0–19–2; Hewitt 8–0–24–4; Blanchett 6–0–22–0; A. G. J. Fraser 6–1–21–1; Dutch 8–0–27–0; Weekes 4–0–17–1.

Middlesex

J. L. Langer lbw b Newport	1	*M. R. Ramprakash not out	23	
†D. C. Nash c Rhodes b Newport	4	L-b 2, w 4, n-b 6	12	
O. A. Shah not out	61			
J. C. Pooley b Sheriyar	19	1/6 2/9 3/57 (3 wkts, 28.5 overs) 120		

P. N. Weekes, K. P. Dutch, A. G. J. Fraser, J. P. Hewitt, I. N. Blanchett and A. R. C. Fraser did not bat.

Bowling: Newport 4–0–17–2; Haynes 6–0–16–0; Moody 5–0–20–0; Sheriyar 5–0–25–1; Illingworth 5.5–0–32–0; Lampitt 3–0–8–0.

Umpires: M. J. Harris and T. E. Jesty.

MIDDLESEX v DURHAM

At Lord's, June 7. Middlesex won by three wickets. Toss: Middlesex.

In a rain-shortened game, Middlesex kept up their habit of winning close finishes – this time with two balls to spare – and went top of the League. Chasing a useful total, Langer batted resolutely, and Nash raised the tempo. Foster was Durham's star. He hammered 70 off 52 balls, hitting a six off Rashid which lodged in the guttering of the pavilion's south turret.

Durham

S. Hutton lbw b Hewitt	9	M. M. Betts c Langer b Weekes	1	
†M. P. Speight c Nash b Hewitt	14	J. Wood not out	1	
N. J. Speak c and b Rashid	36	N. Killeen not out	0	
*D. C. Boon c Hewitt b Fraser	5	B 2, l-b 8, w 5	15	
P. D. Collingwood c Shah b Fraser	3			
J. J. B. Lewis c Nash b Dutch	1	1/26 2/31 3/42 (9 wkts, 34 overs) 160		
M. J. Foster c Nash b Fraser	70	4/54 5/55 6/104		
N. C. Phillips c Dutch b Fraser	5	7/151 8/153 9/158		

Bowling: Hewitt 7–0–25–2; Blanchett 4–1–13–0; Fraser 6–0–19–4; Dutch 6–0–29–1; Rashid 7–0–35–1; Weekes 4–0–29–1.

Middlesex

A. G. J. Fraser b Betts	5	K. P. Dutch not out	1	
*J. L. Langer lbw b Phillips	46	J. P. Hewitt not out	5	
O. A. Shah lbw b Betts	3	L-b 7, w 9	16	
P. N. Weekes c Boon b Foster	24			
J. C. Pooley run out	13	1/15 2/24 3/71 (7 wkts, 33.4 overs) 163		
†D. C. Nash b Betts	33	4/93 5/108		
R. A. Kettleborough run out	17	6/157 7/157		

I. N. Blanchett and U. B. A. Rashid did not bat.

Bowling: Betts 7–0–34–3; Wood 7–0–31–0; Killeen 6.4–0–39–0; Phillips 7–0–30–1; Foster 6–0–22–1.

Umpires: J. C. Balderstone and M. J. Kitchen.

At Derby, June 14. DERBYSHIRE v MIDDLESEX. No result (abandoned).

At Northampton, June 21. MIDDLESEX lost to NORTHAMPTONSHIRE by nine wickets.

At Nottingham, July 5. MIDDLESEX beat NOTTINGHAMSHIRE by 24 runs.

At Guildford, July 19. MIDDLESEX lost to SURREY by one run.

At Hove, July 20. MIDDLESEX lost to SUSSEX by six wickets (D/L method).

MIDDLESEX v YORKSHIRE

At Lord's, July 26. Middlesex won by 57 runs (D/L method). Toss: Yorkshire.

Middlesex surged to an emphatic win, inspired by the batting of Langer and the bowling of two uncapped seamers. Langer, who struck 86 from 79 balls, was in full cry when rain intervened, cutting the match to 28 overs a side. A Duckworth/Lewis calculation meant that Yorkshire needed 186 to tie, 187 to win. Bloomfield and Batt soon had them reeling at 39 for five, and only Parker put up much fight.

Middlesex

*†K. R. Brown c Blakey b McGrath	19	K. P. Dutch not out	7
J. L. Langer lbw b Hutchison	86	B 2, l-b 6, w 4, n-b 4	16
O. A. Shah b Stemp	5		—
R. L. Johnson b McGrath	2	1/42 2/56 (4 wkts, 28 overs)	177
P. N. Weekes not out	42	3/59 4/169	

D. J. Goodchild, D. C. Nash, A. W. Laraman, C. J. Batt and T. F. Bloomfield did not bat.

Bowling: Hoggard 5–0–21–0; Hutchison 6–0–29–1; McGrath 6–1–27–2; Stemp 6–0–42–1; Middlebrook 2–0–19–0; Parker 2–0–18–0; Lehmann 1–0–13–0.

Yorkshire

*D. Byas c Laraman b Batt	18	R. D. Stemp st Brown b Dutch	9
M. P. Vaughan c Langer b Bloomfield	1	M. J. Hoggard c Goodchild b Langer	1
D. S. Lehmann b Bloomfield	5	P. M. Hutchison not out	0
M. J. Wood b Batt	5	L-b 7, w 9, n-b 8	24
A. McGrath c Langer b Batt	2		
B. Parker c Brown b Dutch	33	1/3 2/23 3/30 (24.1 overs)	129
†R. J. Blakey st Brown b Dutch	26	4/35 5/39 6/92	
J. D. Middlebrook c Johnson b Dutch	5	7/112 8/124 9/129	

Bowling: Bloomfield 6–1–13–2; Batt 6–0–26–3; Laraman 3–0–20–0; Johnson 2–0–23–0; Dutch 4–0–22–4; Langer 3.1–0–18–1.

Umpires: J. W. Holder and G. Sharp.

MIDDLESEX v WARWICKSHIRE

At Lord's, August 9. Warwickshire won by six wickets. Toss: Middlesex.

On a highly untrustworthy pitch, the match was virtually settled when Small undermined Middlesex by taking five for 18 – his best League figures, in his 19th season. Warwickshire found scoring equally difficult until Lara hammered 26 in 20 balls, to bring Keith Brown's benefit match to an early, disappointing close. Brown himself was top scorer in the game.

Middlesex

*†K. R. Brown c Piper b Small	28	R. L. Johnson b Small		0
J. L. Langer run out	13	P. C. R. Tufnell not out		5
O. A. Shah c Piper b Giddins	3	T. F. Bloomfield c Small b Giddins		15
P. N. Weekes st Piper b Smith	1	B 8, l-b 5, w 11		24
D. C. Nash lbw b Smith	2			
K. P. Dutch b Small	7	1/30 2/40 3/42	(34.4 overs)	102
D. J. Goodchild c Giles b Small	1	4/57 5/67 6/73		
A. W. Laraman b Small	3	7/76 8/76 9/79		

Bowling: Munton 8–0–25–0; Giddins 6.4–1–22–2; Smith 7–0–20–2; Small 8–0–18–5; Giles 5–2–4–0.

Warwickshire

N. V. Knight b Dutch	23	*B. C. Lara not out		26
N. M. K. Smith c Goodchild				
b Bloomfield	14	B 4, l-b 6, w 1, n-b 4		15
D. L. Hemp c Laraman b Bloomfield	9			
A. Singh b Dutch	0	1/20 2/37	(4 wkts, 23.3 overs)	105
T. L. Penney not out	18	3/54 4/63		

A. F. Giles, †K. J. Piper, G. C. Small, T. A. Munton and E. S. H. Giddins did not bat.

Bowling: Johnson 3–0–20–0; Bloomfield 5–1–15–2; Dutch 8–0–27–2; Tufnell 6–1–17–0; Weekes 1–0–12–0; Laraman 0.3–0–4–0.

Umpires: J. H. Harris and J. F. Steele.

At Southampton, August 30. MIDDLESEX lost to HAMPSHIRE by 12 runs.

At Leicester, September 6. MIDDLESEX lost to LEICESTERSHIRE by 160 runs.

MIDDLESEX v GLOUCESTERSHIRE

At Lord's, September 13. Gloucestershire won by 22 runs. Toss: Middlesex.

Middlesex's unhappy season finally crumbled to dust. Having led the League until mid-July, they failed even to finish in the top half and were destined for the lower division of the National League. Gloucestershire seemed more determined to make the First Division, and took 81 off their last ten overs. Ramprakash failed to rally his dispirited troops, and they sank to their fourth successive League defeat, their eighth in a row including Championship fixtures.

Gloucestershire

R. I. Dawson c Weekes b Dutch	47	A. J. Wright c Goodchild b Weekes		0
M. C. J. Ball c Kettleborough b Hewitt	1	R. J. Cunliffe not out		2
*M. W. Alleyne c Brown b Hewitt	7	L-b 5, w 5, n-b 2		12
M. G. N. Windows c Strauss b Dutch	30			
†R. C. Russell c Goodchild b Weekes	36	1/3 2/17 3/92	(6 wkts, 40 overs)	196
T. H. C. Hancock not out	61	4/99 5/172 6/173		

J. Lewis, A. M. Smith and C. A. Walsh did not bat.

Bowling: Hewitt 8–0–26–2; Fraser 8–1–31–0; Kettleborough 6–0–29–0; Johnson 8–0–45–0; Dutch 8–0–48–2; Weekes 2–0–12–2.

Middlesex

†K. R. Brown c Russell b Lewis	3	R. L. Johnson b Walsh	5
R. A. Kettleborough lbw b Lewis	7	J. P. Hewitt not out	9
*M. R. Ramprakash c Russell b Alleyne	56		
A. J. Strauss c Alleyne b Hancock	15	B 3, l-b 10, w 6, n-b 2	21
P. N. Weekes b Alleyne	29		
O. A. Shah c Dawson b Smith	10	1/4 2/19 3/64 (8 wkts, 40 overs) 174
K. P. Dutch c Windows b Alleyne	1	4/111 5/134 6/137
D. J. Goodchild not out	18	7/138 8/154

A. R. C. Fraser did not bat.

Bowling: Lewis 6–0–21–2; Smith 8–0–28–1; Walsh 8–0–26–1; Hancock 8–0–38–1; Ball 5–0–21–0; Alleyne 5–0–27–3.

Umpires: K. E. Palmer and D. R. Shepherd.

NORTHAMPTONSHIRE

At The Oval, April 19. SURREY v NORTHAMPTONSHIRE. No result.

At Southampton, April 26. NORTHAMPTONSHIRE lost to HAMPSHIRE by three wickets.

NORTHAMPTONSHIRE v YORKSHIRE

At Northampton, May 17. Yorkshire won by 11 runs. Toss: Northamptonshire.

Lehmann, who scored 643 in the League in 1997, was soon back in form; he steadied Yorkshire's innings by sharing a stand of 110 with McGrath. Northamptonshire's tardy over-rate cut their own innings to 38 overs but, with Loye playing fluently for 65, they kept in touch until he was out. Bailey passed Wayne Larkins's county record of 6,068 League runs.

Yorkshire

M. P. Vaughan c Warren b Rose	0	†R. J. Blakey not out	8
C. White c Curran b Penberthy	22	D. Gough not out	8
*D. Byas c Bailey b Rose	4	L-b 3, w 4	7
D. S. Lehmann b Taylor	70		
A. McGrath c Taylor b Snape	52	1/1 2/11 3/35 (6 wkts, 40 overs) 198
B. Parker c Snape b Capel	27	4/145 5/171 6/185

G. M. Hamilton, R. D. Stemp and R. J. Sidebottom did not bat.

Bowling: Rose 8–0–34–2; Penberthy 8–0–25–1; Taylor 8–0–31–1; Snape 8–0–51–1; Capel 8–0–54–1.

Northamptonshire

M. B. Loye c Sidebottom b White	65	J. N. Snape not out	15
†R. J. Warren b Sidebottom	6	J. P. Taylor b White	1
*K. M. Curran b Hamilton	23		
A. L. Penberthy b Gough	21	L-b 7, w 7, n-b 6	20
D. J. Sales c Byas b Vaughan	1		
R. J. Bailey run out	33	1/17 2/78 3/110 (9 wkts, 38 overs) 187
T. C. Walton lbw b Hamilton	1	4/113 5/134 6/141
D. J. Capel c White b Gough	1	7/147 8/180 9/187

F. A. Rose did not bat.

Bowling: Sidebottom 8–0–32–1; Gough 8–0–44–2; White 8–0–31–2; Hamilton 8–0–42–2; Stemp 4–0–20–0; Vaughan 2–0–11–1.

Umpires: J. F. Steele and R. A. White.

At Taunton, May 19. NORTHAMPTONSHIRE beat SOMERSET by seven wickets.

NORTHAMPTONSHIRE v GLAMORGAN

At Northampton, May 25. Glamorgan won by five wickets (D/L method). Toss: Glamorgan.

Northamptonshire made uninspired progress to 99 for six, with half their overs gone, before Snape led a charge which produced 100 runs in the last 11 overs. A recalculation after rain left Glamorgan to score 174 in 24. After they sank to 87 for five, Cottey and Shaw, in a robust partnership of 90, secured their first League victory in 14 matches and moved Glamorgan off the foot of the table.

Northamptonshire

M. B. Loye c Cottey b Cosker	20		J. N. Snape not out	77
R. J. Warren c and b Cosker	39		†D. Ripley not out	27
A. L. Penberthy c Shaw b Parkin	0		B 8, l-b 3, w 7	18
*K. M. Curran c Powell b Parkin	8			
D. J. Sales b Watkin	19		1/45 2/46 3/67	(7 wkts, 40 overs) 239
D. J. Capel c Shaw b Watkin	1		4/96 5/98	
T. C. Walton c Croft b Watkin	30		6/99 7/176	

G. P. Swann and F. A. Rose did not bat.

Bowling: Parkin 8–0–37–2; Butcher 4–0–30–0; Cosker 8–0–26–2; Watkin 8–1–39–3; Croft 8–0–56–0; Dale 4–0–40–0.

Glamorgan

S. P. James b Snape	27		†A. D. Shaw not out	37
R. D. B. Croft c Curran b Penberthy	3			
A. Dale c Loye b Curran	16		L-b 6, w 4	10
*P. A. Cottey not out	77			
M. J. Powell c Warren b Snape	6		1/4 2/52 3/55	(5 wkts, 23.3 overs) 177
G. P. Butcher c Curran	1		4/79 5/87	

A. W. Evans, S. L. Watkin, D. A. Cosker and O. T. Parkin did not bat.

Bowling: Rose 5–0–36–0; Penberthy 5–0–27–1; Curran 5–0–36–2; Snape 5–0–35–2; Capel 2–0–21–0; Swann 1.3–0–16–0.

Umpires: N. G. Cowley and B. Leadbeater.

At Ilford, May 31. NORTHAMPTONSHIRE lost to ESSEX by eight wickets.

NORTHAMPTONSHIRE v LANCASHIRE

At Northampton, June 7. Lancashire won by seven wickets. Toss: Lancashire.

In a rain-affected match, Lancashire won comfortably when Northamptonshire only partially recovered from a disastrous start. Losing wickets to the first two balls of the game, they slumped to 29 for six, before Walton checked the slide. Pacing his innings perfectly, Fairbrother guided Lancashire home, despite having to summon a runner because of a thigh strain.

Northamptonshire

M. B. Loye c Yates b Martin	0		R. J. Bailey b Flintoff	23
†R. J. Warren c Fairbrother b Wasim Akram	17		T. C. Walton not out	51
			J. N. Snape not out	19
D. J. Capel b Martin	0		L-b 3, w 2	5
*K. M. Curran b Austin	0			
A. L. Penberthy b Martin	6		1/0 2/0 3/1 4/12	(7 wkts, 22 overs) 125
D. J. Sales c Lloyd b Green	4		5/23 6/29 7/80	

F. A. Rose and D. Follett did not bat.

Bowling: Martin 5–1–26–3; Austin 4–0–21–1; Wasim Akram 5–0–21–1; Green 4–0–28–1; Flintoff 3–0–11–1; Yates 1–0–15–0.

Lancashire

A. Flintoff b Follett	10
P. C. McKeown c Warren b Rose	0
N. H. Fairbrother not out	58
G. D. Lloyd c Follett b Capel	19

M. Watkinson not out	28
L-b 5, w 2, n-b 5	12
	—
1/3 2/23 3/78 (3 wkts, 20.5 overs)	127

*Wasim Akram, †W. K. Hegg, I. D. Austin, G. Yates, R. J. Green and P. J. Martin did not bat.

Bowling: Rose 4.5–0–30–1; Follett 5–0–27–1; Capel 4–0–30–1; Penberthy 3–0–14–0; Snape 4–0–21–0.

Umpires: M. J. Harris and G. Sharp.

At Chester-le-Street, June 14. DURHAM v NORTHAMPTONSHIRE. No result (abandoned).

NORTHAMPTONSHIRE v MIDDLESEX

At Northampton, June 21. Northamptonshire won by nine wickets. Toss: Middlesex.

Middlesex's hopes of going clear at the top of the table were dashed by a fluent performance from Loye, who switched his epic Championship form into the League by hitting a 112-ball century. Curran helped him secure an easy win. Langer, the acting Middlesex captain, took the responsibility of anchoring the innings and hit no boundaries in his first fifty.

Middlesex

A. G. J. Fraser c Curran b Rose	7
*J. L. Langer not out	87
O. A. Shah c Walton b Penberthy	13
P. N. Weekes b Rose	0
†D. C. Nash c Sales b Curran	23
J. C. Pooley c Bailey b Snape	13
K. P. Dutch b Taylor	25
R. L. Johnson b Taylor	7

J. P. Hewitt b Follett	10
R. A. Kettleborough not out	1
L-b 9, w 8, n-b 2	19
	—
1/14 2/40 3/41 (8 wkts, 40 overs)	205
4/98 5/125 6/175	
7/185 8/200	

T. F. Bloomfield did not bat.

Bowling: Penberthy 6–0–28–1; Rose 8–1–33–2; Taylor 8–1–29–2; Follett 8–0–52–1; Snape 6–0–31–1; Curran 4–0–23–1.

Northamptonshire

M. B. Loye not out	108
†R. J. Warren c Langer b Shah	35
*K. M. Curran not out	54
L-b 3, w 6	9

1/82   (1 wkt, 36.1 overs) 206

A. L. Penberthy, D. J. Sales, R. J. Bailey, T. C. Walton, J. N. Snape, D. Follett, J. P. Taylor and F. A. Rose did not bat.

Bowling: Hewitt 5–0–23–0; Bloomfield 4–0–23–0; Johnson 6–0–23–0; Fraser 6–0–35–0; Weekes 6–0–27–0; Shah 4–0–24–1; Dutch 5–0–44–0; Langer 0.1–0–4–0.

Umpires: A. A. Jones and R. Palmer.

At Worcester, July 5. NORTHAMPTONSHIRE tied with WORCESTERSHIRE.

At Leicester, July 18. NORTHAMPTONSHIRE beat LEICESTERSHIRE by five wickets.

At Cheltenham, July 19. NORTHAMPTONSHIRE beat GLOUCESTERSHIRE by 72 runs.

NORTHAMPTONSHIRE v DERBYSHIRE

At Northampton, July 26. Derbyshire won by 32 runs. Toss: Derbyshire.

Cassar, with 134 off only 108 balls, his maiden one-day century, guided Derbyshire to 286, which was well beyond Northamptonshire. He received support from Slater and DeFreitas, whose 69 included three sixes in an over from Swann. Penberthy and Sales put on 64 in seven overs, but their team-mates could not sustain the pace.

Derbyshire

M. J. Slater c Penberthy b Swann	42	V. P. Clarke not out		15
K. J. Barnett c Warren b Follett	10	G. M. Roberts not out		0
R. M. S. Weston retired hurt	0		B 1, l-b 3, w 3, n-b 4	11
M. E. Cassar c Walton b Curran	134			
P. A. J. DeFreitas c and b Taylor	69	1/19 2/112 3/210	(5 wkts, 40 overs)	286
B. L. Spendlove c Taylor b Swann	5	4/222 5/284		

*†K. M. Krikken, S. J. Lacey and K. J. Dean did not bat.

R. M. S. Weston retired hurt at 19-1.

Bowling: Follett 8–0–47–1; Rose 7–0–47–0; Taylor 8–0–63–1; Curran 4–0–34–1; Swann 5–0–45–2; Snape 8–0–46–0.

Northamptonshire

M. B. Loye c Krikken b Dean	4	F. A. Rose b Lacey		0
†R. J. Warren b Roberts	20	J. P. Taylor b Clarke		19
G. P. Swann c Cassar b DeFreitas	6	D. Follett not out		3
*K. M. Curran c Krikken b Roberts	42		B 1, l-b 11, w 7	19
A. L. Penberthy c Roberts b Dean	71			
D. J. Sales run out	36	1/8 2/20 3/48	(38.2 overs)	254
T. C. Walton c DeFreitas b Clarke	23	4/115 5/179 6/205		
J. N. Snape c Dean b DeFreitas	11	7/223 8/223 9/231		

Bowling: DeFreitas 8–0–48–2; Dean 8–0–45–2; Roberts 8–0–47–2; Lacey 8–0–50–1; Clarke 4.2–0–33–2; Barnett 2–0–19–0.

Umpires: J. C. Balderstone and J. W. Lloyds.

At Nottingham, August 2. NORTHAMPTONSHIRE beat NOTTINGHAMSHIRE by five wickets.

NORTHAMPTONSHIRE v WARWICKSHIRE

At Northampton, August 23. No result (abandoned).

NORTHAMPTONSHIRE v KENT

At Northampton, August 30. Kent won by seven wickets. Toss: Northamptonshire.

The official opening of the County Ground's new indoor school on the old football pitch was a proud moment for Northamptonshire. On the field, their players continued their wretched form. Hooper carried Kent past their modest total with three sixes in an over from Bailey. Overall, he hit five sixes in an unbeaten 65. Earlier, Hooper had found considerable turn with his off-breaks, giving the home batsmen no chance to recover from a languid start.

Northamptonshire

M. B. Loye c Ward b Hooper	27	J. N. Snape c Headley b Patel 23
R. J. Bailey c Hooper b Headley	4	K. J. Innes not out 0
A. L. Penberthy b Phillips	8	L-b 9, w 6, n-b 2 17
D. J. Sales c Ward b Hooper	31	
*K. M. Curran c Marsh b Llong	34	1/9 2/24 3/62 (6 wkts, 40 overs) 168
T. C. Walton not out	24	4/101 5/128 6/160

†D. Ripley, J. P. Taylor and D. Follett did not bat.

Bowling: Headley 7–0–23–1; Phillips 8–1–24–1; Patel 5–0–32–1; Hooper 8–1–19–2; Fleming 5–1–18–0; House 2–0–11–0; Llong 5–0–32–1.

Kent

T. R. Ward b Taylor	15	M. J. Walker not out	30
E. T. Smith b Snape	26	L-b 4, w 4	8
M. V. Fleming c Taylor b Snape	28	
C. L. Hooper not out	65	1/27 2/71 3/75 (3 wkts, 36.4 overs) 172

N. J. Llong, W. J. House, *†S. A. Marsh, B. J. Phillips, D. W. Headley and M. M. Patel did not bat.

Bowling: Follett 7.4–2–31–0; Taylor 6–0–24–1; Curran 3–0–17–0; Snape 8–0–21–2; Penberthy 8–0–35–0; Bailey 4–0–40–0.

Umpires: J. H. Harris and P. Willey.

NORTHAMPTONSHIRE v SUSSEX

At Northampton, September 13. Northamptonshire won by 89 runs. Toss: Sussex.

With only the slightest mathematical chance of either side creeping into the top half of the League, the match lacked edge. After soggy run-ups delayed the start, Northamptonshire set Sussex a target of 182. They quickly collapsed to 30 for four and faded away. The match did produce the League's leading individuals: Loye secured his position as top run-scorer with 650, and Kirtley was leading wicket-taker with 25. Curran passed 5,000 runs in the competition.

Northamptonshire

M. B. Loye c Carpenter b Rao	35	J. N. Snape not out	10
A. L. Penberthy c Martin-Jenkins		G. P. Swann not out	10
b Robinson	17	
*K. M. Curran c Edwards b Bates	42	B 5, l-b 6, w 11	22
D. J. Sales c Bates b Edwards	9	
R. J. Bailey c Robinson b Bates	26	1/51 2/73 3/111 (6 wkts, 36 overs) 181
T. C. Walton c Carpenter b Kirtley	10	4/129 5/144 6/167

†D. Ripley, F. A. Rose and J. P. Taylor did not bat.

Bowling: Kirtley 7–0–30–1; Edwards 7–0–29–1; Robinson 8–1–15–1; Newell 3–0–17–0; Rao 3–0–22–1; Bates 6–0–42–2; Adams 2–0–15–0.

Sussex

R. K. Rao c Penberthy b Rose	3	J. J. Bates not out	2
R. S. C. Martin-Jenkins c Snape		R. J. Kirtley c Loye b Swann	0
b Penberthy	8	M. A. Robinson c Rose b Snape	0
*C. J. Adams c Ripley b Rose	2	
J. R. Carpenter c Snape b Penberthy	1	L-b 8, w 11, n-b 6	25
K. Newell run out	0	
M. T. E. Peirce c Taylor b Swann	29	1/9 2/15 3/22 (29.4 overs) 92
A. D. Edwards c and b Curran	0	4/30 5/59 6/67
†S. Humphries c and b Snape	5	7/90 8/91 9/92

Bowling: Rose 8–1–19–2; Taylor 5–2–6–0; Penberthy 7–0–23–2; Curran 5–0–24–1; Snape 2.4–0–7–2; Swann 2–0–5–2.

Umpires: T. E. Jesty and R. A. White.

NOTTINGHAMSHIRE

At Derby, April 21. NOTTINGHAMSHIRE beat DERBYSHIRE by two wickets.

At Taunton, April 26. NOTTINGHAMSHIRE tied with SOMERSET.

NOTTINGHAMSHIRE v DURHAM

At Nottingham, May 10. Durham won by six wickets (D/L method). Toss: Durham.

In a game shortened by rain, injury-hit Durham – spearheaded by Foster and Speight – reached a target of 135 with three balls to spare. It was their first away League win since 1995. The interruption came in the first over so that, although the Duckworth/Lewis method applied, it had a negligible effect on the outcome. But, technically, Durham had to beat 134.9 rather than 134. So had they ended on one run less, they would have lost, not tied.

Nottinghamshire

J. E. R. Gallian c Boiling b Betts	9	R. T. Bates run out	12
M. P. Dowman c Phillips b Boiling	34	K. P. Evans not out	5
*P. Johnson b Boiling	40	A. R. Oram c Speak b Betts	0
G. F. Archer c Hutton b Boiling	1	B 1, l-b 2, w 3	6
N. A. Gie lbw b Betts	5		—
A. G. Wharf lbw b Boiling	12	1/23 2/86 3/86	(20 overs) 134
P. A. Strang c Betts b Killeen	5	4/89 5/102 6/108	
†W. M. Noon b Boiling	5	7/116 8/117 9/133	

Bowling: Betts 4–0–28–3; Wood 3–0–19–0; Foster 4–0–27–0; Boiling 4–0–23–5; Killeen 4–0–21–1; Phillips 1–0–13–0.

Durham

M. J. Foster c Bates b Oram	53	J. A. Daley not out	0
M. A. Roseberry run out	8	B 2, l-b 6, w 2, n-b 8	18
†M. P. Speight c Gie b Bates	45		—
*N. J. Speak run out	1	1/15 2/116	(4 wkts, 19.3 overs) 135
S. Hutton not out	10	3/124 4/126	

N. C. Phillips, J. Boiling, M. M. Betts, N. Killeen and J. Wood did not bat.

Bowling: Oram 3–0–12–1; Evans 3.3–0–23–0; Wharf 4–0–30–0; Strang 4–0–22–0; Dowman 3–0–24–0; Bates 2–0–16–1.

Umpires: J. W. Lloyds and A. G. T. Whitehead.

NOTTINGHAMSHIRE v SUSSEX

At Nottingham, May 17. Sussex won by 28 runs. Toss: Nottinghamshire.

Adams celebrated his selection for England's one-day squad with a fine hundred and a League victory, his first in four attempts as Sussex captain. Watchful at first, he increased the tempo, ending with three straight sixes off Strang. Although they matched the scoring-rate, Nottinghamshire lost wickets too regularly to sustain a serious challenge.

Sussex

K. Newell c Strang b Evans	2	†S. Humphries not out	1
*C. J. Adams b Franks	100	J. D. Lewry not out	4
M. Newell run out	36	L-b 6, w 10	16
M. G. Bevan run out	39		
J. R. Carpenter st Noon b Archer	0	1/3 2/95 3/181 (7 wkts, 40 overs) 236	
M. T. E. Peirce run out	18	4/182 5/203	
A. D. Edwards c Archer b Evans	20	6/228 7/230	

R. J. Kirtley and M. A. Robinson did not bat.

Bowling: Franks 8–0–41–1; Evans 8–0–57–2; Dowman 8–0–32–0; Tolley 8–0–38–0; Strang 5–0–44–0; Archer 3–0–18–1.

Nottinghamshire

P. R. Pollard c Adams b Kirtley	5	P. J. Franks b Lewry	0
M. P. Dowman c Bevan b Kirtley	14	K. P. Evans not out	23
*P. Johnson c Adams b Edwards	38	R. T. Bates lbw b Robinson	2
G. F. Archer b Edwards	29	B 1, l-b 7, w 10, n-b 4	22
N. A. Gie run out	4		
C. M. Tolley b Robinson	44	1/14 2/42 3/79 (36.1 overs) 208	
P. A. Strang b Edwards	10	4/100 5/116 6/129	
†W. M. Noon lbw b Lewry	17	7/159 8/159 9/199	

Bowling: Lewry 7–0–51–2; Kirtley 6–1–26–2; Robinson 7.1–0–43–2; Edwards 8–0–34–3; K. Newell 8–0–46–0.

Umpires: V. A. Holder and R. Palmer.

NOTTINGHAMSHIRE v GLOUCESTERSHIRE

At Nottingham, May 19. Gloucestershire won by one run. Toss: Gloucestershire. County debut: G. I. Macmillan.

Gloucestershire won a tense match after Nottinghamshire needed 11 off the last over, bowled by Lewis, and four off the last ball. Franks raced through for two but was run out by Hancock attempting a third. Hancock had pulled round the Gloucestershire innings after half the side were out for 58. He scored 73 in 72 balls; thanks mainly to him and Russell, the score was more than doubled in the last ten overs. It was Nottinghamshire's third home defeat in the League in ten days.

Gloucestershire

G. I. Macmillan c Gie b Evans	16	M. C. J. Ball not out	10
R. I. Dawson c Noon b Tolley	17	C. A. Walsh not out	1
*M. W. Alleyne c Dowman b Evans	4		
A. J. Wright b Strang	5	L-b 9, w 1	10
M. J. Church b Bates	8		
†R. C. Russell c Tolley b Franks	40	1/29 2/43 3/44 (8 wkts, 40 overs) 185	
T. H. C. Hancock run out	73	4/56 5/58 6/156	
J. Lewis b Franks	1	7/168 8/183	

J. M. M. Averis did not bat.

Bowling: Franks 8–0–36–2; Evans 8–2–31–2; Tolley 8–0–37–1; Strang 8–1–41–1; Bates 8–0–31–1.

Nottinghamshire

M. P. Dowman c Wright b Alleyne	25	P. J. Franks run out		15
P. R. Pollard c Russell b Walsh	0	K. P. Evans not out		4
*P. Johnson c Macmillan b Alleyne	23			
G. F. Archer run out	26	L-b 8, w 8, n-b 4		20
N. A. Gie run out	57			
C. M. Tolley c Russell b Averis	0	1/1 2/50 3/57	(9 wkts, 40 overs)	184
†W. M. Noon lbw b Averis	4	4/109 5/109 6/115		
P. A. Strang b Walsh	10	7/150 8/177 9/184		

R. T. Bates did not bat.

Bowling: Walsh 8–1–26–2; Lewis 8–2–31–0; Alleyne 8–0–37–2; Averis 8–1–33–2; Macmillan 3–0–18–0; Hancock 5–0–31–0.

Umpires: T. E. Jesty and G. Sharp.

At Birmingham, May 25. NOTTINGHAMSHIRE beat WARWICKSHIRE by seven wickets (D/L method).

At Canterbury, June 21. NOTTINGHAMSHIRE beat KENT by nine wickets.

NOTTINGHAMSHIRE v MIDDLESEX

At Nottingham, July 5. Middlesex won by 24 runs. Toss: Nottinghamshire.

Batsmen struggled on a slow, low pitch. For Middlesex, only Shah looked able to score without grafting. Dowman also rose above the conditions, but the spinners finally stole back the initiative.

Middlesex

*†K. R. Brown c Read b Tolley	34	K. P. Dutch not out		16
J. L. Langer c Strang b Bates	34	B 1, l-b 15, w 6		22
O. A. Shah c Tolley b Strang	42			
P. N. Weekes c Archer b Evans	18	1/63 2/98	(4 wkts, 40 overs)	173
J. C. Pooley not out	7	3/138 4/150		

A. G. J. Fraser, D. C. Nash, J. P. Hewitt, R. L. Johnson and T. F. Bloomfield did not bat.

Bowling: Franks 8–0–29–0; Evans 8–0–31–1; Tolley 8–0–29–1; Bates 8–0–35–1; Strang 8–1–33–1.

Nottinghamshire

M. P. Dowman b Weekes	55	P. A. Strang not out		10
J. E. R. Gallian b Johnson	3	K. P. Evans c and b Bloomfield		10
*P. Johnson c Langer b Johnson	0	R. T. Bates lbw b Weekes		1
G. F. Archer c and b Fraser	28	B 1, l-b 5, w 5, n-b 6		17
N. A. Gie run out	1			
C. M. Tolley lbw b Dutch	7	1/22 2/22 3/83	(35.5 overs)	149
P. J. Franks lbw b Weekes	13	4/86 5/94 6/110		
†C. M. W. Read c Pooley b Bloomfield	4	7/123 8/125 9/144		

Bowling: Johnson 6–1–18–2; Bloomfield 8–0–38–2; Hewitt 2–0–21–0; Fraser 8–1–32–1; Dutch 6–1–17–1; Weekes 5.5–0–17–3.

Umpires: A. Clarkson and J. W. Holder.

NOTTINGHAMSHIRE v GLAMORGAN

At Nottingham, July 12. Glamorgan won by nine runs. Toss: Glamorgan.

Chasing 178 for victory, Nottinghamshire were sustained by Gallian. But the Glamorgan slow bowlers, Croft and Cosker, eventually took control on a grey, blustery day.

Glamorgan

*M. P. Maynard b Tolley	45	A. P. Davies not out		4
A. Dale c Read b Franks	0	D. A. Cosker c Read b Franks		10
P. A. Cottey c Tolley b Evans	10	S. L. Watkin not out		0
M. J. Powell lbw b Strang	27	B 2, l-b 5, w 9, n-b 2		18
R. D. B. Croft b Franks	28			
†I. Dawood c Read b Tolley	25	1/6 2/35 3/80	(9 wkts, 40 overs)	177
G. P. Butcher b Evans	4	4/95 5/132 6/155		
S. D. Thomas run out	6	7/161 8/162 9/175		

Bowling: Evans 8–0–34–2; Franks 8–2–29–3; Tolley 8–0–39–2; Bates 8–0–40–0; Strang 8–0–28–1.

Nottinghamshire

M. P. Dowman b Davies	8	†C. M. W. Read not out		1
J. E. R. Gallian run out	74	K. P. Evans not out		2
R. T. Robinson st Dawood b Cosker	25			
*P. Johnson b Croft	2	B 1, l-b 5, w 7		13
G. F. Archer c Thomas b Cosker	11			
C. M. Tolley c Powell b Thomas	21	1/14 2/63 3/66	(8 wkts, 40 overs)	168
P. A. Strang c Maynard b Watkin	7	4/93 5/130 6/150		
P. J. Franks run out	4	7/161 8/164		

R. T. Bates did not bat.

Bowling: Davies 8–1–33–1; Watkin 8–0–33–1; Thomas 8–0–48–1; Croft 8–1–25–1; Cosker 8–0–23–2.

Umpires: J. H. Harris and R. A. White.

At Scarborough, July 19. NOTTINGHAMSHIRE beat YORKSHIRE by four runs (D/L method).

At Portsmouth, July 26. NOTTINGHAMSHIRE beat HAMPSHIRE by 30 runs.

NOTTINGHAMSHIRE v NORTHAMPTONSHIRE

At Nottingham, August 2. Northamptonshire won by five wickets. Toss: Northamptonshire.

Nottinghamshire, undefeated away, slid passively to their sixth home League defeat of the season on another slow pitch. Northamptonshire settled in with an opening stand of 74, and won comfortably.

Nottinghamshire

*J. E. R. Gallian c Warren b Taylor	12	K. P. Evans not out		20
U. Afzaal run out	12	R. T. Bates not out		1
P. Johnson c Penberthy b Snape	31			
M. P. Dowman b Taylor	8	B 6, l-b 6, w 2, n-b 2		16
G. F. Archer c Curran b Penberthy	13			
C. M. Tolley b Follett	18	1/27 2/27 3/47	(8 wkts, 40 overs)	154
P. A. Strang c Snape b Rose	4	4/80 5/92 6/107		
†C. M. W. Read c Taylor b Follett	19	7/115 8/150		

A. R. Oram did not bat.

Bowling: Follett 8–0–32–2; Rose 8–0–24–1; Taylor 8–1–34–2; Penberthy 8–0–32–1; Snape 8–1–20–1.

Northamptonshire

M. B. Loye c and b Bates	43	J. N. Snape not out	4
R. J. Bailey c Tolley b Bates	32		
*K. M. Curran c Bates b Oram	23	L-b 7, w 4, n-b 6	17
A. L. Penberthy not out	15		—
D. J. Sales b Tolley	18	1/74 2/106 3/110 (5 wkts, 37.2 overs) 155	
T. C. Walton c Oram b Tolley	3	4/142 5/149	

†R. J. Warren, J. P. Taylor, D. Follett and F. A. Rose did not bat.

Bowling: Evans 7–1–16–0; Oram 6.2–0–40–1; Tolley 8–0–26–2; Strang 8–1–28–0; Bates 8–0–38–2.

Umpires: V. A. Holder and A. A. Jones.

At Worcester, August 9. NOTTINGHAMSHIRE lost to WORCESTERSHIRE by seven wickets.

NOTTINGHAMSHIRE v SURREY

At Nottingham, August 23. No result (abandoned).

NOTTINGHAMSHIRE v LEICESTERSHIRE

At Nottingham, August 30. Nottinghamshire won by four runs. Toss: Leicestershire.

Nottinghamshire ended their run of League failures at Trent Bridge in a tight finish. Leicestershire needed 11 off the final over but fell short once Lewis was run out. Lewis was back in the side after being dropped for the Championship match at Worksop for disciplinary reasons, but Simmons was preferred as captain. Although Lewis had one of his good days in all departments on the field, Leicestershire could never quite claw back the advantage after Oram took a wicket in each of his first three overs. Before the game, a minute's silence was observed in honour of Alan Wheelhouse, the Nottinghamshire chairman, who had died two days earlier.

Nottinghamshire

*J. E. R. Gallian c Habib b Mullally	6	K. P. Evans not out	10
P. R. Pollard c Nixon b Mullally	11	R. T. Bates not out	4
P. Johnson c Lewis b Williamson	74		
G. F. Archer c Lewis b Simmons	17	B 2, l-b 10, w 9, n-b 4	25
M. P. Dowman c Maddy b Williamson	30		—
C. M. Tolley b Mullally	32	1/10 2/31 3/70 (8 wkts, 40 overs) 225	
P. A. Strang c Mason b Lewis	8	4/154 5/167 6/199	
†C. M. W. Read run out	8	7/201 8/217	

A. R. Oram did not bat.

Bowling: Mullally 8–0–32–3; Lewis 8–2–31–1; Simmons 7–0–45–1; Wells 6–1–25–0; Williamson 6–0–42–2; Mason 5–0–38–0.

Leicestershire

V. J. Wells lbw b Oram	1	D. Williamson c Read b Evans	12
J. M. Dakin c Archer b Oram	2	A. D. Mullally not out	3
A. Habib lbw b Dowman	71	T. J. Mason not out	2
B. F. Smith c Strang b Oram	4	B 3, l-b 3, w 5, n-b 4	15
*P. V. Simmons c Strang b Bates	45		—
D. L. Maddy c Oram b Strang	29	1/1 2/10 3/14 (9 wkts, 40 overs) 221	
†P. A. Nixon b Strang	3	4/96 5/151 6/158	
C. C. Lewis run out	34	7/171 8/213 9/216	

Bowling: Evans 8–0–46–1; Oram 8–0–44–3; Tolley 4–0–26–0; Bates 8–0–31–1; Strang 8–0–42–2; Dowman 4–0–26–1.

Umpires: M. J. Kitchen and J. F. Steele.

At Chelmsford, September 6. NOTTINGHAMSHIRE beat ESSEX by 51 runs.

NOTTINGHAMSHIRE v LANCASHIRE

At Nottingham, September 9 (day/night). Lancashire won by 52 runs. Toss: Lancashire.

With Nottinghamshire still striving for a place in the top division of the National League and Lancashire already champions, some home supporters thought the opposition might be interested in a quiet night. Instead, Lancashire rubbed home their superiority in ferocious style. They were led by Flintoff, who clubbed 93 off 55 balls with three sixes and 11 fours. Nottinghamshire's sluggishness meant they were docked two overs, so they needed to score more than nine an over. A miserly spell from Martin closed the door, despite a run-a-ball fifty from Johnson. Floodlit cricket at Trent Bridge had got off to a difficult start: rain delayed play until 7 p.m., while high winds prevented the lights being raised to their full height.

Lancashire

*J. P. Crawley b Oram	....	28
M. Watkinson b Evans	....	56
A. Flintoff not out	....	93
G. D. Lloyd not out	....	22
L-b 5, w 5, n-b 12	....	22

1/54 2/146   (2 wkts, 26 overs) 221

M. J. Chilton, N. H. Fairbrother, †W. K. Hegg, I. D. Austin, G. Chapple, G. Yates and P. J. Martin did not bat.

Bowling: Evans 5–0–31–1; Franks 6–0–44–0; Oram 5–0–50–1; Tolley 4–0–40–0; Bates 2–0–26–0; Dowman 4–0–25–0.

Nottinghamshire

*J. E. R. Gallian b Martin	....	3	C. M. Tolley not out	....	30
P. R. Pollard c Martin b Chapple	.....	25	L-b 1, w 12	....	13
P. Johnson not out	....	51			
G. F. Archer c Hegg b Chapple	....	10	1/16 2/43	(4 wkts, 24 overs)	169
M. P. Dowman c Crawley b Flintoff	...	37	3/68 4/122		

†C. M. W. Read, P. J. Franks, K. P. Evans, R. T. Bates and A. R. Oram did not bat.

Bowling: Martin 5–0–17–1; Austin 6–0–38–0; Flintoff 5–0–37–1; Chapple 5–0–45–2; Chilton 2–0–25–0; Yates 1–0–6–0.

Umpires: M. J. Harris and N. T. Plews.

SOMERSET

At Leeds, April 19. SOMERSET lost to YORKSHIRE by 38 runs (D/L method).

SOMERSET v NOTTINGHAMSHIRE

At Taunton, April 26. Tied. Toss: Somerset.

Chasing Nottinghamshire's modest 181, which depended largely on Gallian's 49, Somerset looked out of the hunt at 74 for five with more than half their overs gone. But, when Parsons joined Turner, they hammered 67 from seven overs to restore the run-rate to manageable proportions. Twelve were still wanted from the last over and three from the final ball: Trescothick squeezed it for two before Pierson was run out, leaving the match tied.

Nottinghamshire

M. P. Dowman c Burns b Caddick	....	16	P. J. Franks run out	6
J. E. R. Gallian c and b Pierson	......	49	R. T. Bates c and b Caddick	 3
*P. Johnson c Turner b Trescothick	....	9	M. N. Bowen not out	0
G. F. Archer b Caddick	....	3	L-b 7, w 6, n-b 4	17
N. A. Gie b Burns	....	31		
A. G. Wharf c Trescothick b Pierson	...	1	1/26 2/39 3/52 (38 overs)	181
P. A. Strang run out	....	35	4/110 5/116 6/129	
†W. M. Noon c Pierson b Rose	....	11	7/161 8/169 9/181	

Bowling: Rose 8–0–39–1; Parsons 4–1–4–0; Caddick 8–0–39–3; Trescothick 7–0–34–1; Pierson 7–0–32–2; Burns 4–0–26–1.

Somerset

M. Burns c Noon b Wharf	....	17	M. E. Trescothick not out	 2
P. C. L. Holloway c Noon b Bowen	...	1	A. R. K. Pierson run out	 8
R. J. Harden c Dowman b Franks	....	16		
S. C. Ecclestone c Noon b Gallian	....	23	L-b 6, w 6, n-b 2	14
*P. D. Bowler lbw b Wharf	....	0		
†R. J. Turner c Johnson b Franks	....	60	1/5 2/36 3/45 (9 wkts, 38 overs)	181
K. A. Parsons c Noon b Strang	......	35	4/45 5/74 6/141	
G. D. Rose c Strang b Wharf	....	5	7/160 8/170 9/181	

A. R. Caddick did not bat.

Bowling: Franks 6–0–32–2; Bowen 8–0–38–1; Wharf 7–0–26–3; Strang 8–0–30–1; Bates 5–0–25–0; Gallian 4–0–24–1.

Umpires: T. E. Jesty and M. J. Kitchen.

At Cardiff, May 10. SOMERSET beat GLAMORGAN by eight wickets.

At Lord's, May 17. SOMERSET lost to MIDDLESEX by one run.

SOMERSET v NORTHAMPTONSHIRE

At Taunton, May 19. Northamptonshire won by seven wickets. Toss: Somerset.

Northamptonshire won with four balls to spare, thanks to 79 in 67 balls from Penberthy. Batsmen had the edge throughout, except when Franklyn Rose was bowling. He kept the Somerset score within bounds and gave his batsmen their chance.

Somerset

M. Burns b Capel	....	33	K. A. Parsons c Swann b Rose	 2
P. C. L. Holloway b Swann	....	77	M. E. Trescothick not out	 7
G. D. Rose c Capel b Snape	....	36	B 5, l-b 6, w 7	18
Mushtaq Ahmed c Bailey b Snape	....	10		
M. N. Lathwell c Snape b Taylor	.....	42	1/70 2/137 3/152 (7 wkts, 40 overs)	246
*P. D. Bowler c Warren b Rose	......	14	4/187 5/222	
†R. J. Turner not out	....	7	6/229 7/231	

A. R. Caddick and P. S. Jones did not bat.

Bowling: Rose 8–1–25–2; Penberthy 7–1–44–0; Swann 5–0–42–1; Capel 6–0–28–1; Taylor 8–0–59–1; Snape 6–0–37–2.

Northamptonshire

M. B. Loye c Turner b Trescothick	36		D. J. Sales not out	26
†R. J. Warren run out	27		B 1, l-b 6, w 11, n-b 4	22
*K. M. Curran b Trescothick	59			
A. L. Penberthy not out	79		1/62 2/86 3/210 (3 wkts, 39.2 overs)	249

R. J. Bailey, D. J. Capel, G. P. Swann, J. N. Snape, J. P. Taylor and F. A. Rose did not bat.

Bowling: Parsons 3–1–14–0; Rose 7.2–0–63–0; Caddick 8–0–35–0; Trescothick 8–0–44–2; Mushtaq Ahmed 8–0–56–0; Jones 5–0–30–0.

Umpires: M. J. Harris and R. Palmer.

SOMERSET v SURREY

At Taunton, May 25. Somerset won by seven wickets. Toss: Somerset.
    Asked to bat on a lively pitch, Surrey could not cope with an all-seam attack well led by Caddick: they were 79 for eight before Ward and Salisbury put on 42. Lathwell, going for his shots, was soon in command, and Somerset won without fuss inside 30 overs.

Surrey

M. A. Butcher c Trescothick b Caddick	4		M. P. Bicknell c Lathwell b Parsons	1
A. D. Brown c Parsons b Rose	13		I. D. K. Salisbury c Lathwell b Jones	33
J. D. Ratcliffe lbw b Trescothick	4		J. E. Benjamin b Jones	5
N. Shahid b Caddick	3		L-b 5, w 2	7
*A. J. Hollioake c Burns b Rose	8			
I. J. Ward not out	45		1/14 2/22 3/28 (38.1 overs)	127
B. C. Hollioake b Trescothick	1		4/28 5/46 6/47	
†J. N. Batty lbw b Jones	3		7/78 8/79 9/121	

Bowling: Caddick 8–1–21–2; Rose 8–0–25–2; Trescothick 7–2–14–2; Parsons 8–2–46–1; Jones 7.1–2–16–3.

Somerset

M. Burns c Brown b Bicknell	0		*P. D. Bowler not out	20
P. C. L. Holloway lbw b Ratcliffe	28		L-b 1, w 9, n-b 2	12
G. D. Rose run out	6			
M. N. Lathwell not out	64		1/0 2/22 3/86 (3 wkts, 29.5 overs)	130

†R. J. Turner, K. A. Parsons, M. E. Trescothick, P. S. Jones, Mushtaq Ahmed and A. R. Caddick did not bat.

Bowling: Bicknell 8–2–26–1; Benjamin 5–2–20–0; A. J. Hollioake 3–0–17–0; B. C. Hollioake 4–0–22–0; Ratcliffe 4–2–9–1; Salisbury 4.5–1–31–0; Shahid 1–0–4–0.

Umpires: J. W. Holder and V. A. Holder.

SOMERSET v WARWICKSHIRE

At Taunton, May 31. Somerset won by four wickets. Toss: Somerset.
    Warwickshire captain Lara arrived back from a business trip to Trinidad too late to be included in the team; the county subsequently fined him £2,000. He said he had lost his mobile phone. The team's performance backed up rumours of internal ructions: they were shot out for 96. On a pitch encouraging movement, the Somerset seamers proved almost unplayable, with Jones taking five for one in 19 balls. But, though conditions eased, their own batsmen got themselves out until Parsons steadied the ship.

Warwickshire

*N. V. Knight c Turner b Jones	13	M. A. Sheikh b Jones		0
N. M. K. Smith b Caddick	6	G. C. Small c Trescothick b Caddick		20
D. L. Hemp b Caddick	3	E. S. H. Giddins not out		0
D. P. Ostler c Turner b Jones	3	L-b 6, w 10, n-b 4		20
T. L. Penney lbw b Rose	0			—
D. R. Brown c Turner b Jones	9	1/13 2/25 3/37	(35 overs)	96
A. F. Giles c Parsons b Jones	1	4/40 5/40 6/48		
†K. J. Piper b Mushtaq Ahmed	21	7/51 8/51 9/92		

Bowling: Rose 8–3–15–1; Caddick 8–1–24–3; Jones 8–2–23–5; Trescothick 5–1–12–0; Mushtaq Ahmed 6–1–16–1.

Somerset

M. Burns b Giddins	0	K. A. Parsons not out		18
P. C. L. Holloway c Ostler b Smith	25	Mushtaq Ahmed not out		6
G. D. Rose c Ostler b Sheikh	9	L-b 2, w 7		9
M. N. Lathwell b Piper b Sheikh	11			—
*S. C. Ecclestone c Ostler b Smith	15	1/0 2/29 3/41	(6 wkts, 32.3 overs)	97
†R. J. Turner lbw b Giles	4	4/64 5/69 6/87		

M. E. Trescothick, P. S. Jones and A. R. Caddick did not bat.

Bowling: Giddins 8–0–23–1; Brown 8–3–16–0; Small 3–0–15–0; Sheikh 6–1–21–2; Smith 3–1–8–2; Giles 4.3–1–12–1.

Umpires: J. C. Balderstone and J. F. Steele.

At Manchester, June 14. SOMERSET lost to LANCASHIRE by six wickets.

SOMERSET v ESSEX

At Bath, June 21. Somerset won by seven wickets (D/L method). Toss: Somerset.

Somerset, already nicely placed for victory at 89 for one, returned to chase a simple 34 from six overs, as rain and Duckworth/Lewis reduced their overall target to 123. They stuttered briefly, but won with seven balls to spare. Earlier, Stuart Law had exchanged angry words with the bowler, Rose, and some spectators, after being given out caught behind.

Essex

D. D. J. Robinson c Holloway b Rose	1	M. C. Ilott not out		9
S. G. Law c Turner b Rose	21	P. M. Such run out		0
*P. J. Prichard c Parsons b Jones	60			
R. C. Irani lbw b Caddick	22	L-b 6, w 12, n-b 2		20
A. P. Grayson lbw b Caddick	0			—
S. D. Peters lbw b Trescothick	2	1/4 2/37 3/81	(9 wkts, 40 overs)	209
D. R. Law lbw b Jones	38	4/81 5/84 6/162		
†R. J. Rollins c Jones b Caddick	36	7/163 8/209 9/209		

D. M. Cousins did not bat.

Bowling: Rose 8–2–33–2; Caddick 7–0–38–3; Jones 8–0–35–2; Trescothick 8–0–47–1; Mushtaq Ahmed 2–0–18–0; Parsons 7–0–32–0.

Somerset

M. Burns c Robinson b Such	53	R. J. Harden not out	1
P. C. L. Holloway c Such b Ilott	8	B 1, l-b 3, w 7	11
†R. J. Turner c Robinson b Grayson	43		—
M. N. Lathwell not out	10	1/15 2/108 3/115 (3 wkts, 23.5 overs)	126

G. D. Rose, *Mushtaq Ahmed, K. A. Parsons, M. E. Trescothick, A. R. Caddick and P. S. Jones did not bat.

Bowling: Ilott 5–0–24–1; Cousins 5–0–23–0; Grayson 4.5–0–31–1; Irani 5–1–15–0; S. G. Law 2–0–12–0; Such 2–0–17–1.

Umpires: M. J. Harris and A. G. T. Whitehead.

At Hove, July 5. SOMERSET beat SUSSEX by two wickets.

SOMERSET v HAMPSHIRE

At Taunton, July 19. Somerset won by three wickets. Toss: Hampshire.

Although Hampshire's openers shared a stand of 90, the introduction of Mushtaq Ahmed's taxing leg-spin stifled the innings. He took three for 18, and Stephenson became becalmed on his way to an undefeated 77. Replying, Somerset slipped to 42 for four, but resolute fifties from Bowler and Parsons enabled Mushtaq to hit the winning boundary with two balls to spare.

Hampshire

L. Savident lbw b Mushtaq Ahmed	39	N. A. M. McLean c Bowler b Jones	1
J. P. Stephenson not out	77	P. R. Whitaker not out	12
G. W. White st Burns b Mushtaq Ahmed	0	L-b 8, w 6, n-b 2	16
†A. N. Aymes run out	12		—
W. S. Kendall lbw b Mushtaq Ahmed	5	1/90 2/92 3/115 (6 wkts, 40 overs)	178
A. D. Mascarenhas c Jones b Parsons	16	4/125 5/144 6/152	

*S. D. Udal, P. J. Hartley and C. A. Connor did not bat.

Bowling: Rose 4–0–19–0; Caddick 8–1–53–0; Trescothick 5–0–26–0; Jones 8–2–25–1; Mushtaq Ahmed 8–2–18–3; Parsons 7–0–29–1.

Somerset

†M. Burns lbw b McLean	0	G. D. Rose not out	9
P. C. L. Holloway c White b McLean	5	Mushtaq Ahmed not out	10
R. J. Harden b Connor	7	B 1, l-b 5, w 8, n-b 4	18
M. N. Lathwell c Aymes b Connor	17		—
*P. D. Bowler run out	50	1/0 2/11 3/37 (7 wkts, 39.4 overs)	181
K. A. Parsons c Mascarenhas b Udal	55	4/42 5/137	
M. E. Trescothick b Hartley	10	6/151 7/164	

A. R. Caddick and P. S. Jones did not bat.

Bowling: McLean 7–0–39–2; Connor 8–3–16–2; Hartley 7.4–0–35–1; Udal 8–0–32–1; Stephenson 4–0–26–0; Mascarenhas 5–0–27–0.

Umpires: D. J. Constant and A. A. Jones.

SOMERSET v DURHAM

At Taunton, July 26. Durham won by six runs. Toss: Somerset.

Phillips tilted a fluctuating match Durham's way by taking four wickets just as Somerset seemed well placed. He dismissed Holloway and Bowler, the two top scorers, and opened the door for Wood to finish off the tail in the final over. When Durham had batted, Speak, chastened after running out Boon, crafted an unbeaten 90.

Durham

J. E. Morris c Parsons b Caddick	1	M. J. Foster run out	21
*D. C. Boon run out.	33	L-b 7, w 10, n-b 4	21
N. J. Speak not out.	90		
†M. P. Speight c Burns b Rose.	4	1/2 2/49 3/66 (5 wkts, 40 overs) 218
P. D. Collingwood b Mushtaq Ahmed . .	48	4/178 5/218

J. J. B. Lewis, N. C. Phillips, M. J. Saggers, J. Wood and S. J. Harmison did not bat.

Bowling: Rose 8–1–28–1; Caddick 8–1–56–1; Jones 8–0–35–0; Trescothick 4–0–15–0; Mushtaq Ahmed 8–0–55–1; Parsons 4–0–22–0.

Somerset

†M. Burns c Speight b Saggers.	31	G. D. Rose not out.	9
P. C. L. Holloway st Speight b Phillips .	52	A. R. Caddick lbw b Wood	2
R. J. Harden b Saggers	3	P. S. Jones b Wood.	0
M. N. Lathwell b Saggers	5	L-b 6, w 5.	11
*P. D. Bowler c Saggers b Phillips	44		
Mushtaq Ahmed b Foster.	41	1/46 2/58 3/64 (39.3 overs) 212
K. A. Parsons c Collingwood b Phillips .	0	4/122 5/185 6/185
M. E. Trescothick st Speight b Phillips. .	14	7/185 8/203 9/212

Bowling: Wood 7.3–0–42–2; Harmison 8–2–32–0; Saggers 8–0–35–3; Foster 7–0–32–1; Collingwood 5–0–41–0; Phillips 4–0–24–4.

Umpires: J. H. Harris and B. Leadbeater.

At Leicester, August 9. SOMERSET lost to LEICESTERSHIRE by five runs.

SOMERSET v DERBYSHIRE

At Taunton, August 23. No result (abandoned).

At Bristol, August 25. SOMERSET lost to GLOUCESTERSHIRE by ten wickets (D/L method).

SOMERSET v WORCESTERSHIRE

At Taunton, September 6. No result. Toss: Somerset.
Rain ended play after 19 overs with Somerset in some difficulties at 77 for four.

Somerset

M. Burns b Sheriyar.	8	†R. J. Turner not out	7
M. N. Lathwell st Rhodes b Illingworth .	22	L-b 2, w 6.	8
M. E. Trescothick c Rhodes b Haynes . .	8		
*P. D. Bowler c Catterall b Illingworth. .	11	1/14 2/25 (4 wkts, 19 overs) 77
K. A. Parsons not out	13	3/55 4/58

J. I. D. Kerr, G. D. Rose, A. R. K. Pierson, A. R. Caddick and P. S. Jones did not bat.

Bowling: Sheriyar 3–0–23–1; Haynes 4–2–12–1; Lampitt 5–0–21–0; Illingworth 5–1–10–2; Rawnsley 2–0–9–0.

Worcestershire

W. P. C. Weston, V. S. Solanki, *G. A. Hick, D. A. Leatherdale, †S. J. Rhodes, G. R. Haynes, R. K. Illingworth, S. R. Lampitt, D. N. Catterall, M. J. Rawnsley and A. Sheriyar.

Umpires: J. H. Harris and J. W. Holder.

At Canterbury, September 13. SOMERSET lost to KENT by six wickets (D/L method).

SURREY

SURREY v NORTHAMPTONSHIRE

At The Oval, April 19. No result. Toss: Surrey.

Before the rain intervened, positive play from Loye put pressure on Surrey. He hit 79 from 93 balls until Butcher bowled him with his first delivery.

Northamptonshire

M. B. Loye b Butcher	79	R. J. Bailey not out		13
R. R. Montgomerie lbw b Benjamin	12	A. L. Penberthy not out		2
*K. M. Curran c Thorp		B 4, l-b 4, w 9		17
b B. C. Hollioake	13			
D. J. Capel c Butcher b B. C. Hollioake	0	1/48 2/66 3/66	(5 wkts, 34 overs)	162
D. J. Sales c B. C. Hollioake b Bicknell	26	4/137 5/147		

J. N. Snape, †D. Ripley, J. P. Taylor and G. P. Swann did not bat.

Bowling: Bicknell 8–0–23–1; Benjamin 8–2–17–1; B. C. Hollioake 6–0–28–2; Salisbury 8–0–53–0; A. J. Hollioake 3–0–30–0; Butcher 1–0–3–1.

Surrey

A. D. Brown, M. A. Butcher, N. Shahid, G. P. Thorpe, *A. J. Hollioake, B. C. Hollioake, J. D. Ratcliffe, †J. N. Batty, I. D. K. Salisbury, M. P. Bicknell and J. E. Benjamin.

Umpires: G. I. Burgess and B. Dudleston.

SURREY v WARWICKSHIRE

At The Oval, April 26. Warwickshire won by eight wickets. Toss: Warwickshire.

Smith launched Warwickshire to a comfortable win in a match reduced to a ten-over slog by heavy morning rain. He bludgeoned 48 from 31 balls, scoring all but 11 of an opening stand of 59 with Knight, and his side won with five balls to spare. Surrey had found piercing the field more difficult; Giles's two overs cost only six runs.

Surrey

A. D. Brown b Brown	10	M. A. Butcher not out		1
G. P. Thorpe c Hemp b Brown	4			
†A. J. Stewart c Brown b Giles	17	L-b 4, w 2, n-b 6		12
*A. J. Hollioake b Smith	2			
B. C. Hollioake run out	24	1/13 2/20 3/28	(5 wkts, 10 overs)	81
N. Shahid not out	11	4/53 5/75		

J. D. Ratcliffe, M. P. Bicknell, I. D. K. Salisbury and J. E. Benjamin did not bat.

Bowling: Brown 2–0–16–2; Smith 2–0–11–1; Small 2–0–17–0; Welch 2–0–27–0; Giles 2–0–6–1.

Warwickshire

N. V. Knight not out	25
N. M. K. Smith st Stewart b Salisbury	48
*B. C. Lara c Butcher b B. C. Hollioake	8
D. P. Ostler not out	0
W 1	1

1/59 2/71   (2 wkts, 9.1 overs) 82

D. L. Hemp, T. L. Penney, D. R. Brown, †K. J. Piper, G. Welch, A. F. Giles and G. C. Small did not bat.

Bowling: Bicknell 2–0–14–0; Benjamin 2–0–17–0; B. C. Hollioake 2–0–20–1; A. J. Hollioake 1–0–9–0; Salisbury 1.1–0–13–1; Butcher 1–0–9–0.

Umpires: J. C. Balderstone and D. R. Shepherd.

At Leeds, May 10. SURREY lost to YORKSHIRE by 51 runs (D/L method).

At Southampton, May 17. SURREY lost to HAMPSHIRE by 75 runs.

At Taunton, May 25. SURREY lost to SOMERSET by seven wickets.

At Chelmsford, June 14. SURREY lost to ESSEX by 26 runs (D/L method).

At Manchester, June 17. SURREY lost to LANCASHIRE by four wickets (D/L method).

SURREY v WORCESTERSHIRE

At The Oval, June 28. Worcestershire won by one run. Toss: Worcestershire.

Surrey's slow over-rate ensured their seventh successive League defeat. They lost by a solitary run, having been docked an over for failing to complete their ration in time. Bowlers had the advantage on a pitch of irregular bounce: Hick managed only one boundary in 57 runs. Ben Hollioake, named in the Test squad announced that morning, upped the tempo for Surrey, with 40 off 42 balls. There was an old-fashioned Oval feel to the whole occasion: the sound system had broken down and there was no music to accompany batsmen to the crease.

Worcestershire

*T. M. Moody c A. J. Hollioake b B. C. Hollioake	20
V. S. Solanki b Tudor	29
G. A. Hick b Benjamin	33
D. A. Leatherdale c Tudor b Saqlain Mushtaq	13
G. R. Haynes c Batty b Benjamin	12
W. P. C. Weston run out	23
S. R. Lampitt b A. J. Hollioake	9
†S. J. Rhodes st Batty b Saqlain Mushtaq	3
R. K. Illingworth b A. J. Hollioake	1
M. J. Rawnsley c Saqlain Mushtaq b A. J. Hollioake	0
R. J. Chapman not out	0
L-b 20, w 15, n-b 2	37
	—
1/48 2/68 3/109 4/135 5/136 6/170 7/175 8/180 9/180 (39.1 overs)	180

Bowling: Bicknell 6–0–26–0; Benjamin 8–0–32–2; B. C. Hollioake 8–0–30–1; Tudor 5–0–18–1; Saqlain Mushtaq 7.1–0–39–2; A. J. Hollioake 5–0–15–3.

Surrey

J. D. Ratcliffe c Solanki b Moody	42
A. D. Brown lbw b Haynes	2
G. P. Thorpe c Hick b Chapman	11
I. J. Ward c Hick b Moody	4
*A. J. Hollioake c Rhodes b Moody	1
B. C. Hollioake c Lampitt b Leatherdale	40
†J. N. Batty run out	35
M. P. Bicknell not out	30
A. J. Tudor run out	2
Saqlain Mushtaq run out	1
J. E. Benjamin not out	1
L-b 3, w 5, n-b 2	10
	—
1/9 2/38 3/46 4/52 5/95 6/111 7/164 8/175 9/178 (9 wkts, 39 overs)	179

Bowling: Haynes 8–1–31–1; Chapman 4–0–23–1; Moody 8–1–17–3; Lampitt 6–0–26–0; Illingworth 4–0–32–0; Leatherdale 6–0–32–1; Rawnsley 3–0–15–0.

Umpires: V. A. Holder and A. G. T. Whitehead.

At Swansea, July 5. SURREY lost to GLAMORGAN by 107 runs.

SURREY v LEICESTERSHIRE

At The Oval, July 13. Leicestershire won by 44 runs (D/L method). Toss: Leicestershire.

Leicestershire bounced back from their humiliation by Essex in the Benson and Hedges Cup final the previous day, to inflict a ninth successive defeat on the League's bottom team. Simmons, who scored a boisterous 114, and Smith took command with a partnership of 195 in 30 overs. Ward played boldly as Surrey pursued a rain-revised target of 256 in 38 overs, but it proved too severe a test, though they at least passed 200 at their tenth attempt.

Leicestershire

*P. V. Simmons run out	114	D. Williamson b A. J. Hollioake	1
V. J. Wells c Stewart b Benjamin	1	T. J. Mason b A. J. Hollioake	0
B. F. Smith c Stewart b Tudor	87		
D. L. Maddy c Ward b Tudor	2	L-b 11, w 6, n-b 4	21
†P. A. Nixon c Stewart b Tudor	18		
J. M. Dakin b A. J. Hollioake	0	1/11 2/206 3/212 (9 wkts, 38 overs)	252
A. Habib not out	6	4/237 5/242 6/246	
I. J. Sutcliffe b A. J. Hollioake	2	7/250 8/252 9/252	

M. T. Brimson did not bat.

Bowling: Tudor 6–0–38–3; Benjamin 8–0–38–1; B. C. Hollioake 5–0–29–0; Saqlain Mushtaq 5–0–31–0; A. J. Hollioake 7–0–49–4; Salisbury 6–1–37–0; Ward 1–0–19–0.

Surrey

I. J. Ward c Maddy b Brimson	68	A. J. Tudor c Habib b Brimson	3
A. D. Brown lbw b Simmons	22	Saqlain Mushtaq not out	9
J. D. Ratcliffe c Habib b Williamson	6	J. E. Benjamin not out	2
†A. J. Stewart c and b Mason	25	B 6, l-b 2, w 10	18
B. C. Hollioake run out	24		
*A. J. Hollioake c Nixon b Simmons	27	1/42 2/59 3/111 (9 wkts, 38 overs)	212
N. Shahid c Simmons b Williamson	8	4/147 5/165 6/190	
I. D. K. Salisbury b Brimson	0	7/192 8/194 9/205	

Bowling: Wells 8–0–52–0; Simmons 7–0–30–2; Williamson 8–0–39–2; Mason 8–0–37–1; Brimson 7–0–46–3.

Umpires: T. E. Jesty and J. F. Steele.

SURREY v MIDDLESEX

At Guildford, July 19. Surrey won by one run. Toss: Middlesex. County debut: G. J. Batty.

A festival crowd of 5,000 saw Surrey secure their first AXA League win of the season, in their 11th game, off the final ball of the match. Ward and Shahid shared a run-a-ball stand of 116 as Surrey set a target of 224. Langer responded positively but Middlesex lost their way before Dutch revived hope, with 40 off 24 balls, only to be run out trying to tie the scores.

Surrey

I. J. Ward c Brown b A. G. J. Fraser	91	G. J. Batty lbw b Langer	9
A. D. Brown c Goodchild b Johnson	10	M. A. V. Bell not out	14
N. Shahid c Weekes b Langer	58	J. E. Benjamin not out	2
B. C. Hollioake run out	4	B 1, l-b 2, w 7, n-b 6	16
*A. J. Hollioake c Shah b A. G. J. Fraser	0		
M. A. Butcher st Brown b Langer	5	1/53 2/169 3/171 (9 wkts, 40 overs)	223
J. A. Knott c Shah b Dutch	5	4/171 5/176 6/185	
†J. N. Batty lbw b Dutch	9	7/188 8/204 9/210	

Bowling: A. R. C. Fraser 5–0–30–0; Hewitt 3–1–20–0; Johnson 5–0–18–1; Dutch 8–0–37–2; A. G. J. Fraser 8–0–35–2; Weekes 3–0–29–0; Langer 8–0–51–3.

Middlesex

*†K. R. Brown c G. J. Batty b Benjamin	14	K. P. Dutch run out	40
J. L. Langer c Brown b Butcher	60	R. L. Johnson c Ward b A. J. Hollioake	11
O. A. Shah c A. J. Hollioake		J. P. Hewitt run out	0
b B. C. Hollioake	0	A. R. C. Fraser not out	0
P. N. Weekes run out	6		
D. C. Nash c J. N. Batty b Benjamin	36	L-b 18, w 14	32
A. G. J. Fraser c Butcher			
b A. J. Hollioake	14	1/43 2/44 3/57	(40 overs) 222
D. J. Goodchild c Butcher		4/139 5/151 6/165	
b A. J. Hollioake	9	7/177 8/216 9/222	

Bowling: Benjamin 8–1–29–2; B. C. Hollioake 8–0–46–1; A. J. Hollioake 8–0–35–3; G. J. Batty 6–0–30–0; Bell 6–0–39–0; Butcher 4–0–25–1.

Umpires: J. W. Lloyds and K. E. Palmer.

At Cheltenham, July 26. SURREY lost to GLOUCESTERSHIRE by 22 runs.

SURREY v SUSSEX

At The Oval, August 3 (day/night). Sussex won by eight wickets. Toss: Surrey.

Financially, Surrey had more luck with floodlit cricket than they did at the first attempt a year earlier, which was completely rained off. This time a crowd of almost 7,000 turned up on a dry if blustery night. But Surrey's horrendous form in this competition continued unabated. They struggled to 143 for eight and were then swept aside by Adams and Bevan, who put on 115 to clinch victory with more than 11 overs to spare.

Surrey

I. J. Ward c Bevan b Martin-Jenkins	20	†J. N. Batty not out	23
A. D. Brown c Martin-Jenkins		I. D. K. Salisbury b Edwards	22
b Robinson	19	M. A. V. Bell not out	11
J. D. Ratcliffe c Adams b Robinson	1	L-b 6, w 11	17
M. A. Butcher run out	3		
J. A. Knott c Humphries b K. Newell	6	1/38 2/44 3/44	(8 wkts, 40 overs) 143
N. Shahid c Humphries b Kirtley	15	4/50 5/69 6/84	
*A. J. Hollioake b K. Newell	6	7/84 8/128	

J. E. Benjamin did not bat.

Bowling: Kirtley 7–0–37–1; Martin-Jenkins 8–3–18–1; Robinson 8–2–17–2; Edwards 6–0–25–1; K. Newell 8–0–28–2; Adams 3–0–12–0.

Sussex

R. K. Rao c Salisbury b Butcher	15
R. S. C. Martin-Jenkins lbw b Benjamin	4
*C. J. Adams not out	64
M. G. Bevan not out	39
B 1, l-b 5, w 12, n-b 4	22

1/25 2/29	(2 wkts, 28.5 overs) 144	

M. Newell, J. R. Carpenter, K. Newell, A. D. Edwards, †S. Humphries, R. J. Kirtley and M. A. Robinson did not bat.

Bowling: Benjamin 8–1–29–1; Bell 7–0–39–0; Butcher 6–1–17–1; Salisbury 4–0–21–0; Hollioake 2.5–0–25–0; Knott 1–0–7–0.

Umpires: J. C. Balderstone and R. Julian.

SURREY v DERBYSHIRE

At The Oval, August 5 (day/night). Derbyshire won by 28 runs. Toss: Surrey.

Surrey's second home game under lights in three days produced the same story: a good crowd – about 9,000 – and another defeat. Derbyshire built a testing total around DeFreitas's vibrant 56, and a more circumspect 58 from Slater. Ward and Shahid set off in style but Surrey were derailed by three wickets in four balls from Roberts. Home supporters had to be content with keenly priced Pimm's and the now-traditional hog roast.

Derbyshire

M. J. Slater c Knott b Bicknell	58	V. P. Clarke not out	25
K. J. Barnett c Brown b Bicknell	0	*†K. M. Krikken not out	3
R. M. S. Weston b Hollioake	41	L-b 15, w 8, n-b 6	29
M. E. Cassar c Hollioake b G. J. Batty	7		
P. A. J. DeFreitas c Shahid b Hollioake	56		(7 wkts, 40 overs) 245
B. L. Spendlove run out	6		
I. D. Blackwell c Knott b Bell	20		

G. M. Roberts and K. J. Dean did not bat.

1/1 2/84 3/94 4/178 5/187 6/200 7/217

Bowling: Bicknell 8-0-31-2; Benjamin 8-1-47-0; G. J. Batty 8-1-47-1; Bell 8-0-59-1; Hollioake 8-0-46-2.

Surrey

I. J. Ward c Krikken b Roberts	33	G. J. Batty c Krikken b DeFreitas	37
A. D. Brown c Krikken b Dean	3	M. A. V. Bell c Spendlove b Clarke	16
N. Shahid st Krikken b Roberts	58	J. E. Benjamin not out	1
J. A. Knott b Roberts	0	B 2, l-b 3, w 6	11
J. D. Ratcliffe c and b Blackwell	2		
*A. J. Hollioake st Krikken b Blackwell	12		(39.3 overs) 217
†J. N. Batty run out	40		
M. P. Bicknell c Weston b Blackwell	4		

1/4 2/96 3/96 4/103 5/109 6/129 7/139 8/184 9/202

Bowling: DeFreitas 8-0-42-1; Dean 7-1-41-1; Clarke 4.3-0-32-1; Barnett 4-0-16-0; Roberts 8-0-34-3; Blackwell 8-0-47-3.

Umpires: M. J. Kitchen and R. Palmer.

At Nottingham, August 23. NOTTINGHAMSHIRE v SURREY. No result (abandoned).

SURREY v KENT

At The Oval, September 6. Surrey won by 41 runs. Toss: Kent. First-team debut: C. G. Greenidge.

Opponents are always likely to be intimidated if they see the name C. G. Greenidge on the scorecard at No. 11. And Surrey changed their fortunes after including Carl, son of the former West Indian opener Gordon, who produced seven overs of lively seam bowling. The key player was Hollioake; with Batty, he stabilised Surrey's innings and then took the vital wicket of Hooper on his way to figures of four for 18.

Surrey

D. J. Bicknell b Fleming	23	M. A. V. Bell b Headley	2
I. J. Ward c Marsh b Phillips	4	J. E. Benjamin not out	3
J. D. Ratcliffe c and b Hooper	24		
N. Shahid b McCague	4	L-b 13, w 11	24
A. D. Brown b Phillips	16		
*A. J. Hollioake c Hooper b McCague	32		(8 wkts, 40 overs) 183
†J. N. Batty not out	38		
I. D. K. Salisbury b Fleming	13		

1/17 2/51 3/58 4/79 5/91 6/141 7/156 8/167

C. G. Greenidge did not bat.

Bowling: Headley 8–1–25–1; Phillips 8–0–30–2; McCague 8–1–35–2; Fleming 8–0–43–2; Hooper 8–0–37–1.

Kent

T. R. Ward c Brown b Benjamin	2	M. J. McCague c and b Hollioake	13
E. T. Smith b Bell	31	B. J. Phillips run out	2
R. W. T. Key c Ratcliffe b Salisbury	15	D. W. Headley not out	0
C. L. Hooper b Hollioake	26	L-b 4, w 7, n-b 12	23
M. J. Walker c Ward b Bell	1		
N. J. Llong b Bell	15	1/12 2/38 3/68	(33.3 overs) 142
M. V. Fleming c Shahid b Hollioake	4	4/70 5/96 6/106	
*†S. A. Marsh b Hollioake	10	7/113 8/138 9/141	

Bowling: Benjamin 6–1–12–1; Greenidge 7–0–35–0; Salisbury 7–0–37–1; Bell 8–0–36–3; Hollioake 5.3–0–18–4.

Umpires: A. A. Jones and A. G. T. Whitehead.

At Chester-le-Street, September 13. SURREY beat DURHAM by 101 runs.

SUSSEX

SUSSEX v LANCASHIRE

At Hove, April 21 (day/night). Lancashire won by ten runs. Toss: Sussex. County debut: R. P. Davis.

The first of 14 day/night matches scheduled for the 1998 season was not the disaster many had predicted. Staging the match in April had looked optimistic, but a crowd of around 3,000 turned up. There were rumours that many had been given free tickets. The home side, styled the Sussex Sharks, restricted Lancashire's early efforts but were undone by a robust 62 from Flintoff. Carpenter kept Sussex in the game. The match finished at a chilly 10.35 p.m.

Lancashire

N. T. Wood c Carpenter b Davis	23	G. Yates not out	10
P. C. McKeown b Kirtley	8		
*J. P. Crawley b Martin-Jenkins	30	B 8, l-b 7, w 9, n-b 6	30
G. D. Lloyd b Robinson	7		
A. Flintoff b Martin-Jenkins	62	1/24 2/63 3/84	(6 wkts, 40 overs) 201
†W. K. Hegg lbw b Kirtley	31	4/84 5/165 6/201	

D. J. Shadford, G. Chapple, R. J. Green and P. J. Martin did not bat.

Bowling: Newell 8–1–29–0; Kirtley 8–0–41–2; Davis 8–1–28–1; Robinson 8–0–29–1; Martin-Jenkins 8–0–59–2.

Sussex

W. G. Khan lbw b Martin	0	R. P. Davis b Martin	2
*C. J. Adams c Hegg b Green	19	R. J. Kirtley not out	6
R. K. Rao run out	4	M. A. Robinson not out	3
K. Greenfield run out	48	B 2, l-b 15, w 15	32
J. R. Carpenter c Lloyd b Martin	53		
K. Newell c Hegg b Chapple	3	1/0 2/19 3/35	(9 wkts, 40 overs) 191
R. S. C. Martin-Jenkins b Chapple	21	4/114 5/118 6/175	
†P. Moores c Hegg b Martin	0	7/175 8/177 9/186	

Bowling: Martin 8–1–22–4; Chapple 8–0–33–2; Green 7–0–35–1; Shadford 5–0–29–0; Yates 8–0–34–0; Flintoff 4–0–21–0.

Umpires: M. J. Kitchen and D. R. Shepherd.

At Chelmsford, April 26. SUSSEX lost to ESSEX by 127 runs.

SUSSEX v HAMPSHIRE

At Arundel, May 3. Hampshire won by 76 runs. Toss: Sussex.

Stumbling to their fifth one-day defeat of the season, and their eighth in succession in the League (excluding one washout), Sussex's young side were no match for Hampshire. On a slow pitch, Smith's grafted 47 was enough to put the game out of Sussex's reach.

Hampshire

G. W. White c Moores b Jarvis	14	†A. N. Aymes not out	22
J. S. Laney b Robinson	18	P. J. Hartley c Moores b Lewry	10
*R. A. Smith b Edwards	47		
M. Keech b Robinson	0	B 2, l-b 15, w 19, n-b 2	38
A. D. Mascarenhas c Lewry b Edwards	21		
J. P. Stephenson lbw b Kirtley	11	1/44 2/44 3/45 (9 wkts, 40 overs)	183
S. D. Udal c Moores b Lewry	2	4/104 5/134 6/143	
K. D. James lbw b Kirtley	0	7/144 8/150 9/183	

N. A. M. McLean did not bat.

Bowling: Kirtley 8–0–21–2; Lewry 8–0–38–2; Jarvis 8–1–39–1; Robinson 8–0–37–2; Edwards 8–1–31–2.

Sussex

K. Greenfield b Hartley	21	J. D. Lewry b Mascarenhas	3
*C. J. Adams c Aymes b Hartley	14	R. J. Kirtley not out	0
M. G. Bevan b James	0	M. A. Robinson b Mascarenhas	0
J. R. Carpenter c Keech b Mascarenhas	18	L-b 11, w 11	22
K. Newell b Stephenson	5		
A. D. Edwards lbw b Stephenson	10	1/35 2/40 3/40 (32.4 overs)	107
†P. Moores run out	4	4/53 5/72 6/78	
P. W. Jarvis lbw b Udal	10	7/104 8/106 9/107	

Bowling: Hartley 6–1–10–2; McLean 3–0–25–0; James 8–2–13–1; Stephenson 6–0–22–2; Udal 5–0–14–1; Mascarenhas 4.4–0–12–3.

Umpires: H. D. Bird and B. Dudleston.

At Nottingham, May 17. SUSSEX beat NOTTINGHAMSHIRE by 28 runs.

At Worcester, May 19. SUSSEX beat WORCESTERSHIRE by 103 runs.

SUSSEX v DERBYSHIRE

At Horsham, May 25. Derbyshire won by six wickets. Toss: Derbyshire.

A broken finger, acquired on England one-day duty, spared Adams the embarrassment of this defeat by his former colleagues. Exploiting heavy conditions, Dean swung the ball late and gained an advantage Sussex could not challenge. Slater led Derbyshire to an easy win. Barnett overtook Bill Athey's 7,504 to become the League's second-highest scorer, still more than 1,000 behind Graham Gooch.

Sussex

K. Greenfield b Dean	3	J. D. Lewry run out		1
K. Newell c and b Roberts	42	R. J. Kirtley not out		15
M. Newell b Dean	3	M. A. Robinson c Cassar b DeFreitas		3
*M. G. Bevan b Dean	0	B 1, l-b 6, w 3, n-b 2		12
J. R. Carpenter c Krikken b Roberts	26			—
M. T. E. Peirce lbw b Barnett	25	1/7 2/11 3/11	(38.3 overs)	148
A. D. Edwards c Krikken b Dean	9	4/68 5/95 6/118		
†S. Humphries c Slater b Barnett	9	7/118 8/120 9/132		

Bowling: DeFreitas 6.3–0–22–1; Dean 8–1–26–4; Aldred 6–0–38–0; Cork 2–0–12–0; Roberts 8–0–20–2; Barnett 8–0–23–2.

Derbyshire

M. J. Slater b Lewry	66	*D. G. Cork not out		8
K. J. Barnett st Humphries b Greenfield	25	B 1, l-b 5, w 2, n-b 6		14
A. S. Rollins b Lewry	23			—
P. A. J. DeFreitas c Carpenter b Bevan	4	1/71 2/127	(4 wkts, 37.2 overs)	150
M. E. Cassar not out	10	3/128 4/140		

T. A. Tweats, †K. M. Krikken, P. Aldred, G. M. Roberts and K. J. Dean did not bat.

Bowling: Lewry 8–0–26–2; Kirtley 8–1–24–0; Robinson 8–0–33–0; K. Newell 5–0–16–0; Greenfield 5–0–24–1; Bevan 3.2–0–21–1.

Umpires: A. Clarkson and N. T. Plews.

At Tunbridge Wells, June 7. KENT v SUSSEX. No result.

SUSSEX v WARWICKSHIRE

At Hove, June 21. Warwickshire won by seven runs. Toss: Warwickshire.

While Smith and Lara were piling on 126 for Warwickshire's second wicket, a formidable total looked likely. However, the batting fell away, despite the help of 17 wides. Bevan kept Sussex in touch, but 83 from the last ten overs proved too daunting. Jarvis's three wickets included his 200th in the League.

Warwickshire

N. V. Knight c Humphries b Kirtley	4	G. Welch not out		10
N. M. K. Smith b Kirtley	80	†K. J. Piper not out		2
*B. C. Lara c Kirtley b Jarvis	59	B 2, l-b 13, w 17, n-b 2		34
D. P. Ostler b Lewry	19			—
T. L. Penney run out	6	1/26 2/152 3/175	(8 wkts, 40 overs)	236
D. L. Hemp b Kirtley	18	4/188 5/203 6/215		
A. F. Giles b Jarvis	4	7/215 8/233		
D. R. Brown lbw b Jarvis	0			

G. C. Small did not bat.

Bowling: Lewry 8–0–51–1; Kirtley 8–0–48–3; Bevan 8–0–40–0; Robinson 8–0–48–0; Jarvis 8–0–34–3.

Sussex

W. G. Khan c and b Hemp	33	P. W. Jarvis b Giles		24
*C. J. Adams b Small	10	†S. Humphries not out		4
M. G. Bevan b Giles	56	B 1, l-b 12, w 7, n-b 8		28
M. Newell c Lara b Hemp	32			—
M. T. E. Peirce b Giles	0	1/25 2/85 3/142	(6 wkts, 40 overs)	229
J. R. Carpenter not out	42	4/142 5/163 6/222		

J. D. Lewry, R. J. Kirtley and M. A. Robinson did not bat.

Bowling: Welch 8–0–44–0; Brown 2–0–14–0; Small 8–0–27–1; Smith 8–0–39–0; Hemp 6–0–43–2; Giles 8–0–49–3.

Umpires: M. J. Kitchen and J. W. Lloyds.

SUSSEX v SOMERSET

At Hove, July 5. Somerset won by two wickets. Toss: Somerset.

Sussex batted fitfully on a largely blameless pitch, the only substantial contribution coming from Bevan. His 60 from 64 balls was spread over 31 overs as he was unable to capture the strike. Somerset made heavy weather of the chase but, from 76 for five, the lower order played methodically to secure victory.

Sussex

W. G. Khan run out	14	R. J. Kirtley c Bowler b Parsons	7
R. S. C. Martin-Jenkins c Bowler		J. D. Lewry not out	10
b Caddick	5	M. A. Robinson not out	2
*C. J. Adams b Jones	18		
M. G. Bevan b Caddick	60	L-b 6, w 9, n-b 2	17
M. Newell c Parsons b Trescothick	14		
J. R. Carpenter c Turner b Jones	3	1/7 2/34 3/42 (9 wkts, 40 overs) 165
A. D. Edwards lbw b Parsons	14	4/65 5/76 6/106	
†S. Humphries b Burns	1	7/109 8/134 9/160	

Bowling: Caddick 8–2–28–2; Rose 8–0–32–0; Trescothick 6–1–25–1; Jones 8–0–46–2; Burns 4–0–11–1; Parsons 6–0–17–2.

Somerset

M. Burns lbw b Lewry	0	Mushtaq Ahmed lbw b Kirtley	6
P. C. L. Holloway c Carpenter b Lewry	15	A. R. Caddick not out	12
†R. J. Turner b Lewry	37		
M. N. Lathwell lbw b Kirtley	15	L-b 6, w 9	15
*P. D. Bowler b Robinson	2		
M. E. Trescothick b Bevan	23	1/0 2/52 3/67 (8 wkts, 38.3 overs) 166
K. A. Parsons b Kirtley	24	4/70 5/76 6/113	
G. D. Rose not out	17	7/131 8/150	

P. S. Jones did not bat.

Bowling: Lewry 8–0–19–3; Kirtley 8–0–42–3; Martin-Jenkins 5–0–32–0; Robinson 6–0–22–1; Edwards 8–0–27–0; Bevan 3.3–0–18–1.

Umpires: J. H. Harris and N. T. Plews.

At Cheltenham, July 18. SUSSEX lost to GLOUCESTERSHIRE by 35 runs.

SUSSEX v MIDDLESEX

At Hove, July 20 (day/night). Sussex won by six wickets (D/L method). Toss: Middlesex.

Adams starred under the lights, not only as a batsman but as a destructive bowler. Having taken three wickets in ten years of League cricket, he bowled his little medium-pacers to devastating effect and ripped through the last five Middlesex batsmen for 16. This included a hat-trick that hardly anyone noticed at the time. He bowled Johnson with the last ball of an over, then finished the innings with the wickets of Goodchild and Angus Fraser. Adams followed up with a match-winning 58. The crowd was kept down to 3,000 by a miserable weather forecast, which proved correct. Rain, accompanied by forked lightning, reduced the game to 35 overs a side. Having dismissed Middlesex within the revised allocation of overs, Sussex believed they had a straight run-chase for victory. Mid-innings, they were told that the Duckworth/Lewis system required them to score 133 because the Middlesex innings had been interrupted. Fortunately, it made no difference.

Middlesex

*†K. R. Brown run out	3	R. L. Johnson b Adams	18
J. L. Langer run out	3	J. P. Hewitt not out	3
O. A. Shah c Kirtley b Bevan	37	A. R. C. Fraser lbw b Adams	0
P. N. Weekes lbw b Martin-Jenkins	0	L-b 6, w 9	15
D. C. Nash c Humphries b Bevan	19		
K. P. Dutch b Adams	9	1/5 2/10 3/10	(33.2 overs) 125
D. J. Goodchild b Adams	18	4/70 5/70 6/87	
A. G. J. Fraser lbw b Adams	0	7/87 8/116 9/125	

Bowling: Kirtley 6–2–17–0; Martin-Jenkins 8–2–12–1; Edwards 5–0–28–0; Bevan 4–0–23–2; Robinson 5–0–23–0; Adams 5.2–0–16–5.

Sussex

R. K. Rao lbw b A. R. C. Fraser	38	J. R. Carpenter not out	4
R. S. C. Martin-Jenkins hit wkt b Hewitt	4	L-b 3, w 3, n-b 4	10
*C. J. Adams run out	58		
M. G. Bevan not out	15	1/11 2/109	(4 wkts, 34 overs) 134
M. Newell c Shah b Dutch	5	3/119 4/129	

W. G. Khan, A. D. Edwards, †S. Humphries, R. J. Kirtley and M. A. Robinson did not bat.

Bowling: A. R. C. Fraser 7–1–20–1; Hewitt 5–0–28–1; Johnson 5–0–20–0; A. G. J. Fraser 5–1–18–0; Dutch 7–1–22–1; Langer 5–0–23–0.

Umpires: G. I. Burgess and J. F. Steele.

At The Oval, August 3. SUSSEX beat SURREY by eight wickets.

SUSSEX v DURHAM

At Eastbourne, August 9. Sussex won by seven wickets. Toss: Sussex.

Adams's third successive fifty took Sussex to their third successive win. He hit three sixes in his 73 and got out trying to hit a third six in one over from Wood. Durham's score had been kept down by a spell of three for seven from Bevan at his most tantalising.

Durham

J. E. Morris c Carpenter b K. Newell	41	J. Wood b Kirtley	1
*D. C. Boon lbw b Edwards	2	N. Killeen not out	5
N. J. Speak c Humphries b Edwards	0	S. J. Harmison not out	1
†M. P. Speight c and b Kirtley	31	L-b 8, w 3	11
P. D. Collingwood st Humphries b Bevan	38		
J. J. B. Lewis st Humphries b Adams	17	1/16 2/18 3/65	(9 wkts, 40 overs) 156
M. J. Foster c Martin-Jenkins b Bevan	4	4/98 5/137 6/139	
N. C. Phillips lbw b Bevan	5	7/144 8/147 9/149	

Bowling: Martin-Jenkins 8–0–22–0; Kirtley 8–0–37–2; Edwards 6–3–16–2; K. Newell 3–0–16–1; Robinson 8–0–33–0; Adams 3–0–17–1; Bevan 4–1–7–3.

Sussex

R. K. Rao c Speight b Wood	3	M. Newell not out		15
R. S. C. Martin-Jenkins c Harmison				
b Foster	25	L-b 1, w 5		6
*C. J. Adams b Wood	73			
M. G. Bevan not out	35	1/6 2/69 3/124	(3 wkts, 35.4 overs)	157

J. R. Carpenter, K. Newell, A. D. Edwards, †S. Humphries, R. J. Kirtley and M. A. Robinson did not bat.

Bowling: Harmison 6–0–27–0; Wood 6–0–34–2; Killeen 7.4–0–29–0; Foster 7–2–23–1; Collingwood 4–0–21–0; Phillips 5–0–22–0.

Umpires: H. D. Bird and M. J. Harris.

At Leicester, August 23. LEICESTERSHIRE v SUSSEX. No result (abandoned).

SUSSEX v GLAMORGAN

At Hove, August 30. Glamorgan won by 37 runs. Toss: Sussex.

This match was originally scheduled to be played under floodlights the following Thursday but the plan was abandoned because of lack of sponsorship. With the lower division of the National League beckoning for both sides, the game had no real purpose. Without Bevan, who had joined the Australian Commonwealth Games squad, Sussex were unable to combat an accurate Glamorgan attack. Dale took the vital wicket of Adams in his four for 36.

Glamorgan

*M. P. Maynard c Wilton b Edwards	38	S. D. Thomas c Carpenter b Kirtley		4
W. L. Law c Kirtley b Edwards	15	A. P. Davies not out		0
A. Dale c Wilton b Robinson	8	B 1, l-b 4, w 4, n-b 4		13
P. A. Cottey c Khan b Adams	63			
M. J. Powell c Wilton b K. Newell	32	1/54 2/65 3/66	(7 wkts, 40 overs)	212
R. D. B. Croft not out	37	4/129 5/180		
†A. D. Shaw c Carpenter b Kirtley	2	6/198 7/211		

D. A. Cosker and O. T. Parkin did not bat.

Bowling: Martin-Jenkins 4–0–22–0; Kirtley 6–0–41–2; Edwards 8–1–45–2; Robinson 8–1–28–1; K. Newell 8–0–50–1; Adams 6–0–21–1.

Sussex

R. K. Rao lbw b Davies	4	†N. J. Wilton b Cosker		3
R. S. C. Martin-Jenkins lbw b Thomas	31	R. J. Kirtley c Maynard b Cosker		12
*C. J. Adams b Dale	32	M. A. Robinson run out		1
J. R. Carpenter c Maynard b Dale	20	B 4, l-b 11, w 4		19
M. Newell b Cosker	2			
K. Newell not out	45	1/6 2/61 3/84	(38.4 overs)	175
W. G. Khan c Cosker b Dale	6	4/93 5/110 6/122		
A. D. Edwards lbw b Dale	0	7/122 8/135 9/164		

Bowling: Parkin 6–0–15–0; Davies 4.4–0–24–1; Croft 8–0–25–0; Thomas 5–0–21–1; Dale 8–0–36–4; Cosker 7–0–39–3.

Umpires: R. Julian and K. E. Palmer.

SUSSEX v YORKSHIRE

At Hove, September 6. Sussex won by six wickets. Toss: Yorkshire.

Sussex crushed Yorkshire with 16 overs unused, their first win in this fixture for nine seasons. Yorkshire batted with little resolve on a seamer-friendly pitch; Martin-Jenkins and Kirtley took full advantage, dismissing them for 89. Martin-Jenkins then partnered Rao in an opening stand of 63; despite a mini-collapse, the result was never in doubt.

Yorkshire

C. White b Martin-Jenkins	4	I. D. Fisher c and b Kirtley	4
M. P. Vaughan lbw b Martin-Jenkins	10	M. J. Hoggard lbw b Kirtley	0
M. J. Wood b Kirtley	0	P. M. Hutchison b Kirtley	2
*D. Byas c Adams b Robinson	10	B 1, l-b 2, w 1	4
B. Parker c Carpenter b K. Newell	11		
†R. J. Blakey run out	12	1/6 2/7 3/17	(38 overs) 89
G. M. Hamilton not out	20	4/34 5/42 6/54	
C. E. W. Silverwood b Adams	12	7/78 8/85 9/85	

Bowling: Martin-Jenkins 8–2–12–2; Kirtley 8–0–21–4; Edwards 5–2–7–0; Robinson 8–0–19–1; K. Newell 6–0–17–1; Adams 3–0–10–1.

Sussex

R. K. Rao run out	21	K. Newell not out	12
R. S. C. Martin-Jenkins lbw b Hoggard	44		
*C. J. Adams c Byas b Vaughan	0	L-b 1, n-b 2	3
J. R. Carpenter not out	10		
M. Newell lbw b Hoggard	0	1/63 2/63 3/69 4/69	(4 wkts, 24 overs) 90

W. G. Khan, A. D. Edwards, †S. Humphries, R. J. Kirtley and M. A. Robinson did not bat.

Bowling: Silverwood 4–0–15–0; Hutchison 3–0–15–0; Fisher 4–0–17–0; Hamilton 4–0–16–0; Vaughan 5–0–14–1; Hoggard 4–0–12–2.

Umpires: D. R. Shepherd and J. F. Steele.

At Northampton, September 13. SUSSEX lost to NORTHAMPTONSHIRE by 89 runs.

WARWICKSHIRE

WARWICKSHIRE v DURHAM

At Birmingham, April 19. No result (abandoned).

At The Oval, April 26. WARWICKSHIRE beat SURREY by eight wickets.

WARWICKSHIRE v LEICESTERSHIRE

At Birmingham, May 10. Warwickshire won by 21 runs (D/L method). Toss: Warwickshire.

In a rain-affected match, Warwickshire gained revenge for a Benson and Hedges defeat at Grace Road six days earlier. Warwickshire were interrupted by two showers during their innings, and Duckworth/Lewis rules required Leicestershire to score 172 to win – nine more than the home total. Despite Nixon, who hit three fours in an over off Brown, they fell well short.

Warwickshire

N. V. Knight c Smith b Williamson	40	D. R. Brown not out	11
N. M. K. Smith c Mason b Simmons	38		
*B. C. Lara c Nixon b Simmons	2	B 1, l-b 8, w 2, n-b 8	19
D. L. Hemp c Smith b Williamson	27		
D. P. Ostler not out	23	1/74 2/81 3/110 (5 wkts, 36 overs) 163	
T. L. Penney b Williamson	3	4/128 5/139	

†K. J. Piper, G. Welch, A. F. Giles and E. S. H. Giddins did not bat.

Bowling: Mullally 6–2–11–0; Lewis 4–0–22–0; Simmons 6–1–27–2; Wells 8–1–36–0; Williamson 8–0–34–3; Maddy 4–0–24–0.

Leicestershire

D. L. Maddy lbw b Giddins	6	D. Williamson c Brown b Giles	4
I. J. Sutcliffe c Smith b Welch	11	A. D. Mullally b Giles	0
B. F. Smith c Penney b Smith	34	T. J. Mason not out	0
P. V. Simmons c Piper b Brown	25	L-b 6, w 1, n-b 2	9
V. J. Wells b Smith	1		
A. Habib b Giles	10	1/10 2/32 3/70 (34.2 overs) 151	
†P. A. Nixon run out	44	4/71 5/86 6/110	
*C. C. Lewis run out	7	7/140 8/151 9/151	

Bowling: Giddins 8–0–26–1; Welch 7–1–18–1; Smith 8–1–39–2; Brown 6–0–34–1; Giles 5.2–0–28–3.

Umpires: R. Julian and B. Leadbeater.

At Derby, May 17. WARWICKSHIRE beat DERBYSHIRE by 47 runs.

WARWICKSHIRE v NOTTINGHAMSHIRE

At Birmingham, May 25. Nottinghamshire won by seven wickets (D/L method). Toss: Nottinghamshire. County debut: C. M. W. Read.

The match became 24 overs a side after a two-hour break for rain, but Knight and Lara were already out, and Warwickshire could not set a competitive target. A mad scramble for runs resulted in Strang taking six for 32. The Duckworth/Lewis calculation compensated the home side a little, requiring Nottinghamshire to exceed their opponents' total by 18. But they did that comfortably, led by Johnson.

Warwickshire

N. V. Knight c Robinson b Bates	13	G. C. Small b Strang	0
N. M. K. Smith c Read b Franks	2	†T. Frost not out	1
D. L. Hemp b Strang	21	E. S. H. Giddins not out	6
*B. C. Lara lbw b Tolley	12	L-b 5, w 3	8
D. P. Ostler st Read b Strang	18		
D. R. Brown c Franks b Strang	21	1/6 2/23 3/38 (9 wkts, 24 overs) 102	
A. F. Giles c Archer b Strang	0	4/63 5/74 6/74	
G. Welch st Read b Strang	0	7/95 8/95 9/96	

Bowling: Evans 4–0–12–0; Franks 6–0–10–1; Bates 5–0–17–1; Tolley 2–0–6–1; Strang 4–0–32–6; Dowman 3–0–20–0.

Nottinghamshire

M. P. Dowman c Small b Brown	34	N. A. Gie not out		6
R. T. Robinson b Giddins	6	L-b 4, w 4, n-b 2		10
*P. Johnson c Lara b Giles	47			
G. F. Archer not out	19	1/13 2/90 3/90	(3 wkts, 22.3 overs)	122

C. M. Tolley, †C. M. W. Read, P. A. Strang, P. J. Franks, K. P. Evans and R. T. Bates did not bat.

Bowling: Giddins 5–0–19–1; Smith 5–0–23–0; Welch 3–0–17–0; Small 1–0–10–0; Brown 4.3–0–32–1; Giles 4–0–17–1.

Umpires: G. I. Burgess and A. A. Jones.

At Taunton, May 31. WARWICKSHIRE lost to SOMERSET by four wickets.

At Bristol, June 14. GLOUCESTERSHIRE v WARWICKSHIRE. No result.

At Hove, June 21. WARWICKSHIRE beat SUSSEX by seven runs.

WARWICKSHIRE v LANCASHIRE

At Birmingham, July 1 (day/night). Warwickshire won by 27 runs. Toss: Warwickshire.

The first of Edgbaston's four floodlit League matches was watched by a crowd of about 8,500; they witnessed a home win and some encouraging form by Lara, who batted with great determination to add 111 with Smith. Lancashire were undermined by two early run-outs.

Warwickshire

M. A. Sheikh c Crawley b Martin	2	D. L. Hemp not out		27
N. M. K. Smith run out	47	B 4, l-b 7, w 4, n-b 2		17
*B. C. Lara c Martin b Yates	60			
D. P. Ostler b Yates	9	1/5 2/116	(4 wkts, 40 overs)	181
T. L. Penney not out	19	3/125 4/131		

D. R. Brown, G. Welch, G. C. Small, †K. J. Piper and E. S. H. Giddins did not bat.

Bowling: Martin 8–1–35–1; Austin 6–0–8–0; Wasim Akram 7–0–40–0; Chapple 5–0–33–0; Yates 8–0–26–2; Watkinson 6–0–28–0.

Lancashire

A. Flintoff c Hemp b Welch	6	G. Yates c Piper b Sheikh		0
P. C. McKeown run out	1	G. Chapple run out		3
†J. P. Crawley run out	6	P. J. Martin not out		3
G. D. Lloyd b Sheikh	38	B 1, l-b 14, w 2		17
M. E. Harvey c Ostler b Brown	39			
M. Watkinson c Brown b Giddins	32	1/6 2/11 3/15	(37.4 overs)	154
*Wasim Akram c Giddins b Brown	8	4/80 5/118 6/133		
I. D. Austin b Sheikh	1	7/137 8/137 9/145		

Bowling: Welch 8–1–22–1; Giddins 5.4–3–9–1; Small 6–0–25–0; Brown 7–0–41–2; Sheikh 8–0–32–3; Smith 3–0–10–0.

Umpires: J. C. Balderstone and A. A. Jones.

WARWICKSHIRE v KENT

At Birmingham, July 12. Warwickshire won by five wickets (D/L method). Toss: Warwickshire.

Reduced by rain to 28, and then 27 overs a side, the match tilted Warwickshire's way when they restricted Kent to 159. The innings lacked urgency until Ealham struck 55 off only 33 balls. Knight responded aggressively, and then Smith and Lara added 60 in eight overs.

Kent

T. R. Ward c Penney b Brown	19	*†S. A. Marsh not out		0
R. W. T. Key run out	19	M. J. McCague not out		1
C. L. Hooper c Hemp b Welch	27	L-b 5, w 2		7
A. P. Wells b Giddins	11			—
M. A. Ealham lbw b Giddins	55	1/23 2/63 3/72	(7 wkts, 27 overs)	159
G. R. Cowdrey c Brown b Smith	8	4/79 5/106		
M. J. Walker c and b Smith	12	6/149 7/157		

D. W. Headley and A. P. Igglesden did not bat.

Bowling: Giddins 6–0–26–2; Welch 5–0–32–1; Smith 6–0–32–2; Giles 5–0–34–0; Brown 5–0–30–1.

Warwickshire

N. V. Knight c Walker b McCague	34	A. F. Giles not out		21
N. M. K. Smith b Headley	46			
*B. C. Lara lbw b Ealham	36	L-b 2, w 1, n-b 2		5
D. L. Hemp c Wells b McCague	1			—
T. L. Penney run out	3	1/48 2/108 3/113	(5 wkts, 25.3 overs)	161
D. R. Brown not out	15	4/121 5/125		

G. Welch, †K. J. Piper, G. C. Small and E. S. H. Giddins did not bat.

Bowling: Headley 5–0–18–1; Igglesden 5–0–34–0; Ealham 5.3–0–48–1; McCague 5–0–20–2; Hooper 3–0–26–0; Cowdrey 2–0–13–0.

Umpires: A. Clarkson and B. Dudleston.

WARWICKSHIRE v HAMPSHIRE

At Birmingham, July 14 (day/night). Hampshire won by one wicket. Toss: Warwickshire.

Warwickshire lost their last nine wickets for 59 – and their chance to go clear at the top of the League. White guided Hampshire to a narrow victory, but batting was never easy on another slow, difficult Edgbaston surface. A crowd of around 7,500 were greeted by local residents protesting about the plan to install permanent floodlights.

Warwickshire

N. V. Knight c Udal b Hartley	40	M. A. Sheikh lbw b Stephenson		8
N. M. K. Smith b McLean	10	†K. J. Piper not out		0
*B. C. Lara lbw b Hartley	22	E. S. H. Giddins run out		0
D. L. Hemp c Whitaker b Mascarenhas	1	L-b 3, w 3		6
T. L. Penney lbw b Hartley	1			—
D. R. Brown lbw b Stephenson	20	1/29 2/69 3/70	(35.3 overs)	128
A. F. Giles c and b Udal	13	4/73 5/87 6/112		
G. Welch run out	7	7/112 8/125 9/128		

Bowling: McLean 5–0–24–1; Connor 6–0–18–0; Hartley 8–0–24–3; Mascarenhas 5–0–23–1; Udal 6.3–0–16–1; Stephenson 5–0–20–2.

Hampshire

J. S. Laney lbw b Giddins	4	*S. D. Udal st Piper b Giles	8
J. P. Stephenson b Brown	28	P. J. Hartley b Welch	0
N. A. M. McLean c Lara b Brown	19	C. A. Connor not out	7
G. W. White not out	32	B 1, l-b 10, w 6, n-b 2	19
P. R. Whitaker c Sheikh b Brown	9		
W. S. Kendall lbw b Giddins	2	1/19 2/56 3/61 (9 wkts, 39 overs)	132
A. D. Mascarenhas lbw b Sheikh	2	4/78 5/83 6/90	
†A. N. Aymes lbw b Sheikh	2	7/94 8/113 9/114	

Bowling: Giddins 8–0–47–2; Welch 4–0–11–1; Giles 8–1–15–1; Brown 8–2–15–3; Smith 3–0–14–0; Sheikh 8–2–19–2.

Umpires: R. Julian and J. F. Steele.

WARWICKSHIRE v ESSEX

At Birmingham, July 21 (day/night). Essex won by 17 runs. Toss: Essex.

Ten thousand turned up for an important top-of-the-table game, which left Essex clear leaders. Irani and Stuart Law helped them become the first side to pass 200 at Edgbaston in the League all season. Warwickshire lost three early wickets and could not get back into the contest.

Essex

*P. J. Prichard b Sheikh	19	†R. J. Rollins c Sheikh b Giddins	2
S. G. Law c Welch b Smith	40	A. P. Cowan not out	4
S. D. Peters run out	9	L-b 3, w 2, n-b 2	7
R. C. Irani not out	68		
D. R. Law c Brown b Sheikh	39	1/51 2/66 3/79 (7 wkts, 40 overs)	204
A. P. Grayson c Lara b Giddins	8	4/140 5/161	
G. R. Napier b Giles	8	6/187 7/190	

M. C. Ilott and P. M. Such did not bat.

Bowling: Giddins 8–0–38–2; Welch 5–0–31–0; Sheikh 8–0–44–2; Brown 6–0–24–0; Giles 8–1–38–1; Smith 5–1–26–1.

Warwickshire

N. V. Knight b Ilott	48	G. Welch st Rollins b Grayson	3
N. M. K. Smith c Irani b Cowan	1	†K. J. Piper not out	24
*B. C. Lara c Rollins b Ilott	5	B 4, l-b 9, w 4	17
D. P. Ostler c sub b Cowan	3		
T. L. Penney not out	64	1/2 2/15 3/28 (7 wkts, 40 overs)	187
D. R. Brown c Ilott b Such	2	4/90 5/99	
A. F. Giles b Cowan	20	6/134 7/139	

E. S. H. Giddins and M. A. Sheikh did not bat.

Bowling: Ilott 8–1–26–2; Cowan 8–0–44–3; Irani 8–1–28–0; Such 8–0–31–1; Grayson 8–0–45–1.

Umpires: H. D. Bird and K. E. Palmer.

WARWICKSHIRE v GLAMORGAN

At Birmingham, August 3 (day/night). Glamorgan won by 39 runs (D/L method). Toss: Warwickshire.

Warwickshire's success in staging floodlit cricket was again in direct contrast to their ability to win the games. A crowd of 7,000 saw them go down to their third defeat in three weeks under the Edgbaston lights, making it almost certain they would have to cede their title. Glamorgan were given a good start by James and Maynard. Warwickshire then had to score 185 after their target had been recalculated under Duckworth/Lewis, but they quickly slipped to 32 for three. Lara, batting fourth wicket down, hit four quick boundaries to revive their hopes. But he was run out by Croft from mid-on trying to regain his ground. There was a further demonstration from about 20 residents opposed to the floodlights. One held a placard saying "God created day and night not day and day".

Glamorgan

S. P. James b Sheikh	30	†I. Dawood not out		4
*M. P. Maynard lbw b Munton	43			
A. Dale b Sheikh	43	L-b 11, w 3		14
P. A. Cottey c Knight b Sheikh	0			—
M. J. Powell not out	36	1/80 2/92 3/93	(5 wkts, 36 overs)	172
R. D. B. Croft c and b Giles	2	4/159 5/167		

S. C. B. Tomlinson, A. P. Davies, D. A. Cosker and O. T. Parkin did not bat.

Bowling: Giddins 6–0–34–0; Welch 7–0–27–0; Munton 8–0–30–1; Sheikh 7–0–28–3; Smith 5–0–31–0; Giles 3–0–11–1.

Warwickshire

N. V. Knight c Dawood b Davies	11	M. A. Sheikh not out		3
N. M. K. Smith b Parkin	4	T. A. Munton st Dawood b Cosker		1
G. Welch b Davies	3	E. S. H. Giddins b Dale		0
D. P. Ostler lbw b Croft	14	L-b 11, w 9, n-b 4		24
T. L. Penney b Cosker	27			—
*B. C. Lara run out	30	1/21 2/24 3/32	(32.3 overs)	146
A. F. Giles c Cottey b Cosker	23	4/51 5/101 6/120		
†K. J. Piper b Dale	6	7/141 8/142 9/145		

Bowling: Parkin 8–0–32–1; Davies 5–0–17–2; Croft 6–0–22–1; Dale 6.3–0–22–2; Tomlinson 3–0–24–0; Cosker 4–0–18–3.

Umpires: J. W. Holder and A. G. T. Whitehead.

At Lord's, August 9. WARWICKSHIRE beat MIDDLESEX by six wickets.

At Northampton, August 23. NORTHAMPTONSHIRE v WARWICKSHIRE. No result (abandoned).

WARWICKSHIRE v WORCESTERSHIRE

At Birmingham, August 30. Warwickshire won by four wickets. Toss: Worcestershire.

The Worcestershire openers raced to 43 in seven overs, but the rest of their side capitulated for only 84 more. Lampitt hit back with three important wickets, including Lara for nought. But Penney stopped the rot, securing victory with nine overs unused. During the match, Warwickshire presented a silver salver to batsman Andy Moles, who was retiring.

Worcestershire

W. P. C. Weston c Smith b Small	34	D. N. Catterall c Small b Giles		5
V. S. Solanki c Piper b Munton	25	M. J. Rawnsley c and b Smith		0
E. J. Wilson run out	6	R. J. Chapman c Lara b Giles		1
D. A. Leatherdale c Piper b Small	7	L-b 3, w 9, n-b 2		14
*†S. J. Rhodes c Piper b Brown	6			—
A. Hafeez lbw b Small	7	1/43 2/54 3/64	(32.5 overs)	127
S. R. Lampitt st Piper b Smith	10	4/71 5/87 6/102		
R. K. Illingworth not out	12	7/115 8/124 9/124		

Bowling: Munton 5–1–21–1; Giddins 5–0–31–0; Small 8–0–25–3; Brown 5–0–23–1; Smith 6–1–15–2; Giles 3.5–1–9–2.

Warwickshire

N. V. Knight c Hafeez b Lampitt	19	T. L. Penney not out		36
N. M. K. Smith run out	3	†K. J. Piper not out		8
D. L. Hemp lbw b Lampitt	28	L-b 4, w 3, n-b 2		9
*B. C. Lara c Rhodes b Lampitt	0			—
D. R. Brown c Leatherdale b Chapman	25	1/9 2/53 3/62	(6 wkts, 30.5 overs)	128
A. F. Giles c Rhodes b Chapman	0	4/62 5/116 6/116		

G. C. Small, T. A. Munton and E. S. H. Giddins did not bat.

Bowling: Chapman 5.5–0–33–2; Catterall 7–1–22–0; Lampitt 8–2–16–3; Illingworth 6–0–18–0; Rawnsley 2–0–13–0; Leatherdale 2–0–22–0.

Umpires: M. J. Harris and R. Palmer.

At Leeds, September 13. WARWICKSHIRE beat YORKSHIRE by five wickets.

WORCESTERSHIRE

WORCESTERSHIRE v ESSEX

At Worcester, April 19. No result (abandoned).

At Leicester, April 26. WORCESTERSHIRE lost to LEICESTERSHIRE by 49 runs.

WORCESTERSHIRE v DURHAM

At Worcester, May 3. Worcestershire won by 24 runs. Toss: Worcestershire.

Moody, in his first League game of the season, played the crucial innings, putting on 110 with Solanki for the first wicket. He played stylishly for 80 before being stumped off a leg-side wide. Durham fought their way into a promising position – Lewis and Collingwood added 104 in 14 overs – but the innings fell away.

Worcestershire

*T. M. Moody st Speight b Collingwood	80	†S. J. Rhodes not out		2
V. S. Solanki c Betts b Boiling	44	R. K. Illingworth not out		3
G. A. Hick c Speight b Collingwood	4	B 1, l-b 9, w 12		22
G. R. Haynes c Collingwood b Betts	34			—
D. A. Leatherdale c Boiling b Betts	26	1/110 2/118 3/148	(7 wkts, 40 overs)	235
W. P. C. Weston run out	12	4/199 5/217		
S. R. Lampitt c Morris b Killeen	8	6/227 7/230		

P. J. Newport and A. Sheriyar did not bat.

Bowling: Betts 8–0–39–2; Wood 7–0–43–0; Killeen 8–0–44–1; Boiling 5–0–40–1; Foster 8–0–34–0; Collingwood 4–0–25–2.

Durham

M. A. Roseberry c Rhodes b Newport	5	M. M. Betts not out		1
M. J. Foster c Leatherdale b Illingworth	28	N. Killeen b Leatherdale		0
J. E. Morris b Illingworth	41	J. Wood b Solanki b Sheriyar		0
*D. C. Boon c Rhodes b Newport	1	L-b 11, w 2		13
J. J. B. Lewis b Illingworth	62			—
P. D. Collingwood c Lampitt b Sheriyar	51	1/12 2/59 3/63	(38.2 overs)	211
†M. P. Speight c Weston b Sheriyar	7	4/83 5/187 6/206		
J. Boiling lbw b Leatherdale	2	7/206 8/210 9/210		

Bowling: Newport 8–2–18–2; Haynes 3–0–16–0; Moody 3–0–24–0; Illingworth 8–0–37–3; Lampitt 6–0–46–0; Sheriyar 5.2–0–32–3; Leatherdale 5–0–27–2.

Umpires: R. Palmer and D. R. Shepherd.

WORCESTERSHIRE v SUSSEX

At Worcester, May 19. Sussex won by 103 runs. Toss: Sussex.

A stirring, if confusing, performance by brothers Keith and Mark Newell took Sussex to a comfortable win. They added 181 for the second wicket, before Keith had his century snatched away after it had been applauded. First, he lost two runs because an umpire's signal was amended from six to four, and then three more after a mix-up was sorted out and a scoring stroke was switched to brother Mark. But it was Keith's day, hundred or no hundred. Bowling third change, he took five for 33 as Worcestershire collapsed.

Sussex

K. Greenfield b Sheriyar	16	†S. Humphries not out		7
K. Newell c Moody b Hick	97	J. D. Lewry not out		3
M. Newell run out	77	L-b 13, w 12, n-b 12		37
*M. G. Bevan c Rhodes b Hick	1			
J. R. Carpenter c Lampitt b Leatherdale	16	1/38 2/219 3/223	(7 wkts, 40 overs)	258
M. T. E. Peirce st Rhodes b Hick	2	4/228 5/232		
A. D. Edwards b Hick	2	6/238 7/253		

R. J. Kirtley and M. A. Robinson did not bat.

Bowling: Newport 5–1–41–0; Moody 5–0–32–0; Sheriyar 3–0–20–1; Illingworth 8–0–27–0; Lampitt 6–0–27–0; Hick 8–0–46–4; Leatherdale 5–0–52–1.

Worcestershire

*T. M. Moody c Carpenter b Kirtley	10	R. K. Illingworth lbw b K. Newell		4
V. S. Solanki st Humphries b K. Newell	39	P. J. Newport not out		2
G. A. Hick c Carpenter b Edwards	23	A. Sheriyar st Humphries b Bevan		1
G. R. Haynes c and b K. Newell	32	L-b 11, w 15, n-b 2		28
D. A. Leatherdale b Robinson	1			
W. P. C. Weston c Carpenter b K. Newell	3	1/25 2/64 3/101	(33.1 overs)	155
S. R. Lampitt b Bevan	5	4/102 5/115 6/138		
†S. J. Rhodes c Humphries b K. Newell	7	7/147 8/151 9/153		

Bowling: Lewry 5–1–20–0; Kirtley 4–1–6–1; Robinson 8–0–32–1; Edwards 4–0–33–1; K. Newell 8–0–33–5; Bevan 4.1–0–20–2.

Umpires: D. J. Constant and A. A. Jones.

At Uxbridge, May 25. WORCESTERSHIRE lost to MIDDLESEX by seven wickets (D/L method).

At Cardiff, June 14. WORCESTERSHIRE beat GLAMORGAN by seven wickets.

WORCESTERSHIRE v GLOUCESTERSHIRE

At Worcester, June 21. Worcestershire won by 13 runs. Toss: Gloucestershire.

As England were hurtling to defeat in the Lord's Test, Hick, exiled from the team, scored a commanding hundred. He faced 118 balls, and hit eight fours and three sixes despite an unresponsive pitch. Walsh was absent, fulfilling his role as Jamaica's roving ambassador by supporting their footballers at the World Cup in France.

Worcestershire

*T. M. Moody st Russell b Ball	26	S. W. K. Ellis not out	2	
V. S. Solanki c Russell b Smith	1	†S. J. Rhodes not out	1	
G. A. Hick c Windows b Lewis	116	L-b 4, w 9, n-b 2	15	
D. A. Leatherdale c Ball b Alleyne	3		—	
G. R. Haynes c Russell b Alleyne	5	1/11 2/82 3/93 (7 wkts, 40 overs)	207	
W. P. C. Weston run out	37	4/101 5/173		
S. R. Lampitt c Alleyne b Cawdron	1	6/179 7/204		

R. J. Chapman and R. K. Illingworth did not bat.

Bowling: Smith 8-0-34-1; Lewis 8-0-56-1; Cawdron 8-0-54-1; Alleyne 8-0-31-2; Ball 8-1-28-1.

Gloucestershire

G. I. Macmillan b Chapman	11	J. Lewis not out	19	
R. I. Dawson c and b Moody	30	M. J. Cawdron not out	17	
*M. W. Alleyne b Leatherdale	36			
A. J. Wright c Lampitt b Illingworth	46	L-b 3, w 5, n-b 2	10	
†R. C. Russell c and b Illingworth	9		—	
M. G. N. Windows c and b Leatherdale	15	1/18 2/72 3/102 (8 wkts, 40 overs)	194	
T. H. C. Hancock b Leatherdale	0	4/119 5/153 6/155		
M. C. J. Ball run out	1	7/157 8/163		

A. M. Smith did not bat.

Bowling: Haynes 6-0-34-0; Chapman 4-0-22-1; Lampitt 6-0-24-0; Moody 8-0-37-1; Leatherdale 8-0-42-3; Illingworth 8-0-32-2.

Umpires: H. D. Bird and P. Willey.

At The Oval, June 28. WORCESTERSHIRE beat SURREY by one run.

WORCESTERSHIRE v NORTHAMPTONSHIRE

At Worcester, July 5. Tied. Toss: Northamptonshire. First-team debut: E. J. Wilson.

Northamptonshire, without a Sunday League win at New Road in 21 years, earned a tie when Rose hit the last ball of the match, from Leatherdale, to the boundary. Worcestershire were given a strong start by Moody and Hick. Then their seamers took four quick wickets, but Bailey kept his team in the game.

Worcestershire

*T. M. Moody c Walton b Snape	68	†S. J. Rhodes run out	16	
V. S. Solanki c Warren b Rose	11	R. K. Illingworth not out	3	
G. A. Hick b Follett	36	L-b 8, w 4, n-b 2	14	
D. A. Leatherdale b Follett	0		—	
A. Hafeez c Warren b Snape	0	1/29 2/119 3/119 (8 wkts, 40 overs)	169	
E. J. Wilson b Taylor	15	4/120 5/137 6/150		
S. R. Lampitt b Follett	6	7/155 8/169		

R. J. Chapman and P. J. Newport did not bat.

Bowling: Penberthy 5-1-12-0; Rose 8-0-39-1; Taylor 8-1-27-1; Follett 8-0-26-3; Curran 3-0-20-0; Snape 8-0-37-2.

Northamptonshire

M. B. Loye c Solanki b Chapman	1	J. N. Snape st Rhodes b Lampitt	22
†R. J. Warren b Newport	5	F. A. Rose not out	9
*K. M. Curran c Chapman b Illingworth	51	L-b 6, w 3, n-b 2	11
A. L. Penberthy lbw b Chapman	8		
D. J. Sales c Wilson b Moody	8	1/5 2/10 3/39 (7 wkts, 40 overs) 169	
R. J. Bailey not out	48	4/63 5/90	
T. C. Walton b Illingworth	6	6/111 7/156	

J. P. Taylor and D. Follett did not bat.

Bowling: Newport 6–0–19–1; Chapman 8–0–21–2; Moody 8–1–26–1; Lampitt 8–0–41–1; Illingworth 6–0–34–2; Leatherdale 4–0–22–0.

Umpires: M. J. Kitchen and K. E. Palmer.

At Derby, July 12. WORCESTERSHIRE beat DERBYSHIRE by 48 runs.

At Manchester, July 20. WORCESTERSHIRE lost to LANCASHIRE by one wicket.

WORCESTERSHIRE v YORKSHIRE

At Worcester, August 2. Yorkshire won by 34 runs. Toss: Yorkshire.

A game of two dramatic collapses ended a run of three defeats for Yorkshire. Worcestershire lost nine wickets for 53, first against the back-up bowling of Lehmann and McGrath, and then to Gough, who swept away the tail. But Yorkshire had themselves crumpled, with eight wickets going down for 39. Chapman took five for 30, getting wickets with both the first and last balls of the innings.

Yorkshire

*D. Byas b Chapman	0	D. Gough not out	1
M. P. Vaughan c Weston b Lampitt	21	R. D. Stemp c and b Chapman	0
M. J. Wood c Rawnsley b Lampitt	64		
D. S. Lehmann b Lampitt	59	L-b 8, w 11, n-b 12	31
A. McGrath c Rhodes b Sheriyar	0		
B. Parker c Weston b Chapman	13	1/0 2/52 3/163 (9 wkts, 40 overs) 202	
†R. J. Blakey c Rhodes b Chapman	11	4/165 5/165 6/184	
G. M. Hamilton c Leatherdale b Chapman	2	7/198 8/199 9/202	

P. M. Hutchison did not bat.

Bowling: Chapman 7–1–30–5; Sheriyar 8–0–28–1; Moody 2–0–11–0; Lampitt 8–0–34–3; Rawnsley 8–0–45–0; Hick 3–0–18–0; Leatherdale 4–0–28–0.

Worcestershire

*T. M. Moody b McGrath	47	M. J. Rawnsley lbw b Gough	5
V. S. Solanki c Blakey b Stemp	38	A. Sheriyar c Byas b Gough	1
G. A. Hick c Byas b Lehmann	23	R. J. Chapman not out	1
D. A. Leatherdale c Byas b Lehmann	15	L-b 8, w 7	15
W. P. C. Weston b Gough	13		
E. J. Wilson lbw b McGrath	1	1/74 2/115 3/135 (38 overs) 168	
S. R. Lampitt run out	1	4/135 5/139 6/142	
†S. J. Rhodes b Gough	8	7/156 8/166 9/167	

Bowling: Gough 7–0–30–4; Hutchison 4–0–29–0; Hamilton 6–0–23–0; Stemp 8–0–34–1; Lehmann 8–0–24–2; McGrath 5–0–20–2.

Umpires: B. Dudleston and J. F. Steele.

WORCESTERSHIRE v NOTTINGHAMSHIRE

At Worcester, August 9. Worcestershire won by seven wickets. Toss: Nottinghamshire.

Only two batsmen, Johnson and Solanki, prospered on a pitch that defeated most efforts at strokeplay. Johnson battled 27 overs, without support, to muster 53, which took him past 6,000 League runs. Solanki had help from Moody and Leatherdale, and surged to 88, only to be run out going for the winning run. Weston completed the job.

Nottinghamshire

*J. E. R. Gallian c Rhodes b Lampitt. . .	20	†C. M. W. Read not out	14
U. Afzaal lbw b Chapman	1	K. P. Evans run out	2
M. P. Dowman lbw b Lampitt	17	R. T. Bates run out.	2
P. Johnson run out	53	L-b 4, w 4, n-b 10.	18
G. F. Archer c and b Illingworth	13		
C. M. Tolley b Illingworth	5	1/15 2/38 3/61 (39.4 overs) 154
P. J. Franks c Rawnsley b Illingworth . .	1	4/95 5/119 6/123
P. A. Strang c Rhodes b Chapman.	8	7/132 8/146 9/148

Bowling: Chapman 7.4–0–38–2; Moody 8–0–19–0; Lampitt 7–0–25–2; Rawnsley 8–0–25–0; Illingworth 8–0–27–3; Leatherdale 1–0–16–0.

Worcestershire

V. S. Solanki run out	88	W. P. C. Weston not out	1
E. J. Wilson lbw b Evans	6	W 2, n-b 3.	5
*T. M. Moody c Read b Strang	30		
D. A. Leatherdale not out	25	1/12 2/73 3/154 (3 wkts, 32.3 overs) 155

A. Hafeez, †S. J. Rhodes, S. R. Lampitt, R. K. Illingworth, M. J. Rawnsley and R. J. Chapman did not bat.

Bowling: Evans 6–1–15–1; Franks 6–0–38–0; Tolley 6–0–34–0; Strang 7–0–39–1; Bates 4–0–13–0; Dowman 3–1–15–0; Afzaal 0.3–0–1–0.

Umpires: G. Sharp and R. A. White.

At Canterbury, August 23. KENT v WORCESTERSHIRE. No result.

At Birmingham, August 30. WORCESTERSHIRE lost to WARWICKSHIRE by four wickets.

At Taunton, September 6. SOMERSET v WORCESTERSHIRE. No result.

WORCESTERSHIRE v HAMPSHIRE

At Worcester, September 13. Worcestershire won by four runs. Toss: Worcestershire.

Worcestershire's attack held its nerve to gain victory, and with it First Division status, overtaking Hampshire, who qualified as well. They took control when Illingworth grabbed three important wickets but were then briefly threatened by McLean, who hit 30, which almost atoned for the nine wides he conceded earlier, out of 20 in all. These put the target just beyond Hampshire's reach.

Worcestershire

W. P. C. Weston c Smith b Connor	8	D. N. Catterall not out		11
V. S. Solanki c Aymes b McLean	7	M. J. Rawnsley lbw b Connor		2
*G. A. Hick lbw b Stephenson	32	A. Sheriyar not out		4
D. A. Leatherdale b Mascarenhas	4	B 4, l-b 12, w 20, n-b 4		40
G. R. Haynes c White b Stephenson	8			—
S. R. Lampitt c Smith b Connor	28	1/20 2/20 3/39	(9 wkts, 40 overs)	181
†S. J. Rhodes c Udal b Mascarenhas	7	4/72 5/110 6/124		
R. K. Illingworth c Aymes b Udal	15	7/158 8/163 9/176		

Bowling: McLean 8–0–40–1; Connor 8–0–27–3; James 2–0–14–0; Mascarenhas 8–1–25–2; Stephenson 6–0–31–2; Udal 8–1–28–1.

Hampshire

G. W. White st Rhodes b Illingworth	21	S. D. Udal c Hick b Catterall		17
J. P. Stephenson c Haynes b Sheriyar	6	K. D. James not out		22
*R. A. Smith c Hick b Illingworth	23	C. A. Connor run out		4
W. S. Kendall b Illingworth	22	L-b 11, w 4, n-b 4		19
A. D. Mascarenhas c and b Rawnsley	4			—
M. Keech c Rhodes b Lampitt	8	1/18 2/60 3/61	(40 overs)	177
†A. N. Aymes run out	1	4/72 5/84 6/89		
N. A. M. McLean c Lampitt b Haynes	30	7/119 8/131 9/160		

Bowling: Haynes 8–0–35–1; Sheriyar 4–0–12–1; Catterall 6–0–28–1; Illingworth 8–0–31–3; Rawnsley 8–0–26–1; Lampitt 6–2–34–1.

Umpires: A. Clarkson and A. G. T. Whitehead.

YORKSHIRE

YORKSHIRE v SOMERSET

At Leeds, April 19. Yorkshire won by 38 runs (D/L method). Toss: Somerset. County debut: D. A. Reeve.

Dermot Reeve, the former Warwickshire captain now coaching Somerset, played his first game since 1996. But he had to leave the field in mid-over with a groin strain and could only watch as Somerset fell behind. Yorkshire's 185 was a fair total on a tricky pitch, and three quick wickets from Sidebottom put Somerset's innings in trouble. When the rain, which had interrupted play earlier, finally set in, Somerset were 38 short of their recalculated target.

Yorkshire

M. P. Vaughan c Bowler b Trescothick	52	†R. J. Blakey not out		14
C. White c sub b Parsons	29	L-b 10, w 5		15
*D. Byas not out	46			—
A. McGrath c Trescothick b Parsons	28	1/71 2/107	(4 wkts, 40 overs)	185
B. Parker c Turner b Burns	1	3/157 4/161		

I. D. Fisher, D. Gough, G. M. Hamilton, C. E. W. Silverwood and R. J. Sidebottom did not bat.

Bowling: Reeve 4.4–0–12–0; Rose 8–1–20–0; Parsons 7.2–1–36–2; Caddick 8–0–43–0; Pierson 4–0–19–0; Trescothick 3–0–16–1; Burns 5–0–29–1.

Somerset

*P. D. Bowler c Blakey b Sidebottom	12	M. E. Trescothick not out	10
M. Burns run out	25	G. D. Rose not out	1
R. J. Harden c Blakey b Sidebottom	6	L-b 2, w 3, n-b 2	7
S. C. Ecclestone c Blakey b Sidebottom	10		
†R. J. Turner b White	2	1/38 2/40 3/50	(6 wkts, 20 overs) 79
K. A. Parsons c Silverwood b Hamilton	6	4/57 5/59 6/75	

A. R. K. Pierson, A. R. Caddick and D. A. Reeve did not bat.

Bowling: Silverwood 4–0–18–0; Gough 3–1–10–0; White 7–0–21–1; Sidebottom 5–1–25–3; Hamilton 1–0–3–1.

Umpires: A. Clarkson and B. Leadbeater.

YORKSHIRE v DERBYSHIRE

At Leeds, April 26. Derbyshire won by five wickets (D/L method). Toss: Derbyshire.

In a rain-shortened match, Yorkshire faltered against DeFreitas and Cork on a lively pitch; they were 24 for four when the rain arrived, then 62 for seven, before a partial recovery through McGrath and Hamilton. Duckworth/Lewis calculations reduced Derbyshire's target to 123, and Barnett was more than equal to the task.

Yorkshire

M. P. Vaughan lbw b Cork	3	G. M. Hamilton not out	34
C. White b DeFreitas	1	I. D. Fisher not out	4
*D. Byas b DeFreitas	5		
D. S. Lehmann c Krikken b DeFreitas	0	L-b 6, w 1	7
A. McGrath c Blackwell b Harris	50		
B. Parker lbw b Aldred	5	1/5 2/7 3/8	(8 wkts, 35 overs) 125
†R. J. Blakey c Krikken b Clarke	13	4/15 5/27 6/54	
D. Gough c Cork b Barnett	3	7/62 8/112	

R. J. Sidebottom did not bat.

Bowling: DeFreitas 7–0–12–3; Cork 7–4–11–1; Aldred 7–2–32–1; Harris 6–0–36–1; Clarke 4–0–11–1; Barnett 4–0–17–1.

Derbyshire

A. S. Rollins c Byas b Gough	0	P. A. J. DeFreitas not out	14
*D. G. Cork c Byas b Gough	2		
T. A. Tweats b White	30	L-b 1, w 1, n-b 8	10
K. J. Barnett not out	51		
I. D. Blackwell b Hamilton	16	1/0 2/8 3/56	(5 wkts, 33.1 overs) 123
V. P. Clarke lbw b Hamilton	0	4/97 5/97	

†K. M. Krikken, G. M. Roberts, A. J. Harris and P. Aldred did not bat.

Bowling: Gough 7–0–39–2; Sidebottom 5.1–0–12–0; Hamilton 7–1–22–2; White 7–1–18–1; Fisher 4–0–16–0; Vaughan 3–0–15–0.

Umpires: K. E. Palmer and G. Sharp.

YORKSHIRE v SURREY

At Leeds, May 10. Yorkshire won by 51 runs (D/L method). Toss: Surrey.

On a seam bowler's pitch, Yorkshire struggled to make headway until McGrath and Parker revived the innings. When Surrey replied, a rejected appeal for a catch behind stirred Gough to his devastating best. In the space of 11 balls he took five for two, with international players his first four victims. As the rain swept in, Surrey were well short of a recalculated target of 118.

Yorkshire

M. P. Vaughan c Stewart b Benjamin	7	G. M. Hamilton b A. J. Hollioake	22
C. White c Brown b Bicknell	1	C. E. W. Silverwood not out	6
*D. Byas b Butcher	12	R. J. Sidebottom not out	2
D. S. Lehmann c Benjamin b Butcher	16		
A. McGrath b Benjamin	39	L-b 7, w 8	15
B. Parker c A. J. Hollioake b Bicknell	32		
†R. J. Blakey lbw b Benjamin	1	1/5 2/17 3/38 (9 wkts, 40 overs) 162	
D. Gough c B. C. Hollioake		4/66 5/107 6/109	
b A. J. Hollioake	9	7/125 8/143 9/155	

Bowling: Bicknell 8–1–26–2; Benjamin 8–2–16–3; Butcher 8–0–36–2; A. J. Hollioake 7–0–51–2; Saqlain Mushtaq 8–0–19–0; Ratcliffe 1–0–7–0.

Surrey

A. D. Brown c Blakey b Gough	29	M. P. Bicknell not out	9
†A. J. Stewart lbw b Silverwood	1	I. D. K. Salisbury not out	7
G. P. Thorpe lbw b Gough	6	L-b 3, w 5, n-b 2	10
M. A. Butcher c Byas b Silverwood	2		
*A. J. Hollioake b Gough	3	1/23 2/34 3/37 (7 wkts, 21.3 overs) 67	
B. C. Hollioake c Blakey b Gough	0	4/40 5/40	
J. D. Ratcliffe lbw b Gough	0	6/40 7/45	

Saqlain Mushtaq and J. E. Benjamin did not bat.

Bowling: Silverwood 8–3–23–2; Gough 6–1–25–5; White 4–1–10–0; Hamilton 3–1–2–0; Sidebottom 0.3–0–4–0.

Umpires: M. J. Harris and V. A. Holder.

At Northampton, May 17. YORKSHIRE beat NORTHAMPTONSHIRE by 11 runs.

At Cardiff, May 19. YORKSHIRE beat GLAMORGAN by 37 runs.

At Gloucester, May 25. YORKSHIRE beat GLOUCESTERSHIRE by nine runs.

YORKSHIRE v LEICESTERSHIRE

At Leeds, June 7. Leicestershire won by eight wickets. Toss: Yorkshire.

Yorkshire spurned the chance to go clear at the top of the League with a dismal batting display. Constantly under pressure on a pitch assisting Leicestershire's stingy attack, they almost batted out their overs but managed only 93 runs. Leicestershire found few demons in the wicket or the bowling and eased home in the 23rd over.

Yorkshire

M. P. Vaughan c Nixon b Wells	14	C. E. W. Silverwood lbw b Williamson	0
M. J. Wood c Nixon b Ormond	0	P. M. Hutchison c Dakin b Williamson	1
*D. Byas c Ormond b Lewis	1	R. J. Sidebottom not out	0
C. White c Nixon b Ormond	3	B 1, l-b 3, w 12, n-b 2	18
A. McGrath c Nixon b Ormond	0		
B. Parker c Williamson b Wells	9	1/9 2/10 3/25 (38.1 overs) 93	
†R. J. Blakey c Simmons b Lewis	29	4/25 5/25 6/53	
G. M. Hamilton lbw b Williamson	18	7/78 8/78 9/93	

Bowling: Lewis 8–2–14–2; Ormond 8–2–16–3; Wells 8–1–28–2; Simmons 8–2–19–0; Williamson 6.1–1–12–3.

Leicestershire

P. V. Simmons c Hamilton b Silverwood	16
V. J. Wells c Blakey b Hamilton	38
B. F. Smith not out	15
*C. C. Lewis not out	27

1/53 2/60   (2 wkts, 22.2 overs) 96

D. L. Maddy, A. Habib, J. M. Dakin, †P. A. Nixon, D. Williamson, J. Ormond and T. J. Mason did not bat.

Bowling: Silverwood 6–1–30–1; Hutchison 3–0–17–0; White 3–1–10–0; Hamilton 5.2–1–23–1; Sidebottom 5–1–16–0.

Umpires: D. J. Constant and R. Julian.

YORKSHIRE v HAMPSHIRE

At Leeds, June 14. No result. Toss: Yorkshire.

Rain ended play as Hampshire teetered on the brink at 78 for eight. On a pitch of uneven bounce, Hamilton claimed five for 16 in eight overs.

Hampshire

J. P. Stephenson c Blakey b Silverwood	0	†A. N. Aymes not out	12
N. A. M. McLean c Stemp b Hutchison	4	P. J. Hartley not out	18
G. W. White b Hamilton	22		
*R. A. Smith b Silverwood	3	L-b 3, w 5, n-b 2	10
D. A. Kenway lbw b Hamilton	5		
A. D. Mascarenhas b Hamilton	4	1/0 2/4 3/22 (8 wkts, 30 overs) 78
P. R. Whitaker b Hamilton	0	4/32 5/38 6/38
S. D. Udal b Hamilton	0	7/41 8/52

C. A. Connor did not bat.

Bowling: Silverwood 6–3–5–2; Hutchison 6–0–16–1; Hamilton 8–1–16–5; Sidebottom 6–2–20–0; Stemp 4–0–18–0.

Yorkshire

M. P. Vaughan, M. J. Wood, *D. Byas, A. McGrath, B. Parker, †R. J. Blakey, G. M. Hamilton, C. E. W. Silverwood, P. M. Hutchison, R. D. Stemp and R. J. Sidebottom.

Umpires: M. J. Harris and P. Willey.

At Chester-le-Street, June 21. YORKSHIRE beat DURHAM by six wickets.

At Maidstone, July 5. YORKSHIRE lost to KENT by five wickets.

YORKSHIRE v NOTTINGHAMSHIRE

At Scarborough, July 19. Nottinghamshire won by four runs (D/L method). Toss: Yorkshire.

A crowd of almost 5,000 watched stunned as Yorkshire threw away near-certain victory by losing nine wickets for 37, and their last seven for 12. They were easily heading for a revised target of 124 in 21 overs while Lehmann and Vaughan were batting. But Stemp had to hit the last ball, from Evans, for four. He missed. Nottinghamshire's innings was built entirely round Johnson, who scored 88 out of 138 while he was at the crease.

Nottinghamshire

M. P. Dowman b Silverwood	12		†C. M. W. Read b Gough	6
J. E. R. Gallian st Blakey b Stemp	19		K. P. Evans not out	3
R. T. Robinson c Lehmann b Stemp	4		B 1, l-b 7, w 3	11
*P. Johnson not out	88			
G. F. Archer run out	9		1/17 2/30 3/57	(7 wkts, 33 overs) 168
P. J. Franks run out	12		4/90 5/142	
P. A. Strang c Blakey b Silverwood	4		6/154 7/161	

M. N. Bowen and R. T. Bates did not bat.

Bowling: Silverwood 7–0–27–2; Gough 7–1–16–1; Stemp 7–0–37–2; Sidebottom 6–0–42–0; Hamilton 4–0–28–0; Lehmann 2–0–10–0.

Yorkshire

*D. Byas c Robinson b Franks	3		C. E. W. Silverwood c Bowen b Evans	3
M. P. Vaughan c Archer b Evans	57		R. D. Stemp not out	1
D. S. Lehmann c and b Strang	39		R. J. Sidebottom not out	0
A. McGrath lbw b Strang	0		L-b 6, w 1	7
B. Parker c Gallian b Franks	6			
†R. J. Blakey c Read b Franks	0		1/6 2/83 3/83	(9 wkts, 21 overs) 120
G. M. Hamilton c Gallian b Franks	3		4/108 5/108 6/114	
D. Gough c Gallian b Bowen	1		7/115 8/119 9/120	

Bowling: Franks 5–0–21–4; Evans 4–0–10–2; Bowen 4–0–22–1; Dowman 2–0–15–0; Strang 4–0–34–2; Bates 2–0–12–0.

Umpires: J. C. Balderstone and N. T. Plews.

At Lord's, July 26. YORKSHIRE lost to MIDDLESEX by 57 runs (D/L method).

At Worcester, August 2. YORKSHIRE beat WORCESTERSHIRE by 34 runs.

YORKSHIRE v LANCASHIRE

At Leeds, August 24 (day/night). Lancashire won by 101 runs. Toss: Lancashire.

The excitement of Headingley's first floodlit match, which attracted a crowd of 10,000, was offset by another dreadful Yorkshire collapse. Their batsmen were overwhelmed by Chapple, who took six for 25, the best figures for Lancashire in the League. This upstaged a hat-trick from Gough, who dismissed Wasim Akram, Hegg and Yates, with the last two balls of one over and the first of his next. A resolute 73 from Crawley had looked like taking Lancashire above 200.

Lancashire

J. P. Crawley c Byas b Silverwood	73		G. Yates b Gough	1
M. A. Atherton c McGrath b Fisher	13		G. Chapple not out	1
N. H. Fairbrother c Blakey b Hamilton	32			
G. D. Lloyd b Hamilton	1		L-b 5, w 7	12
A. Flintoff c Byas b Hamilton	21			
*Wasim Akram c Hamilton b Gough	19		1/36 2/86 3/88	(8 wkts, 40 overs) 182
†W. K. Hegg c Hamilton b Gough	4		4/132 5/169 6/175	
I. D. Austin not out	5		7/175 8/181	

P. J. Martin did not bat.

Bowling: Silverwood 8–0–34–1; Hutchison 8–0–35–0; Gough 8–0–25–3; Fisher 5–0–30–1; Hamilton 7–0–33–3; Lehmann 1–0–8–0; McGrath 3–0–12–0.

Yorkshire

*D. Byas c Hegg b Austin	3	C. E. W. Silverwood c Hegg b Chapple	5
M. P. Vaughan c Hegg b Austin	9	I. D. Fisher not out	1
M. J. Wood run out	0	P. M. Hutchison run out	1
D. S. Lehmann c Hegg b Chapple	28	B 4, l-b 8, w 6, n-b 2	20
A. McGrath c Yates b Chapple	6		
†R. J. Blakey c Hegg b Chapple	0	1/5 2/5 3/15	(25 overs) 81
G. M. Hamilton b Chapple	8	4/38 5/53 6/70	
D. Gough lbw b Chapple	0	7/70 8/75 9/80	

Bowling: Martin 5–2–5–0; Austin 6–1–17–2; Chapple 8–1–25–6; Wasim Akram 6–2–22–0.

Umpires: H. D. Bird and N. T. Plews.

YORKSHIRE v ESSEX

At Scarborough, August 30. Yorkshire won by eight wickets. Toss: Essex.

Essex frittered away their ambitions of winning the League with a weak batting display, giving their bowlers little to defend. Only Irani showed the ability to tackle slow left-armers Stemp and Fisher. Wood played with increasing assurance for an unbeaten 65, as Yorkshire won with 12 overs to spare.

Essex

*P. J. Prichard c Blakey b Silverwood	5	A. P. Cowan c Vaughan b Hamilton	4
S. G. Law c Blakey b Hutchison	10	M. C. Ilott not out	9
D. D. J. Robinson b Stemp	9	P. M. Such lbw b Hutchison	0
R. C. Irani lbw b Hamilton	37	L-b 4, w 10	14
D. R. Law st Blakey b Fisher	6		
A. P. Grayson c Hamilton b Fisher	15	1/17 2/21 3/48	(37.3 overs) 129
G. R. Napier c Byas b Fisher	9	4/60 5/84 6/97	
†B. J. Hyam c Fisher b Silverwood	11	7/101 8/113 9/127	

Bowling: Silverwood 7–1–19–2; Hutchison 6.3–0–30–2; Hamilton 8–2–30–2; Stemp 8–0–21–1; Fisher 8–0–25–3.

Yorkshire

C. White b Ilott	6
M. P. Vaughan c Cowan b Irani	25
M. J. Wood not out	65
*D. Byas not out	29
L-b 2, w 4	6

1/17 2/48   (2 wkts, 27.3 overs) 131

B. Parker, †R. J. Blakey, G. M. Hamilton, C. E. W. Silverwood, I. D. Fisher, P. M. Hutchison and R. D. Stemp did not bat.

Bowling: Ilott 5.3–1–23–1; Cowan 8–1–32–0; Such 5–0–20–0; Irani 5–0–33–1; Grayson 4–0–21–0.

Umpires: D. J. Constant and V. A. Holder.

At Hove, September 6. YORKSHIRE lost to SUSSEX by six wickets.

YORKSHIRE v WARWICKSHIRE

At Leeds, September 13. Warwickshire won by five wickets. Toss: Warwickshire.

Dickie Bird's prolonged farewell to umpiring finally reached its conclusion with what was positively his last match after 29 years on the first-class list. The players formed a guard of honour as he took the field. Naturally, there was a Dickie-type incident: he got a bruised knee after being hit by a shot from Parker. Warwickshire secured second place thanks to Knight and Giles, who saved them from an uneasy 125 for five with a match-winning stand. Yorkshire, top of the table in late June, scraped into the First Division for 1999.

Yorkshire

A. McGrath c Giles b Giddins	29		G. M. Fellows lbw b Brown	1
C. White b Brown	14		C. E. W. Silverwood not out	8
M. J. Wood c Frost b Small	27		L-b 11, w 7	18
*D. Byas c and b Small	39			
B. Parker run out	14		1/38 2/47 3/117 (7 wkts, 40 overs)	191
†R. J. Blakey not out	27		4/126 5/143	
G. M. Hamilton lbw b Munton	14		6/178 7/181	

I. D. Fisher and P. M. Hutchison did not bat.

Bowling: Munton 8–0–56–1; Giddins 8–0–26–1; Brown 8–0–41–2; Small 8–1–28–2; Giles 8–0–29–0.

Warwickshire

N. V. Knight not out	92		A. F. Giles not out	38
N. M. K. Smith c Byas b Silverwood	5			
D. L. Hemp lbw b Fisher	13		L-b 5, w 10, n-b 2	17
T. L. Penney c Hamilton b Fisher	8			
*B. C. Lara c White b Fisher	10		1/11 2/57 3/80 (5 wkts, 38.3 overs)	192
D. R. Brown c Byas b Hutchison	9		4/95 5/125	

†T. Frost, G. C. Small, T. A. Munton and E. S. H. Giddins did not bat.

Bowling: Silverwood 6–1–39–1; Hutchison 7–1–28–1; Fisher 8–0–30–3; Hamilton 8–0–31–0; Fellows 5.3–0–36–0; McGrath 4–0–23–0.

Umpires: H. D. Bird and R. Julian.

SUNDAY LEAGUE RECORDS

40 overs available in all games, except for 1993, when teams played 50 overs.

Batting

Highest individual scores: 203, A. D. Brown, Surrey v Hampshire, Guildford, 1997; 176, G. A. Gooch, Essex v Glamorgan, Southend, 1983; 175*, I. T. Botham, Somerset v Northamptonshire, Wellingborough School, 1986.

Most runs: 8,573, G. A. Gooch; 7,794, K. J. Barnett; 7,504, C. W. J. Athey; 7,499, W. Larkins; 7,062, D. W. Randall; 7,040, D. L. Amiss; 6,673, M. W. Gatting; 6,650, C. T. Radley; 6,639, D. R. Turner; 6,603, R. T. Robinson. **In a season:** 917, T. M. Moody, Worcestershire, 1991.

Most hundreds: 14, W. Larkins; 12, G. A. Gooch; 11, C. G. Greenidge; 10, T. M. Moody and R. A. Smith; 9, G. A. Hick, K. S. McEwan and B. A. Richards. 592 hundreds have been scored in the League. The most in one season is 40 in 1990.

Most sixes in an innings: 13, I. T. Botham, Somerset v Northamptonshire, Wellingborough School, 1986. **By a team in an innings:** 18, Derbyshire v Worcestershire, Knypersley, 1985, and Surrey v Yorkshire, Scarborough, 1994. **In a season:** 26, I. V. A. Richards, Somerset, 1977.

Highest total: 375 for four, Surrey v Yorkshire, Scarborough, 1994. **By a side batting second:** 317 for six, Surrey v Nottinghamshire, The Oval, 1993 (50-overs match).

Highest match aggregate: 631 for 13 wickets, Nottinghamshire (314 for seven) v Surrey (317 for six), The Oval, 1993 (50-overs match).

Lowest total: 23 (19.4 overs), Middlesex v Yorkshire, Leeds, 1974.

Shortest completed innings: 16 overs (59), Northamptonshire v Middlesex, Tring, 1974.

Record partnerships for each wicket

239	for 1st	G. A. Gooch and B. R. Hardie, Essex v Nottinghamshire at Nottingham .	1985
273	for 2nd	G. A. Gooch and K. S. McEwan, Essex v Nottinghamshire at Nottingham	1983
223	for 3rd	S. J. Cook and G. D. Rose, Somerset v Glamorgan at Neath.	1990
219	for 4th	C. G. Greenidge and C. L. Smith, Hampshire v Surrey at Southampton .	1987
190	for 5th	R. J. Blakey and M. J. Foster, Yorkshire v Leicestershire at Leicester . . .	1993
137	for 6th	M. P. Speight and I. D. K. Salisbury, Sussex v Surrey at Guildford	1996
132	for 7th	K. R. Brown and N. F. Williams, Middlesex v Somerset at Lord's	1988
110*	for 8th	C. L. Cairns and B. N. French, Nottinghamshire v Surrey at The Oval . .	1993
105	for 9th	D. G. Moir and R. W. Taylor, Derbyshire v Kent at Derby	1984
82	for 10th	G. Chapple and P. J. Martin, Lancashire v Worcestershire at Manchester .	1996

Bowling

Most wickets: 386, J. K. Lever; 368, J. E. Emburey; 346, D. L. Underwood; 307, J. Simmons; 303, S. Turner; 284, N. Gifford; 281, E. E. Hemmings; 267, J. N. Shepherd; 260, A. C. S. Pigott; 256, I. T. Botham; 254, G. C. Small; 249, T. E. Jesty; 244, C. A. Connor. **In a season:** 39, A. J. Holleake, Surrey, 1996.

Best bowling: eight for 26, K. D. Boyce, Essex v Lancashire, Manchester, 1971; seven for 15, R. A. Hutton, Yorkshire v Worcestershire, Leeds, 1969; seven for 16, S. D. Thomas, Glamorgan v Surrey, Swansea, 1998; seven for 39, A. Hodgson, Northamptonshire v Somerset, Northampton, 1976; seven for 41, A. N. Jones, Sussex v Nottinghamshire, Nottingham, 1986; six for six, R. W. Hooker, Middlesex v Surrey, Lord's, 1969; six for seven, M. Hendrick, Derbyshire v Nottinghamshire, Nottingham, 1972; six for nine, N. G. Cowans, Middlesex v Lancashire, Lord's, 1991.

Most economical analysis: 8–8–0–0, B. A. Langford, Somerset v Essex, Yeovil, 1969.

Most expensive analyses: 8–0–96–1, D. G. Cork, Derbyshire v Nottinghamshire, Nottingham, 1993, 8–0–94–2, P. N. Weekes, Middlesex v Leicestershire, Leicester, 1994; 7.5–0–89–3, G. Miller, Derbyshire v Gloucestershire, Gloucester, 1984; 8–0–88–1, E. E. Hemmings, Nottinghamshire v Somerset, Nottingham, 1983.

Hat-tricks: There have been 28 hat-tricks, four of them for Glamorgan.

Four wickets in four balls: A. Ward, Derbyshire v Sussex, Derby, 1970.

Wicket-keeping and Fielding

Most dismissals: 289 (225 ct, 64 st), S. J. Rhodes; 257 (234 ct, 23 st), D. L. Bairstow; 236 (187 ct, 49 st), R. W. Taylor; 223 (184 ct, 39 st), E. W. Jones. **In a season:** 29 (26 ct, 3 st), S. J. Rhodes, Worcestershire, 1988. **In an innings:** 7 (6 ct, 1 st), R. W. Taylor, Derbyshire v Lancashire, Manchester, 1975.

Most catches in an innings: 6, K. Goodwin, Lancashire v Worcestershire, Worcester, 1969; R. W. Taylor, Derbyshire v Lancashire, Manchester, 1975; K. M. Krikken, Derbyshire v Hampshire, Southampton, 1994; and P. A. Nixon, Leicestershire v Essex, Leicester, 1994.

Most stumpings in an innings: 4, S. J. Rhodes, Worcestershire v Warwickshire, Birmingham, 1986 and N. D. Burns, Somerset v Kent, Taunton, 1991.

Most catches by a fielder: 103, V. P. Terry; 101, J. F. Steele; 100, G. A. Gooch; 97, D. P. Hughes; 95, C. W. J. Athey†; 94, G. Cook and P. W. G. Parker. **In a season:** 16, J. M. Rice, Hampshire, 1978. **In an innings:** 5, J. M. Rice, Hampshire v Warwickshire, Southampton, 1978.

† C. W. J. Athey also took two catches as a wicket-keeper.

Results

Largest victory in runs: Somerset by 220 runs v Glamorgan, Neath, 1990.

Victories by ten wickets (32): By Derbyshire, Durham, Essex (four times), Glamorgan (twice), Hampshire (twice), Kent, Leicestershire (twice), Middlesex (twice), Northamptonshire, Nottinghamshire, Somerset (twice), Surrey (three times), Warwickshire, Worcestershire (six times) and Yorkshire (three times). This does not include those matches in which the side batting second was set a reduced target but does include matches where both sides faced a reduced number of overs.

Ties: There have been 49 tied matches. Worcestershire have tied 11 times.

Shortest match: 1 hr 53 min (26.3 overs), Surrey v Leicestershire, The Oval, 1996.

CHAMPIONS 1969-98

John Player's County League
1969 Lancashire

John Player League
1970 Lancashire
1971 Worcestershire
1972 Kent
1973 Kent
1974 Leicestershire
1975 Hampshire
1976 Kent
1977 Leicestershire
1978 Hampshire
1979 Somerset
1980 Warwickshire
1981 Essex
1982 Sussex
1983 Yorkshire

John Player Special League
1984 Essex
1985 Essex
1986 Hampshire

Refuge Assurance League
1987 Worcestershire
1988 Worcestershire
1989 Lancashire
1990 Derbyshire
1991 Nottinghamshire

Sunday League
1992 Middlesex

AXA Equity & Law League
1993 Glamorgan
1994 Warwickshire
1995 Kent
1996 Surrey

AXA Life League
1997 Warwickshire

AXA League
1998 Lancashire

MATCH RESULTS 1969-98

	P	W	L	T	NR	1st	2nd	3rd
			Matches				*League positions*	
Derbyshire	487	204	227	4	52	1	0	1
Durham	119	33	67	3	16	0	0	0
Essex	487	252	185	9	41	3	5*	4
Glamorgan	487	173	256	4	54	1	0	0
Gloucestershire	487	168	254	4	61	0	1	1
Hampshire	487	231	208	7	41	3	1	3
Kent	487	264	171	6	46	4	4	4
Lancashire	487	251	173	9	54	4	2	2
Leicestershire	487	211	212	3	61	2	2*	2
Middlesex	487	217	211	7	52	1	1	3
Northamptonshire	487	190	239	6	52	0	0	1
Nottinghamshire	487	206	233	4	44	1	3	1
Somerset	487	228	207	3	49	1	6*	0
Surrey	487	215	215	4	53	1	0	1
Sussex	487	204	226	5	52	1	2*	1
Warwickshire	487	211	218	6	52	3	2	1
Worcestershire	487	237	194	11	45	3	3	2
Yorkshire	487	218	217	3	49	1	1	1

* Includes one shared 2nd place in 1976.

COUNTY MEMBERSHIP

	1988	1997	1998
Derbyshire	1,594	2,504	2,824
Durham	–	6,438	7,443
Essex	8,599	7,402	7,442
Glamorgan	3,156	11,217	11,072
Gloucestershire	4,464	5,480	5,387
Hampshire	4,000	4,174	4,124
Kent	4,790	5,972	6,256
Lancashire	12,348	13,942	13,445
Leicestershire	3,670	5,363	5,554
Middlesex	8,099	8,957	9,242
Northamptonshire	2,214	4,066	4,286
Nottinghamshire	2,214	5,057	5,341
Somerset	5,038	6,013	6,101
Surrey	6,504	7,533	7,777
Sussex	4,533	6,153	6,299
Warwickshire	8,368	14,333	15,023
Worcestershire	5,145	5,601	5,397
Yorkshire	9,880	9,298	8,804
MCC	19,231	19,851	19,586
	113,847	149,354	151,403

Note: All the first-class counties except three quote their membership in terms of the total number of individuals affiliated to their clubs. Only Derbyshire, Kent and Yorkshire continue to register corporate or joint membership as representing one person.

OXFORD UNIVERSITY 1998

[Bill Smith]

Standing: N. J. Harris (*scorer*), J. A. Claughton, S. H. Khan, D. J. Eadie, R. Garland, M. A. Wagh, D. R. Lockhart, N. G. Pirihi, G. V. Palmer (*coach*).
Seated: D. P. Mather, B. W. Byrne, J. A. G. Fulton (*captain*), J. A. M. Molins, J. P. B. Barnes.

THE UNIVERSITIES IN 1998

OXFORD

President: C. A. Fry (Trinity)
Hon. Treasurer: Dr S. R. Porter (St Cross College)

Captain: J. A. G. Fulton (Eton and Brasenose)
Secretary: J. P. B. Barnes (Canford and Wycliffe Hall)

Captain for 1999: J. A. Claughton (King Edward VI, Southampton, and Keble)
Secretary: J. J. Bull (Oakham and Keble)

Defeat in the Varsity Match for the first time since 1992 was scant reward for Oxford's positive outlook under new coach Gary Palmer. They played their full part in an intriguing contest at Lord's, only to falter in the final session. But they took consolation from the fact that they defeated a first-class county for the second year running, when a century from Mark Wagh inspired a last-ball triumph against a weakened Kent at Canterbury. Wagh, the 1997 captain, was one of seven Blues in residence, but exams restricted him to three first-class games in The Parks. His batting was sorely missed.

For the second successive summer, Oxford opened the campaign with a change of coach. Palmer, the former Somerset player and son of international umpire Ken, was recruited to replace the Zimbabwean Test player Andy Flower, who had stepped down after only one season. Palmer brought with him many inventive ideas. He was big on fitness and motivation, introduced a series of pioneering fielding practices, and also encouraged some one-to-one sessions with a sports psychologist. Yet for all his admirable ideas, Palmer could do nothing about the weather. Three of the shortened programme of six first-class games in The Parks were ruined by rain.

When Wagh was available, his influence was substantial, and never more so than when he scored 126 in the second innings at Canterbury. Although he played in only five of the University's eight first-class fixtures, he was still their leading run-scorer with 271 at 54.20. Only two other batsmen managed to pass 200: the tenacious Australian, Byron Byrne, who often chiselled out his runs in difficult circumstances, and Jason Molins, a member of Ireland's Benson and Hedges Cup squad, who became the first Irish-born and Irish-educated Blue. John Claughton, nephew of the former Oxford and Warwickshire player of the same name, earned Palmer's praise as the most improved batsman over the season, and was appointed captain for 1999. Jez Barnes, studying for Church of England ordination, played competently behind the stumps.

Oxford's bowling attack again toiled for crumbs of comfort. South African seamers David Eadie and Ross Garland both had their moments, and also made useful runs. Garland, in particular, looked far more than a bowler who could bat. The ever-willing Byrne's off-spin was heavily employed, but the best bowling of the campaign was reserved for the Varsity Match, when left-arm swing bowler David Mather, a Blue in 1995 who missed the next two Lord's games, excelled himself. Mather bowled with a consistent line and length throughout the season, and clearly benefited from some fresh self-belief; at Lord's, he enjoyed a match return of ten for 139. It was not enough to spur an Oxford victory, but at least there was a competitive edge to their game, which was more than they showed during a heavy defeat by Cambridge in their one-day meeting in The Parks, six weeks earlier.

In January 1999, Oxford announced an alliance with neighbours Oxford Brookes University; from now on, Brookes students will be eligible to play for Oxford (except in the Varsity Match). The idea was that good cricketers would be encouraged to apply to Brookes, whose entrance requirements are far more lenient. The team will probably be known as Oxford Universities. – MIKE BERRY.

OXFORD UNIVERSITY RESULTS

First-class matches – Played 8: Won 1, Lost 2, Drawn 5.

FIRST-CLASS AVERAGES

BATTING AND FIELDING

	M	I	NO	R	HS	100s	50s	Avge	Ct
M. A. Wagh	5	6	1	271	126	1	1	54.20	2
B. W. Byrne	8	12	4	256	69*	0	1	32.00	4
R. Garland.	8	9	4	158	56*	0	1	31.60	1
J. A. M. Molins . ..	7	10	0	268	73	0	3	26.80	2
J. P. B. Barnes	5	6	3	74	38*	0	0	24.66	8
D. J. Eadie	6	6	2	84	68*	0	1	21.00	2
J. A. Claughton	5	8	1	140	45	0	0	20.00	1
C. G. R. Lightfoot .	3	6	1	98	31	0	0	19.60	1
N. G. Pirihi.	3	5	1	70	23	0	0	17.50	1
J. A. G. Fulton.....	8	12	1	180	78	0	1	16.36	4
J. T. Parker	5	5	0	80	19	0	0	16.00	1
D. R. Lockhart.....	7	11	0	173	35	0	0	15.72	6

Also batted: L. G. Buchanan (2 matches) 2 (1 ct); J. R. Cockcroft (2 matches) 18*; S. H. Ferguson (1 match) 2 (1 ct); S. H. Khan (4 matches) 0, 1; D. P. Mather (7 matches) 0, 0 (4 ct); C. R. C. Parker (1 match) 1*. A. P. Scrini (1 match) did not bat.

* Signifies not out.

BOWLING

	O	M	R	W	BB	5W/i	Avge
D. J. Eadie	113.5	19	434	13	2-34	0	33.38
D. P. Mather	168.5	32	574	17	6-74	1	33.76
B. W. Byrne	174.1	31	583	11	3-103	0	53.00
R. Garland	102	14	452	8	2-64	0	56.50

Also bowled: J. R. Cockcroft 20-1-74-0; S. H. Ferguson 26.2-1-141-3; S. H. Khan 86.4-8-327-2; C. G. R. Lightfoot 38-10-132-2; J. A. M. Molins 1-0-12-1; C. R. C. Parker 10-0-48-0; M. A. Wagh 52-7-148-2.

Note: Matches in this section which were not first-class are signified by a dagger.

OXFORD UNIVERSITY v SUSSEX

At Oxford, April 14, 15, 16. Drawn. Toss: Oxford University. First-class debuts: D. J. Eadie, R. Garland, J. A. M. Molins, J. T. Parker. University debut: D. R. Lockhart. County debuts: C. J. Adams, W. G. Khan.

David Eadie, a post-graduate from Cape Town, came close to recording a hat-trick in his first over in first-class cricket. Introduced for the 16th over of the match, the blond seamer Eadie had Adams, the new Sussex captain, caught at point for 17, and Mark Newell snapped up low down at slip next ball. But Taylor survived the hat-trick and went on to an unbeaten 74. He and Keith Newell rallied Sussex with a century stand for the fifth wicket before rain brought a mercifully early finish on a bone-chilling day. They were unable to build on that, as the springtime deluge prevented any play on days two and three.

Close of play: First day, Sussex 182-4 (N. R. Taylor 74*, K. Newell 52*); Second day, No play.

Sussex

M. T. E. Peirce c Buchanan b Mather	..	14	K. Newell not out	52
W. G. Khan b Garland	....	12		
*C. J. Adams c Byrne b Eadie	....	17	B 1, l-b 4, w 8	13
M. Newell c Wagh b Eadie	....	0		—
N. R. Taylor not out	....	74	1/20 2/42 3/42 4/50 (4 wkts)	182

†P. Moores, A. A. Khan, J. D. Lewry, R. J. Kirtley and M. A. Robinson did not bat.

Bowling: Mather 13.1–5–28–1; Garland 13–2–59–1; Eadie 15–7–34–2; Cockcroft 10–0–27–0; Byrne 9–3–19–0; Wagh 4–0–10–0.

Oxford University

D. R. Lockhart, J. T. Parker, M. A. Wagh, B. W. Byrne, *J. A. G. Fulton, J. A. M. Molins, D. J. Eadie, †L. G. Buchanan, R. Garland, D. P. Mather and J. R. Cockcroft.

Umpires: B. Dudleston and N. A. Mallender.

OXFORD UNIVERSITY v HAMPSHIRE

At Oxford, April 17, 18, 19. Drawn. Toss: Oxford University. County debut: P. J. Hartley.

Hampshire were unable to press home their advantage when the final day was washed out. Laney had scored the first first-class hundred of the season in an opening stand of 195 with White, who batted over five hours for a career-best 150. Smith missed out, caught at slip for one, but Keech chipped in with 70. Next day, Oxford collapsed from 52 for two to 72 for eight; Udal did most of the damage in a spell of three for one in 32 balls. Umpire Willey rang Lord's at lunchtime on the first day to find out if there was any regulation allowing him to suspend play on grounds of cold. There was none; despite a bitter wind and Law 3, which gives the umpires complete discretion, play continued.

Close of play: First day, Hampshire 352-4 (W. S. Kendall 13*, J. P. Stephenson 0*); Second day, Oxford University 101-8 (R. Garland 5*, J. R. Cockcroft 18*).

Hampshire

G. W. White c and b Mather	....	150	†A. N. Aymes not out	 13
J. S. Laney c Mather b Garland	.....	101		
*R. A. Smith c Byrne b Wagh	....	1	B 2, l-b 11, w 10	23
M. Keech b Eadie	....	70		—
W. S. Kendall not out	....	36	1/195 2/213 3/309 (5 wkts dec.)	394
J. P. Stephenson b Eadie	....	0	4/352 5/352	

S. D. Udal, S. J. Renshaw, P. J. Hartley and C. A. Connor did not bat.

Bowling: Mather 32.2–7–90–1; Garland 8–0–48–1; Eadie 30–2–97–2; Byrne 11–1–36–0; Cockcroft 10–1–47–0; Wagh 27–4–63–1.

Oxford University

D. R. Lockhart c Aymes b Hartley	...	6	R. Garland not out	 5
J. A. M. Molins lbw b Hartley	.....	9	†L. G. Buchanan c Laney b Udal	 2
M. A. Wagh c Laney b Stephenson	....	12	J. R. Cockcroft not out	 18
J. T. Parker lbw b Renshaw	.....	16	L-b 4, w 10, n-b 12	 26
B. W. Byrne lbw b Stephenson	....	0		—
*J. A. G. Fulton lbw b Udal	....	7	1/12 2/15 3/52 4/56 5/67 (8 wkts)	101
D. J. Eadie b Udal	....	0	6/69 7/69 8/72	

D. P. Mather did not bat.

Bowling: Connor 16–6–32–0; Hartley 5–1–7–2; Stephenson 15–5–35–2; Udal 15–10–7–3; Renshaw 11–4–15–1; Laney 1–0–1–0.

Umpires: N. A. Mallender and P. Willey.

†At Oxford, April 22. Loughborough Students won by five wickets when rain ended play. Toss: Oxford University. Oxford University 195 for eight (40 overs) (J. A. M. Molins 32, J. A. Claughton 35; D. N. Catterall three for 39); Loughborough Students 98 for five (20 overs) (T. M. B. Bailey 35).

†At Oxford, April 29. Oxford University won by seven wickets. Toss: Wiltshire. Wiltshire 199 (47.1 overs) (D. A. Winter 42; D. J. Eadie four for 22, M. H. Pryor three for 33); Oxford University 202 for three (45.3 overs) (B. W. Byrne 42, C. G. R. Lightfoot 81).

†At Oxford, May 7. Oxfordshire won by two wickets. Toss: Oxfordshire. Oxford University 255 for five (50 overs) (R. Garland 66, B. W. Byrne 68, J. A. Claughton 30 not out; A. Cook three for 42); Oxfordshire 258 for eight (49.4 overs) (C. S. Knightley 82, R. J. Williams 44, I. A. Hawtin 33; S. H. Khan three for 35).

OXFORD UNIVERSITY v WORCESTERSHIRE

At Oxford, May 11, 12, 13. Worcestershire won by 115 runs. Toss: Worcestershire. First-class debuts: J. P. B. Barnes, S. H. Khan; D. J. Pipe.

The University reduced Worcestershire to six for two in four overs, but Hick and Leatherdale responded with 210 for the third wicket. Hick, who scored an unbeaten 164 on his last visit to Oxford, indulged himself with 124 in 132 balls, his 97th first-class hundred. Oxford's innings followed the opposite pattern, collapsing from 84 for two to 162 for eight. Slow left-armer Rawnsley returned a career-best five for 72 and then, after last-morning declarations set the students 242 to win in four hours, improved that to six for 44 – making it 11 for 116 in the match. Oxford had little hope of survival once Byrne, who had made a dogged maiden fifty in the first innings, spooned Rawnsley into the covers for just four.

Close of play: First day, Worcestershire 238-3 (D. A. Leatherdale 97*, A. Hafeez 7*); Second day, Oxford University 162-8 (B. W. Byrne 69*).

Worcestershire

W. P. C. Weston b Mather	0	– not out	32
V. S. Solanki c Pirihi b Khan	2	– not out	59
*G. A. Hick c Mather b Garland	124		
D. A. Leatherdale not out	134		
A. Hafeez not out	33		
B 1, l-b 6, w 6, n-b 4	17	W 2	2

1/0 2/6 3/216	(3 wkts dec.) 310	(no wkt dec.) 93

S. R. Lampitt, S. W. K. Ellis, A. Sheriyar, †D. J. Pipe, M. J. Rawnsley and R. J. Chapman did not bat.

Bowling: *First Innings*—Mather 16–4–51–1; Khan 18–1–77–1; Byrne 15.4–0–86–0; Lightfoot 7–0–33–0; Garland 11–0–56–1. *Second Innings*—Khan 12–1–48–0; Garland 8–2–23–0; Byrne 7–3–15–0; Lightfoot 4–2–7–0.

Oxford University

D. R. Lockhart lbw b Hick	24	– lbw b Rawnsley	22
J. T. Parker c Lampitt b Ellis	11	– b Lampitt	16
N. G. Pirihi c Leatherdale b Rawnsley	23	– c Lampitt b Rawnsley	13
B. W. Byrne not out	69	– c Solanki b Rawnsley	4
C. G. R. Lightfoot c Pipe b Rawnsley	0	– st Pipe b Rawnsley	22
J. A. Claughton lbw b Rawnsley	12	– c sub b Rawnsley	12
*J. A. G. Fulton c Solanki b Rawnsley	2	– c Ellis b Hick	15
R. Garland c Rawnsley b Solanki	10	– c Pipe b Hick	7
†J. P. B. Barnes c Lampitt b Rawnsley	0	– not out	5
S. H. Khan (did not bat)		– c Hafeez b Hick	0
D. P. Mather (did not bat)		– b Rawnsley	0
B 1, l-b 8, n-b 2	11	B 1, l-b 1, n-b 8	10

1/28 2/47 3/84 4/84   (8 wkts dec.) 162   1/23 2/58 3/62 4/66 5/91   126
5/141 6/145 7/162 8/162   6/108 7/121 8/121 9/121

Bowling: *First Innings*—Sheriyar 8–4–7–0; Chapman 7–1–11–0; Lampitt 11–5–13–0; Ellis 12–5–15–1; Rawnsley 29.3–7–72–5; Hick 7–3–10–1; Solanki 10–4–25–1. *Second Innings*—Sheriyar 5–2–14–0; Chapman 6–2–18–0; Lampitt 6–2–16–1; Rawnsley 23–9–44–6; Ellis 3–1–7–0; Hick 15–8–25–3.

Umpires: M. J. Kitchen and K. J. Lyons.

†At Oxford, May 14. Oxford University won by three wickets. Toss: Berkshire. Berkshire 216 (49.5 overs) (G. E. Loveday 35, T. A. Radford 46, T. D. Fray 43; R. Garland three for 33, M. A. Wagh three for 35); Oxford University 217 for seven (49.4 overs) (J. A. M. Molins 70, N. G. Pirihi 31).

†At Oxford, May 16. Cambridge University won by 134 runs. Toss: Cambridge University. Cambridge University 257 for eight (50 overs) (W. J. House 59, G. R. Loveridge 51; S. H. Khan three for 38, R. Garland three for 49); Oxford University 123 (37.3 overs) (W. J. House four for 21).

Cambridge lead 3-1 in the Johnson Fry limited-overs Varsity series.

†At Wormsley, May 17. Drawn. Toss: Oxford University. Oxford University 260 for two dec. (D. R. Lockhart 101 not out, M. A. Wagh 129); Sir Paul Getty's XI 251 for nine (C. H. G. St George 51, T. J. G. O'Gorman 46, R. J. Greatorex 85; C. G. R. Lightfoot three for 80).

OXFORD UNIVERSITY v WARWICKSHIRE

At Oxford, May 18, 19, 20. Drawn. Toss: Warwickshire. First-class debuts: S. H. Ferguson, C. R. C. Parker.

Munton's injury jinx struck again on the second day. The former England seamer, two games into a comeback after missing the entire 1997 season, pulled up with a tweaked hamstring. Before that, Frost's maiden hundred, embracing cover drives, wristy chops and savage pulls, had enabled Warwickshire, without Lara, to reach 307 for seven; debutant seamer Stuart Ferguson collected three wickets. Maiden fifties from Molins and Garland put Oxford in a position to declare 38 behind. Then Ostler and Hemp added 150 in 36 overs to set Oxford 265 on a turning pitch, but their batsmen shut up shop for a draw. With three injured men, Warwickshire needed to find an extra substitute and Darren Altree was summoned. However, after driving round for hours, he was still unable to find the ground and went home instead.

Close of play: First day, Oxford University 26-1 (J. A. M. Molins 18*, N. G. Pirihi 4*); Second day, Warwickshire 64-0 (D. P. Ostler 38*, M. J. Powell 22*).

Warwickshire

M. J. Powell c Barnes b Ferguson	30	– (2) c Lightfoot b Garland........ 26
M. A. Sheikh c Barnes b Byrne	30	
D. L. Hemp c Ferguson b Byrne	9	– not out 59
D. P. Ostler b Ferguson	2	– (1) not out 133
G. Welch lbw b Lightfoot	9	
†T. Frost not out	111	
D. R. Brown b Ferguson	33	
M. D. Edmond c Garland b Byrne	16	
*N. M. K. Smith not out	43	
B 2, 1-b 8, w 6, n-b 8	24	L-b 2, w 6 8

1/71 2/81 3/87 4/93   (7 wkts dec.) 307   1/76   (1 wkt dec.) 226
5/105 6/161 7/218

E. S. H. Giddins and T. A. Munton did not bat.

Bowling: *First Innings*—Garland 10–3–38–0; C. R. C. Parker 7–0–28–0; Ferguson 14.2–0–82–3; Byrne 35–9–103–3; Lightfoot 17–6–46–1. *Second Innings*—C. R. C. Parker 3–0–20–0; Byrne 19–0–71–0; Ferguson 12–1–59–0; Lightfoot 6–1–32–0; Garland 14–3–42–1.

Oxford University

D. R. Lockhart lbw b Munton	4	– (2) c Powell b Giddins 7
J. A. M. Molins b Smith	73	– (1) c Hemp b Powell........ 44
N. G. Pirihi c Ostler b Welch	15	– c sub b Powell............ 5
B. W. Byrne c Frost b Edmond	2	– not out 33
*J. A. G. Fulton c Frost b Welch	5	– c Ostler b Smith........... 2
C. G. R. Lightfoot c Brown b Hemp	14	– not out 27
J. T. Parker c Ostler b Welch	18	
R. Garland not out	56	
†J. P. B. Barnes c Brown b Hemp	18	
S. H. Ferguson c Frost b Smith	2	
C. R. C. Parker not out	1	
B 8, 1-b 27, w 4, n-b 22	61	N-b 6............... 6

1/15 2/66 3/83 4/98 5/134   (9 wkts dec.) 269   1/32 2/57 3/62 4/71   (4 wkts) 124
6/140 7/177 8/253 9/260

Bowling: *First Innings*—Giddins 17–8–31–0; Munton 13.4–6–17–1; Smith 15–4–26–2; Sheikh 4.2–0–18–0; Welch 14–2–24–3; Edmond 13–3–42–1; Hemp 14–2–68–2; Ostler 2–0–8–0. *Second Innings*—Brown 8–1–31–0; Giddins 7–2–23–1; Smith 15–8–17–1; Powell 9–5–16–2; Welch 5–1–11–0; Hemp 4–1–21–0; Ostler 1–0–5–0.

Umpires: N. G. Cowley and N. T. Plews.

†At Arundel, May 21. Earl of Arundel's XI won by five wickets. Toss: Oxford University. Oxford University 189 for nine dec. (D. R. Lockhart 62, D. J. Eadie 34; D. Kotze three for 35); Earl of Arundel's XI 190 for five (R. Macleay 36, R. Thelwell 36, R. Jones 50; G. J. Scrivener four for 82).

†At Oxford, May 27. Drawn. Toss: Harlequins. Harlequins 209 (M. A. Crawley 103; D. J. Eadie three for 45, J. T. Parker three for 12); Oxford University 181 for nine (B. W. Byrne 35, J. A. Claughton 45, D. J. Eadie 30 not out; J. D. Ricketts four for 63).

OXFORD UNIVERSITY v YORKSHIRE

At Oxford, May 29, 30, June 1. Drawn. Toss: Oxford University.

Fulton finally found form after scoring only 31 in five previous innings. It was a good moment, as his team started the final day on 97 for five. But his 78, and a stand of 118 with Barnes, left Yorkshire 291 to win. The county stumbled, and Mather and Byrne had them blocking to a cordon of close catchers, finishing on 209 for seven. On the opening day, fifties from Molins, who went off for X-rays after being hit on the wrist by Sidebottom, and Eadie took Oxford past 250. White and Vaughan responded in kind. Diversions during this game included the scorers complaining that their view was blocked by a sightscreen, and three schoolboys being chased off the pitch at lunchtime after setting up their own impromptu game bowling at the stumps.

Close of play: First day, Yorkshire 19-1 (M. P. Vaughan 11*, D. Byas 4*); Second day, Oxford University 97-5 (C. G. R. Lightfoot 24*, D. J. Eadie 3*).

Oxford University

J. A. M. Molins c Wood b Hoggard	51	– (2) c Chapman b Hoggard	11
D. R. Lockhart c Wood b Hoggard	35	– (1) c Chapman b Hoggard	4
*J. A. G. Fulton c Vaughan b Hamilton	0	– (8) c and b Vaughan	78
B. W. Byrne b Hamilton	10	– c Chapman b Hamilton	24
C. G. R. Lightfoot b Vaughan	4	– lbw b Hoggard	31
R. Garland c Wood b Vaughan	25	– c White b Vaughan	4
J. A. Claughton c White b Vaughan	45	– (3) c Stemp b Vaughan	19
D. J. Eadie not out	68	– (7) c Vaughan b Stemp	8
†J. P. B. Barnes not out	11	– not out	38
L-b 7, n-b 4	11	B 1, l-b 5, n-b 10	16

1/37 2/49 3/69 4/86 (7 wkts dec.) 260
5/116 6/195 7/230

1/10 2/23 3/61 (8 wkts dec.) 233
4/75 5/79 6/111
7/115 8/233

S. H. Khan and D. P. Mather did not bat.

In the first innings J. A. M. Molins, when 31, retired hurt at 37-0 and resumed at 195.

Bowling: *First Innings*—Hoggard 20–5–58–2; Sidebottom 12–4–27–0; Hamilton 16–6–25–2; Stemp 24–8–54–0; Vaughan 22–5–89–3. *Second Innings*—Hoggard 11–0–32–3; Sidebottom 14–4–41–0; Stemp 25–12–25–1; Hamilton 12–3–44–1; Vaughan 20.1–4–73–3; McGrath 1–0–1–0; White 8–3–11–0.

Yorkshire

A. McGrath b Khan	2	– (7) not out	13
M. P. Vaughan c and b Eadie	69	– (4) c Barnes b Lightfoot	59
*D. Byas c Lockhart b Eadie	4	– (1) b Eadie	28
C. White c and b Byrne	80	– (5) c Fulton b Eadie	37
M. J. Wood not out	28	– (2) c Barnes b Mather	6
B. Parker not out	5	– (3) lbw b Mather	3
†C. A. Chapman (did not bat)	–	(6) b Byrne	20
G. M. Hamilton (did not bat)	–	c Lockhart b Byrne	6
R. D. Stemp (did not bat)	–	not out	26
L-b 3, w 10, n-b 2	15	L-b 1, w 2, n-b 8	11

1/11 2/21 (4 wkts dec.) 203
3/125 4/178

1/17 2/37 3/37 4/102 (7 wkts) 209
5/158 6/158 7/173

R. J. Sidebottom and M. J. Hoggard did not bat.

Bowling: *First Innings*—Mather 19–3–71–0; Khan 14–2–41–1; Eadie 10–2–37–2; Byrne 9.2–1–51–1. *Second Innings*—Mather 17–1–76–2; Eadie 8–0–45–2; Khan 9.4–1–38–0; Byrne 14–4–35–2; Lightfoot 4–1–14–1.

Umpires: N. G. Cowley and R. A. White.

†At Oxford, June 3, 4, 5. MCC won by three wickets. Toss: Oxford University. Oxford University 223 for eight dec. (J. A. M. Molins 43, C. G. R. Lightfoot 48 not out) and 270 for eight dec. (D. R. Lockhart 66, J. A. G. Fulton 72, S. H. Ferguson 35 not out, D. P. Mather 30 not out; Z. de Bruyn four for 55, C. Patel three for 55); MCC 180 for one dec. (C. M. Gupte 95, S. A. Richardson 48 not out) and 316 for seven (K. L. T. Arthurton 51, D. J. Capel 63, D. P. Viljoen 96, S. A. Richardson 31 not out).

†At Oxford, June 8, 9. Drawn. Toss: MCC Young Cricketers. MCC Young Cricketers 265 for seven dec. (N. J. Thurgood 34, M. Currie 51, A. J. Clarke 89 not out); Oxford University 195 for three (D. R. Lockhart 64, J. A. M. Molins 50, J. A. G. Fulton 32).

OXFORD UNIVERSITY v MIDDLESEX

At Oxford, June 13, 15, 16. Drawn. Toss: Oxford University. First-class debuts: A. W. Laraman, N. D. Martin. County debut: C. J. Batt.

Vandalism marred the final first-class fixture in The Parks. Night-time intruders scrawled an obscenity on the pitch with a broken bottle and damaged the covers. No play was possible on the first two days, anyway, because of the weather. A new wicket was cut for the final day, and both sides forfeited first innings. Kettleborough missed out on his first century for Middlesex as they declared on 255 for one, off 50 overs. But more rain deprived them of the chance to win, despite a burst of three for eight in three overs from Batt, who played for Sussex against Oxford in 1997. Fulton's 33 led the resistance.

Close of play: First day, No play; Second day, No play.

Middlesex

Middlesex forfeited their first innings.

*M. W. Gatting c Parker b Byrne	.....	62
R. A. Kettleborough not out	....	92
O. A. Shah not out	....	79
B 3, l-b 7, w 10, n-b 2	......	22

1/119   (1 wkt dec.) 255

J. C. Pooley, †D. C. Nash, K. P. Dutch, A. W. Laraman, I. N. Blanchett, N. D. Martin, C. J. Batt and U. B. A. Rashid did not bat.

Bowling: Mather 9–1–34–0; Eadie 9–2–42–0; Khan 8–0–45–0; Wagh 8–0–45–0; Byrne 10–2–45–1; Garland 6–0–34–0.

Oxford University

Oxford University forfeited their first innings.

J. A. M. Molins lbw b Batt	....	0
J. A. Claughton lbw b Batt	....	11
M. A. Wagh b Batt	....	12
B. W. Byrne lbw b Batt	....	0
*J. A. G. Fulton c Gatting b Dutch	....	33
J. T. Parker c Dutch b Martin	....	19
R. Garland not out	....	19
D. J. Eadie not out	....	4
N-b 2	....	2

1/0 2/18 3/18   (6 wkts) 100
4/27 5/65 6/87

†A. P. Scrini, S. H. Khan and D. P. Mather did not bat.

Bowling: Batt 9–1–31–4; Blanchett 6–0–22–0; Dutch 9–0–25–1; Martin 6–1–22–1.

Umpires: M. R. Benson and D. R. Shepherd.

†At Oxford, June 22, 23, 24. Drawn. Toss: Combined Services. Oxford University 278 for seven dec. (N. G. Pirihi 44, J. A. G. Fulton 82, R. Garland 35, J. J. Bull 30, J. P. B. Barnes 31, J. R. Cockcroft 35 not out; Mne A. Procter three for 111) and 318 for three dec. (J. A. Claughton 82, N. G. Pirihi 129, J. A. G. Fulton 41, R. Garland 50 not out); Combined Services 448 (Sgt G. N. Lumb 76, Capt. C. H. G. St George 170, Mne S. Needham 75, Mne G. Owen 42, Mne A. Procter 36; J. J. Bull six for 84).

At Canterbury, June 27, 28, 29. OXFORD UNIVERSITY beat KENT by three wickets.

At Lord's, July 1, 2, 3. OXFORD UNIVERSITY lost to CAMBRIDGE UNIVERSITY by 91 runs.

CAMBRIDGE

President: Professor A. D. Buckingham (Pembroke)

Captain: A. Singh (King Edward's, Birmingham, and Gonville & Caius)
Secretary: Q. J. Hughes (Durham Johnston and St Edmund's)

Captain for 1999: Q. J. Hughes (Durham Johnston and St Edmund's)
Secretary: J. P. Pyemont (Tonbridge and Trinity Hall)

A Varsity Match victory over Oxford, their first win at Lord's since 1992, went a considerable way towards compensating Cambridge for a horrendous Fenner's term. The weather made 1998 one of their most disappointing seasons since the war.

Hopes were high in April, with Cambridge able to boast one of their strongest batting sides since the halcyon days of the later 1950s and early 1960s. Captain Anurag Singh, Ed Smith and Will House, all county-registered, were in their final year; they were joined by James Pyemont, who had appeared for Sussex after topping 1,000 runs at Tonbridge School, and Greg Loveridge, the leg-spinner who played a Test for New Zealand in 1995-96.

But, over the next two months, Cambridge suffered one of the worst springs in living memory. Only two and a half hours' cricket was possible against Northamptonshire in the opening game of the season. Less than an hour was possible in the next match, against Leicestershire. A brief respite during the build-up to examinations enabled games against Durham and Glamorgan to be played virtually without interruption, before the final home fixture, against Derbyshire, was abandoned.

All of this meant that the captain, Singh, who missed the two completed games as he prepared for his finals, finished the Fenner's season without a first-class innings. Smith, who like Singh had scored centuries for Cambridge in each of his two previous seasons, fared only marginally better, batting twice against Glamorgan before he took to his books – a worrying trend. Smith's diligence earned him a first in his history finals. But House also won a first, despite making himself available for all Cambridge games and for the British Universities in their five Benson and Hedges matches, in which Singh played as captain. Their exam successes – Singh recorded a 2:1 in his law finals – showed that sport and academic excellence are compatible, a point the university club will make in seeking to recruit more brainy cricketers.

The bowling, what there was of it, was generally disappointing, although the slow, generally wet, pitches did not help. Loveridge, in particular, suffered. It was not until they arrived at Lord's that Cambridge began to realise their full potential, completing a rare double over Oxford: they had convincingly won their one-day game against them in The Parks.

Smith missed the Varsity Match – when he was available again, he broke a finger batting for British Universities against the South Africans. But a century against Yorkshire at Leeds from Imraan Mohammed, son of former Pakistan and Gloucestershire opener Sadiq, sent Cambridge to Lord's in cheerful mood, enhanced by a sparkling century from Singh on the first day. Oxford responded by declaring behind, and Cambridge sacrificed wickets in the second innings to set a target, confident that Loveridge would be able to bowl out Oxford to win. His first five-wicket haul in England achieved just that.

The appalling weather also hit Cambridge's celebration of 150 years at Fenner's, held in mid-June. The main match, against a Fenner's XI on June 13, was abandoned midway through the first innings; a game against MCC, the first opponents in 1848, was declared a draw when weather intervened minutes before the University would have won. Although the two clubs had agreed to 50 overs a side, the use of the Duckworth/Lewis method to calculate a result had been firmly ruled out by MCC captain Roger Knight. – DAVID HALLETT.

CAMBRIDGE UNIVERSITY RESULTS

First-class matches – Played 6: Won 1, Lost 2, Drawn 3. Abandoned 1.

FIRST-CLASS AVERAGES

BATTING AND FIELDING

	M	I	NO	R	HS	100s	50s	Avge	Ct/St
A. Singh.	4	3	0	178	117	1	0	59.33	0
A. N. Janisch	4	4	2	83	26*	0	0	41.50	0
W. J. House	6	7	0	280	65	0	3	40.00	2
I. Mohammed	6	7	1	237	136	1	0	39.50	0
Q. J. Hughes	6	7	0	217	84	0	1	31.00	4
B. J. Collins	3	5	0	79	36	0	0	15.80	5
J. P. Pyemont	6	7	0	105	54	0	1	15.00	3
G. R. Loveridge	6	7	0	103	41	0	0	14.71	0
P. A. Schaffter	4	3	1	20	12	0	0	10.00	0
P. J. Moffat	5	6	1	34	12	0	0	6.80	0
M. J. Birks	6	7	1	38	13	0	0	6.33	5/2
J. P. Lowe	6	5	2	13	7*	0	0	4.33	1

Also batted: S. J. W. Lewis (1 match) 3, 0; E. T. Smith (3 matches) 44, 27.

* Signifies not out.

BOWLING

	O	M	R	W	BB	5W/i	Avge
P. J. Moffat	91	24	232	7	3-25	0	33.14
G. R. Loveridge	161	31	485	13	5-59	1	37.30
J. P. Lowe	106	27	295	6	2-42	0	49.16

Also bowled: W. J. House 43–8–132–1; Q. J. Hughes 20.5–1–71–1; A. N. Janisch 80–19–253–3; I. Mohammed 12–1–52–1; J. P. Pyemont 2–0–20–0; P. A. Schaffter 44.3–16–118–2; A. Singh 2–0–21–0.

Note: Matches in this section which were not first-class are signified by a dagger.

[Bill Smith]

CAMBRIDGE UNIVERSITY 1998

Standing: D. W. Randall (coach), P. A. Schaffter, B. J. Collins, G. R. Loveridge, J. P. Pyemont, M. J. Birks, P. J. Moffat, J. P. Lowe, E. D. Smith. Seated: W. J. House, Q. J. Hughes, A. N. Janisch, I. Mohammed. Inset: A. R. May (scorer).

†At Cambridge, April 3. Cambridge University v Essex Second XI. Abandoned.

†At Cambridge, April 4. Cambridge University v Essex Second XI. Abandoned.

†At Cambridge, April 7. Cambridge University v Gloucestershire. Abandoned.

†At Cambridge, April 8. Gloucestershire won by seven wickets. Toss: Cambridge University. Cambridge University 135 (49.3 overs) (A. Singh 30; B. W. Gannon three for 27); Gloucestershire 139 for three (29 overs) (T. H. C. Hancock 40 not out).

†At Cambridge, April 9. Cambridge University v Loughborough Students. Abandoned.

†At Cambridge, April 10. Cambridge University v Loughborough Students. Abandoned.

CAMBRIDGE UNIVERSITY v NORTHAMPTONSHIRE

At Cambridge, April 14, 15, 16. Drawn. Toss: Cambridge University. First-class debuts: J. P. Lowe; G. P. Swann. University debuts: G. R. Loveridge, J. P. Pyemont.

Only 150 minutes' play was possible on the first day, after the start was delayed 90 minutes by snow flurries. During that time, Cambridge took three wickets. Rain began falling during the tea interval and the match never restarted.

Close of play: First day, Northamptonshire 122-3 (R. R. Montgomerie 46*, K. M. Curran 41*); Second day, No play.

Northamptonshire

R. R. Montgomerie not out	46	*K. M. Curran not out	41
A. J. Swann b Janisch	1	B 4, l-b 3, w 2, n-b 2	11
M. B. Loye c Birks b Lowe	14		
D. J. Sales c Birks b Schaffter	9	1/15 2/38 3/59 (3 wkts)	122

A. L. Penberthy, D. J. Capel, †D. Ripley, G. P. Swann, S. A. J. Boswell and J. A. R. Blain did not bat.

Bowling: Janisch 7–0–30–1; Lowe 9–2–20–1; Schaffter 10–5–21–1; Loveridge 11–2–32–0; House 4–3–2–0; Mohammed 1–0–10–0.

Cambridge University

J. P. Pyemont, E. T. Smith, Q. J. Hughes, *A. Singh, W. J. House, G. R. Loveridge, I. Mohammed, †M. J. Birks, A. N. Janisch, J. P. Lowe and P. A. Schaffter.

Umpires: P. Carrick and A. G. T. Whitehead.

CAMBRIDGE UNIVERSITY v LEICESTERSHIRE

At Cambridge, April 17, 18, 19. Drawn. Toss: Cambridge University. First-class debut: P. J. Moffat.

The opening day was restricted to less than 16 overs, during which Lowe dismissed England A batsman Maddy. The weather then closed in again and no more play took place.

Close of play: First day, Leicestershire 24-1 (V. J. Wells 10*, I. J. Sutcliffe 7*); Second day, No play.

Leicestershire

V. J. Wells not out	10	
D. L. Maddy b Lowe	2	
I. J. Sutcliffe not out.	7	
B 2, l-b 3	5	

1/5   (1 wkt) 24

*J. J. Whitaker, B. F. Smith, A. Habib, C. C. Lewis, †P. A. Nixon, J. Ormond, T. J. Mason and M. T. Brimson did not bat.

Bowling: Lowe 8–4–10–1; Schaffter 7.3–3–9–0.

Cambridge University

J. P. Pyemont, E. T. Smith, Q. J. Hughes, *A. Singh, W. J. House, G. R. Loveridge, I. Mohammed, †M. J. Birks, P. J. Moffat, J. P. Lowe and P. A. Schaffter.

Umpires: H. D. Bird and A. A. Jones.

†At Cambridge, April 26. Drawn. Toss: Cambridge University. Cambridge University 64 for no wkt (G. R. Loveridge 46 not out) v Cryptics.

†At Cambridge, April 27. Cambridge University won by 38 runs. Toss: Cambridge University. Cambridge University 164 for six (31 overs) (A. Singh 36); Hertfordshire 126 for seven (31 overs) (R. W. Nowell 31 not out).

†At Cambridge, May 3. Free Foresters won by five wickets. Toss: Cambridge University. Cambridge University 208 for seven dec. (Q. J. Hughes 54, C. J. Freeston 38, R. McDowell 41); Free Foresters 209 for five (R. O. Jones 76, C. J. Hollins 82).

†At Cambridge, May 4. Cambridgeshire won by five wickets. Toss: Cambridge University. Cambridge University 197 (52.3 overs) (I. Mohammed 70, R. Khan 65; B. T. P. Donelan five for 31); Cambridgeshire 198 for five (52.1 overs) (R. A. E. Martin 51, M. Yeeles 37, N. T. Gadsby 41 not out).

†At Cambridge, May 5, 6, 7. Cambridge University won by four wickets. Toss: MCC. MCC 276 for six dec. (P. N. Hepworth 71, N. J. Archer 89 not out, B. C. Strang 33 not out; J. P. Lowe three for 67) and 124 (D. P. Viljoen 37; J. P. Lowe four for 36, P. J. Moffat four for 33); Cambridge University 157 (R. Khan 30, M. J. Birks 30; C. M. Pitcher five for 37) and 244 for six (Q. J. Hughes 81, I. Mohammed 94; C. M. Pitcher four for 43).

†At Arundel, May 12. Drawn. Toss: Cambridge University. Cambridge University 240 for seven dec. (I. Mohammed 70, J. C. Hammill 56, A. N. Janisch 30 not out; T. Harrison three for 27); Earl of Arundel's XI 226 for seven (P. Stewart 32, T. Harrison 107 not out; A. N. Janisch three for 31, G. R. Loveridge three for 68).

CAMBRIDGE UNIVERSITY v GLAMORGAN

At Cambridge, May 13, 14, 15. Glamorgan won by 171 runs. Toss: Cambridge University. First-class debuts: S. P. Jones, I. J. Thomas.

Glamorgan started solidly, with Evans scoring a maiden century and sharing successive hundred partnerships with Shaw and Dale. But for once, the University made a good start too: the Tonbridge pair of Pyemont and Smith opened with a stand of 75. Their best batting, however, came from Hughes, captaining Cambridge in a first-class game for the first time. He made a career-best 84 and, helped by a 64-ball fifty from House, was able to declare 72 behind. Cottey and Butcher scored freely in Glamorgan's second innings and Cambridge, set 293 in two sessions, were bowled out for 121 by Parkin and Butcher.

Close of play: First day, Cambridge University 13-0 (J. P. Pyemont 4*, E. T. Smith 7*); Second day, Glamorgan 91-1 (P. A. Cottey 42*, G. P. Butcher 12*).

Glamorgan

†A. D. Shaw c Birks b Moffat	71		
A. W. Evans c Lowe b Loveridge	125		
A. Dale c sub b Lowe	59		
*P. A. Cottey c House b Lowe	4	– (2) c Hughes b Schaffter	71
M. J. Powell not out	21	– (1) c House b Loveridge	27
G. P. Butcher not out	43	– (3) c and b Hughes	82
W. L. Law (did not bat)		– (4) run out	1
I. J. Thomas (did not bat)		– (5) not out	9
B 4, l-b 5, w 2, n-b 8	19	B 4, l-b 8, w 2, n-b 16	30

1/158 2/263 3/274 4/275	(4 wkts dec.) 342	1/73 2/177 (4 wkts dec.) 220
		3/188 4/220

D. A. Cosker, S. P. Jones and O. T. Parkin did not bat.

Bowling: First Innings—Lowe 17–7–42–2; Janisch 17–3–57–0; Schaffter 5–1–22–0; Loveridge 27–0–117–1; Moffat 19–5–56–1; House 6–0–18–0; Mohammed 3–0–21–0. *Second Innings*—Lowe 11–2–34–0; Janisch 10–0–68–0; Loveridge 15–2–45–1; Moffat 4–0–17–0; Schaffter 7–2–33–1; Hughes 3.5–0–11–1.

Cambridge University

J. P. Pyemont c Evans b Dale	54	– c Thomas b Parkin	0
E. T. Smith c Powell b Jones	44	– c Cottey b Cosker	27
*Q. J. Hughes c Thomas b Law	84	– c Evans b Parkin	1
G. R. Loveridge c Butcher b Cosker	7	– lbw b Parkin	7
W. J. House b Law	50	– c Shaw b Cosker	20
I. Mohammed not out	7	– c Law b Jones	9
†M. J. Birks not out	3	– lbw b Butcher	13
A. N. Janisch (did not bat)		– not out	26
P. J. Moffat (did not bat)		– c Shaw b Butcher	2
J. P. Lowe (did not bat)		– lbw b Butcher	0
P. A. Schaffter (did not bat)		– c Cottey b Butcher	8
B 4, l-b 4, n-b 13	21	B 5, l-b 3	8

1/75 2/144 3/161	(5 wkts dec.) 270	1/0 2/4 3/12 4/57 5/64	121
4/253 5/260		6/74 7/97 8/103 9/105

Bowling: First Innings—Parkin 16–6–39–0; Jones 13–1–56–1; Cosker 21–4–57–1; Butcher 12–2–43–0; Dale 12–3–38–1; Law 8–1–29–2. *Second Innings*—Parkin 8–1–19–3; Jones 10–2–28–1; Dale 4–2–15–0; Cosker 17–4–31–2; Law 1–0–6–0; Butcher 8.4–4–14–4.

Umpires: P. Carrick and G. Sharp.

†At Oxford, May 16. CAMBRIDGE UNIVERSITY beat OXFORD UNIVERSITY by 134 runs.

CAMBRIDGE UNIVERSITY v DURHAM

At Cambridge, May 18, 19, 20. Durham won by 95 runs. Toss: Durham. First-class debuts: B. J. Collins; S. J. W. Lewis; M. J. Symington.

Hutton and Gough, in his second first-class match, put on 227 for the first wicket, Durham's third-highest stand for any wicket (the other two were also opening partnerships, against Oxford). That evening, Brown, playing what was to be his only first-class match of 1998, with his damaged knee in a specially constructed brace, took three wickets in seven balls, which he converted into six for 17 next day. A rearguard action by debutant Ben Collins failed by two runs to avert the follow-on. But acting-captain Morris waived it anyway to score an unbeaten century. Cambridge put up more resistance the second time, but still went down to their second successive defeat.

Close of play: First day, Cambridge University 21-3 (J. P. Pyemont 6*, S. J. W. Lewis 0*); Second day, Durham 186-1 (J. E. Morris 110*, P. D. Collingwood 24*).

Durham

S. Hutton c Pyemont b Moffat	100			
M. A. Gough run out	123			
†A. Pratt c Collins b Loveridge	6			
N. Killeen not out	15			
M. J. Symington not out	8			
*J. E. Morris (did not bat)		– (1) not out	110
J. A. Daley (did not bat)		– (2) c Pyemont b Loveridge	47
P. D. Collingwood (did not bat)		– (3) not out	24
B 12, l-b 2, w 4	18	B 4, l-b 1	5

1/227 2/246 3/251   (3 wkts dec.) 270   1/128   (1 wkt dec.) 186

N. C. Phillips, S. J. E. Brown and J. P. Searle did not bat.

Bowling: *First Innings*—Lowe 13–2–41–0; Schaffter 8–2–22–0; Moffat 20–5–57–1; House 15–3–32–0; Loveridge 28–2–83–1; Mohammed 1–0–5–0; Hughes 4–0–16–0. *Second Innings*—Lowe 6–1–21–0; Schaffter 7–3–11–0; Moffat 8–0–20–0; Loveridge 21–5–70–1; House 5–0–28–0; Hughes 9–1–28–0; Mohammed 1–0–3–0.

Cambridge University

J. P. Pyemont c Phillips b Symington	10	– c Daley b Phillips	13
I. Mohammed lbw b Brown	13	– (7) b Phillips	42
†M. J. Birks b Brown	0	– (9) c Gough b Phillips	2
G. R. Loveridge lbw b Brown	2	– lbw b Symington	6
S. J. W. Lewis lbw b Brown	3	– (2) c Phillips b Killeen	0
W. J. House c and b Symington	17	– (5) c Killeen b Brown	65
*Q. J. Hughes c Pratt b Killeen	17	– (3) c Gough b Phillips	27
B. J. Collins c and b Searle	36	– c Pratt b Daley	33
P. J. Moffat lbw b Brown	10	– (6) b Gough	12
J. P. Lowe lbw b Brown	0	– not out	7
P. A. Schaffter not out	0	– c sub b Searle	12
L-b 5, w 2, n-b 4	11	B 7, l-b 12, w 4	23

1/19 2/19 3/21 4/25 5/37   119   1/6 2/34 3/49 4/81 5/135   242
6/61 7/91 8/117 9/117   6/139 7/192 8/206 9/221

Bowling: *First Innings*—Brown 16–8–17–6; Killeen 11–1–47–1; Phillips 15–10–8–0; Symington 6–1–34–2; Searle 7.4–4–8–1. *Second Innings*—Brown 15–4–37–1; Killeen 14.5–27–1; Symington 7–1–27–1; Phillips 24–11–58–4; Searle 14.3–2–58–1; Gough 6–4–4–1; Daley 1–0–12–1.

Umpires: J. C. Balderstone and H. D. Bird.

†At Wormsley, May 31. Drawn. Toss: Sir Paul Getty's XI. Cambridge University 245 for eight dec. (Q. J. Hughes 36, A. Singh 35, D. W. Randall 43, G. R. Loveridge 79, A. N. Janisch 30); Sir Paul Getty's XI 229 for nine (P. A. Wallace 63, S. Elworthy 40; J. P. Lowe three for 62, P. J. Moffat four for 49).

†At Cambridge, June 7. Drawn. Toss: Cambridge University. Cambridge University 213 for five dec. (E. T. Smith 73, Q. J. Hughes 79 not out); Quidnuncs 190 for nine (R. O. Jones 55, J. P. Arscott 46; G. R. Loveridge five for 67).

CAMBRIDGE UNIVERSITY v DERBYSHIRE

At Cambridge, June 10, 11, 12. Abandoned.

Soon after Cambridge won the toss and shortly before the umpires were due to take the field, the rain started. The game was abandoned early on the final morning; Adrian Rollins would have captained his county for the first time.

†At Cambridge, June 13. Drawn. Toss: Cambridge University. Cambridge University 136 for six (E. T. Smith 63) v A Fenner's XI.

†At Cambridge, June 14. Drawn. Toss: MCC. MCC 218 for six dec. (S. J. Dean 56, R. Q. Cake 33, M. A. Crawley 62; P. J. Moffat three for 34); Cambridge University 200 for three (J. P. Pyemont 100 not out).

†At Cambridge, June 18. Cambridge University v Combined Services. Abandoned.

At Leeds, June 27, 28, 29. CAMBRIDGE UNIVERSITY drew with YORKSHIRE.

THE UNIVERSITY MATCH, 1998

OXFORD UNIVERSITY v CAMBRIDGE UNIVERSITY

At Lord's, July 1, 2, 3. Cambridge University won by 91 runs. Toss: Oxford University.

Cambridge won the match for the first time for six years, thanks to positive captaincy. They were put in, and Singh led from the front, scoring a chanceless 117 with 15 fours, after Pyemont was out in the first over. Singh declared that evening, and opened his attack with Loveridge's leg-spin. Next day, Oxford reached 180 for three by mid-afternoon, with fifties from Molins and Wagh. After discussion between the captains, they declared 114 behind, and Cambridge started chasing quick runs. Despite Mather claiming their top three in a 17-ball spell – he finished with six for 74, and ten for 139 in all – the middle order thrived, Singh and House adding 70 in as many balls. But Cambridge were all out early on the final morning, leaving Oxford most of the day to score 291. They moved steadily, but slowly, to 83 for one before three wickets fell in ten balls. Byrne remained undefeated after two and a half hours, but Oxford were bowled out by Loveridge, who took five for 59, with nine overs remaining. In the closing stages, Oxford coach Gary Palmer came out to discuss with the umpires the number of overs in the final hour; he interpreted ECB regulations to specify 16, as in the County Championship, but a footnote stated that, in other first-class matches, it should be 20, as in the Laws. His team's final collapse made it irrelevant.

Close of play: First day, Oxford University 29-0 (J. A. M. Molins 15*, D. R. Lockhart 10*); Second day, Cambridge University 165-8 (G. R. Loveridge 41*, P. J. Moffat 0*).

Cambridge University

J. P. Pyemont (*Tonbridge and Trinity Hall*)
c Barnes b Mather .   0 – lbw b Mather. 17

I. Mohammed (*Karachi GS, Joseph Chamberlain C. and St Catharine's*) c Barnes b Mather .   30 – lbw b Mather. 0

Q. J. Hughes (*Durham Johnston and St Edmund's*)
c Molins b Byrne .   42 – c Barnes b Mather 8

*A. Singh (*King Edward's, Birmingham, and Gonville & Caius*) c Mather b Eadie .   117 – c Eadie b Garland. 31

W. J. House (*Sevenoaks and Gonville & Caius*)
c Fulton b Mather .   33 – c Fulton b Mather. 44

G. R. Loveridge (*Awatapu C., Massey U., New Zealand, and St Edmund's*) run out   10 – c Barnes b Eadie 41

B. J. Collins (*St Albans S. and Girton*)
lbw b Eadie .   6 – lbw b Mather 0

A. N. Janisch (*Abingdon and Trinity*) not out .   22 – c Lockhart b Molins 12

†M. J. Birks (*South Craven CS and Jesus*)
c Fulton b Mather .   13 – c Lockhart b Byrne 1

P. J. Moffat (*Lancaster RGS, Leeds U., and Hughes Hall*) c and b Byrne .   2 – not out 4

J. P. Lowe (*Queen Elizabeth GS, Wakefield, and Girton*) (did not bat) .   – lbw b Mather. 5

B 1, l-b 3, w 5, n-b 10 .   19   L-b 5, w 2, n-b 2 13

1/0 2/45 3/124 4/206 5/228   (9 wkts dec.) 294   1/13 2/20 3/29 4/99 5/123   176
6/255 7/257 8/291 9/294   6/123 7/162 8/165 9/165

Bowling: *First Innings*—Mather 20–4–65–4; Eadie 13–1–64–2; Khan 23–3–71–0; Wagh 3–0–17–0; Byrne 23.1–5–49–2; Garland 6–1–24–0. *Second Innings*—Mather 16.2–1–74–6; Eadie 11–3–39–1; Garland 5–0–34–1; Khan 2–0–7–0; Byrne 3–2–5–1; Molins 1–0–12–1.

Oxford University

J. A. M. Molins (*High School C., Dublin U. and Keble*) lbw b House .   51 – (2) c Birks b Moffat 4

D. R. Lockhart (*Glasgow Academy, Durham U. and Keble*) lbw b Lowe .   12 – (1) c Collins b Loveridge. 26

M. A. Wagh (*King Edward's, Birmingham, and Keble*) not out .   78 – c Birks b Janisch 43

B. W. Byrne (*Esperance HS, Western Australia U. & Balliol*) c Pyemont b Moffat .   19 – not out 41

*J. A. G. Fulton (*Eton and Brasenose*) not out .   10 – c Collins b Loveridge 0

J. A. Claughton (*King Edward VI, Southampton, and Keble*) (did not bat) .   – c Hughes b Loveridge. 26

R. Garland (*Durban HS, Natal U. and Pembroke*) (did not bat) .   – c Collins b Moffat 17

D. J. Eadie (*Diocesan C., Cape Town U. and St Edmund Hall*) (did not bat) .   – b Moffat 0

†J. P. B. Barnes (*Canford, Southampton U. and Wycliffe Hall*) (did not bat) .   – lbw b Janisch 2

S. H. Khan (*Islamabad GS, UCL and Wadham*) (did not bat) .   – st Birks b Loveridge 1

D. P. Mather (*Wirral GS and Green*) (did not bat) .   – lbw b Loveridge. 0

B 6, n-b 4   10   B 10, l-b 7, w 4, n-b 18 . .   39

1/39 2/111 3/161   (3 wkts dec.) 180   1/13 2/83 3/89 4/91 5/141   199
       6/186 7/188 8/194 9/199

Bowling: *First Innings*—Loveridge 12–3–31–0; Moffat 18–7–34–1; House 7–1–34–1; Lowe 14–5–36–1; Janisch 10–0–39–0. *Second Innings*—Moffat 7–1–25–3; Janisch 23–10–36–2; Lowe 15–3–50–0; Loveridge 25–8–59–5; House 4–1–12–0.

Umpires: M. J. Harris and G. Sharp.

OXFORD v CAMBRIDGE, NOTES

The University Match dates back to 1827. Altogether there have been 153 official matches, Cambridge winning 56 and Oxford 48, with 49 drawn. Since the war Cambridge have won ten times (1949, 1953, 1957, 1958, 1972, 1979, 1982, 1986, 1992 and 1998) and Oxford nine (1946, 1948, 1951, 1959, 1966, 1976, 1984, 1993 and 1995). All other matches have been drawn; the 1988 fixture was abandoned without a ball being bowled.

One hundred and four three-figure innings have been played in the University matches, 50 for Oxford and 54 for Cambridge. For the fullest lists see the 1940 and 1993 *Wisdens*. There have been three double-centuries for Cambridge (211 by G. Goonesena in 1957, 201 by A. Ratcliffe in 1931 and 200 by Majid Khan in 1970) and two for Oxford (238* by Nawab of Pataudi, sen. in 1931 and 201* by M. J. K. Smith in 1954). Ratcliffe's score was a record for the match for only one day, before being beaten by Pataudi's. M. J. K. Smith and R. J. Boyd-Moss (Cambridge) are the only players to score three hundreds.

The highest totals in the fixture are 513 for six in 1996, 503 in 1900, 457 in 1947, 453 for eight in 1931 and 453 for nine in 1994, all by Oxford. Cambridge's highest is 432 for nine in 1936. The lowest totals are 32 by Oxford in 1878 and 39 by Cambridge in 1858.

F. C. Cobden, in the Oxford v Cambridge match in 1870, performed the hat-trick by taking the last three wickets and won an extraordinary game for Cambridge by two runs. Other hat-tricks, all for Cambridge, have been achieved by A. G. Steel (1879), P. H. Morton (1880), J. F. Ireland (1911) and R. G. H. Lowe (1926). S. E. Butler, in the 1871 match, took all ten wickets in the Cambridge first innings.

D. W. Jarrett (Oxford 1975, Cambridge 1976), S. M. Wookey (Cambridge 1975-76, Oxford 1978) and G. Pathmanathan (Oxford 1975-78, Cambridge 1983) gained Blues for both Universities.

A full list of Blues from 1837 may be found in Wisdens *published between 1923 and 1939. The lists thereafter were curtailed:* Wisdens *from 1948 to 1972 list Blues since 1880; from 1973 to 1983 since 1919; from 1984 to 1992 since 1946.*

THE HALIFAX BUSA CHAMPIONSHIP, 1998

By GRENVILLE HOLLAND

For the first time in 25 years, there was no champion university. At the end of a short season badly disrupted by the weather, the British University Sports Association (BUSA) final at Luton was ruined by almost two days of incessant rain. A rematch proved impossible, and the title was shared by Durham and Loughborough, who, under the name of Loughborough Colleges, reached the last final to be left undecided, against Leicester in 1973.

There were few surprises in 1998: three of the four semi-finalists could have been predicted before a ball had been bowled. Durham swept through the northern group undefeated, thanks to their all-round strength and the leadership of their captain, Mark Chilton of Lancashire. In the Midlands, Loughborough were equally untroubled and, despite lacking Durham's obvious strengths, still packed enough punch to top their league with ease.

UWIC (University of Wales Institute, Cardiff) are becoming the dominant side in Wales, and their ambition and commitment may be rewarded before long. They were strengthened by the batting of Glamorgan player Steve Tomlinson and by the bowling of off-spinner Tamnay Patnaik, a postgraduate student. Patnaik's best performance came in the opening match against Swansea, when he took four for ten in 45 balls. Nottingham, promoted to the Premier level in 1997, made full use of their elevation to become the fourth semi-finalists. This was thanks largely to the bowling of Anthony Aduhene, whose performances included five for 41 against Worcester.

Cambridge were among the eight teams relegated from the Premier level, which means Oxbridge will be unrepresented in 1999 – a step away from integration with the other cricketing universities.

In the quarter-finals, UWIC enjoyed a comfortable home win against Northumbria, with Tomlinson hitting 71 not out. Exeter were severely disadvantaged when they had to make the long haul to Durham in the middle of exams; their scratch side could muster only 122 on an amiable Racecourse pitch, leaving Durham ample time to reach the target for the loss of two wickets. Nottingham were away to southern-group winners Luton, and reached 286. Luton were dismissed for 134 in reply. Loughborough convincingly defeated Brunel, racking up 323 for three. David Ellis hit 165 not out to put the game beyond Brunel's reach. Loughborough and Durham both won their semi-finals comfortably.

The future direction of university cricket remained in the balance. The ECB continued to consult with BUSA about how best to promote the game at the many institutions that make up higher education. Some have grounds and facilities for training and practice; others lack both. But all are capable of fostering a Test or county cricketer, and so cannot, in terms of the ECB's remit, be neglected.

Lord MacLaurin, the ECB chairman, seemed to favour six university centres of excellence, located strategically around the country, and serviced by either peripatetic or resident coaches. This commendable approach to university cricket must, however, fit into the real world of a modern university system. Trying to fulfil a large fixture list in a summer term of demanding exams places students under considerable pressure and, in the end, they must put their academic commitments first, or perish. To compound the problem, many institutions have introduced "semesters" – two rather than three terms a year – so shrinking the cricket season to little more than a month. In October 1998, tuition fees of £1,000 were introduced, and the maintenance grant all but removed, placing students under a heavy financial burden. Increasingly, they select courses and universities for maximum academic and long-term professional benefit, rather than for sporting opportunities.

BUSA PREMIER GROUP

South

	P	W	L	NR	T	Pts
Luton	5	4	1	0	0	12
Brunel	5	3	2	0	0	9
London	5	3	2	0	0	9
Sussex	5	2	3	0	0	6
Cambridge	5	2	3	0	0	6
Brighton	5	1	4	0	0	0

North

	P	W	L	NR	T	Pts
Durham	5	5	0	0	0	15
Northumbria	5	4	1	0	0	12
Manchester	5	2	2	0	1	7.5
Sheffield	5	2	2	0	1	7.5
Newcastle	5	1	4	0	0	3
Edinburgh	5	0	5	0	0	0

Midlands

	P	W	L	NR	T	Pts
Loughborough	5	4	0	1	0	13
Nottingham	5	4	1	0	0	12
Staffordshire	5	3	2	0	0	9
Birmingham	5	2	3	0	0	6
Chester	5	0	4	1	0	1
Worcester	5	1	4	0	0	0

West

	P	W	L	NR	T	Pts
UWIC	5	4	1	0	0	12
Exeter	5	3	0	1	1	11.5
Southampton	5	3	2	0	0	9
UW Swansea	5	1	2	1	1	5.5
Cheltenham and Gloucester . .	5	1	2	2	0	5
Southampton Institute	5	0	5	0	0	0

Note: Brighton and Worcester were both docked three points for forfeiting games, which were recorded as defeats.

Promoted teams
South: Portsmouth, Reading; *North:* Hull, St Andrews; *Midlands:* Leicester, Liverpool; *West:* Bournemouth, Bristol.

QUARTER-FINALS

Durham beat Exeter by eight wickets; **Loughborough** beat Brunel by 131 runs; **Nottingham** beat Luton by 152 runs; **UWIC** beat Northumbria by four wickets.

SEMI-FINALS

At Christ Church, Oxford, June 8. Loughborough won by 46 runs. Toss: UWIC. Loughborough 211 for nine (60 overs) (N. A. Bourke 60, M. T. Byrne 47; O. Thomas five for 57); UWIC 165 (59.3 overs) (S. C. B. Tomlinson 36).

At Worksop College, June 12. Durham won by 98 runs. Toss: Nottingham. Durham 201 for nine (60 overs) (L. D. Sutton 38, B. L. Hutton 38, E. J. Wilson 61; A. Aduhene five for 53); Nottingham 103 (34.4 overs) (B. L. Hutton four for 25).

FINAL

DURHAM v LOUGHBOROUGH

At Wardown Park, Luton, June 15, 16. No result. Toss: Loughborough.
The final never really got going. From the outset, the weather was threatening and, although some play was possible on the first morning, heavy rain during lunch put paid to any hope of further cricket that day. More overnight rain left the ground and wicket unplayable, and the match was abandoned. It proved impossible to find another date before term ended, and the trophy was shared.

Durham

†L. D. Sutton c T. M. B. Bailey b Leather .	12	
B. L. Hutton c C. D. J. Bailey b Bourke	20	
*M. J. Chilton b Bourke	7	
A. J. Strauss not out	12	

E. J. Wilson not out 9

B 2, l-b 2, w 5 9
                                                      —
1/17 2/33 3/49   (3 wkts, 23 overs) 69

R. C. Driver, R. S. C. Martin-Jenkins, J. A. Ford, J. R. G. Lawrence, S. R. G. Francis and G. D. Franklin did not bat.

Bowling: Leather 5–0–16–1; Catterall 11–3–27–0; Bourke 7–0–22–2.

Loughborough

D. A. Ellis, M. T. Byrne, N. A. Bourke, *†T. M. B. Bailey, J. Sykes, C. D. J. Bailey, J. M. Stainer, D. Leather, D. N. Catterall, I. C. Parkin and M. K. Davies.

Umpires: K. Hopley and A. Slook.

A list of past winners can be found in Wisden 1998, *page 879.*

MCC MATCHES IN 1998

The highlight of MCC's year was the special one-day match played at Lord's in July to mark the 150th anniversary of W. G. Grace's birth, but billed as a Princess Diana memorial. Some 378 other matches were scheduled in Britain against clubs, schools and representative teams. MCC won 176, 67 were lost, 112 drawn, and 23 abandoned without a ball bowled.

Of 69 centuries scored for MCC in 1998, the highest was Tom Newman's 183 not out against the Hampshire Hogs. Both Richard Arscott and Adam Tarrant made three hundreds. For the bowlers, the best return was nine for 56 by Guy Spelman, the former Kent fast bowler, against Millfield School during Western Schools' Week. Former England batsman John Hampshire and his son Ian both made half-centuries against Wickersley School. And two famous South African Test players, Barry Richards and Mike Procter, were reunited to play under the captaincy of Mark Nicholas in an exciting draw against Maidenhead and Bray CC.

The MCC team arriving to play the University of Nottingham were encouraged to find a full car park for their match. They were slightly less impressed to discover that the crowd had come to watch Tim Henman playing next door at the Nottingham Tennis Centre.

When overseas tours are taken into account, MCC exceeded the 400-match mark for the first time. All seven matches were won in the Bahamas in March: Phil Carrick, the former Yorkshire captain, took 24 wickets at 7.87 with his slow left-armers. A tour of Austria in August saw three more wins chalked up (and two draws), including a 146-run victory over the United Nations. In September, MCC were bowled out for 93 at Yokohama, and lost to an All-Japan XI – but they won the other four tour matches. And later in the month another team visited Italy, where they won the four games which were completed; three more were abandoned, two due to rain and one because of an "unfit mat". A strong side also toured East and Central Africa. All 13 matches were won, most by large margins.

In September, Cross Arrows CC returned to their rightful place on the Lord's Nursery Ground, which was unavailable in 1997 because of building work. Fourteen matches were arranged, of which seven were won, three lost, three drawn, and one abandoned. Cross Arrows won their annual match against MCC, reduced this time to a 30-overs game by rain, by 14 runs. – STEVEN LYNCH.

Note: Matches in this section were not first-class.

At Cambridge, May 5, 6, 7. MCC lost to CAMBRIDGE UNIVERSITY by four wickets (See The Universities section).

At Lord's, May 6. MCC Young Cricketers won by one wicket. Toss: MCC. MCC 258 for seven dec. (P. J. Deakin 59, S. P. Henderson 39, J. D. Ricketts 72; P. G. Hudson three for 54); MCC Young Cricketers 262 for nine (G. S. Kandola 53, M. Currie 42, O. A. Dawkins 74, R. East 32; J. D. Ricketts three for 64, D. R. Thomas three for 45).

At Lord's, May 19, 20. Scotland won by five wickets. Toss: Scotland. MCC 212 for two dec. (A. G. Lawson 50, A. A. Metcalfe 36, A. P. Tarrant 69 not out, J. D. Robinson 52 not out) and 149 (P. Farbrace 42; I. M. Stanger three for 36, C. M. Wright four for 56); Scotland 212 for four dec. (B. G. Lockie 54, S. T. Crawley 55, R. A. Parsons 45) and 150 for five (B. G. Lockie 36, M. J. D. Allingham 36; A. R. Whittall three for 46).

At Shenley Park, May 21. Drawn. Toss: Club Cricket Conference. MCC 233 for five dec. (C. J. Rogers 33, H. D. Ackerman 30, A. P. Cole 31, D. M. Lane 101 not out); Club Cricket Conference 192 for eight (M. Fry 34, P. J. Caley 36).

At Finchampstead, June 2. Drawn. Toss: MCC. MCC 165 for five dec. (J. D. Gray 66, Hon. N. R. C. MacLaurin 51 not out; K. Smith three for 44); National Association of Young Cricketers 155 for eight (D. M. Lane three for 38, P. A. W. Heseltine three for 61).

At Lurgan, Belfast, June 3, 4. Drawn. Toss: MCC. Ireland 267 for six dec. (T. Williamson 35, S. G. Smyth 102 not out, D. Heasley 71) and 176 for six dec. (S. G. Smyth 38, P. G. Gillespie 57, P. J. K. Mooney 42); MCC 199 for five dec. (R. J. Boon 81, K. G. Sedgbeer 46 not out) and 187 for eight (G. D. Hodgson 58, N. J. L. Trestrail 75; G. Cooke three for 38, W. K. McCallan four for 33).

At Oxford, June 3, 4, 5. MCC drew with OXFORD UNIVERSITY (See The Universities section).

At Shenley Park, June 10. Drawn. Toss: MCC. MCC 216 for three (35 overs) (J. R. Wileman 78, B. C. Broad 74, S. Mather 38 not out) v Midlands Club Cricket Conference.

At Cambridge, June 14. MCC drew with CAMBRIDGE UNIVERSITY (See The Universities section).

At Durham, June 17, 18, 19. MCC won by three wickets. Toss: Durham University. Durham University 247 (A. J. Strauss 47, R. C. Driver 31, C. Hodgson 41, C. Clark 41; Z. de Bruyn three for 50) and 246 for six dec. (B. L. Hutton 79, M. J. Chilton 56, R. C. Driver 34 not out); MCC 189 (C. J. Rogers 109 not out; S. R. G. Francis three for 45, J. R. G. Lawrence six for 59) and 309 for seven (R. S. M. Morris 41, M. P. W. Jeh 38, D. P. Viljoen 100, P. A. W. Heseltine 47; G. D. Franklin three for 93).

At Arundel, June 28. Drawn. Toss: MCC. MCC 259 for two dec. (G. Morgan 92, A. P. Tarrant 127); Earl of Arundel's XI 255 for nine (C. Abraham 30, P. J. Deakin 68, C. J. Hollins 87; A. M. James five for 75).

At Wilf Slack Memorial Ground, Finchley, June 29, 30, July 1. MCC won by 138 runs. Toss: MCC. MCC 259 for nine dec. (G. W. Flower 38, J. R. Wileman 61, R. J. Greatorex 39; Mohammad Rafiq four for 71) and forfeited second innings; Bangladesh forfeited first innings and 121 (N. G. B. Francis four for 21).

At Swansea, July 13, 14, 15. MCC won by six wickets. Toss: Wales. Wales 62 (E. W. Kidwell three for 14, A. A. Ranade five for 15) and 294 (M. Lear 41, G. D. Hopkins 40, K. M. Bell 48, A. J. L. Barr 43 not out; A. P. Tarrant three for 19); MCC 232 (A. P. Tarrant 116; J. Davies six for 63, G. J. M. Edwards four for 70) and 125 for four (B. J. Debenham 37, A. A. Ranade 50).

At Portsmouth, July 14. Drawn. Toss: MCC. MCC 220 for six dec. (R. J. Greatorex 54, D. R. Thomas 31, J. D. Bean 77; Mne A. Procter three for 59); Combined Services 207 for six (SAC M. Bray 54, Sgt G. N. Lumb 69; R. J. Woods three for 88).

MCC v REST OF THE WORLD XI

At Lord's, July 18. Rest of the World XI won by six wickets. Toss: MCC.

Two strong teams were assembled for this match, played on the 150th anniversary of W. G. Grace's birth, in aid of the Diana, Princess of Wales Memorial Fund, which benefited by some £520,000. Many of the participants were flown in from overseas, while the South African tourists released Donald and McMillan. The innings of the day was played by Tendulkar, the World XI captain, who made a memorable 125 from only 114 balls. Batting with studied nonchalance, he stroked 15 fours and four sixes, being especially severe on Aamir Sohail's occasional left-armers. Tendulkar was almost matched by de Silva, who contributed a twinkling 82 to a stand of 177. Their strokeplay overshadowed Chanderpaul's earlier unbeaten 127, from 144 balls. There seemed to be a gentleman's agreement not to dive in the field, and the fast bowlers operated a little below full throttle, but it was an enjoyable match, free from the tension of most modern-day internationals.

MCC

*M. A. Atherton c sub (H. J. H. Marshall)			B. M. McMillan not out	7
b Cairns .	28			
Aamir Sohail c Flower b Wasim Akram .	12		L-b 5, w 5, n-b 2	12
S. Chanderpaul not out	127			—
M. Azharuddin b Bishop	61		1/29 2/57 (4 wkts, 50 overs)	261
S. C. Ganguly c Bishop b Moody	14		3/204 4/226	

†I. A. Healy, A. Kumble, J. Srinath, A. A. Donald and G. D. McGrath did not bat.

Bowling: Wasim Akram 10–0–46–1; Bishop 10–0–63–1; Cairns 10–1–34–1; Mushtaq Ahmed 10–0–53–0; Moody 10–1–60–1.

Rest of the World XI

S. T. Jayasuriya lbw b Srinath	8		T. M. Moody not out	1
*S. R. Tendulkar b Kumble	125		L-b 4, w 3, n-b 4	11
Saeed Anwar c McGrath b Donald	14			—
P. A. de Silva c and b McGrath	82		1/10 2/54 (4 wkts, 43.3 overs)	262
G. A. Hick not out	21		3/231 4/240	

†A. Flower, C. L. Cairns, Wasim Akram, Mushtaq Ahmed and I. R. Bishop did not bat.

Bowling: McGrath 10–0–50–1; Srinath 9–0–39–1; Donald 7–0–29–1; McMillan 4–0–27–0; Kumble 9.3–0–56–1; Aamir Sohail 2–0–37–0; Ganguly 2–0–20–0.

Umpires: D. R. Shepherd and S. Venkataraghavan.

At Wormsley, July 19. MCC won by 32 runs. Toss: MCC. MCC 213 for seven dec. (B. A. Richards 44, C. M. Taylor 67; D. V. Lawrence three for 39); Sir Paul Getty's XI 181 (M. Azharuddin 68; M. G. Stear three for 26).

At Shenley Park, August 18. MCC won by five wickets. Toss: Margao Cricket Academy. Margao Cricket Academy 183 (A. Bhagwat 42, P. K. Amre 57; J. T. C. Vaughan three for 24, B. T. P. Donelan three for 39); MCC 184 for five (N. R. Gaywood 47, R. A. Flack 52 not out; S. B. Bangar three for 67).

FIFTY YEARS AGO

From WISDEN CRICKETERS' ALMANACK 1949

SIR DONALD BRADMAN By R. C. Robertson-Glasgow – "Don Bradman will bat no more against England, and two contrary feelings dispute within us: relief, that our bowlers will no longer be oppressed by this phenomenon; regret, that a miracle has been removed from among us. So must ancient Italy have felt when she heard of the death of Hannibal."

AUSTRALIANS IN ENGLAND, 1948 By R. J. Hayter – "For the most part, victory followed victory so inevitably for the Australians that at times opponents took on an air of defeat almost before the match had been in progress more than an hour or two. Once or twice that impression extended even to the Tests."

NOTES BY THE EDITOR – The triumph of Glamorgan [1948 county champions] reminds me of the time when St Paul's school, "One and All", and other clubs were tenants at The Oval. My brother, who was at St Paul's, took me for a pick-up game one August morning, and when we were settling down, Shepherd, the groundsman, came to us and said "Now, boys, pull up your stumps, there's a match to-day." "What is it, Shepherd?" "Surrey Club and Ground v. Eighteen of Glamorgan."

OTHER MATCHES, 1998

Note: Matches in this section were not first-class.

HARROGATE FESTIVAL

Costcutter Cup

A 55-over competition contested by an International XI and three other invited teams. Yorkshire were unavailable because of the Benson and Hedges Cup semi-finals.

At Harrogate, June 8. No result. Toss: International XI. Scotland 60 for three (20 overs) (S. T. Crawley 32) v International XI.

Scotland went through to the final on the toss of a coin, conditions being too wet for a bowl-out.

At Harrogate, June 9. Northamptonshire beat Hampshire 2-1 in a bowling contest, after the match was abandoned.

At Harrogate, June 10. **Final:** Scotland beat Northamptonshire 1-0 in a bowling contest, after the match was abandoned.

SECOND XI CHAMPIONS v ENGLAND UNDER-19

At Ramsbottom, June 16, 17, 18, 19. Drawn. Toss: England Under-19. Lancashire Second XI 336 for eight dec. (L. Hilton 54, M. E. Harvey 33, S. P. Titchard 41, P. R. Sleep 84, Extras 57; G. R. Napier three for 17); England Under-19 104 for four (J. Troughton 30, Z. C. Morris 35).

SCARBOROUGH FESTIVAL

At Scarborough, July 10 (Boyes Stores Challenge). Tim Rice's International XI won by five wickets. Toss: Tim Rice's International XI. Yorkshiremen 254 for seven (50 overs) (A. McGrath 60, M. J. Wood 41, D. Byas 70, S. J. Rhodes 50 not out; J. L. Langer four for 39); Tim Rice's International XI 257 for five (49.1 overs) (J. L. Langer 46, M. P. Mott 35, D. C. Boon 36 not out, T. M. Moody 47 not out).

At Scarborough, July 11 (Northern Electric Trophy). Yorkshire won by 53 runs. Toss: Yorkshire. Yorkshire 324 for four (50 overs) (M. P. Vaughan 130, M. J. Wood 44, D. S. Lehmann 93 not out, Extras 34); Durham 271 (47.2 overs) (J. E. Morris 107, N. J. Speak 79; M. J. Hoggard three for 40, D. S. Lehmann three for 55).

At Scarborough, July 13 (Tetley Bitter Shield). Yorkshire won on scoring-rate. Toss: Tim Rice's XI. Tim Rice's XI 242 for six (44.2 overs) (M. B. Loye 40, R. J. Bailey 86, J. C. Adams 32, A. Flower 45); Yorkshire 230 for seven (41.3 overs) (A. McGrath 34, M. J. Wood 66, Extras 43).

TRIPLE CROWN TOURNAMENT

At Greenock, June 30. ECB XI won by 140 runs. Toss: Wales. ECB XI 271 for five (50 overs) (M. J. Roberts 93, S. J. Foster 77; J. Brown three for 75); Wales 131 (43.4 overs) (C. E. Dagnall four for 12, R. G. Halsall three for 26).

At Hamilton Crescent, Glasgow, June 30. Scotland won by nine runs. Toss: Scotland. Scotland 160 for nine (50 overs) (B. M. W. Patterson 79; G. Cooke three for 42, M. D. Dwyer three for 29); Ireland 151 (49.2 overs) (P. G. Gillespie 55, A. R. Dunlop 38; J. E. Brinkley three for 24, I. M. Stanger three for 45).

At Linlithgow, July 1. Ireland won by four runs. Toss: Ireland. Ireland 171 for nine (50 overs) (S. G. Smyth 37, P. G. Gillespie 31, A. R. Dunlop 37; C. E. Dagnall four for 25); ECB XI 167 for nine (50 overs) (J. D. Robinson 47, S. N. V. Waterton 33; R. L. Eagleson three for 33).

At Ayr, July 1. Scotland won by three wickets. Toss: Wales. Wales 164 for nine (50 overs) (K. M. Bell 66; Asim Butt three for 35); Scotland 167 for seven (49.4 overs) (M. J. Smith 41, I. M. Stanger 31 not out; G. J. M. Edwards three for 29, K. M. Bell three for 39).

At Paisley, July 2. Ireland won by 17 runs. Toss: Wales. Ireland 224 for six (50 overs) (W. K. McCallan 100, S. G. Smyth 43); Wales 207 (48.3 overs) (G. C. Hopkins 38, K. M. Bell 48; M. D. Dwyer three for 22, W. K. McCallan four for 53).

At Hamilton Crescent, Glasgow, July 2. ECB XI won by two runs. Toss: Scotland. ECB XI 204 for eight (50 overs) (J. D. Robinson 72; Asim Butt three for 31); Scotland 202 for eight (50 overs) (B. M. W. Patterson 73, G. Salmond 35).

Only nine of Scotland's original squad were fit; they had to seek dispensation to include coach Jim Love and teenager Gregor Maiden.

Final table

	Played	Won	Lost	Points	Avge
ECB XI	3	2	1	4	0.914
Ireland	3	2	1	4	0.686
Scotland	3	2	1	4	0.664
Wales	3	0	3	0	0.346

ECB XI won the Triple Crown on average, as they could not be separated from Ireland and Scotland on head-to-head matches. The average was calculated by dividing teams' scoring-rate (runs scored divided by wickets lost) by their strike-rate (balls bowled divided by wickets taken).

I ZINGARI RESULTS, 1998

Matches 22: Won 4, Lost 8, Drawn 10. Abandoned 4.

April 21	Eton College	Abandoned
May 10	Hampshire Hogs	Drawn
May 16	Eton Ramblers	Drawn
May 17	Stragglers of Asia	Lost by three wickets
May 28	Harrow School	Lost by seven wickets
May 30	Royal Armoured Corps	Won by eight wickets
June 7	Bradfield Waifs	Lost by four wickets
June 7	Earl of Carnarvon's XI	Drawn
June 13	Charterhouse School	Abandoned
June 14	Sandhurst Wanderers	Abandoned
June 20	Guards CC	Lost by four wickets
June 21	Cormorants CC	Won by seven wickets
June 28	Sir Paul Getty's XI	Drawn
June 30	Winchester College	Lost by three wickets
July 5	Hagley CC	Drawn
July 11	Green Jackets Club	Drawn
July 12	Rickling Green CC	Abandoned
July 18	Lord Stafford's XI	Won by five wickets
July 19	Earl of Arundel's XI	Lost by four wickets
July 19	Sir John Starkey's XI	Lost by four wickets
July 25	Hurlingham CC	Drawn
August 2	Band of Brothers	Drawn
August 8, 9	South Wales Hunts XI	Won by six wickets
August 14	Gloucester Gypsies	Lost by six runs
August 23	Willow Warblers	Drawn
September 6	J. H. Pawle's XI	Drawn

THE MINOR COUNTIES IN 1998

By MICHAEL BERRY and ROBERT BROOKE

For the first time in five years, a different name adorned the Minor Counties Championship trophy. But the winners, Staffordshire, were treading familiar territory. Before Devon embarked on their run of four successive Championships between 1994 and 1997, Staffordshire had completed a hat-trick of title wins in the early 1990s. Devon, however, did not finish the season empty-handed: they won the MCC Trophy for the third time in seven seasons.

The year saw some major changes to the Minor Counties programme. In the Championship, three of the nine matches played by each county were played under "grade" rules. These were essentially single-innings games of 120 overs per side, though they would continue into a second innings if time allowed. It was the first season of a two-year experiment, and reaction was mixed. The opportunity for young players to bat longer and to bowl extended spells was welcomed, and the grade game generated many new batting milestones. But spectators accustomed to the active pace of two-day, two-innings matches were disappointed at the loss of tempo.

The scoring system in grade games caused confusion, too. For the first time, points could be gained – and deducted – on *second* innings. In the match between Staffordshire and Hertfordshire, even the umpires apparently could not agree the allocation of the spoils, and it needed a ruling from Lord's to settle the matter. The ECB decided to drop second-innings points for the 1999 season.

MINOR COUNTIES CHAMPIONSHIP, 1998

Eastern Division	Two-Innings Matches					Bonus Points		Grade Matches		Total
	P	W	L	D	NR	Batting	Bowling	M	Points	Points
Staffordshire	6	1	0	4	1	11	13	3	59	104
Buckinghamshire	6	2	0	3	1	5	9	3	38	89
Suffolk	6	1	1	4	0	15	14	3	29	74
Norfolk	6	1	0	4	1	11	8	3	31	71
Bedfordshire	6	1	0	4	1	14	12	3	20	67
Lincolnshire	6	1	3†	2	0	15	15	3	9	60
Northumberland	6	1	0	4	1	9	9	3	20	59
Cambridgeshire	6	0	0	6	0	17	13	3	24	54
Hertfordshire	6	0	2†	3	1	10	10	3	19	49
Cumberland	6	0	2	2	2	6	14	3	17	47

Western Division	Two-Innings Matches					Bonus Points		Grade Matches		Total
	P	W	L	D	NR	Batting	Bowling	M	Points	Points
Dorset	6	2	1†	3	0	15	14	3	39	105
Cheshire	6	1	0	4	1	12	19	3	39	91
Shropshire	6	2	0	3	1	10	13	3	27	87
Herefordshire	6	1	0	5	0	14	11	3	38	79
Devon	6	0	3	3	0	19	15	3	43	77
Cornwall	6	1	0	5	0	8	20	3	33	77
Wiltshire	6	1	1	3	1	4	12	3	34	71
Berkshire	6	0	2	3	1	8	12	3	45	70
Wales	6	1	2†	2	1	8	11	3	15	60
Oxfordshire	6	0	0	3	3	2	8	3	21	46

Final: Staffordshire drew with Dorset, but became champions by virtue of a superior run-rate.

Win = 16 points. No result = 5 points.
 † Includes 5 points gained for losing match reduced to one day.

The MCC Trophy, with a new group format in its early stages, became a 38-county competition by absorbing the 17 first-class Board Elevens (which excludes Glamorgan) plus Huntingdonshire, and also changed from 55 overs per side to 60. Again, there were pros and cons: the failure of Middlesex to fulfil their fixture against Bedfordshire showed that some of the Board Elevens lacked the requisite infrastructure and organisation. Six of the eight groups were won by Minor Counties sides, who shared 43 of the 67 qualifying round wins. The only two Board Elevens to qualify for the knockout stages were Surrey and Kent.

Staffordshire's triumph was their fourth of the decade, and a record tenth (or 11th, if the disputed 1914 title is included). Steve Dean, their captain, and Mark Humphries, the wicket-keeper, were the only survivors of their 1993 title-winning side, and they, together with Laurie Potter, were the key figures in the 1998 team. Dean hit 594 runs in the season, Potter 620, while Humphries, who made a career-best 132 not out against Hertfordshire – and shared a county-record tenth-wicket partnership of 104 – also held 27 catches. Alan Richardson took 31 wickets at 10.87, enough to win him both the Frank Edwards Trophy (for heading the averages for bowlers with 20 wickets or more) and a contract with Warwickshire for 1999. A major reason for Staffordshire's success was that they took 59 points from their three grade matches.

Jason Harrison was **Buckinghamshire's** new captain. He scored 473 runs and, against Norfolk, shared a stand of 322, a county record for any wicket; Harrison made 147, Paul Sawyer 181. Leg-spinner Andy Clarke, formerly of Sussex, collected 18 wickets, and Adam Cole, a pace bowler previously with Norfolk, had figures of 6–5–2–6 in the MCC Trophy win over Sussex.

Suffolk finished third in the Eastern Division, a significant improvement on the previous year's wooden spoon. Going into the final month of the season, they still had a chance of the title, but rain denied them against Cumberland, and then they were beaten by Staffordshire. Adam Seymour, released by Cornwall, blossomed in his new surroundings and struck 540 runs; Glucka Wijesuriya hit 516. Gary Kirk, a 37-year-old seamer, claimed 23 wickets, including a return of six for 35 on his Championship debut against Bedfordshire.

Carl Amos rewrote the **Norfolk** record books. His unbeaten 226 against Lincolnshire in a grade fixture was the highest score in the county's history, surpassing the 222 Geoffrey Stevens hit against Bedfordshire in 1920. It was also the best individual score in the Championship for 43 years. Steve Goldsmith hit 537 in all, and his top score of 157 not out, against Hertfordshire, contributed to a Norfolk fourth-wicket record of 195 with Carl Rogers, who made 88. Paul Newman, the captain, picked up 21 wickets.

David Mercer of **Bedfordshire** topped the national batting averages to win the Wilfred Rhodes Trophy. Mercer, who made 610 runs at 87.14, had also won the award when playing for Berkshire in 1994. Andy Roberts and Wayne Larkins, who both passed 400 runs for the season, gave support with the bat, while John Hughes, like them formerly with Northamptonshire, took 16 wickets in his debut season.

Lincolnshire recruited Gordon Parsons, the former Leicestershire stalwart, but coaching commitments in South Africa both delayed and curtailed his season. In four Championship appearances, he took 16 wickets. Steve Bradford collected 21 and David Christmas 20, but grade cricket did not agree with Lincolnshire: their three matches brought just nine points. Steve Plumb, once of Norfolk, hit 532 runs to extend his career total to 11,486.

Northumberland professional Andrew Golding departed after two years with the county. Golding managed only 14 wickets in a campaign ruined by the weather. Graeme Angus took one more, and Lee Crozier, an off-spinner, finished with ten from four appearances, including a spell of five for eight from 7.3 overs that induced a Cambridgeshire collapse from 44 for two to 64 all out. Chris Clark compiled 329 runs in his debut year, and Wayne Falla made 312.

Cambridgeshire used 23 players, with eight making just one Championship appearance. Brad Donelan, with 401 runs, and Simon Kellett, who hit four fewer, led the way with the bat. More than half Kellett's total came in the game against Bedfordshire, when he scored an undefeated 223, a new county record. It overhauled L. J. Reid's 221 against Hertfordshire in 1909. Ajaz Akhtar, their new captain, shouldered the bulk of the bowling, and took 34 wickets.

David Ward was again **Hertfordshire's** leading run-scorer, with 537. Matt Drury scored 100 not out on his debut against Cumberland, sharing a record fifth-wicket stand of 202 with Andy Griffin, who was unbeaten on 128. Steve Andrew, who spent several years with both Hampshire and Essex, was signed to strengthen the bowling, and he claimed 19 wickets. But he was banned for one game by the county's committee following abuse of an umpire.

In a wet summer in which six Championship matches were completely washed out, **Cumberland** fared worse than most, with the home games against Buckinghamshire and Norfolk both abandoned without a ball being bowled. Ashley Metcalfe, the former Yorkshire and Nottinghamshire batsman, scored 329 runs from five innings and, during his 102 against Hertfordshire, set a fourth-wicket record of 164 with captain Simon Dutton, who made 109. David Pennett claimed 23 wickets.

In the Western Division, **Dorset** ended Devon's dominance. They went top after back-to-back wins over Wales – by one wicket off the last ball – and Berkshire, and stayed there, despite losing their final fixture against Wiltshire. Their collective success was matched by individual honours for both Jon Hardy, their captain, and leg-spinner Vyvian Pike. Hardy was the Championship's leading run-scorer with 693, while Pike took 41 wickets, more than any other bowler.

Rain denied **Cheshire**, leaders of the Western Division for much of the season, the opportunity to overhaul Dorset when their final game with Shropshire was abandoned without a ball bowled. Paul Bryson was their main scorer with 521; Steve Hampson, a slow left-arm bowler, continued his progress after an eye-catching debut in 1997, finishing with 20 wickets.

Bryan Jones took over as **Shropshire's** third captain in less than a year. He scored 667 runs, and, against Berkshire, was instrumental in one of the season's most riveting finishes. Jones, with an undefeated 147, and Matt Turner, who hit 56 not out, steered Shropshire to their target of 326 off 56 overs. They clubbed the last 75 runs off just 28 balls, Turner smashing Jamie Hodgson for 44666 as they won with more than two overs to spare. Asif Din scored 549 runs; he and Gavin Byram both took 15 wickets.

Two recent arrivals scored freely with the bat for **Herefordshire**. Mark Briers, with 449, and Rob Hall with 378, led the way, but the newcomers Chris Boroughs and Jamie Sylvester, the Minor Counties Under-25 captain signed from Berkshire, both passed 300 runs. Kevin Cooper established a new strike partnership with Paul Humphries after Neal Radford's retirement from Championship cricket. Between them, Cooper and Humphries shared 57 wickets.

Devon's fall from grace could in part be attributed to an unsettled side. Of the 27 who appeared, only Nick Folland, Gareth Townsend and Peter Roebuck, the captain, played in every game. Townsend hit 643 runs in the season, but Folland, with 631, took his aggregate for Devon to 8,486, and became their leading scorer, passing the total of 8,153 set by Derek Cole in 1970. Roebuck was the chief wicket-taker with 26, while former Somerset pace bowler Ian Bishop, who is joining Surrey in 1999, claimed 18.

Cornwall's season was dominated by Charlie Shreck and Chris Ellison. Shreck, who bowled at a healthy pace, collected 30 wickets, while Ellison, an 18-year-old slow left-armer, took 24 in five games. On his debut, against Cheshire, Ellison had match figures of 14 for 154, including a hat-trick in his second-innings return of nine for 80. He ended the year by signing a contract with his native Yorkshire. Gary Thomas made 415 runs, Jon Kent 360.

Grade cricket fostered a new record total for **Wiltshire**, who piled up 524 against Cornwall. It bettered their previous highest of 506 for seven against Devon in 1989, the only other 500-plus Championship score since 1951. Jimmy Taylor, hitting 512 runs, and Jamie Glasson, with 464, were Wiltshire's top batsmen, while Richard Bates was the leading wicket-taker with 20.

For **Berkshire** captain Gary Loveday, it was a season full of records. He began with 138 against Herefordshire, in the process overhauling Tony Davis's county record of 6,970 runs. In Loveday's next game, a grade fixture against Wales, he hit 206 not out, sharing a stand of 252 with Toby Radford, a county record for the second wicket. Loveday finished with 562 runs, taking his career total to 7,466. Slow left-armer Neil Kendrick took 30 wickets. Though he played in just five games, Simon Myles scored 322 runs and took 19 wickets.

Wales had a new captain, their third in three years. Roger Clitheroe, a Cambridge Blue, took over from Philip North, but Wales were unable to sustain the improved form that saw them finish second in 1997. No batsman passed 300 runs, but Steve Barwick, formerly of Glamorgan, was his reliable self, claiming 27 victims. Jonathan Davies, a promising 18-year-old left-arm pace bowler, took 16.

Oxfordshire took the wooden spoon in Rupert Evans's last year as captain. Rob Williams, who succeeds Evans, led Oxfordshire's one-day side, and they narrowly missed reaching the MCC Trophy final, losing in an epic semi-final when Shropshire scrambled a bye off the last ball. In the Championship, Oxfordshire mustered just two batting points from their six non-grade games. Bruce Ellison scored 357 runs while Ian Curtis took 20 wickets. Keith Arnold, suspended for one game after a skirmish with Shropshire wicket-keeper William Davies, claimed 19.

LEADING AVERAGES, 1998

BATTING

(Qualification: 8 innings, average 40.00)

	M	I	NO	R	HS	100s	Avge
D. J. M. Mercer (*Bedfordshire*)	9	15	8	610	103*	1	87.14
R. Hall (*Herefordshire*)	9	11	6	378	63*	0	75.60
R. J. Williams (*Oxfordshire*)	5	8	4	271	90*	0	67.75
M. P. Briers (*Shropshire*)	7	10	3	449	98	0	64.14
N. R. Gaywood (*Devon*)	6	8	1	440	174*	2	62.85
P. D. Atkins (*Buckinghamshire*)	6	8	2	372	94*	0	62.00
J. P. Kent (*Cornwall*)	6	9	3	360	112*	1	60.00
D. W. Randall (*Suffolk*)	7	11	3	469	115	1	58.62
C. Amos (*Norfolk*)	8	13	2	632	226*	3	57.45
N. A. Folland (*Devon*)	9	13	2	631	123	1	57.36
D. R. Thomas (*Norfolk*)	7	10	5	281	71	0	56.20
J. B. R. Jones (*Shropshire*)	8	14	2	667	147*	3	55.58
A. J. Pugh (*Devon*)	8	11	3	439	163	1	54.87
A. C. H. Seymour (*Suffolk*)	8	12	2	540	99	0	54.00
D. M. Ward (*Hertfordshire*)	8	12	2	537	131	2	53.70
G. T. J. Townsend (*Devon*)	9	14	2	643	129*	3	53.58
J. J. E. Hardy (*Dorset*)	9	13	0	693	116	2	53.30
B. C. A. Ellison (*Oxfordshire*)	7	9	2	357	122*	1	51.00
Asif Din (*Shropshire*)	8	14	3	549	98	0	49.90
J. R. Wood (*Berkshire*)	5	8	1	346	115*	2	49.42
S. C. Goldsmith (*Norfolk*)	8	13	2	537	157*	2	48.81
S. G. Plumb (*Lincolnshire*)	8	15	4	532	115*	2	48.36
N. D. Hughes (*Hertfordshire*)	6	8	2	287	85*	0	47.83
L. Potter (*Staffordshire*)	10	14	1	620	143*	1	47.69
J. C. Harrison (*Buckinghamshire*)	8	11	1	473	147	1	47.30
K. M. Wijesuriya (*Suffolk*)	9	13	2	516	112	1	46.90
S. J. Dean (*Staffordshire*)	9	15	2	594	131*	1	45.69
C. W. Boroughs (*Herefordshire*)	6	9	1	362	103	1	45.25
P. D. B. Hoare (*Bedfordshire*)	7	10	5	221	53*	0	44.20
K. J. Locke (*Buckinghamshire*)	6	8	4	174	49*	0	43.50
G. E. Loveday (*Berkshire*)	9	14	1	562	206*	2	43.23
M. J. Glasson (*Wiltshire*)	8	12	1	464	86	0	42.18
M. A. Fell (*Lincolnshire*)	8	11	2	363	92*	0	40.33
B. T. P. Donelan (*Cambridgeshire*)	8	14	4	401	70*	0	40.10
P. R. J. Bryson (*Cheshire*)	8	13	0	521	96	0	40.07

BOWLING

(Qualification: 10 wickets, average 24.00)

	O	M	R	W	BB	5W/i	Avge
A. Richardson (*Staffordshire*)....	150.4	60	337	31	6-17	4	10.87
P. R. Clifford (*Wiltshire*)........	35.3	8	126	10	5-53	2	12.60
N. G. Cowley (*Dorset*)........	89.1	23	260	19	7-55	1	13.68
D. R. Thomas (*Norfolk*)......	73.5	28	182	13	7-63	1	14.00
L. J. Crozier (*Northumberland*) ..	53.3	12	144	10	5-8	0	14.40
L. Potter (*Staffordshire*)	109.4	47	210	13	6-63	1	16.15
D. J. Brock (*Staffordshire*)......	96	26	243	15	3-35	0	16.20
Z. A. Sher (*Bedfordshire*)	72.3	14	244	15	5-38	1	16.26
D. B. Pennett (*Cumberland*)	114.2	22	382	23	4-41	0	16.60
T. S. Smith (*Cambridgeshire*)....	81.3	15	239	14	4-19	0	17.07
A. J. Pugh (*Devon*)	71.5	19	173	10	4-36	0	17.30
G. M. Kirk (*Suffolk*)...........	141.2	42	416	23	6-35	1	18.08
A. J. Murphy (*Cheshire*)	74.4	18	206	11	6-43	1	18.72
S. D. Myles (*Berkshire*)	104.2	23	357	19	7-46	2	18.78
K. A. Arnold (*Oxfordshire*)	139.4	33	364	19	6-26	1	19.15
S. A. Stoneman (*Cheshire*)	91.1	15	365	19	5-50	2	19.21
P. J. Humphries (*Herefordshire*) ..	172	33	560	29	6-50	1	19.31
J. Davies (*Wales*)	105	31	316	16	6-75	1	19.75
R. J. Sillence (*Wiltshire*)........	84	22	328	16	6-85	1	20.50
C. J. Ellison (*Cornwall*)	148.1	34	495	24	9-80	2	20.62
J. C. Harrison (*Buckinghamshire*) .	79.1	24	230	11	5-77	1	20.90
G. J. Byram (*Shropshire*)	105	27	316	15	3-51	0	21.06
G. J. Parsons (*Lincolnshire*).....	124	36	339	16	6-50	2	21.18
M. J. O'Sullivan (*Berkshire*)	86	17	319	15	3-24	0	21.26
K. E. Cooper (*Herefordshire*)....	261.2	95	608	28	5-29	1	21.71
K. Donohue (*Devon*)	102.5	23	267	12	4-27	0	22.25
S. R. Barwick (*Wales*)	217.5	51	606	27	5-64	2	22.44
D. J. Rutherford (*Northumberland*)	92.5	19	271	12	5-21	1	22.58
J. G. Hughes (*Bedfordshire*).....	111	28	363	16	6-52	1	22.68
S. F. Stanway (*Buckinghamshire*) .	99	24	297	13	6-39	1	22.84
P. M. Roebuck (*Devon*)	293.2	95	595	26	5-58	1	22.88
M. W. Thomas (*Norfolk*).......	134.4	34	392	17	4-21	0	23.05
C. E. Dagnall (*Cumberland*)	58.3	11	233	10	3-27	0	23.30
A. Akhtar (*Cambridgeshire*)....	257.5	64	807	34	5-67	1	23.73

† *Denotes matches played under "grade" rules, in which a single-innings match is contested over two days, with provision for second innings if time and conditions permit.*

Eastern Division

At Sleaford, May 24, 25. Bedfordshire won by seven wickets. Lincolnshire 223 for seven dec. and 266 (J. G. Hughes six for 52); Bedfordshire 228 for five dec. and 262 for three (A. R. Roberts 112*, D. J. M. Mercer 103*) *Bedfordshire 23 pts, Lincolnshire 4 pts.*

At Marlow, May 26, 27. Drawn. Suffolk 224 for nine dec. and 227 for one dec. (R. J. Catley 130*); Buckinghamshire 202 for six dec. and 179 for six. *Buckinghamshire 7 pts, Suffolk 3 pts.*

†At Askam, May 31, June 1. Drawn (no result). Hertfordshire 442 for four dec. (A. D. Griffin 128*, M. Drury 100*); Cumberland 370 for eight (S. M. Dutton 109, A. A. Metcalfe 102). *Cumberland 8 pts, Hertfordshire 10 pts.*

†At Bourne, May 31, June 1. Staffordshire won by 29 runs on first innings. Staffordshire 239 (S. A. Bradford seven for 81) and 176 for two dec.; Lincolnshire 210 (L. Potter six for 63) and 26 for no wkt. *Staffordshire 18 pts, Lincolnshire 4 pts.*

†At Jesmond, May 31, June 1. Buckinghamshire won by six wickets in one-innings, 20-overs match. Northumberland 103 for eight; Buckinghamshire 105 for four. *Buckinghamshire 12 pts, Northumberland 2 pts.*

At Netherfield, June 2, 3. Abandoned (no result). *Cumberland 5 pts, Buckinghamshire 5 pts.*

At Benwell Hill, June 2, 3. Abandoned (no result). *Northumberland 5 pts, Hertfordshire 5 pts.*

At Barrow, June 8, 9. Abandoned (no result). *Cumberland 5 pts, Norfolk 5 pts.*

At Saffron Walden, June 10, 11. Drawn. Suffolk 226 for nine dec.; Cambridgeshire 227 (S. M. Clements five for 96). *Cambridgeshire 8 pts, Suffolk 8 pts.*

†At Stone, June 10, 11. Staffordshire won by 75 runs in one-innings match. Staffordshire 252 (S. C. Goldsmith seven for 74); Norfolk 177. *Staffordshire 17 pts, Norfolk 5 pts.*

†At Bedford, June 14, 15. Bedfordshire won by two runs in one-innings match. Cumberland 107 (Z. A. Sher five for 38); Bedfordshire 109. *Bedfordshire 14 pts, Cumberland 4 pts.*

†At Grantham, June 14, 15. Abandoned (no result). *Lincolnshire 3 pts, Northumberland 3 pts.*

†At Wisbech, June 16, 17. Northumberland won by 44 runs in one-innings match. Northumberland 108; Cambridgeshire 64 (L. J. Crozier five for eight). *Northumberland 15 pts, Cambridgeshire 4 pts.*

At Longton, June 16, 17. Drawn. Staffordshire 232 for eight dec.; Buckinghamshire 83 (A. Richardson five for 26) and six for no wkt. *Staffordshire 5 pts, Buckinghamshire 3 pts.*

At March, July 1, 2. Drawn. Cambridgeshire 201 for four dec. and 193; Staffordshire 223 for five dec. (S. J. Dean 131*) and 127 for six. *Cambridgeshire 5 pts, Staffordshire 4 pts.*

At Henlow, July 5, 6. Drawn. Northumberland 241 for eight dec. and 227 for six dec.; Bedfordshire 197 for eight dec. and 195 for five. *Bedfordshire 5 pts, Northumberland 4 pts.*

†At Slough, July 5, 6. Drawn (no result). Buckinghamshire 401 for six dec. (P. R. Sawyer 181, J. C. Harrison 147); Norfolk 271 for six (C. Amos 100). *Buckinghamshire 9 pts, Norfolk 8 pts.*

†At Shenley Park, July 5, 6. Drawn (no result). Suffolk 418 for eight dec. (P. J. Caley 109); Hertfordshire 17 for one. *Hertfordshire 6 pts, Suffolk 7 pts.*

At Lincoln, July 5, 6. Lincolnshire won by three wickets. Cumberland 179 (G. J. Parsons five for 49) and 183 (G. J. Parsons six for 50); Lincolnshire 182 and 181 for seven. *Lincolnshire 22 pts, Cumberland 4 pts.*

At Fenner's, Cambridge, July 7, 8. Drawn. Cumberland 242 for eight dec. and 198 for nine dec.; Cambridgeshire 234 (J. M. Fielding six for 68) and 108 for four. *Cambridgeshire 6 pts, Cumberland 6 pts.*

At Long Marston, July 12, 13. Buckinghamshire won by seven runs in one-innings match. Buckinghamshire 262 for two dec. (N. D. Burns 140*); Hertfordshire 255 (D. M. Ward 131; J. C. Harrison five for 77). *Buckinghamshire 16 pts, Hertfordshire 5 pts.*

At Cleethorpes, July 12, 13. Drawn. Lincolnshire 249 for six dec. and 188 for eight dec.; Cambridgeshire 230 for nine dec. (D. A. Christmas six for 45) and 150 for seven. *Lincolnshire 7 pts, Cambridgeshire 5 pts.*

†At Ipswich School, July 12, 13. Suffolk won by eight wickets in one-innings match. Bedfordshire 120 (G. M. Kirk six for 35); Suffolk 121 for two. *Suffolk 15 pts, Bedfordshire 1 pt.*

At Jesmond, July 13, 14. Drawn. Northumberland 220 for five dec. and 288 (C. Clark 108; R. M. Jervis six for 86); Staffordshire 228 for four dec. and 169 for five. *Northumberland 4 pts, Staffordshire 6 pts.*

At Millom, July 15, 16. Drawn. Staffordshire 252 for eight dec. and 272 for three dec. (L. Potter 143*); Cumberland 225 for five dec. and 126 for two. *Cumberland 7 pts, Staffordshire 2 pts.*

†At Fenner's, Cambridge, July 22, 23. Buckinghamshire won by 185 runs on first innings. Cambridgeshire 126 (S. F. Stanway six for 39) and 237 for five; Buckinghamshire 311 for six dec. *Buckinghamshire 17 pts, Cambridgeshire 3 pts.*

At Lakenham, July 22, 23. Norfolk won by 147 runs. Norfolk 245 for four dec. and 308 for five dec. (S. C. Goldsmith 157*); Hertfordshire 226 for one dec. and 180. *Norfolk 20 pts, Hertfordshire 5 pts.*

At Aylesbury, July 26, 27. Drawn. Bedfordshire 202 for six dec. and 275 for five dec.; Buckinghamshire 197 for six dec. and 174 for five. *Buckinghamshire 4 pts, Bedfordshire 5 pts.*

†At Lakenham, July 26, 27. Norfolk won by 287 runs on first innings. Norfolk 420 for six dec. (C. Amos 226*, S. C. Goldsmith 104); Lincolnshire 133 and 109 for two. *Norfolk 18 pts, Lincolnshire 2 pts.*

At Copdock, July 26, 27. Drawn. Suffolk 244 for three dec. (K. M. Wijesuriya 112) and 228 for three dec. (D. W. Randall 115); Northumberland 213 for eight dec. and 227 for nine. *Suffolk 7 pts, Northumberland 3 pts.*

†At Cannock, July 27, 28. Staffordshire won by an innings and 110 runs. Hertfordshire 58 (A. Richardson six for 17) and 140; Staffordshire 308 (M. I. Humphries 132*; S. J. W. Andrew seven for 59). *Staffordshire 24 pts, Hertfordshire 3 pts.*

At Lakenham, July 28, 29. Drawn. Northumberland 231 for six dec.; Norfolk 106 (D. J. Rutherford five for 21) and 243 for three (C. Amos 109*). *Norfolk 2 pts, Northumberland 5 pts.*

At Southill Park, August 2, 3. Drawn. Hertfordshire 207 for six dec. and 267 for six dec. (D. M. Ward 100); Bedfordshire 224 for nine dec. and 208 for six. *Bedfordshire 5 pts, Hertfordshire 5 pts.*

At Lakenham, August 3, 4. Drawn. Cambridgeshire 220 (D. R. Thomas seven for 63) and 224 for eight dec.; Norfolk 212 for three dec. and 206 for nine. *Norfolk 7 pts, Cambridgeshire 1 pt.*

At Ransomes, Ipswich, August 5, 6. Suffolk won by 103 runs. Suffolk 226 for three dec. and 300 for seven dec.; Lincolnshire 227 for two dec. (S. G. Plumb 106*) and 196. *Suffolk 20 pts, Lincolnshire 5 pts.*

At Dunstable, August 9, 10. Drawn. Bedfordshire 201 for six dec. and 342 for eight dec.; Norfolk 239 for five dec. and 289 for eight (C. J. Rogers 118). *Bedfordshire 4 pts, Norfolk 6 pts.*

At Hitchin, August 9, 10. Drawn. Lincolnshire 225 for three dec. (J. Clarke 110) and 262 for one dec. (S. G. Plumb 115*); Hertfordshire 175 for nine dec. and 295 for nine (S. G. Plumb six for 97). *Hertfordshire 3 pts, Lincolnshire 8 pts.*

†At Carlisle, August 11, 12. Drawn (no result). Cumberland 216; Suffolk 87 for two. *Suffolk 7 pts, Cumberland 5 pts.*

At Brewood, August 13, 14. Staffordshire won by ten wickets. Suffolk 199 (A. Richardson five for 62) and 108 (A. Richardson six for 35); Staffordshire 227 for six dec. and 84 for no wkt. *Staffordshire 23 pts, Suffolk 4 pts.*

†At Wardown Park, Luton, August 16, 17. Cambridgeshire won by 213 runs on first innings. Cambridgeshire 403 for seven dec. (S. A. Kellett 223*) and 125 for eight dec.; Bedfordshire 190 (A. Akhtar five for 67) and 66 for one. *Cambridgeshire 17 pts, Bedfordshire 5 pts.*

At Beaconsfield, August 23, 24. Buckinghamshire won by six wickets in one-innings match. Lincolnshire 219 (A. P. Cole six for 77); Buckinghamshire 220 for four. *Buckinghamshire 16 pts, Lincolnshire 5 pts.*

At Balls Park, Hertford, August 23, 24. Drawn. Hertfordshire 298 for three dec.; Cambridgeshire 225 for nine. *Hertfordshire 7 pts, Cambridgeshire 5 pts.*

At Jesmond, August 23, 24. Northumberland won by 35 runs. Northumberland 179 for eight dec. and 124 for five dec.; Cumberland forfeited first innings and 268. *Northumberland 18 pts, Cumberland 3 pts.*

At Leek, August 23, 24. Drawn (no result). Staffordshire 298 for eight dec.; Bedfordshire 145 for three. *Staffordshire 5 pts, Bedfordshire 5 pts.*

At Mildenhall, August 23, 24. Drawn. Norfolk 118 for seven dec. and 147 for two dec.; Suffolk forfeited first innings and 251 for six. *Suffolk 3 pts.*

Western Division

At Hurst, May 24, 25. Drawn. Berkshire 254 for two dec. (G. E. Loveday 138) and 130 (P. J. Humphries six for 50); Herefordshire 221 for seven dec. and 156 for seven. *Berkshire 7 pts, Herefordshire 2 pts.*

At Bovey Tracey, May 24, 25. Drawn. Devon 279 for four dec. and 293 for four dec. (N. R. Gaywood 174*); Dorset 252 for nine dec. and 189 for seven (P. M. Roebuck five for 58). *Devon 8 pts, Dorset 4 pts.*

At Swindon, May 24, 25. Drawn. Wiltshire 183 (S. R. Barwick six for 59) and 263 for eight dec.; Wales 240 for eight dec. (P. R. Clifford five for 53). *Wiltshire 5 pts, Wales 8 pts.*

†At Reading, May 31, June 1. Berkshire won by 185 runs on first innings. Berkshire 386 for six dec. (G. E. Loveday 206*); Wales 201 (N. M. Kendrick five for 52) and 101 for seven. *Berkshire 20 pts, Wales 2 pts.*

†At Kington, May 31, June 1. Herefordshire won by five wickets in one-innings match. Dorset 357; Herefordshire 359 for five (V. J. Pike five for 123). *Herefordshire 18 pts, Dorset 6 pts.*

†At Telford, May 31, June 1. Shropshire won by 105 runs in one-innings match. Shropshire 372 for nine dec. (M. J. Turner 135); Oxfordshire 267. *Shropshire 18 pts, Oxfordshire 7 pts.*

†At Toft, June 2, 3. Cheshire won by 51 runs in one-innings, 40-overs match. Cheshire 251 for seven; Oxfordshire 200 for five. *Cheshire 14 pts, Oxfordshire 6 pts.*

†At Dean Park, Bournemouth, June 14, 15. Dorset won by 113 runs in one-innings match. Dorset 298 (J. J. E. Hardy 113); Shropshire 185. *Dorset 17 pts, Shropshire 5 pts.*

At Banbury, June 14, 15. Abandoned (no result). *Oxfordshire 5 pts, Wales 5 pts.*

†At Corsham, June 14, 15. Wiltshire won by 39 runs in one-innings match. Wiltshire 400 (R. J. Sillence 126); Berkshire 361 (J. R. Wood 102; P. R. Clifford five for 73). *Wiltshire 18 pts, Berkshire 8 pts.*

At Werrington, June 15, 16. Drawn. Cheshire 233 for nine dec. (C. J. Ellison five for 74) and 181 (C. J. Ellison nine for 80); Cornwall 239 for nine dec. (S. W. Hampson five for 65) and 167 for nine (A. J. Murphy six for 43). *Cornwall 7 pts, Cheshire 6 pts.*

At Plymouth, June 17, 18. Cheshire won by three wickets. Devon 227 for eight dec. and 203 for six dec.; Cheshire 185 for seven dec. and 249 for seven. *Cheshire 19 pts, Devon 5 pts.*

†At Colwall, June 28, 29. Devon won by 79 runs in one-innings match. Herefordshire 224 (R. D. Hughes 132); Devon 303 for two (N. R. Gaywood 136, G. T. J. Townsend 113). *Devon 18 pts, Herefordshire 2 pts.*

At Reading, July 5, 6. Drawn. Berkshire 181 for nine dec. and 188 (T. G. Sharp five for 27); Cornwall 178 for six dec. and 176 for six. *Berkshire 2 pts, Cornwall 6 pts.*

At Torquay, July 5, 6. Drawn. Wiltshire 134 and 198 for three; Devon 415 for four dec. (A. J. Pugh 163, G. T. J. Townsend 100). *Devon 8 pts, Wiltshire 1 pt.*

At Newport, July 5, 6. Drawn. Wales 173 for six dec. and 287 for six dec.; Shropshire 200 for six dec. and 109 for three. *Wales 3 pts, Shropshire 5 pts.*

At Christ Church, Oxford, July 7, 8. Drawn. Oxfordshire 158 (T. G. Sharp seven for 75) and 251 for two dec. (B. C. A. Ellison 122*); Cornwall 166 for seven dec. and 214 for eight. *Oxfordshire 3 pts, Cornwall 4 pts.*

At New Brighton, July 12, 13. Drawn. Berkshire 146 (S. A. Stoneman five for 50) and 330 for six dec. (J. Perkins 136); Cheshire 227 for five dec. and 128 for nine. *Cheshire 8 pts, Berkshire 2 pts.*

†At St Austell, July 12, 13. Dorset won by seven wickets in one-innings match. Cornwall 157 for seven dec.; Dorset 203 for eight. *Dorset 16 pts, Cornwall 5 pts.*

At South Wilts CC, July 12, 13. Drawn (no result). Wiltshire 272 for six dec.; Oxfordshire 180 for six. *Wiltshire 5 pts, Oxfordshire 5 pts.*

At Bridgnorth, July 14, 15. Shropshire won by seven wickets. Berkshire 228 for four dec. and 324 for five dec. (J. R. Wood 115*); Shropshire 227 for six dec. and 326 for three (J. B. R. Jones 147*). *Shropshire 21 pts, Berkshire 6 pts.*

At Thame, July 26, 27. Drawn. Devon 233 for three dec. (N. A. Folland 123) and 203 (I. J. Curtis five for 43); Oxfordshire 217 for two dec. and 141 for six. *Oxfordshire 3 pts, Devon 4 pts.*

At Oswestry, July 26, 27. Drawn. Herefordshire 238 for five dec. (C. W. Boroughs 103) and 179 for two dec.; Shropshire 94 for one dec. and 296 for eight (J. B. R. Jones 108). *Shropshire 2 pts, Herefordshire 4 pts.*

†At Swansea, July 26, 27. Cornwall won by two wickets in one-innings match. Wales 258 (J. J. C. Stephens five for 73); Cornwall 269 for eight. *Cornwall 17 pts, Wales 6 pts.*

†At Marlborough, July 26, 27. Cheshire won by 93 runs in one-innings match. Cheshire 348 (R. J. Sillence six for 85); Wiltshire 255 (S. W. Hampson five for 86). *Cheshire 18 pts, Wiltshire 7 pts.*

†At Finchampstead, July 28, 29. Berkshire won by eight runs in one-innings match. Devon 281 (S. D. Myles five for 71); Berkshire 289. *Berkshire 17 pts, Devon 7 pts.*

At Weymouth, July 28, 29. Drawn. Cheshire 201 for eight dec. and 272 for four dec.; Dorset 225 (S. A. Stoneman five for 57) and 151 for five. *Dorset 7 pts, Cheshire 7 pts.*

At Brockhampton, July 28, 29. Drawn. Herefordshire 222 for seven dec. and 274 for seven dec.; Cornwall 280 (I. Mohammed 134) and 116 for five. *Herefordshire 7 pts, Cornwall 6 pts*.

†At Boughton Hall, Chester, August 2, 3. Drawn (no result). Cheshire 314 (J. Davies six for 75) v Wales. *Cheshire 7 pts, Wales 7 pts*.

†At Exmouth, August 2, 3. Devon won by 125 runs on first innings. Shropshire 195 and 94 for three; Devon 320 for eight dec. (G. T. J. Townsend 129*). *Devon 18 pts, Shropshire 4 pts*.

At Dean Park, Bournemouth, August 2, 3. Drawn. Oxfordshire 167 (V. J. Pike six for 63) and 191 for three; Dorset 200 (K. A. Arnold six for 26). *Dorset 7 pts, Oxfordshire 4 pts*.

At Brockhampton, August 2, 3. Drawn. Wiltshire 99 (K. E. Cooper five for 29) and 227 for six dec.; Herefordshire 181 (R. J. Bates six for 73). *Herefordshire 6 pts, Wiltshire 4 pts*.

At Falmouth, August 4, 5. Drawn. Shropshire 252 for seven dec. and 139 for seven dec.; Cornwall 169 for nine dec. and 189 for nine. *Cornwall 3 pts, Shropshire 7 pts*.

†At Camborne, August 9, 10. Drawn (no result). Wiltshire 524 (J. L. Taylor 101, R. H. Wade 100); Cornwall 379 for five (J. P. Kent 112*, S. M. Williams 102). *Cornwall 11 pts, Wiltshire 9 pts*.

†At Aston Rowant, August 9, 10. Herefordshire won by 12 runs in one-innings match. Herefordshire 344 (J. P. J. Sylvester 107; I. J. Curtis five for 113); Oxfordshire 332 (B. J. Thompson 111; B. W. Gannon five for 103). *Herefordshire 18 pts, Oxfordshire 8 pts*.

At Pontarddulais, August 9, 10. Dorset won by one wicket. Wales 197 and 233 (S. H. G. Jenkins 120); Dorset 233 for six dec. and 198 for nine. *Dorset 23 pts, Wales 3 pts*.

At Bowdon, August 16, 17. Drawn. Cheshire 207 for eight dec. (I. Cockbain 100*) and 268 for six dec.; Herefordshire 203 for nine dec. and 252 for seven. *Cheshire 7 pts, Herefordshire 6 pts*.

At Dean Park, Bournemouth, August 16, 17. Dorset won by 45 runs. Dorset 239 for eight dec. (J. J. E. Hardy 116) and 181 for eight dec.; Berkshire 150 for five dec. and 225 (V. J. Pike five for 63). *Dorset 20 pts, Berkshire 3 pts*.

At Wellington, August 16, 17. Shropshire won by two wickets. Wiltshire 191 and 253 for four dec. (R. J. Rowe 110); Shropshire 235 (J. B. R. Jones 112) and 213 for eight (D. P. Moore five for 84). *Shropshire 20 pts, Wiltshire 6 pts*.

At Colwyn Bay, August 16, 17. Wales won by 43 runs. Wales 195 and 261 for six dec.; Devon 206 for seven dec. and 207 (S. R. Barwick five for 64). *Wales 21 pts, Devon 7 pts*.

At Falkland, August 23, 24. Drawn (no result). Berkshire 226 for four dec.; Oxfordshire 128 for nine (S. D. Myles seven for 46). *Berkshire 5 pts, Oxfordshire 5 pts*.

At Alderley Edge, August 23, 24. Abandoned (no result). *Cheshire 5 pts, Shropshire 5 pts*.

At Truro, August 23, 24. Cornwall won by three wickets. Devon 199 for five dec. and 90 for no wkt dec.; Cornwall 30 for no wkt dec. and 260 for seven. *Cornwall 18 pts, Devon 2 pts*.

At Dale's, Leominster, August 23, 24. Herefordshire won by nine wickets in one-innings match. Wales 91; Herefordshire 93 for one. *Herefordshire 16 pts, Wales 5 pts*.

At Westbury, August 23, 24. Wiltshire won by six wickets in one-innings match. Dorset 158 (B. V. Taylor five for 57); Wiltshire 159 for four. *Wiltshire 16 pts, Dorset 5 pts.*

CHAMPIONSHIP FINAL

DORSET v STAFFORDSHIRE

At Dean Park, Bournemouth, September 6, 7. Staffordshire won on superior run-rate. Toss: Dorset.

Despite a second-day collapse in which they lost nine wickets for 56, Staffordshire's dominance on first innings was enough to see them lift the title on run-rate. Potter and Mark Steele, son of former Northamptonshire and England batsman David, held the batting together in the face of a tight Dorset attack, and steered Staffordshire to 177 for six. By the close, Dorset had reached 42 for two. Next morning, though, they crumbled against the pace of Richardson and the left-arm spin of Potter, who took four for six. Wicket-keeper Humphries finished with six catches. In the Staffordshire second innings, Potter made his second fifty of the game before Cowley led a spirited, but vain, fightback with seven for 55.

Man of the Match: L. Potter.

Staffordshire

L. Potter c Swarbrick b Shackleton	58	– c Diment b Pike	52
*S. J. Dean c Rintoul b Shackleton	0	– c Richings b Cowley	59
P. E. Wellings c Reynolds b Pike	15	– c Lamb b Cowley	7
R. Mills c Richings b Pike	12	– lbw b Cowley	1
M. V. Steele not out	40	– c Shackleton b Cowley	0
R. P. Harvey run out	16	– c Cowley b Pike	0
†M. I. Humphries b Cowley	5	– lbw b Cowley	0
D. R. Womble not out	12	– c Lamb b Cowley	20
D. J. P. Boden (did not bat)		– c sub b Cowley	9
D. J. Brock (did not bat)		– not out	2
A. Richardson (did not bat)		– not out	2
B 1, l-b 8, w 2, n-b 8	19	B 12, l-b 2, w 4	18

1/1 2/39 3/73   (6 wkts, 50 overs) 177   1/111 2/123 3/128   (9 wkts) 170
4/112 5/147 6/156   4/128 5/129 6/132
                                  7/133 8/155 9/167

Bowling: *First Innings*—Shackleton 22–6–54–2; Diment 6–2–20–0; Pike 19–1–74–2; Cowley 3–0–20–1. *Second Innings*—Shackleton 9.1–2–17–0; Diment 3–0–16–0; Pike 30–12–68–2; Cowley 26–13–55–7.

Dorset

*J. J. E. Hardy c Humphries b Brock	15	V. J. Pike c Humphries b Potter	10
T. W. Richings c Humphries b Boden	22	S. Diment not out	1
R. J. Scott c Humphries b Richardson	1	J. H. Shackleton c Humphries b Potter	0
†G. D. Reynolds c Dean b Richardson	6		
T. C. Z. Lamb c Potter b Richardson	17	L-b 3, w 2, n-b 2	7
S. W. D. Rintoul c Boden b Potter	5		
N. G. Cowley lbw b Richardson	1	1/41 2/41 3/47 4/58 5/67 (37.5 overs) 92
M. Swarbrick c Humphries b Potter	7	6/70 7/75 8/89 9/92

Bowling: Richardson 18–7–49–4; Brock 11–2–29–1; Boden 1–0–5–1; Potter 7.5–5–6–4.

Umpires: C. T. Puckett and M. K. Reed.

THE MINOR COUNTIES CHAMPIONS

1895 {	Norfolk	1928	Berkshire
	Durham	1929	Oxfordshire
	Worcestershire	1930	Durham
1896	Worcestershire	1931	Leicestershire II
1897	Worcestershire	1932	Buckinghamshire
1898	Worcestershire	1933	Undecided
1899 {	Northamptonshire	1934	Lancashire II
	Buckinghamshire	1935	Middlesex II
	Glamorgan	1936	Hertfordshire
1900 {	Durham	1937	Lancashire II
	Northamptonshire	1938	Buckinghamshire
1901	Durham	1939	Surrey II
1902	Wiltshire	1946	Suffolk
1903	Northamptonshire	1947	Yorkshire II
1904	Northamptonshire	1948	Lancashire II
1905	Norfolk	1949	Lancashire II
1906	Staffordshire	1950	Surrey II
1907	Lancashire II	1951	Kent II
1908	Staffordshire	1952	Buckinghamshire
1909	Wiltshire	1953	Berkshire
1910	Norfolk	1954	Surrey II
1911	Staffordshire	1955	Surrey II
1912	In abeyance	1956	Kent II
1913	Norfolk	1957	Yorkshire II
1914	Staffordshire†	1958	Yorkshire II
1920	Staffordshire	1959	Warwickshire II
1921	Staffordshire	1960	Lancashire II
1922	Buckinghamshire	1961	Somerset II
1923	Buckinghamshire	1962	Warwickshire II
1924	Berkshire	1963	Cambridgeshire
1925	Buckinghamshire	1964	Lancashire II
1926	Durham	1965	Somerset II
1927	Staffordshire	1966	Lincolnshire

1967	Cheshire
1968	Yorkshire II
1969	Buckinghamshire
1970	Bedfordshire
1971	Yorkshire II
1972	Bedfordshire
1973	Shropshire
1974	Oxfordshire
1975	Hertfordshire
1976	Durham
1977	Suffolk
1978	Devon
1979	Suffolk
1980	Durham
1981	Durham
1982	Oxfordshire
1983	Hertfordshire
1984	Durham
1985	Cheshire
1986	Cumberland
1987	Buckinghamshire
1988	Cheshire
1989	Oxfordshire
1990	Hertfordshire
1991	Staffordshire
1992	Staffordshire
1993	Staffordshire
1994	Devon
1995	Devon
1996	Devon
1997	Devon
1998	Staffordshire

† *Disputed. Some sources claim the Championship was never decided.*

MCC TROPHY FINAL

DEVON v SHROPSHIRE

At Lord's, August 26. Devon won by eight wickets. Toss: Devon.

An unbroken third-wicket stand of 156 in 31 overs by Folland and Pugh swept Devon home with more than 18 overs to spare. Shropshire, inserted under gloomy skies, were soon in trouble, losing their first four wickets for 49. Turner and Mark Davies held Devon up, and the tail wagged enough to ensure Shropshire batted their full 60 overs. An epidemic of 42 extras helped them to 201, but a Devon side packed with batting riches had few problems reaching a modest target.

Shropshire

J. V. Anders c Pugh b Bishop	8	A. B. Byram run out	6
*J. B. R. Jones c Williams b Bond	8	A. Shimmons not out	18
Asif Din b Bond	8	R. C. Powell not out	10
J. Ralph c Roebuck b Bishop	6	L-b 7, w 27, n-b 8	42
M. R. Davies c Williams b Donohue	19		
M. J. Turner b Roebuck	36	1/27 2/36 3/47 (9 wkts, 60 overs) 201	
†W. O. Davies c Barrett b Roebuck	16	4/49 5/97 6/118	
G. J. Byram b Cottam	24	7/131 8/158 9/179	

Bowling: Donohue 12–3–32–1; Bishop 12–3–30–2; Bond 12–2–46–2; Pugh 7–0–34–0; Roebuck 12–2–32–2; Cottam 5–0–20–1.

Devon

N. R. Gaywood b Shimmons	11	A. J. Pugh not out	71
G. T. J. Townsend c W. O. Davies		L-b 3, w 25	28
b Shimmons	17		
N. A. Folland not out	77	1/24 2/48 (2 wkts, 41.5 overs) 204	

K. A. O. Barrett, A. C. Cottam, *P. M. Roebuck, †J. I. Williams, I. E. Bishop, I. A. Bond and K. Donohue did not bat.

Bowling: Shimmons 11–0–55–2; G. J. Byram 8–0–46–0; Asif Din 12–1–38–0; Powell 6–1–20–0; A. B. Byram 4–1–31–0; Jones 0.5–0–11–0.

Umpires: D. L. Burden and J. M. Tythcott.

WINNERS 1983-98

1983	Cheshire	1989	Cumberland	1995	Cambridgeshire
1984	Hertfordshire	1990	Buckinghamshire	1996	Cheshire
1985	Durham	1991	Staffordshire	1997	Norfolk
1986	Norfolk	1992	Devon	1998	Devon
1987	Cheshire	1993	Staffordshire		
1988	Dorset	1994	Devon		

UMPIRES FOR 1999

FIRST-CLASS UMPIRES

J. C. Balderstone, G. I. Burgess, A. Clarkson, D. J. Constant, B. Dudleston, J. H. Hampshire, J. H. Harris, M. J. Harris, J. W. Holder, V. A. Holder, T. E. Jesty, A. A. Jones, R. Julian, M. J. Kitchen, B. Leadbeater, J. W. Lloyds, N. A. Mallender, K. E. Palmer, R. Palmer, N. T. Plews, G. Sharp, D. R. Shepherd, J. F. Steele, R. A. White, A. G. T. Whitehead and P. Willey. *Reserves:* P. Adams, M. R. Benson, P. Carrick, N. G. Cowley, J. H. Evans, K. J. Lyons, M. K. Reed and K. Shuttleworth.

MINOR COUNTIES UMPIRES

P. Adams, N. Bainton, S. F. Bishopp, P. Brown, A. R. Bundy, D. L. Burden, P. D. Clubb, K. Coburn, M. Dixon, J. H. Evans, A. J. Hardy, J. Ilott, M. A. Johnson, C. S. Kelly, P. W. Kingston-Davey, S. W. Kuhlmann, D. Lea, G. I. McLean, M. P. Moran, D. Norton, C. T. Puckett, G. P. Randall-Johnson, J. G. Reed, T. R. Riley, G. Ripley, K. S. Shenton, W. E. Smith, J. M. Tythcott, D. J. Warnford, T. G. Wilson and R. Wood. *Reserves:* A. E. Bayley, J. T. Brady, P. G. Burrows, R. G. Eagleton, P. D. Fisher, F. D. Fowler, J. H. James, J. S. Johnson, N. L. Jones, P. W. Joy, C. L. McNamee, C. Megennis, W. Morgan, A. P. Price, C. A. W. Revell, R. M. Sutton, D. G. Tate, K. J. Timpson, G. Watkins and J. Wilkinson.

SECOND ELEVEN CHAMPIONSHIP, 1998

Northamptonshire won their first Second Eleven Championship since 1960, and added the limited-overs AON Trophy to become the third county, after Middlesex and Surrey, to achieve the league and cup double. Their first team may have been in disarray – partly because the strength in depth of their staff created selection dilemmas – but the Second Eleven lost just one game all season.

They averaged almost half a point more than second-placed Sussex, who faltered at the end, having won five consecutive games in mid-season. Northamptonshire all-rounder Kevin Innes was chosen as the Second Eleven Player of the Year.

The outstanding individual performances of the season came from Justin Bates of Sussex and Lancashire's Paddy McKeown. Bates dismissed nine Surrey batsmen for 60 at The Oval, while McKeown became the second batsman to make a triple-hundred in the competition, hitting 306 not out against Gloucestershire at Bristol. The first was Marcus Trescothick of Somerset in 1997. But overall, Lancashire, last season's champions, were thwarted by the weather, won half as many games as in 1997, and had to settle for fifth. They finished behind Somerset – who rose ten places to third – and Gloucestershire, for whom Dominic Hewson made two early double-centuries, and graduated to the first team.

No bowler took fifty wickets, though James Hindson, the Nottinghamshire slow left-armer, came closest with 45, and helped his side to 50 bowling points, more than any other county. Nottinghamshire, who played two games more than any other team, also secured the most batting points. Gloucestershire matched their total of 41 points, thanks largely to Paul Lazenbury, who hit 1,065 runs at 44.37. Nobody else passed 1,000 runs for the season.

The uneven look to the table – Leicestershire and Durham played 12 games, Nottinghamshire 17 – was due to a new rule, whereby each side played a minimum of 12 games, two of which had to be four-dayers. For 1999, each county must play at least six four-day and six three-day games; additional matches, which are optional, may be of either duration.

SECOND ELEVEN CHAMPIONSHIP, 1998

	P	W	L	T	D	A	Bonus points Batting	Bowling	Points	Avge
1 – Northamptonshire (7).	15	9	1	0	4	1	39	46	244	16.27
2 – Sussex (9)	13	7	1	0	4	1	38	41	206	15.85
3 – Somerset (13).	13	6	6	0	1	0	40	43	182	14.00
4 – Gloucestershire (12). .	14	6	5	0	3	0	41	39	185	13.21
5 – Lancashire (1)	14	5	3	0	6	0	39	45	182	13.00
6 – Leicestershire (8) . . .	12	4	3	0	5	0	30	40	149	12.42
7 – Hampshire (5)	14	5	5	0	4	0	38	36	166	11.86
8 – Nottinghamshire (18).	17	5	2	0	10	0	41	50	201	11.82
9 – Yorkshire (2)	15	4	2	0	9	0	37	40	168	11.20
10 – Durham (14)	12	4	3	0	4	1	17	38	134	11.17
11 – Worcestershire (15). .	14	3	4	1	6	0	32	41	145	10.36
12 – Derbyshire (3)	15	3	5	0	7	0	31	41	141	9.40
13 – Kent (16).	14	2	3	0	9	0	33	33	125	8.93
14 – Glamorgan (10)	14	2	4	1	7	0	28	32	119	8.50
15 – Essex (17)	15	2	8	0	5	0	33	43	123	8.20
16 – Warwickshire (4). . . .	14	1	3	0	9	1	36	32	114	8.14
17 – Middlesex (11).	13	1	4	0	8	0	31	30	101	7.77
18 – Surrey (6).	14	1	8	0	5	0	26	45	102	7.29

1997 positions are shown in brackets.

The totals for Glamorgan and Worcestershire include 6 points each for a tied match which began when less than eight hours' playing time remained.

Win = 16 pts; draw = 3 pts.

Derbyshire reached the final of the limited-overs competition for the first time since 1987; it was some consolation for slipping nine places in the Championship. With the first team constantly searching for the right balance, there was plenty of movement between the squads, and Second Eleven results suffered. Even so, Robin Weston, who arrived from Durham in mid-May, and Trevor Smith both made an impact and topped the county's averages. Anthony Woolley, who took 29 wickets and hit 572 runs, was offered a contract for 1999.

Durham had a mixed season, getting off to a promising start, and ending with a total of four wins. But poor first-innings batting – they gained fewer bonus points than any other team – rarely provided a springboard for victory. Senior batsmen Mike Roseberry and Stewart Hutton scored the bulk of the runs, and, in the second innings against Glamorgan, put on an unbeaten 438 for the first wicket, an all-wicket Championship record. Success with the ball was shared around, but off-spinner Jason Searle had the heaviest workload and took most wickets. Three young players, Muazam Ali, Ryan Robinson and Marc Symington, were engaged for the 1999 season.

Essex won two games, one more than in 1997, though they struggled to overcome the club's never-ending injury problems: 46 players turned out during the season. England Under-19 representatives Ian Flanagan, with five fifties in five matches, and Jamie Grove, who took 24 wickets, earned first-team calls, but another Under-19 player, Jonathan Powell, was hampered by injury. Restricted to just eight overs, he concentrated instead on his batting, and hit two centuries. Darren Cousins and Danny Wilson, the most successful bowlers, took 31 wickets each, though neither was retained.

Wicket-keeper Adrian Shaw provided the highlight of **Glamorgan's** season. In the game against Gloucestershire, he took 12 catches, including eight in the second innings, to set two Championship records. Otherwise, an inexperienced side had a tough time, winning only twice. Wayne Law and Lyndon Jones made most progress with the bat but, for the second season running, no bowler managed to take 25 wickets.

Dominic Hewson set **Gloucestershire** off in style, scoring two double-hundreds and ensuring his own promotion to the first team. Paul Lazenbury looked the pick of the younger batsmen in a line-up that gained 41 batting points, while hard-working medium-pacer Ben Gannon took 42 wickets. Gloucestershire finished fourth, eight places up on 1997.

Hampshire placed great emphasis on youth, and enjoyed reasonable reward for their attacking cricket, finishing seventh, with five wins and four draws. Derek Kenway, Jason Laney and Paul Whitaker all scored two hundreds, Laney going on to 241 in the victory over Essex. The form of Alex Morris was intriguing: his bowling average was an unflattering 42.46 but, promoted to the first team, he halved this to 20.08. Simon Francis, from Durham University, bowled with pace and aggression, and collected 28 wickets.

For the sixth season running, **Kent's** leading wicket-taker was a spinner: Darren Scott took 34, but Eddie Stanford, who had led the way in the previous four years, could manage only four. Wicket-keeper Simon Willis had another consistent campaign, adding nearly 600 runs to his 27 dismissals. The rain seemed to come whenever Kent were well-placed, and they won just two games. But they lost only three, and finished 13th, three places higher than in 1997.

The highlight of **Lancashire's** season was an undefeated 306 by Paddy McKeown against Gloucestershire, the first triple-century since the formation of their Second Eleven in 1892. In the same innings, he and Jamie Haynes shared an unbroken partnership of 349 for the fourth wicket, a county record. But despite Mike Smethurst contributing well with the ball, Lancashire failed to recapture the form which made them champions in 1997, and they slipped to fifth.

As **Leicestershire's** first team were storming to the title, the Second Eleven faltered, winning just one of their last four games. First-class calls left resources thin: in the AON Risk match against Middlesex more than half the side were triallists. Even so, Carl Crowe, with 194 against Sussex, and Darren Stevens, who totalled 754 runs, shone with the bat. Making a rare appearance in a season blighted by injury, James Ormond took a hat-trick against Northamptonshire, while Atul Sachdeva took 32 wickets at 16.50 each.

A poor season saw **Middlesex** win just one match, and emulate the first team by finishing 17th. The bowlers suffered a series of injuries and picked up only 30 bonus points, fewer than any other team. Umer Rashid stood out, with 37 wickets, but at a cost of 38.35 each. David Goodchild bucked the trend, though, to score 576 runs in six matches, and wicket-keeper Ben Scott made 23 dismissals, including five catches in an innings against Surrey.

Northamptonshire's Championship season was a team effort: leading run-scorer Kevin Innes was one of four batsmen averaging over 50, along with Mark Powell, David Sales and Richard Montgomerie, while eight bowlers took five wickets in an innings at least once. Three spinners, Jason Brown, Jeremy Snape and Michael Davies, took 86 wickets between them. Alec Swann hit two centuries in the match against Yorkshire.

With four bowlers claiming 30 or more wickets, **Nottinghamshire** had the firepower to gain five wins, and climb into the top half of the table after finishing last in 1997. Despite damp conditions, the spinners held sway: Richard Bates took 36 wickets at less than 20, and James Hindson finished with 45. The batting was solid rather than spectacular. Noel Gie was the most productive, scoring seven fifties, though he reached three figures only once. Mike Newell unexpectedly kept wicket for much of the season as Lindsay Walker and Wayne Noon both suffered injuries.

Somerset, coached by Colin Wells, adopted a positive attitude, and deservedly gained third place in the Championship. Left-arm Matthew Bulbeck converted good second-team form into first-class success, while Jason Kerr, though unable to bowl through injury, responded with eight fifties. Andre van Troost, whose remodelled bowling action gave him greater control, took 30 wickets.

Surrey, after climbing 11 places in 1997, fell 12 in 1998 and finished last. Assistant coach Alan Butcher described a record of one win and eight defeats as very disappointing, and no more than they deserved. Poor form and a spate of injuries resulted in 46 players being used. James Knott lifted some of the gloom with three hundreds, including a match-winning one-day knock against Essex, and 17-year-old Michael Carberry made a promising beginning.

Sussex had their most rewarding season for eight years, and a settled side deserved to finish runners-up. They thrived in the four-day matches, winning all three without declarations or forfeitures. The fielding was excellent, and Keith Greenfield led from the front with 17 catches. Rajesh Rao headed a strong batting line-up, which scored heavily, giving the bowlers scope to attack; the mainstay was Mike Strong, with 40 wickets.

Warwickshire's strength lay in their batting. Tony Frost scored two hundreds in the game against Worcestershire, but the leading light was Michael Powell, who hit three centuries in six matches. They both gained first-team selection. In a toothless attack, spinners Brendan O'Connell and Gavin Franklin showed promise, but could not compensate for the loss of injured strike bowlers Darren Altree and Michael Edmond, and the side finished with just one victory.

Worcestershire waited until mid-July for a win, and only triallist Nathan Batson impressed before reinforcements arrived at the end of the academic year. Ryan Driver overcame a slow start to score heavily – his 214 against Essex was a Worcestershire record – while Elliott Wilson soon earned promotion to the first team. With the exception of slow left-armer Matthew Rawnsley, the bowling resources looked thin; Jason de la Pena took ten wickets in each of his two games, but no one bowled 25.

Yorkshire called on 15 players from their academy, but the exercise was a limited success. The side fell seven places in the table as the youngsters' inexperience was exposed. Even so, the two leading run-makers – Gary Fellows with 922 and Simon Widdup with 701 – were both graduates of the academy. Widdup, in partnership with Colin Chapman, set a Yorkshire first-wicket record of 279, against eventual champions Northamptonshire.

DERBYSHIRE SECOND ELEVEN

Matches 15: Won – Durham, Gloucestershire, Somerset. Lost – Essex, Hampshire, Lancashire, Northamptonshire, Yorkshire. Drawn – Glamorgan, Leicestershire, Middlesex, Nottinghamshire (twice), Sussex, Warwickshire.

Batting Averages

	M	I	NO	R	HS	100s	Avge
R. M. S. Weston	4	4	1	293	100	1	97.66
S. Ahmed	3	5	1	264	178*	1	66.00
I. D. Blackwell	6	7	1	378	68	0	63.00
M. R. May	6	8	1	389	221*	1	55.57
J. W. Cook	6	11	0	549	110	2	49.90
B. L. Spendlove	3	4	0	190	102	1	47.50
C. Brown	3	4	1	114	63	0	38.00
A. P. Woolley	15	23	6	572	77*	0	33.64
T. A. Tweats	6	10	0	319	105	1	31.90
S. D. Stubbings	14	22	1	645	135	1	30.71
*†S. P. Griffiths	13	18	3	444	73*	0	29.60
G. M. Roberts	7	11	0	267	76	0	24.27
S. Patel	4	7	0	156	71	0	22.28
*A. M. Brown	7	7	3	88	30*	0	22.00
L. Nurse	7	11	0	240	43	0	21.81
V. P. Clarke	9	15	0	278	69	0	18.53
T. M. Smith	8	6	2	64	31	0	16.00
M. J. Deane	14	13	9	60	17*	0	15.00
P. A. Thomas	5	5	2	37	13*	0	12.33
M. V. Steele	6	9	0	98	33	0	10.88
S. J. Lacey	6	9	4	52	15*	0	10.40
D. Smit	2	4	0	29	15	0	7.25

Played in two matches: I. C. Parkin 39*, 12, 0. Played in one match: N. A. Brett 5, 33*; J. R. Byrne 0, 4*; P. G. T. Davies 1, 16; L. J. Marland 32, 4; T. R. Menting 0, 6; †D. P. Pavelling 7, 0; †M. D. R. Sutliff 0; P. Aldred and A. J. Harris did not bat.

Bowling Averages

	O	M	R	W	BB	Avge
T. M. Smith	208.1	61	581	24	5-52	24.20
G. M. Roberts	289.2	88	663	26	6-124	25.50
A. P. Woolley	253.5	60	831	29	4-9	28.65
V. P. Clarke	253.5	65	795	27	6-42	29.44
C. Brown	59	13	181	6	3-22	30.16
I. D. Blackwell	129	34	383	11	3-25	34.81
S. Patel	69.4	14	224	5	2-51	44.80
P. A. Thomas	131.3	23	508	11	5-53	46.18
M. J. Deane	263	70	749	16	2-6	46.81
S. J. Lacey	114.1	33	341	6	3-79	56.83

Also bowled: S. Ahmed 3–0–21–0; N. A. Brett 4–0–35–0; J. R. Byrne 17–2–82–2; J. W. Cook 16.1–6–56–2; M. R. May 2–0–23–3; T. R. Menting 24–5–69–0; I. C. Parkin 39–13–112–0; S. D. Stubbings 12–2–95–1; T. A. Tweats 19–2–51–3; R. M. S. Weston 6–0–28–0.

DURHAM SECOND ELEVEN

Matches 12: Won – Essex, Gloucestershire, Kent, Lancashire. Lost – Derbyshire, Nottinghamshire, Sussex. Drawn – Glamorgan, Surrey, Worcestershire, Yorkshire. Abandoned – Northamptonshire.

Batting Averages

	M	I	NO	R	HS	100s	Avge
*M. A. Roseberry	6	10	1	674	238*	3	74.88
S. Hutton	7	14	1	655	165*	2	50.38
M. A. Gough	4	8	0	356	160	1	44.50
J. A. Daley	4	6	0	256	102	1	42.66

	M	I	NO	R	HS	100s	Avge
M. J. Foster	2	4	0	163	69	0	40.75
R. Robinson	4	7	0	233	82	0	33.28
S. Chapman	6	10	3	193	59	0	27.57
P. L. Carlin	5	8	1	191	78	0	27.28
C. J. Hewison	6	11	1	256	70*	0	25.60
D. M. Cox	3	5	0	128	59	0	25.60
G. J. Pratt	2	4	0	89	30	0	22.25
†A. Pratt	9	15	2	263	62*	0	20.23
M. S. Ali	4	6	0	116	43	0	19.33
*A. Walker	9	10	5	71	18	0	14.20
N. Killeen	6	9	0	100	37	0	11.11
S. Lugsden	7	12	5	69	18*	0	9.85
J. P. Searle	9	12	3	73	25	0	8.11
M. J. Saggers	7	12	2	79	15	0	7.90

Played in four matches: M. J. Symington 38, 26*, 10. Played in three matches: I. D. Hunter 2, 5, 6. Played in two matches: J. A. Graham 9; N. G. Hatch 0; J. B. Lewis 3, 10. Played in one match: S. J. Birtwisle 8, 34; †M. R. Duce 14, 6; G. A. Lambert 25; J. P. T. Latham 0, 7*; B. S. Phelps 2, 11; N. C. Phillips 6, 11; A. S. Steele 43, 29; S. J. E. Brown did not bat.

Bowling Averages

	O	M	R	W	BB	Avge
N. Killeen	131.5	44	330	19	5-64	17.36
S. Chapman	120.3	35	324	17	5-131	19.05
M. J. Saggers	147	41	403	20	4-48	20.15
R. Robinson	57	14	201	9	3-10	22.33
M. J. Symington	70	17	264	11	3-71	24.00
J. P. Searle	272	72	752	27	5-62	27.85
S. Lugsden	171	37	647	21	5-73	30.80
I. D. Hunter	60.1	11	267	7	4-93	38.14
D. M. Cox	113.4	37	282	7	2-42	40.28

Also bowled: S. J. E. Brown 36.2–7–147–3; P. L. Carlin 3–0–17–1; M. A. Gough 7–1–20–0; N. G. Hatch 24–3–78–4; C. J. Hewison 12–2–56–0; J. P. T. Latham 14–2–70–1; B. S. Phelps 26.1–6–79–2; N. C. Phillips 29.2–3–96–5.

ESSEX SECOND ELEVEN

Matches 15: Won – Derbyshire, Surrey. Lost – Durham, Glamorgan, Hampshire, Lancashire, Leicestershire, Northamptonshire, Somerset, Worcestershire. Drawn – Gloucestershire, Kent, Middlesex, Warwickshire, Yorkshire.

Batting Averages

	M	I	NO	R	HS	100s	Avge
I. N. Flanagan	5	8	0	477	98	0	59.62
T. P. Hodgson	10	17	1	663	111	2	41.43
G. R. Napier	6	11	0	417	67	0	37.90
†B. J. Hyam	7	10	1	288	112	1	32.00
*J. C. Powell	11	17	2	475	115	2	31.66
†C. J. Warn	3	5	1	111	62*	0	27.75
*A. J. E. Hibbert	12	18	1	453	127	1	26.64
M. Ismail	3	6	0	146	86	0	24.33
†J. G. Foster	6	11	1	239	64	0	23.90
J. O. Grove	9	12	3	179	39*	0	19.88
D. G. Wilson	9	15	1	264	43*	0	18.85
D. M. Cousins	12	17	9	148	42*	0	18.50
*J. H. Childs	9	8	4	70	30*	0	17.50

	M	I	NO	R	HS	100s	Avge
G. S. Kandola	2	4	0	68	37	0	17.00
J. E. Brinkley	7	12	3	127	37	0	14.11
T. J. Phillips	5	8	0	72	27	0	9.00
I. J. Harvey	3	4	1	25	15	0	8.33
N. F. Williams	6	8	0	47	19	0	5.87
J. E. Walford	2	4	0	16	16	0	4.00
D. R. Ellison	3	5	0	5	5	0	1.00

Played in three matches: S. Brown 0*, 2, 15*; S. Mahmood 1, 2, 52*. Played in two matches: R. S. G. Anderson 2, 12, 14; K. A. O. Barrett 9*, 9, 105; R. Hayes 0, 4, 8; W. I. Jefferson 27, 17, 3*; R. S. Marshall 66*, 3, 49; *D. D. J. Robinson 11, 1, 65; †R. J. Rollins 91, 48, 0. Played in one match: A. Agrawalla 27, 20; M. S. Ali 70; S. Awan 0, 0; J. Bishop 1; C. Brown 14, 0; O. Choudhry 5; C. E. Dagnall 34*; R. G. East 1, 38; A. Horsley 2, 0; D. R. Law 31, 4; *P. J. Prichard 24; A. C. Richards 128; W. Ritzema 25, 0; J. Roberts 8; R. Swile 1, 6*; E. J. Wilson 17; N. G. Wrighton 0.

Note: Owing to first-team calls, A. J. E. Hibbert was replaced by J. O. Grove in the match v Derbyshire at Abbotsholme School, Rocester, and J. O. Grove was replaced by D. M. Cousins in the match v Middlesex at Southgate.

Bowling Averages

	O	M	R	W	BB	Avge
C. E. Dagnall	39.4	12	109	5	4-47	21.80
J. H. Childs	172	66	373	17	3-51	21.94
D. G. Wilson	225.4	46	712	31	6-91	22.96
J. O. Grove	140.4	21	600	24	6-29	25.00
R. S. G. Anderson	57	10	194	7	3-65	27.71
N. F. Williams	110.2	30	285	10	3-46	28.50
D. M. Cousins	312	71	957	31	5-29	30.87
J. E. Brinkley	158	32	466	12	4-37	38.83
A. J. E. Hibbert	105.2	24	319	8	3-42	39.87
T. J. Phillips	101.1	26	283	6	2-53	47.16
S. Mahmood	70	16	253	4	2-37	63.25

Also bowled: A. Agrawalla 11–2–41–1; S. Awan 11–3–38–0; C. Brown 28.1–12–51–3; S. Brown 49.5–7–193–3; O. Choudhry 3–0–29–0; R. G. East 29–7–108–2; D. R. Ellison 16–5–53–0; I. N. Flanagan 4–0–24–0; I. J. Harvey 53.1–7–264–3; T. P. Hodgson 34.4–6–108–1; A. Horsley 8–0–40–2; M. Ismail 27–7–104–3; W. I. Jefferson 20–1–79–2; D. R. Law 18–3–49–0; G. R. Napier 22–5–99–2; J. C. Powell 8–2–41–0; J. Roberts 6–1–33–0; D. D. J. Robinson 1–0–8–0; E. J. Wilson 3–0–10–0.

GLAMORGAN SECOND ELEVEN

Matches 14: Won – Essex, Gloucestershire. Lost – Leicestershire, Northamptonshire, Somerset, Surrey. Tied – Worcestershire. Drawn – Derbyshire, Durham, Hampshire, Kent, Middlesex, Warwickshire, Yorkshire.

Batting Averages

	M	I	NO	R	HS	100s	Avge
R. D. Lupton	5	6	1	288	118	1	57.60
L. O. Jones	14	20	8	476	102*	1	39.66
*J. R. A. Williams	5	4	0	151	77	0	37.75
*A. W. Evans	5	9	0	336	98	0	37.33
*†A. D. Shaw	4	8	3	184	63	0	35.46
*†I. Dawood	9	13	0	461	115	1	34.50
W. L. Law	7	10	0	345	118	1	34.50
M. Ismail	4	6	1	168	76*	0	33.60

	M	I	NO	R	HS	100s	Avge
T. J. Hemp	5	9	3	165	45*	0	27.50
D. D. Cherry	4	8	0	202	124	1	25.25
*G. P. Butcher	6	10	0	244	51	0	24.40
I. J. Thomas	14	22	1	510	65	0	24.28
B. M. Morgan	6	8	2	141	35*	0	23.50
C. Brown	9	10	1	190	46	0	21.11
P. S. George	7	10	2	155	41	0	19.37
D. S. Harrison	3	5	0	77	30	0	15.40
O. A. Dawkins	4	7	1	82	29	0	13.66
J. Davies	3	4	1	25	19*	0	8.33
A. P. Davies	6	7	0	54	26	0	7.71
S. C. B. Tomlinson	8	10	1	43	14*	0	4.77
S. P. Jones	8	7	3	8	6	0	2.00

Played in three matches: J. A. Didcote 12*, 3, 9; G. D. Hopkins 0, 16. Played in two matches: D. A. Cosker 0, 9*, 0*. Played in one match: R. V. Almond 0, 49; J. Brooker 29; †N. D. Buttigieg 4, 9*; G. R. Davies 1; M. C. Fletcher 22; G. C. Hopkins 15, 19; B. P. Nash 4; O. T. Parkin 1*; M. J. Powell 83, 69*; †M. A. Wallace 44*, 7*; J. O. Brown did not bat.

Note: In the match v Derbyshire at Pontarddulais, G. P. Butcher, called up for a first-team match, was replaced by P. S. George.

Bowling Averages

	O	M	R	W	BB	Avge
D. A. Cosker	48.5	18	102	8	6-61	12.75
R. D. Lupton	165.4	49	470	18	6-32	26.11
A. P. Davies	197.4	46	574	21	5-88	27.33
J. A. Didcote	116.2	39	291	9	3-116	32.33
L. O. Jones	213	49	606	15	3-35	40.40
G. P. Butcher	132.5	25	456	11	3-82	41.45
S. P. Jones	182.2	20	812	18	5-56	45.11
P. S. George	77	14	269	5	2-31	53.80
C. Brown	263.5	63	769	14	3-40	54.92
O. A. Dawkins	90	8	406	7	3-129	58.00
S. C. B. Tomlinson	119.2	25	431	6	2-57	71.83
B. M. Morgan	136.5	20	513	4	2-57	128.25

Also bowled: J. O. Brown 29–6–113–5; J. Davies 55–13–178–2; D. S. Harrison 20–3–79–1; M. Ismail 18–2–72–2; W. L. Law 34–6–149–0; B. P. Nash 5–0–30–1; O. T. Parkin 33–8–78–3; A. D. Shaw 0.1–0–1–0.

GLOUCESTERSHIRE SECOND ELEVEN

Matches 14: Won – Hampshire, Middlesex, Somerset, Sussex, Warwickshire, Worcestershire. Lost – Derbyshire, Durham, Glamorgan, Northamptonshire, Nottinghamshire. Drawn – Essex, Lancashire, Leicestershire.

Batting Averages

	M	I	NO	R	HS	100s	Avge
*R. J. Cunliffe	6	11	3	548	155	1	68.50
D. R. Hewson	5	10	0	659	226	2	65.90
*N. J. Trainor	7	12	0	685	141	2	57.08
*M. J. Church	8	16	4	627	145*	2	52.25
G. I. Macmillan	6	10	0	522	115	2	52.20
M. A. Hardinges	7	11	3	377	181	1	47.12
*A. J. Wright	3	5	0	231	92	0	46.20
P. S. Lazenbury	14	27	3	1,065	134	3	44.37

	M	I	NO	R	HS	100s	Avge
*R. I. Dawson	6	11	2	351	101	1	39.00
†R. C. J. Williams.	11	17	5	406	86*	0	33.83
M. A. Coombes	14	26	2	776	122	1	32.33
M. J. Cawdron	7	12	0	292	72	0	24.33
C. G. Taylor.	4	6	2	97	54	0	24.25
K. P. Sheeraz	4	4	0	61	38	0	15.25
J. M. M. Averis	10	15	1	200	44	0	14.28
J. D. J. Frith	3	6	0	80	63	0	13.33
†S. P. Pope	3	4	0	46	20	0	11.50
J. P. Rendell.	12	16	7	76	25*	0	8.44
B. W. Gannon	13	12	6	37	17	0	6.16

Played in three matches: D. Forder 5; J. W. White 3, 4*. Played in two matches: D. V. Lawrence 5, 5*. Played in one match: A. N. Bressington 3, 19; N. S. Bressington 0, 3; C. R. J. Budd 10, 5; S. McDonald 0.

Note: In the match v Glamorgan at Usk, A. J. Wright, called up for a first-team match, was replaced by M. J. Cawdron.

Bowling Averages

	O	M	R	W	BB	Avge
N. S. Bressington	25	3	37	5	4-28	7.40
K. P. Sheeraz.	94.4	18	275	11	4-16	25.00
M. J. Cawdron.	196.4	46	630	24	4-60	26.25
D. Forder	62	13	245	8	3-72	30.62
B. W. Gannon	429.1	97	1,429	42	4-75	34.02
J. M. M. Averis	292	63	1,038	25	4-73	41.52
N. J. Trainor	192	27	710	17	5-122	41.76
M. A. Hardinges.	130.2	21	505	12	3-34	42.08
G. I. Macmillan	71	16	215	4	2-29	53.75
J. P. Rendell	343.3	71	1,096	17	4-50	64.47

Also bowled: A. N. Bressington 3–0–24–1; M. J. Church 43–13–155–1; R. J. Cunliffe 1–0–5–0; R. I. Dawson 16.3–1–93–1; D. J. J. Frith 57–15–196–3; D. R. Hewson 19–6–59–4; D. V. Lawrence 41–3–159–1; P. S. Lazenbury 4–0–32–0; S. McDonald 21–3–94–1; C. G. Taylor 3–0–29–0; J. W. White 42–6–161–3.

HAMPSHIRE SECOND ELEVEN

Matches 14: Won – Derbyshire, Essex, Lancashire, Somerset, Surrey. Lost – Gloucestershire, Kent, Northamptonshire, Sussex, Worcestershire. Drawn – Glamorgan, Nottinghamshire, Warwickshire, Yorkshire.

Batting Averages

	M	I	NO	R	HS	100s	Avge
L. Savident	5	6	1	337	96	0	67.40
D. A. Kenway	11	20	4	910	111*	2	56.87
P. R. Whitaker	8	14	2	678	192	2	56.50
J. S. Laney	8	12	0	643	241	2	53.58
W. S. Kendall.	8	12	1	511	137	1	46.45
M. Keech	4	6	0	218	102	1	36.33
*R. J. Maru	5	4	2	70	47*	0	35.00
T. M. Hansen	10	8	3	163	28*	0	32.60
S. R. G. Francis	7	7	5	60	23	0	30.00
*†M. Garaway	13	21	2	482	86	0	25.36
A. C. Morris	6	10	2	178	39*	0	22.25
Z. C. Morris.	10	16	3	268	59*	0	20.61

	M	I	NO	R	HS	100s	Avge
H. J. H. Loudon	13	22	3	311	88	0	16.36
N. J. Makin	12	17	2	164	27	0	10.93
J. R. C. Hamblin	5	7	2	46	23*	0	9.20
R. R. Dibden	10	10	3	63	22*	0	9.00
L. R. Ptittipaul	4	6	0	51	35	0	8.50

Played in three matches: M. R. Pigott 1*, 11*. Played in two matches: S. J. Renshaw 30; L. A. Sears 1, 36, 4. Played in one match: K. Adams 0, 8; G. D. Attenborough 1, 50; C. J. Batt 39; J. D. Francis 0, 4; R. D. McLaren 26, 40; M. A. Richards 7, 6; †I. Brunnschweiler and C. G. van der Gucht did not bat.

Bowling Averages

	O	M	R	W	BB	Avge
P. R. Whitaker	112.3	31	343	17	6-73	20.17
S. R. G. Francis	175.1	40	611	28	6-28	21.82
M. R. Pigott	101	24	332	13	4-54	25.53
J. R. C. Hamblin	119.1	22	445	17	7-31	26.17
T. M. Hansen	191	42	611	23	5-31	26.56
N. J. Makin	172.1	35	673	24	4-50	28.04
R. R. Dibden	244	46	808	22	5-118	36.72
A. C. Morris	180.2	38	552	13	4-52	42.46
Z. C. Morris	230.4	55	775	18	3-39	43.05

Also bowled: K. Adams 30–8–96–2; G. D. Attenborough 16–1–52–0; C. J. Batt 34–6–116–2; J. D. Francis 13–1–35–2; M. Keech 5–1–12–0; W. S. Kendall 38.4–6–137–2; J. S. Laney 5–1–19–1; R. D. McLaren 21–5–64–1; R. J. Maru 78.1–23–150–2; S. J. Renshaw 28–7–80–2; L. Savident 11–5–29–0; L. A. Sears 11–1–57–1; C. G. van der Gucht 12–8–8–2.

KENT SECOND ELEVEN

Matches 14: Won – Hampshire, Surrey. Lost – Durham, Somerset, Sussex. Drawn – Essex, Glamorgan, Lancashire, Leicestershire, Middlesex, Northamptonshire, Nottinghamshire, Warwickshire, Yorkshire.

Batting Averages

	M	I	NO	R	HS	100s	Avge
M. J. Walker	6	10	2	449	87	0	56.12
C. D. Walsh	6	10	0	479	137	2	47.90
W. J. House	6	11	1	405	88	0	40.50
†S. C. Willis	12	17	2	599	139	1	39.93
J. A. Ford	8	14	2	433	134	1	36.08
G. R. Cowdrey	4	7	1	208	49	0	34.66
*N. J. Llong	13	22	1	697	144	3	33.19
J. H. Baldock	8	13	1	397	116	1	33.08
E. J. Stanford	8	11	3	264	65	0	33.00
J. M. de la Pena	9	8	5	89	21*	0	29.66
J. B. Hockley	9	14	1	184	44	0	14.15
M. R. Powell	5	6	2	55	19*	0	13.75
M. M. Patel	3	5	0	52	26	0	10.40
J. B. D. Thompson	8	10	1	93	36	0	10.33
D. A. Scott	13	16	1	154	28	0	10.26
D. D. Masters	14	16	6	86	25	0	8.60

Played in two matches: M. Broadhurst 20, 7*, 12; R. Clinton 60, 0*, 64; S. Iqbal 52*, 35, 40; J. L. Hartley 0, 10, 22*; R. W. T. Key 68, 89, 114; M. J. McCague 4*, 12, 9*; B. J. Phillips 5, 19, 36. Played in one match: M. J. Banes 16, 8; J. P. Booth 0, 34; D. P. Fulton 47, 9; J. M. Golding 30*; A. P. Igglesden 0, 14*; R. M. Rawlings 12; T. R. Ward 47; J. D. Watson 0, 20*.

Bowling Averages

	O	M	R	W	BB	Avge
B. J. Phillips	49	11	125	9	5-26	13.88
M. M. Patel	129	49	248	14	5-35	17.71
J. B. D. Thompson	187	52	472	25	5-27	18.88
D. A. Scott	333.4	95	911	34	4-29	26.79
N. J. Llong	135.4	40	332	12	3-13	27.66
J. A. Ford	60	13	211	7	3-49	30.14
M. Broadhurst	50	9	150	4	2-31	37.50
M. R. Powell	111	20	473	11	4-138	43.00
J. M. de la Pena	221.1	34	806	15	3-76	53.73
D. D. Masters	251	50	833	14	2-78	59.50
E. J. Stanford	158.2	39	492	4	2-55	123.00

Also bowled: G. R. Cowdrey 19.1–1–63–2; J. M. Golding 20–9–47–2; J. B. Hockley 26.4–4–135–2; W. J. House 48–11–159–3; A. P. Igglesden 16–4–37–1; R. W. T. Key 2–0–16–0; M. J. McCague 17.1–1–90–2; M. J. Walker 1–0–1–0; C. D. Walsh 2–1–2–0; J. D. Watson 10–2–44–1.

LANCASHIRE SECOND ELEVEN

Matches 14: Won – Derbyshire, Essex, Leicestershire, Nottinghamshire, Somerset. Lost – Durham, Hampshire, Yorkshire. Drawn – Gloucestershire, Kent, Middlesex, Surrey, Warwickshire, Worcestershire.

Batting Averages

	M	I	NO	R	HS	100s	Avge
M. J. Chilton	7	11	4	441	105*	2	63.00
*P. R. Sleep	14	12	5	426	136*	1	60.85
P. C. McKeown	11	18	2	901	306*	2	56.31
C. P. Schofield	5	6	2	199	100	0	49.75
M. J. Brown	3	5	0	201	85	0	40.20
†J. J. Haynes	14	18	5	506	120*	1	38.92
M. E. Harvey	12	20	4	554	93*	0	34.62
S. P. Titchard	5	8	0	273	63	0	34.12
D. J. Shadford	13	16	3	416	78	0	32.00
N. T. Wood	9	16	0	497	78	0	31.06
R. J. Green	7	8	2	170	50*	0	28.33
M. Watkinson	4	6	0	166	49	0	27.66
G. Yates	6	6	2	88	47*	0	22.00
M. C. Lomas	3	5	1	82	41	0	20.50
M. P. Smethurst	11	6	2	78	22	0	19.50
P. M. Ridgway	10	8	1	123	56	0	17.57
C. J. Hall	11	13	5	108	27*	0	13.50
G. Keedy	7	7	2	52	18*	0	10.40
J. Fearick	3	4	1	9	6	0	3.00

Played in one match: A. Flintoff 30, 25; G. Reynolds 55*, 29; A. Shadford 44*; D. J. Edmundson did not bat.

Note: Owing to first-team calls, J. J. Haynes, G. Keedy and N. T. Wood were replaced by P. C. McKeown, P. M. Ridgway and G. Yates in the match v Durham at Hartlepool, D. J. Shadford was replaced by D. J. Edmundson in the match v Gloucestershire at Bristol, and P. C. McKeown was replaced by C. J. Hall in the match v Somerset at Northern CC.

Bowling Averages

	O	M	R	W	BB	Avge
M. J. Chilton	51	19	136	8	2-19	17.00
R. J. Green	140.4	27	436	21	5-61	20.76
M. P. Smethurst	179	40	653	31	5-60	21.06
C. P. Schofield	166.3	44	523	22	5-33	23.77
G. Keedy	229.3	58	591	22	5-13	26.86
D. J. Shadford	250	42	963	30	8-56	32.10
P. M. Ridgway	157	32	512	14	4-54	36.57
M. Watkinson	83	12	260	7	2-19	37.14
G. Yates	142	33	422	11	4-63	38.36
P. R. Sleep	69.5	19	208	5	1-12	41.60
C. J. Hall	235.3	47	820	18	4-83	45.55

Also bowled: J. Fearick 42–7–179–3; A. Flintoff 4–0–7–0; M. E. Harvey 5–1–21–0; M. C. Lomas 5–0–50–0; G. Reynolds 18–4–36–3; A. Shadford 21–4–60–2; S. P. Titchard 16–3–68–1; N. T. Wood 7–0–75–0.

LEICESTERSHIRE SECOND ELEVEN

Matches 12: Won – Essex, Glamorgan, Northamptonshire, Surrey. Lost – Lancashire, Nottinghamshire, Worcestershire. Drawn – Derbyshire, Gloucestershire, Kent, Sussex, Yorkshire.

Batting Averages

	M	I	NO	R	HS	100s	Avge
*C. D. Crowe	4	7	2	459	194	1	91.80
D. Williamson	8	14	3	566	139*	2	51.45
D. I. Stevens	11	21	2	754	122	1	39.68
*J. M. Dakin	7	13	1	442	115	2	36.83
T. J. Mason	10	17	3	494	136	1	35.28
S. A. Richardson	12	23	1	622	107	1	28.27
J. Ormond	3	5	0	98	81	0	19.60
*P. E. Robinson	9	9	4	97	31*	0	19.40
K. G. Howarth	11	16	3	247	49	0	19.00
A. S. Wright	9	17	1	295	90	0	18.43
†R. D. Whalley	5	10	3	128	38	0	18.28
S. Kirby	6	7	4	53	23*	0	17.66
L. G. Pollard	7	11	3	141	46*	0	17.62
R. A. E. Martin	2	4	0	43	28	0	10.75
A. Sachdeva	6	8	3	46	21	0	9.20

Played in two matches: P. Fisher 0, 25*; G. S. Kandola 84, 51, 13; R. D. McLaren 6, 27; †M. D. R. Sutliff 26, 2, 13. Played in one match: S. J. Adshead 85, 30; M. J. Brown 46; †M. R. Duce 8, 1; S. M. Eaton 1, 10; N. J. C. Kay 10, 23; A. A. Khan 4; D. J. Millns 7, 14; †B. Moore 23, 8; R. Robinson 30*; A. R. Shah 2, 14; K. B. Smith 4, 6; †J. A. Wakeling 0, 8; C. P. Crowe, †C. J. Hellings and C. W. Dodsley did not bat.

Note: In the match v Worcestershire at Hinckley, J. M. Dakin, called up for a first-team match, was replaced by C. P. Crowe.

Bowling Averages

	O	M	R	W	BB	Avge
J. M. Dakin	98.4	37	221	15	5-24	14.73
A. Sachdeva	198.3	61	528	32	5-71	16.50
D. J. Millns	33	10	83	4	3-63	20.75
R. D. McLaren	34	7	105	5	3-24	21.00
J. Ormond	86.3	19	304	13	3-28	23.38
A. A. Khan	45	10	119	5	3-51	23.80
D. Williamson	94	28	213	8	4-44	26.62

	O	M	R	W	BB	Avge
L. G. Pollard	115.5	25	441	16	3-22	27.56
C. D. Crowe	127.4	28	429	15	4-29	28.60
S. Kirby	118.2	24	404	14	3-43	28.85
K. G. Howarth	240.3	49	918	31	4-53	29.61
T. J. Mason	290.2	101	692	23	5-29	30.08

Also bowled: C. P. Crowe 5–1–35–0; C. W. Dodsley 16–1–88–1; P. Fisher 33–4–112–0; G. S. Kandola 2–0–31–0; P. E. Robinson 1–1–0–0; A. R. Shah 12–4–32–0; K. B. Smith 7.1–1–39–0; D. I. Stevens 2–0–5–1; A. S. Wright 2.5–0–14–0.

MIDDLESEX SECOND ELEVEN

Matches 13: Won – Surrey. Lost – Gloucestershire, Sussex, Warwickshire, Yorkshire. Drawn – Derbyshire, Essex, Glamorgan, Kent, Lancashire, Northamptonshire, Nottinghamshire, Worcestershire.

Batting Averages

	M	I	NO	R	HS	100s	Avge
D. J. Goodchild	6	10	2	576	146	2	72.00
G. J. Kennis	3	5	0	300	103	1	60.00
A. J. Strauss	9	16	3	647	95	0	49.76
*J. C. Pooley	6	9	3	252	65*	0	42.00
*J. P. Hewitt	4	6	2	154	72	0	38.50
*†D. C. Nash	4	8	0	301	127	1	37.62
T. D. Fray	2	4	2	75	45	0	37.50
*R. A. Kettleborough	5	7	4	95	29*	0	31.66
S. J. Cook	5	7	4	95	29*	0	31.66
M. J. W. Wright	4	8	2	172	56	0	28.66
A. W. Laraman	9	12	3	226	56	0	25.11
†B. J. M. Scott	9	11	5	146	33	0	24.33
U. B. A. Rashid	13	15	2	299	103	1	23.00
B. L. Hutton	9	16	1	328	74	0	21.86
*K. P. Dutch	4	5	0	109	55	0	21.80
J. K. Maunders	10	19	0	386	120	1	20.31
I. N. Blanchett	7	8	3	82	19	0	16.40
N. D. Martin	11	9	1	117	36	0	14.62
R. S. G. Anderson	5	3	0	23	14	0	7.66

Played in two matches: C. J. Batt 3, 23; *I. J. Gould 19*, 25*, 0; S. Patel 19, 5*. Played in one match: T. F. Bloomfield 10*; O. R. Hutton 2, 12; R. L. Johnson 18; S. P. Naylor 2; L. J. O'Reilly 2; P. R. Sawyer 16, 13; S. A. Selwood 0, 7; †C. P. Coleman, †S. M. Eustace and T. A. Hunt did not bat.

Note: In the match v Nottinghamshire at RAF Vine Lane, Uxbridge, R. A. Kettleborough, called up for a first-team match, was replaced by S. P. Naylor.

Bowling Averages

	O	M	R	W	BB	Avge
R. A. Kettleborough	32	1	151	7	4-103	21.57
K. P. Dutch	117	16	425	14	5-89	30.35
R. S. G. Anderson	74.3	10	283	8	5-94	35.37
J. P. Hewitt	141	30	508	14	4-68	36.28
S. J. Cook	133.2	26	421	11	3-22	38.27
U. B. A. Rashid	469.5	109	1,419	37	6-90	38.35
A. W. Laraman	108.2	15	457	10	2-19	45.70
I. N. Blanchett	137.3	25	452	9	2-25	50.22
N. D. Martin	234	39	1,028	18	3-50	57.11

Also bowled: C. J. Batt 43–11–143–3; T. F. Bloomfield 30–9–93–2; D. J. Goodchild 5–2–13–0; I. J. Gould 7.2–1–40–1; T. A. Hunt 17–5–47–1; B. L. Hutton 24.1–3–89–1; O. R. Hutton 3–0–30–0; R. L. Johnson 5–0–19–0; J. K. Maunders 2.5–0–39–0; S. P. Naylor 2.4–1–11–0; L. J. O'Reilly 4–0–21–0; S. Patel 12–2–43–1; A. J. Strauss 3–0–33–0; M. J. W. Wright 18–1–92–0.

NORTHAMPTONSHIRE SECOND ELEVEN

Matches 15: Won – Derbyshire, Essex, Glamorgan, Gloucestershire, Hampshire, Somerset, Surrey, Warwickshire, Worcestershire. Lost – Leicestershire. Drawn – Kent, Middlesex, Nottinghamshire, Yorkshire. Abandoned – Durham.

Batting Averages

	M	I	NO	R	HS	100s	Avge
M. J. Powell	3	5	2	228	74	0	76.00
D. J. Sales	3	5	0	288	135	1	57.60
R. R. Montgomerie	4	8	2	341	200*	1	56.83
K. J. Innes	11	19	3	874	197	2	54.62
*J. N. Snape	11	18	4	575	106	2	41.07
A. J. Swann	10	20	1	740	131	3	38.94
A. L. Penberthy	2	4	0	155	80	0	38.75
R. J. Warren	6	12	1	423	147	1	38.45
T. C. Walton	11	19	2	508	100	1	29.88
D. J. Capel	4	6	2	115	48*	0	28.75
G. P. Swann	3	5	0	133	68	0	26.60
G. A. White	7	12	0	314	58	0	26.16
†T. M. B. Bailey	9	13	3	253	101*	1	25.30
D. J. Roberts	11	19	1	446	64	0	24.77
M. K. Davies	8	9	3	138	68*	0	23.00
D. L. Iniff	7	7	3	85	32	0	21.25
R. J. Logan	5	6	0	125	67	0	20.83
S. A. J. Boswell	14	17	4	260	115*	1	20.00
J. F. Brown	8	10	4	65	36	0	10.83
D. Follett	7	9	3	54	16	0	9.00

Played in four matches: J. A. R. Blain 0, 1, 0. Played in two matches: A. M. Dobson 0, 19. Played in one match: M. Bamford 0, 41; W. I. Jefferson 64; J. Walker 28; R. White 0, 1; D. E. Malcolm and J. P. Taylor did not bat.

Note: Owing to first-team calls, T. C. Walton was replaced by G. P. Swann in the match v Worcestershire at Worcester, and D. L. Iniff was replaced by D. J. Roberts in the match v Warwickshire at Northampton.

Bowling Averages

	O	M	R	W	BB	Avge
J. F. Brown	275.3	89	662	35	6–74	18.91
J. N. Snape	207.2	64	466	23	5–53	20.26
D. J. Capel	58	12	192	9	5–57	21.33
R. J. Logan	92	16	334	14	5–41	23.85
K. J. Innes	109.4	21	401	16	5–41	25.06
D. L. Iniff	124.3	21	499	19	5–53	26.26
M. K. Davies	294.1	89	739	28	4–62	26.39
S. A. J. Boswell	313.4	58	1,159	38	5–85	30.50
D. Follett	218.1	45	718	23	5–83	31.21
J. A. R. Blain	102.4	22	429	10	3–35	42.90

Also bowled: A. M. Dobson 31–8–92–3; D. E. Malcolm 26–10–64–3; A. L. Penberthy 37–14–83–1; D. J. Roberts 6–0–58–1; D. J. Sales 4–1–20–0; A. J. Swann 7–0–36–0; G. P. Swann 30–11–91–3; J. P. Taylor 23–11–32–2; T. C. Walton 14–4–42–3.

NOTTINGHAMSHIRE SECOND ELEVEN

Matches 17: Won – Durham, Gloucestershire, Leicestershire, Warwickshire, Yorkshire. Lost – Lancashire, Sussex. Drawn – Derbyshire (twice), Hampshire, Kent, Middlesex, Northamptonshire, Somerset, Surrey (twice), Worcestershire.

Batting Averages

	M	I	NO	R	HS	100s	Avge
P. R. Pollard	6	9	2	534	141	3	76.28
M. P. Dowman	5	9	3	439	123*	2	73.16
†C. M. W. Read	4	4	0	282	114	1	70.50
G. F. Archer	5	7	2	275	87	0	55.00
M. N. Bowen	3	4	1	162	76*	0	54.00
†W. M. Noon	5	10	4	320	116*	1	53.33
C. M. Tolley	3	5	1	188	70	0	47.00
J. E. Hindson	16	21	6	532	69	0	35.46
N. A. Gie	14	23	2	733	103*	1	34.90
G. E. Welton	12	20	1	604	128	2	31.78
A. G. Wharf	9	12	1	261	73	0	23.72
J. P. Hart	8	9	1	161	42	0	20.12
J. Clarke	8	14	0	280	56	0	20.00
A. Romaine	3	4	0	74	41	0	18.50
R. W. J. Howitt	8	16	1	277	78	0	18.46
R. T. Bates	9	12	1	199	42	0	18.09
*†M. Newell	16	13	7	104	30*	0	17.33
J. Hemmings	5	6	1	53	21	0	10.60
S. J. Randall	9	8	3	49	25*	0	9.80
D. S. Lucas	13	14	1	108	30	0	8.30
M. J. A. Whiley	6	4	3	6	4*	0	6.00
K. Tate	5	8	0	38	15	0	4.75

Played in three matches: K. P. Evans 20*, 2, 31*. Played in two matches: S. J. Musgrove 97, 36; A. R. Oram 19*, 10; J. W. Shaw 38*, 9. Played in one match: U. Afzaal 127, 5; P. K. Hearle 40; G. S. Kandola 13, 8; T. Roberts 11, 0; A. Steele 30, 11; †J. A. Wakeling did not bat.

Bowling Averages

	O	M	R	W	BB	Avge
G. F. Archer	68	31	113	7	3-6	16.14
R. T. Bates	340.4	130	689	36	5-39	19.13
C. M. Tolley	33	8	87	4	3-52	21.75
S. J. Randall	248	71	694	30	5-18	23.13
M. J. A. Whiley	145	31	361	15	4-31	24.06
D. S. Lucas	308	82	903	35	4-20	25.80
M. N. Bowen	81	26	190	7	4-25	27.14
J. E. Hindson	428.3	116	1,233	45	4-46	27.40
A. G. Wharf	203.1	44	717	24	4-91	29.87
M. P. Dowman	60	19	190	6	2-32	31.66
J. P. Hart	225.3	53	624	17	4-44	36.70
A. R. Oram	64	22	226	6	4-45	37.66
J. Hemmings	109	32	277	7	2-33	39.57
K. P. Evans	79	16	207	5	2-63	41.40

Also bowled: R. W. J. Howitt 15-2-51-1; M. Newell 5-1-10-1; J. W. Shaw 25-5-80-3; G. E. Welton 5-1-16-1.

SOMERSET SECOND ELEVEN

Matches 13: Won – Essex, Glamorgan, Kent, Surrey, Worcestershire, Yorkshire. Lost – Derbyshire, Gloucestershire, Hampshire, Lancashire, Northamptonshire, Sussex. Drawn – Nottinghamshire.

Batting Averages

	M	I	NO	R	HS	100s	Avge
R. J. Harden	3	6	1	416	160	2	83.20
*C. M. Wells	12	20	9	692	106	1	62.90
†M. Burns	5	10	0	489	147	1	48.90
K. A. Parsons	3	6	1	208	92	0	41.60
G. J. Kennis	4	8	2	248	125*	1	41.33
A. R. K. Pierson	4	7	2	206	71	0	41.20
N. R. Boulton	7	14	1	464	177	1	35.69
J. I. D. Kerr	13	25	1	831	110	1	34.62
P. M. Warren	9	16	7	265	67	0	29.44
A. S. Steele	5	10	0	290	101	1	29.00
M. J. Wood	4	8	0	223	49	0	27.87
†L. D. Sutton	6	10	0	238	75	0	23.80
M. P. L. Bulbeck	3	6	1	115	58	0	23.00
P. S. Jones	7	13	0	284	57	0	21.84
O. A. Dawkins	2	4	0	68	34	0	17.00
K. A. O. Barratt	2	4	0	57	28	0	14.25
J. P. Tucker	7	11	0	156	43	0	14.18
B. J. Trott	11	15	4	150	40	0	13.63
K. J. Shine	3	6	1	62	39	0	12.40
C. A. Hunkin	4	5	1	47	22	0	11.75
A. P. van Troost	6	11	0	99	32	0	9.00

Played in three matches: C. M. Gazzard 1, 10, 6. Played in two matches: S. J. Bail 59, 0, 51; D. G. Court 11, 6*; M. T. Gitsham 0, 5. Played in one match: G. R. Armstrong 0, 27; C. Collins 0*, 3; L. A. Cooper 5, 36; C. P. Crowe 0, 8; A. N. Edwards 9, 0; C. J. Hellings 1; P. T. Jacques 36, 18; D. J. Jones 0, 14; J. P. T. Latham 13; S. Mahmood 0, 3; R. J. Parker 23; R. W. Selway 1, 4; J. C. Williams 30, 7; A. D. Cox did not bat.

Bowling Averages

	O	M	R	W	BB	Avge
K. A. Parsons	91.1	24	286	17	5-67	16.82
A. P. van Troost	190	37	656	30	5-40	21.86
J. P. T. Latham	23	5	90	4	2-42	22.50
D. G. Court	33	6	113	5	3-33	22.60
M. P. L. Bulbeck	109	21	384	16	5-41	24.00
A. R. K. Pierson	140.4	40	410	16	4-143	25.62
M. Burns	78.4	11	291	10	3-81	29.10
P. M. Warren	209.2	52	649	22	5-76	29.50
P. S. Jones	197.4	37	681	21	4-35	32.42
B. J. Trott	327.5	56	1,286	37	5-74	34.75
J. P. Tucker	120.1	13	539	12	3-39	44.91

Also bowled: G. R. Armstrong 5–0–26–0; N. R. Boulton 8.5–0–83–1; A. D. Cox 7–1–18–1; C. P. Crowe 7–0–42–0; O. A. Dawkins 19–2–96–0; A. N. Edwards 9–2–28–1; M. T. Gitsham 25.5–5–113–2; C. A. Hunkin 44–5–169–3; P. T. Jacques 12–0–42–0; G. J. Kennis 31–10–71–2; J. I. D. Kerr 11–2–27–1; S. Mahmood 18–5–58–0; R. W. Selway 6–0–23–0; K. J. Shine 57.3–13–187–2; M. J. Wood 3–0–26–1.

SURREY SECOND ELEVEN

Matches 14: Won – Glamorgan. Lost – Essex, Hampshire, Kent, Leicestershire, Middlesex, Northamptonshire, Somerset, Sussex. Drawn – Durham, Lancashire, Nottinghamshire (twice), Warwickshire.

Batting Averages

	M	I	NO	R	HS	100s	Avge
*A. R. Butcher	8	14	7	310	102*	1	44.28
†J. A. Knott	10	18	3	593	119	2	39.53
N. D. Hughes	2	4	0	150	92	0	37.50
S. J. Musgrove	2	4	0	146	66	0	36.50
J. D. Ratcliffe	3	6	1	172	52	0	34.40
G. J. Kennis	4	7	0	235	75	0	33.57
G. J. Batty	8	16	1	460	91	0	30.66
K. A. O. Barratt	6	11	0	325	100	1	29.54
I. E. Bishop	6	10	4	154	49*	0	25.66
N. Shahid	3	6	0	145	45	0	24.16
C. P. R. Hodgson	3	6	0	126	55	0	21.00
†J. N. Batty	4	8	2	123	52*	0	20.50
R. W. Nowell	4	6	0	123	44	0	20.50
M. A. Carberry	5	9	0	180	83	0	20.00
M. A. V. Bell	12	21	1	395	96	0	19.75
M. W. Patterson	6	11	1	196	71	0	19.60
I. J. Ward	3	6	0	111	36	0	18.50
S. J. Ali	3	6	3	53	25*	0	17.66
A. J. Tudor	2	4	0	70	37	0	17.50
P. R. Shaw	3	6	0	104	32	0	17.33
D. M. Lane	3	5	0	83	29	0	16.60
A. D. Patterson	9	16	0	261	59	0	16.31
J. J. McCulley	2	4	0	56	21	0	14.00
C. G. Greenidge	7	12	2	99	37*	0	9.90
R. M. Amin	9	13	4	89	20	0	9.88
W. K. McCallan	2	4	0	34	22	0	8.50
R. S. Clinton	5	9	0	76	19	0	8.44
S. A. Newman	3	5	0	20	8	0	4.00

Played in two matches: A. K. Moon 9, 7, 2*. Played in one match: †D. Alleyne 21, 61; D. J. Bicknell 14, 0; S. B. Brown 1, 0; G. P. Butcher 11, 5; O. Choudhry 8, 14; A. R. Cowan 11, 16; G. J. M. Edwards 0*, 4; E. W. Kidwell 20*, 4; R. J. Mansfield 20; S. R. Mather 0, 19; R. S. A. Mutucumarana 11, 27; S. P. Naylor 16, 5; B. E. A. Preece 1*, 6; N. J. R. Procter 3*; G. D. Puckle 2*; R. Robinson 6, 7; D. Thompson 0, 0.

Note: Owing to first-team calls, J. A. Knott was replaced by R. J. Mansfield in the match v Northamptonshire at The Oval, and M. A. V. Bell was replaced by A. R. Butcher in the match v Somerset at Taunton.

Bowling Averages

	O	M	R	W	BB	Avge
A. R. Cowan	19.3	2	63	5	5-47	12.60
C. G. Greenidge	231.3	47	669	26	6-68	25.73
R. M. Amin	292.5	77	857	31	5-69	27.64
M. A. V. Bell	256	69	889	32	5-93	27.78
A. J. Tudor	52.5	14	149	5	4-51	29.80
G. J. Batty	239.1	64	616	20	5-55	30.80
M. W. Patterson	120.1	16	464	13	3-76	35.69
I. E. Bishop	180.2	30	665	15	5-63	44.33

Also bowled: S. J. Ali 8-0-43-0; S. B. Brown 27-6-67-3; G. P. Butcher 17-1-70-2; G. J. M. Edwards 31-0-141-1; C. P. R. Hodgson 11-1-38-0; E. W. Kidwell 20-2-85-0; J. A. Knott 66-11-249-3; D. M. Lane 35-7-136-2; W. K. McCallan 44-14-105-1; S. R. Mather 4-0-14-0; A. K. Moon 26.5-0-110-2; S. J. Musgrove 14-2-55-1; S. P. Naylor 11-1-49-0; B. E. A. Preece 8-0-60-0; N. J. R. Procter 11-2-56-0; G. D. Puckle 4-0-18-0; J. D. Ratcliffe 17-5-33-3; N. Shahid 14-1-51-1; D. Thompson 13-8-68-1; I. J. Ward 15.3-5-52-1.

SUSSEX SECOND ELEVEN

Matches 13: Won – Durham, Hampshire, Kent, Middlesex, Nottinghamshire, Somerset, Surrey. Lost – Gloucestershire. Drawn – Derbyshire, Leicestershire, Worcestershire, Yorkshire. Abandoned – Warwickshire.

Batting Averages

	M	I	NO	R	HS	100s	Avge
*M. T. E. Peirce	3	5	1	306	132	2	76.50
R. K. Rao	7	12	1	806	207	3	73.27
*N. R. Taylor	3	4	0	244	81	0	61.00
A. D. Edwards	8	11	3	417	146	1	52.12
J. R. Carpenter	7	10	1	426	120	1	47.33
J. P. Pyemont	6	11	2	403	154	1	44.77
A. A. Khan	7	9	2	311	117	1	44.42
*K. Greenfield	10	15	3	466	123	1	38.83
M. R. Strong	11	11	6	149	42	0	29.80
P. W. Jarvis	5	7	2	145	76*	0	29.00
M. Newell	4	8	0	213	104	1	26.62
K. Newell	4	8	1	185	52	0	26.42
†C. M. Mole	4	6	1	129	49	0	25.80
M. H. Yardy	5	8	0	202	87	0	25.25
†N. J. Wilton	9	9	0	149	45	0	16.55
J. J. Bates	8	10	3	100	30	0	14.28
†G. R. A. Campbell	8	12	0	130	30	0	10.83
G. R. Haywood	7	11	1	97	25	0	9.70

Played in three matches: C. J. Ellison 13*, 0, 6. Played in two matches: K. Adams 2; R. S. C. Martin-Jenkins 50, 65, 28. Played in one match: J. N. B. Bovill 17*, 6*; C. G. Greenidge 14*; M. T. Harrison 0, 1; D. Leather 14; L. W. Marshall 17, 10; I. Mohammed 67, 28; N. J. Pont 3, 4; M. A. Hazleton, †S. Humphries and J. Newell did not bat.

Note: In the match v Nottinghamshire at Hove, M. R. Strong, called up for a first-team match, was replaced by J. Newell.

Bowling Averages

	O	M	R	W	BB	Avge
J. N. B. Bovill	55	19	102	9	7-61	11.33
G. R. Haywood	111.2	31	268	17	5-31	15.76
P. W. Jarvis	169	37	534	22	4-40	24.27
M. R. Strong	300	64	986	40	6-71	24.65
A. D. Edwards	177	30	574	23	5-40	24.95
A. A. Khan	311.5	91	757	30	7-98	25.23
C. J. Ellison	83.5	29	165	6	2-19	27.50
M. H. Yardy	63	9	201	7	3-19	28.71
J. J. Bates	294.3	91	841	27	9-60	31.14
R. K. Rao	89	19	233	7	3-61	33.28

Also bowled: K. Adams 28-4-120-3; K. Greenfield 5-1-18-0; C. G. Greenidge 7-1-22-0; M. T. Harrison 14-2-39-0; M. A. Hazleton 9-1-40-1; D. Leather 18-7-66-3; R. S. C. Martin-Jenkins 32-9-105-3; J. Newell 26-9-50-3; K. Newell 40-2-117-1; M. T. E. Peirce 15-0-55-1; N. J. Pont 14-0-52-1.

WARWICKSHIRE SECOND ELEVEN

Matches 14: Won – Middlesex. Lost – Gloucestershire, Northamptonshire, Nottinghamshire. Drawn – Derbyshire, Essex, Glamorgan, Hampshire, Kent, Lancashire, Surrey, Worcestershire, Yorkshire. Abandoned – Sussex.

Batting Averages

	M	I	NO	R	HS	100s	Avge
C. E. Dagnall	5	5	3	147	49	0	73.50
*M. J. Powell	6	11	1	705	151	3	70.50
D. L. Hemp	3	5	0	341	146	2	68.20
M. A. Wagh	2	4	1	185	132	1	61.66
M. A. Sheikh	8	12	3	524	127*	2	58.22
T. L. Penney	4	6	1	268	142	1	53.60
†T. Frost	9	15	1	690	115	2	49.28
*D. P. Ostler	7	11	2	443	108	1	49.22
D. A. T. Dalton	4	8	2	226	59	0	37.66
G. D. Franklin	9	11	3	247	80*	0	30.87
A. Singh	4	7	0	214	125	1	30.57
J. Troughton	7	11	0	325	107	1	29.54
C. R. Howell	8	14	1	340	116	1	26.15
*A. J. Moles	4	6	0	149	51	0	24.83
T. A. Munton	4	4	1	71	28*	0	23.66
D. R. Mudd	3	4	2	39	24	0	19.50
S. Kerby	3	5	1	72	34*	0	18.00
J. N. Webster	4	7	1	102	44*	0	17.00
K. Shah	10	11	4	99	38	0	14.14
K. Ali	3	4	0	54	33	0	13.50
B. W. O'Connell	13	13	5	91	32	0	11.37
I. R. Bell	3	5	0	45	23	0	9.00
†S. Platt	3	4	1	27	13	0	9.00

Played in two matches: A. Richardson 6. Played in one match: *Asif Din 33, 19; R. G. East 46; M. D. Edmond 29, 28; †S. M. Eustace 24; R. D. Hughes 74, 34; S. McDonald 0*; *K. J. Piper 68, 12; N. V. Prabhu 35, 10; N. Sajjad 12*; J. A. Ship 0, 6; G. C. Small 12; A. C. Smyth 14; S. Westergaard 47, 16; D. A. Altree and N. A. Warren did not bat.

Bowling Averages

	O	M	R	W	BB	Avge
N. Sajjad	44	13	119	8	5-56	14.87
T. A. Munton	107	28	243	16	5-33	15.18
C. E. Dagnall	159	42	454	23	4-19	19.73
A. Richardson	54	10	152	6	2-33	25.33
M. J. Powell	48.2	9	161	6	2-25	26.83
J. N. Webster	72.2	20	211	6	3-49	35.16
G. D. Franklin	239	49	739	18	3-56	41.05
M. A. Sheikh	116	19	350	7	2-32	50.00
B. W. O'Connell	431.5	107	1,219	24	3-113	50.79
K. Shah	198.4	42	653	12	2-70	54.41
D. R. Mudd	62	6	264	4	2-47	66.00

Also bowled: K. Ali 51–4–215–3; D. A. Altree 10–0–35–0; Asif Din 3–0–8–0; I. R. Bell 1–1–0–0; D. A. T. Dalton 10–0–44–0; R. G. East 28–5–73–0; M. D. Edmond 21–5–86–0; D. L. Hemp 10–3–40–2; S. Kerby 56.2–7–226–3; D. P. Ostler 37–2–192–3; N. V. Prabhu 9–3–16–0; G. C. Small 26–7–69–3; A. C. Smyth 27–5–114–3; J. Troughton 10–0–41–0; M. A. Wagh 22.1–1–108–3; S. Westergaard 11–2–45–3; N. A. Warren 10–2–28–0.

WORCESTERSHIRE SECOND ELEVEN

Matches 14: Won – Essex, Hampshire, Leicestershire. Lost – Gloucestershire, Northamptonshire, Somerset, Yorkshire. Tied – Glamorgan. Drawn – Durham, Lancashire, Middlesex, Nottinghamshire, Sussex, Warwickshire.

Batting Averages

	M	I	NO	R	HS	100s	Avge
N. E. Batson	8	13	1	666	194	1	55.50
R. J. Chapman	7	9	7	111	35	0	55.50
R. C. Driver	8	13	1	616	214	1	51.33

	M	I	NO	R	HS	100s	Avge
E. J. Wilson	4	7	0	344	156	1	49.14
D. N. Catterall	7	8	2	265	132	1	44.16
R. M. S. Weston	2	4	0	157	94	0	39.25
*S. W. K. Ellis	10	16	1	459	139	1	30.60
C. M. Patel	2	4	1	85	39	0	28.33
†D. J. Pipe	13	20	0	500	69	0	25.00
A. Hafeez	6	10	0	246	119	1	24.60
S. J. Price	2	4	0	90	32	0	22.50
*D. B. D'Oliveira	8	9	2	153	48	0	21.85
A. P. Cole	3	5	0	104	46	0	20.80
G. J. Batty	6	10	0	163	35	0	16.30
R. Nagra	4	6	1	79	49	0	15.80
M. J. Rawnsley	10	16	0	235	60	0	14.68
K. P. Hamilton	3	5	1	51	29	0	12.75
A. Sheriyar	3	4	1	27	22	0	9.00
D. Patel	8	9	5	32	9*	0	8.00
J. Burgoyne	2	2	0	8	7*	0	4.00

Played in three matches: J. S. Trower 27, 8, 6. Played in two matches: J. M. de la Pena 4, 0, 3; *R. K. Illingworth 46, 57, 17; S. R. Lampitt 6, 38, 0; I. J. W. McCarter 4, 48*, 0; C. G. Mason 23, 125, 14; M. M. Mirza 4. Played in one match: †S. J. Adshead 20; S. J. Ali 39*; *C. W. J. Athey 13, 42; I. E. Bishop 8*; N. A. Brett 13, 2; C. Clark 42; G. R. Haynes 8*; L. J. Irish 8, 0; G. J. Kennis 13, 57; J. Khalid 5; C. S. Leaf 15*; A. J. Marsh 5, 17; P. J. Newport 28; N. Patel 0, 20; J. Rasheed 1; P. R. Sawyer 7, 10; J. E. K. Schofield 11; P. R. Shaw 18; B. R. F. Staunton 28, 1; S. M. Trego 1, 14; M. J. Turner 61, 58; T. Wijesinghe 13, 0; A. Wylie 3; R. J. Sillence did not bat.

Note: In the match v Yorkshire at Harrogate, P. J. Newport, called up for a first-team match, was replaced by J. S. Trower.

Bowling Averages

	O	M	R	W	BB	Avge
J. M. de la Pena	80.5	20	224	20	6-52	11.20
I. J. W. McCarter	44.2	12	146	9	6-56	16.22
N. E. Batson	44	11	116	7	4-6	16.57
S. R. Lampitt	80.1	20	221	12	8-39	18.41
R. K. Illingworth	89.3	37	158	8	5-96	19.75
A. P. Cole	45.3	11	130	5	2-18	26.00
A. Sheriyar	81	16	263	10	4-84	26.30
S. W. K. Ellis	77.3	15	294	11	3-71	26.72
G. J. Batty	94	26	276	9	5-62	30.66
K. P. Hamilton	95.1	13	319	9	3-42	35.44
C. M. Patel	40	8	183	5	3-123	36.60
M. J. Rawnsley	310	94	813	22	4-39	36.95
D. N. Catterall	135	22	468	12	5-31	39.00
R. J. Chapman	214.1	57	741	18	4-112	41.16
D. Patel	116.5	18	522	11	3-61	47.45

Also bowled: I. E. Bishop 22–5–84–2; N. A. Brett 8–2–27–0; J. Burgoyne 43.5–9–175–3; R. C. Driver 15–2–56–1; A. Hafeez 29–3–131–0; G. R. Haynes 19–4–54–2; L. J. Irish 32–7–128–3; J. Khalid 14–3–54–0; C. S. Leaf 12–1–43–0; C. G. Mason 10.5–1–52–1; M. M. Mirza 9–0–51–0; R. Nagra 8–2–32–0; P. J. Newport 8–2–12–0; J. Rasheed 14–2–54–0; R. J. Sillence 3.4–0–11–1; J. S. Trower 7–4–10–1; T. Wijesinghe 4–0–24–0; A. Wylie 5–0–42–0.

YORKSHIRE SECOND ELEVEN

Matches 15: Won – Derbyshire, Lancashire, Middlesex, Worcestershire. Lost – Nottinghamshire, Somerset. Drawn – Durham, Essex, Glamorgan, Hampshire, Kent, Leicestershire, Northampton-shire, Sussex, Warwickshire.

Batting Averages

	M	I	NO	R	HS	100s	Avge
S. M. Guy	4	6	4	212	112*	1	106.00
*†C. A. Chapman	10	17	6	592	166	1	53.81
G. M. Fellows	13	23	5	922	150*	1	51.22
C. R. Taylor.	2	4	0	143	83	0	35.75
B. Parker.	8	16	1	518	78	0	34.53
J. D. Middlebrook	9	17	4	429	107*	1	33.00
†S. Widdup	12	22	0	701	122	1	31.86
L. C. Weekes	14	23	3	553	122	1	27.65
G. D. Clough	12	22	0	570	136	1	25.90
R. K. J. Dawson	5	6	2	97	52*	0	24.25
I. D. Fisher	12	11	3	188	58	0	23.50
R. Wilkinson	14	25	4	474	70	0	22.57
J. W. Inglis	9	17	2	311	78*	0	20.73
C. White	4	8	0	156	51	0	19.50
R. C. Towler	10	6	4	35	16	0	17.50
C. J. Ellison	4	6	2	65	23	0	16.25
M. J. Hoggard	7	5	2	2	1	0	0.66

Played in four matches: G. A. Lambert 0, 1. Played in two matches: R. J. Sidebottom 4*, 0; J. A. Smith 11, 5, 4; R. D. Stemp 11, 17. Played in one match: V. J. Craven 10; G. M. Hamilton 34, 0; A. McGrath 92; R. A. Stead 88*; †M. Thewlis 0, 0; M. J. Wood 60, 0.

Bowling Averages

	O	M	R	W	BB	Avge
R. D. Stemp	57.1	24	121	9	4-85	13.44
M. J. Hoggard	169.4	37	503	24	7-63	20.95
J. D. Middlebrook.	254.1	76	587	27	6-53	21.74
L. C. Weekes	306	80	895	38	5-44	23.55
C. White	56	22	147	6	3-46	24.50
G. A. Lambert	56	10	177	6	3-49	29.50
R. C. Towler	190	48	713	21	3-27	33.95
C. J. Ellison	85.2	24	194	5	2-30	38.80
I. D. Fisher	379.3	102	1,020	26	6-82	39.23
G. D. Clough.	95	31	236	6	3-49	39.33
R. K. J. Dawson	152	38	459	10	4-40	45.90

Also bowled: G. M. Fellows 34–8–130–3; G. M. Hamilton 23–7–80–0; A. McGrath 3–1–15–0; R. J. Sidebottom 56–17–131–3; J. A. Smith 24–5–110–3; R. Wilkinson 54–21–182–2.

SECOND ELEVEN CHAMPIONS

1959	Gloucestershire	1973	Essex	1987	{Kent
1960	Northamptonshire	1974	Middlesex		{Yorkshire
1961	Kent	1975	Surrey	1988	Surrey
1962	Worcestershire	1976	Kent	1989	Middlesex
1963	Worcestershire	1977	Yorkshire	1990	Sussex
1964	Lancashire	1978	Sussex	1991	Yorkshire
1965	Glamorgan	1979	Warwickshire	1992	Surrey
1966	Surrey	1980	Glamorgan	1993	Middlesex
1967	Hampshire	1981	Hampshire	1994	Somerset
1968	Surrey	1982	Worcestershire	1995	Hampshire
1969	Kent	1983	Leicestershire	1996	Warwickshire
1970	Kent	1984	Yorkshire	1997	Lancashire
1971	Hampshire	1985	Nottinghamshire	1998	Northamptonshire
1972	Nottinghamshire	1986	Lancashire		

AON TROPHY, 1998

North Zone	Played	Won	Lost	No result	Points	Net run-rate
Derbyshire	8	5	2	1	11	2.96
Yorkshire	8	3	2	3	9	16.06
Lancashire	8	3	3	2	8	−0.70
Nottinghamshire	8	3	4	1	7	−5.71
Durham	8	2	5	1	5	−8.16

Central Zone	Played	Won	Lost	No result	Points	Net run-rate
Northamptonshire	8	7	0	1	15	24.07
Warwickshire	8	3	3	2	8	3.00
Middlesex	8	3	4	1	7	−12.06
Leicestershire	8	2	3	3	7	8.96
Minor Counties	8	1	6	1	3	−19.81

South-West Zone	Played	Won	Lost	No result	Points	Net run-rate
Gloucestershire	8	7	1	0	14	16.94
Hampshire	8	5	3	0	10	14.52
Somerset	8	3	5	0	6	−5.58
Worcestershire	8	3	5	0	6	−11.91
Glamorgan	8	2	6	0	4	−13.68

South-East Zone	Played	Won	Lost	No result	Points	Net run-rate
Sussex	8	5	1	2	12	15.63
Surrey	8	5	2	1	11	−0.58
Kent	8	2	2	4	6*	−7.21
Essex	8	2	5	1	5	−6.32
MCC Young Cricketers	8	1	5	2	4	−3.43

* Kent's total points include a deduction of two points for a breach of regulations.

SEMI-FINALS

At Northampton, August 17. Northamptonshire won by 69 runs. Toss: Northamptonshire. Northamptonshire 223 for nine (50 overs) (T. C. Walton 75, K. J. Innes 55 not out); Sussex 154 (42.5 overs) (J. R. Carpenter 57; M. K. Davies five for 32).

At Derby, August 18. Derbyshire won by four wickets. Toss: Derbyshire. Gloucestershire 241 for eight (50 overs) (R. J. Cunliffe 108, M. A. Coombes 53; G. M. Roberts three for 32); Derbyshire 242 for six (47.5 overs) (S. D. Stubbings 90, G. M. Roberts 33 not out; R. I. Dawson three for 32).

FINAL

NORTHAMPTONSHIRE v DERBYSHIRE

At Northampton, September 7. Northamptonshire won by five wickets. Toss: Northamptonshire.
Man of the Match: A. J. Swann.

Derbyshire

S. D. Stubbings c Roberts b Boswell	18		*†S. P. Griffiths lbw b Logan	1
B. L. Spendlove c Bailey b Follett	0		S. J. Lacey not out	6
M. E. Cassar b Innes	42		T. M. Smith run out	6
T. A. Tweats st Bailey b Davies	27			
I. D. Blackwell b Snape	3		B 2, l-b 15, w 3	20
P. A. J. DeFreitas c and b Snape	58			
V. P. Clarke b Davies	9		1/8 2/22 3/83 4/91 5/107 (50 overs) 199
G. M. Roberts c Snape b Logan	9		6/155 7/174 8/183 9/183

Bowling: Boswell 7–1–28–1; Follett 9–0–30–1; Logan 10–1–24–2; Innes 6–0–30–1; Snape 8–0–37–2; Davies 10–0–33–2.

Northamptonshire

D. J. Roberts c Stubbings b Roberts	...	31	†T. M. B. Bailey not out	17
G. P. Swann b Lacey		46		
A. J. Swann not out		57	B 3, l-b 7, w 7, n-b 2	19
T. C. Walton lbw b Cassar		16		
*J. N. Snape c Griffiths b Cassar		1	1/87 2/88 3/135 (5 wkts, 48 overs)	203
K. J. Innes b Smith		16	4/137 5/179	

S. A. J. Boswell, R. J. Logan, M. K. Davies and D. Follett did not bat.

Bowling: Smith 7–0–27–1; Clarke 10–1–36–0; Blackwell 6–0–32–0; Lacey 6–1–20–1; Roberts 8–0–35–1; DeFreitas 3–0–13–0; Cassar 8–0–30–2.

Umpires: A. Clarkson and T. E. Jesty.

WINNERS 1986-98

1986	Northamptonshire	1991	Nottinghamshire	1996	Leicestershire
1987	Derbyshire	1992	Surrey	1997	Surrey
1988	Yorkshire	1993	Leicestershire	1998	Northamptonshire
1989	Middlesex	1994	Yorkshire		
1990	Lancashire	1995	Leicestershire		

HONOURS' LIST, 1998-99

In 1998-99, the following were decorated for their services to cricket:

Queen's Birthday Honours, 1998: A. J. Stewart (England) MBE.

Barbados Independence Day Honours, 1998: C. C. Hunte (West Indies) Knight of the Order of St Michael.

New Year's Honours, 1999: A. R. C. Fraser (England) MBE, A. R. Owers (lately president of High Roding CC; services to cricket in Essex) MBE.

New Year's Honours (Antigua), 1999: I. V. A. Richards (West Indies) Knight Grand Collar of the Most Distinguished Order of the Nation.

Australia Day Honours, 1999: C. J. McDermott (Australia) OAM.

Australian captain M. A. Taylor was named Australian of the Year, the second cricketer to receive the honour, following A. R. Border in 1989.

ECB TWO-DAY COUNTY BOARD KNOCKOUT CUP

Warwickshire comfortably defeated Sussex in the final of the first-ever ECB County Board Cup. The competition was contested by the Board Elevens of the first-class counties, together with Huntingdonshire, but not including Glamorgan, and formed part of the ECB national development plan. This aimed to increase the length of game played by recreational cricketers, so matches were scheduled to last two days, with 100 overs available for each innings. The final, however, fell victim to the weather: rain meant that it had to be played at Hove rather than Horsham, over one day, not two, and with a maximum of 60 overs a side.

FINAL

At Hove, September 7. Warwickshire won by 85 runs. Toss: Warwickshire. Warwickshire 254 for nine (60 overs) (J. Troughton 73, K. Bray 48, S. McDonald 39 not out, Extras 30; R. G. Halsall three for 52); Sussex 169 (54 overs) (D. Alderman 34; K. Bray three for 19, A. Farooque three for 27).

CAREER FIGURES

Players not expected to appear in county cricket in 1999.

BATTING

	M	I	NO	R	HS	100s	Avge	1,000r/ season
J. Boiling	88	125	38	1,160	69	0	13.33	0
K. R. Brown	247	373	75	10,487	200*	13	35.19	2
G. P. Butcher	40	58	10	1,357	101*	1	28.27	0
C. L. Campbell	2	1	0	7	7	0	7.00	0
D. J. Capel	313	477	66	12,202	175	16	29.68	3
C. A. Connor	221	206	54	1,814	59	0	11.93	0
D. M. Cousins	15	25	5	159	18*	0	7.95	0
G. R. Cowdrey	179	284	29	8,858	147	17	34.73	3
D. M. Cox	17	25	5	535	95*	0	26.75	0
R. P. Davis	169	208	46	2,452	67	0	15.13	0
R. R. Dibden	5	8	2	1	1	0	0.16	0
S. C. Ecclestone	46	74	9	2,277	133	3	35.03	0
S. W. K. Ellis	12	13	5	63	15	0	7.87	0
R. A. Fay	16	25	3	164	26	0	7.45	0
M. W. Gatting	551	861	123	36,549	258	94	49.52	20†
A. J. E. Hibbert	7	12	1	236	85	0	21.45	0
J. E. Hindson	28	36	7	384	53*	0	13.24	0
S. Hutton	66	119	6	3,341	172*	4	29.56	0
A. P. Igglesden	154	170	65	876	41	0	8.34	0
D. V. Lawrence	185	211	38	1,851	66	0	10.69	0
G. I. Macmillan	53	85	9	2,024	122	3	26.63	0
R. J. Maru	229	232	58	2,965	74	0	17.04	0
A. J. Moles	230	416	40	15,305	230*	29	40.70	6
P. Moores	231	345	43	7,351	185	7	24.34	0
M. Newell (Sussex)	23	38	2	857	135*	3	23.80	0
M. W. Patterson	1	2	0	6	4	0	3.00	0
J. C. Pooley	82	137	12	3,811	138*	8	30.48	1
M. J. Saggers	10	17	5	128	18	0	10.66	0
J. P. Searle	4	6	3	7	5*	0	2.33	0
K. P. Sheeraz	13	16	9	27	12*	0	3.85	0
E. J. Stanford	5	6	4	48	32	0	24.00	0
N. R. Taylor	325	551	70	19,031	204	45	39.56	11
S. P. Titchard	76	131	8	3,945	163	4	32.07	0
A. Walker	128	142	63	922	41*	0	11.67	0
T. C. Walton	19	29	3	653	71	0	25.11	0
P. M. Warren	1	0	–	–	–	–	–	–
P. R. Whitaker	37	62	5	1,734	119	1	30.42	0
N. F. Williams	255	302	63	4,457	77	0	18.64	0
D. G. Wilson	3	3	1	31	14*	0	15.50	1
A. J. Wright	287	504	38	13,440	193	18	28.84	6

* Signifies not out.
† Includes 1,029 runs scored overseas in India and Sri Lanka in 1984-85.

BOWLING AND FIELDING

	R	W	BB	Avge	5W/i	10W/m	Ct/St
J. Boiling.	6,633	140	6-84	47.37	4	1	70
K. R. Brown.	276	6	2-7	46.00	–	–	466/33
G. P. Butcher	2,110	54	7-77	39.07	1	0	16
C. L. Campbell.	136	2	1-29	68.00	–	–	0
D. J. Capel.	17,573	546	7-44	32.18	14	0	156
C. A. Connor	19,492	614	9-38	31.74	18	4	61
D. M. Cousins	1,138	27	6-35	42.14	1	0	5
G. R. Cowdrey	872	12	1-5	72.66	–	–	97
D. M. Cox.	1,852	45	5-97	41.15	2	1	4
R. P. Davis.	14,543	414	7-64	35.12	16	2	155
R. R. Dibden	592	8	2-36	74.00	–	–	0
S. C. Ecclestone	1,208	33	4-66	36.60	–	–	22
S. W. K. Ellis.	880	20	5-59	44.00	1	0	8
R. A. Fay.	1,146	31	4-53	36.96	–	–	5
M. W. Gatting.	4,703	158	5-34	29.76	2	0	493
A. J. E. Hibbert	49	3	3-16	16.33	–	–	5
J. E. Hindson	3,045	93	5-42	32.74	7	2	14
S. Hutton	18	0	–	–	–	–	34
A. P. Igglesden	13,488	503	7-28	26.81	23	4	40
D. V. Lawrence.	16,521	515	7-47	32.07	21	1	45
G. I. Macmillan	1,217	23	3-13	52.91	–	–	55
R. J. Maru.	17,714	527	8-41	33.61	15	1	254
A. J. Moles	1,882	40	3-21	47.05	–	–	146
P. Moores	16	0	–	–	–	–	502/44
M. Newell (Sussex)	15	0	–	–	–	–	16
M. W. Patterson	124	7	6-80	17.71	1	0	0
J. C. Pooley	68	0	–	–	–	–	81
M. J. Saggers	769	27	6-65	28.48	2	0	3
J. P. Searle	291	7	3-92	41.57	–	–	2
K. P. Sheeraz	1,104	27	6-67	40.88	2	1	4
E. J. Stanford	388	9	3-84	43.11	–	–	2
N. R. Taylor	891	16	2-20	55.68	–	–	154
S. P. Titchard	171	4	1-11	42.75	–	–	52
A. Walker	9,667	299	8-118	32.33	6	1	43
T. C. Walton.	282	4	1-26	70.50	–	–	5
P. M. Warren	60	0	–	–	–	–	1
P. R. Whitaker	561	13	3-36	43.15	–	–	15
N. F. Williams	20,448	675	8-75	30.29	22	2	67
D. G. Wilson	181	4	1-22	45.25	–	–	1
A. J. Wright	68	1	1-16	68.00	–	–	218

LEAGUE CRICKET IN ENGLAND AND WALES IN 1998

By GEOFFREY DEAN

The ECB's planned reorganisation of league cricket, first mooted in "Raising the Standard" in 1997, gained momentum through the winter of 1998-99. But the Board's hopes of establishing a top tier of some 20 premier leagues by the start of the 1999 season had to be put on hold; only about nine leagues look likely to be in place, but the objective could be reached by 2000. By January 1999, premier leagues had been approved in Cheshire, East Anglia, Essex, Kent, the West of England and Yorkshire, with Middlesex, Surrey and Sussex as possibles.

The criteria for premier status included all-day cricket with declarations and draws – although caps could apply on the length of innings. Those leagues satisfying the preconditions guaranteed their clubs a grant of £1,000 each. The ten clubs making up the new Kent Premier League each received £4,000, as a reward from the Board for taking part in a pilot scheme in 1999. Every match will be a two-day affair spread over two weekends, as in Australian grade cricket. Outright wins, with extra points, will be achieved by bowling a side out twice or by reaching a target in the fourth innings. If a draw cannot be avoided, first-innings points are awarded. In a bizarre departure from convention, the team batting on the first day must adjourn their first innings around teatime if not bowled out, although they will be allowed to continue the same innings the following weekend. This avoids one sided hogging the crease all day. "We think this is an interesting experiment and a good way of making the transition from one to two-day league cricket," said Frank Kemp of the ECB.

The decision by the Board to award bigger grants of £2,000 to clubs forming new regional (as opposed to county) premier leagues seems an entirely logical one. The 12 sides making up the new East Anglia Premier League clearly needed help with the extra costs involved in competing over such a wide area. Another regional league in place for 1999 is a new Western League, drawn from Somerset, Gloucestershire and Wiltshire. This is based on the old Western League, bar the three Welsh clubs who are going their own way, as part of a new structure in Wales.

Smaller ECB grants are to be given to so-called "premier-elect" leagues, which meet some of the Board's criteria for premier status (pyramid structures with promotion and relegation) but not the key one of a time format (a full day's play with around 120 overs). Only Nottinghamshire (six clubs each from the Notts Alliance and Bassetlaw League) and perhaps Northamptonshire were due to be in this category in 1999, although Devon, Derbyshire and others might join them in 2000.

A new Home Counties Premier League (to be drawn from the Thames Valley, Hertfordshire and Cherwell Leagues) is also set to start that year. Similarly, the Southern and the Hampshire Leagues and, at the other end of the country, Northumberland and Durham, were due to amalgamate then.

Not everyone has fallen into line with the ECB's drive to persuade wavering leagues to "think premier". Arguably the strongest league in the country, the Birmingham and District, has refused to change its 55-overs-a-side format. Resistance to the reorganisation has been fiercest in Yorkshire and Lancashire, but the Yorkshire League, which experimented with two-day matches in 1998 (but found problems), came onside just before Christmas. Discussions have been taking place in Lancashire, involving the increasingly powerful Northern League and the Liverpool Competition – but not the two big traditional leagues, the Lancashire and Central Lancashire.

Amid all the politics, and the rain, there was still some cricket in 1998. And Doncaster Town, winners of the National Club Championship, narrowly failed to emulate Walsall in 1996 and score a league and cup double. Against all expectations, they lost their final game of the season to the young Yorkshire Academy side, presenting Harrogate, who were washed out, with the Yorkshire League. A tense finish in the Bradford League saw Bradford & Bingley crowned champions in the final match when opponents Baildon, who had been top for most of the season, failed to beat them. The Indian Amol Muzumdar amassed 976 runs at 70 for Windhill, while Hanging Heaton's John Carruthers finished with 82 wickets at only 11 apiece. Spen Victoria's opening pair, Andy Bethel and Wasim Jaffer, put on 277 against Baildon. Spen won the oldest-surviving trophy in the UK, the Heavy Woollen Cup, beating Hanging Heaton thanks to a century by Jaffer and five wickets from 16-year-old Chris Elstub.

Rain played a decisive part in many leagues' final round of matches. Five sides could have won the Middlesex League on the last Saturday, but only two were able to play. A win for overnight leaders Richmond would have guaranteed them the title, but they were held to a draw by Wembley. This meant that if Southgate could beat South Hampstead they would be champions. But, left with four overs to take their opponents' last two wickets, they managed only one, leaving Richmond on top. Not far away, on the same day, Hertfordshire League leaders Hoddesdon needed to beat Bishop's Stortford to be champions, but they never bowled a ball. Second-placed Langleybury, meanwhile, restricted Watford Town to 89 and cruised home by six wickets to take the title.

In the Northern League, Chorley were condemned to their sixth runners-up spot in eight years, when both they and champions Netherfield were confined to the pavilion on the last day. South African professional Steven Pope of Morecambe fell only 11 short of 1,000 runs, although Kendal's Ross Veenstra topped the batting averages with 687 runs at 62. Former West Indies all-rounder Eldine Baptiste headed the bowling averages with 51 wickets at 13 for St Annes.

Another West Indian, Jimmy Adams, made a critical contribution to Sunbury's charge towards the Surrey Championship title, complementing 1,047 runs with 29 wickets. Peter Richardson and Renee Addabo also played key parts, with 1,089 runs between them and 21 wickets apiece.

West Indies A batsman Keith Semple, playing for Audley, shattered the North Staffs & South Cheshire League run record, passing 1,400 runs. Other overseas players to excel included: Pakistani Naseer Ahmed (45 wickets and a thousand runs for Cornwall League champions St Just) and his compatriot Shahid Nawaz, who set a new Ribblesdale League run record (1,372 for Ribblesdale Wanderers); New Zealand medium-pacer Michael Hayman, who took ten for 21 for Lanchester against Swalwell in the Tyneside Senior League; and South African Chris Mason, who totalled 1,249 runs at 84 for North Yorkshire & South Durham League winners Norton.

Home-grown players also performed notable feats. David Jackson of Consett, aged 44, ended with 120 wickets, beating by six a Tyneside Senior League record that had stood since 1951. In the Derbyshire County League, Quarndon's Kevin Newbold took five wickets in an over against Elvaston, and Steve Stubbings struck an unbeaten 175 off just 144 balls in Langley Mill's record-breaking total of 396 for two against Aston-on-Trent. Former Surrey seamer Tony Murphy claimed all ten Old Whitgiftians wickets for Maori in a Surrey Championship match, while Bromley fast bowler Rupert Staple passed Bert Roebuck's Kent League record of 470 first-team wickets.

There were a growing number of instances of foul play and totally unacceptable behaviour. Ball-tampering was in evidence in the Surrey Championship where both Banstead and Sutton had five points deducted. Sutton's Henderson Clarke admitted scratching one side of the ball, while Neil Kendrick and Matt Patterson were banned by Banstead for scuffing it on the ground. Much more serious were the cases of violence. Players came to blows in a Pembrokeshire League match between Narberth and Lamphey after a batsman was hit in the face by a bouncer. And in Herefordshire, a batsman from Eastnor was banned for life for fighting.

LEAGUE WINNERS, 1998

Airedale & Wharfedale	Adel	**Northants**	Bletchley Town
Bassetlaw	West Indian Cavaliers	**Northern**	Netherfield
Birmingham	Wolverhampton	**North Lancs**	Millom
Bolton	Tonge	**North Staffs & South Cheshire**	Little Stoke
Bradford	Bradford & Bingley	**Northumberland County**	Benwell Hill
Central Yorkshire	Gomersal	**North Wales**	Brymbo
Cherwell	Banbury	**North Yorks & South Durham**	Norton
Cheshire County	Bowdon	**Notts Alliance**	Sandiacre Town
Cornwall	St Just	**Pembrokeshire**	Lamphey
Derbyshire County	Ockbrook & Borrowash	**Ribblesdale**	Padiham
Devon	Exmouth	**Saddleworth**	Hollinwood
Durham County	Tudhoe	**Shropshire**	Wellington
Durham Senior	Durham Academy	**Somerset**	Westlands Sports
Essex	Fives & Heronians	**Southern**	Hungerford
Hertfordshire	Langleybury	**South Wales Association**	Ynysygerwn
Huddersfield	Meltham	**Surrey Championship**	Sunbury
Kent	St Lawrence	**Sussex**	Eastbourne
Lancashire County	Glossop	**Thames Valley**	Hounslow
Leeds	Woodhouse	**Three Counties**	Winget
Leicestershire County	Kibworth	**Two Counties**	Clacton
Lincolnshire	Alkborough	**Tyneside Senior**	Blaydon
Liverpool Competition	New Brighton	**Western**	Bath
Merseyside Competition	Caldy	**West Wales Club Conference**	Llanybydder
Middlesex	Richmond	**Yorkshire**	Harrogate
Norfolk Alliance	Norwich Barleycorns		

Note: To avoid confusion, traditional League names have been given in this list, and sponsors' names omitted.

THE LANCASHIRE LEAGUES, 1998

By CHRIS ASPIN

Some memorable hitting lit up the gloom of a wet and dismal season, which was made worse in the Lancashire League by new rules that caused endless bickering and failed to bring improvements. Teams batting first had the option of facing 55 of the 100 overs, and most did so. Few captains declared early enough to ensure a close finish, and dull draws angered spectators. Equal-overs cricket will return in 1999.

Accrington, who took the wooden spoon in the Lancashire League, provided the season's most exciting cricket when they replied to a Rawtenstall total of 202 for five. Their Australian professional, Ryan Campbell, attacked with such ferocity that they won in 34.2 overs. Campbell hit eight sixes and 17 fours as he plundered an unbeaten 157 off 98 balls. On the same afternoon, Haslingden's professional, Hamish Anthony, hit 120 off 92 balls at Rishton.

There was excitement too when Littleborough beat Walsden by 86 runs in the final of the Central Lancashire League's Lees Wood Cup. After losing Phil Deakin off the first ball of the match, Littleborough reached 271 for three, with Queenslander Clinton Perren scoring 181. He and Steve Kelly put on 240 for the second wicket. It was Littleborough's 12th cup success and they went on to complete the double, topping the table ten points in front of Rochdale. They have now won the championship 17 times.

Perren headed the batting averages with 1,354 runs at 61.54, and Michael Warden of Stand topped 100 wickets for the fourth time in six seasons. The leading amateurs were Peter Wilcock (Rochdale) with 941 runs at 36.19, Les Whittle (Crompton) with 87 wickets at 13.88, and Andrew Smith-Butler (Littleborough) with 85 at 10.17.

The Lancashire League came out on top in the Lees Brewery Trophy competition, winning 11 of the 14 games in the first round. Rochdale kept the CLL flag flying until the semi-finals, when they lost to Haslingden, who beat East Lancs in the final by 13 runs. East Lancs had earlier beaten Colne in the final of the Jennings Worsley Cup and they also finished runners-up to Nelson in the championship.

Nelson's 20th title owed much to former West Indies all-rounder Roger Harper, who bowled virtually unchanged all season (503 overs) to take 96 wickets at 10.13. He scored 767 runs at 47.93. Harper's fellow West Indian, Keith Arthurton of Rawtenstall, was the only player to top 1,000. Mark Lomas (East Lancs) led the amateurs with 645 runs at 32.25. Rawtenstall spinner Keith Roscoe finished with 62 wickets at 14.48.

Ten-year-old John Simpson turned out for Haslingden against Church and fielded for more than two and a half hours when a player fell sick minutes before the start. He joined his father Jack – a wicket-keeping legend in both leagues – who was playing his last game.

The two leagues remained under pressure to form a Premier League, but failed to give way. They believed the existing structure in the county should be built on and supported, rather than being subjected to a radical change which offered no guarantee of success or improvement.

EW CARTONS LANCASHIRE LEAGUE

	P	W	L	D	NR	Bonus Pts	Pts	Professional	Runs	Avge	Wkts	Avge
Nelson	26	11	2	10	3	36	171§	R. A. Harper	767	47.93	96	10.13
East Lancs.	26	10	2	11	3	33	161	B. E. Young	398	28.42	57	12.91
Haslingden .	26	7	6	8	5	24	119§	H. A. G. Anthony	493	27.38	54	15.01
Enfield . . .	26	6	4	9	7	22	114	O. D. Gibson . . .	736	40.88	44	13.86
Bacup	26	5	4	12	5	28	112	B. M. White	766	51.06	66	12.12
Ramsbottom	26	6	3	11	6	16	110	I. J. Harvey	766	51.06	79	11.84
Rishton . . .	26	6	8	7	5	22	106	L. C. R. Jordaan .	160	11.42	77	11.78
Colne	26	4	3	13	5	20	101*	J. C. Scuderi . . .	844	56.26	47	11.78
Todmorden .	26	3	5	9	7	29	97†§	V. C. Drakes . . .	493	30.81	53	15.33
Lowerhouse	26	5	8	9	4	18	94	M. P. Mott	785	43.61	34	21.35
Church . . .	26	3	5	12	5	23	91*§	N. C. McGarrell . .	752	47.00	56	15.14
Rawtenstall.	26	4	7	9	6	18	88	K. L. T. Arthurton	1,156	77.06	27	22.07
Burnley . . .	26	3	8	8	7	19	79	P. Botha	636	37.41	64	15.15
Accrington .	26	3	11	8	4	15	69	R. J. Campbell . . .	824	45.77	37	19.83

Notes: Ten points awarded for a win; five points for a tie; two points for a draw or no-result.

 * Includes five points for a tie; † includes ten points for two ties.
 § Todmorden lost four points and Nelson, Haslingden and Church one each for slow over-rates.

CENTRAL LANCASHIRE LEAGUE

	P	OW	LW	L	D	Pts	Professional	Runs	Avge	Wkts	Avge
Littleborough	30	10	9	2	9	104	C. T. Perren	1,354	61.54	11	38.00
Rochdale	30	6	12	4	8	94	R. M. Baker	1,174	53.36	89	11.19
Crompton . . .	30	3	15	7	5	85	Zafar Iqbal	438	18.25	16	19.40
Royton	30	9	6	10	5	80*	T. B. Arothe	883	36.79	93	12.30
Stand	30	10	3	11	6	74	M. Warden	356	16.18	107	10.19
Oldham	30	9	3	11	7	73†	Sohail Jaffer	996	49.80	14	30.71
Norden	30	7	5	11	7	69	Asif Mujtaba	1,256	50.24	79	15.07
Walsden	30	5	7	11	7	69	R. P. Larkin	955	41.52	58	19.27
Werneth	30	8	3	13	6	64	R. J. Kennedy . . .	458	21.80	79	14.64
Radcliffe	30	4	5	11	10	61*	S. Dearden	810	32.40	58	20.82
Milnrow	30	6	4	13	7	60	J. D. Fitton	959	39.95	49	21.16
Unsworth . . .	30	7	2	15	6	56*	C. P. H. Ramanayake	749	29.96	92	14.59
Middleton . . .	30	4	4	15	7	50	J. D. Batty	680	29.56	42	27.00
Ashton	30	7	0	16	7	49	C. Hillgrove‡	275	21.15	15	22.40
Heywood. . . .	30	3	3	14	10	47	A. Badenhorst . . .	612	23.53	65	17.55
Stockport. . . .	30	4	1	20	5	36†	R. Arshad	714	25.50	21	21.12

Notes: Five points awarded for an outright win; four points for a limited win; two points for a draw. A team achieves an outright win by bowling out the opposition. CLL averages include cup games.

 * Includes three points for a tie; † includes six points for two ties. ‡ Did not play full season.

NATIONAL CLUB CHAMPIONSHIP, 1998

Doncaster Town added their name to the list of club champions when they became the first Yorkshire team to take the title since Scarborough in 1982. They beat Bath in the final at Lord's with four balls to spare, but they were lucky to make it beyond the second round: they squeezed past Sandiacre by one wicket. Chasing 161, Doncaster slumped to 120 for nine. But No. 11 and captain Nick Cowan took his career-best in the competition from four to 32 not out and saw his side through. The quarter-final at Chorley, champions in 1994 and 1995, was watched by a crowd of 1,200. Nineteen-year-old fast bowler Graham Attenborough took four for 13 in nine overs, and scored 36 in a three-wicket victory. He was named man of the match, winning his weight in beer from the sponsors, Abbot Ale.

The semi-final against Yorkshire rivals and the beaten 1997 finalists, Harrogate, also produced a tight finish. Doncaster won by two wickets with two balls to spare and reached their first final. Peter Ellis made 56 and took the first of two consecutive match awards. This had seemed unlikely when, fielding at short leg in a game against Sheffield Collegiate in July, he was knocked out and detained in hospital overnight for a brain scan.

Bath, the beaten finalists, won most of their games by comfortable margins, although they too suffered an early scare, defeating South Wiltshire by two wickets in the first round. Their most impressive victory was a nine-wicket win in the fourth round against Bristol-based Optimists, champions in 1992. Opener Stuart Priscott won match awards for his 84 in the quarter-final at Hastings and 118 in the semi-final against Ealing.

FINAL

BATH v DONCASTER TOWN

At Lord's, August 28. Doncaster Town won by six wickets. Toss: Doncaster Town.

Doncaster, in trouble at 17 for two, recovered to ease to victory. Ellis, missed on 12 by Rupert Swetman, son of former England wicket-keeper Roy, displayed a sound temperament and made the most of a short Grand Stand boundary to score an unbeaten 94 from 101 balls. He shared a century partnership with Widdup before getting further support from the Dawson brothers, Richard and Gareth. Bath had also recovered, from 106 for four, when Staunton and Sage put on 113 for the fifth wicket. Staunton hit an unbeaten 64 off 78 balls, and Sage's 47 included four sixes.

Man of the Match: P. E. Ellis.

Bath

S. M. Priscott run out	33	T. Baker not out		4
D. A. Burton c Widdup b Jones	19			
G. Swinney lbw b Jones	23	B 4, l-b 14, w 9, n-b 2		29
B. R. F. Staunton not out	64			
†R. Swetman c Attenborough b Cowan	10	1/35 2/80 3/84	(5 wkts, 45 overs)	229
M. P. Sage c Farmer b Attenborough	47	4/106 5/219		

*M. J. Roe, M. Thorburn, I. P. Shrubsole and M. R. Howarth did not bat.

Bowling: Attenborough 9–0–39–1; Ellis 6–0–46–0; Jones 9–2–34–2; Stokoe 9–2–18–0; Cowan 7–0–41–1; R. G. Dawson 5–0–33–0.

Doncaster Town

T. Farmer c and b Shrubsole	3	G. Dawson not out	24
G. A. Attenborough c Swetman			
b Shrubsole	6	B 5, l-b 8, w 9, n-b 4	26
†S. Widdup c Thorburn b Shrubsole	53		
P. E. Ellis not out	94	1/12 2/17	(4 wkts, 44.2 overs) 233
R. G. Dawson b Swinney	27	3/134 4/187	

A. Stoves, S. Nicholson, P. Stokoe, D. Jones and *N. W. Cowan did not bat.

Bowling: Priscott 8–0–44–0; Shrubsole 9–0–32–3; Sage 6–0–32–0; Thorburn 3.2–0–31–0; Howarth 9–0–38–0; Swinney 9–0–43–1.

Umpires: J. B. Hamblett and G. Lowden.

WINNERS 1969-98

1969	Hampstead	1979	Scarborough	1989	Teddington
1970	Cheltenham	1980	Moseley	1990	Blackpool
1971	Blackheath	1981	Scarborough	1991	Teddington
1972	Scarborough	1982	Scarborough	1992	Optimists
1973	Wolverhampton	1983	Shrewsbury	1993	Old Hill
1974	Sunbury	1984	Old Hill	1994	Chorley
1975	York	1985	Old Hill	1995	Chorley
1976	Scarborough	1986	Stourbridge	1996	Walsall
1977	Southgate	1987	Old Hill	1997	Eastbourne
1978	Cheltenham	1988	Enfield	1998	Doncaster Town

NATIONAL VILLAGE CHAMPIONSHIP, 1998

Methley, of Yorkshire, won their first National Village Championship, so easing memories of their only previous appearance in the final, in 1992, when they lost to Hursley Park on the last ball. The weather proved the only real obstacle on Methley's path from their home, five miles from Wakefield, to Lord's: after three stoppages for rain, their seventh-round match against Harome of North Yorkshire ended at 8.50 p.m.

Apperley, from Gloucestershire, made less certain progress. With the scores finishing level, they scraped through against Cornwood, winners of the Devon and East Cornwall region, because they had lost nine wickets to Cornwood's ten. Later, they had to call on overseas aid: Hugh Leeke, a key all-rounder who had been working on a carpentry job at Kazakhstan's national airport, flew home 36 hours before the semi-final against Horndon on the Hill of Essex. He took three for 48 and then opened the batting to help Apperley win by six wickets. His busy schedule saw him fly back to Kazakhstan at 4 a.m. the following morning, only to return for the final two weeks later.

The other 653 villages must have breathed a collective sigh of relief when the champions of the last two years, Caldy, from the Wirral, were knocked out in the first round by Port Sunlight. There were also some fine individual performances in the early rounds. Les Sonley, playing for North Yorkshire side Kildale, took five for nine to help bowl out Barton for 114, before the Kildale batsmen collapsed to 91, with seven ducks. In the East Midlands, Jonathan Potter hammered 164 off 89 balls as Nassington amassed a match-winning 322 for five against Great Houghton. Potter had been dismissed first ball the day before, as well as in the same fixture the previous season.

The surprise team of the competition were Grace Dieu Park, a hamlet in Leicestershire boasting a handful of residents. They made the most of their limited resources to reach the final of the Leicestershire and Warwickshire region, where they lost by nine wickets to Bardon Hill. – Andrew Tong.

FINAL

APPERLEY v METHLEY

At Lord's, August 30. Methley won by 61 runs. Toss: Apperley.

Put in to bat, Methley's openers duly played Apperley out of the game. Alec Gilston, fresh from a century in the semi-final, and Steve Rowse put on 152, the best opening stand in the final, beating the previous best of 124 by Brett Saunders and Phil Eymond for Caldy against Langleybury in 1996. Rowse, with 94 off 113 balls, narrowly missed his first hundred for the club when he lost his middle stump, but Methley's total of 238 for three was the second highest in 27 finals, behind Goatacre's 267 for five against Dunstall in 1990. Apperley, losing wickets steadily and falling behind the run-rate, were unable to accelerate with the security their opponents had enjoyed. Ian Coggin batted stylishly before skying a full toss as he went for his fifty off the last ball. Lee Mills collected three wickets in the penultimate over to finish with four for 34.

Methley

†A. Gilston c Coggin b H. M. M. Leeke	62	J. D. Rickers not out.	0	
S. Rowse b J. N. Macpherson.	94	L-b 10, w 4, n-b 1.	15	
P. Oldham not out	37			
N. Lockett run out	30	1/152 2/185 3/236	(3 wkts, 40 overs) 238	

*J. McHale, L. S. Smith, A. Wailes, M. J. Waite, L. Mills and A. J. Waite did not bat.

Bowling: H. M. M. Leeke 9–2–47–1; S. J. Macpherson 9–1–30–0; J. N. Macpherson 9–0–63–1; R. H. Leeke 9–0–51–0; Bubb 4–0–37–0.

Apperley

J. N. Macpherson b Mills	6	J. O. W. Bubb b Mills.	0	
H. M. M. Leeke b M. J. Waite	13	J. D. Scorer b Mills	2	
R. H. Leeke b Oldham	30	C. A. Chatham not out	2	
S. J. Macpherson c and b Oldham. . . .	14	B 1, l-b 10, w 10, n-b 1	22	
P. A. Holbrook c Gilston b Rickers . . .	32			
†I. M. Coggin c McHale b Wailes.	46	1/11 2/43 3/67	(40 overs) 177	
J. R. Hall lbw b McHale	1	4/80 5/132 6/139		
*L. V. Attard c Smith b Mills.	9	7/170 8/170 9/173		

Bowling: McHale 7–1–27–1; Mills 7–1–34–4; M. J. Waite 9–1–37–1; Oldham 9–2–23–2; Rickers 5–0–31–1; A. J. Waite 2–0–11–0; Wailes 1–0–3–1.

Umpires: B. Knight and M. J. Sheehy.

WINNERS 1972-98

1972	Troon (Cornwall)	1986	Forge Valley (Yorkshire)
1973	Troon (Cornwall)	1987	Longparish (Hampshire)
1974	Bomarsund (Northumberland)	1988	Goatacre (Wiltshire)
1975	Gowerton (Glamorgan)	1989	Toft (Cheshire)
1976	Troon (Cornwall)	1990	Goatacre (Wiltshire)
1977	Cookley (Worcestershire)	1991	St Fagans (Glamorgan)
1978	Linton Park (Kent)	1992	Hursley Park (Hampshire)
1979	East Bierley (Yorkshire)	1993	Kington (Herefordshire)
1980	Marchwiel (Clwyd)	1994	Elvaston (Derbyshire)
1981	St Fagans (Glamorgan)	1995	Woodhouse Grange (Yorkshire)
1982	St Fagans (Glamorgan)	1996	Caldy (Cheshire)
1983	Quarndon (Derbyshire)	1997	Caldy (Cheshire)
1984	Marchwiel (Clwyd)	1998	Methley (Yorkshire)
1985	Freuchie (Fife)		

AUSTRALIA A IN SCOTLAND AND IRELAND, 1998

In 1995, a team that was effectively Australia's A side, though it was billed as Young Australia, had toured England with some success but very little attention. This time, they never reached the English counties at all. Planned fixtures against Durham, Kent, Sussex and Somerset were cancelled a few weeks before the Australians were due to arrive, after what the ECB called a "misunderstanding"; the Australian Cricket Board was reported to have expected a greater financial contribution from the ICC development fund. But the trip had always been intended to cover ICC associates Scotland and Ireland as well, and that part of the programme, aimed at encouraging higher playing standards in the junior cricketing countries, went ahead.

Bad weather dogged the tourists. They would probably have won all three of their first-class matches if rain had not arrived on the final day of both Scottish games. Of their one-day fixtures, three were abandoned completely and two others ended without a result. But all the matches played to a conclusion Australia A won with ease.

Their superiority was hardly surprising. Six of the 13-strong squad had played Test cricket – Andy Bichel, Adam Dale, Jason Gillespie, Matthew Hayden, Brendon Julian and Damien Martyn. The captain, Michael Di Venuto, and Brad Young had appeared in one-day internationals, and Colin Miller made his Test debut soon afterwards. Their coach was Australia's most experienced leader, Allan Border. Hayden headed the first-class averages with 241 runs at 80.33, though he was out-scored by Dene Hills of Tasmania, who hit two centuries as he made 264 runs at 66.00. Dale was far and away the most successful bowler, with 18 wickets in six innings at only 10.16.

AUSTRALIA A TOURING PARTY

M. J. Di Venuto (Tasmania) (*captain*), M. L. Hayden (Queensland) (*vice-captain*), A. J. Bichel (Queensland), R. J. Campbell (Western Australia), A. C. Dale (Queensland), J. N. Gillespie (South Australia), D. F. Hills (Tasmania), M. E. Hussey (Western Australia), B. P. Julian (Western Australia), D. R. Martyn (Western Australia), C. R. Miller (Tasmania), A. Symonds (Queensland), B. E. Young (South Australia).

Manager: T. J. Robertson.   *Coach:* A. R. Border.

AUSTRALIA A TOUR RESULTS

First-class matches – Played 3: Won 1, Drawn 2.
Win – Ireland.
Draws – Scotland (2).
Non-first-class matches – Played 9: Won 7, No result 2. Abandoned 3. *Wins* – Scotland XI, Scotland (2), Ireland (4). *No result* – Scotland, Ireland. *Abandoned* – Scotland (2), Ireland.

Note: Matches in this section which were not first-class are signified by a dagger.

†At Forfar, July 31. First unofficial one-day international: Scotland v Australia A. No result (abandoned).

†At Aberdeen, August 2. Australia A won by five wickets. Toss: Scotland XI. Scotland XI 188 for eight (50 overs) (I. L. Philip 100, Extras 38); Australia A 190 for five (47.5 overs) (M. L. Hayden 38, A. Symonds 58 not out).
Philip scored 100 out of 167 while at the crease; the next highest score off the bat was 13.

†At Dundee, August 3. Second unofficial one-day international: Scotland v Australia A. No result (abandoned).

SCOTLAND v AUSTRALIA A

At Raeburn Place, Edinburgh, August 5, 6, 7. Drawn. Toss: Scotland. First-class debut: P. D. Steindl.

Rain denied the Australians: with the whole of the final day to bowl Scotland out, Dale and colleagues had reduced them to 85 for five in 27 overs when the rest of play was lost. The tourists were on top from the moment they were asked to bat. Hills and Di Venuto both hit centuries on the opening day, when they put on 192 for the second wicket. Then their seamers removed four home batsmen that evening. Thanks to Allingham, who batted two and a half hours, the Scots recovered from 93 for six, but still managed less than half the Australian total of 351. Di Venuto waived the follow-on, however, to give his later batsmen practice. They declared again on the final morning, leaving Scotland an impossible target of 394; only Philip resisted before the rain came to the rescue.

Close of play: First day, Scotland 66-4 (M. J. D. Allingham 8*, I. M. Stanger 1*); Second day, Australia A 214-5 (D. R. Martyn 60*, A. C. Dale 3*).

Australia A

D. F. Hills c Salmond b Sheridan	118		
M. L. Hayden b Williamson	50		
*M. J. Di Venuto c Stanger b Sheridan	138		
D. R. Martyn not out	27	– not out	60
A. Symonds (did not bat)		– (1) c Lockie b Stanger	15
†R. J. Campbell (did not bat)		– (2) b Asim Butt	28
B. P. Julian (did not bat)		– (3) c and b Stanger	14
B. E. Young (did not bat)		– (5) c Williamson b Asim Butt	41
C. R. Miller (did not bat)		– (6) c Davies b Stanger	44
A. C. Dale (did not bat)		– (7) not out	3
B 8, l-b 5, n-b 5	18	B 1, l-b 4, w 1, n-b 3	9
1/89 2/281 3/351	(3 wkts dec.) 351	1/41 2/46 3/60 (5 wkts dec.) 214	
		4/124 5/203	

J. N. Gillespie did not bat.

Bowling: First Innings—Asim Butt 20–5–67–0; Steindl 15–6–52–0; Allingham 7–1–33–0; Stanger 10–2–60–0; Williamson 9–1–49–1; Sheridan 18.1–1–77–2. *Second Innings*—Asim Butt 14–3–52–2; Steindl 6–0–46–0; Stanger 16–2–57–3; Williamson 8–0–24–0; Sheridan 9–2–25–0.

Scotland

I. L. Philip c Hills b Gillespie	4	– not out	50
B. G. Lockie lbw b Dale	0	– lbw b Julian	0
D. R. Lockhart b Julian	18	– c Campbell b Dale	4
*G. Salmond c Hills b Gillespie	13	– c Campbell b Dale	3
M. J. D. Allingham st Campbell b Young	29	– lbw b Dale	14
I. M. Stanger c Campbell b Dale	12	– b Miller	6
J. G. Williamson c Young b Julian	6		
†A. G. Davies c Campbell b Miller	14		
P. D. Steindl lbw b Julian	14		
K. L. P. Sheridan not out	12		
Asim Butt c Di Venuto b Young	9		
B 9, l-b 12, w 4, n-b 16	41	B 1, l-b 3, w 2, n-b 2	8
1/7 2/15 3/45 4/65 5/82	172	1/0 2/5 3/30 (5 wkts) 85	
6/93 7/133 8/133 9/156		4/56 5/85	

Bowling: First Innings—Gillespie 7–1–20–2; Dale 16–2–38–2; Julian 17–4–41–3; Miller 14–5–29–1; Young 15.4–8–23–2. *Second Innings*—Dale 12–5–29–3; Julian 6–0–23–1; Miller 8.1–2–29–1.

Umpires: J. Breslin and L. A. Redford.

†At Hamilton Crescent, Glasgow, August 10. Third unofficial one-day international: Australia A won by 149 runs. Toss: Scotland. Australia A 313 for two (50 overs) (M. E. Hussey 136 not out, D. R. Martyn 155 not out); Scotland 164 for eight (50 overs) (Extras 42; C. R. Miller three for 24, B. E. Young three for 31).

Hussey and Martyn shared an unbroken stand of 300 for Australia A's third wicket.

SCOTLAND v AUSTRALIA A

At Linlithgow, August 11, 12, 13. Drawn. Toss: Scotland.

The second three-day match followed a similar pattern to the first, though the Scots gave a better account of themselves. Australia A were put in again, and Hayden hit 21 fours and a six as he scored 123 in three hours before being dismissed by off-spinner Dyer, who took four of the five wickets to fall while conceding only two and a half an over. This time, Scotland reached an encouraging 171 for four before a mini-collapse, and even then Stanger went on to an unbeaten 52, enabling them to declare 24 behind. Hills scored his second hundred in successive first-class matches and added 161 in 142 minutes with Hussey as the Australians took their lead to 267; Dale had collected two cheap Scottish wickets when rain intervened again.

Close of play: First day, Scotland 44-1 (I. L. Philip 27*, D. R. Lockhart 9*); Second day, Australia A 169-1 (M. E. Hussey 55*, D. F. Hills 88*).

Australia A

M. L. Hayden c Philip b Dyer	123		
†R. J. Campbell b Thomson	30	– c Stanger b Thomson	19
*M. J. Di Venuto c Allingham b Dyer	60		
A. Symonds lbw b Dyer	7	– not out	33
D. F. Hills not out	12	– (3) c Davies b Brinkley	110
B. P. Julian b Dyer	25		
A. J. Bichel not out	0	– (5) not out	4
M. E. Hussey (did not bat)		– (1) c Lockhart b Thomson	67
L-b 5, w 1, n-b 2	8	B 2, l-b 6, w 1, n-b 1	10

1/67 2/211 3/224 4/226 5/261 (5 wkts dec.) 265   1/36 2/197 3/225 (3 wkts dec.) 243

B. E. Young, C. R. Miller and A. C. Dale did not bat.

Bowling: First Innings—Brinkley 13–2–51–0; Asim Butt 19–2–83–0; Thomson 10–2–54–1; Stanger 4–0–24–0; Dyer 19–6–48–4. *Second Innings*—Brinkley 17–5–49–1; Asim Butt 3–1–12–0; Thomson 10–1–52–2; Dyer 13.5–1–80–0; Stanger 3–0–26–0; Allingham 3–0–16–0.

Scotland

B. M. W. Patterson lbw b Dale	3	– not out	17
I. L. Philip c Campbell b Dale	28	– c Di Venuto b Dale	1
D. R. Lockhart c Campbell b Young	46	– c Campbell b Dale	0
*G. Salmond lbw b Bichel	16	– not out	9
M. J. D. Allingham lbw b Dale	45		
I. M. Stanger not out	52		
J. E. Brinkley lbw b Dale	0		
†A. G. Davies c Hayden b Julian	1		
K. Thomson c Julian b Bichel	22		
Asim Butt not out	20		
B 4, l-b 2, n-b 2	8	L-b 5, n-b 1	6

1/8 2/61 3/86 4/115 5/171 (8 wkts dec.) 241   1/17 2/21 (2 wkts) 33
6/171 7/172 8/211

N. R. Dyer did not bat.

Bowling: First Innings—Dale 21–7–48–4; Julian 13–2–62–1; Young 17–9–42–1; Miller 10–2–33–0; Bichel 13–4–49–2; Symonds 2–1–1–0. *Second Innings*—Dale 7–4–5–2; Julian 7–1–23–0.

Umpires: D. M. Potter and D. Walker.

†At Raeburn Place, Edinburgh, August 15. Fourth unofficial one-day international: Australia A won by 175 runs. Toss: Australia A. Australia A 291 for six (50 overs) (M. E. Hussey 50, R. J. Campbell 120, A. Symonds 44, D. R. Martyn 34 not out); Scotland 116 (43.1 overs) (A. J. Bichel three for 20).

†At Linlithgow, August 16. Fifth unofficial one-day international: No result. Toss: Scotland. Scotland 206 for eight (50 overs) (D. R. Lockhart 46, I. M. Stanger 74; A. J. Bichel three for 44) v Australia A.

IRELAND v AUSTRALIA A

At Rathmines, Dublin, August 20, 21, 22. Australia A won by 150 runs. Toss: Australia A. First-class debuts: J. A. Bushe, M. D. Dwyer, P. J. K. Mooney, D. M. Olphert.

Australia A began the Irish leg of their tour with a convincing win against a team including their own compatriot, Steve Waugh, Ireland's professional. For once, rain did not prevent them completing victory. On the opening day, it was Hussey's turn to score a hundred, and he remained unbeaten when his team declared at 309. After being troubled by a spinner called Dyer in Scotland, Australia this time lost four wickets to Dwyer, an Irish slow left-armer. But medium-pacer Dale continued his excellent form, and took his haul in three first-class games to 17, as Ireland subsided for 132. Again, Di Venuto declined to enforce the follow-on, and Julian's 60 not out left the Irish a target of 347. Despite 45 from Waugh, they were bowled out on the last day.

Close of play: First day, Ireland 94-4 (S. R. Waugh 22*, P. J. K. Mooney 2*); Second day, Ireland 92-2 (S. G. Smyth 43*, S. R. Waugh 8*).

Australia A

M. L. Hayden lbw b Dwyer	68			
M. E. Hussey not out	125			
*M. J. Di Venuto run out	4	– c Bushe b Mooney	11	
D. R. Martyn c Bushe b Dwyer	26	– b Cooke	43	
D. F. Hills lbw b McCallan	5	– (1) c Bushe b Cooke	19	
†R. J. Campbell st Bushe b Dwyer	53	– (2) lbw b Mooney	6	
B. P. Julian b Dwyer	5	– (5) not out	60	
B. E. Young not out	7	– (6) c Mooney b Dwyer	15	
A. C. Dale (did not bat)		– (7) not out	9	
B 9, l-b 2, w 3, n-b 2	16	L-b 3, w 1, n-b 2	6	

1/115 2/131 3/175   (6 wkts dec.) 309   1/7 2/32 3/67   (5 wkts dec.) 169
4/197 5/286 6/302   4/87 5/137

C. R. Miller and J. N. Gillespie did not bat.

Bowling: *First Innings*—Cooke 8–1–41–0; Mooney 8–2–27–0; Olphert 4–0–28–0; McCallan 20–5–69–1; Dwyer 12–1–57–4; Joyce 10–1–49–0; Waugh 6–1–27–0. *Second Innings*—Mooney 14–2–45–2; Cooke 15–4–49–2; McCallan 9–2–36–0; Dwyer 7–3–27–1; Joyce 2–0–9–0.

Ireland

W. K. McCallan c Julian b Gillespie	0	– (2) c Campbell b Julian	22	
J. A. M. Molins b Dale	33	– (1) lbw b Miller	1	
S. G. Smyth c Campbell b Julian	24	– c Young b Dale	43	
S. R. Waugh c Campbell b Gillespie	31	– c Campbell b Julian	45	
*A. R. Dunlop b Dale	4	– lbw b Gillespie	10	
P. J. K. Mooney lbw b Dale	8	– (7) c and b Young	9	
E. C. Joyce c Martyn b Gillespie	11	– (6) c Hayden b Young	15	
D. M. Olphert lbw b Dale	0	– c Young b Julian	1	
G. Cooke lbw b Dale	5	– run out	12	
†J. A. Bushe not out	4	– c Hayden b Miller	2	
M. D. Dwyer c Hills b Dale	0	– not out	1	
L-b 4, n-b 8	12	B 8, l-b 16, n-b 11	35	

1/11 2/60 3/64 4/74 5/110   132   1/5 2/66 3/102 4/122 5/163   196
6/110 7/122 8/123 9/132   6/167 7/174 8/191 9/193

Bowling: *First Innings*—Gillespie 12–2–49–3; Dale 18.5–8–43–6; Julian 8–1–32–1; Young 1–0–4–0. *Second Innings*—Gillespie 12–1–40–1; Miller 10.3–2–22–2; Julian 12–2–49–3; Young 11–1–41–2; Dale 9–4–20–1.

Umpires: S. Daultrey and L. Keegan.

†At Castle Avenue, Dublin, August 23. First unofficial one-day international: No result. Toss: Australia A. Ireland 168 for seven (50 overs) (S. G. Smyth 39, S. R. Waugh 67) v Australia A.

†At Waringstown, August 25. Second unofficial one-day international: No result (abandoned). *Replayed the following day.*

†At Waringstown, August 26. Third unofficial one-day international: Australia A won by three wickets. Toss: Ireland. Ireland 192 for seven (35 overs) (W. K. McCallan 51, S. R. Waugh 50); Australia A 195 for seven (32.2 overs) (M. J. Di Venuto 33, D. R. Martyn 59 not out; P. J. K. Mooney three for 40).

†At Waringstown, August 27. Fourth unofficial one-day international: Australia A won by eight wickets. Toss: Ireland. Ireland 138 (46.5 overs) (A. R. Dunlop 57; A. J. Bichel three for 32, C. R. Miller four for 28); Australia A 140 for two (30.3 overs) (M. E. Hussey 78 not out).

†At Downpatrick, August 28. Fifth unofficial one-day international: Australia A won by 170 runs. Toss: Australia A. Australia A 268 for eight (50 overs) (D. R. Martyn 98, M. J. Di Venuto 52); Ireland 98 (29.2 overs) (S. G. Smyth 50; A. Symonds four for 13).

†At Beechgrove, August 29. Sixth unofficial one-day international: Australia A won by four wickets. Toss: Australia A. Ireland 128 for eight (50 overs) (S. R. Waugh 36; B. E. Young four for 25); Australia A 131 for six (31.1 overs) (B. P. Julian 53 not out; W. K. McCallan three for 41, M. D. Dwyer three for 19).

ONE HUNDRED YEARS AGO

From JOHN WISDEN'S CRICKETERS' ALMANACK FOR 1899

CRICKET CENTURIES by E. V. Bligh – "It is evident that if cricket is to be in the future, as it has been in the past, a game capable of being played to a finish, *something* must be done to check the centuries. If I may be excused the play upon the word, I will take half a century ago as the basis of my remarks to-day. There was good – rare good cricket then, but there were fewer, far fewer centuries . . . What with a bumpy surface such as even 'Lord's' was, and grass cut only by the scythe, head-balls and shooters prevailed then, perhaps in immediate succession, and would have sorely puzzled (*mutatis mutandis*) our very best modern batsmen. Incontestably something required to be done to make the batsman's tenure more certain by improving the grounds; but it had been well if greater care had been taken not too heavily to handicap the bowler."

PUBLIC SCHOOL CRICKET IN 1898 by W. J. Ford – "There are many pleasant ways of spending a cricket season; the most pleasant to play without ceasing; the next is to haunt the pavilion at Lord's; but there is a third course open, a course which I am convinced would be replete with pleasure; namely to wander from school to school, – of course at 'WISDEN'S' expense – keeping one's eye on the rising generation."

LEICESTERSHIRE IN 1898 – "From the end of May until the third week in August nothing came to break the monotony of defeat save those games ruined by rain . . . undoubtedly weakness in bowling was chiefly responsible for Leicestershire having such an unsuccessful season."

THROWING: A NOTE BY THE EDITOR – "Let it once be understood that new bowlers who do not deliver the ball with strict fairness will be no-balled, and throwing will . . . disappear from first-class cricket."

IRISH CRICKET IN 1998

By DEREK SCOTT

The 1998 season was never going to be easy for Ireland – several senior players had retired after the failure to qualify for the 1999 World Cup – but poor weather and a succession of substandard pitches made it especially difficult for the batsmen to develop. The result was that they won just four of their 22 games, while five were entirely lost to the rain.

The touring team from Bangladesh arrived in June, when the weather was at its worst, and four of the five scheduled limited-overs internationals were washed out. Play was possible, though, at a new venue: Waringstown, in County Down. A marvellous 94 from Peter Gillespie enabled Ireland to beat a target of 230. The South Africans then played two matches, their first visit since 1951: Pollock and Cullinan lit up each of the games but, in Dublin, Ireland's new captain, Angus Dunlop, responded by reaching a hundred with the last man at the crease. It was the first century for Ireland against a Test team since T. G. McVeagh made 102 not out against West Indies in 1928.

The last visitors, Australia A, toured the country in late August. The side contained six Test players – Bichel, Dale, Gillespie, Hayden, Julian and Martyn; a little over a month later, Miller had also played Test cricket. The Australians proved far too good, and it was felt that the tour would have been more beneficial to Ireland if it had been staged earlier in the season, when the home players were in better physical shape. Even so, it was a welcome part of ICC's development plan for Ireland, which will continue with the visit of South Africa A in July 1999.

Steve Waugh succeeded Hansie Cronje as overseas player and turned out against his own compatriots. In the Benson and Hedges Cup, Matt Dwyer, a slow left-arm bowler, made his debut at the age of 39. He finished the season with 31 wickets at 19.19, figures not achieved in Irish cricket since Dermot Monteith in the 1970s. Ireland failed to repeat their great 1997 win over Middlesex, though. Their cause was not helped by the absence of Desmond Curry, who was dropped after failing to attend practice sessions. Stephen Smyth, however, returned after an absence of one season, and hit an unbeaten century against MCC at Lurgan, another new venue. He went on to score a record 703 runs in the season at 37.00, an aggregate challenged only by Dunlop, who made 558 runs at 39.85.

The amateur Triple Crown tournament in Scotland was a great disappointment. Having dismissed Scotland for 160, Ireland got to 127 for four, before they collapsed to lose by nine runs. Wins against the ECB XI and Wales merely emphasised what might have been. Against Wales, Kyle McCallan scored his second century for Ireland. Another let-down was Ireland's failure to defend the European Cup they had won in 1996. Holland were too good for all-comers on their own matting pitches, and Ireland could finish only fourth.

Club highlights included league and cup doubles by Leinster and Cork County, and an extraordinary final in the North-West Cup: Ardmore led Brigade by 64 on first innings, but were then bowled out for 17 to lose by five wickets. However, this was not the lowest score in this cup final: in 1914, City of Derry needed 22 to win, only to be bowled out for 12. The most remarkable individual innings came in the first round of the Royal Liver All Ireland Cup, where Curry hit an unbeaten 260 off 161 balls for Limavady against Catholic Young Men in Dublin with 17 sixes. It was the highest score in a competitive match in Ireland. Limavady declared at 373 for five with nine deliveries of their 50 overs unused, because the opposition had run out of balls.

Winners of Irish Leagues and Cups:
Royal Liver All Ireland Cup: Strabane; **Dublin Senior League:** Leinster; **Munster League:** Cork County; **Munster Cup:** Cork County; **Northern Union:** Ballymena; **Northern Union Cup:** Woodvale; **North-West League:** Limavady; **North-West Cup:** Brigade.

SCOTTISH CRICKET IN 1998

By J. WATSON BLAIR

As Scotland prepared for a crucial season in 1999, when they make their debut in the World Cup, their programme got ever busier. The highlights included visits by the ICC champions, Bangladesh, and Australia A, as well as a historic victory in the NatWest Trophy.

Scotland won the short limited-overs series against Bangladesh, but the Bangladeshis took revenge in a one-day game against a Scotland XI and drew the three-day international. Australia A, coached by Allan Border, were a different proposition, and they easily won the two limited-overs games which survived the rain. The Scots managed to draw the two three-day matches, however, with Iain Philip, who had taken a century off the Australians in an earlier game, and Ian Stanger scoring unbeaten fifties. The annual first-class fixture against Ireland was cancelled because of both sides' unusually heavy schedule.

In the Benson and Hedges, Scotland had chances of winning three of their four games, but failed to convert promising positions into victories. They seemed to have learned from their defeats, however, when they knocked Worcestershire out of the NatWest Trophy at Edinburgh, to record their first win in the competition. Bruce Patterson and Michael Allingham put on 118 – a second-wicket record for Scotland in a one-day game – before Craig Wright destroyed Worcestershire's middle order, taking five for 23 to set up a four-run victory. But Scotland could not repeat their giant-killing in the second round, against Derbyshire.

The other competitions proved largely disappointing. Victory in the Costcutter Cup was tempered by the fact that rain reduced the competition to a series of bowl-outs, and Scotland failed to retain the amateur Triple Crown, losing to the ECB XI by two runs in the vital match. Only nine fit men had turned up for the game, and Scotland had to obtain special dispensation to include teenager Gregor Maiden and coach Jim Love, who were outside their original squad. In the European Cup in Holland, Scotland finished third, but at the Commonwealth Games in Malaysia, the only point they gained was in a rain-ruined match against Pakistan. Before he left for the games, George Salmond, Scotland's energetic captain, had received a special award to mark his 100th appearance, against Australia A. He has been appointed captain for the World Cup as well.

On the domestic scene, Grange repeated their Scottish Cup triumph of 1997, but by the narrowest of margins. Batting first in the final, they scored 212 for six, thanks to 101 from Steve Crawley, the man of the match. In reply, Prestwick were all out for 212. Their tenth wicket fell to a run-out off the last ball of the innings, and so Grange retained the White and Mackay Trophy by losing fewer wickets. Meanwhile, the 31 leading clubs from the recently formed Scottish League and the long-established Western Union were competing in three conferences to decide the make-up of the new three-division Scottish National League in 1999. The conferences were won by Grange, West of Scotland and Ferguslie. They will be joined in the top division by Aberdeenshire, Ayr, Carlton, Greenock, Heriot's FP, Stoneywood Dyce, and West Lothian.

Winners of other Scottish Leagues and Cups:
SCU Trophy: Greenock; **West League Cup:** Greenock; **Border League:** Berwick; **Small Clubs' Cup:** Cults; **Strathmore Union:** Meigle.

PAKISTAN UNDER-19 IN ENGLAND, 1998

By GERALD HOWAT

Although they ended up as losers, Pakistan's Under-19 cricketers presented a much sterner challenge to England than the Zimbabweans had in 1997. Their squad included Test batsman Hasan Raza and eight others who had played first-class cricket. Raza, along with Irfan Fazil and Shoaib Malik, had also toured England in 1997 with Pakistan A. England, winners of the Under-19 World Cup in South Africa in February, were also able to call upon several players with first-class experience and, although they had the edge, the six encounters were well balanced. England won the unofficial Tests 2-1, and the one-day series finished 1-1.

Pakistan's natural strokeplayers adapted to the slow wickets and made some formidable scores as the tour progressed. But Abdul Raqeeb, the manager, and coach Azhar Khan agreed their batsmen often lacked patience, and got themselves out to careless shots as a result. The bowling relied heavily on the seamers, though some of the England batsmen thought it compared well with many county attacks. Shoaib Malik was the only effective spinner – and the nearest the Pakistanis had to an all-rounder. As the Third Test showed, however, the lower order could also make runs, and the batsmen were able to fill in with a few overs of spin to give the fast bowlers a rest.

Even if expectations were not quite fulfilled, Azhar said the tour was "a very good platform for mental strength and attitudes". Hasan Raza, injured early on, registered single figures only in his last innings; he scored quickly and usually dominated the attack to make 730 runs at 81.11. Bazid Khan, son of Majid, was a disappointment in the Tests, but he totalled 644 runs overall at 49.53, and his captaincy improved as the tour went on. Shoaib Malik, by contrast, left his best batting for the two Tests in which he played and, helped by not-outs, averaged 53.83; he also took 23 wickets at 24.82. Taufeeq Umar was, according to Raqeeb, the find of the tour. He opened the batting in the last two Tests, ensuring Pakistan's victory in the Third at Chelmsford. Humayun Farhat was an outstanding wicket-keeper and a flamboyant, if inconsistent, batsman. The seam bowlers all found pace and swing. Irfan Fazil took 39 wickets at 19.51, and made good use of the in-swinging yorker, while left-armer Zahid Saeed finished with 23 at 33.21; support came from the tall Kashif Raza.

England Under-19 cricket has enjoyed a much higher profile over the last couple of years, particularly with the rapid promotion of players such as Ben Hollioake and Andrew Flintoff to the full Test team. The Under-19 manager, John Abrahams, stressed the vital role of this level of cricket in the development of "Team England", and gave credit to those counties who had given players first-team experience. Robert Key of Kent averaged 62.83 in the Tests, while the off-spin of Northamptonshire's Graeme Swann earned him 19 wickets, the most by an English bowler in an Under-19 series, at 18.00. Both were selected for the England A tour of Southern Africa. The captain, Owais Shah, earned praise for his imaginative field-settings, especially in the Second Test, and finished his Under-19 career with an average of 58.53.

PAKISTAN UNDER-19 TOURING PARTY

Bazid Khan (Lahore) (*captain*), Hasan Raza (Karachi/Pakistan Customs) (*vice-captain*), Bilal Asad (Islamabad), Faisal Iqbal (Karachi), Hafiz Majid (Gujranwala), Humayun Farhat (Lahore), Imran Nazir (Lahore), Inam-ul-Haq (Gujranwala), Irfan Fazil (Lahore), Kashif Raza (Lahore), Rizwan Ahmed (Hyderabad), Shakeel Nawaz (Rawalpindi), Shoaib Malik (Gujranwala), Taufeeq Umar (Lahore), Zahid Saeed (Gujranwala), Zayyad Qayyum (Lahore).

Manager: Abdul Raqeeb.   *Coach:* Azhar Khan.

PAKISTAN UNDER-19 TOUR RESULTS

Matches – Played 15: Won 8, Lost 3, Drawn 2, No result 2.

Note: Matches in this section were not first-class.

At Wellington College, July 21. Pakistan Under-19 won by seven wickets. Toss: ECB Under-19 A. ECB Under-19 A 189 for six (50 overs) (J. W. Inglis 95); Pakistan Under-19 190 for three (37.3 overs) (Inam-ul-Haq 39, Hasan Raza 81 not out, Bilal Asad 42 not out).

At Wellington College, July 22. Pakistan Under-19 won by six wickets. Toss: Pakistan Under-19. ECB Under-19 A 188 (48.2 overs) (J. W. Inglis 50; Shoaib Malik three for 35, Rizwan Ahmed three for 36); Pakistan Under-19 189 for four (41.4 overs) (Bazid Khan 70, Hasan Raza 67 not out).

At Eton College, July 23. Pakistan Under-19 won by six wickets. Toss: ECB South Under-19. ECB South Under-19 190 for seven (50 overs) (J. B. Hockley 97, M. H. Yardy 37; Shoaib Malik three for 45); Pakistan Under-19 195 for four (46.4 overs) (Taufeeq Umar 43, Faisal Iqbal 56 not out, Bazid Khan 57 not out).

At Eton College, July 25, 26, 27. Pakistan Under-19 won by eight wickets. Toss: ECB South Under-19. ECB South Under-19 185 (A. G. R. Loudon 35, Extras 43; Bilal Asad four for 43) and 122 (P. R. Sawyer 43 retired hurt; Irfan Fazil three for 41); Pakistan Under-19 236 (Inam-ul-Haq 41, Bazid Khan 86; J. P. Tucker seven for 60) and 74 for two (Humayun Farhat 50).

At Stratford-on-Avon, July 28. Pakistan Under-19 won by six wickets. Toss: Warwickshire Second XI. Warwickshire Second XI 192 (49 overs) (A. Singh 46, M. J. Powell 53; Shoaib Malik three for 28, Rizwan Ahmed three for 35); Pakistan Under-19 195 for four (40.4 overs) (Bazid Khan 95, Bilal Asad 55 not out).

At Harrogate, July 30. First unofficial one-day international: No result. Toss: Pakistan Under-19. England Under-19 195 for seven (35 overs) (S. D. Peters 78, P. J. Franks 37, Extras 33; Kashif Raza four for 46); Pakistan Under-19 39 for no wkt (4.2 overs).
   Rain revised Pakistan's target to 220 in 35 overs under the Duckworth/Lewis method, but then washed out their innings.

At Chester-le-Street, August 1. Second unofficial one-day international: Pakistan Under-19 won by 106 runs. Toss: England Under-19. Pakistan Under-19 245 for six (50 overs) (Humayun Farhat 46, Bilal Asad 47, Imran Nazir 36 not out, Extras 33); England Under-19 139 (30.4 overs) (P. J. Franks 32, Extras 46; Zahid Saeed three for 41, Irfan Fazil four for 26, Bilal Asad three for 30).

At Chester-le-Street, August 3. Third unofficial one-day international: England Under-19 won by four wickets. Toss: England Under-19. Pakistan Under-19 204 for eight (28 overs) (Humayun Farhat 47, Bilal Asad 35; Z. C. Morris four for 40); England Under-19 208 for six (27.5 overs) (O. A. Shah 62 not out).

At Chester-le-Street, August 5, 6, 7. Drawn. Toss: ECB North Under-19. ECB North Under-19 290 for five dec. (J. W. Inglis 73, R. K. L. Dawson 108 not out, M. J. Symington 48, Extras 37) and 136 for seven (R. K. L. Dawson 63; Bazid Khan four for 35); Pakistan Under-19 363 for eight dec. (Hafiz Majid 44, Bazid Khan 83, Hasan Raza 58, Faisal Iqbal 73, Extras 45; M. J. Symington three for 63).

At Kimbolton, August 9, 10, 11. Pakistan Under-19 won by an innings and 46 runs. Toss: ECB Midlands Under-19. ECB Midlands Under-19 141 (J. Troughton 58; Irfan Fazil six for 25) and 254 (J. Adams 106, J. Troughton 31, W. I. Jefferson 46; Irfan Fazil four for 34, Hasan Raza four for 32); Pakistan Under-19 441 for eight dec. (Zayyad Qayyum 78, Inam-ul-Haq 58, Shoaib Malik 40, Bazid Khan 37, Hasan Raza 113 not out, Bilal Asad 30).

ENGLAND UNDER-19 v PAKISTAN UNDER-19

First Unofficial Test

At Worcester, August 14, 15, 16, 17. England Under-19 won by 38 runs. Toss: Pakistan Under-19.

Twenty-five balls were enough for England to take the two wickets they needed on the final morning, which began with Pakistan 55 runs short of victory. After conceding a first-innings deficit of 71, England owed their success to Swann, who took nine for 109 in the match. Shah dominated the opening day, hitting 16 fours and a six in his 96. But when he was out with the score on 200, his colleagues succumbed to the pace and in-swinging yorkers of Irfan Fazil. Pakistan's middle order, led by Hasan Raza, then helped their side into the lead. When England batted again, they were just 88 in front with five wickets down before Peters, who made 72 despite suffering from flu, rescued them. Chasing 199, Pakistan progressed well until Swann took full advantage of some variable bounce. He dismissed five batsmen on the third evening – including three in his last six overs – and another the following morning, to finish with six for 46. Pakistan conceded 93 extras, including 48 in no-balls, ten more than England's margin of victory.

Close of play: First day, Pakistan Under-19 5-0 (Bilal Asad 1*, Inam-ul-Haq 2*); Second day, England Under-19 58-2 (R. W. T. Key 21*, O. A. Shah 16*); Third day, Pakistan Under-19 144-8 (Zahid Saeed 1*).

England Under-19

I. N. Flanagan c Humayun Farhat b Zahid Saeed	2	– c Humayun Farhat b Zahid Saeed .	2
R. W. T. Key c Humayun Farhat b Zahid Saeed	6	– c Bazid Khan b Irfan Fazil	62
M. A. Gough run out	48	– c Humayun Farhat b Zahid Saeed	11
*O. A. Shah c Humayun Farhat b Irfan Fazil	96	– c Kashif Raza b Shoaib Malik	44
S. D. Peters b Inam-ul-Haq b Shoaib Malik	13	– b Irfan Fazil	72
G. P. Swann lbw b Irfan Fazil	0	– c Inam-ul-Haq b Shoaib Malik	0
P. J. Franks c Shoaib Malik b Irfan Fazil	22	– c Humayun Farhat b Zahid Saeed	14
A. W. Laraman b Irfan Fazil	12	– c Humayun Farhat b Kashif Raza	3
C. P. Schofield not out	4	– not out	23
†M. A. Wallace b Irfan Fazil	0	– lbw b Zahid Saeed	2
J. O. Grove lbw b Irfan Fazil	0	– b Zahid Saeed	0
B 11, l-b 16, n-b 30	57	B 10, l-b 7, w 1, n-b 18 .	36

1/11 2/18 3/169 4/200 5/202   260   1/4 2/30 3/121 4/146 5/159   269
6/208 7/243 8/260 9/260   6/194 7/230 8/235 9/269

Bowling: *First Innings*—Irfan Fazil 16.4–6–54–6; Zahid Saeed 13–2–54–2; Kashif Raza 12–3–28–0; Bazid Khan 5–2–17–0; Shoaib Malik 18–4–59–1; Bilal Asad 9–1–21–0. *Second Innings*—Zahid Saeed 17.5–4–75–5; Irfan Fazil 25–1–83–2; Shoaib Malik 14–3–52–2; Kashif Raza 14–8–31–1; Bilal Asad 2–0–11–0.

Pakistan Under-19

Bilal Asad c Wallace b Franks	1	– (6) c and b Swann	1
Inam-ul-Haq c Grove b Franks	52	– (1) c Shah b Franks	10
Hafiz Majid b Key b Grove	12	– (2) c Key b Laraman	16
*Bazid Khan b Swann	9	– (3) b Laraman	31
Hasan Raza lbw b Franks	70	– (4) c Flanagan b Swann	41
Faisal Iqbal c Shah b Franks	50	– (5) lbw b Swann	0
†Humayun Farhat c sub b Grove	39	– c Grove b Swann	28
Shoaib Malik c Peters b Swann	33	– c Shah b Swann	1
Irfan Fazil c and b Swann	4	– (10) c Peters b Swann	12
Zahid Saeed not out	22	– (9) c Wallace b Franks	2
Kashif Raza c Shah b Grove	8	– not out	0
B 12, l-b 5, n-b 14	31	B 1, l-b 17	18

1/7 2/32 3/43 4/96 5/206   331   1/15 2/58 3/61 4/66 5/68   160
6/221 7/260 8/265 9/300   6/124 7/129 8/144 9/152

Bowling: *First Innings*—Grove 23.3–4–72–3; Franks 20–5–70–4; Swann 17–4–63–3; Laraman 15–2–55–0; Schofield 10–1–54–0. *Second Innings*—Grove 9–0–40–0; Franks 14–2–45–2; Laraman 8–3–11–2; Swann 17.4–5–46–6.

Umpires: D. J. Constant and R. Palmer.

At Abergavenny, August 19, 20, 21. Drawn. Toss: ECB Under-18. ECB Under-18 306 (M. A. Carberry 40, G. R. Haywood 66, G. R. Napier 41, A. S. Wright 45, Extras 30; Kashif Raza four for 47, Shakeel Nawaz four for 71) and 275 for four (M. A. Carberry 126 not out, A. S. Wright 30, G. R. Napier 44, J. T. Phillips 43); Pakistan Under-19 479 for six dec. (Taufeeq Umar 38, Bazid Khan 136, Hasan Raza 118, Faisal Iqbal 33, Shoaib Malik 56 not out; R. J. Logan four for 71).

At Taunton, August 23. No result. Toss: Pakistan Under-19. ECB XI 132 for two (22.3 overs) (R. Williams 40 not out) v Pakistan Under-19.

ENGLAND UNDER-19 v PAKISTAN UNDER-19

Second Unofficial Test

At Taunton, August 25, 26, 27, 28. England Under-19 won by seven wickets. Toss: Pakistan Under-19.

England gained an unassailable lead in the series thanks to more magnificent bowling from Swann. On the final morning, he took Pakistan's last six wickets to finish with eight for 118 – the best by an England bowler at this level, surpassing Ryan Sidebottom's seven for 30 against Zimbabwe at Edgbaston in 1997 – and ten for 183 in the match. Even though he would not add to it in the last game, his tally of 19 wickets in the series was another Under-19 record, beating Sidebottom's 16. Pakistan had slumped to 89 for six on the opening morning, victims of their tendency to play across the line and into the hands of Shah's carefully placed leg-side fields. But Imran Nazir and Shoaib Malik then punished some loose bowling to put on 167 for the seventh wicket, the highest partnership of the series. They were helped too by the absence of Bulbeck; a back injury meant he could take little part in his debut, on his home ground. Key replied with a century, and received good support from Peters. Then Gough, batting down the order because of a stiff back, helped England to 430. At 157 for two, Pakistan were still in the game, but Swann secured the crucial wicket of Hasan Raza on the third evening, and mopped up the next day.

Close of play: First day, England Under-19 38-0 (I. N. Flanagan 10*, R. W. T. Key 26*); Second day, England Under-19 332-8 (M. A. Gough 25*, M. A. Wallace 4*); Third day, Pakistan Under-19 178-4 (Faisal Iqbal 16*, Zahid Saeed 0*).

Pakistan Under-19

Inam-ul-Haq b Grove	23	– lbw b Swann	27
Taufeeq Umar c Flanagan b Grove	10	– c Wallace b Franks	59
*Bazid Khan b Franks	2	– c Key b Gough	11
Hasan Raza c Gough b Bulbeck	25	– lbw b Swann	43
Faisal Iqbal c Gough b Bulbeck	8	– c Flanagan b Swann	34
Imran Nazir c Flanagan b Swann	90	– (7) c Flanagan b Swann	0
†Humayun Farhat lbw b Bulbeck	1	– (8) b Swann	46
Shoaib Malik c Wallace b Franks	66	– (9) not out	34
Zahid Saeed not out	6	– (6) b Swann	0
Irfan Fazil lbw b Swann	2	– st Wallace b Swann	4
Kashif Raza c Wallace b Franks	8	– c Flanagan b Swann	0
B 4, l-b 4, n-b 27	35	B 9, l-b 12, w 1, n-b 2	24

1/23 2/44 3/44 4/69 5/88   276   1/65 2/84 3/157 4/173 5/182   282
6/89 7/256 8/260 9/263   6/182 7/217 8/260 9/264

Bowling: *First Innings*—Grove 13–2–48–2; Bulbeck 15–2–72–3; Franks 17.3–4–51–3; Swann 18–3–65–2; Haywood 3–0–24–0; Shah 1–0–8–0. *Second Innings*—Grove 8–2–27–0; Franks 17–4–42–1; Haywood 8–5–6–0; Swann 41.3–13–118–8; Gough 24–7–68–1.

England Under-19

I. N. Flanagan lbw b Zahid Saeed	10	– (2) c sub b Shoaib Malik	25
R. W. T. Key c Hasan Raza b Shoaib Malik	131	– (1) b Hasan Raza	62
G. R. Haywood lbw b Zahid Saeed	0		
*O. A. Shah c Humayun Farhat b Kashif Raza	10	– not out	25
S. D. Peters c Faisal Iqbal b Kashif Raza	64	– not out	10
G. P. Swann lbw b Hasan Raza	18		
P. J. Franks c Bazid Khan b Shoaib Malik	15		
M. A. Gough not out	59	– (3) c sub b Shoaib Malik	0
M. P. L. Bulbeck c Humayun Farhat b Shoaib Malik	2		
†M. A. Wallace lbw b Irfan Fazil	25		
J. O. Grove c Taufeeq Umar b Irfan Fazil	23		
B 22, l-b 7, w 2, n-b 42	73	B 4, l-b 2, n-b 2	8

1/40 2/40 3/95 4/207 5/264   430   1/84 2/84 3/106   (3 wkts) 130
6/280 7/297 8/301 9/382

Bowling: *First Innings*—Irfan Fazil 27.4–5–116–2; Zahid Saeed 29–11–92–2; Kashif Raza 26–4–75–2; Shoaib Malik 43–13–84–3; Hasan Raza 19–7–34–1. *Second Innings*—Zahid Saeed 8–2–18–0; Shoaib Malik 17–5–62–2; Irfan Fazil 4–2–11–0; Inam-ul-Haq 8–0–28–0; Hasan Raza 5.5–4–5–1.

Umpires: J. C. Balderstone and T. E. Jesty.

ENGLAND UNDER-19 v PAKISTAN UNDER-19

Third Unofficial Test

At Chelmsford, August 31, September 1, 2, 3. Pakistan Under-19 won by five wickets. Toss: Pakistan Under-19.

Taufeeq Umar steered Pakistan to a consolation victory with an unbeaten 98, helping his side avoid a whitewash in the three-match series. It was a match with two century last-wicket stands. England had been put into bat and began strongly. But the Pakistani seamers returned to bowl with pace and control, before Logan and Grove added 107 for the last wicket. The 274 needed to prevent the follow-on looked a distant prospect as Pakistan slumped to 30 for three. Hasan Raza returned from injury and played beautifully but, with nine wickets down, they were still 22 short. Irfan Fazil then joined Kashif Raza to put on 107 for the tenth wicket – exactly the same as England's last pair had scored – and reduce the first-innings deficit to 64. In England's second innings, Zahid Saeed took three in seven balls to restrict them to 162. Pakistan, 31 without loss overnight as they chased 227, were initially thwarted by rain on the final day, but scored at six an over until Swann pegged back the run-rate. At 167 for five, they were briefly threatened, but Umar held firm, and only undue caution at the end denied him a century.

Close of play: First day, England Under-19 368-9 (R. J. Logan 53*, J. O. Grove 26*); Second day, Pakistan Under-19 359; Third day, Pakistan Under-19 31-0 (Humayun Farhat 16*, Taufeeq Umar 13*).

England Under-19

I. N. Flanagan lbw b Zahid Saeed	6	– c Imran Nazir b Kashif Raza	4
R. W. T. Key c Inam-ul-Haq b Irfan Fazil	88	– b Irfan Fazil	28
M. A. Gough c Humayun Farhat b Hasan Raza	67	– c Humayun Farhat b Zahid Saeed	13
*O. A. Shah c Humayun Farhat b Zahid Saeed	2	– c Humayun Farhat b Zahid Saeed	29
S. D. Peters c Hasan Raza b Zahid Saeed	10	– c Taufeeq Umar b Zahid Saeed	19
G. P. Swann c Taufeeq Umar b Irfan Fazil	36	– c Bazid Khan b Kashif Raza	1
G. R. Haywood c Humayun Farhat b Irfan Fazil	8	– c Hasan Raza b Kashif Raza	27
P. J. Franks c Imran Nazir b Irfan Fazil	7	– c Humayun Farhat b Zahid Saeed	0
R. J. Logan not out	71	– c and b Hasan Raza	30
†M. A. Wallace c Humayun Farhat b Kashif Raza	0	– not out	7
J. O. Grove c Faisal Iqbal b Inam-ul-Haq	61	– b Kashif Raza	0
B 4, l-b 14, w 1, n-b 48	67	B 1, l-b 1, n-b 2	4

1/25 2/165 3/174 4/183 5/226   423   1/27 2/37 3/52 4/90 5/92   162
6/233 7/256 8/287 9/316   6/96 7/96 8/145 9/159

Bowling: First Innings—Irfan Fazil 27–1–141–4; Zahid Saeed 25–3–105–3; Kashif Raza 19–2–70–1; Bazid Khan 3–0–20–0; Hasan Raza 15–4–50–1; Inam-ul-Haq 4–0–19–1. *Second Innings*—Irfan Fazil 17–2–36–1; Zahid Saeed 18–1–73–4; Kashif Raza 14.4–4–26–4; Hasan Raza 15–6–25–1.

Pakistan Under-19

Inam-ul-Haq c Wallace b Franks	2	– (3) b Haywood	22
Taufeeq Umar run out	38	– not out	98
*Bazid Khan b Grove	8	– (5) c Flanagan b Shah	24
Hasan Raza c Wallace b Haywood	60	– c Wallace b Logan	7
Faisal Iqbal c Shah b Franks	0	– (7) not out	24
Imran Nazir c Shah b Haywood	65	– c Wallace b Shah	1
Zayyad Qayyum lbw b Franks	5		
†Humayun Farhat c Flanagan b Franks	4	– (1) lbw b Franks	30
Zahid Saeed b Shah	33		
Kashif Raza c and b Logan	49		
Irfan Fazil not out	62		
B 11, l-b 6, n-b 16	33	B 6, l-b 7, w 2, n-b 8	23

1/8 2/25 3/30 4/87 5/95   359   1/64 2/112 3/123   (5 wkts) 229
6/101 7/160 8/235 9/252   4/164 5/167

In the first innings Hasan Raza, when 1, retired hurt at 30-2 and resumed at 160.

Bowling: First Innings—Franks 20–3–64–4; Grove 20–2–73–1; Haywood 17–2–91–2; Logan 14.5–1–67–1; Swann 14–5–35–0; Shah 3–0–12–1. *Second Innings*—Franks 15–1–55–1; Grove 5–0–36–0; Swann 7–2–15–0; Haywood 12–0–47–1; Logan 6–1–25–1; Shah 12–3–29–2; Key 0.4–0–9–0.

Umpires: J. H. Harris and B. Leadbeater.

SCHOOLS CRICKET IN 1998

The face of schools cricket – and the Under-19 representative game – changed further in 1998. After 14 years, the Schools Festival at Oxford was consigned to memory, to be replaced by matches played the ECB Under-19 banner. The major schools fixture became a one-off game between the northern and southern schools, played at Shenley Park, MCC's out-ground, as a two-day, 12-a-side game.

The aim of the new structure was to reduce the amount of representative cricket played by the best young cricketers, while still allowing them to compete in high-profile matches. All the cricketing bodies who had previously fielded representative sides were invited to nominate players, as were those counties who played Under-19 cricket. Teams based on these sides later played the Combined Services and the Pakistan Under-19 teams. To link the matches into the ECB's "Development of Excellence" programme, all the teams were trained by national coaches Tim Boon and Paul Farbrace.

ECB SCHOOLS NORTH v ECB SCHOOLS SOUTH

At Shenley Park, July 14, 15. ECB Schools North won by 18 runs. Toss: ECB Schools North.

The North scraped home in the first ECB Schools match after two of the South's players retired hurt, and a third was unable to face a ball. The two-day, 12-a-side game adopted a 100-over format to encourage batsmen to build longer innings, and bowlers to attack. The North chose to bat on a pitch of pace and bounce, and made heavy weather of it. Although five batsmen made starts, none could take advantage of the available time. The bowlers were happier: Webb, with real aggression, and Sethi, hitting a steady line, claimed three wickets each as the North were dismissed for 190. But before the close, Willis-Stovold retired injured, and Fearick removed Fray. Next morning, Cherry was struck on the arm and could not bat on. Fearick then took four more wickets and, when their last fit batsman arrived at the crease, the South still needed 52. The Millfield pair of Hellings and Webb played sensibly, but were 19 short when Webb was bowled.

ECB Schools North

W. I. Jefferson (*Oundle*) c Willis-Stovold b Jordison .	30	†J. G. Foster (*Forest*) c Hellings b Webb	6
V. Craven (*Harrogate GS*) c Jordison b Bressington .	5	D. de Prez (*Bridgewater HS*) b Webb . .	0
J. M. Cornford (*ReaseHeath C.*) c Willis-Stovold b Jordison .	28	J. R. J. Fearick (*St Mary's RC HS, Bolton*) b Sethi	6
C. J. Hewison (*Whickham SFC*) b Sethi .	24	I. D. Hunter (*Durham SFC*) c Cherry b Sethi .	4
*R. K. L. Dawson (*Batley GS*) c Hellings b Webb .	11	G. R. Saxton (*Bradford GS*) not out . . .	0
M. Brown (*Queen Elizabeth GS, Blackburn*) lbw b Sears .	32	L-b 3, w 2, n-b 4	9
M. J. Symington (*Stockton SFC*) c and b Sears .	35		190

1/10 2/57 3/74 4/97
5/117 6/146 7/154
8/154 9/161 10/188

Bowling: Webb 21–4–56–3; Bressington 9–2–25–1; Selwood 5–0–27–0; Jordison 17–8–17–2; Sethi 25–7–40–3; Sears 13.3–2–22–2.

ECB Schools South

N. C. Willis-Stovold (*Clifton C.*) retired hurt	0
L. A. Cooper (*Taunton*) c de Prez b Fearick	9
T. D. Fray (*East Berkshire C.*) b Fearick	1
D. D. Cherry (*Tonbridge*) retired hurt	11
A. N. Bressington (*Marling*) c Saxton b Hunter	20
*L. Sears (*St John's, Southsea*) c Craven b Fearick	39
S. A. Selwood (*Albany C.*) c Dawson b Fearick	18
V. Sethi (*Latymer Upper*) b Saxton	12
†C. J. Hellings (*Millfield*) not out	17
J. R. Jordison (*Trent C.*) lbw b Fearick	3
M. J. Webb (*Millfield*) b Dawson	19
M. S. Ali (*Chigwell*) absent hurt	
B 5, l-b 10, n-b 8	23
	—
1/1 2/14 3/56 4/87 5/114	172
6/135 7/139 8/172	

Bowling: Hunter 23–5–44–1; Fearick 19–6–35–5; de Prez 13–5–19–0; Saxton 12–3–17–1; Symington 11–3–23–0; Jefferson 7–5–4–0; Dawson 7–1–15–1.

Umpires: T. Duckett and B. Knight.

ETON v HARROW

At Lord's, June 26. Drawn. Toss: Eton.

Returning to Lord's after the 1997 washout, the schools agreed that the match should consist of 115 overs, with no more than 65 allowed to the team batting first. This was to avoid the tendency to delay declaring until the second side had no chance of winning. But rain, which arrived in the sixth over and wiped out nearly two hours, reduced the match to 87 overs. When play resumed, it was dominated by Bruce, who took six of the seven Harrow wickets; the other was run out. Figures of six for 40 were the best by an Etonian in this fixture for 13 years. But Harrow were held together by de Rougemont, who hit two sixes and eight fours before Bruce dismissed him for 68 from 77 balls. Eton were finally set 196 in 39 overs. They started slowly and were only 50 at the halfway mark. Then Loudon and Maan added 115 in 20 overs of fading light before running out of time.

Harrow

A. M. A. Andjel c Maan b Bruce	14
A. T. R. Titchener-Barrett c Ross b Bruce	14
†L. F. de Rougemont c Ross b Bruce	68
S. H. Stevens b Bruce	26
W. J. L. Matthews run out	31
*D. R. Hepher c Ross b Bruce	2
J. A. S. Dixon c Bond b Bruce	8
J. S. Weston-Simons not out	8
J. R. F. Cooke-Hurle not out	6
L-b 6, w 6, n-b 6	18
	—
1/30 2/42 3/102 (7 wkts dec.)	195
4/158 5/168	
6/181 7/186	

L. C. L. FitzWilliams and J. M. G. S. Warman did not bat.

Bowling: Bruce 16–2–40–6; Patrick 5–0–26–0; Matheson 6–0–20–0; Maan 8–2–36–0; Bond 3–1–14–0; Loudon 2–0–14–0; Broome 8–1–39–0.

Eton

S. L. J. McL. Hawk b Cooke-Hurle	13
S. E. S. FitzGerald st de Rougemont b Stevens	19
A. F. S. Leslie c Hepher b FitzWilliams	14
*A. G. R. Loudon not out	64
G. G. Maan not out	47
B 2, l-b 4, n-b 2	8
	—
1/28 2/36 3/50 (3 wkts)	165

O. G. C. Broome, C. I. C. Bond, J. T. A. Bruce, †S. J. R. Ross, W. S. L. Patrick and C. M. Matheson did not bat.

Bowling: Warman 10–1–32–0; Weston-Simons 4–1–25–0; Cooke-Hurle 12–2–50–1; Stevens 5–3–8–1; FitzWilliams 8–0–44–1.

Umpires: D. O. Oslear and J. M. Tythcott.

Of the 162 matches played between the two schools since 1805, Eton have won 52, Harrow 44 and 66 have been drawn. Matches during the two world wars are excluded from the reckoning.

The fixture was reduced from a two-day, two-innings-a-side match to one day in 1982. Forty-nine centuries have been scored, the highest being 183 by D. C. Boles of Eton in 1904; M. C. Bird of Harrow is the only batsman to have made two hundreds in a match, in 1907. The highest score since the First World War is 161 not out by M. K. Fosh of Harrow in 1975, Harrow's last victory. Since then Eton have won in 1977, 1985, 1990 and 1991; the 1997 match was abandoned and all other games have been drawn. A full list of centuries since 1918 and results from 1950 can be found in Wisdens prior to 1994.

HIGHLIGHTS FROM THE SCHOOLS

Although the weather was every bit as miserable as the previous year, batsmen coped better with the soggy conditions of the 1998 season; four players passed 1,000 runs, compared with two in 1997. The most prolific were D. B. Wilson of Haberdashers' Aske's, who scored 1,169 runs at 77.93 in 21 innings, and D. A. Cullen of King's, Worcester, who made 1,165 at 72.81 from 22. Close behind were N. J. C. Kay of St Peter's, York, with 1,076 at 59.77, and B. J. Thompson of Magdalen College School, Oxford, whose 1,014 came from 18 innings, at 67.60.

Among those who passed 500 runs, four recorded three-figure averages. For the second year running, R. Clinton of Colfe's led the way with 141.75; D. Jackson of Downside averaged 130.60, while P. J. Furniss of Ellesmere College was fractionally behind with 130.00. T. J. Alldis of West Buckland scored at 122.50. There was only one double-hundred, an undefeated 200 from Kay. The next two highest innings came from Clinton who hit 169 not out and N. R. Boulton of King's College, Taunton, with an unbeaten 166. Four players scored four hundreds: M. J. Banes of Tonbridge, A. R. Duncan of St Paul's, I. S. Pay of King's CS, Wimbledon, and Furniss, who played just ten innings. Dodging the rain better than most, I. Brunnschweiler of King Edward VI, Southampton, recorded 26 innings and 633 runs.

The bowlers acquitted themselves slightly better than last year, with two collecting 60 wickets or more. Brighton College's P. J. S. Spencer took most, with 77 at 8.92 from 300.5 overs – the

Patrick Spencer of Brighton College took 77 wickets, more than any other bowler, and hit 602 runs.

Two leading batsmen: Nick Kay of St Peter's School, York, (left) hit an undefeated double-century, and Daniel Cullen of King's School, Worcester, scored 1,165 runs at 72.81.

greatest number bowled by any player; J. Amin of Haberdashers' Aske's delivered 292.3 overs to dismiss 60 at 9.61. Four others passed 45: G. D. Hicks of Lord Wandsworth College (54 at 10.09), A. A. Hirtenstein of Magdalen College School (52 at 12.38), N. J. K. Creed of Hurstpierpoint (48 at 14.75) and A. T. C. Phillips of King's, Worcester (48 at 17.22).

T. E. Mitzman of King's, Ely, with 42 wickets at 9.73, joined Spencer and Amin as the only bowlers to take 30 wickets with a single-figure average. The outstanding analysis came from H. Smuts-Muller of Glenalmond, who took ten for 37 against Sedbergh; he was the only bowler to take all ten. J. Knox of St George's College, Weybridge, with nine for 19, and G. R. Boyce of Brentwood, with nine for 67, both came close. P. Adshead of St Edmund's, Ware, took seven for six. Of the eight reported hat-tricks, the most remarkable was by R. Johnstone of Christ's College, Finchley, who bowled just once in a season otherwise dedicated to wicket-keeping. Going one better, A. Kelly of Queen Elizabeth GS, Wakefield, grabbed four in four balls against Leeds GS.

In terms of quantity, the leading all-rounders were Spencer, with 602 runs at 37.62 to complement his 77 wickets, B. W. Craft of King Edward VI School, Southampton, with 902 runs at 47.47 and 36 wickets at 14.44, T. J. Phillips of Felsted, with 676 runs at 42.25 and 38 wickets at 16.71, and C. J. Ellerbeck, of St Peter's, York, with 445 runs and 30 wickets. In terms of averages, the best among those with 500 runs and 30 wickets was Spencer.

Of the seven schools that remained unbeaten, Christ's College, Finchley, had the best record, winning 15 of their 18 games. Bromsgrove, Forest, King's College, Taunton, Radley and Woodhouse Grove all won at least half their matches, but St Edward's, Oxford, achieved just one victory to set against nine draws. Bablake put together a most impressive series of results, successful in 12 of their 13 games.

From all regions, schools reported massive interference from the weather, with the West Country worst hit. Truro lost 11 of their 19 fixtures to rain while Kelly College, Kingswood and Plymouth College abandoned half or more of their scheduled games. Elsewhere, however, others were more fortunate; Bancroft's played all but four of their 28 intended matches.

The seven British schools who took part in the 12th Sir Garfield Sobers Schools Cricket Festival, held in Barbados in July, were Aldenham, Bedford, Belfast Academy, Bryanston, Canford, Claysmore and Wilson's. Bedford reached the semi-finals, where they lost to the eventual champions, Dominica Schools.

Details of records broken, other outstanding performances and interesting features of the season may be found in the returns from the schools which follow.

THE SCHOOLS

(Qualification: Batting 150 runs; Bowling 15 wickets)

* On name indicates captain.   * On figures indicates not out.

Note: The line for batting reads Innings–Not Outs–Runs–Highest Score–100s–Average; that for bowling reads Overs–Maidens–Runs–Wickets–Best Bowling–Average.

ABINGDON SCHOOL   *Played 11: W 6, L 3, D 2. A 5*

Master i/c: A. M. Broadbent

Batting—P. J. Edwards 9–4–285–72–0–57.00; T. J. Evans 9–0–219–58–0–24.33; S. C. T. Dexter 10–2–189–66*–0–23.62; P. C. T. Makings 10–0–177–63–0–17.70.

Bowling—R. A. Pike 138–40–361–32–6/23–11.28; *T. W. W. Jones 100–16–284–17–4/34–16.70.

ALDENHAM SCHOOL   *Played 19: W 3, L 12, D 4*

Master i/c: S. D. Thomas

Batting—*A. P. Meara 19–4–634–82*–0–42.26; S. A. Bloom 19–4–260–51*–0–17.33; N. A. M. Densley 17–3–191–35–0–13.64.

Bowling—M. D. S. Calder 92.1–14–287–16–5/29–17.93; J. Rose 77–12–272–15–3/21–18.13; N. A. M. Densley 93–9–344–17–3/19–20.23; M. A. Tennant 186–33–474–15–3/39–31.60.

ALLEYN'S SCHOOL   *Played 15: W 4, L 9, D 2. A 3*

Master i/c: D. J. Tickner   Professional: P. H. Edwards

Batting—D. C. Ellis 10–4–205–57–0–34.16; T. Arul-Pragasam 15–2–292–59*–0–22.46; T. Dasandi 9–0–197–67–0–21.88; S. McGill 14–0–272–41–0–19.42; W. A. C. Bevan 12–0–161–45–0–13.41; B. J. Roberts 14–0–172–40–0–12.28.

Bowling—W. A. C. Bevan 107–15–356–20–3/5–17.80; S. McGill 132.4–21–451–25–4/30–18.04.

AMPLEFORTH COLLEGE   *Played 14: W 3, L 4, D 7*

Master i/c: G. D. Thurman   Professional: D. Wilson

Batting—D. Ansell 13–3–276–61–0–27.60; M. Wilkie 14–1–352–66*–0–27.07; *S. R. Harle 14–0–330–84–0–23.57; J. Melling 12–4–188–41*–0–23.50; S. Phillips 13–2–240–56–0–21.81.

Bowling—M. Wilkie 103–25–346–21–6/26–16.47; H. Murphy 175–34–524–28–5/15–18.71.

ARDINGLY COLLEGE   *Played 13: W 7, L 6, D 0. A 2*

Master i/c: G. Hart   Professional: M. Paterson

Batting—J. Chadburn 12–1–527–95–0–47.90; D. Menzies 9–2–197–58–0–28.14; M. Dewar 11–1–266–51–0–26.60; *N. Strugnell 12–2–198–39–0–19.80.

Bowling—A. Armitage 102–17–327–23–4/56–14.21; D. Macaulay 119–22–376–20–5/16–18.80.

ARNOLD SCHOOL   *Played 9: W 1, L 5, D 3. A 5*

Master i/c: A. Crowther   Professional: I. Wrigglesworth

Batting—*A. E. R. Rawlinson 6–1–199–101*–1–39.80; P. A. R. Willis 8–1–241–61–0–34.42.

Bowling—C. J. P. Moore 116.5–18–418–19–4/34–22.00.

ASHVILLE COLLEGE   *Played 14: W 1, L 1, D 12. A 4*

Master i/c: J. S. Herrington

An undefeated 152 by Matthew Cousen against Bury GS was the highlight of an otherwise undistinguished season. He struck nine sixes and 14 fours in what is believed to be the highest-ever score for the college.

Batting—M. Cousen 12–2–512–152*–2–51.20; P. Crosby 8–4–175–70–0–43.75; A. Boyle 13–2–300–59*–0–27.27.

Bowling—N. Butterfield 121–37–231–17–5/27–13.58; A. Boyle 124–25–378–21–4/15–18.00; J. Oxley 116–22–345–16–5/13–21.56.

BABLAKE SCHOOL   *Played 13: W 12, L 1, D 0. A 3*

Master i/c: B. J. Sutton   Professional: I. Stokes

A successful season included a record number of victories and the retention of the Warwickshire Cup. The only defeat was at the hands of King Edward's, Birmingham. S. P. Byng and A. C. Smyth both turned out for Warwickshire Second Eleven as well as the county Under-17 side, where they played alongside G. R. Drury.

Batting—G. R. Drury 10–3–290–74–0–41.42; *S. P. Byng 10–1–330–86–0–36.66; A. C. Smyth 10–1–306–80–0–34.00; N. Stevens 11–4–155–42*–0–22.14; I. L. Cure 11–2–198–49–0–22.00.

Bowling—A. C. Smyth 61–20–92–15–3/7–6.13; D. M. J. Poole 45.2–5–159–18–5/18–8.83; S. P. Byng 68.3–13–166–17–6/32–9.76; P. R. Jones 89–18–208–19–3/15–10.94.

BANCROFT'S SCHOOL   *Played 24: W 6, L 11, D 7. A 4*

Master i/c: J. K. Lever

A young squad gained valuable experience on a tough winter tour to South Africa, but the season's dreary weather stifled potential, and results were disappointing. The captain, J. R. Davey, led the batting and enjoyed support from the openers R. Gevertz and B. B. Cooper. An array of fast-medium bowlers performed effectively, but the lack of a spinner held the team back.

Batting—*J. R. Davey 24–3–612–110–1–29.14; M. A. Cole 9–1–229–63*–0–28.62; R. Gevertz 19–1–417–70–0–23.16; B. B. Cooper 22–1–360–89–0–17.14; R. G. Ingham 14–2–192–26*–0–16.00; S. Gevertz 15–3–190–40–0–15.83; J. Levis 19–2–265–37–0–15.58; A. E. H. Clark 23–2–293–55–0–13.95.

Bowling—A. E. H. Clark 175–37–604–27–4/6–22.37; A. K. Aggarwal 204.5–40–753–30–4/49–25.10; J. R. Davey 145.4–25–573–15–4/36–38.20.

BANGOR GRAMMAR SCHOOL   *Played 15: W 5, L 7, D 3*

Masters i/c: C. C. J. Harte and D. J. Napier

The captain, Michael Harte, added selection for Ulster Schools to his international Under-18 hockey caps.

Batting—*M. C. W. Harte 14–2–350–98–0–29.16; R. M. Bell 12–2–197–40–0–19.70; S. J. Costley 15–2–231–48–0–17.76.

Bowling—J. A. Robinson 64–13–167–16–4/6–10.43; N. E. R. Boyd 103–22–266–24–4/24–11.08; P. D. McDonald 93.3–23–256–21–5/37–12.19; R. M. Bell 88.5–13–298–16–3/9–18.62.

BARNARD CASTLE SCHOOL *Played 12: W 1, L 6, D 5*

Master i/c: C. P. Johnson

Batting—*S. C. Davies 14–1–442–111–2–34.00; P. E. Clarke 13–1–319–48–0–26.58; G. P. Wilks 13–1–253–51*–0–21.08; A. J. Timmiss 13–0–250–49–0–19.23.

Bowling—G. P. Wilks 161.1–28–498–20–5/48–24.90.

BEDFORD MODERN SCHOOL *Played 18: W 13, L 2, D 3. A 3*

Master i/c: N. Chinneck

The side achieved a school record of 13 wins. Kelvin Locke, who returns in 1999, played for Buckinghamshire in the Minor Counties Championship.

Batting—K. J. Locke 15–5–674–93–0–67.40; M. S. R. Coles 14–4–440–84–0–44.00; *O. J. Clayson 19–4–623–73*–0–41.53; J. R. Wade 19–4–564–95–0–37.60; J. N. Yelland 15–2–428–80–0–32.92; K. Patel 17–4–350–74*–0–26.92.

Bowling—K. Patel 87–10–283–15–3/18–18.86; O. J. Clayson 178–28–633–33–6/85–19.18; N. D. Parsooth 126–27–387–20–5/33–19.35; M. S. R. Coles 135–30–423–21–4/13–20.14; W. J. Liptrot 115–12–428–18–4/74–23.77.

BEDFORD SCHOOL *Played 15: W 6, L 1, D 8. A 2*

Master i/c: J. J. Farrell Professional: R. A. Pick

A successful season was ideal preparation for the Sir Garfield Sobers Schools Cricket Festival, held in Barbados in July. Seven out of eight zonal games were won, but the semi-final brought defeat by eventual winners Dominica Schools.

Batting—E. O'Callaghan 8–3–248–75*–0–49.60; C. Stearn 17–4–565–96*–0–43.46; A. Shankar 15–2–550–112–2–42.30; W. Smith 15–0–483–106–1–32.20; *G. Graham 15–2–417–107*–1–32.07; J. Shaw 9–2–186–63*–0–26.57; A. Dalgleish 13–3–177–32–0–17.70.

Bowling—J. Shaw 237–60–687–33–7/59–20.81; G. Graham 134–33–359–15–4/51–23.93; J. Elphick 144–25–535–16–3/44–33.43.

BEECHEN CLIFF SCHOOL *Played 10: W 2, L 4, D 3, T 1. A 1*

Master i/c: P. J. McKissock

Following encouraging wins against Bristol GS and Queen Elizabeth Hospital, the form of the side became, like the weather, dismal. But Tom Hankins managed to score two hundreds.

Batting—T. Hankins 9–2–459–121*–2–65.57; A. Hulbert 8–0–163–37–0–20.37; R. Wilson 10–0–153–40–0–15.30.

Bowling—No bowler took 15 wickets. The leading bowler was T. Harding 69.4–13–219–12–4/21–18.25.

BERKHAMSTED COLLEGIATE SCHOOL *Played 15: W 8, L 3, D 4. A 2*

Master i/c: J. G. Tolchard Professional: M. R. Herring

Encouraging results were inspired by positive captaincy from Mark Bartholomew, and the all-round contribution from Spencer Fan, who scored three centuries and topped the bowling averages with his leg-spin.

Batting—S. D. Fan 14–2–613–128–3–51.08; *M. A. Bartholomew 13–1–441–89*–0–36.75; C. W. Read 14–1–272–53*–0–20.92; S. N. Mayne 9–0–159–52–0–17.66; A. J. M. McCracken 13–3–157–32–0–15.70.

Bowling—S. D. Fan 118–36–282–22–4/23–12.81; D. A. Horton 96–15–275–16–4/45–17.18; G. H. Wallis 113–28–351–18–4/33–19.50; T. W. Hand 118–22–353–15–4/32–23.53.

BETHANY SCHOOL   *Played 11: W 4, L 4, D 3. A 5*

Master i/c: P. Norgrove   Professional: M. J. McCague

Batting—D. Cheeseman 11–1–393–81*–0–39.30; *T. Golds 11–0–421–105–1–38.27; A. Stevens 11–0–220–44–0–20.00.

Bowling—D. Cheeseman 99–11–373–30–5/18–12.43; A. Stevens 117–26–292–18–4/6–16.22.

BIRKENHEAD SCHOOL   *Played 19: W 11, L 5, D 3. A 2*

Master i/c: G. Prescott

Batting—I. S. Wilson 10–2–383–79–0–47.87; J. J. Pugh 9–3–246–83–0–41.00; A. B. Birley 14–4–314–87–0–31.40; M. J. McGrath 9–0–282–83–0–31.33; G. M. Cashin 19–1–559–74–0–31.05; S. J. Marshall 14–5–232–56*–0–25.77.

Bowling—*S. Cottrell 116.5–36–351–28–4/20–12.53; S. J. Marshall 193–52–538–40–7/36–13.45; G. M. Cashin 166.5–52–431–28–4/7–15.39.

BISHOP'S STORTFORD COLLEGE   *Played 13: W 7, L 5, D 1. A 1*

Master i/c: C. S. Bannister

Batting—*W. A. Defoe 11–0–376–72–0–34.18; S. J. Bunbury 12–1–375–96*–0–34.09; T. S. Bull 12–1–366–81*–0–33.27.

Bowling—G. R. Lindop 167–25–595–27–6/41–22.03; L. A. B. Humphrey 143–20–503–19–4/57–26.47.

BLOXHAM SCHOOL   *Played 9: W 5, L 2, D 2*

Masters i/c: C. N. Boyns and N. C. W. Furley

Batting—C. de Weymarn 9–3–295–114*–1–49.16; A. Deeley 9–1–291–100–1–36.37.

Bowling—C. Stirling 62–16–361–23–7/24–15.69.

BLUNDELL'S SCHOOL   *Played 14: W 4, L 7, D 3*

Master i/c: N. A. Folland

A promising side failed to deliver after the loss of two close matches damaged confidence. However, skipper Mark Vaughan hit an unbeaten century against MCC, and was well supported by Ryan Hopkins in his first year in the team. Tom Wright performed well with bat and ball, taking most wickets for the second season running.

Batting—*G. M. C. Vaughan 12–2–442–102*–2–44.20; R. Hopkins 14–1–468–76–0–36.00; T. A. Wright 13–3–270–72*–0–27.00; P. Arnold 12–2–263–88–0–26.30; B. T. Knott 13–4–229–70–0–25.44; A. I. Chambers 12–0–184–48–0–15.33; J. L. Davies 14–1–185–25*–0–14.23.

Bowling—T. A. Wright 129–26–415–19–4/20–21.84; J. C. R. Day 140.3–24–530–16–4/32–33.12.

BRADFIELD COLLEGE   *Played 14: W 2, L 5, D 7. A 2*

Master i/c: C. C. Ellison   Professional: J. F. Harvey

The highlight of an unremarkable summer was the advance made by several second-year students, notably Sam Tod, who headed the batting averages.

Batting—A. S. G. Tod 5–0–173–55–0–34.60; *A. J. P. Chubb 15–1–392–65–0–28.00; R. F. Dilkes 14–0–312–97–0–22.28; M. D. Clark 11–2–192–47*–0–21.33; J. M. Broad 15–1–283–63–0–20.21.

Bowling—No bowler took 15 wickets. The leading bowler was S. G. Moore 139.4–22–502–14–3/46–35.85.

BRADFORD GRAMMAR SCHOOL   *Played 18: W 7, L 4, D 7. A 4*

Master i/c: A. G. Smith

Though frustrated by the appalling weather, the team, under the captaincy of Guy Saxton, enjoyed a successful season, including a tour of Northern Ireland. Saxton's 39 wickets gave him a career total of 161, a school record. Two young players had outstanding seasons: Ben Graham scored 527 runs, and left-arm spinner Nick Cockcroft took 40 wickets.

Batting—B. R. Graham 17–3–527–106*–1–37.64; N. Pathmanathan 16–3–456–72–0–35.07; C. H. Harper 14–1–359–100*–1–27.61; M. J. Dillingham 15–5–232–59–0–23.20; *G. R. Saxton 16–0–341–129*–1–21.31; A. R. Bates 14–1–226–51–0–17.38; N. Ilyas 12–0–173–49–0–14.41.

Bowling—R. M. Harland 75.5–25–188–18–5/23–10.44; G. R. Saxton 189.5–77–486–39–6/11–12.46; N. R. Cockcroft 160.2–37–532–40–7/56–13.30; M. P. Donovan 168.1–52–479–19–4/43–25.21.

BRENTWOOD SCHOOL   *Played 14: W 6, L 3, D 5. A 3*

Master i/c: B. R. Hardie

In the match against Old Brentwoods, Gareth Boyce, bowling fast-medium, took nine for 67.

Batting—G. R. Boyce 13–1–387–86–0–32.25; T. Robson 13–3–288–59*–0–28.80; A. P. Stanton 12–0–277–70–0–23.08; P. M. Davis 12–3–207–64–0–23.00; *J. D. T. Watkins 12–0–275–78–0–22.91.

Bowling—D. T. Pearce 74–11–278–15–4/16–18.53; N. R. H. Taylor 115–27–369–18–5/37–20.50; G. R. Boyce 149.4–31–502–22–9/67–22.81.

BRIGHTON COLLEGE   *Played 20: W 14, L 1, D 5. A 2*

Master i/c: J. Spencer   Professional: J. D. Morley

Following a successful and enjoyable winter tour of India, the team had an excellent season, undefeated except for one limited-overs game. In a strong batting line-up, three players topped 600 runs. The bowling was dominated by leg-spinner Patrick Spencer, who set a college record with 77 wickets.

Batting—M. J. Prior 17–4–608–81*–0–46.76; C. D. Hopkinson 17–4–604–142*–1–46.46; P. J. S. Spencer 19–3–602–96–0–37.62; P. Sanklecha 11–4–223–74–0–31.85; *A. J. Nichol 16–1–378–60–0–25.20; J. D. Cornthwaite 14–4–242–51*–0–24.20; N. C. F. Woodbridge 14–3–156–44–0–14.18; B. P. Bidwell 13–1–154–63–0–12.83.

Bowling—P. J. S. Spencer 300.5–67–687–77–8/47–8.92; M. S. Wilson 158.3–31–428–28–4/37–15.28; J. T. Barr 149.2–36–366–18–5/15–20.33; C. D. Hopkinson 123–23–347–15–3/10–23.13.

BRISTOL GRAMMAR SCHOOL   *Played 15: W 9, L 3, D 3. A 4*

Master i/c: B. G. Blyth   Professional: C. Bassano

The captain, Daniel Hayward, topped the bowling averages, while younger brother Duncan headed the batting.

Batting—D. W. Hayward 15–2–651–94–0–50.07; N. W. R. Miller 8–2–294–101*–1–49.00; S. Douglas 8–1–230–78–0–32.85; S. J. Scott 10–2–241–61–0–30.12; A. J. T. Winter 11–3–154–40*–0–19.25.

Bowling—*D. R. Hayward 140.1–24–437–36–6/64–12.13; A. J. Staniforth 107.2–15–371–22–4/9–16.86.

BROMSGROVE SCHOOL   *Played 15: W 10, L 0, D 5. A 0*

Master i/c: P. Mullan   Professional: G. Shephard

Batting—*A. Goode 14–1–744–146–2–57.23; N. Reade 15–4–625–102*–1–56.81; M. Williams 7–4–160–41*–0–53.33; B. Steer 14–0–658–143–1–47.00; B. France 13–4–295–60–0–32.77.

Bowling—E. Jenkins 98–6–287–16–3/44–17.93; A. Goode 181–32–586–31–5/32–18.90; B. France 134–30–438–18–3/38–24.33.

BRYANSTON SCHOOL   *Played 12: W 5, L 6, D 1. A 1*

Master i/c: T. J. Hill

The team was over-dependent on the captain, Sam Denning, who carried the batting and was the leading wicket-taker. Results were disappointing at the Sir Garfield Sobers Schools Cricket Festival in Barbados, where the unavailability of several senior players left the batting fragile.

Batting—*S. J. Denning 12–1–519–113*–1–47.18; S. Brenchley 9–2–194–43*–0–27.71; A. Lys 12–0–205–42–0–17.08.

Bowling—S. J. Denning 87–14–292–17–4/17–17.17.

CAMPBELL COLLEGE   *Played 13: W 8, L 4, D 1. A 1*

Master i/c: B. F. Robinson   Professional: W. Haider

Batting—C. Cramett 13–4–282–81*–0–31.33; C. Fuller 14–2–281–55–0–23.41; A. Heasly 14–2–258–61–0–21.50.

Bowling—R. Heasly 106–15–263–26–5/31–10.11; C. Fuller 80–10–314–18–6/35–17.44.

CANFORD SCHOOL   *Played 20: W 11, L 5, D 4*

Master i/c: A. Copp   Professionals: J. J. E. Hardy and J. Shackleton

A rewarding season concluded with participation in the Sir Garfield Sobers Schools Cricket Festival in Barbados.

Batting—N. Stallard 18–4–569–88*–0–40.64; W. McClaren Clark 18–4–483–96–0–34.50; *P. Young 15–2–231–53–0–17.76; J. Mills 14–2–171–34–0–14.25.

Bowling—T. Hodgson 67–11–150–17–4/21–8.82; W. McClaren Clark 166.5–33–523–36–4/6–14.52; S. Haworth 126.1–18–387–23–2/20–16.82; P. Jones 121–15–449–16–3/23–28.06.

CATERHAM SCHOOL   *Played 14: W 5, L 3, D 6. A 1*

Master i/c: R. I. Smith   Professional: Wasim Raja

Unbeaten in their opening eight fixtures, the side, under the captaincy of Richard Jackson, enjoyed more success than in the previous year. Jackson headed the batting and bowling averages and was selected for Sussex Young Cricketers. James Benning was selected to represent England Under-15.

Batting—*R. Jackson 11–1–571–102*–1–63.44; J. Benning 10–1–388–115*–1–43.11; E. Grant 9–1–323–101*–1–40.37; I. Qureshi 14–0–273–63–0–19.50.

Bowling—R. Jackson 130.3–48–333–24–5/37–13.87; I. Qureshi 172.3–37–510–32–5/69–15.93.

CHARTERHOUSE SCHOOL   *Played 15: W 4, L 4, D 7*

Master i/c: P. J. Deakin   Professional: R. V. Lewis

Batting—T. N. G. Savage 13–2–419–81–0–38.09; M. R. Gillespie 13–2–400–108*–1–36.36; *A. P. Hollingsworth 15–2–442–145–1–34.00; H. Nash 14–1–388–108–1–29.84; T. D. Hamblin 10–1–191–51–0–21.22.

Bowling—R. E. Souter 124–30–365–19–3/26–19.21; M. R. Gillespie 155–43–382–16–3/12–23.87.

CHELTENHAM COLLEGE   *Played 13: W 4, L 1, D 8. A 4*

Master i/c: M. W. Stovold

Professional: M. P. Briers

Batting—R. T. J. Howell 13–0–504–108–1–38.76; T. F. G. Richardson 12–4–267–60*–0–33.37; S. H. Fairbairn 12–3–281–70–0–31.22; *S. T. J. Cowley 13–1–366–95–0–30.50; S. E. H. Moore 9–2–156–37–0–22.28.

Bowling—B. E. Annan 45.3–6–143–15–4/15–9.53; S. J. C. Johnston 125.5–22–379–16–2/15–23.68; J. A. D. Brooker 139–26–435–17–4/49–25.58.

CHIGWELL SCHOOL   *Played 12: W 6, L 3, D 3. A 4*

Master i/c: D. N. Morrison

Professional: F. W. Griffiths

Batting—Z. Sharif 10–3–443–85–0–63.28; *M. S. Ali 7–1–290–114*–1–48.33; A. J. Wood 11–1–325–61–0–32.50; S. Samanta 8–2–179–57*–0–29.83; S. Saleem 12–2–227–53–0–22.70.

Bowling—H. P. Barker 100.5–15–344–22–7/94–15.63; Z. Sharif 139.5–28–420–18–4/67–23.33.

CHRIST COLLEGE, BRECON   *Played 10: W 6, L 2, D 1, T 1. A 8*

Master i/c: C. W. Kleiser

Professional: A. Shaw

After a winter tour, the college decided to follow the Australian model of limited-overs games. Despite atrocious weather, exciting cricket ensued, the highlight being a tie, away to Colston's. Two pairs of brothers played: the Prices, Owen and Rhys, and Chris and James Davenport, who headed the bowling and batting averages respectively. At the MCC match, C. W. Kleiser, retiring after 32 years as cricket master, was given a plaque in recognition of his service.

Batting—J. Davenport 10–5–205–52*–0–41.00; *R. J. W. Fish 10–0–399–106–1–39.90; R. Harrington 10–0–174–40–0–17.40; B. Price 10–0–168–43–0–16.80.

Bowling—C. M. P. Davenport 109.5–26–302–19–5/27–15.89.

CHRIST'S COLLEGE, FINCHLEY   *Played 18: W 15, L 0, D 3. A 4*

Master i/c: S. S. Goldsmith

Despite injuries to several senior players, the side enjoyed its most successful season, winning the Middlesex Under-19 Cup. The strength of the team lay in the variety of its attack; talented spinners Murtazar Bukhari and Ritesh Depala complemented the pace of Chris Williams. Leading run-maker Rufus Johnstone kept wicket in all but one match, setting a record with 24 dismissals. In his only bowl of the season he took a hat-trick.

Batting—*C. R. Depala 13–0–372–97–0–28.61; R. Johnstone 15–1–386–104*–1–27.57; A. Brierley 16–3–340–68*–0–26.15; K. Hussain 16–1–383–61–0–25.53; C. C. Spanos 14–3–280–55–0–25.45.

Bowling—N. Morjaria 48.3–9–122–22–4/5–5.54; C. Williams 54–14–164–21–4/5–7.80; M. Bukhari 50–9–131–15–5/51–8.73; C. R. Depala 96.4–14–288–23–4/24–12.52; R. Depala 90–25–232–17–3/22–13.64.

CHRIST'S HOSPITAL   *Played 16: W 6, L 6, D 4*

Master i/c: H. P. Holdsworth

Professional: L. J. Lenham

Batting—F. M. Thomas 16–0–418–115–1–26.12; *D. F. Morley 15–2–339–76*–0–26.07; J. A. M. Owens 15–4–224–47*–0–20.36; C. G. H. White 14–1–152–30–0–11.69.

Bowling—T. H. Fraser-Gausden 104–20–302–25–6/37–12.08; B. F. Geralds 98.5–17–367–21–5/33–17.47; D. F. Morley 165.5–41–503–28–5/50–17.96.

CLAYESMORE SCHOOL   *Played 22: W 10, L 10, D 2*

Master i/c: D. I. Rimmer

Batting—R. Lack 21–1–635–98–0–31.75; M. Harris 20–2–541–76–0–30.05; T. Deighton 12–1–205–37–0–18.63; K. Barker 16–3–216–51–0–16.61; R. Roe 12–2–152–52*–0–15.20; M. Senior 12–0–174–45–0–14.50; C. Toovey 14–1–159–45–0–12.23.

Bowling—K. Barker 41.2–5–175–19–3/12–9.21; M. Senior 88.2–14–306–20–3/10–15.30; J. Gemmell 91.4–6–393–21–4/28–18.71; R. Lack 125.1–23–440–22–3/14–20.00; M. Harris 116.4–7–507–21–4/43–24.14.

CLIFTON COLLEGE   *Played 15: W 5, L 5, D 5. A 3*

Master i/c: D. C. Henderson   Professional: P. W. Romaines

Batting—J. A. Pearson 10–2–200–39*–0–25.00; J. W. T. Aylwin 13–3–230–52–0–23.00; *E. H. Kenworthy 12–1–247–60*–0–22.45; N. C. Willis-Stovold 14–0–267–67–0–19.07; I. D. Simmonds 15–1–265–38–0–18.92; T. C. M. Harris 15–0–249–43–0–16.60.

Bowling—J. A. Pearson 105–23–294–16–3/31–18.37; H. R. Acreman 96–22–281–15–5/45–18.73; M. P. G. Davies 140–28–442–21–4/41–21.04.

COLFE'S SCHOOL   *Played 18: W 7, L 4, D 7. A 4*

Master i/c: G. S. Clinton

Batting—R. Clinton 9–5–567–169*–2–141.75; T. Allen 14–2–337–88–0–28.08; A. Stone 15–2–363–76*–0–27.92; P. Patel 12–2–246–112*–1–24.60; A. Jasquith 13–2–239–50*–0–21.72.

Bowling—A. Jasquith 243–22–852–36–8/48–23.66; E. Cross 272–28–801–28–4/58–28.60; R. Clinton 140–16–527–18–3/27–29.27; M. Taylor 120–15–472–15–3/58–31.46.

CRANBROOK SCHOOL   *Played 15: W 10, L 3, D 2. A 7*

Master i/c: A. J. Presnell

Paul Wicken completed his career with 57 appearances, a school record.

Batting—J. Agar 10–3–337–88–0–48.14; S. Downe 8–4–164–75*–0–41.00; M. Knight 13–0–487–90–0–37.46; M. Bennett 11–2–241–65*–0–26.77; S. Traill 12–4–213–73*–0–26.62; G. Turner 11–2–187–55–0–20.77.

Bowling—B. Dance 145.5–32–325–22–5/20–14.77; P. Wicken 115–15–330–22–4/41–15.00; H. Wacher 140–33–412–22–5/18–18.72.

CRANLEIGH SCHOOL   *Played 16: W 4, L 6, D 6. A 3*

Master i/c: D. C. Williams

The loss of influential captain Dan Scrase to a mid-season injury hampered the progress of a young side. However, wicket-keeper/batsman William Howard performed confidently at the crease and outstandingly behind the stumps. Edward Henderson bowled tirelessly for 34 wickets.

Batting—W. O. F. Howard 16–1–411–107–1–27.40; M. I. Doughty 9–0–245–101–1–27.22; F. J. R. Handcock 16–1–306–68–0–20.40; R. T. Hume 14–1–218–69–0–16.76; D. J. Groenveld 15–0–233–70–0–15.53.

Bowling—E. J. C. Henderson 214–46–604–34–6/21–17.76; R. T. Hume 150.4–35–424–15–3/59–28.26.

CULFORD SCHOOL *Played 12: W 3, L 6, D 3. A 2*

Master i/c: R. P. Shepperson

Batting—M. K. S. Ampomah 8–3–150–52*–0–30.00; T. C. P. Philp 11–0–320–64–0–29.09; J. V. R. Stevenson 9–1–194–79–0–24.25; D. J. Kemp 11–0–243–69–0–22.09; J. R. Tarrant 11–3–169–41*–0–21.12.

Bowling—J. R. Tarrant 144–30–535–17–6/54–31.47.

DARTFORD GRAMMAR SCHOOL *Played 13: W 5, L 6, D 2*

Master i/c: S. R. D. de Winton

While chasing MCC's 204 for four declared, the team recorded seven ducks – but lost by only 18 runs, as E. Tyler made an undefeated 91 and G. Cook 61.

Batting—E. Tyler 7–1–329–91*–0–54.83; *G. Cook 11–0–450–97–0–40.90.

Bowling—No bowler took 15 wickets. The leading bowler was G. Cook 60.5–4–266–14–4/41–19.00.

DAUNTSEY'S SCHOOL *Played 12: W 4, L 6, D 2. A 3*

Master i/c: D. C. R. Baker   Professional: P. Knowles

Batting—B. Darbyshire 7–2–199–61–0–39.80; A. Campbell 11–2–199–56–0–22.11; C. Warde 12–1–206–70*–0–18.72.

Bowling—C. Mortimer 78–10–281–19–5/31–14.78; P. Sutton 86.1–16–285–18–6/10–15.83.

DEAN CLOSE SCHOOL *Played 13: W 3, L 5, D 5. A 4*

Master i/c: C. J. Townsend   Professional: M. Mbangwa

Despite mixed results, it was an encouraging season, with 14 playes who represented the side returning in 1999. The captain, George Lane, played alongside his brother Joseph and brothers Alastair and Thomas Judge.

Batting—*G. D. M. Lane 9–1–285–95–0–35.62; B. D. Mears 12–0–316–87–0–26.33; P. J. Marchand 13–2–245–50*–0–22.27; D. A. Bull 13–0–257–73–0–19.76; A. D. Judge 12–0–211–77–0–17.58.

Bowling—G. A. Walker 79.3–8–339–20–5/19–16.95; O. E. Bretherton 169.5–33–589–32–7/46–18.40.

DENSTONE COLLEGE *Played 13: W 6, L 1, D 6. A 5*

Master i/c: A. N. James

An inexperienced attack exceeded expectations, securing one victory by ten wickets and two by nine. Phillip Cheadle led by example and averaged over 66. He shared a record undefeated second-wicket partnership of 203 with Nottinghamshire Under-16 player P. K. Riley against Wrekin College.

Batting—*P. M. Cheadle 13–3–669–118*–1–66.90; W. J. L. Bagshawe 13–3–534–100*–1–53.40; P. K. Riley 11–3–297–88*–0–37.12; J. A. Blackwell 10–0–257–69–0–25.70.

Bowling—M. C. Webster 103.4–30–288–18–5/21–16.00; P. K. Riley 76–11–277–15–4/12–18.46.

DOVER COLLEGE *Played 11: W 2, L 4, D 5. A 3*

Master i/c: D. C. Butler

The planting of a tree at the college cricket ground commemorates a century or a haul of eight or more wickets in a match. Another sapling was bedded in when Justin Baker claimed an outstanding eight for 12 in the win over The Harvey GS.

Batting—*P. Karafillides 10–2–334–75*–0–41.75; P. C. de M. Thompson 10–0–232–74–0–23.20.

Bowling—J. E. E. Baker 65–17–210–16–8/12–13.12; P. C. de M. Thompson 104.1–20–336–23–4/23–14.60, P. Karafillides 160.4–34–459–25–5/58–18.36.

DOWNSIDE SCHOOL   *Played 13: W 9, L 2, D 2*

Master i/c: A. Smerdon   Professional: D. Perryman

This was, perhaps, the most successful side the school has ever produced. Highlights were a first win against MCC, a long-awaited victory over Blundell's and the defeat of Mount St Mary's, Sheffield, in the final of the Emeriti Trophy. David Jackson had an excellent season, scoring two hundreds and averaging over 130.

Batting—D. Jackson 13–8–653–119*–2–130.60; S. Matthews 10–3–360–71–0–51.42; W. Orr 13–3–304–62–0–30.40.

Bowling—P. Moran 108–30–304–18–4/22–16.88; R. Watts 159.3–38–403–22–5/44–18.31; D. Jackson 102–21–313–16–5/27–19.56.

DUKE OF YORK'S ROYAL MILITARY SCHOOL   *Played 11: W 5, L 1, D 5. A 4*

Master i/c: S. Salisbury   Professional: J. H. Dawes

The team, capably led by Richard Credland, played with considerable maturity, aggression and common sense. Credland bowled well in tandem with fellow-spinner Nathan Fletcher, and together they supported the lively medium-pace of all-rounder Gareth Morris.

Batting—G. B. Morris 9–3–376–110*–1–62.66; J. J. Owen 10–2–253–55–0–31.62; N. I. Barrow 6–1–155–50*–0–31.00.

Bowling—G. B. Morris 83–27–202–18–4/13–11.22; *R. Credland 121–26–279–22–4/35–12.68; N. I. Barrow 93–22–291–15–3/40–19.40; N. D. Fletcher 93.4–30–307–15–4/63–20.46.

DULWICH COLLEGE   *Played 16: W 7, L 1, D 8. A 1*

Master i/c: J. Cooper   Professionals: A. Ransom and A. R. Whittall

Adam Moon, in his third season in the team, was selected to play for Surrey Second Eleven.

Batting—V. H. Kumar 15–3–616–99–0–51.33; N. A. Martin 14–3–482–83–0–43.81; R. L. Barry 14–3–410–112*–1–37.27; A. K. Shah 12–2–356–117*–1–35.60; J. J. Allen 11–4–217–59–0–31.00.

Bowling—B. P. Cooper 138.4–32–248–17–4/21–14.58; A. K. Moon 202.3–44–663–37–5/43–17.91.

DURHAM SCHOOL   *Played 17: W 10, L 1, D 6. A 4*

Master i/c: M. E. Hirsch

Damp conditions restricted the amount of cricket, but the side played positively, losing only to Ampleforth. The team contained four England schoolboys.

Batting—A. C. Beales 13–1–593–100*–1–49.41; C. D. Burdon 13–1–462–100*–1–38.50; J. R. Davidson 11–0–383–62–0–34.81; C. R. Wides 14–0–378–77–0–27.00; J. Pattinson 12–1–235–57*–0–21.36; *M. I. Cannon 16–0–276–94–0–17.25.

Bowling—G. M. Muchall 163–46–458–28–5/40–16.35; C. R. Wides 142–30–462–28–7/22–16.50; J. R. Davidson 104–20–323–19–6/53–17.00; C. D. Burdon 120–21–383–20–5/15–19.15.

EASTBOURNE COLLEGE   *Played 14: W 9, L 2, D 3. A 2*

Masters i/c: N. L. Wheeler and D. A. Stewart   Professional: J. W. Hall

A talented all-round side remained undefeated until the last week of the season. Despite a brilliant 118 from Mark Lock in the final of the Langdale Cup, they lost to Lancing College by two runs. Lock played five years in the team and averaged nearly 50.

Batting—M. J. Lock 12–3–653–118–2–72.55; *H. F. G. Southwell 14–4–575–108*–2–57.50; A. D. Simcox 6–2–152–52–0–38.00; N. T. Sands 13–3–336–75*–0–33.60.

Bowling—A. G. B. Waterlow 114.4–31–280–18–3/12–15.55; N. S. MacLean 92.2–15–332–18–6/17–18.44; J. J. Beer 109–22–332–17–4/38–19.52; S. J. Bessant 113–34–404–18–5/9–22.44.

THE EDINBURGH ACADEMY   *Played 14: W 6, L 4, D 4. A 3*

Master i/c: G. R. Bowe   Professional: S. Dillon

The dreadful weather greatly affected matches and practice but there were excellent wins against Barnard Castle, Loretto and, for the first time, MCC.

Batting—M. R. L. Blair 11–5–228–72–0–38.00; B. J. Leonard 9–1–301–78–0–37.62; *N. J. Hillyard 13–3–292–63–0–29.20; C. M. Hillyard 12–2–232–74–0–23.20; A. G. Moffat 11–1–203–45–0–20.30; J. G. Thomson 3–1–186–58*–0–15.50.

Bowling—D. F. Paterson 154–46–343–32–8/42–10.71; B. J. Leonard 124–36–253–19–6/24–13.31; M. R. L. Blair 133–24–448–24–4/25–18.66.

ELIZABETH COLLEGE, GUERNSEY   *Played 21: W 9, L 9, D 3. A 1*

Master i/c: M. E. Kinder

The side had enjoyed success in island cricket, but faced sterner opposition in two schools' festivals. Although the bowling and fielding remained strong, the batting lacked resilience.

Batting—A. S. Birkett 14–4–332–54–0–33.20; A. D. Shields 14–3–230–103*–1–20.90; H. Ephgrave 18–1–321–67–0–18.88; A. R. Hunter 19–0–347–68–0–18.26; D. P. Walder 12–3–154–58–0–17.11; T. A. le Page 15–3–188–51*–0–15.66.

Bowling—S. P. Queripel 111.4–21–382–24–7/53–15.91; A. G. P. Cooper 157.3–26–472–29–4/12–16.27; A. S. Birkett 113.3–26–323–19–6/54–17.00; D. P. Walder 139.2–20–520–28–7/32–18.57; M. J. S. Betts 105–16–335–18–3/55–18.61; C. J. Blackburn 146.2–22–479–24–5/46–19.95.

ELLESMERE COLLEGE   *Played 11: W 3, L 2, D 6. A 4*

Master i/c: P. J. Hayes   Professional: R. G. Mapp

In tremendous form all season, captain Paul Furniss led from the front. He shared in five century partnerships – four with his brother Robert – and scored three hundreds in his last four innings.

Batting—*P. J. Furniss 10–4–780–135–4–130.00; R. M. Furniss 10–0–284–57–0–28.40; F. G. Walters 9–0–241–91–0–26.77; T. H. Pearson 10–1–218–62–0–24.22.

Bowling—P. F. McCarthy 87.2–16–342–23–7/48–14.86; T. H. Pearson 148.3–34–427–18–5/50–23.72; R. A. Davies 171–32–569–17–4/70–33.47.

ELTHAM COLLEGE   *Played 13: W 2, L 2, D 8, T 1. A 1*

Masters i/c: P. C. McCartney and B. M. Withecombe   Professional: R. W. Hills

The form and confidence of a very young side – the average age was under 16 at the start of the season – was dented by the weather, which denied them victory in several games. Openers Matthew Bainbridge and Paul Clinton were determined and well organised batsmen, while William Goodyear was selected for an England Under-15 trial but denied it by injury.

Batting—M. O. Bainbridge 12–2–384–101–1–38.40; W. J. Goodyear 7–1–203–46–0–33.83; P. Clinton 11–1–222–50–0–22.20; B. Devon 11–0–164–57–0–14.90.

Bowling—A. Ring 58–12–167–16–4/15–10.43.

ENFIELD GRAMMAR SCHOOL   *Played 14: W 4, L 7, D 3. A 7*

Master i/c: M. Alder

Batting—*J. Barber 12–3–452–98–0–50.22; E. Barber 8–1–179–64–0–25.57; A. Herron 12–1–239–73–0–21.72; D. Keerthichandra 13–2–198–44–0–18.00.

Bowling—J. Collard 57–8–185–15–5/50–12.33; J. Barber 132–18–360–24–5/24–15.00.

EPSOM COLLEGE   *Played 14: W 4, L 5, D 5. A 4*

Master i/c: G. A. Jones

Batting—*R. Oram 14–0–429–88–0–30.64; C. Oatway 12–0–346–85–0–28.83; F. Thompson 14–2–314–74–0–26.16; T. Joyce 11–0–265–46–0–24.09.

Bowling—H. Kingham 201–35–668–29–7/73–23.03.

ETON COLLEGE   *Played 13: W 7, L 1, D 5. A 5*

Master i/c: S. J. G. Doggart   Professional: J. M. Rice

A. G. R. Loudon represented ECB South Under-19 against Pakistan Under-19 before going on to captain ECB Under-17.

Batting—*A. G. R. Loudon 10–3–374–64*–0–53.42; S. L. J. McL. Hawk 13–1–516–65*–0–43.00; A. F. S. Leslie 12–4–277–53–0–34.62; S. E. S. FitzGerald 9–1–233–75–0–29.12; O. G. C. Broome 7–1–173–57*–0–28.83; G. G. Maan 9–3–173–68*–0–28.83.

Bowling—A. G. R. Loudon 128.5–35–341–23–5/23–14.82; J. T. A. Bruce 157.1–33–411–26–6/39–15.80; G. G. Maan 108.2–22–310–17–6/24–18.23.

EXETER SCHOOL   *Played 12: W 5, L 5, D 2. A 5*

Master i/c: J. A. Lockwood   Professional: T. A. Roach

Batting—J. P. Cruft 12–0–528–87–0–44.00; *I. P. Gamble 12–1–416–134*–1–37.81; N. J. Saunders 7–0–187–61–0–26.71; T. H. G. Hargraves 12–0–165–43–0–13.75.

Bowling—I. P. Gamble 125.3–27–427–21–3/20–20.33.

FELSTED SCHOOL   *Played 18: W 6, L 5, D 7. A 1*

Master i/c: F. C. Hayes

Although he never quite recaptured the outstanding form of 1997, Tim Phillips remained the dominant player in the side. In a total of 199 against Tonbridge he contributed 127, and of the 144 needed to beat Bishop's Stortford he scored 114. George Finch was the pick of the attack.

Batting—T. J. Phillips 18–2–676–127–2–42.25; M. D. Rath 16–1–493–86–0–32.86; R. A. N. Perkins 16–1–413–94–0–27.53; T. Ballentyne 16–1–283–71–0–18.86; C. J. A. Turtle 18–2–280–50–0–17.50; A. D. Brown 13–0–186–70–0–14.30.

Bowling—G. E. M. Finch 243.4–56–612–39–7/77–15.69; T. J. Phillips 270.4–89–635–38–6/37–16.71.

FETTES COLLEGE   *Played 12: W 3, L 3, D 6*

Master i/c: Rev. R. Marsden   Professional: J. van Geloven

All-rounder Neil Millar represented Scotland at the Under-19 World Cup in South Africa.

Batting—N. Millar 13–2–495–74*–0–45.00; D. J. R. Leckie 11–3–208–50*–0–26.00; T. W. Simpson 13–1–186–38–0–15.50.

Bowling—N. Millar 155–40–385–31–4/21–12.41; J. F. Jackson 142–45–332–17–4/37–19.52.

FOREST SCHOOL   *Played 14: W 10, L 0, D 4. A 6*

Master i/c: S. Turner

Captain and wicket-keeper James Foster played an outstanding role in an undefeated season, and his talents received wider recognition when he was selected for the England Under-19 squad. He represented Essex Second Eleven on several occasions, along with Robert Marshall, who scored 60 on debut.

Batting—*J. Foster 14–6–558–120*–1–69.75; M. Patel 11–4–271–78–0–38.71; R. Marshall 14–3–402–71*–0–36.54; R. McKay 13–0–399–92–0–30.69.

Bowling—A. Jones 59.4–16–155–17–4/14–9.11; R. Smith 166.4–64–414–30–7/14–13.80; M. Orchard-Lisle 167.1–65–356–24–4/22–14.83; C. White 125.3–38–315–16–3/24–19.68.

FOYLE AND LONDONDERRY COLLEGE   *Played 15: W 7, L 7, D 1. A 1*

Master i/c: G. R. McCarter

Batting—I. Donaghey 16–0–339–47–0–21.18; S. Bratton 15–2–229–40–0–17.61; J. Winfield 15–1–175–55*–0–12.50; F. Duddy 14–0–164–24–0–11.71.

Bowling—J. Winfield 132.4–24–342–26–4/10–13.15; D. Braiden 81.2–8–294–15–3/10–19.60; G. Brolly 131–27–363–16–4/36–22.68.

FRAMLINGHAM COLLEGE   *Played 17: W 0, L 13, D 4. A 2*

Master i/c: A. S. Griffiths   Professional: C. Rutterford

Batting—*G. E. Hames 19–2–731–133–2–43.00; M. A. A. Low 16–2–411–90–0–29.35; I. T. K. Tucker 19–2–398–99–0–23.41; P. R. Lewis 15–3–258–59–0–21.50; B. W. Barker 16–2–238–50*–0–17.00; J. C. Jackson 17–2–167–30–0–11.13.

Bowling—M. A. A. Low 119.4–23–405–22–6/29–18.40; P. J. Barker 154.2–16–623–24–5/62–25.95; J. C. Jackson 166–24–688–15–4/69–45.86.

GIGGLESWICK SCHOOL   *Played 8: W 4, L 1, D 3. A 3*

Master i/c: P. Turner   Professional: A. G. Lawson

Batting—J. R. P. Smailes 8–3–237–68*–0–47.40; N. J. Harrison 8–0–262–111–1–32.75; C. Woolsey 8–0–198–45–0–24.75.

Bowling—C. Woolsey 65.5–14–162–18–5/11–9.00; J. R. P. Smailes 81–10–302–16–4/15–18.87; S. J. Langstaff 125–33–382–16–4/66–23.87.

GLENALMOND   *Played 10: W 6, L 1, D 3. A 4*

Master i/c: J. D. Bassett

The first ten-wicket haul for the first team was achieved by Henry Smuts-Muller, who took ten for 37 against Sedbergh.

Batting—H. S. E. Monro 10–1–348–87–0–38.66; J. Burrows 9–2–228–83–0–32.57; J. Murray 10–3–210–58*–0–30.00.

Bowling—M. Thomson 75.1–22–164–15–5/27–10.93; H. Smuts-Muller 148.2–34–311–28–10/37–11.10; D. Hall 123–37–287–18–5/56–15.94.

GORDONSTOUN SCHOOL   *Played 9: W 3, L 2, D 4. A 1*

Master i/c: A. T. Greaves

Batting—A. Morbey 9–1–269–88–0–33.62; W. Brown Douglas 7–0–170–65–0–24.28.

Bowling—T. Illingworth 83–13–196–15–3/19–13.06; M. Broad 71–8–237–16–4/17–14.81.

Jinesh Amin (left) was the second-highest wicket-taker of the summer, with 60; his team-mate from Haberdashers' Aske's School, Dean Wilson, totalled 1,169 runs, more than any other batsman.

GRESHAM'S SCHOOL   *Played 14: W 6, L 6, D 2. A 2*

Master i/c: A. M. Ponder

Batting—A. D. Horsley 11–2–220–64*–0–24.44; M. P. Lintott 11–1–224–53–0–22.40; J. P. E. Rodgers 9–1–157–52*–0–19.62; R. W. Fulford 12–0–235–58–0–19.58; T. G. A. Hedley 12–2–166–45–0–16.60.

Bowling—O. D. Webb 103–21–313–25–5/23–12.52; A. D. Horsley 116–19–427–17–3/35–25.11; *R. D. MacNair 138–22–468–16–4/23–29.25.

HABERDASHERS' ASKE'S SCHOOL   *Played 21: W 9, L 1, D 11. A 3*

Masters i/c: S. D. Charlwood and D. I. Yeabsley

Undefeated by any school, a young side performed well throughout the season, achieving the best results for a decade. Dean Wilson was in excellent form, scoring over 1,000 runs and hitting three centuries. The outstanding bowler was Jinesh Amin, who took 60 wickets – a school record – and gained selection for Middlesex Under-17.

Batting—*D. B. Wilson 21–6–1,169–120–3–77.93; T. J. Hall 12–4–225–66*–0–28.12; J. Amin 14–4–276–83*–0–27.60; I. J. Pryor 13–1–277–91–0–23.08; J. Sethi 10–3–151–60*–0–21.57; J. L. Moore 19–5–274–61*–0–19.57; M. Patel 13–2–194–32–0–17.63.

Bowling—J. Amin 292.3–78–577–60–7/22–9.61; A. Jayaweera 173–34–565–28–4/24–20.17; M. D. East 193–31–623–23–6/49–27.08.

HAILEYBURY   *Played 16: W 1, L 3, D 12. A 2*

Master i/c: M. S. Seymour   Professional: G. D. Barlow

Batting—*C. J. Box 13–4–338–71–0–37.55; J. S. Rixson 15–0–423–100–1–28.20; L. W. L. Molyneux 16–0–441–66–0–27.56; D. A. Raymond 16–0–313–74–0–19.56; M. K. M. Farmiloe 16–3–189–33–0–14.53.

Bowling—M. K. M. Farmiloe 161–43–459–22–4/27–20.86; N. Gauri 308–34–748–24–5/24–31.16.

HAMPTON SCHOOL   *Played 12: W 6, L 2, D 4. A 4*

Master i/c: E. Wesson

At the end of the season, the side enjoyed a six-match tour to Barbados, winning three games.

Batting—G. J. Wilcock 12–0–380–90–0–31.66; R. T. H. Gaines 11–0–337–64–0–30.63; P. C. K. Wood 12–0–361–63–0–30.08; J. M. Evans 10–2–177–65–0–22.12; G. M. Cope 9–2–151–48–0–21.57; E. J. Martin 12–1–200–80–0–18.18.

Bowling—G. J. Wilcock 77–26–228–18–4/14–12.66.

HARROW SCHOOL   *Played 13: W 5, L 4, D 4. A 3*

Master i/c: S. J. Halliday   Professional: R. K. Sethi

A talented side recorded several good victories but did not do themselves justice against stronger schools. The seam bowling was particularly powerful with Jake Warman, Sam Stevens and Sam Weston-Simons all performing well. Warman's eight for 26 at Malvern was a highlight. The batting, however, was over-dependent on Luke de Rougemont.

Batting—L. F. de Rougemont 13–1–526–105*–1–43.83; S. H. Stevens 13–2–363–126*–1–33.00; W. J. L. Matthews 8–1–169–48*–0–24.14; A. T. R. Titchener-Barrett 11–2–171–57–0–19.00; J. A. S. Dixon 11–2–165–54–0–18.33; A. M. A. Andjel 11–0–173–60–0–15.72.

Bowling—S. H. Stevens 113–24–307–24–6/32–12.79; J. M. G. S. Warman 96.2–19–283–19–8/26–14.89; J. S. Weston-Simons 116.3–27–355–22–4/42–16.13; *D. R. Hepher 106.3–24–336–14–4/22–20.87.

THE HARVEY GRAMMAR SCHOOL   *Played 14: W 5, L 4, D 5. A 5*

Masters i/c: P. J. Harding and S. J. Goodfellow

Batting—*A. Towse 13–5–350–68–0–43.75; L. Bill 11–1–331–134–1–33.10; J. Hubbard 10–1–257–82–0–28.55; J. Henderson 11–2–152–37–0–16.88.

Bowling—S. Barlow 115–25–388–23–5/52–16.86; J. Hubbard 107–18–333–16–5/39–20.81.

HEREFORD CATHEDRAL SCHOOL   *Played 16: W 3, L 7, D 5, T 1. A 2*

Master i/c: A. Connop

Batting—R. M. H. Symonds 13–4–450–104*–1–50.00; E. Tomlinson 11–2–182–44*–0–20.22; C. L. Powell 11–1–192–51*–0–19.20; *A. J. Last 13–0–245–67–0–18.84; P. M. Whittal 15–1–239–69–0–17.07; H. W. E. Warren 10–0–157–64–0–15.70.

Bowling—R. M. H. Symonds 117–24–359–28–4/26–12.82; P. A. P. Lloyd 103–21–329–18–6/11–18.27; T. C. Harrison 114–23–322–17–4/31–18.94; G. P. E. Scott 130–14–530–20–4/43–26.50.

HIGHGATE SCHOOL   *Played 10: W 2, L 4, D 4. A 3*

Master i/c: R. J. Davis   Professional: R. E. Jones

Batting—*D. C. Cohen 10–1–285–104–1–31.66; J. R. Edgar 7–0–165–84–0–23.57.

Bowling—S. Dindyal 109–23–347–16–4/69–21.68.

HURSTPIERPOINT COLLEGE   *Played 16: W 8, L 1, D 7. A 2*

Master i/c: M. J. Mance   Professional: D. J. Semmence

An excellent season, with eight wins, could have been even better: both Eastbourne and St John's, Leatherhead, held out with their last pair at the crease. Nicholas Creed had a fine all-round season, scoring 437 runs and taking 48 wickets. Fifteen-year-old Krishana Singh became the youngest boy to score a century for the college.

Batting—K. R. Singh 16–2–491–102*–1–35.07; N. J. K. Creed 15–2–437–82–0–33.61; M. P. Clowes-Tinlin 13–7–175–27–0–29.16; J. N. Taylor 15–2–360–63–0–27.69; *R. K. H. Redford 15–1–370–84–0–26.42; D. M. Gibson 14–2–266–39*–0–22.16; M. J. E. Imber 15–1–262–43–0–18.71; J. I. McKemey 12–3–165–42–0–18.33.

Bowling—D. M. Gibson 160.5–37–431–37–6/44–11.64; N. J. K. Creed 227.4–50–708–48–5/22–14.75; R. K. H. Redford 135–30–431–19–3/15–22.68.

IPSWICH SCHOOL   *Played 17: W 7, L 4, D 6. A 2*

Master i/c: A. K. Golding   Professional: R. E. East

Batting—C. Swallow 16–4–519–140*–1–43.25; T. Jervis 17–1–592–101–1–37.00; R. Mann 16–0–335–57–0–20.93; R. Maddison 16–1–283–52*–0–18.86; T. Debenham 14–1–205–56–0–15.76.

Bowling—G. Ingham 170–32–470–24–3/53–19.58; R. Leeburn 144–15–548–23–4/42–23.82; C. Swallow 210–37–723–26–6/36–27.80; J. Bell 172–29–500–16–3/36–31.25.

THE JOHN LYON SCHOOL   *Played 19: W 4, L 8, D 7. A 2*

Master i/c: I. Parker

Batting—*S. J. Thomas 14–0–351–79–0–25.07; N. J. Jago 14–1–321–61–0–24.69; Z. S. Merali 15–1–275–77–0–19.64; B. A. Rawson-Jones 15–1–258–61–0–18.42; L. W. Wijeratna 17–6–151–48*–0–13.72; D. P. Connolly 13–1–164–38–0–13.66.

Bowling—D. P. Connolly 124.5–19–351–30–6/17–11.70; L. W. Wijeratna 117.5–17–368–18–2/7–20.44.

KELLY COLLEGE   *Played 6: W 4, L 1, D 1. A 6*

Master i/c: T. Ryder

The loss of half the fixtures to the weather prevented a promising side from fulfilling its potential. On slow, low pitches the bowlers had few opportunities to excel. But Ross Schreiber and Simon James led a powerful batting line-up.

Batting—S. W. James 5–2–196–84*–0–65.33; R. T. Schreiber 6–3–166–57*–0–55.33.

Bowling—No bowler took 15 wickets. The leading bowler was S. W. James 40–8–144–12–3/30–12.00.

KIMBOLTON SCHOOL   *Played 13: W 4, L 3, D 6. A 4*

Master i/c: A. G. Tapp   Professional: M. E. Latham

Batting—S. Moore 13–2–318–69–0–28.90; T. Huggins 12–0–300–82–0–25.00; *J. Pepperman 12–1–206–80–0–18.72; C. Hose 11–0–198–54–0–18.00.

Bowling—T. Huggins 105.2–23–323–19–4/32–17.00; C. Binham 161–25–564–30–4/69–18.80; C. Peel 137.2–24–441–22–4/28–20.04.

KING EDWARD VI COLLEGE, STOURBRIDGE   *Played 8: W 4, L 1, D 3. A 7*

Masters i/c: M. L. Ryan and R. A. Williams

The captain, James Burgoyne, was selected as twelfth man for Worcestershire against Oxford University.

Batting—J. Riches 5–1–188–79–0–47.00; *J. Burgoyne 6–2–168–64–0–42.00; M. Foster 8–2–225–55–0–37.50.

Bowling—J. Burgoyne 71.1–21–176–20–6/29–8.80.

KING EDWARD VI SCHOOL, SOUTHAMPTON *Played 26: W 12, L 6, D 8. A 2*

Master i/c: R. J. Putt

Captain and wicket-keeper Iain Brunnschweiler set a record for dismissals in a season with 25 catches and 16 stumpings. Ben Craft hit 902 runs, with a top score of 143, another record.

Batting—J. D. Francis 10–2–437–124*–2–54.62; B. W. Craft 24–5–902–143–1–47.47; R. S. Moore 17–5–420–78–0–35.00; *I. Brunnschweiler 26–1–633–96–0–25.32; B. D. Higgs 20–5–230–51–0–15.33; J. R. N. Warrick 20–0–298–51–0–14.90; G. D. R. Askham 15–2–164–38–0–12.61.

Bowling—B. W. Craft 187–36–520–36–4/29–14.44; B. D. Higgs 215–55–581–40–3/7–14.52; G. D. R. Askham 178–28–561–35–4/14–16.02; S. J. Rigg 79–23–260–15–3/2–17.33; S. E. Hughes 128–14–468–21–3/17–22.28; J. D. R. Tantram 105–21–366–16–5/26–22.87.

KING EDWARD VII SCHOOL, LYTHAM *Played 18: W 3, L 7, D 8. A 3*

Master i/c: A. M. Weston   Professional: E. A. E. Baptiste

Batting—D. R. Finn 19–3–464–60*–0–29.00; M. Q. Wilkinson 19–3–371–62–0–23.18; B. C. Garthwaite 18–4–281–59*–0–20.07; I. F. Battarbee 17–0–290–50–0–17.05; R. N. Cragg 18–7–175–38*–0–15.90; J. M. Hill 20–1–282–54–0–14.84; A. I. Whittle 21–2–268–77*–0–14.10.

Bowling—D. R. Finn 190–34–546–29–5/33–18.82; M. Q. Wilkinson 219.4–57–626–29–4/29–21.58.

KING EDWARD'S SCHOOL, BIRMINGHAM *Played 18: W 4, L 8, D 6. A 2*

Master i/c: M. D. Stead   Professionals: D. Collins and R. J. Newman

Batting—W. R. N. Webb 18–1–452–88–0–26.58; A. M. H. Natkiel 17–0–446–86–0–26.23; R. J. Newman 18–1–318–48*–0–18.70; T. D. S. Owen 16–0–277–57–0–17.31; N. Y. Khan 16–2–212–70*–0–15.14; A. Chatterjee 11–1–150–60–0–15.00.

Bowling—R. P. Cauldwell 97–16–284–15–1/3–18.93; R. J. Newman 86.5–6–357–16–2/16–22.31; G. A. Bhadri 220.1–54–606–26–2/3–23.30; W. R. N. Webb 119.1–25–376–16–3/11–23.50; G. S. Brogal 126–29–384–16–1/2–24.00; D. S. Payne 120–14–419–16–5/28–26.18.

KING EDWARD'S SCHOOL, WITLEY *Played 13: W 2, L 3, D 8. A 2*

Master i/c: D. H. Messenger

Poor weather and a series of injuries to the front-line bowlers restricted progress. The full-strength attack appeared together on only three occasions. However, a successful cricket week included a first-ever fixture against MCC and a convincing victory over the XL Club.

Batting—P. M. McNally 9–3–217–88–0–36.16; M. E. Josling 8–1–222–68*–0–31.71; J. D. Robson 13–2–307–81–0–27.90; J. C. G. Dowdeswell 13–0–285–63–0–21.92; A. J. Brewerton 13–2–205–47*–0–18.63.

Bowling—No bowler took 15 wickets. The leading bowler was W. J. Blake 69.5–10–241–12–5/45–20.08.

KING HENRY VIII SCHOOL, COVENTRY *Played 11: W 4, L 2, D 5*

Master i/c: A. M. Parker

Batting—J. S. Grindal 9–2–353–109*–1–50.42.

Bowling—D. R. Box 99–15–272–15–3/34–18.13.

KING WILLIAM'S COLLEGE   *Played 8: W 3, L 2, D 3*

Master i/c: A. Maree   Professional: D. Mark

Batting—B. Thomas 8–2–240–89–0–40.00; E. Lee 8–2–212–101*–1–35.33; *J. Manuja 8–1–177–53–0–25.28.

Bowling—E. Lee 69–11–230–15–5/10–15.33; E. Craven 87–14–279–16–6/35–17.43.

KING'S COLLEGE, TAUNTON   *Played 11: W 9, L 0, D 2. A 4*

Master i/c: R. J. R. Yeates   Professional: D. Breakwell

The college enjoyed its best-ever season, winning all the games not curtailed by the weather. Highlights were the victories over Millfield and MCC. Captain Nicholas Boulton led the side with distinction and was greatly assisted by Ben Vickers, who bowled with venom throughout the summer.

Batting—*N. R. Boulton 11–2–681–166*–3–75.66; C. J. Stafford 9–4–218–64–0–43.60; J. W. Payn 10–1–355–71–0–39.44; P. D. Lewis 9–2–158–43–0–22.57.

Bowling—B. J. Vickers 96–15–236–23–5/23–10.26.

KING'S COLLEGE SCHOOL, WIMBLEDON   *Played 16: W 9, L 4, D 3. A 2*

Master i/c: G. C. McGinn   Professional: G. J. Kennis

The two highlights of a successful season were the four hundreds scored by Iain Pay, and Ben Woodbridge's six for 61 in the win over a powerful MCC side.

Batting—I. S. Pay 15–2–839–143–4–64.53; *D. A. P. Bowen 14–4–442–81*–0–44.20; Z. Mir 16–6–375–48*–0–37.50; O. J. McGinn 15–0–301–48–0–20.06.

Bowling—S. W. Hammill 162–43–438–32–5/47–13.68; B. H. Woodbridge 164–35–510–29–6/61–17.58; D. A. P. Bowen 130–11–491–16–2/21–30.68; J. R. M. Shelton 105–14–527–17–5/37–31.00.

KING'S SCHOOL, BRUTON   *Played 12: W 5, L 7, D 0. A 3*

Master i/c: P. Platts-Martin

A relatively inexperienced side improved during the season, winning four of their last six matches. Robert Hastings was the backbone of the batting and scored an unbeaten century against Clifton.

Batting—R. W. F. Hastings 12–2–463–134*–1–46.30; M. K. Rogers 12–3–223–71*–0–24.77; E. W. Thomas 11–1–239–65–0–23.90; M. Drewer 12–0–275–60–0–22.91; C. Davis 11–0–167–32–0–15.18; J. Anderson 12–0–180–47–0–15.00.

Bowling—E. W. Thomas 106.4–15–379–17–4/32–22.29.

THE KING'S SCHOOL, CANTERBURY   *Played 11: W 4, L 2, D 5. A 2*

Master i/c: A. W. Dyer   Professional: A. G. E. Ealham

The season started indifferently but ended in style, with four wins in the end-of-term cricket week. Visiting scorers had trouble distinguishing between twins Gareth and Alistair Williams, who batted at No. 3 and No. 4 – and both bowled.

Batting—S. C. Youngman 11–2–325–83–0–36.11; *G. J. R. Williams 11–1–349–88*–0–34.90; A. G. B. Williams 11–2–230–41–0–25.55.

Bowling—H. R. J. Hardy 107.4–31–266–19–4/28–14.00; O. D. Fraser 133.5–27–345–21–6/30–16.42.

THE KING'S SCHOOL, CHESTER   *Played 15: W 13, L 1, D 1. A 2*

Master i/c: S. Neal

The side's all-round ability was illustrated by a record number of wins, and an undefeated last-wicket stand of 76 between Neal Mellor and Christopher Millward, another record. The bowling highlight was Edward Mason's hat-trick against Rydal. David Reeves, James Twiddle and Ned Francis all represented Cheshire at different levels.

Batting—S. P. Barlow 9–4–208–41–0–41.60; *D. J. Reeves 15–0–553–94–0–36.86; I. S. Thistlewood 13–1–307–65*–0–25.58; J. J. Mummé-Young 11–3–160–34*–0–20.00; S. G. Gilchrist 12–3–179–53–0–19.88; J. C. Yates 13–2–211–32–0–19.18; E. W. D. Francis 11–0–157–37–0–14.27.

Bowling—C. S. Ratcliffe 74.5–16–236–23–6/22–10.26; J. J. Mummé-Young 76–12–279–18–4/29–15.50; E. W. Mason 124.1–42–292–15–3/18–19.46.

THE KING'S SCHOOL, ELY   *Played 16: W 9, L 6, D 1. A 2*

Masters i/c: T. Firth and W. J. Marshall

Tim Mitzman's thoughtful captaincy and penetrative bowling took a young side to within one win of the school record. Tom Wilkins, a 13-year-old, took 14 wickets.

Batting—J. J. P. Sayers 14–1–451–94–0–34.69; *T. E. Mitzman 15–1–304–57–0–21.71; F. C. Thorogood 15–1–296–120*–1–21.14.

Bowling—T. E. Mitzman 176–35–409–42–6/29–9.73; J. A. D. Pullen 63–6–232–16–5/35–14.50; A. N. Brett 142.3–26–439–24–6/47–18.29.

THE KING'S SCHOOL, MACCLESFIELD   *Played 19: W 8, L 4, D 7. A 3*

Master i/c: J. D. Nuttall   Professional: S. Moores

An encouraging season for a young side – including a good win against Birkenhead – was epitomised by 16-year-old Daniel Isherwood's seven fifties. A tour of Kenya was planned for the winter.

Batting—D. Isherwood 17–2–610–82–0–40.66; E. Bones 7–2–195–53*–0–39.00; R. Lees 15–4–300–57*–0–27.27; J. Clay 13–0–300–79–0–23.07; *M. Tunwell 9–1–172–55*–0–21.50; R. Emslie 18–3–320–53*–0–21.33; C. Allday 9–0–189–69–0–21.00; N. Jones 11–2–157–40–0–17.44; T. Smith 15–2–192–41*–0–14.76.

Bowling—A. Sharp 124.3–12–459–31–6/41–14.80; M. Jackson 211.4–45–568–36–4/5–15/77; T. Isherwood 75.5–12–253–15–3/19–16.86; M. Tunwell 130–16–468–23–3/25–20.34; O. Rushton 128.1–29–419–19–3/19–22.05; R. Lees 169–34–506–16–3/16–31.62.

KING'S SCHOOL, ROCHESTER   *Played 17: W 5, L 5, D 7. A 3*

Master i/c: G. R. Williams

Brothers Michael and Andrew Maurice were both selected for Kent Under-19.

Batting—J. E. C. Shotter 12–6–152–33*–0–25.33; *S. D. R. Lapthorn 17–2–369–101*–1–24.60; A. M. Maurice 15–1–327–85–0–23.35; M. A. Maurice 14–0–262–54–0–18.71; R. W. Hughes 10–0–163–42–0–16.30; G. E. Clements 16–0–233–43–0–14.56.

Bowling—M. A. Maurice 177.5–44–514–36–7/42–14.27; S. D. R. Lapthorn 118.4–23–451–25–5/9–18.04; A. M. Maurice 115.5–19–386–15–4/51–25/73.

KING'S SCHOOL, TYNEMOUTH   *Played 12: W 6, L 5, D 1. A 7*

Masters i/c: W. Ryan and P. J. Nicholson

The team beat Queen Elizabeth HS, Hexham, in the final of the Northumberland County Cup before leaving to tour Barbados. New Zealander Leighton Hammond averaged over 97, and both he and Marcus Turner hit undefeated centuries.

Batting—L. J. Hammond 5–2–293–103*–1–97.66; M. J. Turner 12–1–383–108*–1–34.81; C. L. Plummer 8–1–151–52*–0–21.57; R. Waller 9–0–164–41–0–18.22.

Bowling—No bowler took 15 wickets. The leading bowler was J. Wall 24–4–111–9–3/11–12.33.

KING'S SCHOOL, WORCESTER   *Played 21: W 10, L 3, D 8. A 3*

Master i/c: D. P. Iddon   Professional: A. A. Gillgrass

A successful side relied heavily on the captain, Daniel Cullen, for the bulk of its runs. He scored a record 1,165 at 72.81. Adam Phillips led the bowling with 48 dismissals, again a record, and received sound support from promising all-rounder Nicholas Dale-Lace.

Batting—*D. A. Cullen 22–6–1,165–140*–2–72.81; E. M. Oliver 8–2–292–62*–0–48.66; N. J. D. Dale-Lace 10–3–263–88*–0–37.57; N. O. S. Major 11–0–237–41–0–21.54; J. W. Robinson 11–1–178–52*–0–17.80.

Bowling—A. T. C. Phillips 275–58–827–48–6/29–17.22; N. J. D. Dale-Lace 207–40–651–31–5/37–21.00; D. J. Harris 190–29–739–27–4/51–27.37.

KINGSTON GRAMMAR SCHOOL   *Played 11: W 5, L 3, D 3. A 5*

Master i/c: M. Collier   Professional: C. Mutucumarana

Imaginative captaincy by Jody Smith and, later in the season, by his younger brother Ollie, meant only three games were drawn. The season's most encouraging aspect was the quality and vigour of the fielding.

Batting—C. Bolton 12–1–298–74–0–27.09; A. Temlett 12–2–222–47–0–22.20; *J. Smith 7–0–153–49–0–21.85; K. Kulendra 12–2–168–40–0–16.80; M. Burns 10–0–166–60–0–16.60.

Bowling—M. Burns 139–31–366–20–6/6–18.30; D. Sandy 98.4–27–283–15–4/12–18.86.

KINGSWOOD SCHOOL   *Played 5: W 0, L 4, D 1. A 6*

Master i/c: G. O. Opie

With more than half the fixtures lost to the appalling weather, a young side struggled to find any form. U. Warmann, the most successful player, leaves after four years in the first team.

Batting—No batsman scored 150 runs. The leading batsman was U. Warmann 4–1–84–52–0–28.00.

Bowling—No bowler took 15 wickets. The leading bowler was *N. Jones 40–4–139–6–3/28–23.16.

LANCING COLLEGE   *Played 16: W 10, L 2, D 4. A 2*

Master i/c: M. Bentley   Professional: R. Davies

Batting—G. Toft 9–4–276–57–0–55.20; G. Price 15–1–727–116–1–51.92; H. Campbell 14–1–484–133*–1–37.23; J. Wood 15–1–344–74–0–24.57; D. Foster 13–2–227–82–0–20.63; N. Wood 13–0–261–73–0–20.07; J. Taylor 14–1–171–46–0–13.15.

Bowling—H. Campbell 170–46–452–27–4/34–16.74; I. Higgins 115–27–323–17–3/24–19.00; G. Price 109.2–27–385–17–3/23–22.64.

LANGLEY PARK SCHOOL   *Played 8: W 3, L 4, D 1*

Master i/c: C. H. Williams

Batting—N. Buddell 6–1–168–80*–0–33.60.

Bowling—A. Ford 66–17–210–15–3/14–14.00.

LEEDS GRAMMAR SCHOOL   *Played 8: W 1, L 3, D 4. A 6*

Master i/c: R. Hill

Batting—A. R. Brown 8–0–151–63–0–18.87.

Bowling—A. R. Wood 110–22–345–18–5/52–19.16; S. D. Kershaw 116–30–333–15–4/32–22.20.

LEIGHTON PARK SCHOOL   *Played 6: W 2, L 2, D 2. A 4*

Master i/c: M. Simmons   Professional: G. Myburgh

Batting—*N. Head 6–2–158–88*–0–39.50; R. Sharma 6–1–173–54–0–34.60; A. Reece-Smith 6–1–151–50*–0–30.20.

Bowling—N. Head 85–18–166–18–8/17–9.22; R. Sharma 79–17–188–16–4/12–11.75; S. Close 86–16–206–15–5/33–13.73.

THE LEYS SCHOOL   *Played 13: W 1, L 9, D 3*

Master i/c: A. R. C. Batterham

Batting—D. Hoy 10–0–207–42–0–20.70; J. Dodkin 12–1–158–38–0–14.36.

Bowling—No bowler took 15 wickets. The leading bowler was J. Welch 64–15–217–14–3/24–15.50.

LIVERPOOL COLLEGE   *Played 10: W 1, L 4, D 4, T 1. A 6*

Master i/c: A. Fox   Professional: B. Mukherjee

Batting—A. Lewis 9–2–287–63–0–41.00; T. Maddison 9–0–156–34–0–17.33.

Bowling—J. Lyons 126.4–31–458–23–5/46–19.91.

LLANDOVERY COLLEGE   *Played 5: W 0, L 4, D 1. A 6*

Master i/c: T. G. Marks

With six matches abandoned and another severely disrupted by rain, the side searched in vain for form, and enthusiasm gradually waned. However, Wales Under-15 player Robert Coles showed great promise as a wicket-keeper/batsman, especially against MCC, when captain Emlyn Morton held the team together with a solid, undefeated 35.

Batting—No batsman scored 150 runs. The leading batsman was E. Morton 5–1–115–35*–0–28.75.

Bowling—No bowler took 15 wickets. The leading bowler was M. Shrivastava 40–7–175–10–6/39–17.50.

LORD WANDSWORTH COLLEGE   *Played 16: W 7, L 4, D 5. A 1*

Master i/c: M. C. Russell

The strength of a successful team was a well-balanced attack, led by captain Guy Hicks. Bowling off-spin, he captured a record 54 wickets and received admirable support from Adrian and Adam Askew, and from Ben Rotheram. William Faulkner, in his first year in the side, batted with maturity and played for England Under-15 against India.

Batting—*G. D. Hicks 15–2–431–106–1–33.15; W. T. Faulkner 12–1–297–73–0–27.00; G. W. Bayer 16–3–260–57–0–20.00; R. A. Black 12–0–226–42–0–18.83.

Bowling—G. D. Hicks 212.4–56–545–54–6/32–10.09; A. P. Askew 182.2–50–503–33–5/39–15.24; B. M. Rotheram 126.1–30–313–20–6/33–15.65.

LORD WILLIAMS'S SCHOOL   *Played 10: W 4, L 4, D 2*

Master i/c: J. E. Fulkes

Batting—*R. Eason 8–1–344–81*–0–49.14; E. Barnett 9–0–243–54–0–27.00; R. Joss 9–2–152–64–0–21.71; S. Lachlan 9–0–176–52–0–19.55.

Bowling—S. Lachlan 92–22–226–20–5/22–11.30.

LOUGHBOROUGH GRAMMAR SCHOOL   *Played 10: W 0, L 5, D 5. A 9*

Master i/c: J. S. Weitzel   Professional: H. T. Tunnicliffe

Batting—J. Carrington 9–1–264–110*–1–33.00; P. C. Stockdale 9–0–240–99–0–26.66; M. Alderson 11–2–213–58–0–23.66.

Bowling—M. P. Kavanagh 164–30–430–18–5/29–23.88.

MAGDALEN COLLEGE SCHOOL   *Played 18: W 10, L 2, D 6. A 3*

Master i/c: P. Askew

Ben Thompson led the side by example, scoring 1,014 runs and guiding his team to ten wins, both records. He played for Oxfordshire in the Minor Counties Championship and hit a century against Herefordshire. Slow left-armer Aaron Hirtenstein broke yet another record when he claimed 52 wickets at under 13.

Batting—*B. J. Thompson 18–3–1,014–139*–3–67.60; P. J. Robinson 19–3–565–74*–0–35.31; J. V. Ellis 16–0–278–46–0–17.37; A. L. Capek 14–2–181–45–0–15.08; P. S. Ellwood 16–0–216–102–1–13.50.

Bowling—A. A. Hirtenstein 262.2–79–644–52–7/36–12.38; B. J. Thompson 111.1–20–394–27–5/17–14.59; K-L. H. E. Noll 207–48–658–44–7/26–14.95; A. I. Robinson 83.2–12–303–16–3/37–18.93; B. B. Crompton 64.2–25–386–18–3/45–21.44.

MALVERN COLLEGE   *Played 15: W 5, L 5, D 5. A 4*

Master i/c: P. Goode   Professional: R. W. Tolchard

The decision to blood more younger players late in the term – after some mediocre performances – transformed the season. Four good wins resulted, the most remarkable occurring in the festival at Rugby. The hosts, needing another 31 off ten overs and with seven wickets standing, fell ten runs short. J. Kontarines took five for one, including a hat-trick, in an eight-ball spell.

Batting—A. Griffiths 15–1–361–67–0–25.78; J. Davis 13–2–273–83*–0–24.81; *R. Neale 13–1–282–76–0–23.50; J. Thompstone 13–1–240–69*–0–20.00; J. Baker 12–2–190–54*–0–19.00; J. Kontarines 12–0–174–35–0–14.50.

Bowling—J. Kontarines 141.4–30–411–25–5/27–16.44; R. Neale 113.1–18–410–19–4/74–21.57; D. Cullen-Jones 142.5–26–437–17–3/28–25.70.

MANCHESTER GRAMMAR SCHOOL   *Played 12: W 4, L 2, D 6. A 5*

Master i/c: D. Moss

After a stuttering start, the side improved, finishing with an impressive victory in a two-day match against Loughborough, and success in a six-a-side competition at Oxford, where they beat Wellington College in the final. Jonathan Lee captained the team with maturity and has scored over 3,000 runs in the first team. All-rounder Mark Leathley and Rana Malook formed a potent new-ball attack, and Nick Murrills bowled his leg-spin with great control. Phil Martin, bowling left-arm spin, took five wickets in each innings on his debut against Loughborough.

Batting—*J. R. M. Lee 10–2–453–118*–2–56.62; S. J. Kotecha 9–2–295–95–0–42.14; M. J. Leathley 7–0–214–97–0–30.57; M. B. Filson 10–1–262–57–0–29.11.

Bowling—N. P. Murrills 149.1–30–443–24–5/93–18.45; R. J. Malook 146.3–33–410–22–5/74–18.63; M. J. Leathley 173.4–37–484–24–6/71–20.16.

MARLBOROUGH COLLEGE   *Played 10: W 1, L 2, D 7. A 6*

Master i/c: N. E. Briers   Professional: R. M. Ratcliffe

Batting—J. F. Caldwell 10–3–166–55*–0–23.71; M. A. L. Bickford 9–2–159–35–0–22.71; *T. E. F. Burne 11–1–225–66*–0–22.50; A. J. R. Bird 10–0–195–54–0–19.50; R. A. E. Stacey 11–0–214–50–0–19.45; M. P. L. Bush 11–1–163–61–0–16.30.

Bowling—T. E. F. Burne 120.2–36–273–26–4/17–10.50; A. J. R. Bird 115.4–19–360–18–5/51–20.00.

MERCHANT TAYLORS' SCHOOL, CROSBY   *Played 15: W 2, L 5, D 8. A 5*

Master i/c: Rev. D. A. Smith   Professional: B. C. Strang

Batting—*C. J. Cheetham 14–2–627–106*–2–52.25; P. A. O'Leary 14–2–467–123*–1–38.91; M. R. Thomas 12–1–228–50*–0–20.72; A. J. Crotty 15–1–200–45–0–14.28.

Bowling—M. S. Cowdy 76–16–249–16–5/32–15.56; J. F. Wildman 114–16–544–22–5/73–24.72.

MERCHANT TAYLORS' SCHOOL, NORTHWOOD   *Played 19: W 7, L 2, D 10*

Master i/c: C. R. Evans-Evans   Professional: H. C. Latchman

Batting—S. G. James 7–5–275–62–0–137.50; A. S. J. Sharland 17–3–759–119–1–54.21; J. Fienberg 17–5–551–112*–1–45.91; S. Noach 12–4–272–82*–0–34.00; *J. G. Wyand 18–1–576–117–1–33.88; S. A. S. Ali 13–4–190–46–0–21.11.

Bowling—P. C. T. Radley 229–43–630–34–6/52–18.52; A. S. J. Sharland 205.4–39–568–30–4/40–18.93.

MERCHISTON CASTLE SCHOOL   *Played 16: W 7, L 2, D 7. A 2*

Master i/c: C. W. Swan   Professional: B. Russell

Unlike 1997, the weather afflicted mid-week practice rather than match days, and a useful side remained undefeated by schools. On a successful tour, King's, Gloucester, and Hereford Cathedral School were both beaten.

Batting—B. T. McKerchar 16–5–326–82–0–29.63; J. A. C. Easton 13–2–301–101–1–27.36; R. D. Allan 13–0–251–49–0–19.30; *M. A. Lawson 17–2–266–51–0–17.73; E. R. Thomson 13–1–201–55–0–16.75.

Bowling—A. J. Lunn 63–9–237–17–4/16–13.94; B. T. McKerchar 185–49–504–34–7/33–14.82; B. J. Yellowlees 242–74–513–33–3/9–15.54; D. P. Barry 140–27–427–18–3/17–23.72.

MILLFIELD SCHOOL   *Played 18: W 7, L 7, D 4. A 4*

Master i/c: R. M. Ellison   Professional: M. R. Davis

In the three-day match against Maritzburg College, Arul Suppiah had match figures of 71–27–131–11.

Batting—W. J. Durston 16–0–592–105–1–37.00; J. M. Macey 18–0–522–80–0–29.00; *J. A. L. Parker 18–4–388–85*–0–27.71; A. V. Suppiah 12–2–258–82–0–25.80; C. J. Hellings 15–2–261–63–0–20.07; T. O. Dann 14–2–224–52–0–18.66; G. J. Cosker 15–0–224–52–0–14.93.

Bowling—A. V. Suppiah 194–56–420–29–6/58–14.48; W. J. Durston 160.3–40–449–29–4/11–15.48; D. J. Standfield 134.1–27–380–23–4/20–16.52; G. E. Morris 113–23–291–16–3/13–18.18; M. J. Webb 156.4–29–441–18–3/54–24.50.

MILL HILL SCHOOL   *Played 11: W 2, L 2, D 7. A 4*

Master i/c: P. H. Edwards   Professional: I. C. J. Hutchinson

Batting—J. Le Fort 11–1–528–121*–3–52.80; S. Bunyard 11–0–374–64–0–34.00; M. Bhimjiyani 11–0–312–72–0–28.36; T. Kalber 11–1–277–56–0–27.70.

Bowling—D. Lewis 154–30–378–25–5/38–15.12; S. Bunyard 94–11–288–18–3/19–16.00; R. Lakhani 132–19–352–20–4/31–17.60; M. Bhimjiyani 75–8–281–15–5/23–18.73.

MILTON ABBEY SCHOOL   *Played 9: W 5, L 1, D 3. A 5*

Master i/c: P. W. Wood

Batting—B. A. A. Clay 9–3–399–137*–1–66.50; T. A. A. Robertson 8–2–151–45–0–25.16.

Bowling—T. A. A. Robertson 105.1–17–343–23–6/26–14.91; J. M. C. Underwood 85–22–247–16–5/56–15.43.

MONMOUTH SCHOOL   *Played 14: W 4, L 4, D 6. A 4*

Master i/c: A. Jones   Professional: G. I. Burgess

In an otherwise moderate season, the Castle Festival was won outright, with victories over Berkhamsted, Framlingham and Kimbolton.

Batting—G. Curtis 13–5–313–63*–0–39.12; N. Jorgenson 11–2–222–54*–0–24.66; A. Fury 15–0–347–100–1–23.13; T. M. Allen 15–0–298–59–0–19.86; A. Mohindru 12–0–197–70–0–16.41.

Bowling—G. Curtis 145–27–379–16–4/25–23.68.

NEWCASTLE-UNDER-LYME SCHOOL   *Played 12: W 3, L 5, D 4. A 3*

Master i/c: S. A. Robson   Professional: M. J. R. Rindel

Fifteen-year-old John James, who scored a century against Bishop Vasey's, was one of four consistent batsmen, but his left-arm spin received little support from the seam bowlers.

Batting—J. W. Allchin 12–0–381–87–0–31.75; V. V. S. Handley 11–3–253–67*–0–31.62; *J. Rodgers 12–4–231–40*–0–28.88; J. W. James 12–0–346–109–1–28.83.

Bowling—J. W. James 118–21–441–24–5/32–18.37; G. E. Wilson 93.2–12–340–18–3/6–18.88.

NOTTINGHAM HIGH SCHOOL   *Played 13: W 3, L 7, D 3. A 1*

Master i/c: J. Lamb   Professional: K. E. Cooper

Batting—G. J. Middleton 10–2–243–69*–0–30.37; T. E. Shacklock 12–2–291–101–1–29.10; *J. E. Hartley 13–2–301–63–0–27.36; R. L. Pilgrim 12–0–325–74–0–27.08; E. I. Storr 13–0–264–55–0–20.30.

Bowling—G. J. Middleton 100.2–18–330–18–4/47–18.33; R. Kitching 165.1–27–618–24–7/65–25.75.

OAKHAM SCHOOL   *Played 15: W 3, L 9, D 3. A 5*

Master i/c: J. Wills   Professional: D. S. Steele

Towards the end of the season, the side was strengthened when several younger players were drafted into the team. Most impressive was David Jackson, who comfortably headed the batting averages, but the bowling remained disappointingly weak. The team entered a six-a-side tournament at St Edward's, Oxford, for the first time.

Batting—D. N. Jackson 8–3–240–76–0–48.00; A. R. Kirk 13–4–276–66*–0–30.66; N. J. Ferraby 10–3–203–71*–0–29.00; T. W. Cassady 9–0–206–79–0–22.88; *A. J. Ward 10–0–226–66–0–22.60; H. Romans 15–0–308–43–0–20.53; C. J. Braddock 13–3–167–41*–0–16.70; B. J. Wheeler 12–0–195–68–0–16.25.

Bowling—No bowler took 15 wickets. The leading bowler was A. R. Kirk 133–17–511–12–3/29–42.58.

THE ORATORY SCHOOL   *Played 11: W 4, L 3, D 4. A 5*

Master i/c: P. L. Tomlinson   Professional: J. B. K. Howell

Batting—D. E. Pike 10–2–273–64*–0–34.12; T. C. Wigley 10–1–272–99–0–30.22; M. I. Wight 10–2–241–52–0–30.12; W. J. Worsdell 10–2–203–56*–0–25.37; S. J. Bird 10–0–245–63–0–24.50; A. P. Orchard 10–1–176–47–0–19.55.

Bowling—S. R. J. Wilson 84–16–326–23–5/42–14.17; M. I. Wight 70–8–272–18–4/30–15.11; D. E. Pike 84–6–365–21–4/17–17.38; T. C. Wigley 56–8–306–17–3/36–18.00; S. J. Bird 85–14–360–18–3/28–20.00.

OUNDLE SCHOOL   *Played 19: W 11, L 2, D 6. A 4*

Master i/c: J. R. Wake   Professional: T. Howorth

The side remained unbeaten by English schools – recording 11 victories overall – thanks to a well-balanced attack and the positive approach of captain and all-rounder William Jefferson. He headed both averages, and was later selected for the ECB Schools Under-19 trials at Shenley. Leading wicket-taker Jonathan Outar took 42 wickets with his chinamen, and was selected for ESCA Midlands and, together with his brother, David, for HMC Under-15 trials.

Batting—W. I. Jefferson 16–3–817–135–2–62.84; S. Lowe 15–5–582–124*–2–58.20; M. Dobson 15–5–392–67–0–39.20; M. Singleton 12–3–244–62–0–27.11; G. Anderson 11–1–226–66–0–22.60.

Bowling—W. I. Jefferson 94.3–18–267–21–4/28–12.71; M. Dobson 152.4–29–418–31–5/19–13.48; J. Outar 178–34–569–42–7/13–13.54; O. Venables 123–39–278–20–5/13–13.90; D. Outar 135–34–387–19–4/4–20.36.

THE PERSE SCHOOL   *Played 14: W 6, L 3, D 5. A 1*

Master i/c: M. A. Judson   Professional: D. C. Collard

Alexis Kay, bowling a mixture of chinamen and googlies, took a hat-trick as The Perse beat Hills Road SFC, Cambridge, in the final of the Cambridgeshire Under-19 Cup.

Batting—C. R. B. Walker 14–3–334–59*–0–30.36; M. G. Moffat 14–3–318–40*–0–28.90; M. D. Mayer 13–0–333–56–0–25.61.

Bowling—J. A. Kay 155.4–27–449–35–5/23–12.82; D. A. Hassall 128.4–15–425–32–5/43–13.28; C. R. B. Walker 149.1–30–406–27–4/25–15.03.

PLYMOUTH COLLEGE   *Played 8: W 1, L 1, D 6. A 9*

Master i/c: T. J. Stevens

The atrocious weather played havoc with the season; nine matches were completely washed out.

Batting—A. Egford 5–0–165–70–0–33.00; *S. Hards 8–1–204–55–0–29.14.

Bowling—No bowler took 15 wickets. The leading bowler was W. Andrews 58–16–185–11–3/22–16.81.

POCKLINGTON SCHOOL   *Played 18: W 6, L 6, D 6. A 3*

Master i/c: R. Smith

Batting—*P. R. Mouncey 17–5–824–121*–3–68.66; R. J. R. Poskitt 15–1–616–125–1–44.00; T. H. S. Hopper 10–3–158–46–0–22.57; B. E. Williams 15–1–307–91–0–21.92; E. D. Townend 15–0–224–54–0–14.93.

Bowling—P. R. Mouncey 236.4–48–692–42–6/34–16.47; E. P. J. M. Heppel 217.2–29–782–39–7/94–20.05; A. N. Mitchell 175.5–35–492–17–3/49–28.94.

PORTSMOUTH GRAMMAR SCHOOL   *Played 17: W 5, L 5, D 7. A 1*

Master i/c: G. D. Payne   Professional: R. J. Parks

Batting—*B. R. Pennells 16–1–529–69–0–35.26; J. B. Grady 11–0–325–89–0–29.54; S. M. Hall 17–4–345–76–0–26.53; S. A. Turner 16–0–237–55–0–14.81; D. S. Fairley 15–0–181–50–0–12.06.

Bowling—A. C. Saunders 74–8–285–21–6/34–13.57; J. H. Stedman 145.5–23–500–23–3/10–21.73; J. J. Owen 159.2–36–463–19–4/40–24.36; S. M. Hall 109.1–21–427–16–3/27–26.68.

PRIOR PARK COLLEGE   *Played 11: W 6, L 3, D 2. A 5*

Master i/c: D. R. Holland   Professional: R. J. Chambers

Batting—A. Owen 11–3–444–91–0–55.50; *P. O'Dea 8–0–283–92–0–35.37; N. Potter 10–3–158–45–0–22.57.

Bowling—E. Gooding 85–21–200–21–4/7–9.52; A. Owen 83–19–250–18–4/11–13.88; D. Gadsden 95–22–289–16–3/36–18.06.

QUEEN ELIZABETH GS, WAKEFIELD   *Played 10: W 4, L 4, D 2. A 4*

Master i/c: T. Barker   Professional: C. Jackson

The highlight of an average season was a record opening partnership of 220 by Richard Sykes and Dominic Castle against William Hulme GS. Both hit undefeated centuries in a comprehensive win. Against Leeds GS, captain Adam Kelly set another record by taking four wickets in four balls.

Batting—D. Castle 8–2–301–100*–1–50.16; R. Sykes 10–1–450–100*–1–50.00; S. Kelly 9–1–226–74–0–28.25; *A. Kelly 8–0–206–46–0–25.75.

Bowling—A. Kelly 81.4–15–272–19–6/18–14.31; R. Sykes 81–16–265–15–6/34–17.66.

QUEEN ELIZABETH'S HOSPITAL, BRISTOL   *Played 10: W 4, L 2, D 4. A 4*

Master i/c: P. Joslin

Batting—*G. P. Parker-Jones 11–2–350–104*–1–38.88; W. R. Humphreys 11–0–265–51–0–24.09; E. Jones 11–1–205–58–0–20.50.

Bowling—E. Jones 102.3–15–324–23–4/37–14.08.

QUEEN'S COLLEGE, TAUNTON   *Played 13: W 8, L 4, D 1*

Master i/c: A. S. Free

A young side played with maturity, though the batting relied heavily on openers Oliver Bailey and Stephen Butt. Sixteen-year-old Matthew Gitsham, who played for Somerset Second Eleven, and William Bates often spun the side into winning positions.

Batting—O. J. Bailey 13–1–574–100*–1–47.83; S. A. Butt 10–1–368–82*–0–40.88; M. T. Gitsham 11–1–255–81–0–25.50; B. P. Turner 10–1–166–34–0–18.44; C. J. Butt 11–2–154–82*–0–17.11.

Bowling—I. S. R. Henry 69–14–206–15–4/17–13.73; M. T. Gitsham 105–24–330–24–4/14–13.75.

RADLEY COLLEGE   *Played 14: W 7, L 0, D 7. A 2*

Master i/c: W. J. Wesson   Professionals: A. G. Robinson and A. R. Wagner

In the last-ball victory over Harrow, Jamie Dalrymple and Charlie van der Gucht put on 123 for the fourth wicket to rescue the team from 21 for three. Dalrymple and Ollie Broom hit three separate century opening partnerships, including 239 against Oxfordshire Under-19.

Batting—J. W. M. Dalrymple 14–2–688–146–3–57.33; O. M. Broom 14–1–624–115–1–48.00; *C. G. van der Gucht 12–2–310–70–0–31.00; O. C. A. Ross 12–2–238–52–0–23.80.

Bowling—O. H. Langton 86.3–22–241–16–3/10–15.06; S. J. Andrews 130.3–31–340– 20–3/17–17.00; C. G. van der Gucht 195.5–64–427–23–4/36–18.56.

RATCLIFFE COLLEGE   *Played 14: W 3, L 6, D 5. A 1*

Master i/c: R. Hughes   Professional: C. Henderson

Batting—B. T. Clarke 11–1–288–71*–0–28.80; J. Kettle 11–1–202–63*–0–20.20; D. J. Howkins 12–0–160–61–0–13.33.

Bowling—R. Wild 78.3–11–298–15–5/19–19.86.

READING SCHOOL   *Played 12: W 2, L 2, D 8*

Masters i/c: R. F. Perkins and J. E. Bonneywell

Batting—M. J. Leary 9–1–463–113–1–57.87; A. S. Bindra 9–2–323–100*–1–46.14; D. R. Leary 11–1–189–48–0–18.90.

Bowling—R. J. Warren 114.2–15–390–15–3/19–26.00.

REIGATE GRAMMAR SCHOOL   *Played 20: W 4, L 8, D 8. A 3*

Master i/c: D. C. R. Jones   Professional: H. Newton

An experienced side never quite recovered from losing their first four games. The batting remained fragile and only seamer Andrew Grave consistently made the most of conditions. But opener Matthew Ross batted soundly and took five wickets against Royal GS, Colchester, with his off-spin, while Daniel Mendis, nephew of Gehan Mendis of Sussex and Lancashire, averaged 40 and took 28 with his left-arm spin; it was enough to gain him selection for Surrey Under-16.

Batting—D. C. Mendis 15–5–400–67*–0–40.00; S. A. Knight 11–3–186–44*–0–23.25; M. P. Ross 19–0–418–69–0–22.00; J. D. Hylton 14–5–185–53–0–20.55; O. J. Jago 18–3–287–106–1–19.13; M. N. Cooper 14–1–248–52*–0–19.07; *I. N. Bezodis 19–1–302–88–0–16.77.

Bowling—S. A. Knight 123.2–44–261–16–5/11–16.31; A. J. Grave 223–57–633–38–5/26–16.65; D. C. Mendis 160.5–23–551–28–4/38–19.67; J. A. R. Brickley 106.5–18–358–17–5/80–21.05; M. P. Ross 117.4–11–525–19–5/64–27.63.

RENDCOMB COLLEGE   *Played 11: W 3, L 3, D 5*

Master i/c: B. L. North

Batting—H. Davies 12–5–481–74*–0–68.71; S. Maylott 13–1–295–59–0–24.58; *A. Taylor 12–2–228–44*–0–22.80; C. Scarth 13–1–242–41–0–20.16; W. Witchell 13–1–218–45–0–18.16.

Bowling—A. Taylor 84–7–265–20–5/22–13.25; N. Stanfield 74.1–10–304–18–4/2–16.88; H. Davies 133.1–8–364–18–4/36–20.22.

REPTON SCHOOL   *Played 10: W 2, L 4, D 4. A 6*

Master i/c: P. Price   Professional: M. K. Kettle

Batting—J. L. Alsop 6–0–274–78–0–45.66; W. T. Wood 10–1–202–72–0–22.44; D. A. Exley 9–0–168–73–0–18.66; A. J. Currie 10–0–186–39–0–18.60.

Bowling—K. J. P. Hall 103.4–20–345–16–5/24–21.56; C. H. M. Standage 83.2–14–325– 15–4/40–21.66.

RICHARD HUISH COLLEGE   *Played 8: W 6, L 2, D 0*

Master i/c: J. W. Davies

Opening batsmen P. Bell and D. Brice performed consistently, and contributed to victories over KES, Totnes, and Britannia Royal Naval College, Dartmouth.

Batting—P. Bell 6–1–169–69–0–33.80; D. Brice 8–1–211–90–0–30.14.

Bowling—No bowler took 15 wickets. The leading bowler was W. Phelps 29–6–84–7–4/19–12.00.

ROSSALL SCHOOL   *Played 16: W 2, L 10, D 4*

Master i/c: A. D. Todd   Professional: K. Higgs

Batting—J. I. Souter 16–1–253–50–0–16.86.

Bowling—G. Dinsdale 182–50–495–27–5/38–18.33; O. J. Barlow 144–15–586–20–4/44–29.30.

THE ROYAL GRAMMAR SCHOOL, COLCHESTER   *Played 22: W 9, L 7, D 6. A 4*

Master i/c: R. L. Bayes

An excellent all-round display from Salman Mohammed, son of the former Pakistan batsman, Sadiq, helped bring about a season of positive cricket and encouraging results. At an enjoyable Royal GS festival, the team defeated both Worcester and Guildford; Mark Gittins also took a hat-trick against the hosts, High Wycombe. Paul Hazell, in his final match for the first team, scored two hundreds in the two-day game against the Old Boys.

Batting—P. B. Hazell 17–3–532–134–2–38.00; S. Mohammed 21–2–697–81–0–36.68; M. Tyler 22–1–433–64–0–20.61; *C. W. Norfolk 20–2–358–53*–0–19.88; M. R. Perrin 18–0–317–96–0–17.61; M. R. Cranley 16–5–179–37–0–16.27; C. H. Dingley 19–3–256–53–0–16.00; M. J. E. Gittins 21–1–314–68*–0–15.70.

Bowling—S. Mohammed 191.5–42–624–29–5/36–21.51; M. Tyler 245–54–848–38–5/34–22.31; M. J. E. Gittins 187.5–27–689–30–4/32–22.96; C. W. Norfolk 128.5–10–510–15–3/31–34.00.

THE ROYAL GRAMMAR SCHOOL, GUILDFORD   *Played 18: W 10, L 5, D 3. A 2*

Master i/c: S. B. R. Shore   Professional: M. A. Lynch

Stuart Peel joined elder brother Duncan in the first team and, in only his fourth innings, scored an unbeaten century against Royal GS, High Wycombe. Earlier in the season, left-arm seamer Tim John took a hat-trick of lbws against John Fisher School, dismissing the first three batsmen.

Batting—S. P. Peel 4–1–171–102*–1–57.00; C. D. Coleman 16–4–372–73–0–31.00; T. W. Hughes 11–4–211–65*–0–30.14; *J. M. Hartfield 18–1–418–70–0–24.58; D. C. Reep 10–2–195–50–0–24.37; D. E. Peel 8–1–165–59–0–23.57; M. C. Roberts 17–4–299–102*–1–23.00; D. J. Williams 13–0–166–38–0–12.76.

Bowling—T. P. A. John 107.1–28–245–19–3/14–12.89; M. C. Roberts 167–34–499–30–5/19–16.63; A. Tucker 96–13–288–15–2/11–19.20; R. A. Bland 167.5–22–584–28–6/62–20.85.

THE ROYAL GRAMMAR SCHOOL, HIGH WYCOMBE   *Played 14: W 4, L 3, D 7. A 2*

Master i/c: P. R. Miles

Batting—A. Melrose 11–0–453–94–0–41.18; S. Crompton 13–0–363–58–0–27.92; A. Shaw 15–0–416–93–0–27.73; C. Dark 13–0–314–73–0–24.15; M. Honeyben 15–1–229–57–0–16.35; S. Rolfs 14–1–182–34–0–14.00.

Bowling—*D. Grant 204–46–642–27–4/30–23.77.

THE ROYAL GRAMMAR SCHOOL, NEWCASTLE   *Played 16: W 10, L 5, D 1. A 1*

Master i/c: D. W. Smith   Professional: C. Craven

Moderate early form gave way to a series of good wins at the Royal GS festival. Fifteen-year-old Nicky Peng again topped the batting, going on to represent England Under-15 and Under-18.

Batting—N. Peng 12–3–416–82*–0–46.22; M. J. Robinson 15–1–329–78–0–23.50; I. D. Nairn 16–0–365–70–0–22.81; J. F. Park 13–1–167–50–0–13.91.

Bowling—W. F. Thompson 66–15–183–15–4/9–12.20; A. Srivastava 72–15–260–21–5/13–12.38; J. M. Gill 130–25–359–21–5/23–17.09; J. W. M. Harte 127.3–23–329–16–4/16–20.56.

THE ROYAL GRAMMAR SCHOOL, WORCESTER   *Played 22: W 8, L 10, D 4. A 3*

Master i/c: B. M. Rees   Professional: F. P. Watson

With his 158 against Pate's GS, captain Nick Cockrell hit the highest-ever innings for the school, breaking a record that had stood since 1910.

Batting—*N. S. A. Cockrell 20–0–615–158–1–30.75; D. L. Andrews 21–2–551–95–0–29.00; L. S. Paton 19–5–365–46*–0–26.07; P. F. Beard 19–4–353–54–0–23.53; R. M. Wilkinson 15–1–308–68–0–22.00; J. Khalid 17–6–170–29–0–15.45.

Bowling—A. Riaz 140.3–15–495–24–5/20–20.62; R. Dovaston 143.3–9–540–25–4/38–21.60; J. S. Smith 114.4–18–363–16–7/24–22.68; J. Khalid 248.2–43–742–28–5/34–26.50; J. A. Hayden 126.5–17–402–15–3/4–26.80.

RUGBY SCHOOL   *Played 14: W 2, L 3, D 9. A 3*

Master i/c: P. J. Rosser   Professional: L. Tennant

Batting—J. Brewer 12–1–304–92–0–27.63; J. C. E. Coulson 14–2–321–77*–0–26.75; P. D. Jones 14–1–272–75–0–20.92; *B. D. R. Maclehose 15–6–183–65*–0–20.33; C. B. Clark 14–1–248–52–0–19.07; N. G. Wilkinson 14–1–247–66*–0–19.00; M. C. Ewer 14–0–243–33–0–17.35.

Bowling—S. W. M. Wolukau-Wanambwa 118.5–18–340–17–4/24–20.00; T. E. M. Jarvis 144.3–25–540–21–4/61–25.71; P. D. Jones 171–40–573–16–4/17–35.81.

RYDAL SCHOOL   *Played 10: W 4, L 3, D 3*

Master i/c: M. T. Leach

The match against King's, Chester, produced two hat-tricks. For Rydal, Gareth van Heerden took the first, all bowled, before Edward Mason struck back for the opposition.

Batting—P. Patel 10–2–373–93–0–46.62; J. Griffiths 10–0–310–70–0–31.00; S. Watkins 8–1–180–40*–0–25.71.

Bowling—G. van Heerden 105.5–18–352–20–6/40–17.60.

RYDE SCHOOL   *Played 11: W 6, L 3, D 2*

Master i/c: M. E. Mairis

A good season included fixtures against visiting South African teams from Cathcart College and Vredenburg High. For two matches the side contained three members of the Baker family, younger brother Daniel joining regulars Conrad and Alex.

Batting—P. Lewis 9–3–332–64*–0–55.33; O. Scadgell 7–3–210–102*–1–52.50; C. Baker 11–0–263–40–0–23.90; J. Down 12–2–166–45–0–16.60.

Bowling—C. Baker 75–6–344–18–5/49–19.11.

ST ALBANS SCHOOL   *Played 15: W 4, L 6, D 5. A 4*

Master i/c: C. C. Hudson   Professional: S. Tyson

The captain, Richard Little, suffered an accident-prone season but still managed to head the batting averages. In a pre-season net he dislocated his knee and missed the early matches; against MCC, he got as far as the toss, but never made it back to the pavilion. Returning from the middle, he misfielded a ball hit by a team-mate and fractured his thumb in three places. He spent the rest of the day in hospital.

Batting—*R. J. Little 8–2–233–70*–0–38.83; M. Warren 13–2–385–87–0–35.00; R. Scase 13–5–218–56*–0–27.25; A. Gocoldas 14–0–182–50–0–13.00.

Bowling—A. Khan 112.1–19–441–25–6/46–17.64; K. O'Reilly 68.1–6–325–15–4/16–21.66.

ST DUNSTAN'S COLLEGE   *Played 11: W 3, L 2, D 6. A 1*

Masters i/c: R. W. Lea and J. Thomas

Batting—B. R. Postma 11–3–449–103*–1–56.12; *R. M. J. Clark 11–2–351–82–0–39.00; P. J. Brightman 10–1–312–96–0–34.66.

Bowling—T. S. Cole 131–24–462–17–3/62–27.17.

ST EDMUND'S COLLEGE, WARE   *Played 11: W 1, L 7, D 3. A 4*

Master i/c: J. D. T. Faithfull

In a generally disappointing season, Paul Adshead, bowling a mixture of off-spin and leg-cutters, had the remarkable figures of 8.4–4–6–7 against adult side ICL.

Batting—J. Norris 11–0–390–116–1–35.45; *P. Adshead 12–0–224–60–0–18.66.

Bowling—P. Adshead 93.4–19–314–23–7/6–13.65; A. Dowling 129.2–17–419–20–4/16–20.95.

ST EDMUND'S SCHOOL, CANTERBURY   *Played 12: W 4, L 4, D 4. A 4*

Master i/c: M. C. Dobson

The side improved steadily during the season, and leading run-scorer Andrew Craig gained valuable support from newcomers Marc Wilkins and Glen Shepherd. The captain, Alex Pitchford, led the attack tirelessly, while Gulam Haji, bowling off-spin and leg-breaks from the front of the hand, was outstanding.

Batting—A. Craig 11–3–310–87*–0–38.75; M. Wilkins 11–3–276–82*–0–34.50; G. Shepherd 11–0–259–41–0–23.54; J. Tinto 10–1–184–55–0–20.44.

Bowling—G. Haji 121–22–378–23–5/43–16.43; *A. Pitchford 117.3–19–448–21–5/38–21.33.

ST EDWARD'S SCHOOL, OXFORD   *Played 10: W 1, L 0, D 9. A 3*

Masters i/c: J. Rae and D. Drake-Brockman   Professional: J. M. Mills

Batting—T. P. Sutton 10–0–374–126–1–37.40; O. D. Martin 10–0–219–62–0–21.90; K. R. J. Bingham 8–0–165–55–0–20.62; M. P. Wingfield Digby 9–0–165–52–0–18.33.

Bowling—N. A. Davey 118–28–365–16–4/30–22.81.

ST GEORGE'S COLLEGE, WEYBRIDGE   *Played 14: W 2, L 6, D 6. A 2*

Master i/c: D. G. Ottley

Batting—A. O'Sullivan 12–3–250–50*–0–27.77; J. Tindall 7–0–172–81–0–24.57; S. Roche 12–0–273–48–0–22.75; J. McInroy 14–0–303–83–0–21.64; O. French 13–0–209–36–0–16.07; T. Frost 10–0–150–37–0–15.00; C. Neill 11–0–162–36–0–14.72.

Bowling—T. Frost 100.4–32–246–15–3/25–16.40; J. Knox 215.2–50–729–32–9/19–22.78; A. Wensley 139–33–464–18–4/68–25.77.

ST JOHN'S SCHOOL, LEATHERHEAD — *Played 15: W 5, L 2, D 8. A·2*

Master i/c: A. B. Gale

All-rounder Joe Porter had a fine season, comfortably heading the batting averages and finishing joint-top wicket-taker with fellow all-rounder Jaycee Smit. Dependable batsman Ben Hudson also had a good season.

Batting—*J. J. Porter 13–6–618–149*–1–88.28; L. R. S. Down 10–6–161–52*–0–40.25; J. C. Smit 14–2–302–63–0–25.16; B. T. Hudson 14–1–300–46–0–23.07; S. J. Fletcher 10–0–159–48–0–15.90; K. Homma 11–0–151–33–0–13.72.

Bowling—J. C. Smit 123.2–16–417–28–6/15–14.89; J. J. Porter 156.2–24–479–28–5/59–17.10.

ST JOSEPH'S COLLEGE, IPSWICH — *Played 15: W 4, L 7, D 4. A 2*

Master i/c: M. Davey

Professional: K. Brooks

Batting—*C. Townrow 16–3–485–110–1–37.30; T. Green 16–3–455–81–0–35.00; M. Minehan 15–5–338–80*–0–33.80; D. Warren 14–4–242–92–0–24.20; A. Mallows 12–2–194–34–0–19.40.

Bowling—J. Westley 100–26–281–24–7/34–11.70; T. Loomes 84.4–9–306–16–4/27–19.12; A. Mallows 124.5–20–425–20–3/15–21.25; N. Jenkins 171.2–12–727–31–6/84–23.45.

ST PAUL'S SCHOOL — *Played 13: W 6, L 2, D 5. A 4*

Master i/c: G. Hughes

Professional: M. Heath

A. R. Duncan established post-war records with an aggregate of 711 runs, average of 88.87, and total of four centuries. He had several effective partnerships with E. G. R. Corner, including a stand of 244 against St Dunstan's.

Batting—A. R. Duncan 12–4–711–122–4–88.87; E. G. R. Corner 11–4–455–120*–2–65.00; A. C. F. Howard 8–3–254–94–0–50.80.

Bowling—S. Kanagathurai 120.4–31–312–26–5/34–12.00; *S. de Villier 77.2–18–239–15–5/25–15.93; C. B. Bennett 122–37–366–16–4/44–22.87.

ST PETER'S SCHOOL, YORK — *Played 22: W 8, L 3, D 11*

Master i/c: D. Kirby

Professional: K. F. Mohan

The captain, Nick Kay, became the first student at St Peter's to score over 1,000 runs in a season. His total of 1,076 included an undefeated 200, from just 154 balls, against Giggleswick, another school record.

Batting—*N. J. C. Kay 23–5–1,076–200*–1–59.77; C. J. Ellerbeck 22–3–445–66*–0–23.42; J. P. Hockin 19–2–350–56*–0–20.58; A. T. Main 17–5–212–30*–0–17.66; J. P. G. Dougherty 20–2–243–46–0–13.50; E. D. Sykes 17–3–164–29–0–11.71.

Bowling—J. P. G. Dougherty 223–62–638–43–6/17–14.83; C. J. Ellerbeck 189–50–552–30–4/13–18.40; G. Mackfall 195–72–470–25–6/40–18.80; M. C. Sigsworth 114.3–20–341–16–4/67–21.31; T. T. Bainbridge 117.3–27–441–16–3/72–27.56.

SEDBERGH SCHOOL — *Played 15: W 3, L 6, D 6. A 2*

Master i/c: N. A. Rollings

Professional: R. E. Veenstra

At the end of a frustrating season in which no batsman was able to dominate in difficult conditions, the side found consolation in an unbeaten tour to the West Indies where they gained satisfying victories over Antigua Under-18 and St Lucia Under-18.

Batting—S. T. Cross 9–2–177–36–0–25.28; R. J. Leather 15–2–302–58–0–23.23; M. M. Wilson 13–1–234–86–0–19.50; M. Blache-Fraser 12–1–161–39–0–14.63; C. R. Winney 14–2–164–36*–0–13.66; M. R. Dinsdale 14–1–176–33–0–13.53.

Bowling—B. M. Wilson 124.4–41–229–29–7/19–7.89; M. Blache-Fraser 150–39–331–24–4/23–13.79; J. C. Hart 118–35–331–22–4/17–15.04; *P. D. Thompson 216.3–60–460–30–5/15–15.33.

SEVENOAKS SCHOOL   *Played 17: W 5, L 2, D 10. A 2*

Master i/c: I. J. B. Walker

Batting—E. W. Grant 14–1–566–88–0–43.53; S. W. Shirreff 14–4–315–82*–0–31.50; I. J. Jenkins 16–1–468–80–0–31.20; C. P. R. Fletcher 13–4–273–57*–0–30.33; *M. A. Soulsby 16–3–286–65*–0–22.00.

Bowling—C. P. R. Fletcher 110.4–34–389–24–5/36–16.20; A. J. G. Miles 133.3–39–322–17–5/39–18.94; I. J. Jenkins 110–26–326–17–3/18–19.17; A. M. Gill 94.5–15–357–18–3/11–19.83.

SHEBBEAR COLLEGE   *Played 11: W 3, L 4, D 3, T 1. A 3*

Master i/c: A. Bryan

Bad weather and a series of injuries to key players limited the success of a promising side, though there were excellent wins against Grenville College and the Old Shebbeareans.

Batting—R. Knapman 7–2–246–78–0–49.20; S. Heal 10–3–275–74*–0–39.28; *R. Bryan 9–2–252–60*–0–36.00.

Bowling—N. Giddy 98–15–321–19–6/44–16.89.

SHERBORNE SCHOOL   *Played 12: W 7, L 3, D 2. A 3*

Master i/c: M. D. Nurton

Batting—J. Adams 13–0–372–117–1–28.61; D. Reece-Smith 13–3–285–53*–0–28.50; M. Shearer 13–0–295–80–0–22.69; T. Fegen 10–1–189–77–0–21.00; N. Chuter 13–0–259–92–0–19.92.

Bowling—P. Harris 82–14–273–20–3/53–13.65; D. Reece-Smith 155.2–36–374–24–4/49–15.58; H. Whipp 124–24–348–19–4/20–18.31; J. Adams 104.5–18–305–16–5/10–19.06.

SHREWSBURY SCHOOL   *Played 15: W 9, L 3, D 3. A 1*

Master i/c: M. J. Lascelles   Professional: A. P. Pridgeon

Batting—*R. G. Hillman 16–2–555–108*–1–39.64; S. T. Corbett 16–5–360–62*–0–32.72; B. J. N. Chapman 15–1–352–84–0–25.14; C. H. C. Marlow 14–0–296–106–1–21.14; A. S. Umpleby 14–2–237–46–0–19.75.

Bowling—A. S. Umpleby 153.4–43–341–34–5/24–10.02; J. Dobbs 259.1–65–652–38–6/45–17.15.

SIMON LANGTON GRAMMAR SCHOOL   *Played 18: W 14, L 2, D 2. A 1*

Master i/c: R. H. Green

A competitive side, expertly led by Tom Bilyard, went one better than last year by winning the Lemon (Kent) Cup. The season also marked the end of the White era: Tim was the last of three brothers to keep wicket for the team.

Batting—S. S. Ramsden 17–4–493–80–0–37.92; *T. Bilyard 17–2–530–91*–0–35.33; S. R. Davies 13–5–246–71*–0–30.75; C. M. Livesey 19–2–360–53*–0–21.17.

Bowling—B. B. Davies 62–15–130–15–3/3–8.66; M. G. Perrin 65.1–12–217–16–4/4–13.56; T. Bilyard 106–11–414–23–4/26–18.00; J. D. Murphy 94.5–15–347–19–3/13–18.26.

SIR ROGER MANWOOD'S SCHOOL   *Played 10: W 3, L 4, D 3*

Master i/c: J. F. Willmott

A young side, with only one player in his last year, made steady progress and reached the semi-finals of the Lemon (Kent) Cup. Tom Shaw was the mainstay of the team: a totally committed captain and aggressive with bat and ball. Kent Under-16 skipper Lewis Jenkins gave the batting stability with some cultured strokeplay while Andrew Dunn's nagging medium-pace claimed 18 wickets.

Batting—*T. Shaw 9–1–395–89*–0–49.37; L. Jenkins 9–0–306–83–0–34.00.

Bowling—A. Dunn 76–12–239–18–4/37–13.27.

SOLIHULL SCHOOL   *Played 14: W 3, L 5, D 6. A 2*

Master i/c: S. A. Morgan   Professional: A. Farooque

Batting—W. J. Gilbert 14–3–530–129*–1–48.18; N. P. Hemming 12–2–286–79*–0–28.60; *J. A. Spires 12–0–316–52–0–26.33; M. S. Travis 13–1–265–51–0–22.08; T. E. Moore 11–0–203–44–0–18.45.

Bowling—N. T. E. Jones 62–9–267–15–4/24–17.80; J. A. Spires 124–27–433–19–5/46–22.78.

SOUTH CRAVEN SCHOOL   *Played 6: W 2, L 4, D 0. A 5*

Master i/c: D. M. Birks

Batting—No batsman scored 150 runs. The leading batsman was *L. Gordon 3–0–94–53–0–31.33.

Bowling—No bowler took 15 wickets. The leading bowler was D. Pollard 54–7–250–12–4/12–20.83.

STAMFORD SCHOOL   *Played 17: W 9, L 2, D 6*

Master i/c: A. Johnston   Professional: J. A. Afford

Batting—H. P. Wickham 16–5–641–96–0–58.27; M. P. Williams 11–3–410–126*–1–51.25; *G. J. Hawkins 7–1–274–85*–0–45.66; M. R. Shepard 16–1–331–50–0–22.06; M. B. Campbell 11–1–183–38–0–18.30; C. D. Fairbairn 16–1–180–45–0–12.00.

Bowling—M. B. Campbell 121–23–437–28–4/23–15.60; D. A. Kearvell 142–19–453–22–3/16–20.59; A. E. Scott 191–64–477–23–4/40–20.73; B. J. E. Tate 156–28–465–22–4/26–21.13; A. P. Williams 148–39–449–17–5/41–26.41.

STOCKPORT GRAMMAR SCHOOL   *Played 8: W 1, L 3, D 4. A 6*

Master i/c: A. Brett   Professional: D. J. Makinson

Batting—D. Foreman 9–0–188–51–0–20.88.

Bowling—No bowler took 15 wickets. The leading bowler was S. Wilkinson 50–8–138–13–4/13–10.61.

STOWE SCHOOL   *Played 8: W 2, L 1, D 5. A 4*

Master i/c: I. Michael   Professional: H. Rhodes

In an enthralling draw with MCC – it ended with the scores level – Robert White and Adam Cottrell opened with a record stand of 203. White had a magnificent season as captain and leading all-rounder. He was well supported by leg-spinner Mark Bowman, especially in the win over the touring Australians from Scotch College.

Batting—*R. A. White 12–1–677–112–3–61.54; T. I. Pearce 12–2–263–72*–0–26.30; T. C. Sleater 12–3–216–58–0–24.00; A. P. Cottrell 11–0–183–91–0–16.63.

Bowling—M. Bowman 55–9–241–17–5/36–14.17; R. A. White 86–18–383–20–4/36–19.15.

STRATHALLAN SCHOOL   *Played 15: W 4, L 3, D 7, T 1*

Master i/c: R. H. Fitzsimmons   Professional: I. L. Philip

Remaining undefeated against Scottish schools and losing only to Royal GS, Lancaster, at the end-of-term festival constituted a most satisfactory season. Another festival match, however, provided the highlight: chasing Dulwich College's 230, and wanting 18 off the last over, Chris Hartley struck two sixes, a four, and scampered a leg-bye off the last ball to tie the game. Hartley, an exchange student from Brisbane Boys' College, scored most runs, kept wicket immaculately and brought Australian know-how to the side. Robin Dicke's season was undermined by illness but, when available, he led the side with calm assurance.

Batting—C. D. Hartley 12–3–615–132*–2–68.33; *R. H. W. J. Dicke 10–3–210–64*–0–30.00; O. Colquhoun 8–1–188–51–0–26.85; I. Stewart 14–2–303–61–0–25.25; A. O. Reed 14–1–243–51–0–18.69.

Bowling—I. Stewart 179.3–59–447–32–6/18–13.96; R. H. W. J. Dicke 119.1–19–358–18–4/35–19.88.

SUTTON VALENCE SCHOOL   *Played 14: W 7, L 1, D 6*

Master i/c: J. H. Kittermaster   Professional: A. Bannerjee

Playing positive and exciting cricket, the side continued to improve. Sixteen-year-old Robert Joseph, a genuine fast bowler, took 41 cheap wickets while all-rounder James Watson was picked for Kent Second Eleven.

Batting—J. Watson 12–3–436–100*–1–48.44; M. Day 13–2–502–102–1–45.63; G. Horton 12–1–247–81–0–22.45; R. Bradstock 9–0–170–56–0–18.88; J. Pavett 10–0–171–67–0–17.10; M. Wooderson 13–2–182–72–0–16.54.

Bowling—R. Joseph 162.3–33–471–41–8/43–11.48; J. Watson 139.2–20–435–17–3/20–25.58; M. Wooderson 110–7–488–16–3/23–30.50.

TAUNTON SCHOOL   *Played 8: W 3, L 4, D 1. A 4*

Master i/c: D. Baty   Professional: A. Kennedy

The highlight was the win against Blundell's; victory came in the penultimate over and with the last pair at the wicket, after L. A. Cooper had made 126.

Batting—L. A. Cooper 6–2–317–126–1–79.25.

Bowling—No bowler took 15 wickets. The leading bowler was S. Lupson 53.5–10–212–9–2/22–23.55.

TIFFIN SCHOOL   *Played 18: W 4, L 9, D 5. A 2*

Master i/c: M. J. Williams

Batting—J. T. Batley 13–1–455–85–0–37.91; R. M. O'Brien 11–1–208–62–0–20.80; T. Mehdi 13–0–253–78–0–19.46; A. J. Lulham 17–2–279–51*–0–18.60; *R. A. Urquhart 16–0–259–67–0–16.18; J. A. Rudofsky 14–4–159–35–0–15.90.

Bowling—A. Tirmizi 160.2–33–508–29–5/25–17.51; J. T. Batley 69.2–7–293–15–6/40–19.53; A. R. Bell 171.1–31–705–33–7/27–21.36; R. A. Urquhart 206.2–37–821–33–4/64–24.87.

Two of Tonbridge School's most prolific batsmen: Dan Cherry (left) scored 871 runs and later played for Glamorgan; Matthew Banes hit four hundreds in the season, taking his total for the school to 11.

TONBRIDGE SCHOOL   *Played 17: W 3, L 4, D 10. A 2*

Master i/c: P. B. Taylor   Professional: C. Stone

Matthew Banes scored four hundreds to take his career total to 11, a school record. In three seasons and an Australian tour, he hit 3,153 runs, with a highest score of 148 not out and an average of 63.06. His final century came against Cambridge University in a pre-Varsity Match warm-up. Dan Cherry was selected for ECB Under-19 and played for Glamorgan's first team.

Batting—*M. J. Banes 18–3–904–148*–4–60.26; D. D. Cherry 19–2–871–115*–2–51.23; J. W. R. Parker 14–2–303–48–0–25.25; O. C. R. Austin 17–3–245–48*–0–17.50; J. E. Knight 14–3–174–60*–0–15.81; T. E. Smitham 12–0–171–43–0–14.25.

Bowling—R. A. Brown 194.5–27–654–34–5/19–19.23; J. W. R. Parker 98.4–18–381–19–5/18–20.05; R. C. Kemp 283.4–78–728–30–4/61–24.26; D. D. Cherry 192.3–24–718–25–5/41–28.72.

TRENT COLLEGE   *Played 14: W 3, L 8, D 3. A 5*

Master i/c: M. McFarland   Professional: G. Miller

With so many matches disrupted by the weather, batsmen struggled for runs, and the team never seemed able to reach or defend targets. However, John Jordison had a rewarding season, clean bowling 17 of his 28 victims. Two touring sides visited: Rodebosch Boys' High School and Sydney GS. A winter tour to Australia was planned.

Batting—J. D. Wilson 14–0–401–65–0–28.64; J. Dove 12–3–201–56–0–22.33; R. J. Hartley 11–2–169–59–0–18.77; S. L. Moore 14–0–261–68–0–18.64; A. J. Allcock 12–0–175–58–0–14.58.

Bowling—J. R. Jordison 139.4–34–383–28–5/21–13.67.

TRINITY SCHOOL, CROYDON   *Played 14: W 2, L 4, D 8. A 5*

Master i/c: C. R. Burke

Batting—*R. Mutucumarana 13–1–709–159–1–59.08; B. Cox 9–1–289–80–0–36.12; R. Piggen 9–1–272–93–0–34.00.

Bowling—R. Piggen 68–15–215–15–5/17–14.33; R. Mutucumarana 153–33–413–21–4/39–19.66; A. Yazdani 142–26–448–21–4/17–21.33.

TRURO SCHOOL   *Played 8: W 4, L 2, D 2. A 11*

Master i/c: D. M. Phillips

The side lost 11 of a possible 19 fixtures to the weather but managed to win half their surviving games.

Batting—B. P. Price 6–2–226–79–0–56.50; P. M. Ellis 7–2–243–96–0–48.60.

Bowling—M. E. Williams 84.3–17–221–16–5/50–13.81.

UNIVERSITY COLLEGE SCHOOL   *Played 13: W 5, L 3, D 5. A 4*

Masters i/c: S. M. Bloomfield and S. A. P. Fitzgerald   Professional: W. G. Jones

Only in a cricket week held after the end of term did the side show its true potential. There was a comprehensive win against local rivals Highgate, and a combative victory when defending a low total against a strong Abingdon side. Daniel Stewart bowled with real speed, and also hit 342 runs.

Batting—*M. K. Floyd 13–2–368–139*–1–33.45; D. M. Stewart 13–2–342–115–1–31.09; D. M. Durban 10–1–258–113*–1–28.66; S. R. Nair 13–1–236–81–0–19.66; J. A. Craig 12–1–168–50–0–15.27.

Bowling—J. Rose 116–26–319–23–6/53–13.86; D. M. Stewart 113–25–293–19–3/16–15.42.

UPPINGHAM SCHOOL   *Played 11: W 1, L 7, D 3. A 4*

Master i/c: I. E. W. Sanders   Professional: B. T. P. Donelan

Batting—L. C. Clancey 11–1–232–66–0–23.20; *N. J. Pont 12–1–254–52–0–23.09; N. C. G. Tom 11–0–254–76–0–23.09; C. W. R. Palmer 9–0–192–51–0–21.33; O. C. W. Williams 11–0–234–60–0–21.27; H. J. G. Waite 8–0–150–41–0–18.75.

Bowling—S. T. P. Pearson 175.4–28–663–22–4/54–30.13.

VICTORIA COLLEGE, JERSEY   *Played 23: W 10, L 3, D 10. A 2*

Master i/c: D. A. R. Ferguson

A change of format in the annual fixture against Elizabeth College, Guernsey, achieved the first positive result in years. Splitting 110 overs – a maximum of 58 for the side batting first and a minimum of 52 for the reply – resulted in a six-wicket win for Victoria. James Mashiter scored most runs, by some margin, including an unbeaten 109 against Clayesmore.

Batting—R. O. Thompson 7–2–267–86*–0–53.40; J. E. Mashiter 21–2–733–109*–1–38.57; B. J. Vautier 20–4–463–68–0–28.93; A. J. D. Laffoley 15–3–324–88–0–27.00; *R. D. Minty 20–1–490–126–1–25.78; J. D. R. Macintosh 12–3–215–50*–0–23.88; R. C. Broughton 12–4–152–37–0–19.00; T. J. Perchard 14–3–195–50–0–17.72.

Bowling—R. C. Broughton 197–60–554–39–5/34–14.20; B. J. Vautier 134–14–571–30–5/24–19.03; B. Stockill 82–13–309–15–4/29–20.60; G. O. Hughes 167–33–511–18–4/53–28.38.

WARWICK SCHOOL   *Played 11: W 6, L 2, D 3. A 3*

Master i/c: G. A. Tedstone

Batting—N. Tarrant 8–6–151–63*–0–75.50; H. Jones 11–2–532–101–1–59.11; *A. Deverell-Smith 13–4–441–87*–0–49.00; N. Moore 10–3–220–58–0–31.42; M. Rowland 11–2–237–53–0–26.33; J. Moffatt 11–1–258–107*–1–25.80; J. Meredith 13–2–259–84–0–23.54.

Bowling—N. Reay 119–30–333–16–4/32–20.81; J. Wall 97–14–357–17–5/40–21.00; D. Lambert 107–21–376–15–4/35–25.06.

WATFORD GRAMMAR SCHOOL   *Played 14: W 2, L 5, D 7. A 1*

Master i/c: R. W. Panter

Batting—F. Samadi 12–3–206–28*–0–22.88; *S. Farrell 14–0–293–48–0–20.92; B. Pugh 14–0–283–65–0–20.21; T. Slade 10–1–164–53*–0–18.22.

Bowling—S. Farrell 70.3–11–267–18–2/4–14.83; M. Rughani 150.5–26–432–26–6/34–16.61; V. Iyengar 111.2–18–386–20–4/19–19.30; T. Slade 99–14–324–16–4/33–20.25.

WELLINGBOROUGH SCHOOL   *Played 18: W 10, L 2, D 6. A 2*

Master i/c: M. H. Askham   Professional: J. C. J. Dye

Batting—R. A. Phipps 8–4–171–59*–0–42.75; J. P. Lilley 17–4–506–85*–0–38.92; M. G. Carter 12–7–152–31–0–30.40; L. L. Jones 17–1–352–58*–0–22.00; T. C. Gee 15–1–284–51–0–20.28; R. Johnson 15–4–222–54–0–20.18.

Bowling—K. M. C. Saville 250.2–52–771–52–6/9–14.82; R. Johnson 229–41–684–43–6/56–15.90.

WELLINGTON COLLEGE   *Played 14: W 2, L 5, D 7. A 2*

Masters i/c: C. M. St. G. Potter and R. I. H. B. Dyer   Professional: P. J. Lewington

Batting—D. P. Cox 14–2–568–126*–2–47.33; J. I. Harper 12–1–331–87–0–30.09; *S. F. Streatfeild 14–1–328–63–0–25.23; J. D. Campbell 11–2–207–48–0–23.00; M. N. F. Brownrigg 10–2–165–35–0–20.62.

Bowling—M. T. Ogboru 151–23–440–23–5/23–19.13; S. E. Massie-Taylor 165–31–487–19–3/49–25.63.

WELLINGTON SCHOOL   *Played 18: W 6, L 7, D 5. A 4*

Master i/c: P. M. Pearce

Batting—T. R. C. Eve 14–1–309–62–0–23.76; B. J. Rogers 17–2–326–74*–0–21.73; L. P. Hawkins 13–1–260–88–0–21.66; T. D. Grabham 11–2–170–65*–0–18.88.

Bowling—S. W. Turner 187.5–34–598–39–6/35–15.33; W. G. Sheppard 63.2–1–370–17–6/29–21.76.

WELLS CATHEDRAL SCHOOL   *Played 9: W 2, L 4, D 3. A 7*

Master i/c: M. Stringer

Batting—*M. Shercliff 10–2–310–87–0–38.75; T. Fogden 9–0–307–71–0–34.11.

Bowling—T. Fogden 113–22–274–15–3/26–18.26.

WEST BUCKLAND SCHOOL   *Played 11: W 6, L 2, D 3. A 8*

Master i/c: L. Whittal-Williams   Professional: J. S. Alldis

The captain, T. J. Alldis, scored three centuries, averaged over 122 and, despite the West Country's appalling weather, led the side through a successful season.

Batting—*T. J. Alldis 12–6–735–122*–3–122.50; O. Smith 6–3–246–152*–1–82.00; T. Shilleto 10–4–318–93*–0–53.00; A. Wallace 6–0–215–68–0–35.83.

Bowling—M. Cann 80–4–312–15–5/25–20.80.

WESTMINSTER SCHOOL   *Played 7: W 2, L 4, D 1*

Master i/c: G. I. Brown   Professional: M. A. Feltham

Batting—No batsman scored 150 runs. The leading batsman was R. Bamford 6–1–110–50*–0–22.00.

Bowling—No bowler took 15 wickets. The leading bowler was R. Daryanani 46–11–122–7–3/34–17.42.

WHITGIFT SCHOOL   *Played 16: W 6, L 3, D 7. A 1*

Master i/c: P. C. Fladgate   Professional: D. M. Ward

Outstanding batsman Nashil Patel scored three centuries – against MCC, The Hague CC Colts and KCS, Wimbledon – to average over 70. He benefited from consistent support from Alex Goward and all-rounder Trevor Clarke, who bowled his leg-spin to great effect. Andy Hooper was the best of the seamers.

Batting—*N. A. Patel 15–4–775–120*–3–70.45; A. Goward 17–1–559–104–1–34.93; T. Clarke 17–1–425–63–0–26.56; D. Watson 12–5–165–28*–0–23.57; D. G. N. Pawan 11–0–214–43–0–19.45.

Bowling—T. Clarke 142.2–29–412–30–5/49–13.73; A. Hooper 158.1–30–507–24–5/64–21.12.

WILSON'S SCHOOL   *Played 20: W 5, L 10, D 5. A 8*

Master i/c: R. C. Wright

Inconsistent batting and poor catching spoiled the season. All-rounder Steven Boswell topped batting and bowling averages, while batsman Gareth Lambe showed some good form.

Batting—S. Boswell 17–2–393–112*–1–26.20; G. Lambe 16–0–359–56–0–22.43; T. Hindley 12–1–202–61–0–18.36; G. Strong 14–2–215–59–0–17.91; R. McCann 14–2–202–58–0–16.83; *M. Lacey 19–0–244–62–0–12.84; F. Mughal 12–0–150–54–0–12.50; D. Lester 19–2–182–76–0–10.70.

Bowling—S. Boswell 85.4–11–320–19–3/4–16.84; G. Strong 115.4–10–477–22–4/36–21.68; V. Shah 86–13–335–15–3/25–22.33; D. Lester 146.2–16–552–24–4/31–23.00.

WINCHESTER COLLEGE   *Played 13: W 7, L 1, D 5. A 5*

Master i/c: C. J. Good   Professional: J. R. Ayling

Batting—E. Witcomb 12–2–452–92–0–45.20; R. Reedhead 10–3–190–53–0–27.14; S. McArthur 12–1–283–59–0–25.72; R. Okeeffe 10–0–255–63–0–25.50; *F. Haycock 11–2–224–81*–0–24.88; T. Moore 12–1–206–41–0–18.72.

Bowling—R. Okeeffe 139–41–385–35–7/9–11.00; N. Holt 117–32–372–20–4/68–18.60; C. Foster 169–29–486–22–6/46–22.09.

WOODBRIDGE SCHOOL   *Played 13: W 0, L 8, D 5*

Master i/c: C. Seal

Batting—S. Harris-Wright 11–4–223–81*–0–31.85; *C. Green 12–2–271–93*–0–27.10; T. Ripman 13–1–319–92–0–26.58; A. Butler 10–1–201–51–0–22.33; E. Parker 13–0–154–31–0–11.84.

Bowling—S. Harris-Wright 127.1–21–496–17–3/11–29.17; E. Parker 137–23–504–17–5/56–29.64.

WOODHOUSE GROVE SCHOOL   *Played 12: W 6, L 0, D 6. A 5*

Master i/c: R. I. Frost

Professional: G. R. J. Roope

A pre-season tour to Zimbabwe led to the first undefeated season for five years. Nick Smith, who played for Yorkshire Senior Schools, batted consistently. He received sound support from all-rounder Stephen Brimacombe, who on occasions worked up genuine pace, and from Yorkshire Schools Under-15 captain Rhodri Jones.

Batting—N. R. Smith 12–1–441–75–0–40.09; R. W. Jones 9–2–241–69*–0–34.42; S. J. Brimacombe 12–0–292–69–0–24.33; *A. J. Brimacombe 12–1–211–35–0–19.18.

Bowling—R. W. Verity 59–16–178–16–5/10–11.12; S. J. Brimacombe 138.2–31–339–28–5/38–12.10; N. R. Smith 78.4–17–255–15–4/31–17.00; N. A. Verity 103.1–16–369–17–4/60–21.70.

WORKSOP COLLEGE   *Played 17: W 7, L 5, D 5. A 1*

Master i/c: C. G. Paton

Professional: A. Kettleborough

Until the pressures of examinations disrupted team selection, the side enjoyed a run of seven successive wins, a school record. Gavin Wilkinson showed great improvement as a seam bowler and may yet follow the success of his twin brothers, who opened the attack in 1994.

Batting—*R. H. Turner 16–1–892–140–2–59.46; H. E. Straw 14–3–404–98*–0–36.72; D. H. Coote 11–3–253–57–0–31.62; B. W. Moore 17–3–358–75*–0–25.57; T. M. Gray 10–3–155–40–0–22.14; S. Clark 12–4–176–43–0–22.00.

Bowling—G. A. H. Wilkinson 126.3–30–351–22–6/33–15.95; K. M. Bonner 153.5–34–414–23–5/19–18.00; F. C. Colton 141.2–17–491–23–3/23–21.34; R. H. Turner 122.1–21–419–19–2/15–22.05; H. E. Straw 119–20–334–15–5/34–22.26.

WREKIN COLLEGE   *Played 13: W 6, L 3, D 4. A 1*

Master i/c: M. de Weymarn

Professional: K. Sharp

An excellent season culminated in a good showing in the festival at Elizabeth College, Guernsey. The side had batting in depth but the bowling was unbalanced by injuries to key players in mid-season.

Batting—M. Tilt 9–5–200–66*–0–50.00; *W. Merrick 13–1–532–113*–1–44.33; P. Snodgrass 13–1–424–100*–1–35.33; L. Wilse-Samson 11–1–251–62–0–25.10; C. Henkel 9–1–151–35–0–18.87; T. Dolby 14–3–195–67–0–17.72.

Bowling—C. Henkel 143–18–511–28–6/27–18.25.

WYGGESTON AND QUEEN ELIZABETH I COLLEGE   *Played 8: W 1, L 3, D 4. A 3*

Master i/c: G. G. Wells

Batting—R. Patel 8–1–161–65*–0–23.00.

Bowling—No bowler took 15 wickets. The leading bowler was K. Jogia 36–4–132–7–4/18–18.85.

YOUTH CRICKET, 1998

UNDER-19 CRICKET

At the instigation of the ECB, the National Association of Young Cricketers voted itself out of existence at its November 1998 AGM. In its 37th and last year, the NAYC had little cricket to oversee. Its two-day competition, which had been due to expand in 1998, was called off; it did organise a one-day tournament and a series of representative matches. With the demise of the NAYC, the role of developing Under-19 cricket now falls exclusively to the ECB. The new North v South schools fixture is reported at the start of the Schools section.

Herefordshire won the last NAYC one-day competition, which took place without the first-class counties. They beat Bedfordshire in the final at Christ Church, Oxford, on August 8 by 114 runs, thanks mainly to their captain Steve Price, who scored 95 out of 260. Herefordshire only came into the competition as late replacements when Shropshire withdrew.

UNDER-17 CRICKET

Durham beat Devon by six wickets in the final of the Texaco Under-17 County Championship. In a two-day match at Canterbury, they reduced Devon to 75 for six, before No. 8 David Court hit 61 not out to ensure a respectable 184; Mark Davies finished with five for 23 from 17 overs. Durham's reply was dominated by opener Gary Pratt, who rushed to 87, and led his side to the brink of victory. Pratt's quick scoring meant Durham reached their target in the 45th over, after Devon had taken 61 overs to compile their total.

UNDER-16 CRICKET

The Britvic Inner Cities Cup, in its third year, was again organised by the Lord's Taverners, with the three-day final event staged at Arundel. Eight teams made it through after the preliminary rounds: Belfast, Bristol, London (North), Manchester, Nottingham, Sunderland, Swansea, and Wolverhampton. They were split into two groups of four, with the winners meeting in the final: London, who failed to win a game in the closing stages in 1997, were undefeated in their group and went on to beat Sunderland by 41 runs in the final. London made 220 for seven in 40 overs, with William Burns hitting 74. Aurfan Raja made 56, and then took six for 36 as Sunderland were bowled out for 179; Philip Shepherd scored 52. As in the previous two competitions, players were only eligible if they lived within a ten-mile radius of their city centre and had not previously played at county or national level.

In the Inter-County Under-16 competition, Cornwall beat Norfolk by six wickets in the final at Shenley Park.

UNDER-15 CRICKET

In August, the national side beat India Under-15 in a three-Test series. In the First Test at Arundel, Nicky Peng made 71 for England in a drawn game, before they won the Second at Shenley Park by eight wickets, despite 68 and four for 60 from Wazid Ali; Peng hit 81. In the final Test at Oundle, Wazid made 102 and took seven wickets in the match, but England held on for a draw to secure the series, with Peng making 53, and captain Damian Sharazi an undefeated 52 off 247 balls. India gained revenge by taking the one-day series, played at Oundle, 2-0.

At the annual Bunbury ESCA Festival, the Midlands repeated their performance of 1997, winning just one of their three games, but finishing as overall champions. They beat the West, who in turn beat the North. All other games – including each of the South's three fixtures – were drawn. Edward Baylis took five for 20 for the Midlands against the West, including a hat-trick, but it was the West who boasted the outstanding batsman of the festival: William Faulkner was awarded the Neil Lloyd Trophy for his tally of 171 runs in three innings. He was closely followed by the South's James Benning (162).

Royal Grammar School, Worcester, won the Lord's Taverners/*Cricketer* Colts Trophy at Trent Bridge, where they beat King's, Taunton by eight wickets. King's chose to bat first, but only Robert Excell, with 40, made any headway against a tight attack, and they were dismissed for 94 in 38.5 overs. Leg-spinner Sam Smith opened the bowling and took three for 13 from ten overs, including a spell of three for two in six, while captain Richard Wilkinson finished with three for 21. Wilkinson then struck 45, as RGS won comfortably with more than seven overs to spare.

Welsh club St Fagans defeated Crewe Rolls Royce by 16 runs in the final of the Sun Life of Canada Under-15 Club Championship at Basingstoke. St Fagans made 103 for eight in their 20 overs, with Owen Price taking three for 17, before restricting Crewe to 87 for eight. Sussex beat Staffordshire by eight wickets in the semi-final of the ESCA/Lord's Taverners Under-15 County Championship, with Chris Nash taking six for 32, before they overcame Yorkshire by nine wickets in the final, thanks to an undefeated 103 from opener Krishna Singh. Hampshire beat Staffordshire in the third-place play-off.

UNDER-13 CRICKET

Oakham School in Rutland hosted the Subaru Under-13 Club Championship for the third successive year, after county competitions and regional finals had established which eight of the original 1,421 entrants would contest the four-day round-robin competition. For the first time, teams consisted of 11 players. Wembdon of Somerset recovered after losing their first game, against Doncaster Town, to win their remaining six matches and take the title. Wolverhampton also won six of their seven matches, but finished second because they had lost their game to Wembdon, by eight wickets. Steve Davis, Daryl Cocks and Andy Halloran all performed well for Wembdon.

The finalists, in finishing order, were: Wembdon, Wolverhampton, Doncaster Town, Billericay, St Fagans, Cambridge Granta and Clydesdale. Though they lost all their games, Clydesdale won the Bill Ainsworth Trophy for being the most sporting side of the tournament.

Whitgift School, Croydon won the Calypso Cup, beating Queen Elizabeth GS, Wakefield by four wickets with one ball to spare in the final at Headingley. In the ECB/ESCA Under-13 Festival, it was the first time that all four regions had selected teams. The Midlands won two of their games and were overall winners, but the outstanding batsman was Tim Rees of the North: his aggregate of 219 runs at 109.50 included an unbeaten century in the draw with the South.

UNDER-11 CRICKET

Twelve sides reached the finals of the HSA Healthcare Under-11 Hardball Competition at Edgbaston. The eventual winners were Millfield of Somerset, who beat Tottington of Bury by 107 runs in the final. Millfield's score of 326 for two was the highest in the competition.

Dale Primary, from Derby, who finished third in the Hardball Competition, again did even better in the Wrigley Softball Cricket Tournament, at Edgbaston. Dale won the competition for the second successive year, beating Wells Central Junior School by nine runs in the final. In both competitions, teams start with 200 runs, and lose six runs every time a wicket is lost; games are eight-a-side, and four pairs bat for three overs each (or four, if there is sufficient time).

WOMEN'S CRICKET, 1998

By CAROL SALMON

AUSTRALIAN WOMEN IN ENGLAND, 1998

England and Australia's women created their own Ashes by burning a miniature bat, autographed by both teams, before their Test series. The trophy was shared, as the three Tests were drawn, but there was no doubt as to the superior team: Australia won all five one-day internationals, and held a clear advantage in the Tests.

They were bowled out only once in 16 fixtures in England and Ireland – by England A, for 596. Their top five batsmen all averaged over 50 in the Tests; Joanne Broadbent scored a double-hundred at Guildford, and there were also centuries for Melanie Jones, Kim Rolton, who scored 327 runs for twice out, and captain Belinda Clark.

England's response was to occupy the crease for as long as possible. Janette Brittin's courage and concentration – she was the leading run-scorer on either side, batting more than 24 hours for an aggregate of 450 – undoubtedly saved them from defeat. Brittin announced her retirement from international cricket after the Third Test, finishing her career as the leading run-scorer in women's Tests, with 1,935 at 49.61 in her 27 matches since 1979.

It was a batsman's series on flat pitches, with 3,002 runs scored for 53 wickets. Cathryn Fitzpatrick took 13 of them for Australia (no one else passed six) and, with proper support, the pressure would have been relentless. A feisty fast bowler, Fitzpatrick produced some of her quickest deliveries late in the day, when she had already bowled more than 30 overs. Bronwen Calver kept line and length, but the third seamer, Charmaine Mason, was injured during the Second Test, hindering Australia's attempts to push home their advantage. They had no such problems in the one-day matches, where Australia followed up their World Cup triumph in India seven months earlier by winning all five, helped by 16 Australian run-outs.

Clark and coach John Harmer led a fit squad completely focused on the job – which included some traditional Aussie sledging. It was hard to imagine any Englishwomen forcing their way into the tourists' line-up; even those with the ability, like Charlotte Edwards, who averaged 63.80 in the Tests, would have needed to work hard to attain the necessary fitness and mental application.

Off the field, the England squad was more secure than ever, thanks to sponsorship from Vodafone, while coverage on Sky television continued to raise their profile. But these hard-earned benefits could be lost if they do not recover their form by the 2000 World Cup in New Zealand. They also need to play with more style: England's scoring-rate of 2.27 an over in the Tests – compared with Australia's 3.34 – was not pretty to watch. Some of the Australian officials said that Test cricket would die in their country if they adopted England's approach. New Zealand have already lost interest in the four-day game, and plan to concentrate on one-day cricket; financial constrictions were likely to force Australia to schedule future series with just one Test and a plethora of limited-overs games.

AUSTRALIAN TOURING PARTY

B. J. Clark (New South Wales) *(captain)*, K. L. Rolton (South Australia) *(vice-captain)*, J. Broadbent (South Australia), B. L. Calver (New South Wales), J. M. Dannatt (Queensland), A. J. Fahey (Western Australia), C. L. Fitzpatrick (Victoria), J. A. Franklin (Victoria), M. A. Goszko (New South Wales), M. Jones (Victoria), L. M. Keightley (New South Wales), O. J. Magno (South Australia), C. L. Mason (Victoria), J. C. Price (Queensland).

Manager: L. A. Larsen.　　*Coach:* J. Harmer.

AUSTRALIAN TOUR RESULTS

Matches – Played 16: Won 12, Drawn 4.

Note: Matches in this section were not first-class.

At Finchley, July 5. Australians won by 167 runs. Toss: England Under-21. Australians 266 for four (50 overs) (B. J. Clark 91, J. Broadbent 67, L. M. Keightley 45, M. Jones 31 not out); England Under-21 99 for seven (50 overs).

At Shenley Park, July 7. Australians won by 102 runs. Toss: Australians. Australians 243 for five (50 overs) (K. L. Rolton 119, J. A. Franklin 75 not out; J. Hawker three for 43); South of England 141 for five (50 overs) (A. Godliman 37, R. Lupton 69).

At Oxton, July 9. Australians won by 187 runs. Toss: Australians. Australians 285 for six (50 overs) (B. J. Clark 35, M. A. Goszko 36, L. M. Keightley 82 not out, B. L. Calver 69; L. McGrother three for 32); North of England 98 for eight (50 overs) (S. Redfern 33 not out; A. J. Fahey three for 23).

At Scarborough, July 12. First one-day international: Australia won on scoring-rate. Toss: Australia. Australia 166 for five (29 overs) (B. J. Clark 95 not out, J. Broadbent 31, K. L. Rolton 31); England 104 for seven (20 overs) (J. A. Brittin 37, K. Smithies 41).
 Clark scored 95 not out in 93 balls and passed 2,000 runs in one-day internationals. England's target was revised to 115 from 20 overs.

At Derby, July 15. Second one-day international: Australia won by 64 runs. Toss: England. Australia 204 for six (50 overs) (L. M. Keightley 59, M. Jones 58); England 140 (47.2 overs) (K. Smithies 44; C. L. Mason four for 24).
 Jones was given out stumped by third umpire Phil Carrick.

At Hove, July 18. Third one-day international: Australia won by 35 runs. Toss: Australia. Australia 237 for four (50 overs) (J. Broadbent 70, K. L. Rolton 67, B. L. Calver 35 not out); England 202 for nine (50 overs) (C. M. Edwards 74, B. A. Daniels 30; O. J. Magno three for 46).

At Southampton, July 19. Fourth one-day international: Australia won by eight wickets. Toss: England. England 102 (49.2 overs); Australia 106 for two (24.5 overs) (L. M. Keightley 56 not out).
 Six England players were run out.

At Lord's, July 21. Fifth one-day international: Australia won by 115 runs. Toss: Australia. Australia 256 for one (50 overs) (B. J. Clark 89, L. M. Keightley 113 not out, J. Broadbent 42 not out); England 141 for seven (50 overs) (K. Smithies 62 not out; C. L. Fitzpatrick five for 47).
 Keightley became the first woman to score a century at Lord's. She hit seven fours in 140 balls and 175 minutes. Australia completed a 5-0 whitewash in the one-day series.

At Trinity College, Dublin, July 24. First one-day international: Australia won by 172 runs. Toss: Ireland. Australia 261 for four (50 overs) (J. A. Franklin 36, M. A. Goszko 45, J. Broadbent 82 not out, B. L. Calver 81 not out); Ireland 89 (44.3 overs) (O. J. Magno three for nine).

At Trinity College, Dublin, July 25. Second one-day international: Australia won by 170 runs. Toss: Australia. Australia 267 for five (50 overs) (B. J. Clark 59, J. C. Price 38, K. L. Rolton 73, M. A. Goszko 40); Ireland 97 for eight (50 overs).

At Merrion CC, Dublin, July 27. Third one-day international: Australia won on scoring-rate. Toss: Australia. Australia 190 for eight (46 overs) (J. M. Dannatt 43, J. Broadbent 33; C. Shillington three for 36); Ireland 90 for eight (41.1 overs).

At Sittingbourne, July 31, August 1, 2. Australians won by an innings and 426 runs. Toss: England A. England A 75 (O. J. Magno five for 15) and 95 (B. L. Calver four for 13, C. L. Mason three for 17); Australians 596 (L. M. Keightley 52, J. Broadbent 46, K. L. Rolton 193, M. A. Goszko 92, B. L. Calver 97 not out, C. L. Mason 49; K. M. Evenson three for 117).

ENGLAND v AUSTRALIA

First Test Match

At Guildford, August 5, 6, 7, 8. Drawn. Toss: England. Test debuts: S. V. Collyer; B. L. Calver, M. Jones.

England regrouped well after their thrashing in the one-day series. Their confident batting performance was led by Jan Brittin, who had broken her finger at Hove three weeks earlier. Here, she survived being dropped on ten to occupy the crease for eight hours and 146 runs. When 110, she became the leading scorer in women's Test cricket, overtaking Rachael Heyhoe-Flint's 1,594. But Australia's reply set records too. Joanne Broadbent was only the second woman to reach a Test double-hundred, following Kirsty Flavell of New Zealand at Scarborough in 1996; she batted 536 minutes and 476 balls and hit 25 fours. Together with Melanie Jones, who made 131, the highest score by a woman on Test debut, she added 220, two short of the fourth-wicket record. Australia finally declared on the fourth day at 569, easily the highest total in women's Tests, beating their own 525 against India in 1983-84.

Close of play: First day, England 257-3 (J. A. Brittin 104*, C. J. Connor 28*); Second day, Australia 99-1 (L. M. Keightley 45*, J. Broadbent 36*); Third day, Australia 393-5 (J. Broadbent 146*).

England

C. M. Edwards c Magno b Calver	53	– b Fitzpatrick	77
J. A. Brittin run out	146	– not out	59
B. A. Daniels c Jones b Magno	31	– not out	17
*K. Smithies lbw b Fitzpatrick	16		
C. J. Connor st Price b Magno	41		
†J. Cassar lbw b Calver	38		
K. M. Leng c Fahey b Magno	34		
S. V. Collyer c Price b Calver	1		
S. Redfern st Price b Magno	10		
C. E. Taylor b Magno	6		
L. C. Pearson not out	5		
B 14, l-b 14, w 4, n-b 1	33	B 3, l-b 3, n-b 1	7

1/94 2/153 3/188 4/288 5/335   414   1/127   (1 wkt) 160
6/359 7/371 8/397 9/403

Bowling: *First Innings*—Fitzpatrick 33-4-103-1; Calver 34-10-62-3; Magno 43-18-87-5; Mason 34-12-64-0; Rolton 12-5-15-0; Fahey 27-9-48-0; Broadbent 5-2-7-0; Clark 1-1-0-0. *Second Innings*—Fitzpatrick 12-5-20-1; Calver 10-5-16-0; Mason 6-1-18-0; Magno 12-2-42-0; Rolton 9-2-29-0; Fahey 6-3-14-0; Clark 4-1-8-0; Broadbent 2-1-5-0; Jones 1-0-2-0.

Australia

*B. J. Clark c Redfern b Pearson	11	†J. C. Price not out	80
L. M. Keightley c and b Edwards	56	O. J. Magno not out	37
J. Broadbent b Smithies	200	B 7, l-b 4, w 10, n-b 1	22
K. L. Rolton lbw b Edwards	4		
M. Jones run out	131		
B. L. Calver b Collyer	28		

1/28 2/136 3/140   (6 wkts dec.) 569
4/360 5/393 6/480

A. J. Fahey, C. L. Fitzpatrick and C. L. Mason did not bat.

Bowling: Taylor 5-4-8-0; Pearson 28-1-101-1; Leng 24-8-61-0; Redfern 21-5-85-0; Connor 16-2-62-0; Edwards 27-7-79-2; Collyer 31-5-88-1; Smithies 28-11-74-1.

Umpires: A. Garton and V. Gibbens.

ENGLAND v AUSTRALIA

Second Test Match

At Harrogate, August 11, 12, 13, 14. Drawn. Toss: Australia.

Australia threw down the gauntlet with a first-day declaration, but England took up the challenge. Charlotte Edwards, dropped in the slips that evening, and Jan Brittin shared their second century partnership in five days, and Brittin scored her fifth and highest Test hundred, which lasted seven and a quarter hours. She eventually became one of four wickets for the pace of Cathryn Fitzpatrick, but England led by 20 runs. Rain wiped out the third evening, causing Australia to delay their declaration; the eventual target was 284 from 43 overs, but more rain ended England's attempt within an hour.

Close of play: First day, England 14-0 (C. M. Edwards 5*, J. A. Brittin 8*); Second day, England 282-5 (J. A. Brittin 148*, K. M. Leng 11*); Third day, Australia 123-1 (L. M. Keightley 61*, J. Broadbent 2*).

Australia

L. M. Keightley c Leng b Edwards	43	– (2) c Smithies b Reynard	90
*B. J. Clark c Smithies b Edwards	76	– (1) c Daniels b Connor	54
J. Broadbent not out	63	– c Connor b Smithies	56
K. L. Rolton c Reynard b Pearson	82	– not out	65
M. Jones not out	19	– c and b Smithies	2
B. L. Calver (did not bat)		– lbw b Leng	24
†J. C. Price (did not bat)		– not out	4
B 16, l-b 2, w 2, n-b 3	23	L-b 5, n-b 3	8

1/125 2/130 3/272   (3 wkts dec.) 306   1/95 2/184 3/224   (5 wkts dec.) 303
4/228 5/291

O. J. Magno, C. L. Fitzpatrick, C. L. Mason and A. J. Fahey did not bat.

Bowling: *First Innings*—Pearson 13.3–2–59–1; Taylor 15–3–59–0; Collyer 23–8–36–0; Leng 5–0–33–0; Reynard 16–4–55–0; Edwards 11–5–28–2; Smithies 9–4–18–0. *Second Innings*—Pearson 8–2–34–0; Taylor 21–6–44–0; Edwards 10–0–32–0; Connor 14–6–30–1; Collyer 16–2–46–0; Reynard 7–0–33–1; Leng 14–1–47–1; Smithies 14–3–32–2.

England

C. M. Edwards run out	48	– not out	42
J. A. Brittin c Rolton b Fitzpatrick	167		
B. A. Daniels c Fitzpatrick b Rolton	22		
*K. Smithies c Magno b Broadbent	26		
C. J. Connor c Price b Fitzpatrick	8		
†J. Cassar run out	0		
K. M. Leng c and b Fitzpatrick	29	– (2) not out	20
M. A. Reynard c Clark b Fitzpatrick	1		
S. V. Collyer not out	4		
C. E. Taylor not out	2		
B 13, l-b 6	19	L-b 2	2

1/103 2/150 3/217 4/241   (8 wkts dec.) 326   (no wkt) 64
5/241 6/318 7/319 8/322

L. C. Pearson did not bat.

Bowling: *First Innings*—Fitzpatrick 43–14–91–4; Calver 42–13–62–0; Mason 8–1–39–0; Rolton 17–5–45–1; Magno 12–1–34–0; Fahey 11–2–22–0; Broadbent 2–1–5–1; Keightley 4–2–9–0. *Second Innings*—Fitzpatrick 8–1–41–0; Calver 7.4–2–21–0.

Umpires: A. Heath and A. Roberts.

At Littleborough, August 17, 18, 19. Drawn. Toss: Australians. Australians 286 for four dec. (K. L. Rolton 144, M. A. Goszko 37, J. M. Dannatt 74 not out); President's XI 128 (A. Godliman 36, H. Lloyd 31) and 121 for six (D. Stock 34 not out).

ENGLAND v AUSTRALIA

Third Test Match

At Worcester, August 21, 22, 23, 24. Drawn. Toss: England. Test debut: J. A. Franklin.

More rain, and the home team's slow scoring, ensured that the Tests ended in stalemate. England took 136 overs to make 243, a total Australia passed in only 65. But the third day was washed out, giving them too little time to build a substantial lead and bowl England out a second time. Despite that, the final day was the most entertaining of the series. After Belinda Clark was dismissed for 136, left-hander Karen Rolton hit the ball ferociously in her maiden Test century; she went from 100 to 150 in 22 balls, and finished with 22 fours and a six in an unbeaten four-hour 176. Australia eventually declared 184 ahead, and Charlotte Edwards responded with some beautiful batting before she tired. Even so, England had only just cleared the arrears as the series drew to a close.

Close of play: First day, England 183-6 (J. Cassar 28*, S. V. Collyer 8*); Second day, Australia 279-1 (B. J. Clark 128*, K. L. Rolton 88*); Third day, No play.

England

C. M. Edwards c Rolton b Fitzpatrick	12	– c Calver b Fahey	87
J. A. Brittin b Fitzpatrick	72	– b Fitzpatrick	6
B. A. Daniels b Franklin	31	– c Broadbent b Clark	38
*K. Smithies b Fahey	10	– c Calver b Fahey	32
C. J. Connor b Calver	11	– b Fitzpatrick	1
†J. Cassar c Magno b Calver	34	– not out	17
M. A. Reynard b Fitzpatrick	0	– c Price b Fitzpatrick	0
S. V. Collyer c Price b Fitzpatrick	14	– not out	6
S. Redfern not out	22		
C. E. Taylor run out	16		
L. C. Pearson c Rolton b Magno	7		
B 5, l-b 8, w 1	14	B 1, l-b 2	3

1/25 2/79 3/102 4/121 5/174   243   1/21 2/111 3/162   (6 wkts) 190
6/174 7/194 8/195 9/221   4/166 5/170 6/174

Bowling: First Innings—Fitzpatrick 40–6–100–4; Rolton 26–12–26–0; Calver 29–14–49–2; Magno 13.4–3–24–1; Fahey 19.4–4–24–1; Franklin 8–4–7–1. *Second Innings*—Fitzpatrick 27–9–58–3; Calver 13–5–27–0; Magno 7–1–34–0; Rolton 4–1–11–0; Franklin 8–4–10–0; Fahey 13–4–37–2; Clark 2–0–10–1.

Australia

L. M. Keightley c Collyer b Smithies	50	B. L. Calver c Edwards b Daniels	28
*B. J. Clark c Daniels b Smithies	136	B 9, l-b 13, w 2, n-b 2	26
K. L. Rolton not out	176		
M. Jones c Connor b Collyer	11	1/127 2/301 3/323 4/427 (4 wkts dec.)	427

J. Broadbent, †J. C. Price, J. A. Franklin, O. J. Magno, C. L. Fitzpatrick and A. J. Fahey did not bat.

Bowling: Pearson 8–0–29–0; Taylor 15–0–84–0; Edwards 9–2–32–0; Redfern 5–0–29–0; Smithies 27–2–83–2; Collyer 16–0–69–1; Reynard 18–4–50–0; Connor 3–0–20–0; Daniels 2.2–0–9–1.

Umpires: A. Fox and J. West.

Women's Test Match Records may be found on page 360.

ENGLISH WOMEN'S CRICKET, 1998

Just short of its 72nd birthday, the Women's Cricket Association was disbanded in 1998. At the end of March, an extraordinary general meeting voted to amalgamate with the England and Wales Cricket Board; an executive committee meeting in June signed a sale and purchase agreement to complete the formalities. The move was not unopposed. Members expressed reservations over the speed of events, and complained of a lack of attention to the finer details. Just before the vote, there was further disquiet when a former ECB receptionist, Theresa Harrild, won an undefended and much-publicised case against the Board at an industrial tribunal. Barbara Daniels, the WCA's executive director, described the case and subsequent publicity about the Board's treatment of women staff as "unhelpful".

Daniels and chair Sharon Bayton were the main driving force behind the amalgamation, and in the end they convinced the membership that there was no alternative but to join forces with the men, taking what Tim Lamb, the chief executive of the ECB, called "a leap of faith". The Sports Council was not prepared to fund two governing bodies for cricket, and the WCA simply lacked the numbers and the financial clout to advance itself on or off the field. Lamb promised the executive committee in June that "the ECB and its management are absolutely committed to the furtherance and promotion of the women's game".

The WCA office at Edgbaston closed in September, and some of its staff moved to the ECB, with Daniels becoming national manager for women's cricket. Paul Farbrace, one of the ECB's national coaches, was assigned to the England team, with special responsibility for the age-group sides.

As with the male game, the growth of women's cricket must depend largely on the performances of the national team. Youngsters require role models, while sponsors and the media soon lose patience if success is not forthcoming. But the numbers taking part continued to grow – even though the touring Australians reported a player base of 23,000 to England's 3,600. Another county, Northumberland, joined the County Championship, bringing the teams up to 18, including three Second Elevens; Lancashire and Cheshire have now split into separate teams, in accordance with the need to align with the ECB's county boards. Leicestershire, Nottinghamshire and Somerset were expected to join in 1999.

In 1998, Yorkshire continued to set the standards. The county won their seventh successive Championship, winning all their five games at Cambridge in July; only Kent put them under any pressure, bowling them out for 149, though Surrey lost to no one except Yorkshire. The previous season's runners-up, West Midlands, never challenged. Yorkshire also won the Under-21 championship, beating Sussex in the final; the Under-17 eight-a-side tournament (to be extended to 11-a-side in 1999) went to The West.

Yorkshire dominated at club level as well: Wakefield won their 11th trophy in nine seasons when they overwhelmed southern champions Shepperton in the National League; they also shared the National Knockout trophy with Nottinghamshire club Thrumpton (previous winners under their former name, Newark & Sherwood) when the final was washed out.

Note: Matches in this section were not first-class.

COUNTY CHAMPIONSHIP

Division One

	Played	Won	Lost	Points
Yorkshire	5	5	0	100
Surrey	5	4	1	82.5
Kent	5	2	3	61
West Midlands	5	2	3	57.5
Thames Valley	5	2	3	55.5
Western Counties	5	0	5	33

Division Two

	Played	Won	Lost	Points
East Midlands	5	4	1	87
Yorkshire Second XI	5	4	1	85
East Anglia	5	3	2	70
Sussex	5	2	3	55
Derbyshire	5	1	4	45
Middlesex	5	1	4	38

Division Three

	Played	Won	Lost	Points
Cheshire	5	5	0	105
Surrey Second XI	5	4	1	89.5
Lancashire	5	3	2	68.5
Hampshire	5	2	3	60.5
Northumberland	5	1	4	40
Sussex Second XI	5	0	5	23

NATIONAL LEAGUE FINAL

At Campbell Park, Milton Keynes, September 6. Wakefield won by ten wickets. Toss: Wakefield. Shepperton 107 (46.3 overs) (K. M. Leng three for 16); Wakefield 108 for no wkt (29.1 overs) (K. M. Leng 58 not out, A. Elder 40 not out).

NATIONAL CLUB KNOCKOUT/PLATE FINALS

At Wolverhampton, September 13. Thrumpton v Wakefield. No result (abandoned). The finalists shared the trophy. The National Knockout Plate final between Ridgeway and Sheffield United, planned for the same date and venue, was also abandoned. The finalists shared the trophy.

WOMEN'S CRICKET FIXTURES, 1999

JULY

6	Manchester	ENGLAND v INDIA (1st one-day international)
9	Northampton	ENGLAND v INDIA (2nd one-day international)
11	Nottingham	ENGLAND v INDIA (3rd one-day international)
15	Shenley Park	ENGLAND v INDIA (Test, 4 days)
24	Cambridge	County Championship (5 days)

AUGUST

15	Colwall	Cricket Week (6 days)

SEPTEMBER

5	Milton Keynes (Campbell Park)	Premier League Final
11	Milton Keynes (Campbell Park)	Under-21 League Final
12	Radlett	National Club Knockout/Plate Finals

PART SIX: OVERSEAS CRICKET IN 1997-98

FEATURES OF 1997-98

Double-Hundreds (38)

340†	S. T. Jayasuriya	Sri Lanka v India (First Test) at Colombo (RPS).
301*	V. V. S. Laxman	Hyderabad v Bihar at Jamshedpur.
265	D. F. Hills§	Tasmania v South Australia at Hobart.
251	S. Abbas Ali	Madhya Pradesh v Railways at Indore.
250	Asif Mahmood	Rawalpindi v Lahore City at Rawalpindi.
242*	A. Jadeja.	Haryana v Services at Faridabad.
241	M. J. Horne	Otago v Auckland at Auckland.
235	J. L. Langer	Western Australia v South Australia at Adelaide.
232*	V. G. Kambli§	Mumbai v Saurashtra at Mumbai.
229*	Narender Singh.	Services v Jammu and Kashmir at Delhi.
225†	R. S. Mahanama	Sri Lanka v India (First Test) at Colombo (RPS).
224*	Rizwan Shamshad	Uttar Pradesh v Rajasthan at Kanpur.
223	M. S. Atapattu§	Sri Lanka v Zimbabwe (First Test) at Kandy.
216	M. D. Bell.	Wellington v Auckland at Auckland.
215	R. Dravid	Karnataka v Uttar Pradesh at Bangalore.
213*	S. Sriram.	Tamil Nadu v Andhra at Vishakhapatnam.
207*	L. D. Harper	Victoria v South Australia at Carlton.
207*	V. G. Kambli§	Mumbai v Railways at Mumbai.
207	M. J. Slater	Australians v Board President's XI at Vishakhapatnam.
206	A. C. Hudson	Natal v Gauteng at Durban.
205	D. F. Hills§	Tasmania v Victoria at Hobart.
204*	Hasan Raza‡	Karachi Whites v Bahawalpur at Karachi.
204*	S. R. Tendulkar.	Mumbai v Australians at Mumbai.
203*	J. C. Adams.	Jamaica v Trinidad & Tobago at St Catherine.
203*	A. C. Gilchrist	Western Australia v South Australia at Perth.
203*	Salim Elahi	Habib Bank v ADBP at Lahore.
203*	G. J. Whittall	Zimbabwe v New Zealand (Second Test) at Bulawayo.
203	J. G. Myburgh	Northerns B v Easterns at Pretoria.
202*	H. D. Ackerman	Western Province v Northerns at Centurion.
202*	S. R. Waugh	New South Wales v Victoria at North Sydney.
202	D. L. Maddy	England A v Kenya at Nairobi.
201*	M. L. Love	Queensland v New Zealanders at Cairns.
201	A. Flower	Mashonaland v Mashonaland A at Harare.
201	G. Kirsten	South Africans v Western Australia at Perth.
201	P. Mullick	Orissa v Tripura at Cuttack.
200*	D. P. M. D. Jayawardene .	Sinhalese SC v Kurunegala Youth CC at Colombo (SSC).
200*	R. S. Sodhi	Punjab v Delhi at Patiala.
200	M. S. Atapattu§	Sinhalese SC v Moors SC at Colombo (SSC).

† S. T. Jayasuriya and R. S. Mahanama scored double-hundreds in the same innings.
‡ Hasan Raza was the youngest player to score a double-hundred in first-class cricket at a recorded age of 15 years 215 days.
§ M. S. Atapattu, D. F. Hills and V. G. Kambli each scored two double-hundreds, Hills in successive innings.

Hundred on First-Class Debut

150†	A. Chopra	Delhi v Services at Delhi.
112	A. Jacobs	North West v Western Province B at Potchefstroom.
144	D. Manohar	Hyderabad v Karnataka at Secunderabad.
105	D. Moffat	Eastern Province B v Natal B at Port Elizabeth.
109	B. B. C. C. Mohapatra . .	Orissa v Assam at Cuttack.

† A. Chopra also scored 100* v Punjab at Patiala in his second match.

Three Hundreds in Successive Innings

Aamir Sohail (Allied Bank/Pakistan)   170 Allied Bank v KRL at Rawalpindi
                                         160 Pakistan v West Indies (Second Test) at Rawalpindi
                                         160 Pakistan v West Indies (Third Test) at Karachi.
Azhar Mahmood (Pakistan) . . . . . .   136 v South Africa (First Test) at Johannesburg
                                         111 v Free State at Bloemfontein
                                         132 v South Africa (Second Test) at Durban.
S. S. Das (Orissa). . . . . 120 v Railways at Cuttack
                                         110 and 131 v Punjab at Berhampur.
P. A. de Silva (Sri Lanka) . . . .   126 v India (First Test) at Colombo (RPS)
                                         146 and 120 v India (Second Test) at Colombo (SSC).
J. J. Martin (Baroda). . . . .   115 v Tamil Nadu at Chennai (1996-97)
                                         104* v Saurashtra at Rajkot
                                         101 v Mumbai at Baroda.
T. M. Moody (Worcs/W. Australia) . .   101 Worcestershire v Derbyshire at Worcester (1997)
                                         180* Worcestershire v Hampshire at Southampton (1997)
                                         101 Western Australia v South Australia at Perth.
Rizwan Shamshad (Uttar Pradesh) . .   134* v Railways at Delhi
                                         224* v Rajasthan at Kanpur
                                         100 v Vidarbha at Allahabad.
A. Symonds (Queensland) . . . .   141 v Tasmania at Hobart
                                         163 and 100* v South Australia at Adelaide.

Hundred in Each Innings of a Match

S. S. Das . . . .   110 131   Orissa v Punjab at Berhampur.
P. A. de Silva . . . . .   146 120   Sri Lanka v India (Second Test) at Colombo (SSC).
G. W. Flower . . . . . .   104 151   Zimbabwe v New Zealand (First Test) at Harare.
B. M. Jadeja . . . . . .   123 112* Saurashtra v Maharashtra at Pune.
A. Symonds . . . .   163 100* Queensland v South Australia at Adelaide.
W. Wiblin . . . .   177 119* Border v Western Province at East London.

Carrying Bat Through Completed Innings

J. Cox . . . .   115* Tasmania (285) v Western Australia at Perth.
G. W. Flower . . . .   156* Zimbabwe (321) v Pakistan (First Test) at Bulawayo.
G. Kirsten . . . .   100* South Africa (239) v Pakistan (Third Test) at Faisalabad.
S. Suresh . . . .   123* Goa (226) v Tamil Nadu at Chennai.
M. A. Taylor . . . .   169* Australia (350) v South Africa (Third Test) at Adelaide.

Batsman Scoring Over 50 Per Cent of Runs in Both Innings

69, 69 . . . .   N. Gaur   Himachal Pradesh (126, 130) v Haryana at Gurgaon.

First-Wicket Partnerships of 100 in Each Innings

118* 179 . . . . R. G. Twose/M. D. Bell, Wellington v Central Districts at Wellington.

In the first innings, the first wicket put on 143, but Bell retired hurt on 71* at 118. Twose and Bell also put on 153 in their next opening stand v Auckland at Auckland.*

Other Notable Partnerships

First Wicket

319 Jitender Singh/N. R. Goel, Haryana v Jammu and Kashmir at Faridabad.
298 Aamir Sohail/Ijaz Ahmed, sen., Pakistan v West Indies (Third Test) at Karachi.
297 D. F. Hills/J. Cox, Tasmania v Victoria at Hobart.
286 M. L. Hayden/M. L. Love, Queensland v New South Wales at Brisbane.

Second Wicket

576† S. T. Jayasuriya/R. S. Mahanama, Sri Lanka v India (First Test) at Colombo (RPS).
287 M. D. Bell/J. D. Wells, Wellington v Auckland at Auckland.
285* M. L. Love/J. P. Maher, Queensland v New Zealanders at Cairns.
283 S. S. Das/P. Mullick, Orissa v Bihar at Cuttack.

Third Wicket

328 Asif Mahmood/Mohammad Wasim, Rawalpindi v Lahore City at Rawalpindi.
323 Aamir Sohail/Inzamam-ul-Haq, Pakistan v West Indies (Second Test) at Rawalpindi.
303 M. T. G. Elliott/L. D. Harper, Victoria v New South Wales at North Sydney.
295 C. B. Wishart/A. Flower, Mashonaland v Mashonaland A at Harare.
279* Ehsan Butt/Atif Rauf, Islamabad v Faislabad at Islamabad.

Fourth Wicket

436 S. Abbas Ali/P. K. Dwevedi, Madhya Pradesh v Railways at Indore.
289 K. C. Wessels/D. J. Callaghan, Eastern Province v Border at Port Elizabeth.
274* D. P. M. D. Jayawardene/R. P. A. H. Wickremaratne, Sinhalese SC v Kurunegala Youth CC at Colombo (SSC).
261 S. S. Bhave/A. V. Kale, Maharashtra v Saurashtra at Pune.

Fifth Wicket

316* L. D. Harper/G. B. Gardiner, Victoria v South Australia at Carlton.
277* M. W. Goodwin/A. Flower, Zimbabwe v Pakistan (First Test) at Bulawayo.
273 T. M. Moody/A. C. Gilchrist, Western Australia v South Australia at Perth.
253 W. Wiblin/S. C. Pope, Border v Western Province at East London.

Sixth Wicket

227* R. S. Gavaskar/S. S. Raul, India A v Pakistan A at Lahore.

Seventh Wicket

261 A. D. R. Campbell/P. A. Strang, Zimbabweans v Canterbury at Timaru.
229 Naeem Ashraf/Abdur Razzaq, Lahore City v Gujranwala at Gujranwala.

Ninth Wicket

195‡ M. V. Boucher/P. L. Symcox, South Africa v Pakistan (First Test) at Johannesburg.
164 B. C. M. S. Mendis/D. Seneviratne, Sebastianites C and AC v Matara SC at Colombo (Braybrooke Place).

Tenth Wicket

160 L. K. Germon/W. A. Wisneski, Canterbury v Northern Districts at Rangiora.
151‡ Azhar Mahmood/Mushtaq Ahmed, Pakistan v South Africa (First Test) at Rawalpindi.

† *World record for second wicket and all-wicket Test record.*
‡ *Test record.*

Eight or More Wickets in an Innings (10)

9-76	J. A. Rennie	Matabeleland v Mashonaland A at Bulawayo.
9-116	Fazl-e-Akbar	ADBP v WAPDA at Sheikhupura.
8-36	B. N. Schultz	Western Province v West Indies A at Cape Town.
8-53	A. G. Botha	Natal B v Northerns B at Centurion.
8-53	A. R. C. Fraser	England v West Indies (Second Test) at Port-of-Spain.
8-71	S. V. Bahutule	Mumbai v Rest of India at Mumbai.
8-74	Shakeel Khan	Habib Bank v Allied Bank at Karachi.
8-77	Shahid Mahboob	Karachi Whites v Bahawalpur at Karachi.
8-95	V. H. K. Ranaweera	Police SC v Bloomfield C and AC at Colombo (Reid Avenue).
8-107	B. J. Walker	Auckland v Canterbury at Auckland.

Twelve or More Wickets in a Match (9)

14-100	Kanwaljit Singh	Hyderabad v Karnataka at Secunderabad.
13-168	S. V. Bahutule	Mumbai v Rest of India at Mumbai.
12-79	Iqbal Siddiqui	Maharashtra v Baroda at Pune.
12-95	A. G. Botha	Natal B v Northerns B at Centurion.
12-103	B. de Silva	Bloomfield C and AC v Colts CC at Colombo (Reid Avenue).
12-113	P. V. Gandhe	Vidarbha v Rajasthan at Jaipur.
12-117	M. Muralitharan	Sri Lanka v Zimbabwe (First Test) at Kandy.
12-119	C. R. Miller	Tasmania v South Australia at Hobart.
12-161	Murtaza Hussain	Bahawalpur v Gujranwala at Rahimyar Khan.

Hat-Tricks

A. Kumble	Karnataka v Orissa at Rourkela.
S. C. G. MacGill	New South Wales v New Zealanders at Newcastle.
K. R. Pushpakumara	Nondescripts CC v Panadura SC at Panadura.
D. Taljard	Border v Pakistanis at East London.

Wicket with First Ball in First-Class Cricket

L. V. Garrick	West Indies A v South Africa A at Bloemfontein.
Shehzad Nazir	Faisalabad v Karachi Blues at Karachi.

Outstanding Innings Analyses

8.2–6–2–5	S. Elworthy	Northerns v Griqualand West at Centurion.
8–6–3–5	R. S. Gavaskar	Bengal v Tripura at Agartala.
4.5–3–4–5	Saeed Ajmal	Faisalabad v Karachi Blues at Karachi.
7–6–1–4	K. Chandrasekhara	Kerala v Andhra at Kochi.

Most Overs Bowled in an Innings

78–8–276–1	R. K. Chauhan	India v Sri Lanka (First Test) at Colombo (RPS).
75–30–174–3	M. Muralitharan	Sri Lanka v India (First Test) at Mohali.

Six or More Wicket-Keeping Dismissals in an Innings

7 ct	K. S. M. Iyer	Vidarbha v Uttar Pradesh at Allahabad.
7 ct	Zahid Umar	WAPDA v Habib Bank at Sheikhupura.
6 ct	D. S. Berry	Victoria v Western Australia at Perth.
6 ct	M. V. Boucher	South Africa v Pakistan (Third Test) at Port Elizabeth.
6 ct	M. V. Boucher	South Africa v Sri Lanka (First Test) at Cape Town.
5 ct, 1 st	E. M. I. Galagoda	Tamil Union C and AC v Sinhalese SC at Colombo (SSC).
6 ct	A. C. Gilchrist	Western Australia v New South Wales at Sydney.
4 ct, 2 st	Mohammad Shafiq	Multan v Islamabad at Sahiwal.
5 ct, 1 st	R. Paul	Tamil Nadu v Uttar Pradesh at Chennai.
6 ct	Rashid Latif	Pakistan v Zimbabwe (First Test) at Bulawayo.
4 ct, 2 st	D. Vitharana	Colts CC v Colombo CC at Colombo (Havelock Park).
6 ct	Wasim Yousufi	Peshawar v Bahawalpur at Peshawar.

Nine or More Wicket-Keeping Dismissals in a Match

11 ct†	Wasim Yousufi	Peshawar v Bahawalpur at Peshawar.
10 ct	A. C. Gilchrist	Western Australia v Victoria at Perth.
7 ct, 2 st	D. S. Berry	Victoria v Queensland at Melbourne.
8 ct, 1 st	M. V. Boucher	South Africa v Pakistan (Third Test) at Port Elizabeth.
9 ct	G. Gopal	Orissa v Assam at Cuttack.
6 ct, 3 st	Mohammad Shafiq	Multan v Islamabad at Sahiwal.
8 ct, 1 st	Zahid Umar	WAPDA v Habib Bank at Sheikhupura.

† National record.

Five Catches in an Innings in the Field

S. P. Fleming†	New Zealand v Zimbabwe (First Test) at Harare.

† Equalling Test record.

Seven Catches in a Match in the Field

S. P. Fleming†	New Zealand v Zimbabwe (First Test) at Harare.
P. W. Gunaratne	Bloomfield C and AC v Police SC at Colombo (Reid Avenue).

† Equalling Test record.

Match Double (100 Runs and 10 Wickets)

U. C. Hathurusinghe .	83, 44; 3-22, 7-55	Moors SC v Antonians SC at Colombo (Braybrooke Place).
Naeem Ashraf	74, 37; 6-56, 4-33	Lahore City v Karachi Blues at Lahore.

Wicket-Keeper's Match Double (100 Runs and 10 Dismissals)

A. C. Gilchrist	109; 5 ct, 5 ct	Western Australia v Victoria at Perth.

No Byes Conceded in Total of 500 or More

R. G. Hart	Northern Districts v Canterbury (524) at Rangiora.
I. A. Healy	Australia v South Africa (517) (Third Test) at Adelaide.
A. C. Parore	New Zealanders v Queensland (571) at Cairns.
R. C. Russell	England v West Indies (500-7 dec.) (Sixth Test) at St John's.

Unusual Dismissal – Timed Out

H. Yadav. . . . .   Tripura v Orissa at Cuttack.

The first such instance in first-class cricket.

Highest Innings Totals

952-6 dec.†	Sri Lanka v India (First Test) at Colombo (RPS).
650-5 dec.	Queensland v New South Wales at Brisbane.
633-5 dec.	India v Australia (Second Test) at Calcutta.
617-9 dec.	Karnataka v Uttar Pradesh at Bangalore.
613	Uttar Pradesh v Haryana at Kanpur.
602-4 dec.	Tamil Nadu v Goa at Chennai.

† *Test record.*

Lowest Innings Totals

33	Andhra v Kerala at Kochi.
54	Windward Islands v Guyana at St Vincent.
55	Goa v Hyderabad at Panaji.
58	Kurunegala Youth CC v Moors SC at Colombo (Braybrooke Place).
62	Allied Bank v Pakistan Customs at Karachi.
64	Northerns B v North West at Fochville.
67	Multan v Islamabad at Sahiwal.
67	Zimbabweans v New Zealand A at Dunedin.
68	Matara SC v Nondescripts CC at Matara.
74	Gauteng v Northerns at Johannesburg.

Highest Fourth-Innings Total

401-3 . . . .   Tasmania v Victoria at Hobart (set 399).

Win after Following On

Allied Bank (62 and 428) beat Pakistan Customs (323 and 80) by 87 runs at Karachi.

Most Extras in an Innings

	b	l-b	w	n-b	
99†	9	10	16	64	Lahore City (502-8 dec.) v Gujranwala at Gujranwala.
84	9	21	4	50	Allied Bank (428) v Pakistan Customs at Karachi.
80	0	10	10	60	Habib Bank (336) v PIA at Karachi.
76	6	20	8	42	PIA (407) v ADBP at Sheikhupura.

† *World record.*

Under experimental rules in domestic matches in Pakistan, two extras were scored for every wide and no-ball, in addition to any runs scored off that ball.

Career Aggregate Milestones

20,000 runs	A. J. Stewart, M. E. Waugh.
15,000 runs	C. L. Hooper.
10,000 runs	Aamir Sohail, M. G. Bevan, M. L. Hayden, D. S. Lehmann, S. V. Manjrekar, J. D. Siddons, S. R. Tendulkar.
1,500 wickets	C. A. Walsh.
1,000 wickets	A. A. Donald.
500 wickets	I. R. Bishop, R. D. B. Croft, A. Kumble, S. K. Warne.

ENGLAND IN THE WEST INDIES, 1997-98

Review by SCYLD BERRY

This was a series which a boxing promoter would have been proud to arrange: a middleweight contest between two well-matched teams, one on the way down, the other gradually on the way up. In one corner, West Indies, sliding rapidly from their position as longstanding unofficial world Test champions. They had recently returned from Pakistan where they had lost all three Tests by wide margins amid rumours of disunity, centred on Brian Lara, who had lost his batting mastery under the captaincy of Courtney Walsh. Indeed, the very future of cricket in the West Indies was perceived to be at crisis-point.

In the other corner, England were making modest progress after winning 2-0 in New Zealand and losing only 3-2 to Australia, instead of disintegrating as usual. But they needed to win a major Test series, which they had not done since beating Australia 11 years earlier, to give their recovery substance. Their captain, Mike Atherton, thought that beating West Indies was a realistic objective, and hinted that he would resign if England did not win.

And resign he did – at the very moment Lara, who displaced Walsh as captain before the series, was parading the Wisden Trophy round the ground in Antigua, the 13th successive occasion the West Indies captain had received it. West Indies won the Test series 3-1 (and the one-day series 4-1), but it was only at the end – after a series of continual drama which lived up to its billing – that their superiority was definitively established. Along the way, the pendulum swung from side to side with each Test. West Indies had the stronger team, if only because they had Curtly Ambrose back to something near his peak form, but the final margin was unjustly wide.

After the two Trinidad Tests had been shared, three crucial pieces of luck all went in the home side's favour. In Guyana, Lara won a toss which allowed West Indies to bat before the Bourda pitch disintegrated; in Barbados, rain washed out most of the last day when an England win or a draw were the only realistic results; then in Antigua, West Indies, having won the toss, were able to bowl when the re-laid pitch was so damp – it had been over-watered for fear that it would crack up prematurely – that three chunks came out of it in the first over. It slowly settled. When all three events went against England, Atherton could sustain his captaincy no longer, and resigned at once even though there were five one-day internationals still to be played; Atherton sat them out forlornly while Adam Hollioake took charge.

The quality of the pitches was a constant theme of the tour from the opening match in Montego Bay, where one ball would kick and the next would shoot; the game would have ended in two days if the umpires had been disposed to grant more than three lbws. England by this stage were desperate for cricket as they had been on tour for nearly a fortnight. They had opted for practice in Antigua, rather than an extra fixture, and even this was hit by rain. Despite a fine pitch for their second match at Chedwin Park, England suspected well before the First Test that Sabina Park was going to be uneven. They could not have guessed how right they would be. After just 56 minutes' cricket the game was abandoned owing to dangerous conditions.

In order to encourage the home fast bowlers, the whole square had just been re-laid – without leaving one old strip in case the process went wrong – with clay from the Appleton sugar estate in Jamaica. There was nothing wrong with the clay (although it may not have been mixed with sufficient good-quality limestone). What was wrong, as a subsequent report by the Jamaica Cricket Association found, was that the Test pitch was "angled and ridged", and that the heavy roller which had been used to lay it was "out of round" and concave in parts. Senior officials of an embarrassed West Indies Cricket Board, and many local supporters, thought the Test had been called off prematurely. Independent assessors, starting with the umpires and the referee, Barry Jarman, believed the historic decision was right.

LONGEST SEQUENCES WITHOUT WINNING A TEST SERIES

Series		
20	New Zealand v England	1929-30 to 1983
13*	**England v West Indies**	**1973 to 1997-98**
11	Pakistan v England	1954 to 1982
10	South Africa v Australia	1902-03 to 1963-64
8	Australia v England	1882-83 to 1890
8	South Africa v England	1938-39 to 1964-65
8	Australia v West Indies	1977-78 to 1992-93

* *Unbroken.*

All dates inclusive   *Research: Robert Brooke*

With commendable despatch, an extra Test match was arranged at a week's notice in Port-of-Spain. A second Test pitch was already being prepared there in case the Guyana Test was cancelled because of political trouble. It was not quite ready for what became the Second Test, however, and too many balls kept low in addition to hitting the batsmen. Thereafter, there was no excuse for the combination of inadequate net facilities, poor pitches and incomplete stands that bedevilled the tour. At its end, ECB chairman Lord MacLaurin made an official complaint to ICC. But while the physical structure of these grounds sometimes fell short of satisfactory, the prevailing spirit was harmonious, and England supporters, who sometimes out-numbered the home spectators on this tour, were warmly received. A carnival atmosphere prevailed as loudspeakers played music during every break in play, however brief.

West Indies, though, still had Ambrose, who defied every prediction that he was finished after his tour of Pakistan. He was particularly effective in Trinidad and Guyana, and against Atherton, whom he dismissed six times in the series. His opening partner Walsh, if not quite so formidable with a new ball, was equally accurate and passionate to win. Secondly, West Indies were re-united, with Lara fully motivated having been granted what he – and the West Indian selectors – had previously thought was his due. (The

Board had earlier vetoed his appointment for the Pakistan tour.) Immediately he was appointed captain – and told by Board president Pat Rousseau that the future of West Indian cricket depended on him – Lara talked to Walsh and Ambrose, to persuade them to carry on. A careless captain might have lost both of his strike bowlers, but Lara introduced a warm, communicative style, and brought the best out of his veterans and the team. Lara's captaincy was innovative in bowling changes and field-placings, a little too much so at times, as he sought to establish a different style from his conventional predecessors. His decision to open England's second innings in the first of the Trinidad Tests without either Walsh or Ambrose was a notable error (and briefly gave England a taste of how easy life might have been had they retired) but on the whole his captaincy was imaginative, and it worked.

If it was predictable that West Indies would have the edge in strike bowling, their superiority in spin was not. While Ambrose and Walsh took 52 wickets, the other four fast bowlers took only 12 between them. But Carl Hooper and, in two Tests, the leg-spinner Dinanath Ramnarine collected 24 at 20 runs each. Hooper shifted to a more attacking line on and outside off stump; Ramnarine offered keenness and a well-controlled leg-break on which to base future variations. He and Nixon McLean were the only two new players that West Indies tried; ten of the 18 players they used were over 30. The former fast bowler Michael Holding called for the West Indian selectors' term to be increased from one year to three years so they would have more of an eye to the long term.

For England, slow left-armer Phil Tufnell took one wicket every 30 overs at 62 runs each, and his presence in all six Tests indicated the extent to which England's strategy relied on containment. It was rational enough that Tufnell should have been defensive at the start of the series, when Dean Headley and Andy Caddick often lapsed from line and length, but not when they tightened up. In effect, Tufnell was reduced to a stock bowler, and seemed all too willing to oblige by bowling over the wicket at a right-hander's legs. This tactic was a major factor in the first West Indian victory, in Trinidad, as it compelled England's increasingly tired and under-prepared seamers to take all the wickets from the other end. While the other spinner, Robert Croft, would not have been such a run-saver, he ventured and gained more in his single Test.

The batting of the two sides was much of a muchness: some fine individual innings were played, but neither team had the collective strength to produce consistently high totals on bowlers' pitches. Alec Stewart was the leading run-scorer in the series, and unequivocally the best batsman in the two Trinidad Tests (and in the Jamaica Test, so far as it went). A strong body of opinion believed that Stewart should have kept wicket, especially after Jack Russell had undergone some confidence-sapping experiences in Trinidad. But England might not have lived with West Indies for so long if he had. For West Indies, the opening pair of Sherwin Campbell and Stuart Williams were as unproductive in the first three proper Tests as Clayton Lambert and Philo Wallace were flamboyantly fruitful in the last two. Whereas Campbell stayed in his crease and had a poor season in all cricket,

his fellow-Barbadian Wallace struck opening bowlers back over their heads, and hooked and cut them with old-time West Indian panache. His new partnership with Lambert, recalled at the age of 36, re-energised the West Indian effort as England tired in the last two back-to-back Tests.

Lara's high-tempo batting suggested that his record-breaking innings might be a thing of the past, but as captain he became the West Indians' leading run-scorer again. He was to benefit greatly from the starts which Lambert and Wallace provided, after being exposed to the new ball early on in Trinidad and dismissed by Angus Fraser on all four occasions. Hooper played the innings of his life to win the first Trinidad Test, without going on from there as a batsman; Shivnarine Chanderpaul was steady as usual, while Jimmy Adams lost his Test place after two landmark decisions by Darrell Hair in Guyana, when he was twice given out for padding the ball away with bat tucked behind pad.

England tried John Crawley and Mark Butcher at No. 3 without finding an answer. Butcher's best work was done down the order in guiding England home in Trinidad: he had the talent, although his shot selection was another matter. Once Mark Ramprakash came good in Guyana, England had a strong middle order with what looked like a long-term future. Ramprakash's 154 in Barbados was a masterpiece and suggested he had shed the over-intensity which had once consumed him. The Test vice-captain, Nasser Hussain, was perhaps the unluckiest batsman on either side in the decisions he received, while Graham Thorpe was dismissed five times by spin, one more reason to suggest that his counter-attacking style would have been more suited to the No. 4 position.

One consequence of the poor pitches in the first half of the series, when the ball frequently did not carry on the bounce, was the poor wicket-keeping on both sides. A second was the effectiveness of Fraser. Almost until the end he matched Ambrose wicket for wicket, while admitting with characteristic self-effacement that, when he took eight for 53, the best figures for any England bowler against West Indies, it was actually the worst spell he bowled in the Trinidad Tests. The thick-seamed ball used in the West Indies allowed him just enough movement, while Headley kept improving (aside from his no-balling), and Caddick continued to permutate on-days and off. With Darren Gough's absence, it was essential to England that their three experienced seamers should stay fit for every Test and, thanks in part to the support staff of physiotherapist Wayne Morton and fitness consultant Dean Riddle, they did. Nevertheless, Gough was still missed for his effervescence, particularly when Hooper and David Williams were knocking off the runs in Trinidad, and for his ability to reverse-swing the old ball.

In the one-day series, as in the Tests, the bottom did not fall out of England's effort until towards the end, though when it did it was spectacular. The idea of having different Test and one-day touring parties was well conceived and executed. Seven one-day players were to be flown out, to join Atherton, Adam Hollioake, Stewart, Thorpe, Croft and Headley, who were selected for both parties, while three places were left open. This arrangement gave the remaining players on the Test tour something to hope and play for, until the end of the Barbados Test, when Fraser, Ramprakash and Russell were nominated as the final three. Russell's selection proved to be a mistake when Thorpe had to fly home with back trouble after the Barbados internationals, and the forlorn Atherton was ignored, leaving England with too little specialist batting. Moreover, England's medium-pacers were better suited to the slow pitches of Sharjah than to containing West Indian strokemakers on their own patch. After Ashley Giles had withdrawn with Achilles trouble from the party of seven reinforcements, a second spinner – even the defensive Tufnell – would have been useful. Still, on all their previous tours of the West Indies since 1973-74, England had collapsed long before the end.

ENGLAND TOURING PARTY

M. A. Atherton (Lancashire) (*captain*), N. Hussain (Essex) (*vice-captain*), M. A. Butcher (Surrey), A. R. Caddick (Somerset), A. P. Cowan (Essex), J. P. Crawley (Lancashire), R. D. B. Croft (Glamorgan), A. R. C. Fraser (Middlesex), D. W. Headley (Kent), A. J. Hollioake (Surrey), M. R. Ramprakash (Middlesex), R. C. Russell (Gloucestershire), C. E. W. Silverwood (Yorkshire), A. J. Stewart (Surrey), G. P. Thorpe (Surrey), P. C. R. Tufnell (Middlesex).

Silverwood was promoted from the England A tour when D. Gough (Yorkshire) withdrew through injury.

After the Test series, Butcher, Caddick, Cowan, Crawley, Hussain, Silverwood and Tufnell flew home. The squad for the one-day series was reinforced by D. R. Brown (Warwickshire), M. A. Ealham (Kent), M. V. Fleming (Kent), G. A. Hick (Worcestershire), B. C. Hollioake (Surrey) and N. V. Knight (Warwickshire). A. F. Giles (Warwickshire) had been selected for the one-day series, but was injured. A. J. Hollioake, originally named as one-day vice-captain, assumed the captaincy when Atherton resigned after the Tests.

Tour manager: R. Bennett. *Coach:* D. Lloyd. *Assistant coach:* J. E. Emburey. *Scorer:* M. N. Ashton. *Physiotherapist:* W. P. Morton. *Fitness consultant:* D. Riddle.

ENGLAND TOUR RESULTS

Test matches – Played 6: Won 1, Lost 3, Drawn 2.
First-class matches – Played 10: Won 2, Lost 3, Drawn 5.
Wins – West Indies, Jamaica.
Losses – West Indies (3).
Draws – West Indies (2), West Indies A, Guyana, Barbados.
One-day internationals – Played 5: Won 1, Lost 4.
Other non-first-class matches – Played 2: Won 1, Drawn 1. *Win* – University of the West Indies Vice-Chancellor's XI. *Draw* – Trinidad & Tobago.

TEST MATCH AVERAGES

WEST INDIES – BATTING

	T	I	NO	R	HS	100s	50s	Avge	Ct
P. A. Wallace	2	3	0	198	92	0	2	66.00	2
C. B. Lambert	2	3	0	188	104	1	1	62.66	3
B. C. Lara	6	9	1	417	93	0	3	52.12	13
C. L. Hooper	6	8	2	295	108*	1	1	49.16	5
S. Chanderpaul	6	9	1	272	118	1	0	34.00	4
I. R. Bishop	3	3	1	62	44*	0	0	31.00	1

	T	I	NO	R	HS	100s	50s	Avge	Ct
S. C. Williams	4	6	0	141	62	0	1	23.50	3
J. C. Adams	4	6	0	113	53	0	1	18.83	2
D. Williams	5	7	0	98	65	0	1	14.00	19
S. L. Campbell	4	6	0	79	28	0	0	13.16	1
C. E. L. Ambrose	6	8	1	83	31	0	0	11.85	2
C. A. Walsh	6	6	4	15	6	0	0	7.50	4
N. A. M. McLean	4	4	1	22	11	0	0	7.33	1
K. C. G. Benjamin	2	4	1	7	6*	0	0	2.33	0

Played in two Tests: R. I. C. Holder 10, 45 (2 ct); D. Ramnarine 0, 19 (2 ct). Played in one Test: J. R. Murray 4 (3 ct); F. A. Rose 2.

* Signifies not out.

BOWLING

	O	M	R	W	BB	5W/i	Avge
C. E. L. Ambrose	205.5	62	428	30	5-25	2	14.26
D. Ramnarine	91	37	148	9	4-29	0	16.44
C. L. Hooper	190.5	61	355	15	5-80	1	23.66
C. A. Walsh	261.2	63	564	22	4-80	0	25.63
N. A. M. McLean	78	15	203	5	2-46	0	40.60

Also bowled: J. C. Adams 15–7–19–1; K. C. G. Benjamin 63–14–166–3; I. R. Bishop 50–7–163–3; S. Chanderpaul 10–3–35–0; C. B. Lambert 1–0–1–0; F. A. Rose 20–6–53–1.

ENGLAND – BATTING

	T	I	NO	R	HS	100s	50s	Avge	Ct/St
M. R. Ramprakash	3	5	1	266	154	1	1	66.50	2
A. J. Stewart	6	11	1	452	83	0	4	45.20	6
G. P. Thorpe	6	11	3	339	103	1	1	42.37	9
N. Hussain	6	11	2	295	106	1	1	32.77	2
M. A. Atherton	6	11	0	199	64	0	1	18.09	5
M. A. Butcher	5	9	1	125	28	0	0	15.62	4
R. C. Russell	5	9	1	90	32	0	0	11.25	12/1
J. P. Crawley	3	4	0	45	22	0	0	11.25	1
D. W. Headley	6	9	2	69	31	0	0	9.85	4
A. R. C. Fraser	6	8	0	44	17	0	0	5.50	1
A. R. Caddick	5	7	0	19	8	0	0	2.71	2
P. C. R. Tufnell	6	8	3	11	6	0	0	2.20	1

Played in two Tests: A. J. Hol250ioake 2, 12. Played in one Test: R. D. B. Croft 26, 14 (1 ct).

* Signifies not out.

BOWLING

	O	M	R	W	BB	5W/i	Avge
A. R. C. Fraser	187.2	50	492	27	8-53	2	18.22
R. D. B. Croft	58.1	18	139	6	3-50	0	23.16
D. W. Headley	171.3	34	546	19	4-77	0	28.73
A. R. Caddick	120	31	388	13	5-67	1	29.84
P. C. R. Tufnell	212.5	69	438	7	2-43	0	62.57

Also bowled: M. A. Butcher 5–1–16–0; A. J. Hol150ioake 5–0–12–0; M. R. Ramprakash 41–9–118–3.

ENGLAND TOUR AVERAGES – FIRST-CLASS AVERAGES

BATTING

	M	I	NO	R	HS	100s	50s	Avge	Ct/St
M. R. Ramprakash	5	8	2	389	154	1	2	64.83	4
G. P. Thorpe	9	15	4	603	103	1	4	54.81	9
A. J. Stewart	9	15	1	538	83	0	5	38.42	10
N. Hussain	10	17	3	529	159	2	1	37.78	5
A. J. Hollioake	6	6	0	182	48	0	0	30.33	2
R. D. B. Croft	3	4	0	90	32	0	0	22.50	3
M. A. Butcher	7	12	1	227	79	0	1	20.63	4
M. A. Atherton	9	16	0	312	64	0	1	19.50	10
R. C. Russell	9	15	3	187	32*	0	0	15.58	23/2
J. P. Crawley	6	8	0	121	41	0	0	15.12	1
D. W. Headley	7	10	3	87	31	0	0	12.42	4
A. R. C. Fraser	8	9	1	53	17	0	0	6.62	1
A. R. Caddick	8	10	0	35	9	0	0	3.50	2
P. C. R. Tufnell	9	9	3	11	6	0	0	1.83	1

Played in three matches: A. P. Cowan 13, 13*, 0 (2 ct). Played in two matches: C. E. W. Silverwood 0, 0*.

* Signifies not out.

BOWLING

	O	M	R	W	BB	5W/i	Avge
A. R. C. Fraser	232.2	60	617	32	8-53	3	19.28
R. D. B. Croft	159.4	48	354	18	6-50	2	19.66
D. W. Headley	200.2	37	592	28	5-32	1	21.14
A. R. Caddick	209	47	690	23	5-67	1	30.00
P. C. R. Tufnell	333.5	99	706	22	5-42	1	32.09

Also bowled: M. A. Butcher 9–3–23–0; A. P. Cowan 72–19–200–1; A. J. Hollioake 22–2–84–1; M. R. Ramprakash 51–13–151–3; C. E. W. Silverwood 39.2–5–155–3; G. P. Thorpe 2–0–13–0.

Note: Matches in this section which were not first-class are signified by a dagger.

JAMAICA v ENGLAND XI

At Montego Bay, January 16, 17, 18. England XI won by an innings and 65 runs. Toss: England XI.

England won their opening match – their first-ever first-class fixture at Jarrett Park – with a day to spare, but victory meant little due to the dreadful pitch. Recently re-laid, using the same soil as the new Test pitch at Sabina Park, it was so uneven that umpire Bucknor was reportedly concerned that the tourists might refuse to play. But, with only two games before the Test, England were just anxious to get on the field. As Jamaica's attack was unusually weak – missing Walsh, Rose and Patterson – and as conditions could only worsen, Atherton batted. He and Crawley negotiated their way to lunch, but England slipped to 78 for four afterwards. They rallied through Thorpe and Hollioake, the only batsmen in this game to escape the twenties. Thorpe batted 333 minutes for 89, though he hit just three fours and a six. The declaration came as he was out, and Headley, English by birth but Jamaican by descent, was soon among the wickets. Caddick followed up with three in nine balls. On the third day, Jamaica followed on 161 behind and were all out again for 96, in just 37.1 overs. This time Headley, who finished with nine wickets, shared the rewards with Tufnell. Russell, in the meantime, had resorted to keeping wicket in a helmet.

Close of play: First day, England XI 179-5 (G. P. Thorpe 41*, R. C. Russell 14*); Second day, Jamaica 108-8 (B. S. Murphy 14*, K. H. Powell 0*).

England XI

*M. A. Atherton c Murphy b Powell . . .	28	A. R. Caddick lbw b Williams	9
A. J. Stewart c Breese b Richards	1	D. W. Headley not out	18
J. P. Crawley run out	25	B 28, l-b 4	32
N. Hussain c Adams b Breese	15		
G. P. Thorpe c Samuels b Murphy . . .	89	1/2 2/55 3/73	(8 wkts dec.) 286
A. J. Hollioake c Coley b Powell	40	4/78 5/139 6/219	
†R. C. Russell c Coley b Williams	29	7/252 8/286	

A. R. C. Fraser and P. C. R. Tufnell did not bat.

Bowling: Powell 24–7–40–2; Richards 19–8–25–1; Williams 33–10–62–2; Breese 24–3–59–1; Murphy 19.3–0–64–1; Adams 1–0–4–0.

Jamaica

L. V. Garrick c Russell b Headley	0	– c Atherton b Headley	2
R. G. Samuels c Russell b Headley	0	– st Russell b Tufnell	26
W. W. Hinds b Headley	18	– c Russell b Caddick	5
*J. C. Adams b Tufnell	18	– c Stewart b Tufnell	9
M. D. Ventura b Caddick	3	– b Headley	0
G. R. Breese b Caddick	6	– lbw b Headley	1
L. R. Williams lbw b Caddick	4	– b Headley	0
†A. N. Coley c Russell b Caddick	10	– b Caddick	7
B. S. Murphy not out	26	– c Stewart b Tufnell	22
K. H. Powell b Headley	0	– c Atherton b Tufnell	1
O. R. Richards b Headley	1	– not out	0
B 15, l-b 3, n-b 21	39	B 9, l-b 4, n-b 10	23

1/6 2/10 3/39 4/69 5/71	**125**
6/75 7/80 8/101 9/112	
1/2 2/21 3/39 4/55 5/55	**96**
6/56 7/63 8/79 9/84	

Bowling: *First Innings*—Caddick 13–4–24–4; Headley 17.5–5–32–5; Fraser 2–0–7–0; Tufnell 20–4–44–1. *Second Innings*—Headley 11–4–14–4; Fraser 5–0–19–0; Caddick 8–3–17–2; Tufnell 13.1–5–33–4.

Umpires: S. A. Bucknor and C. Fletcher.

WEST INDIES A v ENGLAND XI

At St Catherine, January 22, 23, 24, 25. Drawn. Toss: West Indies A.

After the fiasco of Montego Bay, Chedwin Park offered a pitch so slow and true that both teams passed 400 in the first innings, which stretched into the fourth day. England did struggle at the start, when they were asked to bat and slumped to 30 for three. But Hussain and Thorpe combined to add 184 in 63 overs. Hussain shared another century partnership with Hollioake, and finished on 159, with 20 fours. Home captain Holder responded in kind, batting for eight hours and hitting 27 fours in a career-best 183. The Middlesex pair, Fraser and Tufnell, took all the wickets but Holder's; both bowled economically, too, and Fraser's five ensured his return to the Test side. But Hollioake's role was thrown into doubt when he dislocated his right shoulder diving in the field. The draw was inevitable long before England resumed on the last afternoon; there was time for the Guyanese pace bowler King to take another three wickets and give his side a slight moral advantage.

Close of play: First day, England XI 293-4 (N. Hussain 131*, A. J. Hollioake 33*); Second day, West Indies A 156-3 (R. I. C. Holder 57*, R. N. Lewis 0*); Third day, West Indies A 411-7 (L. R. Williams 50*, N. A. M. McLean 24*).

England XI

*M. A. Atherton c sub (K. M. Baker) b McLean	8	– c Hoyte b King	49
A. J. Stewart b King	12	– c Lewis b Collins	21
J. P. Crawley c Semple b King	0	– c Williams b King	41
N. Hussain st Hoyte b Lewis	159	– c Hoyte b King	3
G. P. Thorpe c King b Lewis	81	– not out	36
A. J. Hollioake run out	48		
†R. C. Russell not out	32	– (6) not out	18
A. R. Caddick c Collins b Lewis	5		
A. P. Cowan b King	13		
A. R. C. Fraser not out	9		
B 2, l-b 17, w 4, n-b 10	33	B 6, l-b 2, w 1, n-b 4	13

1/24 2/24 3/30 4/214 5/324   (8 wkts. dec.) 400   1/44 2/103 3/116 4/121   (4 wkts) 181
6/346 7/360 8/386

P. C. R. Tunnell did not bat.

Bowling: *First Innings*—McLean 23–4–86–1; King 21.2–3–84–3; Williams 20–4–46–0; Collins 20–5–62–0; Lewis 37–13–101–3; Hinds 1–0–2–0. *Second Innings*—McLean 9–2–42–0; King 15–5–45–3; Collins 13–2–26–1; Lewis 18–5–34–0; Williams 9–2–23–0; Hinds 1–0–3–0.

West Indies A

L. V. Garrick b Fraser	26	N. A. M. McLean lbw b Fraser	25
W. W. Hinds c Russell b Fraser	12	P. T. Collins c Stewart b Tunnell	3
K. F. Semple b Tunnell	54	R. D. King c Hussain b Tunnell	2
*R. I. C. Holder b Caddick	183		
R. N. Lewis c Stewart b Fraser	11	B 5, l-b 2, n-b 11	18
F. L. Reifer b Fraser	0		
†R. L. Hoyte c Russell b Tunnell	33	1/21 2/59 3/154 4/178 5/186	434
L. R. Williams not out	67	6/277 7/377 8/413 9/426	

Bowling: Caddick 34–6–133–1; Cowan 29–10–75–0; Fraser 38–10–99–5; Tunnell 52.5–14–107–4; Thorpe 2–0–13–0.

Umpires: N. Malcolm and T. Wilson.

WEST INDIES v ENGLAND

First Test Match

At Kingston, January 29. Drawn. Toss: England. Test debut: N. A. M. McLean.

After the third ball of the match flew off a length past the England captain's nose, one alleged sage turned to his neighbour in the press box and whispered: "Well, we can rule out a draw, that's for sure." This was proved wrong with astonishing rapidity. After just 56 minutes' cricket, the contest – which enthusiasts had been looking forward to with relish for months – was called off in sensational and, at this level, unprecedented circumstances because the umpires considered the pitch to be dangerous.

Sixty-one balls (and a no-ball) were bowled in that time, and the England physio Wayne Morton came on to the field six times to attend batsmen who had suffered direct hits from Ambrose and Walsh. Neither bowled exceptionally well, by their standards. It was unnecessary; almost anyone could have propelled a hard ball lethally off such a surface.

Jamaican officials had decided to re-lay the pitch to avoid losing West Indies' traditional advantage over England by playing on the slow, low surface Sabina had become. However, work started less than six months before the game, and there was no time for the soil to bed down. The wicket was not as ugly as the fissured horror of Perth a year earlier, but it never rolled flat, and failed to bind together.

It rapidly became clear that the batsmen were suffering more than the normal terrors England players expect when confronted with a fired-up West Indies attack. They lost three wickets quickly: Butcher for a golden duck. But observers quickly sensed these might be trivial details. The ball was moving so unpredictably that a serious injury looked a near-certainty. Umpire Venkat was on the walkie-talkie to referee Barry Jarman after three overs but, under Law 3, the fitness of the pitch remains the umpires' responsibility whether there is a referee or not, and Jarman could only offer moral support.

After Stewart was hit for the third time and Thorpe for the second, the end was in sight. Atherton, the England captain, came on to the field and got agreement from his opposite number, Lara, that the game could not go on. After ten minutes' discussion, the umpires led the players off and the final decision to abandon came nearly an hour later. Stewart was left on what was widely agreed to be the most heroic nine not out in history.

SHORTEST TEST MATCHES

Balls bowled†

61	**West Indies v England, Kingston**	**1997-98**
72	Sri Lanka v India, Kandy	1993-94
104	England v Australia, Nottingham	1926
216	Pakistan v Sri Lanka, Gujranwala	1991-92
228	England v Australia, Lord's	1902
401	England v South Africa, Manchester	1924
426	England v New Zealand, Manchester	1931
427	India v New Zealand, Madras	1995-96

All the above matches were drawn.

† *Excluding no-balls and wides.*

Research: Robert Brooke

England had chosen to bat in the belief that such a pitch could only get worse. There was loose soil on the top by the time the game ended, so this seems logical enough. We will never know what might have happened had West Indies batted first and faced the far less imposing England attack. It is hard to imagine that Lara, in his first Test as captain, would have cried for mercy in front of a Jamaican crowd, largely hostile to his appointment instead of their hero Walsh. In any case, he would have put England in.

The Sabina crowd, once famously volatile, reacted to the disaster phlegmatically, which was perhaps another signal that, in Kingston, football now excites more passion than cricket. The 4,000 present got their admission fee returned, but that hardly represented a fair deal for the 500 or so who had travelled from England, and legal action was threatened, though it fizzled out. The Jamaican officials who decided to dig up the pitch so soon before the Test were accused of "bungling inadequacy" by local papers.

It took only a few hours to arrange a replacement Test. There was no chance of playing in Jamaica, since there was no alternative stadium. Both Bridgetown and St John's were unavailable, because of work going on there, and there were fears about whether either of these grounds would be ready for their own Tests. Instead, it was

[*Patrick Eagar*

Mark Butcher becomes Sabina's unluckiest victim, falling to his first ball in competitive cricket for four months.

decided to scrap England's first-class game against Trinidad, and play an extra Test at Queen's Park the following week, immediately before the scheduled Test there.

It took several days for ICC to decide that this match existed at all and should count in the records, though all precedent suggested this was the only correct decision and that events which have taken place cannot be expunged. It left Nixon McLean with a peculiar non-event of a debut (luckily, he was picked again and did not emulate J. C. W. MacBryan of England in 1924, who did not bat or bowl in his only Test). And it was rough on the three dismissed batsmen, especially Butcher, who had come in as a late replacement when Russell pulled out with diarrhoea. He had not batted since September, owing to England's poor pre-match planning. It was even rougher on spectators who had saved for years for what they thought would be the holiday of a lifetime rather than an all-time fiasco.

All the consequences took even longer to emerge, but ICC began taking steps to insist on a degree of consultation and supervision designed to make a repetition improbable, if not impossible. – MATTHEW ENGEL.

England

*M. A. Atherton c Campbell b Walsh	2	G. P. Thorpe not out		0
†A. J. Stewart not out	9	B 4, n-b 1		5
M. A. Butcher c S. C. Williams b Walsh	0			
N. Hussain c Hooper b Ambrose	1	1/4 (1) 2/4 (3) 3/9 (4)	(3 wkts)	17

J. P. Crawley, A. J. Hollioake, A. R. Caddick, D. W. Headley, A. R. C. Fraser and P. C. R. Tufnell did not bat.

Bowling: Walsh 5.1–1–10–2; Ambrose 5–3–3–1.

West Indies

S. L. Campbell, S. C. Williams, *B. C. Lara, C. L. Hooper, S. Chanderpaul, J. C. Adams, †D. Williams, I. R. Bishop, C. E. L. Ambrose, N. A. M. McLean and C. A. Walsh.

Umpires: S. Venkataraghavan (India) and S. A. Bucknor. Referee: B. N. Jarman (Australia).

†At Pointe-à-Pierre, February 1, 2. Drawn. Toss: England XI. England XI 351 (M. A. Atherton 61, A. J. Stewart 73, J. P. Crawley 33, N. Hussain 66, R. C. Russell 77; D. Ramnarine five for 72, A. Samaroo four for 91); Trinidad & Tobago 274 (D. Ganga 41, L. A. Roberts 60, P. V. Simmons 78 not out, Extras 34; A. R. Caddick three for 38).

Originally scheduled as a four-day match at Port-of-Spain, but rearranged over two days to accommodate the extra Test.

WEST INDIES v ENGLAND

Second Test Match

At Port-of-Spain, February 5, 6, 7, 8, 9. West Indies won by three wickets. Toss: England.

This match, hastily rearranged after the débâcle of Kingston, did much to restore the tarnished reputation of cricket as the kernel of Caribbean sport. It was a taut, keenly contested game, which fluctuated tantalisingly throughout.

For most of the third and fourth days, England seemed to be on course for victory, but, 20 minutes after lunch on the final day, Hooper stroked the runs that completed a West Indian win by three wickets. Lara, in his first proper Test as the official captain of West Indies, was relieved and triumphant; the England team were desolate. Nothing is so galling in sport as losing a match you should have won. The anguish felt by the senior members of the England party was hauntingly familiar. Fraser and Stewart, who both made outstanding contributions, played, as did Russell, at Port-of-Spain in 1990. Then rain from nowhere allowed West Indies to escape with a draw. The same three were also there on the fourth day in 1994, when England, apparently in control, spurned chances in the field before Ambrose ran amok. This defeat was just as numbing.

It was a game in which the battle-hardened pros, rather than the young whipper-snappers, prevailed. The pitch was untrustworthy (except by Sabina Park standards), producing uneven bounce and substantial lateral movement on the first three days; on such a surface, resolution, know-how and patience were the key virtues. For England, Fraser, who took a career-best eight for 53 in the first innings and 11 for 110 in the match, and Stewart, with two battling half-centuries, showed these qualities in abundance. For West Indies, Ambrose, the tiny wicket-keeper David Williams, and Hooper, whose flawless six-hour innings of 94 not out earned the match award, were the architects of victory.

The toss was again an irrelevance. Atherton batted, Lara would have bowled. Initially, the West Indian pace bowlers were off target and Stewart struck the ball with freedom on the leg side. But, taking their lead from the miserly Ambrose, West Indies restricted England to 175 for eight on the first day. Thorpe's dismissal, edging the first ball of off-spin he received from Hooper, was the softest; Hollioake's the most controversial. He was run out after a mix-up with Hussain. Admittedly, he was yards out of his ground when a bail was removed, but a subsequent replay confirmed Hollioake's polite assertion to umpire Venkat that the keeper had flicked off a bail before taking Chanderpaul's throw from cover. The third umpire, Clyde Cumberbatch, was consulted, but the only replay he viewed gave him what the referee, Barry Jarman, described as "an unplayable lie". Cumberbatch gave Hollioake out anyway.

The second day belonged to Fraser, in his first appearance on the field as an England player for two years. In the morning, he batted stoically for an hour and a half alongside Hussain, who battled five hours for his 61 not out. Then Fraser took five of the seven wickets to fall, including that of Lara, who skied to mid-off for 55. Fraser's method was beautifully simple. Unlike his less experienced partners, he banged the ball down on a length at off stump time and time again. On this pitch, that was enough. The following morning, Fraser's persistence was spectacularly rewarded as he accounted for the last three wickets in 15 balls to give his side an unexpected lead of 23. His figures were the best ever for England against West Indies – beating his own eight for 75, four years earlier.

BEST BOWLING FOR ENGLAND AGAINST WEST INDIES

8-53	**A. R. C. Fraser, Port-of-Spain**	**1997-98**
8-75	A. R. C. Fraser, Bridgetown	1993-94
8-86	A. W. Greig, Port-of-Spain	1973-74
8-103	I. T. Botham, Lord's	1984
7-34	T. E. Bailey, Kingston	1953-54
7-43	D. G. Cork, Lord's	1995
7-44	T. E. Bailey, Lord's	1957
7-44	F. S. Trueman, Birmingham	1963
7-49	J. A. Snow, Kingston	1967-68
7-50	W. E. Hollies, Georgetown	1934-35
7-56	James Langridge, Manchester	1933
7-70	W. Voce, Port-of-Spain	1929-30
7-103	J. C. Laker, Bridgetown	1947-48

Now Lara made an eccentric decision, much appreciated by England's openers. Instead of giving the new ball to Ambrose and Walsh, he tossed it to Benjamin and McLean. England raced to 50 without loss in 13 overs. Again, Stewart was in princely form; he scored 73 before edging to Hooper at first slip via David Williams's forehead. With sturdy contributions from the rest of the batsmen, England held a mighty lead of 242 at the close, with six wickets remaining. The next day, Ambrose intervened, bowling a devastating spell of five for 16 from 7.5 overs as England added just 39. Shades of 1994 – yet West Indies still required the highest total of the match, 282, to win.

Despite a brave 62 by Stuart Williams, Fraser had reduced them to 124 for five when David Williams united with Hooper. For 23 overs on Sunday afternoon and another 25 on Monday morning, they defied the English attack in a partnership of 129. Williams was quick to pull and given ample opportunities by Caddick and Headley. Hooper batted with elegant serenity. Occasionally, he glided down the pitch to drive Tufnell's left-arm spin, but most of the time he kicked the ball away as Tufnell, bowling over the wicket, employed a negative line outside leg stump. Hooper countered the pace bowlers with expert late adjustments, and punished them unerringly whenever they strayed.

England had their chances. Against the first ball of the final day, Williams checked a drive – but Fraser, in his one false move of the game, could not hold the return catch. Off the second new ball, Williams was dropped again, by Russell down the leg-side. Eventually, Headley dismissed him for 65, his highest and most precious Test innings; in Headley's next over, Ambrose was caught behind. But there were no more dramas, just one moment of black comedy: to underline England's plight, a shooter from Fraser passed through Russell's gloves and hit the helmet behind him, thereby conceding five byes.

Russell's return to the England team had been harrowing. He kept poorly, even allowing for a pitch that was tricky for keepers as well as batsmen, and scored few runs. But more worrying for the management was the bowling of Fraser's partners. Even though Headley took four wickets in the game, he was far too inaccurate; so was Caddick, who remained wicketless on a surface well suited to his style of bowling. Moreover, England had only three days to regroup before playing another Test on the same dreaded ground. – VIC MARKS.

Man of the Match: C. L. Hooper.

Close of play: First day, England 175-8 (N. Hussain 44*, A. R. C. Fraser 2*); Second day, West Indies 177-7 (C. E. L. Ambrose 20*, K. C. G. Benjamin 0*); Third day, England 219-4 (G. P. Thorpe 32*, A. J. Holliooke 9*); Fourth day, West Indies 181-5 (C. L. Hooper 40*, D. Williams 36*).

England

*M. A. Atherton c Lara b Ambrose	11	– b Walsh 31
A. J. Stewart lbw b Benjamin	50	– c Hooper b McLean 73
J. P. Crawley c S. C. Williams b Ambrose	17	– lbw b McLean 22
N. Hussain not out	61	– c and b Walsh 23
G. P. Thorpe c D. Williams b Hooper	8	– c Lara b Walsh 39
A. J. Holliooke run out	2	– c Lara b Ambrose 12
†R. C. Russell c S. C. Williams b McLean	0	– lbw b Ambrose 8
A. R. Caddick lbw b Walsh	8	– c D. Williams b Ambrose 0
D. W. Headley c D. Williams b Ambrose	11	– not out 8
A. R. C. Fraser c D. Williams b Benjamin	17	– c Hooper b Ambrose 4
P. C. R. Tufnell c Lara b Benjamin	0	– c D. Williams b Ambrose 6
B 6, l-b 10, n-b 13	29	B 5, l-b 15, w 1, n-b 11 . . 32

1/26 (1) 2/87 (3) 3/105 (3) 4/114 (5) 214 1/91 (1) 2/143 (3) 3/148 (2) 258
5/124 (6) 6/126 (7) 7/143 (8)   4/202 (4) 5/228 (6) 6/238 (7)
8/172 (9) 9/214 (10) 10/214 (11)   7/239 (5) 8/239 (8)
                                               9/246 (10) 10/258 (11)

Bowling: First Innings—Walsh 27-7-55-1; Ambrose 26-16-23-3; McLean 19-7-28-1; Benjamin 24-5-68-3; Hooper 9-3-14-1; Adams 3-0-8-0; Chanderpaul 1-0-2-0. *Second Innings*—Benjamin 15-3-40-0; McLean 12-1-46-2; Ambrose 19.5-3-52-5; Walsh 29-5-67-3; Hooper 19-8-33-0.

West Indies

S. L. Campbell c Russell b Headley	1	– c Stewart b Headley 10
S. C. Williams c Atherton b Fraser	19	– c Crawley b Fraser 62
*B. C. Lara c Atherton b Fraser	55	– c Russell b Fraser 17
C. L. Hooper b Fraser	1	– not out 94
S. Chanderpaul c Thorpe b Fraser	34	– c Thorpe b Tufnell 0
J. C. Adams lbw b Fraser	1	– c Stewart b Fraser 2
†D. Williams lbw b Tufnell	16	– c Thorpe b Headley 65
C. E. L. Ambrose c and b Fraser	31	– c Russell b Headley 1
K. C. G. Benjamin b Fraser	0	– not out 6
N. A. M. McLean c Caddick b Fraser	2	
C. A. Walsh not out	0	
B 12, l-b 5, n-b 14	31	B 10, l-b 8, n-b 7 25

1/16 (1) 2/42 (2) 3/48 (4) 4/126 (5) 191 1/10 (1) 2/68 (3) (7 wkts) 282
5/134 (3) 6/135 (6) 7/167 (7)   3/120 (2) 4/121 (5)
8/177 (9) 9/190 (10) 10/191 (8)   5/124 (6) 6/253 (7) 7/259 (8)

Bowling: First Innings—Headley 22-6-47-1; Caddick 14-4-41-0; Fraser 16.1-2-53-8; Tufnell 21-8-33-1. *Second Innings*—Headley 16-2-68-3; Caddick 16-2-58-0; Tufnell 34.2-9-69-1; Fraser 27-8-57-3; Holliooke 5-0-12-0.

Umpires: S. Venkataraghavan (India) and S. A. Bucknor. Referee: B. N. Jarman (Australia).

WEST INDIES v ENGLAND

Third Test Match

At Port-of-Spain, February 13, 14, 15, 16, 17. England won by three wickets. Toss: England.

Having lost a match they should have won, England achieved a rough sort of parity by winning a match they ought to have lost. The margin was precisely the same as it had been a week earlier and a few feet away. But all the fears that back-to-back Tests on the same ground would be tedious were proved groundless. This was a gloriously tense cricket match, which maintained its fascination until the final ball.

Many observers thought it was yet another case of a bad pitch producing a great game. Perhaps everyone was so conditioned by the previous two Tests that they had forgotten batting could ever be comfortable. However, this was a much kinder strip than its neighbour, a fact masked by a good deal of poor batsmanship. Slow, low, with only the occasional rogue ball, it was not dissimilar to a routine County Championship pitch.

That should have made England feel at home. But on a ground where no visiting team had won a Test in 21 years, where they had been slaughtered by Ambrose four years earlier and just been sandbagged yet again in the Second Test, they seemed to feel instead that the whole place was conspiring against them. That may explain a lot. It cannot explain why West Indies collapsed twice, pretty abjectly.

Both teams, quite consciously, had put off thoughts of team changes until they moved elsewhere, but England were forced into reselection when Hollioake withdrew because of back trouble. Ramprakash missed his chance because of flu, and Butcher came back. Atherton chose to bowl first, believing there would be early dampness. At 93 for one, though, West Indies seemed on the way at last to a regulation sort of Test score.

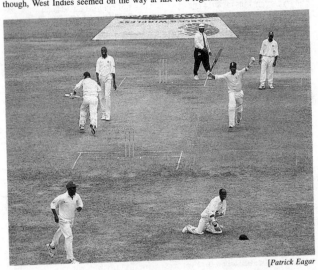

[*Patrick Eagar*

Mark Butcher and Dean Headley run the bye that squares the series.

But Fraser and Caddick induced a barely explicable collapse: nine wickets for 66. Caddick's role was especially inexplicable, since his new-ball bowling had been dreadful. Fraser once again bowled searchingly and with hardly a bad ball in conditions he liked: still, West Indies should not have let him have match figures of nine for 80.

The bad news for England was that they had to face Ambrose before the close. He was at his most searching too, zeroing the ball in towards the right-handers' midriff – and early on the second day the score was 27 for four. Stewart and the middle order effected a minor recovery, but most got out softly, having done the hard work, and Atherton was left with the familiar feeling of being let down. England were left 14 behind; they hit only nine boundaries all innings.

Fraser, however, maintained his remarkable form. After West Indies had again started with a mixture of solidity and, from Lara, exuberance, he led the revival. This time his partner was Headley, who redeemed a hopeless first-day performance with some big-hearted bowling that reduced West Indies to 159 for eight. But Chanderpaul had shown that batsmen other than Lara could play shots. And Adams followed his example, and shepherded the tail to 210. In context, it looked plenty. Few thought that England could summon up the strength of character required to score 225 for victory. But, starting before the close on the third day, they had plenty of time and, in Atherton and Stewart, the men for the job.

MOST TEST WICKETS ON A SINGLE GROUND

		Tests
82	D. K. Lillee, Melbourne	14
76	R. J. Hadlee, Christchurch	14
69	I. T. Botham, Lord's	15
63	F. S. Trueman, Lord's	12
59	Abdul Qadir, Karachi	13
56	Imran Khan, Lahore	11
54	**C. E. L. Ambrose, Port-of-Spain**	**10**
53	R. J. Hadlee, Wellington	12

Statistics: Gordon Vince

They had to see off the front-line assault troops twice – first with the new ball, then again on the fourth morning – but they succeeded, staying together for almost four hours, and wrested the initiative with a remarkable combination of patience, determination and technical merit. But nothing ever seems simple for England. Showers intervened, enabling Ambrose and Walsh to stay fresh (they bowled 71 of the 108 overs); as the weather turned iffy, so did the batting – on this ground, England were superstitiously convinced that something was bound to go wrong. They had to return on the final day to finish the job and, even though only 38 were wanted and six wickets were left, it still seemed daunting. By now, the big crowds and noise of the weekend had long since vanished. But the outward calm masked extraordinary tension as, inch by inch, Butcher, the accidental participant in this match, led England towards victory.

They had been better at fielding and running between the wickets throughout. Fraser won the match award, having been denied it a week earlier; Stewart must have run him close, and Ambrose's abiding power was the most constant feature of a fluctuating contest. He took his total of victims in Queen's Park Tests to 54. On the first three days, crowds touched 20,000, and the ground was dominated by the noise of the Trini Posse, the West Indian answer to the Barmy Army, and their music. A white woman, assumed but never proved to be English, caused enormous offence to local opinion by running on to the field naked, carrying the Trinidadian flag. This is now considered humorous and routine in England, but West Indians were disgusted. – MATTHEW ENGEL.

Man of the Match: A. R. C. Fraser.

Close of play: First day, England 22-2 (A. J. Stewart 16*, D. W. Headley 1*); Second day, West Indies 71-2 (B. C. Lara 30*, K. C. G. Benjamin 0*); Third day, England 52-0 (M. A. Atherton 30*, A. J. Stewart 14*); Fourth day, England 187-4 (G. P. Thorpe 15*, M. A. Butcher 9*).

West Indies

S. L. Campbell c Thorpe b Fraser	28	– lbw b Fraser	13
S. C. Williams c Thorpe b Caddick	24	– c Atherton b Caddick	23
*B. C. Lara c Russell b Fraser	42	– lbw b Fraser	47
C. L. Hooper c Butcher b Fraser	1	– (5) lbw b Headley	5
S. Chanderpaul lbw b Fraser	28	– (6) c Russell b Headley	39
J. C. Adams c Atherton b Caddick	11	– (7) c Atherton b Fraser	53
†D. Williams b Caddick	0	– (8) lbw b Headley	0
C. E. L. Ambrose b Caddick	4	– (9) b Headley	0
K. C. G. Benjamin lbw b Caddick	0	– (4) c Russell b Fraser	1
N. A. M. McLean c Headley b Fraser	11	– c Stewart b Caddick	2
C. A. Walsh not out	5	– not out	1
N-b 5	5	L-b 16, n-b 10	26
	159		**210**

1/36 (2) 2/93 (1) 3/95 (4) 4/100 (3) 1/27 (2) 2/66 (1) 3/82 (4)
5/132 (6) 6/132 (7) 7/140 (8)   4/92 (3) 5/102 (5) 6/158 (6)
8/140 (9) 9/150 (5) 10/159 (10) 7/159 (8) 8/159 (9)
             9/189 (10) 10/210 (7)

Bowling: First Innings—Headley 14-0-40-0; Caddick 22-7-67-5; Fraser 20.4-8-40-5; Tufnell 9-5-11-0; Butcher 2-1-1-0. *Second Innings*—Caddick 19-6-64-2; Fraser 25.3-11-40-4; Headley 26-3-77-4; Tufnell 15-6-13-0.

England

*M. A. Atherton lbw b Ambrose	2	– c D. Williams b Walsh	49
A. J. Stewart c D. Williams b Hooper	44	– c D. Williams b Walsh	83
J. P. Crawley b Ambrose	1	– run out	5
D. W. Headley b Ambrose	1	– (9) not out	7
N. Hussain c D. Williams b Walsh	0	– (4) b Hooper	5
G. P. Thorpe c D. Williams b Hooper	32	– (5) c D. Williams b Ambrose	19
M. A. Butcher c and b Adams	28	– (6) not out	24
†R. C. Russell not out	20	– (7) c Hooper b Ambrose	4
A. R. Caddick run out	0	– (8) c D. Williams b Ambrose	0
A. R. C. Fraser c and b Ambrose	5		
P. C. R. Tufnell lbw b Ambrose	0		
B 1, l-b 4, n-b 7	12	B 2, l-b 15, n-b 12	29
	145	(7 wkts)	**225**

1/5 (1) 2/15 (3) 3/22 (4) 4/27 (5) 1/129 (1) 2/145 (3) (7 wkts)
5/71 (2) 6/101 (6) 7/134 (7)   3/152 (2) 4/168 (4)
8/135 (9) 9/145 (10) 10/145 (11) 5/201 (5) 6/213 (7) 7/213 (8)

Bowling: First Innings—Walsh 17-4-35-1; Ambrose 15.4-5-25-5; McLean 9-2-23-0; Benjamin 13-3-34-0; Hooper 15-3-23-2; Adams 2-2-0-1. *Second Innings*—Walsh 38-11-69-2; Ambrose 33-6-62-3; Benjamin 11-3-24-0; McLean 4-0-17-0; Adams 6-3-5-0; Hooper 16-3-31-1.

Umpires: D. B. Hair (Australia) and E. A. Nicholls. Referee: B. N. Jarman (Australia).

GUYANA v ENGLAND XI

At Everest CC, Georgetown, February 21, 22, 23. Drawn. Toss: Guyana.

This was the first-class debut of the Everest Cricket Ground on Georgetown's seafront. Left-arm spinner Neil McGarrell delighted the home crowd with a career-best seven for 71, but the game was even more important for Ramprakash and Croft, playing their first first-class cricket since September. Croft claimed six wickets on the opening day and 11 in all, while Ramprakash made 77, easily the highest score of the match. Both earned selection for the Fourth Test. Guyana were missing their captain, Hooper, who rejected the West Indian selectors' instruction to play; only a fifty from Vishal Nagamootoo lifted them to the quasi-respectability of 184. England, too, depended heavily on one batsman – Ramprakash – in taking a lead of 55. But, as the Guyanese openers wiped out that deficit, three days seemed inadequate to produce a result. Then the spinners, Croft and Tufnell, took all ten wickets for 60, and England suddenly had a chance to chase 77 in 14 overs. They gave up the idea at 33 for three.

Close of play: First day, England XI 9-0 (M. A. Butcher 7*, M. A. Atherton 0*); Second day, England XI 200-6 (M. R. Ramprakash 68*, R. D. B. Croft 25*).

Guyana

C. B. Lambert c Atherton b Silverwood	4	– c Atherton b Tufnell	35
N. A. De Groot c Russell b Croft	31	– c Hollioake b Tufnell	35
K. F. Semple lbw b Croft	19	– c Hollioake b Croft	3
R. R. Sarwan b Croft	10	– c sub (A. J. Strauss) b Croft	1
*S. Chanderpaul c Russell b Hollioake	26	– c Hussain b Tufnell	34
T. M. Dowlin c Cowan b Croft	1	– lbw b Tufnell	3
N. C. McGarrell c Ramprakash b Croft	8	– b Croft	5
†V. Nagamootoo b Silverwood	55	– c Croft b Tufnell	1
M. V. Nagamootoo c Russell b Croft	0	– lbw b Croft	4
R. D. King c Atherton b Tufnell	0	– (11) not out	0
C. E. L. Stuart not out	11	– (10) lbw b Croft	7
B 9, w 1, n-b 9	19	B 2, l-b 1	3
	184		**131**

1/24 2/50 3/67 4/84 5/91
6/114 7/118 8/122 9/135

1/71 2/72 3/76 4/83 5/86
6/109 7/119 8/120 9/124

Bowling: First Innings—Cowan 10–3–18–0; Silverwood 15.2–1–45–2; Butcher 4–2–7–0; Croft 33–14–50–6; Tufnell 19–5–42–1; Ramprakash 1–1–0–0; Hollioake 5–1–13–1. *Second Innings*—Silverwood 6–2–22–0; Cowan 7–3–13–0; Croft 26.3–6–51–5; Tufnell 16–4–42–5.

England XI

M. A. Butcher lbw b McGarrell	13	– run out	10
*M. A. Atherton c V. Nagamootoo b King	22	– b McGarrell	6
J. P. Crawley b McGarrell	10		
N. Hussain lbw b McGarrell	5	– not out	7
M. R. Ramprakash c V. Nagamootoo b Stuart	77	– not out	2
A. J. Hollioake b McGarrell	35		
†R. C. Russell c Dowlin b M. V. Nagamootoo	10	– (3) run out	1
R. D. B. Croft b McGarrell	32		
A. P. Cowan not out	13		
C. E. W. Silverwood b McGarrell	0		
P. C. R. Tufnell b McGarrell	0		
B 8, l-b 5, w 7, n-b 2	22	B 5, l-b 2	7
	239		**(3 wkts) 33**

1/32 2/44 3/56 4/56 5/131
6/148 7/219 8/231 9/231

1/20 2/21 3/21

Bowling: First Innings—King 20–7–50–1; Stuart 24–5–49–1; McGarrell 40.2–11–71–7; M. V. Nagamootoo 24–9–52–1; Chanderpaul 1–0–1–0; Dowlin 2–0–3–0. *Second Innings*—Stuart 2–0–12–0; McGarrell 5–1–9–1; M. V. Nagamootoo 3–2–5–0.

Umpires: E. Hinds and P. T. L. Montfort.

WEST INDIES v ENGLAND

Fourth Test Match

At Georgetown, February 27, 28, March 1, 2. West Indies won by 242 runs. Toss: West Indies. Test debut: D. Ramnarine.

Notorious for the equatorial rainfall that has repeatedly transformed Bourda from a cricket ground into a lake, Guyana was instead in the grip of the longest drought in living memory. It was attributed to El Niño, the Pacific Ocean weather phenomenon, and was to have as profound an effect on the Test as on the country's sugar and rice crops.

The outfield was arid and bone-hard, and quickly absorbed the water used to prepare the pitch, which became more and more broken as the match went on. Batting was never comfortable after the first day, but neither was it quite as difficult as the last three totals suggested. Indeed, England's last four first-innings wickets added 95 and last man Tufnell batted for over an hour, while Bishop and debutant Dinanath Ramnarine added 70, a record for West Indies' last wicket against England, in their second innings, to put the match conclusively out of England's reach.

The toss was vital, and West Indies made the most of it by accumulating 271 for three on the first day. Yet their comprehensive win also came because they possessed the more penetrative and better balanced bowling. Both teams strengthened their spin attack but, whereas England's replacement of Caddick by Croft left them with only two fast bowlers, Headley and Fraser, West Indies still had Ambrose, Walsh and Bishop, with nearly 850 Test wickets between them, even after introducing the leg-spinner Ramnarine. England's cause was further undermined by several missed chances, notably when Stewart put down Chanderpaul, going to his right at second slip off Fraser, before lunch on the first day. Chanderpaul had made only nine of his eventual 118.

The openers had again fallen cheaply as Headley and Fraser capitalised on the temporary bounce and movement afforded by the little moisture in the pitch. But Chanderpaul and Lara took control in an enterprising partnership of 159. Lara led the way with two sixes and 13 fours from 201 balls until, seven away from repeating his hundred in the same Test four years earlier, he failed to keep down a drive at Croft and was well taken, low down, by Thorpe at extra cover. Hooper announced himself with a straight six off Tufnell third ball, but Chanderpaul commanded the attention as he neared his hundred. When he reached it, ten minutes before the close, he was enveloped by dozens of ecstatic Guyanese who had not seen one of their own score a Test hundred at Bourda since Clive Lloyd's 178 against Australia in 1972-73.

The nature of the game changed dramatically on the second day, on which 13 wickets fell for 168. West Indies lost their last seven for 81, their first three to the second new ball, the last four to spin. Chanderpaul eventually edged Fraser to first slip, having batted all told for just under six and a half hours, with a six and 15 fours. By the close, England were tottering against a similar bowling combination at 87 for six. Ambrose, as usual, triggered the trouble by removing Atherton through a first-slip catch in his second over.

Ramprakash, in the team for the first time in the series to replace Crawley, impressively led England's revival the next morning, in company with Croft, who helped him add 64, and Tufnell, who remained with him long enough to ensure there would be no follow-on. They were aided by Lara's baffling decision not to use Ambrose and to delay taking the second new ball. The game's most feared fast bowler was ignored until after lunch, when Lara was off the field for repairs to a knock on the finger and Hooper was in charge. Ambrose promptly despatched Tufnell, leaving Ramprakash unbeaten after 180 balls of unruffled defiance in difficult circumstances.

With a lead of 182, West Indies set off at frenetic pace in their second innings and were 32 for three before Lara and Hooper recognised the need for more care. Later, four wickets went down for four runs to the off-spin of Croft and Ramprakash in the closing overs. West Indies started the fourth day 309 ahead with their last pair together. It was probably enough even then, but England's mood had been buoyed by their carelessness. It needed the level-headed Bishop, with aid from Ramnarine, who was missed four times, to dash their hopes again.

Set an unlikely 380 on a deteriorating pitch, England started their second innings an over before lunch with the aim of avoiding a humiliating defeat. They were beaten in the last scheduled over of the day, by the biggest margin of runs in a Test between the teams since they lost by 298 in Barbados in 1980-81, sparing Lara the formality of claiming an extra half-hour.

They had no answer to the familiar, dreaded combination of Ambrose, who thundered in, arms and knees pumping like pistons, to generate all of his old pace, and the wily Walsh, who was playing his 100th Test. Ambrose set off the alarm bells with his customary despatch of Atherton, beaten for speed and lbw on the back foot. The only meaningful resistance after that was again provided by Ramprakash, who spent nearly two hours over his 34 before he attracted a wicked leg-cutter off the sixth ball of Walsh's second spell. – TONY COZIER

Man of the Match: S. Chanderpaul.

Close of play: First day, West Indies 271-3 (S. Chanderpaul 100*, C. L. Hooper 36*); Second day, England 87-6 (M. R. Ramprakash 13*, R. D. B. Croft 5*); Third day, West Indies 127-9 (I. R. Bishop 2*).

West Indies

S. L. Campbell c Russell b Headley	10	– c Ramprakash b Fraser	17
S. C. Williams c Thorpe b Fraser	13	– c Stewart b Headley	0
*B. C. Lara c Thorpe b Croft	93	– c Butcher b Tufnell	30
S. Chanderpaul c Thorpe b Fraser	118	– run out	0
C. L. Hooper c Hussain b Headley	43	– lbw b Headley	34
J. C. Adams lbw b Tufnell	28	– lbw b Croft	18
†D. Williams c Croft b Headley	0	– c Butcher b Ramprakash	15
I. R. Bishop c Butcher b Croft	14	– not out	44
C. E. L. Ambrose c Headley b Tufnell	0	– lbw b Croft	2
C. A. Walsh not out	0	– c Russell b Croft	0
D. Ramnarine c Russell b Croft	0	– c Russell b Headley	19
B 4, l-b 14, n-b 12	30	B 1, l-b 11, n-b 6	18

1/16 (2) 2/38 (1) 3/197 (3) 4/295 (5)   352   1/4 (2) 2/32 (1) 3/32 (4)   197
5/316 (4) 6/320 (7) 7/347 (6)   4/75 (3) 5/93 (5) 6/123 (7)
8/349 (9) 9/352 (8) 10/352 (11)   7/123 (6) 8/127 (9)
                                       9/127 (10) 10/197 (11)

Bowling: *First Innings*—Headley 31–7–90–3; Fraser 33–8–77–2; Butcher 3–0–15–0; Croft 36.1–9–89–3; Tufnell 25–10–63–2. *Second Innings*—Fraser 11–2–24–1; Headley 13–5–37–3; Croft 22–9–50–3; Tufnell 24–5–72–1; Ramprakash 2–1–2–1.

England

*M. A. Atherton c Lara b Ambrose	0	– lbw b Ambrose	1
A. J. Stewart c D. Williams b Walsh	20	– lbw b Walsh	12
M. A. Butcher lbw b Bishop	11	– lbw b Hooper	17
N. Hussain lbw b Walsh	11	– c Adams b Walsh	0
G. P. Thorpe c D. Williams b Ramnarine	10	– c Ramnarine b Ambrose	3
M. R. Ramprakash not out	64	– c D. Williams b Walsh	34
†R. C. Russell b Ramnarine	0	– c Lara b Ambrose	17
R. D. B. Croft c Lara b Hooper	26	– c D. Williams b Hooper	14
D. W. Headley c D. Williams b Hooper	0	– c Chanderpaul b Ambrose	9
A. R. C. Fraser c Lara b Ramnarine	0	– c Walsh b Hooper	2
P. C. R. Tufnell c Bishop b Ambrose	2	– not out	0
B 10, l-b 2, n-b 14	26	B 9, l-b 2, w 1, n-b 16	28

1/1 (1) 2/37 (3) 3/41 (2) 4/65 (4)   170   1/6 (1) 2/22 (2) 3/22 (4)   137
5/73 (5) 6/75 (7) 7/139 (8)   4/28 (5) 5/58 (3) 6/90 (6)
8/139 (9) 9/140 (10) 10/170 (11)   7/118 (8) 8/125 (7)
                                         9/135 (10) 10/137 (9)

Bowling: *First Innings*—Walsh 27–7–47–2; Ambrose 12.1–5–21–2; Ramnarine 17–8–26–3; Bishop 13–4–34–1; Adams 3–2–1–0; Hooper 15–5–29–2. *Second Innings*—Ambrose 14.1–3–38–4; Walsh 15–4–25–3; Hooper 18–8–31–3; Bishop 3–1–4–0; Ramnarine 11–5–23–0; Adams 1–0–5–0.

Umpires: D. B. Hair (Australia) and S. A. Bucknor. Referee: B. N. Jarman (Australia).

BARBADOS v ENGLAND XI

At Bridgetown, March 7, 8, 9. Drawn. Toss: Barbados.

Hussain captained England for the first time in a first-class match, but had to sweat it out for a day and a half in the field as Barbados piled up 472 on an excellent pitch before declaring. Their own captain, Wallace, made a successful case for replacing his opening partner, Campbell, in the Test team, and hooked Cowan for a six that landed on the roof of the Kensington Stand, which was being painted at the time. Holder also booked a Test recall with his second big hundred against England on this tour. He had scored 183 for West Indies A in January and added 158 here, batting for six hours and striking 24 fours. But England were undaunted. Butcher and Stewart replied with an opening stand of 117 in 23 overs, and all the top order made runs before the home spinners finished off the innings. The draw was already a foregone conclusion; Barbados played out time, extending their advantage from 90 to 141.

Close of play: First day, Barbados 328-4 (R. I. C. Holder 115*, R. L. Hoyte 19*); Second day, England XI 178-2 (N. Hussain 24*, G. P. Thorpe 3*).

Barbados

S. L. Campbell c Russell b Silverwood	21	– c Russell b Cowan		9
*P. A. Wallace c Croft b Caddick	68	– not out		31
A. F. G. Griffith c Hussain b Caddick	21	– not out		2
R. I. C. Holder run out	158			
F. L. Reifer c Ramprakash b Croft	60			
†R. L. Hoyte c Cowan b Caddick	64			
T. E. Rollock not out	28			
O. D. Gibson not out	24			
L-b 5, w 1, n-b 22	28	L-b 2, n-b 7		9

1/47 2/120 3/124   (6 wkts. dec.) 472   1/22   (1 wkt) 51
4/257 5/401 6/427

P. T. Collins, M. Blagrove and W. E. Reid did not bat.

Bowling: *First Innings*—Caddick 30–3–119–3; Cowan 21–3–71–0; Silverwood 16–2–71–1; Croft 42–10–114–1; Holioake 12–1–59–0; Ramprakash 9–3–33–0. *Second Innings*—Caddick 4–0–9–0; Cowan 5–0–23–1; Silverwood 2–0–17–0.

England XI

M. A. Butcher lbw b Rollock	79	R. D. B. Croft b Rollock	18
A. J. Stewart c Holder b Collins	52	A. R. Caddick lbw b Reid	2
*N. Hussain c Griffith b Blagrove	45	A. P. Cowan c Griffith b Reid	0
G. P. Thorpe c Hoyte b Gibson	58	C. E. W. Silverwood not out	0
M. R. Ramprakash c sub	44	B 6, l-b 6, w 1, n-b 19	32
(H. R. Waldron) b Rollock			
A. J. Holioake st Hoyte b Reid	45	1/117 2/168 3/228 4/286 5/351	382
†R. C. Russell b Rollock	7	6/357 7/371 8/378 9/382	

Bowling: Gibson 24.4–5–79–1; Collins 16–1–80–1; Blagrove 15–1–67–1; Reid 38.2–12–86–3; Rollock 23.3–8–56–4; Reifer 1–0–2–0.

Umpires: D. Holder and M. Jones.

WEST INDIES v ENGLAND

Fifth Test Match

At Bridgetown, March 12, 13, 14, 15, 16. Drawn. Toss: West Indies.

England had needed to summon all their resilience to fight back and square the series in Trinidad. Now, after the rout in Guyana, they were under pressure to do it again. The team responded superbly to the crisis, producing what Atherton said was their best all-round performance under his leadership. But, despite declaring on the fourth evening with a lead of 374, they could not engineer a win. An unseasonal, unrelenting downpour on the fifth morning wasted England's advantage, and ensured that the Wisden Trophy would remain with West Indies for the 13th consecutive series. It was hard on the players, who had given their all, and almost as hard on the estimated 8,000 English supporters who had colonised the island.

There was compensation, though, in the form of an emotional and redemptive maiden Test century from Mark Ramprakash. Coming after 37 innings in his 21 previous Tests had produced only three fifties, his virtuoso 154 proved once and for all that he is capable of reproducing his dominant county form for England. It also transformed him from a fringe player into an outside bet as Atherton's successor.

West Indies dropped four of the men who featured in their convincing victory at Georgetown. Opening batsmen Campbell and Williams were replaced by the 36-year-old Guyanese Lambert and Barbadian captain Wallace. Holder came in for Adams and leg-spinner Ramnarine was replaced by McLean. England brought back Caddick and surprisingly preferred Tufnell to Croft, whose batting might have shortened their overlong tail.

Lara put England in, hoping to take advantage of early life in an otherwise impeccable pitch, and his decision was justified as the top four succumbed for just 53. Before lunch, Ramprakash, on two, survived a caught-and-bowled chance to Ambrose's left hand, and a back spasm left Thorpe lying in a heap.

But a recovery was just around the corner, and it began in a most unlikely way. After the interval, Thorpe chose to be worked over by the physio rather than the quick bowlers, so the out-of-form Russell came to the crease. Fuelled by his rivalry with Gloucestershire team-mate Walsh, he split the field with a series of sweetly timed strokes that gave the innings some much-needed impetus. Thorpe was well enough to return when Russell fell to a bat-pad catch off Hooper before tea, and he found conditions much improved: the pitch was less frolicsome, and the bowlers had been drained by the heat of the afternoon. So began a watchful stand of 205 between Thorpe and Ramprakash that saw both men complete their first centuries against West Indies. They had been batting together (second time round) for 339 minutes when Thorpe finally edged a catch to slip off the persevering Hooper. Then Headley helped England past the 400 mark for the first time since the Ashes opener at Edgbaston, ten Tests previously. Interviewed at the end of the day, Ramprakash said he was "very relieved and very, very happy" to have reached three figures at last.

But England were not safe yet. Lambert and Wallace had sped off at a fearsome pace that evening, racking up 82 runs in barely an hour and a half of flamboyant strokeplay. Wallace was particularly severe on Headley, repeatedly hitting him back over his head, and it might have been sympathy that moved umpire Mitchley to grant a speculative lbw shout just before the close. Still, on 84 for one overnight, West Indies were favourites to take a first-innings lead.

That they ended up with a sizable deficit was testimony to a highly disciplined performance from England's bowlers, who hardly bowled a single four-ball on the third day. West Indies' morale remained heavily dependent on Lara and, after he had driven Headley's away-swinger in the air to cover, nobody else would take responsibility for rescuing the innings. The scoring-rate stagnated so much that only 180 runs were made in the day. Those who tried to lift it – namely Holder and Williams – perished in the attempt.

[*Patrick Eagar*

A happy warrior: Ramprakash reaches a Test hundred at last.

England were 141 ahead when they began their second innings, late on Saturday evening. Atherton and Stewart endured a fearsome couple of overs before the close, but next morning they recorded their fourth century opening partnership against West Indies. Atherton's 64 was also his first Test fifty in his last 17 attempts. Butcher came close to draining the innings of its momentum with an anxious 26 off 69 balls, but he only emphasised the freedom with which Hussain and Thorpe, in particular, tore into the bowling. Ambrose suffered the rare indignity of conceding 16 runs in one over, which included three pulled fours by Thorpe.

A declaration after tea left West Indies needing 375, more than they had ever made in the fourth innings to win a Test, but the English batsmen had just shown that there was nothing wrong with the pitch. Lambert and Wallace were equally adventurous as they provided a reprise of their dramatic first-innings stand. Wallace, driving merrily on the up, was rapidly becoming Headley's personal bugbear, so it was almost inevitable that his skied sweep off Tufnell should fly to Headley at long leg, and that Headley should drop it. West Indies finished the fourth day on 71 without loss, enough to convince the home supporters that they could win the game. England were disappointed, but they knew that their prospects might be improved if West Indies had an outside chance of victory. With any result still possible and a day to go, the game was perfectly poised.

That was the moment when the island's five-month drought, following the age-old precepts of Sod's Law, chose to let up. The rain began in the small hours of Monday morning, and by dawn the roads round Bridgetown had become more like rivers. It did not stop until lunchtime. The parched ground absorbed the moisture fast enough for play to begin at 1 p.m., despite the Barbados Cricket Association's embarrassing inability to locate their motorised whale, but after 18.3 overs another cloud blew over the Kensington Oval and snuffed out England's dying hopes for good. The abandonment of the match was finally announced at ten to four; England's tour would never fully recover from this crushing disappointment. – SIMON BRIGGS.

Man of the Match: M. R. Ramprakash.

Close of play: First day, England 229-5 (G. P. Thorpe 50*, M. R. Ramprakash 80*); Second day, West Indies 84-1 (C. B. Lambert 32*, I. R. Bishop 2*); Third day, England 2-0 (M. A. Atherton 2*, A. J. Stewart 0*); Fourth day, West Indies 71-0 (C. B. Lambert 28*, P. A. Wallace 38*).

England

*M. A. Atherton c Ambrose b Walsh	11	– c Williams b Bishop	64
A. J. Stewart c Williams b Walsh	12	– c Lara b Bishop	48
M. A. Butcher c Hooper b Ambrose	19	– c Lambert b Ambrose	26
N. Hussain c Lara b McLean	5	– not out	46
G. P. Thorpe c Lara b Hooper	103	– not out	36
M. R. Ramprakash c and b McLean	154		
†R. C. Russell c Wallace b Hooper	32		
D. W. Headley c Holder b Hooper	31		
A. R. Caddick c Chanderpaul b Hooper	3		
A. R. C. Fraser c Walsh b Hooper	3		
P. C. R. Tufnell not out	1		
L-b 10, w 2, n-b 17	29	B 1, l-b 6, n-b 6	13

1/23 (2) 2/24 (1) 3/33 (4) 4/53 (3)   **403**   1/101 (2) 2/128 (1)   (3 wkts dec.) **233**
5/131 (7) 6/336 (5) 7/382 (6)   3/173 (3)
8/392 (9) 9/402 (8) 10/403 (10)

In the first innings G. P. Thorpe, when 5, retired hurt at 55 and resumed at 131.

Bowling: *First Innings*—Walsh 34-8-84-2; Ambrose 31-6-62-1; McLean 27-5-73-2; Hooper 37.5-7-80-5; Bishop 20-1-74-0; Chanderpaul 4-0-20-0. *Second Innings*—Walsh 12-1-40-0; Ambrose 12-4-48-1; Hooper 21-5-58-0; Bishop 14-1-51-2; Chanderpaul 5-3-13-0; McLean 7-0-16-0.

West Indies

C. B. Lambert c Russell b Caddick	55	– c Headley b Fraser	29
P. A. Wallace lbw b Headley	45	– lbw b Caddick	61
I. R. Bishop c Russell b Tufnell	4		
*B. C. Lara c Butcher b Headley	31	– (3) not out	13
S. Chanderpaul c Stewart b Fraser	45	– (4) not out	3
R. I. C. Holder b Ramprakash	10		
C. L. Hooper lbw b Fraser	9		
†D. Williams c Ramprakash b Caddick	2		
N. A. M. McLean not out	7		
C. E. L. Ambrose st Russell b Tufnell	26		
C. A. Walsh c and b Headley	6		
B 13, l-b 2, n-b 7	22	B 1, l-b 5	6

1/82 (2) 2/91 (3) 3/134 (4) 4/164 (1)   **262**   1/72 (1) 2/108 (2)   (2 wkts) **112**
5/190 (6) 6/214 (5) 7/221 (8)
8/221 (7) 9/255 (10) 10/262 (11)

Bowling: *First Innings*—Headley 17.3-1-64-3; Fraser 22-5-80-2; Caddick 17-8-28-2; Tufnell 33-15-43-2; Ramprakash 18-7-32-1. *Second Innings*—Caddick 6-1-19-1; Headley 2-0-14-0; Tufnell 16.3-3-37-0; Fraser 11-3-33-1; Ramprakash 2-1-3-0.

Umpires: C. J. Mitchley (South Africa) and E. A. Nicholls. Referee: B. N. Jarman (Australia).

WEST INDIES v ENGLAND

Sixth Test Match

At St John's, March 20, 21, 22, 23, 24. West Indies won by an innings and 52 runs. Toss: West Indies.

The fourth day of this Test was Mike Atherton's 30th birthday, but there was scant chance for England's captain to enjoy the occasion. He walked to the crease with his side 373 runs behind on first innings, and facing the task of having to construct the sort of match-saving innings with which he had rescued England in the past. It was too much to ask of a man in desperate form. Shortly after lunch, Ambrose presented him with a familiar gift, a whistling off-cutter that trapped him leg-before. Ambrose had dismissed him six times in the series, three of them lbw. It was the last significant moment of the Atherton era. The following evening, he resigned the captaincy after four and a half years and a record 52 Tests, England having tumbled to an innings defeat to lose the series 3-1. Poignantly, as Atherton deadpanned his resignation statement in the Recreation Ground pavilion, Brian Lara was receiving the Wisden Trophy and celebrating a triumphant start to his own tenure as captain.

England retained the eleven denied a tilt at victory in Barbados by rain, already knowing the best they could achieve was a share of the series. West Indies made three changes, drafting in leg-spinner Ramnarine and quick bowler Rose for McLean and Bishop, whose poor form finally forced a reluctant Lara to let him go. Williams's shabby series behind the stumps was ended by the recall of Murray.

With 5,000 English supporters at the ground, many of them in the new Richie Richardson Stand, Lara inserted England on a drying pitch relaid just two months previously. Only five balls from Walsh were possible before the first shower of a truncated opening day intervened, but the sight of one of them breaking the surface

[*Patrick Eagar*

On the field, West Indies celebrate winning the Wisden Trophy; inside, Atherton was resigning.

to strike Atherton was enough to start spectators muttering darkly – and incorrectly – of the similarities between this track and the minefield at Sabina Park. Just ten more overs were possible before lunch. Thanks in part to hopelessly inefficient covers, and a ground staff hampered by a broken whale, the players did not emerge again until 4.45 p.m. This third session lasted seven balls. But they came out one last time, and minutes later Atherton and Butcher were back in the pavilion, dismissed in the space of four Ambrose deliveries. England were 35 for two overnight and the die was cast. As one player commented that evening, "We're stuffed now."

Beating demob-happy opponents too late in a series had become something of a habit for Atherton's England. But this time they had no resilience. Suspicious of the surface and distracted by the showers, England were dismissed for a paltry 127. The only notable resistance came from Stewart, who laboured 36 overs over his 22, and top scorer Hussain, who fell for 37 to a gravity-defying diving catch at backward square by Holder; the bowler, Ramnarine, finished with four for 29 in his second Test as the final five wickets fell for 22.

If 127 seemed inadequate when West Indies' pinch-hitting pair Wallace and Lambert strode to the wicket, it looked pitiful by the close, after they had all but extinguished it in a violent, hugely entertaining unbroken stand of 126. Caddick went for 20 off the first two overs of his spell and not even Fraser could staunch the flow. Atherton put down Lambert in the gully in the second over, and several run-out chances were fumbled to complete England's worst day of the series.

The carnage continued on Sunday, as England toiled under unbroken blue skies, and West Indies gorged themselves on a pitch now playing very well indeed. The day saw a wonderful contrast of styles as everyone bar Chanderpaul made quick runs against an England attack utterly without penetration. Wallace reached 92, and Lambert his maiden Test century, having been dropped four times. Then Lara, followed by Hooper, launched an exhibition of strokeplay that even the most partisan England supporters had to applaud. Last time he faced England in Antigua, Lara made a world-record 375. Four years on, he looked certain to add at least 100 more until Stewart, diving goalkeeper-style at mid-wicket, took a catch every bit as good as Holder's. Lara had made 89, ending the series without a hundred. The languid Hooper picked up where his captain had left off, milking both seam and spin as he pleased, and became the second centurion of the match after his fellow-Guyanese Lambert. It was Hooper's ninth Test hundred. Lara declared on 500 for seven, leaving England to negotiate five and a half sessions to achieve a face-saving draw.

Thanks to a stand of 168 between Thorpe and Hussain, they nearly did it. Resuming on the final day on 173 for three, after the morning was lost to rain, they benefited from Ambrose's most wayward bowling of the series. Denied an early breakthrough, Lara turned to Ramnarine and Hooper and, with five men around the bat, waited for a mistake. It finally came at 4.01 p.m., with two hours and 33 overs remaining. Thorpe pushed Ramnarine towards mid-wicket, and Hussain hesitated over the single and was run out for a defiant 106, his sixth Test century. His patience rewarded, Lara called up Walsh to deliver the *coup de grâce* – four of the remaining six wickets – amid heady scenes of local celebration. Once again, the weather was cruel to England: dark clouds, any one of which could have ended play, threatened at intervals through the afternoon, but this time the rain never fell.

It was fitting that Walsh, who had lost the captaincy to Lara in January, should have the final say. He had risen above the disappointment to bowl with total commitment throughout the series, the embodiment of the Caribbean's renewed cricketing unity. England were left to ponder whether their own succession would prove as fruitful. – PAUL KELSO.

Man of the Match: D. Ramnarine.

Close of play: First day, England 35-2 (A. J. Stewart 18*, D. W. Headley 0*); Second day, West Indies 126-0 (C. B. Lambert 46*, P. A. Wallace 67*); Third day, West Indies 451-5 (C. L. Hooper 85*); Fourth day, England 173-3 (N. Hussain 54*, G. P. Thorpe 18*).

England

*M. A. Atherton c Ramnarine b Ambrose	15	– lbw b Ambrose	13
A. J. Stewart b Rose	22	– c Wallace b Hooper	79
M. A. Butcher c Lara b Ambrose	0	– c Murray b Ambrose	0
D. W. Headley c Lara b Ambrose	1	– (8) c Murray b Ramnarine	1
N. Hussain c Holder b Ramnarine	37	– (4) run out	106
G. P. Thorpe lbw b Ramnarine	5	– (5) not out	84
M. R. Ramprakash c Chanderpaul b Walsh	14	– (6) b Ramnarine	0
†R. C. Russell c Lambert b Ramnarine	0	– (7) lbw b Walsh	9
A. R. Caddick c Walsh b Ramnarine	8	– c Murray b Walsh	0
A. R. C. Fraser b Walsh	9	– c Chanderpaul b Walsh	4
P. C. R. Tufnell not out	2	– c Lambert b Walsh	0
B 1, l-b 2, n-b 11	14	B 6, l-b 4, w 1, n-b 14	25

1/27 (1) 2/27 (3) 3/38 (4) 4/57 (2)	127
5/66 (6) 6/105 (5) 7/105 (8)	
8/105 (7) 9/117 (9) 10/127 (10)	

1/45 (1) 2/49 (3) 3/127 (2)	321
4/295 (4) 5/300 (6) 6/312 (7)	
7/313 (8) 8/316 (9)	
9/320 (10) 10/321 (11)	

Bowling: First Innings—Walsh 25.5–8–52–2; Ambrose 17–6–28–3; Ramnarine 17–5–29–4; Hooper 1–1–0–0; Rose 9–4–14–1; Lambert 1–0–1–0. *Second Innings*—Walsh 31.2–7–80–4; Ambrose 20–5–66–2; Rose 11–2–39–0; Ramnarine 46–19–70–2; Hooper 39–18–56–1.

West Indies

C. B. Lambert c Thorpe b Ramprakash	104	F. A. Rose lbw b Caddick	2
P. A. Wallace b Headley	92	C. E. L. Ambrose not out	19
*B. C. Lara c Stewart b Caddick	89	L-b 14, n-b 18	32
S. Chanderpaul lbw b Fraser	5		
C. L. Hooper not out	108	1/167 (2) 2/300 (3) (7 wkts dec.) 500
R. I. C. Holder c and b Caddick	45	3/317 (1) 4/324 (4)
†J. R. Murray c Hussain b Headley	4	5/451 (6) 6/458 (7) 7/465 (8)

D. Ramnarine and C. A. Walsh did not bat.

Bowling: Caddick 26–3–111–3; Fraser 21–3–88–1; Headley 30–4–109–2; Tufnell 35–6–97–0; Ramprakash 19–0–81–1.

Umpires: C. J. Mitchley (South Africa) and S. A. Bucknor.   Referee: B. N. Jarman (Australia).

†At Bridgetown, March 27. England won on run-rate, the University of the West Indies Vice-Chancellor's XI's target having been revised to 278 from 45 overs. Toss: University of the West Indies Vice-Chancellor's XI. England XI 289 for seven (49 overs) (A. J. Stewart 108, A. J. Hollioake 76; F. A. Rose three for 42); University of the West Indies Vice-Chancellor's XI 207 (42 overs) (D. L. Haynes 71, C. G. Greenidge 39).

Retired West Indian Test stars Haynes and Greenidge shared an opening stand of 108 in 21 overs.

†WEST INDIES v ENGLAND

First One-Day International

At Bridgetown, March 29. England won by 16 runs. Toss: West Indies.
Adam Hollioake resumed as England's one-day captain, having been thrust back into office by Atherton's resignation, and won his fifth game in five. His team had only one change from the eleven that triumphed in Sharjah in December: Adam's brother Ben replaced Alistair Brown. Atherton was a forlorn-looking figure in the pavilion. Ben did not bat or bowl, but he did play one vital part – he ran out Lara, when West Indies were well ahead of an asking-rate of nearly six an over, needing 75 from 15. After failing to make a century in the Tests, Lara had scored a dazzling 110 from 106 balls, hitting three sixes and 15 fours, but without him West Indies ran out of wickets. England had relied on a platform of 165 built by Knight and Stewart, who were not separated until the 31st over. Given first use of a good pitch, Knight made 122 from 130 balls, with four sixes and 13 fours; despite Lara's counter-attack, it was enough.
Man of the Match: N. V. Knight.

England

N. V. Knight run out. 122
†A. J. Stewart b Walsh 74
G. A. Hick b Lewis 29
G. P. Thorpe b Simmons 4
*A. J. Holliaoke not out 18
M. A. Ealham b Simmons 20
B. C. Hollioake, D. R. Brown, R. D. B. Croft and D. W. Headley did not bat.

M. V. Fleming not out 22
L-b 4 4

1/165 (2) 2/227 (3)   (5 wkts, 50 overs) 293
3/228 (1) 4/249 (4)
5/271 (6)   Score at 15 overs: 78-0

Bowling: Rose 6–0–31–0; Walsh 10–0–57–1; Ambrose 8–0–42–0; Hooper 10–0–46–0; Lewis 8–0–55–1; Simmons 8–0–58–2.

West Indies

C. B. Lambert c Stewart b Headley . . 11
P. A. Wallace c Hick b Brown 13
*B. C. Lara b Lewis 110
C. L. Hooper c Headley b Fleming . . . 45
S. Chanderpaul c Knight b Croft. 8
P. V. Simmons b A. J. Holliaoke 18
†J. R. Murray c Stewart b Headley . . . 7
R. N. Lewis st Stewart b Ealham 27
F. A. Rose c A. J. Holliaoke b Fleming . 24

C. E. L. Ambrose not out 3
C. A. Walsh b Ealham 0
L-b 7, w 1, n-b 3 11

1/25 (2) 2/27 (1) 3/115 (4)   (46.5 overs) 277
4/145 (5) 5/187 (6)
6/219 (3) 7/222 (7)
8/266 (8) 9/274 (9)
10/277 (11)   Score at 15 overs: 111-2

Bowling: Brown 5–1–32–1; Headley 10–0–63–2; Ealham 7.5–0–37–2; Fleming 7–0–54–2; Croft 10–0–37–1; A. J. Holliaoke 7–1–47–1.

Umpires: B. Morgan and E. A. Nicholls.

†WEST INDIES v ENGLAND

Second One-Day International

At Bridgetown, April 1. West Indies won by one wicket. Toss: West Indies.

West Indies finally passed England with one wicket and one ball to spare. Again, they had charged after their target, scoring far more quickly than England but losing more wickets too. Adam Holliaoke persisted with Headley for seven unchanged overs which went for 68 runs. The heart of the innings came from Williams and Hooper, who put on 132 for the fourth wicket, but five wickets then fell for 25. Ambrose, playing his 150th one-day international, helped take West Indies to 265, two short of victory, and Jacobs finished the job. For England, inserted on a damp pitch, Knight fell just short of a second successive hundred – but had the consolation of his second match award. He shared half-century stands with Ben Hollioake and Ramprakash, who replaced the injured Thorpe, and the later order knocked 96 off the last ten overs.

Man of the Match: N. V. Knight.

England

N. V. Knight lbw b Simmons 90
†A. J. Stewart c Lara b Walsh 3
B. C. Hollioake c and b Rose. 16
G. A. Hick b Lewis 0
M. R. Ramprakash c Ambrose b Lewis . 29
*A. J. Holliaoke run out 11
M. A. Ealham c Ambrose b Simmons . . 45
D. R. Brown b Simmons 21
M. V. Fleming c Williams b Ambrose . . 28

R. D. B. Croft not out 11
D. W. Headley b Ambrose 0
L-b 2, w 9, n-b 1 12

1/21 (2) 2/71 (3) 3/72 (4)   (50 overs) 266
4/131 (5) 5/154 (1)
6/158 (6) 7/206 (8)
8/238 (7) 9/257 (9)
10/266 (11)   Score at 15 overs: 70-1

Bowling: Ambrose 10–0–44–2; Walsh 10–1–51–1; Rose 8–0–50–1; Lewis 10–0–40–2; Simmons 8–0–46–3; Hooper 4–0–33–0.

West Indies

C. B. Lambert run out	25	C. E. L. Ambrose c and b A. J. Hollioake	14
P. A. Wallace c A. J. Hollioake b Brown	22	C. A. Walsh not out	1
*B. C. Lara c Ramprakash b Headley	24		
S. C. Williams c Fleming b A. J. Hollioake	68	L-b 4, w 1, n-b 2	7
C. L. Hooper c Croft b Fleming	66	1/41 (2) 2/54 (1) (9 wkts, 49.5 overs)	267
P. V. Simmons lbw b Fleming	5	3/79 (3) 4/211 (5)	
†R. D. Jacobs not out	28	5/211 (4) 6/221 (6)	
R. N. Lewis run out	24	7/226 (8) 8/236 (9)	
F. A. Rose c A. J. Hollioake b Fleming	3	9/265 (10) Score at 15 overs: 106-3	

Bowling: Brown 8–1–36–1; Headley 7–0–68–1; Croft 10–0–46–0; Ealham 8–0–29–0; Fleming 9–0–41–3; A. J. Hollioake 7.5–0–43–2.

Umpires: B. Morgan and E. A. Nicholls.

†WEST INDIES v ENGLAND

Third One-Day International

At St Vincent, April 4. West Indies won by five wickets. Toss: England.

The teams moved on from Bridgetown to Arnos Vale and West Indies began to pull ahead. They reduced their pace attack to two bowlers – Ambrose and McLean – and reinforced the side with all-rounders, England-fashion. These included Arthurton, who had been ignored since the 1996 World Cup. England chose to bat on a slow pitch, but this time Knight fell cheaply. The best score was 45 from Hick, though he took 85 balls, and West Indies were left needing just 4.2 an over. The openers gave their usual flying start, and the all-rounder policy began to pay off as Hooper contributed the only fifty of the game and then Arthurton and Simmons reached a comfortable victory in the penultimate over.

Man of the Match: C. L. Hooper.

England

N. V. Knight c Wallace b Ambrose	15	D. R. Brown not out	2
†A. J. Stewart c Arthurton b Simmons	33	R. D. B. Croft not out	1
B. C. Hollioake c Wallace b Simmons	35	L-b 7, w 6, n-b 3	16
G. A. Hick c Williams b Arthurton	45		
M. R. Ramprakash b Hooper	1	1/26 (1) 2/84 (3) (8 wkts, 50 overs)	209
*A. J. Hollioake b Lewis	31	3/90 (2) 4/91 (5)	
M. A. Ealham st Jacobs b Lewis	23	5/166 (6) 6/184 (4)	
M. V. Fleming c Williams b Arthurton	7	7/195 (8) 8/208 (7) Score at 15 overs: 62-1	

A. R. C. Fraser did not bat.

Bowling: Ambrose 5–0–12–1; McLean 7–0–33–0; Lewis 10–0–51–2; Simmons 10–0–45–2; Hooper 10–2–30–1; Arthurton 8–0–31–2.

West Indies

C. B. Lambert c Stewart b Fraser	22	P. V. Simmons not out	23
P. A. Wallace b Fleming	33	B 1, l-b 16, w 7, n-b 1	25
*B. C. Lara c A. J. Hollioake b Ealham	21		
C. L. Hooper run out	50	1/33 (1) 2/71 (3) (5 wkts, 48.1 overs)	213
S. C. Williams c Knight b Croft	4	3/112 (2) 4/125 (5)	
K. L. T. Arthurton not out	35	5/173 (4) Score at 15 overs: 73-2	

†R. D. Jacobs, R. N. Lewis, C. E. L. Ambrose and N. A. M. McLean did not bat.

Bowling: Brown 5–0–32–0; Fraser 10–2–35–1; Ealham 7.1–0–41–1; Croft 10–3–18–1; Fleming 9–0–30–1; A. J. Hollioake 5–0–27–0; Hick 2–0–13–0.

Umpires: S. A. Bucknor and W. Doctrove.

†WEST INDIES v ENGLAND

Fourth One-Day International

At St Vincent, April 5. West Indies won by four wickets. Toss: England.

England persisted in batting first, but lost their top three batsmen for a combined total of six runs, two of them to local boy McLean. Despite the efforts of the middle order – in which Russell had replaced Ramprakash in order to introduce a left-hander – they could not recover from this start, and were bowled out with seven balls remaining. Chasing a target of only 150, Lambert scored 52 of his side's first 66 runs. Then Lara, who had dropped down the order because of a bad knee, added his own fifty. When he was out, West Indies were five short of victory; they completed it to secure the series with more than 12 overs in hand.

Man of the Match: B. C. Lara.

England

N. V. Knight c Jacobs b Dillon	3	R. D. B. Croft c Jacobs b Simmons	12
A. J. Stewart c Lara b McLean	1	A. R. C. Fraser not out	12
B. C. Hollioake c Jacobs b McLean	2		
G. A. Hick b McLean	22	L-b 2, w 8	10
*A. J. Hollioake c Hooper b Dillon	23		
†R. C. Russell b Dillon	21	1/7 (2) 2/9 (3) 3/17 (1) (48.5 overs) 149	
M. A. Ealham st Jacobs b Hooper	17	4/33 (4) 5/79 (5) 6/83 (6)	
D. R. Brown c Jacobs b Lewis	19	7/115 (8) 8/120 (7)	
M. V. Fleming b Simmons	7	9/126 (9) 10/149 (10) Score at 15 overs: 60-4	

Bowling: McLean 10–1–44–3; Dillon 10–0–32–3; Hooper 10–1–24–1; Simmons 9.5–0–26–2; Lewis 9–1–21–1.

West Indies

C. B. Lambert c Ealham b Croft	52	K. L. T. Arthurton not out	3
P. A. Wallace b Fraser	4		
S. C. Williams c Knight b Ealham	19	L-b 2, w 1, n-b 2	5
P. V. Simmons lbw b Croft	1		
*B. C. Lara b A. J. Holloake	51	1/18 (2) 2/66 (1) (6 wkts, 37.4 overs) 150	
C. L. Hooper c Fraser b Fleming	15	3/67 (4) 4/104 (3)	
†R. D. Jacobs not out	0	5/137 (6) 6/145 (5) Score at 15 overs: 58-1	

R. N. Lewis, M. Dillon and N. A. M. McLean did not bat.

Bowling: Fraser 6–0–27–1; Brown 4–0–20–0; Croft 9–2–41–2; B. C. Holloake 4–0–18–0; Ealham 4–0–19–1; Fleming 5.4–1–11–1; A. J. Holloake 5–0–12–1.

Umpires: S. A. Bucknor and W. Doctrove.

†WEST INDIES v ENGLAND

Fifth One-Day International

At Port-of-Spain, April 8. West Indies won by 57 runs. Toss: West Indies. International debuts: N. C. McGarrell, C. M. Tuckett.

Returning to Port-of-Spain, West Indies crushed England's campaign with their fourth successive win. They chose to bat for the first time, and Lambert led the way with his maiden century in one-day internationals, scoring 119 from 124 balls, with two sixes and 17 fours. He added 185 in 184 balls with Lara, who just missed his own hundred. Only Fraser could contain the West Indian batting; when Adam Holloake brought himself on, he conceded 19 in his first over and 14 in his second. England needed six an over to win. Despite Knight, who scored 65 at almost a run a ball, and Ramprakash, contributing his first fifty at this level, they might have lost by a three-figure margin but for Fraser. He hit out for 30 from 17 balls, adding 44 with Croft to reduce the deficit to 57, before he became the third run-out victim of debutant McGarrell.

Man of the Match: C. B. Lambert.

West Indies

C. B. Lambert c Stewart		L. R. Williams lbw b Brown	1
b B. C. Hollioake .	119	†R. D. Jacobs not out	5
P. A. Wallace run out	0	B 4, l-b 15, w 3	22
S. C. Williams c Stewart			
b B. C. Hollioake .	27	1/13 (2) 2/67 (3) (5 wkts, 50 overs)	302
*B. C. Lara b Brown	93	3/252 (1) 4/266 (4)	
C. L. Hooper not out	35	5/270 (6) Score at 15 overs: 72-2	

S. Chanderpaul, C. M. Tuckett, N. C. McGarrell and M. Dillon did not bat.

Bowling: Fraser 10–3–28–0; Brown 8–0–49–2; B. C. Hollioake 10–0–43–2; Croft 8–1–33–0; Ealham 5–0–41–0; Fleming 7–0–56–0; A. J. Hollioake 2–0–33–0.

England

N. V. Knight run out	65	M. V. Fleming c L. R. Williams	
†A. J. Stewart c Hooper b Tuckett	12	b S. C. Williams .	10
B. C. Hollioake run out	2	R. D. B. Croft not out	13
G. A. Hick c Chanderpaul b Tuckett	1	A. R. C. Fraser run out	30
M. R. Ramprakash c McGarrell		L-b 6, w 13, n-b 1	20
b Hooper .	51		
*A. J. Hollioake b McGarrell	2	1/41 (2) 2/60 (3) 3/71 (4) (45.5 overs)	245
M. A. Ealham c L. R. Williams		4/109 (1) 5/115 (6) 6/161 (7)	
b Chanderpaul .	26	7/186 (8) 8/196 (5) 9/201 (9)	
D. R. Brown st Jacobs b Hooper.	13	10/245 (11) Score at 15 overs: 77-3	

Bowling: Dillon 5.5–0–41–0; Tuckett 8–0–41–2; L. R. Williams 8–0–32–0; McGarrell 10–0–46–1; Chanderpaul 5–0–23–1; S. C. Williams 4–0–30–1; Hooper 2–0–6–2; Lambert 2–0–8–0; Lara 1–0–12–0.

Umpires: Z. Macuum and E. A. Nicholls. Series referee: R. S. Madugalle (Sri Lanka).

INTERNATIONAL SCHEDULE, 1999-2000

The following tours were arranged as at January 1999.

1999	
August–September	Australians to Zimbabwe
September–October	Australians to Sri Lanka
October	Zimbabweans to South Africa
October–November	West Indians to Pakistan
October–December	New Zealanders to India
November	South Africans to Zimbabwe
November–December	Sri Lankans to Zimbabwe
November–January 2000	England to South Africa
November–January 2000	Pakistanis to Australia
December–February 2000	Indians to Australia

2000	
January–February	West Indians to New Zealand
February	England to Zimbabwe
February–March	Australians to New Zealand
February–March	South Africans to India
February–April	Pakistanis to the West Indies
April–May	New Zealanders to the West Indies
May–July	Zimbabweans to England
May–August	West Indians to England

All fixtures subject to confirmation.

ENGLAND A IN KENYA AND SRI LANKA, 1997-98

By RALPH DELLOR

The brutal economics of staging an A tour, which brings in little revenue, means that there is never a vast choice of venues. Even so, there was questionable wisdom in sending an England team to Kenya in the immediate aftermath of a bitter election, and to Sri Lanka at a time when celebrations to mark the 50th anniversary of independence were a likely target for terrorist activity.

They came through unscathed and a 2-0 series win in the unofficial Test series in Sri Lanka maintained England A's history of success in the subcontinent, where they had beaten Indian and Pakistani A teams in recent seasons. An unbeaten first-class record took their run to 24 matches since their last defeat in a first-class game on any tour, in South Africa four years earlier. They were less successful in their one-day programme, losing the limited-overs series with Sri Lanka A 3-0. But perhaps their decision to stick out the tour was their most important achievement, overcoming the alarm of some of the tourists at a terrorist bomb in Kandy.

It was not the unstable political climate which proved to be a problem in Kenya but the real one. In what was meant to be the dry season, incessant rain disrupted practice and matches alike. Only the first unofficial one-day international escaped entirely unscathed. The second suffered a late start and then an early finish, when some 80 spectators assisted with the removal of the covers and spilled water over vast areas. This caused play to be abandoned, and confusion over the result was not resolved for five days. After lengthy negotiations involving the tour management and both boards, it was declared a no-result, which rather defeats the purpose of limited-overs cricket.

Kenya had been outclassed in the first match and England A would have been disappointed not to win the second had the weather not intervened. In their three-day game against Kenya, they were again in a strong position when the rain returned. The final limited-overs match had already been switched from one ground to another, thought to be drier, but that too was flooded. Even a second change of venue failed to save the game. The unseasonable rains, attributed to El Niño, prevented the Kenyans from getting suitable preparation, which showed in their play. They are better cricketers than these matches suggested, but there was a gulf in class between the desperately enthusiastic amateurs and the young English professionals.

When the tour moved on to Sri Lanka, the weather raised no problems except exhausting heat and humidity. There were, however, other difficulties. Some Test sides have been reluctant to tour Sri Lanka because of doubts about local umpiring. It must be hoped that it is down to nothing more sinister than incompetence, but something has to be done to explode the myth that, to become a good umpire, one merely has to say "not out" in answer to any appeal. This was not a one-sided view. Both managements complained about umpiring standards before the one-day series, and the Sri Lankan Board responded by bringing in their top umpires rather than giving more experience to junior members of their panel.

The Board were also as co-operative as possible on changing the itinerary to avoid potential trouble spots after the bomb at Kandy, which killed 13 people. Originally, England's youngsters appeared to want to leave Sri Lanka on the first available flight. An admirably strong directive from Lord's – and a more determined line from some of the tourists – meant that they stayed to complete a shortened programme, concentrated in the safer southern parts of the island, despite further jitters when another bomb went off in Colombo just before the Second Test.

These negotiations, as well as the discussion over the rain-affected international in Kenya, provided plenty of substance upon which Graham Gooch could cut his managerial teeth. He conducted himself throughout with a suitable blend of authority, diplomacy and tact. His two lieutenants, coach Mike Gatting and physiotherapist Dean Conway, also had good tours.

On the playing side, there was general cause for satisfaction. The party included three Test cricketers, five men fresh from England's one-day triumph in Sharjah and some youngsters with virtually no first-class experience at all. Ben Hollioake began to live up to his potential, and emerged as a genuine Test candidate. He scored his maiden first-class century in the Second Test and followed it up with 163 in the Third. He bowled spells of impressive hostility and, most significantly, realised that he must maintain a high level of fitness if he is to succeed as an all-rounder at the top. After the tour, Hollioake had a setback when a magazine writer implied that they had smoked cannabis together in Sri Lanka. The accusations were vague, and the ECB blamed journalistic perfidy and the player's naivety.

Darren Maddy proved to be a fitness fanatic, as well as a highly promising top-order batsman. A double-hundred, a century, a 99 and five other fifties marked him out as the most consistent batsman of the tour – he scored 687 first-class runs at 68.70 – and were thought at the time to have put him ahead of Nick Knight and Steve James for possible Test honours. Of the other batsmen, Andrew Flintoff made rapid progress, while Owais Shah, who joined the party from South Africa after the Under-19 World Cup, and David Sales gave glimpses of their potential. All-rounders Mark Ealham and Dougie Brown, a late replacement for Chris Silverwood, confirmed what useful cricketers they are, and the two young wicket-keepers, Chris Read and David Nash, will have learned plenty for the future.

The outstanding bowler of the tour was slow left-armer Ashley Giles. Since his last A tour, of Australia the previous year, his action had become smoother while his control and wicket-taking ability had advanced: he collected 25 first-class wickets and appeared ready to step up a class. Fellow left-arm spinner Dean Cosker also made definite progress. Among the quicker bowlers, Paul Hutchison demonstrated good control and swung the ball well. With an extra yard or two in pace, he would be a strong prospect. James Ormond struggled in the early stages of the tour, looking somewhat clumsy, but, as he gained in fitness, his bowling improved; by the end, he was able to come back for penetrative second spells in a climate not best suited to his heavy physique.

Jonathan Powell, like Shah, flew in after the Under-19 World Cup in South Africa. An infected spinning finger kept him out of his first possible match and, when he played in the next, a chronic back injury confined him to one unhappy bowling spell, a short innings and another brief appearance in the field where he dropped a catch. He might have been better served by finishing his winter's cricket on a high note on the Highveld.

Despite the weather, terrorism and umpiring of a doubtful quality, the young players especially will have gained much from this tour – and may even have learned more than they might have done on a less fraught trip. Gooch himself said that results were important, but that the learning process mattered more. In both respects, the expedition offered plenty of opportunities, which were generally accepted.

ENGLAND A TOURING PARTY

N. V. Knight (Warwickshire) (*captain*), S. P. James (Glamorgan) (*vice-captain*), D. R. Brown (Warwickshire), D. A. Cosker (Glamorgan), M. A. Ealham (Kent), A. Flintoff (Lancashire), A. F. Giles (Warwickshire), B. C. Hollioake (Surrey), P. M. Hutchison (Yorkshire), D. L. Maddy (Leicestershire), D. C. Nash (Middlesex), J. Ormond (Leicestershire), C. M. W. Read (Gloucestershire), D. J. Sales (Northamptonshire).

Brown replaced C. E. W. Silverwood (Yorkshire), who was promoted to England's tour of the West Indies. J. C. Powell (Essex) and O. A. Shah (Middlesex) reinforced the party after appearing for England Under-19 in the Under-19 World Cup in South Africa.

Tour manager: G. A. Gooch. *Coach:* M. W. Gatting (Middlesex). *Physiotherapist:* D. O. Conway (Glamorgan).

ENGLAND A TOUR RESULTS

First-class matches – Played 6: Won 3, Drawn 3.
Wins – Board XI, Sri Lanka A (2).
Draws – Kenya, Colts XI, Sri Lanka A.
Non-first-class matches – Played 6: Won 1, Lost 4, No result 1. Abandoned 1. *Win* – Kenya.
  Losses – President's XI, Sri Lanka A (3). *No result* – Kenya. *Abandoned* – Kenya.

ENGLAND A AVERAGES – FIRST-CLASS MATCHES

BATTING

	T	I	NO	R	HS	100s	50s	Avge	Ct
B. C. Holltoake	4	5	0	411	163	2	1	82.20	6
D. L. Maddy	6	10	0	687	202	2	5	68.70	2
A. Flintoff........	3	5	3	99	83	0	1	49.50	5
M. A. Ealham	6	10	3	282	87	0	1	40.28	4
N. V. Knight	6	10	0	361	96	0	3	36.10	10
D. J. Sales........	5	7	2	179	48*	0	0	35.80	5
S. P. James	5	8	0	285	66	0	3	35.62	4
A. F. Giles	6	6	1	155	46	0	0	31.00	4
J. Ormond........	5	4	0	124	49	0	0	31.00	4
C. M. W. Read.....	4	3	0	61	24	0	0	20.33	7
D. A. Cosker	6	6	4	25	13	0	0	12.50	3
D. R. Brown	2	3	0	23	14	0	0	7.66	1
D. C. Nash	2	3	0	21	10	0	0	7.00	5
P. M. Hutchison	4	4	2	13	11*	0	0	6.50	0

Played in one match: J. C. Powell 6; O. A. Shah 23, 11.

* *Signifies not out.*

BOWLING

	O	M	R	W	BB	5W/i	Avge
P. M. Hutchison	68.3	20	195	11	3-43	0	17.72
A. F. Giles	251.2	90	471	25	5-43	1	18.84
D. R. Brown	44	9	116	6	4-50	0	19.33
J. Ormond...........	106	21	373	15	4-76	0	24.86
D. A. Cosker..........	198	54	522	19	3-45	0	27.47
M. A. Ealham	79	25	223	7	3-29	0	31.85
B. C. Holltoake	115.3	30	323	10	3-67	0	32.30

Also bowled: D. L. Maddy 9–1–18–0; J. C. Powell 5–0–28–0.

Note: Matches in this section which were not first-class are signified by a dagger.

†At Aga Khan Sports Club, Nairobi, January 3. First unofficial one-day international: England A won by 148 runs. Toss: England A. England A 221 for nine (50 overs) (A. Flintoff 104; T. Odoyo three for 42, S. O. Tikolo four for 42); Kenya 73 (28.3 overs) (B. C. Holltoake three for 17, A. F. Giles three for seven).

Flintoff's hundred came from 91 balls with five fours and five sixes. His second fifty took only 26 balls.

†At Gymkhana Club, Nairobi, January 4. Second unofficial one-day international: No result. Toss: England A. Kenya 177 for seven (35 overs) (S. O. Tikolo 61, T. Odoyo 50; D. L. Maddy three for 53); England A 147 for three (30.3 overs) (N. V. Knight 66 not out, A. Flintoff 52).

A late start caused the match to be reduced to 35 overs a side and further rain ended England A's reply with 31 needed from 27 balls. England A were originally declared the winners on faster scoring-rate by referee Jasmer Singh. Kenya objected and, after protracted negotiations at Board level, the match was declared a no-result on January 9.

KENYA v ENGLAND A

At Ruaraka Sports Club, Nairobi, January 6, 7, 8. Drawn. Toss: Kenya. First-class debut: C. M. W. Read.

The only first-class match of the African leg of the tour was ruined by rain. Put in by Kenya, England A made their superior class and experience tell from the outset. Though James failed to materialise on a steady start, Knight and Maddy capitalised with 187 for the second wicket. Knight played a tired drive to be caught four runs short of his hundred, but Maddy went on to 202, easily his highest score, taking 227 balls, with 23 fours and four sixes. A second six from Sales over long-on signalled the declaration. Then England A's bowlers worked steadily through the Kenyan order, only Shah and Tikolo showing the resilience to deny them for long. Kenya were still 99 short of avoiding the follow-on, with two wickets standing, when play was rained off after tea on the second day.

Close of play: First day, England A 282-2 (D. L. Maddy 136*, M. A. Ealham 10*); Second day, Kenya 154-8 (L. Onyango 1*, Z. Deen 0*).

England A

S. P. James c Odumbe b Asif Karim . . .	30	A. Flintoff not out 2
*N. V. Knight c Shah b Onyango	96	
D. L. Maddy c Suji b Shah	202	L-b 6, w 1, n-b 4 11
M. A. Ealham c Tikolo b Shah	13	
D. J. Sales not out	48	1/48 2/235 3/297 4/380 (4 wkts dec.) 402

A. F. Giles, J. Ormond, †C. M. W. Read, D. A. Cosker and P. M. Hutchison did not bat.

Bowling: Suji 13–0–53–0; Angara 11–1–46–0; Shah 13.4–2–50–2; Asif Karim 22–4–65–1; Deen 4–0–27–0; Odumbe 7–1–29–0; Patel 5–0–37–0; Tikolo 2–0–16–0; Onyango 11–2–61–1; Vadher 1–0–12–0.

Kenya

†K. Otieno lbw b Hutchison	0	*Asif Karim c Ormond b Giles 24
A. Vadher b Hutchison	5	L. Onyango not out 1
R. Shah c Giles b Ealham	57	Z. Deen not out 0
M. O. Odumbe c Flintoff b Ormond . . .	16	L-b 2, n-b 2 4
S. O. Tikolo c Knight b Giles	43	
A. Suji b Ealham	0	1/1 2/12 3/44 4/91 (8 wkts) 154
B. Patel b Ealham	4	5/91 6/119 7/151 8/154

J. Angara did not bat.

Bowling: Ormond 14–5–34–1; Hutchison 9–0–28–2; Cosker 9–2–48–0; Ealham 10–3–29–3; Giles 5–1–13–2.

Umpires: M. Khan and S. P. Patel.

†At Ruaraka Sports Club, Nairobi, January 10. Third unofficial one-day international: Kenya v England A. No result (abandoned).

England A won the unofficial one-day international series 1-0.

†At Police Park, Bambalapitiya, Colombo, January 17. President's XI won by 40 runs. Toss: President's XI. President's XI 142 (46.2 overs) (A. Rideegammanagedera 31; B. C. Hollioake three for 11, D. A. Cosker three for 37); England A 102 (39 overs) (M. A. Ealham 42; D. Hettiarachchi three for 17).

COLTS XI v ENGLAND A

At Maitland Place, Colombo (NCC), January 19, 20, 21. Drawn. Toss: Colts XI.

Maddy scored another fluent century; this time, Knight went cheaply, and it was James who helped him lay down the foundation for a substantial total in a stand of 95. James was stumped shortly after lunch and Maddy run out, but the bowlers provided useful runs before they got to work with the ball. Ormond followed his 49 with three wickets, and the Colts were made to bat again 171 behind. A stubborn opening partnership held up England A, and a subsequent collapse was halted by Fernando and Mendis, who had already put on 120 for the fourth wicket first time round and now added 63. The Colts were only 12 in front when Fernando was eighth out but, aided by some questionable umpiring decisions, the tail survived and had increased the lead to 38 when stumps were drawn.

Close of play: First day, England A 373-9 (J. Ormond 42*, D. A. Cosker 1*); Second day, Colts XI 208-8 (A. Polonowitta 22*, N. S. Rajan 10*).

England A

S. P. James st Dilshan b Rajan	66	D. R. Brown c Mendis b de Silva	14
*N. V. Knight c Dilshan b A. S. A. Perera	4	A. F. Giles run out	34
D. L. Maddy run out	101	J. Ormond c Rajan b A. S. A. Perera	49
M. A. Ealham c A. S. A. Perera b Rajan	15	D. A. Cosker not out	2
B. C. Hollioake c Dilshan b A. S. A. Perera	33	B 4, l-b 4, w 5, n-b 6	19
D. J. Sales c S. T. Perera b Gallage	42		
†D. C. Nash run out	5	1/17 2/112 3/167 4/224 5/241	384
		6/251 7/284 8/302 9/348	

Bowling: A. S. A. Perera 17.3–7–62–3; Gallage 13–1–65–1; de Silva 24–5–97–1; Rajan 27–6–131–2; Kalawithigoda 10–0–21–0.

Colts XI

P. B. Ediriweera b Ormond	0	– c Hollioake b Giles	27
*S. Kalawithigoda c Knight b Hollioake	4	– b Brown	31
S. T. Perera c Nash b Brown	4	– (4) c Maddy b Brown	0
S. I. Fernando c Sales b Ormond	66	– (6) c Cosker	31
B. C. M. S. Mendis c Nash b Cosker	67	– lbw b Brown	56
A. Polonowitta c Ormond b Hollioake	25	– (3) c Nash b Ealham	15
†T. M. Dilshan lbw b Giles	1	– c Knight b Cosker	0
B. de Silva c Knight b Giles	9	– c Ealham b Brown	9
A. S. A. Perera c Ormond b Cosker	0	– b Hollioake	12
N. S. Rajan c Hollioake b Ormond	11	– not out	8
I. S. Gallage not out	0	– not out	3
B 7, l-b 2, w 1, n-b 16	26	B 3, l-b 9, w 1, n-b 4	17

1/0 2/10 3/21 4/141 5/162   213   1/58 2/62 3/63   (9 wkts) 209
6/163 7/178 8/183 9/210   4/97 5/160 6/161
                                            7/174 8/183 9/201

Bowling: *First Innings*—Ormond 16–5–37–3; Hollioake 12.5–5–27–2; Brown 9–1–29–1; Giles 27–10–47–2; Ealham 6–1–27–0; Cosker 17–6–37–2. *Second Innings*—Ormond 5–0–37–0; Hollioake 14–4–29–1; Brown 18–2–50–4; Giles 17–11–20–1; Ealham 9–5–14–1; Cosker 19–5–47–2.

Umpires: S. Amerasinghe and J. W. K. Boteju.

BOARD XI v ENGLAND A

At P. Saravanamuttu Stadium, Colombo, January 24, 25, 26, 27. England A won by 177 runs. Toss: Board XI.

England A completed their preparations for the unofficial Tests with their opening first-class win of the tour. Put in by Sanjeeva Ranatunga, brother of Test captain Arjuna, their batsmen made full use of their opportunities. James and Maddy maintained their form to share a century stand, and Flintoff scored an 83 which showed he could be selective as well as dominating. Ranatunga was immovable for over five hours in the Board XI's reply. Resuming on the third day, England's top four got valuable time in the middle as they increased their lead to 349. Then the left-arm spinners, Giles and Cosker, bowled them to victory inside 53 overs.

Close of play: First day, England A 305-4 (A. Flintoff 83*, D. J. Sales 36*); Second day, Board XI 204-7 (S. Ranatunga 87*, A. P. Dalugoda 0*); Third day, Board XI 2-0 (G. R. P. Peiris 2*, T. M. Dilshan 0*).

England A

S. P. James c Dilshan b R. L. Perera	57	– c and b N. R. G. Perera	56
*N. V. Knight lbw b Boteju	17	– c Waragoda b N. R. G. Perera	56
D. L. Maddy c and b R. L. Perera	51	– c and b Dalugoda	65
M. A. Ealham c and b Silva b Boteju	33	– not out	40
A. Flintoff c Ranatunga b Lankatilleke	83	– not out	10
D. J. Sales lbw b Boteju	36		
†C. M. W. Read c Ranatunga b N. R. G. Perera	24		
A. F. Giles c N. R. G. Perera b Lankatilleke	6		
J. Ormond c Silva b R. L. Perera	9		
D. A. Cosker not out	2		
P. M. Hutchison c Silva b N. R. G. Perera	0		
B 8, l-b 17, w 1, n-b 9	35	B 10, l-b 3, w 2, n-b 3	18

1/42 2/138 3/139 4/214 5/306 353 1/111 2/130 3/230 (3 wkts dec.) 245
6/308 7/318 8/349 9/353

Bowling: First Innings—R. L. Perera 24-5-70-3; Lankatilleke 18-6-50-2; Boteju 25-6-76-3; Dalugoda 20-4-66-0; N. R. G. Perera 18.5-5-49-2; Ranatunga 6-1-17-0. *Second Innings*—Boteju 5-0-26-0; Lankatilleke 6-0-18-0; R. L. Perera 5-1-17-0; Dalugoda 20-6-51-1; N. R. G. Perera 19-3-76-2; Ranatunga 8-1-34-0; Peiris 1-0-10-0.

Board XI

G. R. P. Peiris c Read b Ormond	6	– c Cosker b Ormond	2
†T. M. Dilshan c Read b Ealham	33	– c James b Hutchison	14
*S. Ranatunga not out	120	– c Sales b Ormond	13
B. C. M. S. Mendis c Flintoff b Giles	22	– c James b Giles	42
S. Silva b Giles	18	– c Ealham b Cosker	6
V. S. K. Waragoda c Read b Hutchison	18	– c and b Giles	29
H. Boteju c Read b Hutchison	4	– b Cosker	0
N. R. G. Perera c Flintoff b Giles	0	– b Giles	51
A. P. Dalugoda c Read b Hutchison	0	– c Flintoff b Giles	4
R. L. Perera run out	4	– c Sales b Cosker	6
A. Lankatilleke b Ormond	8	– not out	0
B 3, l-b 5, w 1, n-b 7	16	B 1, l-b 1, n-b 3	5

1/28 2/62 3/93 4/137 5/166 249 1/3 2/24 3/59 4/81 5/83 172
6/184 7/185 8/204 9/231   6/83 7/121 8/141 9/172

Bowling: First Innings—Ormond 13-2-52-2; Hutchison 19-5-54-3; Ealham 8-2-23-1; Giles 29-9-73-3; Cosker 16-5-39-0. *Second Innings*—Ormond 7-1-25-2; Ealham 8-3-19-0; Giles 19.5-6-54-4; Hutchison 5-1-19-1; Cosker 13-2-53-3.

Umpires: E. K. G. Wijewardene and T. H. Wijewardene.

SRI LANKA A v ENGLAND A

First Unofficial Test

At Kurunegala, January 30, February 1, 2, 3. Drawn. Toss: England A.

Caution consigned the match to a draw. England A's reluctance to take risks on a pitch expected to take spin later on was understandable, but they went too far on the first day, when they scored at barely two an over. Resuming after a day of national mourning for the victims of the bomb in Kandy a week earlier, Ealham and Hollioake lifted the tempo, adding 119 in the morning session before Hollioake was out on the stroke of lunch. With him went all ambition; only 64 runs were added in 33 overs after the interval, a turgid display which made victory improbable. A polished century from Jayawardene made it impossible. He batted for nearly five hours, and shared the limelight on the third day with a snake, said to be five feet long, which was hit by a ball struck to long-on. Sri Lanka A eventually declared 17 behind, and the players thereafter went through the motions.

Close of play: First day, England A 202-4 (M. A. Ealham 30*, B. C. Hollioake 2*); Second day, Sri Lanka A 105-2 (M. S. Atapattu 45*, D. P. M. D. Jayawardene 25*); Third day, Sri Lanka A 341-8 (M. S. Villavarayen 36*, D. Hettiarachchi 9*).

England A

S. P. James c de Silva b Samaraweera	23	– c Nawaz b Samaraweera	15
*N. V. Knight c Atapattu b Samaraweera	85	– c and b Chandana	45
D. L. Maddy b Chandana	50	– c de Silva b Chandana	56
M. A. Ealham c and b Samaraweera	87	– not out	25
A. Flintoff c de Silva b Hettiarachchi	4	– not out	0
B. C. Hollioake c Chandana b Hettiarachchi	67		
A. F. Giles b Hettiarachchi	10		
†C. M. W. Read lbw b Perera	17		
J. Ormond c de Silva b Perera	27		
D. A. Cosker not out	0		
P. M. Hutchison b Perera	0		
B 4, l-b 8, n-b 3	15	L-b 5, n-b 8	13

1/48 (1) 2/144 (3) 3/179 (2) 4/189 (5) **385** 1/36 (1) 2/97 (2) (3 wkts) **154**
5/321 (6) 6/335 (4) 7/337 (5) 8/374 (9) 3/154 (3)
9/385 (8) 10/385 (11)

Bowling: *First Innings*—Villavarayen 14-2-70-0; Perera 14.5-4-35-3; Samaraweera 45-10-106-3; Hettiarachchi 40-11-73-3; Chandana 38-13-76-1; Jayawardene 5-1-13-0. *Second Innings*—Villavarayen 7-2-19-0; Perera 9-1-21-0; Samaraweera 18-2-44-1; Hettiarachchi 11-3-25-0; Chandana 17-5-33-2; Jayawardene 5-0-7-0.

Sri Lanka A

R. P. Arnold c Hollioake b Hutchison	9	M. S. Villavarayen not out	50
*M. S. Atapattu c Flintoff b Ormond	52	D. Hettiarachchi b Cosker	10
S. Ranatunga c James b Ormond	10	A. S. A. Perera not out	10
D. P. M. D. Jayawardene c Cosker b Hutchison	110	B 7, l-b 17, n-b 17	41
M. N. Nawaz b Cosker	31	1/14 (1) 2/43 (3) (9 wkts dec.) 368
†S. K. L. de Silva c Giles b Ealham	33	3/126 (2) 4/183 (5)
U. D. U. Chandana c Read b Hutchison	6	5/254 (4) 6/280 (7) 7/289 (6)
T. T. Samaraweera lbw b Ealham	1	8/296 (8) 9/354 (10)

Bowling: Hollioake 24-5-59-0; Hutchison 17-6-43-3; Ormond 16-2-67-2; Giles 39-12-73-0; Cosker 17-1-52-2; Ealham 15-4-50-2.

Umpires: D. A. S. Dissanayake and G. Pushparajah.

SRI LANKA A v ENGLAND A

Second Unofficial Test

At Matara, February 6, 7, 8, 9. England A won by one wicket. Toss: Sri Lanka A.

The Second Test marked a complete change of mood from the First. Because of the bomb, the venue had been moved from Kandy, and a hastily prepared pitch was still damp, holding up the start for 45 minutes. Left-arm spinners Giles and Cosker made up for lost time by bowling out a much-changed Sri Lankan side cheaply. English batsmen fared little better against the home spinners, Bandaratilleke and the 17-year-old Juniad. But Hollioake, who brought up his maiden first-class century with his second six, over long-on, helped them to a first-innings lead of 89. Led by Arnold, who had replaced Atapattu as captain, Sri Lanka batted with considerably more conviction in the second innings. It was a surprise when he declared, however, leaving England A a target of 192 in 49 overs. The slow bowlers continued to cause problems and, at 51 for four after 18 overs, the tourists appeared to be in difficulties. Hollioake and Sales restored control, until both got out to rash shots, and Giles marshalled the tail with calm nerve. Going into the final over, with two runs required and one wicket left, any one of four results was possible. Giles took a single off the first ball, then last man Hutchison played and missed at two more, got part of his bat to a sweep and scrambled the winning run with two balls to spare.

Close of play: First day, England A 47-1 (S. P. James 23*, D. L. Maddy 22*); Second day, England A 260; Third day, Sri Lanka A 196-3 (P. B. Dassanayake 51*, M. N. Nawaz 13*).

Sri Lanka A

*R. P. Arnold c Nash b Hutchison	15	– c James b Giles	79
D. A. Gunawardene c Knight b Giles	51	– b Cosker	31
M. N. Nawaz c and b Giles	5	– (5) c Nash b Hollioake	24
D. P. M. D. Jayawardene c Knight b Cosker	6	– b Giles	9
B. C. M. S. Mendis c and b Cosker	58	– (6) b Brown	11
S. I. de Saram c Maddy b Cosker	5	– (7) c Brown b Cosker	29
†P. B. Dassanayake c Knight b Giles	2	– (3) lbw b Hollioake	56
H. Boteju c Ealham b Hollioake	10	– c Knight b Giles	9
M. R. C. N. Bandaratilleke not out	10	– b Hollioake	12
R. L. Perera b Giles	4	– not out	0
M. A. Juniad b Hutchison	1		
L-b 1, w 1, n-b 2	4	B 13, l-b 5, n-b 2	20
	171	(9 wkts dec.)	**280**

1/43 (1) 2/70 (2) 3/81 (3) 4/85 (4) 5/97 (6) 6/114 (7) 7/155 (8) 8/157 (5) 9/162 (10) 10/171 (11)

1/57 (2) 2/139 (1) 3/164 (4) 4/208 (5) 5/217 (3) 6/242 (6) 7/260 (8) 8/280 (7) 9/280 (9)

Bowling: *First Innings*—Hutchison 7.3–3–25–2; Hollioake 6–1–29–1; Brown 7–2–18–0; Giles 26–7–52–4; Cosker 26–11–46–3. *Second Innings*—Hutchison 11–5–26–0; Hollioake 23.4–8–67–3; Giles 44–18–61–3; Brown 10–4–19–1; Cosker 32–7–75–2; Ealham 3–0–9–0; Maddy 5–1–5–0.

England A

S. P. James b Bandaratilleke	34	– c Jayawardene b Perera	4
*N. V. Knight lbw b Perera	0	– c and b Jayawardene	12
D. L. Maddy lbw b Juniad	27	– c and b Jayawardene	33
M. A. Ealham lbw b Juniad	6	– b Bandaratilleke	1
D. J. Sales lbw b Bandaratilleke	3	– b Juniad	45
B. C. Hollioake c Mendis b Juniad	103	– st Dassanayake b Bandaratilleke	45
†D. C. Nash lbw b Bandaratilleke	10	– lbw b Juniad	6
D. R. Brown b Bandaratilleke	0	– c Bandaratilleke b Juniad	9
A. F. Giles lbw b Boteju	39	– not out	20
D. A. Cosker c and b Jayawardene	13	– b Juniad	8
P. M. Hutchison not out	11	– not out	2
B 2, l-b 10, w 2	14	B 2, l-b 4, n-b 1	7
	260	(9 wkts)	**192**

1/1 (2) 2/64 (1) 3/64 (3) 4/69 (5) 5/75 (4) 6/122 (7) 7/122 (8) 8/219 (9) 9/229 (6) 10/260 (10)

1/4 (1) 2/36 (2) 3/43 (4) 4/51 (3) 5/137 (5) 6/149 (6) 7/159 (7) 8/162 (8) 9/183 (10)

Bowling: *First Innings*—Perera 11–1–54–1; Boteju 12–3–19–1; Bandaratilleke 33–11–57–4; Juniad 21–3–61–3; Arnold 13–3–22–0; Jayawardene 14–2–35–1. *Second Innings*—Perera 3–0–15–1; Boteju 5–2–5–0; Bandaratilleke 20–0–82–2; Jayawardene 10–1–38–2; Arnold 3–0–18–0; Juniad 7.4–0–28–4.

Umpires: R. N. S. Sirisoma and T. H. Wijewardene.

SRI LANKA A v ENGLAND A

Third Unofficial Test

At Moratuwa, February 13, 14, 15, 16. England A won by seven wickets. Toss: Sri Lanka A.

More changes to the Sri Lankan side brought in five players with 113 Tests between them. One of them, Hathurusinghe, scored 90, though Tillekeratne, the third player to captain the team in three matches, lost a tooth and his wicket in quick succession. Sri Lanka A were 232 for eight before Bandaratilleke and Wickremasinghe added 134 for the ninth wicket. A total of 371 appeared formidable, but England A were to build a lead of 95. Maddy was run out for a heart-breaking 99, while Hollioake followed up his maiden hundred in the previous game with a career-best 163, putting on 154 with Giles. He batted 270 minutes, faced 189 balls and hit 17 fours and ten sixes, though he might have been given out caught behind on ten. Sri Lanka's second innings then fell into unexpected disarray, once more at the hands of the excellent Giles and Cosker, and England were left requiring 74 to win in 18 overs. They seldom looked in difficulty and completed a 2-0 series win with 21 balls to spare.

Close of play: First day, Sri Lanka A 235-8 (M. R. C. N. Bandaratilleke 6*, G. P. Wickremasinghe 0*); Second day, England A 161-2 (D. L. Maddy 92*, M. A. Ealham 23*); Third day, England A 466.

Sri Lanka A

D. P. Samaraweera b Giles	22	– run out	47
U. C. Hathurusinghe c Cosker	90	– c Sales b Giles	7
S. Ranatunga b Ormond	12	– c Hollioake b Ormond	27
*H. P. Tillekeratne c Read b Ormond	11	– b Giles	15
B. C. M. S. Mendis lbw b Hollioake	9	– c Knight b Giles	2
P. R. Hewage c and b Ormond	44	– c Knight b Cosker	42
B. de Silva c Ealham b Hollioake	31	– b Cosker	4
†H. P. W. Jayawardene lbw b Ormond	0	– (10) c Hollioake b Cosker	0
M. R. C. N. Bandaratilleke b Cosker	61	– (8) c Sales b Giles	0
G. P. Wickremasinghe not out	76	– (9) c Hollioake b Giles	12
C. M. Bandara lbw b Hollioake	1	– not out	0
L-b 4, w 2, n-b 8	14	B 4, l-b 2, w 1, n-b 5	12

1/64 (1) 2/91 (3) 3/107 (4) 4/116 (5)   371   1/39 (2) 2/75 (3) 3/97 (4)   168
5/165 (2) 6/225 (6) 7/225 (8) 8/232 (7)   4/102 (1) 5/103 (5) 6/121 (7)
9/366 (9) 10/371 (11)   7/136 (8) 8/156 (6)
     9/156 (10) 10/168 (9)

Bowling: *First Innings*—Hollioake 29–7–95–3; Ormond 24–5–76–4; Ealham 15–4–44–0; Giles 20–4–35–1; Powell 5–0–28–0; Cosker 27–7–80–2; Maddy 3–0–9–0. *Second Innings*—Hollioake 5–1–17–0; Ormond 11–1–45–1; Ealham 5–3–8–0; Giles 24.3–12–43–5; Cosker 22–8–45–3; Maddy 1–0–4–0.

England A

*N. V. Knight lbw b de Silva	18	– c Mendis b Bandara	28
D. L. Maddy run out	99	– c de Silva b Hathurusinghe	3
O. A. Shah c Samaraweera b de Silva	23	– c Tillekeratne b Bandaratilleke	11
M. A. Ealham c Ranatunga b Bandaratilleke	35	– not out	27
D. J. Sales c Samaraweera b de Silva	0	– not out	5
B. C. Hollioake c Mendis b Bandaratilleke	163		
A. F. Giles st Jayawardene b Bandaratilleke	46		
†C. M. W. Read c and b de Silva	20		
J. Ormond st Jayawardene b Bandara	39		
J. C. Powell c Wickremasinghe b Bandaratilleke	6		
D. A. Cosker not out	0		
B 4, l-b 8, w 1, n-b 4	17	B 2	2

1/55 (1) 2/120 (3) 3/176 (2) 4/176 (5)   466   1/16 (2) 2/33 (3) 3/61 (1)   (3 wkts) 76
5/184 (4) 6/338 (7) 7/384 (8) 8/446 (6)
9/466 (9) 10/466 (10)

Bowling: *First Innings*—Wickremasinghe 19–2–65–0; Hewage 7–1–31–0; Bandaratilleke 49.3–21–89–4; Hathurusinghe 8–0–25–0; de Silva 32–3–131–4; Bandara 28–1–113–1. *Second Innings*—Wickremasinghe 4–0–10–0; Hathurusinghe 3–0–17–1; Bandaratilleke 4–0–28–1; de Silva 2–0–14–0; Bandara 1.3–0–5–1.

Umpires: S. Amerasinghe and M. M. Mendis.

†At Moratuwa, February 18. First unofficial one-day international: Sri Lanka A won by 142 runs. Toss: England A. Sri Lanka A 326 for six (50 overs) (U. C. Hathurusinghe 56, D. A. Gunawardene 43, R. P. Arnold 87, D. P. M. D. Jayawardene 52, U. D. U. Chandana 34 not out; A. F. Giles three for 52); England A 184 (35.2 overs) (A. Flintoff 51, M. A. Ealham 48, A. F. Giles 35; H. Boteju four for 33).

†At Matara, February 20. Second unofficial one-day international: Sri Lanka A won by three wickets. Toss: Sri Lanka A. England A 186 (48.3 overs) (O. A. Shah 65; M. R. C. N. Bandaratilleke three for 28, U. D. U. Chandana three for 30); Sri Lanka A 190 for seven (48.5 overs) (R. P. Arnold 88 not out, P. B. Dassanayake 30 not out; D. L. Maddy three for 18).

†At Matara, February 21. Third unofficial one-day international: Sri Lanka A won by 41 runs. Toss: Sri Lanka A. Sri Lanka A 236 for nine (50 overs) (U. C. Hathurusinghe 51, R. P. Arnold 32, R. S. Kalpage 33; A. F. Giles three for 34); England A 195 (47 overs) (S. P. James 39, D. L. Maddy 70; U. D. U. Chandana five for 46).
    Sri Lanka A won the unofficial one-day international series 3-0.

THE INDIANS IN SRI LANKA, 1997-98

By SA'ADI THAWFEEQ

Records and bowlers took a beating in the mini-Test series between Sri Lanka and India, but two high-scoring draws led to stalemate. With both sides rich in batting and short of bowling the only hope of a decisive result would have been a sporting pitch, which neither ground provided.

The series proved that Sri Lanka had durable batsmen capable of batting long hours in the middle with unflagging concentration. No one made the point more emphatically than the indomitable left-handed opener Sanath Jayasuriya. His 799 minutes of un-wavering concentration on a dead-as-a-dodo pitch at R. Premadasa Stadium brought him 340 runs, the fourth-highest innings in Tests and the first triple-hundred by a Sri Lankan in first-class cricket. Jayasuriya proved that, given the pitch and the conditions, he is capable of dominating the bowlers as easily in Tests as he so often does in the abbreviated game. He not only put them to the sword in the First Test, but followed up with 199 in the Second, to finish with an average of 190.33. His three innings combined consumed 1,282 minutes – more than 21 hours – out of the 2,057 minutes Sri Lanka spent at the crease. His phenomenal run made him the first batsman to pass 1,000 Test runs in the 1997 calendar year, on August 12.

Jayasuriya had to share some of his glory with Roshan Mahanama, whose Test career had been on the line because of inconsistent performances – largely due to not being given a permanent place in the batting order. Asked to fill the No. 3 slot after the premature retirement of Asanka Gurusinha, he finally came good with a career-best 225. He helped to rewrite the record books when he and Jayasuriya shared a second-wicket partnership of 576 at the R. Premadasa Stadium – the highest for any wicket in Test cricket. That mammoth stand enabled Sri Lanka to reach the highest total in Tests – 952 for six, beating England's 59-year-old record of 903 for seven against Australia at The Oval. Vice-captain Aravinda de Silva maintained his remarkable consistency on home soil by scoring three consecutive centuries, to add to the three he scored against Pakistan in April, and averaged 130.66.

India could consider themselves lucky to save the Test series (they were white-washed in the one-day internationals). Although their bowlers were pulverised without mercy, their batsmen managed to keep some of their pride. Two of their most experienced cricketers, captain Sachin Tendulkar and Mohammad Azharuddin, scored a couple of hundreds apiece. The tourists' biggest weaknesses were the failure of their key bowlers, Venkatesh Prasad and Anil Kumble, to take wickets consistently, and the lack of guidance for Tendulkar. There were occasions when the 24-year-old captain seemed lost for advice; he was not getting any from his deputy Kumble, nor from his predecessor Azharuddin. India badly missed the wisdom of a manager like Ajit Wadekar, whose fatherly counsel could have been a soothing balm for all their ailments.

Tony Cozier's account of the First Test is in Wisden 1998, *pages 1452-4.*

INDIAN TOURING PARTY

S. R. Tendulkar (Mumbai) (*captain*), A. Kumble (Karnataka) (*vice-captain*), M. Azharuddin (Hyderabad), R. K. Chauhan (Madhya Pradesh), R. Dravid (Karnataka), S. C. Ganguly (Bengal), A. Jadeja (Haryana), V. G. Kambli (Mumbai), G. K. Khoda (Rajasthan), N. M. Kulkarni (Mumbai), A. Kuruvilla (Mumbai), D. S. Mohanty (Orissa), N. R. Mongia (Baroda), B. K. V. Prasad (Karnataka), N. S. Sidhu (Punjab), R. R. Singh (Tamil Nadu).

Manager: R. S. Shetty. *Coach:* Madan Lal.

INDIAN TOUR RESULTS

Test matches – Played 2: Drawn 2.
First-class matches – Played 3: Drawn 3.
Draws – Sri Lanka (2), Board President's XI.
One-day internationals – Played 4: Lost 3, No result 1.
Other non-first-class match – Won v Board President's XI.

Note: Matches in this section which were not first-class are signified by a dagger.

At P. Saravanamuttu Stadium, Colombo, July 29, 30, 31. Drawn. Toss: Indians. Indians 308 (G. K. Khoda 59, N. S. Sidhu 64, S. R. Tendulkar 32, S. C. Ganguly 79, Extras 33; K. J. Silva three for 70, U. D. U. Chandana five for 86) and 255 for five (N. S. Sidhu 100 not out, S. C. Ganguly 62, V. G. Kambli 33); Board President's XI 291 (R. P. Arnold 65, C. Mendis 55, R. S. Kalpage 47, U. D. U. Chandana 38; A. Kuruvilla three for 47, N. M. Kulkarni three for 88).

SRI LANKA v INDIA

First Test Match

At R. Premadasa Stadium, Colombo, August 2, 3, 4, 5, 6. Drawn. Toss: India. Test debuts: D. P. M. D. Jayawardene; N. M. Kulkarni.

On the fifth and final morning, crowds gathered to see a Sri Lankan assault the peak of Test cricket. West Indian Brian Lara's Test record of 375 was under threat from another left-hander, two months his junior: Sanath Jayasuriya. Jayasuriya began the day on 326 and confidently moved to 340 with three fours and two singles. Then an off-break from Chauhan bounced a little more than he expected; he popped a simple catch to silly point to end his hopes of beating Lara. The disappointment was alleviated to some extent by Sri Lanka establishing two other world records. Jayasuriya and Mahanama put on 576, the highest partnership for any Test wicket and only one run short of the all-time first-class record; and Sri Lanka's total of 952 for six was the highest in Test history.

The liaison between Jayasuriya and Mahanama began at the start of the third day, when they added 283 runs together. They carried on throughout the fourth day, adding a further 265. The partnership eventually ended on the morning of the final day, when Mahanama went back to a leg-break from Kumble and was given out lbw for 225, his maiden double-hundred. He had batted 753 minutes, facing 561 balls, and hit 28 fours. Jayasuriya and Mahanama became the second pair of batsmen to bat throughout two consecutive Test days, the first being West Indians Garry Sobers and Frank Worrell, against England at Bridgetown in 1959-60 – but in that case an hour was lost to rain. On this occasion, the Sri Lankan pair surpassed not only the previous Test-best for the second wicket, 451 between Australians Bill Ponsford and Don Bradman, against England in 1934, but also the previous highest for any Test wicket, 467 for the third between New Zealanders Andrew Jones and Martin Crowe against Sri Lanka in 1990-91. Only Vijay Hazare and Gul Mahomed had bettered their eventual 576, adding 577 for Baroda's fourth wicket against Holkar in 1946-47.

Losing Mahanama shook Jayasuriya's concentration; he left at the same score, 615, two balls later, having made 340, the fourth highest innings in Test cricket after Lara's 375, Sobers's 365 not out and Len Hutton's 364. In a chanceless display of 799 minutes – the second longest innings in first-class cricket, after Hanif Mohammad's 970 minutes batting for Pakistan against West Indies at Bridgetown in 1957-58 – Jayasuriya faced 578 balls and hit two sixes and 36 fours. He was also the first Sri Lankan to score a first-class triple-century. He was applauded by all the Indian fielders and received a standing ovation from the crowd.

Even after the double dismissal, India's bowlers had no respite. De Silva, Ranatunga and debutant Mahela Jayawardene continued to flay the bowling. De Silva completed his 12th Test century, batting 293 minutes and hitting 16 fours; with Ranatunga, he added 175 for the fourth wicket in 150 minutes. Yet another century stand – 131 for the fifth wicket between de Silva and Jayawardene – took Sri Lanka past England's Test record total of 903 for seven against Australia in 1938.

"It was a terrible toss to win. We should have batted second," said Indian captain Tendulkar. Even so, his team had dominated the first two days of the Test, piling up an apparently impressive 537 for eight – their highest total in Sri Lanka. After Sidhu had completed his eighth Test century on the opening day, Tendulkar and Azharuddin put on 221 in 242 minutes – a record for India's

MORE THAN 75 RUNS PER WICKET IN A TEST

Runs/wkt	Runs-wkts		
109.30	1,093-10	India v New Zealand at Delhi.................	1955-56
106.35	**1,489-14**	**Sri Lanka v India at Colombo (RPS)**...........	**1997-98**
99.40	994-10	West Indies v New Zealand at Georgetown........	1971-72
86.87	695-8	New Zealand v England at Wellington...........	1987-88
83.25	999-12	Pakistan v Australia at Faisalabad............	1979-80
82.27	905-11	England v Pakistan at Birmingham...........	1992
81.93	1,229-15	West Indies v England at St John's............	1993-94
80.53	1,208-15	Pakistan v India at Lahore................	1989-90
79.53	1,034-13	Pakistan v Sri Lanka at Faisalabad...........	1985-86
78.25	1,252-16	India v West Indies at Calcutta............	1987-88

Note: In 1998-99 at Peshawar, Pakistan and Australia scored a combined total of 1,468 runs for 18 wickets at an average of 81.55.

Research: Robert Brooke

fourth wicket against Sri Lanka. They, too, scored hundreds: Azharuddin's was his 18th in Tests, putting him ahead of Dilip Vengsarkar and in sole second place in the Indian list of century-makers, behind Sunil Gavaskar's all-time record of 34.

The second day ended with debutant left-arm spinner Nilesh Kulkarni becoming the 12th bowler and first Indian to take a wicket with his first ball in Test cricket: he had Atapattu caught behind by Mongia. It was to be the last wicket for twelve and a half hours. This remarkable Test produced 1,489 runs for only 14 wickets, with both teams batting only once on a pitch to break bowlers' hearts.

Man of the Match: S. T. Jayasuriya.

Close of play: First day, India 280-3 (S. R. Tendulkar 65*, M. Azharuddin 18*); Second day, Sri Lanka 39-1 (S. T. Jayasuriya 12*); Third day, Sri Lanka 322-1 (S. T. Jayasuriya 175*, R. S. Mahanama 115*); Fourth day, Sri Lanka 587-1 (S. T. Jayasuriya 326*, R. S. Mahanama 211*).

India

†N. R. Mongia c Jayawardene b Pushpakumara .	7	R. K. Chauhan c Vaas b Jayasuriya	23
N. S. Sidhu c Kaluwitharana b Vaas	111	A. Kuruvilla c Atapattu b Pushpakumara	9
R. Dravid c and b Jayasuriya	69	B 10, n-b 12	22
*S. R. Tendulkar c Jayawardene b Muralitharan .	143		
M. Azharuddin c and b Muralitharan ...	126	1/36 (1) 2/183 (2) (8 wkts dec.)	537
S. C. Ganguly c Mahanama b Jayasuriya	0	3/230 (3) 4/451 (4)	
A. Kumble not out	27	5/451 (6) 6/479 (5)	
		7/516 (8) 8/537 (9)	

N. M. Kulkarni and B. K. V. Prasad did not bat.

Bowling: Vaas 23–5–80–1; Pushpakumara 19.3–2–97–2; Jayawardene 2–0–6–0; Muralitharan 65–9–174–2; Silva 39–3–122–0; Jayasuriya 18–3–45–3; Atapattu 1–0–3–0.

Sri Lanka

S. T. Jayasuriya c Ganguly b Chauhan ..	340	†R. S. Kaluwitharana not out	14
M. S. Atapattu c Mongia b Kulkarni ...	26	W. P. U. J. C. Vaas not out	11
R. S. Mahanama lbw b Kumble	225	B 28, l-b 9, w 7, n-b 14.....	58
P. A. de Silva c Prasad b Ganguly.....	126		
*A. Ranatunga run out	86	1/39 (2) 2/615 (3) (6 wkts dec.)	952
D. P. M. D. Jayawardene c Kulkarni b Ganguly .	66	3/615 (1) 4/790 (5)	
		5/921 (6) 6/924 (4)	

K. J. Silva, M. Muralitharan and K. R. Pushpakumara did not bat.

Bowling: Prasad 24–1–88–0; Kuruvilla 14–2–74–0; Chauhan 78–8–276–1; Kumble 72–7–223–1; Kulkarni 70–12–195–1; Ganguly 9–0–53–2; Tendulkar 2–1–2–0; Dravid 2–0–4–0.

Umpires: S. G. Randell (Australia) and K. T. Francis. Referee: J. R. Reid (New Zealand).

SRI LANKA v INDIA

Second Test Match

At Sinhalese Sports Club, Colombo, August 9, 10, 11, 12, 13. Drawn. Toss: India. Test debut: D. S. Mohanty.

India's deposed captain Azharuddin came to their rescue with a fighting unbeaten century, to force a draw in the Second Test and ensure the short series was shared 0-0.

The Sinhalese Sports Club pitch proved somewhat less unfriendly to the bowlers than Premadasa. Tendulkar called correctly once again; this time, he put the opposition in and bowled them out for 332, with his three fast bowlers sharing eight wickets between them. Most impressive was 21-year-old Debasis Mohanty, the first Test player from the state of Orissa. Among his collection of four wickets were the prize scalps of Jayasuriya, Mahanama and Aravinda de Silva, who batted just over six hours for his 13th Test century.

When India replied, Tendulkar also scored a 13th century – having taken 55 Tests to de Silva's 63 – benefiting from a dropped catch on 34. With the left-hander Ganguly, he put together 150 for the fifth wicket. But after Pushpakumara had Tendulkar caught at extra cover, off-spinner Muralitharan ran through the lower order, taking three for eight to finish with four for 99. Ganguly was last out for a chanceless, Test-best 147, having batted for 426 minutes, reaching the boundary on 19 occasions and clearing it twice. He steered India to a first-innings lead of 43.

Jayasuriya and de Silva resumed their dominance of the Indian bowling, sharing in a third-wicket partnership of 218 in 211 minutes, a Sri Lankan record against any country. In another chanceless display, Jayasuriya hit 21 fours and two sixes in 419 minutes. He faced only 226 balls and, at one stage, was in line to beat the fastest Test double-century recorded in terms of balls – 220, by England's Ian Botham against India in 1982. But he missed his chance and then, one short of the double-hundred, he was bowled off his pads. Earlier in the day, at 85, he had become the first batsman to reach 1,000 Test runs in 1997. De Silva scored a century in each innings for the second time in five months; going back to the series against Pakistan in April, he had scored six hundreds in successive Test innings in Colombo. After a shaky start, when he almost skied a catch to mid-off and was then bowled by a Kuruvilla no-ball, he batted for 267 minutes, hitting 13 fours in his 120.

Ranatunga set India a target of 373 off a minimum of 103 overs, but they slid to 138 for four by mid-afternoon of the final day. Then Azharuddin, helped by some poor Sri Lankan catching – they missed him at 12, 40 and 51 – saw India through to a draw with an unbeaten 108. Ganguly helped them add 110 for the fifth wicket to put the game beyond Sri Lanka's reach.

Man of the Match: P. A. de Silva.   *Man of the Series:* S. T. Jayasuriya.

Close of play: First day, Sri Lanka 316-7 (P. A. de Silva 144*, M. Muralitharan 25*); Second day, India 226-4 (S. R. Tendulkar 117*, S. C. Ganguly 47*); Third day, Sri Lanka 77-1 (S. T. Jayasuriya 34*, R. S. Mahanama 9*); Fourth day, India 49-0 (A. Jadeja 35*, N. S. Sidhu 12*).

Sri Lanka

S. T. Jayasuriya c Tendulkar b Mohanty	32	– b Kuruvilla	199
M. S. Atapattu c Azharuddin b Prasad	19	– c Azharuddin b Kumble	29
R. S. Mahanama c Azharuddin b Mohanty	37	– st Mongia b Kumble	35
P. A. de Silva c Mongia b Mohanty	146	– c sub (V. G. Kambli) b Kumble	120
*A. Ranatunga c Mongia b Ganguly	14	– run out	1
D. P. M. Jayawardene c Mongia b Prasad	16	– (7) c Mongia b Kuruvilla	7
†R. S. Kaluwitharana b Kuruvilla	7	– (6) run out	2
W. P. U. J. C. Vaas b Kuruvilla	10	– not out	5
M. Muralitharan c Azharuddin b Kumble	39		
K. R. Pushpakumara b Mohanty	0		
K. S. C. de Silva not out	0		
B 4, l-b 4, n-b 4	12	B 1, l-b 4, w 1, n-b 11	17

1/53 (1) 2/59 (2) 3/121 (3) 4/192 (5)	332	1/65 (2) 2/145 (3) (7 wkts dec.) 415
5/230 (6) 6/249 (7) 7/274 (8)		3/363 (1) 4/369 (5)
8/322 (4) 9/332 (9) 10/332 (10)		5/374 (6) 6/394 (7) 7/415 (4)

Bowling: *First Innings*—Prasad 26–5–104–2; Kuruvilla 20–5–68–2; Mohanty 20.4–5–78–4; Kumble 25–8–51–1; Ganguly 4–0–23–1. *Second Innings*—Mohanty 16–0–72–0; Prasad 16–1–72–0; Kuruvilla 24–3–90–2; Kumble 38.4–2–156–3; Ganguly 3–0–18–0; Dravid 1–0–2–0.

India

A. Jadeja c Kaluwitharana b Vaas	1	– c Atapattu b K. S. C. de Silva	73
N. S. Sidhu st Kaluwitharana b Muralitharan	29	– c Jayasuriya b Vaas	16
R. Dravid c Vaas b K. S. C. de Silva	2	– c Atapattu b Muralitharan	6
*S. R. Tendulkar c Muralitharan b Pushpakumara	139	– c K. S. C. de Silva b Muralitharan	8
M. Azharuddin c Mahanama b Vaas	22	– not out	108
S. C. Ganguly c Vaas b K. S. C. de Silva	147	– c Kaluwitharana b Muralitharan	45
†N. R. Mongia b Muralitharan	15	– not out	10
A. Kumble c Jayawardene b Muralitharan	0		
A. Kuruvilla c Jayawardene b Muralitharan	0		
B. K. V. Prasad c Kaluwitharana b K. S. C. de Silva	2		
D. S. Mohanty not out	0		
B 2, l-b 3, n-b 13	18	B 1, l-b 7, n-b 7	15

1/2 (1) 2/9 (3) 3/81 (2) 4/126 (5)   375   1/55 (2) 2/75 (3) 3/100 (4)   (5 wkts) 281
5/276 (4) 6/328 (7) 7/334 (8)   4/138 (1) 5/248 (6)
8/342 (9) 9/359 (10) 10/375 (6)

Bowling: *First Innings*—Vaas 27–5–69–2; Pushpakumara 19–3–79–1; K. S. C. de Silva 31.1–6–101–3; Muralitharan 48–17–99–4; Jayasuriya 10–6–15–0; Jayawardene 1–1–0–0; P. A. de Silva 5–2–7–0. *Second Innings*—Vaas 17–3–42–1; K. S. C. de Silva 16–5–32–1; Muralitharan 35–5–96–3; Pushpakumara 14–1–50–0; Jayasuriya 10–4–24–0; Jayawardene 8–1–29–0.

Umpires: R. E. Koertzen (South Africa) and B. C. Cooray. Referee: J. R. Reid (New Zealand).

†At Moratuwa, August 15. Indians won by two wickets. Toss: Indians. Board President's XI 240 for seven (50 overs) (R. P. Arnold 56, D. A. Gunawardene 53, D. P. M. D. Jayawardene 47, H. P. Tillekeratne 33); Indians 243 for eight (49.3 overs) (R. R. Singh 33, R. Dravid 95, V. G. Kambli 35).

†SRI LANKA v INDIA

First One-Day International

At R. Premadasa Stadium, Colombo, August 17 (day/night). Sri Lanka won by two runs. Toss: India.

A world-record fifth-wicket partnership between Azharuddin and Jadeja was not quite enough to bring India victory. Chasing an imposing target of 303, the top four collapsed for 64 in 11 overs. But Azharuddin, who scored 111 not out off 117 balls, and Jadeja, with 119 off 121, put on 223, beating the previous fifth-wicket best of 159, between Australians Ricky Ponting and Michael Bevan against Sri Lanka in 1995-96. India got to 300, just short of victory, before the overs ran out. Sri Lanka had been given a flying start by Atapattu and Jayasuriya, who put on 91 in just 14 overs. Jayasuriya, switching comfortably into one-day mood, smashed 73 off 52 balls, with two sixes and ten fours, while Atapattu completed his maiden century for Sri Lanka. There was controversy in India when TV viewers thought they saw umpire Francis wiping the ball on the Indian flag. After a spate of angry calls to newspaper offices, Francis brought out the offending cloth: a Tennent's Pilsner bar towel – with similar colours – that he had picked up in a Surrey pub.

Man of the Match: A. Jadeja.

Sri Lanka

S. T. Jayasuriya b Prasad	73	H. P. Tillekeratne not out	0
M. S. Atapattu run out	118	L-b 7, w 6, n-b 3	16
R. S. Mahanama c Jadeja b Singh	53		
P. A. de Silva c Kumble b Prasad	34	1/91 2/199 (4 wkts, 50 overs) 302	
*A. Ranatunga not out	8	3/279 4/300	

†S. K. L. de Silva, H. D. P. K. Dharmasena, W. P. U. J. C. Vaas, M. Muralitharan and K. S. C. de Silva did not bat.

Bowling: Chauhan 10-0-64-0; Kuruvilla 9-0-59-0; Prasad 9-0-50-2; Kumble 8-0-50-0; Tendulkar 5-0-28-0; Singh 9-0-44-1.

India

*S. R. Tendulkar c Muralitharan b Vaas	27	R. K. Chauhan c Mahanama b Jayasuriya	1
S. C. Ganguly run out	31	A. Kumble not out	0
R. R. Singh c S. K. L. de Silva b Vaas	1		
R. Dravid run out	1	B 2, l-b 3, w 2, n-b 1	8
M. Azharuddin not out	111		
A. Jadeja c and b Vaas	119	1/58 2/59 3/61 4/64 (7 wkts, 50 overs) 300	
†N. R. Mongia run out	1	5/287 6/294 7/296	

A. Kuruvilla and B. K. V. Prasad did not bat.

Bowling: Vaas 10-0-63-3; K. S. C. de Silva 8-0-49-0; Dharmasena 10-0-40-0; Muralitharan 9-0-51-0; Jayasuriya 7-0-53-1; P. A. de Silva 2-0-14-0; Ranatunga 4-0-25-0.

Umpires: K. T. Francis and P. Manuel.

†SRI LANKA v INDIA

Second One-Day International

At R. Premadasa Stadium, Colombo, August 20 (day/night). Sri Lanka won by seven wickets. Toss: Sri Lanka.

Sri Lanka ensured victory in the series with this comfortable win. Despite a century from Ganguly, his first in one-day internationals, India totalled only 238. They slumped from 212 for four to lose their last six for 26 runs to the spinners. Muralitharan, when he claimed Ganguly's wicket, became the second Sri Lankan (following Jayasuriya) to take 100 wickets in one-day internationals. Jayasuriya once more set the tone for Sri Lanka's reply, with a 56-ball 66, and further half-centuries from Mahanama and Aravinda de Silva saw Sri Lanka to their target in the 42nd over.

Man of the Match: S. T. Jayasuriya.

India

*S. R. Tendulkar lbw b Vaas	6	A. Kumble b Chandana	2
S. C. Ganguly c Dharmasena b Muralitharan	113	R. K. Chauhan st S. K. L. de Silva b Chandana	0
R. R. Singh c and b Dharmasena	42	A. Kuruvilla not out	2
M. Azharuddin st S. K. L. de Silva b Muralitharan	1	B. K. V. Prasad lbw b Jayasuriya	0
R. Dravid c S. K. L. de Silva b Jayasuriya	18	B 2, l-b 3, w 5	10
A. Jadeja c Mahanama b Chandana	28	1/6 2/105 3/106 (49.3 overs) 238	
†N. R. Mongia c P. A. de Silva b Dharmasena	16	4/159 5/212 6/218 7/229 8/235 9/237	

Bowling: Vaas 6-1-38-1; K. S. C. de Silva 7-0-41-0; Dharmasena 10-0-48-2; Muralitharan 10-1-39-2; Jayasuriya 8.3-0-35-2; Chandana 8-0-32-3.

Sri Lanka

S. T. Jayasuriya c Tendulkar b Kumble..	66
M. S. Atapattu lbw b Kuruvilla.......	38
R. S. Mahanama run out............	66
P. A. de Silva not out	52

U. D. U. Chandana not out	4
B 8, l-b 2, w 1, n-b 4	15

1/79 2/130 3/219   (3 wkts, 41.5 overs) 241

*A. Ranatunga, †S. K. L. de Silva, H. D. P. K. Dharmasena, W. P. U. J. C. Vaas, M. Muralitharan and K. S. C. de Silva did not bat.

Bowling: Chauhan 9–0–45–0; Kuruvilla 7–1–35–1; Prasad 9–0–56–0; Kumble 6–0–44–1; Singh 6.5–0–34–0; Jadeja 4–0–17–0.

Umpires: B. C. Cooray and D. N. Pathirana.

†SRI LANKA v INDIA

Third One-Day International

At Sinhalese Sports Club, Colombo, August 23. No result. Toss: Sri Lanka.

India were well on course for their first win of the series when bad weather stopped them short. Robin Singh also missed out on a likely match award. He had scored a maiden one-day international century off 102 balls, with 11 fours and a six, to lead India to a highly respectable total of 291. Then he claimed three wickets for 20, reducing Sri Lanka to 132 for six in the 19th over before the rain ended play. The match was replayed the following day.

India

S. C. Ganguly c Mahanama	
b Pushpakumara .	14
*S. R. Tendulkar c Ranatunga b Liyanage	27
R. R. Singh c Pushpakumara	
b Dharmasena .	100
R. Dravid c Kalpage b P. A. de Silva...	78
M. Azharuddin b P. A. de Silva	34
A. Jadeja st S. K. L. de Silva	
b P. A. de Silva .	6
†N. R. Mongia run out	1

R. K. Chauhan run out	2
A. Kuruvilla run out..............	3
N. M. Kulkarni not out	5
B. K. V. Prasad not out............	2
L-b 6, w 12, n-b 1.......	19

1/30 2/44 3/206   (9 wkts, 50 overs) 291
4/268 5/273 6/274
7/278 8/281 9/288

Bowling: Pushpakumara 6–0–47–1; Liyanage 7–0–26–1; Dharmasena 9–0–51–1; Kalpage 6–0–44–0; Jayasuriya 9–0–40–0; Chandana 3–0–22–0; P. A. de Silva 10–0–55–3.

Sri Lanka

S. T. Jayasuriya c Dravid b Kuruvilla...	68
M. S. Atapattu run out	21
P. A. de Silva c Prasad b Singh	22
*A. Ranatunga c Chauhan b Singh	0
R. S. Mahanama c Dravid b Singh	8
R. S. Kalpage c and b Kulkarni	1

†S. K. L. de Silva not out	6
U. D. U. Chandana not out	0
L-b 2, w 3, n-b 1	6

1/85 2/96 3/97   (6 wkts, 19 overs) 132
4/116 5/122 6/132

D. K. Liyanage, H. D. P. K. Dharmasena and K. R. Pushpakumara did not bat.

Bowling: Chauhan 3–0–31–0; Kuruvilla 5–0–43–1; Prasad 3–0–21–0; Kulkarni 4–1–15–1; Singh 4–0–20–3.

Umpires: K. T. Francis and T. M. Samarasinghe.

†SRI LANKA v INDIA

Fourth One-Day International

At Sinhalese Sports Club, Colombo, August 24. Sri Lanka won by nine runs. Toss: India.

Sri Lanka maintained their one-day dominance with their third win. Aravinda de Silva's ninth one-day century, off 117 balls, with seven fours, helped them to overcome the loss of Jayasuriya and Atapattu for three apiece. Backed up by a maiden fifty from Lanka de Silva, they totalled 264. Still, India were on course to win at 221 for four with Azharuddin and Jadeja together. Both were run out, Azharuddin for 65 off 68 balls. That left 38 to win in five overs. Sri Lanka tightened the screws with some brilliant fielding, and kept India ten short of their target.

Man of the Match: P. A. de Silva.   *Man of the Series:* S. T. Jayasuriya.

Sri Lanka

S. T. Jayasuriya c Jadeja b Kuruvilla	3	H. D. P. K. Dharmasena run out		1
M. S. Atapattu c Azharuddin b Kuruvilla	3	M. Muralitharan c Tendulkar b Kuruvilla		7
R. S. Mahanama b Kulkarni	50	K. S. C. de Silva not out		0
P. A. de Silva c Azharuddin b Kulkarni	104			
*A. Ranatunga b Kulkarni	3	L-b 1, w 1, n-b 5		7
†S. K. L. de Silva c Tendulkar b Kuruvilla	50			
U. D. U. Chandana b Chauhan	16	1/3 2/22 3/105	(49.4 overs)	264
D. K. Liyanage c Jadeja b Tendulkar	20	4/113 5/195 6/226		
		7/254 8/256 9/264		

Bowling: Prasad 6–0–31–0; Kuruvilla 8.4–1–43–4; Kulkarni 10–0–73–3; Chauhan 10–0–43–1; Singh 7–0–32–0; Tendulkar 5–0–22–1; Ganguly 3–0–19–0.

India

*S. R. Tendulkar c S. K. L. de Silva b K. S. C. de Silva	39	R. K. Chauhan c Liyanage b Chandana		4
S. C. Ganguly c and b K. S. C. de Silva	17	A. Kuruvilla c and b Jayasuriya		7
R. R. Singh c sub (R. S. Kalpage) b Muralitharan	28	N. M. Kulkarni not out		3
R. Dravid c Chandana b Jayasuriya	42	B 9, l-b 1, w 2, n-b 2		14
M. Azharuddin run out	65			
A. Jadeja run out	22	1/50 2/78 3/107	(8 wkts, 50 overs)	255
†N. R. Mongia not out	14	4/165 5/221 6/227		
		7/235 8/245		

B. K. V. Prasad did not bat.

Bowling: K. S. C. de Silva 8–0–48–2; Liyanage 5–1–36–0; Dharmasena 9–0–33–0; Muralitharan 10–0–41–1; Jayasuriya 10–0–56–2; Chandana 8–0–31–1.

Umpires: K. T. Francis and T. M. Samarasinghe.   Series referee: J. R. Reid (New Zealand).

THE NEW ZEALANDERS IN ZIMBABWE, 1997-98

By DAVID LEGGAT

New Zealand failed in their ambition to use their second Test tour of Zimbabwe to escape from the cellar of international cricket. They arrived convinced that the home side would play defensively and wait for the New Zealanders to slip up. They were determined not to fall into that trap, and the effect was that neither side grabbed the initiative. Both Tests were drawn yet, with a little more imagination, each team could have claimed a win. And though neither team accepted the notion that Test cricket's wooden spoon was at stake, there was little in the cricket to persuade anyone to the contrary.

Zimbabwe's captain, Alistair Campbell, might have pulled off a win in the First Test at Harare had his team not batted on too long, and too slowly, on the fourth afternoon. An uncharacteristic display of restraint from Chris Cairns enabled New Zealand to see out the final day. Then, at Bulawayo, Campbell made the Kiwis an unexpectedly generous offer: to score 286 on a tame batting pitch in just over two sessions. But New Zealand were not good enough to get home in a last-over finish.

What the tour did produce was some fresh Zimbabwean talent. Leg-spinner Adam Huckle, a cattle-farmer and Heath Streak's next-door neighbour, was called into the Test squad on the basis of just one recent first-class match. But he took 16 wickets in the two Tests, mixing long-hops and full tosses with some highly penetrative bowling. Bespectacled opener Gavin Rennie also caught the New Zealanders off guard. He played in all the matches against the tourists and showed that tenacity and concentration could more than compensate for his limited range of strokes. He formed a highly effective opening partnership with Grant Flower, the player of the series.

Injury deprived the New Zealanders of several leading players, while the experienced Danny Morrison had been prematurely discarded. Left-armer Shayne O'Connor stepped in and made a tidy start to his international career. But Daniel Vettori, already an old hand at 18, was a little disappointing, and much of the New Zealand batting was simply not good enough – the two Chrises, Cairns and Harris, being the big exceptions. Zimbabwe had their disappointments too: Andy Flower had a hard time and Paul Strang's bowling lacked a cutting edge after his long season with Kent. The New Zealand captain Stephen Fleming batted steadily without stamping his authority. But he was the man who summed the tour when it ended: a month of lost opportunities for both teams.

NEW ZEALAND TOURING PARTY

S. P. Fleming (Canterbury) (*captain*), N. J. Astle (Canterbury), C. L. Cairns (Canterbury), H. T. Davis (Wellington), C. Z. Harris (Canterbury), M. J. Horne (Otago), G. R. Larsen (Wellington), C. D. McMillan (Canterbury), S. B. O'Connor (Otago), A. C. Parore (Auckland), B. A. Pocock (Auckland), D. G. Sewell (Otago), C. M. Spearman (Central Districts), D. L. Vettori (Northern Districts), P. J. Wiseman (Otago).

G. I. Allott (Canterbury), S. B. Doull (Northern Districts), A. J. Penn (Central Districts) and B. A. Young (Northern Districts) withdrew from the squad through injury. Sewell replaced Penn and Spearman replaced Young.

Manager: D. J. Graham.   *Coach:* S. J. Rixon.

NEW ZEALAND TOUR RESULTS

Test matches – Played 2: Drawn 2.
First-class matches – Played 3: Drawn 3.
Draws – Zimbabwe (2), Mashonaland.
One-day internationals – Played 3: Won 1, Lost 1, Tied 1.
Other non-first-class match – Won v Zimbabwe Country Districts.

Note: Matches in this section which were not first-class are signified by a dagger.

†At Harare South Country Club, September 12. New Zealanders won by two wickets. Toss: Zimbabwe Country Districts. Zimbabwe Country Districts 190 for six (50 overs) (G. J. Rennie 74, G. K. Bruk-Jackson 44); New Zealanders 194 for eight (42.4 overs) (M. J. Horne 31, C. M. Spearman 42, C. L. Cairns 45 not out, Extras 33; A. G. Huckle four for 38).

At Alexandra Sports Club, Harare, September 13, 14, 15. Drawn. Toss: New Zealanders. New Zealanders 174 (M. J. Horne 35; E. Matambanadzo three for 44, B. C. Strang four for 45) and 336 for five (M. J. Horne 181, S. P. Fleming 42, N. J. Astle 33); Mashonaland 351 (G. W. Flower 55, D. P. Viljoen 35, G. J. Rennie 33, C. B. Wishart 41, D. L. Houghton 59, C. N. Evans 63, Extras 30; S. B. O'Connor three for 58).

ZIMBABWE v NEW ZEALAND

First Test Match

At Harare, September 18, 19, 20, 21, 22. Drawn. Toss: New Zealand. Test debuts: A. G. Huckle, G. J. Rennie; S. B. O'Connor.

This was almost the Happy Families Test. For the first time in Test cricket, three sets of brothers – the Flowers, Rennies and Strangs – played in the same team, while the twelfth man was Andy Whittall, cousin of Guy. It was Grant Flower who dominated the game, becoming the first player to score two hundreds in a Test for Zimbabwe. But Zimbabwe were thwarted on the brink of victory by a member of another cricketing dynasty: Chris Cairns, son of Lance, played a match-saving innings, drawing on reserves of patience few knew he possessed.

Zimbabwe were forced to bat first in humid conditions, and Grant Flower was promptly caught at second slip for nought off a no-ball, one of 24 that Davis produced in the match. Then he was scoreless for 40 minutes. But he broke free and began to play quite fluently: helped by minor contributions from Whittall and Paul Strang, he reached his third Test century in five and a half hours before becoming one of five victims for Cairns.

New Zealand's first four all began steadily, but only Fleming got beyond the twenties, and the leg-spinners, Paul Strang and Huckle, sliced through the tail to give Zimbabwe a 91-run lead. By the close of the third day, this had risen to 206 as the openers capitalised on wayward bowling, and they pressed on next day. Debutant Gavin Rennie scored 57, but Grant Flower pushed on: he reached his second century with a six over third man off Cairns, and his 151 included two other sixes and 12 fours.

On the fourth day, New Zealand chose to slow the game down. They dawdled in the field – for a while the same player was employed at fine leg at both ends – dropping the over-rate as low as ten per hour. Fleming took two catches in the second innings to add to his five in the first, gaining a share of two world records: most catches in a Test innings, and most in a Test match. Campbell unnecessarily batted on past tea, which may have cost his team victory.

Asked to score 403, New Zealand lost their fifth wicket straight after lunch on the last day, when the score was 122, but Cairns and, especially, Parore responded by going on the offensive. For a time, runs came in a flood. Eventually, though, Cairns, with support from the tail, knuckled down for the draw. Batting for 260 minutes, Cairns defied an increasingly excitable Zimbabwe team. Referee Siddath Wettimuny fined Huckle 30 per cent of his match fee, and imposed a suspended one-Test ban for intimidatory appealing.

Man of the Match: G. W. Flower.

Close of play: First day, Zimbabwe 205-4 (G. W. Flower 85*, D. L. Houghton 20*); Second day, New Zealand 91-3 (S. P. Fleming 20*, N. J. Astle 2*); Third day, Zimbabwe 115-0 (G. J. Rennie 45*, G. W. Flower 60*); Fourth day, New Zealand 64-2 (B. A. Pocock 30*, S. P. Fleming 0*).

Zimbabwe

G. J. Rennie c Fleming b Cairns	23	– c Harris b O'Connor	57
G. W. Flower c Parore b Cairns	104	– c Fleming b O'Connor	151
†A. Flower c Spearman b Cairns	8	– c Parore b O'Connor	20
G. J. Whittall c Fleming b O'Connor	33	– run out	4
*A. D. R. Campbell c Pocock b Astle	18	– c Fleming b Davis	21
D. L. Houghton lbw b Davis	23	– c Davis b Astle	1
P. A. Strang c Fleming b Davis	42	– c Horne b Davis	17
H. H. Streak c Fleming b Cairns	0	– run out	0
J. A. Rennie c Fleming b Davis	22	– c and b Astle	16
B. C. Strang lbw b Cairns	1	– not out	4
A. G. Huckle not out	0		
B 1, l-b 5, w 4, n-b 14	24	L-b 12, n-b 8	20

1/47 (1) 2/57 (3) 3/117 (4) 4/144 (5) 298   1/156 (1) 2/218 (3) (9 wkts dec.) 311
5/214 (6) 6/244 (2) 7/244 (8)   3/231 (4) 4/263 (2)
8/295 (7) 9/298 (9) 10/298 (10)   5/264 (6) 6/290 (7)
                                           7/290 (5) 8/290 (8)
                                           9/311 (9)

Bowling: *First Innings*—O'Connor 26–1–104–1; Davis 20–1–57–3; Cairns 28.1–9–50–5; Astle 23–12–40–1; Vettori 4–0–14–0; Harris 13–5–27–0. *Second Innings*—O'Connor 26–3–73–3; Davis 13–2–45–2; Cairns 9–0–44–0; Vettori 13–2–40–0; Harris 5–3–11–0; Astle 25.5–2–86–2.

New Zealand

C. M. Spearman c Campbell b B. C. Strang	23	– (2) c A. Flower b Huckle	33
B. A. Pocock run out	21	– (1) lbw b Streak	52
M. J. Horne c Whittall b Streak	24	– c A. Flower b P. A. Strang	0
*S. P. Fleming c A. Flower b B. C. Strang	52	– lbw b B. C. Strang	27
N. J. Astle c A. Flower b B. C. Strang	7	– c G. W. Flower b B. C. Strang	0
C. L. Cairns run out	12	– not out	71
†A. C. Parore not out	42	– lbw b Huckle	51
C. Z. Harris lbw b Huckle	16	– lbw b Streak	41
D. L. Vettori c J. A. Rennie b P. A. Strang	2	– c G. J. Rennie b Huckle	13
S. B. O'Connor c Houghton b P. A. Strang	2	– not out	1
H. T. Davis c G. J. Rennie b Huckle	1		
B 4, l-b 1	5	B 6, l-b 6, w 1, n-b 2	15

1/44 (2) 2/44 (1) 3/89 (3) 4/96 (5) 207   1/63 (2) 2/64 (3) (8 wkts) 304
5/135 (4) 6/146 (6) 7/189 (8)   3/116 (4) 4/116 (5)
8/198 (9) 9/204 (10) 10/207 (11)   5/122 (1) 6/200 (7)
                                          7/266 (8) 8/296 (9)

Bowling: *First Innings*—Streak 23–2–63–1; J. A. Rennie 8–1–32–0; B. C. Strang 19–10–29–3; P. A. Strang 15–2–31–2; Whittall 5–0–15–0; Huckle 14–3–32–2. *Second Innings*—Streak 21–3–52–2; B. C. Strang 26–10–56–2; Whittall 5–1–19–0; P. A. Strang 42–17–76–1; Huckle 31–9–84–3; J. A. Rennie 3–1–5–0.

Umpires: B. C. Cooray (Sri Lanka) and I. D. Robinson. Referee: S. Wettimuny (Sri Lanka).

ZIMBABWE v NEW ZEALAND

Second Test Match

At Bulawayo, September 25, 26, 27, 28, 29. Drawn. Toss: Zimbabwe. Test debut: D. G. Sewell.
Alistair Campbell shook this game from its torpor and made a dent in Zimbabwe's reputation as a dull team with one of the most unexpected Test-match declarations since Garry Sobers allowed England to win a game and a series in Trinidad almost 30 years earlier.

The first four days were dominated by the bat on a pitch that was too good to produce a result by normal means. And Zimbabwe seemed to be batting with little urgency on the final morning, suggesting they believed a declaration could only benefit New Zealand. Then suddenly Campbell hit out, and set New Zealand 286 in a touch over two sessions. The batsmen took up the challenge and, as Zimbabwe turned to their leg-spinners to keep them in the game, a win for either team became possible. Fleming looked capable of seeing New Zealand home until he was run out in the final push. When Vettori was also run out, leaving 11 to get in four balls with two wickets left, they finally shut the door on a match that, in the end, was almost as exciting as England's draw on the same ground nine months before. Neither side, however, had done enough in the series to prove themselves conclusively superior.

The first half of the contest had belonged to Guy Whittall, who grabbed the opportunity to establish himself as Zimbabwe's No. 4 by scoring an unbeaten 203, with 22 fours and two sixes. He was dropped on five, then stayed for 453 minutes and 359 balls, scoring two-thirds of the runs while he was at the crease. There was already 148 on the board when he came in because the openers Rennie and Grant Flower had carried on where they left off in Harare, with Flower falling 17 short of a third successive century.

New Zealand's bowlers simply lacked the penetration required on such a welcoming batting strip, and the left-arm seamer David Sewell – whose inclusion instead of Davis was as much a punishment for Davis's no-balling as anything else – had a harsh introduction to Test cricket. But the left-arm spinner Vettori was rewarded with four wickets for his perseverance through 58 overs.

For a time on the third day, Zimbabwe had a chance to take a grip: at 162 for six, New Zealand were still 100 short of avoiding the follow-on. But Astle, playing his best innings of the tour, put on 97 with Harris before losing his head, and his wicket, four short of a century. Harris then added a further 112 with Vettori, who scored 90 with remarkable resilience – his previous best in all first-class cricket was 29 not out. Huckle and Paul Strang shared nine wickets, exploiting New Zealand's traditional weakness against leg-spin. Huckle took six for 109, and in the second innings made his match figures 11 for 255, giving him 16 in his first fortnight of Test cricket, and making him the first to take ten or more wickets in a Test for Zimbabwe. He had previously played four first-class matches, three of them in the early 1990s before going to university in South Africa.

Man of the Match: G. J. Whittall. *Man of the Series:* G. W. Flower.

Close of play: First day, Zimbabwe 263-4 (G. J. Whittall 66*, D. L. Houghton 4*); Second day, New Zealand 23-0 (C. M. Spearman 14*, B. A. Pocock 7*); Third day, New Zealand 268-7 (C. Z. Harris 35*, D. L. Vettori 5*); Fourth day, Zimbabwe 152-3 (G. J. Whittall 41*, A. D. R. Campbell 19*).

Zimbabwe

G. J. Rennie c Harris b O'Connor	57	– lbw b Astle 24
G. W. Flower c Fleming b Vettori	83	– run out 49
†A. Flower c Harris b Vettori	39	– c and b Harris 7
G. J. Whittall not out	203	– run out 45
*A. D. R. Campbell c Astle b O'Connor	7	– not out 59
D. L. Houghton b Cairns	32	– c Harris b Vettori 13
P. A. Strang c Harris b Vettori	5	– lbw b Vettori 2
H. H. Streak lbw b Cairns	17	– run out 1
B. C. Strang c Fleming b Cairns	0	– b Cairns 10
A. G. Huckle lbw b Vettori	0	– not out 0
E. Matambanadzo c Fleming b O'Connor	4	
L-b 10, w 2, n-b 2	14	B 2, l-b 7, w 3, n-b 5 17

1/144 (2) 2/148 (1) 3/218 (3) 4/244 (5)   461   1/75 (2) 2/80 (1)   (8 wkts dec.) 227
5/322 (6) 6/343 (7) 7/416 (8)   3/91 (3) 4/172 (4)
8/420 (9) 9/421 (10) 10/461 (11)   5/202 (6) 6/204 (7)
7/205 (8) 8/219 (9)

Bowling: *First Innings*—Sewell 19–3–81–0; O'Connor 27–9–80–3; Cairns 36–11–97–3; Vettori 58–11–165–4; Harris 14–6–13–0; Astle 7–2–15–0. *Second Innings*—Sewell 4–0–9–0; O'Connor 5–0–34–0; Cairns 11–1–49–1; Vettori 18–3–69–2; Astle 9–6–16–1; Harris 17–4–41–1.

New Zealand

C. M. Spearman c Huckle b P. A. Strang	47	– (2) c Campbell b Huckle	27
B. A. Pocock lbw b P. A. Strang	27	– (1) c P. A. Strang b Huckle	62
M. J. Horne lbw b P. A. Strang	5	– c Campbell b Huckle	29
*S. P. Fleming c P. A. Strang b Huckle	27	– run out	75
N. J. Astle c sub (A. R. Whittall) b Huckle	96	– c G. W. Flower b P. A. Strang	21
C. L. Cairns c Rennie b Huckle	0	– c Houghton b Huckle	8
†A. C. Parore c G. W. Flower b Huckle	17	– c Whittall b Huckle	23
C. Z. Harris b Huckle	71	– not out	12
D. L. Vettori c B. C. Strang b Huckle	90	– run out	7
S. B. O'Connor run out	7	– not out	0
D. G. Sewell not out	1		
B 1, l-b 9, n-b 5	15	B 5, l-b 4, n-b 2	11

1/60 (2) 2/76 (3) 3/92 (1) 4/130 (4)   403   1/41 (2) 2/89 (3)   (8 wkts) 275
5/130 (6) 6/162 (7) 7/259 (5)   3/138 (1) 4/207 (5)
8/371 (8) 9/389 (10) 10/403 (9)   5/221 (6) 6/240 (4)
                                      7/260 (7) 8/275 (9)

Bowling: First Innings—Streak 15–5–26–0; Matambanadzo 15–4–52–0; P. A. Strang 47–19–110–3; Huckle 40.4–10–109–6; B. C. Strang 26–12–50–0; Whittall 6–1–14–0; G. W. Flower 10–2–19–0; Campbell 2–0–13–0. *Second Innings*—Matambanadzo 2–0–14–0; B. C. Strang 8–4–15–0; Huckle 32–2–146–5; P. A. Strang 23–1–81–1; G. W. Flower 3–1–10–0.

Umpires: S. Venkataraghavan (India) and R. B. Tiffin. Referee: S. Wettimuny (Sri Lanka).

†ZIMBABWE v NEW ZEALAND

First One-Day International

At Bulawayo, October 1. Tied. Toss: Zimbabwe.

Thrilling hitting from Harris enabled New Zealand to earn a tie as they chased a Zimbabwe total of 233. They needed 30 from the final two overs, 15 from the last, and Larsen was run out at the non-striker's end coming back for what would have been the winning run. Zimbabwe's innings was made up of several useful contributions, but Harris dominated New Zealand's response, scoring an unbeaten 77 from 102 balls. Otherwise it was mostly a poor effort, including four run-outs.

Man of the Match: C. Z. Harris.

Zimbabwe

G. J. Rennie c Fleming b O'Connor	6	P. A. Strang not out	17
G. W. Flower c Larsen b Vettori	66	E. A. Brandes b Cairns	1
*A. D. R. Campbell c Parore b O'Connor	5	J. A. Rennie not out	16
†A. Flower b Larsen	35	L-b 1, n-b 1	2
G. J. Whittall c Spearman b Larsen	24		
D. L. Houghton c sub (P. J. Wiseman) b Astle	40	1/14 2/24 3/101 (8 wkts, 50 overs) 233
C. N. Evans run out	21	4/136 5/139 6/175
A. R. Whittall did not bat.		7/204 8/206

Bowling: O'Connor 8–1–28–2; Cairns 10–0–59–1; Larsen 10–0–42–2; Harris 10–0–40–0; Vettori 6–0–42–1; Astle 6–0–21–1.

New Zealand

C. M. Spearman c A. Flower	C. Z. Harris not out	77
b J. A. Rennie . . 5	D. L. Vettori run out.	18
N. J. Astle c Campbell b J. A. Rennie . . 5	G. R. Larsen run out	17
M. J. Horne run out 55		
*S. P. Fleming c A. Flower	L-b 6, w 2 8	
b G. J. Whittall . 19	—	
C. L. Cairns c Brandes b Evans 26	1/7 2/14 3/49 (9 wkts, 50 overs) 233	
C. D. McMillan run out 2	4/85 5/90 6/100	
†A. C. Parore b Strang 1	7/137 8/178 9/233	

S. B. O'Connor did not bat.

Bowling: Brandes 7–0–42–0; J. A. Rennie 10–2–47–2; G. J. Whittall 2–0–25–1; Strang 10–0–26–1; Evans 8–0–39–1; A. R. Whittall 10–0–36–0; G. W. Flower 3–0–12–0.

Umpires: Q. J. Goosen and R. B. Tiffin.

†ZIMBABWE v NEW ZEALAND

Second One-Day International

At Harare, October 4. Zimbabwe won by three wickets. Toss: New Zealand.

Tight bowling and whole-hearted fielding paved the way for a Zimbabwe victory more convincing than it might appear. Spinners Paul Strang and Andrew Whittall choked New Zealand's run-rate and, while several batsmen began well, none batted on. Gavin Rennie and Campbell were Zimbabwe's main scorers: Rennie built his innings on careful accumulation; Campbell hit out boldly, striking three sixes. The loss of four late wickets was not enough to open the door for the New Zealanders, who were outplayed.

Man of the Match: P. A. Strang.

New Zealand

C. M. Spearman c Campbell	†A. C. Parore c A. Flower b J. A. Rennie 15	
b J. A. Rennie . 1	C. Z. Harris not out	29
N. J. Astle b Strang 36	D. L. Vettori not out.	3
M. J. Horne run out 22	L-b 6, w 14	20
*S. P. Fleming c G. J. Rennie b Evans. . 5	—	
C. L. Cairns c J. A. Rennie b Evans 16	1/6 2/61 3/74 (7 wkts, 50 overs) 185	
C. D. McMillan st A. Flower	4/74 5/116	
b A. R. Whittall . 38	6/143 7/160	

G. R. Larsen and S. B. O'Connor did not bat.

Bowling: Brandes 6–0–28–0; J. A. Rennie 9–1–48–2; G. J. Whittall 5–0–37–0; Strang 10–1–13–1; Evans 10–1–27–2; A. R. Whittall 10–1–26–1.

Zimbabwe

G. J. Rennie lbw b Astle 72	P. A. Strang c and b McMillan	2
G. W. Flower c Cairns b Larsen 4	E. A. Brandes not out	4
†A. Flower c McMillan b O'Connor . . . 5	B 1, l-b 3, w 6, n-b 2	12
G. J. Whittall c O'Connor b Harris 7	—	
*A. D. R. Campbell not out 77	1/12 2/28 3/42 (7 wkts, 48.2 overs) 188	
D. L. Houghton c Vettori b McMillan . . 4	4/165 5/170	
C. N. Evans c O'Connor b Astle 1	6/174 7/180	

J. A. Rennie and A. R. Whittall did not bat.

Bowling: O'Connor 8–0–40–1; Larsen 10–0–32–1; Cairns 7–1–25–0; Harris 6–1–21–1; Vettori 4–0–21–0; Astle 9.2–0–28–2; McMillan 4–0–17–2.

Umpires: G. R. Evans and I. D. Robinson.

†ZIMBABWE v NEW ZEALAND

Third One-Day International

At Harare, October 5. New Zealand won by 83 runs. Toss: New Zealand.

A rearranged batting line-up did the trick for New Zealand. Cairns, promoted to open, and Astle set off at a run a ball, a momentum maintained by Fleming and McMillan, who belted five sixes in an exhilarating 66. The Flower brothers and Guy Whittall tried to match a run-rate of nearly six an over, but wickets fell regularly. New Zealand's last day of the tour was their best.

Man of the Match: C. L. Cairns.   *Man of the Series:* C. Z. Harris.

New Zealand

N. J. Astle c and b J. A. Rennie	33	
C. L. Cairns c G. J. Whittall		C. M. Spearman c Campbell
b A. R. Whittall	71	b B. C. Strang . 0
*S. P. Fleming c A. R. Whittall		†A. C. Parore b B. C. Strang 14
b Evans .	62	D. L. Vettori not out 7
M. J. Horne c and b G. W. Flower	13	L-b 4, w 6 10
C. D. McMillan c A. R. Whittall		
b B. C. Strang .	66	1/58 2/147 3/164 (7 wkts, 50 overs) 294
C. Z. Harris not out	18	4/214 5/263
		6/264 7/287

G. R. Larsen and S. B. O'Connor did not bat.

Bowling: J. A. Rennie 10–0–54–1; B. C. Strang 10–0–66–3; P. A. Strang 10–0–58–0; Evans 6–0–40–1; A. R. Whittall 9–0–48–1; G. W. Flower 5–0–24–1.

Zimbabwe

G. W. Flower c Astle b Cairns	24	J. A. Rennie run out 6
†A. Flower run out	44	B. C. Strang c and b Vettori 15
G. J. Whittall b Astle	49	A. R. Whittall not out 14
*A. D. R. Campbell run out	2	L-b 5, w 2 7
P. A. Strang c Spearman b Vettori	27	
D. L. Houghton run out	1	1/63 2/92 3/116 (44.1 overs) 211
C. N. Evans c Larsen b Vettori	5	4/125 5/126 6/140
G. J. Rennie c Vettori b Larsen	17	7/166 8/176 9/188

Bowling: O'Connor 3–0–22–0; Larsen 7–0–42–1; Cairns 7–1–26–1; Harris 10–0–41–0; Astle 6–0–22–1; Vettori 7.1–0–41–3; McMillan 4–0–12–0.

Umpires: I. D. Robinson and R. B. Tiffin. Series referee: S. Wettimuny (Sri Lanka).

THE SOUTH AFRICANS IN PAKISTAN, 1997-98

By NEIL MANTHORP

This tour was the beginning of important seasons for both teams as they jockeyed for position as the leading Test challengers to Australia. Hansie Cronje encouraged the perception that victories in Pakistan and, on South Africa's next stop, Australia, would make his side world Test champions: "I do not believe that victory in both Pakistan and Australia is an unrealistic goal. I believe we can do it," he said. Meanwhile, Pakistan were celebrating their Golden Jubilee as a country and a cricket union, and had Test series lined up against both South Africa and West Indies, plus a short series against neighbours India and a bumper day-night quadrangular.

But it was the South Africans who were celebrating by the time they departed, having taken the Test series in a startling climax at Faisalabad and beaten all comers in the floodlit spectacular. After they drew on a dead pitch at Rawalpindi and a saturated one at Sheikhupura, a green strip in the final Test saw South Africa concede the advantage, only to fight back to wrap up Pakistan's second innings for 92 – chasing 146 – on the fourth day.

Several heroes emerged in that decisive match. There was 37-year-old off-spinner Pat Symcox – able to get under the skin as well as between bat and pad – who played a vital role as batsman, bowler and team motivator, vice-captain Gary Kirsten, who carried his bat for five hours on the opening day after the rest of the top order folded, and Shaun Pollock, who put the skids under Pakistan at Faisalabad with four wickets in seven balls. His ten wickets in the series and some useful batting contributions also established him as an authentic all-rounder, alongside Brian McMillan and Lance Klusener, increasing South Africa's options for team balance. With Allan Donald leading the attack, fast bowling was still their most potent weapon. Left-arm pace bowler Brett Schultz was grateful for the chance of a third international comeback after nearly a year spent fixing knees, shoulders and other pieces of strained body. But he burst a blood vessel in his bowling shoulder on the first morning of the series and dropped out again. The 20-year-old chinaman and googly bowler Paul Adams achieved little on this trip.

For the hosts, Wasim Akram began the season still recovering from a shoulder injury, and Waqar Younis had only just returned from his physically and emotionally draining Championship-winning season with Glamorgan. The famous fast bowling duo were not to appear together until the final Test. Instead, Pakistan's leading wicket-takers were Mushtaq Ahmed and Saqlain Mushtaq, probably the best pairing of spinners in world cricket, who claimed 23 between them. The batting headlines were stolen by two youngsters, Ali Naqvi and Azhar Mahmood, who became the first pair of debutants to score centuries in the same Test innings.

This was the first time the teams had played a Test in Pakistan; South Africa had won their only previous meeting, a one-off in Johannesburg in January 1995, by a massive 324 runs. But they had toured Pakistan twice for one-day tournaments, which inspired a comprehensive reconnaissance mission by UCB representative Goolam Rajah. This resulted in the cancellation of Quetta as a warm-up venue and the addition of an extra ten days at the start to acclimatise to the extreme heat – but excellent facilities – of Karachi, a decision the team were later to regard as vital. They were afforded the inadvertent luxury of a low-key build-up while India were making their first visit to Pakistan for eight years for three one-day games. Inevitable crowd violence and a 2-1 victory to Pakistan commanded local attention, while South African coach Bob Woolmer was overseeing four-hour training sessions in extreme heat. South Africa's attention to detail also meant that 500 kilograms of pasta, biscuits, sponsors' beer and sweets were flown out with the squad, as well as an extra "coffin" containing 200 videos and various electronic games. All the effort eventually brought reward on the field.

SOUTH AFRICAN TOURING PARTY

W. J. Cronje (Free State) (*captain*), G. Kirsten (Western Province) (*vice-captain*), P. R. Adams (Western Province), A. M. Bacher (Gauteng), D. J. Cullinan (Gauteng), A. A. Donald (Free State), A. C. Hudson (Natal), J. H. Kallis (Western Province), L. Klusener (Natal), B. M. McMillan (Western Province), S. M. Pollock (Natal), J. N. Rhodes (Natal), D. J. Richardson (Eastern Province), B. N. Schultz (Western Province), P. L. Symcox (Natal).

Schultz flew home injured after the First Test. M. V. Boucher (Border) joined the party as cover for the injured Richardson and P. S. de Villiers (Northerns) arrived for the Wills Golden Jubilee Tournament.

Manager: S. K. Reddy. *Coach:* R. A. Woolmer.

SOUTH AFRICAN TOUR RESULTS

Test matches – Played 3: Won 1, Drawn 2.
First-class matches – Played 5: Won 2, Drawn 3.
Wins – Pakistan, Allied Bank.
Draws – Pakistan (2), PCB Combined XI.
One-day internationals – Played 4: Won 4. *Wins* – Pakistan, West Indies, Sri Lanka (2).

TEST MATCH AVERAGES

PAKISTAN – BATTING

	T	I	NO	R	HS	100s	50s	Avge	Ct
Azhar Mahmood....	3	4	2	203	128*	1	1	101.50	1
Mushtaq Ahmed....	3	3	2	63	59	0	1	63.00	3
Ali Naqvi........	3	5	1	181	115	1	0	45.25	1
Moin Khan.......	3	4	1	130	80	0	1	43.33	3
Inzamam-ul-Haq....	3	4	0	165	96	0	2	41.25	0
Waqar Younis.....	2	3	0	79	45	0	0	26.33	0
Ijaz Ahmed, sen. ...	3	4	0	43	16	0	0	10.75	4
Saeed Anwar	3	5	0	40	17	0	0	8.00	1
Saqlain Mushtaq....	3	4	1	6	6	0	0	2.00	1

Played in two Tests: Mohammad Wasim 11, 10 (3 ct, 1 st). Wasim Akram 2, 9. Played in one Test: Aamir Sohail 38, 14 (1 ct); Mohammad Ramzan 29, 7 (1 ct); Ali Hussain Rizvi did not bat.

* *Signifies not out.*

BOWLING

	O	M	R	W	BB	5W/i	Avge
Wasim Akram	40	9	114	6	4-42	0	19.00
Mushtaq Ahmed	140.5	38	386	14	4-57	0	27.57
Waqar Younis	44	11	124	4	2-36	0	31.00
Azhar Mahmood	58.4	8	178	5	2-52	0	35.60
Saqlain Mushtaq........	119	28	322	9	5-129	1	35.77

Also bowled: Ali Hussain Rizvi 18.3–1–72–2.

SOUTH AFRICA – BATTING

	T	I	NO	R	HS	100s	50s	Avge	Ct
G. Kirsten	3	4	1	258	100*	1	2	86.00	1
S. M. Pollock	3	4	1	156	82	0	1	52.00	1
A. M. Bacher	3	4	0	161	96	0	2	40.25	4
P. L. Symcox	3	4	0	158	81	0	2	39.50	1
L. Klusener	2	3	0	114	58	0	1	38.00	0
D. J. Richardson	2	3	1	53	45*	0	0	26.50	6
W. J. Cronje	3	4	0	104	50	0	1	26.00	2
B. M. McMillan	3	4	0	37	21	0	0	9.25	2
D. J. Cullinan	3	4	0	32	16	0	0	8.00	1
A. A. Donald	2	3	0	10	8	0	0	3.33	2
P. R. Adams	2	3	1	4	3*	0	0	2.00	0

Played in one Test: M. V. Boucher 6; J. H. Kallis 61; J. N. Rhodes 11; B. N. Schultz 1.

BOWLING

	O	M	R	W	BB	5W/i	Avge
W. J. Cronje	18.5	4	60	4	2-6	0	15.00
L. Klusener	20	3	57	3	2-30	0	19.00
S. M. Pollock	83	21	232	10	5-37	1	23.20
P. L. Symcox	82.3	22	233	8	3-8	0	29.12
A. A. Donald	67.4	9	226	7	3-108	0	32.28

Also bowled: P. R. Adams 30–9–79–2; D. J. Cullinan 1–0–2–0; J. H. Kallis 14.4–4–36–2; B. M. McMillan 32–7–80–0; B. N. Schultz 15.4–4–58–1.

At National Stadium, Karachi, October 1, 2, 3. Drawn. Toss: South Africans. South Africans 305 for seven dec. (D. J. Cullinan 45, W. J. Cronje 35, J. N. Rhodes 34, J. H. Kallis 52, S. M. Pollock 74 not out; Ali Hussain Rizvi five for 89) and 254 for eight dec. (A. M. Bacher 40, G. Kirsten 61, D. J. Cullinan 44, S. M. Pollock 47 not out; Ali Hussain Rizvi six for 57); PCB Combined XI 132 (Mohammad Ramzan 32, Ali Naqvi 61; P. R. Adams three for 11, P. L. Symcox four for 25) and 237 for four (Ali Naqvi 113, Rana Qayyum 83 not out).

PAKISTAN v SOUTH AFRICA

First Test Match

At Rawalpindi, October 6, 7, 8, 9, 10. Drawn. Toss: Pakistan. Test debuts: Ali Naqvi, Azhar Mahmood, Mohammad Ramzan.

The South Africans took an early advantage and entertained thoughts of victory when Pakistan hobbled to 216 for six on the first day. The truth, however, was soon as bald as the pitch. The bounce was like an old tennis ball on clay, there was no moisture to assist movement, and the clay would not even crack. The contest died, but it was still a memorable Test match, with two of Pakistan's three newcomers taking the starring roles. Ali Naqvi and Azhar Mahmood became the first pair of same-team debutants to score centuries in the same Test.

Naqvi, a 20-year-old opener, stormed to 25 from as many balls on the opening morning before sense and his partners' misfortunes forced him to calm down. He batted on into the evening for his hundred. Congratulations were soon followed by withering sideways glances when, with two overs to go, he rashly slashed at Donald and departed for 115, to be replaced by all-rounder Mahmood. Resuming after a rainy morning, Moin Khan and Saqlain Mushtaq were both lbw, and Pakistan were 231 for eight. South Africa had excelled themselves on a batsman's track.

The last two wickets, however, all but doubled the score. Waqar Younis hit two sixes (including a hook off Donald) and five fours in a Test-best 45 but mostly blocked stoutly, while Mahmood was virtually unnoticeable in his orthodox efficiency. When Waqar fell, though, and last man Mushtaq Ahmed joined him, the accumulator turned aggressor, and Mahmood struck several thumping extra-cover drives, off front and back feet. On the third morning, the last pair added another 111 delicious runs. Mahmood finished unbeaten on 128, his maiden first-class century, after 349 minutes, having struck 11 fours and a six. Mushtaq also gorged on the carcass of South

Africa's shocked attack, lifting off-spinner Symcox for three sixes and a four in one over, on his way to a maiden Test fifty. Between them, they added 151 to equal the tenth-wicket Test record of New Zealanders Brian Hastings and Richard Collinge, who kept Pakistan waiting in Auckland in 1972-73.

Eight sessions remained and Kirsten set out "to bat time, not runs". He was still there at the close, though Saqlain had Bacher well caught at silly point by the third debutant, Mohammad Ramzan. Kirsten went on to bat almost seven hours, virtually assuring the draw, until, two short of his hundred, he edged one of the rare deliveries from Saqlain that turned above ambient pace and bounced as well. At tea, Queen Elizabeth and the Duke of Edinburgh, taking part in Pakistan's 50th anniversary celebrations, met the two teams, cheered by a 15,000-strong crowd that had been admitted free; it was the only time the ground held more than 700 placid spectators.

Having conceded a deficit of 53, Cronje and his bowlers succeeded in their only possible target: "to put them under pressure and win a few psychological points". Pakistan slipped to 80 for five before the determined Mahmood closed the door with an unbeaten fifty.

Man of the Match: Azhar Mahmood.

Close of play: First day, Pakistan 216-6 (Moin Khan 8*, Azhar Mahmood 4*); Second day, Pakistan 345-9 (Azhar Mahmood 72*, Mushtaq Ahmed 6*); Third day, South Africa 139-1 (G. Kirsten 62*, J. H. Kallis 20*); Fourth day, South Africa 359-6 (S. M. Pollock 35*, D. J. Richardson 30*).

Pakistan

*Saeed Anwar c Richardson b Donald	16	– c sub (J. N. Rhodes) b Donald	4
Ali Naqvi c Kirsten b Donald	115	– c Richardson b Kallis	19
Mohammad Ramzan lbw b Pollock	29	– c Cronje b Kallis	7
Ijaz Ahmed, sen. b Symcox	11	– b Symcox	16
Inzamam-ul-Haq c Richardson b Schultz	8	– c Symcox b Cronje	56
Mohammad Wasim c Bacher b Symcox	11	– c Pollock b Symcox	10
†Moin Khan lbw b Donald	12	– (8) not out	6
Azhar Mahmood not out	128	– (7) not out	50
Saqlain Mushtaq lbw b Pollock	0		
Waqar Younis lbw b Pollock	45		
Mushtaq Ahmed b Cronje	59		
B 2, l-b 7, n-b 13	22	B 2, l-b 2, n-b 10	14

1/45 (1) 2/114 (3) 3/135 (4) 4/152 (5)   456   1/5 (1) 2/33 (2)   (6 wkts) 182
5/196 (6) 6/206 (2) 7/230 (7)   3/42 (3) 4/66 (4)
8/231 (9) 9/305 (10) 10/456 (11)   5/80 (6) 6/148 (5)

Bowling: First Innings—Donald 33–3–108–3; Schultz 15.4–4–58–1; Pollock 37–13–74–3; McMillan 17–5–36–0; Symcox 46–11–130–2; Kallis 7–3–15–0; Cronje 7.5–0–26–1. *Second Innings*—Donald 11–4–25–1; Pollock 8–1–22–0; McMillan 8–1–24–0; Kallis 7.4–1–21–2; Symcox 16–2–56–2; Cronje 6–1–28–1; Cullinan 1–0–2–0.

South Africa

G. Kirsten c Ijaz Ahmed b Saqlain Mushtaq	98	
A. M. Bacher c Mohammad Ramzan b Saqlain Mushtaq	50	
J. H. Kallis lbw b Saqlain Mushtaq	61	
D. J. Cullinan lbw b Saqlain Mushtaq	16	
*W. J. Cronje c Ijaz Ahmed b Azhar Mahmood	24	
B. M. McMillan c Ijaz Ahmed b Saqlain Mushtaq	7	
S. M. Pollock c Mohammad Wasim b Azhar Mahmood	48	
†D. J. Richardson not out	45	
P. L. Symcox st Mohammad Wasim b Mushtaq Ahmed	5	
A. A. Donald c Saeed Anwar b Mushtaq Ahmed	0	
B. N. Schultz lbw b Mushtaq Ahmed	1	
B 20, l-b 9, w 4, n-b 15	48	

1/107 (2) 2/221 (3) 3/228 (1)   403
4/249 (4) 5/278 (5) 6/282 (6)
7/388 (7) 8/393 (9)
9/399 (10) 10/403 (11)

Bowling: Waqar Younis 20–8–45–0; Azhar Mahmood 27–1–74–2; Mushtaq Ahmed 58.5–17–126–3; Saqlain Mushtaq 62–13–129–5.

Umpires: S. Venkataraghavan (India) and Javed Akhtar.   Referee: R. S. Madugalle (Sri Lanka).

At Peshawar, October 12, 13, 14. South Africans won by 180 runs. Toss: South Africans. South Africans 367 for four dec. (A. M. Bacher 62, A. C. Hudson 42, J. H. Kallis 134 not out, D. J. Cullinan 87, J. N. Rhodes 30) and 213 for five dec. (B. M. McMillan 34, D. J. Richardson 32 retired hurt, L. Klusener 56; Ata-ur-Rehman three for 49); Allied Bank 275 for three dec. (Aamir Sohail 128, Manzoor Akhtar 117 not out) and 125 (L. Klusener three for 49, P. R. Adams four for 19).

PAKISTAN v SOUTH AFRICA
Second Test Match

At Sheikhupura, October 17, 18, 19, 20, 21. Drawn. Toss: South Africa. Test debuts: Ali Hussain Rizvi; M. V. Boucher.

Monsoon rains, injury and illness starred in this game. Play was possible on only two days. Meanwhile, a groin injury ended wicket-keeper Dave Richardson's unique run of 38 Tests for South Africa since their readmission in 1992; 20-year-old Mark Boucher stepped up after a hasty journey from East London. Klusener played because Donald was injured, and South Africa included both their spinners as Schultz had flown home. After the washed-out first day, Kallis was rushed into hospital with appendicitis and Rhodes replaced him. Pakistan were reinforced by Wasim Akram, after six months off with a bad shoulder, but lost Waqar Younis to a bruised foot. They also added a spinner, Ali Hussain Rizvi.

Both teams stayed amid the big-city comforts of Lahore, and the 90-minute drive meant a 6 a.m. wake-up call for the players, who travelled wrapped in tracksuits and plugged into personal stereos to distract themselves from the journey, which was especially frightful on the first day due to torrential rain. The skies cleared after lunch and nine motley pieces of canvas and tarpaulin were removed to reveal a saturated pitch. There was much gnashing of teeth over this debacle, but no one took responsibility. Referee Ranjan Madugalle did sterling work cajoling the players into action in less than ideal conditions on the second afternoon.

Kirsten and Bacher set off with a second successive strong stand, thanks to aggressive strokeplay and necessary luck against Wasim. Mushtaq Ahmed was bowling his leg-spin by the tenth over. The turn was very slow, but Bacher was still unable to pick it in time. Unable to defend with confidence, he counter-attacked with lofted straight drives and sweeps, striding towards a maiden Test century on a bright third day. Then nerves trapped him on 96, equalling his previous best. Mushtaq, who had passed the bat with nine out of 11 balls, found the edge with the 12th. Cronje raised the tempo with three "slog-sweep" sixes, while Pollock and Klusener added 96 in 18 overs.

Saeed Anwar had expected South Africa to crumble against spin; instead, they made 402. Mushtaq took four for 122 while Saqlain was attacked with some ease and Rizvi, despite a funfair loop and plenty of turn, looked out of his depth. Pakistan passed fifty that evening, losing Anwar just before rain ended play ten overs early. And on the fourth and fifth days, bedraggled bystanders watched the teams driving through drenching rain on a three-hour round trip with no prospect of play. The water buffalo, barely able to keep their nostrils above the rising tide of the fields, emerged on to the road, making the final drive back slower than ever.

Close of play: First day, No play; Second day, South Africa 154-2 (A. M. Bacher 78*, D. J. Cullinan 1*); Third day, Pakistan 53-1 (Ali Naqvi 30*, Saqlain Mushtaq 0*); Fourth day, No play.

South Africa

G. Kirsten b Wasim Akram	56	L. Klusener lbw b Azhar Mahmood	58
A. M. Bacher c Moin Khan		†M. V. Boucher b Azhar Mahmood	6
b Mushtaq Ahmed	96	P. L. Symcox c Mohammad Wasim	
B. M. McMillan c Moin Khan		b Ali Hussain Rizvi	17
b Mushtaq Ahmed	7	P. R. Adams not out	3
D. J. Cullinan c Mohammad Wasim			
b Saqlain Mushtaq	1	B 7, l-b 3, n-b 5	15
*W. J. Cronje c sub (Waqar Younis)			
b Mushtaq Ahmed	50	1/135 (1) 2/152 (3) 3/155 (4)	402
J. N. Rhodes b Mushtaq Ahmed	11	4/179 (2) 5/215 (6) 6/252 (5)	
S. M. Pollock c Ali Naqvi		7/348 (8) 8/356 (9)	
b Ali Hussain Rizvi	82	9/396 (10) 10/402 (7)	

Bowling: Wasim Akram 13–3–26–1; Azhar Mahmood 14–3–52–2; Mushtaq Ahmed 38–12–122–4; Saqlain Mushtaq 32–7–120–1; Ali Hussain Rizvi 18.3–1–72–2.

Pakistan

Ali Naqvi not out	30
*Saeed Anwar b Symcox	17
Saqlain Mushtaq not out	0
B 4, n-b 2	6

1/53 (2)   (1 wkt) 53

Ijaz Ahmed, sen., Inzamam-ul-Haq, Mohammad Wasim, Azhar Mahmood, †Moin Khan, Wasim Akram, Mushtaq Ahmed and Ali Hussain Rizvi did not bat.

Bowling: Pollock 7–1–35–0; Klusener 6–1–14–0; Adams 2–2–0–0; Symcox 2–2–0–1.

Umpires: K. T. Francis (Sri Lanka) and Mohammad Nazir. Referee: R. S. Madugalle (Sri Lanka).

PAKISTAN v SOUTH AFRICA

Third Test Match

At Faisalabad, October 24, 25, 26, 27. South Africa won by 53 runs. Toss: South Africa.

South Africa took the series when they won, quite against the run of play, by bundling Pakistan out for 92 on the fourth day; Symcox played his first match-winning hand in 13 Tests. It was a thrilling game, fought out on a pitch which looked positively emerald by Pakistan's standards: an edict from Majid Khan, the PCB chief executive, had instructed groundsmen to "leave enough grass to encourage results".

Cronje might have preferred to lose the toss; he decided to bat but, with Wasim Akram and Waqar Younis reunited at last, his side capitulated to high-class seam and swing. They left South Africa 30 for four, and Mushtaq Ahmed nipped in with three to shove the innings to the brink of disaster: 99 for seven at lunch. Then Kirsten, bristling with scratchy, scuffling determination, was joined by Symcox, who can really irritate bowlers. His 81, from 94 balls, dominated their stand of 124. Divine intervention seemed to take a hand when he was beaten by a Mushtaq googly that slipped under the bat and passed between off and middle stump. Umpire Dunne gave his spectacles a disbelieving wipe, but the bail was found to be badly cut.

Wasim finally broke through with a slippery in-swinger and Kirsten had to bat on with the dubious help of Adams. He reached his hundred, but this was promptly adjusted back to 99, at which point Adams was out. The scorers then announced that one leg-bye should have been a run for Kirsten. So he finished with an unbeaten 100, becoming the first South African to carry his bat in a Test since Jackie McGlew in 1961-62.

Pakistan's innings followed an eerily similar path to South Africa's, the new ball side-stepping and bouncing eagerly. On the second morning, they were 80 for five before Inzamam-ul-Haq and Moin Khan added 144. At 224 for five, just 15 behind, Pakistan were on top. Cronje, sensing tension and maybe fear in his ranks, brought himself on. Inzamam, on 96, immediately chased a wide away-swinger to second slip. In Cronje's next over, Moin allowed another wobbler to sneak on to off stump. But Aamir Sohail, batting at No. 8 with a damaged finger, and Waqar pushed on to a lead of 69.

The following day Symcox, the night-watchman, reprised his first-innings performance, standing very still and hitting hard anything pitched up to him. This simple form of batting earned him another fifty, including one of his customary sixes over long-on. Mushtaq and Saqlain took seven wickets between them, though, and the confident Pakistanis bedded down on the third evening at four without losing, needing 142 in two days. On the bus back to the hotel, Symcox delivered an impassioned speech to his downcast team-mates about seizing the moment: "This game can be won."

In the morning, Sohail carved Donald for two fours – but his third slash went to point. Then Pollock, bowling with impeccable discipline to a specific plan for each batsman, took four in seven balls. The batsmen played like rabbits but Pollock became the headlights which paralysed them. Lunch was taken at 79 for six – "I don't know how they felt," said Pollock, "but we couldn't eat a thing. We all just sat, staring at the clock, willing the minutes to go by . . ."

Cronje brought Symcox on straight afterwards and the grizzled bear turned cunning fox, tossing the ball up so sweetly it was impossible for the terrified batsmen to hit. He removed Wasim, swatting across the line in panic, and Saqlain, deflecting the ball to short leg. Finally, Moin, after a gutsy 32, pulled him to deep mid-wicket, where Donald took a throat-high catch and sprinted 60 metres to join a celebrating crush of bodies.

Man of the Match: P. L. Symcox. *Men of the Series:* Pakistan – Mushtaq Ahmed; South Africa – G. Kirsten.

Close of play: First day, Pakistan 41-2 (Ijaz Ahmed 15*, Inzamam-ul-Haq 12*); Second day, South Africa 21-2 (B. M. McMillan 2*, P. L. Symcox 0*); Third day, Pakistan 4-0 (Ali Naqvi 4*, Aamir Sohail 0*).

South Africa

A. M. Bacher c sub (Mohammad Wasim) b Wasim Akram .	1	– lbw b Mushtaq Ahmed	14
G. Kirsten not out	100	– c Mushtaq Ahmed b Wasim Akram .	4
B. M. McMillan c sub (Mohammad Wasim) b Wasim Akram .	2	– c Moin Khan b Mushtaq Ahmed ..	21
D. J. Cullinan lbw b Waqar Younis .	0	– (5) lbw b Mushtaq Ahmed	15
*W. J. Cronje lbw b Waqar Younis	9	– (6) c Azhar Mahmood b Waqar Younis .	21
S. M. Pollock c Aamir Sohail b Mushtaq Ahmed	5	– (7) not out	21
†D. J. Richardson c Saqlain Mushtaq b Mushtaq Ahmed .	8	– (8) lbw b Waqar Younis	0
L. Klusener c Ijaz Ahmed b Mushtaq Ahmed .	18	– (9) lbw b Saqlain Mushtaq	38
P. L. Symcox b Wasim Akram .	81	– (4) lbw b Saqlain Mushtaq	55
A. A. Donald c Mushtaq Ahmed b Wasim Akram .	2	– b Saqlain Mushtaq	8
P. R. Adams lbw b Azhar Mahmood .	1	– c and b Mushtaq Ahmed	0
B 4, l-b 3, n-b 5 .	12	B 3, l-b 13, n-b 1 .	17
	239		**214**

1/2 (1) 2/11 (3) 3/12 (4) 4/30 (5)
5/40 (6) 6/64 (7) 7/98 (8)
8/222 (9) 9/230 (10) 10/239 (11)

1/16 (2) 2/21 (1) 3/63 (3)
4/97 (5) 5/140 (4) 6/140 (6)
7/140 (8) 8/187 (9)
9/201 (10) 10/214 (11)

Bowling: *First Innings*—Wasim Akram 16–6–42–4; Waqar Younis 10–1–36–2; Mushtaq Ahmed 22–3–81–3; Azhar Mahmood 10.4–2–36–1; Saqlain Mushtaq 10–2–37–0. *Second Innings*—Wasim Akram 11–0–46–1; Waqar Younis 14–2–43–2; Mushtaq Ahmed 22–6–57–4; Saqlain Mushtaq 15–6–36–3; Azhar Mahmood 7–2–16–0.

Pakistan

Ali Naqvi b Donald	11	– c Cullinan b Pollock	6
*Saeed Anwar lbw b Pollock	3	– (3) c Richardson b Pollock	0
Ijaz Ahmed, sen. lbw b Adams	16	– (4) lbw b Pollock	0
Inzamam-ul-Haq c McMillan b Cronje	96	– (5) c McMillan b Pollock	5
Azhar Mahmood b Klusener.	19	– (6) c Richardson b Klusener	6
Wasim Akram c Richardson b Klusener	2	– (8) c Kirsten b Symcox	0
†Moin Khan b Cronje.	80	– c Donald b Symcox	32
Aamir Sohail c Donald b Pollock	38	– (2) c Bacher b Donald.	14
Saqlain Mushtaq c Bacher b Adams	6	– c Bacher b Symcox.	0
Waqar Younis c Cronje b Donald	34	– b Pollock	0
Mushtaq Ahmed not out	0	– not out	4
L-b 1, w 1, n-b 1 .	3	B 4, l-b 6, w 1, n-b 5 .	16
	308		**92**

1/10 (2) 2/18 (1) 3/42 (3) 4/74 (5)
5/80 (6) 6/224 (4) 7/229 (7)
8/246 (9) 9/304 (8) 10/308 (10)

1/23 (2) 2/24 (3) 3/24 (4)
4/29 (1) 5/31 (5) 6/68 (6)
7/85 (8) 8/87 (9)
9/88 (10) 10/92 (7)

Bowling: *First Innings*—Donald 17.4–1–79–2; Pollock 20–5–64–2; Adams 23–5–69–2; Symcox 9–2–39–0; Klusener 8–1–30–2; McMillan 7–1–20–0; Cronje 5–3–6–2. *Second Innings*—Adams 5–2–10–0; Symcox 9.3–5–8–3; Pollock 11–1–37–5; Donald 6–1–14–1; Klusener 6–1–13–1.

Umpires: R. S. Dunne (New Zealand) and Mian Aslam. Referee: R. S. Madugalle (Sri Lanka).

South Africa's matches v Pakistan, West Indies and Sri Lanka in the Wills Golden Jubilee Tournament (November 2–8) may be found in that section.

THE NEW ZEALANDERS IN AUSTRALIA, 1997-98

By MALCOLM KNOX

Stephen Fleming's young New Zealand side toured in the shadow of the worsening dispute between the Australian first-class players and the Australian Cricket Board. The public squabble paid scant respect to the touring team; it would be difficult to imagine the house being so divided if the opposition had been one of the front-line Test sides.

A truce was called for the First Test in Brisbane, in which New Zealand caught Australia by surprise and sustained a possible winning position from the first morning until the fifth. After Australia stole the game, though, the players' dispute erupted on the first morning of the Second Test in Perth, and the Australians' convincing win was almost incidental to off-field machinations concerning a possible strike.

This uncalculated insult was a disservice to the New Zealanders, who were the reverse of Kiwi teams of the recent past. New Zealand sides have generally comprised canny journeymen who exploited the limits of their modest talents; the 1997-98 squad, by contrast, included a number of gifted cricketers in their twenties (even younger, in Daniel Vettori's case), a group epitomised by Fleming himself, who tried to play expressive, risk-taking cricket. They were far less nondescript than many of their predecessors and were to leave Australia having gained stature, popularity and a good measure of anticipation for their next visit.

Under their coach, former Australian wicket-keeper Steve Rixon, they played a bold, Australian-style game. From the first session of the Brisbane Test, when they took four quick wickets, New Zealand surprised their opponents by refusing, in Fleming's words, to be "the weak little underage side from New Zealand". He insisted: "We have got the ability to match it, whether verbally or aggressively, with them."

Chris Cairns, a target for Australian sledging in 1993-94, was now a harder man and a better cricketer. Adam Parore, settled at last after a long Test apprenticeship, taunted the out-of-form Mark Waugh in Brisbane and mocked Shane Warne's "TV balls" – the leg-spinners that spun too far to do any harm. Craig McMillan made his debut in Brisbane and compiled two fine fifties. He also managed to hit Warne for six in each Test match. Fleming's captaincy was transparently adventurous; his declaration in Hobart, 149 behind on first innings, was emblematic of this team, who preferred a tilt at victory to the dubious honour of a grim draw.

Still, New Zealand failed to breach the class difference; they were unable to win a single first-class match or to reach the finals of the one-day series. Australia had too many good players, every individual making some contribution through the three Test matches. Playing without strike bowler Jason Gillespie for all Tests, and without Glenn McGrath for the Second and Third, Australia proved their strength in depth for an eighth successive series win since 1994. Mark Taylor, who had led them through this extraordinary run, was named Man of the Series, partly for his crucial 112 in the First Test and partly for his team's ensemble performances throughout. Warne, Greg Blewett, Paul Reiffel and Ian Healy were consistent high achievers without controlling more than a session individually.

But, though the game young New Zealanders lost 2-0, as they had on their previous tour, the series ended with them on an upswing.

NEW ZEALAND TOURING PARTY

S. P. Fleming (Canterbury) (*captain*), G. I. Allott (Canterbury), N. J. Astle (Canterbury), C. L. Cairns (Canterbury), H. T. Davis (Wellington), S. B. Doull (Northern Districts), C. Z. Harris (Canterbury), M. J. Horne (Otago), C. D. McMillan (Canterbury), S. B. O'Connor (Otago), A. C. Parore (Auckland), B. A. Pocock (Auckland), D. L. Vettori (Northern Districts), B. A. Young (Northern Districts).

G. R. Larsen (Wellington), D. J. Nash (Northern Districts), C. M. Spearman (Central Districts) and R. G. Twose (Wellington) joined the party for the one-day Carlton & United Series.

Manager: D. J. Graham. *Coach:* S. J. Rixon.

NEW ZEALAND TOUR RESULTS

Test matches – Played 3: Lost 2, Drawn 1.
First-class matches – Played 6: Lost 5, Drawn 1.
Losses – Australia (2), Queensland, New South Wales, Victoria.
Draw – Australia.
One-day internationals – Played 8: Won 2, Lost 6. *Wins* – South Africa, Australia. *Losses* – Australia (3), South Africa (3).
Other non-first-class matches – Played 7: Won 3, Lost 2, Tied 1, No result 1. *Wins* – Australian Country XI, Sutherland, Australia A. *Losses* – Queensland, South Australia. *Tied* – Queensland. *No result* – New South Wales XI.

TEST MATCH AVERAGES
AUSTRALIA – BATTING

	T	I	NO	R	HS	100s	50s	Avge	Ct/St
P. R. Reiffel	3	4	1	178	77	0	2	59.33	0
M. A. Taylor	3	5	1	214	112	1	1	53.50	10
G. S. Blewett	3	5	0	267	99	0	3	53.40	5
I. A. Healy	3	4	0	194	85	0	2	48.50	6/2
M. T. G. Elliott	3	4	0	185	114	1	0	46.25	3
R. T. Ponting	3	4	1	119	73*	0	1	39.66	2
M. E. Waugh	3	5	0	196	86	0	2	39.20	1
S. R. Waugh	3	5	1	130	96	0	1	32.50	4
S. K. Warne	3	3	0	71	36	0	0	23.66	0
M. S. Kasprowicz . .	3	3	1	42	20	0	0	21.00	0

Played in two Tests: S. H. Cook 3*, 0*. Played in one Test: G. D. McGrath 6.

* *Signifies not out.*

BOWLING

	O	M	R	W	BB	5W/i	Avge
S. R. Waugh	15	6	30	4	3-20	0	7.50
G. D. McGrath	49.2	12	128	7	5-32	1	18.28
S. H. Cook	37.2	10	142	7	5-39	1	20.28
S. K. Warne	170.4	36	476	19	5-88	1	25.05
P. R. Reiffel	93	30	226	8	2-27	0	28.25
M. S. Kasprowicz	84	22	233	6	2-40	0	38.83

Also bowled: G. S. Blewett 13–4–30–1; M. T. G. Elliott 1–1–0–0; M. E. Waugh 21–5–54–0.

NEW ZEALAND – BATTING

	T	I	NO	R	HS	100s	50s	Avge	Ct/St
A. C. Parore	3	6	1	229	63	0	1	45.80	5/1
C. L. Cairns	3	6	1	172	64	0	2	34.40	0
C. D. McMillan	3	6	0	174	54	0	2	29.00	1
N. J. Astle	3	6	1	119	40	0	0	23.80	2
B. A. Young	3	6	0	119	45	0	0	19.83	5
B. A. Pocock	2	4	0	76	57	0	1	19.00	1
S. P. Fleming	3	6	0	105	91	0	1	17.50	9
S. B. Doull	3	5	2	30	17	0	0	10.00	1
D. L. Vettori	3	5	1	32	14*	0	0	8.00	2
S. B. O'Connor	2	3	1	14	7	0	0	7.00	2
G. I. Allott	2	4	0	6	4	0	0	2.00	0

Played in one Test: C. Z. Harris 13, 0; M. J. Horne 133, 31; R. G. Twose 2, 29.

* *Signifies not out.*

BOWLING

	O	M	R	W	BB	5W/i	Avge
C. L. Cairns	103.1	31	325	13	4-90	0	25.00
S. B. O'Connor	74.4	17	242	7	3-101	0	34.57
S. B. Doull	111	26	307	8	4-70	0	38.37
D. L. Vettori	112	27	310	6	2-87	0	51.66

Also bowled: G. I. Allott 72.5–10–261–2; N. J. Astle 31–7–91–0; C. Z. Harris 13–1–47–0; C. D. McMillan 15–4–43–1.

Note: Matches in this section which were not first-class are signified by a dagger.

At Cairns, October 22, 23, 24, 25. Queensland won by an innings and 127 runs. Toss: Queensland. New Zealanders 196 (B. A. Pocock 63, S. P. Fleming 57; M. S. Kasprowicz three for 42, A. J. Bichel five for 31) and 248 (B. A. Young 67, S. P. Fleming 62, C. L. Cairns 46; A. C. Dale three for 63); Queensland 571 (M. L. Hayden 73, M. L. Love 201 retired hurt, J. P. Maher 114, G. I. Foley 36, A. C. Dale 55, Extras 33; H. T. Davis three for 113, D. L. Vettori four for 155).
The first first-class match played at Cazaly AFL Ground, Cairns. Love's unbeaten 201 lasted 374 minutes and 281 balls and included 27 fours and three sixes.

†At Cairns, October 26. Queensland won by 127 runs. Toss: Queensland. Queensland 252 for eight (50 overs) (J. P. Maher 72, A. Symonds 75); New Zealanders 125 (36.1 overs) (B. A. Young 46; P. W. Jackson five for 72).

†At Coffs Harbour, October 29. No result. Toss: New South Wales XII. New South Wales XII 156 (49 overs) (C. J. Richards 66; D. L. Vettori three for 27); New Zealanders 68 for three (14.2 overs) (C. L. Cairns 31).
Each team used 12 players.

At Newcastle, October 31, November 1, 2, 3. New South Wales won by an innings and 95 runs. Toss: New South Wales. New South Wales 469 for six dec. (M. J. Slater 137, M. E. Waugh 44, M. G. Bevan 143, G. R. J. Matthews 71 not out); New Zealanders 214 (C. D. McMillan 62, D. L. Vettori 47; S. H. Cook three for 38, S. C. G. MacGill three for 55, including a hat-trick) and 160 (B. A. Pocock 47; S. H. Cook four for 61, S. C. G. MacGill three for 50).

AUSTRALIA v NEW ZEALAND

First Test Match

At Brisbane, November 7, 8, 9, 10, 11. Australia won by 186 runs. Toss: New Zealand. Test debut: C. D. McMillan.
Mark Taylor, carried by his successful team for most of 1997, repaid them with a first-innings century that kept Australia in the match against an unexpectedly competitive New Zealand. Caught by surprise, the Australians just held their ground for four days before the young visitors, mentally spent, capitulated to McGrath and Warne on the fifth morning.
Persistent rain had kept the pitch covered for two days beforehand, and the customary Gabba greenness offered a disproportionate advantage to the team bowling first. Doull and Allott failed to control the new ball, but the arrival of the bristling Cairns in the ninth over enlivened the match. In his first nine overs, Cairns dismissed Elliott, Blewett and the Waugh twins. Australia were 52 for four.

After innings defeats by Queensland and New South Wales, the New Zealanders had predicted that the Test-match atmosphere would lift them. They bowled and fielded with unremitting hostility – while the Australians appeared disengaged, as if needing a shock to raise their competitive hackles.

It fell to Taylor and Healy to retrieve the position with a 117-run partnership. The ironies were plain. Taylor's batting had been so poor for a year that only his strategic role in the team had saved his place. Now, his batting was saving his team from significant embarrassment. At the other end was Healy, who had been vice-captain until Steve Waugh, the ACB's preferred alternative captain, replaced him in case Taylor had been forced to step down on the Ashes tour. Renascent all-rounder Reiffel then scored a Test-best 77, and helped take the total to 373. In reply, Pocock and Fleming grafted for nearly three hours until Pocock pressed forward to a Warne leg-break and edged to Taylor at slip.

New Zealand continued to defy expectations on the third day. Fleming, having reached his 16th Test fifty, was moving smoothly towards only his second Test hundred when Kasprowicz held one up off the pitch and trapped him in front. Undeterred, Cairns and debutant Craig McMillan recorded steady fifties. Warne, on-driven for six by McMillan, ground away for 42 overs and eventually choked back the challenge. When Taylor caught Parore, it was his 39th catch from Warne's bowling in 57 Tests, equalling the Test record for a fielder-bowler combination: c Sobers b Gibbs. Taylor and Warne became the sole record-holders in the second innings.

New Zealand's 349 maintained parity. On the fourth day, they again glimpsed victory when Australia were 105 for four. Mark Waugh recorded another failure after his barren England tour; the extent of New Zealand's cheek was revealed by microphones which picked up Parore murmuring: "It's tough out here, isn't it, Mark?" But Blewett and Ponting enabled Australia to set a target of 319. It took a single delivery on the final morning to start the collapse. Reiffel produced a kicker to find Pocock's edge, Warne increased the pressure, and McGrath moved in for the clean-up, taking five for 32 despite an abdominal strain which would keep him out until after Christmas.

New Zealand's aggressive approach to the first four days, standing toe-to-toe with the world's most feared Test team, turned out to have exhausted them by the fifth. They had miscalculated by playing Harris as a No. 8 who hardly bowled, and their top-order crisis would only be resolved by promoting the stubborn, correct Parore to No. 3. They had played a good Test match, catching a complacent Australia at their most vulnerable. Still, Australia won, and New Zealand had missed their best chance of an upset.

Man of the Match: M. A. Taylor.   *Attendance:* 30,193.

Close of play: First day, Australia 269-6 (I. A. Healy 62*, P. R. Reiffel 23*); Second day, New Zealand 134-3 (S. P. Fleming 49*, D. L. Vettori 0*); Third day, Australia 25-1 (M. T. G. Elliott 7*, I. A. Healy 1*); Fourth day, New Zealand 4-0 (B. A. Pocock 3*, B. A. Young 0*).

Australia

*M. A. Taylor c Young b Doull	112	– (2) c Astle b Cairns	16
M. T. G. Elliott c Young b Cairns	18	– (1) c Fleming b Vettori	11
G. S. Blewett c Vettori b Cairns	7	– (4) c Fleming b Cairns	91
M. E. Waugh c Vettori b Cairns	3	– (5) c Fleming b Vettori	17
S. R. Waugh lbw b Cairns	2	– (6) c Parore b Cairns	23
R. T. Ponting c Pocock b Doull	26	– (7) not out	73
†I. A. Healy b Doull	68	– (3) c Fleming b Allott	25
P. R. Reiffel c Parore b Allott	77	– not out	28
S. K. Warne c Fleming b Vettori	21		
M. S. Kasprowicz not out	13		
G. D. McGrath c Fleming b Doull	6		
B 4, l-b 9, w 1, n-b 6	20	B 1, l-b 4, n-b 5	10

                                                  373   (6 wkts dec.) 294

1/27 (2) 2/46 (3) 3/50 (4) 4/52 (5)   1/24 (2) 2/36 (1)   (6 wkts dec.) 294
5/108 (6) 6/225 (1) 7/294 (7)   3/72 (3) 4/105 (5)
8/349 (9) 9/359 (8) 10/373 (11)   5/163 (6) 6/217 (4)

Bowling: First Innings—Doull 30-6-70-4; Allott 31-3-117-1; Cairns 24-5-90-4; Vettori 21-5-46-1; Astle 11-2-20-0; Harris 4-1-17-0. *Second Innings*—Doull 19-5-44-0; Allott 19.5-4-60-1; Cairns 16-4-54-3; Vettori 36-13-87-2; Harris 9-0-30-0; Astle 1-0-14-0.

New Zealand

B. A. Young c Taylor b Kasprowicz	1	– (2) lbw b McGrath	45
B. A. Pocock c Taylor b Warne	57	– (1) c Taylor b Reiffel	3
N. J. Astle run out	12	– c Blewett b McGrath	14
*S. P. Fleming lbw b Kasprowicz	91	– c Healy b McGrath	0
D. L. Vettori c S. R. Waugh b Blewett	14	– (9) c Taylor b Warne	0
C. D. McMillan lbw b Warne	54	– (5) lbw b McGrath	0
C. L. Cairns b McGrath	64	– (6) b Reiffel	21
†A. C. Parore c Taylor b Warne	12	– (7) not out	39
C. Z. Harris b Warne	13	– (8) b Warne	0
S. B. Doull not out	2	– c Healy b McGrath	2
G. I. Allott c Elliott b McGrath	4	– lbw b Warne	0
B 4, l-b 4, n-b 17	25	L-b 2, n-b 6	8
	349		**132**

1/2 (1) 2/36 (3) 3/134 (2) 4/173 (5)
5/210 (4) 6/279 (6) 7/317 (8)
8/343 (9) 9/343 (7) 10/349 (11)

1/4 (1) 2/55 (3) 3/68 (2)
4/68 (5) 5/69 (4) 6/112 (6)
7/115 (8) 8/117 (9)
9/126 (10) 10/132 (11)

Bowling: *First Innings*—McGrath 32.2–6–96–2; Kasprowicz 24–6–57–2; Warne 42–13–106–4; Reiffel 21–6–53–0; M. E. Waugh 7–2–18–0; Blewett 6–2–11–1. *Second Innings*—McGrath 17–6–32–5; Kasprowicz 8–1–17–0; Reiffel 12–4–27–2; Warne 25–6–54–3.

Umpires: V. K. Ramaswamy (India) and S. G. Randell. Referee: C. W. Smith (West Indies).

At Carlton, November 14, 15, 16, 17. Victoria won by five wickets. Toss: New Zealanders. New Zealanders 82 (D. J. Saker four for 27, D. W. Fleming four for 18) and 173 (B. A. Pocock 44, M. J. Horne 37; D. J. Saker six for 39); Victoria 173 (I. J. Harvey 36; G. I. Allott five for 47, S. B. O'Connor three for 65) and 83 for five (M. T. G. Elliott 34, D. M. Jones 34 not out; D. L. Vettori four for 13).

AUSTRALIA v NEW ZEALAND

Second Test Match

At Perth, November 20, 21, 22, 23. Australia won by an innings and 70 runs. Toss: New Zealand. Test debut: S. H. Cook.

After their scare in Brisbane, Australia were ready for New Zealand's aggressiveness. This time they countered it early, blotting out the visitors' first innings on a true pitch and never relinquishing their advantage, concluding the match before tea on the fourth day. The 2-0 series win was their eighth in succession, discounting the one-off Test loss to India in Delhi in October 1996, and the fifth in succession sealed with at least one Test to play.

Australia's dominance, however, was obscured by the deterioration of the players' relationship with the ACB. Before the First Test, the sides had called a truce; this match, by contrast, was sabotaged on the first morning when the Board leaked a players' association document naming dates for a proposed strike. The Test became a mere backdrop to late-night meetings between the players and their advisers. Captain Mark Taylor used rain delays on the second and third days to arrange secret meetings with ACB chairman Denis Rogers. The players eventually backed down, and, far from being distracted by off-field turmoil, Australia played as if the cricket oval was their refuge, where they could escape from controversy, and do what they do best.

On the field, New Zealand's batsmen continued to show a propensity to lose concentration. Their first-day 217 was a grave disappointment, with no one able to capitalise on a series of good starts in ideal conditions. Parore, promoted to No. 3 after Astle's continuing slump, resisted for nearly two and a half hours, while McMillan and Cairns both carried on their encouraging form from Brisbane. But every time a New Zealander hit the ball in the air – or so it seemed – an Australian hand intercepted it. Mark Waugh, who made an astonishing leap and catch to his right to dismiss Cairns, provided the most memorable moment.

Waugh later said that the catch triggered something in his mind. After averaging only 20.90 in the Ashes series and failing twice in the First Test, he knew his place was in jeopardy. But his 86, in a stand of 153 in 157 minutes with his brother, late on the second day, marked a return to his best. Under the Perth floodlights, which were switched on after tea, the first such use in Tests, he on-drove Vettori more than 130 yards on to the roof of the five-tier Lillee-Marsh Stand, a shot many locals believed to be the biggest six at the WACA ground. Typically, Waugh was out in frustrating fashion, tickling Doull down the leg side.

Australia's old guard – the Waughs, Healy and Reiffel – ground out a 244-run lead. During his innings of 96, Steve Waugh became the seventh Australian to pass 6,000 Test runs, but his dismissal was his seventh score in the nineties, one behind Alvin Kallicharran in this dubious club. Healy, meanwhile, passed Rodney Marsh's 3,633 Test runs and now trailed only Alan Knott (4,389) as Test cricket's highest-run-scoring wicket-keeper.

New Zealand resumed with seven sessions to save the match. But opener Pocock, his right big toe broken by a Ponting hook when he was fielding at square leg, lasted just four balls with a runner and was later ruled out of the Third Test. After that it was down to debutant seamer Simon Cook to provide the flourish, taking the last five wickets of the match. Australia would go to Hobart still without McGrath, but they had proved in Perth that, against this opposition, his absence was inconsequential.

Man of the Match: S. R. Waugh. *Attendance:* 24,991.

Close of play: First day, Australia 32-1 (M. T. G. Elliott 22*, G. S. Blewett 7*); Second day, Australia 235-4 (S. R. Waugh 79*, I. A. Healy 3*); Third day, New Zealand 69-3 (A. C. Parore 42*, S. P. Fleming 0*).

New Zealand

B. A. Young c S. R. Waugh b Kasprowicz	9	– (2) run out	23
B. A. Pocock c Healy b Cook	15	– (1) c Blewett b Kasprowicz	1
†A. C. Parore c Blewett b Reiffel	30	lbw b Kasprowicz	63
*S. P. Fleming c Blewett b Warne	10	– (5) c Blewett b Warne	4
N. J. Astle c Healy b Reiffel	12	– (6) lbw b Cook	19
C. D. McMillan c Taylor b Kasprowicz	54	– (7) lbw b Cook	23
C. L. Cairns c M. E. Waugh b Warne	52	– (8) b Cook	7
D. L. Vettori not out	14	– (4) c Taylor b Warne	1
S. B. Doull c Taylor b Warne	8	– c S. R. Waugh b Cook	17
S. B. O'Connor c S. R. Waugh b Cook	7	– c Taylor b Cook	7
G. I. Allott b Warne	0	– not out	2
L-b 3, n-b 3	6	L-b 2, n-b 5	7
	217		**174**

1/12 (1) 2/31 (2) 3/51 (4) 4/72 (5)
5/87 (3) 6/161 (6) 7/187 (7)
8/197 (9) 9/214 (10) 10/217 (11)

1/2 (1) 2/53 (2) 3/55 (4)
4/84 (5) 5/102 (3) 6/137 (7)
7/145 (8) 8/160 (6)
9/165 (9) 10/174 (10)

Bowling: First Innings—Kasprowicz 20–9–40–2; Reiffel 20–6–46–2; Cook 10–5–36–2; Warne 22.4–3–83–4; Blewett 2–1–9–0. *Second Innings*—Kasprowicz 16–5–43–2; Reiffel 12–4–26–0; Warne 26–4–64–2; Cook 10.2–3–39–5.

Australia

*M. A. Taylor lbw b O'Connor	2	M. S. Kasprowicz run out	9
M. T. G. Elliott c O'Connor b Cairns	42	S. H. Cook not out	3
G. S. Blewett c Astle b O'Connor	14		
M. E. Waugh c Parore b Doull	86	B 6, l-b 5, n-b 7	18
S. R. Waugh b O'Connor	96		—
†I. A. Healy c Fleming b Cairns	85		**461**
R. T. Ponting c Fleming b Cairns	16	1/3 (1) 2/53 (3) 3/71 (2)	
P. R. Reiffel c Fleming b Cairns	54	4/224 (4) 5/262 (5) 6/287 (7)	
S. K. Warne c O'Connor b Vettori	36	7/403 (8) 8/449 (9)	
		9/450 (6) 10/461 (10)	

Bowling: Doull 21–3–78–1; O'Connor 31.4–7–109–3; Cairns 28–9–95–4; Vettori 29–7–84–1; Allott 22–3–84–0.

Umpires: G. Sharp (England) and D. B. Hair.   Referee: C. W. Smith (West Indies).

AUSTRALIA v NEW ZEALAND

Third Test Match

At Hobart, November 27, 28, 29, 30, December 1. Drawn. Toss: Australia.

New Zealand intensified their enterprising approach, this time challenging Australia to a game of risk and reward on the final day, when the rain-affected match appeared doomed to a dull draw. While they lacked the talent to fulfil their competitive instincts, this readiness to gamble won the respect of the Australian team and the admiration of the public. Set 288 to win in two sessions, New Zealand fell 65 short but, to their credit, held out for an exciting draw. Taylor had delayed his declaration until lunch on the final day, an uncustomarily defensive attitude; ultimately, two sessions were not enough for Warne, without McGrath, to force a win.

As in Perth, the cricket was overshadowed by off-field events; on the last day, Australia's Test captain and former vice-captain, Taylor and Healy, were dropped from the limited-overs squad to play New Zealand and South Africa. Hobart's enthusiasm for its biennial Test match was betrayed by its Antarctic weather. Four sessions were lost from the first three days and, with a sluggish pitch holding up both bowlers and batsmen, a draw appeared certain late on the fourth day, when New Zealand were 251 for six – thanks to a quality maiden Test century from Horne – but still 149 behind Australia's 400. Saying "you have to lose one to win one", Fleming called in his batsmen. "We came with the attitude of playing positive cricket," he said after play, "and the fact that our performances in the middle haven't matched that hasn't changed the philosophy."

Taylor responded by bringing out Australia's premier one-day batsman, Mark Waugh, as his opening partner. But after Waugh was out on the last morning, Taylor and later Steve Waugh seemed gripped by fear. Only a sparkling half-century by Blewett gave Taylor enough runs to declare at lunch on 138 for two. New Zealand's one-day record was superior to their Test record, and they chased their target with a freedom they usually lacked. Astle, who in 13 previous tour innings had not passed 22, eclipsed that in 11 balls as he tore into the seamers. Horne repeated his success and helped Astle put on 72 from 52 balls before he was trapped by Reiffel, setting in train a familiar collapse.

When Cairns, promoted to No. 3, Astle and Fleming fell in the space of two runs, New Zealand relinquished their hopes of winning. McMillan and Parore then began to dig in. Both batsmen fell to Warne for six, however: McMillan to a questionable slip catch and Parore to a miraculous catch by Elliott – flinging his hand out as he lost his footing at deep square leg. When Vettori followed, New Zealand had lost their ninth wicket 38 minutes from stumps; Australia's first whitewash of their neighbours loomed. But, having turned a meandering doze into a good match, the New Zealanders did not deserve to lose. Doull and O'Connor had moral force on their side as they resisted Warne and Reiffel until the end.

In Australia's first innings, which stretched into the third afternoon, Elliott scored 114, returning to form after a paltry series. Despite a thousand runs in his first year of Test cricket, Elliott was worried about his place. He said: "I'm a pessimist. It's just my nature." He put on 197 with Blewett, whose 99 was his second in Test cricket, and Mark Waugh scored 81. Their batting was encouragement for Australia as they prepared for what was seen as the summer's main event, the Test series with South Africa.

Man of the Match: G. S. Blewett.   *Man of the Series:* M. A. Taylor.

Attendance: 12,396.

Close of play: First day, Australia 39-0 (M. T. G. Elliott 20*, M. A. Taylor 18*); Second day, Australia 273-5 (M. E. Waugh 21*, I. A. Healy 3*); Third day, New Zealand 15-0 (B. A. Young 11*, M. J. Horne 2*); Fourth day, Australia 14-0 (M. A. Taylor 5*, M. E. Waugh 9*).

Australia

M. T. G. Elliott c Young b McMillan	114		
*M. A. Taylor b O'Connor	18	– (1) not out	66
G. S. Blewett b Doull	99	– b Vettori	56
M. E. Waugh c Parore b O'Connor	81	– (2) lbw b O'Connor	9
S. R. Waugh c McMillan b Doull	7	– (4) not out	2
R. T. Ponting c Parore b Cairns	4		
†I. A. Healy c Young b O'Connor	16		
P. R. Reiffel c Young b Doull	19		
S. K. Warne st Parore b Vettori	14		
M. S. Kasprowicz c Doull b Cairns	20		
S. H. Cook not out	0		
L-b 6, w 1, n-b 1	8	B 4, l-b 1	5
	400	(2 wkts dec.)	138

1/41 (2) 2/238 (1) 3/238 (3) 4/246 (5) 400
5/266 (6) 6/291 (7) 7/326 (8)
8/353 (9) 9/400 (4) 10/400 (10)

1/14 (2) 2/106 (3) (2 wkts dec.) 138

Bowling: *First Innings*—Doull 33–11–87–3; O'Connor 34–8–101–3; Cairns 35.1–13–86–2; Astle 12–5–32–0; McMillan 15–4–43–1; Vettori 12–1–45–1. *Second Innings*—Doull 8–1–28–0; O'Connor 9–2–32–1; Vettori 14–1–48–1; Astle 7–0–25–0.

New Zealand

B. A. Young b Reiffel	31	– (6) c Ponting b Warne	10
M. J. Horne c Elliott b Reiffel	133	– (1) lbw b Reiffel	31
†A. C. Parore lbw b S. R. Waugh	44	– (7) c Elliott b Warne	41
*S. P. Fleming c Healy b S. R. Waugh	0	– st Healy b Warne	0
R. G. Twose lbw b Warne	2	– (8) run out	29
C. D. McMillan lbw b S. R. Waugh	2	– (5) c Taylor b Warne	41
N. J. Astle not out	22	– (2) c Ponting b Reiffel	40
C. L. Cairns not out	10	– (3) st Healy b Warne	18
D. L. Vettori (did not bat)		– c Healy b S. R. Waugh	3
S. B. Doull (did not bat)		– not out	1
S. B. O'Connor (did not bat)		– not out	0
B 1, l-b 2, n-b 4	7	B 2, l-b 7	9
	251	(9 wkts)	223

1/60 (1) 2/192 (3) 3/192 (4) (6 wkts dec.) 251
4/195 (5) 5/198 (6) 6/229 (2)

1/72 (1) 2/93 (3) 3/93 (2) (9 wkts) 223
4/95 (4) 5/137 (6)
6/152 (5) 7/218 (8)
8/221 (7) 9/222 (9)

Bowling: *First Innings*—Kasprowicz 13–1–43–0; Reiffel 14–8–27–2; Warne 27–4–81–1; Cook 13–2–50–0; M. E. Waugh 8–2–17–0; Blewett 5–1–10–0; S. R. Waugh 9–2–20–3; Elliott 1–1–0–0. *Second Innings*—Kasprowicz 3–0–33–0; Reiffel 14–2–47–2; Warne 28–6–88–5; M. E. Waugh 6–1–19–0; Cook 4–0–17–0; S. R. Waugh 6–4–10–1.

Umpires: R. B. Tiffin (Zimbabwe) and S. J. Davis. Referee: C. W. Smith (West Indies).

New Zealand's matches v South Africa and Australia in the Carlton & United Series (December 6–17) may be found in that section.

†At Brisbane, December 13 (day/night). Tied. Toss: New Zealanders. New Zealanders 266 for five (50 overs) (M. J. Horne 102, S. P. Fleming 95 not out; B. N. Creevey three for 35); Queensland 266 for six (50 overs) (M. L. Love 76, A. Symonds 43, C. T. Perren 36, G. I. Foley 49, B. N. Creevey 44).
No-balls were scored as one run; had they been scored as two runs, as regulations suggested, the New Zealanders would have won by four runs.

†At Adelaide, January 4 (day/night). South Australia won by seven runs. Toss: South Australia. South Australia 237 for five (50 overs) (D. A. Fitzgerald 72, B. A. Johnston 53, J. D. Siddons 34, D. S. Webber 36); New Zealanders 230 (49.4 overs) (B. A. Young 53, C. M. Spearman 37, S. P. Fleming 32, N. J. Astle 40; P. Wilson four for 43).

†At Mount Gambier, January 6. New Zealanders won by 164 runs. Toss: New Zealanders. New Zealanders 316 for five (50 overs) (B. A. Young 44, C. M. Spearman 111, M. J. Horne 36, C. D. McMillan 39, C. Z. Harris 33 not out); Australian Country XI 152 (42.1 overs) (A. Jones 70, L. Burns 30; C. D. McMillan four for 22).

†At Caringbah, January 7. New Zealanders won by 103 runs. Toss: New Zealanders. New Zealanders 222 for seven (40 overs) (C. D. McMillan 80, C. Z. Harris 55); Sutherland 119 (35.3 overs) (C. Z. Harris four for 17, N. J. Astle three for 13).

†At Melbourne, January 12 (day/night). New Zealanders won by 21 runs. Toss: New Zealanders. New Zealanders 242 (49.4 overs) (B. A. Young 33, S. P. Fleming 58, C. D. McMillan 37, C. Z. Harris 32; M. S. Kasprowicz four for 21); Australia A 221 (49.1 overs) (J. L. Langer 76, D. R. Martyn 49; S. B. O'Connor four for 39).

New Zealand's matches v South Africa and Australia in the Carlton & United Series (January 9–21) may be found in that section.

INDIVIDUAL TEST RATINGS

Introduced in 1987, the PricewaterhouseCoopers Ratings (originally the Deloitte Ratings, and later the Coopers & Lybrand Ratings) rank Test cricketers on a scale up to 1,000 according to their performances in Test matches. The ratings take into account playing conditions, the quality of the opposition and the result of the matches. In August 1998, a similar set of ratings for one-day internationals was added (see page 1361).

The leading 20 batsmen and bowlers in the Test Ratings after the 1998 Test between England and Sri Lanka which ended on August 31 were:

	Batsmen	Rating		Bowlers	Rating
1.	S. R. Tendulkar (*Ind.*)	858	1.	A. A. Donald (*SA*)	889
2.	B. C. Lara (*WI*)	790	2.	C. E. L. Ambrose (*WI*)	877
3.	S. R. Waugh (*Aus.*)	786	3.	G. D. McGrath (*Aus.*)	808
4.	M. E. Waugh (*Aus.*)	749	4.	M. Muralitharan (*SL*)	786
5.	W. J. Cronje (*SA*)	748	5.	A. R. C. Fraser (*Eng.*)	782
6.	P. A. de Silva (*SL*)	747	6.	S. K. Warne (*Aus.*)	756
7.	R. Dravid (*Ind.*)	744	7.	S. M. Pollock (*SA*)	755
8.	A. J. Stewart (*Eng.*)	741	8.	A. Kumble (*Ind.*)	749
9.	C. L. Hooper (*WI*)	712	9.{	Waqar Younis (*Pak.*)	746
10.	S. Chanderpaul (*WI*)	703		Mushtaq Ahmed (*Pak.*)	746
11.	Saeed Anwar (*Pak.*)	702	11.	Wasim Akram (*Pak.*)	742
12.	N. S. Sidhu (*Ind.*)	684	12.	S. B. Doull (*NZ*)	698
13.{	Inzamam-ul-Haq (*Pak.*)	671	13.	C. A. Walsh (*WI*)	685
	S. C. Ganguly (*Ind.*)	671	14.	H. H. Streak (*Zimb.*)	681
15.	M. Azharuddin (*Ind.*)	660	15.	D. Gough (*Eng.*)	680
16.	S. T. Jayasuriya (*SL*)	659	16.	P. R. Reiffel (*Aus.*)	654
17.	N. Hussain (*Eng.*)	658	17.	J. Srinath (*Ind.*)	653
18.	M. A. Atherton (*Eng.*)	649	18.	J. N. Gillespie (*Aus.*)	632
19.	G. Kirsten (*SA*)	647	19.	I. R. Bishop (*WI*)	616
20.	Azhar Mahmood (*Pak.*)	645	20.	S. L. V. Raju (*Ind.*)	565

THE WEST INDIANS IN PAKISTAN, 1997-98

By FAZEER MOHAMMED

West Indies' sixth Test series in Pakistan was an unqualified disaster. The team's gradual decline from their previous high standards accelerated into freefall and they lost all three Tests by embarrassingly wide margins. Not since their first ever series, in England in 1928, had West Indies experienced such a thorough whitewash. Then, they lost all three matches by an innings. Nearly 70 years later, they came within 12 runs of a similar humiliation.

If the manner and extent of Pakistan's victories – the first two by an innings, the third by ten wickets – shocked the cricketing world, they were not altogether surprising to close followers of Courtney Walsh's team. All that was needed was opposition of the right calibre to expose and capitalise upon their inconsistency, indiscipline and complacency. And this time the Pakistanis, often their own worst enemies, displayed a ruthless efficiency under the inspiring leadership of Wasim Akram, restored to the captaincy after the defeat by South Africa. Wasim himself led the assault, taking 17 wickets, three more than Walsh, who soldiered on manfully with little assistance from his colleagues. By contrast, Wasim had other potent weapons in his arsenal. Leg-spinner Mushtaq Ahmed's 12 wickets included ten in the First Test in Peshawar, while off-spinner Saqlain Mushtaq claimed nine in his only appearance, in the final Test in Karachi. Waqar Younis made an immediate impact on his return to partner Wasim with a spectacular dismissal of Brian Lara in the Second Test in Rawalpindi.

Lara's woes, on and off the field, typified and aggravated West Indies' struggles. Many explanations were sought for his pitiful return of 129 runs at 21.50, most focusing on the dressing-room rather than events in the middle. There were persistent reports of a power struggle between him and Walsh. The West Indies Cricket Board contributed to the furore by not naming an official vice-captain for the tour: Lara had held the position in recent series. Repeated denials by team management, who made him second-in-command anyway, of any rift or general dissension in the ranks failed to quell the almost daily speculation. Manager Clive Lloyd considered it a calculated ploy to unsettle his team. If it was, it worked.

West Indies' batting, so brittle in recent series, plumbed new depths of ineptitude. Only once did they total more than 300 in an innings – and then it was only just. The next best effort was 216, telling a stark tale of players out of their depth, unable – or unwilling – to concentrate for long periods against a challenging attack in testing conditions. Only opener Sherwin Campbell, who scored 248 runs including three half-centuries, suggested any degree of consistency and solidity. Carl Hooper attacked with sublime brilliance for his team's only century of the series, in Karachi, and compiled an equally delightful unbeaten 73 in Rawalpindi. But, typically, his other four scores totalled less than 50. Left-hander Shivnarine Chanderpaul came within five runs of a century in the Second Test yet contributed precious little otherwise. So successful against India in the Caribbean earlier in the year, Chanderpaul found the late swing of Pakistan's pace bowlers an almost insurmountable hurdle.

However, Pakistan's top order weighed in heavily against bowling that was often ordinary and lacking in purpose. An epidemic of dropped catches and generally ragged outcricket only served to ease Pakistan's passage to totals of 381, 471 and 417 in their three completed innings. Aamir Sohail was the prime beneficiary, compiling identical scores of 160 in each of the final two Tests to earn his team's Man of the Series award. Inzamam-ul-Haq topped the averages with 136.50 thanks to a monumental 177 in Rawalpindi after an unbeaten 92 in Peshawar. Not wanting to miss out on the run-feast, Ijaz Ahmed took over the role of opener from the injured Saeed Anwar in Karachi and hit 151. He shared an opening partnership of 298, a record for Pakistan, with Sohail, who had already put on 323 for the third wicket with Inzamam in the previous Test.

Walsh had little support. Aged 35, he bowled 32 more overs than anyone else, but the burden was too much for even him to carry alone. Curtly Ambrose, a destructive force in three previous series against Pakistan, was a shadow of his old self, taking just one wicket for 139 runs in the first two Tests, before injury forced him out of the Third. A few months later he would take out his frustrations on England. In the meantime, Mervyn Dillon filled the breach effectively. But leg-spinner Rawl Lewis disappointed on debut in Peshawar, another step backwards for West Indian slow bowlers. In these circumstances, Walsh's efforts were nothing short of heroic. The obvious choice as West Indies' Man of the Series, he returned home chastened, and on the brink of losing the captaincy, but having built up his Test aggregate to 353 wickets in 96 Tests.

The tourists encountered some of the difficulties associated with a tour of Pakistan, but hardly enough to explain their dreadful performances (they also lost all three of their matches in a quadrangular one-day tournament). The pitches were excellent and, though some local umpires made some highly questionable decisions against them, it mattered little in the final result. The loss of the first-class match scheduled for Hyderabad between the first two Tests was another setback, hindering their hopes of recovery. But none of these was a significant factor. Pakistan gave a rare display of how well they can play when the team's many and varied talents are properly and effectively harnessed.

WEST INDIAN TOURING PARTY

C. A. Walsh (Jamaica) (*captain*), C. E. L. Ambrose (Leeward Islands), I. R. Bishop (Trinidad & Tobago), S. L. Campbell (Barbados), S. Chanderpaul (Guyana), M. Dillon (Trinidad & Tobago), R. I. C. Holder (Barbados), C. L. Hooper (Guyana), B. C. Lara (Trinidad & Tobago), R. N. Lewis (Windward Islands), F. A. Rose (Jamaica), P. V. Simmons (Trinidad & Tobago), P. A. Wallace (Barbados), D. Williams (Trinidad & Tobago), S. C. Williams (Leeward Islands).

Manager: C. H. Lloyd. *Coach:* M. D. Marshall.

WEST INDIAN TOUR RESULTS

Test matches – Played 3: Lost 3.
First-class matches – Played 4: Lost 3, Drawn 1. Abandoned 1.
Losses – Pakistan (3).
Draw – Dr A. Q. Khan's XI.
Abandoned – Habib Bank.
One-day internationals – Played 3: Lost 3. *Losses* – Sri Lanka, South Africa, Pakistan.
Other non-first-class match – Won v National Bank.

TEST MATCH AVERAGES

PAKISTAN – BATTING

	T	I	NO	R	HS	100s	50s	Avge	Ct/St
Inzamam-ul-Haq.	3	3	1	273	177	1	1	136.50	2
Aamir Sohail.	3	3	0	324	160	2	0	108.00	2
Ijaz Ahmed, sen.	3	3	0	226	151	1	1	75.33	2
Azhar Mahmood	3	4	2	69	26*	0	0	34.50	1
Saeed Anwar.	3	3	0	96	65	0	1	32.00	0
Mohammad Wasim . . .	3	4	1	66	28	0	0	22.00	2/1
Moin Khan	3	3	0	64	58	0	1	21.33	5/1
Wasim Akram	3	3	0	16	11	0	0	5.33	2
Mushtaq Ahmed.	3	3	1	5	4	0	0	2.50	3

Played in two Tests: Waqar Younis 2, 12. Played in one Test: Arshad Khan 4; Saqlain Mushtaq 0; Shahid Nazir 18; Shoaib Akhtar 1 (1 ct).

* *Signifies not out.*

BOWLING

	O	M	R	W	BB	5W/i	Avge
Saqlain Mushtaq........	43	15	80	9	5-54	1	8.88
Wasim Akram	107.1	30	294	17	4-42	0	17.29
Azhar Mahmood........	60	16	155	7	4-53	0	22.14
Mushtaq Ahmed........	85.3	20	293	12	5-35	2	24.41
Waqar Younis..........	54	6	195	7	3-99	0	27.85

Also bowled: Arshad Khan 10–3–32–0; Shahid Nazir 17.5–2–59–2; Shoaib Akhtar 22–4–68–2.

WEST INDIES – BATTING

	T	I	NO	R	HS	100s	50s	Avge	Ct/St
C. L. Hooper.......	3	6	0	228	106	1	1	45.60	4
S. L. Campbell	3	6	0	248	78	0	3	41.33	1
S. Chanderpaul	3	6	0	153	95	0	1	25.50	0
D. Williams.........	3	6	1	123	48	0	0	24.60	6/1
B. C. Lara	3	6	0	129	37	0	0	21.50	3
C. E. L. Ambrose....	2	4	1	41	30	0	0	13.66	0
I. R. Bishop	3	6	1	61	21	0	0	12.20	0
S. C. Williams......	3	6	0	60	33	0	0	10.00	1
F. A. Rose	2	4	0	31	13	0	0	7.75	0
C. A. Walsh	3	6	2	16	9*	0	0	4.00	1

Played in one Test: M. Dillon 0, 4; R. I. C. Holder 26, 5; R. N. Lewis 4, 0; P. V. Simmons 1, 1; P. A. Wallace 5, 8 (1 ct).

* Signifies not out.

BOWLING

	O	M	R	W	BB	5W/i	Avge
C. A. Walsh...........	101.1	17	306	14	5-78	2	21.85
M. Dillon	29.4	4	111	5	5-111	1	22.20
F. A. Rose...........	47	8	140	3	3-92	0	46.66
I. R. Bishop...........	68	10	224	4	3-76	0	56.00

Also bowled: C. E. L. Ambrose 44–6–139–1; S. Chanderpaul 7–0–34–1; C. L. Hooper 69–18–185–2; R. N. Lewis 24–6–93–0; P. V. Simmons 2–0–9–0.

Note: Matches in this section which were not first-class are signified by a dagger.

†At Aitchison College, Lahore, October 29. West Indians won by 22 runs. Toss: National Bank. West Indians 234 for seven (45 overs) (S. C. Williams 67, S. Chanderpaul 40, B. C. Lara 38, C. L. Hooper 35; Mohammad Javed three for 46); National Bank 212 for eight (45 overs) (Hanif-ur-Rehman 35, Saeed Azad 73 not out).

West Indies' matches v Sri Lanka, South Africa and Pakistan in the Wills Golden Jubilee Tournament (November 1–4) may be found in that section.

At KRL Cricket Ground, Rawalpindi, November 11, 12, 13, 14. Drawn. Toss: West Indians. West Indians 464 (S. C. Williams 48, S. L. Campbell 76, P. V. Simmons 73, C. L. Hooper 146 not out, R. N. Lewis 41; Abdur Razzaq three for 117, Naeem Akhtar three for 88) and 303 for four dec. (P. A. Wallace 142, S. L. Campbell 54, R. N. Lewis 59); Dr A. Q. Khan's XI 267 (Babar Zaman 62, Mohammad Naved 38, Bazid Khan 39, Naseer Ahmed 49, Extras 33; I. R. Bishop three for 83, F. A. Rose three for 82, M. Dillon three for 65) and 107 for three (Bazid Khan 30 not out, Naseer Ahmed 45).

PAKISTAN v WEST INDIES

First Test Match

At Peshawar, November 17, 18, 19, 20. Pakistan won by an innings and 19 runs. Toss: West Indies. Test debuts: Arshad Khan; R. N. Lewis.

West Indies crashed to what was – for a fortnight – their heaviest ever defeat at the hands of Pakistan, capitulating inside four days by an innings and 19 runs. Coming hard on the heels of their whitewash in the quadrangular limited-overs series, this was another indicator of the decline in Caribbean standards.

Walsh was left to rue his decision to bat first when his team were tottering at 58 for seven just after lunch on the first day. That they reached 151 and a modicum of respectability was due to wicket-keeper David Williams and Ambrose, the top scorers of the innings with 31 and 30 respectively. Williams added 48 for the eighth wicket with Bishop, then Ambrose took up the fight until Mushtaq Ahmed returned to trap him lbw, his fifth victim.

Shahid Nazir had provided the early breakthrough, with two wickets in three balls. Mushtaq held the catch at gully that accounted for Lara, before taking over with the ball himself. He was fortunate to gain lbw and bat-pad decisions against Campbell and Hooper, but Simmons and the debutant Lewis were no match for him and both were bowled looking to drive.

After losing Aamir Sohail before darkness fell on the first day, Pakistan prospered on a bright, cold second morning, through a second-wicket partnership of 133 between Saeed Anwar and Ijaz Ahmed. Both were scoring freely until distracted in mid-afternoon by breaks in play, caused by spectators throwing fruit at West Indian fielders. Hooper promptly had Anwar caught behind and then held Ijaz at slip. When Wasim Akram swung wildly at Hooper and was stumped, the score was 207 for five and the tourists were hopeful of limiting Pakistan's advantage.

Those hopes were dashed by Inzamam-ul-Haq's battling, unbeaten 92, a pugnacious 58 from wicket-keeper Moin Khan and West Indian generosity in the field. Inzamam batted throughout with a runner after being struck painfully on the left ankle while fielding. He was dropped on five, 32 and 88. But when Walsh returned to claim the last two wickets and figures of five for 78, Inzamam was stranded eight short of a first Test century at last.

Trailing by 230, West Indies again lost Stuart Williams and Chanderpaul quickly. Then Lara glittered brilliantly in the gathering gloom, striking eight fluent boundaries off the spinners in his 36, but he failed to prosper against the faster bowlers the next morning. Dropped in the gully off Wasim, he was lbw to Azhar Mahmood in the next over, having added just one to his overnight score. With him went any realistic hope West Indies might have had of making Pakistan bat again, though Campbell made a patient 66 before becoming one of four victims of Wasim's late in-swingers, all lbw.

Mushtaq earned most of the plaudits, completing a second five-wicket haul for match figures of ten for 106 – even if cynics noted that he bowled in both innings at the end where the local umpire, Said Shah, was presiding. Wasim performed the last rites, dismissing Bishop an hour after lunch.

Man of the Match: Mushtaq Ahmed.

Close of play: First day, Pakistan 14-1 (Saeed Anwar 10*, Ijaz Ahmed, sen. 0*); Second day, Pakistan 246-5 (Moin Khan 36*, Azhar Mahmood 14*); Third day, West Indies 99-2 (S. L. Campbell 34*, B. C. Lara 36*).

West Indies

S. C. Williams c Moin Khan b Shahid Nazir . . .	4	– lbw b Wasim Akram 2
S. L. Campbell lbw b Mushtaq Ahmed	15	– lbw b Wasim Akram 66
S. Chanderpaul b Shahid Nazir	0	– c Ijaz Ahmed b Mushtaq Ahmed . . 14
B. C. Lara c Mushtaq Ahmed b Wasim Akram .	3	– lbw b Azhar Mahmood 37
C. L. Hooper c Mohammad Wasim		– c sub (Saqlain Mushtaq)
b Mushtaq Ahmed .	26	b Mushtaq Ahmed . 23
P. V. Simmons b Mushtaq Ahmed	1	– c Wasim Akram b Mushtaq Ahmed 1
†D. Williams b Azhar Mahmood	31	– c Ijaz Ahmed b Mushtaq Ahmed . . 20
R. N. Lewis b Mushtaq Ahmed	4	– lbw b Wasim Akram 0
I. R. Bishop b Azhar Mahmood	20	– lbw b Wasim Akram 21
C. E. L. Ambrose lbw b Mushtaq Ahmed	30	– st Mohammad Wasim
		b Mushtaq Ahmed . 1
*C. A. Walsh not out	9	– not out 6
L-b 6, n-b 2	8	B 9, l-b 4, n-b 7 20

1/9 (1) 2/9 (3) 3/16 (4) 4/29 (2)   151   1/14 (1) 2/56 (3) 3/102 (4)   211
5/45 (6) 6/50 (5) 7/58 (8)   4/145 (5) 5/147 (6) 6/163 (2)
8/106 (7) 9/129 (9) 10/151 (10)   7/167 (8) 8/195 (7)
9/201 (10) 10/211 (9)

Bowling: *First Innings*—Wasim Akram 14–5–29–1; Shahid Nazir 10–1–32–2; Azhar Mahmood 14–2–35–2; Mushtaq Ahmed 18.3–7–35–5; Arshad Khan 4–1–14–0. *Second Innings*—Wasim Akram 23.2–5–65–4; Shahid Nazir 7.5–1–27–0; Azhar Mahmood 10.1–3–17–1; Mushtaq Ahmed 23–5–71–5; Arshad Khan 6–2–18–0.

Pakistan

Saeed Anwar c D. Williams b Hooper . .	65	Arshad Khan c Lara b Bishop 4
Aamir Sohail c Lara b Walsh	4	Shahid Nazir b Walsh 18
Ijaz Ahmed, sen. c Hooper b Bishop . . .	65	Mushtaq Ahmed b Walsh 4
Mohammad Wasim b Walsh	28	B 2, l-b 7, w 2, n-b 11 22
Inzamam-ul-Haq not out	92	
†Moin Khan c Walsh b Bishop	58	1/10 (2) 2/143 (1) 3/145 (3) 4/193 (4) 381
*Wasim Akram st D. Williams b Hooper	5	5/207 (7) 6/250 (8) 7/294 (6)
Azhar Mahmood c Hooper b Walsh	16	8/304 (9) 9/347 (10) 10/381 (11)

Inzamam-ul-Haq, when 13, retired hurt at 184 and resumed at 250.

Bowling: Ambrose 25–4–76–0; Walsh 32–9–78–5; Bishop 29–7–76–3; Simmons 2–0–9–0; Lewis 24–6–93–0; Hooper 20–7–40–2.

Umpires: D. R. Shepherd (England) and Said Shah.   Referee: R. Subba Row (England).

At Hyderabad, November 24, 25, 26. Habib Bank v West Indians. Abandoned.
    The three-day game was cancelled because the West Indians objected to substandard accommodation. A one-day game was arranged for November 26, but was also abandoned because of rain.

PAKISTAN v WEST INDIES
Second Test Match

At Rawalpindi, November 29, 30, December 1, 2, 3. Pakistan won by an innings and 29 runs. Toss: Pakistan. Test debuts: Shoaib Akhtar; P. A. Wallace.
    Pakistan clinched their first series victory over West Indies in 39 years in a most emphatic manner. They improved on their record margin in the First Test by another ten runs, disposing of the visitors within an hour on the final day.
    The match, played on a pitch described by West Indies manager Clive Lloyd as one of the best he had seen, was dominated by a stand of 323 between Inzamam-ul-Haq and Aamir Sohail, the biggest for the third wicket ever conceded by West Indies. That effectively eliminated their hopes of squaring the series after a first-innings total of 303 seemed to herald a batting revival.

West Indies had been in early trouble again at 58 for four, with Pakistan's fast bowlers exploiting heavy, overcast conditions. Waqar Younis signalled his return by removing Lara in a dramatic passage. Lara had sought to impose his dominance on Waqar by taking ten runs off three balls. Waqar had the perfect response, a vicious, late in-swinging yorker that uprooted Lara's leg stump and left him on all fours. Hooper followed without scoring. But the tourists then enjoyed their best partnership of the series. Campbell and Chanderpaul batted with growing assurance into the second morning as they added 147. Campbell finally top-edged a hook to fine leg off Azhar Mahmood, who returned to end the innings after lunch with two wickets in three balls. Chanderpaul's caution in the nineties proved his undoing: he went lbw to Waqar, five short of a second Test century, though David Williams propped up the lower order with 48, his highest Test score.

Pakistan lost two wickets cheaply in reply and, had Lara taken a straightforward chance at first slip from Sohail off Bishop, would have been 76 for three. They paid heavily for the lapse, with Sohail and Inzamam batting through to the final session of the third day and making the most of some very ordinary West Indian bowling and worse fielding. Inzamam finally completed his first Test century in Pakistan, and went on to a Test-best 177, a monumental effort of discipline and composure after his chancy 92 in the First Test. Sohail contributed 160, a timely innings to boost Pakistan and to heal his own relationship with his team-mates, some of whom he had accused earlier in the year of being involved in bribery and match-fixing. Walsh eventually broke the stand, dismissing Sohail on the third evening – the only wicket to fall that day – and Inzamam early next morning. He was to finish with five wickets for the second time running, as a much more determined West Indian effort saw the last seven wickets add only 84. Mohammad Wasim's 26 was the next best score, which only magnified the cost of Lara's miss and the wretched third-day showing.

Pakistan's pace attack soon engineered another early West Indian slide: at 26 for three, a fourth-day finish was in sight. But Campbell soldiered on until he was bowled off his pads by Mushtaq Ahmed. Hooper kept the game going and struck three sixes in one over off Mushtaq to finish unbeaten on 73. This felicitous cameo was little consolation, however, as his team were trounced again.

Man of the Match: Inzamam-ul-Haq.

Close of play: First day, West Indies 179-4 (S. L. Campbell 71*, S. Chanderpaul 66*); Second day, Pakistan 122-2 (Aamir Sohail 62*, Inzamam-ul-Haq 20*); Third day, Pakistan 403-3 (Inzamam-ul-Haq 169*, Mohammad Wasim 3*); Fourth day, West Indies 99-6 (C. L. Hooper 44*, I. R. Bishop 1*).

West Indies

S. L. Campbell c Shoaib Akhtar b Azhar Mahmood .	78	– b Mushtaq Ahmed	34
P. A. Wallace lbw b Wasim Akram	5	– lbw b Waqar Younis	8
S. C. Williams c Mushtaq Ahmed b Waqar Younis .	8	– c Azhar Mahmood b Wasim Akram .	1
B. C. Lara b Waqar Younis	15	– c and b Wasim Akram	1
C. L. Hooper c Moin Khan b Azhar Mahmood . .	0	– not out	73
S. Chanderpaul lbw b Waqar Younis	95	– lbw b Wasim Akram	7
†D. Williams c Moin Khan b Shoaib Akhtar . . .	48	– run out	0
I. R. Bishop b Shoaib Akhtar	10	– run out	2
C. E. L. Ambrose not out	10	– (11) b Waqar Younis	0
F. A. Rose b Azhar Mahmood	7	– (9) c Mushtaq Ahmed b Wasim Akram .	6
*C. A. Walsh lbw b Azhar Mahmood	0	– (10) run out	0
B 1, l-b 16, w 3, n-b 7	27	N-b 7	7
	303		**139**

1/15 (2) 2/37 (3) 3/53 (4) 4/58 (5)   303
5/205 (1) 6/249 (6) 7/264 (8)
8/291 (7) 9/303 (10) 10/303 (11)

1/9 (2) 2/10 (3) 3/26 (4)   139
4/67 (1) 5/98 (6) 6/98 (7)
7/112 (8) 8/126 (9)
9/138 (10) 10/139 (11)

Bowling: First Innings—Wasim Akram 22–6–40–1; Waqar Younis 27–3–99–3; Shoaib Akhtar 15–2–47–2; Azhar Mahmood 20.5–7–53–4; Mushtaq Ahmed 17–3–47–0. *Second Innings*—Wasim Akram 14–5–42–4; Waqar Younis 12–0–44–2; Shoaib Akhtar 7–2–21–0; Azhar Mahmood 2–1–4–0; Mushtaq Ahmed 6–3–28–1.

Pakistan

Saeed Anwar c D. Williams b Ambrose .	16	Waqar Younis b Walsh	2
Aamir Sohail c sub (P. V. Simmons)		Shoaib Akhtar c Hooper b Walsh	1
b Walsh .	160	Mushtaq Ahmed not out	0
Ijaz Ahmed, sen. c Wallace b Rose	10		
Inzamam-ul-Haq c Campbell b Walsh . .	177	B 13, l-b 9, w 6, n-b 25	53
Mohammad Wasim c Hooper b Walsh . .	26		
†Moin Khan c D. Williams b Rose	1	1/41 (1) 2/64 (3) 3/387 (2) 4/414 (4)	471
Azhar Mahmood c D. Williams b Rose .	14	5/415 (6) 6/437 (7) 7/459 (5)	
*Wasim Akram b Bishop	11	8/469 (9) 9/469 (8) 10/471 (10)	

Bowling: Walsh 43.1–6–143–5; Ambrose 19–2–63–1; Bishop 24–3–80–1; Rose 33–7–92–3; Hooper 17–1–71–0.

Umpires: D. R. Shepherd (England) and Javed Akhtar.   Referee: R. Subba Row (England).

PAKISTAN v WEST INDIES

Third Test Match

At Karachi, December 6, 7, 8, 9. Pakistan won by ten wickets. Toss: West Indies.

Pakistan formalised a 3-0 series whitewash with a ten-wicket victory. After trailing on first innings by 201, West Indies forced Pakistan to bat again, for a few minutes on the fourth morning, to avoid a third innings defeat. It was not much solace.

The Test followed a similar course to the previous two. West Indies' batting failed collectively twice, despite a sparkling century from Hooper in his final turn at the crease. Pakistan relied on another massive partnership, this time an opening stand of 298 between Aamir Sohail and Ijaz Ahmed, a national Test record. Wasim Akram was again irresistible with both the new and old ball, while the immediate and telling impact of off-spinner Saqlain Mushtaq emphasised Pakistan's strength in depth. It seemed baffling that Saqlain, who had match figures of nine for 80 and bemused all the batsmen, could have been omitted from the series until then.

On another ideal pitch, and in the best weather so far, West Indies squandered their only good start in all three Tests, sliding from 109 for one to 216 all out. Stuart Williams finally reached double figures, though he wasted his work by being run out; meanwhile, Campbell and Lara picked up runs at leisure off the faster bowlers. But Saqlain changed the game's complexion in mid-afternoon, bowling Lara as he sought to pierce a packed off-side field. Mushtaq Ahmed removed Hooper for a duck and the familiar pattern was restored. Campbell, dropped twice on the way to 50, ran out of luck when an edged cut off Saqlain rebounded from Wasim's knee at second slip into Sohail's hands at first. The tail showed no inclination to hang around and Saqlain finished with five for 54.

Ijaz, opening the batting because Saeed Anwar was injured, embarked on a marathon occupation of the crease which put the squandermania of the opposition's batsmen into perspective. Curbing his natural aggression, he accompanied the more attacking Sohail in a six-hour partnership very reminiscent of the stand between Sohail and Inzamam in the previous Test. There was one difference: here, the West Indians maintained their discipline. But in such batting-friendly conditions, the pair ground on inexorably to big hundreds. Sohail exactly matched his 160 in Rawalpindi before he misplulled a long hop from Chanderpaul on the second evening. Again, the innings declined with relative speed, all ten wickets tumbling for 119. Dillon and Walsh were both rewarded for their perseverance: Dillon completed his first five-wicket haul in his first Test of the series; for Walsh, the first of his four wickets, Moin Khan, was his 350th in 96 Tests. But the total of 417 was still impressive.

Hooper's scintillating 106 off 90 balls ensured that West Indies did regain some dignity. His calculated assault on Mushtaq Ahmed, including three more towering sixes, left Lara an admiring spectator in a third-wicket partnership of 121. It could not last. Lara fell to Saqlain for the second time in the match, and when Wasim returned to bowl Hooper through the gate, the only question was whether West Indies could avoid the innings defeat. They did, but only just. Wasim took the last three wickets on the fourth morning, and Pakistan knocked off the 12 runs needed to complete a historic whitewash.

Man of the Match: Saqlain Mushtaq.   *Men of the Series:* Pakistan – Aamir Sohail; West Indies – C. A. Walsh.

Close of play: First day, Pakistan 34-0 (Aamir Sohail 20*, Ijaz Ahmed 11*); Second day, Pakistan 327-1 (Ijaz Ahmed 127*, Saeed Anwar 15*); Third day, West Indies 198-7 (F. A. Rose 0*, I. R. Bishop 5*).

West Indies

S. L. Campbell c Aamir Sohail			
b Saqlain Mushtaq .	50	– c Inzamam-ul-Haq b Waqar Younis	5
S. C. Williams run out	33	– lbw b Waqar Younis	12
B. C. Lara b Saqlain Mushtaq	36	– c Mohammad Wasim	
		b Saqlain Mushtaq .	37
C. L. Hooper lbw b Mushtaq Ahmed	0	– b Wasim Akram	106
S. Chanderpaul lbw b Wasim Akram	21	– c Moin Khan b Saqlain Mushtaq .	16
R. I. C. Holder b Saqlain Mushtaq	26	– c Aamir Sohail b Saqlain Mushtaq.	5
†D. Williams not out	22	– b Saqlain Mushtaq	2
I. R. Bishop st Moin Khan b Saqlain Mushtaq .	2	– (9) not out	6
F. A. Rose lbw b Wasim Akram	13	– (8) c Moin Khan b Wasim Akram .	5
*C. A. Walsh c Inzamam-ul-Haq			
b Saqlain Mushtaq .	1	– b Wasim Akram	0
M. Dillon b Wasim Akram.	0	– lbw b Wasim Akram	4
B 4, l-b 7, n-b 1	12	B 7, l-b 2, n-b 5.	14

1/47 (2) 2/109 (3) 3/114 (4) 4/126 (1)   216   1/14 (2) 2/19 (1) 3/140 (3)   212
5/160 (5) 6/188 (6) 7/194 (8)   4/182 (4) 5/186 (5) 6/191 (6)
8/209 (9) 9/212 (10) 10/216 (11)   7/193 (7) 8/207 (8)
9/208 (10) 10/212 (11)

Bowling: *First Innings*—Wasim Akram 17.1–2–76–3; Waqar Younis 9–3–21–0; Azhar Mahmood 10–3–14–0; Mushtaq Ahmed 13–2–40–1; Saqlain Mushtaq 24–6–54–5. *Second Innings*—Wasim Akram 16.4–7–42–4; Waqar Younis 6–0–31–2; Azhar Mahmood 3–0–32–0; Mushtaq Ahmed 8–0–72–0; Saqlain Mushtaq 19–9–26–4.

Pakistan

Aamir Sohail lbw b Chanderpaul	160		
Ijaz Ahmed, sen. c D. Williams b Dillon	151		
Saeed Anwar c D. Williams b Dillon	15		
Inzamam-ul-Haq lbw b Dillon	4		
Mohammad Wasim lbw b Dillon	12	– (1) not out	0
†Moin Khan lbw b Walsh	5		
Azhar Mahmood not out	26	– (2) not out	13
*Wasim Akram lbw b Walsh	0		
Saqlain Mushtaq c Lara b Walsh	0		
Mushtaq Ahmed b Walsh	1		
Waqar Younis c S. C. Williams b Dillon	12		
B 3, l-b 9, w 2, n-b 17	31	N-b 2	2

1/298 (1) 2/329 (3) 3/333 (4) 4/359 (5)   417   (no wkt) 15
5/374 (6) 6/388 (2) 7/390 (8)
8/390 (9) 9/396 (10) 10/417 (11)

Bowling: *First Innings*—Walsh 23–2–74–4; Rose 12–1–44–0; Dillon 29.4–4–111–5; Bishop 15–0–68–0; Hooper 32–10–74–0; Chanderpaul 7–0–34–1. *Second Innings*—Walsh 3–0–11–0; Rose 2–0–4–0.

Umpires: C. J. Mitchley (South Africa) and Salim Badar.   Referee: R. Subba Row (England).

THE SRI LANKANS IN INDIA, 1997-98

By CRAIG COZIER

As in their series in Sri Lanka in August, when batting records tumbled, both teams displayed a lack of penetrative bowling. There was further heavy scoring, and three drawn Tests. India held the whip hand throughout the series, and the Sri Lankans were content to leave with a 0-0 scoreline. Their three previous tours of India had resulted in six innings defeats in seven Tests, so to escape without a defeat was an achievement in itself. India's batsmen seized the initiative in all three matches, scoring first-innings totals of 515, 485 and 512. But their bowlers could not dismiss Sri Lanka twice, although they came close in Mohali and Mumbai, and rain robbed them of the opportunity in Nagpur.

Only fast bowler Javagal Srinath, returning after nine months' rehabilitation from a shoulder injury, advertised himself as world-class. Leg-spinner Anil Kumble, reinstated after being rested from the recent one-day tournaments against Pakistan, was never at his best, and off-spinner Rajesh Chauhan was also inconsistent.

The Sri Lankan bowling was even more threadbare. Playing catch-up on many occasions, they often resorted to the negative tactic of pitching in the rough outside leg stump to stem the flow of runs. "We do not have much choice so far as bowling is concerned," said captain Arjuna Ranatunga after the First Test. "We have to make the best use of the available talent. In the circumstances, my bowlers bowled exceedingly well to curb the Indian run-rate."

Left-arm pacer Chaminda Vaas, expected to be Sri Lanka's spearhead, struggled for form, as he had done since a back injury ruled him out of the Caribbean tour earlier in the year. Ravindra Pushpakumara, omitted from the First Test, made the most of his opportunities in the final two matches with aggressive pace, accuracy and swing. Muttiah Muralitharan's off-spin was quickly countered by Navjot Sidhu and company, and Sanath Jayasuriya, more renowned for his boisterous batting, proved the most penetrative of the spinners.

Sourav Ganguly, the Indian left-hander, was the undoubted star with the bat, a notable achievement in a series featuring Jayasuriya, Aravinda de Silva, Sachin Tendulkar and Mohammad Azharuddin. Ganguly continued the rich vein of form which had begun in the second Colombo Test, with 392 runs in four innings, including two centuries and a 99. Rahul Dravid was also impressive, although he was unable to convert any of his three innings over 80 into a second Test hundred. Tendulkar, his captaincy under growing pressure, answered with a quality century in front of his adoring home fans in Mumbai's Wankhede Stadium in the final Test. But his failure to win any of his 12 Tests in 1997 was ultimately to lead to his sacking. Sidhu appeared to have claimed his rightful position as India's premier opening batsman 14 years after his Test debut: he scored his third century of the year among 288 runs at 72.

Sri Lanka's leading batsman again was Aravinda de Silva, whose superb unbeaten century – his seventh in as many Tests – stood between India and victory in Mohali. Marvan Atapattu, whose biography was for so long tarnished by five ducks in his first six Test innings, laid that embarrassment firmly behind him with a maiden century and a stylish 98. A technically correct right-hander with a wide range of strokes, Atapattu complemented the left-handed Jayasuriya at the top of the order, even if Jayasuriya, predictably, could not recapture his golden touch of the preceding series in Colombo.

After a fortnight's break, during which India travelled to Sharjah to take part in the Champions Trophy, the teams reassembled for a three-match one-day series. Even here, the stalemate could not be broken; they won a match apiece, with the middle one controversially called off after three overs because of a dangerous pitch.

SRI LANKAN TOURING PARTY

A. Ranatunga (Sinhalese SC) (*captain*), P. A. de Silva (Nondescripts CC) (*vice-captain*), R. P. Arnold (Nondescripts CC), M. S. Atapattu (Sinhalese SC), K. S. C. de Silva (Nondescripts CC), S. K. L. de Silva (Colombo CC), H. D. P. K. Dharmasena (Bloomfield C and AC), S. T. Jayasuriya (Bloomfield C and AC), D. P. M. D. Jayawardene (Sinhalese SC), R. S. Mahanama (Bloomfield C and AC), M. Muralitharan (Tamil Union C and AC), K. R. Pushpakumara (Nondescripts CC), K. J. Silva (Sinhalese SC), H. P. Tillekeratne (Nondescripts CC), W. P. U. J. C. Vaas (Colts CC), G. P. Wickremasinghe (Sinhalese SC).

U. D. U. Chandana (Tamil Union C and AC) and R. S. Kaluwitharana (Colts CC) replaced Arnold, S. K. L. de Silva, Pushpakumara and Silva for the three one-day internationals.

Team manager: L. R. D. Mendis.   *Coach:* B. Yardley.

SRI LANKAN TOUR RESULTS

Test matches – Played 3: Drawn 3.
First-class matches – Played 4: Drawn 4.
Draws – India (3), Board President's XI.
One-day internationals – Played 3: Won 1, Lost 1, No result 1.
Other non-first-class matches – Played 2: Won 1, Lost 1. *Win* – Indian XI. *Loss* – Indian XI.

TEST MATCH AVERAGES

INDIA – BATTING

	T	I	NO	R	HS	100s	50s	Avge	Ct
S. C. Ganguly	3	4	0	392	173	2	1	98.00	0
R. Dravid	3	4	0	304	93	0	3	76.00	2
N. S. Sidhu	3	4	0	288	131	1	1	72.00	0
S. R. Tendulkar	3	4	0	199	148	1	0	49.75	2
M. Azharuddin	3	4	0	119	62	0	2	29.75	3
A. Kumble	3	4	0	107	78	0	1	26.75	3
N. R. Mongia	3	4	1	78	57	0	1	26.00	2
A. Kuruvilla	3	4	1	41	35*	0	0	13.66	0
J. Srinath	3	4	1	37	15*	0	0	12.33	1
R. K. Chauhan	3	4	0	7	4	0	0	1.75	4

Played in one Test: N. M. Kulkarni 1*; B. K. V. Prasad 3 (1 ct). D. S. Mohanty did not bat.

* *Signifies not out.*

BOWLING

	O	M	R	W	BB	5W/i	Avge
R. K. Chauhan	94	35	164	8	4-48	0	20.50
A. Kuruvilla	64.1	15	180	8	4-88	0	22.50
J. Srinath	92.4	16	299	9	4-92	0	33.22
A. Kumble	122	46	279	6	3-56	0	46.50

Also bowled: M. Azharuddin 1–0–4–0; S. C. Ganguly 7–4–19–0; D. S. Mohanty 35–5–89–0; B. K. V. Prasad 26–9–53–1; S. R. Tendulkar 2–2–0–0.

SRI LANKA – BATTING

	T	I	NO	R	HS	100s	50s	Avge	Ct
P. A. de Silva	3	4	1	227	110*	1	1	75.66	4
M. S. Atapattu	3	4	0	268	108	1	1	67.00	2
S. T. Jayasuriya	3	4	0	157	53	0	2	39.25	0
H. D. P. K. Dharmasena .	2	4	1	110	40	0	0	36.66	3
R. S. Mahanama	3	4	0	108	42	0	0	27.00	4
H. P. Tillekeratne.	3	4	1	66	25	0	0	22.00	3
S. K. L. de Silva	3	4	2	36	20*	0	0	18.00	1
A. Ranatunga	3	4	0	46	30	0	0	11.50	1
W. P. U. J. C. Vaas	3	3	1	6	4	0	0	3.00	1

Played in two Tests: M. Muralitharan 10 (1 ct); K. R. Pushpakumara 0* (2 ct). Played in one Test: K. S. C. de Silva 6; G. P. Wickremasinghe 2. K. J. Silva did not bat.

* *Signifies not out.*

BOWLING

	O	M	R	W	BB	5W/i	Avge
S. T. Jayasuriya	73	16	184	6	2-32	0	30.66
G. P. Wickremasinghe	36.1	10	96	3	2-76	0	32.00
K. R. Pushpakumara	65	8	258	8	5-122	1	32.25
H. D. P. K. Dharmasena . .	94.4	23	266	8	5-57	1	33.25
W. P. U. J. C. Vaas	98.5	19	292	4	2-80	0	73.00
M. Muralitharan	121	39	311	3	3-174	0	103.66

Also bowled: M. S. Atapattu 1–0–4–0; K. S. C. de Silva 28–5–81–1; A. Ranatunga 21–10–43–1; K. J. Silva 28–6–81–0.

Note: Matches in this section which were not first-class are signified by a dagger.

†At Baroda, November 13. Indian XI won by four wickets. Toss: Indian XI. Sri Lankans 187 (39.4 overs) (S. T. Jayasuriya 61, H. P. Tillekeratne 41); Indian XI 191 for six (35.1 overs) (S. R. Tendulkar 69, V. G. Kambli 41, S. V. Manjrekar 35 not out, N. R. Mongia 33; M. Muralitharan three for 40).
Benefit match for A. D. Gaekwad.

At Cuttack, November 14, 15, 16. Drawn. Toss: Board President's XI. Board President's XI 294 (Wasim Jaffer 79, V. V. S. Laxman 112, M. S. K. Prasad 35; K. R. Pushpakumara three for 63, K. J. Silva five for 55) and ten for one dec.; Sri Lankans 198 (H. P. Tillekeratne 77, H. D. P. K. Dharmasena 39; R. Sanghvi four for 60).

INDIA v SRI LANKA

First Test Match

At Mohali, November 19, 20, 21, 22, 23. Drawn. Toss: India. Test debut: S. K. L. de Silva.

A brilliant unbeaten century from Aravinda de Silva, his seventh in seven Tests, denied India a victory that appeared theirs when they reduced Sri Lanka to 106 for five, still 40 behind, at the stroke of lunch on the fifth day. All-rounder Dharmasena helped him add 103 to ensure the draw. De Silva hit 15 fours and a six in just under six and a half hours and passed 1,000 runs for the calendar year. "It was the best of his last seven centuries, keeping in mind the timing and value of this knock for Sri Lankan cricket," said his captain, Ranatunga.

India had created a winning position despite an opening-day century from Sri Lankan opener Atapattu, three days before his 27th birthday. Atapattu's previous two Tests in India had resulted in two pairs, but this time he reached a maiden hundred, in his tenth Test. He was dismissed shortly before the close by Srinath. After nine months on the injury list, Srinath gradually recaptured his pace and was consistently the best of the Indian bowlers. On the second morning, he and Kuruvilla combined to cut down the visitors from a promising 301 for four to 369 all out.

India's laboured reply made it clear that their new coach, Anshuman Gaekwad, and captain Tendulkar were intent on batting just once. They added 91 without loss in 53 overs on the second day and added 202 off 90 on the third to close at 293 for four. The platform was laid by Sidhu, who completed his ninth Test century, his first in his home state of Punjab.

The urgent need for quick runs finally hit home after first-innings lead was achieved, and Ganguly led the charge with a well-paced century, his first in any Test in India. After his first 50 spanned 181 balls, he put his foot on the accelerator and reached his hundred off another 51 deliveries, with nine fours and two sixes. It took him past 1,000 runs in his 15th Test; earlier in the innings, there had also been 1,000-run landmarks for Azharuddin (against Sri Lanka) and Tendulkar (as captain). Ganguly and Kuruvilla provided the most entertaining batting of the match by adding 89 runs, a ninth-wicket record for India against Sri Lanka, off just 70 balls – Kuruvilla clouted three sixes in a Test-best 35.

India tightened their grip when Srinath dismissed Jayasuriya and Mahanama on the fourth afternoon. Next morning, three more wickets fell, with Tillekeratne out for ball before lunch. But India could not close the deal after the break. De Silva unselfishly took an offer of bad light when unbeaten on 98, though the skies brightened long enough for him to complete his hundred.

Man of the Match: P. A. de Silva.

Close of play: First day, Sri Lanka 280-4 (A. Ranatunga 14*, H. P. Tillekeratne 9*); Second day, India 91-0 (N. R. Mongia 41*, N. S. Sidhu 47*); Third day, India 293-4 (M. Azharuddin 23*, S. C. Ganguly 7*); Fourth day, Sri Lanka 61-2 (M. S. Atapattu 26*, P. A. de Silva 6*).

Sri Lanka

S. T. Jayasuriya c Chauhan b Srinath	53	– c Mongia b Srinath	17
M. S. Atapattu lbw b Srinath	108	– c Chauhan b Kuruvilla	31
R. S. Mahanama lbw b Kumble	42	– lbw b Srinath	11
P. A. de Silva b Kuruvilla	33	– not out	110
*A. Ranatunga c Chauhan b Srinath	30	– c Dravid b Kuruvilla	3
H. P. Tillekeratne c Dravid b Kumble	14	– c Tendulkar b Chauhan	9
†S. K. L. de Silva b Kuruvilla	5	– (8) not out	11
H. D. P. K. Dharmasena not out	37	– (7) b Srinath	25
W. P. U. J. C. Vaas b Kuruvilla	2		
M. Muralitharan c Srinath b Kuruvilla	10		
K. S. C. de Silva b Srinath	6		
B 4, l-b 13, n-b 12	29	B 13, l-b 9, n-b 12	34

1/98 (1) 2/202 (3) 3/254 (2) 4/254 (4)   369   1/22 (1) 2/40 (3)   (6 wkts) 251
5/301 (5) 6/307 (7) 7/307 (6)   3/67 (2) 4/82 (5)
8/313 (9) 9/333 (10) 10/369 (11)   5/106 (6) 6/209 (7)

Bowling: *First Innings*—Srinath 27.2–4–92–4; Kuruvilla 27–7–88–4; Mohanty 19–1–57–0; Kumble 34–9–81–2; Ganguly 2–2–0–0; Chauhan 16–2–34–0. *Second Innings*—Srinath 22–3–75–3; Mohanty 16–4–32–0; Kuruvilla 15.1–4–29–2; Kumble 19–5–66–0; Chauhan 18–11–23–1; Ganguly 2–2–0–0; Azharuddin 1–0–4–0.

India

†N. R. Mongia b Muralitharan	57	R. K. Chauhan c Dharmasena		
N. S. Sidhu run out	131	b Muralitharan .	2	
R. Dravid c Ranatunga b Jayasuriya . . .	34	A. Kuruvilla not out	35	
*S. R. Tendulkar c Dharmasena				
b Jayasuriya .	23	B 19, l-b 10, w 6, n-b 8	43	
M. Azharuddin lbw b Vaas.	53		—	
S. C. Ganguly c Tilleteratne b Vaas . . .	109	1/120 (1) 2/214 (3) (9 wkts dec.) 515		
A. Kumble c Dharmasena b Muralitharan	22	3/259 (2) 4/274 (4)		
J. Srinath c Mahanama		5/353 (5) 6/400 (7)		
b K. S. C. de Silva .	6	7/419 (8) 8/426 (9) 9/515 (6)		
D. S. Mohanty did not bat.				

Bowling: Vaas 36.5–11–107–2; K. S. C. de Silva 28–5–81–1; Dharmasena 34–11–65–0; Muralitharan 75–30–174–3; Jayasuriya 30–9–59–2; Ranatunga 3–3–0–0.

Umpires: S. A. Bucknor (West Indies) and S. Venkataraghavan.
Referee: R. B. Simpson (Australia).

INDIA v SRI LANKA

Second Test Match

At Nagpur, November 26, 27, 28, 29, 30. Drawn. Toss: India.

Rain, which announced its presence after just one over, eventually wiped out the final two days and two sessions, limiting action to the 155 overs in which India had convincingly accumulated 485.

Soon after the first interruption, Mongia slapped Pushpakumara, recalled by Sri Lanka, to backward point. But Sidhu and Dravid consolidated, despite the loss of nearly three hours to persistent showers, to build a confident century stand. Sidhu followed up his hundred in the First Test with an aggressive 79. Despite another failure for Tendulkar, India's top order seized the initiative on a sunny second day with some bright strokeplay. Dravid and Azharuddin added 90 for the fourth wicket before Dravid fell eight short of a second Test hundred; like Sidhu, he mis-hit a pull at left-armer Vaas to be caught at backward square leg. Azharuddin scored his second successive fifty but was undone by a fast in-swinger from the pacy Pushpakumara.

Ganguly batted with the confidence back-to-back centuries in Colombo and Mohali had given him. He drove through the off side with his usual flourish and, in partnership with Kumble, took India past 400 just before the second-day close. Their stand realised 159 before Kumble was ruled run out by third umpire Godbole, despite evidence indicating the batsman's desperate dive had got him home. That dismissal sparked a late collapse, five wickets falling for 23 runs. Ganguly was one away from his third hundred in successive Tests when he edged Pushpakumara to the solitary wide slip. His 99 was spiced with 13 boundaries and had lasted five and a quarter hours. Coincidentally, a few minutes later and 6,000 miles away, Greg Blewett was also out for 99 in the Hobart Test. Even as Pushpakumara completed his third five-wicket haul in Tests, the skies darkened and the rain began its ultimate intervention.

Close of play: First day, India 133-1 (N. S. Sidhu 64*, R. Dravid 47*); Second day, India 401-5 (S. C. Ganguly 67*, A. Kumble 42*); Third day, India 485; Fourth day, No play.

India

†N. R. Mongia c Muralitharan		R. K. Chauhan c Vaas c Jayasuriya	1	
b Pushpakumara .	11	A. Kuruvilla lbw b Pushpakumara	0	
N. S. Sidhu c Atapattu b Vaas	79	N. M. Kulkarni not out	1	
R. Dravid c Atapattu b Vaas.	92			
*S. R. Tendulkar b Pushpakumara . . .	15	B 8, l-b 13, w 3, n-b 12	36	
M. Azharuddin lbw b Pushpakumara . . .	62		—	
S. C. Ganguly c Tilleketarne		1/15 (1) 2/152 (2) 3/182 (4)	485	
b Pushpakumara .	99	4/272 (3) 5/303 (5) 6/462 (7)		
A. Kumble run out	78	7/476 (8) 8/484 (9)		
J. Srinath lbw b Jayasuriya	11	9/484 (6) 10/485 (10)		

Bowling: Vaas 31–3–80–2; Pushpakumara 32–3–122–5; Silva 28–6–81–0; Muralitharan 46–9–137–0; Ranatunga 1–0–8–0; Jayasuriya 16–4–32–2; Atapattu 1–0–4–0.

Sri Lanka

S. T. Jayasuriya, M. S. Atapattu, R. S. Mahanama, P. A. de Silva, *A. Ranatunga, H. P. Tillekeratne, †S. K. L. de Silva, W. P. U. J. C. Vaas, K. J. Silva, M. Muralitharan and K. R. Pushpakumàra.

Umpires: C. J. Mitchley (South Africa) and V. K. Ramaswamy.
Referee: R. B. Simpson (Australia).

INDIA v SRI LANKA

Third Test Match

At Mumbai, December 3, 4, 5, 6, 7. Drawn. Toss: Sri Lanka.

India held the upper hand but once again could not produce the incisive bowling to convert their advantage into victory on a tense final day.

Sent in, they slipped to 55 for two before two massive partnerships involving Ganguly, promoted above the out-of-touch Tendulkar, set up a formidable total. With Dravid, he put on 160 to grab the initiative; then he added a dazzling 256 with Tendulkar, an Indian fourth-wicket Test record. Dravid fell in the nineties for the second time running, edging Ranatunga to first slip, but Ganguly followed up his success earlier in the series with another scintillating century, his fifth in Tests. He reached three figures early on the second day, and went on to a Test-best 173, lasting eight hours 36 minutes and 361 balls, with 25 fours and two sixes. Tendulkar, who had laboured 71 minutes scoring eight on the first day, rediscovered his touch to match his partner stroke for stroke. He moved from 87 to 99 with successive sixes off Dharmasena and completed his 14th Test century two balls later; on the way, he brought up his 4,000th run in 58 Tests, and he was only just short of 1,000 runs in 1997, a target he reached in the next innings. But the loss of Ganguly and Tendulkar, in the space of four runs, generated a late collapse that saw seven fall for 41.

Launching Sri Lanka's reply, Jayasuriya raced to his fifty in 41 balls with nine fours. He fought an intriguing battle with Srinath, lashing him for eight fours but also receiving blows to helmet, shoulder and glove. He was caught at slip aiming a big swipe to leg off leg-spinner Kumble just before the close. Batting seemed more leisurely next day, with Atapattu and night-watchman Dharmasena carefully adding 115 before both fell to Chauhan's off-breaks. Atapattu spent almost an hour in the nineties before prodding a catch to silly point.

However, Aravinda de Silva struck another exciting fifty before he succumbed to Chauhan. Wicket-keeper Lanka de Silva was smashed in the face by a bouncer from Srinath which broke through the grille on his helmet; the wound on his left cheek required ten stitches. Srinath would have been more satisfied by his 100th Test wicket – in 30 matches – when he bowled Wickremasinghe to finish off Sri Lanka, 151 behind.

India's quest for quick runs was paced by Dravid and Sidhu, who put on 88 in almost even time. For the 13th time in his 19 Tests, Dravid reached a half-century, but again he fell short of adding to his only hundred. The middle order passed through quickly and Dharmasena secured his second five-wicket haul in Tests.

Sri Lanka were set 333 in 94 overs, and had high hopes when they reached 58 without loss. But wickets began to fall, that of Aravinda de Silva in controversial circumstances. He protested that his catcher, Chauhan, had moved back from square leg while Srinath was on his run-up to deliver the arranged bouncer, something which umpire Bucknor had noticed and checked when it happened a few minutes earlier. But, despite a wearing pitch and fading light, Sri Lanka stood firm until play was called off with 12 overs remaining.

Man of the Match: S. C. Ganguly. *Man of the Series:* S. C. Ganguly.

Close of play: First day, India 247-3 (S. C. Ganguly 92*, S. R. Tendulkar 8*); Second day, Sri Lanka 66-1 (M. S. Atapattu 15*, H. D. P. K. Dharmasena 0*); Third day, Sri Lanka 286-5 (P. A. de Silva 48*, H. P. Tillekeratne 4*); Fourth day, Sri Lanka 6-0 (S. T. Jayasuriya 1*, M. S. Atapattu 5*).

India

†N. R. Mongia b Wickremasinghe	1	– (6) not out	9
N. S. Sidhu c Mahanama b Dharmasena	35	– c Pushpakumara b Jayasuriya	43
R. Dravid c Mahanama b Ranatunga	93	– c P. A. de Silva b Dharmasena	85
S. C. Ganguly c S. K. L. de Silva b Dharmasena	173	– (1) c Tillekeratne b Wickremasinghe	11
*S. R. Tendulkar b Pushpakumara	148	– (4) c P. A. de Silva b Jayasuriya	13
M. Azharuddin lbw b Pushpakumara	0	– (5) c P. A. de Silva b Dharmasena	4
A. Kumble b Pushpakumara	6	– c Mahanama b Dharmasena	1
R. K. Chauhan lbw b Dharmasena	4	– (9) run out	0
A. Kuruvilla c Pushpakumara b Wickremasinghe	6	– (10) c P. A. de Silva b Dharmasena	0
J. Srinath not out	15	– (8) c sub (D. P. M. D. Jayawardene) b Dharmasena	5
B. K. V. Prasad run out	3		
B 3, l-b 15, w 4, n-b 6	28	B 3, l-b 6, n-b 1	10

1/1 (1) 2/55 (2) 3/215 (3) 4/471 (4)　　　　512　　1/15 (1) 2/103 (2)　　(9 wkts dec.) 181
5/475 (5) 6/476 (6) 7/481 (7)　　　　　　　　　　3/136 (4) 4/149 (5)
8/487 (8) 9/502 (9) 10/512 (11)　　　　　　　　　5/173 (3) 6/175 (7)
　　　　　　　　　　　　　　　　　　　　　　　　7/181 (8) 8/181 (9) 9/181 (10)

Bowling: *First Innings*—Vaas 26–4–86–0; Wickremasinghe 28–5–108–3; Pushpakumara 28–5–108–3; Dharmasena 48–12–144–3; Ranatunga 17–7–35–1; Jayasuriya 12–2–45–0. *Second Innings*—Vaas 5–1–19–0; Wickremasinghe 5–0–20–1; Pushpakumara 5–0–28–0; Jayasuriya 15–1–48–2; Dharmasena 12.4–0–57–5.

Sri Lanka

S. T. Jayasuriya c Azharuddin b Kumble	50	– c Tendulkar b Kumble	37
M. S. Atapattu c sub (A. Jadeja) b Chauhan	98	– c Kumble b Chauhan	31
H. D. P. K. Dharmasena c Kumble b Chauhan	40	– (6) c Azharuddin b Kumble	8
R. S. Mahanama c Kumble b Prasad	20	– (3) lbw b Chauhan	35
P. A. de Silva c Mongia b Chauhan	66	– (4) c Chauhan b Srinath	18
*A. Ranatunga c Azharuddin b Chauhan	1	– (5) b Chauhan	12
H. P. Tillekeratne lbw b Kuruvilla	25	– not out	18
†S. K. L. de Silva retired hurt	20	– c Prasad b Kumble	0
W. P. U. J. C. Vaas c sub (N. M. Kulkarni) b Kuruvilla	4	– not out	0
G. P. Wickremasinghe b Srinath	2		
K. R. Pushpakumara not out	0		
B 7, l-b 12, w 4, n-b 12	35	L-b 2, n-b 5	7

1/65 (1) 2/180 (3) 3/219 (4)　　　　　　　　361　　1/58 (2) 2/73 (1)　　　　(7 wkts) 166
4/259 (2) 5/269 (6) 6/312 (5)　　　　　　　　　　3/106 (4) 4/144 (3)
7/351 (7) 8/359 (9) 9/361 (10)　　　　　　　　　5/146 (5) 6/160 (6) 7/166 (8)

In the first innings S. K. L. de Silva retired hurt at 355.

Bowling: *First Innings*—Srinath 28.2–4–107–1; Prasad 18–6–30–1; Kuruvilla 19–2–62–2; Kumble 41–19–76–1; Chauhan 34–13–48–4; Ganguly 3–0–19–0. *Second Innings*—Srinath 15–5–25–1; Prasad 8–3–23–0; Chauhan 26–9–59–3; Kuruvilla 3–2–1–0; Kumble 28–13–56–3; Tendulkar 2–2–0–0.

Umpires: S. A. Bucknor (West Indies) and A. V. Jayaprakash.
Referee: R. B. Simpson (Australia).

†INDIA v SRI LANKA

First One-Day International

At Gauhati, December 22. India won by seven wickets. Toss: India. International debut: S. V. Bahutule.

The two teams resumed combat after a fortnight's break, in which India had visited Sharjah and lost all their three matches in the Champions Trophy. They bounced back here, winning with five overs to spare even after two were trimmed from their allocation because of a slow over-rate. Play had begun 45 minutes late because of mist, and conditions suited the Indian attack. Mohanty collected three early wickets while Srinath tied up the other end. Mahanama batted bravely for 165 minutes, but became one of five victims for Robin Singh. India needed only four an over. Despite the openers going cheaply, Tendulkar settled the issue with 82 in 86 balls; he passed 1,000 one-day international runs in 1997, to go with his 1,000 Test runs.

Man of the Match: R. R. Singh.

Sri Lanka

S. T. Jayasuriya c Jadeja b Mohanty	1	U. D. U. Chandana lbw b Singh	4
M. S. Atapattu c Mongia b Mohanty	8	W. P. U. J. C. Vaas not out	7
R. S. Mahanama c Jadeja b Singh	68	M. Muralitharan b Singh	1
P. A. de Silva c Chauhan b Mohanty	4	K. S. C. de Silva not out	3
*A. Ranatunga c Singh b Ganguly	27	L-b 9, w 6, n-b 2	17
†R. S. Kaluwitharana c Bahutule b Singh	23		
H. D. P. K. Dharmasena c Bahutule b Singh	9		

1/5 2/22 3/30 4/92 5/133 6/152 7/156 8/161 9/167 (9 wkts, 45 overs) 172

Bowling: Srinath 9-4-16-0; Mohanty 9-1-31-3; Chauhan 7-0-30-0; Ganguly 6-0-31-1; Bahutule 9-0-33-0; Singh 5-0-22-5.

India

S. C. Ganguly b Vaas	12	M. Azharuddin not out	28
A. Jadeja run out	7	L-b 1, w 6, n-b 1	8
N. S. Sidhu c Atapattu b Muralitharan	36		
*S. R. Tendulkar not out	82	1/16 2/26 3/94 (3 wkts, 37.5 overs) 173

R. R. Singh, †N. R. Mongia, S. V. Bahutule, J. Srinath, R. K. Chauhan and D. S. Mohanty did not bat.

Bowling: Vaas 7-1-19-1; K. S. C. de Silva 7.5-0-31-0; Dharmasena 5-0-24-0; Muralitharan 7-0-49-1; Jayasuriya 8-0-29-0; Chandana 3-0-20-0.

Umpires: K. S. Giridharan and K. Murali.

†INDIA v SRI LANKA

Second One-Day International

At Indore, December 25. No result. Toss: Sri Lanka. International debut: H. H. Kanitkar.

For the first time, an international match was called off because the pitch was judged unsafe. Both teams had been surprised by its dry and cracked look, but Sri Lanka batted, believing the pitch could only deteriorate with use. They lost Kaluwitharana in the first over and, after off-spinner Chauhan bowled the second, Mahanama was hit on the knuckles by Srinath. At the end of the third over, the batsmen appealed to umpire Porel, who immediately summoned referee Ahmed Ebrahim of Zimbabwe. Play was suspended and, an hour later, called off, on the grounds that the pitch was crumbling so fast that batting was dangerous. Madhya Pradesh officials were upset by the haste of the decision, saying that they had offered to prepare an alternative strip.

Sri Lanka

S. T. Jayasuriya not out	6
†R. S. Kaluwitharana b Srinath	0
R. S. Mahanama not out	5
B 4, w 1, n-b 1	6

1/1 (1 wkt, 3 overs) 17

P. A. de Silva, *A. Ranatunga, H. P. Tillekeratne, U. D. U. Chandana, H. D. P. K. Dharmasena, W. P. U. J. C. Vaas, M. Muralitharan and K. S. C. de Silva did not bat.

Bowling: Srinath 2-0-6-1; Chauhan 1-0-7-0.

India

S. C. Ganguly, A. Jadeja, N. S. Sidhu, *S. R. Tendulkar, M. Azharuddin, R. R. Singh, H. H. Kanitkar, †N. R. Mongia, S. V. Bahutule, J. Srinath and R. K. Chauhan.

Umpires: S. K. Porel and D. Sharma.

†At Indore, December 25. Sri Lankans won by two runs. Toss: Sri Lankans. Sri Lankans 180 for eight (25 overs) (S. T. Jayasuriya 53, R. S. Kaluwitharana 45, M. S. Atapattu 42; S. V. Bahutule four for 17); Indian XI 178 for seven (25 overs) (A. Jadeja 37, H. H. Kanitkar 50, N. R. Mongia 36).

An exhibition match arranged to avoid disappointing a 30,000-crowd when the Indore international was stopped because of the unsafe pitch.

†INDIA v SRI LANKA

Third One-Day International

At Margao, December 28. Sri Lanka won by five wickets. Toss: India.

Sri Lanka levelled the series when Aravinda de Silva led them to victory with ten balls to spare. Arriving in the 13th over, he scored 82 in 90 balls, and shared three successive fifty partnerships. The innings was halted at 205 for four when spectators threw bottles on the field, but they quietened down after an announcement citing Goa's sporting reputation, and Sri Lanka resumed their pursuit of victory ten minutes after the interruption. Earlier, India's openers, Ganguly and Jadeja, had scored 131 in the first 32 overs. But once they fell, in the space of five balls, Sri Lanka did an excellent job of containment.

Man of the Match: P. A. de Silva. *Man of the Series:* R. S. Mahanama.

India

A. Jadeja c Muralitharan b Jayasuriya	. .	53	†N. R. Mongia c Muralitharan		
S. C. Ganguly c Tillekeratne				b K. S. C. de Silva .	14
	b Muralitharan .	61	S. V. Bahutule not out.		0
*S. R. Tendulkar c K. S. C. de Silva				L-b 13, w 20, n-b 1.	34
	b Muralitharan .	6			
M. Azharuddin c and b Muralitharan	. . .	24			___
N. S. Sidhu run out		17	1/131 2/134 3/152	(6 wkts, 50 overs)	228
R. R. Singh not out		19	4/181 5/190 6/223		

J. Srinath, R. K. Chauhan and D. S. Mohanty did not bat.

Bowling: Vaas 9–0–28–0; K. S. C. de Silva 8–0–30–1; Dharmasena 10–0–38–0; Muralitharan 10–2–53–3; Jayasuriya 10–0–52–1; P. A. de Silva 3–0–14–0.

Sri Lanka

S. T. Jayasuriya c Singh b Mohanty. . . .	17	H. D. P. K. Dharmasena not out		5
M. S. Atapattu c Azharuddin b Mohanty.	14			
R. S. Mahanama b Bahutule.	46		L-b 1, w 13, n-b 1.	15
P. A. de Silva not out	82			___
*A. Ranatunga c Jadeja b Srinath	20	1/19 2/51 3/112	(5 wkts, 48.2 overs)	229
†R. S. Kaluwitharana b Mohanty.	30	4/163 5/220		

H. P. Tillekeratne, W. P. U. J. C. Vaas, M. Muralitharan and K. S. C. de Silva did not bat.

Bowling: Srinath 10–1–26–1; Mohanty 10–0–58–3; Singh 5.2–1–29–0; Bahutule 10–0–46–1; Chauhan 9–0–37–0; Ganguly 3–0–25–0; Tendulkar 1–0–7–0.

Umpires: K. Hariharan and R. C. Sharma. Series referee: A. M. Ebrahim (Zimbabwe).

THE SOUTH AFRICANS IN AUSTRALIA, 1997-98

By STEVEN LYNCH

The South Africans arrived with high hopes of recording their first Test series victory over Australia in four attempts since returning to the international fold. In the end, two factors counted against them. A familiar foe, Shane Warne, overcame unseasonal damp weather in the Sydney Test with some wristy magic, which included his 300th Test wicket. And in the Third Test at Adelaide, as the visitors looked set to square the series, uncharacteristically ragged fielding cost them dear. Ten catches went down as Australia just managed to stave off defeat and take the series 1-0.

There was a similar near-miss in the one-day series. South Africa dominated the qualifying stages, winning all four of their matches against Australia and losing only once, to New Zealand. But Australia turned the tables in the best-of-three finals, winning the last two games after another defeat in the first one. The South Africans also failed to win a first-class match on the tour, though they lost only the Test at Sydney.

It seemed almost as if, when pitted against Australia, the South Africans had an inferiority complex – not something they exhibit against other countries nor, indeed, in many other sports. Captaincy came into it too: sometimes, when comparing the thoughtful Mark Taylor with the rather mechanical Hansie Cronje, one was reminded of Dr Who outwitting the Daleks. In the Sydney Test, for example, Cronje delayed posting a short leg during a lightning spell from Allan Donald until after both Waughs had popped up inviting catches there. Later, Taylor positioned Ricky Ponting unusually close at mid-wicket, where he immediately took a sharp low catch to send Adam Bacher back. Good luck – or good judgment?

Their main problem remained the lack of a world-class batsman – a Lara, a Richards (Viv) or, come to that, a Richards (Barry). All their batsmen had workmanlike Test averages in the upper thirties, but none threatened to reach the magic 50 mark. The man most likely to, Daryll Cullinan, ran into trouble against his old nemesis, Warne, and was dropped for the last two Tests. And Cronje let himself down too often with reckless shots after patient starts. Jacques Kallis made an accomplished maiden Test century at Melbourne, and Gary Kirsten, the vice-captain, scored consistently, apart from a double failure in the defeat at Sydney. After the First Test, South African coach Bob Woolmer caused some amusement when he suggested that Bacher had returned to form, moving his feet well in a laboured innings of three in 53 minutes. But the canny Woolmer was proved right when Bacher, who started the tour wretchedly, followed this up with four useful scores.

The tourists had fewer problems in the fast bowling department, although they missed the steadiness of Fanie de Villiers, the match-winner at Sydney four years ago, who was overlooked this time. Donald, who became South Africa's leading Test wicket-taker at Melbourne, was a constant threat. One spell at Sydney, where he bowled after a pain-killing injection in his foot, was as fast as anyone could remember. It was a major blow when he pulled a buttock muscle in the closing stages of the one-day competition and had to miss the final Test. Shaun Pollock responded well in that match, taking seven for 87 on an unhelpful pitch, but Donald's absence probably allowed Australia to stave off defeat. Brian McMillan, who struggled with the bat until the final Test, looked past his best with the ball as well. There were signs of raw promise in Makhaya Ntini, the first black player to play for South Africa. He was given little scope but, in a rare one-day outing, he impressed with his pace with the ball, and, during the Sydney Test, with his fleetness of foot: he took part in an invitation 400-metre race on the outfield. Roared on by his team-mates, he hung on to win.

South Africa's spin reserves remained slender. Pat Symcox was a better-balanced, tighter off-spinner than on the previous visit, but still looked unlikely to run through a Test batting order. And, once they had recovered from the shock of seeing his action, the leading Australians were rarely troubled by Paul Adams, who was commendably accurate but needed to broaden the variety of his left-arm slows to succeed at the highest level.

This series saw the final bow of Dave Richardson, South Africa's polished wicket-keeper. At Melbourne, he broke the national record for Test dismissals, surpassing John Waite, to whom he bears quite a resemblance. There were occasional signs that his keeping had declined, and he made little impact with the bat, but he managed a rare stumping, his second in Tests and, as it turned out, his last. He also took 150 catches in 42 Tests, having missed only one game between South Africa's return and his retirement. His eventual replacement, Mark Boucher, fretted at the limited scope he was allowed on this tour while his rivals were fully employed at home – but he soon took his chance, quite literally with both hands.

Australia did well to complete their ninth successive series win, given the continued absence of Jason Gillespie and the later injuries to Glenn McGrath and Paul Reiffel, which led to a raw new-ball attack taking the field at Adelaide. Warne was unable to bowl South Africa out on the final day at Melbourne, but he made up for it by destroying them at Sydney; and he had a promising new leg-spinning partner at Adelaide, where Stuart MacGill of New South Wales took five wickets on his debut. Australia's batting was again formidable: Taylor almost single-handedly averted a rout by carrying his bat at Adelaide; Mark Waugh made two important and stylish centuries; and Ponting contributed a stroke-studded 105 at Melbourne. Steve Waugh had a near miss, with 96 in his 99th Test, then disappointed his home fans by falling short again in his 100th, at Sydney. Ian Healy became the fourth Australian to join the 100-Test club, at Adelaide, joining Allan Border, David Boon and Steve Waugh.

[*Ben Radford/Allsport*

Shane Warne celebrates his 300th Test wicket during the Second Test at Sydney; Jacques Kallis looks back in despair.

SOUTH AFRICAN TOURING PARTY

W. J. Cronje (Free State) (*captain*), G. Kirsten (Western Province) (*vice-captain*), P. R. Adams (Western Province), A. M. Bacher (Gauteng), M. V. Boucher (Border), D. J. Cullinan (Gauteng), A. A. Donald (Free State), H. H. Gibbs (Western Province), J. H. Kallis (Western Province), L. Klusener (Natal), B. M. McMillan (Western Province), M. Ntini (Border), S. M. Pollock (Natal), J. N. Rhodes (Natal), D. J. Richardson (Eastern Province), P. L. Symcox (Natal).

R. Telemachus (Boland) was originally selected for the tour but withdrew injured, to be replaced by Ntini.

Manager: A. H. Jordaan.   *Coach:* R. A. Woolmer.

SOUTH AFRICAN TOUR RESULTS

Test matches – Played 3: Lost 1, Drawn 2.
First-class matches – Played 6: Lost 1, Drawn 5.
Loss – Australia.
Draws – Australia (2), Western Australia, Tasmania, Australia A.
One-day internationals –.Played 11: Won 8, Lost 3. *Wins:* Australia (5), New Zealand (3). *Losses:* Australia (2), New Zealand.
Other non-first-class matches – Played 3: Won 3. *Wins:* ACB Chairman's XI, Prime Minister's XI, Bradman XI.

TEST MATCH AVERAGES

AUSTRALIA – BATTING

	T	I	NO	R	HS	100s	50s	Avge	Ct/St
M. E. Waugh	3	5	1	279	115*	2	1	69.75	0
M. A. Taylor	3	5	1	265	169*	1	1	66.25	8
P. R. Reiffel	2	3	1	106	79*	0	1	53.00	0
R. T. Ponting.	3	5	0	248	105	1	1	49.60	2
S. R. Waugh	3	5	0	238	96	0	2	47.60	1
G. S. Blewett	3	5	0	107	31	0	0	21.40	3
I. A. Healy.	3	5	1	77	46*	0	0	19.25	9/1
G. D. McGrath	2	3	1	32	18	0	0	16.00	0
M. S. Kasprowicz . . .	2	3	0	36	19	0	0	12.00	0
M. T. G. Elliott	3	5	0	51	32	0	0	10.20	1
S. K. Warne	3	5	1	27	12	0	0	6.75	5

Played in one Test: M. G. Bevan 12; A. J. Bichel 0, 7 (1 ct); S. C. G. MacGill 10 (1 ct).

* *Signifies not out.*

BOWLING

	O	M	R	W	BB	5W/i	Avge
S. K. Warne	187.1	51	417	20	6-34	2	20.85
P. R. Reiffel	68	23	118	5	3-14	0	23.60
S. C. G. MacGill	36	8	134	5	3-22	0	26.80
M. S. Kasprowicz	84.5	16	253	8	3-28	0	31.62
G. D. McGrath.	70	28	136	4	1-8	0	34.00

Also bowled: M. G. Bevan 26–3–74–2; A. J. Bichel 49–12–154–1; G. S. Blewett 30–11–61–2; M. T. G. Elliott 1–0–4–0; M. E. Waugh 47–12–114–2; S. R. Waugh 31–10–74–2.

SOUTH AFRICA – BATTING

	T	I	NO	R	HS	100s	50s	Avge	Ct/St
G. Kirsten	3	6	1	279	108*	1	2	55.80	2
B. M. McMillan	3	5	1	168	87*	0	1	42.00	4
W. J. Cronje	3	6	0	241	88	0	3	40.16	0
J. H. Kallis	3	6	0	207	101	1	0	34.50	1
A. M. Bacher	3	6	0	188	64	0	1	31.33	2
P. L. Symcox	3	5	0	127	54	0	1	25.40	4
H. H. Gibbs	2	4	0	94	54	0	1	23.50	1
S. M. Pollock	3	5	1	84	40	0	0	21.00	3
L. Klusener	2	4	1	55	38	0	0	18.33	0
D. J. Richardson	3	5	0	33	15	0	0	6.60	10/1
A. A. Donald	2	3	2	6	4*	0	0	6.00	0

Played in one Test: P. R. Adams 0, 1* (1 ct); D. J. Cullinan 5, 0 (2 ct); J. N. Rhodes 6, 19*.

* Signifies not out.

BOWLING

	O	M	R	W	BB	5W/i	Avge
A. A. Donald	86.4	19	214	12	6-59	1	17.83
S. M. Pollock	154	42	351	16	7-87	1	21.93
L. Klusener	85	21	247	6	4-67	0	41.16
P. L. Symcox	133.1	29	344	8	4-69	0	43.00

Also bowled: P. R. Adams 38–9–66–1; W. J. Cronje 8–2–26–0; J. H. Kallis 46–18–100–2; B. M. McMillan 66–15–173–2.

Note: Matches in this section which were not first-class are signified by a dagger.

†At Lilac Hill, Perth, November 25. South Africans won by 31 runs. Toss: South Africans. South Africans 282 for five (50 overs) (L. Klusener 40, D. J. Cullinan 101 not out, J. H. Kallis 64); ACB Chairman's XI 251 for seven (50 overs) (M. E. Hussey 62, T. M. Moody 58 not out).
The Chairman's XI included Dennis Lillee, Barry Richards and 53-year-old Graeme Pollock, who briefly faced his nephew, Shaun; he made 18. Brendon Julian broke down after bowling three balls for the Chairman's XI, and was replaced by Simon Katich, who was allowed to bat.

At Perth, November 27, 28, 29, 30. Drawn. Toss: Western Australia. South Africans 468 (G. Kirsten 201, S. M. Pollock 100, P. L. Symcox 54; J. Stewart four for 121) and 167 for three dec. (A. M. Bacher 69 not out, W. J. Cronje 59 not out); Western Australia 347 for eight dec. (M. E. Hussey 59, R. M. Baker 46, D. R. Martyn 54, S. M. Katich 54, J. L. Langer 60 not out, M. P. Atkinson 35; A. A. Donald four for 70, P. L. Symcox three for 59) and 147 for two (M. E. Hussey 74 not out, D. R. Martyn 51).
Kirsten's 201 lasted 505 minutes and 356 balls and included 24 fours and a six. He put on 171 for the sixth wicket with Pollock.

†At Canberra, December 2. South Africans won by 11 runs. Toss: South Africans. South Africans 268 for six (50 overs) (A. M. Bacher 34, H. H. Gibbs 38, D. J. Cullinan 45, J. H. Kallis 50 not out, W. J. Cronje 42 not out); Prime Minister's XI 257 for seven (50 overs) (M. E. Hussey 91, M. J. Slater 70, J. P. Maher 35; B. M. McMillan three for 56).

South Africa's matches v Australia and New Zealand in the Carlton & United Series (December 4–11) may be found in that section.

At Devonport, December 13, 14, 15, 16. Drawn. Toss: Tasmania. Tasmania 535 for five dec. (D. F. Hills 68, J. Cox 73, S. Young 145, D. C. Boon 33, D. J. Marsh 129 not out, Extras 34) and 147 for seven dec. (J. Cox 35, R. J. Tucker 44 not out); South Africans 402 for eight dec. (D. J. Cullinan 30, W. J. Cronje 165, M. V. Boucher 55, A. A. Donald 55 not out; M. W. Ridgway four for 105) and 94 for two (J. H. Kallis 51 not out).

Marsh's 129, his maiden century, took only 132 balls. Cronje's 165 was his first first-class century since December 1995. Donald made his maiden first-class fifty.

At Brisbane, December 19, 20, 21, 22. Drawn. Toss: South Africans. South Africans 458 for nine dec. (G. Kirsten 79, D. J. Cullinan 43, H. H. Gibbs 54, W. J. Cronje 107 not out, D. J. Richardson 55, P. L. Symcox 55 not out; A. C. Dale three for 45) and 220 for seven dec. (J. H. Kallis 35, D. J. Cullinan 83); Australia A 330 (M. J. Slater 80, J. L. Langer 89, D. S. Lehmann 66; S. M. Pollock four for 68, L. Klusener five for 84) and 122 for one (M. J. Slater 64 not out, J. L. Langer 34 not out).

AUSTRALIA v SOUTH AFRICA

First Test Match

At Melbourne, December 26, 27, 28, 29, 30. Drawn. Toss: Australia.

Frequently in recent years, Australia's opponents, set a stiff last-day target, have crumbled in the face of leg-spin sorcery from Warne. This time the magic failed to work, although it was not for want of trying: in the second innings, Warne sent down 44 overs, 35 of them on the last day, when he often seemed to be pushing the ball through a little too quickly. He beat the bat frequently, but with little luck.

Despite the relatively low scoring rates, this was a fascinating match, and the result remained in doubt until the last few deliveries. Appropriately, attendances were high: 73,812 was the third-highest Boxing Day crowd at an MCG Test (behind the 85,661 in 1975-76, against West Indies, and the 77,167 against England the year before that, though none of these compare to the 130,000 who thronged the place for the evangelist Billy Graham in 1959).

South Africa, needing 381 to win or, more realistically, needing to bat through 122 overs, managed to survive. They owed much to an upright 101 from Kallis, his maiden century in his seventh Test, which featured many stylish drives – and an indifference to the sledging of the close fielders that left them wondering if he was deaf. There were still 24 overs remaining when, after nearly six hours, Kallis played on, but the lower order hung around, despite some close lbw calls.

The pitch, at least on the first three days, was low and slow, and inhibited most of the strokemakers, apart from Ponting, whose second Test century included 14 fours to all parts of the ground. A more prosaic 96 from Steve Waugh, who was caught behind off a Donald no-ball when 83, helped Australia to set up a lead of 123. That looked enough, even when Donald took three quick wickets in the second innings. Taylor resisted in typical style until he was unluckily given out caught at slip to a huge turner from Symcox, which missed the bat by some distance. (In equally typical style Taylor marched straight off and refused to criticise the umpire.) It was the only success of the innings for Symcox, who disappointed by pitching too short too often on a helpful surface, on which he had claimed his best Test figures earlier in the game.

Even so, Australia were in some trouble at 128 for seven – only 251 in front. But the tailenders helped Reiffel (whose unbeaten 79 improved his highest Test score from 77 a few weeks before) add another 129. That at least ensured that Australia would not lose. Donald, always a threat, finished with six wickets in the innings and nine in the match. His final scalp, Kasprowicz, was his 171st in Tests and took him past the South African record set by Hugh Tayfield. It was the second South African aggregate record to fall here: when wicket-keeper Richardson ran to catch Elliott's top-edged hook on the first morning, it was his 142nd dismissal, taking him past John Waite.

Man of the Match: J. H. Kallis. *Attendance:* 160,182.

Close of play: First day, Australia 206-4 (S. R. Waugh 87*, R. T. Ponting 56*); Second day, South Africa 94-4 (G. Kirsten 61*, B. M. McMillan 6*); Third day, Australia 67-4 (M. A. Taylor 8*, R. T. Ponting 8*); Fourth day, South Africa 79-1 (A. M. Bacher 34*, J. H. Kallis 40*).

Australia

M. T. G. Elliott c Richardson b Klusener	6	– (2) lbw b Donald	1
*M. A. Taylor c Kirsten b McMillan	20	– (1) c Cullinan b Symcox	59
G. S. Blewett st Richardson b Symcox	26	– c McMillan b Donald	6
M. E. Waugh c Richardson b Donald	0	– b Donald	1
S. R. Waugh c Cullinan b Donald	96	– c Richardson b Pollock	17
R. T. Ponting b Symcox	105	– c and b Pollock	32
†I. A. Healy b Donald	16	– b Donald	4
P. R. Reiffel b Symcox	27	– not out	79
S. K. Warne c and b Pollock	1	– c Symcox b Donald	10
M. S. Kasprowicz c Bacher b Symcox	0	– c Kirsten b Donald	19
G. D. McGrath not out	0	– c McMillan b Pollock	18
B 1, l-b 6, n-b 5	12	B 4, l-b 3, n-b 4	11

1/18 (1) 2/42 (2) 3/44 (4) 4/77 (3)	**309**	1/4 (2) 2/10 (3) 3/12 (4)	**257**
5/222 (5) 6/250 (7) 7/302 (6) 8/309 (8)		4/44 (5) 5/106 (6) 6/128 (1)	
9/309 (9) 10/309 (10)		7/128 (7) 8/146 (9)	
		9/208 (10) 10/257 (11)	

Bowling: *First Innings*—Donald 29–6–74–3; Pollock 28–6–76–1; Klusener 19–3–48–1; McMillan 10–3–19–1; Symcox 27.2–4–69–4; Kallis 4–2–5–0; Cronje 4–2–11–0. *Second Innings*—Donald 27–8–59–6; Pollock 21.2–5–56–3; Symcox 35–9–90–1; McMillan 2–0–6–0; Klusener 9–2–28–0; Cronje 2–0–11–0.

South Africa

A. M. Bacher c Healy b Kasprowicz	3	– (2) c Taylor b Warne	39
G. Kirsten c Healy b M. E. Waugh	83	– (1) b Reiffel	0
J. H. Kallis c Healy b McGrath	15	– b Reiffel	101
D. J. Cullinan run out	5	– b Warne	0
*W. J. Cronje c Blewett b Warne	0	– c Taylor b S. R. Waugh	70
B. M. McMillan c Healy b Kasprowicz	48	– c Taylor b Warne	16
S. M. Pollock lbw b Warne	7	– not out	15
†D. J. Richardson lbw b M. E. Waugh	1	– lbw b McGrath	11
L. Klusener lbw b Warne	11	– not out	6
P. L. Symcox b Kasprowicz	4		
A. A. Donald not out	0		
L-b 2, w 1, n-b 6	9	B 5, l-b 4, n-b 6	15

1/28 (1) 2/62 (3) 3/75 (4) 4/76 (5)	**186**	1/2 (1) 2/88 (2) 3/88 (4)	(7 wkts) **273**
5/138 (2) 6/155 (7) 7/158 (8)		4/211 (5) 5/229 (3)	
8/182 (6) 9/182 (9) 10/186 (10)		6/241 (6) 7/260 (8)	

Bowling: *First Innings*—McGrath 17–9–20–1; Reiffel 14–5–32–0; Kasprowicz 13.5–3–28–3; Warne 42–15–64–3; M. E. Waugh 18–8–28–2; S. R. Waugh 2–0–12–0. *Second Innings*—McGrath 28–11–57–1; Reiffel 18–8–24–2; Kasprowicz 14–1–45–0; Warne 44–11–97–3; M. E. Waugh 10–0–25–0; S. R. Waugh 7–2–12–1; Blewett 1–0–4–0.

Umpires: S. A. Bucknor (West Indies) and S. G. Randell.   Referee: R. S. Madugalle (Sri Lanka).

AUSTRALIA v SOUTH AFRICA

Second Test Match

At Sydney, January 2, 3, 4, 5. Australia won by an innings and 21 runs. Toss: South Africa.

Four years earlier, Warne had taken 12 wickets against South Africa at Sydney, but still lost, as Australia were beaten by five runs after collapsing for 111. There was no mistake this time, though: Warne took 11 wickets, including his 300th in Tests, six years to the day after his first: Ravi Shastri on January 5, 1992. This time the landmark victim was Kallis, bemused by a perfect top-spinner which dipped through his forward lunge. "A quality ball for a quality batsman," Taylor called it. Warne was back to his best here after the disappointments of the First Test: the ball which removed Richardson in the first innings was a near-replica of the famous one which did for Mike Gatting at Old Trafford in 1993. And, with the close fielders backing him up well, another South African escape act proved impossible.

One slight regret for Warne was that few spectators witnessed the final act. Heavy rain on the fourth afternoon sent many home, and it was a surprise when the weather relented enough to allow the players back on. With the floodlights on for the third afternoon running, Australia pushed hard for a four-day victory, claiming the extra half-hour. They were rewarded when, with rain beginning again, Reiffel had Donald caught behind to seal an emphatic innings win.

South Africa had started slowly on a blameless pitch. They managed only 197 in 97 overs on the first day, the highlight being a perky maiden Test fifty from Gibbs, who had replaced Cullinan. Bevan, back in the side for Kasprowicz, looked rusty, but his unpredictable slow left-armers claimed two wickets – one when McMillan obligingly slogged a full toss to mid-on. Cronje lasted 335 minutes for his 88, but Warne worked his way through the lower order and a total of 287 looked at least 100 below par.

The Waughs put South Africa's score in perspective. Steve, in his 100th Test, disappointed his home supporters when he was out for 85, but Mark did complete his century, striking 12 fours and a big six off Symcox. The twins weathered an extremely rapid spell from Donald, who was bowling after a cortisone injection in his left ankle.

The loss of Kirsten and Cronje, the batsmen most likely to stage prolonged resistance, before lunch on the fourth day left South Africa staring at defeat. Apart from Kallis, whose 45 occupied 155 minutes, and Symcox, who enlivened the closing stages, rain was Australia's biggest worry. Thanks to the groundsmen and the floodlights – and the peerless Warne – they completed victory at 7.09 that evening.

The exciting finish made up for an accident-prone start. The match had begun 30 minutes late despite blazing sunshine because a pitch two strips away from the Test wicket had been over-watered by an inexperienced member of the ground staff. Then tenor Brian Gilbertson stopped midway through the South African national anthem, saying he could not hear the music properly and did not want to continue "out of respect to the South Australian (*sic*) team".

"It's amateur hour," groaned Sir Nicholas Shehadie, the former rugby international, now chairman of the SCG Trust. He thought it could get no worse – but he was wrong. Spectators who had been directed to an overflow car park, over a mile from the ground, were told that it would close at 4 p.m. because the attendant had to go home. This was later extended to 6 p.m. – but, because of the late start, play was scheduled to continue until 6.30. And, finally, the drinks buggy broke down on its first visit to the crease, and had to be pushed off by some of the players and umpire Willey.

Man of the Match: S. K. Warne.   *Attendance:* 105,485.

Close of play: First day, South Africa 197-5 (W. J. Cronje 56*, S. M. Pollock 1*); Second day, Australia 174-3 (M. E. Waugh 78*, S. R. Waugh 18*); Third day, Australia 392-9 (I. A. Healy 31*, G. D. McGrath 3*).

South Africa

A. M. Bacher lbw b Blewett	39	– (2) c Ponting b Reiffel	2
G. Kirsten c Taylor b McGrath	11	– (1) lbw b McGrath	0
J. H. Kallis run out	16	– b Warne	45
*W. J. Cronje c Taylor b Warne	88	– c Ponting b Warne	5
H. H. Gibbs c Healy b Bevan	54	– c Blewett b Warne	1
B. M. McMillan c Elliott b Bevan	6	– b Warne	11
S. M. Pollock c Taylor b Warne	18	– c Taylor b Warne	4
†D. J. Richardson b Warne	6	– c and b Warne	0
P. L. Symcox c Healy b Warne	29	– b Reiffel	38
A. A. Donald not out	4	– c Healy b Reiffel	2
P. R. Adams c S. R. Waugh b Warne	0	– not out	1
B 4, l-b 4, w 1, n-b 7	16	B 2, l-b 1, n-b 1	4

1/25 (2) 2/70 (1) 3/70 (3) 4/167 (5)   287   1/1 (1) 2/3 (2) 3/21 (4)   113
5/174 (6) 6/228 (7) 7/236 (8)   4/27 (5) 5/41 (6) 6/55 (7)
8/276 (4) 9/287 (9) 10/287 (11)   7/55 (8) 8/96 (3)
9/112 (9) 10/113 (10)

Bowling: *First Innings*—McGrath 20-6-51-1; Reiffel 24-7-48-0; Warne 32.1-8-75-5; Bevan 23-3-56-2; Blewett 13-5-30-1; S. R. Waugh 8-4-10-0; M. E. Waugh 3-1-5-0; Elliott 1-0-4-0. *Second Innings*—Reiffel 12-3-14-3; McGrath 5-2-8-1; Warne 21-9-34-6; Blewett 2-1-1-0; Bevan 3-0-18-0; M. E. Waugh 10-2-35-0.

Australia

M. T. G. Elliott c McMillan b Symcox	32	S. K. Warne lbw b Pollock	12	
*M. A. Taylor c Richardson b Pollock	11	G. D. McGrath c Richardson b Donald	14	
G. S. Blewett b McMillan	28			
M. E. Waugh lbw b Pollock	100	B 1, l-b 12, n-b 6	19	
S. R. Waugh b Donald	85		—	
R. T. Ponting c and b Adams	62		421	
M. G. Bevan c McMillan b Symcox	12			
†I. A. Healy not out	46			
P. R. Reiffel b Donald	0			

1/35 (2) 2/59 (1) 3/103 (3)
4/219 (4) 5/317 (5) 6/337 (7)
7/354 (6) 8/357 (9)
9/385 (10) 10/421 (11)

Bowling: Donald 30.4–5–81–3; Pollock 33–8–71–3; Symcox 39–11–103–2; Adams 38–9–66–1; McMillan 18–5–55–1; Kallis 8–1–30–0; Cronje 1–0–2–0.

Umpires: P. Willey (England) and D. B. Hair. Referee: R. S. Madugalle (Sri Lanka).

South Africa's matches v Australia and New Zealand in the Carlton & United Series (January 9–27) may be found in that section.

†At Bowral, January 13. South Africans won by 155 runs. Toss: South Africans. South Africans 288 (50 overs) (A. M. Bacher 57, H. H. Gibbs 131; S. Lee three for 51); Bradman XI 133 (34.5 overs) (M. A. Taylor 32; P. R. Adams four for 20).

Gibbs hit 13 fours and five sixes in 127 balls. Taylor bowled the last over of the South African innings, and took two wickets (1–0–3–2), including Makhaya Ntini with the first ball he had faced on the tour, 49 days after the first match.

AUSTRALIA v SOUTH AFRICA

Third Test Match

At Adelaide, January 30, 31, February 1, 2, 3. Drawn. Toss: South Africa. Test debut: S. C. G. MacGill.

Dropped catches – at least ten of them – scuppered South Africa's chances of the victory they needed to square the series. Their failure was felt most keenly by their captain, Cronje, who speared a stump through the door of the umpires' room. Some pundits suggested Cronje should be banned: in the end, a letter of apology seemed to settle the matter. Perhaps the biggest frustration for Cronje was knowing that, had Donald been able to play, even the missed chances would probably not have mattered. Instead, Donald was a rather uncomfortable spectator, nursing a buttock-muscle strain sustained during the one-day series, which South Africa had contrived to lose after dominating the early stages. Adams was dropped, and Klusener and Rhodes returned.

Australia were also handicapped by injuries to McGrath (back) and Reiffel (finger), which meant that Kasprowicz and Bichel opened the bowling. A newcomer was Stuart MacGill, the New South Wales leg-spinner who played one match for Somerset in 1997. A purveyor of shorter, flatter leg-spin than Warne, not unlike Zimbabwe's Paul Strang in appearance and delivery, MacGill outbowled his jaded senior, who was troubled by his shoulder. Openers Bacher and Kirsten, who hit 21 boundaries between them, made the most of the makeshift new-ball attack. They put on 105 in the first session, and 140 in all. However, apart from Cronje, no one else cashed in until McMillan's belated return to form. Pollock and Klusener helped him add 138, then McMillan was almost a bystander as last man Symcox clubbed a rapid fifty from 42 balls.

Australia's reply owed almost everything to Taylor, who played a classic captain's innings. He hit 21 fours from 376 balls, and became the ninth Australian to carry his bat in a Test – the first since David Boon at Auckland in 1985-86. On a pitch offering little help, Pollock did his utmost to make up for Donald's absence. With high pace and not much luck, he took a Test-best seven for 87. But Kasprowicz and MacGill helped Taylor lead Australia past the follow-on. South Africa were left to rue their five dropped catches, a figure they matched in the second innings. Kirsten's sixth Test century – he hit 17 fours and a six – set up a declaration which left Australia 361 in 109 overs.

Elliott went early and Taylor soon followed, after nearly 24 hours on the field, but Pollock was unable to repeat his earlier heroics, and a century from Mark Waugh took Australia to safety. He batted 404 minutes and hit 16 fours, but was the centre of controversy late on: he received a Pollock lifter which hit him on the arm, and walked away as if in disgust; as he did so, his bat brushed the stumps and dislodged a bail. The South Africans appealed vehemently, even though he had clearly finished his stroke and could not therefore have been given out hit wicket under Law 35. The umpires prolonged the agony, consulting the third umpire, Steve Davis. South Africa's misery was compounded when Bacher, at short leg, dropped Waugh next ball. In fact, Waugh was dropped four times, three of them by Bacher.

Richardson announced his retirement after the match, in which his opposite number, Ian Healy, became the fourth Australian to play in 100 Tests. Healy's father, Neville, had died a week before the game, and the Australians wore black armbands in his memory on the first day. Umpire Steve Randell was standing in his 33rd Test, equalling Tony Crafter's Australian record.

Man of the Match: S. M. Pollock. *Man of the Series:* S. K. Warne.

Attendance: 74,346.

Close of play: First day, South Africa 269-4 (W. J. Cronje 70*, D. J. Richardson 0*); Second day, Australia 71-1 (M. A. Taylor 26*, G. S. Blewett 31*); Third day, Australia 327-9 (M. A. Taylor 157*, S. C. G. MacGill 2*); Fourth day, Australia 32-2 (G. S. Blewett 9*, M. E. Waugh 11*).

South Africa

A. M. Bacher c Warne b Bichel	64	– (2) c MacGill b Warne	41
G. Kirsten c Warne b Kasprowicz	77	– (1) not out.	108
J. H. Kallis lbw b MacGill	15	– b Kasprowicz	15
*W. J. Cronje b Warne	73	– c Warne b Kasprowicz	5
H. H. Gibbs c Healy b Blewett	37	– (7) st Healy b MacGill	2
†D. J. Richardson c Taylor b Warne	15		
J. N. Rhodes c Bichel b Kasprowicz	6	– (8) not out.	19
B. M. McMillan not out	87		
S. M. Pollock c Blewett b Kasprowicz	40		
L. Klusener c Warne b MacGill	38	– (5) b MacGill.	0
P. L. Symcox lbw b S. R. Waugh	54	– (6) c Healy b MacGill.	2
L-b 8, w 2, n-b 1	11	N-b 1	1

1/140 (1) 2/148 (2) 3/160 (3) 4/269 (5)   517   1/80 (2) 2/133 (3)   (6 wkts dec.) 193
5/275 (4) 6/286 (7) 7/305 (6)   3/155 (4) 4/155 (5)
8/374 (9) 9/443 (10) 10/517 (11)   5/157 (6) 6/165 (7)

Bowling: *First Innings*—Kasprowicz 39-7-125-3; Bichel 35-10-103-1; Warne 33-6-95-2; MacGill 29-7-112-2; M. E. Waugh 6-1-21-0; Blewett 14-5-26-1; S. R. Waugh 10-3-27-1. *Second Innings*—Kasprowicz 18-5-55-2; Bichel 14-2-51-0; S. R. Waugh 4-1-13-0; Warne 15-2-52-1; MacGill 7-1-22-3.

Australia

*M. A. Taylor not out.	169	– (2) b Klusener	6
M. T. G. Elliott c Kallis b Pollock	8	– (1) c Richardson b Pollock	4
G. S. Blewett c Bacher b Pollock	31	– b Pollock	16
M. E. Waugh c Gibbs b Pollock	63	– not out	115
S. R. Waugh c Richardson b Pollock	6	– c Richardson b Klusener	34
R. T. Ponting b Klusener	26	– c Symcox b Klusener	23
†I. A. Healy c and b Pollock	1	– c Richardson b Kallis	10
A. J. Bichel c Symcox b Pollock	0	– lbw b Klusener.	7
S. K. Warne c Richardson b Pollock	0	– not out	4
M. S. Kasprowicz c Symcox b Kallis	17		
S. C. G. MacGill b Symcox	10		
B 2, l-b 12, n-b 5	19	B 2, n-b 6.	8

1/15 (2) 2/71 (3) 3/197 (4) 4/207 (5)   350   1/6 (1) 2/17 (2) 3/54 (3)   (7 wkts) 227
5/263 (6) 6/273 (7) 7/279 (8)   4/112 (5) 5/185 (6)
8/279 (9) 9/317 (10) 10/350 (11)   6/202 (7) 7/215 (8)

Bowling: *First Innings*—Pollock 41-11-87-7; McMillan 23-5-60-0; Kallis 18-5-45-1; Klusener 27-6-104-1; Symcox 13.5-3-40-1. *Second Innings*—Pollock 30.4-12-61-2; Klusener 30-10-67-4; Kallis 16-10-20-1; Symcox 18-2-42-0; McMillan 13-2-33-0; Cronje 1-0-2-0.

Umpires: D. B. Cowie (New Zealand) and S. G. Randell.
Referee: R. S. Madugalle (Sri Lanka).

THE ZIMBABWEANS IN SRI LANKA AND NEW ZEALAND, 1997-98

By SA'ADI THAWFEEQ and DON CAMERON

Zimbabwe started 1998 with tours of Sri Lanka and New Zealand, playing two Tests against each. It was a disheartening experience: they lost all four Tests, and all but one of the eight accompanying internationals. In fact, Zimbabwe produced some encouraging performances in Sri Lanka, and were convinced they would have won the Second Test but for a string of decisions which went against them. This setback affected their morale, and they lost the ensuing New Zealand Tests by wide margins.

Zimbabwe's mini-Test series in Sri Lanka was their second on the island in 16 months. Although it produced the same result – 2-0 in favour of Sri Lanka – this series was much more closely contested. Whereas both Tests played in September 1996 ended inside four days, Zimbabwe forced these two into a fifth. Their fighting qualities showed as they tackled Sri Lanka's spin kingpin Muttiah Muralitharan in helpful conditions. Zimbabwe were especially unlucky in the Second Test, when they came quite close to achieving their first win overseas. They were the more aggrieved because the umpires had turned down numerous appeals for lbw and for catches at the wicket during the crucial stages of Sri Lanka's run-chase. Coach David Houghton's comments on the umpiring earned him a fine and a two-match suspension.

A double-century by Marvan Atapattu at Kandy and an unbeaten 143 from Aravinda de Silva at Sinhalese Sports Club in Colombo turned out to be the decisive innings for Sri Lanka. Meanwhile off-spinner Muralitharan, with 17 wickets at 15.41, remained Zimbabwe's nemesis – he routed them in the previous series with 14.

The emergence of Murray Goodwin as a solid front-line batsman was one of the plus points for Zimbabwe. Goodwin, who had returned to his native country after playing a couple of seasons for Western Australia, walked straight into the team and scored seventies in both Tests. He took the place of Houghton, who had retired from international cricket to concentrate on coaching the side. Vice-captain Andy Flower confirmed his status as a serious international batsman by scoring the only century for his country in the series.

The ease with which the Sri Lankan batsmen tackled the Zimbabwean spinners put captain Alistair Campbell in a spot. He was forced to fall back on rugged fast bowler Heath Streak for wickets. Streak did not fail him, and gave Zimbabwe an outside chance of victory when he snapped up four cheap wickets in the second innings of the Colombo Test.

While Zimbabwe showed a marked improvement in the longer game, they were completely outplayed by world champions Sri Lanka in one-day cricket, and were whitewashed 3-0. It was the first time in their history that Sri Lanka had made a clean sweep of both Test and one-day series, apart from 1992-93, when they won a one-off Test and two limited-overs games against England. – S.T.

Zimbabwe arrived in New Zealand to contest what was arguably a battle between Test cricket's two weakest nations: frequent reminders of their humble status – at the foot of the Wisden World Championship – had begun to rankle with New Zealand. Having beaten Sri Lanka 2-0 a year before, they felt that, in these two Tests against Zimbabwe, they could show the world that they deserved a higher rating. They duly won the First Test by ten wickets in four days and the Second by an innings in three.

Though the Sri Lankan team they beat in 1996-97 was under-prepared, and the Zimbabweans were below strength, an analysis of Stephen Fleming's first year as captain made encouraging reading for New Zealand. They played nine Tests, won four (all at home), drew three and lost two (both to Australia).

Zimbabwe arrived knowing that their batting line-up was shaky and that they would rely heavily on the seam bowling of Heath Streak and the leg-spin of Paul Strang and Adam Huckle. But Streak was unable to shake off a nagging leg injury and the new-ball attack lacked penetration. In the one-day series, Zimbabwe did better than the margin of 4-1 might suggest, but, in the Tests, the bowlers failed to make a competition of it. To compound matters, Campbell won two important tosses only to make dubious decisions.

There was plenty to encourage the New Zealand team, with several younger players developing well during the series. Matthew Horne followed up his maiden Test hundred in Australia with 44 at Wellington and 157 at Auckland. Craig McMillan, too, built on the promising form he had shown on the Australian tour by scoring his first Test century, full of dazzling strokes, at Basin Reserve. Senior players also regained their touch: Nathan Astle hit an elegant hundred at Eden Park, Simon Doull was clearly back to Test form and Chris Cairns shrugged off his injured ankle. Adam Parore kept wicket tidily and contributed usefully with the bat, while Dion Nash found some of the aggression he had displayed before his back injury, sustained in 1996.

For Zimbabwe, matters were distinctly less encouraging. They had neither the incisive bowling nor the consistent batting demanded by Test cricket. – D.C.

ZIMBABWEAN TOURING PARTY

A. D. R. Campbell (Mashonaland) (*captain*), A. Flower (Mashonaland) (*vice-captain*), G. W. Flower (Mashonaland), M. W. Goodwin (Mashonaland), A. G. Huckle (Matabeleland), E. Matambanadzo (Mashonaland), M. Mbangwa (Matabeleland), H. K. Olonga (Matabeleland), G. J. Rennie (Mashonaland), J. A. Rennie (Matabeleland), P. A. Strang (Mashonaland), B. C. Strang (Mashonaland), H. H. Streak (Matabeleland), A. R. Whittall (Matabeleland), G. J. Whittall (Matabeleland), C. B. Wishart (Mashonaland).

D. P. Viljoen (Mashonaland A) replaced the injured B. C. Strang.

Manager: A. J. Pycroft.   *Coach:* D. L. Houghton.

ZIMBABWEAN TOUR RESULTS

Test matches – Played 4: Lost 4.

First-class matches – Played 7: Won 1, Lost 5, Drawn 1.

Win – Canterbury.

Losses – Sri Lanka (2), New Zealand (2), New Zealand A.

Draw – Board President's XI.

One-day internationals – Played 8: Won 1, Lost 7. *Win* – New Zealand. *Losses* – Sri Lanka (3), New Zealand (4).

Other non-first-class matches – Played 2: Won 1, Lost 1. *Win* – New Zealand Academy XI. *Loss* – Board President's XI.

Note: Matches in this section which were not first-class are signified by a dagger.

At Matara, January 2, 4, 5. Drawn. Toss: Zimbabweans. Zimbabweans 311 for six dec. (G. W. Flower 58, M. W. Goodwin 52, A. Flower 101 not out, A. D. R. Campbell 39; T. T. Samaraweera four for 90); Board President's XI 313 for eight dec. (M. N. Nawaz 111, S. I. de Saram 56).

SRI LANKA v ZIMBABWE

First Test Match

At Kandy, January 7, 8, 9, 10, 11. Sri Lanka won by eight wickets. Toss: Sri Lanka. Test debut: M. W. Goodwin.

Off-spinner Muralitharan returned what were then the best match figures by a Sri Lankan bowler in Test cricket – 12 for 117 – to dismiss Zimbabwe for 140 and 338. Combined with a double-century from Atapattu, that was quite enough to give Sri Lanka a 1-0 lead in the short series. It was their first victory in 12 Tests since they beat Zimbabwe on the previous tour in September 1996.

Zimbabwe had been kept on the field until the final session of the second day, by which time Sri Lanka had taken full advantage of first lease of a pitch expected to help the spinners later in the match. The innings began shakily: Jayasuriya and Mahanama, who had shared a stand of 576 against India in August, both fell in single figures during Streak's opening spell.

But de Silva then joined Atapattu to share a third-wicket stand of 140. De Silva, scorer of seven Test centuries and 1,220 runs in 1997, continued his brilliant progress with an impeccable 75 before mistiming a drive off leg-spinner Huckle. Atapattu had scored his maiden Test century in India seven weeks earlier; now he followed it with a double-hundred in his 13th Test. Batting stylishly and playing strokes straight out of the textbook, he compiled an elegant 223, in 597 minutes and 446 balls, with one six and 29 fours. His only blemish was on 217, when wicket-keeper Andy Flower failed to stump him off Paul Strang. By then, Sri Lanka were well on their way towards a hefty total. Atapattu's was the first double-century made at the Asgiriya Stadium in a Test – the previous highest score was 143 not out by Australia's David Hookes in 1982-83.

Zimbabwe finished the second day at 46 for two, losing Grant Flower and debutant Murray Goodwin cheaply. Next day the slide continued. Only two batsmen made it into double figures: Rennie, who stayed 281 minutes for just 53, and Paul Strang, with 35. Zimbabwe were bowled out for 140, shortly after tea on the third day, as Muralitharan, with his tenth five-wicket haul in Tests, and his fellow-spinner Silva ran through the batting.

Forced to follow on, 329 runs in arrears, Zimbabwe put up sterner resistance. They batted throughout the fourth day, with the fightback being led by 25-year-old Goodwin, who stroked a fine 70 in 191 minutes, and Andy Flower, who batted four hours for 67 but hit only one boundary. The innings was finally terminated in the first hour of the fifth morning. Muralitharan ended up with seven for 94, his best Test figures, giving him 12 in the match. That beat the previous best Test return by a Sri Lankan, ten for 90 by Chaminda Vaas against New Zealand at Napier in 1994-95.

Left with the formality of scoring ten runs for victory, Sri Lanka were mildly embarrassed to lose Jayasuriya and Mahanama again to Streak – for ducks this time – in the first over. But, fittingly, Atapattu and de Silva completed the win in the second.

Man of the Match: M. Muralitharan.

Close of play: First day, Sri Lanka 265-4 (M. S. Atapattu 129*, H. P. Tillekeratne 11*); Second day, Zimbabwe 46-2 (G. J. Rennie 23*, A. Flower 8*); Third day, Zimbabwe 71-2 (M. W. Goodwin 1*, A. R. Whittall 2*); Fourth day, Zimbabwe 289-7 (P. A. Strang 13*, H. H. Streak 6*).

Sri Lanka

S. T. Jayasuriya lbw b Streak	6	– lbw b Streak	0
M. S. Atapattu c Campbell b P. A. Strang	223	– not out	6
R. S. Mahanama c Campbell b Streak	7	– b Streak	0
P. A. de Silva c Whittall b Huckle	75	– not out	4
*A. Ranatunga b Whittall	27		
H. P. Tillekeratne c and b Whittall	44		
†R. S. Kaluwitharana c and b Whittall	29		
W. P. U. J. C. Vaas c Rennie b P. A. Strang	26		
M. Muralitharan c B. C. Strang b P. A. Strang	17		
K. R. Pushpakumara not out	2		
B 2, l-b 2, n-b 9	13		

1/16 (1) 2/33 (3) 3/173 (4)   (9 wkts dec.) 469   1/0 (1) 2/0 (3)   (2 wkts) 10
4/226 (5) 5/321 (6) 6/383 (7)
7/440 (2) 8/461 (8) 9/469 (9)

K. J. Silva did not bat.

Bowling: *First Innings*—Streak 34–11–96–2; B. C. Strang 30–7–78–0; P. A. Strang 35.3–10–123–3; Whittall 30–4–73–3; Huckle 21–3–88–1; Goodwin 4–2–7–0. *Second Innings*—Streak 1–0–4–2; B. C. Strang 0.5–0–6–0.

Zimbabwe

G. J. Rennie c de Silva b Silva	53	– lbw b Muralitharan	24
G. W. Flower b Muralitharan	4	– b de Silva	38
M. W. Goodwin lbw b Silva	2	– b Muralitharan	70
†A. Flower b Vaas	8	– (5) c Mahanama b Muralitharan	67
*A. D. R. Campbell c Mahanama b Pushpakumara	7	– (6) lbw b Vaas	40
C. B. Wishart c Mahanama b Muralitharan	3	– (7) b Muralitharan	0
P. A. Strang c de Silva b Muralitharan	35	– (8) c sub (R. P. Arnold) b Muralitharan	33
H. H. Streak b Muralitharan	5	– (9) c Kaluwitharana b Pushpakumara	13
A. R. Whittall not out	6	– (4) b Muralitharan	14
B. C. Strang b Muralitharan	2	– not out	15
A. G. Huckle lbw b Silva	0	– lbw b Muralitharan	0
B 6, l-b 2, n-b 7	15	B 5, l-b 11, n-b 8	24

1/29 (2) 2/36 (3) 3/46 (4) 4/72 (5)   140   1/68 (2) 2/68 (1) 3/103 (4)   338
5/75 (6) 6/119 (1) 7/127 (7)   4/185 (3) 5/261 (5) 6/261 (7)
8/134 (8) 9/136 (10) 10/140 (11)   7/271 (6) 8/297 (9)
                                                                        9/334 (8) 10/338 (11)

Bowling: *First Innings*—Vaas 17–4–36–1; Pushpakumara 14–5–34–1; Muralitharan 29–18–23–5; Silva 19.4–9–27–3; de Silva 5–0–12–0; Jayasuriya 1–1–0–0. *Second Innings*—Vaas 24–3–65–1; Pushpakumara 19–2–64–1; Muralitharan 42.5–13–94–7; de Silva 13–5–25–1; Silva 11–2–35–0; Jayasuriya 16–0–38–0; Atapattu 1–0–1–0.

Umpires: M. J. Kitchen (England) and B. C. Cooray.   Referee: R. Subba Row (England).

SRI LANKA v ZIMBABWE

Second Test Match

At Sinhalese Sports Club, Colombo, January 14, 15, 16, 17, 18. Sri Lanka won by five wickets. Toss: Zimbabwe.

Sri Lanka's two most experienced cricketers, de Silva and Ranatunga, shared a partnership of 189 – a Sri Lankan sixth-wicket Test record – to reach 326, their highest fourth-innings total to win a Test. De Silva made an undefeated 143, his 16th Test century and first against Zimbabwe, and Ranatunga 87 not out as Sri Lanka took the series 2-0.

But Zimbabwe could consider themselves unlucky, having come close to their first overseas Test victory. After they set Sri Lanka a target of 326 in five sessions, Streak took four wickets to reduce them to 137 for five. Several times during the ensuing de Silva–Ranatunga stand, the Zimbabweans were most unhappy with decisions in the batsmen's favour, from K. T. Francis and Pakistan's Salim Badar. Zimbabwe's captain, Campbell, commented wryly: "I don't think Sri Lanka played all that well to win. We didn't play all that badly to lose." His coach, David Houghton, was more outspoken. "I feel like the umpires raped us," he was quoted as saying. Later he said he did not mind about being fined: "It's worth it to let the world know what really happened." Referee Raman Subba Row was forced to take different action to keep the peace and banned him from the ground during two of the one-day internationals that followed.

De Silva hit two sixes and 16 fours in an innings which must rank as one of his best, because of the pressure. He batted for 459 minutes and faced 313 balls. At 90, he reached 1,000 runs in his ten Tests on the Sinhalese Sports Club ground; his hundred was his fifth in his last six Test innings there. Ranatunga, handicapped by a back strain which kept him off the field during Zimbabwe's second innings, batted more than five hours, mostly with the aid of a runner. He hit 12 fours.

Finding themselves short of spinners to provide contrast to Muralitharan, Sri Lanka had recalled 31-year-old slow left-armer Don Anurasiri for his first Test in four years. He responded with three wickets on the opening day, including top scorer Goodwin. Zimbabwe declined from 110 for one to 251 all out early on the second morning. But before the close, leg-spinner Strang gave them an unlikely first-innings lead of 26: he took four wickets. Jayasuriya and Mahanama failed to reach double figures for the third time running and Sri Lanka's line-up, like Zimbabwe's, managed only two fifties between them.

Zimbabwe built on their narrow lead, thanks chiefly to Andy Flower. He came in when the fourth wicket fell at 117 and batted throughout the rest of the innings, reaching his fourth Test century with a reverse sweep for four to third man. He was to remain unbeaten on 105, in 336 minutes with one six and ten fours. Vaas could not bowl because of measles, but Muralitharan continued to set national records; when he dismissed Wishart, he became the first Sri Lankan to take 150 Test wickets, in his 36th match.

Sri Lanka began their run-chase disastrously when the pace attack removed two batsmen without scoring. Jayasuriya and de Silva stopped the slide with an entertaining 105 runs in 117 minutes. Jayasuriya was dismissed by Streak for the fourth time in four innings, but at least he made runs this time: a hard-hit 68, including two sixes and eight fours. Streak struck twice more to have Sri Lanka struggling, 188 behind with five wickets left. But that was as close as Zimbabwe got to victory; de Silva and Ranatunga took complete control of the game from there onwards.

Man of the Match: P. A. de Silva.   *Man of the Series:* M. Muralitharan.

Close of play: First day, Zimbabwe 251-9 (A. R. Whittall 1*, M. Mbangwa 0*); Second day, Zimbabwe 24-1 (G. W. Flower 10*, A. R. Whittall 0*); Third day, Zimbabwe 241-6 (A. Flower 61*, C. B. Wishart 14*); Fourth day, Sri Lanka 209-5 (P. A. de Silva 87*, A. Ranatunga 29*).

Zimbabwe

G. J. Rennie c Kaluwitharana b Muralitharan	50	– c Kaluwitharana b de Silva	12
G. W. Flower b Pushpakumara	41	– b Jayasuriya	52
M. W. Goodwin b Anurasiri	73	– (4) b Jayasuriya	39
G. J. Whittall run out	11	– (5) c sub (D. P. M. D. Jayawardene) b Muralitharan	17
†A. Flower c and b Anurasiri	8	– (6) not out	105
*A. D. R. Campbell c Kaluwitharana b Vaas	44	– (7) c Kaluwitharana b Anurasiri	37
C. B. Wishart lbw b Muralitharan	2	– (8) c Kaluwitharana b Pushpakumara	18
P. A. Strang c Pushpakumara b Anurasiri	5	– (9) b Muralitharan	3
H. H. Streak b Vaas	3	– (10) run out	1
A. R. Whittall not out	1	– (3) c Tillekeratne b de Silva	2
M. Mbangwa lbw b Pushpakumara	0	– c de Silva b Muralitharan	4
L-b 3, w 1, n-b 9	13	L-b 6, w 1, n-b 2	9
	251		**299**

1/70 (2) 2/110 (1) 3/144 (4) 4/174 (5)   251
5/201 (3) 6/206 (7) 7/223 (8)
8/240 (9) 9/249 (6) 10/251 (11)

1/22 (1) 2/34 (3) 3/104 (4)   299
4/117 (2) 5/129 (5) 6/204 (7)
7/267 (8) 8/284 (9)
9/286 (10) 10/299 (11)

Bowling: First Innings—Vaas 12–1–35–2; Pushpakumara 12.2–2–43–2; de Silva 7–1–33–0; Muralitharan 32–10–72–2; Anurasiri 27–7–65–3. *Second Innings*—Pushpakumara 17–2–54–1; de Silva 23–4–61–2; Muralitharan 37.5–9–73–3; Anurasiri 19–7–41–1; Jayasuriya 29–9–64–2.

Sri Lanka

S. T. Jayasuriya c G. J. Whittall b Streak	5	– c A. Flower b Streak	68
M. S. Atapattu c A. Flower b Strang	48	– c A. Flower b Streak	0
R. S. Mahanama b Mbangwa	8	– lbw b Mbangwa	0
P. A. de Silva c and b Streak	27	– not out	143
*A. Ranatunga c Streak b Strang	52	– (7) not out	87
H. P. Tillekeratne c Rennie b A. R. Whittall	7	– (5) lbw b Streak	0
†R. S. Kaluwitharana c A. Flower b Strang	51	– (6) c Campbell b Streak	4
S. D. Anurasiri not out	3		
M. Muralitharan c A. Flower b Mbangwa	11		
K. R. Pushpakumara b Strang	1		
W. P. U. J. C. Vaas absent ill			
L-b 11, w 1	12	B 11, l-b 13	24

1/12 (1) 2/43 (3) 3/91 (4) 4/91 (2)   **225**   1/1 (2) 2/10 (3) 3/115 (1)   (5 wkts) **326**
5/130 (6) 6/198 (7) 7/213 (5)   4/115 (5) 5/137 (6)
8/224 (9) 9/225 (10)

Bowling: First Innings—Streak 15–5–28–2; Mbangwa 16–4–61–2; G. J. Whittall 3–0–18–0; Strang 19.5–2–77–4; A. R. Whittall 20–6–30–1. *Second Innings*—Streak 25–6–84–4; Mbangwa 14–4–34–1; A. R. Whittall 43–10–93–0; Strang 24–4–75–0; G. J. Whittall 7–1–12–0; Goodwin 0.5–0–4–0.

Umpires: Salim Badar (Pakistan) and K. T. Francis. Referee: R. Subba Row (England).

†At Moratuwa, January 20. Board President's XI won by four wickets. Toss: Zimbabweans. Zimbabweans 244 for six (50 overs) (G. W. Flower 37, A. Flower 67, M. W. Goodwin 41, C. B. Wishart 37); Board President's XI 245 for six (47.1 overs) (S. T. Jayasuriya 55, D. P. M. D. Jayawardene 87 not out, Extras 32).

†SRI LANKA v ZIMBABWE

First One-Day International

At Sinhalese Sports Club, Colombo, January 22. Sri Lanka won by five wickets. Toss: Sri Lanka.

Leg-spinner Chandana justified his selection ahead of batsman Mahela Jayawardene by returning career-best figures of four for 31 to set up a comfortable victory. Sent in first, Zimbabwe were bowled out in the 49th over. Guy Whittall scored 52 off 70 balls, but the rest were tied down by spin. In reply, Jayasuriya and Atapattu hurried to 66 in 14 overs, paving the way for Ranatunga to put the finishing touches with an unbeaten fifty. He passed the target with his second six, hit over mid-wicket.

Man of the Match: A. Ranatunga.

Zimbabwe

G. W. Flower c and b Dharmasena	40	H. H. Streak not out	7
†A. Flower c Mahanama b Pushpakumara	1	J. A. Rennie b Dharmasena	2
M. W. Goodwin c de Silva b Pushpakumara	1	A. R. Whittall lbw b Chandana	5
G. J. Whittall c Mahanama b Jayasuriya	52	L-b 6, w 3, n-b 1	10
*A. D. R. Campbell c and b Chandana	36		
C. B. Wishart b Chandana	41	1/2 2/7 3/67	(48.4 overs) **207**
P. A. Strang c and b Muralitharan	3	4/118 5/173 6/180	
G. J. Rennie lbw b Chandana	9	7/180 8/193 9/198	

Bowling: Vaas 7–0–21–0; Pushpakumara 7–3–30–2; Dharmasena 10–0–29–2; Muralitharan 10–0–55–1; Chandana 7.4–0–31–4; Jayasuriya 7–0–35–1.

Sri Lanka

S. T. Jayasuriya st A. Flower b Strang . .	47	U. D. U. Chandana not out 16
M. S. Atapattu b J. A. Rennie	26	
R. S. Mahanama c Streak b G. W. Flower	39	
P. A. de Silva c and b Strang	5	L-b 2, w 2 4
*A. Ranatunga not out	58	
†R. S. Kaluwitharana c sub (M. Mbangwa)		1/66 2/81 3/91 (5 wkts, 45.2 overs) 210
b G. W. Flower .	15	4/146 5/183

H. D. P. K. Dharmasena, M. Muralitharan, K. R. Pushpakumara and W. P. U. J. C. Vaas did not bat.

Bowling: Streak 7–0–35–0; J. A. Rennie 7–0–25–1; A. R. Whittall 9–0–40–0; Strang 10–2–36–2; Goodwin 5–0–21–0; G. W. Flower 7.2–0–51–2.

Umpires: P. Manuel and D. N. Pathirana.

†SRI LANKA v ZIMBABWE

Second One-Day International

At R. Premadasa Stadium, Colombo, January 24. Sri Lanka won by five wickets. Toss: Zimbabwe.

Once more, Zimbabwe's batsmen struggled against spin. They were restricted to a modest 212, despite a century by Goodwin in only his second one-day international. He scored 111 in 134 balls, and added 105 with Grant Flower. But only one other batsman reached double figures. Jayasuriya and Atapattu once more set the tone of Sri Lanka's reply, opening with 76 in 19 overs, and the home side were never in danger.

Man of the Match: M. W. Goodwin.

Zimbabwe

G. W. Flower b Jayasuriya	51	H. H. Streak run out 4
†A. Flower b Pushpakumara	2	J. A. Rennie not out 4
M. W. Goodwin b Chandana	111	
G. J. Whittall b Chandana	13	L-b 6, w 3, n-b 2 11
*A. D. R. Campbell c Jayasuriya		
b Muralitharan .	6	1/3 2/108 3/143 (8 wkts, 50 overs) 212
C. B. Wishart run out	6	4/165 5/187 6/203
P. A. Strang c Mahanama b Jayasuriya . .	4	7/204 8/212

A. R. Whittall and M. Mbangwa did not bat.

Bowling: Pushpakumara 7–0–26–1; de Silva 4–0–14–0; Dharmasena 10–2–28–0; Muralitharan 10–0–43–1; Jayasuriya 10–0–53–2; Chandana 9–0–42–2.

Sri Lanka

S. T. Jayasuriya c Streak b A. R. Whittall	50	D. P. M. D. Jayawardene not out. 1
M. S. Atapattu c Strang b G. W. Flower.	45	
R. S. Mahanama run out	52	L-b 6, w 4, n-b 1 11
P. A. de Silva st A. Flower b Strang . .	3	
*A. Ranatunga c and b A. R. Whittall . .	43	1/76 2/118 3/127 (5 wkts, 48.2 overs) 213
†R. S. Kaluwitharana not out	8	4/194 5/212

U. D. U. Chandana, H. D. P. K. Dharmasena, M. Muralitharan and K. R. Pushpakumara did not bat.

Bowling: Streak 8–0–37–0; Rennie 10–0–43–0; A. R. Whittall 8.2–0–33–2; Mbangwa 8–0–42–0; Strang 6–0–18–1; G. W. Flower 6–0–22–1; Campbell 2–0–12–0.

Umpires: I. Anandappa and W. A. U. Wickremasinghe.

†SRI LANKA v ZIMBABWE

Third One-Day International

At Sinhalese Sports Club, Colombo, January 26. Sri Lanka won by four wickets. Toss: Zimbabwe. International debuts: D. A. Gunawardene, M. N. Nawaz.

Jayasuriya made a memorable debut as captain of Sri Lanka – after an inauspicious start – scoring a run-a-ball century to ensure a clean sweep. Sri Lanka rested five senior players, including Ranatunga, but their young blood had enough ammunition to overhaul Zimbabwe's best batting of the series. Riding on Grant Flower's maiden one-day international century and a stand of 144 with brother Andy, Zimbabwe rattled up 281 for six. But Sri Lanka responded magnificently. Jayasuriya, who had lost the toss, put down two catches and conceded 66 runs off his ten overs, came good, with his seventh century in 150 one-day internationals. Later, Jayawardene, playing only his second, maintained the momentum with a stylish 74.

Man of the Match: S. T. Jayasuriya.   *Man of the Series:* S. T. Jayasuriya.

Zimbabwe

G. W. Flower c Kalpage b Chandana	...	112
C. B. Wishart c Gunawardene b Kalpage		45
M. W. Goodwin c Chandana b Jayasuriya		18
†A. Flower c Kaluwitharana b Dharmasena	.	68
G. J. Whittall c de Silva b Dharmasena	.	3
*A. D. R. Campbell st Kaluwitharana b Dharmasena		9
P. A. Strang not out	....	6
H. H. Streak not out	....	2
B 2, l-b 8, w 7, n-b 1	......	18

1/82 2/114 3/258   (6 wkts, 50 overs) 281
4/264 5/273 6/274

A. R. Whittall, A. G. Huckle and J. A. Rennie did not bat.

Bowling: Pushpakumara 6–0–34–0; de Silva 6–0–39–0; Dharmasena 10–0–47–3; Kalpage 10–1–34–1; Jayasuriya 10–0–66–1; Chandana 8–0–51–1.

Sri Lanka

*S. T. Jayasuriya st A. Flower b G. J. Whittall	.	102
D. A. Gunawardene b A. R. Whittall	...	12
M. N. Nawaz c Goodwin b Strang	....	5
D. P. M. D. Jayawardene c Huckle b G. W. Flower	.	74
R. S. Kalpage run out	....	37
†R. S. Kaluwitharana c Huckle b G. W. Flower	.	13
H. D. P. K. Dharmasena not out	......	9
U. D. U. Chandana not out	....	14
B 1, l-b 4, w 13, n-b 2	.....	20

1/46 2/87   (6 wkts, 49 overs) 286
3/160 4/233
5/255 6/266

R. P. Arnold, K. S. C. de Silva and K. R. Pushpakumara did not bat.

Bowling: Streak 2–0–21–0; Rennie 5–0–43–0; A. R. Whittall 10–0–46–1; Strang 10–0–54–1; G. W. Flower 7–0–36–2; Huckle 10–0–44–0; G. J. Whittall 4–0–23–1; Campbell 1–0–14–0.

Umpires: P. Manuel and D. M. Samarasinghe.   Series referee: R. Subba Row (England).

†At Taupo, February 3. Zimbabweans won by eight wickets. Toss: Zimbabweans. New Zealand Academy XI 193 (48.3 overs) (C. D. Cumming 41, M. S. Sinclair 51; M. Mbangwa three for 29, A. R. Whittall three for 24); Zimbabweans 195 for two (36.5 overs) (G. W. Flower 54, M. W. Goodwin 66 not out, A. Flower 35 not out).

†NEW ZEALAND v ZIMBABWE

First One-Day International

At Hamilton, February 4. New Zealand won by 40 runs. Toss: New Zealand. International debut:
L. G. Howell.

Llorne Howell, on debut, and Astle put on a lusty 73 in the first 15 overs, but New Zealand
then stumbled until Cairns hit four sixes in his 36-ball innings. He added 75 in 14 overs with
Harris. Zimbabwe also started well and, as long as Andy Flower survived, had the match in their
sights. But Vettori had him stumped in one of two inspired spells of left-arm spin which brought
four wickets and turned things around. Asked to score at ten an over, the tail capitulated.

Man of the Match: C. Z. Harris.

New Zealand

L. G. Howell c and b Strang	24		D. J. Nash c Wishart b Streak		8
N. J. Astle c G. W. Flower b Strang	49		S. B. Doull not out		0
†A. C. Parore c Goodwin b Strang	14		L-b 9, w 7		16
*S. P. Fleming c Rennie b A. R. Whittall	26				—
C. D. McMillan b A. R. Whittall	16		1/73 2/91 3/107	(7 wkts, 50 overs)	248
C. L. Cairns c Goodwin b Mbangwa	43		4/144 5/144		
C. Z. Harris not out	52		6/219 7/240		

D. L. Vettori and S. B. O'Connor did not bat.

Bowling: Streak 10–0–42–1; Mbangwa 9–1–63–1; Rennie 9–0–45–0; Strang 10–0–40–3; A. R.
Whittall 10–0–39–2; G. W. Flower 2–0–10–0.

Zimbabwe

G. W. Flower c and b Harris	32		J. A. Rennie run out		0
C. B. Wishart c Astle b Vettori	37		A. R. Whittall b Vettori		0
M. W. Goodwin c Astle b Vettori	7		M. Mbangwa c Cairns b O'Connor		3
†A. Flower st Parore b Vettori	60		L-b 8, w 4, n-b 2		14
G. J. Whittall c and b Harris	12				—
*A. D. R. Campbell run out	22		1/75 2/75 3/90	(48.2 overs)	208
P. A. Strang c Vettori b Nash	5		4/113 5/170 6/182		
H. H. Streak not out	16		7/189 8/190 9/191		

Bowling: O'Connor 8.2–1–34–1; Cairns 4–1–10–0; Doull 5–0–21–0; Nash 7–0–24–1; Harris
10–0–47–2; Vettori 10–0–49–4; Astle 4–0–15–0.

Umpires: R. S. Dunne and C. E. King.

†NEW ZEALAND v ZIMBABWE

Second One-Day International

At Wellington, February 6. New Zealand won by eight wickets. Toss: New Zealand.

Zimbabwe's top order fell to risky strokes – and New Zealand were soon in control. Despite
a slow recovery from the later batsmen, the total limped to just 138. O'Connor profited from the
erratic batting to take five for 39, and Harris claimed his 100th victim in his 98th one-day
international when he held a return catch from Guy Whittall. Streak counter-attacked with an early
wicket, but a 103-run stand from Astle and Parore carried New Zealand to an easy win.

Man of the Match: S. B. O'Connor.

Zimbabwe

G. W. Flower c and b Doull	11	H. H. Streak c Parore b O'Connor	10
C. B. Wishart c Astle b O'Connor	0	J. A. Rennie b O'Connor	5
M. W. Goodwin c Fleming b O'Connor	3	A. R. Whittall not out	1
†A. Flower c McMillan b Cairns	0	L-b 4, w 5, n-b 1	10
*A. D. R. Campbell c Harris b O'Connor	23		
G. J. Whittall c and b Harris	31	1/1 2/6 3/7	(49 overs) 138
D. P. Viljoen c Parore b Doull	36	4/23 5/48 6/114	
P. A. Strang b Nash	8	7/114 8/131 9/133	

Bowling: O'Connor 10–1–39–5; Cairns 7–2–10–1; Nash 7–1–14–1; Doull 10–1–26–2; Astle 5–1–16–0; Harris 10–2–29–1.

New Zealand

L. G. Howell c Wishart b Streak	7
N. J. Astle run out	67
†A. C. Parore not out	36
*S. P. Fleming not out	17
B 2, 1-b 4, w 5, n-b 1	12

1/18 2/121   (2 wkts, 28.2 overs) 139

C. D. McMillan, C. L. Cairns, C. Z. Harris, D. J. Nash, S. B. Doull, D. L. Vettori and S. B. O'Connor did not bat.

Bowling: Streak 7–0–20–1; Rennie 5–0–27–0; Strang 6–0–30–0; A. R. Whittall 5–0–40–0; G. J. Whittall 5.2–1–16–0.

Umpires: C. E. King and E. A. Watkin.

At Dunedin, February 8, 9, 10. New Zealand A won by an innings and nine runs. Toss: New Zealand A. Zimbabweans 67 (C. J. Drum four for 18, A. R. Tait five for 16) and 195 (M. W. Goodwin 78; C. J. Drum five for 65, H. T. Davis three for 50); New Zealand A 271 for eight dec. (M. D. Bell 50, C. M. Spearman 76, R. G. Twose 69; M. Mbangwa four for 49).

Zimbabwe's total of 67 was the second lowest by a Test-playing nation in New Zealand. The lowest is 64 by England in the Wellington Test of 1977-78.

At Timaru, February 13, 14, 15, 16. Zimbabweans won by an innings and 56 runs. Toss: Canterbury. Canterbury 100 (P. A. Strang four for 20) and 266 (C. D. Cumming 86, H. T. G. James 50, S. J. Pawson 36; P. A. Strang three for 38); Zimbabweans 422 for eight dec. (G. W. Flower 64, A. D. R. Campbell 196, P. A. Strang 93).

In Canterbury's first innings, Strang's full figures were 22–12–20–4. He and Campbell then put on 261 for the Zimbabweans' seventh wicket. After the first day, Glenn Muir replaced Mark Priest, summoned to play a one-day international against Australia, in Canterbury's line-up.

NEW ZEALAND v ZIMBABWE

First Test Match

At Wellington, February 19, 20, 21, 22. New Zealand won by ten wickets. Toss: Zimbabwe.

After rain had cut 24 overs from the first day's play, Campbell unexpectedly chose to bat, presumably hoping that his strong complement of spin bowlers would trouble New Zealand in the fourth innings. But by underestimating the dangers in the moist pitch, he joined the long list of captains to have misread a rain-affected Basin Reserve wicket.

Zimbabwe's cause was not helped by the top order taking extraordinary risks. Against an unexceptional opening attack, batsmen threw away wickets with a series of poor shots. Campbell tried to repair the damage but, after two hours' stubborn resistance, went for a suicidal run and was dismissed for 37. The next morning, Streak helped lift the score to 180, before becoming one of O'Connor's four victims, but this was not the total Campbell had had in mind when he won the toss.

There were 70 overs remaining for New Zealand on the second day, and they made much better use of them. Horne batted solidly for 44, while Parore made an elegant 78. By stumps, New Zealand were comfortably placed at 176 for three. The stage was left for McMillan, the dashing young right-hander, to play his bold strokes on a pitch that had lost all its venom. At lunch, he had moved smartly to 49. Then he began his attack in earnest. He had shown scant regard for Shane Warne in Australia, and he showed even less for the leg-spinners here. McMillan reached his hundred with a six off Huckle (after an agonising wait while the umpire checked it had cleared the ropes). By the time Nash was out, they had added 108 for the seventh wicket. Eventually, Huckle took revenge, but by then McMillan had hit 18 fours and four sixes in his first Test hundred.

Strang came back with three quick wickets at the end, but New Zealand had already established a lead of 231. In the 12 overs remaining before the close, they further strengthened their hold on the match, taking two second-innings wickets for 27.

Goodwin promised to keep Zimbabwe afloat on the fourth day, batting almost four hours for his 72, and Campbell soldiered on doggedly for 56. He and Streak put on 94 for the eighth wicket, but, this partnership aside, wickets fell steadily. Cairns, seemingly untroubled by his ankle injury, took four for 56 as the Zimbabweans struggled to avoid an innings defeat.

Eventually, New Zealand were required to make 20, which they achieved during the extra half-hour of play. Had Zimbabwe fought harder, they might have stretched the Test into the fifth day, when there was heavy rain – and little chance of cricket.

In this game, the New Zealanders quickly became a professional outfit; their bowling was well organised and well directed, and backed by aggressive and accurate fielding. The batting was more variable, but there were several high-quality innings. They had easily done enough to win their third consecutive home Test.

Man of the Match: C. D. McMillan.

Close of play: First day, Zimbabwe 132-8 (H. H. Streak 9*, A. G. Huckle 1*); Second day, New Zealand 176-3 (S. P. Fleming 33*, N. J. Astle 19*); Third day, Zimbabwe 27-2 (A. R. Whittall 4*, M. W. Goodwin 2*).

Zimbabwe

G. J. Rennie b Doull	13	– lbw b Doull	15
G. W. Flower b Nash	38	– c and b Vettori	4
M. W. Goodwin lbw b Vettori	8	– (4) c Fleming b Cairns	72
G. J. Whittall c Parore b O'Connor	6	– (5) c Astle b Nash	22
†A. Flower c Parore b O'Connor	2	– (6) c O'Connor b Vettori	6
*A. D. R. Campbell run out	37	– (7) c Horne b Cairns	56
P. A. Strang c Young b Doull	1	– (8) b Cairns	0
H. H. Streak lbw b O'Connor	39	– (9) not out	43
A. R. Whittall c Parore b Cairns	1	– (3) run out	12
A. G. Huckle c Parore b O'Connor	19	– lbw b Vettori	0
M. Mbangwa not out	0	– lbw b Cairns	0
L-b 4, n-b 6	16	B 6, l-b 14	20
	180		**250**

1/30 (1) 2/53 (3) 3/64 (4) 4/70 (5)
5/78 (2) 6/89 (7) 7/122 (6)
8/131 (9) 9/171 (8) 10/180 (10)

1/18 (2) 2/20 (1) 3/65 (3)
4/110 (5) 5/125 (6) 6/155 (4)
7/155 (8) 8/249 (7)
9/249 (10) 10/250 (11)

Bowling: *First Innings*—Cairns 16–2–50–1; O'Connor 18.3–7–52–4; Doull 17–8–18–2; Nash 14–7–11–1; Vettori 20–10–39–1. *Second Innings*—Cairns 24.3–4–56–4; O'Connor 14–3–39–0; Doull 13–1–47–1; Vettori 41–18–73–3; Nash 9–6–10–1; McMillan 5–1–5–0.

New Zealand

B. A. Young c Strang b Streak	0	– (2) not out	10
M. J. Horne c A. Flower b Mbangwa	44	– (1) not out	9
†A. C. Parore c A. Flower b Huckle	78		
*S. P. Fleming c Campbell b Huckle	36		
N. J. Astle c A. Flower b Streak	42		
C. D. McMillan c A. R. Whittall b Huckle	139		
C. L. Cairns run out	0		
D. J. Nash b Strang	41		
D. L. Vettori b Strang	16		
S. B. Doull c Goodwin b Strang	8		
S. B. O'Connor not out	2		
B 1, l-b 4	5	L-b 1	1

1/0 (1) 2/103 (2) 3/144 (3) 4/179 (4)   411   (no wkt) 20
5/240 (5) 6/254 (7) 7/362 (8)
8/388 (6) 9/397 (10) 10/411 (9)

Bowling: *First Innings*—Streak 22–6–74–2; Mbangwa 17–4–42–1; Strang 49.1–13–126–3; G. J. Whittall 5–2–12–0; A. R. Whittall 12–0–50–0; Huckle 40–10–102–3. *Second Innings*—Streak 2–0–13–0; Huckle 1.5–0–6–0.

Umpires: S. G. Randell (Australia) and R. S. Dunne.   Referee: Hanumant Singh (India).

NEW ZEALAND v ZIMBABWE

Second Test Match

At Auckland, February 26, 27, 28. New Zealand won by an innings and 13 runs. Toss: Zimbabwe.

Traditionally, the first morning of an Eden Park Test rewards seam bowlers. But this pitch looked very similar to one on which a young Auckland leg-spinner, Brooke Walker, had recently taken eight for 107. New Zealand therefore dropped the fast bowler Shayne O'Connor, who had played in the crushing defeat of Zimbabwe at Wellington, for the left-arm spin of Mark Priest. At the age of 36, and almost eight years after his only previous Test, against England at Trent Bridge, Priest now had another chance to add to his single Test wicket (M. A. Atherton c Snedden b Priest 151).

With Streak in patchy form, Zimbabwe were also relying upon the pitch turning on the fourth and fifth days, and stuck to their spin-heavy attack. Campbell again won the toss, and again elected to bat. Perhaps the plan that failed at Wellington would come good here. But it didn't. Mid-way through the second session the Eden Park faithful were rubbing their eyes in disbelief: the new-ball bowlers, Doull in particular, had immediately found devastating form. When the ball was not bouncing sharply from a length, it was whipping away off the seam or swinging wildly.

Even the most talented of players would have struggled to survive in such favourable bowling conditions. Zimbabwe have few world-class batsmen, and their innings was in tatters when Nash and Doull reduced them to 55 for five. In his opening spell, Doull had taken four for 16 in ten overs. Andy Flower and Strang lifted the score to 157 for six but, once Flower had gone, Cairns brushed aside the last three wickets. By the close, New Zealand had reached 69 for two.

Next morning, the pitch had lost much of its life and, although the seamers still found some help, Zimbabwe simply did not have the quicker bowlers needed to put New Zealand under pressure. Instead, Horne and Astle scored freely. Five short of his second Test century, Horne played a rare false stroke: the edge flew over the slips for four. Meanwhile, Astle was dropped at the wicket by Andy Flower when on 68. Both batsmen went on to hundreds. The stand was worth 243 when Astle was out for 114; ten runs later, Horne's long innings ended with a rather tired shot to mid-on.

McMillan then helped extend the New Zealand lead with a brisk 88, before he was last out on the third morning. He fell to the Andy Flower–Paul Strang combination, and these two turned out to be the only batsmen to offer serious resistance when Zimbabwe resumed, 290 in arrears. They lost their fifth wicket at 90; Flower, first with Streak and later with Strang, who scored 67 from 72 balls, led a minor recovery. And then Doull struck again, quickly taking the last three wickets to end the match with eight. With two days unused, the spinners had had little to do, and Priest still had only one Test wicket. But New Zealand were delighted with their 2-0 series win.

Man of the Match: M. J. Horne.

Close of play: First day, New Zealand 69-2 (M. J. Horne 39*, S. P. Fleming 19*); Second day, New Zealand 441-9 (C. D. McMillan 77*, S. B. Doull 0*).

Zimbabwe

G. J. Rennie c Parore b Doull	0	– (2) c Fleming b Cairns	0
G. W. Flower c Parore b Doull	13	– (1) c Young b Nash	32
M. W. Goodwin b Young b Doull	28	– c McMillan b Nash	14
*A. D. R. Campbell c Astle b Doull	11	– c Horne b Vettori	22
†A. Flower c McMillan b Nash	65	– c Parore b Cairns	83
G. J. Whittall c Young b Nash	1	– lbw b Doull	10
H. H. Streak c Fleming b Nash	12	– lbw b Cairns	24
P. A. Strang not out	30	– not out	67
A. R. Whittall lbw b Cairns	4	– c Parore b Doull	3
A. G. Huckle lbw b Cairns	0	– b Doull	13
M. Mbangwa b Cairns	0	– c Fleming b Doull	0
B 1, l-b 3, n-b 2	6	B 1, l-b 6, n-b 2	9

1/1 (1) 2/32 (2) 3/53 (3) 4/54 (4)   170   1/4 (2) 2/29 (3) 3/71 (4)   277
5/55 (6) 6/98 (7) 7/157 (5)   4/71 (1) 5/90 (6) 6/156 (7)
8/168 (9) 9/170 (10) 10/170 (11)   7/227 (5) 8/234 (9)
                                               9/277 (10) 10/277 (11)

Bowling: *First Innings*—Doull 20-6-35-4; Cairns 16.5-4-56-3; Nash 18-4-41-3; Vettori 2-0-15-0; Astle 5-1-15-0; Priest 1-0-4-0. *Second Innings*—Doull 19.4-5-50-4; Cairns 29-9-81-3; Nash 10-5-13-2; Vettori 20-5-60-1; Priest 14-0-51-0; McMillan 2-0-15-0.

New Zealand

B. A. Young b Streak	1	D. L. Vettori c Campbell b Strang	0
M. J. Horne c G. J. Whittall b Mbangwa	157	S. B. Doull not out	6
†A. C. Parore c A. Flower b Mbangwa	10		
*S. P. Fleming c Huckle b Mbangwa	19	B 8, l-b 17, w 1	26
N. J. Astle c G. W. Flower b Streak	114		
C. D. McMillan c A. Flower b Strang	88	1/2 (1) 2/40 (3) 3/69 (4)	460
C. L. Cairns c Strang b Streak	22	4/312 (5) 5/322 (2) 6/382 (7)	
D. J. Nash lbw b Strang	1	7/405 (8) 8/433 (9)	
M. W. Priest c Rennie b Strang	16	9/433 (10) 10/460 (6)	

Bowling: Streak 31-7-105-3; Mbangwa 27-10-78-3; G. J. Whittall 14-3-68-0; Strang 18.1-0-54-4; A. R. Whittall 11-1-37-0; Huckle 13-1-66-0; Goodwin 6-1-27-0.

Umpires: S. G. Randell (Australia) and D. B. Cowie.   Referee: Hanumant Singh (India).

†NEW ZEALAND v ZIMBABWE

Third One-Day International

At Christchurch, March 4 (day/night). Zimbabwe won by one run. Toss: New Zealand.

A month away from one-day action benefited Zimbabwe, who had their first success in a significant match after nine weeks away from home which had contained nine consecutive defeats in Tests and internationals. They set a useful target of 229 on a slow pitch, with Goodwin and Guy Whittall leading the way. New Zealand still seemed to be heading for an easy win when

Howell and Astle opened with 125 at five an over; Howell hit 12 fours and a six in his 71-ball 68. Then the slow bowlers Viljoen and Strang accounted for them both and frustrated the other batsmen. From 168 for six, Harris and Parore launched a recovery. But when Harris was out, the last pair had to get ten from one over. Four were needed off the last ball; Vettori managed two into the covers.

Man of the Match: M. W. Goodwin.

Zimbabwe

G. W. Flower c O'Connor	0	D. P. Viljoen b O'Connor		4
C. B. Wishart b Vettori	28	H. H. Streak not out		2
M. W. Goodwin b Harris	58	L-b 3, w 1		4
*A. D. R. Campbell run out	38			
†A. Flower run out	28	1/0 2/38 3/116 (7 wkts, 50 overs)		228
G. J. Whittall c Horne b Doull	50	4/127 5/197		
P. A. Strang not out	16	6/211 7/221		

J. A. Rennie and A. R. Whittall did not bat.

Bowling: O'Connor 7–1–31–2; Cairns 3–0–23–0; Vettori 10–0–36–1; Doull 5–1–19–1; McMillan 6–0–30–0; Harris 10–0–47–1; Astle 9–0–39–0.

New Zealand

L. G. Howell c sub (H. K. Olonga) b Strang	68	S. B. Doull st A. Flower b Strang		0
N. J. Astle c Campbell b Viljoen	69	D. L. Vettori not out		7
*S. P. Fleming b A. R. Whittall	4	S. B. O'Connor not out		1
M. J. Horne run out	2			
C. D. McMillan c A. Flower b G. W. Flower	15	L-b 1, w 12		13
C. L. Cairns b Viljoen	1	1/125 2/137 3/139 (9 wkts, 50 overs)		227
C. Z. Harris c G. J. Whittall b Strang	22	4/159 5/165 6/168		
†A. C. Parore c Strang b Streak	25	7/218 8/219 9/219		

Bowling: Streak 9–0–57–1; Rennie 4–0–23–0; A. R. Whittall 9–0–45–1; Strang 10–0–44–3; G. W. Flower 6–0–19–1; Goodwin 2–0–7–0; Viljoen 10–0–31–2.

Umpires: B. F. Bowden and C. E. King.

†NEW ZEALAND v ZIMBABWE

Fourth One-Day International

At Napier, March 6 (day/night). New Zealand won by nine wickets. Toss: Zimbabwe.

New Zealand clinched the series with an emphatic victory. Chasing 208, Howell and Astle gave them another blistering start, putting on 147. Howell was caught at long-off, aiming for a third six, but Astle completed his fifth century in one-day internationals. Zimbabwe's batsmen disappointed on a good pitch; ninth-wicket pair Strang and Rennie took them past 200 in an unbeaten stand of 54. New Zealand's performance in the field lost some of its lustre when Parore had to be restrained from charging at umpire Cowie after a disputed call: he was fined half his match fee.

Man of the Match: N. J. Astle.

Zimbabwe

G. W. Flower run out	11	P. A. Strang not out		31
C. B. Wishart c Astle b Harris	41	J. A. Rennie not out		23
M. W. Goodwin c Vettori b Cairns	1			
*A. D. R. Campbell c Astle b O'Connor	18	L-b 7, w 9, n-b 2		18
†A. Flower c Parore b Nash	30			
G. J. Whittall b Nash	18	1/15 2/25 3/56 (8 wkts, 50 overs)		207
D. P. Viljoen c Fleming b Nash	7	4/107 5/122 6/134		
H. H. Streak c and b Harris	9	7/145 8/153		

A. R. Whittall did not bat.

Bowling: O'Connor 10–1–53–1; Cairns 10–1–39–1; Nash 10-2–29–3; Vettori 10–0–49–0; Harris 10–0–30–2.

New Zealand

L. G. Howell c Wishart b Viljoen   66
N. J. Astle not out 104
*S. P. Fleming not out   33
          L-b 3, w 5   8
                                              ___
1/147   (1 wkt, 45.4 overs) 211

M. J. Horne, C. D. McMillan, C. L. Cairns, †A. C. Parore, C. Z. Harris, D. J. Nash, D. L. Vettori and S. B. O'Connor did not bat.

Bowling: Streak 6–1–23–0; Rennie 7–0–35–0; A. R. Whittall 10–0–43–0; Strang 7–0–38–0; Viljoen 6–0–30–1; G. W. Flower 8–0–30–0; Goodwin 1.4–0–9–0.

Umpires: D. B. Cowie and A. L. Hill.

†NEW ZEALAND v ZIMBABWE

Fifth One-Day International

At Auckland, March 8. New Zealand won by two runs. Toss: New Zealand.

Astle scored his fourth consecutive innings over 60 in this series: each time, his was the highest score of the match. When he was out, Harris assumed control, and the last four wickets added 110; Vettori scored a lightning 21 from 13 balls. Zimbabwe started solidly but, when Grant Flower fell at 106 for three, lost momentum – and wickets, as Vettori's accuracy pinned them down. They needed eight from the last over, but Strang, who threatened to steal victory with a lively 23, was run out off the penultimate ball. Andy Whittall had to hit a four; instead, he lobbed to mid-off. The catch was dropped, but a single left Zimbabwe two short.

Man of the Match: D. L. Vettori.   *Man of the Series*: N. J. Astle.

New Zealand

L. G. Howell c Strang b Rennie	1	D. J. Nash c Rennie b Strang	28
N. J. Astle c G. J. Whittall		D. L. Vettori c A. Flower b Streak	21
b G. W. Flower .	62	S. B. Doull not out	5
*S. P. Fleming b A. R. Whittall	27		
M. J. Horne c Rennie b Strang	11	L-b 4, w 8	12
C. D. McMillan c Wishart b Strang	3		___
C. L. Cairns b A. R. Whittall	0	1/3 2/75 3/88 (9 wkts, 50 overs) 231
C. Z. Harris not out	54	4/96 5/96 6/121	
†A. C. Parore c A. Flower b Viljoen . . .	7	7/135 8/181 9/213	

Bowling: Streak 5–0–38–1; Rennie 5–0–45–1; Strang 10–1–44–3; A. R. Whittall 10–1–24–2; Viljoen 10–0–35–1; G. W. Flower 10–0–41–1.

Zimbabwe

G. W. Flower c Fleming b McMillan . . .	55	P. A. Strang run out	23
C. B. Wishart b Cairns	6	J. A. Rennie not out	2
M. W. Goodwin b Harris	27	A. R. Whittall not out	1
†A. Flower b Vettori	27	B 4, l-b 6, w 2, n-b 1	13
*A. D. R. Campbell c Astle b Vettori . .	30		___
G. J. Whittall c Horne b Doull	29	1/19 2/76 3/106 (9 wkts, 50 overs) 229
D. P. Viljoen b Vettori	14	4/143 5/162 6/180	
H. H. Streak b Cairns	2	7/190 8/224 9/228	

Bowling: Doull 7–1–54–1; Cairns 10–0–43–2; Nash 7–0–26–0; Vettori 10–1–29–3; Harris 9–0–42–1; McMillan 7–0–25–1.

Umpires: D. B. Cowie and D. M. Quested.   Series referee: Hanumant Singh (India).

THE PAKISTANIS IN SOUTH AFRICA AND ZIMBABWE, 1997-98

By PAUL WEAVER and GEOFFREY DEAN

A series between Pakistan, the world's most gifted side, and the heroically resilient South Africans always promised momentous cricket. South Africa had just lost a highly competitive series in Australia 1-0, and Pakistan had recently routed West Indies 3-0 at home. But South Africa had achieved the rare feat of winning a series in Pakistan only four months earlier. Some saw the series as deciding the silver medal position in world cricket.

It was certainly a memorable series, fairly drawn 1-1. But, although there was some outstanding cricket, the mood and shape of the contest was directed by incidents off the field. Not for the first time, a Pakistan tour mixed enthralling cricket with mayhem. Even as the teams gathered for the First Test in Johannesburg, there was a strange atmosphere of peevishness in the air.

South African captain Hansie Cronje, who missed the match with a knee injury, had just been obliged to apologise to the Australian Cricket Board after an incident in Adelaide, when the umpires' door was damaged. Pakistan, meanwhile, had arrived in characteristic disarray. Wasim Akram, the captain and inspiration against West Indies, had been omitted from the party, officially for fitness reasons, and Rashid Latif had become their fourth captain in ten months. With allegations of betting and match-fixing still swirling, the appointment of Latif was seen as an attempt by the Pakistan Cricket Board to loosen the grip of the senior pros and repair the side's tarnished image. He had briefly retired three years earlier after complaining about the behaviour of former captain Salim Malik.

A little more tarnish was just round the corner. The First Test was delayed for 24 hours (Pakistan asked for longer) after fast bowler Mohammad Akram and off-spinner Saqlain Mushtaq claimed they had been mugged outside the team hotel. Later reports said they had been seen at two exotically named nightspots, Club 69 and Blue Orchid, and that the injuries had actually been sustained there. The players could not describe their assailants or agree on the time of the attack.

The seeds of mistrust were sown and poisoned the entire series. The immediate effect was to polarise the two camps. Pakistan developed a siege mentality, which can be a healthy attitude for a touring party, but in this case came close to paranoia. In the face of a sceptical press, some senior players favoured returning home.

Ali Bacher, managing director of the United Cricket Board of South Africa, worked and wheedled frantically to keep the tour on course. "I could have written a best-seller to describe what happened on this tour," he said at the end. Meanwhile the Pakistan manager, Asad Aziz, disappeared to his hotel room when difficult questions were asked and went off to an elephant game park when Wasim controversially returned to the fold for the final Test. Given the history of this most talented but mercurial team, it seemed strange to embark on such a serious tour without a strong manager.

The mugging issue was never resolved. South African officials felt they had been hoodwinked, and the players were in danger of being charged with wasting police time. Even on the day of their departure to Zimbabwe there was trouble: coach Haroon Rashid declared that Shoaib Akhtar and Fazl-e-Akbar were to be sent home for late-night partying, but the decision was reversed.

The First Test ended in a miserable and best-forgotten draw. In Durban, Pakistan briefly fulfilled their vast potential, outclassing South Africa to win more emphatically than a margin of 29 runs suggests, before destroying themselves for the final match. Wasim flew in at the personal request of Khalid Mahmood, chairman of the Pakistan Cricket Board, prompting the immediate resignation of Salim Altaf, the chairman of selectors. The arrival of Wasim, a strong personality, divided the team and they under-performed in the final Test. Wasim himself did not look match-fit. There was also a suggestion of racial tension in the series. After the Second Test, the UCB announced that Fanie de Villiers and Pat Symcox, plus fitness trainer Paddy Upton, would appear before a disciplinary committee to explain incidents involving spectators. They were cleared.

The UCB made two experiments. In the Johannesburg Test they tried floodlights, which proved a disaster. Attendance was also poor so, at Durban and Port Elizabeth, they followed the Australian example with a partial blackout of local TV coverage. The move had limited success.

Despite the troubles, there was some fine cricket. On his first Test tour, young all-rounder Azhar Mahmood scored two memorable centuries and was named Man of the Series. Mark Boucher replaced the retired South African wicket-keeper Dave Richardson with some élan. He scored a half-century in each Test and made 18 dismissals to break Richardson's South African record for a three-Test series. At Port Elizabeth, there was some outstanding fast bowling: Waqar Younis took ten in the match for the fifth time, to reach 250 Test wickets in only his 51st match, while Allan Donald claimed eight.

During this final Test, Bacher announced a policy of positive discrimination and the inclusion of black fast bowler Makhaya Ntini for the approaching series against Sri Lanka. "An all-white team is no longer acceptable in modern South Africa," he said. The visit of Pakistan had been momentous to the end. – P.W.

The Pakistanis made the short flight north to Zimbabwe for a three-week tour before returning to South Africa for a one-day tournament. The two Tests were much more evenly contested than expected after Zimbabwe's poor showing in New Zealand – whence they had returned only four days before the First Test – although Pakistan won both one-day internationals with commanding ease.

Zimbabwe were left to rue one, if not two, good opportunities to add to their single Test victory – against Pakistan, three years earlier. In the First Test at Bulawayo, the visitors, needing to bat through the final day, subsided to 80 for four just after lunch. But Alistair Campbell was strangely reluctant to set attacking fields and, on a good batting pitch, Pakistan comfortably held out for a draw. A few days later, Zimbabwe paid heavily for dropped catches which deprived them of an apparently certain first-innings lead. Even in chasing 192 to win, Pakistan lost seven wickets.

For Zimbabwe, there was the consolation of several fine individual performances. In Bulawayo, Grant Flower became the second Zimbabwean to carry his bat in Test cricket, and the first to score five Test hundreds – though his brother Andy caught up in the second innings. Former Western Australian batsman Murray Goodwin, who as a child had emigrated to Perth with his parents, returned to play his first home series in the land of his birth and averaged exactly 100, scoring a maiden Test century in Bulawayo. All-rounder Guy Whittall, whose form with the ball had been poor in New Zealand, bowled particularly well and also ended a lean spell with the bat by scoring a spirited 62 in Harare.

Zimbabwe's lack of first-class cricket meant that they were obliged to blood two young batsmen in the First Test, Dirk Viljoen and Trevor Madondo – the fourth black Zimbabwean to earn a Test cap – despite the fact that neither had a first-class fifty behind them. National coach Dave Houghton had not even seen Madondo play since his school days. Viljoen registered a pair and was dropped for the next Test.

While Zimbabwe badly missed the wrist-spin of the injured Paul Strang in the Second Test, Pakistan were indebted to Waqar Younis, whose tally of 13 wickets on two flat pitches earned him the Man of the Series award. But another strong candidate was Yousuf Youhana, who helped save the First Test and win the Second, with three fifties in four innings.

Despite their eventual success in Zimbabwe, Pakistan's tour ended on a losing note when they returned to South Africa for the triangular tournament. They narrowly beat Sri Lanka into the final, but crashed in that last encounter with South Africa, who beat them by nine wickets. – G.D.

PAKISTANI TOURING PARTY

Rashid Latif (Karachi Blues/Allied Bank) (*captain*), Aamir Sohail (Allied Bank) (*vice-captain*), Ali Naqvi (Karachi Blues), Azhar Mahmood (Islamabad), Ijaz Ahmed, sen. (Lahore), Inzamam-ul-Haq (Faisalabad/Allied Bank), Mohammad Akram (Rawalpindi/Allied Bank), Mohammad Wasim (Rawalpindi/ADBP), Moin Khan (PIA), Mushtaq Ahmed (Lahore/United Bank), Saeed Anwar (ADBP), Saqlain Mushtaq (PIA), Shoaib Akhtar (Rawalpindi/ADBP), Waqar Younis (Multan), Yousuf Youhana (Lahore/WAPDA).

Fazl-e-Akbar (Peshawar/ADBP), Mohammad Hussain (Lahore/United Bank), Shahid Afridi (Karachi Whites/Habib Bank) and Wasim Akram (Lahore/PIA) later reinforced the party.

Manager: Asad Ahmed Aziz. *Coach:* Haroon Rashid.

PAKISTANI TOUR RESULTS

Test matches – Played 5: Won 2, Lost 1, Drawn 2.
First-class matches – Played 8: Won 3, Lost 2, Drawn 3.
Wins – South Africa, Zimbabwe, Griqualand West.
Losses – South Africa, Border.
Draws – South Africa, Zimbabwe, Free State.
One-day internationals – Played 9: Won 4, Lost 5. *Wins* – Zimbabwe (2), Sri Lanka (2).
 Losses – South Africa (4), Sri Lanka.
Other non-first-class matches – Played 2: Drawn 1, No result 1. *Draw* – N. F. Oppenheimer's
 XI. *No result* – Matabeleland Select XI.

TEST MATCH AVERAGES – SOUTH AFRICA v PAKISTAN

SOUTH AFRICA – BATTING

	T	I	NO	R	HS	100s	50s	Avge	Ct/St
S. M. Pollock	3	5	1	166	70*	0	1	41.50	1
M. V. Boucher	3	5	0	188	78	0	3	37.60	17/1
W. J. Cronje	2	4	1	106	85	0	1	35.33	0
J. H. Kallis	3	5	0	159	69	0	1	31.80	4
H. D. Ackerman	2	4	0	121	57	0	1	30.25	0
P. S. de Villiers	2	3	1	54	46*	0	0	27.00	1
G. Kirsten	3	6	1	130	44	0	0	26.00	3
A. M. Bacher	3	6	1	97	46	0	0	19.40	0
A. C. Hudson	3	5	0	87	42	0	0	17.40	3
L. Klusener	2	3	0	14	6	0	0	4.66	2
A. A. Donald	3	4	1	12	11	0	0	4.00	2

Played in one Test: P. R. Adams 2* (1 ct); D. J. Cullinan 16 (1 ct); H. H. Gibbs 4 (1 ct); P. L. Symcox 108.

* Signifies not out.

BOWLING

	O	M	R	W	BB	5W/i	Avge
P. R. Adams	16	8	36	3	3-36	0	12.00
P. S. de Villiers	58.4	15	154	10	6-23	1	15.40
A. A. Donald	80.2	17	262	16	5-79	1	16.37
S. M. Pollock	97.4	26	239	11	6-50	1	21.72
L. Klusener	51	10	192	6	4-93	0	32.00

Also bowled: W. J. Cronje 5–0–20–0; J. H. Kallis 35–8–104–2; P. L. Symcox 5–0–16–0.

PAKISTAN – BATTING

	T	I	NO	R	HS	100s	50s	Avge	Ct/St
Azhar Mahmood	3	5	0	327	136	2	0	65.40	4
Saeed Anwar	3	5	0	236	118	1	1	47.20	0
Mohammad Wasim	2	3	0	61	44	0	0	20.33	3
Moin Khan	3	5	0	94	46	0	0	18.80	4/1
Aamir Sohail	3	5	0	75	36	0	0	15.00	0
Ijaz Ahmed, sen.	3	5	0	75	34	0	0	15.00	0
Mushtaq Ahmed	3	5	1	38	20	0	0	9.50	1
Waqar Younis	3	5	0	26	10	0	0	5.20	0
Shoaib Akhtar	3	5	2	13	6	0	0	4.33	1
Inzamam-ul-Haq	2	3	0	10	6	0	0	3.33	1

Played in one Test: Fazl-e-Akbar 0*, 0 (1 ct); Rashid Latif 0, 0 (4 ct); Saqlain Mushtaq 2; Wasim Akram 30*, 5; Yousuf Youhana 5, 1.

* Signifies not out.

BOWLING

	O	M	R	W	BB	5W/i	Avge
Fazl-e-Akbar	13	4	32	3	2-16	0	10.66
Mushtaq Ahmed	112	29	280	13	6-78	1	21.53
Waqar Younis	105.3	20	354	16	6-78	1	22.12
Wasim Akram	42	11	107	3	3-70	0	35.66
Shoaib Akhtar	78	7	257	6	5-43	1	42.83
Azhar Mahmood	84	19	188	4	3-49	0	47.00

Also bowled: Aamir Sohail 11–2–40–0; Saqlain Mushtaq 12.2–0–47–2.

Note: Matches in this section which were not first-class are signified by a dagger.

†At Randjesfontein, January 29. Drawn. Pakistanis batted first by mutual agreement. Pakistanis 299 for four dec. (Aamir Sohail 41, Mohammad Wasim 73, Inzamam-ul-Haq 107, Yousuf Youhana 38 not out); N. F. Oppenheimer's XI 239 for six (H. H. Dippenaar 35, R. P. Snell 74, D. M. Benkenstein 94; Azhar Mahmood three for 82).

At Kimberley, January 31, February 1, 2, 3. Pakistanis won by 307 runs. Toss: Pakistanis. Pakistanis 418 for eight dec. (Saeed Anwar 117, Inzamam-ul-Haq 57 retired hurt, Azhar Mahmood 59, Rashid Latif 98, Saqlain Mushtaq 39 not out; G. A. Roe three for 98) and 216 for nine dec. (Aamir Sohail 61, Mohammad Wasim 31, Inzamam-ul-Haq 46 not out; G. J. Kruis four for 41, L. L. Bosman three for 25); Griqualand West 218 (J. M. Arthur 33, P. H. Barnard 101; Mushtaq Ahmed six for 63) and 109 (W. Bossenger 39; Mushtaq Ahmed five for 18).

At East London, February 6, 7, 8. Border won by five wickets. Toss: Pakistanis. Pakistanis 232 (Yousuf Youhana 77, Moin Khan 56; M. Ntini three for 99) and 124 (Aamir Sohail 33, Moin Khan 42; M. Ntini three for 45, D. Taljard six for 49); Border 244 (W. Wiblin 82, M. V. Boucher 80; Shoaib Akhtar three for 103, Azhar Mahmood four for 66) and 113 for five (B. M. White 39, P. C. Strydom 41 not out).

Taljard took a hat-trick to set up Border's win with a day to spare.

SOUTH AFRICA v PAKISTAN

First Test Match

At Johannesburg, February 14, 15, 16, 17, 18. Drawn. Toss: Pakistan.

Many observers declared this the most miserable Test they had witnessed, despite some sensational individual performances. Rain and bad light took away more than half the playing time and, when there was cricket, it was usually in overcast and surprisingly cold conditions. It was agreed that the floodlights could be switched on to avoid interruptions for the light. But batsmen complained they could not see the red ball and the umpires could not get a reading on their meters; so the players kept trooping off even with the lights blazing. Above all, it was the first Test to be postponed because of an alleged mugging, and it was played in the dark shadow of suspicion and mistrust. Perhaps a match scheduled to get under way on Friday 13th was fated from the start.

HIGHEST TEST SCORES BY No. 10 BATSMEN

W. W. Read	117	England v Australia at The Oval	1884
P. L. Symcox	**108**	**South Africa v Pakistan at Johannesburg**	**1997-98**
R. A. Duff	104	Australia v England at Melbourne	1901-02
Sarfraz Nawaz	90	Pakistan v England at Lahore	1983-84
R. B. Desai	85	India v Pakistan at Bombay	1960-61
J. G. Bracewell	83*	New Zealand v Australia at Sydney	1985-86
G. G. Macaulay	76	England v Australia at Headingley	1926
J. McC. Blackham	74	Australia v England at Sydney	1894-95
G. F. Lawson	74	Australia v England at Lord's	1989
A. B. C. Langton	73*	South Africa v England at The Oval	1935
D. K. Lillee	73*	Australia v England at Lord's	1975
A. E. Trott	72*	Australia v England at Adelaide	1894-95
M. G. Hughes	72*	Australia v West Indies at Adelaide	1988-89

Both sides had stand-in captains, leading their countries for the first time in Tests. Kirsten led South Africa while Cronje recovered from a cartilage operation, and Aamir Sohail took charge of Pakistan, whose new captain, Rashid Latif, had a neck injury. Sohail chose to bowl on a bouncy but not untrustworthy Wanderers pitch. His decision appeared to have been vindicated when South Africa slid to 166 for eight; Waqar Younis, generating some pace despite a side strain, shared six wickets with leg-spinner Mushtaq Ahmed. Then Boucher, making his home debut, was joined by Symcox, and they lifted South Africa to 296 for eight by the close. Pakistan dropped four simple catches in the afternoon as they surrendered control. Their frustration became evident when Shoaib Akhtar had an angry exchange with Symcox after a near-collision. Referee John Reid made them shake hands and warned both about their behaviour.

On the second day, 37-year-old Symcox and Boucher carried their partnership to 195, a Test record for the ninth wicket. The previous record was 190 between Pakistan's Asif Iqbal and Intikhab Alam, against England at The Oval in 1967. Symcox scored 108, his maiden Test century, in 226 minutes, faced 157 balls and struck 17 fours. He coaxed the tyro Boucher through and played more like an aggressive middle-order batsman than a slogging tailender. Symcox hit the bad balls very hard but defended with great assurance when necessary. He was only the third No. 10 batsman to reach three figures in a Test – and the first for 96 years – and he performed a bat-waving jig of pure delight when he got there, which suggested he had astonished himself as well as everyone else. He was out soon afterwards, shortly followed by Boucher, whose 78 had occupied 265 minutes and included nine fours and a six.

Replying to 364, Pakistan closed on 106 for four; 31 overs were lost to bad light, despite the use of floodlights. An early wicket next morning left them in some danger of following on. But Azhar Mahmood followed his debut hundred, also against South Africa, at Rawalpindi in October, with another thrilling century. He scored 136 in five hours, with 16 fours and two sixes, and was last out, having reduced the deficit to 35, before bad light ended play early. The entire fourth day was washed out and only 63 balls were possible on the fifth.

Man of the Match: P. L. Symcox.   *Attendance:* 32,988.

Close of play: First day, South Africa 296-8 (M. V. Boucher 50*, P. L. Symcox 77*); Second day, Pakistan 106-4 (Ijaz Ahmed, sen. 33*, Moin Khan 5*); Third day, Pakistan 329; Fourth day, No play.

South Africa

A. M. Bacher lbw b Waqar Younis	46	– (2) not out	20
*G. Kirsten c Azhar Mahmood b Waqar Younis	3	– (1) not out	20
J. H. Kallis c Mohammad Wasim b Shoaib Akhtar	15		
D. J. Cullinan b Waqar Younis	16		
A. C. Hudson b Mushtaq Ahmed	33		
H. H. Gibbs lbw b Mushtaq Ahmed	4		
S. M. Pollock c Mushtaq Ahmed b Azhar Mahmood	21		
†M. V. Boucher c Mohammad Wasim b Saqlain Mushtaq	78		
L. Klusener b Mushtaq Ahmed	6		
P. L. Symcox c Shoaib Akhtar b Saqlain Mushtaq	108		
A. A. Donald not out	0		
B 2, l-b 21, w 4, n-b 7	34	L-b 4	4
	364	(no wkt)	**44**

1/14 (2) 2/56 (3) 3/86 (1) 4/91 (4) 5/96 (6) 6/149 (7) 7/157 (5) 8/166 (9) 9/361 (10) 10/364 (8)

Bowling: First Innings—Waqar Younis 23–4–80–3; Shoaib Akhtar 21–1–84–1; Azhar Mahmood 20–1–52–1; Mushtaq Ahmed 27–6–66–3; Saqlain Mushtaq 12.2–0–47–2; Aamir Sohail 1–0–12–0. *Second Innings*—Waqar Younis 5.3–1–18–0; Shoaib Akhtar 5–0–22–0.

Pakistan

Saeed Anwar c Cullinan b Donald	2
*Aamir Sohail c Boucher b Pollock	12
Ijaz Ahmed, sen. c Pollock b Donald	34
Mohammad Wasim c Boucher b Klusener	44
Inzamam-ul-Haq b Klusener	0
†Moin Khan c Gibbs b Klusener	46
Azhar Mahmood c Donald b Pollock	136
Saqlain Mushtaq c Boucher b Kallis	2
Mushtaq Ahmed c Kirsten b Kallis	10
Waqar Younis c Hudson b Klusener	10
Shoaib Akhtar not out	4
B 11, l-b 7, w 3, n-b 8	29
	329

1/15 (2) 2/15 (1) 3/87 (4) 4/91 (5) 5/112 (3) 6/219 (6) 7/230 (8) 8/255 (9) 9/296 (10) 10/329 (7)

Bowling: Donald 23–4–89–2; Pollock 24.1–10–55–2; Klusener 24–6–93–4; Kallis 18–7–58–2; Symcox 5–0–16–0.

Umpires: P. Willey (England) and C. J. Mitchley.   *Referee:* J. R. Reid (New Zealand).

At Bloemfontein, February 21, 22, 23. Drawn. Toss: Free State. Free State 334 for seven dec. (H. H. Dippenaar 45, W. J. Cronje 150 not out, M. N. van Wyk 45, W. J. Smit 44) and 21 for three; Pakistanis 441 (Mohammad Wasim 44, Moin Khan 35, Yousuf Youhana 54, Inzamam-ul-Haq 119, Azhar Mahmood 111; D. Pretorius three for 114, J. F. Venter four for 106).

SOUTH AFRICA v PAKISTAN

Second Test Match

At Durban, February 26, 27, 28, March 1, 2. Pakistan won by 29 runs. Toss: South Africa. Test debuts: H. D. Ackerman; Fazl-e-Akbar, Yousuf Youhana.

For once, Pakistan played to their considerable potential to take a 1-0 lead. South Africa were unable to keep pace with their more gifted opponents, though a less determined side would surely have been overwhelmed by a wider margin.

Cronje returned after his knee injury and was joined in the middle order by debutant Hylton Ackerman, son of the former Northamptonshire batsman of the same name; they replaced Cullinan and Gibbs. The experienced swing bowler de Villiers also came into the side at the expense of off-spinner Symcox, who could feel unfortunate after his heroics at Johannesburg. Pakistan introduced Yousuf Youhana (only the fourth Christian to represent the country in a Test) because Inzamam-ul-Haq had twisted an ankle in practice; there was also a debut for fast-medium bowler Fazl-e-Akbar, replacing Saqlain Mushtaq. South Africa's decision to drop their spinner proved costly. Mushtaq Ahmed, admittedly a better slow bowler than any South Africa had to choose from, was to be the match-winner, with nine wickets.

Pakistan were put in on a two-paced pitch, and Donald and Pollock reduced them to 89 for five. They were rescued by another outstanding hundred from Azhar Mahmood, his third in six Test innings against South Africa. He looked to be much too low at No. 7, as he lifted his side to 259 with an uninhibited innings of 132, 96 of them in boundaries, in 198 minutes. He consistently drove and cut the fast bowlers backward of point and hit Donald back over his head before hooking him in front of square leg. Even more impressive, for a batsman two days short of his 23rd birthday, was the way he protected the tail. In a ninth-wicket stand of 80 with Shoaib Akhtar – who made six – he faced 80 per cent of the deliveries. His second fifty came in only 42 minutes, and he made 96 of Pakistan's last 106 runs.

Then, on the second day, South Africa were troubled by another youngster. Shoaib, carrying a knee injury, was still quicker than Waqar Younis or Donald the previous day – which arguably made him the fastest bowler in the world at this time. He found steep bounce and the reverse swing that comes so easily to many Pakistanis. In his third Test, he captured five for 43 and swept away the lower half of the batting after Kallis and Ackerman had put on 83 for the third wicket. Four of his victims were clean bowled and the other lbw. Despite a fluent, undefeated 70 from Pollock, South Africa were all out shortly after tea, trailing by 28.

On the third day, Saeed Anwar and Aamir Sohail built the first century opening stand against South Africa in 45 Tests since their return to international cricket (the previous best had been 99 for West Indies in the first of the 45). Anwar batted more than five hours for his fifth Test century, which carried him past 2,000 Test runs. But Pakistan lost their last nine wickets for 67. Pollock took five in 43 balls to finish with six for 50.

Set 255 to win, South Africa then faltered against Mushtaq, who used the rough to return figures of six for 78. Once again, they refused to lie down: a ninth-wicket stand of 86 between Boucher and de Villiers gave South Africa sudden, outrageous optimism. But early on the final morning, they suffered their first defeat in six Tests against Pakistan and their first at Kingsmead since England's win in 1964-65.

Man of the Match: Mushtaq Ahmed.   *Attendance:* 35,791.

Close of play: First day, South Africa 23-1 (A. M. Bacher 14*, J. H. Kallis 7*); Second day, Pakistan 11-0 (Saeed Anwar 8*, Aamir Sohail 2*); Third day, Pakistan 222-8 (Mushtaq Ahmed 16*, Shoaib Akhtar 1*); Fourth day, South Africa 186-8 (M. V. Boucher 36*, P. S. de Villiers 26*).

Pakistan

Saeed Anwar lbw b Donald	43	– lbw b Pollock 118
*Aamir Sohail c Boucher b Pollock	17	– c Boucher b Donald 36
Ijaz Ahmed, sen. c de Villiers b Pollock	2	– b de Villiers 24
Mohammad Wasim c Kallis b Donald	12	– run out 5
Yousuf Youhana c Boucher b Donald	5	– c Boucher b Pollock 1
†Moin Khan c Donald b de Villiers	25	– lbw b Pollock 5
Azhar Mahmood b Donald	132	– c Boucher b Pollock 1
Mushtaq Ahmed c Kallis b Klusener	2	– run out 20
Waqar Younis c Hudson b Donald	6	– c Klusener b Pollock 0
Shoaib Akhtar c Boucher b Klusener	6	– not out 1
Fazl-e-Akbar not out	0	– c Klusener b Pollock 0
B 2, l-b 1, w 2, n-b 4	9	L-b 7, w 2, n-b 6 15
	259	**226**

1/35 (2) 2/37 (3) 3/70 (4) 4/82 (5)   259   1/101 (2) 2/159 (3) 3/164 (4)   226
5/89 (1) 6/127 (6) 7/142 (8)   4/182 (5) 5/198 (6) 6/203 (1)
8/153 (9) 9/233 (10) 10/259 (7)   7/212 (7) 8/220 (9)
                                        9/226 (8) 10/226 (11)

Bowling: *First Innings*—Donald 19.2–4–79–5; de Villiers 18–5–55–1; Pollock 18–3–55–2; Klusener 18–3–67–2. *Second Innings*—de Villiers 16–1–51–1; Donald 10–2–20–1; Pollock 22.3–6–50–6; Klusener 9–1–32–0; Cronje 5–0–20–0; Kallis 17–1–46–0.

South Africa

A. M. Bacher c Moin Khan b Fazl-e-Akbar	17	– (2) lbw b Fazl-e-Akbar 0
G. Kirsten c Azhar Mahmood b Fazl-e-Akbar	0	– (1) c sub (Rashid Latif) b Mushtaq Ahmed . 25
J. H. Kallis b Shoaib Akhtar	43	– c Moin Khan b Mushtaq Ahmed . . 22
H. D. Ackerman c Mohammad Wasim b Mushtaq Ahmed	57	– lbw b Mushtaq Ahmed 11
A. C. Hudson lbw b Shoaib Akhtar	0	– c Fazl-e-Akbar b Mushtaq Ahmed . 8
*W. J. Cronje lbw b Mushtaq Ahmed	3	– c Moin Khan b Waqar Younis.... 11
S. M. Pollock not out	70	– st Moin Khan b Mushtaq Ahmed.. 30
†M. V. Boucher b Shoaib Akhtar	2	– b Waqar Younis 52
L. Klusener b Shoaib Akhtar	6	– lbw b Mushtaq Ahmed 2
P. S. de Villiers b Shoaib Akhtar	7	– not out 46
A. A. Donald lbw b Mushtaq Ahmed	11	– lbw b Waqar Younis 0
B 4, l-b 2, w 3, n-b 6	15	L-b 15, n-b 3 18
	231	**225**

1/4 (2) 2/32 (1) 3/115 (4) 4/115 (5)   231   1/2 (2) 2/42 (1) 3/49 (3)   225
5/120 (6) 6/139 (4) 7/154 (8)   4/76 (4) 5/79 (5) 6/114 (6)
8/166 (9) 9/178 (10) 10/231 (11)   7/120 (7) 8/133 (9)
                                        9/219 (8) 10/225 (11)

Bowling: *First Innings*—Waqar Younis 19–3–63–0; Fazl-e-Akbar 8–2–16–2; Shoaib Akhtar 12–1–43–5; Mushtaq Ahmed 32–9–71–3; Azhar Mahmood 17–6–28–0; Aamir Sohail 2–0–4–0. *Second Innings*—Waqar Younis 17.2–2–60–3; Fazl-e-Akbar 5–2–16–1; Shoaib Akhtar 11–0–20–0; Mushtaq Ahmed 37–13–78–6; Azhar Mahmood 11–4–12–0; Aamir Sohail 7–1–24–0.

Umpires: M. J. Kitchen (England) and D. L. Orchard.   Referee: J. R. Reid (New Zealand).

SOUTH AFRICA v PAKISTAN

Third Test Match

At Port Elizabeth, March 6, 7, 8, 9, 10. South Africa won by 259 runs. Toss: Pakistan.
Superficially, Pakistan looked even more powerful going into the final Test. Inzamam-ul-Haq, their finest batsman, had recovered from his ankle injury, and their best player, Wasim Akram, who had been left out of the original tour party, flew in. But this move by the Pakistan Board,

going over the heads of the selectors, appeared to upset the team spirit carefully rebuilt by vice-captain Aamir Sohail in Durban. There was worse. Sohail handed back the captaincy to Rashid Latif, who declared himself fit; but Latif did not appear to possess Sohail's leadership qualities and his authority was not helped when he made a pair and kept wicket erratically. Wasim did not look match-fit, and Inzamam scored six and four. Pakistan imploded and South Africa levelled the series with some ease.

South Africa brought in left-arm wrist-spinner Adams, in place of Klusener, but did not even use him in the first innings. Instead, de Villiers, playing in what he said was his final Test, returned his best figures, six for 23, and had eight for 48 in the match. It was all over 25 minutes into the final day; if rain had not wiped out the second day, Pakistan's humiliation would have been even more obvious.

Latif's delayed debut as a Test captain did not start badly. He put South Africa in and, once again, their batting had to be bailed out by the lower order. Waqar Younis, bowling within himself and pitching the ball well up, took the first two wickets, and South Africa were in some trouble at 122 for five before a stand of 78 between Cronje and Pollock; Cronje scored 85, which included two sixes off Mushtaq Ahmed. Waqar returned to claim his 250th wicket in 51 Tests – de Villiers – and finished with six for 78, but Boucher's third fifty of the series had lifted South Africa to 293 on the third morning, after the second-day washout.

A draw looked likely. But then Donald showed his fondness for the St George's Park ground. Switching ends after three limp overs, he suddenly produced a burst of four for five in 13 deliveries – reducing Pakistan to 29 for four. It inspired a delicious spoonerism from his former team-mate, Dave Richardson, now a TV commentator: "This is a happy grunting hound for Allan," he said. It also proved a happy grunting hound for de Villiers, who took the other six. Pakistan were all out for 106, 187 behind, with Wasim, undefeated on 30, their top scorer. Boucher held six catches to equal Denis Lindsay's South African record.

A solid 69 by Kallis provided the fulcrum of South Africa's second innings, which Cronje declared at 206 for seven. Mushtaq, suffering from a neck injury, did not bowl. Pakistan needed a far-fetched 394 for victory and ended the fourth day on 120 for seven, with defeat inevitable. South Africa needed just 35 balls to complete the job on the final morning; Donald's match figures were eight for 74.

Man of the Match: M. V. Boucher.   *Man of the Series:* Azhar Mahmood.

Attendance: 26,648.

Close of play: First day, South Africa 262-7 (M. V. Boucher 27*, P. S. de Villiers 1*); Second day, No play; Third day, South Africa 94-2 (J. H. Kallis 32*, H. D. Ackerman 0*); Fourth day, Pakistan 120-7 (Azhar Mahmood 30*, Waqar Younis 3*).

South Africa

A. M. Bacher lbw b Waqar Younis	3	– (2) c Rashid Latif b Waqar Younis.	11
G. Kirsten b Waqar Younis	38	– (1) c Rashid Latif b Azhar Mahmood.	44
J. H. Kallis b Waqar Younis	10	– c Rashid Latif b Azhar Mahmood.	69
H. D. Ackerman b Waqar Younis	11	– c Inzamam-ul-Haq b Azhar Mahmood.	42
A. C. Hudson c Moin Khan b Mushtaq Ahmed.	42	– b Waqar Younis.	4
*W. J. Cronje lbw b Waqar Younis	85	– not out.	7
S. M. Pollock c Azhar Mahmood b Wasim Akram.	38	– b Waqar Younis.	7
†M. V. Boucher c Rashid Latif b Wasim Akram	52	– b Waqar Younis.	4
P. S. de Villiers c Azhar Mahmood b Waqar Younis.	1		
A. A. Donald lbw b Wasim Akram	1		
P. R. Adams not out	2		
L-b 3, n-b 7.	10	B 1, l-b 6, w 1, n-b 10.	18
	293	(7 wkts dec.)	**206**

1/3 (1) 2/13 (3) 3/36 (4) 4/81 (2)   1/17 (2) 2/92 (1)   (7 wkts dec.) 206
5/122 (5) 6/200 (7) 7/257 (6)   3/170 (3) 4/185 (5)
8/263 (9) 9/269 (10) 10/293 (8)   5/187 (4) 6/198 (7) 7/206 (8)

Bowling: *First Innings*—Wasim Akram 26–8–70–3; Waqar Younis 23–6–78–6; Azhar Mahmood 21–7–47–0; Shoaib Akhtar 13–4–30–0; Mushtaq Ahmed 16–1–65–1. *Second Innings*—Wasim Akram 16–3–37–0; Waqar Younis 17.4–4–55–4; Shoaib Akhtar 16–1–58–0; Azhar Mahmood 15–1–49–3; Aamir Sohail 1–1–0–0.

Pakistan

Saeed Anwar c Boucher b Donald	18	– c Kallis b Donald	55
Aamir Sohail c Hudson b Donald	3	– (7) lbw b Adams	7
Ijaz Ahmed, sen. c Boucher b Donald	0	– (2) lbw b de Villiers	15
Inzamam-ul-Haq c Boucher b Donald	6	– (3) st Boucher b Adams	4
Moin Khan c Boucher b de Villiers	17	– (4) lbw b Donald	1
Azhar Mahmood c Adams b de Villiers	17	– c Kirsten b Donald	41
Wasim Akram not out	30	– (5) c Boucher b Pollock	5
*†Rashid Latif lbw b de Villiers	0	– c Kallis b Adams	0
Waqar Younis c Kirsten b de Villiers	7	– c Boucher b Donald	3
Shoaib Akhtar c Boucher b de Villiers	0	– b de Villiers	2
Mushtaq Ahmed c Boucher b de Villiers	5	– not out	1
L-b 3	3		

1/21 (1) 2/21 (3) 3/26 (2) 4/29 (4)   106
5/61 (5) 6/62 (6) 7/62 (8)
8/84 (9) 9/84 (10) 10/106 (11)

1/36 (2) 2/67 (3) 3/70 (4)   134
4/75 (1) 5/81 (5) 6/93 (7)
7/101 (8) 8/120 (9)
9/133 (6) 10/134 (10)

Bowling: *First Innings*—Donald 13–3–47–4; Pollock 16–5–33–0; de Villiers 11.5–5–23–6. *Second Innings*—Donald 15–4–27–4; Pollock 17–2–46–1; de Villiers 12.5–4–25–2; Adams 16–8–36–3.

Umpires: R. S. Dunne (New Zealand) and R. E. Koertzen.   Referee: J. R. Reid (New Zealand).

†At Bulawayo Athletic Club, Bulawayo, March 12. No result. Toss: Pakistanis. Pakistanis 118 for five (25.5 overs) (Ali Naqvi 40) v Matabeleland Select XI.

ZIMBABWE v PAKISTAN

First Test Match

At Queens Sports Club, Bulawayo, March 14, 15, 16, 17, 18. Drawn. Toss: Zimbabwe. Test debuts: T. N. Madondo, D. P. Viljoen.

When play finally began after lunch on the first day, under cloudy skies following rain, conditions for swing were ideal. Zimbabwe nevertheless elected to bat, in the hope that the pitch would deteriorate and turn later. In the event, it did neither. Waqar Younis, with out-swing, and Azhar Mahmood, with in-swing, were a difficult proposition early on, but Pakistan badly missed Wasim Akram who was ruled out by fever along with Mushtaq Ahmed. Zimbabwe lost three quick wickets before the Flower brothers restored some order with an excellent stand of 77.

The second day dawned clearer and batting was much easier. Unable to gain any swing, either traditional or reverse, the Pakistanis needed more than 57 overs to take the last five wickets. Streak, equalling his Test best, partnered Grant Flower in a crucial seventh-wicket stand of 109. Flower became the second Zimbabwean after Mark Dekker, at Rawalpindi in 1993-94, to carry his bat, in an outstanding innings, notable for its driving and watertight defence. He gave only one chance in 512 minutes and 329 balls — when 145 — and hit 13 fours and two sixes. Nearly all the Pakistanis got starts, but only the gritty Yousuf Youhana went on to reach fifty, a maiden one in his second Test. Most of the rest were out to careless or ill-disciplined shots against tight bowling on one side of the wicket.

Zimbabwe were armed with their fifth first-innings lead in nine Tests against Pakistan, but they again started badly, losing four wickets for 25 to Waqar and Shoaib Akhtar, who was startlingly fast. But Waqar was soon forced off through injury and, when Saqlain Mushtaq was also injured, Pakistan were left with only two specialist bowlers. This, the excellence of the pitch and the hot weather assisted Goodwin and Andy Flower in building a splendid unbroken partnership of 277 in 68 overs, an all-wicket record for Zimbabwe – overtaking the 269 between Andy and Grant Flower, also against Pakistan, three years earlier. Goodwin reached his maiden Test hundred in

161 balls and then hammered 63 off his next 43, as Zimbabwe sought quick runs for a declaration. His cutting was impressive, as was his use of feet to the spinners. Goodwin hit 17 fours and four sixes; Flower's more measured century contained only six fours.

Left with 105 overs to survive – or an improbable 368 to win – Pakistan were reduced to 80 for four on the final day, thanks to more poor batting. But Youhana and Moin Khan saved the match. They added 110 before the new ball accounted for Youhana, who had batted nearly three hours. Moin batted half an hour longer, but threw away the chance of a fourth Test hundred when he top-edged a sweep off Viljoen, who was bowling left-arm spin into the rough. Surprisingly, Campbell had declined to use his second spinner, Andy Whittall, until after tea; equally surprisingly, he granted Pakistan the draw when 45 balls still remained, with four wickets standing.

Man of the Match: G. W. Flower.

Close of play: First day, Zimbabwe 151-5 (G. W. Flower 69*, T. N. Madondo 11*); Second day, Pakistan 77-1 (Ali Naqvi 24*, Ijaz Ahmed, sen. 16*); Third day, Zimbabwe 15-2 (G. W. Flower 4*); Fourth day, Pakistan 24-0 (Ali Naqvi 7*, Saqlain Mushtaq 6*).

Zimbabwe

G. W. Flower not out	156	– lbw b Waqar Younis	6
D. P. Viljoen c Rashid Latif b Waqar Younis.	0	– lbw b Shoaib Akhtar	0
M. W. Goodwin c Rashid Latif b Waqar Younis.	0	– (4) not out	166
*A. D. R. Campbell c Rashid Latif b Azhar Mahmood .	15	– (5) c Ijaz Ahmed b Waqar Younis .	5
†A. Flower c Rashid Latif b Shoaib Akhtar . . .	44	– (6) not out	100
G. J. Whittall lbw b Waqar Younis	1		
T. N. Madondo c Inzamam-ul-Haq b Waqar Younis .	14		
H. H. Streak c Ijaz Ahmed b Azhar Mahmood .	53		
P. A. Strang c Inzamam-ul-Haq b Shoaib Akhtar	2		
A. R. Whittall c Rashid Latif b Azhar Mahmood	17	– (3) c Yousuf Youhana b Shoaib Akhtar .	6
M. Mbangwa c Rashid Latif b Waqar Younis . .	0		
B 3, l-b 13, w 2, n-b 1	19	L-b 14, w 1, n-b 4	19

1/9 (2) 2/15 (3) 3/38 (4) 4/115 (5)   321   1/0 (2) 2/15 (3)   (4 wkts dec.) 302
5/123 (6) 6/159 (7) 7/268 (8)   3/19 (1) 4/25 (5)
8/272 (9) 9/321 (10) 10/321 (11)

Bowling: *First Innings*—Waqar Younis 28.2–4–106–5; Azhar Mahmood 36–18–56–3; Shoaib Akhtar 27–6–83–2; Saqlain Mushtaq 20–1–60–0; Saeed Anwar 1–1–0–0. *Second Innings*—Waqar Younis 11–5–18–2; Shoaib Akhtar 23.2–5–67–2; Azhar Mahmood 24–1–102–0; Ali Naqvi 2–0–11–0; Saqlain Mushtaq 14.3–0–63–0; Saeed Anwar 4–0–19–0; Inzamam-ul-Haq 1.3–0–8–0.

Pakistan

Saeed Anwar c A. Flower b G. J. Whittall	33	– c Goodwin b Strang	37
Ali Naqvi c Campbell b Mbangwa	27	– c Goodwin b Mbangwa	13
Ijaz Ahmed, sen. c A. Flower b Mbangwa	23	– (7) not out	15
Inzamam-ul-Haq c and b Strang	24	– c A. Flower b Streak	12
Yousuf Youhana b G. J. Whittall	60	– c Viljoen b Streak	64
Moin Khan c A. R. Whittall b G. J. Whittall	12	– c Goodwin b Viljoen	97
Azhar Mahmood lbw b Strang	0		
*†Rashid Latif lbw b Streak	31		
Saqlain Mushtaq lbw b Strang	34	– (3) c A. Flower b Streak	8
Waqar Younis c Strang b G. J. Whittall	0		
Shoaib Akhtar not out	7		
L-b 5	5	B 6, l-b 6	12

1/58 (1) 2/80 (2) 3/99 (3) 4/118 (4)   256   1/28 (3) 2/54 (2)   (6 wkts) 258
5/143 (6) 6/144 (7) 7/205 (8)   3/70 (1) 4/80 (4)
8/230 (5) 9/230 (10) 10/256 (9)   5/190 (5) 6/258 (6)

In the second innings Saeed Anwar, when 7, retired hurt at 10 and resumed at 28.

Bowling: *First Innings*—Streak 24–5–74–1; Mbangwa 23–15–25–2; A. R. Whittall 7–1–29–0; G. J. Whittall 27–9–63–4; Strang 26.1–8–54–3; G. W. Flower 1–0–3–0; Goodwin 1–0–3–0. *Second Innings*—Streak 18–6–42–3; Mbangwa 22–13–29–1; Strang 27–5–69–1; G. J. Whittall 18–5–61–0; A. R. Whittall 8–3–28–0; Goodwin 2–0–3–0; Viljoen 3.3–0–14–1.

Umpires: D. R. Shepherd (England) and I. D. Robinson.   Referee: G. T. Dowling (New Zealand).

ZIMBABWE v PAKISTAN

Second Test Match

At Harare Sports Club, Harare, March 21, 22, 23, 24, 25. Pakistan won by three wickets. Toss: Zimbabwe.

But for some crucial missed chances, Zimbabwe might well have won an enthralling match. Shortly before the end of the second day, Mohammad Wasim was dropped, on 81, by Mbangwa; next morning, he was put down again, in the slips off Bryan Strang, when he was 125 and Pakistan were 236 for eight, still 41 behind. Neither chance was difficult. He went on to reach 192, batting 560 minutes and masterminding a critical ninth-wicket stand of 147 with Mushtaq Ahmed. Instead of surrendering a first-innings deficit, Pakistan gained an unlikely lead of 77. Once Zimbabwe lost three second-innings wickets for 38, Pakistan's victory was virtually inevitable. It was much more comfortable than a three-wicket margin would suggest, for they gave wickets away whenever the game looked won.

The seeds of Pakistan's success could be traced to a remarkable last half-hour before tea on the first day, when Zimbabwe lost five wickets in as many overs to slip from 141 for two to 153 for seven. The Pakistani bowlers deserve credit for inducing the collapse, although they were helped by a poor shot (Goodwin, caught at deep square leg), a bad umpiring decision (Andy Flower) and a needless run-out. The fact that Strang, previously without a Test fifty, was able to make one from just 78 balls, and shared an eighth-wicket stand of 110 with Guy Whittall, showed what was possible on a pitch that played well throughout. Strang, only picked because his brother Paul was injured, counter-attacked gamely, hitting Mushtaq for two straight fours and a six. Whittall pulled anything remotely short and hit 13 fours, three off successive balls from Wasim Akram.

Pakistan's batsmen, most of them out of form, lacked the patience to graft on a pitch discouraging strokeplay. The Zimbabwean seamers embraced the ploy of bowling on a length, wide of off stump, trying to frustrate them into giving wickets away. Several did, but Mohammad Wasim's watchfulness, combined with his ability to put the bad ball away, proved all-important. Mushtaq, who also capitalised on some indifferent bowling to score a sensible fifty, was the perfect foil for 49 overs. Mohammad was last out for a career-best 192, having hit 23 fours in 407 balls.

Needing a good start to their second innings, Zimbabwe ran into early problems as the new ball swung. Conditions eased after that and Goodwin and Andy Flower slowly added 95 for the fourth wicket. Goodwin showed excellent temperament and technique by batting for nearly six hours until Waqar took the new ball and immediately dismissed him for 81. Some lusty blows from Streak at least gave Zimbabwe something to bowl at, but it was not enough. They made Pakistan's task all the easier on the final day with some ill-directed bowling. Saeed Anwar scored 65 in 89 balls, and Pakistan needed only 54 overs to make 192. Youhana fell for 52 with victory in sight.

Man of the Match: Mohammad Wasim.   *Man of the Series:* Waqar Younis.

Close of play: First day, Pakistan 18-0 (Saeed Anwar 9*, Ali Naqvi 6*); Second day, Pakistan 190-8 (Mohammad Wasim 96*, Mushtaq Ahmed 0*); Third day, Zimbabwe 82-3 (M. W. Goodwin 25*, A. Flower 25*); Fourth day, Pakistan 58-1 (Saeed Anwar 37*, Mohammad Wasim 8*).

Zimbabwe

G. W. Flower c Rashid Latif b Azhar Mahmood	39	– lbw b Wasim Akram	6
G. J. Rennie c Rashid Latif b Azhar Mahmood	13	– c Yousuf Youhana b Waqar Younis.	0
M. W. Goodwin c Inzamam-ul-Haq b Mushtaq Ahmed	53	– c Inzamam-ul-Haq b Waqar Younis	81
*A. D. R. Campbell c Yousuf Youhana b Mushtaq Ahmed	23	– lbw b Azhar Mahmood	14
†A. Flower lbw b Waqar Younis	1	– c Inzamam-ul-Haq b Mushtaq Ahmed	49
G. J. Whittall c Inzamam-ul-Haq b Wasim Akram	62	– c Rashid Latif b Azhar Mahmood	15
T. N. Madondo run out	0	– c Rashid Latif b Azhar Mahmood	2
H. H. Streak c Mohammad Wasim b Waqar Younis	6	– not out	37
B. C. Strang c and b Waqar Younis	53	– c Yousuf Youhana b Mushtaq Ahmed	21
A. G. Huckle b Waqar Younis	0	– b Wasim Akram	0
M. Mbangwa not out	2	– lbw b Wasim Akram	3
B 6, l-b 14, w 1, n-b 4	25	B 13, l-b 15, n-b 12	40

1/47 (2) 2/75 (1) 3/141 (4) 4/142 (5)   277   1/7 (1) 2/9 (2) 3/38 (4)   268
5/143 (3) 6/144 (7) 7/153 (8)   4/133 (5) 5/166 (6) 6/175 (7)
8/263 (9) 9/263 (10) 10/277 (6)   7/205 (3) 8/255 (9)
     9/255 (10) 10/268 (11)

Bowling: First Innings—Wasim Akram 20.5–6–67–1; Waqar Younis 20–8–47–4; Mushtaq Ahmed 20–2–74–2; Azhar Mahmood 22–6–69–2. *Second Innings*—Wasim Akram 33–8–70–3; Waqar Younis 25–3–60–2; Azhar Mahmood 16–7–26–3; Mushtaq Ahmed 37–6–84–2.

Pakistan

Saeed Anwar lbw b G. J. Whittall	15	– c sub (A. R. Whittall) b G. J. Whittall	65
Ali Naqvi c A. Flower b G. J. Whittall	13	– (7) c A. Flower b Huckle	8
Mohammad Wasim c Mbangwa b G. J. Whittall	192	– run out	8
Inzamam-ul-Haq c and b Strang	13	– st A. Flower b Huckle	10
Yousuf Youhana c A. Flower b Mbangwa	9	– c Goodwin b G. J. Whittall	52
Moin Khan b Strang	12	– c Campbell b Streak	21
Azhar Mahmood c G. J. Whittall b Mbangwa	20	– (2) c Campbell b Streak	9
Wasim Akram c Rennie b Mbangwa	0	– not out	12
*†Rashid Latif c sub (A. R. Whittall) b Strang	4	– not out	1
Mushtaq Ahmed c Campbell b Streak	57		
Waqar Younis not out	8		
L-b 8, w 1, n-b 2	11	B 2, l-b 3, n-b 1	6

1/31 (1) 2/46 (2) 3/61 (4) 4/88 (5)   354   1/14 (2) 2/59 (3) 3/77 (4)   (7 wkts) 192
5/119 (6) 6/169 (7) 7/169 (8)   4/105 (1) 5/138 (6)
8/187 (9) 9/334 (10) 10/354 (3)   6/162 (7) 7/186 (5)

Bowling: First Innings—Streak 31–8–83–1; Mbangwa 33–12–56–3; Strang 28–10–65–3; G. J. Whittall 32.5–4–78–3; Huckle 21–7–55–0; Goodwin 2–0–9–0. *Second Innings*—Streak 13–5–40–2; G. J. Whittall 15–4–35–2; Mbangwa 2–0–11–0; Huckle 18.5–1–81–2; Strang 5–0–20–0.

Umpires: S. G. Randell (Australia) and R. B. Tiffin. Referee: G. T. Dowling (New Zealand).

†ZIMBABWE v PAKISTAN

First One-Day International

At Harare Sports Club, Harare, March 28. Pakistan won by four wickets. Toss: Pakistan.

Campbell promoted himself to open with Grant Flower and they put on 72 in 14 overs, but Zimbabwe then slumped. All of the top order bar Andy Flower got starts, but none went on to play a long innings. Strang helped set a target but, once Aamir Sohail and Ijaz Ahmed steadied Pakistan's reply after a poor start, the outcome was a virtual formality against unimpressive home bowling. Strang was not yet fully fit and played only as a batsman. In the closing stages, Shahid Afridi smashed 30 off 20 balls.

Man of the Match: Aamir Sohail.

Zimbabwe

G. W. Flower c Rashid Latif		H. H. Streak not out	48
b Azhar Mahmood .	32	C. N. Evans c Rashid Latif	
*A. D. R. Campbell		b Aamir Sohail .	5
c and b Azhar Mahmood .	36	P. A. Strang not out	15
M. W. Goodwin b Shahid Afridi	35		
†A. Flower c Rashid Latif		L-b 6, w 9, n-b 3	18
b Shoaib Akhtar .	5		—
G. J. Whittall c Ijaz Ahmed		1/72 2/80 3/95 (6 wkts, 50 overs) 236	
b Shahid Afridi .	42	4/154 5/171 6/187	

D. P. Viljoen, A. R. Whittall and M. Mbangwa did not bat.

Bowling: Wasim Akram 10–0–52–0; Waqar Younis 8–0–55–0; Azhar Mahmood 9–1–34–2; Shoaib Akhtar 5–0–10–1; Shahid Afridi 10–1–45–2; Aamir Sohail 8–0–34–1.

Pakistan

Aamir Sohail c Campbell b Evans	77	Shahid Afridi c Evans b Goodwin	30
Inzamam-ul-Haq c Mbangwa b Streak	0	Azhar Mahmood c Evans b G. J. Whittall	13
Mohammad Wasim c A. R. Whittall		Wasim Akram not out	2
b G. J. Whittall .	3	B 2, l-b 1, w 7	10
Ijaz Ahmed, sen. c G. W. Flower			—
b Evans .	43	1/15 2/27 3/121 (6 wkts, 47.4 overs) 237	
Yousuf Youhana not out	59	4/137 5/198 6/226	

*†Rashid Latif, Shoaib Akhtar and Waqar Younis did not bat.

Bowling: Streak 10–0–48–1; Mbangwa 10–1–34–0; G. J. Whittall 9.4–1–35–2; A. R. Whittall 4–0–27–0; Evans 9–0–50–2; G. W. Flower 2–0–15–0; Goodwin 1–0–13–1; Viljoen 2–0–12–0.

Umpires: K. C. Barbour and I. D. Robinson.

†ZIMBABWE v PAKISTAN

Second One-Day International

At Harare Sports Club, Harare, March 29. Pakistan won by four wickets. Toss: Pakistan.

On another good pitch, Zimbabwe started more slowly, making only 71 in their first 20 overs. Campbell, who had scored at nearly a run a ball the previous day, laboured 41 balls over 12 this time, but Grant Flower, well supported by Goodwin, upped the tempo. From the last 11 overs, Whittall and Streak plundered 89, to reach a useful total of 272. Shahid Afridi continued as he had left off, with three sixes in his 20-ball 32. He got his side off to a flier, but then three wickets fell for eight runs. Mohammad Wasim and Yousuf Youhana swung the match in a stand of 144 in 28 overs, and Mohammad Hussain ensured an early finish with 31 off 20 balls. Zimbabwe again bowled poorly.

Man of the Match: Mohammad Wasim.   *Man of the Series:* G. J. Whittall.

Zimbabwe

G. W. Flower st Rashid Latif		G. J. Whittall not out	53
b Mohammad Hussain .	81	H. H. Streak not out	26
*A. D. R. Campbell st Rashid Latif		B 1, l-b 13, w 18	32
b Mohammad Hussain .	12		—
M. W. Goodwin run out	47	1/64 2/149	(4 wkts, 50 overs) 272
†A. Flower b Waqar Younis	21	3/177 4/183	

C. B. Wishart, C. N. Evans, P. A. Strang, A. G. Huckle and M. Mbangwa did not bat.

Bowling: Wasim Akram 10–0–51–0; Waqar Younis 10–1–39–1; Azhar Mahmood 10–1–45–0; Shahid Afridi 10–0–63–0; Mohammad Hussain 10–0–60–2.

Pakistan

Saeed Anwar c Streak b Whittall	25	Azhar Mahmood not out	14
Shahid Afridi c A. Flower b Streak	32	Mohammad Hussain not out	31
Mohammad Wasim c Strang			
b G. W. Flower .	76	L-b 7, w 9, n-b 2	18
Ijaz Ahmed, sen. lbw b Whittall	4		—
Yousuf Youhana b Streak	66	1/57 2/60 3/65	(6 wkts, 46.4 overs) 276
Moin Khan lbw b Goodwin	10	4/209 5/225 6/227	

*†Rashid Latif, Wasim Akram and Waqar Younis did not bat.

Bowling: Streak 8–0–36–2; Mbangwa 10–0–72–0; Whittall 8–0–41–2; Huckle 10–0–45–0; Evans 5.4–0–35–0; G. W. Flower 3–0–25–1; Goodwin 2–0–15–1.

Umpires: G. R. Evans and R. B. Tiffin. Series referee: G. T. Dowling (New Zealand).

Pakistan's matches v South Africa and Sri Lanka in the Standard Bank International One-Day Series (April 3–23) may be found in that section.

INTERNATIONAL UMPIRES' PANEL

On December 21, 1993, the International Cricket Council announced the formation of an international umpires' panel, backed by sponsorship from National Grid. Each full member of ICC was to nominate two officials – apart from England, who named four, because of their large number of professional umpires and the fact that most Tests take place during the English winter. A third-country member of the panel was to stand with a "home" umpire, not necessarily from the panel, in every Test staged from February 1994. Teams would have no right of objection to appointments. In 1997, National Grid renewed their sponsorship until 2000.

The following umpires were on the panel from September 1998: S. A. Bucknor (West Indies), D. B. Cowie (New Zealand), R. S. Dunne (New Zealand), K. T. Francis (Sri Lanka), D. B. Hair (Australia), D. J. Harper (Australia), Javed Akhtar (Pakistan), M. J. Kitchen (England), R. E. Koertzen (South Africa), P. Manuel (Sri Lanka), E. A. Nicholls (West Indies), D. L. Orchard (South Africa), V. K. Ramaswamy (India), I. D. Robinson (Zimbabwe), Salim Badar (Pakistan), G. Sharp (England), D. R. Shepherd (England), R. B. Tiffin (Zimbabwe), S. Venkataraghavan (India), P. Willey (England).

Note: Compared with the 1997-98 list, D. J. Harper has replaced S. G. Randell, P. Manuel has replaced B. C. Cooray, E. A. Nicholls has replaced L. H. Barker, and D. L. Orchard has replaced C. J. Mitchley.

THE AUSTRALIANS IN INDIA, 1997-98

By DICKY RUTNAGUR

Australia's sequence of nine victorious Test series, starting with the 1994-95 Ashes, was ended by India, who had not lost a series on home soil for exactly 11 years. There had been one blip in Australia's record before this, also involving India, when they lost a one-off Test in Delhi in October 1996. But India's 2-1 victory – the Australian win came in the dead last game – was only the second time they had had the better of Australia over a Test series. The last was in 1979-80, during the Packer era, when the Australian team was gravely weakened.

Their 1997-98 successors were not at full strength either. Two frontline fast bowlers, Glenn McGrath and Jason Gillespie, were left at home recovering from injuries. Then Paul Reiffel, one of only two experienced seam bowlers in the party, suffered a recurrence of his shoulder injury; he played no further part after the First Test. Michael Kasprowicz was forced to play the dual role of strike and stock bowler. These misfortunes explain Australia's inability to win, until the very end, but not the two heavy defeats. Their batsmen were the best they could call on, yet they failed time and again against an attack as limited as their own. The two Australian centuries, by Mark Waugh and Mark Taylor, were scored after the series was settled; Michael Slater, too, was slow to make an impact.

The fact that the last series Australia lost was in Pakistan, in 1994-95, suggested that they are still not at ease touring the subcontinent. But there were no overt signs of unhappiness, except that Shane Warne could not manage the cuisine and had cans of baked beans and spaghetti flown out. A more plausible explanation for the poor performance was tiredness, exacerbated by extreme heat and humidity. In the 17 months since their last visit to India, Australia had played 20 Tests – five against West Indies, six against South Africa, six against England and three against New Zealand. They had also played 33 one-day internationals, culminating with four in New Zealand just before arriving here.

Pre-series hype concentrated on the head-to-head contest between India's batting champion, Sachin Tendulkar, and Warne, the greatest contemporary bowler. The two jousted five times during the Tests and only once was Warne the winner. Of the Indian bowlers savaged by Don Bradman in the first-ever series between the two countries, in 1947-48, a handful survive: watching Tendulkar blasting away at Warne *et al* might have left them with a sense that vengeance had come at last. The 446 runs Tendulkar scored in the series, at a strike-rate of 80.65 per hundred balls received and a Bradmanesque average of 111.50, were the product of sheer genius. The Australians had been given a warning of the storm to come in their opening fixture against Mumbai, when Tendulkar made 204 not out from 192 balls. Warne's ten wickets in the series cost 54 runs apiece; his career average previously was 23.81. The Indians, using their feet, played him expertly. But the limitations of the pace department and the inexperience of his fellow spinner, Gavin Robertson (ironically, Australia's main wicket-taker), thrust on him the colossal burden of holding the fort as well as attacking. And the figures were unkind: there were times when he bowled really well, though at a slower pace than usual and without trying to turn his leg-break extravagantly.

Tendulkar's dramatic return to top form probably owed something to his loss of the captaincy. Mohammad Azharuddin had been reinstated in January, a move not universally approved at first. But he seemed more committed than for a long time, while Tendulkar, far from brooding, revelled in freedom from the onus of leadership. In the field, he often volunteered advice, and Azharuddin often sought it.

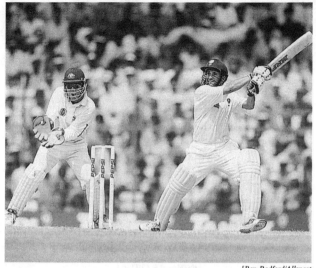

[Ben Radford/Allsport

Ian Healy watches open-mouthed as Sachin Tendulkar dominates the Australian bowling on his
way to 155 not out during the First Test at Chennai.

India's other batsmen were by no means eclipsed. Tendulkar had scope to flourish
because he invariably went in with the innings well established, thanks to Navjot Sidhu,
who was only once dismissed for less than 50, and the solidity of Rahul Dravid at
No. 3. In the Second Test, Azharuddin cut loose with a vengeance to score 163 not
out. V. V. S. Laxman returned in the same match with 95, pressing his claim to the
opener's spot, while Mongia, almost faultless with the gloves, did his bit with the bat
too. India's bowling strength did not run as deep: they were completely reliant on
Javagal Srinath and Anil Kumble. Although the pitches were not amenable to pace,
Srinath was hostile, willing and intelligent. His absence from the Third Test through
injury weakened his side badly. Kumble, cutting down on his pace and harnessing
variations to spin and bounce, rose to great heights and finished with 23 wickets.
Venkatapathy Raju, the left-arm spinner, took six wickets in the First Test but was
ineffectual afterwards. While Australia's fielding sometimes fell below its usual high
level, India's had improved, especially close in, where Dravid and Laxman were
brilliant.

The series was played in congenial spirit. However, the referee, Peter van der Merwe,
twice took punitive action for dissent: against Mongia in the First Test, and Ganguly
– suspended for one match – in the last. Crowds for the Chennai and Calcutta Tests
were large and exuberant but well behaved, and the conspicuous camaraderie between
the locals and a substantial group of visiting Australian supporters was most heart-
warming.

AUSTRALIAN TOURING PARTY

M. A. Taylor (New South Wales) (*captain*), S. R. Waugh (New South Wales) (*vice-captain*), G. S. Blewett (South Australia), A. C. Dale (Queensland), I. A. Healy (Queensland), M. S. Kasprowicz (Queensland), D. S. Lehmann (South Australia), S. C. G. MacGill (South Australia), R. T. Ponting (Tasmania), P. R. Reiffel (Victoria), G. R. Robertson (South Australia), M. J. Slater (New South Wales), S. K. Warne (Victoria), M. E. Waugh (New South Wales), P. Wilson (South Australia).

D. W. Fleming (Victoria) replaced Wilson, who returned home injured. M. G. Bevan (New South Wales) reinforced the team when S. R. Waugh was injured.

A. C. Gilchrist, D. R. Martyn and T. M. Moody (all Western Australia) replaced Taylor, Blewett, Dale, Healy, MacGill, Reiffel and Slater for the one-day triangular series. S. R. Waugh took over the captaincy.

Tour manager: Dr A. C. Battersby.   *Team manager:* S. R. Bernard.   *Coach:* G. R. Marsh.

AUSTRALIAN TOUR RESULTS

Test matches – Played 3: Won 1, Lost 2.
First-class matches – Played 6: Won 1, Lost 3, Drawn 2.
Win – India.
Losses – India (2), Mumbai.
Draws – Board President's XI, India A.
One-day internationals – Played 5: Won 3, Lost 2. *Wins* – Zimbabwe (2), India. *Losses* – India (2).

TEST MATCH AVERAGES

INDIA – BATTING

	T	I	NO	R	HS	100s	50s	Avge	Ct
S. R. Tendulkar	3	5	1	446	177	2	1	111.50	2
M. Azharuddin.	3	5	1	311	163*	1	1	77.75	6
N. S. Sidhu.	3	5	0	341	97	0	4	68.20	0
N. R. Mongia	3	5	2	136	58	0	1	45.33	7
R. Dravid	3	5	0	223	86	0	3	44.60	6
V. V. S. Laxman	2	3	0	116	95	0	1	38.66	4
S. C. Ganguly	3	5	1	131	65	0	1	32.75	2
A. Kumble	3	5	0	78	39	0	0	26.00	2
S. L. V. Raju	3	3	0	7	5	0	0	2.33	1
Harvinder Singh.	2	3	1	0	0*	0	0	0.00	0

Played in two Tests: R. K. Chauhan 3; J. Srinath 1 (3 ct). Played in one Test: Harbhajan Singh 4*, 0 (1 ct).

* *Signifies not out.*

BOWLING

	O	M	R	W	BB	5W/i	Avge
S. C. Ganguly	19.4	3	47	3	3-28	0	15.66
A. Kumble	191	51	416	23	6-98	2	18.08
J. Srinath	59.3	13	179	8	3-44	0	22.37
S. L. V. Raju	132	32	302	7	3-31	0	43.14
R. K. Chauhan.	76.4	16	228	4	2-66	0	57.00

Also bowled: Harbhajan Singh 29–2–136–2; Harvinder Singh 23–4–98–2; V. V. S. Laxman 2–0–2–0; S. R. Tendulkar 13.2–1–47–1.

AUSTRALIA – BATTING

	T	I	NO	R	HS	100s	50s	Avge	Ct
M. E. Waugh	3	6	2	280	153*	1	1	70.00	1
I. A. Healy	3	5	1	165	90	0	1	41.25	6
S. R. Waugh	2	4	0	152	80	0	1	38.00	2
M. A. Taylor	3	6	1	189	102*	1	0	37.80	3
M. J. Slater	3	6	0	162	91	0	1	27.00	0
R. T. Ponting	3	5	0	105	60	0	1	21.00	3
S. K. Warne	3	5	0	105	35	0	0	21.00	0
G. R. Robertson	3	5	0	90	57	0	1	18.00	1
M. S. Kasprowicz. . . .	3	5	1	54	25	0	0	13.50	1
G. S. Blewett	3	6	0	48	25	0	0	8.00	2

Played in one Test: A. C. Dale 5; D. S. Lehmann 52 (2 ct); P. R. Reiffel 15, 8 (1 ct); P. Wilson 0*, 0*.

* Signifies not out.

BOWLING

	O	M	R	W	BB	5W/i	Avge
A. C. Dale	28	7	92	3	3-71	0	30.66
G. R. Robertson	111.4	13	413	12	4-72	0	34.41
M. S. Kasprowicz	116	29	312	8	5-28	1	39.00
S. K. Warne	167	37	540	10	4-85	0	54.00

Also bowled: G. S. Blewett 45–8–152–2; D. S. Lehmann 7–1–27–1; P. R. Reiffel 24–5–59–0; M. E. Waugh 32–1–149–2; S. R. Waugh 12–1–38–0; P. Wilson 12–2–50–0.

At Mumbai, February 24, 25. 26. Mumbai won by ten wickets. Toss: Australians. Australians 305 for eight dec. (M. J. Slater 98, G. S. Blewett 47, R. T. Ponting 53, P. R. Reiffel 30; R. V. Pawar three for 59) and 135 (G. S. Blewett 50, R. T. Ponting 37; N. M. Kulkarni five for 23); Mumbai 410 for six dec. (A. A. Pagnis 50, S. V. Manjrekar 39, S. R. Tendulkar 204 not out, A. A. Muzumdar 42, R. Sutar 45) and 31 for no wkt.

Manjrekar announced that this would be his final first-class appearance. Tendulkar's 204 not out, his maiden double-hundred, lasted 269 minutes and 192 balls and included 25 fours and two sixes.

At Vishakhapatnam, March 1, 2, 3. Drawn. Toss: Board President's XI. Board President's XI 329 for four dec. (S. Ramesh 58, V. V. S. Laxman 85, H. H. Kanitkar 102 not out, V. Pratap 59 not out); Australians 567 for eight (M. J. Slater 207, G. S. Blewett 57, R. T. Ponting 155, M. E. Waugh 52, Extras 35; A. Kuruvilla three for 105).

Slater's 207 lasted 236 balls and included 22 fours and six sixes. He added 206 with Ponting.

INDIA v AUSTRALIA

First Test Match

At Chennai (formerly Madras), March 6, 7, 8, 9, 10. India won by 179 runs. Toss: India. Test debuts: Harvinder Singh; G. R. Robertson.

The head-to-head contest between Sachin Tendulkar and Shane Warne was the key to this opening encounter. Warne's quick conquest of Tendulkar in the first innings gave Australia the initial advantage. But Tendulkar retaliated so devastatingly in the second, scoring 155 not out, that India were able to declare with a lead of 347, and 105 overs to bowl Australia out on a spinners' pitch. They had three men out overnight and won in comfort on the final afternoon.

On the first day, Tendulkar had been as much a victim of Warne's guile as of his own daring. He drove his first ball with scorching power past the bowler. But the fifth dipped as he rushed forward, and turned to take the edge of his flailing bat; Taylor completed a marvellous slip catch. In the second innings, however, when Tendulkar scored his third and highest century in seven Tests against Australia, he was as severe on Warne as on the rest. Warne followed up his first-innings four for 85 with a deflating one for 122. Tendulkar's belligerence was awesome and his shot-placement enthralling.

Both sides batted erratically at their first attempt. After an opening stand of 122 between Sidhu and Mongia, three Indian wickets went down for eight and the last five for ten. They were saved because Dravid batted four hours and built respectable stands with Azharuddin and Kumble. On a bare pitch of little pace, the quick bowlers could only contain. But it readily offered purchase to spin and was so generous with lift that Mongia was wearing a helmet to keep to Kumble by the second day. Warne and the tall debutant off-spinner Gavin Robertson skilfully exploited the batsmen's indiscretions. Each picked up four wickets; Robertson struck back admirably after being severely mauled by Sidhu in his maiden Test spell.

In reply, Australia stumbled to 137 for six: only Mark Waugh, who lasted three hours, batted with distinction. They were hauled back into the game by the indomitable Healy. He made a fighting 90, and put on 96 with Robertson, splendidly accomplished for a No. 10. They looked so much at ease as they set up a lead of 71 that the pitch seemed to have dozed off.

This impression stayed when India resumed on the third evening. Warne had already been softened up by Sidhu before Tendulkar came in at 115 for two. He and Dravid almost doubled that. Then, when Australia rather fortuitously prised Dravid out, Azharuddin joined Tendulkar to pound a wilting attack for another 127 runs in even time, a stand reminiscent of their epic in Cape Town 14 months earlier. In all, Tendulkar batted for 286 minutes and 191 balls, and struck 14 fours and four sixes.

Azharuddin's declaration gave Australia 15 overs on the fourth evening, in which India grabbed three wickets. Slater drove expansively at Srinath and played on; Kumble had Blewett caught at silly point; and Taylor bottom-edged a pull on to his pad and was caught on the ricochet.

These disasters extinguished Australia's hopes of winning. But a calm start on the final morning did raise their prospects for survival before four wickets fell for 42 runs. All four batsmen looked displeased and television suggested three decisions were harsh and the fourth dubious. The umpires did have a difficult task with the ball turning and fielders clustered round the bat; referee van der Merwe, who had reprimanded Mongia for "excessive appealing" earlier, took no action now, attributing the Australians' reactions to mere disappointment.

But with seven down at lunch, Australia were sunk. Again, Healy batted as if to gag the proverbial fat lady; he was undefeated after an hour and a half when Kumble completed victory with his eighth wicket of the match.

Man of the Match: S. R. Tendulkar.

Close of play: First day, India 232-5 (R. Dravid 42*, A. Kumble 19*); Second day, Australia 193-7 (I. A. Healy 31*, S. K. Warne 13*); Third day, India 100-1 (N. S. Sidhu 55*, R. Dravid 18*); Fourth day, Australia 31-3 (P. R. Reiffel 0*).

India

†N. R. Mongia c Healy b Kasprowicz	58	– lbw b Blewett	18
N. S. Sidhu run out	62	– c Ponting b Robertson	64
R. Dravid c Robertson b Warne	52	– c Healy b Warne	56
S. R. Tendulkar c Taylor b Warne	4	– not out	155
*M. Azharuddin c Reiffel b Warne	26	– c S. R. Waugh b M. E. Waugh	64
S. C. Ganguly lbw b Robertson	3	– not out	30
A. Kumble c S. R. Waugh b Robertson	30		
J. Srinath c Taylor b Warne	1		
R. K. Chauhan c Healy b Robertson	3		
Harvinder Singh not out	0		
S. L. V. Raju b Robertson	0		
B 8, l-b 6, n-b 4	18	B 18, l-b 6, n-b 7	31

1/122 (1) 2/126 (2) 3/130 (4) 4/186 (5)   257   1/43 (1) 2/115 (2)   (4 wkts dec.) 418
5/195 (6) 6/247 (7) 7/248 (8)   3/228 (3) 4/355 (5)
8/253 (9) 9/257 (3) 10/257 (11)

Bowling: *First Innings*—Kasprowicz 21–8–44–1; Reiffel 15–4–27–0; Warne 35–11–85–4; Robertson 28.2–4–72–4; M. E. Waugh 1–0–4–0; S. R. Waugh 4–1–11–0. *Second Innings*—Kasprowicz 14–6–42–0; Reiffel 9–1–32–0; Robertson 27–4–92–1; Warne 30–7–122–1; Blewett 10–2–35–1; M. E. Waugh 9–0–44–1; S. R. Waugh 8–0–27–0.

Australia

*M. A. Taylor c Mongia b Harvinder Singh	12	– (2) c Srinath b Kumble	13
M. J. Slater c David b Kumble	11	– (1) b Srinath	13
M. E. Waugh c Ganguly b Raju	66	– (5) c David b Kumble	18
S. R. Waugh b Kumble	12	– (6) c David b Raju	27
R. T. Ponting c Mongia b Raju	18	– (7) lbw b Raju	2
G. S. Blewett lbw b Chauhan	9	– (3) c David b Kumble	5
†I. A. Healy c Ganguly b Raju	90	– (8) not out	32
P. R. Reiffel c David b Kumble	15	– (4) c Azharuddin b Raju	8
S. K. Warne c Tendulkar b Kumble	17	– c Kumble b Chauhan	35
G. R. Robertson c Mongia b Srinath	57	– b Chauhan	0
M. S. Kasprowicz not out	11	– c Kumble b Kumble	4
B 1, l-b 6, n-b 3	10	B 4, l-b 3, n-b 4	11

1/16 (2) 2/44 (1) 3/57 (4) 4/95 (5)   328   1/18 (1) 2/30 (3) 3/31 (2) 4/54 (5)   168
5/119 (6) 6/137 (3) 7/173 (8)   5/79 (4) 6/91 (7) 7/96 (6)
8/201 (9) 9/297 (7) 10/328 (10)   8/153 (9) 9/153 (10) 10/168 (11)

Bowling: *First Innings*—Srinath 17.3–3–46–1; Harvinder Singh 11–4–28–1; Kumble 45–10–103–4; Chauhan 25–3–90–1; Raju 32–8–54–3. *Second Innings*—Srinath 6–4–9–1; Harvinder Singh 2–0–9–0; Chauhan 22–7–66–2; Kumble 22.5–7–46–4; Raju 15–4–31–3.

Umpires: G. Sharp (England) and S. Venkataraghavan.
Referee: P. L. van der Merwe (South Africa).

At Jamshedpur, March 13, 14, 15. Drawn. Toss: India A. India A 216 for nine dec. (D. Manohar 30, V. Rathore 36, J. J. Martin 45, V. Dahiya 42; P. Wilson three for 51, S. C. G. MacGill four for 67) and 241 for two (A. R. Khurasia 117 not out, J. J. Martin 52 not out); Australians 391 (M. A. Taylor 57, G. S. Blewett 57, S. R. Waugh 107, D. S. Lehmann 76, P. R. Reiffel 33; B. K. V. Prasad three for 89, K. N. A. Padmanabhan three for 71).

INDIA v AUSTRALIA

Second Test Match

At Calcutta, March 18, 19, 20, 21. India won by an innings and 219 runs. Toss: Australia. Test debut: P. Wilson.

Rather than make amends for their batting failures in the First Test, Australia plumbed new depths. They could not blame the pitch; in between their innings of 233 and 181, India amassed 633 for five, their biggest total ever against Australia and the highest total at Eden Gardens. No Indian was dismissed for less than 65, while only two Australians passed 45. Australia had bad luck with injuries and umpiring errors. But so vast was the chasm that it made little difference as they surrendered the series.

Azharuddin scored his fifth century in six Tests on this ground, and it was one of his masterpieces: 163 not out in 310 minutes with 18 fours and three sixes. But with the pitch so amiable, it was apt that a bowler was named Man of the Match – and that it was Srinath, rather than Kumble, whose bag was fuller by two wickets, for Srinath's strikes made the bigger impact. He bowled with pace and accuracy, cutting the ball back and, in the second innings, reverse-swinging it menacingly.

In the first over of the match, Srinath, producing extra bounce from a length, had Slater caught at short leg. His next ball bowled Blewett, and within half an hour he had Mark Waugh lbw. Taylor could not locate the middle of his bat and, having made only three in 49 overs, sliced one that Ganguly – sharing the new ball because India had dropped Harvinder Singh – slanted across him.

India's ascendancy, established in that first over, was challenged only during a partnership of 112 between Steve Waugh and Ponting, which had its roots in a miserable 29 for four. It would have been 51 for five had Ponting not got away with a snick off Kumble to Mongia, who missed nothing else. But for two and a half hours, they batted with an air of permanence until Ponting pulled at a ball from Kumble that was not short enough. Waugh, who had strained his groin, was out when his runner, Blewett, failed to make his ground. His disability notwithstanding, he had batted with poise for a flawless 80, with 13 fours. Resistance thereafter was confined to a ninth-wicket stand of 54 between Robertson and Kasprowicz.

India had picked Laxman at the last minute, from outside their squad of 12, to open the batting with Sidhu. The pairing was a triumph: they put on 191 in only 40 overs. Australia had also made one change, because of an injury to Reiffel's shoulder, but Paul Wilson had a disappointing debut as their latest opening bowler. His leg-stump line invited punishment from Laxman, who is strong off his legs, but neither he nor Kasprowicz pitched the ball up as Srinath did. Both openers fell just short of a hundred, Sidhu missing a deflection at Mark Waugh and Laxman edging a square-cut. Tendulkar launched an immediate assault. He bent the bowling to his will, reaching 50 off only 60 balls, but a lapse of concentration cost him his wicket on 79, including 12 fours and two sixes. Kasprowicz and Warne checked the scoring next morning and Dravid, impatient for his century, fell to Blewett. But once the bowlers tired, Azharuddin cut loose and Ganguly joined in the plunder.

In Australia's second innings, Taylor began to bat soundly at last, but was run out by agile fielding from Laxman at short leg. Healy and the injured Steve Waugh resisted for a while until they, like Blewett, were out to dubious lbw decisions which expedited Australia's demise on the fourth evening.

Man of the Match: J. Srinath.

Close of play: First day, Australia 233; Second day, India 369-3 (R. Dravid 76*, M. Azharuddin 9*); Third day, Australia 38-1 (M. A. Taylor 11*, G. S. Blewett 19*).

Australia

M. J. Slater c Dravid b Srinath	0	– (2) b Srinath	5
*M. A. Taylor c Mongia b Ganguly	3	– (1) run out	45
G. S. Blewett b Srinath	0	– lbw b Srinath	25
M. E. Waugh lbw b Srinath	10	– c Laxman b Kumble	0
S. R. Waugh run out	80	– (7) lbw b Kumble	33
R. T. Ponting b Kumble	60	– (5) c Srinath b Kumble	9
†I. A. Healy c Laxman b Kumble	1	– (6) b Srinath	38
S. K. Warne c Azharuddin b Kumble	11	– c and b Kumble	9
G. R. Robertson lbw b Ganguly	29	– c Azharuddin b Kumble	0
M. S. Kasprowicz c Azharuddin b Ganguly	25	– c Raju b Chauhan	10
P. Wilson not out	0	– not out	0
L-b 2, n-b 12	14	B 1, l-b 3, n-b 3	7

1/1 (1) 2/1 (3) 3/15 (4) 4/29 (2)   233   1/7 (2) 2/55 (4) 3/56 (3) 4/81 (5)   181
5/141 (6) 6/151 (7) 7/168 (8)   5/91 (1) 6/133 (6) 7/158 (8)
8/178 (5) 9/232 (10) 10/233 (9)   8/158 (9) 9/181 (7) 10/181 (10)

Bowling: *First Innings*—Srinath 17–0–80–3; Ganguly 13.4–3–28–3; Kumble 28–11–44–3; Tendulkar 2–0–6–0; Raju 17–2–42–0; Chauhan 11–2–30–0; Laxman 1–0–1–0. *Second Innings*—Srinath 19–6–44–3; Ganguly 4–0–9–0; Kumble 31–10–62–5; Chauhan 18.4–4–42–1; Raju 16–7–20–0.

India

V. V. S. Laxman c Healy b Robertson	95	†N. R. Mongia not out		30
N. S. Sidhu lbw b M. E. Waugh	97			
R. Dravid c and b Blewett	86	B 2, l-b 7, n-b 9		18
S. R. Tendulkar c Blewett b Kasprowicz	79			
*M. Azharuddin not out	163	1/191 (2) 2/207 (1)	(5 wkts dec.)	633
S. C. Ganguly c sub (D. S. Lehmann)		3/347 (4) 4/400 (3)		
b Robertson	65	5/558 (6)		

A. Kumble, J. Srinath, R. K. Chauhan and S. L. V. Raju did not bat.

Bowling: Kasprowicz 34–6–122–1; Wilson 12–2–50–0; Blewett 20–3–65–1; Warne 42–4–147–0; Robertson 33–2–163–2; M. E. Waugh 18–1–77–1.

Umpires: B. C. Cooray (Sri Lanka) and K. Parthasarathy.
Referee: P. L. van der Merwe (South Africa).

INDIA v AUSTRALIA

Third Test Match

At Bangalore, March 25, 26, 27, 28. Australia won by eight wickets. Toss: India. Test debuts: Harbhajan Singh; A. C. Dale, D. S. Lehmann.

Few Tests – at least in the modern era of covered pitches – have ended decisively after both sides have scored 400 in the first innings, and fewer still inside four days to boot. Though India batted poorly the second time, the positive approach of both teams contributed to the speedy finish.

Australia's victory was especially laudable given their growing injury list. Steve Waugh, their staunchest batsman, had not recovered after the Second Test and was replaced by newcomer Darren Lehmann. Reiffel and Wilson had returned home for treatment and Damien Fleming, who had been flown out, fell ill; Adam Dale, a fast-medium bowler, filled the vacancy. India had one fitness problem, but a major one: Srinath had a side strain, so Harvinder Singh returned. India also omitted Chauhan and picked another off-spinner, 17-year-old Harbhajan Singh.

Although India, batting first on a slow pitch, formed only two substantial partnerships, they ran up 424 in a little over four sessions. Impetus and substance came from Sidhu, who hit eight fours and three sixes, and then Tendulkar, who scored 177 out of 281 added while he was in, with 29 fours and three sixes. He put on 139 with an indisposed Azharuddin, who was, by his standards, subdued. But Tendulkar was impossible to contain, especially on the second morning, when he scored 60 in 64 balls. He fell to his own excesses, when he tried to hoist a straight ball from Dale to mid-wicket and was bowled. Dale had earlier accounted for Ganguly, who was suspended for one match after showing his disapproval when given lbw.

Taylor called on seven bowlers, but depended heavily on Kasprowicz, who bowled a fuller length than previously, and Warne, who bowled well even though the pitch was short of pace and bounce. Warne's dismissal of Dravid – which made him Test cricket's most successful spinner, carrying him past Lance Gibbs's 309 wickets – was a classic. The ball drifted and dipped on to leg stump, then spun away to hit off. Minutes earlier, he had bowled Sidhu, and he added Mongia through a magnificent catch at cover by Ponting.

Australia replied with urgency matching India's, and the pattern of their innings was remarkably similar; they, too, had only three major contributions, with Mark Waugh's delightful 153 not out the highest. The fact that Waugh had a gastric disorder added to the merit of his innings. He batted responsibly, yet was free with all manner of strokes, hitting 13 fours and four sixes. Lehmann, who joined him at an awkward 143 for three, appeared admirably unbothered for a debutant, and made 52 with élan. Earlier, Taylor, caught behind square-cutting, and Blewett, bowled allowing for non-existent turn, had failed again. But Slater, using his feet to the spinners, excelled at last with a boisterous 91 off 117 balls, including 15 fours and two sixes.

It helped that, without Srinath, most of India's attack was mediocre. Kumble, who took six for 98, was both hostile and economical, however, and young Harbhajan, bravely faced the aggression of Slater and Waugh. Azharuddin took his 100th catch in his 91st Test. Beginning their second innings after tea, just 24 ahead, India finished the third day on 99 for three wickets, all lost in search of quick runs. Within 45 minutes next morning, Kasprowicz swung the balance in Australia's favour. He caught and bowled Tendulkar with a slower ball and bowled Azharuddin with a yorker, throwing the Indians into disarray; later, he returned to rout the tail. Australia were left 194 to win, and their openers knocked off 91 of them. Taylor ended a dreadful series in style, with an accomplished 102 not out that guaranteed a consolation victory.

Man of the Match: M. S. Kasprowicz. _Man of the Series:_ S. R. Tendulkar.

Close of play: First day, India 290-4 (S. R. Tendulkar 117*, S. C. Ganguly 17*); Second day, Australia 209-3 (M. E. Waugh 58*, D. S. Lehmann 35*); Third day, India 99-3 (S. R. Tendulkar 27*, M. Azharuddin 4*).

India

V. V. S. Laxman c Taylor b Kasprowicz	6	– c Ponting b Warne	15
N. S. Sidhu b Warne	74	– c Lehmann b Warne	44
R. Dravid b Warne	23	– c Healy b Robertson	6
S. R. Tendulkar b Dale	177	– c and b Kasprowicz	31
*M. Azharuddin c Healy b Lehmann	40	– b Kasprowicz	18
S. C. Ganguly lbw b Dale	17	– b Robertson	16
†N. R. Mongia c Ponting b Warne	18	– not out	12
A. Kumble c Waugh b Robertson	39	– lbw b Robertson	9
Harvinder Singh lbw b Dale	0	– lbw b Kasprowicz	0
S. L. V. Raju c Lehmann b Robertson	5	– b Kasprowicz	2
Harbhajan Singh not out	4	– lbw b Kasprowicz	0
B 6, l-b 6, n-b 9	21	B 5, l-b 5, n-b 6	16
	424		**169**

1/24 (1) 2/109 (2) 3/110 (3) 4/249 (5)   424
5/294 (6) 6/353 (7) 7/390 (4)
8/390 (9) 9/415 (10) 10/424 (8)

1/50 (1) 2/61 (2) 3/92 (3)   169
4/111 (4) 5/127 (5) 6/144 (6)
7/158 (8) 8/159 (9)
9/163 (10) 10/169 (11)

Bowling: _First Innings_—Kasprowicz 29-4-76-1; Dale 23-6-71-3; Warne 35-9-106-3; Blewett 14-3-50-0; Robertson 11.2-1-58-2; Waugh 4-0-24-0; Lehmann 7-1-27-1. _Second Innings_—Kasprowicz 18-5-28-5; Dale 5-1-21-0; Warne 25-6-80-2; Robertson 12.2-2-28-3; Blewett 1-0-2-0.

Australia

M. J. Slater c Mongia b Harvinder Singh	91	– (2) c Azharuddin b Tendulkar	42
*M. A. Taylor c Mongia b Kumble	14	– (1) not out	102
G. S. Blewett b Harbhajan Singh	4	– lbw b Kumble	5
M. E. Waugh not out	153	– not out	33
D. S. Lehmann c Laxman b Harbhajan Singh	52		
R. T. Ponting c Tendulkar b Kumble	16		
†I. A. Healy c Mongia b Kumble	4		
S. K. Warne c Harbhajan Singh b Raju	33		
G. R. Robertson c Azharuddin b Kumble	4		
M. S. Kasprowicz lbw b Kumble	4		
A. C. Dale c Laxman b Kumble	5		
B 12, l-b 5, n-b 3	20	B 8, l-b 5	13
	400	(2 wkts)	**195**

1/68 (2) 2/77 (3) 3/143 (1) 4/249 (5)   400
5/274 (6) 6/286 (7) 7/350 (8)
8/378 (9) 9/394 (10) 10/400 (11)

1/91 (2) 2/114 (3)   (2 wkts) 195

Bowling: _First Innings_—Harvinder Singh 7-0-44-1; Ganguly 2-0-10-0; Kumble 41.3-8-98-6; Raju 37-7-118-1; Harbhajan Singh 23-1-112-2; Laxman 1-0-1-0. _Second Innings_—Harvinder Singh 3-0-17-0; Kumble 22.4-5-63-1; Raju 15-4-37-0; Harbhajan Singh 6-1-24-0; Tendulkar 11.2-1-41-1.

Umpires: D. R. Shepherd (England) and V. K. Ramaswamy.
Referee: P. L. van der Merwe (South Africa).

Australia's matches v India and Zimbabwe in the Pepsi Triangular Series (April 1–14) may be found in that section.

THE SRI LANKANS IN SOUTH AFRICA, 1997-98

By COLIN BRYDEN

The Sri Lankans' tour of South Africa was in distinct contrast to their visit three years earlier, when they had just two first-class matches and made up the numbers in a quadrangular limited-overs tournament. They had been lightly regarded by the fixture planners and did not play at South Africa's two major grounds, Wanderers and Newlands. Arjuna Ranatunga's team now returned as World Cup champions and were fêted accordingly.

Their results, however, were disappointing. Sri Lanka were beaten in both Tests and won only two out of six matches in a triangular limited-overs tournament against South Africa and Pakistan, failing to reach the final. South African spectators, though, warmed to the visitors. At the end of an arduous season, they provided some of the most entertaining cricket of the summer. One Sri Lankan paper suggested the players' own entertainments contributed to their poor results, but excessive socialising was not apparent to those who followed the tour.

For the home side, the pressure was less than it had been in the series against Pakistan and Australia. The selectors decided that now was the time to blood Makhaya Ntini, the 20-year-old fast bowler from Border, who became the first black African to play Test cricket for South Africa. Sri Lanka's batting did not quite live up to expectations, although the tourists reached 300 in each of their first three Test innings. They had an excellent chance to square the series when they took a 103-run first-innings lead at Centurion, but succumbed to inspired fast bowling by Allan Donald. Even then, they had a slight chance of winning when South Africa, needing 226 to win, were 99 for three and struggling against the off-spin of Muttiah Muralitharan. But Hansie Cronje swung the match decisively South Africa's way with a brutal assault on Sri Lanka's only bowler with match-winning potential.

Perhaps Centurion summed up the relative strengths of the teams. South Africa always seemed to have something in reserve when it mattered, whereas Sri Lanka lacked resilience in both batting and bowling. They had a wealth of experience, but there were signs of leg-weariness, notably from Aravinda de Silva among their batsmen. Marvan Atapattu, the newest of the regulars in the top six, had a good tour, showing sound technique and temperament against the fast bowlers. His opening partner, Sanath Jayasuriya, did not live up to expectations on bouncy pitches and was seldom granted the width to indulge his favourite off-side strokes. Ranatunga played only one substantial Test innings, 73 at Centurion, but showed his quality in the limited-overs games.

Sri Lanka's bowling relied far too much on Muralitharan, who was outstanding. The South Africans found him an even more awkward opponent than in the first series between the two countries in Sri Lanka in 1993-94, when he took 16 wickets in three Tests. Muralitharan, who has developed variations on his sharply turning off-breaks, again took 16 wickets, nine more than Jayasuriya, who was a useful rather than a consistently threatening left-arm slow bowler. The pace bowling was mediocre. Its limited firepower was further reduced by a foot injury which hampered Chaminda Vaas throughout.

South Africa's wins in both Tests enabled them to finish the season with four wins and two defeats from 11 matches. They won a series away and shared one at home against Pakistan, and were beaten in Australia. Daryll Cullinan, having been dropped twice during the season, came back strongly with two centuries which re-established him at No. 4, while Gary Kirsten and Cronje averaged better than 50. Donald was again his country's best bowler. At Centurion, in his 42nd match, he became the first South African to take 200 Test wickets.

SRI LANKAN TOURING PARTY

A. Ranatunga (Sinhalese SC) (*captain*), P. A. de Silva (Nondescripts CC) (*vice-captain*), R. P. Arnold (Nondescripts CC), M. S. Atapattu (Sinhalese SC), U. D. U. Chandana (Tamil Union C and AC), K. S. C. de Silva (Nondescripts CC), H. D. P. K. Dharmasena (Bloomfield C and AC), S. T. Jayasuriya (Bloomfield C and AC), D. P. M. D. Jayawardene (Sinhalese SC), R. S. Kaluwitharana (Colts CC), R. S. Mahanama (Bloomfield C and AC), M. Muralitharan (Tamil Union C and AC), K. R. Pushpakumara (Nondescripts CC), H. P. Tillekeratne (Nondescripts CC), W. P. U. J. C. Vaas (Colts CC), G. P. Wickremasinghe (Sinhalese SC).

D. N. T. Zoysa (Sinhalese SC) joined the party as cover for Vaas, who was injured during the First Test.

Manager: L. R. D. Mendis.   *Coach:* B. Yardley.

SRI LANKAN TOUR RESULTS

Test matches – Played 2: Lost 2.
First-class matches – Played 4: Lost 3, Drawn 1.
Losses – South Africa (2), Gauteng.
Draw – Boland.
One-day internationals – Played 6: Won 2, Lost 4. *Wins* – South Africa, Pakistan. *Losses* – South Africa (2), Pakistan (2).
Other non-first-class match – Won v North West.

Note: Matches in this section which were not first-class are signified by a dagger.

At Johannesburg, March 7, 8, 9. Gauteng won by 118 runs. Toss: Gauteng. Gauteng 296 for seven dec. (N. D. McKenzie 135, D. J. Cullinan 47, D. N. Crookes 67; U. D. U. Chandana four for 80) and 203 for eight dec. (A. J. Seymore 52, N. Pothas 40, R. P. Snell 44, Extras 33; W. P. U. J. C. Vaas three for 51, G. P. Wickremasinghe three for 42); Sri Lankans 243 for eight dec. (S. T. Jayasuriya 38, R. S. Mahanama 52, H. P. Tillekeratne 66 not out, R. S. Kaluwitharana 42, Extras 30; R. P. Snell three for 42, J. T. Mafa three for 53) and 138 (R. S. Kaluwitharana 42; E. W. Kidwell three for 53, R. P. Snell three for 51).

†At Fochville, March 11. Sri Lankans won by 93 runs. Toss: Sri Lankans. Sri Lankans 295 for eight (50 overs) (R. P. Arnold 113, A. Ranatunga 80, R. S. Kaluwitharana 30, Extras 37); North West 202 (47.2 overs) (H. M. de Vos 30, M. J. Lavine 51, E. G. Poole 35; P. A. de Silva five for 44).

At Paarl, March 14, 15, 16. Drawn. Toss: Boland. Boland 178 (J. M. Henderson 33; M. Muralitharan four for 40) and 160 for seven dec. (J. M. Henderson 61 not out, R. G. Arendse 38; M. Muralitharan five for 30); Sri Lankans 213 for four dec. (R. S. Mahanama 82, H. P. Tillekeratne 52 not out, M. S. Atapattu 30 not out; R. Telemachus three for 26) and 48 for five (R. Telemachus four for 30).

SOUTH AFRICA v SRI LANKA

First Test Match

At Cape Town, March 19, 20, 21, 22, 23. South Africa won by 70 runs. Toss: South Africa. Test debut: M. Ntini.

The selection of Makhaya Ntini was a significant event for South African cricket. The 20-year-old son of a domestic servant from a small village in the Eastern Cape, he was the first product of South Africa's development programme to make the Test team. He had been weaned on mini-cricket, a soft-ball game for children, and attended Dale College, a strong sporting school, on a cricket scholarship. Ntini's own debut performance was patchy, but he slotted well into a successful team as, for the second season in succession, Newlands hosted the most entertaining Test match of the South African summer. The pitch, one of the worst in the country two seasons earlier, had been transformed by successive groundsmen, Andy Atkinson and Christo Erasmus, into arguably the best, offering pace and consistent bounce.

Kirsten adopted his usual phlegmatic approach to batting, but Cullinan rejoiced in his recall with a stroke-filled innings that took him to his fourth Test hundred; 113 from 160 balls with 13 fours and a six. Cronje was aggressive but he, Kallis and Cullinan fell in quick succession. Pollock and Boucher batted through to the close and took their seventh-wicket stand to 95 on the second morning. Pollock batted with elegance and confidence, but again found himself too low in the order to sustain hopes of a century. As in Sheikhupura, where he made 82 against Pakistan, he was the last man out, this time for 92.

At the start of the Sri Lankan innings Jayasuriya hit three fours, but was living dangerously. He slashed and missed at Donald and was caught behind in the same over. After Mahanama became Donald's second victim, Atapattu and de Silva steadied the innings. Ntini's first spell in Test cricket was expensive, yielding 32 off four overs as he pitched too short and was punished by de Silva. He came back later, downwind this time, and was hit for further boundaries by de Silva before producing a good bouncer. De Silva ducked it but was caught off his glove for 77, made off 99 balls with 13 fours. Boucher took six catches in the innings, for the second Test running.

Starting their second innings after lunch on the third day with a lead of 112, South Africa lost both openers for 18. Kallis and Cullinan put on 116 with sensible batting but both fell before the close. On the fourth day, the spin bowlers, Muralitharan and Jayasuriya, bowled unchanged for 47 overs. Cronje hit three sixes but his team-mates struggled, with only 98 runs being added as six wickets fell. Nevertheless, the target of 377 in 132 overs required Sri Lanka to make their highest fourth-innings total to win.

With Jayasuriya and Mahanama out cheaply, Cronje was able to give left-arm spinner Adams plenty of bowling. Wickets fell steadily enough, and though Kaluwitharana and Wickremasinghe batted audaciously, they had no real prospect of snatching victory. Ntini yorked Wickremasinghe to end the match before tea.

Man of the Match: S. M. Pollock.   *Attendance:* 45,010.

Close of play: First day, South Africa 298-6 (S. M. Pollock 15*, M. V. Boucher 12*); Second day, Sri Lanka 212-5 (H. P. Tillekeratne 2*, R. S. Kaluwitharana 13*); Third day, South Africa 155-4 (W. J. Cronje 11*, M. V. Boucher 6*); Fourth day, Sri Lanka 120-3 (M. S. Atapattu 50*, A. Ranatunga 14*).

South Africa

A. M. Bacher c Mahanama b Wickremasinghe	6	– (2) c Kaluwitharana b Vaas	0
G. Kirsten lbw b Vaas	62	– (1) c Mahanama b Vaas	15
H. D. Ackerman c and b Muralitharan	23	– (7) lbw b Muralitharan	8
D. J. Cullinan b Wickremasinghe	113	– c Tillekeratne b Muralitharan	68
*W. J. Cronje c Mahanama b Vaas	49	– c Muralitharan b Jayasuriya	74
J. H. Kallis c Ranatunga b Muralitharan	3	– (3) st Kaluwitharana b Jayasuriya	49
S. M. Pollock lbw b Wickremasinghe	92	– (8) st Kaluwitharana b Jayasuriya	6
†M. V. Boucher run out	33	– (6) c Jayasuriya b Muralitharan	10
A. A. Donald b Muralitharan	12	– c Pushpakumara b Jayasuriya	18
P. R. Adams st Kaluwitharana b Muralitharan	2	– c Kaluwitharana b Muralitharan	3
M. Ntini not out	3	– not out	0
L-b 8, n-b 12	20	B 4, l-b 3, w 1, n-b 5	13

1/20 (1) 2/60 (3) 3/155 (2) 4/251 (5)　　　　418　　　1/5 (2) 2/18 (1) 3/134 (3)　　　　264
5/260 (6) 6/272 (4) 7/367 (8)　　　　　　　　　　　　　4/146 (4) 5/166 (6) 6/188 (7)
8/402 (9) 9/414 (10) 10/418 (7)　　　　　　　　　　　7/219 (8) 8/256 (5)
　　　　　　　　　　　　　　　　　　　　　　　　　　　9/260 (10) 10/264 (9)

Bowling: First Innings—Vaas 21-2-75-2; Pushpakumara 20-3-81-0; Wickremasinghe 28.4-7-75-3; Muralitharan 45-8-135-4; Jayasuriya 6-1-29-0; de Silva 4-0-15-0. *Second Innings*—Vaas 11-3-41-2; Pushpakumara 8-0-24-0; Wickremasinghe 8-1-24-0; Muralitharan 41-10-108-4; de Silva 1-1-0-0; Jayasuriya 33-7-53-4; Atapattu 1-0-7-0.

Sri Lanka

S. T. Jayasuriya c Boucher b Donald	17	– lbw b Donald	0
M. S. Atapattu c Cullinan b Adams	60	– c and b Adams	71
R. S. Mahanama c Boucher b Donald	9	– c Kallis b Pollock	11
P. A. de Silva c Boucher b Ntini	77	– c Kallis b Adams	37
*A. Ranatunga c Ackerman b Adams	20	– c Kirsten b Kallis	43
H. P. Tillekeratne c Boucher b Pollock	22	– lbw b Donald	13
†R. S. Kaluwitharana lbw b Pollock	13	– b Pollock	45
W. P. U. J. C. Vaas c Boucher b Donald	30	– c Boucher b Donald	0
G. P. Wickremasinghe c sub (L. Klusener)		– b Ntini	51
b Pollock	11		
M. Muralitharan not out	15	– run out	10
K. R. Pushpakumara c Boucher b Donald	4	– not out	9
B 8, l-b 7, w 1, n-b 12	28	B 5, l-b 3, n-b 8	16

1/20 (1) 2/36 (3) 3/165 (4) 4/194 (5)   306   1/3 (1) 2/27 (3) 3/98 (4)   306
5/195 (2) 6/219 (7) 7/241 (6)   4/171 (2) 5/175 (5) 6/234 (6)
8/270 (9) 9/300 (8) 10/306 (11)   7/234 (8) 8/239 (7)
    9/287 (10) 10/306 (9)

Bowling: *First Innings*—Donald 21.3–7–66–3; Pollock 10–1–57–1; Kallis 7–1–23–0; Adams 20–2–62–2. *Second Innings*—Donald 20.4–6–64–3; Pollock 23–3–77–2; Kallis 15–5–45–1; Ntini 5.3–0–17–1; Adams 27–3–90–2; Cronje 5–3–5–0.

Umpires: R. S. Dunne (New Zealand) and D. L. Orchard. Referee: J. R. Reid (New Zealand).

SOUTH AFRICA v SRI LANKA

Second Test Match

At Centurion, March 27, 28, 29, 30. South Africa won by six wickets. Toss: Sri Lanka. Test debut: G. F. J. Liebenberg.

Sri Lanka played themselves into a strong position, only to be destroyed by Donald's pace and craft in the second innings. He had to perform without the assistance of Pollock, who had bowled only 43 balls in the match before breaking down with a groin injury. But a Sunday crowd of 14,000 roared Donald on, and Sri Lanka – 103 ahead on first innings – collapsed to 42 for six and 122 all out.

The early stages had gone very differently. The star batsman in the first innings was South African, but his team still fell far behind. Four Sri Lankans scored half-centuries in a total of 303; Jayasuriya hit out early for 51 off 77 balls but, after he and de Silva were both out to Ntini in the space of five balls, the others, led by Ranatunga, put safety first.

Gerry Liebenberg, who had replaced Bacher, was then out first ball on his debut, pushing half-forward to the otherwise innocuous Pushpakumara, and South Africa relied almost entirely on Cullinan to make a respectable reply. He scored more than half his side's total and dominated the innings before he was eighth man out. While Cullinan stroked 13 boundaries, his team-mates were bemused by Muralitharan.

Sri Lanka were on course for a rare victory on foreign soil. But then Donald raced in. He bowled Jayasuriya off an inside edge as he played defensively, his 200th Test and 1,000th first-class wicket. Mahanama was lbw next ball and Atapattu was caught behind off a bottom edge. Cronje replaced Donald and struck with his third and ninth deliveries, Ranatunga jabbing at a ball which reared up and Tillekeratne falling to a splendid catch at point by Derek Crookes, substituting for Pollock. Three balls later, Crookes made a diving save at backward point; with de Silva committed to the run, Kaluwitharana sacrificed his own wicket. Sri Lanka were 42 for six.

Aided by Wickremasinghe, de Silva doubled the total, but he too was run out when, shortly before the close of the third day, wicket-keeper Boucher slid to stop a leg glance and threw down the wicket at the bowler's end. Ntini joined Pollock on the injury list and was unable to bowl on the fourth day after suffering a side strain. But Donald wrapped up the innings, leaving South Africa with 226 to win. Liebenberg batted attractively as he and Kirsten got South Africa off to the best start by either side in the series, before Muralitharan caused alarm when he spun out three men for the addition of ten runs.

This, however, brought Cronje to the crease. And the captain took command, square-cutting Muralitharan for four and lofting him for six in the second over the spinner bowled to him. Another six and some exquisitely timed strokes against both Muralitharan and Jayasuriya followed before he went to his fifty in sensational fashion, hitting Muralitharan for 4666 off successive balls. With three men on the leg-side boundary, Cronje lifted his arms in triumph as the third six sailed into the crowd. He had reached the second-fastest half-century in Test cricket in terms of balls: 31, just one more than Kapil Dev needed for India against Pakistan at Karachi in 1982-83.

Ranatunga admitted afterwards that he had no choice but to continue bowling Muralitharan, as he considered him the only man likely to win the match for Sri Lanka. The 19-year-old left-arm seamer Nuwan Zoysa, replacement for the injured Vaas, had broken down, further reducing the options. Cronje took South Africa within 11 runs of their victory before being caught at long-on; in all, he had hit 82 from 63 balls with eight fours and six sixes.

Man of the Match: A. A. Donald. *Man of the Series:* D. J. Cullinan. *Attendance:* 29,725.
Close of play: First day, Sri Lanka 165-3 (R. S. Mahanama 44*, A. Ranatunga 40*); Second day, South Africa 75-3 (D. J. Cullinan 42*, W. J. Cronje 0*); Third day, Sri Lanka 93-7 (G. P. Wickremasinghe 16*, D. N. T. Zoysa 6*).

Sri Lanka

S. T. Jayasuriya c Boucher b Ntini	51	– b Donald 16
M. S. Atapattu run out	12	– c Boucher b Donald 7
R. S. Mahanama c Kallis b Cronje	50	– lbw b Donald 0
P. A. de Silva c Adams b Ntini	1	– run out 41
*A. Ranatunga lbw b Donald	73	– c Boucher b Cronje 0
H. P. Tillekeratne c Kirsten b Cronje . . .	55	– c sub (D. N. Crookes) b Cronje . . 0
†R. S. Kaluwitharana c Boucher b Donald	9	– run out 0
G. P. Wickremasinghe c Adams b Donald	10	– b Adams 21
D. N. T. Zoysa lbw b Kallis	0	– c Boucher b Donald 14
M. Muralitharan c Boucher b Cronje . . .	11	– c Kirsten b Donald 15
K. R. Pushpakumara not out	0	– not out 0
B 6, l-b 14, w 3, n-b 8	31	L-b 5, n-b 3 8
	303	**122**

1/53 (2) 2/66 (1) 3/68 (4) 4/186 (3)   303   1/19 (1) 2/19 (3) 3/40 (2)   122
5/228 (5) 6/240 (7) 7/254 (8)   4/40 (5) 5/42 (6) 6/42 (7)
8/255 (9) 9/290 (10) 10/303 (6)   7/85 (4) 8/98 (8)
                                                  9/118 (9) 10/122 (10)

Bowling: *First Innings*—Donald 33–10–73–3; Pollock 7.1–3–9–0; Kallis 19–7–42–1; Adams 22–6–77–0; Ntini 22.5–7–61–2; Cronje 14.3–3–21–3. *Second Innings*—Donald 13.3–2–54–5; Ntini 6–2–13–0; Kallis 7–3–12–0; Cronje 8–3–13–2; Adams 7–1–25–1.

South Africa

G. F. J. Liebenberg lbw b Pushpakumara	0	– (2) lbw b Muralitharan 45
G. Kirsten b Muralitharan	13	– (1) not out 75
H. D. Ackerman b Zoysa	7	– b Muralitharan 2
D. J. Cullinan c Wickremasinghe b Jayasuriya .	103	– lbw b Muralitharan 0
*W. J. Cronje st Kaluwitharana b Muralitharan .	10	– c de Silva b Jayasuriya 82
J. H. Kallis c Kaluwitharana b Wickremasinghe .	12	– not out 0
S. M. Pollock b Muralitharan	1	
†M. V. Boucher c Jayasuriya b Muralitharan . .	13	
A. A. Donald b Muralitharan	6	
P. R. Adams c and b Jayasuriya	12	
M. Ntini not out	2	
B 1, l-b 6, w 6, n-b 8	21	B 8, l-b 3, n-b 11 22
	200	**(4 wkts) 226**

1/0 (1) 2/11 (3) 3/75 (2) 4/103 (5)   200   1/89 (2) 2/99 (3)   (4 wkts) 226
5/122 (6) 6/137 (7) 7/170 (8)   3/99 (4) 4/215 (5)
8/182 (4) 9/186 (9) 10/200 (10)

Bowling: *First Innings*—Pushpakumara 16–2–55–1; Zoysa 12–2–29–1; Wickremasinghe 15–2–36–1; Muralitharan 30–8–63–5; Jayasuriya 5–2–10–2. *Second Innings*—Pushpakumara 7–2–27–0; Zoysa 2–0–11–0; Wickremasinghe 6–1–7–0; de Silva 5–1–14–0; Muralitharan 23.5–4–94–3; Jayasuriya 19–6–62–1.

Umpires: Javed Akhtar (Pakistan) and R. E. Koertzen (South Africa). Referee: H. A. B. Gardiner (Zimbabwe).

Sri Lanka's matches v South Africa and Pakistan in the Standard Bank International One-Day Series (April 5–19) may be found in that section.

THE NEW ZEALANDERS IN SRI LANKA, 1997-98

By MARTIN DAVIDSON

New Zealand knew their seven-week tour of Sri Lanka was likely to be a severe test of their cricketing character. But the preparation of pitches ideally suited to the formidable Sri Lankan spin attack seemed to take them by surprise.

A youngish tour party left home talking up their chances. They were buoyant after destroying Zimbabwe at the end of the domestic season and believed the tough lessons learned in Australia before Christmas would stand them in good stead. Their confidence appeared well placed when they won the First Test, at the Premadasa Stadium, comfortably. However, the pitches for the other two Tests were simply below the standard expected. New Zealand captain Stephen Fleming called the surface in Galle a dungheap. Sri Lanka won the series 2-1.

To their credit, Fleming and coach Steve Rixon refused to blame defeat on the pitches. Instead, they displayed growing maturity by blaming themselves for not adapting to the harsh conditions, and accepting the ploy as the right of the home team. Sri Lanka, though, must review the strategy if they wish to grow as a Test nation. Their captain, Arjuna Ranatunga, agreed the authorities should aim to encourage pace and spin alike. However, he believed that it could only happen once Sri Lanka had the fast bowlers to take advantage.

As it was, Sri Lanka did not miss injured left-arm fast bowlers Chaminda Vaas and Nuwan Zoysa, and were content to direct their attack around the brilliant off-spinner, Muttiah Muralitharan, and a highly promising newcomer, left-arm spinner Niroshan Bandaratilleke. These two proved the dominant force: Muralitharan won the series award for his 19 wickets at less than 20, and Bandaratilleke, aged 23, hinted at a bright future with 16.

The New Zealand spinners, headed by 19-year-old slow left-armer Daniel Vettori, had their moments, but could not match their rivals' consistency. Vettori continued his cricketing education; in the Third Test, his best figures yet, six for 64, included his 50th wicket in only his 14th Test. He completed the series with 17 wickets. The 28-year-old off-spinner Paul Wiseman of Otago made pleasing progress after a shoulder injury and a questionable bowling action had held him back on his first overseas tour, to Zimbabwe in late 1997. He surprised the Sri Lankans in the First Test, his maiden appearance at this level, when he took seven wickets; thereafter the home team attacked him early on to unsettle his rhythm. They succeeded, although Wiseman learned a lot from the experience.

Most encouragingly for New Zealand, Fleming made strides both as the team's principal batsman and as captain. He topped the batting averages for both teams with 357 at 71.40, while his leadership abilities suggested he had a difficult job for as long as he wanted it. New Zealand also failed in the rain-hit triangular tournament with India. But while the players understandably grew frustrated, they lost neither their sense of humour nor their appreciation of the Sri Lankans' outstanding hospitality. They left for home with their tails between their legs but smiles on their faces.

NEW ZEALAND TOUR PARTY

S. P. Fleming (Canterbury) (*captain*), N. J. Astle (Canterbury), C. L. Cairns (Canterbury), S. B. Doull (Northern Districts), C. Z. Harris (Canterbury), M. J. Horne (Otago), C. D. McMillan (Canterbury), D. J. Nash (Northern Districts), S. B. O'Connor (Otago), A. C. Parore (Auckland), M. W. Priest (Canterbury), C. M. Spearman (Central Districts), D. L. Vettori (Northern Districts), P. J. Wiseman (Otago), B. A. Young (Northern Districts).

Doull and O'Connor returned home injured. A. R. Tait (Northern Districts) replaced O'Connor. *Manager:* D. J. Graham. *Coach:* S. J. Rixon.

NEW ZEALAND TOUR RESULTS

Test matches – Played 3: Won 1, Lost 2.
First-class matches – Played 5: Won 1, Lost 2, Drawn 2.
Win – Sri Lanka.
Losses – Sri Lanka (2).
Draws – Sri Lankan Board XI (2).
One-day internationals – Played 4: Lost 2, No result 2. Abandoned 2.
Other non-first-class matches – Played 2: Won 2. *Wins* – Sri Lankan Board XI (2).

TEST MATCH AVERAGES

SRI LANKA – BATTING

	T	I	NO	R	HS	100s	50s	Avge	Ct/St
D. P. M. D. Jayawardene ..	3	5	0	300	167	1	2	60.00	4
R. S. Kaluwitharana	3	5	0	230	88	0	2	46.00	4/3
A. Ranatunga.	3	5	0	162	64	0	1	32.40	1
H. P. Tillekeratne	2	3	0	93	43	0	0	31.00	6
P. A. de Silva	3	5	0	125	71	0	1	25.00	1
S. T. Jayasuriya.	3	5	0	111	59	0	1	22.20	9
M. S. Atapattu	3	5	0	104	48	0	0	20.80	2
M. Muralitharan	3	5	3	38	26*	0	0	19.00	2
G. P. Wickremasinghe	3	5	1	63	27	0	0	15.75	1
H. D. P. K. Dharmasena. . .	2	3	0	34	12	0	0	11.33	0
M. R. C. N. Bandaratilleke.	3	5	0	52	20	0	0	10.40	0

Played in one Test: C. M. Bandara 0*, 0 (1 ct); R. S. Kalpage 6, 16 (3 ct).

* Signifies not out.

BOWLING

	O	M	R	W	BB	5W/i	Avge
H. D. P. K. Dharmasena ..	58.1	10	137	8	6-72	1	17.12
M. Muralitharan	155	41	374	19	5-30	2	19.68
P. A. de Silva	35.5	10	82	4	3-30	0	20.50
M. R. C. N. Bandaratilleke.	160	45	339	16	5-36	1	21.18
G. P. Wickremasinghe	42.3	8	114	4	2-7	0	28.50

Also bowled: C. M. Bandara 21–3–79–0; S. T. Jayasuriya 20–1–71–1; D. P. M. D. Jayawardene 3–0–10–0; R. S. Kalpage 30–6–100–2.

NEW ZEALAND – BATTING

	T	I	NO	R	HS	100s	50s	Avge	Ct
S. P. Fleming	3	6	1	357	174*	1	2	71.40	2
A. C. Parore	3	6	1	151	67	0	1	30.20	6
N. J. Astle.	3	6	0	162	53	0	1	27.00	2
C. D. McMillan	3	6	0	159	142	1	0	26.50	0
B. A. Young.	3	6	0	124	46	0	0	20.66	5
M. J. Horne.	3	6	0	101	35	0	0	16.83	4

	T	I	NO	R	HS	100s	50s	Avge	Ct
C. Z. Harris	2	4	1	46	19	0	0	15.33	2
C. L. Cairns	3	6	0	74	26	0	0	12.33	1
P. J. Wiseman	3	5	2	32	23	0	0	10.66	0
D. L. Vettori	3	5	0	23	20	0	0	4.60	4

Played in one Test: S. B. Doull 1* (1 ct); S. B. O'Connor 0*, 0 (1 ct); M. W. Priest 12, 2; C. M. Spearman 4, 22 (1 ct).

* Signifies not out.

BOWLING

	O	M	R	W	BB	5W/i	Avge
D. L. Vettori	159	52	361	17	6-64	1	21.23
C. L. Cairns	73.4	7	280	10	5-62	1	28.00
P. J. Wiseman	112.5	30	288	10	5-82	1	28.80
C. D. McMillan	55	18	146	5	2-27	0	29.20

Also bowled: N. J. Astle 10–3–22–0; S. B. Doull 15.2–2–58–0; C. Z. Harris 36.4–8–99–1; S. B. O'Connor 4–0–13–0; M. W. Priest 35.5–11–77–2.

Note: Matches in this section which were not first-class are signified by a dagger.

At P. Saravanamuttu Stadium, Colombo, May 18, 19, 20. Drawn. Toss: New Zealanders. New Zealanders 274 (C. M. Spearman 39, N. J. Astle 42, C. D. McMillan 34, A. C. Parore 53; M. R. C. N. Bandaratilleke four for 80) and 178 for five dec. (N. J. Astle 32, C. D. McMillan 35, A. C. Parore 35 not out; M. R. C. N. Bandaratilleke three for 46); Sri Lankan Board XI 204 (U. A. Fernando 36, D. P. M. D. Jayawardene 38, S. Ranatunga 32; D. L. Vettori three for 55, P. J. Wiseman five for 65) and 157 for five (U. A. Fernando 37, D. P. M. D. Jayawardene 40).

At Kandy, May 22, 23, 24. Drawn. Toss: Sri Lankan Board XI. Sri Lankan Board XI 300 for nine dec. (S. T. Jayasuriya 83, D. P. M. D. Jayawardene 67, R. P. Hewage 30, S. K. L. de Silva 32; M. W. Priest four for 90) and 82 for one (S. I. Fernando 42 not out); New Zealanders 344 for nine dec. (B. A. Young 32, M. J. Horne 92, C. D. McMillan 71, A. C. Parore 43, C. Z. Harris 42; C. M. Bandara three for 100, D. P. M. D. Jayawardene four for 29).

SRI LANKA v NEW ZEALAND

First Test Match

At R. Premadasa Stadium, Colombo, May 27, 28, 29, 30, 31. New Zealand won by 167 runs. Toss: New Zealand. Test debuts: C. M. Bandara, M. R. C. N. Bandaratilleke; P. J. Wiseman.

New Zealand shocked the home team by outplaying them in every department to set up a big win. Once Fleming won the toss and chose to bat, everything went right for his side, although their first-innings 305 was fifty short of what they wanted. The captain, who made 78, revealed his well-known absent-mindedness twice – once when he rushed back to the dressing-room to retrieve his box, and later when he played a lazy stroke to bring about his own dismissal. But with wicket-keeper Parore stroking an elegant 67, the New Zealanders at least had a score to bowl to.

Sri Lanka started poorly, with the loss of two quick wickets, before Jayawardene and Kaluwitharana lifted them to within 20 of the opposition. The course of the match was decided when Fleming and McMillan shared an outstanding partnership of 240 in just 222 minutes for the fourth wicket. Fleming scored a career-best 174 not out and McMillan, still 21 but with a mature cricketing mind, offered great support by hitting 142. The Sri Lankan spinners were nullified by decisive footwork and clarity of stroke. New Zealand had ended the third day already strongly placed at 260 for three, with Fleming on 106. He pushed on next morning, adding another 68 runs to his overnight score and watching McMillan go to three figures off just 140 balls. McMillan eventually fell, having hit 13 fours and six sixes in his 179 deliveries. Fleming's innings could yet prove a turning point in his career. Too often he had promised much only to lose concentration.

But now he displayed hardened resolve to hit a big century, only the second – compared to 17 fifties – he had mustered in 35 Tests.

Asked to score 465, Sri Lanka had four and a half sessions to bat in conditions they knew well: a docile pitch beginning to take spin. They ended the fourth day on 111 for two. Before de Silva departed for 71 to the first ball after lunch, they looked to have made the game safe. Then came the rot: their last seven wickets fell for just 81 runs. Wiseman, playing his first Test at the age of 28, who collected five for 82 from a marathon spell of 46.5 overs to end the game shortly after tea.

Man of the Match: S. P. Fleming.

Close of play: First day, New Zealand 282-7 (A. C. Parore 67*, D. L. Vettori 9*); Second day, Sri Lanka 251-7 (G. P. Wickremasinghe 9*, M. R. C. N. Bandaratilleke 8*); Third day, New Zealand 260-3 (S. P. Fleming 106*, C. D. McMillan 64*); Fourth day, Sri Lanka 111-2 (D. P. M. D. Jayawardene 13*, P. A. de Silva 19*).

New Zealand

B. A. Young c Kaluwitharana b Muralitharan	30	– lbw b Bandaratilleke	11
M. J. Horne b Bandaratilleke	15	– c Ranatunga b Muralitharan	35
*S. P. Fleming c Jayasuriya b Kalpage	78	– not out	174
N. J. Astle c Jayawardene b Kalpage	30	– c Kaluwitharana b Jayasuriya	34
C. D. McMillan lbw b Muralitharan	0	– c Kalpage b Muralitharan	142
†A. C. Parore c Jayasuriya b Wickremasinghe	67	– c Kalpage b Muralitharan	1
C. L. Cairns b Bandara b Muralitharan	20	– c Jayasuriya b Muralitharan	6
C. Z. Harris lbw b Wickremasinghe	19	– not out	14
D. L. Vettori c Kalpage b Muralitharan	20		
P. J. Wiseman c Jayawardene b Muralitharan	6		
S. B. Doull not out	1		
L-b 9, w 1, n-b 9	19	B 5, l-b 10, n-b 12	27
	305	(6 wkts dec.)	**444**

1/25 (2) 2/97 (1) 3/141 (4) 4/141 (5) 5/188 (3) 6/229 (7) 7/269 (8) 8/282 (6) 9/296 (10) 10/305 (9)

1/11 (1) 2/68 (2) 3/160 (4) 4/400 (5) 5/404 (6) 6/416 (7)

Bowling: *First Innings*—Wickremasinghe 14–2–55–2; Jayawardene 3–0–10–0; Bandaratilleke 22–6–51–1; Muralitharan 38.2–9–90–5; Kalpage 15–2–49–2. *Second Innings*—Wickremasinghe 7–0–21–0; Bandaratilleke 39–8–105–1; de Silva 2–0–14–0; Muralitharan 36–5–137–4; Bandara 8–0–38–0; Kalpage 15–4–51–0; Jayasuriya 16–0–63–1.

Sri Lanka

S. T. Jayasuriya c Parore b Cairns	10	– c Young b Wiseman	59
M. S. Atapattu c Parore b Cairns	0	– c Horne b Wiseman	16
D. P. M. D. Jayawardene c Vettori b Wiseman	52	– c Horne b Wiseman	54
P. A. de Silva c Doull b McMillan	37	– lbw b Vettori	71
*A. Ranatunga c Cairns	49	– c and b Vettori	9
†R. S. Kaluwitharana b Vettori	72	– c Parore b McMillan	39
R. S. Kalpage b Wiseman	6	– c Young b Vettori	16
G. P. Wickremasinghe lbw b Vettori	27	– (9) c Young b Cairns	0
M. R. C. N. Bandaratilleke run out	20	– (8) c Horne b Wiseman	16
M. Muralitharan b Vettori	0	– not out	9
C. M. Bandara not out	0	– lbw b Wiseman	0
L-b 8, n-b 4	12	B 1, l-b 4, n-b 3	8
	285		**297**

1/6 (2) 2/21 (1) 3/101 (4) 4/105 (3) 5/206 (5) 6/221 (7) 7/237 (6) 8/284 (8) 9/284 (10) 10/285 (9)

1/70 (2) 2/89 (1) 3/194 (4) 4/216 (5) 5/216 (3) 6/239 (7) 7/277 (6) 8/279 (9) 9/289 (8) 10/297 (11)

Bowling: *First Innings*—Doull 12.2–2–43–0; Cairns 15–0–59–3; Harris 7–1–27–0; Vettori 24–8–56–3; Wiseman 20–4–61–2; McMillan 12–4–31–1. *Second Innings*—Doull 3–0–15–0; Cairns 19–6–64–1; Wiseman 46.5–17–82–5; Vettori 51–23–101–3; McMillan 6–4–12–1; Harris 4–1–16–0; Astle 2–0–2–0.

Umpires: R. E. Koertzen (South Africa) and K. T. Francis. Referee: Talat Ali (Pakistan).

SRI LANKA v NEW ZEALAND

Second Test Match

At Galle, June 3, 4, 5, 6, 7. Sri Lanka won by an innings and 16 runs. Toss: New Zealand.

This was the first Test played at the stunningly beautiful Galle International Stadium, dominated by the 17th-century Dutch fort. Before Galle became the 79th Test venue – and the seventh in Sri Lanka – facilities were upgraded at vast expense, though the pitch and outfield were seemingly ignored. This oversight marred the game as a spectacle, but allowed the Sri Lankans to square the series with one to play.

Poor drainage and leaking covers meant that seven hours of play were lost on the first two days. With the ball turning square from the first over, New Zealand never found it easy to cope with the Sri Lankan spinners. They struggled to 96 for four by the close of the first day, slow left-armer Bandaratilleke taking three for ten in 15 overs. During the 55 minutes of play on the second day, he added a fourth wicket. And on the third day, Dharmasena, who had opened the bowling with his rapid off-spin, completed Test-best figures of six for 72. New Zealand were all out for 193, Astle top-scoring with a dour 53.

By stumps, the inadequacy of New Zealand's total had become clear: Sri Lanka were ahead with seven wickets in hand. The 21-year-old Jayawardene, showing remarkable technique and control, was undefeated on 88. Next day, his captain, Ranatunga, nursed him through the nineties to a magnificent maiden Test century that sparked off wild celebrations. The players hugged in mid-pitch, a policeman set off a rocket and, with remarkable timing, a hot-dog vending machine blew up, sending clouds of smoke across the pavilion.

However, Jayawardene, in only his fourth Test, was not finished yet, pushing on to a superb 167. The true test of his ability would come on hard, bouncy pitches, but he seemed to have the temperament and personality to succeed on the international stage. The next highest score was in the thirties.

New Zealand had to survive more than four sessions to save the match, but failed even to hit the 130 necessary to make Sri Lanka bat again. At 94 for five at the close of the fourth day, the cause was hopeless. When their prayers for rain on the final day went unanswered, the end came swiftly; New Zealand surrendered their last five wickets for 20 runs in 43 minutes. This capitulation shattered the confidence gained from victory in the First Test. Spin accounted for all but one of the tourists' wickets – the exception being a run-out. Bandaratilleke ended with a match haul of nine for 83 from 62 overs.

Man of the Match: D. P. M. D. Jayawardene.

Close of play: First day, New Zealand 96-4 (N. J. Astle 30*, C. D. McMillan 2*); Second day, New Zealand 122-5 (N. J. Astle 42*, A. C. Parore 3*); Third day, Sri Lanka 197-3 (D. P. M. D. Jayawardene 88*, A. Ranatunga 33*); Fourth day, New Zealand 94-5 (A. C. Parore 25*, C. L. Cairns 16*).

New Zealand

B. A. Young c Jayasuriya b Bandaratilleke	46	– c Tillekeratne b Bandaratilleke	11
M. J. Horne c Kaluwitharana b Bandaratilleke	1	– lbw b Bandaratilleke	3
*S. P. Fleming lbw b Dharmasena	14	– lbw b Muralitharan	10
N. J. Astle c Tillekeratne b Dharmasena	53	– b de Silva	13
D. L. Vettori c Tillekeratne b Bandaratilleke	0	– (9) run out	0
C. D. McMillan b Bandaratilleke	13	– (5) c Jayasuriya b Bandaratilleke	1
†A. C. Parore c Jayasuriya b Dharmasena	30	– (6) not out	32
C. L. Cairns c Jayasuriya b Dharmasena	0	– (7) c Tillekeratne b Bandaratilleke	16
C. Z. Harris c Wickremasinghe b Dharmasena	4	– (8) c Jayawardene b Muralitharan	9
P. J. Wiseman st Kaluwitharana b Dharmasena	23	– c Tillekeratne b Bandaratilleke	2
S. B. O'Connor not out	0	– c Jayasuriya b Muralitharan	0
L-b 7, n-b 2	9	B 7, l-b 7, w 1, n-b 2	17

1/5 (2) 2/21 (3) 3/90 (1) 4/90 (5)   193   1/18 (2) 2/21 (1) 3/40 (3)   114
5/110 (6) 6/137 (4) 7/137 (8)   4/41 (5) 5/69 (4) 6/94 (7)
8/147 (9) 9/190 (10) 10/193 (10)   7/103 (8) 8/106 (9)
                                                         9/109 (10) 10/114 (11)

Bowling: *First Innings*—Wickremasinghe 7–1–20–0; Dharmasena 24.1–4–72–6; Bandaratilleke 38–13–47–4; Muralitharan 23–9–33–0; Jayasuriya 4–1–8–0; de Silva 5–2–6–0. *Second Innings*—Wickremasinghe 2–0–6–0; Bandaratilleke 24–9–36–5; de Silva 7–1–18–1; Dharmasena 6–0–16–0; Muralitharan 16–7–24–3.

Sri Lanka

S. T. Jayasuriya c Harris b Vettori	21
M. S. Atapattu c Vettori b Wiseman . . .	35
D. P. M. D. Jayawardene lbw b Harris . .	167
P. A. de Silva lbw b Vettori	10
*A. Ranatunga c O'Connor b Vettori . . .	36
H. P. Tillekeratne b Wiseman	10
†R. S. Kaluwitharana run out	3
H. D. P. K. Dharmasena run out	12
G. P. Wickremasinghe c Harris b Vettori.	12

M. R. C. N. Bandaratilleke run out	4
M. Muralitharan not out	2
L-b 9, n-b 2	11
	323

1/44 (1) 2/106 (2) 3/135 (4)
4/211 (5) 5/262 (6) 6/271 (7)
7/301 (3) 8/315 (8)
9/319 (9) 10/323 (10)

Bowling: O'Connor 4–0–13–0; Cairns 5–0–20–0; Wiseman 30–3–95–2; Vettori 26–4–88–4; Harris 25.4–6–56–1; McMillan 11–3–30–0; Astle 5–3–12–0.

Umpires: D. L. Orchard (South Africa) and B. C. Cooray.   Referee: Talat Ali (Pakistan).

SRI LANKA v NEW ZEALAND

Third Test Match

At Sinhalese Sports Club, Colombo, June 10, 11, 12, 13. Sri Lanka won by 164 runs. Toss: Sri Lanka.

After Sri Lanka had spun them out cheaply at Galle, New Zealand fielded three slow bowlers – Priest, Vettori and Wiseman – for the first time since 1985-86. It was a sensible move by the tourists, though ironically it was their sole fast bowler, Chris Cairns, who claimed five for 62. In his 33rd Test, he emulated his father, Lance, by reaching 100 Test wickets. Never before in Test cricket have a father and son both achieved this feat. He also became only the third New Zealander, after Sir Richard Hadlee and John Bracewell, to record the Test double of 100 wickets and 1,000 runs.

Tight bowling restricted Sri Lanka to 206, but again the New Zealand batsmen squandered their chances, despite a resolute 78 from Fleming. At the close of the second day, with the home team enjoying a lead of just 13 on first innings, the game hung nicely in the balance. The next morning, Sri Lanka stumbled to 36 for four on a deteriorating pitch before Ranatunga and Tillekeratne added 102 for the fifth wicket.

New Zealand, in turn, fought back, and seemed to have earned themselves a realistic chance of victory when Sri Lanka were 211 for nine, 224 ahead. But Kaluwitharana, who punished the bowling mercilessly, and No. 11 Muralitharan produced a match-winning last-wicket stand of 71, a record between the two countries. Vettori, claiming Test-best figures of six for 64, was the only bowler to impress. He showed great control and variation, but there was scant support from the other end. When he bowled Tillekeratne for 40, it was his 50th Test wicket in 14 matches; he was still only 19. Meanwhile, 36-year-old Priest advanced his total to three in three Tests.

Facing a target of 296 in six sessions and 22 minutes, New Zealand were ten without loss overnight, but succumbed meekly for 131. Muralitharan and Bandaratilleke snapped up nine wickets between them as all ten fell to spin, as in the first innings at Galle. The New Zealand coach Steve Rixon was so upset by his team's performance that he could not bring himself to talk about it after the match. A series that had started promisingly for New Zealand ended with two hefty defeats, which could not be blamed wholly on the pitches.

Man of the Match: R. S. Kaluwitharana.   *Man of the Series*: M. Muralitharan.

Close of play: First day, Sri Lanka 200-8 (G. P. Wickremasinghe 20*, M. R. C. N. Bandaratilleke 4*); Second day, New Zealand 193; Third day, New Zealand 10-0 (B. A. Young 7*, C. M. Spearman 1*).

Sri Lanka

S. T. Jayasuriya c Young b Cairns	13	– c Parore b Cairns	8
M. S. Atapattu c Vettori b Wiseman	48	– lbw b Vettori	5
D. P. M. D. Jayawardene c Parore b Cairns	16	– c Horne b Vettori	11
P. A. de Silva c Spearman b Cairns	4	– c Astle b Vettori	3
*A. Ranatunga run out	4	– c Cairns b Priest	64
H. P. Tillekeratne c Young b McMillan	43	– b Vettori	40
†R. S. Kaluwitharana b McMillan	28	– lbw b Priest	88
H. D. P. K. Dharmasena c Parore b Cairns	11	– b McMillan	7
G. P. Wickremasinghe not out	24	– c Fleming b Vettori	0
M. R. C. N. Bandaratilleke lbw b Vettori	5	– c Fleming b Vettori	7
M. Muralitharan c Astle b Cairns	1	– not out	26
B 1, l-b 8	9	B 8, l-b 10, n-b 1	19

1/24 (1) 2/52 (3) 3/56 (4) 4/70 (5)	206
5/102 (2) 6/156 (7) 7/163 (6)	
8/196 (8) 9/201 (10) 10/206 (11)	

1/12 (1) 2/16 (2) 3/24 (4)	282
4/36 (3) 5/138 (5) 6/140 (6)	
7/188 (8) 8/193 (9)	
9/211 (10) 10/282 (7)	

Bowling: *First Innings*—Cairns 17.4–1–62–5; Vettori 25–7–52–1; Priest 24–11–35–0; Wiseman 10–4–21–1; McMillan 12–5–27–2. *Second Innings*—Cairns 17–0–75–1; Vettori 33–10–64–6; Astle 3–0–8–0; Wiseman 6–2–29–0; McMillan 14–2–46–1; Priest 11.5–0–42–2.

New Zealand

B. A. Young c Atapattu b Bandaratilleke	2	– st Kaluwitharana b Muralitharan	24
C. M. Spearman c de Silva b Wickremasinghe	4	– c and b Muralitharan	22
*S. P. Fleming b Wickremasinghe	78	– lbw b Dharmasena	3
N. J. Astle c Atapattu b Dharmasena	2	– c and b Muralitharan	16
M. J. Horne c Tillekeratne b de Silva	35	– c Kaluwitharana b Bandaratilleke	12
C. D. McMillan st Kaluwitharana b de Silva	2	– c Jayawardene b Muralitharan	1
†A. C. Parore lbw b de Silva	19	– b Bandaratilleke	2
C. L. Cairns run out	6	– b Bandaratilleke	26
M. W. Priest c sub (A. S. A. Perera) b Muralitharan	12	– b Bandaratilleke	2
D. L. Vettori c Jayasuriya b Muralitharan	0	– b Muralitharan	3
P. J. Wiseman not out	1	– not out	0
B 11, l-b 2, n-b 5	18	B 6, l-b 10, n-b 4	20

1/5 (2) 2/7 (1) 3/30 (4) 4/94 (5)	193
5/98 (6) 6/128 (7) 7/143 (8)	
8/181 (9) 9/183 (10) 10/193 (3)	

1/44 (1) 2/57 (2) 3/63 (3)	131
4/82 (5) 5/84 (6) 6/93 (7)	
7/105 (4) 8/128 (8)	
9/131 (9) 10/131 (10)	

Bowling: *First Innings*—Wickremasinghe 6.3–3–7–2; Bandaratilleke 20–6–48–1; Dharmasena 18–4–35–1; de Silva 18.5–7–30–3; Muralitharan 23.1–3–60–2. *Second Innings*—Wickremasinghe 6–2–5–0; Bandaratilleke 17–3–52–4; de Silva 3–0–14–0; Dharmasena 10–2–14–1; Muralitharan 18.3–8–30–5.

Umpires: V. K. Ramaswamy (India) and P. Manuel. Referee: Talat Ali (Pakistan).

†At Kurunegala, June 16. New Zealanders won by 32 runs. Toss: New Zealanders. New Zealanders 240 for eight (50 overs) (N. J. Astle 57, S. P. Fleming 52, M. J. Horne 40; R. P. Arnold three for 45); Sri Lankan Board XI 208 for nine (50 overs) (D. A. Gunawardene 96; S. B. O'Connor three for 25, C. D. McMillan three for 34).

†At Moratuwa, June 18. New Zealanders won by 81 runs. Toss: Sri Lankan Board XI. New Zealanders 281 for six (50 overs) (B. A. Young 108 retired hurt, M. J. Horne 43, A. C. Parore 32 not out, C. Z. Harris 35); Sri Lankan Board XI 200 for eight (50 overs) (S. I. Fernando 75, U. C. Hathurusinghe 32, B. C. M. S. Mendis 31).

New Zealand's matches v Sri Lanka and India in the Singer Akai Nidahas Trophy (June 21–July 5) may be found in that section.

PEPSI ASIA CUP, 1997-98

By SA'ADI THAWFEEQ

World Cup holders Sri Lanka added the Asia Cup to their growing list of one-day titles when they ended India's stranglehold on the competition in comprehensive fashion. India had won four of the five previous Asia Cups; Sri Lanka won in 1985-86, the last time they hosted it, but on that occasion India had withdrawn. This time the Indians were thoroughly outplayed by Arjuna Ranatunga's men, who won the final with more than 13 overs to spare. Sri Lanka went through the tournament with a 100 per cent record, beating India twice, Pakistan and Bangladesh. They were led admirably by Ranatunga, referred to as "Captain Cool" by ICC referee John Reid; with an aggregate of 272 runs for only two dismissals, he was named Man of the Series. The key to Sri Lanka's success was their fitness, demonstrated in some spectacular fielding. Pakistan's disappointing record in the Asia Cup continued; they bowed out when India pushed past them on net run-rate, hitting the Bangladeshi attack for 132 in 15 overs. Bangladesh, who qualified as the fourth team through winning the Asian Cricket Council tournament, failed to win a single game.

Note: Matches in this section were not first-class.

SRI LANKA v PAKISTAN

At R. Premadasa Stadium, Colombo, July 14. Sri Lanka won by 15 runs. Toss: Pakistan.
Sri Lanka got off to a confident start, making better use of a slow pitch than Pakistan. Atapattu scored 80 in 114 balls, the nucleus of a total of 239. But Pakistan struggled throughout against the spinners, especially Jayasuriya, who took four for 49, three of them coming from excellent outfield catches by Kalpage.
Man of the Match: M. S. Atapattu.

Sri Lanka

S. T. Jayasuriya c Ramiz Raja			H. D. P. K. Dharmasena st Moin Khan	
b Kabir Khan .	33		b Saqlain Mushtaq .	25
M. S. Atapattu run out	80		W. P. U. J. C. Vaas run out	0
P. A. de Silva c Saqlain Mushtaq			M. Muralitharan not out	2
b Aamir Sohail .	34		K. S. C. de Silva b Aqib Javed	6
*A. Ranatunga c Ramiz Raja			L-b 4, w 7, n-b 1	12
b Arshad Khan .	28			
R. S. Mahanama lbw b Shahid Afridi . .	3		1/46 2/111 3/160	(49.5 overs) 239
†R. S. Kaluwitharana lbw b Kabir Khan .	1		4/168 5/169 6/199	
R. S. Kalpage run out	15		7/209 8/216 9/232	

Bowling: Aqib Javed 7.5–0–37–1; Kabir Khan 8–1–49–2; Saqlain Mushtaq 10–0–38–1; Shahid Afridi 4–0–25–1; Arshad Khan 10–0–48–1; Aamir Sohail 10–1–38–1.

Pakistan

Saeed Anwar b Vaas	27		Saqlain Mushtaq c Kalpage b Jayasuriya .	5
Aamir Sohail c Ranatunga			Aqib Javed c Kalpage b Jayasuriya	0
b K. S. C. de Silva .	6		Arshad Khan not out	6
Shahid Afridi c Muralitharan			Kabir Khan not out	1
b K. S. C. de Silva .	16			
*Ramiz Raja st Kaluwitharana			B 3, l-b 2, w 9, n-b 1	15
b Jayasuriya .	29			
Inzamam-ul-Haq run out	48		1/32 2/36 3/51	(9 wkts, 50 overs) 224
Salim Malik b Dharmasena	57		4/102 5/165 6/205	
†Moin Khan c Kalpage b Jayasuriya . . .	14		7/214 8/216 9/216	

Bowling: Vaas 6–1–30–1; K. S. C. de Silva 6–0–26–2; Dharmasena 10–0–33–1; Muralitharan 10–0–44–0; Jayasuriya 10–0–49–4; Kalpage 8–0–37–0.

Umpires: S. K. Bansal and S. Venkataraghavan.

BANGLADESH v PAKISTAN

At R. Premadasa Stadium, Colombo, July 16. Pakistan won by 109 runs. Toss: Pakistan. International debut: Sheikh Salahuddin.

Pakistan recovered magnificently to run up 319 for five, the highest total ever in the Asia Cup. The previous best was their own 284 for three off five fewer overs, also against Bangladesh, at Chittagong in 1988-89. Aamir Sohail went for a duck to his first ball, but Saeed Anwar defied a fever to hit 90 off 94 balls, with 11 fours; the other main batsmen put the game beyond Bangladesh's reach. Off-spinner Saqlain Mushtaq took five wickets to dismiss Bangladesh for 210, a total depending heavily on opener Ather Ali Khan and captain Akram Khan.

Man of the Match: Saeed Anwar.

Pakistan

Saeed Anwar c Habib-ul-Bashar b Enam-ul-Haque .	90	†Moin Khan not out	21
Aamir Sohail c Khaled Masud b Hasib-ul-Hassan .	0	Shahid Afridi not out	4
*Ramiz Raja c and b Minhaz-ul-Abedin .	52	B 1, l-b 2, w 9, n-b 1	13
Inzamam-ul-Haq c Habib-ul-Bashar b Sheikh Salahuddin .	77		
Salim Malik c Amin-ul-Islam b Saif-ul-Islam .	62	1/13 2/136 (5 wkts, 50 overs) 319	
		3/166 4/275	
		5/315	

Saqlain Mushtaq, Aqib Javed, Arshad Khan and Kabir Khan did not bat.

Bowling: Hasib-ul-Hassan 4–0–47–1; Saif-ul-Islam 7–0–45–1; Ather Ali Khan 5–0–27–0; Sheikh Salahuddin 10–0–50–1; Naim-ur-Rahman 8–0–49–0; Minhaz-ul-Abedin 10–0–51–1; Enam-ul-Haque 6–0–47–1.

Bangladesh

Ather Ali Khan st Moin Khan b Saqlain Mushtaq .	82	Hasib-ul-Hassan b Aqib Javed	10
Naim-ur-Rahman lbw b Kabir Khan. . . .	8	Saif-ul-Islam c Moin Khan b Saqlain Mushtaq .	7
Habib-ul-Bashar b Kabir Khan	0	Sheikh Salahuddin not out	0
Amin-ul-Islam c Kabir Khan b Saqlain Mushtaq .	14	Minhaz-ul-Abedin absent ill	
*Akram Khan c Ramiz Raja b Saqlain Mushtaq .	59	L-b 7, w 9, n-b 2	18
Enam-ul-Haque c Aamir Sohail b Aqib Javed .	8	1/13 2/13 3/61 (49.3 overs) 210	
†Khaled Masud c Moin Khan b Saqlain Mushtaq .	4	4/171 5/184 6/188	
		7/199 8/209 9/210	

Bowling: Aqib Javed 9–3–18–2; Kabir Khan 5–1–23–2; Saqlain Mushtaq 9.3–1–38–5; Shahid Afridi 9–0–36–0; Arshad Khan 7–0–24–0; Aamir Sohail 6–0–35–0; Salim Malik 4–0–29–0.

Umpires: S. K. Bansal and B. C. Cooray.

SRI LANKA v INDIA

At R. Premadasa Stadium, Colombo, July 18. Sri Lanka won by six wickets. Toss: Sri Lanka.
International debut: S. K. L. de Silva.

Ranatunga scored 131 not out, which he later described as one of his best innings, to steer Sri
Lanka into the final. It was his third and highest hundred in 215 one-day internationals, and he
needed all his experience to rescue the side from nine for two in the third over. Ranatunga faced
152 balls and struck 17 fours, sharing century partnerships with Atapattu and debutant Lanka de
Silva. India had also suffered early setbacks and were 51 for three in 18 overs before Dravid and
Azharuddin added 117, guiding them to a respectable 227.

Man of the Match: A. Ranatunga.

India

*S. R. Tendulkar b Vaas	21	A. Jadeja st S. K. L. de Silva
S. C. Ganguly c Dharmasena		b Jayasuriya . 3
b K. S. C. de Silva .	11	A. Kumble not out 16
†S. S. Karim c S. K. L. de Silva		
b Dharmasena .	12	W 3, n-b 1 4
R. Dravid b Jayasuriya	69	
M. Azharuddin not out	81	1/32 2/35 3/51 (6 wkts, 50 overs) 227
R. R. Singh c P. A. de Silva b Vaas. . . .	10	4/168 5/189 6/201

N. A. David, A. Kuruvilla and B. K. V. Prasad did not bat.

Bowling: Vaas 8–1–35–2; K. S. C. de Silva 7–0–30–1; Muralitharan 10–1–30–0; Dharmasena
10–1–52–1; Jayasuriya 10–0–52–2; Kalpage 5–0–28–0.

Sri Lanka

S. T. Jayasuriya c Dravid b Prasad	0	†S. K. L. de Silva not out 37
M. S. Atapattu lbw b Singh	31	L-b 6, w 12, n-b 3 21
P. A. de Silva c Karim b Prasad	6	
*A. Ranatunga not out	131	1/0 2/9 (4 wkts, 44.4 overs) 231
R. S. Mahanama c Karim b Singh	5	3/117 4/125

R. S. Kalpage, H. D. P. K. Dharmasena, W. P. U. J. C. Vaas, M. Muralitharan and K. S. C.
de Silva did not bat.

Bowling: Prasad 8–0–44–2; Kuruvilla 7–0–35–0; Kumble 10–0–38–0; David 8–0–36–0;
Ganguly 3–0–19–0; Singh 4–0–29–2; Jadeja 4–0–18–0; Tendulkar 0.4–0–6–0.

Umpires: Mohammad Nazir and Salim Badar.

INDIA v PAKISTAN

At Sinhalese Sports Club, Colombo, July 20. No result. Toss: India.

India were unlucky that bad weather came to Pakistan's aid at a dismal 30 for five. Sent in to
bat in heavy, overcast conditions – the match had already been reduced to 33 overs – Pakistan's
batsmen struggled against the moving ball. Their top order succumbed to Prasad, who took a
career-best four for 17. The match was to be replayed the following day (a request from Pakistan
to move to the Premadasa Stadium was rejected). But rain washed out the new game without a
ball bowled.

Pakistan

Saeed Anwar lbw b Prasad	0	Shahid Afridi not out 0
Aamir Sohail lbw b Prasad	1	
*Ramiz Raja c Azharuddin b Kuruvilla .	5	L-b 3, w 6, n-b 1 10
Inzamam-ul-Haq c Dravid b Prasad	0	
Salim Malik c Azharuddin b Prasad. . . .	10	1/3 2/10 3/10 (5 wkts, 9 overs) 30
†Moin Khan not out.	4	4/23 5/29

Saqlain Mushtaq, Aqib Javed, Arshad Khan and Kabir Khan did not bat.

Bowling: Prasad 5–1–17–4; Kuruvilla 4–0–10–1.

India

*S. R. Tendulkar, S. C. Ganguly, N. S. Sidhu, R. Dravid, M. Azharuddin, A. Jadeja, R. R. Singh, †S. S. Karim, A. Kumble, A. Kuruvilla and B. K. V. Prasad.

Umpires: B. C. Cooray and K. T. Francis.

SRI LANKA v BANGLADESH

At Sinhalese Sports Club, Colombo, July 22. Sri Lanka won by 103 runs. Toss: Bangladesh. International debut: Mafiz-ur-Rahman.

Jayasuriya slammed an 83-ball century as Sri Lanka completed the preliminaries with an unbeaten record. He hit three sixes and 14 fours and shared an opening stand of 171 (a Sri Lankan record) with Atapattu. Ranatunga continued his fine form with a fifty which carried him to 6,000 runs in one-day internationals. Bangladesh began promisingly with an opening stand of 76 in 17 overs. But they then lost wickets regularly.

Man of the Match: S. T. Jayasuriya.

Sri Lanka

S. T. Jayasuriya c Mafiz-ur-Rahman b Sheikh Salahuddin	108	R. S. Mahanama not out	39
M. S. Atapattu c Amin-ul-Islam b Minhaz-ul-Abedin	60	†S. K. L. de Silva not out	10
P. A. de Silva c Khaled Masud b Minhaz-ul-Abedin	15	L-b 4, w 9	13
*A. Ranatunga c Naim-ur-Rahman b Sheikh Salahuddin	51	1/171 2/177 (4 wkts, 46 overs) 296 3/213 4/284	

R. S. Kalpage, U. D. U. Chandana, D. K. Liyanage, M. Muralitharan and K. S. C. de Silva did not bat.

Bowling: Saif-ul-Islam 6–0–34–0; Hasib-ul-Hassan 8–0–50–0; Mafiz-ur-Rahman 6–0–37–0; Akram Khan 2–0–34–0; Sheikh Salahuddin 8–0–48–2; Minhaz-ul-Abedin 9–0–43–2; Naim-ur-Rahman 7–0–46–0.

Bangladesh

Ather Ali Khan b Muralitharan	42	Mafiz-ur-Rahman c K. S. C. de Silva b P. A. de Silva	6
Naim-ur-Rahman c Kalpage b K. S. C. de Silva	47	†Khaled Masud not out	5
Habib-ul-Bashar run out	6	Hasib-ul-Hassan run out	2
Amin-ul-Islam run out	29	B 3, l-b 6, w 12, n-b 2	23
*Akram Khan st S. K. L. de Silva b Chandana	32	1/76 2/95 3/117 (8 wkts, 46 overs) 193	
Minhaz-ul-Abedin c K. S. C. de Silva b Muralitharan	1	4/167 5/177 6/178 7/190 8/193	

Saif-ul-Islam and Sheikh Salahuddin did not bat.

Bowling: Liyanage 3–0–10–0; K. S. C. de Silva 4–0–17–1; P. A. de Silva 9–0–39–1; Ranatunga 2–0–16–0; Muralitharan 10–0–29–2; Chandana 9–0–38–1; Kalpage 9–1–35–0.

Umpires: Salim Badar and S. Venkataraghavan.

BANGLADESH v INDIA

At Sinhalese Sports Club, Colombo, July 24. India won by nine wickets. Toss: India. International debut: Zakir Hassan.

Tendulkar won a vital toss in this rain-affected match. His team restricted Bangladesh to a moderate total of 130 in 43 overs. But India needed to pass that score inside 20 overs to displace Pakistan on run-rate and qualify for the final. They used just 15, left-hander Ganguly stroking an elegant unbeaten 73 off 52 balls.

Man of the Match: S. C. Ganguly.

Bangladesh

Ather Ali Khan lbw b Tendulkar	33	Hasib-ul-Hassan lbw b Singh	0
Naim-ur-Rahman lbw b Kuruvilla	0	Sheikh Salahuddin not out	3
Minhaz-ul-Abedin c Karim b Prasad	3		
Amin-ul-Islam c Kumble b Singh	30	L-b 15, w 2, n-b 2	19
*Akram Khan c Jadeja b Kumble	11		
†Khaled Masud c Ganguly b Singh	12	1/2 2/12 3/57 (8 wkts, 43 overs) 130
Enam-ul-Haque run out	4	4/79 5/92 6/100	
Mafiz-ur-Rahman not out	15	7/104 8/104	

Zakir Hassan did not bat.

Bowling: Prasad 7–1–15–1; Kuruvilla 6–0–28–1; Kumble 10–3–17–1; Ganguly 6–1–24–0; Tendulkar 5–0–18–1; Singh 9–2–13–3.

India

S. C. Ganguly not out	73
*S. R. Tendulkar b Enam-ul-Haque	28
M. Azharuddin not out	23
B 4, l-b 1, w 2, n-b 1	8

1/54   (1 wkt, 15 overs) 132

N. S. Sidhu, R. Dravid, A. Jadeja, R. R. Singh, †S. S. Karim, A. Kumble, A. Kuruvilla and B. K. V. Prasad did not bat.

Bowling: Hasib-ul-Hassan 3–0–25–0; Zakir Hassan 2–0–17–0; Sheikh Salahuddin 3–0–22–0; Enam-ul-Haque 3–0–34–1; Mafiz-ur-Rahman 2–0–16–0; Minhaz-ul-Abedin 2–0–13–0.

Umpires: K. T. Francis and Mohammad Nazir.

QUALIFYING TABLE

	Played	Won	Lost	No result	Points	Net run-rate
Sri Lanka	3	3	0	0	6	1.03
India	3	1	1	1	3	1.40
Pakistan	3	1	1	1	3	0.94
Bangladesh	3	0	3	0	0	–2.89

India reached the final on net run-rate, their head-to-head match with Pakistan having been a no-result. Net run-rate was calculated by subtracting runs conceded per over from runs scored per over.

FINAL

SRI LANKA v INDIA

At R. Premadasa Stadium, Colombo, July 26. Sri Lanka won by eight wickets. Toss: India. International debut: N. M. Kulkarni.

Jayasuriya and Atapattu ensured a one-sided final, wiping out more than half a target of 240 with an opening partnership of 137 off 109 balls. Sri Lanka won with more than 13 overs to spare, to regain the Asia Cup after 11 years. India fielded only three front-line bowlers, and paid dearly; Jayasuriya raced to 63 off 52 balls and Ranatunga finished the job with an unbeaten 62 off 67. Atapattu, meanwhile, played the anchor role to perfection. India's total revolved around their most experienced pair, Tendulkar and Azharuddin, who added 109. Azharuddin scored 81 but hit only one four and two sixes, while Tendulkar made 53 with two fours. A stunning Sri Lankan fielding display featured five marvellous outfield catches.

Man of the Match: M. S. Atapattu.   *Man of the Series:* A. Ranatunga.

India

S. C. Ganguly c P. A. de Silva b Dharmasena .	34	
N. S. Sidhu c Muralitharan b K. S. C. de Silva .	10	
R. Dravid c Mahanama b Vaas	7	
*S. R. Tendulkar c Kalpage b Muralitharan .	53	
M. Azharuddin c Muralitharan b Dharmasena .	81	
A. Jadeja run out	22	
R. R. Singh c P. A. de Silva b Vaas....	9	
A. Kumble not out .	7	
†S. S. Karim not out.	1	
B 1, l-b 8, w 5, n-b 1	15	

1/32 2/51 3/59 (7 wkts, 50 overs) 239
4/168 5/215
6/225 7/234

B. K. V. Prasad and N. M. Kulkarni did not bat.

Bowling: Vaas 8–1–32–2; K. S. C. de Silva 9–1–44–1; Dharmasena 10–1–54–2; Muralitharan 10–1–38–1; Jayasuriya 10–0–46–0; Kalpage 3–0–16–0.

Sri Lanka

S. T. Jayasuriya c Sidhu b Kulkarni....	63	
M. S. Atapattu not out	84	
P. A. de Silva c and b Ganguly.	6	
*A. Ranatunga not out	62	
L-b 10, w 13, n-b 2	25	

1/137 2/144 (2 wkts, 36.5 overs) 240

R. S. Mahanama, †S. K. L. de Silva, R. S. Kalpage, H. D. P. K. Dharmasena, W. P. U. J. C. Vaas, M. Muralitharan and K. S. C. de Silva did not bat.

Bowling: Prasad 4–0–43–0; Singh 3–0–26–0; Kumble 8–0–54–0; Tendulkar 3–0–20–0; Kulkarni 10–0–48–1; Ganguly 5–0–25–1; Dravid 2–0–6–0; Jadeja 1.5–0–8–0.

Umpires: Mohammad Nazir and Salim Badar. Series referee: J. R. Reid (New Zealand).

SAHARA CUP, 1997-98

By TONY COZIER

India put behind them a miserable sequence of seven defeats in their last eight completed one-day internationals to triumph over Pakistan in the second Sahara Cup. The tournament had been inaugurated in the unlikely setting of the Toronto Cricket, Skating & Curling Club in 1996, specifically for the benefit of a satellite television channel covering south-east Asia. The previous year, Pakistan won the final match to secure the Cup 3-2. Now, India reeled off four straight victories before spirited Pakistan batting earned them belated consolation.

Ironically, attention was diverted from the cricket by just the sort of incident that the distant location was chosen to avoid. In the second match, the heavy-set Pakistani Inzamam-ul-Haq was repeatedly taunted about his size by a spectator using a megaphone. "Aloo", Hindi for potato, was reportedly the offensive word. Inzamam charged into the stand wielding a bat, handed to him on the boundary by the twelfth man, to accost his tormentor. Although play was suspended for more than half an hour, the scuffle was quickly quelled by ground security and there was no further trouble. In the end, the repercussions were no more serious than the two-match suspension handed down against Inzamam by referee Jackie Hendriks "for conduct unbecoming an international cricketer and for bringing the game into disrepute", and the charges of assault, subsequently dropped, brought against both Inzamam and the spectator, a Toronto resident of Indian descent.

India's star was Sourav Ganguly, unquestionably Man of the Series after earning the individual award in four of the matches. He had already been recognised for his stylish left-handed batting, which brought him 222 runs. Here, his right-arm medium-pace swing, for which he was less well-known, was encouraged by helpful pitches and earned him 15 wickets; he had taken only one in 42 previous one-day internationals.

Pakistan were missing three of their best players. Captain Wasim Akram, filling the role of television commentator instead, and leg-spinner Mushtaq Ahmed were both injured; Waqar Younis was helping Glamorgan to the County Championship. The experienced Ramiz Raja led the team but failed with the bat; he was replaced when the two teams travelled to Pakistan for a three-match series immediately afterwards.

Note: Matches in this section were not first-class.

INDIA v PAKISTAN

First One-Day International

At Toronto, September 13. India won by 20 runs. Toss: Pakistan. International debut: Harvinder Singh.

Heavy overnight dew left the pitch so damp that the start was delayed for half an hour. Conditions encouraged seam and swing, though bowlers found control so difficult that they delivered 43 wides. When they did bowl on target, the ball repeatedly found the edge of uncertain bats or beat them altogether. India's critical partnership was 91 off 108 balls between Azharuddin and Jadeja, who hit four sixes. Saqlain Mushtaq's clever off-spin caused a late collapse of six for nine, and he also figured with the bat, adding 64 with Salim Malik after Pakistan declined to 107 for seven. But once he ran himself out, the possibility of an unlikely win disappeared.

Man of the Match: A. Jadeja.

India

*S. R. Tendulkar c Mohammad Akram b Azhar Mahmood .	17	
S. C. Ganguly c Shahid Afridi b Mohammad Akram .	17	
R. Dravid c Ijaz Ahmed b Shahid Afridi.	23	
M. Azharuddin st Moin Khan b Saqlain Mushtaq .	52	
A. Jadeja c Mohammad Akram b Saqlain Mushtaq .	49	
R. R. Singh b Saqlain Mushtaq .	16	
†S. S. Karim b Aqib Javed .	3	

R. K. Chauhan b Aqib Javed 0
A. Kuruvilla c Saeed Anwar
      b Saqlain Mushtaq . 1
Harvinder Singh c Aqib Javed
      b Saqlain Mushtaq . 1
D. S. Mohanty not out 0
      B 1, l-b 3, w 22, n-b 3. 29

1/52 2/52 3/85   (50 overs) 208
4/176 5/199 6/202
7/203 8/207 9/208

Bowling: Aqib Javed 10-3-39-2; Mohammad Akram 9-1-41-1; Azhar Mahmood 10-1-28-1; Saqlain Mushtaq 10-0-45-5; Shahid Afridi 10-0-43-1; Salim Malik 1-0-8-0.

Pakistan

Saeed Anwar b Mohanty 2
*Ramiz Raja c Azharuddin b Kuruvilla . 1
Ijaz Ahmed, sen. c Azharuddin
      b Ganguly . 24
Inzamam-ul-Haq c Jadeja b Kuruvilla. . . 13
Shahid Afridi c Azharuddin
      b Harvinder Singh . 13
Salim Malik c Chauhan
      b Harvinder Singh . 64
†Moin Khan c R. R. Singh b Ganguly . . 0

Azhar Mahmood c Azharuddin
      b Harvinder Singh . 9
Saqlain Mushtaq run out 29
Aqib Javed run out. 2
Mohammad Akram not out. 0
      B 1, l-b 4, w 21, n-b 5. 31

1/4 2/6 3/32   (44.2 overs) 188
4/57 5/82 6/84
7/107 8/171 9/188

Bowling: Kuruvilla 8–2–27–2; Mohanty 7–0–22–1; R. R. Singh 10–1–35–0; Harvinder Singh 8.2–0–44–3; Ganguly 7–0–27–2; Tendulkar 2–0–13–0; Chauhan 2–0–15–0.

Umpires: S. A. Bucknor and R. E. Koertzen.

INDIA v PAKISTAN

Second One-Day International

At Toronto, September 14. India won by seven wickets. Toss: Pakistan.

India's emphatic victory was overshadowed by the fracas in which Inzamam-ul-Haq accosted a spectator who had been taunting him using a megaphone. Play was held up for 35 minutes and referee Jackie Hendriks suspended Inzamam for two matches. Assault charges against Inzamam and the spectator, Shiva Kumar Thind, were subsequently dropped. India bowled superbly and fielded impeccably in helpful conditions to dismiss Pakistan for 116. Mohanty removed the first three wickets and conceded just 15 from seven overs. The two Singhs and Ganguly ensured there was no recovery, in spite of Salim Malik's cultured 36. Ganguly then led the cruise to victory.

Man of the Match: S. C. Ganguly.

Pakistan

Saeed Anwar c Harvinder Singh b Mohanty .	12	Saqlain Mushtaq c Karim b Kuruvilla . .	21		
Shahid Afridi b Mohanty	0	Azhar Mahmood c Azharuddin b Ganguly	8		
*Ramiz Raja c Mohanty b R. R. Singh .	8	Aqib Javed c Azharuddin b Kuruvilla . .	0		
Ijaz Ahmed, sen. c Azharuddin b Mohanty .	4	Kabir Khan not out	1		
Inzamam-ul-Haq c Karim b R. R. Singh .	10	L-b 4, w 6, n-b 5	15		
Salim Malik c and b Ganguly	36	1/7 2/17 3/26	(45 overs) 116		
†Moin Khan run out	1	4/41 5/50 6/66			
		7/91 8/115 9/115			

Bowling: Kuruvilla 10–0–29–2; Mohanty 7–1–15–3; Harvinder Singh 8–2–19–0; R. R. Singh 6–2–22–2; Ganguly 9–2–16–2; Kulkarni 5–0–11–0.

India

S. C. Ganguly c Inzamam-ul-Haq b Saqlain Mushtaq .	32	M. Azharuddin not out	21
†S. S. Karim b Azhar Mahmood	9	B 1, l-b 2, w 6, n-b 7	16
R. Dravid run out.	14		
*S. R. Tendulkar not out	25	1/34 2/63 3/69 (3 wkts, 34.4 overs) 117	

A. Jadeja, R. R. Singh, A. Kuruvilla, N. M. Kulkarni, Harvinder Singh and D. S. Mohanty did not bat.

Bowling: Aqib Javed 10–1–46–0; Kabir Khan 0.3–0–0–0; Azhar Mahmood 9.3–1–28–1; Ijaz Ahmed 5–0–11–0; Saqlain Mushtaq 8–2–24–1; Shahid Afridi 1–0–3–0; Saeed Anwar 0.4–0–2–0.

Umpires: S. A. Bucknor and S. G. Randell.

INDIA v PAKISTAN

Third One-Day International

At Toronto, September 17. No result. Toss: India.

Two down with three matches to go, Pakistan had built the foundations of a demanding total when rain ended their innings. Saeed Anwar was left on 74 not out off 84 balls. India were set a revised target of 141 from 25 overs, but never attempted it as the match was aborted, forcing a replay.

Pakistan

Saeed Anwar not out	74	Hasan Raza c and b Ganguly	1
Shahid Afridi c Karim b Harvinder Singh	47	L-b 1, w 8, n-b 3	12
*Ramiz Raja retired hurt	34		—
Salim Malik b Ganguly	1	1/71 2/158 3/169 (3 wkts, 31.5 overs)	169

†Moin Khan, Azhar Mahmood, Saqlain Mushtaq, Mohammad Hussain, Aqib Javed and Mohammad Akram did not bat.

Ramiz Raja retired hurt at 156.

Bowling: Kuruvilla 6–0–30–0; Mohanty 8–1–44–0; Harvinder Singh 3–0–22–1; Ganguly 7.5–0–39–2; R. R. Singh 3–0–16–0; Tendulkar 4–0–17–0.

India

S. C. Ganguly, †S. S. Karim, R. Dravid, *S. R. Tendulkar, M. Azharuddin, A. Jadeja, R. R. Singh, A. Kuruvilla, N. M. Kulkarni, Harvinder Singh and D. S. Mohanty.

Umpires: R. E. Koertzen and S. G. Randell.

INDIA v PAKISTAN

Fourth One-Day International

At Toronto, September 18. India won by 34 runs. Toss: Pakistan.

India made sure of the Cup with a resilient performance, and Ganguly won the match award for his bowling, after scoring only two. Having to bat first on a bowler-friendly pitch, India could raise only 182 for six – a strong recovery from 23 for three, when Tendulkar went for nought in the 12th over. Azharuddin charted a course through choppy waters, while Jadeja and Robin Singh, who hit 32 off 29 balls, provided late momentum. As Shahid Afridi smashed six fours in 44 off 38 balls, a Pakistan victory seemed assured. But complacency led to reckless strokes – all ten wickets fell to catches – and they were undone by Ganguly, who claimed five for 16.

Man of the Match: S. C. Ganguly.

India

S. C. Ganguly c Ijaz Ahmed		A. Jadeja c Moin Khan	
b Azhar Mahmood .	2	b Mohammad Akram .	20
†S. S. Karim c Moin Khan b Aqib Javed	2	R. R. Singh not out	32
R. Dravid c Saeed Anwar b Salim Malik	25	A. Kuruvilla not out	1
*S. R. Tendulkar c Moin Khan		B 1, l-b 12, w 19, n-b 1	33
b Mohammad Akram .	0		—
M. Azharuddin c Azhar Mahmood		1/12 2/12 3/23 (6 wkts, 50 overs)	182
b Saqlain Mushtaq .	67	4/89 5/133 6/164	

N. M. Kulkarni, Harvinder Singh and D. S. Mohanty did not bat.

Bowling: Aqib Javed 10–4–17–1; Azhar Mahmood 9–0–30–1; Mohammad Akram 10–0–28–2; Shahid Afridi 5–0–20–0; Salim Malik 6–1–26–1; Saqlain Mushtaq 10–0–48–1.

Pakistan

Saeed Anwar c Dravid b Mohanty	22	Saqlain Mushtaq c Mohanty b Kuruvilla	11
Shahid Afridi c Tendulkar b Kuruvilla	44	Azhar Mahmood c Karim b Mohanty	6
*Ramiz Raja c Ganguly		Aqib Javed c Kuruvilla b Ganguly	11
b Harvinder Singh .	11	Mohammad Akram not out	2
Ijaz Ahmed, sen. c sub (V. G. Kambli)		L-b 6, w 4, n-b 5	15
b Ganguly .	13		—
Salim Malik c Tendulkar b Ganguly	6	1/52 2/79 3/87 (36.5 overs)	148
Hasan Raza c Jadeja b Ganguly	0	4/103 5/103 6/116	
†Moin Khan c R. R. Singh b Ganguly	7	7/118 8/126 9/141	

Bowling: Kuruvilla 8.5–1–26–2; Mohanty 8–0–43–2; Harvinder Singh 5–0–41–1; Ganguly 10–3–16–5; R. R. Singh 5–1–16–0.

Umpires: R. E. Koertzen and S. G. Randell.

INDIA v PAKISTAN

Fifth One-Day International

At Toronto, September 20. India won by seven wickets. Toss: India.

Again, Ganguly dominated a tense match, reduced by almost half because the outfield was soaked. His medium-pace swing helped contain Pakistan to 159 for six: he then opened India's batting and remained to the pulsating end, with three balls remaining (their allocation had been reduced by two overs through their tardy over-rate). Ganguly's run-a-ball 75, including a six and eight fours, controlled a decisive partnership of 108 off 106 balls with Jadeja. As India closed in, Pakistan seemed overcome by both tension and the cold: the temperature had dropped to 12 degrees Centigrade. Moin Khan missed a stumping off Jadeja, Mohammad Akram converted a catch off Ganguly into a six by stepping over the boundary, and three run-out chances were muffed.

Man of the Match: S. C. Ganguly.

Pakistan

Saeed Anwar b Kuruvilla	30	Azhar Mahmood not out		33
Shahid Afridi c Karim b Mohanty	2	Saqlain Mushtaq not out		0
*Ramiz Raja c Karim b Ganguly	20			
Ijaz Ahmed, sen. c Jadeja b Harvinder Singh	15	L-b 8, w 10, n-b 1		19
Salim Malik c R. R. Singh b Ganguly	17			
†Moin Khan c Tendulkar b Harvinder Singh	23	1/31 2/46 3/72 4/95 5/107 6/155	(6 wkts, 28 overs)	159

Aqib Javed, Shahid Nazir and Mohammad Akram did not bat.

Bowling: Kuruvilla 6–0–29–1; Mohanty 5–0–35–2; Harvinder Singh 5–0–25–2; R. R. Singh 6–0–33–0; Ganguly 6–2–29–2.

India

*S. R. Tendulkar c Moin Khan b Shahid Nazir	6	A. Jadeja not out		37
S. C. Ganguly not out	75			
R. R. Singh c Mohammad Akram b Shahid Nazir	16	B 1, l-b 5, w 13, n-b 2		21
M. Azharuddin c Ijaz Ahmed b Shahid Nazir	7	1/8 2/41 3/54	(3 wkts, 25.3 overs)	162

V. G. Kambli, R. Dravid, †S. S. Karim, A. Kuruvilla, Harvinder Singh and D. S. Mohanty did not bat.

Bowling: Aqib Javed 4.3–0–35–0; Shahid Nazir 6–0–38–3; Mohammad Akram 5–0–27–0; Azhar Mahmood 5–0–25–0; Saqlain Mushtaq 5–0–31–0.

Umpires: S. A. Bucknor and R. E. Koertzen.

INDIA v PAKISTAN

Sixth One-Day International

At Toronto, September 21. Pakistan won by five wickets. Toss: Pakistan.

Batsmen at last enjoyed themselves in bright sunshine on the first true pitch of the tournament. Tendulkar, finding something like his real form, and Ganguly prospered in a stand of 98, then

Ganguly and Azharuddin capitalised to add 104. Azharuddin completed his third fifty but Ganguly fell trying to bring up his hundred, to a catch at deep extra cover; he had hit two sixes and five fours. Opening instead of Saeed Anwar, who was ill, Ijaz Ahmed joined Shahid Afridi in a breath-taking assault that yielded 99 from the first ten overs. Ijaz's 60 came off 42 balls, Afridi's 39 off 30; one of his two sixes landed in an adjoining car park. Later, Inzamam-ul-Haq, ending his suspension, and the teenager Hasan Raza steadily guided Pakistan to a consolation victory.

Man of the Match: S. C. Ganguly.   *Man of the Series:* S. C. Ganguly.

India

*S. R. Tendulkar lbw b Azhar Mahmood	51	R. R. Singh c and b Aqib Javed		9
S. C. Ganguly c Azhar Mahmood		R. Dravid not out		3
b Saqlain Mushtaq	96			
V. G. Kambli c Saqlain Mushtaq		L-b 5, w 8, n-b 4		17
b Azhar Mahmood	1			
M. Azharuddin run out	50	1/98 2/102 3/206 (5 wkts, 50 overs)		250
A. Jadeja not out	23	4/214 5/237		

†S. S. Karim, A. Kuruvilla, Harvinder Singh and D. S. Mohanty did not bat.

Bowling: Aqib Javed 10–3–40–1; Shahid Nazir 10–0–66–0; Azhar Mahmood 10–1–27–2; Saqlain Mushtaq 10–1–51–1; Salim Malik 1–0–13–0; Shahid Afridi 9–0–48–0.

Pakistan

Shahid Afridi c Tendulkar b Ganguly	39	Hasan Raza c Karim b Mohanty		41
Ijaz Ahmed, sen. c Tendulkar		†Moin Khan not out		3
b Harvinder Singh	60	B 2, l-b 9, w 14, n-b 4		29
Salim Malik c Karim b Harvinder Singh	8			
*Ramiz Raja b Ganguly	0	1/109 2/109 3/111 (5 wkts, 41.5 overs)		251
Inzamam-ul-Haq not out	71	4/127 5/240		

Azhar Mahmood, Saqlain Mushtaq, Aqib Javed and Shahid Nazir did not bat.

Bowling: Kuruvilla 9.5–0–80–0; Mohanty 9–1–66–1; Harvinder Singh 8–0–33–2; Ganguly 9–1–33–2; R. R. Singh 4–0–15–0; Jadeja 2–0–13–0.

Umpires: S. A. Bucknor and S. G. Randell.   Series referee: J. L. Hendriks (West Indies).

WILLS CHALLENGE SERIES, 1997-98

The Indians had not toured Pakistan since 1989-90 because of political tensions, though they had continued to meet regularly for one-day internationals, usually on neutral territory, such as Sharjah. In fact they had played each other only a week earlier, in Toronto, where India won the Sahara Cup 4-1. They finally returned to Pakistan for a short one-day series which opened their neighbours' Golden Jubilee celebrations. Pakistan took revenge for their Canadian setback, with Saeed Anwar leading them to a 2-1 victory (Ramiz Raja, the previous week's captain, had already been dropped). The crowds were mostly welcoming, though there was trouble during the second match, in Karachi, when the Indian fielders were stoned by some spectators, causing an abrupt end to Pakistan's innings. That resulted in Pakistan's only defeat, but a stunning century from Ijaz Ahmed at Lahore brought the series to a triumphant conclusion.

Note: Matches in this section were not first-class.

PAKISTAN v INDIA

First One-Day International

At Hyderabad, September 28. Pakistan won by five wickets. Toss: India.

Tendulkar chose to bat on a pitch which was less friendly than it looked and soon had cause to regret it: Waqar Younis, who had just returned from bowling Glamorgan to the County Championship, dismissed him and Ganguly in his first two overs. The middle order advanced to 166 for four, but the innings fell apart when six wickets went down for four runs, with Aqib Javed bowling four of them. Pakistan's openers, Saeed Anwar and Shahid Afridi, made a determined reply, scoring 70 in 13 overs on a surface which grew ever more awkward. After a mid-innings wobble, Inzamam-ul-Haq, who batted steadily for an hour and a half, saw his side home with time to spare.

Man of the Match: Aqib Javed.

India

*S. R. Tendulkar b Waqar Younis	2	R. K. Chauhan c Ijaz Ahmed	
S. C. Ganguly c Hasan Raza		b Saqlain Mushtaq	0
b Waqar Younis	0	A. Kuruvilla b Aqib Javed	1
R. R. Singh b Saqlain Mushtaq	20	N. M. Kulkarni b Aqib Javed	0
M. Azharuddin b Shahid Afridi	31	D. S. Mohanty not out	1
R. Dravid b Aqib Javed	50	B 1, l-b 8, w 13, n-b 2	24
A. Jadeja b Aqib Javed	41		
†S. S. Karim c Ijaz Ahmed		1/2 2/3 3/61 4/77 5/166 (49 overs) 170	
b Saqlain Mushtaq	0	6/167 7/167 8/169 9/169	

Bowling: Waqar Younis 7–1–21–2; Aqib Javed 8–0–29–4; Azhar Mahmood 9–0–35–0; Saqlain Mushtaq 9–3–13–3; Shahid Afridi 10–0–38–1; Ijaz Ahmed 6–0–25–0.

Pakistan

*Saeed Anwar lbw b Kulkarni	30	†Moin Khan not out	12
Shahid Afridi lbw b Kulkarni	45		
Ijaz Ahmed, sen. c Tendulkar b Singh	22	B 2, l-b 6, w 5, n-b 1	14
Salim Elahi run out	8		
Inzamam-ul-Haq not out	35	1/70 2/87 3/106 (5 wkts, 44.3 overs) 171	
Hasan Raza c Tendulkar b Kulkarni	5	4/113 5/138	

Azhar Mahmood, Saqlain Mushtaq, Waqar Younis and Aqib Javed did not bat.

Bowling: Kuruvilla 8–1–23–0; Mohanty 4–0–23–0; Chauhan 10–2–40–0; Kulkarni 10–2–27–3; Singh 5–0–14–1; Ganguly 4–0–21–0; Tendulkar 3–1–11–0; Jadeja 0.3–0–4–0.

Umpires: Said Shah and Salim Badar.

PAKISTAN v INDIA

Second One-Day International

At Karachi, September 30. India won by four wickets. Toss: Pakistan.

Stone-throwing from the crowd interrupted Pakistan's innings four times, and perhaps cost them the match. When Ganguly became the fifth Indian fielder to be hit, Tendulkar told referee Madugalle he could not risk his players any longer, and Madugalle agreed. Pakistan were halted in mid-over and their disappointed supporters murmured that, with Inzamam-ul-Haq unbeaten on 74, India might have faced a target much stiffer than 266 from 47 had he continued to hit out for another three overs. Pakistan's initial momentum came from Shahid Afridi, who struck 72 in 56 balls, with nine fours and a six. Ganguly was almost as forceful in reply. He hit 89 off 96 balls, with 11 fours. India then stumbled, losing four quick wickets, two to run-outs. But Robin Singh, with a run-a-ball 31, and Karim fought back in a stand of 62. Off-spinner Saqlain Mushtaq suddenly went for 33 in three overs, perhaps suffering from the mix-up when a worn ball which had gone out of shape was replaced by a brand new one. Even then, Karim's dismissal might have ended India's challenge, but Chauhan hit a six in the final over to ensure victory.

Man of the Match: S. C. Ganguly.

Pakistan

*Saeed Anwar c and b Chauhan	18	†Moin Khan not out	31
Shahid Afridi c Kuruvilla b Kulkarni	72		
Ijaz Ahmed, sen. c Azharuddin		L-b 7, w 9, n-b 5	21
b Kulkarni	31		
Inzamam-ul-Haq not out	74	1/55 2/126	(4 wkts, 47.2 overs) 265
Salim Elahi c Kulkarni b Chauhan	18	3/148 4/197	

Hasan Raza, Azhar Mahmood, Saqlain Mushtaq, Waqar Younis and Aqib Javed did not bat.

Bowling: Kuruvilla 7.2–0–50–0; Mohanty 3–0–25–0; Chauhan 10–0–48–2; Kulkarni 10–0–66–2; Ganguly 10–0–39–0; Singh 6–0–23–0; Tendulkar 1–0–7–0.

India

*S. R. Tendulkar c Moin Khan		R. R. Singh not out	31
b Azhar Mahmood	21	†S. S. Karim b Waqar Younis	26
S. C. Ganguly c Shahid Afridi		R. K. Chauhan not out	8
b Waqar Younis	89	L-b 7, w 12, n-b 5	24
V. G. Kambli run out	53		
M. Azharuddin run out	6	1/71 2/169 3/179	(6 wkts, 46.3 overs) 266
A. Jadeja c Ijaz Ahmed b Shahid Afridi	8	4/185 5/195 6/257	

A. Kuruvilla, N. M. Kulkarni and D. S. Mohanty did not bat.

Bowling: Waqar Younis 9–0–36–2; Aqib Javed 10–0–73–0; Azhar Mahmood 9–0–56–1; Saqlain Mushtaq 9.3–1–46–0; Shahid Afridi 9–0–48–1.

Umpires: Mian Aslam and Salim Badar.

PAKISTAN v INDIA

Third One-Day International

At Lahore, October 2 (day/night). Pakistan won by nine wickets. Toss: Pakistan.

An astonishing century from Ijaz Ahmed enabled Pakistan to secure the series with 23 overs to spare. Promoted to open under the Lahore floodlights, Ijaz hit an unbeaten 139 from only 84 balls, winning the match with his ninth six – on top of ten fours. His opening partner, Shahid Afridi, struck 47 in 23 balls as they put on 80 in eight overs. Mohanty was hit especially hard, going for 24 in one over. India had struggled when asked to bat, and had to be rescued from 77 for five by Jadeja, who scored 76 in a comparatively stately 109 balls, and there was a late run-a-ball flourish from Chauhan. But 217 in 49 overs (Pakistan were deprived of one for a slow over-rate) proved quite indefensible against what Tendulkar called one of the greatest one-day innings.

Man of the Match: Ijaz Ahmed.

India

*S. R. Tendulkar c Inzamam-ul-Haq		R. K. Chauhan c Mohammad Hussain	
b Aqib Javed	7	b Waqar Younis	32
S. C. Ganguly c Mohammad Hussain		A. Kuruvilla run out	6
b Saqlain Mushtaq	26	N. M. Kulkarni c sub (Hasan Raza)	
R. R. Singh b Azhar Mahmood	17	b Aqib Javed	2
M. Azharuddin c Moin Khan		D. S. Mohanty not out	0
b Azhar Mahmood	6		
V. G. Kambli c Moin Khan		L-b 5, w 11, n-b 2	18
b Azhar Mahmood	6		
A. Jadeja c Inzamam-ul-Haq		1/12 2/53 3/56	(49.2 overs) 216
b Waqar Younis	76	4/66 5/77 6/130	
†S. S. Karim b Mohammad Hussain	20	7/206 8/206 9/215	

Bowling: Waqar Younis 8.2–0–33–2; Aqib Javed 7–0–35–2; Azhar Mahmood 9–0–34–3; Saqlain Mushtaq 10–0–46–1; Shahid Afridi 5–0–26–0; Mohammad Hussain 10–0–37–1.

Pakistan

Ijaz Ahmed, sen. not out	139
Shahid Afridi c Tendulkar b Kulkarni. . .	47
Mohammad Wasim not out	27
L-b 2, w 4	6

1/80   (1 wkt, 26.2 overs) 219

*Saeed Anwar, Inzamam-ul-Haq, †Moin Khan, Azhar Mahmood, Mohammad Hussain, Saqlain Mushtaq, Waqar Younis and Aqib Javed did not bat.

Bowling: Kuruvilla 6–1–42–0; Mohanty 3–0–38–0; Kulkarni 8–0–57–1; Chauhan 5–0–30–0; Ganguly 2.2–0–28–0; Singh 2–0–22–0.

Umpires: Javed Akhtar and Mohammad Nazir.   Series referee: R. S. Madugalle (Sri Lanka).

PRESIDENT'S CUP, 1997-98

By UTPAL SHUVRO

This tournament, the second senior one-day international competition to be staged in Nairobi, staggered from disaster to fiasco as arrangement after arrangement went awry. The idea was simple: a contest involving one or more of the world's top limited-overs teams to mark the new standing of the hosts, Kenya, who, along with Bangladesh, had been given a special status allowing them to play full one-day internationals and first-class cricket but not Tests.

The Kenya Cricket Association, the organisers, hoped to secure either India (guaranteeing lucrative TV rights) or the World Cup holders Sri Lanka, or both. In the end, the poor relations of world cricket – Kenya, Bangladesh and Zimbabwe – contested a private affair among themselves; spectators and television cameras both stayed away. For one fixture between the two visiting teams there were just 32 paying customers. The games, shifted from their original dates in the hope of attracting the Indians, caught the start of Kenya's rainy season. Then the third match of the finals was moved again to maximise attendance on a public holiday – only for Zimbabwe's emphatic victories in the first two to rule out the need for a decider.

Nor was the cricket especially exciting. Kenya set two world partnership records, for the first and seventh wickets in one-day internationals, but Zimbabwe – led by the Flower brothers – were overall much too professional for their opponents and won the trophy with considerable ease, underlining the gulf that both Kenya and Bangladesh must bridge before ICC awards them full Test status. Kenya seemed closer to their goal than the Bangladeshis, who barely put up a fight in any of their four matches. Their coach, Gordon Greenidge, said they performed "like a bunch of schoolboys".

Note: Matches in this section were not first-class.

KENYA v BANGLADESH

At Nairobi Gymkhana, Nairobi, October 10. Kenya won by 150 runs. Toss: Bangladesh.
International debuts: Mohammad Sheikh; A. Vadher; Shahriar Hossain.

With both teams having received official one-day international status only in June, national
records were inevitable. But no one expected the highest opening partnership in 1,239 one-day
internationals: the stand of 225 between Dipak Chudasama and Kennedy Otieno surpassed the
212 between Australians Geoff Marsh and David Boon at Jaipur in 1986-87. Kenya's 347 was
the highest total by a non-Test side and Chudasama, a dentist by profession, became the first
Kenyan to make a one-day international century, though Otieno soon overtook him, and finished
with 144. At 100 for two, Bangladesh looked to have made a reasonable start, but the Kenyan
captain, Asif Karim, took wickets throughout the innings to finish with five for 33. Only Ather
Ali Khan, with 61, offered any resistance. For the Kenyans, who had lost the ICC Trophy final
to Bangladesh in Malaysia the previous April, revenge was sweet.

Man of the Match: K. Otieno.

Kenya

D. Chudasama c and b Hasib-ul-Hassan .	122	T. Odoyo not out		18
†K. Otieno b Hasib-ul-Hassan	144	B 1, l-b 3, w 12		16
S. O. Tikolo b Mohammad Rafiq	32			
M. O. Odumbe not out	15	1/225 2/309 3/316	(3 wkts, 50 overs)	347

*Asif Karim, A. Vadher, Hitesh Modi, Mohammad Sheikh, Rajab Ali and M. Suji did not bat.

Bowling: Saif-ul-Islam 6.3–0–35–0; Hasib-ul-Hassan 10–1–68–2; Ather Ali Khan 4–0–29–0;
Sheikh Salahuddin 10–0–80–0; Mohammad Rafiq 10–0–71–1; Minhaz-ul-Abedin 4–0–24–0;
Akram Khan 3.3–0–22–0; Amin-ul-Islam 2–0–14–0.

Bangladesh

Ather Ali Khan c and b Asif Karim. . . .	61	Sheikh Salahuddin st Otieno	
Shahriar Hossain b Rajab Ali	14	b Mohammad Sheikh .	3
Jahangir Alam b Asif Karim	3	Saif-ul-Islam absent hurt	
Amin-ul-Islam b Tikolo	37		
*Akram Khan lbw b Asif Karim	16	B 4, l-b 7, w 8, n-b 2	21
Minhaz-ul-Abedin b Asif Karim	1		—
Mohammad Rafiq c and b Tikolo	19	1/55 2/90 3/100	(43.4 overs) 197
†Khaled Masud c Tikolo b Asif Karim . .	1	4/123 5/124 6/163	
Hasib-ul-Hassan not out.	21	7/166 8/176 9/197	

Bowling: Suji 5–0–35–0; Rajab Ali 7–1–20–1; Odoyo 3–0–18–0; Asif Karim 10–2–33–5;
Odumbe 7–0–37–0; Tikolo 6–0–31–2; Mohammad Sheikh 4.4–1–12–1; Hitesh Modi 1–1–0–0.

Umpires: R. E. Koertzen and Salim Badar.

BANGLADESH v ZIMBABWE

At Nairobi Gymkhana, Nairobi, October 11. Zimbabwe won by 48 runs. Toss: Zimbabwe.
International debut: Shafiuddin Ahmed.

After their disappointing performance against Kenya, the Bangladeshi batsmen put up more of
a fight against tougher opposition. However, their bowlers again struggled. The Flower brothers,
Grant and Andy, gave Zimbabwe an excellent start, putting on 161 for the first wicket, and Guy
Whittall later hit an undefeated 79. Bangladesh were chasing 300 for the second successive match;
a fourth-wicket partnership of 87 between Habib-ul-Bashar and Akram Khan, the captain, hinted
at a surprise. Once they were parted it was all downhill, though Bangladesh's 257 was their highest
total in one-day internationals.

Man of the Match: G. W. Flower.

Zimbabwe

G. W. Flower c and b Amin-ul-Islam	79		G. J. Rennie not out	17
†A. Flower c Akram Khan				
b Amin-ul-Islam	81		B 8, w 8, n-b 4	20
C. N. Evans c and b Amin-ul-Islam	0			
G. J. Whittall not out	79		1/161 2/161 (4 wkts, 50 overs)	305
*A. D. R. Campbell b Mohammad Rafiq	29		3/188 4/265	

C. B. Wishart, P. A. Strang, A. G. Huckle, A. R. Whittall and E. Matambanadzo did not bat.

Bowling: Hasib-ul-Hassan 9–1–60–0; Shafiuddin Ahmed 9–0–50–0; Mafiz-ur-Rahman 2–0–19–0; Ather Ali Khan 6–0–38–0; Minhaz-ul-Abedin 4–0–25–0; Mohammad Rafiq 10–0–48–1; Amin-ul-Islam 10–0–57–3.

Bangladesh

Ather Ali Khan run out	32		†Khaled Masud c Evans b Strang	6
Shahriar Hossain c Evans			Mafiz-ur-Rahman run out	16
b Matambanadzo	10		Hasib-ul-Hassan c G. W. Flower b Strang	4
Habib-ul-Bashar c A. R. Whittall			Shafiuddin Ahmed not out	0
b G. W. Flower	70			
Amin-ul-Islam c Campbell b Evans	16		B 1, l-b 5, w 16, n-b 5	27
*Akram Khan c Rennie b G. W. Flower	59			
Minhaz-ul-Abedin run out	16		1/35 2/72 3/96 (47.1 overs)	257
Mohammad Rafiq c G. J. Whittall			4/183 5/221 6/224	
b A. R. Whittall	1		7/231 8/242 9/257	

Bowling: Matambanadzo 5–0–24–1; G. J. Whittall 5–0–38–0; Strang 9.1–1–32–2; A. R. Whittall 10–0–62–1; Evans 5–0–30–1; Huckle 6–0–35–0; G. W. Flower 7–0–30–2.

Umpires: M. J. Kitchen and R. E. Koertzen.

KENYA v ZIMBABWE

At Nairobi Gymkhana, Nairobi, October 12. Zimbabwe won by six wickets, their target having been revised to 244 from 47 overs. Toss: Kenya.

At 206 for four from 43.1 overs, Zimbabwe were progressing steadily towards their target of 250. Then came a brief shower and they had to get 38 from 23 balls. With two overs left they still needed 20. But 16 came from the penultimate over, bowled by Asif Karim, and Zimbabwe won with three balls to spare. For Kenya, Otieno continued his excellent form to score 87, but he had little support.

Man of the Match: G. J. Whittall.

Kenya

D. Chudasama b G. J. Whittall	31		A. Vadher not out	13
†K. Otieno c Evans b A. R. Whittall	87		M. Suji not out	2
S. O. Tikolo c Evans b P. A. Strang	17			
M. O. Odumbe c B. C. Strang			B 1, l-b 12, w 13, n-b 1	27
b G. W. Flower	23			
Hitesh Modi c Wishart b B. C. Strang	31		1/51 2/95 (8 wkts, 50 overs)	249
T. Odoyo b P. A. Strang	4		3/149 4/197	
*Asif Karim run out	10		5/216 6/216	
Mohammad Sheikh c A. R. Whittall			7/224 8/242	
b P. A. Strang	4			

Rajab Ali did not bat.

Bowling: B. C. Strang 9–0–35–1; A. R. Whittall 10–0–44–1; G. J. Whittall 4–1–13–1; P. A. Strang 10–1–38–3; Evans 5–0–38–0; G. W. Flower 7–0–40–1; Huckle 5–0–28–0.

Zimbabwe

G. W. Flower c Hitesh Modi b Suji	7	C. B. Wishart not out	18
†A. Flower c Otieno b Odumbe	72		
G. J. Rennie run out	1	B 3, l-b 6, w 3, n-b 4	16
G. J. Whittall c Mohammad Sheikh b Odoyo	83	1/12 2/30 (4 wkts, 46.3 overs)	244
*A. D. R. Campbell not out	47	3/162 4/180	

C. N. Evans, P. A. Strang, B. C. Strang, A. G. Huckle and A. R. Whittall did not bat.

Bowling: Suji 8–2–28–1; Rajab Ali 4–0–22–0; Odoyo 10–0–51–1; Asif Karim 7–0–41–0; Odumbe 8.3–1–39–1; Tikolo 5–0–34–0; Mohammad Sheikh 4–0–20–0.

Umpires: M. J. Kitchen and Salim Badar.

BANGLADESH v ZIMBABWE

At Aga Khan Sports Club, Nairobi, October 14. Zimbabwe won by 192 runs. Toss: Zimbabwe.

After three high-scoring contests at the Gymkhana, the teams moved on to the Aga Khan club, where the Bangladeshi batsmen struggled; no one passed 18 in either of their innings there. Zimbabwe's scorecard had a familiar look, however: Andy Flower and Whittall scored fifties for the third game running. Bangladesh's batting was undone by the left-arm medium-pace of Bryan Strang. His figures of six for 20 were the seventh-best in all one-day internationals – and the best for Zimbabwe, beating his brother Paul's five for 21 against Kenya in the 1996 World Cup. Bangladesh's 92 was their lowest-ever total.

Man of the Match: B. C. Strang.

Zimbabwe

G. W. Flower c Khaled Masud b Shafiuddin Ahmed	15	C. B. Wishart c Khaled Masud b Hasib-ul-Hassan	30
†A. Flower c Shahriar Hossain b Sheikh Salahuddin	70	P. A. Strang b Shafiuddin Ahmed	33
		B. C. Strang run out	3
C. N. Evans c Khaled Masud b Shafiuddin Ahmed	1	A. G. Huckle run out	1
G. J. Whittall lbw b Mohammad Rafiq	52	M. Mbangwa not out	0
*A. D. R. Campbell b Hasib-ul-Hassan	40	L-b 9, w 9, n-b 6	24
G. J. Rennie st Khaled Masud b Mohammad Rafiq	15	1/37 2/55 3/150 4/160 5/186 (50 overs) 6/237 7/257 8/275 9/284	284

Bowling: Hasib-ul-Hassan 10–0–63–2; Shafiuddin Ahmed 10–0–42–3; Ather Ali Khan 3–0–19–0; Akram Khan 3–0–23–0; Sheikh Salahuddin 8–0–37–1; Mohammad Rafiq 10–0–65–2; Habib-ul-Bashar 6–0–26–0.

Bangladesh

Ather Ali Khan b B. C. Strang	9	†Khaled Masud lbw b B. C. Strang	0
Shahriar Hossain c P. A. Strang b B. C. Strang	0	Mohammad Rafiq lbw b Huckle	2
		Sheikh Salahuddin not out	6
Habib-ul-Bashar c A. Flower b B. C. Strang	2	Hasib-ul-Hassan c Rennie b Huckle	16
Minhaz-ul-Abedin c A. Flower b P. A. Strang	18	Shafiuddin Ahmed b P. A. Strang	11
		B 4, l-b 4, w 4, n-b 4	16
Jahangir Alam lbw b B. C. Strang	1	1/3 2/14 3/20 4/22 5/33 (32.3 overs) 6/38 7/53 8/57 9/77	92
*Akram Khan c Wishart b B. C. Strang	11		

Bowling: B. C. Strang 10–2–20–6; Mbangwa 6.3–0–15–0; P. A. Strang 9–1–22–2; Huckle 7–1–27–2.

Umpires: R. E. Koertzen and Salim Badar.

KENYA v BANGLADESH

At Aga Khan Sports Club, Nairobi, October 15. Kenya won by eight wickets. Toss: Bangladesh.

Bangladesh fared little better against Kenya. Having chosen to bat in a rain-shortened match, they managed just 100, Extras top-scoring with 19. Martin Suji, one of eight survivors from the Kenyan team that famously defeated West Indies in the 1996 World Cup, took four for 24 and the match award. Kenya wobbled slightly early on – Hasib-ul-Hassan took two wickets in successive deliveries – but thereafter had no trouble. Otieno maintained his good form, and Kenya won with 29 overs to spare.

Man of the Match: M. Suji.

Bangladesh

Ather Ali Khan c Otieno b M. Suji	0	Sheikh Salahuddin	
Mohammad Rafiq c Hitesh Modi		hit wkt b Mohammad Sheikh .	12
b M. Suji .	1	Hasib-ul-Hassan c Vadher b Odumbe ...	8
Habib-ul-Bashar b A. Suji	4	Shafiuddin Ahmed not out	0
Shahriar Hossain c Tikolo b Odoyo	16		
*Akram Khan c Odoyo b M. Suji	7	L-b 2, w 10, n-b 7.........	19
Minhaz-ul-Abedin c Odoyo b M. Suji ..	5		
†Khaled Masud c Vadher b Asif Karim .	12	1/1 2/9 3/10 (41.2 overs)	100
Mafiz-ur-Rahman c Mohammad Sheikh		4/28 5/40 6/51	
b Asif Karim .	16	7/63 8/88 9/100	

Bowling: M. Suji 10–1–24–4; A. Suji 6–0–19–1; Odoyo 9–2–15–1; Asif Karim 9–1–21–2; Odumbe 5.2–1–16–1; Mohammad Sheikh 2–0–3–1.

Kenya

D. Chudasama c Shahriar Hossain		A. Vadher not out	42
b Hasib-ul-Hassan .	4	L-b 2, w 8, n-b 4	14
†K. Otieno not out	42		
S. O. Tikolo b Hasib-ul-Hassan.......	0	1/11 2/11 (2 wkts, 17 overs)	102

M. O. Odumbe, Hitesh Modi, T. Odoyo, *Asif Karim, A. Suji, M. Suji and Mohammad Sheikh did not bat.

Bowling: Hasib-ul-Hassan 6–0–54–2; Shafiuddin Ahmed 4–0–18–0; Mohammad Rafiq 4–0–15–0; Sheikh Salahuddin 2–0–12–0; Mafiz-ur-Rahman 1–0–1–0.

Umpires: M. J. Kitchen and R. E. Koertzen.

KENYA v ZIMBABWE

At Aga Khan Sports Club, Nairobi, October 16. Zimbabwe won by seven wickets. Toss: Zimbabwe.

Both teams had already qualified and Kenya's top order showed little sign of caring about the outcome; only Otieno reached double figures. When Tony Suji joined Odoyo at 68 for six, a three-figure total seemed improbable. But Kenya, who had established a one-day international record for the first wicket six days earlier, now repeated the feat for the seventh wicket. Odoyo and Suji added 119. The previous record, 115, was jointly held by Jeff Dujon and Malcolm Marshall of West Indies, and Adam Parore and Lee Germon of New Zealand. A total of 207 ensured respectability, though not victory: Grant and Andy Flower gave Zimbabwe another century stand in reply, and Zimbabwe coasted in.

Man of the Match: A. Flower.

Kenya

D. Chudasama c A. Flower b Mbangwa .	5
†K. Otieno c Rennie b Mbangwa	34
S. O. Tikolo c Evans b B. C. Strang . .	6
A. Vadher c A. Flower b G. J. Whittall .	9
M. O. Odumbe c G. J. Whittall	
b Evans .	2
Hitesh Modi lbw b G. J. Whittall	1
T. Odoyo c Rennie b B. C. Strang . .	41
A. Suji c and b G. J. Whittall	67

*Asif Karim st A. Flower	
b A. R. Whittall .	5
M. Suji not out	9
Mohammad Sheikh not out	5
B 4, l-b 3, w 10, n-b 6	23
1/22 2/35 3/64 (9 wkts, 50 overs) 207	
4/64 5/68 6/68	
7/187 8/188 9/200	

Bowling: B. C. Strang 10–1–48–2; Mbangwa 8–3–24–2; G. J. Whittall 10–1–43–3; Evans 2–1–3–1; P. A. Strang 8–1–18–0; A. R. Whittall 8–0–41–1; G. W. Flower 4–0–23–0.

Zimbabwe

G. W. Flower lbw b Mohammad Sheikh .	71
†A. Flower c sub (J. Angara) b Tikolo .	66
G. J. Rennie c Odoyo b Asif Karim. . . .	27
G. J. Whittall not out	20

*A. D. R. Campbell not out	5
B 7, l-b 5, w 5, n-b 4	21
1/124 2/170 3/200 (3 wkts, 41.2 overs) 210	

C. B. Wishart, C. N. Evans, P. A. Strang, B. C. Strang, A. R. Whittall and M. Mbangwa did not bat.

Bowling: M. Suji 5–0–22–0; A. Suji 2–0–9–0; Odoyo 6–0–38–0; Asif Karim 10–0–39–1; Odumbe 4–0–19–0; Tikolo 4.2–0–29–1; Mohammad Sheikh 10–0–42–1.

Umpires: R. E. Koertzen and Salim Badar.

QUALIFYING TABLE

	Played	Won	Lost	Points	Net run-rate
Zimbabwe	4	4	0	8	1.52
Kenya	4	2	2	4	1.33
Bangladesh	4	0	4	0	–2.91

Net run-rate was calculated by subtracting runs conceded per over from runs scored per over.

KENYA v ZIMBABWE

First Final Match

At Nairobi Gymkhana, Nairobi, October 18. Zimbabwe won by 82 runs, Kenya's target having been revised to 255 from 40 overs. Toss: Zimbabwe.

Rain brought Kenya's reply to a close ten overs early, when they were 109 adrift with just three wickets remaining. Their target was retrospectively revised to 255, so they had fallen 83 short. Odumbe alone had troubled the bowlers for any length of time. In Zimbabwe's innings, the Flower brothers scored their third century stand of the tournament. From this base, the other batsmen were able to play freely, and Campbell contributed a run-a-ball 51.

Man of the Match: A. Flower.

Zimbabwe

G. W. Flower b Tikolo	69
†A. Flower st Otieno	
b Mohammad Sheikh .	79
G. J. Rennie c Vadher b Tikolo.	13
G. J. Whittall c M. Suji b Tikolo	17
*A. D. R. Campbell c A. Suji b Odumbe	51
C. B. Wishart c M. Suji b Odumbe	18
C. N. Evans b Odoyo	9

P. A. Strang not out	10
B. C. Strang b Odoyo	3
A. R. Whittall not out	2
L-b 4, w 3, n-b 3	10
1/154 2/154 3/179 (8 wkts, 50 overs) 281	
4/193 5/246 6/262	
7/268 8/279	

A. G. Huckle did not bat.

Bowling: M. Suji 8–0–36–0; Odumbe 6–0–48–2; A. Suji 7–0–32–0; Asif Karim 3–0–22–0; Odoyo 6–0–44–2; Tikolo 10–0–41–3; Mohammad Sheikh 10–0–54–1.

Kenya

D. Chudasama b B. C. Strang	2		T. Odoyo c A. Flower b G. W. Flower	18
†K. Otieno b G. J. Whittall	34		A. Suji not out	3
S. O. Tikolo run out	28		M. Suji not out	0
M. O. Odumbe c A. R. Whittall			B 1, l-b 3, w 2, n-b 3	9
b G. W. Flower	67			
A. Vadher b P. A. Strang	5		1/3 2/57 3/83 (7 wkts, 40 overs)	172
Hitesh Modi st A. Flower			4/104 5/127	
b G. J. Whittall	6		6/168 7/172	

*Asif Karim and Mohammad Sheikh did not bat.

Bowling: B. C. Strang 8–2–35–1; A. R. Whittall 7–1–22–0; P. A. Strang 8–0–29–1; G. J. Whittall 8–0–40–2; Huckle 5–1–18–0; Evans 2–0–18–0; G. W. Flower 2–0–6–2.

Umpires: M. J. Kitchen and R. E. Koertzen.

KENYA v ZIMBABWE

Second Final Match

At Nairobi Gymkhana, Nairobi, October 19. Zimbabwe won by 82 runs. Toss: Zimbabwe. International debut: J. Angara.

The two most reliable batsmen in the tournament, Andy Flower and Otieno – averaging 73.60 and 85.25 respectively – both failed in this match. That apart, matters largely followed the script, despite drab weather. Grant Flower compensated for his brother's lapse, sharing a partnership of 150 with Rennie. Then Evans hit 48 off 43 balls. Kenya fell quickly into crisis: Andrew Whittall claimed the first three wickets and the seventh fell at 71. Hitesh Modi and Asif Karim stayed together and threatened yet another one-day international partnership record: but, after adding 100, they fell 19 short. There was little more resistance and Zimbabwe won by 82 runs to claim the President's Cup.

Man of the Match: A. R. Whittall.   *Man of the Series:* A. Flower.

Zimbabwe

G. W. Flower run out	78		C. N. Evans not out	48
†A. Flower c Otieno b Suji	7		P. A. Strang not out	3
G. J. Rennie lbw b Mohammad Sheikh	76		B 3, l-b 12, w 4, n-b 3	22
G. J. Whittall run out	7			
*A. D. R. Campbell c Otieno b Odoyo	28		1/18 2/168 3/175 (6 wkts, 49 overs)	272
C. B. Wishart st Otieno b Odumbe	7		4/178 5/193 6/241	

B. C. Strang, A. R. Whittall and A. G. Huckle did not bat.

Bowling: Suji 8–0–40–1; Angara 6–0–34–0; Odoyo 4–0–47–1; Asif Karim 6–0–29–0; Tikolo 10–0–38–0; Mohammad Sheikh 9–0–43–1; Odumbe 6–0–26–1.

Kenya

D. Chudasama b A. R. Whittall	6		A. Suji run out	2
†K. Otieno b A. R. Whittall	15		*Asif Karim run out	53
S. O. Tikolo b A. R. Whittall	23		Mohammad Sheikh lbw b G. W. Flower	1
M. O. Odumbe c sub (D. P. Viljoen)			J. Angara not out	3
b P. A. Strang	14			
Hitesh Modi c B. C. Strang			L-b 7, w 6	13
b G. W. Flower	57			
A. Vadher c Campbell b P. A. Strang	0		1/21 2/29 3/62 (46.1 overs)	190
T. Odoyo c sub (D. P. Viljoen)			4/62 5/62 6/66	
b P. A. Strang	3		7/71 8/171 9/175	

Bowling: B. C. Strang 6–0–25–0; A. R. Whittall 10–2–23–3; P. A. Strang 10–2–37–3; G. W. Flower 9.1–0–44–2; Huckle 6–0–38–0; G. J. Whittall 5–0–16–0.

Umpires: R. E. Koertzen and Salim Badar.   Series referee: P. L. van der Merwe.

WILLS GOLDEN JUBILEE TOURNAMENT, 1997-98

By CRAIG COZIER

South Africa finally won a limited-overs tournament in the subcontinent at their seventh attempt. As in their last two visits, for the World Cup and the Titan Cup, both held in 1996, they won all their qualifying games, and this time they held their nerve for the final as well, deservedly beating Sri Lanka at the scene of their World Cup triumph 20 months earlier. The Wills Golden Jubilee tournament, held under floodlights at Lahore's Gaddafi Stadium to celebrate Pakistan's 50 years of independence, was devalued somewhat by heavy night dew and swarms of insects, both of which left the team fielding second at a distinct disadvantage. The white ball was likened to a bar of soap because it became soggy and discoloured even after numerous ball changes. Courtney Walsh, who lost all West Indies' three tosses and matches, fielding last, deemed it "quite impossible".

But the South Africans, inspired by the all-round skill of Lance Klusener, the consistency of Gary Kirsten and Hansie Cronje and the new-ball penetration of Shaun Pollock, defied all obstacles. They even won twice with the handicap of bowling second, and their professionalism shone through in the final.

In whipping West Indies and Pakistan in their first two matches, Sri Lanka stretched their unbeaten run of limited-overs matches to ten, including one no-result. They let down their guard in the last preliminary against South Africa, having already reached the final, and could not regain their edge. Pakistan, with Wasim Akram restored to the captaincy in place of Saeed Anwar, were embarrassingly outplayed by Sri Lanka when they had to win to advance to the final; their only success came against the winless West Indies. For West Indies, it was an ominous sign of what was to come in the Test series against Pakistan.

Even though their team did not appear in the final, the Pakistanis ended the competition in style. There was a dazzling fireworks display and the country's living Test captains – with the notable exception of Imran Khan, who pleaded political commitments – were paraded in horse-drawn carriages and honoured with gold medallions at a glitzy on-field ceremony.

Note: Matches in this section were not first-class.

SRI LANKA v WEST INDIES

At Lahore, November 1 (day/night). Sri Lanka won by seven wickets. Toss: Sri Lanka. International debut: R. N. Lewis.

Sri Lanka coasted home with 10.2 overs to spare, thanks to an unbeaten stand of 171 between Mahanama and Ranatunga. It was a record for Sri Lanka's fourth wicket in limited-overs internationals: Mahanama hit 94 off 112 balls, and Ranatunga 87 off 90 balls. Given a bigger target, both could have reached centuries. West Indies' top order paced their innings well: Lara added a cautious 82 with Chanderpaul and a run-a-ball 74 with Hooper. But then five wickets fell for 16 runs. Vaas claimed his 100th wicket in one-day internationals when he removed Simmons.

Man of the Match: A. Ranatunga.

West Indies

S. C. Williams c Ranatunga b Vaas	5	R. I. C. Holder run out	2
S. Chanderpaul lbw b P. A. de Silva	42	†D. Williams b K. S. C. de Silva	2
B. C. Lara b Jayasuriya	80		
C. L. Hooper c S. K. L. de Silva		L-b 5, w 4, n-b 4	13
b K. S. C. de Silva	68		
P. V. Simmons c Muralitharan b Vaas	20	1/16 2/98 3/172 (8 wkts, 50 overs)	237
C. E. L. Ambrose not out	4	4/221 5/228 6/229	
F. A. Rose run out	1	7/232 8/237	

R. N. Lewis and *C. A. Walsh did not bat.

Bowling: Vaas 10–0–35–2; K. S. C. de Silva 10–2–31–2; Dharmasena 10–0–55–0; Muralitharan 6–0–46–0; Jayasuriya 8–0–33–1; P. A. de Silva 6–0–32–1.

Sri Lanka

S. T. Jayasuriya c Lewis b Hooper	24	*A. Ranatunga not out	87
M. S. Atapattu c Hooper b Walsh	1	L-b 4, w 9, n-b 8	21
R. S. Mahanama not out	94		
P. A. de Silva c Chanderpaul b Rose	13	1/17 2/56 3/69 (3 wkts, 39.4 overs)	240

H. P. Tillekeratne, †S. K. L. de Silva, H. D. P. K. Dharmasena, W. P. U. J. C. Vaas, M. Muralitharan and K. S. C. de Silva did not bat.

Bowling: Ambrose 8–0–52–0; Walsh 9–1–41–1; Hooper 8–0–31–1; Rose 7–0–64–1; Lewis 5–0–24–0; Simmons 2.4–0–24–0.

Umpires: Javed Akhtar and Salim Badar.

PAKISTAN v SOUTH AFRICA

At Lahore, November 2 (day/night). South Africa won by nine runs. Toss: Pakistan.

Given that South Africa lost their third wicket at 192 and Pakistan at nought, this was an extraordinarily close finish. Pollock jolted Pakistan's pursuit of 272 with the wickets of Saeed Anwar, Aamir Sohail and Ijaz Ahmed for ducks in his opening over. He added Shahid Afridi in the fifth over, leaving Pakistan a desperate nine for four. But Inzamam-ul-Haq and Moin Khan, playing as a batsman while Rashid Latif returned behind the stumps, launched a rearguard action, adding 133 in 29 overs. And then Azhar Mahmood hit a blistering 59 not out off 43 balls to carry Pakistan within ten runs of victory. South Africa's total centred on Kirsten, who shared successive stands of 90 with Klusener and 98 with Cullinan. But Wasim Akram clean bowled the last three batsmen in an over to prevent a late assault.

Man of the Match: S. M. Pollock.

South Africa

A. C. Hudson lbw b Wasim Akram	2	P. L. Symcox b Wasim Akram	0
G. Kirsten lbw b Azhar Mahmood	89	P. S. de Villiers b Wasim Akram	1
L. Klusener b Saqlain Mushtaq	45	A. A. Donald b Wasim Akram	0
D. J. Cullinan run out	51		
*W. J. Cronje run out	35	L-b 9, w 8, n-b 1	18
J. N. Rhodes lbw b Saqlain Mushtaq	5		
S. M. Pollock c Ijaz Ahmed		1/4 2/94 3/192 (48 overs)	271
b Saqlain Mushtaq	15	4/221 5/241 6/254	
†D. J. Richardson not out	10	7/264 8/269 9/271	

Bowling: Wasim Akram 8–0–33–4; Waqar Younis 10–0–59–0; Saqlain Mushtaq 9–1–34–3; Azhar Mahmood 7–0–57–1; Aamir Sohail 4–0–23–0; Shahid Afridi 10–0–56–0.

Pakistan

Saeed Anwar c Hudson b Pollock	0	†Rashid Latif c and b Klusener	14
Shahid Afridi b Pollock	7	Saqlain Mushtaq c Rhodes b Donald	11
Aamir Sohail lbw b Pollock	0	Waqar Younis not out	6
Ijaz Ahmed, sen. lbw b Pollock	0	L-b 4, w 8	12
Inzamam-ul-Haq c Cronje	85		
Moin Khan lbw b de Villiers	59	1/0 2/0 3/0 (9 wkts, 50 overs)	262
*Wasim Akram run out	9	4/9 5/142 6/152	
Azhar Mahmood not out	59	7/180 8/206 9/247	

Bowling: Pollock 10-2-49-4; de Villiers 10-1-49-1; Donald 10-1-44-1; Cronje 8-0-38-1; Klusener 8-0-50-1; Symcox 4-0-28-0.

Umpires: R. S. Dunne and I. D. Robinson.

SOUTH AFRICA v WEST INDIES

At Lahore, November 3 (day/night). South Africa won by five wickets. Toss: South Africa.

South Africa made light work of what had seemed a formidable West Indies total of 293 for eight. Kirsten laid the foundations with 64 and, after they slipped to 81 for three, Cronje helped him add 112. Cronje was out for a run-a-ball 94 but a frantic 53 off 39 balls by Rhodes sealed the win. Struggling to control the slippery ball, West Indies conceded 11 wides and 13 no-balls. Earlier, Hooper scored his fourth one-day international century, off 101 balls, to lead a fluent batting display. Lara hit another delightful half-century, flavoured with ten fours and a six, which carried him past 5,000 runs, while Chanderpaul's 47 took just 40 balls.

Man of the Match: W. J. Cronje.

West Indies

S. C. Williams run out	26	C. E. L. Ambrose b de Villiers	6
S. L. Campbell c Cullinan b Pollock	0	†D. Williams b de Villiers	0
B. C. Lara run out	68	B 1, l-b 10, w 4, n-b 1	16
C. L. Hooper c Cullinan b Donald	105		
S. Chanderpaul c de Villiers b Cronje	47	1/1 2/87 3/131 (8 wkts, 50 overs)	293
P. V. Simmons not out	18	4/214 5/270 6/283	
R. N. Lewis c de Villiers b Donald	7	7/293 8/293	

M. Dillon and *C. A. Walsh did not bat.

Bowling: Pollock 9-0-52-1; de Villiers 10-1-40-2; Donald 10-0-58-2; Klusener 7-0-42-0; Symcox 10-0-52-0; Cronje 4-0-38-1.

South Africa

A. C. Hudson c Lewis b Ambrose	6	S. M. Pollock not out	11
G. Kirsten run out	64		
L. Klusener b Hooper	17	B 1, l-b 4, w 11, n-b 13	29
D. J. Cullinan b Lewis	23		
*W. J. Cronje run out	94	1/10 2/47 3/81 (5 wkts, 48.1 overs)	297
J. N. Rhodes not out	53	4/193 5/259	

†D. J. Richardson, P. L. Symcox, P. S. de Villiers and A. A. Donald did not bat.

Bowling: Ambrose 10-0-52-1; Walsh 10-0-56-0; Hooper 10-1-49-1; Lewis 8.1-0-55-1; Dillon 9-0-68-0; Simmons 1-0-12-0.

Umpires: Javed Akhtar and Said Shah.

PAKISTAN v WEST INDIES

At Lahore, November 4 (day/night). Pakistan won by eight wickets. Toss: Pakistan.

West Indies sank to their third straight defeat as left-handers Saeed Anwar and Aamir Sohail returned to form together in an undefeated third-wicket stand of 164. Anwar took 129 balls over his 13th century in limited-overs internationals, lashing 13 fours. Waqar Younis and Saqlain Mushtaq pegged back West Indies by claiming four top-order wickets between them, after Walsh lost his third successive toss. Stuart Williams and Simmons added 74 to lift the visitors in mid-innings but, with a suspect tail, their freedom was restricted and their total was the lowest of the preliminary round.

Man of the Match: Saeed Anwar.

West Indies

S. C. Williams b Azhar Mahmood	75	†D. Williams c and b Azhar Mahmood	13
S. L. Campbell c Rashid Latif		I. R. Bishop not out	15
b Waqar Younis	6	F. A. Rose not out	7
B. C. Lara b Waqar Younis	7		
C. L. Hooper c Shahid Afridi		B 5, l-b 11, w 5	21
b Saqlain Mushtaq	1		
S. Chanderpaul lbw b Saqlain Mushtaq	0	1/24 2/51 3/54 (7 wkts, 50 overs)	215
P. V. Simmons st Rashid Latif		4/56 5/130	
b Saqlain Mushtaq	70	6/166 7/204	

M. Dillon and *C. A. Walsh did not bat.

Bowling: Wasim Akram 8–0–35–0; Waqar Younis 10–1–42–2; Saqlain Mushtaq 10–0–35–3; Shahid Afridi 8–0–41–0; Aamir Sohail 5–1–20–0; Azhar Mahmood 9–1–26–2.

Pakistan

Shahid Afridi b Walsh	17
Saeed Anwar not out	108
Ijaz Ahmed, sen. lbw b Bishop	5
Aamir Sohail not out	71
L-b 3, w 6, n-b 9	18
1/34 2/55 (2 wkts, 40.4 overs)	219

Inzamam-ul-Haq, Moin Khan, *Wasim Akram, Azhar Mahmood, †Rashid Latif, Saqlain Mushtaq and Waqar Younis did not bat.

Bowling: Walsh 7.4–1–43–1; Rose 7–1–41–0; Dillon 8–1–37–0; Bishop 5–0–42–1; Hooper 9–1–29–0; Chanderpaul 1–0–5–0; Simmons 3–0–19–0.

Umpires: R. S. Dunne and I. D. Robinson.

PAKISTAN v SRI LANKA

At Lahore, November 5 (day/night). Sri Lanka won by eight wickets. Toss: Sri Lanka.

Needing another win to advance to the final, Pakistan were torn apart by sizzling centuries from Jayasuriya and Aravinda de Silva which made a target of 281 look puny. They added 213, a Sri Lankan one-day record for the third wicket, and charged to victory by scoring at seven runs an over. Jayasuriya reached his hundred in 86 balls, de Silva in 87; all told, Jayasuriya hit 13 fours and three sixes and de Silva 12 fours. Pakistan's total of 280 was set up by a third-wicket stand of 122 between Aamir Sohail and Ijaz Ahmed.

Man of the Match: S. T. Jayasuriya.

Pakistan

Shahid Afridi b Vaas	39	Azhar Mahmood c S. K. L. de Silva	
Saeed Anwar c Ranatunga b Vaas	26	b K. S. C. de Silva	15
Aamir Sohail c and b Muralitharan	70	†Rashid Latif c S. K. L. de Silva b Vaas	1
Ijaz Ahmed, sen. c sub (U. D. U.		Waqar Younis b K. S. C. de Silva	1
Chandana) b K. S. C. de Silva	94	Saqlain Mushtaq not out	1
Inzamam-ul-Haq c P. A. de Silva		L-b 6, w 3	9
b Jayasuriya	8		
*Wasim Akram c S. K. L. de Silva		1/66 2/73 3/195 (49.4 overs)	280
b Muralitharan	6	4/205 5/214 6/234	
Moin Khan run out	10	7/269 8/278 9/278	

Bowling: Vaas 10–0–59–3; K. S. C. de Silva 9.4–1–58–3; Dharmasena 10–1–41–0; Muralitharan 10–0–37–2; Jayasuriya 6–0–54–1; P. A. de Silva 4–0–25–0.

Sri Lanka

S. T. Jayasuriya not out	134	P. A. de Silva not out	102
M. S. Atapattu run out	23	L-b 6, w 13, n-b 3	22
R. S. Mahanama c Aamir Sohail			
b Azhar Mahmood	0	1/65 2/68	(2 wkts, 40 overs) 281

*A. Ranatunga, H. P. Tillekeratne, †S. K. L. de Silva, H. D. P. K. Dharmasena, W. P. U. J. C. Vaas, M. Muralitharan and K. S. C. de Silva did not bat.

Bowling: Wasim Akram 8–0–44–0; Waqar Younis 6–0–49–0; Saqlain Mushtaq 8–0–55–0; Azhar Mahmood 8–0–53–1; Aamir Sohail 5–0–32–0; Shahid Afridi 5–0–42–0.

Umpires: R. S. Dunne and I. D. Robinson.

SOUTH AFRICA v SRI LANKA

At Lahore, November 6 (day/night). South Africa won by 66 runs. Toss: Sri Lanka.

With both teams already qualified for the final, South Africa claimed the psychological edge with a convincing victory over Sri Lanka, who had rested Vaas, Muralitharan and Jayasuriya. Quickfire fifties from Kirsten – his third in three games – Klusener, off 41 balls with nine fours and a six, and Cronje, off 45 balls with three sixes, helped the South Africans to blaze the highest total of the tournament. Klusener returned to slice through the top order, earning career-best figures of six for 49. Despite the handicap of bowling second, South Africa reduced Sri Lanka to an embarrassing 72 for six; half-centuries from Lanka de Silva and Dharmasena restored some respectability.

Man of the Match: L. Klusener.

South Africa

A. C. Hudson c S. K. L. de Silva		P. L. Symcox not out	22
b Liyanage	10	P. S. de Villiers b K. S. C. de Silva	6
G. Kirsten c Arnold b P. A. de Silva	50	P. R. Adams not out	0
L. Klusener c Atapattu b Dharmasena	54		
D. J. Cullinan c Liyanage b Chandana	36	B 5, l-b 2, w 7, n-b 3	17
*W. J. Cronje c Chandana			
b P. A. de Silva	50		
J. N. Rhodes c and b Dharmasena	24	1/12 2/90 3/154	(9 wkts, 50 overs) 311
S. M. Pollock c Arnold b Dharmasena	37	4/165 5/200	
†D. J. Richardson c Ranatunga		6/272 7/274	
b K. S. C. de Silva	5	8/299 9/308	

Bowling: Liyanage 9–0–57–1; K. S. C. de Silva 9–1–51–2; Dharmasena 10–0–46–3; Chandana 10–0–65–1; P. A. de Silva 8–0–61–2; Arnold 4–0–24–0.

Sri Lanka

M. S. Atapattu c Pollock b Klusener	25	U. D. U. Chandana c Rhodes b Klusener	2
R. P. Arnold c Richardson b Pollock	11	D. K. Liyanage c and b Klusener	22
R. S. Mahanama lbw b Klusener	9	K. S. C. de Silva not out	5
P. A. de Silva c Symcox b Klusener	6	L-b 9, w 17, n-b 4	30
H. P. Tillekeratne run out	9		
*A. Ranatunga lbw b Klusener	0	1/35 2/46 3/55	(9 wkts, 50 overs) 245
†S. K. L. de Silva lbw b de Villiers	57	4/61 5/62 6/72	
H. D. P. K. Dharmasena not out	69	7/165 8/172 9/227	

Bowling: Pollock 10–0–37–1; de Villiers 9–2–38–1; Klusener 10–0–49–6; Adams 6–0–35–0; Symcox 4–0–25–0; Cronje 10–0–49–0; Hudson 1–0–3–0.

Umpires: Mian Aslam and Mohammad Nazir.

QUALIFYING TABLE

	Played	Won	Lost	Points	Net run-rate
South Africa	3	3	0	6	0.59
Sri Lanka	3	2	1	4	0.38
Pakistan	3	1	2	2	−0.06
West Indies	3	0	3	0	−0.91

Net run-rate was calculated by subtracting runs conceded per over from runs scored per over.

FINAL

SOUTH AFRICA v SRI LANKA

At Lahore, November 8 (day/night). South Africa won by four wickets. Toss: South Africa.

The platform for South Africa's dominance was laid in a superb fielding and bowling display. A brilliant running catch from mid-on by Symcox to dismiss the dangerous Jayasuriya set the pattern. Klusener was equally spectacular, clutching both Aravinda de Silva, who had become the fourth batsman to score 7,000 runs in one-day internationals, at fine leg and Ranatunga at third man. The Sri Lankans were restricted to 209, the lowest total of the tournament. Klusener then followed up his catches with 99 off 96 balls, hitting 11 fours and two sixes. He added 79 with captain Cronje to pull his team from the uncertainty of 109 for four and chart a course for victory, which they achieved with more than nine overs in hand.

Man of the Match: L. Klusener.   *Man of the Tournament:* L. Klusener.

Sri Lanka

S. T. Jayasuriya c Symcox b de Villiers .	14	H. D. P. K. Dharmasena not out	24
M. S. Atapattu c Cronje b Klusener....	27	W. P. U. J. C. Vaas not out	18
R. S. Mahanama c Hudson b Donald ...	26		
P. A. de Silva c Klusener b Donald	24	L-b 8, w 11, n-b 1.........	20
*A. Ranatunga c Klusener b Pollock ...	32		—
H. P. Tillekeratne c Richardson b Pollock	28	1/29 2/66 3/95 (7 wkts, 50 overs) 209	
†S. K. L. de Silva c Richardson		4/101 5/155	
b Pollock .	1	6/157 7/173	

M. Muralitharan and K. S. C. de Silva did not bat.

Bowling: Pollock 10–0–42–3; de Villiers 8–1–28–1; Donald 10–0–46–2; Klusener 7–0–29–1; Symcox 10–0–37–0; Cronje 5–0–19–0.

South Africa

A. C. Hudson lbw b Vaas	11	J. N. Rhodes not out.............	5
G. Kirsten run out	7	S. M. Pollock not out	10
L. Klusener c and b K. S. C. de Silva ..	99		
P. L. Symcox b K. S. C. de Silva	15	W 3, n-b 7.............	10
D. J. Cullinan st S. K. L. de Silva			—
b P. A. de Silva .	20	1/18 2/40 (6 wkts, 40.4 overs) 210	
*W. J. Cronje c Tillekeratne		3/71 4/109	
b Dharmasena .	33	5/188 6/197	

†D. J. Richardson, P. S. de Villiers and A. A. Donald did not bat.

Bowling: Vaas 6–1–34–1; K. S. C. de Silva 6–0–48–2; Muralitharan 10–0–34–0; Dharmasena 8.4–0–47–1; P. A. de Silva 5–0–25–1; Jayasuriya 5–0–22–0.

Umpires: Javed Akhtar and Salim Badar.   Series referee: A. M. Ebrahim (Zimbabwe).

THE CARLTON & UNITED SERIES, 1997-98

By ROBERT CRADDOCK

Australia's home one-day season featured all the emotional turmoil and lingering unrest of a divorce – because that is precisely what it was. After 26 years of regarding one-day cricket and Test matches as bedfellows, Australia decided it was time for a split in the family.

Having won only one in three of their limited-overs matches since the 1996 World Cup, Australia embraced and enhanced a new world trend. The Australian Cricket Board told the selectors to pick a specialist one-day side who could be moulded into a world-beating force for the 1999 World Cup. And, amid enormous controversy, they chose separate captains for the Test and one-day teams.

A universal rating as Test cricket's most dynamic captain did not save Mark Taylor from the sack; wicket-keeper Ian Healy was also axed. Steve Waugh became Australia's new one-day captain and, with his brother Mark, and Shane Warne, formed the experienced core of a team which, on occasion, featured as few as four regular Test players. The side took time to gel, and the plan looked doomed when Australia lost two of their first three games. A Sydney newspaper put mug shots of Australia's three selectors on its back page under the headline "Wanted for incompetence". But Australia rallied late to win the competition, coming from behind to beat South Africa in the best-of-three finals.

For most of the series, it seemed South Africa's one-day team had the "we can win from anywhere" feel that characterises Australia's Test team; while Australia's one-day side had the "we just can't quite get over the line" mentality that dripped off South Africa in the Test series. But such are the vagaries of a three-team competition that Australia managed to win the trophy despite losing six games and winning only five – beating South Africa who won eight, lost only three and defeated Australia the first five times they played. This was one of those rare summers when winning didn't justify everything.

Not for the first time, South Africa paid the price for trying to field their top team in every game, ignoring the chance to introduce fresh, high-quality replacements. The schedule wore them down but they were, without doubt, the best team of the one-day summer. Opener Gary Kirsten was named Man of the Tournament.

Though they won only two games – their first, against South Africa, and their last, against Australia, New Zealand put up a good fight throughout. They were pipped by one run, two runs and with two balls to spare in desperate finishes which drained their morale without ever quite driving them to despair.

Note: Matches in this section were not first-class.

AUSTRALIA v SOUTH AFRICA

At Sydney, December 4 (day/night). South Africa won by 67 runs. Toss: South Africa. International debut: I. J. Harvey.

South African captain Cronje threatened to take his side off the field after Symcox was pelted with golf balls, fruit and a stuffed barbecued chicken from the boundary. The crowd were much harsher on him than Australia's timid batsmen were, as they laboured against his well-flighted off-spin and his vibrant and intimidating repertoire of grunts, groans, stares and stomps. No batsman from either side topped 45 on a slow, turning deck as Australia, bowled out in 38 overs, batted poorly, as they were to do often again. Cullinan danced into the arms of his team-mates after removing his nemesis, Warne, with his district-standard off-breaks. Earlier, Australian seamer Ian Harvey bowled Rhodes with his second ball in international cricket.

Man of the Match: P. L. Symcox.   *Attendance:* 36,562.

South Africa

G. Kirsten c McGrath b M. E. Waugh	44	†D. J. Richardson lbw b Bichel	0
J. H. Kallis c Harvey b McGrath	8	P. L. Symcox not out	27
L. Klusener b McGrath	3	A. A. Donald c Gilchrist b McGrath	11
D. J. Cullinan run out	33	L-b 11, w 1, n-b 4	16
*W. J. Cronje c and b Bichel	21		
J. N. Rhodes b Harvey	12	(50 overs) 200	
S. M. Pollock run out	6	1/28 2/37 3/96	
B. M. McMillan c Warne b Bichel	19	4/98 5/113 6/124	
		7/153 8/153 9/160	

Bowling: McGrath 10–1–40–3; Reiffel 8–3–25–0; Bichel 9–0–46–3; Warne 10–0–33–0; M. E. Waugh 3–0–12–1; Harvey 10–1–33–1.

Australia

M. J. Di Venuto c Rhodes b Pollock	1	S. K. Warne lbw b Cullinan	17
M. E. Waugh b Symcox	45	A. J. Bichel run out	3
G. S. Blewett c Rhodes b Donald	15	G. D. McGrath not out	0
*S. R. Waugh lbw b Symcox	1	B 5, l-b 1, w 3, n-b 1	10
M. G. Bevan st Richardson b Symcox	16		
†A. C. Gilchrist c and b Cullinan	4	(38 overs) 133	
I. J. Harvey c Kallis b Symcox	4	1/6 2/61 3/64	
P. R. Reiffel c Kirsten b Klusener	17	4/71 5/78 6/89	
		7/92 8/122 9/133	

Bowling: Pollock 6–1–12–1; Klusener 7–0–34–1; Cronje 2–0–9–0; Donald 5–0–13–1; Symcox 10–1–28–4; Cullinan 8–0–31–2.

Umpires: D. J. Harper and S. G. Randell.

NEW ZEALAND v SOUTH AFRICA

At Adelaide, December 6 (day/night). New Zealand won by 47 runs. Toss: South Africa.

The last of Australia's five great grounds having finally got lit up, Adelaide's first day/night international delivered an upset, with New Zealand securing their first win in nine matches of a hitherto tormented tour. South Africa, brimming with adrenalin and passion against Australia, could not reach the same emotional high against lesser opposition. New Zealand had three batting heroes – Cairns halted an early wobble with 55 off 54 balls, while youngster McMillan, with 86, and all-rounder Harris shared a stand of 124. Then each of New Zealand's six-man seam attack chipped in to bowl South Africa out for 177.

Man of the Match: C. D. McMillan.   *Attendance:* 9,642.

New Zealand

M. J. Horne c Rhodes b Pollock	4	C. Z. Harris not out	52
N. J. Astle run out	0	†A. C. Parore not out	2
C. L. Cairns c Richardson b Donald	55	B 1, l-b 8, w 5	14
*S. P. Fleming b Richardson b Pollock	10		
C. D. McMillan c Symcox b Pollock	86	(6 wkts, 50 overs) 224	
R. G. Twose lbw b Donald	1	1/6 2/6 3/58	
		4/89 5/93 6/217	

D. L. Vettori, G. R. Larsen and S. B. O'Connor did not bat.

Bowling: Pollock 10–2–36–3; Klusener 9–0–56–0; Cronje 10–0–57–0; Donald 10–3–17–2; Symcox 4–0–20–0; McMillan 7–1–29–0.

South Africa

G. Kirsten st Parore b Astle	35	P. L. Symcox c and b Harris	9
J. H. Kallis c Astle b O'Connor	14	†D. J. Richardson not out	21
L. Klusener c Horne b O'Connor	25	A. A. Donald b Cairns	4
D. J. Cullinan b Larsen	13	L-b 1, n-b 1	2
*W. J. Cronje c Parore b Cairns	11		
J. N. Rhodes lbw b Larsen	3	1/23 2/52 3/85	(47.5 overs) 177
S. M. Pollock c Horne b McMillan	37	4/91 5/94 6/113	
B. M. McMillan b Astle	3	7/126 8/141 9/161	

Bowling: O'Connor 7–1–36–2; Cairns 9.5–1–29–2; Larsen 10–0–31–2; Harris 10–0–32–1; Astle 9–0–31–2; McMillan 2–0–17–1.

Umpires: S. J. Davis and R. A. Emerson.

AUSTRALIA v NEW ZEALAND

At Adelaide, December 7 (day/night). Australia won by three wickets. Toss: New Zealand.

Mark Waugh purred to his 11th one-day century, 104 off 113 balls, which should have set up a comfortable win. But Australia lost wickets regularly after his opening stand of 156 with Di Venuto, and eventually sneaked home with two balls to spare, when Bichel late-cut his first ball for four. This was a victory for Australia's young talent brigade: Di Venuto scored 77 off 74 balls, form he never reproduced again in the season, while Gilchrist batted steadily and Harvey bowled well under pressure. New Zealand's top order started well, reaching 186 for two, but the later batting fell away.

Man of the Match: M. E. Waugh.   *Attendance:* 30,049.

New Zealand

M. J. Horne lbw b Warne	31	C. Z. Harris not out	9
N. J. Astle c Warne b Bichel	66	G. R. Larsen not out	0
*S. P. Fleming c Harvey b Bichel	61	L-b 4, w 9, n-b 2	15
C. D. McMillan c Harvey b Warne	43		
C. L. Cairns c Gilchrist b McGrath	0	1/77 2/146 3/186	(7 wkts, 50 overs) 260
†A. C. Parore b Harvey	9	4/190 5/220	
R. G. Twose c Bevan b Warne	26	6/227 7/259	

D. L. Vettori and S. B. O'Connor did not bat.

Bowling: McGrath 10–1–53–1; Dale 6–0–41–0; Warne 10–0–48–3; Harvey 10–0–39–1; M. E. Waugh 4–0–23–0; Bichel 10–1–52–2.

Australia

M. E. Waugh c Parore b Harris	104	S. K. Warne b Larsen	5
M. J. Di Venuto st Parore b Vettori	77	A. J. Bichel not out	4
†A. C. Gilchrist run out	29	L-b 5, w 3, n-b 1	9
G. S. Blewett b Larsen	0		
I. J. Harvey c Parore b Astle	3	1/156 2/202 3/209	(7 wkts, 49.4 overs) 263
*S. R. Waugh lbw b Larsen	7	4/221 5/221	
M. G. Bevan not out	25	6/249 7/259	

A. C. Dale and G. D. McGrath did not bat.

Bowling: O'Connor 4–1–23–0; Cairns 8–0–54–0; Harris 10–2–34–1; Astle 6–1–35–1; Larsen 9.4–0–56–3; Vettori 9–0–47–1; McMillan 3–0–9–0.

Umpires: D. B. Hair and T. A. Prue.

AUSTRALIA v SOUTH AFRICA

At Melbourne, December 9 (day/night). South Africa won by 45 runs. Toss: South Africa.

A bouncy MCG pitch yielded just enough seam to make batsmen mistrust their instincts. It says much about the quality of South Africa's bowling that they had beaten Australia twice without any of their batsmen reaching 50. Klusener's pace drew a stream of edges and excellent figures of five for 24, enabling South Africa to bowl Australia out for 125. The economical Symcox continued to slip through the Australians' guard and under their skin. Mark Waugh hit him 15 rows into the Great Southern Stand, but Symcox took revenge when Waugh top-edged a cut to backward point. Reiffel twinged a hamstring, weakening Australia's pace attack still further.

Man of the Match: L. Klusener.   *Attendance:* 55,673.

South Africa

G. Kirsten c Warne b Reiffel	0	†D. J. Richardson not out	18
H. H. Gibbs run out	15	P. L. Symcox not out	4
L. Klusener c Gilchrist b Moody.	17		
*W. J. Cronje run out	2	L-b 5, w 8, n-b 1	14
J. H. Kallis c Gilchrist b M. E. Waugh .	27		
J. N. Rhodes run out.	42	1/1 2/36 3/40 (8 wkts, 50 overs)	170
S. M. Pollock c Moody b M. E. Waugh .	18	4/44 5/105 6/125	
B. M. McMillan run out	13	7/140 8/161	

A. A. Donald did not bat.

Bowling: Reiffel 10–1–18–1; Bichel 5–0–26–0; Moody 8–3–10–1; Harvey 7–0–36–0; Warne 10–0–36–0; M. E. Waugh 10–0–39–2.

Australia

M. J. Di Venuto c Pollock b Klusener . .	6	P. R. Reiffel run out	1
M. E. Waugh c Pollock b Symcox.	45	S. K. Warne c Gibbs b Klusener.	5
*S. R. Waugh c Richardson b Klusener .	0	A. J. Bichel c McMillan b Klusener . . .	0
R. T. Ponting c Kirsten b Klusener	15	L-b 3, n-b 1	4
M. G. Bevan c Rhodes b McMillan. . . .	19		
†A. C. Gilchrist not out.	29	1/11 2/12 3/38 (39.1 overs)	125
T. M. Moody lbw b Symcox	0	4/79 5/97 6/97	
I. J. Harvey lbw b McMillan	1	7/100 8/104 9/123	

Bowling: Pollock 8–1–25–0; Klusener 7.1–0–24–5; Donald 6–0–26–0; McMillan 8–0–29–2; Symcox 10–2–18–2.

Umpires: D. J. Harper and P. D. Parker.

NEW ZEALAND v SOUTH AFRICA

At Hobart, December 11. South Africa won by one run. Toss: South Africa.

A slow, low pitch spread a wet blanket over this game, the only one of the tournament to be played entirely in daylight. Dashers were unable to hit their stride in a dreadfully dull contest – until Harris and Vettori set up the tightest of finishes. Watching New Zealand score 100 in 35 overs was like watching a dentist pull teeth, and they seemed to be right out of it at 111 for seven. But Harris and Vettori whittled the target down to 35 off five overs, 16 off two and six off the final ball – which Harris edged for four. South Africa's unsung hero was keeper Richardson, who moved smartly to stop two edges sneaking by in the last three overs. Had either passed him, they would probably have lost. Klusener's burst of form continued, claiming New Zealand's top three plus 37 runs.

Man of the Match: L. Klusener.   *Attendance:* 4,018.

South Africa

G. Kirsten b O'Connor	6	B. M. McMillan b Cairns	1
H. H. Gibbs c Vettori b O'Connor	12	†D. J. Richardson not out	9
L. Klusener run out	37	W 4	4
P. L. Symcox c and b Harris	15		
*W. J. Cronje run out	0		—
J. H. Kallis c and b Harris	45	1/14 2/41 3/71 (9 wkts, 50 overs) 174	
J. N. Rhodes b Vettori	14	4/72 5/73 6/99	
S. M. Pollock c Larsen b Cairns	31	7/153 8/156 9/174	

A. A. Donald did not bat.

Bowling: O'Connor 7–0–42–2; Cairns 10–2–26–2; Harris 10–0–36–2; Larsen 8–1–23–0; Vettori 6–1–17–1; Astle 9–0–30–0.

New Zealand

M. J. Horne lbw b Klusener	3	C. Z. Harris not out	37
N. J. Astle c McMillan b Klusener	1	D. L. Vettori not out	25
C. L. Cairns b Klusener	29	L-b 8, w 3	11
*S. P. Fleming c Pollock b Symcox	32		
C. D. McMillan c Kirsten b Symcox	18	1/5 2/6 3/45 (7 wkts, 50 overs) 173	
R. G. Twose c Kirsten b Pollock	11	4/83 5/89	
†A. C. Parore run out	6	6/97 7/111	

G. R. Larsen and S. B. O'Connor did not bat.

Bowling: Pollock 10–2–24–1; Klusener 10–0–46–3; Donald 10–2–32–0; McMillan 10–1–28–0; Symcox 10–1–35–2.

Umpires: A. J. McQuillan and S. G. Randell.

AUSTRALIA v NEW ZEALAND

At Melbourne, December 17 (day/night). Australia won by six wickets. Toss: New Zealand. International debut: P. Wilson.

Two pace bowlers who had risen from oblivion to represent Australia provided the twin engines of the victory their country so desperately needed. Paul Wilson, who once drove halfway across Australia to plead his way into the Cricket Academy, and Adam Dale, who has flourished with Queensland after being an anonymous grade cricketer in Victoria, helped skittle New Zealand for 141. Their recovery from 45 for six owed everything to Harris, who had scored 310 runs in his last eight one-day international innings without being dismissed. Australia faltered in the chase, Cairns reducing them to 22 for three before Bevan, ever the cool head, scored a nerveless 42.

Man of the Match: M. G. Bevan.   *Attendance:* 31,097.

New Zealand

M. J. Horne c Gilchrist b Dale	3	D. L. Vettori c Warne b Bevan	14
N. J. Astle c Gilchrist b Dale	20	G. R. Larsen c S. R. Waugh b Bevan	0
C. L. Cairns b Wilson	0	S. B. O'Connor run out	8
*S. P. Fleming c Bevan b Wilson	6	L-b 4, w 5, n-b 5	14
C. D. McMillan c Harvey b Warne	9		
R. G. Twose run out	0	1/5 2/9 3/19 (49.3 overs) 141	
†A. C. Parore c Bichel b Wilson	5	4/45 5/45 6/45	
C. Z. Harris not out	62	7/75 8/108 9/108	

Bowling: Wilson 10–0–39–3; Dale 10–2–22–2; Warne 10–2–25–1; Bevan 10–0–26–2; Bichel 9–0–17–0; Harvey 0.3–0–8–0.

Australia

M. J. Di Venuto c Astle b Cairns	7	†A. C. Gilchrist not out 11
M. E. Waugh c Parore b Cairns	9	L-b 4, w 8, n-b 1 13
R. T. Ponting not out	60	
*S. R. Waugh c Parore b Cairns	0	1/17 2/22 (4 wkts, 38.5 overs) 142
M. G. Bevan c Astle b Cairns	42	3/22 4/117

I. J. Harvey, S. K. Warne, A. J. Bichel, A. C. Dale and P. Wilson did not bat.

Bowling: O'Connor 10–0–43–0; Cairns 10–3–40–4; Vettori 9–1–32–0; Harris 9.5–1–23–0.

Umpires: R. A. Emerson and D. B. Hair.

NEW ZEALAND v SOUTH AFRICA

At Brisbane, January 9 (day/night). South Africa won by two runs. Toss: South Africa.

This was one of the best limited-overs games seen in Australia. Chasing 301, New Zealand were out of the game at 124 for six in the 31st over. But Cairns, who hit 64 off 54 balls, Parore, with 67 off 48, and Nash almost pulled off the comeback of the summer. Off the second last ball, Nash slashed Pollock towards the third-man fence. The ball hit the boundary rope on the full and was rightly called four, but it was bad luck that it landed where the rope overlapped itself, presenting a wider target. Had the ball carried a centimetre or two further, it would have been six, levelling the scores with one ball to play. As it was, they needed three and Nash was caught in the deep. Kirsten won the match award with his 103 off 116 balls, while Donald was so precise he was given the rare luxury of three slips in the 20th over.

Man of the Match: G. Kirsten.   *Attendance:* 14,219.

South Africa

G. Kirsten c Nash b Harris	103	S. M. Pollock not out 14
L. Klusener b Nash	50	P. L. Symcox not out 12
J. H. Kallis c Parore b Vettori	31	L-b 5, w 5 10
*W. J. Cronje c Harris b McMillan	55	
H. H. Gibbs lbw b Harris	2	1/100 2/167 3/231 (6 wkts, 50 overs) 300
J. N. Rhodes c Nash b McMillan	23	4/241 5/269 6/277

B. M. McMillan, †D. J. Richardson and A. A. Donald did not bat.

Bowling: O'Connor 6–0–50–0; Cairns 7–0–37–0; Nash 10–1–52–1; Harris 10–0–41–2; Vettori 7–0–46–1; Astle 5–0–42–0; McMillan 5–0–27–2.

New Zealand

C. M. Spearman c Symcox b Pollock...	11	D. J. Nash c Klusener b Pollock 38
N. J. Astle c Richardson b Donald....	29	D. L. Vettori not out............. 11
M. J. Horne c McMillan b Kallis	42	
*S. P. Fleming c Richardson b Donald ..	2	B 3, 1-b 11, w 4, n-b 2 20
C. D. McMillan c Richardson b Donald .	4	
C. Z. Harris c McMillan b Kallis	10	1/24 2/84 3/88 (9 wkts, 50 overs) 298
C. L. Cairns run out..............	64	4/94 5/97 6/124
†A. C. Parore c Symcox b Donald	67	7/197 8/266 9/298

S. B. O'Connor did not bat.

Bowling: Pollock 10–1–58–2; Klusener 10–0–55–0; Donald 10–1–43–4; McMillan 8–0–52–0; Kallis 8–1–49–2; Symcox 4–0–27–0.

Umpires: S. J. Davis and A. J. McQuillan.

AUSTRALIA v SOUTH AFRICA

At Brisbane, January 11 (day/night). South Africa won by five wickets. Toss: Australia.

South Africa gave Australia a third successive one-day thumping, while a hip injury to captain Steve Waugh caused them further anguish. Waugh failed again with the bat – he had scored only

12 in five innings – and Bevan's 45 was the best offering on a flat pitch against a string of in-form bowlers. Australia's total looked 30 shy, and Kirsten confirmed that as he earned his second match award in three days, giving South Africa a pacy start and crunching two mighty fours in Warne's first over. Cronje, who exchanged words with Steve Waugh after receiving a short ball from him before he was ready, steered his side into the finals with a run-a-ball fifty.

Man of the Match: G. Kirsten.   *Attendance:* 20,671.

Australia

M. E. Waugh c Richardson b Donald	37	S. K. Warne run out	8
S. G. Law c Richardson b Donald	27	A. J. Bichel not out	9
R. T. Ponting c and b Symcox	31		
D. S. Lehmann c Rhodes b Kallis	34	L-b 6, w 6, n-b 2	14
*S. R. Waugh c Symcox b Kallis	4		
M. G. Bevan not out	45	1/68 2/75 3/131 (8 wkts, 50 overs)	235
†A. C. Gilchrist c Donald b Pollock	21	4/140 5/140 6/192	
P. R. Reiffel c Rhodes b Donald	5	7/203 8/217	

P. Wilson did not bat.

Bowling: Pollock 8–1–32–1; Klusener 9–0–65–0; McMillan 6–0–25–0; Donald 10–0–37–3; Symcox 10–0–38–1; Kallis 7–0–32–2.

South Africa

G. Kirsten c Warne b S. R. Waugh	89	J. N. Rhodes not out	14
L. Klusener c Bevan b Wilson	15		
P. L. Symcox run out	6	L-b 3, w 1	4
J. H. Kallis lbw b Wilson	47		
*W. J. Cronje not out	59	1/41 2/72 3/151 (5 wkts, 47.3 overs)	236
H. H. Gibbs b Bichel	2	4/189 5/192	

S. M. Pollock, B. M. McMillan, †D. J. Richardson and A. A. Donald did not bat.

Bowling: Wilson 10–1–50–2; Reiffel 8–1–39–0; Warne 10–0–47–0; Bichel 10–0–47–1; Bevan 2.3–0–25–0; S. R. Waugh 4–0–14–1; M. E. Waugh 3–0–11–0.

Umpires: D. J. Harper and P. D. Parker.

AUSTRALIA v NEW ZEALAND

At Sydney, January 14 (day/night). Australia won by 131 runs. Toss: Australia. International debut: J. P. Maher.

Playing without either Waugh twin for the first time in 11 years (Steve had a pulled muscle, Mark a virus), Australia were led to a convincing victory by Warne. Dozens of flash bulbs went off in the crowd when he bowled his first ball as captain, in the 21st over; by then, New Zealand were all but gone at 81 for four. Ponting, who had continued his breakthrough in one-day cricket with 84 in 103 balls, followed up with some world-class fielding. He picked off Spearman and McMillan with direct hits: to remove McMillan as captain, he made a challenging tumble and throw from backward point look routine. Australia blooded left-hander James Maher, on the strength of his Queensland form, but he failed here and at Perth. Rain shortened Australia's allocation to 48 overs.

Man of the Match: R. T. Ponting.   *Attendance:* 36,476.

Australia

J. P. Maher c Vettori b O'Connor	8	P. R. Reiffel c Fleming b O'Connor	17
S. G. Law c Parore b Cairns	12	*S. K. Warne not out	0
I. J. Harvey c Nash b O'Connor	11	P. Wilson run out	0
R. T. Ponting b McMillan	84	L-b 7, w 5, n-b 1	13
D. S. Lehmann c Young b McMillan	52		
M. G. Bevan c and b Harris	25	1/18 2/22 3/36 (47.5 overs)	250
†A. C. Gilchrist c McMillan b O'Connor	28	4/168 5/190 6/217	
T. M. Moody c and b Harris	0	7/217 8/250 9/250	

Bowling: O'Connor 9.5–0–51–4; Cairns 7–0–29–1; Nash 10–0–56–0; Harris 10–0–42–2; Vettori 6–0–35–0; McMillan 5–0–30–2.

New Zealand

C. M. Spearman run out	6	D. J. Nash b Warne		5
B. A. Young b Moody	22	D. L. Vettori c Bevan b Warne		4
M. J. Horne c Gilchrist b Wilson	14	S. B. O'Connor not out		0
*S. P. Fleming c Bevan b Harvey	28	L-b 4, w 9, n-b 4		17
C. D. McMillan run out	10			
C. L. Cairns c Warne b Harvey	5	1/11 2/51 3/53	(33.1 overs)	119
C. Z. Harris run out	8	4/78 5/86 6/99		
†A. C. Parore c Ponting b Harvey	0	7/101 8/109 9/118		

Bowling: Wilson 8–0–29–1; Reiffel 6–0–28–0; Moody 6–1–22–1; Harvey 7–1–17–3; Warne 6.1–0–19–2.

Umpires: S. J. Davis and P. D. Parker.

NEW ZEALAND v SOUTH AFRICA

At Perth, January 16 (day/night). South Africa won by 67 runs. Toss: South Africa. International debut: M. Ntini.

Fast bowler Makhaya Ntini took a few large steps for himself but greater ones for his country when he became the first black cricketer to represent South Africa. With surprising pace and cunning for a player who first picked up a ball five years before, Ntini unsettled every batsman who faced him. His first ball was a fine in-swinging yorker and his first wicket a gem: an away-seamer which Fleming edged defensively, coincidentally giving keeper Boucher his first international scalp. Kallis, the epitome of style and balance, scored his maiden century at this level, 111 from 140 balls, and the innings lost a cylinder when he was caught in the deep in the 42nd over.

Man of the Match: J. H. Kallis.   *Attendance:* 10,794.

South Africa

G. Kirsten run out	44	S. M. Pollock not out		22
L. Klusener c Vettori b O'Connor	4	P. L. Symcox not out		5
J. H. Kallis c Nash b McMillan	111	L-b 2, w 3		5
D. J. Cullinan c Harris b Cairns	26			
H. H. Gibbs c and b Harris	8	1/7 2/98 3/171	(7 wkts, 50 overs)	233
*W. J. Cronje c O'Connor b Cairns	6	4/194 5/199		
J. N. Rhodes c O'Connor b Astle	2	6/203 7/211		
†M. V. Boucher and M. Ntini did not bat.				

Bowling: O'Connor 6–0–27–1; Cairns 10–1–50–2; Nash 8–0–41–0; Harris 10–0–39–1; Astle 9–0–39–1; Vettori 4–0–22–0; McMillan 3–0–13–1.

New Zealand

B. A. Young c Ntini b Symcox	34	D. J. Nash c Gibbs b Kallis		15
C. M. Spearman c Rhodes b Pollock	13	D. L. Vettori run out		4
*S. P. Fleming c Boucher b Ntini	26	S. B. O'Connor not out		2
C. D. McMillan c Gibbs b Symcox	11	L-b 3, w 10, n-b 1		14
N. J. Astle c Cullinan b Pollock	18			
C. L. Cairns c Gibbs b Pollock	17	1/30 2/60 3/86	(45.1 overs)	166
C. Z. Harris lbw b Kallis	4	4/89 5/124 6/127		
†A. C. Parore c Boucher b Ntini	8	7/138 8/144 9/151		

Bowling: Pollock 10–0–28–3; Klusener 8–1–41–0; Symcox 8–0–37–2; Ntini 10–0–31–2; Kallis 9.1–1–26–2.

Umpires: R. A. Emerson and A. J. McQuillan.

AUSTRALIA v SOUTH AFRICA

At Perth, January 18 (day/night). South Africa won by seven wickets. Toss: Australia. International debut: B. E. Young.

South Africa simply overwhelmed Australia, who were inept in all departments. Australia's batting was so dreadful and South Africa's bowling so expectant of an edge that the fast men occasionally had three slips during the dying overs. Donald, relishing the WACA's famous bounce, swept away the middle order like a horse swishing a fly. South Africa made a mockery of a target of 166, bagging it in just 28.2 overs. They hit or cleared the fence 20 times compared with Australia's six. New spinner Brad Young was treated with total contempt and yielded seven an over. Cronje summed up the proceedings when he won the match with a cover-driven six.

Man of the Match: A. A. Donald.   *Attendance:* 27,052.

Australia

S. G. Law c Richardson b Pollock	1	B. E. Young c Richardson b Donald		5
J. P. Maher c Cronje b Klusener	13	A. J. Bichel not out		27
R. T. Ponting c Kallis b Symcox	16	P. Wilson b Donald		0
D. S. Lehmann c Rhodes b Donald	10	L-b 6, w 8, n-b 4		18
*S. R. Waugh c Richardson b Donald	0			
M. G. Bevan c Cullinan b McMillan	26	1/3 2/27 3/46	(48.2 overs)	165
†A. C. Gilchrist c Donald b Symcox	6	4/46 5/54 6/70		
I. J. Harvey run out	43	7/93 8/108 9/165		

Bowling: Pollock 10–1–35–1; Symcox 10–1–33–2; Donald 9.2–0–29–4; Klusener 9–1–27–1; McMillan 8–3–27–1; Kallis 2–0–8–0.

South Africa

G. Kirsten run out	44	*W. J. Cronje not out		39
L. Klusener c Law b Wilson	11	N-b 3		3
J. H. Kallis c Wilson b Bichel	38			
D. J. Cullinan not out	35	1/34 2/80 3/100	(3 wkts, 28.2 overs)	170

J. N. Rhodes, S. M. Pollock, P. L. Symcox, B. M. McMillan, †D. J. Richardson and A. A. Donald did not bat.

Bowling: Wilson 9.2–2–41–1; Bichel 8–0–55–1; Harvey 4–0–25–0; Young 7–0–49–0.

Umpires: D. B. Hair and T. A. Prue.

AUSTRALIA v NEW ZEALAND

At Melbourne, January 21 (day/night). New Zealand won by four wickets. Toss: Australia.

A brilliantly paced century from Fleming enabled his team to finish with an exceptional win. It could not lift them into the finals, but was New Zealand's only victory over Australia throughout their tour. Bookmakers made them 20 to 1 when they limped to 42 for three and, when they dawdled past 100 in the 30th over, a target of 252 looked like Everest. But they pruned it from 83 off ten overs to 61 off seven and 18 off three. Five were needed – and taken – off the last over, from Warne. McMillan's explosive 26 off 14 balls complemented the stylish fluency of Fleming. Earlier, Ponting took his aggregate to 306 in six innings with a smooth hundred.

Man of the Match: S. P. Fleming.   *Attendance:* 27,722.

Australia

T. M. Moody c O'Connor b Harris	19	I. J. Harvey not out		4
M. E. Waugh c Nash b Vettori	31	W 6		6
R. T. Ponting c O'Connor b Cairns	100			
D. S. Lehmann run out	46	1/51 2/65	(4 wkts, 50 overs)	251
*S. R. Waugh not out	45	3/153 4/246		

M. G. Bevan, †A. C. Gilchrist, P. R. Reiffel, S. K. Warne and P. Wilson did not bat.

Bowling: O'Connor 4–0–23–0; Cairns 10–2–46–1; Vettori 10–0–41–1; Harris 10–0–50–1; Astle 7–0–35–0; Nash 3–0–24–0; McMillan 6–0–32–0.

New Zealand

C. M. Spearman c Gilchrist b Wilson. . .	10	C. L. Cairns c sub (S. G. Law) b Wilson	4
N. J. Astle c sub (S. G. Law) b Wilson .	13	C. Z. Harris not out	13
B. A. Young c M. E. Waugh b Moody . .	8	B 1, l-b 5, w 9, n-b 2	17
*S. P. Fleming not out	116		
†A. C. Parore c and b Moody	46	1/25 2/26 3/42 (6 wkts, 49.1 overs)	253
C. D. McMillan lbw b Warne	26	4/178 5/219 6/226	

D. J. Nash, D. L. Vettori and S. B. O'Connor did not bat.

Bowling: Wilson 10-1-39-3; Reiffel 8-1-31-0; Moody 10-1-52-2; Harvey 8-0-42-0; Warne 8.1-0-50-1; Bevan 5-0-33-0.

Umpires: T. A. Prue and S. G. Randell.

QUALIFYING TABLE

	Played	Won	Lost	Points	Net run-rate
South Africa	8	7	1	14	0.61
Australia	8	3	5	6	-0.10
New Zealand	8	2	6	4	-0.51

Net run-rate was calculated by subtracting runs conceded per over from runs scored per over.

AUSTRALIA v SOUTH AFRICA

First Final Match

At Melbourne, January 23 (day/night). South Africa won by six runs. Toss: South Africa.

Just when Australia seemed poised for victory – they needed 36 runs from 35 balls with six wickets in hand – they buckled under a withering onslaught from Donald, lost five wickets for 14 and fell seven short. Attacking and defending at the same time, Donald took two for four in the 47th and 49th overs. Pollock finished the job. Life had looked rosy when Steve Waugh and Bevan were adding 101 in a stand which ticked over with the smoothness of a grandfather clock. Earlier, South Africa had chosen to bat and pulled a surprise by opening with Cullinan, an attempt to short-circuit his problems with Warne. The plan worked for a while as he thumped 26 off 22 balls. But Warne dismissed him for the 11th time when a pumped-up Cullinan roared out of his crease on a death-or-glory mission and was stumped.

Man of the Match: A. A. Donald.　　　　*Attendance:* 44,321.

South Africa

D. J. Cullinan st Gilchrist b Warne	26	B. M. McMillan lbw b Warne	2
G. Kirsten st Gilchrist b M. E. Waugh . .	70	†D. J. Richardson not out	11
L. Klusener c Bevan b Moody	0		
J. H. Kallis c Gilchrist b Wilson	33	W 2, n-b 1	3
*W. J. Cronje c Bevan b Lehmann	29		
J. N. Rhodes c Gilchrist b Lehmann . . .	21	1/55 2/62 3/126 (9 wkts, 50 overs)	241
S. M. Pollock c Bevan b Warne	36	4/137 5/178 6/186	
P. L. Symcox b M. E. Waugh	10	7/203 8/210 9/241	

A. A. Donald did not bat.

Bowling: Wilson 9-0-52-1; Reiffel 3-0-18-0; Warne 10-1-52-3; Moody 5-0-24-1; Harvey 9-0-39-0; M. E. Waugh 10-0-45-2; Lehmann 4-0-11-2.

Australia

M. E. Waugh run out	3	P. R. Reiffel c Richardson b Donald	1
†A. C. Gilchrist c Symcox b Pollock	20	S. K. Warne b Pollock	0
R. T. Ponting c Richardson b Donald	33	P. Wilson not out	1
D. S. Lehmann run out	31	L-b 6, w 5, n-b 3	14
*S. R. Waugh c Richardson b McMillan	53		
M. G. Bevan run out	57	1/15 2/37 3/94	(49.5 overs) 235
T. M. Moody run out	15	4/105 5/206 6/221	
I. J. Harvey b Donald	7	7/231 8/233 9/234	

Bowling: Pollock 9.5–1–39–2; Klusener 7–0–36–0; Symcox 10–1–56–0; Donald 10–0–36–3; McMillan 9–1–39–1; Kallis 4–0–23–0.

Umpires: D. B. Hair and S. G. Randell.

AUSTRALIA v SOUTH AFRICA

Second Final Match

At Sydney, January 26 (day/night). Australia won by seven wickets. Toss: South Africa.

The match was postponed from the previous day, when more than 35,000 had turned up but the game was abandoned because of overnight rain. When the weather improved, Australia scorched to victory on the back of Gilchrist's maiden one-day century, arguably Australia's best innings of the competition. Gilchrist had been invited to open in the previous game by captain Steve Waugh, who acted on a hunch during the dinner break. He made only 20 then, but this time took just 32 overs to reach his century, studded with all manner of strokes from robust drives to feather-wristed late cuts just wide of the keeper. He hit ten fours and a six in 104 balls. The match became an unexpected farewell for Donald; a buttock strain forced him out of the third final and the last Test.

Man of the Match: A. C. Gilchrist.   *Attendance:* 26,293.

South Africa

D. J. Cullinan c Warne b M. E. Waugh	3	S. M. Pollock lbw b Reiffel	3
G. Kirsten c Gilchrist b Wilson	14	P. L. Symcox not out	5
L. Klusener c Harvey b Reiffel	31	L-b 4, w 3	7
J. H. Kallis c Ponting b Reiffel	10		
*W. J. Cronje b Bevan b Warne	73	1/7 2/35 3/55	(6 wkts, 50 overs) 228
J. N. Rhodes not out	82	4/64 5/198 6/211	

B. M. McMillan, †D. J. Richardson and A. A. Donald did not bat.

Bowling: Wilson 10–0–39–1; M. E. Waugh 5–0–17–1; Reiffel 10–1–32–3; Moody 8–0–28–0; Warne 10–0–52–1; Harvey 4–0–27–0; Lehmann 3–0–29–0.

Australia

†A. C. Gilchrist b McMillan	100	D. S. Lehmann not out	17
M. E. Waugh b Klusener	25	B 4, l-b 2, w 5, n-b 2	13
R. T. Ponting lbw b Klusener	47		
I. J. Harvey not out	27	1/51 2/177 3/184	(3 wkts, 41.5 overs) 229

*S. R. Waugh, M. G. Bevan, T. M. Moody, P. R. Reiffel, S. K. Warne and P. Wilson did not bat.

Bowling: Pollock 8–0–39–0; Klusener 10–0–57–2; Donald 3–0–17–0; Symcox 9–0–39–0; McMillan 8–0–45–1; Cullinan 2–0–17–0; Cronje 1.5–0–9–0.

Umpires: D. B. Hair and S. G. Randell.

AUSTRALIA v SOUTH AFRICA

Third Final Match

At Sydney, January 27 (day/night). Australia won by 14 runs. Toss: Australia.

After losing their first five meetings with South Africa in this tournament, Australia did the improbable and beat them 2-1 in the finals. No one savoured the win more than Steve Waugh, who followed six successive failures with successive fifties and put on 102 with Ponting. Waugh likened the recovery to Australia's unforgettable back-from-the-dead World Cup win against West Indies at Mohali in 1996. After South Africa slipped to 64 for three chasing 248, they always needed a special innings. Instead, when Australia wanted a wicket most, they always got one. As usual, South Africa fought all the way down to brazen No. 11 Paul Adams, who reverse-swept Warne and hit him inside-out over cover. That prompted Cronje to say: "He's got some explaining to do ... I have been trying that for four years and haven't managed it once."

Man of the Match: R. T. Ponting.   *Man of the Tournament:* G. Kirsten.   *Attendance:* 19,008.

Australia

M. E. Waugh b Klusener	21	I. J. Harvey c Bacher b McMillan	1
†A. C. Gilchrist b McMillan	6	P. R. Reiffel not out	11
R. T. Ponting st Richardson b Adams	76	L-b 4, w 10, n-b 1	15
D. S. Lehmann c Rhodes b Symcox	10		
*S. R. Waugh run out	71	1/11 2/58 3/79 (7 wkts, 50 overs) 247	
M. G. Bevan not out	36	4/181 5/210	
T. M. Moody c Bacher b McMillan	0	6/210 7/212	

S. K. Warne and P. Wilson did not bat.

Bowling: Pollock 10-1-33-0; McMillan 10-0-47-3; Kallis 3-0-23-0; Klusener 10-0-59-1; Symcox 10-0-35-1; Adams 7-0-46-1.

South Africa

G. Kirsten run out	3	B. M. McMillan run out	15
A. M. Bacher c Gilchrist b Reiffel	45	†D. J. Richardson c Ponting b Reiffel	1
J. H. Kallis hit wkt b Reiffel	14	P. R. Adams not out	15
*W. J. Cronje st Gilchrist b Warne	5	B 3, l-b 6, w 1	10
J. N. Rhodes c and b M. E. Waugh	29		
S. M. Pollock st Gilchrist b Bevan	28	1/25 2/63 3/64 (48.1 overs) 233	
L. Klusener c S. R. Waugh b Moody	46	4/72 5/122 6/139	
P. L. Symcox run out	22	7/191 8/202 9/204	

Bowling: Wilson 10-1-55-0; M. E. Waugh 6-0-31-1; Reiffel 9-0-40-3; Moody 9-1-26-1; Warne 9.1-0-43-1; Bevan 5-0-29-1.

Umpires: S. J. Davis and D. B. Hair.
Series referees: C. W. Smith (West Indies) and R. S. Madugalle (Sri Lanka).

AKAI SINGER CHAMPIONS TROPHY, 1997-98

By MIKE SELVEY

Hindsight will show that Abdul Rahman Bukhatir's cricket ground in the desert was the starting point for England's build-up to the 1999 World Cup. For years, England selectors had failed to recognise that one-day international cricket was no longer just a novelty, money-spinning adjunct to Test matches, but a parallel branch of the game deserving of full and separate attention. Humiliating results over the previous two winters in South Africa, the World Cup, Zimbabwe and New Zealand inspired a strategic rethink, led by chairman of selectors David Graveney. So, after a decade of tearing up invitations to the Gulf, English administrators finally relented, acknowledging that they had to compete to improve.

The most radical move was to appoint a captain specifically to lead a one-day side, a job viewed as requiring a dynamism and reactive instinct not so fundamental to captaining the Test team. There are doubts that he would have made a specialist side for Sharjah's conditions on merit, but Mike Atherton's unavailability made the decision easier in any case, and Adam Hollioake was given the chance to state his credentials as a potential leader in the World Cup.

In the event, the brief tour exceeded expectations. Chosen specifically for the task, with the accent on all-rounders and depth to the batting order, England's team entered the competition mindful of the need to learn and to adapt to conditions in which two of the four contestants – India and Pakistan – were effectively playing in front of home crowds. Progress was expected, but winning was not quite on the agenda. However, an unchanged eleven won all four of their games, including a thrilling final against West Indies, and supplemented established stars, like Alec Stewart, with new ones such as Kent's 33-year-old all-rounder Matthew Fleming, whose nine wickets made him the leading bowler along with Pakistan's Saqlain Mushtaq. Hollioake's performance as captain was exemplary both on the field, where he showed himself to be astute and unflappable, and off it. His players proved just as enthusiastic and amenable (including the three who never appeared, Ashley Giles, Ben Hollioake and Peter Martin).

The tournament proved even more of a turning point for the other three nations. All of them changed captains during the following three weeks. Though West Indies' success in reaching the final was in contrast to a string of dreadful performances in Pakistan, where they had just been whitewashed in the Tests and one-day tournament, it was to mark the end of Courtney Walsh's reign; he was soon replaced by Brian Lara. Pakistan and India, despite their "home" advantage, were eliminated in the round robin. India, who lost all their games, axed six players (including one who had not played a match) and transferred the captaincy back from Sachin Tendulkar to his predecessor, Mohammad Azharuddin. Meanwhile, Wasim Akram announced that he had had to give up leading Pakistan because of death threats, and was then controversially omitted from the squad to tour South Africa.

Note: Matches in this section were not first-class.

ENGLAND v INDIA

At Sharjah, December 11 (day/night). England won by seven runs. Toss: India. International debuts: D. R. Brown, M. V. Fleming.

In Sharjah's first match under lights, Stewart hit a superb 116 from 111 deliveries to provide the bedrock for the successful start of Adam Hollioake's career as an international captain. Timing the ball impeccably on a slow pitch, he hit nine fours and a six, sharing substantial stands with Knight and Hick before eight wickets fell for 41 in the last 11 overs. Strangely, India kept their best player, Tendulkar, down the order, but still they appeared to have the game under control while he and Jadeja were adding 108 for the fifth wicket. However, medium-pacer Matthew Fleming, making his international debut on the eve of his 33rd birthday, kept a cool head, dismissing Jadeja for 50 and effectively winning the game when Tendulkar, attempting to hit him square on the off side, yorked himself and was stumped by Stewart, for an 87-ball 91. Fleming finished off India with four for 45.

Man of the Match: A. J. Stewart.

England

A. D. Brown c Ganguly b Kuruvilla	18		D. R. Brown c Tendulkar b Srinath	6
†A. J. Stewart c Azharuddin b Kumble	116		R. D. B. Croft c Kuruvilla b Srinath	6
N. V. Knight c Kumble b Chauhan	42		D. W. Headley not out	1
G. A. Hick b Kuruvilla	32		L-b 3, w 1	4
*A. J. Hollioake b Kuruvilla	4			
M. A. Ealham run out	9		1/42 2/131 3/209	(49.5 overs) 250
G. P. Thorpe run out	3		4/211 5/215 6/218	
M. V. Fleming c Karim b Srinath	9		7/232 8/237 9/248	

Bowling: Srinath 8.5–0–37–3; Kuruvilla 10–0–50–3; Kumble 10–0–53–1; Singh 6–0–34–0; Ganguly 2–0–14–0; Chauhan 9–0–35–1; Tendulkar 4–0–24–0.

India

†S. S. Karim c Croft b Headley	29		R. K. Chauhan b Fleming	12
S. C. Ganguly b Ealham	29		J. Srinath b Headley	3
N. S. Sidhu c Hollioake b Ealham	3		A. Kuruvilla not out	1
*S. R. Tendulkar st Stewart b Fleming	91		L-b 3, w 3, n-b 2	8
M. Azharuddin c Headley b Hollioake	3			
A. Jadeja c Thorpe b Fleming	50		1/60 2/64 3/65	(49.3 overs) 243
R. R. Singh lbw b Fleming	12		4/74 5/182 6/207	
A. Kumble run out	2		7/221 8/232 9/237	

Bowling: D. R. Brown 7–0–44–0; Headley 9–0–38–2; Ealham 10–0–43–2; Hollioake 9–1–38–1; Croft 5–0–32–0; Fleming 9.3–0–45–4.

Umpires: S. A. Bucknor and K. T. Francis.

PAKISTAN v WEST INDIES

At Sharjah, December 12 (day/night). West Indies won by 43 runs. Toss: West Indies. International debut: Akhtar Sarfraz.

West Indies' comfortable victory belied their recent disastrous tour of Pakistan. Only the off-spin of Saqlain Mushtaq and the late charge of Wasim Akram put any brake on the scoring, and Pakistan were let down by some of the shoddiest catching imaginable. The chief beneficiary was Stuart Williams, who went on to 77, but the impetus came from Lara, with 88 from 80 balls, including seven fours and three sixes, before he clipped a catch to deep square leg. A containing spell from Walsh and an imaginative one from Lewis, who bowled his leg-spin into the rough from around the wicket, pegged Pakistan back. Despite a slow start, Shahid Afridi's explosive hitting brought him 67 from 56 balls with six fours and four sixes. But he was one of three run-outs as the innings disintegrated.

Man of the Match: B. C. Lara.

West Indies

P. A. Wallace c Inzamam-ul-Haq b Saqlain Mushtaq	32		S. Chanderpaul not out	16
S. C. Williams c Wasim Akram b Shahid Afridi	77		F. A. Rose b Wasim Akram	2
B. C. Lara c Azhar Mahmood b Wasim Akram	88		†D. Williams c and b Wasim Akram	0
C. L. Hooper st Moin Khan b Saqlain Mushtaq	17		R. N. Lewis not out	1
P. V. Simmons c Aamir Sohail b Saqlain Mushtaq	22		B 1, l-b 6, w 12, n-b 1	20
			1/81 2/160 3/217	(7 wkts, 50 overs) 275
			4/243 5/266	
			6/271 7/271	

M. Dillon and *C. A. Walsh did not bat.

Bowling: Wasim Akram 10–0–62–3; Waqar Younis 10–0–53–0; Saqlain Mushtaq 10–0–35–3; Azhar Mahmood 10–0–61–0; Shahid Afridi 10–0–57–1.

Pakistan

Aamir Sohail c Lewis b Rose	17	Azhar Mahmood c Simmons b Walsh	4
Shahid Afridi run out	67	Saqlain Mushtaq not out	2
Saeed Anwar c Lara b Dillon	22	Waqar Younis c Wallace b Hooper	1
Ijaz Ahmed, sen. c Hooper b Lewis	12	L-b 8, w 7, n-b 4	19
Inzamam-ul-Haq run out	33		
Akhtar Sarfraz lbw b Simmons	25	1/24 2/91 3/124 (46 overs)	232
*Wasim Akram c Chanderpaul b Walsh	22	4/135 5/178 6/204	
†Moin Khan run out	8	7/222 8/229 9/230	

Bowling: Walsh 8–0–14–2; Rose 6–0–47–1; Dillon 8–0–45–1; Hooper 9–0–56–1; Lewis 8–1–31–1; Simmons 7–0–31–1.

Umpires: B. C. Cooray and C. J. Mitchley.

ENGLAND v WEST INDIES

At Sharjah, December 13 (day/night). England won by four wickets. Toss: West Indies.

Dougie Brown bowled Wallace with the first ball of the match and had Lara lbw with the third, but thereafter England had to work hard. Hooper grafted his way to a century from the final ball of the innings. This was England's second match on a pitch growing ever slower: runs were at a premium against disciplined bowling. All their bowlers did well, especially Ealham, and Fleming again showed skill at the death. England found batting equally uncomfortable against tight bowling and some inspired fielding (Chanderpaul's full-length dive and direct hit to run out Hick, after a full-blooded carve to extra cover, verged on the supernatural). At 123 for five, they appeared in trouble. There are few players more pragmatic than Thorpe, however. He hit only two fours in his 57 but added 50 with Ealham, who finished the job with Brown's help; they had 25 balls to spare.

Man of the Match: C. L. Hooper.

West Indies

P. A. Wallace b D. R. Brown	0	R. N. Lewis b Fleming	13
S. C. Williams c Thorpe b Headley	22	F. A. Rose not out	11
B. C Lara lbw b D. R. Brown	0	N-b 2	2
C. L. Hooper not out	100		
S. Chanderpaul lbw b Ealham	16	1/0 2/0 3/50 (7 wkts, 50 overs)	197
P. V. Simmons c Croft b Hollioake	29	4/77 5/143	
†D. Williams run out	4	6/151 7/181	

M. Dillon and *C. A. Walsh did not bat.

Bowling: D. R. Brown 7–1–28–2; Headley 7–1–24–1; Ealham 10–1–28–1; Croft 10–0–40–0; Hollioake 8–0–41–1; Fleming 8–1–36–1.

England

A. D. Brown c Lewis b Walsh	10	M. A. Ealham not out	28
†A. J. Stewart c Walsh b Rose	23	D. R. Brown not out	16
N. V. Knight c D. Williams b Dillon	10	L-b 7, w 4, n-b 6	17
G. A. Hick run out	28		
G. P. Thorpe c D. Williams b Hooper	57	1/21 2/45 3/53 (6 wkts, 45.5 overs)	198
*A. J. Hollioake c Chanderpaul b Dillon	9	4/100 5/123 6/173	

M. V. Fleming, R. D. B. Croft and D. W. Headley did not bat.

Bowling: Walsh 9.5–1–51–1; Rose 10–0–38–1; Dillon 10–0–38–2; Lewis 6–0–34–0; Simmons 2–0–8–0; Hooper 8–1–22–1.

Umpires: B. C. Cooray and K. T. Francis.

INDIA v PAKISTAN

At Sharjah, December 14 (day/night). Pakistan won by four wickets. Toss: India. International debut: Manzoor Akhtar.

Until a sixth-wicket stand of 82 between Saeed Anwar and Moin Khan, this was an even contest. Pakistan had been 144 for five against a spin attack finding spiteful turn in a wearing pitch, but could thank India's generosity in feeding Anwar's leg-side strokes. He made 104 from 128 balls, his 14th century in limited-overs internationals and his seventh in Sharjah, and most of his eight fours and one six went through the area between mid-wicket and fine leg. Having won the toss, India really should have taken the game. Sidhu's 54 and a well-constructed 90, including three sixes, from Ganguly ought to have set up a challenging total. The loss of three prime wickets in seven balls proved vital. Again, Tendulkar was held back, and he did not get to the crease until the 31st over. That was too late for India's best batsman to introduce himself.

Man of the Match: Saeed Anwar.

India

†S. S. Karim run out	18	A. Jadeja b Saqlain Mushtaq	6
S. C. Ganguly b Wasim Akram	90	A. Kumble not out	11
N. S. Sidhu run out	54		
R. R. Singh c Moin Khan b Azhar Mahmood	0	L-b 11, w 4, n-b 3	18
*S. R. Tendulkar c Inzamam-ul-Haq b Manzoor Akhtar	3	1/31 2/143 3/143 (7 wkts, 50 overs)	239
M. Azharuddin c Wasim Akram b Saqlain Mushtaq	39	4/147 5/200	
		6/224 7/239	

R. K. Chauhan, J. Srinath and A. Kuruvilla did not bat.

Bowling: Wasim Akram 10–1–34–1; Aqib Javed 10–0–49–0; Azhar Mahmood 10–0–40–1; Saqlain Mushtaq 10–0–55–2; Manzoor Akhtar 10–0–50–1.

Pakistan

Saeed Anwar c Karim b Srinath	104	†Moin Khan not out	49
Shahid Afridi c and b Chauhan	19	*Wasim Akram not out	9
Ijaz Ahmed, sen. lbw b Kumble	16	L-b 8, w 6, n-b 1	15
Akhtar Sarfraz c Azharuddin b Chauhan	7		
Manzoor Akhtar lbw b Kumble	5	1/48 2/79 3/93 (6 wkts, 47.2 overs)	243
Inzamam-ul-Haq c Karim b Ganguly	19	4/102 5/144 6/226	

Azhar Mahmood, Saqlain Mushtaq and Aqib Javed did not bat.

Bowling: Srinath 10–0–43–1; Kuruvilla 8–1–43–0; Chauhan 9.2–0–47–2; Kumble 10–1–44–2; Ganguly 7–0–39–1; Singh 3–0–19–0.

Umpires: S. A. Bucknor and C. J. Mitchley.

ENGLAND v PAKISTAN

At Sharjah, December 15 (day/night). England won by eight runs. Toss: England.

A pulsating finish forced England to dig deeper than before. Alistair Brown and Stewart had opened with 71 in 14 overs, before the innings was stifled by the spin of Saqlain Mushtaq and Manzoor Akhtar, who took four each, and Mushtaq Ahmed. Despite a worn pitch staging its third match in five days, a target of 216 should not have been too testing for batting as versatile and flamboyant as Pakistan's. But Dougie Brown bowled the dangerous Shahid Afridi with his second delivery and Headley bowled Aamir Sohail with his first. Though Saeed Anwar and Ijaz Ahmed added 94, the bowlers held their ranks. Crucial breakthroughs came from Croft, who bowled Anwar, and Ealham, whose next delivery had Ijaz caught at mid-off. Ealham conceded 16 from his second over but just 19 from his final eight, backed up by superlative outcricket. Manzoor still threatened, until Knight ran him out spectacularly from backward point.

Man of the Match: Manzoor Akhtar.

England

A. D. Brown c Moin Khan b Saqlain Mushtaq .	41	M. V. Fleming c and b Saqlain Mushtaq .	0	
†A. J. Stewart b Manzoor Akhtar	47	R. D. B. Croft c Ijaz Ahmed b Saqlain Mushtaq .	6	
N. V. Knight b Manzoor Akhtar	18	D. W. Headley not out	6	
G. A. Hick b Manzoor Akhtar	40			
G. P. Thorpe run out	3	B 1, l-b 4, w 7, n-b 1	13	
*A. J. Hollioake c Shahid Afridi b Manzoor Akhtar .	17	1/71 2/108 3/121 (9 wkts, 50 overs) 215		
M. A. Ealham c and b Saqlain Mushtaq .	6	4/129 5/168 6/180		
D. R. Brown not out	18	7/185 8/185 9/203		

Bowling: Wasim Akram 6–1–34–0; Azhar Mahmood 7–1–31–0; Saqlain Mushtaq 10–1–26–4; Mushtaq Ahmed 10–0–43–0; Manzoor Akhtar 10–0–50–4; Shahid Afridi 7–0–26–0.

Pakistan

Aamir Sohail b Headley	1	Azhar Mahmood c Stewart b Hollioake .	12	
Shahid Afridi b D. R. Brown	0	Saqlain Mushtaq run out	9	
Saeed Anwar b Croft	54	Mushtaq Ahmed not out	0	
Ijaz Ahmed, sen. c Croft b Ealham	41			
Akhtar Sarfraz b Croft	20	L-b 5, w 5, n-b 2	12	
Manzoor Akhtar run out	44			
†Moin Khan c Knight b Fleming	10	1/1 2/5 3/99 (49 overs) 207		
*Wasim Akram c D. R. Brown b Hollioake .	4	4/99 5/134 6/152		
		7/177 8/185 9/207		

Bowling: D. R. Brown 5–0–29–1; Headley 8–0–33–1; Ealham 10–1–39–1; Croft 10–1–39–2; Hollioake 10–0–35–2; Fleming 6–0–27–1.

Umpires: S. A. Bucknor and K. T. Francis.

INDIA v WEST INDIES

At Sharjah, December 16 (day/night). West Indies won by 41 runs. Toss: India.

An unbeaten century from Stuart Williams, his first in limited-overs internationals, and fine all-round cricket from Hooper completed a miserable week for India. The sound of selectors' axes was soon heard in the subcontinent. Having gone against convention by putting West Indies in, Tendulkar saw Williams bat throughout the innings, hitting ten fours in 149 balls. India could still have qualified by winning in 45 overs. An opening stand of 87 between Ganguly and Sidhu put them well on the way. Instead, they were undone by the three spinners, and a death wish that saw first Tendulkar, who reached the crease this time in the 29th over, and then Azharuddin run out by Lewis. More than seven overs remained when Hooper bowled Prasad.

Man of the Match: S. C. Williams.

West Indies

P. A. Wallace c Ganguly b Srinath	8	F. A. Rose b Srinath	14	
S. C. Williams not out	105	R. N. Lewis not out	1	
B. C. Lara c Kumble b Chauhan	23	L-b 5, n-b 3	8	
C. L. Hooper c Azharuddin b Ganguly .	38			
S. Chanderpaul c Jadeja b Chauhan	16	1/26 2/63 3/134 (6 wkts, 50 overs) 229		
P. V. Simmons b Kumble	16	4/164 5/202 6/227		

†D. Williams, M. Dillon and *C. A. Walsh did not bat.

Bowling: Srinath 9–1–48–2; Prasad 10–1–39–0; Kumble 10–0–52–1; Chauhan 10–1–30–2; Ganguly 7–0–38–1; Tendulkar 4–0–17–0.

India

S. C. Ganguly st D. Williams b Hooper .	70
N. S. Sidhu c Wallace b Lewis	25
R. Dravid b Hooper	31
*S. R. Tendulkar run out	1
M. Azharuddin run out	4
A. Jadeja b Hooper	8
†S. S. Karim b Chanderpaul	26
A. Kumble c and b Chanderpaul	6

J. Srinath b Chanderpaul	4
R. K. Chauhan not out	0
B. K. V. Prasad b Hooper	1
B 1, l-b 5, w 4, n-b 2	12

1/87 2/126 3/127   (42.2 overs) 188
4/136 5/140 6/162
7/177 8/187 9/187

Bowling: Walsh 7–1–24–0; Rose 6–0–35–0; Dillon 6–0–30–0; Lewis 10–0–38–1; Hooper 8.2–0–37–4; Chanderpaul 5–0–18–3.

Umpires: B. C. Cooray and C. J. Mitchley.

QUALIFYING TABLE

	Played	Won	Lost	Points	Net run-rate
England	3	3	0	6	0.23
West Indies	3	2	1	4	0.43
Pakistan	3	1	2	2	−0.23
India	3	0	3	0	−0.43

Net run-rate was calculated by subtracting runs conceded per over from runs scored per over.

FINAL

ENGLAND v WEST INDIES

At Sharjah, December 19 (day/night). England won by three wickets. Toss: West Indies.

England's decision to play a clutch of all-rounders paid its dividend when Dougie Brown, batting No. 9, hit his first delivery to the boundary to secure victory with 11 balls to spare. The win, owing much to the team's all-round depth, might have been beyond them a few months earlier. With less than nine overs remaining, England, chasing 236 for victory, were 165 for six, despite 51 from Stewart. But Thorpe, working the ball well, took control and added 70 in seven overs with Fleming – who had shown great instinct throughout the series. With the scores level, Fleming was run out, for 33 from 27 balls; Thorpe remained unbeaten at the finish. West Indies paid for some dreadful fielding and conceded 31 extras. Earlier, the medium-pacers had put a brake on their batsmen after an opening stand of 97 between Stuart Williams and Chanderpaul. Ealham bowled with superb discipline: his ten overs cost just 26 and he had Lara cannily stumped by Stewart as he pushed forward and unwittingly dragged his back foot. Only Simmons, scoring 39 from 37 balls in the closing overs, lent the total a competitive edge.

Man of the Match: G. P. Thorpe. *Man of the Tournament:* C. L. Hooper.

West Indies

S. C. Williams c A. D. Brown b Croft .	55
S. Chanderpaul run out	76
B. C. Lara st Stewart b Ealham	2
C. L. Hooper lbw b Fleming	34
P. V. Simmons not out	39
R. I. C. Holder lbw b Fleming	0
R. N. Lewis b Fleming	16

F. A. Rose run out	0
†D. Williams not out	9
L-b 3, w 1	4

1/97 2/101 3/164   (7 wkts, 50 overs) 235
4/174 5/174
6/200 7/200

M. Dillon and *C. A. Walsh did not bat.

Bowling: D. R. Brown 5–0–35–0; Headley 7–0–39–0; Ealham 10–1–26–1; Hol-lioake 10–0–50–0; Croft 10–0–40–1; Fleming 8–0–42–3.

England

A. D. Brown c Chanderpaul b Rose	...	1	M. V. Fleming run out 33
†A. J. Stewart b Hooper	....	51	D. R. Brown not out 4
N. V. Knight run out	....	24	B 1, l-b 16, w 5, n-b 9 31
G. A. Hick c Hooper b Lewis	....	9	──
G. P. Thorpe not out	....	66	1/14 2/89 3/107 (7 wkts, 48.1 overs) 239
*A. J. Hollioake st D. Williams b Hooper		16	4/107 5/152
M. A. Ealham b Walsh	....	4	6/165 7/235

R. D. B. Croft and D. W. Headley did not bat.

Bowling: Walsh 9.1–1–39–1; Rose 10–0–36–1; Dillon 6–0–36–0; Simmons 4–0–25–0; Lewis 9–0–51–1; Hooper 10–0–35–2.

Umpires: K. T. Francis and C. J. Mitchley.   Series referee: P. J. Burge.

SILVER JUBILEE INDEPENDENCE CUP, 1997-98

Bangladesh's second official limited-overs international tournament – the first was the Asia Cup, nine years earlier – was held as a slightly belated celebration of 25 years' independence. The guests of honour were their neighbours, India and Pakistan, who played most of the cricket. There were only three qualifying matches to establish who would contest the best-of-three finals, and Bangladesh were unable to stage an upset in either of their two games.

India won both their preliminaries, and went on to beat Pakistan 2-1 in the finals. It was a satisfying return to captaincy for Mohammad Azharuddin, who had just regained the job he had lost to Sachin Tendulkar in August 1996. But it was also a satisfying return to form for Tendulkar. Both scored more than 250 runs. The leading run-scorer of the tournament, however, was Saeed Anwar of Pakistan, who made 315 in his five innings, culminating with 140 in the climactic final. He and Ijaz Ahmed shared a world record third-wicket stand of 230, only to see India surge to the highest total ever made to win a one-day international batting second. Pakistan also had the leading wicket-taker in off-spinner Saqlain Mushtaq.

Bangladesh put up a decent fight in their opening game against India, but were completely outclassed by Pakistan. And there was a persistent problem with the venue, the National Stadium in Dhaka; five of the six matches had to be shortened because of fog.

Note: Matches in this section were not first-class.

BANGLADESH v INDIA

At Dhaka, January 10. India won by four wickets. Toss: India. International debuts: Khaled Mahmud, Sanuar Hossain, Sharif-ul-Haq.

Azharuddin, India's newly-restored captain, and Tendulkar, who had held the post for the past 17 months, combined to set up their team's victory. They put on 121 in 28 overs; Azharuddin scored 84, his 50th innings of 50 or more in 268 one-day internationals. But a few late wickets meant that India got home with only ten balls to spare. Bangladesh had recovered well from 22 for four, with Amin-ul-Islam scoring a maiden fifty and adding 109 with Khaled Mahmud. They reached a respectable 190 in an innings cut to 48 overs by fog. Srinath returned career-best figures of five for 23.

Man of the Match: J. Srinath.

Bangladesh

Shahriar Hossain c Tendulkar b Srinath	1	
Javed Omar lbw b Mohanty	4	
Sanuar Hossain c Tendulkar b Srinath	9	
Amin-ul-Islam not out	69	
*Akram Khan c and b Mohanty	2	
Khaled Mahmud run out	47	
Mohammad Rafiq b Srinath	20	
†Khaled Masud c Srinath b Mohanty	8	

Hasib-ul-Hassan b Srinath 3
Shafiuddin Ahmed b Srinath 0
Sharif-ul-Haq run out 10
     B 1, l-b 7, w 6, n-b 3 17
                        ——
1/4 2/16 3/19   (48 overs) 190
4/22 5/131 6/158
7/171 8/179 9/179

Bowling: Srinath 10–4–23–5; Mohanty 10–1–30–3; Bahutule 8–0–43–0; Ganguly 5–1–13–0; Kanitkar 7–1–27–0; Singh 6–0–33–0; Tendulkar 2–0–13–0.

India

S. C. Ganguly c Khaled Masud		
b Shafiuddin Ahmed	11	
N. S. Sidhu run out	0	
*M. Azharuddin c Akram Khan		
b Shafiuddin Ahmed	84	
S. R. Tendulkar c and b Mohammad Rafiq	54	
A. Jadeja b Hasib-ul-Hassan	10	

R. R. Singh run out 8
H. H. Kanitkar not out 13
†N. R. Mongia not out 0
     L-b 1, w 8, n-b 2 11
                        ——
1/0 2/14 3/135   (6 wkts, 46.2 overs) 191
4/162 5/167 6/190

S. V. Bahutule, J. Srinath and D. S. Mohanty did not bat.

Bowling: Hasib-ul-Hassan 9.2–2–37–1; Shafiuddin Ahmed 10–1–40–2; Khaled Mahmud 9–0–38–0; Sharif-ul-Haq 3–0–21–0; Mohammad Rafiq 10–0–42–1; Amin-ul-Islam 5–0–12–0.

Umpires: D. B. Cowie and R. B. Tiffin.

INDIA v PAKISTAN

At Dhaka, January 11. India won by 18 runs. Toss: Pakistan. International debut: Fazl-e-Akbar.

Latif's debut as Pakistan captain ended in failure as India stepped up a gear. Tendulkar and Azharuddin shared another century stand, but this one was much quicker: 112 in 14 overs, with Tendulkar hitting 67 in 44 balls. Like Azharuddin the previous day, he reached his 50th fifty, but in just 175 matches. Azharuddin carried on to his fifth century in one-day internationals, falling in the last over of their fog-shortened innings. Pakistan's hopes of scoring 6.64 an over rested chiefly on Inzamam-ul-Haq, who scored 77 from 69 balls. But he was caught and bowled by Tendulkar, who claimed his 50th wicket at this level and equalled the Indian record of four catches in a match.

Man of the Match: M. Azharuddin.

India

S. C. Ganguly c Inzamam-ul-Haq		
b Aqib Javed	13	
S. R. Tendulkar st Rashid Latif		
b Saqlain Mushtaq	67	
*M. Azharuddin c Azhar Mahmood		
b Saqlain Mushtaq	100	
N. S. Sidhu c and b Azhar Mahmood	36	
A. Jadeja c Manzoor Akhtar		
b Saqlain Mushtaq	6	
R. R. Singh c Saeed Anwar b Aqib Javed	1	

S. V. Bahutule c Shahid Afridi
     b Saqlain Mushtaq . 1
†N. R. Mongia not out 1
J. Srinath not out 0
     L-b 9, w 7, n-b 4 20
                        ——
1/14 2/126 3/215   (7 wkts, 37 overs) 245
4/236 5/239
6/243 7/243

Harvinder Singh and D. S. Mohanty did not bat.

Bowling: Aqib Javed 6–0–34–2; Fazl-e-Akbar 2–0–19–0; Azhar Mahmood 7–0–65–1; Saqlain Mushtaq 8–0–41–4; Shahid Afridi 8–0–38–0; Aamir Sohail 1–0–9–0; Manzoor Akhtar 5–0–30–0.

Pakistan

Shahid Afridi c Tendulkar b Mohanty	5	*†Rashid Latif not out	14
Ijaz Ahmed, sen. b Harvinder Singh	18	Saqlain Mushtaq b Srinath	11
Aamir Sohail c Tendulkar b Srinath	19	Fazl-e-Akbar run out	7
Saeed Anwar c and b Harvinder Singh	13	L-b 4, w 3, n-b 1	8
Inzamam-ul-Haq c and b Tendulkar	77		
Manzoor Akhtar run out	39	1/5 2/44 3/44 (9 wkts, 37 overs)	227
Azhar Mahmood c Tendulkar		4/62 5/146 6/185	
b Harvinder Singh	16	7/197 8/214 9/227	

Aqib Javed did not bat.

Bowling: Srinath 8–0–40–2; Mohanty 3–0–31–1; Harvinder Singh 8–0–47–3; R. R. Singh 6–0–20–0; Bahutule 7–0–53–0; Ganguly 1–0–8–0; Tendulkar 4–0–24–1.

Umpires: D. B. Cowie and R. E. Koertzen.

BANGLADESH v PAKISTAN

At Dhaka, January 12. Pakistan won by nine wickets. Toss: Pakistan.

Pakistan crushed Bangladesh with 16 overs to spare. Again, fog had intervened, reducing the game to 41 overs. When Rashid Latif asked Bangladesh to bat, they could not last even that long. The spinners, led by Saqlain Mushtaq, tied them up so that only Mohammad Rafiq reached 20. Saeed Anwar then hit 13 fours in an unbeaten 73 from 69 balls as Pakistan coasted into the final.

Man of the Match: Saqlain Mushtaq.

Bangladesh

Javed Omar b Mushtaq Ahmed	17	Mohammad Rafiq b Saqlain Mushtaq	29
Habib-ul-Bashar c sub (Mohammad		†Khaled Masud c and b Saqlain Mushtaq	3
Hussain) b Saqlain Mushtaq	15	Hasib-ul-Hassan b Aqib Javed	7
Sanuar Hossain st Rashid Latif		Shafiuddin Ahmed not out	6
b Mushtaq Ahmed	13	Zakir Hassan lbw b Aqib Javed	0
Amin-ul-Islam run out	6	L-b 7, w 4, n-b 1	12
*Akram Khan c Rashid Latif			
b Shahid Afridi	7	1/33 2/38 3/52 (39.3 overs)	134
Khaled Mahmud c Rashid Latif		4/59 5/76 6/100	
b Shahid Afridi	19	7/116 8/126 9/134	

Bowling: Aqib Javed 7.3–1–27–2; Azhar Mahmood 8–1–22–0; Saqlain Mushtaq 8–0–33–3; Mushtaq Ahmed 8–0–20–2; Shahid Afridi 8–1–25–2.

Pakistan

Saeed Anwar not out	73		
Shahid Afridi c Sanuar Hossain			
b Shafiuddin Ahmed	11		
Aamir Sohail not out	37		
B 1, l-b 1, w 12, n-b 1	15		
1/43 (1 wkt, 24.2 overs)	136		

Ijaz Ahmed, sen., Inzamam-ul-Haq, Manzoor Akhtar, Azhar Mahmood, *†Rashid Latif, Saqlain Mushtaq, Mushtaq Ahmed and Aqib Javed did not bat.

Bowling: Hasib-ul-Hassan 6–0–26–0; Shafiuddin Ahmed 6–0–42–1; Zakir Hassan 4–0–18–0; Khaled Mahmud 2–0–19–0; Mohammad Rafiq 5–1–18–0; Amin-ul-Islam 1.2–0–11–0.

Umpires: R. E. Koertzen and R. B. Tiffin.

QUALIFYING TABLE

	Played	Won	Lost	Points	Net run-rate
India................	2	2	0	4	0.32
Pakistan.............	2	1	1	2	1.05
Bangladesh..........	2	0	2	0	–0.98

Net run-rate was calculated by subtracting runs conceded per over from runs scored per over.

INDIA v PAKISTAN

First Final Match

At Dhaka, January 14 (day/night). India won by eight wickets. Toss: Pakistan.

A comfortable victory, with nine overs in hand, gave India a 1-0 lead in the best-of-three finals. Tendulkar starred again, smashing 95 from 78 balls, with five sixes and six fours. He shared an opening stand of 159 in 25 overs with Ganguly, and on the way he became the youngest player to pass 6,000 runs in limited-overs internationals, at 24 years 265 days. Earlier, he had also taken three wickets, though the bowler who did most to restrict Pakistan was Robin Singh. Most of their top-order batsmen made starts, but no one got to 40.

Man of the Match: S. R. Tendulkar.

Pakistan

Saeed Anwar c Ganguly b Bahutule....	38	*†Rashid Latif c Azharuddin b Srinath..	1
Shahid Afridi c Ganguly		Saqlain Mushtaq not out	7
b Harvinder Singh .	29	Mushtaq Ahmed not out	10
Aamir Sohail c Mongia b Mohanty	10		
Ijaz Ahmed, sen. st Mongia b Tendulkar.	34	L-b 4, w 7.............	11
Inzamam-ul-Haq c Harvinder Singh			
b Tendulkar .	33	1/45 2/73 3/95 (8 wkts, 46 overs) 212	
Azhar Mahmood b Srinath..........	30	4/142 5/155 6/172	
Manzoor Akhtar st Mongia b Tendulkar .	9	7/173 8/197	

Aqib Javed did not bat.

Bowling: Srinath 9–1–40–2; Mohanty 9–0–46–1; Harvinder Singh 5–0–20–1; Bahutule 7–0–31–1; R. R. Singh 9–0–26–0; Tendulkar 7–0–45–3.

India

S. C. Ganguly lbw b Mushtaq Ahmed ..	68
S. R. Tendulkar b Shahid Afridi	95
*M. Azharuddin not out	30
A. Jadeja not out	11
L-b 2, w 6, n-b 1	9

1/159 2/182   (2 wkts, 37.1 overs) 213

N. S. Sidhu, R. R. Singh, †N. R. Mongia, S. V. Bahutule, J. Srinath, Harvinder Singh and D. S. Mohanty did not bat.

Bowling: Aqib Javed 4–1–24–0; Azhar Mahmood 4–0–26–0; Saqlain Mushtaq 10–0–53–0; Mushtaq Ahmed 9–0–48–1; Shahid Afridi 9–0–49–1; Manzoor Akhtar 1.1–0–11–0.

Umpires: D. B. Cowie and R. B. Tiffin.

INDIA v PAKISTAN

Second Final Match

At Dhaka, January 16 (day/night). Pakistan won by six wickets. Toss: India.

Pakistan pulled level in the only match of the tournament unaffected by fog. Azhar Mahmood gave them the ideal start by bowling Tendulkar in the second over, and only Azharuddin reached 50. Most of the damage was done by slow left-armer Mohammad Hussain, who took four wickets, and off-spinner Saqlain Mushtaq, who took his 150th wicket in only his 78th one-day international, a record for any bowler. Pakistan passed their target of 190 in 32 overs – they needed only 13 to reach three figures, as Saeed Anwar raced to 51 in 40 balls.

Man of the Match: Mohammad Hussain.

India

S. C. Ganguly c and b Mohammad Hussain	26	S. V. Bahutule st Rashid Latif		
S. R. Tendulkar b Azhar Mahmood	1	b Saqlain Mushtaq .	11
*M. Azharuddin c Aqib Javed		J. Srinath b Aqib Javed	12
b Mohammad Hussain .	66	Harvinder Singh not out	3
N. S. Sidhu c Azhar Mahmood		D. S. Mohanty c Ijaz Ahmed		
b Mohammad Hussain .	6	b Saqlain Mushtaq .	4
A. Jadeja c and b Aqib Javed	34	L-b 3, w 5, n-b 3	11
R. R. Singh c Shahid Afridi			
b Mohammad Hussain .	5	1/5 2/82 3/96	(49.5 overs) 189
†N. R. Mongia c Aamir Sohail		4/116 5/124 6/151	
b Saqlain Mushtaq .	10	7/167 8/182 9/184	

Bowling: Aqib Javed 10–0–49–2; Azhar Mahmood 7–1–28–1; Saqlain Mushtaq 9.5–0–36–3; Mohammad Hussain 10–1–33–4; Shahid Afridi 10–2–21–0; Manzoor Akhtar 3–0–19–0.

Pakistan

Saeed Anwar c Ganguly		Mohammad Hussain not out	0
b Harvinder Singh .	51		
Shahid Afridi c Bahutule b Srinath	21	L-b 2, w 1, n-b 2	5
Aamir Sohail c Azharuddin b R. R. Singh	36		
Ijaz Ahmed, sen. not out	40	1/31 2/105	(4 wkts, 31.3 overs) 193
Inzamam-ul-Haq c Sidhu b R. R. Singh .	40	3/123 4/189	

Azhar Mahmood, Manzoor Akhtar, *†Rashid Latif, Saqlain Mushtaq and Aqib Javed did not bat.

Bowling: Srinath 7–1–38–1; Mohanty 2–0–26–0; Harvinder Singh 5–0–33–1; Bahutule 5–0–53–0; R. R. Singh 9–3–24–2; Tendulkar 3.3–0–17–0.

Umpires: D. B. Cowie and R. E. Koertzen.

INDIA v PAKISTAN

Third Final Match

At Dhaka, January 18 (day/night). India won by three wickets. Toss: India. International debut: R. Sanghvi.

India took the series in a breathless climax under floodlights. They had to score 315, more than any team had ever made batting second to win a one-day international (Sri Lanka managed 313 to beat Zimbabwe in the 1992 World Cup). Thanks to an early burst from Tendulkar – 41 in 26 balls – and a 179-run stand in 30 overs between Ganguly and pinch-hitter Robin Singh, they reached 250 in 38 overs with one wicket down. But in the last ten overs (bad light having trimmed two from each innings), six more wickets fell; Kanitkar hit the winning four with one ball to go. Pakistan's batsmen had also put up a record-breaking performance. Saeed Anwar, who scored 140, his 15th one-day international century, from 132 balls, and Ijaz Ahmed, who made 117 in 112, added 230 – a third-wicket record, six more than Dean Jones and Allan Border for Australia against Sri Lanka in 1984-85. Border's record of 273 one-day internationals was equalled in this game by the victorious captain, Azharuddin.

Man of the Match: S. C. Ganguly. *Man of the Series:* S. R. Tendulkar.

Pakistan

Saeed Anwar c Azharuddin b Harvinder Singh .	140
Shahid Afridi c R. R. Singh b Harvinder Singh .	18
Aamir Sohail c Mongia b Harvinder Singh .	14
Ijaz Ahmed, sen. c Sidhu b Srinath	117

Azhar Mahmood c Azharuddin b Tendulkar .	10
Mohammad Hussain not out	2
L-b 6, w 6, n-b 1	13
1/30 2/66 3/296 (5 wkts, 48 overs)	314
4/302 5/314	

Inzamam-ul-Haq, Manzoor Akhtar, *†Rashid Latif, Saqlain Mushtaq and Aqib Javid did not bat.

Bowling: Srinath 10-0-61-1; Harvinder Singh 10-0-74-3; R. R. Singh 8-0-47-0; Ganguly 2-0-5-0; Kanitkar 6-0-34-0; Tendulkar 7-0-49-1; Sanghvi 5-0-38-0.

India

S. C. Ganguly b Aqib Javed	124
S. R. Tendulkar c Azhar Mahmood b Shahid Afridi .	41
R. R. Singh c Aqib Javed b Mohammad Hussain .	82
*M. Azharuddin c Aamir Sohail b Saqlain Mushtaq .	4
A. Jadeja b Saqlain Mushtaq	8
N. S. Sidhu lbw b Saqlain Mushtaq	5

H. H. Kanitkar not out	11
†N. R. Mongia run out	9
J. Srinath not out	5
B 1, l-b 11, w 12, n-b 3	27
1/71 2/250 3/268 (7 wkts, 47.5 overs)	316
4/274 5/281	
6/296 7/306	

Harvinder Singh and R. Sanghvi did not bat.

Bowling: Aqib Javed 9.2-0-63-1; Azhar Mahmood 8-0-55-0; Shahid Afridi 6.4-0-56-1; Saqlain Mushtaq 9.5-0-66-3; Mohammad Hussain 10-0-40-1; Manzoor Akhtar 4-0-24-0.

Umpires: R. E. Koertzen and R. B. Tiffin.   Series referee: M. H. Denness (England).

THE AUSTRALIANS IN NEW ZEALAND, 1997-98

By DON CAMERON

Just before their Test tour of India, Australia played four one-day internationals in New Zealand. They were without Shane Warne, who was resting an injured right shoulder before the Indian expedition. However, when the Australians won handsomely in both Christchurch and Wellington to take a 2-0 lead, no one seemed to notice his absence: captain Steve Waugh was happily talking of a clean sweep.

But New Zealand, led from the front by Stephen Fleming, won an emphatic victory in the third match, and fought hard from an unpromising position in the fourth to square the series. The main talking point of the tour was the behaviour of the crowd at Wellington, where they reacted to the home team's performance by hurling missiles at the Australian outfielders.

Note: Matches in this section were not first-class.

NEW ZEALAND v AUSTRALIA

First One-Day International

At Christchurch, February 8 (day/night). Australia won by seven wickets. Toss: New Zealand.
Showing the sort of explosive form that ousted Ian Healy from the one-day team, Adam Gilchrist led Australia to an easy victory over a lacklustre New Zealand. Howell scored a steady fifty, but no one else in the New Zealand team found much rhythm against intelligent, restrictive bowling.

Harris and Nash put on 66 for the seventh wicket, but 212 still proved far too little. Gilchrist hit 118 in 117 balls, with ten fours and five sixes, and with Mark Waugh put on 146 in 26 overs; the Australians raced in with almost 12 overs to spare.

Man of the Match: A. C. Gilchrist.

New Zealand

L. G. Howell b Robertson	50	D. J. Nash not out		39
N. J. Astle b Moody	23	S. B. Doull not out		0
†A. C. Parore c Bevan b Robertson	29	L-b 7, w 4		11
*S. P. Fleming c and b Robertson	2			—
C. D. McMillan run out	4	1/40 2/104 3/109	(7 wkts, 50 overs)	212
C. L. Cairns c Dale b S. R. Waugh	16	4/109 5/119		
C. Z. Harris c Law b Moody	38	6/136 7/202		

D. L. Vettori and S. B. O'Connor did not bat.

Bowling: Wilson 7–1–39–0; Dale 8–0–34–0; Moody 8–2–36–2; Robertson 10–0–32–3; S. R. Waugh 10–1–24–1; M. E. Waugh 3–0–19–0; Law 4–0–21–0.

Australia

†A. C. Gilchrist c Cairns b McMillan	118	D. S. Lehmann not out		0
M. E. Waugh c Nash b Vettori	65	B 2, l-b 1, w 1, n-b 1		5
T. M. Moody b McMillan	17			—
R. T. Ponting not out	10	1/146 2/173 3/208	(3 wkts, 38.2 overs)	215

*S. R. Waugh, M. G. Bevan, S. G. Law, G. R. Robertson, A. C. Dale and P. Wilson did not bat.

Bowling: O'Connor 4–0–31–0; Doull 4–0–25–0; Cairns 4–0–16–0; Harris 8–0–43–0; Vettori 10–0–44–1; Astle 2–0–15–0; McMillan 6.2–0–38–2.

Umpires: D. B. Cowie and D. M. Quested.

NEW ZEALAND v AUSTRALIA

Second One-Day International

At Wellington, February 10. Australia won by 66 runs. Toss: Australia.

On a true Basin Reserve pitch, Australia came close to 300, a total that was always beyond New Zealand's reach. All the Australian top order, bar Gilchrist, the hero of Christchurch, contributed, Mark Waugh leading the way with 85. Chasing 298, Fleming experimented with promoting the big-hitting Cairns to No. 3. The ploy itself worked – Cairns hit 67 – but the other recognised batsmen gave little support. Harris, playing his 100th limited-overs international, batted well without much hope of success. With the home team heading for defeat again, some of the 12,000 capacity crowd expressed their frustration by hurling missiles, including fruit and golf balls, on to the pitch. Law was struck by a full sauce bottle, an incident likened by Steve Waugh to the stabbing of the tennis player Monica Seles; he demanded greater security for his players.

Man of the Match: M. E. Waugh.

Australia

M. E. Waugh c Howell b Astle	85	S. G. Law not out		13
†A. C. Gilchrist c McMillan b O'Connor	0	T. M. Moody not out		12
R. T. Ponting c Fleming b Nash	26	L-b 5, w 3, n-b 5		13
D. S. Lehmann c Vettori b O'Connor	62			—
M. G. Bevan run out	39	1/1 2/46 3/168	(6 wkts, 50 overs)	297
*S. R. Waugh c Fleming b O'Connor	47	4/191 5/265 6/277		

A. J. Bichel, G. R. Robertson and A. C. Dale did not bat.

Bowling: O'Connor 9–0–55–3; Cairns 9–0–55–0; Nash 10–0–52–1; Doull 4–1–16–0; Harris 6–0–31–0; Vettori 7–0–49–0; Astle 5–0–34–1.

New Zealand

L. G. Howell c Lehmann b Dale	1	D. L. Vettori c M. E. Waugh		
N. J. Astle st Gilchrist b Robertson	37	b S. R. Waugh	4	
C. L. Cairns lbw b S. R. Waugh	67	S. B. Doull not out	9	
*S. P. Fleming run out	3	S. B. O'Connor run out	4	
†A. C. Parore run out	0	B 4, l-b 2, w 7	13	
C. D. McMillan c Robertson b Bevan	25			
C. Z. Harris b Bevan	45	1/1 2/82 3/86 4/89 5/132 (47.3 overs) 231		
D. J. Nash c Gilchrist b Bevan	23	6/142 7/193 8/209 9/219		

Bowling: Bichel 6–0–28–0; Dale 5–1–23–1; Robertson 9–0–40–1; Moody 8–1–34–0; Bevan 10–1–54–3; S. R. Waugh 9.3–0–46–2.

Umpires: D. M. Quested and E. A. Watkin.

NEW ZEALAND v AUSTRALIA

Third One-Day International

At Napier, February 12 (day/night). New Zealand won by seven wickets. Toss: Australia.

Cairns took five for 42, his best return in one-day internationals, to extinguish a promising Australian innings and set up a big home win. At 209 for four, with almost eight overs remaining, the tourists were well set – until a devastating spell from Cairns brought him four wickets in eight balls and reduced them to 215 for eight. Outclassed until now, New Zealand displayed new resolve by weathering an early-innings wobble to win handsomely. Fleming himself led the charge with an unbeaten 111 and shared successive century stands with Astle and McMillan.

Man of the Match: S. P. Fleming.

Australia

†A. C. Gilchrist c Cairns b Nash	40	A. J. Bichel c Fleming b Cairns	0	
M. E. Waugh c Parore b Vettori	42	G. R. Robertson not out	11	
R. T. Ponting c Fleming b Harris	30	P. Wilson c Fleming b Cairns	2	
D. S. Lehmann c Parore b Cairns	44	L-b 6, w 4, n-b 1	11	
T. M. Moody b Vettori	3			
*S. R. Waugh c Parore b Cairns	42	1/60 2/98 3/136 (48.4 overs) 236		
M. G. Bevan run out	10	4/141 5/209 6/210		
S. G. Law c Nash b Cairns	1	7/214 8/215 9/226		

Bowling: O'Connor 5–0–20–0; Cairns 7.4–0–42–5; Doull 7–0–28–0; Nash 6–0–37–1; Vettori 10–0–35–2; Astle 3–0–16–0; Harris 10–0–52–1.

New Zealand

L. G. Howell c Gilchrist b Wilson	4	C. D. McMillan not out	53	
N. J. Astle run out	55	B 1, l-b 6, w 3, n-b 7	17	
†A. C. Parore b Bichel	0			
*S. P. Fleming not out	111	1/4 2/5 3/121 (3 wkts, 48.2 overs) 240		

C. L. Cairns, C. Z. Harris, D. J. Nash, D. L. Vettori, S. B. Doull and S. B. O'Connor did not bat.

Bowling: Wilson 6.2–0–42–1; Bichel 10–0–42–1; Moody 10–0–39–0; Robertson 10–1–38–0; S. R. Waugh 10–0–56–0; Law 2–0–16–0.

Umpires: B. F. Bowden and E. A. Watkin.

NEW ZEALAND v AUSTRALIA

Fourth One-Day International

At Auckland, February 14. New Zealand won by 30 runs. Toss: Australia.

Neither side was able to take advantage of a slow pitch, but New Zealand, battling as doggedly as they had at Napier, successfully defended a low total to square the series. Their batsmen squandered the start given them by Howell – his 51 came from 54 balls – and had to be rescued by Harris and Nash, who put on 89 for the seventh wicket. Similarly, Australia failed to build on Gilchrist's brisk opening innings and their progress, never comfortable, was hampered by a leg injury to Steve Waugh. He resumed with a runner, but was unable to arrest the Australian decline, caused principally by Doull.

Man of the Match: C. Z. Harris.

New Zealand

L. G. Howell lbw b Robertson	51	D. J. Nash not out		31
N. J. Astle c Robertson b Bichel	20			
†A. C. Parore c Ponting b Robertson	32	W 5, n-b 1		6
*S. P. Fleming c Gilchrist b Robertson	13			
C. D. McMillan b Lehmann	13	1/46 2/85 3/107	(7 wkts, 50 overs)	223
C. L. Cairns c S. R. Waugh b Bevan	2	4/120 5/132		
C. Z. Harris run out	55	6/134 7/223		

M. W. Priest, S. B. Doull and S. B. O'Connor did not bat.

Bowling: Wilson 4–0–25–0; Dale 6–0–33–0; Bichel 7–0–33–1; Robertson 10–0–29–3; M. E. Waugh 2–0–11–0; Bevan 10–0–37–1; Lehmann 9–0–37–1; Law 2–0–18–0.

Australia

†A. C. Gilchrist c Parore b Nash	42	G. R. Robertson c Nash b Doull		7
M. E. Waugh lbw b Doull	4	A. C. Dale c Nash b Cairns		6
R. T. Ponting b Doull	10	P. Wilson not out		1
D. S. Lehmann c Astle b Priest	26			
*S. R. Waugh c sub (S. J. Peterson) b Priest	23	L-b 4, w 4, n-b 1		9
S. G. Law c Fleming b McMillan	7	1/26 2/48 3/60	(49.1 overs)	193
M. G. Bevan c Nash b Doull	37	4/105 5/107 6/147		
A. J. Bichel c Cairns b Harris	21	7/176 8/183 9/190		

S. R. Waugh, when 14, retired hurt at 88 and resumed at 147.

Bowling: O'Connor 2–0–21–0; Cairns 9.1–0–32–1; Doull 8–1–25–4; Nash 5–0–23–1; Priest 10–0–31–2; Harris 10–0–33–1; McMillan 3–0–14–1; Astle 2–0–10–0.

Umpires: B. F. Bowden and R. S. Dunne. Series referee: Hanumant Singh (India).

PEPSI TRIANGULAR SERIES, 1997-98

Hopes for a home victory in this tournament were understandably high; India had just convincingly defeated the Australian tourists in a three-match Test series, and were better suited to cope with both the searing heat of summer and the demanding travel schedules. Indian supporters were delighted when their team won all four qualifying matches. Only in their second match, against Zimbabwe at Baroda, did they come close to losing. But in the final, Australia turned the tables to take the trophy.

In their four earlier wins, India had found the tournament's most consistent batsman – and also an unexpected bowling hero. Ajay Jadeja finished the competition with an average of 354, having lost his wicket just once in five innings. In the opening match, Sachin Tendulkar, who had torn apart the Australian bowlers in the Test series, now gave them a lesson in how it should be done, claiming five for 32. The seven matches also produced a new record for any partnership in one-day internationals, when Jadeja and Mohammad Azharuddin added 275 against Zimbabwe, and made Azharuddin the world's most experienced player in this form of cricket; he overtook Allan Border's 273 appearances in the opening match and finished the tournament on 278, with power to add.

Australia's progress to the final was hardly ideal, but it sufficed. Only Ricky Ponting of the batsmen hit anything like consistent form, and none of the bowlers managed to find much of a rhythm. In the final, however, Australia won with some ease, yet again showing their ability to play when it mattered. Zimbabwe's recent one-day results had been poor; Alistair Campbell and his team arrived in India after losing nine of their ten one-day internationals in 1998. In the event, they threatened to win three of their four matches (losing by 13, 13 and 16 runs in high-scoring contests), but failed to challenge the supremacy of the other two nations.

Such is the proliferation of these tournaments that the finalists were due to play each other again – in a different competition and on a different continent – only five days later.

Note: Matches in this section were not first-class.

INDIA v AUSTRALIA

At Kochi (Cochin), April 1. India won by 41 runs. Toss: India. International debut: A. B. Agarkar.

There were high expectations of Tendulkar, who had averaged 111.50 in the Test series against Australia, but he fell for just eight when he lofted a cover drive. Azharuddin (who passed Allan Border's record of 273 one-day international appearances in this match) and Jadeja then restored the impetus with a century partnership. Supported late on in the innings by Kanitkar, Jadeja took India to 309, their second-highest one-day score behind their 316 for seven against Pakistan earlier in 1998. But Australia set off at a rate of knots and, at 202 for three in the 32nd over, were well placed. Enter Tendulkar, bowling a mixture of off-spin and medium-pace. His five for 32 wrested the game from the visitors and the match award from Jadeja.

Man of the Match: S. R. Tendulkar.

India

N. S. Sidhu c Gilchrist b Kasprowicz...	1	H. H. Kanitkar lbw b Martyn........	57
S. R. Tendulkar c Ponting b Kasprowicz.	8	†N. R. Mongia not out	2
*M. Azharuddin c M. E. Waugh		L-b 11, w 8, n-b 2.........	21
b Kasprowicz .	82		
V. G. Kambli lbw b Fleming	33	1/11 2/19 3/80 (5 wkts, 50 overs)	309
A. Jadeja not out	105	4/184 5/305	

A. B. Agarkar, A. Kumble, J. Srinath and D. S. Mohanty did not bat.

Bowling: Fleming 10–0–61–1; Kasprowicz 8.2–2–50–3; Moody 10–0–60–0; Warne 10–0–42–0; Bevan 5–0–34–0; Martyn 3.4–0–30–1; M. E. Waugh 3–0–21–0.

Australia

M. E. Waugh c Agarkar b Srinath	28	S. K. Warne c Kanitkar b Kumble.....	0
†A. C. Gilchrist c Azharuddin b Agarkar	61	M. S. Kasprowicz not out	6
R. T. Ponting c Azharuddin b Kanitkar..	12	D. W. Fleming c Kumble b Srinath	5
M. G. Bevan st Mongia b Tendulkar ...	65	B 4, l-b 12, w 7, n-b 9......	32
*S. R. Waugh c and b Tendulkar	26		
D. S. Lehmann lbw b Tendulkar	8	1/101 2/105 3/142 (45.5 overs)	268
T. M. Moody c Mongia b Tendulkar ...	23	4/202 5/222 6/239	
D. R. Martyn c Srinath b Tendulkar....	2	7/253 8/254 9/259	

Bowling: Srinath 7.5–1–41–2; Mohanty 5–0–51–0; Agarkar 5–0–31–1; Kumble 10–0–51–1; Kanitkar 8–0–46–1; Tendulkar 10–2–32–5.

Umpires: S. K. Bansal and A. V. Jayaprakash.

AUSTRALIA v ZIMBABWE

At Ahmedabad, April 3. Australia won by 13 runs. Toss: Australia.

Australia kept their heads to win a tight match despite a late onslaught from Campbell, the Zimbabwean captain. At 212 for three from 42 overs, Australia were looking at a sizeable total. But the bowlers, finding considerable reverse swing, stuck to their task and restricted them to 252. In reply, Zimbabwe also made an encouraging start, but then it all went wrong. From 143 for one in the 30th over, they subsided to 192 for eight in the 42nd. Fleming, with three wickets in 14 balls, and Moody destroyed the lower order, and Campbell's heroics – he was last man out, for 102 – counted for nothing.

Man of the Match: A. D. R. Campbell.

Australia

†A. C. Gilchrist lbw b Streak	12		S. K. Warne not out	11
M. E. Waugh lbw b A. R. Whittall	37		G. R. Robertson not out	5
R. T. Ponting run out	53		B 1, l-b 3, w 9	13
M. G. Bevan c Streak b Evans	65			—
*S. R. Waugh b G. J. Whittall	48		1/19 2/87 3/142 (7 wkts, 50 overs)	252
D. S. Lehmann b Streak	6		4/212 5/232	
T. M. Moody run out	2		6/234 7/238	

D. W. Fleming and A. C. Dale did not bat.

Bowling: Streak 10–0–48–2; G. J. Whittall 10–0–56–1; Huckle 10–0–47–0; A. R. Whittall 10–1–45–1; Viljoen 4–0–26–0; Evans 6–0–26–1.

Zimbabwe

G. W. Flower c Bevan b Warne	35		D. P. Viljoen c Gilchrist b Moody	0
*A. D. R. Campbell b Moody	102		A. R. Whittall c Warne b Dale	5
M. W. Goodwin b Warne	55		A. G. Huckle not out	1
†A. Flower lbw b Fleming	1		B 5, l-b 4, w 7, n-b 3	19
G. J. Whittall lbw b Fleming	0			—
H. H. Streak b Fleming	5		1/52 2/143 3/149 (49.5 overs)	239
C. B. Wishart b Dale	11		4/149 5/163 6/181	
C. N. Evans c Gilchrist b Moody	5		7/192 8/192 9/209	

Bowling: Fleming 10–0–30–3; Dale 8–0–50–2; Warne 10–0–45–2; Moody 9.5–1–39–3; M. E. Waugh 5–0–24–0; Robertson 5–0–28–0; Bevan 2–0–14–0.

Umpires: R. Desraj and B. A. Jamula.

INDIA v ZIMBABWE

At Baroda, April 5. India won by 13 runs. Toss: Zimbabwe.

When Tendulkar and Azharuddin were out to successive balls, leaving India 17 for two, Campbell's decision to insert them seemed vindicated. But Jadeja – scoring at more than a run a ball on a day when the thermometer touched 43 degrees Centigrade – and Ganguly, returning after a one-match suspension, then took advantage of loose bowling (which included 14 wides). Chasing 275, Grant Flower and Campbell got off to an ideal start, hitting 121 for the first wicket. At 212 for three from 36 overs, Azharuddin was contemplating defeat. But the inexperienced spinners Sanghvi and Kanitkar (who held a spectacular return catch to dismiss Goodwin) rewarded his faith – and Zimbabwe had thrown away another winning position.

Man of the Match: H. H. Kanitkar.

India

S. C. Ganguly c Wishart b G. J. Whittall	82	†N. R. Mongia not out 4
S. R. Tendulkar run out	5	
*M. Azharuddin c Campbell b Streak . . .	0	L-b 13, w 14, n-b 3 30
V. G. Kambli run out	39	───
A. Jadeja not out	79	1/17 2/17 3/95 (5 wkts, 50 overs) 274
H. H. Kanitkar lbw b Streak	35	4/168 5/246

A. B. Agarkar, A. Kumble, B. K. V. Prasad and R. Sanghvi did not bat.

Bowling: Streak 10–1–42–2; Mbangwa 8–0–28–0; G. J. Whittall 9–0–70–1; A. R. Whittall 7–0–38–0; Evans 10–0–50–0; Huckle 6–0–33–0.

Zimbabwe

G. W. Flower c Jadeja b Tendulkar	57	A. R. Whittall b Agarkar 8
*A. D. R. Campbell st Mongia		M. Mbangwa run out 2
b Kanitkar .	60	A. G. Huckle run out 0
M. W. Goodwin c and b Kanitkar	11	
C. N. Evans st Mongia b Sanghvi	46	B 5, l-b 10, w 6, n-b 2 23
†A. Flower c Azharuddin b Kumble . . .	25	───
G. J. Whittall c and b Sanghvi	9	1/121 2/136 3/146 (48.3 overs) 261
H. H. Streak not out	16	4/212 5/224 6/226
C. B. Wishart c and b Streak	4	7/232 8/246 9/260

Bowling: Prasad 8–0–43–0; Agarkar 8.3–0–57–1; Ganguly 3–0–17–0; Kumble 9–0–27–1; Kanitkar 7–0–37–2; Sanghvi 8–0–29–3; Tendulkar 5–0–36–1.

Umpires: Jasbir Singh and G. A. Pratap Kumar.

INDIA v AUSTRALIA

At Kanpur, April 7. India won by six wickets. Toss: Australia.

Australia never recovered from the loss of Mark Waugh in the third over and India won a one-sided contest to secure their place in the final. Agarkar, bowling at a lively pace, took four wickets, including those of Ponting and Moody, the only batsmen to hit decent scores. India raced towards their target and, at 28 overs, had reached 175 without loss, their record first-wicket stand against Australia. Warne, struggling to find any form, did then manage to dismiss Tendulkar, but only after he had reached his 13th century in one-day internationals. Tendulkar struck seven sixes and five fours in his 89-ball innings.

Man of the Match: S. R. Tendulkar.

Australia

M. E. Waugh c Mongia b Prasad	6	G. R. Robertson lbw b Agarkar 15
†A. C. Gilchrist c Azharuddin b Agarkar	11	M. S. Kasprowicz not out 2
R. T. Ponting c Kanitkar b Agarkar	84	D. W. Fleming not out 3
M. G. Bevan b Kanitkar	16	L-b 11, w 7, n-b 3 21
D. S. Lehmann b Sanghvi	18	───
*S. R. Waugh st Mongia b Kanitkar	0	1/12 2/35 3/71 (9 wkts, 50 overs) 222
T. M. Moody b Agarkar	44	4/106 5/108 6/185
S. K. Warne c Mongia b Kumble	2	7/190 8/216 9/218

Bowling: Prasad 6–0–33–1; Agarkar 10–0–46–4; Kumble 10–0–42–1; Kanitkar 10–1–33–2; Sanghvi 10–1–38–1; Tendulkar 4–0–19–0.

India

S. C. Ganguly c Gilchrist b Kasprowicz .	72	H. H. Kanitkar not out 7
S. R. Tendulkar c sub (D. R. Martyn)		
b Warne .	100	L-b 3, w 12, n-b 3 18
*M. Azharuddin c and b Kasprowicz . . .	3	───
V. G. Kambli b Bevan	17	1/175 2/183 (4 wkts, 44.3 overs) 223
A. Jadeja not out	6	3/197 4/212

†N. R. Mongia, A. Kumble, A. B. Agarkar, B. K. V. Prasad and R. Sanghvi did not bat.

Bowling: Fleming 9–0–42–0; Kasprowicz 10–1–39–2; Robertson 7.3–0–34–0; Moody 3–0–26–0; Lehmann 4–0–28–0; Warne 9–0–43–1; Bevan 2–0–8–1.

Umpires: C. K. Sathe and M. R. Singh.

INDIA v ZIMBABWE

At Cuttack, April 9. India won by 32 runs. Toss: Zimbabwe.

India continued their impressive form to set a daunting target, despite languishing at 26 for three in the ninth over. When Jadeja joined Azharuddin the nature of the contest changed abruptly. Neither batsman gave a chance, though Azharuddin, just after reaching his century, pulled a no-ball from Huckle to deep mid-wicket. He walked, only to be recalled a moment later. In ferocious heat, the pair then extended their unbroken partnership to 275, an all-wicket one-day international record, beating the 263 added by Aamir Sohail and Inzamam-ul-Haq for Pakistan against New Zealand in 1993-94. Azharuddin's eventual 153 not out took 150 balls and included 17 fours and a six. In Zimbabwe's reply, Grant Flower scored a gritty century, but wickets fell with regularity – and India were never threatened.

Man of the Match: M. Azharuddin.

India

S. C. Ganguly c A. Flower b Streak ...	13	A. Jadeja not out	116	
S. R. Tendulkar c A. Flower b Mbangwa	1	L-b 2, w 14, n-b 2	18	
V. V. S. Laxman lbw b Mbangwa	0			
*M. Azharuddin not out	153	1/8 2/8 3/26 (3 wkts, 50 overs)	301	

H. H. Kanitkar, †N. R. Mongia, A. B. Agarkar, B. K. V. Prasad, D. S. Mohanty and R. Sanghvi did not bat.

Bowling: Streak 10–0–56–1; Mbangwa 9–0–47–2; Whittall 8–0–68–0; Brent 5–0–26–0; Huckle 8–1–42–0; Evans 6–0–39–0; G. W. Flower 4–0–21–0.

Zimbabwe

G. W. Flower c and b Sanghvi	102	G. B. Brent b Kanitkar	24	
*A. D. R. Campbell c Azharuddin		M. Mbangwa c Prasad b Kanitkar	8	
b Prasad ..	11	A. G. Huckle not out	0	
M. W. Goodwin c Kanitkar b Agarkar ..	47			
†A. Flower b Agarkar	3	L-b 6, w 9, n-b 4	19	
G. J. Whittall run out	13			
H. H. Streak b Ganguly	30	1/23 2/92 3/104 (48.4 overs)	269	
P. A. Strang run out	8	4/121 5/188 6/204		
C. N. Evans b Ganguly	4	7/211 8/255 9/269		

Bowling: Prasad 7–0–40–1; Mohanty 10–0–54–0; Agarkar 8–0–45–2; Ganguly 8–0–34–2; Sanghvi 7–0–44–1; Kanitkar 6.4–0–26–2; Tendulkar 2–0–20–0.

Umpires: N. Menon and R. Nagarajan.

AUSTRALIA v ZIMBABWE

At Delhi, April 11. Australia won by 16 runs. Toss: Zimbabwe.

By beating Zimbabwe in the last qualifying match, Australia ensured their place in the final and gained much-needed confidence. Mark Waugh and Ponting put on 219 for the second wicket to wrest the initiative from the bowlers; Guy Whittall was hit for 52 from his five overs. Ponting's aggressive innings – more than half his runs came in boundaries – equalled the highest one-day international score by an Australian: Dean Jones had also made 145, against England at Brisbane in 1990-91. For the umpteenth time, Zimbabwe failed to capitalise on a steady start: the Flower brothers took them to 219 for two in the 41st over but the rest faded.

Man of the Match: R. T. Ponting.

Australia

†A. C. Gilchrist c A. Flower b Mbangwa	1	D. R. Martyn not out	8
M. E. Waugh b Streak	87		
R. T. Ponting c Mbangwa			
b G. J. Whittall	145	L-b 6, w 13, n-b 1	20
M. G. Bevan not out	33	1/2 2/221 3/268 (3 wkts, 50 overs)	294

*S. R. Waugh, D. S. Lehmann, S. K. Warne, G. R. Robertson, D. W. Fleming and M. S. Kasprowicz did not bat.

Bowling: Streak 10–0–64–1; Mbangwa 10–0–58–1; G. J. Whittall 5–0–52–1; Huckle 8–0–45–0; A. R. Whittall 10–1–31–0; Evans 5–0–29–0; Goodwin 2–0–9–0.

Zimbabwe

G. W. Flower b Warne	89	P. A. Strang lbw b Fleming	2
*A. D. R. Campbell c S. R. Waugh		A. R. Whittall b Fleming	0
b Kasprowicz	1	M. Mbangwa b Kasprowicz	0
M. W. Goodwin c Kasprowicz		A. G. Huckle not out	5
b S. R. Waugh	46	L-b 10, w 7, n-b 5	22
†A. Flower run out	73		
C. N. Evans run out	6	1/2 2/98 3/219 (9 wkts, 50 overs)	278
G. J. Whittall c Warne b Lehmann	7	4/226 5/227 6/246	
H. H. Streak not out	27	7/256 8/256 9/260	

Bowling: Fleming 10–1–39–2; Kasprowicz 10–1–47–2; Warne 10–0–54–1; S. R. Waugh 10–0–55–1; Robertson 4–0–31–0; Bevan 3–0–19–0; Martyn 2–0–15–0; Lehmann 1–0–8–1.

Umpires: S. Dandapani and O. Krishna.

QUALIFYING TABLE

	Played	Won	Lost	Points	Net run-rate
India	4	4	0	8	0.59
Australia	4	2	2	4	–0.21
Zimbabwe	4	0	4	0	–0.37

Net run-rate was calculated by subtracting runs conceded per over from runs scored per over.

FINAL

INDIA v AUSTRALIA

At Delhi, April 14. Australia won by four wickets. Toss: India.

Producing hostile bowling and responsible batting when it really mattered, Australia exacted revenge for their defeats in the qualifying matches. With the top six all getting in, the Indian innings promised much, but delivered only 227. Early on, Fleming and Kasprowicz found bounce – Tendulkar edged a ball that was heading for his throat – though others, such as Azharuddin and Sidhu, fell to rash shots. Ponting and Bevan steered the Australian reply towards victory and, with ten overs to go, they were 169 for four. Whereas India – 168 for four at the same stage – lost their last six wickets for another 59, the Australians coasted home.

Man of the Match: S. R. Waugh. *Man of the Tournament:* A. Jadeja.

India

S. C. Ganguly c Gilchrist b Moody	29	A. Kumble not out	1
S. R. Tendulkar c Gilchrist b Fleming	15	B. K. V. Prasad b Kasprowicz	1
*M. Azharuddin c Bevan b S. R. Waugh	44	R. Sanghvi run out	0
N. S. Sidhu c Fleming b S. R. Waugh	38	B 2, l-b 6, w 6, n-b 1	15
A. Jadeja c and b Kasprowicz	48		
H. H. Kanitkar b Fleming	18	1/37 2/58 3/128	(49.3 overs) 227
A. B. Agarkar c S. R. Waugh b Warne	4	4/144 5/177 6/185	
†N. R. Mongia c Bevan b Fleming	14	7/218 8/225 9/227	

Bowling: Fleming 10–1–47–3; Kasprowicz 9.3–0–43–2; Moody 10–0–40–1; Warne 10–0–35–1; S. R. Waugh 7–0–42–2; Lehmann 3–0–12–0.

Australia

M. E. Waugh b Kumble	20	T. M. Moody c Jadeja b Agarkar	4
†A. C. Gilchrist b Agarkar	1	D. S. Lehmann not out	6
R. T. Ponting st Mongia b Sanghvi	41	L-b 6, w 5, n-b 2	13
M. G. Bevan not out	75		
S. K. Warne b Prasad	14	1/6 2/56 3/84	(6 wkts, 48.4 overs) 231
*S. R. Waugh b Kumble	57	4/111 5/210 6/219	

D. R. Martyn, D. W. Fleming and M. S. Kasprowicz did not bat.

Bowling: Prasad 7–0–43–1; Agarkar 10–1–53–2; Kumble 9.4–2–36–2; Kanitkar 7–0–35–0; Sanghvi 10–0–45–1; Tendulkar 5–0–13–0.

Umpires: V. Chopra and V. K. Ramaswamy.
Series referee: P. L. van der Merwe (South Africa).

STANDARD BANK INTERNATIONAL ONE-DAY SERIES, 1997-98

By QAMAR AHMED

South Africa deservedly won another limited-overs tournament, having dominated it from start to finish. They were undoubtedly the best all-round side, fielding superbly, bowling magnificently and batting sensibly to outplay Pakistan and World Cup holders Sri Lanka. Though they started the competition without their first-choice attack of Shaun Pollock, who was injured, and Allan Donald, attending the birth of his second child, understudies Roger Telemachus and Lance Klusener were more than adequate to their task, collecting 23 wickets between them, while Jacques Kallis and Jonty Rhodes both topped 200 runs.

Their only defeat was at the hands of Sri Lanka, who recovered from a disastrous start – three straight defeats – to fall just short of winning a place in the final. Arjuna Ranatunga and Marvan Atapattu played some excellent innings, though Sanath Jayasuriya and Aravinda de Silva failed to strike form. Muttiah Muralitharan took 14 wickets, second only to Wasim Akram, with 15, who played a key role in Pakistan's two victories over Sri Lanka. Pakistan were weakened by the loss of several players to injury during their recent visit to Zimbabwe. But thanks to Wasim and occasional flashes of brilliance from the batsmen, they outplayed Sri Lanka long enough to reach the final – only to collapse when they got there.

Note: Matches in this section were not first-class.

SOUTH AFRICA v PAKISTAN

At Durban, April 3 (day/night). South Africa won by 52 runs. Toss: South Africa. International debuts: S. Elworthy, R. Telemachus.

Kallis and Rhodes combined at 97 for four to set South Africa on the road to victory. Kallis scored 109 from 114 balls and Rhodes 94 from 95; their unbroken stand of 183 was a South African record for the fifth wicket. Then debutants Steve Elworthy and Roger Telemachus, sharing the new ball because Donald and Pollock were absent, put the skids under Pakistan's top order, who collapsed to 75 for seven. The last three wickets trebled the score. Moin Khan and Wasim Akram added 53, while Abdur Razzaq and Waqar Younis put on 72 for the last wicket, but they had been left too much to do. Razzaq's unbeaten 46 was the highest score by a No. 10 in one-day internationals.

Man of the Match: J. H. Kallis.   Attendance: 21,162.

South Africa

G. Kirsten c Mohammad Wasim b Wasim Akram .	0	*W. J. Cronje run out 34
M. J. R. Rindel c Moin Khan b Waqar Younis .	17	J. H. Kallis not out 109
D. J. Cullinan c Mohammad Wasim b Wasim Akram .	16	J. N. Rhodes not out. 94
		B 4, l-b 2, w 2, n-b 2 10
		1/1 2/26 3/48 4/97 (4 wkts, 50 overs) 280

L. Klusener, †M. V. Boucher, S. Elworthy, P. L. Symcox and R. Telemachus did not bat.

Bowling: Wasim Akram 10–0–39–2; Waqar Younis 10–0–73–1; Azhar Mahmood 10–0–59–0; Abdur Razzaq 5.2–0–15–0; Shahid Afridi 9.4–0–52–0; Aamir Sohail 5–0–36–0.

Pakistan

Saeed Anwar lbw b Elworthy	0	Wasim Akram b Symcox 27
Shahid Afridi c Cullinan b Elworthy . . .	19	Abdur Razzaq not out 46
*Aamir Sohail b Telemachus	8	Waqar Younis b Telemachus 33
Mohammad Wasim c and b Cronje . . .	9	B 2, l-b 6, w 5, n-b 7 20
Ijaz Ahmed, sen. c Cronje b Klusener . .	5	
Yousuf Youhana run out	15	1/1 2/18 3/37 (47.4 overs) 228
†Moin Khan b Klusener	45	4/45 5/63 6/72
Azhar Mahmood c Kallis b Klusener . . .	1	7/75 8/128 9/156

Bowling: Elworthy 8–0–25–2; Telemachus 8.4–0–40–2; Cronje 9–0–31–1; Klusener 10–2–31–3; Kallis 5–0–50–0; Symcox 7–0–43–1.

Umpires: W. A. Diedricks and D. L. Orchard.

SOUTH AFRICA v SRI LANKA

At Johannesburg, April 5. South Africa won by 57 runs. Toss: South Africa.

Left-handed opener Rindel set up South Africa's innings, sharing half-century stands with Kirsten and Klusener, and Rhodes kept up the momentum with a brisk 43 from 51 balls. A target of 5.4 an over was not beyond Sri Lanka's celebrated line-up, especially while Jayasuriya was adding a quickfire 65 with de Silva. Jayasuriya hit six fours and one six, interspersed with a couple of chances, but, once Cronje broke the stand, the innings fell apart. Crookes and Telemachus cleaned up the lower order, though last man Muralitharan denied Telemachus a hat-trick.

Man of the Match: R. Telemachus.   Attendance: 30,630.

South Africa

M. J. R. Rindel st Kaluwitharana		D. N. Crookes c Wickremasinghe	
b Muralitharan .	59	b Dharmasena .	26
G. Kirsten b de Silva	29	†M. V. Boucher b Jayasuriya	6
L. Klusener b de Silva	26	S. Elworthy not out	14
D. J. Cullinan b Chandana	24	L-b 11, w 1	12
*W. J. Cronje c de Silva			—
b Chandana .	22	1/67 2/117 3/121 (8 wkts, 50 overs) 266	
J. H. Kallis c Vaas b Chandana	5	4/160 5/169 6/172	
J. N. Rhodes not out	43	7/218 8/243	

R. Telemachus did not bat.

Bowling: Vaas 7–0–33–0; Wickremasinghe 6–0–32–0; Dharmasena 6–0–37–1; de Silva 6–0–26–2; Muralitharan 10–0–39–1; Chandana 10–1–48–3; Jayasuriya 5–0–40–1.

Sri Lanka

S. T. Jayasuriya c Crookes b Cronje	68	U. D. U. Chandana c Klusener	
M. S. Atapattu c Rhodes		b Elworthy .	26
b Telemachus .	4	W. P. U. J. C. Vaas b Telemachus	8
R. S. Mahanama c Kirsten b Elworthy	11	G. P. Wickremasinghe b Telemachus	0
P. A. de Silva c Rindel b Cronje	28	M. Muralitharan not out	13
†R. S. Kaluwitharana c Boucher		B 3, l-b 3, w 3, n-b 2	11
b Telemachus .	19		—
*A. Ranatunga c Boucher b Crookes	0	1/12 2/51 3/116 (46.3 overs) 209	
H. D. P. K. Dharmasena c Rindel		4/127 5/127 6/151	
b Crookes .	21	7/169 8/182 9/182	

Bowling: Elworthy 8.3–1–34–2; Telemachus 10–0–43–4; Cronje 9–0–43–2; Klusener 9–0–46–0; Crookes 10–1–37–2.

Umpires: S. B. Lambson and C. J. Mitchley.

PAKISTAN v SRI LANKA

At Kimberley, April 7. Pakistan won by four wickets. Toss: Sri Lanka.

Pakistan batted gloriously in perfect conditions to score more than a run a ball. They had one over docked, because of their slow over-rate, but soared to 300 with six balls to spare. Inzamam-ul-Haq, who arrived after both openers fell cheaply, hit a hurricane 116 from 110 balls. His fifth century at this level included four sixes and four fours, and he was backed up by Ijaz Ahmed, who also hit four sixes, and Moin Khan. Earlier, Sri Lanka's openers punished ragged fielding and bowling in a stand of 107. Kaluwitharana scored 54 off 52 balls; oddly, he hit no boundaries, while Jayasuriya's slower 57, taking 71 balls, included seven fours and a six. De Silva and Ranatunga put on 142 to set up a total of 295, which they must have thought quite enough.

Man of the Match: Inzamam-ul-Haq.   *Attendance:* 7,156.

Sri Lanka

S. T. Jayasuriya c Rashid Latif		U. D. U. Chandana run out	1
b Abdur Razzaq .	57	H. D. P. K. Dharmasena not out	1
†R. S. Kaluwitharana run out	54		
P. A. de Silva b Wasim Akram	62	L-b 2, w 12, n-b 4	18
*A. Ranatunga c Azhar Mahmood			—
b Wasim Akram .	86	1/107 2/128 3/270 (7 wkts, 50 overs) 295	
R. S. Mahanama b Wasim Akram	10	4/287 5/287	
D. P. M. D. Jayawardene run out	6	6/291 7/295	

W. P. U. J. C. Vaas, K. R. Pushpakumara and M. Muralitharan did not bat.

Bowling: Wasim Akram 10–1–53–3; Waqar Younis 10–1–68–0; Abdur Razzaq 8–0–51–1; Azhar Mahmood 9–0–60–0; Mohammad Hussain 10–0–40–0; Ijaz Ahmed 3–0–21–0.

Pakistan

Saeed Anwar c Mahanama	Azhar Mahmood c Pushpakumara
b Pushpakumara . 17	b Muralitharan . 2
Abdur Razzaq c and b Pushpakumara . . 15	Wasim Akram not out 19
Ijaz Ahmed, sen. c Pushpakumara	
b Dharmasena . 59	B 1, l-b 11, w 5, n-b 1 18
Inzamam-ul-Haq not out 116	
Moin Khan c Vaas b Dharmasena 34	1/31 2/46 3/126 (6 wkts, 48 overs) 300
Mohammad Hussain b Vaas 20	4/212 5/260 6/269

Yousuf Youhana, *†Rashid Latif and Waqar Younis did not bat.

Bowling: Vaas 10–0–58–1; Pushpakumara 8–0–56–2; de Silva 1–0–11–0; Dharmasena 10–0–35–2; Muralitharan 10–0–61–1; Chandana 6–0–42–0; Jayasuriya 3–0–25–0.

Umpires: D. F. Becker and R. E. Koertzen.

PAKISTAN v SRI LANKA

At Paarl, April 9 (day/night). Pakistan won by 110 runs. Toss: Pakistan.

Sri Lanka went down to their third defeat in three games, and their heaviest yet: they were skittled for 139 inside 35 overs, apparently hindered by floodlights that failed to reach full power. Wasim Akram and Waqar Younis led the assault, removing the first four wickets for 54. After electing to bat first, Pakistan made a brisk start, thanks to Saeed Anwar and Ijaz Ahmed, who scored 65 in 79 balls in his 200th one-day international. But a middle-order slump saw three wickets fall for one run, and it was only the wagging tail which lifted them to 249.

Man of the Match: Wasim Akram. *Attendance:* 7,428.

Pakistan

Saeed Anwar c Jayasuriya b Muralitharan 53	Wasim Akram c and b P. A. de Silva . . . 22
Shahid Afridi c Dharmasena	Abdur Razzaq c Jayawardene
b K. S. C. de Silva . 17	b P. A. de Silva . 22
Ijaz Ahmed, sen. run out 65	Mohammad Hussain c Mahanama
Inzamam-ul-Haq c Kaluwitharana	b P. A. de Silva . 10
b Muralitharan . 9	Waqar Younis not out 2
Yousuf Youhana st Kaluwitharana	
b Muralitharan . 0	L-b 4, w 6, n-b 3 13
Azhar Mahmood c Mahanama	
b Chandana . 0	1/31 2/111 3/141 (48.5 overs) 249
*†Rashid Latif c K. S. C. de Silva	4/141 5/142 6/164
b P. A. de Silva . 36	7/214 8/214 9/240

Bowling: Pushpakumara 8–0–46–0; K. S. C. de Silva 6–0–41–1; Dharmasena 10–0–49–0; Muralitharan 10–0–29–3; Chandana 4–0–19–1; Jayasuriya 3–0–16–0; P. A. de Silva 7.5–0–45–4.

Sri Lanka

S. T. Jayasuriya lbw b Waqar Younis . . . 8	M. Muralitharan c Shahid Afridi
†R. S. Kaluwitharana c Rashid Latif	b Azhar Mahmood . 0
b Wasim Akram . 18	K. R. Pushpakumara b Azhar Mahmood . 0
R. S. Mahanama lbw b Wasim Akram . . 7	K. S. C. de Silva not out 0
P. A. de Silva b Abdur Razzaq 31	
*A. Ranatunga lbw b Waqar Younis . . 2	L-b 6, w 15, n-b 1 22
D. P. M. D. Jayawardene run out 11	
H. D. P. K. Dharmasena c Yousuf Youhana	1/19 2/39 3/47 (34.2 overs) 139
b Mohammad Hussain . 17	4/54 5/91 6/93
U. D. U. Chandana c Rashid Latif	7/128 8/132 9/132
b Wasim Akram . 23	

Bowling: Wasim Akram 7.2–1–24–3; Waqar Younis 7–0–41–2; Azhar Mahmood 10–1–27–2; Abdur Razzaq 5–0–16–1; Mohammad Hussain 5–0–25–1.

Umpires: W. A. Diedricks and C. J. Mitchley.

SOUTH AFRICA v PAKISTAN

At East London, April 11. South Africa won by three wickets. Toss: Pakistan.

This was South Africa's tenth successive one-day win over Pakistan, a sequence stretching back to January 1995. Rindel and Pollock made sixties after Wasim Akram struck early – by bowling Kallis, he became the first bowler to take 350 wickets in one-day internationals, in his 244th game. But it was Cronje who ensured victory with three overs to spare, scoring 52 from 53 balls with five sixes and a four. Cronje had also taken two cheap wickets to set back Pakistan. They were helped to a respectable 250 by some purposeful batting by Inzamam-ul-Haq and Yousuf Youhana, followed by a belligerent 57 from Wasim.

Man of the Match: W. J. Cronje.   *Attendance:* 12,122.

Pakistan

Saeed Anwar c Gibbs b Cronje	28		*†Rashid Latif run out	3
Azhar Mahmood c Cronje b Pollock	14		Mohammad Hussain not out	26
Ijaz Ahmed, sen. c Boucher b Cronje	0		L-b 7, w 13, n-b 2	22
Inzamam-ul-Haq lbw b Klusener	52			—
Yousuf Youhana c Kallis b Crookes	39		1/37 2/41 3/56 (8 wkts, 50 overs)	250
Wasim Akram run out	57		4/142 5/162 6/189	
Moin Khan b Elworthy	9		7/197 8/250	

Abdur Razzaq and Waqar Younis did not bat.

Bowling: Pollock 10–0–47–1; Elworthy 9–0–70–1; Cronje 10–2–17–2; Klusener 10–0–50–1; Crookes 9–0–43–1; Kallis 2–0–16–0.

South Africa

M. J. R. Rindel b Abdur Razzaq	64		J. N. Rhodes c Rashid Latif	
J. H. Kallis b Wasim Akram	6		b Azhar Mahmood	10
H. H. Gibbs c Mohammad Hussain			D. N. Crookes not out	3
b Waqar Younis	5		L. Klusener not out	5
D. J. Cullinan b Waqar Younis	11		L-b 9, w 17, n-b 6	32
S. M. Pollock c Inzamam-ul-Haq				—
b Azhar Mahmood	66		1/11 2/34 3/83 4/122 (7 wkts, 46.2 overs)	254
*W. J. Cronje b Azhar Mahmood	52		5/211 6/230 7/242	

†M. V. Boucher and S. Elworthy did not bat.

Bowling: Wasim Akram 10–1–40–1; Waqar Younis 10–1–47–2; Azhar Mahmood 10–0–50–3; Abdur Razzaq 6.2–0–33–1; Ijaz Ahmed 4–0–35–0; Mohammad Hussain 6–0–40–0.

Umpires: S. B. Lambson and D. L. Orchard.

SOUTH AFRICA v SRI LANKA

At Port Elizabeth, April 13. Sri Lanka won by six wickets. Toss: South Africa.

South Africa suffered their only defeat of the tournament as Sri Lanka celebrated their first win. It looked an unlikely outcome when Sri Lanka lost their first three wickets for 17, chasing 232. But that brought in Ranatunga, to share successive century stands with Atapattu and Mahanama. He finished unbeaten on 93, including nine fours and a six, as his team won with 20 balls to spare. South Africa, by contrast, started well but declined from 78 without loss to 104 for four. Despite the efforts of Gibbs and Rhodes, the innings never really took off against some tight bowling.

Man of the Match: A. Ranatunga.   *Attendance:* 10,643.

South Africa

M. J. R. Rindel b Vaas	35	J. H. Kallis lbw b Jayasuriya	1
G. Kirsten c Atapattu b Muralitharan	46	†M. V. Boucher lbw b Vaas	14
P. L. Symcox c Muralitharan		L. Klusener c Atapattu b Vaas	18
b Dharmasena	13	R. Telemachus not out	1
H. H. Gibbs c Muralitharan b Jayasuriya	33		
*W. J. Cronje c Ranatunga		B 1, l-b 9, w 2	12
b Muralitharan	0		—
J. N. Rhodes st Kaluwitharana		1/78 2/94 3/104 (49.5 overs) 231	
b Muralitharan	36	4/104 5/150 6/186	
S. M. Pollock c de Silva b Chandana	22	7/189 8/201 9/230	

Bowling: Vaas 7.5–0–33–3; Wickremasinghe 6–0–28–0; Dharmasena 10–0–37–1; Muralitharan 10–1–47–3; Chandana 9–0–42–1; Jayasuriya 7–0–34–2.

Sri Lanka

S. T. Jayasuriya c Cronje b Telemachus	7	R. S. Mahanama not out	46
†R. S. Kaluwitharana lbw b Telemachus	4	L-b 9, w 7, n-b 2	18
M. S. Atapattu b Kallis	63		—
P. A. de Silva b Pollock	1	1/8 2/15 (4 wkts, 46.4 overs) 232	
*A. Ranatunga not out	93	3/17 4/125	

H. D. P. K. Dharmasena, U. D. U. Chandana, W. P. U. J. C. Vaas, G. P. Wickremasinghe and M. Muralitharan did not bat.

Bowling: Pollock 8–0–29–1; Telemachus 7–1–37–2; Klusener 8–0–47–0; Cronje 7.4–0–36–0; Kallis 7–0–30–1; Symcox 9–0–44–0.

Umpires: D. F. Becker and R. E. Koertzen.

PAKISTAN v SRI LANKA

At Benoni, April 15. Sri Lanka won by 115 runs. Toss: Pakistan.

Sri Lanka's revival continued as Pakistan's batting let them down again. They had no hope of reaching 289 once the strike bowlers reduced them to 44 for four. Though Saeed Anwar held firm to score 59, he became one of five victims for Muralitharan, and Pakistan were bowled out in the 40th over. Sri Lanka had wobbled slightly at 94 for three, but Atapattu and Ranatunga assumed control in a stand of 138. Ranatunga scored 78 from 72 balls before being bowled by Wasim Akram, who added Wickremasinghe next ball. Mahanama averted the hat-trick.

Man of the Match: M. S. Atapattu. *Attendance:* 5,122.

Sri Lanka

S. T. Jayasuriya b Azhar Mahmood	30	H. D. P. K. Dharmasena c Shahid Afridi	
†R. S. Kaluwitharana c Mushtaq Ahmed		b Waqar Younis	20
b Wasim Akram	33	W. P. U. J. C. Vaas run out	4
M. S. Atapattu b Wasim Akram	94	M. Muralitharan not out	1
P. A. de Silva b Abdur Razzaq	2		
*A. Ranatunga b Wasim Akram	78	L-b 12, w 12	24
G. P. Wickremasinghe c Waqar Younis			—
b Wasim Akram	0	1/56 2/91 3/94 (49.4 overs) 288	
R. S. Mahanama run out	2	4/232 5/232 6/238	
D. P. M. D. Jayawardene c Rashid Latif		7/238 8/281 9/286	
b Waqar Younis	0		

Bowling: Wasim Akram 9.4–1–43–4; Waqar Younis 10–0–86–2; Abdur Razzaq 9–1–50–1; Azhar Mahmood 10–0–33–1; Mushtaq Ahmed 9–0–46–0; Shahid Afridi 2–0–18–0.

Pakistan

Saeed Anwar b Muralitharan	59	Wasim Akram st Kaluwitharana	
Shahid Afridi run out	6	b Muralitharan .	13
Ijaz Ahmed, sen. c Kaluwitharana		*†Rashid Latif b Muralitharan	6
b Vaas .	8	Waqar Younis c Vaas b Muralitharan	17
Abdur Razzaq b Vaas	0	Mushtaq Ahmed not out	1
Inzamam-ul-Haq c Kaluwitharana		L-b 12, w 6	18
b Wickremasinghe	3		
Yousuf Youhana run out	29	1/11 2/32 3/33 (39.2 overs) 173	
Azhar Mahmood c Dharmasena		4/44 5/108 6/126	
b Muralitharan .	13	7/142 8/151 9/156	

Bowling: Vaas 7–0–33–2; Wickremasinghe 7–1–23–1; Dharmasena 8–0–30–0; Jayawardene 3–0–17–0; Muralitharan 9.2–0–23–5; Jayasuriya 5–0–35–0.

Umpires: S. B. Lambson and C. J. Mitchley.

SOUTH AFRICA v PAKISTAN

At Centurion, April 17. South Africa won by seven wickets. Toss: Pakistan.

South Africa ensured their place in the finals in a tediously one-sided game, needing only 42 overs to bundle out Pakistan and a mere 36 to overtake a paltry total of 145. Pakistan's batsmen were frustrated by South Africa's pace attack, which included Donald, playing his 100th one-day international and his first since he was injured in the Second Test against Sri Lanka. But three Pakistanis fell to run-outs, brilliantly executed by Kallis, Crookes and Rhodes. Though opener Rindel fell for nought, Kallis shared half-century stands with Kirsten and Cullinan to steer his side to a predictable win.

Man of the Match: J. H. Kallis.   *Attendance:* 15,291.

Pakistan

Saeed Anwar c Rhodes b Klusener	3	*†Rashid Latif not out	6
Azhar Mahmood c Cullinan b Klusener	20	Abdur Razzaq b Elworthy	0
Mohammad Wasim c Crookes b Donald	18	Mushtaq Ahmed run out	0
Ijaz Ahmed, sen. b Elworthy	2	B 2, 1-b 4, w 5, n-b 1	12
Inzamam-ul-Haq run out	33		
Moin Khan c Cronje b Elworthy	25	1/10 2/25 3/31 (41.5 overs) 145	
Wasim Akram b Rindel	12	4/57 5/95 6/114	
Mohammad Hussain run out	14	7/135 8/142 9/142	

Bowling: Elworthy 9–1–28–3; Klusener 7.5–0–27–2; Cronje 6–0–18–0; Donald 8–0–22–1; Rindel 7–0–23–1; Crookes 4–0–21–0.

South Africa

M. J. R. Rindel c Rashid Latif		*W. J. Cronje not out	7
b Wasim Akram .	0		
G. Kirsten b Azhar Mahmood	35		
J. H. Kallis not out	79	B 4, 1-b 5, w 2, n-b 3	14
D. J. Cullinan c Azhar Mahmood			
b Mohammad Hussain .	14	1/1 2/65 3/116 (3 wkts, 35.3 overs) 149	

J. N. Rhodes, †M. V. Boucher, L. Klusener, D. N. Crookes, S. Elworthy and A. A. Donald did not bat.

Bowling: Wasim Akram 8–0–26–1; Mohammad Hussain 10–1–51–1; Azhar Mahmood 5–1–19–1; Mushtaq Ahmed 10–0–31–0; Abdur Razzaq 2.3–0–13–0.

Umpires: W. A. Diedricks and R. E. Koertzen.

SOUTH AFRICA v SRI LANKA

At Bloemfontein, April 19. South Africa won by five wickets. Toss: South Africa.

At the start of this match, Sri Lanka were level on points with Pakistan. But they threw away their chance of entering the final by crashing for 105 in just 36 overs. Telemachus and Pollock grabbed four wickets for 12 runs and Sri Lanka, tied up by tight bowling and electrifying fielding, never really recovered from the shock. Though the South African openers went early, Kallis and Cullinan made sure of victory. It was all over by 3.35 p.m., so, to entertain the disappointed crowd, the teams staged a double-wicket contest. South Africa won this, too, Crookes and Klusener beating Dharmasena and Chandana.

Man of the Match: R. Telemachus.   *Attendance:* 11,663.

Sri Lanka

S. T. Jayasuriya c Gibbs b Telemachus . .	7	U. D. U. Chandana c Kirsten b Kallis . .	5
†R. S. Kaluwitharana c Kirsten		W. P. U. J. C. Vaas not out	10
b Telemachus .	11	G. P. Wickremasinghe c Cronje b Kallis .	0
M. S. Atapattu b Pollock	4	M. Muralitharan c Pollock b Symcox . .	0
P. A. de Silva c Boucher b Pollock	0	L-b 8, w 10, n-b 1	19
*A. Ranatunga c Boucher b Donald . . .	13		—
R. S. Mahanama c Boucher b Cronje . .	22	1/14 2/23 3/23	(36 overs) 105
H. D. P. K. Dharmasena c Kallis		4/26 5/50 6/71	
b Pollock .	14	7/93 8/95 9/104	

Bowling: Pollock 8–2–21–3; Telemachus 8–1–23–2; Donald 6–0–12–1; Cronje 6–1–23–1; Kallis 6–1–16–2; Symcox 2–0–2–1.

South Africa

G. Kirsten b Wickremasinghe	0	J. N. Rhodes not out	23
H. H. Gibbs c Kaluwitharana		S. M. Pollock not out	2
b Wickremasinghe .	10	L-b 2, w 6, n-b 1	9
J. H. Kallis c Atapattu b Muralitharan . .	39		—
D. J. Cullinan c and b Dharmasena	18	1/7 2/24 3/74	(5 wkts, 26.3 overs) 106
†M. V. Boucher run out	5	4/80 5/91	

*W. J. Cronje, P. L. Symcox, A. A. Donald and R. Telemachus did not bat.

Bowling: Vaas 5–0–30–0; Wickremasinghe 8–2–22–2; Muralitharan 8.3–1–34–1; Dharmasena 5–0–18–1.

Umpires: D. F. Becker and D. L. Orchard.

QUALIFYING TABLE

	Played	Won	Lost	Points	Net run-rate
South Africa	6	5	1	10	1.03
Pakistan	6	2	4	4	−0.47
Sri Lanka	6	2	4	4	−0.55

Pakistan qualified for the final ahead of Sri Lanka because they had won two of their three head-to-head games. Net run-rate was calculated by subtracting runs conceded per over from runs scored per over.

FINAL

SOUTH AFRICA v PAKISTAN

At Cape Town, April 23. South Africa won by nine wickets. Toss: South Africa.

Rain forced the final to be abandoned on April 22 and replayed the next day. South Africa easily maintained their dominance over Pakistan in one-day cricket, taking their winning streak to 12 games. On a bouncy pitch, they dismissed them for 114 and then cantered home, losing only Rindel as Kirsten scored an unbeaten fifty. Pakistan collapsed from 84 for three to lose seven wickets for 30, five of them to Klusener, who seamed and swung the ball to great effect. Saeed Anwar hit three sixes in his 30 runs, but only three others reached double figures, including Inzamam-ul-Haq, who was unlucky to be given caught behind by umpire Mitchley.

Man of the Match: L. Klusener.   *Man of the Series:* J. N. Rhodes.
Attendance: 14,554.

Pakistan

Saeed Anwar c Boucher b Klusener	30	Abdur Razzaq c Kallis b Klusener	6
Mohammad Wasim run out	8	Waqar Younis c Kallis b Telemachus	15
Ijaz Ahmed, sen. c Kirsten b Telemachus	0	Mushtaq Ahmed not out	0
Inzamam-ul-Haq c Boucher b Cronje	21	L-b 1, w 8, n-b 1	10
Moin Khan c Rindel b Klusener	19		
Wasim Akram run out	2	1/26 2/27 3/54	(37.1 overs) 114
Azhar Mahmood b Klusener	0	4/84 5/87 6/87	
*†Rashid Latif c Rhodes b Klusener	3	7/90 8/93 9/113	

Bowling: Pollock 8–1–13–0; Telemachus 10–1–31–2; Donald 6–1–27–0; Klusener 7.1–1–25–5; Cronje 6–1–17–1.

South Africa

M. J. R. Rindel c Rashid Latif b Wasim Akram	20
G. Kirsten not out	52
J. H. Kallis not out	28
L-b 4, w 6, n-b 5	15
1/54	(1 wkt, 27.4 overs) 115

D. J. Cullinan, *W. J. Cronje, J. N. Rhodes, S. M. Pollock, †M. V. Boucher, L. Klusener, A. A. Donald and R. Telemachus did not bat.

Bowling: Wasim Akram 10–1–29–1; Waqar Younis 9–1–32–0; Azhar Mahmood 4–0–17–0; Abdur Razzaq 2–0–17–0; Mushtaq Ahmed 2.4–0–16–0.

Umpires: R. E. Koertzen and C. J. Mitchley.   Series referee: J. R. Reid (New Zealand).

COCA-COLA CUP (SHARJAH), 1997-98

Three days before the start of this three-nation competition, India and Australia had been contesting the final of another, the Pepsi Triangular Series, in Delhi. The similarities between the two events extended beyond the sponsors' products. In India, the home team went undefeated until losing the final to Australia: in Sharjah, it was Australia's turn to win all the qualifying matches, only to succumb to India when it mattered.

And, in both events, one Indian batsman stood out above the others. Where Ajay Jadeja had shone in India, so Sachin Tendulkar did in Sharjah. He particularly relished the Australian bowling, with scores of 80, 143 and 134 – each hit at more than a run a ball. In five innings he amassed 435 runs at 87.00. His genius pulled India through into the final and then guided them to victory. The other batsman to enjoy his stint in the desert was Michael Bevan. Until Tendulkar's flourish in the last two matches, he had hogged the batting headlines with a run of consistent scores, accumulating 276 at 92.00.

Unlike the other two teams, New Zealand had no great batting hero. Their fielding was magnificent, but a lack of nerve meant that promising positions were squandered. Batting conditions improved steadily throughout the tournament, ensuring that no bowler ever got on top. Damien Fleming came closest and was pronounced the bowler of the series for taking ten wickets at 15.60.

This was the first Sharjah tournament in ten years not to include Pakistan. Worries over attendance were partly justified for the games not involving India, but 90,000 were thought to have attended the seven matches, including a record 24,000 for the final.

Note: Matches in this section were not first-class.

INDIA v NEW ZEALAND

At Sharjah, April 17 (day/night). India won by 15 runs. Toss: India.

At 170 for four in the 39th over, New Zealand were within easy reach of their modest target. They had done the hard work first by restricting India to 220, despite a dogged hundred from Ganguly, and then by recovering from a poor start which had seen them struggling at 33 for three. But Agarkar, bowling at pace, removed both Fleming and McMillan, who had added 85 for the fifth wicket. The tail offered little resistance, and the Indians had salvaged a victory from an indifferent performance, their first win after five consecutive Sharjah defeats.

Man of the Match: A. B. Agarkar.

India

S. R. Tendulkar c Doull b Harris	40	A. Kumble not out	3
S. C. Ganguly b Nash	105	B. K. V. Prasad run out	5
*M. Azharuddin run out	31	Harbhajan Singh not out	0
N. S. Sidhu lbw b McMillan	4	L-b 2, w 2, n-b 1	5
A. Jadeja c Horne b Nash	17		
H. H. Kanitkar c Doull b Nash	1	1/76 2/148 3/157 (9 wkts, 50 overs)	220
A. B. Agarkar b Cairns	9	4/190 5/195 6/211	
†N. R. Mongia c Howell b Nash	0	7/212 8/212 9/219	

Bowling: Doull 6–1–25–0; Cairns 10–0–47–1; Nash 10–1–38–4; Harris 10–0–45–1; Priest 5–0–29–0; McMillan 9–0–34–1.

New Zealand

L. G. Howell c Mongia b Agarkar	0	D. J. Nash b Agarkar	2
N. J. Astle c Mongia b Prasad	24	M. W. Priest c Jadeja b Kumble	0
C. L. Cairns b Prasad	4	S. B. Doull b Kumble	10
*S. P. Fleming c Kumble b Agarkar	75		
M. J. Horne st Mongia b Harbhajan Singh	16	L-b 5, w 6, n-b 1	12
C. D. McMillan lbw b Agarkar	49	1/0 2/24 3/33 (47.5 overs)	205
C. Z. Harris c Mongia b Kumble	4	4/85 5/170 6/184	
†A. C. Parore not out	9	7/186 8/189 9/190	

Bowling: Agarkar 10–2–35–4; Prasad 8–0–48–2; Kumble 9.5–0–39–3; Harbhajan Singh 10–0–32–1; Ganguly 1–0–4–0; Kanitkar 7–0–29–0; Tendulkar 2–0–13–0.

Umpires: S. A. Bucknor and Javed Akhtar.

AUSTRALIA v NEW ZEALAND

At Sharjah, April 18 (day/night). Australia won by six wickets. Toss: New Zealand.

A listless, one-sided affair saw Australia coast home with six wickets and 13 overs to spare. New Zealand, electing to bat, soon had to dig themselves out of another hole; both openers were gone by the time the score was 28. The captain, Stephen Fleming, again pulled things round with a steady 59, but enjoyed only laboured support. Harris, a naturally exuberant strokeplayer, took 69 balls for his 26. As against India, the lower order capitulated – the last five wickets totalled 16. Damien Fleming finished with four for 28. Gilchrist and Ponting set about the paltry target with alacrity and, although three wickets later fell for nine runs, the result was never in doubt.

Man of the Match: D. W. Fleming.

New Zealand

L. G. Howell lbw b Fleming	13	D. J. Nash not out		2
N. J. Astle run out	7	M. W. Priest c Gilchrist b Fleming		2
C. L. Cairns c and b Moody	19	S. B. O'Connor lbw b Fleming		0
*S. P. Fleming b Robertson	59	L-b 7, w 4		11
M. J. Horne c Moody b Warne	14			
C. D. McMillan c Lehmann b Warne	1	1/20 2/28 3/61	(48.4 overs)	159
C. Z. Harris c Lehmann b M. E. Waugh	26	4/90 5/92 6/143		
†A. C. Parore b Fleming	5	7/153 8/155 9/159		

Bowling: Fleming 9.4–1–28–4; Kasprowicz 6–0–24–0; Moody 5–0–16–0; Warne 10–1–28–2; Robertson 10–0–30–1; M. E. Waugh 8–0–26–1.

Australia

†A. C. Gilchrist c Astle b Harris	57	D. S. Lehmann not out		11
M. E. Waugh c Fleming b O'Connor	11	L-b 6, w 3, n-b 2		11
R. T. Ponting c Horne b Harris	52			
M. G. Bevan not out	15	1/35 2/125	(4 wkts, 36.5 overs)	160
*S. R. Waugh lbw b McMillan	3	3/131 4/134		

T. M. Moody, S. K. Warne, G. R. Robertson, M. S. Kasprowicz and D. W. Fleming did not bat.

Bowling: O'Connor 5–0–31–1; Cairns 5–0–24–0; Nash 4–1–15–0; Harris 10–2–31–2; Priest 9.5–1–42–0; McMillan 3–0–11–1.

Umpires: Javed Akhtar and I. D. Robinson.

AUSTRALIA v INDIA

At Sharjah, April 19 (day/night). Australia won by 58 runs. Toss: Australia.

India were without Agarkar, their match-winner two days earlier, through a thigh injury, and his replacement, Harvinder Singh, proved costly. Most of the Australians got runs and, although no one dominated, a respectable score resulted, thanks in part to substandard fielding. Bevan, the master of the limited-overs game, made 58, a wily innings that contained no boundaries. With the confidence of youth, the 17-year-old off-spinner Harbhajan Singh bravely gave the ball air – and was rewarded with three for 41. In reply, Tendulkar alone offered resistance and, when he departed in the 33rd over with another 104 still needed, so did any chance of an Indian victory.

Man of the Match: S. R. Tendulkar.

Australia

M. E. Waugh run out	16	D. R. Martyn run out		30
†A. C. Gilchrist c Kanitkar		S. K. Warne c Harbhajan Singh b Prasad		19
b Harbhajan Singh	25	M. S. Kasprowicz not out		0
R. T. Ponting b Kumble b Kanitkar	48			
T. M. Moody c Azharuddin		L-b 2, w 7		9
b Harbhajan Singh	39			
M. G. Bevan c Jadeja b Kumble	58	1/33 2/46 3/110	(9 wkts, 50 overs)	264
*S. R. Waugh b Harvinder Singh	8	4/156 5/173 6/196		
D. S. Lehmann b Harbhajan Singh	12	7/227 8/259 9/264		
D. W. Fleming did not bat.				

Bowling: Prasad 8–0–41–1; Harvinder Singh 8–0–50–1; Harbhajan Singh 10–0–41–3; Kumble 10–0–57–1; Kanitkar 10–0–52–1; Tendulkar 4–0–21–0.

India

S. C. Ganguly b Kasprowicz	8	B. K. V. Prasad c M. E. Waugh		
S. R. Tendulkar c Gilchrist b Fleming	80	b S. R. Waugh		2
*M. Azharuddin c Gilchrist b Fleming	9	Harbhajan Singh b S. R. Waugh		4
N. S. Sidhu c Lehmann b Moody	11			
A. Jadeja st Gilchrist b Warne	14			
H. H. Kanitkar lbw b S. R. Waugh	35	L-b 6, w 3		9
†N. R. Mongia c Ponting b Kasprowicz	19			
A. Kumble not out	14	1/15 2/48 3/63	(44 overs)	206
Harvinder Singh c M. E. Waugh		4/94 5/161 6/161		
b S. R. Waugh	1	7/192 8/196 9/198		

Bowling: Fleming 8–0–35–2; Kasprowicz 8–0–40–2; Moody 10–0–40–1; Warne 8–1–37–1; S. R. Waugh 9–0–40–4; Bevan 1–0–8–0.

Umpires: S. A. Bucknor and I. D. Robinson.

INDIA v NEW ZEALAND

At Sharjah, April 20 (day/night). New Zealand won by four wickets. Toss: India. International debut: P. J. Wiseman.

Tight bowling and the suicidal tendency of the Indian top order brought New Zealand their first win of the tournament. After a bright start – 60 for nought in the 13th over – India's three most experienced batsmen all perished to a combination of atrocious running and inspired fielding. Wickets continued to fall regularly and cheaply, and 181 was insufficient even against a side with its own fallibilities. McMillan and Fleming, top scorers for New Zealand in their earlier encounter, set up victory, and raised the prospect of India – effectively the home nation – not reaching the final.

Man of the Match: C. D. McMillan.

India

S. R. Tendulkar run out	38	Harvinder Singh b Cairns		0
S. C. Ganguly c Fleming b Cairns	31	B. K. V. Prasad c Wiseman b Astle		8
*M. Azharuddin run out	11	Harbhajan Singh not out		3
A. Jadeja run out	11	L-b 3, w 8		11
V. V. S. Laxman c O'Connor b Priest	23			
†N. R. Mongia c McMillan b Cairns	22	1/60 2/82 3/85	(49.3 overs)	181
H. H. Kanitkar b Priest	13	4/100 5/131 6/153		
A. Kumble b Astle	10	7/161 8/162 9/172		

Bowling: Doull 5–0–20–0; O'Connor 4–0–29–0; McMillan 6–0–25–0; Cairns 10–1–26–3; Harris 10–2–24–0; Priest 10–1–44–2; Astle 4.3–0–10–2.

New Zealand

M. J. Horne c Azharuddin b Harvinder Singh	4	C. Z. Harris not out	9
N. J. Astle c Mongia b Prasad	14	M. W. Priest not out	2
*S. P. Fleming b Kumble	33		
C. D. McMillan c Mongia b Tendulkar	59	L-b 8, w 5, n-b 3	16
C. L. Cairns c Laxman b Prasad	19		
†A. C. Parore c Harvinder Singh b Kumble	27	(6 wkts, 49 overs)	183

1/18 2/22 3/82 4/116 5/165 6/168

S. B. Doull, P. J. Wiseman and S. B. O'Connor did not bat.

Bowling: Prasad 10–0–34–2; Harvinder Singh 5–0–25–1; Kumble 10–0–26–2; Harbhajan Singh 10–1–30–0; Kanitkar 2–0–12–0; Tendulkar 7–0–28–1; Ganguly 5–0–20–0.

Umpires: S. A. Bucknor and Javed Akhtar.

AUSTRALIA v NEW ZEALAND

At Sharjah, April 21 (day/night). Australia won by five wickets. Toss: New Zealand.

Australia rested three key players – Fleming, Kasprowicz and Ponting – but still ran out convincing winners to ensure their place in the final. In extreme heat, the bowlers suffered as the ball came on enticingly. Determined strokeplay, notably from Astle and Cairns, who lofted Warne for six only to fall to his next delivery, set New Zealand on their way, and 30 came from the last 14 balls. However, it was not enough as Moody and Bevan both hit assured fifties. With no team from the subcontinent involved, the crowd was small.

Man of the Match: T. M. Moody.

New Zealand

L. G. Howell b Harvey	2	C. Z. Harris not out	26
N. J. Astle c and b Harvey	78		
*S. P. Fleming c and b Dale	20	L-b 5, w 6, n-b 1	12
C. D. McMillan run out	43		
C. L. Cairns st Gilchrist b Warne	56	1/9 2/56 3/138 (5 wkts, 50 overs)	259
†A. C. Parore not out	22	4/179 5/229	

D. J. Nash, M. W. Priest, S. B. Doull and P. J. Wiseman did not bat.

Bowling: Dale 10–1–30–1; Harvey 10–0–59–2; Robertson 10–0–41–0; Warne 10–0–56–1; Moody 4–0–21–0; Lehmann 2–0–9–0; S. R. Waugh 4–0–38–0.

Australia

D. S. Lehmann b McMillan	26	†A. C. Gilchrist not out	11
D. R. Martyn c Harris b Doull	16	B 2, l-b 14, w 6	22
*S. R. Waugh lbw b Wiseman	32		
T. M. Moody c Doull b Nash	63		
M. G. Bevan c Parore b Nash	57	1/39 2/59 3/115 (5 wkts, 47.5 overs)	261
M. E. Waugh not out	34	4/188 5/228	

I. J. Harvey, S. K. Warne, G. R. Robertson and A. C. Dale did not bat.

Bowling: Doull 10–0–48–1; Cairns 8.5–0–52–0; Nash 9–1–39–2; McMillan 3–0–14–1; Harris 4–0–28–0; Priest 6–0–25–0; Wiseman 6–0–31–1; Astle 1–0–8–0.

Umpires: Javed Akhtar and I. D. Robinson.

AUSTRALIA v INDIA

At Sharjah, April 22 (day/night). Australia won by 25 runs, India's target having been revised to 276 from 46 overs. Toss: Australia.

At stake was whether India or New Zealand would join Australia in the final. Spectators and organisers were eager to avoid an all-Antipodean final, but Australia were less keen to oblige. Bevan, scoring his third century in one-day internationals, and Mark Waugh took advantage of a true pitch and slipshod fielding. India then had two targets: 285 to win the match, 254 to qualify on run-rate. After a dust storm accounted for four overs, these were revised to 276 and 237. Their success was thanks to a glorious 143 from Tendulkar. His highest score in limited-overs internationals (and the third highest for India) took 131 balls and included nine fours and five sixes. India lost the match, but achieved their main objective.

Man of the Match: S. R. Tendulkar.

Australia

†A. C. Gilchrist c Mongia b Harvinder Singh	11	D. S. Lehmann b Prasad	26
M. E. Waugh c Ganguly b Tendulkar	81	T. M. Moody c Azharuddin b Prasad	5
R. T. Ponting st Mongia b Harbhajan Singh	31	S. K. Warne not out	7
D. R. Martyn b Kumble	1	L-b 4, w 6, n-b 1	11
M. G. Bevan not out	101		
*S. R. Waugh run out	10	1/17 2/84 3/87 (7 wkts, 50 overs)	284

M. S. Kasprowicz and D. W. Fleming did not bat.

4/177 5/197
6/250 7/271

Bowling: Prasad 8–0–41–2; Harvinder Singh 7–0–44–1; Kumble 10–0–41–1; Harbhajan Singh 8–0–63–1; Ganguly 2–0–15–0; Kanitkar 6–0–33–0; Laxman 4–0–16–0; Tendulkar 5–0–27–1.

India

S. C. Ganguly lbw b Fleming	17	H. H. Kanitkar not out	5
S. R. Tendulkar c Gilchrist b Fleming	143		
†N. R. Mongia c M. E. Waugh b Moody	35	L-b 5, w 3, n-b 4	12
*M. Azharuddin b Moody	14		
A. Jadeja c Gilchrist b S. R. Waugh	1	1/38 2/107 3/135 (5 wkts, 46 overs)	250
V. V. S. Laxman not out	23	4/138 5/242	

A. Kumble, Harvinder Singh, B. K. V. Prasad and Harbhajan Singh did not bat.

Bowling: Fleming 10–0–46–2; Kasprowicz 9–0–55–0; Warne 9–0–39–0; Moody 9–0–40–2; S. R. Waugh 9–0–61–1.

Umpires: S. A. Bucknor and I. D. Robinson.

QUALIFYING TABLE

	Played	Won	Lost	Points	Net run-rate
Australia	4	4	0	8	0.78
India	4	1	3	2	–0.33
New Zealand	4	1	3	2	–0.40

India reached the final ahead of New Zealand on net run-rate, having shared the points in their head-to-head matches. Net run-rate was calculated by subtracting runs conceded per over from runs scored per over.

FINAL

AUSTRALIA v INDIA

At Sharjah, April 24 (day/night). India won by six wickets. Toss: India.

India overturned the form of the past week to win the final at a canter. They began well: by the fifth over both Mark Waugh and Ponting had been caught behind. When Moody was given out in similar fashion, Australia were 26 for three. The third umpire confirmed that the ball had indeed carried; the fact that it had not struck Moody's bat was outside his remit. Australia rallied and, thanks to Steve Waugh and Lehmann, who added 103 from 96 balls, set a stiff target. But, to the delight of the partisan spectators, Tendulkar celebrated his 25th birthday by hitting a second successive century, his 15th in one-day internationals. Earlier, Prasad took his 100th one-day international wicket when he dismissed Kasprowicz.

Man of the Match: S. R. Tendulkar.   *Man of the Series:* S. R. Tendulkar.

Australia

M. E. Waugh c Mongia b Agarkar	7	S. K. Warne not out		6
†A. C. Gilchrist c Mongia b Kanitkar	45	M. S. Kasprowicz c Kanitkar b Prasad		0
R. T. Ponting c Mongia b Prasad	1	D. W. Fleming not out		1
T. M. Moody c Mongia b Agarkar	1	B 4, l-b 3, w 2, n-b 1		10
M. G. Bevan run out	45			
*S. R. Waugh c Agarkar b Kanitkar	70	1/18 2/19 3/26	(9 wkts, 50 overs)	272
D. S. Lehmann c Sanghvi b Kumble	70	4/85 5/121 6/224		
D. R. Martyn run out	16	7/255 8/263 9/264		

Bowling: Prasad 10-1-32-2; Agarkar 8-0-61-2; Kumble 10-1-46-1; Kanitkar 10-0-58-2; Sanghvi 10-0-45-0; Laxman 1-0-11-0; Tendulkar 1-0-12-0.

India

S. C. Ganguly c Moody b Fleming	23	H. H. Kanitkar not out		6
S. R. Tendulkar lbw b Kasprowicz	134	B 1, l-b 7, w 5, n-b 2		15
†N. R. Mongia c Gilchrist b Fleming	28			
*M. Azharuddin c Gilchrist b Kasprowicz	58	1/39 2/128	(4 wkts, 48.3 overs)	275
A. Jadeja not out	11	3/248 4/261		

V. V. S. Laxman, A. B. Agarkar, A. Kumble, B. K. V. Prasad and R. Sanghvi did not bat.

Bowling: Fleming 10-1-47-2; Kasprowicz 10-0-48-2; Warne 10-0-61-0; Moody 9.3-0-63-0; M. E. Waugh 3-0-20-0; S. R. Waugh 6-0-28-0.

Umpires: S. A. Bucknor and Javed Akhtar.   Series referee: Talat Ali.

COCA-COLA CUP (INDIA), 1997-98

India, to no one's surprise, ran out easy winners in this triangular tournament with two junior nations, though there were a couple of notable results on the way to the one-sided final. Bangladesh won their first senior one-day international, at the 23rd attempt, when a fine all-round effort from Mohammad Rafiq guided them to a convincing victory over Kenya, though their other form was disappointing.

A much bigger talking point was Kenya's 69-run success against India. For India, who had already qualified for the final, it was a dead match, but Kenya, at last realising the potential of their batting, wholly outplayed them. Ravindu Shah made an impressive entrance to international cricket, hitting three fifties in his first four innings and ending up with 213 runs in all, and another Kenyan, Steve Tikolo, was named Man of the Series.

That one defeat aside, India were rarely troubled. They got away with giving some younger players a chance – 23 men were used in the five matches – and Tendulkar was rested for two games before coming back to score a century in the final. The most competitive aspect of the tournament came beforehand and involved the giant cola companies rather than the cricketers.

A contract between Pepsi-Cola and the Board of Control for Cricket in India had effectively barred their rivals Coca-Cola from sponsoring any of the hugely popular one-day series currently proliferating in India. But before the previous one-day competition, which pitted India against Australia and Zimbabwe, the Board, hoping to instigate a bidding war, had claimed that the agreement with Pepsi did not cover triangular events. After losing the court battle, the Board arranged this series and assumed Pepsi would be obliged to sponsor it. However, they baulked at a competition with limited potential for media exposure, citing a clause in their contract that stipulated matches had to be against full ICC members. Coca-Cola stepped in for an undisclosed sum.

Note: Matches in this section were not first-class.

INDIA v BANGLADESH

At Mohali, May 14 (day/night). India won by five wickets. Toss: India. International debuts: G. K. Khoda, M. S. K. Prasad; Maharab Hossain, Morshed Ali Khan.

India, at half-throttle and without Tendulkar, still proved too good for Bangladesh. Agarkar struck early, taking two wickets. Bangladesh never fully recovered, though stand-in captain Amin-ul-Islam hit a measured 70 before becoming Agarkar's third victim. In pursuit of a modest 185, India also set off slowly. After 28 overs, they were only 105 for four and in need of a steadying innings: Jadeja duly provided it.

Man of the Match: A. Jadeja.

Bangladesh

Ather Ali Khan c Mohanty b Agarkar . .	15
Sanuar Hossain b Agarkar	0
Minhaz-ul-Abedin c Dravid b Singh . . .	14
*Amin-ul-Islam b Agarkar	70
Maharab Hossain b Sanghvi	6
Naim-ur-Rahman c Azharuddin b Sanghvi	25
Khaled Mahmud run out	31
Mohammad Rafiq c Mohanty b Kanitkar	1
Hasib-ul-Hassan run out	1
†Khaled Masud not out	0
L-b 7, w 9, n-b 5	21

Morshed Ali Khan did not bat.

1/2 2/33 3/52   (9 wkts, 50 overs) 184
4/61 5/132 6/163
7/172 8/182 9/184

Bowling: Agarkar 8–1–41–3; Mohanty 7–1–18–0; Singh 10–0–32–1; Sanghvi 10–0–35–2; Ganguly 6–0–21–0; Kanitkar 9–1–30–1.

India

S. C. Ganguly c and b Morshed Ali Khan	7
G. K. Khoda c Khaled Masud b Ather Ali Khan .	26
*M. Azharuddin c Khaled Masud b Khaled Mahmud .	31
A. Jadeja c Khaled Masud b Hasib-ul-Hassan .	73
R. Dravid c and b Ather Ali Khan	5
R. R. Singh not out	27
H. H. Kanitkar not out	1
L-b 7, w 8	15

†M. S. K. Prasad, A. B. Agarkar, D. S. Mohanty and R. Sanghvi did not bat.

1/12 2/55 3/85   (5 wkts, 45.2 overs) 185
4/105 5/183

Bowling: Hasib-ul-Hassan 9–0–44–1; Morshed Ali Khan 10–0–31–1; Khaled Mahmud 9.2–1–35–1; Ather Ali Khan 10–0–33–2; Mohammad Rafiq 7–0–35–0.

Umpires: K. N. Raghavan and I. Shivaram.

BANGLADESH v KENYA

At Hyderabad, May 17 (day/night). Bangladesh won by six wickets. Toss: Kenya. International debut: Ravindu Shah.

Bangladesh's first one-day international victory came after Kenya had overcome a poor start – 29 for two, then 89 for four – to muster 236, thanks largely to a brisk fifty from Ravindu Shah, in his first international. Bangladesh began their reply encouragingly, not losing a wicket until Ather Ali Khan was run out in the 26th over, by which time the arrears were under a hundred. Mohammad Rafiq, dropped twice on 14, rode his luck to add 77 runs to the three wickets he had taken with his left-arm spin.

Man of the Match: Mohammad Rafiq.

Kenya

D. Chudasama run out	36	A. Suji b Mohammad Rafiq	22
†K. Otieno c Hasib-ul-Hassan		*Asif Karim st Khaled Masud	
b Morshed Ali Khan	5	b Mohammad Rafiq	5
S. O. Tikolo b Khaled Mahmud	13	M. Suji run out	3
M. O. Odumbe c Hasib-ul-Hassan		Mohammad Sheikh not out	1
b Enam-ul-Haque	20	L-b 8, w 12, n-b 1	21
Hitesh Modi lbw b Enam-ul-Haque	40		
Ravindu Shah b Khaled Mahmud	52	1/13 2/29 3/84 (49 overs) 236	
T. Odoyo st Khaled Masud		4/89 5/156 6/193	
b Mohammad Rafiq	18	7/209 8/221 9/234	

Bowling: Hasib-ul-Hassan 4–0–16–0; Morshed Ali Khan 7–1–26–1; Khaled Mahmud 7–0–38–2; Enam-ul-Haque 10–0–45–2; Naim-ur-Rahman 10–1–42–0; Ather Ali Khan 1–0–5–0; Mohammad Rafiq 10–0–56–3.

Bangladesh

Ather Ali Khan run out	47	*Akram Khan c Mohammad Sheikh	
Mohammad Rafiq c Otieno		b Odumbe	39
b Mohammad Sheikh	77	Naim-ur-Rahman not out	4
Minhaz-ul-Abedin		B 1, l-b 5, w 23, n-b 7	36
lbw b Mohammad Sheikh	14		
Amin-ul-Islam not out	20	1/137 2/157 3/166 4/230 (4 wkts, 48 overs) 237	

Khaled Mahmud, Enam-ul-Haque, Hasib-ul-Hassan, †Khaled Masud and Morshed Ali Khan did not bat.

Bowling: M. Suji 4–1–14–0; Tikolo 10–0–40–0; Odoyo 4–0–19–0; Odumbe 9–0–42–1; Asif Karim 10–0–56–0; Mohammad Sheikh 10–0–46–2; Hitesh Modi 1–0–14–0.

Umpires: C. R. Mohite and S. K. Sharma.

INDIA v KENYA

At Bangalore, May 20 (day/night). India won by four wickets. Toss: India.

Steve Tikolo, sharing half-century stands with Chudasama and Odumbe, gave the Kenyans a confident start. Before he holed out to deep square leg for a sparkling 77, Kenya were 152 for two. But from there the innings lost impetus. Gagan Khoda, in his second limited-overs international, led India's reply. His partnerships with Dravid and Jadeja took them to the brink of victory. Then Jadeja, in charge while Azharuddin attended the ICC captains' meeting at Lord's, departed to a fine catch in the covers by Tikolo. Three more wickets followed, in the space of 12 runs, but the wobble did not quite turn into a collapse.

Man of the Match: G. K. Khoda.

Kenya

D. Chudasama b Singh	32		*Asif Karim b Singh	6
†K. Otieno b Agarkar	0		M. Suji not out	1
S. O. Tikolo c Laxman b Sanghvi	77		Mohammad Sheikh not out	2
M. O. Odumbe c Prasad b Agarkar	47		L-b 6, w 2, n-b 3	11
Hitesh Modi b Sanghvi	17			
Ravindu Shah c and b Kanitkar	21		1/7 2/70 3/152 (9 wkts, 50 overs)	223
T. Odoyo c Dravid b Kanitkar	1		4/175 5/186 6/199	
A. Suji run out	8		7/211 8/215 9/220	

Bowling: Agarkar 10–2–36–2; Mohanty 9–0–44–0; Singh 8–0–24–2; Sanghvi 10–0–52–2; Kanitkar 10–0–46–2; Ganguly 3–0–15–0.

India

G. K. Khoda c and b Tikolo	89		R. R. Singh not out	2
S. C. Ganguly b M. Suji	9		†M. S. K. Prasad not out	11
R. Dravid b Asif Karim	49			
*A. Jadeja c Tikolo b Mohammad Sheikh	50		B 2, l-b 2, w 8	12
H. H. Kanitkar run out	1			
V. V. S. Laxman c and b Mohammad Sheikh	1		1/21 2/119 3/197 (6 wkts, 47 overs) 4/200 5/207 6/209	224

A. B. Agarkar, R. Sanghvi and D. S. Mohanty did not bat.

Bowling: M. Suji 7–0–22–1; Tikolo 10–0–46–1; Odoyo 7–0–34–0; Asif Karim 10–0–39–1; Odumbe 6–0–38–0; Mohammad Sheikh 7–0–41–2.

Umpires: A. Bhattacharya and D. Sharma.

BANGLADESH v KENYA

At Chennai (formerly Madras), May 23 (day/night). Kenya won by 27 runs, Bangladesh's target having been revised to 226 from 49 overs. Toss: Kenya.

Kenya, who had to win to maintain hopes of reaching the final, began well. Otieno and Ravindu Shah scored at four an over, before the experienced pair of Tikolo and Odumbe took charge. The Kenyans collapsed, though, losing three wickets on 203. A partial power failure (all matches in this tournament were played under lights, to avoid the summer heat) interrupted the Bangladesh reply. It looked well set at 171 for five in the 41st over, but Tikolo added a couple of late wickets to his 65 runs and gave Kenya victory.

Man of the Match: S. O. Tikolo.

Kenya

†K. Otieno c Enam-ul-Haque b Naim-ur-Rahman	21		T. Odoyo b Mohammad Rafiq	0
Ravindu Shah c Amin-ul-Islam b Enam-ul-Haque	62		A. Vadher not out	11
			L. Onyango b Khaled Mahmud	2
S. O. Tikolo c Enam-ul-Haque b Hasib-ul-Hassan	65		*Asif Karim b Khaled Mahmud	0
M. O. Odumbe c Morshed Ali Khan b Hasib-ul-Hassan	40		M. Suji not out	3
			L-b 11, w 10, n-b 1	22
Hitesh Modi c Enam-ul-Haque b Mohammad Rafiq	0		1/76 2/99 3/193 (8 wkts, 50 overs) 4/203 5/203 6/203 7/212 8/212	226

Mohammad Sheikh did not bat.

Bowling: Hasib-ul-Hassan 10–0–44–2; Morshed Ali Khan 6–0–28–0; Khaled Mahmud 4–0–20–2; Enam-ul-Haque 10–0–35–1; Naim-ur-Rahman 10–1–43–1; Mohammad Rafiq 10–0–45–2.

Bangladesh

Ather Ali Khan c Ravindu Shah b Suji. .	0	†Khaled Masud c Odumbe b Tikolo. . . .	5
Mohammad Rafiq c Mohammad Sheikh		Enam-ul-Haque run out	4
b Odoyo .	23	Hasib-ul-Hassan b Asif Karim	2
Minhaz-ul-Abedin c Tikolo		Morshed Ali Khan not out	2
b Mohammad Sheikh .	45		
Amin-ul-Islam c and b Odoyo	6	B 1, l-b 3, w 10, n-b 5.	19
*Akram Khan run out	23		
Naim-ur-Rahman c Ravindu Shah		1/0 2/57 3/64	(46.2 overs) 198
b Asif Karim .	41	4/102 5/115 6/171	
Khaled Mahmud b Tikolo	28	7/189 8/192 9/194	

Bowling: Suji 7–0–21–1; Onyango 2–0–20–0; Odoyo 7–1–31–2; Asif Karim 9–0–28–2; Tikolo 8.2–0–37–2; Mohammad Sheikh 7–0–27–1; Odumbe 6–0–30–0.

Umpires: S. Asnani and S. Shastri.

INDIA v BANGLADESH

At Mumbai, May 25 (day/night). India won by five wickets. Toss: Bangladesh.

Despite being gifted 21 wides, Bangladesh struggled to set a three-figure target. They managed, thanks to a 44-run partnership between the watchful Khaled Masud and the more aggressive Hasib-ul-Hassan, who had come together at 71 for eight. Kumble took three for 17. India began at a sprint until Tendulkar, returning after a two-match rest to play before his home crowd, was first out in the tenth over – with the score already 72. His departure abruptly changed the game; it took India almost 20 more overs, and four more wickets, to reach the target. Bangladesh had needed a large total to boost their run-rate; their qualification now depended upon a titanic Kenyan collapse in the last qualifier.

Man of the Match: A. Kumble.

Bangladesh

Ather Ali Khan b Mhambrey	0	Enam-ul-Haque c Karim b Kumble	0
Mohammad Rafiq c Karim b Prasad . . .	6	Hasib-ul-Hassan b Tendulkar	21
Minhaz-ul-Abedin c Laxman b Prasad . .	0	Anis-ur-Rehman c Dravid b Tendulkar . .	0
Amin-ul-Islam c Jadeja b Kumble	18	L-b 8, w 21, n-b 5	34
*Akram Khan c and b R. R. Singh	8		
Naim-ur-Rahman c Laxman b Kumble . .	6	1/17 2/18 3/21	(36.3 overs) 115
Khaled Mahmud c Karim b Prasad	7	4/53 5/55 6/70	
†Khaled Masud not out	15	7/71 8/71 9/115	

Bowling: Prasad 9–2–26–3; Mhambrey 6–1–22–1; R. R. Singh 6–1–16–1; Kumble 10–4–17–3; Harbhajan Singh 4–0–18–0; Tendulkar 1.3–0–8–2.

India

N. S. Sidhu lbw b Khaled Mahmud	41	†S. S. Karim c Naim-ur-Rahman	
S. R. Tendulkar c Amin-ul-Islam		b Mohammad Rafiq .	8
b Ather Ali Khan .	33	R. R. Singh not out	1
R. Dravid b Mohammad Rafiq	1	L-b 3, w 8, n-b 1	12
*A. Jadeja not out	16		
V. V. S. Laxman c Khaled Masud		1/72 2/84 3/90	(5 wkts, 29.2 overs) 116
b Khaled Mahmud .	4	4/98 5/107	

A. Kumble, B. K. V. Prasad, P. L. Mhambrey and Harbhajan Singh did not bat.

Bowling: Hasib-ul-Hassan 5–0–30–0; Anis-ur-Rehman 3–0–26–0; Ather Ali Khan 4–0–24–1; Mohammad Rafiq 10–5–21–2; Khaled Mahmud 7.2–2–12–2.

Umpires: R. T. Ramachandran and B. K. Sadashiv.

INDIA v KENYA

At Gwalior, May 28 (day/night). Kenya won by 69 runs. Toss: Kenya. International debuts: N. Chopra, J. V. Paranjpe.

Kenya sailed confidently into the final with an emphatic victory against an Indian side already certain of their place. It was their fifth win at this level, and their second over a Test nation. Ravindu Shah, notching his third fifty in only his fourth one-day international, dominated the first phase of the innings. When he fell for 70 – including 50 in boundaries – the score was 93. For once, Kenya built on their sound start. Odumbe peppered his 91-ball 83 with five sixes, while Hitesh Modi contributed a run-a-ball fifty. In India's reply, eight batsmen made it to double figures, but none beyond 33. Odumbe followed his biggest score in one-day internationals with his best bowling, taking three for 14 with his off-spin.

Man of the Match: M. O. Odumbe.

Kenya

†K. Otieno c Kumble b Prasad	8	T. Odoyo not out		11
Ravindu Shah c and b Kumble	70			
S. O. Tikolo run out	21	L-b 4, w 4		8
M. O. Odumbe c Sidhu b Kumble	83			
Hitesh Modi c Dravid b Chopra	51	1/26 2/93 3/109	(5 wkts, 50 overs)	265
A. Vadher not out	13	4/209 5/250		

M. Suji, J. Angara, *Asif Karim and Mohammad Sheikh did not bat.

Bowling: Prasad 6–1–28–1; Singh 5–1–18–0; Kulkarni 10–0–60–0; Tendulkar 5–0–34–0; Kumble 8–2–27–2; Chopra 10–1–65–1; Dravid 6–0–29–0.

India

N. S. Sidhu run out	27	A. Kumble b Odumbe		20
S. R. Tendulkar c Asif Karim b Suji	18	B. K. V. Prasad b Odumbe		19
*M. Azharuddin b Angara	9	N. M. Kulkarni not out		1
R. Dravid c Vadher b Tikolo	33	L-b 3, w 3, n-b 1		7
R. R. Singh c Ravindu Shah b Tikolo	11			
J. V. Paranjpe c and b Tikolo	27	1/34 2/47 3/62	(47.1 overs)	196
†N. R. Mongia c Tikolo b Odumbe	21	4/97 5/106 6/150		
N. Chopra run out	3	7/155 8/155 9/189		

Bowling: Suji 9–0–50–1; Asif Karim 8–1–33–0; Angara 6–1–19–1; Tikolo 10–0–29–3; Mohammad Sheikh 6–0–24–0; Odoyo 4–0–24–0; Odumbe 4.1–0–14–3.

Umpires: S. Banerjee and R. Seth.

QUALIFYING TABLE

	Played	Won	Lost	Points	Net run-rate
India	4	3	1	6	0.26
Kenya	4	2	2	4	0.36
Bangladesh	4	1	3	2	–0.66

Net run-rate was calculated by subtracting runs conceded per over from runs scored per over.

FINAL

INDIA v KENYA

At Calcutta, May 31 (day/night). India won by nine wickets. Toss: Kenya.

India exacted revenge for their defeat three days earlier when they cruised to a simple win. After eight overs had brought two wickets each for Prasad and Agarkar, Kenya were reeling at 23 for four. Ravindu Shah had gone for eight – his first failure in five innings. But Hitesh Modi and Otieno gamely set about repairing the damage. Otieno assumed the anchor role while Modi, compiling a fluent 71 from 93 balls, played his shots. Prasad later took two more wickets to claim four for 23. For India, Tendulkar hit 100 in 103 balls, his 16th century in one-day internationals. He and Jadeja saw their team home with 15 overs unused.

Man of the Match: S. R. Tendulkar.   *Man of the Series:* S. O. Tikolo.

Kenya

D. Chudasama c Azharuddin b Agarkar .	10	M. Suji c Mongia b Prasad	4
Ravindu Shah c Kanitkar b Prasad	8	Mohammad Sheikh not out	6
S. O. Tikolo c Mongia b Agarkar	3	J. Angara c and b Agarkar	3
M. O. Odumbe b Prasad	0	B 2, l-b 13, w 12, n-b 2	29
Hitesh Modi c Kanitkar b Singh	71		
†K. Otieno lbw b Kumble	28	1/13 2/19 3/21	(46.3 overs) 196
T. Odoyo b Kumble	21	4/23 5/105 6/142	
*Asif Karim c Mongia b Prasad	13	7/164 8/180 9/185	

Bowling: Prasad 10–2–23–4; Agarkar 9.3–0–31–3; Singh 6–0–41–1; Kumble 10–0–34–2; Sanghvi 7–0–26–0; Kanitkar 2–0–15–0; Ganguly 1–0–7–0; Tendulkar 1–0–4–0.

India

S. C. Ganguly b Angara	36
S. R. Tendulkar not out	100
A. Jadeja not out	50
L-b 1, w 9, n-b 1	11
1/77	(1 wkt, 35 overs) 197

*M. Azharuddin, H. H. Kanitkar, R. R. Singh, †N. R. Mongia, A. Kumble, A. B. Agarkar, B. K. V. Prasad and R. Sanghvi did not bat.

Bowling: Suji 5–0–30–0; Asif Karim 5–0–27–0; Angara 6–0–37–1; Odoyo 8–0–38–0; Tikolo 3–0–17–0; Odumbe 2–0–15–0; Mohammad Sheikh 5–0–27–0; Ravindu Shah 1–0–5–0.

Umpires: A. V. Jayaprakash and K. Parthasarathy.   Series referee: R. S. Madugalle (Sri Lanka).

SINGER AKAI NIDAHAS TROPHY, 1997-98

By MARTIN DAVIDSON

This tournament was staged in honour of the Golden Jubilee of Sri Lankan independence (*nidahas* in Sinhalese). India and New Zealand were the two guest teams, Australia having turned down an invitation. But local celebrations were dampened first by monsoon rains, which prevented results in two Colombo games and washed out all three in Galle, and then by the Indians.

Sri Lanka, who were less often affected by the weather in the league stage, headed the table, but lost a close-fought final to give India their fourth one-day title since Mohammad Azharuddin reclaimed the captaincy in January. New Zealand were never in the same class. They did not manage a single victory and owed all their points to washouts.

Home favourite Aravinda de Silva was named Man of the Series for his 368 runs in five innings, while Indian master Sachin Tendulkar was not far behind with 263 in four. Both scored centuries in the final, when Tendulkar and Sourav Ganguly shared an opening stand of 252, a first-wicket record in all one-day internationals. Ajit Agarkar of India was the leading bowler of the tournament, with 12 wickets.

Note: Matches in this section were not first-class.

SRI LANKA v INDIA

At R. Premadasa Stadium, Colombo, June 19 (day/night). India won by eight wickets. Toss: Sri Lanka. International debut: A. S. A. Perera.

India began the series in style with a thoroughly convincing win over their hosts. Sri Lanka's only significant stand came from Atapattu and de Silva, who put on 145 in 30 overs. But after that, the home batting was restricted to 48 runs off the last ten. India were asked to chase 244 and strolled to victory with more than six overs to spare, helped immeasurably by a rollicking start of 115 in 18 overs from Ganguly and Tendulkar. Ganguly contributed 80 from 114 balls and Tendulkar 65 from 50, quickly reducing the game to a no contest.

Man of the Match: S. C. Ganguly.

Sri Lanka

S. T. Jayasuriya b Agarkar	12	D. P. M. D. Jayawardene not out	1
†R. S. Kaluwitharana c Agarkar b Harbhajan Singh	29	H. D. P. K. Dharmasena not out	2
M. S. Atapattu b Kumble	70	B 1, l-b 5, w 1	7
P. A. de Silva c Azharuddin b Agarkar	97		
*A. Ranatunga c Azharuddin b Kumble	25	1/16 2/50 3/195 (6 wkts, 50 overs)	243
R. S. Mahanama run out	0	4/236 5/238 6/238	

G. P. Wickremasinghe, M. Muralitharan and A. S. A. Perera did not bat.

Bowling: Agarkar 9–0–38–2; Prasad 7–0–32–0; Harbhajan Singh 10–0–45–1; R. R. Singh 8–0–30–0; Kumble 10–0–56–2; Kanitkar 4–1–19–0; Tendulkar 2–0–17–0.

India

S. C. Ganguly c Jayawardene b Muralitharan	80	A. Jadeja not out	22
S. R. Tendulkar c Atapattu b Muralitharan	65	L-b 8, w 14, n-b 2	24
*M. Azharuddin not out	55	1/115 2/211 (2 wkts, 43.4 overs)	246

R. R. Singh, H. H. Kanitkar, †N. R. Mongia, A. B. Agarkar, A. Kumble, B. K. V. Prasad and Harbhajan Singh did not bat.

Bowling: Wickremasinghe 5–0–36–0; Perera 10–0–58–0; Dharmasena 9.4–0–57–0; Muralitharan 10–0–48–2; Jayasuriya 9–0–39–0.

Umpires: K. T. Francis and P. Manuel.

SRI LANKA v NEW ZEALAND

At R. Premadasa Stadium, Colombo, June 21 (day/night). Sri Lanka won by seven wickets. Toss: New Zealand.

Sri Lanka bounced back quickly from their defeat against India. Young scored 55 from 52 balls for the visitors in an opening stand of 71, but they declined from 107 for one to 200 for nine, their last six wickets falling for 20. Jayasuriya provided his customary fast start, 57 from 62 balls; then Atapattu again combined with de Silva, and their partnership of 95 saw Sri Lanka most of the way home.

Man of the Match: M. S. Atapattu.

New Zealand

B. A. Young c Chandana b Dharmasena	55		C. Z. Harris b Dharmasena	7
N. J. Astle b Muralitharan	33		D. J. Nash run out	1
*S. P. Fleming run out	47		D. L. Vettori not out	4
M. J. Horne st Kaluwitharana b Dharmasena	1		S. B. O'Connor not out	6
C. D. McMillan c Muralitharan b Chandana	26		L-b 9, w 3	12
C. L. Cairns c Atapattu b Chandana	7		1/71 2/107 3/112 (9 wkts, 50 overs)	200
†A. C. Parore c Kaluwitharana b Chandana	1		4/169 5/171 6/176	
			7/179 8/186 9/189	

Bowling: Wickremasinghe 6–0–35–0; Bandaratilleke 10–0–41–0; Dharmasena 10–0–40–3; Muralitharan 10–1–24–1; Jayasuriya 7–0–27–0; Chandana 7–1–24–3.

Sri Lanka

S. T. Jayasuriya c McMillan b Vettori	57		*A. Ranatunga not out	6
†R. S. Kaluwitharana hit wkt b O'Connor	2		B 4, l-b 3, w 4	11
M. S. Atapattu not out	83			
P. A. de Silva b Astle	42		1/3 2/85 3/180 (3 wkts, 40 overs)	201

R. S. Mahanama, U. D. U. Chandana, H. D. P. K. Dharmasena, G. P. Wickremasinghe, M. R. C. N. Bandaratilleke and M. Muralitharan did not bat.

Bowling: O'Connor 4–0–21–1; Nash 6–0–25–0; Cairns 5–0–24–0; Harris 10–0–50–0; Vettori 8–0–41–1; McMillan 4–0–31–0; Astle 3–2–2–1.

Umpires: B. C. Cooray and D. N. Pathirana.

INDIA v NEW ZEALAND

At R. Premadasa Stadium, Colombo, June 23 (day/night). No result. Toss: India.

Fleming's team were in the firing line again when their 219 for eight – only Astle got to 50 – was put into perspective by Tendulkar and Azharuddin. Tendulkar raced to his fifty off 33 balls, and Azharuddin had reached a run-a-ball 53. But with India comfortably placed on 131 for two, the heavens opened. Twenty-five overs – another four balls – would have had to be bowled for a result to stand. Incredibly, India would have been declared losers; the rules for interrupted matches stated that they needed 147 from 25 overs.

New Zealand

B. A. Young b Kumble	23		C. Z. Harris c and b Agarkar	3
N. J. Astle c Kanitkar b Harbhajan Singh	81		M. W. Priest not out	4
*S. P. Fleming c Prasad b Harbhajan Singh	5		D. L. Vettori not out	1
C. D. McMillan c Jadeja b Tendulkar	23		L-b 3, w 10, n-b 1	14
M. J. Horne lbw b Prasad	44		1/65 2/73 3/122 (8 wkts, 50 overs)	219
C. L. Cairns c Mongia b Agarkar	20		4/185 5/204 6/209	
†A. C. Parore lbw b Agarkar	1		7/212 8/215	

P. J. Wiseman did not bat.

Bowling: Agarkar 9–0–52–3; Prasad 7–1–21–1; Harbhajan Singh 9–0–30–2; R. R. Singh 2–1–8–0; Kumble 8–0–31–1; Kanitkar 9–0–42–0; Tendulkar 6–0–32–1.

India

S. C. Ganguly c Parore b Cairns	4
S. R. Tendulkar c and b Harris	53
*M. Azharuddin not out	53
A. Jadeja not out	17
W 3, n-b 1	4

1/20 2/78   (2 wkts, 24.2 overs) 131

H. H. Kanitkar, R. R. Singh, †N. R. Mongia, A. B. Agarkar, A. Kumble, B. K. V. Prasad and Harbhajan Singh did not bat.

Bowling: Cairns 5–0–36–1; Vettori 6.2–0–32–0; Harris 6–0–40–1; Astle 4–0–12–0; Wiseman 3–0–11–0.

Umpires: K. T. Francis and T. M. Samarasinghe.

SRI LANKA v INDIA

At Galle, June 25. No result (abandoned).
    Galle's first one-day international (Sri Lanka and New Zealand had played a Test there earlier in June) was called off at 10.30 a.m., to the disappointment of a sell-out crowd.

SRI LANKA v NEW ZEALAND

At Galle, June 27. No result (abandoned).

INDIA v NEW ZEALAND

At Galle, June 29. No result (abandoned).
    After all three fixtures in Galle were washed out by heavy rain, Sri Lanka proposed that they should be replayed in Colombo, using the rest days between the remaining scheduled matches. New Zealand were willing, but India argued that four league games in six days would be too strenuous.

SRI LANKA v INDIA

At Sinhalese Sports Club, Colombo, July 1. Sri Lanka won by eight runs. Toss: India.
    Returning to Colombo, Sri Lanka avenged their earlier defeat by the in-form Indians. The game was delayed for three hours by a wet patch on the pitch and eventually reduced to 36 overs each. After his side lost three early wickets, de Silva played a fluent 62, lifting them to 171 for eight; impressive young pace bowler Agarkar claimed three for 38. Anxious to run up a winning total in 25 overs, in case of further rain, India batted wildly and slumped to 75 for six. Robin Singh and Agarkar rallied the side but, once Jayasuriya dismissed them both, the Indian challenge dissolved against tight bowling and enthusiastic fielding. Next day, Kumar Dharmasena took advantage of a rare day off to get married; all three teams were invited to the wedding.
    Man of the Match: P. A. de Silva.

Sri Lanka

S. T. Jayasuriya c Kanitkar b Prasad ... 23	H. D. P. K. Dharmasena c Tendulkar
D. A. Gunawardene c Azharuddin	b Kumble . 11
b Agarkar . 0	G. P. Wickremasinghe not out 5
M. S. Atapattu c R. R. Singh b Agarkar . 12	M. Muralitharan not out 3
P. A. de Silva c Azharuddin b Prasad... 62	
*A. Ranatunga c Jadeja	L-b 4, w 2, n-b 5 11
b Harbhajan Singh . 11	———
†R. S. Kaluwitharana st Mongia	1/1 2/30 3/38 (8 wkts, 36 overs) 171
b Harbhajan Singh . 7	4/77 5/90 6/132
U. D. U. Chandana c Agarkar 26	7/160 8/164
A. S. A. Perera did not bat.	

Bowling: Agarkar 7–0–38–3; Prasad 7–0–34–2; R. R. Singh 7–0–38–0; Harbhajan Singh 7–0–35–2; Kumble 8–0–22–1.

India

S. C. Ganguly c de Silva b Perera..... 26	A. Kumble st Kaluwitharana b Jayasuriya 4
S. R. Tendulkar c and b Dharmasena ... 17	B. K. V. Prasad not out............ 1
†N. R. Mongia c Ranatunga b Perera... 2	Harbhajan Singh st Kaluwitharana
*M. Azharuddin c Ranatunga	b Jayasuriya . 0
b Dharmasena . 8	
A. Jadeja run out 0	B 4, l-b 5, w 6, n-b 1 16
H. H. Kanitkar c Ranatunga b de Silva . 9	———
R. R. Singh c sub (D. P. M. D. Jayawardene)	1/41 2/48 3/57 (35.4 overs) 163
b Jayasuriya . 50	4/57 5/58 6/75
A. B. Agarkar b Jayasuriya 30	7/138 8/162 9/163

Bowling: Wickremasinghe 3–0–26–0; Perera 6–0–25–2; Dharmasena 7–0–29–2; Muralitharan 8–0–29–0; de Silva 6–0–27–1; Jayasuriya 5.4–0–18–4.

Umpires: I. Anandappa and B. C. Cooray.

INDIA v NEW ZEALAND

At Sinhalese Sports Club, Colombo, July 3. No result. Toss: New Zealand.

More rain ensured that all three matches between these two teams ended without a result. New Zealand's innings was halted with nearly 19 overs to go; most of their batsmen made starts, but were unable to consolidate. Play was called off before India could make their reply.

New Zealand

B. A. Young st Mongia b Kumble 26	C. L. Cairns not out 19
N. J. Astle c Kumble b Prasad 15	†A. C. Parore not out 9
*S. P. Fleming c Tendulkar	L-b 3, w 10 13
b Harbhajan Singh . 20	———
C. D. McMillan c Ganguly b Kanitkar . . 26	1/28 2/57 3/85 (5 wkts, 31.1 overs) 128
M. J. Horne st Mongia b Harbhajan Singh 0	4/89 5/111

C. Z. Harris, D. J. Nash, D. L. Vettori and P. J. Wiseman did not bat.

Bowling: Agarkar 7–0–39–0; Prasad 5–1–23–1; Harbhajan Singh 8–0–26–2; Kumble 6–1–15–1; Kanitkar 5–0–21–1; R. R. Singh 0.1–0–1–0.

India

S. C. Ganguly, S. R. Tendulkar, *M. Azharuddin, A. Jadeja, H. H. Kanitkar, R. R. Singh, †N. R. Mongia, A. B. Agarkar, A. Kumble, B. K. V. Prasad and Harbhajan Singh.

Umpires: B. C. Cooray and D. N. Pathirana.

SRI LANKA v NEW ZEALAND

At Sinhalese Sports Club, Colombo, July 5. Sri Lanka won by 87 runs. Toss: New Zealand.

Although they had not yet won a game, New Zealand had enough no-result points to have a faint chance of booking a berth in the final on net run-rate. But, after Sri Lanka stormed to 293, they had to beat the target in 41.4 overs, a near-impossible task. After the home openers reached 69 in the 13th over, Ranatunga struck 102 from 98 balls, with two sixes and six fours – only his fourth century in 240 one-day internationals – and added 132 with de Silva. New Zealand's only hope was to lash out and Astle scored 74 in 76 balls. But losing Fleming was a serious blow, and they expired in the 40th over.

Man of the Match: A. Ranatunga.

Sri Lanka

S. T. Jayasuriya c Cairns b Vettori	24	M. S. Atapattu not out 6
†R. S. Kaluwitharana c Astle b Harris	54	L-b 6, w 12 18
P. A. de Silva c Fleming b Harris	62	
*A. Ranatunga c Fleming b McMillan	102	1/69 2/92 (4 wkts, 50 overs) 293
U. D. U. Chandana not out	27	3/224 4/282

R. S. Mahanama, H. D. P. K. Dharmasena, M. R. C. N. Bandaratilleke, M. Muralitharan and A. S. A. Perera did not bat.

Bowling: Cairns 7–0–52–0; Nash 5–0–30–0; Vettori 10–0–53–1; Harris 10–1–44–2; Wiseman 6–0–32–0; McMillan 7–0–38–1; Astle 5–0–38–0.

New Zealand

B. A. Young c Mahanama b Perera	3	†A. C. Parore not out 28
N. J. Astle c de Silva b Chandana	74	C. Z. Harris b Jayasuriya 2
*S. P. Fleming c Dharmasena		D. J. Nash c Chandana b Muralitharan 3
b Bandaratilleke	20	D. L. Vettori b Jayasuriya 0
C. D. McMillan c Muralitharan		P. J. Wiseman c Dharmasena b Chandana 16
b Bandaratilleke	5	L-b 10, w 12, n-b 1 23
M. J. Horne c Kaluwitharana		
b Muralitharan	4	1/11 2/78 3/86 (39.1 overs) 206
C. L. Cairns c Kaluwitharana		4/106 5/152 6/154
b Jayasuriya	28	7/163 8/172 9/176

Bowling: Perera 4–0–34–1; Bandaratilleke 9–0–34–2; Dharmasena 2–0–24–0; Muralitharan 10–0–50–2; Jayasuriya 8–0–28–3; Chandana 6.1–0–26–2.

Umpires: P. Manuel and T. M. Samarasinghe.

QUALIFYING TABLE

	Played	Won	Lost	No result	Points	Net run-rate
Sri Lanka	6	3	1	2	8	0.62
India	6	1	1	4	6	0.31
New Zealand	6	0	2	4	4	–1.42

Net run-rate was calculated by subtracting runs conceded per over from runs scored per over.

FINAL

SRI LANKA v INDIA

At R. Premadasa Stadium, Colombo, July 7 (day/night). India won by six runs. Toss: India.

Tendulkar and Ganguly gave India an enormous advantage in this match when they ran up 252 in 43 overs for the first wicket, a world record in limited-overs internationals. Ganguly scored 109 from 136 balls, with two sixes and six fours; Tendulkar's share was 128 from 131 balls, and he hit two sixes and eight fours. It was Tendulkar's 17th century at this level, equalling Desmond

Haynes's record; he also became the second Indian to pass 7,000 one-day international runs, in his 196th match. India left Sri Lanka an imposing target of 308. But de Silva was not to be outdone. Fighting against a groin strain (he needed a runner), he made 105, from 94 balls. Sri Lanka fell only seven runs short of victory in the final over; Agarkar again proved himself with four wickets.

Man of the Match: S. R. Tendulkar. *Man of the Series:* P. A. de Silva.

India

S. C. Ganguly c and b Muralitharan	109	A. B. Agarkar run out	5
S. R. Tendulkar st Kaluwitharana		H. H. Kanitkar not out	5
b Jayasuriya	128	L-b 3, w 12	15
*M. Azharuddin b Chandana	5		
A. Jadeja b Jayasuriya	25	1/252 2/252 3/262 (6 wkts, 50 overs)	307
R. R. Singh run out	15	4/297 5/297 6/307	

†N. R. Mongia, A. Kumble, B. K. V. Prasad and Harbhajan Singh did not bat.

Bowling: Wickremasinghe 7–0–43–0; Bandaratilleke 5–0–36–0; Dharmasena 10–0–67–0; Muralitharan 8–0–51–1; Jayasuriya 9–0–42–2; de Silva 6–0–32–0; Chandana 5–0–33–1.

Sri Lanka

S. T. Jayasuriya c Ganguly b Agarkar	32	H. D. P. K. Dharmasena lbw b Prasad	2
†R. S. Kaluwitharana b Agarkar	24	G. P. Wickremasinghe run out	5
P. A. de Silva c Harbhajan Singh		M. R. C. N. Bandaratilleke run out	0
b Agarkar	105	M. Muralitharan not out	1
M. S. Atapattu c Prasad		B 1, l-b 5, w 4, n-b 2	22
b Harbhajan Singh	39		
*A. Ranatunga c Mongia b Agarkar	23	1/59 2/73 3/160 (49.3 overs)	301
R. S. Mahanama run out	44	4/197 5/272 6/280	
U. D. U. Chandana b Kumble	4	7/287 8/295 9/298	

Bowling: Agarkar 10–0–53–4; Prasad 10–0–56–1; Kumble 9.3–0–57–1; Harbhajan Singh 10–0–57–1; R. R. Singh 5–0–25–0; Kanitkar 4–0–24–0; Tendulkar 1–0–13–0.

Umpires: B. C. Cooray and K. T. Francis. Series referee: C. W. Smith (West Indies).

ONE-DAY INTERNATIONAL COMPETITIONS, 1997-98

Competition	Winners	Runners-up	Others
Pepsi Asia Cup in Sri Lanka	**Sri Lanka**	India	Bangladesh, Pakistan
President's Cup in Kenya	**Zimbabwe**	Kenya	Bangladesh
Wills Golden Jubilee in Pakistan	**South Africa**	Sri Lanka	Pakistan, West Indies
Carlton & United Series in Australia	**Australia**	South Africa	New Zealand
Akai Singer Champions Trophy in Sharjah	**England**	West Indies	India, Pakistan
Silver Jubilee Independence Cup in Bangladesh	**India**	Pakistan	Bangladesh
Pepsi Triangular Series in India	**Australia**	India	Zimbabwe
Standard Bank International Series in South Africa	**South Africa**	Pakistan	Sri Lanka
Coca-Cola Cup in Sharjah	**India**	Australia	New Zealand
Coca-Cola Cup in India	**India**	Kenya	Bangladesh
Singer Akai Nidahas Trophy in Sri Lanka	**India**	Sri Lanka	New Zealand

Note: Only competitions held during the 1997-98 season and involving three or more teams are included.

COMMONWEALTH GAMES, 1998

By JIM TUCKER

There was no rich pot of rand, rupees or dollars for the winning team at the Commonwealth Games in Kuala Lumpur. For most, the lure of cricket's first gold medal was reward enough. The steely South Africans, led by Shaun Pollock, and Steve Waugh's Australians certainly thought so, and it was fitting they should fight out the final of this 16-team, one-day tournament. In the end, it was the South Africans who took gold.

Many players wondered quite what they were doing there, since team events had not been included in the previous 15 Games. Cricket's last appearance in a multi-sports festival on this scale was at the Paris Olympics in 1900, when a collection of Devon and Somerset club cricketers won the gold medal for England; their only opposition was France. Now the sport was part of an international jamboree embracing more than 4,000 athletes from 69 nations.

The rationale for including cricket was partly to encourage the development of emerging nations such as Kenya, Bangladesh and hosts Malaysia, who have set themselves the target of playing Tests by 2020. But cricket was also seen as a means of broadening the appeal of the Commonwealth Games, especially within the Indian subcontinent.

Unfortunately, not all the Test-playing nations were whole-hearted in their support. India and Pakistan could not work out whether they wanted to be in Kuala Lumpur or in Toronto for the lucrative Sahara Cup. Most of the leading players went to Toronto, though Sachin Tendulkar, the world's pre-eminent one-day batsman, rushed between both. In three innings at Kuala Lumpur, he made barely a mark before flying to Canada to join the No. 1 team for their last game.

The Sri Lankans, fresh from their triumphant tour of England, arrived without their core of Jayasuriya, Ranatunga and de Silva. England, indeed, declined to take any part in the competition, and were roundly criticised for it. Their problem was that the domestic season was reaching its climax as the Games got under way. The ECB were prepared to send a weakened team, but the English Commonwealth Games authorities insisted it was a full-strength squad or nothing.

The teams reflected the nations recognised by the Games, rather than by international cricket, so Antigua, Barbados and Jamaica took part separately, as did Northern Ireland, since the Irish Republic is not a member of the Commonwealth. This was one reason why ICC refused to grant the matches official one-day international status.

For all the complications, the tournament had far more meaning than most of the one-day frolics that litter the international cricket calendar. Viv Richards, coaching the Antigua and Barbuda team, confessed to a lump in his throat when he carried the national flag at the opening ceremony. The Barbados team chose to shave their heads as a form of bonding ritual. Their technical director, Joel Garner, promised to do the same if his side reached the final. He kept his hair.

Waugh led the patriotic fervour for Australia, even appearing at the pool with green-and-gold face paint to cheer his country's swimmers. "When you watch the Olympics or Commonwealth Games, you can't help thinking that winning a gold medal and hearing your anthem playing would be the ultimate," he said. "As a cricketer it has always been an impossible dream – until now." With the bat, he could have done no more to make it happen. In sapping humidity, he hit an unbeaten hundred, and wrenched the key preliminary match from India after Australia had collapsed to 84 for five. But the innings Waugh rated as his "most satisfying in one-day cricket" will never make official records. The hat-trick taken by Australian spinner Brad Young as New Zealand were routed for 58 in the semi-final, over by lunch, suffers the same fate.

Despite this ignominious defeat, New Zealand won the bronze medal, beating the other losing semi-finalists, Sri Lanka. In the final, Waugh hit a defiant 90 not out as Australia reached 183 after Pollock had made deep inroads. Malaysia's 76-year-old king, the Yang di-Pertuan Agong Tuanku Ja'afar, applauded generously, but it was around the necks of Pollock's team that he hung the gold medals. Openers Mike Rindel and Andrew Hudson set a base that assured an unexpected win by four wickets. Typically, the South Africans had picked themselves up off the canvas: in their semi-final, pursuing Sri Lanka's meagre 130, they were 96 for nine before last pair Alan Dawson and Nicky Boje put on 35 to steal victory.

While several matches developed into compelling contests, too many were made non-events by afternoon storms, uneven or damp pitches, and mismatched sides. The final drew around 7,000 fans to the marquees and grassy vantage-points around the PKNS ground, but it remained unclear whether such a day would ever be repeated. Three decisions remained to be made in 1999: whether any team events would form part of the next Commonwealth Games, in Manchester in 2002; if so, whether cricket would be among them; and then what form of cricket should be played – the normal one-day game or the so-called "third generation" quickfire format. ICC has come out in favour of the quickfire option.

Group A
Zimbabwe beat Jamaica.
Sri Lanka beat Malaysia.
Sri Lanka beat Jamaica.
Zimbabwe beat Malaysia.
Jamaica beat Malaysia.
Sri Lanka beat Zimbabwe.

Sri Lanka 6 pts, Zimbabwe 4 pts,
Jamaica 2 pts, Malaysia 0 pts.

Group B
Antigua and Barbuda v India: no result.
Australia beat Canada.
Australia beat Antigua and Barbuda.
India beat Canada.
Antigua and Barbuda beat Canada.
Australia beat India.

Australia 6 pts, Antigua and Barbuda 3 pts,
India 3 pts, Canada 0 pts.

Group C
Barbados beat Bangladesh.
South Africa beat Northern Ireland.
South Africa beat Bangladesh.
Barbados beat Northern Ireland.
Northern Ireland beat Bangladesh.
South Africa beat Barbados.

South Africa 6 pts, Barbados 4 pts,
Northern Ireland 2 pts, Bangladesh 0 pts.

Group D
Pakistan v Scotland: no result.
New Zealand beat Kenya.
Pakistan beat Kenya.
New Zealand beat Scotland.
Kenya beat Scotland.
New Zealand beat Pakistan.

New Zealand 6 pts, Pakistan 3 pts,
Kenya 2 pts, Scotland 1 pt.

SEMI-FINALS

At PKNS, September 16. South Africa won by one wicket. Toss: South Africa. Sri Lanka 130 (44 overs) (D. A. Gunawardene 53; N. Boje four for 16); South Africa 131 for nine (47 overs).

At Tenaga Sports Ground (Kilat Kelab), September 17. Australia won by nine wickets. Toss: Australia. New Zealand 58 (26.4 overs) (D. W. Fleming three for 23, B. E. Young four for four); Australia 62 for one (10.4 overs) (A. C. Gilchrist 42 not out).

BRONZE MEDAL PLAY-OFF

At Tenaga Sports Ground (Kilat Kelab), September 18. New Zealand won by 51 runs. Toss: Sri Lanka. New Zealand 212 for seven (50 overs) (N. J. Astle 56, C. Z. Harris 56 not out, Extras 34); Sri Lanka 161 (44.4 overs) (D. A. Gunawardene 30, U. C. Hathurusinghe 34, A. S. A. Perera 45; D. L. Vettori three for 33).

FINAL

AUSTRALIA v SOUTH AFRICA

At PKNS, September 19. South Africa won by four wickets. Toss: South Africa.

Australia

M. E. Waugh c Boucher b Pollock	2	G. R. Robertson lbw b Boje		2
†A. C. Gilchrist c Rindel b Pollock	15	M. S. Kasprowicz run out		12
R. T. Ponting c Dawson b Pollock	2	D. W. Fleming run out		1
M. G. Bevan run out	13			
*S. R. Waugh not out	90	B 1, l-b 2, w 11, n-b 1		15
D. S. Lehmann c Boucher b Pollock	26			—
T. M. Moody st Boucher b Adams	3	1/10 2/16 3/28 4/58 5/121	(49.3 overs)	183
B. E. Young c Benkenstein b Adams	2	6/124 7/142 8/157 9/177		

Bowling: Pollock 9–2–19–4; Kallis 6–1–21–0; Dawson 8.1–1–27–0; Crookes 10–0–43–0; Boje 8–0–36–1; Adams 8–0–33–2; Benkenstein 0.2–0–1–0.

South Africa

A. C. Hudson c Bevan b Robertson	36	*S. M. Pollock c Young b Lehmann		2
M. J. R. Rindel c M. E. Waugh		†M. V. Boucher not out		0
b Lehmann	67			
D. N. Crookes c Moody b Robertson	3	B 6, l-b 1, w 10, n-b 4		21
J. H. Kallis c Gilchrist b Lehmann	44			—
H. H. Gibbs b Fleming	9	1/73 2/86 3/158	(6 wkts, 46 overs)	184
D. M. Benkenstein not out	2	4/172 5/181 6/183		

N. Boje, P. R. Adams and A. C. Dawson did not bat.

Bowling: Fleming 10–1–44–1; Kasprowicz 5–0–34–0; Young 10–3–31–0; Robertson 10–2–28–2; Moody 4–0–15–0; Bevan 3–0–11–0; Lehmann 4–1–14–3.

Umpires: S. A. Bucknor and K. T. Francis.   Referee: J. R. Reid.

WORLD CUP FOR THE BLIND, 1998

The inaugural World Cup for the blind was won by South Africa, who beat Pakistan by ten wickets in the final at Delhi. It was a tournament completely dominated by batsmen, once they realised that the ball was hardly bouncing by the time it reached them, and that they could flat-bat it along the ground. Players were divided into three categories: B1 (totally blind), B2 (partially blind) and B3 (partially sighted); the B3s scored 20 centuries and the B2s 11. In the next World Cup, runs scored by B1 players will count double.

Teams had to include at least four B1s and three B2s, and were allowed a maximum of four B3s. Innings lasted 40 overs; no one could bowl more than eight, and B1s had to bowl a minimum of 16. All deliveries were underarm, and the ball had to bounce twice before reaching the batsman – once in the first half of the pitch and again in the second. The ball – the same size as a standard cricket ball – contained ball-bearings to help batsmen locate it.

Seven teams took part, competing in a round-robin league to determine the four semi-finalists. England won two of their six league games, and could finish only fifth. South Africa began disastrously, losing their first three matches, but recovered to qualify for the semi-finals in fourth place. There, they beat hosts India, who had won all six group games, by ten wickets, with brothers Scott and Rury Field, the captain, sharing an unbroken partnership of 336 for the first wicket, a world record they would break again in the final.

In the other semi-final, Pakistan ran up 342 for six with Ashraf Bhatti scoring 166 not out against Australia, who finished on 334 for five, including an undefeated 129 from Chris Backstrom. In the final, Pakistan were put in to bat, and scored 372 for five. Masood Jan, who had hit a competition-record 262 in the group game between the two sides, scored 146, and put on 254 for the first wicket with Noor Queresh, who made 82. But the Field brothers again embarked on a record-breaking partnership, reaching the target without being parted with 17 balls to spare: Scott finished on 159, his sixth century of the competition, with Rury on 193. – LAWRENCE BOOTH.

MTN UNDER-19 WORLD CUP, 1998

By JOHN STERN

England were the unexpected winners of the Under-19 World Cup in South Africa. The only previous tournament of its kind was held ten years earlier and won by hosts Australia, whose team included Stuart Law and Alan Mullally. But Jagmohan Dalmiya, the president of the International Cricket Council, announced that it was to be a biennial event henceforth.

Support for many of the matches was good, largely because of the efforts of the various provincial unions, who encouraged local schoolchildren to attend. India's game against Pakistan in Durban attracted a crowd of more than 10,000 and the final in Johannesburg between England and New Zealand was watched by about 6,000. Had South Africa qualified, their presence would have doubled the numbers at least.

In terms of cricketing "globalisation" – one of the buzzwords at the pre-tournament press conference – the World Cup was a bold and exciting venture. In addition to the nine Test-playing nations, there were teams from Bangladesh, Kenya and Scotland, the three countries who had qualified for the adult World Cup in 1999, plus Ireland, Denmark, Namibia and Papua New Guinea. The teams were divided into four pools, named after famous cricketers, and the top two sides from each progressed to two Super League pools, whose winners advanced to the final. In order to give everyone a decent amount of cricket, the non-qualifiers competed in a Plate League (with pools named after Mike Procter and South African selector Rushdie Majiet), won by Bangladesh, who beat West Indies in the final.

The spread of competitors naturally led to some mismatches, though one of the biggest wins was achieved by Denmark. Namibia scored only 78 against them in the Plate, having given away 87 in Extras. Papua New Guinea provided the most touching story of the tournament. They arrived in South Africa with only two leather bags of cricket equipment between them – as opposed to the sponsored "coffins" of many other teams. But after the Gauteng players heard of their plight, they received four coffins of kit donated by Ken Rutherford, the Gauteng captain, and his team-mates. Despite this help, they were predictably well beaten in all their matches. They were the only team West Indies beat in the Cowdrey Pool.

West Indies failed to qualify for the Super League after a fiasco concerning the composition of their squad. They arrived with seven players who contravened the age restrictions for the tournament, which required players from Test nations to be under 19 on September 1, 1997 (players from the other countries could be eight months older). The West Indian authorities had observed the less stringent qualification rule that applied in their domestic Under-19 tournament. As a result, they had to fly in seven new players and their opening game was postponed for two days. It still came as a surprise when, after losing to Australia, they also succumbed to Zimbabwe and failed to go through.

The opening game of the tournament was played at the Wanderers between South Africa and India. After an opening ceremony between the innings, South Africa won by four wickets, with their wicket-keeper Morné van Wyk making a disciplined 86 not out. Both teams won their remaining games against Kenya and Scotland to qualify from the Gavaskar Pool. As expected, Pakistan headed the Bradman Pool, qualifying with Sri Lanka, whom they beat by seven wickets. In that match, Test player Hasan Raza made an unbeaten 90 for Pakistan, though his overall form was disappointing.

The eventual finalists, England and New Zealand, also met in the first match of the Sobers Pool; England won by four wickets in a closely fought game. But they lost their final match to Bangladesh, who received fanatical support from a small number of expatriates. Had Bangladesh scored the 224 they needed in 38 rather than 44 overs, they, and not England, would have qualified for the Super League. As it was, England and New Zealand went through on net run-rate and Bangladesh had to settle for the Plate.

The Super League, in which every game was covered live on South African satellite television, also threw up a number of shocks and tense finishes; both pools came down to net run-rate at the finish. England, from being down and almost out, beat Pakistan, who surprisingly lost all three of their games, but lost a rain-affected match to India.

Meanwhile, Australia had beaten India and Pakistan and were favourites to reach the final. Only a massive defeat by England could deny them: but that is precisely what they suffered. In front of a crowd of about 6,000 at Newlands, the England pace bowlers bowled better than at any stage of the tournament or, indeed, of their two-month tour of South Africa. Australia's prolific batsmen did not know what had hit them and were bowled out for only 147. England learned that, if they could reach the target in 33 overs or less, they would overhaul Australia on net run-rate. Aggressive hitting from Paul Franks and Stephen Peters took them there with nearly four overs to spare. It then emerged that the Australians and their coach, former Test captain Allan Border, had been unaware of the run-rate ramifications. England had to wait two days to be sure of their place in the final; but India, despite beating Pakistan to tie on points, failed to score quickly enough to pull ahead.

In the other pool, South Africa had beaten Zimbabwe easily and New Zealand less easily, needing another mature innings from van Wyk to get home. New Zealand, however, had beaten Sri Lanka, demolished Zimbabwe by ten wickets, and, thanks to opener James Marshall, did it speedily enough to boost their net run-rate. South Africa were still confident of beating Sri Lanka, which would make these calculations irrelevant. They scored 240, but their pace bowlers, who had been so disciplined thus far, succumbed to the pressure. A third-wicket partnership of 142 between Pradeep Hewage and Chamara Silva took Sri Lanka to 217 for three and, despite a late collapse, the winning boundary came off the penultimate ball. That ensured New Zealand joined England in the final, where a century from England's Peters won the day.

Three batsmen scored 300 runs in the tournament; Christopher Gayle, one of West Indies' seven replacements, made 364, Marshall of New Zealand 325 and Sri Lankan captain Hewage 316 at 105.33. Muleki Nkala of Zimbabwe and Ramnaresh Sarwan of West Indies led the bowlers with 16 wickets each. Most teams contained a wrist-spinner; Goolam Bodi, the South African "chinaman" bowler, was one of the most impressive. Abdur Razzaq, of Pakistan, and the Indian Amit Bhandari were two of the more successful pace bowlers. Thomas Odoyo of Kenya was the leading all-rounder, with 293 runs and 15 wickets.

Note: Matches in this section were not first-class.

Gavaskar Pool

At Johannesburg, January 11. South Africa won by four wickets. India 197 (49.2 overs) (M. Kaif 31, V. Sehwag 38, R. Shanbal 43; V. P. Mpitsang three for 27, J. Rudolph three for 42); South Africa 201 for six (46.4 overs) (M. N. van Wyk 86 not out, Extras 32; A. Bhandari three for 31).

At Soweto, January 12. Kenya won by eight wickets. Scotland 202 (50 overs) (F. Watts 45, G. Butchart 31, N. Millar 30, Extras 32; J. Ababu three for 42); Kenya 208 for two (35.5 overs) (A. Janmohammed 80, T. Odoyo 96 not out).

At Lenasia, January 13. India won by seven wickets. Scotland 103 (48 overs) (S. Singh three for 15, V. Sehwag three for four); India 104 for three (26.3 overs) (M. Kaif 48 not out; G. Maiden three for 37).

At Soweto, January 13. South Africa won by 80 runs. South Africa 283 for eight (50 overs) (M. Lumb 52, J. C. Kent 102, M. Street 52; T. Odoyo three for 71); Kenya 203 for eight (50 overs) (A. Janmohammed 38, T. Odoyo 42, E. Mboya 57; J. Rudolph three for 38).

At Azaadville, January 15. India won by 175 runs. India 253 for nine (50 overs) (R. S. Sodhi 126, M. Kaif 50; A. Mboya five for 47); Kenya 78 (28.2 overs) (Harbhajan Singh three for five, A. Solanki three for 22).

At Potchefstroom, January 15. South Africa won by eight wickets. Scotland 110 (38.1 overs) (W. Samsodien three for 20); South Africa 111 for two (19.2 overs) (M. Lumb 51 not out, M. N. van Wyk 54 not out).

South Africa 6 pts, India 4 pts, Kenya 2 pts, Scotland 0 pts. South Africa and India qualified for the Super League.

Sobers Pool

At Centurion (Laudium Oval), January 12. Bangladesh won by four wickets. Namibia 105 (43 overs); Bangladesh 109 for six (28.1 overs).

At Pretoria (St Alban's College), January 12. England won by four wickets. New Zealand 180 (47.1 overs) (J. A. H. Marshall 35, L. Vincent 33); England 181 for six (43.2 overs) (G. P. Swann 39, G. R. Haywood 39).

At Pretoria (University), January 13. New Zealand won by 99 runs. New Zealand 278 for eight (50 overs) (J. A. H. Marshall 40, D. Kelly 88, P. Ingram 82; Shabbir Khan three for 57); Bangladesh 179 (46.3 overs) (Al-Shahrian Rokon 40, Mushfiq-ur-Rahman 33; R. M. West three for 33, B. Martin three for 52).

At Randjesfontein, January 13. England won by three wickets. Namibia 161 for nine (50 overs) (B. Kotze 38, D. Viljoen 33, Extras 35; P. J. Franks three for 19); England 162 for seven (33.4 overs) (R. W. T. Key 35, O. A. Shah 40, Extras 34; R. Scholtz five for 29).

At Pretoria (Will Hofmeyr Oval), January 15. Bangladesh won by three wickets. England 223 (49.3 overs) (P. J. Franks 65, C. P. Schofield 34; Mushfiq-ur-Rahman three for 36); Bangladesh 225 for seven (44 overs) (Maharab Hossain 62, Al-Shahriar Rokon 48).

At Pretoria (University), January 15. New Zealand won by 212 runs. New Zealand 372 for seven (50 overs) (D. Kelly 77, J. A. H. Marshall 164 not out, P. McGlashan 46, Extras 32); Namibia 160 (43.5 overs) (R. Walters 48, B. Kotze 31; T. Anderson three for 19, P. Ingram three for 12).

England 4 pts, New Zealand 4 pts, Bangladesh 4 pts, Namibia 0 pts. England and New Zealand qualified for the Super League on net run-rate.

Bradman Pool

At Boksburg (CBC Old Boys), January 12. Denmark won by two wickets. Ireland 160 (44 overs) (B. Dunlop 57, Extras 37; A. Khan three for 23, J. Larsen three for 18); Denmark 161 for eight (48.3 overs) (D. Christiansen 36, Extras 30; D. McGerrigle five for 26).

At Benoni, January 12. Pakistan won by seven wickets. Sri Lanka 168 (47 overs) (P. R. Hewage 80 not out; Abdur Razzaq three for 23, Waqas Ahmed three for 32); Pakistan 169 for three (46.5 overs) (Hasan Raza 90 not out, Bazid Khan 41 not out).

At Boksburg (CBC Old Boys), January 13. Pakistan won by 277 runs. Pakistan 348 for seven (50 overs) (Hafiz Majid 37, Bazid Khan 106, Abdur Razzaq 84, Humayun Farhat 56, Extras 42; T. Nielsen four for 58); Denmark 71 for seven (50 overs).

At Boksburg (CBC School), January 13. Sri Lanka won by two wickets. Ireland 159 for nine (45 overs) (S. Carruthers 35, C. Hosford 33); Sri Lanka 163 for eight (48 overs) (U. A. Fernando 49, I. C. Zoysa 31 not out).

At Kempton Park (Barnard Stadium), January 15. Sri Lanka won by seven wickets. Denmark 97 (49.2 overs); Sri Lanka 100 for three (18.5 overs) (P. R. Hewage 35 not out).

At Kempton Park (Avion Park), January 15. Pakistan won by 139 runs. Pakistan 292 for eight (50 overs) (Inam-ul-Haq 84, Saeed Anwar, jun. 51, Hasan Raza 65); Ireland 153 (48.3 overs) (Shoaib Malik three for 20).

Pakistan 6 pts, Sri Lanka 4 pts, Denmark 2 pts, Ireland 0 pts. Pakistan and Sri Lanka qualified for the Super League.

Cowdrey Pool

At Potchefstroom, January 12. Australia won by 103 runs. Australia 352 for eight (50 overs) (D. Thornley 126, M. North 115, B. Oliver 35; M. L. Nkala three for 59); Zimbabwe 249 (41.4 overs) (A. Maregwede 59, M. A. Vermeulen 69, G. Barrett 41; S. Busbridge three for 55).

At Potchefstroom, January 13. Australia won by 71 runs. Australia 299 for eight (50 overs) (J. Hopes 105, T. Anderson 30, B. Oliver 33, M. Miller 30, Extras 40; A. Jan three for 30); West Indies 228 for seven (50 overs) (C. Gayle 65, D. Ganga 32, R. R. Sarwan 35, R. Hinds 33, M. Graham 30 not out).

At Klerksdorp (Recreation Centre), January 13. Zimbabwe won by 147 runs. Zimbabwe 290 for eight (50 overs) (L. S. Malloch-Brown 62, N. A. Ferreira 32, M. A. Vermeulen 112; R. Dikana three for 41); Papua New Guinea 143 (39 overs) (J. Iga 30; M. L. Nkala four for 20, D. Mutendera five for 25).

At Klerksdorp (Manzil Park), January 14. West Indies won by ten wickets. Papua New Guinea 59 (26 overs) (S. John four for 17, R. R. Sarwan three for 12); West Indies 60 for no wkt (10.5 overs).

At Orkney, January 15. Australia won by 259 runs. Australia 398 for six (50 overs) (L. Stevens 35, C. Davies 40, S. Kremerskothen 164, T. Anderson 36, M. Klinger 56); Papua New Guinea 139 (34.3 overs) (J. Iga 36, R. Dikana 32; S. Busbridge four for 38, S. Tubb three for 28).

At Potchefstroom, January 15. Zimbabwe won by five wickets. West Indies 234 for eight (50 overs) (R. Hinds 77, S. C. Joseph 48, R. R. Sarwan 63; M. L. Nkala five for 51); Zimbabwe 236 for five (45.1 overs) (G. Barrett 67, M. A. Vermeulen 63, D. Ebrahim 48 not out).

Australia 6 pts, Zimbabwe 4 pts, West Indies 2 pts, Papua New Guinea 0 pts. Australia and Zimbabwe qualified for the Super League.

SUPER LEAGUE

Pollock Pool

At Port Elizabeth, January 21. South Africa won by seven wickets. Zimbabwe 177 (50 overs) (D. Ebrahim 60 not out, Extras 33); South Africa 181 for three (38.2 overs) (M. Lumb 33, J. C. Kent 84 not out).

At Port Elizabeth, January 22. New Zealand won by 41 runs. New Zealand 180 (48.5 overs) (J. I. Englefield 54; C. M. Bandara four for 20); Sri Lanka 139 (46.5 overs) (U. A. Fernando 36; B. Martin three for 12).

At Cape Town, January 25. South Africa won by five wickets. New Zealand 194 (45.2 overs) (L. Vincent 55, J. Franklin 55, Extras 43; G. H. Bodi four for 26); South Africa 196 for five (46 overs) (M. N. van Wyk 51 not out, G. D. Elliott 36, M. W. Creed 32 not out).

At East London, January 26. Sri Lanka won by four wickets. Zimbabwe 137 for nine (50 overs) (M. L. Nkala 33; N. S. H. Ratwatte three for 27, C. M. Bandara three for 48); Sri Lanka 138 for six (42 overs) (P. R. Hewage 80 not out; M. L. Nkala four for 26).

At Bloemfontein, January 28. New Zealand won by ten wickets. Zimbabwe 97 (31.2 overs) (K. Mills four for 32, J. Franklin four for 20); New Zealand 98 for no wkt (12.2 overs) (D. Kelly 46 not out, J. A. H. Marshall 39 not out).

At Durban, January 30. Sri Lanka won by three wickets. South Africa 240 (50 overs) (A. I. Gait 31, J. C. Kent 55, M. Street 35, G. D. Elliott 45; C. M. Bandara three for 44); Sri Lanka 244 for seven (49.5 overs) (P. R. Hewage 83, P. C. Silva 85).

New Zealand 4 pts, South Africa 4 pts, Sri Lanka 4 pts, Zimbabwe 0 pts. New Zealand qualified for the final on net run-rate.

D'Oliveira Pool

At Centurion, January 19. England won by 18 runs. England 251 (49.3 overs) (S. D. Peters 92, R. W. T. Key 35; Imran Tahir four for 54); Pakistan 233 (48.5 overs) (Humayun Farhat 34, Hafiz Majid 49, Shoaib Malik 33; G. R. Napier three for 40).

At Centurion, January 20. Australia won by six wickets. India 174 (49.2 overs) (M. Kaif 60, S. Singh 38); Australia 175 for four (29.3 overs) (C. Davies 31, J. Hopes 51, T. Anderson 30 not out).

At Kimberley, January 23. Australia won by 27 runs. Australia 253 for eight (50 overs) (J. Hopes 71, M. Klinger 64, B. Oliver 40); Pakistan 226 (45.5 overs) (Hafiz Majid 31, Bazid Khan 32, Abdur Razzaq 34, Saeed Anwar, jun. 60 not out; M. Miller three for 53, S. Busbridge three for 35).

At Benoni, January 24. India won by 51 runs, England's target having been revised to 204 from 39 overs. India 252 for eight (50 overs) (A. A. Pagnis 99, V. Sarvanan 34 not out); England 152 (33.5 overs) (R. W. T. Key 57, P. J. Franks 31; V. Sehwag three for 32).

At Cape Town, January 27. England won by six wickets. Australia 147 (47.2 overs) (M. Klinger 62 not out); England 151 for four (29.1 overs) (S. D. Peters 51, P. J. Franks 41).

At Durban, January 29. India won by five wickets. Pakistan 188 (47 overs) (Humayun Farhat 43, Inam-ul-Haq 45 not out; A. Bhandari four for 49, R. S. Sodhi three for 13); India 191 for five (40.1 overs) (A. A. Pagnis 52, M. Kaif 53 not out, A. Solanki 34 not out).

England 4 pts, Australia 4 pts, India 4 pts, Pakistan 0 pts. England qualified for the final on net run-rate.

PLATE LEAGUE

Majiet Pool

At Potchefstroom, January 19. Bangladesh won by three wickets. Kenya 132 (45.5 overs) (F. Otieno 39, T. Odoyo 44; Al-Shahriar Rokon four for seven); Bangladesh 134 for seven (40.2 overs) (Fahim Muntasir 38 not out, S. Choudhury 33 not out; T. Odoyo four for 34).

At Lenasia, January 19. Ireland won by six wickets. Papua New Guinea 118 (40.5 overs) (D. Alu 32 not out; K. Spelman five for 16); Ireland 119 for four (29.5 overs) (J. Bushe 48, C. Hosford 33).

At Johannesburg (St John's College), January 20. Bangladesh won by 161 runs. Bangladesh 263 (48.3 overs) (Reza-ul-Haque 50, Towhid Hossain 64, Al-Shahriar Rokon 46, Extras 31); Papua New Guinea 102 (40.5 overs) (Tanvir-ul-Islam five for 29).

At Fochville, January 20. Kenya won by four wickets. Ireland 191 (48.5 overs) (C. Hosford 47, Extras 44; T. Odoyo five for 32); Kenya 195 for six (48.4 overs) (F. Otieno 70 not out, T. Odoyo 46).

At Benoni, January 22. Bangladesh won by three wickets. Ireland 169 (48.4 overs) (E. C. Joyce 67 not out; Shabbir Khan four for 23, Tanvir-ul-Islam three for 42); Bangladesh 173 for seven (42.5 overs) (Al-Shahriar Rokon 46, Fahim Muntasir 31; S. Harrison three for 47).

At Johannesburg (St Stithian's College), January 22. Kenya won by 50 runs. Kenya 211 (49.4 overs) (A. Janmohammed 72, T. Odoyo 40, F. Karmali 37; T. Dai five for 16); Papua New Guinea 161 (46 overs) (R. Leka 34 not out; F. Otieno three for 15).

Bangladesh 6 pts, Kenya 4 pts, Ireland 2 pts, Papua New Guinea 0 pts. Bangladesh qualified for the final.

Procter Pool

At Pretoria (St Alban's College), January 19. West Indies won by 200 runs. West Indies 307 for six (50 overs) (D. Ganga 58, C. Gayle 69, R. Hinds 64, R. R. Sarwan 54 not out; T. Thogersen three for 57); Denmark 107 (30.4 overs) (R. R. Sarwan three for 16).

At Kempton Park (Avion Park), January 19. Scotland won by 156 runs. Scotland 244 for nine (50 overs) (G. Butchart 128 not out, Extras 38; B. Kotze three for 36); Namibia 88 (32.2 overs) (J. Blain three for 19, R. Mitchison three for eight).

At Kempton Park (Avion Park), January 20. Scotland won by 82 runs. Scotland 222 for seven (38 overs) (G. Butchart 53, N. Millar 72, A. Speirs 32); Denmark 140 (37.3 overs) (A. Khan 30; G. Maiden three for 21).

At Boksburg (CBC Old Boys), January 20. West Indies won by eight wickets. Namibia 94 (38.3 overs) (R. R. Sarwan three for 14; C. Gayle three for 14); West Indies 95 for two (17.4 overs) (Extras 30).

At Johannesburg (Wanderers Oval 3), January 22. Denmark won by 227 runs. Denmark 305 for five (50 overs) (J. Hensen 50, D. Christiansen 90 not out, B. Hensen 34 not out, Extras 87; W. Slabbert three for 33); Namibia 78 (30.5 overs) (D. Christiansen four for 27, T. Nielsen three for nought).

At Fochville, January 22. West Indies won by five wickets. Scotland 144 (48.1 overs) (G. Maiden 30); West Indies 148 for five (37.3 overs) (C. Gayle 55, R. Hinds 33).

West Indies 6 pts, Scotland 4 pts, Denmark 2 pts, Namibia 0 pts. West Indies qualified for the final.

Plate Final

At Fochville, January 24. Bangladesh won by six wickets. West Indies 243 for eight (50 overs) (C. Gayle 141 not out, M. N. Samuels 33; Mushfiq-ur-Rahman three for 48); Bangladesh 245 for four (46.5 overs) (Reza-ul-Haque 34, Maharab Hossain 63, Al-Shahriar Rokon 90 not out).

ENGLAND UNDER-19 TOUR RESULTS

Matches – Played 17: Won 7, Lost 5, Drawn 5. Abandoned 1.

Note: Matches in this section were not first-class.

At Cape Town, December 3, 4, 5. Drawn. Toss: Western Cape Academy. Western Cape Academy 262 (D. Barns 43, K. Blakely 77 not out, S. Conrad 39, Extras 50; R. J. Logan three for 45) and 129 for seven dec. (A. G. Puttick 30, D. Barns 37 not out; G. P. Swann three for 45); England Under-19 148 (G. P. Swann 30; D. Henry four for 56, N. Kruger three for 37) and 109 for four (M. A. Gough 34 not out).

At Paarl, December 6, 7, 8. Drawn. Toss: England Under-19. England Under-19 293 (S. D. Peters 33, I. N. Flanagan 68, G. P. Swann 31, G. R. Haywood 52, A. W. Laraman 38; W. du Toit four for 81) and 191 for three dec. (S. D. Peters 55, R. W. T. Key 78, G. R. Napier 56); Boland Under-19 253 (R. Arendse 67, J. L. Ontong 50, G. Strydom 52, Extras 40; C. P. Schofield five for 82, G. P. Swann three for 39) and 83 for one (S. van der Merwe 54 not out).

SOUTH AFRICA UNDER-19 v ENGLAND UNDER-19

First Unofficial Test

At Cape Town, December 11, 12, 13, 14. Drawn. Toss: South Africa Under-19.
England salvaged a draw after a thrilling finish in which they followed on and were bowled out again only 38 ahead. That left South Africa two overs to chase 39. Creed, promoted to open, hooked Logan's first ball for six, but the task was beyond them. Despite a century opening stand in England's second innings between Peters and Key, only Gough, of the remaining nine batsmen, made more than 19. He batted more than four hours for his 32 not out, having been dropped at second slip by Elliott on five. On the first two days, Elliott had exhibited tremendous concentration and temperament in making 201 not out, assisting South Africa's recovery from 171 for five at tea on the first day. His captain, Street, batted sensibly for a three-hour 79. Franks bowled with admirable control and stamina, but only Swann provided decent support. Swann also drove sweetly in England's first innings for 75, which included 11 fours and two sixes, but most of the batting was irresponsible.

Close of play: First day, South Africa Under-19 285-6 (G. D. Elliott 85*, J. Rudolph 19*); Second day, England Under-19 155-5 (G. R. Haywood 12*, R. J. Logan 0*); Third day, England Under-19 96-0 (S. D. Peters 48*, R. W. T. Key 42*).

South Africa Under-19

A. G. Puttick c Peters b Franks	4		
A. I. Gait c Flanagan b Swann	55	– (3) not out	2
J. de Nobrega b Franks	0	– (2) not out	8
*M. Street c and b Swann	79		
†M. N. van Wyk b Franks	15		
G. D. Elliott not out	201		
M. Lumb b Swann	11		
J. Rudolph b Franks	28		
M. W. Creed b Haywood	61	– (1) c Flanagan b Logan	6
R. Peterson not out	15		
B 8, l-b 12, w 5, n-b 10	35	B 2. l-b 1	3

1/12 2/12 3/131 4/154 5/164   (8 wkts dec.) 504   1/6   (1 wkt) 19
6/203 7/302 8/450

V. P. Mpitsang did not bat.

Bowling: *First Innings*—Logan 29.5–5–104–0; Franks 35–9–65–4; Napier 14–1–71–0; Schofield 17–1–69–0; Swann 43–6–139–3; Haywood 7–0–36–1. *Second Innings*—Logan 1–0–9–1; Franks 1–0–7–0.

England Under-19

S. D. Peters c Gait b Creed	4	– c van Wyk b Mpitsang	92
R. W. T. Key c Street b Lumb	39	– c Mpitsang b Creed	51
I. N. Flanagan c Puttick b Creed	11	– run out	2
G. P. Swann c Street b Peterson	75	– lbw b Rudolph	12
M. A. Gough c van Wyk b Lumb	0	– not out	32
G. R. Haywood c Creed b Lumb	30	– c van Wyk b Creed	6
R. J. Logan c Elliott b Mpitsang	3	– (11) c Elliott b Rudolph	0
G. R. Napier c Elliott b Mpitsang	40	– (7) lbw b de Nobrega	19
*P. J. Franks c Lumb b Mpitsang	20	– (8) c Gait b Mpitsang	6
C. P. Schofield c Mpitsang b Creed	18	– (9) c Gait b Creed	6
†N. J. Wilton not out	6	– (10) lbw b Mpitsang	1
B 10, l-b 5, w 7, n-b 18	40	B 3, l-b 9, w 4, n-b 13	29
	286		**256**

1/14 2/44 3/90 4/106 5/154   286   1/105 2/121 3/159 4/176 5/185   256
6/162 7/215 8/236 9/253   6/222 7/233 8/244 9/255

Bowling: *First Innings*—Mpitsang 24–6–69–3; Creed 21.4–5–69–3; Lumb 20–1–74–3; Peterson 19–4–45–1; Rudolph 5–1–14–0. *Second Innings*—Creed 21–8–64–3; Mpitsang 28–11–36–3; Lumb 20–7–59–0; Peterson 15–7–32–0; Rudolph 37.1–18–45–2; de Nobrega 7–4–8–1.

Umpires: J. C. Paleker and P. J. Reypert.

At Port Elizabeth (University), December 17, 18, 19. Drawn. Toss: South African Students. South African Students 315 for nine dec. (D. Moffat 130, G. King 78, A. Jacobs 32; J. C. Powell four for 42) and 140 for two dec. (D. Moffat 72 not out); England Under-19 192 (G. P. Swann 44, C. P. Schofield 34; M. K. Holmes three for 50, G. T. Love three for 53) and 166 for eight (G. R. Napier 110; N. Evans four for 53, G. T. Love three for 49).
   Moffat was dropped six times and caught once off a no-ball in making 202 runs in the match.

At Port Elizabeth (University), December 20. South African Students won by three wickets. Toss: England Under-19. England Under-19 194 (48.4 overs) (R. W. T. Key 105 not out; G. T. Love three for 26); South African Students 195 for seven (48 overs) (J. M. Henderson 56, A. Jacobs 33, C. T. Enslin 36 not out; J. C. Powell three for 24).

At Zwide, December 22. England Under-19 won by 28 runs. Toss: England Under-19. England Under-19 265 for nine (50 overs) (G. P. Swann 47, C. P. Schofield 35 not out, Extras 49; S. Bosch four for 45, K. Peterson three for 52); South African Schools Colts 237 for nine (50 overs) (J. Kreusch 57, D. Makalima 77; J. C. Powell three for 40).
   Swann hit four sixes in five balls from Peterson. Makalima hit seven sixes, four of them in one over from Swann.

At Port Elizabeth (St George's Park), December 23. England Under-19 won by 47 runs. Toss: England Under-19. England Under-19 268 (50 overs) (P. J. Franks 41, O. A. Shah 57, G. P. Swann 40, J. C. Powell 36, Extras 31; G. H. Bodi three for 42); South African Schools 221 (44.5 overs) (M. Lumb 30, J. C. Kent 58, M. N. van Wyk 60; G. R. Napier four for 43, J. C. Powell three for 46).
   South African Schools' innings was restricted to 48 overs because of their slow over-rate.

SOUTH AFRICA UNDER-19 v ENGLAND UNDER-19

Second Unofficial Test

At Fochville, December 27, 28, 29, 30. Drawn. Toss: South Africa Under-19.
   South Africa took first use of an excellent pitch and, despite two early wickets, climbed above 500 for the second match running. England used eight bowlers but only Swann, who took four wickets and conceded barely two an over, had much effect. Van Wyk, already, at 18, the first-choice Free State wicket-keeper, played a marvellously mature innings of 188 in six and a half

hours, hitting 29 fours and a six. England's reply got off to a dreadful start, and they were 128 for eight after 80 minutes of the third day. However, Franks, playing straight and with good judgment, remained unbeaten for 246 minutes. He added 75 with Wilton and a further 88 in even time with Grove. England had three and a half sessions to negotiate and in the end saved the game comfortably, with Shah and Gough sharing a third-wicket stand of 149. It helped that the South African bowlers were exhausted.

Close of play: First day, South Africa Under-19 311-6 (M. N. van Wyk 120*, M. W. Creed 2*); Second day, England Under-19 77-5 (G. R. Napier 11*); Third day, England Under-19 36-0 (S. D. Peters 21*, R. W. T. Key 8*).

South Africa Under-19

J. G. Myburgh c Wilton b Swann	64	G. H. Bodi c and b Swann	69
A. I. Gait b Grove	6	W. Samsodien not out	29
J. C. Kent c Wilton b Napier	17	V. P. Mpitsang not out	4
*M. Street c Wilton b Franks	24	B 7, l-b 7, w 3, n-b 5	22
†M. N. van Wyk c Key b Gough	188		—
G. D. Elliott c Key b Powell	39	1/9 2/36 3/99	(9 wkts dec.) 506
J. Rudolph c Shah b Swann	20	4/140 5/238 6/291	
M. W. Creed lbw b Swann	24	7/358 8/420 9/496	

Bowling: Grove 13–1–63–1; Franks 23–5–66–1; Schofield 20–5–83–0; Napier 7–1–34–1; Powell 33–6–118–1; Swann 42–15–90–4; Gough 10–2–38–1; Shah 1–1–0–0.

England Under-19

S. D. Peters c van Wyk b Creed	16	– b Bodi	55
R. W. T. Key c Bodi b Creed	4	– b Bodi	36
M. A. Gough lbw b Rudolph	19	– b Bodi	54
*O. A. Shah b Samsodien	13	– not out	104
G. P. Swann b Bodi	5	– not out	5
G. R. Napier c Street b Rudolph	32		
J. C. Powell b Mpitsang	1		
C. P. Schofield b Rudolph	21		
P. J. Franks not out	119		
†N. J. Wilton c Street b Samsodien	23		
J. O. Grove c van Wyk b Creed	12		
B 4, l-b 8, w 2, n-b 12	26	B 5, l-b 6, n-b 9	20
	—		—
1/5 2/25 3/48 4/63 5/77	291	1/97 2/98 3/247	(3 wkts) 274
6/87 7/117 8/128 9/203			

Bowling: *First Innings*—Mpitsang 18–3–57–1; Creed 15.4–3–56–3; Samsodien 16–2–49–2; Rudolph 39–17–62–3; Bodi 20–6–41–1; Kent 4–0–14–0. *Second Innings*—Creed 13–2–41–0; Mpitsang 21–6–43–0; Samsodien 14–3–30–0; Rudolph 19–2–54–0; Bodi 20–7–51–3; Kent 15–3–44–0.

Umpires: K. Hurter and A. O'Connor.

At Benoni, January 3. First unofficial one-day international: No result (abandoned).

At Benoni, January 4. Second unofficial one-day international: South Africa Under-19 won by seven wickets. Toss: South Africa Under-19. England Under-19 171 (47.4 overs) (S. D. Peters 57, N. J. Wilton 33; M. W. Creed three for 27); South Africa Under-19 172 for three (31.4 overs) (J. G. Myburgh 80).

At Centurion, January 6. Third unofficial one-day international: South Africa Under-19 won by 50 runs. Toss: South Africa Under-19. South Africa Under-19 252 for nine (50 overs) (M. N. van Wyk 45); England Under-19 202 (44.5 overs) (M. A. Gough 56 not out, C. P. Schofield 49; M. Lumb four for 43).

England Under-19's matches in the MTN Under-19 World Cup (January 12–February 1) may be found in that section.

HERO HONDA WORLD CUP, 1997

By CAROL SALMON

India hosted the biggest Women's World Cup to date – with 11 teams taking part – in December 1997. Australia claimed their fourth title in six tournaments, and did it so convincingly that their failure to reach the final in the last competition, in England in 1993, could be written off as a temporary aberration. Of their 46 World Cup games since 1974, they have won 39 and lost only four, with one tie and two abandoned.

Here, they won all their seven matches after the first fixture was washed out; on the way, they ran up 412 for three against Denmark, the highest total in World Cup history, with captain Belinda Clark scoring 229 not out, the first double-century by any individual, female or male, in a one-day international. But Australia's triumph was essentially one of teamwork.

As in 1993, the runners-up were New Zealand, who were also unbeaten until the final, though they were held to a tie by India during the group matches. Their best player was 35-year-old opener Debbie Hockley, who amassed 456 runs at 76.00, to become the leading run-scorer in the history of the World Cup with a total of 1,351, shading her long-time rival, England's Janette Brittin, on 1,314.

England's hopes of retaining the title they won at home four years earlier were high when they won their opening four games. In Pune, Charlotte Edwards celebrated her 18th birthday with 173 not out against the persevering but limited Irish attack – a World Cup record, until Clark overtook it the same day. But their optimism was tempered when Australia beat them out of sight in a group match in Nagpur. The seam of Cathryn Fitzpatrick and the leg-spin of Olivia Magno dismissed them for 95, which Australia sailed past in 27 overs. England won their quarter-final, against Sri Lanka, easily enough, only to encounter New Zealand, their fellow-finalists in 1993, at Chennai (formerly Madras). This match was overshadowed by controversy when England were docked an over for failing to complete their allocation of 50 within three hours.

Coach Megan Lear argued that the umpires had not allowed for two five-minute drinks breaks taken during New Zealand's innings because of the baking heat, let alone for the amusing stick-flailing antics of one of the ground staff trying to clear basking dogs off the outfield. England believed they had won their case but, while batting, discovered that the over had been removed again. Two angry trips to the middle by captain Karen Smithies were in vain, and her team were bowled out 20 short in what was now the penultimate over. Hosts India lost two overs in similar circumstances in the other semi-final in Delhi. After rain shortened the match to 32 overs, they managed to keep Australia down to 123. Chasing 124 in 30, India were handicapped by a string of run-outs, and they fell well short. Captain Pramila Bhatt subsequently announced her retirement.

The four semi-finalists had also been the top four teams in the previous World Cup, and the expansion of the competition to 11 (it would have been 12, but for Canada's late withdrawal) led to some gross mismatches in the opening rounds. In any case, the group games had little significance, as only three teams were eliminated before the quarter-finals. Of the three new entrants, South Africa and Sri Lanka performed respectably and should be a real force by the next tournament, due to be held in New Zealand in 2000, but Pakistan's World Cup debut was a disaster.

The team was weakened by a dispute between two bodies claiming to be the true national representatives – the Pakistan Women's Cricket Control Association and the Pakistan Women's Cricket Association, which was further divided into two factions. All three groups sent officials to the meeting of the International Women's Cricket Council in Calcutta coinciding with the tournament. IWCC eventually decided to recognise the PWCCA, represented by Shaiza and Sharmeen Khan, dubbed the "super-rich sisters" by the Indian press. Their father provided financial backing for the team, in which they were the leading players. But they lost all their five matches, usually heavily, and were bowled out for 27 inside 14 overs by Australia, the lowest total in World Cup history. When they played Ireland at Gurgaon, 15,000 were reported to have turned up – the biggest crowd outside the final – to barrack them.

To address the problem of one-sided matches, IWCC ruled that only the eight quarter-finalists (Australia, England, Holland, India, Ireland, New Zealand, South Africa and Sri Lanka) would be accepted for the 2000 World Cup, and introduced a qualifying competition to precede the 2004 tournament in South Africa. But Pakistan and Sri Lanka were accorded full membership of IWCC, with Canada and Japan (who had also withdrawn from this tournament) made associates. Bangladesh's application was put on hold. IWCC now has 11 full members, and hopes to integrate with its male counterpart, the International Cricket Council.

The tournament was not without the odd organisational hiccup. India found a sponsor, Hero Honda, only at the eleventh hour, and there was some horrendous travelling for the teams. England had any number of 3 a.m. wake-up calls and seven-hour coach journeys, but this had little impact on the sharp end as they had ample time to prepare for the one game that really counted – the semi-final in Chennai. Several teams failed to attend the opening dinner because they were becalmed in Delhi traffic jams, and the IWCC hierarchy missed the closing dinner because their taxi got lost.

But overall the organisers' efforts in arranging grounds, travel and accommodation for 11 teams and 33 games were highly commendable. Coloured clothing and trousers were worn by all teams, for the first time. And the final at Eden Gardens in Calcutta was a memorable occasion, with at least 50,000 in the crowd – some estimates said 65,000. The turnout was politically contrived, the West Bengal government having commandeered 1,600 buses (somewhat to the annoyance of local commuters) in order to ferry schoolgirls to the match. But the girls responded enthusiastically to the occasion, adopted Australia as their own and cheered them on to victory.

Note: Matches in this section were not first-class.

Group A

At Chennai, December 10. Australia v Ireland. No result (abandoned).

At Bangalore, December 10. Denmark won by eight wickets. Pakistan 65 (30.4 overs) (S. Nielsen four for nine, J. Jonsson three for 22); Denmark 66 for two (29.3 overs).

At Hyderabad, December 10. England won by seven runs. England 94 for seven (20 overs) (C. M. Edwards 38); South Africa 87 for nine (20 overs) (K. Smithies three for 26, C. M. Edwards three for 15).

At Bangalore, December 12. Australia won by ten wickets. South Africa 163 for nine (50 overs) (L. Olivier 51); Australia 166 for no wkt (28.5 overs) (B. J. Clark 93 not out, J. Broadbent 61 not out).

At Chennai, December 12. Ireland won by nine wickets. Denmark 56 for seven (23 overs) (B. McDonald three for 12); Ireland 57 for one (19.1 overs).

At Vijayawada, December 12. England won by 230 runs. England 376 for two (50 overs) (J. A. Brittin 138, H. C. Plimmer 36, B. A. Daniels 142 not out, J. S. Metcalfe 35 not out); Pakistan 146 for three (47 overs) (Shaiza Khan 41, Sharmeen Khan 35 not out).
Brittin and Daniels added 203 for England's second wicket. Pakistan were penalised three overs because of their slow over-rate.

At Hyderabad, December 14. Australia won by nine wickets. Pakistan 27 (13.4 overs) (J. M. Dannatt three for five, O. J. Magno three for nought); Australia 28 for one (6.1 overs).
   Pakistan's total of 27 was the lowest ever in the World Cup. The match lasted only 19.5 overs.

At Hyderabad, December 14. England won by 194 runs. England 301 for four (50 overs) (C. M. Edwards 72, H. C. Plimmer 87, J. A. Brittin 51, J. Cassar 43 not out); Denmark 107 for seven (50 overs) (K. Mikkelsen 39 not out).

At Pune, December 14. South Africa won by nine wickets. Ireland 155 (43.1 overs) (M. Grealey 57, Extras 39; D. J. Reid three for 27); South Africa 156 for one (27.5 overs) (L. Olivier 78 not out).

At Mumbai, December 16. Australia won by 363 runs. Australia 412 for three (50 overs) (B. J. Clark 229 not out, L. M. Keightley 60, K. L. Rolton 64, Extras 31); Denmark 49 (25.5 overs) (K. L. Rolton three for nine).
   Clark's 229 not out, from 157 balls with 23 fours, was the first double-hundred in any one-day international. She reached 100 in 64 balls, breaking her own record for the fastest century at this level. The total of 412 was a World Cup record. In Denmark's reply, only Extras reached double figures.

At Pune, December 16. England won by 208 runs. England 324 for three (50 overs) (C. M. Edwards 173 not out, J. A. Brittin 37, J. Cassar 50 not out, Extras 31); Ireland 116 (41.1 overs) (C. Beggs 49; M. A. Reynard four for six).
   On her 18th birthday, Edwards scored 173 not out from 155 balls, with 19 fours. It was the second highest score in the World Cup, after Clark's 229 not out scored the same day.

At Baroda, December 16. South Africa won by 149 runs. South Africa 258 for seven (50 overs) (L. Olivier 49, A. Kotze 30, A. Kuylaars 74 not out); Pakistan 109 (39.4 overs) (Sharmeen Khan 48; C. E. Eksteen three for 28).

At Nagpur, December 18. Australia won by eight wickets. England 95 (49.4 overs) (C. L. Fitzpatrick three for 25, O. J. Magno four for ten); Australia 96 for two (26.5 overs) (B. J. Clark 40, M. A. Goszko 51 not out).

At Baroda, December 18. South Africa won by 99 runs. South Africa 213 for six (50 overs) (L. Olivier 51, D. Terblanche 48); Denmark 114 (46.2 overs) (Extras 38).

At Gurgaon, December 18. Ireland won by 182 runs. Ireland 242 for seven (50 overs) (C. Beggs 31, M. Grealey 62, C. O'Neill 45, C. O'Leary 48 not out, Extras 34; Shaiza Khan three for 42); Pakistan 60 (30.3 overs) (C. O'Neill four for ten, A. Spence three for four).

Australia 27 pts, England 24 pts, South Africa 18 pts, Ireland 15 pts, Denmark 6 pts, Pakistan 0 pts.

Group B

At Agra, December 9. Holland v West Indies. No result (abandoned).

At Delhi, December 9. India v Sri Lanka. No result (abandoned).

At Ghaziabad, December 11. New Zealand won by eight wickets. Holland 48 for eight (20 overs); New Zealand 49 for two (8.1 overs).

At Delhi, December 11. Sri Lanka won by six wickets. West Indies 79 (29.4 overs) (Extras 32; T. Gunaratne four for six); Sri Lanka 81 for four (30.3 overs).

At Faridabad, December 13. India won by 62 runs. India 145 for seven (40 overs) (A. Jain 42, S. Harikrishna 34, Extras 30); West Indies 83 (33.2 overs) (P. Choudhary five for 21).

At Chandigarh, December 13. New Zealand won by 165 runs. New Zealand 236 for three (50 overs) (D. A. Hockley 100 not out, K. M. Withers 57 not out, Extras 38); Sri Lanka 71 (47.4 overs).

At Ghaziabad, December 15. India won by 93 runs. India 175 for eight (40 overs) (A. Jain 35, Extras 33; A. van Noortwijk four for 25); Holland 82 for nine (40 overs).

At Chandigarh, December 15. New Zealand won by 198 runs. New Zealand 253 for nine (50 overs) (D. A. Hockley 100, M. A. M. Lewis 39, Extras 46; D. Luke three for 57); West Indies 55 (28.4 overs) (K. M. Withers four for five).
Withers's full bowling analysis was 10–6–5–4.

At Delhi, December 17. Holland won by 47 runs. Holland 138 (45.3 overs) (N. Payne 55; C. Seneviratne three for 19, S. Sivanathan four for 18); Sri Lanka 91 (45.2 overs) (A. A. Indralatha 32; S. Kottman four for 24).

At Indore, December 17. Tied. New Zealand 176 for nine (50 overs) (D. A. Hockley 44, E. C. Drumm 69; P. Rau three for 35); India 176 (49.1 overs) (A. Jain 61, C. Aheer 30).
India tied after losing their last six wickets for 24 in seven overs.

New Zealand 21 pts, India 18 pts, Holland 9 pts, Sri Lanka 9 pts, West Indies 3 pts.

Ninth-place play-off

At Delhi, December 20. West Indies won by 101 runs. West Indies 229 for five (45 overs) (C-A. James 95 not out, R. Scott 66); Denmark 128 (40 overs) (M. Frost 36; G. Smith three for 21, E. Gregg three for 36, C-A. James three for 16).

Quarter-finals

At Lucknow, December 20. Australia won by 115 runs. Toss: Australia. Australia 223 for four (50 overs) (B. L. Calver 74, M. Jones 43); Holland 108 for six (50 overs).

At Mohali, December 21. England won by nine wickets. Toss: Sri Lanka. Sri Lanka 104 (43.2 overs) (V. Bowen 38; C. M. Edwards three for 21); England 105 for one (22.1 overs) (C. M. Edwards 57 not out).
Reduced by rain to 46 overs a side. Edwards's three victims were all stumped by Jane Cassar.

At Patna, December 22. India won by five wickets. Toss: South Africa. South Africa 80 (43.1 overs); India 81 for five (28 overs).

At Mumbai, December 23. New Zealand won by 139 runs. Toss: New Zealand. New Zealand 244 for three (50 overs) (D. A. Hockley 70, E. C. Drumm 60, S. Fruin 33, K. M. Withers 32 not out, Extras 35); Ireland 105 for nine (50 overs).

Semi-finals

At Delhi, December 24. Australia won by 19 runs. Toss: India. Australia 123 for seven (32 overs) (B. J. Clark 31, J. Broadbent 33; K. S. P. Bhatt three for 25); India 104 for nine (30 overs) (C. Aheer 48; C. L. Fitzpatrick three for 18).
Rain shortened the match to 32 overs, and India were penalised two overs for their slow over-rate.

At Chennai, December 26. New Zealand won by 20 runs. Toss: New Zealand. New Zealand 175 for six (50 overs) (D. A. Hockley 43, K. M. Withers 35; K. Smithies three for 40); England 155 (47.5 overs) (J. A. Brittin 32, B. A. Daniels 30).
England were penalised one over for their slow over-rate, though they protested that the umpires had not allowed for two drinks breaks.

FINAL

AUSTRALIA v NEW ZEALAND

At Calcutta, December 29. Australia won by five wickets. Toss: New Zealand.

Australia regained the World Cup they had lost in 1993, with a convincing victory at Eden Gardens. They took control from the start despite losing the toss; Calver made two early strikes, and no one except Hockley was able to stand up to the Australian attack. She batted into the 47th over of the innings, when she was eighth out for 79, having taken her aggregate for the tournament to 456. But Australian captain Clark almost caught up with that record – the 52 she scored as she led the run-chase left her only 11 runs behind Hockley, and her average of 148.33 was almost twice as high. A target of 3.3 an over hardly stretched Australia; Clark and Goszko put on 71 to set up victory with 14 balls to spare. In an emotional presentation ceremony, both teams and a crowd of more than 50,000 bused in by the state government joined in singing "We shall overcome". Hockley had the compensation of the individual award, being officially declared "Eve of the Match".

Player of the Match: D. A. Hockley.   *Player of the Series:* B. J. Clark.

New Zealand

D. A. Hockley b Fitzpatrick	79	C. A. Campbell not out		3
E. C. Drumm b Calver	6	K. D. Brown run out		1
S. Fruin c Clark b Calver	8			
K. M. Withers c Price b Mason	5	L-b 10, w 13		23
*M. A. M. Lewis lbw b Magno	10			
K. Ramel run out	1	1/14 (2) 2/36 (3) 3/49 (4) (49.3 overs)		164
C. M. Nicholson lbw b Rolton	2	4/87 (5) 5/99 (6) 6/104 (7)		
S. McLauchlan st Price b Rolton	8	7/125 (8) 8/155 (1)		
†R. Rolls c Calver b Mason	18	9/157 (9) 10/164 (11)		

Bowling: Fitzpatrick 10–2–23–1; Calver 10–1–29–2; Mason 9.3–0–31–2; Magno 6–1–28–1; Rolton 6–1–25–2; Fahey 8–1–18–0.

Australia

*B. J. Clark c and b Campbell	52	O. J. Magno not out		0
J. Broadbent c Lewis b Ramel	15	B 5, l-b 4, w 3, n-b 1		13
M. A. Goszko b Withers	37			
K. L. Rolton c Brown b Ramel	24	1/36 (2) 2/107 (3) (5 wkts, 47.4 overs)		165
M. Jones b Withers	17	3/117 (1) 4/153 (5)		
B. L. Calver not out	7	5/160 (4)		

C. L. Mason, †J. C. Price, C. L. Fitzpatrick and A. J. Fahey did not bat.

Bowling: Withers 10–2–23–2; Nicholson 10–3–26–0; Brown 1–0–10–0; Ramel 4.4–0–23–2; Campbell 10–1–36–1; McLauchlan 9–0–26–0; Hockley 3–0–12–0.

Umpires: A. Bhattacharya and S. Chowdhury.

WORLD CUP WINNERS

1973	England	1981-82	Australia	1993	England
1977-78	Australia	1988-89	Australia	1997-98	Australia

CRICKET IN AUSTRALIA, 1997-98

By JOHN MACKINNON

Colin Miller

For the third year running, Western Australia reached the Sheffield Shield final, and it proved to be third time lucky. After their previous two failures, they made short work of Tasmania, winning with a day to spare. It was a happy finale to the 50th anniversary of their debut in the competition, in 1947-48, when they won the Shield at their first attempt.

As usual, Western Australia were tough opponents on their own ground, winning all their home Shield games except for the day/night match with Queensland. The side suffered less than most from international calls and were at full strength for the final.

Tom Moody led by example with bat and ball. A century and five for 20 in their opening fixture provided an auspicious start; a century and the Shield-winning hit in the final a satisfying climax. For good measure, he was a regular, though not especially successful, member of Australia's one-day squad. Adam Gilchrist launched his season with a double-century, but selection as Australia's one-day wicket-keeper ahead of Ian Healy aroused a measure of national resentment. Gilchrist's eventual success as a one-day opener effectively silenced the critics. He was also the country's leading first-class keeper, for the fourth season running, with 49 dismissals.

Ryan Campbell took the gloves when Gilchrist was away; he retained his volatile batting style, but one of his three hundreds, 177 in Sydney, showed he had learned how to consolidate an innings. His opening partner, Michael Hussey, was conservative by comparison but rather more consistent. For all their individual achievements, however, they managed only one century partnership, 155 in the final.

For a number of years, Justin Langer and Damien Martyn have been on the fringes of the Australian team. Langer's early-season double-century in Adelaide suggested a serious challenge for more permanent recognition. But he was selected only for Australia A, against the touring South Africans. Perhaps Langer was a victim of his own intensity. He was, nevertheless, along with Mark Taylor and the Tasmanian Dene Hills, one of only three players to score 1,000 runs. Martyn had a useful Shield season but really excelled in the one-day Mercantile Mutual series. However, by the time Western Australia had played their first match, in December, Australia were already three games into the one-day international campaign, so Martyn's run came too late. Brendon Julian had a late flourish with the bat as well, underlining a prodigious but unpredictable talent. He and Jo Angel were formidable bowlers on the Perth wicket, with Moody and latterly Mark Atkinson almost equally effective.

Tasmania's season started slowly, with just four points from four games by mid-December. But their luck changed after a successful chase for 399 against a Victorian attack including Shane Warne. That set them up for a run of six consecutive victories and, ultimately, a place in the final in Perth. The catalyst for the win over Victoria came from the long-standing opening pair of Hills and Jamie Cox, who shared a monumental partnership of 297. In the final they opened together in the Shield for the 89th time, beating a record previously held by Trevor Barsby and Matthew Hayden of Queensland. After Cox's great year in 1996-97, Hills became the dominant partner by dint of consecutive double-hundreds – 205 in the Victorian game and 265 off South Australia. Two more centuries, 1,220 runs in all and some brilliant fielding at short leg made him the Sheffield Shield Player of the Year.

David Boon's captaincy was also a big factor in a remarkable team performance, but no one responded more passionately than 34-year-old Colin Miller. Miller's career started in Melbourne back in 1985-86 and continued for a time in Adelaide before his move to Hobart in 1992-93. This season, bowling an intriguing mix of medium-pace and off-breaks, he sent down 150 overs more than any other Australian bowler, finishing with 70 wickets, including 67 in the Shield, an all-time record. The players voted him Lord's Taverners Player of the Year. The supporting cast of bowlers was never less than honest, encouraged by a pitch at the Bellerive Oval that at last had something in it for them.

The batting line-up was one of the best in the competition. The state's premier batsman, Ricky Ponting, enjoyed a flying start to the season, but figured in only the first of the six wins. And on the very day his colleagues were being taken apart in Perth, a drunken Ponting was having his own problems in a Calcutta nightclub, resulting in a hefty fine and much adverse publicity. Michael Di Venuto broke into international one-day cricket, though his only century, a brilliant 189 in the final, came after the match was well out of Tasmania's reach.

Queensland's mid-season surge raised northern hopes of a third title in four years. Successive wins over Tasmania, Western Australia and Victoria were followed by an inexplicable failure under lights against South Australia and then no points at all in the last three games. Ironically, it was during this period that Andrew Symonds at last realised his potential for the benefit of Australian spectators and hit three consecutive hundreds. He and opener Hayden were far and away Queensland's best batsmen. But it was the fast bowlers, led by the lion-hearted Michael Kasprowicz, who gave the side their best days. Andy Bichel and Adam Dale made the most of limited opportunities and there was plenty of quality among the reserves. Paul Jackson and the all-rounder Geoff Foley provided contrasting spin, but Foley's action twice fell foul of umpire Ross Emerson; in the first match, his cause was not helped by the antics of Dean Jones, who mimicked a throw to prompt the umpire. At least Queensland could celebrate winning the one-day Mercantile Mutual Cup.

A visit to Melbourne marked the season's turning point for New South Wales. After they had amassed 532 for nine and reduced Victoria to 166 for seven, their poor fielding and indifferent bowling allowed the Victorians to reach 387, avoiding the follow-on and eventually holding out for a draw – instead of New South Wales's fourth successive win. A six-point certainty was converted to a mere two, and then their form plummeted, with not a point to show for their last four games. Once again, the reserve players showed spasmodic promise. Too often, New South Wales capitulated pathetically, not only in Perth (as is now customary), but also twice to Tasmania. On the credit side, before the season turned sour, New South Wales enjoyed an epic win over eventual champions Western Australia. Inspired by Michael Bevan and Rodney Davison, they rallied from a first-innings deficit of 223, and then 26-year-old leg-spinner Stuart MacGill bowled Western Australia out. MacGill already had a hat-trick against the New Zealand tourists under his belt. His antagonistic demeanour had previously overshadowed his bowling ability but, with Warne's fitness an increasing concern, his 50 wickets took on national significance. He made his Test debut against South Africa. There were several splendid individual performances, especially the batting of Bevan and Davison, who scored three hundreds in successive matches. But the end-of-season collapse highlighted a lack of reserve talent or commitment or both. All told, nine New South Welshmen represented their country, with off-spinner Gavin Robertson taken to India after playing just one first-class match during the season. Seemingly lost to the game was Greg Matthews who, at 37, trod on a ball in a warm-up, broke his foot and never regained his place.

Victoria's lacklustre run – in the last three seasons, they have finished sixth, fifth and fifth – continued. They did even worse in the Mercantile Mutual Cup: they came seventh after succumbing to Australian Capital Territory, who joined the competition for the first time. Off-field dissensions surfaced when the chairman of selectors, John Grant, resigned. Matthew Elliott, Australia's batting star in England a few months earlier, seemed beset with personal problems and finally lost his place in the Australian side. Graeme Vimpani and Ian Harvey, from whom much was expected, were both dropped. Even Dean Jones found the pressures of batting at No. 3 too much and took refuge lower down the order. It was, however, good to see Damien Fleming coming back from injury in style and bowling Victoria to a couple of belated wins. Laurie Harper, a 27-year-old left-hander, came of age with a splendid 160 at North Sydney. His confidence established, he went on to become the side's leading batsman. His continued good form will now be more vital: Jones made a tearful and apparently final exit from the game at a post-season press conference. He had played a record 124 games for Victoria and leads their run-scorers with 10,412; his 9,622 in the Shield put him second only to his former team-mate Jamie Siddons, now with South Australia.

Jones's retirement brought to an end a 40-year dynasty in Victorian cricket, started in senior club ranks by his competitive and outspoken father Barney, and extended into the state and international forums by the more talented but no less forthright Dean. Towards the end, it seemed as though his popularity grew with the public as it diminished with the administrators and fellow-players. As an emotional Jones left the press conference he was ushered away by Ken Jacobs, the Victorian chief executive, who looked not merely unemotional but distinctly relaxed. Tony Dodemaide, who also retired, was as popular a stalwart as you could find. In 15 years he took 534 wickets, 281 of them in the Shield; only Alan Connolly, with 297, has taken more Shield wickets for Victoria.

Andrew Sincock's coaching term with South Australia lasted just one year; the side won only one match and finished last for the second year running. They had to make do for the most part without Greg Blewett, Darren Lehmann (on international duty) and Jason Gillespie, whose unsuccessful return from injury was as big a setback for his country as it was for his state. Paul Wilson, a strong, bullocking sort of fast bowler, came to the fore, and earned selection for the Australian one-day squad, while Brad Young's left-arm spin deserved praise for its persistence, but player resources were alarmingly thin. The captain, Siddons, virtually carried the batting with his usual mix of brilliance and recklessness. At the end of the season, he surrendered the captaincy to Lehmann, while Greg Chappell took on an administrative coaching position.

Off the field, the season was overshadowed by the tortuous debate between the Australian Cricket Board and the Australian Cricketers' Association over pay and other conditions for first-class players. The threat of a strike during the one-day internationals eventually fizzled out. The issue of one-day team squads versus Test squads also remained contentious. Test captain Mark Taylor, having had teams disrupted by players being sent home early during tours of South Africa and India, was an outspoken critic – even before he became a victim himself. Taylor was very publicly opposed to the policy of appointing separate Test and one-day captains, but eventually accepted the reality that his own style of play had no place in the regime of limited-overs specialists. Steve Waugh took over the one-day side. However, as the number of one-day tournaments grew to inordinate proportions, it was hard to justify the selection of Warne for a triangular one-day tournament in India, and then another, also involving India, a week later in Sharjah. Sachin Tendulkar and friends gave him no respite from a relentless battering, which seemed dubious therapy for his chronic shoulder problem.

On the domestic front, the Sheffield Shield's drain on the ACB's finances, estimated at \$A6 million a season, has made a review of format an urgent need. Floodlit first-class matches failed to attract the crowds, and both New South Wales and Victoria gave up on them. For years, many myopic observers have complacently claimed the Sheffield Shield as the best domestic competition in the world. Yet Australia's humiliation in the Tests in India at the end of the season, coupled with the indifference of sponsors, ought to bring some sense of reality to the administration. Why should a sponsor part with \$A1 million to a competition in which the top players participate at best in one third of the matches?

Tours to Pakistan and the Caribbean sandwiching home Ashes and limited-overs series made sure that the 1998-99 Shield was again deprived of its prime attractions. Meanwhile, big scores on bland pitches, scored off second-string bowlers, will continue to inflate reputations, averages and hopes at about the same rate as they deflate the exchequer. The Mercantile Mutual Cup did undergo reform, of a kind to horrify purists; teams were increased to 12, of whom one was designated a non-batsman, with only 11 allowed on the field at any time.

FIRST-CLASS AVERAGES, 1997-98

BATTING

(Qualification: 500 runs, average 40.00)

	M	I	NO	R	HS	100s	Avge
T. M. Moody (*WA*)	8	13	4	702	160	3	78.00
M. G. Bevan (*NSW*)	9	14	4	738	153	3	73.80
R. T. Ponting (*Tas*)	9	15	4	697	129*	3	63.36
J. L. Langer (*WA*)	12	20	3	1,075	235	3	63.23
D. F. Hills (*Tas*)	12	23	1	1,220	265	4	55.45
S. R. Waugh (*NSW*)	10	17	4	720	202*	1	55.38
M. A. Taylor (*NSW*)	13	21	2	1,021	169*	3	53.73
D. M. Jones (*Vic*)	11	21	4	896	151*	3	52.70
R. J. Davison (*NSW*)	7	14	2	630	169	3	52.50
J. D. Siddons (*SA*)	9	17	1	838	117	2	52.37
L. D. Harper (*Vic*)	11	21	2	992	207*	4	52.21
M. J. Slater (*NSW*)	9	17	1	831	137	2	51.93
M. E. Waugh (*NSW*)	11	17	2	747	115*	2	49.80
M. J. Di Venuto (*Tas*)	10	18	1	845	189	2	49.70
M. L. Hayden (*Qld*)	11	19	0	934	181	4	49.15
M. E. Hussey (*WA*)	12	21	2	915	134	3	48.15
A. Symonds (*Qld*)	11	18	1	809	163	4	47.58
M. L. Love (*Qld*)	10	17	2	713	201*	2	47.53
D. C. Boon (*Tas*).	12	18	2	707	146	1	44.18
S. Lee (*NSW*).	11	17	4	574	183*	1	44.15
J. Cox (*Tas*)	12	23	3	860	126	2	43.00
D. R. Martyn (*WA*)	12	20	1	813	141*	2	42.78
G. S. Blewett (*SA*).	13	24	0	969	111	1	40.37

* *Signifies not out.*

BOWLING

(Qualification: 20 wickets)

	O	M	R	W	BB	5W/i	Avge
D. W. Fleming (*Vic*)	326.5	98	705	39	6-35	2	18.07
M. P. Atkinson (*WA*)	158	34	493	24	5-92	1	20.54
J. Angel (*WA*)	304.1	78	800	36	4-45	0	22.22
D. A. Freedman (*NSW*)	339	89	915	38	7-106	3	24.07
J. H. Dawes (*Qld*)	158.2	35	485	20	4-27	0	24.25
A. J. Bichel (*Qld*)	269	63	758	31	5-31	1	24.45
M. S. Kasprowicz (*Qld*)	432.4	113	1,157	47	4-22	0	24.61
A. C. Dale (*Qld*)	244.1	74	571	23	5-19	1	24.82
C. R. Miller (*Tas*)	649.2	172	1,749	70	7-49	5	24.98
B. P. Julian (*WA*)	324.3	74	988	39	7-39	2	25.33
S. H. Cook (*NSW*)	249.2	62	756	29	5-39	1	26.06
D. J. Saker (*Vic*)	382.1	99	1,044	38	6-39	1	27.47
S. C. G. MacGill (*NSW*)	444.3	104	1,443	50	6-64	4	28.86
S. K. Warne (*Vic*)	498.5	115	1,381	47	6-34	3	29.38
T. M. Moody (*WA*)	256.4	73	665	22	5-20	1	30.22
M. W. Ridgway (*Tas*)	309.3	83	1,005	33	6-50	1	30.45
B. S. Targett (*Tas*)	262.1	68	791	23	4-143	0	34.39
D. J. Marsh (*Tas*)	317.2	89	906	26	7-57	1	34.84
B. E. Young (*SA*)	457.1	98	1,329	34	5-64	2	39.08

SHEFFIELD SHIELD, 1997-98

	Played	Won	Lost	Drawn	1st-inns Points	Points	Quotient
Western Australia	10	6	3	1	4	40	1.324
Tasmania	10	6	3	1	4	40	1.271
Queensland	10	3	4	3	4	22	1.043
New South Wales	10	3	3	4	2	20	0.987
Victoria	10	2	4	4	6	18	0.887
South Australia	10	1	4	5	8	14	0.649

Final: Western Australia beat Tasmania by seven wickets.

Western Australia finished ahead of Tasmania by virtue of their superior quotient.

> *Outright win = 6 pts; lead on first innings in a drawn or lost game = 2 pts.*
> *Quotient = runs per wkt scored divided by runs per wkt conceded.*

Under Australian Cricket Board playing conditions, two extras are scored for every no-ball bowled whether scored off or not. Any runs scored off the bat are credited to the batsman, while byes and leg-byes are counted as no-balls, in accordance with Law 24.9, in addition to the initial penalty.

*In the following scores, * by the name of a team indicates that they won the toss.*

At Brisbane, October 15, 16, 17, 18. Drawn. New South Wales 464 (M. A. Taylor 124, M. G. Bevan 153, G. R. J. Matthews 35, P. A. Emery 50; M. S. Kasprowicz four for 129, A. C. Dale three for 77) and 191 for three (M. A. Taylor 55, M. E. Waugh 69 not out); Queensland* 650 for five dec. (M. L. Hayden 181, M. L. Love 129, J. P. Maher 44, S. G. Law 107 retired hurt, A. Symonds 63, G. I. Foley 70 not out, Extras 37; G. R. J. Matthews three for 197). *Queensland 2 pts.*

In New South Wales's first innings, Taylor and Bevan added 200 for the fourth wicket. Hayden and Love opened with 286 for Queensland's first wicket.

At Adelaide, October 15, 16, 17, 18. Drawn. Tasmania* 301 (D. F. Hills 35, M. J. Di Venuto 68, S. Young 58, D. C. Boon 38, M. N. Atkinson 33 not out; P. Wilson four for 53) and 396 for five dec. (M. J. Di Venuto 94, R. T. Ponting 121, D. C. Boon 73 not out); South Australia 381 (G. S. Blewett 41, D. S. Lehmann 138, J. D. Siddons 87; C. R. Miller six for 77) and 207 for six (D. A. Fitzgerald 41, M. P. Faull 71, G. S. Blewett 38). *South Australia 2 pts.*

Siddons reached 10,000 first-class runs, in his 139th match, when 32.

At North Sydney, October 22, 23, 24, 25. Drawn. Victoria* 509 for six dec. (M. T. G. Elliott 187, G. R. Vimpani 30, L. D. Harper 160, G. B. Gardiner 50 not out, Extras 30; S. C. G. MacGill three for 139) and 279 for eight dec. (G. B. Gardiner 56, I. J. Harvey 109; A. M. Stuart three for 44, S. C. G. MacGill three for 93); New South Wales 407 for four dec. (S. R. Waugh 202 not out, M. E. Waugh 72, S. Lee 81 not out) and 225 for three (M. A. Taylor 50, M. J. Slater 85, S. R. Waugh 60 not out). *Victoria 2 pts.*

The first Shield match played at North Sydney Oval. In Victoria's first innings, Elliott and Harper (who was dropped first ball) added 303 for the third wicket. Steve Waugh's 202 not out lasted 389 minutes and 304 balls and included 24 fours.

At Perth, October 23, 24, 25, 26. Western Australia won by an innings and 77 runs. Western Australia* 477 for five dec. (M. E. Hussey 38, R. J. Campbell 47, T. M. Moody 101, A. C. Gilchrist 203 not out, Extras 44); South Australia 142 (G. S. Blewett 34; J. Angel three for 34, T. M. Moody five for 20) and 258 (G. S. Blewett 76, D. S. Lehmann 40, J. D. Siddons 69; M. S. Garnaut three for 31, B. P. Julian six for 45). *Western Australia 6 pts.*

Gilchrist's 203 not out, his maiden double-hundred, lasted 339 minutes and 293 balls and included 25 fours and two sixes. He added 273 for Western Australia's fifth wicket with Moody. South Australian captain Siddons described the pitch as the worst he had played on in 12 years.

At Hobart, October 31, November 1, 2, 3. Western Australia won by six wickets. Tasmania 366 for five dec. (J. Cox 35, M. J. Di Venuto 87, R. T. Ponting 129 not out, S. Young 51, D. C. Boon 38) and 101 for five dec. (S. Young 31 not out; J. Angel four for 45); Western Australia* 101 for three dec. (J. Angel 52) and 367 for four (M. E. Hussey 108, D. R. Martyn 101, T. M. Moody 73 not out, A. C. Gilchrist 37 not out). *Western Australia 6 pts, Tasmania 2 pts.*

After the first two days were washed out, reciprocal declarations set Western Australia 367 in 79 overs; they won with 7.4 to spare.

At Melbourne, October 31, November 1, 2, 3. Drawn. Queensland* 231 (M. L. Hayden 53, J. P. Maher 50, A. J. Bichel 34 not out, A. C. Dale 39; I. J. Harvey four for 27, S. K. Warne three for 70) and 313 for nine dec. (M. L. Hayden 76, J. P. Maher 77, A. Symonds 37, G. I. Foley 33, M. P. Mott 44; D. J. Saker three for 70); Victoria 318 for nine dec. (D. M. Jones 151 not out, D. S. Berry 30, P. R. Reiffel 60; P. W. Jackson three for 89) and 30 for one. *Victoria 2 pts.*

In his 115th match for Victoria – a state record – Jones scored the slowest century recorded at the MCG, reaching three figures in 406 minutes; he batted 510 minutes in all and hit only six fours. Berry made seven catches and two stumpings in the match. Umpire Emerson called Foley for throwing.

At Newcastle, November 14, 15, 16. New South Wales won by nine wickets. Queensland* 187 (M. L. Love 74, I. A. Healy 33 not out; D. A. Freedman six for 43) and 172 (M. L. Hayden 38, I. A. Healy 30; D. A. Freedman four for 55, S. C. G. MacGill five for 54); New South Wales 325 (M. J. Slater 50, M. A. Taylor 73, S. R. Waugh 53, M. G. Bevan 61 not out; M. S. Kasprowicz three for 71, A. C. Dale four for 69) and 35 for one. *New South Wales 6 pts.*

Queensland captain Healy said Newcastle should be taken off the first-class schedule "until the wicket, practice facilities and outfield come up to scratch". Emery became the first New South Wales wicket-keeper to make 300 Shield dismissals, in his 93rd match.

At Adelaide, November 14, 15, 16, 17. Drawn. South Australia* 452 for nine dec. (D. A. Fitzgerald 62, G. S. Blewett 53, D. S. Lehmann 54, J. D. Siddons 84, D. S. Webber 70 not out, T. J. Nielsen 38, Extras 36; T. M. Moody three for 60) and 190 for six (D. A. Fitzgerald 85; J. Stewart three for 68); Western Australia 593 (M. E. Hussey 134, R. J. Campbell 37, J. L. Langer 235, D. R. Martyn 51, T. M. Moody 78, Extras 30; P. E. McIntyre five for 175, B. E. Young four for 128). *Western Australia 2 pts.*

Langer's 235 lasted 509 minutes and 359 balls and included 18 fours and three sixes. He shared successive partnerships of 223 with Hussey, 110 with Martyn and 165 with Moody.

At Sydney, November 20, 21, 22, 23. New South Wales won by 60 runs. New South Wales* 138 (R. J. Davison 47; B. P. Julian seven for 39) and 477 for five dec. (R. J. Davison 113, M. J. Slater 43, M. G. Bevan 132, K. J. Roberts 78 not out, P. A. Emery 51 not out; J. Stewart three for 134); Western Australia 361 (R. J. Campbell 177, J. L. Langer 39, D. R. Martyn 90; A. M. Stuart seven for 76) and 194 (M. E. Hussey 46, R. J. Campbell 51, A. C. Gilchrist 44; D. A. Freedman three for 38, S. C. G. MacGill five for 87). *New South Wales 6 pts, Western Australia 2 pts.*

Julian and Stuart both returned career-best figures during the first innings. Campbell, who hit 20 fours and two sixes in his 177, his highest score, and Martyn added 204 for Western Australia's third wicket before eight wickets fell for 58. In New South Wales's second innings, Davison and Bevan added 218 for the third wicket. Western Australia were dismissed with two overs to spare when debutant Brett Lee bowled last man Bret Mulder.

At Brisbane, November 27, 28, 29, 30. Queensland won by six wickets. Tasmania 307 (D. F. Hills 38, J. Cox 45, D. J. Marsh 82 not out, M. N. Atkinson 47; S. A. Muller five for 73, J. H. Dawes three for 63) and 179 (R. J. Tucker 77; S. A. Muller four for 55, J. H. Dawes four for 27); Queensland* 237 (J. P. Maher 71; C. R. Miller three for 73, B. S. Targett three for 56) and 252 for four (M. L. Hayden 117, S. G. Law 56 not out). *Queensland 6 pts, Tasmania 2 pts.*

At Carlton, November 27, 28, 29, 30. Drawn. South Australia* 452 (D. A. Fitzgerald 81, D. S. Lehmann 42, J. D. Siddons 60, D. S. Webber 69, B. E. Young 66; B. A. Williams three for 120); Victoria 285 (D. M. Jones 58, L. D. Harper 57, G. B. Gardiner 32; P. Wilson four for 72, B. E. Young three for 65, B. E. Young three for 96) and 393 for four (L. D. Harper 207 not out, G. B. Gardiner 133 not out). *South Australia 2 pts.*

When 54, Siddons passed David Hookes's record of 9,364 Shield runs, taking 128 games to Hookes's 120. Jones became the fourth player to reach 9,000 Shield runs in his 103rd game. Harper's 207 not out, his maiden double-hundred, lasted 463 minutes and 389 balls and included 11 fours. Victoria were following on, and lost their fourth wicket when still 90 behind, but Harper and Gardiner, who completed a maiden hundred, added 316 in six hours.

At Perth, December 5, 6, 7, 8. Western Australia won by 185 runs. Western Australia 404 for nine dec. (M. E. Hussey 36, J. L. Langer 76, T. M. Moody 160, S. M. Katich 42) and 314 for nine dec. (R. J. Campbell 61, J. L. Langer 113, D. R. Martyn 50, T. M. Moody 42; B. S. Targett three for 36, P. J. Hutchinson four for 34); Tasmania* 360 for eight dec. (D. F. Hills 61, D. C. Boon 146, S. Young 81; D. R. Martyn three for 39) and 173 (M. W. Ridgway 35; J. Angel four for 47, M. S. Garnaut three for 61). *Western Australia 6 pts.*

At Adelaide, December 19, 20, 21, 22. New South Wales won by ten wickets. South Australia* 366 (D. A. Fitzgerald 57, B. A. Johnson 33, D. S. Webber 145, T. J. Nielsen 40, B. E. Young 46; S. H. Cook four for 86) and 168 (D. S. Webber 30, B. E. Young 41 not out; G. R. Robertson five for 37); New South Wales 519 (M. A. Taylor 50, R. J. Davison 137, M. E. Waugh 47, S. Lee 183 not out, P. A. Emery 42, Extras 35; G. S. Blewett three for 85, B. E. Young three for 173) and 16 for no wkt. *New South Wales 6 pts.*

Webber scored his first century for four years, having had laser surgery to improve his sight. South Australian Test bowler Jason Gillespie played his first match of the season after a back injury, but managed only 11 overs.

At Hobart, December 19, 20, 21, 22. Tasmania won by seven wickets. Victoria* 180 for nine dec. (M. T. G. Elliott 35, D. M. Jones 42; C. R. Miller four for 67) and 348 (L. D. Harper 152, I. J. Harvey 83, D. S. Berry 38; S. Young three for 69, D. J. Marsh three for 49); Tasmania 130 (R. T. Ponting 38; D. J. Saker four for 42, I. J. Harvey three for one) and 401 for three (D. F. Hills 205, J. Cox 95, M. J. Di Venuto 53). *Tasmania 6 pts, Victoria 2 pts.*

Harvey's first-innings analysis was 5.4–5–1–3. Hills's 205 lasted 335 minutes and 270 balls and included 32 fours. Chasing 399 to win, he and Cox opened Tasmania's second innings with a stand of 297 in 308 minutes, breaking their own state first-wicket record of 215, also against Victoria at Hobart, the previous season.

At Perth, December 19, 20, 21 (day/night). Queensland won by eight wickets. Western Australia* 184 (S. M. Katich 47, G. B. Hogg 31, M. P. Atkinson 31; M. S. Kasprowicz three for 42, S. A. Muller three for 44) and 186 (S. M. Katich 93 not out, M. P. Atkinson 32; M. S. Kasprowicz three for 36, A. J. Bichel four for 52); Queensland 341 (M. L. Love 37, A. Symonds 88, G. I. Foley 82, I. A. Healy 42; J. Angel four for 85, S. R. Cary three for 75) and 33 for two. *Queensland 6 pts.*

At Melbourne, January 7, 8, 9, 10. Drawn. New South Wales* 532 for nine dec. (M. J. Slater 137, R. J. Davison 169, C. J. Richards 67, S. Lee 47; B. J. Hodge four for 92) and 188 for four dec. (R. J. Davison 60, C. J. Richards 30, R. Chee Quee 40, S. Lee 42 not out); Victoria 387 (B. J. Hodge 47, D. S. Berry 166 not out, D. J. Saker 30, Extras 44; S. H. Cook four for 60, D. A. Freedman three for 97) and 281 for nine (M. T. G. Elliott 42, D. M. Jones 57, B. J. Hodge 47, S. A. J. Craig 52; S. C. G. MacGill six for 99). *New South Wales 2 pts.*
  Slater and Davison put on 219 for New South Wales's first wicket. At the end of Victoria's first innings, Berry and debutant Mathew Inness added 118 for the tenth wicket. In the second innings, last man Inness and Brad Williams survived 25 balls to draw the match.

At Hobart, January 15, 16, 17, 18. Tasmania won by an innings and 151 runs. South Australia 264 (B. A. Johnson 32, J. D. Siddons 105, B. N. Wigney 31; C. R. Miller six for 64) and 154 (D. A. Fitzgerald 33, J. D. Siddons 41; C. R. Miller six for 55, B. S. Targett three for 23); Tasmania* 569 for six dec. (D. F. Hills 265, J. Cox 73, M. J. Di Venuto 34, S. Young 105). *Tasmania 6 pts.*
  Hills's 265, his second double-hundred in successive innings and the highest score for Tasmania in the Sheffield Shield, lasted 618 minutes and 490 balls and included 23 fours and two sixes. He put on 150 in 173 minutes with Cox for Tasmania's first wicket and 243 in 232 minutes with Young for the third. Tasmania's total of 569 was the highest at Bellerive Oval. Miller took 12 for 119, the best match analysis for Tasmania in Shield cricket. The margin of victory was also Tasmania's biggest in the Shield.

At Brisbane, January 23, 24, 25. Queensland won by an innings and 140 runs. Queensland 408 (M. L. Love 34, A. Symonds 100, I. A. Healy 50, A. J. Bichel 110, P. W. Jackson 37; D. W. Fleming five for 68, M. W. H. Inness four for 80); Victoria* 170 (L. D. Harper 40, D. J. Saker 42 not out; M. S. Kasprowicz four for 45, A. J. Bichel four for 33) and 98 (A. C. Dale five for 19, M. S. Kasprowicz four for 22). *Queensland 6 pts.*
  Bichel hit a maiden hundred, including 107 runs between tea and stumps on the first day. The match ended 25 minutes into the third morning.

At Melbourne, February 3, 4, 5, 6. Victoria won by 82 runs. Victoria* 391 for nine dec. (J. L. Arnberger 36, L. D. Harper 118, D. M. Jones 116, S. A. J. Craig 71 not out) and 247 for nine dec. (L. D. Harper 34, B. J. Hodge 57, D. M. Jones 70; J. Angel three for 46); Western Australia 327 for seven dec. (S. M. Katich 90, R. M. Baker 33, B. P. Julian 121 not out; D. W. Fleming three for 47) and 229 (M. E. Hussey 40, J. L. Langer 48, R. M. Baker 30, G. B. Hogg 37, B. P. Julian 38; J. M. Davison four for 84). *Victoria 6 pts.*
  Victoria's first Shield win for 12 months. When 63 in their first innings, Jones became the first batsman to score 10,000 runs for the state.

At Sydney, February 4, 5, 6, 7. Tasmania won by 80 runs. Tasmania* 202 (J. Cox 38, D. C. Boon 61 not out; S. C. G. MacGill six for 64, D. A. Freedman four for 65) and 347 (D. C. Boon 64, R. J. Tucker 99, D. J. Marsh 50, M. N. Atkinson 31; D. A. Freedman seven for 106); New South Wales 200 (M. J. Slater 47, M. A. Taylor 66; D. J. Marsh seven for 57) and 269 (M. J. Slater 89, C. J. Richards 57, S. Lee 33; M. W. Ridgway six for 50, C. R. Miller three for 98). *Tasmania 6 pts.*

At Brisbane, February 4, 5, 6 (day/night). South Australia won by four wickets. Queensland 236 (M. L. Hayden 59, J. P. Maher 38, P. W. Jackson 41; B. N. Wigney three for 47, B. E. Young five for 64) and 154 (J. P. Maher 49, G. I. Foley 46; M. A. Harrity three for 49, B. N. Wigney five for 37); South Australia* 218 (G. S. Blewett 36, J. D. Siddons 37, D. S. Webber 34, J. C. Scuderi 43; M. S. Kasprowicz three for 65, J. H. Dawes four for 46) and 173 for six (D. A. Fitzgerald 42, G. S. Blewett 33). *South Australia 6 pts, Queensland 2 pts.*

At Adelaide, February 10, 11, 12, 13. Victoria won by four wickets. Victoria* 442 for four dec. (M. T. G. Elliott 122, J. L. Arnberger 74, B. J. Hodge 116 not out, D. M. Jones 82, S. A. J. Craig 36 not out) and 178 for six (J. L. Arnberger 53, D. M. Jones 53 not out, L. D. Harper 34 not out; B. E. Young four for 62); South Australia 205 (G. S. Blewett 111; D. W. Fleming six for 35) and 414 (B. A. Johnson 39, G. S. Blewett 97, G. R. Parker 37, C. J. Davies 35, T. J. Nielsen 115, M. J. P. Minagall 43; D. W. Fleming four for 72). *Victoria 6 pts.*

In South Australia's second innings, Nielsen and Brad Wigney added 103 for the ninth wicket.

At Hobart, February 11, 12, 13, 14. Tasmania won by ten wickets. Queensland 175 (G. I. Foley 37, B. N. Creevey 52; M. W. Ridgway four for 44, C. R. Miller three for 42) and 318 (A. Symonds 141, G. I. Foley 37, I. A. Healy 37; M. W. Ridgway three for 93, C. R. Miller four for 89); Tasmania* 292 (D. F. Hills 72, J. Cox 34, D. C. Boon 52, R. J. Tucker 52; J. H. Dawes three for 90, B. N. Creevey five for 51) and 204 for no wkt (D. F. Hills 121 not out, J. Cox 71 not out). *Tasmania 6 pts.*

Hills and Cox shared their third century opening stand in four Shield matches. Umpire Emerson called Foley for throwing, as he had at Melbourne in November.

At Perth, February 14, 15, 16. Western Australia won by an innings and 137 runs. Western Australia* 470 for seven dec. (M. E. Hussey 120, R. J. Campbell 66, J. L. Langer 46, D. R. Martyn 141 not out, Extras 50); New South Wales 150 (M. A. Taylor 61, Extras 30; J. Angel three for 30, B. P. Julian three for 39) and 183 (P. A. Emery 43 not out). *Western Australia 6 pts.*

At Adelaide, March 5, 6, 7, 8. Drawn. Queensland* 268 (A. Symonds 163; M. A. Harrity three for 48, P. E. McIntyre four for 83) and 349 for seven dec. (M. L. Love 44, M. L. Hayden 101, A. Symonds 100 not out, A. J. Bichel 66; B. E. Young five for 69); South Australia 302 (D. A. Fitzgerald 41, J. D. Siddons 63, C. J. Davies 55, T. J. Nielsen 30, B. E. Young 40, P. E. McIntyre 43; A. J. Bichel four for 66, G. J. Rowell three for 73, J. H. Dawes three for 71) and 241 for seven (J. D. Siddons 117, B. E. Young 36 not out; A. J. Bichel four for 44). *South Australia 2 pts.*

Symonds scored a hundred in each innings, to complete four in his last seven innings. Hayden passed 10,000 first-class runs in his 118th match.

At Hobart, March 5, 6, 7, 8. Tasmania won by nine wickets. New South Wales* 332 (C. J. Richards 164, M. G. Bevan 58, K. J. Geyer 41; C. R. Miller four for 88) and 226 (C. J. Richards 35, M. G. Bevan 65, S. Lee 39; C. R. Miller six for 75); Tasmania 468 for nine dec. (J. Cox 126, M. J. Di Venuto 47, S. Young 50, R. J. Tucker 39, D. J. Marsh 70, M. N. Atkinson 38 not out, C. R. Miller 38; D. A. Freedman five for 77) and 94 for one (D. F. Hills 43, J. Cox 38 not out). *Tasmania 6 pts.*

At Perth, March 5, 6, 7, 8. Western Australia won by 112 runs. Western Australia* 196 (T. M. Moody 31, A. C. Gilchrist 109; D. J. Saker four for 56, M. W. H. Inness four for 42) and 388 for eight dec. (M. E. Hussey 44, R. J. Campbell 100, J. L. Langer 101, T. M. Moody 64 not out; I. J. Harvey three for 82); Victoria 157 (J. L. Arnberger 45; B. P. Julian three for 63, M. P. Atkinson four for 36) and 315 (B. J. Hodge 95, D. M. Jones 46, D. S. Berry 33, D. W. Fleming 45 not out; S. R. Cary four for 96, M. P. Atkinson four for 60). *Western Australia 6 pts.*

In the first innings, Gilchrist came in with Western Australia on 35 for five; he scored 109 out of 157 while he was at the wicket. Later, he took ten catches in the match.

At Newcastle, March 12, 13, 14, 15. Drawn. South Australia 352 (D. A. Fitzgerald 65, M. P. Faull 58, J. M. Vaughan 61, J. D. Siddons 54, C. J. Davies 33, T. J. Nielsen 32; B. E. McNamara three for 47, S. Lee three for 26) and 258 for seven dec. (M. P. Faull 103, B. E. Young 64); New South Wales* 284 (C. J. Richards 61, S. Lee 48, B. E. McNamara 68 not out; P. E. McIntyre four for 92) and 63 for one (R. J. Davison 31 not out). *South Australia 2 pts.*

At Brisbane, March 12, 13, 14, 15. Western Australia won by five wickets. Queensland 197 (M. L. Love 62, J. P. Maher 31; J. Angel three for 33, T. M. Moody three for 37) and 313 (M. L. Hayden 124, W. A. Seccombe 54 not out, A. J. Bichel 50; T. M. Moody three for 45, D. R. Martyn four for 46); Western Australia* 405 for eight dec. (M. E. Hussey 61, J. L. Langer 67, D. R. Martyn 60, S. M. Katich 80, B. P. Julian 94; A. J. Bichel four for 104) and 106 for five (R. J. Campbell 36, J. L. Langer 31). *Western Australia 6 pts.*

At Melbourne, March 12, 13, 14, 15. Tasmania won by 120 runs. Tasmania* 373 for nine dec. (D. F. Hills 128, M. J. Di Venuto 61, S. Young 81, D. C. Boon 50; D. W. Fleming four for 59) and 200 (M. J. Di Venuto 82, D. C. Boon 33; D. J. Saker four for 44, J. M. Davison four for 94); Victoria 317 for six dec. (M. T. G. Elliott 32, L. D. Harper 41, B. J. Hodge 36, D. M. Jones 100 not out, D. J. Saker 50 not out) and 136 (M. T. G. Elliott 31, B. J. Hodge 39; C. R. Miller seven for 49). *Tasmania 6 pts.*

Tasmania's sixth successive Shield win. Hills was taken to hospital on the first day after batting for four and a half hours in temperatures of around 40 degrees Centigrade. Miller's career-best seven for 49 took him to 64 Shield wickets for the season, passing Les Fleetwood-Smith's record of 60 for Victoria in 1934-35. Jones followed up his first-innings 100 not out with a duck; in May, he announced his retirement from first-class cricket, having scored 19,188 runs in 245 matches at 51.85.

FINAL

WESTERN AUSTRALIA v TASMANIA

At Perth, March 20, 21, 22, 23. Western Australia won by seven wickets. Toss: Tasmania.

Western Australia made sure of the Shield with a day to spare, avenging their defeat by Queensland the previous season. The Tasmanians had arrived in Perth fresh from six consecutive wins. For half a day, the momentum continued as Hills, Cox and Di Venuto capitalised on some wayward seam bowling. A two-hour rain-break transformed the match: Tasmania collapsed from 174 for two to 285 all out, with their middle-order batsmen – notably Boon – playing some rash strokes. Only Cox showed the discipline required, carrying his bat for a six-hour century: the first time a Tasmanian had achieved the feat in the Shield and anyone had done it in the final. When Western Australia replied, Campbell expunged memories of his pair in last year's final with a flamboyant hundred. Martyn and Moody took command to put Western Australia in the lead, but it was Julian's arrival, at 397 for seven, which finally extinguished Tasmania's hopes. His fifty came up from 27 balls, his hundred from 76, with three sixes and 15 fours. Trailing by 286, Tasmania lost three wickets on the third evening, including Cox, their first-innings hero, for nought. Di Venuto, however, hit out ferociously. Dropped second ball in the gully by Julian, he reached 100 in 105 balls, and struck 30 fours in his 189 before miscuing a pull to mid-on. Boon and later the 5 ft 5 in wicket-keeper Mark Atkinson defended resolutely but, when Atkinson fell to his larger namesake, also Mark Atkinson, his reluctance to go cost him A$500 for dissent. Atkinson the bowler, by contrast, took five in an innings for the first time. In spite of a small flurry of wickets, Western Australia cruised to victory on the fourth evening.

Man of the Match: B. P. Julian.

Close of play: First day, Tasmania 244-8 (J. Cox 96*, M. W. Ridgway 0*); Second day, Western Australia 323-5 (T. M. Moody 54*); Third day, Tasmania 92-3 (M. J. Di Venuto 59*).

Tasmania

D. F. Hills lbw b Moody	49	– b Atkinson	17
J. Cox not out	115	– c Gilchrist b Angel	0
M. J. Di Venuto c Langer b Angel	34	– c Campbell b Atkinson	189
S. Young c Moody b Angel	13	– lbw b Julian	7
*D. C. Boon c Gilchrist b Atkinson	7	– c Julian b Moody	39
R. J. Tucker c Gilchrist b Atkinson	0	– c Julian b Atkinson	6
D. J. Marsh c Langer b Julian	13	– c Moody b Atkinson	12
†M. N. Atkinson c Campbell b Julian	7	– c Gilchrist b Atkinson	39
B. S. Targett c Moody b Julian	7	– c Gilchrist b Angel	0
M. W. Ridgway c Gilchrist b Julian	6	– lbw b Julian	5
C. R. Miller c and b Angel	11	– not out	9
L-b 7, n-b 16	23	L-b 5, w 2, n-b 18	25

1/80 2/136 3/174 4/193 5/195   285   1/2 2/42 3/92 4/189 5/200   348
6/216 7/230 8/242 9/266   6/245 7/329 8/330 9/338

Bowling: First Innings—Angel 24.2–4–62–3; Julian 28–6–89–4; Moody 21–1–80–1; Atkinson 15–5–47–2. *Second Innings*—Angel 23–3–74–2; Atkinson 25–5–92–5; Moody 24–7–68–1; Julian 18.4–0–83–2; Oldroyd 9–2–26–0.

Western Australia

M. E. Hussey c Hills b Miller	44	– not out	39
R. J. Campbell c Tucker b Young	104	– c Di Venuto b Ridgway	4
J. L. Langer lbw b Targett	19	– c Atkinson b Ridgway	12
D. R. Martyn lbw b Ridgway	83	– c Atkinson b Targett	7
*T. M. Moody c Marsh b Targett	125	– not out	1
J. Angel c Atkinson b Ridgway	1		
S. M. Katich c Ridgway b Targett	22		
†A. C. Gilchrist c Miller b Targett	8		
B. P. Julian lbw b Miller	124		
M. P. Atkinson not out	9		
B. J. Oldroyd b Miller	2		
B 4, l-b 15, w 1, n-b 10	30		

1/155 2/163 3/229 4/311 5/323   571   1/7 2/31 3/46   (3 wkts) 63
6/376 7/397 8/533 9/563

Bowling: *First Innings*—Ridgway 29–7–107–2; Miller 47.3–12–145–3; Young 25–7–92–1; Targett 39–6–143–4; Marsh 11–4–50–0; Tucker 4–0–15–0. *Second Innings*—Ridgway 8–1–45–2; Miller 5–0–13–0; Targett 2.1–1–5–1.

Umpires: D. B. Hair and D. J. Harper.

SHEFFIELD SHIELD WINNERS

1892-93	Victoria	1930-31	Victoria
1893-94	South Australia	1931-32	New South Wales
1894-95	Victoria	1932-33	New South Wales
1895-96	New South Wales	1933-34	Victoria
1896-97	New South Wales	1934-35	Victoria
1897-98	Victoria	1935-36	South Australia
1898-99	Victoria	1936-37	Victoria
1899-1900	New South Wales	1937-38	New South Wales
1900-01	Victoria	1938-39	South Australia
1901-02	New South Wales	1939-40	New South Wales
1902-03	New South Wales	1940-46	No competition
1903-04	New South Wales	1946-47	Victoria
1904-05	New South Wales	1947-48	Western Australia
1905-06	New South Wales	1948-49	New South Wales
1906-07	New South Wales	1949-50	New South Wales
1907-08	Victoria	1950-51	Victoria
1908-09	New South Wales	1951-52	New South Wales
1909-10	South Australia	1952-53	South Australia
1910-11	New South Wales	1953-54	New South Wales
1911-12	New South Wales	1954-55	New South Wales
1912-13	South Australia	1955-56	New South Wales
1913-14	New South Wales	1956-57	New South Wales
1914-15	Victoria	1957-58	New South Wales
1915-19	No competition	1958-59	New South Wales
1919-20	New South Wales	1959-60	New South Wales
1920-21	New South Wales	1960-61	New South Wales
1921-22	Victoria	1961-62	New South Wales
1922-23	New South Wales	1962-63	Victoria
1923-24	Victoria	1963-64	South Australia
1924-25	Victoria	1964-65	New South Wales
1925-26	New South Wales	1965-66	New South Wales
1926-27	South Australia	1966-67	Victoria
1927-28	Victoria	1967-68	Western Australia
1928-29	New South Wales	1968-69	South Australia
1929-30	Victoria	1969-70	Victoria

1970-71	South Australia	1984-85	New South Wales
1971-72	Western Australia	1985-86	New South Wales
1972-73	Western Australia	1986-87	Western Australia
1973-74	Victoria	1987-88	Western Australia
1974-75	Western Australia	1988-89	Western Australia
1975-76	South Australia	1989-90	New South Wales
1976-77	Western Australia	1990-91	Victoria
1977-78	Western Australia	1991-92	Western Australia
1978-79	Victoria	1992-93	New South Wales
1979-80	Victoria	1993-94	New South Wales
1980-81	Western Australia	1994-95	Queensland
1981-82	South Australia	1995-96	South Australia
1982-83	New South Wales	1996-97	Queensland
1983-84	Western Australia	1997-98	Western Australia

New South Wales have won the Shield 42 times, Victoria 25, Western Australia 14, South Australia 13, Queensland 2, Tasmania 0.

MERCANTILE MUTUAL INSURANCE CUP

Note: Matches in this section were not first-class.

One-day 50-over tournament between the six states and Australian Capital Territory. Top four in league qualify for semi-finals. Teams included 12 players, one of whom was not allowed to bat; only 11 players were allowed in the field at any time.

At North Sydney, October 5. New South Wales won by 37 runs. New South Wales* 319 for seven (50 overs) (M. J. Slater 37, S. R. Waugh 72, M. E. Waugh 76, M. G. Bevan 56, S. Lee 35); South Australia 282 (47.4 overs) (G. S. Blewett 45, D. A. Fitzgerald 49, J. D. Siddons 58, G. R. Parker 36).

At Brisbane, October 12. New South Wales won by one wicket. Queensland* 230 (47.4 overs) (G. I. Foley 34, S. A. Prestwidge 35, M. S. Kasprowicz 33); New South Wales 232 for nine (49.2 overs) (M. A. Taylor 70, M. G. Bevan 65 not out; A. C. Dale three for 38, S. A. Prestwidge three for 55).

At Adelaide, October 19. South Australia won by 69 runs. South Australia 278 for seven (50 overs) (G. S. Blewett 56, N. T. Adcock 57, J. D. Siddons 57; D. G. Wright three for 44); Tasmania* 209 (45.5 overs) (J. Cox 75, R. J. Tucker 68; P. Wilson three for 27, G. S. Blewett three for 27).

At North Sydney, October 26. New South Wales won by 37 runs. New South Wales 275 for nine (50 overs) (M. J. Slater 68, M. E. Waugh 57, M. G. Bevan 62 not out, C. J. Richards 32; S. K. Warne three for 43); Victoria* 238 (44.4 overs) (B. J. Hodge 53, P. R. Reiffel 44, D. S. Berry 64 not out; S. Lee three for 49).

At Canberra, November 2. South Australia won by 11 runs. South Australia* 237 (49 overs) (G. S. Blewett 97, N. T. Adcock 51; M. A. Higgs three for 39); Australian Capital Territory 226 (49.3 overs) (P. L. Evans 37, P. J. Solway 41, M. A. Higgs 36).

At Hobart, November 16. Tasmania won by four wickets. Australian Capital Territory* 213 for eight (49 overs) (M. R. J. Veletta 49, P. J. Solway 56; M. G. Farrell four for 51); Tasmania 214 for six (42.2 overs) (J. Cox 99, S. Young 37).

At Bendigo, November 23. Australian Capital Territory won by 15 runs. Australian Capital Territory 250 (50 overs) (P. J. Solway 73, B. J. Haddin 89; D. J. Saker three for 34); Victoria* 235 (50 overs) (D. M. Jones 64, L. D. Harper 36, B. J. Hodge 61; M. A. Higgs three for 28).

At Brisbane, December 5 (day/night). Queensland won by seven wickets. Victoria* 200 for nine (50 overs) (M. T. G. Elliott 30, G. B. Gardiner 33; S. A. Muller five for 43); Queensland 202 for three (34.5 overs) (M. L. Hayden 59, J. P. Maher 41, S. G. Law 32, A. Symonds 37 not out; S. A. J. Craig three for 56).

At Perth, December 12 (day/night). Western Australia won by 136 runs. Western Australia* 285 for five (50 overs) (R. J. Campbell 72, D. R. Martyn 34, A. C. Gilchrist 59, T. M. Moody 71 not out); South Australia 149 (34.4 overs) (G. S. Blewett 61, J. D. Siddons 38; K. M. Harvey four for 35).

At Canberra, December 14. New South Wales won by five wickets, their target having been revised to 191 from 48 overs. Australian Capital Territory* 192 (49 overs) (P. J. Solway 34; G. R. Robertson three for 31); New South Wales 192 for five (43.5 overs) (R. Chee Quee 40, M. A. Taylor 45, C. J. Richards 31, K. J. Roberts 33 not out).

At Perth, January 2 (day/night). Western Australia won by 152 runs. Western Australia* 278 for six (50 overs) (R. J. Campbell 48, D. R. Martyn 78, J. L. Langer 86); Australian Capital Territory 126 (32.2 overs) (M. R. J. Veletta 50; K. M. Harvey four for eight).

At Melbourne, January 4. Tasmania won by six wickets. Victoria* 239 for eight (50 overs) (S. A. J. Craig 38, D. M. Jones 91 not out, B. J. Hodge 58); Tasmania 242 for four (47.1 overs) (D. F. Hills 50, M. J. Di Venuto 60, J. Cox 30, R. J. Tucker 51).

At Adelaide, January 10. Queensland won by 11 runs. Queensland* 260 for eight (50 overs) (J. P. Maher 126, M. L. Love 46; J. N. Gillespie four for 61); South Australia 249 (48.5 overs) (D. A. Fitzgerald 61, J. D. Siddons 52; M. S. Kasprowicz three for 35).

At Brisbane, January 17 (day/night). Western Australia won by one wicket. Queensland* 209 for nine (50 overs) (S. A. Prestwidge 53, G. I. Foley 46, C. T. Perren 42; K. M. Harvey three for 37); Western Australia 210 for nine (46.3 overs) (D. R. Martyn 93; S. A. Muller three for 41).

At Perth, January 23 (day/night). New South Wales won by 98 runs. New South Wales* 283 for three (50 overs) (M. J. Slater 63, M. A. Taylor 51, R. Chee Quee 47, S. Lee 99 not out); Western Australia 185 (42.1 overs) (J. L. Langer 96; S. C. G. MacGill four for 32).

At Canberra, January 31. Queensland won by 48 runs. Queensland* 275 for seven (50 overs) (M. L. Hayden 35, J. P. Maher 70, M. L. Love 48, A. Symonds 44, B. N. Creevey 31 not out); Australian Capital Territory 227 (44.5 overs) (B. J. Haddin 52, M. A. Higgs 34; G. I. Foley three for 45).

At Hobart, January 31. Western Australia won by 219 runs. Western Australia 310 for six (50 overs) (R. J. Campbell 55, D. R. Martyn 140, A. C. Gilchrist 41, M. E. Hussey 49); Tasmania* 91 (29.4 overs) (J. Cox 30; K. M. Harvey four for 23).

At Melbourne, February 7. Victoria won on scoring-rate, Western Australia's target having been retrospectively set as 211 from 43 overs. Victoria* 223 for five (47 overs) (S. A. J. Craig 60, D. M. Jones 57, B. J. Hodge 33; D. R. Martyn three for 31); Western Australia 188 for one (43.2 overs) (J. L. Langer 83 not out, D. R. Martyn 99 not out).

At Sydney, February 8. New South Wales won by seven wickets. Tasmania* 187 (48.4 overs) (R. J. Tucker 66, D. J. Marsh 30; S. R. Clark four for 26); New South Wales 191 for three (42.4 overs) (K. J. Geyer 92 not out, S. Lee 35, C. J. Richards 35 not out).

At Adelaide, February 14. South Australia won by 141 runs. South Australia* 307 for seven (50 overs) (D. A. Fitzgerald 92, G. S. Blewett 83, B. A. Johnson 40, G. R. Parker 30; I. J. Harvey three for 60); Victoria 166 (32.1 overs) (M. T. G. Elliott 32, D. M. Jones 43; M. A. Harrity five for 42).

At Hobart, February 15. Queensland won by 12 runs. Queensland 233 (50 overs) (J. P. Maher 68, M. L. Love 42, C. T. Perren 52; Tasmania* 221 (47.3 overs) (J. Cox 52, R. J. Tucker 75; A. Symonds three for 32, G. I. Foley three for 31).

New South Wales 12 pts, Western Australia 8 pts, Queensland 8 pts, South Australia 6 pts, Tasmania 4 pts, Australian Capital Territory 2 pts, Victoria 2 pts.

Semi-finals

At Perth, February 21. Queensland won by three wickets. Western Australia 283 for six (50 overs) (J. L. Langer 51, R. J. Campbell 35, D. R. Martyn 50, T. M. Moody 63 not out, Extras 37); Queensland* 284 for seven (46.5 overs) (M. L. Hayden 31, J. P. Maher 56, M. L. Love 75, B. N. Creevey 32; J. Angel three for 39).

At Sydney, February 22. New South Wales won by 69 runs. New South Wales* 212 for eight (50 overs) (M. G. Bevan 74, P. A. Emery 48; M. A. Harrity three for 41); South Australia 143 (41.1 overs) (J. C. Scuderi 32 not out).

Final

At Sydney, March 1. Queensland won by two wickets. New South Wales* 166 (49.3 overs) (P. A. Emery 38; A. J. Bichel three for 25, S. A. Prestwidge three for 25); Queensland 167 for eight (47.5 overs) (S. A. Prestwidge 42 not out, A. J. Bichel 30).
  New South Wales's only defeat in the tournament.

SHEFFIELD SHIELD FINALS

1982-83	NEW SOUTH WALES* beat Western Australia by 54 runs.
1983-84	WESTERN AUSTRALIA beat Queensland by four wickets.
1984-85	NEW SOUTH WALES beat Queensland by one wicket.
1985-86	NEW SOUTH WALES drew with Queensland.
1986-87	WESTERN AUSTRALIA drew with Victoria.
1987-88	WESTERN AUSTRALIA beat Queensland by five wickets.
1988-89	WESTERN AUSTRALIA drew with South Australia.
1989-90	NEW SOUTH WALES beat Queensland by 345 runs.
1990-91	VICTORIA beat New South Wales by eight wickets.
1991-92	WESTERN AUSTRALIA beat New South Wales by 44 runs.
1992-93	NEW SOUTH WALES beat Queensland by eight wickets.
1993-94	NEW SOUTH WALES beat Tasmania by an innings and 61 runs.
1994-95	QUEENSLAND beat South Australia by an innings and 101 runs.
1995-96	SOUTH AUSTRALIA drew with Western Australia.
1996-97	QUEENSLAND* beat Western Australia by 160 runs.
1997-98	WESTERN AUSTRALIA beat Tasmania by seven wickets.

Note: The team that finishes top of the table has home advantage against the runners-up. The home team wins the Shield in a drawn match.

  * *Denotes victory for the away team.*

SHEFFIELD SHIELD PLAYER OF THE YEAR

The Sheffield Shield Player of the Year Award for 1997-98 was won by Dene Hills of Tasmania. The Award, instituted in 1975-76, is adjudicated by the umpires over the course of the season. Each of the two umpires standing in each of the 30 Sheffield Shield matches (excluding the final) allocated marks of 3, 2 and 1 to the three players who most impressed them during the game. Hills earned 23 votes in 11 matches, three ahead of Andrew Symonds of Queensland. Colin Miller, also of Tasmania, won the Player of the Year award sponsored by Lord's Taverners and decided by his fellow players. The Mercantile Mutual Player of the Year was Damien Martyn of Western Australia.

CRICKET IN SOUTH AFRICA, 1997-98

By COLIN BRYDEN and ANDREW SAMSON

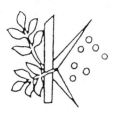

H. D. Ackerman

South Africans have long been aware that politics or, more realistically, normal life, cannot be kept separate from cricket. The racial policies of the former South African government had a devastating impact on the country's cricketers, and it was a certainty that the implications of the post-apartheid era would affect the game. The most contentious issue in a season with no shortage of discussion points was the "fast-tracking" of black cricketers, culminating in the selection of Makhaya Ntini for two Test matches against Sri Lanka. He became the first black African to play Test cricket for South Africa.

The race issue resurfaced some four years after South Africa's first fully inclusive general election in April 1994. "The euphoria of the new South Africa two or three years ago has worn off," noted Ali Bacher, managing director of the United Cricket Board. "People are impatient and they want to see results." Unlike rugby, cricket has remained in tune with the Government's aspirations, and leading figures, including President Nelson Mandela and Archbishop Desmond Tutu, have been among the most enthusiastic supporters of the national team. Millions of rands have been spent on developing the game and providing facilities in black areas. Yet the continued "white" look of the team attracted criticism from a parliamentary sports committee and some vocal spectators during the Second Test against Pakistan in Durban. There was a small demonstration in Port Elizabeth before the Third Test against Pakistan, leading to a meeting between Bacher and protest leaders. "In 1998, you cannot have an all-white national team," Bacher said afterwards.

The cynical might read an over-abundance of coincidence into the events which happened quickly thereafter. Bacher made his statement on the first day of the Test match. Fanie de Villiers, 33, announced his retirement the following day, citing family priorities, a lucrative offer to commentate on TV, and a long struggle against injuries. He took Test-best figures of six for 23 on the day after that. It was the worst-kept secret in South Africa that Ntini would play in South Africa's next Test, the first against Sri Lanka, at Newlands less than two weeks later. On the last day of the Newlands game, a delegation from the United Cricket Board had a largely amicable meeting with the parliamentary sports committee.

Bacher outlined the choice for cricket in an article in the Sunday Times, South Africa's largest-selling newspaper. "Either we take the majority of South Africans with us or we alienate them," he wrote. He insisted, though, that standards would not be compromised. "We must have excellence," he said in a separate interview. "Although cricket is a team game, you are alone when you have a bat or a ball in your hand.

There is no place to hide an inferior player. We want our national team to be truly representative, but there are a lot of pressures, especially on the individuals in contention."

The issue is peculiarly South African and needs to be seen against the background of a country in which whites for decades enjoyed inordinate privileges in employment, education and sporting opportunities. In the new South Africa, there has been an active policy of affirmative action throughout society, with many top jobs being awarded to black people. Affirmative action has been applied either officially or unofficially at various levels of cricket since the formation of the United Cricket Board in 1991. In the case of players from underprivileged backgrounds, potential is as important as performance. Ntini, from a small village near King William's Town in the Eastern Cape, had been noticed while playing soft-ball Mini Cricket, which has introduced many thousands of youngsters to the game. Because of his cricketing ability, Ntini was awarded a scholarship to Dale College, a school with a strong cricket tradition. He quickly proved himself a fine schoolboy fast bowler and won selection to the senior Border provincial team in 1995-96, making his debut against England. His first victim was Alec Stewart. National Under-15 and Under-19 teams have long reflected the demographics of the "rainbow nation", with Ntini one of many to be exposed at the highest junior level.

Bacher put the onus on provinces to take the process further. "The selectors cannot be expected to pick black players for the national team when hardly any are playing at provincial level. The problem is not with the national selectors, it is with the provincial A teams. Not enough black players are getting opportunities." The UCB currently has an affirmative action policy up to provincial B level. That, Bacher indicated, may be extended to senior teams. "We are not a normal country. Nobody must delude themselves. Changes must be immediate."

It was agreed last season that the selectors should have the option of expanding national touring parties by one to make room for a promising player. Thus Roger Telemachus of Boland was selected to tour Australia in 1997-98. When he failed a fitness test shortly before departure he was replaced by Ntini, who impressed his team-mates and the tour management with his ability and attitude. No fewer than seven black or coloured cricketers were chosen for the senior tour of England or the South Africa A tour of Sri Lanka during 1998, all with the ability at least to justify their inclusion. While in England, Bacher also announced that three black members would be added to the Board itself.

The need to provide opportunities for black players was one of the reasons why the United Cricket Board had decided to increase the number of teams in the senior first-class competition, the Supersport Series, from eight to nine from 1996-97, by adding Griqualand West. And at least one young man grabbed his chance: Loots Bosman made 96 on his debut for Griquas in 1997-98, and went on to win selection for South Africa A.

In general, however, there was concern at the poor standard of domestic provincial cricket. It was originally decided at the end of the season that, from 1999-2000, the Supersport Series would be split into two sections. This plan was abandoned when it was realised that it would hinder the progress of the very players South Africa are most desperate to encourage. Provinces were also anxious about the potential loss of status, sponsors and income. It was agreed that Easterns and North West should be promoted to the Supersport Series in 1999-2000, as first planned, but in a single division of 11. Meanwhile, in 1998-99, a five-day final was to be contested between the two teams finishing highest in the round-robin competition. A drawn final would mean a shared trophy.

Had such a system operated in 1997-98 it could have resulted in a travesty of justice for Free State. They dominated the Supersport Series and clinched their third title in six years when they drew their penultimate game with nearest challengers Eastern Province. Free State finished with six wins in eight matches, despite minimal participation by their most famous players. Hansie Cronje did not appear in any of their Supersport matches (he scored an unbeaten 150 against the Pakistani tourists), while Allan Donald played just once, in a comeback after an injury suffered in Australia. It was a remarkable achievement for a small province.

Free State's cause was helped by the preparation of lively pitches at Springbok Park in Bloemfontein, which in previous seasons had been renowned as a batsman's paradise. It was two away wins, however, that set them on their way to the title, when they beat Western Province and Gauteng convincingly. Free State were well captained by Gerhardus Liebenberg, while their former player Corrie van Zyl had developed into an influential coach. Liebenberg was able to call on a varied attack, with the left-arm spin of Nicky Boje and off-spin of Kosie Venter supplementing the disciplined seam of Herman Bakkes, Chris Craven, Sarel Cilliers and Chrisjan Vorster. In successive outings, the medium-paced Craven had match returns of nine for 50 against Gauteng and nine for 52 against the defending champions, Natal; he also scored two centuries. Boje and Bakkes proved their worth as all-rounders. Of the specialist batsmen, Louis Wilkinson scored freely while wicket-keeper Morné van Wyk announced himself as a highly promising young player.

Natal fell away badly and finished fourth in the standings. National calls and injuries decimated their bowling, and off-spinning all-rounder Derek Crookes departed for Gauteng. The attack was carried by Gary Gilder, though the emergence of his fellow left-arm fast bowler Shaun Adam and left-arm spinner Craig Tatton signified hope for the future. Natal's batting was disappointing with the exception of Andrew Hudson, who scored freely at provincial level after being dropped from the national team, and opening batsman Mark Bruyns.

Eastern Province were the closest challengers to Free State, with 40-year-old Kepler Wessels continuing to score heavily, topping the Supersport averages with 847 runs at 84.70 and setting a competition record for Eastern Province. But a distinguished association ended in acrimony when he was not offered a new contract and signed up with Griqualand West for 1998-99. Dave Callaghan, who enjoyed another prolific batting season, will take over the captaincy from Wessels while Graham Barlow, the former England player, will coach.

Northerns (formerly Northern Transvaal) had a much-improved season, finishing third in the Supersport Series after being last the previous year. They had a potent pace bowling attack, spearheaded by Steve Elworthy, Fanie de Villiers and the left-armer Greg Smith. De Villiers and Smith were responsible for one of the most sensational episodes of the season when they sent Gauteng plummeting from 12 for no wicket to 12 for seven in the space of 34 deliveries at the Wanderers. Although Northerns were unable to retain their title in the Standard Bank League limited-overs competition, they were a creditable second, remaining unbeaten until their final match when they lost away to Western Province in the series decider. Northerns were also runners-up in the Standard Bank knockout, losing the final to Gauteng.

Gauteng, formerly Transvaal, were disappointing apart from that triumph in the Standard Bank Cup. Inconsistent batting was their biggest problem, though Ken Rutherford, the captain, had a fine season. Injuries again affected the bowling, which was often carried by Clive Eksteen, the left-arm spinner.

Boland won three matches despite a fragile batting order which relied too heavily on Kenny Jackson. The bowling of Telemachus, Henry Williams and Claude Henderson was steady. But Boland suffered two blows at the end of the season: the retirement of their captain, Adrian Kuiper, and Henderson's decision to move to Western Province. Border were delighted that two of their players, Mark Boucher and Ntini, won national honours, but otherwise had little to show. Wayne Wiblin scored heavily, while Piet Botha, Vasbert Drakes and Dion Taljard were the most successful bowlers.

Western Province were the major disappointments. Despite their depth of talent and financial resources, they plummeted to eighth place in the four-day competition, although they won the Standard Bank League. The absence of their national players and injuries to bowlers Craig Matthews and Eric Simons meant they had a weak attack, and the lack of reliable opening batsmen was also a problem. H. D. Ackerman, however, had a remarkable season, scoring 866 runs in the Supersport Series at 66.61, including five centuries. Ackerman went on to break the 24-year-old record of Barry Richards for the most first-class runs by a home player in a season, scoring 1,373 at 50.85. Being selected against West Indies A as well as in four Tests against Pakistan and Sri Lanka, he played 16 matches in all, four more than Richards who made 1,285 at 80.31 in 1973-74.

Griqualand West won only one match but it was a notable triumph: they beat neighbours and eventual champions Free State by eight wickets. Henderson Bryan, their West Indian import, took ten for 120 in that game but otherwise did not live up to expectations, while the rest of the Griquas' bowling was weak. Martyn Gidley had another consistent season with the bat, Piet Barnard had some success and Bosman showed promise.

North West threw away the form book in the UCB Bowl's first-class division. Since being admitted to the Bowl as Western Transvaal in 1991-92, they had previously recorded only one first-class win. This time they took the title, winning three of their five matches. Griqualand West B won promotion from the non-first-class division. The future of the Bowl was in doubt, however. There seemed no justification for another first-class tournament, especially as North West and Easterns, the only provincial affiliates not currently playing in the premier competition, will be included by 1999-2000. – C.B.

FIRST-CLASS AVERAGES, 1997-98

BATTING

(Qualification: 8 innings, average 35.00)

	M	I	NO	R	HS	100s	Avge
K. C. Wessels (*E. Province*)	9	15	4	899	179*	4	81.72
D. J. Cullinan (*Gauteng*)	6	10	1	663	172	4	73.66
W. J. Cronje (*Free State*)	6	10	2	511	150*	1	63.87
N. Boje (*Free State*)	11	16	4	683	105*	2	56.91
G. C. Victor (*E. Province B*)	5	9	0	501	138	1	55.66
A. C. Hudson (*Natal*)	10	16	2	779	206	3	55.64
J. G. Myburgh (*Northerns B*)	5	10	2	427	203	1	53.37
A. G. Lawson (*North West*)	5	10	3	371	110	1	53.00
H. D. Ackerman (*W. Province*)	16	29	2	1,373	202*	5	50.85
M. van Jaarsveld (*Northerns*)	9	16	2	709	139*	2	50.64
E. A. E. Baptiste (*E. Province*)	6	8	4	196	53	0	49.00
K. R. Rutherford (*Gauteng*)	8	13	2	532	143	2	48.36
W. Wiblin (*Border*)	9	17	2	688	177	2	45.86
M. N. van Wyk (*Free State*)	7	11	3	366	121	1	45.75
D. J. Callaghan (*E. Province*)	9	15	2	548	132	2	42.15
A. G. Prince (*W. Province/E. Province B*)	7	11	0	447	116	1	40.63
H. C. Bakkes (*Free State*)	8	9	1	319	101	1	39.87
S. M. Pollock (*Natal*)	6	9	1	319	92	0	39.87
J. Kemp (*E. Province*)	7	10	3	274	81*	0	39.14
L. J. Koen (*E. Province*)	9	15	1	519	174*	2	37.07
M. I. Gidley (*Griqualand W.*)	9	18	0	658	134	2	36.55
K. C. Jackson (*Boland*)	9	18	2	579	102*	1	36.18
P. C. Strydom (*Border*)	9	16	1	541	106	1	36.06
L. J. Wilkinson (*Free State*)	9	14	3	396	89	0	36.00
C. F. Craven (*Free State*)	6	8	0	286	105	2	35.75
P. J. R. Steyn (*Northerns*)	9	16	1	536	141	2	35.73
J. M. Henderson (*Boland*)	6	12	2	355	135	1	35.50
N. C. Johnson (*Natal*)	10	14	2	421	100	1	35.08

* *Signifies not out.*

BOWLING

(Qualification: 20 wickets)

	O	M	R	W	BB	5W/i	Avge
C. F. Craven (*Free State*)	71	26	165	21	5-25	2	7.85
P. S. de Villiers (*Northerns*)	240.1	59	708	47	7-80	3	15.06
D. J. Pryke (*North West*)	133.1	33	314	20	6-43	2	15.70
S. Abrahams (*E. Province*)	226.3	59	533	33	6-39	3	16.15
A. A. Donald (*Free State*)	199.2	49	583	35	5-54	2	16.65
A. Badenhorst (*E. Province*)	150.2	37	429	23	5-48	1	18.65
R. Telemachus (*Boland*)	220	45	676	34	5-43	2	19.88
H. C. Bakkes (*Free State*)	202.2	46	484	24	5-70	1	20.16
S. M. Pollock (*Natal*)	181.5	49	449	22	6-50	1	20.40
G. M. Gilder (*Natal*)	193.1	42	538	25	4-54	0	21.52
C. E. Eksteen (*Gauteng*)	511	167	1,145	51	6-54	2	22.45
M. W. Pringle (*E. Province*)	309.4	74	801	35	7-78	1	22.88
A. G. Botha (*Natal*)	226	44	605	26	8-53	1	23.26
C. R. Tatton (*Natal*)	233.2	68	493	21	4-60	0	23.47
V. C. Drakes (*Border*)	240.1	64	592	25	5-75	1	23.68
P. J. Botha (*Border*)	324.5	79	788	33	6-32	1	23.87
E. W. Kidwell (*Gauteng*)	189	24	742	31	7-58	2	23.93
D. Taljard (*Border*)	243.4	69	700	29	6-49	2	24.13
H. S. Williams (*Boland*)	232.4	66	489	20	4-65	0	24.45
G. A. Roe (*Griqualand W.*)	312.3	83	663	27	4-35	0	24.55
M. Hayward (*E. Province*)	374.4	68	1,156	47	6-51	1	24.59
J. F. Venter (*Free State*)	245.4	65	731	29	5-123	1	25.20
A. C. Dawson (*W. Province*)	273.2	82	686	27	5-80	1	25.40
N. Boje (*Free State*)	440.5	146	913	35	6-34	2	26.08
G. J. Smith (*Northerns*)	246.3	51	788	30	6-35	1	26.26
C. W. Henderson (*Boland*)	355.4	124	749	28	4-39	0	26.75
P. R. Adams (*W. Province*)	299.5	72	836	30	7-69	2	27.86
G. J. Kruis (*Griqualand W.*)	297.4	64	900	32	7-58	1	28.12
M. F. George (*W. Province*)	260.4	46	901	32	6-61	1	28.15
H. R. Bryan (*Griqualand W.*)	223	37	683	23	6-71	1	29.69
S. Elworthy (*Northerns*)	265	65	776	25	5-2	2	31.04
B. T. Player (*W. Province*)	269.2	63	696	20	4-8	0	34.80

SUPERSPORT SERIES, 1997-98

	Played	Won	Lost	Drawn	Bonus Points Batting	Bonus Points Bowling	Points
Free State	8	6	1	1	26	26	112
Eastern Province	8	4	1	3	20	25	85
Northerns	8	3	3	2	21	28	79
Natal	8	3	1	4	20	25	75
Boland	8	3	4	1	8	31	69
Gauteng	8	2	4	2	21	27	68
Border	8	2	3	3	16	21	57
Western Province	8	2	3	3	12	18	50
Griqualand West	8	1	6	1	15	23	48

Outright win = 10 pts.

Bonus points are awarded for the first 100 overs of each team's first innings. One batting point is awarded for the first 150 runs and for every subsequent 50. One bowling point is awarded for the third wicket taken and for every subsequent two.

In the following scores, * by the name of a team indicates that they won the toss.

At Paarl, November 14, 15. Border won by ten wickets. Boland* 85 (V. C. Drakes four for 17, D. Taljard three for 37) and 145 (S. J. Palframan 45, R. Telemachus 30; P. J. Botha six for 32); Border 221 (B. M. White 46, S. C. Pope 57 not out; R. Telemachus three for 66, C. W. Henderson four for 47) and 13 for no wkt. *Border 16 pts, Boland 4 pts.*

At Kimberley, November 14, 15, 16, 17. Eastern Province won by 154 runs. Eastern Province* 307 for nine dec. (C. C. Bradfield 103, A. V. Birrell 57, M. Hayward 32 not out; H. R. Bryan four for 82) and 270 for five dec. (G. T. Love 43, K. C. Wessels 122 not out); Griqualand West 226 (M. I. Gidley 103; M. W. Pringle three for 65, E. A. E. Baptiste four for 37) and 197 (P. H. Barnard 47; M. W. Pringle four for 75, M. Hayward three for 58). *Eastern Province 18 pts, Griqualand West 6 pts.*

At Durban, November 14, 15, 16. Natal won by an innings and five runs. Northerns* 209 (G. Dros 35, M. van Jaarsveld 37, M. J. R. Rindel 62; S. M. Pollock three for 18, Zahir Shah four for 56) and 198 (G. Dros 49, M. van Jaarsveld 39; Zahir Shah five for 67); Natal 412 (E. L. R. Stewart 60, A. C. Hudson 74, N. C. Johnson 100, S. M. Pollock 54; G. J. Smith four for 99). *Natal 18 pts, Northerns 5 pts.*

At Cape Town, November 14, 15, 16, 17. Free State won by six wickets. Free State 387 (G. F. J. Liebenberg 72, L. J. Wilkinson 81, J. F. Venter 86, N. Boje 76; C. R. Matthews four for 71) and 61 for four; Western Province* 193 (J. H. Kallis 52, J. B. Commins 44, B. M. McMillan 37; C. J. Vorster three for 49) and 253 (H. D. Ackerman 82, J. B. Commins 30, B. T. Player 30, P. Kirsten 31; S. A. Cilliers three for 54). *Free State 17 pts, Western Province 3 pts.*
   On the second day, play was halted because of an overpoweringly bad smell from the nearby brewery. (See Wisden 1998, page 1385.)

At East London, November 21, 22, 23, 24. Drawn. Border* 341 (B. M. White 83, P. C. Strydom 51, S. C. Pope 61; G. M. Gilder three for 83) and 265 for seven dec. (P. C. Strydom 106, S. C. Pope 83; G. M. Gilder three for 59); Natal 350 (A. C. Hudson 125, D. M. Benkenstein 102; V. C. Drakes three for 73, D. Taljard three for 92). *Border 4 pts, Natal 6 pts.*

At Port Elizabeth, November 21, 22, 23, 24. Drawn. Eastern Province* 293 (L. J. Koen 42, D. J. Callaghan 35, M. W. Rushmere 35, M. W. Pringle 30, M. Hayward 55 not out; H. S. Williams four for 65) and 232 for six dec. (K. C. Wessels 130 not out); Boland 274 (K. C. Jackson 81, C. Grainger 68, A. P. Kuiper 30; M. W. Pringle three for 50, D. J. Callaghan three for 25) and 157 for six (E. J. Ferreira 32, A. P. Kuiper 32 not out). *Eastern Province 6 pts, Boland 6 pts.*

At Bloemfontein, November 21, 22, 23, 24. Griqualand West won by eight wickets. Free State* 237 (H. C. Bakkes 62, C. J. Vorster 45; H. R. Bryan six for 71) and 227 (G. F. J. Liebenberg 43, M. N. van Wyk 42, N. Boje 43 not out; M. Strydom three for 54, H. R. Bryan four for 49); Griqualand West 362 (J. M. Arthur 42, P. H. Barnard 146, L. L. Bosman 96; H. C. Bakkes five for 70, J. F. Venter three for 102) and 106 for two (M. I. Gidley 33). *Griqualand West 17 pts, Free State 3 pts.*

At Cape Town, November 21, 22, 23, 24. Drawn. Western Province* 267 for seven (J. B. Commins 40, P. Kirsten 91 not out, C. R. Matthews 41 not out) v Gauteng. *Western Province 3 pts, Gauteng 3 pts.*

At Kimberley, November 27, 28, 29, 30. Border won by 51 runs. Border* 278 (W. Wiblin 43, V. C. Drakes 98; G. A. Roe four for 35) and 192 (W. Wiblin 40, P. C. Strydom 68, S. C. Pope 34; G. A. Roe three for 23, M. Strydom four for 33); Griqualand West 257 (J. M. Arthur 35, L. L. Bosman 77, G. J. Kruis 34, G. A. Roe 31 not out; A. J. Swanepoel 39; B. M. White three for 23) and 162 (W. M. Dry 30, M. Strydom 32; P. A. N. Emslie three for 55, I. L. Howell four for 35). *Border 17 pts, Griqualand West 5 pts.*

At Johannesburg, November 28, 29, 30, December 1. Free State won by seven wickets. Gauteng* 89 (N. D. McKenzie 38; H. C. Bakkes three for 22, C. F. Craven five for 26) and 183 (S. G. Koenig 32, K. R. Rutherford 36, R. P. Snell 33; C. J. Vorster three for 72, C. F. Craven four for 24); Free State 205 (C. F. Craven 40, L. J. Wilkinson 44; S. Jacobs five for 55) and 70 for three (L. J. Wilkinson 30 not out). *Free State 16 pts, Gauteng 4 pts.*

At Durban, November 28, 29, 30, December 1. Drawn. Eastern Province 238 for six dec. (K. C. Wessels 65, J. Kemp 51 not out, E. A. E. Baptiste 33 not out); Natal* 33 for two.

Rain prevented play on the first three days, so the match was played as a single-innings game with no bonus points.

At Centurion, November 28, 29. Northerns won by an innings and 29 runs. Boland 100 (J. B. Mackey 32; P. S. de Villiers four for 35, M. J. R. Rindel four for 17) and 84 (P. S. de Villiers five for 30); Northerns* 213 (G. Dros 45, S. Elworthy 89; C. K. Langeveldt four for 70, J. D. Albanie three for 32). *Northerns 16 pts, Boland 4 pts.*

At Paarl, December 12, 13, 14, 15. Boland won by 67 runs. Boland* 165 (A. P. Kuiper 36; B. N. Schultz four for 42, A. C. Dawson four for 42) and 265 (J. B. Mackey 45, A. P. Kuiper 30, K. M. Curran 67, S. J. Palframan 40; A. C. Dawson four for 51); Western Province 121 (R. Telemachus four for 36, C. W. Henderson three for 39) and 242 (L. D. Ferreira 69, E. O. Simons 48, C. R. Matthews 40 not out; R. Telemachus five for 52, C. W. Henderson three for 88). *Boland 15 pts, Western Province 4 pts.*

At Bloemfontein, December 12, 13. Free State won by an innings and 36 runs. Natal 106 (C. J. Vorster four for 34, C. F. Craven four for 27) and 127 (A. C. Hudson 36; H. C. Bakkes four for 33, C. F. Craven five for 25); Free State* 269 (H. H. Dippenaar 42, J. F. Venter 50, N. Boje 55, J. Beukes 52, C. J. Vorster 33; G. M. Gilder four for 70, N. C. Johnson three for 38). *Free State 17 pts, Natal 4 pts.*

Craven took nine wickets for the second match running.

At Johannesburg, December 12, 13, 14, 15. Gauteng won by 163 runs. Gauteng* 361 (M. R. Benfield 36, K. R. Rutherford 143, N. Pothas 76; V. C. Drakes five for 75, P. J. Botha three for 68) and 253 for five dec. (M. R. Benfield 35, K. R. Rutherford 35, D. N. Crookes 106 not out, Z. de Bruyn 45); Border 216 (P. J. Botha 32, P. C. Strydom 82; D. J. Terbrugge three for 62, C. E. Eksteen four for 36) and 235 (B. M. White 51, W. Wiblin 38, B. C. Fourie 57; D. J. Terbrugge three for 44, C. E. Eksteen four for 85). *Gauteng 18 pts, Border 5 pts.*

At Centurion, December 12, 13, 14. Northerns won by nine wickets. Northerns 328 (P. J. R. Steyn 58, G. Dros 96, M. van Jaarsveld 53, M. J. R. Rindel 88 not out; G. A. Roe three for 57, G. J. Kruis seven for 58) and 89 for one (P. J. R. Steyn 36 not out, M. van Jaarsveld 35); Griqualand West* 104 (G. J. Kruis 34 not out; P. S. de Villiers four for 49, S. Elworthy five for two) and 310 (M. I. Gidley 134, P. H. Barnard 53, W. Bossenger 54; P. S. de Villiers four for 105, S. Elworthy five for 82). *Northerns 17 pts, Griqualand West 2 pts.*

At East London, January 16, 17, 18, 19. Drawn. Border* 375 (W. Wiblin 177, S. C. Pope 100; A. C. Dawson five for 80) and 270 for eight dec. (W. Wiblin 119 not out, P. C. Strydom 33, C. C. van der Merwe 34; B. T. Player four for 96); Western Province 395 (H. D. Ackerman 114, F. Davids 61, P. Kirsten 37; D. Taljard three for 50, P. A. N. Emslie three for 94) and 106 for three (L. D. Ferreira 56 not out). *Border 6 pts, Western Province 5 pts.*

Wiblin scored a hundred in each innings; in the first innings, he added 253 for the fifth wicket with Pope.

At Port Elizabeth, January 16, 17, 18, 19. Eastern Province won by 117 runs. Eastern Province* 401 for five dec. (L. J. Koen 104, K. C. Wessels 79, J. Callaghan 111 not out, E. A. E. Baptiste 51 not out) and 259 for six dec. (M. W. Rushmere 42, C. C. Bradfield 49, J. Kemp 81 not out, E. A. E. Baptiste 53; C. E. Eksteen four for 97); Gauteng 307 (M. R. Benfield 31, K. R. Rutherford 45, D. N. Crookes 90, Z. de Bruyn 43, R. E. Veenstra 35; M. W. Pringle seven for 78) and 236 (M. R. Benfield 59, D. N. Crookes 31, Z. de Bruyn 35; M. W. Pringle three for 53, M. Hayward four for 49). *Eastern Province 18 pts, Gauteng 6 pts.*

At Bloemfontein, January 16, 17, 18, 19. Free State won by 197 runs. Free State* 380 (G. F. J. Liebenberg 79, C. F. Craven 105, N. Boje 104 not out; G. J. Smith three for 82) and 218 for five dec. (H. H. Dippenaar 100 not out, L. J. Wilkinson 89); Northerns 298 (P. J. R. Steyn 33, M. van Jaarsveld 82, D. J. J. de Vos 31, S. Elworthy 31, A. G. Davis 33 not out; N. Boje five for 84, J. F. Venter three for 111) and 103 (P. J. R. Steyn 33; N. Boje six for 34, J. F. Venter three for 27). *Free State 17 pts, Northerns 6 pts.*

At Kimberley, January 16, 17, 18, 19. Boland won by six wickets. Griqualand West* 184 (W. Bossenger 63, C. V. English 60; H. S. Williams three for 41, K. M. Curran four for 17) and 147 (L. L. Bosman 69 not out; C. W. Henderson four for 39); Boland 166 (C. Grainger 41, K. M. Curran 30; G. A. Roe three for 38, G. J. Kruis three for 43, A. J. Swanepoel three for 23) and 169 for four (E. J. Ferreira 50, K. C. Jackson 53 not out, K. M. Curran 33 not out; G. A. Roe three for 26). *Boland 15 pts, Griqualand West 5 pts.*

At Johannesburg, January 23, 24, 25, 26. Northerns won by 236 runs. Northerns* 235 (D. J. J. de Vos 64, M. J. G. Davis 42, G. J. Smith 51 not out; E. W. Kidwell seven for 58) and 277 for seven dec. (M. van Jaarsveld 134, D. J. J. de Vos 54; C. E. Eksteen four for 63); Gauteng 202 for seven dec. (K. R. Rutherford 78 not out; S. Elworthy three for 51, G. J. Smith three for 62) and 74 (P. S. de Villiers four for 11, G. J. Smith three for 16). *Northerns 15 pts, Gauteng 6 pts.*
    In Gauteng's second innings, the first seven wickets all fell with the score on 12. This is thought to be the first time seven wickets had fallen at the same total since MCC lost seven on nought against Surrey in 1872.

At Durban, January 23, 24, 25, 26. Natal won by seven wickets. Natal* 500 for five dec. (M. L. Bruyns 135, D. J. Watson 145, E. L. R. Stewart 51, A. C. Hudson 119 not out) and 25 for three (D. G. Payne three for ten); Western Province 205 (L. D. Ferreira 41, E. O. Simons 41, P. Kirsten 47; G. M. Gilder four for 54, C. R. Tatton four for 60) and 319 (J. de Nobrega 30, H. D. Ackerman 131, B. A. Murphy 41, P. Kirsten 32; R. B. MacQueen five for 125, C. R. Tatton three for 84). *Natal 18 pts, Western Province 2 pts.*
    Natal beat Western Province for the first time since 1981-82.

At Paarl, January 30, 31, February 1. Boland won by nine wickets. Gauteng* 235 (A. J. Seymore 96, R. P. Snell 40, C. E. Eksteen 32; R. Telemachus five for 43) and 166 (M. R. Benfield 73; H. S. Williams three for 42, A. P. Kuiper three for 36); Boland 228 (K. C. Jackson 79, C. W. Henderson 33 not out; C. E. Eksteen six for 56) and 174 for one (J. M. Henderson 51 not out, K. C. Jackson 102 not out). *Boland 16 pts, Gauteng 6 pts.*

At Port Elizabeth, January 30, 31, February 1, 2. Eastern Province won by an innings and 150 runs. Border 220 (B. M. White 40, W. Wiblin 36; E. A. E. Baptiste three for 33, D. J. Callaghan three for 19) and 144 (B. M. White 40, P. A. N. Emslie 31; E. A. E. Baptiste four for 28, G. T. Love four for 56); Eastern Province* 514 for five dec. (M. W. Rushmere 65, C. C. Bradfield 33, L. J. Koen 33, K. C. Wessels 179 not out, D. J. Callaghan 132). *Eastern Province 17 pts, Border 3 pts.*
    Wessels and Callaghan added 289 for Eastern Province's fourth wicket.

At Bloemfontein, February 6, 7, 8. Free State won by an innings and 129 runs. Boland 184 (K. C. Jackson 33, C. Grainger 41, A. P. Kuiper 31; N. Boje three for 30) and 158 (E. J. Ferreira 32, K. C. Jackson 65; A. A. Donald three for 25, J. F. Venter four for 26); Free State* 471 (C. F. Craven 100, N. Boje 50, M. N. van Wyk 86, H. C. Bakkes 101; K. M. Curran three for 31). *Free State 19 pts, Boland 4 pts.*

At Durban, February 6, 7, 8, 9. Drawn. Natal* 434 (D. J. Watson 62, A. C. Hudson 206, K. A. Forde 61; E. W. Kidwell six for 115) and 220 (M. L. Bruyns 58, A. C. Hudson 79; C. E. Eksteen six for 54, D. N. Crookes three for 86); Gauteng 333 (M. R. Benfield 35, D. J. Cullinan 103, K. R. Rutherford 125; S. M. Adam five for 57, N. C. Johnson three for 34) and 100 for three (D. J. Cullinan 35 not out). *Natal 9 pts, Gauteng 6 pts.*
    Hudson's 206, his maiden double-hundred, lasted 315 minutes and 259 balls and included 30 fours and one six.

At Cape Town, February 6, 7, 8, 9. Western Province won by 123 runs. Western Province* 145 (L. D. Ferreira 34; M. Hayward three for 20, J. Kemp four for 12) and 427 for eight dec. (H. H. Gibbs 152, H. D. Ackerman 100, B. T. Player 53 not out, P. R. Adams 38); Eastern Province 204 (M. W. Rushmere 31, C. C. Bradfield 34, J. Kemp 30; M. F. George three for 33, E. O. Simons three for 39) and 245 (L. J. Koen 52, K. C. Wessels 40, D. J. Callaghan 37, J. Kemp 38; P. R. Adams six for 90, B. T. Player three for 84). *Western Province 14 pts, Eastern Province 6 pts.*

At Cape Town, February 13, 14, 15, 16. Western Province won by an innings and 45 runs. Griqualand West* 239 (J. M. Arthur 31, W. Bossenger 85, M. Strydom 43; M. F. George six for 61, A. C. Dawson three for 65) and 216 (M. I. Gidley 88; P. R. Adams seven for 69); Western Province 500 for six dec. (A. G. Prince 60, H. D. Ackerman 174, E. O. Simons 157 not out). *Western Province 16 pts, Griqualand West 3 pts.*

At Paarl, February 20, 21, 22, 23. Natal won by six wickets. Boland 177 (C. Grainger 47, J. L. Ontong 42; N. C. Johnson three for 38, C. R. Tatton three for 24) and 253 (A. P. Kuiper 30, C. Grainger 37, S. J. Palframan 71; S. M. Adam three for 44, N. C. Johnson four for 64); Natal* 190 (D. J. Watson 47, J. N. Rhodes 41) and 242 for four (M. L. Bruyns 107, A. C. Hudson 31, J. N. Rhodes 69 not out). *Natal 15 pts, Boland 5 pts.*

At Centurion, February 20, 21, 22, 23. Eastern Province won by 148 runs. Eastern Province 169 (D. J. Callaghan 58, Q. Ferreira 31; P. S. de Villiers four for 63, G. J. Smith four for 48) and 431 for four dec. (M. W. Rushmere 124, C. C. Bradfield 43, L. J. Koen 174 not out, D. J. Callaghan 39, J. Kemp 32); Northerns* 233 (D. J. J. de Vos 60, D. J. Smith 40; M. W. Pringle three for 98, A. Badenhorst three for 36, Q. Ferreira three for 44) and 219 (P. J. R. Steyn 35, M. van Jaarsveld 32, D. J. J. de Vos 47, S. Elworthy 49; S. Abrahams four for 101). *Eastern Province 15 pts, Northerns 6 pts.*

At East London, February 26, 27, 28, March 1. Drawn. Northerns 326 (R. F. Pienaar 56, G. Dros 47, M. van Jaarsveld 34, M. J. R. Rindel 39, D. J. Smith 46; D. Taljard five for 54, M. Ntini three for 101); Border* 199 for eight (S. C. Pope 70, V. C. Drakes 59). *Border 4 pts, Northerns 6 pts.*

At Port Elizabeth, February 26, 27, 28, March 1. Drawn. Eastern Province* 382 (M. W. Rushmere 55, K. C. Wessels 133, D. J. Callaghan 42, S. Abrahams 50); Free State 250 for five dec. (G. F. J. Liebenberg 68, J. F. Venter 40 not out, N. Boje 31; M. Hayward three for 57). *Eastern Province 5 pts, Free State 5 pts.*

At Kimberley, March 6, 7, 8, 9. Drawn. Natal* 379 (D. J. Watson 42, E. L. R. Stewart 47, D. M. Benkenstein 96, N. C. Johnson 54, A. G. Botha 52; G. A. Roe four for 98, G. J. Kruis three for 89) and 239 for four dec. (M. L. Bruyns 43, D. J. Watson 44, E. L. R. Stewart 61, J. N. Rhodes 60 not out); Griqualand West 425 for nine dec. (M. I. Gidley 55, C. V. English 34, P. H. Barnard 37, W. Bossenger 124 not out, H. R. Bryan 71; C. R. Tatton three for 85) and 165 for five (J. M. Arthur 58; C. R. Tatton four for 62). *Griqualand West 5 pts, Natal 5 pts.*

At East London, March 13, 14, 15. Free State won by an innings and 75 runs. Border* 120 (S. A. Cilliers three for ten, N. Boje three for 30) and 264 (W. Wiblin 42, S. C. Pope 30, P. C. Strydom 39, V. C. Drakes 53; J. F. Venter five for 123, N. Boje three for 65); Free State 459 (H. H. Dippenaar 46, M. N. van Wyk 121, L. J. Wilkinson 45, W. J. Cronje 40, J. F. Venter 70, H. C. Bakkes 74; D. Taljard three for 77). *Free State 18 pts, Border 2 pts.*

At Johannesburg, March 13, 14, 15. Gauteng won by an innings and 96 runs. Gauteng* 431 (A. J. Seymore 41, N. D. McKenzie 84, D. J. Cullinan 172, D. N. Crookes 41, C. E. Eksteen 33; H. R. Bryan three for 85, G. J. Kruis three for 81); Griqualand West 207 (M. I. Gidley 93; K. Ingram four for 43, A. J. Hall three for 48) and 128 (H. R. Bryan 31 not out; E. W. Kidwell four for 52, C. E. Eksteen three for 27). *Gauteng 19 pts, Griqualand West 5 pts.*

At Centurion, March 13, 14, 15, 16. Drawn. Northerns* 483 for eight dec. (P. J. R. Steyn 141, G. Dros 38, M. van Jaarsveld 139 not out, P. de Bruyn 50; A. C. Dawson three for 80) and 120 for five; Western Province 153 (P. Kirsten 47; G. J. Smith six for 35) and 581 for seven dec. (G. Kirsten 32, J. H. Kallis 111, H. H. Gibbs 63, H. D. Ackerman 202 not out, B. M. McMillan 64, A. G. Prince 42; D. J. J. de Vos three for 117). *Northerns 8 pts, Western Province 3 pts.*

Ackerman's 202 not out, his maiden double-hundred, lasted 359 minutes and 294 balls and included 25 fours.

CHAMPIONS

Currie Cup			
1889-90	Transvaal	1965-66	Natal/Transvaal (Tied)
1890-91	Kimberley	1966-67	Natal
1892-93	Western Province	1967-68	Natal
1893-94	Western Province	1968-69	Transvaal
1894-95	Transvaal	1969-70	Transvaal/W. Province (Tied)
1896-97	Western Province	1970-71	Transvaal
1897-98	Western Province	1971-72	Transvaal
1902-03	Transvaal	1972-73	Transvaal
1903-04	Transvaal	1973-74	Natal
1904-05	Transvaal	1974-75	Western Province
1906-07	Transvaal	1975-76	Natal
1908-09	Western Province	1976-77	Natal
1910-11	Natal	1977-78	Western Province
1912-13	Natal	1978-79	Transvaal
1920-21	Western Province	1979-80	Transvaal
1921-22	Transvaal/Natal/W. Prov. (Tied)	1980-81	Natal
1923-24	Transvaal	1981-82	Western Province
1925-26	Transvaal	1982-83	Transvaal
1926-27	Transvaal	1983-84	Transvaal
1929-30	Transvaal	1984-85	Transvaal
1931-32	Western Province	1985-86	Western Province
1933-34	Natal	1986-87	Transvaal
1934-35	Transvaal	1987-88	Transvaal
1936-37	Natal	1988-89	Eastern Province
1937-38	Natal/Transvaal (Tied)	1989-90	E. Province/W. Province (Shared)
1946-47	Natal		
1947-48	Natal	*Castle Cup*	
1950-51	Transvaal	1990-91	Western Province
1951-52	Natal	1991-92	Eastern Province
1952-53	Western Province	1992-93	Orange Free State
1954-55	Natal	1993-94	Orange Free State
1955-56	Western Province	1994-95	Natal
1958-59	Transvaal	1995-96	Western Province
1959-60	Natal		
1960-61	Natal	*Supersport Series*	
1962-63	Natal	1996-97	Natal
1963-64	Natal	1997-98	Free State

Transvaal have won the title outright 24 times, Natal 20, Western Province 15, Orange Free State/Free State 3, Eastern Province 2, Kimberley 1. The title has been shared five times as follows: Transvaal 4, Natal and Western Province 3, Eastern Province 1.

UCB BOWL, 1997-98

Division 1

	Played	Won	Lost	Drawn	Bonus Points Batting	Bowling	Points
North West	5	3	0	2	19	18	67
Northerns B	5	2	2	1	18	19	57
Western Province B	5	2	2	1	19	15	54
Eastern Province B	5	2	1	2	18	18	51†
Natal B	5	1	2	2	18	15	42†
Easterns	5	0	3	2	11	15	23†

Division 2 (not first-class)

	Played	Won	Lost	Drawn	Bonus Points Batting	Bonus Points Bowling	Points
Griqualand West B........	6	3	0	3	22	20	71†
Border B..............	6	3	1	2	15	23	68
Gauteng B.............	6	1	0	5	23	22	52†
Zimbabwe Board XI......	6	1	0	5	22	19	50†
Boland B.............	6	1	2	3	18	19	47
Free State B............	6	1	3	2	18	17	39†
Namibia..............	6	0	4	2	17	20	37

Griqualand West B were promoted, but Easterns remained in Division 1.

Outright win = 10 pts.

Bonus points are awarded for the first 85 overs of each team's first innings. One batting point is awarded for the first 100 runs and for every subsequent 50. One bowling point is awarded for the second wicket taken and for every subsequent two up to eight.

† Points deducted for slow over-rate. Eastern Province B also had four points deducted for a substandard pitch.

Note: First innings closed at 100 overs.

In the following scores, * by the name of a team indicates that they won the toss.

Division 1

At Cape Town, October 30, 31, November 1. Western Province B won by four wickets. Natal B 324 (K. D. Donaldson 50, U. H. Goedeke 124, J. L. Cooke 37; R. Munnik four for 63) and 212 (J. Buxton-Forman 43, W. R. Wingfield 39, A. M. Amla 57; M. F. George three for 37, D. M. Koch four for 35); Western Province B* 296 for two dec. (R. Maron 65, J. de Nobrega 64, H. Pangarker 128 not out) and 241 for six (R. Maron 40, D. M. Koch 46 not out, M. T. Solomons 59 not out; R. M. Nienaber three for 58). *Western Province B 18 pts, Natal B 6 pts.*

At Centurion, November 13, 14, 15. Drawn. Northerns B* 322 for nine dec. (P. de Bruyn 103, E. de Bruyn 41, J. Rudolph 56; R. Munnik three for 58, F. Davids three for 47) and 217 for nine dec. (L. L. Gamiet 39, D. J. Smith 59, J. Rudolph 55; M. F. George four for 39); Western Province B 245 (R. Maron 59, S. Hofmeyr 31, F. Davids 36, N. Adams 36; R. T. Coetzee seven for 74) and 181 for six (S. Hofmeyr 35, N. Adams 81 not out). *Northerns B 8 pts, Western Province B 6 pts.*

At Durban (Northwood Crusaders Club), November 21, 22, 23. Drawn. North West* 166 (A. G. Lawson 57) and 270 for seven dec. (L. P. Vorster 89 not out, M. J. Lavine 86; R. M. Nienaber three for 88); Natal B 228 for eight (A. G. Botha 39, C. B. Sugden 89, W. R. Wingfield 40). *Natal B 6 pts, North West 5 pts.*

At Port Elizabeth, November 27, 28, 29. Eastern Province B won by an innings and 26 runs. Eastern Province B 429 for eight dec. (D. Moffat 105, A. K. Prince 116, G. C. Victor 138; A. N. W. Tweedie three for 81); Natal B* 276 (A. G. Botha 94, M. Badat 33, K. A. Forde 66, U. H. Goedeke 34; A. Badenhorst four for 53, A. L. Hobson five for 103) and 127 (W. R. Wingfield 41; S. Abrahams four for 33). *Eastern Province B 20 pts, Natal B 6 pts.*

Moffat scored 105 on first-class debut.

At Belville, December 11, 12, 13. Eastern Province B won by five wickets. Western Province B* 290 (F. Davids 109 not out, B. T. Player 79; W. Walker four for 70, S. Abrahams five for 71) and 305 for nine dec. (S. Hofmeyr 31, B. T. Player 56, D. M. Koch 54, M. F. George 42 not out; S. Abrahams six for 93); Eastern Province B 339 for eight (C. C. Bradfield 34, G. C. Victor 36, D. W. Murray 103 not out, Q. Ferreira 38; B. T. Player four for eight) and 257 for five (G. C. Victor 85, J. D. C. Bryant 63, C. C. Bradfield 40 not out, S. Abrahams 33 not out). *Eastern Province B 18 pts, Western Province B 7 pts.*

At Fochville, December 12, 13, 14. North West won by eight wickets. Easterns* 236 (M. J. Mitchley 75, G. White 34, W. R. Radford 39; M. J. Lavine three for 44, D. Rossouw three for 72) and 248 (G. W. Myburgh 50, N. Martin 46, J. Uys 34; L. C. R. Jordaan six for 67); North West 361 for nine (A. G. Lawson 110, G. M. Hewitt 96, L. P. Vorster 47, M. J. Lavine 41; G. P. Cooke three for 58) and 124 for two (A. G. Lawson 44 not out, M. C. Venter 50 not out). *North West 18 pts, Easterns 5 pts.*

At Benoni, January 16, 17, 18. Drawn. Eastern Province B* 160 (G. C. Victor 54, A. Badenhorst 34 not out; A. Nel four for 41) and 231 (A. G. Prince 48, G. C. Victor 43, G. V. Grace 31; A. Nel five for 74, A. G. Pollock three for 56); Easterns 166 (G. W. Myburgh 37; A. Badenhorst five for 48, Q. Ferreira three for 56) and 175 for nine (C. R. Norris 83, G. W. Myburgh 49; A. Badenhorst three for 48, Q. Ferreira four for 17). *Easterns 6 pts, Eastern Province B 6 pts.*

At Port Elizabeth, February 6, 7, 8. Northerns B won by 32 runs. Northerns B* 182 (J. G. Myburgh 38, P. de Bruyn 33; S. Abrahams six for 39) and 111 (Q. Ferreira three for 24, S. Abrahams three for 30); Eastern Province B 164 (M. G. Beamish 56, J. D. C. Bryant 65; D. H. Townsend four for 26, P. de Bruyn five for 36) and 97 (D. H. Townsend four for 43, P. Joubert four for 27). *Northerns B 16 pts, Eastern Province B 6 pts.*
Eastern Province B later lost four points for a substandard pitch.

At Benoni, February 6, 7, 8. Western Province B won by 23 runs. Western Province B 308 (M. J. Crosoer 38, H. Pangarker 55, R. Munnik 32, M. T. Solomons 35, M. van Olst 54; A. Nel three for 63, C. Kruger four for 50, J. Uys three for 77) and 244 for eight dec. (M. J. Crosoer 64, S. Hofmeyr 41, A. Paleker 46; J. Uys five for 87); Easterns* 303 (J. S. Lerm 112, N. A. Fusedale 34, C. R. Norris 53; D. G. Payne three for 65, R. Munnik three for 55) and 226 (M. J. Mitchley 37, J. S. Lerm 41, G. White 32). *Western Province B 17 pts, Easterns 8 pts.*

At Port Elizabeth (University), February 20, 21, 22. Drawn. Eastern Province B* 280 (M. G. Beamish 32, G. C. Victor 48, J. D. C. Bryant 104 not out; L. C. R. Jordaan five for 69) and 266 for four dec. (M. G. Beamish 43, G. V. Grace 112 not out, G. C. Victor 65); North West 259 for six (S. Nicolson 79, A. G. Lawson 78, L. P. Vorster 46 not out, E. G. Poole 31; J. September four for 30) and 178 for four (L. P. Vorster 43 not out, M. J. Lavine 60). *Eastern Province B 6 pts, North West 7 pts.*

At Pretoria (University), February 20, 21, 22. Northerns B won by ten wickets. Easterns 112 (C. R. Norris 38; R. E. Bryson three for 26, P. de Bruyn four for 31) and 255 (G. W. Myburgh 50, G. White 66, J. Uys 48; R. E. Bryson five for 63, Q. R. Still three for 20); Northerns B* 351 for nine dec. (J. G. Myburgh 203, D. Jordaan 60; C. Kruger four for 74, C. R. Norris four for 75) and 17 for no wkt. *Northerns B 19 pts, Easterns 4 pts.*
Johan Myburgh's 203, his maiden hundred, lasted 393 minutes and 264 balls and included 26 fours and one six. He was the youngest South African to score a first-class double-hundred, at 17 years 122 days, in his third match.

At Centurion, February 27, 28, March 1. Natal B won by one wicket. Northerns B* 256 (D. Jordaan 80, Q. R. Still 32, J. Rudolph 32; A. G. Botha eight for 53) and 147 (D. Jordaan 46, G. Morgan 48 not out; T. Bosch three for 28, A. G. Botha four for 42); Natal B 200 (A. G. Botha 64; P. de Bruyn three for 35, J. Rudolph three for 46) and 205 for nine (W. R. Wingfield 32, J. C. Kent 44, G. S. Katz 34; J. Rudolph three for 47). *Natal B 17 pts, Northerns B 8 pts.*

At Potchefstroom, March 5, 6, 7. North West won by nine wickets. Western Province B* 284 (R. Maron 75, R. Munnik 57; D. J. Pryke five for 38, E. F. J. Wyma three for 44) and 151 (H. Pangarker 78, M. van Olst 41; D. J. Pryke six for 43); North West 373 for nine (S. Nicolson 42, H. M. de Vos 101, A. Jacobs 112, M. J. Lavine 43, D. Rossouw 37 not out; D. G. Payne four for 93) and 64 for one (H. M. de Vos 30 not out). *North West 19 pts, Western Province B 6 pts.*
Jacobs scored 112 on first-class debut.

At Durban, March 6, 7, 8. Drawn. Easterns 142 (M. J. Mitchley 63; J. E. Bastow six for 37) and 196 for six (M. J. Mitchley 79, C. R. Norris 33; K. G. Storey three for 23); Natal B* 310 for seven dec. (K. D. Donaldson 54, A. Mall 85, G. S. Katz 77). *Natal B 8 pts, Easterns 3 pts.*

At Fochville, March 13, 14, 15. North West won by ten wickets. Northerns B* 291 for eight (J. G. Myburgh 60 retired hurt, D. Jordaan 107; M. J. Lavine three for 58) and 64 (C. T. Enslin three for 15, M. J. Lavine four for 31); North West 338 (S. Nicolson 58, L. P. Vorster 115, M. J. Lavine 39, C. T. Enslin 51; R. E. Bryson three for 97, J. Rudolph five for 98) and 20 for no wkt. *North West 18 pts, Northerns B 6 pts.*

OTHER FIRST-CLASS MATCHES

West Indies A in South Africa

At Johannesburg, November 14, 15, 16, 17. Drawn. Gauteng XI* 372 for seven dec. (S. G. Koenig 69, N. Pothas 138, N. D. McKenzie 85, G. Toyana 44 not out) and 141 for eight dec. (R. E. Veenstra 37); West Indies A 250 (L. V. Garrick 82, Extras 43; R. P. Snell five for 56) and 58 for two.

At Centurion, November 21, 22, 23, 24. West Indies A won by 67 runs. West Indies A* 293 (R. G. Samuels 55, L. V. Garrick 42, J. C. Adams 123 not out; P. S. de Villiers seven for 80) and 202 (R. G. Samuels 57, S. Ragoonath 48; P. S. de Villiers three for 31, D. H. Townsend five for 68); Northerns President's XI 175 (M. J. G. Davis 36, P. S. de Villiers 46; R. D. King five for 63) and 253 (P. J. R. Steyn 105, M. van Jaarsveld 40, D. J. Smith 39; R. D. King three for 69, P. T. Collins four for 58).

At Cape Town, November 28, 29, 30, December 1. West Indies A won by 23 runs. West Indies A* 290 (J. C. Adams 52, L. R. Williams 110, N. B. Francis 46; M. F. George four for 79) and 174 (L. V. Garrick 35, J. C. Adams 53, W. W. Hinds 32; B. N. Schultz eight for 36); Western Province 199 (H. D. Ackerman 47, P. Kirsten 63; O. D. Gibson four for 36, D. Ramnarine three for 25) and 242 (H. Pangarker 53, H. D. Ackerman 72; O. D. Gibson five for 85, D. Ramnarine three for 55).

At Bloemfontein, December 4, 5, 6, 7. First Unofficial Test: South Africa A won by six wickets. West Indies A* 187 (R. G. Samuels 76, R. R. Sarwan 32, O. D. Gibson 37; B. N. Schultz three for 62, C. E. Eksteen three for 35, M. Hayward three for 45) and 314 (F. L. Reifer 62, J. C. Adams 129, L. R. Williams 34, O. D. Gibson 41; M. Hayward three for 67); South Africa A 306 (G. F. J. Liebenberg 84, H. D. Ackerman 85, N. Pothas 30, M. Hayward 30; O. D. Gibson three for 76, R. D. King three for 34, L. R. Williams three for 56) and 199 for four (D. J. Watson 30, N. D. McKenzie 31, H. D. Ackerman 53 not out, D. M. Benkenstein 52).

At Port Elizabeth, December 12, 13, 14. Drawn. West Indies A 289 (W. W. Hinds 63, R. L. Hoyte 72, N. B. Francis 38; A. Badenhorst four for 69) and 192 for six dec. (S. Ragoonath 76, R. R. Sarwan 34 not out); Eastern Province* 140 (M. G. Beamish 45, K. C. Wessels 52; N. A. M. McLean six for 28, D. Ramnarine three for 50) and 51 for three.

At East London, December 19, 20, 21, 22. Second Unofficial Test: South Africa A won by an innings and 28 runs. South Africa A* 474 for eight dec. (N. C. Johnson 89, A. G. Prince 71, D. M. Benkenstein 70, P. J. Botha 60; O. D. Gibson four for 104); West Indies A 280 (S. Ragoonath 77, W. W. Hinds 115, R. R. Sarwan 33 not out; M. Hayward six for 51) and 166 (J. C. Adams 63; D. N. Crookes six for 50).

At Cape Town, December 26, 27, 28, 29. Third Unofficial Test: South Africa A won by 19 runs. South Africa A* 129 (N. C. Johnson 34, D. M. Benkenstein 36; N. A. M. McLean three for 27) and 301 (G. F. J. Liebenberg 53, A. G. Prince 44, H. D. Ackerman 69, D. M. Benkenstein 66; N. A. M. McLean four for 77, P. T. Collins four for 61); West Indies A 164 (W. W. Hinds 33, L. R. Williams 45, N. A. M. McLean 39 not out; R. Telemachus three for 50, P. J. Botha three for 41) and 247 (S. Ragoonath 36, L. R. Williams 84, R. L. Hoyte 38; M. Hayward three for 82, P. J. Botha three for 37).

South Africa A won the unofficial Test series 3-0. They also won the ensuing one-day series 2-0.

New Zealand Academy in South Africa

At Chatsworth, August 15, 16, 17, 18. Drawn. South African Academy* 327 (M. L. Bruyns 33, M. Strydom 73, G. Morgan 87, T. Odoyo 55; S. B. O'Connor three for 46, P. J. Wiseman three for 96) and 211 for seven dec. (M. L. Bruyns 88, D. R. Gain 49; D. L. Vettori three for 69); New Zealand Academy 275 (M. E. Parlane 32, L. G. Howell 52, C. D. McMillan 63, D. L. Vettori 32; N. Boje three for 62, A. G. Botha three for 22) and 191 for five (C. D. McMillan 62, M. S. Sinclair 35 not out).

At Centurion, August 22, 23, 24, 25. New Zealand Academy won by 147 runs. New Zealand Academy 242 (L. G. Howell 32, M. S. Sinclair 37, A. J. Penn 70; D. J. Terbrugge three for 36) and 291 for nine dec. (M. D. Bell 76, L. G. Howell 67, M. S. Sinclair 45); South African Academy* 201 (A. J. Hall 59; D. G. Sewell six for 40) and 185 (N. Boje 105 not out, A. J. Hall 30; D. L. Vettori five for 45).

At Krugersdorp, August 27, 28, 29, 30. New Zealand Academy won by six wickets. South African Academy* 324 (M. Strydom 49, J. M. Henderson 135, N. Boje 54; S. B. O'Connor four for 66, P. J. Wiseman three for 71) and 190 for six dec. (R. Maron 47, A. J. Hall 62 not out); New Zealand Academy 256 (M. E. Parlane 43, C. D. McMillan 32, M. S. Sinclair 59, S. B. O'Connor 34 not out; E. O. Moleon five for 62, R. B. MacQueen three for 84) and 261 for four (M. E. Parlane 58, M. D. Bell 105 not out, C. D. McMillan 57; A. G. Botha three for 64).

Note: Matches in the following two competitions were not first-class.

STANDARD BANK LEAGUE, 1997-98

	Played	Won	Lost	No Result	Points
Western Province	10	9	1	0	18
Northerns	10	9	1	0	18
Eastern Province	10	6	3	1	13
Gauteng	10	5	5	0	10
Free State	10	5	5	0	10
Boland	10	5	5	0	10
Border	10	4	5	1	9
Natal	10	3	4	3	9
Easterns	10	3	5	2	8
North West	10	1	8	1	3
Griqualand West	10	1	9	0	2

Western Province finished ahead of Northerns by virtue of winning their head-to-head match. Gauteng, Free State and Boland finished in that order by virtue of results in matches between them.

STANDARD BANK CUP, 1997-98

Quarter-finals

At Cape Town, January 9, 10. Free State won by 74 runs. Free State* 204 for nine (39 overs) (J. F. Venter 40, G. F. J. Liebenberg 31, W. J. Smit 43 not out; A. C. Dawson three for 26); Western Province 130 (32.5 overs) (H. D. Ackerman 38, E. O. Simons 31; H. C. Bakkes five for 28).

At Paarl, January 10. Boland won by 25 runs. Boland* 274 for four (45 overs) (J. M. Henderson 36, K. C. Jackson 93, A. P. Kuiper 95 not out); Eastern Province 249 (42.5 overs) (L. J. Koen 41, J. D. C. Bryant 59, E. A. E. Baptiste 65; H. S. Williams four for 37).

At Centurion, January 11. Northerns won by 40 runs. Northerns* 217 for six (45 overs) (M. J. R. Rindel 41, D. Jordaan 96); Zimbabwe A 177 for eight (45 overs) (A. H. Shah 39, D. P. Viljoen 30).

At Johannesburg, January 14. Gauteng won by eight wickets. Kenya* 134 for nine (45 overs) (K. Otieno 37, A. Suji 30 not out); Gauteng 135 for two (26.2 overs) (A. J. Seymore 52 not out, K. R. Rutherford 37 not out).

Semi-finals

At Johannesburg, February 4. Gauteng won by nine wickets. Free State* 87 (28.1 overs) (D. N. Crookes three for seven); Gauteng 89 for one (19 overs) (K. R. Rutherford 74 not out).

At Paarl, February 11. Northerns won by six wickets. Boland* 181 for nine (45 overs) (K. M. Curran 63, S. J. Palframan 34; P. S. de Villiers three for 32, S. Elworthy three for 16); Northerns 182 for four (39.3 overs) (M. J. R. Rindel 45, R. F. Pienaar 78 not out).

Final

At Centurion, March 4. Gauteng won by three wickets. Northerns* 192 (40.5 overs) (M. J. R. Rindel 70, M. van Jaarsveld 61; K. Ingram four for 39, C. E. Eksteen three for 49); Gauteng 193 for seven (43.2 overs) (D. J. Cullinan 62, D. N. Crookes 42).

THE DUCKWORTH/LEWIS METHOD

In 1997, the ECB's limited-overs competitions adopted a new method to revise targets in interrupted games, devised by Frank Duckworth of the Royal Statistical Society and Tony Lewis of the University of the West of England. The system aims to preserve any advantage that one team has established before the interruption. It uses the idea that teams have two resources from which they make runs – an allocated number of overs and ten wickets. It also takes into account when the interruption occurs, because of the different scoring-rates typical of different stages of an innings. Traditional run-rate calculations relied only on the overs available, and ignored wickets lost.

After modifications, the system now uses one table with 50 rows, covering matches of any length up to 50 overs, and ten columns, from nought to nine wickets down. Each figure in the table gives the percentage of the total runs in an innings that would, on average, be scored with a certain number of overs left and wickets lost.

If overs are lost, the table is used to calculate the percentage of runs the team would be expected to score in those missing overs. This is obtained by reading off the figure for the number of overs left and wickets down when play stops and subtracting from it the corresponding figure for the number of overs remaining when it resumes.

If the first innings is complete and the second innings is interrupted, the target to be beaten is reduced by the percentage of the innings lost. If the suspension occurs between innings, as in the ICC Trophy final between Bangladesh and Kenya at Kuala Lumpur in April 1997, only one figure is required: the percentage of the innings remaining for the reduced number of overs with no wicket lost. Kenya scored 241 from 50 overs, but rain restricted Bangladesh to 25 overs. On the traditional average run-rate, losing half their overs would have halved the target to 121. But they had all ten wickets, so had more than half their run-scoring resources. The table showed that, on average, 25 overs should yield 68.7 per cent of a 50-over total. Bangladesh's target was set at 166 (68.7 per cent of 241 = 165.56), which they reached off the final ball.

The system also covers interruptions to the first innings, multiple interruptions and innings terminated by rain. Outside England, it has been adopted by South Africa, New Zealand, India, Pakistan, Zimbabwe and Bangladesh, and is under consideration by West Indies.

CRICKET IN THE WEST INDIES, 1997-98

BY TONY COZIER

Jimmy Adams

The twin triumphs over England towards the end of the home season – 3-1 in the Tests, 4-1 in the one-day internationals – came as a timely and immense relief for West Indies cricket. For several months it had been consumed by chaos, confusion and controversy off the field and catastrophe on it. It seemed to be in self-destruct mode, undermined by a succession of administrative blunders and divisions, and shamed by heavy defeats sustained by its teams at all levels. To have faltered against England, opponents with an unflattering record, would have been a devastating reversal for a sport already beginning to lose its exalted status in the English-speaking Caribbean.

The game plunged back into crisis later in the year when the star players effectively went on strike for a week over pay and conditions, before finally agreeing to start the 1998-99 tour of South Africa. Most of the immediate troubles could be traced to the financial losses incurred by the West Indies Cricket Board in its grandiose schemes of the previous year and to the contentious debate over the captaincy. The decision to extend the 1996-97 season by doubling the number of matches in the first-class tournament, the Red Stripe Cup, playing home and away, and by hosting, for the first time, two separate Test series, proved a serious drain on funds. The retention of 22 players on year-long contracts increased the liability when the relevant governments reneged on pledges of support. Operating profits of over $US4 million the previous year were transformed into a loss of $US267,000. The players' contracts were not renewed and the 1997-98 regional tournament reverted to its one-round format. There was a further setback when it could not find a sponsor; Red Stripe transferred its support to the limited-overs competition, previously the Shell/Sandals Trophy, which became the Red Stripe Bowl.

The Bowl in October was a prelude to the senior team's tour of Pakistan and Sharjah, and the A team's trip to South Africa. Both proved disastrous. Every international match in Pakistan was lost, including all three Tests, the first time since their inaugural series in England in 1928 that West Indies had suffered such an indignity. They did reach the final of the Champions' Trophy in Sharjah, only to be beaten by England. At the same time, the A team was struggling in South Africa, where they went down in all three representative matches plus the one-day series. No new player enhanced his reputation and only the well-established Jimmy Adams, appointed captain after being dropped from the senior side, achieved much.

West Indies hoped for some salvation in the Under-19 World Cup in South Africa in January. Instead, an alarming administrative lapse scuppered their chances even before the tournament started: seven players were discovered to be over-age. Explaining that it had observed its own domestic qualifications, rather than ICC's, the embarrassed

WICB hurriedly despatched replacements. The team was beaten by Australia and Zimbabwe in the first round, failed to qualify for the Super League and lost to Bangladesh in the Plate final, finishing tenth out of 16.

As awkward as all this was, it was overshadowed by the acrimonious debate over the captaincy. It was public knowledge that the Board had overridden the selectors' recommendation that Brian Lara, a Trinidadian, take over from Courtney Walsh, a Jamaican, for the tours of Pakistan and Sharjah. This rejection was angrily resented by the Trinidad & Tobago Board, which issued a statement alleging "a calculated plot to tarnish [Lara's] image and international reputation using past indiscretions as the basis for sowing the seeds of destruction". Lara was heckled by Jamaicans during the Red Stripe Bowl and there were repeated claims of tension within the team – vehemently denied – in Pakistan and Sharjah.

Eventually, Lara was, indeed, appointed in January for the series against England, his accession eased by Walsh's magnanimity and continuing commitment to the team. It was a significant factor in their success. Yet the problems were not over. West Indies made another entry in the ledger of infamy when the First Test had to be abandoned because of the treacherous and ill-prepared Sabina Park pitch. It was an unwelcome first in Test cricket's history – and, as a substitute Test was hurriedly arranged, a further disruption to the first-class domestic tournament, which halted during international games.

The effect was that the President's Cup started on January 9 and did not finish until April 20, when Leeward Islands and Guyana won their final games and thus shared the championship. As in 1996-97, public interest had been drained by the Test series and the length of the season. For the joint champions, 20 scheduled days of Cup cricket had been stretched across more than three months.

While only 20 points separated the champions from Barbados and Trinidad & Tobago, who shared fourth position, Windward Islands yet again foundered in last place. They lost all five matches in spite of former Test captain Richie Richardson, a Leeward Islander, who was brought in to bolster the weak batting. They lost to the Leewards by ten wickets in only two days, and their stock hit rock bottom when they crumbled to 54 all out, their lowest total in regional first-class cricket, in their final match, against Guyana. Concerned that a chain is only as strong as its weakest link, the WICB decided to give the Windwards priority in its development programme. It was not before time: the group, comprising the islands of Dominica, Grenada, St Lucia and St Vincent, had finished last in eight of the previous 11 years, and never higher than fourth out of six.

After a meeting with the West Indies Players Association, the WICB agreed on yet another change in format for 1998-99. After an initial round-robin league, four teams would advance into semi-finals, culminating in a championship final.

Once more, most of the names at the top of the batting and bowling lists were well known. It was cause for concern that the players of the future again failed to advance. Adams, who scored 449 runs for Jamaica at 112.25, and another Test left-hander, Shivnarine Chanderpaul of Guyana (471 at 67.28), were the leading scorers in the President's Cup. Each compiled three centuries, with Adams's unbeaten 203 against Trinidad & Tobago the highest of the season. Thanks to his form with the A team, Adams regained his Test place for four games against England but was discarded again in favour of the in-form Roland Holder.

Barbados captain and opener Philo Wallace was the only other batsman to top 400 runs, enough to earn him a belated, and profitable, Test call-up. Clayton Lambert – recalled by West Indies aged 36 – and Carl Hooper of Guyana, Keith Arthurton of the Leewards, Adrian Griffith of Barbados and Junior Murray of the Windwards were the other Test players who aggregated 300 runs. The only two non-internationals to pass the standard were Tony Powell, the Jamaican left-hander, and Richard Smith, the stylish Trinidadian in his eighth season.

As West Indian pitches have come to dictate, spinners were the most used and most successful of the bowlers. They accounted for four of the five with 20 or more Cup wickets, the odd man out being the Leewards fast bowler Kenny Benjamin, whose 25, at just over 17 each, were enough to gain him his first Test in over a year.

Left-arm spinners Neil McGarrell of Guyana, Barbados's evergreen 35-year-old Winston Reid, and young leg-spinners Mahendra Nagamootoo of Guyana and Brian Murphy of Jamaica were the others above the 20-wicket mark. Yet the one summoned to add variety to the attack against England was Dinanath Ramnarine, whose leg-spin had earned him wickets and respect since his days in the West Indies youth team and who had bowled tidily for the A team in South Africa.

Back in October, the new-look Bowl had introduced the modern razzmatazz of one-day cricket to West Indies. Coloured uniforms, white balls and black sightscreens were used, and the semi-finals and final were televised live throughout the Caribbean and into North America, another innovation. There was an outcry from the other territories when the WICB announced that the semi-finals and final would be held in Jamaica for the five years of the deal on the insistence of Red Stripe, brewers of "the great Jamaican beer". Some saw a conflict of interest: WICB president Pat Rousseau was also chairman of Red Stripe.

One of the first-round matches had to be put back a day because the coloured clothing was held up in Trinidad on its way from Jamaica to Guyana. A later match, in upcountry Guyana, was delayed nearly an hour because the white balls had been left in Georgetown. But, apart from disruption by rain in Jamaica, the tournament proceeded with few subsequent setbacks. Because the pitch was being relaid – inadequately as it turned out – Sabina Park in Kingston was unavailable, and matches in Jamaica were staged in country areas unaccustomed to major cricket; the picturesque Kaiser Sports Club in Discovery Bay on the north coast hosted the semi-finals and final. Four centres, in addition to the Test ground, Bourda, were also used in Guyana, a welcome feature.

Leeward Islands and Guyana advanced to the final, where the Leewards comfortably secured the Bowl, inflicting Guyana's first defeat of the tournament. ICC associates Canada and Bermuda took part for the second time although, once more, neither won a match. The outstanding individual was Arthurton, the Leewards' all-rounder: he scored two centuries, one of them in the final, his slow-medium bowling was economical and his fielding, as always, breathtaking.

In addition to their success at senior level, Guyana continued their domination of youth cricket, claiming the Under-19 Nortel championship for the sixth successive time when they hosted it in August 1997, and the Under-15 Carib Cement title in its third year, in Jamaica in April 1998. The WICB's decision to hold the 1998 Nortel tournament in Trinidad in July, one of the wettest months of the year, proved ill-considered, but it was only in keeping with its recent administration. Predictably, the weather forced a change of format from three-day matches to limited-overs and, even then, several games, including the final, were left incomplete.

FIRST-CLASS AVERAGES, 1997-98

BATTING

(Qualification: 200 runs)

	M	I	NO	R	HS	100s	Avge
C. L. Hooper (*Guyana*)	10	14	3	620	108*	2	56.36
K. L. T. Arthurton (*Leeward I.*)	5	6	0	332	93	0	55.33
P. A. Wallace (*Barbados*)	8	15	2	710	129	1	54.61
R. I. C. Holder (*Barbados*)	8	12	1	583	183	2	53.00
T. O. Powell (*Jamaica*)	5	8	1	351	100*	1	50.14
C. B. Lambert (*Guyana*)	8	14	2	589	108	3	49.08
J. C. Adams (*Jamaica*)	9	14	2	589	203*	3	49.08

	M	I	NO	R	HS	100s	Avge
S. Chanderpaul (*Guyana*)	12	18	1	803	125	4	47.23
R. L. Hoyte (*Barbados*)	5	6	1	232	76*	0	46.40
R. D. Jacobs (*Leeward I.*)	5	6	1	230	76	0	46.00
D. Ganga (*T & T*)	3	6	0	264	138	1	44.00
B. C. Lara (*T & T*)	9	14	1	536	93	0	41.23
R. A. M. Smith (*T & T*)	5	10	2	319	108*	1	39.87
A. F. G. Griffith (*Barbados*)	6	12	2	358	186	1	35.80
F. L. Reifer (*Barbados*)	5	8	1	244	102	1	34.85
S. Ragoonath (*T & T*)	5	10	0	346	98	0	34.60
J. R. Murray (*Windward I.*)	6	11	1	325	86	0	32.50
S. C. Williams (*Leeward I.*)	8	13	2	344	108*	1	31.27
C. Wright (*Jamaica*)	5	9	1	240	95*	0	30.00
N. A. De Groot (*Guyana*)	6	11	1	292	54*	0	29.20
K. F. Semple (*Guyana*)	6	10	1	250	81	0	27.77
B. M. Watt (*Windward I.*)	5	10	1	238	86*	0	26.44
S. L. Campbell (*Barbados*)	10	18	1	392	65	0	23.05
N. A. M. McLean (*Windward I.*) . .	9	13	2	205	52	0	18.63

* Signifies not out.

BOWLING

(Qualification: 12 wickets)

	O	M	R	W	BB	5W/i	Avge
N. C. McGarrell (*Guyana*)	302.4	113	505	34	7-71	4	14.85
C. E. L. Ambrose (*Leeward I.*) . .	276.5	80	595	38	5-25	2	15.65
W. K. L. Quinn (*Leeward I.*)	99.2	18	289	16	5-38	1	18.06
K. C. G. Benjamin (*Leeward I.*) . .	205.2	44	592	28	6-39	1	21.14
W. E. Reid (*Barbados*)	341	136	664	31	5-48	2	21.41
R. D. King (*Guyana*)	103.2	30	303	14	3-45	0	21.64
D. Ramnarine (*T & T*)	249.3	73	548	25	5-57	1	21.92
C. A. Walsh (*Jamaica*)	364.2	88	817	36	6-46	1	22.69
C. L. Hooper (*Guyana*)	280.5	80	540	23	5-80	1	23.47
O. D. Gibson (*Barbados*)	99.4	17	324	13	4-76	0	24.92
F. A. Rose (*Jamaica*)	117.3	25	344	13	5-67	1	26.46
B. S. Murphy (*Jamaica*)	221.2	50	596	21	7-48	2	28.38
M. V. Nagamootoo (*Guyana*)	237.4	50	662	22	5-103	1	30.09
C. E. L. Stuart (*Guyana*)	128.2	25	401	13	3-51	0	30.84
P. I. C. Thompson (*Barbados*) . . .	130	26	444	14	4-48	0	31.71
L. R. Williams (*Jamaica*)	169	41	481	14	5-105	1	34.35
I. R. Bishop (*T & T*)	194.5	22	656	19	5-32	1	34.52
M. Dillon (*T & T*)	124.3	22	444	12	4-51	0	37.00
N. A. M. McLean (*Windward I.*) .	206.3	40	657	17	4-67	0	38.64

PRESIDENT'S CUP, 1997-98

	Played	Won	Lost	Drawn	1st-inns Points	Points
Leeward Islands	5	3	1	1	4	56
Guyana	5	3	0	2	0	56
Jamaica	5	1	1	3	12	40
Barbados	5	2	2	1	0	36
Trinidad & Tobago	5	2	2	1	0	36
Windward Islands	5	0	5	0	10	10

Win = 16 pts; draw = 4 pts; 1st-innings lead in a drawn match = 4 pts; 1st-innings lead in a lost match = 5 pts.

In the following scores, * by the name of a team indicates that they won the toss.

At Sabina Park, Kingston, January 9, 10, 11, 12. Drawn. Barbados 135 (S. L. Campbell 33, C. O. Browne 30; C. A. Walsh six for 46, K. H. Powell four for 43) and 291 for nine dec. (S. L. Campbell 40, R. I. C. Holder 87, H. R. Waldron 31, C. O. Browne 32, Extras 51; C. A. Walsh four for 56, F. A. Rose five for 67); Jamaica* 222 (T. O. Powell 38, A. N. Coley 33, B. S. Murphy 39 not out, Extras 37; P. I. C. Thompson four for 48, W. E. Reid four for 72) and 110 for four (C. Wright 37). *Jamaica 8 pts, Barbados 4 pts.*

The first match played on the relaid pitch was an ominous prelude to the First Test against England, later in the month. Barbados manager Tony Howard said: *"There were loads of ridges, cracks and corrugations and even before a ball was bowled our dressing-room was concerned."*

At Webster Park, The Valley (Anguilla), January 9, 10, 11, 12. Drawn. Guyana 186 (C. L. Hooper 63, V. Nagamootoo 30, Extras 34; W. K. L. Quinn three for 30) and 166 for one (N. A. De Groot 54 not out, K. F. Semple 81); Leeward Islands* 339 for six dec. (S. C. Williams 63, J. Mitchum 57, K. L. T. Arthurton 63, R. D. Jacobs 50 not out, C. M. Tuckett 54, Extras 34; M. V. Nagamootoo five for 103). *Leeward Islands 8 pts, Guyana 4 pts.*

At Guaracara Park, Pointe-à-Pierre, January 15, 16, 17, 18. Trinidad & Tobago won by six wickets. Windward Islands 234 (J. R. Murray 40, R. A. Marshall 32, R. N. Lewis 46; I. R. Bishop four for 90) and 143 (R. B. Richardson 62 not out; I. R. Bishop five for 32); Trinidad & Tobago* 196 (A. Balliram 62, R. A. M. Smith 55, N. B. Francis 30; C. A. Davis three for 33, R. A. Marshall four for 46) and 182 for four (B. C. Lara 52, R. A. M. Smith 52 not out, Extras 38). *Trinidad & Tobago 16 pts, Windward Islands 5 pts.*

Richardson, the former Leeward Islands and West Indies captain, was out for a first-ball duck in his first innings for Windwards.

At Kensington Oval, Bridgetown, January 16, 17, 18, 19. Barbados won by eight wickets. Leeward Islands* 224 (K. L. T. Arthurton 50, R. D. Jacobs 56; P. T. Collins three for 58, W. E. Reid four for 49) and 191 (D. R. E. Joseph 68, C. M. Tuckett 64; W. E. Reid five for 48); Barbados 278 (F. L. Reifer 102, R. L. Hoyte 76 not out, Extras 36; C. E. L. Ambrose three for 58, K. C. G. Benjamin four for 71) and 139 for two (S. L. Campbell 48 not out, P. A. Wallace 34). *Barbados 16 pts.*

At Kensington Oval, Bridgetown, January 22, 23, 24, 25. Guyana won by six wickets. Guyana 435 (C. B. Lambert 108, S. Chanderpaul 115, C. L. Hooper 61; O. D. Gibson three for 72, W. E. Reid five for 100) and 99 for four (C. L. Hooper 35 not out); Barbados* 269 (A. F. G. Griffith 37, H. R. Waldron 80, T. E. Rollock 40, C. O. Browne 35; M. V. Nagamootoo four for 99, C. L. Hooper three for 30) and 259 (P. A. Wallace 129; C. L. Hooper four for 61, N. C. McGarrell four for 66). *Guyana 16 pts.*

At Queen's Park Oval, Port-of-Spain, January 22, 23. Leeward Islands won by ten wickets. Trinidad & Tobago* 125 (K. C. G. Benjamin six for 39) and 87 (C. M. Tuckett four for 17); Leeward Islands 175 (K. L. T. Arthurton 72, R. D. Jacobs 31; M. Dillon four for 51, I. R. Bishop four for 45) and 38 for no wkt. *Leeward Islands 16 pts.*

At Windsor Park, Roseau (Dominica), January 22, 23, 24. Jamaica won by ten wickets. Windward Islands 211 (R. B. Richardson 33, R. A. Marshall 33, B. M. Watt 86 not out, V. Dumas 31; F. A. Rose three for 74) and 152 (R. A. Marshall 42; C. A. Walsh three for 46, B. S. Murphy seven for 48); Jamaica* 192 (T. O. Powell 54, A. N. Coley 37; V. Dumas four for 36) and 176 for no wkt (C. Wright 95 not out, R. G. Samuels 72 not out). *Jamaica 16 pts, Windward Islands 5 pts.*

At Chedwin Park, St Catherine (Jamaica), February 19, 20, 21, 22. Drawn. Trinidad & Tobago 288 (S. Ragoonath 61, D. Ganga 68, P. V. Simmons 51 not out, B. C. Lara 37) and 274 for four (A. Balliram 35, S. Ragoonath 74, R. A. M. Smith 108 not out); Jamaica* 455 for seven dec.

(C. Wright 40, L. V. Garrick 73, J. C. Adams 203 not out, B. S. Murphy 54 not out; D. Ramnarine three for 138). *Jamaica 8 pts, Trinidad & Tobago 4 pts.*

Smith's hundred was his first in eight seasons of first-class cricket; Adams's double-hundred, which lasted 469 minutes and 334 balls and included 23 fours, was his highest score for Jamaica.

At Tanteen, St George's (Grenada), February 20, 21, 22, 23. Barbados won by seven wickets. Windward Islands* 319 (A. L. Crafton 30, R. B. Richardson 34, J. R. Murray 35, R. N. Lewis 34, C. A. Davis 54, N. A. M. McLean 52; O. D. Gibson four for 80) and 270 (J. R. Murray 86, N. A. M. McLean 43 not out; O. D. Gibson four for 76, W. E. Reid four for 92); Barbados 435 for eight dec. (P. A. Wallace 87, A. F. G. Griffith 186, T. E. Rollock 30, O. D. Gibson 45) and 155 for three (P. A. Wallace 79 not out, R. I. C. Holder 34). *Barbados 16 pts.*

At Enmore, Demerara, March 5, 6, 7, 8. Guyana won by 21 runs. Guyana* 450 for eight dec. (C. B. Lambert 106, N. A. De Groot 49, S. Chanderpaul 111, C. L. Hooper 104, Extras 36; M. Dillon three for 101, M. Persad three for 123) and 64 for one dec. (C. B. Lambert 34 not out); Trinidad & Tobago 211 (S. Ragoonath 68, Extras 41; N. C. McGarrell five for 61, M. V. Nagamootoo three for 62) and 282 (S. Ragoonath 98, D. Ganga 33, P. V. Simmons 52, Extras 34; N. C. McGarrell five for 53). *Guyana 16 pts.*

At Webster Park, The Valley (Anguilla), March 5, 6. Leeward Islands won by ten wickets. Windward Islands 151 (J. R. Murray 40; K. C. G. Benjamin four for 39) and 112 (R. B. Richardson 31; A. Lake three for six); Leeward Islands* 257 (F. A. Adams 53, K. L. T. Arthurton 54, D. R. E. Joseph 65, Extras 31; N. A. M. McLean four for 67, R. N. Lewis four for 66) and eight for no wkt. *Leeward Islands 16 pts.*

At Bourda, Georgetown, April 11, 12, 13, 14. Drawn. Jamaica* 148 (T. O. Powell 41; C. E. L. Stuart three for 51, M. V. Nagamootoo three for 25) and 318 for four dec. (W. W. Hinds 55, J. C. Adams 108 not out, T. O. Powell 100 not out); Guyana 114 (V. Nagamootoo 40; B. S. Murphy five for 44) and 335 for six (C. B. Lambert 64, N. A. De Groot 52, S. Chanderpaul 89, C. L. Hooper 62, Extras 31; L. R. Williams five for 105). *Guyana 4 pts, Jamaica 8 pts.*

The umpires stopped the match in fading light with three overs left and Guyana needing 18 to win.

At Guaracara Park, Pointe-à-Pierre, April 11, 12, 13, 14. Trinidad & Tobago won by one wicket. Barbados* 285 (S. L. Campbell 65, A. F. G. Griffith 37, R. L. Hoyte 30, T. E. Rollock 33, Extras 34; M. Dillon three for 82, D. Ramnarine three for 64) and 254 (S. L. Campbell 41, P. A. Wallace 61, F. L. Reifer 42, V. C. Drakes 32; D. Ramnarine four for 57); Trinidad & Tobago 332 (D. Ganga 138, P. V. Simmons 47, R. A. M. Smith 50, Extras 30; V. C. Drakes five for 78, P. I. C. Thompson three for 70) and 208 for nine (A. Balliram 30, P. V. Simmons 31, L. A. Roberts 40; H. R. Bryan five for 51). *Trinidad & Tobago 16 pts.*

At Grove Park, Charlestown (Nevis), April 17, 18, 19, 20. Leeward Islands won by nine wickets. Jamaica* 142 (T. O. Powell 35, G. R. Breese 42; W. K. L. Quinn five for 38) and 323 (J. C. Adams 112, T. O. Powell 62, Extras 43; K. C. G. Benjamin three for 88, W. D. Phillip three for 97, A. Lake three for 58); Leeward Islands 306 (K. L. T. Arthurton 93, D. R. E. Joseph 51, R. D. Jacobs 76; B. S. Murphy three for 79, G. R. Breese four for 82) and 160 for one wkt (S. C. Williams 108 not out, F. A. Adams 48). *Leeward Islands 16 pts.*

At Arnos Vale, St Vincent, April 17, 18, 19, 20. Guyana won by an innings and 51 runs. Windward Islands 202 (J. R. Murray 54, B. M. Watt 72; R. D. King three for 45, N. C. McGarrell five for 31) and 54 (N. C. McGarrell four for 15); Guyana* 307 (C. B. Lambert 33, T. M. Dowlin 48, S. Chanderpaul 125, Extras 44; N. A. M. McLean three for 67, V. Dumas four for 41). *Guyana 16 pts.*

Windward Islands' 54 was their lowest total in regional cricket, undercutting their 94 against Barbados in 1985-86.

REGIONAL CHAMPIONS

Shell Shield			
1965-66	Barbados	1983-84	Barbados
1966-67	Barbados	1984-85	Trinidad & Tobago
1967-68	No competition	1985-86	Barbados
1968-69	Jamaica	1986-87	Guyana
1969-70	Trinidad		
1970-71	Trinidad	*Red Stripe Cup*	
1971-72	Barbados	1987-88	Jamaica
1972-73	Guyana	1988-89	Jamaica
1973-74	Barbados	1989-90	Leeward Islands
1974-75	Guyana	1990-91	Barbados
1975-76 {	Trinidad	1991-92	Jamaica
	Barbados	1992-93	Guyana
1976-77	Barbados	1993-94	Leeward Islands
1977-78	Barbados	1994-95	Barbados
1978-79	Barbados	1995-96	Leeward Islands
1979-80	Barbados	1996-97	Barbados
1980-81	Combined Islands		
1981-82	Barbados	*President's Cup*	
1982-83	Guyana	1997-98 {	Leeward Islands
			Guyana

Barbados have won the title outright 14 times, Guyana 5, Jamaica 4, Leeward Islands and Trinidad/Trinidad & Tobago 3, Combined Islands 1. Barbados, Guyana, Leeward Islands and Trinidad have also shared the title.

RED STRIPE BOWL, 1997-98

Zone A (in Jamaica)

At Chedwin Park, St Catherine, October 4. Trinidad & Tobago won by 184 runs. Trinidad & Tobago* 300 for five (50 overs) (B. C. Lara 110, P. V. Simmons 59, R. A. M. Smith 44 not out); Bermuda 116 (43.3 overs) (A. B. Steede 33; M. Dillon four for 22).

At Melbourne CC, Kingston, October 4. No result. Windward Islands 215 for nine (50 overs) (D. A. Joseph 71, J. A. R. Sylvester 38); Jamaica* 72 for five (15 overs) (L. V. Garrick 42 not out; N. A. M. McLean three for 21).

At Melbourne CC, Kingston, October 5. Windward Islands won by 125 runs. Windward Islands* 332 for four (50 overs) (D. A. Joseph 153 not out, A. L. Crafton 63, J. A. R. Sylvester 40); Bermuda 207 for four (50 overs) (C. J. Smith 100 not out, A. Amory 39, W. A. E. Manders 35).
   Joseph's 153 not out was a record for the regional one-day tournament. Smith scored Bermuda's first hundred in the tournament.

At Chedwin Park, St Catherine, October 5. Jamaica won by three wickets. Trinidad & Tobago* 84 (42.3 overs) (P. V. Simmons 34; F. A. Rose three for 24, C. A. Walsh four for 15); Jamaica 85 for seven (33.4 overs).

At Alpart SC, St Elizabeth, October 8. Jamaica won by eight wickets. Bermuda 87 (41.2 overs) (L. R. Williams six for 19); Jamaica* 88 for two (21.1 overs) (W. W. Hinds 33 not out).

At Melbourne CC, Kingston, October 8. Trinidad & Tobago won by seven wickets, their target having been revised to 139 from 45 overs. Windward Islands* 144 (39.2 overs) (D. A. Joseph 59; N. B. Francis three for 43); Trinidad & Tobago 141 for three (35.1 overs) (D. Ganga 53 not out, R. A. M. Smith 63 not out).

Jamaica 5 pts, Trinidad & Tobago 4 pts, Windward Islands 3 pts, Bermuda 0 pts.

Zone A Quarter-finals

At Melbourne CC, Kingston, October 11. No result. Bermuda 193 for seven (50 overs) (C. J. Smith 101 not out); Jamaica* seven for no wkt (0.5 overs).

At Chedwin Park, St Catherine, October 11. Trinidad & Tobago v Windward Islands. No result (abandoned).

Jamaica and Trinidad & Tobago qualified for the semi-finals by virtue of leading the preliminary round table.

Zone B (in Guyana)

At Hampton Court, Essequibo, October 4. Guyana won by seven wickets. Canada 179 (50 overs) (P. Prashad 61; N. C. McGarrell three for 32); Guyana* 180 for three (40 overs) (C. B. Lambert 74, A. Gonsalves 54).

At Enmore, Demerara, October 5. Leeward Islands won by 21 runs. Leeward Islands 202 for eight (50 overs) (K. L. T. Arthurton 50, S. C. Joseph 84 not out; O. D. Gibson three for 43); Barbados* 181 (45.1 overs) (P. A. Wallace 47, F. L. Reifer 80; R. M. Powell four for 27).
The match was postponed for a day because of the late arrival of the players' coloured clothing.

At Uitvlugt, Demerara, October 7. Barbados won by 103 runs. Barbados 258 for eight (47 overs) (P. A. Wallace 64, A. F. G. Griffith 48, R. L. Hoyte 62 not out); Canada* 155 (40.5 overs) (A. Varadarajan 43; D. K. Marshall three for 44).
The match was reduced to 47 overs a side because of the late arrival of white balls.

At Albion, Berbice, October 7. Guyana won by five wickets. Leeward Islands 225 for four (50 overs) (S. C. Williams 73, K. L. T. Arthurton 80 not out); Guyana* 226 for five (47.3 overs) (C. B. Lambert 74, C. L. Hooper 57 not out, Extras 39).

At Albion, Berbice, October 9. Leeward Islands won by 62 runs. Leeward Islands* 325 for seven (50 overs) (S. C. Williams 76, L. A. Harrigan 31, D. R. E. Joseph 82, S. C. Joseph 38; A. Pittman three for 69); Canada 263 for five (50 overs) (A. Varadarajan 42, M. Diwan 130, Extras 31).
Diwan scored Canada's first hundred in the tournament.

At Bourda, Georgetown, October 9. Guyana won by 66 runs. Guyana 296 for five (50 overs) (C. B. Lambert 151, S. Chanderpaul 37, Extras 30; J. H. Williams three for 54); Barbados* 230 for nine (50 overs) (A. F. G. Griffith 66, R. I. C. Holder 38, I. D. S. Bradshaw 46 not out).

Guyana 6 pts, Leeward Islands 4 pts, Barbados 2 pts, Canada 0 pts.

Zone B Quarter-finals

At Albion, Berbice, October 11. Leeward Islands won by seven wickets. Barbados 237 for nine (50 overs) (R. L. Hoyte 39, I. D. S. Bradshaw 76 not out, Extras 30; K. C. G. Benjamin three for 34); Leeward Islands* 238 for three (44.3 overs) (S. C. Williams 47, K. L. T. Arthurton 103 not out, S. C. Joseph 55).

At Bourda, Georgetown, October 11. Guyana won by seven wickets. Canada* 223 for six (50 overs) (P. Prashad 58, A. Glegg 47, S. Thuraisingham 30 not out); Guyana 226 for three (47.4 overs) (C. B. Lambert 31, A. Gonsalves 33, K. F. Semple 71 not out, S. Chanderpaul 58).

Semi-finals

At Kaiser SC, Discovery Bay, Jamaica, October 17. No result; Guyana had been set a revised target of 147 from 25 overs. Trinidad & Tobago 219 for nine (50 overs) (S. Ragoonath 69, A. Lawrence 30; S. Chanderpaul three for 11); Guyana* 72 for no wkt (11 overs) (C. B. Lambert 41 not out).
Guyana qualified for the final by virtue of heading their preliminary group; Trinidad & Tobago were second in theirs.

At Kaiser SC, Discovery Bay, Jamaica, October 18. Leeward Islands won by eight wickets. Jamaica 214 (49.4 overs) (L. V. Garrick 69; K. L. T. Arthurton four for 43); Leeward Islands* 215 for two (38.4 overs) (S. C. Williams 33, L. A. Harrigan 85, K. L. T. Arthurton 56 not out).

Final

At Kaiser SC, Discovery Bay, Jamaica, October 20. Leeward Islands won by 30 runs. Leeward Islands 245 (49.4 overs) (K. L. T. Arthurton 100, S. C. Joseph 50; M. V. Nagamootoo three for 56); Guyana* 215 for nine (50 overs) (A. R. Percival 38, R. R. Sarwan 42; K. C. G. Benjamin three for 30).

THE STRANGE EVENTS AT THE EXCELSIOR HOTEL

In November 1998, cricket had its most dramatic modern industrial dispute, which almost led to the cancellation of West Indies' first ever tour of South Africa. It was solved only after the West Indian players spent nearly a week holed up in a hotel near Heathrow airport.

The furore erupted immediately after the Mini World Cup in Dhaka. The players picked for the South African tour flew from Dhaka to Bangkok, where they were supposed to catch a connecting flight. But the captain and vice-captain, Brian Lara and Carl Hooper, went to London instead. They were unhappy with their tour payments – £32,000 for senior players, £23,000 or less for others – and their general treatment by the West Indies Cricket Board. They met the remaining members of the tour party, on their way out from the Caribbean, and persuaded them to stay put at the Excelsior Hotel.

Two days later, the Board voted to sack Lara and Hooper, fined the other rebels ten per cent of their tour fee and ordered them to go to South Africa. It was a futile response: no one obeyed. Instead, the seven players already in Johannesburg went to London. They were not the only ones making the journey. Ali Bacher, managing director of the South African Board, and Clive Lloyd, the West Indies tour manager, also arrived and checked in at another airport hotel.

There was one ace up Bacher's sleeve – or so he thought. He carried with him 16 copies – one for each player – of a letter signed by South African President Nelson Mandela personally urging them to tour. Bacher had to wait more than an hour before Courtney Walsh, president of the West Indies Players' Association, would even come downstairs to see him. The players all wanted to tour, Walsh later insisted to the press, but the West Indies Board had to come to London and talk to them. "This is not just about money," he said. "It's to do with generalised conditions, the future of West Indies cricket, and safeguarding the younger guys who are coming in."

On November 7, Pat Rousseau, the West Indies Board president, duly arrived at the head of a three-man delegation. There were 19 hours of talks. Two days later, Rousseau finally emerged with a deal: no pay increase as such, but the salary bands would be adjusted, and the Board would take "all practical steps" to improve players' pay. He said the sacking of Lara and Hooper had been "a misunderstanding". A week after it all began, they were reinstated.

The tour was on: only the opening match was cancelled, the country house game against Nicky Oppenheimer's XI. The proceeds for that were supposed to go towards cricket for South Africa's disadvantaged. Tons of lobsters, prawns and strawberries reportedly went to waste. There was no record of Mr Oppenheimer's reaction to the idea that they should be sent to the townships instead. For West Indies, the tour turned into a playing disaster – they lost the series 5-0 – but that's another story. – JULIAN GUYER.

CRICKET IN NEW ZEALAND, 1997-98

By TERRY POWER

Alex Tait

The New Zealand team had a mixed season, with unreliable batting the keynote. But after struggling abroad they improved in a brief home stint, when Simon Doull, Chris Cairns and Dion Nash – who had not bowled together before – looked a high-class pace combination. Other, less prominent, sides had very healthy summers. The women's and youth teams both reached World Cup finals, though both fell at the last hurdle. The Academy XI, on their maiden overseas tour, beat their South African counterparts 2-0 in their "Tests". And New Zealand won the first international series of Cricket Max – the ten-over slog – against England 2-1.

Conference cricket, featuring first-class and limited-overs competitions for the best players of three regions, was established early in the season. Though it had a stuttering first run-through – thanks to minimal promotion, neither four-day nor one-day finals attracted good crowds – it showed promise as a means of testing national contenders. Conference and Max both helped towards the goal of enabling players to make a living from the sport between November and March. Many cricketers, tired by their mid-twenties of living at student levels, retire prematurely; it was hoped that decent prospects would keep them playing into their thirties, and still allow them to take out mortgages.

But, as New Zealand Cricket's chief executive, Christopher Doig, has repeatedly pointed out, public perceptions of the sport depend on the performance of just one team. New Zealand captain Stephen Fleming had a ready wit in adversity. After heavy defeats in Australia, he was asked about the team's need for fine-tuning. "Fine-tuning?" he replied. "We haven't got anything to fine-tune, we're still looking for a station and all we're getting is static." But humour goes only a small distance towards compensating for failure. The fact that New Zealand did better at home, against Australia and Zimbabwe, should not obscure many poor performances in Zimbabwe, Australia and Sri Lanka.

The problem lay largely with the selectors. They opted for unadulterated combinations of risk-taking strokemakers, ignoring the grafters essential for the five-day game. Their selections did not all flop as individuals, but as a unit they demonstrated a lack of solidity, especially after the customary poor start. Newcomers like Matt Horne and Craig McMillan had considerable success. Horne scored 1,114 first-class runs at home and overseas between September and March, including four first-class centuries – two of them Test hundreds against Australia and Zimbabwe – displaying fluency, athleticism and leg-side strength. McMillan, diabetic but Aussie-confident, reached his maiden Test fifty (off Warne) and century with sixes, and averaged just over 50 in his first five Tests. But their strokeplay needed to be anchored by batsmen such as Blair

Pocock, discarded after playing the key innings in New Zealand's win over Sri Lanka in March 1997. Matthew Bell, potentially the best – and most secure – opener to appear since Glenn Turner, was never given a chance. New Zealand had, in Adam Parore, a wicket-keeper capable of batting with courage and dedication. Chris Cairns and Dion Nash are pace bowlers who bat. Daniel Vettori emerged, during a Test 90 at Bulawayo, as a spinner who bats. But they did not field a specialist batting line-up who batted, at any rate not consistently enough.

The innovation of the season was Conference cricket. The six first-class teams formed three pairs – Northern Conference (Auckland/Northern Districts), Central Conference (Central Districts/Wellington) and Southern Conference (Canterbury/Otago) – and competed with Bangladesh in round-robin four-day and one-day series running through November and December, each ending in a final. There were problems. The national team was abroad and Bangladesh proved weaker than expected. A format of one-day games on Sundays, four-day games from Monday to Thursday (played in coloured clothing) and then a split back to six provincial teams for Cricket Max on Friday nights made too many conflicting demands, especially on batsmen. But the intention, to provide a stepping stone between provincial and international cricket, was good, and lessons were learned for 1998-99.

Led by Nash, whose return to fitness and improved batting were bright spots in the season, Northern did the Conference double. The region's superiority was reinforced when Northern Districts took the one-day Shell Cup and the Max title. Pleasingly, all their players in the Shell Cup final had graduated through the province's junior teams, the majority hailing from farms or small townships. Medium-pacer Alex Tait who, a year before, had become the first New Zealander to take 16 wickets in a match, offered as a spectacular encore a quadruple-wicket maiden to swing the cup final against Canterbury. His 38 wickets at 17 made him the highest placed non-international bowler in the first-class averages. Mark Bailey, another man who was ignored, scored 786 runs, the highest aggregate of the home season, including three first-class centuries.

Former Test left-arm spinner Matt Hart played second fiddle to Vettori – who, in Colombo, reached 50 Test wickets at 19 years 136 days – but began to look a full-scale all-rounder, as did Nash. Hart's younger brother Robert captained the team maturely and again looked next-best to Parore in a strong wicket-keeping field. Simon Doull, mostly away with New Zealand, was a top-drawer fast-medium swing bowler when he appeared. Less conspicuous, and used as a spare part in his first season, Gareth Hopkins showed potential as a batsman/wicket-keeper with superior timing.

Canterbury had their revenge on Northern Districts in the first-class Shell Trophy, beating them handsomely in the final at Rangiora to retain their title. Cairns, Fleming, Astle and McMillan all performed well when not on international duty. Warren Wisneski rivalled Tait's claim to be the best non-international stock bowler. Craig Cumming, a 22-year-old opener from Timaru, displayed great promise – and also led the side in the absence of Germon, the ex-national captain who retired, aged 29, after winning the final. It was Germon's third Shell Trophy, on top of five Shell Cups. The most remarkable story belonged to 36-year-old Mark Priest. The outstanding spinner in New Zealand domestic cricket – until Vettori's arrival – Priest had never had a chance to add to Mike Atherton's wicket, which he took in his only Test back in 1990. But when Vettori was injured before the last one-day international against Australia, Priest was awoken at 11.30 p.m. and told he was playing next morning more than 1,000 kilometres away. A successful return in a New Zealand victory earned him a tour of Sri Lanka. Ironically, Priest had contributed less than usual for Canterbury.

Wellington's major gain was Bell, who moved from Northern Districts, though Jason Wells, helped by five not-outs, topped the batting averages (despite being picked as an off-spinner). They thrashed Canterbury – the champions' only defeat – but found it hard to take wickets at reasonable cost. Mark Jefferson, an earlier migrant from Northern Districts, might solve this problem as his left-arm spin gains in guile. On Boxing Day, wicket-keeper Chris Nevin hit 149, a one-day record for Wellington, against Central Districts, and shared a national record one-day stand of 216 with Wells. Phil DeFreitas was imported from England but never played because of an injured shoulder.

Central Districts captain Mark Greatbatch scored more than a third of his runs in one of his 12 innings, as what used to be a chorus demanding his international recall faded away. Similarly, Craig Spearman scored one big hundred and was lucky to be taken to Sri Lanka. At 22, the consistent Matthew Sinclair may have more of a future. Carl Bulfin, a solidly built fast bowler of ever-changing hair colour, bowled occasional deadly deliveries, while left-armer David Blake, outstandingly talented as a youngster and given little opportunity since, looked dangerous.

Auckland were awful. The most populous and best resourced of the major associations finished bottom of both Cup and Trophy tables. They fielded four captains (making ten in under six years) and had the services of Graeme Hick in the Cup, as well as the guidance of three experienced internationals: coach Tony Blain plus managers John Bracewell and Jeremy Coney. It was all to no avail. Both Blain and Coney thought they had fielded the best possible teams – there was a simple shortage of talent willing to get stuck in. They have paid heavily for allowing Horne, Paul Wiseman and, earlier, Mark Richardson, none of whom could gain a secure place, to migrate to Otago, where they were better appreciated; Horne and Wiseman graduated to the Test side.

Matthew Maynard, the captain of county champions Glamorgan, had a second season as Otago's player-coach. Again, he was disappointing, and the news that he was returning early to Wales was badly received. But he hit a Shell Cup 50 in 22 deliveries as Otago ran up a record 294 for six against Auckland. Left-arm opening bowlers Shayne O'Connor and David Sewell both made the Test team (Sewell became Oamaru's first home-grown international). Pitching the ball well up, O'Connor was more successful, if inclined to bowl too much driving-fodder. Off-spinner Wiseman was the outstanding domestic spinner and Horne was brilliantly fluent when available.

New Zealand cricket now lies in the hands of captain Fleming, and the administrators Doig and Sir John Anderson, the banker and board chairman who is almost invisible day-to-day but believed to be highly effective behind the scenes and at ICC level. They seem the most intelligent and eloquent leaders the national game has had in the late twentieth century. But at lower levels, there can be a shortage of competence and plain common sense. It was a good idea to publish a pop-newsletter, aimed largely at youngsters. It was less clever to bring it out two months after the season ended.

Terry Power, Wisden's New Zealand correspondent since 1994, died in October 1998. We will greatly miss his forthright contributions to the Almanack, and all his help.

FIRST-CLASS AVERAGES, 1997-98

BATTING

(Qualification: 5 innings, average 35.00)

	M	I	NO	R	HS	100s	Avge
J. D. Wells (*Wellington*)............	5	7	5	259	115	1	129.50
A. C. Parore (*Auckland*)...........	4	6	1	349	111*	1	69.80
M. J. Horne (*Otago*)...............	6	10	1	625	241	2	69.44
S. P. Fleming (*Canterbury*)........	6	8	1	407	95	0	58.14
C. D. McMillan (*Canterbury*)........	6	7	0	380	139	1	54.28
M. D. Bailey (*N. Districts*).........	11	16	1	786	180*	3	52.40
M. D. Bell (*Wellington*)...........	9	14	1	661	216	1	50.84
D. J. Nash (*N. Districts*)...........	7	8	0	385	125	2	48.12
B. A. Pocock (*Auckland*)...........	5	9	2	327	114*	2	46.71

	M	I	NO	R	HS	100s	Avge
N. J. Astle (*Canterbury*)	5	6	0	272	114	1	45.33
S. R. Mather (*Wellington*)	5	8	1	298	170	1	42.57
M. S. Sinclair (*C. Districts*)	9	14	1	529	95	0	40.69
R. G. Twose (*Wellington*)	7	12	2	405	109	1	40.50
M. N. Hart (*N. Districts*)	10	14	0	553	82	0	39.50
R. D. Burson (*Canterbury*)	3	6	4	78	41*	0	39.00
C. D. Cumming (*Canterbury*)	10	17	2	580	103	1	38.66
M. H. Richardson (*Otago*)	9	17	4	494	162*	1	38.00
M. J. Greatbatch (*C. Districts*)	8	12	1	411	139*	1	37.36
M. E. Parlane (*N. Districts*)	10	14	0	494	190	2	35.28
L. K. Germon (*Canterbury*)	6	8	0	281	80	0	35.12

* Signifies not out.

BOWLING

(Qualification: 15 wickets, average 30.00)

	O	M	R	W	BB	5W/i	Avge
C. L. Cairns (*Canterbury*)	167.4	50	425	25	6-55	1	17.00
S. B. O'Connor (*Otago*)	120.4	32	362	21	6-31	2	17.23
A. R. Tait (*N. Districts*)	229.2	69	675	38	6-73	3	17.76
B. K. Walker (*Auckland*)	115.3	19	373	20	8-107	1	18.65
P. J. Wiseman (*Otago*)	351.1	95	836	44	6-53	2	19.00
K. P. Walmsley (*Auckland*)	169.4	36	464	24	6-49	2	19.33
S. B. Doull (*N. Districts*)	154.4	43	394	20	4-35	0	19.70
R. J. Kennedy (*Otago*)	131.4	31	380	19	6-61	1	20.00
C. J. Drum (*Auckland*)	201.1	62	551	27	5-65	1	20.40
M. J. Haslam (*Auckland*)	205.3	69	433	21	5-25	1	20.61
W. A. Wisneski (*Canterbury*)....	353	104	865	41	4-37	0	21.09
M. J. Mason (*C. Districts*)......	130.3	34	344	16	4-22	0	21.50
C. E. Bulfin (*Canterbury*)	167.4	43	471	21	5-99	1	22.42
D. G. Sewell (*Otago*)	287.5	66	838	36	5-34	2	23.27
M. N. Hart (*N. Districts*)	197.1	61	448	19	4-30	0	23.57
D. L. Vettori (*N. Districts*)	186.3	59	509	20	5-22	2	25.45
D. R. Tuffey (*N. Districts*)	157	42	420	16	3-37	0	26.25
M. W. Priest (*Canterbury*)......	279	64	716	25	4-24	0	28.64
M. R. Jefferson (*Wellington*)	218.3	57	585	20	5-42	1	29.25
G. R. Jonas (*Wellington*)	180.4	44	506	17	5-102	1	29.76

SHELL CONFERENCE, 1997-98

	Played	Won	Lost	Drawn	1st-inns Points	Points
Northern	3	2	0	1	2	14
Southern	3	2	1	0	0	12
Central	3	1	1	1	0	6
Bangladesh	3	0	3	0	0	0

Final: Northern drew with Southern, but took the title by virtue of heading the table.

Outright win = 6 pts; lead on first innings in a drawn or lost game = 2 pts.

Under New Zealand Cricket playing conditions, two extras are scored for every no-ball bowled whether scored off or not. Any runs scored off the bat are credited to the batsman, while byes and leg-byes are counted as no-balls, in accordance with Law 24.9, in addition to the initial penalty.

In the following scores, * by the name of a team indicates that they won the toss.

At Victoria Park, Wanganui, November 17, 18, 19. Southern won by one wicket. Central 103 (M. S. Sinclair 45; D. G. Sewell three for 34, W. A. Wisneski four for 37) and 211 (M. S. Sinclair 50, M. D. J. Walker 38; W. A. Wisneski three for 49, D. G. Sewell three for 59); Southern* 159 (M. H. Richardson 67; C. E. Bulfin three for 46, S. J. Hotter five for 65) and 159 for nine (C. J. M. Furlong four for 66). *Southern 6 pts.*

At Seddon Park, Hamilton, November 17, 18, 19. Northern won by an innings and 151 runs. Northern* 408 (M. E. Parlane 58, M. D. Bailey 148, M. N. Hart 65, D. J. Nash 75; Shafiuddin Ahmed three for 95, Hasib-ul-Hassan six for 143); Bangladesh 125 (Javed Omar 48; C. J. Drum three for 19, M. N. Hart four for 30) and 132 (Sanuar Hossain 30, Akram Khan 52; K. P. Walmsley five for 23, M. J. Haslam five for 25). *Northern 6 pts.*
   Bangladesh's first first-class match.

At Basin Reserve, Wellington, November 24, 25. Central won by an innings and 17 runs. Bangladesh* 120 (Akram Khan 39 not out; M. R. Jefferson three for five) and 174 (Sanuar Hossain 44, Khaled Masud 41; C. J. M. Furlong four for 95, M. R. Jefferson five for 42); Central 311 (M. S. Sinclair 95, M. J. Greatbatch 63, R. G. Hart 57; Shafiuddin Ahmed three for 59, Saifullah Khan three for 85). *Central 6 pts.*

At Hagley Park, Christchurch, November 24, 25, 26. Northern won by 86 runs. Northern* 235 (R. A. Jones 40, A. C. Barnes 45, M. N. Hart 50; W. A. Wisneski three for 48, P. J. Wiseman four for 36) and 150 (M. N. Hart 66, K. P. Walmsley 39 not out; W. A. Wisneski three for 35, D. G. Sewell five for 38); Southern 109 (C. J. Drum three for 43, M. J. Haslam four for 11) and 190 (L. G. Howell 32, C. B. Gaffaney 51; M. N. Hart three for 36). *Northern 6 pts.*

At Eden Park Outer Oval, Auckland, December 1, 2, 3, 4. Drawn. Northern 351 (P. J. B. Chandler 35, M. E. Parlane 64, M. N. Hart 39, D. J. Nash 107, A. R. Tait 33; G. R. Jonas five for 102) and 108 for four (P. J. B. Chandler 47 not out, G. J. Hopkins 40 not out); Central* 206 for eight dec. (M. W. Douglas 51, R. G. Hart 52 not out; A. R. Tait four for 57). *Northern 2 pts.*

At Carisbrook, Dunedin, December 1, 2, 3, 4. Southern won by seven wickets. Bangladesh* 286 for nine dec. (Sanuar Hossain 54, Amin-ul-Islam 30, Al-Shahriar Rokon 102, Khaled Masud 45; P. J. Wiseman four for 101) and 244 (Javed Omar 89, Sanuar Hossain 47, Al-Shahriar Rokon 32, Khaled Masud 30; W. A. Wisneski three for 52, P. J. Wiseman three for 68); Southern 366 for six dec. (C. B. Gaffaney 33, C. D. Cumming 103, M. H. Richardson 34, G. R. Stead 96, W. A. Wisneski 46 not out; Saifullah Khan three for 91) and 165 for three (C. B. Gaffaney 35, D. J. Murray 58, C. D. Cumming 49 not out). *Southern 6 pts.*
   Though Bangladesh went down to their third successive defeat, Al-Shahriar Rokon scored their first first-class century.

Final

At Eden Park Outer Oval, Auckland, December 14, 15, 16, 17. Drawn. Northern* 504 (P. J. B. Chandler 59, B. A. Pocock 108, M. D. Bailey 121, G. E. Bradburn 62, M. N. Hart 69, D. J. Nash 33; P. J. Wiseman four for 118, M. H. Richardson three for 61); Southern 354 (D. J. Murray 110, C. D. Cumming 48, G. R. Stead 44, A. J. Gale 57, Extras 37; C. J. Drum three for 35) and 76 for three (L. G. Howell 32 not out, M. H. Richardson 36 not out).
   Pocock and Bailey added 132 in 147 minutes for Northern's second wicket on the opening day. Rain restricted the third day to 29 overs. Northern took the inaugural Shell Conference title by virtue of heading the league table.

SHELL TROPHY, 1997-98

	Played	Won	Lost	Drawn	1st-inns Points	Points
Canterbury...........	5	4	1	0	0	24
Northern Districts.......	5	3	1	1	2	20
Wellington...........	5	3	1	1	0	18
Otago...............	5	3	2	0	0	17†
Central Districts........	5	1	4	0	4	9†
Auckland	5	0	5	0	2	0†

Final: Canterbury beat Northern Districts by an innings and 56 runs.

Outright win = 6 pts; lead on first innings in a drawn or lost game = 2 pts.
† Points deducted for slow over-rate.

In the following scores, * by the name of a team indicates that they won the toss.

At Eden Park, Auckland, January 28, 29, 30. Canterbury won by 172 runs. Canterbury* 232 (S. P. Fleming 89, L. K. Germon 60; K. P. Walmsley three for 56) and 275 (G. R. Stead 33, D. J. Murray 35, S. P. Fleming 76, C. Z. Harris 61; B. K. Walker eight for 107); Auckland 176 (J. C. Forrest 48, I. S. Billcliff 30; M. W. Priest three for 66, R. D. Burson six for 35) and 159 (A. C. Parore 63; M. W. Priest four for 70, C. Z. Harris three for 33). *Canterbury 6 pts.*
Leg-spinner Brooke Walker, 18, took eight in an innings in his first match for Auckland, and second in first-class cricket.

At Queen Elizabeth Park, Masterton, January 28, 29, 30. Northern Districts won by an innings and 64 runs. Northern Districts 403 (M. D. Bailey 55, G. E. Bradburn 50, D. J. Nash 125, A. R. Tait 77; C. E. Bulfin five for 99); Central Districts* 197 (M. S. Sinclair 55, M. J. Greatbatch 37, C. J. M. Furlong 49 not out; S. B. Doull three for 30, D. L. Vettori three for 63) and 142 (M. J. Greatbatch 53; A. R. Tait three for 73, D. L. Vettori five for 28). *Northern Districts 6 pts.*
Nash and Tait added 136, a Northern Districts seventh-wicket record.

At Basin Reserve, Wellington, January 28, 29, 30, 31. Otago won by 158 runs. Otago 231 for nine dec. (M. J. Horne 90, M. P. Maynard 84; H. T. Davis four for 74) and 157 for five dec. (M. H. Richardson 30 not out, D. J. Reekers 33 not out, Extras 34; H. T. Davis four for 38); Wellington* 128 (P. J. B. Chandler 53; P. J. Wiseman six for 53) and 102 (J. D. Wells 40 not out; S. B. O'Connor six for 31). *Otago 6 pts.*

At Hagley Park, Christchurch, February 2, 3, 4. Wellington won by an innings and 104 runs. Wellington* 544 (M. D. Bell 48, S. R. Mather 170, T. A. Boyer 79, R. G. Petrie 31, M. R. Jefferson 114; W. A. Wisneski four for 91); Canterbury 183 (G. R. Stead 35, R. D. Burson 41 not out; R. G. Twose three for 16) and 257 (B. J. K. Doody 77, D. J. Murray 38, R. M. Frew 58; M. R. Jefferson three for 58). *Wellington 6 pts.*

At Seddon Park, Hamilton, February 14, 15, 16, 17. Northern Districts won by three wickets. Auckland* 249 (B. A. Pocock 32, I. S. Billcliff 94, B. K. Walker 44; D. R. Tuffey three for 37) and 117 (A. C. Barnes 32; A. R. Tait three for 27, G. E. Bradburn three for 20); Northern Districts 167 (M. D. Bailey 40, A. R. Tait 38 not out) and 202 for seven (B. A. Young 33, M. N. Hart 55; K. P. Walmsley six for 49). *Northern Districts 6 pts, Auckland 2 pts.*

At Carisbrook, Dunedin, February 14, 15, 16. Otago won by three wickets. Central Districts* 135 (M. W. Douglas 75; D. J. Reekers three for 25, P. J. Wiseman three for 19) and 287 (C. M. Spearman 64, M. S. Sinclair 81, C. J. M. Furlong 39 not out; R. J. Kennedy three for 67, D. J. Reekers three for 35); Otago 108 (A. J. Gale 35; L. J. Hamilton four for 37, M. J. Mason four for 22) and 317 for seven (M. H. Richardson 162 not out, M. J. Sale 38; M. J. Mason four for 87). *Otago 6 pts, Central Districts 2 pts.*
On first-class debut, Matthew Sale equalled the Otago wicket-keeping record of seven dismissals in a match.

At ..toria Park, ... (34 overs) (D. J. Murray); Central* 129 for five (32.2 overs).

At Seddon Park, Hamilton, November 16. Northern v Bangladesh. No result (abandoned).

At Basin Reserve, Wellington, November 23. Central won by 93 runs. Central 256 for five (50 overs) (M. D. Bell 48, R. G. Twose 105 not out, G. R. Larsen 35; Hasib-ul-Hassan three for 49); Bangladesh* 163 for nine (50 overs) (Akram Khan 33, Mohammad Hasannuzzaman 46; R. G. Twose four for 18).

At Lancaster Park, Christchurch, November 23. Northern won by 33 runs. Northern* 191 (49.5 overs) (M. E. Parlane 51; A. J. Gale four for 21); Southern 158 (44.3 overs) (L. G. Howell 42, R. A. Lawson 34; C. Pringle three for 18, A. C. Barnes three for 34).

At Eden Park Outer Oval, Auckland, November 30. Central won by nine wickets. Northern 131 (43.1 overs) (M. D. Bailey 31; R. G. Petrie three for 26); Central* 134 for one (24.3 overs) (C. M. Spearman 68 not out, M. D. Bell 56).

At Carisbrook, Dunedin, December 30. No result. Bangladesh 48 for three (14.4 overs) v Southern*.

Central 6 pts, Northern 3 pts, Bangladesh 2 pts, Southern 1 pt.

Final

At Basin Reserve, Wellington, November 7. Northern won by 80 runs. Northern* 216 (48.5 overs) (M. D. Bailey 35, P. J. B. Chandler 39, A. R. Tait 44, G. E. Bradburn 32); Central 136 (42.3 overs) (R. G. Petrie 31; G. E. Bradburn three for 35, C. Pringle three for 23).

SHELL CUP, 1997-98
Play-offs

At Seddon Park, Hamilton, January 17. Northern Districts won by four wickets. Canterbury* 96 (36.3 overs) (S. B. Doull three for 28); Northern Districts 97 for six (33.1 overs) (R. D. Burson three for 24).
Both sides lost their sixth wicket at 53; Canterbury subsided to their lowest Shell Cup total, but for Northern Districts, Alex Tait and Scott Styris, with 28 not out each, added a match-winning 44.

At Basin Reserve, Wellington, January 17. Wellington won by four wickets. Central Districts 230 for eight (50 overs) (M. W. Douglas 40, M. S. Sinclair 32, M. J. Greatbatch 51); Wellington* 234 for six (49 overs) (C. J. Nevin 43, J. D. Wells 46, R. G. Twose 64 not out).

At Lancaster Park, Christchurch, January 20. Canterbury won by seven wickets. Wellington* 172 (49.1 overs) (P. J. B. Chandler 42, R. G. Petrie 41; M. B. Owens four for 26); Canterbury 173 for three (33.2 overs) (L. G. Howell 64, D. J. Murray 69).

Final

At Seddon Park, Hamilton, January 24. Northern Districts won by 55 runs. Northern Districts 189 for nine (50 overs) (D. J. Nash 45; W. A. Wisneski four for 42); Canterbury* 134 (33.1 overs) (S. P. Fleming 48; A. R. Tait four for 29).
At 117 for five, Tait bowled a four-wicket maiden, with three of his victims caught by wicket-keeper Robert Hart.

The visitors went away winless and often outclassed, though the three home teams were lacking their international players, who were simultaneously struggling in Australia. As national selection convener Ross Dykes said, Bangladesh played to district association (second-class) standard.

Their background, overwhelmingly in one-day play, was quickly obvious. Even in a country whose own batsmen are over-inclined to adventurism, Bangladeshi batsmen stood out for the frequency with which they played suicidal one-day shots early in first-class innings. Al-Shahriar Rokon had his nation's inaugural first-class century, 102 (of his 169 in six innings) against Southern at Carisbrook, but, apart from Maharab Hossain, who scored 85 runs in his only match, nobody averaged more than Rokon's 28.16.

The bowling lacked sting early and awkward turn later, labouring to take 36 first-class wickets in four matches at 47.16 each. Right-arm stock bowler Hasib-ul-Hassan worked hard to take six for 143 off 37.4 overs against Northern, the only five-wicket bag. His partner Shafiuddin Ahmed returned the best average, 33.75 from eight wickets.

Two one-dayers were rain-ruined but, even more disappointingly given Bangladesh's previous record, those completed brought no comfort, being lost by 93 and 112 runs. New Zealand Cricket, who before the tour had indicated that Kenya would follow Bangladesh in 1998-99, changed tack. They lined up Pakistan A, England A and India A as the fourth teams to join Northern, Southern and Central in Conference cricket for the following three seasons.

Other Bangladesh Tour Matches

At Hagley Park, Christchurch, December 7 (not first-class). Canterbury won by 112 runs. Canterbury 266 for nine (50 overs) (L. G. Howell 58, C. D. Cumming 58, G. R. Stead 36, Extras 32; Hasib-ul-Hassan three for 51, Shafiuddin Ahmed four for 37); Bangladesh* 154 (42.4 overs) (Akram Khan 51 not out, Mafiz-ur-Rahman 30; W. W. Stead three for 23, M. B. Owens three for 19).

At Lincoln Green, Christchurch, December 9, 10, 11. New Zealand Academy won by an innings and 115 runs. Bangladesh* 130 (Akram Khan 39; D. G. Sewell five for 34, D. R. Tuffey three for 57) and 203 (Maharab Hossain 81; D. G. Sewell four for 47, B. K. Walker four for 36); New Zealand Academy 448 for seven dec. (C. B. Gaffaney 112, M. E. Parlane 190, H. D. Barton 53, G. J. Hopkins 47).

Lincoln Green, at Lincoln University, south of Christchurch, became New Zealand's 53rd first-class venue. Gaffaney and Parlane put on 213 for the Academy's first wicket. Maharab Hossain scored 81 on first-class debut, after retiring hurt on four.

CRICKET IN INDIA, 1997-98

By R. MOHAN and SUDHIR VAIDYA

Rahul Dravid

For the first time in the 64 seasons of the Ranji Trophy, two teams were debarred from the competition. Tamil Nadu and Delhi were both disqualified after the pitch was scuffed up during a drinks break in their match at Chennai in February. It seemed safe to assume that one of Tamil Nadu's players was responsible, as they had both motive and opportunity: they had a big score on the board, and the Delhi batsmen, who were wearing rubber-soled shoes, were with the umpires as they took refreshments. The referee ordered that the pitch should be repaired so that play could resume on the final day, a decision some questioned. But the Delhi captain, Ajay Sharma, simply refused to continue the pursuit of Tamil Nadu's score of 473.

It took several months for the Board of Control for Cricket in India to find out who was to blame. Eventually, the Tamil Nadu wicket-keeper Reuben Paul was named, and initially banned for life from first-class cricket. This was later reduced to a one-year ban, and then to nothing. In the meantime, rough and ready justice had been administered: Tamil Nadu were suspended for tampering with the pitch, and Delhi for refusing to resume. The innocent players on both sides were the losers.

Their disappearance left Uttar Pradesh with a straightforward path into the quarter-finals, where they crushed Haryana by an innings, after which they scored an unexpected win over defending champions Mumbai to qualify for the final. Meanwhile, Karnataka, who had skipped the quarter-finals as the most successful team in any of the three Super League groups, won a tough battle against Hyderabad in their semi, scraping past the target with the last pair of batsmen at the crease.

They had no such difficulty in the final. It took just one fiery over from Test opening bowler Javagal Srinath to set the pattern: left behind while India were playing in Sharjah, on grounds of fitness, he fired out two batsmen in his first over – just as he had done to Australia in the Calcutta Test. Uttar Pradesh never quite recovered from those blows. Srinath did not bowl much after that, but he did not need to, as left-arm spinner Sunil Joshi picked up four wickets. Rahul Dravid, also left out of the national squad, demonstrated that there was nothing wrong with the pitch by scoring a double-century as Karnataka mercilessly piled on the runs – their 617 was the highest total of the domestic season. Uttar Pradesh had their day in the sun second time around, reaching 416 for seven to force a draw. But Karnataka took the title, thanks to a first-innings lead of 483.

It was Karnataka's fifth Ranji championship, and their second in three years; t.. had had a disastrous season in 1996-97, when heavy international calls saw them fail to qualify for the Super League. This time, they were closer to full strength, with leg-spinner Anil Kumble and pace bowler Venkatesh Prasad the only absentees in Sharjah during the final. India's star slow bowler B. S. Chandrasekhar, a member of two victorious Karnataka sides but now confined to a wheelchair after a road accident, presented the trophy to Dravid.

It was a fitting gesture, enhancing the image of the inter-state Ranji Trophy as the senior tournament to the inter-zone Duleep Trophy. The reformed Ranji format introduced in 1996-97 — 15 teams in three Super Leagues producing six qualifiers for the knockout stages – was appreciated by the players, who also felt more comfortable representing their state sides than the regional zones. By returning to the Duleep's old knockout format the previous season, after three years staging it as a league, the Board saved considerably on expenses and logistics. But the players have been denied opportunities at a higher level, and also the chance to impress the selectors – the tournament used to be played before the international season opened. However, the expansion of the international season, which now occupies India for close to nine months in the year, has detracted from its significance and taken even more of the limelight from domestic cricket.

In 1997-98, the Duleep Trophy also suffered from the monsoon, which curtailed play badly in the semis and the final. For only the second time in its 37 years, the trophy was shared. Title-holders Central Zone, who had reached the final after beating East Zone on run-quotient, were in dire straits at 36 for five on the last day, replying to the 384 amassed by West Zone before three days were lost to the weather. But a washout spared them: as the innings was never completed, West Zone could not claim the lead, and the two team names went on the cup together.

The Irani Cup survived as the traditional season opener. It provided a tight finish in which Mumbai, the 1996-97 Ranji champions, weathered a spirited fightback by the Rest of India. Mumbai seemed to have the match sewn up when a century from Jatin Paranjpe helped them to a first-innings lead of 194. Then Kumble, the Rest's captain, bowled them out for 93 on a wearing pitch. But his team were denied by another leg-spinner, Sairaj Bahutule, who returned career-best figures of eight for 71. Mumbai had another triumph towards the end of the season, when they won the limited-overs Wills Trophy, beating a Board President's XI.

Their leading batsman, Sachin Tendulkar, dominated the averages with 1,256 first-class runs in 13 innings at 114.18. More than half of those came in Tests: he played only three matches for his state team. Tendulkar was just outscored by Dravid, who made 1,264 from eight more innings. Being ignored by India in the later one-day games did at least allow Dravid to assist Karnataka's title challenge, notably when he scored 215 in the final. Vinod Kambli, Tendulkar's team-mate, and Sandagoppan Ramesh of Tamil Nadu also averaged over 100, while V. V. S. Laxman of Hyderabad came close to 1,000 runs thanks to his triple-hundred against Bihar, which lasted ten hours. Kumble, with 85 wickets (29 in Tests) at 16.23, was easily the leading bowler; apart from him, seamer Paras Mhambrey of Mumbai and slow left-armer Utpal Chatterjee of Bengal reached 50 wickets.

The drastic trimming of the Duleep Trophy has only enhanced the preponderance of the limited-overs format, which now runs to four senior competitions. The Wills Trophy is preceded by the Ranji one-day league, whose results arouse considerable indifference: the five zonal winners, however, accompanied by two scratch teams and Bangladesh, provide the Wills quarter-finalists. Then there is the Deodhar Trophy, a one-day tournament for the zonal teams. It was won by North Zone, who tied on points with West (unlike its first-class equivalent, the competition was played in a league format), but had beaten them in their head-to-head clash. Meanwhile, India Seniors won the three-team floodlit Challenger Trophy. This overcrowding of the one-day arena reflects the craze for the limited-overs game – at first-class cricket's expense. – R.M.

FIRST-CLASS AVERAGES, 1997-98

BATTING

(Qualification: 500 runs)

	M	I	NO	R	HS	100s	Avge
S. R. Tendulkar (*Mumbai*)	10	13	2	1,256	204*	6	114.18
V. G. Kambli (*Mumbai*)	9	11	3	890	232*	3	111.25
S. Ramesh (*Tamil Nadu*)	6	6	0	614	187	3	102.33
V. V. S. Laxman (*Hyderabad*)	12	14	3	986	301*	3	89.63
S. S. Karim (*Bengal*)	8	9	2	602	111	1	86.00
J. V. Paranjpe (*Mumbai*)	7	11	1	821	174	3	82.10
S. Sharath (*Tamil Nadu*)	9	10	2	586	129	3	73.25
S. Sriram (*Tamil Nadu*)	7	10	3	505	213*	2	72.14
A. Chopra (*Delhi*)	6	9	1	554	150	2	69.25
Rizwan Shamshad (*Uttar Pradesh*)	12	13	3	640	224*	3	64.00
R. Dravid (*Karnataka*)	15	21	1	1,264	215	2	63.20
S. A. Shukla (*Uttar Pradesh*)	9	11	1	615	189	2	61.50
C. S. Pandit (*Madhya Pradesh*)	8	10	1	525	104	2	58.33
P. Mullick (*Orissa*)	8	13	1	698	201	2	58.16
Rajiv Kumar (*Bihar*)	8	15	1	805	126	3	57.50
D. Gandhi (*Bengal*)	10	15	2	740	176	2	56.92
J. J. Martin (*Baroda*)	9	14	3	623	107	3	56.63
N. S. Sidhu (*Punjab*)	11	15	0	842	131	1	56.13
M. Azharuddin (*Hyderabad*)	10	13	1	664	163*	1	55.33
S. C. Ganguly (*Bengal*)	8	12	1	604	173	2	54.90
Jitender Singh (*Haryana*)	11	18	2	872	175	4	54.50
R. V. Bharadwaj (*Karnataka*)	11	15	1	739	164	3	52.78
Jyoti P. Yadav (*Uttar Pradesh*)	12	13	1	619	145*	2	51.58
S. S. Das (*Orissa*)	8	13	0	662	164	4	50.92
A. A. Muzumdar (*Mumbai*)	13	19	2	788	113	1	46.35
Tariq-ur-Rehman (*Bihar*)	10	15	3	546	70*	0	45.50
N. R. Mongia (*Baroda*)	13	18	5	585	88	0	45.00
C. C. Williams (*Baroda*)	8	13	0	526	94	0	40.46
A. Kumble (*Karnataka*)	13	16	1	592	113	1	39.46
S. Somasunder (*Karnataka*)	12	18	2	629	97	0	39.31
J. Arun Kumar (*Karnataka*)	11	17	1	604	111	3	37.75
D. Manohar (*Hyderabad*)	10	14	0	501	144	1	35.78

* Signifies not out.

BOWLING

(Qualification: 25 wickets)

	O	M	R	W	BB	5W/i	Avge
A. Kumble (*Karnataka*)	610.2	188	1,380	85	7-33	9	16.23
P. L. Mhambrey (*Mumbai*)	380.3	105	929	54	7-42	5	17.20
B. Ramprakash (*Kerala*)	256.3	65	487	28	5-113	1	17.39
N. M. Kulkarni (*Mumbai*)	367.1	127	811	45	5-23	2	18.02
S. V. Bahutule (*Mumbai*)	228.3	49	601	29	8-71	4	20.72
P. Jain (*Haryana*)	455	146	918	44	4-22	0	20.86
M. S. Kulkarni (*Maharashtra*)	208.5	46	545	26	5-47	3	20.96
U. Chatterjee (*Bengal*)	561.2	189	1,070	51	7-59	5	20.98
Kanwaljit Singh (*Hyderabad*)	351.1	116	739	35	7-38	2	21.11
Obaid Kamal (*Uttar Pradesh*)	250.5	87	551	25	5-58	1	22.04

	O	M	R	W	BB	5W/i	Avge
S. B. Joshi (*Karnataka*)	484	133	1,092	46	5-25	1	23.73
B. Vij (*Punjab*)	254.3	56	690	28	5-67	1	24.64
S. Pandey (*Madhya Pradesh*). . . .	230.2	38	730	29	5-67	1	25.17
J. Srinath (*Karnataka*)	250.1	43	799	31	4-92	0	25.77
T. B. Arothe (*Baroda*)	236.2	45	652	25	6-53	2	26.08
A. W. Zaidi (*Uttar Pradesh*)	272.2	53	866	33	7-99	3	26.24
P. Thakur (*Haryana*)	467.3	123	1,157	43	7-107	2	26.90
A. Kuruvilla (*Mumbai*).	239.1	41	818	30	4-88	0	27.26
V. Jain (*Haryana*)	277.1	69	796	29	6-55	1	27.44
A. R. Kapoor (*Punjab*).	271.2	58	788	28	5-98	1	28.14
S. L. V. Raju (*Hyderabad*)	560.2	172	1,210	42	5-49	3	28.80
K. V. P. Rao (*Bihar*)	427.4	91	993	33	5-33	2	30.09
Harbhajan Singh (*Punjab*)	303	78	799	26	4-66	0	30.73
N. D. Hirwani (*Madhya Pradesh*).	335.2	82	854	27	5-64	1	31.62
Avinash Kumar (*Bihar*).	348.4	75	866	25	5-185	1	34.64

*In the following scores, * by the name of a team signifies that they won the toss.*

IRANI CUP, 1997-98

Ranji Trophy Champions (Mumbai) v Rest of India

At Wankhede Stadium, Mumbai, October 1, 2, 3, 4, 5. Mumbai won by 54 runs. Mumbai* 473 (Wasim Jaffer 83, J. V. Paranjpe 113, A. A. Muzumdar 97, S. V. Bahutule 71; A. Kumble four for 140) and 93 (A. Kumble seven for 33); Rest of India 279 (G. K. Khoda 59, S. Sharath 59, N. R. Mongia 78 not out; S. V. Bahutule five for 97, R. V. Pawar three for 78) and 233 (V. V. S. Laxman 35, A. R. Kapoor 50, A. Kumble 46 not out; S. V. Bahutule eight for 71).

Leg-spinners Kumble and Bahutule took 24 wickets between them.

DULEEP TROPHY, 1997-98

Quarter-final

At Gymkhana Ground, Secunderabad, December 1, 2, 3, 4, 5. East Zone won by five wickets. North Zone* 295 (V. Rathore 94, A. Chopra 63, Harvinder Singh 31; U. Chatterjee three for 93) and 279 for eight dec. (V. Rathore 48, A. Chopra 69, P. Dharmani 41; U. Chatterjee five for 102); East Zone 346 (S. Saikia 32, N. Haldipur 103, R. S. Gavaskar 55, S. S. Karim 45, Tariq-ur-Rehman 31; Harbhajan Singh three for 74) and 232 for five (R. F. Morris 58, S. S. Karim 80 not out).

Semi-finals

At M. Chinnaswamy Stadium, Bangalore, December 7, 8, 9, 10, 11. Drawn. Central Zone were declared winners by virtue of their superior run-quotient. East Zone* 337 (N. Haldipur 34, D. Gandhi 158, S. Raul 31, R. F. Morris 34; S. Pandey three for 57); Central Zone 295 for seven (G. K. Khoda 31, Jyoti P. Yadav 145 not out; S. Raul three for 68).

At Ukku Stadium, Vishakhapatnam, December 9, 10, 11, 12, 13. Drawn. West Zone were declared winners by virtue of their first-innings lead. West Zone* 321 (Wasim Jaffer 133, J. J. Martin 54, J. V. Paranjpe 46, Extras 31; D. J. Johnson three for 94, S. B. Joshi three for 58) and 101 for three (A. A. Muzumdar 46); South Zone 262 (V. V. S. Laxman 46, S. Sharath 111, Extras 31; S. V. Bahutule four for 79, H. H. Kanitkar three for 26).

Final

At M. A. Chidambaram Stadium, Chennai, December 17, 18, 19, 20, 21. Drawn. Central and West Zones shared the Duleep Trophy. West Zone* 384 for seven dec. (Wasim Jaffer 40, A. A. Muzumdar 43, J. J. Martin 72, J. V. Paranjpe 55, A. B. Agarkar 56 not out, P. L. Mhambrey 30, N. M. Kulkarni 34 not out, Extras 36); Central Zone 36 for five.

DULEEP TROPHY WINNERS

1961-62	West Zone	1974-75	South Zone	1987-88	North Zone
1962-63	West Zone	1975-76	South Zone	1988-89	{ North Zone
1963-64	West Zone	1976-77	West Zone		West Zone
1964-65	West Zone	1977-78	West Zone	1989-90	South Zone
1965-66	South Zone	1978-79	North Zone	1990-91	North Zone
1966-67	South Zone	1979-80	North Zone	1991-92	North Zone
1967-68	South Zone	1980-81	West Zone	1992-93	North Zone
1968-69	West Zone	1981-82	West Zone	1993-94	North Zone
1969-70	South Zone	1982-83	North Zone	1994-95	North Zone
1970-71	South Zone	1983-84	North Zone	1995-96	South Zone
1971-72	Central Zone	1984-85	South Zone	1996-97	Central Zone
1972-73	West Zone	1985-86	West Zone	1997-98	{ Central Zone
1973-74	North Zone	1986-87	South Zone		West Zone

RANJI TROPHY, 1997-98

Central Zone

At Karnail Singh Stadium, Delhi, October 19, 20, 21, 22. Drawn. Railways 159 (S. B. Bangar 55, J. Zaman 33; A. W. Zaidi four for 45, Mohammad Said three for 34) and 231 for six (S. B. Bangar 95, Y. Gowda 44, Extras 32); Uttar Pradesh* 346 for six dec. (Jyoti P. Yadav 100, Rizwan Shamshad 134 not out, Extras 46; M. Kartik three for 50). *Railways 3 pts, Uttar Pradesh 5 pts.*

At Mansarovar Stadium, Jaipur, October 19, 20, 21, 22. Drawn. Rajasthan 341 (V. Joshi 109, A. S. Parmar 42, P. Krishnakumar 89, Extras 32; P. V. Gandhe six for 63) and 149 (P. K. Amre 48, N. Negi 33; P. V. Gandhe six for 50); Vidarbha* 212 (L. S. Rajput 49, M. S. Doshi 52 not out; Mohan Singh three for 68, P. R. Yadav four for 54) and 157 for four (P. Sutane 72, L. S. Rajput 39 not out). *Rajasthan 5 pts, Vidarbha 3 pts.*

At Digvijay Stadium, Rajnandgaon, October 27, 28, 29, 30. Drawn. Madhya Pradesh* 206 for five (P. K. Dwevedi 102 not out, Raja Ali 57 not out) v Uttar Pradesh. *Madhya Pradesh 2 pts, Uttar Pradesh 2 pts.*

At VCA Ground, Nagpur, October 27, 28, 29, 30. Drawn. Railways* 300 (S. Yadav 139, V. Sharma 68, Extras 40; P. V. Gandhe five for 88, P. Sadhu four for 104); Vidarbha 200 (P. Sutane 48, L. S. Rajput 34, U. V. Gandhe 34 not out, Extras 32; K. S. Parida three for 49, M. Kartik four for 28). *Vidarbha 3 pts, Railways 5 pts.*

At Karnail Singh Stadium, Delhi, November 5, 6, 7, 8. Railways won by an innings and one run. Rajasthan 189 (G. K. Khoda 111; J. Zaman four for 52, K. S. Parida four for 35) and 184 (G. K. Khoda 39, N. Negi 33; M. Kartik six for 35); Railways* 374 for nine dec. (S. Yadav 35, Y. Gowda 49, P. S. Rawat 144, Arvind Kumar 37, Extras 36; D. Pal Singh four for 81). *Railways 8 pts.*

At VCA Ground, Nagpur, November 5, 6, 7, 8. Madhya Pradesh won by nine wickets. Vidarbha* 277 (L. S. Rajput 112, U. V. Gandhe 38, T. A. Gonsalves 34, Extras 34; S. Pandey five for 67, N. D. Hirwani three for 59) and 267 (P. K. Hedaoo 41, L. S. Rajput 41, U. V. Gandhe 48 not out; S. Pandey four for 74, S. S. Lahore three for 42); Madhya Pradesh 508 for six dec. (Jai P. Yadav 40, K. K. Patel 61, D. Bundela 37, S. Abbas Ali 98, C. S. Pandit 83, Raja Ali 56 not out, R. K. Chauhan 78 not out, Extras 35) and 37 for one. *Madhya Pradesh 8 pts.*

At Maharani Ushadevi Cricket Ground, Indore, November 14, 15, 16, 17. Drawn. Madhya Pradesh* 571 for eight dec. (S. Abbas Ali 251, P. K. Dwevedi 189, Extras 52; Zakir Hussain three for 83, K. S. Parida three for 140); Railways 282 (S. Yadav 41, Y. Gowda 95 not out, P. S. Rawat 49, Extras 38; S. Pandey four for 72, N. D. Hirwani four for 106) and 165 for three (S. B. Bangar 73, S. Yadav 32). *Madhya Pradesh 5 pts, Railways 3 pts.*

   Abbas Ali's 251 lasted 592 minutes and 471 balls and included 24 fours and five sixes. He added 436 with Dwevedi for Madhya Pradesh's fourth wicket.

At Green Park, Kanpur, November 14, 15, 16, 17. Drawn. Uttar Pradesh 577 for five dec. (M. S. Mudgal 54, Jyoti P. Yadav 45, Rizwan Shamshad 224 not out, R. V. Sapru 55, G. K. Pandey 68, S. A. Shukla 53 not out, Extras 50; D. Pal Singh three for 150); Rajasthan* 334 (Kuldip Singh 81, V. Yadav 39, V. Joshi 32, P. K. Amre 99, Extras 32; A. W. Zaidi six for 105) and 21 for no wkt. *Uttar Pradesh 5 pts, Rajasthan 3 pts.*

Rizwan Shamshad's 224 not out lasted 622 minutes and 437 balls and included 13 fours.

At Mansarovar Stadium, Jaipur, November 22, 23, 24, 25. Drawn. Madhya Pradesh 309 (A. R. Khurasia 88, C. S. Pandit 104, P. K. Dwevedi 33; Samsher Singh five for 97, S. Yadav three for 66); Rajasthan* 159 (A. Jain 47; H. S. Sodhi four for 69, S. Pandey four for 58) and 241 for six (Kuldip Singh 32, G. K. Khoda 83, P. Krishnakumar 35 not out, D. Pal Singh 32 not out; S. S. Lahore three for 62). *Rajasthan 3 pts, Madhya Pradesh 5 pts.*

At Madan Mohan Malaviya Stadium, Allahabad, November 28, 29, 30, December 1. Drawn. Uttar Pradesh 352 (R. Sharma 110, Rizwan Shamshad 100, A. W. Zaidi 74 not out; T. A. Gonsalves five for 128, Y. P. Chandurkar four for 98); Vidarbha* 130 for four (L. S. Rajput 57 not out; Obaid Kamal three for 39). *Uttar Pradesh 2 pts, Vidarbha 2 pts.*

Rizwan Shamshad's 100 was his third century in successive innings. Vidarbha wicket-keeper K. S. M. Iyer made seven catches.

Madhya Pradesh 20 pts, Railways 19 pts, Uttar Pradesh 14 pts, Rajasthan 11 pts, Vidarbha 8 pts. Madhya Pradesh, Railways and Uttar Pradesh qualified for the Super League.

East Zone

At North-East Frontier Railway Stadium, Maligaon, Gauhati, November 6, 7, 8, 9. Assam won by six wickets. Tripura* 231 (R. Chowdhary 31, V. Prajapati 62, T. Chanda 30, G. Banik 43; Sukhbinder Singh three for 35) and 107 (Iqbal Khan five for 34, S. S. Sawant three for 21); Assam 293 (P. Dutta 52, Rajinder Singh 66, Sukhbinder Singh 33; S. Roy five for 83, H. Yadav four for 78) and 101 for four (Rajinder Singh 36 not out, Sukhbinder Singh 31). *Assam 8 pts.*

At Permit Padia, Balasor, November 6, 7, 8, 9. Bengal won by eight wickets. Orissa* 165 (P. Jayachandra 45, P. Mullick 30; U. Chatterjee seven for 59) and 158 (P. Mullick 55; U. Chatterjee three for 55, S. Singh four for 47); Bengal 176 (S. S. Karim 46, R. S. Gavaskar 44; D. S. Mohanty three for 29, S. Khan three for 42) and 151 for two (S. C. Ganguly 30, D. Gandhi 78 not out). *Bengal 8 pts.*

At Keenan Stadium, Jamshedpur, November 14, 15, 16, 17. Bihar won by 119 runs. Bihar* 242 (V. Khullar 39, Rajiv Kumar 126; G. Dutta five for 56) and 190 (C. M. Jha 56, Tariq-ur-Rehman 69; Iqbal Khan four for 56, S. S. Sawant four for 32); Assam 224 (S. S. Sawant 66; K. V. P. Rao four for 59) and 89 (Avinash Kumar four for 27, K. V. P. Rao five for 33). *Bihar 8 pts.*

At Keenan Stadium, Jamshedpur, November 22, 23, 24, 25. Drawn. Bengal* 460 for eight dec. (A. Varma 64, N. Haldipur 117, S. S. Karim 111, G. Shome 54; Avinash Kumar five for 185, K. V. P. Rao three for 143); Bihar 243 (Sunil Kumar 92, S. Arfi 47; U. Chatterjee seven for 88) and 187 for five (Sunil Kumar 32, Tariq-ur-Rehman 59 not out, Rajiv Kumar 42). *Bihar 3 pts, Bengal 5 pts.*

At Barabati Stadium, Cuttack, November 22, 23, 24. Orissa won by an innings and 234 runs. Orissa* 511 (P. Jayachandra 80, B. B. C. C. Mohapatra 109, P. Mullick 96, R. F. Morris 91, G. Gopal 62; Sukhbinder Singh four for 133); Assam 119 (S. Saikia 34, Rajinder Singh 49; R. F. Morris four for 46, S. Raul three for 13) and 158 (N. Bordoloi 47, V. R. Samant 46 not out; R. F. Morris five for 35). *Orissa 8 pts.*

Mohapatra scored 109 on first-class debut. Wicket-keeper Gopal made nine catches in the match.

At Barabati Stadium, Cuttack, December 17, 18, 19, 20. Drawn. Orissa* 521 for eight dec. (P. Mullick 201, S. Raul 139, R. R. Parida 50, R. F. Morris 35, G. Gopal 30, Extras 55; A. Shukla four for 136); Tripura 235 (S. Lahiri 46, V. Prajapati 46, G. Banik 42, V. Bhatnagar 35; D. S.

Mohanty five for 48) and 187 for three (R. Chowdhary 92, S. Lahiri 54, Extras 33). *Orissa 5 pts, Tripura 3 pts.*

Mullick's 201 lasted 495 minutes and 437 balls and included 15 fours and one six. Tripura No. 11 Hemulal Yadav became the first player ever to be given timed out, under Law 31, in first-class cricket. A drinks interval had been called at the fall of Tripura's ninth wicket, during which Yadav sat near the boundary, but the umpires said that he made no attempt to come to the crease after the break and they upheld Orissa's appeal against him.

At Barabati Stadium, Cuttack, December 26, 27, 28, 29. Drawn. Orissa* 534 for five dec. (S. S. Das 164, P. Mullick 141, S. Raul 100 not out, R. R. Parida 45; Rakesh Kumar three for 112); Bihar 320 (Sunil Kumar 49, Rajiv Kumar 92, C. M. Jha 61, V. Saxena 37; S. Khan five for 99) and 122 for two (D. Chakraborty 54 not out, C. M. Jha 51 not out). *Orissa 5 pts, Bihar 3 pts.*
Das and Mullick added 283 for Orissa's second wicket.

At Polytechnic Ground, Agartala, December 26, 27, 28, 29. Drawn. Bengal* 263 (N. Haldipur 30, R. S. Gavaskar 80, G. Shome 56, R. Dutta 38; R. Deb-Burman three for 95, S. Roy five for 95) and 211 for six dec. (D. Gandhi 58, A. Sarkar 30); Tripura 181 (R. Chowdhary 52, S. Lahiri 88; M. Lodhgar three for 26, A. Varma six for 56) and 115 for eight (R. Chowdhary 60; R. S. Gavaskar five for three). *Tripura 3 pts, Bengal 5 pts.*
Gavaskar's full second-innings analysis was 8–6–3–5.

At Eden Gardens, Calcutta, January 3, 4, 5, 6. Drawn. Assam* 360 (S. Saikia 35, Rajinder Singh 143, Iqbal Khan 74, G. Dutta 38; U. Chatterjee five for 101, A. K. Das three for 49) and 211 (Rajinder Singh 63, V. R. Samant 47; U. Chatterjee four for 81, A. Varma three for 26); Bengal 255 (R. S. Gavaskar 42, A. K. Das 35, U. Chatterjee 56, H. Feroze 46; G. Dutta six for 70) and 118 for three (D. Gandhi 54 not out). *Bengal 2 pts, Assam 5 pts.*

At Polytechnic Ground, Agartala, January 3, 4, 5, 6. Drawn. Bihar* 370 (C. M. Jha 77, Tariq-ur-Rehman 50, S. Arfi 101, S. Prakash 32, V. Saxena 33; R. Deb-Burman five for 134); Tripura 166 (S. Lahiri 78; K. V. P. Rao five for 48, Avinash Kumar three for 51) and 27 for one. *Tripura 3 pts, Bihar 5 pts.*

Bengal 21 pts, Bihar 19 pts, Orissa 18 pts, Assam 13 pts, Tripura 9 pts. Bengal, Bihar and Orissa qualified for the Super League.

North Zone

At Feroz Shah Kotla Ground, Delhi, October 19, 20, 21, 22. Drawn. Haryana 203 (Shafiq Khan 48, P. Thakur 43, P. Jain 30; A. Mehra three for 51) and 284 for nine dec. (Jitender Singh 111, A. S. Kaypee 62; R. Singh six for 70); Delhi* 261 (R. Lamba 30, M. Minhas 51, D. Sharma 44, Extras 45; V. Jain six for 55) and 112 for five (R. Lamba 38, Ajay Sharma 33). *Delhi 5 pts, Haryana 3 pts.*

At Indira Stadium, Una, October 19, 20, 21, 22. Drawn. Himachal Pradesh* 383 (N. Gaur 97, R. Nayyar 45, S. Chandel 30, Chetan Kumar 58, Jaswant Rai 49, Shakti Singh 36, Extras 32; Vijay Sharma five for 70, A. Gupta four for 106); Jammu and Kashmir 227 (R. Gill 31, Kanwaljit Singh 35, A. Gupta 35, Vivek Sharma 35; Shakti Singh five for 75, Jaswant Rai four for 72) and 81 for one (R. Gill 58). *Himachal Pradesh 5 pts, Jammu and Kashmir 3 pts.*

At PCA Stadium, Mohali, Chandigarh, October 19, 20, 21. Punjab won by an innings and 54 runs. Punjab* 339 for nine dec. (N. S. Sidhu 83, A. R. Kapoor 38, Sandeep Sharma 33, Harvinder Singh 65 not out; M. V. Rao five for 68); Services 78 (B. Vij four for 32, A. R. Kapoor three for six) and 207 (Sarabjit Singh 41, S. Mishra 32; B. Vij five for 67, A. R. Kapoor three for 63). *Punjab 8 pts.*

At Nahar Singh Stadium, Faridabad, October 26, 27, 28, 29. Haryana won by nine wickets. Jammu and Kashmir* 159 (Kanwaljit Singh 31, Vivek Sharma 47; P. Jain four for 22) and 309 (A. Gupta 112, S. Sharma 56, P. Bali 39; V. Jain three for 88, Dhanraj Singh four for 36); Haryana 445 for five dec. (Jitender Singh 175, N. R. Goel 143, A. Jadeja 32) and 26 for one. *Haryana 8 pts.*
Jitender Singh and Goel put on 319 for Haryana's first wicket.

At PCA Stadium, Mohali, Chandigarh, October 26, 27, 28, 29. Punjab won by nine wickets. Himachal Pradesh 119 (R. Nayyar 36; B. Bhushan five for 53, Sandeep Sharma three for 35) and 119 (Jaswant Rai 43 not out; Harvinder Singh seven for 51); Punjab* 219 (N. S. Sidhu 34, D. Mongia 32, A. R. Kapoor 65; Shakti Singh four for 87, P. Sharma five for 99) and 20 for one. *Punjab 8 pts.*

At Air Force Complex, Palam, Delhi, October 26, 27, 28, 29. Delhi won by an innings and 30 runs. Delhi* 444 (R. Chopra 34, A. Chopra 150, A. Malhotra 56, M. Minhas 115; M. V. Rao three for 135, P. Maitreya five for 117); Services 210 (A. Nadkarni 58, S. Dutta 48; R. Singh six for 85) and 204 (Narender Singh 41, A. E. Samy 32; F. Ghayas four for 56, R. Sanghvi five for 96). *Delhi 8 pts.*
   Chopra scored 150 on first-class debut.

At MLSN Ground, Sunder Nagar, November 2, 3, 4, 5. Services won by six wickets. Himachal Pradesh* 163 (N. Gaur 53; M. V. Rao three for 60, Arun Sharma four for 32) and 100 (M. V. Rao six for 46); Services 101 (Shakti Singh seven for 37) and 164 for four (Sarabjit Singh 62 not out, P. Maitreya 35; Shakti Singh four for 59). *Services 8 pts.*

At Dhruv Pandove Stadium, Patiala, November 2, 3, 4, 5. Drawn. Delhi* 311 (Ajay Sharma 59, A. Malhotra 42, M. Minhas 65, D. Sharma 31; Harbhajan Singh four for 66, B. Vij four for 88) and 270 for four (A. Chopra 100 not out, Ajay Sharma 31, A. Malhotra 87); Punjab 488 for eight dec. (R. S. Sodhi 200 not out, N. S. Sidhu 89, P. Dharmani 80, B. Vij 33; Ajay Sharma three for 96). *Punjab 5 pts, Delhi 3 pts.*
   Chopra scored his second century in his second first-class match. Sodhi's 200 not out lasted 635 minutes and 422 balls and included 19 fours and two sixes.

At Nahar Singh Stadium, Faridabad, November 9, 10, 11, 12. Haryana won by an innings and two runs. Haryana* 413 (N. R. Goel 42, A. Jadeja 242 not out, V. S. Yadav 43; M. V. Rao three for 157, Arun Sharma three for 72); Services 234 (P. Maitreya 51, A. Nadkarni 43, S. Dutta 32; P. Jain three for 64, Dhanraj Singh four for 34) and 177 (Narender Singh 58, Sarabjit Singh 45; P. Thakur three for 62, P. Jain four for 59). *Haryana 8 pts.*
   Jadeja's 242 not out lasted 497 minutes and 438 balls and included 17 fours and five sixes.

At Indira Stadium, Una, November 9, 10, 11, 12. Himachal Pradesh v Delhi. Abandoned due to rain. *Himachal Pradesh 2 pts, Delhi 2 pts.*

At Burlton Park, Jalandhar, November 9, 10, 11, 12. Punjab v Jammu and Kashmir. Abandoned due to rain. *Punjab 2 pts, Jammu and Kashmir 2 pts.*

At Nehru Stadium, Gurgaon, November 16, 17, 18. Haryana won by an innings and 115 runs. Himachal Pradesh 126 (N. Gaur 69; V. Jain three for 27, P. Jain three for 41, P. Thakur three for 41) and 130 (N. Gaur 69; P. Jain three for 24, P. Thakur three for 47); Haryana* 371 for six dec. (Jitender Singh 127, Shafiq Khan 38, A. S. Kaypee 80, S. Dalal 56 not out, Dhanraj Singh 38). *Haryana 8 pts.*
   Gaur scored more than half Himachal Pradesh's runs in both innings.

At Air Force Complex, Palam, Delhi, November 16, 17, 18. Services won by an innings and 185 runs. Services* 429 for nine dec. (Narender Singh 229 not out, Sarabjit Singh 58, A. Nadkarni 45; Abdul Qayyum three for 118); Jammu and Kashmir 137 (Abdul Qayyum 35; Harpreet Singh six for 38, Arun Sharma four for 27) and 107 (Ishfaq Ahmed 41; M. V. Rao three for 28, S. K. Kulkarni five for 19). *Services 8 pts.*
   Narender Singh's 229 not out lasted 560 minutes and 360 balls and included 29 fours.

At Feroz Shah Kotla Ground, Delhi, November 23, 24, 25, 26. Drawn. Jammu and Kashmir* 183 (A. Bhatti 33, Vijay Sharma 33; A. Mehra four for 45) and 151 for four (R. Gill 47; A. Mehra three for 65); Delhi 140 (Extras 35; Raj Kumar three for 39, Vijay Sharma four for 41). *Delhi 3 pts, Jammu and Kashmir 5 pts.*

At Nehru Stadium, Gurgaon, November 23, 24, 25, 26. Drawn. Punjab* 286 (R. S. Sodhi 40, P. Dharmani 97, R. Saini 35; P. Thakur seven for 107) and 89 for two (R. S. Sodhi 39 not out); Haryana 189 (V. S. Yadav 61, P. Thakur 50; B. Bhushan four for 29). *Haryana 3 pts, Punjab 5 pts.*

Haryana 30 pts, Punjab 28 pts, Delhi 21 pts, Services 16 pts, Jammu and Kashmir 10 pts, Himachal Pradesh 7 pts. Haryana, Punjab and Delhi qualified for the Super League.

South Zone

At Ukku Stadium, Vishakhapatnam, October 21, 22, 23, 24. Drawn. Andhra* 202 (R. V. C. Prasad 54, V. Vinay Kumar 33; S. Mahesh three for 43, M. Venkataramana three for 43) and 389 for five (A. Pathak 56, M. S. K. Prasad 123 not out, R. V. C. Prasad 49, V. Vinay Kumar 41, N. Veerabrahman 78); Tamil Nadu 485 for four dec. (S. Ramesh 123, W. V. Raman 36, S. Sriram 213 not out, S. Sharath 80; Y. S. Ranganath three for 150). *Andhra 3 pts, Tamil Nadu 5 pts.*
  Sriram's 213 not out lasted 444 minutes and 307 balls and included 16 fours and two sixes.

At M. Chinnaswamy Stadium, Bangalore, October 21, 22, 23, 24. Karnataka won by an innings and 23 runs. Kerala 181 (S. Oasis 46, B. Ramprakash 30; B. K. V. Prasad three for 25, S. B. Joshi four for 33) and 141 (S. Shankar 60, S. Oasis 45; A. Kumble six for 32); Karnataka* 345 (S. Somasunder 37, J. Arun Kumar 111, R. V. Bharadwaj 35, K. Sriram 44, A. Kumble 58; K. N. A. Padmanabhan three for 111, B. Ramprakash four for 78). *Karnataka 8 pts.*

At Gymkhana Ground, Secunderabad, October 29, 30, 31, November 1. Drawn. Hyderabad 284 (M. Azharuddin 82, V. Pratap 56, Yuvraj Singh 45; H. Ramkishen three for 79, N. Madhukar four for 79); Andhra* 278 for nine (A. Pathak 32, M. S. K. Prasad 81, B. S. Naik 67, R. V. C. Prasad 44; Kanwaljit Singh three for 65). *Hyderabad 2 pts, Andhra 2 pts.*

At M. Chinnaswamy Stadium, Bangalore, October 29, 30, 31. Karnataka won by ten wickets. Goa 152 (V. B. Chandrasekhar 44; A. Kumble three for 31, D. J. Johnson four for 57) and 127 (V. B. Chandrasekhar 39, J. Gokulkrishnan 38 not out; S. B. Joshi five for 25); Karnataka* 211 (R. V. Bharadwaj 42, K. Sriram 30, A. Kumble 34; S. Khalid four for 46) and 70 for no wkt (S. Somasunder 55 not out). *Karnataka 8 pts.*

At Gymkhana Ground, Secunderabad, November 6, 7, 8, 9. Drawn. Hyderabad* 433 (G. A. Shetty 70, D. Manohar 144, V. V. S. Laxman 67, V. Pratap 44, M. Azharuddin 63, Extras 30; A. Kumble six for 73); Karnataka 446 for nine dec. (R. Dravid 99, R. V. Bharadwaj 68, S. B. Joshi 42, A. Kumble 113, A. Katti 31 not out, Extras 37). *Hyderabad 3 pts, Karnataka 5 pts.*
  Manohar scored 144 on first-class debut.

At Nehru Stadium, Kochi, November 6, 7, 8, 9. Drawn. Andhra* 180 (R. V. C. Prasad 50; B. Ramprakash four for 47) and 33 (K. Chandrasekhara four for one); Kerala 163 (S. M. Manoj 34, K. Chandrasekhara 36; N. Madhukar three for 26, K. Chakradhar Rao three for 40) and 41 for eight (H. Ramkishen five for 21). *Kerala 3 pts, Andhra 5 pts.*
  Chandrasekhara's full second-innings analysis was 7–6–1–4.

At South-Eastern Railway Stadium, Vishakhapatnam, November 14, 15, 16, 17. Goa won by seven wickets. Andhra* 201 (A. Pathak 50, P. Srihari Rao 50; J. Gokulkrishnan three for 39) and 157 (V. Nagini Kumar 35, A. Pathak 67; S. Suresh four for 35); Goa 237 (V. V. Kolambkar 69, R. R. Naik 74, S. Y. Dhuri 33; N. Madhukar four for 50) and 125 for three (S. Suresh 85 not out; Y. S. Ranganath three for 45). *Goa 8 pts.*

At Nehru Stadium, Kochi, November 14, 15, 16, 17. Drawn. Hyderabad* 272 (G. A. Shetty 141, D. Manohar 34, M. V. Sridhar 43; C. T. K. Masood four for 78, B. Ramprakash four for 82) and 56 for five (B. Ramprakash four for 24); Kerala 163 (S. M. Manoj 42; S. L. V. Raju five for 60, Kanwaljit Singh four for 36). *Kerala 3 pts, Hyderabad 5 pts.*

At M. Chinnaswamy Stadium, Bangalore, November 15, 16, 17, 18. Drawn. Tamil Nadu* 281 (W. V. Raman 56, H. K. Badani 85 not out, T. Jabbar 32, D. Vasu 31; D. Ganesh four for 63, D. S. Ananth three for 37) and 233 for five dec. (R. C. Vasant Kumar 103 not out, T. Jabbar 41, R. R. Singh 35); Karnataka 146 (S. Somasunder 31, S. B. Joshi 43; D. Vasu five for 26, M. Venkataramana three for 54). *Karnataka 3 pts, Tamil Nadu 5 pts.*

At IGMC Stadium, Vijayawada, November 22, 23, 24, 25. Drawn. Karnataka* 381 for four dec. (S. Somasunder 97, J. Arun Kumar 101, R. V. Bharadwaj 101 not out; H. Ramkishen three for 102) and 51 for two; Andhra 247 (A. Pathak 138, P. Srihari Rao 49, Extras 34; D. J. Johnson five for 65). *Andhra 3 pts, Karnataka 5 pts.*

At Gymkhana Ground, Panaji, November 22, 23, 24, 25. Drawn. Goa 339 (R. R. Naik 133, V. Jaisimha 100, J. Gokulkrishnan 30; B. Ramprakash three for 83) and 176 for five (V. B. Chandrasekhar 87); Kerala* 291 (K. N. A. Padmanabhan 96, S. Oasis 57, B. Ramprakash 37; J. Gokulkrishnan six for 79). *Goa 5 pts, Kerala 3 pts.*

At M. A. Chidambaram Stadium, Chennai, November 22, 23, 24, 25. Drawn. Hyderabad 30 for two dec.; Tamil Nadu* 33 for one. *Tamil Nadu 5 pts, Hyderabad 3 pts.*
Play was possible only in two short sessions on the first and third days.

At Gymkhana Ground, Panaji, December 30, 31, January 1. Hyderabad won by an innings and 76 runs. Goa 55 (N. P. Singh seven for 24) and 166 (S. Suresh 62, S. V. Kamat 34; N. P. Singh three for 24, D. Manohar three for 50, N. A. David three for 30); Hyderabad* 297 (V. V. S. Laxman 145 not out, M. Azharuddin 87; J. Gokulkrishnan four for 49, P. M. Kakade four for 68). *Hyderabad 8 pts.*

At M. A. Chidambaram Stadium, Chennai, December 31, January 1, 2, 3. Drawn. Kerala* 323 (S. Oasis 134, A. S. Kudva 49, K. N. A. Padmanabhan 74; D. Vasu three for 63, M. Venkataramana four for 70) and 256 (A. S. Kudva 124 not out, Feroz Rashid 37; S. Sriram three for 51); Tamil Nadu 466 (S. Ramesh 187, S. Sharath 129, R. R. Singh 51; C. T. K. Masood four for 142, B. Ramprakash five for 113) and eight for one. *Tamil Nadu 5 pts, Kerala 3 pts.*

At M. A. Chidambaram Stadium, Chennai, January 7, 8, 9, 10. Tamil Nadu won by an innings and 116 runs. Goa* 260 (S. Suresh 55, V. B. Chandrasekhar 98, S. Upadhyaya 30; T. Kumaran five for 61) and 226 (S. Suresh 123 not out, V. B. Chandrasekhar 47; T. Kumaran three for 33, M. Venkataramana four for 92); Tamil Nadu 602 for four dec. (S. Ramesh 182, W. V. Raman 54, R. C. Vasant Kumar 151, S. Sriram 129, S. Sharath 58 not out). *Tamil Nadu 8 pts.*
Suresh carried his bat through Goa's second innings.

Karnataka 29 pts, Tamil Nadu 28 pts, Hyderabad 21 pts, Andhra 13 pts, Goa 13 pts, Kerala 12 pts. Karnataka, Tamil Nadu and Hyderabad qualified for the Super League.

West Zone

At Sardar Patel Stadium, Valsad, November 6, 7, 8. Mumbai won by an innings and 68 runs. Gujarat 182 (K. R. Patdiwala 50, M. H. Parmar 53, B. N. Mehta 39; P. L. Mhambrey seven for 42) and 161 (B. N. Mehta 36; A. Kuruvilla three for 34, P. L. Mhambrey four for 46); Mumbai* 411 for eight dec. (V. G. Kambli 43, S. R. Tendulkar 177, S. V. Manjrekar 46, A. A. Muzumdar 68; B. N. Mehta four for 111). *Mumbai 8 pts.*

At Municipal Ground, Rajkot, November 6, 7, 8, 9. Drawn. Saurashtra* 469 (J. D. Motivaras 99, S. S. Tanna 52, S. H. Kotak 77, B. M. Jadeja 30, P. J. Bhatt 85, M. M. Parmar 49, K. C. Mehta 30; D. Mulherkar four for 161, R. A. Swarup four for 90); Baroda 509 (M. Kadri 68, R. A. Swarup 165, C. C. Williams 76, J. J. Martin 104 not out, T. B. Arothe 37; H. J. Parsana five for 147). *Saurashtra 3 pts, Baroda 5 pts.*

At Brabourne Stadium, Mumbai, November 16, 17, 18, 19. Mumbai won by 311 runs. Mumbai 426 (A. A. Pagnis 56, A. A. Muzumdar 31, V. G. Kambli 39, J. V. Paranjpe 91, R. V. Sutar 49, S. K. Kulkarni 33, A. B. Agarkar 43; M. S. Kulkarni five for 72) and 208 for three dec. (V. G. Kambli 78 not out, S. V. Manjrekar 81); Maharashtra* 201 (A. V. Kale 39, S. S. Sugwekar 70; S. Saxena four for 61) and 122 (A. B. Agarkar four for 38, R. V. Pawar four for 33). *Mumbai 8 pts.*

At Municipal Ground, Rajkot, November 16, 17, 18, 19. Saurashtra won by six wickets. Gujarat* 147 (N. D. Modi 56; H. J. Parsana three for 40, H. J. Parsana five for 50) and 259 (A. S. Kotecha 47, N. D. Modi 48, P. H. Patel 32, U. S. Belsare 56, H. D. Patel 47; Y. Bambhania four for 70, H. J. Parsana three for 91); Saurashtra 290 (S. S. Tanna 31, S. H. Kotak 77, P. K. Khakhar 60; B. N. Mehta five for 119, H. D. Patel four for 56) and 119 for four (P. J. Bhatt 43). *Saurashtra 8 pts.*

At IPCL Ground, Baroda, November 30, December 1, 2, 3. Drawn. Baroda 382 (C. C. Williams 55, J. J. Martin 101, T. B. Arothe 123; A. B. Agarkar three for 92, S. V. Bahutule six for 122) and 282 for five (C. C. Williams 42, R. A. Swarup 54, A. P. Bhohite 37, A. C. Bedade 103 not out); Mumbai* 380 (S. K. Kulkarni 39, J. V. Paranjpe 135, V. G. Kambli 39, A. A. Muzumdar 43, A. B. Agarkar 31, S. V. Bahutule 36 not out; R. A. Swarup three for 123, T. B. Arothe three for 103). *Baroda 5 pts, Mumbai 3 pts.*
  Martin's 101 was his third century in successive first-class innings, going back to February 1997.

At Sardar Patel Stadium, Ahmedabad, November 30, December 1, 2, 3. Drawn. Maharashtra* 367 (S. S. Bhave 49, H. H. Kanitkar 125, A. V. Kale 76 not out; J. J. Patel three for 53, B. N. Mehta five for 110) and 51 for three; Gujarat 214 (T. N. Varsania 40, H. D. Patel 47; M. S. Kulkarni three for 51, M. V. Sane six for 58) and 242 (N. Patel 62, T. N. Varsania 34, A. S. Kotecha 30, H. D. Patel 40; I. A. Kamtekar three for 81, M. V. Sane five for 68). *Gujarat 3 pts, Maharashtra 5 pts.*

At IPCL Ground, Baroda, December 30, 31, January 1, 2. Baroda won by an innings and one run. Gujarat* 248 (T. N. Varsania 93, B. N. Mehta 58 not out; T. B. Arothe four for 56) and 213 (A. S. Kotecha 35, M. H. Parmar 77, B. N. Mehta 72; R. A. Swarup three for 45, T. B. Arothe six for 57); Baroda 462 for eight dec. (M. Kadri 76, R. A. Swarup 73, J. J. Martin 107, D. Mulherkar 42, N. R. Mongia 76 not out, Extras 41; B. N. Mehta three for 143). *Baroda 8 pts.*

At Nehru Stadium, Pune, December 30, 31, January 1, 2. Drawn. Saurashtra 327 (S. H. Kotak 131, B. M. Jadeja 123; M. S. Kulkarni five for 66) and 259 for eight (S. S. Tanna 53, B. M. Jadeja 112 not out, Extras 31; Iqbal Siddiqui four for 66); Maharashtra* 439 (S. S. Bhave 156, S. S. Sugwekar 76, A. V. Kale 126; R. R. Garsondia four for 101). *Maharashtra 5 pts, Saurashtra 3 pts.*
  Jadeja scored a century in each innings.

At Poona Club, Pune, January 6, 7, 8. Maharashtra won by 180 runs. Maharashtra* 171 (H. A. Kinikar 34, S. S. Sugwekar 63; D. Mulherkar four for nine) and 238 (H. A. Kinikar 35, A. V. Kale 61, S. V. Jedhe 35, M. V. Sane 49; M. Kadri four for 34); Baroda 151 (Iqbal Siddiqui seven for 49) and 78 (M. S. Kulkarni five for 47, Iqbal Siddiqui five for 30). *Maharashtra 8 pts.*

At Wankhede Stadium, Mumbai, January 7, 8, 9, 10. Drawn. Mumbai 538 for five dec. (S. K. Kulkarni 51, J. V. Paranjpe 174, V. G. Kambli 232 not out, A. B. Agarkar 54 not out) and 290 for five dec. (S. V. Manjrekar 74, V. G. Kambli 31, A. A. Muzumdar 113, A. B. Agarkar 43); Saurashtra* 386 (S. H. Kotak 45, B. J. Dutta 48, P. J. Bhatt 81, H. J. Parsana 102; P. L. Mhambrey five for 78) and nine for two. *Mumbai 5 pts, Saurashtra 3 pts.*
  Kambli's 232 not out lasted 297 minutes and 253 balls and included 17 fours and six sixes.

Mumbai 24 pts, Baroda 18 pts, Maharashtra 18 pts, Saurashtra 17 pts, Gujarat 3 pts. Mumbai, Baroda and Maharashtra qualified for the Super League.

Super League Group A

At M. Chinnaswamy Stadium, Bangalore, February 5, 6, 7, 8. Karnataka won by 262 runs. Karnataka* 298 (S. Somasunder 58, R. Dravid 38, F. Khaleel 35, A. Kumble 44, Extras 38; A. R. Kapoor three for 62, Harbhajan Singh three for 50) and 254 for nine dec. (S. Somasunder 42, R. Dravid 55, R. V. Bharadwaj 57; B. Vij three for 48); Punjab 157 (P. Dharmani 32; S. B. Joshi three for 27, A. Kumble five for 51) and 133 (V. Rathore 31, D. Mongia 35; J. Srinath three for 20). *Karnataka 8 pts.*

At Wankhede Stadium, Mumbai, February 5, 6, 7. Mumbai won by an innings and 176 runs. Railways 124 (P. S. Rawat 40; A. Kuruvilla three for 47, P. L. Mhambrey four for 43) and 197 (V. Sharma 48, S. S. Bhatia 40, M. Suresh Kumar 34; A. Kuruvilla three for 61, N. M. Kulkarni three for 14); Mumbai* 497 for four dec. (A. A. Pagnis 30, S. K. Kulkarni 45, S. V. Manjrekar 30, S. R. Tendulkar 95, V. G. Kambli 207 not out, A. A. Muzumdar 63 not out). *Mumbai 8 pts.*
  Kambli's 207 not out lasted 270 minutes and 196 balls and included 22 fours and six sixes.

At M. Chinnaswamy Stadium, Bangalore, February 14, 15, 16, 17. Karnataka won by six wickets. Karnataka* 462 for eight dec. (S. Somasunder 37, R. Dravid 65, R. V. Bharadwaj 164, A. Kumble 59, S. Siriguppi 37 not out, Extras 44; K. S. Parida three for 116) and 22 for four (Zakir Hussain three for 15); Railways 269 (S. B. Bangar 54, Z. Zuffri 99, Extras 31; A. Kumble four for 81, S. B. Joshi four for 57) and 213 (S. B. Bangar 36, V. Sharma 42, Y. Gowda 54; A. Kumble six for 69). *Karnataka 8 pts.*

At Wankhede Stadium, Mumbai, February 14, 15, 16. Mumbai won by an innings and 46 runs. Orissa 150 (R. R. Parida 54; P. L. Mhambrey six for 45, N. M. Kulkarni four for 36) and 297 (P. Jayachandra 40, S. S. Das 35, R. R. Parida 71, G. Gopal 58, Extras 36; N. M. Kulkarni five for 74); Mumbai* 493 for seven dec. (S. V. Manjrekar 126, S. R. Tendulkar 135, V. G. Kambli 48, A. A. Pagnis 64 not out, S. Dahad 59, Extras 34). *Mumbai 8 pts.*

At Ispat Stadium, Rourkela, February 23, 24, 25. Karnataka won by an innings and 123 runs. Orissa* 183 (P. Jayachandra 45; A. Kumble five for 34, S. B. Joshi three for 46) and 92 (A. Kumble five for nine); Karnataka 398 for nine dec. (S. Somasunder 67, R. Dravid 138, R. V. Bharadwaj 41, A. Kumble 38, Extras 45; P. Jayachandra five for 64). *Karnataka 8 pts.*
In the second innings, Kumble took a hat-trick.

At PCA Stadium, Mohali, Chandigarh, February 23, 24, 25, 26. Drawn. Railways* 300 (P. S. Rawat 49, A. Kapoor 54, J. Alam 36, Extras 42; Sandeep Sharma three for 69); Punjab 276 (V. Rathore 95, M. Mehra 37; P. S. Rawat three for 72). *Punjab 3 pts, Railways 5 pts.*

At Barabati Stadium, Cuttack, March 4, 5, 6, 7. Orissa won by 116 runs. Orissa* 218 (P. Mullick 98 not out, S. S. Das 37; Zakir Hussain three for 59) and 265 for five dec. (B. B. C. C. Mohapatra 57, S. S. Das 120); Railways 113 (P. Jayachandra three for 18, S. Satpathy five for 25) and 254 (Jaswinder Singh 71, P. S. Rawat 43, S. S. Bhatia 37; S. Satpathy five for 95, S. Khan three for 76). *Orissa 8 pts.*

At PCA Stadium, Mohali, Chandigarh, March 4, 5, 6, 7. Drawn. Punjab* 272 (P. Dharmani 96, Amit Sharma 46, A. R. Kapoor 34; P. L. Mhambrey three for 54, N. M. Kulkarni four for 77) and 73 for eight (R. V. Pawar three for nine); Mumbai 280 (A. A. Pagnis 56, S. S. More 46, V. G. Kambli 86; A. R. Kapoor five for 98, B. Vij three for 43). *Punjab 3 pts, Mumbai 5 pts.*

At Wankhede Stadium, Mumbai, March 13, 14, 15, 16. Drawn. Mumbai 467 (A. A. Pagnis 72, V. G. Kambli 151, A. A. Muzumdar 41, M. D. Phadke 114; D. J. Johnson three for 129) and 196 for one dec. (A. A. Pagnis 47, S. S. More 82 not out, A. A. Muzumdar 53 not out); Karnataka* 313 (J. Arun Kumar 48, F. Khaleel 49, R. V. Bharadwaj 58, S. B. Joshi 55, D. S. Ananth 35; A. Kuruvilla three for 70, P. L. Mhambrey three for 78, N. M. Kulkarni four for 107) and 177 for six (F. Khaleel 83, S. B. Joshi 30 not out). *Mumbai 5 pts, Karnataka 3 pts.*

At Berhampur Stadium, Berhampur, March 13, 14, 15, 16. Drawn. Orissa* 261 (S. S. Das 110; B. Vij four for 60) and 305 for six dec. (P. Jayachandra 35, S. S. Das 131, R. R. Parida 99; B. Vij three for 92); Punjab 145 (Harvinder Singh 40; R. F. Morris three for 32, S. Satpathy three for 55) and 88 for nine (R. S. Rickey 34; S. Satpathy three for 25, J. Das three for 28). *Orissa 5 pts, Punjab 3 pts.*
S. S. Das's 110 and 131 were his second and third centuries in successive innings.

Karnataka 27 pts, Mumbai 26 pts, Orissa 13 pts, Punjab 9 pts, Railways 5 pts. Karnataka, as the team with most points in all three Super League Groups, and Mumbai, as defending champions, advanced directly to the semi-finals.

Super League Group B

At Feroz Shah Kotla Ground, Delhi, February 5, 6, 7, 8. Drawn. Delhi* 300 (Ajay Sharma 101, A. Malhotra 38, N. Chopra 84; S. C. Ganguly six for 87) and 194 for six (R. Lamba 36, A. Chopra 65, M. Minhas 31 not out; S. C. Ganguly three for 48); Bengal 527 for six dec. (A. Varma 75, A. Lahiri 87, D. Gandhi 176, S. S. Karim 97, S. C. Ganguly 47, Extras 35). *Points cancelled.*

At M. A. Chidambaram Stadium, Chennai, February 5, 6, 7, 8. Drawn. Uttar Pradesh* 460 (S. A. Shukla 164, G. K. Pandey 62, R. V. Sapru 99, M. S. Mudgal 41; T. Kumaran five for 96, D. Vasu three for 81); Tamil Nadu 269 (S. Sriram 39, S. Chandramouli 51, H. K. Badani 58, D. Vasu 44; A. Jaffer three for 65, M. Raza three for 73) and 215 for three (S. Sriram 65, S. Sharath 108 not out). *Points cancelled.*

Tamil Nadu wicket-keeper R. Paul made five catches and a stumping in Uttar Pradesh's innings.

At M. A. Chidambaram Stadium, Chennai, February 14, 15, 16, 17. Drawn. Tamil Nadu* 473 (S. Ramesh 47, W. V. Raman 67, D. Vasu 148, H. K. Badani 57, S. Mahesh 77, Extras 32; N. Chopra three for 104); Delhi 183 for four (A. Chopra 34, Ajay Sharma 55 not out).

Both teams were suspended from the tournament after the pitch was tampered with during a drinks break on the third day; Tamil Nadu were held responsible, but Delhi were punished for refusing to continue after pitch repairs. All points in the matches they had already played were cancelled.

At Ordnance Stadium, Kanpur, February 14, 15, 16, 17. Drawn. Maharashtra* 383 (H. H. Kanitkar 126, A. V. Kale 32, I. A. Kamtekar 30, S. M. Kondhalkar 68, M. V. Sane 30, Extras 35; A. W. Zaidi seven for 99); Uttar Pradesh 498 for nine (R. Sharma 84, Jyoti P. Yadav 39, S. A. Shukla 33, G. K. Pandey 67, R. V. Sapru 37, M. S. Mudgal 37, M. Saif 104 not out, M. Raza 43, Extras 31; M. S. Kulkarni three for 87, Iqbal Siddiqui three for 110). *Uttar Pradesh 5 pts, Maharashtra 3 pts.*

At Calcutta Cricket & Football Club, Calcutta, March 4, 5, 6, 7. Drawn. Bengal* 525 (A. Varma 45, A. Lahiri 94, D. Gandhi 91, G. Shome 45, S. S. Karim 93, S. J. Kalyani 76; M. S. Kulkarni three for 97, M. V. Sane three for 92); Maharashtra 301 (H. A. Kinikar 30, S. S. Bhave 140, R. R. Kanade 42, Iqbal Siddiqui 48; U. Chatterjee five for 77, A. K. Das four for 67) and 127 for four (H. A. Kinikar 71 not out). *Bengal 5 pts, Maharashtra 3 pts.*

At Calcutta Cricket & Football Club, Calcutta, March 13, 14, 15, 16. Drawn. Uttar Pradesh 293 (R. Sharma 68, Jyoti P. Yadav 82, R. V. Sapru 50 not out; S. T. Banerjee four for 63, U. Chatterjee three for 65); Bengal* 159 for five (A. Varma 73, G. Shome 44). *Bengal 2 pts, Uttar Pradesh 2 pts.*

Bengal 7 pts, Uttar Pradesh 7 pts, Maharashtra 6 pts, Delhi 0 pts, Tamil Nadu 0 pts. Bengal and Uttar Pradesh qualified for the quarter-finals.

Super League Group C

At IPCL Sports Complex Ground, Baroda, February 5, 6, 7. Haryana won by nine wickets. Baroda* 240 (C. C. Williams 40, S. Parab 48, D. Mulherkar 35; P. Thakur three for 63) and 88 (M. Kadri 48; M. K. Shakalkar four for 21, P. Jain four for 25); Haryana 289 (Jitender Singh 37, R. Puri 143, A. S. Kaypee 58; A. R. Tandon five for 39, M. Kadri three for 49) and 43 for one. *Haryana 8 pts.*

At Keenan Stadium, Jamshedpur, February 5, 6, 7, 8. Hyderabad won by an innings and 152 runs. Hyderabad* 529 for eight dec. (D. Manohar 35, V. V. S. Laxman 301 not out, M. V. Sridhar 33, S. L. V. Raju 30, N. P. Singh 34 not out); Bihar 248 (Rajiv Kumar 33, Tariq-ur-Rehman 70 not out, S. Panda 39; S. L. V. Raju five for 69) and 129 (Rajiv Kumar 51; R. Sridhar three for 43, S. L. V. Raju four for 51). *Hyderabad 8 pts.*

Laxman's 301 not out lasted 609 minutes and 434 balls and included 28 fours. None of his team-mates passed 35.

At Nahar Singh Stadium, Faridabad, February 14, 15, 16, 17. Drawn. Haryana* 308 (P. Sharma 37, Shafiq Khan 34, V. S. Yadav 72, P. Thakur 85; S. Panda four for 68, K. V. P. Rao three for 43) and 231 for four dec. (Jitender Singh 92, P. Sharma 38, A. S. Kaypee 61 not out; Avinash Kumar three for 81); Bihar 323 (Sunil Kumar 76, Rajiv Kumar 106, Tariq-ur-Rehman 38; P. Jain four for 65, P. Thakur five for 109) and 107 for one (Sunil Kumar 38 not out, Rajiv Kumar 53 not out). *Haryana 3 pts, Bihar 5 pts.*

At Digvijay Stadium, Rajnandgaon, February 14, 15, 16, 17. Drawn. Madhya Pradesh* 596 for eight dec. (Jai P. Yadav 63, K. K. Patel 79, A. R. Khurasia 195, C. S. Pandit 104, Raja Ali 59; R. A. Swarup three for 149); Baroda 305 (M. Kadri 56, C. C. Williams 43, N. R. Mongia 60, A. C. Bedade 81; R. K. Chauhan four for 103, S. S. Lahore three for 46) and 176 for six (N. R. Mongia 88, R. A. Swarup 36 not out). *Madhya Pradesh 5 pts, Baroda 3 pts.*

At Moin-ul-Haq Stadium, Patna, February 22, 23, 24, 25. Drawn. Baroda* 389 (M. Kadri 53, C. C. Williams 72, A. C. Bedade 54, T. B. Arothe 72, K. S. More 34; Avinash Kumar four for 107, K. V. P. Rao three for 66); Bihar 229 (Rajiv Kumar 73, S. Arfi 36, V. Saxena 32; A. R. Tandon six for 87) and 123 for six (Tariq-ur-Rehman 46; A. R. Tandon four for 38). *Bihar 3 pts, Baroda 5 pts.*

At Jayanti Stadium, Bhilai, February 23, 24, 25, 26. Drawn. Hyderabad 536 for six dec. (G. A. Shetty 32, D. Manohar 31, V. V. S. Laxman 92, V. Pratap 51, M. V. Sridhar 108, A. Nandakishore 136, Yuvraj Singh 42 not out; S. S. Lahore three for 102); Madhya Pradesh* 225 (Jai P. Yadav 31, K. K. Patel 48, N. Patwardhan 51, R. K. Chauhan 35; S. L. V. Raju five for 49, Kanwaljit Singh three for 64) and 226 for four (Jai P. Yadav 106 not out, K. K. Patel 35, A. R. Khurasia 30). *Madhya Pradesh 3 pts, Hyderabad 5 pts.*

At Nahar Singh Stadium, Faridabad, March 4, 5, 6, 7. Drawn. Hyderabad 263 (S. Yadav 68, Yuvraj Singh 54, T. Pawan Kumar 34, Extras 40; P. Thakur three for 50, P. Jain three for 37); Haryana* 280 for seven (Dhanraj Singh 83, A. S. Kaypee 48 not out, V. S. Yadav 68; R. Sridhar three for 81, D. Manohar three for ten). *Haryana 5 pts, Hyderabad 3 pts.*

At Roop Singh Stadium, Gwalior, March 4, 5, 6, 7. Drawn. Bihar 356 (N. Ranjan 78, Rajiv Kumar 108, Tariq-ur-Rehman 44, Extras 35; H. S. Sodhi five for 120, S. Pandey four for 90) and 163 for three (Rajiv Kumar 55, Tariq-ur-Rehman 61 not out); Madhya Pradesh* 395 for eight dec. (D. Bundela 56, K. K. Patel 38, C. S. Pandit 42, N. Patwardhan 121 not out, H. S. Sodhi 41, Extras 34; K. V. P. Rao four for 71). *Madhya Pradesh 5 pts, Bihar 3 pts.*

At Nahar Singh Stadium, Faridabad, March 13, 14, 15, 16. Drawn. Madhya Pradesh* 298 (Jai P. Yadav 51, K. K. Patel 40, D. Bundela 34, C. S. Pandit 82, H. S. Sodhi 32; P. Jain four for 75, P. Thakur three for 89) and 242 for nine dec. (Jai P. Yadav 72, D. Bundela 33, N. Patwardhan 31, C. S. Pandit 36; V. Jain four for 82); Haryana 232 (P. Sharma 54, A. S. Kaypee 84; N. D. Hirwani five for 64) and 196 for six (P. Sharma 79 not out, I. Ganda 47; N. D. Hirwani three for 74). *Haryana 3 pts, Madhya Pradesh 5 pts.*

At Gymkhana Ground, Secunderabad, March 13, 14, 15, 16. Drawn. Baroda* 337 (C. C. Williams 94, H. R. Jadhav 51, T. B. Arothe 91) and 167 for six dec. (C. C. Williams 30, H. R. Jadhav 80 not out); Hyderabad 222 (T. Ravikumar 45, V. Pratap 50, S. Yadav 58 not out; T. B. Arothe six for 53) and 104 for four (A. Nandakishore 39). *Hyderabad 3 pts, Baroda 5 pts.*

Haryana 19 pts, Hyderabad 19 pts, Madhya Pradesh 18 pts, Baroda 13 pts, Bihar 11 pts. Hyderabad and Haryana qualified for the quarter-finals.

Quarter-finals

At Gymkhana Ground, Secunderabad, March 30, 31, April 1, 2, 3. Hyderabad won by 44 runs. Hyderabad* 209 (D. Manohar 44, A. Nandakishore 44; S. T. Banerjee three for 64, A. Varma four for 31) and 244 (D. Manohar 66, N. A. David 59, A. Nandakishore 30; S. T. Banerjee five for 58); Bengal 243 (S. S. Karim 69, S. J. Kalyani 39, C. Singh 51; N. P. Singh seven for 103) and 166 (S. S. Karim 59 not out, U. Chatterjee 30; S. L. V. Raju three for 45, D. Manohar four for 48).

At Ordnance Stadium, Kanpur, March 30, 31, April 1, 2, 3. Uttar Pradesh won by an innings and 34 runs. Haryana 156 (Obaid Kamal three for 37, M. Saif three for 58) and 423 (Jitender Singh 149, P. Sharma 34, R. Puri 49, Shafiq Khan 61, Dhanraj Singh 78; A. W. Zaidi four for 111); Uttar Pradesh* 613 (M. Kaif 100, Jyoti P. Yadav 51, S. A. Shukla 189, Rizwan Shamshad 44, G. K. Pandey 36, M. S. Mudgal 65, A. W. Zaidi 39, Extras 41; Dhanraj Singh three for 77, P. Jain three for 146)

Semi-finals

At Gymkhana Ground, Secunderabad, April 9, 10, 11, 12, 13. Karnataka won by one wicket. Hyderabad* 283 (G. A. Shetty 58, D. Manohar 47, V. Pratap 53, M. V. Sridhar 51; D. Ganesh five for 74, M. A. Khan three for 84) and 179 (M. V. Sridhar 35, A. Nandakishore 39; D. Ganesh four for 74); Karnataka 309 (S. Somasunder 51, J. Arun Kumar 85, F. Khaleel 38, R. Dravid 71, S. B. Joshi 48; Kanwaljit Singh seven for 62) and 157 for nine (F. Khaleel 51; Kanwaljit Singh seven for 38).

Kanwaljit Singh took 14 for 100 in the match.

At Wankhede Stadium, Mumbai, April 9, 10, 11, 12. Uttar Pradesh won by three wickets. Mumbai* 94 (J. V. Paranjpe 42, A. A. Muzumdar 31; A. W. Zaidi six for 29) and 328 (J. V. Paranjpe 83, A. A. Muzumdar 87, S. V. Bahutule 44 not out; Obaid Kamal five for 58, M. Saif three for 86); Uttar Pradesh 293 (S. A. Shukla 30, Rizwan Shamshad 64, G. K. Pandey 109; P. L. Mhambrey three for 48, N. M. Kulkarni three for 63, R. V. Pawar three for 73) and 135 for seven (G. K. Pandey 45 not out; N. M. Kulkarni four for 46).

Final

At M. Chinnaswamy Stadium, Bangalore, April 19, 20, 21, 22, 23. Drawn. Karnataka were declared champions by virtue of their first-innings lead. Uttar Pradesh* 134 (Jyoti P. Yadav 36, M. Kaif 30; S. B. Joshi four for 37) and 416 for seven (R. Sharma 65, Jyoti P. Yadav 73, S. A. Shukla 91, R. V. Sapru 39 not out, M. Kaif 62, G. K. Pandey 55; S. B. Joshi three for 112); Karnataka 617 for nine dec. (S. Somasunder 68, J. Arun Kumar 104, F. Khaleel 31, R. Dravid 215, R. V. Bharadwaj 122, S. Siriguppi 31; Obaid Kamal four for 99).

Dravid's 215 lasted 511 minutes and 346 balls and included 26 fours and two sixes. He added 257 for the fourth wicket with Bharadwaj.

RANJI TROPHY WINNERS

1934-35	Bombay	1956-57	Bombay	1978-79	Delhi
1935-36	Bombay	1957-58	Baroda	1979-80	Delhi
1936-37	Nawanagar	1958-59	Bombay	1980-81	Bombay
1937-38	Hyderabad	1959-60	Bombay	1981-82	Delhi
1938-39	Bengal	1960-61	Bombay	1982-83	Karnataka
1939-40	Maharashtra	1961-62	Bombay	1983-84	Bombay
1940-41	Maharashtra	1962-63	Bombay	1984-85	Bombay
1941-42	Bombay	1963-64	Bombay	1985-86	Delhi
1942-43	Baroda	1964-65	Bombay	1986-87	Hyderabad
1943-44	Western India	1965-66	Bombay	1987-88	Tamil Nadu
1944-45	Bombay	1966-67	Bombay	1988-89	Delhi
1945-46	Holkar	1967-68	Bombay	1989-90	Bengal
1946-47	Baroda	1968-69	Bombay	1990-91	Haryana
1947-48	Holkar	1969-70	Bombay	1991-92	Delhi
1948-49	Bombay	1970-71	Bombay	1992-93	Punjab
1949-50	Baroda	1971-72	Bombay	1993-94	Bombay
1950-51	Holkar	1972-73	Bombay	1994-95	Bombay
1951-52	Bombay	1973-74	Karnataka	1995-96	Karnataka
1952-53	Holkar	1974-75	Bombay	1996-97	Mumbai
1953-54	Bombay	1975-76	Bombay	1997-98	Karnataka
1954-55	Madras	1976-77	Bombay		
1955-56	Bombay	1977-78	Karnataka		

Bombay/Mumbai have won the Ranji Trophy 33 times, Delhi 6, Karnataka 5, Baroda and Holkar 4, Bengal, Hyderabad, Madras/Tamil Nadu and Maharashtra 2, Haryana, Nawanagar, Punjab and Western India 1.

CRICKET IN PAKISTAN, 1997-98

By ABID ALI KAZI

Fazl-e-Akbar

The Golden Jubilee season of Pakistani cricket was one of the busiest ever for the international team. Between July 1997 and April 1998, they played 11 Tests in four series, and 32 one-day internationals in eight tournaments. To commemorate the 50th anniversary of Pakistan's independence, there were two home Test series, three one-day games with neighbours India, and a quadrangular tournament with South Africa, Sri Lanka and West Indies.

Results were mixed. The high point of the season was a 3-0 whitewash of West Indies, who had not suffered such a humiliation since 1928. But, shortly before, Pakistan had lost 1-0 to South Africa, only their second defeat in a home Test series since 1980-81. The return series in South Africa was drawn, though Pakistan did win in Zimbabwe. Their one-day form was disappointing; they won against India and Zimbabwe, but reached only two finals in the larger tournaments and lost them both.

In August 1998, the coaching of the team was passed from Haroon Rashid to former captain Javed Miandad. During the season, Pakistan had got through five captains: Ramiz Raja, Saeed Anwar, Wasim Akram, Rashid Latif and Aamir Sohail. Most of these were discarded because of poor results, but the case of Wasim was especially controversial. He gave up the captaincy shortly after leading Pakistan to their triumph over West Indies, was dropped for the tour of South Africa, then reinstated by the Pakistan Cricket Board chairman, Khalid Mahmood; Salim Altaf, chairman of the selectors, resigned in protest. In September, Wasim faced further trouble when an interim PCB enquiry implicated him, together with Salim Malik and Ijaz Ahmed, in the continuing allegations of match-fixing; he furiously denied all charges. This story remained a strong undercurrent to the flow of Pakistani cricket.

On the domestic scene, the main tournaments' rules and formats were tinkered with for the umpteenth time. An experimental regulation awarded a two-run penalty for no-balls and wides – which resulted in Gujranwala conceding a world record of 99 extras in an innings to Lahore City. The semi-finals of both the Quaid-e-Azam and the Patron's Trophy were abolished, with the top two teams in the league table advancing to the final. The schedule of fixtures was altered so that the two first-class tournaments, instead of being played one after the other, with some overlap, were played in alternation: two rounds of the Quaid-e-Azam, two rounds of the Patron's Trophy, repeated until the end of the programme. The PCB said this was to make sure that the leading players would be available both to the city associations who contest the Quaid-e-Azam and to the commercial teams of the Patron's Trophy. The Pepsi Junior Under-19 championship also ran concurrently.

The first-class Grade I of the Quaid-e-Azam Trophy had been limited to eight teams the previous season, but in 1997-98 it reverted to ten because bottom-placed Bahawalpur were not relegated and two teams were promoted. Bahawalpur responded to their reprieve by springing up to third place, despite a bizarre start to the season when two rival squads, representing different factions in the Bahawalpur Cricket Association, arrived for the opening match with Karachi Blues. (Oddly enough, four years earlier Karachi Blues had been awarded a match when Bahawalpur did not turn up at all). Peshawar, next to bottom in 1996-97, made an even more striking recovery, heading the table to reach the final for the first time. But they missed out on the crown when second-placed Karachi Blues beat them on first-innings lead to regain the Trophy after a one-year gap; it was the 16th time a Karachi team had won this title. Grade II was won by Sargodha, who thus earned promotion, while Multan went down again after just one season.

In the Patron's Trophy, the 1997-98 champions, United Bank, had had to withdraw; their players were made redundant in the Prime Minister's austerity drive, though they were given golden handshakes. In their absence, Habib Bank won the Trophy for the first time in five years when they beat Allied Bank in the final. At the bottom of the table, WAPDA, the previous season's Grade II champions, went down, trading places again with PNSC, who bounced back after a year's relegation.

Allied Bank did retain the one-day Wills Cup, beating PIA in the floodlit final at Lahore. Bangladesh took part again, and Malaysia also joined in, but neither had much success. The Pepsi Junior Under-19 championship was won by Lahore City Whites, who beat Rawalpindi.

Asif Mujtaba, of Karachi Blues and PIA, was the leading run-scorer for the second season running, with 1,084, and headed the averages for the third time running, at 67.75. Azam Khan, also of Karachi Blues, and PIA, was the only other batsman to reach 1,000 runs, though Asif Mahmood of Rawalpindi and KRL, who scored 250, the highest individual innings of the season, was only 45 short. The leading wicket-taker was 17-year-old Fazl-e-Akbar of Peshawar and ADBP, who took 86 wickets at 17.65 apiece, including the best analysis of the season: nine for 116 against WAPDA. Another Peshawar player, Sajid Shah, who also appeared for Habib Bank, was close behind with 82 wickets. Bilal Rana, of Multan and Allied Bank, headed the bowling averages with 25 wickets at 12.32. For the second successive year, Wasim Yousufi of Peshawar was the leading wicket-keeper, with 31 dismissals in 11 matches – thanks largely to the 11 he made against Bahawalpur, a national record.

FIRST-CLASS AVERAGES, 1997-98

BATTING

(Qualification: 500 runs)

	M	I	NO	R	HS	100s	Avge
Asif Mujtaba (*Karachi Blues/PIA*)	14	21	5	1,084	191	2	67.75
Yousuf Youhana (*Lahore City/WAPDA*)	9	15	4	727	163*	2	66.09
Aamir Sohail (*Allied Bank*).	8	11	0	720	170	4	65.45
Shahid Afridi (*Karachi Whites/Habib Bank*). . .	10	15	1	685	123	2	48.92
Bilal Asad (*Islamabad*)	6	11	0	534	117	2	48.54
Salim Elahi (*Lahore City/Habib Bank*)	14	22	2	890	203*	2	44.50
Azam Khan (*Karachi Blues/Pakistan Customs*).	14	25	2	1,014	136	2	44.08
Asif Mahmood (*Rawalpindi/KRL*)	15	23	0	955	250	2	41.52
Akhtar Sarfraz (*Peshawar/National Bank*)	16	25	6	750	125	2	39.47
Mohammad Wasim (*Rawalpindi/ADBP*)	11	15	2	501	165	2	38.53
Mujahid Hameed (*Rawalpindi/ADBP*)	12	18	3	556	133*	1	37.06

	M	I	NO	R	HS	100s	Avge
Wajahatullah Wasti (*Peshawar/Allied Bank*) . . .	14	23	4	690	87	0	36.31
Shakeel Ahmed (*Gujranwala/Habib Bank*)	14	23	0	818	148	2	35.56
Manzoor Akhtar (*Karachi Blues/Allied Bank*) . .	12	18	2	558	117*	2	34.87
Aamer Hanif (*Karachi Whites/Allied Bank*) . . .	13	21	2	650	153	2	34.21
Taimur Khan (*Peshawar/Allied Bank*)	14	23	5	612	111	1	34.00
Aamer Bashir (*Bahawalpur/Pakistan Customs*) .	14	24	2	744	173*	2	33.81
Naseer Ahmed (*Rawalpindi/KRL*)	16	24	2	729	152*	1	33.13
Farhan Adil (*Karachi Whites/Habib Bank*)	14	18	1	544	100*	1	32.00
Zafar Iqbal (*Karachi Blues/National Bank*) . . .	13	18	2	511	110	1	31.93
Rana Qayyum (*Gujranwala/Pakistan Customs*) .	14	26	2	690	83*	0	28.75
Murtaza Hussain (*Bahawalpur/KRL*)	15	22	3	530	67*	0	27.89
Sohail Jaffer (*Karachi Blues/PIA*)	11	20	1	524	100	1	27.57
Zahoor Elahi (*Lahore City/ADBP*)	13	21	1	529	78	0	26.45
Azhar Shafiq (*Bahawalpur/Pakistan Customs*) .	17	31	1	671	104*	1	22.36

* *Signifies not out.*

BOWLING

(Qualification: 25 wickets)

	O	M	R	W	BB	5W/i	Avge
Bilal Rana (*Multan/Allied Bank*)	136.1	48	308	25	6-29	4	12.32
Aqib Javed (*Allied Bank*)	222.2	43	661	42	7-77	4	15.73
S. John (*Islamabad*)	156.2	47	451	28	6-19	2	16.10
Wasim Akram (*Lahore City/PIA*)	178.1	52	464	28	4-42	0	16.57
Fazl-e-Akbar (*Peshawar/ADBP*)	427.2	68	1,518	86	9-116	7	17.65
Mohammad Akram (*Rawalpindi/Allied Bank*) . .	162.4	36	607	34	7-73	3	17.85
Mohammad Zahid (*Bahawalpur/Allied Bank*) . .	391	149	786	42	6-50	2	18.71
Naeem Ashraf (*Lahore City/National Bank*) . . .	375	93	1,016	54	7-41	4	18.81
Sajid Shah (*Peshawar/Habib Bank*)	497.5	93	1,607	82	6-56	7	19.59
Shahid Nazir (*Faisalabad/Habib Bank*)	142.2	22	532	27	6-76	2	19.70
Murtaza Hussain (*Bahawalpur/KRL*)	633	176	1,570	76	7-95	7	20.65
Ali Gauhar (*Karachi Blues/PIA*)	353	63	1,164	56	6-76	3	20.78
Shakeel Ahmed (*Rawalpindi/KRL*)	478	150	1,113	50	7-91	4	22.26
Mohammad Asif (*Lahore City/ADBP*)	349.3	100	765	34	4-19	0	22.50
Jaffer Nazir (*Rawalpindi/KRL*)	368.3	86	1,177	52	7-42	4	22.63
Azhar Shafiq (*Bahawalpur/Pakistan Customs*) .	391.4	85	1,162	51	5-23	2	22.78
Zafar Iqbal (*Karachi Blues/National Bank*) . . .	252.5	43	908	39	6-18	2	23.28
Kashif Ibrahim (*Karachi Whites*)	193.2	38	688	29	5-63	2	23.72
Ali Raza (*Karachi Blues/Pakistan Customs*) . . .	244.1	40	740	31	7-117	1	23.87
Akram Raza (*Faisalabad/Habib Bank*)	272.3	58	697	29	7-102	1	24.03
Nadeem Ashraf (*Faisalabad/Pakistan Customs*)	172.5	30	657	27	7-59	2	24.33
Nadeem Khan (*Karachi Blues/PIA*)	354.2	78	968	39	5-36	2	24.82
Lal Faraz (*Karachi Blues/Pakistan Customs*) . .	198.2	33	725	29	6-63	1	25.00
Shabbir Ahmed (*Multan/WAPDA*)	277.3	79	780	31	5-31	1	25.16
Ata-ur-Rehman (*Lahore City/Allied Bank*) . . .	306.4	68	1,054	41	7-20	1	25.70
Arshad Khan (*Peshawar/Allied Bank*)	551.1	136	1,294	50	4-25	0	25.88
Mushtaq Ahmed (*Pakistan*)	226.2	58	679	26	5-35	2	26.11
Naeem Akhtar (*Rawalpindi/KRL*)	321.1	74	912	33	6-52	2	27.63
Ali Hussain Rizvi (*Karachi Blues/Pak.Customs*)	407.3	97	1,117	39	6-57	3	28.64
Shoaib Akhtar (*Rawalpindi/ADBP*)	298.3	38	1,278	42	6-136	4	30.42
Abdur Razzaq (*Lahore City/KRL*)	259	28	1,214	38	5-73	1	31.94

QUAID-E-AZAM TROPHY, 1997-98

	Played	Won	Lost	Drawn	1st-inns Points	Points
Peshawar.............	9	5	0	4	14	64
Karachi Blues..........	9	5	1	3	10	60
Bahawalpur...........	9	5	2	2	8	58
Lahore City...........	9	3	1	5	8	38
Karachi Whites........	9	3	3	3	4	34
Rawalpindi...........	9	1	0	8	14	24
Gujranwala...........	8	1	5	2	4	14
Faisalabad...........	9	1	5	3	4	14
Islamabad............	8	1	3	4	2	12
Multan..............	9	1	6	2	2	12

Note: The match between Islamabad and Gujranwala was abandoned.

Outright win = 10 pts; lead on first innings in a won or drawn game = 2 pts.

Final: Karachi Blues beat Peshawar by virtue of their first-innings lead.

Under Pakistan Cricket Board playing conditions, two extras are scored for every no-ball or wide bowled whether scored off or not. Any runs scored off the bat are credited to the batsman, while byes and leg-byes are counted as no-balls or wides, in accordance with Laws 24.9 and 25.6, in addition to the initial penalty.

In the following scores, * by the name of a team indicates that they won the toss.

At Bohranwala Ground, Faisalabad, October 3, 4, 5, 6. Peshawar won by eight wickets. Faisalabad 136 (Fazl-e-Akbar four for 28, Arshad Khan four for 37) and 167 (Wasim Haider 35, Extras 30; Fazl-e-Akbar six for 60); Peshawar* 246 (Jahangir Khan, sen. 52, Akhtar Sarfraz 32, Wajahatullah Wasti 72; Akram Raza seven for 102, Naved Nazir three for 61) and 58 for two. *Peshawar 12 pts.*

At Municipal Stadium, Gujranwala, October 3, 4, 5, 6. Drawn. Gujranwala 240 for seven dec. (Zahid Fazal 41 retired hurt, Majid Saeed 68; Mohammad Siddiq three for 46, Nadeem Naazar three for 54); Multan* 135 for eight (Arshad Hayat 31, Ali Rafi 53 not out; Aleem Dar three for 42, Aamer Wasim four for 20).
The second and third days were lost to rain.

At Chaudhry Rehmat Ali Cricket Ground, Islamabad, October 3, 4, 5, 6. Drawn. Islamabad 275 (Qaiser Mahmood 109 not out, Kamran Siddiqi 30, Extras 43; Jaffer Nazir three for 58, Shakeel Ahmed four for 71); Rawalpindi* 276 for three (Naved Ashraf 54, Asif Mahmood 77, Mujahid Hameed 63 not out, Naseer Ahmed 58 not out; Alamgir Khan three for 72). *Rawalpindi 2 pts.*

At Asghar Ali Shah Stadium, Karachi, October 3, 4, 5, 6. Drawn. Bahawalpur* 401 (Naved Latif 32, Sajid Ali 71, Bilal Moin 91, Aamer Bashir 94, Rehan Rafiq 34 not out, Tariq Sarwar 30, Extras 37; Lal Faraz four for 69) and 64 for three; Karachi Blues 395 (Shoaib Mohammad 45, Sohail Jaffer 32, Asif Mujtaba 119, Zafar Iqbal 110; Murtaza Hussain five for 114). *Bahawalpur 2 pts.*

Due to a dispute within the Bahawalpur Cricket Association, two Bahawalpur squads arrived; after consulting the PCB, the match referee chose the team managed by Ghulam Abbas. There was further controversy because they fielded Sajid Ali, a Karachi Blues reserve.

At LCCA Ground, Lahore, October 3, 4, 5, 6. Drawn. Karachi Whites 149 (Aamer Hanif 48, Extras 32; Wasim Akram three for 30, Mohammad Asif four for 22); Lahore City* 104 for two (Zahoor Elahi 35).
Wasim Akram played his first first-class match for Lahore City since 1985-86. There was no play on the last two days due to rain.

At Bohranwala Ground, Faisalabad, October 10, 11, 12, 13. Drawn. Faisalabad 262 (Fida Hussain 99, Shahid Nazir 35, Extras 53; Shoaib Akhtar three for 101, Jaffer Nazir four for 57); Rawalpindi* 284 for five (Sabih Azhar 31, Naseer Ahmed 152 not out, Shahid Javed 41). *Rawalpindi 2 pts.*

At Municipal Stadium, Gujranwala, October 10, 11, 12, 13. Karachi Blues won by eight wickets. Gujranwala 211 (Zahid Fazal 42, Extras 52; Ali Gauhar four for 65, Zafar Iqbal five for 64) and 151 (Extras 32; Ali Gauhar three for 44, Zafar Iqbal three for 25); Karachi Blues* 239 (Basit Ali 55, Ahmed Zeeshan 42, Extras 44; Ameem Abbas four for 101, Shoaib Malik four for 66) and 127 for two (Shadab Kabir 55, Sohail Jaffer 31 not out). *Karachi Blues 12 pts.*

At Chaudhry Rehmat Ali Cricket Ground, Islamabad, October 10, 11, 12, 13. Drawn. Peshawar 168 (Hameed Gul 59 not out; Ehsan Butt three for 23, Fahad Khan three for 26) and 238 for five (Jahangir Khan, sen. 45, Abdus Salam 60, Taimur Khan 57 not out); Islamabad* 203 (Naved Ahmed 39, Asif Mahmood 38 not out, Alamgir Khan 33, Extras 40; Shahid Hussain seven for 55). *Islamabad 2 pts.*

At National Stadium, Karachi, October 10, 11, 12, 13. Karachi Whites won by ten wickets. Bahawalpur 402 (Azhar Shafiq 42, Aamer Bashir 122, Saifullah 80, Extras 43; Baqar Rizvi five for 86) and 202 (Faisal Elahi 46, Murtaza Hussain 64; Shahid Mahboob eight for 77); Karachi Whites* 521 for three dec. (Shahid Afridi 118, Hasan Raza 204 not out, Iqbal Saleem 70, Farhan Adil 100 not out) and 86 for no wkt (Shahid Afridi 62 not out). *Karachi Whites 12 pts.*

Shahid Afridi scored his 118 in 72 balls. Hasan Raza's 204 not out lasted 450 minutes and 315 balls and included 24 fours and one six. He was the youngest player to score a double-hundred, at 15 years 215 days.

At Montgomery Cricket Club Ground, Sahiwal, October 10, 11, 12, 13. Drawn. Multan 152 (Aqeel Aziz 34, Extras 43; Abdur Razzaq four for 52, Sajjad Akbar three for 33); Lahore City* 76 for eight (Azhar Abbas four for 29).

There was no play on the first two days due to rain.

At Mahmood Stadium, Rahimyar Khan, October 31, November 1, 2. Bahawalpur won by six wickets. Multan* 144 (Mohammad Zahid three for 58, Murtaza Hussain six for 44) and 177 (Arshad Hayat 49, Masroor Hussain 38; Mohammad Zahid four for 47, Murtaza Hussain four for 40); Bahawalpur 183 (Naved Latif 47, Kamran Hussain 40; Shakir Qayyum six for 53) and 139 for four (Javed Sami 30, Naved Latif 53 not out; Shakir Qayyum three for 62). *Bahawalpur 12 pts.*

At Municipal Stadium, Gujranwala, October 31, November 1, 2. Lahore City won by four wickets. Gujranwala 129 (Rana Qayyum 33, Extras 32; Abdur Razzaq four for 40, Naeem Ashraf three for 29, Irfan Fazil three for 44) and 431 (Shakeel Ahmed 89, Inam-ul-Haq 66, Majid Saeed 107, Ameem Abbas 37, Extras 73; Abdur Razzaq four for 182, Mohammad Asif three for 35); Lahore City* 502 for eight dec. (Salim Elahi 81, Shahid Nawaz 33, Naeem Ashraf 139, Abdur Razzaq 103 not out, Extras 99; Tahir Mughal six for 83) and 60 for six (Tahir Mughal four for 29). *Lahore City 12 pts.*

In Lahore City's first innings, Naeem Ashraf and Abdur Razzaq added 229 for the seventh wicket. In the same innings, Gujranwala conceded a world record 99 extras – b 9, l-b 10, w 16, n-b 64 – though the figure was inflated by experimental rules awarding two runs each for wides and no-balls. They conceded only three in the second innings, to total 102, while Lahore conceded 105 extras over two innings. Tahir Mughal took ten wickets on first-class debut.

At Chaudhry Rehmat Ali Cricket Ground, Islamabad, October 31, November 1, 2, 3. Drawn. Islamabad 195 (Ghaffar Kazmi 103; Shahid Nazir six for 76, Nadeem Ashraf three for 38) and 350 for two (Qaiser Mahmood 40, Ehsan Butt 102 not out, Atif Rauf 155 not out, Extras 37); Faisalabad* 196 (Mohammad Nawaz, sen. 100; S. John four for 56, Fahad Khan four for 64). *Faisalabad 2 pts.*

At Asghar Ali Shah Stadium, Karachi, October 31, November 1, 2, 3. Karachi Blues won by eight wickets. Karachi Whites* 183 (Mohammad Farrukh 40, Hasan Raza 34, Extras 33; Ali Hussain Rizvi five for 46) and 291 (Hasan Raza 43, Nasir Ali 47, Iqbal Sikandar 41, Mohammad Shakeel 31 not out, Extras 48; Ali Raza four for 80); Karachi Blues 247 (Asim Kamal 81, Rizwan Qureshi 57, Extras 34; Kashif Ibrahim five for 63) and 230 for two (Kashif Ahmed 73 not out, Shadab Kabir 54, Azam Khan 82 not out). *Karachi Blues 12 pts.*

At Gymkhana Club Ground, Peshawar, October 31, November 1, 2, 3. Drawn. Rawalpindi* 104 (Extras 37; Sajid Shah five for 44) and 415 (Naseer Ahmed 76, Shahid Javed 100, Tasawwar Hussain 39, Mujahid Hameed 43, Shakeel Ahmed 43, Extras 69; Fazl-e-Akbar four for 103); Peshawar 321 (Nadeem Younis 30, Akhtar Sarfraz 125, Wajahatullah Wasti 50, Hameed Gul 36, Extras 42; Shoaib Akhtar five for 127) and 116 for four (Wajahatullah Wasti 52 not out). *Peshawar 2 pts.*

At Mahmood Stadium, Rahimyar Khan, November 7, 8, 9. Bahawalpur won by six wickets. Lahore City 252 (Shahid Anwar 33, Mansoor Rana 61, Abdur Razzaq 51; Mohammad Zahid six for 52) and 162 (Zahoor Elahi 33, Mansoor Rana 38; Murtaza Hussain five for 62, Mohammad Zahid four for 30); Bahawalpur* 229 (Azhar Shafiq 38, Aamer Bashir 82, Extras 41) and 190 for four (Azhar Shafiq 61, Sajid Ali 35, Aamer Bashir 50 not out). *Bahawalpur 10 pts.*

At National Stadium, Karachi, November 7, 8, 9. Karachi Whites won by eight wickets. Islamabad 142 (Atif Rauf 32, Aaley Haider 37, Extras 33; Shahid Mahboob five for 40) and 261 (Bilal Asad 73, Atif Rauf 46, Azhar Mahmood 64, Extras 37; Shahid Mahboob three for 74, Aamer Hanif three for 55); Karachi Whites* 293 (Farhan Adil 70, Aamer Hanif 33, Mohammad Javed 45, Extras 55; Azhar Mahmood three for 85, S. John three for 92) and 111 for two (Saeed Azad 41 not out). *Karachi Whites 12 pts.*

At Montgomery Cricket Club Ground, Sahiwal, November 7, 8, 9. Multan won by eight wickets. Faisalabad 135 (Fida Hussain 55 not out; Nadeem Iqbal three for 32, Imran Idrees six for 32) and 217 (Mohammad Salim 45, Fida Hussain 40, Ijaz Ahmed, jun. 37, Nadeem Ashraf 31; Imran Idrees three for 74, Bilal Rana five for 46); Multan* 288 (Arshad Hayat 34, Tariq Mahboob 55, Masroor Hussain 37, Bilal Rana 35, Mohammad Shafiq 46; Mohammad Wasim four for 51, Naved Nazir three for 62) and 65 for two (Arshad Hayat 35). *Multan 12 pts.*

At Gymkhana Club Ground, Peshawar, November 7, 8, 9. Peshawar won by eight wickets. Gujranwala 110 (Fazl-e-Akbar five for 44) and 231 (Shakeel Ahmed 56, Ameem Abbas 35, Khalid Mahmood 41 not out; Fazl-e-Akbar three for 85, Sajid Shah six for 85); Peshawar* 280 (Wasim Yousufi 103, Shahid Hussain 66, Extras 40; Zahid Saeed three for 51, Shoaib Malik three for 28) and 62 for two. *Peshawar 12 pts.*

At Pindi Cricket Stadium, Rawalpindi, November 7, 8, 9, 10. Drawn. Rawalpindi 278 (Mohammad Wasim 111 not out, Jaffer Nazir 36, Extras 48; Ali Gauhar three for 57, Lal Faraz three for 92); Karachi Blues* 195 (Asif Mujtaba 42, Extras 48; Jaffer Nazir seven for 42). *Rawalpindi 2 pts.*
   There was no play on the last two days due to rain.

At Mahmood Stadium, Rahimyar Khan, November 29, 30, December 1, 2. Bahawalpur won by 39 runs. Bahawalpur* 183 (Javed Sami 50, Rehan Rafiq 51; Alamgir Khan three for 50, Khalid Zafar five for 43) and 215 (Azhar Shafiq 34, Murtaza Hussain 42, Mohammad Zahid 41; Fahad Khan three for 55, Alamgir Khan three for 63, Khalid Zafar three for 68); Islamabad 250 (Zaheer Abbasi 30, Asif Ali 47, Qaiser Mahmood 64, Shakeel Sajjad 31; Murtaza Hussain seven for 110, Mohammad Zahid three for 83) and 109 (Zaheer Abbasi 46; Murtaza Hussain three for 17, Mohammad Altaf three for 21, Mohammad Zahid four for 40). *Bahawalpur 10 pts.*

At Iqbal Stadium, Faisalabad, November 29, 30, December 1. Faisalabad won by nine wickets. Faisalabad 299 (Mohammad Nawaz, sen. 34, Mohammad Ramzan 46, Fida Hussain 72 not out, Bilal Ahmed 52, Shahid Nazir 32, Extras 48; Tahir Mughal five for 69) and 61 for one (Ijaz Mahmood 36 not out); Gujranwala* 147 (Ansaar Ahmed 31, Extras 34; Shahid Nazir four for 57, Saadat Gul five for 36) and 207 (Ameem Abbas 50, Extras 34; Shahid Nazir three for 46, Saadat Gul three for 56). *Faisalabad 12 pts.*

At Gaddafi Stadium, Lahore, November 29, 30, December 1, 2. Lahore City won by 176 runs. Lahore City 278 (Yousuf Youhana 44, Naeem Ashraf 74, Extras 74; Ali Gauhar five for 72) and 236 (Yousuf Youhana 60, Naeem Ashraf 37; Ali Gauhar four for 70, Zafar Iqbal three for 68); Karachi Blues* 194 (Mahmood Hamid 33, Zafar Iqbal 34, Ali Raza 30 not out, Extras 34; Ata-ur-Rehman three for 87, Naeem Ashraf six for 56) and 144 (Shadab Kabir 34, Ghulam Ali 33, Extras 32; Ata-ur-Rehman three for 60, Naeem Ashraf four for 33, Shahid Nawaz three for eight). *Lahore City 12 pts.*

At Arbab Niaz Stadium, Peshawar, November 29, 30. Peshawar won by an innings and 12 runs. Multan 92 (Fazl-e-Akbar three for 22, Sajid Shah five for 46) and 113 (Fazl-e-Akbar five for 61, Arshad Khan three for 12); Peshawar* 217 (Abdus Salam 35, Wajahatullah Wasti 81, Taimur Khan 30; Rehan Adil three for 54, Shakir Qayyum three for 29). *Peshawar 12 pts.*

At KRL Cricket Ground, Rawalpindi, November 29, 30, December 1, 2. Drawn. Rawalpindi 337 (Asif Mahmood 101, Mohammad Nadeem 125, Extras 30; Asim Zaidi five for 78) and 273 (Arif Butt 85, Mohammad Nadeem 30, Sabih Azhar 45, Naeem Akhtar 36; Kashif Ibrahim three for 74, Ahmer Saeed three for 70); Karachi Whites* 286 (Shahid Afridi 123, Farhan Adil 47; Mohammad Akram seven for 73) and 60 for one. *Rawalpindi 2 pts.*

At Mahmood Stadium, Rahimyar Khan, December 6, 7, 8, 9. Bahawalpur won by an innings and 23 runs. Gujranwala 275 (Shehzad Malik 59, Hasan Adnan 64, Iqbal Zahoor 62 not out, Extras 32; Murtaza Hussain seven for 95) and 139 (Hasan Adnan 34, Iqbal Zahoor 40; Azhar Shafiq three for 25, Murtaza Hussain five for 66); Bahawalpur* 437 (Javed Sami 45, Bilal Hashmi 35, Aamer Bashir 173 not out, Rehan Rafiq 69, Murtaza Hussain 67; Tahir Mughal three for 127, Zulfiqar Butt three for 98). *Bahawalpur 12 pts.*

At UBL Sports Complex, Karachi, December 6, 7, 8, 9. Karachi Blues won by 99 runs. Karachi Blues 225 (Asim Kamal 37, Asif Mujtaba 86, Extras 32; S. John three for 46, Ehsan Butt three for 38) and 270 (Azam Khan 51, Majid Mujtaba 44, Zafar Iqbal 76, Extras 31; S. John six for 99); Islamabad* 204 (Bilal Asad 78, Extras 33; Ali Gauhar five for 59, Zafar Iqbal three for 47) and 192 (Ali Raza 64, Bilal Asad 48; Lal Faraz six for 63). *Karachi Blues 12 pts.*

At LCCA Ground, Lahore, December 6, 7, 8, 9. Lahore City won by an innings and 72 runs. Lahore City* 332 (Zahoor Elahi 53, Mansoor Rana 30, Shahid Nawaz 58, Iftikhar Hussain 48, Javed Hayat 59; Ijaz Mahmood three for 74, Shahid Ali three for 54); Faisalabad 173 (Javed Iqbal 46; Mohammad Asif four for 31, Javed Hayat three for 28) and 87 (Mohammad Asif four for 19, Javed Hayat three for four). *Lahore City 12 pts.*

At Montgomery Cricket Club Ground, Sahiwal, December 6, 7, 8, 9. Rawalpindi won by 16 runs. Rawalpindi 158 (Asif Mahmood 68, Mohammad Nadeem 38; Azhar Abbas three for 41, Bilal Rana six for 29) and 209 (Asif Mahmood 41, Shahid Tanvir 49; Azhar Abbas four for 44, Bilal Rana three for 53); Multan* 151 (Mohammad Shafiq 40; Naeem Akhtar six for 52) and 200 (Tariq Mahboob 36, Majid Inayat 37; Shakeel Ahmed six for 72). *Rawalpindi 12 pts.*

At Arbab Niaz Stadium, Peshawar, December 6, 7, 8. Peshawar won by seven wickets. Karachi Whites 295 (Shahid Afridi 88, Mohammad Masroor 40, Kashif Ibrahim 48; Fazl-e-Akbar three for 77, Arshad Khan four for 97) and 110 (Mohammad Shakeel 34; Fazl-e-Akbar five for 54, Arshad Khan three for 23); Peshawar* 342 (Taimur Khan 111, Sajid Shah 43, Shahid Hussain 55, Fazl-e-Akbar 32 not out; Kashif Ibrahim five for 119, Asim Zaidi five for 109) and 67 for three. *Peshawar 12 pts.*

At Iqbal Stadium, Faisalabad, December 27, 28, 29, 30. Drawn. Faisalabad 298 (Javed Iqbal 43, Ijaz Ahmed, jun. 94, Saadat Gul 39; Kashif Ibrahim four for 52); Karachi Whites* 25 for no wkt. *There was no play on the first two days due to rain.*

At Chaudhry Rehmat Ali Ground, Islamabad, December 27, 28, 29, 30. Islamabad v Gujranwala. Abandoned.
    Rain prevented any play.

At National Stadium, Karachi, December 27, 28, 29, 30. Karachi Blues won by ten wickets. Multan 190 (Mohammad Shafiq 71, Extras 32; Ali Gauhar three for 78, Lal Faraz three for 46, Zafar Iqbal four for 42) and 230 (Majid Inayat 55, Nadeem Iqbal 39, Extras 40; Ali Gauhar four for 43, Lal Faraz three for 90); Karachi Blues* 382 (Asif Mujtaba 97, Azam Khan 119, Kamal Merchant 67 not out, Extras 36; Nadeem Iqbal four for 98, Shabbir Ahmed three for 84) and 39 for no wkt. *Karachi Blues 12 pts.*

At Arbab Niaz Stadium, Peshawar, December 27, 28, 29, 30. Drawn. Lahore City 126 (Fazl-e-Akbar three for 44, Sajid Shah five for 41) and 120 for three (Javed Hayat 42 not out); Peshawar* 204 for six dec. (Taimur Khan 52 not out, Wasim Yousufi 37 not out, Extras 31; Naeem Ashraf five for 88). *Peshawar 2 pts.*

At Pindi Cricket Stadium, Rawalpindi, December 27, 28, 29, 30. Drawn. Bahawalpur 244 (Rehan Rafiq 72 not out, Mohammad Tayyab 38, Mohammad Zahid 45, Extras 31; Jaffer Nazir six for 94, Naeem Akhtar three for 64) and 26 for one; Rawalpindi* 342 (Arif Butt 54, Asif Mahmood 63, Mohammad Wasim 33, Naseer Ahmed 35, Sabih Azhar 41, Extras 66; Azhar Shafiq three for 102, Aamer Bashir three for 32). *Rawalpindi 2 pts.*

At Mahmood Stadium, Rahimyar Khan, January 3, 4, 5, 6. Bahawalpur won by one wicket. Faisalabad* 141 (Mohammad Nawaz, sen. 37, Umar Tanvir 35; Mohammad Altaf three for 42, Mohammad Zahid six for 50) and 303 (Mohammad Ramzan 94, Mohammad Nawaz, jun. 61; Azhar Shafiq three for 41, Mohammad Altaf three for 58); Bahawalpur 171 (Mohammad Wasim four for 58) and 275 for nine (Azhar Shafiq 104 not out, Mohammad Tayyab 34, Rehan Rafiq 54; Farooq Iqbal three for 43, Mohammad Nawaz, jun. three for 39). *Bahawalpur 12 pts.*

At Municipal Stadium, Gujranwala, January 3, 4, 5, 6. Drawn. Rawalpindi* 211 (Shakeel Ahmed 32 not out, Extras 74; Asadullah Butt three for 46, Shafiq Ahmed three for 36) and 268 for eight (Asif Mahmood 87, Naeem Akhtar 30, Extras 33; Tahir Mughal three for 78); Gujranwala 220 (Shehzad Malik 69, Hasan Adnan 64 not out; Mohammad Akram three for 73, Shakeel Ahmed five for 41). *Gujranwala 2 pts.*

At Chaudhry Rehmat Ali Ground, Islamabad, January 3, 4, 5, 6. Drawn. Islamabad* 274 (Bilal Asad 36, Abdul Basit 41, Azhar Mahmood 52, Extras 42; Mohammad Asif four for 70, Shahid Mahmood four for 58) and 275 for eight (Bilal Asad 105, Ghaffar Kazmi 58; Javed Hayat three for 42); Lahore City 430 (Salim Elahi 113, Yousuf Youhana 120, Shahid Nawaz 72, Mohammad Asif 33 not out, Extras 44; Azhar Mahmood five for 115). *Lahore City 2 pts.*

At Asghar Ali Shah Stadium, Karachi, January 3, 4, 5, 6. Drawn. Peshawar* 472 (Asmatullah Mohmand 63, Jahangir Khan, sen. 175, Taimur Khan 43, Arshad Khan 50 not out, Extras 47; Nadeem Khan four for 112, Ali Hussain Rizvi three for 155) and 92 for five; Karachi Blues 480 (Ali Naqvi 38, Manzoor Akhtar 47, Asif Mujtaba 191, Azam Khan 74, Rashid Latif 91; Sajid Shah four for 120, Arshad Khan three for 121). *Karachi Blues 2 pts.*

At National Stadium, Karachi, January 3, 4, 5, 6. Karachi Whites won by five wickets. Multan 214 (Arshad Hayat 31, Mohammad Shafiq 70; Arif Mahmood four for 54) and 241 (Arshad Hayat 46, Mohammad Shafiq 48, Tariq Mahboob 31, Nadeem Iqbal 35; Kashif Ibrahim three for 48, Shahid Afridi five for 53); Karachi Whites* 128 (Shahid Afridi 44, Farhan Adil 34; Shabbir Ahmed four for 33, Imran Idrees three for 23) and 328 for five (Farhan Adil 95, Hasan Raza 54, Aamer Hanif 113 not out, Iqbal Imam 55). *Karachi Whites 10 pts.*

At National Stadium, Karachi, January 17, 18, 19. Karachi Blues won by six wickets. Faisalabad 262 (Fida Hussain 57, Abdur Rehman 38, Extras 47; Lal Faraz three for 36, Nadeem Khan five for 36) and 132 (Zafar Iqbal six for 18); Karachi Blues* 157 (Basit Ali 30, Zafar Iqbal 57, Extras 48; Shahid Nazir three for 47, Saeed Ajmal five for four) and 238 for four (Ali Naqvi 43, Munir-ul-Haq 60, Basit Ali 53 not out, Extras 35). *Karachi Blues 10 pts.*
In Karachi Blues' first innings, Saeed Ajmal's bowling analysis was 4.5–3–4–5. Faisalabad's Shehzad Nazir took a wicket with his first ball in first-class cricket.

At Faisal Base Sports Ground, Karachi, January 17, 18, 19. Gujranwala won by five wickets. Karachi Whites 153 (Shahid Naqi 34, Farhan Adil 31; Aamer Wasim four for 39, Abdur Rehman four for 59) and 186 (Farhan Adil 44, Aamer Hanif 37, Irfanullah 48 not out; Aamer Wasim six for 80); Gujranwala* 224 (Hasan Adnan 93; Taufeeq Badaruddin three for 54, Tahir Andy four for 64) and 116 for five (Hasan Adnan 43 not out; Taufeeq Badaruddin three for 45). *Gujranwala 12 pts.*
Faisal Base Sports Ground became the 69th first-class ground in Pakistan and the 15th in Karachi. Three brothers – Aamer, Abid and Rashid Hanif – played for Karachi Whites.

At Montgomery Cricket Club Ground, Sahiwal, January 17, 18, 19, 20. Islamabad won by 99 runs. Islamabad 123 (Bilal Asad 51; Waqar Younis six for 16) and 307 (Bilal Asad 117, Khalid Zafar 54, Zaheer Abbasi 36, Extras 35; Shabbir Ahmed three for 57); Multan* 264 (Arshad Hayat 59, Mohammad Shafiq 30, Bilal Rana 78, Extras 38; S. John three for 57, Taimur Ali four for 84) and 67 (S. John six for 19, Taimur Ali three for 28). *Islamabad 10 pts.*
Multan wicket-keeper Mohammad Shafiq made four catches and two stumpings in Islamabad's first innings and nine dismissals in the match.

At Arbab Niaz Stadium, Peshawar, January 17, 18, 19, 20. Peshawar won by 35 runs. Peshawar 205 (Wajahatullah Wasti 87, Sajid Shah 30 not out; Azhar Shafiq five for 25) and 211 for nine dec. (Akhtar Sarfraz 103 not out, Arshad Khan 31; Azhar Shafiq four for 78, Kamran Hussain four for 79); Bahawalpur* 190 (Bilal Moin 72 not out; Sajid Shah three for 74, Waqar Ahmed six for 45) and 191 (Sher Ali 42, Zia-ul-Hasan 33; Sajid Shah four for 51, Waqar Ahmed four for 64). *Peshawar 12 pts.*

Peshawar wicket-keeper Wasim Yousufi set a national record with 11 dismissals (all caught) in the match – six in the first innings and five in the second. Bahawalpur wicket-keeper Saifullah also took five catches in Peshawar's first innings.

At KRL Cricket Ground, Rawalpindi, January 17, 18, 19, 20. Drawn. Rawalpindi 588 for six dec. (Asif Mahmood 250, Mohammad Wasim 165, Naseer Ahmed 44, Extras 65; Naeem Ashraf three for 147) and 127 for five (Azeem Mansoor 32; Naeem Ashraf three for 55); Lahore City* 264 (Salim Elahi 88, Faisal Butt 41, Naeem Ashraf 33; Shoaib Akhtar five for 95, Shakeel Ahmed three for 71). *Rawalpindi 2 pts.*

Asif Mahmood's 250 lasted 486 minutes and 358 balls and included 27 fours and one six. He added 328 runs for Rawalpindi's third wicket with Mohammad Wasim.

Final

At National Stadium, Karachi, March 1, 2, 3, 4, 5. Drawn. Karachi Blues were declared champions by virtue of their first-innings lead. Karachi Blues 394 (Shoaib Mohammad 66, Azam Khan 136, Zafar Iqbal 46, Extras 51; Kabir Khan four for 73, Humayun Hussain three for 104, Arshad Khan three for 110) and 287 for seven dec. (Shadab Kabir 35, Sohail Jaffer 100, Manzoor Akhtar 58 not out, Zafar Iqbal 41; Waqar Ahmed three for 103, Arshad Khan three for 72); Peshawar* 211 (Moin-ul-Atiq 35, Wajahatullah Wasti 48, Wasim Yousufi 60; Ali Gauhar four for 67, Nadeem Khan four for 41) and 153 for three (Wasim Yousufi 30, Asmatullah Mohmand 47 not out, Moin-ul-Atiq 55).

QUAID-E-AZAM TROPHY WINNERS

1953-54 Bahawalpur	1972-73 Railways	1985-86 Karachi
1954-55 Karachi	1973-74 Railways	1986-87 National Bank
1956-57 Punjab	1974-75 Punjab A	1987-88 PIA
1957-58 Bahawalpur	1975-76 National Bank	1988-89 ADBP
1958-59 Karachi	1976-77 United Bank	1989-90 PIA
1959-60 Karachi	1977-78 Habib Bank	1990-91 Karachi Whites
1961-62 Karachi Blues	1978-79 National Bank	1991-92 Karachi Whites
1962-63 Karachi A	1979-80 PIA	1992-93 Karachi Whites
1963-64 Karachi Blues	1980-81 United Bank	1993-94 Lahore City
1964-65 Karachi Blues	1981-82 National Bank	1994-95 Karachi Blues
1966-67 Karachi	1982-83 United Bank	1995-96 Karachi Blues
1968-69 Lahore	1983-84 National Bank	1996-97 Lahore City
1969-70 PIA	1984-85 United Bank	1997-98 Karachi Blues
1970-71 Karachi Blues		

PCB PATRON'S TROPHY, 1997-98

	Played	Won	Lost	Drawn	1st-inns Points	Points
Allied Bank.	7	4	2	1	6	46
Habib Bank.	7	2	1	4	8	28
National Bank	7	2	0	5	6	26
KRL	7	1	1	5	10	20
PIA	7	1	1	5	6	16
ADBP	7	1	2	4	2	12
Pakistan Customs	7	1	5	1	0	10
WAPDA	7	0	0	7	6	6

Outright win = 10 pts; lead on first innings in a won or drawn game = 2 pts.

Final: Habib Bank beat Allied Bank by 160 runs.

Under Pakistan Cricket Board playing conditions, two extras are scored for every no-ball or wide bowled whether scored off or not. Any runs scored off the bat are credited to the batsman, while byes and leg-byes are counted as no-balls or wides, in accordance with Laws 24.9 and 25.6, in addition to the initial penalty.

In the following scores, * by the name of a team indicates that they won the toss.

At National Stadium, Karachi, October 17, 18, 19, 20. Drawn. National Bank 309 (Shahid Anwar 41, Akhtar Sarfraz 63, Mohammad Javed 46, Extras 67; Shahid Nazir five for 100) and 223 for seven (Shahid Anwar 106 not out, Naeem Ashraf 46; Akram Raza three for 54); Habib Bank* 446 (Shakeel Ahmed 132, Asadullah Butt 58, Salim Malik 124, Extras 64; Naeem Ashraf four for 97). *Habib Bank 2 pts.*

At KRL Cricket Ground, Rawalpindi, October 17, 18, 19, 20. Drawn. ADBP 181 (Manzoor Elahi 81 not out, Extras 30; Abdur Razzaq five for 73, Murtaza Hussain four for 17) and 276 for two (Nadeem Younis 38, Zahoor Elahi 43, Atif Rauf 98 not out, Mujahid Hameed 71 not out); KRL* 299 (Naved Ashraf 39, Iftikhar Hussain 36, Murtaza Hussain 56, Abdur Razzaq 67, Extras 34; Mohammad Asif four for 86). *KRL 2 pts.*

At Gaddafi Stadium, Lahore, October 17, 18, 19, 20. Drawn. WAPDA 253 (Adil Nisar 61, Extras 53; Adnan Naeem three for 62, Nadeem Khan three for 61) and 124 for two (Tariq Aziz 33 not out, Yousuf Youhana 34 not out, Extras 32); PIA* 153 (Asif Mujtaba 61 not out, Extras 49; Shabbir Ahmed five for 31). *WAPDA 2 pts.*

At UBL Sports Complex, Karachi, October 18, 19, 20, 21. Allied Bank won by 87 runs. Pakistan Customs 323 (Ameeruddin 50, Rana Qayyum 30, Azam Khan 92, Saad Wasim 52, Extras 59; Aqib Javed five for 77, Aamir Nazir three for 81) and 80 (Aqib Javed five for 31, Ata-ur-Rehman four for 32); Allied Bank* 62 (Nadeem Iqbal five for 14, Azhar Shafiq five for 23) and 428 (Manzoor Akhtar 64, Aamer Hanif 153, Rashid Latif 34, Extras 84; Ali Raza seven for 117). *Allied Bank 10 pts.*

Allied Bank won after following on 261 behind.

At Sheikhupura Stadium, Sheikhupura, October 24, 25, 26, 27. Drawn. PIA* 407 (Ghulam Ali 54, Sohail Jaffer 98, Asif Mujtaba 45, Aamer Malik 30, Ayaz Jilani 46, Extras 76; Shoaib Akhtar six for 136) and 151 for five dec. (Babar Zaman 54, Mahmood Hamid 32 not out); ADBP 325 (Zahoor Elahi 78, Mujahid Hameed 65, Javed Hayat 89, Extras 42; Nadeem Afzal three for 113, Nadeem Khan five for 132) and 76 for one (Zahoor Elahi 33 not out). *PIA 2 pts.*

At UBL Sports Complex, Karachi, October 24, 25, 26. Allied Bank won by an innings and 29 runs. Habib Bank 152 (Aqib Javed four for 47, Ata-ur-Rehman three for 53, Humayun Hussain three for 17) and 196 (Mujahid Jamshed 49, Farhan Adil 42, Tahir Rashid 44; Aqib Javed six for 59, Humayun Hussain three for 53); Allied Bank* 377 (Bilal Rana 32, Ijaz Ahmed, jun. 45, Manzoor Akhtar 113, Aamer Hanif 73, Extras 36; Shakeel Khan eight for 74). *Allied Bank 12 pts.*

At Municipal Stadium, Gujranwala, October 24, 25, 26, 27. Drawn. KRL 472 for eight dec. (Abdul Basit 43, Iftikhar Hussain 129, Naseer Ahmed 57, Nadeem Abbasi 82, Murtaza Hussain 67 not out, Extras 50); WAPDA* 265 (Tariq Aziz 76, Yousuf Youhana 34, Shahid Mansoor 52 not out, Extras 46; Abdur Razzaq three for 113, Jaffer Nazir five for 68) and 193 for four (Ijaz Mahmood 39, Adil Nisar 51, Yousuf Youhana 30 not out, Extras 39; Shakeel Ahmed three for 22). *KRL 2 pts.*

At National Stadium, Karachi, October 24, 25, 26. National Bank won by six wickets. Pakistan Customs 110 (Rana Qayyum 34; Athar Laeeq five for 26, Mohammad Javed four for 11) and 271 (Ameeruddin 73, Rana Qayyum 58, Saad Wasim 50; Naeem Ashraf four for 37); National Bank* 146 (Tahir Shah 53, Akhtar Sarfraz 30; Nadeem Ashraf seven for 59, Azhar Shafiq three for 27) and 238 for four (Tariq Mohammad 45, Saeed Azad 48, Akhtar Sarfraz 34 not out, Mohammad Javed 54 not out, Extras 38). *National Bank 12 pts.*

At Sheikhupura Stadium, Sheikhupura, November 14, 15, 16, 17. Drawn. ADBP 368 (Zahoor Elahi 61, Mansoor Rana 66, Mujahid Hameed 133 not out, Extras 45; Naseer Shaukat three for 73, Anwar Ali four for 93) and 228 for eight dec. (Zahoor Elahi 64, Mohammad Asif 45 not out; Shabbir Ahmed four for 96); WAPDA* 277 (Adil Nisar 36, Yousuf Youhana 72, Shahid Mansoor 36, Shahid Aslam 50, Extras 46; Fazl-e-Akbar nine for 116) and 298 for nine (Adil Nisar 79, Tariq Aziz 44, Yousuf Youhana 69, Extras 33). *ADBP 2 pts.*

At Gaddafi Stadium, Lahore, November 14, 15. National Bank won by eight wickets. Allied Bank 90 (Athar Laeeq five for 39, Naeem Ashraf three for 29) and 168 (Manzoor Akhtar 31, Aamer Hanif 32, Extras 55; Naeem Ashraf seven for 41); National Bank* 229 (Shahid Anwar 40, Sajid Ali 48, Extras 67; Aqib Javed seven for 77, Mohammad Akram three for 49) and 33 for two. *National Bank 12 pts.*

At UBL Sports Complex, Karachi, November 14, 15, 16, 17. Drawn. Habib Bank 336 (Shakeel Ahmed 40, Salim Elahi 86, Naved Anjum 69, Extras 80; Nadeem Afzal three for 97, Nadeem Khan three for 72, Ashfaq Ahmed three for 75) and 252 for eight dec. (Mujahid Jamshed 58, Salim Malik 97, Extras 32; Ashfaq Ahmed three for 75); PIA* 241 (Asif Mujtaba 54, Aamer Malik 32, Extras 64; Sajid Shah four for 65) and 270 for four (Rizwan-uz-Zaman 50, Asif Mujtaba 67 not out, Aamer Malik 36, Mahmood Hamid 51 not out, Extras 32). *Habib Bank 2 pts.*

At Iqbal Stadium, Faisalabad, November 16, 17, 18, 19. KRL won by six wickets. KRL 404 (Naved Ashraf 61, Asif Mahmood 48, Maqsood Ahmed 32, Abdur Razzaq 117, Extras 47; Nadeem Ashraf five for 104, Azhar Shafiq three for 111) and 75 for four; Pakistan Customs* 210 (Azam Khan 37, Aamer Iqbal 64; Abdur Razzaq three for 81, Jaffer Nazir five for 88) and 268 (Rana Qayyum 78, Azam Khan 77, Aamer Iqbal 37; Murtaza Hussain four for 64). *KRL 12 pts.*

At Sheikhupura Stadium, Sheikhupura, November 19, 20, 21, 22. Drawn. Habib Bank 190 (Shakeel Ahmed 44, Naved Anjum 34; Naseer Shaukat three for 22) and 345 for eight (Shakeel Ahmed 75, Mujahid Jamshed 115, Naved Anjum 33, Extras 31; Ameem Abbas three for 102, Adil Nisar four for 57); WAPDA* 346 (Adil Nisar 30, Yousuf Youhana 163 not out, Naseer Shaukat 42; Akram Raza four for 72, Shahid Mahmood four for 96). *WAPDA 2 pts.*
   WAPDA wicket-keeper Zahid Umar made seven catches in Habib Bank's first innings and nine dismissals in the match.

At Iqbal Stadium, Faisalabad, November 22, 23, 24, 25. ADBP won by 194 runs. ADBP 156 (Javed Hayat 43 not out, Mohammad Ali 34; Ali Raza three for 26, Azhar Shafiq three for 49) and 347 for eight dec. (Zahoor Elahi 40, Mujahid Hameed 51, Mansoor Rana 107, Atif Rauf 35, Extras 48; Nadeem Ashraf four for 63); Pakistan Customs* 168 (Azam Khan 36, Extras 47; Fazl-e-Akbar six for 57) and 141 (Azam Khan 47, Extras 36; Fazl-e-Akbar four for 40, Shoaib Akhtar three for 46, Javed Hayat three for six). *ADBP 10 pts.*

At KRL Cricket Ground, Rawalpindi, November 22, 23, 24. Allied Bank won by seven wickets. Allied Bank* 308 (Aamir Sohail 170, Ehsan Butt 44; Murtaza Hussain three for 106, Shakeel Ahmed seven for 91) and 24 for three; KRL 158 (Naeem Akhtar 58, Murtaza Hussain 35; Bilal Rana five for 59, Mohammad Zahid four for 39) and 173 (Iftikhar Hussain 70, Naeem Akhtar 30; Bilal Rana five for 42). *Allied Bank 12 pts.*

At Gaddafi Stadium, Lahore, November 22, 23, 24, 25. Drawn. PIA 287 (Rizwan-uz-Zaman 91, Asif Mujtaba 38, Extras 51; Naeem Ashraf six for 69) and 211 for four (Babar Zaman 48, Rizwan-uz-Zaman 65, Asif Mujtaba 50); National Bank* 306 (Hanif-ur-Rehman 61, Tariq Mohammad 51, Akhtar Sarfraz 69, Tahir Shah 53; Nadeem Afzal four for 107, Sohail Jaffer three for 39). *National Bank 2 pts.*

At Gaddafi Stadium, Lahore, December 13, 14, 15. Allied Bank won by four wickets. ADBP 135 (Mohammad Akram six for 49, Aamir Nazir four for 26) and 92 (Ata-ur-Rehman seven for 20, Aamir Nazir three for 17); Allied Bank* 132 (Extras 39; Fazl-e-Akbar six for 58, Mohammad Ali three for 26) and 96 for six (Taimur Khan 37 not out; Fazl-e-Akbar three for 35, Shoaib Akhtar three for 32). *Allied Bank 10 pts.*

At Sheikhupura Stadium, Sheikhupura, December 13, 14, 15, 16. Habib Bank won by seven wickets. Pakistan Customs 109 (Rana Qayyum 31; Nadeem Ghauri five for 39) and 138 (Azhar Shafiq 36, Azam Khan 34; Sajid Shah four for 42, Akram Raza three for 37, Nadeem Ghauri three for 31); Habib Bank* 209 (Tahir Rashid 57, Extras 53; Azhar Shafiq three for 27, Haaris Khan five for 59) and 44 for three. *Habib Bank 12 pts.*

At UBL Sports Complex, Karachi, December 13, 14, 15, 16. Drawn. PIA 318 for eight dec. (Babar Zaman 60, Sohail Jaffer 72, Asif Mujtaba 64 not out, Zahid Fazal 30, Extras 40; Jaffer Nazir four for 113, Naeem Akhtar three for 88) and 107 for nine dec. (Asif Mujtaba 39 not out; Jaffer Nazir four for 50, Naeem Akhtar five for 38); KRL* 184 (Iftikhar Hussain 80 not out, Murtaza Hussain 42; Nadeem Afzal three for 44, Hasnain Kazim six for 73) and 122 for seven (Naved Ashraf 31; Ali Gauhar four for 63, Nadeem Afzal three for 13). *PIA 2 pts.*

At Municipal Stadium, Gujranwala, December 13, 14, 15. 16. Drawn. WAPDA 329 for seven dec. (Adil Nisar 98, Yousuf Youhana 56, Fida Hussain 40 not out, Extras 64); National Bank* 173 for eight (Tahir Shah 41, Zafar Iqbal 32 not out, Extras 43; Irfan-ul-Haq five for 89).

At Municipal Stadium, Gujranwala, December 20, 21, 22, 23. Drawn. National Bank 376 (Shahid Anwar 103, Hanif-ur-Rehman 40, Akhtar Sarfraz 71, Mohammad Javed 39 not out, Wasim Arif 33, Extras 52; Mohammad Asif three for 78); ADBP* 24 for two.

At Sheikhupura Stadium, Sheikhupura, December 20, 21, 22, 23. Drawn. WAPDA 134 (Extras 35; Mohammad Akram five for 33, Ata-ur-Rehman four for 44) and 86 for five (Ata-ur-Rehman three for 21); Allied Bank* 214 (Iqbal Saleem 45, Arshad Khan 50; Shabbir Ahmed three for 33). *Allied Bank 2 pts.*

At KRL Cricket Ground, Rawalpindi, December 20, 21, 22, 23. Drawn. KRL 276 (Naved Ashraf 38, Asif Mahmood 55, Maqsood Ahmed 64, Extras 33; Shahid Afridi six for 101) and 128 for five (Naseer Ahmed 33, Maqsood Ahmed 36 not out); Habib Bank* 256 (Salim Elahi 30, Mujahid Jamshed 86 not out, Tahir Rashid 46; Jaffer Nazir four for 96, Naeem Akhtar four for 49). *KRL 2 pts.*

At National Stadium, Karachi, December 20, 21, 22, 23. Pakistan Customs won by seven wickets. PIA* 334 (Sohail Jaffer 61, Zahid Fazal 132, Zahid Ahmed 57; Ali Raza four for 74, Azhar Shafiq three for 74) and 228 (Aamer Malik 47, Zahid Ahmed 65; Mohammad Zahid five for 73, Ali Raza three for 68); Pakistan Customs 263 (Azhar Shafiq 40, Rana Qayyum 64, Aamer Bashir 47; Ali Gauhar six for 76) and 300 for three (Ameeruddin 84, Azhar Shafiq 82, Rana Qayyum 63 not out, Azam Khan 34 not out). *Pakistan Customs 10 pts.*

At Gaddafi Stadium, Lahore, January 10, 11, 12, 13. Habib Bank won by an innings and 70 runs. ADBP 120 (Mohammad Nadeem 30; Naved Anjum three for 16, Sajid Shah six for 56) and 242 (Asif Ali 39, Mohammad Wasim 35, Mohammad Nadeem 43, Mohammad Ali 36; Sajid Shah five for 89); Habib Bank* 432 for seven dec. (Shakeel Ahmed 36, Salim Elahi 203 not out, Salim Malik 63, Naved Anjum 37, Extras 58; Shoaib Akhtar five for 166). *Habib Bank 12 pts.*
Salim Elahi's 203 not out lasted 498 minutes and 323 balls and included 26 fours.

At National Stadium, Karachi, January 10, 11, 12, 13. PIA won by four wickets. Allied Bank 266 (Ata-ur-Rehman, jun. 80, Bilal Rana 32, Extras 41; Hasnain Kazim four for 101, Ali Gauhar three for 87) and 227 (Raj Hans 40, Taimur Khan 42, Ata-ur-Rehman, sen. 43; Ali Gauhar four for 63, Nadeem Khan three for 54); PIA* 325 (Moin Khan 129, Wasim Akram 59, Extras 63; Mohammad Akram three for 93, Aamir Nazir five for 104) and 170 for six (Zahid Fazal 78 not out; Mohammad Akram three for 59, Aamir Nazir three for 70). *PIA 12 pts.*

At KRL Cricket Ground, Rawalpindi, January 10, 11, 12, 13. Drawn. National Bank* 169 (Akhtar Sarfraz 51, Naeem Ashraf 45; Shakeel Ahmed five for 52, Murtaza Hussain five for 73) and 98 for nine (Shakeel Ahmed four for 33); KRL 239 (Naseer Ahmed 50, Nadeem Abbasi 87 not out; Salman Fazal five for 98, Naeem Tayyab four for 74). *KRL 2 pts.*

At Niaz Stadium, Hyderabad, January 10, 11, 12, 13. Drawn. Pakistan Customs* 199 (Aamer Iqbal 62, Haaris Khan 54 not out; Tariq Rasheed three for 55, Anwar Ali three for 50) and 356 (Ameeruddin 60, Mohammad Ramzan 91, Aamer Bashir 49, Aamer Iqbal 45, Tauseef Ahmed 49; Shabbir Ahmed three for 75, Anwar Ali four for 128); WAPDA 277 (Adil Nisar 64, Tariq Aziz 57, Shahid Mansoor 30, Zahid Umar 39, Extras 36; Tauseef Ahmed four for 57, Haaris Khan five for 78) and 25 for two. *WAPDA 2 pts.*

Final

At Gaddafi Stadium, Lahore, February 18, 19, 20, 21, 22. Habib Bank won by 160 runs. Habib Bank 399 (Salim Elahi 38, Shakeel Ahmed 148, Salim Malik 43, Naved Anjum 70, Extras 45; Arshad Khan four for 72, Taimur Khan three for 21) and 187 (Salim Elahi 31, Naved Anjum 32, Extras 35; Arshad Khan four for 25); Allied Bank* 175 (Wajahatullah Wasti 45; Sajid Shah three for 32, Shakeel Khan three for 41, Akram Raza three for 32) and 251 (Wajahatullah Wasti 55, Ijaz Ahmed, jun. 46, Extras 36; Sajid Shah five for 107, Shakeel Khan three for 41).

WINNERS

Ayub Trophy		1973-74	Railways	1986-87	National Bank
1960-61	Railways-Quetta	1974-75	National Bank	1987-88	Habib Bank
1961-62	Karachi	1975-76	National Bank	1988-89	Karachi
1962-63	Karachi	1976-77	Habib Bank	1989-90	Karachi Whites
1964-65	Karachi	1977-78	Habib Bank	1990-91	ADBP
1965-66	Karachi Blues	1978-79	National Bank	1991-92	Habib Bank
1967-68	Karachi Blues	†1979-80	IDBP	1992-93	Habib Bank
1969-70	PIA	†1980-81	Rawalpindi	1993-94	ADBP
		†1981-82	Allied Bank	1994-95	Allied Bank
BCCP Trophy		†1982-83	PACO		
1970-71	PIA	1983-84	Karachi Blues	*PCB Patron's Trophy*	
1971-72	PIA	1984-85	Karachi Whites	1995-96	ADBP
		1985-86	Karachi Whites	1996-97	United Bank
BCCP Patron's Trophy				1997-98	Habib Bank
1972-73	Karachi Blues				

† *The competition was not first-class between 1979-80 and 1982-83, when it served as a qualifying competition for the Quaid-e-Azam Trophy.*

OTHER FIRST-CLASS MATCHES

India A in Pakistan

At National Stadium, Karachi, February 3, 4, 5. Drawn. Karachi 338 for nine dec. (Zafar Iqbal 38, Shahid Afridi 66, Basit Ali 133; M. Kartik three for 76); India A 382 for five (Wasim Jaffer 90, G. K. Khoda 95, J. V. Paranjpe 115).
The third day was cancelled because of Kashmir Solidarity Day.

At Arbab Niaz Stadium, Peshawar, February 8, 9, 10. Drawn. India A* 180 (N. Haldipur 35; Kabir Khan three for 40, Fazl-e-Akbar three for 36, Sajid Shah three for 53) and 343 for six dec. (J. V. Paranjpe 37, S. S. Raul 114 not out, A. B. Agarkar 109 not out; Sajid Shah three for 68); Peshawar 203 (Taimur Khan 58, Wasim Yousufi 43, Kabir Khan 46 not out; A. B. Agarkar six for 75) and 89 for three (Jahangir Khan, sen. 55).

At Rawalpindi Cricket Stadium, Rawalpindi, February 13, 14, 15, 16. First Unofficial Test: Drawn. Pakistan A 112 (Salim Elahi 39; D. S. Mohanty three for 47, A. B. Agarkar five for 34); India A* 43 for three.
The last three days were lost to rain.

At Rawalpindi Cricket Stadium, Rawalpindi, February 19, 20, 21. Drawn. India A 234 for six dec. (Wasim Jaffer 37 retired out, G. K. Khoda 36 retired out, R. S. Gavaskar 63 retired out, S. Abbas Ali 60 retired out); Rawalpindi* 216 for seven (Asif Mahmood 33, Naseer Ahmed 34, Nadeem Abbasi 31 not out, Naeem Akhtar 39; S. V. Bahutule three for 61, N. A. David three for 61).

At Arbab Niaz Stadium, Peshawar, February 24, 25, 26, 28. Second Unofficial Test: Pakistan A v India A. Abandoned.

At Gaddafi Stadium, Lahore, March 1, 2, 3, 4. Third Unofficial Test: Drawn. India A* 557 for five dec. (Wasim Jaffer 34, G. K. Khoda 189, S. Abbas Ali 76, R. S. Gavaskar 115 not out, S. S. Raul 115 not out; Ali Hussain Rizvi three for 183); Pakistan A 69 for three.
   The last four sessions were lost to rain.

At National Stadium, Karachi, March 7, 8, 9, 10. Fourth Unofficial Test: India A won by 58 runs. India A 260 (M. S. K. Prasad 64, S. S. Raul 42, S. V. Bahutule 43, Extras 32; Aqib Javed four for 70, Abdur Razzaq four for 61) and 180 (R. S. Gavaskar 48, M. S. K. Prasad 54; Aqib Javed three for 32, Murtaza Hussain four for 52); Pakistan A* 212 (Salim Elahi 42, Hasan Raza 48; A. B. Agarkar six for 72, S. V. Bahutule three for 33) and 170 (Shahid Afridi 65; A. B. Agarkar three for 62, S. V. Bahutule four for 26).
   India A won the unofficial Test series 1-0, but Pakistan A won the ensuing one-day series 3-0.

WILLS CUP, 1997-98

Note: Matches in this section were not first-class.

Semi-finals

At Gaddafi Stadium, Lahore, April 1 (day/night). Allied Bank won by 115 runs. Allied Bank 302 for six (50 overs) (Mohammad Nawaz, sen. 82, Wajahatullah Wasti 37, Ramiz Raja 41, Manzoor Akhtar 39, Ata-ur-Rehman 37); Karachi Blues* 187 for nine (50 overs) (Zafar Jadoon 37, Javed Miandad 38, Munir-ul-Haq 50 not out, Arif Mahmood 30).
   Former Test captain Javed Miandad, aged 40, made his only appearance of the season.

At Gaddafi Stadium, Lahore, April 2 (day/night). PIA won by eight wickets. KRL 220 (49.2 overs) (Asif Mahmood 58, Naseer Ahmed 73; Mahmood Hamid three for 30); PIA* 224 for two (41.2 overs) (Babar Zaman 35, Ghulam Ali 70, Zahid Fazal 63 not out, Asif Mujtaba 31 not out).

Final

At Gaddafi Stadium, Lahore, April 4 (day/night). Allied Bank won by 32 runs. Allied Bank 248 (48 overs) (Ramiz Raja 68, Manzoor Akhtar 68, Ijaz Ahmed, jun. 30, Extras 37; Zahid Ahmed three for 47); PIA* 216 (48.3 overs) (Zahid Fazal 57, Asif Mujtaba 40; Ata-ur-Rehman three for 41).

CRICKET IN SRI LANKA, 1997-98

By GERRY VAIDYASEKERA and SA'ADI THAWFEEQ

Chandika Hathurusinghe

Sri Lanka's national side had a long but encouraging season. They began in July 1997 by winning the one-day Asia Cup, proceeded to rewrite several Test records against India, won Test series against Zimbabwe and New Zealand, and concluded in August 1998 with another one-day success, against England and South Africa, and victory over England in the Oval Test. There were disappointments, notably losing two Tests away to South Africa. But the win over England provided an optimistic conclusion.

The ever-expanding international programme kept the top players away from their clubs. Aravinda de Silva headed the averages with 766 runs, all scored in the seven home Tests, but never appeared for Nondescripts, while Muttiah Muralitharan took 45 of his 51 wickets, easily the biggest aggregate, in Tests, playing only once for Tamil Union. Even so, it was the commitment of Sinhalese Sports Club's international players which helped to win the P. Saravanamuttu Trophy. Test stars Arjuna Ranatunga, Marvan Atapattu and Mahela Jayawardene all turned out for Sinhalese in the April final, shortly after returning from South Africa, whereas only Kumar Dharmasena of the touring party joined their arch-rivals Bloomfield: Sanath Jayasuriya and Roshan Mahanama chose to rest.

Though Dharmasena scored 109 in Bloomfield's first-innings total of 313, that was soon overshadowed. Helped by some butter-fingered fielding, Atapattu and Ranatunga added 259 for Sinhalese's fourth wicket; Atapattu, who was dropped three times, hit 179, and Ranatunga 192. That helped Sinhalese to 582, the highest total of the domestic season, and a decisive 269-run advantage. Though Bloomfield reached 295 for four on resuming, first-innings lead was enough to give Sinhalese their fourth outright title since the P. Saravanamuttu Trophy became first-class in 1988-89. They have also shared the trophy twice, most recently with Bloomfield in 1994-95, when they contested the last final.

In the two intervening seasons, the first-class Segment A of the tournament had been staged as a single round-robin league for 15 teams, with no final. Partly because of heavy international commitments, the Sri Lankan Board reverted to dividing the teams into two groups, of eight and seven – effectively halving the number of games. This time, they added semi-finals for the top two teams from each group (a similar proposal to add semi-finals to the non-first-class Segment B was overruled, amid some controversy). At the end of March, Sinhalese, who had headed Group B with four outright wins, defeated Group A runners-up Colombo on first-innings lead, thanks to 151 from Arjuna Ranatunga's younger brother, Sanjeeva. But Bloomfield, winners of Group A, had to wait a fortnight to know who their semi-final opponents would be. Moors had finished half a point ahead of Tamil Union, who argued that there had been a discrepancy in the reckoning. The tournament committee upheld Moors' position, but it hardly mattered: on the field, seamer Pulasthi Gunaratne took five wickets to dismiss them for 298, 53 behind, enough to see defending champions Bloomfield through.

It was not the only grudge between Moors and Tamil Union. Former Test opener Chandika Hathurusinghe had left Tamil after a dispute over the captaincy, moved to Moors and enjoyed one of his best seasons. He was third both in the batting averages, with 590 runs at 65.55, and in the bowling, with 35 wickets at 16.17, easily claiming the prize for best all-rounder.

Atapattu was the leading run-scorer with 1,046 – the third time in four seasons he had reached four figures. Jayasuriya was close behind with 985, thanks to his 340 against India in August, when Sri Lanka compiled 952 for six, the biggest total in Test history. But the most encouraging feature was the emergence of 20-year-old Mahela Jayawardene, a stylish right-hander from Sinhalese. He made his Test debut in that match and went on to score 926 runs, including an unbeaten 200 against Kurunegala in the P. Sara Trophy, and 167 against New Zealand at Galle in June.

There was another promising newcomer in left-arm spinner Niroshan Bandaratilleke of Tamil Union. He was the leading wicket-taker, after Muralitharan, with 44 at 18.86, and, having established his claim to provide the foil to Muralitharan's off-spin, was capped against New Zealand. Like Jayawardene, he put in a decisive performance in the Test victory at Galle, where he took nine for 83.

Galle won the non-first-class Segment B of the P. Sara Trophy, after some anxious moments. In their qualifying group, they tied on points with Nomads and went through to the final on a net runs-per-wicket formula. Then they slumped to 30 for six against Kalutara Town. Chandragupta Hewamanna fought back with a sparkling century, and off-spinner Hasitha Rajapakse took six wickets to dismiss Kalutara for 129 in the run-chase.

Nondescripts won the Division One limited-overs competition, beating Tamil Union by five wickets in a low-scoring final. But they lost the final of the inaugural J. R. Jayawardene Memorial Challenge Trophy, a 45-over competition, to Sinhalese, whose younger players picked up the club's third title of 1997-98 when they won the Under-24 tournament. Bloomfield and Air Force were joint winners of the Inter-Club Six-a-Side tournament after a washed-out final. And, in the Inter-District tournament, there was a hopeful development for peace on an ethnically divided island: a team from Jaffna, in the war-torn north, came to Galle, in the south, for the first time since 1976.

Although Sri Lanka did not reach the final of the Under-19 World Cup in South Africa in January, they provided some of the tournament's brightest stars in Pradeep Hewage, who averaged 105.33, wicket-keeper Prasanna Jayawardene and leg-spinner Malinga Bandara. Jayawardene later toured England with the senior squad.

At home, Colombo North beat Kurunegala by ten wickets in the Inter-District Under-19 limited-overs final, while St Thomas's of Mount Lavinia won the Inter-School Coca-Cola Cup, beating fancied Ananda by one run. Sajith Rupasinghe of Ananda was judged the competition's best bowler, and Chamara Soysa of Dharmasoka the best batsman. Other notable schoolboy performances included 247 by Lakshaman Fernando of Ananda against St Anthony's in the Under-15 semi-finals, twin centuries by Priyasad Seneviratne of De Mazenod against St Anne's, and six hundreds in successive matches – including four in four innings – by 14-year-old Chanaka Wijesinghe, of St Sylvester's in Kandy.

Among the bowlers, Sarath Wasantha of Sri Chandrasekera Vidyalala took 13 wickets for 18 in an Under-13 game against St John's of Panadura, including eight for six in the second innings. Shinnan Warnakula of St Joseph's College, Colombo, captured 50 wickets for the fourth season running. All-rounder twins Malintha Madushanka Jayatissa and Tarindu Trivanka Jayatissa led the first and third Under-13 sides of Thurstan College. And Trinity College, Kandy, beat Royal College of Colombo for the first time since 1945 – by one run, with one ball to spare.

FIRST-CLASS AVERAGES, 1997-98

BATTING

(Qualification: 400 runs)

	M	I	NO	R	HS	100s	Avge
P. A. de Silva (*Sri Lanka*)	7	12	2	766	146	4	76.60
S. T. Jayasuriya (*Bloomfield C and AC*)	9	15	0	985	340	3	65.66
U. C. Hathurusinghe (*Moors SC*)	6	10	1	590	125	1	65.55
R. P. Arnold (*Nondescripts CC*)	6	9	1	503	149	2	62.87
A. Ranatunga (*Sinhalese SC*)	9	14	1	807	192	2	62.07
M. S. Atapattu (*Sinhalese SC*)	11	18	1	1,046	223	3	61.52
R. S. Kalpage (*Bloomfield C and AC*)	10	13	2	669	189	3	60.81
S. I. Fernando (*Colts CC*)	9	15	3	713	102	1	59.41
R. P. A. H. Wickremaratne (*Sinhalese SC*)	9	15	3	679	132*	3	56.58
R. S. Mahanama (*Bloomfield C and AC*)	5	8	0	416	225	2	52.00
D. P. Samaraweera (*Colts CC*)	8	13	1	621	140*	2	51.75
D. P. M. D. Jayawardene (*Sinhalese SC*)	13	19	1	926	200*	3	51.44
C. Mendis (*Colts CC*)	8	10	0	471	66	0	47.10
B. C. M. S. Mendis (*Sebastianites C and AC*)	8	16	1	704	160	1	46.93
S. K. L. de Silva (*Colombo CC*)	10	14	1	609	154	2	46.84
N. R. G. Perera (*Sebastianites C and AC*)	6	11	1	447	102	1	44.70
M. T. Gunaratne (*Bloomfield C and AC*)	8	13	2	473	108	2	43.00
M. N. Nawaz (*Bloomfield C and AC*)	11	16	0	678	111	2	42.37
P. B. Ediriweera (*Colombo CC*)	9	13	0	542	154	2	41.69
N. S. Bopage (*Colombo CC*)	8	11	1	411	108*	1	41.10
S. Ranatunga (*Sinhalese SC*)	10	16	2	551	151	2	39.35
S. T. Perera (*Bloomfield C and AC*)	10	17	2	414	95	0	27.60

* Signifies not out.

BOWLING

(Qualification: 20 wickets, average 30.00)

	O	M	R	W	BB	5W/i	Avge
S. D. Anurasiri (*Panadura SC*)	204	76	349	23	7-73	1	15.17
S. Madanayake (*Burgher RC*)	151.5	30	375	24	5-19	2	15.62
U. C. Hathurusinghe (*Moors SC*)	202.1	58	566	35	7-55	2	16.17
D. Hettiarachchi (*Colts CC*)	218.5	60	519	32	7-41	2	16.21
M. M. de Silva (*Singha SC*)	180.1	41	492	30	5-28	3	16.40
M. R. C. N. Bandaratilleke (*Tamil Union C and AC*)	374.2	114	830	44	5-36	2	18.86
K. G. Perera (*Antonians SC*)	180	51	456	24	6-46	2	19.00
A. S. A. Perera (*Sinhalese SC*)	220.3	61	605	31	4-15	0	19.51
W. C. Labrooy (*Burgher RC*)	167.4	34	504	24	6-40	2	21.00
B. de Silva (*Bloomfield C and AC*)	479.4	133	1,094	51	7-94	4	21.45
M. Muralitharan (*Tamil Union C and AC*)	149.3	27	472	22	5-53	1	21.45
P. W. Gunaratne (*Bloomfield C and AC*)	225.4	66	558	26	5-46	2	21.46
P. K. Serasinghe (*Police SC*)	197	35	662	30	5-40	2	22.06
M. J. H. Rushdie (*Colombo CC*)							

	O	M	R	W	BB	5W/i	Avge
M. S. Villavarayen (*Tamil Union C and AC*).....	207.1	49	606	27	5-26	1	22.44
P. P. Wickremasinghe (*Bloomfield C and AC*).....	197.3	52	500	22	4-55	0	22.72
S. H. S. M. K. Silva (*Sinhalese SC*)...........	226.5	48	706	31	5-74	1	22.77
V. H. K. Ranaweera (*Police SC*)...............	217.1	54	647	28	8-95	1	23.10
D. P. M. C. Waidyaratne (*Matara SC*)...........	182	37	561	24	6-60	3	23.37
K. J. Silva (*Sinhalese SC*)..................	274.1	74	743	31	5-76	1	23.96
T. T. Samaraweera (*Colts CC*)................	311.2	74	747	31	5-60	1	24.09
R. Herath (*Kurunegala Youth CC*).............	192.4	35	659	27	5-93	1	24.40
I. S. Gallage (*Colombo CC*)..................	232.5	45	591	24	5-80	1	24.62
R. S. Priyadarshana (*Moors SC*)..............	201.2	32	694	26	5-88	1	26.69
U. D. U. Chandana (*Tamil Union C and AC*)....	202.4	48	573	21	5-86	1	27.28

P. SARAVANAMUTTU TROPHY, 1997-98

Group A

	Played	Won	Lost	Drawn	1st-inns Wins	Points
Bloomfield C and AC	7	3	0	4	2	104.00
Colombo CC...........	7	2	0	5	3	88.50
Colts CC	7	1	0	6	4	86.50
Nondescripts CC	7	3	0	4	1	86.00
Police SC	7	1	1	5	2	58.50
Panadura SC	7	0	2	5	3	48.50
Sebastianites C and AC ...	7	1	4	2	0	43.00
Matara SC	7	0	4	3	0	29.00

Group B

	Played	Won	Lost	Drawn	1st-inns Wins	Points
Sinhalese SC...........	6	4	0	2	1	109.00
Moors SC............	6	3	1	2	1	88.50
Tamil Union C and AC ...	6	3	1	2	1	88.00
Burgher RC..........	6	2	2	2	0	65.00
Singha SC...........	6	0	2	4*	3	50.00
Antonians SC	6	1	3	2*	1	44.50
Kurunegala Youth CC	6	0	4	2	0	16.50

* *Includes one abandoned match.*

Semi-finals: Sinhalese SC beat Colombo CC by virtue of their first-innings lead; Bloomfield C and AC beat Moors SC by virtue of their first-innings lead.

Final: Sinhalese SC beat Bloomfield C and AC by virtue of their first-innings lead.

In the following scores, * by the name of a team indicates that they won the toss.

Group A

At Reid Avenue, Colombo, January 2, 3, 4. Drawn. Colts CC* 203 (S. Janaka 54, S. I. Fernando 93; R. S. Kalpage three for 61, B. de Silva six for 63) and 176 (S. I. Fernando 32, M. T. Sampath 36, D. P. Samaraweera 31; B. de Silva six for 40, M. T. Gunaratne three for 25); Bloomfield C and AC 165 (K. E. A. Upashantha three for 50, D. Hettiarachchi four for 44) and 14 for two.

At Maitland Place, Colombo (NCC), January 2, 3, 4. Drawn. Nondescripts CC 217 (S. Warusamana 57, A. Rideegammanagedera 40, C. D. U. S. Weerasinghe 44; P. K. Serasinghe five for 46); Police SC* 124 for three (H. A. Priyantha 33, R. C. Liyanage 51).

At Moratuwa Stadium, Moratuwa, January 2, 3, 4. Drawn. Sebastianites C and AC* 281 (W. D. J. Abeywardene 37, P. Salgado 78, S. Silva 43, M. Peiris 47 not out; K. C. Silva three for 35, S. D. Anurasiri three for 61); Panadura SC 254 for eight (B. P. Perera 61, S. N. Liyanage 115).

At Havelock Park, Colombo (Colts), January 9, 10, 11. Drawn. Colts CC 279 (C. Mendis 54, M. T. Sampath 49, T. Samaraweera 85; W. N. M. Soysa three for 21) and 248 for nine (D. P. Samaraweera 73, C. Mendis 46, S. I. Fernando 32, M. T. Sampath 40 not out; P. K. Serasinghe five for 62); Police SC* 221 (P. S. Gunaratne 90, W. N. M. Soysa 43; S. Alexander five for 62).

At Maitland Place, Colombo (NCC), January 9, 10, 11. Drawn. Bloomfield C and AC* 308 (P. B. Dassanayake 32, M. N. Nawaz 61, S. T. Perera 32, P. P. Wickramasinghe 32 not out; A. Rideegammanagedera four for 65, C. Fernando three for 44) and 86 for two; Nondescripts CC 310 (G. R. P. Peiris 84, C. D. U. S. Weerasinghe 38, S. Warusamana 43, A. Pathirana 44; P. W. Gunaratne three for 54, R. L. Perera three for 65).

At Panadura Esplanade, Panadura, January 9, 10, 11. Drawn. Panadura SC* 217 (B. P. Perera 61, S. N. Liyanage 73, S. D. Anurasiri 33; M. J. H. Rushdie three for 37, N. S. Rajan six for 38); Colombo CC 262 (C. P. Handunnettige 67, D. Arnolda 42, I. S. Gallage 31 not out, Extras 33; C. Perera four for 52, M. Jayasena three for 39).

At Reid Avenue, Colombo, January 16, 17, 18. Bloomfield C and AC won by an innings and 95 runs. Bloomfield C and AC 367 (R. S. Kalpage 189, M. T. Gunaratne 51, P. P. Wickramasinghe 44, R. Palliyaguru 59; V. H. K. Ranaweera eight for 95); Police SC* 143 (P. P. Wickramasinghe three for 24, H. D. P. K. Dharmasena three for 17) and 129 (R. C. Liyanage 36; H. D. P. K. Dharmasena six for 40).
Bloomfield were six for five before Kalpage and Gunaratne added 151 for the sixth wicket. Pulasthi Gunaratne of Bloomfield took seven catches in the field during the match.

At Maitland Crescent, Colombo (CCC), January 16, 17, 18. Colombo CC won by an innings and 18 runs. Colombo CC 402 for four dec. (N. S. Bopage 89, P. B. Ediriweera 154, A. Polonowitta 49, C. P. Handunnettige 35 not out, S. K. L. de Silva 40); Sebastianites C and AC* 85 (M. J. H. Rushdie three for 32) and 299 (B. C. M. S. Mendis 84, N. R. G. Perera 102; S. H. Alles four for 57, D. Arnolda three for 104).

At Havelock Park, Colombo (Colts), January 16, 17, 18. Drawn. Panadura SC 334 (A. K. D. A. S. Kumara 132, M. Jayasena 51, Extras 36; S. Alexander three for 50, T. Mathews three for 57, T. T. Samaraweera three for 52) and 144 (M. P. Silva 39, D. Wickremanayake 44; T. T. Samaraweera five for 60, S. I. Fernando four for 32); Colts CC* 326 (D. P. Samaraweera 41, C. Mendis 64, S. I. Fernando 91, M. T. Sampath 40, N. Ranatunga 39; M. Jayasena seven for 109) and 48 for one.

At Uyanwatte Stadium, Matara, January 16, 17, 18. Nondescripts CC won by an innings and 14 runs. Matara SC 68 (K. S. C. de Silva five for 17, D. Samarasinghe four for 29) and 192 (S. M. Faumi 36, G. Lanka 33 not out; K. S. C. de Silva three for 66, L. E. Hannibal three for 48); Nondescripts CC* 274 (A. Pathirana 51, P. K. Rajapakse 61, C. D. U. S. Weerasinghe 58; P. I. W. Jayasekera three for 47, N. R. C. K. Guruge three for 35).

At Reid Avenue, Colombo, January 23, 24, 25. Bloomfield C and AC won by 272 runs. Bloomfield C and AC* 273 (S. T. Perera 44, B. de Silva 38, R. Palliyaguru 51 not out; Anusha Perera three for 56) and 259 for five dec. (M. N. Nawaz 44, S. T. Perera 95, R. Palliyaguru 60 not out); Sebastianites C and AC 182 (M. P. A. Cooray 95; P. P. Wickramasinghe four for 67, B. de Silva three for 40) and 78 (A. Fernando 46; R. Palliyaguru four for 31).

At Maitland Place, Colombo (NCC), January 23, 24, 25. Drawn. Nondescripts CC* 298 (R. P. Arnold 149, C. D. U. S. Weerasinghe 63, A. Pathirana 32; T. T. Samaraweera four for 75, D. Hettiarachchi four for 66) and 120 for eight (C. D. U. S. Weerasinghe 32; D. Hettiarachchi seven for 41); Colts CC 374 (D. P. Samaraweera 104, C. Mendis 66, S. I. Fernando 54, S. Alexander 54 not out; A. Rideegammanagedera four for 74).

At Panadura Esplanade, Panadura, January 23, 24, 25. Drawn. Panadura SC 209 (S. N. Liyanage 55, S. D. Anurasiri 50; D. P. M. C. Waidyaratne six for 60) and 97 for five dec. (D. P. M. C. Waidyaratne three for 31); Matara SC* 113 (C. Perera three for 27, S. D. Anurasiri four for 11) and 78 for five (S. Kulatunga 35 not out).

At Police Park, Colombo, January 23, 24, 25. Drawn. Colombo CC* 166 (P. B. Ediriweera 40, C. P. Handunettige 41; V. H. K. Ranaweera three for 39, D. Nanayakkara three for 19) and 205 for six (S. K. L. de Silva 39, C. P. Handunettige 55 not out; W. N. M. Soysa three for 55); Police SC 229 (S. Gunaratne 86; M. J. H. Rushdie four for 45, S. H. Alles three for 46).

At Havelock Park, Colombo (Colts), February 6, 7, 8. Drawn. Colts CC* 349 (C. Mendis 40, S. I. Fernando 40, J. Kulatunga 54, D. P. Samaraweera 61, S. Alexander 72, D. Vitharana 37 not out; Anusha Perera five for 101) and 258 for one dec. (D. P. Samaraweera 140 not out, C. Mendis 60, S. I. Fernando 39 not out); Sebastianites C and AC 264 (W. D. J. Abeywardene 33, Anusha Perera 67; S. Alexander three for 49) and 239 for seven (D. Bodiyabaduge 47, Sanjeewa Silva 49, A. Fernando 71 not out; S. Alexander three for 41).
    In Colts' first innings, Alexander and Vitharana added 105 for the last wicket.

At Maitland Place, Colombo (NCC), February 6, 7, 8. Drawn. Nondescripts CC 234 for nine dec. (H. P. Tillekeratne 50, K. Sangakkara 34, S. Jayaratne 44 not out; I. S. Gallage four for 45) and 189 for four (S. Warusamana 64, H. P. Tillekeratne 51 not out); Colombo CC* 398 (P. B. Ediriweera 47, S. K. L. de Silva 154, A. Polonowitta 47, D. Arnolda 77, Extras 35; G. R. P. Peiris four for 33).

At Reid Avenue, Colombo, February 13, 14, 15. Drawn. Bloomfield C and AC* 340 (S. T. Jayasuriya 31, R. S. Mahanama 104, H. D. P. K. Dharmasena 104; I. S. Gallage five for 80) and 251 for six (S. T. Jayasuriya 110, H. D. P. K. Dharmasena 58); Colombo CC 263 (S. B. Ediriweera 110, A. P. Dalugoda 38; P. P. Wickremasinghe four for 55).

At Havelock Park, Colombo (Colts), February 13, 14, 15. Colts CC won by an innings and 188 runs. Matara SC* 153 (P. Rangana 34; K. E. A. Upashantha three for 42, D. Hettiarachchi four for 47, T. T. Samaraweera three for 17) and 105 (D. Hettiarachchi three for 21, S. I. Fernando three for 27); Colts CC 446 for nine dec. (S. I. Fernando 102, M. T. Sampath 78, J. Kulatunga 76, T. T. Samaraweera 77, K. E. A. Upashantha 46; D. P. M. C. Waidyaratne four for 79).

At Panadura Esplanade, Panadura, February 13, 14, 15. Nondescripts CC won by eight wickets. Panadura SC* 217 (M. P. Wijesuriya 33, A. K. D. A. S. Kumara 102 not out; K. R. Pushpakumara four for 56, K. S. C. de Silva three for 44) and 140 (F. N. Jayalath 31; K. R. Pushpakumara five for 40); Nondescripts CC 263 (R. P. Arnold 112; S. D. Anurasiri seven for 73) and 95 for two (R. P. Arnold 39, R. G. P. Peiris 45).
    Pushpakumara took a hat-trick – all lbw – in the second innings.

At Moratuwa Stadium, Moratuwa, February 20, 21, 22. Police SC won by six wickets. Sebastianites C and AC* 173 (Anusha Perera 31 not out; V. H. K. Ranaweera three for 51) and 177 (W. D. J. Abeywardene 36, N. R. G. Perera 76; V. H. K. Ranaweera three for 46); Police SC 233 (R. C. Liyanage 70, W. N. M. Soysa 75, I. D. Gunawardene 34; N. D. Priyaratne four for 46) and 118 for four (W. N. M. Soysa 40 not out).

At Panadura Esplanade, Panadura, February 27, 28, March 1. Drawn. Panadura SC* 287 (D. Wickremanayake 30, M. P. Silva 36, A. K. D. A. S. Kumara 33, M. Jayasena 76 not out; P. K. Serasinghe three for 73) and 202 for six (F. N. Jayalath 38, D. Wickremanayake 42, A. K. D. A. S. Kumara 40 not out, K. C. Silva 40 not out); Police SC 208 (W. N. M. Soysa 57, M. N. C. Silva 30, R. R. Wimalasiri 72 not out; S. D. Anurasiri three for 59).

At Braybrooke Place, Colombo (Moors), February 27, 28, March 1. Sebastianites C and AC won by 176 runs. Sebastianites C and AC 268 (B. C. M. S. Mendis 160, D. Seneviratne 41; A. Lankatilleke three for 75) and 272 for three dec. (W. D. J. Abeywardene 72, P. Salgado 37, N. R. G. Perera 78 not out, B. C. M. S. Mendis 76); Matara SC* 212 (T. D. Munasinghe 57, S. M. Faumi 57, L. S. Suwandaratne 31; W. D. J. Abeywardene three for 27, N. R. G. Perera four for 75) and 152 (N. R. G. Perera seven for 66)
    In Sebastianites' first innings, Mendis and Seneviratne added 164 for the ninth wicket.

At Reid Avenue, Colombo, March 6, 7, 8. Bloomfield C and AC won by an innings and 161 runs. Bloomfield C and AC* 517 for seven dec. (S. K. Perera 62, M. T. Gunaratne 108, S. T. Perera 73, R. S. Kalpage 100 not out, R. Palliyaguru 62, Extras 46; K. C. Silva three for 144); Panadura SC 191 (D. Wickremanayake 34, K. C. Silva 80 not out, M. H. Fernando 31; P. W. Gunaratne four for 45) and 165 (C. Perera 49, D. Wickremanayake 60; P. W. Gunaratne four for 34).

At Havelock Park, Colombo (Colts), March 6, 7, 8. Drawn. Colombo CC* 352 (N. S. Bopage 39, S. K. L. de Silva 75, A. Polonowitta 48, C. P. Handunettige 47, D. Arnolda 95; K. E. A. Upashantha five for 108, D. Hettiarachchi five for 84) and 176 for two (N. S. Bopage 108 not out); Colts CC 296 (D. P. Samaraweera 66, C. Mendis 43, S. I. Fernando 33, M. T. Sampath 33, J. Kulatunga 55; I. S. Gallage three for 62, A. P. Dalugoda three for 84).

Colts wicket-keeper D. Vitharana made four catches and two stumpings in Colombo's first innings.

At Moratuwa Stadium, Moratuwa, March 6, 7, 8. Nondescripts CC won by six wickets. Sebastianites C and AC* 246 (S. Silva 60, N. R. G. Perera 53, C. Liyanage 32; L. E. Hannibal three for 42, A. T. Weerappuli four for 75) and 256 (S. Silva 75, B. C. M. S. Mendis 95; L. E. Hannibal four for 36); Nondescripts CC 417 (S. Warusamana 69, A. Rideegammanagedera 121, P. K. Rajapakse 30, C. Fernando 93; C. Liyanage four for 59, N. R. G. Perera three for 142) and 89 for four (C. Liyanage three for 31).

At Reid Avenue, Colombo, March 13, 14, 15. Drawn. Matara SC 203 (N. R. C. K. Guruge 46, S. M. Faumi 50; R. Palliyaguru three for 20) and 233 for six (T. D. Munasinghe 71, P. Siriwardene 35, N. R. C. K. Guruge 39; P. P. Wickremasinghe three for 44); Bloomfield C and AC* 566 for seven dec. (S. K. Perera 52, M. T. Gunaratne 36, M. N. Nawaz 109, R. S. Kalpage 42, P. B. Dassanayake 66, P. P. Wickremasinghe 121 not out, R. Palliyaguru 61, B. de Silva 54 not out).

At Maitland Crescent, Colombo (CCC), March 20, 21, 22. Colombo CC won by 85 runs. Colombo CC 241 (P. B. Ediriweera 32, S. K. L. de Silva 41, D. Arnolda 35, A. P. Dalugoda 31; D. P. M. C. Waidyaratne five for 87, P. I. W. Jayasekera three for 37) and 212 (N. S. Bopage 92, P. B. Ediriweera 35; P. Siriwardene seven for 48); Matara SC* 254 (S. Kulatunga 45, L. S. Suwandaratne 62, P. I. W. Jayasekera 46; M. J. H. Rushdie five for 74, S. H. Alles three for 56) and 114 (M. S. Ramzan 32; I. S. Gallage three for 15, M. J. H. Rushdie five for four).

At Braybrooke Place, Colombo (Moors), March 27, 28, 29. Drawn. Matara SC 147 (V. H. K. Ranaweera three for 59, I. D. Gunawardene five for 35) and 355 for six (N. R. C. K. Guruge 60, S. M. Faumi 127, L. S. Suwandaratne 63 not out, G. Lanka 41 not out); Police SC* 301 for eight dec. (R. C. Liyanage 91, M. N. C. Silva 54, R. R. Wimalasiri 66 not out).

Group B

At Panadura Esplanade, Panadura, January 2, 3, 4. Antonians SC v Singha SC. Abandoned.

At Havelock Park, Colombo (BRC), January 2, 3, 4. Moors SC won by six runs. Moors SC* 174 (U. C. Hathurusinghe 42; A. P. Ranaweera three for 46, S. Madanayake five for 19) and 185 (N. de Silva 70; D. Rajapakse three for 16); Burgher RC 154 (A. P. Ranaweera 36, W. C. Labrooy 31; U. C. Hathurusinghe four for 25, A. S. Jayasinghe three for 27) and 199 (C. R. Perera 66, D. Rajapakse 52; R. S. Priyadarshana three for 24, M. R. Farouk three for 27).

At Maitland Place, Colombo (SSC), January 2, 3, 4. Drawn. Tamil Union C and AC* 262 (V. Wijegunawardene 33, U. D. U. Chandana 65, D. N. Nadarajah 35, C. P. H. Ramanayake 47, A. Weerakoon 45 not out; G. R. K. Wijekoon three for 27, K. J. Silva five for 76) and 223 (E. M. I. Galagoda 44, V. Wijegunawardene 49, D. N. Nadarajah 40, N. Shiroman 30; K. J. Silva three for 46, S. H. S. M. K. Silva four for 50); Sinhalese SC 246 (R. P. A. H. Wickremaratne 101; M. S. Villavarayen three for 51).

Tamil Union wicket-keeper Galagoda made five catches and a stumping in SSC's innings.

At Havelock Park, Colombo (BRC), January 9, 10, 11. Drawn. Singha SC* 220 (S. Jayantha 77, R. R. K. Wimalasena 49, A. D. B. Ranjith 36; W. C. Labrooy four for 57, I. Amerasinghe three for 43) and 172 (T. M. Dilshan 46; D. D. Madurapperuma five for 43); Burgher RC 178 (C. R. Perera 47, D. D. Madurapperuma 52; M. M. de Silva five for 57) and 83 for six (M. M. de Silva five for 28).

At Welagedera Stadium, Kurunegala, January 9, 10, 11. Tamil Union C and AC won by 180 runs. Tamil Union C and AC 236 (D. N. Nadarajah 91, V. S. K. Waragoda 59, S. Weerakoon 37 not out; M. W. Kumara five for 48) and 146 for seven dec. (E. M. I. Galagoda 59, S. I. de Saram 30; A. W. Ekanayake three for 44); Kurunegala Youth CC* 112 (P. K. Aluwihare 31; M. S. Villavarayen five for 26) and 90 (N. Jaymon 41; M. S. Villavarayan four for 41, U. D. U. Chandana four for 18).

At Havelock Park, Colombo (BRC), January 16, 17, 18. Burgher RC won by five wickets. Tamil Union C and AC 95 (C. P. H. Ramanayake 37; I. Amerasinghe four for 17) and 185 (S. I. de Saram 64, Extras 30; W. C. Labrooy three for 48, S. Madanayake four for 54); Burgher RC* 143 (N. Shiroman three for 31) and 139 for five (M. Rajapakse 38, D. Rajapakse 53 not out).

At Braybrooke Place, Colombo (Moors), January 16, 17, 18. Moors SC won by 212 runs. Moors SC 315 (U. C. Hathurusinghe 125, M. S. Sampan 89, R. S. Priyadarshana 51; M. W. Kumara five for 104) and 183 for five dec. (A. S. Jayasinghe 55, S. Wijesiri 44, U. C. Hathurusinghe 51 not out; R. Herath three for 72); Kurungela Youth CC* 58 (U. C. Hathurusinghe five for eight) and 228 (R. R. Jaymon 55, S. Malmewala 38, A. W. R. Madurasinghe 61 not out; R. Jayasinghe three for 55).

At Havelock Park, Colombo (BRC), January 23, 24, 25. Drawn. Sinhalese SC 208 (A. A. W. Gunawardene 54, S. Kalawithigoda 77; A. P. Ranaweera three for 46, S. Madanayake five for 40) and 230 for seven dec. (A. A. W. Gunawardene 102, M. Perera 30, H. Jayasuriya 40); Burgher RC* 207 (C. U. Jayasinghe 53, D. Rajapakse 38, S. K. B. Tennekoon 43, Extras 32; G. P. Wickremasinghe four for 44, S. H. S. M. K. Silva three for 61, H. Jayasuriya three for 27) and 101 for four (C. U. Jayasinghe 58 not out).

At Welagedera Stadium, Kurunegala, January 23, 24, 25. Drawn. Kurunegala Youth CC* 248 (R. Kariyawasam 78, N. Munasinghe 37, H. Liyanage 38; A. D. B. Ranjith six for 63) and 260 for nine (R. R. Jaymon 58, A. W. R. Madurasinghe 51; M. M. de Silva five for 86); Singha SC 402 (C. Galappathy 32, N. T. Thenuwara 107, A. S. Wewalwala 94, S. Jayantha 38, A. D. B. Ranjith 40, H. Premasiri 52).

At Welagedera Stadium, Kurunegala, February 6, 7, 8. Drawn. Antonians SC 350 for eight dec. (S. K. Silva 65, W. A. M. P. Perera 106, P. N. Wanasinghe 79; A. W. Ekanayake three for 100, R. Kariyawasam three for 56) and 165 (W. A. M. P. Perera 30, E. F. M. U. Fernando 30, M. A. Fernando 33; R. Herath three for 31); Kurunegala Youth CC* 214 (R. R. Jaymon 55, A. W. Ekanayake 40; N. S. Samarawickrame five for 43).

At Braybrooke Place, Colombo (Moors), February 6, 7, 8. Drawn. Tamil Union C and AC* 216 (V. S. K. Waragoda 32, U. D. U. Chandana 42, C. P. H. Ramanayake 57; A. S. Jayasinghe three for 42, U. C. Hathurusinghe four for 67) and 271 for seven (B. Jaganathan 31, N. Shiroman 69, V. S. K. Waragoda 46, U. D. U. Chandana 63; U. C. Hathurusinghe three for 67); Moors SC 440 (A. Hettiarachchi 64, U. C. Hathurusinghe 60, A. S. Jayasinghe 92, M. S. Sampan 36, R. S. Priyadarshana 35, K. Jayasinghe 48 not out, Extras 44; M. S. Villavarayen four for 90).

At Maitland Place, Colombo (SSC), February 6, 7, 8. Sinhalese SC won by 236 runs. Sinhalese SC* 314 (S. Kalawithigoda 38, R. P. A. H. Wickremaratne 42, S. H. S. M. K. Silva 36, A. S. A. Perera 45 not out, G. P. Wickremasinghe 48; S. Sanjeewa four for 78, M. M. de Silva three for 48) and 272 for four dec. (A. A. W. Gunawardene 51, R. P. A. H. Wickremaratne 62 not out, U. N. K. Fernando 101 not out); Singha SC 132 (S. H. S. M. K. Silva four for 30) and 218 (N. T. Thenuwara 44, A. S. Wewalwala 63, S. Jayantha 30; A. S. A. Perera three for 45, H. Jayasuriya three for 36).

At Havelock Park, Colombo (BRC), February 13, 14, 15. Antonians SC won by one wicket. Burgher RC* 231 (M. Rajapakse 78, S. Mackay 36, S. Madanayake 52 not out; K. G. Perera four for 86) and 155 (D. Rajapakse 40, S. Madanayake 33; T. Dammika six for 40, K. G. Perera three for 33); Antonians SC 173 (M. A. Fernando 51, Extras 31; I. Amerasinghe three for 25, S. Madanayake four for 52) and 214 for nine (W. A. M. P. Perera 44, Y. N. Tillekeratne 44, Extras 32; A. P. Ranaweera three for 22).

At Braybrooke Place, Colombo (Moors), February 13, 14, 15. Drawn. Singha SC* 278 (T. M. Dilshan 36, N. T. Thenuwara 35, S. Jayantha 53, A. D. B. Ranjith 55; R. S. Priyadarshana four for 70) and 290 for eight dec. (T. M. Dilshan 124, H. Premasiri 40, S. Sanjeewa 57 not out); Moors SC 216 (M. S. Sampan 36, K. Jayasinghe 54; A. D. B. Ranjith three for 89, M. M. de Silva three for 38) and 210 for five (A. S. Jayasinghe 127 not out, A. Hettiarachchi 32).

At Maitland Place, Colombo (SSC), February 13, 14, 15. Sinhalese SC won by 392 runs. Sinhalese SC 443 for three dec. (M. S. Atapattu 42, S. Kalawithigoda 77, D. P. M. D. Jayawardene 200 not out, R. P. A. H. Wickremaratne 100 not out) and 204 for eight dec. (M. S. Atapattu 83, H. Jayasuriya 39; M. W. Kumara three for 72, R. Herath five for 93); Kurungela Youth CC* 143 (A. S. A. Perera four for 43) and 112 (A. S. A. Perera four for 43, K. J. Silva four for 17).

In SSC's first innings, Jayawardene and Wickremaratne added 274 unbroken runs for the fourth wicket.

At Maitland Place, Colombo (SSC), February 20, 21, 22. Sinhalese SC won by 282 runs. Sinhalese SC* 439 for five dec. (M. S. Atapattu 200, A. Ranatunga 103, R. P. A. H. Wickremaratne 55, M. Perera 36 not out) and 251 for seven dec. (M. S. Atapattu 35, A. A. W. Gunawardene 37, S. Ranatunga 52, A. Ranatunga 83; R. S. Priyadarshana five for 88); Moors SC 215 (M. S. Sampan 41, K. Jayasinghe 43 not out; G. P. Wickremasinghe four for 65, S. H. S. M. K. Silva four for 57) and 193 (N. de Silva 40, A. S. Jayasinghe 34; S. H. S. M. K. Silva five for 74, K. J. Silva three for 62).

At P. Saravanamuttu Stadium, Colombo, February 20, 21, 22. Tamil Union C and AC won by an innings and 108 runs. Antonians SC* 236 (W. B. Ekanayake 35, P. N. Wanasinghe 39, Y. N. Tillekeratne 76; M. S. Villavarayen three for 65, M. Muralitharan four for 82) and 99 (C. P. H. Ramanayake five for 30); Tamil Union C and AC 443 for eight dec. (E. M. I. Galagoda 44, N. Shiroman 97, S. I. de Saram 97, V. S. K. Waragoda 54, V. Wijegunawardene 65; M. A. Fernando four for 82).

At P. Saravanamuttu Stadium, Colombo, February 27, 28, March 1. Tamil Union C and AC won by 166 runs. Tamil Union C and AC 233 (N. Shiroman 55, V. S. K. Waragoda 59, V. Wijegunawardene 47; S. Sanjeewa four for 94, A. S. Wewalwala three for 39) and 258 for nine dec. (E. M. I. Galagoda 31, N. Shiroman 33, V. S. K. Waragoda 44, V. Wijegunawardene 39, D. N. Nadarajah 35; S. Sanjeewa three for 89, M. M. de Silva four for 40); Singha SC* 147 (S. Jayantha 36, G. Sanjeewa 35; M. R. C. N. Bandaratilleke three for 37) and 178 (H. Premasiri 65; M. S. Villavarayen four for 58, M. R. C. N. Bandaratilleke five for 48).

At Welagedera Stadium, Kurungela, March 6, 7, 8. Burgher RC won by 71 runs. Burgher RC* 219 (C. R. Perera 32, S. K. B. Tennekoon 47, S. Madanayake 40; R. Herath four for 41) and 254 for nine dec. (C. U. Jayasinghe 36, C. R. Perera 71, D. Rajapakse 31, S. K. B. Tennekoon 31, Extras 34; R. Herath three for 68, R. Kariyawasam three for 40); Kurungela Youth CC 157 (R. Herath 44; I. Amerasinghe four for 46) and 245 (R. R. Jaymon 63, S. Malmewala 33, A. W. Ekanayake 38 not out, Extras 33; W. C. Labrooy three for 53, I. Amerasinghe three for 38).

At Braybrooke Place, Colombo (Moors), March 6, 7, 8. Moors SC won by seven wickets. Antonians SC* 118 (R. S. Priyadarshana three for 35, U. C. Hathurusinghe three for 22) and 252 (S. K. Silva 57, E. F. M. U. Fernando 56, P. N. Wanasinghe 57; U. C. Hathurusinghe seven for 55); Moors SC 262 (U. C. Hathurusinghe 83, R. S. Priyadarshana 80; T. Dammika three for 76) and 109 for three (U. C. Hathurusinghe 44).

At St Thomas's Ground, Mount Lavinia, March 12, 13, 14. Sinhalese SC won by 81 runs. Sinhalese SC* 257 (A. A. W. Gunawardene 36, M. Perera 39, S. Ranatunga 39, U. N. K. Fernando 46, H. Jayasuriya 30; K. G. Perera five for 65, K. Dharmasena four for 75) and 111 (K. G. Perera six for 46); Antonians SC 201 (E. F. M. U. Fernando 38, P. N. Wanasinghe 88; H. Jayasuriya four for 25) and 86 (A. S. A. Perera four for 15).

Semi-finals

At Reid Avenue, Colombo, March 27, 28, 29. Drawn. Sinhalese SC were declared winners by virtue of their first-innings lead. Sinhalese SC* 321 (S. Ranatunga 151, H. Jayasuriya 61; S. H. Alles five for 72) and 263 for four (M. Perera 37, R. P. A. H. Wickremaratne 132 not out, S. Ranatunga 34 not out; A. P. Dalugoda three for 72); Colombo CC 271 (S. K. L. de Silva 119, D. Arnolda 37; S. Arunakumara five for 79).

At Maitland Place, Colombo (SSC), April 17, 18, 19. Drawn. Bloomfield C and AC were declared winners by virtue of their first-innings lead. Bloomfield C and AC* 351 (S. K. Perera 75, M. T. Gunaratne 66, M. N. Nawaz 40, R. S. Kalpage 58; R. S. Priyadarshana three for 105, U. C. Hathurusinghe three for 88) and 262 for five (M. T. Gunaratne 64, M. N. Nawaz 93, S. T. Perera 39); Moors SC 298 (M. Shiyam 33, U. C. Hathurusinghe 74, N. de Silva 38, K. Jayasinghe 49; P. W. Gunaratne five for 53).

Final

At Maitland Place, Colombo (SSC), April 30, May 1, 2, 3. Drawn. Sinhalese SC won the P. Saravanamuttu Trophy by virtue of their first-innings lead. Bloomfield C and AC* 313 (M. T. Gunaratne 31, M. N. Nawaz 34, H. D. P. K. Dharmasena 109, P. W. Gunaratne 42, Extras 35) and 295 for four (S. T. Perera 53, R. S. Kalpage 120 not out, M. N. Nawaz 68); Sinhalese SC 582 (M. S. Atapattu 179, A. Ranatunga 192, R. P. A. H. Wickremaratne 60; R. L. Perera three for 94, R. Palliyaguru three for 75, R. S. Kalpage three for 127).

Atapattu and Ranatunga added 259 for SSC's fourth wicket.

CHAMPIONS

Lakspray Trophy		1992-93	Sinhalese SC
1988-89	{ Nondescripts CC Sinhalese SC	1993-94	Nondescripts CC
1989-90	Sinhalese SC	1994-95	{ Bloomfield C and AC Sinhalese SC
P. Saravanamuttu Trophy		1995-96	Colombo CC
1990-91	Sinhalese SC	1996-97	Bloomfield C and AC
1991-92	Colts CC	1997-98	Sinhalese SC

INDIVIDUAL ONE-DAY INTERNATIONAL RATINGS

The PricewaterhouseCoopers One-Day International Ratings, introduced in August 1998, follow similar principles to the Test Ratings (see page 1093).

The leading ten batsmen and bowlers in the One-Day International Ratings after the Emirates Triangular Tournament which ended on August 21 were:

	Batsmen	Rating		Bowlers	Rating
1.	S. R. Tendulkar (*Ind.*)	845	1.	M. Muralitharan (*SL*)	862
2.	B. C. Lara (*WI*)	837	2.	Saqlain Mushtaq (*Pak.*)	831
3.	M. G. Bevan (*Aus.*)	810	3.	A. A. Donald (*SA*)	821
4.	S. T. Jayasuriya (*SL*)	798	4.	D. Gough (*Eng.*)	809
5.	Saeed Anwar (*Pak.*)	765	5.	C. E. L. Ambrose (*WI*)	801
6.	P. A. de Silva (*SL*)	777	6.	S. M. Pollock (*SA*)	798
7.	N. J. Astle (*NZ*)	749	7.	Wasim Akram (*Pak.*)	782
8.	{ W. J. Cronje (*SA*) { R. T. Ponting (*Aus.*)	727 727	8.	C. Z. Harris (*NZ*)	729
			9.	A. Kumble (*Ind.*)	722
10.	M. E. Waugh (*Aus.*)	705	10.	A. R. C. Fraser (*Eng.*)	720

CRICKET IN ZIMBABWE, 1997-98

By JOHN WARD

Adam Huckle

After their improvement the previous season, Zimbabwe confidently expected that 1997-98 would be the year in which they established themselves on the international stage. However, it became the most disappointing since the country gained Test status. As New Zealand and Sri Lanka have found in the past, victories beget victories. The first few wins are the hardest to achieve, before the team learns self-belief and the technique of forcing home advantage. Luck also plays a part, and Zimbabwe had little of it. A remarkable number of fairly close matches swung on small hinges; several times it seemed that Zimbabwe had done everything right, only for the opposition to pull something extra out of the bag.

But there were also times when the team let the opposition off the hook. Their catching close to the wicket, so brilliant in the past, proved fallible. Then again, Zimbabwe were constantly frustrated by a single individual standing in the gap to deny them. But for Chris Harris, Zimbabwe could have won both Test and one-day series at home to New Zealand, and, but for Yousuf Youhana, they would probably have beaten Pakistan as well.

There was one more damaging factor. During the Second Test at Colombo, Zimbabwe had built a winning position with tremendous determination, and Sri Lanka found themselves 189 short of victory with their last two recognised batsmen together. At this point the umpires, who had received virulent local criticism for earlier decisions against the home side, stopped giving decisions at all. Several catches were disallowed, and numerous lbw appeals rejected. De Silva and Ranatunga secured victory, but Zimbabwe were convinced that weak umpiring had denied them a second Test win. Team coach Dave Houghton was fined and suspended for his comments; he sent videotapes of crucial decisions to ICC with little apparent effect. Instead of having their confidence boosted, Zimbabwe were left fighting anger, bitterness and frustration. On an unhappy tour of New Zealand, they put up their poorest performance in six seasons of Test cricket.

There is no telling how long this decline might have lasted but for Grant Flower. Zimbabwe went into their third series without a break when they entertained Pakistan at home. At Bulawayo, Zimbabwe faced cheap dismissal, but Flower stood in the breach and carried his bat for 156. Thereafter Zimbabwe were back to normal: strong competitors, but lacking the self-belief and technique to force victory. This was confirmed during a triangular one-day competition in India, involving Australia. They lost all four matches by narrow margins batting second.

The most satisfying part of the season had been another triangular series, in October, with Kenya and Bangladesh. For once, Zimbabwe had no disadvantage in assurance and experience: they won all six matches with ease, illuminating the large gap between Test nations and the rest.

After twenty years of marvellous service, Houghton retired, aged 40, from the first-class game, mainly because of niggling injuries. He played at home against New Zealand but, while his strokeplay looked as strong as ever, he often fell to poor shot selection. Zimbabwe missed not only his batting but also his tactical awareness on the field. Retirement enabled him to contribute more as national coach, and he was anxious to establish a cricket academy, on the Australian model, where promising youngsters would enjoy intensive training. He spent June on a sponsored walk from Bulawayo to Harare, and hoped to raise enough money to open the Academy in 1999.

Two newcomers making their debuts as Houghton departed were batsman Murray Goodwin and leg-spinner Adam Huckle. Both grew up in Zimbabwe, but Goodwin emigrated to Australia as a child, and Huckle attended university in South Africa. Both returned at the start of the season; Huckle became the first Zimbabwean to take ten wickets in a Test – going on to 11 – in his second match, while Goodwin launched himself with a batting average of 55 in six Tests.

Financial constraints and the amateur status of all but the leading international players mean that Zimbabwean cricketers still play much less domestic first-class cricket than other nations – a mere two possible matches each, down from three the previous year. The Logan Cup competition had been expanded from two teams to three, with the addition of Mashonaland A, probably the best solution until the provinces have greater depth of talent. But the total number of matches remained at three, and the competition was still very one-sided, as the Zimbabwe Cricket Union decided that Mashonaland A should be virtually a second eleven. Predictably, Mashonaland proved much too strong and trounced Mashonaland A and Matabeleland by an innings apiece. The competition set some sort of bizarre record, being decided just nine days into the season which, for the first time, started in August. The idea was to give the international players match practice before the New Zealand series, but its value was debatable given that the cricket was so uncompetitive. No change was expected in 1998-99, except that the Logan Cup was scheduled for January. Again, only one round was planned.

The club scene was dominated by Universals of Harare, who won two national and two provincial trophies. They were captained by Ali Shah, who enjoyed a vintage season with the bat at the age of 38. Universals were formerly an all-Asian club, but they now aim for a multiracial team, and fielded current national captain Alistair Campbell and his predecessor Andy Flower. Eddo Brandes opened the batting successfully after injury prevented him from bowling, and the attack was based on the pace trio of Antiguan Colin Joseph, David Mutendera and Bernard Pswarayi. The club's cricket chairman, Macsood Ebrahim, said their success proved that cricket in Zimbabwe can best progress when teams are fully multi-racial. Furthering this philosophy, Andy Flower was to move in 1998-99 to second-league team Winstonians, which consists mainly of keen young black players. Flower hoped to help them fight their way to first-league status.

Political events in Zimbabwe also cast some uncertainty over cricket. The cash-strapped Zimbabwe Cricket Union could ill-afford further economic difficulties. The government drastically reduced the amount of money put into its schools, and it was feared that many would no longer be able to afford the kit. The farming community, keen cricket supporters who run a strong winter league, were also threatened by government proposals to redistribute their farms.

At the ZCU prize-giving and awards ceremony, Grant Flower deservedly won the Player of the Season award for the second successive year, while Mutendera, believed by many to be a future Test player, won the Bob Nixon Trophy for the best Under-21 player. Mluleki Nkala, who impressed on the 1997 Under-19 tour to England, was selected for the annual scholarship to the Australian Academy.

The team which had toured England was clearly inexperienced, but showed they had learned fast in the first round of the Under-19 World Cup in South Africa, where they beat the West Indian team to progress to the Super League. It is regrettable that financial constraints prevent the country's young players from enjoying more than the occasional tour, home or abroad. The development programme continues, not as quickly as anybody would like, but once again constrained by lack of money. The ZCU rightly believes that the emphasis, when a choice is necessary, should be on quality rather than quantity, and visitors, including David Richards, chief executive of ICC, have been impressed by what they have seen.

In August 1998, ZCU chief executive Don Arnott retired after five years in the job, to be replaced by David Ellman-Brown, who had masterminded Zimbabwe's promotion to Test status, but resigned after being made a partner in the accountancy firm Coopers & Lybrand. Retirement from business left him free to return to cricket, where his ability as an administrator is legendary. Zimbabwe cricket keenly looked forward to a new era of progress under his leadership.

FIRST-CLASS AVERAGES, 1997-98

BATTING

(Qualification: 200 runs)

	M	I	NO	R	HS	100s	Avge
M. W. Goodwin (*Mashonaland A*)	3	6	1	456	166*	1	91.20
G. W. Flower (*Mashonaland*)	7	11	1	762	156*	3	76.20
A. Flower (*Mashonaland*)	6	10	1	585	201	3	65.00
G. J. Whittall (*Matabeleland*)	6	11	1	496	203*	1	49.60
G. J. Rennie (*Mashonaland A*)	5	9	0	358	101	1	39.77
H. H. Streak (*Matabeleland*)	6	11	2	322	81	0	35.77

* Signifies not out.

BOWLING

(Qualification: 10 wickets)

	O	M	R	W	BB	5W/i	Avge
J. A. Rennie (*Matabeleland*)	69.3	17	189	12	9-76	1	15.75
B. C. Strang (*Mashonaland*)	171	68	356	19	5-49	1	18.73
G. W. Flower (*Mashonaland*)	114.2	35	223	11	5-37	1	20.27
A. G. Huckle (*Matabeleland*)	208.3	45	689	22	6-109	2	31.31
P. A. Strang (*Mashonaland*)	180.1	52	421	11	3-54	0	38.27
H. H. Streak (*Matabeleland*)	160	36	440	11	3-42	0	40.00

LONRHO LOGAN CUP, 1997-98

The three contesting teams played each other once. No match points were awarded. Mashonaland were declared winners by virtue of beating the other two teams outright.

*In the following scores, * by the name of a team indicates that they won the toss.*

At Harare South Country Club, Harare South, August 28, 29. Mashonaland won by an innings and 146 runs. Mashonaland A* 181 (G. J. Rennie 101; U. Ranchod three for 34, G. C. Martin three for 39) and 158 (G. J. Rennie 50; G. W. Flower five for 37, U. Ranchod three for 42); Mashonaland 485 for eight dec. (C. B. Wishart 144, A. Flower 201, G. K. Bruk-Jackson 32; A. M. Blignaut three for 140, D. P. Viljoen three for 93).

Andy Flower's 201, his maiden double-hundred, lasted 345 minutes and 281 balls and included 26 fours. He and Wishart added 295 for the third wicket, a Zimbabwean record.

At Old Hararians Sports Club, Harare, September 4, 5. Mashonaland won by an innings and 36 runs. Mashonaland* 307 (G. W. Flower 89, A. Flower 116; J. A. Rennie three for 52, A. R. Whittall three for 52, A. G. Huckle three for 77); Matabeleland 129 (H. H. Streak 61 not out; E. Matambanadzo three for 27, B. C. Strang five for 49) and 142 (G. J. Whittall 42, H. H. Streak 41).

Huckle made his first appearance in Zimbabwean first-class cricket since 1991-92; his next match was the First Test against New Zealand.

At Bulawayo Athletic Club, Bulawayo, October 23, 24, 25. Drawn. Mashonaland A* 312 (T. G. Bartlett 33, M. W. Goodwin 78, T. L. Penney 76, K. J. Davies 43; J. A. Rennie nine for 76) and 279 for five dec. (M. A. Vermeulen 35, T. G. Bartlett 40, M. W. Goodwin 78, T. L. Penney 44 not out, D. J. R. Campbell 32 not out); Matabeleland 300 for seven dec. (J. R. Craig 76, M. D. Abrams 34, H. H. Streak 81, K. A. Burki three for 24) and 277 for nine (G. J. Whittall 61, J. A. Rennie 64, A. R. Whittall 39; A. M. Blignaut three for 56).

John Rennie became only the third bowler in Zimbabwean cricket to take nine wickets in an innings, after Mike Procter (1972-73) and Stephen Peall (1995-96), but could not add a tenth in the second innings. Goodwin, who had previously played for Western Australia, made his first-class debut in Zimbabwe and scored 78 off 46 balls.

LONRHO LOGAN CUP WINNERS

1993-94	Mashonaland Under-24
1994-95	Mashonaland
1995-96	Matabeleland
1996-97	Mashonaland
1997-98	Mashonaland

CRICKET IN BANGLADESH, 1997-98

By UTPAL SHUVRO

Bangladesh turned into a land of fiesta after their victory in the ICC Trophy in April 1997. Cricket emerged as a new dream, and the cricketers became national heroes. But they failed to fulfil heightened expectations in the season that followed. After the success in Kuala Lumpur, the national squad continued to frustrate their fans.

Bangladesh had their busiest-ever season in 1997-98, thanks to the granting of one-day international status, along with the right to play first-class cricket, after their ICC Trophy success. They toured Kenya, India, Pakistan, New Zealand and finally the British Isles, but could not generate much optimism about their likely performance in the 1999 World Cup in England.

Moreover, problems between national coach Gordon Greenidge and the Bangladesh Cricket Control Board became public knowledge when Greenidge, the former West Indian opener awarded honorary citizenship after the ICC Trophy triumph, told a local newspaper that he was not getting proper co-operation from the Board. His outburst came after vice-president Syed Ashraful Haq called him a "rookie" as a coach. The Board took rapid action: Greenidge was not sent with the national side to the Commonwealth Games in Kuala Lumpur, and his position became increasingly difficult, though he was eventually confirmed as coach for the World Cup.

Bangladesh did reach one or two memorable landmarks during the season. They had started playing one-day internationals in 1985-86, but could not register a win in any of their first 22 games. The much-cherished victory came at last in the 23rd match, against Kenya in the Coca-Cola Cup in India in May 1998, although it was over-shadowed by poor results in the rest of the tournament. The disappointing performances of the Bangladesh team had started in the three-nation President's Cup in Kenya in October 1997. They conceded two heavy defeats to Kenya, the team they had beaten to win the ICC Trophy final (which did not have senior international status) six months earlier, and succumbed for a paltry 92 against Zimbabwe – their lowest score in one-day internationals.

The team made its first-class debut during the New Zealand tour in November. But they lost all four first-class matches, three of them by an innings, and two one-day games. The only notable feat was Bangladesh's maiden first-class century, scored by the talented but enigmatic Al-Shahriar Rokon. Bangladesh's first team took part in Pakistan's domestic one-day tournament, the Wills Cup, while the second string was sent to India. The national side later toured the UK for nearly two months, learning to adapt to English conditions as part of its preparation for the World Cup in 1999. But defeats by Ireland and Scotland, previously considered much weaker than Bangladesh, added to the team's heartache.

It would be unfair to blame only the players for the frustrating results. The selectors should also be held responsible. From the ICC Trophy in March 1997 until the Coca-Cola Cup in May 1998, they experimented with 30 or so players, which meant the side could never find a settled look. Questions could also be asked of the team management, in which Greenidge had a permanent presence.

The Board encountered further difficulties in reforming domestic cricket. To realise their dream of winning Test status, it was a must to play the longer version of the game as well as the one-day cricket already well-established in the country. But the Board's efforts met with resistance from the leading clubs, who said they could not afford it. Eventually, the Dhaka Premier League, the country's largest, agreed to switch to a format of 80 overs a side.

In fact, Bangladesh's greatest achievement in 1997-98 came when they successfully hosted the three-nation Silver Jubilee Independence Cup, marking 25 years of independence, in January. Although Bangladesh could not register any upset against their two mighty neighbours, India and Pakistan, Dhaka entered the record books as India beat Pakistan by scoring 316, the highest total to win a one-day international chasing a target. This was a prelude to the first Mini World Cup tournament, played among the nine Test nations, in October 1998. There was local disappointment that Bangladesh were not allowed to take part, but the presence of most of the world's greatest players in Dhaka – only a month after Bangladesh had suffered some of its worst floods in memory – did a great deal to restore national morale and the unprecedented enthusiasm for cricket created by the ICC Trophy win. It also established Dhaka as a popular and welcoming international venue.

Unfortunately, the 1997-98 season was marred by a terrible incident. The former Indian Test cricketer, Raman Lamba, who played for Abahani, sustained a head injury while fielding at short leg in a league match against Mohammedans. He died in hospital three days later. Lamba was a very popular figure in Bangladesh, and a pioneer in cricket's revival. The country was shocked and saddened.

For the second season running, Abahani won the Dhaka Premier League. Arch rivals Mohammedans could not achieve success despite hiring the services of Sri Lankan captain Arjuna Ranatunga and Pakistani Test batsman Basit Ali. They were not even runners-up, being displaced by Brothers Union. Mohammedans had to be satisfied with winning the Victory Day tournament. Abahani also retained the Damal Memorial Tournament, the season's curtain-raiser.

CRICKET IN KENYA, 1998

By JASMER SINGH

After an eventful two years in which Kenya defeated West Indies in the World Cup, finished second in the ICC Trophy in Malaysia and were granted one-day international status, the national side set about trying to consolidate their position.

They went some way to achieving this in May when they beat India by 69 runs under the floodlights in Gwalior to reach the final of the Coca-Cola Cup, a triangular competition also involving Bangladesh. It was Maurice Odumbe's day: he hit 83 and took three wickets. Though India had little to play for – they had already qualified for the final, where they took revenge – the result was significant because it effectively confirmed Kenya as the best of the non-Test-playing nations, ahead of Bangladesh.

This helped make up for other disappointments during the year, the humiliating defeat against Gauteng in the quarter-final of the Standard Bank Cup in South Africa, when Kenya managed only 134 in their 45 overs, and lost by eight wickets. The team also failed to do themselves justice when a strong England A team visited for a week marred by bad weather. In September, they lost to New Zealand and Pakistan in the Commonwealth Games in Malaysia, but they did beat Scotland, one of the other qualifiers for the 1999 World Cup. Then, in October, they competed in the first African Cup in Namibia, along with Botswana, Lesotho, Namibia, Uganda, and Zambia plus the development teams from South Africa and Zimbabwe. Kenya won all their matches and the trophy, taking particular pleasure from the wins over the big two. Hitesh Modi scored 84 against Botswana, 70 not out against Uganda and an unbeaten 104 against Zimbabwe, and was named man of the match in all three games.

Unfortunately, financial constraints and the heavy schedules of the Test-playing countries preparing for the World Cup prevented Kenya from staging an international tournament in 1998. Instead, to give their players much-needed experience, they sent nine of them abroad to play league cricket: six to South Africa, three to England.

In the major domestic league, reigning champions Nairobi Gymkhana, fielding six national players, finished second behind the Sir Ali Muslim Club. Two players passed 1,000 runs: Pakistani professional Tariq Javed, playing for SAMC, scored 1,276, and

Steve Tikolo of Nairobi Gymkhana made 1,027. Shakil Khan was the leading wicket-taker with 35, while Asif Karim headed the averages, taking 25 wickets at 7.60. Nairobi Gymkhana won the cup competition, beating the Aga Khan Club in the final by six wickets with 13 overs to spare.

There were three significant appointments in 1998. Kenya's most successful captain, Maurice Odumbe, swapped roles with vice-captain Asif Karim. Alvin Kallicharran, the former West Indian batsman, was appointed national coach. And in July, Jimmy Rayani was appointed chairman of the ICC's associate members.

Kenya, conscious of its growing stature in world cricket, is making strides to develop the game at all levels – from primary schools right up to international matches. Professionalism is growing, and the days of staging social cricket on a voluntary basis are all but over. The World Cup will be a huge test, and Kenya's aim will be to achieve not just another great win, but an all-round consistency that has so far eluded them.

CRICKET IN DENMARK, 1998

By PETER S. HARGREAVES

The high point of the Danish season came at the European Championship in The Hague. Coached by their former star fast bowler Ole Mortensen, Denmark recovered from a poor start to beat Ireland and Scotland, and make it to the final, only to lose to Holland by five wickets. With better luck, they might have won the competition: the captain, Peer Jensen, was attending the birth of his child, while Denmark's two players on county books – Søren Westergaard of Warwickshire, and Hampshire's Thomas Hansen – were troubled by injury. Hansen made it through the tournament, but Westergaard was eventually dropped. The side had begun their preparation for the Championship with a successful tour of Namibia, which included an innings of 197 by 21-year-old Carsten Petersen in a drawn three-day match.

Svanholm again dominated the domestic scene, winning both the knockout cup, where they beat Herning in the final, and the league. Glostrup came second, as they had in 1997, while KB finished third, their highest place for 40 years. The Pakistani club, Ishøj, were relegated from the top division, to be replaced by Skanderborg, but Herning survived, after winning a play-off against Chang-Aalborg of the second division. Muktar Butt of Nørrebro scored most runs – 464 – but Mickey Lund of Svanholm topped the averages with 89.00. Glostrup's Søren Sørensen headed the bowling averages with 26 wickets at 11, while 17-year-old Amjad Khan of KB took most wickets – 27. He made a fine debut for Denmark in the European Championship, leading to interest from two counties.

The Under-19 men's team took part in the World Cup in South Africa and, though they lost to Sri Lanka and Pakistan, defeats of Ireland and Namibia helped them finish 13th out of 16. The women's team, in their World Cup in India, were drawn in much the harder pool and scored just one win, over Pakistan. But they managed to draw a two-match series at home to Holland in July, having lost both games the previous year. The Dansk XL Club won the annual Forty Clubs' triangular tournament, held in England.

The turf wickets at Brøndby were expected to be ready for Denmark's first appearance in the NatWest Trophy, but the ECB will not allow the new pitch to be used until after a thorough inspection, so Denmark's home debut will be delayed until at least 2000. One notable first for Danish cricket occurred in 1997: the two matches against British Combined Services – both of which Denmark won – were broadcast almost in their entirety on national television.

CRICKET IN THE NETHERLANDS, 1998

By DAVID HARDY

After disappointing results in 1997, Holland recovered their self-respect in 1998 with a well-deserved victory in the European Cricket Championship on home soil – or rather matting. Held in The Hague at three clubs – HCC, HBS and Quick – the event was a resounding success. Ten teams were split, according to strength, into two groups. Holland won the stronger Group A convincingly, beating Denmark, Ireland, Scotland and an ECB XI.

Luuk van Troost, a burly all-rounder from the Excelsior club in Schiedam and brother of Somerset's Andre, twice won the match award in the group section: against Denmark he made 82 and took three for 24, while against Scotland he hit 64 not out and claimed five for 27. Other leading performers were captain and all-rounder Tim de Leede, Klaas Jan van Noortwijk, a stylish batsman, and opener Roger Bradley from New Zealand, the one remnant of the policy to include foreign-born professionals in the Dutch team. Old rivals Denmark, who were runners-up in Group A, were the opposition in the final, and de Leede saved his best for last, scoring 33 and taking four for 20. But van Troost delighted a 1,500-strong crowd with a quickfire 29 to help seal victory for Holland by five wickets, and was named man of the tournament.

Holland had benefited enormously from their short tour of Western Province in South Africa. But they remained inconsistent, as performances either side of the European Championship showed. In June, Holland gave their worst display in the NatWest Trophy since entering the competition in 1995: Somerset bowled them out for 117 and got the runs in 17.4 overs. South Africa arrived for a one-day game the following month, and won comfortably. Then, in August, the visit by an Indian A team proved an acute embarrassment: in a series of one and two-day matches, an under-strength Holland capitulated for 56, 73, 95 and 96. Their lack of professional status was cruelly exposed as many of their big names were unavailable: almost all the players either study or have full-time jobs and, at the end of a busy season, they were not granted any more leave to play. The Indians were so insulted by the standard of the opposition that, in the last two-day game, they ground out a meaningless 505 for eight.

On the domestic scene, VRA of Amstelveen, one of only two clubs in Holland with a grass wicket, won the Premier League (*Hoofdklasse*) for the first time since 1981. The title race went down to the penultimate over of the final match, when VRA beat closest rivals VOC of Rotterdam by one wicket. VRA won 13 of their 18 matches, finishing two points ahead of VOC (the points system is simple – two for a win, one for a tie, and none for a loss, with all games 55 overs a side). Two New Zealanders were central to VRA's success: Craig Cumming was the League's leading scorer, with 862 runs, while former Test player Shane Thomson finished sixth in the batting averages and fourth in the bowling. Also prominent were three young Dutch internationals who had recently transferred from other clubs – Bas Zuideent, Maurits Houben and Jaap Leemhuis.

But it was Guyanese-born former Dutch international Rupert Gomes, now well into his 40s and playing for the Gandhi club, who topped the batting averages with 772 runs at 70.18. The leading bowlers were both Australians: Colin Miller headed the averages with 35 wickets at 9.05 for Rood en Wit, Haarlem; while VOC's Peter McIntyre had most victims, with 45. A few weeks later, Miller followed McIntyre in winning a Test cap.

Voorburg CC were relegated from the *Hoofdklasse*, to be replaced in 1999 by Koninklijke UD of Deventer, who won 17 of their 18 matches in the first division (*Eerste Klasse*). Their return to the elite should be of wider benefit to the game in Holland as they possess the country's only other grass wicket. 1999 is also important for Dutch cricket, because it marks the first-ever World Cup match in continental Europe, when South Africa play Kenya on the grass pitch at VRA.

CRICKET ROUND THE WORLD, 1998

ASIAN CRICKET COUNCIL TROPHY

Rejoicing in their status as a fully fledged member of the limited-overs international fraternity, Bangladesh easily overpowered the lesser nations of the region to win the second Pepsi ACC Trophy held in Kathmandu, Nepal, in October 1998. Their victory over Malaysia, the surprise finalists, qualified them to contest the next Asia Cup with the major subcontinental powers in Dhaka. The biennial ACC carnival is growing in popularity; and for the first time the semi-finals and final were televised. The United Arab Emirates and Hong Kong lost in the semi-finals; Singapore, Papua New Guinea, Japan, Thailand, the Maldives and Nepal also took part.

Mostly, the standard of cricket was modest. But clearly a culture of cricket is developing in some countries in the region – most notably in Malaysia and Singapore. The game has long had royal patronage in Malaysia, and His Highness Tunku Imran, president of the Malaysian Cricket Association, was on hand to restate his belief that his country could attain Test match status by 2020. He also talked about his idea of an "East Indies" team to play one-day internationals, drawing on the finest players from the Asian countries which do not have Test status.

Though the tournament was played on turf, the quality of pitches left much to be desired, especially at the two minor venues. Conditions were better at the principal venue of Tribhuvan University, though the steadfast refusal of curator Prem Chand Sharma to cross-roll the pitch resulted in an uneven surface. Nepalese officials believe the ground can become an alternative venue to Sharjah and Toronto for matches between the game's leviathans. With its steep grass embankments, chenar trees and outlook over the foothills of the Kathmandu Valley, it would be a very attractive one. – Mike Coward.

Mike Coward is cricket columnist of The Australian.

BELGIUM

Big hitters prospered in Belgian cricket in 1998, as much rain and grassy outfields favoured the brave. For the first time a club did the double: Pakistan Greens CC won both the league and the cup, losing only one game all season. The best individual performance came from David Steele, who hit an unbeaten 100 out of 130 for Royal Brussels against Twelve Stars. Steele is no relation to the former England cricketer, and is both younger and plumper. He has similar dedication, though: he travels each weekend for his cricket from his job in eastern Germany. New clubs from Geel and Hasselt acquitted themselves well in the second division, and Ostend CC look likely to join this Flemish contingent in 1999. As well as the increasingly healthy geographical spread, the game continues to attract women and youngsters. Royal Brussels Ladies played what amounted to a Test series against the Luxembourg Maidens, and mixed teams have made evening social cricket popular. The Belgians like the gear; the expats like the beer. – Colin Wolfe.

BRUNEI DARUSSALAM

When the players of Brunei and Sarawak trudged off the field on November 8, 1998, a 36-week cricket season came to an end. It had been interrupted just after it started, for health reasons. The longest drought in living memory led to major bush and scrub fires. As air quality deteriorated, the authorities issued warnings about engaging in outside physical activity, and when one fit young batsman was forced to retire ill, it was time to call a halt. The league competition was finally completed, with Cavaliers narrowly winning the title. Yachties won the Galfar Cup, however. Cavaliers' hopes of a double foundered when they were shot out for 33 in the semi-final by lowly Manggis. Brunei hosted the triangular tournament with Sabah and Sarawak for the Borneo Cup, which Sabah won. – Derek Thursby.

CANADA

Canada continues to work for one-day international status by 2000. One success already achieved was beating strong competition from the US and Ireland for the right to stage the next ICC Trophy in 2001. We now have six turf wickets, including the Toronto Cricket Club, where India and Pakistan play for the Sahara Cup. Canada failed to win a game in the Commonwealth Games, but the Under-19 squad performed creditably in their first visit to the Caribbean for the Nortel Championships. The inaugural Harmony Festival, the North American Cup and numerous touring teams made for a busy summer from British Columbia to Nova Scotia. – Geoff Edwards.

EUROPEAN CHAMPIONSHIP

Holland beat Denmark in the final of the European Championships in The Hague to cap a successful tournament in which the Dutch team's unbeaten run brought in good crowds and substantial local media interest. The competition involved associate members of ICC plus Germany and the England ECB XI, divided into two divisions based on merit. Holland's match-winner was already in evidence on the first day; the tall, left-handed all-rounder Luuk van Troost, brother of the Somerset player Andre, who was absent with a broken wrist. Van Troost led them to victory over Denmark, and these two finished at the head of the group, clear of Scotland, Ireland and England. Holland and Denmark met again in the final, where the Dutch captain Tim de Leede and van Troost were the most effective with bat and ball in a five-wicket win, along with Klaas Jan van Noortwijk, who made 54 not out. The week's sensation, however, came in the challenge match between the English team, bottom of the first group, and Italy, winners of the second group, ahead of Germany, France, Israel and Gibraltar. England made 242 for eight off 50 overs but were blown away by Italy's Australian-born opener Joe Scuderi, who hit 106 with six sixes. The opening pair put on 183 and Italy won by five wickets with seven overs to spare. The next tournament will be in Scotland in 2000. – Peter S. Hargreaves.

FALKLAND ISLANDS

The annual match between the Governor's XI and the Forces resulted in a thrilling one-run win for the Governor's XI, reducing the Forces' lead in the series to 4-3. The contest is played on the world's southernmost cricket field, Mount Pleasant Oval, for a handsome trophy, mounted on rock, representing a penguin's beak emerging from an egg. The Oval can hold the entire population of the Falkland Islands: 4,000. The matting wicket traditionally favours bowlers, but only when they have the wind behind them. Those bowling into the wind regularly struggle to reach the opposite end. – Richard Heller.

FRANCE

France's promotion to ICC associate status could not quite match the soccer World Cup as the French sporting highlight of 1998. But both the BBC and Sky were sufficiently interested to send crews to Liettres, near Calais, for a celebration of what is claimed to be the first written mention of cricket. A 1478 petition in the Archives Nationales records how "Gunner Estievenet Le Grant left the castle in Liettres . . . and arrived at a spot where people were playing with a ball near a stake at *criquet*". A plaque was unveiled, a street renamed Allée du Criquet, and a paying crowd of 450 saw France defeat the Kent 50+ team by 52 runs on the field beneath Le Grant's castle. The year also saw the establishment of a network of regional development officers, and a French translation of the Laws. France avenged their defeat by Italy in the European Championships with two wins at Chauny a month later. Paris Université retained the national championship, and Gymkhana won the French Cup. – Simon Hewitt.

GERMANY

Mark Brodersen booked his place in German cricket history when he became the first German-born player to score an international century: 104 not out against Gibraltar during the European Championships at The Hague. Four days later, Gerrit Müller became the second, with 119 not out against France. Germany were the only affiliate member who joined the ICC associates in this tournament, and came seventh out of ten. They were not admitted by ICC to join the associates in 1998, but were to be reconsidered for 1999. DSSC Berlin successfully defended the German Championship by beating Hassloch Cosmopolitans. – Brian Fell.

GIBRALTAR

Gibraltar had a disappointing showing in the European Championships against rivals who fielded more experienced teams. In contrast, Gibraltar took a young squad, including two 17-year-olds and four in their early 20s, all products of Gibraltar's development programme. Domestically, Gibraltar CC lifted the Senior League for the fourth consecutive season. However, they were deprived of the double when UKCC beat them in the Murto Cup final. More and more youngsters are moving up the ranks, as evidenced by the form of Calpe CC, in their second season and mainly made up of teenagers, who came second in the Senior League. – T. J. Finlayson.

HONG KONG

Despite concerns about the resilience of the game after the change of sovereignty in June 1997, Hong Kong cricket has continued to flourish. The usual busy season took place during 1997-98, and there was international competition at Under-13, 15, 19 and 23 levels; the vast majority of the three younger groups were locally born, boding well for the future. The sixth Hong Kong International Sixes event was held in 1997, and was won by Pakistan for the third time. Attendance, though, was disappointing: the lack of star names and TV revenues led to an overall loss. The event was due to be replaced in September 1998 by an International Super-Max Eights competition, representing the "third generation" form of the game. Unfortunately, due to lack of sponsorship arising from the Asian economic downturn, it was postponed until 1999. – John Cribbin.

ISRAEL

If one is to gauge the standard of cricket in Israel by the performance of the national team, then 1998 was an upbeat year. Since 1997 we have won five games out of ten. At the European Championships, Israel lost the first three games, but came back strongly against Gibraltar. The fielding and fitness of the team improved markedly and the bowling showed more guile and enterprise. The batting, however, needs to become more resilient. Lions Lod again won the league title with a well-balanced bowling attack and depth in their batting. Neve Yonathan beat Netanya in the knockout final; Abe Daniels scored 86. Two new innovations were an Israeli version of Super Eights (won by Lions Lod) and a Friday league for observant cricketers unable to play on the Sabbath. Roland Lefebvre, our national coach, did outstanding work with both the seniors and juniors. Special tribute must be paid to Raymond Abrahams who has finally retired from cricket, aged 75. His father, the late Ben Abrahams, was the founder of cricket in Israel in 1948. And in those 50 years Raymond has always been involved in the game, either as player, umpire, coach or administrator. – Stanley Perlman.

ITALY

Italian cricket made further progress in 1998. In a week at the European Championship the *Azzurri* beat Gibraltar, France, Israel, Germany and the England ECB XI to gain fifth place and promotion to the A Pool for Scotland in 2000. Youth cricket was the other theme of the season, with an Under-18 tour of England the highlight: the policy of investing in coaches produced a new wave of *cricketari* all over the peninsula. Pianoro, from the Apennines, retained the pennant, beating Bologna in the finals 2-0, the second match being umpired by Darrell Hair. They also won the Under-15 Championship but lost in the semi-finals of the Italian cup, played under Cricket Max rules, to Grosseto, the eventual winners. In 1999 competitive cricket is due to be introduced to Sicily. Not even Lord Nelson got beyond Naples! – Simone Gambino.

JAPAN

In September, MCC visited us under the captaincy of their secretary Roger Knight, with four ex-professionals, nine very able players, and one congenial umpire. The first two games comfortably went to MCC. By the third, the Japanese were starting to show the benefits of listening to Roger and watching. The fourth made the history books. Batting first, the MCC could not find the gaps as before: catches were held and fielding was tight: they were soon 48 for nine. A 90-minute lunch break with a member of the Japanese Imperial family gave them a chance to regroup, and Andrew Wingfield Digby and Harry Latchman put on 45 for the last wicket. But 93 was never going to be enough. The young Japanese openers began confidently, facing up to Peter Hacker without flinching, and the All-Japan XI – comprising only Japanese, with no expatriates – beat the might of Marylebone by five wickets. Two weeks later, the team came down to earth when they were bowled out for 18 by Hong Kong in the Asian Cricket Council tournament; Hong Kong knocked off the runs in just 15 balls. But two days later, Japan bowled out the United Arab Emirates, the former ICC champions. Even though the batting let them down again, the all-round improvement is clear. The rising sun is now truly a cricket ball. – Trevor Bayley.

LUXEMBOURG

The admission of Luxembourg, one of the least likely of cricketing nations, to the giddy heights of affiliate status of ICC raised eyebrows in some quarters in 1998. The Grand Duchy is six times the size of Barbados but would fit into Australia 3,000 times, and it is scarcely known for its wild enthusiasm for the game. It has essentially one team, of minor-club standard, made up entirely of expatriates working either for the European Union or for one of the country's many banks. The chances of participation in anything like regular international matches for this small country, wedged between France, Germany and Belgium, must be remote indeed.

As an affiliate member, Luxembourg can observe at meetings and get a ticket allocation for the World Cup. One of Luxembourg cricket's senior figures, Anthony Dunning, said: "This is a milestone event. We are now members of the official worldwide fraternity of cricketing nations. It is a recognition that we exist on the cricketing map of the world."

However, no adult Luxembourgeois has ever been known to play the sport. The head of state, Grand Duke Jean, could at least have watched the game while he was a schoolboy at Ampleforth. It is rumoured that he used his influence to persuade the local commune at Walferdange to allow a recreation ground to be used by the cricket club, aptly called the Optimists.

Luxembourg now has a cricket federation – a qualifying requirement of ICC membership – but only by stretching a point, since a federation needs more than one team. It therefore counts two evening teams of Eurocrats and the Optimists' women's team to make up the numbers. To put it kindly, the federation was formed to give cricket official status with the sports ministry and the *Comité Olympique et Sportif du Luxembourg*. It now gets about £800 a year from the government, most of which is spent on sending representatives to meetings at Lord's. Appropriately, given Luxembourg's financial reputation, its most cogent contribution so far has been a suggestion that the European Cricket Council should hold its meetings on Fridays, instead of midweek, so delegates can qualify for cheaper weekend fares.

The Optimists, founded in the late 1970s after Britain joined the Common Market and started sending civil servants to Luxembourg, have to travel more than 130 miles to reach their nearest away fixture and, although the team has in the past won the Belgian League, last summer it sometimes struggled to raise a side. There are 35 players, but only 15 or so play regularly.

And things are getting harder. Luxembourg is no longer such a hub for EU institutions: the now-aging bureaucrats who arrived in the 1970s are not being supplemented by much new young blood, while the bankers nowadays tend to find the pressures of their jobs allow little time for cricket. There are young New Zealanders who play for the local rugby club, but they tend to want to spend their summer weekends touring Europe rather than cricketing. A few years ago, the Optimists were thrilled to find an Antipodean batsman who scored a century every time he played for them. The only trouble was that he could spare time from sightseeing only four times in two seasons before he too moved on.

The Luxembourgeois themselves tend to look towards American sports – they were liberated by General Patton in 1944 and remained in the American sector thereafter – and schools give little time to any games. The Optimists' chief hope for home-grown talent comes from the five sons of a team member who has married a local woman.

Robert Deed, club chairman, sighed: "We're called the Optimists, but I have to accept that cricket will remain an expatriate game. It is difficult to find people with time and energy to take the game to the local community. Unlike in Belgium, they can't even see it on television." – Stephen Bates.

Stephen Bates is Brussels correspondent of The Guardian.

MALAYSIA

Malaysian cricket has had an eventful two years, culminating in the Commonwealth Games in September 1998, and a place in the final of the Asian Cricket Council Trophy in Nepal. We have a young national team already and now have separate Under-15 and Under-19 national leagues, as well as the two-division Carlsberg National League; 24 teams took part in the Under-12 tournament in the northern town of Ipoh. As a result of the Commonwealth Games, we now have in the Klang Valley eight good turf wickets with clubhouses, and hope to hire foreign curators to look after them. We also send teams at five different age levels to the South-East Asian tournament, the Tunku Ja'afar Cup. This eats heavily into our budget, but we feel it is a worthy cause. – C. Sivanandan.

MALTA

Malta, who became an ICC affiliate in 1998, celebrate the centenary of cricket at the Marsa Oval in 1999. The game is played all year on an artificial pitch with a large, watered outfield: there is a match every Saturday, with fixtures against touring teams in midweek. The Hague were among the visiting clubs in 1998, and Malta is keen to welcome other teams and tourists on holiday who want to join us for a Saturday game. – Pierre Naudi.

MOROCCO

The Moroccan Cricket Club had an active season in 1997-98, and Moroccan cricketers, all young and with quick reflexes, have picked up the game swiftly without formal coaching. They won the Morocco–Pakistan Friendship Cup by six wickets after bowling out a Diplomatic Corps XI for 42 on the rugby ground in Rabat. Another fixture was played, in front of a large and curious crowd, on the lovely ground at Khemisset. Unfortunately, the talented captain, Idrissi Mohamed, whose medium-fast bowling was largely responsible for the win in Rabat, has now gone abroad, but hopes are pinned on his replacement, Amine Nejjati, a promising all-rounder. His brother Karim also plays, and his sister Asmae is the scorer. – S. Azmat Hassan, Pakistani Ambassador.

NAMIBIA

Cricket continued its momentum in Namibia, partly due to the appeal of the game on TV. Enough country towns entered the league to allow it to split into three regions for 1998-99: the huge distance between centres made the game expensive and difficult for teams who had to travel up to 900 km for a match. The highlight of the previous year was a four-wicket victory in a one-day match over the Danish national team, who had finished ten places higher than Namibia at the ICC Trophy. Namibia also took part in the South African Bowl competition, but failed to win any of their games. – Laurie Pieters.

NEPAL

As well as the successful Asian Cricket Council tournament (reported above), national cricket also grew in Nepal, and tournaments were held in eight different centres, including the remote village of Gunj Bhanwanipur. Thirty years ago, I went there on an elephant's back; this time I went by jeep but wished they had sent an elephant instead. In the final, Motihari from India beat the local team from Kaliya, watched by more than 6,000 people. Sixteen districts took part in the main competition, the Jai Trophy: Banke were the winners ahead of Rupendehi. – Jai Kumar Shah.

NORWAY

It was a successful season in Norway, despite Oslo experiencing its worst summer in 40 years: this is an especially serious problem when there is only one wicket in the entire country available for competition. The good news is that negotiations for a new wicket are well advanced. Sentrum CC won both the preliminary league, in which all nine teams in the country compete, and the top-six play-offs, to become Norwegian champions for the sixth successive year. The surprise club of the year was Drammen CC, who reached the last four in only their second year. This was just reward for their enterprise in building a concrete/mat wicket, which they cannot use for league matches but is clearly an invaluable practice facility. Another encouraging development was the formation of Stavanger CC, thanks to the presence of oil workers. – Bob Gibb.

QATAR

The elite cricketers of India and Pakistan staged two unofficial matches for their expatriate supporters in the Qatari capital of Doha in August 1998. Mohammad Azharuddin's Indian XI won the first match against Rashid Latif's Pakistanis by 16 runs at the Al Arabi Stadium, but lost the return at the Al Wakra Stadium by 141 runs. As with an earlier game in nearby Dubai, the matches were played on artificial surfaces on soccer fields. The Qatari games attracted crowds of 5,000 and were beamed live to the subcontinent. Further matches between the rivals are planned for Muscat and, possibly, Kuwait. – Mike Coward.

SLOVENIA

One of the least-known and prettiest parts of Europe has begun playing cricket. Slovenia – the peaceful and prosperous northern end of what was Yugoslavia – acquired a team when the Royal Hague Cricket Club of Holland were looking for fixtures. Even though cricket had never been played here, a motley crew of expatriates and one brave Slovene rose to the challenge. We cheekily asked the President of Slovenia, Milan Kucan, if we could use his name. He not merely agreed but attended the match, and I explained to him the origin of various cricketing phrases. "Oh," he replied, "so you might say the American attitude to our application to join NATO is not quite cricket." The game was the lead sports item on national TV, and led to a fixture in Austria. The next challenge is to find our own ground near Ljubljana. – Francis King.

SOUTH KOREA

The main topic of conversation among cricketers during the autumn was terrorism. Who could cricketers terrorise? This arose from a decision by the American authorities to discontinue cricket at the UN compound following the bombings of their embassies in Kenya and Tanzania. The Autumn Sixes competition had to be abandoned. And, instead of playing on grass, we had to move on to shale school pitches, where we compete with other sports for space; on one occasion, baseball was being practised in one corner, basketball behind the bowler's arm and soccer at mid-on. There were also wandering parents, children, roller-bladers, and the odd motorcycle and car. Courtesy of a local elementary school, whose vice-principal spent some time in Australia, we have now settled in a more suitable environment. Our frustration is real, but cricket is hardly a priority for the Americans. The Rest of the World team, led by Canadian Tony James, swept all the spring competitions, and we have fitted in tours to Japan and Hong Kong. – Olivier de Braekeleer.

SPAIN

Financial restrictions are still holding back Spanish cricket. Despite a three-year agreement to provide a budget for the sport, nothing has been forthcoming from the Government. We still managed to complete a full national league and cup programme, with help from Royal & Sun Alliance, even though teams often had to travel eight hours to fulfil fixtures. Spain was unable to turn out a national team, but a Select XI beat Portugal in Malaga. The most hopeful aspect is the development of youth games, with Kwik Cricket equipment, on the Costa Blanca. – Ken Sainsbury.

TURKEY

The Turkish museum on the Gallipoli peninsula that commemorates the 1915 campaign contains an aging photograph entitled *Kricket Oynuyor*. Anzac forces are shown playing cricket on Shell Green, a modest, flat basin secured at a cost of many lives. Despite the "ground" being overlooked by Turkish guns – hence the name – those shown in the photograph appear to be playing with typical vigour. On Anzac Day 1998 (April 25), there was a dawn service at 5.00 a.m., the time the original landings took place. A commemorative match was then arranged for Shell Green between the Anzacs and the Rest of the World. Hundreds of young Australians and New Zealanders sought to play for the Anzac team. The Rest of the World was more difficult to finalise, and it is not known whether it was to include any Turks. Sadly, the heavens opened and the match was abandoned before a ball could be bowled. – Anthony Bradbury.

UNITED STATES

Like a runner on a treadmill, American cricket has worked up quite a sweat just staying upright in recent years and, although 1998 produced a new constitution and a new administration, real progress remains difficult to measure. Months after tense elections, even some on the new board – supposedly a union of the old US Cricket Association and the rebel US Cricket Federation – wondered if the whole exercise, conducted at ICC's behest, was merely a shuffling of the deck.

Priorities remain confused over the most basic issues, such as whether experience or education should carry American cricket to the next level. Some touted the nation's debut in the West Indies' Red Stripe Bowl one-day competition in October as a Neil Armstrong-like step despite three thumping defeats, by 242 runs, ten wickets and seven wickets. Others attacked it as reckless indulgence with half the game's annual income of around $50,000 spent on a team consisting largely of expatriate West Indians, Pakistanis and Indians. US cricket has always been a battleground between egos and evangelists.

Until the game can pay for a full-time administration, it will remain in the charge of volunteers – in a country where baseballers and basketballers make millions of dollars are not enough. Even so, there seems cause for hope, if not yet optimism, with more than 10,000 registered players in the US. The overwhelming majority are imports, in large part thanks to the burgeoning computer industry, but there is at least a growing amount of second-generation immigrants who are in the US to stay. They have a thirst for cricket information, partially sated via the Internet. The playing resources, not to mention the commercial potential of the growing US market, make the US a front-runner for cricketing development. Already there are moves from ICC for an America's Cup of cricket, with the US pitted against the likes of Argentina, Cayman Islands and Canada, rather than providing fodder for comparative giants such as Barbados and Jamaica.

Perhaps more significantly, ICC is back in negotiations with the Disney Corporation for a field of international standard at the entertainment company's Orlando base, with a possible launch date in 2000 for the second Mini World Cup. The date is no accident: the US administration's contract with WorldTel, widely held to have scuppered ICC's earlier plans for Disney, will have expired.

Television rights for internationals staged in Florida would provide a ready pool for grassroots development in the US, which has got about as far as curing the common cold. To reinforce the point, there is believed to be just one professional coach in the US working with school-age players. That man, working his way along the West Coast, is former Glamorgan spinner Malcolm Nash, who, if nothing else, can empathise with the US team's recent experience in the Caribbean. It was he, of course, whom Sir Garry Sobers sent for six sixes in an over. – Trent Bouts.

Trent Bouts, former cricket correspondent of The Australian, *now lives in North Carolina.*

PART SEVEN:
ADMINISTRATION AND LAWS

INTERNATIONAL CRICKET COUNCIL

On June 15, 1909, representatives of cricket in England, Australia and South Africa met at Lord's and founded the Imperial Cricket Conference. Membership was confined to the governing bodies of cricket in countries within the British Commonwealth where Test cricket was played. India, New Zealand and West Indies were elected as members on May 31, 1926, Pakistan on July 28, 1952, Sri Lanka on July 21, 1981, and Zimbabwe on July 8, 1992. South Africa ceased to be a member of ICC on leaving the British Commonwealth in May, 1961, but was elected as a Full Member on July 10, 1991.

On July 15, 1965, the Conference was renamed the International Cricket Conference and new rules were adopted to permit the election of countries from outside the British Commonwealth. This led to the growth of the Conference, with the admission of Associate Members, who were each entitled to one vote, while the Foundation and Full Members were each entitled to two votes, on ICC resolutions. On July 12, 13, 1989, the Conference was renamed the International Cricket Council and revised rules were adopted.

On July 7, 1993, ICC ceased to be administered by MCC and became an independent organisation with its own chief executive, the headquarters remaining at Lord's. The category of Foundation Member, with its special rights, was abolished. On October 1, 1993, Sir Clyde Walcott became the first non-British chairman of ICC.

On June 16, 1997, ICC became an incorporated body, with an executive board and a president instead of a chairman. Jagmohan Dalmiya became ICC's first president.

Officers

President: J. Dalmiya.　*Chief Executive:* D. L. Richards.

Chairman of Committees: Cricket: Sir Clyde Walcott; *Development:* Dr A. Bacher; *Finance and Marketing:* E. Mani.

Executive Board: The five officers listed above sit on the board *ex officio*. They are joined by Sir John Anderson (New Zealand), J. Buzaglo (Gibraltar), P. Chingoka (Zimbabwe), S. H. Chowdhury (Bangladesh), Raj Singh Dungarpur (India), HRH Tunku Imran (Malaysia), Lord MacLaurin (England), Khalid Mahmood (Pakistan), D. W. Rogers (Australia), P. H. O. Rousseau (West Indies), T. Sumathipala (Sri Lanka), R. C. White (South Africa).

General Manager: R. M. G. Hill. *Cricket Operations Manager:* C. D. Hitchcock. *Development Manager:* R. M. Turner. *Executive Assistant:* D. C. Jamieson.

Constitution

President: Each Full Member has the right, by rotation, to appoint ICC's president. In 1997, India named J. Dalmiya to serve until 2000. Australia has nominated M. A. Gray to serve from 2000 to 2003. Subsequent presidents will serve for two years.

Chief Executive: Appointed by the Council. D. L. Richards was appointed in 1993; his contract has been extended until 2003.

Membership

Full Members: Australia, England, India, New Zealand, Pakistan, South Africa, Sri Lanka, West Indies and Zimbabwe.

Associate Members*: Argentina (1974), Bangladesh (1977), Bermuda (1966), Canada (1968), Denmark (1966), East and Central Africa (1966), Fiji (1965), France (1998), Gibraltar (1969), Hong Kong (1969), Ireland (1993), Israel (1974), Italy (1995), Kenya (1981), Malaysia (1967), Namibia (1992), Nepal (1996), Netherlands (1966), Papua New Guinea (1973), Scotland (1994), Singapore (1974), Uganda (1998), United Arab Emirates (1990), USA (1965) and West Africa (1976).

Affiliate Members*: Austria (1992), Bahamas (1987), Belgium (1991), Belize (1997), Brunei (1992), Cayman Islands (1997), Germany (1991), Greece (1995), Japan (1989), Kuwait (1998), Luxembourg (1998), Malta (1998), Portugal (1996), Spain (1992), Sweden (1997), Switzerland (1985), Thailand (1995) and Vanuatu (1995).

* *Year of election shown in parentheses.*

The following governing bodies for cricket shall be eligible for election.

    Full Members: The governing body for cricket recognised by ICC of a country, or countries associated for cricket purposes, or a geographical area, from which representative teams are qualified to play official Test matches.

    Associate Members: The governing body for cricket recognised by ICC of a country, or countries associated for cricket purposes, or a geographical area, which does not qualify as a Full Member but where cricket is firmly established and organised.

    Affiliate Members: The governing body for cricket recognised by ICC of a country, or countries associated for cricket purposes, or a geographical area (which is not part of those already constituted as a Full or Associate Member) where ICC recognises that cricket is played in accordance with the Laws of Cricket. Affiliate Members have no right to vote or to propose or second resolutions at ICC meetings.

ENGLAND AND WALES CRICKET BOARD

The England and Wales Cricket Board (ECB) became responsible for the administration of all cricket – professional and recreational – in England and Wales on January 1, 1997. It took over the functions of the Cricket Council, the Test and County Cricket Board and the National Cricket Association which had run the game in England and Wales since 1968. The Management Board is answerable to the First-Class Forum on matters concerning the first-class game and to the Recreational Forum on matters concerning the non-professional game. Each of the forums elects four members to the Management Committee.

Officers

Chairman: Lord MacLaurin of Knebworth. *Chief Executive:* T. M. Lamb.

Management Board: Lord MacLaurin (*chairman*), D. L. Acfield, J. B. Bolus, D. G. Collier, B. G. K. Downing, P. J. Edwards, F. H. Elliott, B. G. Ford, P. W. Gooden, R. Jackson, R. D. V. Knight, F. D. Morgan, J. B. Pickup.

Chairmen of Committees: First-Class Forum: F. D. Morgan; *Recreational Forum:* J. B. Pickup; *Cricket Advisory Committee:* D. L. Acfield; *England Management Advisory Committee:* J. B. Bolus; *Finance Advisory Committee:* B. G. Ford; *Marketing Advisory Committee:* B. G. K. Downing; *Discipline Standing Committee:* G. Elias QC; *Registration Standing Committee:* D. S. Kemp.

Deputy Chief Executive and Finance Director: C. A. Barker; *Director of Cricket Operations:* J. D. Carr; *Marketing Director:* T. D. M. Blake; *Corporate Affairs Director:* R. Peel; *Technical Director:* H. Morris; *National Development Manager:* K. R. Pont; *International Teams Director:* S. J. Pack; *Cricket Operations Manager (First-Class):* A. Fordham; *Cricket Operations Manager (Recreational):* F. Kemp; *National Manager of Women's Cricket:* B. A. Daniels.

THE MARYLEBONE CRICKET CLUB

The Marylebone Cricket Club evolved out of the White Conduit Club in 1787, when Thomas Lord laid out his first ground in Dorset Square. Its members revised the Laws in 1788 and gradually took responsibility for cricket throughout the world. However, it relinquished control of the game in the UK in 1968 and the International Cricket Council finally established its own secretariat in 1993. MCC still owns Lord's and remains the guardian of the Laws. It calls itself "a private club with a public function" and aims to support cricket everywhere, especially at grassroots level and in countries where the game is least developed.

Patron: HER MAJESTY THE QUEEN

Officers

President: 1998-2000 – A. R. Lewis.

Treasurer: M. E. L. Melluish.   *Chairman of Finance:* D. L. Hudd.

Trustees: Lord Cowdrey, D. R. W. Silk, J. C. Woodcock.

Hon. Life Vice-Presidents: Sir Donald Bradman, Lord Bramall, D. G. Clark, Lord Cowdrey, G. H. G. Doggart, Lord Griffiths, D. J. Insole, F. G. Mann, C. H. Palmer, E. W. Swanton, J. J. Warr.

Secretary: R. D. V. Knight.

Assistant Secretaries: A. I. C. Dodemaide (Head of Cricket), J. A. Jameson (Assistant Secretary of Cricket), C. A. Lewis (Head of Finance), C. W. W. Rea (Marketing and Public Affairs). *Personal Assistant to Secretary:* Miss S. A. Lawrence. *Curator:* S. E. A. Green.

MCC Committee, elected members 1998-99: D. J. C. Faber, C. A. Fry, Sir Michael Jenkins, D. R. Male, M. C. J. Nicholas, T. J. G. O'Gorman, D. A. Peck, D. Rich, O. H. J. Stocken, M. O. C. Sturt, J. A. F. Vallance, A. W. Wreford.

Chairmen of main sub-committees: E. R. Dexter (Cricket); B. M. Thornton (Estates); R. V. C. Robins (General Purposes).   *Chairmen of specialist sub-committees:* R. P. Hodson (Players and Fixtures); B. A. Sharp (Tennis and Squash); T. M. B. Sissons (Marketing); Lord Alexander (Arts and Libraries).

PROFESSIONAL CRICKETERS' ASSOCIATION

The Professional Cricketers' Association was formed in 1967 (as the Cricketers' Association) to represent the first-class county playing staffs, and to promote and protect professional players' interests. During the 1970s, it succeeded in establishing pension schemes and a minimum wage. In 1995, David Graveney became the Association's general secretary and first full-time employee; in 1998, he became chief executive. In 1997, the organisation set up its own management company to raise regular revenue and fund improved benefits for members of the PCA during and after their playing careers.

President: M. W. Gatting.   *Chairman:* M. V. Fleming.   *Chief Executive:* D. A. Graveney. *Managing Director, PCA Management:* R. H. Bevan.   *Directors:* H. Goldblatt, D. A. Graveney, T. J. G. O'Gorman.   *Communications Manager:* S. C. Ecclestone.

EUROPEAN CRICKET COUNCIL

On June 16, 1997, the eight-year-old European Cricket Federation was superseded by the European Cricket Council, bringing together all European ICC members, plus Israel. In 1998, the Council consisted of England (Full Member); Denmark, France, Gibraltar, Ireland, Israel, Italy, Netherlands and Scotland (Associate Members); and Austria, Belgium, Germany, Greece, Luxembourg, Malta, Portugal, Spain, Sweden and Switzerland (Affiliate Members).

Chairman: D. J. Insole.   *European Development Officer:* N. E. F. Laughton.

ADDRESSES

INTERNATIONAL CRICKET COUNCIL

D. L. Richards, The Clock Tower, Lord's Cricket Ground, London NW8 8QN (0171-266 1818; fax 0171-266 1777).

Full Members

AUSTRALIA: Australian Cricket Board, M. Speed, 90 Jolimont Street, Jolimont, Victoria 3002 (00 61 3 9653 9999; fax 00 61 3 9653 9911).
ENGLAND: England and Wales Cricket Board, T. M. Lamb, Lord's Ground, London NW8 8QZ (0171-432 1200; fax 0171-289 5619).
INDIA: Board of Control for Cricket in India, J. Y. Lele, Sanmitra, Anandpura, Baroda 390 001 (00 91 265 431233; fax 00 91 265 428833).
NEW ZEALAND: New Zealand Cricket Inc., C. Doig, PO Box 958, 109 Cambridge Terrace, Christchurch (00 64 3 366 2964; fax 00 64 3 365 7491).
PAKISTAN: Pakistan Cricket Board, Majid Khan, Gaddafi Stadium, Ferozepur Road, Lahore 54600 (00 92 42 575 4737/9936; fax 00 92 42 571 1860).
SOUTH AFRICA: United Cricket Board of South Africa, Dr A. Bacher, PO Box 55009, Northlands 2116 (00 27 11 880 2810; fax 00 27 11 880 6578).
SRI LANKA: Board of Control for Cricket in Sri Lanka, D. Ranatunga, 35 Maitland Place, Colombo 7 (00 94 1 691439/681601; fax 00 94 1 697405).
WEST INDIES: West Indies Cricket Board, G. S. Camacho, Factory Road, PO Box 616 W, Woods Centre, St John's, Antigua (00 1 268 460 5462/5465; fax 00 1 268 460 5452/5453).
ZIMBABWE: Zimbabwe Cricket Union, D. Ellman-Brown, PO Box 2739, Harare (00 263 4 704616/704617/704618; fax 00 263 4 729370).

Associate and Affiliate Members

ARGENTINA: Argentine Cricket Association, B. C. Roberts, ACA Sede Central, J. M. Gutierrez 3829, 1425 Buenos Aires (00 54 1 802 6166; fax 00 54 1 802 6692).
AUSTRIA: Österreichischer Cricket Verband, A. Simpson-Parker, Apollogasse 3/42, A-1070 Vienna (00 43 1 524 9366; fax 00 43 1 524 9367).
BAHAMAS: Bahamas Cricket Association, S. Deveaux, Government House, PO Box 1001, Nassau (00 1 242 322 1875; fax 00 1 242 322 4659).
BANGLADESH: Bangladesh Cricket Board, S. H. Chowdhury, Bangabandhu National Stadium, Dhaka 1000 (00 880 2 955 6343; fax 00 880 2 966 6808/955 4271).
BELGIUM: Belgian Cricket Federation, M. O'Connor, Koningin Astridlaan 98, B-2800 Mechelen (00 32 15 331 635; fax 00 32 15 331 639).
BELIZE: Belize National Cricket Association, Mrs V. Parks, Burnham Manse, 88 Albert Street, PO Box 619, Belize City (00 501 2 72201; fax 00 501 2 30936).
BERMUDA: Bermuda Cricket Board of Control, R. Outerbridge, PO Box HM992, Hamilton HM DX (00 1 441 292 8958; fax 00 1 441 292 8959).
BRUNEI: Brunei Darussalam National Cricket Association, S. Langton, PO Box 667, MPC, Badar Seri Begawan 3706, Brunei Darussalam (00 673 2 452889; fax 00 673 2 452890).
CANADA: Canadian Cricket Association, G. Edwards, 46 Port Street East, Mississauga, Ontario L5G 1C1 (00 1 905 278 5000; fax 00 1 905 278 5005).
CAYMAN ISLANDS: Cayman Islands Cricket Association, J. Powell, PO Box 1201 GT, George Town, Grand Cayman (00 1 345 945 5589; fax 00 1 345 945 5558).
DENMARK: Danish Cricket Association, J. Holmen, Idraettens Hus, 2605 Brøndby (00 45 4326 2160; fax 00 45 4326 2163).
EAST AND CENTRAL AFRICA: East and Central African Cricket Conference, T. B. McCarthy, PO Box 34321, Lusaka 1010, Zambia (00 260 1 226 228; fax 00 260 1 224 454/235 450).
FIJI: Fiji Cricket Association, P. I. Knight, PO Box 300, Suva (00 679 301 499/300 321; fax 00 679 301 618).

FRANCE: France Cricket, D. Marchois, La Saunerie, Manzac-sur-Vern, 24110 Saint Astier (00 33 5 5354 2783; also fax).

GERMANY: Deutscher Cricket Bund, B. Fell, Luragogasse 5, D-94032 Passau (00 49 851 34307; fax 00 49 851 32815).

GIBRALTAR: Gibraltar Cricket Association, T. J. Finlayson, 23 Merlot House, Vineyards Estate (00 350 79461; fax 00 350 41706).

GREECE: Greek Cricket Federation, C. Evangelos, Cat. Pappa 8, Corfu 49100 (00 30 661 47753; fax 00 30 661 47754).

HONG KONG: Hong Kong Cricket Association, J. A. Cribbin, Room 1019, Sports House, 1 Stadium Path, So Kon Po, Causeway Bay (00 852 250 48101; fax 00 852 257 78486).

IRELAND: Irish Cricket Union, J. Wright, The Diamond, Malahide, Co Dublin (00 353 1 845 0710; fax 00 353 1 845 5545).

ISRAEL: Israel Cricket Association, S. Perlman, PO Box 65085, Tel-Aviv 61650 (00 972 3 642 5529; fax 00 972 3 641 7271).

ITALY: Federazione Italiana Cricket, S. Gambino, Via S. Ignazio 9, 00186 Roma (00 39 6 689 6989; fax 00 39 6 687 8684).

JAPAN: Japan Cricket Association, T. Bayley, Nankitsu Machi 15-5, Maebashi City 371-0043 (00 81 272 37 3323; fax 00 81 272 37 3324).

KENYA: Kenya Cricket Association, M. Jaffer, PO Box 45870, Nairobi (00 254 2 221992; fax 00 254 2 213240).

KUWAIT: Kuwait Cricket Association, Abdul Muttaleb Ahmad, PO Box 6706, Hawalli-32042 (00 965 572 6600/573 4972; fax 00 965 573 4973).

LUXEMBOURG: Federation Luxembourgeoise de Cricket, T. Dunning, 87 rue de Dr Lucius Stroos, Reimberg L-8614 (00 352 430 132964; fax 00 352 430 132795).

MALAYSIA: Malaysian Cricket Association, K. Selveratnam, 1st Floor, Wisma OCM, Jalan Hang Jebat, 50150 Kuala Lumpur (00 60 3 201 6761; fax 00 60 3 201 3878).

MALTA: Malta Cricket Association, P. Naudi, c/o Marsa Sports and Country Club, Marsa HMR 15 (00 356 233 851; fax 00 356 231 809).

NAMIBIA: Namibia Cricket Board, L. Pieters, PO Box 457, Windhoek 9000 (00 264 61 263128/263129; fax 00 264 61 215149).

NEPAL: Cricket Association of Nepal, B. R. Pandey, PO Box 1432, Kantipath, Kathmandu (00 977 1 224782; fax 00 977 1 231166/226692).

NETHERLANDS: Royal Netherlands Cricket Board, A. de la Mar, Nieuwe Kalfjeslaan 21-B, 1182 AA Amstelveen (00 31 20 645 1705; fax 00 31 20 645 1715).

PAPUA NEW GUINEA: Papua New Guinea Cricket Board of Control, W. Satchell, PO Box 83, Konedobu NCD (00 675 321 1070; fax 00 675 321 7974).

PORTUGAL: Cricket Association of Portugal, J. Simonson, Largo de Academia Nacional de Belas Artes 16, Lisboa P-1200 (00 351 1 346 2277; fax 00 351 1 346 5079).

SCOTLAND: Scottish Cricket Union, R. W. Barclay, Caledonia House, South Gyle, Edinburgh EH12 9DQ (0131 317 7247; fax 0131 317 7103).

SINGAPORE: Singapore Cricket Association, A. Kalaver, 15 Stadium Road, National Stadium, Singapore 397718 (00 65 348 6566; fax 00 65 348 6506).

SPAIN: Asociacion Española de Cricket, K. Sainsbury, Casa Desiderata, AA 153, Javea E-03737, Alicante (00 34 96 579 4948; also fax).

SWEDEN: Sweden Cricket Board, Mrs I. Persson, Enskedevägen 81 12238, Enskede (00 46 8 6496167; fax 00 46 40 911467).

SWITZERLAND: Swiss Cricket Association, B. Pattison, 9 Chemin du Bois-Contens, CH-1291 Commugny (00 41 22 767 2923; fax 00 41 22 767 9191).

THAILAND: Thailand Cricket League, T. Sharma, 25-27 Soi 32/1, Charoen Nakhorn Road, Klongsan, Bangkok 10600 (00 66 2 862 7101; fax 00 66 2 862 4407).

UGANDA: Uganda Cricket Association, C. Azuba, c/o National Council of Sports, Lugogo Stadium, PO Box 8346, Kampala (00 256 41 220375; fax 00 256 41 223311).

UNITED ARAB EMIRATES: Emirates Cricket Board, M. Khan, Sharjah Cricket Stadium, PO Box 88, Sharjah (00 971 6 322 991; fax 00 971 6 334 741).

USA: United States of America Cricket Association, S. Caesar, 1689 Gilberto Street, Glendale Heights, Illinois 60139 (00 1 630 665 5582; also fax).

VANUATU: Vanuatu Cricket Association, M. Stafford, c/o Stafford and Associates, PO Box 734, Port Vila, Vanuatu (00 678 26104; fax 00 678 26105).

WEST AFRICA: West Africa Cricket Conference, Mrs Tayo Oreweme, Tafawa Balewa Square, Cricket Pavilion, Race Course, Lagos, Nigeria (00 234 1 261 4152; fax 00 234 1 261 4960).

UK ADDRESSES

ENGLAND AND WALES CRICKET BOARD: T. M. Lamb, Lord's Ground, London NW8 8QZ (0171-432 1200; fax 0171-289 5619).

MARYLEBONE CRICKET CLUB: R. D. V. Knight, Lord's Ground, London NW8 8QN (0171-289 1611; fax 0171-289 9100. Tickets 0171-432 1066; fax 0171-432 1061. Administration 0171-432 1046. Membership 0171-432 1026).

First-Class Counties

DERBYSHIRE: County Ground, Nottingham Road, Derby DE21 6DA (01332-383211; fax 01332-290251).

DURHAM: County Ground, Riverside, Chester-le-Street, County Durham DH3 3QR (0191-387 1717; fax 0191-387 1616).

ESSEX: County Ground, New Writtle Street, Chelmsford CM2 0PG (01245-252420; fax 01245-491607).

GLAMORGAN: Sophia Gardens, Cardiff CF1 9XR (01222-343478; fax 01222-377044).

GLOUCESTERSHIRE: Phoenix County Ground, Nevil Road, Bristol BS7 9EJ (0117-924 5216; fax 0117-924 1193).

HAMPSHIRE: Northlands Road, Southampton SO15 2UE (01703-333788; fax 01703-330121).

KENT: St Lawrence Ground, Old Dover Road, Canterbury CT1 3NZ (01227-456886; fax 01227-762168).

LANCASHIRE: County Cricket Ground, Old Trafford, Manchester M16 0PX (0161-282 4000; fax 0161-282 4100).

LEICESTERSHIRE: County Ground, Grace Road, Leicester LE2 8AD (0116-283 2128; fax 0116-244 0363).

MIDDLESEX: Lord's Cricket Ground, London NW8 8QN (0171-289 1300; fax 0171-289 5831).

NORTHAMPTONSHIRE: County Ground, Wantage Road, Northampton NN1 4TJ (01604-514455; fax 01604-514488).

NOTTINGHAMSHIRE: County Cricket Ground, Trent Bridge, Nottingham NG2 6AG (0115-982 3000; fax 0115-945 5730).

SOMERSET: County Ground, St James's Street, Taunton TA1 1JT (01823-272946; fax 01823-332395).

SURREY: The Oval, London SE11 5SS (0171-582 6660; fax 0171-735 7769).

SUSSEX: County Ground, Eaton Road, Hove BN3 3AN (01273-827100; fax 01273-771549).

WARWICKSHIRE: County Ground, Edgbaston, Birmingham B5 7QU (0121-446 4422; fax 0121-446 4544).

WORCESTERSHIRE: County Ground, New Road, Worcester WR2 4QQ (01905-748474; fax 01905-748005).

YORKSHIRE: Headingley Cricket Ground, Leeds LS6 3BU (0113-278 7394; fax 0113-278 4099).

Minor Counties

MINOR COUNTIES CRICKET ASSOCIATION: D. J. M. Armstrong, Thorpe Cottage, Mill Common, Ridlington, North Walsham NR28 9TY (01692-650563).

BEDFORDSHIRE: D. J. F. Hoare, "Gyr", 1a Falcon Avenue, Bedford MK41 7DS (01234-266648).

BERKSHIRE: J. A. W. Carlisle, 29 Oaken Grove, Newbury, Berkshire RG14 6DX (01635-46251 home; 01635-49175 business).

BUCKINGHAMSHIRE: K. A. Beaumont, 49 Amersham Road, Little Chalfont, Amersham, Buckinghamshire HP6 6SW (01494-763516).

CAMBRIDGESHIRE: P. W. Gooden, The Redlands, Oakington Road, Cottenham, Cambridge CB4 4TW (01954-250429).

CHESHIRE: J. B. Pickup, 2 Castle Street, Northwich, Cheshire CW8 1AB (01606-74970 home, 01606-74301 business; fax 01606-871034).

CORNWALL: The Rev. Canon Kenneth Rogers, 25 Paul's Row, Truro, Cornwall TR1 1HH (01872-261007).

CUMBERLAND: K. Ion, 47 Beech Grove, Stanwix, Carlisle, Cumbria CA3 9BG (01228-528858).

DEVON: G. R. Evans, Blueberry Haven, 20 Boucher Road, Budleigh Salterton, Devon EX9 6JF (01395-445216 home, 01392-258406 business; fax 01392-411697).

DORSET: K. H. House, The Barn, Higher Farm, Bagber Common, Sturminster Newton, Dorset DT10 2HB (01258-473394).

HEREFORDSHIRE: P. Sykes, 5 Dale Drive, Holmer Grange, Hereford HR4 9RF (01432-264703

HERTFORDSHIRE: D. S. Dredge, "Trevellis", 38 Santers Lane, Potters Bar, Hertfordshire EN6 2BX (01707-658377 home, 0171-359 3579 business).

LINCOLNSHIRE: C. A. North, "Koorah", Whisby Road, Whisby Moor, Lincoln LN6 9BY (01522-681636).

NORFOLK: S. J. Skinner, 27 Colkett Drive, Old Catton, Norwich NR6 7ND (01603-485940 home – weekend, 01354-659026 – midweek, 01733-412152 business).

NORTHUMBERLAND: A. B. Stephenson, Northumberland County Cricket Club, Osborne Avenue, Jesmond, Newcastle-upon-Tyne NE2 1JS (0191-281 2738).

OXFORDSHIRE: P. R. N. O'Neill, 4 Brookside, Thame, Oxfordshire OX9 3DE (01844-260439, also fax; 0411-943449 mobile).

SHROPSHIRE: N. H. Birch, Four Winds, 24 Ridgebourne Road, Shrewsbury, Shropshire SY3 9AB (01743-233650).

STAFFORDSHIRE: W. S. Bourne, 10 The Pavement, Brewood, Staffordshire ST19 9BZ (01902-850325 home, 01384-230001 business).

SUFFOLK: T. J. Pound, 94 Henley Road, Ipswich IP1 4NJ (01473-213288 home, 01473-232121 business).

WALES MINOR COUNTIES: W. Edwards, 59a King Edward Road, Swansea SA1 4LN (01792-462233; fax 01792-643931).

WILTSHIRE: C. R. Sheppard, 18 Bath Road, Swindon SN1 4BA (07071-221293 mobile).

Other Bodies

ASSOCIATION OF CRICKET UMPIRES AND SCORERS: G. J. Bullock, PO Box 399, Camberley, Surrey GU16 5ZJ (01276-27962).

BRITISH UNIVERSITIES SPORTS ASSOCIATION: J. Ellis, 8 Union Street, London SE1 1SZ (0171-357 8555).

CLUB CRICKET CONFERENCE: D. Franklin, 361 West Barnes Lane, New Malden, Surrey KT3 6JF (0181-949 4001).

COMBINED SERVICES: Major R. W. K. Ross-Hurst, c/o Army Sports Control Board, Clayton Barracks, Aldershot, Hampshire GU11 2BG.

ENGLISH SCHOOLS' CRICKET ASSOCIATION: K. S. Lake, 38 Mill House, Woods Lane, Cottingham, Hull HU16 4HQ.

EUROPEAN CRICKET COUNCIL: N. E. F. Laughton, Europe Office, Lord's Ground, London NW8 8QN (0171-432 1019; fax 0171-432 1018).

LEAGUE CRICKET CONFERENCE: N. Edwards, 1 Longfield, Freshfield, Formby, Merseyside.

MIDLAND CLUB CRICKET CONFERENCE: D. R. Thomas, 4 Silverdale Gardens, Wordsley, Stourbridge, W. Midlands DY8 5NU.

PROFESSIONAL CRICKETERS' ASSOCIATION: D. A. Graveney, Suite 210, 68 Lombard Street, London EC3V 9LJ (0171-868 1610: fax 0171-868 1803). PCA MANAGEMENT: R. H. Bevan, Hawkstone Park, Weston-under-Redcastle, Shrewsbury, Shropshire SY4 5UY (01939-200202; fax 01939-200699).

SCARBOROUGH CRICKET FESTIVAL: Colin T. Adamson, Cricket Ground, North Marine Road, Scarborough, North Yorkshire YO12 7TJ.

Cricket Associations and Societies

COUNCIL OF CRICKET SOCIETIES, THE: B. Rickson, 31 Grange Avenue, Cheadle Hulme, Cheshire SK8 5EN.

COUNTY CRICKET SUPPORTERS ASSOCIATION: Miss F. J. Walker, 12 Grasmere Drive, Linton Croft, Wetherby, West Yorkshire LS22 6GP.

CRICKET MEMORABILIA SOCIETY: A. Sheldon, 29 Highclere Road, Crumpsall, Manchester M8 4WH.

CRICKET SOCIETY, THE: E. R. Budd, 16 Storey Court, 39 St John's Wood Road, London NW8 8QX.

CRICKET STATISTICIANS AND HISTORIANS, ASSOCIATION OF: P. Wynne-Thomas, 3 Radcliffe Road, West Bridgford, Nottingham NG2 5FF.

NATIONAL CRICKET MEMBERSHIP SCHEME: c/o Cricket Lore, 22 Grazebrook Road, London N16 0HS.

SCOTLAND, CRICKET SOCIETY OF: A. J. Robertson, 5 Riverside Road, Eaglesham, Glasgow G76 0DQ.

WOMBWELL CRICKET LOVERS' SOCIETY: M. Pope, 59 Wood Lane, Treeton, Rotherham, South Yorkshire S60 5QR.

THE LAWS OF CRICKET

(1980 CODE)

As updated in 1992. World copyright of MCC and reprinted by permission of MCC. Copies of the "Laws of Cricket" may be obtained from Lord's Cricket Ground.

INDEX OF THE LAWS

LAW 1. THE PLAYERS

1. Number of Players and Captain

A match is played between two sides each of 11 players, one of whom shall be captain. In the event of the captain not being available at any time, a deputy shall act for him.

2. Nomination of Players

Before the toss for innings, the captain shall nominate his players, who may not thereafter be changed without the consent of the opposing captain.

Note

(a) **More or Less than 11 Players a Side**
A match may be played by agreement between sides of more or less than 11 players, but not more than 11 players may field.

LAW 2. SUBSTITUTES AND RUNNERS: BATSMAN OR FIELDSMAN LEAVING THE FIELD: BATSMAN RETIRING: BATSMAN COMMENCING INNINGS

1. Substitutes

In normal circumstances, a substitute shall be allowed to field only for a player who satisfies the umpires that he has become injured or become ill during the match. However, in very exceptional circumstances, the umpires may use their discretion to allow a substitute for a player who has to leave the field for other wholly acceptable reasons, subject to consent being given by the opposing captain. If a player wishes to change his shirt, boots, etc., he may leave the field to do so (no changing on the field), but no substitute will be allowed.

2. Objection to Substitutes

The opposing captain shall have no right of objection to any player acting as substitute in the field, nor as to where he shall field; however, no substitute shall act as wicket-keeper.

3. Substitute not to Bat or Bowl

A substitute shall not be allowed to bat or bowl.

4. A Player for whom a Substitute has Acted

A player may bat, bowl or field even though a substitute has acted for him.

5. Runner

A runner shall be allowed for a batsman who, during the match, is incapacitated by illness or injury. The person acting as runner shall be a member of the batting side and shall, if possible, have already batted in that innings.

6. Runner's Equipment

The player acting as runner for an injured batsman shall wear the same external protective equipment as the injured batsman.

7. Transgression of the Laws by an Injured Batsman or Runner

An injured batsman may be out should his runner break any one of Laws 33 (Handled the Ball), 37 (Obstructing the Field) or 38 (Run Out). As striker he remains himself subject to the Laws. Furthermore, should he be out of his ground for any purpose and the wicket at the wicket-keeper's end be put down he shall be out under Law 38 (Run Out) or Law 39 (Stumped), irrespective of the position of the other batsman or the runner, and no runs shall be scored.

When not the striker, the injured batsman is out of the game and shall stand where he does not interfere with the play. Should he bring himself into the game in any way, then he shall suffer the penalties that any transgression of the Laws demands.

8. Fieldsman Leaving the Field

No fieldsman shall leave the field or return during a session of play without the consent of the umpire at the bowler's end. The umpire's consent is also necessary if a substitute is required for a fieldsman, when his side returns to the field after an interval. If a member of the fielding side leaves the field or fails to return after an interval and is absent from the field for longer than 15 minutes, he shall not be permitted to bowl after his return until he has been on the field for at least that length of playing time for which he was absent. This restriction shall not apply at the start of a new day's play.

9. Batsman Leaving the Field or Retiring

A batsman may leave the field or retire at any time owing to illness, injury or other unavoidable cause, having previously notified the umpire at the bowler's end. He may resume his innings at the fall of a wicket, which for the purposes of this Law shall include the retirement of another batsman.

If he leaves the field or retires for any other reason he may resume his innings only with the consent of the opposing captain.

When a batsman has left the field or retired and is unable to return owing to illness, injury or other unavoidable cause, his innings is to be recorded as "retired, not out". Otherwise it is to be recorded as "retired, out".

10. Commencement of a Batsman's Innings

A batsman shall be considered to have commenced his innings once he has stepped on to the field of play.

Note

(a) Substitutes and Runners
For the purpose of these Laws, allowable illnesses or injuries are those which occur at any time after the nomination by the captains of their teams.

LAW 3. THE UMPIRES

1. Appointment

Before the toss for innings, two umpires shall be appointed, one for each end, to control the game with absolute impartiality as required by the Laws.

2. Change of Umpires

No umpire shall be changed during a match without the consent of both captains.

3. Special Conditions

Before the toss for innings, the umpires shall agree with both captains on any special conditions affecting the conduct of the match.

4. The Wickets

The umpires shall satisfy themselves before the start of the match that the wickets are properly pitched.

5. Clock or Watch

The umpires shall agree between themselves and inform both captains before the start of the match on the watch or clock to be followed during the match.

6. Conduct and Implements

Before and during a match the umpires shall ensure that the conduct of the game and the implements used are strictly in accordance with the Laws.

7. Fair and Unfair Play

The umpires shall be the sole judges of fair and unfair play.

8. Fitness of Ground, Weather and Light

(a) The umpires shall be the sole judges of the fitness of the ground, weather and light for play.

    (i) However, before deciding to suspend play, or not to start play, or not to resume play after an interval or stoppage, the umpires shall establish whether both captains (the batsmen at the wicket may deputise for their captain) wish to commence or to continue in the prevailing conditions; if so, their wishes shall be met.

    (ii) In addition, if during play the umpires decide that the light is unfit, only the batting side shall have the option of continuing play. After agreeing to continue to play in unfit light conditions, the captain of the batting side (or a batsman at the wicket) may appeal against the light to the umpires, who shall uphold the appeal only if, in their opinion, the light has deteriorated since the agreement to continue was made.

(b) After any suspension of play, the umpires, unaccompanied by any of the players or officials, shall, on their own initiative, carry out an inspection immediately the conditions improve and shall continue to inspect at intervals. Immediately the umpires decide that play is possible they shall call upon the players to resume the game.

9. Exceptional Circumstances

In exceptional circumstances, other than those of weather, ground or light, the umpires may decide to suspend or abandon play. Before making such a decision the umpires shall establish, if the circumstances allow, whether both captains (the batsmen at the wicket may deputise for their captain) wish to continue in the prevailing conditions; if so, their wishes shall be met.

10. Position of Umpires

The umpires shall stand where they can best see any act upon which their decision may be required.

Subject to this over-riding consideration, the umpire at the bowler's end shall stand where he does not interfere with either the bowler's run-up or the striker's view.

The umpire at the striker's end may elect to stand on the off instead of the leg side of the pitch, provided he informs the captain of the fielding side and the striker of his intention to do so.

11. Umpires Changing Ends

The umpires shall change ends after each side has had one innings.

12. Disputes

All disputes shall be determined by the umpires, and if they disagree the actual state of things shall continue.

13. Signals

The following code of signals shall be used by umpires who will wait until a signal has been answered by a scorer before allowing the game to proceed.

Boundary   – by waving the arm from side to side.
Boundary 6 – by raising both arms above the head.
Bye   – by raising an open hand above the head.
Dead Ball   – by crossing and re-crossing the wrists below the waist.
Leg-bye   – by touching a raised knee with the hand.
No-ball   – by extending one arm horizontally.
Out   – by raising the index finger above the head. If not out, the umpire shall call "not out".
Short Run   – by bending the arm upwards and by touching the nearer shoulder with the tips of the fingers.
Wide   – by extending both arms horizontally.

14. Correctness of Scores

The umpires shall be responsible for satisfying themselves on the correctness of the scores throughout and at the conclusion of the match. See Law 21.6 (Correctness of Result).

Notes

(a) Attendance of Umpires
The umpires should be present on the ground and report to the ground executive or the equivalent at least 30 minutes before the start of a day's play.

(b) Consultation between Umpires and Scorers
Consultation between umpires and scorers over doubtful points is essential.

(c) Fitness of Ground
The umpires shall consider the ground as unfit for play when it is so wet or slippery as to deprive the bowlers of a reasonable foothold, the fieldsmen, other than the deep-fielders, of the power of free movement, or the batsmen of the ability to play their strokes or to run between the wickets. Play should not be suspended merely because the grass and the ball are wet and slippery.

(d) Fitness of Weather and Light
The umpires should suspend play when they consider that the conditions are so bad that it is unreasonable or dangerous to continue.

LAW 4. THE SCORERS

1. Recording Runs

All runs scored shall be recorded by scorers appointed for the purpose. Where there are two scorers they shall frequently check to ensure that the score-sheets agree.

2. Acknowledging Signals

The scorers shall accept and immediately acknowledge all instructions and signals given to them by the umpires.

LAW 5.   THE BALL

1. Weight and Size

The ball, when new, shall weigh not less than 5½ ounces/155.9g, nor more than 5¾ ounces/163g; and shall measure not less than 8¹³/₁₆ inches/22.4cm, nor more than 9 inches/22.9cm in circumference.

2. Approval of Balls

All balls used in matches shall be approved by the umpires and captains before the start of the match.

3. New Ball

Subject to agreement to the contrary, having been made before the toss, either captain may demand a new ball at the start of each innings.

4. New Ball in Match of Three or More Days' Duration

In a match of three or more days' duration, the captain of the fielding side may demand a new ball after the prescribed number of overs has been bowled with the old one. The governing body for cricket in the country concerned shall decide the number of overs applicable in that country, which shall be not less than 75 six-ball overs (55 eight-ball overs).

5. Ball Lost or Becoming Unfit for Play

In the event of a ball during play being lost or, in the opinion of the umpires, becoming unfit for play, the umpires shall allow it to be replaced by one that in their opinion has had a similar amount of wear. If a ball is to be replaced, the umpires shall inform the batsman.

Note

    (a) Specifications
    The specifications, as described in 1 above, shall apply to top-grade balls only. The following degrees of tolerance will be acceptable for other grades of ball.

      (i) *Men's Grades 2–4*
        Weight: 5⁵/₁₆ ounces/150g to 5¹³/₁₆ ounces/165g.
        Size: 8¹¹/₁₆ inches/22.0cm to 9¹/₁₆ inches/23.0cm.

      (ii) *Women's*
        Weight: 4¹⁵/₁₆ ounces/140g to 5⁵/₁₆ ounces/150g.
        Size: 8¼ inches/21.0cm to 8⅞ inches/22.5cm.

      (iii) *Junior*
        Weight: 4¹¹/₁₆ ounces/133g to 5¹/₁₆ ounces/143g.
        Size: 8¹/₁₆ inches/20.5cm to 8¹¹/₁₆ inches/22.0cm.

LAW 6.   THE BAT

1. Width and Length

The bat overall shall be not more than 38 inches/96.5cm in length; the blade of the bat shall be made of wood and shall not exceed 4¼ inches/10.8cm at the widest part.

Note

    (a) The blade of the bat may be covered with material for protection, strengthening or repair. Such material shall not exceed ¹/₁₆ inch/1.56mm in thickness.

LAW 7.   THE PITCH

1. Area of Pitch

The pitch is the area between the bowling creases – see Law 9 (The Bowling and Popping Creases). It shall measure 5 feet/1.52m in width on either side of a line joining the centre of the middle stumps of the wickets – see Law 8 (The Wickets).

2. Selection and Preparation

Before the toss for innings, the executive of the ground shall be responsible for the selection and preparation of the pitch; thereafter the umpires shall control its use and maintenance.

3. Changing Pitch

The pitch shall not be changed during a match unless it becomes unfit for play, and then only with the consent of both captains.

4. Non-Turf Pitches

In the event of a non-turf pitch being used, the following shall apply:

(a) Length: That of the playing surface to a minimum of 58 feet/17.68m.

(b) Width: That of the playing surface to a minimum of 6 feet/1.83m.

See Law 10 (Rolling, Sweeping, Mowing, Watering the Pitch and Re-marking of Creases) Note (a).

LAW 8. THE WICKETS

1. Width and Pitching

Two sets of wickets, each 9 inches/22.86cm wide, and consisting of three wooden stumps with two wooden bails upon the top, shall be pitched opposite and parallel to each other at a distance of 22 yards/20.12m between the centres of the two middle stumps.

2. Size of Stumps

The stumps shall be of equal and sufficient size to prevent the ball from passing between them. Their tops shall be 28 inches/71.1cm above the ground, and shall be dome-shaped except for the bail grooves.

3. Size of Bails

The bails shall be each 4⅞ inches/11.1cm in length and when in position on the top of the stumps shall not project more than ½ inch/1.3cm above them.

Notes

(a) **Dispensing with Bails**
In a high wind the umpires may decide to dispense with the use of bails.

(b) **Junior Cricket**
For junior cricket, as defined by the local governing body, the following measurements for the wickets shall apply:

Width – 8 inches/20.32cm.
Pitched – 21 yards/19.20m.
Height – 27 inches/68.58cm.
Bails – each 3⅞ inches/9.84cm in length and should not project more than ½ inch/1.3cm above the stumps.

LAW 9. THE BOWLING, POPPING AND RETURN CREASES

1. The Bowling Crease

The bowling crease shall be marked in line with the stumps at each end and shall be 8 feet 8 inches/2.64m in length, with the stumps in the centre.

2. The Popping Crease

The popping crease, which is the back edge of the crease marking, shall be in front of and parallel with the bowling crease. It shall have the back edge of the crease marking 4 feet/1.22m from the centre of the stumps and shall extend to a minimum of 6 feet/1.83m on either side of the line of the wicket.

The popping crease shall be considered to be unlimited in length.

3. The Return Crease

The return crease marking, of which the inside edge is the crease, shall be at each end of the bowling crease and at right angles to it. The return crease shall be marked to a minimum of 4 feet/1.22m behind the wicket and shall be considered to be unlimited in length. A forward extension shall be marked to the popping crease.

LAW 10.   ROLLING, SWEEPING, MOWING, WATERING THE PITCH AND RE-MARKING OF CREASES

1. Rolling

During the match the pitch may be rolled at the request of the captain of the batting side, for a period of not more than seven minutes before the start of each innings, other than the first innings of the match, and before the start of each day's play. In addition, if, after the toss and before the first innings of the match, the start is delayed, the captain of the batting side may request to have the pitch rolled for not more than seven minutes. However, if in the opinion of the umpires the delay has had no significant effect upon the state of the pitch, they shall refuse any request for the rolling of the pitch.

The pitch shall not otherwise be rolled during the match.

The seven minutes' rolling permitted before the start of a day's play shall take place not earlier than half an hour before the start of play and the captain of the batting side may delay such rolling until ten minutes before the start of play should he so desire.

If a captain declares an innings closed less than 15 minutes before the resumption of play, and the other captain is thereby prevented from exercising his option of seven minutes' rolling or if he is so prevented for any other reason, the time for rolling shall be taken out of the normal playing time.

2. Sweeping

Such sweeping of the pitch as is necessary during the match shall be done so that the seven minutes allowed for rolling the pitch, provided for in 1 above, is not affected.

3. Mowing

(a) Responsibilities of Ground Authority and of Umpires
All mowings which are carried out before the toss for innings shall be the responsibility of the ground authority; thereafter they shall be carried out under the supervision of the umpires. See Law 7.2 (Selection and Preparation).

(b) Initial Mowing
The pitch shall be mown before play begins on the day the match is scheduled to start, or in the case of a delayed start on the day the match is expected to start. See 3(a) above (Responsibilities of Ground Authority and of Umpires).

(c) Subsequent Mowings in a Match of Two or More Days' Duration
In a match of two or more days' duration, the pitch shall be mown daily before play begins. Should this mowing not take place because of weather conditions, rest days or other reasons, the pitch shall be mown on the first day on which the match is resumed.

(d) Mowing of the Outfield in a Match of Two or More Days' Duration
In order to ensure that conditions are as similar as possible for both sides, the outfield shall normally be mown before the commencement of play on each day of the match, if ground and weather conditions allow. See Note (b) to this Law.

4. Watering

The pitch shall not be watered during a match.

5. Re-marking Creases

Whenever possible the creases shall be re-marked.

6. Maintenance of Foot-holes

In wet weather, the umpires shall ensure that the holes made by the bowlers and batsmen are cleaned out and dried whenever necessary to facilitate play. In matches of two or more days' duration, the umpires shall allow, if necessary, the re-turfing of foot-holes made by the bowler in his delivery stride, or the use of quick-setting fillings for the same purpose, before the start of each day's play.

7. Securing of Footholds and Maintenance of Pitch

During play, the umpires shall allow either batsman to beat the pitch with his bat and players to secure their footholds by the use of sawdust, provided that no damage to the pitch is so caused, and Law 42 (Unfair Play) is not contravened.

Notes

(a) Non-turf Pitches

The above Law 10 applies to turf pitches.

The game is played on non-turf pitches in many countries at various levels. Whilst the conduct of the game on these surfaces should always be in accordance with the Laws of Cricket, it is recognised that it may sometimes be necessary for governing bodies to lay down special playing conditions to suit the type of non-turf pitch used in their country.

In matches played against touring teams, any special playing conditions should be agreed in advance by both parties.

(b) Mowing of the Outfield in a Match of Two or More Days' Duration

If, for reasons other than ground and weather conditions, daily and complete mowing is not possible, the ground authority shall notify the captains and umpires, before the toss for innings, of the procedure to be adopted for such mowing during the match.

(c) Choice of Roller

If there is more than one roller available, the captain of the batting side shall have a choice.

LAW 11.   COVERING THE PITCH

1. Before the Start of a Match

Before the start of a match, complete covering of the pitch shall be allowed.

2. During a Match

The pitch shall not be completely covered during a match unless prior arrangement or regulations so provide.

3. Covering Bowlers' Run-up

Whenever possible, the bowlers' run-up shall be covered, but the covers so used shall not extend further than 4 feet/1.22m in front of the popping crease.

Note

(a) Removal of Covers

The covers should be removed as promptly as possible whenever the weather permits.

LAW 12.   INNINGS

1. Number of Innings

A match shall be of one or two innings of each side according to agreement reached before the start of play.

2. Alternate Innings

In a two-innings match each side shall take their innings alternately except in the case provided for in Law 13 (The Follow-on).

3. The Toss

The captains shall toss for the choice of innings on the field of play not later than 15 minutes before the time scheduled for the match to start, or before the time agreed upon for play to start.

4. Choice of Innings

The winner of the toss shall notify his decision to bat or to field to the opposing captain not later than ten minutes before the time scheduled for the match to start, or before the time agreed upon for play to start. The decision shall not thereafter be altered.

5. Continuation after One Innings of Each Side

Despite the terms of 1 above, in a one-innings match, when a result has been reached on the first innings, the captains may agree to the continuation of play if, in their opinion, there is a prospect of carrying the game to a further issue in the time left. See Law 21 (Result).

Notes

   (a) **Limited Innings – One-innings Match**
   In a one-innings match, each innings may, by agreement, be limited by a number of overs or by a period of time.
   (b) **Limited Innings – Two-innings Match**
   In a two-innings match, the first innings of each side may, by agreement, be limited to a number of overs or by a period of time.

LAW 13.   THE FOLLOW-ON

1. Lead on First Innings

In a two-innings match the side which bats first and leads by 200 runs in a match of five days or more, by 150 runs in a three-day or four-day match, by 100 runs in a two-day match, or by 75 runs in a one-day match, shall have the option of requiring the other side to follow their innings.

2. Day's Play Lost

If no play takes place on the first day of a match of two or more days' duration, 1 above shall apply in accordance with the number of days' play remaining from the actual start of the match.

LAW 14.   DECLARATIONS

1. Time of Declaration

The captain of the batting side may declare an innings closed at any time during a match, irrespective of its duration.

2. Forfeiture of Second Innings

A captain may forfeit his second innings, provided his decision to do so is notified to the opposing captain and umpires in sufficient time to allow seven minutes' rolling of the pitch. See Law 10 (Rolling, Sweeping, Mowing, Watering the Pitch and Re-marking of Creases). The normal ten-minute interval between innings shall be applied.

LAW 15.   START OF PLAY

1. Call of Play

At the start of each innings and of each day's play, and on the resumption of play after any interval or interruption, the umpire at the bowler's end shall call "play".

2. Practice on the Field

At no time on any day of the match shall there be any bowling or batting practice on the pitch.

No practice may take place on the field if, in the opinion of the umpires, it could result in a waste of time.

3. Trial Run-up

No bowler shall have a trial run-up after "play" has been called in any session of play, except at the fall of a wicket when an umpire may allow such a trial run-up if he is satisfied that it will not cause any waste of time.

LAW 16.   INTERVALS

1. Length

The umpire shall allow such intervals as have been agreed upon for meals, and ten minutes between each innings.

2. Luncheon Interval – Innings Ending or Stoppage within Ten Minutes of Interval

If an innings ends or there is a stoppage caused by weather or bad light within ten minutes of the agreed time for the luncheon interval, the interval shall be taken immediately.

The time remaining in the session of play shall be added to the agreed length of the interval but no extra allowance shall be made for the ten-minute interval between innings.

3. Tea Interval – Innings Ending or Stoppage within 30 Minutes of Interval

If an innings ends or there is a stoppage caused by weather or bad light within 30 minutes of the agreed time for the tea interval, the interval shall be taken immediately.

The interval shall be of the agreed length and, if applicable, shall include the ten-minute interval between innings.

4. Tea Interval – Continuation of Play

If, at the agreed time for the tea interval, nine wickets are down, play shall continue for a period not exceeding 30 minutes or until the innings is concluded.

5. Tea Interval – Agreement to Forgo

At any time during the match, the captains may agree to forgo a tea interval.

6. Intervals for Drinks

If both captains agree before the start of a match that intervals for drinks may be taken, the option to take such intervals shall be available to either side. These intervals shall be restricted to one per session, shall be kept as short as possible, shall not be taken in the last hour of the match, and in any case shall not exceed five minutes.

The agreed times for these intervals shall be strictly adhered to, except that if a wicket falls within five minutes of the agreed time then drinks shall be taken out immediately.

If an innings ends or there is a stoppage caused by weather or bad light within 30 minutes of the agreed time for a drinks interval, there will be no interval for drinks in that session.

At any time during the match the captains may agree to forgo any such drinks interval.

Notes

   (a) **Tea Interval – One-day Match**
   In a one-day match, a specific time for the tea interval need not necessarily be arranged, and it may be agreed to take this interval between the innings of a one-innings match.

   (b) **Changing the Agreed Time of Intervals**
   In the event of the ground, weather or light conditions causing a suspension of play, the umpires, after consultation with the captains, may decide in the interests of time-saving to bring forward the time of the luncheon or tea interval.

LAW 17.   CESSATION OF PLAY

1. Call of Time

The umpire at the bowler's end shall call "time" on the cessation of play before any interval or interruption of play, at the end of each day's play, and at the conclusion of the match. See Law 27 (Appeals).

2. Removal of Bails

After the call of "time", the umpires shall remove the bails from both wickets.

3. Starting a Last Over

The last over before an interval or the close of play shall be started provided the umpire, after walking at his normal pace, has arrived at his position behind the stumps at the bowler's end before time has been reached.

4. Completion of the Last Over of a Session

The last over before an interval or the close of play shall be completed unless a batsman is out or retires during that over within two minutes of the interval or the close of play or unless the players have occasion to leave the field.

5. Completion of the Last Over of a Match

An over in progress at the close of play on the final day of a match shall be completed at the request of either captain, even if a wicket falls after time has been reached.

If, during the last over, the players have occasion to leave the field, the umpires shall call "time" and there shall be no resumption of play and the match shall be at an end.

6. Last Hour of Match – Number of Overs

The umpires shall indicate when one hour of playing time of the match remains according to the agreed hours of play. The next over after that moment shall be the first of a minimum of 20 six-ball overs (15 eight-ball overs), provided a result is not reached earlier or there is no interval or interruption of play.

7. Last Hour of Match – Intervals between Innings and Interruptions of Play

If, at the commencement of the last hour of the match, an interval or interruption of play is in progress or if, during the last hour, there is an interval between innings or an interruption of play, the minimum number of overs to be bowled on the resumption of play shall be reduced in proportion to the duration, within the last hour of the match, of any such interval or interruption.

The minimum number of overs to be bowled after the resumption of play shall be calculated as follows:

   (a) In the case of an interval or interruption of play being in progress at the commencement of the last hour of the match, or in the case of a first interval or interruption, a deduction shall be made from the minimum of 20 six-ball overs (or 15 eight-ball overs).

   (b) If there is a later interval or interruption, a further deduction shall be made from the minimum number of overs which should have been bowled following the last resumption of play.

   (c) These deductions shall be based on the following factors:

      (i) The number of overs already bowled in the last hour of the match or, in the case of a later interval or interruption, in the last session of play.

      (ii) The number of overs lost as a result of the interval or interruption allowing one six-ball over for every full three minutes (or one eight-ball over for every full four minutes) of interval or interruption.

      (iii) Any over left uncompleted at the end of an innings to be excluded from these calculations.

(iv) Any over of the minimum number to be played which is left uncompleted at the start of an interruption of play to be completed when play is resumed and to count as one over bowled.

(v) An interval to start with the end of an innings and to end ten minutes later; an interruption to start on the call of "time" and to end on the call of "play".

(d) In the event of an innings being completed and a new innings commencing during the last hour of the match, the number of overs to be bowled in the new innings shall be calculated on the basis of one six-ball over for every three minutes or part thereof remaining for play (or one eight-ball over for every four minutes or part thereof remaining for play); or alternatively on the basis that sufficient overs be bowled to enable the full minimum quota of overs to be completed under circumstances governed by (a), (b) and (c) above. In all such cases the alternative which allows the greater number of overs shall be employed.

8. Bowler Unable to Complete an Over during Last Hour of the Match

If, for any reason, a bowler is unable to complete an over during the period of play referred to in 6 above, Law 22.7 (Bowler Incapacitated or Suspended during an Over) shall apply.

LAW 18. SCORING

1. A Run

The score shall be reckoned by runs. A run is scored:

(a) So often as the batsmen, after a hit or at any time while the ball is in play, shall have crossed and made good their ground from end to end.

(b) When a boundary is scored. See Law 19 (Boundaries).

(c) When penalty runs are awarded. See 6 below.

2. Short Runs

(a) If either batsman runs a short run, the umpire shall call and signal "one short" as soon as the ball becomes dead and that run shall not be scored. A run is short if a batsman fails to make good his ground on turning for a further run.

(b) Although a short run shortens the succeeding one, the latter, if completed, shall count.

(c) If either or both batsmen deliberately run short the umpire shall, as soon as he sees that the fielding side have no chance of dismissing either batsman, call and signal "dead ball" and disallow any runs attempted or previously scored. The batsmen shall return to their original ends.

(d) If both batsmen run short in one and the same run, only one run shall be deducted.

(e) Only if three or more runs are attempted can more than one be short and then, subject to (c) and (d) above, all runs so called shall be disallowed. If there has been more than one short run the umpires shall instruct the scorers as to the number of runs disallowed.

3. Striker Caught

If the striker is caught, no run shall be scored.

4. Batsman Run Out

If a batsman is run out, only that run which was being attempted shall not be scored. If, however, an injured striker himself is run out, no runs shall be scored. See Law 2.7 (Transgression of the Laws by an Injured Batsman or Runner).

5. Batsman Obstructing the Field

If a batsman is out Obstructing the Field, any runs completed before the obstruction occurs shall be scored unless such obstruction prevents a catch being made, in which case no runs shall be scored.

6. Runs Scored for Penalties

Runs shall be scored for penalties under Laws 20 (Lost Ball), 24 (No-ball), 25 (Wide-ball), 41.1 (Fielding the Ball) and for boundary allowances under Law 19 (Boundaries).

7. Batsman Returning to Wicket he has Left

If, while the ball is in play, the batsmen have crossed in running, neither shall return to the wicket he has left, even though a short run has been called or no run has been scored as in the case of a catch. Batsmen, however, shall return to the wickets they originally left in the cases of a boundary and of any disallowance of runs and of an injured batsman being, himself, run out. See Law 2.7 (Transgression by an Injured Batsman or Runner).

Note

(a) Short Run

A striker taking stance in front of his popping crease may run from that point without penalty.

LAW 19. BOUNDARIES

1. The Boundary of the Playing Area

Before the toss for innings, the umpires shall agree with both captains on the boundary of the playing area. The boundary shall, if possible, be marked by a white line, a rope laid on the ground, or a fence. If flags or posts only are used to mark a boundary, the imaginary line joining such points shall be regarded as the boundary. An obstacle, or person, within the playing area shall not be regarded as a boundary unless so decided by the umpires before the toss for innings. Sightscreens within, or partially within, the playing area shall be regarded as the boundary and when the ball strikes or passes within or under or directly over any part of the screen, a boundary shall be scored.

2. Runs Scored for Boundaries

Before the toss for innings, the umpires shall agree with both captains the runs to be allowed for boundaries, and in deciding the allowance for them, the umpires and captains shall be guided by the prevailing custom of the ground. The allowance for a boundary shall normally be four runs, and six runs for all hits pitching over and clear of the boundary line or fence, even though the ball has been previously touched by a fieldsman. Six runs shall also be scored if a fieldsman, after catching a ball, carries it over the boundary. See Law 32 (Caught) Note (a). Six runs shall not be scored when a ball struck by the striker hits a sightscreen full pitch if the screen is within, or partially within, the playing area, but if the ball is struck directly over a sightscreen so situated, six runs shall be scored.

3. A Boundary

A boundary shall be scored and signalled by the umpire at the bowler's end whenever, in his opinion:

(a) A ball in play touches or crosses the boundary, however marked.

(b) A fieldsman with ball in hand touches or grounds any part of his person on or over a boundary line.

(c) A fieldsman with ball in hand grounds any part of his person over a boundary fence or board. This allows the fieldsman to touch or lean on or over a boundary fence or board in preventing a boundary.

4. Runs Exceeding Boundary Allowance

The runs completed at the instant the ball reaches the boundary shall count if they exceed the boundary allowance.

5. Overthrows or Wilful Act of a Fieldsman

If the boundary results from an overthrow or from the wilful act of a fieldsman, any runs already completed and the allowance shall be added to the score. The run in progress shall count provided that the batsmen have crossed at the instant of the throw or act.

Note

(a) Position of Sightscreens

Sightscreens should, if possible, be positioned wholly outside the playing area, as near as possible to the boundary line.

LAW 20.   LOST BALL

1. Runs Scored

If a ball in play cannot be found or recovered, any fieldsman may call "lost ball" when six runs shall be added to the score; but if more than six have been run before "lost ball" is called, as many runs as have been completed shall be scored. The run in progress shall count provided that the batsmen have crossed at the instant of the call of "lost ball".

2. How Scored

The runs shall be added to the score of the striker if the ball has been struck, but otherwise to the score of byes, leg-byes, no-balls or wides as the case may be.

LAW 21.   THE RESULT

1. A Win – Two-innings Matches

The side which has scored a total of runs in excess of that scored by the opposing side in its two completed innings shall be the winner.

2. A Win – One-innings Matches

(a) One-innings matches, unless played out as in 1 above, shall be decided on the first innings, but see Law 12.5 (Continuation after One Innings of Each Side).

(b) If the captains agree to continue play after the completion of one innings of each side in accordance with Law 12.5 (Continuation after One Innings of Each Side) and a result is not achieved on the second innings, the first-innings result shall stand.

3. Umpires Awarding a Match

(a) A match shall be lost by a side which, during the match, (i) refuses to play, or (ii) concedes defeat, and the umpires shall award the match to the other side.

(b) Should both batsmen at the wickets or the fielding side leave the field at any time without the agreement of the umpires, this shall constitute a refusal to play and, on appeal, the umpires shall award the match to the other side in accordance with (a) above.

4. A Tie

The result of a match shall be a tie when the scores are equal at the conclusion of play, but only if the side batting last has completed its innings.

If the scores of the completed first innings of a one-day match are equal, it shall be a tie but only if the match has not been played out to a further conclusion.

5. A Draw

A match not determined in any of the ways as in 1, 2, 3 and 4 above shall count as a draw.

6. Correctness of Result

Any decision as to the correctness of the scores shall be the responsibility of the umpires. See Law 3.14 (Correctness of Scores).

If, after the umpires and players have left the field in the belief that the match has been concluded, the umpires decide that a mistake in scoring has occurred, which affects the result, and provided time has not been reached, they shall order play to resume and to continue until the agreed finishing time unless a result is reached earlier.

If the umpires decide that a mistake has occurred and time has been reached, the umpires shall immediately inform both captains of the necessary corrections to the scores and, if applicable, to the result.

7. Acceptance of Result

In accepting the scores as notified by the scorers and agreed by the umpires, the captains of both sides thereby accept the result.

Notes

(a) Statement of Results

The result of a finished match is stated as a win by runs, except in the case of a win by the side batting last when it is by the number of wickets still then to fall.

(b) Winning Hit or Extras

As soon as the side has won, see 1 and 2 above, the umpire shall call "time", the match is finished, and nothing that happens thereafter other than as a result of a mistake in scoring (see 6 above) shall be regarded as part of the match.

However, if a boundary constitutes the winning hit – or extras – and the boundary allowance exceeds the number of runs required to win the match, such runs scored shall be credited to the side's total and, in the case of a hit, to the striker's score.

LAW 22.   THE OVER

1. Number of Balls

The ball shall be bowled from each wicket alternately in overs of either six or eight balls according to agreement before the match.

2. Call of "Over"

When the agreed number of balls has been bowled, and as the ball becomes dead or when it becomes clear to the umpire at the bowler's end that both the fielding side and the batsmen at the wicket have ceased to regard the ball as in play, the umpire shall call "over" before leaving the wicket.

3. No-ball or Wide-ball

Neither a no-ball nor a wide-ball shall be reckoned as one of the over.

4. Umpire Miscounting

If an umpire miscounts the number of balls, the over as counted by the umpire shall stand.

5. Bowler Changing Ends

A bowler shall be allowed to change ends as often as desired, provided only that he does not bowl two overs consecutively in an innings.

6. The Bowler Finishing an Over

A bowler shall finish an over in progress unless he be incapacitated or be suspended under Law 42.8 (The Bowling of Fast Short-pitched Balls), 9 (The Bowling of Fast High Full Pitches), 10 (Time Wasting) and 11 (Players Damaging the Pitch). If an over is left incomplete for any reason at the start of an interval or interruption of play, it shall be finished on the resumption of play.

7. Bowler Incapacitated or Suspended during an Over

If, for any reason, a bowler is incapacitated while running up to bowl the first ball of an over, or is incapacitated or suspended during an over, the umpire shall call and signal "dead ball" and another bowler shall be allowed to bowl or complete the over from the same end, provided only that he shall not bowl two overs, or part thereof, consecutively in one innings.

8. Position of Non-striker

The batsman at the bowler's end shall normally stand on the opposite side of the wicket to that from which the ball is being delivered, unless a request to do otherwise is granted by the umpire.

LAW 23.   DEAD BALL

1. The Ball Becomes Dead

When:

    (a) It is finally settled in the hands of the wicket-keeper or the bowler.

    (b) It reaches or pitches over the boundary.

    (c) A batsman is out.

    (d) Whether played or not, it lodges in the clothing or equipment of a batsman or the clothing of an umpire.

    (e) A ball lodges in a protective helmet worn by a member of the fielding side.

    (f) A penalty is awarded under Law 20 (Lost Ball) or Law 41.1 (Fielding the Ball).

    (g) The umpire calls "over" or "time".

2. Either Umpire Shall Call and Signal "Dead Ball"

When:

    (a) He intervenes in a case of unfair play.

    (b) A serious injury to a player or umpire occurs.

    (c) He is satisfied that, for an adequate reason, the striker is not ready to receive the ball and makes no attempt to play it.

    (d) The bowler drops the ball accidentally before delivery, or the ball does not leave his hand for any reason other than in an attempt to run out the non-striker (See Law 24.5 – Bowler Attempting to Run Out Non-striker before Delivery).

    (e) One or both bails fall from the striker's wicket before he receives delivery.

    (f) He leaves his normal position for consultation.

    (g) He is required to do so under Law 26.3 (Disallowance of Leg-byes), etc.

3. The Ball Ceases to be Dead

When:

    (a) The bowler starts his run-up or bowling action.

4. The Ball is Not Dead

When:

    (a) It strikes an umpire (unless it lodges in his dress).

    (b) The wicket is broken or struck down (unless a batsman is out thereby).

    (c) An unsuccessful appeal is made.

    (d) The wicket is broken accidentally either by the bowler during his delivery or by a batsman in running.

    (e) The umpire has called "no-ball" or "wide".

(a) Ball Finally Settled

Whether the ball is finally settled or not – see 1(a) above – must be a question for the umpires alone to decide.

(b) Action on Call of "Dead Ball"

(i) If "dead ball" is called prior to the striker receiving a delivery, the bowler shall be allowed an additional ball.

(ii) If "dead ball" is called after the striker receives a delivery, the bowler shall not be allowed an additional ball, unless a "no-ball" or "wide" has been called.

LAW 24. NO-BALL

1. Mode of Delivery

The umpire shall indicate to the striker whether the bowler intends to bowl over or round the wicket, overarm or underarm, right or left-handed. Failure on the part of the bowler to indicate in advance a change in his mode of delivery is unfair and the umpire shall call and signal "no-ball".

2. Fair Delivery – The Arm

For a delivery to be fair the ball must be bowled, not thrown – see Note (a) below. If either umpire is not entirely satisfied with the absolute fairness of a delivery in this respect he shall call and signal "no-ball" instantly upon delivery.

3. Fair Delivery – The Feet

The umpire at the bowler's wicket shall call and signal "no-ball" if he is not satisfied that in the delivery stride:

(a) The bowler's back foot has landed within and not touching the return crease or its forward extension; or

(b) Some part of the front foot whether grounded or raised was behind the popping crease.

4. Bowler Throwing at Striker's Wicket before Delivery

If the bowler, before delivering the ball, throws it at the striker's wicket in an attempt to run him out, the umpire shall call and signal "no-ball". See Law 42.12 (Batsman Unfairly Stealing a Run) and Law 38 (Run Out).

5. Bowler Attempting to Run Out Non-striker before Delivery

If the bowler, before delivering the ball, attempts to run out the non-striker, any runs which result shall be allowed and shall be scored as no-balls. Such an attempt shall not count as a ball in the over. The umpire shall not call "no-ball". See Law 42.12 (Batsman Unfairly Stealing a Run).

6. Infringement of Laws by a Wicket-keeper or a Fieldsman

The umpire shall call and signal "no-ball" in the event of the wicket-keeper infringing Law 40.1 (Position of Wicket-keeper) or a fieldsman infringing Law 41.2 (Limitation of On-side Fieldsmen) or Law 41.3 (Position of Fieldsmen).

7. Revoking a Call

An umpire shall revoke the call "no-ball" if the ball does not leave the bowler's hand for any reason. See Law 23.2 (Either Umpire Shall Call and Signal "Dead Ball").

8. Penalty

A penalty of one run for a no-ball shall be scored if no runs are made otherwise.

9. Runs from a No-ball

The striker may hit a no-ball and whatever runs result shall be added to his score. Runs made otherwise from a no-ball shall be scored no-balls.

10. Out from a No-ball

The striker shall be out from a no-ball if he breaks Law 34 (Hit the Ball Twice) and either batsman may be run out or shall be given out if either breaks Law 33 (Handled the Ball) or Law 37 (Obstructing the Field).

11. Batsman Given Out off a No-ball

Should a batsman be given out off a no-ball the penalty for bowling it shall stand unless runs are otherwise scored.

Notes

(a) Definition of a Throw

A ball shall be deemed to have been thrown if, in the opinion of either umpire, the process of straightening the bowling arm, whether it be partial or complete, takes place during that part of the delivery swing which directly precedes the ball leaving the hand. This definition shall not debar a bowler from the use of the wrist in the delivery swing.

(b) No-ball Not Counting in Over

A no-ball shall not be reckoned as one of the over. See Law 22.3 (No-ball or Wide-ball).

LAW 25. WIDE-BALL

1. Judging a Wide

If the bowler bowls the ball so high over or so wide of the wicket that, in the opinion of the umpire, it passes out of reach of the striker, standing in a normal guard position, the umpire shall call and signal "wide-ball" as soon as it has passed the line of the striker's wicket.

The umpire shall not adjudge a ball as being wide if:

(a) The striker, by moving from his guard position, causes the ball to pass out of his reach.

(b) The striker moves and thus brings the ball within his reach.

2. Penalty

A penalty of one run for a wide shall be scored if no runs are made otherwise.

3. Ball Coming to Rest in Front of the Striker

If a ball which the umpire considers to have been delivered comes to rest in front of the line of the striker's wicket, "wide" shall not be called. The striker has a right, without interference from the fielding side, to make one attempt to hit the ball. If the fielding side interfere, the umpire shall replace the ball where it came to rest and shall order the fieldsmen to resume the places they occupied in the field before the ball was delivered.

The umpire shall call and signal "dead ball" as soon as it is clear that the striker does not intend to hit the ball, or after the striker has made an unsuccessful attempt to hit the ball.

4. Revoking a Call

The umpire shall revoke the call if the striker hits a ball which has been called "wide".

5. Ball Not Dead

The ball does not become dead on the call of "wide-ball" – see Law 23.4 (The Ball is Not Dead).

6. Runs Resulting from a Wide

All runs which are run or result from a wide-ball which is not a no-ball shall be scored wide-balls, or if no runs are made one shall be scored.

7. Out from a Wide

The striker shall be out from a wide-ball if he breaks Law 35 (Hit Wicket), or Law 39 (Stumped). Either batsman may be run out and shall be out if he breaks Law 33 (Handled the Ball), or Law 37 (Obstructing the Field).

8. Batsman Given Out off a Wide

Should a batsman be given out off a wide, the penalty for bowling it shall stand unless runs are otherwise made.

Note

> **(a) Wide-ball Not Counting in Over**
> A wide-ball shall not be reckoned as one of the over – see Law 22.3 (No-ball or Wide-ball).

LAW 26.   BYE AND LEG-BYE

1. Byes

If the ball, not having been called "wide" or "no-ball", passes the striker without touching his bat or person, and any runs are obtained, the umpire shall signal "bye" and the run or runs shall be credited as such to the batting side.

2. Leg-byes

If the ball, not having been called "wide" or "no-ball", is unintentionally deflected by the striker's dress or person, except a hand holding the bat, and any runs are obtained the umpire shall signal "leg-bye" and the run or runs so scored shall be credited as such to the batting side.

Such leg-byes shall be scored only if, in the opinion of the umpire, the striker has:

> (a) Attempted to play the ball with his bat; or
>
> (b) Tried to avoid being hit by the ball.

3. Disallowance of Leg-byes

In the case of a deflection by the striker's person, other than in 2(a) and (b) above, the umpire shall call and signal "dead ball" as soon as one run has been completed or when it is clear that a run is not being attempted, or the ball has reached the boundary.

On the call and signal of "dead ball" the batsmen shall return to their original ends and no runs shall be allowed.

LAW 27.   APPEALS

1. Time of Appeals

The umpires shall not give a batsman out unless appealed to by the other side which shall be done prior to the bowler beginning his run-up or bowling action to deliver the next ball. Under Law 23.1 (g) (The Ball Becomes Dead), the ball is dead on "over" being called; this does not, however, invalidate an appeal made prior to the first ball of the following over provided "time" has not been called – see Law 17.1 (Call of Time).

2. An Appeal "How's That?"

An appeal "How's That?" shall cover all ways of being out.

3. Answering Appeals

The umpire at the bowler's wicket shall answer appeals before the other umpire in all cases except those arising out of Law 35 (Hit Wicket) or Law 39 (Stumped) or Law 38 (Run Out) when this occurs at the striker's wicket.

When either umpire has given a batsman not out, the other umpire shall, within his jurisdiction, answer the appeal or a further appeal, provided it is made in time in accordance with 1 above (Time of Appeals).

4. Consultation by Umpires

An umpire may consult with the other umpire on a point of fact which the latter may have been in a better position to see and shall then give his decision. If, after consultation, there is still doubt remaining the decision shall be in favour of the batsman.

5. Batsman Leaving his Wicket under a Misapprehension

The umpires shall intervene if satisfied that a batsman, not having been given out, has left his wicket under a misapprehension that he has been dismissed.

6. Umpire's Decision

The umpire's decision is final. He may alter his decision, provided that such alteration is made promptly.

7. Withdrawal of an Appeal

In exceptional circumstances the captain of the fielding side may seek permission of the umpire to withdraw an appeal provided the outgoing batsman has not left the playing area. If this is allowed, the umpire shall cancel his decision.

LAW 28.   THE WICKET IS DOWN

1. Wicket Down

The wicket is down if:

> (a) Either the ball or the striker's bat or person completely removes either bail from the top of the stumps. A disturbance of a bail, whether temporary or not, shall not constitute a complete removal, but the wicket is down if a bail in falling lodges between two of the stumps.

> (b) Any player completely removes with his hand or arm a bail from the top of the stumps, provided that the ball is held in that hand or in the hand of the arm so used.

> (c) When both bails are off, a stump is struck out of the ground by the ball, or a player strikes or pulls a stump out of the ground, providing that the ball is held in the hand(s) or in the hand of the arm so used.

2. One Bail Off

If one bail is off, it shall be sufficient for the purpose of putting the wicket down to remove the remaining bail, or to strike or pull any of the three stumps out of the ground in any of the ways stated in 1 above.

3. All the Stumps Out of the Ground

If all the stumps are out of the ground, the fielding side shall be allowed to put back one or more stumps in order to have an opportunity of putting the wicket down.

4. Dispensing with Bails

If, owing to the strength of the wind, it has been agreed to dispense with the bails in accordance with Law 8, Note (a) (Dispensing with Bails), the decision as to when the wicket is down is one for the umpires to decide on the facts before them. In such circumstances and if the umpires so decide, the wicket shall be held to be down even though a stump has not been struck out of the ground.

Note

> **(a) Remaking the Wicket**
> If the wicket is broken while the ball is in play, it is not the umpire's duty to remake the wicket until the ball has become dead – see Law 23 (Dead Ball). A member of the fielding side, however, may remake the wicket in such circumstances.

LAW 29.   BATSMAN OUT OF HIS GROUND

1. When out of his Ground

A batsman shall be considered to be out of his ground unless some part of his bat in his hand or of his person is grounded behind the line of the popping crease.

LAW 30.   BOWLED

1. Out Bowled

The striker shall be out *Bowled* if:

> (a) His wicket is bowled down, even if the ball first touches his bat or person.
>
> (b) He breaks his wicket by hitting or kicking the ball on to it before the completion of a stroke, or as a result of attempting to guard his wicket. See Law 34.1 (Out Hit the Ball Twice).

Note

> **(a) Out Bowled – Not lbw**
> The striker is out bowled if the ball is deflected on to his wicket even though a decision against him would be justified under Law 36 (lbw).

LAW 31.   TIMED OUT

1. Out Timed Out

An incoming batsman shall be out *Timed Out* if he wilfully takes more than two minutes to come in – the two minutes being timed from the moment a wicket falls until the new batsman steps on to the field of play.

If this is not complied with and if the umpire is satisfied that the delay was wilful and if an appeal is made, the new batsman shall be given out by the umpire at the bowler's end.

2. Time to be Added

The time taken by the umpires to investigate the cause of the delay shall be added at the normal close of play.

Notes

> **(a) Entry in Scorebook**
> The correct entry in the scorebook when a batsman is given out under this Law is "timed out", and the bowler does not get credit for the wicket.
>
> **(b) Batsmen Crossing on the Field of Play**
> It is an essential duty of the captains to ensure that the in-going batsman passes the out-going one before the latter leaves the field of play.

LAW 32. CAUGHT

1. Out Caught

The striker shall be out *Caught* if the ball touches his bat or if it touches below the wrist his hand or glove, holding the bat, and is subsequently held by a fieldsman before it touches the ground.

2. A Fair Catch

A catch shall be considered to have been fairly made if:

(a) The fieldsman is within the field of play throughout the act of making the catch.

(i) The act of making the catch shall start from the time when the fieldsman first handles the ball and shall end when he both retains complete control over the further disposal of the ball and remains within the field of play.

(ii) In order to be within the field of play, the fieldsman may not touch or ground any part of his person on or over a boundary line. When the boundary is marked by a fence or board the fieldsman may not ground any part of his person over the boundary fence or board, but may touch or lean over the boundary fence or board in completing the catch.

(b) The ball is hugged to the body of the catcher or accidentally lodges in his dress or, in the case of the wicket-keeper, in his pads. However, a striker may not be caught if a ball lodges in a protective helmet worn by a fieldsman, in which case the umpire shall call and signal "dead ball". See Law 23 (Dead Ball).

(c) The ball does not touch the ground even though a hand holding it does so in effecting the catch.

(d) A fieldsman catches the ball, after it has been lawfully played a second time by the striker, but only if the ball has not touched the ground since being first struck.

(e) A fieldsman catches the ball after it has touched an umpire, another fieldsman or the other batsman. However, a striker may not be caught if a ball has touched a protective helmet worn by a fieldsman.

(f) The ball is caught off an obstruction within the boundary provided it has not previously been agreed to regard the obstruction as a boundary.

3. Scoring of Runs

If a striker is caught, no run shall be scored.

Notes

(a) **Scoring from an Attempted Catch**
When a fieldsman carrying the ball touches or grounds any part of his person on or over a boundary marked by a line, six runs shall be scored.

(b) **Ball Still in Play**
If a fieldsman releases the ball before he crosses the boundary, being struck the ball will be considered to be still in play and it may be caught by another fieldsman. However, if the original fieldsman returns to the field of play and handles the ball, a catch may not be made.

LAW 33. HANDLED THE BALL

1. Out Handled the Ball

Either batsman on appeal shall be out *Handled the Ball* if he wilfully touches the ball while in play with the hand not holding the bat unless he does so with the consent of the opposite side.

Note

(a) **Entry in Scorebook**
The correct entry in the scorebook when a batsman is given out under this Law is "handled the ball", and the bowler does not get credit for the wicket.

LAW 34.   HIT THE BALL TWICE

1. Out Hit the Ball Twice

The striker, on appeal, shall be out *Hit the Ball Twice* if, after the ball is struck or is stopped by any part of his person, he wilfully strikes it again with his bat or person except for the sole purpose of guarding his wicket: this he may do with his bat or any part of his person other than his hands, but see Law 37.2 (Obstructing a Ball From Being Caught).

For the purpose of this Law, a hand holding the bat shall be regarded as part of the bat.

2. Returning the Ball to a Fieldsman

The striker, on appeal, shall be out under this Law if, without the consent of the opposite side, he uses his bat or person to return the ball to any of the fielding side.

3. Runs from Ball Lawfully Struck Twice

No runs except those which result from an overthrow or penalty – see Law 41 (The Fieldsman) – shall be scored from a ball lawfully struck twice.

Notes

  (a) Entry in Scorebook
  The correct entry in the scorebook when the striker is given out under this Law is "hit the ball twice", and the bowler does not get credit for the wicket.

  (b) Runs Credited to the Batsman
  Any runs awarded under 3 above as a result of an overthrow or penalty shall be credited to the striker, provided the ball in the first instance has touched the bat, or, if otherwise, as extras.

LAW 35.   HIT WICKET

1. Out Hit Wicket

The striker shall be out *Hit Wicket* if, while the ball is in play:

  (a) His wicket is broken with any part of his person, dress, or equipment as a result of any action taken by him in preparing to receive or in receiving a delivery, or in setting off for his first run, immediately after playing, or playing at, the ball.

  (b) He hits down his wicket whilst lawfully making a second stroke for the purpose of guarding his wicket within the provisions of Law 34.1 (Out Hit the Ball Twice).

Notes

  (a) Not Out Hit Wicket
  A batsman is not out under this Law should his wicket be broken in any of the ways referred to in 1(a) above if:
    (i) It occurs while he is in the act of running, other than in setting off for his first run immediately after playing at the ball, or while he is avoiding being run out or stumped.
    (ii) The bowler after starting his run-up or bowling action does not deliver the ball; in which case the umpire shall immediately call and signal "dead ball".
    (iii) It occurs whilst he is avoiding a throw-in at any time.

LAW 36.   LEG BEFORE WICKET

1. Out lbw

The striker shall be out *lbw* in the circumstances set out below:

  (a) Striker Attempting to Play the Ball
  The striker shall be out lbw if he first intercepts with any part of his person, dress or equipment a fair ball which would have hit the wicket and which has not previously touched his bat or a hand holding the bat, provided that:

(i) The ball pitched in a straight line between wicket and wicket or on the off side of the striker's wicket, or was intercepted full pitch; and

(ii) The point of impact is in a straight line between wicket and wicket, even if above the level of the bails.

(b) Striker Making No Attempt to Play the Ball

The striker shall be out lbw even if the ball is intercepted outside the line of the off stump if, in the opinion of the umpire, he has made no genuine attempt to play the ball with his bat, but has intercepted the ball with some part of his person and if the other circumstances set out in (a) above apply.

LAW 37.   OBSTRUCTING THE FIELD

1. Wilful Obstruction

Either batsman, on appeal, shall be out *Obstructing the Field* if he wilfully obstructs the opposite side by word or action.

2. Obstructing a Ball From Being Caught

The striker, on appeal, shall be out should wilful obstruction by either batsman prevent a catch being made.

This shall apply even though the striker causes the obstruction in lawfully guarding his wicket under the provisions of Law 34. See Law 34.1 (Out Hit the Ball Twice).

Notes

(a) Accidental Obstruction

The umpires must decide whether the obstruction was wilful or not. The accidental interception of a throw-in by a batsman while running does not break this Law.

(b) Entry in Scorebook

The correct entry in the scorebook when a batsman is given out under this Law is "obstructing the field", and the bowler does not get credit for the wicket.

LAW 38.   RUN OUT

1. Out Run Out

Either batsman shall be out *Run Out* if in running or at any time while the ball is in play – except in the circumstances described in Law 39 (Stumped) – he is out of his ground and his wicket is put down by the opposite side. If, however, a batsman in running makes good his ground he shall not be out run out if he subsequently leaves his ground, in order to avoid injury, and the wicket is put down.

2. "No-ball" Called

If a no-ball has been called, the striker shall not be given run out unless he attempts to run.

3. Which Batsman Is Out

If the batsmen have crossed in running, he who runs for the wicket which is put down shall be out; if they have not crossed, he who has left the wicket which is put down shall be out. If a batsman remains in his ground or returns to his ground and the other batsman joins him there, the latter shall be out if his wicket is put down.

4. Scoring of Runs

If a batsman is run out, only that run which is being attempted shall not be scored. If, however, an injured striker himself is run out, no runs shall be scored. See Law 2.7 (Transgression of the Laws by an Injured Batsman or Runner).

Notes

(a) Ball Played on to Opposite Wicket

If the ball is played on to the opposite wicket, neither batsman is liable to be run out unless the ball has been touched by a fieldsman before the wicket is broken.

(b) Entry in Scorebook

The correct entry in the scorebook when a batsman is given out under this Law is "run out", and the bowler does not get credit for the wicket.

(c) Run Out off a Fieldsman's Helmet

If, having been played by a batsman, or having come off his person, the ball rebounds directly from a fieldsman's helmet on to the stumps, with either batsman out of his ground, the batsman shall be "not out".

LAW 39. STUMPED

1. Out Stumped

The striker shall be out *Stumped* if, in receiving the ball, not being a no-ball, he is out of his ground otherwise than in attempting a run and the wicket is put down by the wicket-keeper without the intervention of another fieldsman.

2. Action by the Wicket-keeper

The wicket-keeper may take the ball in front of the wicket in an attempt to stump the striker only if the ball has touched the bat or person of the striker.

Note

(a) Ball Rebounding from Wicket-keeper's Person

The striker may be out stumped if, in the circumstances stated in 1 above, the wicket is broken by a ball rebounding from the wicket-keeper's person or equipment other than a protective helmet or is kicked or thrown by the wicket-keeper on to the wicket.

LAW 40. THE WICKET-KEEPER

1. Position of Wicket-keeper

The wicket-keeper shall remain wholly behind the wicket until a ball delivered by the bowler touches the bat or person of the striker, or passes the wicket, or until the striker attempts a run.

In the event of the wicket-keeper contravening this Law, the umpire at the striker's end shall call and signal "no-ball" at the instant of delivery or as soon as possible thereafter.

2. Restriction on Actions of the Wicket-keeper

If the wicket-keeper interferes with the striker's right to play the ball and to guard his wicket, the striker shall not be out except under Laws 33 (Handled the Ball), 34 (Hit the Ball Twice), 37 (Obstructing the Field) and 38 (Run Out).

3. Interference with the Wicket-keeper by the Striker

If, in the legitimate defence of his wicket, the striker interferes with the wicket-keeper, he shall not be out, except as provided for in Law 37.2 (Obstructing a Ball From Being Caught).

LAW 41. THE FIELDSMAN

1. Fielding the Ball

The fieldsman may stop the ball with any part of his person, but if he wilfully stops it otherwise, five runs shall be added to the run or runs already scored; if no run has been scored five penalty runs shall be awarded. The run in progress shall count provided that the batsmen have crossed at the instant of the act. If the ball has been struck, the penalty shall be added to the score of the striker, but otherwise to the score of byes, leg-byes, no-balls or wides as the case may be.

2. Limitation of On-side Fieldsmen

The number of on-side fieldsmen behind the popping crease at the instant of the bowler's delivery shall not exceed two. In the event of infringement by the fielding side the umpire at the striker's end shall call and signal "no-ball" at the instant of delivery or as soon as possible thereafter.

3. Position of Fieldsmen

Whilst the ball is in play and until the ball has made contact with the bat or the striker's person or has passed his bat, no fieldsman, other than the bowler, may stand on or have any part of his person extended over the pitch (measuring 22 yards/20.12m × 10 feet/3.05m). In the event of a fieldsman contravening this Law, the umpire at the bowler's end shall call and signal "no-ball" at the instant of delivery or as soon as possible thereafter. See Law 40.1 (Position of Wicket-keeper).

4. Fieldsmen's Protective Helmets

Protective helmets, when not in use by members of the fielding side, shall be placed, if above the surface, only on the ground behind the wicket-keeper. In the event of the ball, when in play, striking a helmet whilst in this position, five penalty runs shall be awarded as laid down in Law 41.1 and Note (a).

Note

(a) **Batsmen Changing Ends**
The five runs referred to in 1 and 4 above are a penalty and the batsmen do not change ends solely by reason of this penalty.

LAW 42.   UNFAIR PLAY

1. Responsibility of Captains

The captains are responsible at all times for ensuring that play is conducted within the spirit of the game as well as within the Laws.

2. Responsibility of Umpires

The umpires are the sole judges of fair and unfair play.

3. Intervention by the Umpire

The umpires shall intervene without appeal by calling and signalling "dead ball" in the case of unfair play, but should not otherwise interfere with the progress of the game except as required to do so by the Laws.

4. Lifting the Seam

A player shall not lift the seam of the ball for any reason. Should this be done, the umpires shall change the ball for one of similar condition to that in use prior to the contravention. See Note (a).

5. Changing the Condition of the Ball

Any member of the fielding side may polish the ball provided that such polishing wastes no time and that no artificial substance is used. No one shall rub the ball on the ground or use any artificial substance or take any other action to alter the condition of the ball.

In the event of a contravention of this Law, the umpires, after consultation, shall change the ball for one of similar condition to that in use prior to the contravention.

This Law does not prevent a member of the fielding side from drying a wet ball, or removing mud from the ball. See Note (b).

6. Incommoding the Striker

An umpire is justified in intervening under this Law and shall call and signal "dead ball" if, in his opinion, any player of the fielding side incommodes the striker by any noise or action while he is receiving a ball.

7. Obstruction of a Batsman in Running

It shall be considered unfair if any fieldsman wilfully obstructs a batsman in running. In these circumstances the umpire shall call and signal "dead ball" and allow any completed runs and the run in progress, or alternatively any boundary scored.

8. The Bowling of Fast Short-pitched Balls

The bowling of fast short-pitched balls is unfair if, in the opinion of the umpire at the bowler's end, it constitutes an attempt to intimidate the striker. See Note (d).

Umpires shall consider intimidation to be the deliberate bowling of fast short-pitched balls which by their length, height and direction are intended or likely to inflict physical injury on the striker. The relative skill of the striker shall also be taken into consideration.

In the event of such unfair bowling, the umpire at the bowler's end shall adopt the following procedure:

(a) In the first instance the umpire shall call and signal "no-ball", caution the bowler and inform the other umpire, the captain of the fielding side and the batsmen of what has occurred.

(b) If this caution is ineffective, he shall repeat the above procedure and indicate to the bowler that this is a final warning.

(c) Both the above caution and final warning shall continue to apply even though the bowler may later change ends.

(d) Should the above warnings prove ineffective the umpire at the bowler's end shall:

(i) At the first repetition call and signal "no-ball" and when the ball is dead direct the captain to take the bowler off forthwith and to complete the over with another bowler, provided that the bowler does not bowl two overs or part thereof consecutively. See Law 22.7 (Bowler Incapacitated or Suspended during an Over).

(ii) Not allow the bowler, thus taken off, to bowl again in the same innings.

(iii) Report the occurrence to the captain of the batting side as soon as the players leave the field for an interval.

(iv) Report the occurrence to the executive of the fielding side and to any governing body responsible for the match, who shall take any further action which is considered to be appropriate against the bowler concerned.

9. The Bowling of Fast High Full Pitches

Any high full-pitched ball (regardless of its pace) which passes or would have passed above waist height of the batsman standing upright at the crease shall be called and signalled "no-ball" by the umpire at the bowler's end.

In the event of a bowler bowling a "fast" high full-pitched ball (i.e. a beamer), the umpire at the bowler's end shall adopt the procedure of caution, final warning, action against the bowler and reporting as set out in Law 42.8. However, if the umpire at the bowler's end considers that such a fast high full pitch has been bowled deliberately at the batsman, he shall call and signal "no-ball" and direct the captain of the fielding side to take the bowler off forthwith without adopting the procedure of caution and final warning.

10. Time Wasting

Any form of time wasting is unfair.

(a) In the event of the captain of the fielding side wasting time or allowing any member of his side to waste time, the umpire at the bowler's end shall adopt the following procedure:

(i) In the first instance he shall caution the captain of the fielding side and inform the other umpire of what has occurred.

(ii) If this caution is ineffective he shall repeat the above procedure and indicate to the captain that this is a final warning.

(iii) The umpire shall report the occurrence to the captain of the batting side as soon as the players leave the field for an interval.

(iv) Should the above procedure prove ineffective the umpire shall report the occurrence to the executive of the fielding side and to any governing body responsible for that match, who shall take appropriate action against the captain and the players concerned.

(b) In the event of a bowler taking unnecessarily long to bowl an over the umpire at the bowler's end shall adopt the procedures, other than the calling of "no-ball", of caution, final warning, action against the bowler and reporting as set out in 8 above.

(c) In the event of a batsman wasting time (See Note (e)) other than in the manner described in Law 31 (Timed Out), the umpire at the bowler's end shall adopt the following procedure:

   (i) In the first instance he shall caution the batsman and inform the other umpire at once, and the captain of the batting side, as soon as the players leave the field for an interval, of what has occurred.

   (ii) If this proves ineffective, he shall repeat the caution, indicate to the batsman that this is a final warning and inform the other umpire.

   (iii) The umpire shall report the occurrence to both captains as soon as the players leave the field for an interval.

   (iv) Should the above procedure prove ineffective, the umpire shall report the occurrence to the executive of the batting side and to any governing body responsible for that match, who shall take appropriate action against the player concerned.

11. Players Damaging the Pitch

The umpires shall intervene and prevent players from causing damage to the pitch which may assist the bowlers of either side. See Note (c).

(a) In the event of any member of the fielding side damaging the pitch, the umpire shall follow the procedure of caution, final warning and reporting as set out in 10(a) above.

(b) In the event of a bowler contravening this Law by running down the pitch after delivering the ball, the umpire at the bowler's end shall first caution the bowler. If this caution is ineffective the umpire shall adopt the procedures, other than the calling of "no-ball", as set out in 8 above.

(c) In the event of a batsman damaging the pitch the umpire at the bowler's end shall follow the procedures of caution, final warning and reporting as set out in 10(c) above.

12. Batsman Unfairly Stealing a Run

Any attempt by the batsman to steal a run during the bowler's run-up is unfair. Unless the bowler attempts to run out either batsman – see Law 24.4 (Bowler Throwing at Striker's Wicket before Delivery) and Law 24.5 (Bowler Attempting to Run Out Non-striker before Delivery) – the umpire shall call and signal "dead ball" as soon as the batsmen cross in any such attempt to run. The batsmen shall then return to their original wickets.

13. Player's Conduct

In the event of a player failing to comply with the instructions of an umpire, criticising his decisions by word or action, or showing dissent, or generally behaving in a manner which might bring the game into disrepute, the umpire concerned shall, in the first place, report the matter to the other umpire and to the player's captain, requesting the latter to take action. If this proves ineffective, the umpire shall report the incident as soon as possible to the executive of the player's team and to any governing body responsible for the match, who shall take any further action which is considered appropriate against the player or players concerned.

Notes

(a) **The Condition of the Ball**
Umpires shall make frequent and irregular inspections of the condition of the ball.

(b) **Drying of a Wet Ball**
A wet ball may be dried on a towel or with sawdust.

(c) **Danger Area**
The danger area on the pitch, which must be protected from damage by a bowler, shall be regarded by the umpires as the area contained by an imaginary line 4 feet/1.22m from the popping crease, and parallel to it, and within two imaginary and parallel lines drawn down the pitch from points on that line 1 foot/30.48cm on either side of the middle stump.

(d) Fast Short-pitched Balls

As a guide, a fast short-pitched ball is one which pitches short and passes, or would have passed, above the shoulder height of the striker standing in a normal batting stance at the crease.

(e) Time Wasting by Batsmen

Other than in exceptional circumstances, the batsman should always be ready to take strike when the bowler is ready to start his run-up.

CHANGE IN THE LAWS

The following change in the Laws of Cricket has been made since the publication of *Wisden* in 1998.

Law 42.9 (Unfair Play: The Bowling of Fast High Full Pitches) has been amended so that the umpire at the bowler's end is solely responsible for no-balling high full pitches. This umpire is now authorised to have the bowler taken off forthwith, without the procedure of caution and final warning, if he considers that a fast high full pitch has been bowled deliberately at the batsman.

REGULATIONS OF THE INTERNATIONAL CRICKET COUNCIL

Extracts

1. Standard Playing Conditions

In 1998, the ICC Cricket Committee revised its standard playing conditions of 1995 to apply to all Tests and one-day internationals for a further three years. These include the following:

Duration of Test Matches

Test matches shall be of five days' scheduled duration. The two participating countries may:

(a) Provide for a rest day during the match, and/or a reserve day after the scheduled days of play.

(b) Play on any scheduled rest day, conditions and circumstances permitting, should a full day's play be lost on any day prior to the rest day.

(c) Play on any scheduled reserve day, conditions and circumstances permitting, should a full day's play be lost on any day. Play shall not take place on more than five days.

(d) Make up time lost in excess of five minutes in each day's play owing to circumstances outside the game, other than acts of God.

Hours of Play and Minimum Overs in the Day in Test Matches

1. Start and cessation times shall be determined by the home board, subject to there being six hours scheduled for play per day (Pakistan a minimum of five and a half hours).

(a) Play shall continue on each day until the completion of a minimum number of overs or until the scheduled or rescheduled cessation time, whichever is the later. The minimum number of overs to be completed, unless an innings ends or an interruption occurs, shall be:

(i) on days other than the last day – a minimum of 90 overs.

(ii) on the last day – a minimum of 75 overs (or 15 overs per hour) for playing time other than the last hour when a minimum of 15 six-ball overs shall be bowled. All calculations with regard to suspensions of play or the start of a new innings shall be based on one over for each full four minutes. (Fractions are to be ignored in all calculations except where there is a change of innings in a day's play, when the over in progress at the conclusion shall be rounded up.) If, however, at any time after 30 minutes of the last hour have elapsed both captains (the batsmen at the wicket may act for their captain) accept that there is no prospect of a result to the match, they may agree to cease play at that time.

(iii) Subject to weather and light, except in the last hour of the match, in the event of play being suspended for any reason other than normal intervals, the playing time on that day shall be extended by the amount of time lost up to a maximum of one hour. The minimum number of overs to be bowled shall be in accordance with the provisions of this clause and the cessation time shall be rescheduled accordingly.

(iv) *Experimental Condition, subject to both Boards' agreement before the tour:* If any time is lost and cannot be made up under (a)(iii), additional time of up to a maximum of one hour per day shall be added to the scheduled playing hours for the next day, and subsequent day(s) as required. Of this additional time, the first 30 minutes (or less) shall be added before the scheduled start of the first session and the remainder to the last session.

(b) When an innings ends, a minimum number of overs shall be bowled from the start of the new innings. The number of overs to be bowled shall be calculated at the rate of one over for each full four minutes to enable a minimum of 90 overs to be bowled in a day. The last hour of the match shall be excluded from this calculation (see (a) (ii)).

Where a change of innings occurs during a day's play, in the event of the team bowling second being unable to complete its overs by the scheduled cessation time, play shall continue until the required number of overs have been completed.

2. The umpires may decide to play 30 minutes (a minimum eight overs) extra time at the end of any day (other than the last day) if requested by either captain if, in the umpires' opinion, it would bring about a definite result on that day. If the umpires do not believe a result can be achieved, no extra time shall be allowed. If it is decided to play such extra time, the whole period shall be played out even though the possibility of finishing the match may have disappeared before the full period has expired. Only the actual amount of playing time up to the maximum 30 minutes' extra time by which play is extended on any day shall be deducted from the total number of hours of play remaining and the match shall end earlier on the final day by that amount of time.

Use of Lights: Experimental Condition for one year from September 1, 1998, subject to both Boards' agreement before the tour

If, in the opinion of the umpires, natural light is deteriorating to an unfit level, they shall authorise the ground authorities to use the available artificial lighting so that the match can continue in acceptable conditions.

The lights are only to be used to enable a full day's play to be completed as provided for in Clause 1 above. In the event of power failure or lights malfunction, the existing provisions of Clause 1 shall apply.

Once the lights have been turned on, they must remain on for the remainder of the day's play.

The Bowling of Fast, Short-Pitched Balls: Law 42.8

1. A bowler shall be limited to two fast, short-pitched deliveries per over.

2. A fast, short-pitched ball is defined as a ball which passes or would have passed above the shoulder height of the batsman standing upright at the crease.

3. In the event of a bowler bowling more than two fast, short-pitched deliveries in an over, either umpire shall call and signal "no-ball" on each occasion.

4. The penalty for a fast, short-pitched no-ball shall be one run, plus any runs scored from the delivery.

5. The umpire shall call and signal "no-ball" and then raise the other arm across the chest.

Where a bowler delivers a third fast, short-pitched ball in one over which is also a no-ball under Law 24, e.g. a front-foot no-ball, the penalty will be one run plus any runs scored from that delivery, i.e. the greater penalty will apply. The umpire shall also adopt the procedures of caution, final warning, action against the bowler and reporting as set out in Law 42.8.

The above Regulation is not a substitute for Law 42.8 (as amended below), which umpires are able to apply at any time:

The bowling of fast, short-pitched balls is unfair if the umpire at the bowler's end considers that, by their repetition and taking into account their length, height and direction, they are likely to inflict physical injury on the striker, irrespective of the protective clothing and equipment he may be wearing. The relative skill of the striker shall also be taken into consideration.

The umpire at the bowler's end shall adopt the procedures of caution, final warning, action against the bowler and reporting as set out in Law 42.8.

New Ball: Law 5.4

The captain of the fielding side shall have the choice of taking a new ball any time after 80 overs have been bowled with the previous ball.

Judging a Wide: Law 25.1

Law 25.1 will apply, but in addition

For bowlers whom umpires consider to be bowling down the leg side as a negative tactic, the one-day international wide interpretation will be applied. A ball landing clearly outside the leg stump going further away shall be called wide.

Ball Lost or Becoming Unfit for Play: Law 5.5

In the event of a ball during play being lost or, in the opinion of the umpires, being unfit for play through normal use, the umpires shall allow it to be replaced by one that in their opinion has had a similar amount of wear. However, if the ball needs to be replaced after 110 overs for any of the reasons above, it shall be replaced by a new ball. If the ball is to be replaced, the umpires shall inform the batsmen.

Practice on the Field: Law 15.2

At no time on any day of the match shall there be any bowling or batting practice on the pitch or the square, except in official netted practice pitch areas. In addition, there shall be no bowling or batting practice on any part of the square or the area immediately parallel to the match pitch after the commencement of play on any day. Any fielder contravening this Law may not bowl his next over.

No practice may take place on the field if, in the opinion of the umpires, it could result in a waste of time.

Fieldsman Leaving the Field: Law 2.8

No fieldsman shall leave the field or return during a session of play without the consent of the umpire at the bowler's end. The umpire's consent is also necessary if a substitute is required for a fieldsman at the start of play or when his side returns to the field after an interval.

If a member of the fielding side does not take the field at the start of play, leaves the field, or fails to return after an interval and is absent from the field longer than eight minutes, he shall not be permitted to bowl in that innings after his return until he has been on the field for at least that length of playing time for which he was absent. In the event of a follow-on, this restriction will, if necessary, continue into the second innings. Nor shall he be permitted to bat unless or until, in the aggregate, he has returned to the field and/or his side's innings has been in progress for at least that length of playing time for which he has been absent or, if earlier, when his side has lost five wickets. The restrictions shall not apply if he has suffered an external blow (as opposed to an internal injury such as a pulled muscle) while participating earlier in the match and consequently been forced to leave the field, nor if he has been absent for exceptional and acceptable reasons (other than injury or illness) and consent for a substitute has been granted by the opposing captain.

2. Classification of First-Class Matches

1. Definitions

A match of three or more days' duration between two sides of 11 players played on natural turf pitches on international standard grounds and substantially conforming with standard playing conditions shall be regarded as a first-class fixture.

2. Rules

    (a) Full Members of ICC shall decide the status of matches of three or more days' duration played in their countries.

(b) In matches of three or more days' duration played in countries which are not Full Members of ICC, except Bangladesh and Kenya (see 2.3 (k) below):

    (i) If the visiting team comes from a country which is a Full Member of ICC, that country shall decide the status of matches.

    (ii) If the visiting team does not come from a country which is a Full Member of ICC, or is a Commonwealth team composed of players from different countries, ICC shall decide the status of matches.

Notes

    (a) Governing bodies agree that the interest of first-class cricket will be served by ensuring that first-class status is *not* accorded to any match in which one or other of the teams taking part cannot on a strict interpretation of the definition be adjudged first-class.

    (b) In case of any disputes arising from these Rules, the Chief Executive of ICC shall refer the matter for decision to the Council, failing unanimous agreement by postal communication being reached.

3. First-Class Status

The following matches shall be regarded as first-class, subject to the provisions of 2.1 (Definitions) being complied with:

    (a) **In Great Britain and Ireland:** (i) County Championship matches. (ii) Official representative tourist matches from Full Member countries unless specifically excluded. (iii) MCC v any first-class county. (iv) Oxford v Cambridge and either University against first-class counties. (v) Scotland v Ireland.

    (b) **In Australia:** (i) Sheffield Shield matches. (ii) Matches played by teams representing states of the Commonwealth of Australia between each other or against opponents adjudged first-class.

    (c) **In India:** (i) Ranji Trophy and Shell Conference matches. (ii) Duleep Trophy matches. (iii) Irani Trophy matches. (iv) Matches played by teams representing state or regional associations affiliated to the Board of Control between each other or against opponents adjudged first-class. (v) All three-day matches played against representative visiting sides.

    (d) **In New Zealand:** (i) Shell Trophy and Shell Conference matches. (ii) Matches played by teams representing major associations affiliated to New Zealand Cricket, between each other or against opponents adjudged first-class.

    (e) **In Pakistan:** (i) Quaid-e-Azam Trophy (Grade 1) matches. (ii) PCB Patron's Trophy (Grade 1) matches. (iii) PCB Pentangular Trophy matches. (iv) Matches played by teams representing divisional associations affiliated to the Pakistan Cricket Board, between each other or against teams adjudged first-class.

    (f) **In South Africa:** (i) Supersport Series four-day matches between Boland, Border, Eastern Province, Free State, Gauteng, Griqualand West, KwaZulu-Natal, Northerns, Western Province. (ii) The United Cricket Board Bowl competition three day matches between Easterns, North West and the B teams of Eastern Province, Griqualand West, KwaZulu-Natal, Northerns and Western Province.

    (g) **In Sri Lanka:** (i) Matches of three days or more against touring sides adjudged first-class. (ii) Inter-Club Division I tournament matches played over three or more days for the Premier Championship.

    (h) **In West Indies:** Matches played by teams representing Barbados, Guyana, Jamaica, the Leeward Islands, Trinidad & Tobago and the Windward Islands, either for the Busta Cup or against other opponents adjudged first-class.

    (i) **In Zimbabwe:** (i) Matches of three days or more against touring sides adjudged first-class. (ii) Logan Cup competition three-day matches between Mashonaland, Mashonaland A and Matabeleland.

    (j) **In all Full Member countries represented on the Council:** (i) Test matches and matches against teams adjudged first-class played by official touring teams. (ii) Official Test Trial matches. (iii) Special matches between teams adjudged first-class by the governing body or bodies concerned.

    (k) **In Bangladesh and Kenya:** (i) Matches between a Full Member and either country. (ii) Matches between teams adjudged first-class and either country. (iii) Matches between both countries.

3. Classification of One-Day International Matches

The following shall be classified as one-day internationals:

(a) All matches played in the official World Cup competition, including matches involving Associate Member countries.

(b) All matches played between the Full Member countries of ICC as part of an official tour itinerary.

(c) All matches played as part of an official tournament by Full Member countries. These need not necessarily be held in a Full Member country.

(d) All matches between the Full Members and Bangladesh or Kenya.

(e) Matches between Bangladesh and Kenya on natural turf pitches conforming with standard playing conditions.

Note: Matches involving the A team of a Full Member country shall not be classified as one-day internationals.

4. Qualification Rules for Test Matches and One-Day International Matches

Qualification by Birth

A cricketer is qualified to play in Tests, one-day internationals or any other representative cricket match for the country of his birth provided he has not played in Tests, one-day internationals or, after October 1, 1994, in any other representative cricket match for any other Member country during the two immediately preceding years.

Qualification by Residence

A cricketer is qualified to play in Tests, one-day internationals or in any other representative cricket match for any Full or Associate Member country in which he has resided for at least 183 days in each of the four immediately preceding years provided that he has not played in Tests, one-day internationals or, after October 1, 1994, in any other representative cricket match for any other Member country during that period of four years.

However, cricketers qualified for Associate and Affiliate countries can continue to represent that country without negating their eligibility or interrupting their qualification period for a Full Member country until the cricketer has played for the Full Member country at Under-19 level or above.

Exceptional Circumstances

Should a player be deemed ineligible under the above qualifications and his Board believe that there are exceptional circumstances requiring consideration, a detailed written application shall be made to the Chief Executive of ICC. The application will be referred to the Chairman of the Cricket Committee whose decision shall be final.

Notes: "Representative cricket match" means any cricket match in which a team representing a Member country at Under-19 level or above takes part, including Tests and one-day internationals.

The governing body for cricket of any Member country may impose more stringent qualification rules for that country.

ICC CODE OF CONDUCT

1. The captains are responsible at all times for ensuring that play is conducted within the spirit of the game as well as within the Laws.

2. Players and team officials shall not at any time engage in conduct unbecoming to an international player or team official which could bring them or the game into disrepute.

3. Players and team officials must at all times accept the umpire's decision. Players must not show dissent at the umpire's decision.

4. Players and team officials shall not intimidate, assault or attempt to intimidate or assault an umpire, another player or a spectator.

5. Players and team officials shall not use crude or abusive language (known as "sledging") nor make offensive gestures.

6. Players, umpires and team officials shall not use or in any way be concerned in the use or distribution of illegal drugs.

7. Players, umpires and team officials shall not disclose or comment upon any alleged breach of the Code or upon any hearing, report or decision arising from such breach.

8. Players, umpires and team officials shall not make any public pronouncement or media comment which is detrimental either to the game in general; or to a particular tour in which they are involved; or about any tour between other countries which is taking place; or to relations between the Boards of the competing teams.

9. Players, umpires and team officials shall not engage, directly or indirectly, in betting, gambling or any form of financial speculation on the outcome of any cricket match to which this Code applies and in which the player is a participant or with which a team official is associated or on any event which, in the opinion of the referee, shall be connected with any such cricket match the purpose (or pretended purpose) of which is to benefit such player or team official either directly or indirectly whether financially or otherwise. Players, umpires and team officials shall not accept any form of inducement which is considered by the referee to be likely to affect the performance of any player involved in any such cricket match adversely.

CRIME AND PUNISHMENT

ICC Code of Conduct – Breaches and Penalties in 1997-98

N. S. Sidhu   India v Sri Lanka, one-day international at Colombo (RPS).
Commercial logo on pads. Fined 20 per cent of match fee, with further 20 per cent fine suspended for six months, by J. R. Reid.

Inzamam-ul-Haq   Pakistan v India, one-day international at Toronto.
Clashed with spectator. Suspended for two one-day internationals, with further one-match ban suspended for three and a half months, by J. L. Hendriks.

A. D. R. Campbell   Zimbabwe v New Zealand, 1st Test at Harare.
Verbal abuse of dismissed batsman. Reprimanded by S. Wettimuny.

A. G. Huckle   Zimbabwe v New Zealand, 1st Test at Harare.
Attempted intimidation of umpire and offensive gesture to dismissed batsman. Fined 30 per cent of match fee, with one-match ban suspended for six months, by S. Wettimuny.

P. L. Symcox   South Africa v Pakistan, 1st Test at Rawalpindi.
Dissent when bat-pad appeal rejected and offensive gesture to dismissed batsman. Fined 50 per cent of match fee by R. S. Madugalle.

G. J. Whittall   Zimbabwe v Sri Lanka, 2nd Test at Colombo (SSC).
Dissent when catch by wicket-keeper rejected. Fined 50 per cent of match fee by R. Subba Row.

D. L. Houghton
(Zimbabwean coach)   Zimbabwe v Sri Lanka, 2nd Test at Colombo (SSC).
Public criticism of umpires. Barred from ground for two one-day internationals by R. Subba Row.

Saqlain Mushtaq   Pakistan v South Africa, 1st Test at Johannesburg.
Coloured armguard. Fined 20 per cent of match fee by J. R. Reid.

Asad Aziz
(Pakistani manager)   Pakistan v South Africa, 1st Test at Johannesburg.
Allowed Saqlain Mushtaq to play with coloured armguard. Severely reprimanded by J. R. Reid.

C. E. L. Ambrose   West Indies v England, 4th Test at Georgetown.
Dissent when given out. Severely reprimanded by B. N. Jarman.

A. C. Parore   New Zealand v Zimbabwe, one-day international at Napier.
Dissent when appeal for catch rejected. Fined 50 per cent of match fee by Hanumant Singh.

S. P. Fleming   New Zealand v Zimbabwe, one-day international at Napier.
Dissent when appeal for catch rejected. Severely reprimanded by Hanumant Singh.

N. R. Mongia   India v Australia, 1st Test at Chennai.
Dissent when given out. Fined 50 per cent of match fee, with one-Test ban suspended for rest of
series, by P. L. van der Merwe.

P. R. Adams   South Africa v Sri Lanka, 1st Test at Cape Town.
Gesture to dismissed batsman. Reprimanded by H. Gardiner.

G. P. Thorpe   England v West Indies, 6th Test at St John's.
Dissent when given out. Severely reprimanded by B. N. Jarman.

S. C. Ganguly   India v Australia, 3rd Test at Bangalore.
Dissent when given out. Suspended for one one-day international by P. L. van der Merwe.

M. J. R. Rindel   South Africa v Pakistan, one-day international at Durban.
Coloured armguard. Fined ten per cent of match fee by J. R. Reid.

A. H. Jordaan
(South African manager)   South Africa v Pakistan, one-day international at Durban.
Allowed Rindel to play with coloured armguard. Reprimanded by J. R. Reid.

S. C. Ganguly   India v Zimbabwe, one-day international at Baroda.
Excessive coloured piping on pads. Fined 35 per cent of match fee by P. L. van der Merwe.

Harbhajan Singh   India v Australia, one-day international at Sharjah.
Offensive gesture and abuse of dismissed batsman (Ponting). Fined 50 per cent of match fee, with
one-match ban suspended for 40 days, by Talat Ali.

R. T. Ponting   Australia v India, one-day international at Sharjah.
Offensive gesture to bowler (Harbhajan Singh) when given out. Fined 20 per cent of match fee
by Talat Ali.

Inzamam-ul-Haq   Pakistan v South Africa, one-day international at Cape Town.
Dissent when given out. Fined 50 per cent of match fee, with one-match ban suspended for eight
months, by J. R. Reid.

M. R. Ramprakash   England v South Africa, 2nd Test at Lord's.
Dissent when given out. Fined 25 per cent of match fee, with one-Test ban suspended for six
months, by Javed Burki.

A. A. Donald South Africa v England, 4th Test at Nottingham.
Public criticism of umpires. Fined 50 per cent of match fee, with one-match ban suspended for
one year, by A. M. Ebrahim.

REGULATIONS FOR FIRST-CLASS MATCHES IN BRITAIN, 1998

Hours of Play

Four-day matches:

1st, 2nd, 3rd days . . . 11.00 a.m. to 6.30 p.m.
4th day . . . . 11.00 a.m. to 6.00 p.m.

Three-day matches:

1st, 2nd days . . . . . . 11.30 a.m. to 6.30 p.m. (11.00 a.m. to 6.30 p.m. in tourist matches and
                         Oxford v Cambridge)
3rd day . . . . 11.00 a.m. to 6.00 p.m.

Intervals

Lunch: 1.15 p.m. to 1.55 p.m. (1st, 2nd [3rd] days) in Championship and tourist matches and
Oxford v Cambridge, 1.30 p.m. to 2.10 p.m. in others
1.00 p.m. to 1.40 p.m. (final day)
Where an innings concludes or there is a break in play within ten minutes of the scheduled
lunch interval, the interval will commence at that time and be limited to 40 minutes.

Tea: (Championship matches) A tea interval of 20 minutes shall normally be taken at 4.10 p.m.
(3.40 p.m. on final day), or when 32 overs or less remain to be bowled (except on the
final day or in tourist matches). The over in progress shall be completed unless a batsman
is out or retires during that over within two minutes of the interval or the players have
occasion to leave the field.

If an innings ends or there is a stoppage caused by weather within 30 minutes of the
scheduled time, the tea interval shall be taken immediately. There will be no tea interval
if the scheduled timing for the cessation of play is earlier than 5.30 p.m.

(Other matches) 4.10 p.m. to 4.30 p.m. (1st, 2nd [3rd] days), 3.40 p.m. to 4.00 p.m. (final
day).

Note: The hours of play, including intervals, are brought forward by half an hour for matches
scheduled to start in September.

(i) Play shall continue on each day until the completion of a minimum number of overs or
until the scheduled cessation time, whichever is the later. The minimum number of overs,
unless an innings ends or an interruption occurs, shall be 104 on days other than the last
day, and 80 on the last day before the last hour.

(ii) Where there is a change of innings during the day (except during an interval or suspension
of play or during the last hour of domestic matches), two overs will be deducted from
the minimum number, plus any over in progress at the end of the completed innings (in
domestic matches).

(iii) If interruptions for weather or light occur, other than in the last hour of the match, the
minimum number of overs shall be reduced by one over for each full 3¾ minutes of the
aggregate playing time lost.

(iv) On the last day, if any of the minimum of 80 overs, or as recalculated, have not been
bowled when one hour of scheduled playing time remains, the last hour of the match
shall be the hour immediately following the completion of those overs.

(v) Law 17.6 and 17.7 will apply except that a minimum of 16 six-ball overs shall be bowled
in the last hour, and *all* calculations with regard to suspensions of play or the start of
a new innings shall be based on one over for each full 3¾ minutes. If, however, at
5.30 p.m. both captains accept that there is no prospect of a result or (in Championship
games) of either side gaining any further first-innings bonus points, they may agree to
cease play at that time or at any time after 5.30 p.m.

(vi) The captains may agree or, in the event of disagreement, the umpires may decide to play
30 minutes (a minimum eight overs) extra time at the end of any day other than the last
day if, in their opinion, it would bring about a definite result on that day. In tourist
matches, either captain may make the decision. The whole period shall be played out
even though the possibility of finishing the match may have disappeared before the full

period has expired. The time by which play is extended on any day shall be deducted from the total number of hours remaining, and the match shall end earlier on the last day by the amount of time by which play was extended.

(vii) Notwithstanding any other provision, there shall be no further play on any day, other than the last day, if a wicket falls or a batsman retires, or if the players leave the field during the last minimum over within two minutes of the scheduled cessation time or thereafter.

(viii) An over completed on resumption of a new day's play shall be disregarded in calculating minimum overs for that day.

(ix) The scoreboard shall show the total number of overs bowled with the ball in use and the minimum number remaining to be bowled in a day. In Championship matches, it shall show the number of overs up to 120 in each side's first innings and subsequently the number bowled with the current ball.

Substitutes

(Domestic matches only) Law 2.1 will apply, but in addition:

No substitute may take the field until the player for whom he is to substitute has been absent from the field for five consecutive complete overs, with the exception that if a fieldsman sustains an obvious, serious injury or is taken ill, a substitute shall be allowed immediately. In the event of any disagreement between the two sides as to the seriousness of an injury or illness, the umpires shall adjudicate. If a player leaves the field during an over, the remainder of that over shall not count in the calculation of the five complete overs.

A substitute shall be allowed by right immediately in the event of a cricketer currently playing in a Championship match being required to join the England team for a Test match (or one-day international). Such a substitute may be permitted to bat or bowl in that match, subject to the approval of the ECB. The cricketer who is substituted shall take no further part in the match, even though he may not be required by England. If batting at the time, he shall retire "not out" and his substitute may be permitted to bat later in that innings subject to the approval of the ECB.

Fieldsman Leaving the Field

ICC regulations apply (see page 1416) but, in domestic matches, the fielder is permitted to be absent for 15 minutes; there is no mention of the follow-on and it is explained that "external blow" should include, but not be restricted to, collisions with boundary boards, clashes of heads, heavy falls etc.

New Ball

The captain of the fielding side shall have the choice of taking the new ball after 100 overs (80 in tourist matches) have been bowled with the old one.

Covering of Pitches and Surrounding Areas

(Domestic matches) The whole pitch shall be covered:

(a) The night before the match and, if necessary, until the first ball is bowled; and whenever necessary and possible at any time prior to that during the preparation of the pitch.

(b) On each night of the match and, if necessary, throughout any rest days.

(c) In the event of play being suspended on account of bad light or rain, during the specified hours of play.

The bowler's run-up shall be covered to a distance of at least ten yards, with a width of four yards, as will the areas ten feet either side of the length of the pitch.

Declarations

Law 14 will apply, but, in addition, a captain may also forfeit his first innings, subject to the provisions set out in Law 14.2. If, due to weather conditions, a County Championship match has not started when less than eight hours' playing time remains, the first innings of each side shall automatically be forfeited and a one-innings match played.

MEETINGS AND DECISIONS IN 1998

MCC SPECIAL GENERAL MEETING

On February 24, a resolution that women should be eligible for membership of MCC received 6,969 votes with 5,538 against. But those in favour represented only 55.7 per cent of the members who voted, falling short of the required two-thirds majority.

WOMEN'S CRICKET ASSOCIATION

Members of the 71-year-old Women's Cricket Association met on March 29 and voted by a large majority to merge with the England and Wales Cricket Board. Barbara Daniels, the executive director of the WCA, was to become an ECB employee with special responsibility for women's cricket.

ENGLAND CAPTAINS' APPOINTMENT

On May 5, Alec Stewart was appointed to lead England in the summer's six Tests, following the resignation of Mike Atherton in March. His Surrey team-mate, Adam Hollioake, remained England's one-day captain for the Texaco Trophy series against South Africa. On July 19, however, before the Triangular Tournament with South Africa and Sri Lanka in August, the selectors announced that Stewart would also take over as one-day captain.

MCC ANNUAL GENERAL MEETING

The 211th annual general meeting of the Marylebone Cricket Club was held on May 6. The President, Colin Ingleby-Mackenzie, announced that his successor for two years from October 1 would be Tony Lewis, the former England captain. The club confirmed that members would have to pay to attend World Cup matches at Lord's, and announced that it would be sending a questionnaire to members to find out whether their concerns about the admission of women to MCC could be answered. Membership of the club on December 31, 1997, was 19,746, made up of 17,065 full members, 1,974 associate members, 595 honorary members and 112 senior members, with 29 out-match members. There were 9,200 candidates awaiting election. In 1997, 447 vacancies arose. Following the AGM, a special general meeting approved a change to Law 42.9 of the Laws of Cricket, regarding the bowling of fast high full pitches.

PROFESSIONAL CRICKETERS' ASSOCIATION

At its AGM on May 11, the Professional Cricketers' Association voted by a majority of more than five-to-one against the existing single-division County Championship. Most of them favoured the idea of two divisions. They also voted, by an even wider margin, against the List system of registration for players, which restricts transfers between counties, and called for the ECB to recognise the PCA as a "19th county" for the distribution of funds.

ECB ANNUAL REPORT

The ECB presented its first Annual Report on May 12. Board revenue was £65 million, with profits of £174,000 before tax. With three sponsorship deals – involving Britannic Assurance, AXA and Texaco – coming to an end, the ECB was anxious to maximise revenue from television and urged that Test cricket should be removed from the list of sporting events reserved for terrestrial channels. It proposed to commit more resources to personnel management in the wake of the Theresa Harrild sex discrimination case.

ECB MEETINGS

On May 15, the ECB announced the formation of a review body to examine employment and contractual arrangements for England cricketers. It was to be chaired by Don Trangmar, the joint chairman of Sussex; current Test player Angus Fraser was among its nine members. The body was to present its findings to the Management Board in the autumn.

ICC CRICKET COMMITTEE MEETING

The ICC cricket committee, chaired by Sir Clyde Walcott, met on May 19–20 and decided that, before another Test or one-day international could take place at Indore in India, or Kingston in Jamaica – where international matches were cancelled in 1997-98 due to substandard pitches – an ICC-approved person would be sent to inspect the venues. Several changes to playing conditions were agreed. Umpires were to be authorised to apply, in Tests, the stricter limited-overs interpretation of a wide to curb the negative tactic of bowling into the rough outside the leg stump. Players leaving the field would have to return after two overs (eight minutes, rather than 15) to avoid being penalised. If a ball became unfit, or lost, after 110 overs, it would be replaced by a new ball rather than one of similar condition. Concerns were also expressed about increases in the amount of appealing in internationals, and in the number of drinks breaks.

ICC ANNUAL CONFERENCE

ICC announced on June 16, after its annual conference, that the ninth World Cup in 2007 would be staged in the West Indies. It was decided that the Under-19 World Cup would be staged every two years, following the success of the event in South Africa early in 1998. Canada was chosen to host the next ICC Trophy in 2001. ICC delayed making a decision about a Test World Championship. Bangladesh's application for Test status was again deferred, but France and Uganda were granted Associate status, and Kuwait, Luxembourg and Malta became Affiliates.

THE CRICKET FOUNDATION

In July, the Cricket Foundation announced awards totalling £2,550,000 in support of the ECB's development policies. The money would be distributed to grass-roots cricket via the boards of the 38 first-class and minor counties. It would be used to forge stronger links between schools and clubs; extend Kwik Cricket in primary schools and introduce cricket into secondary schools; expand the ECB's network of 65 cricket development officers; increase playing opportunities for girls, women and disabled people; provide more non-turf pitches and better coaching for youngsters, and increased training for teachers, coaches, ground staff, umpires and scorers.

MCC SPECIAL GENERAL MEETING

On September 28, MCC held its second special general meeting of the year to vote on the eligibility of women for membership. This time, the resolution was passed by 9,394 to 4,072; 69.8 per cent of the members voting were in favour – sufficient for it to be adopted. It was expected that MCC would name a few honorary female members shortly, with playing members being added in coming seasons; others would join the waiting list of over 9,000.

FIRST-CLASS FORUM

Meeting on October 13–14, the ECB's First-Class Forum approved a new programme for England of seven Tests and ten one-day internationals (presumed to be a triangular tournament, with England having a minimum of seven fixtures) each home season from 2000. It was also agreed, in principle, that the England squad should be contracted to the ECB; this was to be discussed further in March 1999. The forum decided that matches in the two-division National League to be introduced in 1999 would consist of 45 overs a side, rather than 50 as proposed in 1997, and that the NatWest Trophy would be reduced from 60 to 50 overs a side. Further investigation of the two-division County Championship proposal was agreed with a view to a decision in December.

ECB TELEVISION DEAL

On October 15, the ECB announced television agreements with Channel 4 and Sky TV to cover all major cricket matches and competitions in the UK (excluding the 1999 World Cup, to be shown on BBC and Sky) up to and including 2002. The deal, worth £103 million, ended the BBC's 60 years of covering major cricket in England. Channel 4 would cover all but one of England's home Tests; the other would be shown only on Sky, who would continue to broadcast home one-day internationals, and have the rights to the County Championship, as well as the new National League, women's cricket, Under-19 internationals, the Super Cup and a tourist match.

FIRST-CLASS FORUM

On December 3, the First-Class Forum voted by 15-1 with three abstentions for a two-division County Championship, to start in 2000. The counties would be assigned to their divisions on 1999 placings. Each county would play the other eight in its division twice, home and away, and three teams would be relegated and promoted. The Super Cup would be continued for another year in 2000, providing further incentive for counties to perform well in the final season of the single Championship in 1999. The forum agreed that in 1999 a Championship victory would be worth 12 points, not 16 as before, and a draw four, not three. In addition, the forum decided to introduce a free hit for no-balls in the new National League. The minimum number of four-day Second Eleven Championship matches would be increased from two to six, but a proposal to play Second Eleven games on uncovered pitches was narrowly defeated.

MEETING IN 1999

ICC EXECUTIVE BOARD

In Christchurch, New Zealand, on January 10–11, 1999, ICC's executive board agreed to set up a Code of Conduct Commission empowered to deal with allegations of match-fixing, and other matters arising from the ICC Code of Conduct. The commission was to consist of three members independent of the cricket boards that form ICC's membership; one of them would have a legal background. Their immediate brief would be to consider the findings of the Pakistani and Australian inquiries into allegations of betting, match-fixing and bribery. They would have powers to require member boards to carry out a review of allegations made against any player, umpire or official and, if not satisfied, to require a further comprehensive investigation in co-ordination with the relevant board. The commission would be empowered to review any board's findings in future, including the penalties imposed. ICC was to establish uniform penalties for match-fixing and bribery at its annual conference in June 1999.

ICC again postponed deciding on a Test World Championship, pending a full review of the international tours schedule; a progress report would be made in June. England and Australia were assured any Championship plans would not threaten the future of five-Test Ashes series. It was agreed to appoint six referees for the 1999 World Cup, along with 12 umpires – two from England, one from each of the other eight Full Members, and two more from the current international panel. Bangladesh, Kenya and Scotland, the Associates taking part, would nominate one umpire each, to officiate in warm-up matches and act as back-up umpire in some World Cup games. The executive board decided to send Bob Simpson, Andy Pycroft and Nasim-ul-Ghani to Bangladesh in March 1999; they would report back, before the annual meeting in June, on whether Bangladesh's application to become the tenth Test nation should be considered further.

The next Under-19 World Cup, now a biennial event, would be held in Sri Lanka in January 2000 and feature 16 teams. ICC were to write to the Commonwealth Games Federation supporting the inclusion of cricket in the Manchester Games in 2002, and recommending Super Max Cricket, rather than 50-over matches, as the most suitable form for this purpose.

The meeting decided to charge umpire Darrell Hair under the Code of Conduct, for detrimental remarks in his autobiography concerning the bowling action of Sri Lankan off-spinner Muttiah Muralitharan. A detailed report from ICC was to be sent to the Australian Cricket Board who would hold an independent hearing. Hair was the first umpire to face charges under the code.

PART EIGHT: MISCELLANEOUS

CHRONICLE OF 1998

JANUARY

2 Steve Waugh plays 100th Test match. Sachin Tendulkar replaced by Mohammad Azharuddin as captain of India. **5** David Bairstow found hanged. Shane Warne takes 300th Test wicket. Wasim Akram resigns as captain of Pakistan. **7** Courtney Walsh replaced by Brian Lara as captain of West Indies. **18** India successfully chase 315 to win one-day international against Pakistan in Dhaka. **20** Geoffrey Boycott given suspended sentence by French court for assault. **24** Zimbabwe coach Dave Houghton suspended for criticising umpires in Sri Lanka. **29** West Indies–England Test in Kingston abandoned after 56 minutes' play because the pitch was dangerous. **30** Ian Healy becomes first wicket-keeper to play 100 Tests.

FEBRUARY

1 England win Under-19 World Cup in South Africa. **13** Johannesburg Test postponed for 24 hours because two Pakistani players were allegedly mugged. **17** England beat West Indies in Port-of-Spain, their first Test defeat on the ground since 1977. **23** Former Indian Test player Raman Lamba dies in Dhaka after being hit while fielding at short leg. **24** Proposal to admit women to MCC fails to get necessary two-thirds majority.

MARCH

5 Australian players' dispute with the Board settled. **6** Rashid Latif becomes fifth Pakistan captain in 12 months. **8** Fanie de Villiers takes six for 23 in Port Elizabeth Test against Pakistan the day after announcing his retirement. **11** Former ECB receptionist who accused the Board of sex discrimination wins case. **18** Makhaya Ntini becomes South Africa's first black Test player. **21** Australia lose the Calcutta Test by an innings and 219, their biggest defeat in 60 years. **23** Western Australia win the Sheffield Shield. **24** England lose the Antigua Test, and the series 3-1; West Indies secure the Wisden Trophy for the 13th successive time; Mike Atherton resigns as England captain.

APRIL

1 Azharuddin appears in his 274th one-day international, breaking Allan Border's record.

MAY

5 Alec Stewart appointed England Test captain. **24** Mal Loye and David Ripley of Northamptonshire put on 401 against Glamorgan, an English fifth-wicket record. **25** Dean Jones announces retirement. **28** Kenya beat India in

a one-day international at Gwalior, their second win over a Test country.
31 Graeme Hick scores his 100th hundred.

JUNE

21 Alex Tudor of Surrey concedes 38 in an over against Andrew Flintoff of
Lancashire. South Africa win Lord's Test by ten wickets.

JULY

4 England batsmen booed off field after collapsing on Saturday of Old
Trafford Test. **6** England save Old Trafford Test. **12** Essex bowl Leicestershire
out for 76 to win last Benson and Hedges Cup final by 192 runs. **18** 150th
anniversary of W. G. Grace's birth. Sri Lankans bowled out for 54 by
Glamorgan at Cardiff, their lowest total in Britain. Leicestershire score 204
in 19.1 overs to win Championship match against Northamptonshire. **21**
Australian Lisa Keightley becomes the first woman to score a century at
Lord's. **27** England win Trent Bridge Test to level series.

AUGUST

6 Alan Butcher, 44, returns to the Surrey team after 12 years – the day his
son Mark scores his maiden Test century. **10** England win Headingley Test,
and the series 2-1. **16** Aamir Sohail appointed Pakistan captain. **31** Sri Lanka
achieve first Test win in England, in one-off game at The Oval; Muttiah
Muralitharan takes 16 for 220, the fifth-best Test analysis ever.

SEPTEMBER

7 Lancashire, led by Wasim Akram, win the last Sunday League, having
won the NatWest final 24 hours earlier. **9** Pakistan judge recommends interim
ban on three players, including Wasim Akram, on suspicion of match-fixing.
11 Andrew Caddick becomes first England-qualified bowler since 1991 to
take 100 wickets in a season. **13** Dickie Bird retires as a first-class umpire.
Wasim announces retirement from international cricket to clear his name.
19 South Africa win first Commonwealth Games cricket gold medal.
Leicestershire win County Championship for the second time in three years.
20 Mike Gatting retires from first-class cricket. **27** Wasim included in
Pakistan squad to face Australia. **28** MCC admit women: proposal finally
gets required two-thirds majority.

OCTOBER

4 Ian Healy beats Rod Marsh's wicket-keeping record of 355 Test victims.
5 Australia win a Test in Pakistan for the first time in 39 years. **6** Mark
Taylor and Mark Waugh give evidence to Pakistani inquiry on match-fixing.
10 Zimbabwe achieve their second-ever Test victory, against India in Harare.

14 English counties agree to new fixture structure of seven Tests and ten one-day internationals per summer. **15** BBC lose rights to televise Tests in England to Channel 4 and Sky TV. **16** Yorkshire abandon plans to leave Headingley. In Peshawar, Mark Taylor equals Don Bradman's 334, the highest Test score by an Australian. **17** Taylor declares, giving away chance of breaking world-record individual Test score. **26** Australia win series in Pakistan, also for the first time in 39 years. **28** Azharuddin plays his 300th one-day international.

NOVEMBER

1 South Africa win Mini World Cup in Dhaka. **4** Brian Lara sacked as West Indian captain after pay dispute. **9** Lara reinstated and dispute settled after week in which the team is holed up in London hotel. **10** West Indies arrive in South Africa six days late. Boycott's assault conviction confirmed after retrial. **17** National Bank of Pakistan bowled out for 20 by Customs in Karachi, the lowest first-class score anywhere since 1983. **20** Mark Taylor plays his 100th Test match. **28** South Africa win the first World Cup for the Blind in Delhi. **30** Zimbabwe score their first away Test win, in Peshawar. Australia beat England in the Perth Test in three days. In Johannesburg, South Africa score their first Test win over West Indies.

DECEMBER

3 English counties agree to two-division Championship from 2000. **8** Mark Waugh and Shane Warne admit taking money from an Indian bookmaker in 1994. **10** Aamir Sohail withdraws from Lahore Test against Zimbabwe; Moin Khan becomes captain. **14** ICC promises inquiry into bribes and match-fixing. **15** Australia win the Adelaide Test, and thus the Ashes for the sixth consecutive series. **20** Faisalabad Test abandoned because of fog, giving Zimbabwe their first series win. **29** England beat Australia in Melbourne by 12 runs to reduce deficit to 2-1. South Africa win Third Test against West Indies in Durban to take an unassailable 3-0 lead.

The following were also among items reported in the media during 1998:

Arjuna Ranatunga was chosen as Man of the Year 1997 by the Colombo paper *Midweek Mirror*, ahead of Sri Lanka's President and other politicians. Sanath Jayasuriya had been picked the previous year. "Why me?" Ranatunga asked on being given the news. (*Midweek Mirror*, Colombo, January 7)

Players at the annual Reedybrook Ashes, in the Queensland outback, killed several pythons and one Taipan snake while looking for lost balls. (*Australian Cricket*, January)

A 23-year-old Sri Lankan man, Ramasinghe Premadasa, drank insecticide and died after his father told him to give up playing cricket and look for a job. (*The Island*, Colombo, January 8)

Magistrates in Gampaha, Sri Lanka, were told that Mrs Thushanee Priyadarshani was forced to stay under the bed for several hours at a stretch because she refused to worship her husband's favourite pictures, showing a film star, and Test player Roshan Mahanama. (*The Island*, Colombo, January 8)

Nizanjan Sarkar, a tailor from Gauhati, Assam, died from heart failure, apparently overcome by excitement while watching the close one-day game between India and Pakistan in Dhaka. (*The Hindu*, January 19)

The disgruntled parents of a teenage boy stopped play at a school tournament to protest against his omission from the Tamil Nadu team. They held up the start of the inter-state Under-14 tournament in Chennai for nearly 40 minutes by sitting on the pitch. "Injustice has been done to my son Pramod Doss," said his father Deva Doss. "It surprises me how a boy good enough to be in the Under-16 city squad cannot find a place in the Under-14 state XI." They were finally persuaded to leave by officials. (*The Hindu*, January 31)

The Prince of Wales declared himself "absolutely knackered" after facing three balls from a schoolboy at the Sinhalese Sports Club on a royal visit to Colombo today. (*Evening Standard*, February 5)

Four teenagers playing cricket were killed by a bomb in the Indian city of Coimbatore when they went to investigate the contents of a bag left in a nearby bush. They were among at least 60 people killed in a wave of explosions in the city. Police believed the bag had been hidden there by the terrorists during the searches which followed earlier blasts. (*Times of India*, February 18)

A 13-year-old boy, Chanminoa Panagodage, fell three storeys to his death in Colombo after he climbed up the outside of a school building to get a piece of wood to use as a cricket bat. Pupils had been banned from bringing bats to school. (*The Hindu*, February 28)

Former Test player Chetan Chauhan was returned to the Indian parliament when he won the Amroha seat for the BJP, the Hindu nationalist party, with a 65,000 majority. Ranjib Biswal, a past captain of the national Under-19 team, and the former Board President, Madhavrao Scindia, were elected on Congress tickets. (*Times of India/The Hindu*, March 6)

The British Psychological Society was told that fielders could quadruple their success rate at catching by practising under ultra-violet light. Dr Simon Bennett of Manchester Metropolitan University said it cut out distractions and enabled people to concentrate. (*Evening Standard*, March 27)

Rosemary, Dowager Countess of Darnley, the 82-year-old daughter-in-law of the Hon. Ivo Bligh, who was given the Ashes urn in 1883, said it contains the burnt remains not of a bail, but of a veil her mother-in-law wore when she watched her future husband play in Australia. She said no one had asked her before. Stephen Green, curator of the Lord's museum, said he had never heard this version before and added: "I've never had the courage to open the urn." (*Evening Standard*, April 15/*The Guardian* April 16)

An Under-13 team from the Baranagar Ramakrishna Mission, batting one man short, were bowled out for nought by the Bournvita team in a match between rival cricket coaching centres in Calcutta. The innings lasted just 18 minutes. Sayak Ghosh took six of the wickets, including a hat-trick, then hit the winning boundary from the second ball. (*The Hindu*, May 11/*Wisden Cricket Monthly*, July)

Richard Shotton, 32, took a hat-trick with his first three balls for his new team, Hengrove Second Eleven, in a Bristol and District League match against Pucklechurch. Shotton, a part-time bowler, had only recently moved into the area. (*Evening Post*, Bristol, May 15)

Keith Hookway, 60, from Bexhill, has played his 600th consecutive match for St John's in Sussex, having never missed a game in the club's 22-year history. (*Summer Sports Argus*, Brighton, May 16)

The Earl's Croome club near Worcester have been allowed to use a disused 18th-century stately home, Croome Court, as their new headquarters. They play on the back lawn and serve teas in the 90ft long Pink Gallery, designed by Robert Adam. John Rudge, a partner in the development firm that has bought the house, said: "We love the fact that a classic English scene takes place there." (*Daily Telegraph*, May 21)

Ten-year-old Michael Andrews scored 241 not out in 100 minutes for Birchfield Prep School, Shropshire, against Belmont School from Surrey. He hit 11 sixes and 30 fours, and was rewarded by being let off his homework. His mother said that both Michael and his 12-year-old brother John Philip are cricket-crazy. "They eat, sleep and drink cricket. Whenever there's an English batting collapse, friends say to the boys 'Hurry up and get in the team.'" (*Daily Mail*, May 22)

Stan Rudder, at 63 believed to be the oldest player in the competition, hit the last ball of the match for four to give Waterlooville a one-wicket win over Hambledon in the National Club Championship. (*The Times*, May 28)

The Thames Valley League banned Marlow's new strip, which had a gold top, a blue band and their sponsors' name across the back. "It's a head in the sand attitude," said club secretary Alan Tierney. (*Sunday Telegraph*, May 31)

A team of Blanks played a match against Staffordshire club Cannock Wood, when Alan Blank, a member of the club, put together an eleven entirely composed of his relatives. It filled in a blank day in the club fixture list.

There were eight Blanks and three relations with a different surname. Two of the team, father and son, were both called David Blank. Another Blank umpired, and other clan members provided what the club said was a record attendance. (*Express & Star*, Wolverhampton, June 1)

A magpie stopped play at Ryde on the Isle of Wight. It swooped and stole the keys from the ignition of a motorised roller which was about to roll the pitch. The start was delayed until a tractor could tow the roller away. (*The Times*, June 3)

MCC received a letter addressed to a Mr O. F. Time, who had been selected to be one of the first to receive a brochure "full of beautiful items for home or boardroom". Stephen Green, curator of the Lord's museum, presumed that the letter was intended for Old Father Time, who he regretted was unable to enter into any correspondence. (*The Times*, June 8)

Nottinghamshire have been granted a licence to conduct marriages at Trent Bridge. (*The Sun*, June 12)

Village cricketers at Over, Cambridgeshire, continued playing in honour of lifelong supporter Sid Wright who died, aged 86, while watching a game. "It's what Sid would have wanted," said a club spokesman. (*Daily Mail*, June 12)

Jennifer Christian drove on to the field in the middle of a match in Dorset, slid to a halt, flung her car keys at the man fielding in the gully and ran off, leaving their two children strapped in the car. Her husband Eric drove off after her and took no further part in the game, between the Dorchester Third Eleven and the Parley Montys from Wimborne. He refused to comment, but team-mates believed he had promised to look after the children that afternoon. (*Daily Mail*, June 19)

Alex Mannock, 16, scored two double-centuries in successive weeks for Billericay in the 40-over Raffingers Matchplay competition: 227 against Roding Valley and 200 not out against Bentley. (*Billericay Gazette*, June 25)

The chief executive of South African cricket, Ali Bacher, failed to make a planned speech in the President's Box at the Lord's Test, because he was trapped in the ladies' toilet. He had wandered in there in error to read through his notes. (*The Express*, June 28)

The Old Alcovians, a team of Northampton businessmen, have found it almost impossible to arrange away fixtures. All their opponents want to play at their new home ground: Earl Compton's ancestral home, Castle Ashby. They were allowed to move there after both the Castle Ashby club and the team from the local village, Yardley Hastings, disbanded. (*Chronicle and Echo*, Northampton, June 29)

Teenager Mark Tomlinson agreed to play for Glazebury Second Eleven against Rylands until 4.30 p.m. when he had to leave for the airport to fly off on holiday with his parents. He took four for 44 as the opposition were bowled out for 67, then hit an unbeaten 51 to win the game. Luckily, his home adjoins the ground, and he leapt back over the garden fence with a minute to spare. (*League Cricket Review*, July)

A match between Hoveringham and the Inland Revenue in Nottinghamshire was stopped for more than five minutes when a naked woman drove across the outfield on a quad bike. (*The Times*, July 1)

Krishana Singh, 15, scored 158 out of a team total of 188 in a house match at Hurstpierpoint College. Twenty-four of the other runs were extras. (*Evening Argus*, Brighton, July 3)

Play in a Suffolk Premier League match was stopped by two police cars chasing a drunken moped rider across the outfield. Deben Valley were batting against the Ipswich and East Suffolk team at Woodbridge when the rider appeared, waving at the police and taunting them. He eventually fell off and was arrested. (*Daily Mail*, July 7)

Thirteen-year-old American Nicholas de la Motte took eight wickets for nought for Hurstpierpoint College, bowling medium-pace, less than three months after joining the school and playing his first match. Stoke Brunswick were bowled out for 15. Nicholas said he wanted to take up cricket as a career and play for Sussex and England. (*Evening Argus*, Brighton, July 8)

A league match in Cornwall was abandoned because of a punch-up between two players on the same side. There was a run-out with both batsmen out of their ground. Neither would leave the field, and they had to be separated by fielders after they began fighting. The batsmen, from the Barripper team, were playing a Mining Division Evening League match against Camborne. The Camborne players walked off and the game was finally abandoned when there was another incident involving the batsmen in the dressing-room. (*Falmouth Packet*, July 18)

Cambridge University student Adam Bidwell, 23, hit six sixes in an over for Old Brightonians off Old Whitgiftian off-spinner Charlton Lamb. His score moved from 75 to 111. (*Sports Argus*, Brighton, July 25)

A cricket injury which left a policeman in a coma for three days may have saved his life, doctors said, as they discovered he had a potentially fatal brain condition. Brain scans showed that Robert Newham, 36, from Elston, Nottinghamshire, had a malformation which would probably have killed him within 15 years. (*Daily Telegraph*, August 1)

Flying ants forced the abandonment of the Worcestershire Borders League game at Alvechurch against Dominies & Guild. Fifteen-year-old Dominies batsman Richard Wilkinson was forced to flee the crease when the ants began to emerge from a nest next to him. Play resumed after a kettle of boiling water was poured on the nest but, ten minutes later, the ants returned and the game was called off. "The whole wicket turned silver," said Dominies captain Glyn Wilks. "Every time anyone went near the wicket they just flew up in a storm." The ants probably saved his team: they were 98 for five chasing 241. (*Worcester Evening News*, August 10)

At a celebration match to open the new pavilion at Buckie in north-east Scotland, Fraser McBean had his car window broken by a six from another player. When McBean batted himself, he hit a six into the hole that was already there. (*The Scottish Cricketer*, September)

A Sri Lankan inquest decided that R. G. Ranasinghe, of Wattegama, had died from "a heart attack caused by excessive happiness" after watching Sri Lanka beat England in the Oval Test. (*The Island*, Colombo, September 4)

Chris Purdie of Tilford dropped Gary Cox off the first ball of his over in a match against Redingensians in Surrey, and went on to concede 40 from the over. The dropped catch went for four, and Cox hit the next six balls for six. This included a no-ball, called when Purdie switched to bowling round the wicket without warning. (*Daily Telegraph*, September 4)

Lymington Second Eleven tied three successive matches in Division One of the Hampshire League. First, they matched 177 by Winchester KS Second Eleven; the following week, Tim Hunter hit 17 off the final over to equal Penton's 274 for five; then they batted first, scoring 167 for nine, against Sparsholt, who were all out off the final ball – for 167. (*Daily Echo*, Southampton, September 5)

Cricket is as dangerous as skiing, according to research by David Ball of Middlesex University. For every 100,000 participants, 130 require hospital treatment in Britain every year. This makes the game the third most risky, behind only rugby and soccer, and equal with hockey and skiing. However, there were only two recorded fatalities among cricketers between 1988 and 1992. (*The Times*, September 14)

A 26-year-old Rawalpindi man was allegedly shot dead by his uncle for supporting India against Pakistan in a one-day international. Muzaffar Ahmed died in hospital of his wounds. His uncle, Arbab Ahmed, was arrested. "It is a sad incident," said the officer in charge of the case, "but it proves how much people love their country and the national cricket team." (*The Hindu*, September 22)

Neil Carey, 24, from Bath, failed to get a batting average after scoring 531 in the season for St Stephen's without being dismissed. (*Bath Chronicle*, October 14)

An impromptu game of cricket in the gents' toilet at the Dutch Open Championships led to English badminton internationals Peter Knowles and Colin Haughton being suspended for ten weeks and six weeks respectively. They played with a cleaners' brush and a bar of soap; Knowles reacted angrily when there were complaints. (*Daily Telegraph*, October 20)

A leading Hindu sage has called on India to give up cricket because the manufacture of balls involves the slaughter of nine cows, which are sacred to Hindus, every day. Swami Nischalananda Saraswati Maharaj, custodian of the temple at Puri, said an alternative to cowhide should be found if the game was to continue. (*Daily Telegraph*, November 5)

A nine-year-old Melbourne boy took a hat-trick in the first three balls of an innings. Thomas Macready-Bryan, playing for Kew Under-12s, bowled all three. (*Herald Sun*, Melbourne, November 19)

The family of a sick woman in Colombo said her life had been saved by the Sri Lankan TV channel showing the Mini World Cup in Dhaka. An urgent call for an A-negative blood donor was flashed on to the screen. (*Sunday Times*, Colombo, November 22)

A batsman in Hyderabad, Pakistan, died after being hit in the neck by a bouncer. Iftikhar Ahmed, playing for Nazimabad Gymkhana, was trying to hook fast bowler Ahmed Ali Jafri of Ghauri Sports Club. The ball was declared a no-ball because it was above head height. (*The Hindu*, November 24)

Two former Sheffield Shield players, Scott Hookey and Neil Maxwell, have been suspended after an alleged fight during a Sydney grade match. Hookey apparently blamed Maxwell, formerly the New South Wales marketing manager, for not including him in a state team photograph. (*Inside Edge*, December)

The treasurer of Builth Wells Cricket Club in Wales, sent out to buy a strimmer to keep the ground under control, bought two goats for £20 to do the job instead. (*Daily Telegraph*, December 11)

A psychologist who studied 33 county cricketers found that they played better when they were feeling cheerful. Peter Totterdell of the University of Sheffield said there was a difference in performance of between six and 16 per cent. (*The Guardian*, December 16)

Contributions from readers for this feature are very welcome, particularly if the items are from local or non-UK newspapers. The relevant cutting is essential. Please send cuttings to the editor at The Oaks, Newton St Margarets, Herefordshire HR2 0QN, England (Fax: 01981-510308) with the title and date of publication clearly marked.

CRICKET BOOKS, 1998

By MARK LAWSON

The plays of Tom Stoppard specialise in unexpected literary encounters – between, for example, James Joyce and Lenin in *Travesties* and A. E. Housman and Oscar Wilde in *The Invention of Love* – but Trent Bridge last August hosted an oddball bookish conversation which even the cricket-loving Stoppard would have hesitated to invent.

In the pavilion during a rained-off Sunday League match, the umpire Dickie Bird was introduced to Stephen King, the world's top-selling horror novelist. With little obviously in common except a tendency to imagine the worst, the men had been brought together by their shared publisher Hodder & Stoughton, being respectively the company's biggest-selling non-fiction and fiction writers of the moment. Bird's book, *My Autobiography*, was already a phenomenon, and by the start of 1999 had sold 670,000 (mostly in hardback, which was reprinting even after the appearance of the paperback). Stoppard's version of the meeting might outstrip reality. King, when I interviewed him the following morning for BBC Radio 4, said that, as a baseball fanatic, he had been keen to make a comparative visit to the English bat-and-glove game. But the significance of the encounter was that it symbolised the strength of the cricket books market, at least for major titles. Bird's book had given him equal weight in the industry with one of the most successful authors in history.

No book published during 1998 could lift a finger to Bird's sales achievement of the previous year – though Hodder & Stoughton had another best-seller with **Anything But . . . An Autobiography**, the gently disingenuous title of the memoirs of Richie Benaud (60,000 hardback sales by the start of 1999). The book takes its name from a warning given to Benaud by a friend on being told that he had signed up to write another book, his eighth.

In terms of potential material, Benaud technically had the advantage over Bird, a moderate batsman who became a super-umpire, in that both his playing and post-playing careers were unusually illustrious. A fabled Australian captain, he became a cricket commentator of such status that he was the only element of the BBC coverage which Channel 4 moved instantly to poach last autumn on winning the rights to televise Tests in England.

Benaud's impeccable commentaries, however, held a clue to what prove to be his deficiencies as a memoirist. His television work is marked by reticence and objectivity. While many commentators seem frightened if there is no fresh saliva on their lip-mike, Benaud sometimes risks unadorned pictures for so long that the viewer starts to fret about technical problems. Also, though Sydney-born and an icon of Australian cricket, he has maintained throughout England v Australia Test series, and all others, a sense of impartiality which would impress a BBC political editor. Unfortunately, while long pauses and fairness have served him well at the mike, they are limitations at the laptop. Silences work less well on page than screen. In a

year when the American President's penis has been a topic of daily conversation, it seems antique to encounter an autobiographer (or even a non-autobiographer) who reveals upheavals in his private life only with the briefest explanation when the name of his wife changes between one paragraph and the next.

Amid a great deal of late-late-late-edition match reporting ("We lost Alan Davidson in the fourth over with a torn hamstring"), the book is at its best, unexpectedly, when it becomes a version of the year's hit genre in mainstream publishing: the medical confessional. Benaud successively suffers two bouts of facial reconstruction following fielding accidents, dengue fever contracted while touring Pakistan, and a tonsillectomy at the unusually late age of 30. Then there is the split spinning finger which threatens to curtail his career and is semi-miraculously cured by a pharmacist in the tiny New Zealand town of Timaru, who prescribes boracic acid powder and sandpaper.

The reader is left with a strong sense of a driven man (when a career in journalism beckoned in his playing twilight, Benaud commendably insisted on training as a news reporter) who is temperamentally unwilling to reveal the nature of the engine.

Three other titles might be read as companion volumes to the Benaud. Cricketing geneticists and psychologists, for example, may enjoy comparing it with **Matters of Choice: A Test Selector's Story**, by John Benaud ("JB" throughout his brother's book). This is a lively work which gives intriguing insights into the mixture of statistical chicanery, personal friendships, regional politics, hunches and finger-crossing which decides the identities of Test elevens in most parts of the world. It is a pity the book's press date prevents coverage of the splitting of the Australian captaincy between Tests and one-dayers (one of the few things RB becomes really animated about in his book), and non-Australian readers may find the book over-detailed on such local controversies as whether Dean Jones and Michael Slater should have been selected for various matches.

The two other volumes appropriate for bringing on at the other end of the bookshelf to Richie Benaud's belong to the expanding genre of commentator memoirs. After last year's *Over to You, Aggers*, another member of the *Test Match Special* team offers **Cakes And Bails: Henry Blofeld's Cricket Year**. It is not clear what virus is affecting 1998 books, but this too is surprisingly medical: "Blowers" at one point goes in for emergency knee surgery on a poisoned joint. Otherwise, the work preserves Blofeld's verbal style: happy, chatty, packed with references to exotic vintages and locations.

The good-sport tone begins to seem inadequate, though, when one of the author's co-commentators, Geoffrey Boycott, begins to suffer the legal manoeuvres over an allegation of violence towards a girlfriend which would dominate the year for him. You also have to wonder whether even devoted *TMS* listeners may not feel they are due some new anecdotes soon. CMJ's lateness, the tendency of Aggers to send fellow commentators faxes from "Hugh Jarse", Bill Frindall's irascibility: all are here, again, suggesting that the moral of these *TMS* books may be that farce repeats itself the fourth time as ancient history.

The author who first alerted the publishing world to the sales potential of books related to *Test Match Special* is again represented in book lists almost five years after his death. **Brian Johnston: Letters Home** is edited by Barry Johnston, the broadcaster's son. This is a collection of letters, found in a trunk in Johnston's study after his death, which he sent to his "Dearest Mummy" between 1926 and 1945. It covers the period from Etonian schoolboy to soldier returning home from the Second World War: from "I was 3rd in French and 1st in Maths last fortnight and 6th in Greek" to "This is German paper I'm writing on: we've also got a lot of champagne they had looted in Brussels", the latter despatches occasionally bearing the editing marks of a military censor.

The effect of the letters is curious. Compelling as social history – a repository of upper middle-class speech and attitudes across two decades – they would work perfectly as one of those Radio 4 morning readings, although for maximum impact the soldier would be unknown. The fame of the correspondent becomes an obstacle. It is questionable whether – as might be the case with a writer or artist – Johnston has reached the stage where absolutely any detail of his life is compelling and relevant. The letters rarely connect with the central cause of his celebrity. Although Johnston writes from Hamburg at the end of the war to ask his mother to send his wicket-keeping gloves out in a parcel, and at another point he receives *Wisden* while on manoeuvres, there are relatively few references to cricket. In this sense, it's somewhat like reading Monty's letters on cricket or Wordsworth's on war. Though the public demand for Johnstoniana clearly exists, his executors should be wary of slicing the cake too thinly.

With so many cricket books rushed out to take advantage of the visibility of contemporary players and commentators – the publishing equivalent of declaration bowling, looking for an easy hit – it is good to find some authors operating on a fuller length historically. Managing an appearance in the general best-seller charts, **W. G. Grace: A Life**, by the broadcaster and poet Simon Rae, marked the 150th anniversary of the birth of a man who has become the touchstone for discussion of cricket much as Olivier became in acting and Lincoln in politics.

The writer Martin Amis once said that the test of a good biography was whether it gave you "a sense of what it was like to be in a room with that person". To adapt that analogy, the reader wants Rae to show us what it was like to be at the crease with W.G. This he admirably achieves, drawing contemporary reports and memoirs together to form his own crisp and immediate narrative.

Rae isolates, for example, a moment – in the Gentlemen of the South against the Players of the South game at The Oval in 1866 – when the singularity of Grace's talent became clear. "The Oval authorities had given him a presentation bat, complete with silver plate, and this he now called for. There had been no time to knock it in but careless of the consequences Grace was soon blazing away, hitting James Lillywhite for two all-run sixes. As the professionals watched him sprinting up and down the wicket, with the silver plate on his bat glinting in the sunshine, they must have sensed that they were witnessing the transformation of the game as they knew it."

Rae's book makes it clear that, in appearing for the Gentlemen in that encounter, Grace was both legally and temperamentally playing for the wrong team. The author establishes that Grace, despite playing as an amateur, made "a minimum of £30,000 a year out of domestic cricket in today's terms during the 1870s", and considerably more on two lucrative tours of Australia. An organiser of tours to Scotland was quoted at the time as saying "It takes a lot of money to bring Grace down."

On the matter of non-gentlemanly behaviour on the pitch, Rae finds some support for the stories all schoolboys are told about Grace's bullying of umpires and reluctance to leave the crease when dismissed.

It intrigued me that many of the cricket writers who reviewed Rae's book, particularly those correspondents of the older school and the venerable broadsheets, seemed keen to treat Grace's cheating and financial deceit as a bit of fun, and unsurprising for the time. But – rather as Thomas Jefferson's sex life provides a useful historical counterpoint to Bill Clinton's – part of the importance of Rae's work is that, at a time when international cricketers are being held to very high moral standards by the media, it usefully questions the existence of a golden age of integrity and fairness. There are also glancing historical revelations, including the fact that *Lillywhite's Companion* (a cricket reference book of the period) always toadyingly placed the Prince of Wales at the top of the batting averages, whatever his performance; he once headed the charts with an average of one.

Dr Grace is also treated in another original and diverting work by Simon Wilde, a versatile young sports writer now deservedly promoted to cricket correspondent of the *Sunday Times*. **Number One: The World's Best Batsmen and Bowlers** has the clever idea of running Test cricket's computer-ratings system – which has brought to cricket a ranking method previously confined to pop music and world tennis – on the statistics of players from the pre-computer age.

The aim is to establish who were the number one batsmen and bowlers in the world from the 1770s (John Small with the bat, Edward "Lumpy" Stevens with the ball) to the 1990s (Steve Waugh taking guard, Shane Warne running up.) Those start and end points certainly chart the curve of supremacy in the game away from England and towards Australia, although it is irritating that the Waugh–Warne encounter is only possible in infrequent state games or, future schedules and shoulders allowing, in English county cricket.

Wilde's book is clearly intended to start arguments, and it seems improbable to me that my childhood hero Geoffrey Boycott was never at any point the number one batsman in the world. But the author's encapsulations of the players selected by the computer – each is described in five or six pages – are highly impressive. The lethal swagger of a Viv Richards innings, for example, is fascinatingly attributed to the influence of boxing, which he took up when banned for two years as a youngster (this, again, a key biographical detail) after disputing an umpire's verdict in an inter-island game. Wilde convincingly suggests that Richards's "desire to duel may have stemmed from his passion for boxing ... He possessed a boxer's powerful shoulders and quickness of foot and he liked to punch the ball hard. He timed his entrances into the 'ring' as dramatically as any heavyweight ..."

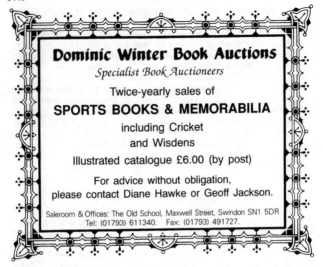

Some might argue that this is an example of the biographical fallacy (the view that everything in a person's life connects) but, like all the best critical writing, it makes you think again about what you saw. Wilde faces a harder task with players witnessed by neither him nor the reader, but these early essays succeed through well-placed detail, such as the fact that David Harris (the best bowler of 1783 to 1798) forced batsmen to develop the forward defensive stroke because he bowled a fuller length than had previously been common.

Another of the backward-glancing volumes is **Cricketing Falstaff: A Biography of Colin Milburn** by Mark Peel. The choice of subject may seem slightly surprising for the head of politics at Fettes College, Milburn's only obvious connection with the political being the incorrectness by contemporary standards of his lifestyle for one playing sport at the highest level. Peel sometimes seems sloppy on cricket, confusing, for example, Jim Watts with Peter Watts. But his short book manages, by the Martin Amis yardstick quoted above, to give you a sense of what it was like to be in a room with Milburn: the room would soon be spinning. Without judgmentalism, Peel describes drinking and eating bouts which would seem likely to leave even a spectator of cricket unable to perform. There is a tawdry story of a curried-and-lagered Milburn vomiting on the wicket during a televised Sunday League match, leaving the twelfth man rushing for sawdust and John Arlott informing viewers that Milburn had been "taken ill".

It seems obvious that Milburn could not have lived and played the same way today. He could not have met the personal fitness targets now handed to England players before tours, and the tabloid press would have made him a Gazza of the summer game, recording his alcohol consumption under the pretence of urging him to get help.

That Milburn was able to play so well – and so explosively – despite the regime described by Peel can only be attributed to an exceptional eye. In that respect, of course, Milburn's life story notoriously turned out to have been scripted by Sophocles. Peel's account of the May 1969 car crash, in which Milburn was thrown through the windscreen of his car while driving back into Northampton late at night, comes across as cricket's equivalent of the events in Paris of August 31, 1997, in the sense of how much difference to history a mere seat-belt might have made.

The book's final third – covering Milburn's brave but doomed attempt to play the game with one eye, and then the post-cricket years of reminiscing in bars with a cheeriness which he cannot have felt inside – brings to cricketing literature a bleakness which has not been reached except in David Frith's study of the game's suicides.

Peel is helped by the fact that his narrative has a genuinely tragic shape. In comparison, standard lives of past players can seem routine, but **Jim Laker: A Biography** by Alan Hill and **On The Spot: Derek Shackleton** by David Matthews are efficient career reconstructions, largely consisting of descriptions of matches which are then represented numerically in appendices in the final pages. It is sometimes hard to see how this division of cricket writing can long survive in the age of video, which will always be better at historical match-reporting. Many younger readers may feel that a book like the one on Laker needs more spin.

If biographies of past stars could do with a few more edges, books written by (which is to say, usually written for) current players are increasingly, like a No. 11's innings, all edge and swipe. Now traditionally published in the period between retirement from Test cricket (to avoid the strong censorship clauses in international players' contracts) and retirement from county cricket (to ensure that the cricketer still has public pulling power), these volumes are designed to provoke headlines and serialisations in the sports pages.

You Guys Are History! by Devon Malcolm and **Wasim** by Wasim Akram are classic examples of books which stage a fight in public in the hope of attracting a crowd of media bystanders. The BBC's Patrick Murphy has become associated with holding the coats of cricketers on these occasions (he served Jack Russell last year) and his tape-recorder has captured the raw material from both Malcolm and Wasim.

Spookily similar Acknowledgements pages feature the England pace bowler thanking Murphy for having "battered his way through the Midlands traffic network" while the Pakistan fast man thanks the ghost for his willingness to "negotiate the M6 motorway". You get the impression that Murphy has been beginning interview sessions by complaining about the traffic. Maybe he was late a lot. If so, perhaps he's simply assisting too many autobiographical cricketers at once.

In Malcolm's book, the chapter on his historic nine for 57 against South Africa at The Oval is as blandly platitudinous as an after-match interview on TV: "Then I really got one to swing to have Dave Richardson lbw." The sections which won the headlines on publication, dealing with rows with England selectors and bowling coaches, read tediously even a few months later. The one really vivid line – the remark made by Malcolm before avenging himself on the South Africans for being bounced while batting – is used up in the title.

The Wasim Akram book, looking no further for its title than the cricketer's birth certificate, is more inviting because its own carefully-planted bombshells – death threats in Pakistan after defeats in 1998, and Wasim's response to long-term allegations of ball-tampering – have a longer aftershock than complaints about being dropped from Test matches.

Mad Dogs and Englishwomen sees the welcome recruitment to cricket-writing (although it is probably temporary) of one of the most original sports authors, Pete Davies. A political novelist who came to greater prominence with *All Played Out* – a book based on deep access to the England football squad in the World Cup of Gazza's tears – Davies has always seemed to me the man to tell the truth about English cricket: a kind of Simon Hughes-plus, in that he would not be constrained by any professional friendships. Davies, though, seems currently to be directing his sharp and pitiless eye towards a feminist agenda. After a book about women footballers, he now follows England's female cricketers at their World Cup in India in December 1997. Davies will hate this being said, but many male readers will surely struggle to summon interest in the detailed reports of matches.

The pleasures of the book, as always with Davies, come from his gift for putting a person on the page in one well-heard phrase, or a place through a well-seen detail. It is fascinating to discover that the women's favourite adjective of abuse is "mingeing" and, switching on TV in his hotel room, the reporter notes a message which is worthy of a scene in a book by his obvious model as a writer, Dr Hunter S. Thompson: "Don't Believe Rumours. Situation In The City Is Quite Normal And Peaceful. Commissioner of Police."

An increasingly popular genre in flannel publishing is the diary. Since the success of Simon Hughes's *A Lot Of Hard Yakka* last year, most members of the England team and several of each summer's tourists are signed up by publishers or newspapers as prospective Boswells. **Postcards from the Beach** is Phil Tufnell's day-by-day account of the 1997-98 England tour of the West Indies, with help from Peter Hayter, and depends heavily on teasing the reader with the spinner's bad-boy reputation.

"Bumped into the Judge last night. No, no, don't panic. Not that kind of judge," he begins one entry, hoping that readers will not immediately recognise the nickname of Robin Smith of Hampshire. The problem with this volume is that it's rather like reading one of Brian Johnston's wartime letters in the book reviewed above. We are always aware that a censor (in this case from the England and Wales Cricket Board) has been through the text. There is, though, one very funny story. Choosing for some reason to make a will before he leaves for the West Indies, Tufnell is teased by the solicitor with the idea that he thinks he's going to be killed by the bowling of Ambrose and Walsh.

Recent English squads have at least included an unusual kind of diarist, who seems unlikely to be replaced unless Alec Stewart or Warren Hegg is keeping very quiet about membership of the Royal Academy. **The Art of Jack Russell: Caught on Canvas** collects the sketches and watercolours of the only England wicket-keeper with whom reference to "a Turner" was likely to prompt an art history lecture rather than remarks about spin bowling.

The landscapes – from Gloucestershire to Barbados – are most impressive. Russell comes off less well when he goes head to head with the press photographers. His painting of himself in conversation with Mike Atherton during their epic stand at Johannesburg in 1995 is oddly less evocative than what the daily smudgers got, presumably because Russell was unable to observe the scene. The growing volume of the pictures he was able to produce during the more recent overseas tours is one of the more oblique but eloquent commentaries on the decline of the specialist wicket-keeper.

Two books, their sales surely heavily weighted towards Wales, record Glamorgan's Championship summer of 1997. **To Lord's With A Title** by Hugh Morris, a leading figure in that campaign, is cutely named for this market – it refers to Morris's retirement to take up an administrative job with the ECB – but otherwise consists of not very animated match reports, most chapters beginning with the Championship table at the start of the relevant match.

The problem is that there can never be any tension about the outcome, except to a non-cricketing Martian, who would probably not make this his

first withdrawal from the British Library anyway. **Daffodil Days** by Grahame Lloyd seems similarly restricted in its appeal and, as with the Morris volume, you have the strong sense that video would be a better medium for memento works of this kind.

The word from within the publishing industry last year was that, while books by the game's major personalities (Bird, Benaud, Botham, Boycott) can now sell at unprecedented levels, sales of lower-order titles, lacking a big name or promotional campaign, were losing appeal. The market needs another Dickie Bird. Or Stephen King's encounter with him might inspire his first cricket horror novel: *Bloody Stumps*, perhaps.

Mark Lawson is a columnist for The Guardian *and presenter of* Front Row *on BBC Radio 4 and the BBC TV programme* Late Review. *He grew up in Leeds and was given a Geoffrey Boycott pillowcase one Christmas in the 1970s.*

ADDITIONAL REVIEWS

Matthew Engel writes: The year also produced two important reference works which pose obvious difficulties for any *Wisden* reviewer. In November, there emerged (dressed in green) the first edition of **Wisden Cricketers' Almanack Australia**, a little brother for this almanack after a mere 135 years.

The new book is published independently, by the Melbourne firm Hardie Grant Books. But it is licensed and supervised by John Wisden and Co, our publishers. *Wisden Australia* is a sibling, not a clone, and none of the material duplicates this Almanack.

The year also produced the fourth edition of Bill Frindall's masterful compilation, **The Wisden Book of Cricket Records**, now immodestly clad in imperial purple. This contains detail that cannot possibly be printed every year in *Wisden*. It is accepted as authoritative. Enough said.

It was also a special year for the best of all county publications: the stylish and dignified **Yorkshire County Cricket Club Yearbook** reached its centenary edition in 1998. The editor, Derek Hodgson, marked the occasion by asking eight non-Yorkshiremen for their memoirs of the county; we were all appropriately respectful.

A Century of Great Cricket Quotes by David Hopps constitutes another potential classic. It is less useful than it ought to be as a reference due to the absence of an index. But it is a wonderful book to dip into. John Woodcock, who has resolutely refused to write his memoirs, has gone between hard covers with **The Times One Hundred Greatest Cricketers**, a well-illustrated version of his original newspaper series; the list appeared in *Wisden* 1998.

A Dictionary of Cricket Terminology by Keith Foley is the best-researched book of its type I have seen. It is not clear to me who might buy it, but cricket historians a century hence will be glad to hunt it down.

BOOKS RECEIVED IN 1998

GENERAL

Allen, Peter **The Invincibles: The Legend of Bradman's 1948 Australians** Foreword by Thomas Kenneally (Allen & Kemsley Publishing, Australia, \$A39.95; in UK from John Wisden & Co Ltd: for details ring 01483-570358, or write to 25 Down Road, Guildford, Surrey GU1 2PY)

Baxter, Peter and McNeill, Phil **Cricket's Big Day Out: The Benson and Hedges Cup 1972-1998** (Andre Deutsch, £14.99)

Beckles, Hilary McD. ed. **A Spirit of Dominance: Cricket and Nationalism in the West Indies** Essays in honour of Viv Richards on the 21st anniversary of his Test debut (Canoe Press, University of the West Indies, 1A Aqueduct Flats, Mona, Kingston 7, Jamaica, price varies)

Benaud, John **Matters of Choice: A Test Selector's Story** (Swan Publishing, Perth; in UK from Sportspages, 94-96 Charing Cross Road, London WC2H 0JG and Barton Square, St Ann's Square, Manchester M2 7HA, £16.95)

Blofeld, Henry **Cakes and Bails: Henry Blofeld's Cricket Year** (Simon & Schuster, £16.99)

Booth, Keith **Knowing the Score: The Past, Present and Future of Cricket Scoring** (Two Heads Publishing, Freepost LON 6708, London N19 3BR, £9.99 inc. p&p)

Craven, Nico **Sunday, Monday or All Days** Foreword by David Lemmon (The Coach House, Ponsonby, Seascale, Cumbria CA20 1BX, £6.66)

Davies, Pete **Mad Dogs and Englishwomen** (Abacus, £9.99, paperback)

Hargreaves, Peter S. **A Man and His Cricket** (from J. W. McKenzie, 12 Stoneleigh Park Road, Ewell, Epsom, Surrey KT19 0QT, £5)
Reminiscences of Wisden's Danish correspondent.

Hartland, Peter **The Balance of Power in Test Cricket 1877-1998** (Field Publishing, 17 Tollwood Park, Crowborough, East Sussex TN6 2XR, £12.95 inc. p&p)

Hartman, Rodney **Hansie and the Boys: The making of the South African cricket team** (Zebra Press, 32 Thora Crescent, Wynberg, Sandton, South Africa, price not given)

Johnston, Barry ed. **Brian Johnston: Letters Home 1926-45** (Weidenfeld & Nicolson, £20)

Lloyd, Grahame **Daffodil Days: Glamorgan's Glorious Summer** (Gomer Press, Llandysul, Ceredigion SA44 4BQ, £16.99)

McDonald, Ian and Ugra, Shanda **Anyone for Cricket? Equal opportunities and changing cricket cultures in Essex and East London** (University of East London, Longbridge Road, Dagenham, Essex RM8 2AS, £9.95)

Morris, Hugh with Andy Smith **To Lord's With A Title: The Inside Story of Glamorgan's Championship** (Mainstream, £14.99)

Rajan, Sunder **Lord Harris Shield Cricket Tournament: Commemoration volume 1897-1997** Foreword by Raj Singh Dungarpur (Marine Sports, Mumbai; in UK from J. W. McKenzie, address as above)

Stoddart, Brian and Sandiford, Keith ed. **The Imperial Game: Cricket, Culture and Society** (Manchester University Press, price not given)

Tufnell, Phil with Peter Hayter **Postcards from the Beach** (Collins Willow, £6.99, paperback)

Wallish, E. A. "Ned" **The Great Laurie Nash** Foreword by Keith Miller (Ryan Publishing, Melbourne, \$A29.95; in UK from Sportspages, addresses as above, £15.99)

Waugh, Mark with Grantlee Keiza **A Year to Remember** (Random House Australia; in UK from Sportspages, addresses as above, £16.95)

Webber, J. R. **The Chronicle of W.G.** (ACS, 3 Radcliffe Road, West Bridgford, Nottingham NG2 5FF, £50 limited edition, £60 with hard case)

Wilde, Simon **Number One: The World's Best Batsmen and Bowlers** (Gollancz, £16.99)

Woodcock, John **The Times One Hundred Greatest Cricketers** Foreword by Mike Brearley (Macmillan, £16.99)

ANTHOLOGY

Wright, Graeme ed. **Wisden on Bradman: 90th Birthday Edition** (Hardie Grant Books, Melbourne, \$A29.95; in UK from Penguin Direct, Bath Road, Harmondsworth, Middlesex UB7 0DA, £14.99, tel 0181-899 4036)

AUTOBIOGRAPHY

Benaud, Richie **Anything But . . . An Autobiography** (Hodder & Stoughton, £17.99)
Malcolm, Devon with Patrick Murphy **You Guys Are History!** (Collins Willow, £16.99)
Wasim Akram with Patrick Murphy **Wasim** (Piatkus Books, £16.99)

BIOGRAPHY

Hill, Alan **Jim Laker: A Biography** (Andre Deutsch, £17.99)
Matthews, David **On The Spot: Derek Shackleton: A Biography** Foreword by Colin Ingleby-Mackenzie (Blackberry Downs Books, Lincombe, Lee, Devon EX34 8LL, £15.95 inc. p&p)
Meher-Homji, Kersi **The Waugh Twins** Foreword by Bob Simpson (Kangaroo Press, Sydney, \$A24.95; in UK through Hi Marketing, tel 0171-738 7751)
Peel, Mark **Cricketing Falstaff: A Biography of Colin Milburn** (Andre Deutsch, £17.99)
Rae, Simon **W. G. Grace: A Life** (Faber and Faber, £20)

PICTORIAL

Russell, Jack **The Art of Jack Russell: Caught on Canvas** (HarperCollins, £19.99)

REFERENCE

Foley, Keith **A Dictionary of Cricket Terminology** (Edwin Mellen Press, Lampeter, Wales SA48 8LT, £69.95. Limited offer to individuals £35, tel 01570-423356)
Frindall, Bill ed. **The Wisden Book of Cricket Records: Fourth Edition** Completely revised and updated to end of 1997 English season (Headline, £40)
Hopps, David **A Century of Great Cricket Quotes** (Robson Books, £16.95)
Vaidyanathan, P. V. comp. **Indian Cricket 1997: 51st edition** (Kasturi & Sons, Chennai 600002, India, Rs65)
Wisden Cricketers' Almanack Australia 1998: First edition (Hardie Grant Books, Melbourne, \$A39.95; in UK from Penguin Direct, Bath Road, Harmondsworth, Middlesex UB7 0DA, £19.99, tel 0181-899 4036)

STATISTICAL

Bailey, Philip J. comp. **Sri Lanka First-Class Matches 1994-95** and **1995-96** (ACS, 3 Radcliffe Road, West Bridgford, Nottingham NG2 5FF, £5 and £7.50)
Croudy, Brian and Bartlett, Kit **D. C. S. Compton: His Record Innings-by-Innings** (ACS, address as above, £6.95)
Gerrish, Keith **Gloucestershire County Cricket Club First-Class Records 1870-1997** (Limlow Books, Blue Bell House, 2-4 Main Street, Scredington, Sleaford, Lincs NG34 0AE, £9.25 + 50p p&p)
Griffiths, Peter **Complete First-Class Match List: Volume 4 1963-1980/81** (ACS, address as above, £7)
Griffiths, Peter **Subject Index to the Cricket Statistician 1973 to 1997: Issues No 1 to 100** (ACS, address as above, £7)
Heald, Brian and Ambrose, Don comp. **1863: A Statistical Survey** (ACS, address as above, £4.50)
Hudd, Gerald **Tom Graveney: His Record Innings-by-Innings** (ACS, address as above, £7.95)
Ledbetter, Jim ed. **First-Class Cricket: A Complete Record 1932** (Limlow Books, address as above, £17.95 + £1.50 p&p)
Lodge, Jerry **T. G. Evans: His Record Innings-by-Innings** (ACS, address as above, £6)
Milton, Howard **F. E. Woolley: His Record Innings-by-Innings: Second Edition** (ACS, address as above, £8.95)
Powell, William A. **London County Cricket Club First-Class Records** (Limlow Books, address as above, £25 limited edition)
Richardson, Michael **Neil Harvey: His Record Innings-by-Innings** (ACS, address as above, £5.50)
Sandiford, Keith A. P. **Gary Sobers: His Record Innings-by-Innings** (ACS, address as above, £7)

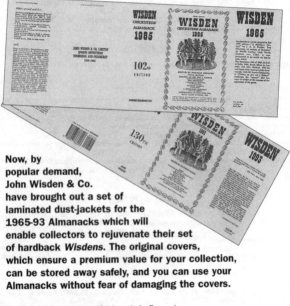

Snow, E. E. **Country House Cricket Grounds of Leicestershire and Rutland** (ACS, address as above, £3.50)

Thorn, Philip and Bailey, Philip comp. **European Cricketers in India, Ceylon and Burma** (ACS, address as above, £6)

TECHNICAL

Know the Game: Cricket Produced in collaboration with MCC (A&C Black, £4.99)

Steen, Rob **Cricket: Inside the Game** (Icon Books, £9.99 inc. p&p)

FIRST-CLASS COUNTY YEARBOOKS. 1998

Derbyshire (£5), Durham (£6), Essex (£7), Glamorgan (£6), Gloucestershire (£5), Hampshire (£7), Kent (£4.99), Lancashire (£6.50), Leicestershire (£6.95), Middlesex (£8), Northamptonshire (£8.50), Nottinghamshire (£4.50), Somerset (£7), Surrey (£5), Sussex (£6), Warwickshire (£5), Worcestershire (£6), Yorkshire (£13). 1999 prices may change. Some counties may add charges for p&p.

OTHER HANDBOOKS AND ANNUALS

Bader, Nauman ed. **The Pakistan Cricketers' Who's Who 1997** (from Limlow Books, Blue Bell House, 2-4 Main Street, Scredington, Sleaford, Lincs NG34 0AE, £25 inc. p&p in UK)

Bader, Nauman ed. **PCB Paktel Cricket Annual 1997-98** (from Limlow Books, address as above, £21 inc. p&p in UK)

Bailey, Philip comp. **ACS International Cricket Year Book 1998** (ACS, 3 Radcliffe Road, West Bridgford, Nottingham NG2 5FF, £9.95)

Bryden, Colin ed. **Mutual & Federal South African Cricket Annual 1998** (UCBSA/Mutual & Federal, PO Box 1120, Johannesburg 2000, no price given)

Il Cricket italiano 1998 (from Federazione Cricket Italiana, Via S. Ignazio 9, 00186 Roma)

Frindall, Bill ed. **NatWest Playfair Cricket Annual 1998** (Headline, £4.99)

Hatton, Les comp. **First-Class Counties Second Eleven Annual 1998** (ACS, address as above, £4.95)

Lemmon, David ed. **Benson and Hedges Cricket Year: 17th Edition** Foreword by Mike Procter (Bloomsbury, £20)

Maxwell, Jim ed. **ABC Cricket Book 1998-99** (ABC/Fairfax Press, $A5.50)

Miller, Allan ed. **Allan's Australian Cricket Annual 1998** (from Allan Miller, PO Box 974, Busselton, WA 6280, $A35; in UK from Sport in Print, 3 Radcliffe Road, West Bridgford, Nottingham NG2 5FF, £17.50)

Ward, John ed. **Zimbabwe Cricket Year 1998** (Pangolin Press, Helena Close, Marlborough, Harare, Zimbabwe; in UK from Limlow Books, address as above, £13 + 50p p&p)

REPRINTS AND UPDATES

Agnew, Jonathan **Over to You, Aggers** Paperback edition (Vista, £6.99)

Botham, Ian **The Botham Report** Paperback edition with extra chapter on England's 1997-98 tour (Collins Willow, £6.99)

Bradman, Sir Donald **The Art of Cricket** Prefaces by Richie Benaud and E. W. Swanton (Robson Books, £16.95)

Cartwright, Phill **90+: A Study of Scores of 90-99 in Test Cricket** (from the author, 14 Warren Close, Pilsley, Derbys, £2.50)

Foot, David **Wally Hammond: The Reasons Why** Paperback edition (Robson Books, £10.99)

Heller, Richard **A Tale of Ten Wickets** (Oval Publishing, 30 Crewdson Road, London SW9 0LJ)
Novel, first published 1994.

John Wisden's Cricketers' Almanack for 1904 and 1905 Facsimile editions (Willows Publishing, 17 The Willows, Stone, Staffs ST15 0DE, fax 01785-615867, £48 inc. p&p for each volume in UK, £2 extra overseas postage; £5 extra for version with facsimile of original hard cloth cover)

Lillywhite, Frederick **Frederick Lillywhite's Cricket Scores and Biographies** Volume III 1841-1848 and Volume IV 1849-1854 (Facsimile edition, from Roger Heavens, 2 Lowfields, Little Eversden, Cambs CB3 7HJ; limited edition of 500, £50 each + £3.50 p&p)
Volume III is the rarest volume of Scores and Biographies: *most of the pages were apparently thrown into a furnace before they could be bound.*

Low, Robert **W.G.: A Life of W. G. Grace** Paperback edition (Richard Cohen Books, £8.99)

Mote, Ashley ed. **John Nyren's The Cricketers of My Time** (Robson Books, £14.95)

Russell, Jack with Murphy, Pat **Unleashed** Updated paperback (Collins Willow, £6.99)

Trueman, Fred with Mosey, Don **Fred Trueman Talking Cricket** Paperback edition (Coronet, £6.99)

PERIODICALS

The Cricketer International (monthly) ed. Peter Perchard (Beech Hanger, Ashurst, Tunbridge Wells, Kent TN3 9ST, £2.75)

The Cricketer Quarterly: Facts and Figures ed. Richard Lockwood (The Cricketer International, address as above, £2.90)

Cricket Lore (ten per volume, frequency variable) ed. Richard Hill (Cricket Lore, 22 Grazebrook Road, London N16 0HS, £35 per volume)

The Cricket Statistician (quarterly) ed. Philip J. Bailey (ACS, 3 Radcliffe Road, West Bridgford, Nottingham NG2 5FF, £2.50, free to ACS members)

Cricket World Monthly (very erratic) editorial director Michael Blumberg (157 Praed Street, London W2 1RL, £2.35)

Inside Edge (Australia, monthly) managing editor Norman Tasker (ACP Publishing, 54 Park Street, Sydney 2000, NSW, $A5.20)

The Journal of the Cricket Society (twice yearly) ed. Clive W. Porter (from P. Ellis, 63 Groveland Road, Beckenham, Kent BR3 3PX, £5 to non-members)

League Cricket Review (six issues a year) ed. Andy Searle (Empire Publications, 62 Charles Street, Manchester M1 7DF, £1.80)

The New Ball (twice yearly) ed. Rob Steen (Two Heads Publishing, £8.99)
Collections of new cricket writing. First edition concentrates on England v Australia.

Red Stripe Caribbean Quarterly ed. Tony Cozier (Cozier Publishing, PO Box 40W, Worthing, Christ Church, Barbados, annual subscription £14 Europe, $BDS25 Barbados, $BDS32/$US16 rest of West Indies, $US20 US, $Can28 Canada, $US28 elsewhere)

SA Cricket Action (nine issues a year) ed. Chris Whales (PO Box 1144, Cape Town 8000, R9.95. Subscriptions (00 27) 21 461 9752)

The Scottish Cricketer (three issues a year) editorial director Terry Brennan (4 Belhaven Terrace, Dowanhill, Glasgow G12 0TF, £1.50)

Wisden Cricket Monthly ed. Tim de Lisle (The New Boathouse, 136-142 Bramley Road, London W10 6SR, £2.70. Subscriptions 01795-414895)

SELECTED LOCAL HISTORIES

250 Years of Cricket in Bearsted Foreword by E. W. Swanton (Bearsted CC, PO Box 556, Maidstone, Kent ME14 4QY, £5)

Lillywhite, George **A Tickle to Leg: The History of Upton-by-Southwell and its Cricketers 1855-1901** (Moorley's Publishing, 23 Park Road, Ilkeston, Derbys, DE7 5DA, £5.95)

Pearce, Roy ed. **Matches, Meetings and Memories: Wirksworth Cricket Club 1849-1999** (from the author, 3 Summer Lane, Wirksworth, Derbys DE4 4EB, £3.50 +50p p&p)

MISCELLANEOUS

Poster of Australian Test Cricketers 1876-77 to 1997-98 (Jack Pollard Pty Ltd, Kingsgrove Sports Centre, Locked Bag 4000, Kingsgrove NSW 1480, $A55 inc. p&p worldwide)
Portraits of 378 Test players.

DIRECTORY OF BOOKSELLERS

AARDVARK BOOKS, "Copperfield", High Street, Harmston, Lincoln LN5 9SN. Tel: 01522-722671. Peter Taylor specialises in *Wisdens*. Send SAE for list. Restoration service available for *Wisdens* and other books. *Wisdens* also purchased.

TIM BEDDOW, 62a Stanmore Road, Edgbaston, Birmingham B16 9TB. Tel: 0121-420 3466; fax: 0121-429 2184; e-mail: timbeddowsports@btinternet.com. Large stock of cricket/football books, programmes and signed material. Items purchased. SAE for catalogue. Stall at Thwaite Gate, Edgbaston, every first-team match.

BODYLINE BOOKS. Specialist dealer in cricket books of all vintages. Scorecards, signed ephemera. Catalogues issued on receipt of 38p stamp to: **150A Harbord Street, London SW6 6PH. Tel: 0171-385 2176; e-mail: cricket@dircon.co.uk.** Collections purchased.

BOUNDARY BOOKS, Southlands, Sandy Lane, Goostrey, Cheshire CW4 8NT. Tel: 01477-533106; fax: 01477-544529; e-mail: mike@boundary-books.demon.co.uk. Second-hand and antiquarian cricket books and autographs. Catalogues issued. Viewing by appointment.

IAN DYER CRICKET BOOKS: Specialists in antiquarian books and *Wisdens*. Catalogue/bookfair list from: **29 High Street, Gilling West, Richmond, North Yorkshire DL10 5JG. Tel/fax: 01748-822786; e-mail: iandyercricketbooks@btinternet.com; web site: www.cricketbooks.co.uk.**

K. FAULKNER, 65 Brookside, Wokingham, Berkshire RG41 2ST. Tel: 0118-978 5255. Cricket books, *Wisdens*, memorabilia bought and sold. Telephone enquiries welcome. Display in Gloucestershire CCC Shop, Nevil Road, Bristol BS7 9EJ. Open all year. Catalogues issued.

E. O. KIRWAN, 3 Pine Tree Garden, Oadby, Leicestershire LE2 5UT. Tel: 0116-271 4267 (evenings and weekends only). Second-hand and antiquarian cricket books, *Wisdens*, autograph material and cricket ephemera of all kinds.

*J. W. McKENZIE, 12 Stoneleigh Park Road, Ewell, Epsom, Surrey KT19 0QT. Tel: 0181-393 7700; fax: 0181-393 1694. Specialists in antiquarian second-hand cricket books, particularly *Wisdens*, since 1969. Catalogues sent on request. Publishers of rare cricket books. Shop premises open regular business hours.

ROGER PAGE, 10 Ekari Court, Yallambie, Victoria 3085, Australia. Tel: (03) 9435-6332; fax: (03) 9432-2050. Dealer in new and second-hand cricket books. Distributor of overseas cricket annuals and magazines. Agent for Cricket Statisticians and Cricket Memorabilia Society.

*PENGUIN DIRECT. New *Wisdens* for 1991-98 and the first edition of *Wisden Australia* available from *Wisden's* mail-order supplier. Prices from £9.99 including p&p. **Tel: 0181-899 4036.**

RED ROSE BOOKS, 196 Belmont Road, Bolton BL1 7AR. Tel: 01204-596118; fax: 01204-598080; e-mail: redrosebooks@btinternet.com; web site: www.redrosebooks.co.uk. Specialist dealer in second-hand and antiquarian cricket books. Catalogue sent on request.

WILLIAM H. ROBERTS, The Crease, 113 Hill Grove, Salendine Nook, Huddersfield, West Yorkshire HD3 3TL. Tel/fax: 01484-654463. Second-hand/antiquarian cricket books, *Wisdens*, autograph material and memorabilia bought and sold. Catalogues sent on request.

*CHRISTOPHER SAUNDERS, Orchard Books, Kingston House, High Street, Newnham on Severn, Gloucestershire GL14 1BB. Tel: 01594-516030; fax: 01594-517273. Office/bookroom by appointment. Second-hand/antiquarian cricket books and memorabilia bought and sold. Full-time bookseller for 18 years.

*SPORTSPAGES, Caxton Walk, 94-96 Charing Cross Road, London WC2H 0JG. Tel: 0171-240 9604; fax: 0171-836 0104. Barton Square, St Ann's Square, Manchester M2 7HA. Tel: 0161-832 8530; fax: 0161-832 9391. New cricket books, audio and video tapes, including imports, especially from Australasia; retail and mail order service.

STUART TOPPS, 40 Boundary Avenue, Wheatley Mills, Doncaster, South Yorkshire DN2 5QU. Tel: 01302-366044. Our 100-page catalogue of cricket books, *Wisdens*, booklets, brochures and county yearbooks is always available.

WILEC LTD, 164 Old Christchurch Road, Bournemouth BH1 1NU. Established 1905. Second-hand and antiquarian books, *Wisdens* and *Vanity Fair* specialists. Books and collections purchased. Catalogues sent on request.

*WILLOWS PUBLISHING CO., 17 The Willows, Stone, Staffordshire ST15 0DE. Tel: 01785-814700. *Wisden* Reprints 1879–1906, plus 1916–1919. Some years still available. Send SAE for list.

WISTERIA BOOKS, Wisteria Cottage, Birt Street, Birtsmorton, Malvern WR13 6AW. Tel: 01684-833578. Visit our family-run stall at county grounds for new, second-hand, antiquarian cricket books and ephemera, or contact Grenville Simons at the address above. Send SAE for catalogue.

MARTIN WOOD, 2 St John's Road, Sevenoaks, Kent TN13 3LW. Tel/fax: 01732-457205. Since 1970 Martin Wood has posted 27,000 parcels of cricket books worldwide; stocks still increasing. Send first-class stamp for catalogue.

AUCTIONEERS

*CHRISTIE'S inaugural cricket sale was the MCC Bicentenary Sale of 1987. Since then sales have been held on a regular basis at London, South Kensington, with May 21 as the planned date for this year's sale.

*PHILLIPS have held specialised cricket auctions since 1978, highlighted by the celebrated Hal Cohen Collection in 1995. Free valuations and collection undertaken by Mike Ashton on **01222-396453.**

*T. VENNETT-SMITH, 11 Nottingham Road, Gotham, Nottinghamshire NG11 0HE. Tel: 0115-983 0541. Auctioneers and valuers. Twice-yearly auctions of cricket and sports memorabilia. The cricket auction run by cricketers for cricket lovers worldwide.

*DOMINIC WINTER, Specialist Book Auctioneers & Valuers, The Old School, Maxwell Street, Swindon SN1 5DR. Tel: 01793-611340; fax: 01793-491727. Twice-yearly auction sales of sports books and memorabilia, including *Wisdens*.

Asterisks indicate businesses that have display advertisements elsewhere in the Almanack. See page 1496 for more details.

THE CRICKET SOCIETY LITERARY AWARD

The Cricket Society Literary Award has been presented since 1970 to the author of the cricket book judged as best of the year. The 1999 award, sponsored by PricewaterhouseCoopers, went to Simon Rae for **W. G. Grace: A Life** and to J. R. Webber for **The Chronicle of W.G.** It was the first time a joint award had been made.

CRICKET VIDEOS IN 1998

By SIMON BRIGGS

"As a rule, any debate on the greatest bowler in the history of the game is soon over: Sydney Barnes is returned *nem. con.*" So writes John Woodcock, placing Barnes at No. 6 in his list of greatest cricketers. But despite his hyper-extended career – Barnes was still opening the bowling for Staffordshire at 62 – the only thing many cricket-lovers know about him is that he had an astonishing record: 189 wickets in 27 Tests.

Legends of Cricket: Sydney Barnes offers a more rounded view: it features footage of Barnes in his seventies, still landing the ball on a sixpence in a benefit match, and uses photographs to suggest what he must have been like at his peak, launching rapid off-cutters and leg-breaks with a textbook follow-through. Barnes's various clashes with authority are also covered, and the cussed, contrary nature that reputedly caused A. C. MacLaren to announce, on the way home from Australia: "At least if we go down we'll take that bugger Barnes down with us."

There is even less debate when it comes to the greatest batsman in history. He crops up again this year in a video with an identity crisis: the sleeve is labelled **Don Bradman – 90 Not Out**, but what flashes up on screen is **Don Bradman – 87 Not Out**. In fact, an interview was conducted in 1995, and repackaged in time for The Don's 90th birthday in 1998.

Despite its age, this is the best of a bunch of recent Bradman videos. It includes an appearance from the late Lady Bradman, and from one of her husband's old willows, as he demonstrates the evils of modern coaching. The most (unintentionally) amusing moment comes from Dickie Bird at his most Tykeish: "My father walked 38 miles from Barnsley to Headingley to watch Don Bradman bat, queued for miles and miles, and then walked 38 miles back home. He did that every day." On modern maps, Barnsley is only 18 miles from Headingley, but maybe it was further in those days.

The pile of winsome Dickie-ana grew taller still with the addition of **A Bird's Eye View of Cricket**, described on the cover as "Hilarious cricketing moments which will hit you for six". Dickie never found it easy to maintain the umpire's traditional Olympian perspective: as this video shows, he was always being hit by the ball, colliding with players, or shouting at innocent box-holders. But even his misadventures don't run to 57 minutes, so there's padding in the form of Dennis Lillee's infamous row with Javed Miandad, plus film of various batsmen being hit in the groin. The resulting mess can be recommended only to the most devoted of fans.

The **Cover Point** video magazine changed its frequency from monthly to quarterly, extended its length from an hour to around 100 minutes, and put its price up to £25 an issue. It remains an invaluable and far-ranging survey of world cricket, featuring international footage that can be found nowhere else. All the English content has been stitched together into Cover Point's **Story of the 1998 Cricket Season**, which includes the summer's Test and county action, and represents good value at £13.99.

To zoom in on the England–South Africa Test series alone, try **England's Glory**, a Cover Point collaboration with VCI videos. Or, for a close-up of Leicestershire's Championship-winning season, James Whitaker presents **Amazing Grace**, a collection of match clips and interviews.

Amazing Grace (Cover Point, £16.99 inc. p&p, Cover Point Ltd, 113 Upper Tulse Hill, London SW2 2RD)
Bradman – 90 Not Out (Green Umbrella, £12.99)
Cover Point Video magazine (£25 inc. p&p, Cover Point Ltd, as above)
Dickie Bird – A Bird's Eye View of Cricket (VCI, £14.99)
England's Glory (VCI, £13.99)
Legends of Cricket: Sydney Barnes (Action Sports International, £12.99)
Story of the 1998 Cricket Season (Cover Point, £13.99 from WH Smith or £15.99 inc. p&p from Cover Point Ltd, as above)

COMPUTER GAMES IN 1998

There were high-profile launches for two very different cricket simulations. **Brian Lara Cricket '98** was a refinement of the original Brian Lara game, which enjoyed such unexpected success when released on the Sega Mega Drive in 1996 that it outsold Sonic the Hedgehog.

The new game offers superbly realistic graphics, generated by "data capture" – a system in which a real batsman's movements are scanned into a computer's memory and then replayed on screen. But the rather simplistic playing technique has not been developed: you still receive an advance warning of where the ball will land, choose a shot, and press the "hit" button as the bowler lets go. Bowling is even less complicated. On Lara '96, working up a good pace required some skill. Now all you have to do is point and shoot – although there is a "slower ball" button, in line with current tactical fashion.

Empire Sports' **International Cricket Captain** (officially endorsed by *Wisden*) is a much more cerebral affair: this is a management simulation in which you start at a county club, selecting and even coaching your players throughout a Championship campaign. If you perform well enough, you step up to international level. You can make bowling changes and set the field but, as Graham Gooch is prone to say, once the players cross that white line, they're on their own. International Cricket Captain is a little slow and unwieldy at times; but, personally, I found it far more addictive than its racier rival. – SIMON BRIGGS.

Brian Lara Cricket '98 (Codemasters, £44.99 PlayStation, £34.99 PC CD-ROM)
International Cricket Captain (Empire Sports, £34.95 PC CD-ROM)

CRICKET AND THE MEDIA IN 1998

By MARCUS BERKMANN

Two thousand years after the birth of Christ, and after nearly as long with the BBC, English cricket bravely threw in its lot with Channel 4, who out-negotiated the Beeb for the new TV contract by promising to attract a younger audience to the game with "bright" and "multicultural" coverage (i.e. lots of adverts).

The problem the authorities have is not only that young people don't watch the game, but that they are the ones who play it. This can be very distressing. "Ben Hollioake, the brightest young star of English cricket, has been reprimanded by the game's authorities after a magazine article implied that he smoked cannabis during a tour of Sri Lanka by the England A team," raged the *Sunday Telegraph*. The article, in the men's magazine *GQ*, and painted a predictably lurid portrait of the tourists' laddish behaviour, though it had not directly accused the young all-rounder of inhaling illegal sub-stances. The writer did claim to have overheard Hollioake describe himself as "badgered, mongoosed and babooned", which, the *Sunday Times* informed us, "are alternative words for being under the influence of drugs". Hollioake denied everything. "He's misheard or misinterpreted the sort of stuff you talk about when you're in the middle of nowhere with nothing much to do," he said.

"Holli-mania" was a brief but entertaining burst of hype that lasted until the team for the First Test was announced. By then, *Now* magazine (a sort of downmarket *Hello!*) had already published a special issue devoted to "The World's Most Beautiful People" featuring the elder of the heart-throb brothers. Adam Hollioake, we were told, had a "taut, powerful body" and was "a cross between Keanu Reeves and George Clooney". In *Company* ("the magazine for your freedom years"), Natalie Meddings went bodysurfing with the brothers and drooled over their hunky frames. Noting that Adam wore a 55-carat diamond bangle on his wrist, she wrote, "On anyone else it would look lairy, but on him it looks cool." Lairy?

England's new Test captain, Alec Stewart, could not command this sort of attention. Indeed, Ivo Tennant of *The Times* was more interested in interviewing Sheila Stewart, wife of former England manager Mickey, and Alec's mum: "Sheila settled on two strategies to ensure her three children ate and drank properly. 'I told them all that they could drink alcohol if they wanted to, but that if they did not touch it until they were 21, I would give them each £50, which was a lot of money at the time. Alec was about seven at the time and he was the only one who won it,' she said.

"When I wanted him to eat green vegetables, I told him: 'You won't like this because it's grown-up food,' so of course he ate it. Mickey is a meat-and-two-veg man and Alec has followed that: he is fond of steak and kidney pie and roast dinners." It's possible that virtually everything you need to know about Alec Stewart is contained in those two paragraphs.

Michael Parkinson, now ensconced as the *Telegraph's* resident Mr Angry, had a good year. After England's narrow-squeak draw in the Old Trafford Test, he went cheerfully off the deep end, spurred by David Graveney's pronouncement that the South Africans would be disappointed and think they had lost: "The chairman of selectors is a bigger spinner of fairy-tales than he was of a cricket ball . . . England were completely, totally and embarrassingly outplayed . . .

"Graveney's response was typical of the rearguard action being fought by the ECB and those commentators who remain unconvinced there is anything wrong with the game. It is as if the rest of us are imagining the public apathy, the reluctance of sponsors, the whimsical ways of our cricketers, the evidence of our own eyes." Virtually everyone wrote this piece at one time or other, but no one could rival Parkinson for sheer fury. The fact that Graveney turned out to be right is, of course, irrelevant.

Umpiring controversies dominated the second half of the season, and no piece was more quietly influential than Simon Hughes's *Daily Telegraph* column on July 30, just after the Trent Bridge Test. "On Monday afternoon, in the lee of the Radcliffe Road stand, a dejected figure crept quietly to his car . . . It was Merv Kitchen. 'Can't say I enjoyed that Test match,' he muttered, reflecting on a couple of errors highlighted by television. 'I think it will be my last, I'm afraid.'

"Having sympathised, I asked why. 'I don't think I feel up to the job any more,' said the man from Nailsea. 'I could have sworn there was a woody noise when Kallis and Rhodes played their shots, then I looked at the replays later and I realised I'd made a mistake. It's terribly depressing, and I've had some awful mail – offers of special prescription glasses, hearing aids – which just makes it worse.'"

South African commentators became increasingly vehement. BBC viewers had to put up with Barry Richards's rising fury every time a decision went against his country. ("That's out," he said whenever the ball hit an English pad.) And a cartoon in the Afrikaans daily *Beeld* depicted an umpire flipping a coin to answer an appeal by the South Africans. Eddie Barlow in the *Cape Times* wrote: "Between Steve Dunne, Merv Kitchen and Javed Akhtar, I have not seen so many poor decisions ever. Did they play a role? Without a doubt." Kitchen, like the others, remained a Test umpire.

Sri Lanka's victory at The Oval was less controversial. "The subject that is imperative today is the warmest congratulations to Sri Lanka for as conclusive a victory as could be imagined, the details of which to English eyes and ears hold sad, salutary lessons," wrote E. W. Swanton, as you had probably realised well before the middle of that sentence. "In these sophisticated, deeply analytical days of 'counselling' and over-emphasis on physical fitness their attitude was refreshing to a degree." Like a stately galleon, his prose rolls serenely along, unaffected by the passing centuries.

When David Lloyd implied Muttiah Muralitharan was a chucker, everyone agreed this was unworthy. For instance, John Woodcock in *The Times*: "When, in 1960, the Imperial Cricket Conference, as it then was, held a special meeting at Lord's to consider the growing problem of throwing . . . it was agreed that 'the bowler shall be at liberty to use the wrist freely in the delivery action' and that, it seems to me, is all that Murali does. Should it ever be decided otherwise and he is banned, the game will be the loser, so salutary is his influence, so marvellous his dexterity, so refreshing his success. For the great majority of spinners, life is so unrewarding in the modern game that it would not be entirely inexpedient to allow them to throw." Only Woodcock could conceal such a controversial suggestion within this thicket of qualifiers and multiple negatives.

The Sri Lankan press, though, celebrated as freely as their batsmen had smashed English bowling to all corners of Kennington. "England 'stewed' in Oval pot" ran the front page headline of the Colombo *Evening Observer* on September 1. "True, England won the battle of Waterloo in the fields of Eton defeating Napoleon," wrote Ian Jayasinha. "But alas! Those who colonised us and brought the Bible in one hand and the cricket bat in the other with them had to cook their own Christmas goose.

"Fragments of Kipling's era were obvious on the field played by flannelled fools in this gentlemen's game. The English captain Alec Stewart made unsavoury remarks to some of our cricketers. Not cricket old chap! . . . Murali's name will go down in *Wisden* in gold letters." Elmo Rodrigopulle, writing in the Colombo *Daily News*, talked of Stewart's men "grovelling and biting the Oval dust".

How much more humiliating, though, to bite your tongue, the prospect which faced Geoffrey Boycott. Convicted in a French appeal court of beating up his girlfriend, the so-called Greatest Living Yorkshireman was instantly sacked by the BBC, Sky TV and *The Sun*, while Channel 4 hinted that they would be looking elsewhere for an expert summariser. At least they didn't say he wasn't "bright" or "multicultural" enough.

Marcus Berkmann is a freelance writer and author of Rain Men: the Madness of Cricket.

CRICKETANA IN 1998

By GORDON PHILLIPS

There were notable anniversaries in 1998 for cricket's twin colossi, W. G. Grace (the 150th anniversary of his birth) and Sir Donald Bradman (his 90th birthday). They were accorded proper recognition with predictable issues of books, chinaware and first-day covers. Most noteworthy, however, was the outright sale of the late Geoffrey Copinger's library.

With some 16,000 items, mainly books, this was the largest known collection of cricketana in private hands. It was bought by an anonymous London businessman for a reported £250,000, though informed sources placed the figure much lower. The sale dismayed many collectors and dealers, who had hoped for the chance to secure cherished titles. Others, though, were content in the knowledge that the collection was to remain secure and intact, and there were hopes that scholars would eventually be allowed access.

Another disconcerting development for some English collectors was the increasing influence (and affluence) of Australian auctions. And a surprise

move by the Australian authorities to protect national movable cultural treasures raised eyebrows. A cricket ball (with several signatures) that had been crashed around the Melbourne Cricket Ground in 1911, along with a 1902 pocket diary and other top collectables associated with the magical name of Trumper, were the first sporting items to be refused export licences.

So how does the cricketana market stand? Confronted by the regular deluge of temptation, one can only generalise wildly. The market seems to be rising in the following: enamelled vesta cases, inscribed tobacco paraphernalia, desk sets, clocks, any W.G.-related items (contracts with promoters, cast-iron tables bearing his effigy), cabinet photographs of early Australians (£1,000 for Trumper; £500 for the others), and the highly desirable Royal Doulton "All Black" series and their more modern "Bunnykins" series.

Bodyline and Timeless Test material retains a firm hold, as do *Wisdens* and other endlessly appealing items. These include the Coalport "Century of Centuries" plates, signed programmes, scorecards, autographed photographs, sheet music and records, Staffordshire pottery figures of Caesar and Parr, the wonderful menu cards of 1912 illustrated by Hillyard Swinstead (when signed by a galaxy of immortals from the Triangular series) and Doulton Lambeth jugs and beakers, which are collected by non-cricket lovers as well.

On the way down may be glassware, modern Coalport china, cigarette cards, modern signed limited-edition books, winners' medals from the one-day game, and the full wardrobe of cricket attire – unless it was associated with a very big name. With advertising posters, time will tell. But a life-size bronze sculpture of Bradman has been bought for £27,000 by an Australian businessman to lend lustre to his office. It will do just that, whatever happens to its value.

CRICKET EQUIPMENT IN 1998

By NORMAN HARRIS

Manufacturers must at last be getting things right, such was the lack of controversy on the bat and ball front in 1998. The only debate surrounded the white ball, and even that seemed to disappear after a little corrective action.

Early in the Triangular Tournament last August, the Sri Lankans complained that the Dukes balls being used were too hard on the bat, and there was also a feeling that they swung too much. The manufacturers were at pains to point out that the composition of these white balls was identical to that of comparable red ones. "The only difference is in a urethane skin we put on it to retain the whiteness," Dilip Jajodia, managing director of the makers, British Cricket Balls, explained. "If we didn't, the grease and dirt which is absorbed by the leather of the red ball would soon turn the white ball black, so we toughen it up with this urethane polish, which gives it a protective skin."

That protection, though, was also applied to the seam, which arguably stayed stiffer for longer. Jajodia agreed that this could marginally affect the microsecond of action as the bowler's finger-tips released the ball, as well as the ball's aerodynamics. So tests were conducted with balls on which the polish was *not* applied to the stitching. "These balls didn't swing at all," Jajodia said, "and neither did they when we supplied such balls for the final two triangular matches." He hoped there would be no complaints during the 1999 World Cup, which was to use the Dukes ball.

As for bats, there was the comforting sight of a Test batsman, Nasser Hussain, using a bat with strips of tape down both edges. Lesser players who have been using the same bats for years could identify with that. The professionals sometimes seem to be using bats almost like disposable razors, with one in use, one ready to use, and one being knocked in – and all of them being used up in the course of a season's 40 or 50 innings. But Hussain's Gray-Nicolls blade was evidently something of an old warhorse. Whether a material with a thickness akin to masking tape will actually protect a bat's edges from a hard cricket ball is perhaps open to question, but players will do anything which might be thought to prolong the life of what they call "an absolute gun".

Many innovations these days seem to come from South Africa, including the instant (and, at last, accurate) measurement of bowling speeds which diverted crowds at the summer's Tests (see pages 39–40). Another is a coaching aid called the WicketMaster, a ball with coloured markings that show a youngster where to place fingers and thumb. There was a Spin Ball and a Pace Ball, each of which showed different variations – such as the flipper or the seam bowler's slower ball. A simple idea, really, and surprising that no one had thought of it sooner.

Also from South Africa came the Panasonic cameras dedicated to adjudication of run-out and stumping decisions. Four were installed at Lord's, aligned precisely with the creases, unlike the TV camera. Ali Bacher, who oversaw their introduction in South Africa, had described them as giving "pictures so accurate you could go to court with them". But their debut in the Second Test must have been a disappointment for MCC, who had decided to pay £150,000 for them rather than engage in a sponsorship deal, as in South Africa. They were called into action early on in the Test, with a run-out appeal when the wicket was broken by a ball ricocheting from the forward short-leg fielder. But the zoom proved to be too "tight" to show all the action – and the decision was made via the BBC's usual camera on a slight angle at "high square". Ironically, no further replays were called for in this Test, and the Panasonic cameras seemed to be little used during subsequent matches at Lord's.

UMPIRING IN 1998

By JACK BAILEY

Although you still get the impression that first-class umpires generally enjoy their work – being part of the game and its bonhomie – there is little doubt that the demands imposed by the all-seeing eye of the television camera have knocked off a sizable amount of gilt from the gingerbread.

Witness Mervyn Kitchen's unguarded words to Simon Hughes of the *Daily Telegraph*, when he wondered aloud whether he was up to the job after a poorish day during the England v South Africa Test at Trent Bridge. The erosion of the umpire's confidence during this match was so complete that nothing was done about the intimidatory bowling levelled by Donald at Atherton when he had been given not out caught off his glove. The Donald/Atherton duel was of riveting intensity and millions thrilled to it. But the Laws were temporarily suspended while it went on.

The final match against South Africa raised criticism of ICC's method of appointing umpires. Javed Akhtar was drafted in for this crucial game with only one Test outside Pakistan behind him, and recent experience of just one rain-affected Second Eleven match at Uxbridge. A number of seemingly arbitrary decisions, the majority to the South Africans' disadvantage, caused one critic to liken the whole thing to a game of Russian roulette. Since then, Akhtar has umpired in the Pakistan v Australia series and earned much praise.

Akhtar had in fact stood in 16 Tests before Headingley. In any case, ICC say they have to give relatively inexperienced Test umpires every chance to do themselves justice. They strive to give them two warm-up games before a Test and at least two Tests in a series. Neither happened in the summer of 1998; weather and scheduling problems were blamed.

The method of selecting umpires has evolved since the early days when ICC strove to do something about constant complaints of home bias. The system of one home umpire and one visiting umpire has been established since 1994. (No home umpires were being used at all in the Asian Test Championship early in 1999.) But the 20-man National Grid international panel – two from each Test-playing country with an extra two from England – now includes an elite band, headed by David Shepherd, Steve Bucknor and Venkat, who are constantly on the go. They are supplemented by those of lesser experience; the aim is to pair the tyro with a senior umpire. The logistical problems are such that the system will never be perfect. But ten out of ten for effort.

CRICKET SOCIETIES IN 1998

By MURRAY HEDGCOCK

The cricket society movement, like the game itself, faces one urgent problem as it heads for the new millennium – how to attract the next generation. Thirty societies, mostly in England, provide off-season entertainment and information for thousands of members. The movement is growing too. New societies have been formed in both Worcestershire (whose local hero Tom Graveney has replaced the late Lord Howell as president of The Council of Cricket Societies) and neighbouring Herefordshire; Kent and Wales are trying to get started.

But membership tends to be like that of county clubs – aging, traditionalist, happy to see their beloved game continue much as they have known it most of their lives. Societies increasingly seek to become "more relevant", often inviting current players to talk about the game they know. However, such speakers often ask fees beyond a movement with many pensioner members.

One comparatively new society, just outside London, invited a well-known former international in his benefit year, the time when players are most receptive. Yes, he would be delighted to speak – for £4,000. As the society had a membership below 100, and attendances often were no more than 20, the reply indicated the speaker would be welcome if he trimmed two noughts from the sum. The rest was silence. Other societies complain that even young players waiting for their county cap tend to respond "Talk to my agent", which usually means a demand beyond the society's resources.

In a bid to make the movement more positive, and to attract younger members, the Australian Cricket Society, at its Melbourne base, has launched a series of initiatives under a lively new president, Lancashire-born academic J. Neville Turner. In a stimulating paper, "The Role of the Society", he argued that the ACS should seek to educate youngsters, offering its own speakers to talk on cricket at local schools. It should also introduce panels at its meetings, encouraging discussion among members.

ERRATA

WISDEN, 1980

Page 1152   Eddie Paynter died at Idle, not Keighley.

WISDEN, 1984

Page 1016   In South Australia's second innings against Tasmania, J. Garner was c Reid b Clough for 10 and K. J. Wright did not bat.

WISDEN, 1998

Page 37   In the case *Bolton* v *Stone*, Cheetham Cricket Club was in Manchester, not in Kent.

Page 389   England and Australia have played 24 Tests, not 23, at Lord's in the 20th century.

Page 571   In Northamptonshire's team photograph, the insets of R. J. Logan and G. P. Swann have been transposed; Logan is second left, Swann is on the right.

Page 1014   B. A. Pocock's fifty off 239 balls was not the slowest recorded in Tests; T. E. Bailey took 350 balls to reach the mark for England v Australia at Brisbane in 1958-59, and A. R. Border took 262 balls for Australia v West Indies at Sydney in 1988-89.

Page 1115   D. L. Houghton's double-hundred for Zimbabwe v Sri Lanka, at Bulawayo in 1994-95, took 524 minutes and 433 balls, not the other way round, and so was not the second-slowest recorded in terms of balls received. G. W. Flower reached his double-hundred for Zimbabwe v Pakistan, at Harare in 1994-95, in 654 minutes and 520 balls.

Page 1428   D. C. S. Compton's average for the Commonwealth XI was 53.33.

CRICKET GROUNDS IN 1998

Several English counties have been talking about new headquarters. In 1998, one took the plunge: Hampshire sold their Northlands Road ground to Berkeley Homes, and are now committed to move to a new setting in West End, near Southampton, for the 2001 season. A nine-hole golf course which is part of the same complex is due to open this summer.

The main cricket square (there will be a nursery ground as well) is already under the loving care of head groundsman Nigel Gray, and there were hopes of an inaugural match in 1999 with regular Second Eleven cricket in 2000. Facilities for spectators may be spartan for those early games and, even after the initial opening, capacity will be kept relatively low. However, there is enough space to put in large quantities of temporary seating. Hampshire's early attempts to find a "name sponsor" for the ground to defray the costs – and irritate the membership – were unsuccessful, and the title of the new ground remained uncertain.

Hampshire, like other teams, have been encouraged by the planned expansion of Test and one-day international cricket in England, which could mean big fixtures going away from the six traditional big grounds. This news has also whetted the appetite of administrators at both Essex and Sussex.

Essex have been watching events next door to their cramped Chelmsford HQ, where the old Chelmsford City football ground has been sold to Country-wide Properties. Countrywide hoped to build houses on the site, and perhaps extend the plan to embrace the cricket ground as well. They told Essex that in return they would be willing to hand over – and develop – a site for a new cricket stadium on the A12, where there is enough land to build something very impressive indeed. Their initial application for the football ground houses was rejected by Chelmsford council; an appeal was being heard early in 1999.

Meanwhile, once-sleepy Hove was becoming the first cricket ground in the country to install permanent floodlights. Sussex beat Warwickshire, whose scheme to put in lights at Edgbaston had run into opposition from residents and councillors, and expected to have them operational in 1999. Even so, Sussex were still "assessing the options" about a possible new ground, though they now appear to have given up the idea of a ground-share with their local football club.

In contrast, Yorkshire in 1998 finally kissed goodbye to their dreams of moving to Wakefield. They found themselves unable to get out of the lease which commits the club to Headingley and, as they wrestled with that problem, the funding for a new ground slipped away. The club were hoping to get funds from the National Lottery to support an £11 million re-development plan at Headingley instead. Meanwhile, time ticks by, and the ground gets ever greyer and more uninviting.

CRICKET AND THE WEATHER, 1998

By PHILIP EDEN

Bad light *will* stop play on Wednesday, August 11, 1999, in all cricket matches taking place in southern England between approximately 11 a.m. and half past. There is no Championship cricket that day, and the tourist match between Middlesex and the New Zealanders will not be affected, thanks to the foresight of the ECB who have rescheduled the playing hours so that the teams will take the field at noon.

Such a confident prediction does not, of course, have anything to do with the weather. August 11 is the day Britain experiences the first ever total eclipse of the sun to occur in playing hours during its first-class cricket season. Totality, however, will not be seen from any first-class venue; only people in Cornwall and south Devon will enjoy that awesome spectacle. The next summer eclipse in Britain, in case you are waiting, will be on June 14, 2151.

The eclipse apart, no one can tell you what kind of weather the summer will bring. But we can delve back into the statistical archives to compare the weather of past seasons one with another, and to contrast the climates of the different county grounds. We can also make certain predictions. 1998 began with El Niño in charge. This phenomenon, a reversal of ocean currents in the tropical Pacific, has a major impact in countries bordering the south Pacific, with diminishing ripples further afield. In these regions, including Guyana but excluding most of the Caribbean islands, there is a tendency (we should put it no more strongly than that) for less rain in El Niño years than at other times. Much of Australia and South Africa had a dry summer, and this was reflected in the Test series in both countries.

England's visit to the Caribbean was less favoured. Interruptions at Port-of-Spain are par for the course, for it rains here (little or much) on 15 days in an average February. By contrast, the Guyana Test was played in a drought even though Georgetown ranks alongside Colombo as the world's wettest international venue. Barbados has a moist climate, but February, March and April are easily the driest months of the year, and the Bridgetown Test often escapes with minimal interruption. Not so in 1998: almost two months' worth of rain fell in 48 hours, ruining the end of the match.

The 1998 English summer was vilified in the media as the worst for many years, but the statistics are less damning. It was far from being a good summer, and June was a foul month with more than double the normal amount of rain; but May and August were both warmer, drier and sunnier than average. The bare statistics, averaged over England and Wales, were as follows:

	Average max temperature (°C)	Difference from normal for 1961-90	Total rainfall (mm)	% of normal	Total sunshine (hours)	% of normal
April (second half) . . .	12.9	−0.1	36	126	57	71
May	17.8	+1.9	29	45	242	122
June	18.4	−0.5	131	202	158	78
July	19.9	−0.8	56	88	156	86
August	20.8	+0.4	47	55	214	123
September (first half). .	18.8	+0.4	70	171	66	89
1998 cricket season . .	**18.6**	**+0.2**	**369**	**104**	**893**	**98**

Anyone who has read a school geography textbook knows that, on average, northern and western parts of the country are cooler and wetter than the south and east. Each summer has slightly different regional variations and, in 1998, the contrast between the warm, dry Home Counties and the cold, damp north-west of England was greater than usual. We can make a simple and useful comparison by devising a "summer index", incorporating rainfall amount and frequency, sunshine and temperature in a single figure. The formula for the index (*I*) can be written as:

$$I = 20(Tx - 12) + (S - 400)/3 + 2Rd + (250 - R/3)$$

Tx is the average maximum temperature, *S* is the total sunshine, *Rd* is the number of dry days, and *R* is the total rainfall, covering the period May 1 to August 31. The formula may look complicated, but it is designed so that temperature, sunshine, rainfall frequency and rainfall amount each contribute roughly 25 per cent of the total, while the final index ranges from zero for the theoretical worst possible summer to 1,000 for the theoretical best. The score for an average summer ranges from 510 at Chester-le-Street and 515 at Old Trafford to 645 at Hove and Lord's, and 650 at The Oval. Broadly speaking, an index over 650 indicates a good summer whereas one below 500 clearly describes a poor summer.

Values for each county for the summer of 1998 against the average value for the standard reference period 1961-90 are as follows:

	1998	Normal	Variation		1998	Normal	Variation
Derbyshire	568	565	+3	Middlesex	664	645	+19
Durham	461	510	−49	Northamptonshire.	584	595	−11
Essex	648	620	+28	Nottinghamshire .	579	575	+4
Glamorgan	489	540	−51	Somerset	599	605	−6
Gloucestershire .	560	575	−15	Surrey	668	650	+18
Hampshire	695	625	+70	Sussex	719	645	+74
Kent	686	630	+56	Warwickshire . . .	527	525	+2
Lancashire	441	515	−74	Worcestershire. . .	586	595	−9
Leicestershire . .	570	570	0	Yorkshire	498	545	−47

Thus it can be seen that Sussex and Hampshire fared comparatively well last season, while Lancashire were particularly hard done by.

This summer index can also be used to compare one summer with another. Averaged over the whole of England and Wales, the results for the last 20 cricket seasons are:

1998	565	1993	573	1988	507	1983	634
1997	601	1992	556	1987	444	1982	564
1996	663	1991	538	1986	568	1981	541
1995	777	1990	746	1985	568	1980	542
1994	651	1989	770	1984	602	1979	546

Average for 1961-1990: 568; Highest this century (1976): 812; Lowest this century (1954): 413.

So, although the summer of 1998 was statistically average, it was actually the poorest since 1992, thanks to a run of good years (which may or may not be connected with global warming). This, perhaps, is why last summer was perceived to be bad, even in the south-east.

Philip Eden is weather expert for BBC Radio Five Live, and the Daily *and* Sunday Telegraph.

CHARITIES IN 1998

THE LORD'S TAVERNERS, founded in 1950, and accredited by the ECB as cricket's national charity for the recreational game, distributed £1.5 million during 1998. This was raised to give young people, particularly those with special needs, a sporting chance. Over half the funds were disbursed to promote grassroots cricket, and was administered with the help of the ECB. The rest of the money was used to provide 25 specially adapted minibuses for disabled children, and to support projects to help disabled young people participate in many other sports. The Taverners will be celebrating their 50th anniversary in 2000, when a special appeal will be launched.

The Secretary, 10 Buckingham Place, London SW1E 6HX. Telephone: 0171-821 2828. Fax: 0171-821 2829.

THE BRIAN JOHNSTON MEMORIAL TRUST was launched in 1995. Its objectives are to support a) youth cricket in schools and clubs in deprived areas through Brian Johnston Awards, b) young cricketers of exceptional promise in need of financial assistance through Brian Johnston Scholarships, and c) sport for the disabled, especially cricket for the blind. There were 27 awards and scholarships presented in 1998, along with other grants. Cricket enthusiasts are invited to join the Johnners Club, and clubs all over the country to participate in the Charity Cricket Club Challenge, which will take place throughout the 1999 season, in support of the Trust.

Chief Executive: Chris Atkinson, 71 Baker Street, London W1M 1AH. Telephone: 0171-224 1005. Fax: 0171-224 0431.

THE PRIMARY CLUB, which was one of Brian Johnston's favourite charities, raises money for sporting and recreational facilities for the blind and partially sighted. Membership is nominally restricted to anyone who has been dismissed first ball in any form of cricket. Started in 1955, the club raises money by donations and a wide variety of members' activities – both in the UK and overseas. In 1998, it sponsored the British Blind Sport cricket knockout final on the Nursery Ground at Lord's, and the first Cricket World Cup for the blind, in India. A radio station for pupils of Dorton House School in Kent was nearing completion.

Hon. Secretary: Robert Fleming, PO Box 12121, London NW1 9WS. Telephone: 0171-267 3316. Fax: 0171-485 6808.

THE HORNSBY PROFESSIONAL CRICKETERS FUND was established in 1928, from the estate of J. H. J. Hornsby, who played for Middlesex, MCC and the Gentlemen. It provides money to assist "former professional cricketers [not necessarily first-class] or their wives, widows until remarriage, children and other dependants, provided the persons concerned shall be in necessitous circumstances". Assistance is given by monthly allowances, special grants or, in certain cases, loans. Donations, requests for help or information about potential recipients are all welcome.

Clerk to the Trustees: A. K. James, Dunroamin, 65 Keyhaven Road, Milford-on-Sea, Lymington, Hampshire SO41 0QX. Telephone: 01590-644720.

THE PROFESSIONAL CRICKETERS' ASSOCIATION CHARITY was founded in 1983 to relieve financial hardship among present or former members of the Association, anyone who has played cricket for a first-class county or their "wives, widows, children, parents and dependants". It is becoming the custom for cricketers in their benefit year to donate half of one per cent of their proceeds to the fund. Donations are welcome, as are requests for help and information about cricketers who may be in need.

Chairman of the Trustees: Harold Goldblatt, 60 Doughty Street, London WC1N 2LS. Telephone: 0171-405 9855.

THE CRICKET SOCIETY TRUST was founded in 1958, and became a registered charity in 1992. It helps young cricketers by providing remedial and recreational facilities, and, in 1998, made donations to schools and clubs, as well as to organisations for blind cricket. The aim is to target specific small projects and problems not always reached by bigger donors.

Hon. Secretary: K. F. C. Merchant, 16 Louise Road, Rayleigh, Essex SS6 8LW.

THE CRICKET FOUNDATION was reconstituted in 1996 with the help of £10 million of funding promised by the first-class game over a four-year period. The Foundation exists to support youth and grassroots cricket, mainly by helping training and education in all aspects of the game. It is run from the ECB offices but operates independently of the Board, with Ossie Wheatley as chairman of the trustees.

Secretary: Terry Bates, ECB, Lord's Ground, London NW8 8QZ.

GRANT AID FOR CRICKET

Since it began in 1994, Britain's National Lottery has made a substantial impact on the development of the game. In all, there have been 455 awards to cricket organisations, totalling £54.6 million. This money has been used for projects costing a total of £98.3 million; applicants are required to provide at least 35 per cent of the overall budget for themselves. Cricket has received more capital awards than any other sport, and benefited from many multi-sport grants which include provision for cricket.

The biggest grant during 1998 was the £1.2 million given to Northamptonshire CCC for a new cricket centre at the County Ground – a project costing £1.9 million.

The Sports Grounds Initiative, which began in 1996, and is funded by the Foundation for Sports and Arts, has provided a total of £2,028,000 for county cricket clubs. The Initiative provides support for safety-related developments in county cricket, rugby union and rugby league grounds.

For further information on these and other potential donors – several of which will consider grants for much smaller projects – consult the booklet *Sources of Grant Aid for Cricket*, which is available from the ECB at Lord's. Mike Turner, author of the booklet, is available to give advice to clubs on 0116-283 1615.

CRICKET AND THE LAW IN 1998

HARRILD v ECB

Theresa Harrild, 32, received "substantial" compensation from the England and Wales Cricket Board after an industrial tribunal decided on March 11, 1998, that the Board had breached the Sex Discrimination Act by dismissing her. Miss Harrild, a £14,000-a-year receptionist at the ECB's Lord's office, claimed she had been made pregnant by a colleague, pressured into having an abortion and then sacked.

Miss Harrild painted a picture of attitudes at Lord's that caused a media uproar. She said the atmosphere was sexist, and quoted Tim Lamb, the Board chief executive, referring to the England women cricketers – then on the brink of merging their organisation with the ECB – in derogatory terms. She claimed he said: "We want our good dykes on board so that we can get more lottery money."

Soon after joining the Board in 1996, Miss Harrild had embarked on a romance with a junior executive at the Board, Nick Marriner. She said that after she became pregnant, Lamb told her that a child would make promotion impossible. Pressure was put on her to have an abortion, she said, and the ECB gave her £400 in a brown envelope to pay for it. Although she returned to work, she suffered from depression and subsequently took two overdoses. Cliff Barker, Lamb's deputy, then visited her at her home to dismiss her. He also made a sexual pass at her, she said.

The tribunal chairman, Christopher Carstairs, said his panel unanimously accepted that her evidence was entirely truthful. The ECB did not attend the hearing, saying that Miss Harrild had "exploited" the forum provided by the tribunal when the matter could have been settled privately. The Board issued a statement saying: "The culture of the ECB bears no resemblance to the description put forward. This is a new organisation which is committed to delivering equality across the game." On May 1, it was announced that Miss Harrild had received an apology and "a substantial sum" of compensation and costs. The ECB also assured her that it "had no intention of suggesting that she had done other than provide an honest recollection of events".

GEOFFREY BOYCOTT

Geoffrey Boycott was given a three-month suspended prison sentence and fined 50,000 francs (about £5,000) by a court in Grasse, France, on January 20, 1998, for assaulting his former mistress, Margaret Moore, who was awarded one franc in damages. This followed what Mrs Moore said was a "brutal and caddish" attack that left her with two black eyes.

The incident had happened in a hotel room at Antibes on the French Riviera in 1996. "He grabbed me by the arm and hit me 20 times or more. He is very strong. I was screaming and screaming," Mrs Moore said. Boycott did not attend the trial, but sent a fax denying the allegation and stating that Mrs Moore became hysterical because he would not marry her. "I tried to restrain her and she slipped and fell, hitting the right side of her head on the floor." Mrs Moore's lawyer rejected this, saying: "She would have had to fall on one eye and then the other."

On being told that Boycott was absent because he was commentating on a cricket match, the court president, Marc Joando, remarked sarcastically: "How can we interrupt so noble an activity as cricket?" Boycott later said he had received legal advice that his attendance had been unnecessary.

He appealed and was granted a retrial, which took place on October 20. This time he not merely attended, but took a team of expert and character witnesses to support his claim that he had never been violent in his life. However, Boycott complained: "It's very difficult. Everyone's talking French". At one point, he told everyone to shut up.

On November 10, the judge, Dominique Haumant-Daumas, issued a seven-page ruling, upholding the original decision: "His arguments did not support the theory of an accidental fall." She added: "The accused did not hesitate to interrupt Mrs Moore's barrister, thereby undermining the image of the perfect gentleman which so many of his old friends and witnesses had come to support." Boycott said afterwards he was not surprised by the decision, "after the way the court hearing was conducted", and added: "I was on a hiding to nothing". *The Sun*, under the headline BOYCOTT THE BRUTE, said it was dropping his ghosted columns; other news media which employed him soon followed.

In the *Mail on Sunday*, Patrick Collins wrote that the hiding-to-nothing remark "proved he has no awareness of his own absurdity". In the *Sunday Telegraph*, Norman Lebrecht said Boycott was being stripped of his livelihood "in a frenzy of media self-righteousness".

League officials in north-east England used new laws designed to control stalkers to end a campaign by an angry club chairman. Colin Orr, 67, the former chairman of Silksworth in the Durham Coast League, admitted four charges of harrassment in a private prosecution brought by the League on September 17, 1998. He had bombarded officials with more than 300 letters after Silksworth had to forfeit a match when their pitch was vandalised. He accused them of a "jackboot mentality". Orr's counsel agreed that his client was "fairly obsessive". Orr was given a two-year conditional discharge by Sunderland magistrates, ordered not to approach anyone connected to the league, and to pay £500 costs.

Derek and Barbara Sheffield of Rolvenden, Kent, lost a case against the Rolvenden Cricket Club at Ashford County Court on March 24, 1998, claiming damages done for balls hit into their garden and against their house. Mr Sheffield said normal life was impossible when matches were being played on the village green, and that the club had been slow to respond to complaints. The club had erected a 6ft net in 1997, but Mr Sheffield wanted a bigger one. However, his next-door neighbour Anne Cox, 86, said her property had never been damaged in her 28 years there: "Country activities should be encouraged," she said. Judge Edwina Millward said the plaintiffs were aware when they bought the house that cricket was played on the green.

AUSTRALIAN CRICKETERS OF THE YEAR

When *Wisden Cricketers' Almanack Australia* came out for the first time in 1998, it named one Cricketer of the Year for 1997-98, rather than five. And the brash newcomer immediately did something *Wisden* had never done by choosing a woman, Belinda Clark.

At the same time, the Australian almanack commissioned the cricket writer and historian Gideon Haigh to choose a player who might have been the Australian Cricketer of the Year for the century or so when *Wisden Australia* could have existed but didn't. Haigh considered Australian players' feats at home and abroad, and overseas players' feats in Australia, while sticking to the ancient rule: no one to be chosen twice. This is his list:

1892-93	G. Giffen	1929-30	D. G. Bradman	1965-66	K. D. Walters
1893-94	C. T. B. Turner	1930-31	C. V. Grimmett	1966-67	G. D. McKenzie
1894-95	T. Richardson	1931-32	H. Ironmonger	1967-68	G. A. R. Lock
1895-96	T. R. McKibbin	1932-33	H. Larwood	1968-69	I. M. Chappell
1896-97	H. Trumble	1933-34	W. M. Woodfull	1969-70	A. N. Connolly
1897-98	J. Darling	1934-35	S. J. McCabe	1970-71	J. A. Snow
1898-99	C. Hill	1935-36	W. J. O'Reilly	1971-72	D. K. Lillee
1899-00	M. A. Noble	1936-37	L. O'B. Fleetwood-Smith	1972-73	G. S. Chappell
1900-01	A. E. Trott			1973-74	S. C. Trimble
1901-02	C. J. Eady	1937-38	W. A. Oldfield	1974-75	J. R. Thomson
1902-03	V. T. Trumper	1938-39	W. A. Brown	1975-76	I. R. Redpath
1903-04	W. Rhodes	1939-40	A. L. Hassett	1976-77	D. W. Hookes
1904-05	V. S. Ransford	1940-41	S. G. Barnes	1977-78	I. J. Brayshaw
1905-06	J. R. M. Mackay	1945-46	C. G. Pepper	1978-79	R. M. Hogg
1906-07	S. E. Gregory	1946-47	K. R. Miller	1979-80	I. V. A. Richards
1907-08	W. W. Armstrong	1947-48	D. Tallon	1980-81	K. J. Hughes
1908-09	A. Marshal	1948-49	A. R. Morris	1981-82	T. M. Alderman
1909-10	W. Bardsley	1949-50	W. A. Johnston	1982-83	G. F. Lawson
1910-11	G. A. Faulkner	1950-51	L. Hutton	1983-84	R. W. Marsh
1911-12	S. F. Barnes	1951-52	A. L. Valentine	1984-85	M. D. Marshall
1912-13	R. J. A. Massie	1952-53	R. R. Lindwall	1985-86	A. R. Border
1913-14	J. N. Crawford	1953-54	R. N. Harvey	1986-87	B. C. Broad
1914-15	F. A. Tarrant	1954-55	F. H. Tyson	1987-88	D. C. Boon
1919-20	H. L. Collins	1955-56	J. W. Burke	1988-89	C. E. L. Ambrose
1920-21	J. M. Gregory	1956-57	G. E. Tribe	1989-90	M. A. Taylor
1921-22	C. G. Macartney	1957-58	R. Benaud	1990-91	C. J. McDermott
1922-23	A. A. Mailey	1958-59	C. C. McDonald	1991-92	Imran Khan
1923-24	W. H. Ponsford	1959-60	N. C. O'Neill	1992-93	B. C. Lara
1924-25	M. W. Tate	1960-61	A. K. Davidson	1993-94	S. K. Warne
1925-26	E. A. McDonald	1961-62	W. M. Lawry	1994-95	S. R. Waugh
1926-27	L. P. D. O'Connor	1962-63	G. S. Sobers	1995-96	M. E. Waugh
1927-28	A. F. Kippax	1963-64	B. C. Booth	1996-97	G. D. McGrath
1928-29	W. R. Hammond	1964-65	R. B. Simpson		

CRICKET PEOPLE IN 1998

By SIMON BRIGGS

One familiar Aussie voice was missing from the 1998-99 Ashes series. NEVILLE OLIVER, head of sport on both ABC Radio and Television, was also *Test Match Special*'s overseas player in the last three Ashes series in England. But in March, he suddenly announced his resignation, cleared his desk within three days and, at 53, was out of a job.

"It had been mulling over in my mind for a year or 18 months," he says. "There comes a time when you have to look at a wider expanse of life than just tootling around doing cricket. By that stage I was also in a senior management position at the ABC. I won't say I despised a lot of the people around me, but I certainly didn't agree with them, and I'm a fairly forthright person. That made my decision easier, put it that way."

Oliver stood as a Labor candidate for the Tasmanian state parliament in August, but narrowly missed election. Instead, he is spending most days at his local golf club in Hobart, where he is the honorary secretary: "It fills in my time, but I'm looking for something more meaningful than that, I can assure you."

Oliver says he will miss seeing his friends around the world, but when it was suggested that he might feel a pang of regret at missing the World Cup, he laughed. "Anyone who has listened to me for long will know my very deep loathing of one-day cricket and all that it stands for. To miss any kind of one-day tournament strikes me as more of a reward than a fine."

In contrast, ALAN CURTIS, one-time voice of English Test cricket, finally achieved a lifelong ambition in the winter by watching an Ashes series in Australia. Curtis, a noted pantomime stalwart, usually spent his Christmases playing either Captain Hook or the Sheriff of Nottingham. Then his acting career was cut short by a serious stroke in 1995. Now 68, he has emerged from a period of convalescence with his John Arlott impression intact.

Curtis first worked at Lord's in 1968, when Dick Morris, head of light entertainment at the BBC, nominated a panel of four actors and broadcasters to operate the public address system, including John Snagge, the wartime newsreader and voice of the Boat Race. But Curtis was in sole occupation a year later. "The others were more experienced than me, but I think I was better at remembering the players' names."

Throughout the 1970s, he handed over to his deputy Johnny Dennis (now the main announcer) whenever a film offer came in. Curtis appeared in *Carry On Henry*, *Carry On Abroad*, and Alfred Hitchcock's *Frenzy*, among others, and his c.v. boasts that "he was the original Phantom Raspberry Blower of Old London Town". He also manned the mike at 138 Test matches before the ECB dispensed with his services, immediately after his stroke. Curtis responded by going to an industrial tribunal: the case was settled privately. But he hasn't completely left Lord's: spectators at various Middlesex and MCC games can still hear his catchphrase, honed to perfection in endless performances of *Robin Hood* and *Peter Pan*: "Good morning, ladies and gentlemen, boys and girls".

[Winston Bynorth

Dave Houghton

[Patrick Eagar

Neville Oliver

Bitter ethnic conflict has raged in Sri Lanka since 1983, but at least the national cricket team provides a small oasis of harmony. Tamils and Sinhalese alike rejoice when Sri Lanka win. The cadres of the LTTE (Liberation Tigers of Tamil Eelam, better known simply as the Tamil Tigers) are said to celebrate by firing their rifles in the air. Even their leader VELUPILLAI PRABHAKARAN, described by *Asiaweek* magazine as a "ruthless and single-minded autocrat", is not immune. He apparently kept his lieutenants waiting in the front of his house while he watched the conclusion of an international between Sri Lanka and India.

ANGELA EAGLE, the first woman to play for the Lords and Commons cricket team, moved in July 1998 from the Department of the Environment to become a junior minister in Social Security. Angela and her twin sister Maria learned the game from their father, "when we were about two". Now, aged 37, they are both Labour MPs: for Wallasey and Liverpool Garston respectively. "We were allowed to practise with the boys at primary school," Angela says, "but not to play in any real games." Both sisters did represent Lancashire when they were 16, however. Ministerial commitments have limited Angela's appearances recently, but she enjoyed the coaching she received as part of the Lords and Commons team: "We never had any proper coaching when we were younger," she says, "which I really regret." On the other hand, she had to put up with single-sex changing facilities, and male confusion at parliamentary etiquette: "They never knew whether to bounce me, or bowl me gentle donkey drops."

Cricketers may not walk in the old-fashioned way when they edge a catch, but the tradition of long-distance walking exemplified by Ian Botham's marathons lives on. DAVE HOUGHTON, Zimbabwe's coach and former captain, trekked almost 300 miles in June 1998 between Bulawayo and Harare to try to raise funds for the Zimbabwean cricket academy. "Botham gave me the inspiration," he said. Every day, Houghton was accompanied by a different group of schoolchildren. The result: a million Zimbabwean dollars, at that time £40,000, a substantial amount in a poor country. There were a couple of worrying moments with speeding traffic, and one with a puff adder, which Houghton nearly trod on. But he was sufficiently enthused to contemplate Part Two: an east–west walk finishing at Lake Kariba. The academy is scheduled to open in 1999.

Commentators at the final Ashes Test were perplexed when the SCG's electronic scoreboard flashed up the England XI, followed by the name "King". Alan Mullally was the official twelfth man, but Alec Stewart had arranged for THEO KING, England's dressing-room helper, to bring out the drinks in England's first innings. King describes his role as "looking after the mundane stuff, so the players don't have to". In practice, this means anything from manning the dressing-room door to bowling in the nets. He used to take the new ball for West Bromwich Dartmouth in the Birmingham League, so he's no pushover. King, 39, is a PE teacher at Wolverhampton Grammar School, where he has "a very understanding headmaster". He has been helping out at Edgbaston for ten years but, since David Lloyd took over as England coach, he has been invited to join the players at every home Test, and a handful of overseas ones. "It's a dream come true," he says.

Another candidate for the title of best backroom bowler must be JEEVANLAL PAUL, the masseur and dressing-room attendant at Calcutta's Eden Gardens for over 35 years. Now 59, Paul claimed some notable scalps in the nets as a young man, sending down medium-paced swingers to the great names of world cricket. "The two Vijays, Hazare and Manjrekar, would specifically insist I bowl to them," he says. Two future knights of the game were surprised when Paul, switching to off-breaks, dismissed them at pre-match practice: Sir Colin (now Lord) Cowdrey, on the eve of the 1964 Test, and Sir Garry Sobers, a few hours before the Second Test of the 1966-67 series. Paul was a fine all-round sportsman who represented George Telegraph and Sporting Union in Calcutta's soccer leagues. Alf Gover offered him a place at his coaching school in London. "I just didn't have the resources to travel. Who's there to support masseurs and servants?"

The plans being hatched at Lord's to turn the top amateur leagues into feeders for the first-class counties received a boost when Middlesex recruited a talented seam bowler from Stanmore CC. However, ALASTAIR FRASER wasn't exactly new to county cricket. The younger brother of Angus, he had been on the staff at Middlesex from 1986 to 1990, and then Essex until 1993, when a serious shoulder injury forced him to leave the professional game. Fraser, 31, has worked in Amtrak Express Parcels' marketing department ever since, but Middlesex approached him before the season with an offer of match-by-match employment. "I caught their eye because I had a tremendous summer for Stanmore in 1997," Fraser says. The Amtrak office is less busy in the summer, and his bosses were amenable, so Fraser was able to play 11 one-day games, picking up 15 wickets at 22.53. On his second appearance, a Benson and Hedges game against Essex, he took four for 45 to claim the Gold Award. It was a first for the family: Angus had never won one in 15 years.

Additional research: Lokendra Pratap Sahi

OBITUARY

ADAMS, GEOFFREY COKER ARDING, MBE, who died on February 10, 1998, aged 88, was a Cambridge rugby Blue but failed to make the cricket team. He did, however, play 18 matches for Hampshire in his vacations and captained them in one match against Essex in 1930. He had modest success as both middle-order batsman and change bowler. After the war, he emigrated to Australia and built up a newspaper group in rural Victoria.

ALMADI, VASANT R., who died on July 10, 1998, aged 79, was an all-rounder for Bombay from 1947-48 to 1952-53. He made a century against Sind on his Ranji Trophy debut.

ATKINSON, ERIC ST EVAL, who died after a long illness on May 29, 1998, aged 70, played eight Tests for West Indies in the late 1950s. He made his debut as a 30-year-old opening bowler at Bridgetown in 1957-58, alongside his older and better-known brother Denis, playing his last Test. The Atkinsons were the third pair of brothers to play together for West Indies, after the Grants and the Stollmeyers; there have been none since. In his second game, at Sabina Park a month later, Eric took five for 42, a performance that was somewhat overshadowed by Garry Sobers's 365 not out. A tearaway bowler in his youth, Atkinson was not very successful when he first played for Barbados: three wickets in his first nine matches. But he had settled down to bowl fast-medium swing by the time he got into the Test team; he was said to have used reverse swing long before anyone had a name for it. Atkinson was chosen to tour the subcontinent a year later and, in his last Test, helped set up victory at Lahore with figures of 12–8–15–3, as Pakistan were bowled out for 104.

BALL, GEORGE ARMSTRONG, who died on December 20, 1997, aged 83, was a club cricketer from Barwell. He stepped up to play 11 matches as a batsman for Leicestershire between 1933 and 1936, and made 44 not out against Glamorgan on debut.

BARNWELL, CHARLES JOHN PATRICK, died on September 4, 1998, aged 84. John Barnwell played 69 matches for Somerset as an amateur batsman either side of the war. He was correct, but rarely effective at county level, though he did once take four fours in an over off Bill Voce. He occasionally deputised as captain, and might have been considered for the post full-time, had he not run a demanding business breeding silver foxes. He was awarded his county cap in 1937, though apparently no one bothered to tell him.

BEARDMORE, CARLIN, who died on February 19, 1998, aged 86, was an accountant who scored for Derbyshire from 1970 to 1981. He was also the club's treasurer from 1977 to 1981.

BEESLEY, RAYMOND, who died on December 7, 1997, aged 81, was a left-arm seam bowler for Border. He took 82 wickets in a career lasting 15 years from 1938-39. Three of these came in a remarkable hat-trick, against Griqualand West at Queenstown in 1946-47, all caught by the same fielder, Cyril White at short leg. It was almost four in a row: White got his fingertips to the next ball. Beesley finished with four for 11 off 15 overs.

BERNARD, Dr JOHN RICHARD, died on February 23, 1998, aged 59. Dr Richard Bernard was a popular Bristol family doctor descended from another well-known Bristol medical family: E. M. Grace, W.G.'s brother, was his great-grandfather. *Wisden* 1956 called Bernard "the most promising cricketer Clifton have had for some years", and he won a Cambridge Blue three years running as a hard-hitting middle-order batsman and medium-pace change bowler. He made his debut for Gloucestershire as a 17-year-old, though he played only 11 county matches in all: he was rather shocked by the intensity of county cricket. But he remained besotted by the game, and his surgery timetable would be thrown into chaos whenever another enthusiast was a patient.

BEVERIDGE, ROBERT, died in New Zealand on March 5, 1998, aged 88. Bob Beveridge was a slow left-arm bowler who played 41 times for the weak Middlesex team of the early 1930s. In his third match, at Leicester, he took six for 66, but after that achieved little. He went to coach in Cairo before emigrating to New Zealand, and was groundsman at Eden Park in the 1960s and 1970s.

BIRKETT, LIONEL SYDNEY, who died on January 16, 1998, aged 93, was vice-captain on West Indies' first tour of Australia, in 1930-31. He made 64, opening the batting at Adelaide on his debut, but his form deteriorated, and he did not play in the last Test when West Indies scored a surprise win. Birkett had attracted attention by making 253 for Trinidad against British Guiana a year earlier, and his batting – learned among the Barbadian elite at Harrison College – was always elegant. But his cricket had to be fitted in with his peripatetic work in the sugar business: his career comprised 26 first-class matches spread over 20 years, for Barbados, Trinidad and British Guiana as well as the West Indians. After the Australian tour, Birkett did not play again until 1937. He was the oldest living Test player before he died, a title taken over by Alf Gover of England.

BOON, RONALD WINSTON, who died in New Zealand on August 3, 1998, aged 89, was a batsman who played 11 matches for Glamorgan in 1931 and 1932 without obvious success. He was better-known for his rugby, winning 12 caps for Wales as a winger: in January 1933, he scored all the points – a try and a drop goal – in Wales's 7-3 win over England, their first-ever victory at Twickenham. There were three other Glamorgan cricketers in the team: Vivian Jenkins, Maurice Turnbull and Wilf Wooller, who were all making their debuts.

BRAY, ELAINE JOY, who died on January 10, 1998, aged 57, was an all-rounder who played in the Australian team that lost the final of the first women's World Cup and won the second. She later became a well-known breeder of cairn terriers.

CAWSTON, EDWARD, died on September 5, 1998, aged 87. Ted Cawston was a gifted schoolboy all-rounder picked for Sussex in 1928 while still in his penultimate year at Lancing. Cawston played five more county matches over the next three seasons, and won his Cambridge Blue in 1932. He had an unspectacular match at Lord's but, playing for the university the previous week at Eastbourne, he had bowled out Leveson-Gower's XI, taking seven for 53 with his briskish medium-pace, and then scored 93, putting on 171 in 90 minutes with J. H. Human. After leaving Cambridge, he played mainly for Berkshire and Suffolk, and became headmaster of Orwell Park School.

CHRIST, CHARLES PERCIVAL, died on January 22, 1998, aged 86. "Chilla" Christ was a slow left-armer who was chosen to play for Queensland against Victoria in 1930-31 when they were short of players. Rain caused the complete abandonment of the fixture and he had to wait seven years for his debut. After that, he established himself as an effective bowler in a struggling team. He took 56 wickets in 24 first-class matches; Ginty Lush of New South Wales was both his first and last victim.

COLE, JOHN WAVELL, who died on March 4, 1998, aged 75, was a leading figure in Canadian cricket. Born in Surrey, he emigrated just after the war, began playing for Grace Church in Toronto, and rapidly became one of Ontario's senior cricket administrators. He was President of the Canadian Cricket Association from 1967 to 1978. Cole taught classics at the University of Toronto for 40 years.

COPINGER, GEOFFREY ARTHUR, who died on May 9, 1998, aged 87, owned the world's largest private collection of cricket books: about 12,000. They dominated every room of his house in Hampstead, neatly arranged by height in glass-fronted bookcases, double-parked to save space. Copinger even segregated books depending on how the title was positioned on their spine: upwards, downwards, or horizontal. In the dining room, as an aesthetic refinement for his wife's benefit, he arranged them by colour as well. He also had thousands of items of cricketana. E. W. Padwick, compiler of *A Bibliography of Cricket*, made 23 visits to Copinger's house for his first edition. The collection was sold to an anonymous buyer in a deal arranged just before his death. A figure of £250,000 was reported, but is understood to be exaggerated. Copinger was a fount of knowledge on cricket from his prep school days, and in his spare time while working as a banker he was chief statistician for *Wisden* from 1947 to 1963. For 35 years, between 1947 and 1982, he compiled the first-class averages used in almost all the national papers.

COSTORPHIN, COLIN JOHN, who died on September 4, 1998, after a long illness, aged 44, played three matches for Victoria as a seam bowler. Costorphin would have played in 1973-74 but his debut was delayed for three years by a back injury. He took four or five in an innings in each of his first-class matches, finishing with 14 wickets at 29.14.

DALLING, HARRY WILLIAM, who died on December 10, 1998, aged 77, was a member of the extraordinary Dalling dynasty inextricably associated with Trent Bridge. From 1949 to 1991, he served as Nottinghamshire's ground superintendent, a sort of general factotum "responsible for everything beyond the boundary rope". He succeeded his father Frank, who had done the same job since 1920; meanwhile Harry's brother, another Frank, was head groundsman and responsible for everything inside the rope; Frank's son – yet another Frank – is still on the ground staff and was briefly head groundsman himself. Until 1955, Harry lived in a basement flat under the pavilion before the area was commandeered for toilets, and he moved a few streets away. Even in retirement, he did a variety of jobs for the county, including the public address announcements. He was featured as one of the "Alternative Five" in the 1995 *Wisden*.

DESAI, RAMAKANT BHIKAJI, died in a Mumbai hospital on April 27, 1998, aged 58, while awaiting heart surgery. "Tiny" Desai was only 5ft 4in tall but, from a supple run-up, generated sufficient pace to sustain the Indian attack in the 1960s, when it desperately needed sustenance, and usually got it only from spin bowlers. He was drafted into the side as a 19-year-old for the Delhi Test in 1958-59, and had to bowl 49 overs in West Indies' only innings, taking four for 169; he promptly took over the leadership of the attack for the 1959 tour of England. At Lord's he had England in deep trouble at 80 for six, and finished with five for 89 in the innings. *Wisden* praised his "rare ability", "endless courage", and his out-swinger, though the team was hopelessly overmatched, and he was over-bowled. That was often the way: he was on the winning side in only four of his 28 Tests. But he played a crucial role in blunting the threat of Hanif Mohammad in the 1960-61 series against Pakistan. Hanif had some trouble against Desai's deceptive bouncer, and was dismissed by him four times in nine innings: the Indians joked that he was "Ramakant's bakra" – the Hindi equivalent of rabbit. With the older ball, Desai was especially effective. His finest hour arguably came in that series, at the Brabourne Stadium in the opening Test, when he scored 85, batting No. 10; his ninth-wicket stand of 149 with P. G. Joshi remains an Indian Test record. He also scored a crucial 32 not out at Dunedin in 1967-68, continuing to bat after his jaw was broken. India won, but he never played Test cricket again. In 53 Ranji matches for Bombay, he took 239 wickets at 15.61, and he retired completely in 1969, aged only 30. Desai returned to the front line in 1996 when he was appointed chairman of selectors, and he was responsible for the appointment – and the dismissal – of Sachin Tendulkar as captain. It was not a happy term of office, and his natural sense of loyalty and reticence, combined with increasing ill-health, made it difficult for him both in committee and in his dealings with the media. He resigned the month before he died.

DULDIG, LANCE DESMOND, who died on September 14, 1998, aged 76, was an attractive batsman for South Australia in the 1940s and early 1950s, and toured New Zealand with the Australian B team in 1949-50. He had made his debut on his 19th birthday, in the state's last match before the war intervened. His unbeaten 70 against MCC in 1950-51 was described in one British paper as "far from a dull dig".

DUNCAN, Colonel ANTHONY ARTHUR, OBE, died on January 3, 1998, aged 83. Tony Duncan was a successful schoolboy bat at Rugby, and scored 58 and 94 against Marlborough at Lord's in 1933. He played twice without distinction for Glamorgan the following year, and once for Oxford in 1935, but made his name as an amateur golfer, reaching the final of the 1939 Amateur Championship and captaining the British Walker Cup team in 1953.

FARMER, STUART CAREY STEDMAN, died in September, aged 77. "Stephen" Farmer was an outstanding schoolboy wicket-keeper at Cheltenham College. He was commissioned into the Gloucestershire Regiment straight after leaving school, and was posted to Jamaica after the war. In 1947-48 he was put on standby for the MCC team touring the West Indies when Godfrey Evans was injured. But the Army posted him to British Guiana, where there was a threat of hostilities.

FEATHERSTONE, JOHN, who died from a heart attack on his way to a football match on February 14, 1998, aged 59, was a cricketing enthusiast. He was secretary of the Council of Cricket Societies and of the Women's Cricket Association. He also edited *White Rose*, Yorkshire's club newspaper.

FORD, Group Captain WALTER RONALD, CBE, died on October 7, 1998, aged 84. Ronnie Ford was a left-handed batsman and wicket-keeper who played four matches for Combined Services just after the war. He was assistant secretary (administration) of MCC from 1973 to 1977.

FRASER, THOMAS CAMPBELL, who died on May 20, 1998, aged 80, played irregularly for Otago between 1937 and 1953; against Wellington in 1939-40, he made a match-winning 118. Fraser later became a successful businessman and owner of the *Otago Daily Times*.

FREER, FREDERICK WILLIAM, who died on November 2, 1998, aged 82, bowled Cyril Washbrook in his first over of Test cricket. Freer was a Victorian swing bowler who had been drafted into the Australian side at Sydney for the Second Test of the 1946-47 series when Ray Lindwall had chicken-pox. Batting No. 9, he scored a rapid 28 not out before Australia declared at 659 for eight. In the second innings, he dismissed both Compton and Ikin, but bowled only 20 overs in a match dominated by Australia's spinners. When Lindwall returned, he was relegated to twelfth man for two Tests, and was not called on again. Freer was already 31; he had entered first-class cricket in Victoria's first game after the war when he took seven for 29 against Queensland. In

1948 he came to England and played for Rishton, carrying them to their first Lancashire League title in 36 years; he lived near the ground and reputedly hit a six into his own garden.

GADKARI, Lt-Col CHANDRASEKHAR VAMAN, who died on January 11, 1998, aged 69, played six Tests for India in the early 1950s: three on the 1952-53 tour of the West Indies, and three more in Pakistan two years later. He was a batsman who bowled occasional seamers, but his position in the Test match order varied between No. 3 and No. 10. India were 183 for seven when he went in at Georgetown, but he held out against Ramadhin and Valentine to score an unbeaten 50. Gadkari's first-class career lasted until 1959-60, when he made his career-best – 145 for Services v Railways – but cricket came second to his army career, and his appearances were spasmodic.

GHULAM AHMED, who died on October 28, 1998, aged 76, was a harbinger of the great Indian spin bowling tradition. He bowled off-breaks with a high, handsome action, sometimes compared to Jim Laker's, and on the right wicket could be just as effective. Ghulam made his Test debut at Calcutta in 1948-49, when Everton Weekes scored twin hundreds. But Ghulam dismissed him both times, and took four for 94 in the first innings. Against England in 1951-52 he was highly successful, and was instrumental in India's maiden victory at Madras, before becoming by far the most potent member of a weak attack on the 1952 tour of England. "He had days when he looked in the highest world class," said *Wisden*, "but on other occasions he lacked bite." Later that year he helped Mankad bowl India to victory in Pakistan's first Test match, at Delhi, and – improbably – scored 50, sharing a last-wicket stand of 109 with H. R. Adhikari, still an Indian record. His subsequent career was deeply involved with shifts in local cricket politics. In 1955-56, Ghulam captained India against New Zealand in his home town of Hyderabad, then mysteriously resigned. A year later, he bowled Australia out at Calcutta, taking seven for 49, only to be eclipsed by Richie Benaud. In 1958-59, against West Indies, he was captain again but, after two hefty defeats, he stood down for reasons that never became clear. "By his action," wrote one Indian observer, "he strengthened the belief of his critics that he was not a fighter." This belief does not wholly accord with his record: he took four for 245 in 92.3 overs for Hyderabad against Holkar in 1950-51, and bowled 85 overs in an innings three years earlier. Ghulam became a prominent administrator: he was secretary of the Indian Board from 1975 to 1980, and served twice as a selector; when India won the 1983 World Cup he was chairman. Asif Iqbal, who played for Pakistan, is his nephew.

GREEN, BERNARD, died on June 22, 1998, aged 70. Benny Green was a jazz musician, broadcaster, writer and wit who had the rare ability to make unexpected connections between his various enthusiasms, and delighted millions of people in the process. Among those enthusiasms were cricket – he grew up watching Compton at Lord's – and, most specifically, *Wisden*, which he regarded as a work of glorious social history. He reviewed the Almanack one year in *The Spectator*, and suggested there ought to be an anthology. There was only one candidate for the job. In 1979 he began work, reading the entire canon cover-to-cover before slimming down the first 119 editions into four (chunky) volumes, brought alive by Green's eye for telling and quirky detail. This turned into a cottage industry: spin-offs included *The Wisden Book of Obituaries* (1986), *The Wisden Papers* (1989) and *The Concise Wisden* (1990), originally published two years earlier especially for Marks & Spencer, a very Green-ish connection itself. His various introductions are mini-classics. He also published a number of other cricket books, including a notably eclectic non-*Wisden* anthology, *The Cricket Addict's Archive* (later retitled *Benny Green's Cricket Archive*). He talked about everything with an auto-didact's zest, and in an unchanging Cockney accent. "The effect," wrote Dave Gelly in *The Observer*, "was as though a particularly grumpy taxi-driver had started quoting Dr Johnson while sorting out your change."

GREENHALGH, ERIC WASHINGTON, who died on July 2, 1996, aged 86, was a stocky middle-order batsman and occasional medium-pace bowler who played 14 matches for Lancashire in the late 1930s.

GRIEVESON, RONALD EUSTACE, OBE, died on July 24, 1998, aged 88. Ronnie Grieveson was South Africa's wicket-keeper in the Timeless Test at Durban in 1938-39, conceding only eight byes in three days while England scored 654 in their second innings. He made 75 and 39 himself, batting No. 8. It was his second and last game for South Africa: he had played in the previous Test at Johannesburg and taken five catches, three of them off Norman Gordon. (Following the death of Doug Wright later in 1998, Gordon became the last survivor from the Durban game, one of the most famous cricket matches of all.) Grieveson played for Transvaal from 1929-30 until the war, not always keeping wicket – the province had the great Jock Cameron until his death in 1935 – but his batting made him worth his place. He hit 107 not out opening against Griqualand West in 1933-34, and the following year averaged nearly 50. He was awarded the OBE for his wartime service, when he reached the rank of major.

HARDY, DONALD WRIGHTSON, who died on January 17, 1998, aged 71, played for Durham from 1948 to 1967 and captained the Minor Counties against the South Africans at Jesmond in 1965, his only first-class match.

HEYN, Major-General BERTRAM RUSSEL, who died on February 5, 1998, captained Ceylon at both cricket and hockey. His finest moment came when he dismissed Don Bradman for 20 during the Australians' stopover on the way to England in 1948. The Australians, who had been highly suspicious all along, later measured the pitch and found it was two yards short. Heyn also scored a century in 35 minutes in a wartime match for the Ceylon Defence Force against The Rest.

HORTON, HENRY, who died on November 2, 1998, aged 75, was a Hampshire stalwart for most of the 1950s and 1960s, such a fixture that to everyone in the club he was just "H". He went in first wicket down in the team that memorably won the Championship in 1961, and was the most reliable run-getter in the side. His stance attracted regular derision: the crouch was so pronounced it was compared to "squatting on the loo". It was effective, but more for defence than attack. "He could get out of first gear," recalled his captain, Colin Ingleby-Mackenzie, "but he didn't really have second gear. Just now and again he would go into fourth, and start hitting over the top." Above all, Horton was brave, both against fast bowling and at short leg. He played 405 times for the county (having earlier played 11 games for Worcestershire), made 21,669 runs and 32 hundreds. He passed 2,000 runs three times. Originally, Horton had chosen to become a footballer, and Southampton paid Blackburn £10,000 to sign him as a battling wing-half in 1951, but, with the encouragement of Hampshire coach Arthur Holt, he slowly switched over to cricket. He later coached Worcestershire and became a first-class umpire. Away from the crease, "H" remained a cautious man: he drank halves, and never married, going back to his home town – Colwall in Herefordshire – to live with his sisters.

HORTON, JOSEPH, died on November 6, 1998, aged 83, four days after his younger brother Henry. Joe Horton had a more textbook method than his brother, and was inclined to be exasperated by Henry's eccentric stance. But he failed to make the same impact, despite playing 62 matches for Worcestershire before the war. His highest score was 70 against Glamorgan in 1938.

HOWELL, Baron, died on April 19, 1998, aged 74. Denis Howell was a Labour politician and Britain's first Minister for Sport. He became so identified with the job that he was widely assumed to be in office long after Labour had lost power. Howell played a crucial role in the negotiations in which the Government effectively forced Lord's to cancel the 1970 South African tour. He was an affable Brummie, also remembered for his appointment as Minister for Drought in 1976, which was greeted by a deluge. He was also a League football referee, and a keen follower of Warwickshire.

IBBOTSON, DOUGLAS GEORGE, died on November 26, 1998, aged 71. Doug Ibbotson was one of the *Daily Telegraph* team of cricket writers for nearly two decades. He was a gentle, wry man who covered county matches with what his colleague John Mason called "a kindly eye and a telling phrase": he is believed to have been responsible for christening the County Ground at Northampton "Coronation Street with grass". He worked for the *News Chronicle* and the London *Evening News* before both papers folded; for the *Evening News* he wrote sports features and covered major events, including three Olympic Games, before settling into a quieter existence on the cricket and rugby circuit. "Ibbo" was always an early arriver and would make himself comfortable in the press box with his pipe, sandwiches and Thermos, but still retained his sense of adventure: in his late sixties he obtained a pilot's licence.

IRISH, ARTHUR FRANK, who died on July 17, 1997, aged 78, played Minor Counties cricket for Devon over three decades, and a solitary season for Somerset in 1950. Frank Irish appeared in 16 first-class matches for them, with a top score of 76 against Glamorgan. But he did not care for the professional game, and returned to Sidmouth, where he was a forthright and combative captain of the town club and ran a barber's shop-cum-tobacconist.

JINKS, ALLAN, who died in Melbourne on November 7, 1997, aged 83, was an off-spinner whose first-class career was curtailed by the presence in the Victorian team of Ian Johnson. In his eight first-class matches before and after the war, he twice claimed five wickets in an innings against Queensland. He took 569 wickets in club cricket for Carlton.

JOHNSON, IAN WILLIAM, CBE, who died on October 9, 1998, aged 80, captained Australia in 17 of his 45 Tests. Unfortunately for him, he took over in the mid-1950s, when Australian cricket was decidedly inferior to England's for the first time since before the Bradman era, and he became the first 20th-century captain to lead Australia to defeats in successive Ashes series. His problems were worsened because he had been controversially preferred to Keith Miller, and many Australians regarded him almost as a usurper. Inter-state rivalry had played a part in Johnson's selection, but it was also a rather English sort of decision: Johnson, who had something of an amateur's bearing, appealed more to many members of the Australian establishment than the more wayward Miller. But he was a fine cricketer and, in some respects, a visionary.

Johnson made his debut for Victoria as an 18-year-old and emerged, after wartime service, as a mainstay of Australia's attack. He was an off-spinner in a country traditionally keener on wrist-spin and, according to E. W. Swanton, "probably the slowest bowler to achieve any measure of success in Test cricket". His action was compared to a corkscrew (and occasionally had its legality queried), but in the right circumstance his flight and dip could not merely tantalise batsmen, but madden them. Against England at Sydney in 1946-47, he floated the ball into the breeze to take six for 42 in 30.1 eight-ball overs. Though he did little in the Tests in England in 1948, Johnson reasserted himself in South Africa in 1949-50, taking five for 34 to help win the Durban Test. But his form declined after that, and he failed to make the 1953 tour of England. Later that year, he succeeded Lindsay Hassett as captain of Victoria, but there seemed little chance of him playing for Australia again. That changed after a pep-talk from Hassett himself at a New Year's Eve party, when he hinted that Johnson could be captain of Australia if only he put his mind to it. By the end of the year, the prophecy had come true. Johnson can hardly be remembered as a great Test captain: of his nine Ashes Tests in charge, in 1954-55 and 1956, Australia lost four and won just two. But his finest hour came in between those series when he led their first Test tour of the Caribbean, only 12 months after a notably bad-tempered visit by England. They won not merely the series but the people's hearts, with a charm offensive that led to much favourable comparison with the stand-offish English: "Ian did the best PR job of any captain I've ever seen," said Alan Davidson. But Johnson's own form was patchy, and this worsened the dressing-room tensions: some malcontents called him "myxomatosis" because he only bowled when the rabbits were in, and he was seen by others as dictatorial. The 1956 tour was unwinnable, and impossible to survive. After an epilogue in the subcontinent on the way home had mixed results, he retired.

The following year Johnson began the second half of his career. He was chosen ahead of 44 other candidates to be secretary of the Melbourne Cricket Club. This really did cement his place in the Australian establishment, but he was a progressive administrator: the MCG remained the beating heart of Australian sport, and Johnson was there, mostly smiling, through 26 years of dramatic change. For 56 years he was married to Lal, daughter of Roy Park, who played one Test for Australia. He had a knack for getting things right: on his South African tour in 1949-50 he wrote a series of pieces for the local paper, the *Sunday Express*. One touched on the racial question. "You're living in something of a fool's paradise," he warned.

KAYE, MICHAEL ARTHUR CHADWICK PORTER, TD, DL, who died on September 22, 1998, aged 82, was a medium-pace all-rounder and a Cambridge Blue in 1938. Batting No. 10, he hit 78 in 43 minutes for the University against MCC at Lord's in 1938, then went out and dismissed the first four MCC batsmen, including Compton for a duck. He played first-class cricket for Free Foresters after the war.

KELLY, EDWARD ARTHUR, died on October 7, 1998, aged 65. Ted Kelly was a fast-medium bowler who played four matches for Lancashire in 1957. He then lost both his out-swinger (apparently after taking advice) and his place, and returned to club cricket in Chorley.

KEMPSTER, MICHAEL EDMUND IVOR, QC, who died on May 28, 1998, aged 74, unsuccessfully represented the cricketing authorities in the High Court in the case brought by Tony Greig after the 1977 World Series Cricket schism. Shortly afterwards, he went to practise in Hong Kong, and became a judge. His favourite sport was beagling.

KING, LESTER ANTHONY, who died on July 9, 1998, aged 59, of a liver complaint, was one of West Indies' leading fast bowlers of the 1960s. Unfortunately for him, the presence of Hall, Griffith and the multi-talented Sobers confined him to just two Tests. But in 1961-62 he made perhaps the most sensational of all entries into international cricket, aged 23, after just two matches for his native Jamaica. He was called in to open the bowling with Wes Hall against India at Sabina Park, and took five wickets in his first four overs. That left India 26 for five, and he finished with five for 46. King took two more quick wickets in the second innings, and West Indies completed a 5-0 series win. But they played no more Tests until they visited England more than a year later, and by then King had been superseded by the more hostile Charlie Griffith. Though he took 47 first-class wickets at 27.31 on the tour, he was actually tenth in the tour bowling averages that remarkable year. King pulled out of the 1966 trip through injury and, though he went to India and Australasia subsequently, never got the chance to play an overseas Test. He was called back in to replace Griffith for the final Test against England at Georgetown in 1967-68, taking two further wickets, but his second chance was his last. King was nowhere near as fast as many modern West Indian bowlers, but he had command of swing and cut. He was a clean tail-end hitter, and his cheerful disposition kept him going through the various disappointments. He played a season for Bengal, and also for Rawtenstall in the Lancashire League.

KUBUNAVANUA, PETERO, who died on November 20, 1997, became a first-class cricketer retrospectively when the Fijian tour of New Zealand in 1947-48 was given first-class status more than 30 years later. He was a dashing left-handed bat and spectacular outfielder whose saves and spear-like throwing, barefoot and with his *sulu* (knee-length skirt) flying, delighted the crowds. His fielding action was depicted on a postage stamp to mark the centenary of cricket in Fiji. Kubunavanua had a fine solo voice and performed in concert halls on the tour; he made an impressive sight as well, with a ferocious countenance under a bush of hair. After fighting the Japanese in the Solomon Islands, he served in Malaya. Fielding at square leg in a state match there, he was irritated by a swallow flying round him, stuck out his hand, and put the bird in his *sulu* pocket.

LAITT, DAVID JAMES, who died on June 27, 1998, aged 67, played two first-class matches for the Minor Counties in 1959 and 1960. But his medium-paced leg-cutters were a legend on the Minor County circuit, and he took 670 wickets for Oxfordshire between 1952 and 1972.

LAMBA, RAMAN, the former Indian Test player, died in a Dhaka hospital on February 23, 1998, aged 38. Three days earlier he had been hit on the temple while fielding, without a helmet, at short leg in front of a substantial crowd at a big club match at the Bangabandhu Stadium. Lamba walked off the field and the injury appeared not to be serious, but he suffered an internal haemorrhage and his condition worsened dramatically. A neurosurgeon was flown in from Delhi but it was already too late. The news caused widespread grief in both India and Bangladesh. Lamba was a popular cricketer in India, but in Bangladesh he was a legend. He first went there to play club cricket in 1991, and was a key figure in the revival of interest in the game there. "I am the Don of Dhaka," he would joke to his Indian friends. The tragedy happened in Dhaka's traditional local derby between Mohammedans and Abahani, when Maharab Hossain, the Mohammedans' opener, played a full-blooded pull shot. Lamba had only moved in from the outfield that delivery and it was reported that he had already signalled for a helmet. Lamba was known to be fearless, though, as well as an exceptionally committed and enthusiastic player. The commitment sometimes went too far: he was banned for ten months after provoking Rashid Patel, who charged after him brandishing a stump in the 1990-91 Duleep Trophy final. Critics also pointed to his technical shortcomings, but he always hoped for a recall to the Indian team after his four indifferent Tests in the late 1980s: "Runs I am going to make," he would say, "then we shall see." And he did make runs. His career average was over 50: in 1996-97, his 19th season, he scored 1,034 runs in just 14 innings for Delhi in the Ranji Trophy. He was one of only two Indians (with Vijay Hazare) to score two triple-centuries: 320 for North Zone in the 1987-88 Duleep Trophy final, and 312 for Delhi against Himachal Pradesh in 1994-95. He had been chosen to tour England in 1986, but failed to make the Test team. He did, however, establish a lasting rapport with Ulster: he played club cricket there for 12 years, appeared four times for Ireland, and married an Irish girl. They had two children. "I admired his guts," said his former team-mate Maninder Singh. "He never believed he could be defeated." Only two cricketers are known to have died as a result of on-field injuries in a first-class fixture. Both were hit while batting: George Summers of Nottinghamshire on the head at Lord's

Raman Lamba fields close to the bat while playing for Ardmore in Northern Ireland in 1991.

in 1870; and Abdul Aziz, the Karachi wicket-keeper, over the heart in the 1958-59 Quaid-e-Azam final. The last first-class cricketer to die after being hit in any match was Ian Folley of Lancashire, playing for Whitehaven in 1993.

LEMMON, DAVID HECTOR, who died on October 25, 1998, aged 67, was a schoolteacher who turned into the most industrious of the writers to emerge from the great cricket-book boom of the 1980s. At his peak, there could be four Lemmons a year, and there were about 50 in all: inevitably, the quantity sometimes overwhelmed the quality. He wrote best about his enthusiasms, which in cricket meant anything to do with Essex. The *Benson and Hedges Cricket Year* (formerly the *Pelham Cricket Year*) was a remarkable annual achievement, and he had almost completed the 17th just before his final illness. He was a genial, chatty man and a good companion.

LESTER, GERALD, who died on January 26, 1998, aged 82, was one of Leicestershire cricket's most devoted sons. Gerry Lester was born in the county, at Long Whatton, and during his lifetime served the county club as a player (in 373 first-class matches), Second Eleven captain, coach and committee man. He joined the staff in 1937 and, after the war, turned into a reliable opening bat. Instinctively, he was a free-scoring player, but the pressures of professional cricket turned him into one of the circuit's stodgier batsmen. If he was rarely entertaining, he was always brave, and would take regular blows on the body, stuffing a few pound notes in his pocket to serve as an impromptu thigh pad. Lester was also a gifted leg-spin and googly bowler who could find substantial turn, but rarely got a bowl when the county could call on Jack Walsh and Vic Jackson. As a coach, he tried to instil his own work ethic: "Get stuck in" was his catchphrase. He was still watching cricket at Grace Road the summer before he died.

LISTER, WILLIAM HUBERT LIONEL, died on July 29, 1998, aged 86. Lionel Lister captained Lancashire from 1936 to 1939, when the county was in retreat after a decade of success, and was sometimes criticised for unwise declarations and failing to show command. But, overall, he is remembered as a good leader of a declining team, notably short of fast bowling, and was much liked by his men. He was also a batsman of spasmodic magnificence. He scored a century against Middlesex in his second match for the county, in 1933, and made 96 in 100 minutes at Worcester later that season. In 1934 he played an innings of great courage at Trent Bridge when being pummelled by Larwood and Voce. As captain, the great innings were infrequent, though Neville Cardus was ecstatic when Lister made just 34 in the 1937 Roses match at Sheffield: "boundaries as good as any cricketer could wish to make or to see . . . a brave and dashing and good-looking innings". In August 1939, Lister was padded up at Northampton when he was summoned to join his territorial regiment. He said goodbye to his team-mates (he was recorded as "absent . . . 0"), and never played another first-class match, though some were amazed that he was not contacted when Lancashire were desperate for a captain in 1946; he was still only 34. Lister was the son of the managing director of Cunard, and had been a successful batsman at Malvern. At Cambridge, he failed to get a cricket Blue, but won a soccer Blue three times, and four amateur international caps as a wing-half. He was a brigade-major in the Normandy landings, though his moneyed background enabled him to live a post-war life of some ease. This included plenty of golf and regular visits to Old Trafford.

LIVINGSTON, LEONARD, died on January 16, 1998, aged 77. "Jock" Livingston was among the best of the Australians who gave up all hope of playing Test cricket by joining an English county after the war. Livingston played five matches for New South Wales between 1941 and 1947, making a century against Queensland, and might have been a contender for the 1948 tour of England. But a much younger left-hander, Neil Harvey, was chosen, and Livingston came to England to make a living. The Northamptonshire coach Jack Mercer spotted him playing for Royton while on a mission to spy on an opposing bowler who Livingston kept hooking. He signed for Northamptonshire in 1950 when already 30, and immediately began to play a vital role in the county's revival under Freddie Brown, just missing 2,000 runs in his first season. He did pass 2,000 three years running, 1954 to 1956, and finished his career with 34 centuries and an average of 45.01. But Livingston made another, even more vital, contribution to Northamptonshire, taking on the role of recruiting-sergeant himself, and encouraging the county to sign both Keith Andrew and his fellow-Australian, George Tribe. Livingston was a thrilling bat – perhaps the best left-hander in county cricket at the time – who could murder slow bowling and was especially quick to get back and lash anything wide: "he was like lightning on his feet," Andrew recalled. At Northampton, he once hit three sixes off Jim Laker against the spin, every one landing on the bowling green next door. At Wellingborough in 1955, Northamptonshire were set an apparently ungenerous 332 in 217 minutes by Essex: Livingston scored an unbeaten 172 in 160 minutes as his team won with seven wickets and 15 minutes to spare. He was also a brilliant cover fielder and, when necessary, a very capable wicket-keeper. Jock was a teetotaller but was always chirpy, even voluble, which did not endear him to all his colleagues. But he loved the game and for many years remained a presence on the English circuit as a sales executive for the batmakers Gray-Nicolls, before he returned to Sydney. His ashes were flown back to be buried in Royton.

McCAULLY, BARRY DESMOND ANSELM, who died on November 16, 1998, aged 65, after a long illness, was a leading statistician. He was a Home Counties solicitor who took over the *Wisden* record section in 1983 and did the job for three years; he was associated with the *Cricketer Quarterly* from its inception in 1973, and was a contributor to many other publications.

Jackie McGlew: sweeping Fred Titmus at Arundel in 1960.

McGLEW, DERRICK JOHN, died from a blood disorder in Pretoria on June 9, 1998, aged 69. Jackie McGlew became synonymous with South African cricket in the 1950s. His batting fitted his name: he was a sticker, and concentration, discipline, commitment and athleticism were the abiding virtues of his own game, and that of his team. He became famous – or notorious – for some of Test cricket's slowest innings. He batted nine hours 35 minutes for 105 against Australia at Durban in 1957-58; his 545-minute century remained the slowest in first-class cricket for 20 years. "Although as a feat of endurance and concentration it was remarkable," said *Wisden*, "it is doubtful whether South Africa benefited by it." They led by 221 on first innings but could not bowl Australia out.

McGlew grew up in Natal, and was pictured waving a bat as a four-year-old. He went on to captain the province's schoolboys, and made his debut for Natal in 1947-48. In 1951 he was picked to tour England on the strength of 138 in a 12-a-side (and thus non-first-class) Test trial at Kingsmead. He hit 40 when South Africa won at Trent Bridge but failed in his next three innings, and was dropped. But he scored consistently in the county games, and his agile fielding in the deep was widely noted. When the young South Africa team stunned Australia by drawing their series 18 months later, McGlew was established as the opening bat and, aged only 23, as vice-captain. Though he missed the crucial win at the MCG through injury, he returned in New Zealand with 255 not out in eight hours 54 minutes, then South Africa's highest Test score. He was on the field throughout the match. Back in England in 1955, he scored centuries in both South Africa's Test wins, at Manchester and Leeds, having bagged a pair at Lord's the game before. McGlew was captain in both games because Jack Cheetham was injured; South Africa lost the other three Tests. McGlew was a Cricketer of the Year; *Wisden* noted both his dourness at the crease and his vitality in the field. "Attrition is not a popular method of progress. McGlew himself has not always batted this way, but circumstances wrought the change of style."

A shoulder injury forced him to miss all but one Test against England in 1956-57, when he had been appointed captain, and his deputy Clive van Ryneveld kept the job for the home series against Australia a year later, though McGlew stood in for him in the opening Test, and scored another century. By the end of the decade, much of the zest that had characterised Cheetham's side had gone from South Africa's cricket. They came back to England in 1960, with McGlew now entrenched in the captaincy. But it was a grim series in a wet summer – "The Sad Season" according to *Wisden* – dominated inside the grounds by the throwing controversy, with small and, as yet, little-noticed demonstrations against apartheid outside the grounds. McGlew himself had a very poor series, which might have been a mercy given that attendances were declining rapidly anyway. He finished his Test career against New Zealand in 1961-62 with a century in his penultimate Test, and a dislocated shoulder in the last. He continued playing for Natal for another five seasons. McGlew also bowled leg-breaks very occasionally, and took only 35 wickets in his career, but three came in a hat-trick, spread over two innings for Natal v Transvaal in 1963-64 – his best bowling figures were actually two for four.

South Africa's next cricketing generation was more charismatic, but doomed to isolation: McGlew had been a supporter of apartheid and agreed to stand as a National Party candidate in provincial elections in 1969 before withdrawing for business reasons. He later backed away from politics, and retreated into religion. When South Africa made its first tentative steps back into the real world in 1991-92, McGlew was chosen as manager of the ground-breaking Under-19 team to the West Indies. He was a rather intense man, at his best enthusing youngsters with his delight in the game, and when the chips were down on the field. "He had such guts," said his friend Johnny Waite. "Jackie never flinched or turned a hair."

MEAKIN, DOUGLAS, who died on February 13, 1998, aged 68, was a fast bowling all-rounder who played four first-class matches for Combined Services between 1959 and 1962 while in the RAF. He appeared regularly for Bedfordshire.

MEHTA, SORABHJII RUSTOMIJI, who died on May 2, 1998, aged 84, was a member of the Hyderabad team which won the Ranji Trophy in 1937-38. Mehta played for Hyderabad over 14 seasons as an off-spinning all-rounder. While still in the team, he became secretary of the Hyderabad Cricket Association.

MORLEY, COLLEEN, who died after a short illness on April 11, 1998, aged 56, was the first woman umpire to officiate in the Yorkshire League. She was also secretary of the Wombwell Cricket Lovers' Society.

NAGARWALLA, NUSSERWANJEE DORAB, who died on September 10, 1998, aged 88, umpired five Tests in India, mainly in the 1950s. He had played for Maharashtra and scored 98, going in No. 10, in a stand of 245 with V. S. Hazare against Baroda in 1939-40, the fourth highest ninth-wicket stand of all time; Hazare scored 316 not out.

NELSON, Major PETER MAURICE, who died on February 12, 1998, aged 84, was a successful schoolboy batsman at Marlborough who scored 62 in his only first-class match, for The Army v Cambridge University at Fenner's in 1939, and played with Douglas Jardine for the Royal Berkshire Regiment. Nelson became a well-known racehorse trainer, and trained Snow Knight, the 50-1 winner of the 1974 Derby.

OAKLEY, HECTOR HERBERT, who died on December 19, 1998, aged 89, scored three Sheffield Shield centuries for Victoria, all against South Australia at the MCG, in the early 1930s. He was made twelfth man for the Australian XI against MCC in

1932-33, but his form fell away. After three years out of the state side, Oakley was recalled to lead a second-string team against Tasmania in 1938-39, and at Hobart scored 162 in 175 minutes; on the strength of that he was brought back for two more Shield matches that season.

OSBORNE, JOHN, who died of cancer on November 7, 1998, aged 57, was commercial manager of Worcestershire from 1986 to 1995. He was better known as the West Bromwich Albion goalkeeper, and won a FA Cup winner's medal in 1968.

OSWALD, DENIS GEOFFREY, who died on February 5, 1998, aged 87, was a batsman who played two matches for Oxford University in 1931. He is thought to be the only first-class cricketer born on the Falkland Islands.

PARIS, CECIL GERARD ALEXANDER, who died on April 4, 1998, aged 86, was the first chairman of the Test and County Cricket Board. He was a Southampton lawyer who held the post from 1968 to 1975, and then became President of MCC. Paris used his legal expertise, fair-mindedness and pleasant manner to help smooth the administrative transition from MCC control to the new era. He was a conscientious rather than high-profile or dynamic administrator; the major crisis of his term, involving South Africa, was handled by the Cricket Council rather than the TCCB, and Paris played a subsidiary role. His major work was done on such subjects as county registration and benefits. As a player, he had been low-key as well, appearing in 98 matches for Hampshire between 1933 and 1948; he was captain in 1938. His batting was mostly defensive, though he hit a fast unbeaten 134 against Northamptonshire at Bournemouth in 1935. "He possessed the rare talent of making others feel good about themselves," wrote Jack Bailey, "while pursuing his own rightful objectives with much skill and determination."

PHEBEY, ARTHUR HENRY, who died on June 28, 1998, aged 73, was a mainstay of Kent's batting through the 1950s. He became ensconced as the opening bat in 1952, first with Arthur Fagg then Bob Wilson. Though Kent were a poor side, they often had good starts. The word most used about Phebey was "meticulous". His sleeves were rolled up inch-perfect; his strokes were graceful, yet careful. He played 327 matches in all, scored 14,643 runs at 25.91, and passed 1,000 runs every year from 1952 to 1960: of his 13 centuries, his first, last and highest (157) all came against Gloucestershire; none came at Canterbury. Phebey had been a fine amateur footballer yet was considered a moderate fielder, perhaps because he was not all that strong physically. Later, he became a successful property developer, and ran *Building* magazine. He was also a keen golfer.

PITMAN, RAYMOND WALTER CHARLES, died on June 5, 1998, aged 65. Ray Pitman was an aggressive batsman who played 50 games for Hampshire in the 1950s without quite making the grade. He scored 77 against Derbyshire in 1958, and went on to be coach and groundsman at Rydal School.

POWER, TERRENCE JOHN, died on October 23, 1998, aged 59, after a short illness. Terry Power had been the *Wisden* correspondent in New Zealand since 1994, and for *Wisden Cricket Monthly* since the magazine began in 1979. He also wrote widely for local publications. Power's reports for *Wisden* were pleasingly trenchant, especially when he was detailing administrative bungles. As a former schoolteacher, he never lost his enthusiasm for school sport, or for New Zealand country cricket, and was an especially gifted obituarist. His well-researched and lovingly crafted anecdotes of old-time Kiwi farm-boy players will be greatly missed.

PRICE, COLIN MICHAEL, died on October 23, 1998, from a heart attack while on holiday in Kenya, aged 50. He was rugby correspondent and No. 2 cricket writer for the *Daily Mirror* – having earlier worked for the *Daily Star*. At the major cricket matches, he was usually the "quotes man", a job that sometimes shades into the less reputable end of journalism, but Price's charm and smile won him far more friends than enemies. David Graveney and Clive Woodward, the England rugby coach, were both among the mourners at his funeral, though they did not speak. "In life," wrote his old colleague Paul Weaver, "Pricey would not have allowed them such a luxury."

PRIEM, WILLIAM CHARLES, who died on April 11, 1998, aged 79, was a Brisbane-based umpire who stood in 19 first-class matches over ten seasons from 1962-63. In his second game, he called Ian Meckiff for throwing.

RADCLIFFE, HAROLD TALBOT, died in May 1998 aged 90. Toll Radcliffe created his own privately owned ground at Bodedern in Anglesey after the war. At the golden jubilee game against MCC in 1997, Radcliffe ordered his gamekeeper to shoot 11 ducks and hang them on the opposition's pegs. He was a famous breeder of English springer spaniels.

RANASINGHE, ANURA NANDANA, who died suddenly in his sleep on November 9, 1998, aged 42, represented Sri Lanka in the 1975 World Cup as an 18-year-old schoolboy. Nearly seven years later, when Sri Lanka played their inaugural Test, he was squeezed out of a place in the team by Arjuna Ranatunga, but was chosen later that year, for one game each against Pakistan and India. In Faisalabad he opened the bowling with his left-arm medium-pace; in Madras he scored 77. However, Ranasinghe's career stuttered to a halt when he joined the 1982-83 Sri Lankan rebel tour to South Africa and, along with 13 others, was banned for 25 years. Only in his last year, when he became a coach at the Bloomfield club, did he start to return to the game. Ranasinghe could bowl slow left-arm as well, and was an effective fielder; he played nine one-day internationals and, but for the ban, that figure would have been far higher. He is the second Sri Lankan Test player to die, after Sridharan Jeganathan.

RANSOM, VICTOR JOSEPH, who died on September 22, 1998, aged 81, was an amateur all-rounder. He made 34 appearances for Hampshire between 1947 and 1950, batting aggressively and bowling fast-medium, and was capped in 1949. He later played twice for Surrey and captained their Second Eleven.

REVILL, ALAN CHAMBERS, who died on July 6, 1998, aged 75, was hardly the best-known cricketer of the immediate post-war era, but many of his contemporaries considered him the most charismatic. He epitomised county cricket as a way of life – and a wonderful one at that – rather than just a profession. Revill spent the first 12 seasons after the war with Derbyshire, then had three years with Leicestershire. He was a very decent batsman, passing 1,000 runs nine times in a flamboyant style which was successful enough, except against really quick bowling. On the circuit, he was better-known for two other attributes. One was his fielding: in the days before any restrictions, he was an amazing leg slip; flanked by Donald Carr and Derek Morgan, he was at the heart of a formidable leg-trap which snapped up any edge created by Cliff Gladwin's in-swingers. Revill had a long reach and was a phenomenal catcher, if rather inclined to let his team-mates chase anything that did get past him. But, above all, he was a talker. Since he was funny, wholly without malice, and thoroughly sporting, opponents used to enjoy the experience as much as his team-mates. "The perfect companion," Morgan called him. His love for cricket never diminished: he played on, for Berkshire and any touring side he could find. In later years, he was usually at Lord's, holding court in the bar, supping ale and dispensing cricketing lore and wit. "He could talk the leg off an iron pot," wrote Michael Parkinson.

RICHARDSON, ALLEN, who died on September 20, 1998, aged 71, was a tall fast bowler from north Nottinghamshire. He made a promising home debut for the county in 1949 with figures of three for 25 in 16 overs against Hampshire. He had natural pace, but failed to progress, not helped by the bland Trent Bridge wickets. Injury forced him out of the game in 1951.

RIDDINGTON, ANTHONY, died on February 25, 1998, aged 86. Tony "Pant" Riddington was a left-handed bat and left-arm slowish bowler from Countesthorpe who played 128 matches for Leicestershire between 1931 and 1950. He scored a stylish 104 not out at Northampton in 1946 and, two days later, began an epic match against Yorkshire. He returned first-innings figures of 27.2–8–34–5, and then saved the match in a 35-minute last-wicket stand with 18-year-old Vic Munden. Most of Riddington's cricket was in the leagues, though, especially in Scotland; while with Kilmarnock he did the double of 1,000 runs and 100 wickets. He later became coach at Uppingham.

RIDINGS, PHILIP LOVETT, AO, died on September 13, 1998, aged 80. Phil Ridings was captain of South Australia for 12 years, starting as Bradman's deputy and then taking the job in his own right; he exemplified what remains a tradition of aggressive South Australian captains. Later, he was both an ally and a successor of Bradman as one of Australia's leading administrators. Ridings was one of four brothers who dominated the West Torrens club, one of Adelaide's finest: his brother Ken, who was thought likely to play for Australia, was killed in the war. His father was an umpire, and was standing when Phil made his first-class debut. Ridings became an effective middle-order bat, and scored nine centuries, including an unbeaten 186 against Victoria in 1947-48. Five years later, he took South Australia to the Shield without losing a game. He toured New Zealand with a non-Test team in 1949-50, and was sometimes talked about as a Test possible. He may have been in contention for the 1953 tour of England, but made himself unavailable (reports vary) either out of delicacy because he was himself a selector or because his business was just taking off. When Bradman retired as a selector in 1971, Ridings again replaced him; he rapidly became chairman and remained in the post until 1984. From 1980 to 1983 he was also chairman of the Australian Cricket Board. He cut a confident figure in everything he did.

ROBINSON, ELLIS PEMBROKE, who died on November 10, 1998, aged 87, was the last surviving regular from the great Yorkshire team of 1939. He was an off-spinner who played in six Championship-winning teams in nine seasons before and after the war. And in the last pre-war Roses match, at Headingley, he finished the game by taking eight for 35. "Robinson looked a terrifying bowler," wrote Neville Cardus. "I have seen no more impossible, more devastating off-spin since Parkin's heyday." It was seven years before he had the chance to show similar form again, but he took 167 wickets on the wet pitches of 1946, and finished with 1,009 in his career. Always a big spinner of the ball, on less friendly pitches Robinson would often bowl too short. But allied to his batting was his catching: he took six, still a Yorkshire record, in an hour when Leicestershire collapsed at Bradford in 1938. After Brian Close emerged, he finished his career with three seasons at Somerset, and had match figures of 15 for 78 against Sussex at Weston-super-Mare in 1951. But the Robinsons came from the mining village of Denaby, and he did not care much for exile.

ROSS, KENNETH HULME, who died on February 24, 1998, aged 86, was a left-handed opening bat and the last survivor of the 1936 Canadian touring team to England. He scored 42 not out for Montreal against the 1939 West Indians, when they went home from England early due to the war.

ROWAN, ATHOL MATTHEW BURCHELL, who died on February 21, 1998, aged 77, was one of South Africa's best off-spinners. He played 15 Tests, all against England, between 1947 and 1951, and made a speciality of dismissing Len Hutton: 11 times in all, including five in a row at the end of the 1948-49 series and the First Test of 1951. Morally, the figure might be 12: he was the bowler at The Oval when Hutton was given out for obstruction after impeding wicket-keeper Russell Endean as he tried to take a simple catch. Hutton rated Rowan almost as high as Laker. Rowan's achievements were the more remarkable since his leg was damaged by a wartime explosion: he was unable to put his full weight on the front foot, often bowled in pain, and sometimes in leg irons. In his way, he was as courageous as his famously older brother Eric, but Athol's way was more good-humoured and quiet. He also suffered slightly different privations on the 1947 tour: England was still in the grip of rationing, and Rowan was a famous trencherman. Before the war, he had bowled fast-medium. When he came back, having escaped from the Germans when taken prisoner in the Western desert, he turned into an off-spinner while retaining something more like a seam bowler's grip. His most dramatic performance came at The Wanderers in 1949-50, when he took nine for 19 as Transvaal bowled the mighty Australians out for 84. Set 69 to win, Transvaal were bowled out for 53 themselves. But Rowan's captain, Dudley Nourse, singled out his performance against England at Port Elizabeth a year earlier when he bowled almost unchanged for figures of 60–9–167–5. "It had to be seen to be appreciated," wrote Nourse. "As I called on his reserve of energy he unfailingly gave his best without ever a murmur . . . A wholehearted bowler is Athol Rowan, but not a lucky one." He missed the Tests against Australia through injury, and the pain forced him to retire after the 1951 tour of England.

SANSOM, DESMOND ARTHUR, who died on June 28, 1998, aged 64, was the only umpire to give a player out for obstruction in a South African first-class match. The victim was Trevor Quirk at East London in 1978-79, when he deflected an attempted run-out by hitting the ball with his bat.

SARJOO, NEVILLE, was shot dead outside his currency-exchange business in Georgetown on May 30, 1998, aged 52. Sarjoo was treasurer of the Guyana Cricket Board and an enthusiastic administrator, credited with the revival of the game in the East Bank Demerara area.

SHEPHERD, DONALD ARTHUR, OBE, who died on May 29, 1998, aged 82, was captain of the Leeds Grammar School team and played a solitary first-class match as an Oxford undergraduate. Though he was not good enough for the university team, Shepherd played for Yorkshire at The Parks in 1938, when Arthur Mitchell was injured, and they needed a Yorkshire-born replacement in a hurry. He was out for nought and did not bowl or take a catch. Shepherd did, however, have a few games for the second team later that summer and did a little better. He became a civil servant in the Colonial Service.

SHERMAN, HUGH PETER, MBE, died on June 15, 1998, aged 76. Peter Sherman scored 64 not out at Lord's in 1939 for Marlborough against Rugby. He became a district commissioner in Sudan, wearing, according to *The Times*, "the traditional bush jacket, long shorts and topi with ostrich feather . . . dispensing justice among the Dinka tribesmen and their chiefs, who wore nothing at all except, for important occasions, pork pie hats." Sherman later became a director of MI5.

SKINNER, DAVID ANTHONY, who died on January 17, 1998, aged 77, played occasionally for Derbyshire in the late 1940s and captained them in 1949. The side badly missed George Pope, and dropped from sixth to 15th. Skinner, a useful club player, contributed little except for enthusiastic fielding, mainly at cover point, and resigned after the season. His elder brother Alan had played for the county before the war and – unusually even for that era – captained Northamptonshire in his only game for them, against the New Zealanders in 1949, the day after they had beaten Derbyshire, led by David.

SMITH, KENNETH DESMOND, who died on May 31, 1998, aged 76, was a batsman who played regularly for Leicestershire in 1950 and 1951. He made an unbeaten 70 at Northampton in 1950. His sons David (also K. D.) and Paul both played for Warwickshire.

SNOW, EDWARD ERIC, died on September 18, 1998, aged 88, the day before his beloved Leicestershire won the County Championship. Eric Snow served the club in many non-playing capacities, including 40 years as librarian and 30 years on the committee, and wrote two histories of the club. He also wrote a history of Sir Julien Cahn's XI. He was a fount of knowledge on Leicestershire lore, cricketing and general. His elder brother was C. P. (later Lord) Snow the writer; his younger brother Philip represented Fiji on ICC.

SOPER, Rev. Baron, died on December 22, 1998, aged 95. Donald Soper was a Methodist preacher and orator of enormous power, a staunch pacifist, and one of Britain's most famous 20th-century churchmen. As a schoolboy, at Aske's, Hatcham, just after the First World War, he was a bowler of considerable pace. In a school match, a ball bowled by Soper bounced and hit the batsman over the heart. The boy died. William Purcell wrote in *A Portrait of Soper*: "The degree to which this upset Donald at the time and the persistence of the memory of it – he was recalling it 50 years later – suggest an abhorrence of violence which was possibly an unconscious ingredient of his later pacifism."

SUTCLIFFE, WILLIAM HERBERT HOBBS, died on September 16, 1998, aged 71. Billy Sutcliffe captained Yorkshire in 1956 and 1957; he was also the son of the great Herbert Sutcliffe. These two facts were widely held to be connected, which made Sutcliffe's task more difficult than it already was. He took over Yorkshire at what was, by their then standards, a very low ebb, with Surrey dominating county cricket. In his first season in charge they fell to seventh and, though they rose to third in 1957, there was clear disunity in the dressing-room, and Sutcliffe was considered too lax. Many spectators could never forgive him for not being as good a bat as his father. But when Sutcliffe was appointed, he was well worth his place in the side: in 1955 he had scored three centuries and come second in the county averages behind Willie Watson. Given the (now quaint-seeming) notion that the captain had to be an amateur, Sutcliffe was the obvious choice. But his form fell away completely. It returned only when he resigned and went back to club cricket: he was the first batsman to make 1,000 runs in a Yorkshire League season. "He was a damn good cricketer," wrote Don Mosey, "who might have become better but for the millstone of his parentage." He remained a committee man, and was often in the thick of the club's many traumas over the next three decades before being swept from office in the pro-Geoff Boycott landslide at the committee elections of 1984. In 1969 and 1970, he was a Test selector and was thus partly responsible for handing the England captaincy to Ray Illingworth, the epitome of the Yorkshire professional.

SWANTON, ANN MARION, who died on November 23, 1998, aged 87, had been married to the cricket writer E. W. Swanton for 40 years. She was a gifted golfer, musician and artist.

TRICKER, DUDLEY D. L., who was killed in a car crash in the Eastern Cape on May 10, 1998, aged 53, played 18 matches as a batsman for Border in the 1960s. Tricker's finest hour came in 1969-70 when, in a remarkable match against Orange Free State, he and Ray Watson-Smith shared a seventh-wicket stand of 208. Watson-Smith was making his debut, and scored 310 in three matches before being dismissed in first-class cricket. Tricker made 68. There were claims that Border might have done even better had not one of the umpires been a Free State selector.

TWISELTON, FRANK J., who died on August 31, 1998, aged 79, was chairman (1973-75) and president (1990-92) of Gloucestershire. He was also a patron of cricket through his management job at Whitbread brewery.

WEEKES, KENNETH HUNNELL, died on February 9, 1998, aged 86. "Bam Bam" Weekes played one of the great early Test innings for West Indies when he enthralled the crowd at The Oval just two weeks before the outbreak of the Second World War. Weekes put on 163 in 100 minutes with Vic Stollmeyer, 43 coming in four overs against the new ball, with Weekes hitting four consecutive fours off Reg Perks. He finished with 137 in two and a quarter hours. Two months earlier at Lord's, Neville Cardus had declared him "hopelessly short of aim and eyesight", and thought he shaped like a left-hander batting the wrong way round. Weekes was dropped, then recalled after scoring 146 against Surrey; Cardus later admitted that he could "hit like a mule". These were the only two Tests Weekes played (and he thus had an average of 57.66) though he continued to play for Jamaica until 1947. He was brought up in Jamaica, his mother's home island, and his father was Barbadian, but he was born in Boston, Massachussetts. He went back to the US after the war, worked as a nurse, and died in New York, the father of six children. He claimed no kinship with Everton Weekes.

WHEELHOUSE, ALAN, who died from cancer on August 28, 1998, aged 64, had been chairman of Nottinghamshire since 1994; he was one of the most influential figures in English cricket administration. His stature was such that he was elected to the management board of the ECB as a representative of the 12 counties who do not stage Test cricket, even though he came from a county which does stage Tests. He won a Blue at Cambridge in 1959 and played one match for Nottinghamshire in 1961, opening the bowling against Glamorgan, and taking four wickets in a style which E. W. Swanton once likened to "an arthritic centipede". Thereafter, Wheelhouse concentrated on his career in the law and was senior partner in a large Nottingham legal practice. Lord MacLaurin, the ECB chairman, called his contribution "immense".

WILLIAMS, CECIL BEAUMONT, OBE, died on September 20, 1998, aged 72. "Monty" or "Boogles" Williams was a Barbadian leg-spinning all-rounder who made a dramatic entry to regional cricket in 1948-49, with six for 28, and 108, in his first two matches, both against Trinidad. He was chosen for the 1950 tour of England but found himself wholly overshadowed by his fellow slow bowlers Ramadhin and Valentine. Against a powerful MCC team at Lord's, Williams took seven for 55, but he made few runs anywhere, and failed to make the Test team. His finest hour may have come in 1955-56 when he captained Barbados against E. W. Swanton's XI, and took 133 off an attack headed by Frank Tyson. Later he became a diplomat, and was High Commissioner to London and Ottawa, and Ambassador to Washington. His brother is Chief Justice of Barbados.

WORDSWORTH, CHRISTOPHER WILLIAM VAUGHAN, who died on October 15, 1998, aged 83, epitomised the breed of eccentrics who used to report county cricket for the posher Sunday papers. In his younger days he was an adventurer who tried to eke out a living in Wales by his skill as a fly-fisherman; later he eked out an even more precarious living reviewing books for *The Guardian* and *The Observer*. On

Saturdays, he would write erudite and literate reports on rugby or cricket, dictated in a booming voice, and was a familiar, shambling figure on the county circuit, liked by his colleagues, except by those who remembered him as The Man Who Broke The Only Phone At Horsham.

WRIGHT, DOUGLAS VIVIAN PARSON, died on November 13, 1998, aged 84, after several years of ill-health. Doug Wright was the finest English leg-spinner, perhaps the most dangerous of all English bowlers, in the years just before and after the war. A Kentishman, from Sidcup, he made his debut for the county in 1932 aged 17, but did not become a regular for another four years until "Tich" Freeman's final season. By 1938, he was in the Test team against Australia, and at Leeds came close to bowling them to a remarkable victory, dismissing Bradman, McCabe and Hassett as Australia sought a mere 105 for victory. For most of his 34 Tests, he was bowling in difficult circumstances with little support. Often he *was* the spin attack, as in Australia in 1946-47 when he and Bedser bowled almost 500 eight-ball overs between them. Against South Africa at Lord's in 1947, he took ten for 175, but there were many more days of abject frustration.

Wright began as a quick bowler who liked to turn his wrist and slip in the odd spinner; later he reversed the proportions. But his quicker ball remained so fast that Godfrey Evans had to signal the slips to move deeper, and even his stock ball had a rare fizz to it. Everyone agreed – and Bradman and Hammond were among his chief admirers – that on his day Wright was unplayable. But he gave the batsmen a chance to score too. "With his technique," wrote David Frith, "running in from over 15 yards, hopping and skipping as he went, and whipping over a wristy and finger-spun ball that would dip, bounce and deviate crazily off the pitch, to expect long-term accuracy was to display a dismal ignorance of physics." "He never ever bowled a ball defensively," said Lord Cowdrey, his team-mate at Kent. "Every ball was bowled to take a wicket."

He took seven hat-tricks, more than anyone else in history, and 100 wickets in a season ten times. In 1954, Doug Wright became Kent's first professional captain, though his natural diffidence did not obviously lend itself to leadership and, as so often in his career, he had a weak team around him: Kent slid nearer the bottom each season. At the end of each day, he would take his shoes and socks off and apologise to his poor old feet. "Sorry, boys," he would say, "but you're going to be needed again tomorrow." He retired aged 43, and in 1959 succeeded George Geary as coach at Charterhouse. Everyone liked Doug Wright. Cowdrey remembers him being asked about the best over he ever bowled. "Bowling to the Don at Lord's," he said. "Every ball came out of my hand the way I wanted and pitched where I wanted. I beat him twice. It went for 16."

CAREER FIGURES OF TEST CRICKETERS

	Tests				First-class			
	Runs	Avge	Wkts	Avge	Runs	Avge	Wkts	Avge
Atkinson, E. St E...	126	15.75	25	23.56	696	21.75	61	26.72
Birkett, L. S.	136	17.00	1	71.00	1,295	33.20	9	56.00
Desai, R. B.......	418	13.48	74	37.31	2,384	18.19	468	24.10
Freer, F. W.	28	–	3	24.66	1,284	32.10	104	27.75
Gadkari, C. V.	129	21.50	0	–	3,024	40.32	48	30.47
Ghulam Ahmed.	192	8.72	68	30.17	1,379	14.36	407	22.57
Grieveson, R. E....	114	57.00	–	–	1,130	33.23	0	–
Johnson, I. W.	1,000	18.51	109	29.19	4,905	22.92	619	23.30
King, L. A.	41	10.25	9	17.11	1,404	20.64	142	31.42
Lamba, C.	102	20.40	–	–	8,776	53.84	6	70.50
McGlew, D. J.	2,440	42.06	0	–	12,170	45.92	35	26.62
Ranasinghe, A. N...	88	22.00	1	69.00	1,664	23.77	39	42.64
Rowan, A. M. B...	290	17.05	54	38.59	1,492	24.06	273	23.47
Weekes, K. H.	173	57.66	–	–	1,731	40.25	12	38.66
Wright, D. V. P. ...	289	11.11	108	39.11	5,903	12.34	2,056	23.98

DIRECTORY OF CRICKET SUPPLIERS

BOWLING MACHINES

STUART & WILLIAMS (BOLA), 6 Brookfield Road, Cotham, Bristol BS6 5PQ; e-mail: info@bola.co.uk; web site: www.bola.co.uk. Manufacturers of bowling machines and ball throwing machines for all sports. Machines for recreational and commercial application. UK and overseas.

COMPUTER DATABASES

RIC FINLAY. Test cricket, standard and professional, ODI, Sheffield Shield for IBM-compatible computers. **214 Warwick Street, West Hobart, Tasmania, Australia 7000. Tel/fax: +61 3623 10193; e-mail: ricf@netspace.net.au.**

GORDON VINCE. The Cricket Statistics System is used worldwide to produce the widest range of averages and statistics, from Test to village level. Also available with an extensive range of up-to-date databases of matches from around the world. **5 Chaucer Grove, Camberley, Surrey GU15 2XZ.**

CRICKET EQUIPMENT

DUNCAN FEARNLEY DISTRIBUTION, Mill Race Lane, Stourbridge, West Midlands DY8 1JN. Tel: 01384-370898; fax: 01384-444969. Makers of the finest hand-made English willow bats, and suppliers of a complete range of cricket equipment, including pads, gloves, clothing, footwear and accessories.

NOMAD BOX COMPANY, Rockingham Road, Market Harborough, Leicestershire LE16 7QE. Tel: 01858-464878. Manufacturer of the original "cricket coffin", available in ten colours. Also aluminium framed cases with or without wheels.

PEAK SPORTS, Unit 4, Ford Street, Brinksway, Stockport SK3 0BT. Suppliers of quality PS cricket equipment and clothing. UK agents for Wimbledon Unreal Grass, the professional's choice for practice and play. **Tel: 0161-480 2502; fax: 0161-480 1652** for colour brochure.

PLATYPUS (UK) LTD. Suppliers of genuine hand-stitched quality Australian leather cricket balls. For shops and clubs. **Web site: www.lexicon.net/platypus/platypus.htm; 31 Cotswold Avenue, Wrose, Shipley, West Yorkshire BD18 1LS. Tel: 01274-826758; fax: 01274-598696.**

READERS, Teston, Kent ME18 5AW. Tel: 01622-812230. Leading manufacturer of cricket balls. The Sovereign is claimed to be the best ball available. Major supplier to senior/premier leagues throughout the country. BSI approved.

CRICKET TOURS

ALL-WAYS PACIFIC SPORTS TRAVEL, 4 The Green, Chalfont St Giles, Buckinghamshire HP8 4QF. Tel: 01494-875757; fax: 01494-874747. Specialist tour operators to the South Pacific. Worldwide cricket supporters' tours include Australia, New Zealand and South Africa.

***SPORT ABROAD**, the official travel agent for the ECB, are the acknowledged experts in arranging cricket supporters' tours (South Africa v England 1999-2000), corporate hospitality and club and school tours, at home and overseas. **Tel/fax: 01306-744345/744380.**

SUN LIVING, 10 Milton Court, Ravenshead, Nottingham NG15 9BD. Tel: 01623-795365; fax: 01623-797421. Worldwide specialists in cricket tours for all levels and ages, plus our ever popular supporters' tours. ABTA and ATOL bonded.

WISDEN ENGLAND SUPPORTERS' TOURS, in association with **Sunsport Tours, 66 Palmerston Road, Northampton NN1 5EX. Tel/fax: 01604-631626/631628; e-mail: paul@sunsport.co.uk.** Millennium tours for Tests and safaris in South Africa and Zimbabwe, November 1999–February 2000.

ELECTRONIC CRICKET SCOREBOARDS

EUROPEAN TIMING SYSTEMS, Oldbury-on-Severn, Bristol BS35 1PL. Tel: 01454-413606; fax: 01454-415139. New installations or modifying existing manual boards. Easy to operate, portable plug-in controllers for remote operation or from inside the scorebox.

LIMITED-EDITION PRINTS

DD DESIGNS, 40 Willowbank, Tamworth, Staffordshire B78 3LS. Tel: 01827-69950. Specialists in signed limited edition prints. Official producer of *Wisden's* "Cricketers of the Year" sets and other art portfolios.

MAIL-ORDER/RETAIL CRICKET SPECIALISTS

FORDHAM SPORTS CRICKET EQUIPMENT SPECIALIST, 81 Robin Hood Way, Kingston Vale, London SW15 3PW. Largest range of branded stock in UK at discount prices. 1,000 bats in stock. **Free catalogue 0181-974 5654.**

PAVILION AND GROUND EQUIPMENT

E. A. COMBS LIMITED, Pulteney Works, London E18 1PS. Tel: 0181-530 4216. Pavilion clocks for permanent and temporary siting. Wide choice of sizes and styles to suit any ground.

POWER PRECISION & FABRICATION LTD, Greenhill, Gunnislake, Cornwall PL18 9AS. Tel: 01822-832608. The Poweroll range of new Sportsfield Rollers weigh 800–2800kg, using water as ballast. Reconditioned machines also available.

STADIA SPORTS INTERNATIONAL LIMITED, Ely, Cambridgeshire CB6 3NW, England. Tel: 01353-668686. Manufacturer of quality sightscreens, scoreboxes and faces, net cages, synthetic wickets and wicket covers. Full colour catalogue available.

STUART CANVAS PRODUCTS, Warren Works, Hardwick Grange, Warrington, Cheshire WA1 4RF. Tel: 01925-814525; fax: 01925-831709. Designers, manufacturers and suppliers of ground covering equipment, sold throughout the world, including Test and county grounds.

TILDENET LTD, Hartcliffe Way, Bristol BS3 5RJ. Tel: 0117-966 9684; fax: 0117-923 1251. Mobile and static practice nets, sightscreens, ball stop and perimeter netting, mobile and layflat covers. Automatic pitch cover (protection in three minutes), Groundsman's Mate (wicket preparation and marking), germination sheets.

PITCHES (NON-TURF)

CLUB SURFACES LIMITED, The Barn, Bisham Grange, Marlow, Buckinghamshire SL7 1RS. Tel: 01628-485969; fax: 01628-471944. ClubTurf, world-leading pitch since 1978, with 4,500 installations, including Lord's, Old Trafford. Contact Derek Underwood for information pack.

NOTTS SPORT, Cricket Division, Launde House, Harborough Road, Oadby, Leicester LE2 4LE. Tel: 0116-272 0222; fax: 0116-272 0617; e-mail: info@nottssport.com. World-renowned pitch systems. Clients include ICC, MCC, ECB and many national and regional bodies.

PITCHES (TURF)

C. H. BINDER LTD, Moreton, Ongar, Essex CM5 0HY. Tel: 01277-890246; fax: 01277-890105. Sole producers of Ongar Loam™ top dressing for cricket pitches, grass seed, fertilisers etc. Catalogue and quotations on request. Collections available.

SOCIETIES

CRICKET MEMORABILIA SOCIETY. Hon. Secretary, Tony Sheldon, 29 Highclere Road, Crumpsall, Manchester M8 4WH. Tel/fax: 0161-740 3714. For collectors worldwide – meetings, speakers, auctions, magazines, directory, merchandise, but most of all friendship.

TIES AND CLOTHING

LUKE EYRES, Freepost, Denny Industrial Estate, Pembroke Avenue, Waterbeach, Cambridge CB5 8BR. Tel: 01353-863125. 100% wool, cotton or acrylic sweaters as supplied to major county clubs, international cricket teams and schools.

WILLIAM TURNER & SON, 95 Ann Street, Reddish, Stockport SK5 7PP. Tel: 0161-480 8582; fax: 0161-480 0985; e-mail: sales@ties-scarves.co.uk; web site: www.william-turner.co.uk. Manufacturers of cricket and club ties for 30 years.

Asterisks indicate businesses that have display advertisements elsewhere in the Almanack. See below for more details.

INDEX OF ADVERTISEMENTS

Roman numerals refer to the colour section between pages 48 and 49.

INDEX OF TEST MATCHES

WEST INDIES v ENGLAND, 1997-98

SOUTH AFRICA v PAKISTAN, 1997-98

NEW ZEALAND v ZIMBABWE, 1997-98

INDIA v AUSTRALIA, 1997-98

ZIMBABWE v PAKISTAN, 1997-98

SOUTH AFRICA v SRI LANKA, 1997-98

SRI LANKA v NEW ZEALAND, 1997-98

ENGLAND v SOUTH AFRICA, 1998

ENGLAND v SRI LANKA, 1998

TEST MATCHES, 1998-99

Full details of these Tests, and others too late for inclusion, will appear in the 2000 edition of *Wisden*.

PAKISTAN v AUSTRALIA

First Test: At Rawalpindi, October 1, 2, 3, 4, 5. Australia won by an innings and 99 runs. Toss: Pakistan. Pakistan 269 (Saeed Anwar 145, Moin Khan 39; S. C. G. MacGill five for 66) and 145 (Salim Malik 52 not out; S. C. G. MacGill four for 47); Australia 513 (M. J. Slater 108, S. R. Waugh 157, D. S. Lehmann 98, I. A. Healy 82, Extras 30; Wasim Akram three for 111).

Australia won a Test in Pakistan for the first time since 1959-60. Healy reached a world record 356 Test dismissals (331 catches, 25 stumpings), passing Rodney Marsh's 355. Colin Miller made his Test debut aged 34 and dismissed Malik with his fifth ball.

Second Test: At Peshawar, October 15, 16, 17, 18, 19. Drawn. Toss: Australia. Australia 599 for four dec. (M. A. Taylor 334 not out, J. L. Langer 116, M. E. Waugh 42, R. T. Ponting 76 not out) and 289 for five (M. A. Taylor 92, M. E. Waugh 43, S. R. Waugh 49 not out, R. T. Ponting 43); Pakistan 580 for nine dec. (Saeed Anwar 126, Aamir Sohail 31, Ijaz Ahmed, sen. 155, Inzamam-ul-Haq 97, Salim Malik 49, Mushtaq Ahmed 48 not out; G. D. McGrath three for 131).

Taylor equalled the highest Test score by an Australian (Don Bradman at Leeds in 1930), batting for 720 minutes and 564 balls with 32 fours and a six. He passed 7,000 Test runs in his 98th match and added 279 with Langer, an Australian all-wicket record v Pakistan, but declared on the third morning. Taylor's match aggregate of 426 had been bettered only by Graham Gooch, with 333 plus 123 runs v India at Lord's in 1990.

Third Test: At Karachi, October 22, 23, 24, 25, 26. Drawn. Toss: Australia. Australia 280 (M. J. Slater 96, J. L. Langer 30, I. A. Healy 47; Arshad Khan three for 72, Shahid Afridi five for 52) and 390 (M. A. Taylor 68, J. L. Langer 51, M. E. Waugh 117, G. R. Robertson 45; Shakeel Ahmed four for 91); Pakistan 252 (Aamir Sohail 133, Wasim Akram 35; G. D. McGrath three for 66, S. C. G. MacGill three for 64) and 262 for five (Ijaz Ahmed, sen. 120 not out, Moin Khan 75; C. R. Miller three for 82).

Australia secured their first series victory in Pakistan since 1959-60. Shahid Afridi played his first Test after playing 66 one-day internationals – beating Robin Singh's record set 15 days earlier. Salim Malik bagged a pair in his 99th Test.

ZIMBABWE v INDIA

Only Test: At Harare, October 7, 8, 9, 10. Zimbabwe won by 61 runs. Toss: India. Zimbabwe 221 (G. J. Rennie 47, M. W. Goodwin 42, A. Flower 30; J. Srinath three for 59, A. Kumble three for 42) and 293 (G. J. Rennie 84, C. B. Wishart 63, M. W. Goodwin 44, A. Flower 41 not out; Harbhajan Singh three for 64, A. Kumble four for 87); India 280 (R. Dravid 118, S. R. Tendulkar 34, S. C. Ganguly 47; H. H. Streak three for 62, H. K. Olonga five for 70) and 173 (R. Dravid 44, S. C. Ganguly 36; N. C. Johnson three for 41).

Zimbabwe won their second Test victory, following their win over Pakistan in 1994-95. Andy Flower became the first Zimbabwean to score 2,000 Test runs; he and captain Alistair Campbell were now Zimbabwe's only ever-presents in their 31 Tests, Grant Flower having dropped out with a broken finger. Johnson, Zimbabwean-born but formerly registered with South Africa, was cleared to play 48 hours before the match. Robin Singh made his Test debut after 60 one-day internationals, breaking Gavin Larsen's record of 55 before playing a Test. Kumble was the fourth Indian to reach 200 Test wickets, in his 47th Test.

AUSTRALIA v ENGLAND

First Test Match

At Brisbane, November 20, 21, 22, 23, 24. Drawn. Toss: Australia.

Australia

*M. A. Taylor c Hussain b Cork	46	– (2) b Cork	0
M. J. Slater c Butcher b Mullally	16	– (1) c and b Fraser	113
J. L. Langer lbw b Gough	8	– c Mullally b Croft	74
M. E. Waugh c Stewart b Mullally	31	– not out	27
S. R. Waugh c Stewart b Mullally	112	– not out	16
R. T. Ponting c Butcher b Cork	21		
†I. A. Healy c Mullally b Fraser	134		
M. S. Kasprowicz c Stewart b Mullally	0		
D. W. Fleming not out	71		
S. C. G. MacGill c Stewart b Mullally	20		
G. D. McGrath c Atherton b Croft	5		
L-b 14, w 1, n-b 6	21	B 1, l-b 1, n-b 5	7
	485	(3 wkts dec.)	**237**

1/30 2/59 3/106 4/106 5/178   1/20 2/182 3/199
6/365 7/365 8/420 9/445

Bowling: *First Innings*—Gough 34–4–135–1; Cork 31–6–98–2; Mullally 40–10–105–5; Croft 23–6–55–1; Fraser 28–7–76–1; Ramprakash 2–1–2–0. *Second Innings*—Gough 6–0–50–0; Cork 5–0–18–1; Mullally 14–4–38–0; Fraser 15–1–52–1; Croft 20–2–71–1; Ramprakash 2–0–6–0.

England

M. A. Butcher c and b M. E. Waugh	116	– lbw b MacGill	40
M. A. Atherton c M. E. Waugh b McGrath	0	– c Fleming b McGrath	28
N. Hussain c Healy b Kasprowicz	59	– b MacGill	47
*†A. J. Stewart c Kasprowicz b MacGill	8	– c Ponting b M. E. Waugh	3
G. P. Thorpe c Langer b McGrath	77	– c Langer b M. E. Waugh	9
M. R. Ramprakash not out	69	– st Healy b MacGill	14
D. G. Cork c MacGill b McGrath	0	– not out	21
R. D. B. Croft b Kasprowicz	23	– not out	4
D. Gough lbw b McGrath	0		
A. D. Mullally c Kasprowicz b McGrath	0		
A. R. C. Fraser c M. E. Waugh b McGrath	1		
B 1, l-b 9, n-b 12	22	L-b 3, w 1, n-b 9	13
	375	(6 wkts)	**179**

1/11 2/145 3/168 4/240 5/315   1/46 2/96 3/103
6/319 7/360 8/373 9/373   4/133 5/148 6/161

Bowling: *First Innings*—McGrath 34.2–11–85–6; Fleming 27–5–83–0; Kasprowicz 29–7–82–2; MacGill 24–4–70–1; S. R. Waugh 3–0–17–0; Ponting 3–0–10–0; M. E. Waugh 8–1–18–1. *Second Innings*—McGrath 16–6–30–1; Kasprowicz 8–3–28–0; Fleming 7–2–12–0; MacGill 22–4–51–3; M. E. Waugh 14–0–55–2; Ponting 1–1–0–0.

Umpires: K. T. Francis (Sri Lanka) and D. B. Hair.   Referee: J. R. Reid (New Zealand).

Taylor became the fifth Australian to play in 100 Tests. Fleming, batting at No. 9, made his highest first-class score. Butcher scored his second Test hundred – after totalling nine in his previous five innings. England, chasing 348 in 98 overs, were saved by rain and bad light; they had declined to use floodlights under ICC's experimental regulation.

AUSTRALIA v ENGLAND

Second Test Match

At Perth, November 28, 29, 30. Australia won by seven wickets. Toss: Australia.

England

M. A. Butcher c Healy b Fleming	0	– c Ponting b Fleming	1
M. A. Atherton c Healy b McGrath	1	– c Taylor b Fleming	35
N. Hussain c Healy b McGrath	6	– lbw b Fleming	1
*†A. J. Stewart b McGrath	38	– c Taylor b Fleming	0
M. R. Ramprakash c Taylor b Fleming	26	– not out	47
J. P. Crawley c M. E. Waugh b Gillespie	4	– c Langer b Miller	15
G. A. Hick c Healy b Gillespie	0	– c Ponting b Gillespie	68
D. G. Cork c Taylor b Fleming	2	– lbw b Gillespie	16
A. J. Tudor not out	18	– c Healy b Gillespie	0
D. Gough c M. E. Waugh b Fleming	11	– lbw b Gillespie	0
A. D. Mullally c Healy b Fleming	0	– b Gillespie	0
L-b 2, w 2, n-b 2	6	N-b 8	8

1/2 2/4 3/19 4/62 5/74   112   1/5 2/11 3/15 4/40 5/67   191
6/74 7/81 8/90 9/108   6/158 7/189 8/189 9/189

Bowling: *First Innings*—McGrath 16–4–37–3; Fleming 14–3–46–5; Gillespie 7–0–23–2; Miller 2–0–4–0. *Second Innings*—McGrath 26–10–47–0; Fleming 19–7–45–4; Gillespie 15.2–2–88–5; Miller 10–4–11–1.

Australia

*M. A. Taylor c Stewart b Cork	61	– (2) c Hick b Mullally	3
M. J. Slater c Butcher b Gough	34	– (1) c and b Gough	17
J. L. Langer c Crawley b Ramprakash	15	– c Atherton b Tudor	7
M. E. Waugh c Butcher b Tudor	36	– not out	17
J. N. Gillespie c Stewart b Mullally	11		
S. R. Waugh b Tudor	33	– (5) not out	15
R. T. Ponting c Stewart b Tudor	11		
†I. A. Healy lbw b Gough	12		
D. W. Fleming c Hick b Gough	0		
C. R. Miller not out	3		
G. D. McGrath c Cork b Tudor	0		
B 1, l-b 10, n-b 13	24	L-b 3, n-b 2	5

1/81 2/115 3/138 4/165 5/209   240   1/16 2/24 3/36   (3 wkts) 64
6/214 7/228 8/228 9/239

Bowling: *First Innings*—Gough 25–9–43–3; Cork 21–5–49–1; Tudor 20.2–5–89–4; Mullally 21–10–36–1; Ramprakash 2–0–12–1. *Second Innings*—Gough 9–5–18–1; Mullally 9–0–24–1; Tudor 5–0–19–1.

Umpires: S. Venkataraghavan (India) and D. J. Harper.   Referee: J. R. Reid (New Zealand).

Australia won in two and a half days after England succumbed for their lowest total in Perth on the opening day and lost their last four wickets for two runs in 12 balls on the third morning; Gillespie claimed all four. Taylor reached 150 Test catches, in his 101st game, and Stewart completed 1,000 Test runs in 14 matches in 1998.

AUSTRALIA v ENGLAND

Third Test Match

At Adelaide, December 11, 12, 13, 14, 15. Australia won by 205 runs. Toss: Australia.

Australia

M. J. Slater c Stewart b Headley	17	– (2) lbw b Gough	103
*M. A. Taylor c Hussain b Such	59	– (1) lbw b Such	29
J. L. Langer not out	179	– c sub (B. C. Hollioake) b Such	52
M. E. Waugh c and b Such	7	– not out	51
S. R. Waugh c Hick b Gough	59	– c Hick b Headley	7
R. T. Ponting c Hick b Gough	5	– b Gough	10
†I. A. Healy c Ramprakash b Headley	13	– not out	7
D. W. Fleming lbw b Headley	12		
S. C. G. MacGill b Such	0		
C. R. Miller lbw b Headley	11		
G. D. McGrath c Stewart b Gough	10		
L-b 6, n-b 13	19	L-b 12, w 1, n-b 6	19
	391	(5 wkts dec.)	**278**

1/28 2/140 3/156 4/264 5/274 6/311 7/338 8/339 9/354

1/54 2/188 3/216 4/230 5/268

Bowling: *First Innings*—Gough 29.5–4–103–3; Mullally 26–5–59–0; Headley 23–1–97–4; Such 38–8–99–3; Ramprakash 9–1–27–0. *Second Innings*—Gough 22–2–76–2; Mullally 16–6–18–0; Headley 18–1–78–1; Such 29–5–66–2; Ramprakash 12–1–27–0; Hick 1–0–1–0.

England

M. A. Butcher lbw b Miller	6	– c Healy b Fleming	19
M. A. Atherton c Taylor b MacGill	41	– c M. E. Waugh b Miller	5
N. Hussain not out	89	– lbw b Miller	41
*†A. J. Stewart b Miller	0	– (6) not out	63
M. R. Ramprakash c M. E. Waugh b McGrath	0	– (4) b Fleming	57
J. P. Crawley b McGrath	5	– (7) c M. E. Waugh b McGrath	13
G. A. Hick c Taylor b MacGill	0	– (8) c Ponting b McGrath	0
D. W. Headley lbw b MacGill	0	– (5) c M. E. Waugh b Miller	2
D. Gough c Healy b MacGill	7	– c Healy b McGrath	3
A. D. Mullally b Fleming	0	– c Healy b Fleming	4
P. M. Such lbw b Fleming	0	– lbw b McGrath	0
B 1, l-b 3, w 1, n-b 5	10	B 7, l-b 9, n-b 14	30
	227		**237**

1/18 2/83 3/84 4/187 5/195 6/210 7/210 8/226 9/227

1/27 2/31 3/120 4/122 5/163 6/221 7/221 8/231 9/236

Bowling: *First Innings*—McGrath 18–4–48–2; Fleming 10.5–2–34–2; Miller 23–6–71–2; MacGill 28–6–53–4; M. E. Waugh 3–0–17–0. *Second Innings*—McGrath 17–0–50–4; Fleming 21–3–56–3; Miller 24–1–57–3; MacGill 25–8–55–0; S. R. Waugh 2–1–3–0.

Umpires: S. A. Bucknor (West Indies) and S. J. Davis. Referee: J. R. Reid (New Zealand).

Australia retained the Ashes for the sixth consecutive series on December 15 – the earliest date by which the Ashes had been settled on Australian soil. Taylor completed 1,000 Test runs in 11 matches in 1998 and overtook David Boon's total of 7,422 to become Australia's second-highest run-scorer. Atherton passed 6,000 Test runs in his 87th Test. Mullally finally got off the mark in his fifth innings of the series.

AUSTRALIA v ENGLAND

Fourth Test Match

At Melbourne, December 26, 27, 28, 29. England won by 12 runs. Toss: Australia.

England

M. A. Atherton c Healy b McGrath	0	– b Fleming	0
*A. J. Stewart b MacGill	107	– c Slater b MacGill	52
M. A. Butcher c Langer b McGrath	0	– c Slater b MacGill	14
N. Hussain c Healy b Nicholson	19	– (5) c Slater b Nicholson	50
M. R. Ramprakash c McGrath b S. R. Waugh	63	– (6) b Nicholson	14
G. A. Hick c Fleming b MacGill	39	– (7) b Fleming	60
†W. K. Hegg c Healy b S. R. Waugh	3	– (8) c MacGill b Nicholson	9
D. W. Headley c Taylor b McGrath	14	– (4) b McGrath	1
D. Gough b MacGill	11	– c Slater b MacGill	4
A. R. C. Fraser not out	0	– not out	7
A. D. Mullally lbw b MacGill	0	– c and b McGrath	16
L-b 7, w 1, n-b 6	14	B 2, l-b 4, n-b 11	17
	270		**244**

1/0 2/4 3/81 4/200 5/202
6/206 7/244 8/266 9/270

1/5 2/61 3/66 4/78 5/127
6/178 7/202 8/221 9/221

Bowling: *First Innings*—McGrath 22–5–64–3; Fleming 19–3–71–0; Nicholson 10–0–59–1; MacGill 19–2–61–4; S. R. Waugh 6–2–8–2. *Second Innings*—McGrath 20.2–5–56–2; Fleming 17–4–45–2; Nicholson 15–4–56–3; MacGill 27–3–81–3; M. E. Waugh 1–1–0–0.

Australia

*M. A. Taylor c Hick b Gough	7	– (2) c Headley b Mullally	19
M. J. Slater lbw b Gough	1	– (1) lbw b Headley	18
J. L. Langer c Hussain b Gough	44	– c Ramprakash b Mullally	30
M. E. Waugh lbw b Fraser	36	– c Hick b Headley	43
S. R. Waugh not out	122	– not out	30
D. S. Lehmann c Hegg b Gough	13	– c Hegg b Headley	4
†I. A. Healy c Headley b Fraser	36	– c Hick b Headley	0
D. W. Fleming c Hick b Mullally	12	– lbw b Headley	0
M. J. Nicholson b Gough	5	– c Hegg b Headley	9
S. C. G. MacGill c Hegg b Mullally	43	– b Gough	0
G. D. McGrath b Mullally	0	– lbw b Gough	0
B 4, l-b 6, n-b 11	21	B 4, l-b 1, n-b 4	9
	340		**162**

1/13 2/26 3/98 4/127 5/151
6/209 7/235 8/252 9/340

1/31 2/41 3/103 4/130 5/140
6/140 7/140 8/161 9/162

Bowling: *First Innings*—Gough 28–7–96–5; Headley 25–3–86–0; Mullally 21.3–5–64–3; Ramprakash 2–0–6–0; Fraser 22–0–78–2. *Second Innings*—Gough 15.4–2–54–2; Headley 17–5–60–6; Mullally 10–4–20–2; Fraser 4–0–23–0.

Umpires: S. A. Bucknor (West Indies) and D. J. Harper.   Referee: J. R. Reid (New Zealand).

The first day was lost to rain, and subsequent days were extended by an hour (subject to bad light); the fourth and final day lasted eight hours and three minutes, after Australia claimed the extra half-hour as well. Steve Waugh reached 7,000 Test runs, in his 110th Test, and overtook Bradman's 6,996 to become Australia's fifth-highest run-scorer; in the next match, he passed Greg Chappell's 7,110 to go fourth. Atherton made the first pair of his Test career. Mark Waugh completed 1,000 Test runs in 12 matches in 1998. Australia, needing 175 to win, were bowled out inside 47 overs.

AUSTRALIA v ENGLAND

Fifth Test Match

At Sydney, January 2, 3, 4, 5. Australia won by 98 runs. Toss: Australia.

Australia

*M. A. Taylor c Hick b Headley	2	– (2) c Stewart b Gough	2
M. J. Slater c Hegg b Headley	18	– (1) c Hegg b Headley	123
J. L. Langer c Ramprakash b Tudor	26	– lbw b Headley	1
M. E. Waugh c Hegg b Headley	121	– c Ramprakash b Headley	24
S. R. Waugh b Such	96	– (7) b Headley	8
D. S. Lehmann c Hussain b Tudor	32	– (5) c Crawley b Such	0
†I. A. Healy c Hegg b Gough	14	– (6) c Crawley b Such	5
S. K. Warne not out	2	– c Ramprakash b Such	8
S. C. G. MacGill b Gough	0	– c Butcher b Such	6
C. R. Miller b Gough	0	– not out	3
G. D. McGrath c Hick b Headley	0	– c Stewart b Such	0
L-b 2, n-b 9	11	B 3, l-b 1	4
	322		**184**

1/4 2/52 3/52 4/242 5/284   322   1/16 2/25 3/64 4/73 5/91   184
6/319 7/321 8/321 9/321   6/110 7/141 8/180 9/184

Bowling: *First Innings*—Gough 17–4–61–3; Headley 19.3–3–62–4; Tudor 12–1–64–2; Such 24–6–77–1; Ramprakash 15–0–56–0. *Second Innings*—Headley 19–7–40–4; Gough 15–3–51–1; Such 25.5–5–81–5; Tudor 5–2–8–0.

England

M. A. Butcher lbw b Warne	36	– st Healy b Warne	27
*A. J. Stewart c Warne b McGrath	3	– st Healy b MacGill	42
N. Hussain c M. E. Waugh b Miller	42	– c and b MacGill	53
M. R. Ramprakash c MacGill b McGrath	14	– c Taylor b MacGill	14
G. A. Hick c Warne b MacGill	23	– b MacGill	7
J. P. Crawley c Taylor b MacGill	44	– lbw b Miller	5
†W. K. Hegg b Miller	15	– c Healy b MacGill	3
A. J. Tudor b MacGill	14	– b MacGill	3
D. W. Headley c McGrath b MacGill	8	– c Healy b MacGill	16
D. Gough lbw b MacGill	0	– not out	7
P. M. Such not out	0	– c and b MacGill	2
B 8, l-b 8, w 1, n-b 4	21	L-b 5, w 1, n-b 3	9
	220		**188**

1/18 2/56 3/88 4/137 5/139   220   1/57 2/77 3/110 4/131 5/150   188
6/171 7/204 8/213 9/213   6/157 7/162 8/175 9/180

Bowling: *First Innings*—McGrath 17–7–35–2; Miller 23–6–45–2; MacGill 20.1–2–57–5; Warne 20–4–67–1. *Second Innings*—McGrath 10–1–40–1; Miller 17–1–50–1; MacGill 20.1–4–50–7; Warne 13–3–43–1.

Umpires: R. S. Dunne (New Zealand) and D. B. Hair. Referee: J. R. Reid (New Zealand).

Taylor won his fifth toss of the series, and later took his 157th Test catch, passing Allan Border's world record of 156. Four weeks later, Taylor announced his retirement from Test cricket, finishing with 7,525 runs at 43.49 in 104 matches. Gough claimed a hat-trick, the first for England in an Ashes Test in the 20th century. McGrath took his 200th Test wicket, in his 45th match. Mark Waugh made his 100th Test catch. Slater scored 67 per cent of Australia's second-innings runs, and reached his seventh century in 16 Ashes Tests. McGrath bagged his second successive pair. Australia took the series 3-1.

SOUTH AFRICA v WEST INDIES

First Test: At Johannesburg, November 26, 27, 28, 29, 30. South Africa won by four wickets. Toss: West Indies. West Indies 261 (S. Chanderpaul 74, C. L. Hooper 44, S. C. Williams 35; A. A. Donald three for 91, S. M. Pollock five for 54) and 170 (C. B. Lambert 33, R. D. Jacobs 42, C. L. Hooper 34; S. M. Pollock four for 49, P. L. Symcox three for 43); South Africa 268 (G. Kirsten 62, J. H. Kallis 53, W. J. Cronje 41; C. A. Walsh four for 66) and 164 for six (J. H. Kallis 57 not out, D. J. Cullinan 35, W. J. Cronje 31; C. A. Walsh three for 45).

This was only the second Test between South Africa and West Indies, who won the first in 1991-92. In his 26th match, Pollock became the second South African, after Trevor Goddard, to reach 1,000 Test runs and 100 wickets. Walsh passed Malcolm Marshall's West Indian record of 376 Test wickets and moved up to fourth on the all-time wicket-takers' list.

Second Test: At Port Elizabeth, December 10, 11, 12. South Africa won by 178 runs. Toss: West Indies. South Africa 245 (J. H. Kallis 30, P. L. Symcox 36, A. A. Donald 34; C. A. Walsh four for 87) and 195 (J. N. Rhodes 64, S. M. Pollock 42; C. E. L. Ambrose six for 51, C. A. Walsh three for 58); West Indies 121 (S. C. Williams 37, N. A. M. McLean 31; S. M. Pollock five for 43, D. J. Terbrugge three for 27) and 141 (B. C. Lara 39; A. A. Donald five for 49).

Walsh rose to third on the wicket-takers' list, overtaking Ian Botham's 383. West Indies' first innings lasted 37.3 overs, their second 38.2. They lost in three days.

Third Test: At Durban, December 26, 27, 28, 29. South Africa won by nine wickets. Toss: South Africa. West Indies 198 (B. C. Lara 51, R. D. Jacobs 39; J. H. Kallis three for 18, W. J. Cronje three for 19) and 259 (S. Chanderpaul 75, B. C. Lara 79; A. A. Donald three for 62, S. M. Pollock five for 83); South Africa 312 (H. H. Gibbs 35, D. J. Cullinan 40, W. J. Cronje 30, J. N. Rhodes 87, S. M. Pollock 30; F. A. Rose seven for 84) and 147 for one (G. Kirsten 71 not out, H. H. Gibbs 49).

Donald reached 250 Test wickets in his 50th match; only Dennis Lillee had reached the milestone in fewer matches – 48. South Africa took an unbeatable 3-0 lead.

Fourth Test: At Cape Town, January 2, 3, 4, 5, 6. South Africa won by 149 runs. Toss: South Africa. South Africa 406 for eight dec. (H. H. Gibbs 42, J. H. Kallis 110, D. J. Cullinan 168, J. N. Rhodes 34; M. Dillon three for 99) and 226 for seven dec. (J. H. Kallis 88 not out, W. J. Cronje 54; N. A. M. McLean three for 53); West Indies 212 (C. L. Hooper 86, O. D. Gibson 37; A. A. Donald three for 20) and 271 (B. C. Lara 33, R. D. Jacobs 69 not out, N. A. M. McLean 39, M. Dillon 36; J. H. Kallis five for 90).

Ambrose dismissed Kirsten with the first ball of the match. Kallis became the eighth player in Test history to hit a hundred, a fifty, and take five wickets in an innings in the same Test.

Fifth Test: At Centurion, January 15, 16, 17, 18. South Africa won by 351 runs. Toss: West Indies. South Africa 313 (J. H. Kallis 83, M. V. Boucher 100; C. A. Walsh six for 80) and 399 for five dec. (G. Kirsten 134, H. H. Gibbs 51, W. J. Cronje 58, J. N. Rhodes 103 not out; C. L. Hooper three for 117); West Indies 144 (S. Chanderpaul 38, B. C. Lara 68; A. A. Donald five for 49) and 217 (S. Chanderpaul 44, R. D. Jacobs 78, N. A. M. McLean 33; P. R. Adams four for 64).

South Africa became the seventh team in Test history to win a series 5-0; three of the previous winners had been West Indies, now the victims. Rhodes scored the fastest Test century in South Africa in terms of balls – 95. Kirsten played his 50th consecutive Test. Walsh finished with 397 Test wickets after breaking down in the second innings.

PAKISTAN v ZIMBABWE

First Test: At Peshawar, November 27, 28, 29, 30. Zimbabwe won by seven wickets. Toss: Zimbabwe. Pakistan 296 (Saeed Anwar 36, Ijaz Ahmed, sen. 87, Yousuf Youhana 75; H. H. Streak four for 93, M. Mbangwa three for 40) and 103 (Saeed Anwar 31, Wasim Akram 31; H. K. Olonga four for 42, M. Mbangwa three for 23); Zimbabwe 238 (N. C. Johnson 107; Wasim Akram five for 53, Waqar Younis four for 78) and 162 for three (G. W. Flower 31, M. W. Goodwin 73 not out; Wasim Akram three for 47).

Zimbabwe won their first overseas Test victory. Streak became the first Zimbabwean to reach 100 Test wickets, in 25 Tests, and Grant Flower the second to score 2,000 Test runs, in his 31st match, seven weeks after his brother Andy. Wasim took his 350th Test wicket in his 82nd Test.

Second Test: At Lahore, December 10, 11, 12, 13, 14. Drawn. Toss: Pakistan. Zimbabwe 183 (A. Flower 60 not out; Waqar Younis four for 54, Saqlain Mushtaq five for 32) and 48 for no wkt; Pakistan 325 for nine dec. (Saeed Anwar 75, Naved Ashraf 32, Yousuf Youhana 120 not out; H. K. Olonga three for 63).

Fog shortened play on each of the first four days and prevented any on the fifth. Salim Malik became the second Pakistani, after Javed Miandad, to play in 100 Tests.

Third Test: At Faisalabad, December 17, 18, 19, 20, 21. Abandoned.

This was the first Test in Pakistan to be abandoned without a ball bowled; fog enveloped the stadium on all five days. The draw gave Zimbabwe their first overseas Test series win.

NEW ZEALAND v INDIA

First Test: At Dunedin, December 18, 19, 20, 21, 22. Abandoned.

Rain caused the match to be abandoned one day after fog wiped out the Faisalabad Test between Pakistan and Zimbabwe.

Second Test: At Wellington, December 26, 27, 28, 29, 30. New Zealand won by four wickets. Toss: India. India 208 (S. R. Tendulkar 47, M. Azharuddin 103 not out; S. B. Doull seven for 65) and 356 (N. S. Sidhu 34, S. C. Ganguly 48, S. R. Tendulkar 113, M. Azharuddin 48; D. J. Nash three for 20); New Zealand 352 (M. J. Horne 38, S. P. Fleming 42, N. J. Astle 56, D. J. Nash 89 not out, D. L. Vettori 57, Extras 37; A. Kumble four for 83) and 215 for six (M. J. Horne 31, C. D. McMillan 74 not out, C. L. Cairns 61; J. Srinath three for 82).

Doull, who took the first seven wickets to fall in India's first innings, returned New Zealand's fourth-best analysis in Tests. Nash and Vettori added 137, a record for New Zealand's eighth wicket.

Third Test: At Hamilton, January 2, 3, 4, 5, 6. Drawn. Toss: India. New Zealand 366 (M. J. Horne 63, R. G. Twose 87, C. D. McMillan 92, Extras 40; J. Srinath five for 95) and 464 for eight dec. (C. D. McMillan 84, A. C. Parore 50, C. L. Cairns 126, D. J. Nash 63, D. L. Vettori 43 not out); India 416 (R. Dravid 190, S. R. Tendulkar 67, J. Srinath 76, B. K. V. Prasad 30 not out; S. B. Doull three for 64, C. L. Cairns four for 107) and 249 for two (R. Dravid 103 not out, S. C. Ganguly 101 not out).

New Zealand won the series 1–0, their third successive home series win. Dravid became the third Indian to score two centuries in a Test.

INDIA v PAKISTAN

First Test: At Chennai, January 28, 29, 30, 31. Pakistan won by 12 runs. Toss: Pakistan. Pakistan 238 (Yousuf Youhana 53, Moin Khan 60, Wasim Akram 38; J. Srinath three for 63, A. Kumble six for 70) and 286 (Shahid Afridi 141, Inzamam-ul-Haq 51, Salim Malik 32; B. K. V. Prasad six for 33); India 254 (S. Ramesh 43, R. Dravid 53, S. C. Ganguly 54; Saqlain Mushtaq five for 94, Shahid Afridi three for 31) and 258 (S. R. Tendulkar 136, N. R. Mongia 52, Extras 36; Wasim Akram three for 80, Saqlain Mushtaq five for 93)

India and Pakistan met in a Test series for the first time since 1989-90; the venue had to be switched from Delhi after Hindu extremists dug up the pitch there. India were 82 for five, then 254 for six, chasing 271; when Tendulkar was out, the last four wickets fell for four runs.

Second Test: At Delhi, February 4, 5, 6, 7. India won by 212 runs. Toss: India. India 252 (S. Ramesh 60, V. V. S. Laxman 35, R. Dravid 33, M. Azharuddin 67; Saqlain Mushtaq five for 94) and 339 (S. Ramesh 96, S. C. Ganguly 62 not out, J. Srinath 49, Extras 31; Wasim Akram three for 43, Saqlain Mushtaq five for 122); Pakistan 172 (Shahid Afridi 32, Salim Malik 31; Harbhajan Singh three for 30, A. Kumble four for 75) and 207 (Saeed Anwar 69, Shahid Afridi 41, Wasim Akram 37; A. Kumble ten for 74).

On the hastily repaired pitch, Saqlain Mushtaq took five in an innings for the third and fourth time running in this series and the fifth time in three Tests. Wasim Akram became Pakistan's leading wicket-taker, overtaking Imran Khan's 362 in 88 Tests with 363 in 85. Kumble became only the second bowler to take ten wickets in a Test innings, following Jim Laker's ten for 53 for England v Australia in 1956; Kumble's full figures were 26.3–9–74–10.

FIXTURES, 1999

World Cup Fixtures

World Cup fixtures and warm-up matches between World Cup teams and counties may be found on pages 61-62.

Fixtures for women's cricket may be found on page 1014.

All County Championship matches are of four days' duration; tourist matches are four days unless stated; and other first-class matches are three days unless stated.   † Not first-class.

Thursday, April 8

Cambridge	Cambridge U. v Lancs
Oxford	Oxford U. v Worcs

Monday, April 12

Nottingham	Notts v Cambridge U.

Tuesday, April 13

Chester-le-Street	Durham v Worcs
Chelmsford	Essex v Leics
Manchester	Lancs v Sussex
Lord's	Middx v Kent
The Oval	Surrey v Glos

Wednesday, April 14

Birmingham	Warwicks v Northants
Oxford	Oxford U. v Hants

Thursday, April 15

Cambridge	Cambridge U. v Somerset

Saturday, April 17

†National League, Division One (1 day)

Leicester	Leics v Hants

Sunday, April 18

†National League, Division One (1 day)

Canterbury	Kent v Lancs

†National League, Division Two (1 day)

Chester-le-Street	Durham v Surrey
Lord's	Middx v Notts

Monday, April 19

Birmingham	Warwicks v Somerset

Tuesday, April 20

Derby	Derbys v Glam
Leicester	Leics v Notts
Lord's	Middx v Lancs
Worcester	Worcs v Surrey

Wednesday, April 21

Southampton	Hants v Kent
Hove	Sussex v Northants
Leeds	Yorks v Glos
Cambridge	Cambridge U. v Essex

Saturday, April 24

†National League, Division Two (1 day)

Taunton	Somerset v Durham

Sunday, April 25

†National League, Division One (1 day)

Chelmsford	Essex v Lancs
Southampton	Hants v Kent
Birmingham	Warwicks v Worcs
Leeds	Yorks v Glos

†National League, Division Two (1 day)

Lord's	Middx v Glam
The Oval	Surrey v Northants
Hove	Sussex v Derbys

Wednesday, April 28

Chester-le-Street	Durham v Hants
Chelmsford	Essex v Warwicks
Cardiff	Glam v Sussex
Bristol	Glos v Middx
Canterbury	Kent v Derbys
Leicester	Leics v Lancs
Northampton	Northants v Surrey
Nottingham	Notts v Worcs

Thursday, April 29

Taunton	Somerset v Yorks

Monday, May 3

†National League, Division One (1 day)

Bristol	Glos v Lancs
Southampton	Hants v Warwicks
Canterbury	Kent v Leics
Worcester	Worcs v Yorks

†National League, Division Two (1 day)

Chester-le-Street	Durham v Middx
Cardiff	Glam v Derbys

Northampton	Northants v Sussex
Nottingham	Notts v Surrey

†NatWest Trophy – First Round (1 day)
(see pages 1514-1515)

Tuesday, May 4

Wednesday, May 5

Oxford	Oxford U. v Notts

Sunday, May 9

Cambridge	Cambridge U. v Northants

Friday, May 14

Stockton-on-Tees	Durham v Kent
Cardiff	Glam v Glos
Southampton	Hants v Worcs
Manchester	Lancs v Northants
Nottingham	Notts v Somerset
The Oval	Surrey v Essex
Birmingham	Warwicks v Derbys
Leeds	Yorks v Middx

Sunday, May 16

Cambridge	†Cambridge U. v Oxford U. (1 day)

Wednesday, May 19

Derby	Derbys v Northants
Chelmsford	Essex v Yorks
Manchester	Lancs v Notts
Lord's	Middx v Hants
Taunton	Somerset v Leics
Hove	Sussex v Glos
Birmingham	Warwicks v Worcs
Oxford	Oxford U. v Glam

†NatWest Trophy – Second Round (1 day)
(see pages 1514-1515)

Thursday, May 20

Cambridge	Cambridge U. v Kent

Sunday, May 23

†National League, Division One (1 day)

Chelmsford	Essex v Yorks
Manchester	Lancs v Worcs
Birmingham	Warwicks v Kent

†National League, Division Two (1 day)

Derby	Derbys v Durham
Taunton	Somerset v Surrey
Hove	Sussex v Glam

Tuesday, May 25

Oxford	Oxford U. v Warwicks

Dunstable	†Northants (2nd XI champions) v England Under-19 (4 days)

Wednesday, May 26

Gloucester	Glos v Essex
Canterbury	Kent v Leics
Lord's	Middx v Sussex
The Oval	Surrey v Somerset
Worcester	Worcs v Glam

Thursday, May 27

Nottingham	Notts v Hants
Leeds	Yorks v Durham

Monday, May 31

†National League, Division One (1 day)

Gloucester	Glos v Worcs
Leicester	Leics v Lancs
Birmingham	Warwicks v Essex
Leeds	Yorks v Hants

†National League, Division Two (1 day)

Cardiff	Glam v Northants
Lord's	Middx v Sussex
Nottingham	Notts v Somerset
The Oval	Surrey v Derbys

Wednesday, June 2

Derby	Derbys v Yorks
Chester-le-Street	Durham v Somerset
Ilford	Essex v Hants
Bristol	Glos v Lancs
Tunbridge Wells	Kent v Surrey
Leicester	Leics v Glam
Northampton	Northants v Notts
Horsham	Sussex v Worcs
Birmingham	Warwicks v Middx

Sunday, June 6

†National League, Division One (1 day)

Ilford	Essex v Glos
Tunbridge Wells	Kent v Worcs
Leicester	Leics v Warwicks

†National League, Division Two (1 day)

Derby	Derbys v Glam
Chester-le-Street	Durham v Somerset
Northampton	Northants v Middx

Monday, June 7

Chester-le-Street	†Durham v New Zealanders (1 day)

Unless New Zealand in World Cup Super Six.

Wednesday, June 9

Chelmsford	Essex v Derbys
Cardiff	Glam v Middx
Basingstoke	Hants v Yorks
Southport	Lancs v Warwicks
Leicester	Leics v Surrey
Northampton	Northants v Durham
Bath	Somerset v Glos
Hove	Sussex v Kent
Worcester	Worcs v New Zealanders

Unless New Zealand in World Cup Super Six.

Sunday, June 13

†National League, Division One (1 day)

Chelmsford	Essex v Kent
Bristol	Glos v Leics
Basingstoke	Hants v Yorks
Birmingham	Warwicks v Lancs

†National League, Division Two (1 day)

Northampton	Northants v Surrey
Bath	Somerset v Notts
Hove	Sussex v Durham
Cardiff	†Glam v New Zealanders (1 day)

Unless New Zealand in World Cup Super Six.

Tuesday, June 15

Southampton	Hants v Leics
Canterbury	Kent v Glam
Nottingham	Notts v Warwicks
The Oval	Surrey v Lancs
Worcester	Worcs v Somerset
Leeds	Yorks v Sussex
Chelmsford	Essex v Oxford U.
Bristol	Glos v New Zealanders

One-day match on June 18 if New Zealand reach World Cup Super Six but not semi-final.

Wednesday, June 16

Cambridge	Cambridge U. v Middx

Saturday, June 19

†National League, Division One (1 day)

Southampton	Hants v Leics
Worcester	Worcs v Glos
Leeds	Yorks v Essex

†National League, Division Two (1 day)

Chester-le-Street	Durham v Northants
Nottingham	Notts v Middx
Taunton	Somerset v Derbys
The Oval	Surrey v Glam

Sunday, June 20

Lord's	†WORLD CUP FINAL (1 day)
Oxford	British Universities v New Zealanders

One-day match on June 23 if New Zealand in World Cup Final.

Wednesday, June 23

†NatWest Trophy – Third Round (1 day)
(see pages 1514-1515)

Friday, June 25

Taunton	Somerset v New Zealanders
Lord's	Oxford U. v Cambridge U.

†Benson and Hedges Super Cup – 1st and 2nd Quarter-finals (1 day)

Manchester	Lancs v Sussex
Leeds	Yorks v Hants

Saturday, June 26

†Benson and Hedges Super Cup – 3rd Quarter-final (1 day)

Leicester	Leics v Warwicks

Sunday, June 27

†Benson and Hedges Super Cup – 4th Quarter-final (1 day)

Bristol	Glos v Surrey

Monday, June 28

†National League, Division Two (1 day)

Hove	Sussex v Northants (day/night)

Tuesday, June 29

Manchester	Lancs v Essex

†National League, Division One (1 day)

Leicester	Leics v Yorks (day/night)
Lord's	†Eton v Harrow (1 day)
Dublin	†Triple Crown Tournament (3 days)

Wednesday, June 30

Swansea	Glam v Hants
Bristol	Glos v Notts
Maidstone	Kent v Warwicks
Lord's	Middx v Derbys
Northampton	Northants v Worcs
Taunton	Somerset v Sussex
The Oval	Surrey v Durham

Thursday, July 1

| Birmingham | ENGLAND v
NEW ZEALAND
(1st Cornhill Test,
5 days) |
| Leicester | Leics v Yorks |

Saturday, July 3

†**National League, Division One** (1 day)

| Manchester | Lancs v Essex
(day/night) |

Sunday, July 4

†**National League, Division One** (1 day)

| Maidstone | Kent v Warwicks |
| Worcester | Worcs v Hants |

†**National League, Division Two** (1 day)

Derby	Derbys v Surrey
Swansea	Glam v Sussex
Lord's	Middx v Durham
Northampton	Northants v Notts
Oakham School	ECB XI v Sri Lanka A (3 days)

Wednesday, July 7

†**NatWest Trophy – Fourth Round** (1 day)
(see pages 1514-1515)

| Milton Keynes
(Campbell Park) | †New Zealanders v
Sri Lanka A (1 day) |

Friday, July 9

Derby	Derbys v Somerset
Chester-le-Street	Durham v Notts
Cardiff	Glam v Essex
Lord's	Middx v Northants
Worcester	Worcs v Kent
Southampton or Leeds	Hants or Yorks v New Zealanders
Manchester or Hove	Lancs or Sussex v Sri Lanka A

Subject to involvement in Benson and Hedges Super Cup semi-finals.

Saturday, July 10

†**Benson and Hedges Super Cup –
1st Semi-final** (1 day)

Sunday, July 11

†**Benson and Hedges Super Cup –
2nd Semi-final** (1 day)

Tuesday, July 13

| Birmingham | Warwicks v Yorks |

†**National League, Division Two** (1 day)

| Chester-le-Street | Durham v Derbys
(day/night) |

Wednesday, July 14

Southend	Essex v Middx
Cheltenham	Glos v Worcs
Blackpool	Lancs v Glam
Guildford	Surrey v Hants
Arundel	Sussex v Leics

Thursday, July 15

Chester-le-Street	Durham v Derbys
Canterbury	Kent v New Zealanders
Northampton	Northants v Sri Lanka A

Saturday, July 17

†**National League, Division One** (1 day)

| Birmingham | Warwicks v Yorks |

Sunday, July 18

†**National League, Division One** (1 day)

| Southend | Essex v Hants |
| Cheltenham | Glos v Yorks |

†**National League, Division Two** (1 day)

Nottingham	Notts v Glam
Guildford	Surrey v Somerset
Arundel	Sussex v Middx

Monday, July 19

†**National League, Division One** (1 day)

| Manchester | Lancs v Warwicks
(day/night) |
| Cheltenham | †Glos v Sri Lanka A
(1 day) |

Tuesday, July 20

| Scarborough | Yorks v Northants |

†**National League, Division One** (1 day)

| Worcester | Worcs v Leics
(day/night) |

Wednesday, July 21

Derby	Derbys v Sussex
Cheltenham	Glos v Durham
Portsmouth	Hants v Lancs
Nottingham	Notts v Kent
Taunton	Somerset v Middx
Birmingham	Warwicks v Surrey
Chelmsford	Essex v Sri Lanka A

Thursday, July 22

Lord's	ENGLAND v NEW ZEALAND (2nd Cornhill Test, 5 days)
Worcester	Worcs v Leics

Sunday, July 25

†National League, Division One (1 day)

Cheltenham	Glos v Warwicks
Portsmouth	Hants v Lancs
Scarborough	Yorks v Kent

†National League, Division Two (1 day)

Derby	Derbys v Northants
Pontypridd	Glam v Surrey
Cleethorpes	Notts v Sussex
Taunton	Somerset v Middx

Monday, July 26

Chester-le-Street	†Durham v Sri Lanka A (1 day)

Wednesday, July 28

†NatWest Trophy – Quarter-finals (1 day)

Derby or Bristol	†Derbys or Glos v New Zealanders (1 day)
Chester-le-Street or Leeds or Leicester	†First-Class Counties Select v Sri Lanka A (1 day)

Subject to involvement in NatWest Trophy quarter-finals.

Friday, July 30

Cardiff	Glam v Durham
Northampton	Northants v Essex
Nottingham	Notts v Derbys
Leicester or Birmingham	Leics or Warwicks v New Zealanders
Bristol or The Oval	Glos or Surrey v Sri Lanka A
Canterbury	†England Under-19 v Australia Under-19 (1st 1-day)

Saturday, July 31

Chelmsford	†England Under-19 v Australia Under-19 (2nd 1-day)

Sunday, August 1

Lord's	†BENSON AND HEDGES SUPER CUP FINAL (1 day)

†National League, Division One (1 day)

Worcester	Worcs v Kent

Monday, August 2

Hove	†England Under-19 v Australia Under-19 (3rd 1-day)

Tuesday, August 3

†National League, Division One (1 day)

Bristol	Glos v Hants (day/night)
Lord's	†MCC v Wales (2 days)

Wednesday, August 4

Derby	Derbys v Lancs
Chester-le-Street	Durham v Sussex
Canterbury	Kent v Essex
Southgate	Middx v Notts
Northampton	Northants v Somerset
The Oval	Surrey v Glam
Leeds	Yorks v Worcs

†National League, Division One (1 day)

Birmingham	Warwicks v Leics (day/night)

Thursday, August 5

Manchester	ENGLAND v NEW ZEALAND (3rd Cornhill Test, 5 days)
Bristol	Glos v Hants
Lord's	†MCC v Ireland (2 days)

Friday, August 6

Leicester	Leics v Warwicks

Sunday, August 8

†National League, Division One (1 day)

Canterbury	Kent v Essex
Leeds	Yorks v Worcs

†National League, Division Two (1 day)

Chester-le-Street	Durham v Sussex
Southgate	Middx v Somerset
Northampton	Northants v Derbys
The Oval	Surrey v Notts

Tuesday, August 10

†National League, Division One (1 day)

Southampton	Hants v Essex
Manchester	Lancs v Glos
Leicester	Leics v Kent

†**National League, Division Two** (1 day)

Cardiff	Glam v Durham
Southgate	Middx v Derbys
Nottingham	Notts v Northants (day/night)
Hove	Sussex v Somerset (day/night)
Worcester	Worcs v Sri Lanka A

Wednesday, August 11

Southgate	†Middx v New Zealanders (1 day)

Thursday, August 12

†**National League, Division One** (1 day)

Chelmsford	Essex v Leics
Bristol	Glos v Kent (day/night)
Leeds	Yorks v Lancs (day/night)

†**National League, Division Two** (1 day)

Derby	Derbys v Somerset
Chester-le-Street	Durham v Notts
Northampton	Northants v Glam
Hove	Sussex v Surrey (day/night)

Friday, August 13

Chelmsford or Northampton	Essex or Northants v New Zealanders

Saturday, August 14

†**NatWest Trophy – 1st Semi-final** (1 day)

Sunday, August 15

†**NatWest Trophy – 2nd Semi-final** (1 day)

Taunton or Hove	†Somerset or Sussex v Sri Lanka A (1 day)

Monday, August 16

†**AON Trophy Semi-finals** (1 day)

Tuesday, August 17

Southampton	Hants v Warwicks
Northampton	Northants v Glos
Shenley Park	MCC v Sri Lanka A

†**National League, Division One** (1 day)

Manchester	Lancs v Yorks (day/night)

†**AON Trophy Semi-finals** (1 day)
(if not played on August 16)

Birmingham	†England Under-19 v Australia Under-19 (1st Unofficial Test,

Wednesday, August 18

Colchester	Essex v Durham
Colwyn Bay	Glam v Notts
Southgate	Middx v Leics
Taunton	Somerset v Kent
Hove	Sussex v Surrey
Kidderminster	Worcs v Derbys

Thursday, August 19

The Oval	ENGLAND v NEW ZEALAND (4th Cornhill Test, 5 days)
Manchester	Lancs v Yorks

Saturday, August 21

Downpatrick	Ireland v Scotland

Sunday, August 22

†**National League, Division One** (1 day)

Colchester	Essex v Warwicks
Southampton	Hants v Glos
Leicester	Leics v Worcs

†**National League, Division Two** (1 day)

Colwyn Bay	Glam v Notts
Southgate	Middx v Northants
Taunton	Somerset v Sussex

Monday, August 23

Bristol	†England Under-19 v Australia Under-19 (2nd Unofficial Test, 4 days)

Tuesday, August 24

Derby	Derbys v Surrey
Chester-le-Street	Durham v Middx
Chelmsford	Essex v Somerset
Cardiff	Glam v Warwicks
Portsmouth	Hants v Sussex
Canterbury	Kent v Northants
Leicester	Leics v Glos
Nottingham	Notts v Yorks
Worcester	Worcs v Lancs

Sunday, August 29

Lord's	†NATWEST TROPHY FINAL (1 day)

†**National League, Division One** (1 day)

Canterbury	Kent v Yorks
Manchester	Lancs v Leics
Worcester	Worcs v Essex

†**National League, Division Two** (1 day)

Nottingham	Notts v Derbys
The Oval	Surrey v Durham

Monday, August 30

†**National League, Division One** (1 day)

Canterbury	Kent v Hants
Leicester	Leics v Glos
Worcester	Worcs v Warwicks

†**National League, Division Two** (1 day)

Derby	Derbys v Notts
Cardiff	Glam v Somerset
Northampton	Northants v Durham

Tuesday, August 31

Eastbourne	Sussex v Essex

†**National League, Division One** (1 day)

Birmingham	Warwicks v Glos (day/night)

†**National League, Division Two** (1 day)

Lord's	Middx v Surrey
Taunton	Somerset v Glam (day/night)

Wednesday, September 1

Manchester	Lancs v Durham
Leicester	Leics v Derbys
Northampton	Northants v Hants
The Oval	Surrey v Notts
Scarborough	Yorks v Kent
Chester-le-Street	†England Under-19 v Australia Under-19 (3rd Unofficial Test, 4 days)
Lord's	†ECB 38-County Final

Thursday, September 2

Taunton	Somerset v Glam
Birmingham	Warwicks v Glos

Friday, September 3

Lord's	†National Club Championship Final (1 day)

Sunday, September 5

†**National League, Division One** (1 day)

Chelmsford	Essex v Worcs
Scarborough	Yorks v Leics

†**National League, Division Two** (1 day)

Derby	Derbys v Middx
Lord's	†National Village Championship Final (1 day)

Monday, September 6

†**National League, Division One** (1 day)

Manchester	Lancs v Hants (day/night)

†**National League, Division Two** (1 day)

The Oval	Surrey v Sussex (day/night)

†**AON Trophy Final** (1 day)

Tuesday, September 7

†**National League, Division Two** (1 day)

The Oval	Surrey v Middx (day/night)

Wednesday, September 8

Chester-le-Street	Durham v Warwicks
Chelmsford	Essex v Worcs
Bristol	Glos v Derbys
Southampton	Hants v Somerset
Manchester	Lancs v Kent
Northampton	Northants v Leics
Leeds	Yorks v Glam

†**National League, Division Two** (1 day)

Hove	Sussex v Notts (day/night)

Thursday, September 9

Lord's	Middx v Surrey

Friday, September 10

Hove	Sussex v Notts

Sunday, September 12

†**National League, Division One** (1 day)

Bristol	Glos v Essex
Southampton	Hants v Worcs
Manchester	Lancs v Kent
Leeds	Yorks v Warwicks

†**National League, Division Two** (1 day)

Chester-le-Street   Durham v Glam
Northampton   Northants v Somerset

†**Minor Counties Final** (3 days)

Wednesday, September 15

Derby	Derbys v Hants
Cardiff	Glam v Northants
Canterbury	Kent v Glos
Leicester	Leics v Durham
Nottingham	Notts v Essex
Taunton	Somerset v Lancs
The Oval	Surrey v Yorks
Birmingham	Warwicks v Sussex
Worcester	Worcs v Middx

Sunday, September 19

†**National League, Division One** (1 day)

Canterbury	Kent v Glos
Leicester	Leics v Essex
Birmingham	Warwicks v Hants
Worcester	Worcs v Lancs

†**National League, Division Two** (1 day)

Derby	Derbys v Sussex
Cardiff	Glam v Middx
Nottingham	Notts v Durham
Taunton	Somerset v Northants

†NATWEST TROPHY, 1999

All matches are of one day's duration.

First Round – Tuesday, May 4

1	Koninklijke UD, Deventer	Holland v Cambs
2	Cheam	Surrey Board XI v Norfolk
3	Bury St Edmunds	Suffolk v Hants Board XI
4	Sleaford	Lincs v Wales
5	Linlithgow	Scotland v Notts Board XI
6	Maidstone	Kent Board XI v Denmark
7	Netherfield	Cumberland v Cornwall
8	Northampton	Northants Board XI v Wilts
9	Luton	Beds v Hunts
10	Reading	Berks v Warwicks Board XI
11	Radlett	Herts v Leics Board XI
12	Hatherley & Reddings, Cheltenham	Glos Board XI v Yorks Board XI
13	Jesmond	Northumberland v Ireland
14	Hartlepool	Durham Board XI v Oxon

Second Round – Monday, May 17

| 15 | Taunton | Somerset Board XI v Match 9 Winner |

Second Round – Wednesday, May 19

16	Liverpool	Lancs Board XI v Match 1 Winner
17	Guildford or Lakenham	Match 2 Winner v Cheshire
18	Wellington	Salop v Match 3 Winner
19	Dunstall	Derbys Board XI v Match 4 Winner
20	Hamilton Crescent, Glasgow or Boots Ground, Nottingham	Match 5 Winner v Dorset
21	Maidstone or away*	Match 6 Winner v Worcs Board XI
22	Southgate	Middx Board XI v Match 7 Winner
23	Brockhampton	Herefordshire v Match 8 Winner
24	Torquay	Devon v Match 10 Winner
25	Hertfort or Oakham School	Match 11 Winner v Sussex Board XI
26	Hatherley & Reddings, Cheltenham or Sheffield	Match 12 Winner v Bucks
27	Jesmond or Belfast	Match 13 Winner v Essex Board XI
28	Gateshead Fell or Challow & Childrey	Match 14 Winner v Staffs

* If Denmark qualify, they will play away.

Third Round – Wednesday, June 23

29	Taunton or Luton or Kimbolton School	Match 15 Winner v Derbys
30	Lytham or KUD, Deventer or March	Match 16 Winner v Durham
31	Guildford or Lakenham or Bowdon	Match 17 Winner v Kent
32	St Georges, Telford or Bury St Edmunds or Portsmouth	Match 18 Winner v Glam
33	Derby or Grantham or Swansea	Match 19 Winner v Somerset
34	Raeburn Place, Edinburgh or Boots Ground, Nottingham or Bournemouth	Match 20 Winner v Surrey
35	Canterbury or away* or Kidderminster	Match 21 Winner v Hants
36	Southgate or Netherfield or Truro	Match 22 Winner v Sussex
37	Kington or Old Northamptonians or South Wilts CC	Match 23 Winner v Yorks
38	Exmouth or Finchampstead or Birmingham	Match 24 Winner v Worcs
39	Radlett or Leicester or Hove	Match 25 Winner v Lancs
40	Bristol or Harrogate or Marlow	Match 26 Winner v Warwicks
41	Jesmond or Castle Avenue, Dublin or Chelmsford	Match 27 Winner v Leics
42	Chester-le-Street or Challow & Childrey or Leek	Match 28 Winner v Glos
43	Northampton	Northants v Essex
44	Nottingham	Notts v Middx

* If Denmark qualify, they will play away.

Fourth Round – Wednesday, July 7

45	Match 38 Winner v Match 34 Winner	49	Match 35 Winner v Match 39 Winner
46	Match 37 Winner v Match 41 Winner	50	Match 30 Winner v Match 31 Winner
47	Match 32 Winner v Match 40 Winner	51	Match 42 Winner v Match 29 Winner
48	Match 43 Winner v Match 44 Winner	52	Match 36 Winner v Match 33 Winner

Quarter-finals to be played on Wednesday, July 28.

1st Semi-final to be played on Saturday, August 14;
2nd Semi-final to be played on Sunday, August 15.

Final to be played on Sunday, August 29, at Lord's.

†MINOR COUNTIES CHAMPIONSHIP, 1999

Unless otherwise indicated, all matches are of two days' duration.

MAY

23—Cornwall v Wales (Truro); Herefordshire v Berks (Colwall).

30—Cumberland v Beds (Carlisle); *Dorset v Herefordshire (Bournemouth); *Lincs v Herts (Sleaford); Wilts v Devon (Corsham).

JUNE

6—Beds v Bucks (Luton); Herts v Norfolk (Tring Park).

9—*Bucks v Staffs (Campbell Park, Milton Keynes); *Cambs v Lincs (Wisbech).

13—Beds v Suffolk (Bedford); Cheshire v Wilts (Alderley Edge); Cumberland v Lincs (Millom); Dorset v Wales (Bournemouth); *Northumberland v Norfolk (Jesmond); Oxon v Salop (Shipton-under-Wychwood).

15—Berks v Salop (Reading CC); Cambs v Norfolk (March).

20—Bucks v Cambs (Marlow); *Oxon v Wilts (Challow & Childrey); Wales v Cheshire (Colwyn Bay).

JULY

4–*Herts v Beds (Hertford); Lincs v Suffolk (Lincoln Lindum); Salop v Devon (St Georges, Telford).

6–Cheshire   v   Devon   (Bowdon); *Northumberland v Suffolk (Jesmond).

8–*Staffs v Cambs (Cannock).

11–Beds v Staffs (Southill Park); *Berks v Dorset (Finchampstead); *Bucks v Cumberland (Beaconsfield); *Herts v Northumberland (Shenley Park); Wales v Oxon (Pontarddulais); Wilts v Herefordshire (South Wilts CC).

13–Bucks v Northumberland (Beaconsfield); Herts v Cumberland (Stevenage).

18–Berks v Wilts (Hurst CC); Devon v Wales (Exmouth); Northumberland v Lincs (Jesmond); Oxon v Dorset (Christ Church, Oxford).

19–*Cheshire v Cornwall (Oxton).

20–Staffs v Northumberland (Brewood).

21–Cambs v Herts (Cambridge); *Salop v Cornwall (Bridgnorth).

22–Norfolk v Suffolk (Lakenham).

25–*Dorset v Devon (Weymouth); *Herefordshire v Cheshire (Kington); Herts v Staffs (Long Marston); Lincs v Bucks (Grimsby); *Norfolk v Beds (Lakenham); Oxon v Berks (Banbury); *Salop v Wales (Oswestry); Wilts v Cornwall (Marlborough).

AUGUST

1–*Beds v Lincs (Dunstable); *Devon v Oxon (Torquay); Dorset v Cornwall (Bourne-

mouth); *Norfolk v Cumberland (Lakenham); *Suffolk v Bucks (Ransomes, Ipswich); *Wales v Herefordshire (Newport).

3–Cornwall v Oxon (Falmouth); Norfolk v Bucks (Lakenham); Suffolk v Cumberland (Ransomes, Ipswich).

8–Cumberland   v   Northumberland (Netherfield); Herefordshire v Salop (Luctonians CC); *Oxon v Cheshire (Thame).

9–Norfolk v Staffs (Lakenham).

10–Berks v Cheshire (Falkland CC); *Wilts v Salop (Westbury).

11–Cambs v Beds (Cambridge); *Suffolk v Staffs (Ipswich School).

15–*Cornwall v Berks (Camborne); Devon v Herefordshire (Bovey Tracey); Northumberland v Cambs (Jesmond); Salop v Dorset (Shifnal); Suffolk v Herts (Mildenhall); *Wales v Wilts (Swansea).

17–Cheshire v Dorset (Neston); Cornwall v Herefordshire (St Austell); *Cumberland v Cambs (Barrow); *Devon v Berks (Mount Wise, Plymouth); Staffs v Lincs (Stone).

22–Bucks v Herts (Wormsley); Devon v Cornwall (Budleigh Salterton); Dorset v Wilts (Bournemouth); Herefordshire v Oxon (Brockhampton); Lincs v Norfolk (Grantham); Northumberland v Beds (Jesmond); Salop v Cheshire (Wellington); Staffs v Cumberland (Leek); Suffolk v Cambs (Bury St Edmunds); Wales v Berks (St Fagans).

SEPTEMBER

12–Final (3 days).

* *Played under "grade" rules, in which a single-innings match is contested over two days, with provision for second innings if time and conditions permit.*

†ECB 38-COUNTY COMPETITION (FOR THE MCC TROPHY)

All matches are of one day's duration.

Teams are County Board XIs and do not include first-class counties.

MAY

5–Lancs v Cheshire (Middleton).

9–Beds v Surrey (Bedford); Cornwall v Somerset (Helston); Dorset v Devon (Bournemouth); Salop v Derbys (Shrewsbury); Wales v Herefordshire (Abergavenny).

16–Berks v Bucks (Hungerford); Cumberland v Cheshire (Penrith); Dorset v Cornwall (Sherborne School); Herefordshire v Wilts (Brockhampton); Leics v Notts (Hinckley Town); Lincs v Durham (Cleethorpes); Norfolk v Cambs (Lakenham); Northants v

Suffolk (Great Oakley); Oxon v Hunts (Thame); Warwicks v Wales (King Edward's School, Birmingham); Yorks v Northumberland (Dunnington).

23–Bucks v Hants (Ascott Park); Cheshire v Salop (Boughton Hall); Devon v Glos (Sidmouth); Durham v Lincs (Ropery Lane, Chester-le-Street); Hunts v Leics (Kimbolton School); Norfolk v Suffolk (Lakenham); Oxon v Staffs (Aston Rowant); Sussex v Kent (Hastings & St Leonards); Worcs v Wilts (Halesowen).

26–Cheshire v Derbys (New Brighton).

27–Cumberland v Lancs (Askam); Surrey v Middx (Metropolitan Police CC).

30–Cambs v Essex (Saffron Walden); Kent v Hants (Ashford); Northants v Norfolk (Finedon Dolben); Somerset v Glos (Taunton); Wales v Worcs (Ynysygerwn).

JUNE

6–Berks v Sussex (Slough); Essex v Northants (Chelmsford); Glos v Cornwall (Bristol University); Lincs v Yorks (Bourne); Notts v Oxon (Boots Ground, Nottingham); Somerset v Dorset (Bath); Staffs v Leics (Porthill Park); Suffolk v Cambs (Exning); Warwicks v Herefordshire (King Edward's School, Birmingham); Wilts v Wales (Swindon).

8–Durham v Northumberland (Chester-le-Street).

Some venues were subject to confirmation when Wisden went to press.

9–Lancs v Salop (Blackpool).

10–Surrey v Herts (Metropolitan Police CC); Yorks v Durham (Elland).

13–Bucks v Kent (Aylesbury); Devon v Somerset (Instow); Hants v Sussex (Cove CC); Herefordshire v Worcs (Dales CC); Hunts v Notts (Kimbolton School); Middx v Herts (Shenley Park).

17–Derbys v Lancs (Denby); Middx v Beds (Richmond).

20–Cornwall v Devon (Penzance); Essex v Norfolk (Chelmsford); Hants v Berks (Southampton); Herts v Beds (Shenley Park); Northumberland v Lincs (Jesmond); Notts v Staffs (Boots Ground, Nottingham); Salop v Cumberland (Whitchurch); Worcs v Warwicks (Bromsgrove).

27–Beds v Middx (Dunstable); Cambs v Northants (March); Derbys v Cumberland (Denby); Glos v Dorset (Bristol University); Herts v Surrey (Shenley Park); Kent v Berks (Canterbury); Leics v Oxon (Oakham School); Northumberland v Yorks (Jesmond); Staffs v Hunts (Longton); Suffolk v Essex (Copdock CC); Sussex v Bucks (Horsham); Wilts v Warwicks (Warminster).

Quarter-finals to be played on July 16.

Semi-finals to be played on July 29.

Final to be played on September 1 at Lord's.

---

†SECOND ELEVEN CHAMPIONSHIP, 1999

Unless otherwise stated, all matches are of three days' duration

APRIL

20–Durham v Northants (Chester-le-Street; 4 days); Kent v Somerset (Canterbury; 4 days); Notts v Middx (Nottingham; 4 days).

21–Glam v Essex (Cardiff); Glos v Worcs (Bristol).

27–Hants v Kent (Southampton; 4 days); Surrey v Essex (The Oval; 4 days).

28–Sussex v Glos (Hove); Warwicks v Notts (Knowle & Dorridge); Worcs v Leics (Worcester); Yorks v Somerset (York).

MAY

5–Derbys v Sussex (Cheadle); Durham v Glos (Chester-le-Street, Ropery Lane); Lancs v

Glam (Haslingden); Somerset v Essex (North Perrott); Yorks v Middx (Leeds).

10–Kent v Essex (Maidstone; 4 days); Sussex v Durham (Eastbourne).

11–Lancs v Yorks (Middleton; 4 days).

12–Derbys v Hants (Abbotsholme School, Rocester); Warwicks v Glos (Moseley).

16–Glam v Worcs (Panteg).

17–Sussex v Lancs (Middleton-on-Sea).

18–Yorks v Derbys (Harrogate; 4 days).

19–Kent v Middx (Ashford); Notts v Somerset (Boots Ground, Nottingham); Surrey v Warwicks (Cheam).

25–Sussex v Surrey (Hove; 4 days); Yorks v Derbys (Rotherham; 4 days).

26–Glos v Notts (Bristol); Lancs v Kent (Blackpool); Middx v Glam (Ealing).

JUNE

1–Derbys v Middx (Dunstall; 4 days); Glos v Glam (Cheltenham College; 4 days); Hants v Northants (Southampton; 4 days); Somerset v Sussex (Taunton; 4 days); Worcs v Warwicks (Kidderminster; 4 days).

2–Essex v Leics (Saffron Walden); Kent v Durham (Canterbury).

7–Leics v Surrey (Hinckley Town).

8–Durham v Glam (Hartlepool); Kent v Sussex (Maidstone; 4 days); Notts v Derbys (Boots Ground, Nottingham; 4 days); Somerset v Worcs (Taunton; 4 days); Yorks v Lancs (Middlesbrough; 4 days).

9–Glos v Northants (Bristol); Hants v Warwicks (Bournemouth).

14–Durham v Yorks (Chester-le-Street; 4 days); Leics v Glam (Hinckley Town; 4 days).

15–Hants v Notts (Finchampstead); Northants v Worcs (Northampton; 4 days); Warwicks v Lancs (Stratford-upon-Avon; 4 days).

16–Surrey v Derbys (Oxted).

21–Essex v Warwicks (Chelmsford; 4 days); Glam v Hants (Abergavenny; 4 days); Lancs v Leics (Manchester).

22–Glos v Derbys (Bristol); Surrey v Notts (The Oval; 4 days); Yorks v Kent (Elland).

23–Northants v Somerset (Oundle School); Worcs v Middx (Worcester).

JULY

13–Essex v Derbys (Coggeshall; 4 days); Glos v Hants (Bristol; 4 days); Middx v Sussex (Eton College; 4 days); Surrey v Somerset (The Oval; 4 days); Worcs v Yorks (Kidderminster; 4 days).

14–Glam v Kent (Ammanford); Notts v Northants (Nottingham High School).

19–Northants v Yorks (Northampton; 4 days).

20–Derbys v Leics (Heanor; 4 days); Durham v Notts (Darlington; 4 days); Glam v Somerset (Cardiff; 4 days); Hants v Worcs (Southampton; 4 days); Warwicks v Middx (Walmley).

21–Surrey v Lancs (The Oval).

26–Lancs v Durham (Crosby; 4 days); Leics v Kent (Oakham School; 4 days).

27–Hants v Essex (Bournemouth); Middx v Glos (Vine Lane, Uxbridge; 4 days); Yorks v Warwicks (Castleford; 4 days).

28–Northants v Surrey (Campbell Park, Milton Keynes); Notts v Worcs (Boots Ground, Nottingham); Somerset v Derbys (Clevedon).

AUGUST

2–Derbys v Durham (Chesterfield; 4 days).

3–Essex v Middx (Chelmsford; 4 days); Glam v Surrey (Usk; 4 days); Somerset v Glos (Taunton; 4 days); Sussex v Leics (Hove; 4 days); Worcs v Lancs (Worcester; 4 days).

4–Hants v Yorks (Southampton); Notts v Kent (Worksop College).

9–Durham v Surrey (South Shields); Leics v Notts (Oakham School; 4 days); Sussex v Hants (Hastings; 4 days).

10–Glos v Essex (Hatherley & Reddings); Warwicks v Northants (Studley; 4 days).

11–Glam v Yorks (Pontarddulais); Somerset v Lancs (Taunton).

18–Essex v Durham (Halstead); Glos v Yorks (Bristol); Kent v Warwicks (Folkestone); Leics v Northants (Hinckley Town); Surrey v Hants (Whitgift School); Worcs v Sussex (Worcester).

23–Lancs v Derbys (Lytham; 4 days).

24–Essex v Notts (Saffron Walden); Glos v Leics (Bristol; 4 days); Middx v Surrey (Vine Lane, Uxbridge; 4 days); Northants v Kent (Northampton; 4 days); Warwicks v Glam (Birmingham; 4 days).

25–Yorks v Sussex (Leeds).

30–Lancs v Glos (Liverpool; 4 days).

31–Essex v Worcs (Colchester); Hants v Somerset (Southampton); Notts v Yorks (Nottingham; 4 days).

SEPTEMBER

1–Kent v Surrey (Eltham); Middx v Northants (Harrow); Warwicks v Derbys (Kenilworth Wardens).

7–Worcs v Durham (Worcester; 4 days).
To be played on September 8 if Durham or Worcs reach AON final.

8–Derbys v Glam (Derby); Essex v Northants (Wickford); Leics v Yorks (Leicester); Middx v Lancs (Southgate); Notts v Surrey (Boots Ground, Nottingham; 4 days); Sussex v Warwicks (Horsham).

13–Lancs v Hants (Manchester); Northants v Derbys (Northants).

Some venues were subject to confirmation when Wisden *went to press.*

†AON TROPHY, 1999

All matches are of one day's duration.

APRIL

26–Glos v Glam (Bristol).

MAY

10–Hants v Glam (Portsmouth).

24–Glam v Glos (Cardiff); MCC Young Cricketers v Essex (Shenley Park); Yorks v Derbys (Doncaster).

25–Minor Counties Under-25 v Middx (Campbell Park, Milton Keynes).

28–Warwicks v Minor Counties Under-25 (Solihull).

31–Derbys v Yorks (Duffield); Worcs v Glos (Worcester).

JUNE

1–Essex v MCC Young Cricketers (Saffron Walden).

7–Minor Counties Under-25 v Northants (Dunstable); Somerset v Glos (Bath).

8–Minor Counties Under-25 v Warwicks (Banbury).

14–Glos v Hants (Hatherley & Reddings); MCC Young Cricketers v Surrey (Shenley Park); Middx v Northants (Harrow).

15–Middx v Minor Counties Under-25 (Harrow).

21–Glos v Worcs (Bristol).

25–MCC Young Cricketers v Sussex (Shenley Park); Yorks v Lancs (Todmorden).

28–Essex v Surrey (Chelmsford); Hants v Somerset (Southampton); Lancs v Durham (Fleetwood); Northants v Leics (Campbell Park, Milton Keynes); Notts v Yorks (Unity Casuals, Nottingham), Sussex v MCC Young Cricketers (Middleton-on-Sea); Worcs v Glam (Halesowen).

29–Glam v Somerset (Cardiff); Leics v Middx (Lutterworth); MCC Young Cricketers v Kent (Shenley Park); Notts v Derbys (Farnsfield); Yorks v Durham (Marske).

30–Hants v Glos (Southampton); Kent v Essex (Canterbury); Lancs v Derbys (Littleborough); Sussex v Surrey (Hove); Warwicks v Middx (Coventry & North Warwicks); Worcs v Somerset (Ombersley).

JULY

1–Durham v Derbys (Seaton Carew); Glam v Worcs (Newport); Leics v Warwicks (Lutterworth); Yorks v Notts (Bingley).

2–Derbys v Lancs (Repton School); Durham v Notts (Chester-le-Street); Kent v Surrey (Canterbury); Sussex v Essex (Hove); Worcs v Hants (Barnt Green).

5–Durham v Yorks (Boldon); Glos v Somerset (Bristol); Hants v Worcs (Southampton); Kent v Sussex (Canterbury); Lancs v Notts (Manchester); Middx v Leics (Ealing); Surrey v Essex (The Oval).

6–Derbys v Notts (Belper Meadows); Somerset v Worcs (Taunton); Surrey v Kent (The Oval); Warwicks v Leics (West Bromwich Dartmouth).

7–Glam v Hants (Ebbw Vale); Lancs v Yorks (Manchester); Middx v Warwicks (Ealing); Notts v Durham (Welbeck); Sussex v Kent (Haywards Heath).

8–Derbys v Durham (Glossop); Northants v Minor Counties Under-25 (Isham); Notts v Lancs (Worksop College); Somerset v Glam (Taunton); Surrey v MCC Young Cricketers (The Oval).

9–Essex v Sussex (Billericay); Kent v MCC Young Cricketers (Maidstone); Minor Counties Under-25 v Leics (North Runcton); Somerset v Hants (Taunton); Warwicks v Northants (Leamington).

12–Essex v Kent (Coggeshall); Northants v Warwicks (Northampton).

13–Leics v Northants (Leicester).

15–Durham v Lancs (Sunderland); Leics v Minor Counties Under-25 (Leicester).

19–Surrey v Sussex (The Oval).

26–Northants v Middx (Wellingborough School).

Semi-finals to be played on August 16 or 17.

Final to be played on September 6 (reserve day September 7).

Fixtures for women's cricket may be found on page 1014.

ENGLAND IN SOUTH AFRICA AND ZIMBABWE, 1999-2000

NOVEMBER

1	Randjesfontein	†v N. F. Oppenheimer's XI (1 day)
2	Benoni	†v Easterns (1 day)
5	Cape Town	v Combined Western Province/Boland XI (4 days)
12	Bloemfontein	v Combined Free State/Griqualand West XI (4 days)
18	Centurion	v Combined Northerns/Gauteng XI (4 days)
25	Johannesburg	v SOUTH AFRICA (1st Test, 5 days)

DECEMBER

1	Lenasia	†v Gauteng Invitation XI (1 day)
3	Durban	v KwaZulu-Natal (4 days)
9	Port Elizabeth	v SOUTH AFRICA (2nd Test, 5 days)
16	Alice	†v Combined Eastern Province/Border Invitation XI (1 day)
18	East London	v Combined Eastern Province/Border XI (4 days)
26	Durban	v SOUTH AFRICA (3rd Test, 5 days)

JANUARY

| 2 | Cape Town | v SOUTH AFRICA (4th Test, 5 days) |

9	Port Elizabeth	v South Africa Invitation XI (3 days)
14	Centurion	v SOUTH AFRICA (5th Test, 5 days)
20	Potchefstroom	†v North West (1 day, day/night)

Triangular Tournament (1 day)

23	Bloemfontein	†v South Africa
26	Cape Town	†v South Africa (day/night)
28	Paarl	†v Zimbabwe (day/night)
30	Kimberley	†v Zimbabwe

FEBRUARY

3	Centurion	†v Zimbabwe (day/night)
5	East London	†v South Africa
9	Johannesburg	† **Triangular Tournament Final** (day/night)
12	Bulawayo	†v District XI (1 day)
13	Bulawayo	†v Zimbabwe (1st 1-day international)
16	Harare	†v Zimbabwe (2nd 1-day international)
19	Harare	†v Zimbabwe (3rd 1-day international)
20	Harare	†v Zimbabwe (4th 1-day international)

World Cup Fixtures, 1999

World Cup fixtures and warm-up matches may be found on pages 61-62.

INDEX OF UNUSUAL OCCURRENCES